PASSWORD

ENGLISH DICTIONARY FOR SPEAKERS OF SPANISH

Originally published as *Harrap's Easy English Dictionary.*
First published in Great Britain 1980
by Harrap Ltd, 19-23 Ludgate Hill, London EC4M 7PD.

Kernerman Semi-Bilingual Dictionaries

This semi-bilingual edition (1991) published by
Ediciones SM by arrangement with Harrap Ltd.

Password
English Dictionary for Speakers of Spanish

Traducción: Recaredo Sainz-Ezquerra
Revisión: Fernando Villaverde
Cubierta: Alfonso Ruano
Dirección editorial: Javier Odriozola

ISBN: 84-348-3365-4
Depósito legal: M. 8383-1991
Printed in Spain
Imprenta SM. Joaquín Turina, 39. 28044 Madrid

PASSWORD

ENGLISH DICTIONARY FOR SPEAKERS OF SPANISH

ediciones sm Joaquín Turina 39 28044 Madrid

KERNERMAN SEMI-BILINGUAL DICTIONARIES

Preface

About one billion people, or one fifth of the world's population, can speak English. About one third of these speak it as their mother tongue or first language, one third use it as their second language, and one third use it as a foreign language. Several hundred million more are currently learning it as a second or foreign language. In most countries of the world English is either a compulsory subject of study or the most popular option.

These figures are astounding, but no less so is the fact that English is used as the world's chief language of communication — not only among its native speakers — but among non-native speakers. Not only statistically, but in the most important fields — science and technology, medicine, diplomacy, international business, publishing, sport, pop music and entertainment, English is dominant in all six continents.

English, then, is no longer a national language spoken internationally, but a truly international language. It is no longer the monopoly of the English-speaking people, but has become common property of all people — a world language.

In the Spanish speaking world, today, English enjoys the status of being the main foreign language — in international relations, in business, and as a school subject. There is a tremendous thirst for qualified teachers and for appropriate textbooks. A dictionary is required that satisfies the need of the communicative method of foreign language learning, while at the same time fulfilling the user's desire to know the Spanish translation. This semi-bilingual dictionary satisfies both of these demands.

Bilingual dictionaries (English-Spanish) have the drawbacks of not inducing the user to think in English, as well as providing ambiguous meanings. Monolingual dictionaries (English-English), while giving accurate meanings, are difficult for foreign language learners to use and do not satisfy their desire to know the Spanish translation.

This semi-bilingual dictionary gives the meaning in easy English, with examples of usage, and has the exact equivalent in Spanish of each usage of each entry. It encourages the user to read the definition in the target language, while providing a brief translation in the mother tongue for confirmation and reinforcement.

We are certain that this dictionary will contribute considerably to the advancements of Spanish speaking students who are learning English as a second or foreing language.

LIONEL KERNERMAN

Prefacio

Alrededor de mil millones de personas, es decir una quinta parte de la población mundial, habla inglés. Aproximadamente un tercio de ellos lo habla como lengua materna o primera lengua, un tercio lo utiliza como segunda lengua y el otro tercio lo utiliza como lengua extranjera. Varios cientos de millones más lo están aprendiendo como segunda lengua o lengua extranjera. En la mayoría de los países del mundo el inglés es una asignatura de estudio obligatorio o la opción más popular.

Estas cifras son impresionantes, pero no lo es menos el hecho de que el inglés se utilice como la principal lengua de comunicación, no sólo entre sus hablantes nativos, sino entre los no nativos también. El inglés domina en todos los continentes no sólo estadísticamente sino en los campos más importantes: ciencia y tecnología, medicina, diplomacia, comercio internacional, edición, deporte, música moderna y espectáculos.

Por lo tanto, el inglés no es ya una lengua nacional hablada internacionalmente, sino una lengua auténticamente internacional. Ya no es monopolio de los hablantes nativos de inglés, sino que se ha convertido en propiedad común de todo el mundo: una lengua mundial.

En el mundo de habla española, hoy en día, el inglés disfruta del status de ser la principal lengua extranjera; en las relaciones internacionales, los negocios y como asignatura escolar. Hay una enorme demanda de profesores cualificados y libros de texto apropiados. Se requiere también un diccionario que se adapte a las necesidades de los métodos comunicativos de aprendizaje de lenguas extranjeras, mientras que a la vez satisfaga el deseo del alumno de conocer la traducción española. Este diccionario semi-bilingüe cumple ambas demandas.

Los diccionarios bilingües (Inglés-Español) tienen las desventajas de no inducir al usuario a pensar en inglés y además proporcionar significados ambiguos. Los diccionarios monolingües (Inglés-Inglés), a pesar de proporcionar significados precisos, resultan difíciles de usar para los estudiantes de lenguas extranjeras y no satisfacen su deseo de conocer la traducción española.

Este diccionario semi-bilingüe da el significado en un inglés sencillo, con ejemplos de uso, y tiene el equivalente exacto en español para cada acepción de cada palabra. Anima al usuario a leer la definición en la lengua extranjera, a la vez que proporciona una traducción breve en la lengua materna como confirmación y refuerzo.

Estamos seguros de que este diccionario contribuirá significativamente al progreso de los estudiantes de habla española que están aprendiendo inglés como segunda lengua o lengua extranjera.

Lionel Kernerman

International Phonetic Symbols used in the Dictionary

Vowels

i	bit	below	ɔ	bottom	block
iː	bee	beast	ɔː	bought	board
iə	beer	bleary	ɔi	boy	boil
e	bet	belch	ou	bold	blow
ei	bay	bait	u	bull	book
ɛə	bear	blare	uː	boot	boom
æ	bat	back	uə	boor	bourgeois
ai	buy	bible	ʌ	but	blood
aː	barn	blanch	əː	burn	berth
au	bough	blouse	ə	banana	balloon

Consonants

p	pat	m	man	s	some	ʃ	shall
b	bat	n	nice	z	zoo	ʒ	vision
t	today	l	laugh	h	have	tʃ	church
d	dog	r	ride	w	witch	dʒ	jet
k	catch	f	fat	θ	thin	ŋ	bang
g	good	v	vat	ð	there	j	yet

Abbreviations used in the Dictionary

adj.	adjetive	*inf.*	informal
adv.	adverb	*inter.*	interjection
Am.	American	*n.*	noum
approx.	approximately	*pl.*	plural
def.	definite	*prep.*	preposition
e.g.	for example	*sl.*	slang
esp.	especially	*usu.*	usually
indef.	indefinite	*v.*	verb

A,a

A, a [ei] first letter of the alphabet. □ **A, a**
A1, in very good condition. □ **de primera**
a, an [*stressed* ei, æn; *unstressed* ə, ən] (***a*** before words beginning with a consonant, and before words beginning with ***u*** pronounced [ju:] ***an*** before ***a, e, i, o*** or ***u*** and before ***h*** where ***h*** is not pronounced: *a house, an empty house, an hour, an adult, a one-way street, a useful knife*) *indefinite article* **1** one: *give me a stamp and an envelope* (for emphasis on the number: *give me one stamp*). □ **un, una**
2 not a particular one: *he has a big nose; she's still a little girl.* □ **un, una**
3 for each one/in each one: *thirty kilometres an hour; eighty pence a kilo.* □ **por**
4 a certain: *I know a Dr Smith who works in London.* □ **un tal**
aback [ə'bæk] *adv.* ***to be taken aback,*** to be surprised, usually unpleasantly. □ **por sorpresa**
abacus ['æbəkəs] *n.* (*pl. abacuses*) device for counting, made of small beads which slide along rods in a frame. □ **ábaco**
abandon [ə'bændən] *v.* **1** to leave: *the crew abandoned the sinking ship.* □ **abandonar (para siempre)**
2 to give up: *I've had to abandon the idea of becoming a farmer.* □ **renunciar**
abashed [ə'bæʃt] *adj.* ashamed. □ **avergonzado**
abate [ə'beit] *v.* to become less strong: *when the storm abated.* □ **disminuir, amainar**
abattoir ['æbətwɑ:] *n.* slaughterhouse, place where animals are killed for meat. □ **matadero**
abbess ['æbes] *n.* (*pl. abbesses*) woman in charge of nuns in a convent. □ **abadesa**
abbey ['æbi] *n.* large Christian religious establishment with living quarters, hospital, etc., grouped round a church. □ **abadía**
abbot ['æbət] *n.* man in charge of monks in an abbey. □ **abad**
abbreviate [ə'bri:vieit] *v.* to shorten: *'Company' is usually abbreviated to 'Co.' in the names of firms.* □ **abreviar**
abbreviation [əbri:vi'eiʃn] *n.* group of letters which represent a larger word: *'etc.' is the abbreviation for 'et cetera'.* □ **abreviatura**
ABC [eibi:'si:] *n.* the letters of the alphabet. □ **abecedario**
as easy as ABC, extremely easy. □ **muy fácil**
abdicate ['æbdikeit] *v.* (*of king or queen*) to give up the throne: *he abdicated in favour of his son.* □ **abdicar**
abdication [æbdi'keiʃn] *n.* giving up (of a throne): *there was a crisis at the time of the king's abdication.* □ **abdicación**
abdomen ['æbdəmen] *n.* lower part of the body, containing the stomach, bowels, etc. □ **abdomen**
abdominal [æb'dɔminl] *adj.* referring to the abdomen: *he was rushed to hospital with abdominal pains.* □ **abdominal**
abduct [æb'dʌkt] *v.* to remove (someone) by force: *robbers abducted the wife of the bank manager.* □ **secuestrar**
abduction [æb'dʌkʃn] *n.* removal by force. □ **secuestro**
aberration [æbə'reiʃn] *n.* **1** change from what is usual. □ **desviación**
2 sudden attack of forgetfulness.
mental aberration, slight confusion: *did I call you John? - it must have been a mental aberration on my part.* □ **lapsus**
abet [ə'bet] *v.* (*he abetted*) ***to aid and abet someone,*** to be someone's accomplice in a crime: *he was accused of aiding and abetting.* □ **inducir; apoyar**
abeyance [ə'beiəns] *n.* **1** suspension (of a law, etc.). □ **suspensión**
2 *the rule is temporarily **in abeyance,*** it is not being applied at present. □ **en suspenso**
abhor [əb'hɔ:] *v.* (*he abhorred*) to feel hatred/horror for something: *I abhor smelly trains.* □ **detestar**
abhorrent [əb'hɔrənt] *adj.* disgusting, which makes you shudder: *the whole idea is quite abhorrent to me.* □ **detestable**
abide [ə'baid] *v.* **1** ***to abide by,*** to stick to; to follow: *to abide by a promise,* to stand by what you have promised; *I will abide by your decision.* □ **atenerse; acatar**
2 (*usually only with negative*) to like: *I can't abide the smell of garlic.* □ **soportar**
ability [ə'biliti] *n.* **1** (*pl. abilities*) power to do something; capability: *he's a man of great ability,* he's a very capable man. □ **competencia; talento**
2 *I'll do it **to the best of my ability,*** as best I can. □ **lo mejor que pueda**
abject ['æbdʒekt] *adj.* **1** very miserable: *they live in abject poverty.* □ **abyecto**
2 cowardly; extremely humble: *he made an abject apology.* □ **cobarde**
ablaze [ə'bleiz] *adv.* in flames: *soon the whole house was ablaze.* □ **en llamas**
able ['eibl] *adj.* **1** having the ability to do something: *he wasn't able to breathe; will you be able to come?* □ **capaz (no podía; ¿podrás?)**
able seaman, first class seaman in the Royal Navy. □ **marinero de primera**
2 *he's a very able man,* he can do many things well. □ **competente, capaz**
ably ['eibli] *adv.* very efficiently: *the singer was ably accompanied by Miss Smith at the piano.* □ **bien, con eficacia**
ablutions [ə'blu:ʃənz] *n. pl.* (*formal*) washing (face/hands, etc.): *have you done your ablutions yet?* □ **abluciones**
abnormal [əb'nɔ:ml] *adj.* not normal: *there is something abnormal about that family.* □ **anormal**
abnormally *adv.* not normally; unusually: *the winter has been abnormally mild.* □ **anormalmente**
abnormality [æbnɔ:'mæliti] *n.* (*pl. abnormalities*) being abnormal; unusualness/peculiarity. □ **anormalidad**
aboard [ə'bɔ:d] *adv.* and *prep.* on/in (a ship/aircraft/train/bus): *the passengers went aboard the liner; if everyone is aboard, we'll cast off.* □ **a bordo**
abode [ə'boud] *n.* (*formal*) home: *come into my humble abode.* □ **residencia**
of no fixed abode, with no permanent address. □ **domicilio**
abolish [ə'bɔliʃ] *v.* to cancel/to remove: *capital punishment has been abolished; this school has abolished examinations.* □ **abolir**
abolition [æbə'liʃn] *n.* act of abolishing: *the abolition of capital punishment.* □ **abolición**
abominable [ə'bɔminəbl] *adj.* horrible; disgusting: *abominable treatment of patients; this soup/this weather is absolutely abominable.* □ **abominable**

abominate [ə'boumineit] *v.* to dislike intensely. □ **abominar**
abomination *n.* unpleasant/nasty thing. □ **abominación**
aborigine [æbə'ridʒini] *n.* member of a race which was living in a country before the country was colonized; original inhabitant: *the Australian aborigines.* □ **aborigen**
aboriginal *adj.* referring to aborigines: *aboriginal art.* □ **primitivo**
■ *n.* aborigine. □ **aborigen**
abortion [ə'bɔːʃn] *n.* (deliberate) miscarriage of an unborn child: *she had an abortion in the clinic.* □ **aborto**
abort *v.* **1** to cause an abortion to (someone). □ **hacer abortar**
2 to stop (a project) taking place: *to abort a rocket launch; in the end the whole plan was aborted by the central office.* □ **abortar**
abortive *adj.* unsuccessful: *he made an abortive attempt to commit suicide.* □ **infructuoso**
abound [ə'baund] *v.* to be full of: *the whole book abounds with mistakes; a country abounding in wild life.* □ **abundar**
about [ə'baut] *adv.* and *prep.* **1** in various places: *they left tea cups lying about on the floor; there's a lot of flu about at this time of year.* □ **por, por aquí**
2 concerning: *tell me about your holiday; there's something odd about this cheque; what do you want to speak to me about?; they quarrelled about the wallpaper in the bedroom.* □ **sobre, acerca de**
what about me?, have you forgotten me? □ **¿ y yo qué?**
how about *a cup of tea?,* would you like a cup of tea? □ **¿y qué tal...?**
3 round; facing the opposite direction.
about turn!, (*in the army*) turn round to face the opposite way. □ **media vuelta**
about-turn: *the government did a complete about-turn over prices,* changed its mind completely. □ **cambio de opinión**
4 approximately: *the room is about three metres square; the last train is at about four o'clock.* □ **aproximadamente (unos...)**
5 on the point (of doing something): *I was just about to go out when you phoned.* □ **a punto de**
6 in the process of doing something: *while you're about it, can you post this letter for me?* □ **ya que...**
above [ə'bʌv] *adv.* and *prep.* **1** higher than (something): *the plane was flying above the clouds; the temperature was above 40°.* □ **por encima de**
2 louder than: *I can only just hear you above the noise of the engine.* □ **por encima de**
3 *they're living above their means,* more extravagantly than they can afford. □ **por encima de sus posibilidades**
4 earlier on (in a book); higher up (on a page): *see paragraph 6 above.* □ **arriba, atrás**
above-board *adj.* open/honest; not corrupt: *the whole affair is completely above-board.* □ **abierto, limpio**
abracadabra [æbrəkə'dæbrə] *n.* traditional magic spell. □ **abracadabra**
abrasion [ə'breiʒn] *n.* scraping off (of the skin): *although his car was travelling very fast when it hit the tree, he only suffered minor cuts and abrasions.* □ **abrasión**
abrasive [ə'breiziv] *adj.* **1** grinding (substance). □ **abrasivo**
2 sharp; rude: *my boss is a pleasant man, but he can be very abrasive at times; he made some very abrasive comments about the Prime Minister.* □ **duro, hiriente**
■ *n.* rough substance for smoothing a surface. □ **abrasivo**
abreast [ə'brest] *adv.* **1** in a row; level (with something). □ **en línea**
2 *they were cycling three abreast,* the three bicycles were side by side. □ **en línea**
3 ***to keep abreast of,*** (i) *I can hardly keep abreast of all the changes in the staff,* I can hardly keep up with/keep track of all the changes. □ **estar al día**
(ii) *my salary hasn't kept abreast of the cost of living,* has not risen as fast as the cost of living. □ **acorde con**
abridged [ə'bridʒd] *adj.* shortened: *this is an abridged edition of 'War and Peace'.* □ **abreviado**
abridgement *n.* shortened version (of a long book). □ **versión abreviada**
abroad [ə'brɔːd] *adv.* in or to another country: *he has gone to live abroad; we are going abroad on holiday.* □ **en el/al extranjero**
abrogate ['æbrəgeit] *v.* (*formal*) to end (a law). □ **abolir, revocar**
abrupt [ə'brʌpt] *adj.* sudden (departure); brusque (way of speaking). □ **brusco**
abruptly *adv.* suddenly; brusquely. □ **bruscamente**
abruptness *n.* suddenness; brusqueness. □ **brusquedad**
abscess ['æbses] *n.* (*pl. abscesses*) collection of pus in the body: *I've got an abscess under my tooth.* □ **absceso**
abscond [əb'skɔnd] *v.* to run away: *before the trial could begin, the prisoner had absconded.* □ **fugarse**
absence ['æbsəns] *n.* **1** not being there: *in the absence of the chairman, Mr Smith will take the chair; she was sentenced in her absence to a year in prison,* she was not there to receive the sentence. □ **ausencia**
2 lack: *in the absence of a map of the town, we had to ask a postman how to find the house.* □ **falta**
absent ['æbsənt] *adj.* not present: *half the class was absent through illness; he is always absent on Friday afternoons.* □ **ausente**
■ *v.* ***to absent oneself,*** to stay away (from class/from a meeting) deliberately. □ **ausentarse**
absentee [æbsən'tiː] *n.* person who is absent: *have we any absentees today?* □ **ausente**
absentee landlord, landowner who does not live near his land and takes no interest in it. □ **absentista**
absenteeism *n.* deliberately staying away from work: *absenteeism is very noticeable on Monday mornings; the factory has a bad record of absenteeism.* □ **absentismo**
absent-minded *adj.* forgetful: *he is so absent-minded he left for work in his slippers.* □ **distraído, despistado**
absent-mindedly *adv.* forgetfully: *he absent-mindedly sprinkled salt in his cocoa.* □ **distraídamente**
absent-mindedness *n.* being frequently forgetful: *his absent-mindedness is so well known that people make jokes about it.* □ **distracción**
absolute ['æbsəluːt] *adj.* **1** unlimited: *the president assumed absolute power,* became a dictator. □ **absoluto**
2 *the government has an* ***absolute majority*** *of ten,* has a majority of ten over all the other parties in Parliament. □ **mayoría absoluta**
3 complete: *she's an absolute idiot,* is completely idiotic. □ **completo**
absolutely *adv.* totally: *you're absolutely right!* □ **absolutamente**
absolution [æbsə'luːʃn] *n.* giving of blessing by a

priest to forgive sin. □ **absolución**

absolve [əb'zɔlv] *v.* to remove blame for a sin from (someone); to release (someone) from a promise. □ **absolver**

absorb [əb'zɔ:b] *v.* **1** to soak up (liquid); to deaden (a shock); to accept (a strange person/outside body) into a group: *the paper quickly absorbed the watercolour.* □ **absorber**

2 *we have absorbed the loss into our company accounts,* our company accounts have covered the loss. □ **absorber**

3 *he was absorbed in the newspaper,* he was so busy reading the newspaper that he noticed nothing. □ **absorto**

4 *it's an absorbing story,* a story that holds your attention. □ **absorbente**

absorbent *adj.* which absorbs: *absorbent bandage.* □ **absorbente**

absorbent cotton, *Amer.* cotton wool/fluffy cotton stuff, used for cleaning wounds, etc. □ **algodón hidrófilo**

absorber *n.* ***shock absorber,*** part of a car which softens the shock of a bump to the passengers. □ **amortiguador**

absorption [əb'zɔ:pʃn] *n.* act of absorbing. □ **absorción**

abstain [əb'stein] *v.* not to do something deliberately: *I abstained from making any comment; there were four votes for the motion and two against, but Mr Smith abstained,* refused to vote. □ **abstenerse**

abstemious [əb'sti:miəs] *adj.* not drinking (or eating) too much: *he's very abstemious - he only has one meal a day.* □ **abstemio**

abstemiousness *n.* not drinking (or eating) too much. □ **sobriedad**

abstention [əb'stenʃn] *n.* **1** refusal to do something. □ **abstención**

2 *in the vote on government spending there were several abstentions,* there were several people who did not vote. □ **abstenciones**

abstinence ['æbstinəns] *n.* not drinking (or eating) to excess. □ **abstinencia, sobriedad**

total abstinence, not drinking any alcohol. □ **abstinencia total**

abstract ['æbstrækt] *adj.* not concrete; (painting) which does not reproduce something recognizable: *he is an abstract painter.* □ **abstracto**

■ *n.* **1** quality of not being concrete. □ **abstracción**

2 *we should discuss this point* ***in the abstract,*** without mentioning specific cases. □ **en abstracto**

3 abstract picture: *he has a fine collection of twentieth century abstracts.* □ **pintura abstracta**

4 summary: *I'll send you an abstract of my research paper.* □ **extracto**

■ *v.* **1** to remove; to steal: *he apparently abstracted several important documents from the office.* □ **sustraer**

2 to summarize. □ **extractar**

abstracted *adj.* vague/dreamy; thoughtful: *he had an abstracted look about him as if he were half asleep.* □ **abstraído**

abstraction *n.* **1** removing; stealing: *the abstraction of documents was only one of his crimes.* □ **sustracción**

2 vague idea. □ **abstracción**

abstruse [əb'stru:s] *adj.* very difficult to understand: *she is doing some sort of abstruse research into mushrooms.* □ **abstruso**

absurd [əb'sə:d] *adj.* very odd; ridiculous. □ **absurdo**

that's absurd!, that's nonsense.

absurdity *n.* (*pl. absurdities*) the fact of being absurd. □ **absurdo**

absurdly *adv.* ridiculously: *they have just bought an absurdly expensive car.* □ **absurdamente**

abundant [ə'bʌndənt] *adj.* in large quantity. □ **abundante**

abundance *n.* large quantity: *Christmastime always brings an abundance of good food.* □ **abundancia**

abundantly *adv.* copiously; very much. □ **abundantemente**

abuse [ə'bju:s] *n.* **1** wrong use/bad use: *it's an abuse of my time to have to answer all your questions.* □ **abuso**

2 evil: *corruption is a major abuse in local politics; the police are doing all they can to stamp out such abuses.* □ **mal**

3 rude words/insults: *when he was arrested the murderer let out a torrent of abuse.* □ **insultos**

term of abuse, rude/insulting word: *in some societies the word 'dog' is a term of abuse.* □ **palabra injuriosa**

■ *v.* **1** to put to wrong use: *he abused my confidence,* he took advantage of my confidence. □ **abusar de**

2 to insult: *you are abusing the memory of your dead father.* □ **ofender**

3 to ill-treat (someone). □ **maltratar**

abusive [ə'bju:siv] *adj.* insulting: *he used abusive language.* □ **insultante**

abut [ə'bʌt] *v.* (*it abutted*) *to abut on a property,* (*formal*) be next to a property. □ **lindar**

abysmal [ə'bizml] *adj.* **1** very deep: *abysmal ignorance; she showed an abysmal lack of interest in politics.* □ **abismal**

2 *the weather was abysmal,* very bad. □ **pésimo**

abyss [ə'bis] *n.* (*pl. abysses*) very deep hole which appears to have no bottom; very deep part of the sea. □ **abismo; zona abisal**

acacia [ə'keiʃə] *n.* common tropical tree which produces gum. □ **acacia**

academic [ækə'demik] *adj.* **1** abstract (idea): *the question is only academic,* it will never be put into practice; *he did it out of purely academic interest,* not for any practical purpose. □ **teórico**

2 relating to study, especially at a university: *psychology has become an academic discipline,* it is a subject studied seriously at university. □ **académico**

academic staff, teaching staff at university. □ **personal académico; profesorado**

academic textbook, book used at university. □ **manual universitario**

academic training, study at university. □ **enseñanza superior**

the academic community, university teachers. □ **comunidad académica**

■ *n.* university teacher: *the Minister of Education is not liked by academics.* □ **profesor universitario**

academically *adv.* referring to academic matters/to teaching at university: *he is an unpleasant man, but brilliant academically.* □ **académicamente**

academy [ə'kædəmi] *n.* (*pl. academies*) **1** specialized teaching establishment; (*in Scotland*) selective secondary school. □ **academia**

military academy, training school for army officers. □ **academia militar**

academy of music, school for musicians. □ **conservatorio**

2 society for the promotion of art/science, etc. □ **academia**

accede [ək'si:d] *v.* **1** *to accede to the throne,* to become king or queen. □ **subir**

2 *to accede to a request,* to agree. □ **acceder**

accelerate [æk'seləreit] *v.* to make something go faster; to go faster: *instead of slowing down at the cross-*

roads he accelerated. □ **acelerar**

acceleration [ækselə'reiʃn] *n.* going faster: *the rate of acceleration of a rocket is enormous.* □ **aceleración**

accelerator *n.* pedal (in a car) which allows more petrol into the engine, and therefore increases speed: *he put his foot down on the accelerator.* □ **acelerador**

accent ['æksənt] *n.* **1** way of pronouncing: *he speaks with an Irish accent.* □ **acento**

2 small sign over a letter to show that it is pronounced differently: *acute accent* (é). □ **acento**

3 stress: *the accent today is on youth.* □ **énfasis**

accentuate [ək'sentjueit] *v.* to stress/to make more obvious: *when he spoke in public, his German accent was accentuated; the background music accentuates the drama of the scene.* □ **acentuar**

accept [ək'sept] *v.* **1** to take (something which is offered): *he had no cash, but the salesman accepted a cheque; I would like you to accept this small gift; he has accepted a job in the Post Office.* □ **aceptar**

2 to agree (to do something): *I have invited thirty people to the party and they have all accepted.* □ **aceptar**

3 *it is an accepted custom,* it is something which is usually done. □ **costumbre aceptada**

acceptable *adj.* which you can easily accept: *she received a very acceptable little cheque.* □ **agradable**

acceptance *n.* **1** receiving (of something offered). □ **aceptación**

2 agreement (to do something): *he wrote back immediately with his acceptance of the invitation; she signed a copy of the contract to signify her acceptance of the terms.* □ **aceptación**

access ['ækses] *n.* **1** way of getting to someone, somewhere. □ **acceso**

access road, road leading off a main road to buildings. □ **acceso, entrada**

to have easy access to something, to be able to get it easily. □ **tener fácil acceso a algo**

2 *the island is very **easy of access,*** it is easy to get to the island. □ **de fácil acceso**

3 *I have access to all the files on your case,* I can consult all the files. □ **acceso**

accessible [ək'sesibl] *adj.* able to be reached: *the sparking plugs are easily accessible; she is a very accessible sort of person,* one can easily see and talk to her. □ **accesible**

accession [ək'seʃn] *n.* ***accession (to the throne),*** becoming king or queen. □ **subida (al trono)**

accessions *n. pl.* new books added to a library. □ **adquisiciones**

accessory [ək'sesəri] *n.* (*pl. accessories*) **1** piece of minor equipment which is added to main items of equipment: *he has bought a complete skiing outfit with all the accessories; a camera with its accessories.* □ **accesorio**

accessory bag, bag for carrying extra items to attach to a camera. □ **bolsa de accesorios**

2 non-essential items of clothing: *she has a brown suit with matching accessories,* handbag, gloves, hat, etc. which match the suit in colour and style. □ **complementos**

3 *he was charged with being an accessory to the crime,* with helping to commit the crime. □ **cómplice**

■ *adj.* non-essential: *accessory items.* □ **accesorio**

accident ['æksidənt] *n.* something which happens by chance, often with unfortunate results: *my meeting her at the bus stop was a pure accident; I discovered the documents quite by accident; a road accident held up traffic for two hours; fatal accident,* accident where someone is killed; *drive carefully - make sure you don't have an accident.* □ **accidente**

accidental [æksi'dentl] *adj.* by accident: *our meeting was quite accidental; accidental death.* □ **casual; accidental**

■ *n.* (*in music*) additional sharp, flat, or natural. □ **accidente**

accidentally *adv.* by accident; not on purpose: *I accidentally gave away the secret; she accidentally knocked over a vase; he was killed accidentally.* □ **sin querer; por/en accidente**

accident-prone *adj.* (person) who is likely to have a lot of accidents. □ **propenso a los accidentes**

acclaim [ə'kleim] *n.* great shout of praise: *he was chosen sportsman of the year by popular acclaim.* □ **aclamación**

■ *v.* to greet with a shout of praise: *he was acclaimed the hero of the match.* □ **aclamar**

acclamation [æklə'meiʃn] *n.* act of acclaiming: *the queen bowed to the acclamation of the crowd.* □ **aclamación**

acclimatize [ə'klaimətaiz] *Amer.* **acclimate** [ə'klaimət] *v.* to make (something/someone) used to a new climate or a new way of living: *it is difficult for some people to become acclimatized to living in hot countries/to working at night.* □ **aclimatar**

acclimatization [əklaimətai'zeiʃn] *Amer.* **acclimation** [əklai'meiʃn] *n.* act of becoming acclimatized. □ **aclimatación**

accolade ['ækəleid] *n.* sign of praise; giving of a knighthood to someone. □ **acolada**

accommodate [ə'kəmədeit] *v.* **1** to adapt; to supply (someone) with something. □ **acomodar**

2 to provide lodging for (someone): *the hotel can accommodate sixty visitors.* □ **alojar**

accommodating *adj.* helpful; giving satisfaction: *they're very accommodating in this shop,* they do everything they can to help the customers; *he's very accomodating,* he is always ready to help. □ **complaciente; servicial**

accommodation [əkəmə'deiʃn] *n.* **1** place to live/to sleep: *we have no sleeping accommodation; all the accommodation in the town has been booked; at the time of the Olympic Games, visitors found it difficult to get accommodation.* □ **alojamiento**

2 agreement/compromise: *they came to an accommodation,* they settled their differences. □ **acuerdo**

accompany [ə'kʌmpni] *v.* (*accompanied; accompanying*)

1 to go with: *will you accompany me to the Post Office? there is a white sauce to accompany the fish,* the sauce is to be served with the fish. □ **acompañar**

2 to play (usually the piano) while someone sings or plays another instrument: *the singer accompanied herself on the harp,* she sang and played the harp at the same time. □ **acompañar**

accompaniment *n.* **1** something which accompanies. □ **acompañamiento**

2 music played to accompany a singer, etc.: *the piano accompaniment was so loud you couldn't hear the soloist.* □ **acompañamiento**

accompanist *n.* person who accompanies a singer, etc.: *the piano accompanist was a little girl of twelve.* □ **acompañante**

accomplice [ə'kʌmplis] *n.* person who helps another person commit a crime. □ **cómplice**

accomplish [ə'kʌmpliʃ] *v.* to finish/to carry out (a plan, etc.): *what have you accomplished by all these changes?,* what has been the result of the changes? *he has worked for years, but accomplished nothing.*

□ **realizar; lograr**
accomplished *adj.* gifted/talented; skilled: *he is an accomplished pianist; all his children are very accomplished.* □ **consumado; dotado**
accomplishments *n. pl.* talents: *he has many accomplishments,* he is talented in many ways. □ **dotes**
accord [əˈkɔːd] *n.* **1** agreement. □ **acuerdo**
with one accord, all together/in agreement: *with one accord the members of Parliament attacked the proposal.* □ **de común acuerdo**
2 ***of your own accord,*** spontaneously/with no prompting: *of his own accord he gave up his job and became a priest.* □ **espontáneamente**
accordance *n.* ***in accordance with*** *your instructions,* following your instructions; *in accordance with rule 23, he was not allowed to vote.* □ **de acuerdo con**
accordingly *adv.* in consequence: *I read my instructions and acted accordingly,* I did what the instructions said; *accordingly the play was cancelled.* □ **en consecuencia**
according to *adv.* **1** as someone says or writes; as stated by someone: *according to the police, Mr Jones left the country on Friday; according to the instructions, you simply push this button; according to Shakespeare, Richard III killed the little princes.* □ **según**
2 by/in relation to: *separate the children into groups according to their ages; pile up the books according to size.* □ **según**
accordion [əˈkɔːdiən] *n.* **(*piano*)** ***accordion,*** small musical instrument with a bellows and a keyboard. □ **acordeón**
accordionist *n.* person who plays an accordion. □ **acordeonista**
accost [əˈkɔst] *v.* to go/to come up to and speak to (someone): *the girl accosted me in the street.* □ **abordar**
account [əˈkaunt] *n.* **1** story/description: *the newspaper carried a full account of the accident.* □ **narración, versión**
by all accounts, *it was a very difficult meeting,* according to what everyone said. □ **a decir de todos**
2 statement of money: *they send their account at the end of the month.* □ **saldo**
bank account, money deposited in a bank: *I want to open a bank account; I've only got $10 in my account.* □ **cuenta bancaria**
current account, account from which you can draw money without giving notice, but which does not pay interest. □ **cuenta corriente**
deposit account, account where you leave money for some time and on which interest is paid. □ **cuenta a plazo**
expense account, money which a businessman is allowed to spend on entertainment and personal expenses which are paid for by his firm. □ **cuenta de gastos**
savings account, account where you put money regularly. □ **cuenta de ahorros**
3 *to have an account with a shop,* to have an arrangement where the shop allows you credit on items bought and sends you a total bill every month; *put it on my account; charge it to my account.* □ **cuenta**
4 *to pay a sum of money* ***on account,*** to pay part of the total bill in advance. □ **a cuenta**
5 ***accounts*** *(of a firm),* statement showing the financial position of a firm: *the sum is put down as a loss in the company accounts.* □ **cuentas**
6 *he turned the accident to account,* he was able to profit from the accident. □ **ventaja**
7 ***to call to account:*** *he was called to account,* he was asked to explain. □ **pedir cuentas**
8 *she gave a good account of herself,* she came out of the game/examination, etc., very well. □ **salir bien parado**
9 ***to take something into account,*** to make allowances for something: *you have to take into account the fact that he is almost blind.* □ **tener algo en cuenta**
10 ***on account of,*** because of: *aircraft could not take off on account of the snow-storm; I was worried on her account,* I was afraid something might happen to her. □ **por; a causa de**
11 ***on no account*** *must you go into the garden,* do not go into the garden under any circumstances. □ **de ninguna manera**
12 *he is acting* ***on his own account,*** he is working on his own initiative/for himself. □ **por su cuenta**
■ *v.* to explain: *can you account for the discrepancies between the two sets of figures?* □ **explicar**
there's no accounting for taste, people's tastes differ and you should not try to explain why. □ **sobre gustos no hay nada escrito**
accountable *adj.* responsible: *he is accountable to the directors for all the cash.* □ **responsable**
accountancy *n.* theory/profession of being an accountant: *when he left school he took up accountancy; she is taking examinations in accountancy.* □ **contabilidad**
accountant *n.* person who deals with the accounts (of a company): *Mr Smith is the chief accountant.* □ **contable**
chartered accountant, person who has passed high-level examinations in accountancy. □ **censor jurado de cuentas**
accounting *n.* accountancy. □ **contabilidad**
accoutrements [əˈkuːtrəmənts] *n. pl.* (usually bulky or complicated) equipment which is carried. □ **pertrechos**
accredit [əˈkredit] *v.* to authorize: *he is our accredited representative; the ambassador is accredited to the Russian Government,* he has been authorized by his own government to represent them in Russia. □ **acreditar**
accretion [əˈkriːʃn] *n.* increase in size by gradual additions. □ **aumento gradual**
accrue [əˈkruː] *v.* to increase by addition: *accrued interest.* □ **acumular**
accumulate [əˈkjuːmjuleit] *v.* to pile up: *he accumulated a fortune; the ice had accumulated on the wings.* □ **acumular**
accumulation [əkjuːmjuˈleiʃn] *n.* act of accumulating; pile/heap: *his only interest was the accumulation of money; the accumulation of ice on the wings forced the plane to land.* □ **acumulación**
accumulator *n.* electric battery which can be recharged. □ **acumulador**
accurate [ˈækjurət] *adj.* completely correct: *the time signal on the radio is always accurate.* □ **exacto**
accuracy *n.* being accurate; complete correctness: *he hit the target with remarkable accuracy; I am beginning to doubt the accuracy of that statement.* □ **exactitud**
accurately *adv.* very correctly: *he accurately describes life in the back streets of London.* □ **exactamente, con precisión**
accuse [əˈkjuːz] *v.* to say that someone has done something wrong: *the police accused him of stealing the car.* □ **acusar**
accusation [ækjuˈzeiʃn] *n.* saying that someone has done something wrong: *the accusation of corruption*

is quite unjustified. □ **acusación**
accusative [ə'kju:zətiv] *adj.* and *n.* (*in grammar*) case which shows the object of a verb: *in the phrase 'he hit her,' 'her' is in the accusative.* □ **acusativo**
accused *n.* person who has been accused of a crime: *will the accused please stand.* □ **acusado**
accuser *n.* person who accuses someone: *at last he turned to face his accusers.* □ **acusador**
accusing *adj. she answered in an accusing tone,* as if she was accusing. □ **acusatorio**
accusingly *adv.* as if accusing: *he pointed at her accusingly.* □ **en forma acusadora**

accustom [ə'kʌstəm] *v.* to make (someone) used to (something): *he was accustomed to having servants about the house; you must accustom yourself to working in a noisy office; are you getting accustomed to the smell? I'm quite accustomed to long train journeys.* □ **acostumbrar(se)**

ace [eis] *n.* **1** playing card which shows only one spot: *the ace of diamonds.* □ **as**
2 person who is very brilliant at doing something: *he is an ace pilot; John Smith, the American ace.* □ **as**
3 (*in tennis*) a shot which your opponent cannot return: *he served two aces in a row.* □ **'ace'**

acerbity [ə'sə:biti] *n.* (*formal*) sharpness (of flavour/character): *he answered the letter with some acerbity.* □ **acritud**

acetate ['æsiteit] *n.* type of manmade fibre. □ **acetato**

acetic [ə'si:tik] *adj.* referring to vinegar: *acetic acid.* □ **acético**

acetone ['æsitəun] *n.* colourless liquid, used to dissolve solids. □ **acetona**

acetylene [ə'setili:n] *n.* gas which burns with a very bright light. □ **acetileno**
acetylene welding, welding using acetylene. □ **soldadura de acetileno**
acetylene torch, torch used for acetylene welding. □ **soplete oxiacetilénico**

ache [eik] *n.* **1** pain: *I've got a tummy ache,* a pain in my stomach: (*see* **toothache, headache,** *etc.*). □ **dolor**
2 *I'm full of aches and pains,* I feel pains all over. □ **lleno de goteras**
■ *v.* to hurt: *my back aches.* □ **doler**
aching *adj.* which hurts: *my aching feet; an aching tooth.* □ **dolorido**

achieve [ə'tʃi:v] *v.* to succeed (in doing something); to reach (a goal): *he achieved popular success only late in life; he will never achieve anything; he achieved the miracle of scoring four goals in ten minutes.* □ **lograr, conseguir**
achievement *n.* what you achieve; successful undertaking/exploit: *we are reading about the achievements of nineteenth century explorers; the scientific achievements of the Russians.* □ **éxito; logro**

Achilles' heel [ə'kili:z'hi:l] *n.* weak spot. □ **talón de Aquiles**

acid ['æsid] *n.* usually liquid chemical substance which contains hydrogen, corrodes some metals, and turns litmus paper red: *sulphuric acid; nitric acid.* □ **ácido**
acid drops, boiled sweets with a sharp taste. □ **caramelos ácidos**
the acid test, test which will show the true value of something. □ **prueba de fuego**
■ *adj.* **1** bitter/unpleasant: *he made some very acid remarks.* □ **ácido**
2 *acid soil,* soil with much acid. □ **suelo ácido**
acidity [ə'siditi] *n.* **1** acid contents: *the acidity of the soil.* □ **acidez**
2 bitterness. □ **amargura**

acknowledge [ək'nɔlidʒ] *v.* **1** to admit (that something is true): *I acknowledge that he's a charming man; he acknowledged he was beaten/he acknowledged defeat.* □ **reconocer**
2 to reply: *have you acknowledged this letter?,* have you replied to say that you have received this letter? □ **acusar recibo**
acknowledgement *n.* admission (that something is true); reply stating that you have received something: *my letter has not had any acknowledgement,* no one has replied to it. □ **reconocimiento; acuse de recibo**
acknowledgements, (*at the beginning of a book*) the list of people the author wants to thank for their help. □ **agradecimientos**

acme ['ækmi] *n.* highest point: *the acme of perfection.* □ **apogeo**

acne ['ækni] *n.* skin disease, with spots on the face/neck, etc. □ **acné**

acolyte ['ækəlait] *n.* person who helps a priest during religious ceremonies. □ **acólito**

aconite ['ækənait] *n.* small spring flower which is poisonous. □ **acónito**

acorn ['eikɔ:n] *n.* fruit of an oak tree. □ **bellota**

acoustic [ə'ku:stik] *adj.* referring to sound. □ **acústico**
acoustic guitar, ordinary guitar (as opposed to an electric guitar). □ **guitarra acústica**
■ *n.* ***acoustics,*** (i) study of sound. □ **acústica**
(ii) ability to carry sound without distortion: *the acoustics in the concert hall are perfect.* □ **acústica**

acquaint [ə'kweint] *v.* **1** to inform: *to acquaint someone with the facts; are you acquainted with the real reason for the divorce?* □ **informar**
2 ***to be acquainted with someone/something,*** to know someone/something: *I'm slightly acquainted with her,* I know her slightly. □ **conocer**
3 *we must* ***get acquainted,*** we must get to know each other better. □ **conocerse**
acquaintance *n.* **1** knowing: *you must make the acquaintance of our new bank manager; when did you first make her acquaintance?* □ **(conocer)**
2 person you know: *he's one of my acquaintances; they have a wide circle of acquaintances,* they know a lot of people. □ **conocido**

acquiesce [ækwi'es] *v.* (*formal*) to agree: *he acquiesced to the kidnappers' demands.* □ **consentir**
acquiescence *n.* agreement. □ **aquiescencia**

acquire [ə'kwaiə] *v.* to obtain/to get into your possession: *he has acquired a house in the country; she acquired the habit of smoking a pipe.* □ **adquirir**
acquisition [ækwi'ziʃn] *n.* **1** act of acquiring. □ **adquisición**
2 thing which you have acquired: *let me show you my latest acquisition.* □ **adquisición**
acquisitive [ə'kwizitiv] *adj.* always ready to acquire things. □ **ávido**

acquit [ə'kwit] *v.* (*he acquitted*) **1** to decide that someone is innocent: *he was acquitted of the charge of murder.* □ **absolver**
2 *he acquitted himself well,* he did well. □ **defenderse bien**
acquittal *n.* decision that a person is innocent. □ **absolución**

acre *n.* unit for measuring the area of land (4,840 square yards or 0.4 hectare). □ **acre**
acreage ['eikridʒ] *n.* area in acres: *what is the acreage of this farm?* □ **área en acres**

acrid ['ækrid] *adj.* bitter/pungent (smell). □ **acre**

acrimonious [ækri'mouniəs] *adj.* bitter (argument): *the discussion became acrimonious.* □ **agrio**
acrimony ['ækriməni] *n.* bitterness (of argument). □ **acritud**
acrobat ['ækrəbæt] *n.* person who does spectacular physical exercises (especially in a circus/on a tightrope). □ **acróbata**
acrobatic [ækrə'bætik] *adj.* referring to spectacular exercises (as on a tightrope): *they executed a very acrobatic dance.* □ **acrobático**
acronym ['ækrənim] *n.* word (like *NATO*) formed from the initials of other words. □ **sigla**
across [ə'krɔs] *adv.* and *prep.* **1** from one side to the other: *don't run across the road; the bridge goes across the river; go across the bridge.* □ **a través de**
2 *the lake is 500 metres across,* 500 metres wide. □ **de ancho**
3 on the other side: *the church is just across the road; he lives across the street from us.* □ **al otro lado de**
4 *to come/run across: I came/ran across this in a junk shop,* I found it in a junk shop. □ **encontrarse**
acrostic [ə'kroustik] *n.* poem/puzzle in which the first letters of each line form a word. □ **acróstico**
acrylic [ə'krilik] *adj.* and *n.* (synthetic material/ paint) made from acid: *to paint in acrylics; acrylic fibre.* □ **acrílico**
act [ækt] *n.* **1** something which is done: *act of kindness.* □ **acto**
to catch someone in the act: *we caught him in the act,* as he was doing it. □ **'con las manos en la masa'**
2 *Act (of Parliament),* law voted by Parliament. □ **ley**
3 large section of a play: *most of Shakespeare's plays have five acts.* □ **acto**
■ *v.* **1** to play (a part in a play): *he once acted in 'Hamlet' at school.* □ **actuar**
2 *he's only* ***play-acting,*** only pretending. □ **...haciendo teatro**
3 *stop acting the fool,* stop being silly. □ **deja de hacer el tonto**
4 to do something: *you must act at once or your father will be put in prison.* □ **actuar**
5 *I'm acting on behalf of the road-safety committee,* I'm representing the committee. □ **representar a...**
to act as *she's acting as my secretary,* she's doing the work of a secretary for me. □ **hacer de**
6 to behave: *he started acting very strangely.* □ **comportarse**
7 to take effect/to work: *this medicine acts very quickly.* □ **actuar**
acting *adj. acting chairman,* person who is taking the place of the chairman. □ **en funciones**
■ *n.* profession of an actor: *she's decided on acting as a career.* □ **interpretación (teatro, cine)**
action ['ækʃn] *n.* **1** doing: *I knew she was a good cook, but I'd never seen her in action before.* □ **acción**
out of action: *our television is out of action,* it is not working. □ **averiado**
2 thing done: *he is beginning to regret his action.* □ **acción**
actions speak louder than words, it is better to do something than just to talk about it. □ **obras son amores, que no buenas razones**
3 *the action of the play,* what happens in the play. □ **argumento, acción**
action!, (*when filming*) start acting. □ **¡acción!**
4 *this watch has a ten-jewel action,* mechanism. □ **mecanismo**
5 lawsuit: *he is bringing an action for libel against the newspaper.* □ **pleito**
6 warfare: *our troops have been in action against the guerillas; they saw action in the Near East,* they fought in the Near East; *he was killed in action,* he was killed on the battle-field. □ **combate**
actionable *adj.* (something) for which someone could bring a lawsuit against you: *I think the newspaper report is actionable.* □ **procesable**
active ['æktiv] *adj.* **1** vigorous/agile: *he has an active brain; even though he's only got one leg, he's still very active; he took an active part in the demonstration.* □ **activo**
2 *active volcano,* which still erupts. □ **en actividad**
3 *he's on active service,* (*of a soldier*) he is on the battlefront. □ **activo**
activate ['æktiveit] *v.* to put into action. □ **activar**
activist *n.* person who actively supports a political policy. □ **activista**
activity [æk'tiviti] *n.* (*pl. activities*) **1** movement/ being active. □ **actividad**
2 *there is a lot of activity in the street,* there are a great many people coming and going. □ **actividad**
3 occupation: *spare time activities.* □ **ocupación**
actor ['æktə] **actress** ['æktrəs] *n.* person who acts in the theatre/films/on television. □ **actor, actriz**
actual ['æktjuəl] *adj.* real: *I want the actual figures, not just the estimates.* □ **real**
in actual fact, really. □ **en realidad**
actuality [æktju'æliti] *n.* reality. □ **realidad**
actually *adv.* really: *he works as a teacher, but actually he is a spy; what I actually said was....* □ **de hecho; realmente**
actuary ['æktjuəri] *n.* (*pl. actuaries*) person who calculates insurance rates. □ **actuario**
actuarial [æktju'ɛəriəl] *adj. actuarial tables,* tables showing statistics of risk (for insurance calculations). □ **tablas actuariales**
actuate ['æktjueit] *v.* to set in motion/to start off: *she was actuated by insane jealousy.* □ **impulsar**
acumen ['ækju:men] *n.* ability to make shrewd decisions: *business acumen.* □ **agudeza**
acupuncture ['ækjupʌŋktʃə] *n.* way of healing and curing by pricking the body with needles. □ **acupuntura**
acute [ə'kju:t] *adj.* **1** very sharp (angle): *acute-angled triangle.* □ **agudo**
2 sudden serious (illness/pain): *he has acute appendicitis.* □ **agudo**
3 perceptive: *she has a very acute sense of hearing.* □ **fino**
acuteness *n.* sharpness (of pain); seriousness (of illness); clearness (of hearing). □ **intensidad; gravedad; agudeza**
ad [æd] *n.* (*informal*) advertisement: *put an ad in the paper.* □ **anuncio**
small ads, small advertisements for staff/articles for sale, etc. □ **anuncios por palabras**
AD ['ei'di:] *abbreviation for* Anno Domini (*Latin for* in the year of our Lord) (used to indicate dates after the birth of Christ): *William I became king in 1066 AD.* □ **d.C. (después de Cristo)**
Adam ['ædəm] *n. I don't know him from Adam,* (*informal*) I haven't any idea who he is. □ **no le conozco ni por asomo**
Adam's apple, lump in the front of a man's neck, below the chin. □ **nuez**
adamant ['ædəmənt] *adj.* fixed in your opinion/intentions: *she's adamant about it,* she will not change her mind. □ **inflexible**
adapt [ə'dæpt] *v.* **1** to change (something) so that it fits; to make (something) more suitable: *to adapt a novel for television,* write a television script based on a novel. □ **adaptar**

2 *he adapts easily,* he can easily change his way of life/way of working to fit new circumstances. □ **adaptarse**
adaptability [ədæptə'biliti] *n.* ease of adapting yourself to new circumstances. □ **adaptabilidad**
adaptable *adj. he is very adaptable,* he can easily change to fit new circumstances. □ **adaptable**
adaptation [ædæp'teiʃn] *n.* written work which is adapted from another: *he was working on an adaptation of 'War and Peace' for a TV serial.* □ **adaptación**
adapter/adaptor *n.* electric plug which allows several plugs to be fitted to the same socket; small disc which allows a record with a large central hole to be fitted on a turntable. □ **adaptador**
add [æd] *v.* **1** to join (something to something else): *to add an extension to a house; this just adds further problems to our accounts; add some more water to the soup.* □ **añadir**
2 to say/to write something more: *she added a note at the end of her letter; the policeman said Mr Jones was speeding, and added that his lights were not working either.* □ **agregar**
3 to make a total: *can you add these numbers together? if you add two and two you get four.* □ **sumar**
addendum [ə'dendəm] *n.* (*pl. addenda*) piece added, as at the end of a book. □ **apéndice**
adding machine *n.* machine for adding figures. □ **calculadora**
add up *v.* **1** to make a total of figures: *if you add up the figures you should get a thousand.* □ **sumar**
2 *these figures don't add up,* the total given is incorrect. □ **cuadrar**
3 ***to add up to:*** *all this doesn't add up to very much,* it is not very important. □ **significar**
adder ['ædə] *n.* viper, a poisonous snake. □ **víbora**
addict ['ædikt] *n.* person who cannot stop himself from doing something (usually which is harmful to himself). □ **adicto**
drug addict, someone who cannot stop taking a drug. □ **drogadicto**
TV addict, someone who is always watching television. □ **teleadicto**
addicted [ə'diktid] *adj.* **1** (person) who cannot stop (taking a drug): *she's addicted to gin.* □ **adicto**
2 *I'm addicted to cartoons,* I like them very much. □ **enviciado con...**
addiction [ə'dikʃn] *n. drug addiction,* inability to stop taking a drug. □ **adicción**
addictive *adj.* which causes addiction. □ **adictivo**
addition [ə'diʃn] *n.* **1** act of adding: *he enlarged his house by the addition of two bedrooms.* □ **adición**
in addition, added to this; also: *in addition we must save more money.* □ **además**
2 thing added: *we have two new additions to the staff.* □ **incorporación**
additional *adj.* **1** further: *an additional reason.* □ **adicional**
2 *additional staff,* more staff. □ **personal adicional**
additive ['æditiv] *n.* substance, usually chemical, which is added. □ **aditivo**
addled ['ædld] *adj.* rotten (egg). □ **podrido**
address [ə'dres] *n.* (*pl. addresses*) **1** number of house, name of street, town, county, etc., where a person lives/where an office is situated, etc.: *my address is 15 Vale Road.* □ **dirección**
address book, book containing a list of addresses. □ **agenda**
2 formal speech: *the Mayor gave an address at the prizegiving ceremony.* □ **discurso**
■ *v.* **1** to write the name and address of the person/the firm to whom something is being sent: *the letter is addressed to me; you haven't addressed the envelope properly.* □ **dirigir, poner la dirección**
2 to speak to someone: *he addressed the crowd in fluent French.* □ **dirigirse**
addressee [ædre'si:] *n.* person to whom a letter is addressed. □ **destinatario**
adduce [ə'dju:s] *v.* (*formal*) to bring added proof (of something). □ **aducir**
adenoids ['ædənɔidz] *n. pl.* small growths in the back of the throat. □ **vegetaciones (adenoideas)**
adept ['ædept] *adj.* clever: *he's adept at opening bottles.* □ **experto**
■ *n.* person who is clever at doing something: *she's an adept in/at swimming.* □ **experto**
adequate ['ædikwət] *adj.* enough: *do you think the salary is adequate? I simply do not get adequate help.* □ **suficiente**
adequately *adv.* enough: *he has been adequately punished.* □ **suficientemente**
adhere [əd'hiə] *v.* to stick: *the paper doesn't adhere to the walls; he adheres to his decision; do you still adhere to your promise?* □ **adherirse**
adherence *n.* sticking/attachment. □ **adherencia**
adherent *n.* person who belongs to (a society, etc.): *he is an adherent of a small religious sect.* □ **miembro**
adhesion [əd'hi:ʒn] *n.* attachment/sticking; ability to stick: *the glue lacks adhesion.* □ **adhesión**
adhesive [əd'hi:ziv] *adj.* which sticks. □ **adhesivo**
adhesive tape, plastic tape which sticks. □ **cinta adhesiva**
adhesive plaster, material which is used to stick bandages to cover wounds. □ **esparadrapo**
■ *n.* glue: *have you another pot of adhesive?* □ **cola**
ad hoc [æd'hɔk] *adj.* which applies to a particular case: *an ad hoc meeting,* meeting called specially to discuss a particular problem. □ **ad hoc**
adipose ['ædipous] *adj.* fatty: *adipose tissue.* □ **adiposo**
adjacent [ə'dʒeisənt] *adj.* next to/touching/side by side: *adjacent land; his garden is adjacent to mine.* □ **adyacente, contiguo**
adjective ['ædʒəktiv] *n.* word used to describe a noun: *in the phrase 'a big green door', 'big' and 'green' are adjectives.* □ **adjetivo**
adjectival [ædʒek'taivl] *adj.* used like an adjective. □ **adjetival**
adjectivally *adv.* like an adjective: *in the phrase 'watch strap' the word 'watch' is used adjectivally.* □ **adjetivadamente**
adjoin [ə'dʒɔin] *v.* to be next to something/to touch something: *he leapt over the fence into the adjoining garden; they got up and went into the adjoining room.* □ **estar contiguo**
adjourn [ə'dʒə:n] *v.* **1** to put off (a meeting) to a later date: *we will adjourn the discussion until next Thursday.* □ **aplazar**
2 *the meeting adjourned at 13.45,* the meeting stopped at 13.45 (but would meet again later). □ **...se aplazó...**
3 *let's adjourn to the bar,* let's stop talking here and continue in the bar. □ **pasemos al bar**
adjournment *n.* putting off (a meeting) to a later date. □ **aplazamiento**
adjudicate [ə'dʒu:dikeit] *v.* to give a decision (in a dispute); to be the judge (in a competition). □ **dictaminar**
adjudication [ədʒu:di'keiʃn] *n.* decision (in a dispute); judging (of a competition). □ **fallo; dictamen**
adjudicator [ə'dʒu:dikeitə] *n.* judge (in a show). □ **jurado**

adjunct ['ædʒʌŋkt] *n.* something additional (to something). □ **adjunto**

adjust [ə'dʒʌst] *v.* to put right by making a slight change: *please adjust your watches as the time in London is one hour behind Paris; she adjusted her scarf.* □ **ajustar**

adjustable *adj.* which can be changed slightly: *adjustable lamp; adjustable chair.* □ **ajustable**

adjustment *n.* slight change to (a mechanism, etc.): *I have to make some adjustments to the engine; the government is proposing adjustments to the tax structure.* □ **ajuste**

adjutant ['ædʒətənt] *n.* army officer who assists in administration. □ **asistente**

ad-lib ['æd'lib] *v.* (*he ad-libbed*) (*informal*) to speak without a script. □ **improvisar**

administer [əd'ministə] *v.* **1** to govern/to rule (a country/an office); to run (a company/an estate). □ **administrar**

2 *to administer an oath to someone,* to make someone swear an oath. □ **tomar juramento**

3 *to administer justice,* to give justice. □ **administrar justicia**

administration [ədmini'streiʃn] *n.* ruling (of a country): *under the present administration,* under the present government. □ **administración**

administrative *adj.* which administers: *she has excellent administrative qualities.* □ **administrativo**

administrator *n.* someone who rules/governs: *he's an excellent administrator.* □ **administrador**

admirable ['ædmərəbl] *adj. see* **admire.**

admiral ['ædmərəl] *n.* highest ranking officer in the navy. □ **almirante**

red admiral, type of red and black butterfly. □ **nínfalo**

the Admiralty *n.* the British government department dealing with the navy. □ **Almirantazgo**

admire [əd'maiə] *v.* to look at (something) with pleasure: *he was admiring my new car; I admire his courage.* □ **admirar**

admirable ['ædmərəbl] *adj.* remarkable; excellent: *she showed admirable restraint.* □ **admirable**

admirably *adv.* remarkably; excellently: *the meal was admirably served.* □ **admirablemente**

admiration [ædmə'reiʃn] *n.* feeling of pride/pleasure: *I have nothing but admiration for his work.* □ **admiración**

admirer [əd'maiərə] *n.* person who admires: *I think she's got a secret admirer.* □ **admirador**

admiring *adj.* showing admiration: *she gave him an admiring look.* □ **admirativo**

admiringly *adv.* full of pride and pleasure: *she looked admiringly at her son.* □ **admirativamente**

admission [əd'miʃn] *n.* **1** being allowed to enter: *admission to the show is free.* □ **admisión; entrada**

no admission, no one can enter. □ **prohibida la entrada**

2 saying that something is true: *his admission that he had lied.* □ **reconocimiento**

admissible [əd'misibl] *adj.* (evidence) that can be admitted. □ **admisible**

admit [əd'mit] *v.* (*he admitted*) **1** to allow to enter: *ticket which admits one person; children are not admitted to this film.* □ **admitir**

2 to say that something is true: *he admitted he was wrong.* □ **reconocer**

3 to accept (evidence/idea, etc.). □ **admitir**

admittance *n.* entrance: *no admittance except on business; he gained admittance by bribing the doorkeeper.* □ **entrada**

admittedly *adv.* according to general opinion: *admittedly, he is something of a crook.* □ **cierto es que...**

admixture [æd'mikstʃə] *n.* something which is added to make a mixture. □ **ingrediente**

admonish [əd'mɔniʃ] *v.* to scold someone/to tell someone off: *the judge admonished the prisoner.* □ **amonestar**

admonition [ædmə'niʃn] *n.* scolding. □ **amonestación**

ado [ə'du:] *n.* ***without any more ado,*** without making any more fuss. □ **alharaca; bulla**

much ado about nothing, a lot of fuss for nothing. □ **mucho ruido y pocas nueces**

adolescence [ædə'lesns] *n.* period between childhood and being an adult. □ **adolescencia**

adolescent *adj.* and *n.* (referring to) young person between child and adult. □ **adolescente**

adopt [ə'dɔpt] *v.* **1** to take (someone) legally as your son or daughter: *they have adopted two children; he has two daughters and an adopted son.* □ **adoptar**

2 to follow/to take up (a line of argument); to put on (an air): *he adopted the line that the money should not have been spent in the first place; she adopted a supercilious air.* □ **adoptar**

3 to prescribe (a book) for use in class. □ **mandar, poner**

adoption [ə'dɔpʃn] *n.* **1** legal taking of a child as your own. □ **adopción**

2 prescribing (of a book) for use in class. □ **elección (de texto)**

adoptive *adj.* who has (been) adopted: *his adoptive son; her adoptive father.* □ **adoptivo**

adore [ə'dɔ:] *v.* to love very strongly: *she adores her son; I adore the smell of roses.* □ **adorar**

adorable *adj.* pretty/lovely: *what an adorable little house!* □ **adorable**

adoration [ædə'reiʃn] *n.* strong love/worship. □ **adoración**

adorer *n.* person who adores. □ **adorador**

adorn [ə'dɔ:n] *v.* to cover with ornaments/to decorate: *the church was adorned with flowers.* □ **adornar**

adornment *n.* ornament. □ **adorno**

adrenalin [ə'drenəlin] *n.* secretion which is produced by a gland when someone is excited/afraid: *driving fast on the motorway sends the adrenalin rushing round your system.* □ **adrenalina**

adrift [ə'drift] *adv.* **1** *to cast a boat adrift,* to let a boat float without control. □ **a la deriva**

2 *to cut yourself adrift,* to separate yourself. □ **separarse**

adroit [ə'drɔit] *adj.* skilful/clever (with your hands). □ **diestro, hábil**

adroitly *adv.* smartly. □ **hábilmente**

adulation [ædju'leiʃn] *n.* wild praise/excessive flattery: *the emperor basked in the adulation of the masses.* □ **adulación**

adult ['ædʌlt, ə'dʌlt] *adj.* and *n.* grown-up; fully grown: *he captured an adult gorilla and two young; the entrance fee for adults is $1.* □ **adulto**

adulterate [ə'dʌltəreit] *v.* to water down; to add something of inferior quality (to a substance). □ **adulterar**

adulterer [ə'dʌltərə] **adulteress** [ə'dʌltərəs] *n.* married person who has sexual intercourse with someone to whom he/she is not married. □ **adúltero(a)**

adultery *n.* (*of married person*) having sexual intercourse with someone to whom he/she is not married: *she was granted a divorce on account of her husband's adultery with his secretary.* □ **adulterio**

advance [əd'vɑ:ns] *n.* **1** forward movement: *the advance of modern technology; the battalion made an*

advance into enemy territory. □ **avance**
advance guard, troops sent forward to prepare the way for the main force. □ **avanzadilla**
2 *to arrive* ***in advance,*** to arrive early; *you must pay in advance; have you booked your room in advance? send your luggage in advance,* before you travel. □ **previamente; de antemano**
3 ***to make advances to someone,*** to try to attract someone. □ **hacer proposiciones**
4 payment made early: *can I have an advance on my salary?* □ **anticipo**
■ *v.* **1** to go forward: *the army advanced to the town.* □ **avanzar**
2 to put forward. □ **proponer**
3 *he advanced me $10,* he gave me $10 as an early payment. □ **adelantar**
advanced *adj.* **1** *advanced student,* student who has studied for several years. □ **avanzado**
2 *advanced book,* book for students who have studied for several years; *advanced biology; advanced engineering.* □ **avanzado**
3 *the season is well advanced,* the season is coming to an end; *in an advanced state of decay,* very decayed. □ **avanzado**
advancement *n.* progress (of science, etc.). □ **progreso**
advantage [əd'vɑːntidʒ] *n.* **1** something useful which will help you to be successful: *it's an advantage if you know how to type.* □ **ventaja**
to ***take advantage of:*** *he took advantage of the good weather,* he profited from the good weather. □ **aprovechar**
to take advantage of someone, to cheat someone for your own benefit. □ **aprovecharse de alguien**
2 *her dress shows off her figure* ***to advantage,*** makes her figure look perfect. □ **hacer destacar**
advantageous [ædvən'teidʒəs] *adj.* profitable/useful: *he made me an advantageous offer.* □ **ventajoso**
advent ['ædvent] *n.* **1** coming; arrival: *with the advent of value added tax, prices went up.* □ **llegada**
2 *Advent,* church season before Christmas. □ **Adviento**
adventure [əd'ventʃə] *n.* new, exciting and dangerous experience: *our boating trip was quite an adventure; he experienced many adventures on his expedition across the desert.* □ **aventura**
adventurer *n.* person who aims to make a fortune by taking risks with his money or by illegal means. □ **aventurero**
adventurous *adj.* bold (person); exciting: *he leads an adventurous life.* □ **arriesgado**
adverb ['ædvəːb] *n.* word used to describe a verb/an adjective/another adverb: *in the phrase 'he drives quickly', the word 'quickly' is an adverb.* □ **adverbio**
adverbial [əd'vəːbiəl] *adj.* used as an adverb. □ **adverbial**
adversary ['ædvəsri] *n. (pl. adversaries)* person you are fighting against. □ **adversario**
adverse ['ædvəːs] *adj.* **1** contrary. □ **adverso**
adverse winds, winds which blow against your line of travel. □ **viento de cara / en contra**
2 bad; unfavourable: *due to adverse weather conditions,* because of bad weather. □ **adverso**
adversely *adv.* badly: *the poll was adversely affected by the Minister's speech.* □ **adversamente**
adversity [əd'vəːsiti] *n.* (*pl. adversities*) difficulty: *in the end he triumphed over adversity,* he overcame the difficulties. □ **adversidad; infortunio**
advert ['ædvəːt] *n.* (*informal*) advertisement. □ **anuncio**
advertise ['ædvətaiz] *v.* **1** to show that something is for sale/to publicize something: *I'm advertising my car in the paper; he advertised for a new secretary,* put an advertisement in the paper asking people to apply for the job; *they are advertising cheap holidays in France.* □ **anunciar, poner un anuncio**
2 *there's no need to advertise the fact,* there's no need to tell everyone the secret. □ **dar publicidad**
advertisement [əd'vəːtismənt] *n.* announcement that something is for sale/is wanted: *have you seen the advertisement for washing machines? I am putting an advertisement in the paper; he answered the advertisement for a chef at the hotel.* □ **anuncio**
advertiser *n.* person who advertises something. □ **anunciante**
advertising *n.* action of announcing the sale of something; business of describing goods for sale. □ **publicidad**
advertising agency, firm which designs and places advertisements. □ **agencia de publicidad**
advice [əd'vais] *n.* **1** suggestion as to what should be done: *my advice to you is to take a long holiday; he followed my advice and went on holiday; let me give you a piece of advice.* □ **consejo**
2 ***advice note,*** paper which tells you that goods have been shipped. □ **aviso, notificación**
advise [əd'vaiz] *v.* to suggest what should be done: *the doctor advised me to take a long holiday; I would advise against it,* I would suggest that this should not be done. □ **aconsejar**
advisable *adj.* which you would recommend: *it is advisable to take plenty of warm clothing.* □ **aconsejable**
advisedly *adv.* after a lot of thought: *I say this advisedly.* □ **con conocimiento de causa**
adviser, advisor *n.* person who gives advice. □ **consejero, asesor**
advisory *adj. in an advisory capacity,* as an adviser. □ **como asesor**
advocacy ['ædvəkəsi] *n.* pleading for: *his advocacy of the cause of free speech,* his support for the cause. □ **defensa**
advocate ['ædvəkət] *n.* **1** person who pleads for a cause: *he is a great advocate of hot baths.* □ **defensor**
2 (*in Scotland*) lawyer who pleads in court. □ **procurador**
■ *v.* to recommend/to plead: *I always advocate a hot drink before going to bed.* □ **recomendar**
adze [ædz] *n.* axe with the blade at right angles to the handle. □ **azuela**
aegis ['iːdʒis] *n.* ***under the aegis of,*** (*formal*) supported by/patronized by. □ **égida**
aeon ['iːoun] *n.* very long time. □ **eón; eternidad**
aerial ['ɛəriəl] *adj.* referring to the air: *aerial bombardment,* bombardment from the air; *aerial reconnaissance.* □ **aéreo**
■ *n.* device for sending or receiving radio or television signals: *we have a TV aerial fixed to our roof.* □ **antena**
aerie ['iəri] *n. Amer. see* **eyrie.**
aerodrome ['ɛərədroum] *n.* small airfield. □ **aeródromo**
aerodynamics ['ɛərə'dai'næmiks] *n.* (usually with singular verb) science of movement of flying bodies in the air: *he's an aerodynamics specialist.* □ **aerodinámica**
aeronautical [ɛərə'nɔːtikl] *adj.* referring to aircraft flying. □ **aeronáutico**
aeronautics *n.* (*usually with singular verb*) science of flying aircraft. □ **aeronáutica**
aeroplane ['ɛərəplein] *n.* machine that flies: *the aeroplane landed at a small airfield.* □ **avión**

aerosol ['ɛərəsɔl] *n.* canister filled with a liquid and a gas under pressure, which sends out a spray when the button is pushed: *aerosol spray; aerosol paint.* □ **aerosol**
aerospace ['eərəuspeis] *n.* the space around the earth, including the atmosphere. □ **atmósfera terrestre**
aesthete ['i:sθi:t] *n.* person who appreciates beauty in art. □ **esteta**
aesthetic [i:s'θetik] *adj.* pleasing from an artistic point of view. □ **estético**
aesthetically *adv.* from an artistic point of view: *I find the painting aesthetically satisfying.* □ **estéticamente**
afar [ə fɑ:] *adv.* ***from afar,*** from a long way away. □ **desde lejos**
affable ['æfəbl] *adj.* pleasant/courteous. □ **afable**
affably *adv.* in a pleasant/friendly way: *he greeted me very affably.* □ **afablemente**
affability [æfə'biliti] *n.* pleasantness/courtesy. □ **afabilidad**
affair [ə'fɛə] *n.* **1** business: *this affair is keeping him occupied; that's my affair,* it's my business and not yours; *his affairs seem very complicated,* his business deals seem very complicated. □ **asunto; negocio**
2 *he's having an affair with her,* he's her lover. □ **aventura**
3 *in the present state of affairs,* as things are at present. □ **situación**
affect [ə'fekt] *v.* **1** to pretend/to put on: *he affected stupidity,* he pretended to be stupid. □ **fingir**
2 to touch/to change something: *the climate has affected his health; the new law affects small businesses; measles can affect the eyes.* □ **afectar**
affectation [æfek'teiʃn] *n.* pretence: *his accent is just an affectation,* his accent is put on. □ **afectación**
affected *adj.* pretended/put on: *he has a very affected style of writing.* □ **afectado**
affecting *adj.* touching/which makes you feel emotion: *what an affecting scene!* □ **conmovedor**
affection [ə'fekʃn] *n.* liking/love: *she has a great affection for her cat.* □ **afecto, cariño**
affectionate *adj.* showing love or fondness for someone: *he is a very affectionate dog.* □ **afectuoso**
affidavit [æfi'deivit] *n.* written sworn statement: *he signed an affidavit that she was his daughter.* □ **declaración jurada**
affiliate [ə'filieit] *v.* to link (a small group to a larger one): *our union is affiliated to the miners' union.* □ **afiliar**
affiliation [əfili'eiʃn] *n. political affiliation,* political link. □ **afiliación**
affinity [ə'finiti] *n.* (*pl. affinities*) closeness/similarity of character; strong attraction. □ **afinidad**
affirm [ə'fə:m] *v.* **1** to state: *he affirmed that he was at home on the night of the fire.* □ **afirmar**
2 to make a statement (in court, instead of taking the oath). □ **aseverar**
affirmation [æfə'meiʃn] *n.* statement. □ **afirmación**
affirmative [ə'fə:mətiv] *adj.* agreeing: *he gave an affirmative reply,* he said yes. □ **afirmativo**
■ *n. the answer is in the affirmative,* the answer is yes. □ **afirmativa**
affirmatively *adj. he answered affirmatively,* he answered yes. □ **afirmativamente**
afflict [ə'flikt] *v.* to torture/to torment: *he is afflicted with rheumatism.* □ **afligir**
affliction [ə'flikʃn] *n.* torment; cause of distress: *blindness is a greater affliction than deafness.* □ **aflicción**
affluence ['æfluəns] *n.* wealth. □ **riqueza**
affluent *adj.* rich. □ **acaudalado, rico**
affluent society, society where most people have enough money. □ **la sociedad opulenta**
afford [ə'fɔ:d] *v.* **1** to have enough money to pay for something: *I can't afford two holidays a year; you can't afford $20,* you haven't enough money to pay $20; *he can afford to run two cars.* □ **permitirse**
2 *I can afford to wait,* I don't mind waiting. □ **poder**
afforestation [æfɔri'steiʃn] *n.* planting of trees to make a forest. □ **forestación**
affray [ə'frei] *n.* (*formal*) fight between several people in public. □ **riña**
affront [ə'frʌnt] *n.* offence: *it's an affront to any decent person,* it offends any decent person. □ **afrenta**
■ *v.* to insult. □ **afrentar**
afield [ə'fi:ld] *adv.* ***to go far afield,*** to go a long way. □ **lejos**
aflame [ə'fleim] *adj.* (*formal*) on fire. □ **en llamas**
afloat [ə'flout] *adv.* floating: *the ship is still afloat,* the ship has not sunk yet. □ **a flote**
afoot [ə'fut] *adv.* **1** *there's a plan afoot,* a plan is being prepared. □ **en marcha**
2 *there's something afoot,* something is being plotted. □ **se está tramando algo**
afraid [ə'freid] *adj.* **1** frightened (by): *she's afraid of the dark; are you afraid of snakes?* □ **(tener) miedo**
2 sorry to have to say: *I'm afraid it is time to go; I'm afraid she's ill; I was afraid you'd be out.* □ **(temer, sentir)**
afresh [ə'freʃ] *adv.* again: *we must start afresh,* we must start all over again. □ **de nuevo**
Africa ['æfrikə] *n.* large continent between the Atlantic and Indian Oceans. □ **Africa**
African *adj.* and *n.* (person) from Africa. □ **africano**
aft [ɑ:ft] *adv.* at the back of a ship. □ **a popa**
to go aft, to go towards the stern. □ **retroceder**
after ['ɑ:ftə] *adv.* next/later: *you speak first, I'll speak after; I never spoke to him after; the day after,* the next day; *the week after.* □ **después; siguiente**
■ *prep.* **1** next to/following: *if today is Monday, the day after tomorrow is Wednesday; it's after five o'clock.* □ **después de**
2 *the police are after you,* the police are looking for you. □ **detrás de**
what's he after?, what does he want? □ **¿ qué es lo que busca?**
after you, please go first. □ **usted primero**
***after you with** the salt,* please pass me the salt when you have taken some. □ **páseme... cuando acabe**
one after the other, one following another. □ **uno detrás de otro**
■ *conj.* following the time when: *the grass turned green after the rain had fallen.* □ **después de que...**
afterbirth *n.* placenta which comes out of the womb after the birth of young. □ **placenta**
aftercare *n.* care for people after an operation, etc. □ **atención postoperatoria**
aftereffects *n. pl.* effects that follow on something: *I hope all that drink didn't have any aftereffects.* □ **efectos secundarios, consecuencias**
aftermath *n.* what takes place after a catastrophe: *in the aftermath of the typhoon hundreds of people were made homeless.* □ **repercusiones**
afternoon *n.* part of the day between 12 noon and evening: *I'll come to see you this afternoon; tomorrow afternoon; at 3 o'clock in the afternoon.* □ **tarde**
afters *n. pl.* (*in a meal*) (*informal*) sweet pudding/dessert. □ **postre**
aftersales service *n.* maintenance (of a car/a washing machine, etc.) by the manufacturer/the agent after it has been sold. □ **servicio postventa**

aftershave *n.* ***aftershave (lotion)***, lotion for soothing the face after shaving. □ **(loción) para después del afeitado**
afterthought *n.* something which you think of later: *he added, as an afterthought, that his house was for sale.* □ **ocurrencia tardía**
afterwards *adv.* after that; next/later: *we'll go shopping first, and come to see you afterwards.* □ **más tarde, después**
again [ə'gein, ə'gen] *adv.* **1** once more: *I'll sing the song again.* □ **nuevamente**
2 ***once again,*** another time. □ **una vez más**
3 *she shouted* ***again and again,*** several times. □ **una y otra vez**
4 ***now and again,*** sometimes: *he's back home again now.* □ **de vez en cuando**
5 *you must come to see us again,* you must come back to see us another time. □ **otra vez**
6 ***come again?,*** could you repeat that? □ **¿cómo? ¿qué?**
against [ə'genst] *prep.* **1** touching: *he hit his head against the branch; the ladder was leaning against the wall.* □ **con, en**
2 contrary: *it's against the rules,* it's contrary to the rules. □ **contra**
3 *he's against lending her any more money,* he's opposed to lending her money. □ **contra**
4 in contrast to: *it shows up well against a white background.* □ **sobre**
agaric [ə'gærik] *n.* type of fungus. □ **agárico**
agate ['ægət] *n.* semi-precious stone, usually with bands of different colours. □ **ágata**
age [eidʒ] *n.* **1** number of years you have lived: *what's your age next birthday? he was twelve years of age; he's still under age,* he is still below the legal age (to do something); *old age; old-age pension; age limit; she comes into the 20 to 29 age group.* □ **edad**
2 period: *the Stone Age; the Middle Ages; it is the age of the transistor radio.* □ **edad**
3 *I've been waiting here for ages,* for a very long time; *it's ages since I went to France.* □ **hace siglos**
■ *v.* to become old: *he's aged a lot since I last saw him.* □ **envejecer**
aged [eidʒd] *adj. he died last year - aged 74,* when he was 74 years old. □ **de... años de edad**
■ ['eidʒid] *adj.* very old: *an aged man.* □ **anciano**
■ ['eidʒid] *n.* ***the aged,*** old people. □ **los viejos**
agency ['eidʒənsi] *n.* **1** which represents a larger firm/which works on behalf of another firm: *travel agency.* □ **agencia**
2 *we have the agency for Ford cars,* we are the distributors for Ford cars in our neighbourhood. □ **distribución**
3 means: *I'm contacting him through the agency of his local priest.* □ **por medio de**
agenda [ə'dʒendə] *n.* list of things to be discussed at a meeting; timetable: *what's on the agenda today? I'm afraid my agenda is fairly heavy,* has many items. □ **orden del día, programa**
agent ['eidʒənt] *n.* **1** someone who represents someone else: *he's our agent in West Africa.* □ **representante; agente**
secret agent, spy. □ **agente secreto**
2 substance which has an effect on another: *cleaning agent.* □ **agente**
agglomeration [əglɔmə'reiʃn] *n.* large urban area. □ **aglomeración**
aggravate ['ægrəveit] *v.* to make worse: *it only aggravates the situation.* □ **agravar; empeorar**
aggravating *adj.* (*informal*) annoying. □ **irritante**
aggravation [ægrə'veiʃn] *n. (informal)* worsening (of a quarrel); annoyance. □ **agravamiento; exasperación**
aggregate ['ægrigət] *n.* **1** total: *what is the aggregate of all these sales?* □ **total**
in the aggregate, as a total. □ **en total, en conjunto**
2 mixture of sand, gravel, etc., with cement. □ **hormigón**
aggression [ə'greʃn] *n.* hostility; attacking: *an act of aggression,* an attack. □ **agresión**
aggressive [ə'gresiv] *adj.* hostile; attacking: *aggressive stance,* menacing position. □ **agresivo**
aggressively *adv.* violently. □ **agresivamente**
aggressor *n.* attacker: *it was difficult to decide which of the two countries was the aggressor,* which attacked the other first. □ **agresor**
aggrieved [ə'gri:vd] *adj.* upset: *he feels very aggrieved over the report in the paper.* □ **agraviado**
aggro ['ægrou] *n.* (*no pl.*) (*slang*) violent quarrelling/disagreement. □ **riña**
aghast [ə'gɑ:st] *adj.* horrified: *I was aghast when I found out what had happened.* □ **horrorizado**
agile ['ædʒail] *adj.* lightfooted; (animal/person) who can climb/swing/run, etc., very easily: *monkeys are extremely agile.* □ **ágil**
agility [ə'dʒiliti] *n.* state of being agile. □ **agilidad**
agitate ['ædʒiteit] *v.* to stir up public opinion: *they are agitating for a shorter working week; the parents are agitating against the closure of the school.* □ **agitar**
agitated *adj.* bothered; worked up: *he got more and more agitated as the meeting continued.* □ **agitado**
agitation [ædʒi'teiʃn] *n.* **1** worry. □ **preocupación**
2 *political agitation,* political unrest. □ **agitación, política**
agitator ['ædʒiteitə] *n.* person who stirs up political unrest. □ **agitador**
agnostic [æg'nɔstik] *adj.* and *n.* (person) who believes that nothing can be known about god. □ **agnóstico**
ago [ə'gou] *adv.* in the past: *three years ago; a long time ago; I saw him twenty minutes ago; it was as long ago as last year.* □ **hace...**
agog [ə'gɔg] *adj. she's all agog to know what happened,* she's very eager to know what happened. □ **ansioso**
agonized ['ægənaizd] *adj.* as if in pain/in agony: *he let out an agonized yell.* □ **desesperado**
agonizing ['ægənaiziŋ] *adj.* **1** very sharp (pain): *I am suffering from agonizing pains in my knee.* □ **terrible**
2 upsetting: *they had to make an agonizing decision about selling their shop.* □ **doloroso**
agony ['ægəni] *n.* (*pl. agonies*) extreme pain/extreme discomfort: *she's in agony with her twisted ankle; the journey was a total agony; he's suffering agonies of remorse.* □ **gran dolor; tormento**
agony column, letters and advice about personal problems in a newspaper. □ **anuncios personales**
agoraphobia [ægərə'foubiə] *n.* irrational fear of public spaces. □ **agorafobia**
agrarian [ə'grɛəriən] *adj.* dealing with the land: *agrarian reforms.* □ **agrario**
agree [ə'gri:] *v.* **1** to say that you think the same way: *I agree with you that the colours are too bright; I don't agree with spending all this money on food.* □ **estar de acuerdo con...**
2 to say yes: *we asked him to be the chairman and he agreed; I agree that we should write a letter of complaint; 'let's go for a picnic' - 'agreed'.* □ **parecer bien, aceptar**
3 *the hot weather doesn't agree with him,* the hot

weather makes him feel ill; *eggs don't agree with me.* □ **sentar bien**

agreeable *adj.* **1** pleasant: *he's a very agreeable person.* □ **agradable**

2 in agreement: *are you agreeable to this suggestion?*, do you agree? □ **de acuerdo con...**

agreeably *adv.* pleasantly: *I was agreeably surprised by his reaction.* □ **agradablemente**

agreement *n.* **1** act of saying yes: *he nodded his head to show his agreement.* □ **acuerdo, conformidad**

2 *everyone was* ***in agreement,*** they all thought the same. □ **acuerdo**

agriculture ['ægrikʌltʃə] *n.* use of the land for growing crops/raising animals, etc.: *the agriculture of the country is based on growing coffee and cocoa.* □ **agricultura**

agricultural [ægri'kʌltʃərəl] *adj.* relating to agriculture: *the Government's agricultural policy; agricultural machinery.* □ **agrícola**

aground [ə'graund] *adv.* no longer afloat: *the ship went aground on the sandbank; the tanker ran aground off the French coast.* □ **encallado**

ahead [ə'hed] *adv.* **1** in front. □ **delante**

2 *the time here is two hours* ***ahead of*** *London,* two hours in advance of London time. □ **de adelanto**

3 ***full speed ahead!*** go forward as quickly as possible. □ **¡adelante a toda máquina!**

4 *the police motorcycles went ahead of the president's car; the opposing team gradually drew ahead,* went into the lead; *go on ahead and find a good place for the picnic.* □ **por delante de; adelante**

5 *you must always try* ***to think ahead,*** to foresee what may happen. □ **prever**

ahoy [ə'hɔi] *interjection used by sailors to call a ship.* □ **¡ah del barco!**

aid [eid] *n.* **1** help. □ **ayuda**

first aid, help to injured/sick people. □ **primeros auxilios**

first-aid kit, box with bandages/medicines, etc. □ **botiquín**

in aid of, to help: *we are taking a collection in aid of the old people's home.* □ **en ayuda de**

what's this all in aid of?, what is this all about? □ **¿para qué sirve esto?**

2 instrument to help something: *a hearing aid.* □ **ayuda**

■ *v.* to help: *the villagers aided in the rescue.* □ **ayudar**

aide [eid] *n.* assistant: *one of the president's aides.* □ **ayudante**

aide-de-camp [eiddə'kɑŋ] *n.* (*pl. aides-de-camp*) officer who assists a senior officer. □ **edecán, ayudante de campo**

aileron ['eilərɔn] *n.* flap on the edge of an aircraft's wing □ **alerón**

ailing ['eiliŋ] *adj.* sick. □ **enfermo**

ailment ['eilmənt] *n.* minor illness: *he keeps on telling me about his ailments.* □ **indisposición**

aim [eim] *n.* **1** target; what you are trying to do: *our aim is to save enough money to go on holiday.* □ **objetivo**

2 *he took aim and fired,* he pointed his gun at the target. □ **apuntar**

■ *v.* **1** to plan/to intend to do: *we aim to collect enough money to go on holiday; he's aiming at leaving school next year.* □ **planear, ir a**

2 to point at: *the guns were aimed at the enemy tanks; the new law is aimed at shopkeepers who charge too high prices.* □ **apuntar**

aimless *adj.* with no particular plan. □ **sin propósito fijo**

aimlessly *adv.* with no particular plan: *the crowd wandered aimlessly round the streets.* □ **sin rumbo**

air [ɛə] *n.* **1** mixture of gases (chiefly oxygen and nitrogen) which we breathe, and which surrounds the earth: *in the cave the air felt cold; the balloon floated up into the air.* □ **aire**

2 ***by air*** *are you travelling by air?,* are you going in an aircraft? □ **por avión**

3 ***there's something in the air,*** there is something being plotted. □ **...en el ambiente**

4 *it's still* ***in the air,*** it hasn't been decided yet. □ **en el aire**

5 ***air attack,*** attack by aircraft. □ **ataque aéreo**

6 *you're* ***on the air,*** you're speaking live on TV/on radio. □ **en el aire; en directo**

7 little tune. □ **aire**

8 appearance/feeling: *there's a comfortable air about this house; there's an air of wealth about him.* □ **aire de...**

■ *v.* **1** to freshen something by giving more air: *to air a room,* to open the windows to let in fresh air. □ **airear**

2 *to air laundry,* to warm clean sheets, etc.. □ **guardar la ropa en un sitio caliente**

airing cupboard, warm cupboard for keeping sheets and blankets in. □ **armario para ropa**

3 *he's fond of airing his views,* he likes showing off his opinions. □ **alardear**

airbase *n.* military airfield. □ **base aérea**

airbed *n.* inflatable plastic/rubber mattress. □ **colchón inflable**

airborne *adj.* carried in the air: *airborne invasion; we were airborne five minutes after we had got on to the plane.* □ **aerotransportado; volando**

airbrake *n.* **1** movable part on an aircraft to slow it down. □ **freno aerodinámico**

2 brake (on trucks) which works by compressed air. □ **freno neumático**

air-conditioned [ɛəkən'diʃnd] *adj.* whose air is cooled by an air conditioner: *the restaurant is air-conditioned; he sat in the air-conditioned luxury of his office.* □ **de/con aire acondicionado**

air-conditioner *n.* machine which keeps a room at the right temperature. □ **acondicionador de aire**

air-conditioning *n.* cooling of the air by an air-conditioner: *we're having air-conditioning installed.* □ **aire acondicionado**

aircooled *adj.* (engine) which is cooled by air, not by water. □ **refrigerado por aire**

aircraft *n.* (*pl. aircraft*) machine which flies: *two enemy aircraft came down in the sea.* □ **avión**

aircraft carrier *n.* large warship which carries aircraft and has a long deck for landing and taking off. □ **portaaviones**

aircraftman, aircraftwoman *n.* (*pl. aircraftmen, aircraftwomen*) lowest rank in the Air Force. □ **miembro sin graduación de las fuerzas aéreas**

aircrew *n.* the crew of an aircraft. □ **tripulación**

airfield *n.* small private or military aerodrome. □ **aeródromo**

air force *n.* military air defence organization: *the French Air Force.* □ **fuerzas aéreas**

airgun *n.* gun which shoots pellets using compressed air. □ **pistola de aire comprimido**

air hostess *n.* (*pl. air hostesses*) woman who works on a passenger aircraft, serving meals and looking after the passengers. □ **azafata**

airily ['ɛərili] *adv.* vaguely/not seriously: *he airily promised to lend me a thousand pounds.* □ **a la ligera**

airless *adj.* with no air or wind; stuffy. □ **cargado; sin aire**

air letter *n.* very light piece of paper for writing letters which, when folded and stuck down becomes its own envelope. □ **aerograma**
airlift *n.* transport of emergency supplies/people by air: *they organized an airlift of supplies to the area cut off by floods.* □ **puente aéreo**
■ *v.* to transport emergency supplies/people by air: *food was airlifted to the disaster area.* □ **aerotransportar**
airline *n.* company which runs passenger or cargo air services. □ **compañía aérea**
airlock *n.* blockage in the flow of a liquid in a pipe (caused by air). □ **burbuja de aire**
airmail *n.* and *adv.* (mail) sent by air: *I'll send it to you airmail.* □ **correo aéreo**
airman *n.* (*pl. airmen*) man serving in an air force. □ **aviador**
air mattress *n.* (plastic) mattress which can be inflated. □ **colchón neumático**
airplane *n. Amer.* machine which flies. □ **avión**
air pocket *n.* sudden turbulence in air. □ **bache**
airport *n.* commercial installation with customs facilities, where passenger and cargo planes land and take off: *we're flying from London Airport to Paris.* □ **aeropuerto**
air raid *n.* attack by military aircraft. □ **ataque aéreo**
airship *n.* large inflated balloon driven by an engine. □ **dirigible**
airsick *adj.* sick because of travelling by air. □ **mareado (en avión)**
airsickness *n.* feeling of sickness which you get when travelling by air. □ **mareo (en avión)**
airstrip *n.* small runway where planes can land and take off: *they cut an airstrip out of the jungle.* □ **pista de aterrizaje**
air terminal *n.* station in a town where air passengers can take buses to an airport. □ **terminal aéreo**
airtight *adj.* not letting in any air: *is this box airtight?* □ **hermético**
air traffic control *n.* control of the movement of aircraft by people on the ground. □ **control de tráfico aéreo**
airworthiness *n.* safety of an aircraft for use: *has the aircraft a certificate of airworthiness?* □ **navegabilidad**
airy *adj.* (*airier, airiest*) **1** full of air: *the church was light and airy.* □ **ventilado**
2 vague (promise). □ **vago**
airy-fairy *adj.* impractical (plan). □ **etéreo**
aisle [ail] *n.* gangway; side part in a church, parallel to the nave: *you're not allowed to stand in the aisles while the film is on.* □ **pasillo; nave lateral**
ajar [ə'dʒɑ:] *adj.* (*of door/window*) half-open: *leave the door ajar.* □ **entreabierto**
akimbo [ə'kimbou] *adv. she stood **with** her **arms akimbo**,* with her hands on her hips. □ **en jarras**
akin [ə'kin] *adj.* similar: *he experienced a feeling akin to terror; it is a disease somewhat akin to chickenpox.* □ **parecido**
alabaster ['æləbɑ:stə] *n.* smooth white stone (especially used for making statues). □ **alabastro**
à la carte [ælæ'kɑ:t] *adv.* and *adj.* (meal) made up of several dishes ordered separately from a menu. □ **a la carta**
alacrity [ə'lækriti] *n.* speed: *he carried out the instructions with alacrity.* □ **prontitud**
à la mode [ælæ'mɔd] *adv. Amer.* served with ice cream: *apple pie à la mode.* □ **a la moda**
alarm [ə'lɑ:m] *n.* something which gives a loud warning: *he gave the alarm/he raised the alarm; false alarm,* warning signal which is false. □ **alarma**
fire alarm, bell which rings when a fire breaks out. □ **alarma**
alarm (clock), clock which rings at a certain time. □ **despertador**
■ *v.* to warn (someone); to frighten (someone): *I am rather alarmed at the increase in our expenditure.* □ **alarmar**
alas [ə'læs] *interjection* showing sadness: *alas, both children died of cholera.* □ **¡ay!**
albatross ['ælbətrɔs] *n.* (*pl. albatrosses*) very large white sea bird. □ **albatros**
albino [æl'bi:nou] *n.* animal or person born with pale skin, white hair, and pink eyes. □ **albino**
album ['ælbəm] *n.* **1** large book for sticking things in: *stamp album; photograph album.* □ **álbum**
2 long playing record with several songs on it. □ **álbum**
albumen ['ælbjumən] *n.* white part of an egg. □ **albúmina**
alchemy ['ælkəmi] *n.* medieval chemistry, aimed at converting metals to gold. □ **alquimia**
alchemist *n.* person who studied alchemy. □ **alquimista**
alcohol ['ælkəhɔl] *n.* intoxicating liquid distilled from a fermented mixture: *this camping stove runs on alcohol; he drinks a lot of alcohol,* he drinks alcoholic drinks, especially spirits. □ **alcohol**
alcoholic [ælkə'hɔlik] *adj.* referring to alcohol: *what is the alcoholic content of this beer?* □ **alcohólico**
■ *n.* person who is addicted to drinking alcohol. □ **alcohólico**
alcoholism *n.* addiction to drinking alcohol. □ **alcoholismo**
alcove ['ælkouv] *n.* small recess in a wall: *we can put a cupboard in the alcove by the fireplace.* □ **hueco**
alder ['ɔ:ldə] *n.* tree which often grows near water. □ **aliso**
ale [eil] *n.* type of beer: *pale ale.* □ **cerveza (espesa y amarga)**
alert [ə'lə:t] *adj.* watchful; lively: *he's very alert even if he is over ninety.* □ **despierto; alerta**
■ *n.* **1** ***to be on the alert,*** to be watchful/to watch out for something. □ **estar alerta**
2 *he gave the alert,* he gave a warning signal. □ **alarma**
alertness *n.* watchfulness; promptness (in doing something). □ **vigilancia; prontitud**
alfresco [æl'freskou] *adj.* and *adv.* in the open air: *we had an alfresco meal on the patio.* □ **al aire libre**
algae ['ældʒi:] *n. pl.* tiny water plants with no stems or leaves. □ **algas**
algebra ['ældʒibrə] *n.* branch of mathematics where numbers are replaced by letters. □ **álgebra**
algebraic [ældʒi'breiik] *adj.* referring to algebra: *an algebraic equation.* □ **algebraico**
alias ['eiliəs] *adv.* otherwise known as: *here is John Smith alias 'the terror of the tennis courts'.* □ **alias**
■ *n.* (*pl. aliases*) *in his criminal career he used several aliases,* he used several assumed names. □ **apodos**
alibi ['ælibai] *n.* proof that you were somewhere else when a crime was committed: *he can't have committed the burglary - he has a cast-iron alibi.* □ **coartada**
alien ['eiliən] *adj.* foreign: *alien citizens; the whole idea is alien to the British way of life.* □ **extranjero, ajeno**
■ *n.* foreigner: *aliens must register every week with the police.* □ **extranjero**
alienate ['eiliəneit] *v.* to turn away/to repel: *he has alienated all his supporters,* made them all go away

because of his behaviour. □ **alejar**
alienation [eiliə'neiʃn] *n.* turning away/repelling. □ **alejamiento**
alight [ə'lait] *v.* ***to alight from,*** (*formal*) to get off (a train/bus, etc.): *alight here for St Paul's Cathedral.* □ **apearse**
■ *adj.* on fire: *the fire is hardly alight; he set the barn alight.* □ **en llamas**
align [ə'lain] *v.* to put (yourself/something) in line; to put (yourself) on the same side as: *he aligned himself with the radical politicians; all the African states aligned themselves behind Nigeria,* they all followed the same policies as Nigeria. □ **alinearse**
alignment *n.* row (of objects); putting (countries) on the same side. □ **alineamiento**
alike [ə'laik] *adv.* almost the same: *the two brothers look alike; they were dressed alike.* □ **del mismo modo, casi igual**
alimentary [æli'mentəri] *adj.* which feeds. □ **alimenticio**
the alimentary canal, tube by which your food goes into the stomach, and passes through and out of the body. □ **tubo digestivo**
alimony ['æliməni] *n.* (*pl. alimonies*) money paid regularly by a husband to his divorced wife. □ **pensión alimenticia**
alive [ə'laiv] *adj.* **1** living/not dead: *the fish is still alive, although it was taken out of the water some time ago; when the barn caught fire, the animals were burnt alive.* □ **vivo**
2 aware: *I am very alive to the possibility that our sales will fall.* □ **consciente**
3 lively. □ **vivo**
alkali ['ælkəlai] *n.* substance which will neutralize an acid, and which turns litmus paper blue. □ **álcali**
alkaline *adj.* not acid: *an alkaline solution.* □ **alcalino**
all [ɔːl] *adj.* and *pron.* **1** everything; everyone: *all tomatoes are red; the children are all here; all our family are tall; is this all your luggage? at all hours (of the day or night),* all the time; *all of us prefer beer to wine; they all sang songs; that is all.* □ **todo; todos**
2 *sing it **all together,*** everyone at the same time. □ **todos juntos**
3 *fifteen all,* (*in tennis*) fifteen points each. □ **iguales**
4 ***once (and) for all,*** for the last time. □ **por última vez**
5 ***not at all,*** certainly not: *he was not at all bothered by the fact that his trousers had a hole in them,* not in any way bothered. □ **en absoluto; de ninguna manera**
6 ***all but,*** nearly: *it is all but impossible to find a hotel room vacant in August,* it is practically impossible. □ **casi; prácticamente**
■ *adv.* **1** completely: *she was dressed all in blue; you will be all the better for a couple of weeks' holiday.* □ **completamente**
2 ***all at once/all of a sudden,*** suddenly. □ **de repente**
3 *sometimes I wonder if he's **all there,*** if he is sane. □ **...en sus cabales**
all in [ɔːl'rait] *adj.* **1** (*informal*) worn out: *I've been climbing since 6 o'clock in the morning and now I'm all in.* □ **agotado**
2 *all-in,* including everything: *all-in price.* □ **todo incluido**
all-night *adj.* which goes on for the whole night: *all-night bar,* bar which is open all night. □ **...toda la noche**
all-out *adj. we must make an all-out effort to eradicate corruption,* we must do everything. □ **supremo; total**
all right *adj.* fine; well: *I was sick yesterday but I am all right now; is it all right for me to take an extra day's holiday? 'can you go to the Post Office for me? - 'all right',* yes I will. □ **de acuerdo**
all-round *adj.* **1** general. □ **completo**
2 *all-round athlete,* person who is good at all sorts of sports. □ **atleta polivalente**
all-rounder *n.* person who can do anything; especially cricketer who can play in any position. □ **persona completa; jugador polivante (cricket)**
all-star *adj.* with many stars appearing: *all-star show.* □ **de/con primeras figuras**
all-time *adj. sales have reached an all-time high,* sales are higher than they have ever been before. □ **nunca visto/alcanzado**
allay [ə'lei] *v.* to calm (fear/anger). □ **calmar**
allegation [æli'geiʃn] *n.* suggestion as if it were fact: *I must refute the allegation that I spent vast sums of money as bribes.* □ **alegato, suposición**
allege [ə'ledʒ] *v.* to suggest (as a fact that): *he alleges that you were there.* □ **alegar**
alleged *adj.* suggested: *at the time of the alleged attack I was asleep in bed.* □ **supuesto**
allegedly [ə'ledʒidli] *adv.* as is alleged. □ **supuestamente**
allegiance [ə'liːdʒəns] *n.* faithfulness: *the generals swore allegiance to the President,* they swore to obey his orders. □ **lealtad**
allegory ['æligəri] *n.* (*pl. allegories*) piece of writing where the characters represent abstract qualities or defects. □ **alegoría**
allegorical [æli'gɔrikl] *adj.* referring to allegory. □ **alegórico**
allegro [ə'legrou] *adv.* and *adj.* (*in music*) played quite fast. □ **allegro**
allergy ['ælədʒi] *n.* (*pl. allergies*) illness caused by a reaction to irritant substances. □ **alergia**
allergic [ə'ləːdʒik] *adj.* reacting badly against: *I am allergic to grass pollen; he is allergic to cats; she is allergic to anything by Shakespeare,* she dislikes intensely anything by Shakespeare. □ **alérgico**
alleviate [ə'liːvieit] *v.* to lessen/to soften: *we must try to alleviate the conditions of the prisoners.* □ **aliviar**
alleviation [əliːvi'eiʃn] *n.* lessening. □ **alivio**
alley ['æli] *n.* **1** narrow street or path. □ **callejón**
2 ***skittle alley/bowling alley,*** long narrow area for playing skittles. □ **bolera**
alliance [ə'laiəns] *n.* link between two groups or countries: *an alliance between the radicals and the conservatives; the Anglo-French alliance; Britain has signed an alliance with France.* □ **alianza**
allied ['ælaid] *adj.* **1** linked by an alliance: *the allied powers,* western countries linked against communist states. □ **aliado**
2 linked: *the plastics and allied industries.* □ **relacionadas**
alligator ['æligeitə] *n.* large flesh-eating reptile living in tropical rivers. □ **caimán**
alliteration [əlitə'reiʃn] *n.* use of repeated consonants at the beginning of words in poetry. □ **aliteración**
allocate ['æləkeit] *v.* to give (something) as a share (for a particular purpose): *I have allocated funds to each of the departments.* □ **asignar**
allocation [ælə'keiʃn] *n.* division/giving as a share. □ **asignación**
allot [ə'lɔt] *v.* (*he allotted*) to split up between (several people). □ **repartir**
allotment *n.* **1** splitting up. □ **reparto**
2 small plot of land leased by a town to a citizen (especially for growing vegetables). □ **parcela; lote**

allow [ə'lau] *v.* **1** to let someone do something: *are dogs allowed into the shop? are we allowed to walk on the grass? my parents allow me to stay up until 11 o'clock.* □ **permitir**
2 to give: *we will allow you six weeks to pay; I will allow you fifty per cent discount.* □ **conceder**
allowable *adj.* which is permitted. □ **admisible**
allowable expenses, expenses which are allowed against tax. □ **gastos deducibles**
allowance *n.* **1** money paid regularly: *my son gets a small allowance each week.* □ **cantidad fija, 'paga'**
family allowance, money paid each week by the State to families with children. □ **prestación familiar**
2 *you must* ***make allowance for*** *his inexperience,* you must take his inexperience into account. □ **tener en cuenta**
alloy ['ælɔi] *n.* mixture of two or more metals: *bronze is an alloy of copper and tin.* □ **aleación**
allude [ə'lu:d] *v.* ***to allude to something,*** to refer to something indirectly or briefly: *he alluded to the high cost of travel.* □ **aludir**
allure [ə'ljuə] *v.* to attract. □ **atraer**
alluring *adj.* attractive. □ **atractivo**
allusion [ə'lu:ʒn] *n.* slight reference: *I didn't understand his allusion to fairies at the bottom of the garden.* □ **alusión**
alluvial [ə'lu:viəl] *adj.* (soil/land) which has been deposited by rivers. □ **aluvial**
alluvium *n.* soil which has been deposited by a river. □ **terreno de aluvión**
ally ['ælai] *n.* (*pl. allies*) person/country who is on the same side as you in a quarrel or war: *he is my main ally in the argument over higher salaries; the United States and Britain were allies during the Second World War.* □ **aliado**
■ *v.* (*allied; allying*) ***to ally oneself to,*** to join forces with/to support: *he allied himself to the left wing of the party.* □ **aliarse**
almanac ['ɔ:lmənæk] *n.* calendar which also contains advice or information. □ **almanaque**
almighty [ɔ:l'maiti] *adj. (informal)* very powerful: *the car made an almighty row,* it made a very loud noise. □ **todopoderoso; enorme**
■ *n.* ***the Almighty,*** God. □ **El Todopoderoso**
almond ['ɑ:mənd] *n.* nut from a tree of the peach family. □ **almendra**
almoner ['ɑ:mənə] *n.* person in a hospital who sees that the patients are happy and well fed. □ **asistente social**
almost ['ɔ:lmoust] *adv.* nearly; not quite: *he is almost as tall as his father; I am almost 15 - my birthday is next week.* □ **casi**
alms [ɑ:mz] *n. pl.* formerly, a gift to old/sick/poor people. □ **limosna**
almshouses *n. pl.* houses formerly built as homes for the old. □ **asilos**
aloe ['ælou] *n.* desert plant with thick leaves and bitter juice. □ **áloe**
aloft [ə'lɔft] *adv.* (*formal*) high up (in the air). □ **arriba, en alto**
alone [ə'loun] *adj.* **1** with no one else: *he was all alone in the house; can I speak to you alone?* □ **solo**
2 *I would* ***leave well alone*** *if I were you,* I wouldn't get involved if I were you. □ **dejar en paz**
3 *I can't speak Russian* ***let alone*** *read it,* I can't speak it, so I can't possibly try to read it. □ **...y menos**
along [ə'lɔŋ] *prep.* from one end to the other: *there are trees along both sides of the road; I am going for a walk along the street/along the river bank,* for some distance down the street/on the bank of the river. □ **a lo largo de**
■ *adv.* **1** *come along with me,* come with me; *we all went along to the police station,* we went together. □ **con; juntos**
2 *I knew what would happen* ***all along,*** I knew from the beginning what would happen. □ **desde el principio**
3 ***to get along:*** *they don't get along very well together,* they do not agree. □ **entenderse**
alongside *adv.* and *prep.* beside (on water): *we tied the boat up alongside the quay.* □ **junto a**
aloof [ə'lu:f] *adv.* and *adj.* **1** coldly/unfriendly. □ **distante**
2 *they always kept aloof,* they did not mix with other people because they looked down on them. □ **distante**
aloofness *n.* cold superciliousness. □ **reserva**
aloud [ə'laud] *adv.* loud enough to be heard; in a loud voice: *he was reading the newspaper aloud in the bath.* □ **en voz alta**
alp [ælp] *n.* mountain meadow in Switzerland. □ **montaña, prado montañoso**
alphabet ['ælfəbet] *n.* letters used to write words, set out in conventional order (A, B, C, D, E, etc.): *A is the first letter of the alphabet.* □ **alfabeto**
alphabetical [ælfə'betikl] *adj. in alphabetical order,* in order based on the first letter of each word; *Aberdeen, Bath, Dover and Southampton are in alphabetical order; some of the words in the index are out of alphabetical order.* □ **alfabético**
alphabetically *adv.* in alphabetical order: *he called out the names alphabetically.* □ **alfabéticamente**
alpine ['ælpain] *adj.* and *n.* referring to high mountain (plant/animal) which grows or lives on high mountains. □ **alpino**
already [ɔ:l'redi] *adv.* by now: *it's already 10 o'clock; have you finished already? the car has already broken down again, when it was only mended yesterday.* □ **ya**
alright [ɔ:l'rait] *adj. (informal) all right.* □ **de acuerdo**
Alsatian [æl'seiʃn] *n.* large dog (of German origin) often used as a guard dog. □ **pastor alemán**
also ['ɔ:lsou] *adv.* as well/at the same time: *he is a doctor and also a dentist; his wife is also French.* □ **también**
altar ['ɔltə] *n.* table in church/temple for religious ceremonies. □ **altar**
alter ['ɔltə] *v.* to change: *I would like to alter the time of my appointment; when he came out of prison he had altered completely.* □ **alterar**
alteration [ɔltə'reiʃn] *n.* change: *you cannot make any alterations to the arrangements.* □ **alteración**
altercation [ɔ:ltə'keiʃn] *n.* (*formal*) argument. □ **altercado**
alternate [ɔ:l'tə:nət] *adj.* every other/missing one each time: *I go to the pictures on alternate Mondays,* on Monday every other week; *there are maps on alternate pages of the book.* □ **alterno**
■ *v.* to put (something) in place of something else, and then switch them round; to follow by turns: *I alternate between going to work by bus and by car,* one day (or for a period) I go by bus, then I change to the car, then back to the bus again; *they alternate as driver and navigator.* □ **alternar**
alternately [ɔ:l'tə:nətli] *adv.* in turns; one first and then the other. □ **alternativamente**
alternating *adj.* (electric current) which flows one

way and then the other. □ **alterna**
alternative [ɔl'tə:nətiv] *n.* **1** something in place of another: *if you cannot go by car, the only alternative is to take the bus.* □ **alternativa**
2 *he has no alternative,* he cannot do anything else, he has no choice. □ **alternativa**
■ *adj.* in place of something else: *is there no alternative transport to the village?* □ **alternativo, otro**
alternatively *adv.* on the other hand: *you can walk, or alternatively, I'll drive you there in the car.* □ **si no**
alternator ['ɔ:ltəneitə] *n.* device which produces alternating current. □ **alternador**
although [ɔ:l'ðou] *conj.* in spite of the fact that: *although it was windy, it was still very hot; although he's quite old, he can still run fast.* □ **aunque**
altimeter ['æltimi:tə] *n.* instrument (especially in an aircraft) for measuring altitude. □ **altímetro**
altitude ['æltitju:d] *n.* height (measured above the level of the sea): *they climbed to an altitude of 5,000 metres before they turned back; he parachuted from an altitude of 5,000 metres.* □ **altitud**
alto ['æltou] *n.* (*pl. altos*) (man with a) high-pitched voice; (woman with a) low-pitched voice. □ **alto**
altogether [ɔ:ltə'geðə] *adv.* considering everything together: *the shirt is $6 and the shoes $30 - that makes $36 altogether; how much do I owe you altogether?* □ **en total**
altruism ['æltruizəm] *n.* being unselfish. □ **altruismo**
altruistic *adj.* unselfish. □ **altruista**
aluminium [ælju'minjəm] *Amer.* **aluminum** [ə'lu:minəm] *n.* (*chemical element:* Al) light white metal, used for kitchen equipment, etc. □ **aluminio**
alumnus [ə'lʌmnəs] *n.* (*pl. alumni*) *Amer.* graduate (of a college/university). □ **antiguo alumno**
always ['ɔ:lweiz] *adv.* every time/all the time: *she's always late; in the desert it's nearly always hot.* □ **siempre**
alyssum ['ælisəm] *n.* low garden plant with masses of small white flowers. □ **especie de alhelí**
am [æm] *v. see* **be.**
a.m. ['ei'em] *adv.* in the morning: *I am catching the 9 a.m. train.* □ **de la mañana**
amalgam [ə'mælgəm] *n.* (*formal*) mixture of substances. □ **amalgama**
amalgamate [ə'mælgəmeit] *v.* to mix together/to link up: *the two clubs have decided to amalgamate.* □ **amalgamar**
amalgamation [əmælgə'meiʃn] *n.* linking/mixing. □ **amalgamación**
amass [ə'mæs] *v.* to pile up: *he amassed a fortune by selling paintings.* □ **acumular, amontonar**
amateur ['æmətə:] *n.* and *adj.* (person) who is not paid to do something; (person) who does something because he likes doing it: *an amateur footballer; she is an amateur violinist; amateur theatre company.* □ **'amateur', aficionado**
amateurish *adj.* not very well done: *his painting is a bit amateurish.* □ **de aficionado**
amaze [ə'meiz] *v.* to surprise: *it amazes me how he can drive so fast.* □ **asombrar**
amazed *adj.* surprised: *the travellers were amazed at the beauty of the lake.* □ **asombrado**
amazement *n.* surprise: *she stopped still in amazement at the scene.* □ **asombro**
amazing *adj.* **1** very surprising: *it's amazing how much she can eat.* □ **asombroso**
2 *he's an amazing man,* he's unusually gifted. □ **maravilloso**
ambassador [æm'bæsədə] **ambassadress** [æm'bæsədres] *n.* person who represents his country in another country: *the British Ambassador; the Russian Ambassador.* □ **embajador**
amber ['æmbə] *n.* hard orange-coloured stone made of fossilized resin. □ **ámbar**
■ *adj.* orange: *the traffic lights turn from green to amber before going red.* □ **ámbar**
ambidextrous [æmbi'dekstrəs] *adj.* (person) who can use either right or left hand equally well. □ **ambidextro**
ambience ['æmbiəns] *n.* surroundings. □ **ambiente**
ambiguous [æm'bigjuəs] *adj.* which has two possible meanings; vague: *the wording of the contract is ambiguous.* □ **ambiguo**
ambiguity [æmbi'gju:iti] *n.* state of having two possible meanings; vagueness: *I want to make sure there is no ambiguity about the order.* □ **ambigüedad**
ambition [æm'biʃn] *n.* desire to improve your status in the world: *his ambition is to be Prime Minister one day.* □ **ambición**
ambitious *adj.* **1** wanting to get on in the world. □ **ambicioso**
2 *ambitious project,* very grandiose project which may prove too difficult to carry out. □ **ambicioso**
ambivalent [æm'bivələnt] *adj.* undecided/with two points of view: *his attitude to working wives is still ambivalent.* □ **ambivalente**
amble ['æmbl] *v. he was ambling along,* he was walking slowly along. □ **deambular**
ambulance ['æmbjuləns] *n.* vehicle for taking sick people to hospital: *the injured were taken away in ambulances.* □ **ambulancia**
ambush ['æmbuʃ] *n.* (*pl. ambushes*) surprise attack: *guerilla group walked into an ambush laid for them by government forces.* □ **emboscada**
■ *v.* to attack by surprise: *the troops were ambushed as they drove along the narrow track.* □ **emboscar**
ameliorate [ə'mi:ljəreit] *v.* (*formal*) to make better. □ **mejorar**
amelioration [əmi:ljə'reiʃn] *n.* becoming better: *I detect a slight amelioration in her condition.* □ **mejora**
amen [ɑ:'men, ei'men] *interjection* **1** word (*ng* let this be so) which is used at the end of Christian prayers. □ **amén**
2 ***I say amen to that,*** I agree entirely. □ **amén**
amenable [ə'mi:nəbl] *adj.* **1** docile/easy-going. □ **dócil**
2 *he is always amenable to new ideas,* he accepts new ideas easily. □ **abierto**
amend [ə'mend] *v.* to change (for the better): *we will have to amend the text.* □ **enmendar**
amendment *n.* change, especially suggested change to a proposal: *he proposed an amendment to clause 3 of the agreement.* □ **enmienda**
amends *n.* ***to make amends for something,*** to compensate for an injury, etc. □ **compensar, reparar**
amenity [ə'mi:niti] *n.* (*pl. amenities*) **1** pleasantness (of a place). □ **amenidad, atractivo**
amenity bed, bed in a separate room in a public hospital. □ **cama en habitación privada**
2 sport and entertainment facility: *civic amenities.* □ **complejo deportivo, de recreo**
amenity centre, building which houses (for example) a cinema, auditorium, gymnasium, swimming pool, etc. □ **centro recreativo**
America [ə'merikə] *n.* **1** one of two continents, lying between the Pacific and Atlantic Oceans: *North America; South America.* □ **América**
2 country in North America, the United States. □ **Estados Unidos**
American *adj.* referring to America. □ **americano,**

estadounidense
American plan, full board (in a hotel). □ **pensión completa**
■ *n.* person from the United States. □ **estadounidense**
amethyst ['æməθist] *n.* purple precious stone. □ **amatista**
amiable ['eimiəbl] *adj.* pleasant. □ **amable**
amiably *adv.* pleasantly: *they chatted amiably for several minutes.* □ **amablemente**
amicable ['æmikəbl] *adj.* friendly. □ **amigable**
amicably *adv.* in a friendly way: *they settled their dispute quite amicably.* □ **amigablemente**
amid(st) [ə'mid(st)] *prep.* in the middle of: *amidst all the crowd two people stood out; the explorer stood amid the snowy wastes of the South Pole.* □ **entre**
amidships *adv.* and *prep.* in the middle of a ship: *the torpedo struck the ship amidships.* □ **en medio del barco**
amino acid [ə'mi:nou 'æsid] *n.* acid found in protein, necessary for growth. □ **aminoácido**
amiss [ə'mis] *adv.* and *adj.* **1** ***to take something amiss:*** *don't take it amiss if I say you have been silly,* don't be hurt. □ **a mal**
2 ***something is amiss,*** something has gone wrong. □ **impropio**
ammeter ['æmitə] *n.* device for measuring electricity in amperes. □ **amperímetro**
ammonia [ə'mouniə] *n.* gas made of hydrogen and nitrogen, which has a strong smell. □ **amoniaco**
ammonite ['æmənait] *n.* fossil shell like that of a large snail. □ **amonita**
ammunition [æmju'niʃn] *n.* (*no pl.*) bullets/shells, etc., for using in warfare/hunting, etc.: *they had to stop firing when they ran out of ammunition.* □ **munición**
amnesia [æm'ni:ziə] *n.* medical state when you forget everything (because of shock). □ **amnesia**
amnesty ['æmnəsti] *n.* (*pl. amnesties*) pardon (to criminals): *the new government offered a general amnesty to its opponents.* □ **amnistía**
amoeba [ə'mi:bə] *n.* (*pl. amoebas, amoebae*) tiny organism consisting of a single cell. □ **ameba**
amok [ə'mɔk] *adv.* ***to run amok,*** to run wild killing people. □ **volverse loco (matando o destruyendo)**
among(st) [ə'mʌŋ(st)] *prep.* **1** in the middle of: *the birds were hiding amongst the leaves.* □ **entre**
2 between: *divide the money among you.* □ **entre**
3 out of: *she is the only one among my friends who can knit.* □ **entre, de**
amoral [ei'mɔrəl] *adj.* with no sense of morality. □ **amoral**
amorous ['æmərəs] *adj.* tending to fall in love; showing (sexual) love. □ **enamoradizo**
amorphous [ə'mɔ:fəs] *adj.* having no particular shape. □ **amorfo**
amortize ['æmɔ:taiz] *v.* to write off (a debt): *we will amortize the sum over five years.* □ **amortizar**
amount [ə'maunt] *n.* **1** quantity: *my mother drinks a huge amount of tea; you can take any amount of apples,* as many apples as you like. □ **cantidad**
2 sum (of money): *have you got the right amount?* □ **importe**
■ *v.* to add up (to): *the bill amounts to $10.* □ **ascender a**
amount to (i) *it amounts to the same thing,* it means the same thing. □ **significar, equivaler**
(ii) *it amounts to slander,* it is a case of slander. □ **significar, equivaler**
amp [æmp] **ampere** ['æmpɛə] *n.* quantity of electricity flowing in a current: *a 5 amp fuse,* fuse which can stand a current of 5 amps. □ **amperio**
ampersand ['æmpəsænd] *n.* printing sign (&) meaning 'and'. □ **signo de &; y**
amphetamine [æm'fetəmi:n] *n.* drug which stimulates and excites. □ **anfetamina**
amphibian [æm'fibiən] *n.* **1** animal which lives both in water and on land. □ **anfibio**
2 (military) vehicle that runs in water and on land. □ **anfibio**
amphibious *adj.* which lives/travels in water and on land. □ **anfibio**
amphitheatre ['æmfiθiətə] *n.* Greek or Roman circular theatre with the stage in the centre; lecture hall with rows of seats rising in tiers. □ **anfiteatro**
amphora ['æmfərə] *n.* (*pl. amphorae*) Greek or Roman wine jar. □ **ánfora**
ample ['æmpl] *adj.* **1** large: *she clutched him to her ample bosom.* □ **amplio**
2 enough/sufficient: *we have an ample supply of food; you have ample time to catch the train.* □ **suficiente**
amply *adv.* in large quantity: *they were amply rewarded.* □ **ampliamente**
amplify ['æmplifai] *v.* (*amplified; amplifying*) **1** to make (a sound, etc.) louder. □ **amplificar**
2 to develop in more detail: *would you like to amplify your statement?* □ **ampliar**
amplification [æmplifi'keiʃn] *n.* development; making louder. □ **amplificación**
amplifier *n.* machine for making sound louder: *the music goes from the turntable through the amplifier to the loudspeakers.* □ **amplificador**
amputate ['æmpjuteit] *v.* to cut off (a limb): *he had to have his leg amputated.* □ **amputar**
amputation [æmpju'teiʃn] *n.* cutting off. □ **amputación**
amuse [ə'mju:z] *v.* to give (someone) pleasure: *to amuse yourself,* to spend time happily; *he amused his son by playing trains with him; they amused themselves by doing a jigsaw puzzle; she was not at all amused by the joke.* □ **divertir(se)**
amusement *n.* pleasure: *to his great amusement everybody danced in big boots.* □ **diversión**
amusement arcade, hall with slot machines for playing games, shooting, etc. □ **salón recreativo**
amusement park, open air park with roundabouts, swings, etc.. □ **parque de atracciones**
amusing *adj.* which makes you laugh: *the amusing thing is that he didn't realize they had pinned the notice to his back.* □ **gracioso**
an [æn, ən] *see* **a.**
anachronism [ə'nækrənizəm] *n.* **1** thing which is out of keeping with the period: *a jet aircraft is an anachronism in a play about Napoleon.* □ **anacronismo**
2 *he is something of an anachronism,* he is a bit out of date. □ **anacrónico**
anachronistic [ənækrə'nistik] *adj.* which is not in keeping with the period. □ **anacrónico**
anaemia [ə'ni:miə] *Amer.* **anemia** *n.* illness caused by lack of iron in the blood. □ **anemia**
anaemic [ə'ni:mik] *adj.* looking pale; suffering from anaemia. □ **anémico**
anaesthetic [ænəs'θetik] *Amer.* **anesthetic** *n.* substance which makes you lose consciousness: *the patient is given an anaesthetic before an operation.* □ **anestésico**
local anaesthetic, substance which numbs part of the body. □ **anestesia local**
anaesthesia [ænis'θi:ziə] *n.* loss of consciousness

from being given an anaesthetic. □ **anestesia**
anaesthetist [ə'ni:sθətist] *n.* doctor who gives anaesthetics. □ **anestesista**
anaesthetize [ə'ni:sθətaiz] *v.* to give (someone) an anaesthetic. □ **anestesiar**
anagram ['ænəgræm] *n.* word or phrase containing the letters of another word or phrase jumbled up (for example *Cathy* and *yacht*). □ **anagrama**
anal ['einl] *adj.* referring to the anus: *an anal infection.* □ **anal**
analgesic [ænəl'dʒi:zik] *adj.* and *n.* (drug) which relieves pain. □ **analgésico**
analogous [ə'næləgəs] *adj.* similar/parallel: *an analogous case.* □ **análogo**
analogy [ə'nælədʒi] *n.* (*pl. analogies*) similarity/parallel: *he draws an analogy between American and French literature.* □ **analogía**
analyse ['ænəlaiz] *v.* to examine closely to see how something is formed: *the police pharmacist analysed the contents of the glass; I have just analysed last month's sales figures.* □ **analizar**
analysis [ə'nælisis] *n.* (*pl. analyses*) examination: *a chemical analysis; we have made an analysis of the blood samples; here is the analysis of the car performance tests.* □ **análisis**
analyst ['ænəlist] *n.* **1** person who carries out analyses. □ **analista**
2 psychoanalyst. □ **psicoanalista**
analytical [ænə'litikl] *adj.* which examines closely in detail: *he has an analytical brain; I wish you wouldn't use this analytical approach to the study of poetry.* □ **analítico**
anarchy ['ænəki] *n.* total lack of order or government: *after the fall of the emperor, a period of anarchy followed; it is absolute anarchy the way this place is being run.* □ **anarquía**
anarchic [ə'nɑ:kik] *adj.* lacking in order. □ **anárquico**
anarchist *n.* person who believes in lack of order or government: *the Foreign Minister was killed by anarchists.* □ **anarquista**
anathema [ə'næθəmə] *n.* curse; something you dislike intensely: *long Russian novels are an absolute anathema to him.* □ **anatema**
anatomy [ə'nætəmi] *n.* (*pl. anatomies*) structure of something (especially a body): *a fish's anatomy is very different from a mammal's.* □ **anatomía**
anatomical [ænə'tɔmikl] *adj.* relating to the structure of the body: *anatomical diagram.* □ **anatómico**
ancestor ['ænsestə] *n.* member of your family many generations ago: *my ancestors originally came from Germany.* □ **antepasado**
ancestral [æn'sestrəl] *adj. ancestral house,* home of a family for many generations. □ **ancestral**
ancestry ['ænsestri] *n.* (*pl. ancestries*) origin (of a family): *he is of German ancestry.* □ **ascendencia**
anchor ['æŋkə] *n.* **1** heavy metal hook dropped to the bottom of the sea to hold a ship in one place: *the ship dropped anchor in the harbour; the ship was at anchor.* □ **ancla**
2 thing which holds secure/which gives security. □ **apoyo**
■ *v.* to drop anchor: *there were three ships anchored in the harbour.* □ **anclar**
anchorage *n.* place where ships can safely drop anchor: *the bay is a safe anchorage.* □ **fondeadero**
anchovy ['æntʃəvi, æn'tʃouvi] *n.* (*pl. anchovies*) small fish with a strong taste. □ **anchoa**
ancient ['einʃənt] *adj.* very old: *an ancient Welsh custom.* □ **antiguo**
the Ancient World, the world of the Greeks and Romans. □ **la Antigüedad clásica**
ancillary [æn'siləri] *adj.* secondary. □ **secundario**
ancillary services, services which are attached to main services. □ **auxiliar**
ancillary workers, cleaners/porters, etc., in hospitals. □ **personal de servicios**
and [ænd, ənd] *conj.* (showing connection between two things): *chair and two tables; seven hundred and two; he was running and singing at the same time; the juice was cold and sweet; the clouds got bigger and bigger,* continued to grow; *wait and see.* □ **y**
try and *sing,* try to sing □ **intenta cantar**
android ['ændrɔid] *adj.* shaped like a man. □ **androide**
anecdote ['ænikdout] *n.* short humorous story told by someone: *he was telling me an anecdote about his father.* □ **anécdota**
anemia [ə'ni:miə] *n. Amer. see* **anaemia.**
anemone [ə'neməni] *n.* small flower. □ **anémona**
sea anemone, animal living in salt water which looks like a flower. □ **anémona de mar**
aneroid ['ænərɔid] *adj.* ***aneroid barometer,*** barometer which measures atmospheric pressure by the movement of a vacuum box. □ **aneroide**
anesthetic [ænis'θetik] *n. Amer. see* **anaesthetic.**
anew [ə'nju:] *adv.* (*formal*) again. □ **de nuevo**
angel ['eindʒl] *n.* **1** heavenly being with wings. □ **ángel**
2 ***be an angel*** *and pass me the ashtray,* (*informal*) be a kind person. □ **ángel**
angelic [æn'dʒelik] *adj.* looking innocent/like an angel: *the two boys looked angelic but they weren't.* □ **angelical**
angelica [æn'dʒelikə] *n.* sweet smelling plant of which the green stalks are preserved in sugar and used to decorate cakes and desserts. □ **angélica**
anger ['æŋgə] *n.* great annoyance: *in his anger he hit her with his stick.* □ **ira; cólera**
■ *v.* to make (someone) annoyed: *his behaviour angered his father.* □ **encolerizar**
angle ['æŋgl] *n.* **1** corner: *a square has four right angles,* angles of 90°; *a triangle has three angles.* □ **ángulo**
acute angle, angle of less than 90°. □ **ángulo agudo**
obtuse angle, angle of more than 90°. □ **ángulo obtuso**
2 point of view: *I want you to write about this from the consumer's angle.* □ **punto de vista**
■ *v.* **1** to kick a ball/to shoot at an angle and not straight. □ **tirar a la escuadra**
2 *to angle for a rise,* to try to get an increase in salary by dropping hints. □ **ir a la caza de...**
angler *n.* person who fishes with a rod. □ **pescador (de caña)**
angling *n.* fishing with a rod: *angling club; sea angling.* □ **pesca con caña**
anglicism ['æŋglisizm] *n.* way of saying something which is English or influenced by English. □ **anglicismo**
Anglo- ['æŋglou] *prefix meaning* English/between England and another country: *Anglo-Swedish cooperation.* □ **anglo**
angora [æŋ'gɔ:rə] *n.* and *adj.* (animal) with thick very soft wool: *angora cat; angora rabbit; angora jumper.* □ **angora, de angora**
angry ['æŋgri] *adj.* very annoyed: *he was very angry with the staff when they laughed at his hat; don't make him angry; he was getting angrier and angrier.* □ **enfadado**

angrily *adv.* in an angry way: *he slammed the telephone down angrily.* □ **enfadado**

anguish ['æŋgwiʃ] *n.* great suffering: *he's in anguish with his toothache.* □ **angustia**

anguished *adj.* showing great suffering: *an anguished letter asking for more money.* □ **angustiado**

angular ['æŋgjulə] *adj.* (*of rock*) sharp/with sharp angles; (*of person*) with prominent bones. □ **anguloso; huesudo**

aniline ['æniliːn] *n.* liquid produced from coal, used to make paint and plastics. □ **anilina**

animal ['æniml] *n.* living creature which is not a plant: *cats and dogs are both animals; there is a great deal of animal life in this field,* there are many wild animals. □ **animal**

animate ['ænimeit] *v.* **1** to make lively. □ **animar**
2 to draw on a film a series of cartoon figures, each with slightly different poses, so that when the film is projected the figures appear to move. □ **hacer dibujos animados**

animated *adj.* **1** lively: *as the evening wore on, the discussion became extremely animated.* □ **animado**
2 *animated cartoon,* cartoon film where the figures appear to move. □ **dibujos animados**

animation [æni'meiʃn] *n.* **1** liveliness/vivacity. □ **animación**
2 act of making an animated cartoon. □ **animación**

animosity [æni'mɔsiti] *n.* unfriendly attitude/hostility to someone: *he has a great feeling of animosity towards his boss.* □ **animosidad**

aniseed ['ænisiːd] *n.* plant whose seeds are used to flavour sweets and drinks. □ **anís**

ankle ['æŋkl] *n.* part of your body joining the foot to the leg. □ **tobillo**
ankle socks, short socks which stop just above the ankles. □ **calcetines**
ankle-deep: *we were ankle-deep in mud,* we were up to our ankles in mud. □ **...hasta los tobillos**

annals ['ænlz] *n. pl.* written yearly account of events/discoveries, etc., which have taken place. □ **anales**

annex [ə'neks] *v.* to join (one country to another). □ **anexar**

annexation [ænek'seiʃn] *n.* joining of one country to another. □ **anexión**

annexe ['æneks] *n.* building attached to another building: *the restaurant is in the annexe.* □ **anexo**

annihilate [ə'naiəleit] *v.* to destroy something completely: *the population of the town was completely annihilated.* □ **aniquilar**

annihilation [ənaiə'leiʃn] *n.* complete destruction: *the oil from the tanker caused the annihilation of thousands of seabirds.* □ **aniquilación**

anniversary [æni'vəːsəri] *n.* (*pl. anniversaries*) **1** day which falls on the same date as an important event in the past: *June 15th is the anniversary of the signing of the Magna Carta.* □ **aniversario**
2 *today is our tenth* ***wedding anniversary,*** we were married ten years ago today. □ **aniversario**

annotate ['ænəteit] *v.* to make notes (on something). □ **anotar**
annotated edition *of a book,* edition with the text and notes. □ **edición anotada**

announce [ə'nauns] *v.* to tell publicly: *the mayor announced the result of the election; I am happy to announce that my daughter is getting married.* □ **anunciar**

announcement *n.* public statement: *here is an announcement from the police headquarters; I have two announcements to make.* □ **anuncio, declaración**

announcer *n.* person on radio or television who announces programmes, reads the news, etc. □ **locutor**

annoy [ə'nɔi] *v.* to make someone angry: *he annoyed her by saying that she was getting fat.* □ **enojar**

annoyance *n.* state of being annoyed: *she showed her annoyance by marching out of the room and slamming the door.* □ **enojo; enfado**

annoyed *adj.* angry: *he's annoyed because no one has given him a Christmas present.* □ **enfadado**

annual ['ænjuəl] *adj.* which happens once a year: *we're closed for our annual holidays.* □ **anual**
■ *n.* plant that lives for one year only; book which comes out in a new edition each year, especially a children's book published for Christmas. □ **anual**

annually *adv.* every year: *the money is paid twice annually.* □ **anualmente**

annuity [ə'njuiti] *n.* (*pl. annuities*) sum of money which is paid annually. □ **anualidad**

annul [ə'nʌl] *v.* (*he annulled*) to end/to cancel: *their marriage was annulled,* their marriage was legally ended. □ **anular**

annulment *n.* cancellation. □ **anulación**

anode ['ænoud] *n.* positive electric terminal. □ **ánodo**

anodyne ['ænədain] *adj.* and *n.* (medicine) which makes pain less strong; (something) which stops you worrying. □ **anodino**

anoint [ə'nɔint] *v.* to put oil on (a person) as part of a religious ceremony. □ **ungir**

anomaly [ə'nɔməli] *n.* something which is unusual/which does not fit into the pattern: *his job is something of an anomaly.* □ **anomalía**

anomalous *adj.* abnormal/strange. □ **anómalo**

anon [ə'noun] *adv.* soon: *you will have further news anon.* □ **pronto**

anonymous [ə'nɔniməs] *adj.* (person) who does not give his name: *he received an anonymous letter,* a letter which had no signature. □ **anónimo**

anonymity [ænə'nimiti] *n.* hiding of your name: *to preserve his anonymity he wrote all the letters with his left hand.* □ **anonimato**

anonymously *adv.* without giving your name: *he gave $50 to charity anonymously.* □ **anónimamente**

anorak ['ænəræk] *n.* waterproof jacket with a hood. □ **anorak**

anorexia nervosa [ænə'reksiə nəː'vousə] *n.* illness where you refuse to eat because of worry that you may become fat. □ **anorexia**

another [ə'nʌðə] *adj.* and *pron.* **1** (one) more: *would you like another glass of beer? in another two years we should have finished building the house.* □ **otro**
2 a different one: *he arrived in one car, his wife in another; I'll put on another dress; they fell down one after another.* □ **otro**
3 ***one another,*** each other: *we like to be near one another; the best advice is to help one another.* □ **uno a otro**

answer ['ɑːnsə] *n.* reply: *I telephoned the doctor, but there was no answer; can you tell me the answer to this maths question? I am writing in answer to your letter.* □ **respuesta, contestación**
■ *v.* **1** to reply: *the nurse answered the telephone; why didn't you answer my letter?* □ **contestar**
2 *I don't like children who* ***answer back,*** who reply rudely. □ **responder**
3 ***answer the door*** open the door in answer to a knock or ring. □ **abrir la puerta**

answerable *adj.* **1** responsible: *he isn't answerable for his actions.* □ **responsable**
2 *he isn't answerable to anybody,* he is independent. □ **no responde ante nadie**

answering *adj. an answering shout,* a shout in an-

swer. □ **de respuesta**
answering service, recorded message on the telephone which answers automatically for someone who is out. □ **contestador automático**
ant [ænt] *n.* small insect living in large communities. □ **hormiga**
ants' nest, nest of thousands of ants. □ **hormiguero**
anteater *n.* animal which eats ants. □ **hormiguero**
anthill *n.* mound of earth containing an ants' nest. □ **hormiguero**
antagonize [æn'tægənaiz] *v.* to arouse someone's hostility: *don't antagonize him,* do not make him furious. □ **enemistar**
antagonism *n.* hostility/opposition: *the government's plans provoked the antagonism of the teachers.* □ **antagonismo**
antagonist *n.* opponent. □ **antagonista**
antarctic [æn'tɑːktik] *adj.* and *n.* (referring to) the area around the South Pole: *an antarctic expedition.* □ **antártico**
Antarctica *n.* the region around the South Pole. □ **Antártida**
ante ['ænti] *n.* money gambled by a player at the beginning of a game of poker. □ **apuesta inicial**
ante- ['ænti] *prefix meaning* before. □ **antes de, ante**
antecedent [ænti'siːdənt] *n.* earlier form of something; something which comes before. □ **antecedente**
antedate ['æntideit] *v.* to put an earlier date on (a cheque); to happen earlier: *this must have antedated our conversation last Wednesday,* this must have happened earlier than our conversation. □ **preceder**
antediluvian [æntidi'luːviən] *adj.* very ancient. □ **antediluviano**
antelope ['æntiloup] *n.* type of deer found in Africa. □ **antílope**
antenatal [ænti'neitl] *adj.* before birth. □ **prenatal**
antenatal clinic, clinic for pregnant women. □ **maternidad**
antenna [æn'tenə] *n.* **1** (*pl. antennae*) feeler/sensitive apparatus for sensing: *a butterfly has two antennae.* □ **antena**
2 (*pl. antennas*) *Amer.* ***television antenna,*** television aerial. □ **antena**
anterior [æn'tiːəriə] *adj.* which comes earlier. □ **anterior**
anteroom ['æntiruːm] *n.* small room leading to a larger room. □ **antesala**
anthem ['ænθəm] *n.* choral music (to celebrate a special occasion). □ **himno**
national anthem, official music of a country, played to honour the state: *'God save the Queen' is the British national anthem.* □ **himno nacional**
anther ['ænθə] *n.* tip of a stamen which carries pollen. □ **antera**
anthology [æn'θɔlədʒi] *n.* (*pl. anthologies*) collection of poems/stories, etc., by various people in one book. □ **antología**
anthracite ['ænθrəsait] *n.* hard coal which gives off a lot of heat but not much smoke or flame. □ **antracita**
anthropoid ['ænθrəpɔid] *adj.* and *n.* (ape) which is like a man. □ **antropoide**
anthropology [ænθrə'pɔlədʒi] *n.* study of man. □ **antropología**
anthropological [ænθrəpə'lɔdʒikl] *adj.* referring to the study of man: *anthropological expedition to study cannibals.* □ **antropológico**
anthropologist [ænθrə'pɔlədʒist] *n.* scientist who studies man. □ **antropólogo**
anti- ['ænti] *prefix meaning* against. □ **anti**
anti-tank gun, gun used against tanks. □ **antitanque**
anti-malaria tablet, tablet used to prevent malaria. □ **antimalaria**
antibiotic [æntibai'ɔtik] *adj.* and *n.* (drug) which kills bacteria: *he is taking antibiotics three times a day.* □ **antibiótico**
antibody ['æntibɔdi] *n.* (*pl. antibodies*) chemical substance built up in the human body to fight a particular disease. □ **anticuerpo**
anticipate [æn'tisipeit] *v.* **1** to act because you see something is about to happen: *the brewery anticipated a rise in demand, and so increased production.* □ **prever**
2 to expect something to happen: *I anticipated that the weather would soon turn hot.* □ **prever**
anticipation [æntisi'peiʃn] *n.* expectation that something will happen. □ **previsión**
anticlimax [ænti'klaimæks] *n.* (*pl. anticlimaxes*) feeling of being let down when something exciting does not happen: *the final tennis match was an anticlimax.* □ **decepción**
anticlockwise [ænti'klɔkwaiz] *adj.* and *adv.* in the opposite direction to the hands of a clock: *you turn the screwdriver anticlockwise to unscrew screws.* □ **en sentido contrario a las agujas del reloj**
antics ['æntiks] *n. pl.* playing around; fooling: *the children laughed at the antics of the clowns.* □ **travesuras**
anticyclone [ænti'saikloun] *n.* area of high atmospheric pressure. □ **anticiclón**
antidote ['æntidout] *n.* something which counteracts the effects of a poison/of something bad. □ **antídoto**
antifreeze ['æntifriːz] *n.* liquid put in the radiator of a car to prevent it freezing in cold weather. □ **anticongelante**
antihistamine [ænti'histəmiːn] *n.* medicine which prevents allergies. □ **antihistamínico**
antimony ['æntiməni] *n.* (*chemical element*: Sb) white metal used to make alloys. □ **antimonio**
antipathy [æn'tipəθi] *n.* (*pl. antipathies*) feeling of not liking someone/something: *his antipathy towards the Welsh.* □ **antipatía**
antipodes [æn'tipədiːz] *n. pl.* opposite side of the earth, especially Australia and New Zealand. □ **antípodas**
antiquary [æn'tikwəri] *n.* (*pl. antiquaries*) person who collects, studies or sells antiques. □ **anticuario**
antiquarian [ænti'kwɛəriən] *adj. antiquarian bookseller,* bookseller who sells old books. □ **librero de viejo**
antiquated ['æntikweitid] *adj.* old (and decrepit): *he arrived on an antiquated bicycle.* □ **anticuado**
antique [æn'tiːk] *adj.* very old (and valuable): *I have bought an antique bookcase.* □ **antiguo**
■ *n.* old and valuable object. □ **antigüedad**
antique shop, shop which sells old objects. □ **anticuario, tienda de antigüedades**
antiquity [æn'tikwiti] *n.* **1** ancient times. □ **Antigüedad**
2 *its origin is lost in the mists of antiquity,* it is so old, no one knows what its origin is. □ **antigüedad**
antirrhinum [ænti'rainəm] *n.* summer flower, the snapdragon. □ **antirrino**
antiseptic [ænti'septik] *adj.* and *n.* (substance) which prevents a wound becoming septic: *put some antiseptic on that cut.* □ **antiséptico**
antisocial [ænti'souʃl] *adj.* disliking society; bad for society: *smoking is antisocial; he's an antisocial character.* □ **antisocial**
antithesis [æn'tiθəsis] *n.* (*pl. antitheses*) opposite: *she's the antithesis of her mother.* □ **antítesis**

antitoxin [ænti'touksin] *n.* substance which counteracts the effect of a toxin. □ **antitoxina**
antler ['æntlə] *n.* horn (on deer). □ **asta, cornamenta**
antonym ['æntənim] *n.* word which means the opposite of another word. □ **antónimo**
anus ['einəs] *n.* (*pl. anuses*) hole through which animals produce waste matter from the bowels. □ **ano**
anvil ['ænvil] *n.* large block on which a blacksmith beats hot metal. □ **yunque**
anxiety [æŋ'zaiəti] *n.* (*pl. anxieties*) **1** great worry: *she was sick with anxiety before her examinations.* □ **ansiedad, gran preocupación**
2 eagerness: *he fell down the stairs in his anxiety to get to the door.* □ **afán**
anxious ['æŋkʃəs] *adj.* **1** very worried: *I am anxious about my brother's health; she became anxious when her daughter didn't come back home.* □ **muy preocupado**
2 eager: *he is anxious to start work; I am anxious to meet her.* □ **deseoso de...**
anxiously *adv.* worriedly: *he looked anxiously at his watch; she watched the sick child's face anxiously.* □ **con gran preocupación**
any ['eni] *adj.* and *pron.* **1** it does not matter which: *you can wear any dress you like; come and see me any day next week; any doctor will tell you his illness is incurable; take any two cards from the pack; which one should I take? - take any.* □ **cualquier(a)**
2 some: *have you any sugar left? give me some coffee - I haven't got any; he hasn't any money; if any of those people should see him.* □ **(un poco de...)**
■ *adv.* **1** *I can't go any further,* I can go no further. □ **más lejos**
2 *have you any more cake?,* have you any cake left? □ **más**
anybody ['enibɔdi] *pron.* **1** it does not matter who: *anybody can learn French; anybody would think he was mad.* □ **cualquiera**
2 some person: *has anybody seen John?* □ **alguien**
3 *I didn't meet anybody else,* I met nobody else. □ **...a nadie**
4 *there was hardly anybody in the room,* there were very few people. □ **nadie**
anyhow ['enihau] *adv.* carelessly: *he laid the table anyhow,* he laid the table in a slapdash way; *she had her hat on all anyhow,* her hat was not straight. □ **de cualquier modo/manera**
■ *conj.* = **anyway.**
anyone ['eniwʌn] *pron.* = **anybody.**
anything ['eniθiŋ] *pron.* **1** it does not matter what: *our dog will eat anything; you can have anything you like.* □ **cualquier cosa, de todo, lo que quieras**
2 something: *is anything worrying you? can I do anything to help? has anything happened to them?* □ **algo**
3 *he hardly ate anything,* he ate almost nothing. □ **nada**
4 *it's raining* ***like anything,*** it's pouring down. □ **...como nunca**
anyway ['eniwei] *adv.* and *conj.* in any case: *we were late, anyway the film wasn't very good.* □ **de todos modos**
anywhere ['eniwɛə] *prep.* **1** it does not matter where: *just put those books anywhere.* □ **en cualquier parte**
2 somewhere: *can you see it anywhere?* □ **...en algún sitio**
aorta [ei'ɔ:tə] *n.* main artery taking blood from the heart. □ **aorta**
apart [ə'pɑ:t] *adv.* **1** separated: *how far apart were the two cars? the two accidents were only a few hours apart.* □ **¿qué separación...?; en un intervalo de pocas horas**
2 separate: *we planted the trees wide apart.* □ **muy separados**
3 to pieces: *the watch came apart in my hands; they are taking the engine apart.* □ **desmontar, en piezas**
4 *can you* ***tell*** *them* ***apart?,*** can you say which is which? □ **por separado**
5 ***apart from,*** except: *everyone had something to eat apart from me.* □ **aparte de**
apartheid [ə'pɑ:tait] *n.* policy in South Africa for segregating the black and white sections of the population. □ **segregación racial**
apartment [ə'pɑ:tmənt] *n.* **1** set of rooms in a large building, as a separate living unit. □ **piso**
2 *Amer.* flat. □ **apartamento**
apartment block, block of flats. □ **bloque de pisos**
apathy ['æpəθi] *n.* lack of interest: *the campaign failed because of public apathy.* □ **apatía**
apathetic [æpə'θetik] *adj.* uninterested. □ **apático**
ape [eip] *n.* large man-like monkey with no tail. □ **simio**
aperient [ə'piəriənt] *adj.* and *n.* substance which makes the bowels work. □ **laxante**
aperitif [ə'periti:f] *n.* drink taken before a meal to give you an appetite. □ **aperitivo**
aperture ['æpətʃə] *n.* hole; opening. □ **abertura**
apex ['eipeks] *n.* (*pl. apexes*) top (of a triangle). □ **vértice**
aphid ['eifid] **aphis** ['eifis, 'æfis] *n.* small insect which sucks the sap from plants. □ **áfido**
aphorism ['æfərizəm] *n.* short wise saying. □ **aforismo**
aphrodisiac [æfrə'diziæk] *n.* substance which increases sexual desire. □ **afrodisiaco**
apiary ['eipiəri] *n.* (*pl. apiaries*) place where bees are kept. □ **colmenar**
apiculture ['æpikʌltʃə] *n.* keeping of bees (for honey). □ **apicultura**
apiece [ə'pi:s] *adv.* each: *these apples cost 10p apiece; the children were given two bars of chocolate apiece.* □ **cada uno**
aplomb [ə'plɔm] *n.* calmness; self-confidence. □ **aplomo**
apocalyptic [əpɔkə'liptik] *adj.* which prophesies doom and destruction. □ **apocalíptico**
apocryphal [ə'pɔkrifl] *adj.* probably untrue. □ **apócrifo**
apogee ['æpədʒi:] *n.* highest point (in the orbit of a planet/ in the career of a statesman, etc.). □ **apogeo**
apologetic [əpɔlə'dʒetik] *adj.* making excuses; saying you are sorry: *he was quite apologetic about the accident,* he said he was sorry for the accident. □ **apologético (excusarse, lamentar)**
apologetically *adv. she smiled apologetically,* she smiled to say she was sorry. □ **excusándose**
apologize [ə'pɔlədʒaiz] *v.* to say you are sorry: *he apologized for keeping us waiting; the waiter apologized to the customers for the slow service.* □ **disculparse**
apology *n.* saying you are sorry: *my apologies for being late,* I'm sorry I'm late. □ **disculpas**
apoplexy ['æpəpleksi] *n.* (*pl. apoplexies*) sudden inability to move caused by a stroke. □ **apoplejía**
apoplectic [æpə'plektik] *adj.* **1** referring to apoplexy. □ **apoplético**
2 red-faced. □ **furioso**
apostle [ə'pɔsl] *n.* one of the twelve men who were the original disciples of Jesus. □ **apóstol**
apostrophe [ə'pɔstrəfi] *n.* printing sign (') which shows either that a letter has been left out (*weren't*)

or with *s* to show possession (*a boy's coat, the girls' team*). □ **apóstrofo**

appal [ə'pɔːl] *v.* (*he is appalled*) to frighten/to make horrified: *I am appalled at the wastage of food.* □ **horrorizar**

appalling *adj.* horrible/frightening: *there were appalling scenes of destruction during the bombing of the town.* □ **horroroso**

appallingly *adv.* frighteningly: *the traffic is appallingly slow on Saturday afternoons.* □ **horrorosamente**

apparatus [æpə'reitəs] *n.* (*no pl.*) equipment (for doing scientific tests, etc.): *have you got your own apparatus for developing films?* □ **aparato**

apparel [ə'pærəl] *n.* (*formal*) clothes. □ **vestiduras**

apparent [ə'pærənt] *adj.* which seems: *his apparent lack of concern.* □ **aparente**

apparently *adv.* as it seems: *the car apparently skidded on the patch of oil,* it seems that the car skidded. □ **aparentemente**

apparition [æpə'riʃn] *n.* ghost; something which seems strange. □ **aparición**

appeal [ə'piːl] *n.* **1** asking for (help, etc.): *he made an appeal for money to help the victims of the earthquake.* □ **llamamiento**

2 request to the law courts to reconsider a verdict: *the prisoner has lodged an appeal against his sentence.* □ **apelación**

3 ***sex appeal,*** physical attraction. □ **atractivo sexual**

■ *v.* **1** to ask for: *the victims of the earthquake appealed for help.* □ **pedir**

2 to attract: *does the idea of going for a picnic appeal to you? it doesn't appeal to me,* I don't like it. □ **atraer**

appealing *adj.* attractive; as if asking for help: *he asked in an appealing tone; the dog has such appealing eyes.* □ **atractivo**

appear [ə'piə] *v.* **1** to come into sight: *the ship suddenly appeared out of the mist.* □ **aparecer**

2 to be present at: *he had to appear in court.* □ **comparecer**

3 *he is appearing in 'Waiting for Godot',* he is acting in the play. □ **actuar**

4 to seem: *he appeared to be waving a flag; it appears that no one was in charge of the money.* □ **parecer**

appearance *n.* **1** how a thing or person looks: *his dirty appearance; you could tell from his appearance that he hadn't washed for days.* □ **aspecto**

2 *we must **keep up appearances,*** we must keep up our standards. □ **apariencia**

3 *you must **put in an appearance** at the church fete,* you must attend. □ **presencia**

4 *this is her **first appearance** on the London stage,* this is the first time she has acted in London. □ **aparición**

appease [ə'piːz] *v.* to try to avoid/to soothe: *this present is to appease the anger of the headmaster.* □ **apaciguar**

appeasement *n.* policy of avoiding conflict. □ **apaciguamiento**

append [ə'pend] *v.* to attach/to join. □ **añadir**

appendage *n.* something attached. □ **añadido**

appendix [ə'pendiks] *n.* **1** (*pl. appendixes*) small tube attached to main intestine: *he's had his appendix out,* he's had an operation to remove his appendix. □ **apéndice**

2 (*pl. appendices*) section at the back of a book sometimes giving information which is additional to the text: *look up the table of weights and measures in the appendix.* □ **apéndice**

appendectomy [æpen'dektəmi] *n.* operation to remove the appendix. □ **apendectomía**

appendicitis [əpendi'saitis] *n.* illness caused by inflammation of the appendix: *he was rushed to hospital with acute appendicitis.* □ **apendicitis**

appertain [æpə'tein] *v.* (*formal*) to be relevant: *the documents appertaining to the case.* □ **relacionarse con**

appetite ['æpitait] *n.* desire to eat, etc.: *a swim before breakfast will give you an appetite; he has a good appetite,* he eats a lot; *she has an insatiable appetite for work.* □ **apetito; ganas de**

appetizer *n.* snack taken with drinks before the main meal. □ **aperitivo**

appetizing *adj.* which makes you want to eat: *a very appetizing smell came from the kitchen.* □ **apetitoso**

applaud [ə'plɔːd] *v.* to clap or cheer to show you appreciate something: *the audience applauded the pianist.* □ **aplaudir**

applause *n.* clapping and cheering: *the applause at the end of the play went on for ten minutes.* □ **aplauso**

apple ['æpl] *n.* common hard fruit, growing on a tree: *apple pie; stewed apples; eating apples; cooking apple,* sour green apple for cooking. □ **manzana**

apple (***tree***), tree which bears apples. □ **manzano**

appliance [ə'plaiəns] *n.* **1** machine/device: *electrical appliances.* □ **aparato**

household appliances, cooker, refrigerator, washing machine, etc. □ **electrodomésticos**

2 *three appliances went to the fire,* three fire engines went to the fire. □ **coche de bomberos**

appliqué [ə'pliːkei] *n.* decoration made by sewing shaped pieces of cloth onto a larger piece. □ **aplicación**

apply [ə'plai] *v.* (*applied; applying*) **1** to put something on something: *apply two coats of paint; he applied the brakes too sharply.* □ **aplicar**

2 to be relevant: *it doesn't apply in his case; does it apply to you?,* does this refer to you? □ **ajustarse; referirse**

3 to ask someone for something (especially a job): *I have applied for a job as a teacher; for further information, please apply to the head office.* □ **solicitar, dirigirse**

4 ***to apply yourself,*** to work hard. □ **aplicarse**

applicable [ə'plikəbl] *adj.* which refers to: *is this rule applicable in your case?* □ **aplicable**

applicant ['æplikənt] *n.* person who applies for a job; candidate. □ **aspirante**

application [æpli'keiʃn] *n.* **1** action of putting something on something: *application of oil to the wheels; for external application only,* only to be used on the outside of the body. □ **aplicación; uso**

2 asking for (a job, etc.): *I have sent in my application for a job in his office.* □ **solicitud**

application form, form to be filled in when applying for a job. □ **impreso de solicitud**

appoint [ə'pɔint] *v.* to give (someone) a job (as): *Mr Smith has been appointed manager; we are going to appoint a new salesman.* □ **designar**

appointed *adj.* arranged/stated: *we must be there at the appointed time,* at the time we have arranged. □ **convenido**

appointment *n.* **1** being given a job: *he has just heard of his appointment as manager.* □ **nombramiento**

2 meeting time which has been agreed: *I have an appointment with the dentist at 2 o'clock; he couldn't keep his appointment,* he was not able to be there at the right time. □ **cita**

apportion [ə'pɔːʃn] *v.* (*formal*) to divide up/to share out. □ **repartir**
apposite ['æpəzit] *adj.* fitting/appropriate (remark). □ **apropiado**
appraise [ə'preiz] *v.* to judge the value of (something). □ **valorar, tasar**
appraisal *n.* evaluation. □ **valoración, tasación**
appreciate [ə'priːʃieit] *v.* **1** to feel the value of (something): *his telegram was greatly appreciated; she certainly appreciates good music.* □ **apreciar**
2 to increase in value: *gold has appreciated in value.* □ **aumentar de valor**
appreciable *adj.* which can be felt or noticed: *there was an appreciable fall in the temperature; there was an appreciable quantity of snow,* there was quite a large quantity of snow. □ **apreciable**
appreciably *adv.* in a way which could be felt: *the temperature grew appreciably colder.* □ **apreciablemente**
appreciation [əpriːʃi'eiʃn] *n.* **1** estimation (of the value of something). □ **apreciación**
2 increase in value. □ **aumento de valor**
appreciative [ə'priːʃjətiv] *adj.* **1** praising. □ **elogioso**
2 *there was a very appreciative audience,* the audience was very enthusiastic. □ **entusiasta**
apprehend [æpri'hend] *v.* to arrest (a criminal). □ **detener**
apprehension [æpri'henʃn] *n.* fear. □ **aprensión**
apprehensive *adj.* afraid/nervous: *he's feeling a bit apprehensive about meeting her mother.* □ **aprensivo**
apprentice [ə'prentis] *n.* youth who works for a skilled man to learn from him. □ **aprendiz**
apprenticeship *n.* time you spend as an apprentice: *he has to serve a seven year apprenticeship before he will be qualified.* □ **aprendizaje**
approach [ə'proutʃ] *n.* (*pl. approaches*) **1** way of dealing (with a problem): *her approach to the problem of money is very direct.* □ **enfoque**
2 *he made approaches to her to join his firm,* he contacted her to ask her to join his firm. □ **proposiciones**
3 way into: *the approaches to London,* roads leading to London; *an approach road,* a road leading to a main road. □ **acceso; vía de acceso; los accesos...**
■ *v.* **1** to go near: *we're approaching Paris; the train was approaching the station when the accident happened.* □ **acercarse**
2 to deal with (a question): *it is best to approach the problem by concentrating on the details.* □ **abordar, enfocar**
approachable *adj.* easy to talk to: *he is a very approachable person.* □ **accesible**
approaching *adj.* which is coming closer: *the approaching storm.* □ **...que se acerca**
approbation [æprə'beiʃn] *n.* (*formal*) approval. □ **aprobación**
appropriate [ə'proupriət] *adj.* suitable/which fits: *he chose an appropriate moment, and then asked her to marry him; I'm trying to think of an appropriate joke to start my speech.* □ **apropiado**
■ *v.* to seize (something which belongs to someone else): *the general appropriated the army stores.* □ **apropiarse**
appropriation [əproupri'eiʃn] *n.* **1** seizure: *the appropriation of land by the dictator.* □ **apropiación**
2 money voted to a budget. □ **asignación**
approve [ə'pruːv] *v.* to express agreement with something; to allow: *has the editor approved the text?* □ **aprobar**
to approve of something, to be in agreement with something: *I don't approve of smoking.* □ **aprobar**
approval *n.* **1** allowing (something): *she nodded approval,* she nodded to show that she agreed. □ **aprobación; asentimiento**
2 *he has bought the cooker **on approval,*** on trial. □ **a prueba**
approving *adj.* which shows agreement: *he cast an approving glance round the room.* □ **aprobatorio**
approximate [ə'prɔksimət] *adj.* rough (calculation): *the approximate cost will be $25.* □ **aproximado**
■ *v.* to be nearly correct. □ **aproximarse**
approximately *adv.* roughly: *the books are worth approximately $10; the train arrived at approximately 9 o'clock; the car was travelling at approximately 50 miles per hour.* □ **aproximadamente**
approximation [əprɔksi'meiʃn] *n.* rough estimate. □ **aproximación**
appurtenance [ə'pəːtənəns] *n.* (*formal*) thing which is connected to or belongs to something else. □ **accesorio**
apricot ['eiprikɔt] *n.* yellow fruit with large stone grown in warm countries; tree which bears apricots. □ **albaricoque; albaricoquero**
April ['eiprəl] *n.* fourth month of the year: *April 30th is the last day of the month.* □ **abril**
April Fool *n.* person who is tricked on April 1st. □ **inocente**
April Fool's Day *n.* April 1st/day when people are tricked. □ **día de los Santos Inocentes**
apron ['eiprən] *n.* **1** piece of cloth/plastic, etc., worn over clothes to protect them when doing housework. □ **delantal**
2 area in an airport where aircraft are parked. □ **pista**
apse [æps] *n.* rounded end of a church. □ **ábside**
apt [æpt] *adj.* **1** which fits well: *he used a very apt expression to describe his aunt.* □ **adecuado**
2 likely: *he is apt to lose his temper; the car is apt to break down on hills.* □ **probable**
aptitude *n.* ability: *you must take an aptitude test,* a test to see if you are fitted for the job. □ **aptitud**
aptly *adv.* fittingly: *William was aptly named the Conqueror.* □ **apropiadamente**
aptness *n.* fitness (of an expression): *the aptness of his descriptions of rural life.* □ **lo apropiado**
aqualung ['ækwəlʌŋ] *n.* skindiver's portable oxygen apparatus. □ **botella de oxígeno**
aquamarine [ækwəmə'riːn] *adj.* dark blue-green. □ **de color verde mar**
aquarium [ə'kwɛəriəm] *n.* **1** tank for keeping fish. □ **acuario**
2 exhibition (usually part of a zoo) where fish are displayed. □ **acuario**
Aquarius [ə'kwɛəriəs] *n.* one of the signs of the Zodiac, shaped like a man carrying water. □ **Acuario**
aquatic [æ'kwætik] *adj.* which lives in water: *aquatic plants.* □ **acuático**
aqueduct ['ækwidʌkt] *n.* channel which takes water over land. □ **acueducto**
aquiline ['ækwilain] *adj.* hooked (nose). □ **aguileño**
Arab ['ærəb] *adj.* and *n.* *see* **Arabia.**
arabesque ['ærəbesk] *n.* complicated design of leaves/flowers, etc. □ **arabesco**
Arabia [ə'reibiə] *n.* area in the Near East. □ **Arabia**
Arab ['ærəb] *adj.* referring to Arabia: *the Arab States.* □ **árabe**
■ *n.* Muslim person living in Arabia or some other Near Eastern countries. □ **árabe**
Arabian *adj.* referring to Arabia. □ **árabe**
Arabic ['ærəbik] *n.* language spoken by Arabs. □ **árabe**

■ *adj. arabic numerals,* signs for numbers written 1, 2, 3, 4, etc. □ **...arábigos**
arable ['ærəbl] *adj.* (land) which is good for growing crops. □ **cultivable**
arachnid [ə'ræknid] *n.* type of animal with eight legs, such as a spider. □ **arácnido**
arbitrate ['ɑːbitreit] *v.* to judge: *to arbitrate between two parties in a quarrel.* □ **arbitrar**
arbitrarily *adv.* at random: *he was arbitrarily dismissed.* □ **arbitrariamente**
arbitrary *adj.* taken at random: *everyone was surprised by his arbitrary decision to sell the shop.* □ **arbitrario**
arbitration [ɑːbi'treiʃn] *n.* judgement in a dispute. □ **arbitraje**
arbitrator ['ɑːbitreitə] *n.* person who judges a dispute. □ **árbitro**
arboratum [ɑːbə'riːtəm] *n.* collection of trees grown for botanical study. □ **jardín botánico**
arc [ɑːk] *n.* **1** part of a circle: *the plane turned in a wide arc overhead.* □ **arco**
2 electric spark jumping between two points. □ **arco voltaico**
arc-lamp *n.* very bright light. □ **lámpara de arco**
arcade [ɑː'keid] *n. **shopping arcade,*** row of shops covered by a roof. □ **galería comercial**
arcane [ɑː'kein] *adj.* mysterious/secret. □ **arcano**
arch [ɑːtʃ] *n.* (*pl. arches*) **1** vault/rounded structure forming a roof, or top of a door: *Norman churches have round arches but Gothic churches have pointed ones.* □ **bóveda; arco**
2 ***triumphal arch,*** large construction with a rounded vault over a carriageway, usually built to celebrate a victory. □ **arco triunfal**
3 *arch of the foot,* rounded part under the foot. □ **puente**
■ *v* to make round: *the cat arched its back.* □ **arquear**
■ *adj.* wicked and playful. □ **travieso**
arched *adj.* made of an arch: *an arched doorway.* □ **en arco**
archway *n.* passage covered with an arch. □ **arcada**
arch- [ɑːtʃ] *prefix meaning* greatest: *arch-enemy.* □ **archi**
archaeology [ɑːki'ɔlədʒi] *n.* study of ancient civilization: *he is an expert in Egyptian archaeology.* □ **arqueología**
industrial archaeology, study of old machinery/factories/mines, etc. □ **arqueología industrial**
archaeological [ɑːkiə'lɔdʒikl] *adj.* referring to archaeology: *archaeological remains; the archaeological site is being excavated.* □ **arqueológico**
archaeologist [ɑːki'ɔlədʒist] *n.* person who studies ancient civilizations. □ **arqueólogo**
archaic [ɑː'keiik] *adj.* very ancient. □ **arcaico**
archangel ['ɑːkeindʒl] *n.* highest rank of angel. □ **arcángel**
archbishop *n.* [ɑːtʃ'biʃəp] very important bishop/leader of bishops. □ **arzobispo**
archer ['ɑːtʃə] *n.* person who shoots with a bow and arrow: *the king was killed by an arrow shot by the French archers.* □ **arquero**
archery *n.* sport of shooting with a bow and arrow at a target. □ **tiro con arco**
archetype ['ɑːkitaip] *n.* original version from which other versions can be copied. □ **arquetipo**
archetypal *adj.* original; perfect (example). □ **arquetípico**
archipelago [ɑːki'peləgou] *n.* (*pl. archipelagos*) group of islands. □ **archipiélago**
architect ['ɑːkitekt] *n.* person who designs buildings. □ **arquitecto**
architecture *n.* design of buildings: *the parliament building is in the classical style of architecture.* □ **arquitectura**
archives ['ɑːkaivz] *n. pl.* collection of documents, especially public or historical records. □ **archivo**
archivist ['ɑːkivist] *n.* librarian who looks after archives. □ **archivero**
arctic ['ɑːktik] *adj.* and *n.* **1** (referring to) the area around the North Pole. □ **ártico**
2 *we're having really arctic weather these days,* it's extremely cold. □ **polar**
ardent ['ɑːdənt] *adj.* very strenuous; keen: *he is an ardent supporter of proportional representation.* □ **ardiente**
ardently *adv.* strenuously/fiercely: *she ardently opposed the proposal to demolish the old houses.* □ **ardientemente**
ardour ['ɑːdə] *Amer.* **ardor** *n.* violence (of emotions). □ **fervor**
arduous ['ɑːdjuəs] *adj.* very difficult/hard (task). □ **arduo**
arduously *adv.* with great difficulty: *after we had arduously collected all these statistics, no one bothered to read them.* □ **arduamente**
are [ɑː] *v. see* **be.**
area ['ɛəriə] *n.* **1** space; measure of the surface of something: *the area of this room is four square metres; how do you measure the area of a circle?* □ **área**
2 region: *the London area,* the part of the country round London. □ **área**
the sterling area, the countries where the $ sterling is the main exchange currency. □ **zona de ...**
3 general subject: *the company is weak in the area of exports.* □ **campo de...**
arena [ə'riːnə] *n.* space where sports and fights take place. □ **arena**
Argentina [ɑːdʒən'tiːnə] *n.* country in South America. □ **Argentina**
Argentinian *adj.* referring to Argentina. □ **argentino**
■ *n.* person from Argentina. □ **argentino**
argue ['ɑːgjuː] *v.* to discuss without agreeing; to quarrel: *they argued over who should pay for the damage; we argued about politics for hours; don't argue with me,* don't discuss it, do as I say. □ **discutir**
arguable *adj.* which is open to discussion: *whether it is better to save money or to spend it in times of inflation is arguable.* □ **discutible**
argument *n.* **1** quarrel/discussion without agreement: *I got into an argument with the waiter about the bill.* □ **discusión**
2 reasoning: *his argument is very weak.* □ **razonamiento**
argumentative [ɑːgju'mentətiv] *adj.* (person) who likes to quarrel. □ **discutidor**
aria ['ɑːriə] *n.* long solo song in opera. □ **aria**
arid ['ærid] *adj.* very dry. □ **árido**
aridity *n.* extreme dryness. □ **aridez**
Aries ['ɛəriːz] *n.* one of the signs of the Zodiac, shaped like a ram. □ **Aries**
arise [ə'raiz] *v.* (*it arose; it has arisen*) **1** to appear; to start: *a storm arose; an argument arose over the bill.* □ **surgir, empezar**
2 to result from: *the misunderstanding has arisen from the wording of the letter.* □ **originarse**
aristocrat ['æristəkræt] *n.* person who is born into a high rank of society. □ **aristócrata**
aristocracy [æri'stɔkrəsi] *n.* top rank (by birth) of

society. □ **aristocracia**

aristocratic [ærɪstə'krætɪk] *adj.* referring to the aristocracy; superior: *he adopted a very aristocratic attitude towards his staff.* □ **aristocrático**

arithmetic [ə'rɪθmetɪk] *n.* calculations with figures: *addition, subtraction, multiplication and division are all parts of arithmetic.* □ **aritmética**

arithmetical [ærɪθ'metɪkl] *adj.* referring to arithmetic. □ **aritmético**

arm [ɑːm] *n.* **1** part of the body between hand and shoulder: *put your arms above your head; my right arm is stiff after playing tennis.* □ **brazo**

2 *they were walking **arm in arm**,* with their arms linked. □ **del brazo**

3 *they welcomed me **with open arms**,* they gave me a warm welcome. □ **...con los brazos abiertos**

4 something shaped like an arm; piece at the side of a chair to rest your arms on: *he sat on the arm of my chair.* □ **brazo**

5 narrow stretch of sea running inland. □ **brazo de mar**

6 *arms,* weapons. □ **armas**

small arms, pistols/rifles, etc., which can be carried easily. □ **armas portátiles**

arms race, race between countries to equip themselves with superior weapons. □ **carrera de armamentos**

up in arms, very angry/furious. □ **poner el grito en el cielo**

■ *v.* to equip with weapons: *the soldiers were armed with machine guns.* □ **armar**

armaments *n. pl.* heavy weapons/war equipment. □ **armamento**

armband *n.* piece of cloth which you put round your arm: *the ambulance crew were wearing Red Cross armbands.* □ **brazalete**

armchair *n.* chair with arms. □ **sillón**

armed *adj.* equipped with weapons: *watch out - the man is armed!* □ **armado**

the armed forces, the army, navy and air force. □ **las fuerzas armadas**

armful *n.* load carried in your arms: *the children were carrying armfuls of flowers.* □ **brazada**

armhole *n.* hole in a piece of clothing through which you put your arm. □ **manga (interior)**

armour *n.* (*no pl.*) metal protective clothes for medieval soldiers: *the knight wore a suit of armour.* □ **armadura**

armoured *adj.* protected by metal. □ **blindado**

armoured car, military car made of thick metal which carries a small gun. □ **vehículo blindado**

armour-plated *adj.* protected by thick metal plates. □ **blindado; acorazado**

armoury *n.* (*pl. armouries*) place where weapons are kept. □ **arsenal**

armpit *n.* part of your body under where your arm joins the shoulder. □ **axila**

army *n.* (*pl. armies*) all the soldiers of a country: *he's in the army,* he's a soldier. □ **ejército**

armada [ɑː'mɑːdə] *n.* fleet of warships. □ **armada**

armadillo [ɑːmə'dɪləu] *n.* small South American animal covered with a flexible shell. □ **armadillo**

armistice ['ɑːmɪstɪs] *n.* decision to stop fighting temporarily. □ **armisticio**

aroma [ə'roumə] *n.* (pleasant) smell (of coffee/wine, etc.). □ **aroma**

aromatic [ærə'mætɪk] *adj.* which smells strongly: *aromatic herbs.* □ **aromático**

arose [ə'rouz] *v. see* **arise.**

around [ə'raund] *adv.* **1** surrounding a place: *all around was an expanse of white snow,* everywhere surrounding the area. □ **alrededor**

2 in an indefinite place: *the newspaper must be somewhere around.* □ **por algún lado**

■ *prep.* **1** surrounding: *there was water all around the house; the area around London.* □ **alrededor de**

2 approximately: *the car cost around $2,000.* □ **alrededor de, unos...**

arouse [ə'rauz] *v.* **1** to wake: *he was aroused by the sound of the fire alarm.* □ **despertar**

2 to excite: *his temper was aroused by the speech.* □ **excitar**

arpeggio [ɑː'pedʒɪəu] *n.* chord, with the notes played one after the other and not all together. □ **arpegio**

arrange [ə'reɪndʒ] *v.* **1** to put in order: *the words in this book are arranged in alphabetical order; the books are arranged according to size; she's expert at flower arranging.* □ **ordenar**

2 to adapt (a piece of music): *this piece is arranged for solo violin.* □ **adaptar**

3 to organize: *I have arranged to stay three nights in Oslo; she would like to arrange the meeting for Friday; have you arranged for a car to meet us at the airport?* □ **disponer**

arrangement *n.* **1** way in which something is laid out: *I don't like the arrangement of the chairs; flower arrangement,* flower decoration. □ **disposición; decoración**

2 organizing: *all the arrangements for my trip to Africa have been made by my secretary.* □ **arreglos**

3 agreement: *I'll leave it to you to come to some arrangement over the price.* □ **acuerdo**

array [ə'reɪ] *n.* display: *he has a wonderful array of medals.* □ **colección**

■ *v.* **1** to set out in order. □ **ordenar**

2 (*formal*) to dress (in fine costume). □ **ataviar**

arrears [ə'rɪəz] *n. **to be in arrears,*** to be late (in doing something): *he is in arrears with the rent; don't get into arrears with the payments.* □ **atrasado**

arrest [ə'rest] *n.* being held (by the police) on a charge: *he is under arrest.* □ **detención**

cardiac arrest, stoppage of the heart. □ **paro cardiaco**

■ *v.* to hold (someone) for breaking the law: *the police arrested the burglars.* □ **arrestar**

arrive [ə'raɪv] *v.* to reach (a place): *we arrived in England on Monday; the plane from Tokyo arrives at 3 o'clock; after a lot of haggling we arrived at a price,* we agreed on a price. □ **llegar**

arrival *n.* **1** reaching (a place): *our time of arrival in New York is 15.00 hours; his arrival changed our whole way of working.* □ **llegada**

2 person who has arrived: *a new arrival,* person who has just arrived. □ **llegado**

arrogant ['ærəgənt] *adj.* very proud. □ **arrogante**

arrogance *n.* being very proud; thinking that you are superior. □ **arrogancia**

arrogantly *adv.* proudly. □ **arrogantemente**

arrow ['ærou] *n.* **1** long stick with a sharp point which is shot by a bow. □ **flecha**

2 sign showing the way to a place. □ **flecha**

arrowroot *n.* flour made from the root of an American plant. □ **arruruz**

arse [ɑːs] *n.* (*vulgar*) buttocks. □ **culo**

arsenal ['ɑːsənl] *n.* store of weapons. □ **arsenal**

arsenic ['ɑːsnɪk] *n.* (*chemical element*: As) powerful poison. □ **arsénico**

arson ['ɑːsn] *n.* criminal act of setting fire to a property: *after the offices were burnt down, the police suspected the manager of arson.* □ **incendio premeditado**

art [ɑːt] *n.* painting, drawing, sculpture and music. □ **arte**
work of art, painting/drawing, etc., which is considered valuable. □ **obra de arte**
art exhibition, show of art. □ **exposición**
art gallery, museum of paintings, sculptures, etc. □ **museo de bellas artes, galería**
arts subjects, subjects (such as languages, history, etc.) which are not sciences. □ **humanidades; letras**
artful *adj.* clever; up to all the latest tricks. □ **ingenioso**
artless ['ɑːtləs] *adj.* natural; not forced; naive: *he answered with an artless smile.* □ **natural**
artefact ['ɑːtifækt] *n.* object (usually a tool) made by man. □ **artefacto**
arteriosclerosis [ɑːtiːəriousklə'rousis] *n.* hardening of the arteries (especially in old age). □ **arteriosclerosis**
artery ['ɑːtəri] *n.* (*pl. arteries*) **1** tube that blood flows through from the heart to other parts of the body. □ **arteria**
2 important road. □ **arteria**
arterial [ɑː'tiəriəl] *adj.* referring to an artery: *arterial disease; an arterial road.* □ **arterial**
artesian [ɑː'tiːʒn] *adj.* ***artesian well,*** well drilled in the soil which does not require a pump to make the water rise. □ **artesiano**
arthritis [ɑː'θraitis] *n.* illness where joints become swollen and stiff. □ **artritis**
arthritic [ɑː'θritik] *adj.* stiff from arthritis: *he has an arthritic knee.* □ **artrítico**
artichoke ['ɑːtitʃouk] *n.* **1** (*globe*) *artichoke,* green vegetable like the flower of a thistle. □ **alcachofa**
2 (*Jerusalem*) *artichoke,* root vegetable like a bumpy potato. □ **cotufa, pataca**
article ['ɑːtikl] *n.* **1** clause (in agreement): *under the terms of article 14.* □ **artículo**
2 piece of writing in a newspaper, etc.: *have you read the article on drugs?* □ **artículo**
3 thing/object: *article of clothing,* piece of clothing. □ **artículo; prenda de vestir**
4 part of speech: *'the' is a definite article; 'a' is an indefinite article.* □ **artículo**
articulate [ɑː'tikjuleit] *v.* **1** to speak (a word): *he does not articulate very clearly.* □ **articular**
2 to join. □ **unir, enlazar**
articulated lorry, lorry with a trailer. □ **camión articulado**
■ *adj.* clear-speaking: *he is barely articulate.* □ **inteligible**
artificial [ɑːti'fiʃl] *adj.* which is imitated/not the real thing: *artificial wood; he has an artificial leg.* □ **artificial**
artillery [ɑː'tiləri] *n.* (*pl. artilleries*) section of the army concerned with guns: *the artillery,* the guns; *you could hear the artillery bombardment quite distinctly.* □ **artillería**
artilleryman *n.* (*pl. artillerymen*) soldier working on guns. □ **artillero**
artisan [ɑːti'zæn] *n.* person who makes things by hand; workman/craftsman. □ **artesano**
artist ['ɑːtist] *n.* person who draws, paints, or plays music: *Picasso is a world famous artist.* □ **artista**
artistic *adj.* (person) who has a feeling or skill for art; (thing) which looks good because it is made by someone with good taste: *an artistic flower arrangement.* □ **artístico**
artistically *adv.* with art: *she has decorated her room most artistically.* □ **artísticamente**
artistry ['ɑːtistri] *n.* skill in art: *he drew the old women's face with great artistry.* □ **arte**
artiste [ɑː'tiːst] *n.* performer in a theatre (especially dancer/acrobat, etc.). □ **artista**
arty ['ɑːti] *adj.* (*informal*) pretending to be artistic. □ **que se las da de artista**
as [æz, əz] *conj.* **1** like: *as small as a mouse; he's as tall as me.* □ **tan... como**
2 because: *as you can't come, I'll take your place; as you're here, you might as well stay for lunch.* □ **como; ya que**
3 at the same time that: *as he opened the door, a bucket of water fell on his head.* □ **cuando**
4 doing the job of; acting the part of: *he started work as an office boy; she's got a job as a secretary; he acts as a father to me; did you ever see him as Hamlet?* □ **como**
5 in a certain way: *do as you think fit; leave it as it is.* □ **como**
6 ***as for,*** referring to/concerning: *as for you, I'll deal with you later.* □ **en cuanto a...**
7 ***as from,*** starting from: *as from tomorrow, all salaries rise by 10%; as from last Wednesday he is no longer working here.* □ **a partir de...**
8 ***as if/as though,*** like/seeming: *it looks as if the train is late; he went on eating as though nothing had happened.* □ **como si**
9 ***as long as,*** on condition that: *I'll let you come with me as long as you promise to be good.* □ **siempre y cuando**
10 ***as soon as,*** immediately: *as soon as you get home telephone the doctor.* □ **tan pronto como**
11 ***as to,*** referring to: *I want to question him as to his whereabouts on the evening of 21st July.* □ **en cuanto a..., por**
12 ***as well as,*** in addition to: *we had cheese as well as dessert.* □ **y también...; así como**
asbestos [æs'bestəs] *n.* mineral substance which is fireproof: *you should surround the fire with asbestos sheeting.* □ **amianto**
asbestosis [æsbe'stousis] *n.* lung disease caused by breathing in particles of asbestos. □ **asbestosis**
ascend [ə'send] *v.* **1** (*formal*) to go up. □ **ascender**
2 *he ascended the throne,* he became king. □ **subir a**
ascendancy *n.* influence: *his ascendancy over his father.* □ **ascendiente**
ascendant *n.* **1** rising. □ **ascendente**
2 *the pop group is **in the ascendant,*** is becoming very popular. □ **...va en ascenso**
ascension [ə'senʃn] **ascent** [ə'sent] *n.* going up: *the ascent of Everest.* □ **ascensión**
ascertain [æsə'tein] *v.* (*formal*) to check/to find out the facts. □ **verificar**
ascetic [ə'setik] *adj.* (way of life) where you do not allow yourself any comfort or pleasure: *he leads an ascetic existence.* □ **ascético**
ascorbic [æ'skɔːbik] *adj.* ***ascorbic acid,*** vitamin occurring in oranges, vegetables, etc. □ **ascórbico**
ascot ['æskət] *n. Amer.* cravat/scarf worn round the neck in place of a tie. □ **pañuelo de cuello**
ascribe [æ'skraib] *v.* to attribute (something to someone). □ **atribuir**
aseptic [ə'septik] *adj.* sterilized/with no infection. □ **aséptico**
ash [æʃ] *n.* (*pl. ashes*) **1** common tree in northern countries; wood of this tree: *an ash stick.* □ **fresno**
2 dust left after something has burnt: *they left cigarette ash all over the carpet.* □ **ceniza**
3 ***ashes,*** remains of a person's body after cremation: *he was cremated and his ashes were scattered at sea.* □ **cenizas**
ashcan *n. Amer.* container for putting rubbish in; dustbin. □ **cubo de la basura**

ashen ['æʃən] *adj.* very pale: *he has an ashen complexion.* □ **ceniciento**
ashpan *n.* (*in a stove*) box for collecting ash. □ **recipiente para la ceniza**
ashtray *n.* small bowl for putting ash from cigarettes, etc. □ **cenicero**
ashamed [ə'ʃeimd] *adj.* sorry because of something wrong: *he was ashamed of his dirty clothes; aren't you ashamed of yourself, hitting a little girl like that?* □ **avergonzado**
ashlar ['æʃlə] *n.* (*no pl.*) building stones cut square. □ **sillar**
ashore [ə'ʃɔ:] *adv.* on land: *the passengers came ashore; we went ashore at Marseilles.* □ **a/en tierra**
Asia ['eiʃə] *n.* very large continent stretching from Europe to the Far East. □ **Asia**
Asia Minor, Turkey. □ **Asia Menor**
Asian *adj.* and *n.* (person) from Asia. □ **asiático**
Asiatic [eisi'ætik] *adj.* referring to Asia. □ **asiático**
aside [ə'said] *adv.* to one side: *he put his glass aside; she stood aside to let the children pass; I took him aside to say a few words about his behaviour.* □ **a un lado**
aside from, *Amer.* apart from: *aside from a mild attack of flu he has not been ill this winter.* □ **aparte de**
■ *n.* words spoken in a play which the other characters are not supposed to hear: *in an aside to the audience.* □ **aparte**
asinine ['æsinain] *adj.* stupid: *he will keep on making asinine comments.* □ **necio**
ask [ɑ:sk] *v.* **1** to put a question: *if you're lost, ask a policeman to show you the way; the tourist asked the way to the museum; I want to ask about holidays in France,* I want some information on holidays in France. □ **preguntar**
to ask after: *he was asking after your mother,* he was inquiring about your mother's health. □ **preguntar por**
2 ***to ask for,*** to request/to want (something) to be given to you: *he is asking $100 for his old car,* he is trying to sell his car for $100; *the man at the door is asking for your father,* he wants to see your father; *I have asked for a new bicycle for my birthday.* □ **pedir**
to ask for something back, to demand the return of something which has been borrowed: *he borrowed my lawnmower two weeks ago - I must ask him for it back.* □ **pedir que se devuelva**
3 *I've asked her to the party,* I've invited her to come to the party. □ **invitar**
asking *n.* ***it's yours for the asking,*** you only have to ask for it and you will be given it. □ **a pedir de boca**
askance [ə'skɑ:ns] *adv.* ***to look at something/someone askance,*** to be suspicious of something/someone. □ **mirar de soslayo**
askew [ə'skju:] *adv.* not straight: *his tie was all askew.* □ **torcido**
asleep [ə'sli:p] *adj.* sleeping: *at midnight everyone in the house was asleep.* □ **dormido**
to fall asleep: *he fell asleep reading the newspaper,* he went to sleep while reading the newspaper. □ **dormirse**
asparagus [ə'spærəgəs] *n.* cultivated plant of which you eat the new shoots as a vegetable. □ **espárrago**
aspect ['æspekt] *n.* **1** direction which a house faces: *this house has a northerly aspect.* □ **orientación**
2 side; way of looking at something: *you have to consider all the aspects of the problem; this shows up yet another aspect of the question.* □ **aspecto**
aspen ['æspn] *n.* small tree with little leaves which tremble in the wind. □ **álamo temblón**
asperity [æ'speriti] *n.* sharpness: *the asperity of his remarks to his wife.* □ **aspereza**
aspersions [ə'spə:ʃnz] *n. pl.* bad comments (on someone): *he is casting aspersions on my talents as a musician.* □ **difamación**
asphalt ['æsfælt] *n.* mixture of tar and sand which is used for surfacing roads. □ **asfalto**
■ *v.* to cover with asphalt: *an asphalted playground.* □ **asfaltar**
asphyxiate [əs'fiksieit] *v.* to stifle/to kill (someone) by preventing them from breathing: *the baby was asphyxiated in his cot.* □ **asfixiar**
asphyxia, asphyxiation [əsfiksi'eiʃn] *n.* being unable to breathe. □ **asfixia**
aspic ['æspik] *n.* meat jelly. □ **gelatina**
aspidistra [æspi'distrə] *n.* type of indoor plant. □ **aspidistra**
aspirate ['æspirət] *adj.* and *n.* (sound) which has to be breathed: *the letter 'h' is aspirate in 'horse' but silent in 'hour'.* □ **aspirado**
aspire [ə'spaiə] *v.* to have the ambition to do something: *he aspires to being a politician.* □ **aspirar**
aspiration [æspi'reiʃn] *n.* ambition. □ **aspiración**
aspiring *adj.* ambitious/hopeful: *an aspiring politician.* □ **ambicioso**
aspirin ['æsprin] *n.* (tablet of) common drug taken to stop headaches/colds, etc.: *if you've got a headache, take an aspirin.* □ **aspirina**
ass [æs] *n.* (*pl. asses*) **1** donkey. □ **burro**
2 ***to make an ass of yourself,*** make a fool of yourself. □ **ponerse en ridículo**
3 *don't be an ass,* don't be an idiot. □ **tonto**
4 *Amer.* (*slang*) buttocks. □ **culo**
assailant [ə'seilənt] *n.* someone who attacks (someone): *in the dark she couldn't see her assailant clearly.* □ **asaltante**
assassinate [ə'sæsineit] *v.* to kill (someone) for political reasons: *he was assassinated by terrorists.* □ **asesinar**
assassin *n.* person who kills for political reasons. □ **asesino**
assassination [əsæsi'neiʃn] *n.* political murder. □ **asesinato**
assault [ə'sɔ:lt] *n.* **1** attack: *the troops took part in the assault on the enemy stronghold.* □ **asalto**
2 *the young men were charged with assault,* with an attack on someone. □ **agresión**
assault course, ground where soldiers practise attacks. □ **campo de prácticas**
■ *v.* to attack: *the postmistress was assaulted by two men who tried to rob the post office.* □ **atacar**
assay [ə'sei] *n.* test to see how pure metal is. □ **ensayo**
■ *v.* to test (metal) to see how pure it is. □ **ensayar**
assemble [ə'sembl] *v.* to get together; to put together: *the crowd quickly assembled outside the palace; Parliament assembles again next week,* Parliament meets again after a holiday; *I'm learning how to assemble this car engine.* □ **congregarse; reunirse; montar**
assembly *n.* **1** meeting: *the United Nations Assembly.* □ **asamblea**
morning assembly, meeting of all the children in a school at the beginning of the day for prayers. □ **reunión matinal**
2 putting together. □ **montaje**
assembly line, continuous moving line in a factory, where cars/washing machines, etc., are put together. □ **cadena de montaje**

assent [ə'sent] *n.* agreement: *he withheld his assent,* he refused to agree. □ **asentimiento**
■ *v.* to agree: *he assented to the proposal.* □ **asentir**
assert [ə'sə:t] *v.* **1** to state firmly: *you must assert your authority,* you must make your authority felt. □ **afirmar**
assert yourself, take a firm position. □ **imponerse**
2 *he asserted that,* he stated that. □ **aseverar**
assertion [ə'sə:ʃn] *n.* statement (of rights). □ **reivindicación**
assertive *adj.* forceful. □ **enérgico**
assess [ə'ses] *v.* **1** to calculate the amount of damages/of tax which should be paid. □ **estimar**
2 to value: *the property is assessed for rates at $300; damages were assessed at $10,000.* □ **valorar**
3 to estimate: *how do you assess our chances of winning?* □ **juzgar, valorar**
assessment *n.* **1** calculation of damages/of tax. □ **tasación**
2 calculation of value. □ **valoración**
3 estimate. □ **estimación**
assessor *n.* person who assesses. □ **tasador**
asset ['æset] *n.* **1** valuable thing which belongs to you: *the firm has assets of over $1 million.* □ **activo**
2 *his greatest asset is his ability to calculate rapidly,* his most valuable talent. □ **ventaja**
assiduous [ə'sidjuəs] *adj.* regular and very careful. □ **asiduo**
assiduity [æsi'dju:iti] *n.* regularity of work. □ **asiduidad**
assiduously *adv.* regularly and very carefully; without fail: *he assiduously sends me a birthday card each year.* □ **asiduamente**
assign [ə'sain] *v.* **1** to appoint (someone to do something): *he was assigned the task of dealing with the complaints.* □ **asignar**
2 to transfer something to someone. □ **ceder**
assignation [æsig'neiʃn] *n.* **1** transfer (of property). □ **cesión**
2 lovers' meeting. □ **cita**
assignment *n.* **1** delegation (of a task to someone). □ **misión**
2 work which you have been told to do. □ **tarea, cometido**
assimilate [ə'simileit] *v.* to digest (food); to learn and understand (facts). □ **asimilar**
assimilation *n.* act of assimilating food or information. □ **asimilación**
assist [ə'sist] *v.* to help (someone): *the lifeboat, assisted by a helicopter, took the crew off the sinking ship.* □ **asistir**
assistance *n.* **1** help. □ **asistencia**
2 *can I be of assistance?,* can I help? □ **ayuda**
assistant *n.* person who helps: *ask the shop assistant if they have any white shoes; she is Professor Smith's assistant; laboratory assistant; library assistant.* □ **ayudante, asistente**
■ *adj.* deputy: *assistant manager.* □ **subdirector**
assizes [ə'saiziz] *n. pl.* local courts held in various parts of England and Wales at regular intervals. □ **tribunal de lo criminal**
associate [ə'sousieit] *v.* to link with someone/to be linked to someone/something: *he associated with criminals; his name is associated with relief work for refugees.* □ **asociarse**
■ *n.* person who is linked to someone: *he is my associate,* he is my partner. □ **socio**
association [əsousi'eiʃn] *n.* group/society: *I am a member of the dental association; the horticultural association groups together people who are interested in gardening.* □ **asociación**
assorted [ə'sɔ:tid] *adj.* **1** matched: *they're an oddly assorted couple.* □ **encajado, avenido**
2 mixed: *I'll have a pound of assorted chocolates.* □ **surtido**
assortment *n.* collection/mixture: *assortment of chocolates; there was an odd assortment of people in the hall.* □ **variedad**
assuage [ə'sweidʒ] *v.* (*formal*) to calm/to soothe. □ **mitigar**
assume [ə'sju:m] *v.* **1** to take upon yourself: *when the director was ill his deputy assumed responsibility for the management of the factory; the general assumed power in 1968,* he took control of the country. □ **asumir; tomar**
2 to suppose: *I assume the story is true; I assume we are going to see my sister as usual on Tuesday?* □ **suponer**
assumed *adj.* false: *assumed name,* false name; *I am not taken in by his assumed anger.* □ **supuesto; falso**
assumption [ə'sʌmpʃn] *n.* **1** *assumption of office,* taking up office. □ **toma de posesión**
2 belief that something is true, even if it has not been proved: *they acted on the assumption that the police would not interfere.* □ **suposición**
assure [ə'ʃuə] *v.* **1** to make safe/certain: *the job of the bodyguard is to assure the protection of the president.* □ **asegurar**
2 to state/to affirm: *I can assure you that the parcel will leave here today.* □ **afirmar**
assurance *n.* **1** promise: *I have his assurance that no harm will come to our men.* □ **promesa**
2 ***life assurance,*** insurance against death. □ **seguro de vida**
3 calm; feeling of certainty: *he answered the question with complete assurance.* □ **seguridad**
assured *adj. his success is assured,* his success is certain. □ **asegurado**
assuredly [ə'ʃuərədli] *adv.* certainly. □ **ciertamente**
aster ['æstə] *n.* garden flower with star-shaped flowers in many colours. □ **aster**
asterisk ['æstərisk] *n.* sign (*) to indicate some special note, etc. □ **asterisco**
astern [ə'stə:n] *adv.* behind a ship. □ **a popa**
to go astern (*of ship*), to go backwards. □ **ir hacia atrás**
asteroid ['æstərɔid] *n.* very small planet. □ **asteroide**
asthma ['æsmə] *n.* wheezing, usually caused by allergy: *he suffers a lot from asthma in damp weather.* □ **asma**
asthmatic [æs'mætik] *adj.* and *n.* (person) who suffers from asthma. □ **asmático**
astigmatism [ə'stigmətizəm] *n.* condition of the eyes where the image focuses correctly at one angle but not at another. □ **astigmatismo**
astigmatic [æstig'mætik] *adj.* referring to differing focal angles in the eyes. □ **astigmático**
astonish [ə'stɔniʃ] *v.* to surprise: *you astonish me.* □ **asombrar**
astonished *adj.* surprised: *I am astonished she has not had an accident before now; she was astonished when I told her of my marriage.* □ **asombrado**
astonishing *adj.* surprising: *the astonishing thing is that she never knew about it.* □ **asombroso**
astonishingly *adv.* surprisingly: *he is astonishingly knowledgeable about old china.* □ **asombrosamente**
astonishment *n.* surprise: *a look of astonishment appeared on his face; if he was surprised, he certainly did not show any astonishment.* □ **asombro**
astound [ə'staund] *v.* to surprise completely: *you astound me.* □ **pasmar**

astounding *adj.* very surprising: *have you heard the astounding news?* □ **pasmoso**
astrakhan [æstrə'kæn] *n.* dark fur from the skin of black lambs. □ **astracán**
astray [ə'strei] *adv.* lost: *he went astray,* he got lost. □ **perdido**
to lead someone astray, to lead someone into bad habits. □ **descarriar**
astride [ə'straid] *prep.* with your legs on either side: *he sat astride the branch; he stood astride the path.* □ **a horcajadas**
astringent [ə'strindʒənt] *adj.* harsh/severe (comments, etc.). □ **severo**
■ *n.* cosmetic for closing pores. □ **astringente**
astrology [ə'strɔlədʒi] *n.* art of foretelling events from the stars and planets. □ **astrología**
astrologer *n.* person who gives advice based on reading the position of the stars. □ **astrólogo**
astronaut ['æstrənɔːt] *n.* person who travels in a spacecraft. □ **astronauta**
astronomy [ə'strɔnəmi] *n.* science of studying the stars, the sun and the universe. □ **astronomía**
astronomer *n.* person who studies the stars, the sun and the universe. □ **astrónomo**
astronomical [æstrə'nɔmikl] *adj.* **1** referring to astronomy. □ **astronómico**
2 *(informal)* very large: *our debts this year have reached astronomical proportions.* □ **astronómico**
astronomically *adv.* **1** using astronomy. □ **astronómicamente**
2 *(informal)* enormously: *his watch is astronomically expensive.* □ **enormemente**
astute [ə'stjuːt] *adj.* clever/wise. □ **astuto**
astutely *adv.* cleverly. □ **astutamente**
asylum [ə'sailəm] *n.* **1** place of refuge. □ **asilo**
2 *he asked for* ***political asylum,*** he asked to be allowed to stay in the country as he was politically undesirable in his own country. □ **asilo político**
3 formerly, a mental hospital. □ **manicomio**
asymmetrical [æsi'metrikl] *adj.* not symmetrical. □ **asimétrico**
at [æt, ət] *prep.* **1** (showing time or place): *at the corner of the street; at ten o'clock; at home; at the post office; at sea; at night.* □ **en**
2 (showing speed or rate): *the train was going at 100 miles an hour; we sell these apples at 20p a pound; come in two at a time.* □ **a**
3 (showing cause): *she laughed at my old coat.* □ **de**
4 busy: *they are all at work.* □ **en**
to be at it, (i) *he is at it again,* he is doing it again. □ **en**
(ii) *while you're at it, could you do something for me?,* while you are doing that. □ **en**
5 ***at first,*** at the beginning: *at first I thought he was going to hit me.* □ **al principio**
at last, finally: *after a long delay, at last we reached home.* □ **por fin**
6 ***at once,*** immediately: *I'll do it at once.* □ **al instante**
ate [et] *v. see* **eat.**
atheism ['eiθiizəm] *n.* believing there is no god. □ **ateísmo**
atheist *n.* person who believes there is no god. □ **ateo**
athlete ['æθliːt] *n.* person who takes part in sport, in particular, running, jumping, throwing: *the parade of the athletes at the opening of the Olympic Games.* □ **atleta**
athlete's foot, skin infection on the feet. □ **pie de atleta**
athletic [æθ'letik] *adj.* referring to sport: *she is a very athletic woman,* she does a lot of sport. □ **atlético**
athletics *n.* (*usually with singular verb*) organized sports where you run, jump or throw: *I'm in the school athletics team.* □ **atletismo**
Atlantic [ət'læntik] *n.* ***the Atlantic (Ocean),*** ocean separating Europe and Africa from North and South America. □ **Atlántico**
atlas ['ætləs] *n.* (*pl. atlases*) book of maps. □ **atlas**
atmosphere ['ætməsfiə] *n.* **1** air which surrounds the earth: *the earth's atmosphere.* □ **atmósfera**
2 general feeling (in a party, etc.): *there's a very happy atmosphere in the office; the atmosphere became electric,* the general feeling became very tense. □ **ambiente**
atmospheric [ætməs'ferik] *adj.* referring to the atmosphere: *atmospheric pressure.* □ **atmosférico**
atmospherics *n.* electric disturbances which interfere with radio or TV signals. □ **interferencias**
atoll ['ætɔl] *n.* tropical coral island. □ **atolón**
atom ['ætəm] *n.* **1** basic particle of matter: *to split the atom; a hydrogen atom.* □ **átomo**
2 very small thing: *there isn't an atom of truth in what he says.* □ **pizca**
atomic [ə'tɔmik] *adj.* referring to physical atoms: *atomic particle; atomic bomb; atomic energy.* □ **atómico**
atomic number, number of protons in one atom of a chemical element. □ **número atómico**
atomize ['ætəmaiz] *v.* to reduce to very fine particles. □ **pulverizar**
atomizer *n.* device for reducing something to very fine particles, especially a spray for scent. □ **pulverizador**
atone [ə'toun] *v. to atone for a sin,* to make amends for a sin. □ **expiar**
atonement *n.* making amends (for a sin). □ **expiación**
atrocious [ə'trouʃəs] *adj.* very bad: *an atrocious crime; what atrocious weather! he writes well, but his spelling is atrocious.* □ **atroz**
atrociously *adv.* very badly: *he drives atrociously.* □ **atrozmente**
atrocity [ə'trɔsiti] *n.* (*pl. atrocities*) very wicked deed: *the enemy committed atrocities against the civilian population.* □ **atrocidad**
atrophy ['ætrəfi] *n.* wasting away (of a limb). □ **atrofia**
■ *v.* to waste away. □ **atrofiar(se)**
attach [ə'tætʃ] *v.* **1** to fasten: *the cheque is attached to the letter; the trailer is attached to the car with a chain; he attached the papers to the contract with a pin.* □ **unir, adjuntar**
2 ***to be attached to:*** *he is very attached to his mother,* he is very fond of his mother. □ **...unido a...**
attaché [ə'tæʃei] *n.* specialized member of the staff of an embassy: *a commercial attacheBPY1; a military attaché.* □ **agregado**
attaché case *n.* small case for carrying papers. □ **maletín**
attachment *n.* **1** device which is attached to something else: *the camera has a whole range of attachments.* □ **accesorio**
2 affection. □ **cariño**
attack [ə'tæk] *n.* **1** starting to fight: *they made an attack on the castle; our forces are under attack,* they are being attacked; *when are we going into the attack?* □ **ataque**
2 sudden start of a disease: *he had an attack of bronchitis.* □ **ataque**

heart attack, sudden pain as the heart fails to work properly. □ **ataque al corazón**
■ *v.* to start fighting (someone): *the enemy has attacked our tanks; the old lady was attacked by robbers; how are you going to attack the problem of unemployment?* □ **atacar**
attacker *n.* person who attacks: *the girl did not recognize her attacker.* □ **atacante**
attain [ə'tein] *v.* to reach: *he has attained the ripe old age of 92; she has attained her ambition of becoming a pop star.* □ **alcanzar**
attainable *adj.* which can be reached: *a sales increase of 20% is easily attainable.* □ **alcanzable**
attainment *n.* **1** reaching: *attainment of an ambition.* □ **logro**
2 (*pl.*) talents/intellectual capacities: *he is a man of remarkable attainments.* □ **dotes**
attempt [ə'tempt] *n.* try: *he has made three attempts to swim the Channel; she did it at the first/second attempt,* she did it the first/second time she tried; *he tried to climb Mount Everest, but had to give up the attempt; his attempt to break the world record has failed.* □ **intento**
■ *v.* to try: *he is attempting to swim across the English Channel; she attempted to murder her husband; he is going to attempt his sixth win in succession,* he will try to winR again for the sixth time; *she is attempting the impossible,* she is trying to do what cannot be done. □ **intentar**
attend [ə'tend] *v.* **1** ***to attend to someone,*** to look after someone: *are you being attended to?* □ **atender**
2 to be present at: *is he going to attend the meeting tomorrow? he cannot attend school because his sister has an infectious disease.* □ **asistir**
attendance *n.* being present: *he has a prize for good attendance,* for not missing school; *there was a good attendance at the meeting,* there were a lot of people at the meeting; *attendance at the lectures is down on last year,* fewer people go to the lectures than last year. □ **asistencia**
attendant *n.* person (in a museum) who guards the exhibits; person who is on duty (in a public lavatory in a theatre): *could you call the attendant, this lady is feeling ill.* □ **encargado**
attention [ə'tenʃn] *n.* **1** careful thought about something: *he did not pay attention to what the doctor said, we must now turn our attention to the question of income tax; she attracts attention wherever she goes,* everyone looks at her. □ **atención**
2 *to stand to attention,* (*of soldiers*) to stand straight with heels together. □ **firmes**
attentive [ə'tentiv] *adj.* **1** paying attention; careful: *he is very attentive to details.* □ **atento**
2 taking care (of someone): *nurses have to be attentive to their patients.* □ **atento**
attentively *adv.* with attention: *he listened attentively to the complaints; she looks after her mother very attentively.* □ **atentamente**
attenuate [ə'tenjueit] *v.* (*formal*) to make thinner/weaker. □ **atenuar**
attenuating circumstances, circumstances which reduce the blame attached to a crime. □ **atenuantes**
attest [ə'test] *v.* (*formal*) to say that something is true. □ **atestiguar**
attic ['ætik] *n.* room under the roof of a house. □ **buhardilla**
attire [ə'taiə] *n.* (*formal*) clothing: *he was wearing clerical attire,* he was dressed as a priest. □ **atuendo**
attitude ['ætitju:d] *n.* **1** way of standing/sitting, etc.: *he was sitting in an attitude of despair.* □ **actitud, postura**
2 way of thinking: *she adopted an attitude of defiance; what is your attitude towards vandalism by teenagers?* □ **postura, actitud**
attorney [ə'tə:ni] *n.* **1** *(especially Amer.)* lawyer. □ **abogado**
2 ***power of attorney,*** power to act on behalf of someone else. □ **poder de procuración**
attract [ə'trækt] *v.* to make something come towards you: *magnets attract iron; flowers attract bees; she attracts admiring glances.* □ **atraer**
attraction [ə'trækʃn] *n.* **1** pull: *the gravitational attraction of the earth; the attraction of a magnet.* □ **atracción**
2 ability to attract (someone)/to make (someone) interested: *the attraction of an ice cream van on a hot day; I cannot see what the attraction is in watching cricket.* □ **el atractivo**
3 thing which attracts people: *what are the main tourist attractions in Stockholm?,* what are the main monuments visited by tourists? *the circus's star attraction is the lion tamer.* □ **atracción**
attractive *adj.* pleasant-looking:. *it's a very attractive town; she's the most attractive girl I know.* □ **atractivo**
attractively *adv.* in such a way as to attract: *she's very attractively dressed.* □ **atractivamente**
attribute ['ætribju:t] *n.* **1** quality: *what are the main attributes of the Prime Minister?* □ **atributo**
2 symbol: *the balance is the attribute of justice.* □ **atributo**
■ *v.* to say that something belongs to someone: *this saying is attributed to Churchill; the church is attributed to a famous 17th century architect; painting wrongly attributed to Rembrandt.* □ **atribuir**
attributable [ə'tribjutəbl] *adj.* which can be attributed to someone: *that story is attributable to a gossip columnist on the local newspaper.* □ **atribuible**
attrition [ə'triʃn] *n.* wearing down. □ **desgaste**
war of attrition, war to be won by wearing down your enemy's forces. □ **guerra de desgaste**
aubergine ['óubədʒi:n] *n.* eggplant/purple-skinned fruit eaten as a vegetable. □ **berenjena**
auburn ['ɔ:bən] *adj.* reddish chestnut-coloured (hair). □ **castaño**
auction ['ɔ:kʃn] *n.* sale where the item is sold to the highest bidder: *we bought this table at an auction; we are putting our house up for auction.* □ **subasta**
■ *v.* to sell something to the highest bidder: *he auctioned off his stock,* he got rid of it by auction. □ **subastar**
auctioneer [ɔ:kʃə'ni:ə] *n.* person who is in charge of an auction. □ **subastador**
auction rooms *n. pl.* place where auctions are carried out. □ **sala de subastas**
audacious [ɔ:'deiʃəs] *adj.* very daring. □ **audaz**
audaciously *adv.* daringly: *he very audaciously offered to cross the street on a tightrope.* □ **audazmente**
audacity [ɔ:'dæsiti] *n.* daring: *he had the audacity to wear pink socks to the funeral.* □ **audacia**
audible ['ɔ:dibl] *adj.* which can be heard: *his whispered comments were quite audible.* □ **audible**
audibility [ɔ:di'biliti] *n.* capacity for being heard. □ **audibilidad**
audibly *adv.* in a way which can be heard: *he was audibly sick in the bathroom.* □ **audiblemente**
audience ['ɔ:diəns] *n.* **1** people listening to a concert/watching a film or play, etc.: *the audience clapped loudly at the end of the song.* □ **el público**
studio audience, people in a studio watching a programme being televised/listening to a programme

being recorded. □ **público**
2 hearing: *to grant someone an audience,* to allow someone to speak to you. □ **audiencia**
audio-visual [ɔ:djou'vizjuəl] *adj.* referring to a method of teaching using sounds (on tape) and pictures (on film): *an audio-visual language course.* □ **audiovisual**
audit ['ɔ:dit] *n.* checking of accounts: *we have an annual audit of accounts.* □ **auditoría**
■ *v.* to check accounts: *this firm is auditing our company's accounts.* □ **auditar**
auditor *n.* expert accountant who checks a company's accounts. □ **auditor**
audition [ɔ:'diʃn] *n.* testing of the suitability of actors/dancers, etc., for a job: *I have been asked to go to an audition for Hamlet.* □ **prueba**
■ *v.* to test the suitability of an actor/dancer, etc., for a job: *she was auditioned for the new musical.* □ **hacer una prueba**
auditorium [ɔ:di'tɔ:riəm] *n.* huge hall for meetings/concerts, etc. □ **auditorio**
augment [ɔ:g'ment] *v.* to increase: *salaries have been augmented by 10%.* □ **aumentar**
augmentation [ɔ:gmen'teiʃn] *n.* increase. □ **aumento**
augur ['ɔ:gə] *v.* to be a sign for the future: *this doesn't augur well for the future,* things probably will go badly in future. □ **augurar**
August ['ɔ:gəst] *n.* eighth month of the year: *August 10th is my birthday.* □ **agosto**
auk [ɔ:k] *n.* large black and white sea bird. □ **alca**
aunt [ɑ:nt] *n.* sister of your mother or father; wife of an uncle: *I have three aunts; Aunt Margaret is on the telephone.* □ **tía**
auntie, aunty *n.* (*pl. aunties*) familiar name for an aunt. □ **tía; tiíta**
au pair [ou'pɛə] *adj.* and *n.* (*pl. au pairs*) *she is going to France as an au pair* (*girl*), she is going to live with a French family to do light housework (and learn French). □ **'au pair'**
aura ['ɔ:rə] *n.* general feeling surrounding a person/a place: *there is an aura of respectability about him.* □ **aura**
auricle ['ɔ:rikl] *n.* space in the heart which fills up with blood and then pumps it out into the ventricles. □ **aurícula**
aurora [ə'rɔ:rə] *n.* ***aurora borealis,*** the Northern lights/bright lights seen in the sky in the far North. □ **aurora boreal**
auspices ['ɔ:spisiz] *n. pl.* **1** forecast/signs of the future: *the auspices are not very good.* □ **auspicios**
2 patronage: *the meeting is being held under the auspices of the new cultural agreement.* □ **auspicios**
auspicious [ɔ:'spiʃəs] *adj.* favourable/lucky: *this is a particularly auspicious occasion; the meeting got off to an auspicious start.* □ **propicio**
auspiciously *adv.* favourably. □ **favorablemente**
Aussie ['ɔzi] *n.* and *adj.* *(informal)* Australian. □ **australiano**
austere [ɔ:'stiə] *adj.* cold/severe; without luxury: *he is a very austere man; the church has an austere look about it.* □ **austero**
austerity [ɔ:'steriti] *n.* absence of luxury: *in times of austerity,* in periods of restrictions. □ **austeridad**
austerity campaign, campaign to cut spending. □ **campaña de austeridad**
Australia [ɔ'streiliə] *n.* continent and country in the south Pacific. □ **Australia**
Australasia [ɔstrə'leiziə] *n.* Australia and the countries and islands around it, including New Zealand. □ **Australasia**
Australian *adj.* referring to Australia. □ **australiano**
■ *n.* person from Australia. □ **australiano**
Austria ['ɔstriə] *n.* European country south of Germany and east of Switzerland. □ **Austria**
Austrian *adj.* referring to Austria. □ **austriaco**
■ *n.* person from Austria. □ **austriaco**
authentic [ɔ:'θentik] *adj.* real; genuine: *this is an authentic Roman coin; he is an authentic descendant of Charles Dickens.* □ **auténtico**
authenticate [ɔ:'θentikeit] *v.* to swear that something is true. □ **autentificar**
authenticity [ɔ:θen'tisiti] *n.* being authentic: *I doubt the authenticity of this piece of furniture,* I doubt that it is as antique as it looks; *he can vouch for the authenticity of my story,* he can swear that my story is true. □ **autenticidad**
author ['ɔ:θə] *n.* person who writes books, etc.: *who is the author of 'Animal Farm'?* □ **autor**
authorship *n.* identity of the author: *the authorship of some of Shakespeare's plays has been disputed.* □ **paternidad literaria**
authority [ɔ:'θɔriti] *n.* (*pl. authorities*) **1** power: *he has no authority over the crew; this will undermine the authority of the headmaster; who is in authority here?,* who is in charge here? □ **autoridad**
2 permission: *by whose authority did he get into the building?* □ **permiso**
3 source: *I have it on good authority that he is about to be divorced.* □ **lo sé de buena fuente...**
4 *he is the world authority on pigeons,* he knows more about them than anyone else. □ **autoridad**
5 ruling committee or group: *the authorities are trying to clamp down on vandalism.* □ **autoridades**
6 *local education authority,* part of the local administration responsible for education in their area. □ **autoridades**
authoritarian [ɔ:θɔri'tɛəriən] *adj.* exercising strict control: *authoritarian regime,* regime that governs strictly and undemocratically. □ **autoritario**
authoritative [ɔ:'θɔritətiv] *adj.* **1** commanding: *he spoke in an authoritative way.* □ **autoritario**
2 which sounds as if it is correct: *this is an authoritative document.* □ **autorizado**
authoritatively *adv.* **1** in a commanding way. □ **autoritariamente**
2 *he spoke authoritatively about the Second World War,* he spoke in a way which showed he knew what he was talking about. □ **con autoridad**
authorize ['ɔ:θəraiz] *v.* to give (someone) permission: *he is authorized to enter the bank vaults.* □ **autorizar**
authorization [ɔ:θərai'zeiʃn] *n.* permission: *he has no authorization to sign cheques.* □ **autorización**
autistic [ɔ:'tistik] *adj.* suffering from a mental illness which makes you withdrawn and unable to communicate with other people. □ **autista**
auto- ['ɔ:tou] *prefix meaning* self: *automatic; automobile.* □ **auto**
autobiography [ɔ:təbai'ɔgrəfi] *n.* (*pl. autobiographies*) life story of a person written by himself. □ **autobiografía**
autobiographical [ɔ:təbaiə'græfikl] *adj.* referring to the life of the writer: *there is a lot of autobiographical detail in this novel.* □ **autobiográfico**
autocracy [ɔ:'tɔkrəsi] *n.* (*pl. autocracies*) system of government by one man. □ **autocracia**
autocrat ['ɔ:təkræt] *n.* dictator/person who does not allow anyone else to rule him. □ **autócrata**
autocratic [ɔ:tə'krætik] *adj.* ruled by one man. □ **autocrático**

autocratically *adv.* like a dictator: *the director runs the factory very autocratically.* □ **autocráticamente**
autocue ['ɔːtoukjuː] *n.* screen with the text printed on it to help television announcers to speak while looking into the camera. □ **'autocue' (apuntador visual)**
autograph ['ɔːtəgrɑːf] *n.* signature (of a famous person): *the boys were crowding round the tennis stars asking for autographs.* □ **autógrafo**
■ *v.* to write your signature for someone: *after the dinner the guests autographed the menu.* □ **poner el autógrafo**
automatic [ɔːtə'mætik] *adj.* and *n.* **1** (device) which works by itself: *automatic record changer; an automatic (pistol).* □ **automático**
2 *his new car is an automatic,* car where the gears change automatically. □ **automático**
automatically *adv.* working by itself: *the record changes automatically.* □ **automáticamente**
automation [ɔːtə'meiʃn] *n.* installation of machinery to make a process more automatic: *when they introduced automation, several hundred workers lost their jobs.* □ **automatización**
automaton [ɔː'tɔmətən] *n.* (*pl. automata*) doll which moves with a motor inside it; person who acts like a robot. □ **autómata**
automobile ['ɔːtəməbiːl] *n. (especially Amer.)* car. □ **automóvil**
autonomy [ɔː'tɔnəmi] *n.* self-government. □ **autonomía**
autonomous *adj.* (region) which governs itself. □ **autónomo**
autopsy ['ɔːtɔpsi] *n.* (*pl. autopsies*) cutting up a dead body to discover the cause of death: *the pathologist carried out an autopsy on the victim.* □ **autopsia**
autumn ['ɔːtəm] *n.* season of the year when the leaves fall off the trees: *Americans call autumn the fall.* □ **otoño**
autumnal [ɔ'tʌmnl] *adj.* referring to autumn: *autumnal smell of dead leaves.* □ **otoñal**
auxiliary [ɔːg'ziljəri] *n.* (*pl. auxiliaries*) helper: *a nursing auxiliary.* □ **auxiliar**
■ *adj.* (person/machine) which helps: *an auxiliary motor.* □ **auxiliar**
avail [ə'veil] *v.* to use: *he availed himself of the opportunity to go to Russia; she didn't avail herself of the offer.* □ **aprovecharse de...**
■ *n.* ***it's of no avail,*** it's no use. □ **es inútil...**
to no avail, uselessly; unsuccessfully: *they banged on the door, and rang the bell, but all to no avail, as no one came to answer.* □ **inútilmente**
availability [əveilə'biliti] *n.* readiness to be used: *what is the availability of this car?,* how long do you have to wait for this car to be ready? □ **disponibilidad**
available *adj.* ready to be used; which can be obtained: *how many cars have we got available? he has quite a sum of money available for investment; he's never available when you want him,* he's never there/never free when he is needed. □ **disponible**
avalanche ['ævəlɑːnʃ] *n.* fall of snow down a mountain side. *The road was blocked by an avalanche.* □ **avalancha**
avarice ['ævəris] *n.* state of not wanting to spend money. □ **avaricia**
avaricious [ævə'riʃəs] *adj.* wanting to hoard money and not to spend it. □ **avaricioso**
avenge [ə'vendʒ] *v.* to pay someone back for a crime: *her brother will avenge her death,* he will try to kill the person who killed her. □ **vengar**
avenger *n.* person who pays back a crime. □ **vengador**
avenue ['ævənjuː] *n.* **1** wide, tree-lined, road in a city. □ **avenida**
2 two parallel rows of trees: *an avenue of chestnuts.* □ **camino entre árboles**
3 way of approaching a problem: *the governments are exploring several avenues to reach a peace agreement.* □ **vía**
average ['ævəridʒ] *n.* **1** middle figure out of two or more: *to calculate an average, add all the figures together and divide by the number of figures you have added; the average of 5, 6, and 10 is 7; it falls below the national average.* □ **promedio**
2 ***on average,*** as a general rule: *on average ten people are drowned here every summer.* □ **por término medio**
the law of averages, probability: *by the law of averages you ought to win the jackpot this time.* □ **ley de probabilidades**
■ *adj.* general; ordinary: *their son is of above average intelligence; take an average household; the average commuter.* □ **común, medio**
■ *v.* to work out as an average: *she averages six hours work a day; pay rises averaged 8% this year.* □ **(...) por término medio**
averse [ə'vəːs] *adj. he is averse to hard work,* he dislikes hard work; *I am not averse to a glass of beer from time to time,* I rather like a glass of beer. □ **contrario**
aversion [ə'vəːʃn] *n.* **1** dislike: *she has an aversion to spiders; the dog has taken an aversion to the postman,* he has started to dislike the postman. □ **aversión; antipatía**
2 *he's my pet aversion,* he's the person I dislike most at the moment. □ **bestia negra**
avert [ə'vəːt] *v.* **1** to turn away: *she averted her eyes.* □ **desviar**
2 to prevent: *his action averted the strike.* □ **impedir**
aviary ['eiviəri] *n.* (*pl. aviaries*) building for keeping birds in. □ **pajarera**
aviation [eivi'eiʃn] *n.* art/technology of flying (aircraft): *he is studying aviation technology.* □ **aviación**
aviation fuel, fuel used by aircraft. □ **combustible para aviones**
avid ['ævid] *adj.* eager/enthusiastic: *he is an avid reader of detective stories.* □ **ávido**
avidly *adv.* eagerly: *she avidly looked through the job advertisements.* □ **ávidamente**
avocado (pear) [ævə'kɑːdou ('pɛə)] *n.* (*pl. avocados*) green tropical fruit with a large stone in the middle, eaten as a vegetable. □ **aguacate**
avoid [ə'vɔid] *v.* **1** to try not to do something: *he is trying to avoid paying customs duty; he has been charged with avoiding paying income tax.* □ **no (hacer)**
2 to keep away from something: *do your Christmas shopping early and avoid the crowds; the escaped prisoner is still avoiding capture.* □ **evitar**
avoidable *adj.* which you could have avoided: *the argument was really quite avoidable.* □ **evitable**
avoidance *n.* act of avoiding: *her avoidance of me is very annoying; he was charged with avoidance of tax.* □ **el evitar; impago de impuestos**
avoirdupois [ævədə'pɔiz] *n.* commercial weight: *it weighs 10 pounds avoirdupois.* □ **'avoirdupois' (sistema de pesas)**
avowal [ə'vauəl] *n.* (*formal*) admission. □ **confesión**
avowed [ə'vaud] *adj.* stated: *his avowed intention.* □ **declarado**
avuncular [ə'vʌŋkjulə] *adj.* like an uncle. □ **de tío**

await [ə'weit] *v.* to wait for: *we are awaiting his instructions; these parcels are awaiting collection.* □ **esperar**
awake [ə'weik] *v.* (*he awoke; he was awoken*) **1** to wake (someone) up: *he was awoken by the sound of breaking glass; she awoke at 10 o'clock.* □ **despertar(se)**
2 to become aware of: *they have only just awoken to the danger of losing money.* □ **ser consciente de**
■ *adj.* not sleeping: *although it was midnight he was still wide awake,* completely awake; *are you still awake?* □ **despierto**
awaken [ə'weikn] *v.* to wake/to arouse: *we must not awaken his suspicions.* □ **levantar sospechas**
awakening *n. he had **a rude awakening**,* he had a sharp shock. □ **el despertar**
award [ə'wɔ:d] *n.* prize: *he has received an international award for peace.* □ **premio**
■ *v.* to give (a prize, etc.): *he was awarded the Nobel Prize; the first prize has been awarded to Mrs Smith.* □ **conceder**
aware [ə'wɛə] *adj.* knowing: *he was not aware of the fact that his watch had been stolen; are you aware of the importance of reading the instructions? she is aware that the train has been cancelled.* □ **consciente**
not that I am aware of, not as far as I know. □ **...que yo sepa**
awareness *n.* state of being aware: *his awareness of the importance of obeying the rules.* □ **conciencia**
awash [ə'wɔʃ] *adj.* covered with a liquid. □ **inundado**
away [ə'wei] *adv.* **1** not here/far: *they have all gone away on holiday; the nearest shops are miles away; go away! far away in the distance; when her husband is away on business.* □ **fuera; lejos**
2 *she is away sick today,* she is not at work, etc., today because she is ill. □ **estar ausente**
3 *our team isn't playing at home - they're playing away,* at another team's ground; *(also adj.) this Saturday we have an away match,* we are playing a match at another team's ground. □ **...en campo contrario**
4 *the birds were singing away,* they were going on singing. □ **...seguían cantando**
5 *I'll do it **right away**,* immediately. □ **en seguida**
awe [ɔ:] *n.* fear/terror: *they all stand in awe of the headmaster,* they are all frightened of him. □ **temor**
awe-inspiring, awesome *adj.* **1** frightening. □ **impresionante**
2 *an awe-inspiring sight,* wonderful and amazing sight. □ **impresionante**
awful ['ɔ:fl] *adj.* **1** very frightening. □ **horrible**
2 very bad/very strong; unpleasant: *what an awful smell; I've got awful earache; the weather has been awful this summer.* □ **horroroso**
awfully *adv. (informal)* very: *I'm awfully sorry; I know it sounds awfully rude, but could you lend me some money?* □ **terriblemente, muy**
awhile [ə'wail] *adv.* for a short time: *just wait here awhile.* □ **por un rato**
awkward ['ɔ:kwəd] *adj.* **1** difficult: *this is an awkward place to find; he's an awkward man to deal with; he's getting himself into a very awkward situation.* □ **difícil**
2 embarrassing: *it was very awkward for me to have to tell her to go away.* □ **violento**
3 clumsy: *she's at the awkward age,* period when children are entering puberty and are clumsy and gauche. □ **torpe (edad del pavo)**
awkwardly *adv.* with difficulty; inconveniently: *this house is very awkwardly situated.* □ **difícilmente, incómodamente**
awkwardness *n.* **1** embarrassment: *there was a moment of awkwardness when she met her former husband.* □ **incomodidad**
2 difficulty: *the awkwardness of having to go there, and then return here, just to fetch their dog.* □ **incomodidad**
awl [ɔ:l] *n.* tool used for making small holes. □ **lezna**
awning ['ɔ:niŋ] *n.* canvas roof stretched out to protect from the sun or rain. □ **toldo**
awoke [ə'wouk] **awoken** [ə'woukn] *v. see* **awake.**
awry [ə'rai] *adv.* **1** not straight: *she came in with her hat on all awry.* □ **torcido**
2 *their plans have gone awry,* have gone wrong. □ **...salido mal**
axe [æks] *Amer.* **ax** *n.* instrument with a sharp metal head for chopping wood. □ **hacha**
to have an axe to grind, to have a particular point of view to put across. □ **tener intereses personales**
■ *v.* to reduce (expenditure); to sack (staff): *the budget for the school libraries has been axed; as part of the economy campaign we had to axe 10% of the staff.* □ **recortar**
axiom ['æksiəm] *n.* well-known saying/obviously true statement. □ **axioma**
axiomatic [æksiə'mætik] *adj.* obvious; well-known. □ **axiomático**
axis ['æksis] *n.* (*pl. axes*) imaginary line through centre of a sphere: *the earth turns on its axis.* □ **eje**
axle ['æksl] *n.* rod going through the middle of a wheel: *the wheel turns on its axle; my rear axle has snapped.* □ **eje**
ayatollah [æjə'toulə] *n.* Muslim leader. □ **ayatola**
aye [ai] *n.* yes. □ **sí**
the ayes have it, more people have voted yes than no. □ **mayoría de votos a favor**
azalea [ə'zeiliə] *n.* small shrub (of eastern origin) with showy pink and orange scented flowers. □ **azalea**
azure ['eizə] *adj.* blue like the sky. □ **azul celeste**

B,b

B, b [bi:] second letter of the alphabet. □ **B, b**
babble ['bæbl] *n.* **1** trickling sound (of water): *the babble of a brook.* □ **murmullo**
2 chatter. □ **charla**
■ *v* **1** to make a trickling sound: *the babbling brook.* □ **murmurante**
2 to chatter/to jabber: *stop babbling! he was babbling on about his golf handicap.* □ **charlar**
babe [beib] *n.* (*formal*) baby. □ **nene, niño**
babel ['beibl] *n.* loud noise of talking: *the discussion afterwards was an absolute babel.* □ **guirigay**
baboon [bə'bu:n] *n.* large African monkey. □ **babuino**
baby ['beibi] *n.* (*pl. babies*) **1** very young child: *babies start to walk when they are about 12 months old; I've known her since she was a baby; she is having the baby in Grace Hospital,* she will give birth to the baby there; *he is the baby of the family,* he is the youngest of the children. □ **niño**
to be left holding the baby: *he was left holding the baby,* he had to sort out all the problems left to him by others. □ **cargar con el muerto**
to throw out the baby with the bathwater, get rid of good things when you try to get rid of useless ones. □ **ser peor el remedio que la enfermedad; tirar lo bueno con lo malo**
2 small animal: *baby elephant; baby giraffe.* □ **cachorro**
3 small object: *baby grand* (*piano*). □ **pequeño**
baby carriage *n. Amer.* pram/cot with large wheels and a hood for pushing babies about in. □ **coche de niño**
baby carrier *n.* canvas cot with handles for carrying a baby. □ **moisés**
babyish *adj.* like a baby. □ **infantil**
baby-sit *v.* (*he baby-sat*) to look after children while their parents are out: *he's baby-sitting tonight.* □ **cuidar niños**
baby-sitter *n.* person who stays in a house to look after the children while the parents are out. □ **canguro**
bachelor ['bætʃələ] *n.* **1** unmarried man: *he is still a bachelor although he is over 40.* □ **soltero**
bachelor pad, small flat for a single person. □ **piso de soltero**
bachelor girl, unmarried woman. □ **soltera**
2 holder of a first degree from a university: *a Bachelor of Science.* □ **licenciado**
bacillus [bə'siləs] *n.* (*pl. bacilli*) type of bacterium. □ **bacilo**
back [bæk] *n.* **1** part of body down the spine between neck and buttocks: *she carried the baby on her back; lie down flat on your back; I've got pains in my back; they were standing back to back.* □ **espalda**
2 ***do something behind someone's back:*** *he did it behind my back,* without my knowing; *the government went behind the backs of the employers and negotiated direct with the unions.* □ **a espaldas de...**
3 *I'd* ***be glad to see the back of*** *him,* I will be glad to see him go. □ **librarse de...**
4 *everything I do seems* ***to put his back up,*** seems to annoy him. □ **...parece picarlo**
5 ***to break the back of:*** *I think we've broken the back of the work,* we have done most of the work. □ **...hemos hecho la parte más difícil...**
6 opposite part/side to the front: *look on the back of the piece of paper; he worked out the sum on the back of an envelope; the index is in the back of the book; could you go round to the back of the house? this dress fastens at the back; there was a large stain on the back of the sofa; it's awkward getting into the back of this car.* □ **en la parte de atrás**
7 *I* ***know*** *London* ***like the back of*** *my* ***hand,*** very well indeed. □ **...como la palma de su mano**
8 *I have an idea at the back of my mind,* I have the beginnings of an idea. □ **fondo**
9 *he lives* ***in the back of beyond,*** way out of a town/ in an inaccessible place. □ **...en el quinto pino**
10 ***back to front,*** the wrong way round: *he's put his trousers on back to front.* □ **al revés**
11 sportsman who plays in a defensive position in football/hockey, etc.: *the England backs.* □ **zaguero; defensa**
■ *adj.* **1** referring to the rear: *there's someone at the back door; he's sleeping in the back room; she grew up in the back streets of London,* in small streets in poor areas of London; *I have a puncture in the back tyre; she was sitting in the back seat.* □ **de atrás**
2 *he's had* ***to take a back seat,*** he's had to take a less prominent position. □ **pasar a segundo plano**
back seat driver, passenger in a car who offers the driver unwanted advice on how to drive. □ **entrometido**
3 in arrears: *back pay,* pay which is owed to someone; *I owe $50 in back payments on my TV set,* I'm $50 in arrears in paying the instalments on my TV. □ **estar atrasado**
■ *adv.* **1** to the rear: *stand back,* move backwards. □ **atrás**
2 *our house stands well back from the road,* our house has a long front garden. □ **...está muy retranqueada...**
3 *please sit back, I can't see,* please lean backwards in your chair. □ **hacia atrás**
4 in return: *I must pay you back for the lunch; when everyone thought he was finished, he suddenly hit back with accusations of corruption; can you put the car back into the garage? go back to bed!* □ **volver a...**
5 *I'll* ***call*** *you* ***back*** *after six,* I'll phone you again. □ **volver a...**
6 *as soon as I* ***get back*** *to the office,* as soon as I return to the office. □ **...de vuelta**
7 ago: *a few years back.* □ **atrás**
as far back as *the 1920's,* as long ago as the 1920's. □ **ya en...**
■ *v.* **1** to reverse: *can you back the car into the garage?* □ **ir marcha atrás; alejarse retrocediendo**
he backed away from the madman.
2 to support (with money): *he is backed by one of the large banks.* □ **respaldar**
3 to gamble (on a horse): *I'm backing Black Beauty to win.* □ **apostar**
backache *n.* pain in the back. □ **dolor de espalda**
back bencher *n.* ordinary member of parliament who has no political office. □ **diputado común**
backbiting *n.* sharp criticism. □ **maledicencia**
backbone *n.* spine/column of bones forming the main support for the back. □ **columna vertebral**

backbreaking *adj.* very hard (work). □ **matador**
backcloth *n.* (in theatre) painted sheet at the back of the stage. □ **telón de fondo**
backdate *v.* to put an earlier date than true (on a cheque): *I'll backdate the invoice to last month.* □ **antedatar**
back down *v.* to retreat from your former position: *he demanded an increase of $1,000, but in the face of the manager's refusal had to back down.* □ **dar marcha atrás**
backer *n.* **1** person who supports something with money. □ **patrocinador**
2 person who gambles money on horse racing. □ **apostante**
backfire *v.* **1** *the car backfired,* the car made a small bang, due to misfiring of the ignition. □ **petardear**
2 *their plan backfired on them,* the plan went wrong - with unfortunate consequences for them. □ **...les salió el tiro por la culata**
backgammon *n.* game like draughts played on a special board. □ **'backgammon'**
background *n.* **1** the back part of a painting against which the foreground stands out: *the figure of the clown stands out against a grey background; our new curtains have little red flowers on a blue background; the house looked gloomy against a background of grey hills.* □ **fondo**
2 *he comes from a working class background,* his family is working class. □ **origen**
3 *he is the head of the firm, but prefers **to keep in the background,*** he prefers not to play a dominant role. □ **...no destacar**
background music, music played quietly in a film or in a restaurant. □ **...de fondo**
backhand *adj.* and *n.* (tennis/table tennis shot) played with the back of the racket/bat. □ **de revés**
backhanded *adj. he paid her a rather **backhanded compliment,*** a grudging compliment/a compliment that could be taken also as an insult. □ **ambiguo**
backhander *n.* **1** blow/shot with the back of the hand. □ **revés**
2 (*slang*) bribe. □ **mordida; soborno**
backing *n.* **1** material used on the back of something to strengthen it: *the picture has a plywood backing.* □ **refuerzo**
2 musical accompaniment to a singer or instrument. □ **acompañamiento**
3 support: *he has the backing of the mayor; she has a considerable financial backing from her husband.* □ **apoyo**
4 reversing (of a car). □ **marcha atrás**
backlash *n.* reverse effect (of a political or social move): *his support for old people has created a backlash among the youth clubs.* □ **reacción (contraria)**
white backlash, reaction among white people against measures taken to protect black people. □ **reacción blanca**
backless *adj.* (dress, etc.) with no back. □ **escotado (en la espalda)**
backlog *n.* work not done/bills not paid: *I have a backlog of correspondence I must deal with.* □ **acumulación, retraso**
back number *n.* old copy of a magazine or newspaper; person who is no longer in fashion. □ **atrasado**
back out *v.* **1** to reverse out: *he backed (the car) out of the garage.* □ **salir marcha atrás**
2 to decide not to continue (with a project): *although she promised to come, she had to back out at the last minute.* □ **echarse atrás**
backpack *n.* bag carried on a walker's back. □ **mochila**
backpacker *n.* person who travels carrying only a backpack. □ **excursionista**
backpacking *n.* going on a journey on foot carrying clothes, tent, etc., in a backpack. □ **excursión a pie**
backpedal *v.* (*he backpedalled*) **1** to pedal backwards. □ **pedalear hacia atrás**
2 to reverse your opinions: *the council had promised more housing, but because of the cost is backpedalling fast.* □ **volverse atrás**
backside *n. (informal)* buttocks: *get up off your backside and do some useful work; if I meet that man he'll get a kick in the backside.* □ **culo; trasero**
backsliding *n.* going back to a bad habit after. □ **reincidencia**
backstage *adv.* and *adj.* in the parts of a theatre where the audience can't go; behind the scenes/hidden from view: *there must have been a lot of backstage negotiations before they signed the agreement.* □ **bastidores**
backstairs *n.* stairs (for servants) in the back part of a large house. □ **escalera de servicio**
backstroke *n.* style of swimming on your back with arms moving over your head. □ **espalda**
back up *v.* **1** to support (someone): *if you propose the formation of the committee, I'll back you up; he backed up his proposal with a mass of evidence.* □ **respaldar**
2 *Amer.* to reverse a car. □ **ir marcha atrás**
backward *adj.* **1** slow/retarded: *backward child,* child who is less advanced than others of the same age. □ **atrasado**
backward countries, countries which are not industrially advanced. □ **atrasado**
2 *he is rather backward in paying his bills,* he is slow in paying. □ **moroso; remiso**
backwardness *n.* slowness/retardedness. □ **tardanza, atraso**
backwards *adv.* **1** in reverse/towards the rear: *he fell backwards over the cliff; the soldiers took one step backwards; the car ran backwards down the hill.* □ **hacia atrás**
2 *they were walking **backwards and forwards** along the street,* they were walking up and down. □ **arriba y abajo**
to know something backwards: *he's sung it so many times he knows the song backwards,* extremely well. □ **...al dedillo**
backwater *n.* **1** small slow-moving branch of a river. □ **remanso**
2 quiet/old-fashioned place. □ **lugar apartado y tranquilo**
backwoods *n. pl.* **1** *especially Amer.* forest. □ **lugar remoto y silvestre**
2 *they live in the backwoods,* they live far from other houses. □ **...en el quinto pino (aislado)**
backyard *n.* small paved area behind a house. □ **patio trasero**
bacon ['beikn] *n.* (*no pl.*) pork which has been salted or smoked. □ **tocino entreverado; 'bacon'**
to save one's bacon: *it saved his bacon,* it got him out of the difficult situation. □ **salvar el pellejo**
bacterium [bæk'tiəriəm] *n.* (*pl. bacteria*) microscopic organism which produces germs or decay. □ **bacteria**
bacteriological [bæktiəriə'lɔdʒikl] *adj.* referring to bacteria: *bacteriological warfare,* method of conducting war by using bacteria to kill the enemy. □ **bacteriológico**
bacteriologist [bæktiəri'ɔlədʒist] *n.* scientist who

specializes in the study of bacteria. □ **bacteriólogo**
bacteriology *n.* study of bacteria. □ **bacteriología**

bad [bæd] *adj.* **1** not good: *she is good at maths, but bad at English; he's a bad driver; too much butter is bad for you.* □ **malo**
not bad: *this cake isn't bad at all,* is quite good really. □ **...no está nada mal**
2 *bad meat,* rotten meat. □ **carne podrida**
3 *bad food,* unappetizing food. □ **comida desagradable**
to go bad: *this pie has gone bad,* it has become rotten. □ **estropearse**
4 *bad translation,* translation which is not correct. □ **mala traducción**
5 wicked: *he's a bad man; you're a bad boy!* □ **malo**
6 unpleasant: *I have some bad news for you; he's got a very bad cold; she's always in a bad temper; it's too bad you can't come to the party.* □ **mal, malo**
7 serious: *he had a bad accident last year; it was a very bad mistake to lend him so much money.* □ **grave**
8 ill: *I've got a bad leg; she's got a bad finger and can't write.* □ **malo**
■ *n.* **1** *there's a lot of bad in these potatoes,* a lot of rotten bits. □ **(trozos...) malos**
2 ***to go to the bad:*** *he has gone to the bad,* he has developed bad habits. □ **echarse a perder**
3 *I'm $100* ***to the bad,*** I've lost $100. □ **de pérdida**
baddy *n.* (*pl. baddies*) (*informal*) wicked person: *at the end of the film all the baddies were killed.* □ **los malos**
badly *adv.* (*worse, worst*) **1** not well (done): *he did badly in his driving test; the foundations of the house were badly laid; business is going badly.* □ **mal**
2 seriously: *he was badly wounded in the war; the church was badly damaged by the fire.* □ **gravemente**
3 *he needs a shave badly,* he needs one very much. □ **ya; con urgencia**

bade [bæd] *v. see* **bid.**

badge [bædʒ] *n.* small sign worn to show that you belong to a group, or simply as a decoration: *he was wearing his club badge; when she came back from holiday she had badges from every country she had visited.* □ **insignia, 'chapa'**

badger ['bædʒə] *n.* wild animal with striped black and white head which lives underground and comes out at night. □ **tejón**
■ *v.* to bother (someone): *he badgered me into giving him $5 as a present.* □ **fastidiar, acosar**

badminton ['bædmintən] *n.* game for two or four people, played with rackets and a feathered shuttlecock. □ **badminton**

baffle ['bæfl] *n.* shield (to cut out noise). □ **pantalla acústica**
■ *v.* **1** to puzzle: *the detectives are baffled by the mystery.* □ **desconcertar**
2 to frustrate: *they baffled the attempts of the spies to find out about nuclear secrets.* □ **frustrar**

bag [bæg] *n.* **1** something made of paper/cloth/plastic which you can carry things in: *a bag of potatoes; put the apples in a paper bag; have you a plastic bag I can put this rubbish in?* □ **bolsa**
carrier bag, bag made of stiff paper with two handles for shopping. □ **bolsa**
shopping bag, large bag for carrying shopping. □ **bolsa para la compra**
string bag, bag made of string like a net for carrying shopping. □ **bolsa de cuerda, red**
2 ***bags:*** *he's got bags of money,* (*informal*) lots of money; *there's bags of time,* (*informal*) lots of time. □ **montones de...; montón de...**
3 *bags under the eyes,* puffy layer of skin beneath the eyes, often showing that you are ill or tired. □ **ojeras, bolsas**
4 ***it's in the bag,*** (*informal*) the deal is agreed/the contract is signed. □ **está en el saco**
■ *v.* (*he bagged*) to catch: *I bagged three rabbits.* □ **cazar**
bags I *go first,* (*informal*) I claim the right to go first. □ **yo el primero**
baggy *adj.* (*baggier, baggiest*) too big; hanging in folds: *baggy trousers.* □ **holgado, que hace bolsas**

bagatelle [bægə'tel] *n.* **1** game where small metal balls are sent round a board, aiming to make them fall in holes or cages which give certain points. □ **billar inglés**
2 something unimportant. □ **bagatela**

baggage ['bægidʒ] *n.* (*no pl.*) luggage; cases/trunks, etc., which are taken when travelling: *send the baggage on in advance.* □ **equipaje**

bagpipes ['bægpaips] *n. pl.* musical instrument made of an air sack attached to pipes. □ **gaita**

bail [beil] *n.* **1** small piece of wood resting on the top of stumps in cricket. □ **varilla, travesaño**
2 money paid to a court as surety for a prisoner's temporary release: *he was released on bail of $500; when the accused did not return to the court he forfeited his bail.* □ **fianza**
■ *v.* **1** to pay money to let a prisoner out temporarily between hearings: *I had to bail my brother out.* □ **pagar una fianza**
2 *to bail out a boat,* to scoop water out of a boat: *the water came in so fast we were all bailing it out.* □ **achicar**
bailer *n.* scoop for removing water from a boat. □ **achicador**

bailiff ['beilif] *n.* **1** court official who can seize property in payment of debts. □ **alguacil**
2 landowner's agent on an estate. □ **administrador**

bairn ['bɛən] *n.* (*in Scotland*) child. □ **niño**

bait [beit] *n.* fly, worm, meat, etc., used to attract fish or animals: *he was fishing using worms as bait; I must put down some bait to catch the rats.* □ **cebo**
■ *v.* to attach bait to a hook or trap: *the mousetrap was baited with cheese.* □ **poner cebo**

baize [beiz] *n.* green cloth made of wool. □ **tapete**

bake [beik] *v.* to cook (in an oven): *don't come into the kitchen, I'm baking cakes; baked potatoes,* potatoes cooked in an oven. □ **cocer al horno**
bakehouse *n.* building with ovens for baking. □ **tahona**
baker *n.* person who makes bread and cakes: *go to the baker's and buy me a loaf.* □ **panadero**
baker's dozen, thirteen. □ **docena del fraile**
bakery *n.* (*pl. bakeries*) shop and workshop of a baker. □ **panadería**
baking *n.* cooking (in an oven). □ **cocción; hornada**
baking dish, fireproof dish which is used for cooking meat, etc.. □ **cazuela; fuente para horno**
baking tray, flat sheet of metal for baking cakes/biscuits etc. on. □ **bandeja de horno**
■ *adv.* ***baking hot,*** extremely hot: *it was baking hot in the sun.* □ **calor terrible**
baking powder *n.* powder which when added to a cake mix helps it to rise. □ **levadura**

balaclava [bælə'klɑːvə] *n.* ***balaclava (helmet),*** knitted woollen helmet covering the whole head and neck, with a round opening for the face. □ **pasamontañas**

balance ['bæləns] *n.* **1** machine which weighs. □ **balanza**
2 *the result hangs* ***in the balance,*** you cannot tell

which way the result will turn out. □ **...está en juego**
3 staying steady. □ **equilibrio**
to keep/lose one's balance: *although he slipped on the tightrope, he managed to keep his balance,* he managed not to fall off; *he lost his balance,* he fell off. □ **mantener/perder el equilibrio**
the balance of power, the division of power between countries. □ **equilibrio de fuerzas**
4 what remains after all payments have been made: *we have a balance of $25 in the bank.* □ **saldo**
balance in hand, money left in an account after payments have been made. □ **saldo disponible**
balance of payments, difference between money obtained from exports and money paid for imports by a country: *our balance of payments rose last month.* □ **balanza de pagos**
balance sheet, statement drawn up at the end of a year showing the payments and receipts of a company. □ **balance**
■ *v.* **1** to remain in one position without falling: *he was balancing on top of the fence.* □ **hacer equilibrios**
2 to make something stand without falling: *he balanced the jug of water on his head.* □ **poner en equilibrios**
3 to counteract the effect of something: *the profit we make in one shop balances the loss in the other one.* □ **contrarrestar**
4 *to make the accounts balance,* to make the totals of income and expenditure cancel each other out. □ **cuadrar**
balanced *adj.* level/not excessive; sensible: *a balanced diet; she's a well balanced person.* □ **equilibrado**

balcony ['bælkəni] *n.* (*pl. balconies*) small terrace jutting out from the upper floor of a building where you can walk about: *we were sitting on the balcony drinking coffee.* □ **balcón**

bald [bɔːld] *adj.* **1** with no hair: *my brother is going bald already although he's younger than me.* □ **calvo**
2 not elaborate; with no frills: *it is just a bald statement of fact.* □ **desnudo, estricto**
balding *adj.* becoming bald. □ **que se está quedando calvo**
baldly *adv.* with no frills/drily: *he baldly announced that he had sold the family shop.* □ **sin remilgos**
baldness *n.* lack of hair: *he wears a wig to hide his baldness.* □ **calvicie**

bale [beil] *n.* large bundle: *bale of straw.* □ **paca; fardo**
■ *v.* ***to bale out,*** to jump out of a crashing aircraft with the help of a parachute. □ **saltar en paracaídas**

baleful ['beilful] *adj.* threatening/unpleasant: *a baleful look.* □ **siniestro**

balk [bɔːlk] *v.* **1** to prevent someone from doing something: *we balked his plans for selling the shop.* □ **desbaratar**
2 to refuse to do something: *the horse balked at the fence,* the horse refused to jump over the fence; *I balk at having to take work home every day.* □ **negarse**

ball [bɔːl] *n.* **1** round object for playing games: *ping-pong ball; tennis ball; golf ball; he passed the ball to the wing; the goalkeeper dived on a low ball.* □ **pelota; bola**
2 ***keep the ball rolling,*** keep up the action/keep everything moving. □ **no dejar decaer...**
3 *I'll* ***start the ball rolling,*** I'll start things off. □ **empezar**
4 *he's very much* ***on the ball,*** he knows his job very well/he is up to date with the latest developments. □ **estar al tanto**
5 *they won't* ***play ball,*** they won't co-operate with us. □ **cooperar**
6 thing with a round shape: *a ball of wool; he screwed the paper up into a little ball.* □ **ovillo (de lana); bola**
7 formal dance: *an end-of-term ball.* □ **baile**
8 *Amer.* baseball. □ **béisbol**
ball park, area set aside for playing baseball. □ **campo de ...**
ball-and-socket *adj.* (joint) where a ball at the end of one rod/bone fits a socket at the end of another. □ **articulación de rótula**
ballcock *n.* mechanism with a valve operated by a floating ball (for filling cisterns). □ **llave de bola**
ballpoint *adj.* ***ballpoint pen,*** pen with a tiny ball which is automatically coated with ink from a tube. □ **bolígrafo**
ballroom *n.* large room for formal dances. □ **salón de baile**
ballroom dancing, formal dancing. □ **baile de etiqueta**

ballad ['bæləd] *n.* romantic popular song or poem telling a story. □ **balada**

ballast ['bæləst] *n.* **1** material carried in ship/balloon to give extra weight. □ **lastre**
2 stones used to bed down railway sleepers. □ **balasto**

ballet ['bælei] *n.* **1** dancing as a spectacle for public performance: *classical ballet; modern ballet; ballet dancer.* □ **ballet**
2 danced piece for performance: *she danced in the ballet 'Swan Lake'.* □ **ballet**
3 company which performs ballets: *the Russian Ballet.* □ **ballet**
ballerina [bælə'riːnə] *n.* woman ballet dancer. □ **bailarina**

ballistic [bə'listik] *adj.* *ballistic missile,* missile which has an engine but which falls to its target by gravity. □ **balístico**
ballistics [bə'listiks] *n.* (*usually with singular verb*) science of shooting bullets or shells. □ **balística**

balloon [bə'luːn] *n.* large round object which is inflated: *we are blowing up the balloons for the Christmas party.* □ **globo**
hot-air balloon, large passenger-carrying balloon inflated with hot air. □ **globo aerostático**
ballooning *n.* sport of racing large passenger-carrying balloons. □ **aerostación**

ballot ['bælət] *n.* voting by pieces of paper: *a secret ballot,* election where the votes of individual voters are not disclosed. □ **votación**
postal ballot, election where voters can send their votes by post. □ **votación por correo**
ballot paper, paper with names of candidates against which the voter makes a cross. □ **papeleta de voto**
ballot box, sealed box for putting ballot papers in. □ **urna**
■ *v.* to vote by pieces of paper: *they balloted for the offices of president and secretary.* □ **votar**

ballyhoo [bæli'huː] *n.* *Amer.* energetic publicizing (during an election campaign, etc.). □ **propaganda sensacionalista**

balmy ['bɑːmi] *adj.* (*balmier; balmiest*) fragrant/soft (air/breeze). □ **balsámico**

balsa ['bɔːlsə] *n.* very light wood (used for making models). □ **balsa**

balsam ['bɔːlsəm] *n.* fragrant flowering plant. □ **bálsamo**

balustrade [bælə'streid] *n.* stone fence made of small carved pillars along the edge of terrace/bal-

cony, etc. □ **balaustrada**
baluster ['bæləstə] *n.* small pillar. □ **balaustre**
bamboo [bæm'bu:] *n.* tropical plant which provides tall, strong, jointed canes: *bamboo furniture; bamboo shoots,* young shoots of bamboo which can be eaten □ **bambú**
bamboozle [bæm'bu:zl] *v.* to trick/to puzzle (someone). □ **embaucar**
ban [bæn] *n.* law/instruction which forbids something: *a ban on smoking in cinemas; ban on the export of antiques; nuclear test ban.* □ **prohibición**
■ *v.* (*he banned*) to forbid (something): *the headmaster has banned comics in school; the government has banned the use of firearms; they are campaigning to ban night flying.* □ **prohibir**
banal [bə'nɑ:l] *adj.* ordinary/trivial: *he can expand the most banal incident into a major crisis.* □ **banal**
banality [bə'næliti] *n.* ordinariness. □ **banalidad**
banana [bə'nɑ:nə] *n.* long yellow tropical fruit. □ **plátano**
band [bænd] *n.* **1** thin loop of material for tying things together: *the papers were held together with an elastic band.* □ **cinta**
2 *bands,* strips of white cloth worn round the neck by lawyers/clergymen. □ **alzacuello**
3 group of frequencies in radio transmission. □ **banda**
4 group of people: *the looters were roaming the streets in bands; bands of soldiers crossed the border.* □ **banda**
5 group of musicians, especially playing brass and percussion instruments: *a brass band; the band of the Royal Marines.* □ **banda**
■ *v.* to form into a group: *they banded together for safety.* □ **juntarse**
bandmaster *n.* leader of a brass band. □ **director de banda**
bandsman *n.* musician playing in a band. □ **músico de banda**
bandstand *n.* small stage (in public gardens) for outdoor concerts. □ **quiosco de música**
bandwagon *n.* ***to jump on the bandwagon,*** to join a popular movement/to start to do something which is already proving popular. □ **seguir la corriente**
bandage ['bændidʒ] *n.* piece of cloth to tie round a wound/round a twisted ankle, etc.: *the soldier had a bandage round his head.* □ **venda; vendaje**
■ *v.* to tie a cloth round a wound: *his leg is all bandaged up.* □ **vendar**
bandit ['bændit] *n.* robber/brigand: *the travellers were attacked by bandits.* □ **bandido**
bandy ['bændi] *adj.* *he has bandy legs,* when he stands with feet together, his knees do not touch. □ **patizambo**
■ *v.* (*he bandied*) to shout words (to each other): *they were bandying jokes about.* □ **intercambiar**
bane [bein] *n.* *it's the bane of my life,* it's what annoys me most. □ **me ha amargado la vida**
bang [bæŋ] *n.* **1** loud noise: *the bomb went off with a loud bang.* □ **estruendo**
supersonic bang, loud noise made when an aircraft goes faster than the speed of sound. □ **onda de choque**
2 sharp blow: *he had a bang on the head.* □ **flequillo**
■ *v.* to make a bang (by hitting something): *he was banging on the table with his fist; she banged the door shut; I banged my head on the low beam.* □ **golpear**
■ (*interjection showing noise of an explosion*): *bang! bang! you're dead; the gun suddenly went bang.* □ **¡pum!; ¡bang!**
bang in the middle, right in the middle: *he suddenly laughed out loud, bang in the middle of the sermon.* □ **justo en el medio de...**
banger *n.* **1** firework that goes bang. □ **petardo**
2 *(slang)* old car. □ **cacharro**
3 *(informal)* sausage. □ **salchicha**
banging *n.* noise of repeated bangs: *there is a great deal of bumping and banging going on outside.* □ **detonaciones**
bangle ['bæŋgl] *n.* bracelet made of metal or rigid material. □ **brazalete**
banish ['bæniʃ] *v.* to send (someone) away; to exile (someone): *he was banished to a small island in the Mediterranean; this spray banishes nasty smells in the kitchen.* □ **desterrar**
banishment *n.* sending away; exile: *he suffered twenty years' banishment.* □ **destierro**
banisters ['bænistəz] *n. pl.* set of vertical rods with a handrail along the side of stairs. □ **barandilla**
banjo ['bændʒou] *n.* (*pl. banjos*) stringed instrument with a round body. □ **banjo**
bank [bæŋk] *n.* **1** long mound of earth/sand/snow, etc.: *let's sit on this bank and eat our sandwiches.* □ **montículo**
2 edge of a river or canal: *he ran along the bank of the river.* □ **ribera, orilla**
3 row (of lights). □ **hilera**
4 institution for keeping or lending money: *I put my money in a savings bank; how much have you got in your bank account? my bank manager wouldn't agree to lend me any more money.* □ **banco**
merchant bank, bank which deals with lending large sums of money to businesses. □ **banco de negocios**
clearing banks, banks which issue cheques. □ **bancos (de compensación)**
bank holiday, public holiday when the banks are closed: *May 1st is a bank holiday.* □ **día festivo**
■ *v.* **1** to pile up in a long mound. □ **amontonar**
2 *they banked up the side of the canal,* they reinforced the canal banks. □ **reforzar**
3 *the snow banked up along the road,* the wind blew the snow into banks. □ **amontonarse**
4 to roll to one side: *the aircraft banked and flew away.* □ **ladearse**
5 to put money into a bank; to use a bank: *I'm banking the money I won on the races; where do you bank?,* which bank do you use? □ **depositar; utilizar un banco**
6 ***to bank on:*** *I'm banking on taking two weeks off next month,* I'm counting on/relying on taking two weeks off. □ **contar con**
banker *n.* **1** person who directs a bank. □ **banquero**
2 (*in Australia*) river which is full of water. □ **río en crecida**
banking *n.* the profession of being a banker: *he is training to go into merchant banking.* □ **banca**
banknote *n.* paper money issued by a bank. □ **billete de banco**
bankrupt *adj.* and *n.* (person) whose debts exceed his assets and who has been declared incapable of meeting his debts: *he has gone bankrupt; he has been declared bankrupt.* □ **en quiebra**
bankruptcy *n.* state of being unable to meet your debts. □ **quiebra, bancarrota**
bankruptcy court, court which decides if someone should be declared bankrupt. □ **tribunal de lo económico (quiebras)**
banner ['bænə] *n.* **1** long flag: *the knights advanced with banners flying.* □ **estandarte**
banner headlines, headlines in a newspaper in very large type. □ **grandes titulares**

2 large piece of material with a slogan written on it, carried in a procession or protest march. □ **pancarta**
banns [bænz] *n. pl.* official statement in church of intention to marry: *to publish the banns of marriage between Mr Smith and Miss Jones.* □ **amonestaciones**
banquet ['bæŋkwit] *n.* large formal dinner: *the Prime Minister gave a banquet for the visiting president.* □ **banquete**
bantam ['bæntəm] *n.* very small race of chicken. □ **gallina Bantam**
bantamweight *n.* light weight in boxing between flyweight and featherweight. □ **peso gallo**
banter ['bæntə] *n.* sarcastic teasing comments: *I get fed up with this continual banter.* □ **burlas**
bantering *adj. bantering tone,* tone of voice used when making light sarcastic comments. □ **tono burlón**
bap [bæp] *n.* soft flat white bread roll. □ **panecillo**
baptize [bæp'taiz] *v.* to admit someone to the church and give him a Christian name: *the baby is going to be baptized next Sunday.* □ **bautizar**
baptism ['bæptizəm] *n.* church ceremony where someone is given a Christian name. □ **bautismo**
bar [bɑː] *n.* **1** long piece (of metal/chocolate, etc.): *the prison windows had iron bars to stop the prisoners escaping; he ate a bar of chocolate; I have put a new bar of soap in the bathroom.* □ **barra; tableta; pastilla**
2 obstacle: *there is no bar to your applying for the job,* there is nothing to stop you applying. □ **obstáculo**
harbour bar, ridge of sand at the entrance to a harbour. □ **barra**
colour bar, objection to persons because of the colour of their skin. □ **segregación racial**
3 place where drinks are served: *let's have a drink in the bar; he was leaning on the bar,* leaning on the counter where drinks are served; *are you going to drink at the bar or in the lounge?* □ **barra**
saloon bar, room in a pub with carpets and comfortable chairs. □ **bar (sector elegante)**
public bar, room in a pub which is less comfortable than the saloon bar. □ **bar (sector normal)**
milk bar/snack bar/sandwich bar, counter/shop where milk/snacks/sandwiches are served. □ **bar/ establecimiento de...**
4 place where a prisoner stands in court. □ **estrado**
the prisoner at the bar, the person who is accused of the crime. □ **estrado**
5 officially recognized lawyers. □ **colegio de abogados**
to be called to the bar: *he was called to the bar,* he became a barrister. □ **ser admitido para ejercer la abogacía**
6 division (in music): *this piece has three beats to the bar.* □ **barra; compás**
■ *v.* (*he barred*) **1** to block (a road); to stop (someone doing something). □ **interceptar**
2 *he was barred from the club,* he was no longer allowed into the club. □ **excluir**
■ *prep.* ***bar none,*** with no exceptions: *he's the greatest golfer bar none.* □ **sin excepción (de todos)**
barring *prep.* **1** excepting. □ **salvo**
2 *he is the greatest golfer* ***barring none,*** with no exceptions. □ **sin excepción (de todos)**
3 *barring accidents, we should arrive on Friday afternoon,* unless we have an accident. □ **salvo**
barb [bɑːb] *n.* small tooth (on a fish-hook/arrow). □ **lengüeta**
barbed *adj.* **1** with sharp points. □ **de púas**
2 *barbed comment,* sharp critical comment. □ **mordaz**
barbed wire, wire (for fences) with sharp spikes. □ **alambre de espino**
barbarian [bɑː'bɛəriən] *n.* wild/uncivilized person. □ **bárbaro**
barbaric [bɑː'bærik] *adj.* cruel/uncivilized. □ **bárbaro**
barbarity [bɑː'bæriti] *n.* (*pl. barbarities*) cruelty. □ **barbaridad**
barbarous ['bɑːbərəs] *adj.* cruel/uncivilized: *barbarous treatment of prisoners.* □ **bárbaro**
barbecue ['bɑːbikjuː] *n.* **1** charcoal fire/grill for cooking food outdoors. □ **barbacoa**
2 meal cooked on a charcoal grill outdoors: *we often have a barbecue in the garden at weekends; come and have a barbecue supper on the beach.* □ **parrillada**
■ *v.* to cook on a charcoal grill: *barbecued pork.* □ **asar a la parrilla**
barber ['bɑːbə] *n.* man who cuts men's hair: *I must go to the barber's - my hair is getting long.* □ **peluquero**
barbiturate [bɑː'bitjurət] *n.* drug which sends you to sleep. □ **barbitúrico**
bard [bɑːd] *n.* poet (especially in Wales). □ **bardo**
bare ['bɛə] *adj.* **1** naked/not covered with clothes or leaves: *in the winter the branches of the trees are bare; she was not allowed into the church with bare arms.* □ **desnudo; sin mangas**
2 not more than; only: *he earns a bare living,* he earns just enough to live. □ **gana lo justo para vivir**
bare necessities, absolutely essential items for existence. □ **lo imprescindible**
3 *they were elected with a bare majority,* with a very small majority. □ **mayoría muy escasa**
■ *v.* to strip naked. □ **desnudar**
to bare one's soul/heart: *he bared his soul,* he told all his innermost thoughts. □ **descubrir**
bareback *adj.* and *adv.* riding a horse with no saddle: *bareback rider; she rode the horse bareback.* □ **a pelo**
barefaced *adj.* crude/cynical: *it's a barefaced lie.* □ **descarada**
barefoot *adv.* with no shoes on: *they ran around barefoot.* □ **descalzo**
barefooted *adj.* with no shoes on: *barefooted children.* □ **descalzo**
bareheaded *adv.* and *adj.* with no hat on: *they stood bareheaded in the pouring rain.* □ **descubierto**
barely *adv.* hardly/scarcely: *there was barely enough food to go round; he barely had time to sit down before the telephone rang; I barely had enough money to pay the bill.* □ **apenas**
bareness *n.* nakedness: *the bareness of the hills.* □ **desnudez**
bargain ['bɑːgin] *n.* **1** something bought; sale agreed: *we struck a bargain,* we agreed on the sale. □ **compra; trato**
to drive a hard bargain: *he drives a hard bargain,* he is a tough negotiator/he does not allow himself to be forced to make concessions. □ **imponer duras condiciones**
2 something bought more cheaply than it usually is: *a ticket to New York for only $50 is a real bargain.* □ **ganga**
3 *he paid my expenses* ***into the bargain,*** as well as everything else. □ **además**
bargain offer, special offer of goods at low prices. □ **saldos, rebajas**
■ *v.* **1** to negotiate a sale. □ **negociar**

2 ***bargain for:*** *I got more than I bargained for,* more than I expected. □ **esperar**
3 to haggle: *he's bargaining with the shopkeeper over the discount.* □ **regatear**
bargaining *n.* discussion about prices/wages, etc. □ **negociación, regateo**
bargaining team, union representatives discussing salaries with management. □ **negociadores**
barge [bɑ:dʒ] *n.* large flat-bottomed cargo boat on inland waters: *the tug was towing three barges down the river.* □ **barcaza**
■ *v.* to bump heavily (into something). □ **irrumpir**
to barge in: *what did you come barging in for?,* why did you come to interfere? □ **entrometerse**
bargee [bɑ:'dʒi:] *n.* man who is in charge of a barge. □ **gabarrero**
barge pole *n.* long pole for moving a barge along. □ **bichero**
I wouldn't touch it with a barge pole, (*informal*) I don't recommend getting involved with it in any way. □ **no lo cogería ni con pinzas**
baritone ['bæritoun] *adj.* and *n.* (singer with a) voice between tenor and bass. □ **barítono**
barium ['bɛəriəm] *n.* (*chemical element:* Ba) white soft metal. □ **bario**
barium meal, liquid which you drink before having your stomach X-rayed, which will show up clearly on the X-ray. □ **papilla de bario**
bark [bɑ:k] *n.* **1** outer part of a tree: *the Indians make canoes out of birch bark.* □ **corteza**
2 loud call made by dog. □ **ladrido**
his bark is worse than his bite, he is not as terrifying as he sounds. □ **perro ladrador, poco mordedor**
■ *v.* **1** *he barked his shin on the rock,* he scraped the skin off his shin. □ **raspar**
2 to make a loud call like a dog: *the sergeant barked out an order; the guard dogs bark every time anyone comes near the fence.* □ **ladrar**
to bark up the wrong tree: *he's barking up the wrong tree,* he's on the wrong track/he's got the wrong idea. □ **equivocarse**
barking *n.* continuous calls of dogs: *I was woken by loud barking from the garden.* □ **ladridos**
barley ['bɑ:li] *n.* cereal crop. □ **cebada**
pearl barley, grains of barley used in cooking. □ **cebada perlada**
barley sugar, sweet made of boiled sugar. □ **azúcar cande**
barley wine, very strong beer. □ **cerveza de mucho grado**
barmaid ['bɑ:meid] *n.* woman who serves drinks in a bar. □ **camarera**
barman ['bɑ:mən] *n.* (*pl. barmen*) man who serves drinks in a bar. □ **barman, camarero**
barmy ['bɑ:mi] *adj.* (*barmier, barmiest*) (*informal*) mad/crazy. □ **chiflado**
barn [bɑ:n] *n.* large farm building for storing grain or hay. □ **granero**
barnyard *n.* yard in a farm. □ **corral**
barnacle ['bɑ:nəkl] *n.* **1** small shellfish which clings to the bottoms of ships/to submerged wooden posts, etc. □ **lapa**
2 *barnacle goose,* common northern goose. □ **barnacla**
barometer [bə'rɔmitə] *n.* instrument for measuring atmospheric pressure, and therefore for forecasting the weather: *the barometer showed 'very dry'.* □ **barómetro**
barometric [bærə'metrik] *adj.* referring to a barometer: *barometric pressure.* □ **barométrico**
baron ['bærən] *n.* lowest rank of hereditary peers, now also title of life peers. □ **barón**
baroness *n.* wife of a baron, now also title of life peeresses. □ **baronesa**
baronet *n.* hereditary knight. □ **baronet**
baroque [bə'rɔk] *adj.* in the ornate style of architecture of the late 17th and 18th centuries. □ **barroco**
barrack ['bærək] *n.* ***barracks,*** buildings where soldiers, sailors or airmen are housed; army/naval base (usually in a town). □ **cuartel**
confined to barracks, punishment for military personnel which consists of not being allowed outside the barracks. □ **estar arrestado**
barrack room, dormitory for soldiers, etc. □ **dormitorio de tropa**
■ *v.* to make a loud noise showing displeasure: *they barracked our football team.* □ **abuchear**
barrage ['bærɑ:ʒ] *n.* **1** dam across a river, etc. □ **presa**
2 rapid fire from many guns: *anti-aircraft barrage; he had to face a barrage of questions from the newspaper reporters.* □ **andanada**
barrel ['bærəl] *n.* **1** large wooden container (for wine/oil/fish/oysters, etc.). □ **barril; cuba**
2 firing tube (on a gun): *the barrel of a revolver was pointing at him from behind the curtain.* □ **cañón**
3 *he's got me* ***over a barrel,*** (*informal*) in a very awkward position. □ **con el agua al cuello**
4 ***barrel organ,*** machine for making music when a handle is turned. □ **organillo**
barren ['bærən] *adj.* unproductive (land); (woman/animal) who cannot have young; (tree) which does not produce fruit. □ **estéril; yermo**
barrenness *n.* being unproductive; not being able to have young. □ **esterilidad**
barricade [bæri'keid] *n.* makeshift heap of cars/rubbish, etc., made to block a street: *the revolutionaries were manning the barricades,* were in position behind the barricades. □ **barricada**
■ *v.* to block (a street/a door): *he barricaded himself in his room.* □ **bloquear**
barrier ['bæriə] *n.* something which stops you moving forward: *the police put up barriers to keep the football crowd under control.* □ **barrera**
barrister ['bæristə] *n.* lawyer who speaks in court. □ **abogado**
barrow ['bærou] *n.* **1** small wheeled truck which is pushed by hand: *he makes a living selling fruit from a barrow.* □ **carretilla**
2 mound of earth piled over a prehistoric tomb. □ **túmulo**
barter ['bɑ:tə] *n.* exchange (of one product for another). □ **trueque**
■ *v.* to exchange (one product for another): *he bartered his chickens for a sack of potatoes.* □ **cambiar**
basalt ['bæsɔ:lt] *n.* black volcanic rock. □ **basalto**
base [beis] *n.* **1** bottom part: *the jug has a flat base.* □ **base**
2 military camp: *air force base; submarine base; rocket base.* □ **base**
3 substance which is the main part of a mixture. □ **base**
4 chemical compound which reacts with an acid to form a salt. □ **base**
■ *v.* to use as a base; to use a basis (for a theory): *I have based my theory on the research carried out by Professor Smith; his play is based on a novel by Tolstoy.* □ **basar**
■ *adj.* low/cheap. □ **despreciable**
base metal, not a precious metal. □ **de baja ley**
baseball ['beisbɔ:l] *n.* American team game played

with a bat and ball. □ **béisbol**
baseboard *n. Amer.* skirting board, decorative board running along the bottom edge of a wall in a room. □ **zócalo**
baseless *adj.* (accusation) without any basis in fact. □ **infundado**
basement *n.* floor beneath the ground floor: *our garage is in the basement; the household department is in the basement.* □ **sótano**
bash [bæʃ] *n.* (*pl. bashes*) **1** *your car has had a bash,* something has bumped into your car. □ **golpe**
2 *go on, **have a bash,*** (*informal*) go on, try to do it. □ **...inténtalo**
■ *v.* to hit hard: *someone bashed into my car; give me all your money or I'll bash your face in; she got bashed about in the fight.* □ **golpear**
bashful ['bæʃful] *adj.* shy/modest: *he is rather bashful about his exam successes.* □ **modesto**
bashfully *adv.* shyly. □ **tímidamente**
basic ['beisik] *adj.* **1** elementary: *the basic principles of engineering,* principles on which the rest of the science is based. □ **básico**
2 *basic vocabulary,* most commonly used words. □ **básico**
basically *adv.* at bottom: *basically he is a very shy person.* □ **en el fondo**
basil ['bæzl] *n.* type of scented herb. □ **albahaca**
basin ['beisn] *n.* large bowl (used in cooking). □ **fuente**
wash basin, bowl in a bathroom with taps giving running water for washing the hands, etc. □ **lavabo**
basis ['beisis] *n.* (*pl. bases*) (scientific) reason for something: *what is the basis of this theory? I am making changes on the basis of your report.* □ **base**
bask [bɑ:sk] *v.* to lie (in the sun/in glory). □ **tomar el sol, disfrutar de**
basket ['bɑ:skit] *n.* container made of woven straw/cane, etc.: *wastepaper basket; shopping basket.* □ **cesto**
basket chair, chair made of woven cane. □ **sillón de mimbre**
basketball ['bɑ:skitbɔl] *n.* team game where the object is to throw a ball into a small net high up. □ **baloncesto**
basketwork *n.* making of baskets; woven straw/cane, etc. □ **cestería**
bas-relief ['bæsrili:f] *n.* type of carving in stone where the figures stand out against (but are joined to) the background. □ **bajorrelieve**
bass [beis] *adj.* and *n.* (*pl. basses*) (singer with a) low/deep voice; very low (music). □ **bajo**
double bass, instrument like a very large cello. □ **contrabajo**
bass guitar/trombone, large guitar/trombone tuned to play low notes. □ **bajo**
the bass clef, the notation in music covering the lower part of the scale. □ **clave de fa**
basset ['bæsit] *n.* ***basset (hound),*** breed of dog with short legs and long ears. □ **perro basset**
bassoon [bə'su:n] *n.* wind instrument playing lower notes than an oboe or clarinet. □ **fagot**
bastard ['bɑ:stəd] *adj.* and *n.* **1** (person) not born of married parents; (something) which is not pure: *a bastard form of Greek.* □ **bastardo**
2 *(slang)* a nasty person. □ **bastardo**
3 *it's a bastard, (slang)* it's very difficult. □ **duro**
baste [beist] *v.* **1** to sew material loosely. □ **hilvanar**
2 to spread juices over (meat which is cooking). □ **rociar**
bastion ['bæstiən] *n.* fortified part/stronghold. □ **bastión**
bat [bæt] *n.* **1** small mammal which flies by night and hangs upside down in caves/church towers, etc. □ **murciélago**
2 instrument for hitting a ball (in some games): *cricket bat; table tennis bat; baseball bat.* □ **bate**
3 *he did it **off his own bat,*** he did it on his own initiative. □ **por su cuenta**
■ *v.* (*he batted*) **1** to be one of the two batsmen (in cricket); (*of a cricket team*) to have the turn to strike: *Kent are batting; he batted for five hours.* □ **batear**
2 *she never batted an eyelid,* she did not register any surprise. □ **...sin parpadear**
batsman *n.* (*pl. batsmen*) cricketer who is at the wicket/whose turn it is to strike. □ **bateador**
batch [bætʃ] *n.* (*pl. batches*) quantity of bread/cakes baked at one time; group of letters/goods taken together: *I've made two batches of cakes today; we've had another batch of complaints about the service.* □ **hornada; grupo, tanda**
bated ['beitid] *adj.* *we listened **with bated breath,*** we held our breath as we listened. □ **pasmado**
bath [bɑ:θ] *n.* **1** large container for washing all the body: *is the bath clean?* □ **bañera**
2 container for a liquid; container full of a liquid: *acid bath; bath of developer.* □ **baño**
3 act of washing all the body: *cold baths are supposed to be good for you; go upstairs straight away and have a bath.* □ **baño**
4 bath full of water: *will you run my bath for me?,* will you fill the bath with water for me? *I like to lie in a hot bath.* □ **baño**
5 ***baths,*** large (public) building with a swimming pool: *public baths.* □ **baños**
■ *v.* to wash (someone/yourself) all over: *he is bathing the baby.* □ **bañar(se)**
bathmat *n.* small mat to step on as you get out of the bath. □ **alfombra de baño**
bath oil *n.* scented oil to put in a bath. □ **aceite de baño**
bathrobe *n.* **1** loose coat of towelling worn before or after a bath. □ **albornoz**
2 *Amer.* man's dressing-gown. □ **batín**
bathroom *n.* room with a bath, wash basin and sometimes a toilet. □ **cuarto de baño**
bathsalts *n. pl.* scented crystals to put in a bath. □ **sales de baño**
bathtowel *n.* very large towel for drying yourself after a bath. □ **toalla de baño**
bathtub *n. especially Amer.* bath, container for washing all the body. □ **bañera**
bathe [beið] *n.* swim: *I am going for a bathe in the river.* □ **baño**
■ *v.* **1** to swim: *they are over there bathing by the rocks.* □ **bañarse (en el mar, río o piscina)**
2 to wash (a wound) carefully: *you ought to bathe your knee with antiseptic.* □ **lavar**
3 *Amer.* to have a bath. □ **tomar un baño**
bather *n.* person who is swimming. □ **bañista**
bathing *n.* swimming (in the sea, river or a pool). □ **baño (en el mar, río o piscina)**
bathing costume, piece of clothing worn when swimming: *I'm going to change into my bathing costume.* □ **traje de baño**
bathos ['beiθɔs] *n.* sudden drop from a serious subject to a trivial one. □ **(paso a una) trivialidad**
bathysphere ['bæθisfiə] *n.* round pressurized cabin for exploring deep parts of the sea. □ **batisfera**
baton ['bætn] *n.* stick (of conductor of orchestra); truncheon (of policeman). □ **batuta; porra**

battalion [bə'tæliən] *n.* part of the army often commanded by a lieutenant colonel. □ **batallón**
batten ['bætn] *n.* thin strip of wood. □ **listón**
■ *v.* (on ship) ***to batten down the hatches,*** to close down the hatch covers before a storm. □ **asegurar las escotillas con listones**
batter ['bætə] *n.* thin liquid mixture of flour/eggs/milk, for making pancakes, etc. □ **pasta**
■ *v.* to hit hard: *they were battering on the wall; the police battered down the door to enter the house.* □ **apalear**
battered *adj.* **1** which has been hit hard: *battered face of a boxer; battered babies/wives,* babies/wives who have been constantly ill-treated. □ **magullado; maltratado**
2 *battered old hat,* shapeless old hat. □ **ajado**
battery ['bætəri] *n.* (*pl. batteries*) **1** group of artillery guns. □ **batería**
2 container with a cell or several cells charged with electricity: *the car won't start - the battery must be flat; have you put a new battery into the torch? battery-powered shaver.* □ **batería, pila**
3 hut with cages for raising large numbers of chickens. □ **batería de...**
4 ***assault and battery,*** criminal charge of attacking someone with violence: *he was charged with assault and battery.* □ **agresión**
battle ['bætl] *n.* **1** important fight between large enemy forces: *the Battle of Trafalgar; the Battle of Britain.* □ **batalla**
2 *being fit is* ***half the battle,*** being fit means you are halfway to reaching your aim. □ **medio camino (recorrido)**
3 *there is going to be a* ***battle royal*** *over the elections to the committee,* there will be a great struggle over the elections. □ **batalla**
■ *v.* to fight: *they battled against huge waves.* □ **batallar**
battlefield *n.* site of a battle: *this is the battlefield of Waterloo.* □ **campo de batalla**
battlefront *n.* line along which fighting is taking place. □ **el frente**
battlements *n. pl.* top part of a castle wall, with a walk for soldiers. □ **almenas**
battleship *n.* very large warship. □ **acorazado**
bauble ['bɔ:bl] *n.* (*formal*) cheap piece of jewellery. □ **baratija**
baulk [bɔ:lk] *v. see* **balk.**
bauxite ['bɔ:ksait] *n.* mineral from which aluminium is produced. □ **bauxita**
bawdy ['bɔ:di] *adj.* rude/coarse: *the Rugby team sang bawdy songs.* □ **obsceno**
bawl [bɔ:l] *v.* to shout loudly: *the football fans were bawling out a song.* □ **gritar**
bay [bei] *n.* **1** fragrant shrub whose leaves are used in cooking: *bay tree; bay leaf.* □ **laurel**
2 large rounded inlet in the coast: *the Bay of Biscay.* □ **bahía, golfo**
3 arch of a bridge; section of a medieval church between pillars. □ **vano**
bay window, window which projects from an outside wall. □ **ventana salediza**
4 special section set back from the road. □ **zona retranqueada**
parking bay, place marked for parking. □ **estacionamiento**
loading bay, place where lorries can be parked with high platform for loading. □ **muelle de carga**
5 light brown horse. □ **caballo castaño**
6 ***to be at bay,*** to be attacked/encircled by hunters. □ **estar acorralado**
7 *he held up a stick* ***to keep*** *his attackers* ***at bay,*** to keep them away. □ **...a raya**
■ *v.* (*of hunting dog*) to bark. □ **ladrar**
bayonet ['beiənət] *n.* sharp blade attached rifle. □ **bayoneta**
bazaar [bə'zɑ:] *n.* **1** oriental market. □ **bazar**
2 market selling goods for charity: *they are holding a bazaar in aid of the old people's home.* □ **venta benéfica**
BC ['bi:'si:] *abbreviation for* before Christ: *Julius Caesar died in 44 BC.* □ **antes de Cristo**
be [bi:] *v.* (*I am, you are, he is, we/they are; I/he was, we/you/they were; he has been*) **1** (describing a person or thing): *the house is big; the town is near the river; he is my brother; if I were you.* □ **ser; estar**
2 to add up to: *two twos are four; two and three are five.* □ **ser**
3 to exist/to live: *I was at the meeting,* I was present at the meeting; *where are we? there he is; how are you today? tomorrow is Friday.* □ **ser; estar**
4 to feel: *I am cold; they are hungry; she is afraid of spiders.* □ **tener**
5 to go: *have you ever been to New York? she still has not been to the dentist; where have you been all day? the police had been into every room.* □ **estar, ir**
6 (showing time): *it is late; it is four o'clock; it is a fortnight since I saw him.* □ **ser**
7 (showing future): *he is to see the doctor tomorrow.* □ **ir a + inf.**
■ (*used to make part of verbs*) **1** *I am coming; she was going; she is not eating; he has been waiting for hours.* □ **estar**
2 (passive use): *he was killed by a train; are we allowed to smoke?* □ **ser**
being *adj.* ***for the time being,*** temporarily/for now. □ **por el momento**
■ *n.* **1** existence: *the association came into being in 1946,* was founded in 1946. □ **existencia**
2 ***human being,*** person: *human beings are very highly developed.* □ **ser humano**
beach [bi:tʃ] *n.* (*pl. beaches*) stretch of sand/pebbles by the side of the sea: *we like sitting on the beach; in the summer the Mediterranean beaches are very crowded.* □ **playa**
■ *v.* to bring (a boat) on to the beach. □ **varar**
beachcomber *n.* person who collects things thrown up on the beach by the sea. □ **raquero**
beachhead *n.* small area occupied by troops at the beginning of an invasion from the sea: *they established a beachhead before the main landings began.* □ **cabeza de playa**
beachwear *n.* (*no pl.*) clothes to wear on the beach. □ **ropa de playa**
beacon ['bi:kən] *n.* light (used as a signal). □ **baliza**
radio beacon, radio transmitter which guides aircraft into an airport. □ **radiofaro**
Belisha beacon, orange globe light which marks a zebra crossing. □ **luz intermitente en el paso zebra**
bead [bi:d] *n.* **1** small ornament with a hole so that it can be threaded: *she wore nothing but a string of beads.* □ **abalorio**
2 small drop of liquid: *beads of perspiration.* □ **gotita**
beading *n.* thin strip of wood (usually carved in a pattern) used to decorate the edge of a table, the sides of a panel, etc. □ **moldura**
beady *adj. beady eyed,* with eyes small and bright like beads. □ **ojos vivos**
beagle ['bi:gl] *n.* breed of dog used for hunting. □ **sabueso**

beak [biːk] *n.* hard covering of a bird's mouth: *the parrot nipped me with its beak.* □ **pico**
beaker ['biːkə] *n.* metal/plastic cup, usually with no handle; glass container used in scientific experiments. □ **cubeta**
beam [biːm] *n.* **1** large block of wood used in building: *the ceilings in the old house are so low you can easily hit your head on a beam.* □ **viga**
2 ray (of light/sound): *the aircraft was picked out by the beam from the searchlight.* □ **rayo**
radio beam, wavelength for radio transmission. □ **onda dirigida**
3 *he's a bit **off beam,** (informal)* he's mad/he's doing something in the wrong way. □ **equivocado**
4 width of a ship. □ **manga**
5 *he's **broad in the beam,** (informal)* rather fat. □ **ancho de caderas**
■ *v.* **1** to send out rays: *the sun beamed through the window.* □ **irradiar**
2 *he beamed at his daughter,* he gave her a radiant smile. □ **sonreír**
to beam in on: *we beamed in on the enemy station,* our target was the enemy station. □ **tener como blanco**
beaming *adj.* radiant (sunshine/smile/face). □ **radiante**
bean [biːn] *n.* **1** vegetable with edible seeds (and pods). □ **judía**
broad beans, *Amer.* ***Lima beans,*** beans with large pale green seeds. □ **haba**
runner beans, green beans which climb up poles. □ **judía de enrame**
French beans, green beans with edible pods. □ **judías verdes**
baked beans, dish of dried beans cooked with tomato sauce. □ **judías blancas con salsa de tomate**
2 *he's **full of beans,** (informal)* he's full of vigour. □ **rebosar de vitalidad**
3 ***coffee beans,*** fruit of the coffee plant which, when roasted and ground, are used to make coffee. □ **granos de café**
bear ['bɛə] *n.* **1** large furr animal. □ **oso**
polar bear, large white bear living in Arctic regions. □ **oso polar**
teddy bear, toy bear. □ **oso de peluche**
2 person who believes the stock market prices will fall. □ **bajista**
■ *v.* (*he bore; he has borne*) **1** to carry; to produce: *this tree has borne fruit every year; she bore him three children,* she was the mother of his three children; *banknotes bear the signature of the Governor of the Bank; the deposit bears interest at 5%.* □ **dar; llevar**
2 to stand/to put up with: *I can't bear standing in bus queues; he can't bear to watch.* □ **aguantar**
3 to support: *will this branch bear my weight?* □ **soportar**
4 to turn: *bear right at the next crossroads.* □ **doblar**
5 to aim: *the enemy brought their guns to bear on our ship; can you bring your mind to bear on the problem of overpopulation?* □ **dirigir**
bearable *adj.* which you can put up with. □ **soportable**
bear down *v.* to advance heavily towards (someone): *the bus bore down on the lady with a pram.* □ **abalanzarse**
bearer *n.* person who carries something. □ **portador**
beargarden *n. don't turn the place into a beargarden,* don't make a row and mess everywhere. □ **casa de locos**
bearing *n.* **1** ***ball bearings,*** set of small balls around an axle to spread the weight evenly and make the wheel turn smoothly. □ **cojinete de bolas**
2 *to get your bearings,* to find out where you are; *to lose your bearings,* to lose all idea of where you are. □ **orientarse; desorientarse**
3 *stately bearing,* stately way of standing/walking. □ **porte**
bear out *v.* to confirm: *the results bear out my feeling that the team is weak.* □ **corroborar**
bear up *v.* to survive cheerfully: *how are things? - bearing up!* □ **soportar con buen ánimo**
bear with *v.* to endure patiently: *just bear with me for another minute.* □ **tener paciencia con**
beard ['biəd] *n.* hair on the lower part of a man's face: whiskers on a mussel/oyster, etc.: *Henry VIII had a red beard; Father Christmas has a red coat and a long white beard.* □ **barba**
bearded *adj.* with a beard. □ **barbudo**
beardless *adj.* with no beard/clean-shaven. □ **imberbe**
beast [biːst] *n.* **1** wild animal. □ **bestia**
beast of burden, donkey/horse, etc., trained to carry loads. □ **bestia de carga**
2 nasty person: *you revolting beast!* □ **bestia**
beastliness *n.* nastiness (of person). □ **bestialidad**
beastly *adj.* nasty: *what beastly weather!* □ **de perros**
beat [biːt] *n.* **1** regular sound: *drum beat.* □ **golpe**
2 *heart beat,* noise made by the heart. □ **latido**
3 regular measure in music: *he tapped his foot in time to the beat of the music.* □ **ritmo**
4 regular area patrolled by a policeman: *PC Jones has been transferred to another beat.* □ **ronda**
■ *v.* (*he beat; he has beaten*) **1** to hit hard several times: *he beat his wife with a stick; he was beating a drum.* □ **golpear**
2 *she **beat time** with her foot,* tapped her foot in time to the music. □ **marcar el compás**
3 *we **beat a hasty retreat,*** we went away very quickly. □ **batirse en retirada**
4 ***to beat about the bush:*** *don't beat about the bush,* get to the point quickly/do it straight away. □ **andarse con rodeos**
5 ***beat it!,*** *(slang)* go away! □ **largarse**
6 to defeat: *our football team beat the Scots by 4 goals to 1.* □ **ganar**
that beats everything!, we could never find another like that/nothing could be better than that. □ **eso es el colmo**
to beat the record: *he beat the world record,* he did better than the record. □ **batir el récord...**
7 to stir vigorously: *beat the eggs and sugar together.* □ **batir**
beat back *v.* to push back. □ **rechazar**
beat down *v.* **1** *the rain beat down the corn,* flattened the corn. □ **acamar**
2 *I beat down his price,* I reduced the price he was asking by haggling; *he beat me down,* he made me reduce my price. □ **bajar regateando**
3 *the sun beats down on the desert,* the sun strikes hard on the desert. □ **caer de plomo**
beaten *adj. the beaten track,* commonly used road; *our house is rather off the beaten track.* □ **...está retirada**
beating *n.* **1** act of hitting: *the boys got such a beating.* □ **paliza**
2 *our team took a beating,* our team was defeated. □ **paliza**
beat off, *v.* to ward off (an attack). □ **rechazar**
beat up *v.* **1** to whip (cream). □ **batir**

2 to attack (someone): *he was beaten up by football fans.* □ **atacar**

beatify [bi:'ætifai] *v.* to declare (someone) blessed (as the first step to declaring someone a saint). □ **beatificar**

beautiful ['bju:tiful] *adj.* very pleasing to look at: *look at the beautiful sunset; she's a beautiful girl; my mother made a beautiful Christmas cake.* □ **hermoso**

beaut *n.* (*especially Australian*) a beautiful thing/person. □ **una belleza**

beautician *n.* person who makes people beautiful (by applying makeup, etc.). □ **'esthéticienne'**

beautifully *adv.* in a very pleasing way: *he played the last piece of music beautifully.* □ **bellamente**

beautify *v.* to make something beautiful. □ **embellecer**

beauty *n.* (*pl. beauties*) state of being beautiful: *even in old age she has a radiant beauty; he doesn't appreciate the beauty of the scenery.* □ **belleza**

beauty salon, clinic specializing in women's appearance (hair/skin/hands, etc.). □ **salón de belleza**

beauty spot, (i) famous beautiful natural place: *the Lake District is a famous beauty spot.* □ **sitio pintoresco** (ii) dark spot usually on the face. □ **lunar**

beaver ['bi:və] *n.* small American mammal which lives in water and makes dams with trees which it gnaws down. □ **castor**

■ *v.* ***to beaver away at something,*** to work hard at something. □ **esforzarse**

becalmed [bi:'kɑ:md] *adj.* (*of a sailing ship*) not able to move because there is no wind. □ **encalmado**

became [bi'keim] *v. see* **become.**

because [bi'kɔz] *conj.* for the reason that; due to; owing to the fact that: *I am late because I missed my train.* □ **porque**

because of *prep.* on account of: *the trains are not running because of the strike.* □ **a causa de**

beck [bek] *n.* **1** (*in North of England*) mountain stream. □ **arroyo**

2 *she is always **at his beck and call,*** she always does exactly what he wants her to do. □ **estar sometido a la voluntad de...**

beckon ['bekən] *v.* to make a sign (to someone) to come (by bending the first finger): *I beckoned him over to my chair.* □ **hacer señas**

become [bi'kʌm] *v.* (*he became; he has become*) **1** to change into something different: *it was becoming dark; he became very deaf in his old age; she became a bus driver.* □ **llegar a ser, convertirse, hacerse, ponerse**

2 *what became of him?,* what happened to him? □ **¿qué fue de él?**

becoming *adj. her dress is very becoming,* her dress suits her very well. □ **favorecedor**

bed [bed] *n.* **1** piece of furniture for sleeping on: *lie down on my bed; he was sitting up in bed reading the newspaper; to get into bed; to get out of bed.* □ **cama**

double bed, bed for two people. □ **cama de matrimonio**

single bed, bed for one person. □ **cama individual**

to go to bed, to lie down in bed to sleep for the night. □ **irse a la cama**

to take to one's bed: *he took to his bed,* he was ill and so had to lie in bed. □ **acostarse**

to make the bed, to arrange the bedclothes ready for someone to sleep. □ **hacer la cama**

2 bottom (of a river). □ **lecho**

oyster bed, collection of oysters at the bottom of the sea. □ **banco de ostras**

watercress bed, mass of watercress growing in a river. □ **berros**

3 area of garden kept for plants: *rose bed; flower bed; onion bed.* □ **macizo de...**

■ *v.* (*he bedded*) **1** *to bed down horses,* to give horses fresh straw. □ **hacer la cama a los animales**

2 *to bed down railway sleepers,* to lay them on ballast. □ **colocar traviesas**

3 *to bed out plants,* to put out plants in a flower bed. □ **sacar del semillero, trasplantar**

bedclothes *n. pl.* sheets/blankets, etc., on a bed: *he woke up freezing because his bedclothes had slipped off.* □ **ropa de cama**

bedcover *n.* piece of cloth which covers a bed during the daytime. □ **colcha**

bedding *n.* **1** bedclothes (mattress/pillows, etc.); straw (for horses). □ **ropa de cama; lecho**

2 *bedding out,* putting out (of plants) into flower beds. □ **trasplante**

bedding plants, plants suitable for putting into flower beds. □ **plantas trasplantables**

bedjacket *n.* warm jacket worn in bed. □ **mañanita**

bedpan *n.* bowl for passing waste water into when sick in bed. □ **bacinilla**

bedridden *adj.* forced to stay in bed because of illness. □ **postrado en cama**

bedrock *n.* bottom rock beneath various mineral seams. □ **roca firme**

bedroom *n.* room for sleeping in. □ **dormitorio**

bedside *n.* **1** side of a bed: *she sat at his bedside,* she sat beside his bed: *bedside table; bedside lamp.* □ **a la cabecera; mesilla de noche; lámpara de cama**

2 *the doctor has a good **bedside manner,*** he has a comforting way with patients who are in bed. □ **trato gentil**

bed-sitting room [bed'sitiŋ ru:m] *(informal)* **bed-sitter, bedsit** *n.* bedroom and living room combined: *she is living in a bed-sitter in Oxford.* □ **salón-dormitorio**

bedsore *n.* sore which is caused by lying in bed for long periods. □ **úlcera de decúbito**

bedspread *n.* decorative cloth to put over a bed. □ **cobertor; colcha**

bedstead *n.* solid frame of a bed. □ **armazón**

bedtime *n.* time to go to bed: *it's past your bedtime,* it's later than the time you usually go to bed. □ **hora de acostarse**

bedevilled [bi'devld] *adj.* surrounded (with difficulties). □ **complicado**

bedlam ['bedləm] *n.* loud noise; chaos. □ **alboroto**

bedraggled [bi'drægld] *adj.* wet and dirty. □ **enlodado**

bee [bi:] *n.* small insect which makes honey. □ **abeja**

beehive *n.* box (in which a colony of bees lives). □ **colmena**

beekeeper *n.* person who keeps bees. □ **apicultor**

beekeeping *n.* keeping of bees (for honey). □ **apicultura**

beeline *n.* straight line. □ **línea recta**

to make a beeline for: *he made a beeline for the drinks,* he went straight to the drinks. □ **ir derecho a algo**

beeswax *n.* wax produced by bees used as a polish. □ **cera**

beech [bi:tʃ] *n.* (*pl. beeches*) large northern tree; wood of this tree: *the table is made of beech.* □ **haya**

copper beech, beech tree with reddish leaves. □ **haya roja**

beef [bi:f] *n.* meat from a bull or cow: *we are having roast beef for dinner.* □ **carne de vaca**

corned beef, beef which has been salted. □ **cecina**

beefburger ['bi:fbə:gə] *n.* round flat cake of minced

beef. □ **hamburguesa**
beefy *adj.* (*beefier, beefiest*) very strong. □ **fornido**
beer ['biə] *n.* **1** alcoholic drink made from malt, flavoured with hops: *can I have a glass of beer please? what I want is a cold beer.* □ **cerveza**
2 *two beers, please,* two glasses of beer. □ **cerveza**
beery *adj.* referring to beer: *a beery smell.* □ **...a cerveza**
beet [bi:t] *n.* **1** root vegetable. □ **remolacha**
sugar beet, beet grown for processing into sugar. □ **remolacha azucarera**
2 beetroot. □ **remolacha**
beetroot *n.* dark red root vegetable: *he turned as red as a beetroot.* □ **remolacha**
beetle ['bi:tl] *n.* small winged insect with a hard cover over its wings. □ **escarabajo**
befall [bi'fɔ:l] *v.* (*it befell; it has befallen*) (*formal*) to happen (to): *an accident befell him.* □ **acontecer**
before [bi'fɔ:] *adv.* **1** in front: *look at the page before.* □ **anterior**
2 earlier: *I think I have met him before; he didn't come yesterday, he came the day before.* □ **antes**
■ *prep.* **1** in front of: *before my very eyes,* right in front of me; *he stood trembling before the judge.* □ **ante**
2 earlier than; prior to: *make sure you arrive before 10.30; Henry VII was the King before Henry VIII; always wash your hands before meals.* □ **antes de**
3 *his house is just before the traffic lights,* just before you reach the traffic lights. □ **antes de**
■ *conj. before you sit down could you pass me the bread?,* pass me the bread, and then sit down; *before answering, think carefully; come and see me before you leave.* □ **antes de/de que**
beforehand *adv.* in advance: *it's always useful to know beforehand the sort of questions you will be asked.* □ **por adelantado**
befriend [bi'frend] *v.* to be friendly to and help (someone). □ **favorecer**
beg [beg] *v.* (*he begged*) **1** to ask for money: *the old man was begging at the church door.* □ **mendigar**
2 to ask: *to beg a favour of someone,* to ask someone a favour; *I beg you not to go there alone; I beg your pardon,* excuse me. □ **rogar; suplicar**
beggar *n.* person who asks for money: *the tourists were surrounded by a crowd of beggars.* □ **mendigo**
poor beggar, poor chap/poor fellow. □ **pobre tipo**
lucky beggar!, (*informal*) what a lucky person! **¡qué suerte tiene el tío!**
beggarly *adj.* small/poor: *beggarly wage.* □ **miserable**
begging *n.* asking for money: *she was arrested for begging.* □ **pedir limosna**
begin [bi'gin] *v.* (*he began; he has begun*) to start: *she began to cry before she got to school; the rain was beginning to fall quite fast; the story begins with a description of the railway station.* □ **empezar**
begin again, start from the beginning. □ **empezar de nuevo**
beginner *n.* person who is starting to do something: *Russian for beginners,* Russian language for people who have never learnt any Russian. □ **principiante**
beginning *n.* first part/start: *read the beginning of the letter again; at the beginning,* to start with. □ **principio; comienzo**
begonia [bi'gəuniə] *n.* pot plant with large bright flowers. □ **begonia**
begrudge [bi'grʌdʒ] *v.* to feel resentment because of something someone has or does: *I don't begrudge him his money.* □ **envidiar**
beguile [bi'gail] *v.* to make (time) pass quickly and pleasantly. □ **entretener**
behalf [bi'hɑ:f] *n.* **1** *I am speaking on behalf of the old sailors' association,* I am speaking to get support for the association. □ **en favor de**
2 *Mr Jones will act on my behalf,* will act for me. □ **en nombre de**
3 *don't worry on my behalf,* do not worry about me. □ **por mí**
behave [bi'heiv] *v.* **1** to act: *the children behaved very well/very badly; he just does not know how to behave,* he does not know how to conduct himself. □ **comportarse**
2 *behave yourself,* be good; *if you don't behave, you will be sent to bed,* if you are naughty. □ **compórtate**
behaved *adj.* ***well-behaved*** *child,* polite/quiet child. □ **educado**
badly-behaved *child,* child who is rude/dirty/noisy. □ **maleducado**
behaviour *Amer.* **behavior** *n.* conduct/way of acting: *the behaviour of the football fans was appalling.* □ **conducta**
to be on one's best behaviour, to try to be as good as possible. □ **comportarse lo mejor posible**
behavioural *adj.* concerning the behaviour of human beings: *behavioural science.* □ **de la conducta**
behead [bi'hed] *v.* to cut off someone's head: *Charles I was beheaded.* □ **decapitar**
behind [bi'haind] *adv.* **1** after; back: *he stayed behind,* he stayed at the place everyone started from; *we had gone ten miles when we realized we had left the picnic things behind,* we had forgotten them. □ **detrás; atrás**
2 late: *I am very behind with my work.* □ **atrasado**
■ *prep.* **1** at the back of: *let's hide behind this door; what is really behind it all?,* what is the real cause of it all? □ **detrás**
2 *I'm behind you completely,* I'm in full support. □ **te apoyo por completo**
3 late/retarded (by comparison with someone else); less advanced than (someone): *as far as technology goes we are years behind the Americans.* □ **por detrás de**
■ *n.* buttocks: *he just sits on his behind all day and does nothing useful; he'll get a kick in the behind if I catch him stealing apples.* □ **trasero**
behindhand *adv.* late: *I am getting behindhand with my work.* □ **atrasado**
behold [bi'hould] *v.* (*he beheld*) (*formal*) to see. □ **percibir**
beholden [bi'houldən] *adj.* (*formal*) grateful: *I am beholden to you for this information.* □ **agradecido**
beige [beiʒ] *adj.* pale fawn colour. □ **beige**
belated [bi'leitid] *adj.* late: *one or two belated travellers; he sent a rather belated apology.* □ **tardío**
belatedly *adv.* late. □ **tarde**
belch [beltʃ] *n.* (*pl. belches*) noise made when bringing up gas from the stomach. □ **eructo**
■ *v.* **1** to make a noise by bringing up gas from the stomach through the mouth. □ **eructar**
2 to pour out (smoke, flames, etc.): *the chimney was belching smoke; flames were belching out of the windows.* □ **arrojar; salir**
beleaguered [bi'li:gəd] *adj.* in a difficult position; surrounded by enemies. □ **sitiado**
belfry ['belfri] *n.* (*pl. belfries*) tower for bells. □ **campanario**
Belgium ['beldʒəm] *n.* European country between France and Holland. □ **Bélgica**
Belgian ['beldʒən] *adj.* referring to Belgium.

□ **belga**
■ *n.* person from Belgium. □ **belga**
believe [bi'li:v] *v.* to feel sure of something, without any proof; to suppose: *I believe I am right; I don't believe we have met before; I believe so,* I think that is correct; *you don't believe what he says, do you?,* you don't think that what he says is true, do you? *he doesn't believe in God; do you believe in ghosts?* do you think there are such things as ghosts? □ **creer**
belief *n.* feeling sure of something/conviction: *it is my belief that he is a thief; belief in God.* □ **creencia; fe**
believable *adj.* which one can believe: *the story is quite believable.* □ **creíble**
believer *n.* person who believes in something, especially God: *he is a great believer in physical exercise.* □ **creyente**
belittle [bi'litl] *v.* to make something seem small or unimportant: *do not belittle the achievements of the nineteenth century explorers.* □ **minimizar**
bell [bel] *n.* metal cup-shaped object which makes a ringing sound when hit; mechanism to make a ringing sound: *door bell; bicycle bell; church bell; the postman rang the bell twice.* □ **campana**
ring a bell: *that rings a bell,* that reminds me of something. □ **eso me suena**
bellboy *Amer.* **bellhop** *n.* messenger boy employed in a hotel. □ **botones**
bellpush *n.* button which rings a bell when pushed. □ **pulsador; timbre**
bell tower *n.* tower with bells. □ **campanario**
bellicose ['belikous] *adj.* (*formal*) warlike. □ **belicoso**
belligerent [bə'lidʒərənt] *adj.* warlike. □ **beligerante**
■ *n.* country fighting a war. □ **país beligerante**
belligerency *n.* being belligerent. □ **beligerancia**
bellow ['belou] *n.* loud cry (of bull/angry person). □ **bramido**
■ *v.* to make a loud cry. □ **bramar**
bellows ['belouz] *n. pl.* apparatus for blowing air into a fire to make it burn brightly. □ **fuelle**
belly ['beli] *n.* (*pl. bellies*) (*informal*) abdomen: *he got a punch in the belly.* □ **tripa; panza**
bellyache *n.* pain in the stomach. □ **dolor de tripa**
■ *v.* (*informal*) to complain bitterly: *he's always bellyaching about something.* □ **quejarse**
bellyflop *n. to do a bellyflop,* (*informal*) to fall flat on to the water instead of diving into it. □ **panzada**
bellyful *n. I've had a bellyful of his complaints,* (*informal*) I've had as many of his complaints as I can stand. □ **panzada**
belly landing *n.* landing of an aircraft on the underside of its body (because the undercarriage has failed). □ **aterrizaje forzoso (sobre la panza)**
belong [bi'lɔŋ] *v.* **1** to be someone's property: *this hat belongs to my sister; who does this car belong to?* □ **pertenecer**
2 to be a member (of a club): *do you belong to the sports club?* □ **pertenecer**
3 *you shouldn't have touched that book - put it back where it belongs,* put it back in the right place on the shelf. □ **en su sitio**
belongings *n. pl.* personal property: *the case came open and all my belongings fell on to the platform.* □ **pertenencias**
beloved [bi'lʌvid] *adj.* whom someone loves: *he was carrying his beloved teddy bear.* □ **amado**
■ *n.* person whom someone loves. □ **querido**
below [bi'lou] *adv.* **1** lower down: *he stood on the hill and looked down into the valley below.* □ **abajo**
2 *if you look three lines below,* three lines further on from the one you are reading. □ **abajo**
■ *prep.* lower than: *the temperature never goes below 25°; if you look below the surface; you shouldn't have hit him below the belt; his marks were considerably below (the) average.* □ **(por) debajo de**
belt [belt] *n.* **1** strap which goes round your waist: *tighten your belt if you don't want your trousers to fall down.* □ **cinturón**
seat belt, belt in a car or aircraft which holds you in place and protects against sudden shocks. □ **cinturón de seguridad**
2 zone. □ **cinturón**
green belt, area round a town where building is not permitted. □ **cinturón verde**
■ *v.* **1** ***to belt along,*** (*slang*) to go very fast. □ **ir a toda pastilla**
2 ***belt up!,*** (*informal*) shut up/keep quiet! □ **¡cierra el pico!**
3 *they were belting out a song,* (*informal*) singing the song very loudly. □ **cantar a voz en grito**
bemoan [bi'məoun] *v.* (*formal*) to complain about (something). □ **lamentarse**
bemused [bi'mju:zd] *adj.* bewildered/puzzled. □ **perplejo**
bench [bentʃ] *n.* (*pl. benches*) **1** long hard seat (for several people): *park bench; he slept on a bench in the park.* □ **banco**
2 *bench of magistrates,* group of magistrates who try cases in court; *he came up before the bench,* he had to appear before the magistrates. □ **los magistrados; tribunal**
3 table (for working): *work bench.* □ **banco**
bend [bend] *n.* **1** curve: *the road makes several bends.* □ **curva**
S-bend, double curve in a pipe. □ **recodo**
2 *he's* ***round the bend,*** (*informal*) he's quite mad. □ **majareta**
3 ***the bends,*** illness in divers caused by coming up from a deep dive too quickly. □ **aeroembolia**
■ *v.* (*he bent*) to make a straight object curved; to curve: *this piece of meat is so tough it's bent my fork; the road bends around the side of the mountain; this pipe has been bent out of shape,* it no longer has its proper shape because it has been bent. □ **curvar; torcer**
bend down *v.* to stoop: *he bent down to tie up his shoelaces.* □ **inclinarse**
beneath [bi'ni:θ] *adv.* underneath/below: *he looked out of the plane at the mountains beneath.* □ **abajo**
■ *prep.* **1** under: *have you looked beneath the cooker?* □ **debajo de**
2 *he thinks it is beneath him,* he thinks it is too insignificant/too unimportant for him to deal with. □ **él piensa que es indigno de él....**
benediction [beni'dikʃn] *n.* blessing (in church). □ **bendición**
benefactor ['benifæktə] **benefactress** ['benifæktrəs] *n.* person who gives someone/a society money. □ **benefactor**
beneficent [bi'nefisənt] *adj.* (*formal*) (person) who does good. □ **benéfico**
beneficial [beni'fiʃl] *adj.* which does good; useful: *you will find it beneficial to take three vitamin tablets in the morning.* □ **provechoso**
beneficiary [beni'fiʃəri] *n.* (*pl. beneficiaries*) person who inherits something from a person who has died. □ **beneficiario**
benefit ['benifit] *n.* **1** profit: *you didn't get much benefit from approaching the manager.* □ **beneficio**
2 payment. □ **prestación, subsidio**

maternity benefit, payment to a woman who has had a baby. □ **prestación por...**
unemployment benefit, payment (by the state) to unemployed people. □ **subsidio de desempleo**
■ *v.* to be of profit: *he benefited from his uncle's will to the tune of $5,000; the building of the shopping centre has benefited our whole community.* □ **beneficiar(se)**
benevolence [bə'nevələns] *n.* goodness/charity. □ **benevolencia**
benevolent *adj.* good/charitable: *benevolent dictatorship,* dictatorship which provides for the well-being of the people. □ **benévolo**
benign [bi'nain] *adj.* **1** pleasant (person). □ **benigno**
2 non-malignant/inoffensive (growth). □ **benigno**
bent [bent] *adj.* **1** curved: *he used a bent pin instead of a hook.* □ **curvo**
2 ***bent on:*** *he is bent on becoming a sailor,* he is very keen to become a sailor. □ **decidido**
3 (*slang*) dishonest. □ **deshonesto**
■ *n. she has a natural bent to be a nurse,* she has an instinct to become a nurse. □ **inclinación**
■ *v. see also* **bend.**
benzene ['benzi:n] *n.* liquid obtained from coal, which is used as a fuel. □ **benceno**
benzine ['benzi:n] *n.* liquid mixture obtained from petroleum, and used to clean clothing. □ **bencina**
bequeath [bi'kwi:ð] *v.* to leave (property/money) to someone when you die: *he bequeathed his art collection to the museum.* □ **legar**
bequest [bi'kwest] *n.* property left to someone. □ **legado**
bereaved [bi'ri:vd] *n.* (*no pl.*) widow/widower; family of a person who has died. □ **desconsolado...**
bereavement *n.* loss of member of the family through death: *I am very sorry to hear of your bereavement,* to hear that a member of your family has died. □ **pérdida**
beret ['berei] *n.* round cloth or felt cap with no peak. □ **boina**
beriberi [beri'beri] *n.* tropical disease of the nervous system. □ **beriberi**
berry ['beri] *n.* (*pl. berries*) fruit of a shrub. □ **baya**
berserk [bə'zə:k] *adj.* ***to go berserk,*** to go wild. □ **frenético**
berth [bə:θ] *n.* **1** place where a ship ties up to a quay. □ **atracadero**
to give something a wide berth, to avoid something at all costs. □ **evitar a alguien**
2 bed (in a ship/train): *a four-berth cabin,* cabin with bunks for four people. □ **litera**
■ *v.* to tie up (a ship): *the liner berthed two hours late.* □ **atracar**
beseech [bi'si:tʃ] *v.* (*he beseeched/besought*) (*formal*) *to ask; to plead: I beseech you to help find my child.* □ **suplicar**
beset [bi'set] *v.* (*he beset*) to surround causing problems: *they were beset by many problems.* □ **acosar**
besetting sin *n.* defect which is always present: *his besetting sin is a tendency to criticize.* □ **gran pecado, defecto dominante**
beside [bi'said] *prep.* **1** at the side of: *sit down here beside me; put the kettle beside the teapot.* □ **junto a**
2 ***it's beside the point,*** it's irrelevant/it's nothing to do with the subject. □ **no viene al caso...**
3 ***to be beside oneself (with),*** *he was beside himself with rage,* extremely angry. □ **estar fuera de sí**
besides [bi'saidz] *prep.* other than: *have you any pets besides the cat? besides my parents, there were only two other guests.* □ **además de**
■ *adv.* also/in any case: *I cannot come out because I have a cold - besides, it is pouring down.* □ **además**
besiege [bi'si:dʒ] *v.* to surround (with troops/newspaper reporters, etc.): *the camp was besieged by guerrillas for two months; the film star was besieged by journalists.* □ **sitiar**
besought [bi'sɔ:t] *v. see* **beseech.**
bespoke [bi'spouk] *adj. bespoke tailor,* tailor who makes clothes to measure. □ **a la medida**
best [best] *adj.* and *n.* **1** very good; better than anyone/anything else: *this is the best film I have ever seen; what is the best way to get to the station from here?* □ **mejor**
2 ***best man,*** friend of the bridegroom who is in attendance on him at a wedding. □ **padrino**
3 *all dressed up in his* ***Sunday best,*** wearing smart clothes kept for special occasions. □ **endomingarse**
4 ***the best of it*** *is that,* the most interesting/funniest part of the story is that. □ **lo mejor**
5 ***do your best,*** do as well as you can: *she did her best to keep a straight face.* □ **haz todo lo posible**
6 *she spoke for* ***the best part*** *of an hour,* for almost a whole hour. □ **durante casi...**
7 ***at best,*** *the prices are no higher than last year,* the most you can say is that prices are no higher. □ **en el mejor de los casos**
8 *he did it* ***to the best of his ability,*** as well as he could. □ **...lo mejor que pudo**
9 ***to the best of my knowledge,*** as far as I know. □ **que yo sepa**
■ *adv.* **1** in a way which is better than anyone else: *who plays the piano best?* □ **¿quién toca mejor el piano?**
2 *I struggled through the speech* ***as best*** *I could,* as well as I could. □ **...lo mejor que pude**
3 ***best-dressed,*** wearing the most fashionable clothes. □ **a la última**
bestseller *n.* book/article that sells in very large numbers. □ **éxito editorial**
bestial ['bestjəl] *adj.* like a beast. □ **bestial**
bestir [bi'stə:] *v.* ***to bestir yourself,*** (*formal*) to get the energy to do something. □ **esforzarse**
bestow [bi'stəou] *v.* (*formal*) to give. □ **otorgar**
bet [bet] *n.* money put down as a pledge when you try to forecast the result of a race, etc., and which you lose if you guess wrongly: *you must place your bets before the race starts.* □ **apuesta**
■ *v.* (*he bet*) **1** to offer to pay money if what you think will happen does not happen: *he bet me $10 the Prime Minister would lose the next general election.* □ **apostar**
2 *I bet he's going to be late,* I am quite sure he's going to be late. □ **apostar**
betting *n.* placing of bets. □ **el apostar**
betting shop, office where you can wager money on horse races. □ **oficina de apuestas**
betray [bi'trei] *v.* to reveal a secret about (someone) to his enemies/to give (someone) away: *the spy was betrayed to the secret service; an informer betrayed the whereabouts of the murderer; by asking a stupid question, he betrayed his ignorance of the geography of the Mediterranean.* □ **entregar, revelar (un secreto)**
betrayal *n.* act of giving someone up to his enemies. □ **traición**
betroth [bi'trouð] *v.* (*formal*) to make someone engaged to marry someone. □ **prometer en matrimonio**
better ['betə] *adj.* superior; of higher quality; less ill; finer (weather): *have you got a better photograph than this one? he is a better man than you are; I was*

ill last week, but I'm better now, in good health; *the weather is better than last week.* □ **mejor**
■ *adv.* **1** *I'm feeling better,* I'm feeling less ill. □ **mejor**
2 ***to think better of:*** *he thought better of it,* he decided not to do what he had planned. □ **cambió de plan, lo pensó mejor**
3 ***had better:*** *you'd better be going,* it's time you went; *he'd better stay here,* he would be wiser to stay here/he ought to stay. □ **sería mejor que**
4 *he's* ***better off*** *where he is,* he's in a better position where he is. □ **está mucho mejor...**
■ *v.* ***to better oneself/one's position,*** to improve one's position. □ **mejorar**
between [bi'twi:n] *prep.* with things on both sides: *there is a fence between my garden and his; the boat sails between Calais and Dover; come and see me any time between 4 and 6; I can't tell the difference between butter and margarine; between now and Monday evening we must reach a decision,* we must reach a decision by Monday evening. □ **entre**
between you and me, privately/confidentially. □ **entre**
in between, in the middle of: *we have breakfast at 8 and lunch at 1, and I often have a snack in between.* □ **entremedias**
bevel ['bevl] *n.* angled edge of a flat surface. □ **chaflán; bisel**
■ *v.* (*he bevelled*) to give a flat surface an angled edge: *the table has a bevelled edge.* □ **biselar**
beverage ['bevərid3] *n.* (something to) drink. □ **bebida**
bevy ['bevi] *n.* (*pl. bevies*) group (especially of girls). □ **una pandilla de...**
bewail [bi'weil] *v.* (*formal*) to complain about (something). □ **quejarse**
beware [bi'wɛə] *v.* to watch out for: *you must beware of large black snakes; beware of the dog.* □ **tener cuidado con**
bewilder [bi'wildə] *v.* to puzzle: *I had a bewildering choice of places to go on holiday; the old lady was bewildered by the noise of the party; I am completely bewildered when I try to sort out who is who in their family.* □ **desconcertar**
bewilderment *n.* puzzle/surprise: *he stood with his mouth open in bewilderment at the scene.* □ **desconcierto**
bewitch [bi'witʃ] *v.* to charm/to cast a spell on. □ **encantar**
bewitching *adj.* charming (girl). □ **encantador**
beyond [bi'jɔnd] *adv.* further; on the other side: *I can see the chimney, but I can't see anything beyond.* □ **más allá**
■ *prep.* **1** further than; on the other side of: *his house is just beyond the traffic lights; you have to go at least ten kilometres beyond the farm to find her cottage.* □ **más allá de, al otro lado de**
2 *it's getting beyond a joke,* it's no longer funny. □ **te estás pasando**
3 *the whole thing is beyond me,* I cannot understand anything about it. □ **...está fuera de mi comprensión**
biannual [bai'ænjuəl] *adj.* which happens twice a year. □ **semestral**
biannually *adv.* twice a year. □ **semestralmente**
bias ['baiəs] *n.* **1** *to cut material on the bias,* slantwise/across the run of threads. □ **bies**
bias binding, narrow strip of material cut on the bias, used for hemming raw edges. □ **al sesgo**
2 slant; strong opinion in one direction: *he showed particular bias towards the English,* he favoured the English. □ **inclinación**
3 tendency to turn in one direction (of a bowl in a game of bowls). □ **descentramiento**
biased *adj.* showing strong opinion in one direction/prejudiced: *he is biased against anyone who has not been to university.* □ **tener prejuicio en contra de...**
bib [bib] *n.* small cloth tied under a baby's chin. □ **babero**
bible ['baibl] *n.* **1** book of Christian or Jewish scriptures. □ **Biblia**
2 important book of reference: *that dictionary is his bible.* □ **biblia**
biblical ['biblikl] *adj.* referring to the bible. □ **bíblico**
bibliography [bibli'ɔgrəfi] *n.* (*pl. bibliographies*) list of books/articles referring to a special subject. □ **bibliografía**
bibliographical [bibliə'græfikl] *adj.* (details) referring to a particular subject. □ **bibliográfico**
bibliophile ['biblioufail] *n.* person who loves books. □ **bibliófilo**
bicarbonate [bai'kɑ:bənət] *n.* ***bicarbonate of soda,*** chemical used as a medicine for stomach pains or as an ingredient in cooking. □ **bicarbonato**
bicentenary [baisen'ti:nəri] *n.* (*pl. bicentenaries*) anniversary of 200 years (since the birth/death of someone): *1991 is the bicentenary of Mozart's death.* □ **bicentenario**
bicentennial [baisen'teniəl] *adj.* referring to a bicentenary. □ **bicentenario**
biceps ['baiseps] *n.* large muscle in the top part of the arm. □ **bíceps**
bicker ['bikə] *v.* to quarrel: *they are always bickering among themselves.* □ **discutir**
bicycle ['baisikl] *n.* two-wheeled vehicle driven by pedals: *he goes to school on his bicycle; can you ride a bicycle?* □ **bicicleta**
■ *v.* to ride on a bicycle: *they were bicycling happily along.* □ **montar en bicicleta**
bid [bid] *n.* **1** offer/attempt: *his bid of $50 was too low to buy the statue.* □ **oferta**
2 *he made a bid for power,* he tried to seize power. □ **intento**
takeover bid, attempt to take over a company. □ **oferta de absorción**
■ *v.* **1** (*he bid/he bade: he has bidden*) to wish: *he bade me farewell.* □ **decir adiós**
2 (*he bid*) to make an offer at an auction: *I bid $50 for it; what am I bid for this valuable painting?* □ **pujar**
bidder *n.* person who makes an offer at an auction: *the chair was sold to the highest bidder.* □ **postor**
bidding *n.* **1** command: *I did it at his bidding,* I did it because he told me to do it. □ **orden**
2 offers made at an auction: *the bidding started at $5.* □ **puja**
bier [bi:ə] *n.* table/hearse for carrying a coffin: *the mourners followed the bier.* □ **andas**
bifocal [bai'foukl] *adj.* and *n.* ***bifocal spectacles/bifocals,*** spectacles with two types of lens in each frame, one for reading and one for long distance: *he has to wear bifocals.* □ **bifocal**
bifurcate ['baifəkeit] *v.* to split. □ **bifurcar**
bifurcation *n.* splitting (of a road). □ **bifurcación**
big [big] *adj.* (*bigger, biggest*) large: *ours is the biggest house in the road; I don't want a small ice cream, I want a big one; he is bigger than me,* he is taller/larger than I am. □ **grande**
big game, large animals (lions/elephants, etc.) which are hunted for sport. □ **caza mayor**
■ *adv.* ***to talk big:*** *he always talks big,* he pretends

to be important. □ **fanfarronear**
bighead *n.* (*informal*) person who is proud of himself and shows off. □ **engreído**
bigamy ['bigəmi] *n.* action of illegally marrying a second wife/husband, when the first is still alive and has not been divorced. □ **bigamia**
bigamist *n.* person who is illegally married to two people at the same time. □ **bígamo**
bigamous *adj. bigamous marriage,* illegal marriage when you are already married to someone else. □ **bígamo**
bight [bait] *n.* **1** loop of a rope. □ **gaza**
2 wide curved bay. □ **cala**
bigot ['bigət] *n.* person with a narrow-minded attitude to religion/politics; fanatic. □ **fanático**
bigoted *adj.* with very unbending ideas about religion/politics, etc. □ **intolerante**
bigotry *n.* narrow-minded attitude to religion/politics, etc. □ **fanatismo**
bike [baik] *n.* (*informal*) bicycle: *I came by bike/on my bike; can you ride a bike?* □ **bici**
bikini [bi'ki:ni] *n.* brief two-piece bathing costume for women. □ **bikini**
bilateral [bai'lætərəl] *adj.* on two sides: *bilateral agreement,* agreement between two sides. □ **bilateral**
bilberry ['bilbəri] *n.* (*pl. bilberries*) small edible blue berry growing in northern mountains. □ **arándano**
bile [bail] *n.* bitter fluid produced by the liver to digest fat. □ **bilis**
bilge [bildʒ] *n.* **1** dirty water (in a ship's hull). □ **sentina**
2 *don't talk bilge,* don't talk rubbish. □ **...idioteces**
bilingual [bai'liŋgwəl] *adj.* using two languages; (person) who can speak two languages equally fluently: *bilingual secretary; he's completely bilingual in French and Chinese.* □ **bilingüe**
bilious ['biliəs] *adj.* sick: *he had a bilious attack,* he was sick. □ **biliar**
bill [bil] *n.* **1** hard covering of a bird's mouth: *the canary picks up seeds with its bill.* □ **pico**
2 note showing the amount of money you have to pay: *after inviting me for dinner he left me to pay the bill; our telephone bill is very large this month.* □ **cuenta; factura**
3 *Amer.* banknote: *a two-dollar bill.* □ **billete**
4 poster (showing what is on at a theatre). □ **cartel**
5 ***to top the bill,*** to be mentioned at the top of a list as the most important item. □ **encabezar el reparto**
6 *that will* ***fill the bill*** *nicely,* it will be very suitable. □ **eso servirá...**
7 ***bill of fare,*** menu. □ **menú**
8 *he got a* ***clean bill of health,*** the doctor said he was fit. □ **buenos resultados médicos**
9 proposed act of Parliament before it is voted. □ **proyecto de ley**
billboard *n. Amer.* large wooden panel for posters. □ **tablón de anuncios, cartelera**
billfold *n. Amer.* wallet for banknotes. □ **billetero**
billhook *n.* large hooked knife, used for cutting small branches. □ **podadera**
billet ['bilit] *n.* lodgings (for soldiers). □ **alojamiento**
■ *v.* to lodge (soldiers): *she had three soldiers billeted on her.* □ **alojar**
billiards ['biljədz] *n.* game involving hitting balls with a long rod on a smooth green-covered table: *billiard ball,* ball used in playing billiards; *billiard table; billiard room.* □ **billar**
billion ['biljən] *n.* **1** one million millions; *Amer.* one thousand millions. □ **billón; en Amér., mil millones**
2 *we have billions of letters,* a great many letters. □ **...cientos de...**
billow ['bilou] *n.* large wave. □ **oleada**
■ *v.* to move in large waves: *billowing clouds of smoke.* □ **oleadas de humo**
billy can ['bilikæn] *n.* small can used (especially by hikers) for cooking. □ **cazo**
billy goat ['biligout] *n.* male goat. □ **macho cabrío**
bin [bin] *n.* storage box. □ **recipiente**
pedal bin, rubbish container which opens with a pedal. □ **cubo de la basura con pedal**
bread bin, plastic/metal box for keeping bread fresh. □ **panera**
binary ['bainəri] *adj.* in twos: *binary system,* where numbers are shown by the figures 1 and 0 only. **binario**
bind [baind] *n.* (*slang*) bother: *what a bind!* □ **¡qué rollo!**
■ *v.* (*he bound*) **1** to tie: *they bound his hands behind his back; the nurse bound up his wounds.* □ **atar; vendar**
2 to cover a book: *the book is bound with leather.* □ **encuadernar**
3 *this contract binds him to work for us for seven years,* the contract ties him to work for us. □ **comprometer**
binder *n.* stiff cover for holding and protecting loose sheets of paper/magazines. □ **cubierta, carpeta**
binding *adj. this contract is binding on both parties,* both parties have to do what it says. □ **vinculante**
■ *n.* outside cover of a book: *book with a leather binding.* □ **encuadernación**
bindweed *n.* type of climbing weed. □ **enredadera**
binge [bindʒ] *n.* (*informal*) wild drunken party: *they went on a binge.* □ **ir de parranda**
bingo ['biŋgou] *n.* game (played in public) where the aim is to cover up all the numbers on a card as they are called out. □ **bingo**
binocular [bi'nɔkjulə] *adj. binocular vision,* ability to see the same object with two eyes, and therefore to judge distance. □ **binocular**
■ *n. pl.* ***binoculars,*** double glasses for seeing long distances: *he was watching the birds through his binoculars.* □ **prismáticos**
biochemistry [baiou'kemistri] *n.* science of the chemical constituents of animals or plants. □ **bioquímica**
biochemist *n.* person who studies the chemical composition of animals or plants. □ **bioquímico**
biodegradable [baioudi'greidəbl] *adj.* which decomposes naturally to form harmless material. □ **biodegradable**
biography [bai'ɔgrəfi] *n.* (*pl. biographies*) story of the life of someone: *he is writing a biography of Shakespeare.* □ **biografía**
biographer *n.* person who writes a life story of someone. □ **biógrafo**
biographical *adj.* referring to a biography. □ **biográfico**
biology [bai'ɔlədʒi] *n.* study of living things. □ **biología**
biological [baiə'lɔdʒikl] *adj.* referring to living things: *a biological drawing.* □ **biológico**
biological warfare, war in which germs are used. □ **guerra biológica**
biologist *n.* person who studies living things. □ **biólogo**
bionic [bai'ɔnik] *adj.* with powers reinforced by electronic devices. □ **biónico**

biophysics [baiou'fiziks] *n.* (*usually with singular verb*) science of physics of living things. □ **biofísica**
biopsy ['baiɔpsi] *n.* operation to remove a growth. □ **biopsia**
biorhythms ['baiouriðmz] *n. pl.* cycles of activity which are said to recur regularly in each person's life. □ **biorritmo**
biped ['baiped] *n.* animal with two legs. □ **bípedo**
biplane ['baiplein] *n.* aircraft with two sets of wings, one above the other. □ **biplano**
birch [bəːtʃ] *n.* (*pl. birches*) *silver birch,* northern tree with white bark. □ **abedul**
■ *v.* to beat with a bundle of twigs: *the criminal was birched.* □ **azotar**
bird [bəːd] *n.* **1** animal with wings and feathers: *the birds were singing in the trees.* □ **pájaro**
2 (*informal*) person: *he's a curious old bird.* □ **tipo**
3 (*informal*) girl. □ **chavala**
bird's-eye view *n.* view from high up looking down. □ **vista de pájaro**
bird watcher *n.* ornithologist, person who studies birds. □ **ornitólogo**
bird watching *n.* study of birds. □ **ornitología**
biro ['bairou] *n.* (*pl. biros*) trademark for a ballpoint pen. □ **bolígrafo**
birth [bəːθ] *n.* **1** being born. □ **nacimiento**
2 *he is French by birth,* he has French nationality because his parents are French. □ **...de nacimiento**
birth certificate, official document showing date and place of someone's birth. □ **certificado de nacimiento**
birth control, method of preventing pregnancy. □ **control de la natalidad**
birth rate, average number of children born per thousand population. □ **tasa de natalidad**
to give birth, to have a child/to produce young. □ **dar a luz**
birthday *n.* date on which you were born: *my birthday is June 15th; birthday cake/party,* special cake/party to celebrate someone's birthday. □ **cumpleaños**
in his birthday suit, naked/with no clothes on. □ **como Dios le trajo al mundo**
birthmark *n.* mark on the skin which is there from birth. □ **mancha de nacimiento**
birthplace *n.* place (house or town) where someone was born. □ **lugar de nacimiento**
biscuit ['biskit] *n.* small hard cake, usually sweet: *would you like a biscuit with your coffee? a packet of biscuits; cheese and biscuits,* cheese with dry unsweetened biscuits. □ **galleta**
water biscuits, biscuits made of flour and water. □ **galleta**
bisect [bai'sekt] *v.* to cut into two equal parts: *the line bisects the circle.* □ **bisecar**
bishop ['biʃəp] *n.* **1** church leader in charge of a diocese: *the Bishop of Exeter; here is Bishop Smith.* □ **obispo**
2 piece in chess shaped like a bishop's hat. □ **alfil**
bishopric *n.* post of bishop: *he was offered the bishopric of Durham.* □ **obispado**
bismuth ['bizməθ] *n.* (*chemical element*: Bi) white metal used in medicine. □ **bismuto**
bison ['baisn] *n.* (*no pl.*) large wild ox-like animal. □ **bisonte**
bistro ['biːstrou] *n.* (*pl. bistros*) small restaurant serving continental food. □ **bistro**
bit [bit] *n.* **1** small piece: *I've had two bits of cake; tie up the parcel with this bit of string.* □ **trozo**
2 *let him sleep **a bit** longer,* a little while longer; *you look a bit worried; can you wait a bit?* □ **un poquito; un ratito**
3 ***to bits:*** *the chair has come to bits,* has fallen apart; *he took my watch to bits,* he undid my watch into its component parts; *he wore his shoes until they fell to bits,* wore themselves to pieces. □ **...se ha venido abajo; desmontar**
4 *she's thrilled to bits,* very pleased. □ **contento**
5 *he is **a bit of** a nuisance,* he is rather a nuisance. □ **un poco pesado**
6 *he built his house **bit by bit,*** in stages. □ **poco a poco**
7 *this machine is **not a bit of** use,* it is of no use at all. □ **no sirve absolutamente para nada**
8 *he's **every bit as** ugly as you said,* just as ugly. □ **exactamente tan feo**
9 *I've had **a bit of** luck,* I've been lucky. □ **un poco de...**
10 *he has a bit part in a play,* just a small part. □ **pequeño papel**
11 piece of metal for making holes which is placed in a drill. □ **broca**
12 piece of metal going through a horse's mouth which the reins are attached to. □ **bocado**
13 *v. see also* **bite.**
bitch [bitʃ] *n.* (*pl. bitches*) **1** female dog. □ **perra**
2 (*informal*) unpleasant woman. □ **zorra**
■ *v.* (*informal*) to complain: *she was bitching about her salary.* □ **quejarse**
bite [bait] *v.* (*he bit; he has bitten*) **1** to cut with teeth: *our dog bit the postman; I've been bitten by a mosquito.* □ **morder**
2 ***to bite someone's head off:*** *I said hello and he bit my head off,* he replied angrily and in a bad temper. □ **...y me echó una bronca**
3 ***be bitten with:*** *he's been bitten with the idea of sailing round the world,* he's suddenly got the idea of sailing round the world. □ **...le ha picado el gusanillo de...**
4 to attack: *the acid bites into the metal.* □ **morder**
5 *the government's financial measures are beginning to bite,* are beginning to take effect. □ **...a hacer efecto**
■ *n.* **1** mouthful: *I took a big bite of cake.* □ **bocado**
2 place where you have been bitten: *he is covered with mosquito bites.* □ **picaduras**
biting *adj.* sharp (wind); piercing (cold); sharp (remark). □ **cortante**
bitten ['bitn] *v. see* **bite.**
bitter ['bitə] *adj.* **1** not sweet; sour: *lemons are very bitter.* □ **amargo**
2 resentful/cruel: *she had a bitter smile; he learnt through bitter experience.* □ **amargo**
3 *we stayed at the party **to the bitter end,*** right to the very end. □ **...hasta el final**
4 very cold: *a bitter wind.* □ **intenso**
■ *n.* light-coloured beer which is not sweet. □ **'bitter'**
bitterly *adv.* sharply/resentfully: *she was bitterly disappointed; it was bitterly cold.* □ **amargamente**
bitterness *n.* resentment: *there was a lot of bitterness when the firm closed down.* □ **amargura**
bitumen ['bitjumən] *n.* black substance, like tar. □ **betún**
bivalve ['baivælv] *n.* shellfish with two shells hinged together. □ **bivalvo**
bivouac ['bivuæk] *v.* (*he bivouacked*) to camp out in the open without a tent. □ **acampar al raso**
bizarre [bi'zɑː] *adj.* very strange. □ **extraño**
blab [blæb] *v.* (*he blabbed*) (*informal*) to talk too much. □ **parlotear**

black [blæk] *adj.* (*blacker, blackest*) **1** of a very dark colour, the opposite of white: *at night the sky is black; big black clouds appeared on the horizon; black coffee,* coffee with no milk or cream in it. □ **negro**
2 *he got a* ***black eye,*** he was hit in the eye which made the skin round the eye turn black. □ **le pusieron el ojo morado**
3 ***black ice,*** dangerous layer of thin ice on a road. □ **placas de hielo**
4 ***to be in someone's black books,*** not have his favour or approval. □ **...en su lista negra**
5 ***black box,*** device which stores information about an aircraft's flight. □ **caja negra**
6 ***black market,*** selling illegally, at high prices, products which are not normally available: *he bought his coffee on the black market; there is a thriving black market in English magazines.* □ **mercado negro**
7 bad: *a black day for peace.* □ **negro**
black spot, place where traffic accidents often happen. □ **punto negro**
■ *n.* **1** very dark colour, opposite to white: *she looks very smart in black.* □ **negro**
to be in the black, to have money in a bank account/ to be in profit. □ **tener fondos**
2 person whose skin is very dark-coloured. □ **negro**
■ *v.* to refuse to handle goods in support of a strike: *the shipment has been blacked by the dockers.* □ **boicotear**
blackbeetle *n.* large beetle living in houses. □ **cucaracha**
blackberry *n.* (*pl. blackberries*) common wild fruit, growing on long prickly stems; the bush which bears this fruit. □ **zarzamora**
blackbird *n.* common northern bird, the male of which has black feathers and yellow beak. □ **mirlo**
blackboard *n.* (*in school*) a board on the wall which can be written on: *a green blackboard.* □ **pizarra**
blackcurrant *n.* common black soft fruit grown in the garden; the bush which bears this fruit. □ **grosella negra**
blacken *v.* to make black. □ **ennegrecer**
blackfly *n.* (*pl. blackfly* or *blackflies*) small black aphis. □ **jején**
blackguard ['blægɑːd] *n.* scoundrel/wicked person. □ **canalla**
blackhead *n.* blocked pore which shows up as a black dot on the skin. □ **espinilla**
blackish *adj.* rather black. □ **negruzco**
blackleg *n.* person who goes to work in spite of orders to go on strike. □ **esquirol**
blacklist *n.* list of undesirable things or people: *he is on the police blacklist.* □ **lista negra**
■ *v.* to put someone's name on a list of undesirable people. □ **poner en la lista negra**
blackmail *n.* act of making someone pay money by threatening to reveal some unpleasant detail about them. □ **chantaje**
■ *v.* to make someone pay money by threatening to reveal some unpleasant or shameful detail about them. □ **chantajear**
blackmailer *n.* person who blackmails. □ **chantajista**
blackness *n.* total darkness. □ **negrura**
black out *v.* **1** to wipe off/to cover up (a name). □ **tachar**
2 to faint; to lose consciousness. □ **desmayarse**
3 to cut off the electricity: *the storm blacked out half the country.* □ **producir un apagón**
blackout *n.* **1** loss of consciousness: *he's had a blackout.* □ **desmayo**
2 sudden stoppage of electricity supply. □ **apagón**
blacksmith *n.* man who makes horseshoes, who shoes horses and who makes gates, etc., out of metal. □ **herrero**
bladder ['blædə] *n.* **1** bag in the body where urine is stored. □ **vejiga**
2 bag inside a ball which is inflated. □ **cámara de aire**
blade [bleid] *n.* **1** cutting part of knife, etc.: *this kitchen knife has a very sharp blade.* □ **hoja**
2 thin leaf of grass. □ **brizna**
3 one arm of a propeller. □ **aspa**
4 flat part at the end of an oar. □ **pala**
blame [bleim] *n.* criticism of someone for having done something: *who got the blame for the broken window?,* who was said to be responsible for the broken window? □ **culpa**
■ *v.* to say that something was caused by (someone/ something): *she blamed the rain for making the house smell damp; he blamed the neighbour's cat for killing his goldfish; don't blame me if you catch a cold; I don't blame you,* I think you were quite right. □ **culpar**
to be to blame for: *he is in no way to blame for the accident,* he has absolutely no responsibility for the accident. □ **en absoluto es culpable...**
blameless *adj.* pure/innocent. □ **inocente**
blanch [blɑːntʃ] *v.* **1** to put quickly into boiling water. □ **escaldar**
2 to turn white. □ **blanquear**
blancmange [blə'mɔnʒ] *n.* dessert like a cream jelly flavoured with chocolate/strawberry, etc. □ **crema de chocolate, etc.**
bland [blænd] *adj.* smooth; not striking: *he gave a bland smile; the sauce needs some spices - it's too bland.* □ **suave**
blandishments ['blændiʃmənts] *n. pl.* attractive flattery. □ **halago**
blank [blæŋk] *adj.* (*blanker, blankest*) **1** (paper, etc.) with nothing on it. □ **en blanco**
blank cheque, cheque where the figures are not written in. □ **cheque en blanco**
2 ***blank verse,*** poetry which does not rhyme. □ **blanco**
3 *he looked blank,* he looked lost/surprised. □ **sin expresión**
4 *an expression of blank despair,* of total despair. □ **total**
5 *blank cartridge,* with no bullet in it. □ **cartucho de fogueo**
■ *n.* **1** white space (with nothing printed on it): *fill up the blanks; leave blanks if you cannot think of the answer.* □ **espacio en blanco**
2 *my mind is a blank,* I cannot remember anything. □ **...se ha quedado en blanco**
3 ***to draw a blank,*** fail to make any progress; to be unsuccessful. □ **se llevó un chasco**
4 cartridge with no bullet in it: *the police fired blanks over the heads of the crowd.* □ **cartucho de fogueo**
blankly *adv.* with a vacant expression: *he stared blankly at the wall.* □ **con la mirada vacía**
blanket ['blæŋkit] *n.* thick woollen bed covering: *he was sleeping wrapped up in a blanket.* □ **manta**
electric blanket, electrically heated pad to warm a bed. □ **manta eléctrica**
blanket order, order which covers many items. □ **pedido general**
blare [blɛəː] *n.* loud noise. □ **estruendo**

■ *v.* to make a loud noise: *the radio was blaring away all the time.* □ **resonar**

blasé ['blɑːzei] *adj.* bored because you have done something so often: *he's crossed the Atlantic so many times he's blasé about flying.* □ **hastiado**

blaspheme [blæs'fiːm] *v.* to swear; to talk without respect for God. □ **blasfemar**

blasphemer *n.* person who swears. □ **blasfemo**

blasphemous ['blæsfəməs] *adj.* showing no respect for religion; anti-religious (talk). □ **blasfematorio**

blasphemy *n.* disrespect for religion; swearing: *it is blasphemy to talk of leaving the association,* you must not/it is not thought right to talk of leaving the association. □ **blasfemia**

blast [blɑːst] *n.* **1** sharp blowing of wind: *he sheltered from the icy blast.* □ **ráfaga**

2 short whistle: *there was a warning blast on the siren.* □ **toque; sirenazo**

3 *everything is going **full blast**,* everything is working flat out. □ **a toda máquina**

4 explosion; shock wave from an explosion: *he was knocked down by the blast; the blast could be heard three miles away.* □ **sacudida**

■ *v.* **1** to blow up: *the explosion blasted a huge hole in the wall; the burglars blasted their way into the bank.* □ **abrir**

2 to ruin: *his hopes were blasted by the letter from the director.* □ **arruinar**

blast furnace *n.* furnace used to make steel. □ **alto horno**

blast-off *n.* departure of a rocket: *three, two, one, blast-off!* □ **despegue**

blatant ['bleitənt] *adj.* obvious/unmistakable: *a blatant violation of the traffic regulations.* □ **flagrante**

blaze [bleiz] *n.* **1** fierce fire: *the blaze quickly destroyed the store.* □ **incendio**

2 *she worked **like blazes,*** she worked extremely hard. □ **trabajó como una negra**

3 white mark made by cutting away the bark of a tree; white mark on the forehead of an animal. □ **marca; mancha**

■ *v.* **1** to burn fiercely: *the roof of the store was already blazing when the firemen arrived.* □ **arder**

2 ***to blaze a trail,*** to mark a path by cutting the bark on trees/to be the first to do something. □ **señalar/abrir camino**

blazing *adj.* **1** fiery. □ **abrasador**

2 *they had a blazing row,* they had a violent quarrel. □ **violento**

blazer ['bleizə] *n.* (dark) jacket often worn with a badge to show membership of a club/school, etc. □ **'blazer'**

blazon ['bleizn] *n.* coat of arms. □ **blasón**

■ *v.* to proclaim (something). □ **proclamar**

bleach [bliːtʃ] *n.* (*pl. bleaches*) substance which takes the colour out of something: *put some bleach in the water when you are washing sheets.* □ **lejía**

■ *v.* to take the colour out of something: *she has bleached her hair.* □ **aclarar**

bleachers *n. pl. Amer.* raised tiers of seats at a sports stadium. □ **gradas**

bleak [bliːk] *adj.* **1** cold/inhospitable: *the bleak landscape of the North Pole.* □ **desolado**

2 *prospects for an increase in profits are looking very bleak,* are looking very unlikely. □ **poco prometedor**

bleary ['bliəri] *adj.* (*blearier, bleariest*) watery/dim (eyes): *he rubbed his bleary eyes and peered out from the tent.* □ **nublado; turbio**

bleary-eyed *adj.* with watery eyes. □ **vista nublada**

bleat [bliːt] *n.* noise made by a sheep or goat. □ **balido**

■ *v.* **1** to call (like a goat/sheep); to make a noise like a goat/sheep. □ **balar**

2 *what is he bleating on about?,* what does he keep on complaining about? □ **¿de qué se está quejando?**

bleating *n.* noise of sheep/goat calling. □ **balido**

bleed [bliːd] *n. a nose bleed,* loss of blood from the nose. □ **hemorragia nasal**

■ *v.* (*he bled*) **1** to lose blood: *when he cut his thumb it bled; after he hit me my nose began to bleed; have you a towel, his finger's bleeding?* □ **sangrar**

2 *my heart bleeds for you,* I am very sorry for you. □ **mi corazón sufre por...**

bleep [bliːp] *n.* small noise made by a radio/a radar screen. □ **señal**

■ *v.* (*of a radio*) to make a small noise: *the intercom bleeped twice.* □ **emitir una señal**

bleeper *n.* machine which makes a bleep. □ **buscador**

blemish ['blemiʃ] *n.* (*pl. blemishes*) imperfection; mark: *there is a blemish on this apple.* □ **mancha**

■ *v.* to spoil: *his reputation was blemished by his behaviour at the party.* □ **echar a perder**

blend [blend] *n.* mixture (of coffee/tea/tobacco). □ **mezcla**

■ *v.* to mix: *the colours blend together; the zebra blended into the background.* □ **mezclar**

bless [bles] *v.* to make sacred; to bring happiness/wealth to (someone): *he is blessed with wonderful health; she is blessed with a family of six boys.* □ **bendecir**

well I'm blessed!, I am surprised. □ **¡caramba!**

bless you!, (*informal*) (*phrase said when someone sneezes*). □ **¡Jesús!**

blessed ['blesid] *adj.* **1** protected by God: *the blessed saints.* □ **bendito**

2 (*informal*) cursed/annoying: *I had to write the whole blessed thing out again; he talked for the whole blessed day.* □ **bendito**

blessing *n.* **1** something which is useful/which brings happiness: *the blessings of an efficient bus service.* □ **ventaja, bendición**

it's a blessing in disguise, it doesn't look like it, but it is very useful/convenient. □ **no hay mal que por bien no venga**

2 short prayer, especially before or after a meal. □ **bendición**

blew [bluː] *v. see* **blow.**

blight [blait] *n.* fungus disease (attacking vegetables/leaves, etc.): *potato blight.* □ **roya, añublo**

■ *v.* to spoil/to ruin: *it blighted his chances of winning first prize.* □ **arruinar**

blind [blaind] *n.* **1** covering (over a window): *roller blind.* □ **persiana**

Venetian blind, blind made of many horizontal flat strips of wood or plastic. □ **persiana de lamas**

2 ***the blind,*** people who cannot see. □ **los ciegos**

■ *adj.* not able to see: *some blind people carry white sticks.* □ **ciego**

to turn a blind eye: *he turned a blind eye to the stealing that went on in the shop,* he pretended not to notice/did not bother about the stealing. □ **se hizo el loco...**

blind alley, (i) alley with no way out. □ **callejón sin salida**

(ii) position with no prospect of progress. □ **callejón sin salida**

blind spot, (i) part of the road which a motorist cannot see. □ **punto ciego**

(ii) something which someone is incapable of understanding. □ **punto negro**

■ *v.* to prevent someone from seeing: *he was blinded*

by the white light. □ **fue cegado...**
blindfold *n.* bandage put over someone's eyes to prevent him from seeing. □ **venda**
■ *v.* to put a bandage over someone's eyes: *she was blindfolded by the kidnappers.* □ **vendar los ojos**
blindly *adv.* without being able to see: *they groped blindly in the dark cellar.* □ **ciegamente**
blindness *n.* not being able to see: *his approaching blindness.* □ **ceguera**
blink [bliŋk] *v.* to close your eyelids very quickly: *he blinked in the bright light.* □ **pestañear**
blinkers *n.* shades put on a horse's eyes to prevent it from looking sideways. □ **anteojeras**
blip [blip] *n.* small dot of light on a radar screen. □ **punto de luz**
bliss [blis] *n.* great happiness: *sitting here eating strawberries is just sheer bliss.* □ **felicidad**
blissful *adj.* extremely happy. □ **dichoso**
blissfully *adv.* happily: *he was blissfully ignorant of what was going on.* □ **felizmente**
blister ['blistə] *n.* bump on the skin (with water underneath) made by rubbing, etc.: *I have a blister on my heel; my new shoes have given me a blister.* □ **ampolla**
■ *v.* to make bumps on the surface: *the paint is blistering in the heat.* □ **levantar ampollas**
blithely ['blaiðli] *adv.* in a happy carefree way. □ **alegremente**
blithering ['bliðəriŋ] *adj.* (*informal*) awful: *you blithering idiot!* □ **¡tonto de capirote!**
blitz [blits] *n.* (*pl. blitzes*) **1** bombing (of a town). □ **bombardeo aéreo**
2 (*informal*) sudden campaign to clear up something: *I'm having a blitz on the garden rubbish.* □ **limpieza a fondo**
■ *v.* to bomb: *the town was blitzed by the enemy.* □ **bombardear**
blizzard ['blizəd] *n.* heavy snowstorm with strong winds. □ **ventisca**
bloated ['bloutid] *adj.* full; too fat: *I've eaten too much pudding - I feel bloated.* □ **inflado**
bloater ['bloutə] *n.* dried salt herring. □ **arenque ahumado**
blob [blɔb] *n.* large spot: *a blob of paint.* □ **mancha**
bloc [blɔk] *n.* (political) group: *the Soviet bloc.* □ **bloque**
block [blɔk] *n.* **1** piece/lump (of stone or wood): *the baby is playing with wooden blocks; a large block of chocolate.* □ **bloque**
2 large building: *block of offices/block of flats; he lives two blocks down the street,* (*Amer.*) there are two crossroads between here and his house. □ **bloque de...**
3 group: *block of shares.* □ **grupo**
block vote, vote by a group voting together. □ **voto en bloque**
4 *block capitals/letters,* capital letters: *please fill in your surname in block letters.* □ **letras mayúsculas**
5 ***block and tackle,*** arrangement of pulleys and ropes for lifting heavy objects. □ **aparejo de poleas**
■ *v.* to prevent something going past: *the water is overflowing, the pipe must be blocked; the overturned lorry blocked the road for two hours.* □ **bloquear**
blockade [blɔ'keid] *n.* preventing supplies being brought into a place. □ **bloqueo**
■ *v.* to prevent supplies being brought into a place: *the enemy blockaded our ports.* □ **bloquear**
blockage *n.* blocking: *there was a blockage in the narrow street.* □ **obstrucción**
block up *v.* to stop (a hole), to fill (a pipe): *they blocked up the doorway with bricks.* □ **cegar**
bloke [blouk] *n.* (*informal*) man. □ **tío**
blond, blonde [blɔnd] *adj.* and *n.* (person) with fair hair: *she's got blond hair; his sister's a blonde.* □ **rubio**
blood [blʌd] *n.* red liquid in the body: *blood is pumped around the body by the heart; blood poisoning.* □ **sangre**
blood group, letters (A, B, AB and O) showing the type of blood a person has. □ **grupo sanguíneo**
blood donor, person who gives blood to be used in operations. □ **donante de sangre**
blood pressure, pressure at which the heart pumps blood: *he is suffering from high blood pressure.* □ **tensión**
to make someone's blood boil: *it makes my blood boil,* it makes me very angry. □ **...que me hierva la sangre**
to make someone's blood run cold, to scare him: *the sound of footsteps in the dark made his blood run cold.* □ **se le heló la sangre**
new blood: *we need to recruit new blood into the association,* new energetic members. □ **...nueva savia...**
bloodbath *n.* massacre: *the fighting in the town turned into a bloodbath.* □ **baño de sangre**
bloodcurdling *adj.* very frightening: *there was a bloodcurdling howl.* □ **espeluznante**
bloodhound *n.* dog trained to follow tracks. □ **sabueso**
bloodless *adj.* **1** with no blood: *bloodless corpse.* □ **exangüe**
2 *bloodless revolution,* revolution where no one was killed. □ **incruenta**
bloodshed *n.* killing: *was there much bloodshed during the battle?* □ **derramamiento de sangre**
bloodshot *adj.* red (eyes). □ **inyectado en sangre**
bloodstain *n.* stain caused by blood: *she tried to remove the bloodstains by washing.* □ **mancha de sangre**
bloodstained *adj.* stained with blood: *the police took away a bloodstained coat as evidence.* □ **manchado de sangre**
bloodstream *n.* flow of blood round the body: *the poison entered his bloodstream.* □ **sangre**
blood test *n.* test to show the condition of the blood. □ **análisis de sangre**
bloodthirsty *adj.* liking gory details. □ **ávido de sangre**
bloody *adj.* (*bloodier, bloodiest*) **1** covered with blood; where much blood has been shed: *a bloody battle.* □ **sangriento**
2 (*slang*) awful: *what a bloody liar! it's bloody hot in here I can tell you.* □ **maldito**
bloody-minded *adj.* (*informal*) awkward/uncooperative. □ **puñetero; de mala sombra**
bloom [bluːm] *n.* **1** flower. □ **flor**
2 *the apple trees are* ***in full bloom,*** all the apple flowers are out. □ **en flor**
3 velvety skin (of a peach); dust (on skin of a grape). □ **pelusa; vello**
4 *bloom of youth,* healthy glow of a young person. □ **en la flor de la vida**
■ *v.* to flower: *the roses are blooming; it is a flower that only blooms once and then dies; how is she? - she's blooming,* she's doing very well. □ **florecer**
blossom ['blɔsəm] *n.* flowers (on trees): *blossom in the hedgerow; apple blossom.* □ **flor**
■ *v.* to flower: *the apple trees are blossoming.* □ **florecer**
blot [blɔt] *n.* dirty spot; drop (of ink on paper). □ **borrón**

■ *v.* (*he blotted*) to drop a spot (of ink) on something; to dry the ink on a letter. □ **emborronar**
blotter *n.* pad of blotting paper. □ **secante**
blotting paper *n.* thick absorbent paper for drying ink. □ **papel secante**
blotch [blɔtʃ] *n.* large patch of colour. □ **mancha**
blotchy *adj.* (face) with patches of red. □ **con ronchas**
blouse [blauz] *n.* (woman's) shirt. □ **blusa**
blow [blou] *n.* **1** knock/punch: *he knocked him out with a blow on the jaw.* □ **puñetazo**
2 *this must have come as a blow to him,* it must have shocked him. □ **...como una bofetada para él**
■ *v.* (*he blew: he has blown*) **1** to make air move; (*of air*) to move: *he blew on his soup to make it cool; it's blowing hard,* there is a strong wind; *the window suddenly blew open.* □ **soplar**
2 *he blew his nose,* he cleared his nose by blowing down it into a handkerchief. □ **se sonó los mocos**
3 *I have just blown a fuse,* I have burnt out a fuse by overloading it. □ **quemar**
blow away *v.* to move (something) away by blowing: *the wind blew the clouds away.* □ **arrastrar**
blow down *v.* to fall down/to make (something) fall down by blowing: *half the trees in the park have been blown down; our fence has blown down.* □ **derribar**
blower *n.* **1** device which blows. □ **sopladora**
2 (*slang*) telephone. □ **teléfono**
blowfly *n.* (*pl. blowflies*) large blue-green fly that is attracted by meat. □ **moscón**
blowlamp *n.* lamp with strong gas jet for stripping old paint. □ **soplete**
blow off *v.* to move (something) off by blowing: *his hat was blown off; three tiles were blown off our roof; the wind blew the leaves off the trees.* □ **volarse**
blow out *v.* to go out/to make (something) go out by blowing: *he blew out the candles on his birthday cake; the candle has blown out; half my papers blew out of the window.* □ **apagar**
blowout *n.* **1** (*informal*) huge meal. □ **comilona**
2 bursting (of a car tyre). □ **reventón**
blow over *v.* to get calm; to knock down by blowing: *the storm has blown over; the crisis has blown over; the statue was blown over by the bomb blast.* □ **calmarse; derribar**
blow up *v.* **1** to explode: *the grenade blew up in his hand.* □ **explotar**
2 to destroy by explosives: *the terrorists blew up the railway line.* □ **volar**
3 to inflate: *can you help me blow up all these balloons for the party?* □ **inflar**
4 to enlarge (a photograph). □ **ampliar**
5 to arrive with a wind: *a sudden storm blew up.* *levantarse*
blowy *adj.* windy. □ **ventoso**
blubber ['blʌbə] *n.* fat (of a whale/seal). □ **grasa de ballena**
■ *v.* to cry noisily. □ **lloriquear**
bludgeon ['blʌdʒən] *n.* large stick for hitting people. □ **cachiporra**
■ *v.* to beat someone with a stick: *he was bludgeoned to death.* □ **apalear**
blue [blu:] *adj.* (*bluer, bluest*) **1** coloured like the sky: *the door of our house is painted dark blue; he was wearing pale blue socks.* □ **azul**
blue baby, baby with blue skin caused by heart disease. □ **niño azul**
once in a blue moon, very seldom. □ **de Pascuas a Ramos**
2 pornographic: *they were watching blue movies.* □ **pornográfico**
3 sad: *I'm feeling blue.* □ **estoy melancólico**
■ *n.* **1** colour like that of the sky: *have you a blue that is darker than this?* □ **azul**
2 *the offer came to him **out of the blue,*** as a complete surprise. □ **...como llovido del cielo**
3 ***blues,*** sad slow jazz music. □ **'blues'**
bluebell *n.* common blue wild flower/wild hyacinth. □ **campanilla azul**
blueberry *n.* (*pl. blueberries*) *Amer.* small blue berry used in pies. □ **arándano**
bluebottle *n.* large blue-green fly that is attracted to meat. □ **moscón**
blue collar worker *n.* manual worker (in industry). □ **obrero**
blue-eyed *adj.* **1** with blue eyes. □ **de ojos azules**
2 *he's her blue-eyed boy,* he is her favourite. □ **él es la niña de sus ojos**
blueprint *n.* detailed plan: *I think the whole thing is a blueprint for disaster.* □ **proyecto**
bluish *adj.* rather blue. □ **azulado**
bluff [blʌf] *n.* **1** steep rocky hill. □ **risco**
2 trick. □ **farol**
to call someone's bluff, to claim (successfully) that someone is tricking/is lying. □ **hacer que alguien descubra sus cartas**
■ *adj.* down-to-earth/straightforward (person): *he has a bluff hearty manner.* □ **campechano**
■ *v.* to trick/to pretend: *he's only bluffing - he'll never sack you.* □ **intimidar**
blunder ['blʌndə] *n.* mistake: *he made a terrible blunder.* □ **disparate**
■ *v.* **1** to make a mistake. □ **meter la pata**
2 ***to blunder into someone,*** to bump into someone. □ **tropezar con alguien**
blundering *adj.* clumsy: *you blundering idiot!* □ **¡idiota de remate!**
blunt [blʌnt] *adj.* **1** not sharp: *this knife is so blunt it will hardly cut butter.* □ **romo, desafilado**
2 straightforward/almost rude: *he has a blunt way of expressing himself; the blunt facts of the issue.* □ **franco, brusco**
■ *v.* to make blunt: *you've blunted this knife by using it to open tins.* □ **desafilar**
bluntly *adv.* frankly/almost rudely: *he bluntly told them he would not pay out any more money.* □ **sin rodeos**
bluntness *n.* frankness/rudeness. □ **franqueza, brusquedad**
blur [blə:] *n.* indistinct picture: *last night's party is all a blur.* □ **impresión borrosa**
■ *v.* (*he blurred*) to make indistinct: *the picture is rather blurred,* out of focus. □ **desenfocar**
blurb [blə:b] *n.* piece of publicity describing a book. □ **anuncio**
blurt [blə:t] *v. he blurted out the secret,* he let out the secret. □ **dejar escapar**
blush [blʌʃ] *n.* (*pl. blushes*) red shade (on skin). □ **rubor**
■ *v.* to go red (with embarrassment): *he blushed when the teacher praised his work.* □ **ruborizarse**
bluster ['blʌstə] *n.* swaggering talk; air of defiance. □ **jactancia**
■ *v.* to swagger/to show off. □ **fanfarronear**
blustery *adj.* strong (wind/gale). □ **violento**
boa ['bouə] *n.* ***boa constrictor,*** large tropical snake which kills animals by wrapping itself round them and squeezing them. □ **boa**
boar [bɔəd] *n.* male pig, usually wild. □ **verraco**
board [bɔ:d] *n.* **1** large flat piece of wood, etc. □ **tabla**

ironing board, narrow table for ironing. □ **tabla de planchar**
2 *I'm afraid your holiday will have **to go by the board,*** will have to be cancelled. □ **...por la borda**
3 food. □ **comida**
board and lodging, food and housing. □ **comida y casa**
full board, bed and all meals (in a hotel). □ **pensión completa**
4 group of people: *board of examiners; board (of directors); board of enquiry.* □ **tribunal; junta; consejo (de administración)**
5 *to go on board,* to go on to a ship/into an aircraft. □ **a bordo**
■ *v.* to go on to a ship/bus/into an aircraft: *the passengers can now board the plane; the flight is now boarding,* passengers are now going on to the plane; *he boarded the bus at the stop by the Post Office.* □ **subir a bordo**
boarder *n.* child who lives at school. □ **interno**
boarding *adj.* **1** *boarding card,* card which allows you to go into an aircraft. □ **tarjeta de embarque**
2 ***boarding house,*** house where you can pay to lodge. □ **pensión**
boarding school, school where the children live during term. □ **internado**
boardroom *n.* room where a board of directors meets. □ **sala de juntas**
board up *v.* to cover (windows/doors) with boards to prevent burglars getting into an empty house. □ **cerrar con tablones**
boast [boust] *n.* act of boasting. □ **alarde**
■ *v.* **1** to talk about how clever/strong/handsome, etc., you are: *he boasted that he could jump higher than anyone else; he's always boasting about his money; that's nothing to boast about,* it's not something you should be proud of. □ **alardear de**
2 to possess, and be proud: *the city boasts the largest town hall in the north.* □ **presumir de tener**
boastful *adj.* very proud; always boasting. □ **presumido**
boat [bout] *n.* **1** (small) ship: *sailing boat; rowing boat; they came by boat; we will take the boat across the bay.* □ **barco, bote**
boat train, train which connects with a boat. □ **tren que enlaza con un barco**
2 *we're **all in the same boat,*** we're all in equal circumstances. □ **en el mismo barco/caso**
boater *n.* flat straw hat. □ **sombrero de paja**
boathouse *n.* shed for rowing boats. □ **cobertizo para botes**
boating *n.* rowing (for pleasure). □ **paseo en barco**
boating pool, lake where you can hire rowing boats. □ **estanque para remar**
boatswain ['bousn] *n.* (*at sea*) man in charge of the crew. □ **contramaestre**
bob [bɔb] *v.* (*he bobbed*) **1** to move quickly up and down: *the cork was bobbing up and down on the water.* □ **balancearse**
2 *the duck dived and then bobbed up again,* came back up again. □ **aparecer**
bobbin ['bɔbin] *n.* small reel for holding thread (for a sewing machine/a spinning machine). □ **bobina**
bobby ['bɔbi] *n.* (*pl. bobbies*) (*informal*) policeman. □ **poli**
bobby-pin *n. Amer.* flat hairpin. □ **horquilla**
bobby-socks *n. pl. Amer.* girls' ankle socks. □ **calcetines tobilleros**
bobsleigh ['bɔbslei] *n.* sledge with two runners, used for racing. □ **'bobsleigh'**
bodice ['bɔdis] *n.* top part (of a dress). □ **corpiño**
bodkin ['bɔdkin] *n.* large thick needle used for threading tape or elastic. □ **punzón**
body ['bɔdi] *n.* (*pl. bodies*) **1** main structure of an animal or person; main part of an animal or person not including the head and limbs. □ **cuerpo**
dead body, corpse. □ **cadáver**
2 group of people: *I am speaking on behalf of two bodies; a large body of people were waiting outside the palace.* □ **grupo, órgano**
3 main part (of a building/a car, etc.). □ **cuerpo del edificio; carrocería del coche**
4 strength (of wine): *here is a wine with some body to it.* □ **cuerpo**
bodily *adj.* of the body: *to supply someone's bodily needs; to cause someone grievous bodily harm,* to attack someone and beat them up. □ **corporal**
■ *adv. they carried him bodily out of the meeting,* they lifted him up and carried him. □ **...en andas**
bodyguard *n.* **1** soldier/person who guards someone: *the president was surrounded by his bodyguards.* □ **guardaespaldas**
2 group of soldiers who guard someone: *the president's bodyguard of loyal soldiers.* □ **guardia personal**
bodywork *n.* outer covering of a car: *the bodywork is a bit scratched.* □ **carrocería**
bog [bɔg] *n.* **1** area of marshland. □ **ciénaga**
2 (*slang*) toilet. □ **cagadero**
■ *v.* (*bogged*) ***to get bogged down,*** (i) to get stuck (in mud). □ **atascarse**
(ii) *the discussion got bogged down in details,* they got stuck in details. □ **...se atascó...**
boggy *adj.* marshy. □ **pantanoso**
bogey (man) ['bougi(mæn)] *n.* ghost/thing which frightens children. □ **coco**
boggle ['bɔgl] *v.* to be reluctant (to do something): *the mind boggles,* it is impossible to imagine. □ **vacilar**
bogie ['bougi] *n.* pivoted set of wheels on a railway carriage. □ **vagoneta**
bogus ['bougəs] *adj.* false: *the man who knocked at the door was a bogus police inspector.* □ **falso**
boil [bɔil] *n.* **1** swelling in the body full of infected matter. □ **furúnculo**
2 *the kettle is on the boil,* the water is boiling; *bring the water to the boil,* make the water boil; *the soup has come to the boil,* the soup is boiling. □ **hervor; ebullición**
3 *you must try **to keep** everything **on the boil,*** try to keep all the projects working at full speed. □ **...a toda máquina**
■ *v.* **1** to heat a liquid until it bubbles: *the soup is boiling; can you put the kettle on to boil?* □ **hervir**
2 to cook in boiling water: *boil the cabbage for ten minutes; boiled eggs.* □ **cocer**
hard-boiled egg, egg which has been cooked until it is solid (usually eaten cold). □ **huevo duro**
boil away *v.* to evaporate (through boiling): *the water has all boiled away.* □ **evaporarse**
boil down *v.* **1** to evaporate (through boiling); to reduce (a piece of writing): *the article is a boiled-down version of a longer piece written last year.* □ **consumirse; versión abreviada**
2 to be reduced to: *it all boils down to whether he will resign willingly or not,* the main question is, will he resign willingly or not. □ **todo se reduce a si...**
boiler *n.* large metal receptacle for boiling water; main heater for central heating: *they stoked the engines until the boilers burst.* □ **caldera**
boiler suit, blue overalls. □ **mono**
boiling *n.* action of heating a liquid until it bubbles.

□ **ebullición**
boiling point, the temperature at which a liquid boils. □ **punto de ebullición**
boiling fowl, chicken to be cooked in boiling water. □ **gallina para guisar**
■ *adj.* **1** (liquid) which is boiling or very hot. □ **hirviente**
2 *it is boiling in this room,* it is very hot. □ **hace mucho calor**
■ *adv.* ***boiling hot,*** very hot. □ **muy caliente**
boil over *v.* to rise in a pan when boiling, and run over the sides: *the milk has boiled over.* □ **salirse**
boisterous ['bɔistrəs] *adj.* noisy/violent (crowd/wind/sea, etc.). □ **tempestuoso**
boisterousness *n.* noise/violence. □ **bullicio**
bold [bould] *adj.* daring/brave: *he made a bold attack on the enemy tanks.* □ **valiente, audaz**
boldly *adv.* bravely/defiantly: *he boldly went up to the headmaster.* □ **audazmente**
boldness *n.* daring/bravery. □ **audacia**
bole [boul] *n.* tree trunk. □ **tronco**
bolero [bə'leərou] *n.* **1** type of Spanish dance. □ **bolero**
2 short sleeveless jacket worn by women. □ **bolero**
bollard ['bɔlɑːd] *n.* low post on a quay for a ship's rope, or in the road to indicate where traffic should go. □ **bolardo**
bolshie ['bɔlʃi] *adj.* (*informal*) difficult/uncooperative (person). □ **'borde'**
bolster ['boulstə] *n.* long pillow going right across a bed. □ **cabezal**
■ *v.* to support (someone who is falling): *the army is bolstering up the unpopular regime.* □ **apoyar**
bolt [boult] *n.* **1** flash of lightning with thunder. □ **relámpago**
2 *it came as **a bolt from the blue,*** it came as a complete surprise. □ **cayó como una bomba**
3 metal rod which slides into a hole to secure a door: *she slid back the bolts.* □ **cerrojo**
4 metal rod with a screw which fastens with a nut. □ **perno**
5 ***to make a bolt for:*** *they made a bolt for the door,* they rushed towards the door. □ **se fueron como un rayo hacia...**
■ *v.* **1** to run fast/to escape: *the horse bolted,* the horse got out of control. □ **desbocarse**
2 to eat quickly and with big mouthfuls: *he bolted his dinner and ran out.* □ **engullir**
3 to fasten a door with a bolt: *the door is bolted.* □ **echar el cerrojo**
4 to fasten with a bolt and nut: *the seats are bolted to the floor of the car.* □ **empernar**
■ *adv. he was sitting bolt upright,* he was sitting straight upright. □ **derecho**
bomb [bɔm] *n.* large explosive weapon, often dropped from an aircraft: *atom bomb; they planted a bomb under his car; bomb disposal,* removing the fuse from an unexploded bomb. □ **bomba**
to go like a bomb, to go very well: *the party went like a bomb.* □ **ir de miedo**
■ *v.* to drop bombs on (a target): *the enemy aircraft bombed the bridge.* □ **bombardear**
bombard [bɔm'bɑːd] *v.* to attack (repeatedly with shells): *the ships bombarded the port; the speaker was bombarded with questions.* □ **bombardear**
bombardment *n.* attack (with bombs/shells/questions). □ **bombardeo**
bomber *n.* special aircraft for dropping bombs. □ **bombardero**
bombing *n.* attack (with bombs): *the bombing of the naval base.* □ **bombardeo**
bombshell *n.* great (unpleasant) surprise: *the news came like a bombshell; it was a bombshell to everyone.* □ **una bomba**
bombastic [bɔm'bæstik] *adj.* flowery/boasting (way of speaking). □ **rimbombante**
bona fide ['bounə'faidi] *adj.* in good faith: *this is a bona fide offer.* □ **de buena fe**
■ *n. the police are checking on his bona fides,* they are checking that he is speaking the truth. □ **sinceridad**
bonanza [bə'nænzə] *n.* great wealth (discovered suddenly): *an oil bonanza.* □ **riqueza repentina**
bond [bɔnd] *n.* **1** link; joining together: *bonds of friendship; does this glue make a good bond?* □ **vínculo**
2 paper showing that money has been lent to the government. □ **bono del Estado**
premium bonds, bonds which are eligible to win a lottery. □ **bonos con premio**
3 contract. □ **compromiso**
my word is my bond, when I give my word it is as good as having a signed contract. □ **te doy mi palabra de honor**
4 ***to be in bond,*** to be in a customs warehouse: *whisky in bond.* □ **estar en depósito**
■ *v.* to link/to join (with glue): *the two surfaces have bonded very well.* □ **unir**
bondage *n.* slavery. □ **servidumbre**
bone [boun] *n.* **1** one of the solid white pieces which make up the framework of the body: *do you know how many bones you have in each foot? he broke his collar-bone playing rugby.* □ **hueso**
2 *chicken **off the bone,*** chicken meat with the bones removed. □ **deshuesado**
3 ***bone dry,*** completely dry. □ **más seco que una pasa**
4 *he's just **bone idle,*** he's completely lazy. □ **vagazo**
5 ***to make no bones about:*** *he made no bones about complaining,* he did not hesitate to complain. □ **no dudar en**
6 ***I have (got) a bone to pick with*** *you,* I want to complain about something which you've done. □ **tengo que ajustarte las cuentas**
■ *v.* to take the bones out of (meat, fish). □ **deshuesar**
boneless *adj.* with no bones. □ **deshuesado; sin espinas**
bony *adj.* (*bonier, boniest*) **1** with big bones: *his bony knees.* □ **huesudo**
2 *bony fish,* fish with many bones. □ **lleno de espinas**
bonfire ['bɔnfaiə] *n.* outdoor fire for burning rubbish or as a celebration: *we will make a bonfire of all the dead leaves.* □ **hoguera**
bonnet ['bɔnit] *n.* **1** child's/woman's hat, with a brim framing the face, often tied under the chin. □ **gorro**
2 hinged cover for the front part of a car: *have a look under the bonnet.* □ **capó**
bonus ['bounəs] *n.* (*pl. bonuses*) extra money. □ **prima**
cost-of-living bonus, extra pay to counteract the increased cost of living. □ **plus de carestía de vida**
no claim bonus, (*on motor insurance*) reduced payment if you have never made a claim. □ **bonificación por falta de siniestros**
boo [buː] *interjection* call to show disapproval or to surprise: *a man at the back of the audience shouted 'boo'.* □ **¡fuera!**
■ *v.* to show disapproval by saying 'boo': *the audience booed the speaker.* □ **abuchear**
boob [buːb] *n.* (*slang*) **1** mistake. □ **patochada**
2 breast. □ **teta**

booby ['bu:bi] *n.* (*pl. boobies*) silly person. □ **bobo**
booby prize *n.* (silly) prize given to the last person in a competition. □ **premio para el último**
boobytrap *n.* trap to catch someone unawares: *the terrorists set a boobytrap in the car.* □ **trampa explosiva**
■ *v.* (*he boobytrapped*) to set a trap (in a place): *the car may be boobytrapped.* □ **puede que le hayan puesto una bomba**

book [buk] *n.* **1** printed pages attached together with a cover: *the library has more than 1,000 books; have you read this book on gardening? a friend of mine has written a book about horses; school book; reference book.* □ **libro**
book club, club whose members buy books cheaply. □ **club de libro**
2 *exercise book,* book of blank pages with lines for writing on. □ **cuaderno**
cheque book, book of blank cheques. □ **talonario**
bank book, book showing money in a deposit/savings account. □ **libreta de ahorros**
to be in someone's bad books: *I'm in his bad books,* he disapproves of me. □ **estar en su lista negra**
3 script (of musical): *book and lyrics by John Smith.* □ **libreto**
4 *book of tickets,* several tickets fastened together and sold as a unit. □ **taco de billetes**
5 *book of matches,* cardboard matches fastened together in a card holder. □ **caja de cerillas de solapa**
■ *v.* **1** to reserve a place/seat/table (on plane/in theatre/in restaurant): *I want to book three seats for Saturday night; have you booked?,* have you made a reservation in advance? *I've booked a table for 8.30; I'm sorry but we're fully booked.* □ **reservar**
2 *I was booked for speeding,* the police have made a charge against me for speeding. □ **multar**
bookable *adj.* which can be reserved in advance: *all seats are bookable.* □ **reservable**
bookbinder *n.* person who puts covers on printed sheets to make a book. □ **encuadernador**
bookbinding *n.* art of binding books. □ **encuadernación**
bookcase *n.* cabinet/set of shelves for keeping books. □ **librería**
bookie *n.* (*informal*) person who collects bets before a race. □ **corredor de apuestas**
book in *v.* to register: *we booked in at the hotel.* □ **inscribirse**
booking *n.* **1** reservation (of seats/places). □ **reserva**
booking office, office (at theatre) where you can book seats in advance. □ **despacho de billetes**
2 arrangement (for actor, etc.) to appear at a theatre. □ **contratación**
bookish *adj.* learned/studious. □ **empollón**
book-keeper *n.* person who works in the accounts department (in a firm). □ **contable**
book-keeping *n.* keeping of accounts. □ **contabilidad**
booklet *n.* small book with only a few pages. □ **folleto**
booklover *n.* person who loves (and collects) books. □ **bibliófilo**
bookmaker *n.* person who collects bets before a race. □ **corredor de apuestas**
bookmark(er) *n.* long, narrow, piece of card/cloth/leather used to keep your place in a book which you are reading. □ **marcador**
bookmobile ['bukməbi:l] *n.* travelling library. □ **biblioteca ambulante**
bookseller *n.* person who sells books. □ **librero**
bookshelf *n.* (*pl. bookshelves*) shelf for keeping books. □ **estantería; repisa**
bookshop *n.* shop selling books. □ **librería**
bookstall, bookstand *n.* kiosk (in railway station) selling books and magazines. □ **quiosco de prensa/libros**
book trade *n.* the book producing and selling industry. □ **industria editorial**
book up *v.* to reserve: *we couldn't get tickets for the play as it was fully booked up.* □ **reservar (todo vendido)**
bookworm *n.* person who reads many books. □ **ratón de biblioteca**

boom [bu:m] *n.* **1** floating barrier across a harbour. □ **barrera**
2 long rod (for holding a microphone over speakers' heads). □ **jirafa**
3 low muffled sound (of wind/distant thunder/supersonic aircraft, etc.). □ **retumbo**
4 sudden increase (in value/sales/general prosperity): *the boom years; there was a boom on the Stock Exchange.* □ **'boom'**
■ *v.* **1** to make a low muffled sound: *cannon were booming in the distance.* □ **retumbar**
2 to increase suddenly/to become more prosperous: *business is booming; sales are booming.* □ **estar en auge**

boomerang ['bu:məræŋ] *n.* curved piece of wood which, when thrown, comes back to the thrower. □ **bumerang**
■ *v.* to backfire/to rebound: *his plan boomeranged,* turned against him. □ **ser contraproducente**

boon [bu:n] *n.* advantage/blessing: *the new dishwasher is a real boon.* □ **bendición**

boor [bɔ:, 'buə] *n.* rough/uncouth man. □ **patán**
boorish *adj.* rude/uncouth: *they criticized him for his boorish behaviour.* □ **tosco**

boost [bu:st] *n.* help/publicity: *the television commercial gave his sales a boost; his policy got a boost from the Americans.* □ **impulso**
■ *v.* **1** to help/to promote: *his reputation was boosted by his first film performances; sales were boosted by the Christmas publicity campaign.* □ **impulsar**
2 to increase voltage (in electricity cable). □ **elevar**
booster *n.* apparatus for increasing voltage. □ **elevador de voltaje**
booster rocket, rocket which helps keep up the speed of main rocket. □ **cohete acelerador**
booster shot, injection which keeps up the protection given by a former injection. □ **inyección de refuerzo**

boot [bu:t] *n.* **1** footwear which goes above the ankle: *ankle boots,* boots which just cover the ankles; *knee boots,* boots which come up to the knees; *to put on/take off your boots; footballers wear boots, but athletes do not.* □ **bota; botín**
the boot is on the other foot, the situation is just the opposite. □ **se ha dado la vuelta a la tortilla**
2 back part of a car (where the luggage can be put). □ **maletero**
■ *v.* **1** to kick: *he booted the ball into the net.* □ **dar patadas**
2 *the manager booted him out,* dismissed him. □ **despedir**
bootee *n.* small knitted boot for babies. □ **patuco**
bootlaces *n. pl.* very long laces for boots. □ **cordones**

booth [bu:ð] *n.* **1** (covered) stall at a market/fair. □ **puesto**
2 small enclosed space for one person: *telephone booth; polling booth.* □ **cabina**

booty ['bu:ti] *n.* treasure captured in war: *the soldiers pillaged the town and took a vast quantity of booty.* □ **botín**
booze [bu:z] *n.* (*informal*) alcoholic drink: *he's always on the booze.* □ **copas**
■ *v.* (*informal*) to drink (alcohol): *he's always boozing.* □ **siempre está chispa**
boozer *n.* (*informal*) **1** person who drinks a lot. □ **bebedor**
2 bar; public house: *let's go along to the boozer.* □ **bar**
boracic [bə'ræsik] *adj.* chemical substance used in ointments: *boracic ointment/powder.* □ **bórico**
borax ['bɔ:ræks] *n.* white powder used in making glass and as an antiseptic. □ **bórax**
border ['bɔ:də] *n.* frontier/edge: *the border between France and Germany; handkerchief with lace along the border.* □ **frontera**
flower border, edging of flowers along a flower bed. □ **ribete, remate de flores**
■ *v.* ***to border on*** **1** *France borders on Germany,* France touches Germany. □ **limitar**
2 *it is a film which borders on the indecent,* which is almost indecent. □ **es una película que raya...**
bordering *adj.* close to: *a statement bordering on slander; countries bordering on Switzerland.* □ **rayano, limítrofe**
borderline *n.* line between two surfaces. □ **frontera**
borderline case, case which is on the dividing line (between two types). □ **caso dudoso**
bore [bɔ:] *n.* **1** width of a tube: *a small-bore rifle.* □ **calibre**
2 person/thing which makes you fed up: *don't listen to that old bore; I don't want to be a bore, but,* I don't want to be a nuisance, but; *what a bore,* what a nuisance. □ **pelmazo; pesado**
3 wave in a river caused by the tide. □ **ola**
■ *v.* **1** to make a hole: *they bored a well; they are boring for oil; he bored a hole right through the wall.* □ **perforar**
2 to make (someone) fed up (with you): *I was bored by the film; she said he bored her to tears; I'm bored stiff,* very bored. □ **aburrir**
3 *see also* **bear.**
boredom *n.* being bored, having no interest: *she was dying of boredom in the little village in the mountains.* □ **aburrimiento**
borehole *n.* exploratory hole made to see if there are any mineral/oil deposits in the ground. □ **perforación**
boring *adj.* which makes you lose interest completely: *what a boring book.* □ **aburrido**
born [bɔ:n] *adj.* **1** *he was born in 1962,* his birth took place in 1962. □ **nacido**
2 *she's a born actress,* she has always had a gift for acting. □ **es una actriz nata**
3 ***I wasn't born yesterday,*** I'm not as stupid as you think. □ **no nací ayer**
borne [bɔ:n] *v. see* **bear.**
boron ['bɔ:rɔn] *n.* (*chemical element*: B) brown powder which resists high temperatures and is used to make borax. □ **boro**
borough ['bʌrə] *n.* large town (with a governing council). □ **municipio**
borrow ['bɔrou] *v.* to take something for a short time with the owner's permission; to take money (from a bank, etc.) for a time, usually paying interest on it: *I have lost my pen, can I borrow yours? he wants to borrow our lawnmower.* □ **tomar prestado**
borrower *n.* person who borrows (money, etc.): *the bank is raising the interest rate to borrowers.* □ **prestatario**
borrowing *n.* **1** act of borrowing money. □ **el tomar en préstamo**
2 money borrowed: *the firm's borrowings exceeded one million dollars.* □ **préstamo**
bosom ['buzəm] *n.* breast. □ **pecho**
bosom companion, close friend. □ **amigo íntimo**
boss [bɔs] *n.* (*pl. bosses*) (*informal*) **1** person who is in charge: *if you want more holiday you must ask the boss.* □ **jefe**
2 round knob. □ **tirador**
■ *v.* (*informal*) **1** to command/to give orders: *he bosses the whole show,* he is in charge of the whole business. □ **dirigir**
2 *she bosses him around,* she is always telling him what to do. □ **dominar**
boss-eyed *adj.* (*slang*) squinting. □ **bizco**
bossy *adj.* (*bossier, bossiest*) (person) always giving orders: *what a bossy little girl!* □ **mandón**
bosun ['bousn] *n.* (*at sea*) man in charge of the crew. □ **contramaestre**
botany ['bɔtəni] *n.* study of plants. □ **botánica**
botanical *adj.* relating to plants: *botanical gardens,* gardens scientifically arranged to show different species of plants. □ **botánico**
botanist ['bɔtənist] *n.* person who studies plants. □ **botánico**
botch [bɔtʃ] *v.* to ruin/to make a mess of (a job): *they planned a big hold-up but botched the whole affair; he botched the job of mending the bathroom pipes.* □ **hacer chapuzas**
both [bouθ] *adj.* and *pron.* two persons/objects together: *I cannot say which film I liked best - I liked them both; both these socks have holes in them; we both like playing tennis; hold the ladder in both hands.* □ **ambos; los dos**
■ *adv.* at the same time: *she both attracts and repels me; I was both amused and horrified.* □ **al mismo tiempo; a la vez**
bother ['bɔðə] *n.* worry/annoyance: *what's all the fuss and bother about?* □ **molestia**
■ *v.* **1** to annoy: *stop bothering him, he's trying to work.* □ **molestar**
2 to take trouble: *he can't be bothered to pay the rent,* it is too much of an effort for him to pay the rent; *don't bother to come to the door; he didn't even bother to send a postcard.* □ **molestarse**
bothered *adj.* worried/embarrassed: *she's all hot and bothered.* □ **molesto**
bottle ['bɔtl] *n.* tall glass/plastic container for liquids: *wine bottle; milk bottle; shall I open the bottle of wine? medicine bottles should be kept out of the reach of children.* □ **botella**
bottle party, party where the guests each bring a bottle of alcohol. □ **reunión (cada invitado se lleva su botella)**
hot water bottle, rubber container for hot water which is used for warming beds. □ **bolsa de agua caliente**
■ *v.* to put into a bottle. □ **embotellar**
bottled fruit, fruit which has been preserved in sealed jars. □ **fruta en conserva**
bottle-feeding *n.* feeding of babies by a bottle, not at the breast. □ **con biberón**
bottleneck *n.* **1** narrow part of a bottle. □ **gollete**
2 narrow road (where traffic often gets jammed). □ **embotellamiento**
bottle up *v.* **1** to hold back (one's feelings): *his anger was bottled up inside him.* □ **reprimir**
2 to jam (traffic): *the traffic was bottled up at the narrow bridge.* □ **se produjo un atasco...**

bottling *n.* putting into bottles, especially preserving fruit in sealed jars. □ **conserva**
bottling jar, special jar with a rubber seal for preserving fruit. □ **tarro de conserva**
bottom ['bɔtəm] *n.* **1** lowest part; base: *there was water at the bottom of the well; they pulled the car out of the bottom of the lake; the shed is at the bottom of the garden,* at the end of the garden furthest from the house: *the notes are at the bottom of the page; prices have touched rock bottom,* they are at their lowest. □ **fondo**
2 *he came bottom of the class,* he had the worst marks. □ **el último de la clase**
3 *the detective is trying* ***to get to the bottom of*** *the mystery.* □ **...al fondo del**
4 *the bottom has fallen out of the stock market,* the prices of shares have collapsed. □ **la Bolsa se ha hundido**
5 *the suitcase has a* ***false bottom,*** a double bottom to conceal smuggled goods. □ **doble fondo**
6 buttocks: *he just sits on his bottom and does nothing; if you do that again I'll smack your bottom.* □ **culo**
■ *adj.* lowest: *it is in the bottom drawer; look on the bottom shelf.* □ **... de abajo**
bottomless *adj.* with no bottom: *a bottomless pit.* □ **sin fondo**
botulism ['bɔtju:lizəm] *n.* illness caused by bacteria in food. □ **botulismo**
boudoir ['bu:dwɑ:] *n.* small private room for a woman. □ **tocador**
bough [bau] *n.* large branch (of a tree). □ **rama**
bought [bɔ:t] *v. see* **buy.**
boulder ['bouldə] *n.* large rock. □ **canto rodado de gran tamaño**
bounce [bauns] *n.* **1** spring: *the bed has a lot of bounce in it; the ball shot up into the air with a big bounce.* □ **bote**
2 *he's got a lot of bounce,* he has a lot of energy. □ **vitalidad**
■ *v.* **1** to spring up and down; to make (something) spring up and down: *he bounced up and down on the bed; the ball bounced down the stairs; the harder you throw a ball the higher it will bounce; she was bouncing a ball in the road.* □ **botar**
2 *his cheque bounced,* (*informal*) there was not enough money in the account to pay the sum on the cheque. □ **cheque devuelto**
bouncer *n.* **1** (*in cricket*) ball which bounces very high. □ **golpe alto**
2 person who throws undesirable customers out of a restaurant/club, etc. □ **gorila**
bouncing *adj.* **1** (ball) which bounces. □ **que bota**
2 *bouncing baby,* healthy-looking baby. □ **robusto**
bouncy *adj.* **1** which bounces well: *a very bouncy ball.* □ **de mucho bote**
2 (person) who is full of energy. □ **enérgico**
bound [baund] *n.* leap: *the dog raced across the field with great bounds.* □ **salto**
■ *adj.* **1** *the ship is bound for South America,* is leaving for/on the way to South America; *homeward bound,* on the way home. □ **el barco se dirige; de vuelta a casa**
2 tied up: *the burglars left him bound and gagged.* □ **amarrado; atado**
3 obliged: *he is bound by the rules to attend the meeting.* □ **obligado**
4 very likely: *they are bound to be late; it was bound to happen sooner or later.* □ **seguro que**
5 *see also* **bind.**
■ *v.* to leap: *the dog bounded towards him; he bounded into the room.* □ **saltar**
boundless *adj.* without any limits: *he has boundless energy.* □ **ilimitado**
bounds *n.* **1** limits/edges. □ **límites**
out of bounds, (place) where people are not allowed to go: *the town is out of bounds to the soldiers from the camp.* □ **...en zona prohibida...**
2 *to keep expenses within bounds,* to limit expenses. □ **dentro de un límite**
boundary ['baundri] *n.* (*pl. boundaries*) frontier/outer limit of something: *rivers and mountains form natural boundaries.* □ **frontera**
to hit a boundary, (*in cricket*) to hit the ball beyond the edge of the field. □ **golpear fuera del campo**
bounty ['baunti] *n.* **1** giving (of money). □ **generosidad**
2 money given as a reward or in excess of usual wages. □ **gratificación**
bountiful *adj.* generous. □ **generoso**
bouquet [bu'kei] *n.* artistically arranged bunch of flowers. □ **ramillete**
bourbon ['bə:bən] *n. Amer.* corn whisky. □ **'bourbon'**
bourgeois ['buəʒwɑ:] *adj.* and *n.* middle-class (person). □ **burgués**
bourgeoisie [bu:əʒwɑ'zi:] *n.* the middle class. □ **burguesía**
bout [baut] *n.* **1** sports contest: *wrestling bout; boxing bout.* □ **combate**
2 attack (of illness): *he has recurrent bouts of fever; he's had a bout of flu.* □ **ataque**
boutique [bu:'ti:k] *n.* small shop selling fashionable clothes/perfume, etc.; small specialized clothing department in a large store. □ **boutique**
bovine ['bouvain] *adj.* referring to cows and bulls. □ **bovino**
bow[1] [bou] *n.* **1** long piece of wood with taut string joining both ends, used for shooting arrows. □ **arco**
2 wooden rod with hair stretched taut between its ends, used for playing a violin or other stringed instrument. □ **arco**
3 knot of ribbon/tie arranged to look like a butterfly. □ **lazo**
bow-legged *adj.* with legs which curve apart at the knee. □ **patizambo**
bow tie *n.* short necktie tied in a bow. □ **pajarita**
bow window *n.* window projecting out from the wall in a curve. □ **mirador**
bow[2] [bau] *n.* **1** salute made by bending the body forward: *he made a deep bow,* he bent very far forward in salute. □ **reverencia**
2 (usually *bows*) front part of a ship: *he stood in the bows of the ship with a rope in his hand.* □ **proa**
3 rower who sits nearest the bow of a rowing boat. □ **proel**
■ *v.* to bend forward: *he bowed his head in shame; he bowed to the Queen.* □ **inclinar**
bowels ['bauəlz] (sometimes **bowel**) *n.* **1** intestines: *he has a bowel infection,* he has an infection in the intestines. □ **intestinos**
2 *in the bowels of the earth,* deep down underground. □ **en las entrañas...**
bower ['baou] *n.* shelter covered by trees or plants. □ **emparrado**
bowl [boul] *n.* **1** wide china/plastic/wooden container: *a bowl of soup.* □ **tazón**
a soup bowl, a bowl specially made for soup. □ **tazón de sopa**
washing-up bowl, large plastic bowl for washing up. □ **barreño de plástico**
2 wooden ball for playing game of bowls. □ **bolo**
3 ***bowls,*** game where wooden balls are rolled to try

to get nearest to small target ball: *they were playing (a game of) bowls.* □ **bolos**
■ *v.* **1** to throw a ball, especially in cricket. □ **lanzar**
2 to roll a bowl (in a game of bowls). □ **lanzar**
bowler *n.* **1** person who plays bowls. □ **jugador de bolos**
2 (*in cricket*) person who throws the ball to the opposing batsman. □ **lanzador**
3 ***bowler (hat),*** black round-topped man's hat. □ **sombrero hongo**
bowling *n.* **1** game of bowls. □ **bolos**
bowling green, grass pitch for playing bowls. □ **campo de bolos**
2 game of knocking down skittles with a large ball. □ **bolos**
bowling alley, hall for bowling. □ **bolera**
bowl over *v.* to knock down/to surprise. □ **derribar**
box [bɔks] *n.* (*pl. boxes*) **1** container with a lid: *a box of biscuits; a box of matches.* □ **caja**
letter box/pillar box, box in the street for posting letters: *can you put this card in the letter box?* □ **buzón**
letter box, slit in a door for delivering letters/newspapers: *the postman pushed two letters through our letter box.* □ **buzón**
box number, number of a box in the post office/newspaper office where letters will be kept for you and delivered in bulk. □ **Apartado de Correos**
2 small tree, with very hard wood: *a box hedge.* □ **boj**
3 small balcony room in a theatre; cubicle for a horse; place where a witness gives evidence in court. □ **palco; 'box'; estrado**
4 smack (on the ear): *I'll give you a box on the ear.* □ **bofetón**
■ *v.* **1** ***to box someone's ears,*** to smack someone on the ears. □ **abofetear**
2 to fight an opponent in the boxing ring: *he is boxing well tonight.* □ **boxear**
boxer *n.* **1** man who practises the sport of boxing. □ **boxeador**
2 breed of large dog with short hair. □ **bóxer**
boxful *n.* quantity contained in a full box. □ **una caja**
boxing *n.* sport of fighting with gloves in a ring: *boxing ring/gloves/match.* □ **boxeo**
Boxing Day, day after Christmas Day, 26th December. □ **26 de diciembre**
box office *n.* office in a theatre where you buy tickets for a performance. □ **taquilla**
boxroom *n.* small room for keeping boxes, cases, unused objects. □ **trastero**
box spanner *n.* spanner with a ring-shaped end which fits over nuts. □ **llave de tubo**
boy [bɔi] *n.* male child: *the boys were playing football in the yard.* □ **muchacho, chico**
old boy, old friend/feeble old man/former pupil of a school. □ **compadre; antiguo alumno**
paper boy, boy who delivers newspapers. □ **repartidor de periódicos**
boyfriend *n.* young male friend: *she has gone out with her boyfriend.* □ **novio; amigo**
boyhood *n.* youth/time of life when you are a boy. □ **(segunda) infancia**
boyish *adj.* like a boy: *she has a boyish look.* □ **infantil**
Boy Scouts *n.* social/educational organization for boys: *he's joining the Boy Scouts.* □ **Boy Scouts**
boycott ['bɔikɔt] *n.* act of refusing to have anything to do with someone/something: *they are organizing a boycott of imported goods.* □ **boicoteo**
■ *v.* to refuse to have anything to do with someone/something: *they boycotted the meeting,* they refused to attend; *they want to boycott imported goods.* □ **boicotear**
bra [brɑː] *n.* (*informal*) brassiere/woman's undergarment for supporting the breasts. □ **sujetador**
braless *adj.* not wearing a bra. □ **sin sujetador**
brace [breis] *n.* **1** support; (*on teeth*) metal clamp to make teeth grow straight. □ **abrazadera; aparato de ortodoncia**
2 ***braces,*** elastic straps over the shoulders to hold up trousers. □ **tirantes**
3 pair: *a brace of grouse,* two grouse. □ **un par**
4 tool for holding a bit to drill holes: *he drilled a hole with a brace and bit.* □ **berbiquí**
■ *v.* **1** to support/to strengthen. □ **reforzar**
2 *he braced himself for the ordeal,* he stiffened his muscles to prepare himself for the ordeal. □ **fortalecerse**
bracing *adj.* invigorating/healthy (climate). □ **vigorizante**
bracelet ['breislət] *n.* ornamental chain/band worn round the wrist. □ **brazalete, pulsera**
bracken ['brækən] *n.* wild fern growing often in open country. □ **helecho**
bracket ['brækit] *n.* **1** support (for shelf, etc., against a wall). □ **soporte, ménsula**
2 printing symbol showing that something is separated from the rest of the text: *put the next two words in brackets; round brackets* =(T); *square brackets* =[T]. □ **paréntesis; corchetes**
3 (administrative) group: *people in the middle-income bracket.* □ **categoría**
■ *v.* **1** to put words into brackets: *he bracketed the three words together.* □ **poner entre paréntesis**
2 to link: *his name was bracketed with that of the mayor.* □ **relacionar**
brackish ['brækiʃ] *adj.* salty/undrinkable water. □ **salobre**
bract [brækt] *n.* part of a plant which is shaped like a leaf but can be coloured like a flower. □ **bráctea**
bradawl ['brædɔːl] *n.* boring tool for making holes (in leather, etc.). □ **punzón**
brag [bræg] *v.* (*he bragged*) to boast: *he is always bragging about his success with women.* □ **jactarse**
bragging *n.* boasting. □ **jactancia**
brahmin ['brɑːmin] *n.* highest-ranking Hindu; very important person (especially in the civil service). □ **brahmán**
braid [breid] *n.* plaited decoration: *the commissionaire's uniform was covered with gold braid.* □ **...galón de oro**
■ *v.* to plait hair (with ribbon). □ **trenzar**
braille [breil] *n.* system of raised dots on paper for the blind to read by touch: *he can read braille; this book is printed in braille.* □ **braille**
brain [brein] *n.* **1** nervous centre of the head which thinks and directs the body: *some dinosaurs had very small brains; the human brain is extremely complex; use your brain,* think hard. □ **cerebro**
2 ***to have something on the brain:*** *he's got model trains on the brain,* (*informal*) he's madly interested in model trains.□ **...metido en la cabeza**
3 *I'm racking my brains to think of a way of doing it,* I'm thinking hard to find a way of doing it. □ **me estoy devanando los sesos...**
4 *she's got brains,* she's intelligent. □ **es inteligente**
5 *he was the brains behind the series of burglaries,* he was the organizer of the burglaries. □ **era el cerebro...**
brain drain, departure of highly intelligent people

to other countries in order to work for higher salaries. □ **fuga de cerebros**
■ *v.* to kill someone by hitting them on the head. □ **romper la crisma**
brainchild *n.* original idea/plan thought up by someone. □ **idea genial**
braininess *n.* intelligence. □ **ingenio**
brainless *adj.* idiotic/stupid. □ **memo; tonto**
brainpower *n.* intelligence/ability to think or reason. □ **capacidad intelectual**
brainwash *v.* to indoctrinate someone/to make someone think in a totally different manner than before: *housewives have been brainwashed by TV commercials; the prisoners had been brainwashed by the secret services.* □ **lavar el cerebro**
brainwashing *n.* act of changing someone's way of thinking. □ **lavado de cerebro**
brainwave *n.* brilliant idea: *I've had a brainwave.* □ **idea luminosa**
brainy *adj.* (*brainier, brainiest*) (*informal*) intelligent. □ **listo**
braise [breiz] *v.* to cook (meat/vegetables) in a covered pot with very little liquid: *braised steak.* □ **cocinar a fuego lento, 'brasear'**
brake [breik] *n.* mechanism for stopping a car/bicycle, etc.; *hand brake,* brake operated by a hand lever: *he put on/applied the brakes; he released the brake; he drove away with the brake on.* □ **freno**
■ *v.* to stop/to slow down by applying the brakes: *as the cyclist came out from the side street, I had to brake hard.* □ **frenar**
braking *n.* putting on the brakes. □ **frenado**
braking distance, distance a car travels after the brakes are applied before it comes to a halt. □ **distancia de frenado**
bramble ['bræmbl] *n.* wild blackberry; bush which bears this fruit. □ **zarzamora; zarza**
bran [bræn] *n.* skins of wheat seeds which are separated from the flour. □ **salvado**
branch [brɑːntʃ] *n.* (*pl. branches*) **1** limb of a tree: *the squirrels jump from branch to branch.* □ **rama**
2 offshoot: *branch of a river.* □ **brazo**
3 ***branch line,*** minor railway line. □ **ramal**
4 *he is from the Norfolk branch of our family,* the part of the family which lives in Norfolk. □ **rama**
5 office (of a bank, etc.); store (of a chain of stores): *we have branches all over the country.* □ **sucursal**
■ *v.* **1** ***to branch out,*** to spread out/to diversify: *he is branching out into selling records,* he is adding record selling to his activities. □ **ramificarse**
2 *the road you want branches off this one about a mile away,* splits off from this one. □ **ramificarse**
brand [brænd] *n.* **1** identification mark made (on cattle) by a hot iron. □ **marca**
2 sort of product made by one manufacturer: *I like this brand of tea; I only buy superior brands of coffee; they have an excellent brand image,* the reputation of their brand is excellent; *they have their own brand name for their products.* □ **marca**
■ *v.* **1** to mark (cattle) with a hot iron. □ **marcar**
2 *he was branded as a thief,* he was called a thief. □ **tildar de**
branded *adj.* **1** marked (cattle, etc.). □ **marcado**
2 (goods) with a brand name. □ **de marca**
branding *n.* marking (of cattle) with a hot iron. □ **marcado**
brand-new *adj.* completely new. □ **flamante**
brandish ['brændiʃ] *v.* to wave about: *he was brandishing a spear.* □ **blandir**
brandy ['brændi] *n.* (*pl. brandies*) strong alcohol distilled from wine; glass of this alcohol: *he drank two brandies.* □ **brandy, coñac**
cherry brandy, alcohol distilled from cherries. □ **aguardiente de cerezas**
brandy snap, thin rolled biscuit flavoured with ginger. □ **bizcochito de gengibre**
brash [bræʃ] *adj.* vulgar and pushing (person). □ **insolente**
brass [brɑːs] *n.* **1** yellow metal made from copper and zinc: *a brass bowl; the candlestick is made of brass.* □ **latón**
the top brass, the directors/high-ranking officers, etc. □ **los jefazos**
2 *let's **get down to brass tacks,*** let's discuss the basic problem. □ **vayamos al grano**
3 musical instruments made of brass: *the brass section of an orchestra; a brass band.* □ **el cobre, metal**
4 (*informal*) money: *he's made plenty of brass in his time.* □ **pasta**
5 (*pl. brasses*) (*in church*) memorial plate made of brass. □ **placa conmemorativa**
brass rubbing *n.* method of getting a reproduction of a brass plate by covering it with paper and rubbing with wax; the reproduction itself. □ **calco**
brassy *adj.* (*brassier, brassiest*) **1** (noise) like that of brass instruments. □ **estridente**
2 rude, loud-mouthed (person). □ **descarado**
brassiere ['bræziə] *n.* woman's undergarment for supporting the breasts. □ **sujetador**
brat [bræt] *n.* rude child. □ **mocoso**
bravado [brə'vɑːdou] *n.* reckless bravery: *he did it in a fit of bravado.* □ **bravata**
brave [breiv] *adj.* (*braver, bravest*) not afraid; courageous: *the brave policeman saved the boy from drowning.* □ **valiente**
■ *v.* to defy: *he braved the storm; she braved the anger of the crowd.* □ **desafiar**
■ *n.* male American Indian fighter. □ **guerrero indio**
bravely *adv.* with courage: *he bravely went into the burning house to rescue the old woman.* □ **valientemente**
bravery *n.* courage: *he received a medal for his bravery during the fire.* □ **valor; valentía**
bravo [brɑː'vou] *interjection* showing approval. □ **¡bravo!**
brawl [brɔːl] *n.* wild fight: *the police stopped the brawl among the drinkers in the pub.* □ **alboroto**
■ *v.* to fight wildly: *the rival gangs were brawling in the streets.* □ **pelearse**
brawler *n.* person who is fighting wildly. □ **camorrista**
brawn [brɔːn] *n.* **1** chopped meat mixed with jelly to form a loaf. □ **carne picada en rollo**
2 muscle power: *he's got more brawn than brain.* □ **músculo**
brawny *adj.* muscular/strong: *a brawny rugby player.* □ **fornido**
bray [brei] *v.* to make a loud raucous call like a donkey. □ **rebuznar**
brazen ['breizn] *adj.* **1** like or made of brass. □ **de latón**
2 shameless: *a brazen lie.* □ **descarado**
■ *v.* ***to brazen it out:*** *he brazened it out,* he impudently got through the awkward situation. □ **lo aguantó con descaro**
Brazil [brə'zil] *n.* **1** country in South America. □ **Brasil**
2 ***Brazil (nut),*** large tropical nut. □ **nuez del Brasil**
Brazilian *adj.* referring to Brazil. □ **brasileño**
■ *n.* person from Brazil. □ **brasileño**
breach [briːtʃ] *n.* (*pl. breaches*) **1** crack (in a defence/dam): *the soldiers poured through the breach in the*

walls. □ **brecha**
2 breaking (of a law/promise). □ **violación**
breach of faith, going back on what has been promised. □ **incumplimiento**
breach of promise, refusing to marry someone after having promised to do so. □ **incumplimiento de la palabra de casamiento**
3 disagreement; separation: *we are trying to heal the breach between the two sides of the family.* □ **enfrentamiento**
■ *v.* to split: *this agreement has breached the government's pay policy.* □ **abrir una brecha**

bread [bred] *n.* (*no pl.*) **1** food made from flour and water and yeast baked in an oven: *you buy bread at the baker's; can I have two loaves of bread? would you like another piece of bread and butter?* □ **pan**
bread bin, metal/plastic container for keeping bread fresh. □ **panera**
bread sauce, thick white sauce made from soft white breadcrumbs. □ **salsa de pan**
brown bread, bread made from unrefined flour. □ **pan moreno**
wholemeal bread, bread made from flour which contains the whole grain. □ **pan integral**
2 *he wrote a **bread-and-butter letter,*** letter written to say thank you for hospitality. □ **carta de agradecimiento**
breadcrumbs *n. pl.* bread broken up into very small pieces: *the cutlet was coated with breadcrumbs.* □ **migajas**
breaded *adj.* covered with breadcrumbs. □ **empanado**
breadline *n. he's **on the breadline,*** he has very little money/he has hardly enough to live on. □ **vive en la miseria**
breadwinner *n.* person who earns money to feed the family: *she's the breadwinner in the family.* □ **el que gana el pan**

breadth [bredθ] *n.* **1** measurement of how broad or wide something is: *the table is three feet in breadth.* □ **anchura**
2 *he swam three breadths,* he swam across the swimming pool three times. □ **nadó tres anchos**
3 wideness (of views): *he is remarkable for the breadth of his knowledge.* □ **amplitud**

break [breik] *n.* **1** split/crack (where two parts have broken): *a break in the clouds; break in a journey; he spoke for three hours without a break.* □ **claro; descanso**
2 *break in transmission,* gap in transmitting a radio/television programme. □ **interrupción**
3 quarrel: *there has been a break between the two friends.* □ **riña**
4 *break in the weather,* change in the weather. □ **cambio**
5 rest period: *coffee break,* period where you stop work for a cup of coffee; *morning break,* short period of recreation during the morning at school. □ **descanso; recreo**
6 *he had a lucky break,* his bad luck changed. □ **racha de suerte**
7 *at break of day,* at dawn. □ **al amanecer**
■ *v.* (*he broke; he has broken*) **1** to fall to pieces/to smash into pieces: *the plate slipped off the table and broke; he broke two cups while he was doing the washing up; she broke her arm.* □ **romper(se)**
2 *we'll break our journey at Edinburgh,* we'll stop for a while/for the night at Edinburgh. □ **haremos una parada en ...**
3 *my watch is broken,* my watch has stopped working. □ **estropeado**
4 ***to break someone's heart:*** *it broke her heart to see the house sold,* she was extremely upset. □ **partir el corazón de**
5 *he has been broken by his debts,* he has been ruined. □ **ha quedado destrozado...**
6 *he intends **to break the record** for the high jump,* to jump higher than anyone has ever done before. □ **superó el récord...**
7 ***to break even:*** *we are breaking even,* we are not making a loss or a profit. □ **ni ganamos ni perdemos**
8 not to keep (a promise): *he has broken his word; you are breaking the law.* □ **ha roto su palabra**
9 *the storm broke,* the storm suddenly started; *the day was breaking over the battlefield,* daylight was coming. □ **la tormenta estalló; amanecía sobre...**
10 (*of boy's voice*) to become deeper as the boy grows older: *I can't sing now, my voice has broken.* □ **mudar la voz**
11 to cushion (a fall): *the bushes broke his fall.* □ **amortiguar**
breakable *adj.* which can easily be broken. □ **rompible**
breakables *n. pl.* fragile objects (glasses/cups, etc.). □ **objetos frágiles**
breakages *n. pl.* breaking (of glass, etc.); things which have been broken: *you will have to pay for all the breakages.* □ **estropicios**
break away *v.* to escape/to be detached: *the prisoner broke away from the policemen; an iceberg broke away from the iceflow.* □ **escapar, soltarse**
breakaway *adj.* which has become detached: *the breakaway nationalist party,* the nationalist party which has split off from a larger party. □ **escindido**
break down *v.* **1** to smash: *the attackers broke down the door; we must break down prejudices.* □ **derribar**
2 to collapse/to go wrong: *his health has broken down completely; she broke down and cried; my car broke down on the motorway; the discussions have broken down.* □ **deteriorarse; derrumbarse; averiarse; fracasar**
3 to list: *he broke down the sales under three main headings.* □ **desglosar**
breakdown *n.* **1** collapse: *the breakdown in negotiations; a breakdown in the television service.* □ **fracaso; avería**
2 *he has had a **nervous breakdown,*** he has become severely depressed. □ **crisis nerviosa**
3 list under various headings: *give me a breakdown of our sales over the last three months.* □ **desglose**
4 *we had a breakdown on the motorway,* our car stopped working; *garage with a 24-hour breakdown service.* □ **avería**
breakdown truck, truck which tows away cars which do not work. □ **grúa**
breaker *n.* **1** big wave which is breaking: *we could hear the breakers pounding on the rocks.* □ **ola que rompe**
2 person who buys old cars, etc., to take them to bits and sell the parts: *breaker's yard.* □ **desguazador**
breakfast ['brekfəst] *n.* first meal of the day: *we have toast and coffee for breakfast; they have breakfast every day at 7.30.* □ **desayuno**
breakfast cup, large cup. □ **tazón**
wedding breakfast, meal after a wedding (often lunch). □ **banquete de bodas**
continental breakfast, breakfast of bread and coffee. □ **desayuno continental**
English breakfast, breakfast with cereals, bacon and eggs, toast and coffee or tea. □ **desayuno inglés**
■ *v.* to eat the first meal of the day: *have you break-*

fasted yet? □ **desayunar**
break in *v.* **1** to smash in: *the burglars broke in.* □ **irrumpir**
2 to interrupt: *excuse me if I break in for a moment.* □ **interrumpir**
3 to train (a horse). □ **domar**
break-in *n.* burglary: *there has been a spate of break-ins around us recently.* □ **robo**
breaking *n.* **1** action of smashing/falling to pieces. □ **rotura**
2 ***breaking and entering,*** crime of breaking into someone's property. □ **allanamiento de morada**
break into *v.* to smash in order to enter: *someone has broken into the safe; our house has been broken into twice this year.* □ **forzar**
break loose *v.* to escape: *the prisoners broke loose.* □ **fugarse**
breakneck *adj. at breakneck speed,* extremely fast. □ **a toda prisa**
break off *v.* **1** to split away/to crack: *he broke off another piece of chocolate; a large piece of ice has broken off from the glacier.* □ **partir; desprenderse**
2 to stop: *their engagement has been broken off; they have broken off negotiations.* □ **romper**
break open *v.* to smash (in order to open): *they used dynamite to break open the safe.* □ **abrir**
break out *v.* **1** to start: *war has broken out; fighting broke out in the crowd.* □ **estallar**
2 to escape: *three prisoners broke out from prison.* □ **escapar**
breakout *n.* escape: *there was a mass breakout at the prison,* a lot of prisoners escaped. □ **evasión**
break through *v.* to smash in order to go through: *we had to break through the hedge; the sun is breaking through the clouds.* □ **atravesar**
breakthrough *n.* sudden success (in science): *the discovery of radium was a breakthrough in the fight against cancer.* □ **gran avance**
break up *v.* **1** to smash to pieces: *he broke up the concrete slab with a hammer; they broke up the demonstration; the crowd is beginning to break up; the ship was breaking up on the rocks.* □ **deshacer**
break it up!, stop fighting. □ **¡separaos!**
2 *they had a quarrel and broke up,* did not work/live together any more. □ **...y se separaron**
3 to go on holiday: *school breaks up on Tuesday.* □ **finalizar**
4 (*of weather*) to get worse. □ **empeorar**
breakup *n.* coming to pieces/falling apart: *the breakup of a marriage.* □ **ruptura**
breakwater *n.* wall/fence going into the sea to prevent waves from battering the coast. □ **rompeolas**
bream [bri:m] *n.* type of fat edible fish. □ **brema**
breast [brest] *n.* **1** one of two milk-giving organs in a woman's body. □ **pecho**
breast feeding, feeding of a child with milk which he sucks from the breast: *both her children were breast-fed.* □ **dar el pecho**
2 chest/front part of the top of the body. □ **pecho**
breast pocket, pocket on the front of a jacket. □ **bolsillo del pecho**
breast stroke, swimming stroke where both arms stretch out together and are brought back to the chest. □ **braza de pecho**
3 white meat (on a chicken). □ **pechuga**
breath [breθ] *n.* **1** air which goes into and out of the body: *take a deep breath before you dive.* □ **respiración, aire**
2 *he ran so fast he was* ***out of breath,*** he was panting. □ **se quedó sin resuello**
3 *at the end of the climb we were gasping for breath,* we were having difficulty in breathing; *after a few moments' rest, she got her breath back.* □ **...estábamos jadeando**
4 ***to waste one's breath:*** *don't waste your breath on them,* don't waste time talking to them. □ **no gastes saliva en balde**
5 ***take one's breath away:*** *when he mentioned the price it took my breath away,* I was completely astonished. □ **...me dejó sin aliento**
6 *he muttered* ***under his breath,*** quietly. □ **...en voz baja**
7 *there wasn't a breath of wind,* not the slightest breeze. □ **...ni un soplo de aire**
breathalyser ['breθəlaizə] *n.* instrument for testing if a driver has drunk too much alcohol. □ **alcohómetro**
breathless *adj.* out of breath/panting. □ **sin aliento**
breathlessly *adv.* in a rush/without taking time to breathe. □ **en un santiamén**
breathtaking *adj.* so exciting/beautiful that it takes your breath away: *a breathtaking view.* □ **imponente**
breathe [bri:ð] *v.* **1** to suck air in or out through the nose or mouth: *breathe deeply,* take a deep breath; *the mountain was so high we had difficulty in breathing; he breathed a sigh of relief.* □ **respirar**
2 *you mustn't breathe a word about it!,* you mustn't say anything about it. □ **no debes decir ni una palabra**
breather *n.* **1** rest period. □ **descanso**
2 *I'm going out for a breather,* I'm going out to get some fresh air. □ **respiro, a tomar un poco el aire**
breathing *n.* act of taking air in and out of the body. □ **respiración**
breathing apparatus, mask, etc., which allows you to breathe in gas/smoke, etc.: *the firemen were wearing breathing apparatus.* □ **máscara de oxígeno**
breathing space, rest period: *we had a welcome breathing space between games.* □ **descanso**
bred [bred] *v. see* **breed.**
breech [bri:tʃ] *n.* (*pl. breeches*) **1** back part of a gun where the ammunition is loaded. □ **recámara**
2 ***breech birth,*** birth in which the baby's buttocks appear first. □ **nacimiento de nalgas**
3 ***breeches,*** trousers which come down to below the knees and are tight over the lower leg: *riding breeches.* □ **pantalones de montar**
breeches buoy, device, like a canvas seat, used to rescue people at sea. □ **salvavidas**
breed [bri:d] *n.* particular race of animal: *there are several breeds of sheep with black faces.* □ **raza**
■ *v.* (*he bred*) **1** to produce young animals/plants: *rabbits breed very quickly; we are trying to breed very fat pigs.* □ **criar**
2 *I was* ***born and bred*** *in the country,* I was born and grew up in the country. □ **nací y me crié...**
well-bred *person,* someone who is polite/who has been well educated. □ **bien educado**
breeder *n.* **1** person who breeds (animals): *a cat breeder.* □ **criador**
2 ***(fast) breeder reactor,*** nuclear machine which makes a surplus of nuclear material. □ **reactor, reproductor rápido**
breeding *n.* **1** production of animals: *he has gone in for pig breeding.* □ **cría**
2 training in good manners: *it is a sign of good breeding not to shout.* □ **educación**
breeze [bri:z] *n.* slight wind: *the breeze made waves on the lake; there was a stiff breeze blowing,* quite a strong wind was blowing. □ **brisa**
■ *v. he breezed into the restaurant,* he rushed into the restaurant looking very pleased with himself.

□ **entró con cara de satisfecho**
breeze-block *n.* block of concrete used for building inside walls. □ **viga de hormigón**
breezy *adj.* **1** windy. □ **ventoso**
2 happy-go-lucky: *he has a breezy manner.* □ **despreocupado**
breviary ['bri:vjəri] *n.* book of Roman Catholic prayers. □ **breviario**
brevity ['breviti] *n.* conciseness/shortness. □ **brevedad**
brew [bru:] *n.* liquid which has been brewed: *your tea is a very curious brew.* □ **infusión**
■ *v.* **1** to make (beer/tea). □ **elaborar**
2 *the tea is brewing,* is being left to stand until it is strong enough. □ **el té está reposando**
3 *there's trouble brewing,* there is trouble coming. □ **algo se está tramando**
brewer *n.* person who makes beer. □ **cervecero**
brewer's yeast, yeast used in brewing beer, and taken in tablet form as a source of vitamin B. □ **levadura de cerveza**
brewery *n.* (*pl. breweries*) place where beer is made. □ **fábrica de cerveza**
briar ['braiə] *n.* prickly (rose) bush. □ **zarza**
briar pipe *n.* pipe made from briar wood. □ **pipa de brezo**
bribe [braib] *n.* money given illegally to someone to get something done: *I had to give the agent a bribe to get a visa.* □ **soborno**
■ *v.* to give someone money illegally to get something done: *I bribed the doorkeeper to let me in.* □ **sobornar**
bribery *n.* giving money illegally to get something done. □ **soborno**
bric-a-brac ['brikəbræk] *n.* (*no pl.*) ornaments or furniture of little value. □ **baratijas**
brick [brik] *n.* block of baked clay, used for building: *the house is built of brick; a brick wall.* □ **ladrillo**
to drop a brick: *he dropped a brick,* he made an unfortunate remark by mistake. □ **metió la pata**
■ *v. they bricked up the door,* they filled in the doorway with a wall of bricks. □ **tapiaron la puerta con ladrillos**
brick-built *adj.* built of bricks. □ **de ladrillo**
bricklayer *n.* person who builds with bricks. □ **albañil**
brickwork *n.* bricks built up into a wall. □ **enladrillado**
bride [braid] *n.* woman who is about to get married or who has just got married: *the bride is wearing white.* □ **novia**
bridal *adj.* referring to a wedding. □ **nupcial**
bridal bouquet, bouquet carried by the bride. □ **ramo de novia**
bridegroom *n.* man who is about to get married or who has just got married. □ **novio**
bridesmaid *n.* unmarried woman who is the bride's attendant at a wedding. □ **dama de honor**
bridge [bridʒ] *n.* **1** construction across a river/road/railway line: *the road crosses the river by a very long bridge; a railway bridge.* □ **puente**
2 top part of a ship where a captain stands. □ **puente**
3 top of the nose. □ **caballete**
4 type of card game for four people: *we were having a game of bridge; do you play bridge?* □ **bridge**
■ *v.* **1** to put a bridge across (a river, etc.). □ **tender un puente sobre**
2 *we are finding it difficult* ***to bridge the gap,*** to fill in the gap. □ **llenar un vacío**
bridgehead *n.* preliminary position held by attackers who have attacked across water □ **cabeza de puente**
bridge roll *n.* small long soft roll of white bread. □ **panecillo**
bridle ['braidl] *n.* reins (attached to a horse's bit): *he was leading his horse by the bridle.* □ **brida**
■ *v.* **1** to hold back (a horse). □ **retener**
2 to take offence: *he bridled when we mentioned his salary.* □ **ofenderse**
bridlepath, bridleway *n.* path for horseriders. □ **camino de herradura**
brief [bri:f] *adj.* short: *he sent me a brief note; the meeting was very brief.* □ **breve**
in brief, *he is against the deal,* in short/to sum up, he is against the deal. □ **en resumen**
■ *n.* **1** papers concerning a legal case. □ **expediente**
2 instructions: *his brief is to increase sales in Europe.* □ **instrucciones**
3 *the envoy has been given a very wide brief,* authority to deal with many problems. □ **mandato**
4 ***briefs,*** short knickers/underpants. □ **braguitas/calzoncillos**
■ *v.* to give a case to a lawyer; to give someone information/instructions: *have they briefed you on the background to the case? let me brief you on what has happened so far.* □ **informar**
briefcase *n.* small case for carrying papers. □ **cartera**
briefing *n.* conference where information is given. □ **sesión informativa**
briefly *adv.* shortly/without speaking for a long time: *he thanked them all briefly and went to bed.* □ **brevemente**
brigade [bri'geid] *n.* **1** army group, smaller than a division. □ **brigada**
2 ***fire brigade,*** group of people whose job is to fight fires. □ **bomberos**
brigadier [brigə'diə] *n.* officer in charge of a brigade in the army; rank in the army above colonel. □ **general de brigada**
brigand ['brigənd] *n.* robber. □ **bandido**
bright [brait] *adj.* (*brighter, brightest*) **1** shining very strongly/having a very vivid colour: *the bright sunshine made the water sparkle; he has painted his car bright red.* □ **brillante**
2 *you have* ***to look on the bright side (of things),*** you must be optimistic. □ **...el lado bueno de las cosas**
3 intelligent: *his children are both very bright; I've had a bright idea.* □ **listo; brillante**
brighten *v.* **1** to make bright: *his appearance brightened a rather dull evening.* □ **iluminar, dar brillo**
2 *she brightened up when she saw him,* she became more lively/more cheerful. □ **ella se animó...**
3 *the weather is brightening up,* it is getting finer. □ **el tiempo mejora**
brightly *adv.* **1** *the lights were shining brightly,* with a strong light. □ **brillantemente**
2 *she answered brightly,* in an intelligent/cheerful tone of voice. □ **ingeniosamente**
brightness *n.* strength (of light); intelligence (of person). □ **brillo/inteligencia**
brill [bril] *n.* type of flat white edible sea fish. □ **rodaballo**
brilliant ['briljənt] *adj.* **1** very shiny: *a brilliant light.* □ **brillante**
2 very intelligent: *he's a brilliant scientist; I've had a brilliant idea.* □ **brillante**
■ *n.* diamond. □ **brillante**
brilliance *n.* brightness; intelligence. □ **brillantez**
brim [brim] *n.* edge: *fill the glasses up to the brim; he*

turned down the brim of his hat. □ **borde; ...ala del sombrero**
■ *v.* (*he brimmed*) *the glass was brimming over with wine,* the glass was overflowing. □ **rebosar**
to brim over with: *he is brimming over with new ideas,* he is full of new ideas. □ **está rebosante de ideas**
brimful *adj.* very full/full to overflowing. □ **rebosante**
brindled ['brindld] *adj.* (*of animals*) brown with streaks of another colour. □ **berrendo**
brine [brain] *n.* salt water. □ **salmuera**
bring [briŋ] *v.* (*he brought; he has brought*) **1** to take (something/someone) to this place: *bring the money to me here; he brought his girlfriend with him; I hope it brings you luck.* □ **traer**
2 *he can't bring himself to say 'no',* he cannot make himself say no. □ **no se resigna a decir ...**
bring about *v.* to cause/to make (something) happen: *it brought about the fall of the Roman Empire.* □ **causar**
bring along *v.* to bring with you: *bring along your Beatles record.* □ **traer consigo**
bring-and-buy *n.* type of market where people bring and buy homemade goods. □ **rastrillo**
bring back *v.* **1** to return (here): *don't forget to bring back the bottles.* □ **devolver**
2 *seeing that picture brings it all back to me,* makes me remember it all. □ **...me trae el recuerdo**
bring down *v.* to make (something/someone) fall down; to lower (something): *I have brought my suitcase down myself; he brought down the opposing forward,* he held him so that he fell down. □ **bajar; abatir**
bring forward *v. to bring forward the date of the meeting,* to arrange an earlier date for the meeting. □ **adelantar**
bring in *v.* to make (something/someone) come in: *bring the suspect in here; my job doesn't bring in much money.* □ **haz entrar al sospechoso; mi empleo no me da mucho...**
bring off *v.* to succeed in: *he brought it off,* he did it successfully. □ **lograr**
bring on *v.* **1** to produce/to make grow: *the flowers bring on my hayfever.* □ **producir**
2 *you've brought it on yourself,* it's your own fault. □ **te lo has buscado tú mismo**
bring out *v.* **1** to make something/someone come out: *he is bringing out a new book of poetry,* he is publishing a new book. □ **sacar, publicar**
2 *it brings out the colour of the curtains,* it makes the colour of the curtains more noticeable/more effective. □ **resaltar**
bring round *v.* **1** to carry (something) round: *can you bring round your ladder?* □ **llevar**
2 to revive (someone) who is unconscious: *the sip of whisky brought him round.* □ **hacer volver en sí**
bring up *v.* **1** to raise (a subject): *I told him not to bring up the question of money.* □ **sacar a colación**
2 to vomit. □ **vomitar**
3 to educate in manners: *he has been badly brought up.* □ **educar**
brink [briŋk] *n.* **1** edge (of cliff). □ **borde**
2 *she is **on the brink of** a nervous breakdown,* she is very close to having a nervous breakdown. □ **al borde de**
brisk [brisk] *adj.* rapid: *he walked along at a brisk pace; he did a brisk trade in tourist souvenirs.* □ **rápido**
briskly *adv.* rapidly. □ **rápidamente**
brisket ['briskit] *n.* beef from the breast of an animal. □ **falda**
bristle ['brisl] *n.* short stiff hair (on animal/brush): *brush with nylon bristles.* □ **cerda**
■ *v.* to take offence. □ **enfadarse**
bristly *adj.* covered with short stiff hair. □ **hirsuto**
Britain ['britn] *n.* (*also **Great Britain***) country formed of England, Wales and Scotland. □ **Gran Bretaña**
British ['britiʃ] *adj.* and *n.* referring to Great Britain: *the British Isles.* □ **británico**
the British, the people of Great Britain. □ **los británicos**
Briton ['britn] *n.* person from Great Britain. □ **británico**
brittle ['britl] *adj.* which breaks easily. □ **quebradizo**
brittleness *n.* fragility. □ **fragilidad**
broach [broutʃ] *v.* **1** to open (a cask of wine, etc.). □ **espitar**
2 to start talking (about a problem): *he didn't dare broach the subject of holidays,* didn't dare mention holidays. □ **mentar**
broad [brɔːd] *adj.* **1** (*broader, broadest*) very wide: *the street is very broad in front of the church; a table 2 metres broad.* □ **ancho**
2 *the burglar went into the house in broad daylight,* in full daylight. □ **...en pleno día**
3 *a broad Scottish accent,* a strong accent. □ **un acento marcado**
broadcast *n.* radio/television programme: *we try to listen to BBC broadcasts.* □ **emisión**
outside broadcast, radio/television programme recorded in the open air, not in a studio. □ **emisión al aire libre**
■ *v.* (*he broadcast*) **1** to sow (by throwing seed by hand). □ **sembrar a voleo**
2 to send out by radio/television: *they broadcast an appeal to the people.* □ **emitir**
3 to tell (everyone) the news: *don't broadcast the fact,* keep it a secret. □ **divulgar**
■ *adv.* (sowing) by throwing the seed by hand: *they sowed the seed broadcast.* □ **...a voleo**
■ *adj.* sent by radio/television: *a broadcast message.* □ **un mensaje por radio/televisión**
broadcaster *n.* person who speaks on the radio/television. □ **locutor**
broadcasting *n.* sending out of radio/television programmes. □ **emisión**
broaden *v.* **1** to make wider. □ **ampliar**
2 *travel broadens the mind,* travel makes your knowledge/interest more extensive. □ **viajar te ensancha la mente**
broadloom *adj.* (carpet) woven in a very wide strip. □ **alfombra**
broadly *adv. broadly speaking,* in a general way. □ **en términos generales**
broadminded *adj.* tolerant; not easily taking offence. □ **abierto**
broad-shouldered *adj.* with wide shoulders. □ **ancho de espaldas**
broadside *n.* **1** firing of all the guns on one side of a ship. □ **andanada**
2 sharp written or spoken criticism. □ **crítica corrosiva**
3 *broadside on,* with the side towards. □ **de costado**
brocade [brə'keid] *n.* thick cloth with a raised pattern. □ **brocado**
broccoli ['brɔkəli] *n.* (*no pl.*) cabbage-like vegetable of which the flower-heads are eaten. □ **brécol**
brochure ['brouʃə] *n.* small book; small publicity pamphlet. □ **folleto**
brogue [broug] *n.* **1** heavy shoe with patterned

leather top. □ **zapato calado y abotinado inglés**
2 accent (usually Irish). □ **deje de un irlandés al hablar inglés**
broil [brɔil] *v.* to grill: *the broiling sun.* □ **asar a la parrilla**
broiler *n.* chicken specially bred for roasting. □ **pollo tomatero**
broke [brouk] *adj.* ***to be flat broke,*** (*informal*) to have no money; *see also* **break.** □ **estar sin blanca**
broken ['broukən] *adj.* **1** in pieces: *a broken plate.* □ **roto**
a broken home, home where the parents have separated. □ **un hogar destrozado**
2 spoken with a bad accent and with many mistakes: *he spoke a few words of broken English.* □ **...un inglés macarrónico**
3 not working: *a broken-down car; see also* **break.** □ **averiado**
broken-hearted *adj.* very upset: *she was broken-hearted when her cat died.* □ **corazón partido**
broker ['broukə] *n.* person who deals in shares/insurance. □ **corredor de bolsa/agente de seguros**
brokerage *n.* fee charged by a broker for his work. □ **corretaje**
brolly ['brɔli] *n.* (*pl. brollies*) (*informal*) umbrella. □ **paraguas**
bronchial ['brɔŋkiəl] *adj.* referring to the respiratory tubes: *bronchial asthma,* asthma in the lungs. □ **bronquial**
bronchitis [brɔŋ'kaitis] *n.* disease of the respiratory tubes. □ **bronquitis**
bronze [brɔnz] *n.* metal made from copper and tin: *a bronze helmet.* □ **bronce**
Bronze Age, prehistoric period when men used weapons of bronze. □ **Edad de Bronce**
bronzed *adj.* tanned: *he was looking bronzed and healthy.* □ **bronceado**
brooch [broutʃ] *n.* (*pl. brooches*) ornament to pin on to clothing. □ **broche**
brood [bru:d] *n.* group of chicks/small children. □ **pollada/prole**
■ *v.* **1** to have gloomy thoughts. □ **cavilar**
2 *she's brooding over a plan to redecorate the kitchen,* she is turning over a plan/pondering a plan. □ **darle vueltas a...**
broody *adj.* **1** (hen) preparing to sit on a clutch of eggs; (woman) who wants to have a baby. □ **gallina clueca/mujer maternal**
2 (person) who has gloomy thoughts. □ **melancólico**
brook [bruk] *n.* small stream. □ **arroyo**
■ *v.* to allow/to accept. □ **tolerar**
broom [bru:m] *n.* **1** shrub with yellow flowers. □ **retama**
2 brush with long handle for sweeping the floor. □ **escoba**
broomstick *n.* long handle of a broom. □ **palo de la escoba**
broth [brɔθ] *n.* light soup. □ **caldo**
Scotch broth, thick soup with barley, vegetables and lamb. □ **caldo escocés**
brothel ['brɔθl] *n.* house of prostitutes. □ **burdel**
brother ['brʌðə] *n.* **1** male child of the same parents as another child: *there are three children in our family - myself and my two brothers.* □ **hermano**
2 man belonging to a monastic order. □ **hermano**
brotherhood *n.* fraternity. □ **hermandad**
brother-in-law *n.* (*pl. brothers-in-law*) brother of your husband or wife; husband of your sister; husband of the sister of your husband or wife. □ **cuñado**
brotherly *adj.* as of brothers: *brotherly love.* □ **fraternal**
brought [brɔ:t] *v. see* **bring.**
brow [brau] *n.* **1** forehead/top part of the face above the eyes. □ **frente**
2 line of hair above each eye. □ **ceja**
3 rounded top of a hill: *the soldiers appeared over the brow of the hill.* □ **cumbre**
browbeat *v.* (*he browbeat; he has browbeaten*) to intimidate (someone): *he refused to be browbeaten.* □ **intimidar**
brown [braun] *adj.* (*browner, brownest*) coloured like the colour of wood or soil: *in autumn the leaves turn brown and fall off the trees; brown bread; you are very brown - you must have been sitting in the sun.* □ **marrón**
brown sugar, unrefined sugar. □ **azúcar moreno**
■ *n.* colour of wood or soil: *brown doesn't suit me.* □ **marrón**
■ *v.* **1** to go brown; to make brown. □ **dorarse**
2 *brown the meat in fat,* cook it until it turns brown. □ **dorar**
3 *I'm **browned off** with all this waiting,* I'm fed up with all this waiting. □ **me fastidia toda esta espera**
brownie *n.* **1** girl in the younger section of the Girl Guides. □ **niña guía exploradora**
2 *Amer.* small chocolate cake. □ **bizcocho de chocolate y nueces**
brownish *adj.* rather brown. □ **pardusco**
browse [brauz] *v.* **1** (*of animal*) to wander about eating grass: *the cattle are browsing in the meadow.* □ **pacer**
2 (*of person*) to wander round a shop looking at goods for sale. □ **curiosear**
browser *n.* person who is browsing in a shop. □ **curioso**
bruise [bru:z] *n.* mark made on the skin by a blow: *his legs are covered with bruises.* □ **magulladura**
■ *v.* to get marks on the skin from a blow: *I bruised my elbow; peaches bruise easily.* □ **magullarse**
brunch [brʌntʃ] *n.* large meal (as a combination of breakfast and lunch) taken in the middle of the morning. □ **almuerzo**
brunette [bru:'net] *adj.* and *n.* (woman) with brown hair. □ **morena/una morena**
brunt [brʌnt] *n.* ***to bear the brunt of something,*** to suffer most from something: *he bore the brunt of the expense,* he paid most of the expense; *the town will bear the brunt of the attack,* most of the attack will be centred on the town. □ **soportar lo más arduo de**
brush [brʌʃ] *n.* (*pl. brushes*) **1** instrument with a handle and hair/wire/nylon bristles for painting or cleaning: *use a stiff brush to get the mud off your shoes; he uses a very fine brush to paint the thin lines; scrubbing brush; clothes brush.* □ **brocha/cepillo**
2 scrub land: *the wolves ran off into the brush.* □ **maleza**
3 cleaning with a brush: *his coat needs a good brush.* □ **un buen cepillado**
4 short argument with an opponent: *after his brush with the police.* □ **roce**
■ *v.* **1** to clean with a brush: *did you brush your teeth this morning? let me brush your shoes.* □ **cepillar**
2 to go past something touching it gently: *he brushed against her in the crowd; they brushed past the doorkeeper.* □ **pasar rozando**
brush aside *v.* to reject: *he brushed aside their invitation.* □ **rechazar**
brush away *v.* to clear away with a brush. □ **quitar con un cepillo**

brush down *v.* to brush something vigorously. □ **cepillar con fuerza**
brush off *v.* to clean (something) off with a brush: ***he brushed the dust off his shoes.*** □ **limpiar con un cepillo**
brush-off *n.* ***to give someone the brush-off,*** (*informal*) to send someone away without agreeing to what they want. □ **despedir con cajas destempladas**
brush up *v.* **1** to make (yourself) smart. □ **acicalar/acicalarse**
2 to improve: *he is brushing up his German,* he is revising his German. □ **refrescar (sus conocimientos de...)**
brushwood *n.* low undergrowth. □ **maleza**
brusque [bru:sk] *adj.* abrupt/impolite. □ **brusco**
brusquely *adv.* rudely. □ **bruscamente**
brute [bru:t] *n.* **1** rude/violent person: *he is a brute.* □ **bruto**
2 *this engine is a brute to start,* (*informal*) is very difficult to start. □ **chungo**
■ *adj.: he always wants to use brute force,* he wants to use rough methods. □ **fuerza bruta**
brutal *adj.* violent: *brutal murder.* □ **brutal**
brutality [bru:'tæliti] *n.* violent action. □ **brutalidad**
brutally *adv.* violently: *he was brutally murdered.* □ **brutalmente**
bryony ['braiəni] *n.* type of climbing wild plant, usually with poisonous berries. □ **brionia**
bubble ['bʌbl] *n.* small amount of air (trapped in liquid). □ **burbuja**
soap bubble, ball of air caught in a film of soapy water. □ **pompa de jabón**
■ *v.* to make bubbles: *the water is bubbling in the pan.* □ **borbotear**
bubbly *adj.* with bubbles. □ **burbujeante**
■ *n.* (*informal*) champagne. □ **champán**
buck [bʌk] *n.* **1** male deer/rabbit. □ **macho**
2 *Amer.* (*informal*) dollar. □ **dólar, pavo**
3 ***to pass the buck,*** (*informal*) to hand responsibility on to someone else. □ **echarle el muerto a uno**
■ *v.* (*of horse*) to jump in the air (with rounded back). □ **corcovear**
bucked *adj.* (*informal*) very pleased and encouraged. □ **animado**
buckteeth *n. pl.* teeth which stick out in front. □ **dientes salientes**
buck up *v.* **1** *the medicine bucked him up,* (*informal*) made him feel more lively. □ **reanimar**
2 *buck up,* (*informal*) hurry up/cheer up. □ **¡date prisa!/¡espabílate!**
bucket ['bʌkit] *n.* round container with an open top and a handle: *can you get a bucket of water from the river?* □ **cubo**
■ *v. to bucket down,* (*informal*) (*of rain*) to pour down. □ **llover a cántaros**
bucketful *n.* quantity contained in a bucket: *they brought up bucketfuls of mud.* □ **cubo**
buckle ['bʌkl] *n.* metal fastener for attaching a belt/strap/shoe. □ **hebilla**
■ *v.* **1** to attach with a metal clasp: *he buckled on his holster.* □ **abrochar**
2 to bend/to collapse: *the metal sheet buckled under the strain.* □ **combarse**
buckwheat ['bʌkwi:t] *n.* dark grain, giving a brown flour. □ **alforfón**
bucolic [bju:'kɔlik] *adj.* referring to the countryside. □ **bucólico**
bud [bʌd] *n.* point on a plant where a new shoot is appearing; flower not yet opened: *the roses are in bud,* the flowers are not open yet. □ **brote; ...en capullo**
■ *v.* (*he budded*) **1** to make buds: *the roses are budding.* □ **las rosas están saliendo**
2 to graft a bud. □ **injertar en escudete**
budding *adj.* **1** (flower) not yet open: *a budding rose.* □ **un capullo de rosa**
2 *he is a budding concert pianist,* he hopes to be a concert pianist, but isn't one yet. □ **...en ciernes**
Buddhism ['budizəm] *n.* religion following the teaching of Buddha. □ **budismo**
Buddhist *adj.* and *n.* (person) who follows the teaching of Buddha. □ **budista**
buddy ['bʌdi] *n.* (*pl. buddies*) *Amer.* (*informal*) friend. □ **amiguete**
budge [bʌdʒ] *v.* to move: *I asked him to make some room, but he wouldn't budge.* □ **correrse**
budgerigar ['bʌdʒərigɑ:] *n.* small blue or green tropical bird, often kept in a cage. □ **periquito**
budget ['bʌdʒit] *n.* list of proposed expenditure. □ **presupuesto**
household budget, list of spending in a household. □ **presupuesto doméstico**
the Budget, the government's declaration of proposals for tax and expenditure. □ **el presupuesto nacional**
■ *v.* to plan how to spend money: *I have budgeted for an expenditure of $100 on holidays.* □ **presupuestar**
budgie ['bʌdʒi] *n.* (*informal*) budgerigar. □ **perico**
buff [bʌf] **1** *adj.* and *n.* (of a) pale yellowy-brown colour: *a buff envelope.* □ **amarillento; sobre manila**
2 *n.* (*slang*) enthusiast: *film buffs.* □ **entusiasta**
■ *v.* to polish/to shine. □ **dar brillo**
buffalo ['bʌfəlou] *n.* (*pl. buffaloes/buffalo*) large wild ox or cow (in America and tropical countries). □ **búfalo**
buffer ['bʌfə] *n.* **1** shock-absorbing pad, especially at end of railway line. □ **tope**
buffer zone, area between two areas of fighting. □ **área desmilitarizada**
2 ***old buffer,*** (*slang*) old man. □ **carcamal**
buffet ['bufei] *n.* **1** self-service snack bar (in railway station, etc.). □ **cantina**
buffet car, railway coach containing a buffet. □ **vagón restaurante**
2 self-service meal: *after the ceremony there will be a cold buffet in the garden.* □ **bufé**
3 sideboard. □ **aparador**
buffet ['bʌfit] *v.* to bang/to jolt: *the ship was buffeted by the waves.* □ **zarandear**
buffoon [bə'fu:n] *n.* fool. □ **bufón**
buffoonery *n.* foolish action. □ **payasada**
bug [bʌg] *n.* **1** small insect which sucks. □ **chinche**
2 *Amer.* any small insect. □ **bicho**
3 germ. □ **microbio**
4 *he's caught a bug from somewhere,* he's got a mild illness. □ **enfermedad leve**
5 hidden microphone. □ **micrófono oculto**
■ *v.* (*he bugged*) **1** to install a hidden microphone: *the room has been bugged.* □ **espiar con micrófono oculto**
2 *what's bugging you?,* (*informal*) what's bothering you? □ **¿qué te preocupa?**
bugbear *n.* thing which you hate. □ **pesadilla**
bugle ['bju:gl] *n.* military trumpet. □ **corneta**
bugler *n.* person who blows a bugle. □ **el corneta**
build [bild] *n.* size/shape (of person): *he is a man of very powerful build.* □ **figura**
■ *v.* (*he built: he has built*) to construct; to make by putting pieces together: *they're building a new school; the house is built on very solid foundations; he built a boat out of matchsticks.* □ **construir**

builder *n.* person who constructs (houses, etc.). □ **constructor**
building *n.* **1** constructing: *building land,* land for construction of houses. □ **construcción**
2 construction; house/office block: *hundreds of buildings were destroyed in the explosion.* □ **edificio**
building society, society which lends money to people to buy houses. □ **sociedad de préstamo inmobiliario**
build up *v.* **1** to construct; to create: *he has built up a reputation for efficiency.* □ **crearse**
2 *traffic is building up on the motorway,* is becoming greater; *pressure was building up in the kettle.* □ **aumentar**
built-in *adj.* (cupboards, etc.) which are constructed as part of the building of the house. □ **empotrado**
built-up *adj.* ***built-up area,*** area of a town where there are many buildings. □ **zona urbanizada**
bulb [bʌlb] *n.* **1** fleshy underground stem of a plant, which produces leaves and flowers in spring: *daffodils and hyacinths have bulbs.* □ **bulbo**
2 glass globe full of gas which produces light when an electric current passes through it: *a 60 watt bulb.* □ **bombilla**
bulbous *adj.* fat and rounded. □ **bulboso**
bulge [bʌldʒ] *n.* swelling: *there was an ominous bulge in his coat.* □ **bulto**
■ *v.* to swell out: *his pockets were bulging with sweets.* □ **...llenos de caramelos**
bulk [bʌlk] *n.* large quantity; size. □ **volumen**
bulk shipment/shipment in bulk, shipment of a large quantity (of a product). □ **...a granel**
bulk purchase, purchase in very large quantities. □ **compra al por mayor**
the bulk of *our sales,* most of our sales. □ **la mayor parte**
■ *v.* ***to bulk large,*** to be important; to take up a lot of room. □ **tener un puesto importante**
bulkhead *n.* dividing wall in a ship or aircraft. □ **mamparo**
bulky *adj.* (*bulkier, bulkiest*) very large/taking up an inconvenient amount of room. □ **voluminoso**
bull [bul] *n.* **1** male ox. □ **toro**
2 male of certain species: *bull elephant.* □ **macho**
3 person who believes the stock market prices will rise. □ **'bull'; alcista**
4 official pronouncement by the pope. □ **bula**
bulldog *n.* breed of squat, flatfaced dogs. □ **buldog**
bulldoze *v.* **1** to knock down/to clear using a bulldozer: *to bulldoze a path through a jungle.* □ **abrir, despejar**
2 to force: *he bulldozed his proposal through the committee,* forced them to agree to it. □ **forzar**
bulldozer *n.* large tractor with a shovel in front for moving earth. □ **excavadora**
bullfight *n.* entertainment in Spain, where a man fights a bull. □ **corrida de toros**
bullfighter *n.* man who fights bulls. □ **torero**
bullfinch *n.* small finch with a red breast. □ **pinzón real**
bullfrog *n.* large frog. □ **rana toro**
bullock *n.* castrated bull. □ **buey**
bullring *n.* arena where bullfights take place. □ **ruedo**
bull's-eye *n.* centre point of a target: *he scored a bull's-eye.* □ **diana**
bullet ['bulit] *n.* piece of metal fired from a revolver or small gun. □ **bala**
bullet-proof *adj.* (waistcoat/window, etc.) specially made so that bullets cannot pierce it. □ **a prueba de balas**
bulletin ['bulitin] *n.* piece of information; report on a situation. □ **comunicado**
news bulletin, list of news items read on the radio/television. □ **boletín informativo**
bullion ['buljən] *n.* gold or silver bars. □ **lingote**
bully ['buli] *n.* (*pl. bullies*) person who frightens people who are weaker than he is. □ **matón**
bully boys, thugs. □ **macarras**
■ *v.* (*bullies, bullying*) to intimidate (someone); to beat (someone) up. □ **intimidar**
bulrush ['bulrʌʃ] *n.* (*pl. bulrushes*) tall reed with a brown furry head. □ **junco**
bulwark ['bulwək] *n.* side of a ship which rises higher than the deck. □ **borda**
bum [bʌm] *n.* (*informal*) **1** buttocks. □ **culo**
2 *Amer.* tramp; someone who loafs about doing nothing. □ **vago**
■ *v.* (*he bummed*) ***to bum off someone,*** (*informal*) to live at someone's expense. □ **gorronear**
bumblebee ['bʌmblbi:] *n.* large furry bee. □ **abejorro**
bumf [bʌmf] *n.* (*slang*) paper (usually useless documents); toilet paper. □ **papeleo; papel higiénico**
bump [bʌmp] *n.* **1** slight shock from hitting something lightly: *the plane landed with a bump.* □ **topetón; choque**
2 small bulge on the body (from being hit): *I've got a bump on the back of my head.* □ **chichón**
■ *v.* **1** to hit something (lightly): *as he turned the corner he bumped into someone coming the other way; he reversed the car and bumped into a lamppost.* □ **chocar**
2 *I bumped into him at the station,* I met him by chance. □ **toparse**
bump off *v.* (*informal*) to murder. □ **cargarse a alguien**
bumpy *adj.* (*bumpier, bumpiest*) uneven (path/flight). □ **lleno de baches**
bumper ['bʌmpə] *n.* **1** something very large: *we've got a bumper crop of apples this year.* □ **cosecha abundante**
2 metal or rubber strip at front and rear of a car to protect it when it is hit. □ **parachoques**
bumptious ['bʌmpʃəs] *adj.* (person) full of his own importance. □ **engreído**
bun [bʌn] *n.* **1** small cake: *currant bun; sticky bun.* □ **bollo**
2 hair wound round in a knot at the back of the head. □ **moño**
bunch [bʌntʃ] *n.* (*pl. bunches*) **1** cluster (of things) tied together: *bunch of flowers; bunch of grapes/radishes; bunch of keys.* □ **ramo; racimo; manojo**
the pick of the bunch, the best out of the group. □ **la flor y nata de...**
2 group (of racing cyclists). □ **pelotón**
■ *v.* (in sport) to form a group: *the leaders in the race are all bunched together.* □ **agrupar**
bundle ['bʌndl] *n.* roughly tied parcel: *bundle of laundry; bundle of papers.* □ **lío de ropa; fajo de papeles**
■ *v.* **1** to tie (several things) together: *he bundled the papers together.* □ **atar**
2 *he bundled everything into a cupboard,* he pushed everything hurriedly into a cupboard; *she was bundled into a car.* □ **amontonar**
bung [bʌŋ] *n.* stopper; something which stops up a hole (in a cask). □ **tapón; bitoque**
■ *v.* **1** to block/to stop up a hole: *my nose is all bunged up,* my nose is blocked. □ **taponar**
2 *bung it in the wastepaper basket,* (*informal*) throw it in the wastepaper basket. □ **tíralo a la papelera**
bungalow ['bʌŋgəlou] *n.* house with only a ground floor. □ **'bungalow'**

bungle ['bʌŋgl] *v.* to do something badly: *the whole job has been bungled.* □ **chapucear**
bungler *n.* person who has done a job badly. □ **chapucero**
bungling *n.* action of doing something badly: *it's your bungling that ruined the whole deal.* □ **chapucería**
bunion ['bʌnjən] *n.* painful swelling at the base of the big toe. □ **juanete**
bunk [bʌŋk] *n.* **1** bed attached to a wall: *there are two bunks in the cabin; bunk beds,* two beds, one on top of the other. □ **litera**
2 ***to do a bunk,*** (*informal*) to run away. □ **poner pies en polvorosa**
bunker ['bʌŋkə] *n.* **1** coalhole. □ **carbonera**
2 sandy pit on a golf course. □ **bunker**
3 fortified gun emplacement. □ **bunker**
bunny ['bʌni] *n.* (*pl. bunnies*) child's name for a rabbit. □ **conejito**
bunting ['bʌntiŋ] *n.* **1** type of small singing bird. □ **pinzón**
2 (*no pl.*) strings of small flags. □ **banderas**
buoy [bɔi] *n.* floating marker showing a channel (in a river/at the entrance to a harbour). □ **boya**
■ *v.* ***to buoy someone up,*** to cheer someone. □ **animar**
buoyancy *n.* ability to float. □ **flotabilidad**
buoyancy aid, type of life jacket made of blocks of light substance, worn by yachtsmen, etc. □ **chaleco salvavidas**
buoyant *adj.* **1** which can float easily. □ **flotante**
2 full of vigour. □ **boyante**
burble ['bəːbl] *n.* low murmur. □ **murmullo**
■ *v.* to murmur softly. □ **murmurar**
burden ['bəːdn] *n.* heavy load. □ **carga**
beast of burden, animal (like a donkey) used to carry loads. □ **animal de carga**
to make someone's life a burden, to make things difficult for someone. □ **hacer la vida imposible a alguien**
■ *v.* to load: *he is burdened with crippling debts.* □ **está agobiado con...**
bureau ['bjuərou] *n.* (*pl. bureaux*) **1** office. □ **oficina**
information bureau, office which collects and hands out information. □ **oficina de...**
tourist bureau, office dealing with tourists. □ **oficina de turismo**
2 (antique) desk; *Amer.* chest of drawers. □ **cómoda**
bureaucracy [bjuə'rɔkrəsi] *n.* (*pl. bureaucracies*) rule by civil servants: *the country is run by the bureaucracy.* □ **burocracia**
bureaucrat ['bjuərəkræt] *n.* civil servant. □ **burócrata**
bureaucratic *adj.* referring to the civil service. □ **burocrático**
burgeon ['bəːdʒn] *v.* to increase rapidly. □ **desarrollarse**
burglar ['bəːglə] *n.* person who enters a house to steal. □ **ladrón**
burglar alarm, electric alarm which rings if a burglar attempts to enter the house. □ **alarma antirrobo**
burglary *n.* (*pl. burglaries*) stealing from a house. □ **robo en una casa**
burgle *v.* to steal (from a house): *the flat has been burgled.* □ **desvalijar**
burial ['beriəl] *n.* act of burying (a dead body). □ **entierro**
burial ground, cemetery. □ **cementerio**
burlesque [bəː'lesk] *adj.* and *n.* light satirical (play). □ **burlesco; obra burlesca**
■ *v.* to satirize. □ **parodiar**
burly ['bəːli] *adj.* (*burlier, burliest*) strong/solid (man). □ **corpulento**
Burma ['bəːmə] *n.* country in the Far East. □ **Birmania**
Burmese *adj.* coming from Burma. □ **birmano**
■ *n.* **1** person from Burma. □ **birmano**
2 language spoken in Burma. □ **birmano**
burn [bəːn] *n.* **1** place (on the body) which has been burnt: *his arm was covered with burns.* □ **quemadura**
2 (*in Scotland*) mountain stream. □ **arroyo**
■ *v.* (*he burnt/burned; he has burnt/burned*) **1** to destroy by fire: *he is burning rubbish in the garden; dry wood burns easily; he's burnt the sausages,* cooked them too much; *they rescued a girl from the burning house.* □ **quemar, arder**
2 *there must be someone in the house as the lights are all burning,* the lights are all on. □ **...encendidas**
3 ***to burn one's fingers:*** *he burnt his fingers,* he suffered a loss/he did not do at all as well as he expected. □ **se pilló los dedos**
4 ***to burn one's boats/bridges:*** *he's burnt his bridges,* he can't go back now. □ **ha quemado las naves**
5 to use as a fuel: *a wood-burning stove.* □ **estufa de leña**
burn down *v.* to destroy (house, etc.) by fire. □ **incendiar(se)**
burner *n.* apparatus for burning. □ **quemador**
burn out *v. the fire has burnt itself out,* the fire has gone out because there was nothing left to burn. □ **extinguirse**
burnt *adj.* which has gone black with fire: *burnt toast.* □ **quemado**
burnish ['bəːniʃ] *v.* to make (something) shine by rubbing. □ **bruñir**
burp [bəːp] *n.* noise made when bringing up gas from the stomach through the mouth. □ **eructo**
■ *v.* to make a noise by bringing up gas from the stomach through the mouth. □ **eructar**
burr [bəː] *n.* prickly part of a plant, containing seeds, which clings to clothes, etc. □ **cubierta espinosa, 'piojo de señorita'**
burrow ['bʌrou] *n.* hole in the ground where rabbits live. □ **madriguera**
■ *v.* to make a long hole underground: *the rabbits have burrowed into the hill.* □ **excavar**
bursar ['bəːsə] *n.* (*pl. bursaries*) person in charge of the finances of a school/college. □ **tesorero**
bursary *n.* scholarship/money given to a student to help him pay for his studies. □ **beca**
burst [bəːst] *n.* **1** explosion: *burst of gunfire; burst of laughter.* □ **estallido**
2 sudden attack: *a burst of effort.* □ **arranque**
3 *he put on a burst of speed,* he suddenly ran faster. □ **sprint**
■ *v.* (*he burst; he has burst*) **1** to explode/to break open: *shells were bursting all around the soldiers; the bag burst and sugar came out everywhere; he burst all the balloons with a pin.* □ **estallar**
2 *she* ***burst into*** *the room,* she rushed into the room. □ **irrumpió en ...**
3 *the boy* ***burst into tears,*** he started to cry. □ **rompió a llorar**
4 *he was bursting to tell everyone the secret,* he was dying/eagerly waiting to tell the secret. □ **se estaba muriendo por...**
burst open *v.* to come open with a bang: *the police burst open the door; the bag burst open and all the sweets fell on the floor.* □ **abrirse de golpe**

burst out *v.* to explode: *he burst out laughing in the middle of the speech.* □ **echarse a reír**

bury ['beri] *v.* (*buried; burying*) to put (something) into a hole in the ground: *the dead man was buried yesterday; the squirrel buries nuts; buried treasure.* □ **enterrar**

burying *n.* putting into the ground. □ **entierro**

bus [bʌs] *n.* (*pl. buses*) motor vehicle for carrying passengers: *buses do not always run on time; take a bus - it is cheaper than the train; I go to work by bus; he missed the last bus and had to walk home; bus stop; bus route; bus driver; school bus,* bus which takes children to school. □ **autobús**

■ *v.* (*he bussed*) to take children to school in a different part of the town in order to mix racial groups. □ **ir a otro colegio en favor de la integración racial**

busman *n.* (*pl. busmen*) **1** person who works on a bus. □ **conductor**

2 *he's taking a **busman's holiday**,* is spending his spare time doing something similar to his normal job. □ **trabajar en lo mismo en el tiempo libre**

bussing *n.* action of sending children to school in a different part of the town in order to mix racial groups. □ ***véase* bus (verbo)**

bus stop *n.* place where a bus stops regularly to let people on or off. □ **parada de autobús**

busby ['bʌzbi] *n.* tall fur hat worn by some soldiers. □ **gorro alto de piel**

bush [buʃ] *n.* (*pl. bushes*) **1** plant which is smaller than a tree: *a currant bush; rose bush.* □ **arbusto**

bush rose, rose which grows in a compact form and does not climb. □ **zarzarrosa**

2 ***the bush,*** wild uncultivated land (in Africa/Australia). □ **la sabana**

bushman *n.* (*pl. bushmen*) native of the bush. □ **bosquimano**

bushy *adj.* (*bushier, bushiest*) growing thickly: *he has bushy eyebrows.* □ **tupido**

business ['biznəs] *n.* (*businesses*) **1** affair: *it's my business to ask everyone what they are doing; it's none of your business,* it has nothing to do with you. □ **asunto**

2 commercial work: *he is in the painting business; she is going on a business trip to South America; we do business with several European countries,* we trade with several European countries. □ **negocio**

to mean business: *do you think he means business?,* do you think he is serious? □ **¿crees que habla en serio?**

3 commercial firm: *he runs a car-hire business.* □ **negocio, empresa**

businesslike *adj.* practical/serious. □ **serio**

businessman, businesswoman *n.* (*pl. businessmen/businesswomen*) person who works in a commercial company. □ **hombre/mujer de negocios**

busker ['bʌskə] *n.* person who sings/plays a musical instrument, etc., to entertain people in the street. □ **músico ambulante**

bust [bʌst] *n.* **1** sculpture of head and shoulders. □ **busto**

2 breasts: *she's got a small bust; she has a 36 inch bust,* she measures 36 inches round the breasts. □ **pecho; busto**

■ *adj.* (*informal*) broken: *the clock's bust.* □ **el reloj está hecho una porquería**

to go bust: *the firm went bust,* the firm went bankrupt. □ **quebrar**

■ *v.* (*he busted/bust*) (*informal*) to break: *my watch has bust.* □ **romperse**

bustle ['bʌsl] *n.* rushing around: *there was a great bustle in the kitchen.* □ **bullicio**

■ *v.* to rush around: *the cooks were bustling about.* □ **ir y venir**

busy ['bizi] *adj.* (*busier, busiest*) occupied with doing something: *he is busy mending the vacuum cleaner; a busy street,* street with lots of pedestrians and traffic; *the doctor is busy at the moment and can't see you.* □ **ocupado; concurrido**

busily *adv.* in a busy way: *he was busily putting pieces of paper on each desk.* □ **afanosamente**

busybody *n.* (*pl. busybodies*) person who interferes in other people's affairs. □ **entrometido**

but [bʌt] *conj., adv.* and *prep.* **1** (suggesting the opposite/a reservation): *he is tall but his sister is short; I would like to come, but I am going out with someone else that evening.* □ **pero**

2 *he is **anything but** a hero,* he is nothing like a hero. □ **es todo menos...**

3 *he is **nothing but** a little boy,* he is only a little boy. □ **es sólo un chiquillo**

4 ***but for*** *his letter, we would not have known he was here,* if it had not been for his letter. □ **de no haber sido por su carta...**

butane ['bju:tein] *n.* gas (often used for cooking or heating). □ **butano**

butcher ['butʃə] *n.* **1** person who prepares and sells meat: *to buy a pound of beef at the butcher's.* □ **carnicero**

2 ***butcher's,*** (*slang*) look: *let's have a butcher's at it.* □ **vistazo**

■ *v.* to kill in cold blood: *the soldiers butchered the prisoners.* □ **...hicieron una carnicería con...**

butchery *n.* massacre/brutal killing. □ **carnicería**

butler ['bʌtlə] *n.* main male servant who is in charge of wines and spirits in a large house. □ **mayordomo**

butt [bʌt] *n.* **1** large barrel for keeping water. □ **tonel**

2 end of a cigarette. □ **colilla**

3 handle end of a rifle. □ **culata**

4 place where you practise shooting. □ **campo de tiro**

5 person who is often teased. □ **el blanco de...**

6 push (with the head). □ **cabezazo**

■ *v.* **1** to push (someone) with your head: *the goat butted him.* □ **topar**

2 ***to butt in,*** to interrupt a conversation. □ **entrometerse**

butter ['bʌtə] *n.* solid yellow fat made from cream: *he spread some butter on his slice of bread.* □ **mantequilla**

peanut butter, paste made of crushed peanuts. □ **...de cacahuete**

■ *v.* to spread butter on (something): *I like hot buttered toast.* □ **untar con mantequilla**

to know on which side one's bread is buttered, to know where you are best looked after. □ **saber lo que a uno le conviene**

to butter someone up, to flatter someone. □ **hacer la pelota a...**

buttercup *n.* common bright yellow wild flower. □ **ranúnculo**

butterfingers *n.* person who can't catch/who drops things. □ **manazas**

butterfly *n.* (*pl. butterflies*) insect with brightly coloured wings. □ **mariposa**

butterscotch *n.* sweet made from butter and sugar. □ **caramelo de mantequilla**

buttock(s) ['bʌtək(s)] *n.* fleshy part of the body which you sit on: *he had an injection in his right buttock.* □ **nalga; culo**

button ['bʌtn] *n.* small round object stitched to

clothes for attaching one part of clothing to another: *you have two buttons undone; do up all your buttons.* □ **botón**

button mushroom, small round mushroom which is not fully grown. □ **champiñón pequeño**

■ *v.* to attach with buttons: *this dress buttons down the back; button up your coat.* □ **abrocharse**

buttonhole *n.* **1** hole for putting a button through. □ **ojal**

2 flower stuck in the hole in a lapel. □ **flor en el ojal**

■ *v. **to buttonhole someone,*** to trap someone and talk to them at length. □ **enganchar**

buttress ['bʌtrəs] *n.* supporting pillar (reinforcing a wall). □ **contrafuerte**

■ *v.* to support. □ **apuntalar**

butty ['bʌti] *n.* (*pl. butties*) (*slang*) sandwich. □ **bocata**

buxom ['bʌksəm] *adj.* fat and attractive (woman). □ **rolliza**

buy [bai] *v.* (*he bought: he has bought*) to get by paying money: *I bought three apples on my way home; he bought a car from my brother.* □ **comprar**

■ *n.* something which you have bought/which you might buy: *that's a good buy,* a bargain. □ **compra**

buyer *n.* person who buys, especially person who buys stock for a large store. □ **comprador**

buy out *v.* to buy a partner's share in a business. □ **comprar la parte de un socio**

buzz [bʌz] *n.* (*pl. buzzes*) noise like a bee: *there was a buzz of conversation in the room.* □ **zumbido**

■ *v.* **1** to make a noise like a bee: *bees were buzzing round the flowers.* □ **zumbar**

2 (of aircraft) to fly close to another aircraft to force it to go away. □ **pasar rozando**

buzzer *n.* device which makes a buzzing noise. □ **zumbador**

buzzing *n.* noise like a bee: *I can hear the buzzing of the bees.* □ **zumbido**

buzz off *v.* (*informal*) to go away. □ **largarse; pirarse**

buzzard ['bʌzəd] *n.* kind of bird of prey. □ **águila ratonera**

by [bai] *prep.* **1** near: *the house is right by the railway line; by the sea, the weather is often cooler than inland.* □ **junto a**

2 before: *be sure to get there by four o'clock; we have to finish by next Tuesday.* □ **antes de**

3 using: *send the letter by airmail; are you coming by car? what time is it by your watch?* □ **por avión; ...en coche**

4 *a painting by Rembrandt,* which Rembrandt painted; *a play by Shakespeare,* which Shakespeare wrote; *a song by the school choir,* which the choir sang/will sing. □ **de; por**

5 ***by yourself,*** alone: *I'm all by myself; he did it by himself.* □ **solo; por sí solo/mismo**

■ *adv.* **1** near: *I was standing close by.* □ **cerca**

2 ***put** some money **by** for a rainy day,* put money to one side/save money. □ **aparta algo de dinero...**

3 past: *he drove by without stopping.* □ **pasó conduciendo sin detenerse**

by-election *n.* election to fill a place left vacant by the death/resignation of a representative. □ **elección parcial**

bygone *adj.* past/former: *in bygone times.* □ **pasado**

■ *n.* thing which comes from the past. □ **cosa pasada**

let bygones be bygones, forget past insults. □ **lo pasado, pasado está**

by-law *n.* law which is passed by a municipal council, etc. □ **ordenanza municipal**

bypass *n.* (*pl. bypasses*) road which goes round a town. □ **carretera de circunvalación**

■ *v.* to go round (a town), avoiding the centre; to avoid (something) by going round it. □ **circunvalar**

by-product *n.* secondary product made as a result of manufacturing something else: *tar is a by-product of oil refining.* □ **subproducto**

by-road *n.* small local road. □ **carretera comarcal**

bystander *n.* person standing near the scene of action. □ **espectador**

byword *n.* famous example: *he is a byword for hard work.* □ **prototipo**

bye [bai] *n.* (*in cricket*) run scored without the batsman having hit the ball. □ **punto; tanto**

to have a bye, to pass to the next round of a sporting tournament without having to play. □ **pasar directamente a la segunda eliminatoria**

bye(-bye) [bai(bai)] *interjection* used when leaving someone. □ **¡adiós!**

bye for now, (*informal*) goodbye until we meet again. □ **hasta ahora**

C,c

C, c [siː] third letter of the alphabet. □ **C, c**
cab [kæb] *n.* taxi. □ **taxi**
cab-driver *n.* person who drives a taxi. □ **taxista**
cabaret ['kæbərei] *n.* entertainment (such as singing or telling jokes) given in a restaurant or club. □ **cabaret**
cabbage ['kæbidʒ] *n.* green leafy vegetable: *boiled cabbage.* □ **col, repollo**
red cabbage, variety of cabbage with red leaves. □ **lombarda**
cabbage white, common type of white butterfly, of which the caterpillars eat cabbages. □ **mariposa de la col**
cabin ['kæbin] *n.* **1** small room on a ship: *two berth cabin,* cabin for two people. □ **camarote**
2 small hut. □ **cabaña**
3 interior of an aircraft. □ **cabina**
cabin crew, air hostesses and stewards. □ **tripulación**
cabinet ['kæbinət] *n.* **1** piece of furniture with shelves: *kitchen cabinet.* □ **armario**
china cabinet, cabinet with shelves and glass doors for displaying rare china. □ **vitrina**
2 central committee of ministers in a government: *cabinet meeting,* meeting of the cabinet. □ **gabinete**
shadow cabinet, committee formed by the main opposition party to parallel the actual cabinet. □ **gabinete en la sombra**
cable ['keibl] *n.* **1** thick rope/wire. □ **cable**
2 telegraph wire for sending messages under the sea: *send us a cable when you arrive,* send us a message by telegraph. □ **telegrama**
■ *v.* to send a message by telegraph: *he cabled that he would be late.* □ **cablegrafiar**
cacao [kə'kɑːou] *n.* tropical tree, of which the seeds provide cocoa and chocolate. □ **cacao**
cache [kæʃ] *n.* hidden store: *the police found a cache of arms in the loft.* □ **escondrijo**
cackle ['kækl] *n.* noise made by hens. □ **cacareo**
cut the cackle, (*slang*) stop chattering. □ **corta el rollo**
■ *v.* to chatter: *the hens were cackling.* □ **cacarear**
cackling *n.* noise made by hens. □ **cacareo**
cactus ['kæktəs] *n.* (*pl. cacti*) prickly plant which grows in the desert. □ **cactus**
cad [kæd] *n.* unpleasant/dishonest person. □ **sinvergüenza**
cadaverous [kə'dævərəs] *adj.* looking like a corpse. □ **cadavérico**
caddie ['kædi] *n.* person who carries the clubs for a golfer. □ **caddie**
caddis fly ['kædisflai] *n.* insect living near water. □ **frígano**
caddy ['kædi] *n.* box for keeping tea in. □ **cajita para el té**
cadence ['keidəns] *n.* rhythm (of music/poetry). □ **cadencia**
cadet [kə'det] *n.* young person training for the armed services. □ **cadete**
cadge [kædʒ] *v.* to scrounge/to try to get something without having to pay for it. □ **gorronear**
cadmium ['kædmiəm] *n.* (*chemical element*: Cd) grey metal which can be poisonous to human beings. □ **cadmio**
caesarean [si'zɛəriən] *n.* operation on a pregnant woman to deliver her baby through the wall of the womb: *she had a caesarean; her baby was born by caesarean.* □ **cesárea**
café ['kæfei] *n.* small restaurant where you can eat snacks or light meals, but which does not serve alcoholic drinks. □ **café**
cafeteria [kæfi'tiəriə] *n.* self-service restaurant. □ **restaurante de autoservicio**
caffeine ['kæfiːn] *n.* stimulating substance found in coffee and tea. □ **cafeína**
cage [keidʒ] *n.* enclosure of wire or with metal bars for keeping birds or animals: *I think it's wrong to keep tigers in cages.* □ **jaula**
■ *v.* to put in a cage. □ **enjaular**
caged birds, birds (like budgerigars/canaries) which are kept in cages. □ **pájaros enjaulados**
cagey ['keidʒi] *adj.* secretive/unwilling to reveal something: *he is cagey about his real salary.* □ **reservado**
cahoots [kə'huːts] *n.* ***to be in cahoots with someone,*** (*informal*) to work with someone, against another person. □ **estar conchabado con...**
cairn [kɛən] *n.* heap of stones to mark an important spot. □ **mojón**
cajole [kə'dʒoul] *v.* to persuade someone by flattering: *they tried to cajole him into agreeing to lend them money.* □ **engatusar**
cake [keik] *n.* **1** cooked food made of eggs, flour and sugar, usually eaten cold: *birthday cake,* cake specially made to celebrate someone's birthday; *Christmas cake.* □ **tarta, pastel**
it's a piece of cake, (*slang*) it is very easy. □ **está chupado**
you can't have your cake and eat it, you can't benefit from two quite opposite things. □ **no se puede estar en misa y repicando**
fish cake/potato cake, cake made from cooked fish/potatoes. □ **pastel de pescado, etc...**
2 block of soap. □ **pastilla de jabón**
■ *v.* **1** to form a dry crust: *the mud was caked on his boots.* □ **apelmazarse**
2 *he came back from the rugby game caked with mud,* covered with dried mud. □ **con barro hasta las orejas**
calamine ['kæləmain] *n.* ***calamine lotion,*** pink liquid put on skin to soothe and stop itching. □ **calamina**
calamity [kə'læmiti] *n.* disaster. □ **calamidad**
calamitous *adj.* very unfortunate/disastrous. □ **calamitoso**
calcium ['kælsiəm] *n.* (*chemical element*: Ca) grey metal; white substance found in water, lime, etc., and which forms bones. □ **calcio**
calculate ['kælkjuleit] *v.* **1** to work out (a sum); to estimate (quite accurately): *I calculated that we had spent more on food than on petrol; have you calculated the distance between here and London?* □ **calcular**
2 *calculated insult,* deliberate insult. □ **insulto intencionado**
calculable *adj.* which can be calculated. □ **calculable**
calculation [kælkju'leiʃn] *n.* sum: *according to my calculations he owes us $10.* □ **cálculo**
calculator *n.* electronic machine for doing sums: *can you work out these percentages on your calculator? a pocket calculator.* □ **calculadora**
calculus *n.* mathematical way of calculating. □ **cálculo**

caldron ['kɔldrən] *n. Amer. see* **cauldron.**
□ **caldera**
calendar ['kælendə] *n.* sheet showing the days and months of a year: *I have a calendar pinned up on the wall of my office.* □ **calendario**
calf [kɑ:f] *n.* (*pl. calves*) **1** young cow/bull; young (of elephant, etc.): *the calves were lying in the grass.* □ **ternero**
2 leather (from cow's skin). □ **cuero**
3 fleshy back part of the leg above the ankle and below the knee. □ **pantorrilla**
calibre ['kælibə] *Amer.* **caliber** *n.* **1** interior diameter of a gun: *22 mm calibre gun.* □ **calibre**
2 standing/intellectual ability: *he does not earn much for a man of his calibre.* □ **...de su calibre**
calibrate *v.* to mark degrees on a thermometer/to mark units on a scale. □ **calibrar**
caliph *n.* title once used by some Moslem rulers who were successors of Muhammad. □ **califa**
call [kɔ:l] *n.* **1** shout/cry: *did you hear a call for help? bird call,* song of a bird; *the call of an owl; lunch is ready - give your father a call,* shout to him; *I want a call at 7 o'clock,* I want to be woken at 7 o'clock. □ **llamada**
to be on call, to be available at all times. □ **estar disponible**
2 conversation on the telephone: *I have to make a call to New York; long distance call; local calls do not cost much.* □ **llamada**
3 visit: *we must pay a call on the vicar.* □ **hacer una visita**
■ *v.* **1** to shout: *I called to her across the street; the drowning man was calling for help; can you call me at 7 o'clock?,* can you wake me at 7 o'clock? *can you call me a taxi?/ can you call a taxi for me?,* can you hail a taxi? □ **llamar**
2 to telephone: *call the doctor - she looks very ill; I called you yesterday but there was no answer.* □ **llamar por teléfono**
3 to give someone a name: *his son is called Peter; they called their dog Pablo; they live in a house called 'The Gables'; Tolstoy called his book 'War and Peace'.* □ **llamar**
4 to visit: *I must call at the baker's on my way home; the doctor called on my mother this afternoon; the cruise ship calls at Bermuda.* □ **pasar; visitar; hacer escala**
call back *v.* **1** to telephone in reply; to telephone again: *I will call you back tomorrow; can you call back in half an hour?* □ **volver a llamar**
2 to come back: *I will call back to fetch the piano tomorrow.* □ **volver**
callbox *n.* street telephone box. □ **cabina telefónica**
callboy *n.* **1** young man in a theatre who tells performers when it is time for them to go on stage. □ **traspunte**
2 young man in a hotel who runs messages. □ **botones**
caller *n.* **1** person who comes to visit. □ **visita**
2 person who telephones. □ **usuario**
call for *v.* **1** *he called for help,* he shouted to ask for help. □ **pedir**
2 ***to call for someone,*** to go to someone's house to collect them. □ **ir a recoger a alguien**
3 to need/to require: *this calls for a government inquiry.* □ **exigir**
call-girl *n.* prostitute who can be called by telephone. □ **prostituta**
call in *v.* to shout to someone to make them come in. □ **hacer pasar**
calling *n.* vocation; job. □ **vocación; profesión**
call off *v.* to cancel: *they called off the meeting.* □ **cancelar**
call on *v.* **1** to visit. □ **visitar**
2 to appeal to someone: *I call on you for your support.* □ **acudir**
call out *v.* to shout. □ **gritar**
call up *v.* **1** to telephone. □ **telefonear**
2 to mobilize troops: *he was called up at the beginning of the war.* □ **movilizar**
call-up *n.* mobilization. □ **movilización**
call-up papers, documents telling you to join your regiment/ship, etc. □ **documentos de incorporación a filas**
calligraphy [kə'ligrəfi] *n.* art of fine handwriting. □ **caligrafía**
callipers ['kælipəz] *n. pl.* **1** instrument for measuring the diameter of something round (like a pipe). □ **calibrador**
2 metal frame to support the legs of a handicapped or injured person. □ **aparato ortopédico**
callous ['kæləs] *adj.* hard/unfeeling. □ **insensible**
callously *adv.* cruelly. □ **cruelmente**
calm [kɑ:m] *adj.* quiet; not rough: *the sea is very calm tonight.* □ **calmado**
■ *n.* period of quiet. □ **calma**
■ *v.* to become/to make quiet: *the storm calmed down; she succeeded in calming him down.* □ **calmar(se)**
calmness *n.* period of quiet. □ **calma**
calorie ['kæləri] *n.* measure of heat/of energy-giving value of food: *you really only need to consume 2,000 calories per day.* □ **caloría**
calumny ['kæləmni] *n.* lie/false statement. □ **calumnia**
calumniate *v.* to tell lies about someone. □ **calumniar**
calve [kɑ:v] *v.* to give birth to a calf. □ **parir**
■ *n. see* **calf.**
calypso [kə'lipsou] *n.* type of topical song sung in the West Indies. □ **calipso**
calyx ['kæliks] *n.* outer covering of a flower bud. □ **cáliz**
camber ['kæmbə] *n.* **1** bend/curve (in a surface). □ **combadura**
2 *the camber of a road,* the way in which the road slopes. □ **el peralte de la carretera**
cambered *adj.* sloping/rounded (surface). □ **combado**
came [keim] *v. see* **come.**
camel ['kæml] *n.* desert animal with one or two humps, used for riding. □ **camello**
camel-hair *n.* thick pale brown wool, used for making coats, etc. □ **pelo de camello**
camellia [kə'mi:liə] *n.* evergreen bush with pink or white flowers. □ **camelia**
cameo ['kæmiou] *n.* **1** small stone with a design of a head which stands out. □ **camafeo**
2 small but sharply defined part in a play/film: *a cameo role.* □ **papel breve, 'cameo'**
camera ['kæmərə] *n.* **1** machine for taking photographs.□ **cámara**
cine camera, machine for taking moving films: *she objected to undressing in front of the cameras,* in front of the cine cameras. □ **cámara**
2 *the case will be heard in camera,* in closed session/in secret. □ **...a puerta cerrada**
cameraman *n.* (*pl. cameramen*) man who operates a cine camera. □ **cámara**
camomile ['kæməmail] *n.* fragrant plant, of which

the dried flowers are used for making hot drinks. □ **manzanilla**

camouflage ['kæməflɑːʒ] *n.* hiding something by means of colouring, so that it is difficult to see against the background: *the zebra's stripes are a form of camouflage.* □ **camuflaje**

■ *v.* to hide something so that it is difficult to distinguish it against the background: *the tanks were camouflaged with branches.* □ **camuflar**

camp [kæmp] *n.* place where people live in tents or cabins in the open: *army camp; to pitch camp,* to set up tents. □ **campamento**

to strike camp, to take down tents. □ **levantar el campamento**

camp bed, folding bed. □ **catre de tijera**

camp fire, bonfire round which campers sit at night. □ **fuego de campamento**

holiday camp, place where people spend holidays in cabins and enjoy organized entertainment. □ **campamento de verano**

■ *v.* to live (on holiday) in a tent: *we always go camping in the summer; the refugees camped out in the desert.* □ **ir de cámping; acampar**

■ *adj.* in an affected (often humorously homosexual) style. □ **amanerado**

camper *n.* **1** person who lives in a tent or caravan. □ **campista**

2 *Amer.* small van equipped with beds, tables, cooking facilities, etc. □ **caravana**

camping *n.* going on holiday with a tent or caravan: *camping equipment; camping site,* area specially laid out for tents and caravans. □ **cámping**

campsite *n.* area specially laid out for tents and caravans. □ **cámping**

campaign [kæm'pein] *n.* **1** organized military movement: *the campaign in the North African desert.* □ **campaña**

2 organized method of working: *we are running a publicity campaign for our new brand of soap,* general organization of publicity; *political campaign/election campaign,* organized appeal to voters at the time of an election; *campaign to prevent a new airport being built; campaign for more money for schools.* □ **campaña**

■ *v.* **1** to take part in a war: *the battalion campaigned in North Africa.* □ **hacer una campaña**

2 to work in an organized fashion to achieve an end: *she's campaigning for equal pay; they are campaigning to prevent the airport being built; the party is campaigning on the theme of stability,* is appealing to voters to vote for their candidates as promoters of stability. □ **hacer una campaña**

camphor ['kæmfə] *n.* strong smelling substance which comes from certain trees. □ **alcanfor**

camphor balls, small white balls impregnated with camphor which prevent moths from attacking clothes. □ **bolas de...**

campus [kæmpəs] *n.* land on which a university/polytechnic is built: *the students mainly live on (the) campus.* □ **campus**

camshaft ['kæmʃɑːft] *n.* (*in an engine*) shaft with projecting rings which open and close pistons in turn. □ **árbol de levas**

can [kæn] *n.* **1** round metal box for preserving food or drink: *open a can of beer; there were empty cans all over the floor.* □ **lata; bote**

2 *watering can,* bucket with a long spout for watering plants. □ **regadera**

■ *v.* **1** (*I/he can;* negative *cannot;* short form *can't;* past *I/he could;* negative *could not;* short form *couldn't*) able to do something/knowing how to do something: *can you swim? can you hold your breath for a minute? it is so dark I can't see anything; it was so dark, he couldn't see anything.* □ **poder; saber**

2 *can I leave the room please?,* will you give me permission to leave the room? □ **puedo...**

3 (*he canned*) to put fruit/vegetables, etc., into cans to preserve them for sale: *canning factory.* □ **enlatar**

canned *adj.* in a metal box: *canned peas; I only have canned beer, not bottles.* □ **en lata; enlatado**

canned music, recorded music. □ **música grabada**

Canada ['kænədə] *n.* country in North America, north of the United States. □ **Canadá**

Canadian [kə'neidjən] *adj.* referring to Canada. □ **canadiense**

■ *n.* person from Canada. □ **canadiense**

canal [kə'næl] *n.* artificial waterway: *the Suez Canal; the Panama Canal.* □ **canal**

canary [kə'nɛəri] *n.* small yellow singing bird. □ **canario**

cancel ['kænsl] *v.* (*he cancelled*) **1** to stop something which had been planned: *my train has been cancelled; we have cancelled the dinner party.* □ **cancelar**

2 to cross out a postage stamp with a rubber stamp. □ **matar**

3 *the two forces* ***cancel each other out,*** are equal and, therefore, neither can win. □ **anular**

cancellation [kænsə'leiʃn] *n.* act of cancelling; seat/ticket which is on sale because a purchaser cannot use it. □ **anulación**

cancer ['kænsə] *n.* **1** disease of the blood or tissue: *lung cancer; cancer research,* research into possible cures for cancer; *he died of cancer.* □ **cáncer**

2 *Cancer,* one of the signs of the Zodiac, shaped like a crab. □ **Cáncer**

Tropic of Cancer, imaginary line 23° north of the equator. □ **Trópico de Cáncer**

cancerous *adj.* referring to cancer: *a cancerous growth.* □ **canceroso**

candid ['kændid] *adj.* frank/open: *I want you to give me your candid opinion.* □ **sincero**

candidly *adv.* in a frank way/honestly: *candidly, I don't think he will win the election.* □ **sinceramente**

candidate ['kændidət] *n.* person standing for election; person who has entered for a competition/an examination: *the socialist candidate for our constituency; candidates should write their names at the top of the paper.* □ **candidato**

candidature *n.* act of standing as a candidate. □ **candidatura**

candied ['kændid] *adj.* dried and sugared: *candied peel,* dried orange/lemon peel. □ **escarchado**

candle ['kændl] *n.* stick of wax with a wick in the centre: *she lit/blew out the candles on the birthday cake; candles were once used for lighting, but now they are mainly decorative.* □ **vela**

to burn the candle at both ends, to work hard during the day and enjoy yourself late into the night. □ **trabajar mucho de día y trasnochar**

candlelight *n.* light from a candle: *during the electricity strike we had to work by candlelight.* □ **luz de una vela**

candlelit *adj.* lit by candles. □ **con luz de vela**

candlestick *n.* wood/metal holder for a candle. □ **candelabro**

candlewick *n.* cotton material for bedcovers, with patterns of tufts. □ **tela guateada**

candour ['kændə] *Amer.* **candor** *n.* frankness/openness. □ **franqueza**

candy ['kændi] *n. Amer.* sweet. □ **caramelo**

candy store, sweet shop. □ **confitería**

candyfloss *n.* molten sugar spun to make a fluffy mass. □ **algodón de azúcar**
candy-striped *adj.* with stripes of colour on a white background like certain sweets. □ **a rayas**
cane [kein] *n.* **1** stem (especially of jointed plants like bamboo): *raspberry cane; sugar cane.* □ **caña**
2 stick (cut from such plants): *tie your tomato plants to canes; the officer carried a short cane.* □ **caña; vara**
■ *v.* to hit with a cane: *the boy was caned by the headmaster.* □ **pegar con la palmeta**
caning *n.* beating with a cane. □ **castigo con la palmeta**
canine ['keinain] *adj.* referring to dogs. □ **canino**
■ *n.* round pointed tooth: *each person has four canines.* □ **canino**
canister ['kænistə] *n.* round metal box. □ **lata redonda**
canker ['kæŋkə] *n.* disease/sore which eats into flesh/into wood of trees. □ **llaga gangrenosa/cancro (en un árbol)**
cannabis ['kænəbis] *n.* plant which can be smoked to give a pleasant feeling of relaxation. □ **cáñamo**
cannibal ['kænibl] *n.* person who eats people: *he was killed and eaten by cannibals.* □ **caníbal**
cannibalism *n.* custom of eating people. □ **canibalismo**
cannibalize *v.* to take pieces of old machinery to repair another machine. □ **aprovechar piezas de repuesto ya usadas en otra parte**
cannon ['kænən] *n.* **1** (*no pl.*) large gun; gun in an aircraft. □ **cañón**
2 (*in billiards*) hitting of one ball off the other two. □ **carambola**
■ *v.* to bounce off (another ball/the cushion); to bump into something. □ **chocar**
cannonball *n.* large metal ball fired by a cannon. □ **bala de cañón**
cannot ['kænət] *v. see* **can.**
canny ['kæni] *adj.* wise/clever. □ **astuto**
canoe [kə'nuː] *n.* boat propelled by one or more people with paddles: *Indian canoe.* □ **canoa**
■ *v.* (*he canoed*) to travel in a canoe. □ **ir en canoa**
canoeing *n.* sport of going in a canoe. □ **piragüismo**
canoeist *n.* person who paddles a canoe. □ **piragüista**
canon ['kænən] *n.* **1** religious rule or instructions. □ **canon**
canon law, the church's laws. □ **derecho canónico**
2 clergyman attached to a cathedral. □ **canónigo**
canonize *v.* to declare someone a saint: *St Bernadette was canonized in 1933.* □ **canonizar**
canopy ['kænəpi] *n.* small roof over a platform/balcony, etc. □ **dosel**
cant [kænt] *n.* **1** hypocrisy/insincere language. □ **hipocresía**
2 jargon/language of a certain group of people: *thieves' cant.* □ **jerga**
can't [kɑːnt] *v. see* **can.**
cantankerous [kæn'tæŋkrəs] *adj.* bad-tempered. □ **malhumorado**
cantankerousness *n.* continual bad temper. □ **malhumor**
cantata [kæn'tɑːtə] *n.* musical piece for several voices and orchestra (usually on a religious theme). □ **cantata**
canteen [kæn'tiːn] *n.* **1** private self-service restaurant: *works' canteen; I am going to have a cup of coffee in the canteen.* □ **cantina**
2 *canteen of cutlery,* wooden box containing knives, forks and spoons. □ **cubertería**
3 portable flask for water. □ **cantimplora**
canter ['kæntə] *n.* **1** gentle gallop. □ **medio galope**
2 *the horse won* ***at a canter,*** won easily. □ **...ganó holgadamente**
■ *v.* to go at a gentle gallop. □ **ir a medio galope**
to canter home, to win easily. □ **ganar con facilidad**
cantilever ['kæntiliːvə] *n.* projecting support which holds up a balcony/a bridge. □ **voladizo**
cantilevered *adj.* held up by a cantilever. □ **en voladizo**
canvas ['kænvəs] *n.* **1** thick cloth (for making tents/sails, or for painting on). □ **lona, lienzo**
2 *holiday* ***under canvas,*** camping holiday. □ **...en tienda de campaña**
3 *a canvas by Rembrandt,* a painting by Rembrandt. □ **lienzo**
canvass ['kænvəs] *v.* to try to persuade people to vote for someone/to buy something: *the candidates are out canvassing; I'm canvassing support for a petition against the new road.* □ **solicitar votos de...**
canvasser *n.* person who goes from door to door to persuade people to vote for a political candidate. □ **agente electoral**
canvassing *n.* going from door to door to persuade people to vote: *canvassing is only allowed in the three weeks before an election.* □ **campaña electoral**
canyon ['kænjən] *n.* (*in America*) large valley with perpendicular sides: *the Grand Canyon.* □ **cañón**
cap [kæp] *n.* **1** hat with a peak: *soldier's cap; jockey's cap; he was wearing a cloth cap.* □ **gorra**
cap and gown, hat and robes worn by graduates of a university. □ **toga y bonete**
2 top/cover: *cap on a bottle/a bottle cap; he unscrewed the cap on his pen.* □ **chapa; capuchón**
3 small piece of paper with gunpowder: *this toy pistol fires caps.* □ **pistón**
■ *v.* (*he capped*) **1** to top with a cap: *to cap a pipe,* to fix a cover on a pipe to stop it leaking; *to cap an oil well.* □ **recubrir**
2 to name someone to a national side (in football/rugby/cricket): *he has been capped six times for England.* □ **seleccionar**
3 to surpass/to do better than: *I can cap that,* I can do better than that. □ **superar**
capable ['keipəbl] *adj.* competent/able: *he's a capable worker; is he capable of really hard work?* can he work really hard? □ **capaz**
capability [keipə'biliti] *n.* ability: *it is quite above his capabilities,* it is too difficult for him to do. □ **capacidad**
capably *adv.* competently/efficiently. □ **competentemente**
capacity [kə'pæsiti] *n.* **1** amount which a container can hold: *what is the capacity of this tank?* □ **capacidad**
2 *seating capacity,* number of seats (in a bus/cinema, etc.). □ **capacidad; aforo**
3 *engine capacity,* power of an engine. □ **cilindrada**
4 ability to do something: *his capacity for work.* □ **capacidad de trabajo**
5 position: *I am speaking to you in my capacity as manager.* □ **...en calidad de...**
capacitor *n.* device for storing an electric charge. □ **condensador**
capacious [kə'peiʃəs] *n.* very large/which contains a lot: *a capacious suitcase.* □ **espacioso**
cape [keip] *n.* **1** long cloak. □ **capa**
2 headland jutting into the sea. □ **cabo**
Cape Horn, the tip of South America. □ **Cabo de Hornos**
Cape of Good Hope, southern tip of Africa. □ **Cabo de Buena Esperanza**

caper ['keipə] *n.* **1** jumping/leaping. □ **cabriola**
2 small bitter seed used in cooking. □ **alcaparra**
3 (*informal*) trick: *that's an old caper.* □ **truco**
■ *v.* to jump/to leap: *he capered about all over the place.* □ **brincar**

capillary [kə'piləri] *adj.* and *n.* very thin (tube); very thin blood vessel. □ **capilar**
capillary attraction, physical phenomenon where water is drawn up a thin tube. □ **capilaridad**

capital ['kæpitl] *n.* **1** decorated stone on the top of a column. □ **capitel**
2 large letter: *a capital A; write your name in capitals.* □ **letra mayúscula**
3 main city of a country/a state, etc.: *Paris is the capital of France; a provincial capital.* □ **capital**
4 money which is invested: *he has put all his capital into the shop.* □ **capital**
5 ***capital punishment,*** execution/legal killing of a criminal. □ **pena capital**
■ *adj.* very important: *capital error.* □ **capital**
capitalism *n.* economic system based on ownership of resources by individuals or companies and not by the state. □ **capitalismo**
capitalist *adj.* and *n.* (person) who supports the theory of capitalism; businessman: *the capitalist system.* □ **capitalista**
capitalization [kæpitəlai'zeiʃn] *n.* amount of capital invested in a company. □ **capitalización**
capitalize ['kæpitəlaiz] *v.* **1** (*of a company*) to have money invested in it: *the company is capitalized at $10,000.* □ **capitalizar**
2 *the company is **under-capitalized,*** has insufficient capital. □ **descapitalizada**
3 to take advantage of something: *he capitalized on his opponent's weakness.* □ **sacar provecho de**

capitation [kæpi'teiʃn] *n.* amount of money allowed to a school for spending on books and equipment for each pupil. □ **asignación por cabeza**

capitulate [kə'pitjuleit] *v.* to give in/to surrender. □ **capitular**
capitulation [kəpitju'leiʃn] *n.* surrendering. □ **capitulación**

capon ['keipɒn] *n.* fat castrated chicken. □ **capón**

caprice [kə'pri:s] *n.* whim/sudden fancy. □ **capricho**
capricious [kə'priʃəs] *adj.* whimsical/prone to change your mind. □ **caprichoso**
capriciousness *n.* tendency to change your mind suddenly. □ **antojo; capricho**

Capricorn ['kæprikɔ:n] *n.* one of the signs of the Zodiac, shaped like a goat. □ **Capricornio**
Tropic of Capricorn, imaginary line 23° south of the equator. □ **Trópico de Capricornio**

capsize [kæp'saiz] *v.* (of boats) to turn over: *the boat capsized in the storm.* □ **zozobrar**

capstan ['kæpstən] *n.* machine which turns to haul in a rope or anchor. □ **cabrestante**

capsule ['kæpsju:l] *n.* enclosed case; small case for a dose of medicine which melts when swallowed: *he swallowed two capsules of antihistamine.* □ **cápsula**
space capsule, living compartment in a space rocket. □ **cápsula espacial**

captain ['kæptn] *n.* **1** officer in charge of a ship or aircraft: *Captain Jones; the captain is on the bridge.* □ **capitán**
2 rank in the army above lieutenant; rank in the navy above commander. □ **capitán**
3 leader of a sports team: *the English captain; Evans has been selected as captain of the Welsh team.* □ **capitán**
■ *v.* to lead (an expedition/a team): *he has captained England on three occasions.* □ **capitanear**
captaincy *n.* **1** rank of captain (in army/navy). □ **capitanía**
2 post of leader of a sports team. □ **puesto de capitán**

caption ['kæpʃn] *n.* phrase printed beneath a picture: *the photograph has the caption 'Too late?'* □ **pie**

captivate ['kæptiveit] *v.* to charm/to seduce. □ **cautivar**

captive ['kæptiv] *n.* prisoner: *the guerrillas took three soldiers captive; he was held captive by the guerrillas.* □ **cautivo**
captivity [kæp'tiviti] *n.* **1** imprisonment. □ **cautividad**
2 *animals in captivity,* animals in zoos. □ **cautividad**
captor *n.* person who captures someone. □ **capturador**

capture ['kæptʃə] *n.* taking of someone/something captive: *the capture of the enemy fortress.* □ **captura, toma**
■ *v.* **1** to take someone/something captive: *they captured six enemy tanks.* □ **capturar**
2 *they have captured 10% of the market,* they have taken 10% of the possible sales. □ **se han hecho con...**

car [kɑ:] *n.* **1** private motor vehicle: *I have parked my car outside the bank; he was driving his wife's car.* □ **coche**
car park, special parking place for cars. □ **aparcamiento**
2 railway wagon. □ **vagón**
dining car, railway carriage for eating in. □ **coche restaurante**
buffet car, railway carriage with a self-service buffet. □ **...cafetería autoservicio**
sleeping car, railway carriage with separate bedrooms for travellers. □ **coche cama**
carport *n.* shelter for a car. □ **cobertizo**
carsick *adj.* feeling ill when travelling by motor vehicle: *he gets carsick.* □ **mareado**

carafe [kə'ræf] *n.* glass jar for serving wine. □ **frasca**

caramel ['kærəmel] *n.* **1** sweet made with sugar and butter. □ **caramelo (con leche)**
2 sugar which has been melted. □ **azúcar quemada**
caramel custard, pudding of egg custard topped with browned sugar. □ **flan al caramelo**

carat ['kærət] *n.* **1** measure for purity of gold: *18-carat gold.* □ **quilate**
2 weight of a diamond: *18-carat diamond.* □ **quilate**

caravan ['kærəvæn] *n.* **1** shelter on wheels, with beds, table, washing facilities, etc., which can be towed by a car: *we are taking the caravan to Scotland this year.* □ **caravana**
2 group of vehicles/animals travelling together (especially across a desert). □ **caravana**
caravanning *n.* going on holiday in a caravan. □ **ir de vacaciones con la caravana**

caraway ['kærəwei] *n.* spicy seed used to flavour cakes and biscuits. □ **alcaravea**

carbohydrate [kɑ:bou'haidreit] *n.* chemical substance containing carbon, hydrogen and oxygen: *she eats too many carbohydrates,* too much fattening food. □ **hidrato de carbono**

carbolic [kɑ:'bɒlik] *adj.* referring to an acid used to disinfect: *carbolic soap.* □ **carbólico**

carbon ['kɑ:bən] *n.* (*chemical element*: C) substance found in charcoal, soot, diamonds. □ **carbono**
carbon dioxide, colourless gas (CO_2) in the atmosphere. □ **anhídrido carbónico**
carbon monoxide, colourless poisonous gas (CO) in the atmosphere, also present in car exhaust fumes. □ **monóxido de carbono**

carbon paper, paper with black substance on one side, used to make copies in typing. □ **papel carbón**
carbon copy, identical copy. □ **copia**
carbonate *n.* salt of carbonic acid. □ **carbonato**
carbonic [kɑ:'bɔnik] *adj* ***carbonic acid,*** acid formed when carbon dioxide is dissolved in water. □ **ácido carbónico**
carboniferous [kɑ:bə'nifərəs] *adj.* coal-bearing. ***the Carboniferous period,*** prehistoric period when jungle flourished which later formed coal seams. □ **carbonífero**
carbonize *v.* to make into carbon; to burn up. □ **carbonizar**

carboy ['kɑ:bɔi] *n.* very large glass container for carrying liquids. □ **bombona**

carbuncle ['kɑ:bʌŋkl] *n.* **1** red precious stone. □ **carbúnculo**
2 large inflamed spot on the skin. □ **carbunco**

carburettor [kɑ:bə'retə] *n.* device in a car for changing liquid petrol into vapour. □ **carburador**

carcase/carcass ['kɑ:kəs] *n.* **1** body of a dead cow/pig/lamb ready for the butcher; bones left after you have eaten a cooked bird. □ **canal; huesos**
2 body (of a person). □ **cuerpo**

carcinogen [kɑ:'sinədʒən] *n.* substance which causes cancer. □ **carcinógeno**

card [kɑ:d] *n.* **1** small rectangle of stiff paper for writing on: *I'll send you a card from Paris,* I will send you a postcard. □ **postal**
birthday card/Christmas card, decorative card sent to someone on their birthday/at Christmas. □ **felicitación de cumpleaños/crisma**
2 rectangle of stiff paper with a design on it, used for playing games: *pack of cards.* □ **carta**
playing cards, ordinary cards, marked in four designs (diamonds, hearts, clubs, spades). □ **naipes**
card games, games using packs of special cards: *they were playing cards,* they were playing games of cards (for money). □ **...a las cartas**
3 (***visiting***) ***card,*** small piece of stiff paper with your name and address printed on it. □ **tarjeta de visita**
4 ***identity card,*** card with photograph, (and sometimes fingerprints) and biographical details. □ **documento de identidad**
5 ***embarkation card,*** card filled in when leaving a country. □ **tarjeta de control**
6 ***banker's card/cheque card,*** plastic card given by a bank which guarantees payment of a cheque. □ **tarjeta de crédito**
7 *cards,* official record of an employee. □ **ficha**
to get one's cards: *he got his cards,* he was told to leave. □ **le mandaron irse**
■ *v.* to comb raw wool. □ **cardar**
cardboard *n.* thick card, used for packing: *we packed the books into cardboard boxes.* □ **cartón**
card-index *n.* series of small cards classified into alphabetical or numerical order. □ **fichero**
■ *v.* to classify (something) on to small filing cards. □ **clasificar**
card sharper *n.* person who cheats at cards to win money. □ **jugador tramposo**

cardiac ['kɑ:diæk] *adj.* referring to the heart: *cardiac arrest,* brief heart attack. □ **cardiaco**

cardigan ['kɑ:digən] *n.* woollen jacket which buttons at the front. □ **rebeca**

cardinal ['kɑ:dinl] *adj.* **1** very important: *a cardinal rule.* □ **esencial**
2 *cardinal numbers,* numbers which show quantity (1, 2, 3, etc.). □ **...cardinales**
■ *n.* **1** high dignitary of the Catholic church. □ **cardenal**
2 bright red North American bird. □ **cardenal**

cardiogram ['kɑ:diəgræm] *n.* chart showing heart beats. □ **cardiograma**
cardiograph *n.* machine for recording heart beats in the form of cardiograms. □ **cardiógrafo**
cardiology [kɑ:di'ɔlədʒi] *n.* study of the heart and its diseases. □ **cardiología**
cardiologist *n.* doctor specializing in the study of the heart. □ **cardiólogo**

care ['kɛə] *n.* **1** worry: *he hasn't a care in the world.* □ **preocupación**
2 looking after someone or something: *the monument is in the care of the historical monuments department.* □ **cuidado**
to take care, to watch out/to be careful: *take care when you play in the road; he took care not to spend all his money.* □ **tener cuidado**
3 *Mr White* ***care of*** *Mrs Green,* (*on a letter*) Mr White, at Mrs Green's house. □ **en casa de**
■ *v.* **1** to worry: *I don't care if I never see you again; he couldn't care less,* it does not matter to him at all. □ **importar**
2 to like: *would you care for a piece of cake?* □ **apetecer**
3 ***to care for someone,*** to look after someone: *he was cared for by his sister.* □ **cuidar**
carefree *adj.* without any worries. □ **despreocupado**
careful *adj.* cautious/taking care: *be careful when you lean out of the window; the burglar was careful not to make any noise.* □ **cuidadoso**
carefully *adv.* with care: *we wrapped all the glasses very carefully in tissue paper.* □ **cuidadosamente**
careless *adj.* not paying attention/not taking care: *he was careless about his clothes; she made several careless mistakes.* □ **descuidado**
carelessly *adv.* without taking care: *he carelessly threw the china cups into a box.* □ **descuidadamente**
carelessness *n.* negligence; not taking care: *the accident was due to his carelessness.* □ **descuido**
caretaker *n.* person who looks after a building: *the office caretaker; a school caretaker.* □ **vigilante**

career [kə'riə] *n.* **1** life of professional work: *he has decided to make his career as an architect; she has started on a nursing career.* □ **carrera**
2 forward rush. □ **carrera**
■ *v.* to rush forward out of control: *the car careered into a lamp-post; he was careering along on his bicycle.* □ **ir a toda velocidad**

caress [kə'res] *n.* gentle touch. □ **caricia**
■ *v.* to stroke gently. □ **acariciar**

cargo ['kɑ:gou] *n.* (*pl. cargoes*) goods carried (especially on a ship). □ **carga**
cargo boat, ship which carries only goods and no passengers. □ **barco mercante**

caricature ['kærikətjuə] *n.* amusing drawing which satirizes by emphasizing someone's particular features. □ **caricatura**
■ *v.* to satirize by emphasizing someone's bad features. □ **caricaturizar**

caries ['kɛəri:z] *n.* (*no pl.*) decayed place in a tooth. □ **caries**

carmine ['kɑ:min] *adj.* and *n.* bright red (colour). □ **carmín**

carnage ['kɑ:nidʒ] *n.* bloodshed/massacre/killing. □ **carnicería**

carnal ['kɑ:nl] *adj.* referring to the body. □ **carnal**

carnation [kɑ:'neiʃn] *n.* strongly scented flower often worn as a buttonhole. □ **clavel**

carnival ['kɑ:nivl] *n.* festival often with dancing and eating in the open air. □ **carnaval**

carnivore ['kɑːnivɔː] *n.* animal which eats meat: *a cow is not a carnivore.* □ **carnívoro**
carnivorous [kɑː'nivərəs] *adj.* (animal) which eats meat: *lions and tigers are carnivorous animals.* □ **carnívoro**

carol ['kærəl] *n.* special song sung at a particular time of year: *Christmas carol.* □ **villancico**
■ *v.* (*he carolled*) to sing Christmas carols: *they went out carolling in the snow.* □ **cantar villancicos**
carol-singer *n.* person singing Christmas carols (to collect money for charity). □ **villanciquero**
carol-singing *n.* singing of carols. □ **canto de...**

carp [kɑːp] *n.* (*no pl.*) fat edible fish often bred in captivity for eating. □ **carpa**
■ *v.* to keep on finding fault with things. □ **quejarse**

carpenter ['kɑːpəntə] *n.* person who works with wood, especially in building. □ **carpintero**
carpentry *n.* art of working with wood: *he has taken up carpentry.* □ **carpintería**

carpet ['kɑːpit] *n.* woven or knotted covering for the floor: *don't wipe your dirty shoes on the carpet; Persian carpet.* □ **alfombra**
stair carpet, narrow piece of carpet for covering stairs. □ **...de escalera**
■ *v.* to cover as with a carpet: *the ground was carpeted with dead leaves.* □ **alfombrar**
carpeting *n.* covering with a carpet. □ **alfombrado**
wall-to-wall carpeting, carpet which covers the entire floor area of a room. □ **moqueta**

carriage ['kæridʒ] *n.* **1** action of carrying goods. □ **transporte**
carriage paid, the price includes payment for transport. □ **porte pagado**
2 open vehicle pulled by a horse. □ **carruaje**
3 ***railway carriage,*** passenger wagon on a train. □ **vagón**
4 way of walking. □ **andares**
5 movable part on a typewriter which goes from side to side. □ **carro**
carriageway *n.* surface of the road on which traffic moves. □ **calzada**
dual carriageway, road separated into two parts by a central grass bank or fence. □ **carretera de doble calzada**

carrier ['kæriə] *n.* **1** thing/person who carries. □ **transportista**
luggage carrier, grid on the back of a bicycle for carrying parcels. □ **portaequipajes**
carrier pigeon, pigeon specially trained for carrying messages. □ **paloma mensajera**
carrier bag, large paper or plastic bag with handles. □ **bolsa**
2 person who carries the germ of a disease and can infect others with it. □ **portador**
3 ***aircraft carrier,*** ship which carries aircraft. □ **portaaviones**

carrion ['kæriən] *n.* rotting meat. □ **carroña**

carrot ['kærət] *n.* bright orange root vegetable. □ **zanahoria**

carry ['kæri] *v.* **1** to lift something up and move it from one place to another: *he carried the old lady out of the burning house; the lorry was carrying a load of wood; this bus carries seventy passengers; this cable carries the main electricity supply to the house; foxes can carry rabies.* □ **llevar**
2 to win (a vote): *the motion was carried.* □ **ganar**
3 to be heard at a distance: *the sound of the church bells carries for miles.* □ **oírse a lo lejos**
4 to keep (in a shop): *we only carry a small stock of chocolates.* □ **tener en existencia**
carry along *v.* to transport unwillingly: *we were carried along by the crowd; large cars were carried along by the floodwater.* □ **arrastrar**
carry away *v.* **1** to take away/to demolish: *the chicken house was carried away in the storm.* □ **llevarse**
2 ***to get carried away,*** to get overcome with emotion/excitement. □ **entusiasmarse**
carry-cot *n.* rectangular box with handles for carrying a baby. □ **moisés**
carry forward *v.* (*in book-keeping*) to take a sum on to the next page or column. □ **suma y sigue**
carry off *v.* **1** to win/to take away: *he carried off three first prizes; all the treasures were carried off by the attackers.* □ **llevarse**
2 *he carried it off very well,* he got through a potentially embarrassing situation very well. □ **salir bien parado**
carry on *v.* **1** to continue/to go on: *he carried on talking even though everyone had told him to keep quiet; they carried on a correspondence for ten years.* □ **continuar**
carry on!, don't stop! □ **¡sigue!**
2 (*informal*) to be very angry: *when she discovered he was already married she started to carry on dreadfully.* □ **estar de morros**
carry out *v.* **1** to lift and take out: *he was carried out of the house on a stretcher.* □ **llevar, sacar**
2 to do something successfully: *they carried out a nuclear test; I carried out all your instructions.* □ **llevar a cabo**
carry through *v.* to bring something to a finish. □ **llevar a cabo**

cart [kɑːt] *n.* vehicle pulled by a horse: *farm cart.* □ **carro; carreta**
to put the cart before the horse, not to put first things first. □ **empezar la casa por el tejado**
■ *v.* to carry (something heavy): *what are you carting that box around with you for?* □ **acarrear**
carter *n.* person who drives a cart. □ **carretero**
carthorse *n.* large strong horse. □ **caballo de tiro**
cartload *n.* quantity carried in a cart. □ **carretada**
cartwheel *n.* **1** wheel of a cart. □ **rueda de carro**
2 ***to turn cartwheels,*** to turn sideways on your outstretched hands and feet, over and over like a wheel. □ **dar volteretas**

cartilage ['kɑːtilidʒ] *n.* strong flexible material which acts as a cushion in joints in the body: *the nose is made of bone and cartilage.* □ **cartílago**

cartographer [kɑː'tɔgrəfə] *n.* person who draws maps. □ **cartógrafo**
cartography *n.* science of drawing maps. □ **cartografía**

carton ['kɑːtən] *n.* cardboard box: *a carton of cigarettes.* □ **cartón**

cartoon [kɑː'tuːn] *n.* **1** funny (often political) drawing: *the paper has a cartoon of the Prime Minister.* □ **chiste**
2 film made of moving drawings: *they were watching a cartoon about a cat and two mice.* □ **dibujos animados**
cartoonist *n.* person who draws (political) cartoons. □ **dibujante de chistes**

cartridge ['kɑːtridʒ] *n.* **1** tube packed with gunpowder and a bullet for firing from a gun. □ **cartucho**
2 film/recording tape enclosed in a plastic case which fits directly into the camera/tape recorder; tube of ink which fits into a pen. □ **cartucho; recambio (para pluma)**
3 part of a record player which holds the stylus. □ **portaagujas**

4 ***cartridge paper,*** good quality white paper. □ **papel de calidad**

carve [kɑːv] *v.* **1** to cut meat up at table: *shall I carve the chicken?* □ **trinchar**
2 to cut stone/wood to make a shape: *he has carved a statue of his son.* □ **labrar, tallar**
carver *n.* **1** person who carves. □ **escultor, tallista**
2 carving knife. □ **trinchante**
3 dining chair with arms. □ **silla de caderas**
carving *n.* **1** cutting up cooked meat. □ **arte cisoria**
carving knife, large sharp knife for cutting meat. □ **trinchante**
2 art of cutting stone/wood into shapes. □ **labra, talla**
3 statue which has been carved: *I bought a Japanese carving of an old man.* □ **escultura, talla**

cascade [kæs'keid] *n.* (artificial) waterfall. □ **cascada**
■ *v.* to fall: *the water cascaded down the steps.* □ **caer en cascada**

case [keis] *n.* **1** box (of goods): *a case of wine.* □ **caja**
2 protective box: *spectacle case; cigarette case.* □ **funda; petaca**
3 ***pillow case,*** linen bag for covering a pillow. □ **funda**
4 suitcase: *have you packed your cases yet?* □ **maleta**
5 way in which something happens; example: *that's often the case.* □ **...el caso**
in any case, anyway: *there is nothing on TV, in any case I'm too tired to stay up.* □ **de cualquier manera**
in case of *fire,* if fire breaks out; ***in case*** *you are hungry I have made some sandwiches.* □ **en caso de**
just in case, to guard against a possible emergency: *it's sunny, but I am taking my umbrella just in case; I always carry a thick stick just in case.* □ **por si acaso**
6 sick person: *we treat six cases of food poisoning each week.* □ **caso**
case history, details of a patient's progress. □ **historial médico**
7 legal affair: *he has won every case he has defended; he is the judge in a murder case; it is a case of murder.* □ **caso**

casement ['keismənt] *n.* window that opens on hinges; frame around such a window. □ **ventana de bisagras**

cash [kæʃ] *n.* money (in coins and notes): *can you lend me some money - I have run out of cash? are you paying cash or by cheque?* □ **efectivo**
cash box, metal box for keeping money. □ **caja**
cash desk, place in a shop where you pay. □ **caja**
cash register, machine which shows the amount to be paid and has a drawer for keeping money. □ **caja registradora**
■ *v.* ***to cash*** *a cheque,* to change a cheque into cash: *can I cash some travellers' cheques?* □ **cobrar**
to cash in on: *he cashed in on the craze for skateboards,* he made a lot of money by profiting from the craze. □ **sacar partido de**
cash flow *n.* rate at which money comes into and is paid out of a business. □ **'cash flow'**

cashew [kə'ʃuː] *n.* small sweetish nut, often eaten salted. □ **anacardo**

cashier [kə'ʃiːə] *n.* person who deals with money: *she works as a cashier in a dress shop.* □ **cajero**
■ *v.* to expel (an officer) from the armed forces. □ **expulsar**

cashmere ['kæʃmiə] *adj.* and *n.* (made of) fine soft goat's wool; *a cashmere sweater.* □ **cachemir**

casing ['keisiŋ] *n.* hard covering which protects something. □ **cubierta**

casino [kə'siːnou] *n.* building where you can gamble. □ **casino**

cask [kɑːsk] *n.* large barrel. □ **tonel**

casket ['kɑːskit] *n.* **1** ornamental box (for jewels). □ **cofre; joyero**
2 *Amer.* coffin. □ **ataúd**

casserole ['kæsəroul] *n.* **1** oven-proof covered dish. □ **cacerola**
2 food cooked in a covered dish in the oven: *a casserole of chicken; beef casserole.* □ **...a la cazuela**

cassette [kə'set] *n.* **1** magnetic tape in a plastic case which can fit directly into a playing or recording machine. □ **casete**
cassette player, machine for playing cassettes. □ **el casete**
cassette recorder, machine for recording and playing back cassettes. □ **grabadora**
2 film in a plastic case which fits directly into a camera. □ **cartucho**

cassock ['kæsək] *n.* long, usually black, gown worn by priests, choirboys, etc. □ **sotana**

cast [kɑːst] *n.* **1** throwing (of a fishing line). □ **lanzamiento**
2 plaster shape made from a mould. □ **vaciado**
3 ***worm cast,*** small pile of earth thrown up by a worm. □ **montículo**
4 list of actors in a play/film; all the actors in a play/film. □ **reparto**
5 ***cast of mind,*** way of thinking. □ **mentalidad**
6 squint (in an eye). □ **ligero estrabismo**
■ *v.* (*he cast; he has cast*) **1** to throw: *he cast a glance over the newspaper; he cast his line into the river.* □ **echar (una mirada/el sedal)**
2 to mould metal/plaster: *they cast a bell.* □ **vaciar**
3 to choose actors for a play/film. □ **elegir reparto**
■ *adj.* **1** which has been cast in a mould: *cast bronze; cast iron.* □ **fundido**
2 *she has a* ***cast-iron*** *excuse,* a perfect excuse. □ **convincente**
cast about *v.* to look for: *he cast about for a suitable excuse.* □ **buscar**
cast adrift *v.* to abandon a boat/a family. □ **abandonar**
cast aside *v.* to throw away: *he cast aside all caution.* □ **desechar**
cast away *v.* **1** to throw away. □ **arrojar**
2 *she was cast away on a desert island,* she was shipwrecked on a desert island. □ **arrojar**
castaway *n.* person who has been shipwrecked. □ **náufrago**
cast down *v. they were cast down,* they were miserable. □ **abatidos**
casting *n.* **1** moulding of a shape; thing which has been moulded: *they make metal castings.* □ **pieza de fundición**
2 choosing of actors. □ **elección del reparto**
■ *adj.* ***casting vote,*** vote which decides when the other votes are equal: *the chairman has the casting vote.* □ **voto de calidad**
cast off *v.* **1** to calculate roughly the number of pages in a book, before it is printed. □ **cálculo tipográfico**
2 to untie the ropes holding a boat: *they cast off from the quay.* □ **soltar amarras**
3 (*in knitting*) to finish stitches: *cast off three stitches.* □ **cerrar**
cast-off clothing, cast-offs *n. pl.* clothes which someone has thrown away. □ **ropas de desecho**
cast on *v.* to put stitches on to the needles when knitting. □ **echar puntos**

castanets [kæstə'nets] *n. pl.* hollow clappers made of wood which are held in the hand and clicked in time to music by Spanish dancers. □ **castañuelas**
caste [kɑːst] *n.* hereditary class (in Indian society). □ **casta**
castigate ['kæstigeit] *v.* (*formal*) to punish/to beat someone as a punishment; to criticize someone sharply. □ **castigar**
castle ['kɑːsl] *n.* **1** large fortified building: *the army retreated into the castle.* □ **castillo**
2 piece in chess which looks like a castle. □ **torre**
castor/caster ['kɑːstə] *n.* **1** *sugar castor,* pot with holes in the lid for sprinkling sugar. □ **azucarero**
castor sugar, fine sugar. □ **azucar blanco**
2 wheel screwed on to the leg of a chair. □ **ruedecilla**
castor oil *n.* oil from a palm which is used as a laxative. □ **aceite de ricino**
castrate [kæ'streit] *v.* to remove the testicles from a male animal. □ **castrar**
castration [kæ'streiʃn] *n.* removing the testicles from a male animal. □ **castración**
casual ['kæʒjuəl] *adj.* **1** not formal. □ **informal**
casual dress, informal dress. □ **ropa informal**
casual labour, workers taken on for very short periods. □ **temporeros**
2 not serious: *a casual attitude to his work.* □ **despreocupado**
casually *adv.* by chance; in an informal way: *he casually strolled into the shop.* □ **por casualidad**
casualness *n.* lack of seriousness. □ **informalidad**
casualty ['kæʒjuəlti] *n.* **1** person injured or killed in a battle/an accident: *how many casualties were there when the plane crashed?* □ **víctima**
casualty department, section of a hospital for accident victims. □ **urgencias**
2 *the new town hall was a casualty of the government cutbacks,* the projected new town hall was abandoned because of government cutbacks. □ **víctima**
cat [kæt] *n.* furry domestic pet, which purrs and has a long tail. □ **gato**
the cat family, all felines: *lions and tigers are members of the cat family.* □ **felinos**
the big cats, lions and tigers. □ **grandes felinos**
cat burglar, burglar who climbs walls or drainpipes to enter a house. □ **ladrón escalador**
to let the cat out of the bag, (*informal*) reveal the secret. □ **irse de la lengua**
catcall *n.* whistle/hoot (to show displeasure). □ **rechifla**
catfish *n.* large ugly freshwater fish with whiskers. □ **siluro**
catgut *n.* string made from the insides of animals used for musical instruments. □ **cuerda de tripa**
cat's eyes *n.* small glass reflectors showing the centre or sides of a road. □ **reflectores**
catwalk *n.* open metal gangway running along the outside of a ship/building. □ **pasarela**
cataclysm ['kætəklizm] *n.* disaster. □ **cataclismo**
catacombs ['kætəkuːmz] *n. pl.* underground rooms (used in ancient times for burying the dead). □ **catacumbas**
catalepsy ['kætəlepsi] *n.* state where someone becomes unconscious and stiff. □ **catalepsia**
catalogue ['kætəlɔg] *Amer.* **catalog** *n.* list of things for sale/in a library/in a museum: *I can't find this book in the catalogue.* □ **catálogo**
■ *v.* to make a list of books in a library/of treasures in a museum/of things for sale. □ **catalogar**
cataloguer *n.* person who specializes in the making of catalogues. □ **catalogador**
catalyst ['kætəlist] *n.* chemical substance which helps to produce a chemical reaction; anything which helps something to take place. □ **catalizador**
catamaran [kætəmə'ræn] *n.* boat with two parallel hulls. □ **catamarán**
catapult ['kætəpʌlt] *n.* strong elastic band on a forked stick, used for throwing stones. □ **catapulta**
catapult launching gear, mechanism on an aircraft carrier for sending an aircraft into the air. □ **lanzador de catapulta**
■ *v.* to send (an aircraft, etc.) into the air: *when the rope snapped he was catapulted six feet into the air.* □ **catapultar**
cataract ['kætərækt] *n.* **1** waterfall on a river. □ **catarata**
2 film which grows over the eye and eventually prevents you from seeing. □ **catarata**
catarrh [kə'tɑː] *n.* type of cold caused by inflammation of the nose and bronchial tubes. □ **catarro**
catarrhal [kə'tɑːrəl] *adj.* referring to catarrh: *catarrhal cold.* □ **catarral**
catastrophe [kə'tæstrəfi] *n.* disaster. □ **catástrofe**
catastrophic *adj.* disastrous: *a catastrophic summer for the farmers.* □ **catastrófico**
catch [kætʃ] *n.* **1** things which have been caught. □ **captura**
2 *we had a good catch,* we caught a lot of fish. □ **captura**
3 *he's a good catch,* he is a good prospective husband/worker. □ **un buen partido/fichaje**
4 action of catching (a ball, etc.): *he made a wonderful catch; he dropped an easy catch.* □ **parada**
5 thing which fastens a door/window, etc. □ **pestillo**
6 awkwardness/hitch: *there must be a catch in it somewhere,* there must be something wrong with it/there must be a trap. □ **pega, truco**
catch 22, vicious circle which cannot be escaped from. □ **trampa**
■ *v.* (*he caught*) **1** to grab hold of something (which is moving): *he caught the ball in his left hand; did the police ever catch the burglar? how many fish did you catch?* □ **coger; atrapar**
2 *I had to run to catch the bus,* to get on the bus. □ **tomar**
3 *I didn't catch what you said,* I was not able to hear. □ **no cogí lo que...**
to catch someone's eye: *try and catch the waiter's eye,* try to attract his attention. □ **llama al camarero**
4 to get (a disease): *he has caught mumps from the children; she caught a cold from standing in the rain.* □ **coger**
5 to find someone by surprise: *he was caught in the act,* as he was committing the crime; *they caught him red-handed.* □ **le cogieron con las manos en la masa**
catching *adj.* (disease) which can be caught/which is infectious: *is it catching?* □ **¿es contagioso?**
catchment area *n.* **1** land from which a river gets its water. □ **zona de captación**
2 area around a school from which all the pupils in the school must come. □ **zona escolar**
catch on *v.* **1** to understand. □ **caer en la cuenta**
2 to become fashionable: *short skirts have caught on quickly.* □ **ponerse de moda**
catch out *v.* to find that someone has made a mistake: to ask someone a question to which he does not know the answer. □ **coger a alguien**
catch phrase *n.* popular phrase, usually associated with an entertainer or advertisement. □ **frase hecha; tópico**
catch up *v.* to move faster than someone so as to

draw level with him: *I had to run fast to catch up with the postman; I must try to catch up on the backlog of work.* □ **alcanzar al cartero; ponerse al día en el trabajo**
catchword *n.* popular phrase. □ **lema; eslogan**
catchy *adj.* (tune) which is easy to remember. □ **pegadizo**
catechize ['kætikaiz] *v.* to ask questions. □ **preguntar**
catechism ['kætikizm] *n.* book of religious instruction; religious classes. □ **catecismo**
category ['kætigəri] *n.* classification of things/people: *we classify books into six main categories.* □ **categoría**
categorical [kæti'gɔrikl] *adj.* straightforward/definite: *he gave a categorical denial.* □ **categórico**
categorically *adv.* definitely: *he denied everything categorically.* □ **categóricamente**
cater ['keitə] *v.* to supply food and drink (at a party, etc.). □ **proveer**
caterer *n.* person who supplies food. □ **proveedor**
cater for *v.* to look after: *we cater for the needs of a small group of scientists; the shop tries to cater for all tastes.* □ **atender, satisfacer**
catering *n.* supplying of food. □ **servicio de comidas; 'catering'**
caterpillar ['kætəpilə] *n.* insect larva which turns into a moth or butterfly. □ **oruga**
caterpillar track, endless metal belt running round a pair of wheels (on a tank, etc.). □ **oruga**
caterpillar tractor, tractor which runs on endless belts around the wheels. □ **tractor oruga**
caterwaul ['kætəwɔːl] *v.* to howl (like cats at night). □ **maullar**
cathedral [kə'θiːdrəl] *n.* large church which is the seat of a bishop. □ **catedral**
catherine wheel ['kæθrinwiːl] *n.* firework which spins round and round. □ **girándula**
catheter ['kæθitə] *n.* very thin tube which can be inserted into the body to remove fluid. □ **catéter**
cathode ['kæθoud] *n.* negative electric pole. □ **cátodo**
cathode ray tube, tube (as in a television set) where a stream of electrons hits a screen. □ **tubo de rayos catódicos**
catholic ['kæθlik] *adj.* **1** wide/general: *he has a catholic taste in wine,* he likes all sorts of wine. □ **persona a la que le gusta de todo**
2 referring to the Roman Catholic church: *a Catholic church; a Catholic priest.* □ **católico**
■ *n.* member of the Roman Catholic Church: *all his family are Catholics.* □ **católico**
catholicism [kə'θɔlisizm] *n.* beliefs of the Catholic church. □ **catolicismo**
catkin ['kætkin] *n.* flower of a willow or hazel tree. □ **amento**
catsup ['kætsəp] *n. Amer.* ketchup. □ **'catsup'**
cattle ['kætl] *n.* (*no pl.*) animals of the cow family (such as bulls, calves, oxen, etc.). □ **ganado vacuno**
cattle shed, shed for keeping cows. □ **vaqueriza**
cattle show, agricultural show. □ **feria**
cattle market, market for live animals. □ **mercado**
catty ['kæti] *adj.* nasty/sharp-tongued (woman). □ **chismoso**
caucus ['kɔːkəs] *n.* group of party members who plan electoral strategy and choose candidates. □ **comité electoral**
caught [kɔːt] *v. see* **catch.**
cauldron ['kɔːldrən] *Amer.* **caldron** *n.* large deep pan for cooking. □ **caldera**
cauliflower ['kɔliflauə] *n.* cabbage-like vegetable with a large white flower head which is eaten. □ **coliflor**
caulk ['kɔːk] *v.* to fill the cracks in a boat's hull to make it watertight. □ **calafatear**
cause [kɔːz] *n.* **1** thing which makes something happen: *what was the cause of the accident? the cause of his death was poisoning; he died from natural causes,* he died naturally, and was not killed in an accident or murdered. □ **causa**
2 reason for doing something: *he did it with good cause.* □ **causa**
3 noble aim/charity to which it is good to give money: *it's all in a good cause; we are all fighting for the cause of freedom.* □ **causa**
■ *v.* to make something happen: *what caused the explosion? his death was caused by faulty electric wiring.* □ **causar**
causal *adj.* referring to a cause. □ **causal**
causeway ['kɔːzwei] *n.* road/path built up on a bank above marshy ground. □ **carretera elevada**
caustic ['kɔːstik] *adj.* **1** burning: *caustic soda,* chemical used in the kitchen for cleaning. □ **cáustico**
2 sharp (wit). □ **cáustico**
caustically *adv.* in a sharp/witty way. □ **cáusticamente**
cauterize ['kɔːtəraiz] *v.* to burn a wound to stop infection. □ **cauterizar**
cauterization [kɔːtərai'zeiʃn] *n.* burning of a wound to stop infection. □ **cauterización**
caution ['kɔːʃn] *n.* care/precaution: *you must drive with caution when the roads are icy.* □ **cautela**
■ *v.* to warn: *the policeman cautioned the two boys.* □ **amonestar**
cautious *adj.* careful/prudent. □ **cauto**
cautiously *adv.* carefully: *the soldiers went forward cautiously because of the possibility of mines.* □ **cautamente**
cautiousness *n.* carefulness. □ **cautela**
cavalcade ['kævəlkeid] *n.* procession (usually of horseriders). □ **cabalgata**
cavalier [kævə'liə] *adj.* high-handed/with no respect for other people or customs. □ **arrogante**
cavalry ['kævəlri] *n.* soldiers on horseback. □ **caballería**
cave [keiv] *n.* large hole in rock or earth: *thousands of years ago primitive man lived in caves.* □ **cueva**
cave bears, prehistoric bears which lived in caves. □ **oso de las cavernas**
cave paintings, paintings on walls of caves done by primitive man. □ **pinturas rupestres**
■ *v.* ***to cave in,*** to collapse: *the roof of the tunnel caved in; the English defence caved in.* □ **derrumbarse**
caveman *n.* (*pl. cavemen*) primitive man who lived in caves. □ **hombre de las cavernas**
cavern ['kævən] *n.* very large cave. □ **caverna**
cavernous *adj.* like a cavern. □ **cavernoso**
caviar(e) [kævi'ɑː] *n.* very expensive delicacy consisting of the eggs of a sturgeon. □ **caviar**
cavil ['kævil] *v.* (*he cavilled*) ***to cavil at something,*** to object to something. □ **poner peros a**
cavity ['kæviti] *n.* hole: *beetles live in cavities in tree trunks; the dentist said I had several cavities which needed filling.* □ **cavidad; caries**
cavity wall, wall made of two rows of bricks with a gap in between. □ **pared con cámara**
cavort [kə'vɔːt] *v.* to rush about in excitement. □ **retozar**
caw [kɔː] *v.* to make a croaking sound like a crow. □ **graznar**

cayenne ['keien] *n.* type of hot red pepper. □ **cayena**
cayman ['keimən] *n.* alligator. □ **caimán**
cease [si:s] *v.* to stop: *I have ceased worrying about the expense; they ceased work at 12 noon.* □ **dejar de**
ceasefire *n.* agreement to stop shooting (in a war): *the ceasefire was signed yesterday; the ceasefire was broken almost immediately.* □ **alto el fuego**
ceaseless *adj.* without stopping: *the ceaseless roar of the waves on the rocks.* □ **incesante**
ceaselessly *adv.* without stopping: *she ceaselessly twisted her handkerchief in her hands.* □ **sin cesar**
cedar ['si:də] *n.* large evergreen tree, with sweet-smelling wood; wood from this tree: *a cedar chest.* □ **cedro**
cede [si:d] *v.* to pass property/land to someone else: *the territory was ceded to France.* □ **ceder**
ceiling ['si:liŋ] *n.* **1** inside roof over a room: *a room has four walls, a floor and a ceiling.* □ **techo**
2 upper limit: *we have set a ceiling of $10,000 on expenditure.* □ **techo, límite**
celebrate ['selibreit] *v.* to remember a special day with parties and feasts: *they celebrated his birthday by going to the theatre; how do you usually celebrate the New Year? the police arrested some football fans who had been celebrating their club's win.* □ **celebrar**
celebrated *adj.* very famous: *the celebrated German singer is giving a recital.* □ **célebre**
celebration [seli'breiʃn] *n.* **1** festivity. □ **celebración**
2 *I'm going to get married - this calls for a celebration,* we must have a drink to celebrate. □ **celebración**
celebrity [sə'lebriti] *n.* **1** famous person. □ **celebridad**
2 being famous. □ **celebridad**
celery ['seləri] *n.* white or green stemmed plant, eaten as a vegetable, especially raw as a salad. □ **apio**
celestial [sə'lestjəl] *adj.* (*formal*) heavenly/referring to the sky. □ **celestial**
celibate ['selibət] *adj.* not married: *Catholic priests must remain celibate.* □ **célibe**
celibacy *n.* state of not being married. □ **celibato**
cell [sel] *n.* **1** room in a prison/in a monastery: *the prisoner escaped from his cell by climbing out of the window.* □ **celda**
condemned cell, cell for a person who has been condemned to death. □ **celda de los condenados a muerte**
2 basic unit of an organism: *the body is made up of different cells.* □ **célula**
3 part of an electric battery. □ **elemento**
cellular *adj.* made up of many small cells; (cloth) with open holes in it. □ **celular**
cellar ['selə] *n.* underground room or rooms beneath a house: *we keep our bicycles in the cellar.* □ **sótano**
cello ['tʃelou] *n.* large stringed musical instrument, smaller than a double bass. □ **violoncelo**
cellist *n* person who plays the cello. □ **violoncelista**
cellophane ['seləfein] *n.* trade mark for transparent plastic sheet for wrapping or covering. □ **celofán**
cellulose ['seljulous] *n.* chemical substance found in plants, used for making paper and paint. □ **celulosa**
Celsius ['selsiəs] *adj.* and *n.* (scale for) measuring heat where the boiling point of water is 100° and the freezing point is 0°: *the temperature outside was only 6° Celsius (6 °C).* □ **Celsio**
Celt [kelt] *n.* descendant of a European race now found in Scotland, Ireland, Wales, Britanny, etc. □ **celta**
Celtic *adj.* referring to ancient or modern Celts. □ **céltico**

cement [si'ment] *n.* **1** powder made from limestone heated with clay, which when mixed with water dries hard: *you need cement, water and sand to make concrete.* □ **cemento**
2 wet concrete: *don't walk on the cement, it isn't dry yet.* □ **hormigón blando**
3 strong glue. □ **cola**
balsa cement, special glue for making models out of balsa wood. □ **cola para balsa**
■ *v.* **1** to stick together with cement: *they cemented the bricks into the wall.* □ **unir con cemento**
2 to strengthen/to make closer: *to cement the friendship between the two countries.* □ **fortalecer, estrechar**
cement-mixer *n.* machine for mixing wet concrete. □ **hormigonera**
cemetery ['semətri] *n.* burial ground. □ **cementerio**
cenotaph ['senətɑ:f] *n.* war memorial; empty tomb. □ **cenotafio**
censer ['sensə] *n.* (*in church*) metal receptacle on a chain for burning incense. □ **incensario**
censor ['sensə] *n.* official who inspects letters/newspaper articles/plays/books, etc., to see if they can be sent or published: *all our reports have to be vetted by the censor; the censor cut ten minutes out of the film.* □ **censor**
■ *v.* to forbid the publication of something because it may be obscene or may reveal secrets. □ **censurar**
censorious [sen'sɔ:riəs] *adj.* critical/which criticizes. □ **criticón**
censorship *n.* office of censor; act of censoring: *all reports have to pass the official censorship; the government has imposed strict censorship.* □ **censura**
censure ['senʃə] *n.* condemnation/criticism (of a government/an official): *Parliament passed a vote of censure on the government.* □ **censura**
■ *v.* to condemn/to criticize someone: *he was censured by the committee for using bad language.* □ **censurar**
census ['sensəs] *n.* official counting of the population of a country: *the government has proposed taking a census.* □ **censo**
cent [sent] *n.* small coin/one-hundredth part of a dollar: *this pencil costs twenty five cents (25c).* □ **centavo; céntimo**
centenary [sen'ti:nəri] *n.* hundredth anniversary: *1978 was the centenary of the Salvation Army; centenary celebrations.* □ **centenario**
centenarian [senti'nεəriən] *n.* person who is 100 years old or more. □ **centenario**
centennial [sen'tenjəl] *adj.* referring to a centenary: *the centennial celebrations.* □ **del centenario**
centigrade ['sentigreid] *adj.* and *n.* (scale for) measuring temperature where the boiling point of water is 100° and the freezing point 0°: *the temperature outside was only six degrees centigrade (6 °C).* □ **centígrado**
centilitre ['sentili:tə] *Amer.* **centiliter** *n.* liquid measure, one hundredth part of a litre. □ **centilitro**
centimetre ['sentimi:tə] *Amer.* **centimeter** *n.* measure of length, one hundredth part of a metre: *there are ten millimetres in a centimetre; the table is ninety centimetres (90cm) wide.* □ **centímetro**
centipede ['sentipi:d] *n.* creeping animal with a large number of legs. □ **ciempiés**
centre ['sentə] *Amer.* **center** *n.* **1** middle: *he stood in the centre of the stage; centuries ago people used to believe that the earth was the centre of the universe; the centre of the town is the business district.* □ **centro**
centre party, political party in the centre, neither

right nor left. □ **partido del centro**
2 large building. □ **centro**
sports centre, building with various sports facilities. □ **polideportivo**
arts centre, building with various cultural institutions (library/cinema/art gallery/museum, etc.). □ **centro cultural**
shopping centre, group of several shops linked together with covered walks. □ **centro comercial**
■ *v.* **1** to place in the centre. □ **centrar**
2 to put the main emphasis on: *the main criticism of the film is centred on the character of the hero; the accusation centres on his handling of the firm's money.* □ **centrarse**
central *adj.* in the middle: *the station is very central,* is in the middle of the town. □ **central**
central heating, heating for a whole house which comes from one heating apparatus. □ **calefacción central**
the central nervous system, main nervous system. □ **sistema nervioso central**
centralize *v.* to put under the control of a central system. □ **centralizar**
centrally *adv.* in the middle: *the house is very centrally situated.* □ **en el centro**
centre forward *n.* (*in football*) player in the centre of the forward line. □ **delantero centro**

centrifugal [sentri'fju:gl] *adj.* which tends to go away from the centre: *centrifugal force.* □ **centrífugo**

centripetal [sentri'pi:tl] *adj.* which tends to go towards the centre. □ **centrípeto**

century ['sentʃəri] *n.* **1** hundred years: *the period from 1800 to 1899 is the nineteenth century.* □ **siglo**
2 (*in games*) score of one hundred. □ **ciento**

ceramic [sə'ræmik] *adj.* made of pottery: *a ceramic tile.* □ **cerámico**
ceramics *n.* art of working in pottery. □ **cerámica**

cereal ['siəriəl] *n.* grain crop such as wheat, barley, maize, etc. □ **cereal**
cereals *n. pl. (breakfast) cereals,* grain foods eaten with sugar and milk for breakfast. □ **cereales**

cerebral ['seribrəl] *adj.* **1** referring to the brain. □ **cerebral**
2 intellectual (rather than emotional). □ **cerebral**

ceremony ['seriməni] *n.* official occasion; the trappings of an official occasion: *the prize-giving ceremony will be held in the hall; he was buried quietly without ceremony.* □ **ceremonia**
to stand on ceremony, to follow the formal rules of behaviour: *don't stand on ceremony,* be informal. □ **no seas tan cumplido**
ceremonial [seri'mouniəl] *adj.* referring to a ceremony. □ **ceremonial**
ceremonial robes, robes specially worn at ceremonies. □ **trajes de gala**
ceremonially *adv.* with ceremony. □ **ceremonialmente**
ceremonious *adj.* with a lot of ceremony. □ **ceremonioso**
ceremoniously *adv.* with a lot of ceremony. □ **ceremoniosamente**

cert [sə:t] *n.* (*informal*) certainty: *it's a dead cert,* it is bound to happen. □ **certeza**

certain ['sə:tn] *adj.* **1** sure: *I'm certain he stole the money; this horse is certain to win the race; before you go on holiday make certain that your house is properly locked up.* □ **seguro**
2 particular: *I want to speak to a certain Mr. Smith.* □ **...a un tal Mr...**
3 ***a certain amount,*** some: *we do a certain amount of business with Communist countries; mending the watch will take a certain amount of time.* □ **una cierta cantidad**
certainly *adv.* of course: *I will certainly try to go to his wedding.* □ **desde luego**
certainty *n.* **1** being certain. □ **certeza**
2 sure/certain thing: *it is a certainty that it will rain tomorrow.* □ **tengo la certeza...**

certificate [sə:'tifikət] *n.* official document which proves/shows something: *if you are ill, you must have a doctor's certificate to show you can't go to work; death certificate.* □ **certificado**
birth certificate, piece of paper showing when and where you were born. □ **partida de nacimiento**
savings certificate, paper showing you have invested money in National Savings. □ **título de inversión**
certify ['sə:tifai] *v.* to write a certificate; to put in writing an official declaration: *he was certified insane.* □ **certificar**

certitude ['sə:titju:d] *n.* certainty. □ **certidumbre**

cervix ['sə:viks] *n.* neck, especially the neck of the womb. □ **cerviz, cuello del útero**
cervical *adj.* referring to the cervix. □ **cervical**

cessation [se'seiʃn] *n.* stopping: *cessation of hostilities.* □ **cese**

cession ['seʃn] *n.* passing of property/land to someone else: *the cession of the territory to France.* □ **cesión**

cesspit ['sespit] **cesspool** ['sespu:l] *n.* underground tank for collecting sewage: *the house is not on main drainage and has a cesspit in the garden.* □ **pozo negro**

chafe [tʃeif] *v.* **1** to rub/to wear out by rubbing: *these new shoes have chafed my heel.* □ **rozar**
2 to become irritated/annoyed. □ **irritarse**

chaff [tʃɑ:f] *n.* **1** dried corn stalks left after the grain is extracted. □ **paja**
2 good-humoured teasing. □ **chanza**

chaffinch ['tʃæfintʃ] *n.* common pink-breasted finch. □ **pinzón**

chagrin ['ʃægrin] *n.* annoyance/sadness: *to his chagrin, he did not get first prize.* □ **disgusto**

chain [tʃein] *n.* **1** series of rings joined together: *she wore a medal on a gold chain round her neck; we keep the dog on a chain; each prisoner was attached to the wall by a chain.* □ **cadena**
chain reaction, events/chemical reaction which build up rapidly. □ **reacción en cadena**
2 row (of mountains). □ **cordillera**
3 ***chain store,*** group of shops belonging to the same company: *a supermarket chain.* □ **cadena de...**
■ *v.* to attach with a chain: *the horse was chained to the post; we have to keep the dog chained up.* □ **encadenar**
chain-smoke *v.* to smoke (cigarettes) one after the other. □ **fumar como una chimenea**
chain-smoker *n.* person who smokes cigarettes one after the other. □ **fumador empedernido**

chair ['tʃɛə] *n.* **1** piece of furniture for one person to sit on: *pull up a chair and have some supper.* □ **silla**
easy chair, soft comfortable chair. □ **poltrona**
2 position of chairman at a meeting; position of professor at a university: *she has been appointed to the chair of French.* □ **presidencia; cátedra**
to be in the chair, to be in charge of a meeting. □ **presidir**
■ *v. **to chair** a meeting,* to be in charge of a meeting. □ **presidir**
chairlift *n.* chairs on a cable which take skiers, etc., up a mountain. □ **telesilla**
chairman *n.* (*pl. chairmen*) person who is in charge

of a meeting; head of a company. □ **presidente**
chairmanship *n.* art of being a chairman. □ **presidencia**
chairperson *n.* person who is in charge of a meeting. □ **presidente**
chalet ['ʃælei] *n.* small (holiday) house, usually made of wood. □ **chalé**
chalice ['tʃælis] *n.* metal cup in which wine is offered at a communion service. □ **cáliz**
chalk [tʃɔ:k] *n.* **1** soft white rock: *chalk hills are only good for growing grass.* □ **creta**
2 stick of white or coloured material for writing on a blackboard. □ **tiza**
■ *v.* to mark or write with chalk: *he chalked up the results on the board.* □ **marcar/escribir con tiza**
chalky *adj.* white like chalk; gritty like chalk. □ **blanco/arenoso como la tiza**
challenge ['tʃæləndʒ] *n.* invitation to fight: *the challenge of a new job,* the way in which a new job makes you fight to show you are good; *the challenge of climbing Everest; he took up the challenge,* he accepted the invitation to fight. □ **reto**
■ *v.* to ask someone to fight; to ask someone to prove that they are right: *he challenged his brother to a boxing match; he challenged me to prove it; I would challenge these computer figures.* □ **retar**
challenger *n.* person who challenges: *the challenger for the heavyweight title,* boxer who is fighting the man who holds the title. □ **retador; aspirante**
challenging *adj.* provocative: *a book with the challenging title 'Are men the weaker sex?'* □ **desafiante**
chamber ['tʃeimbə] *n.* **1** room/hall. □ **habitación, sala, cámara**
council chamber, room where a town council meets. □ **salón de sesiones**
chamber of commerce, official group of businessmen in a town. □ **cámara de comercio**
lawyer's chambers, offices of a lawyer. □ **bufete**
2 space in a piece of machinery, especially one of the spaces for cartridges in a revolver. □ **recámara**
3 ***chamber music,*** music for a few instruments which was originally played in a small room. □ **música de cámara**
chambermaid *n.* woman who cleans rooms in a hotel. □ **camarera**
chamberpot *n.* pot in which you can urinate, and which is usually kept in the bedroom. □ **orinal**
chameleon [kə'mi:liən] *n.* lizard which changes its colour according to its natural surroundings. □ **camaleón**
chammy-leather ['ʃæmileðə] *n.* very soft leather used for washing windows, etc. □ **gamuza**
chamois ['ʃæmi] *n.* very soft leather. □ **gamuza**
champ [tʃæmp] *n.* (*informal*) champion. □ **campeón**
■ *v.* to chew hard and noisily. □ **mascar con ruido**
to champ at the bit, to be impatient; be eager. □ **impacientarse**
champagne [ʃæm'pein] *n.* sparkling French white wine. □ **champán**
champion ['tʃæmpiən] *n.* best person/animal in a particular competition: *he is the world motorcycle champion; a champion bull.* □ **campeón**
■ *v.* to support a cause strenuously: *he championed the cause of peace.* □ **abogar**
championship *n.* **1** support of a cause: *his championship of the human rights movement.* □ **apoyo**
2 contest to determine who is the champion: *a world heavyweight championship.* □ **campeonato**
chance [tʃɑ:ns] *n.* **1** luck: *it was pure chance that they won the game; it was quite a chance that I happened to meet him.* □ **suerte**
games of chance, games where you gamble on the possibility of winning. □ **juegos de azar**
2 ***to take a chance:*** *I am not taking any chances,* I am not risking anything. □ **no quiero correr ningún riesgo**
3 possibility: *do you think you have a chance of winning? is there any chance of getting a cup of tea? there was no chance that he might turn up; give her another chance,* let her try again. □ **posibilidad; oportunidad**
■ *adj.* accidental: *a chance discovery,* a discovery made unexpectedly. □ **fortuito**
■ *v.* **1** to happen unexpectedly: *I chanced to look up at the window.* □ **por casualidad miré por la...**
2 *I chanced upon this book in an antique shop,* I found this book unexpectedly in an antique shop. □ **encontré por casualidad...**
3 to risk: *I think we can chance it.* □ **arriesgar**
chancy *adj.* (*informal*) risky. □ **arriesgado**
chancel ['tʃɑ:nsl] *n.* part of a church near the altar where a choir sits. □ **presbiterio**
chancellery ['tʃɑ:nsəlri] *n.* office of a chancellor; office attached to an embassy. □ **cancillería**
chancellor ['tʃɑ:nsələ] *n.* **1** government minister; (*in Germany/Austria*) = Prime Minister. □ **canciller**
Chancellor of the Exchequer, British minister who deals with finance. □ **Ministro de Hacienda**
2 titular head of a university. □ **rector**
chandelier [ʃændə'liə] *n.* lightfitting hanging from the ceiling with several branches for holding lights. □ **araña**
chandler ['tʃɑ:ndlə] *n.* person who supplies stores for ships. □ **comerciante de efectos navales**
change [tʃeindʒ] *n.* **1** difference from what was before: *I like a change of scenery; we usually go on holiday in August, but this year we are going in July for a change; he thinks the new design is a change for the worse/for the better; have you brought a change of clothes?,* a new set of clothes to wear. □ **cambio**
to ring the changes, (i) to ring peals of bells. □ **repicar el carillón**
(ii) to try several alternatives to see which works best. □ **agotar todas las posibilidades**
2 money given back when you pay a larger amount than the price asked: *the bill comes to $6.50, so you have $3.50 change out of $10.* □ **cambio; vuelta**
3 ***(small) change,*** money in coins: *have you got nothing smaller than that note? - I have no change at all.* □ **suelto**
■ *v.* **1** to make (something) different; to become different: *he has changed since I last saw him,* he looks different; *London has changed a lot in the last ten years.* □ **cambiar**
2 to put on different clothes: *if you want me to mend the car, I'll have to change into my old clothes.* □ **cambiarse**
changing room, room where you can change into sports clothes. □ **vestuario**
3 to give something in place of something else: *can you change a $5 note?,* give me $5 in smaller notes or coins? *I must change the car tyres,* put on new tyres in place of the old ones; *she wants to change her travellers' cheques,* exchange the cheques for money. □ **cambiar**
4 *you will have to change (trains) at Birmingham,* get off one train to catch another which will take you to your destination. □ **hacer transbordo**
changeable *adj.* which changes often/is likely to change: *the weather is changeable.* □ **variable**
changeless *adj.* which never changes. □ **invariable**

channel ['tʃænl] *n.* **1** piece of water connecting two seas. □ **canal**
the English Channel, stretch of water between England and France. □ **Canal de la Mancha**
the Channel Islands, the British islands in the English Channel. □ **islas del Canal de la Mancha**
2 bed (of a stream); ditch/gutter along which liquid can flow. □ **cauce**
3 means/ways: *channels of communication,* ways of communicating; *he heard through official channels that he was being awarded a medal.* □ **canal**
4 frequency band for radio or television. □ **(radio); canal (TV), banda**
■ *v.* (*he channelled*) to direct/to persuade to take a certain direction: *we have to channel his energies into productive work; our job is to channel the information to the right people.* □ **canalizar**
chant [tʃɑːnt] *n.* regular singing of a repeated phrase; monotonous song: *the crowd took up the chant of 'down with the police'.* □ **melopea**
■ *v.* to sing to a regular beat: *the fans chanted the name of the goalkeeper.* □ **corear**
chaos ['keiɔs] *n.* confusion. □ **caos**
chaotic *adj.* confused/disorderly. □ **caótico**
chap [tʃæp] *n.* (*informal*) man: *he's a nice chap.* □ **tío; tipo**
chapel ['tʃæpl] *n.* **1** small church; part of a large church with a separate altar; place of worship for nonconformists. □ **capilla**
2 branch of a trades union (in the printing and publishing industry). □ **gremio**
chaperon ['ʃæpəroun] *n.* older woman who goes around with a young girl on social visits. □ **carabina**
■ *v.* to protect a young girl who is going to a social occasion. □ **hacer de carabina**
chaplain ['tʃæplin] *n.* priest (attached to a private individual or in the armed services). □ **capellán**
chapped [tʃæpt] *adj.* cracked (with cold): *chapped lips.* □ **labios cortados**
chapter ['tʃæptə] *n.* **1** division of a book: *the exciting part comes in chapter nine.* □ **capítulo**
2 *a chapter of accidents,* a series of accidents. □ **serie de...**
3 group of priests who administer a cathedral. □ **cabildo**
char [tʃɑː] *n.* **1** (*informal*) woman who does the housework for someone else. □ **chacha; asistenta**
2 (*informal*) tea. □ **té**
■ *v.* (*he charred*) **1** to do housework for someone: *she goes out charring.* □ **trabajar de asistenta**
2 to burn black: *the charred remains of the barn.* □ **carbonizar**
character ['kærəktə] *n.* **1** central being of a person which makes him an individual who is different from all others: *he has got a very strong character; she is a sweet character.* □ **carácter**
2 person in a play/novel: *he is the leading character in the play.* □ **personaje**
3 odd person: *he is a curious character.* □ **personaje**
4 letter/symbol used in writing or printing: *Chinese characters.* □ **caracteres chinos**
characteristic [kærəktə'ristik] *adj.* special/typical: *characteristic behaviour; this attitude is characteristic of teenagers today.* □ **característico**
■ *n.* special/typical feature: *it is a characteristic of young monkeys.* □ **característica**
characteristically *adv.* typically. □ **característicamente**
characterize ['kærəktəraiz] *v.* to be a typical feature of something: *modern society is characterized by lack of moral standards.* □ **caracterizar**
characterless *adj.* ordinary/with no special features. □ **ordinario**
charade [ʃə'rɑːd] *n.* **1** game where spectators have to guess a word from a scene acted by others. □ **acertijo**
2 action which has no meaning/which is simply a pretence. □ **gesto vacío**
charcoal ['tʃɑːkoul] *n.* black material formed by partly burnt wood: *a charcoal grill; charcoal drawing.* □ **carbón vegetal; carboncillo**
charcoal grey, dark dull grey colour. □ **gris negruzco**
chard [tʃɑːd] *n.* green vegetable like spinach. □ **acelga**
charge [tʃɑːdʒ] *n.* **1** money to be paid: *there is no charge for admission,* you do not have to pay to go in; *you get service free of charge; there is a 10% service charge.* □ **cargo**
2 care (of someone/something): *who's in charge of these children?* □ **¿quién está al cuidado de estos...?**
to take charge of: *he has taken charge of the tickets,* he is dealing with the tickets. □ **se ha encargado de los...**
3 accusation: *he has been arrested on a charge of murder.* □ **cargo**
4 attack (by soldiers running forward): *bayonet charge,* attack with bayonets; *the charge of the Light Brigade.* □ **carga**
5 amount of gunpowder in a cartridge/bomb: *the terrorists planted an explosive charge in the hotel.* □ **carga**
6 amount of electric current: *the cable carries a charge of 3,000 volts.* □ **carga**
■ *v.* **1** to make someone pay: *they charged us $1 for two glasses of orange juice; how much do you charge for changing the oil in a car?* □ **cobrar**
2 to accuse: *the police charged him with murder.* □ **acusar**
3 to put a cartridge in a gun; to put electricity into a battery. □ **cargar**
4 to attack (by running forward): *the soldiers charged the enemy gun emplacements.* □ **atacar**
5 *he charged out of the room,* he rushed out making a lot of noise. □ **salir corriendo**
6 to entrust: *he was charged with the task of writing to the mayor.* □ **encargar**
chargeable *adj.* which can be charged. □ **imputable**
charger *n.* **1** battle horse. □ **caballo de guerra**
2 device for putting electricity into a car battery. □ **cargador**
chargé d'affaires [ʃɑːʒeidæ'fɛə] *n.* deputy of an ambassador. □ **encargado de negocios**
charisma [kə'rizmə] *n.* personal appeal: *somehow the Prime Minister lacks charisma.* □ **carisma**
charismatic [kæriz'mætik] *adj.* which appeals to the people. □ **carismático**
charity ['tʃæriti] *n.* **1** organization which collects money to distribute to the poor; giving of money to the poor: *he gave all his money to charity; I'm collecting on behalf of a local charity.* □ **institución benéfica**
2 kindness (to the poor/the oppressed): *he did it out of charity.* □ **caridad**
charitable *adj.* **1** which refers to a charity: *a charitable organization.* □ **benéfico**
2 kind; not critical: *we have to take a charitable view of his management of the organization.* □ **...una visión comprensiva...**
charitably *adv.* in a charitable way. □ **comprensivamente**

charlady ['tʃɑːleidi] *n.* woman who does housework for someone. □ **asistenta**
charlatan ['ʃɑːlətən] *n.* person who says he is an expert, but really is not. □ **charlatán**
charm [tʃɑːm] *n.* **1** supposedly magic object: *a lucky charm.* □ **amuleto**
charm bracelet, bracelet hung with little silver/gold ornaments. □ **pulsera de colgantes**
2 attractiveness: *he put on all his charm; the charm of the English countryside.* □ **encanto**
■ *v.* **1** to bewitch/to put under a spell: *he has a charmed life,* he is very lucky. □ **encantar**
2 to attract/to make someone pleased: *I was charmed by her singing; she has a charming voice.* □ **encantar**
chart [tʃɑːt] *n.* **1** map of the sea, a river or lake. □ **carta marina; mapa cartográfico**
2 diagram showing statistics: *sales chart,* graph which shows sales; *a chart showing the petrol consumption of different models of cars.* □ **gráfico**
3 *is their record in the* ***charts?*** in the list of most popular records. □ **listas**
■ *v.* **1** to make a map of (the sea, a river or lake): *the explorers charted the coast of South America.* □ **levantar un mapa**
2 to make a diagram; to show information in a diagram. □ **hacer un gráfico**
charter ['tʃɑːtə] *n.* **1** aircraft hired for a particular flight: *we took a charter flight because it was cheaper; we went by charter.* □ **vuelo 'charter'**
2 legal document giving rights or privileges to (a town/a university). □ **carta**
■ *v.* to hire (an aircraft or boat). □ **fletar**
chartered *adj.* (accountant, etc.) who has passed his examinations. □ **jurado**
charwoman ['tʃɑːwumən] *n.* (*pl. charwomen*) woman who does housework for someone. □ **mujer de la limpieza; asistenta**
chary ['tʃɛəri] *adj.* reluctant to do something/cautious: *I am chary of putting too much faith in statistics.* □ **reacio**
chase [tʃeis] *n.* hunt: *we've given up the chase,* stopped chasing. □ **caza**
to give chase to something, to run after it to try to catch it: *the stolen car drove off, and the police car gave chase.* □ **dar caza a alguien**
wild goose chase, useless search for something. □ **búsqueda inútil**
■ *v.* **1** to run after (someone) to try to catch them: *the police chased the burglar.* □ **perseguir**
2 *I am trying to chase away these flies,* to wave away the flies. □ **ahuyentar**
chaser *n.* strong alcoholic drink such as beer, drunk after another, stronger, alcoholic drink. □ **bebida alcohólica tras otra más fuerte**
chasm ['kæzəm] *n.* huge hole in the ground; vast cave. □ **abismo**
chassis ['ʃæsi] *n.* (*pl. chassis*) metal framework of a car. □ **chasis**
chaste [tʃeist] *adj.* (sexually) pure. □ **casto**
chastity *n.* virginity/state of being a virgin. □ **castidad**
chasten ['tʃeisn] *v.* to reprimand; to make (someone) less proud. □ **reprender; bajar los humos**
chastened *adj.* meek; less proud. □ **dócil**
chastise [tʃæ'staiz] *v.* (*formal*) to punish. □ **castigar**
chastisement *n.* punishment. □ **castigo**
chat [tʃæt] *n.* casual friendly talk: *we had a chat over a cup of coffee.* □ **charla**
■ *v.* (*he chatted*) **1** to talk in a casual and friendly way: *they were chatting away in the restaurant.* □ **charlar**
2 *he tried* ***to chat up*** *the girl he met at the bus stop,* (*informal*) to get into conversation/to flirt with. □ **dar palique**
chatty *adj.* (letter) full of unimportant news. □ **llena de noticias banales**
chattel ['tʃætl] *n.* object which you possess: *all your goods and chattels.* □ **enseres**
chatter ['tʃætə] *n.* quick talking. □ **cháchara**
■ *v.* **1** to talk quickly and not seriously: *the children were chattering away in the classroom.* □ **parlotear**
2 *his teeth were chattering,* were rattling because of cold. □ **castañetear**
chatterbox *n.* person who cannot stop talking. □ **parlanchín**
chauffeur ['ʃoufə] *n.* person who is paid to drive a car for someone else: *a chauffeur-driven Rolls.* □ **chófer**
chauvinism ['ʃouvinizm] *n.* excessive pride in your native country. □ **chauvinismo**
chauvinist *n.* person who is excessively proud of his native country. □ **chauvinista**
male chauvinist, man who feels that men are superior to women. □ **machista**
chauvinistic [ʃouvi'nistik] *adj.* nationalistic. □ **patriotero**
cheap [tʃiːp] *adj.* **1** not costing a lot of money: *this coat is much cheaper than that one; cheap jewellery; cheap hotel; he is trying to do it on the cheap,* in the cheapest possible way; *I got it cheap from a man I know at work.* □ **barato**
2 low/sly: *a cheap joke at someone's expense.* □ **un chiste mal intencionado**
cheapen *v.* to reduce the value of something. □ **abaratar**
cheaply *adv.* not expensively; for a low price. □ **a bajo precio**
cheapness *n.* low cost. □ **baratura**
cheat [tʃiːt] *n.* person who tricks someone so that he loses. □ **tramposo**
■ *v.* **1** to trick (someone) so that he loses: *I never play cards with Paul - he always cheats.* □ **hacer trampas**
2 *he cheated me out of $10,* he made me lose $10 by tricking me. □ **estafar**
cheating *n.* act of trickery. □ **trampa**
check [tʃek] *n.* **1** making sure; examination/test: *no check was made on who went into the office; the car has to go to the garage for a check.* □ **comprobación; revisión**
2 sudden halt: *a slight check to our progress.* □ **parón**
3 (*in chess*) a state where your opponent has to move to protect his king. □ **jaque**
4 pattern of squares in different colours: *check shirt; check tablecloth.* □ **a/de cuadros**
5 ticket: *baggage check,* ticket for baggage which has been handed to someone. □ **resguardo**
6 *Amer.* bill (in a restaurant). □ **cuenta**
7 *Amer.* = **cheque.** □ **cheque**
■ *v.* **1** to make sure; to examine: *could you check if we have paid the right amount? I asked the garage to check the brakes.* □ **comprobar**
2 to bring (someone) to a halt: *our progress was checked by the rain; the shipping strike checked our sales overseas.* □ **detener**
3 (*in chess*) to put the opponent's king in danger. □ **dar jaque**
4 to hold back: *she tried to check her tears.* □ **contener**
5 *Amer.* to tick/to mark with a sign to show that

something is correct. □ **poner el visto bueno**
checked *adj.* with a squared pattern: *checked shirt; checked tablecloth.* □ **a cuadros**
checkers *n. Amer.* = **draughts.** □ **juego de damas**
check in *v.* **1** to register when you arrive at a hotel/at an airport; to register when you arrive at work. □ **registrarse**
2 to hand in luggage for safe keeping. □ **facturar**
checklist *n.* list which is used for checking: *a checklist of British birds.* □ **lista de control**
checkmate *n.* (*in chess*) position where the king cannot move. □ **jaque mate**
■ *v.* to put your opponent's king in a position from which he cannot escape. □ **dar jaque mate**
check out *v.* **1** to leave a hotel; to take luggage out of the keeping of someone. □ **pagar la cuenta y marcharse**
2 *Amer.* to verify/to see if something is correct. □ **verificar**
checkout *n.* cash desk in a supermarket. □ **salida de caja**
check over *v.* to look over something to make sure it is all there/all in working order. □ **comprobar**
checkroom *n. Amer.* cloakroom. □ **guardarropa**
check up on *v.* to verify/to see if something is correct. □ **verificar**
checkup *n.* complete medical examination; general examination (of a car). □ **chequeo; revisión**
cheek [tʃi:k] *n.* **1** fat side of the face on either side of the nose and below the eye: *she has got red cheeks.* □ **mejilla**
2 (*informal*) rudeness. □ **descaro**
what cheek!, how rude. □ **¡qué cara!**
■ *v.* (*informal*) to be rude to someone. □ **tener caradura con**
cheekily *adv.* in a rude way. □ **descaradamente**
cheekiness *n.* rudeness. □ **descaro**
cheeky *adj.* rude. □ **descarado**
cheep [tʃi:p] *n.* little cry, like that made by a baby bird. □ **piada**
■ *v.* to make a little cry. □ **piar**
cheer ['tʃiə] *n.* shout of praise or encouragement: *three cheers for the boss - hip! hip! hooray! the winner of the marathon entered the stadium to the cheers of the crowd.* □ **vivas**
cheers!, (i) (*when drinking*) here's to you. □ **a tu salud**
(ii) (*when receiving something*) thank you. □ **gracias**
■ *v.* **1** to shout encouragement: *the crowd cheered when their team scored a goal.* □ **vitorear**
2 to comfort: *the good news cheered his mother.* □ **alegrar**
3 ***to cheer up,*** to make/become happier: *cheer up!,* do not be miserable; *he cheered up considerably when he had had a drink.* □ **animarse**
cheerful *adj.* happy: *I am cheerful because I am going on holiday tomorrow.* □ **alegre**
cheerfully *adv.* happily/gaily. □ **alegremente**
cheerfulness *n.* happiness. □ **alegría**
cheerily *adv.* gaily. □ **alegremente**
cheering *n.* cheers of encouragement. □ **gritos de entusiasmo**
cheerleader *n.* person who directs the cheering of a crowd. □ **animador**
cheerless *adj.* gloomy/sad. □ **melancólico**
cheery *adj.* happy/gay. □ **jovial**
cheese [tʃi:z] *n.* solid food made from milk: *a piece of cheese; we always have cheese as the last course in a meal.* □ **queso**
a cheese, a whole round cheese. □ **un queso**
cream cheese, rich soft cheese. □ **requesón**
processed cheese, soft cheese which has been chemically treated. □ **queso tratado**
toasted cheese, cheese on bread cooked under a grill. □ **tostada de queso fundido**
cheese biscuits, biscuits flavoured with cheese; plain dry biscuits which you eat with cheese. □ **galletas de queso**
cheesecake *n.* tart made of sweet pastry and cream cheese with fruit. □ **tarta de queso**
cheesecloth *n.* thin cotton cloth such as cheeses are wrapped in (often used for light shirts). □ **estopilla**
cheesed *adj. I'm feeling* ***cheesed off,*** (*informal*) I am fed up. □ **estoy hasta el gorro**
cheesemonger *n.* person who specializes in selling cheese. □ **quesero**
cheeseparing *n.* meanness/miserliness. □ **mezquindad**
cheetah ['tʃi:tə] *n.* type of leopard which can run very fast. □ **onza**
chef [ʃef] *n.* (chief) cook (in a restaurant). □ **jefe de cocina**
chemical ['kemikl] *adj.* referring to chemistry. □ **químico**
■ *n.* substance (either natural or man-made) which is formed by reactions between elements: *it takes a very strong chemical to try to clear the blocked drain.* □ **sustancia/producto químico**
chemist ['kemist] *n.* **1** person who specializes in chemistry. □ **químico**
2 person who makes or sells medicines: *go along to the chemist's to get some cough medicine.* □ **farmacéutico; farmacia**
chemistry *n.* science of chemical substances, elements, compounds, and their reactions. □ **química**
inorganic chemistry, study of elements which are not part of living bodies. □ **...inorgánica**
organic chemistry, study of elements which form part of living bodies. □ **...orgánica**
cheque [tʃek] *Amer.* **check** *n.* note to a bank asking them to pay money from one account to another: *can I pay by cheque? I wrote him a cheque for $100.* □ **cheque**
cheque book, book of about 30 blank cheques. □ **talonario**
blank cheque, cheque which has no details filled in. □ **cheque en blanco**
crossed cheque, cheque which can only be paid through a bank. □ **cheque cruzado**
chequers ['tʃekəz] *n. pl.* squares in a pattern. □ **cuadros**
chequered *adj.* **1** laid out in a pattern of squares: *chequered tablecloth.* □ **a cuadros**
2 varied/with good and bad parts: *he has had a chequered career.* □ **...con altibajos**
cherish ['tʃeriʃ] *v.* to love/to treat kindly; to nourish (a hope): *I cherish the hope that he will come back home one day.* □ **querer; abrigar (una esperanza)**
cheroot [ʃə'ru:t] *n.* long thin cigar with both ends open. □ **palma**
cherry ['tʃeri] *n.* small summer fruit, growing at the end of a long stalk. □ **cereza**
flowering cherry, cherry tree, grown for its flowers, not fruit. □ **cerezo de flor**
cherry (tree), tree which bears cherries. □ **cerezo**
cherry stone, stone in a cherry. □ **pipo de cereza**
cherub ['tʃerəb] *n.* small fat child-like angel; child who looks like an angel. □ **querubín**
cherubic [tʃe'ru:bik] *adj.* round and innocent (face). □ **de angelito**
chess [tʃes] *n.* game for two people played on a black and white squared board with sixteen pieces

on each side. □ **ajedrez**
chessboard *n.* squared board you play chess on. □ **tablero de...**
chessmen *n.* pieces used for playing chess. □ **piezas**
chest [tʃest] *n.* **1** piece of furniture, like a large box: *he keeps his papers in an old oak chest.* □ **cofre**
chest of drawers, piece of furniture with several drawers for keeping clothes in. □ **cómoda**
chest freezer, freezer of which the top is a lid. □ **congelador de caja**
2 top front part of the body, where the heart and lungs are: *he has a cold on the chest,* he has a wheezy cough; *she has a weak chest,* she is always getting coughs or bronchitis. □ **pecho**
to get something off your chest, to speak frankly about something which is worrying you. □ **desahogarse**
chestnut ['tʃesnʌt] *n.* **1** bright red-brown nut; large tree which grows these nuts: *chestnut tree.* □ **castaña; castaño (árbol)**
sweet chestnut, edible chestnut. □ **castaña**
2 red-brown colour. □ **castaño**
3 red-brown horse. □ **alazán**
4 (*informal*) old joke; cliché. □ **chiste viejo**
chew [tʃuː] *v.* to make something soft with your teeth: *this meat is too tough to chew.* □ **masticar**
chewing gum *n.* sweet gum which you chew but do not swallow. □ **chicle**
chic [ʃiːk] *adj.* elegant: *a very chic hat; she lives at a chic address,* an address in one of the smart areas of the town. □ **'chic'**
radical chic, fashionable left-wing opinions or people who hold them. □ **progre**
chick [tʃɪk] *n.* baby bird, especially hen. □ **polluelo**
chicken ['tʃikin] *n.* young farmyard bird, especially young hen; meat from a (young) hen: *the farmer's wife was feeding the chickens; roast chicken.* □ **pollo**
■ *v.* ***to chicken out,*** to back out of a fight/argument because you are afraid. □ **rajarse**
chickenfeed *n.* (*informal*) not much money/profit. □ **una miseria**
chicken-livered *adj.* scared/frightened. □ **cagado de miedo**
chickenpox *n.* disease (usually of children) which gives red itchy spots. □ **varicela**
chicory ['tʃikəri] *n.* vegetable of which the leaves are used for salads, and the roots are dried and ground to mix with coffee to make it bitter. □ **achicoria**
chief [tʃiːf] *adj.* most important: *chief engineer; the chief cause for complaint.* □ **jefe**
commander-in-chief, commander above all other officers. □ **comandante en jefe**
■ *n.* leader: *he is the chief of the tribe.* □ **jefe**
chiefly *adv.* mainly. □ **principalmente**
chieftain ['tʃiːftən] *n.* leader of a tribe. □ **cacique**
chiffon ['ʃifɔn] *n.* type of very thin material. □ **'chiffon', gasa**
chignon ['ʃiːnjɔn] *n.* hair tied together in a knot at the back of the head. □ **moño**
chilblain ['tʃilblein] *n.* painful swelling on hands, ears and feet caused by the cold. □ **sabañón**
child [tʃaild] *n.* (*pl. children*) young boy or girl: *the children came running out of school; how many children have you got?,* how many sons and daughters have you got? □ **niño; hijo**
it's child's play, it's very easy. □ **...juego de niños**
childbirth *n.* act of giving birth to a child: *she died in childbirth.* □ **parto**
childhood *n.* state of being a child; time when you are a child (between birth and about 12 years old). □ **niñez; infancia**
childish *adj.* like a child; silly/foolish. □ **infantil**
childishness *n.* silliness. □ **niñería**
childless *adj.* with no children. □ **sin hijos**
childlike *adj.* innocent like a child. □ **inocente**
Chile ['tʃili] *n.* country in South America. □ **Chile**
Chilean *adj.* referring to Chile. □ **chileno**
■ *n.* person from Chile. □ **chileno**
chill [tʃil] *n.* **1** coldness in the air. □ **frío**
to take the chill off something, to warm it up a little. □ **quitar el frío**
2 illness caused by cold: *I think he caught a chill standing in the rain.* □ **enfriamiento**
■ *v.* **1** to cool: *chilled wine.* □ **enfriar**
2 *I am chilled to the bone,* I am cold. □ **helado hasta los huesos**
chilliness *n.* coldness. □ **frío; frialdad**
chilly *adj.* **1** cold: *a chilly morning.* □ **fresco**
2 *a chilly reception,* not a very welcoming reception. □ **fría**
chilli ['tʃili] *Amer.* **chili** *n.* dried seed pod of the pepper plant, used to make very hot sauces. □ **chile**
chime [tʃaim] *n.* ringing of bells. □ **repique**
■ *v.* to ring: *the bells chimed out on Christmas morning; the clock chimed six.* □ **repicar; dar**
chimney ['tʃimni] *n.* tall tube or brick column for taking smoke away from a fire: *the factory has six tall chimneys.* □ **chimenea**
chimney pot *n.* round top to a chimney on a house. □ **sombrerete**
chimney stack *n.* tall chimney rising above the roof of a factory; group of chimneys on the roof of a house. □ **chimenea**
chimney sweep *n.* person who cleans chimneys. □ **deshollinador**
chimpanzee [tʃimpæn'ziː] (*informal*) **chimp** [tʃimp] *n.* type of intelligent ape from Africa. □ **chimpancé**
chin [tʃin] *n.* front part of the bottom jaw: *I hit him on the chin.* □ **mentón; barbilla**
China ['tʃainə] *n.* **1** very large country in Asia. □ **China**
2 *china,* porcelain; cups, plates, etc., made out of fine white clay: *a china teapot; English china.* □ **porcelana**
chine [tʃain] *v.* to cut the rib bones from the backbone of a joint of meat. □ **deshuesar**
Chinese [tʃai'niːz] *adj.* referring to China. □ **chino**
■ *n.* **1** person from China. □ **chino**
2 language spoken in China. □ **chino**
chink [tʃiŋk] *n.* **1** little crack: *the door was open a chink.* □ **grieta**
2 noise of metal objects, etc., hitting each other: *the chink of coins.* □ **tintineo**
■ *v.* to make a noise by knocking metal objects, etc., together: *he chinked the coins in his pocket.* □ **hacer tintinear**
chintz [tʃints] *n.* thick cotton cloth with bright flower patterns, used for upholstery. □ **chintz**
chip [tʃip] *n.* **1** little piece of wood/stone, etc.: *as he chiselled away at the statue, the chips flew in all directions.* □ **viruta, trocito**
2 *there is a chip in this plate,* a place where a small piece has broken off. □ **desportilladura**
3 ***to have a chip on your shoulder about something,*** to be permanently indignant about something where you feel you have been treated unfairly. □ **tener una espina clavada**
4 long piece of potato fried in oil: *I want meat pie and chips.* □ **patata frita**
5 *Amer.* potato crisp. □ **patata frita**
■ *v.* (*he chipped*) to break off a small piece: *the plate isn't broken, only chipped.* □ **desportillarse**

chipboard *n.* thick board made of small chips of wood glued together, and used in building. □ **aglomerado**
chip in *v.* to contribute; to interrupt. □ **compartir gastos; interrumpir**
chip off *v.* to break off: *the paint is chipping off.* □ **desconcharse**
chipped *adj. chipped potatoes,* long pieces of potato fried in oil. □ **patatas fritas**
chippings *n. pl.* small bits of stone used to make roads. □ **casquijo**
chipmunk ['tʃipmʌŋk] *n.* small North American animal, like a striped squirrel. □ **ardilla listada**
chipolata [tʃipə'lɑ:tə] *n.* long thin sausage. □ **longaniza**
chiropodist [ki'rɔpədist] *n.* person who specializes in the treatment of feet. □ **pedicuro**
chiropody *n.* treatment of feet. □ **quiropodia**
chirp [tʃə:p] *n.* sharp short call of birds/grasshoppers. □ **gorjeo**
■ *v.* (*of birds/grasshoppers*) to call. □ **gorjear**
chirpy *adj.* (*informal*) bright and cheerful. □ **alegre**
chisel ['tʃizl] *n.* metal tool for cutting small pieces of wood/stone, when hit with a hammer. □ **formón (madera); cincel (piedra)**
■ *v.* (*he chiselled*) **1** to cut wood/stone with a chisel: *he chiselled out a hole for the joint.* □ **escoplar; cincelar**
2 (*slang*) to swindle. □ **timar**
chit [tʃit] *n.* **1** note/small invoice. □ **nota**
2 young girl. □ **jovencita**
chitchat ['tʃittʃæt] *n.* gossip/talk. □ **cháchara**
chivalrous ['ʃivəlrəs] *adj.* courteous/very polite. □ **caballeroso**
chivalry *n.* politeness/courtesy. □ **caballerosidad**
the age of chivalry, medieval period when knights fought in tournaments. □ **caballería**
chives [tʃaivz] *n. pl.* onion-like plant with small green leaves. □ **cebollino**
chlorine ['klɔ:ri:n] *n.* (*chemical element*: Cl) greenish gas used to disinfect swimming pools, etc. □ **cloro**
chlorinate ['klɔ:rineit] *v.* to disinfect with chlorine: *the swimming pool smells of chlorinated water.* □ **clorar**
chloroform ['klɔrəfɔ:m] *n.* chemical, whose vapour when breathed makes you unconscious: *dentists used to give people chloroform before pulling out their teeth.* □ **cloroformo**
■ *v.* to make someone unconscious with chloroform. □ **cloroformizar**
chlorophyll ['klɔrəfil] *n.* green substance which makes plants green. □ **clorofila**
chock [tʃɔk] *n.* small block of wood which prevents wheels turning. □ **calzo, cuña**
chock-a-block, chock-full *adj.* completely full: *the room was chock-a-block for the auction.* □ **...lleno hasta los topes**
chocolate ['tʃɔklət] *n.* **1** food made from cacao tree seeds: *a bar of chocolate; chocolate cake; chocolate sauce; his carpet is chocolate colour.* □ **chocolate**
plain chocolate, bitter chocolate. □ **sin leche**
milk chocolate, sweet chocolate made with milk. □ **...con leche**
2 *a drink of hot chocolate,* a hot drink made of powdered chocolate. □ **...a la taza**
3 small sweet made from chocolate: *a box of chocolates.* □ **chocolatina, bombón**
choice [tʃɔis] *n.* **1** something you choose: *the shop has a wonderful choice of shoes,* a great many shoes to choose from. □ **elección; surtido**
2 *I haven't any choice,* I have to do it. □ **alternativa**
■ *adj. choice peaches,* peaches which have been specially selected. □ **selecto**
choir ['kwaiə] *n.* **1** group of people singing together: *church choir.* □ **coro**
2 part of the church where the choir sits. □ **coro**
choirboy *n.* boy who sings in a church choir. □ **niño de coro**
choirmaster *n.* person who conducts and rehearses a choir. □ **director de coro**
choke [tʃouk] *n.* **1** blockage in the throat. □ **ahogo**
2 (*in a car engine*) valve which increases the flow of air to the engine; knob on the dashboard which activates this valve: *to start the car you should have the choke full out.* □ **regulador del aire**
3 central inedible part of a globe artichoke. □ **heno**
■ *v.* **1** to block (a pipe, etc.). □ **obturar**
2 to stop breathing because you have swallowed something: *he choked on his sandwich; the smoke makes you choke.* □ **atragantarse; ahogarse**
choke back *v.* to hold back (tears). □ **contener**
choker *n.* piece of ribbon, etc., worn tightly round the neck. □ **gargantilla**
choking *adj.* stifling: *choking fog; the firemen struggled in choking clouds of smoke.* □ **asfixiante**
cholera ['kɔlerə] *n.* serious infectious disease causing severe diarrhoea: *a cholera epidemic.* □ **cólera**
cholesterol [kə'lesterɔl] *n.* substance in fats and eggs which is said to deposit fat in the arteries. □ **colesterol**
choose [tʃu:z] *v.* (*he chose; he has chosen*) to decide to take something/to do one particular thing: *I can't make up my mind what colour shirt to choose; have you chosen what you want on the menu? In the end he chose not to go to Norway.* □ **escoger, elegir**
choosing *n.* act of making a choice. □ **elección**
choosy *adj.* difficult to please. □ **quisquilloso**
chop [tʃɔp] *n.* piece of meat with a rib bone: *lamb chops and peas.* □ **chuleta**
■ *v.* (*he chopped*) to cut into small pieces with an axe/a knife: *he chopped the wood to bits.* □ **trocear**
chop down *v.* to cut down (a tree) with an axe. □ **talar**
chop off *v.* to cut off. □ **cortar**
chopper *n.* **1** axe for cutting meat. □ **tajadera**
2 (*slang*) helicopter. □ **helicóptero**
choppy *adj.* quite rough (sea). □ **picado**
chop up *v.* to cut up into little bits: *I am chopping up wood for the fire.* □ **partir (leña); picar (carne)**
chopsticks ['tʃɔpstiks] *n. pl.* small sticks used by oriental people for eating food. □ **palillos**
choral ['kɔ:rəl] *adj.* referring to a choir: *choral music; choral society.* □ **coral**
chord [kɔ:d] *n.* **1** several notes played together in harmony. □ **acorde**
2 line which joins two points on the circumference of a circle. □ **cuerda**
chore [tʃɔ:] *n.* piece of routine work, especially housework. □ **faena**
choreography [kɔri'ɔgrəfi] *n.* art of working out the steps for a ballet. □ **coreografía**
choreographer *n.* person who works out the steps for a ballet. □ **coreógrafo**
chorister ['kɔristə] *n.* person who sings in a choir. □ **miembro de un coro**
chortle ['tʃɔ:tl] *v.* to chuckle loudly. □ **reír entre dientes**
chorus ['kɔ:rəs] *n.* **1** group of people who sing or dance together: *the chorus to an opera.* □ **coro**

2 part of a song which is repeated by everyone together. □ **estribillo**
■ *v.* to say something all together: *'Oh no' they all chorused.* □ **corear**
chorus-girl *n.* girl who appears as a member of a chorus in a variety show. □ **corista**
chose [tʃouz] **chosen** [tʃouzn] *v. see* **choose**
chowder ['tʃaudə] *n. Amer.* fish soup. □ **sopa de pescado**
christen ['krisn] *v.* **1** to give a name to (a baby) in church; to give a name to a ship/a bell, etc., at a ceremony: *she has been christened Anne.* □ **bautizar como, poner nombre**
2 to use something for the first time. □ **estrenar**
christening *n.* ceremony in church where a baby is given a name. □ **bautismo**
Christian ['kristʃən] *n.* person who believes in Jesus Christ. □ **cristiano**
■ *adj.* referring to Jesus Christ: *the Christian Church.* □ **cristiano**
Christian name, first name given at a ceremony in church. □ **nombre de pila**
Christianity [kristi'æniti] *n.* doctrine preached by Christ and followed by Christians ever since. □ **cristianismo**
Christmas ['krisməs] *n.* Christian festival held on December 25th: *Christmas cake; Christmas pudding; Christmas dinner.* □ **Navidad**
Christmas Day, December 25th. □ **día de Navidad**
Father Christmas, man dressed in red robes with a long white beard who is believed to bring gifts to children on Christmas Day. □ **Papá Noel**
chrome [kroum] *n.* chromium/hard shiny metal. □ **cromo**
chrome yellow, bright yellow. □ **amarillo de cromo**
chromium ['kroumiəm] *n.* (*chemical element*: Cr) hard shiny metal which does not rust: *chromium-plated handles.* □ **cromo**
chromosome ['krouməsoum] *n.* one of several elements which form a biological cell, and which carries the genes. □ **cromosoma**
chronic ['krɔnik] *adj.* very serious/continual/repeating (illness, etc.): *chronic iron deficiency; chronic lack of communications.* □ **crónico**
chronicle ['krɔnikl] *n.* record of things which take place; news story: *chronicle of events of the past two years.* □ **crónica**
■ *v.* to write the history of events in the order in which they took place: *he chronicled the downfall of the Roman Empire.* □ **hacer la crónica de**
chronicler *n.* person who writes a chronicle. □ **cronista**
chronological [krɔnə'lɔdʒikl] *adj.* in order of when the events happened: *put these treaties in chronological order; list of presidents in chronological order.* □ **cronológico**
chronologically *adv.* in chronological order. □ **cronológicamente**
chronometer [krə'nɔmitə] *n.* very correct watch (as used for timing races). □ **cronómetro**
chrysalis ['krisəlis] *n.* hard-cased stage through which a caterpillar passes before turning into a butterfly or moth. □ **crisálida**
chrysanthemum [kri'sænθəməm] *n.* bright-coloured autumn flower. □ **crisantemo**
chubby ['tʃʌbi] *adj.* quite plump. □ **regordete**
chuck [tʃʌk] *n.* **1** part of a drill which holds the bit. □ **portabroca**
2 type of beef steak. □ **paletilla**
■ *v.* (*informal*) **1** to throw: *stop chucking stones at cars.* □ **tirar**
2 *he was chucked out of his job,* thrown out/dismissed. □ **le pusieron de patitas en la calle**
3 *he chucked up his job,* he gave up his job/resigned. □ **mandó a paseo su trabajo**
chucker-out *n.* person whose job is to throw undesirable people out of night-clubs, etc. □ **matón**
chuckle ['tʃʌkl] *n.* quiet laugh. □ **risita**
■ *v.* to give a quiet laugh. □ **reírse entre dientes**
chug [tʃʌg] *v.* (*he chugged*) to make a regular puffing noise like a steam engine. □ **resoplar**
chum [tʃʌm] *n.* (*informal*) friend. □ **amiguete**
chump [tʃʌmp] *n.* ***chump chop,*** large lamb chop. □ **chuleta**
chunk [tʃʌŋk] *n.* large piece: *give me a chunk of bread.* □ **pedazo**
church [tʃə:tʃ] *n.* **1** large building for Christian religious ceremonies: *do you go to church every Sunday?* □ **iglesia**
2 group of Christians together. □ **Iglesia**
the Roman Catholic Church, all Roman Catholics. □ **...Apostólica y Romana**
the Orthodox Church, all Eastern Christians. □ **...Ortodoxa**
churchgoer *n.* person who goes to church (regularly). □ **practicante**
churchwarden *n.* senior member of a parish. □ **mayordomo**
churchyard *n.* cemetery round a church. □ **patio de la iglesia**
churlish ['tʃə:liʃ] *adj.* rude: *it would be churlish of me to refuse.* □ **grosero**
churlishness *n.* rudeness. □ **grosería**
churn [tʃə:n] *n.* large metal container for milk; container in which cream is turned to make butter. □ **lechera; mantequera**
■ *v.* **1** to turn cream to make butter. □ **hacer mantequilla**
2 *the cars churned up the mud,* mixed up/stirred up the mud. □ **...removieron el barro**
churn out *v.* (*informal*) to produce in a series: *he churns out newspaper articles at a rate of two a week.* □ **hacer como churros**
chute [ʃu:t] *n.* **1** slide into water (in a swimming pool). □ **tobogán**
2 slide for sending things to a lower level. □ **tolva**
chutney ['tʃʌtni] *n.* pickle (usually made with tomatoes, onions and spices). □ **salsa picante**
CIA [si:ai'ei] *abbreviation for* Central Intelligence Agency. □ **CIA**
CID [si:ai'di:] *abbreviation for* Criminal Investigation Department. □ **CID**
cider ['saidə] *n.* alcoholic drink made from fermented apple juice. □ **sidra**
cigar [si'gɑ:] *n.* tight roll of tobacco leaves which you can light and smoke: *the businessman was smoking a large cigar.* □ **puro**
cigarette [sigə'ret] *n.* chopped tobacco rolled in very thin paper which you can light and smoke: *how many cigarettes do you smoke a day?* □ **cigarrillo**
cigarette case *n.* special case for holding cigarettes. □ **pitillera**
cigarette end *n.* end of a cigarette which has been smoked. □ **colilla**
cigarette holder *n.* holder for putting cigarettes in to smoke. □ **boquilla**
cinders ['sindəz] *n. pl.* lumps of coarse ash left after coal has been burnt. □ **cenizas**
cinder track *n.* race track covered with cinders. □ **pista de ceniza**
cinema ['sinəmə] *n.* **1** theatre for showing films: *what is on at the cinema this week? we go to the cinema*

every Friday. □ **cine**
2 art of making moving pictures: *the cinema industry; the French cinema of the 1930's.* □ **cine**
cinematographic [sinəmætə'græfik] *adj.* referring to the cinema. □ **cinematográfico**
cinnamon ['sinəmən] *n.* spice made from the bark of a tropical tree. □ **canela**
cipher ['saifə] *n.* **1** code/secret message: *I am sending a message in cipher.* □ **clave**
2 monogram/initials of a name linked together artistically. □ **monograma**
3 zero. □ **cero**
4 *he is a mere cipher,* he is of no importance. □ **es un cero a la izquierda**
circa ['sə:kə] *prep.* about: *he died circa 1250.* □ **hacia**
circle ['sə:kl] *n.* **1** line forming a round shape: *we sat in a circle and sang songs; draw a circle 10 cm in diameter.* □ **círculo**
2 *the wheel has* ***come full circle,*** events have returned to their original starting point. □ **...al punto de partida**
3 row of seats above the stalls in a theatre: *dress circle; upper circle.* □ **entresuelo**
4 group of people/society: *he moves in artistic circles.* □ **círculo**
■ *v.* to go round in a ring: *the aircraft circled the airport for an hour; vultures circled round the dead antelope.* □ **dar vueltas alrededor de...**
circuit ['sə:kit] *n.* **1** trip around something: *they made a circuit of the town; the winning racing driver made the fastest circuit of the course.* □ **circuito**
2 area visited by a judge who travels from court to court. □ **circuito**
3 path of electricity. □ **circuito**
short circuit, fault (caused by crossed wires, etc.) when electricity follows a shorter path than usual. □ **cortocircuito**
closed circuit television, private television operating over a short area by cable. □ **circuito cerrado**
circuitous [sə'kjuitəs] *adj.* roundabout (way). □ **sinuoso**
circular ['sə:kjulə] *adj.* and *n.* (something) round in shape; publicity leaflet given out to many people: *I have had a circular from the gas people saying that charges are going up.* □ **circular**
circulate ['sə:kjuleit] *v.* **1** to distribute/to pass round. □ **hacer circular**
2 to move round: *visitors were circulating freely round the exhibition.* □ **circular**
circulation [sə:kju'leiʃn] *n.* **1** movement of blood round the body: *she has poor circulation.* □ **circulación**
2 number of copies of a newspaper which are sold. □ **circulación**
circumcise ['sə:kəmsaiz] *v.* to remove the foreskin of a male person. □ **circuncidar**
circumference [sə'kʌmfərəns] *n.* (distance round) the edge of a circle. □ **circunferencia**
circumnavigate [sə:kəm'nævigeit] *v.* (*formal*) to sail round (the world). □ **circunnavegar**
circumscribe [sə:kəm'skraib] *v.* (*formal*) to draw a line round something; to set limits to something: *his powers are circumscribed by parliament.* □ **circunscribir**
circumscription [sə:kəm'skripʃən] *n.* limiting; a limited area. □ **circunscripción**
circumstances ['sə:kəmstənsiz] *n. pl.* **1** way in which something took place: *what were the circumstances of his death?* □ **circunstancias**
under no circumstances, not at all. □ **bajo ninguna circunstancia**
in the circumstances, as things have turned out like this/as it happens: *it's a pity it's pouring down, but in the circumstances it doesn't matter so much as there is plenty to do indoors.* □ **en estas circunstancias**
2 state of your finances: *he is in easy circumstances; they are in tight circumstances.* □ **situación**
circumstantial [sə:kəm'stænʃl] *adj.* giving a lot of details. □ **detallado**
circumstantial evidence, evidence which indirectly leads to the criminal but does not offer firm proof. □ **indirecto**
circumvent [sə:kəm'vent] *v.* to avoid: *he tried to circumvent the customs regulations.* □ **burlar; circunvenir**
circus ['sə:kəs] *n.* **1** travelling show given under a large tent, with animals, clowns, etc. □ **circo**
2 busy roundabout in the centre of a large town. □ **glorieta**
cirrhosis [si'rousis] *n.* disease of the liver caused especially by alcohol. □ **cirrosis**
cirrus ['sirəs] *n.* small very high fleecy cloud. □ **cirro**
cissy ['sisi] *n.* (*informal*) man/boy who acts like a girl. □ **mariquita**
cistern ['sistən] *n.* water tank. □ **cisterna**
citadel ['sitədəl] *n.* fort guarding a town. □ **ciudadela**
cite [sait] *v.* **1** to quote a reference as proof: *to justify his action he cited two other people who had done the same thing.* □ **citar**
2 to call someone to appear in court: *to cite a witness.* □ **citar**
citation [sai'teiʃn] *n.* **1** official document recognizing an act of bravery. □ **citación**
2 quotation of something as a reference or proof. □ **cita**
3 summons to appear in court. □ **citación**
citizen ['sitizn] *n.* **1** inhabitant of a town: *the citizens of London are called Londoners.* □ **ciudadano**
2 person with full rights as an inhabitant of a country: *he was born in India but is a British citizen.* □ **súbdito, ciudadano**
citizenship *n.* state of being a citizen: *does she have French citizenship?* □ **ciudadanía**
citric ['sitrik] *adj.* ***citric acid,*** acid found in citrus fruit. □ **cítrico**
citrus ['sitrəs] *n.* ***citrus fruit,*** fruit such as oranges, lemons or grapefruit. □ **cítricos**
city ['siti] *n.* **1** very large town: *what is the largest city in Germany?* □ **ciudad**
2 town created by charter, often with a cathedral. □ **ciudad**
the City, the old self-governing town of London, now the main business district. □ **'City' londinense**
civet ['sivət] *n.* type of African wild cat, which provides a substance used in making perfume. □ **civeta**
civic ['sivik] *adj.* referring to a city. □ **cívico**
civic centre, social/sports centre run by a city. □ **centro cultural**
civic authorities, leaders of a city. □ **autoridades municipales**
civics *n.* study of municipal affairs. □ **estudio de la política municipal**
civil ['sivl] *adj.* **1** belonging to the general public, not to the army. □ **civil**
civil service, the government bureaucracy. □ **administración pública; funcionariado**
2 referring to the ordinary citizen. □ **civil**
civil action, court action brought by one citizen against another. □ **procedimiento civil**
civil defence, defence by ordinary citizens, not the army. □ **defensa civil**

civil engineer, person who designs roads, bridges, etc. □ **ingeniero de caminos**
civil law, law referring to the citizen, not to criminals. □ **derecho civil**
civil rights, the rights of a citizen. □ **derechos civiles**
civil rights movement, campaign to ensure that all citizens have equal rights. □ **movimiento por los derechos civiles**
civil war, war between groups in the same country. □ **guerra civil**
3 polite: *he did not answer in a very civil tone.* □ **cortés**
civilian [si'viljən] *adj.* and *n.* (person) not belonging to the armed forces; private citizen: *during the war many civilians were killed by enemy attacks; back in civilian life,* out of the army. □ **civil**
civility *n.* politeness. □ **cortesía**
civilly *adv.* politely. □ **cortésmente**
civilize ['sivilaiz] *v.* **1** to educate (primitive people) to a higher level of society: *the invaders tried to civilize the natives.* □ **civilizar**
2 to make (someone) less rude/uncouth: *his wife is a civilizing influence.* □ **educar**
civilization [sivilai'zeiʃn] *n.* regular civilized way of conducting one's life: *Roman civilization spread over most of Western Europe.* □ **civilización**
clad [klæd] *adj.* covered (with clothes): *you should be warmly clad if you're going mountain climbing.* □ **vestido; abrigado**
cladding *n.* material for insulating walls against cold. □ **aislamiento térmico**
claim [kleim] *n.* **1** demand: *he put in a claim for more money.* □ **petición**
2 statement/assertion: *his claim is that he is related to me; does she have a claim to further state benefits?* □ **afirmación**
to lay claim to: *they laid claim to this territory,* they stated it was theirs. □ **reivindicación**
■ *v.* **1** to demand: *she claimed the prize.* □ **exigir**
2 to state/to assert (without any proof): *he claims he is a relative of mine.* □ **pretender, afirmar**
3 to say you own something which has been left/lost: *does anybody claim this watch? she claimed her luggage at the left luggage office.* □ **reclamar**
claimant *n.* person who claims a right. □ **demandante**
clairvoyant [kleə'vɔiənt] *n.* person who can see mentally things which are happening elsewhere/who can foretell the future. □ **clarividente**
clairvoyance *n.* act of communicating with spirits/of foretelling the future. □ **clarividencia**
clam [klæm] *n.* large shellfish with a hinged shell. □ **almeja**
clamber ['klæmbə] *v.* to climb with difficulty: *the soldiers clambered over the wall.* □ **trepar, gatear**
clammy ['klæmi] *adj.* wet and cold: *he has clammy hands.* □ **frío y húmedo**
clamour ['klæmə] *Amer.* **clamor** *n.* shouting: *a clamour arose for more food.* □ **clamor**
■ *v.* to shout/to demand loudly: *they clamoured to be heard; they were clamouring for food.* □ **pedir a voces**
clamorous *adj.* noisy/shouting. □ **clamoroso**
clamp [klæmp] *n.* metal pieces which are screwed tightly to hold something together: *put a clamp round the pieces of wood until the glue dries.* □ **abrazadera**
■ *v.* **1** to hold tight with a clamp. □ **sujetar con abrazadera**
2 ***to clamp down on,*** to stop (petty crime, etc.): *the police are clamping down on people who exceed the speed limit.* □ **tratar de acabar con...**
clampdown *n.* severe action to stop something: *there has been a clampdown on late night parties.* □ **batida**
clan [klæn] *n.* Scottish family tribe: *the clan MacDonald; the MacDonald clan.* □ **clan**
clannish *adj.* loyal to the clan; supporting your own group. □ **con espíritu de clan**
clannishness *n.* loyalty to one's tribe. □ **lealtad**
clansman *n.* (*pl. clansmen*) member of a clan. □ **miembro de un clan**
clandestine [klæn'destin] *adj.* secret/undercover: *clandestine making of alcohol.* □ **clandestino**
clang [klæŋ] *n.* loud noise of metal ringing: *the clang of the bell.* □ **sonido metálico**
■ *v.* to make a loud ringing noise: *the bell clanged.* □ **sonar**
clanger *n.* ***to drop a clanger,*** (*informal*) to make a very bad mistake. □ **meter la pata**
clank [klæŋk] *n.* loud noise of metal hitting metal: *the clank of chains.* □ **ruido metálico**
■ *v.* to make a noise of metal hitting other metal: *the chains clanked; the knight in armour clanked his way up the stairs.* □ **hacer ruido metálico**
clap [klæp] *n.* **1** beating of hands against each other to show pleasure: *give him a big clap.* □ **aplauso**
2 friendly tap (with the hand): *a clap on the shoulder.* □ **palmada**
3 loud noise (of thunder). □ **estruendo**
■ *v.* (*he clapped*) **1** to beat your hands together to show your are pleased: *at the end of the concert the audience clapped and cheered.* □ **aplaudir**
2 to give someone a friendly tap with the hand: *he clapped him on the shoulder.* □ **dar una palmada a...**
3 to put suddenly: *he was clapped in prison.* □ **meter en la...**
to clap eyes on: *the first time I clapped eyes on him,* the first time I saw him. □ **poner los ojos en**
clapped out *adj.* (*slang*) worn out/broken-down (car, etc.). □ **para el arrastre**
clapper *n.* swinging metal bar inside a bell which strikes the bell. □ **badajo**
clapperboard *n.* black board with a striped hinged section at the top, used in film making to indicate the start of a new scene. □ **claqueta**
clapping *n.* applause: *the clapping went on for five minutes after the end of the concert.* □ **aplausos**
claptrap ['klæptræp] *n.* (*informal*) rubbish: *don't talk claptrap.* □ **chorradas**
claret ['klærət] *n.* red Bordeaux wine. □ **vino tinto de Burdeos**
clarify ['klærifai] *v.* **1** to make clear: *to clarify a question; can you clarify my position as regards tax?* □ **aclarar**
2 *to clarify butter,* to heat it until it becomes transparent. □ **clarificar...**
clarification [klærifi'keiʃn] *n.* making clear/explanation: *his statement needs clarification.* □ **aclaración**
clarinet [klæri'net] *n.* wind instrument in the woodwind group. □ **clarinete**
clarinettist *n.* person who plays a clarinet. □ **clarinetista**
clarity ['klæriti] *n.* clearness. □ **claridad**
clash [klæʃ] *n.* **1** loud noise of things hitting each other: *the clash of cymbals; clash of glasses.* □ **estrépito**
2 battle/conflict: *a clash between two armed mobs; a border clash,* conflict across a frontier. □ **choque**
3 *clash between two colours,* shock of two colours seen side by side. □ **contraste**
4 *a clash of interests,* where interests of two people/firms are in conflict. □ **conflicto de intereses**

■ *v.* **1** to bang together making a loud noise. □ **chocar con ruido**
2 not to agree; to be in conflict: *the dates of the two meetings clash,* the meetings are held on the same day, so you cannot attend both; *the colours clash,* they give a shock when seen side by side; *do not wear that tie, it clashes with your shirt; the interests of the two firms clash.* □ **desentonar, no coincidir**
3 to fight: *the mobs clashed with police; the frontier patrols have clashed on several occasions.* □ **chocar**

clasp [klɑːsp] *n.* **1** device for holding something shut: *clasp on a purse; clasp on a necklace.* □ **cierre**
2 brooch. □ **broche**
3 act of holding in your hand. □ **apretón (de mano)**
■ *v.* to hold something tight: *he clasped a stick in his right hand; she clasped my hand.* □ **agarrar**
claspknife *n.* (*pl. claspknives*) pocket knife which folds shut. □ **navaja**

class [klɑːs] *n.* **1** group of people with the same position in society. □ **clase**
middle class, class of professional people/bourgeoisie. □ **clase media**
working class, class of people who do mainly manual labour. □ **clase obrera**
upper class, the rich/the aristocracy. □ **clase alta**
2 group of people (usually children) who study together: *there are thirty children in my son's class; I go to evening classes on Thursdays to learn German; she goes to a woodwork class.* □ **clase**
3 category/group into which things are classified: *class of mammal.* □ **clase...**
4 *he travels everywhere **first class,*** in the most expensive seats. □ **en primera clase**
first class, very good. □ **de primera clase**
tourist class/economy class, less expensive seats on aircraft and ships. □ **clase...**
classification [klæsifi'keiʃn] *n.* way of ordering things into categories: *classification of books in a library; classification of butterflies.* □ **clasificación**
classify ['klæsifai] *v.* to arrange things into groups: *to classify books in a library.* □ **clasificar**
classified information, information which is officially secret. □ **materia reservada**
class-room *n.* room in which a class is taught. □ **aula**
classy *adj.* chic/expensive-looking. □ **con clase**

classic ['klæsik] *n.* **1** great book/play/piece of music/writer/composer, etc.: *the classics of Japanese literature; Molière, Corneille and other French classics; jazz classics.* □ **clásico**
2 ***the classics,*** Ancient Greek and Roman literature, culture, etc. □ **los clásicos**
■ *adj.* **1** (style) which is elegant and based on that of Greek or Roman architecture/literature, etc. □ **clásico**
2 typical: *it's a classic case of bureaucratic muddle.* □ **clásico**
classical *adj.* **1** referring to classics: *the classical period in Chinese poetry.* □ **clásico**
2 serious (music): *do you really prefer classical music to pop songs?* □ **clásica**

clatter ['klætə] *n.* noise of things hitting together: *clatter of plates; clatter of clogs on the cobblestones; stop making that clatter.* □ **estrépito**
■ *v.* to make a noise: *he was clattering the plates in the kitchen; they clattered downstairs when the bell rang.* □ **hacer ruido**

clause [klɔːz] *n.* **1** paragraph in a treaty or legal document: *we do not agree to clause 8 in the proposed contract.* □ **cláusula**
2 part of a sentence. □ **oración**
main clause, the central part of a sentence. □ **oración principal**
subordinate clauses, clauses which depend on the main clause. □ **oración subordinada**

claustrophobia [klɔstrə'foubiə] *n.* abnormal terror of being shut inside a closed place. □ **claustrofobia**

clavicle ['klævikl] *n.* collarbone/bone which runs from the shoulder to the top of the ribs. □ **clavícula**

claw [klɔː] *n.* **1** nail (of animal/bird): *the cat scratched the table with her claws.* □ **garra**
2 pincer/part of a crab or lobster which pinches. □ **pinza**
■ *v.* to scratch with a claw: *the cat clawed at the bird cage.* □ **arañar**
claw hammer *n.* hammer with the back of the head curved and split for removing nails. □ **martillo de orejas**

clay [klei] *n.* stiff soil found in river valleys; stiff earth used for making bricks or china. □ **arcilla**
clayey *adj.* containing clay: *our garden has a very clayey soil.* □ **arcilloso**

clean [kliːn] *adj.* **1** not dirty: *have you got a clean handkerchief? give me a clean glass.* □ **limpio**
2 *a clean break,* a complete break. □ **una rotura limpia**
3 ***to come clean,*** to confess (to a crime). □ **confesar**
■ *adv.* completely: *I clean forgot; they got clean away.* □ **enteramente; se escaparon sin dejar rastro**
■ *v.* to remove dirt: *don't forget to clean your shoes; have you cleaned your teeth today? to clean up the mess after a party.* □ **limpiar**
cleaner *n.* person/something that removes dirt. □ **limpiador**
vacuum cleaner, machine for sucking up dirt. □ **aspiradora**
(*dry*) ***cleaner's,*** shop where clothes can be taken to be cleaned: *I am taking my winter coat to the cleaner's.* □ **tintorería**
oven cleaner, strong substance for cleaning dirty ovens. □ **limpiahornos**
cleaning *n.* removing dirt. □ **limpieza**
cleanliness ['klenlinəs] **cleanness** ['kliːnnəs] *n.* state of being clean. □ **limpieza; aseo**
cleanshaven *adj.* with no beard or moustache. □ **bien afeitado**

cleanse [klenz] *v.* to make very clean. □ **limpiar**
cleansing cream, cream for removing make-up. □ **crema limpiadora**
cleanser *n.* material which removes dirt. □ **producto para la limpieza**

clear ['kliə] *adj.* **1** pure; transparent: *on a clear day; clear blue sky; clear glass.* □ **claro; transparente**
2 with nothing in the way: *a clear view; can you see your way clear to joining the committee?* □ **claro**
3 obvious: *a clear case of bribery.* □ **claro**
4 easily understood: *have I made myself clear? you should have given clearer instructions.* □ **¿está claro?**
5 complete: *he made $100 clear profit; we have three clear days in Paris,* three whole days; *the government has a clear majority.* □ **completo; claro**
6 free: *the ship is clear of the rocks; the streets are clear of litter.* □ **libre; limpio de...**
■ *adv.* **1** in a clear way. □ **claramente**
2 *I can hear you loud and clear,* very clearly. □ **claramente**
3 *stand clear of the door,* stand away from the door; *I would steer clear of his brother,* keep away from him. □ **apartarse de; evitar**
■ *v.* **1** to remove (obstacles): *can you clear this rubbish out of the passage? to clear the streets of debris.*

□ **limpiar**
2 *to clear the table,* remove dirty china and cutlery. □ **quitar la mesa**
3 *he cleared his throat,* he coughed slightly to get ready for speaking. □ **carraspear**
4 to make clear/pure; to become clear/pure: *the fog is clearing.* □ **aclarar**
5 to show that someone is innocent: *he was cleared of the charge of murder.* □ **demostrar la inocencia de**
6 not to hit: *he cleared 2 metres in the high jump.* □ **saltar, salvar**
clearance *n.* **1** act of removing obstacles: *snow clearance; slum clearance.* □ **despeje; supresión del chabolismo**
clearance sale, sale where all the goods are reduced in price to clear them from the shelves. □ **liquidación**
2 space for something to pass through. □ **espacio libre**
clear away *v.* to remove (something) which is in the way; to remove (dirty dishes) from a table. □ **quitar**
clear-cut *adj.* definite/distinct. □ **claro; inequívoco**
clear-headed *adj.* clever/with a sharp understanding. □ **de ideas claras**
clearing *n.* **1** act of removing obstacles. □ **despeje**
2 area in a wood where the trees have been cut down. □ **desmonte; calvero**
3 ***clearing bank,*** bank which issues cheques. □ **banco (de compensación)**
clearly *adv.* **1** in a way which is easily understood or heard: *speak clearly.* □ **claramente**
2 obviously: *he clearly had nothing to do with the murder.* □ **evidentemente**
clearness *n.* pureness/sharpness (of a picture). □ **claridad**
clear off *v.* **1** to pay off one's debts. □ **liquidar**
2 to run away. □ **largarse**
clear out *v.* **1** to throw out rubbish: *I am going to clear out the boot of the car.* □ **limpiar**
2 to go away. □ **irse; largarse**
clear up *v.* **1** to make clear/pure: *you must clear up the mess.* □ **ordenar**
2 *to clear up a problem,* to solve a problem. □ **resolver**
3 to become brighter: *the weather is finally clearing up.* □ **despejarse; aclararse**
clearway *n.* road where no parking is allowed. □ **donde está prohibido estacionar**
cleavage ['kli:vidʒ] *n.* space between the breasts. □ **canal**
cleaver ['kli:və] *n.* large axe used by butchers. □ **cuchilla**
clef [klef] *n.* sign at the beginning of a piece of music which shows whether it is bass or treble. □ **clave**
cleft [kleft] *adj.* and *n.* **1** split: *a cleft in the rocks.* □ **fisura**
cleft palate, split roof of the mouth. □ **fisura del paladar**
2 *he's* ***in a cleft stick,*** he is in an awkward situation. □ **está entre la espada y la pared**
clematis [klə'meitis] *n.* climbing garden plant with large purple or pink flowers. □ **clemátide**
clement ['klemənt] *adj.* (*formal*) kind/soft (weather). □ **clemente, suave**
clemency *n.* mercy (to a criminal): *in an act of clemency the president freed all political prisoners.* □ **clemencia**
clementine ['klemənti:n] *n.* small sweet orange with a skin which is easily removed. □ **clementina**
clench [klentʃ] *v.* to close tightly: *they waved their clenched fists at the police; he clenched his teeth.* □ **apretar**
clergy ['klə:dʒi] *n.* priests: *the bishops and clergy.* □ **clero**
clergyman *n.* (*pl. clergymen) Anglican priest.* □ **clérigo**
clerical *adj.* **1** referring to a clerk. □ **de oficina**
clerical work, filing/typing, etc. □ **trabajo de oficina**
2 referring to clergy: *clerical dress,* black suit and stiff white collar fastening at the back. □ **clerical**
clerk [klɑ:k] *n.* person who works in an office: *filing clerk; bank clerk,* person who works in a bank. □ **oficinista; empleado**
town clerk, person in charge of the records of a town. □ **secretario**
clever ['klevə] *adj.* **1** intelligent/able to learn quickly: *he is a clever thief; she is very clever at business.* □ **listo**
2 *he is clever with his hands,* he is good at making things. □ **hábil**
cleverly *adv.* in a clever way. □ **con inteligencia**
cleverness *n.* intelligence. □ **inteligencia**
cliché ['kli:ʃei] *n.* saying/phrase which is frequently used. □ **lugar común**
click [klik] *n.* short sharp sound: *the box shut with a click.* □ **clic; chasquido**
■ *v.* **1** to make a short sharp sound: *the box clicked shut.* □ **chasquear**
2 *to click one's heels,* to bring the heels of one's boots together to make a noise. □ **taconear**
3 *it suddenly clicked,* it was suddenly understood. □ **de repente caí en lo...**
client ['klaiənt] *n.* person with whom you do business/to whom you give a service: *he is one of my best clients.* □ **cliente**
clientele [kliɔn'tel] *n.* all the customers (of a shop). □ **clientela**
cliff [klif] *n.* high rock face, usually by the sea. □ **acantilado**
cliffhanger *n.* **1** suspense story. □ **relato de suspense**
2 *it was a cliffhanger,* we did not know what the outcome would be until the last moment. □ **de suspense**
climate ['klaimət] *n.* general weather conditions: *the climate in the mountains is cool and wet.* □ **clima**
climatic [klai'mætik] *adj.* referring to climate: *climatic conditions.* □ **climático**
climatology [klaimə'tɔlədʒi] *n.* study of climate. □ **climatología**
climax ['klaimæks] *n.* peak/greatest amount/highest point: *the noise reached a climax.* □ **clímax**
climb [klaim] *n.* act of going up; place where you go up: *a stiff climb,* a steep slope; *the plane went into a steep climb,* rose steeply. □ **subida**
■ *v.* to go up: *he climbed a ladder to get in through a bedroom window; the first men to climb Everest; the plane climbed sharply.* □ **subir (escalera/avión); escalar**
climb down *v.* **1** to come down a mountain/a ladder. □ **descender**
2 to give in: *he refused to apologize for some time, but in the end climbed down.* □ **rendirse**
climber *n.* person who climbs; plant which climbs. □ **escalador**
climbing *n.* sport of climbing mountains. □ **montañismo**
clinch [klintʃ] *n.* **1** (*in boxing*) a position where both boxers hold on to each other: *they got into a clinch.* □ **cuerpo a cuerpo**

2 (*informal*) close embrace. □ **abrazo**
■ *v.* **1** (*in boxing*) to hold tight to the other boxer. □ **engancharse en un cuerpo a cuerpo**
2 to settle a deal: *that clinched the deal.* □ **cerrar**

cling [kliŋ] *v.* (*he clung*) to hold tight to something: *the baby monkey clung to its mother; after the shipwreck, the sailors clung to the wreckage.* □ **agarrarse**

clinic ['klinik] *n.* specialized medical office or hospital: *baby clinic; TB clinic.* □ **clínica**
clinical *adj.* **1** medical. □ **clínico**
clinical thermometer, thermometer for taking a person's temperature. □ **termómetro clínico**
2 ***to take a clinical view of something,*** to look at it coolly. □ **desapasionado**

clink [kliŋk] *n.* **1** noise of glasses/metal objects hitting each other. □ **tintineo**
2 (*slang*) prison. □ **trena; chirona**
■ *v.* to make a noise: *they clinked glasses,* they hit their glasses gently together in a toast. □ **hacer tintinear**

clinker ['kliŋkə] *n.* waste material after coal has been burnt. □ **escoria**

clip [klip] *n.* **1** piece of bent wire for attaching papers, etc., together: *paper clip.* □ **clip**
2 (*informal*) smack: *he will get a clip round the ear.* □ **bofetada**
3 *they were going at a good clip,* (*informal*) quite fast. □ **...a toda pastilla**
■ *v.* (*he clipped*) **1** to attach (papers) together: *can you clip these papers together?* □ **unir con clip**
2 to cut with scissors or shears: *she clipped the article out of the newspaper; he is clipping the dead flowers off the rose bushes.* □ **recortar**
3 *the conductor clipped the tickets,* punched a little hole in them to show they had been used. □ **picar**
clippers *n. pl.* small scissors; instrument with a movable blade for cutting hair. □ **maquinilla para el pelo**
clipping *n.* small piece cut out of a newspaper, cut off a hedge, etc. □ **recorte**

clique [kli:k] *n.* small select group of people. □ **élite**

cloak [klouk] *n.* **1** long outer coat with no sleeves: *the spy wore dark glasses and a long black cloak.* □ **capa**
2 *under the cloak of darkness,* hidden by the dark. □ **al amparo de...**
■ *v.* to cover/to hide as if with a cloak: *cloaked in secrecy.* □ **ocultar**
cloakroom *n.* **1** place where you leave your coat in a restaurant/theatre, etc. □ **guardarropa**
2 toilet. □ **servicios**

clobber ['klɔbə] *n.* (*informal*) belongings. □ **trastos**
■ *v.* (*informal*) to hit/to tax: *commuters have been clobbered by fare increases.* □ **sacudir**

cloche [klɔʃ] *n.* small glass or polythene tent used in gardening for covering young plants. □ **invernadero**

clock [klɔk] *n.* machine for telling the time: *the church clock has stopped; our clock is five minutes fast.* □ **reloj**
grandfather clock, clock which works by long chains and weights and is enclosed in a tall wooden case. □ **reloj de caja**
alarm clock, clock which rings a bell to wake you up. □ **despertador**
round/around the clock, all day and all night. □ **de sol a sol**
■ *v.* ***to clock in/out, on/off,*** to record your time of arrival or departure at work. □ **fichar**
clock golf *n.* game like golf where you hit the ball into a central hole from points round a circle. □ **variante de golf**
clockwise *adv.* in the same direction as the hands of a clock: *turn the screw clockwise to tighten it.* □ **en el sentido de las agujas del reloj**
clockwork *n.* **1** machine which works on a spring which is wound up with a key: *the engine has a clockwork motor.* □ **mecanismo de cuerda**
2 *it is going **like clockwork,*** it is working smoothly. □ **como un reloj**

clod [klɔd] *n.* large lump of earth. □ **terrón**

clog [klɔg] *n.* wooden shoe. □ **zueco**
■ *v.* (*he clogged*) to block: *the weeds are clogging the river.* □ **atascar**

cloister ['klɔistə] *n.* (*in a monastery*) covered walk round a courtyard where monks can meditate or walk. □ **claustro**
cloistered *adj.* shut up (as in a monastery): *she lives a cloistered existence.* □ **enclaustrado**

clone [kloun] *n.* plant/animal which is grown from a piece of another plant/animal, and not from a seed. □ **clon**

close [klous] *adj.* **1** very near: *our house is close to the post office; a close friend.* □ **cercano; íntimo**
to keep a close watch on someone, to watch someone attentively. □ **someter a una estrecha vigilancia a...**
2 *close finish,* near finish. □ **casi terminado**
3 *a close election,* election where the winner is separated from the loser by only a small number of votes. □ **elección por escaso margen**
4 shut. □ **cerrado**
close season, season when hunting is forbidden. □ **veda**
5 stuffy: *it's close in here; it's close today.* □ **mal ventilado; cargado**
■ *adv.* near: *to follow close behind someone; they were standing close together; she is close on forty.* □ **cerca de**
■ *n.* gardens and houses round a cathedral; small road with houses. □ **recinto; calle**
close-fisted *adj.* miserly. □ **tacaño**
close-fitting *adj.* tight (dress). □ **ceñido**
closely *adv.* **1** attentively: *he follows the horse race results closely.* □ **atentamente**
2 tightly: *closely packed in a tin.* □ **muy apretado**
closeness *n.* **1** nearness. □ **proximidad**
2 stuffiness. □ **mala ventilación**
close-up *n.* photograph taken at very close range. □ **primer plano**

close [klouz] *n.* end: *the year is drawing to a close; at close of play,* when the game ends. □ **fin**
■ *v.* **1** to shut: *close the window; would you mind closing the door? the Post Office is closed on Saturday afternoons; he closed the book he was reading.* □ **cerrar**
2 to end (an argument/a debate). □ **concluir**
3 *the list of nominations is closed,* no more nominations can be accepted. □ **...está cerrada**
4 to fight with someone: *the policeman closed with the robber.* □ **enfrentarse**
closed *adj.* shut: *the doors are closed; road closed.* □ **cerrado**
closed shop, system whereby a firm can only employ members of a certain trade union. □ **empresa que sólo contrata gente sindicada**
close down *v.* to shut a shop, etc., (permanently); to stop transmitting radio/TV programmes: *the factory had to close down after the fire.* □ **cerrar**
close in *v.* **1** *the days are closing in,* the days are becoming shorter. □ **hacerse más cortos**
2 ***to close in on someone,*** to run someone to earth/to come close to one's prey: *the police are closing in on the escaped prisoner.* □ **rodear a uno**
closing *adj.* final: *the closing day of a sale.*

□ **último día**
closing bid, last bid at an auction. □ **última puja**
■ *n.* shutting (of a shop, etc.). □ **cierre**
early closing day, day when a shop is shut in the afternoon. □ **tarde que cierra**
closing time, time when a pub, etc., closes. □ **hora de cierre**
closure ['klouʒə] *n.* shutting: *the closure of three factories.* □ **cierre**

clot [klɔt] *n.* lump of solidified blood, etc. □ **coágulo**
■ *v.* (*it clotted*) to form lumps: *he was given a drug to prevent his blood clotting.* □ **coagular**
clotted cream, cream which has been heated until it solidifies. □ **crema cuajada**

cloth [klɔθ] *n.* **1** piece of woven material: *have you a cloth for wiping the table? floor cloth.* □ **trapo**
dish cloth, cloth for washing dishes. □ **estropajo, bayeta**
2 woven material: *the book is bound in cloth; a cloth cap.* □ **tela; paño**

clothe [klouð] *v.* to dress: *climbers have to be warmly clothed; their children are always poorly clothed.* □ **vestirse**

clothes [klouðz] *n. pl.* things you wear: *he took off his clothes and plunged into the river; have you got any clean clothes to wear?* □ **ropa**
clothes brush, brush for cleaning clothes. □ **cepillo de ropa**
clothes line, long rope for hanging wet clothes to dry. □ **cuerda para tender**
clothes horse, wooden or metal frame for hanging wet clothes to dry. □ **tendedero**
clothes peg, *Amer.* ***clothes pin,*** small plastic or wooden clip for attaching wet clothes to a clothes line. □ **pinza**

clothing [klouðiŋ] *n.* (*no pl.*) clothes: *you should wear light clothing in summer.* □ **ropa**
the clothing trade, the industry which manufactures clothes. □ **industria de la confección**

cloud [klaud] *n.* **1** mass of vapour/smoke (in the air): *big black clouds came up with the storm; clouds of smoke poured out of the house; there were clouds of flies around the dead lion.* □ **nube**
2 *he's* ***under a cloud,*** he is unpopular with the authorities. □ **bajo sospecha**
■ *v.* to hide with a cloud: *the windows are clouded with steam; the sky clouded over.* □ **empañar (ventana); nublarse**
cloudburst *n.* sudden downpour of rain. □ **chaparrón**
cloud-capped *adj.* (mountain) topped with clouds. □ **coronado de nubes**
cloudiness *n.* state of being covered with clouds; state of not being transparent. □ **nubosidad**
cloudless *adj.* (sky) with no clouds. □ **despejado**
cloudy *adj.* covered with clouds; not clear/not transparent: *a cloudy day; the water in the glass turned cloudy.* □ **nuboso; turbio**

clout [klaut] *n.* **1** blow (with the fist). □ **tortazo**
2 (*informal*) power/influence: *he has more clout than I have.* □ **influencia**
■ *v.* to give (someone) a blow with the fist. □ **dar un tortazo**

clove [klouv] *n.* **1** spice formed by small dried flower buds of a tropical tree. □ **clavo**
2 piece of garlic. □ **diente (de ajo)**

cloven ['klouvn] *adj.* split. □ **partido**

clover ['klouvə] *n.* common weed, used as fodder for cattle. □ **trébol**
to be in clover, to live very comfortably. □ **vivir a cuerpo de rey**
clover leaf intersection, crossroads formed by two motorways and their linking roads, which when seen from above looks like the leaf of a clover. □ **raqueta**

clown [klaun] *n.* **1** man who makes people laugh in a circus. □ **payaso**
2 stupid fool. □ **tonto**
■ *v.* to play the fool: *he is always clowning around.* □ **hacer payasadas**

cloy [klɔi] *v.* to be sickly sweet: *a cloying taste.* □ **empalagar**

club [klʌb] *n.* **1** large stick: *he hit him on the head with a club.* □ **palo**
golf club, long stick with which you hit the ball when playing golf. □ **palo de golf**
2 one of the four suits in a pack of cards: *the six of clubs.* □ **bastos**
3 group of people who allow others to join them (usually on payment of a fee): *golf club; football club.* □ **club**
youth club, group for entertaining young people often run by a church or local authority. □ **club juvenil**
■ *v.* (*he clubbed*) **1** to hit with a club: *the young seals are clubbed by the hunters.* □ **apalear**
2 to put all your money together: *they clubbed together and bought a caravan.* □ **reunir**
clubfoot *n.* deformed foot. □ **pie zopo**
clubhouse *n.* house where members of a club meet. □ **sede del club**

cluck [klʌk] *v.* (*of hen*) to make a low noise in the throat. □ **cloquear**

clue [klu:] *n.* information which helps you solve a mystery: *there were no clues as to how the burglars got into the house; the police examined the car looking for clues; clues to a crossword puzzle.* □ **pista**
not have a clue: *I haven't a clue,* I do not know at all. □ **...ni idea**
clued up *adj.* (*informal*) expert/knowing a great deal: *he's all clued up on how to avoid paying tax.* □ **enterado**
clueless *adj.* (*informal*) stupid. □ **estúpido**

clump [klʌmp] *n.* group of shrubs, trees, etc.: *a clump of primroses.* □ **mata**
■ *v.* to move making a dull noise: *he was clumping about in the room upstairs; they clumped downstairs in their boots.* □ **andar con paso pesado**

clumsy ['klʌmzi] *adj.* not graceful; frequently breaking things: *the clumsy fool broke my vase.* □ **torpe**
clumsily *adv.* in an awkward way: *he steered his bike clumsily through the crowd.* □ **torpemente**
clumsiness *n.* awkward habits. □ **torpeza**

clung [klʌŋ] *v. see* **cling.**

clunk [klʌŋk] *n.* noise of heavy metal objects hitting each other. □ **sonido metálico sordo**

cluster ['klʌstə] *n.* group of small objects together: *a cluster of stars; a cluster of flowers in a vase.* □ **conjunto; ramo**
■ *v.* to group together: *the bees clustered round the hive.* □ **apiñarse**

clutch [klʌtʃ] *n.* **1** several eggs laid together in a nest. □ **nidada**
2 clasp. □ **agarrón**
3 *do not let your money fall into his* ***clutches,*** do not let him get his hands on your money. □ **...en sus garras**
4 mechanism for changing the gears in a car: *clutch pedal,* pedal which works the clutch; *to let in the clutch,* to make the gears connect; *to let out the*

clutch, to disengage the engine from the gears. □ **embrague**
■ *v.* to grab: *the drowning man clutched at a plank of wood.* □ **agarrarse**

clutter ['klʌtə] *n.* mass of things left lying about: *I want to try to clear up the clutter in the room.* □ **desorden**
■ *v.* to fill (a room) with rubbish: *the place is cluttered up with old books.* □ **llenar, atestar**

co- [kou] *prefix meaning* together. □ **co-**

co. [kou, 'kʌmpəni] *abbreviation for* company. □ **cía.**

coach [koutʃ] *n.* **1** large bus for long distance travelling: *we went on a coach tour of Scotland; when does the coach leave for London?* □ **autocar**
2 passenger wagon (on a train): *the train has only four coaches.* □ **vagón**
3 person who trains sportsmen, etc.: *a football coach; a tennis coach.* □ **entrenador**
■ *v.* **1** to train sportsmen: *he is coaching the English team.* □ **entrenar**
2 to give private lessons: *she is coaching my daughter in maths.* □ **dar clases particulares**

coagulate [kou'ægjuleit] *v.* to form into lumps/to cake. □ **coagularse**
coagulation [kouægju'leiʃn] *n.* forming into lumps/caking. □ **coagulación**

coal [koul] *n.* black mineral used as fuel: *coal merchant; coal-fired boiler,* boiler which is heated by coal. □ **carbón**
coalfield *n.* area of coal underground. □ **cuenca carbonífera**
coalhole *n.* space in a cellar for storing coal; hole in the ground, through which coal can be delivered into a cellar. □ **carbonera**
coalmine *n.* mine where coal is dug. □ **mina de carbón**
coal scuttle *n.* box for keeping coal near a fireplace. □ **cubo del carbón**

coalesce [kouə'les] *v.* to join together. □ **unirse**
coalescence *n.* joining together. □ **unión; fusión**

coalition [kouə'liʃn] *n.* joining together; combination of political parties forming a government. □ **coalición**

coarse [kɔːs] *adj.* **1** not fine/rough: *coarse cloth; coarse sandpaper.* □ **basto**
2 rude: *he gave a coarse laugh.* □ **ordinario**
coarsely *adv.* rudely. □ **groseramente**
coarseness *n.* **1** roughness (of cloth). □ **basteza**
2 rudeness. □ **ordinariez**

coast [koust] *n.* land by the sea: *the south coast has been ruined by oil from the wrecked tanker.* □ **costa**
from coast to coast, across an area of land from one sea to another: *he crossed Africa from coast to coast.* □ **de costa a costa**
■ *v.* **1** to ride (a vehicle) without using the engine or the pedals: *the car coasted to a stop; he coasted downhill on his bike.* □ **ir en punto muerto (coche); ir sin pedalear (bici)**
2 to sail along the coast. □ **costear**
coastal *adj.* referring to the coast: *coastal navigation.* □ **costero**
coaster *n.* **1** ship which sails from port to port along the coast. □ **barco de cabotaje**
2 flat dish or small mat for standing a bottle/glass on. □ **salvamantel; posavaso**
coastguard *n.* person who guards a piece of coast (watching out for wrecks/smugglers, etc.). □ **guardacostas**
coastline *n.* line of the coast: *the heavily indented coastline of Norway.* □ **litoral**

coat [kout] *n.* **1** long article of clothing which covers the top part of the body and which is worn out of doors: *put on your winter coat; she was wearing an expensive fur coat.* □ **abrigo**
2 fur of an animal: *our cat has a beautiful soft coat.* □ **pelo**
3 layer: *I have given the door two coats of paint.* □ **capa**
4 ***coat of arms,*** symbolic design on the shield of a family/town, etc. □ **escudo de armas**
■ *v.* to cover (something) with a layer: *the blade is coated with oil; chocolate-coated biscuits.* □ **cubrir**
coat-hanger *n.* piece of wood/wire/plastic on which you hang clothes. □ **percha**
coat-hook *n.* hook (on a wall/door) for hanging a coat. □ **percha**

coax [kouks] *v.* to persuade someone to do something. □ **engatusar**

cob [kɔb] *n.* seed head (of corn/maize, etc.). □ **mazorca**
cob nut, hazel nut. □ **avellana**

cobalt ['koubɔːlt] *n.* (*chemical element*: Co) white metal; blue colour obtained from the metal. □ **cobalto**

cobble (stone) ['kɔbl(stoun)] *n.* rounded stone formerly used for paving streets. □ **guijarro (redondo); adoquín (cuadrado)**

cobbler ['kɔblə] *n.* person who mends shoes. □ **zapatero**

cobra ['kɔbrə] *n.* large poisonous tropical snake. □ **cobra**

cobweb ['kɔbweb] *n.* net of fine thread made by a spider. □ **telaraña**

cocaine [kə'kein] *n.* painkilling drug, also used as a stimulant. □ **cocaína**

coccyx ['kɔksiks] *n.* small bones at the end of the spine. □ **coxis**

cochineal [kɔtʃi'niːl] *n.* red colouring used in cooking. □ **tinde de cochinilla**

cock [kɔk] *n.* **1** male bird (especially a domestic chicken): *a cock sparrow; a hen and a cock.* □ **gallo; un gorrión macho**
2 tap. □ **grifo**
3 hammer on a gun which fires the cartridge. □ **percutor**
■ *v.* **1** to prick up (your ears). □ **aguzar**
2 to put (your head) to one side. □ **ladear**
3 to set a gun ready for firing. □ **montar**
cock-a-doodle doo! *interjection* showing the noise made by a cock. □ **quiquiriquí**
cock-a-hoop *adj.* triumphant. □ **jubiloso**
cock-crow *n.* early morning: *you have to be up at cock-crow.* □ **al cantar el gallo**

cockade [kɔ'keid] *n.* rosette of ribbons worn attached to a hat. □ **escarapela**

cockatoo [kɔkə'tuː] *n.* type of large parrot. □ **cacatúa**

cockchafer ['kɔktʃeifə] *n.* large beetle. □ **escarabajo**

cocker ['kɔkə] *n.* type of spaniel. □ **cocker**

cockerel ['kɔkrəl] *n.* young cock. □ **pollo**

cock-eyed ['kɔkaid] *adj.* **1** askew. □ **torcido**
2 *that's a cock-eyed idea,* that is a pretty odd idea. □ **disparatado**

cockle ['kɔkl] *n.* small edible shellfish with a double shell. □ **berberecho**
■ *v.* (of paper) to curl up. □ **arrugar(se)**

cockney ['kɔkni] *adj.* and *n.* (person) who comes from the east part of London; way of speaking of a person from the east part of London. □ **'cockney'**

cockpit ['kɔkpit] *n.* place where the pilot sits in an aircraft or boat. □ **carlinga, cabina**

cockroach ['kɔkroutʃ] *n.* large brown or black insect which lives in kitchens. □ **cucaracha**
cocksure [kɔk'ʃuə] *adj.* very sure/self-confident. □ **presuntuoso**
cocktail ['kɔkteil] *n.* mixed alcoholic drink. □ **cóctel**
cocktail lounge, smart lounge bar in a hotel. □ **bar**
cocktail snacks/cocktail onions, snacks/onions which are eaten with drinks. □ **aperitivos salados; ...en vinagre**
fruit cocktail/prawn cocktail, mixture of fruit/prawns in salad. □ **macedonia; cóctel de gambas**
cock-up ['kɔkʌp] *n.* (*slang*) mistake/badly carried out work. □ **chapuza**
cocky ['kɔki] *adj.* unpleasantly proud and conceited. □ **engreído**
cocoa ['koukou] *n.* brown powder ground from the seeds of the cacao tree, used for making a drink; drink made in this way: *I always have a cup of cocoa before going to bed.* □ **cacao**
coconut ['koukənʌt] *n.* large nut from a palm tree. □ **coco**
coconut shy, stall at a fair where you try to hit coconuts with a ball. □ **tipo de tiro al blanco**
coconut ice, sweet made from the inside of a coconut mixed with sugar. □ **dulce de coco**
coconut matting, rough matting made from the outer fibres of a coconut. □ **estera**
cocoon [kə'ku:n] *n.* protective case of thread made by a larva before it turns into a moth or butterfly. □ **capullo**
cod [kɔd] *n.* (*no pl.*) large sea fish. □ **bacalao**
cod liver oil, oil extracted from the livers of cod, which is very rich in vitamins. □ **aceite de hígado de bacalao**
c.o.d. [si:ou'di:] *abbreviation for* cash on delivery. □ **pago contra entrega**
coda ['koudə] *n.* last part of a piece of music. □ **coda**
coddle ['kɔdl] *v.* **1** to spoil/to pamper (someone). □ **mimar**
2 to cook (eggs) in warm, but not boiling water. □ **cocer a fuego lento**
code [koud] *n.* **1** set of laws/of rules of behaviour: *the Highway Code,* rules for drivers; *the Boy Scouts' code of conduct.* □ **código**
2 secret signs agreed in advance for sending messages. □ **clave**
the Morse code, series of dots and dashes used for sending telegraphic messages. □ **alfabeto Morse**
code word, secret agreed word. □ **contraseña; santo y seña**
■ *v.* to write (a message) in code. □ **cifrar**
codeine ['koudi:n] *n.* drug used to relieve pain and produce sleep. □ **codeína**
codicil ['koudisil] *n.* additional clause to a will. □ **codicilo**
codify ['koudifai] *v.* to write rules of conduct/laws. □ **codificar**
co-director [koudai'rektə] *n.* one of two or more directors. □ **codirector**
co-educational [kouedju'keiʃənl] *adj.* (school) where boys and girls are taught together. □ **mixto**
co-ed *adj.* (school) where boys and girls are taught together. □ **mixto**
■ *n.* girl who goes to a co-educational school. □ **alumna de colegio mixto**
coefficient [koui'fiʃənt] *n.* factor in mathematics. □ **coeficiente**
coelacanth ['siləkænθ] *n.* prehistoric type of fish which is not extinct. □ **celacanto**
coerce [kɔu'ə:s] *v.* to force: *he was coerced into joining the party.* □ **coercer, obligar**
coercion [kou'ə:ʃn] *n.* force. □ **coerción**
coexist [kouig'zist] *v.* to exist/to live together. □ **coexistir**
coexistence *n.* living together: *peaceful coexistence,* where countries with different types of government exist side by side in peace. □ **coexistencia**
coffee ['kɔfi] *n.* **1** brown seeds of a tropical plant, which are roasted and ground to make a drink: *a pound of coffee.* □ **café**
2 drink made from these beans: *do you want black or white coffee?,* do you want your coffee without milk or with milk? *coffee cup; coffee pot.* □ **café**
instant coffee, powdered extract of coffee which makes coffee when hot water is poured on it. □ **...instantáneo**
coffee table, low table for putting cups/glasses, etc., on. □ **mesa de centro**
coffee table book, large colourful art book. □ **libro de arte**
coffers ['kɔfəz] *n. pl.* money chests. □ **cofre; arca**
coffin ['kɔfin] *n.* long wooden box in which a dead person is buried. □ **ataúd**
cog [kɔg] *n.* tooth (on a toothed wheel). □ **diente**
cog-wheel *n.* wheel with teeth round the edge which fit into the teeth on another wheel and make it turn. □ **rueda dentada**
cogent ['koudʒənt] *adj.* valid (argument); powerful (reason). □ **convincente**
cogitate ['kɔdʒiteit] *v.* to ponder/to think deeply. □ **meditar**
cognate ['kɔgneit] *adj.* (*formal*) with the same origin. □ **cognado, afín**
cognizance ['kɔgnizəns] *n.* knowledge (of a fact). □ **conocimiento**
cohabit [kou'hæbit] *v.* to live together as man and wife, especially when not married. □ **cohabitar**
cohere [kou'hiə] *v.* to hold together; to form a whole. □ **adherirse**
coherence *n.* links/connection between ideas. □ **coherencia**
coherent *adj.* clear/logical ideas. □ **coherente**
coherently *adv.* clearly/logically: *after the accident he couldn't speak coherently.* □ **coherentemente**
cohesion [kou'hi:ʒn] *n.* sticking together. □ **cohesión**
cohesive [kou'hi:siv] *adj.* which stick together. □ **cohesivo**
cohort ['kouhɔ:t] *n.* large group of people. □ **cohorte**
coiffure [kwæ'fjuə] *n.* hairstyle. □ **peinado**
coil [kɔil] *n.* **1** roll (of rope); loop (in a rope). □ **rollo (de la cuerda); lazo**
2 *coils of smoke,* round wreaths of smoke. □ **espiral**
3 *electric coil,* wire wrapped round a shaft which produces electricity. □ **bobina**
■ *v.* to roll up; to make loops: *the rope was neatly coiled on the deck; the snake coiled itself round the branch.* □ **enrollar**
coin [kɔin] *n.* piece of metal money: *most countries have currency in both coins and notes.* □ **moneda**
■ *v.* **1** to strike/to produce metal money. □ **acuñar**
to coin it: *he is coining it,* (*informal*) he is making a lot of money. □ **se está forrando**
2 to invent a new word. □ **acuñar**
coinage *n.* **1** system of money (of a country). □ **sistema monetario**
2 new word. □ **acuñación**
coincide [kouin'said] *v.* to happen (by chance) at the same time as something else: *his birthday happens to coincide with the national holiday.* □ **coincidir**
coincidence [kou'insidəns] *n.* two things which happen together/chance: *what a coincidence!*

□ **coincidencia**
coincidental [kouinsi'dentl] *adj.* happening by chance. □ **fortuito; casual**
coke [kouk] *n.* **1** fuel processed from coal, which gives a very fierce heat. □ **coque**
2 (*informal*) Coca-Cola/trademark for a type of soft drink. □ **coca**
colander ['kɔləndə] *n.* metal/plastic bowl with holes in it for draining water off vegetables, etc. □ **escurridor, colador**
cold [kould] *adj.* **1** not hot: *he has a cold shower every day; it is very cold outside; are you cold? my feet are cold.* □ **frío**
to get cold feet, to lose courage: *he was going to apply for the job but he got cold feet.* □ **se acobardó**
cold war, fight for power between countries without actually using weapons. □ **guerra fría**
2 unfriendly: *we had a very cold reception.* □ **fría**
■ *n.* **1** state of being cold: *she can't stand the cold.* □ **el frío**
2 *he was left* ***out in the cold,*** left on one side. □ **...al margen**
3 infectious illness when you sneeze and cough: *don't come near me - I've got a cold; he caught a cold by standing in the rain.* □ **resfriado**
cold-blooded *adj.* **1** (animal such as fish) with blood whose temperature varies with its surroundings. □ **de sangre fría**
2 with no feelings. □ **despiadado**
coldness *n.* state of being cold. □ **frialdad, frío**
coleslaw ['koulslɔ:] *n.* cabbage salad. □ **ensalada de col**
coley ['kouli] *n.* type of sea fish. □ **tipo de pez marino**
colic ['kɔlik] *n.* severe pain in the stomach. □ **cólico**
colitis [kə'laitis] *n.* infection of the colon. □ **colitis**
collaborate [kə'læbəreit] *v.* to work together: *they collaborated in carrying out the experiments.* □ **colaborar**
collaboration [kəlæbə'reiʃn] *n.* working together. □ **colaboración**
collapse [kə'læps] *n.* falling down/ruin: *the collapse of the Roman Empire; several people were trapped in the collapse of the building.* □ **caída; derrumbamiento**
■ *v.* to fall down in a heap: *the wall suddenly collapsed; the old lady collapsed on the pavement.* □ **desplomarse**
collapsible *adj.* which can be folded up: *a collapsible stand; a collapsible boat.* □ **plegable**
collar ['kɔlə] *n.* part of clothing which goes round the neck: *he buttoned up his shirt collar; she turned up her coat collar to keep out the wind; our dog has his name written on his collar; what's your collar size?* □ **cuello**
■ *v.* to grab/to catch someone. □ **prender por el cuello**
collarbone *n.* bones on either side of the neck going from the top of the ribs to the shoulder blades. □ **clavícula**
collate [kə'leit] *v.* to compare texts. □ **cotejar**
collation [kə'leiʃn] *n.* **1** (*formal*) light cold lunch. □ **colación; refacción**
2 comparison of texts. □ **cotejo**
collator *n.* someone who compares texts. □ **cotejador**
collateral [kə'lætərəl] *adj.* and *n.* parallel; (security) which is used as an additional guarantee. □ **paralelo; garantía subsidiaria**
colleague ['kɔli:g] *n.* person who works with you: *I am having lunch with two of my colleagues.* □ **colega**
collect [kə'lekt] *v.* **1** to fetch and bring together: *my wife collects the children from school at 4 o'clock; a crowd collected when the two men started to fight; do you collect stamps?* □ **recoger; congregarse; coleccionar**
2 *I am collecting for the old people's home,* I am collecting money to give to the home. □ **hacer una colecta**
3 ***to call collect,*** *Amer.* to ask the person you are phoning to pay for the call. □ **...de cobro revertido**
collected *adj.* calm/not flustered. □ **sosegado**
collection *n.* **1** group of objects brought together: *a stamp collection; a collection of seventeenth-century paintings.* □ **colección**
2 gathering of money; money which has been gathered: *we are taking a collection in aid of the old people.* □ **colecta; cuestación**
collective *adj.* brought together. □ **colectivo**
collective farm, farm where everything belongs to and is run by the workers on behalf of the state. □ **explotación agrícola colectiva**
collective bargaining, negotiations for new salaries carried out between union and management. □ **negociación colectiva**
collector *n.* person who collects: *stamp collector; tax collector.* □ **coleccionista; recaudador**
ticket collector, person who takes the tickets from the passengers as they leave a railway station. □ **empleado que recoge los billetes**
college ['kɔlidʒ] *n.* teaching establishment (for adults and adolescents): *to go to college; technical college.* □ **colegio; escuela técnica**
college of further education, college for study after secondary school. □ **colegio universitario; universidad (en EE.UU.)**
college of education, college for training teachers. □ **escuela universitaria**
collegiate [kə'li:dʒiət] *adj.* referring to a college. □ **colegiado; universitario (en EE.UU.)**
collide [kə'laid] *v.* to bump into: *the two planes collided in mid air; the car went out of control and collided with a lorry.* □ **chocar**
collie ['kɔli] *n.* type of sheepdog. □ **'collie'**
collier ['kɔliə] *n.* **1** coal miner. □ **minero**
2 ship which carries coal. □ **barco carbonero**
colliery ['kɔljəri] *n.* coalmine. □ **mina de carbón**
collision [kə'liʒən] *n.* bumping into something: *the collision resulted in an explosion.* □ **colisión**
colloquial [kə'loukwiəl] *adj.* as is commonly spoken; conversational: *colloquial Italian.* □ **coloquial**
colloquialism *n.* colloquial expression. □ **expresión coloquial**
colloquially *adv.* as in conversational speech. □ **coloquialmente**
collusion [kə'lu:ʒn] *n.* secret illegal agreement: *they acted in collusion.* □ **en connivencia**
colon ['koulən] *n.* **1** large part of the intestines. □ **colon**
2 punctuation sign (:) to show a break in a sentence. □ **dos puntos**
colonel ['kə:nl] *n.* officer in charge of a regiment; rank in the army above lieutenant-colonel. □ **coronel**
colonnade [kɔlə'neid] *n.* row of columns. □ **columnata**
colony ['kɔləni] *n.* **1** territory ruled by another country. □ **colonia**
2 group of animals/humans living together: *a colony of ants; a nudist colony.* □ **colonia**
colonial [kə'louniəl] *adj.* referring to a colony/the colonies. □ **colonial**
colonialism *n.* exploitation of colonies.

□ **colonialismo**
colonialist *n.* person who advocates colonialism. □ **colonialista**
colonist ['kɔlənist] *n.* person sent from the home country to settle in a colony. □ **colono**
colonization [kɔlənai'zeiʃn] *n.* act of making a colony out of a territory. □ **colonización**
colonize *v.* to occupy (a territory) and make it a colony. □ **colonizar**
color ['kʌlə] *n.* and *v. Amer. see* **colour.**
Colorado beetle [kɔlərɑːdou'biːtl] *n.* striped beetle which attacks potato plants. □ **escarabajo de la patata**
colossal [kə'lɔsl] *adj.* **1** very large/huge. □ **colosal**
2 splendid. □ **colosal**
colossally *adv.* greatly/enormously. □ **colosalmente**
colossus *n.* huge statue; huge man. □ **coloso**
colour ['kʌlə] *Amer.* **color** *n.* **1** shade/tint which an object has in light: *the primary colours are red, yellow and blue; her dress was a dark green colour.* □ **color**
2 *colour film/colour photograph/colour TV,* not black and white. □ **...en color**
colour scheme, arrangement of colours (as in the furnishing of a room). □ **combinación de colores**
to be /feel off colour: *she is off colour today,* she is feeling unwell. □ **indispuesto**
3 shade (of a person's skin). □ **color**
colour bar, bar to someone because of the colour of his skin. □ **barrera racial**
4 paint. □ **color**
water colours, paint which has to be mixed with water □ **acuarela**
5 ***colour(s)*** = flag. □ **bandera**
6 *he passed his examination* ***with flying colours,*** he passed with high marks. □ **con muy buenas notas**
7 *he finally showed himself* ***in his true colours,*** as he really was. □ **...como era en realidad**
■ *v.* to paint with colour; to make (something) coloured: *you have to colour in the details of the picture.* □ **colorear**
colour-blind *adj.* unable to distinguish some colours (usually red and green). □ **daltoniano**
colour-blindness *n.* inability to distinguish colours (such as red and green). □ **daltonismo**
coloured *adj.* **1** (illustration) in colour. □ **en color**
2 *adj.* and *n.* (person) whose skin is not white. □ **de color**
colourful *adj.* brightly coloured; picturesque/full of local colour. □ **pintoresco**
colouring *n.* way in which something is coloured; substance which gives colour to something (such as food). □ **colorido; colorante**
colourless *adj.* pale/uninteresting. □ **sin color**
colt [koult] *n.* young male horse. □ **potro**
column ['kɔləm] *n.* **1** tall pillar: *Nelson's Column is in Trafalgar Square; the church has rows of columns separating the nave from the aisles.* □ **columna**
2 something which is round and long. □ **columna**
spinal column, backbone. □ **columna vertebral**
control column/steering column, shaft with a wheel on top for steering an aircraft/a car. □ **columna de dirección**
3 line of soldiers: *a column of infantry/tanks paraded through the town.* □ **columna**
4 ***fifth column,*** subversive elements working behind the enemy lines to weaken the morale of the population. □ **quinta columna**
5 long thin block of printing on a page: *these pages are printed in two columns; the paper has a three-column article about the guerrilla attacks.* □ **columna**
columnist ['kɔləmist] *n.* journalist (especially one who writes a regular column for a paper). □ **columnista**
coma ['koumə] *n.* state of unconsciousness: *after the accident she was in a coma for ten days.* □ **coma**
comatose ['koumətous] *adj.* **1** in a coma. □ **comatoso**
2 sleepy/half awake. □ **adormilado**
comb [koum] *n.* **1** long-toothed instrument for disentangling hair. □ **peine**
2 red crest on the head of a bird (such as a cock). □ **cresta**
3 honeycomb/construction of wax cells in which bees store honey. □ **panal**
■ *v.* **1** to disentangle hair: *have you brushed and combed your hair today?* □ **peinar**
2 to search: *the police are combing the countryside for the escaped prisoners.* □ **peinar**
combat ['kɔmbæt] *n.* fighting: *unarmed combat.* □ **combate**
■ *v.* to fight: *the police are combating crime.* □ **combatir**
combatant ['kɔmbətənt] *adj.* and *n.* (someone) who takes part in a fight. □ **combatiente**
combative *adj.* quarrelsome/argumentative. □ **combativo**
combine ['kɔmbain] *n.* **1** financial/commercial group. □ **consorcio, cártel**
2 ***combine (harvester***), large machine for cutting and threshing grain. □ **cosechadora**
■ *v.* to join together: *I am combining business with pleasure,* I am working on business but having a holiday at the same time. □ **combinar**
combination [kɔmbi'neiʃn] *n.* **1** several things joined together: *the disaster was caused by a combination of errors.* □ **combinación**
2 series of numbers which open a lock: *a combination lock; do you know the combination of the safe?* □ **combinación**
3 ***motorcycle combination,*** motorcycle with sidecar. □ **moto con sidecar**
4 ***combinations,*** long one-piece winter underwear. □ **combinación**
combustion [kəm'bʌstʃən] *n.* burning. □ **combustión**
combustible *adj.* and *n.* (substance) which can easily catch fire and burn. □ **combustible**
come [kʌm] *v.* (*he came; he has come*) **1** to arrive here: *I come to the office on my bicycle; there was a knock at the door - 'come in', he said; come and see us again soon; come up to my room for a cup of coffee.* □ **venir; entre**
2 to happen: *the murder comes in the first chapter of the book; my shoelace has come undone; how does the door come to be open?* □ **suceder (asesinato); desatarse (cordón); llegar a abrirse**
how come?, (*informal*) why/how did it happen? □ **¿cómo es eso?**
3 to add up to: *how much does it all come to? it comes expensive,* it costs a lot. □ **resultar caro**
come to that, by the way/while we are talking of that: *come to that, why did you stay behind?* □ **a propósito**
4 ***to come,*** in the future: *generations to come will bless the discovery of penicillin; in years to come.* □ **futuro, venidero**
come across *v.* to find: *I came across this book in a secondhand shop.* □ **encontrarse con**
come after *v.* to follow: *what letter comes after X in the alphabet?* □ **seguir**

come along *v.* to arrive. □ **llegar**
come along!, hurry up. □ **¡venga!**
come back *v.* to return: *he came back home after the war.* □ **volver**
comeback *n.* **1** repercussions: *has there been any comeback after our proposals?* □ **reacción**
2 return (of a singer/sportsman) after retirement: *after six years out of the boxing ring he staged an unsuccessful comeback.* □ **reaparición**
come by *v.* to obtain: *where did he come by all this money?* □ **conseguir**
come down *v.* to descend: *prices never seem to come down; he came down the stairs in his pyjamas.* □ **bajar**
comedown *n.* humiliation: *what a comedown after the life of luxury they used to lead!* □ **bajón**
come into *v.* **1** to enter: *he came into the room.* □ **entrar**
2 to inherit: *he came into some property when his grandfather died.* □ **heredar**
come off *v.* **1** to fall off: *the button has come off my shirt.* □ **caerse**
2 to result: *he came off badly,* the result was bad for him. □ **salir**
come on *v.* **1** to hurry: *come on!* □ **¡vamos!; ¡venga!**
2 to arrive: *there's a storm coming on; I think I have a cold coming on.* □ **venirse encima**
come out *v.* **1** to move outside: *are you coming out to play?* □ **salir**
2 (*of photography, etc.*) to result/to show: *the holiday pictures have all come out well,* are all successful. □ **salir**
3 *to come out* (*on strike*), to strike. □ **declararse en huelga**
come over *v.* **1** to cross: *he came over the road to say 'hello'.* □ **cruzar**
2 to start to feel: *he came over funny,* he began to feel ill. □ **ponerse**
3 *what has come over him?,* what is the matter with him? □ **¿qué le pasa?**
comer *n.* person who comes: *late comers; all comers.* □ **el que llega**
come round *v.* **1** to visit: *come round for a cup of tea at three o'clock.* □ **pasarse**
2 to recover (from unconsciousness). □ **volver en sí**
3 to change one's way of thinking: *he refused to let me see his daughter, but I think he is coming round; she is finally coming round to my point of view.* □ **ceder, aceptar**
come to *v.* to recover (from unconsciousness): *when he came to he was in a dark cell.* □ **volver en sí**
coming *adj.* approaching: *the coming year; their coming marriage.* □ **el año próximo; venidero**
■ *n.* arrival: *there were lots of comings and goings.* □ **llegada**

comedy ['kɔmədi] *n.* play or film which makes you laugh; funny aspect (of an event). □ **comedia**
comedian [kə'miːdiən] *n.* person who tells jokes to make people laugh. □ **comediante**

comet ['kɔmit] *n.* stream of gas which moves visibly through the sky with a bright tail. □ **cometa**

comfort ['kʌmfət] *n.* **1** something which helps to relieve suffering: *it is not much comfort to me to know that everyone else has money problems too.* □ **consuelo**
2 ease of living: *I like a bit of comfort.* □ **'confort'; bienestar**
comfort station, *Amer.* public toilet. □ **servicios**
■ *v.* to relieve the suffering (of someone who is miserable, etc.). □ **consolar**
comfortable *adj.* soft/relaxing: *what a comfortable armchair!* □ **confortable, cómodo**
make yourself comfortable, choose a soft chair, etc. □ **póngase cómodo**
comfortably *adv.* **1** in a soft/relaxing way. □ **cómodamente**
2 *they are comfortably off,* they have plenty of money to live on. □ **viven con desahogo**
comforter *n.* **1** person who comforts. □ **consolador**
2 long woolly scarf. □ **bufanda**
3 *Amer.* eiderdown/quilted covering for a bed. □ **edredón**
comforting *adj.* consoling. □ **reconfortante**
comfortless *adj.* harsh/hard: *a comfortless prison cell.* □ **incómodo**
comfy *adj.* (*informal*) comfortable. □ **cómodo**

comic ['kɔmik] *adj.* funny. □ **cómico**
■ *n.* **1** person who tells jokes to make people laugh. □ **cómico**
2 children's paper which only has cartoon stories: *my father reads all my comics.* □ **tebeo**
comical *adj.* funny: *he could not see the comical side of the situation.* □ **cómico**

comma ['kɔmə] *n.* punctuation mark (,) showing a break in a sentence around a clause. □ **coma**
inverted commas ("'"), printing signs showing speech: *open the inverted commas* ("); *close the inverted commas* ("). □ **comillas**

command [kə'mɑːnd] *n.* **1** order: *the soldiers did not hear the command to cease fire.* □ **orden**
command performance, play/film put on at the command of the king/queen. □ **representación/proyección solicitada por el soberano**
second-in-command, officer/person who is directly under the main commander/director. □ **subjefe**
2 *he is in command of a regiment,* in charge of. □ **está al mando de...**
3 knowledge (of a language): *he has a good command of German.* □ **dominio**
■ *v.* **1** to order: *the officer commanded the troops to cease fire.* □ **ordenar**
2 to be in charge of: *he commanded a regiment at the age of 30.* □ **mandar**
3 to demand: *paintings by Picasso command a high price.* □ **venderse a**
commandant [kɔmən'dænt] *n.* officer in charge of a camp, etc. □ **comandante**
commandeer [kɔmən'diːə] *v.* to order that something should be given over to the armed forces: *the soldiers commandeered every available lorry and car.* □ **requisar**
commander [kə'mɑːndə] *n.* officer in charge (of a corps/ship); rank in the navy below captain. □ **capitán de fragata**
commanding *adj.* **1** in command: *commanding officer.* □ **al mando**
2 *in a commanding tone of voice,* in an authoritarian tone. □ **autoritario**
commandment *n.* rule. □ **mandamiento**
the Ten Commandments, rules given by God to Moses. □ **los Diez Mandamientos**
commando *n.* member of a group of specially trained shock troops: *commando tactics; commando attack.* □ **comando**

commemorate [kə'meməreit] *v.* to celebrate (the memory of something/a special occasion, etc.): *today we commemorate the death of Nelson.* □ **conmemorar**
commemoration [kəmemə'reiʃn] *n.* celebration/remembrance of an anniversary. □ **conmemoración**
commemorative *adj.* which commemorates. □ **conmemorativo**

commence [kə'mens] *v.* (*formal*) to begin: *now we commence operations; let the festivities commence.* □ **comenzar**
commencement *n.* **1** beginning. □ **comienzo**
2 *Amer.* day when degrees are awarded at a university. □ **ceremonia de entrega de diplomas**
commend [kə'mend] *v.* to praise someone: *he was highly commended for his bravery.* □ **alabar**
commendable *adj.* praiseworthy. □ **loable**
commendably *adv.* in a praiseworthy way: *he spoke in a commendably forthright way.* □ **de manera loable**
commendation [kɔmen'deiʃn] *n.* official praise. □ **elogio**
commendatory [kə'mendətri] *adj.* which praises. □ **elogioso**
commensurate [kə'mensjurət] *adj.* in proportion to: *he has a salary commensurate with his responsibilities.* □ **proporcionado**
comment ['kɔment] *n.* remark/what you feel about something: *no comments please,* do not make rude remarks (about it). □ **comentario**
no comment, I refuse to discuss the matter. □ **sin comentarios**
■ *v.* to make remarks about something: *the police commented on the boy's behaviour; he commented that it was quite unusual.* □ **comentar**
commentary *n.* **1** remarks about a book, etc. □ **comentario**
2 spoken report on a football match/horse race, etc. □ **crónica**
commentator *n.* person who reports on events on the radio or television: *sports commentator.* □ **comentarista**
commerce ['kɔmə:s] *n.* business transactions. □ **comercio**
chamber of commerce, association of businessmen. □ **cámara de comercio**
commercial [kə'mə:ʃl] *adj.* dealing with business. □ **comercial**
commercial vehicle, vehicle used for business purposes. □ **vehículo industrial**
■ *n.* piece of publicity on television. □ **anuncio**
commercialize *v.* to make something into a business proposition: *sport has been commercialized.* □ **comercializar**
commiserate [kə'mizəreit] *v.* to sympathize (with someone). □ **compadecerse**
commissar [kɔmi'sɑ:] *n.* political leader (in a communist state). □ **comisario**
commission [kə'miʃn] *n.* **1** group of people which investigates problems of national importance. □ **comisión**
2 document naming someone an officer: *he got his commission at the beginning of the war.* □ **nombramiento**
3 order for something to be made/to be used: *the architect got the commision to design the new town hall; the ship was put into commission.* □ **encargo**
4 *my car is* ***out of commission,*** has broken down. □ **averiado**
5 percentage of sales given to the salesman: *you will get 10% commission on each sale you make.* □ **comisión**
■ *v.* **1** to authorize (someone) to be an officer/to authorize (an artist/architect, etc.) to do a piece of work; to put (a ship) into commission. □ **comisionar**
2 to authorize (a piece of work) to be done: *he commissioned a portrait of his wife.* □ **encargar**
commissionaire [kəmiʃə'nεə] *n.* doorkeeper (in a hotel/office block). □ **portero**
commissioner [kə'miʃnə] *n.* **1** representative of authority: *commissioner of police,* highest ranking police officer. □ **comisario**
High Commissioner ambassador of a Commonwealth country. □ **alto comisario**
2 *commissioner for oaths,* solicitor who can take sworn statements. □ **notario público**
commit [kə'mit] *v.* (*he committed*) **1** to carry out (a crime): *he committed murder; she committed perjury in the witness box.* □ **cometer**
2 *to commit someone for trial,* to send someone to the courts for trial. □ **citar ante los tribunales**
3 ***to commit oneself,*** to promise to do something: *he wouldn't commit himself; without committing myself,* without promising anything. □ **comprometerse**
committed *adj.* firmly believing in (something): *he's a committed Christian.* □ **comprometido**
commitment *n.* **1** promise. □ **promesa**
2 agreement to do something: *I have to refuse your invitation because of other commitments.* □ **compromiso**
3 promise to pay money: *the firm couldn't meet its commitments,* couldn't pay its debts. □ **compromiso**
committal *n.* sending of prisoner to the courts for trial. □ **envío a juicio**
committee [kə'miti] *n.* official group of people who organize or discuss on behalf of a larger body: *to be on a committee,* to be a member of it. □ **comisión, comité**
commodious [kə'moudiəs] *adj.* spacious/large (room/house, etc.). □ **espacioso**
commodity [kə'mɔditi] *n.* merchandise; thing sold. □ **mercancía**
basic commodities, basic foodstuffs and raw materials. □ **productos básicos**
commodore ['kɔmədɔ:] *n.* **1** rank in the Navy above captain. □ **comodoro**
2 person who directs a yacht club. □ **comodoro**
common ['kɔmən] *adj.* **1** belonging to everyone/to the public in general. □ **común**
2 *it is common knowledge,* everyone knows it. □ **es sabido de todos**
3 belonging to two or more people: *he and I have two things in common: we both have red hair and we both wear glasses.* □ **en común**
the Common Market, organization linking several European countries for purposes of trade. □ **Mercado Común**
4 *we have a common goal,* the same goal. □ **objetivo común**
5 ordinary/which happens frequently: *accidents are quite common on this stretch of road; writing 'recieve' is a very common mistake; an expression in common usage.* □ **común**
6 vulgar: *what a common little boy!* □ **vulgar**
■ *n.* land which belongs to a community: *we have a fair on the common every summer.* □ **ejido**
commoner *n.* ordinary citizen; not a noble. □ **plebeyo**
commonly *adv.* frequently. □ **frecuentemente**
common-or-garden *adj.* ordinary: *it's not serious just a common-or-garden cold.* □ **simple resfriado**
commonplace *adj.* and *n.* (thing) which happens frequently. □ **lugar común**
commons *n.* **1** *we are on short commons,* we have a small ration of food. □ **a media ración**
2 *the House of Commons,* the lower (elected) house

of the British parliament: *he sits in the Commons for Richmond,* he is the member of Parliament for Richmond. □ **Cámara de los Comunes**
common-sense *n.* **1** ordinary good sense. □ **sentido común**
2 *a common-sense solution,* a practical solution. □ **lógica**
commonwealth *n.* a republic; a group of states. □ **mancomunidad de estados**
the (British) Commonwealth, association of countries which were formerly colonies of Britain but which are now independent. □ **Commonwealth**
commotion [kə'mouʃən] *n.* confusion/trouble: *there was some commotion in the store when they caught a shoplifter.* □ **alboroto**
communal [kə'mju:nəl] *adj.* (property) held in common/belonging to several people. □ **común**
commune ['kɔmju:n] *n.* group of people who work together sharing everything. □ **comuna**
■ *v.* to be in touch with someone/something in spirit: *he was communing with nature,* he was sitting outside meditating. □ **estar en comunión**
communicate [kə'mju:nikeit] *v.* **1** to pass information to someone/to be in touch with someone: *they communicated by letter; the decree from the government was communicated to him by a special messenger.* □ **comunicar**
2 ***communicating rooms,*** rooms with a connecting door. □ **...que se comunican**
communicating door, door which links two rooms. □ **puerta de comunicación**
communication [kəmju:ni'keiʃn] *n.* **1** act of communicating/passing of information: *the quickest means of communication is the telephone; to get into communication with someone.* □ **comunicación**
2 *to pull the* ***communication cord,*** to pull the alarm signal on a train. □ **alarma de parada**
communicative [kə'mju:nikətiv] *adj.* talkative; (person) who is willing to give information. □ **comunicativo**
communion *n.* **1** fellowship with someone. □ **comunión**
2 ***Holy Communion,*** central religious ceremony in the Christian day, celebrating the Last Supper. □ **la Eucaristía**
communiqué [kə'mju:nikei] *n.* official news item given to the press. □ **comunicado**
communism ['kɔmjunizəm] *n.* political doctrine whereby the state owns all industry and land. □ **comunismo**
communist *adj.* referring to communism: *the communist state; the Communist Party.* □ **comunista**
■ *n.* **1** person who believes in communism. □ **comunista**
2 member of the Communist Party. □ **comunista**
community [kə'mju:niti] *n.* **1** group of people living in one place: *an urban community,* a town and its inhabitants. □ **comunidad**
community centre, sports/arts centre belonging to a town. □ **centro cultural**
the European Community, the Common Market. □ **la Comunidad Europea**
religious community, group of monks or nuns. □ **comunidad religiosa**
2 the population as a whole: *for the good of the community.* □ **la comunidad**
commute [kə'mju:t] *v.* **1** to reduce (a legal penalty): *his death sentence has been commuted to life imprisonment.* □ **conmutar**
2 to travel to work in town every day: *I commute in from the country every day; I am looking for a house within commuting distance of London.* □ **viajar diariamente**
commutation [kɔmju:'teiʃn] *n.* act of commuting a sentence. □ **conmutación**
commuter *n.* person who travels to work in town every day. □ **viajero diario**
commuter train, train for commuters. □ **tren de cercanías**
commuter belt, area round a town where commuters live. □ **extrarradio**
compact ['kɔmpækt] *n.* **1** agreement. □ **pacto**
2 small box for carrying face powder. □ **polvera**
3 *Amer.* small car. □ **utilitario**
■ *adj.* small; tight/close together: *this tool set fits into a very compact space.* □ **pequeño**
compactly *adv.* tightly/close together: *the tent folds down compactly.* □ **de modo compacto**
companion [kəm'pænjən] *n.* **1** person who travels or lives with someone. □ **compañero**
2 handbook. □ **manual**
companionable *adj.* friendly. □ **sociable**
companionship *n.* friendship. □ **compañerismo**
companionway *n.* stairway on a ship. □ **escalera de toldilla**
company ['kʌmpəni] *n.* **1** being together with other people. □ **compañía**
to keep someone company: *will you keep me company?,* will you come with me to stop me being lonely? □ **¿me harás compañía?**
to be good company, to be an entertaining companion: *he is very good company,* he is a very entertaining companion. □ **es una buena compañía**
to part company, to split up. □ **separarse**
to get into bad company, to get in with bad companions. □ **ir con malas compañías**
2 group of soldiers within a battalion; crew of a ship. □ **compañía; tripulación**
3 *theatrical company,* group of actors who play together: *touring company.* □ **compañía teatral**
4 (usually written *Co.* in names) commercial firm: *John Smith* and *Co.* (*Company*); *she works for an engineering company.* □ **empresa**
compare [kəm'pɛə] *v.* **1** to put two things side by side to see how they differ: *try on both pairs of shoes to compare them; you can't compare tinned peaches with/to fresh ones; compared with/to the rest of the family he is very small.* □ **comparar**
2 *he very rudely compared our homemade bread to a lump of concrete,* he said it was like a lump of concrete. □ **comparar**
3 *his work doesn't compare very well with his brother's,* is not as good as his brother's. □ **...no se puede comparar con...**
comparable ['kɔmprəbl] *adj.* which can be compared. □ **comparable**
comparative [kəm'pærətiv] *adj.* relative: *he is a comparative stranger; you have to look at the comparative cost of gas central heating against that of electricity.* □ **relativo; comparativo**
■ *n.* form of an adjective/adverb showing an increase in level: *'better', 'sillier' and 'more stupidly' are the comparatives of 'good', 'silly' and 'stupidly'.* □ **grado comparativo**
comparatively *adv.* more or less; relatively: *he is comparatively unknown.* □ **comparativamente**
comparison *n.* **1** act of comparing. □ **comparación**
2 ***there is no comparison*** *between butter and margarine,* you cannot compare them, one is so much better than the other. □ **no hay comparación...**
compartment [kəm'pɑ:tmənt] *n.* division inside a

box; separate section in a railway carriage/in a ship: *first-class compartment; watertight compartment.* □ **departamento; compartimiento**

compass ['kʌmpəs] *n.* **1** device which indicates the north by means of a needle: *can you find your way through the forest using a compass?* □ **brújula**
2 *a pair of compasses,* instrument for drawing a circle. □ **compás**

compassion [kəm'pæʃn] *n.* pity: *to have compassion on someone,* to take pity on someone. □ **compasión**
compassionate *adj.* merciful/pitying. □ **compasivo**
compassionate leave, extra holiday given to someone to visit a sick member of his family, etc. □ **permiso por motivos familiares/humanitarios**

compatible [kəm'pætəbl] *adj.* able to fit with something: *the two recording systems are not compatible.* □ **compatible**
compatibility [kəmpætə'biliti] *n.* ability to fit together. □ **compatibilidad**

compatriot [kəm'pætriət] *n.* person who comes from the same country. □ **compatriota**

compel [kəm'pel] *v.* (*he compelled*) to force: *he was compelled to resign; I can't compel you to sell me your house.* □ **obligar**
compelling *adj.* which forces; very exciting (story/film). □ **apremiante; irresistible**

compensate ['kɔmpenseit] *v.* to pay (someone) for damage done; to pay for a loss: *can I compensate you for the trouble I have caused you?* □ **indemnizar; compensar**
compensation [kɔmpen'seiʃn] *n.* payment for damage: *he was awarded $20,000 compensation.* □ **indemnización; compensación**

compère ['kɔmpɛə] *n.* host/person who introduces a show. □ **presentador**
■ *v.* to act as host in a show/to introduce different acts. □ **presentar**

compete [kəm'pi:t] *v.* to try to beat others in a race/a game/a business: *he was competing against two champions; six teams are competing for the prize; two firms are competing for the contract.* □ **competir**

competent ['kɔmpitənt] *adj.* able (to do something)/capable (of doing something); efficient: *a competent accountant.* □ **competente**
competence *n.* **1** capability/efficiency. □ **competencia**
2 professional responsibilities: *the case is outside the competence of this court.* □ **competencia**
competently *adv.* in a capable/efficient way. □ **con eficacia**

competition [kɔmpə'tiʃn] *n.* **1** game where several teams or people try to win: *a chess competition; a crossword competition; she went in for a competition to guess the weight of a pig.* □ **competición**
2 commercial rivalry/trying to sell more than another firm: *the strongest competition to the home car industry comes from Japan.* □ **competencia**
competitive [kəm'petitiv] *adj.* (person) who likes entering competitions; (sport) which is based on competitions; (prices) which aim to compete with those of rival firms. □ **competitivo**
competitor *n.* person who goes in for a competition; rival firm: *there are sixty competitors in the marathon race; our main competitor is J. Smith and Co.* □ **competidor**

compile [kəm'pail] *v.* to draw up (a list); to make a collection (of poetry); to write (a dictionary). □ **compilar**
compilation [kɔmpi'leiʃn] *n.* act of compiling; work which has been compiled. □ **compilación**
compiler [kəm'pailə] *n.* person who compiles. □ **compilador**

complacent [kəm'pleisnt] *adj.* self-satisfied: *he looked around him with a complacent smile.* □ **complaciente**
complacency *n.* contentment/self-satisfaction. □ **complacencia**
complacently *adv.* in a self-satisfied way. □ **de manera complaciente**

complain [kəm'plein] *v.* to grumble because something is wrong: *he complained about the smell; she complains of pains in her feet; they complained to the police about the noise from the nightclub.* □ **quejarse**
complaint *n.* **1** grumble/statement that something is wrong: *her constant complaint is that he is permanently drunk.* □ **queja**
2 illness: *rheumatism is a very common complaint among old people.* □ **enfermedad**

complement ['kɔmplimənt] *n.* **1** number of people needed to fill something. □ **dotación**
2 something which adds to or fits in with something else. □ **complemento**
■ *v.* to complete/to fit in with: *the colours complement each other.* □ **complementar**
complementary [kɔmpli'mentəri] *adj.* which fills/completes something. □ **complementario**

complete [kəm'pli:t] *adj.* **1** full/whole: *the complete book has over one thousand pages; I have a complete set of the new German stamps.* □ **completo**
2 finished: *all our preparations are now complete.* □ **concluido**
■ *v.* **1** to finish: *he completed the job in two days.* □ **acabar**
2 to fill in: *the form has to be completed and returned to the tax office.* □ **rellenar**
completely *adv.* wholly. □ **completamente**
completeness *n.* fullness (of success). □ **totalidad**
completion [kəm'pli:ʃn] *n.* **1** finishing; finish: *the building is nearing completion.* □ **terminación**
2 *completion of a contract,* signing of a contract. □ **firma de un contrato**

complex ['kɔmpleks] *adj.* complicated. □ **complejo**
■ *n.* **1** series of buildings: *an industrial complex; the arts centre complex.* □ **complejo**
2 repressed emotions/obsessions: *she has a complex about her hair,* she is obsessed with her hair. □ **complejo; obsesión**
inferiority complex, feeling that you are inferior. □ **complejo de inferioridad**
Oedipus complex, feeling of hatred for one's father and love for one's mother. □ **complejo de Edipo**
complexity [kəm'pleksiti] *n.* complicated nature. □ **complejidad**

complexion [kəm'plekʃn] *n.* colour of the skin on your face: *she has a beautiful olive complexion.* □ **tez**

complicate ['kɔmplikeit] *v.* to make things complicated. □ **complicar**
complicated *adj.* with many small details/difficult to understand: *a very complicated operation; flying a large jet aircraft is a very complicated job.* □ **complicado**
complication [kɔmpli'keiʃn] *n.* **1** being complicated/difficult to understand. □ **complicación**
2 *after the operation, complications set in,* the patient's state became considerably worse because of further developments. □ **...surgieron complicaciones**

complicity [kəm'plisiti] *n.* being an accomplice to a crime. □ **complicidad**

compliment ['kɔmplimənt] *n.* **1** praise: *the winner re-*

ceived the compliments of the judges. □ **felicitación**
2 *send him my compliments,* send him my good wishes. □ **saludos**
■ *v.* to praise: *the winner of the piano competition was complimented on his technique.* □ **alabar**
complimentary [kɔmpli'mentəri] *adj.* **1** which praises: *a complimentary review in the paper.* □ **elogioso**
2 *complimentary ticket,* free ticket. □ **entrada de favor**
comply [kəm'plai] *v.* to observe (a rule); to obey (an order): *he complied with the request to leave the country.* □ **cumplir; obedecer**
compliance *n.* agreement to do something. □ **conformidad**
compliant *adj.* (person) who agrees to do something/who obeys the rules. □ **sumiso, obediente**
component [kəm'pounənt] *adj.* and *n.* (piece) which forms part of something: *the component parts of a car; half the components are unobtainable.* □ **componente**
compose [kəm'pouz] *v.* **1** to make up (music); to write (a letter/a poem). □ **componer**
2 ***compose yourself,*** be calm. □ **serénate**
composed *adj.* calm/unflustered. □ **sereno**
composer *n.* person who writes music. □ **compositor**
composite ['kɔmpəzit] *adj.* made of several different parts. □ **compuesto**
composition [kɔmpə'ziʃn] *n.* **1** way in which something is formed: *what is the chemical composition of this plastic?* □ **composición**
2 piece of music/poem/long essay. □ **'composición**
3 artificial substance. □ **compuesto**
compositor [kəm'pɔzitə] *n.* person who sets type for printing. □ **cajista**
composure [kəm'pouʒə] *n.* calmness. □ **compostura**
compost ['kɔmpɔst] *n.* rotted vegetable matter used in gardening. □ **abono vegetal**
compound ['kɔmpaund] *adj.* made up of several parts. □ **compuesto**
compound fracture, fracture where the broken bone pierces the skin. □ **fractura abierta**
compound interest, interest calculated each year on the total sum including the previous year's interest. □ **interés compuesto**
■ *n.* **1** chemical made up of two or more elements. □ **compuesto**
2 yard enclosed by a fence. □ **cercado**
■ *v.* [kəm'paund] **1** to come to an agreement with people to whom you owe money. □ **llegar a un acuerdo, liquidar en parte**
2 to keep information about a crime hidden. □ **encubrir**
3 to increase/to aggravate (a crime). □ **agravar**
comprehend [kɔmpri'hend] *v.* **1** to understand. □ **comprender**
2 to include. □ **comprender**
comprehensible *adj.* which can be understood/understandable. □ **comprensible**
comprehension *n.* understanding. □ **comprensión**
comprehensive *adj.* **1** which includes everything. □ **global**
2 *comprehensive knowledge,* knowledge which covers all fields. □ **...de gran amplitud**
comprehensive (***school***), school for children of different abilities. □ **instituto de bachillerato**
comprehensive education, system of education where all children go to the same type of school without any selection. □ **general**
comprehensiveness *n.* wide range (of knowledge, etc.). □ **amplitud**
compress ['kɔmpres] *n.* pad of material put on a bruise/sore. □ **bayeta**
■ *v.* [kəm'pres] to squeeze into a small space. □ **comprimir**
compressed air, air under pressure. □ **aire comprimido**
compressor *n.* machine which compresses air/gas, etc. □ **compresor**
comprise [kəm'praiz] *v.* to be formed of: *the book comprises three main sections.* □ **constar de**
compromise ['kɔmprəmaiz] *n.* agreement of two opposing points of view, where each side gives way to some extent: *after three hours of discussion we reached a compromise; in the end we agreed on a compromise resolution.* □ **transacción**
■ *v.* **1** to come to an agreement by giving way: *you want $20, I'm offering $10. let's compromise on $15.* □ **llegar a una transacción**
2 to embarrass/to put in a difficult position: *the position of the prime minister was compromised when his brother was found guilty of bribery.* □ **comprometer**
compromising *adj.* embarrassing: *he was put in a compromising situation.* □ **comprometedor**
compulsion [kəm'pʌlʃn] *n.* force/urge: *there is no compulsion for you to attend the trial.* □ **obligación**
compulsive *adj.* (person) who cannot stop himself doing something: *he is a compulsive gambler.* □ **compulsivo**
compulsory *adj.* which you are forced to do: *military service is compulsory in some countries.* □ **obligatorio**
compunction [kəm'pʌŋkʃn] *n.* remorse/regret: *he did it without any compunction,* he did not hesitate to do it. □ **...sin escrúpulos**
compute [kəm'pju:t] *v.* to calculate. □ **computar**
computation *n.* calculation. □ **cómputo**
computer *n.* electronic machine which calculates and keeps information automatically: *all our sales information is on computer,* is held in a computer; *the census figures are being processed by computer.* □ **ordenador**
computerize *v.* to process by computer: *the payment system is all computerized.* □ **procesar, informatizar**
comrade ['kɔmreid] *n.* friend/companion; fellow member of a socialist or communist party. □ **camarada**
comradeship *n.* fellowship/friendliness. □ **camaradería**
con [kɔn] *n.* (*informal*) deception: *con trick.* □ **engaño**
con man, trickster. □ **estafador**
■ *v.* (*he conned*) (*informal*) to deceive/to trick someone. □ **estafar**
concave [kɔn'keiv] *adj.* (surface) which is hollowed in the middle like a spoon: *a concave lens.* □ **cóncavo**
conceal [kən'si:l] *v.* to hide: *the smuggler had drugs concealed in the heels of his shoes.* □ **ocultar**
concealed *adj.* hidden: *concealed entrance,* entrance which is difficult to see; *concealed lighting.* □ **oculto**
concealment *n.* **1** hiding. □ **ocultación**
2 *place of concealment,* hiding place. □ **escondrijo**
concede [kən'si:d] *v.* **1** to admit (that you are wrong). □ **reconocer**
2 to admit that you have lost: *he conceded defeat; after the fiftieth move the challenger conceded.* □ **darse por vencido**

conceit [kən'si:t] *n.* high opinion of oneself. □ **engreimiento**
conceited *adj.* (person) who thinks too much of himself. □ **engreído**
conceive [kən'si:v] *v.* **1** to become pregnant. □ **concebir**
2 to think up (an idea): *he conceived (of) a plan to dam the river.* □ **concebir**
conceivable *adj.* which can be imagined: *it is hardly conceivable that he can survive so many years in prison.* □ **concebible**
concentrate ['kɔnsəntreit] *n.* concentrated substance: *tomato concentrate.* □ **concentrado**
■ *v.* **1** to pay great attention to something: *I am concentrating on learning German; the teacher concentrated on the student's mistakes; I can't concentrate when you are practising the violin.* □ **concentrarse**
2 to put all one's resources together in one place: *the general concentrated the attack on one hill; we must concentrate our efforts on increasing sales in Japan.* □ **concentrar**
concentrated *adj.* very strong (after water has been extracted): *concentrated orange juice.* □ **concentrado**
concentration [kɔnsən'treiʃn] *n.* **1** attentiveness. □ **concentración**
2 putting all your resources into one area. □ **concentración**
3 ***concentration camp,*** camp where many political prisoners are held in captivity. □ **campo de concentración**
concentric [kən'sentrik] *adj.* (circles) inside each other, each with the same central point. □ **concéntrico**
concept ['kɔnsept] *n.* idea/philosophical notion: *the concept of space.* □ **concepto**
conception [kən'sepʃn] *n.* **1** becoming pregnant. □ **concepción**
2 idea: *he has no conception of punctuality; I have no conception of what it feels like to be a baby.* □ **no tiene ni idea...**
concern [kən'sə:n] *n.* **1** worry: *his health is a source of great concern.* □ **preocupación**
2 business/interest: *it is no concern of yours,* it is none of your business. □ **asunto**
3 firm/business: *he is the manager of a big industrial concern.* □ **empresa**
■ *v.* **1** to deal with. □ **tener que ver con**
2 *this letter concerns you,* is about you. □ **referirse**
3 *that does not concern him,* it has nothing to do with him. □ **concernir**
as far as** money **is concerned, with reference to money. □ **por lo que al dinero se refiere**
as far as I am concerned, *he is an idiot,* my feeling is that he is an idiot. □ **por lo que a mí se refiere...**
4 to worry: *he was very concerned about your health.* □ **preocuparse**
concerning *prep.* about/referring to: *I want to speak to you concerning your bank account.* □ **sobre**
concert ['kɔnsət] *n.* programme of music played in public: *we went to a concert last night; the orchestra is giving a concert tomorrow.* □ **concierto**
concerted [kən'sə:tid] *adj.* done or planned jointly: *a concerted attack.* □ **concertado**
concert hall *n.* large hall for giving concerts. □ **sala de conciertos**
concertina [kɔnsə'ti:nə] *n.* portable musical instrument with bellows and a set of keys at either end. □ **concertina**
■ *v.* to become crushed/crumpled: *the front of the car concertinaed under the impact.* □ **arrugarse**
concerto [kən'tʃɛətou] *n.* piece of music for a solo instrument and orchestra, or for a small group of instruments: *a piano concerto.* □ **concierto**
concession [kən'seʃn] *n.* act of conceding/of admitting something: *as a concession to public opinion, we are removing the poster,* because people did not like it, we are removing the poster; *to make a concession,* to change what you planned to fit in with someone else's wishes. □ **concesión**
conch [kɔntʃ] *n.* type of sea shell, like a large snail shell. □ **caracola**
conchology [kɔn'kɔlədʒi] *n.* study of shells. □ **conquiliología**
conciliate [kən'silieit] *v.* to win over (someone) who was previously unfriendly; to reconcile. □ **reconciliarse**
a conciliating gesture, a gesture aimed at reducing tension. □ **gesto conciliador**
conciliation [kənsili'eiʃn] *n.* act of conciliating: *a gesture of conciliation.* □ **reconciliación**
conciliation board, committee set up to arbitrate in industrial disputes. □ **tribunal de conciliación laboral**
conciliator [kən'silieitə] *n.* person who tries to reconcile people of opposing views. □ **conciliador**
conciliatory [kən'siliətri] *adj.* which is aimed at conciliating: *he sent a very conciliatory letter.* □ **conciliatorio**
concise [kən'sais] *adj.* short; saying a lot, but using few words: *he gave me a concise report on what had happened.* □ **conciso**
concisely *adv.* in a concise way. □ **concisamente**
conciseness, concision [kən'siʒn] *n.* briefness: *his letter was a model of concision.* □ **concisión**
conclave ['kɔŋkleiv] *n.* religious assembly, especially meeting of cardinals to elect a pope. □ **cónclave**
conclude [kən'klu:d] *v.* **1** to come to an end: *the evening's entertainment concluded with a song by the president.* □ **concluir**
2 to deduce/to come to an opinion: *as he did not come to the interview, I concluded that he did not want the job.* □ **sacar la conclusión**
3 to arrange (a treaty). □ **concertar**
concluding *adj.* final: *the concluding chapter of a book.* □ **final**
conclusion [kən'klu:ʒn] *n.* **1** end. □ **conclusión**
in conclusion, *I would like to say,* as an end to my speech, I would like to say. □ **en conclusión**
2 opinion reached by reasoning: *he came to the conclusion that the man had drowned.* □ **conclusión**
a foregone conclusion, something which is inevitable. □ **resultado inevitable**
conclusive *adj.* decisive/which offers firm proof: *the tests on the bloodstains were conclusive evidence that the dead man had been carried in the boot of the car.* □ **concluyente**
conclusively *adv.* in a decisive way: *it proves conclusively that she could not have committed the crime.* □ **definitivamente**
concoct [kən'kɔkt] *v.* **1** to make a dish of food: *what on earth have you been concocting?* □ **preparar**
2 to make up/to invent a story. □ **urdir**
concoction *n.* curious mixture of food or drink. □ **mixtura (comida); brebaje (bebida)**
concord ['kɔŋkɔ:d] *n.* harmony/peace. □ **concordia**
concordance [kən'kɔ:dəns] *n.* alphabetical list of words used in a book: *concordance to Shakespeare's plays.* □ **concordancias**
concordat [kɔn'kɔ:dæt] *n.* agreement (between secular and temporal powers). □ **concordato**
concourse ['kɔŋkɔ:s] *n.* **1** crowd/mass of people.

□ **concurrencia**
2 large open space inside a railway station/concert hall, etc. □ **vestíbulo**
concrete ['kɔŋkri:t] *adj.* real/firm: *a concrete proposal.* □ **concreto**
■ *adj.* and *n.* (made of) a hard stone-like substance made by mixing sand, cement and water: *many buildings are built of concrete; a concrete pavement.* □ **hormigón**
concrete mixer *n.* machine for mixing concrete. □ **hormigonera**
concubine ['kɔŋkjubain] *n.* woman whom a man lives with as a second wife, but who is not married to him. □ **concubina**
concur [kən'kə:] *v.* (*he concurred*) to agree. □ **estar de acuerdo**
concurrence [kən'kʌrəns] *n.* agreement. □ **acuerdo**
concurrent [kən'kʌrənt] *adj.* which happen at the same time. □ **concurrente**
concurrently *adv.* happening at the same time: *the two jail sentences are to run concurrently,* the criminal is sentenced for two crimes, but the judge asks for the two sentences not to follow one after the other. □ **al mismo tiempo**
concussion [kən'kʌʃn] *n.* shock to the brain caused by being hit on the head. □ **conmoción cerebral**
concussed *adj.* in a state of concussion. □ **conmocionado**
condemn [kən'dem] *v.* **1** to blame; to sentence a criminal: *he was condemned to death.* □ **condenar**
2 *these blocks of flats have been condemned,* local authorities have said that no one may live in them. □ **...han sido declarados en ruina**
condemnation [kɔndem'neiʃn] *n.* blame. □ **censura**
condense [kən'dens] *v.* **1** to reduce the size of something: *condensed report,* report which has been shortened. □ **condensar**
condensed milk, milk which has been concentrated and sweetened. □ **leche condensada**
2 (*of steam*) to form drops of water: *water condensed on the panes of glass.* □ **condensarse**
condensation [kɔnden'seiʃn] *n.* act of condensing; steam which has formed into a film on a cold surface: *wipe the condensation off the bathroom mirror.* □ **condensación**
condenser *n.* part of a machine which turns gas into liquid. □ **condensador**
condescend [kɔndi'send] *v.* to speak/to act as if you are superior to someone else: *the teacher condescended to speak to the parents.* □ **condescender**
condescending *adj.* unpleasantly superior (voice/smile, etc.). □ **condescendiente**
condescension *n.* acting with a feeling of superiority. □ **condescendencia**
condiment ['kɔndimənt] *n.* seasoning for food, such as salt, pepper, mustard. □ **condimento**
condition [kən'diʃn] *n.* **1** state: *the bicycle is in very good condition; weather conditions are appalling.* □ **estado**
2 term (of a bargain): *I will come on condition that you pay for me,* provided that you pay for me; *there are various conditions attached to the agreement.* □ **con la condición de que...**
3 bad state: *he has a heart condition,* he has a weak heart. □ **afección**
■ *v.* **1** to put into good condition. □ **arreglar, acondicionar**
2 to make (someone) used to something. □ **acostumbrar**
conditional *adj.* and *n.* provided that certain things happen; part of a verb which shows this: *'I would come' is a conditional form of 'to come'.* □ **condicional**
conditionally *adv.* under certain conditions: *he was set free conditionally.* □ **condicionalmente**
conditioner *n.* lotion which puts something (especially hair) into good condition. □ **acondicionador**
condole [kən'doul] *v.* ***to condole with someone,*** to express your regrets for some tragedy which has happened. □ **dar el pésame**
condolences *n. pl.* expressions of regret (at the death of someone). □ **le acompaño en el sentimiento**
condominium [kɔndə'miniəm] *n.* joint ownership. □ **condominio**
condone [kən'doun] *v.* to excuse (a crime, etc.): *he condoned the action against the terrorists.* □ **disculpar**
conducive [kən'dju:siv] *adj.* favourable: *conditions are not conducive to peace.* □ **conducente**
conduct ['kɔndʌkt] *n.* way of behaving: *she got full marks for good conduct; his conduct at the party was appalling.* □ **conducta**
■ *v.* [kən'dʌkt] **1** to lead/to guide: *conducted tour,* tour led by a guide; *he is conducting the local orchestra in tonight's concert.* □ **dirigir**
2 *metal conducts electricity,* allows electricity to pass along it. □ **conducir**
3 ***to conduct yourself,*** to behave. □ **comportarse**
conduction [kən'dʌkʃn] *n.* passing of heat/electricity. □ **conducción**
conductor *n.* **1** substance (such as metal) which conducts heat/electricity. □ **conductor**
conductor rail, rail which conducts electricity for electric trains. □ **carril conductor**
2 person who directs an orchestra. □ **director**
3 ***bus conductor,*** person who collects money from the passengers on a bus. □ **cobrador**
4 *Amer.* railway guard. □ **revisor**
conductress *n.* woman who collects money from passengers on a bus. □ **cobradora**
conduit ['kɔndit] *n.* tube along which liquids can be passed. □ **conducto**
cone [koun] *n.* **1** geometrical figure, round at the base, rising to a point. □ **cono**
2 *ice cream cone,* cone made of biscuit for holding ice cream. □ **helado de cucurucho; cono**
3 ***fir cone,*** fruit of a fir tree. □ **piña**
4 ***nose cone,*** pointed end of a rocket. □ **morro**
cone-shaped *adj.* shaped like a cone. □ **coniforme**
confab ['kɔnfæb] *n.* (*informal*) chat/discussion. □ **palique**
confection [kən'fekʃən] *n.* food made of a mixture of sweet things. □ **confite**
confectionery [kən'fekʃənri] *n.* sweets and cakes. □ **repostería**
confectioner's *n.* shop selling sweets and cakes. □ **confitería; pastelería**
confederate [kən'fedərət] *n.* someone who has joined with others (usually to do a crime). □ **cómplice**
confederacy *n.* joining together. □ **confederación**
confederation [kənfedə'reiʃn] *n.* group (of states/trade unions, etc.). □ **confederación**
confer [kən'fə:] *v.* (*he conferred*) **1** to discuss: *I must confer with my colleagues before giving an answer.* □ **consultar**
2 *to confer an honour on someone,* to award someone an honour. □ **conferir**
conference ['kɔnfərəns] *n.* discussion; meeting of a group/society: *the annual conference of the Mathematical Association.* □ **conferencia**
press conference, meeting where a person in the news answers questions from members of the press: *the*

president gave a press conference on his return from the summit meeting. □ **conferencia de prensa**

confess [kən'fes] *v.* to admit that you have done something wrong: *the boy confessed to having stolen the chocolate.* □ **confesar**

confession [kən'feʃn] *n.* **1** admission of fault. □ **confesión**

2 *to make your confession,* to admit your sins to a priest. □ **confesarse**

confessional *n.* small private box in a church where a priest hears confessions. □ **confesionario**

confessor *n.* priest who hears confessions. □ **confesor**

confetti [kən'feti] *n.* small pieces of coloured paper which are thrown over the bride and bridegroom after a wedding. □ **confeti**

confidant, confidante [kɔnfi'dænt] *n.* person you tell secrets to. □ **confidente**

confide [kən'faid] *v.* to tell someone a secret: *he confided in me.* □ **hacer confidencias**

confidence ['kɔnfidəns] *n.* **1** feeling sure: *I have complete confidence in him.* □ **confianza**

2 secrecy: *he told me this in confidence,* he told it to me as a secret. □ **en confianza**

3 ***confidence trick,*** trick whereby a trickster gains someone's confidence to steal money from him. □ **timo**

confident *adj.* sure (of yourself): *I am confident we shall win; I am confident of success.* □ **confiado**

confidently *adv.* in a sure way: *he confidently expects to make a lot of money.* □ **lleno de confianza**

confidential [kɔnfi'denʃl] *adj.* **1** secret: *the spy photographed confidential documents.* □ **confidencial**

2 private: *a confidential secretary.* □ **una secretaria de confianza**

confidentially *adv.* secretly/in a confidential way: *confidentially, I am told he will be getting an award for his work.* □ **confidencialmente**

confine [kən'fain] *v.* **1** to restrict/to shut up: *I will confine myself to a few short remarks; she does not like being in a confined space.* □ **limitar**

2 *he was confined to bed,* the doctor told him to stay in bed. □ **tuvo que guardar cama**

confinement *n.* **1** imprisonment. □ **prisión**

2 *he was kept in* ***solitary confinement*** *for four years,* in a prison cell by himself. □ **estuvo incomunicado...**

3 period when a woman gives birth to a baby. □ **de parto**

confirm [kən'fə:m] *v.* **1** to make definite/to make sure: *I will confirm the booking of the hotel room by letter; he confirmed that the price had gone up.* □ **confirmar**

2 to be made a full member of a church. □ **confirmar**

confirmation [kɔnfə'meiʃn] *n.* **1** making sure: *I received his letter of confirmation,* letter in which he confirmed what we had agreed. □ **confirmación**

2 ceremony in which someone is made a full member of the church. □ **confirmación**

confirmed *adj.* **1** permanent. □ **inveterado**

2 *he is a confirmed bachelor,* he will never get married. □ **... un solterón empedernido**

confiscate ['kɔnfiskeit] *v.* to take away someone's possessions as a punishment: *the teacher confiscated the boy's catapult.* □ **confiscar**

confiscation [kɔnfis'keiʃn] *n.* act of taking away. □ **confiscación**

conflagration [kɔnflə'greiʃn] *n.* (*formal*) big fire. □ **conflagración**

conflict ['kɔnflikt] *n.* battle/fight: *the conflict in the Middle East.* □ **conflicto**

■ *v.* to clash/to contradict: *we had conflicting reports about what had happened,* we had different reports which told opposite stories. □ **chocar, contradecirse**

conform [kən'fɔ:m] *v.* to fit in with a pattern/to act in the same way as other people: *you must conform to the rules of the club.* □ **ajustarse**

conformist *n.* person who conforms. □ **conformista**

conformity *n.* being the same/acting in the same way as other people. □ **conformidad**

confound [kən'faund] *v.* to confuse/to bother: *the success of the play confounded the critics.* □ **desconcertar**

confront [kən'frʌnt] *v.* **1** to face up to (a danger). □ **enfrentarse con**

2 *to confront someone with witnesses,* to bring someone face to face with witnesses. □ **confrontar**

confrontation [kɔnfrʌn'teiʃn] *n.* bringing face to face; meeting between opposing sides. □ **confrontación**

confuse [kən'fju:z] *v.* to mix/to muddle: *stop asking him so many questions, it only confuses him; I always confuse Portsmouth with Plymouth; it confuses the issue,* it attracts attention away from the main problem. □ **confundir**

confused *adj.* mixed up/muddled. □ **confuso**

confusedly [kən'fju:zidli] *adv.* in a muddled way. □ **confusamente**

confusing *adj.* muddling. □ **desconcertante**

confusion [kən'fju:ʒn] *n.* muddle/disorder: *in the confusion, the bank robbers escaped.* □ **confusión**

congeal [kən'dʒi:l] *v.* to set solid; to become solid (as of dried blood). □ **coagular**

congenial [kən'dʒi:niəl] *adj.* sympathetic/friendly. □ **agradable**

congenital [kən'dʒenitl] *adj.* (illness/defect) present in a person since birth. □ **congénito**

conger eel ['kɔŋgəi:l] *n.* very large type of eel. □ **congrio**

congested [kən'dʒestid] *adj.* blocked/crowded: *the narrow streets are very congested on market day.* □ **congestionado**

congestion [kən'dʒeʃtʃn] *n.* blocking of streets; filling (of the lungs) with liquid: *the centre of the town suffers from traffic congestion.* □ **congestión**

conglomeration [kəngləmə'reiʃn] *n.* mass of things heaped together. □ **conglomeración**

conglomerate [kən'glɔmərət] *n.* many subsidiary companies linked together in a large company. □ **conglomerado de empresas**

Congo ['kɔŋgou] *n.* country in West Africa. □ **Congo**

Congolese *adj.* and *n.* (person) from the Congo. □ **congoleño**

congratulate [kən'grætjuleit] *v.* to give (someone) good wishes on a special occasion; to praise (someone) for some achievement: *I congratulated him on winning first prize.* □ **felicitar**

congratulations [kəngrætju'leiʃnz] *n.* good wishes: *give him my congratulations on his success.* □ **enhorabuena; felicidades**

congratulatory [kən'grætjulətri] *adj.* which gives good wishes: *congratulatory telegram.* □ **de felicitación**

congregate ['kɔŋgrigeit] *v.* to gather together: *voters congregated in front of the parliament building.* □ **congregarse**

congregation [kɔŋgri'geiʃn] *n.* people gathered together; people meeting together in a church. □ **congregación**

congress ['kɔŋgres] *n.* meeting of a group of people. □ **congreso**

Trades Union Congress, general meeting of representatives of all trade unions. □ **congreso de los sindicatos**
Congress, the elected legislative body of the United States. □ **Congreso**
congressional *adj.* referring to the US Congress. □ **del Congreso**
congressman *n.* (*pl. congressmen*) member of the Congress of the United States. □ **congresista**
conical ['kɔnikl] *adj.* shaped like a cone. □ **cónico**
conifer ['kɔnifə] *n.* tree which bears cones. □ **conífera**
coniferous *adj.* referring to conifers: *coniferous forest.* □ **conífero, de coníferas**
conjecture [kən'dʒektʃə] *n.* guess: *to hazard a conjecture,* to guess. □ **conjetura**
■ *v.* to guess. □ **hacer conjeturas**
conjectural *adj.* possible/which has been guessed at. □ **conjetural**
conjugal ['kɔndʒugl] *adj.* referring to marriage/to the married state: *conjugal rights.* □ **conyugal**
conjugate ['kɔndʒugeit] *v.* to show the different parts of a verb (I am, you are, he is, etc.). □ **conjugar**
conjugation [kɔndʒu'geiʃn] *n.* way in which a verb changes according to tense and person. □ **conjugación**
conjunction [kən'dʒʌŋkʃn] *n.* word which links different parts of a sentence. □ **conjunción**
in conjunction with someone, together with someone. □ **conjuntamente con**
conjunctivitis [kəndʒʌŋkti'vaitis] *n.* inflammation of the eyes. □ **conjuntivitis**
conjuncture [kən'dʒʌŋktʃə] *n.* circumstances. □ **coyuntura**
conjure ['kʌndʒə] *v.* **1** to do tricks with cards/rabbits, etc. □ **hacer aparecer**
2 to call up (a spirit/a picture): *the word 'Provence' conjures up images of sun and sea.* □ **conjurar**
conjurer, conjuror *n.* person who does tricks. □ **prestidigitador**
conjuring *n.* magic tricks: *he does conjuring tricks.* □ **juegos de manos; ilusionismo**
conker ['kɔŋkə] *n.* (*informal*) horse chestnut. □ **castaño de Indias**
connect [kə'nekt] *v.* **1** to join/to link: *the cooker is connected to the gas pipe; can you connect the hose to the tap? this train connects with the 13.56 from London,* this train arrives in time for you to get off it and catch the 13.56; *do not play with the wires - they are all connected up.* □ **conectar**
2 *they are connected to the Williams family of Cardiff,* they are related to them. □ **están emparentados con...**
connected *adj.* **1** joined/linked. □ **conectado**
2 *he is well connected,* he has influential friends and relations. □ **está muy relacionado**
connection, connexion *n.* **1** join/link: *is there any connection between your visit and his letter?* □ **conexión**
in connection with *your visit to Africa,* with reference to/concerning your visit. □ **con respecto a**
2 *there is a connection to London,* there is a train which connects with this one for London. □ **enlace**
3 *he has* ***connections*** *in the theatre,* he has friends/relations in the theatre. □ **relaciones**
conning tower ['kɔniŋtauə] *n.* highest part of a submarine. □ **torreta**
connive [kə'naiv] *v.* ***to connive at something,*** to allow it/to take no notice of it. □ **hacer la vista gorda a**
connivance *n. connivance at something,* tolerating/taking no notice of it. □ **connivencia**
connoisseur [kɔnə'sə:] *n.* expert: *he is a connoisseur of good wine.* □ **entendido**
connote [kə'nout] *v.* to imply something in addition. □ **connotar**
conquer ['kɔŋkə] *v.* to defeat by force: *the country was conquered by the invading armies.* □ **conquistar**
conquering *adj.* triumphant/victorious: *a conquering hero.* □ **victorioso**
conqueror *n.* person who leads the invasion of a country; state which captures another country: *William the Conqueror.* □ **conquistador**
conquest ['kɔŋkwest] *n.* **1** capturing of something: *the conquest of Spain.* □ **conquista**
2 thing/country which has been captured. □ **conquista**
conscience ['kɔnʃəns] *n.* feeling which tells you if you have done right or wrong: *he has a guilty conscience.* □ **conciencia**
conscience-stricken *adj.* ashamed. □ **lleno de remordimientos**
conscientious [kɔnʃi'enʃəs] *adj.* who works carefully and well: *he is a very conscientious employee.* □ **concienzudo**
conscientious objector, person who refuses to join the services because he feels war is wrong. □ **objetor de conciencia**
conscientiously *adv.* in a conscientious way. □ **concienzudamente**
conscious ['kɔnʃəs] *adj.* **1** aware of things around you: *I became conscious of a feeling of hostility.* □ **darse cuenta de**
2 *the victim only became conscious two days after the attack,* woke up after being in a coma for two days. □ **la víctima volvió en sí...**
3 *a conscious decision,* a deliberate decision. □ **deliberado**
consciously *adv.* in a conscious way. □ **conscientemente**
consciousness *n.* **1** awareness of what is happening. □ **consciencia**
2 *he lost consciousness as soon as the car hit the tree,* he became unconscious; *he regained consciousness a few minutes later,* he woke again after being unconscious. □ **conocimiento**
conscript ['kɔnskript] *n.* person who has been ordered to join the services. □ **recluta**
■ *v.* to order people to join the services. □ **reclutar**
conscription [kən'skripʃn] *n.* legal obligation to join the services. □ **servicio militar**
consecrate ['kɔnsikreit] *v.* **1** to bless (a new church/a king). □ **consagrar**
2 *to consecrate your life to helping the blind,* to devote all your life to helping the blind. □ **consagrar**
consecration [kɔnsi'kreiʃn] *n.* blessing; devoting (of your life). □ **consagración**
consecutive [kən'sekjutiv] *adj.* following one after the other: *on three consecutive days,* on three days following after each other. □ **consecutivo**
consecutively *adv.* in order. □ **sucesivamente**
consensus [kən'sensəs] *n.* generally agreed opinion. □ **consenso**
consent [kən'sent] *n.* agreement: *she ran away without her parents' consent.* □ **consentimiento**
■ *v.* to agree: *has he consented to his daughter's marriage?* □ **consentir**
consequence ['kɔnsikwəns] *n.* **1** result: *he ran out of money, with the consequence that he couldn't buy any food; she broke her leg and as a consequence she couldn't drive for three months.* □ **consecuencia**
2 importance: *it is of no consequence,* it does not matter. □ **importancia**

consequent *adj.* ***consequent on,*** resulting from. □ **consiguiente; consecutivo a**
consequential [kɔnsi'kwenʃl] *adj.* resulting. □ **consiguiente**
consequently *adv.* because of this/for this reason. □ **por consiguiente**
conserve [kən'səːv] *v.* to save: *we must try to conserve energy.* □ **conservar**
conservation [kɔnsə'veiʃn] *n.* preservation/saving (of natural resources/old buildings, etc.). □ **conservación**
conservative [kən'səːvətiv] *adj.* **1** not wanting to change: *he dresses in a very conservative way,* he does not follow the latest fashions. □ **conservador**
2 *at a conservative estimate,* at the lowest/most moderate estimate. □ **cálculo moderado**
3 ***Conservative party,*** political party which does not want to change the existing system of government, and which does not favour state control of industry. □ **partido conservador**
a Conservative, member of the Conservative Party. □ **un conservador**
conservatively *adv.* moderately: *the crowd was conservatively estimated at ten thousand,* the estimate (probably low) of the crowd was ten thousand. □ **moderadamente**
conservatory *n.* **1** room with large windows, where you keep tropical flowers and plants. □ **invernadero**
2 academy of music. □ **conservatorio**
consider [kən'sidə] *v.* to think deeply about something: *he is considering emigrating to Canada; just consider the expense; we have to consider the feelings of the workers,* we have to pay attention to their feelings; *my considered opinion is that we should sell the building.* □ **considerar**
considerable *adj.* quite large: *he lost a considerable sum of money; she has put a considerable amount of effort into her shop.* □ **considerable**
considerably *adv.* to a great extent: *he speaks French considerably better than he used to.* □ **considerablemente**
considerate *adj.* full of feeling/understanding towards someone. □ **considerado**
considerately *adv.* thoughtfully. □ **con consideración**
consideration [kənsidə'reiʃn] *n.* **1** being thought about: *the suggestion is under consideration.* □ **...se está estudiando**
to take into consideration, to take into account: *you must take into consideration the age of the criminal.* □ **...tomar en consideración...**
2 small sum of money: *he will show you round the castle for a consideration.* □ **gratificación**
considering *prep.* when you think of; taking into account: *he is very agile considering his age; considering the amount of money it cost, I don't think the meal was very good.* □ **...teniendo en cuenta...**
consign [kən'sain] *v.* to give (goods) into someone's care. □ **consignar**
consignment *n.* **1** sending of goods. □ **envío**
2 goods which have been sent: *we are waiting for a consignment of cheese from France.* □ **remesa**
consist [kən'sist] *v.* to be made up of: *the class consists of ten Germans and two Belgians; she had a snack consisting of a biscuit and a glass of milk.* □ **consistir**
consistency *n.* **1** being the same throughout: *the book lacks consistency - some parts are good, but others are boring.* □ **coherencia**
2 thickness (of a paste, etc.): *beat the milk, eggs and flour to a smooth consistency.* □ **consistencia**
consistent *adj.* which does not contradict; always the same/unchanging. □ **coherente**
consistently *adv.* always/permanently: *he is consistently late for work.* □ **sistemáticamente**
console ['kɔnsoul] *n.* **1** flat table with the keyboard (of an organ/telex machine, etc.). □ **consola**
2 cabinet for a TV set. □ **mueble para el televisor**
■ *v.* to comfort someone (for a loss): *he was consoled by the thought that others had lost more money than he had.* □ **consolar**
consolation [kɔnsə'leiʃn] *n.* comfort: *it is no consolation to know that most of the other boats capsized too.* □ **consuelo**
consolation prize, prize given to someone who did not win, but who tried hard. □ **premio de consolación**
consolidate [kən'sɔlideit] *v.* to make firm/solid. □ **consolidar**
consolidation [kənsɔli'deiʃn] *n.* **1** making firm. □ **consolidación**
2 grouping together of small packets from different sources into one large shipment. □ **agrupamiento**
consommé [kən'sɔmei] *n.* thin clear soup. □ **consomé**
consonant ['kɔnsənənt] *n.* letter which is not a vowel: *'p' and 'z' are consonants, but 'e' and 'o' are not.* □ **consonante**
consort ['kɔnsɔːt] *n.* husband or wife (of a queen or king). □ **consorte**
■ *v.* to go around with someone. □ **ir con**
consortium [kən'sɔːtiəm] *n.* group of companies who work together: *the tunnel is being built by a British and German consortium.* □ **consorcio**
conspicuous [kən'spikjuəs] *adj.* **1** very obvious. □ **evidente, llamativo**
2 *he was conspicuous by his absence,* everyone noticed that he was not there. □ **brilló por su ausencia**
conspire [kən'spaiə] *v.* **1** to plot to do something: *they conspired to overthrow the government.* □ **conspirar**
2 *everything conspired against us,* everything seemed to go wrong. □ **volverse**
conspiracy [kən'spirəsi] *n.* plot: *the conspiracy of the generals against the king.* □ **conspiración**
conspirator *n.* plotter. □ **conspirador**
conspiratorial [kənspirə'tɔːriəl] *adj.* like someone who is plotting: *in a conspiratorial tone,* in a whisper. □ **conspiratorio**
constable ['kʌnstəbl] *n.* policeman: *Constable Smith was on duty at the crossroads.* □ **policía**
constabulary [kən'stæbjuləri] *n.* police force of a district. □ **policía**
constant ['kɔnstənt] *adj.* **1** not changing or stopping: *I cannot work with constant interruptions; the machine makes a constant whistle.* □ **constante**
2 faithful. □ **leal**
constancy *n.* faithfulness. □ **fidelidad**
constantly *adv.* all the time: *he is constantly changing his mind.* □ **constantemente**
constellation [kɔnstə'leiʃn] *n.* group of stars forming a pattern in the sky. □ **constelación**
consternation [kɔnstə'neiʃn] *n.* shock/surprise: *they looked at each other in consternation.* □ **consternación**
constipated ['kɔnstipeitid] *adj.* unable to empty the bowels regularly. □ **estreñido**
constipation [kɔnsti'peiʃn] *n.* slow working of the bowels. □ **estreñimiento**
constituent [kən'stitjuənt] *adj.* (part) which makes up a whole. □ **componente**
■ *n.* person who may vote in an electoral area: *our*

MP is very good at looking after the interests of his constituents. □ **votante**
constituency *n.* area which elects a member of Parliament: *she represents one of the northern constituencies in Parliament.* □ **circunscripción**
constitute ['kɔnstitju:t] *v.* to make up; to establish: *does this constitute a new record?* □ **constituir**
constitution [kɔnsti'tju:ʃn] *n.* **1** bodily health: *a brisk walk is good for the constitution.* □ **forma física**
2 laws and principles which form the basis of a country's organization: *the new French constitution was drawn up in 1958.* □ **constitución**
constitutional *adj.* referring to the legal basis of a state: *a constitutional crisis,* crisis which threatens the basis of a country's existence. □ **constitucional**
constitutional monarchy, monarchy where the power is held by an elected government. □ **constitucional**
■ *n.* short walk which is supposed to be good for the health. □ **paseo**
constrain [kən'strein] *v.* to force. □ **constreñir**
constraint *n.* force. □ **fuerza**
constrict [kən'strikt] *v.* to squeeze/to strangle. □ **estrechar, estrangular**
constriction [kən'strikʃn] *n.* squeezing/strangling. □ **constricción**
construct [kən'strʌkt] *v.* to build: *he constructed a shelter of branches and leaves.* □ **construir**
construction [kən'strʌkʃn] *n.* **1** act of building: *the construction of the suspension bridge took ten years.* □ **construcción**
2 *the construction of the novel is very strange,* the way in which the novel is made up. □ **construcción**
3 something which has been built: *the whole construction collapsed in a gale.* □ **construcción**
constructive *adj.* which aims at improving: *constructive criticism.* □ **constructivo**
constructor *n.* builder/person who constructs. □ **constructor**
construe [kən'stru:] *v.* to take to mean. □ **interpretar**
consul ['kɔnsəl] *n.* country's representative abroad, particularly looking after the personal affairs of his fellow-countrymen. □ **cónsul**
consular ['kɔnsjulə] *adj.* referring to a consul: *consular department, (of an embassy)* department which looks after passports and visas. □ **consular**
consulate *n.* house/offices of a consul. □ **consulado**
consult [kən'sʌlt] *v.* to ask for advice: *she consulted her doctor about her headaches; I will consult the telephone directory to try and find his address.* □ **consultar**
consultant *n.* specialist who gives advice, especially medical specialist attached to a hospital. □ **especialista**
consultation [kɔnsʌl'teiʃn] *n.* act of consulting. □ **consulta**
consultative *adj.* which gives advice: *a consultative assembly,* assembly to advise the government. □ **consultivo**
consulting *n.* asking for advice. □ **consultante**
consulting room, doctor's office. □ **consultorio**
consume [kən'sju:m] *v.* **1** to eat or drink: *the children consumed a dozen peanut butter sandwiches and two bottles of orange juice.* □ **consumir**
2 to use up: *the amount of electricity consumed by the car industry.* □ **consumir**
consumer *n.* person who uses goods or eats food: *consumers must be protected against dishonest shopkeepers.* □ **consumidor**
consumer goods, goods which are bought by ordinary members of the public (and not by industry). □ **bienes de consumo**
consummate [kən'sʌmit] *adj.* **1** perfect. □ **consumado**
2 *a consummate musician,* a musician who is a master at his craft. □ **consumado**
■ *v.* ['kɔnsəmeit] **1** to complete. □ **consumar**
2 *to consummate a marriage,* to have sexual intercourse for the first time after marriage. □ **consumar**
consummation [kɔnsə'meiʃn] *n.* completion; end. □ **consumación**
consumption [kən'sʌmpʃn] *n.* act of consuming; quantity consumed: *the petrol consumption of this car is quite high,* it uses quite a lot of petrol. □ **consumo**
consumptive *adj.* looking as though one is suffering from tuberculosis: *a consumptive youth.* □ **tísico**
contact ['kɔntækt] *n.* **1** touch: *the wires must have been in contact with a metal surface,* they must have been touching a metal surface. □ **contacto**
to be in contact with someone, to correspond with someone/to be able to telephone someone. □ **estar en contacto con...**
contact lenses, tiny lenses which cover the eyeball, replacing glasses. □ **lentes de contacto, lentillas**
2 person whom you know/whom you have contacted: *I have a contact in the town hall.* □ **contacto**
■ *v.* to get into communication with (someone): *I will try and contact you over the weekend.* □ **ponerse en contacto**
contagious [kən'teidʒəs] *adj.* (disease) which is transmitted by touching. □ **contagioso**
contain [kən'tein] *v.* **1** to hold: *this box contains two pounds of chocolates; the bottle contains one litre.* □ **contener**
2 to hold back/to restrain: *can we contain the enemy attack? she could hardly contain her fury.* □ **contener**
container *n.* **1** box/bottle, etc., which holds something else: *make sure the container is clean before putting food into it.* □ **recipiente**
2 large case for easy loading on a ship. □ **contenedor**
container ship, specially designed ship for carrying containers. □ **barco portacontenedores**
contaminate [kən'tæmineit] *v.* to make bad/dirty: *don't eat contaminated food.* □ **contaminar**
contamination [kəntæmi'neiʃn] *n.* act of making bad/dirty: *there is a risk of contamination of the drinking water.* □ **contaminación**
contemplate ['kɔntempleit] *v.* **1** to look at something intently: *to contemplate the scenery.* □ **contemplar**
2 to plan to do something: *he is contemplating making a trip to the USA.* □ **proyectar**
contemplation [kɔntem'pleiʃn] *n.* meditation/deep thought. □ **contemplación**
contemplative [kən'templətiv] *adj.* which meditates. □ **contemplativo**
contemporary [kən'temprəri] *adj.* and *n.* **1** (person) who lives at the same time as another; (thing) which dates back to the same period as another thing. □ **contemporáneo**
2 *they were contemporaries at school,* they went to the same school together. □ **amigo del colegio**
3 *he is my contemporary,* he and I are about the same age. □ **coetáneo**
4 *exhibition of contemporary art,* exhibition of art by artists who are still alive. □ **...de arte contemporáneo**
5 *contemporary furniture/dance,* modern/up-to-date furniture/dance. □ **moderno**
contemporaneous [kəntempə'reiniəs] *adj.* of the same date/period. □ **contemporáneo**

contempt [kən'tempt] *n.* feeling of hatred/disrespect for someone: *he is beneath contempt,* he is so unpleasant that you cannot even dislike him. □ **desprecio**
contempt of court, conduct which a judge rules is offensive to a court. □ **desacato al tribunal**
contemptible *adj.* which deserves contempt: *his contemptible behaviour.* □ **despreciable**
contemptuous *adj.* scornful: *she is very contemptuous of my attempts to learn French.* □ **desdeñoso**
contend [kən'tend] *v.* **1** to fight: *travellers have to contend with tropical diseases.* □ **luchar**
2 to state/to believe: *he contends that the war could have been prevented.* □ **sostener**
contender *n.* person who challenges someone to a fight; person who fights: *the British contender for the heavyweight title.* □ **contendiente**
content [kən'tent] *adj.* satisfied/happy: *not content with getting more money he asked for longer holidays too.* □ **contento**
■ *n.* **1** satisfaction. □ **satisfacción**
2 *you can play around* ***to your heart's content,*** as much as you like. □ **...hasta quedar harto**
3 something which is contained/which is in a container: *he turned the box upside down and tipped the contents on the floor.* □ **contenido**
4 ***table of contents,*** list of chapters/sections in a book. □ **índice de materias**
5 *the contents of the letter seemed to please her,* what was written in it. □ **contenido**
6 *mineral content of water,* percentage of minerals in water. □ **contenido**
■ *v.* to satisfy: *he contented himself with saying a few rude words and going away.* □ **contentar**
contented *adj.* satisfied/happy: *she is very contented with her way of life; the cows are looking contented.* □ **satisfecho**
contentedly *adv.* in a satisfied way. □ **con satisfacción**
contentedness *n.* satisfaction. □ **contento**
contention [kən'tenʃn] *n.* **1** dispute. □ **contienda**
a bone of contention, a source of argument. □ **...motivo de disputa**
2 statement/belief: *it is my contention that Russian is the most difficult language to learn.* □ **opinión**
contentious [kən'tenʃəs] *adj.* **1** (person) who likes arguments. □ **peleón**
2 *a contentious issue,* problem which is a frequent source of dispute. □ **un contencioso**
contest ['kɔntest] *n.* fight; competition: *at the end of the contest the judges decide who has won; he has entered for a music contest.* □ **concurso, competición**
■ *v.* **1** to fight: *he is going to contest the election,* to stand as a candidate in the election. □ **luchar**
2 to query: *I will contest the will,* I will argue that the will is invalid. □ **impugnar**
contestant *n.* competitor/person who enters a contest. □ **concursante**
context ['kɔntekst] *n.* **1** phrase in which a word occurs, which helps show its meaning: *you must look at each word in its context; you have taken the phrase out of context,* by quoting the phrase without the surrounding text, you are changing its meaning. □ **contexto**
2 *consider the treaty in the context of the Middle European political situation,* against the background of the political situation. □ **contexto**
continent ['kɔntinənt] *n.* **1** large mass of land: *Africa, Asia and America are continents.* □ **continente**
2 *on the Continent,* in Europe. □ **en el continente (Europa)**
continental [kɔnti'nentl] *adj.* **1** referring to a continent. □ **continental**
2 referring to Europe (excluding the British Isles). □ **continental, europeo**
a Continental, a European (but not an inhabitant of the British Isles). □ **continental, europeo**
continental breakfast, coffee and rolls or bread. □ **desayuno continental**
continental quilt, duvet/bag stuffed with feathers, used as the only covering for a bed. □ **edredón**
contingent [kən'tindʒənt] *adj.* which depends on something. □ **contingente**
■ *n.* group of soldiers, etc. □ **contingente**
contingency *n.* emergency: *to provide for contingencies; contingency plan.* □ **emergencia**
continue [kən'tinju:] *v.* to go on doing something: *we will continue this discussion tomorrow; the discussion continued late into the night; the rain continued to pour down for three days.* □ **continuar**
continual *adj.* which goes on all the time without stopping: *a continual process.* □ **continuo**
continually *adv.* very frequently; all the time: *I am continually being interrupted in my work.* □ **continuamente**
continuation [kəntinju'eiʃn] *n.* **1** going on without stopping. □ **continuación**
2 extension/thing which has been continued: *continuation of a wall; the continuation of the story will appear in our next issue.* □ **continuación**
continuity [kɔnti'njuiti] *n.* state of continuing without a break. □ **continuidad**
continuity girl, girl who ensures that each scene in a film follows on smoothly. □ **secretaria de rodaje**
continuous [kən'tinjuəs] *adj.* with no break. □ **continuo**
continuous performance, film show where there are no breaks between the films. □ **sesión continua**
continuously *adv.* one after the other with no break in between: *he worked continuously for six weeks at his painting.* □ **continuamente**
contort [kən'tɔ:t] *v.* to twist unnaturally: *her face was contorted with pain.* □ **retorcer**
contortion [kən'tɔ:ʃn] *n.* twisting unnaturally. □ **contorsión**
contortionist *n.* person in a show who twists his body into odd shapes. □ **contorsionista**
contour ['kɔntu:ə] *n.* shape of the outline of something: *the contours of the mountain were clear against the sky.* □ **contorno**
contour (line), line on a map drawn through points at the same height above sea level: *the contours are shown in brown.* □ **curva de nivel**
contraband ['kɔntrəbænd] *n.* (*no pl.*) goods on which customs duty has not been paid. □ **contrabando**
contraception [kɔntrə'sepʃn] *n.* prevention of pregnancy. □ **anticoncepción**
contraceptive *adj.* and *n.* (thing) which prevents pregnancy: *contraceptive pill.* □ **anticonceptivo**
contract ['kɔntrækt] *n.* **1** legal agreement: *we signed the contract last week; according to the terms of the contract.* □ **contrato**
2 (*in north of England*) bus or train season ticket. □ **bonobús; bonotrén**
■ *v.* **1** to get smaller; to make smaller; to tighten. □ **contraer**
2 to sign an agreement to do some work: *the company contracted for the purchase of a new machine.* □ **firmar un contrato**
3 to catch (a disease). □ **contraer**
contraction [kən'trækʃn] *n.* shortening; shrinking. □ **contracción**

contractor *n.* person who does work according to a signed agreement: *building contractor; haulage contractor.* □ **contratista**
contractual *adj.* according to a contract: *a contractual agreement.* □ **contractual**
contradict [kɔntrə'dikt] *v.* to deny what someone else says: *children ought not to contradict their teachers.* □ **contradecir**
contradiction [kɔntrə'dikʃn] *n.* saying the opposite. □ **contradicción**
contradiction in terms, two terms which mutually contradict each other: *an ugly Swedish girl is a contradiction in terms,* all Swedish girls are beautiful. □ **contradicción**
contradictory *adj.* which says the opposite: *we had contradictory reports of the battle.* □ **contradictorio**
contralto [kən'træltou] *n.* (woman with a) low-pitched singing voice. □ **contralto**
contraption [kən'træpʃn] *n.* machine/device: *he built himself a bamboo contraption for catching butterflies.* □ **artilugio**
contrary ['kɔntrəri] *adj.* **1** opposite: *contrary winds,* winds blowing in the opposite direction to the one you want. □ **contrario**
2 rude; always doing the opposite of what you want: *he is a contrary child.* □ **niño que siempre lleva la contraria**
■ *n.* **1** ***the contrary,*** the opposite. □ **lo contrario**
2 ***on the contrary,*** quite the opposite. □ **por el contrario**
3 *unless you hear* ***to the contrary,*** *we will meet at 6 p.m.,* unless you have different instructions before then. □ **en contra**
■ *adv.* in an opposite way: *contrary to what is generally thought.* □ **contrariamente**
contrariness [kən'trɛərinəs] *n.* always doing the opposite of what people want/awkwardness (of a child). □ **espíritu de contradicción**
contrast ['kɔntrɑːst] *n.* sharp difference: *the red roofs make a pleasant contrast against the blue sky; after the Mozart let's hear some jazz by way of a contrast.* □ **contraste**
■ *v.* [kən'traːst] **1** to show up the differences between: *he contrasted life in Greece with that in Italy.* □ **contrastar**
2 *contrasting colours,* colours which are very different. □ **contrastante**
contravene [kɔntrə'viːn] *v.* to break the law/the regulations. □ **contravenir**
contravention [kɔntrə'venʃn] *n.* breaking of a law: *the prisoner was not allowed to see his consul in contravention of international agreements.* □ **contravención**
contribute [kən'tribjuːt] *v.* **1** to help towards. □ **contribuir**
2 *he contributes articles to the local paper,* he writes articles. □ **escribir**
3 to give money (to a charity): *she contributed $10 to the building of the new swimming pool.* □ **aportar**
contribution [kɔntri'bjuʃn] *n.* **1** articles submitted to a newspaper. □ **colaboración**
2 money, etc., given to help something. □ **aportación**
contributor [kən'tribjutə] *n.* helper; journalist. □ **colaborador**
contributory *adj.* which helps: *contributory factors,* factors which have helped produce the situation. □ **que contribuye**
contrite ['kɔntrait] *adj.* who is sorry. □ **contrito**
contrition *n.* regret. □ **contrición**
contrive [kən'traiv] *v.* to manage; to plan: *he contrived a scheme for sending old people to the country on holiday; she contrived to lock herself out of the house.* □ **idear**
contrivance *n.* machine/device. □ **aparato**
control [kən'troul] *n.* **1** authority/power; keeping in order: *she has no control over the children; because of circumstances beyond our control; the firemen had difficulty in bringing the fire under control.* □ **control**
2 ***everything is under control,*** everything is in order. □ **todo está bajo control**
3 ***birth control,*** limiting of the number of babies born. □ **control de natalidad**
4 ***the controls,*** the gears/levers, etc., for directing a machine: *the champion racing driver is at the controls.* □ **los mandos**
5 standard with which the results of an experiment can be compared. □ **control**
■ *v.* (*he controlled*) **1** to direct: *to control the traffic; the firemen had difficulty in controlling the fire.* □ **controlar**
2 to limit/to regulate: *to control the imports of foreign cars.* □ **limitar**
controller *n.* person who controls. □ **controlador**
controversy [kən'trɔvəsi] *n.* violent discussion. □ **controversia; polémica**
controversial [kɔntrə'vəːʃl] *adj.* (subject) which provokes violent discussions: *the question of nuclear power stations is still controversial.* □ **polémico**
contusion [kən'tjuːʒn] *n.* (*formal*) bruise. □ **contusión**
conundrum [kə'nʌndrəm] *n.* riddle. □ **acertijo**
conurbation [kɔnə'beiʃn] *n.* very large spread of a built-up area. □ **conurbación**
convalesce [kɔnvə'les] *v.* to recover after an illness/an operation. □ **convalecer**
convalescence *n.* period when you are recovering from an illness/an operation. □ **convalecencia**
convalescent *adj.* and *n.* (person) who is convalescing. □ **convaleciente**
convalescent home, rest home for people who are convalescing. □ **clínica de reposo**
convection [kən'vekʃn] *n.* movement of heat in air/liquid. □ **convección**
convector *n.* ***convector heater,*** heater which warms the air moving through it. □ **calentador de convección**
convene [kən'viːn] *v.* to call together (a meeting). □ **convocar**
convenor *n.* person who calls meetings together. □ **convocante**
convenience [kən'viːniəns] *n.* **1** suitableness. □ **conveniencia**
at your earliest convenience, as soon as it suits you. □ **tan pronto como puedas**
2 public toilet. □ **servicios**
3 *all modern conveniences,* all modern comforts (in a house). □ **comodidades**
convenient *adj.* suitable; practical: *when it is convenient,* when it is suitable for you. □ **conveniente**
conveniently *adv.* handily: *the shops are conveniently close.* □ **cómodamente**
convent ['kɔnvənt] *n.* religious house for women. □ **convento**
convention [kən'venʃn] *n.* **1** custom/usual way of doing things: *according to the convention of the association.* □ **convención**
2 contract. □ **convenio**
3 congress/general meeting of an association/political party. □ **convención**
conventional *adj.* **1** ordinary/usual. □ **convencional**
2 *conventional weapons,* ordinary weapons (not nuclear weapons). □ **armas convencionales**

conventionally *adv.* in an ordinary/usual way: *he was very conventionally dressed.* □ **muy normal**
converge [kən'vəːdʒ] *v.* to come together at a certain place: *the police converged on the guerrillas' headquarters.* □ **converger**
convergence *n.* meeting. □ **convergencia**
convergent *adj.* meeting at a certain point. □ **convergente**
conversant [kən'vəːsənt] *adj.* familiar: *is he conversant with the subject?,* does he know the subject well? □ **familiarizado; versado; enterado**
converse ['kɔnvəːs] *n.* the opposite. □ **contrario**
■ *v.* to talk: *they conversed for a while in Spanish.* □ **conversar**
conversation [kɔnvə'seiʃn] *n.* talk: *they had a long conversation before the meeting.* □ **conversación**
conversion [kən'vəːʃn] *n.* **1** changing (of one thing into another): *conversion of water into steam; conversion of francs into marks; conversion of a house into offices.* □ **conversión**
2 turning of a person to another religion: *conversion of pagans to Christianity.* □ **conversión**
3 (*in Rugby*) kicking the ball over the crossbar between the goal posts after a try has been scored. □ **transformación**
convert ['kɔnvəːt] *n.* person who has changed religion: *a Moslem convert.* □ **converso**
■ *v.* [kən'vəːt] **1** to turn someone from one religion to another: *Paul was converted to Christianity.* □ **convertir**
2 to change: *to convert water into steam; to convert a house into flats.* □ **convertir**
3 *to convert a goal,* (*in Rugby*) to kick the ball over the crossbar between the goal posts after a try has been scored. □ **transformar**
converter *n.* machine which converts. □ **convertidor**
convertibility [kənvəːti'biliti] *n.* easiness of change of one currency to another. □ **convertibilidad**
convertible [kən'vəːtəbl] *adj.* which can easily be changed (especially of a currency). □ **convertible**
■ *n.* car with a roof which folds back. □ **descapotable**
convex ['kɔnveks] *adj.* (surface) which is rounded outwards like the back of a spoon: *a convex lens.* □ **convexo**
convey [kən'vei] *v.* to transport/to carry: *please convey my best wishes to your father; the lorry was conveying dangerous acid when the accident occurred.* □ **transmitir; transportar**
conveyance *n.* **1** transporting: *the conveyance of goods by sea.* □ **transporte**
2 means of transport: *what is the commonest conveyance in India?* □ **medio de transporte**
3 transfer of property from one owner to another. □ **traspaso**
conveyancing *n.* transferring of property. □ **escritura de traspaso**
conveyor *n.* person who transports/thing which transports. □ **transportista**
conveyor belt, long moving surface used in a factory to move products through the production processes. □ **cinta transportadora**
convict ['kɔnvikt] *n.* criminal who has been sentenced to prison. □ **convicto**
■ *v.* [kən'vikt] to find someone guilty; to sentence a criminal to prison: *he was convicted of murder.* □ **condenar**
conviction [kən'vikʃn] *n.* **1** being found guilty. □ **condena**
2 firm belief: *it is my conviction that the earth is flat.* □ **convicción**
convince [kən'vins] *v.* to persuade/to make someone believe something: *he is convinced I know his brother,* he is sure I know his brother. □ **convencer**
convincing *adj.* which persuades: *convincing argument.* □ **convincente**
convincingly *adv.* in a way which makes you believe: *he told his story very convincingly.* □ **convincentemente**
convivial [kən'viviəl] *adj.* lively/jolly. □ **alegre**
conviviality *n.* liveliness. □ **alegría**
convoke [kən'vouk] *v.* to call a meeting. □ **convocar**
convocation *n.* **1** calling of a meeting. □ **convocatoria**
2 meeting of a church assembly/university. □ **claustro**
convolvulus [kən'vɔlvjuləs] *n.* common climbing weed. □ **convólvulo**
convoy ['kɔnvoi] *n.* group of ships/lorries travelling together in line under protection: *the lorries were travelling in convoy.* □ **convoy**
■ *v.* to escort/to protect (especially a line of merchant ships). □ **escoltar**
convulse [kən'vʌls] *v.* **1** to make something shake. □ **convulsionar**
2 *they were convulsed with laughter,* they were shaking with laughter. □ **dislocarse de risa**
3 *the crowd was convulsed with terror,* was shaking with fright. □ **descomponerse**
convulsion *n.* violent shaking of the body: *the baby has convulsions,* has violent spasms which make it twitch. □ **convulsión**
convulsive *adj.* which causes violent shaking. □ **convulsivo**
coo [kuː] *v.* to make soft noises (like a pigeon). □ **arrullar**
cooing *n.* noise made by a pigeon. □ **arrullo**
cook [kuk] *n.* person who prepares food by heating it: *she's a very good cook; the school is advertising for a new cook.* □ **cocinero**
■ *v.* **1** to prepare food by heating: *how do you cook artichokes? I am cooking breakfast; a cooked breakfast,* a hot breakfast. □ **cocinar, hacer**
2 ***to cook the books/the accounts,*** (*informal*) to falsify the entries in account books. □ **falsificar**
cookbook *n.* book of recipes. □ **libro de cocina**
cooker *n.* **1** stove for cooking. □ **cocina**
2 sour apple for cooking. □ **manzana para cocinar**
cookery *n.* (*no pl.*) art of cooking. □ **cocina**
cookery book, book of recipes. □ **libro de cocina**
cookie *n. Amer.* biscuit. □ **galleta**
cooking *n.* action of preparing food, usually by heating: *cooking time is ten minutes.* □ **cocción**
cooking apple, sour green apple for cooking. □ **manzana para cocinar**
cool [kuːl] *adj.* **1** quite cold: *a cool drink on a hot day; keep in a cool place; the weather is getting cooler; it is quite cool outside.* □ **fresco**
2 calm: *keep cool; cool, calm and collected,* very sure of yourself. □ **tranquilo**
3 unfriendly: *he got a cool reception at the meeting.* □ **frío**
■ *n.* **1** state of being cool; place where it is cool: *keep the bottle of wine in the cool; in the cool of the evening.* □ **fresco**
2 calmness: *she lost her cool,* she lost her temper. □ **tranquilidad**
■ *v.* to make cool; to become cool. □ **refrescar(se)**
coolant *n.* substance (usually water) used to keep car engines, etc., cool. □ **líquido refrigerante**
cool down *v.* **1** to become cool. □ **enfriarse**
2 to become calm: *he was furious, but he cooled*

down after a few minutes. □ **calmarse**
cooler *n.* **1** thing/machine which cools. □ **refrigerador**
2 (*slang*) prison. □ **trena**
cooling *adj.* refreshing (drink, etc.). □ **refrescante**
■ *n.* action of becoming cool. □ **refrigerante**
coolly *adv.* in a cool/calm way. □ **con tranquilidad**
coolness *n.* **1** being cool: *the coolness of the evening.* □ **frescor**
2 calmness. □ **tranquilidad**
3 unfriendliness (of a reception, etc.). □ **frialdad**
cool off *v.* to become cooler: *after a game of squash it is pleasant to cool off under a shower.* □ **refrescarse**
coop [ku:p] *n.* cage for chickens. □ **gallinero**
■ *v. **to be cooped up,*** to be shut up inside: *I don't like being kept cooped up in this office.* □ **enjaular**
co-op ['kouɔp] *n.* (*informal*) cooperative stores: *I bought it at the co-op.* □ **cooperativa**
cooperate [kou'ɔpəreit] *v.* to work with someone: *the two committees are cooperating to find a solution to the drug problem.* □ **cooperar**
cooperation [kouɔpə'reiʃn] *n.* working together: *I got no cooperation from him at all,* he was no help at all. □ **cooperación**
cooperative [kou'ɔprətiv] *adj.* and *n.* (shop, etc.) which works on a profit-sharing basis: *cooperative stores.* □ **cooperativa**
■ *adj.* willing to work with someone: *he was not very cooperative when I asked him to help.* □ **cooperativo**
co-opt [kou'ɔpt] *v.* to ask someone to join a committee without being formally elected to it. □ **cooptar**
co-ordinate [kou'ɔ:dinət] *n.* **1** set of figures which fix a point on a map/graph. □ **coordenada**
2 *co-ordinates,* matching outer clothes for women. □ **conjuntados**
■ *v.* to make things work together/fit in with each other: *he is co-ordinating the relief work in the disaster area.* □ **coordinar**
co-ordination [kouɔ:di'neiʃn] *n.* working together/fitting together: *the work suffers because of a lack of co-ordination between the various departments.* □ **coordinación**
coot [ku:t] *n.* black water bird with a white forehead. □ **focha común**
cop [kɔp] *n.* (*informal*) policeman. □ **poli**
cope [koup] *n.* long coloured cloak worn by a priest. □ **capa**
■ *v.* **1** to deal with: *can you cope with the cooking for all these people?* □ **poder con**
2 *she will cope all right,* she will manage. □ **arreglárselas**
copilot ['koupailət] *n.* pilot who is second in command to the captain of an aircraft. □ **copiloto**
coping ['koupiŋ] *n. **coping stone,*** top stone on a wall, which protects the wall from the weather. □ **piedra de albardilla**
copious ['koupiəs] *adj.* plentiful/in good supply: *he washed down his meal with copious amounts of beer; she took copious notes throughout the lecture.* □ **copioso, abundante**
copper ['kɔpə] *n.* **1** (*chemical element*: Cu) reddish metal which turns green when exposed to air: *copper piping; copper sulphate.* □ **cobre**
2 large pan for boiling water and washing clothes. □ **caldera**
3 (*informal*) policeman. □ **poli**
4 small coin made of copper or other brown metal. □ **calderilla**
coppice ['kɔpis] **copse** [kɔps] *n.* wood of young trees. □ **soto**
copulate ['kɔpjuleit] *v.* to have sexual intercourse. □ **copular**
copy ['kɔpi] *n.* **1** an imitation/reproduction: *it's not a real Rembrandt, it is only a copy; can you type this letter with two copies?* □ **copia**
2 a book; a newspaper: *I have yesterday's copy of the 'Times'; he has lost his copy of Shakespeare's plays.* □ **periódico; ejemplar**
3 material to be used in a newspaper article/in an advertisement, etc.: *she writes very good copy.* □ **texto**
■ *v.* to imitate/to make a reproduction: *he is copying his father's way of walking; she was copying the letter on the photocopier.* □ **copiar**
copying *n.* imitation. □ **copia**
copyright *n.* right to publish a book/put on a play, etc. and not to have it copied without permission: *is this poem still in copyright?,* still protected by the laws of copyright? □ **propiedad literaria; 'copyright'**
copywriter *n.* person who writes copy for advertisements. □ **redactor; 'copywriter'**
coral ['kɔrəl] *n.* **1** rock-like substance formed of the skeletons of tiny animals in tropical waters: *coral island; coral reef.* □ **coral**
2 light red colour. □ **coral**
cord [kɔ:d] *n.* **1** string/thin rope.□ **cuerda; cordón**
2 string-like part of the body: *spinal cord; vocal cords.* □ **médula espinal; cuerdas vocales**
3 ***cords,*** (*informal*) corduroy trousers. □ **pantalones de pana**
cordial ['kɔ:diəl] *adj.* friendly: *a cordial greeting.* □ **cordial**
■ *n.* concentrated juice of a fruit to which water is added. □ **zumo concentrado**
cordiality [kɔ:di'æliti] *n.* friendliness. □ **cordialidad**
cordially *adv.* warmly/in a friendly way. □ **cordialmente**
cordite ['kɔ:dait] *n.* type of explosive. □ **cordita**
cordon ['kɔ:dən] *n.* **1** barrier to prevent someone escaping; line of police/soldiers surrounding a point. □ **cordón**
2 fruit tree grown as a single stem, with side shoots cut back. □ **rama madre**
■ *v. **to cordon off** a street,* to put up barriers to prevent people going into the street. □ **acordonar**
corduroy ['kɔ:djurɔi] *n.* velvet-like cloth with ribs: *corduroy trousers.* □ **pana**
core [kɔ:] *n.* **1** central part: *the core of the earth; an apple core.* □ **núcleo; centro; corazón**
rotten to the core, rotten right through. □ **podrido hasta la médula**
2 *to take a core sample,* to cut a long round sample of rock with a drill. □ **tomar una muestra**
■ *v. to core an apple,* to scoop out the core of an apple. □ **quitar el corazón de**
corgi ['kɔ:gi] *n.* breed of small dogs, with short hair and pointed faces. □ **perro galés**
cork [kɔ:k] *n.* **1** (material made from) very light bark of a type of oak tree. □ **corcho**
cork oak, oak tree with very light bark. □ **alcornoque**
cork tiles, tiles made of very light bark. □ **planchas de corcho**
2 stopper of cork which closes wine bottles: *to take the cork out,* to open a bottle. □ **corcho**
■ *v. to cork a bottle,* to put a cork into a bottle. □ **encorchar**
corkage *n.* charge made by a restaurant for taking the cork out of a bottle of wine which a customer

has brought with him. □ **recargo**
corked *adj.* (wine) which has an unpleasant taste because of a rotting cork. □ **que sabe a corcho**
corkscrew *n.* special screwing device for taking corks out of bottles. □ **sacacorchos**
corm [kɔ:m] *n.* fat root which can be planted like a bulb and from which a flower grows. □ **cormo**
cormorant ['kɔ:mərənt] *n.* large dark seabird which eats fish. □ **cormorán**
corn [kɔ:n] *n.* **1** cereal crops: *corn-producing area.* □ **grano; cereales**
2 maize. □ **maíz**
sweet corn, maize grown for human consumption. □ **maíz**
corn cob, head of maize with many seeds: *to eat corn on the cob.* □ **mazorca**
3 painful hard growth (on a toe). □ **callo**
cornflakes *n. pl.* breakfast cereal of crisp pieces of toasted maize. □ **'cornflakes'**
cornflour *n.* maize powder, used in cooking. □ **harina de maíz**
cornflower *n.* blue flower growing in corn fields. □ **aciano**
cornstarch *n. Amer.* maize powder used in cooking. □ **maicena**
corny *adj.* (*informal*) old/out-of-date (joke). □ **chiste muy viejo**
cornea ['kɔ:niə] *n.* transparent covering of the eyeball. □ **córnea**
corneal *adj.* referring to the cornea: *corneal graft.* □ **corneal**
corned [kɔ:nd] *adj.* salted/preserved (beef). □ **acecinado**
corner ['kɔ:nə] *n.* **1** angle made by two flat surfaces joining: *at the corner of the street; in the far corner of the room; the car took the corner on two wheels,* went round the bend on two wheels. □ **esquina; rincón**
to turn the corner: *she has turned the corner,* she is beginning to recover from an illness. □ **está saliendo de...**
to drive (someone) into a corner: *he was driven into a corner,* put into a position from which he could not escape. □ **arrinconar**
2 (*in football*) free kick taken from the corner of the pitch. □ **saque de esquina**
■ *v.* **1** to turn a corner: *the car corners well; he had to corner sharply.* □ **tomar una curva**
2 to monopolize: *the company has cornered the market in sugar.* □ **monopolizar**
3 to drive into a corner: *we have cornered him.* □ **arrinconar**
cornet ['kɔ:nit] *n.* **1** cone-shaped biscuit for holding ice cream. □ **cucurucho**
2 trumpet-like brass musical instrument. □ **corneta**
cornice ['kɔ:nis] *n.* decorated moulding round a ceiling/round the eaves (of a building). □ **cornisa**
corollary [kə'rɔləri] *n.* natural result/something which follows naturally. □ **corolario**
corona [kə'rounə] *n.* ring of light: *the sun's corona,* ring of light visible when the sun is totally eclipsed. □ **corona; halo**
coronary ['kɔrənri] *adj.* referring to the arteries to the heart. □ **coronario**
coronary thrombosis, heart attack caused by blocking of an artery: *he's had a coronary,* he has had a heart attack. □ **trombosis coronaria**
coronation [kɔrə'neiʃn] *n.* crowning (of a king/queen/emperor, etc.). □ **coronación**
coroner ['kɔrənə] *n.* person who directs a court to investigate murders or sudden or accidental deaths. □ **juez forense**
coronet ['kɔrənət] *n.* small crown. □ **diadema**
corporal ['kɔ:prəl] *adj.* referring to the body: *corporal punishment,* beating/whipping/caning. □ **corporal**
■ *n.* non-commissioned rank in the army below sergeant. □ **cabo**
corporate ['kɔ:pərət] *adj.* **1** forming a body. □ **corporativo**
2 *corporate feeling,* feeling of fraternity. □ **sentimiento colectivo**
3 *corporate plan,* overall plan for a whole company. □ **plan general de una empresa**
corporation [kɔ:pə'reiʃn] *n.* **1** ***municipal corporation,*** town council. □ **corporación**
a corporation rubbish van, rubbish van belonging to a town council. □ **camión municipal de la basura**
2 large firm. □ **empresa, corporación**
corps [kɔ:] *n.* (*pl. corps* [kɔ:z]) military or organized group: *the Pay Corps; the Diplomatic Corps.* □ **cuerpo**
corpse [kɔ:ps] *n.* dead body. □ **cadáver**
corpulent ['kɔ:pjulənt] *adj.* fat. □ **corpulento**
corpulence *n.* fatness □ **corpulencia**
corpuscle ['kɔ:pʌsl] *n.* cell in blood: *blood contains both white and red corpuscles.* □ **glóbulo**
correct [kə'rekt] *adj.* accurate/right/true: *what is the correct time please? if you give correct answers to all six questions you will win a prize.* □ **correcto**
■ *v.* to show the mistakes in something; to remove the mistakes from something: *the teacher corrected our homework; she corrected my pronunciation; the technicians corrected a fault in the ship's steering.* □ **corregir**
correction [kə'rekʃn] *n.* making correct: *correction of homework.* □ **corrección**
corrective *adj.* and *n.* (thing) which corrects. □ **correctivo**
correctly *adv.* accurately: *if she answers all the questions correctly, she will win the prize; Cambridge lies to the north, or more correctly to the north east, of London.* □ **correctamente**
correctness *n.* accuracy (of answer, etc.); rightness (of clothes). □ **exactitud; corrección**
correlate ['kɔrəleit] *v.* **1** to correspond to/to be linked to. □ **correlacionar**
2 *how can you correlate these facts?,* how can you show the link between them? □ **correlacionar**
correlation [kɔrə'leiʃn] *n.* correspondence/link: *what is the correlation between speed and petrol consumption?* □ **correlación**
correspond [kɔri'spɔnd] *v.* **1** to fit in with; to match: *does this correspond to your requirements?* □ **corresponder**
2 to write letters; to exchange letters with someone: *we correspond regularly.* □ **cartearse**
correspondence *n.* **1** matching. □ **correspondencia**
2 exchange of letters; letters which have come: *I must open my correspondence.* □ **correspondencia**
correspondence course, course of study taken at home with lessons sent by post. □ **curso por correspondencia**
correspondent *n.* person who writes letters; journalist who writes articles for newspapers on particular subjects: *report from our special correspondent in Washington; the gardening correspondent.* □ **corresponsal**
corresponding *adj.* which fits/matches: *heavy rainfall and corresponding flooding.* □ **correspondiente**
correspondingly *adv.* fittingly/in a similar way: *the*

countryside is flat and correspondingly dull. □ **correspondientemente**
corridor ['kɔridɔː] *n.* long, narrow passage. □ **corredor**
corroborate [kə'rɔbəreit] *v.* to confirm (a statement). □ **corroborar**
corroboration [kərɔbə'reiʃn] *n.* confirmation of a statement: *the garage proprietor gave evidence in corroboration of the motorist's statement.* □ **corroboración**
corrode [kə'roud] *v.* to rot (metal)/to rust: *the iron pillars were corroded by sea water.* □ **corroer**
corrosion [kə'rouʒn] *n.* rusting/eating away (of metal). □ **corrosión**
corrosive [kə'rousiv] *adj.* and *n.* (substance) which eats away metal. □ **corrosivo**
corrugated ['kɔrəgeitid] *adj.* bent into waves: *corrugated iron; corrugated paper.* □ **ondulado**
corrupt [kə'rʌpt] *adj.* not honest: *a corrupt judge,* judge who takes bribes. □ **corrupto**
■ *v.* to make dishonest/to bribe: *he tried to corrupt the jury before the trial.* □ **corromper**
corruptible *adj.* (person) who can be bribed. □ **corruptible**
corruption [kə'rʌpʃn] *n.* dishonesty/bribery. □ **corrupción**
corset ['kɔːsit] *n.* tight underwear worn by women to hold in their bodies. □ **corsé**
cortisone ['kɔːtizoun] *n.* hormone medicine used against skin allergies/arthritis, etc. □ **cortisona**
cosh [kɔʃ] *n.* (*informal*) short stick for hitting. □ **cachiporra**
■ *v.* (*informal*) to hit someone on the head. □ **aporrear**
cos lettuce ['kɔz'letis] *n.* type of tall green plant used for salads. □ **lechuga romana**
cosmetic [kɔz'metik] *adj.* and *n.* (substance) used in beautifying the face, etc.: *cosmetic powder.* □ **cosmético**
cosmic ['kɔzmik] *adj.* referring to the universe. □ **cósmico**
cosmonaut *n.* Soviet astronaut/person who travels into outer space. □ **cosmonauta**
cosmopolitan [kɔzmə'pɔlitən] *adj.* **1** made up of people from different parts of the world: *London is a very cosmopolitan city.* □ **cosmopolita**
2 at ease in different cities/with people of different nationalities: *he is very cosmopolitan.* □ **cosmopolita**
cosset ['kɔsit] *v.* to spoil someone with comfort. □ **mimar**
cost [kɔst] *n.* **1** amount which you have to pay for something: *the cost of living.* □ **precio; coste**
at all costs, at no matter what price. □ **a toda costa**
2 what is suffered or lost to get another thing; price: *after the battle was over, they reckoned up the cost in human lives.* □ **precio**
■ *v.* (*it cost*) **1** to have a price of: *apples cost 20p a pound; petrol seems to cost more each month; it cost me $20; writing novels costs a lot of effort.* □ **costar**
2 to calculate the price for something: *we have costed it at $2.* □ **calcular el coste de**
costing *n.* calculation of a selling price. □ **cálculo del coste**
costliness *n.* expensiveness. □ **carestía**
costly *adj.* expensive. □ **costoso**
co-star ['koustɑː] *n.* famous actor/actress starring in a film/play with other famous actors/actresses. □ **coprotagonista**
■ *v.* (*he co-starred*) to act in a play/film as a co-star. □ **coprotagonizar**
costume ['kɔstjuːm] *n.* **1** set of clothes. □ **traje**
bathing/swimming costume, woman's swimsuit. □ **traje de baño**
costume jewellery, cheap imitation jewellery. □ **bisutería**
2 set of clothes for the theatre: *he was wearing his costume for Hamlet.* □ **vestuario**
cosy ['kouzi] *adj.* warm and comfortable: *it is nice and cosy in here.* □ **cómodo, acogedor**
cosily *adv.* comfortably/warmly. □ **cómodamente**
cot [kɔt] *n.* child's bed with sides. □ **cuna**
cottage ['kɔtidʒ] *n.* little house in the country. □ **casa de campo**
weekend cottage, house in the country where you can go for the weekend. □ **casa de campo**
cottage pie, minced meat cooked with mashed potatoes on top. □ **pastel de carne picada y puré de patatas**
cotton ['kɔtn] *n.* **1** fibre from the downy seed heads of a tropical plant: *a bale of cotton.* □ **algodón**
2 cloth made of this fibre: *a cotton shirt.* □ **tela de algodón**
3 thread: *a reel of cotton.* □ **algodón**
■ *v.* ***to cotton on,*** (*informal*) to understand: *he cottoned on quite fast; she hasn't cottoned on yet.* □ **coger**
cotton candy *n. Amer.* candyfloss/molten sugar spun to make a fluffy mass. □ **algodón de azúcar**
cotton wool *n.* fluffy cotton stuff, used for wiping wounds, applying ointment, etc. □ **algodón hidrófilo**
cotyledon [kɔti'liːdən] *n.* first leaf on a seedling. □ **cotiledón**
couch [koutʃ] *n.* sofa/low bed. □ **sofá**
couch grass *n.* weedlike grass which spreads from underground roots. □ **grama**
couchette [kuː'ʃet] *n.* folding bed in a train. □ **litera**
cough [kɔf] *n.* sending air out of the lungs suddenly because of an irritation in the throat: *I have got a cough.* □ **tos**
cough pastille, medicated sweet sucked to relieve irritation in the throat. □ **pastilla para la tos**
■ *v.* to send air out of the lungs suddenly because of irritation: *the smoke made us all cough; he coughs a lot at night.* □ **toser**
to cough up, (*slang*) to pay. □ **soltar la pasta**
coughing *n.* series of coughs: *a fit of coughing.* □ **tos**
could [kud] **couldn't** [kudnt] *v. see* **can.**
council ['kaunsl] *n.* elected committee. □ **consejo**
a town council, elected committee which runs the affairs of a town. □ **ayuntamiento**
council house, house belonging to a town council and rented out. □ **vivienda protegida**
council estate, group of council houses or flats laid out in a special area. □ **viviendas protegidas**
council chamber, room in which a town council meets. □ **salón de plenos**
councillor *n.* elected member of a town council. □ **concejal**
counsel ['kaunsl] *n.* **1** advice. □ **consejo**
2 lawyer/barrister: *we are awaiting for counsel's report on the case.* □ **abogado**
■ *v.* (*he counselled*) to advise: *he counselled caution,* he advised us to go cautiously. □ **aconsejar**
counsellor *n.* adviser. □ **consejero**
count [kaunt] *n.* **1** action of counting/adding figures: *at the last count the population was 10,000.* □ **recuento/cuenta**
to lose count, to have no longer any idea of what the total is: *I have lost count of the times I have had to borrow money.* □ **perder la cuenta**
blood count, calculation of the amount of cor-

puscles in the blood. □ **recuento globular**
2 accusation: *he was found guilty on all four counts.* □ **cargo**
■ *v.* **1** to add up a total: *they are counting the votes; have you counted the cost?* □ **contar**
2 to say numbers in order: *count up to ten; he can't count.* □ **contar**
3 to rely: *I'm counting on you to wake me up in the morning.* □ **contar con**
4 to be important: *every second counts; it is the thought that counts,* it is the intention in giving a present which is important, not the present itself. □ **contar**
count down *v.* to count backwards (9, 8, 7, 6, etc.) before pressing a button to set off an explosion/to launch a rocket. □ **contar hacia atrás**
countdown *n.* counting backwards: *the countdown has begun.* □ **cuenta atrás**
counting *n.* action of adding up a total: *the counting of the votes.* □ **recuento**
countless *adj.* which cannot be counted/numerous. □ **incontable**
countenance ['kauntnəns] *n.* (*formal*) face: *a smiling countenance.* □ **semblante**
■ *v.* (*formal*) to approve of someone's action: *I cannot countenance such excessive spending.* □ **aprobar**
counter ['kauntə] *n.* **1** machine which counts: *revolution counter.* □ **cuentarrevoluciones**
2 small round disc used in games. □ **ficha**
3 long flat surface in a shop for displaying goods, or in a bank for placing money: *he is sitting behind the counter.* □ **mostrador**
■ *adj., adv.* and *prefix.* opposite: *it goes counter to the instructions we were given.* □ **contra**
■ *v.* **1** to stop/to block: *we countered the enemy attack.* □ **repeler**
2 to reply with an opposing response: *he countered the lawyer's criticism with criticisms of his own.* □ **contestar**
counteract *v.* to neutralize/to stop the effects of something: *this antidote will counteract the effects of the poison.* □ **contrarrestar**
counter-attack *n.* attack in return/attack against someone who has just attacked you. □ **contraataque**
■ *v.* to attack in return. □ **contraatacar**
counter-attraction *n.* attraction aimed at luring customers away from a rival. □ **atracción rival**
counterbalance *v.* to compensate for a force in one direction by going in the opposite direction. □ **compensar**
counterblast *n.* strong written or spoken reply to an attack. □ **réplica**
countercharge *n.* accusation against someone who has just accused you. □ **recriminación**
counter-demonstration *n.* rival/opposed demonstration in reply to a demonstration. □ **contramanifestación**
counter-espionage *n.* secret service working against spies. □ **contraespionaje**
counterfeit ['kauntəfit] *adj.* false/forged (money). □ **falso; falsificado**
■ *v.* to forge/to make false money. □ **falsificar**
counterfoil *n.* slip of paper which you retain after giving someone a cheque/an invoice, etc. □ **matriz**
countermand *v.* to say that (an order) should not be carried out. □ **revocar**
countermeasure *n.* way of stopping the effects of something. □ **contramedida**
counterpane *n.* bedcover. □ **cubrecama; colcha**
counterpart *n.* person who has a similar job/is in a similar situation; parallel thing: *he is my counterpart in our French office; this is the German counterpart of a Post Office Savings Bank.* □ **colega, equivalente**
counterpoint *n.* combination of melodies in a piece of music. □ **contrapunto**
counterpoise *n.* heavy weight which counter-balances. □ **contrapeso**
counter-productive *adj.* which produces a contrary effect to the one intended. □ **contraproducente**
counter-revolution *n.* revolt against a revolution. □ **contrarrevolución**
counter-revolutionary *adj.* and *n.* (person who is) in revolt against a revolution. □ **contrarrevolucionario**
countersign *v.* to sign a document which someone else has signed in order to authorize it. □ **refrendar**
countersink *v.* (*he countersank; he has countersunk*) to make a hole for the head of a nail or screw to fit into so that it is level with the surface. □ **avellanar**
country ['kʌntri] *n.* **1** political or geographical unit of land: *the countries of the Common Market; Scotland is the country to the north of England.* □ **país**
2 region: *the West Country; open country; hilly country.* □ **región**
3 not town: *we live in the country; he has a house in the country.* □ **campo**
countryside *n.* the country/the land (excluding towns and cities). □ **campo**
county ['kaunti] *n.* small administrative district. □ **condado**
county town, main town of a county. □ **capital de un condado**
coup [ku:] *n.* (*pl. coups* [ku:z]) **1** armed overthrow of a government: *there has been a coup and a new president has been sworn in.* □ **golpe**
2 success: *he scored quite a coup; getting the Prime Minister to come to the party was quite a coup.* □ **éxito**
coup d'état [ku:dei'tɑ:] *n.* armed overthrow of a government. □ **golpe de estado**
coupé ['ku:pei] *n.* car with two doors and a fixed roof. □ **cupé**
couple [kʌpl] *n.* **1** pair/two things/two people together: *I'll have a couple of bottles of white wine.* □ **par**
2 *a couple of minutes,* not long. □ **par**
3 *they are a very devoted couple,* a husband and wife who adore each other. □ **pareja**
■ *v.* to link together. □ **emparejar**
couplet *n.* two lines of poetry which rhyme. □ **pareado**
coupling *n.* metal links for joining two pieces of machinery/two wagons together. □ **enganche**
coupon ['ku:pɒn] *n.* piece of paper which acts in place of money/in place of a ticket. □ **cupón**
free gift coupon, piece of paper which if presented entitles you to a free gift. □ **vale**
football coupon, form on which you fill up your forecast for the football pools. □ **boleto**
courage ['kʌridʒ] *n.* bravery: *to show courage.* □ **valor**
to pluck up courage, to steel oneself to do something. □ **armarse de valor**
courageous [kə'reidʒəs] *adj.* brave. □ **valiente**
courageously *adv.* bravely. □ **valientemente**
courgette [kuə'ʒet] *n.* very small marrow. □ **calabacín**
courier ['kuriə] *n.* person who carries messages; a guide with a package tour. □ **correo**

course [kɔːs] *n.* **1** passing of time: *in the course of the last few years; in the course of his long career.* □ **curso**
in due course, eventually. □ **a su debido tiempo**
2 road; direction: *the ship's course was due north.* □ **rumbo**
3 *of course,* naturally. □ **por supuesto; desde luego**
as a matter of course, in the usual way. □ **naturalmente**
4 series of lessons; book/series of books for studying: *I am taking a course in needlework; he is the author of a very successful maths course.* □ **curso**
5 series of treatments for an illness: *he is on a course of antibiotics.* □ **tratamiento**
6 dish of food for a meal: *the main course is roast chicken; what is the first course? are we having a sweet course?* □ **plato**
7 track (for racing): *the horses are lining up on the course; the car spun off the course.* □ **pista**
8 *golf course,* area of land specially designed for playing golf. □ **campo de golf**
9 line of bricks (in a wall). □ **hilada**
■ *v.* to flow fast. □ **correr**

court [kɔːt] *n.* **1** tribunal where a judge (and jury) try criminals: *magistrate's court; court of appeal.* □ **tribunal**
2 group of people living round a king or queen. □ **corte**
3 area where a game of tennis/squash, etc., is played. □ **cancha**
■ *v.* **1** to try to persuade a woman to marry you. □ **cortejar**
2 to look for; to try to win (praise, etc.): *he is courting disaster,* he is risking a disaster. □ **buscarse**
courteous ['kəːtjəs] *adj.* very polite. □ **cortés**
courteously *adv.* politely. □ **cortésmente**
courtesy ['kəːtəsi] *n.* politeness. □ **cortesía**
by courtesy of, with the kind permission of. □ **por cortesía de**
courtesy car, free car waiting for hotel guests at an airport. □ **coche a la disposición del cliente**
courtier ['kɔːtjə] *n.* member of a king's court. □ **cortesano**
court-martial [kɔːt'mɑːʃl] *n.* trial of a soldier by other soldiers. □ **consejo de guerra**
■ *v.* to try a soldier: *he was court-martialled.* □ **juzgar en consejo de guerra**
courtroom *n.* room where a trial is held. □ **sala de un tribunal**
courtship *n.* attentions paid to a woman with a view to marriage. □ **cortejo**
courtyard *n.* square yard surrounded by buildings. □ **patio**

cousin ['kʌzn] *n.* son or daughter of an uncle or aunt. □ **primo**

cove [kouv] *n.* small bay. □ **cala; ensenada**

coven ['kʌvn] *n.* group of witches. □ **aquelarre**

covenant ['kʌvənənt] *n.* contract/agreement. □ **convenio**
deed of covenant, official signed agreement (to pay someone a sum each year). □ **convenio oficial**
■ *v.* to agree by contract: *I have covenanted to pay $10 a year to the church.* □ **pactar**

Coventry ['kɔvəntri] *n. to send someone to Coventry,* to refuse to speak to someone. □ **hacer el vacío a alguien**

cover ['kʌvə] *n.* **1** thing which is put over something to protect it. □ **cubierta; tapa**
loose cover, removable protective cloth which is put on chairs. □ **funda**
under cover of night, under the protection of the dark. □ **al amparo de la noche**
2 lid: *put the cover on the pan.* □ **tapa**
3 (cardboard) binding of a book; outer pages of a magazine. □ **cubierta; portada**
4 shelter. □ **refugio**
to take cover: we took cover in a shop doorway, we sheltered. □ **nos refugiamos...**
5 protection (guaranteed by insurance). □ **cobertura**
■ *v.* **1** to put something over (something) to protect it: *cover the floor with newspaper before you start painting the ceiling.* □ **cubrir**
2 to travel a certain distance: *he covered the 1,000 metres in less than four minutes.* □ **recorrer**
3 to point a gun at: *they covered the prisoners with their machine guns.* □ **apuntar**
4 to be enough to pay for: *will $6 cover the bill?* □ **cubrir**
5 to deal with: *the report covers all aspects of the problem.* □ **abarcar**
6 to protect with insurance: *were you covered at the time of the accident?* □ **cubrir**
7 to be a reporter at an event: *he is covering the cricket season for the local paper.* □ **cubrir la información**
coverage *n.* amount of space/time devoted to an event in a newspaper/on TV: *the attempted murder got front page coverage.* □ **alcance; cobertura**
covering *n.* thing which covers: *the ground had a covering of snow.* □ **capa**
■ *adj. covering letter,* explanatory letter sent with a form/with another letter, etc. □ **carta explicatoria**
cover up *v.* to hide completely: *they tried to cover up the scandal.* □ **encubrir**
cover-up *n.* hiding (of a scandal). □ **encubrimiento**

coverlet ['kʌvələt] *n.* cover for a bed. □ **colcha**

covet ['kʌvit] *v.* to want something which belongs to someone else. □ **codiciar**
covetous *adj.* wanting something which belongs to someone else. □ **codicioso**

cow [kau] *n.* **1** female animal of the bull family kept to give milk: *he was milking his cow.* □ **vaca**
2 female of certain animals: *cow elephant; cow whale.* □ **...hembra**
■ *v.* to frighten: *he was not at all cowed by the presence of the chief of police.* □ **acobardar**
cowboy *n.* man who drives herds of cattle in America. □ **vaquero**
cowhand, cowherd, cowman *n.* man who looks after cattle. □ **vaquero**
cowpat *n.* round flat cake of cow dung. □ **boñiga**
cowshed *n.* shed where cows are kept in winter or at night. □ **establo**

coward ['kauəd] *n.* person who is not brave. □ **cobarde**
cowardice *n.* lack of bravery. □ **cobardía**
cowardly *adj.* not brave. □ **cobardemente**

cower ['kauə] *v.* to crouch down because of fear: *the mouse was cowering under a chair.* □ **encogerse de miedo**

cowl [kaul] *n.* hood (for a monk's habit); cover for a chimney. □ **capucha; sombrerete de chimenea**

cowslip ['kauslip] *n.* common yellow wild flower. □ **prímula**

cox [kɔks] *n.* person who steers a rowing boat. □ **timonel**
■ *v.* to steer a rowing boat. □ **gobernar**

coxswain ['kɔksn] *n.* **1** officer in charge of a boat. □ **patrón**
2 person who steers a rowing boat. □ **timonel**

coy [kɔi] *adj.* timid; shy. □ **tímido**

coyly *adv.* in a timid way; shyly. □ **tímidamente**
coyness *n.* shyness. □ **timidez**
coyote [kɔ'jouti] *n.* small American wolf. □ **coyote**
coypu ['kɔipu:] *n.* small animal like a beaver. □ **coipo**
crab [kræb] *n.* edible ten-footed crustacean with large pincers, which walks sideways. □ **cangrejo**
to catch a crab, to miss a stroke when rowing. □ **dar un falso golpe con el remo**
crab apple, bitter wild apple. □ **manzana silvestre**
crabbed *adj.* (handwriting) which is difficult to read. □ **ilegible**
crack [kræk] *n.* **1** sharp dry sound: *the crack of a whip; the crack of a pistol.* □ **crujido; chasquido; estallido**
2 sharp blow: *he got a crack on the head.* □ **golpe**
3 thin break; split: *this plate has a crack in it; we watched them through a crack in the fence.* □ **raja**
at crack of dawn, at daybreak. □ **al romper el alba**
4 ***to have a crack at something,*** (*informal*) to try to do something. □ **intentar**
■ *adj.* (*informal*) first-class: *crack regiment; crack shot.* □ **de primera**
■ *v.* **1** to make a sharp sound: *he cracked his whip.* □ **restallar**
2 to make a thin split in something: *he cracked the window with a stone; this glass is cracked; he cracked a bone in his foot.* □ **resquebrajar**
3 *to crack jokes,* to tell jokes. □ **contar chistes**
4 ***get cracking!,*** (*informal*) start (working, etc.). □ **ponte a (trabajar, etc.)**
crack down *v.* (*informal*) to campaign against: *the police are cracking down on traffic offenders.* □ **acosar**
cracker *n.* **1** small firework which makes a bang. □ **buscapiés**
2 paper tube which makes a little explosion when it is pulled at Christmas parties. □ **triquitraque**
3 dry unsweetened biscuit. □ **'cracker', galleta**
crack up *v.* (*informal*) **1** to praise something extravagantly. □ **dar bombo a**
it's not all it's cracked up to be, it is not as good as they say. □ **no es tan bueno como la gente dice**
2 to collapse: *after six months' non-stop work, he just cracked up.* □ **desplomarse**
crackle ['krækl] *n.* small explosive sounds. □ **crepitación**
■ *v.* to make little explosive sounds: *the log fire was crackling merrily.* □ **crepitar**
crackling *n.* hard cooked pork skin. □ **chicharrón**
cradle ['kreidl] *n.* **1** baby's bed which can be rocked. □ **cuna**
2 support (for a piece of machinery). □ **soporte**
■ *v.* to rock (in your arms). □ **mecer**
craft [krɑ:ft] *n.* **1** artistry; skill: *the watchmaker is very proud of his craft.* □ **arte; destreza**
2 *rural crafts,* types of work which used to be common in the country before mechanization. □ **oficios rurales**
3 ship. □ **navío**
4 cunning; slyness. □ **astucia**
craftily *adv.* cunningly. □ **astutamente**
craftiness *n.* cunning; slyness. □ **astucia**
craftsman *n.* (*pl. craftsmen*) artist; someone who is expert in using his hands. □ **artesano**
crafty *adj.* sly. □ **astuto**
crag [kræg] *n.* steep rock cliff. □ **despeñadero**
cram [kræm] *v.* (*he crammed*) **1** to squeeze into: *he crammed the papers into his briefcase; they all crammed into the little car.* □ **meter(se) a la fuerza**
2 to learn facts hurriedly before an examination. □ **empollar a última hora**
cramfull *adj.* very full; overflowing. □ **atestado**
cramp [kræmp] *n.* sudden pain where the muscles tighten up and cannot be relaxed: *he got cramp when swimming and drowned.* □ **calambre**
■ *v.* to hinder; to squeeze tight. □ **obstaculizar; apretar**
crampon *n.* metal hook/spike attached to boots for climbing in ice and snow. □ **crampón**
cranberry ['krænbəri] *n.* wild red edible berry. □ **arándano**
crane [krein] *n.* **1** tall metal construction for lifting heavy weights: *they hoisted the boiler up with a crane.* □ **grúa**
2 long-legged tropical bird. □ **grulla**
■ *v.* to stretch one's neck: *he craned his neck to get a better view.* □ **estirar**
cranium ['kreiniəm] *n.* bones covering the head/top part of the skull. □ **cráneo**
crank [kræŋk] *n.* **1** winch; geared lever for lifting a heavy weight. □ **manivela**
2 very odd person. □ **excéntrico**
cranky *adj.* odd/bizarre (person). □ **excéntrico**
cranny ['kræni] *n.* small crack/small gap. □ **grieta**
crash [kræʃ] *n.* **1** loud noise: *crash of thunder.* □ **estrépito**
2 accident: *car crash.* □ **choque**
crash helmet, helmet worn by motorcyclists to protect them in case of a crash. □ **casco**
crash barrier, strong fence by the side of a road to prevent cars from running off the road. □ **quitamiedos**
3 financial collapse. □ **'crash'**
■ *v.* **1** to explode; to make a great noise: *the tree crashed on to the house; the herd of elephants came crashing through the forest.* □ **caer; abrirse camino arrollando**
2 to hit in an accident: *the car crashed into the wall; the plane crashed,* hit the ground. □ **estrellarse**
3 to collapse financially. □ **quebrar**
■ *adj.* urgent: *a crash course in German,* very rapid course; *a crash programme of austerity.* □ **de emergencia; intensivo**
crash-land *v.* to land heavily, without using the undercarriage, so that the aircraft is damaged: *the jet crash-landed in a potato field.* □ **hacer un aterrizaje forzoso**
crate [kreit] *n.* large rough wooden box. □ **cajón**
■ *v.* to put into a crate. □ **embalar**
crater ['kreitə] *n.* hole at the top of a volcano; hole made by a bomb. □ **cráter**
cravat [krə'væt] *n.* type of scarf worn by men knotted round the neck in place of a tie. □ **pañuelo de cuello**
crave [kreiv] *v.* to want something very much. □ **ansiar**
craving *n.* strong desire: *I have a craving for milk chocolate.* □ **ansia**
crawl [krɔ:l] *n.* **1** creeping on hands and knees. □ **arrastramiento**
2 fast swimming stroke with arms going overarm. □ **nadar a 'crawl'**
3 very slow progress: *there was so much traffic that we were reduced to a crawl.* □ **andar a paso de tortuga**
■ *v.* **1** to move around on hands and knees: *the baby is crawling but cannot walk.* □ **gatear**
2 to creep along slowly. □ **avanzar paso a paso**
3 to be covered with creeping things: *the place is crawling with ants.* □ **estar lleno de**

crayfish ['kreifiʃ] *n.* kind of fresh-water crustacean like a small lobster. □ **cangrejo de río**
crayon ['kreiɔn] *n.* stick of coloured material for drawing. □ **pastel**
craze [kreiz] *n.* mania (for something): *it's the latest craze.* □ **moda**
crazily *adv.* madly. □ **locamente**
craziness *n.* madness. □ **locura**
crazy *adj.* mad: *he drives me crazy.* □ **loco; me vuelve loco**
crazy paving, different-shaped paving stones placed irregularly. □ **pavimento irregular**
creak [kri:k] *n.* squeaky cracking noise: *the floorboards made a creak.* □ **crujido**
■ *v.* to make a squeaky cracking noise: *the stairs creak.* □ **crujir**
creaky *adj.* which make a squeaky cracking noise: *creaky shoes; creaky hinges.* □ **que cruje**
cream [kri:m] *n.* **1** rich fatty part of milk: *single cream,* runny cream; *double cream,* thick cream. □ **nata; crema**
cream cheese, a soft white smooth cheese made from milk or cream. □ **queso de nata**
the cream of *the undergraduates,* the top few undergraduates. □ **la flor y nata de...**
2 smooth paste: *face cream; shoe cream.* □ **crema**
■ *adj.* coloured like cream; very pale fawn: *he was wearing a cream shirt and green tie.* □ **crema**
■ *v.* **1** to take away the best: *the best pupils have been creamed off into the sixth form.* □ **seleccionar**
2 to whip into a smooth paste: *cream the butter and sugar together; creamed potatoes.* □ **batir**
creamery *n.* dairy. □ **lechería**
creamy *adj.* smooth; full of cream: *creamy milk; thick creamy paste.* □ **cremoso**
crease [kri:s] *n.* fold made by ironing; fold made accidentally: *he has a beautiful crease in his trousers; after the train journey her dress was full of creases.* □ **arruga**
■ *v.* **1** to iron a fold into something: *beautifully creased trousers.* □ **hacer la raya de los pantalones**
2 to make folds accidentally: *this material is guaranteed not to crease.* □ **arrugarse**
create [kri'eit] *v.* **1** to make; to invent: *he created a masterpiece; the museum was created on the orders of the king.* □ **crear**
2 (*informal*) to make a disturbance/a fuss. □ **armar jaleo**
creation [kri'eiʃn] *n.* **1** thing which has been made. □ **creación**
2 *his latest creation,* the latest style of fashion which he has invented. □ **creación**
creative *adj.* full of ideas; always making something. □ **creativo**
creativity [kriei'tiviti] *n.* aptitude for creating. □ **creatividad**
creator *n.* person who makes/invents something: *Disney, the creator of Mickey Mouse.* □ **creador**
creature ['kri:tʃə] *n.* animal; person: *he is a creature of habit; all living creatures.* □ **criatura**
creache [kreʃ] *n.* nursery where babies can be left while their parents are at work. □ **guardería infantil**
credentials [kri'denʃəlz] *n. pl.* papers which prove your identity or rank so that people can trust you. □ **credenciales**
credible ['kredibl] *adj.* which can be believed: *his story is perfectly credible.* □ **creíble**
credibility [kredi'biliti] *n.* ability to be believed: *he suffers from a credibility gap,* people do not believe him. □ **credibilidad**
credibly *adv.* reliably. □ **creíblemente**
credit ['kredit] *n.* **1** merit; recognition of quality: *I gave him credit for more sense than that,* I thought he had more sense. □ **crédito, reconocimiento**
2 ***to do (someone) credit:*** *it does you credit,* you are to be praised for it. □ **puedes enorgullecerte de ello**
3 *he's a credit to the school,* he has made the school proud of him. □ **hace honor al**
4 belief; faith: *to give credit to a rumour,* to make it seem that the rumour is correct. □ **crédito**
5 time given to pay: *I gave him six months' credit.* □ **plazo**
credit card, card which allows you to buy goods without having to pay immediately. □ **tarjeta de crédito**
6 *to buy something* ***on credit,*** without paying immediately. □ **a crédito**
7 side of an account showing money in hand or which is owed to you: *the credit side; my bank account is in credit,* I do not owe the bank any money. □ **haber; saldo positivo**
credit note, note showing that money is owed you. □ **nota de crédito**
8 ***credits,*** list of actors'/directors' names which appear at the beginning or end of a film/TV programme. □ **títulos de crédito**
■ *v.* **1** to attribute a quality to (someone): *he is credited with having discovered the North Pole; I credited him with more sense than that,* I thought he had more sense. □ **acreditar, atribuir**
2 to believe: *I don't credit his story.* □ **dar crédito**
3 to promise to pay (someone); to pay money into: *my account has been credited with $3,000.* □ **abonar en cuenta**
creditable *adj.* honourable (deed). □ **encomiable**
creditably *adv.* honourably: *he acquitted himself very creditably in the cricket match,* he played quite well. □ **honrosamente**
creditor *n.* person who is owed money. □ **acreedor**
credulous ['kredjuləs] *adj.* (person) who believes anything easily. □ **crédulo**
credulity [kre'djuliti] **credulousness** *n.* belief/trust. □ **credulidad**
credulously *adv.* without questioning; trustingly. □ **crédulamente**
creed [kri:d] *n.* statement of what you believe. □ **credo**
the Apostles' Creed, the statement of Christian faith. □ **credo**
creek [kri:k] *n.* little inlet of the sea; *Amer.* small river. □ **cala; riachuelo**
creep [kri:p] *n. pl. he gives me the creeps,* he makes me shudder. □ **me pone la carne de gallina**
■ *v.* (*he crept*) **1** to move around stealthily: *he crept into the cellar; she crept downstairs in the dark.* □ **ir cautelosamente**
2 *the police crept up on the burglar,* they surprised him from behind. □ **acercarse sigilosamente a**
3 ***creeping plant,*** plant which spreads close to the ground/which climbs up a wall. □ **trepadora**
4 *it made my flesh creep,* it made me shudder. □ **me puso la carne de gallina**
creeper *n.* plant which climbs over walls. □ **enredadera**
creepy *adj.* (*informal*) which makes you shudder. □ **espeluznante**
cremate [kri'meit] *v.* to burn a dead body. □ **incinerar**
cremation *n.* burning of a dead body. □ **incineración**
crematorium [kremə'tɔ:riəm] *n.* (*pl. crematoria*) place where bodies are burnt. □ **crematorio**

creosote ['kriəsout] *n.* dark brown liquid, used for protecting wood from rotting.□ **creosota**
■ *v.* to paint with creosote. □ **creosotar**
crepe [kreip] *n.* **1** *crepe paper,* slightly crinkly coloured paper. □ **papel de China**
crepe bandage, bandage made of wrinkled elastic cloth. □ **venda elástica**
2 *crepe soles,* thick rubber soles for shoes. □ **suela de crepé**
crept [krept] *v. see* **creep.**
crescent ['kresnt] *n.* **1** curved shape, like a new moon. □ **creciente**
2 street which forms a semicircle. □ **calle en semicírculo**
cress [kres] *n.* small green salad plant, usually eaten with seedlings of mustard. □ **berro**
crest [krest] *n.* **1** (a) top (of hills/waves). □ **cresta**
2 plumes/fleshy growth on the head of a bird. □ **cresta**
3 coat of arms. □ **escudo de armas; blasón**
crestfallen *adj.* discouraged/depressed. □ **alicaído**
cretin ['kretin] *n.* person who is mentally weak; (*informal*) very stupid person. □ **cretino**
crevasse [kri'væs] *n.* deep crack in a glacier. □ **grieta**
crevice ['krevis] *n.* small crack in rock/wall. □ **grieta**
crew [kru:] *n.* **1** people who work a boat/aircraft/bus, etc.: *a ship's crew; the bus crews went on strike.* □ **tripulación**
2 gang. □ **banda**
crewcut *n.* very short haircut. □ **corte de pelo a cepillo**
crib [krib] *n.* **1** manger/box for food for horses or cows. □ **pesebre**
2 baby's bed. □ **cuna**
3 model of the scene of the first Christmas displayed in a church at Christmas time. □ **nacimiento**
4 word-for-word translation to help a bad student with homework. □ **chuleta**
■ *v.* (*he cribbed*) to copy. □ **copiar**
crick [krik] *n. crick in the neck,* sprain/pulled muscle in the neck. □ **tortícolis**
■ *v. I've cricked my neck,* I have pulled a muscle in my neck. □ **dar tortícolis**
cricket ['krikit] *n.* **1** small jumping insect, like a grasshopper. □ **grillo**
2 game of English origin, played between two teams of eleven players using bats, hard balls and wickets as targets: *a cricket match.* □ **críquet**
cricketer *n.* person who plays cricket. □ **jugador de críquet**
crime [kraim] *n.* illegal act: *he committed a crime.* □ **delito**
criminal ['kriminl] *adj.* referring to an illegal act. □ **criminal**
■ *n.* person who commits a crime. □ **delincuente**
criminally *adv.* so bad as to be against the law: *criminally negligent.* □ **criminalmente**
criminology *n.* study of crime. □ **criminología**
crimson ['krimzn] *adj.* and *n.* deep red colour. □ **carmesí**
cringe [krindʒ] *v.* **1** to bend to avoid a blow: *he cringed as the man raised his stick.* □ **agacharse**
2 to be excessively humble. □ **humillarse**
crinkle ['kriŋkl] *v.* to fold making many small creases: *crinkled paper.* □ **ondular, arrugar**
crinkly *adj.* **1** with many creases. □ **arrugado**
2 *crinkly hair,* hair with tight curls. □ **rizado**
cripple ['kripl] *n.* person who is disabled or lame. □ **lisiado**
■ *v.* **1** to make (someone) disabled: *he is crippled with arthritis.* □ **lisiar**
2 to prevent a machine/a factory from working: *the ship was crippled by an explosion; the steel industry was hit by crippling strikes.* □ **paralizar**
crisis *n.* (*pl. crises*) critical moment; turning point: *government crisis,* when a government loses a vote of confidence; *a Middle East crisis,* moment when it looks as though war might break out in the Middle East. □ **crisis**
crisp [krisp] *adj.* **1** dry and brittle; sharp/cold (air): *a crisp biscuit.* □ **churruscante**
2 *a crisp lettuce,* a crunchy lettuce. □ **lechuga crujiente**
■ *n.* (***potato***) ***crisps,*** thin slices of potato fried until they are crisp. □ **patatas fritas (a la inglesa)**
crispness *n.* brittleness/freshness (of biscuit/lettuce); sharpness (of air). □ **carácter de crujiente; frescor**
criss-cross ['kriskrɔs] *adj.* with lines crossing in two directions: *tablecloth with a criss-cross pattern.* □ **entrecruzado**
■ *v.* to go backwards and forwards in different directions: *the mountain is criss-crossed with paths.* □ **entrecruzar**
criterion [krai'tiəriən] *n.* (*pl. criteria*) standard by which things are judged: *his criteria are very high,* he is a very severe judge. □ **criterio**
critic ['kritik] *n.* **1** person who examines something and comments on it: *theatre/film critic,* journalist who goes to the theatre/the cinema and writes comments on new plays and films for a newspaper. □ **crítico**
2 person who comments unfavourably on something/who finds fault with something: *he is one of the government's sharpest critics.* □ **crítico**
critical *adj.* **1** dangerous (situation); extremely urgent/important: *unemployment has reached a critical level.* □ **crítico**
2 unfavourable (comment): *he made some very critical remarks about her dress.* □ **crítico**
critically *adv.* **1** dangerously: *he is critically ill in hospital.* □ **críticamente**
2 unfavourably: *she commented critically on his latest book.* □ **críticamente**
criticism ['kritisizəm] *n.* **1** comment: *literary criticism,* comment on a work of literature. □ **crítica**
2 unfavourable comment: *she can't stand criticism of her piano playing.* □ **crítica**
criticize *v.* to comment unfavourably on something: *he criticized the minister for smoking in public.* □ **criticar**
croak [krouk] *n.* hoarse noise (like that made by frogs). □ **croar**
■ *v.* to make a hoarse sound: *'Get out', he croaked.* □ **gruñir**
croaky *adj.* hoarse (voice). □ **gruñona**
crochet ['krouʃei] *n.* type of knitting where you use only one needle with a hook at the end. □ **ganchillo**
■ *v.* (*she crocheted: crocheting*) to make something (using a hooked needle): *she is crocheting a tablecloth.* □ **hacer labor de ganchillo**
crochet-hook *n.* hooked needle for crocheting. □ **ganchillo**
crock [krɔk] *n.* **1** rough earthenware pot. □ **cántaro**
2 (*informal*) brokendown car or person. □ **trasto (coche); carcamal (persona)**
crockery *n.* rough pottery tableware. □ **loza**
crocodile ['krɔkədail] *n.* **1** large meat-eating reptile living in rivers in Africa. □ **cocodrilo**
2 *she wept* ***crocodile tears,*** she pretended to cry when she was not in any way sad. □ **lágrimas de cocodrilo**

3 long line of schoolchildren walking in pairs: *they walked in a crocodile along to school.* □ **...en fila de a dos**

crocus ['kroukəs] *n.* purple, yellow or white spring flower. □ **azafrán**

croft [krɔft] *n.* (*in Scotland*) small farm held by a tenant. □ **pequeña explotación agrícola arrendada**

crofter *n.* farmer who holds a croft. □ **arrendatario**

crony ['krouni] *n.* old friend: *one of my father's cronies.* □ **amigote**

crook [kruk] *n.* **1** bend: *the crook of your arm.* □ **curva; pliegue del codo**

2 long stick with a bent top: *a shepherd's crook.* □ **cayado**

3 (*informal*) criminal. □ **chorizo**

crooked ['krukid] *adj.* **1** bent. □ **curvado**

2 dishonest. □ **poco limpio**

crookedly *adv.* in a bent way; not straight: *he put his hat on crookedly.* □ **torcidamente**

croon [kru:n] *v.* to sing in a low voice. □ **canturrear**

crop [krɔp] *n.* **1** vegetables/grain, etc., grown for food: *root crops; we have got a good crop of tomatoes; the rice crop has failed.* □ **cosecha**

2 part of a bird's throat shaped like a bag. □ **buche**

3 small whip used by a rider. □ **fusta**

4 short haircut. □ **corte de pelo corto**

■ *v.* (*he cropped*) **1** to cut (a hedge/someone's hair). □ **cortar**

2 to eat (grass) so that it is very short: *the sheep had cropped the grass.* □ **cortar**

cropper *n.* ***to come a cropper,*** (*informal*) (i) to fall badly. □ **darse un batacazo**

(ii) to fail completely. □ **fracasar**

crop up *v.* to occur: *problems like this crop up from time to time.* □ **aflorar**

croquet ['kroukei] *n.* lawn game played with hoops, balls and mallets. □ **croquet**

croquette [krə'ket] *n.* small ball of mashed potato, covered with breadcrumbs and fried. □ **croqueta**

cross [krɔs] *n.* **1** shape with two lines cutting across each other at right angles: *he wrote a cross on the ballot paper.* □ **cruz**

2 shape of a vertical line, with another cutting across it at right angles, forming the symbol of the Christian church; wooden construction of this shape. □ **cruz**

the Red Cross, international rescue and medical organization. □ **la Cruz Roja**

3 mixture of two breeds: *a mule is a cross between a donkey and a horse.* □ **cruce**

■ *v.* **1** *to cross oneself,* to make a sign of the cross on oneself. □ **santiguarse**

2 *to cross a cheque,* to put two lines across a cheque so that it can only be paid into the bank account of the person to whom it is made out. □ **cruzar un cheque**

3 to go across; to place across: *he crossed the street; the road crosses the river by a suspension bridge; in the afternoon we crossed into France,* we crossed the border into France. □ **cruzar**

4 *the main roads cross in the centre of the town,* go across each other; *she sat down and crossed her legs.* □ **cruzar**

crossed line, telephone connection where you can hear other people talking. □ **cruce de lineas**

5 to breed two animals/plants together: *he tried to cross the two breeds of cattle.* □ **cruzar**

■ *adj.* **1** opposed/contrary. □ **opuesto**

2 *they are **at cross purposes**,* they are in disagreement. □ **contrario**

to talk at cross purposes, to misunderstand what each other is saying. □ **hablar sin entenderse uno al otro**

3 bad-tempered: *why are you so cross today? you mustn't be cross with him,* you mustn't be angry. □ **enfadado**

crossbar *n.* beam which goes across a space, especially beam between the posts in a football goal, or bar between front and back pillars of a man's bicycle. □ **travesaño; barra (en una bici)**

crosscheck *v.* to check again to make sure. □ **volver a comprobar**

cross-country *adj.* and *n.* (race) across fields and along roads, not on a track. □ **a campo través**

cross-examination *n.* searching questioning by an opposing lawyer. □ **interrogatorio**

cross-examine *v.* to ask someone searching questions. □ **interrogar**

crosseyed *adj.* (person) whose eyes do not face forward; (person) with a squint. □ **bizco**

cross-fertilize *v.* to fertilize one plant with another variety. □ **fecundar por fecundación cruzada**

crossfire *n.* gunfire from two directions, so that the fire crosses. □ **fuego cruzado**

cross-grained *adj.* bad-tempered. □ **intratable**

crossing *n.* **1** act of going across: *the Channel crossing was very rough.* □ **travesía**

2 place where you cross. □ **cruce**

pedestrian crossing, place where pedestrians can cross a street. □ **paso para peatones**

level crossing, place where a road crosses a railway line. □ **paso a nivel**

crosslegged *adj.* and *adv.* with one ankle over the other: *he was sitting crosslegged.* □ **con las piernas cruzadas**

cross off, cross out *v.* to draw a line through something written. □ **tachar**

cross-question *v.* to ask someone searching questions. □ **interrogar**

cross-questioning *n.* questioning by an opposing lawyer. □ **interrogatorio**

cross-reference *n.* line in a reference book telling you to look in another section for further information. □ **referencia cruzada**

crossroads *n. pl.* place where two roads cross. □ **cruce**

cross-section *n.* **1** diagram as if a cut had been made across something: *a cross-section of a coalmine.* □ **sección transversal**

2 sample: *a good cross-section of the population.* □ **muestra representativa**

crosswalk *n.* *Amer.* pedestrian crossing/place where pedestrians can cross a street. □ **cruce**

crosswind *n.* wind blowing across a road, etc. □ **viento de costado**

crossword *n.* puzzle where small squares have to be filled with words to which clues are given. □ **crucigrama**

crotch [krɔtʃ] *n.* space between the two legs. □ **entrepierna**

crotchet ['krɔtʃit] *n.* note in music lasting two quavers or half as long as a minim. □ **negra**

crotchety *adj.* **1** bad-tempered. □ **de mal genio**

2 odd/slightly mad. □ **excéntrico**

crouch [krautʃ] *v.* to bend down low: *the soldiers crouched behind the wall.* □ **ponerse en cuclillas**

croupier ['kru:piə] *n.* person who is in charge of a gaming table. □ **'croupier'**

crow [krou] *n.* large common black bird. □ **cuervo**

as the crow flies, in a straight line. □ **en línea recta**

■ *v.* **1** to call (of a cockerel). □ **cacarear**

2 ***to crow over someone,*** to exclaim happily because

you have beaten someone. □ **cantar victoria**
crowbar *n.* large metal lever for opening boxes. □ **palanca**
crow's-feet *n.* little wrinkles round the eyes. □ **patas de gallo**
crow's nest *n.* platform on top of a mast for a lookout. □ **atalaya**
crowd [kraud] *n.* mass of people. □ **multitud**
■ *v.* **1** to group together: *the hall was crowded (with people); don't all crowd together.* □ **apiñarse**
2 *the people crowded into the exhibition,* they went into the exhibition in crowds. □ **agolparse**
crown [kraun] *n.* **1** gold and jewelled headdress for a king/queen, etc. □ **corona**
2 symbol of monarchy. □ **corona**
counsel for the crown, lawyer representing the state. □ **abogado del estado**
3 top: *crown of the head; crown of a tooth.* □ **coronilla; corona**
4 type of coin. □ **corona**
■ *v.* **1** to make someone king/queen/emperor, etc.: *he was crowned in the cathedral.* □ **coronar**
2 (*informal*) to hit someone on the head. □ **dar un golpe en la cabeza a**
3 to reward: *their efforts were crowned with success.* □ **coronar**
4 to put a false top on a tooth. □ **poner una corona**
crown cork *n.* metal and cork cap on a bottle. □ **cápsula**
crucial ['kru:ʃl] *adj.* extremely important/critical: *it is crucial that the report should be on time.* □ **crucial**
crucially *adv.* vitally/critically: *a crucially important meeting.* □ **crucialmente**
crucible ['kru:sibl] *n.* small pot used for heating substances in chemical experiments. □ **crisol**
crucifix ['kru:sifiks] *n.* statue representing Jesus Christ on the cross. □ **crucifijo**
crucifixion [kru:si'fikʃn] *n.* killing by nailing to a cross. □ **crucifixión**
crucify *v.* to kill (someone) by nailing to a cross. □ **crucificar**
crude [kru:d] *adj.* **1** unpurified: *crude oil.* □ **crudo**
2 rude/ill-mannered: *he used very crude language.* □ **ordinario**
crudely *adv.* in a rude/straightforward way: *to put it crudely he hates my guts.* □ **llanamente**
crudeness, crudity *n.* rudeness/bluntness (of an expression). □ **ordinariez**
cruel ['kruəl] *adj.* which causes pain/suffering: *a cruel tyrant.* □ **cruel**
cruelly *adv.* **1** savagely/unkindly. □ **cruelmente**
2 *he was cruelly disappointed,* bitterly/badly disappointed. □ **cruelmente**
cruelty *n.* savage treatment of someone: *he was accused of cruelty to his children.* □ **crueldad**
cruet ['kru:it] *n.* set of containers for putting on a table containing salt, pepper, mustard, etc. □ **vinagreras**
cruise [kru:z] *n.* long pleasure voyage in a ship calling at different ports: *he went for a cruise round the Mediterranean.* □ **crucero**
■ *v.* **1** to go about steadily (in a boat) visiting places: *they went cruising in the Mediterranean.* □ **hacer un crucero**
2 to travel at an even speed: *we were cruising along at 70 miles per hour.* □ **ir a velocidad de crucero**
cruiser *n.* large warship, smaller than a battleship. □ **crucero**
cabin cruiser, motor boat with a cabin for living in. □ **yate de recreo**
crumb [krʌm] *n.* small piece (of bread, etc.). □ **migaja**
crumble ['krʌmbl] *n.* dessert made of fruit covered with a mixture of flour, fat and sugar: *apple crumble.* □ **pastel**
■ *v.* to break into small pieces: *he crumbled the cake into a bowl.* □ **desmigajar**
crumbly *adj.* which easily falls to pieces: *this cheese is very crumbly.* □ **desmenuzable**
crumpet ['krʌmpit] *n.* thick round batter cake, served toasted with butter. □ **bollo**
crumple ['krʌmpl] *v.* to crush/to screw up into a ball: *she crumpled up the letter.* □ **arrugar**
crunch [krʌntʃ] *n.* **1** sound of something crisp being crushed: *the crunch of feet on the snow.* □ **crujido**
2 (*informal*) crisis point: *when it comes to the crunch, will he be able to manage alone?* □ **punto crítico**
■ *v.* to crush (something crisp); to chew (something hard): *the dog crunched up the bones; the snow crunched beneath his feet.* □ **ronzar; crujir (nieve)**
crunchy *adj.* hard and crisp: *crunchy biscuits.* □ **crujiente**
crusade [kru:'seid] *n.* **1** medieval campaign by Christians against Moslems who occupied the Holy Land. □ **cruzada**
2 campaign: *he is leading a crusade against legalizing abortion.* □ **cruzada**
■ *v.* to campaign/to fight against or for: *they are crusading for a new school; we are crusading against the new airport.* □ **hacer una campaña**
crusader *n.* person who went on a crusade. □ **cruzado**
crush [krʌʃ] *n.* **1** drink made of fruit juice. □ **refresco de fruta**
2 mass of people squeezed together: *he lost his hat in the crush.* □ **aglomeración**
■ *v.* to squash: *we tried to crush all the clothes into one suitcase; I sat on her hat and crushed it flat.* □ **comprimir; aplastar**
crust [krʌst] *n.* hard exterior (of bread/cake/the earth, etc.). □ **corteza**
crusty *adj.* (bread) with a hard crust. □ **de corteza dura**
crustacean [krʌ'steiʃn] *n.* one of many types of animals with hard shells, mainly living in the sea, such as lobsters, crabs, etc. □ **crustáceo**
crutch [krʌtʃ] *n.* **1** lame person's long stick which goes under the armpit. □ **muleta**
2 place between the two legs. □ **entrepierna**
crux [krʌks] *n.* central point of a problem: *the crux of the matter is does she want to marry him?* □ **quid**
cry [krai] *n.* **1** act of crying/making tears: *she sat in the corner and had a good cry.* □ **llanto; lloro**
2 shout; exclamation (especially of pain): *no one heard his cries for help.* □ **grito**
3 call (of a bird/animal). □ **reclamo**
■ *v.* **1** to make tears: *when she cut her finger she cried.* □ **llorar**
2 to shout; to exclaim (in pain): *'that's not true', he cried.* □ **gritar**
crying *adj.* scandalous/which needs putting right: *it is a crying shame; a crying injustice.* □ **que clama al cielo**
cry off *v.* to decide not to do something which you had promised to do: *he said he would play in the match on Saturday, but at the last minute he cried off.* □ **echarse atrás**
crypt [kript] *n.* cellar under a church. □ **cripta**
cryptic ['kriptik] *adj.* secret; mysterious. □ **enigmático**
crystal ['kristl] *n.* **1** chemical formation of regular-shaped solids: *crystals of copper sulphate; sugar*

crystals. □ **cristal**
2 very clear bright glass: *crystal wine glasses.* □ **cristal**
crystalline *adj.* shaped like a crystal; clear as a crystal. □ **cristalino**
crystallization [kristəlai'zeiʃn] *n.* formation of crystals. □ **cristalización**
crystallize ['kristəlaiz] *v.* **1** to form crystals. □ **cristalizar**
2 to preserve fruit in sugar: *crystallized fruit.* □ **escarchar**
3 to take shape: *his ideas are crystallizing.* □ **cristalizarse**
crystallography [kristə'lɔgrəfi] *n.* study of crystals. □ **cristalografía**
cub [kʌb] *n.* **1** young animal: *fox cub; bear cub; lion cub.* □ **cachorro**
2 ***Cub Scout,*** young Boy Scout. □ **niño Boy Scout**
Cuba ['kju:bə] *n.* country on an island in the Caribbean Sea. □ **Cuba**
Cuban *adj.* and *n.* referring to Cuba; person from Cuba. □ **cubano**
cubby-hole ['kʌbihoul] *n.* small dark cupboard/hiding place. □ **chiribitil**
cube [kju:b] *n.* **1** geometric solid shape where all six sides are square and join each other at right angles: *sugar cube.* □ **cubo**
2 the result where a number is multiplied by itself twice: *twenty seven is the cube of three.* □ **cubo**
cube root, number which when multiplied by itself twice gives another number: *three is the cube root of twenty seven.* □ **raíz cúbica**
■ *v.* **1** to multiply a number by itself twice: *eight is two cubed.* □ **elevar al cubo**
2 *cubed sugar,* sugar in square lumps. □ **terrón**
cubic *adj.* solid. □ **cúbico**
cubic capacity, capacity to hold something. □ **capacidad cúbica**
cubic centimetre, cube where each side measures one centimetre; the volume of this size: *engine with a 1,300 cubic centimetre (cc) capacity.* □ **centímetro cúbico**
cubicle ['kju:bikl] *n.* small room (in a dormitory); changing room (in a shop/at swimming baths). □ **cubículo**
cubism ['kju:bizəm] *n.* art movement where geometric shapes predominate. □ **cubismo**
cubist *adj.* and *n.* (painter) using geometric shapes. □ **cubista**
cuckoo ['kuku:] *n.* **1** common bird in the summer, which lays its eggs in other birds' nests. □ **cuclillo**
2 (*informal*) stupid: *he's completely cuckoo.* □ **lelo**
cuckoo clock *n.* clock where a small bird makes a noise like a cuckoo to call the time. □ **reloj de cuco**
cucumber ['kju:kʌmbə] *n.* long vegetable used in salads or for pickling. □ **pepino**
cud [kʌd] *n.* food chewed a second time: *the cows were chewing the cud.* □ **bolo alimenticio**
cuddle ['kʌdl] *n.* a hug. □ **abrazo**
■ *v.* to hug and kiss (someone). □ **abrazar**
to cuddle up: *she cuddled up close to him,* she moved very close to him. □ **arrimarse**
cuddly *adj.* warm and soft: *a cuddly doll.* □ **blando**
cudgel ['kʌdʒl] *n.* large stick for hitting people with. □ **garrote**
to take up cudgels on someone's behalf, to go to defend someone. □ **salir en defensa de**
cue [kju:] *n.* **1** (*in a play*) the line which indicates that you speak or act next: *when she collapses on the floor, that is your cue for coming in through the window.* □ **entrada**
to take your cue from someone, to follow someone closely/to do as someone does. □ **seguir el ejemplo de**
2 long stick for playing billiards. □ **taco**
cuff [kʌf] *n.* **1** end of the sleeve round the wrist. □ **puño**
2 *he was speaking* ***off the cuff,*** without any notes; making an impromptu speech. □ **...improvisando**
3 *Amer.* folded part at the bottom of each leg of a pair of trousers. □ **vuelta**
4 smack (with an open hand). □ **bofetada**
■ *v.* to give someone a smack. □ **abofetear**
cuff-links *n. pl.* fasteners linked with a chain for attaching shirt cuffs. □ **gemelos**
cuisine [kwi'zi:n] *n.* style of cooking. □ **cocina**
cul-de-sac ['kʌldəsæk] *n.* small street open at only one end. □ **callejón sin salida**
culinary ['kʌlinəri] *adj.* referring to cooking. □ **culinario**
cull [kʌl] *v.* to kill some animals in a herd when there are too many of them. □ **sacrificar**
culminate ['kʌlmineit] *v.* to end; to reach a climax: *the evening culminated in a firework display.* □ **culminar**
culmination [kʌlmi'neiʃn] *n.* final point/grand ending. □ **culminación**
culpable ['kʌlpəbl] *adj.* guilty. □ **culpable**
culpability *n.* guilt. □ **culpabilidad**
culprit ['kʌlprit] *n.* person who has done something wrong: *someone has stolen my ruler - now who is the culprit?* □ **culpable**
cult [kʌlt] *n.* **1** religious or semi-religious worship: *cult of the sun.* □ **culto**
2 *he is a* ***cult hero,*** he is worshipped by a group of admirers. □ **héroe de culto**
cultivate ['kʌltiveit] *v.* **1** to dig and water the land to grow plants; to grow plants: *cultivated land; cultivated raspberries,* raspberries which are grown for fruit. □ **cultivar**
2 to do everything to win (someone's friendship). □ **cultivar**
cultivated *adj.* (person) who has been educated/who is civilized. □ **culto**
cultivation [kʌlti'veiʃn] *n.* **1** act of cultivating. □ **cultivo**
2 education. □ **cultura**
cultivator *n.* **1** farmer/person who cultivates. □ **agricultor**
2 small motor-powered plough. □ **mula mecánica**
culture ['kʌltʃə] *n.* **1** cultivation of plants/pearls: *plants suitable for greenhouse culture.* □ **cultivo**
2 growing (of germs in a laboratory). □ **cultivo**
3 civilization: *French culture.* □ **cultura**
cultural *adj.* referring to culture. □ **cultural**
cultured *adj.* **1** civilized; well educated (person). □ **civilizado; educado**
2 (pearl) which has been artificially grown. □ **perla cultivada**
cumbersome ['kʌmbəsəm] *adj.* large and heavy. □ **voluminoso**
cumulative ['kju:mjulətiv] *adj.* which accumulates; which grows by adding new parts. □ **acumulativo**
cumulus ['kju:mjuləs] *n.* type of large white cloud; rounded masses of clouds. □ **cúmulo**
cuneiform ['kju:nifɔ:m] *adj.* and *n.* type of very old writing done on wet clay with a stick. □ **cuneiforme**
cunning ['kʌniŋ] *n.* **1** cleverness. □ **astucia**
2 trickery. □ **picardía**
■ *adj.* **1** clever: *it is a cunning trick.* □ **ingenioso**
2 tricky/sly: *the cunning old fox.* □ **astuto**
cup [kʌp] *n.* **1** bowl with a handle for drinking tea

or coffee, etc.: *tea cup; coffee cup; would you like a cup of tea?* □ **taza**
2 silver goblet or vase given as a prize in sporting events/competitions, etc.. □ **copa**
cup final, final match for a football championship. □ **final de copa**
cup tie, preliminary match for a football championship. □ **encuentro de clasificación**
■ *v.* (*he cupped*) to put in the shape of a cup: *she cupped her hands.* □ **ahuecar**
cupful *n.* quantity held by a cup: *add a cupful of sugar.* □ **taza**
cupboard ['kʌbəd] *n.* large piece of furniture with shelves and doors; alcove in a wall with shelves and doors: *put the flour in the cupboard.* □ **armario**
cupidity [kjuː'piditi] *n.* greed; desire for something. □ **codicia**
curate ['kjuərət] *n.* minor priest who helps the parish priest. □ **coadjutor**
curator [kju'reitə] *n.* person in charge of a museum. □ **director, conservador**
curb [kəːb] *n.* **1** = **kerb.** □ **bordillo**
2 brake/something which holds you back: *to impose a curb on exports to certain countries.* □ **freno**
■ *v.* to brake; to hold back: *he tried to curb his desire to hit her.* □ **frenar**
curd [kəːd] *n.* solid food made from sour milk. □ **cuajada**
curdle ['kəːdl] *v.* to go sour: *the milk has curdled.* □ **cortarse**
cure ['kjuə] *n.* **1** making better: *he had a complete cure.* □ **cura**
2 remedy: *I know a cure for loneliness.* □ **cura**
■ *v.* **1** to make better: *he was completely cured.* □ **curar**
2 to preserve (fish/pork, etc.) by salting/smoking, etc.; to preserve (skins) to make leather. □ **curar**
curable *adj.* which can be cured. □ **curable**
curfew ['kəːfjuː] *n.* period when no one is allowed on the streets: *the curfew starts at 10 p.m.* □ **toque de queda**
curio ['kjuəriou] *n.* odd/rare object. □ **curiosidad**
curiosity [kjuəri'ɔsiti] *n.* **1** desire for knowledge: *I went into the cellar out of sheer curiosity.* □ **curiosidad**
2 odd/rare object. □ **rareza**
curious ['kjuəriəs] *adj.* **1** wanting to know: *I am curious to find out if they are married.* □ **curioso**
2 odd/peculiar: *he has a curious habit of pulling the end of his nose.* □ **curioso**
curiously *adv.* oddly. □ **curiosamente**
curl [kəːl] *n.* lock of wavy twisted hair: *she has her hair in curls.* □ **rizo**
■ *v.* **1** to make hair wave/twist: *she is having her hair curled.* □ **rizar**
2 to grow in waves/twists naturally: *his hair curls naturally; the piece of paper curled in the heat; smoke curled up from the bonfire.* □ **rizarse**
curler *n.* small tube for wrapping hair round to make it curl: *she answered the door in curlers.* □ **rulo**
curling *n.* team game where heavy weights are slid across ice towards a target. □ **'curling'**
curl up *v.* to roll up into a ball: *the cat was curled up on a cushion; I like to curl up in an armchair with a good book.* □ **acurrucarse**
curly *adj.* with natural waves, twists: *he has a thick curly beard; curly lettuce,* lettuce with crinkly leaves. □ **rizado**
curlew ['kəːljuː] *n.* brown wading bird with a long curved beak. □ **zarapito**
currant ['kʌrənt] *n.* **1** small soft fruit of various sorts: *black currant.* □ **grosella**
2 small dried grape. □ **pasa de Corinto**
currency ['kʌrənsi] *n.* **1** (system of) money: *foreign currency.* □ **moneda**
hard currency, money which can be easily exchanged internationally: *I want $100 in French currency.* □ **moneda fuerte**
2 being well known: *the rumour gained currency,* became more frequently heard. □ **circulación**
current ['kʌrənt] *n.* flow of water/air/electricity: *the current in the river is strong; the bather was washed away by the current; electric current; the glider soared upwards in a current of hot air.* □ **corriente**
■ *adj.* of the present time; frequent: *the current number of a magazine; it is a word which is in current use in the north of Germany.* □ **el último número (revista); uso actual (palabra)**
current affairs, things which are happening at the present moment. □ **asuntos del momento**
current account, bank account from which you can draw money without giving notice, but which does not pay interest. □ **cuenta corriente**
currently *adv.* at the present time; frequently. □ **actualmente**
curriculum [kə'rikjuləm] *n.* list of subjects studied in a school, etc.: *English is on the curriculum.* □ **plan de estudios**
curriculum vitae, summary of biographical details, especially details of education and work experience. □ **curriculum vitae**
curry ['kʌri] *n.* hot spice; dish made with hot spice: *chicken curry; curry powder.* □ **curry**
■ *v.* **1** to cook with hot spices: *curried chicken.* □ **cocinar con curry**
2 to brush down (a horse). □ **almohazar**
3 ***to curry favour with someone,*** to try to make someone favour you. □ **buscar el favor de alguien**
currycomb *n.* stiff brush for brushing a horse. □ **almohaza**
curse [kəːs] *n.* **1** evil magic spell. □ **hechizo maligno**
2 swear word. □ **¡maldita sea!**
3 calamity/evil: *alcoholism is the curse of that family.* □ **mal**
■ *v.* **1** to cast an evil spell: *he was cursed with permanent bad health.* □ **afligir**
2 to swear: *he cursed when he dropped the stone on his foot.* □ **maldecir, blasfemar**
cursory ['kəːsəri] *adj.* rapid/superficial (inspection/glance). □ **rápido**
cursorily *adv.* rapidly. □ **rápidamente**
curt [kəːt] *adj.* abrupt: *the only answer she got was a curt 'no'.* □ **seco**
curtly *adv.* abruptly. □ **bruscamente**
curtail [kəː'teil] *v.* to shorten; to reduce: *I had to curtail my holidays; you ought to try to curtail your expenses.* □ **acortar; reducir**
curtain ['kəːtn] *n.* long piece of material hanging by hooks from a pole, covering a window or cutting off the stage in a theatre. □ **cortina; telón (teatro)**
behind the Iron Curtain, in Eastern Europe. □ **detrás del Telón de Acero**
Iron Curtain countries, Communist countries of Eastern Europe. □ **países del Telón de Acero**
■ *v.* ***to curtain off,*** to hide/to cover with a curtain. □ **tapar con cortinas**
curtain-call *n.* calling of an actor to take a bow after the end of a performance. □ **llamada a escena**
curtain-rod *n.* rod on which a curtain is hung. □ **riel**
curtsy ['kəːtsi] *n.* respectful movement made by

women/girls, by bending the knees and putting one foot forward. □ **reverencia**
■ *v. to curtsy to someone,* to make someone a movement of respect. □ **hacer una reverencia**

curve [kəːv] *n.* rounded shape like a semi-circle: *curve in a road; the car takes the curves very well; the plane flew round in a wide curve.* □ **curva**
■ *v.* to make a rounded shape: *the road curves round the mountain.* □ **rodear**
curvature ['kəːvətʃə] *n.* **1** bending of something into a curve: *the curvature of the earth,* roundness visible in the horizon when at sea. □ **curvatura**
2 *curvature of the spine,* abnormal bending of the spine. □ **encorvamiento**
curved *adj.* rounded. □ **curvado**

cushion ['kuʃn] *n.* bag filled with feathers or foam rubber for sitting/leaning on: *a sofa with comfortable cushions.* □ **cojín**
■ *v.* to soften a blow: *a thick bed of moss cushioned his fall.* □ **amortiguar**

cushy ['kuʃi] *adj.* (*informal*) easy (job). □ **cómodo**

cussed ['kʌsid] *adj.* (*informal*) awkward and contrary. □ **terco**
cussedness ['kʌsidnəs] *n.* (*informal*) awkwardness/contrariness. □ **terquedad**

custard ['kʌstəd] *n.* cream made with eggs, milk and sugar; also with a special powder and milk. □ **natillas**
custard tart *n.* small pastry case filled with custard and baked. □ **tarta**

custody ['kʌstədi] *n.* **1** keeping. □ **custodia**
2 *in custody,* in prison; *he was taken into custody,* he was arrested. □ **bajo custodia; fue detenido**
custodian [kʌ'stoudiən] *n.* person who keeps something safe; guardian of an ancient monument. □ **custodia; guardián**

custom ['kʌstəm] *n.* **1** habit: *it is the custom in that country to marry the children off before they are six years old.* □ **costumbre**
2 using of a shop: *he is losing his custom because his prices are too high.* □ **clientela**
3 *he will not get my custom again,* I will not go to his shop again. □ **no me tendrá por cliente otra vez**
4 ***custom-built/custom-made,*** made to special order. □ **hecho de encargo**
customarily *adv.* usually. □ **habitualmente**
customary *adj.* habitual: *he was having his customary six o'clock drink,* the drink he always has at six o'clock. □ **habitual; de costumbre**
customer *n.* client/person who buys in a shop. □ **cliente**
customs *n.* **1** tax on goods imported into a country. □ **derechos de aduana**
2 the government department/office which inspects imports: *when you enter the country you have to go through the customs; a customs officer inspects your luggage.* □ **aduana**

cut [kʌt] *n.* **1** reduction (in salary); breaking off (electricity supply): *a power cut.* □ **reducción; corte**
2 opening made with a sharp blade; small wound: *he had a cut in his right thumb.* □ **corte**
3 ***short cut,*** way which is shorter than usual; a quicker way of getting to your destination: *there are no short cuts to becoming a doctor.* □ **atajo**
4 way in which a suit/jacket, etc., is made. □ **corte**
5 piece/slice of meat. □ **corte**
■ *v.* (*he cut; he has cut*) **1** to make an opening using a sharp blade; to wound (with a knife); to shorten; to reduce: *she cut the cloth in two; he has cut his finger; when are you going to get your hair cut? they have cut his salary by half; the hours of work have been cut to 35 per week; prices have been cut by 50% during the sale.* □ **cortar; reducir**
2 to split a pack of playing cards in half. □ **cortar la baraja**
3 not to look at someone whom you know: *he cut me dead.* □ **pasar sin saludar a un conocido**
4 *to cut a lecture,* to miss a lecture. □ **perderse una conferencia**
■ *adj.* which has been cut: *cut glass; well cut suit.* □ **cristal tallado; bien cortado**
cut down *v.* to chop down (a tree); to reduce (amount). □ **cortar (un árbol); reducir (una cantidad)**
cut in *v.* to interrupt a conversation; to move in quickly in front of another car in traffic. □ **interrumpir; meterse (un coche)**
cut off *v.* to disconnect (electricity supply); to remove; to stop (someone) reaching a place: *they were cut off by the tide.* □ **cortar; llevarse; cortar el paso**
cut out *v.* **1** to stop (eating, etc.): *I have cut out cigarettes.* □ **dejar de...**
2 *the engine cut out,* stopped. □ **pararse**
3 to remove by cutting a small piece out of a large piece (of paper, etc.). □ **recortar**
4 *he is not* ***cut out for*** *the army,* he does not fit in with/is not suitable for the army. □ **no está hecho para el ejército**
cut-price *adj.* cheap: *cut-price petrol.* □ **a precio reducido**
cutter *n.* **1** person who cuts. □ **cortador**
2 machine which cuts. □ **cortadora**
3 small, fast boat. □ **cúter**
cut-throat *adj.* vicious/intense: *cut-throat competition,* bitter competition. □ **implacable**
cutting *adj.* **1** which cuts: *cutting edge of a knife; a cutting wind.* □ **cortante**
2 *cutting remarks,* cruel/sarcastic remarks. □ **comentario hiriente**
■ *n.* **1** small piece of paper cut out of a newspaper. □ **recorte**
2 little piece of a plant which will take root if stuck in the ground. □ **esqueje**
cut up *v.* **1** to make into small pieces by cutting. □ **cortar en pedazos**
2 *she was very cut up,* (*informal*) very upset. □ **estaba muy cabreada**

cute [kjuːt] *adj. Amer.* (*informal*) nice. □ **lindo**
cuteness *n.* niceness. □ **monería**

cuticle ['kjuːtikl] *n.* skin round a fingernail or toenail. □ **cutícula**

cutlery ['kʌtləri] *n.* knives, forks and spoons. □ **cubertería**

cutlet ['kʌtlət] *n.* **1** thin slice of meat (usually with the rib bone attached). □ **chuleta**
2 fried meat patty. □ **croqueta**

cyanide ['saiənaid] *n.* strong poison. □ **cianuro**

cybernetics [saibə'netiks] *n.* science of the communication of information. □ **cibernética**

cyclamen ['sikləmən] *n.* common indoor plant with pink flowers which grow from a corm. □ **ciclamen**

cycle ['saikl] *n.* **1** period during which something returns: *the cycle of the seasons; the life cycle of a frog.* □ **ciclo**
2 series of songs or poems: *a song cycle.* □ **ciclo**
3 bicycle. □ **bicicleta**
■ *v.* to go on a bicycle: *he cycles to school every day.* □ **montar en bicicleta**
cyclic, cyclical ['seklik(l)] *adj.* occuring in cycles. □ **cíclico**
cycling *n.* riding a bicycle as a sport. □ **ciclismo**
cyclist *n.* person who rides a bicycle. □ **ciclista**

cyclone ['saikloun] *n.* tropical storm. □ **ciclón**
cygnet ['signət] *n.* baby swan. □ **pollo de cisne**
cylinder ['silində] *n.* **1** shape like a tube. □ **cilindro** **2** *a four-cylinder engine,* engine with four pistons which move up and down in four cylinders. □ **motor de cuatro cilindros**
cylindrical [si'lindrikl] *adj.* tube-shaped. □ **cilíndrico**
cymbals ['simbəlz] *n. pl.* pair of round metal plates which are banged together to make a loud noise in music. □ **palillos**
cynic ['sinik] *n.* person who mocks/who doubts that anything is good. □ **cínico**
cynical *adj.* referring to a cynic: *a cynical reply,* a reply which shows the speaker does not believe anything is good. □ **cínico**
cynically *adv.* in a cynical, mocking way. □ **cínicamente**
cynicism ['sinisizm] *n.* doubt about the goodness of anything. □ **cinismo**
cypress ['saiprəs] *n.* tall evergreen tree. □ **ciprés**
Cyprus ['saiprəs] *n.* country on an island in the Mediterranean Sea. □ **Chipre**
Cypriot ['sipriət] *adj.* referring to Cyprus. □ **chipriota**
■ *n.* person from Cyprus. □ **chipriota**
cyst [sist] *n.* small growth on or inside the body. □ **quiste**
cystitis *n.* inflammation of the bladder. □ **cistitis**
Czechoslovakia *n.* country in Eastern Europe. **Checoslovaquia**
Czech *adj.* referring to Czechoslovakia. **checoslovaco**
■ *n.* person from Czechoslovakia. □ **checoslovaco**

D,d

D, d [diː] fourth letter of the alphabet. □ **D, d**
dab [dæb] *n.* **1** light tap. □ **golpecito**
2 *he's a **dab hand** at poker,* (*informal*) he is very good at playing poker. □ **es un hacha al póquer**
3 small flat fish. □ **gallo**
4 small quantity: *a dab of butter.* □ **pizca**
■ *v.* (*he dabbed*) to give (something) a light tap: *she was dabbing her eyes with a handkerchief.* □ **dar un toquecito, retocar**
dabble ['dæbl] *v.* **1** to paddle (in water). □ **salpicar**
2 *he dabbles in politics,* he does a little political work. □ **meterse en política**
dabchick ['dæbtʃik] *n.* common small dark water-bird with a red forehead. □ **somormujo**
dace [deis] *n.* (*no pl.*) small edible freshwater fish. □ **albur**
dachshund ['dækshund] *n.* breed of long low dog (originally from Germany). □ **'dachshund'**
dad [dæd] **daddy** ['dædi] *n.* (*informal*) father. □ **papá**
daddy-long-legs *n.* insect with very long legs. □ **típula**
dado ['deidou] *n.* (*pl. dadoes*) lower part of a wall, which is panelled or painted differently from the upper part. □ **friso**
daffodil ['dæfədil] *n.* spring flower in shades of yellow, with a trumpet-shaped centre. □ **narciso**
daft [dɑːft] *adj.* (*informal*) silly: *don't be daft.* □ **tonto**
dagger ['dægə] *n.* **1** short knife. □ **daga**
2 *they are **at daggers drawn,*** they are bitter enemies. □ **estar a matar**
dahlia ['deiliə] *n.* autumn garden flower (produced from a bulbous root). □ **dalia**
daily ['deili] *adj.* every day: *the 'Guardian' is a daily paper; daily exercises are supposed to keep you fit.* □ **diario**
■ *adv. take the tablets twice daily,* two times a day. □ **al día**
■ *n.* (*pl. dailies*) **1** newspaper published every weekday. □ **(periódico) diario**
2 woman who comes to a house every day to do housework. □ **asistenta**
dainty ['deinti] *adj.* (*daintier, daintiest*) delicate; small. □ **delicado, fino**
daintily *adv.* delicately: *she eats her food daintily.* □ **finamente**
dairy ['dɛəri] *n.* (*pl. dairies*) place where milk, cream and butter are processed or sold. □ **lechería**
dairy produce, milk, butter, cream and cheese. □ **productos lácteos**
dairy ice cream, ice cream with a large percentage of milk. □ **helado**
dairy farm, farm which produces milk. □ **vaquería**
dairy farming, milk production. □ **producción láctea**
dairyman *n.* (*pl. dairymen)* man who looks after dairy cows. □ **vaquero**
dais ['deiis] *n.* (*pl. daises*) low platform (in large hall). □ **estrado**
daisy ['deizi] *n.* (*pl. daisies*) small pink and white summer flower (growing as a weed in grass). □ **margarita**
dale [deil] *n.* (*in north of England*) valley. □ **valle**
up hill and down dale, across the country. □ **a campo traviesa**
dally ['dæli] *v.* to idle; to spend time doing nothing. □ **remolonear; perder el tiempo**
Dalmatian [dæl'meiʃn] *n.* large white dog with black spots. □ **dálmata**
dam [dæm] *n.* **1** wall (of earth or concrete) blocking a river, etc.: *the dam across the Zambezi.* □ **presa**
2 female mammal which is a mother. □ **madre**
■ *v.* (*he dammed*) to build a wall across a river, etc.: *the engineers dammed the river to make a lake.* □ **embalsar**
damage ['dæmidʒ] *n.* **1** harm (done to things, not to people): *no one was killed but the fire caused a lot of damage; storm damage/flood damage,* destruction caused by a storm/by a flood. □ **daño**
2 ***damages,*** payment ordered by a court to a victim: *she was awarded $20,000 damages; after he was knocked down by a car he claimed damages from the driver.* □ **daños y perjuicios**
■ *v.* to spoil or harm something: *the wind and rain damaged the wheat crop; the car was badly damaged in the accident.* □ **dañar**
damask ['dæməsk] *n.* kind of patterned material, used especially for tablecloths, etc. □ **damasco**
dame [deim] *n.* **1** (*in a pantomime*) old woman (usually played by a man). □ **vieja**
2 *Amer.* (*informal*) woman. □ **tía**
3 title given to women (equivalent to Sir for men). □ **dama**
damn [dæm] *n.* curse. □ **maldición**
I don't give a damn, I don't mind at all. □ **no me importa un comino**
■ *v.* to condemn; to curse; to criticize: *the report damned the part played by the committee.* □ **condenar**
damnation [dæm'neiʃn] *n.* state of being eternally condemned. □ **condenación**
damned *adj.* (*informal*) very annoying: *it's a damned shame.* □ **maldito**
damning *adj.* which shows that something is wrong: *damning evidence,* evidence which proves that someone is in the wrong. □ **irrecusable**
damp [dæmp] *n.* wetness. □ **humedad**
rising damp, humidity which creeps up walls of a house. □ **humedad**
damp course, strip of material inserted in a wall to prevent damp rising. □ **aislante hidrófugo**
■ *adj.* (*damper, dampest*) wet: *after weeks of sunshine the weather turned damp and cold.* □ **húmedo**
■ *v.* **1** to wet. □ **humedecer**
2 ***to damp down** someone's enthusiasm,* to reduce someone's enthusiasm by being unenthusiastic yourself. □ **rebajar**
damper *n.* **1** gloom. □ **pesimismo**
***to put a damper on** the proceedings,* to make everyone gloomy. □ **apagar el ánimo**
2 plate at the back of a fireplace which regulates the draught. □ **regulador de tiro**
dampness *n.* state of being wet. □ **humedad**
damp-proof *adj.* resistant to wet. □ **a prueba de humedad**
damson ['dæmzən] *n.* small purple plum; tree which bears this fruit. □ **ciruela damascena; ciruelo (árbol)**
dance [dɑːns] *n.* **1** way of moving to music: *the waltz is an old-fashioned dance; African tribal dances.* □ **baile, danza**
dance music, music specially written for dancing. □ **música de baile**
dance hall, large room where people dance.

□ **sala de baile**
2 evening entertainment where people dance: *I'm going to a dance on Friday.* □ **baile**
■ *v.* **1** to move (in time to music): *he is dancing with my sister; they were dancing to the music of the band; can you dance the waltz?* □ **bailar**
2 to jump up and down: *he danced for joy.* □ **saltar**
dancer *n.* person who dances. □ **persona que baila**
ballet dancer, person who dances in ballet. □ **bailarín de ballet**
dandelion ['dændilaiən] *n.* wild plant with yellow flowers and bitter sap. □ **diente de león**
dandruff ['dændrʌf] *n.* small pieces of dry skin (in the hair). □ **caspa**
dandy ['dændi] *n.* (*pl. dandies*) man who is too interested in clothes. □ **dandi**
Dane [dein] *n.* person from Denmark. □ **danés**
Great Dane, breed of very large short-haired dogs. □ **gran danés**
danger ['deindʒə] *n.* risk; possibility of harm or death: *when the weather is hot and dry there is a danger of forest fires; to be in danger,* to be at risk; *he is in danger of losing his job; she is out of danger/she is off the danger list,* she is no longer likely to die. □ **peligro**
dangerous *adj.* which can cause injury or death: *don't touch those wires, they are dangerous; it is dangerous to walk on railway lines.* □ **peligroso**
dangle ['dæŋgl] *v.* to hang limply: *the boys were sitting on the bridge dangling pieces of string into the stream.* □ **colgar**
Danish ['deiniʃ] *adj.* referring to Denmark. □ **danés**
Danish pastry, sweet piece of flaky pastry with jam or fruit folded in it. □ **pasta danesa**
■ *n.* language spoken in Denmark. □ **danés**
dank [dæŋk] *adj.* cold and damp. □ **húmedo, frío**
daphne ['dæfni] *n.* small shrub with pink flowers which appear very early in spring. □ **adelfa**
dapper ['dæpə] *adj.* smart/elegant. □ **apuesto**
dappled ['dæpld] *adj.* covered with patches of light and dark colour. □ **moteado**
dare [dɛə] *n.* act of daring someone to do something: *he ran across the railway line for a dare.* □ **reto**
■ *v.* **1** to be brave enough to do something: *I would never dare to jump with a parachute; she dare not go out of the house for fear of burglars; how dare you be so rude!* □ **atreverse**
I dare say, perhaps/probably. □ **a mi parecer; quizá**
2 to persuade someone to do something by suggesting it is cowardly not to do it: *he dared the other boys to run across the railway line in front of the train.* □ **desafiar**
daring *adj.* brave but foolish: *he made a daring escape from the enemy castle.* □ **osado**
■ *n.* foolish bravery. □ **osadía**
dark [dɑːk] *adj.* (*darker, darkest*) **1** with little or no light: *during the storm it turned quite dark; the sky at night is dark and full of stars; it is getting dark – switch the light on.* □ **oscuro**
2 not a light colour: *his shirt is dark green; his sister is fair but he is dark,* he has dark brown or black hair. □ **oscuro; moreno**
dark horse, someone/something which succeeds though not expected to do so. □ **ganador no favorito**
Dark Ages, period between the end of the Roman civilization in Northern Europe and the Middle Ages. □ **Alta Edad Media**
3 *keep it dark,* keep it a secret. □ **guárdalo en secreto**
4 gloomy: *she's in one of her dark moods.* □ **triste**
■ *n.* **1** absence of light: *I am not afraid of the dark.* □ **oscuridad**
after dark *the streets were quite empty,* after night fell. □ **después de oscurecer...**
2 ***to keep someone in the dark,*** to keep something a secret from someone. □ **ocultar algo a alguien**
darken *v.* to become dark. □ **oscurecer**
darkness *n.* absence of light: *the house was in complete darkness,* there were no lights on in the house. □ **oscuridad**
darkroom *n.* room with no light, in which you can develop films. □ **cuarto oscuro**
darling ['dɑːliŋ] *n.* and *adj.* (person) loved; lovable: *my darling; what a darling little cottage/boy! she's a darling,* everyone loves her. □ **querido; encanto**
darn [dɑːn] *v.* to mend holes in clothes: *he was darning his socks.* □ **zurcir**
■ *n.* place where clothes have been mended: *his socks are full of darns.* □ **zurcido**
darning *n.* action of mending: *I have piles of darning to do,* there are piles of clothes which have to be mended. □ **zurcido(s)**
darning needle, large needle for mending. □ **aguja de zurcir**
dart [dɑːt] *n.* **1** light arrow with a sharp point. □ **saeta**
2 small heavy arrow with feathers (for playing a game with). □ **dardo**
darts, game where two teams throw small heavy arrows at a round target: *he likes playing darts; let's have a game of darts.* □ **(juego de) dardos**
darts match, competition at darts between two teams. □ **partida de dardos**
3 small tuck sewn into a garment to make it fit. □ **pinza**
4 quick rush: *he made a dart across the road.* □ **como una flecha**
■ *v.* to run fast: *she darted across the road without looking; she darted into the shop, bought a packet of sweets and darted out again.* □ **(ir) como una flecha**
dartboard *n.* round target at which darts are thrown. □ **diana**
dash [dæʃ] *n.* (*pl. dashes*) **1** small amount: *add a dash of mustard; a dash of colour.* □ **pizca**
2 little line: *the Morse Code is made up of dots and dashes.* □ **raya**
3 sudden rush: *he made a dash for the door.* □ **se precipitó hacia la puerta**
■ *v.* **1** to rush: *I must dash,* I am in a hurry. □ **correr**
2 *he dashed off a letter to the newspaper,* he wrote a letter very quickly. □ **escribir a toda prisa**
dashboard *n.* instrument panel in a car. □ **salpicadero**
dashing *adj.* very smart and energetic (person). □ **dinámico**
dastardly ['dɑːstədli] *adj.* cowardly and unpleasant. □ **ruin, vil**
data ['deitə] *n.* statistical information: *he has collected a lot of data; the data shows that a chemical change takes place.* □ **datos**
data processing *n.* analysis of statistical information using a computer. □ **proceso de datos**
date [deit] *n.* **1** number of a day, month or year: *what is the date today? what was the date of your driving test? do you know the date of the Battle of Hastings? give me Napoleon's dates,* tell me the years of his birth and death. □ **fecha**
2 ***up to date,*** recent: *the telephone directory is completely up to date; keep me up to date with your progress; he is bringing the book up to date,* he is revising the book to put in the most recent information. □ **actualizado, al día**

out of date, not modern: *the book is three years out of date.* □ **anticuado**
3 agreed meeting time: *I have a date with my dentist tomorrow; let's make a date for next Tuesday.* □ **hora; cita**
4 small, very sweet brown fruit of a date palm. □ **dátil**
■ *v.* **1** to write the number of the day on (something): *the letter is dated June 1st.* □ **fechar**
2 *Amer.* to agree to meet someone (of the opposite sex) at a particular time: *he is dating my sister,* he often meets my sister. □ **salir con**
3 *this house dates from the 16th century,* this house has existed since the 16th century; *this church dates back to the Roman period.* □ **datar**
4 *his style is beginning to date,* his style is beginning to seem old-fashioned. □ **pasarse de moda**
5 *that dates you,* that shows how old you are. □ **eso indica tu edad**
dated *adj.* old-fashioned. □ **anticuado**
dateless *adj.* with no date. □ **sin fecha**
date palm *n.* palm growing in desert countries which provides small, very sweet fruit. □ **palmera datilera**

daub [dɔːb] *n.* bad painting: *you expect me to pay $1,000 for that daub.* □ **pintarrajo**
■ *v.* to smear with paint/with mud, etc. □ **pintarrajear**

daughter ['dɔːtə] *n.* female child (of a parent). □ **hija**
daughter-in-law *n.* (*pl. daughters-in-law*) son's wife. □ **nuera**

daunt [dɔːnt] *v.* to discourage: *he was not in any way daunted by the task.* □ **desalentar**
nothing daunted, not frightened. □ **sin inmutarse**
dauntless *adj.* fearless. □ **intrépido**

davenport ['dævənpɔːt] *n.* **1** *Amer.* sofa/comfortable soft seat for two or more people. □ **sofá**
2 small writing desk. □ **escritorio**

davit ['dævit] *n.* (*on a ship*) small crane for lowering the lifeboats into the sea. □ **pescante**

dawdle ['dɔːdl] *v.* to walk slowly and aimlessly: *he was dawdling on his way to school.* □ **andar despacio**

dawn [dɔːn] *n.* **1** beginning of day, when the sun rises: *I must be up at dawn.* □ **amanecer**
the dawn chorus, singing of birds as the day breaks. □ **canto de la mañana**
2 beginning: *the dawn of civilization.* □ **albores**
■ *v.* **1** to begin: *a new era is dawning.* □ **alborear**
2 *at last it dawned on him that she was stealing his money,* at last he realized that she was stealing his money. □ **caer en la cuenta**

day [dei] *n.* **1** period of time lasting 24 hours: *there are 365 days in the year; June has 30 days; Christmas Day is the 25th day of December; what day of the month is it? the day before yesterday; the day after tomorrow; the day after my birthday.* □ **día**
every other day, once every two days. □ **cada dos días**
day after day, regularly for a long period: *day after day he would wait for the postman to come.* □ **día tras día**
day by day, progressively: *day by day the flood waters rose.* □ **día a día**
2 period of time from morning to night: *I have been working all day in the garden; he works a seven hour day; it will take me five days to finish; all day long the bulldozers worked on the demolition.* □ **día**
3 light: *the day was just breaking,* the light was just beginning to appear. □ **día**
4 ***a day,*** every day: *you must take your tablets twice a day; he drinks a bottle of milk a day.* □ **al día**
5 ***one day/some day,*** sometime in the future: *I hope to visit India one day; one day you will be grown up.* □ **algún día**
6 period (in the past): *in the days of the Romans; the good old days,* good times in the past; *in those days we lived in Denmark,* at that time. □ **tiempos, época**
daybreak *n.* early morning when the sun is about to rise: *I will have to be up at daybreak.* □ **amanecer**
daydream *n.* dream which you have during the day when you are not asleep. □ **sueño**
■ *v.* to think about other things; not to concentrate. □ **soñar despierto**
daylight *n.* and *adj.* **1** light of day: *the robbers attacked the train in broad daylight; daylight hours.* □ **luz del día**
2 *it's* ***daylight robbery,*** (*informal*) it's far too expensive. □ **es un robo a todas luces**
daytime *n.* ***in the daytime,*** during the day. □ **durante el día**
daytime flight, flight during the hours of daylight. □ **vuelo diurno**

daze [deiz] *n.* state of not being mentally alert: *after hearing the news, he wandered around in a daze.* □ **aturdimiento**
■ *v.* to make mentally unalert: *she was dazed by a blow on the head.* □ **aturdir**

dazzle ['dæzl] *v.* to blind (temporarily): *he was dazzled by the lights of the on-coming cars.* □ **cegar**
dazzling *adj.* very bright (light): *dazzling sunshine; dazzling lights of the city.* □ **cegador**

deacon ['diːkən] *n.* minor priest. □ **diácono**

dead [ded] *adj.* **1** not alive: *my grandparents are all dead; dead fish were floating in the river.* □ **muerto**
2 *the line went dead,* the telephone line stopped working. □ **...se cortó**
3 complete: *dead silence; the car came to a dead stop; he's a dead loss,* he's no good. □ **completo; total; en seco**
4 no longer used: *Latin is a dead language.* □ **(lengua) muerta**
■ *n.* **1** dead people: *the dead were piled by the side of the road.* □ **(los) muertos**
2 *at dead of night,* in the middle of the night. □ **en plena noche**
■ *adv.* **1** completely: *I'm dead tired; to go dead slow; the car stopped dead; we arrived dead on time.* □ **completamente; en seco; justo (a tiempo)**
2 exactly: *to go dead straight; you are dead right; the line is dead level.* □ **ir al grano; tienes toda la razón; a nivel**
dead and alive *adj.* small/uninteresting (town). □ **aburrido**
dead beat *adj.* (*informal*) tired out. □ **hecho polvo**
deaden *v.* to make (a sound) silent; to make (a blow) soft. □ **amortiguar**
dead end *n.* (street/way) leading nowhere. □ **callejón sin salida**
dead heat *n.* race where two people come in equal first. □ **empate**
deadline *n.* date by which something has to be done: *the deadline for finishing this work is Monday week.* □ **fecha tope, plazo**
deadlock *n.* state where two sides cannot agree: *the discussions soon reached a state of deadlock.* □ **punto muerto**
■ *v.* to (cause to) be unable to agree: *the two sides were deadlocked over clause three.* □ **estar en punto muerto**
deadly *adj.* (*deadlier, deadliest*) so strong as to kill: *deadly poison.* □ **mortal**

deadpan *adj.* not showing any emotion: *he paid the money with a deadpan expression.* □ **inexpresivo**

deaf [def] *adj.* unable to hear; having difficulty in hearing: *when you speak to Mr Jones you have to shout because he's deaf.* □ **sordo**
■ *n. **the deaf,*** people who cannot hear. □ **los sordos**
deaf-aid *n.* small device which helps a deaf person to hear. □ **audífono**
deafen *v.* to make deaf (by a loud noise). □ **ensordecer**
deafening *adj.* so loud as to make you deaf: *a deafening clap of thunder.* □ **ensordecedor**
deafness *n.* state of being deaf. □ **sordera**

deal [di:l] *n.* **1** large quantity or degree: *I have wasted a good deal of time; he made a great deal of money; he is a good deal better now,* he is much better now. □ **gran cantidad; mucho**
2 handing out (playing cards): *whose deal is it?,* whose turn is it to hand out the cards? □ **reparto**
3 (business) affair: *we made a deal to supply them with steel tubes.* □ **trato**
it's a deal!, it's agreed! □ **trato hecho**
4 wood from a pine tree. □ **madera de pino**
■ *v.* (*he dealt*) **1** to hand out: *he was dealing the cards; whose turn is it to deal? this will deal a blow to his hopes of promotion.* □ **repartir; dar**
2 to organize things to solve a problem: *do not worry about your luggage - I will deal with it; the housing problem is the worst one we have to deal with.* □ **ocuparse de**
3 to buy and sell: *he deals in secondhand furniture.* □ **tratar, comerciar**
dealer *n.* person who buys and sells: *he is a dealer in old silver.* □ **comerciante**
dealings *n. pl.* affairs: *have you had any dealings with a man called Small?* □ **tratos**

dean [di:n] *n.* person in charge of lecturers or priests. □ **deán**

dear ['diə] (*dearer, dearest*) **1** well liked; loved: *a very dear friend; dear old Mrs Jones; my dear James.* □ **querido**
2 (addressing someone at the beginning of a letter): *Dear Mr Smith; Dear Sir.* □ **Estimado...; Muy señor mío**
3 expensive: *oranges are dearer than apples; why do you always order the dearest thing on the menu?* □ **caro**
■ *interjection*: ***oh dear!,*** how annoying! □ **¡Dios mío!**
dearly *adv.* tenderly; very much: *he dearly loves his bottle of beer.* □ **cariñosamente, mucho**

dearth [də:θ] *n.* scarcity: *there is no dearth of apples this year.* □ **escasez**

death [deθ] *n.* act of dying: *his sudden death shocked his family; on the death of William I his son became King; I am sick to death of hearing your complaints.* □ **muerte**
death duty, tax paid on money left by dead person. □ **derechos de sucesión**
death rate, number of people who die (as a percentage of the population). □ **tasa de mortalidad**
deathbed *n.* bed on which someone is dying: *on his deathbed he forgave his son.* □ **lecho de muerte**
deathly *adv.* (*deathlier, deathliest*) **1** as if dead: *deathly pale.* □ **mortalmente**
2 *deathly hush,* complete silence. □ **silencio sepulcral**
deathtrap *n.* dangerous place: *this road junction is a real deathtrap.* □ **trampa mortal**

debâcle [dei'bɑ:kl] *n.* sudden defeat/collapse. □ **desastre**

debar [di'bɑ:] *v.* (*he debarred*) to forbid (someone to do something): *he was debarred from playing football for a month.* □ **prohibir**

debase [di'beis] *v.* to degrade; to reduce the value of (something): *to debase the coinage,* to reduce the value of the metal in coins. □ **degradar; alterar**

debate [di'beit] *n.* formal discussion: *we will hold a debate on women's rights.* □ **debate**
■ *v.* to discuss: *we debated the question 'can justice exist?'; they were debating whether to go to the beach.* □ **debatir**
debatable *adj.* not absolutely certain: *it is debatable whether there is life on Mars.* □ **discutible**

debauched [di'bɔ:tʃt] *adj.* (person) who spends his time in wild living and enjoys immoral pleasures. □ **libertino**
debauchery [di'bɔ:tʃəri] *n.* (*pl. debaucheries*) wild living. □ **libertinaje**

debenture [di'bentʃə] *n.* agreement to repay a debt, and to pay a fixed interest on it. □ **obligación**

debilitate [di'biliteit] *v.* to make weak. □ **debilitar**
debility *n.* weakness. □ **debilidad**

debit ['debit] *n.* (money) which is owed. □ **débito, debe**
on the debit side, against (a proposal). □ **contra**
■ *v.* to deduct money (from an account): *please debit my account with this sum.* □ **adeudar**

debonair [debə'nɛə] *adj.* carefree/ relaxed (air). □ **jovial**

debrief ['di:'bri:f] *v.* to ask someone questions to get all possible information about a job which he has done. □ **pedir cuentas**
debriefing *n.* getting information about a task (such as an air raid) which has just been finished. □ **petición de cuentas**

debris ['debri:] *n.* (*no pl.*) pieces (of a demolished building/crashed aircraft, etc.): *the ground was littered with debris after the explosion.* □ **escombros**

debt [det] *n.* **1** money owed to someone. □ **deuda**
2 *he is **in debt,*** he owes money. □ **tener deudas**
3 *he is **out of debt,*** he no longer owes any money. □ **no tener deudas**
debtor *n.* person who owes money. □ **deudor**

debunk [di'bʌŋk] *v.* (*informal*) to disprove: *he debunked the theory that men used to have tails.* □ **refutar**

debut ['deibju:] *n.* first appearance (of an artist/actor, etc.). □ **debut**

decade ['dekeid] *n.* period of ten years. □ **década**

decadence ['dekədəns] *n.* decline in moral values. □ **decadencia**
decadent *adj.* declining in moral values. □ **decadente**

decaffeinated [di:'kæfineitid] *adj.* (coffee) which has had the caffeine removed. □ **descafeinado**

decal ['di:kæl] *n. Amer.* sticker/piece of plastic or paper with a pattern or slogan which you can stick to a surface as a decoration. □ **pegatina**

decant [di'kænt] *v.* to pour liquid (especially wine) from a bottle into another container. □ **decantar**
decanter *n.* glass bottle which wine is poured into before serving. □ **frasca**

decapitate [di'kæpiteit] *v.* to cut off the head of (someone). □ **decapitar**

decathlon [di'kæθlən] *n.* sporting competition where each athlete has to compete in ten different types of sport. □ **decatlón**

decay [di'kei] *n.* falling into ruin; rotting. □ **descomposición**
dental decay, rotting of teeth. □ **caries**
■ *v.* to fall into ruin; to rot: *there was a smell of decaying vegetation.* □ **descomponerse**

decease [di'si:s] *n.* (*formal*) death. □ **fallecimiento**
deceased *n.* (*no pl.*) dead person. □ **difunto**
deceit [di'si:t] *n.* trickery: *he took all her money away by deceit.* □ **engaño**
deceitful *adj.* tricking. □ **engañoso**
deceive [di'si:v] *v.* to trick; to make (someone) believe something which is not true: *he deceived the bank manager completely.* □ **engañar**
December [di'sembə] *n.* twelfth month of the year: *Christmas Day is December 25th; his birthday is in December/is on December 4th.* □ **diciembre**
decent ['di:sənt] *adj.* **1** honest: *he is a decent sort of person.* □ **decente**
2 quite good: *you can get a decent meal there.* □ **bastante bueno, decente**
decency *n.* honour; good morals: *he had the decency to apologize.* □ **decencia**
decentralize [di:'sentrəlaiz] *v.* to move authority/offices, etc., from the centre. □ **descentralizar**
deception [di'sepʃn] *n.* fraud; making someone believe something which is not true. □ **engaño**
deceptive *adj.* not as it looks: *the distance is very deceptive,* it is further/nearer than it looks. □ **engañoso**
deceptively *adv.* in a way which deceives. □ **engañosamente**
decibel ['desibel] *n.* unit of measurement of noise. □ **decibelio**
decide [di'said] *v.* to make up your mind (to do something): *have you decided what to do yet? nothing has been decided; they decided to go home; he decided not to accept.* □ **decidir**
decided *adj.* **1** firm: *'no,' she said in a decided tone.* □ **decidido**
2 certain/obvious: *there is a decided difference between the two sorts of cheese.* □ **clara**
decidedly *adv.* **1** in a firm manner. □ **decididamente**
2 certainly: *it is decidedly embarrassing.* □ **claramente**
deciduous [di'sidjuəs] *adj.* (tree) which loses its leaves in winter. □ **de hoja caduca, caducifolio**
decimal ['desiml] *adj.* system of mathematics based on the number 10. □ **decimal**
decimal point, dot indicating the division between units and parts which are less than one unit (such as 2.05). □ **coma de decimales**
■ *n.* figure expressed on the base of 10: *a half is .5 in decimals.* □ **decimal**
decimate *v.* to remove one out of ten; to cut down/to remove/to kill in large numbers. □ **diezmar**
decipher [di'saifə] *v.* to make out something badly written, or written in code: *I can hardly decipher the address.* □ **descifrar**
decision [di'siʒn] *n.* making up your mind; ability to make up your mind: *the players argued with the referee's decision; the judge came to a decision very quickly,* made up his mind very quickly. □ **decisión**
decisive [di'saisiv] *adj.* which brings about a result: *a decisive battle,* battle which wins the war. □ **decisivo**
deck [dek] *n.* **1** floor (of ship/bus). □ **cubierta; piso**
below deck, inside a ship. □ **en la bodega**
flight deck, (i) control cabin (of plane). □ **cabina**
(ii) flat surface of an aircraft carrier where aircraft land and take off. □ **cubierta de aterrizaje**
2 *Amer.* pack (of playing cards). □ **baraja**
3 apparatus for playing records, tapes, cassettes. □ **cadena**
deckchair *n.* collapsible canvas chair (for sitting in the sun). □ **tumbona**
decked *adj.* decorated/covered with: *a table decked with flowers.* □ **engalanado**
deckle-edged [dekl'edʒd] *adj.* with a ragged/torn edge. □ **con borde de barbas**
declaim [di'kleim] *v.* to recite in a loud voice: *he was declaiming 'the Charge of the Light Brigade'.* □ **declamar**
declare [di'klɛə] *v.* to state (officially): *the chairman declared the meeting open; Britain declared war on Spain;* (at customs) *have you anything to declare?* □ **declarar**
declaration [dekla'reiʃn] *n.* **1** (official) statement. □ **declaración**
2 *customs declaration form,* paper on which you list items bought abroad and which may be subject to customs duty. □ **impreso de declaración**
decline [di'klain] *n.* downward trend: *the decline of the Roman Empire.* □ **decadencia**
■ *v.* **1** to refuse (an invitation). □ **declinar**
2 to become weaker. □ **debilitarse**
declutch [di'klʌtʃ] *v.* to disconnect the clutch in a car, etc., by pushing down the clutch pedal. □ **desembragar**
decode [di:'koud] *v.* to translate (a message) out of code. □ **descodificar**
decompose [di:kəm'pouz] *v.* to rot: *the road was lined with decomposing bodies.* □ **descomponer**
decompression [di:kəm'preʃn] *n.* reducing the pressure in something. □ **descompresión**
decompression chamber, room where divers stay to get used to normal pressures after working in very deep water. □ **cámara de...**
decongestant [di:kən'dʒestənt] *n.* medicine which unblocks, especially a blocked nose. □ **descongestivo**
decontaminate [di:kən'tæmineit] *v.* to remove infection/radioactivity from (something). □ **descontaminar**
decor ['deikɔ:] *n.* **1** scenery (for a play). □ **decorado**
2 interior decoration (of a room). □ **decoración**
decorate ['dekəreit] *v.* **1** to paint (building); to put new wallpaper in (a room); to put up flags/lights (to celebrate an occasion): *the square was decorated with Christmas trees.* □ **decorar**
2 to award (someone) a medal. □ **condecorar**
decorations [dekə'reiʃnz] *n. pl.* **1** flags/lights, etc., used to celebrate an occasion: *Christmas decorations.* □ **decoración**
2 medals. □ **condecoraciones**
decorator *n.* person who paints houses. □ **pintor (de brocha gorda)**
interior decorator, person who designs ways of decorating the inside of buildings. □ **decorador**
decorative ['dekərətiv] *adj.* pleasant to look at; serving as decoration. □ **decorativo**
decorum [di'kɔ:rʌm] *n.* being well-behaved. □ **decoro**
decorous ['dekərəs] *adj.* very well-behaved. □ **decoroso**
decoy ['di:kɔi] *n.* object to attract and trap something: *the policewoman acted as a decoy to trap the murderer; duck decoy,* wooden duck to attract ducks which can then be shot. □ **señuelo**
■ *v.* to attract and trap. □ **atraer**
decrease ['di:kri:s] *n.* fall: *the decrease in the cost of living; cigarette smoking is on the decrease,* is less frequent. □ **disminución**
■ *v.* to fall; to become less: *the exchange rate has decreased by 2%.* □ **disminuir**
decree [di'kri:] *n.* legal order which has not been

voted by Parliament: *presidential decree.* □ **decreto**
decree nisi/absolute decree, granting by a judge of a provisional/complete divorce. □ **sentencia provisional/definitiva de divorcio**
decrepit [di'krepit] *adj.* falling to pieces; old and feeble (person). □ **decrépito**
decrepitude *n.* state of being decrepit. □ **decrepitud**
dedicate ['dedikeit] *v.* to place (a church) under the patronage of a saint; to write a book for/to offer a book to someone; to spend (all your life) on something: *the church is dedicated to St Francis; he dedicated his life to the service of the poor; she dedicated the book of poems to her brother.* □ **dedicar**
dedication [dedi'keiʃn] *n.* **1** devotion: *he looked after his wife with dedication.* □ **dedicación**
2 inscription at the beginning of a book showing to whom it is dedicated. □ **dedicatoria**
deduce [di'dju:s] *v.* to conclude (from examining evidence). □ **deducir**
deduct [di'dʌkt] *v.* to remove (from a sum of money): *I am going to deduct 10% from your salary.* □ **deducir**
deduction [di'dʌkʃn] *n.* **1** something which is deduced; conclusion. □ **deducción**
2 something which is deducted; sum of money which is taken away. □ **deducción**
deed [di:d] *n.* **1** (noble) act: *the knight performed many brave deeds.* □ **hazaña**
2 legal document: *the deeds of a house,* papers showing who owns the house. □ **escritura**
deem [di:m] *v.* (*formal*) to consider: *I deem it an honour to be asked to speak to you today.* □ **considerar**
deep [di:p] *adj.* (*deeper, deepest*) **1** which goes down a long way: *be careful if you can't swim, the river is very deep; this is the deepest coalmine in Europe; he dived into the deep end of the swimming pool; she gave a deep sigh.* □ **profundo**
2 rich/dark: *deep brown.* □ **oscuro**
3 low-pitched/bass (voice). □ **bajo**
■ *adv.* a long way down: *the mine went deep into the ground.* □ **profundamente**
■ *n.* ***the deep,*** the sea. □ **el mar, piélago**
deepen *v.* to go further down; to become deeper; to make (something) deeper: *they felt the deepening gloom.* □ **profundizar**
deep-freeze *n.* refrigerator for freezing food and keeping it frozen. □ **congelador**
deeply *adv.* profoundly; very much: *I deeply regret the way I behaved.* □ **profundamente**
deep-rooted *adj.* which goes down a long way. □ **profundamente arraigado**
deep-seated *adj.* solid/firm: *deep-seated suspicion.* □ **sólido**
deer [diə] *n.* (*pl. deer*) wild animal which runs fast, and of which the male usually has horns: *a herd of deer.* □ **ciervo**
deface [di'feis] *v.* to spoil the surface of (something); to write on (a wall); to mutilate (a statue). □ **desfigurar**
de facto [di:'fæktou] *adj.* existing in fact/real: *a de facto government.* □ **de hecho**
defamation [defə'meiʃn] *n. defamation of character,* saying bad things about someone. □ **difamación**
defamatory [di'fæmətri] *adj.* which says bad things about someone. □ **difamatorio**
default [di'fɔ:lt] *n.* **1** failing to carry out the terms of a contract. □ **incumplimiento**
2 *he won the game by default,* because his opponent withdrew. □ **...por no presentarse su adversario**
3 ***in default of*** *payment,* since payment has not been made. □ **por falta de pago**
■ *v.* to fail to carry out the terms of a contract: *he defaulted on his hire purchase payments.* □ **incumplir**
defaulter *n.* person who defaults; (*in the army*) soldier who is being punished. □ **persona que incumple; militar culpable de una ofensa militar**
defeat [di'fi:t] *n.* loss (of battle/vote): *the defeat of the English at the Battle of Hastings; the Government had another defeat over its pay policy.* □ **derrota**
■ *v.* to beat (someone in a battle/vote): *the candidate was defeated in the election; Napoleon was defeated at the Battle of Waterloo; Wales defeated Scotland in the international rugby match.* □ **derrotar**
defeatism *n.* feeling sure that you will lose. □ **derrotismo**
defeatist *adj.* sure that you will lose. □ **derrotista**
defecate ['defəkeit] *v.* to pass waste matter from the bowels. □ **defecar**
defect ['di:fekt] *n.* fault: *there is a defect in the car's steering system.* □ **defecto**
■ *v.* to leave (the army/your country); to go over to the enemy side. □ **desertar**
defection *n.* going over to the side of the enemy. □ **deserción**
defective *adj.* faulty: *the police found that the car's brakes were defective.* □ **defectivo**
defector *n.* person who leaves his country to go to an enemy country. □ **desertor**
defence [di'fens] *Amer.* **defense** *n.* **1** protection: *they built strong defences round the town; we must spend more on defence.* □ **defensa**
2 *the defence,* lawyers who speak on behalf of an accused person. □ **la defensa**
defenceless *adj.* unprotected. □ **indefenso**
defensive *adj.* which protects: *defensive weapons.* □ **defensivo**
■ *n. he is always* ***on the defensive,*** he feels he always has to justify himself. □ **a la defensiva**
defend [di'fend] *v.* **1** to protect (from attack): *the frontier is defended by two armies.* □ **defender**
2 to speak on behalf of (an accused person): *he is being defended by two lawyers.* □ **defender**
defendant *n.* person who is accused of doing something illegal/person who is sued in a civil law suit. □ **acusado**
defensible *adj.* which can be defended. □ **defendible**
defer [di'fə:] *v.* (*he deferred*) **1** to put off/to put back: *the decision has been deferred until next week.* □ **aplazar**
2 ***defer to*** *someone/to someone's opinion,* to accept the advice of someone who knows better. □ **remitirse a**
deference ['defərəns] *n.* respect. □ **deferencia**
deferential *adj.* respectful. □ **respetuoso**
deferment *n.* postponement. □ **aplazamiento**
defiance [di'faiəns] *n.* acting against (law/authority): *defiance of the law.* □ **desafío**
defiant *adj.* very proud and antagonistic. □ **desafiante**
deficiency [di'fiʃənsi] *n.* (*pl. deficiencies*) lack: *the baby is suffering from vitamin deficiency.* □ **falta**
deficient *adj.* **1** lacking (something): *the diet is deficient in vitamins.* □ **deficiente**
2 *mentally deficient,* below normal intelligence. □ **deficiente mental**
deficit ['defisit] *n.* amount by which expenditure is larger than receipts (in a firm's/a country's accounts). □ **déficit**

defile ['di:fail] *n.* narrow pass between mountains. □ **desfiladero**
■ *v.* to dirty/to pollute. □ **ensuciar**
define [di'fain] *v.* **1** to explain clearly: *'love' is a difficult word to define.* □ **definir**
2 to state the boundary of something: *well defined limits.* □ **determinar**
definite ['definət] *adj.* very clear: *I want you to give me a definite answer.* □ **claro**
definite article, 'the' (as opposed to the indefinite article, 'a' or 'an'). □ **definido**
definitely *adv.* certainly: *I'm definitely not going to the theatre.* □ **claramente**
definition [defi'niʃn] *n.* **1** clear explanation (of a word). □ **definición**
2 clearness (of a picture). □ **claridad**
definitive [di'finitiv] *adj.* final/which cannot be improved: *a definitive history of the Second World War.* □ **definitivo**
deflate [di'fleit] *v.* **1** to let the air out of a tyre. □ **desinflar**
2 to reduce the inflation in the economy. □ **deflacionar**
deflation [di'fleiʃn] *n.* reducing the inflation of the economy. □ **deflación**
deflect [di'flekt] *v.* to turn aside (an arrow/a bullet, etc.). □ **desviar**
deformed [di'fɔ:md] *adj.* badly shaped. □ **deforme**
deformity *n.* (*pl. deformities*) badly shaped part of the body. □ **deformidad**
defraud [di'frɔ:d] *v.* to cheat: *he was defrauded of all his money.* □ **defraudar**
defray [di'frei] *v. to defray the costs,* to pay the costs. □ **sufragar**
defreeze [di:'fri:z] *v.* to thaw (frozen food). □ **descongelar**
defrost [di:'frɔst] *v.* to melt the ice on (the inside of a refrigerator). □ **descongelar**
deft [deft] *adj.* very agile/clever (with your hands). □ **diestro**
defunct [di'fʌŋkt] *adj.* dead (person); (law) which is no longer applied. □ **difunto (persona); que no se aplica ya (ley)**
defuse [di:'fju:z] *v.* **1** to take the fuse out of (a bomb) so that it cannot explode. □ **desactivar**
2 *to defuse the situation,* to make a situation less tense. □ **quitar hierro al asunto**
defy [di'fai] *v.* (*defied; defying*) **1** to refuse to obey (law): *he defied the policeman's order.* □ **desafiar**
2 to challenge someone to do something: *he defied me to phone the police.* □ **retar**
3 to present great difficulty: *it defies description.* □ **resistirse a**
degenerate [di'dʒenerət] *adj.* which has degenerated/become depraved. □ **degenerado**
■ *v.* **1** to become depraved. □ **degenerar**
2 to get worse. □ **empeorar**
degrading [di'greidiŋ] *adj.* lowering; which humiliates/which makes a person like an animal: *what a degrading spectacle!* □ **degradante**
degradation [degrə'deiʃn] *n.* becoming like an animal. □ **degradación**
degree [di'gri:] *n.* **1** scientific division of an angle or scale: *a circle has 360 degrees; this taxi can turn in 180 degrees; the temperature is 20 degrees centigrade (20 °C).* □ **grado**
2 level; amount. □ **etapa; nivel**
to a certain degree, to some extent. □ **hasta cierto punto**
3 diploma (of a university): *he has a degree in American history.* □ **título**
dehydrate [dihai'dreit] *v.* to remove water from (something). □ **deshidratar**
deice [di:'ais] *v.* to remove the ice (from something). □ **deshelar**
deify ['deiifai] *v.* to make something/someone into a god. □ **deificar**
deign [dein] *v.* to condescend (to do something): *he did not deign to reply.* □ **dignarse a**
deity ['deiiti] *n.* (*pl. deities*) god. □ **deidad**
dejected [di'dʒektid] *adj.* depressed/unhappy: *he had a very dejected look when he failed his examinations.* □ **abatido**
dejectedly *adv.* in a gloomy way. □ **con abatimiento**
dejection [di'dʒekʃn] *n.* gloom/depression. □ **abatimiento**
delay [di'lei] *n.* time during which one is late: *after a delay of twenty minutes; I am sorry for the delay in answering your letter.* □ **retraso**
■ *v.* to make late; to wait; to put off until later: *the plane was delayed by fog.* □ **demorarse**
delayed-action bomb, bomb which goes off some time after it has been dropped or set. □ **bomba de acción retardada**
delectable [di'lektəbl] *adj.* very pleasant; very attractive. □ **delicioso**
delegate ['deligət] *n.* person who represents others at a meeting. □ **delegado**
■ *v.* ['deligeit] to pass (authority/responsibility) on to a subordinate. □ **delegar**
delegation [deli'geiʃn] *n.* **1** group of representatives. □ **delegación**
2 passing of authority to a subordinate. □ **delegación**
delete [di'li:t] *v.* to cross out (a word). □ **tachar**
deletion *n.* word/phrase which has been crossed out. □ **supresión**
deliberate [di'liberət] *adj.* **1** done on purpose: *this was a deliberate attempt to kill the president.* □ **deliberado**
2 slow and thoughtful (speech/manner). □ **premeditado**
■ *v.* [di'libəreit] to debate/to discuss. □ **deliberar**
deliberately *adv.* **1** on purpose: *he deliberately set fire to the shed.* □ **deliberadamente**
2 slowly and thoughtfully. □ **premeditadamente**
deliberation [dilibə'reiʃn] *n.* **1** thought; consideration: *after due deliberation.* □ **reflexión**
2 *the deliberations of a meeting,* the debate/discussion. □ **deliberación**
delicacy ['delikəsi] *n.* (*pl. delicacies*) **1** sensitivity. □ **delicadeza**
2 state of being delicate. □ **delicadeza**
3 rare thing to eat. □ **manjar exquisito**
delicate *adj.* **1** easily damaged; very thin: *be careful with these glasses, they are very delicate; if you use a thin brush you can draw very delicate lines.* □ **delicado**
2 liable to get illnesses: *a delicate state of health.* □ **delicado**
3 very fine: *delicate carving.* □ **fino, delicado**
delicately *adv.* with care. □ **delicadamente**
delicatessen [delikə'tesn] *n.* shop selling cold meat and foreign food, etc. □ **'delicatessen'**
delicious [di'liʃəs] *adj.* which tastes very good: *the ice cream is delicious.* □ **delicioso**
delight [di'lait] *n.* pleasure: *he takes delight in showing me my mistakes; our cat's greatest delight is sleeping in front of the fire.* □ **deleite (encantar)**
■ *v.* to take pleasure: *he delights in being rude to women.* □ **deleitarse, encantar**

delighted *adj.* very pleased: *she was delighted with her present; I shall be delighted to come to your party.* □ **encantado**
delightful *adj.* very pleasant. □ **encantador**
delineate [di'linieit] *v.* to draw. □ **delinear**
delinquency [di'liŋkwənsi] *n.* minor crime. □ **delincuencia**
juvenile delinquency, crimes committed by young people. □ **delincuencia juvenil**
delinquent *adj.* and *n.* criminal. □ **delincuente**
delirious [di'liriəs] *adj.* mad with fever/with happiness. □ **delirante**
delirium *n.* madness caused by fever. □ **delirio**
deliver [di'livə] *v.* **1** to bring (something) to someone: *the postman delivers the mail; can you deliver a message for me?* □ **entregar**
2 to make (a speech): *he delivered an attack on the Government,* in a speech he attacked the Government. □ **pronunciar**
3 *to deliver a baby,* to help the mother give birth. □ **dar a luz**
delivery *n.* (*pl. deliveries*) **1** bringing something to someone: *the next postal delivery is at 10 o'clock.* □ **entrega**
cash on delivery, payment for goods when they are delivered. □ **pago a la entrega**
2 birth (of a child). □ **parto**
delphinium [del'finiəm] *n.* garden plant with tall blue flowers. □ **espuela de caballero**
delta ['deltə] *n.* land around the mouth of a river made of mud brought by the river. □ **delta**
delta wing aircraft, with wings forming a triangle. □ **con ala delta**
delude [di'lju:d] *v.* to make someone believe something which is wrong: *do not delude yourself.* □ **engañar**
delusion [di'lu:ʒn] *n.* wrong belief: *he was under the delusion that she loved him,* he believed wrongly that she loved him. □ **engaño; ilusión**
deluge ['delju:dʒ] *n.* flood. □ **diluvio**
■ *v.* to flood: *the office was deluged with inquiries.* □ **inundar**
de luxe [di'lʌks] *adj.* very expensive; of very high quality: *we can't afford the de luxe model.* □ **de lujo**
delve [delv] *v.* to dig (into the past/into archives, etc.). □ **indagar**
demagogue ['deməgɔg] *n.* politician who appeals to the crowd for support. □ **demagogo**
demand [di'mɑ:nd] *n.* **1** asking for something. □ **petición**
2 *this book is in great demand,* people often ask for this book. □ **demanda**
final demand, last reminder that you must pay a bill. □ **última reclamación**
■ *v.* to ask insistently for something: *she demanded an apology; he demanded to see the manager.* □ **exigir**
demanding *adj.* (job) which takes up much time and energy. □ **absorbente**
demarcation [di:mɑ:'keiʃn] *n.* showing of boundaries. □ **demarcación**
demarcation dispute, dispute between workers over who should be responsible for a certain type of work. □ **conflicto de atribuciones**
demean [di'mi:n] *v.* ***to demean yourself,*** to make yourself appear undignified or contemptible. □ **rebajarse**
demeanour [di'mi:nə] *n.* behaviour/manner. □ **proceder**
demented [di'mentid] *adj.* mad. □ **demente**
demerara [demə'rɛərə] *n.* type of coarse brown sugar. □ **azúcar terciado**
demilitarized [di:'militəraizd] *adj.* (zone) which has no armed forces in it. □ **desmilitarizado**
demise [di'maiz] *n.* (*formal*) death. □ **defunción**
demister [di:'mistə] *n.* blower (on a car) to prevent the windows misting up. □ **antivaho**
demobilize [di:'moubilaiz] *v.* to release (someone) from the armed forces. □ **desmovilizar**
democracy [di'mɔkrəsi] *n.* (*pl. democracies*) system of government by freely elected representatives of the people: *Great Britain and the USA are democracies.* □ **democracia**
democrat ['deməkræt] *n.* person who believes in democracy. □ **demócrata**
democratic [demə'krætik] *adj.* referring to democracy. □ **democrático**
demography [di'mɔgrəfi] *n.* study of population figures. □ **demografía**
demographic *adj.* referring to population figures. □ **demográfico**
demolish [di'mɔliʃ] *v.* to knock down: *the workmen demolished several houses to make way for the new road.* □ **demoler**
demolition [demə'liʃn] *n.* knocking down: *the new town plan involved the demolition of some shops.* □ **demolición**
demon ['di:mən] *n.* devil. □ **demonio**
demonstrate ['demənstreit] *v.* **1** to show: *I will demonstrate how the car works.* □ **demostrar**
2 to form a crowd to protest against something. □ **manifestarse**
demonstrable *adj.* which can be demonstrated. □ **demostrable**
demonstration [demən'streiʃn] *n.* **1** showing: *the salesman gave a demonstration of the new hair dryer.* □ **demostración**
2 march to protest against something; crowd which is protesting against something: *the police broke up the anti-government demonstration.* □ **manifestación**
demonstrator *n.* person who marches/who forms part of a crowd to protest against something. □ **manifestante**
demonstrative [di'mɔnstrətiv] *adj.* (person) who shows his feelings openly. □ **expansivo**
demoralize [di'mɔrəlaiz] *v.* to lower the morale/confidence of (someone). □ **desmoralizar**
demoralization [dimɔrəlai'zeiʃn] *n.* lowering of morale. □ **desmoralización**
demoralized *adj.* doubtful that you can win: *the demoralized soldiers ran away from the battle.* □ **desmoralizado**
demote [di:'mout] *v.* to give (someone) a less important job. □ **degradar**
demur [di'mə:] *v.* (*he demurred*) to object (to something). □ **poner pegas (a algo)**
demure [di'mjuə] *adj.* quiet and serious (girl). □ **recatada**
den [den] *n.* **1** place to hide away in: *a lion's den.* □ **guarida**
2 (*informal*) small room where you can hide away to work. □ **estudio**
denial [di'naiəl] *n.* statement that something is not right: *the Government issued a denial of the newspaper report.* □ **mentís**
denigrate ['denigreit] *v.* to say that something is worse than it is. □ **denigrar**
denim ['denim] *n.* thick cotton cloth. □ **dril; mahón**
denims, clothes made of this cloth. □ **tela vaquera**

denizen ['denizən] *n.* (*formal*) inhabitant of a particular place. □ **habitante**
Denmark ['denmɑ:k] *n.* country in Northern Europe. □ **Dinamarca**
denomination [dinɔmi'neiʃn] *n.* **1** unit of money (on a banknote/coin). □ **valor**
2 religious sect; church. □ **secta, confesión**
denominational *adj.* belonging to a particular sect. □ **sectario; confesional**
denominator [di'nɔmineitə] *n.* figure beneath the line in a fraction. □ **denominador**
denote [di'nout] *v.* (*formal*) to mean. □ **denotar**
denounce [di'nauns] *v.* to blame/to accuse (someone/something) openly: *he was denounced to the police by his accomplices.* □ **denunciar**
dense [dens] *adj.* (*denser, densest*) **1** very thick; crowded together: *we drove in dense fog.* □ **denso**
2 stupid. □ **duro de mollera**
densely *adv.* thickly: *the South of England is a densely populated area.* □ **densamente**
density *n.* (*pl. densities*) **1** physical degree of mass per unit of volume: *what is the density of uranium?* □ **densidad**
2 *Hong Kong has a high density of population,* Hong Kong has many people per unit of area. □ **densidad**
dent [dent] *n.* slight hollow (as made by a blow): *he hit the car with a stick and made a dent in the bonnet.* □ **abolladura**
■ *v.* to make a slight hollow (in something): *he hit a tree and dented the rear bumper.* □ **abollar**
dentist ['dentist] *n.* person who looks after teeth: *my teeth are hurting again - I must go to the dentist.* □ **dentista**
dental *adj.* referring to teeth. □ **dental**
dental surgery, dentist's office. □ **consulta de dentista**
dentistry *n.* work of a dentist. □ **odontología**
dentures ['dentʃəz] *n. pl.* false teeth. □ **dentadura postiza**
denude [di'nju:d] *v.* to make (something) bare; to remove all the covering from (something). □ **despojar**
denunciation [dinʌnsi'eiʃn] *n.* public accusation/blame. □ **denuncia**
deny [di'nai] *v.* (*denied; denying*) to state that something is not correct: *he denied that he had stolen the car; he denied stealing the car; I don't deny it,* I admit it. □ **negar**
deodorant [di'oudərənt] *n.* preparation which removes unpleasant smells. □ **desodorante**
deodorize *v.* to remove unpleasant smells from (something). □ **desodorizar**
depart [di'pɑ:t] *v.* to go away: *the plane was ready to depart.* □ **partir**
departed *n.* ***the departed,*** the dead. □ **el difunto**
departure [di'pɑ:tʃə] *n.* leaving: *when is your departure time? arrivals and departures.* □ **salida**
departure lounge, large waiting room at an airport for passengers about to leave. □ **sala de embarque**
department [di'pɑ:tmənt] *n.* section of a large organization: *if you want to buy cheese, you must go to the food department; the accounts department looks after money; she teaches in the French department in the local school.* □ **departamento**
department store, large shop with many different sections. □ **grandes almacenes**
Department of Education, government ministry dealing with education. □ **Ministerio de Educación**
depend [di'pend] *v.* **1** to be decided according to something: *whether she goes to university depends on her exam results.* □ **depender**
that depends, that may or may not be true: *I don't know if I'll go to the party - that all depends.* □ **eso depende**
2 to rely on: *I'm depending on you to help me.* □ **contar con**
dependable *adj.* that can be relied on. □ **fiable**
dependant *n.* member of family supported by another. □ **persona a cargo**
dependency *n.* (*pl. dependencies*) country which is ruled by another. □ **posesión; colonia**
dependent *adj.* supported by someone else; relying on someone else: *dependent relatives.* □ **dependiente**
depict [di'pikt] *v.* to show. □ **representar**
depilatory [di'pilətri] *adj.* and *n.* (substance) which removes hair from the body. □ **depilatorio**
deplete [di'pli:t] *v.* to run down/to use up (stores). □ **agotar**
deplore [di'plɔ:] *v.* to be extremely sorry that something has happened; to dislike an action/an attitude: *I deplore his statement to the crowd.* □ **deplorar**
deplorable *adj.* very bad: *deplorable behaviour.* □ **deplorable**
deploy [di'plɔi] *v.* to spread out (soldiers, etc.) so that they can fight effectively. □ **desplegar**
depopulate [di:'pɔpjuleit] *v.* to reduce the number of people living in an area: *the slump in agricultural prices has depopulated the whole countryside.* □ **despoblar**
deport [di'pɔ:t] *v.* to expel (someone) from a country. □ **deportar**
deportation [di:pɔ:'teiʃn] *n.* expulsion (of a foreigner). □ **deportación**
deportment *n.* way of walking/sitting. □ **movimientos, porte**
depose [di'pouz] *v.* **1** to force (someone) to leave his position; to force (a king, etc.) to give up his office. □ **deponer**
2 to state (in court). □ **declarar**
deposition [depə'ziʃn] *n.* **1** forcing someone to leave their position. □ **deposición**
2 statement (by a witness). □ **declaración**
deposit [di'pɔzit] *n.* **1** placing money (in a bank); giving money to secure something you want to buy: *if you leave a deposit, we will keep the watch until you have enough money to pay for it.* □ **depósito**
deposit account, bank account where you leave money for some time to earn interest. □ **cuenta de depósito**
2 mineral layer (in the ground); sediment/chemical left at the bottom of a container. □ **depósito**
■ *v.* to put (money) in a bank. □ **depositar**
depositor *n.* person with money in a bank. □ **depositante**
depository *n.* place for storing furniture, etc. □ **almacén, guardamuebles**
depot ['depou] *n.* central warehouse; central garage; central barracks for a regiment: *bus depot.* □ **almacén; parque móvil; depósito; cochera**
depraved [di'preivd] *adj.* corrupted/wicked. □ **depravado**
depravity [di'prævitі] *n.* state of living a wicked life. □ **depravación**
deprecate ['deprəkeit] *v.* to disapprove of: *I deprecate his rudeness.* □ **desaprobar**
depreciate [di'pri:ʃieit] *v.* to lose value. □ **depreciar**
depreciation [dipriʃi'eiʃn] *n.* regular loss in value. □ **depreciación**
depredation [deprə'deiʃn] *n.* attack/ruining. □ **estragos**
depress [di'pres] *v.* **1** to make miserable. □ **deprimir**
2 to push down (a button). □ **apretar**

depressed *adj.* miserable: *I am feeling depressed.* □ **deprimido**
depressing *adj.* gloomy: *what depressing weather!* □ **deprimente**
depression [di'preʃn] *n.* **1** miserable feeling: *she got into a state of depression.* □ **depresión**
2 low pressure area bringing bad weather. □ **depresión**
3 economic crisis. □ **depresión**
4 hollow (in the ground). □ **depresión, hondonada**

deprive [di'praiv] *v.* to take something away from someone: *he has been deprived of the right to see his family.* □ **privar**
deprivation [depri'veiʃn] *n.* being deprived of something. □ **privación**
deprived *adj.* (person) who has not enjoyed any of society's benefits. □ **desheredado**

depth [depθ] *n.* **1** how deep something is; distance downwards: *what is the depth of the pool at the deep end?* □ **profundidad**
out of one's depth: *I'm out of my depth,* (i) the water is too deep for me to stand up. □ **no hago pie**
(ii) it is too complicated for me to understand. □ **no entiendo nada**
depth charge, large bomb which explodes under water. □ **carga de profundidad**
2 very deep point. □ **abismo**
3 *in the depths of winter,* in the middle of winter; *the depths of the forest.* □ **lo más crudo del invierno**

deputation [depju'teiʃn] *n.* group of people who speak on behalf of others: *the deputation of union leaders met the president.* □ **delegación**
depute *n.* (*in Scotland*) deputy. □ **delegado**
■ *v.* to give responsibility to someone: *he was deputed to speak to the visitors.* □ **delegar**
deputize ['depjutaiz] *v.* to stand in for someone: *he deputized for me in my absence.* □ **sustituir**
deputy ['depjuti] *n.* (*pl. deputies*) person who can take the place of another person: *deputy mayor; deputy chairman.* □ **delegado; teniente de alcalde; vicepresidente**

derail [di'reil] *v.* to make (a train) leave the rails: *the train was derailed by a concrete post on the line.* □ **descarrilar, hacer descarrilar**
derailment *n.* leaving the rails. □ **descarrilamiento**

deranged [di'reinʒd] *adj.* mad. □ **trastornado**

derby ['dɑːbi] *n.* **1** sporting contest between local teams. □ **derby**
2 *Amer.* round-topped man's hat. □ **hongo**

derelict ['derəlikt] *adj.* ruined and abandoned. □ **abandonado**
dereliction [derə'likʃən] *n.* neglecting (to do your duty). □ **negligencia**

derestricted [diːri'striktid] *adj.* (road) with no speed limit. □ **sin límite de velocidad**

deride [di'raid] *v.* to laugh at (someone). □ **mofarse de**
derision [di'riʒn] *n.* mockery. □ **irrisión, mofa**
derisive *adj.* mocking: *derisive laughter.* □ **burlón**
derisory [di'raizəri] *adj.* laughable: *a derisory sum of money.* □ **irrisorio**

derive [di'raiv] *v.* to come originally from something: *his income is derived from interest on his savings; the word 'school' is derived from the Latin word 'schola'.* □ **derivar**
derivation [deri'veiʃn] *n.* origin (of a word). □ **derivación**
derivative [di'rivətiv] *n.* thing which is derived: *what are the derivatives of carbon dioxide?* □ **derivado**

dermatitis [dəːmə'taitis] *n.* disease of the skin. □ **dermatitis**

derogatory [di'rɔgətri] *adj.* showing contempt. □ **despectivo**

derrick ['derik] *n.* large metal construction (like a crane). □ **estructura metálica (grúa)**
oil derrick, metal frame which holds the drilling equipment for an oil well. □ **torre de perforación**

derv [dəːv] *n.* fuel used in diesel engines. □ **gasóleo**

descant ['deskænt] *n.* musical part which is played/sung much higher than the rest. □ **contrapunto**

descend [di'send] *v.* **1** to go down (a staircase, etc.). □ **descender**
2 *he is descended from Queen Victoria,* Queen Victoria is one of his ancestors. □ **desciende de...**
3 ***to descend upon someone,*** to attack: *my aunt descended on us last week,* (*informal*) came to stay with us unexpectedly. □ **caer sobre**
descendant *n.* person whose family goes back to a certain ancestor: *the descendants of the Pilgrim Fathers.* □ **descendiente**
descent *n.* **1** going down. □ **descenso**
2 *he is of Irish descent,* his family was Irish. □ **descendencia**

describe [di'skraib] *v.* to say what something/someone is like: *can you describe the man who attacked you?* □ **describir**
description [di'skripʃn] *n.* picture in words of what something is like: *she gave a description of the car which had been stolen.* □ **descripción**
descriptive *adj.* which says what something is like: *a descriptive passage in a novel.* □ **descriptivo**

desecrate ['desikreit] *v.* to use (a church, a grave) in a disrespectful way. □ **profanar**

desert ['dezət] *adj.* and *n.* very dry, usually sandy (place): *the Sahara Desert in North Africa; a desert island.* □ **desierto**
■ *v.* [di'zəːt] to leave the armed forces without permission; to leave someone alone. □ **desertar, abandonar**
deserted *adj.* abandoned; with no inhabitants: *deserted castle; deserted village.* □ **abandonado**
deserter *n.* person who leaves the armed forces without permission. □ **desertor**

deserve [di'zəːv] *v.* to merit (something): *he deserved to be punished.* □ **merecer**
deservedly [di'zəːvidli] *adv.* in a way which is right: *he was quite deservedly awarded a medal for bravery.* □ **merecidamente**
deserving *adj.* which ought to be supported/helped: *a deserving cause.* □ **meritorio**

desiccate ['desikeit] *v.* **1** to dry. □ **desecar**
2 *dessicated coconut,* dried coconut, used in cooking. □ **coco rallado**

design [di'zain] *n.* plan; drawing of something, before it is constructed: *design for a new house; this is the latest in car design; there is something wrong with the design of this machine.* □ **diseño**
■ *v.* to plan (something): *the architect designed a new school; the conference is designed to unite the two groups.* □ **diseñar, concebir**
designer *n.* artist who plans something: *dress designer.* □ **diseñador**
interior designer, person who plans ways of decorating the interior of houses. □ **decorador**

designate ['dezigneit] *v.* to appoint someone (to a post). □ **designar, nombrar**
■ *adj.* who has been appointed but has not started work: *the ambassador-designate.* □ **nombrado**

desire [di'zaiə] *n.* want: *I have a great desire to travel.* □ **deseo**

■ *v.* to want. □ **desear**
it leaves a lot to be desired, it is not satisfactory. □ **deja mucho que desear**
desirability *n.* being desirable. □ **atractivo**
desirable *adj.* which a lot of people want. □ **deseable**
desist [di'sist] *v.* (*formal*) to stop doing something. □ **dejar de**
desk [desk] *n.* table for writing: *my desk is covered with papers.* □ **escritorio**
cash desk, place where you pay for what you have bought. □ **caja**
desolate ['desələt] *adj.* bleak/inhospitable (place). □ **desolado**
desolation [desə'leiʃn] *n.* bleakness; ruin (of a place): *after the war there were scenes of total desolation.* □ **desolación**
despair [di'spɛə] *n.* hopelessness: *I am driven to despair,* I have lost all hope; *in despair she went to the police,* because she had given up all hope of finding a solution she went to the police. □ **desesperación**
■ *v. he despaired of ever being rescued,* he had given up all hope of being rescued. □ **perder la esperanza**
desperate ['desprət] *adj.* **1** hopeless: *his condition is desperate.* □ **desesperado**
2 wild (through being in despair): *a desperate attempt to escape from prison.* □ **desesperado**
desperately *adv.* urgently; wildly: *he desperately wants to get a job.* □ **desesperadamente**
desperation [despə'reiʃn] *n.* hopelessness: *in desperation, he phoned the police/he phoned the police out of sheer desperation,* because he didn't know what else to do. □ **desesperación**
despicable [di'spikəbl] *adj.* worthless/which you can look down on. □ **despreciable**
despise [di'spaiz] *v.* to look down on/to think (someone) is not worth much. □ **despreciar**
despite [di'spait] *prep.* in spite of: *despite the weather, we will still be playing football tomorrow.* □ **a pesar de**
despondency [di'spɔndənsi] *n.* (*no pl.*) discouragement: *he had a fit of despondency,* he felt discouraged. □ **desánimo**
despondent *adj.* discouraged: *our team was very despondent after they lost the game.* □ **desanimado**
despot ['despɔt] *n.* tyrant/dictator. □ **déspota**
despotic *adj.* like a dictator. □ **despótico**
despotism *n.* tyranny/dictatorship. □ **despotismo**
dessert [di'zə:t] *n.* sweet course (in a meal): *what have we got for dessert?* □ **postre**
dessert spoon, spoon for eating dessert. □ **cuchara de postre**
destination [desti'neiʃn] *n.* place a person/vehicle is going to: *what is your destination?,* where are you travelling to? □ **destino**
destine ['destin] *v.* to aim someone in a certain direction: *his son is destined to go to university,* his intention is that his son will go to university. □ **destinar**
destiny *n.* (*pl. destinies*) what may happen in the future: *what does destiny have in store for us?,* what is going to happen to us in the future? *her destiny was to die young.* □ **destino**
destitute ['destitju:t] *adj.* with no money or belongings: *he is utterly destitute.* □ **indigente**
destroy [di'strɔi] *v.* to remove/to kill/to ruin completely: *the bombs destroyed the centre of the town.* □ **destruir**
destroyer *n.* medium-sized naval ship. □ **destructor**
destruction [di'strʌkʃn] *n.* complete ruining: *the destruction caused by the Great Fire of London.* □ **destrucción**
destructive [di'strʌktiv] *adj.* **1** which destroys. □ **destructivo**
2 *he is a destructive child,* he breaks everything he touches. □ **destructivo**
destructiveness *n.* tendency to want to destroy things: *the destructiveness of teenage vandals.* □ **espíritu de destrucción**
desultory ['dezəltri] *adj.* with no connecting links: *desultory conversation,* conversation which continues by fits and starts. □ **sin orden**
detach [di'tætʃ] *v.* to separate: *please detach the guarantee card and return it to the maker.* □ **separar**
detached house, house which is not attached to another. □ **casa exenta**
semi-detached house, house which is joined to another similar house on one side, but not on the other. □ **casa adosada por un solo lado**
detachable *adj.* which you can separate. □ **separable**
detachment *n.* **1** indifference; lack of immediate interest. □ **indiferencia, desapego**
2 small group of servicemen, etc. □ **destacamento**
detail ['di:teil] *n.* small item: *I will not go into details,* I will not describe absolutely everything about it; *the policeman listed all the details of the crime.* □ **detalle**
■ *v.* to list all the small items: *he gave a detailed description of the burglar.* □ **detallar**
detain [di'tein] *v.* **1** to keep (someone in prison). □ **detener**
2 to hold (someone) back; to stop (someone) from leaving: *the police detained three people for questioning; I will not detain you for very long.* □ **detener**
detainee [di:tei'ni:] *n.* person who is being held in prison: *a political detainee.* □ **detenido, preso**
detect [di'tekt] *v.* to discover; to notice: *can you detect any sign of life on Mars? the pathologist detected traces of poison in the body.* □ **detectar**
detection [di'tekʃn] *n.* discovery: *his fraud escaped detection for several weeks,* his fraud was not found out for several weeks. □ **descubrimiento**
detective *n.* policeman who investigates crimes. □ **detective**
detective story, story about solving a crime. □ **novela policiaca**
private detective, person (not a policeman) employed privately to solve crimes. □ **detective privado**
detector *n.* instrument which discovers something: *metal detector; mine detector.* □ **detector**
détente [dei'tɑ:nt] *n.* friendly atmosphere between two formerly hostile countries. □ **distensión**
detention [di'tenʃn] *n.* imprisonment; keeping someone from leaving: *he was sentenced to sixty days' detention; the whole class was kept in detention after school.* □ **arresto**
detention centre, place where young criminals are imprisoned for a short time. □ **centro penitenciario para jóvenes**
deter [di'tə:] *v.* (*he deterred*) to discourage: *the bad weather did not deter them from playing golf.* □ **desalentar, desanimar**
detergent [di'tə:dʒənt] *n.* chemical used instead of soap for washing clothes or dishes. □ **detergente**
deteriorate [di'tiəriəreit] *v.* to go bad; to get worse: *relations between the manager and his staff are deteriorating.* □ **deteriorar**
deterioration [ditiəriə'reiʃn] *n.* worsening: *the deterioration in weather conditions.* □ **deterioro**
determine [di'tə:min] *v.* **1** to fix: *they determined the date for the party.* □ **fijar**

2 to decide finally: *he determined to go on an expedition to the North Pole.* □ **decidir**
determination [ditəːmi'neiʃn] *n.* firm intention: *she is a person of great determination,* once she has decided to do something, nothing will stop her doing it. □ **determinación**
determined *adj.* resolved: *he is determined to learn to fly,* he has made up his mind he will learn to fly. □ **resuelto**
deterrent [di'terənt] *n.* something which discourages. □ **freno, algo que disuade**
nuclear deterrent, nuclear weapon which it is hoped will discourage the enemy from attacking. □ **fuerza de disuasión nuclear**
detest [di'test] *v.* to dislike intensely. □ **detestar**
detestable *adj.* which is very unpleasant. □ **detestable**
detonate ['detəneit] *v.* to set off (an explosive). □ **hacer detonar**
detonation [detə'neiʃn] *n.* explosion. □ **detonación**
detonator *n.* small explosive charge which will set off a large explosion. □ **detonador**
detour ['diːtuə] *n.* roundabout road taken to avoid an obstacle/to see something not on the direct route: *we made a detour through the village to see the church; instead of taking the motorway, we'll make a detour through the mountains.* □ **desvío**
detract [di'trækt] *v.* to remove part of something/to make something less important: *nothing must detract from the carrying out of the plan.* □ **quitar, deslucir**
detriment ['detrimənt] *n.* hurt; damage: *his speech was to the detriment of good race relations,* his speech damaged good race relations. □ **detrimento**
detrimental [detri'mentl] *adj.* which damages/hurts. □ **perjudicial**
deuce [djuːs] *n.* **1** score in tennis when both players are at 40 points. □ **cuarenta iguales**
2 score of two (in cards). □ **dos**
deuterium [djuː'tiəriəm] *n.* heavy form of hydrogen. □ **deuterio**
devalue [diː'væljuː] *v.* to reduce value of currency in relationship to that of other countries: *the pound was devalued by 10% against the dollar.* □ **devaluar**
devaluation [diːvælju'eiʃn] *n.* reducing the international value of currency. □ **devaluación**
devastate ['devəsteit] *v.* to wreck/to lay waste (countryside): *the storm devastated wide areas of farmland.* □ **devastar**
devastating *adj.* overwhelming: *he has a devastating way of quoting figures.* □ **devastador**
devastation [devə'steiʃn] *n.* widespread damage. □ **devastación**
develop [di'veləp] *v.* **1** to use to good purpose: *the council has plans to develop the land near the railway station.* □ **ordenar, urbanizar**
2 to expand: *he does exercises to develop his muscles.* □ **desarrollar**
3 to start (a disease, etc.): *she developed measles; he developed a liking for chocolates.* □ **contraer (enfermedad); adquirir (gusto)**
4 to produce and fix a photograph from film: *can you develop this film please?* □ **revelar**
5 to grow: *he has developed into a tall, strong man.* □ **desarrollarse**
developer *n.* liquid for developing photographs. □ **revelador**
developing *adj.* growing. □ **en desarrollo**
developing countries, countries which are becoming industrialized. □ **países en desarrollo**
development *n.* **1** growth. □ **desarrollo**
2 *we are awaiting new developments,* we are waiting to see what happens. □ **...acontecimientos**
deviate ['diːvieit] *v.* to swerve/to turn away (from a direct line). □ **desviarse**
deviation *n.* moving away from a direct or normal line. □ **desviación**
deviance *n.* deviation from normal human behaviour. □ **desviación**
deviant *adj.* and *n.* (person) who deviates from normal human behaviour. □ **inadaptado**
device [di'vais] *n.* **1** small (useful) machine: *I have fitted a device to my car which opens the garage doors automatically.* □ **dispositivo**
2 ***leave someone to his own devices:*** *he was left to his own devices,* he was left to do whatever he wanted. □ **le dejaron hacer lo que le diera la gana**
3 motto (on a coat of arms). □ **lema**
devil ['devl] *n.* **1** evil spirit. □ **diablo**
what the devil *are you doing?,* (*informal*) what on earth/in heaven's name are you doing? □ **¿qué demonios...?**
2 (*informal*) person: *he's a lucky devil!* □ **demonio**
devilish *adj.* referring to the devil. □ **diabólico**
devious ['diːviəs] *adj.* not straightforward; roundabout: *by devious means he managed to get an invitation to the party.* □ **tortuoso**
devise [di'vaiz] *v.* to think up; to invent: *he devised a plan for making twice as much money.* □ **concebir**
devoid [di'vɔid] *adj.* empty: *his speech was devoid of any sense.* □ **desprovisto**
devolution [divə'ljuːʃn] *n.* removing of power from the centre. □ **descentralización**
devolve [di'vɔlv] *v.* to pass on (responsibility) to a deputy. □ **delegar**
devote [di'vout] *v.* to spend (time) on something: *I try to devote three minutes every morning to my exercises.* □ **dedicar**
devoted *adj.* **1** (person) who spends all his time on something: *he is devoted to his work.* □ **dedicado**
2 *they are a devoted couple,* they love each other very much. □ **son una pareja feliz**
devotion [di'vouʃn] *n.* **1** (religious) attachment. □ **devoción**
2 *devotion to duty,* doing one's duty. □ **cumplimiento del deber**
devotee [dəvə'tiː] *n.* person who is very enthusiastic about something. □ **devoto**
devour [di'vauə] *v.* (*formal*) to eat (greedily): *the giant devoured the cakes.* □ **devorar**
devout [di'vaut] *adj.* pious; deeply concerned with religion: *she is a very devout Catholic.* □ **devoto**
dew [djuː] *n.* water which forms at night on objects in the open air. □ **rocío**
dexterity [dek'sterəti] *n.* skill (with hands). □ **destreza**
diabetes [daiə'biːtiːz] *n.* (*no pl.*) illness where the sugar content of the blood rises because of lack of insulin. □ **diabetes**
diabetic [daiə'betik] *adj.* referring to diabetes: *diabetic food,* food with a low sugar content which can be eaten by people suffering from diabetes. □ **diabético**
■ *n.* person suffering from diabetes. □ **diabético**
diabolical [daiə'bɔlikl] *adj.* referring to the devil; evil. □ **diabólico**
diaeresis [dai'iərisis] *n.* two dots (¨) put over a vowel to show that it is pronounced separately from another: *naïve can be written with a diaeresis.* □ **diéresis**
diagnose [daiəg'nouz] *v.* to identify (an illness): *the doctor diagnosed measles; the doctor diagnosed the*

disease as measles. □ **diagnosticar**
diagnosis *n.* (*pl. diagnoses*) identification (of an illness): *I do not agree with the doctor's diagnosis.* □ **diagnóstico**
diagnostic [daiəg'nɔstik] *adj.* referring to diagnosis. □ **diagnóstico**
diagonal [dai'ægənl] *adj.* and *n.* (line) going from one corner to another slantwise. □ **diagonal**
diagonally *adv.* slantwise. □ **en diagonal**
diagram ['daiəgræm] *n.* sketch/plan: *he drew a diagram of the way the engine worked.* □ **diagrama, esquema**
diagrammatic [daiəgrə'mætik] *adj.* in the form of a diagram. □ **esquemático**
dial ['daiəl] *n.* round face (of a clock/meter/telephone): *the pilot watched the dials in front of him; the clock dial is illuminated at night.* □ **esfera (reloj); disco (teléfono)**
■ *v.* (*he dialled*) to make a telephone number: *can you dial this number for me? to call the police you must dial 999.* □ **marcar (un número)**
dialling *n.* making a number on the telephone. □ **marcado**
dialling tone, sound on the telephone which shows that you can dial. □ **señal**
dialling code, number which you dial to call a particular town or country: *the dialling code is 013.* □ **prefijo**
dialect ['daiəlekt] *n.* variety of a language spoken in a particular area. □ **dialecto**
dialectic [daiə'lektik] *n.* reasoned investigation of philosophical truth. □ **dialéctica**
dialogue ['daiəlɔg] *n.* conversation between two people/two groups. □ **diálogo**
dialysis [dai'ælisis] *n.* cleaning of a person's blood by passing it through a filter. □ **diálisis**
diameter [dai'æmitə] *n.* distance across the centre of a circle: *the tube is six centimetres in diameter.* □ **diámetro**
diametrically [daiə'metrikli] *adv. diametrically opposed to something,* completely against/opposite. □ **diametralmente**
diamond ['daiəmənd] *n.* **1** very hard transparent precious stone: *a diamond ring.* □ **diamante**
diamond wedding, 60th wedding anniversary. □ **bodas de diamante**
2 one of the four suits in a pack of cards: *the three of diamonds.* □ **diamantes**
diaper ['daiəpə] *n. Amer.* cloth used to wrap round a baby's bottom. □ **pañal**
diaphragm ['daiəfræm] *n.* **1** thin sheet which vibrates with noise. □ **diafragma**
2 thin wall of muscle separating the chest and the abdomen. □ **diafragma**
diarrhoea [daiə'riə] *Amer.* **diarrhea** *n.* illness of the intestines where your bowel movements are very fluid. □ **diarrea**
diary ['daiəri] *n.* (*pl. diaries*) **1** description of what has happened in your life day by day: *a diary of life in London at the time of the plague; he has kept a diary for years.* □ **diario**
2 small book in which you write notes/appointments for each day of the week. □ **agenda**
diatribe ['daiətraib] *n.* violent spoken or written criticism. □ **diatriba**
dice [dais] *n.* (*no pl.*) small cube with one to six dots on each face (for games). □ **dado**
■ *v.* to cut up (vegetables, etc.) into very small cubes. □ **cortar en cuadraditos**
dicey *adj.* (*informal*) dangerous/difficult. □ **peligroso**
dichotomy [dai'kɔtəmi] *n.* splitting into two (usually contradictory) parts. □ **dicotomía**
dicotyledon [daikɔti'li:dən] *n.* plant whose seedlings have two fleshy leaves. □ **dicotiledónea**
dictate [dik'teit] *v.* **1** to speak to someone who writes down your words: *he was dictating letters to his secretary.* □ **dictar**
2 to tell someone what to do: *the President dictates the country's foreign policy.* □ **dictar**
dictation [dik'teiʃn] *n.* act of dictating (something to be written down): *his secretary is good at answering the telephone but not very good at dictation; he took it down at my dictation.* □ **dictado**
dictator *n.* person who rules a country alone. □ **dictador**
dictatorial [diktə'tɔ:riəl] *adj.* with sole powers. □ **dictatorial**
dictatorship *n.* rule of a country by one person. □ **dictadura**
diction ['dikʃn] *n.* way of speaking. □ **dicción**
dictionary ['dikʃənri] *n.* (*pl. dictionaries*) book which lists words in alphabetical order, giving their meanings or translations. □ **diccionario**
did [did] *v. see* **do.**
didactic [dai'dæktik] *adj.* which teaches. □ **didáctico**
diddle ['didl] *v.* (*informal*) to trick/to cheat (someone). □ **timar**
die [dai] *n.* metal stamp for making coins. □ **troquel**
■ *v.* (*died; dying*) **1** to stop living: *my father died three years ago; she died of typhus.* □ **morir**
2 *I'm dying to read his book,* (*informal*) I am very eager to read his book. □ **me muero por...**
3 *I'm dying for a cup of tea,* I'd love a cup of tea. □ **me muero por...**
to die away: *the sound died away,* became fainter. □ **irse apagando**
to die down: *the wind died down,* became less strong. □ **amainar**
to die out: *the old customs are dying out,* not being continued. □ **desaparecer**
diesel ['di:zl] *n.* ***diesel engine,*** engine which runs on thicker fuel than petrol. □ **diésel**
diesel oil, oil used in diesel engines. □ **gasóleo**
diet ['daiət] *n.* **1** kind of food you eat: *I am too fat — I must go on a diet.* □ **dieta, régimen**
2 (*in some countries*) parliament. □ **dieta**
■ *v.* to eat less food/only one sort of food. □ **ponerse a régimen**
dietician [daiə'tiʃn] *n.* person who specializes in the study of diets. □ **dietólogo**
differ ['difə] *v.* not to be the same as: *he differed from the rest of the family in that he was left-handed.* □ **diferir**
I beg to differ, I must disagree. □ **siento disentir**
difference ['difrəns] *n.* way in which two things are not the same: *there is no real difference between them; can you tell the difference between butter and margarine?* □ **diferencia**
it doesn't make any difference, it does not alter the situation. □ **da lo mismo**
different *adj.* not the same: *living in a village is different from living in a town; he went to six different shops; that is quite a different thing,* it is not at all the same. □ **diferente**
differential [difə'renʃl] *adj.* showing up the difference: *differential equation.* □ **diferencial**
■ *n.* **1** part of the axle of a car which allows wheels to turn at different speeds at corners. □ **diferencial**
2 difference in salary between different grades of jobs. □ **diferencial**
differentiate *v.* to make/to tell the difference: *he*

cannot differentiate between good and evil. □ **diferenciar**
differently *adv.* not in the same way: *he dresses differently from you.* □ **de manera diferente.**
difficult ['difikʌlt] *adj.* not easy: *the examination was very difficult; it is difficult to find somewhere to park.* □ **difícil**
difficulty *n.* **1** thing which is not easy: *the difficulty with this car is getting it to start,* the problem; *do you have difficulty in getting up in the morning?* □ **dificultad**
2 *she got into difficulties when swimming,* she was in danger of drowning; *he is in financial difficulties,* he has problems to do with money. □ **apuro**
diffidence ['difidəns] *n.* shyness; lack of confidence. □ **timidez**
diffident *adj.* shy; lacking confidence. □ **tímido**
diffidently *adv.* shyly. □ **tímidamente**
diffraction [di'frækʃn] *n.* splitting up of light into its different colours. □ **difracción**
diffuse [di'fju:s] *adv.* **1** vague/unclear. □ **difuso**
2 *diffuse lighting,* soft lighting, not giving any sharp shadows. □ **luz difusa**
■ *v.* to spread out; to send out. □ **difundir**
dig [dig] *n.* **1** poke: *he gave me a dig in the ribs,* he nudged me with his elbow. □ **golpe; codazo**
2 satirical attack: *that is a dig at the Prime Minister.* □ **pulla**
3 archaeological excavation. □ **excavación**
■ *v.* (*he dug; he has dug*) **1** to make a hole in the ground: *he dug a tunnel with his bare hands; they used a mechanical digger to dig the foundations of the office block.* □ **excavar**
2 *we dug up a Roman coin in the garden,* we found the coin when digging. □ **desenterrar**
digger *n.* person/machine that digs. □ **excavador**
digging *n.* action of making a hole in the ground. □ **excavación, cava**
dig in *v.* **1** to bury (manure) in the ground. □ **abonar**
2 (*informal*) to eat a lot. □ **atiborrarse**
dig in!, start eating! □ **¡empieza a comer!**
digs *n. pl.* (*informal*) furnished room(s) (let to students, etc.). □ **pensión**
digest ['daidʒest] *n.* summary. □ **resumen**
■ *v.* [dai'dʒest] **1** to turn food into energy (in the stomach and intestine): *I cannot digest my dinner,* I am feeling unwell after my dinner. □ **digerir**
2 to ponder over (a piece of information). □ **reflexionar sobre**
digestible *adj.* which can be digested: *babies have to be given easily digestible food.* □ **digerible**
digestion *n.* action of turning food into energy: *a quick walk after a meal helps the digestion.* □ **digestión**
digestive *adj.* which helps you to digest. □ **digestivo**
digestive biscuit, sweet biscuit made of wholemeal. □ **galleta integral**
digit ['didʒit] *n.* **1** figure: *977-7904 is a seven-digit telephone number.* □ **dígito**
2 finger or toe. □ **dedo**
digital *adj.* which involves figures: *digital watch,* watch where the time is shown by figures (such as 16.52). □ **digital**
dignified ['dignifaid] *adj.* solemn/important-looking. □ **solemne**
dignify *v.* to honour (with a title); to give dignity to (someone). □ **otorgar un título**
dignitary *n.* (*pl. dignitaries*) important person: *civic dignitaries,* the mayor, councillors, etc., of a town. □ **dignatario**
dignity *n.* **1** solemn/serious way of behaving: *his dignity at the trial was praised.* □ **dignidad**
2 *it is **beneath his dignity** to clean his own shoes,* he is far too superior to clean his shoes. □ **no se digna...**
3 title (given to someone as an honour). □ **dignidad**
digress [dai'gres] *v.* to wander away from the subject when speaking. □ **hacer una digresión**
digression *n.* speech/writing which does not deal with the subject. □ **digresión**
dihedral [dai'hi:drəl] *n.* angle at which an aircraft's wing rises above the horizontal: *model aircraft with a 10 centimetre dihedral.* □ **diedro**
dike [daik] *n.* **1** long wall of earth to keep out water. □ **dique**
2 long ditch. □ **zanja**
dilapidated [di'læpideitid] *adj.* falling into ruin. □ **derruido**
dilapidation *n.* being in ruins. □ **estado ruinoso**
dilate [dai'leit] *v.* to make (eyes) grow larger; (*of the eyes*) to grow larger. □ **dilatar; dilatarse**
dilatory ['dilətəri] *adj.* slow (to act). □ **lento**
dilemma [di'lemə] *n.* serious problem, where a choice has to be made between several bad alternatives: *I am in a dilemma,* I do not know which course of action to follow. □ **dilema**
dilettante [dili'tænti] *n.* person who is interested in a subject, but not very seriously. □ **diletante**
diligence ['dilidʒəns] *n.* hard work. □ **diligencia**
diligent *adj.* hard-working. □ **diligente**
dill [dil] *n.* herb, used for flavouring fish and pickles. □ **eneldo**
dilly-dally ['dilidæli] *v.* to hang back; to loiter. □ **entretenerse, perder el tiempo**
dilute [dai'lju:t] *v.* to add water to another liquid to make it weaker. □ **diluir**
■ *adj.* with water added: *dilute sulphuric acid.* □ **diluido**
dim [dim] *adj.* (*dimmer, dimmest*) **1** weak (light). □ **pálido; débil**
2 *I have **a dim recollection** of it,* I can remember it vaguely. □ **vago**
3 rather stupid. □ **lerdo**
■ *v.* (*he dimmed*) **1** to turn down (a light). □ **poner a media luz**
2 *the house lights dimmed,* the lights in the theatre were turned down (as the play started). □ **apagarse poco a poco**
dimly *adv.* vaguely; unclearly. □ **débilmente**
dimmer *n.* light switch which dims a light gradually instead of turning it off. □ **regulador de voltaje**
dimness *n.* weakness (of light); vagueness (of memory). □ **penumbra (luz); lo borroso**
dime [daim] *n. Amer.* ten cent coin. □ **moneda de 10 centavos de dólar**
dimension [di'menʃn] *n.* measurement (in figures): *what are the dimensions of this table?* □ **dimensión**
dimensional *adj.* ***two-dimensional,*** having two dimensions, flat. □ **relativo a la dimensión, de dos dimensiones**
three-dimensional, having three dimensions/in the round. □ **tridimensional**
diminish *v.* to make smaller; to become smaller: *his influence is diminishing.* □ **disminuir**
diminution *n.* becoming smaller. □ **disminución**
diminutive *adj.* very small. □ **diminuto**
■ *n.* word used to show that something is small: *'booklet' is a diminutive of 'book'; 'Kate' is a diminutive of 'Catherine'.* □ **diminutivo**
dimple ['dimpl] *n.* small hollow (in the cheeks/in babies' fat elbows, etc.). □ **hoyuelo**
din [din] *n.* loud noise. □ **estrépito**
■ *v.* (*he dinned*) to force (a piece of information)

into someone's head by frequently repeating it. □ **machacar**

dine [dain] *v.* to eat an evening meal. □ **cenar**
to dine out: *we are dining out,* we are having dinner away from home. □ **cenar fuera**
diner *n.* **1** person eating dinner. □ **comensal**
2 restaurant car on a train. □ **coche restaurante**
3 *Amer.* small restaurant selling hot food. □ **restaurante barato**
dining car *n.* restaurant car (on a train). □ **coche restaurante**
dining room *n.* room where people usually eat. □ **comedor**

ding-dong ['diŋdɔŋ] *n.* sound made by a bell. □ **talán-talán**
■ *adj.* vigorous (argument): *a ding-dong battle.* □ **reñido**

dinghy ['diŋgi] *n.* (*pl. dinghies*) small boat: *rubber dinghy.* □ **bote; 'zodiac'**

dingy ['dindʒi] *adj.* (*dingier, dingiest*) dirty: *a dingy café.* □ **sucio**
dinginess *n.* dirt. □ **suciedad**

dinner ['dinə] *n.* main meal (usually the evening meal): *it is dinner time; we always have dinner at 7.45; we have got friends coming to dinner.* □ **cena**
school dinner, meal served to children in school in the middle of the day. □ **comida**
dinner break, school break at the middle of the day. □ **hora de la comida**
dinner jacket, formal (usually black) jacket worn for dinner with a black bow tie. □ **esmoquin**
dinner party, dinner to which guests are invited. □ **cena con invitados**
dinner service, set of plates for eating a main meal. □ **vajilla**
dinner table, table (where people eat). □ **mesa de comedor**

dinosaur ['dainəsɔː] *n.* prehistoric reptile, usually very large. □ **dinosaurio**

dint [dint] *n.* ***by dint of,*** through: *he passed his examinations by dint of much hard work.* □ **a fuerza de**

diocese ['daiəsis] *n.* area under the charge of a bishop. □ **diócesis**

dioxide [dai'ɔksaid] *n.* oxide with two parts of oxygen to one part of another substance. □ **dióxido**

dip [dip] *n.* **1** quick covering with liquid: *I am going for a quick dip in the sea.* □ **baño**
2 sudden drop (of a road/of land). □ **depresión**
3 savoury paste, into which biscuits, etc., can be dipped as cocktail snacks: *cheese dip.* □ **pasta**
■ *v.* (*he dipped*) **1** to put something quickly into a liquid: *the painter was dipping his brush into the paint; she dipped her toes into the water.* □ **mojar**
2 to dive: *the road dips sharply into the village.* □ **descender**
3 *I have only dipped into this book,* I have only looked at a few pages. □ **hojear**
4 *to dip your headlights,* to lower the beam of your headlights when another car is approaching. □ **quitar las luces largas**
dipper *n.* **1** *big dipper,* fairground railway which goes up and down steep slopes. □ **motaña rusa**
2 small brown bird which dives into water. □ **mirlo acuático**
dipstick *n.* rod (in the engine of a car) which shows the level of oil in the engine. □ **varilla de nivel**

diphtheria [dif'θiəriə] *n.* (*no pl.*) serious infectious disease of babies. □ **difteria**

diphthong ['difθɔŋ] *n.* two vowel sounds which are pronounced together. □ **diptongo**

diploma [di'ploumə] *n.* certificate showing that you have passed an examination: *he is studying for a diploma in engineering.* □ **diploma, título**

diplomacy [di'plouməsi] *n.* art of negotiating between different parties, especially between different countries. □ **diplomacia**
diplomat ['dipləmæt] *n.* person (such as an ambassador) who represents his country abroad. □ **diplomático**
diplomatic [diplə'mætik] *adj.* **1** representing one's country: *the diplomatic service.* □ **diplomático**
2 careful not to give offence: *he gave a very diplomatic reply.* □ **diplomático**
diplomatist [di'ploumətist] *n.* person (such as an ambassador) who represents his country abroad. □ **diplomático**

dipsomania [dipsə'meiniə] *n.* habitual drinking of alcohol. □ **dipsomanía**
dipsomaniac *n.* person who wants to drink alcohol all the time. □ **dipsómano**

dire ['daiə] *adj.* **1** very serious. □ **extremo**
2 *dire necessity,* urgent necessity. □ **necesidad apremiante**

direct [dai'rekt/di'rekt] *v.* **1** to aim towards a point: *the policeman was directing the traffic; can you direct me to the post office? I must direct your attention to paragraph 3.* □ **dirigir**
2 to tell someone to do something: *I am directed to inform you; medicine to be taken as directed by the doctor.* □ **indicar**
3 *the film was directed by an Australian,* an Australian was in charge of it. □ **dirigir**
■ *adj.* **1** straight: *the road goes in a direct line towards the town; a direct answer; direct hit,* hit on the target. □ **...recto; ...directo**
2 *direct taxation,* taxes which you pay to the tax office. □ **impuestos directos**
3 *there is a direct flight to London,* the plane does not stop between here and London. □ **directo**
■ *adv.* straight: *I flew direct to London,* I flew without stopping. □ **directamente**
direction [dai'rekʃn] *n.* **1** point to which you are going/at which you are aiming: *is the station in this direction? turn round - you're going in the wrong direction; bottles were flying in all directions at the football match.* □ **dirección**
2 instruction: *I cannot make this thing work because there are no directions as to how to switch it on.* □ **instrucción**
3 guiding (of the making of a film). □ **dirección**
directive *n.* official instruction. □ **directiva**
directly *adv.* immediately; straight: *he went directly to the police; the house is directly opposite the post office.* □ **directamente**
■ *conj. I will write the letter directly I get home,* as soon as I get home. □ **tan pronto como**
directness *n.* frankness (of a reply). □ **franqueza**
director [dai'rektə] *n.* **1** person who is appointed by the shareholders to help run a firm. □ **director**
managing director, person who is in charge of a firm. □ **director gerente**
2 person in charge of making a film/a play. □ **director**
directory *n.* (*pl. directories*) list of people/businesses showing their telephone numbers and addresses; book giving lists of people/businesses with their addresses and telephone numbers: *telephone directory; a directory of local estate agents.* □ **guía telefónica; directorio**
classified directory, telephone directory where firms

are classified into various groups. □ **'páginas amarillas'**
dirge [dəːdʒ] *n.* funeral song. □ **canto fúnebre**
dirigible [di'ridʒibl] *n.* large airship which can be steered. □ **dirigible**
dirt [dəːt] *n.* mud; earth; filth: *pigs love to wallow in dirt; people were shocked at the dirt in the slum areas.* □ **lodo; tierra; suciedad**
dirt cheap, extremely cheap. □ **tirado**
dirtiness *n.* state of being dirty/of not being clean. □ **suciedad**
dirt-track *n.* cinder-covered track for racing. □ **pista de ceniza**
dirty *adj.* (*dirtier, dirtiest*) **1** not clean; covered with dirt: *if you lie on the ground you will get your clothes dirty.* □ **sucio**
2 *dirty weather,* grey, drizzly, weather. □ **tiempo desapacible**
3 *that's a dirty trick,* that is a low, unpleasant, trick. □ **...mala jugada**
■ *v.* to cover with dirt: *he has dirtied all his clothes.* □ **ensuciar**
disability [disə'biliti] *n.* (*pl. disabilities*) physical handicap. □ **minusvalía (física)**
disabled [dis'eibld] *adj.* physically handicapped: *this is a school for seriously disabled children.* □ **minusválido (físico)**
■ *n.* ***the disabled,*** physically handicapped people. □ **los minusválidos (físicos)**
disabuse [disə'bjuːz] *v.* to make (someone) see that they were wrong. □ **desengañar**
disadvantage [disəd'vɑːntidʒ] *n.* handicap; drawback; lack of advantage: *if you want to work in Germany it is a disadvantage not to be able to speak German; the football team was at a disadvantage because two of their best players were ill.* □ **desventaja**
disadvantageous [disædvɑːn'teidʒəs] *adj.* which does not give an advantage; unfavourable. □ **desventajoso**
disaffected [disə'fektid] *adj.* discontented/rebellious. □ **descontento**
disagree [disə'griː] *v.* **1** not to agree: *I said Hong Kong is hotter than Singapore, but he disagreed; the goalkeeper disagreed with the referee's decision.* □ **estar en desacuerdo, discrepar**
2 *cabbage disagrees with me,* makes me feel ill. □ **no me sienta bien el...**
disagreeable *adj.* unpleasant. □ **desagradable**
disagreement *n.* lack of agreement: *the work came to a halt because of a disagreement between the manager and his staff.* □ **desacuerdo**
disallow [disə'lau] *v.* **1** to refuse to accept. □ **no aceptar**
2 *the team's second goal was disallowed,* was not counted. □ **...fue anulado**
disappear [disə'piə] *v.* to vanish: *the pickpockets disappeared into the crowd.* □ **desaparecer**
disappearance *n.* vanishing: *the police are puzzled by the disappearance of the main witness.* □ **desaparición**
disappoint [disə'pɔint] *v.* to let (someone) down; not to turn out as expected: *he is disappointed with his new car, she was disappointed by her examination results.* □ **decepcionar**
disappointing *adj.* unsatisfactory; not coming up to expectations. □ **decepcionante**
disappointment *n.* sadness because what was expected did not take place: *to her great disappointment she failed her driving test.* □ **decepción**
disapprove [disə'pruːv] *v.* not to approve: *I disapprove of men with long hair.* □ **desaprobar**
disapproval *n.* lack of approval: *he met with the disapproval of his family.* □ **desaprobación**
disapprovingly *adv.* in a way which shows you do not approve: *she looked at the little boy disapprovingly.* □ **con desaprobación**
disarm [dis'ɑːm] *v.* to remove weapons from someone: *he managed to disarm his attacker.* □ **desarmar**
disarmament *n.* abolition of weapons by a country. □ **desarme**
disarming *adj.* charming (manner) which prevents people from criticizing. □ **que desarma**
disarrange [disə'reinʒ] *v.* to put into disorder: *she disarranged all the books in the bookcase.* □ **desordenar**
disarray [disə'rei] *n.* lack of order: *the soldiers were in disarray.* □ **desorden**
disaster [di'zɑːstə] *n.* catastrophe; very bad accident: *air disaster,* crash of an aircraft killing many people. □ **desastre**
disastrous *adj.* very bad/catastrophic: *a disastrous fire.* □ **desastroso**
disastrously *adv.* very badly: *the play failed disastrously.* □ **desastrosamente**
disband [dis'bænd] *v.* to send soldiers in an army back home; to split up (a group of soldiers/musicians, etc.). □ **licenciar; disolver**
disbelief [disbi'liːf] *n.* lack of belief. □ **incredulidad**
disbeliever *n.* person who does not believe. □ **incrédulo**
disbud [dis'bʌd] *v.* (*he disbudded*) to remove some of the buds from (a plant). □ **desyemar**
disburse [dis'bəːs] *v.* to pay out (money). □ **desembolsar**
disc [disk] *n.* round flat object, especially a record for playing on a record-player. □ **disco**
slipped disc, painful condition where one of the cushioning discs in the spine has become displaced. □ **hernia discal**
disc brakes, brakes in a car which are in the form of discs. □ **frenos de disco**
disc jockey, person who plays records on the radio/in a club, etc. □ **pinchadiscos**
discard [dis'kɑːd] *v.* to put on one side; to reject. □ **descartar**
discern [di'səːn] *v.* to see/to make out. □ **discernir**
discernible *adj.* which can be seen: *a barely discernible puff of smoke.* □ **discernible**
discerning *adj.* (person) who has good judgement: *a discerning art critic.* □ **perspicaz, entendido**
discernment *n.* ability to judge correctly. □ **discernimiento**
discharge ['distʃɑːdʒ] *n.* **1** liquid (coming out of a pipe, etc.); pus (coming out of a wound). □ **desagüe; supuración (pus)**
2 payment (of a debt). □ **pago**
3 release (of a prisoner). □ **puesta en libertad**
■ *v.* [dis'tʃɑːdʒ] **1** to unload (a cargo); to let off (a gun). □ **descargar**
2 to send someone away. □ **despedir**
3 *he was discharged from hospital,* he was allowed to go home because he was better. □ **dar de alta**
4 to pay (a debt). □ **pagar**
discharged bankrupt, person who has paid off his debts according to the requirements of the court. □ **fallido rehabilitado**
disciple [di'saipl] *n.* follower (of a religious leader): *Jesus had twelve disciples.* □ **discípulo**
discipline ['disiplin] *n.* keeping people under control: *there is no discipline in our school.* □ **disciplina**
■ *v.* to control/to punish someone: *he was disciplined for bad conduct on the football field.*

□ **disciplinar**
disciplinarian [disipli'nɛəriən] *n.* person who believes in strict discipline. □ **ordenancista**
disciplinary [disi'plinəri] *adj.* (action) which keeps someone under control. □ **disciplinario**
disclaim [dis'kleim] *v.* not to admit; to deny: *he disclaims all knowledge of the payment,* he says he knows nothing about the payment. □ **negar**
disclaimer *n.* statement in which you disclaim all knowledge of something. □ **negación**
disclose [dis'klouz] *v.* to reveal (a secret). □ **revelar**
disclosure [dis'klouʒə] *n.* revealing (of a secret): *the newspaper has published some startling disclosures about the minister.* □ **revelación**
disco ['diskou] *n.* (*pl. discos*) (*informal*) discotheque; place where people dance to recorded music; equipment used to play records in a discotheque. □ **discoteca**
discolour [dis'kʌlə] *Amer.* **discolor** *v.* to change colour: *his socks have become discoloured in the wash.* □ **descolorar**
discomfort [dis'kʌmfət] *n.* lack of comfort. □ **incomodidad**
disconcert [diskən'sə:t] *v.* to surprise/to embarrass. □ **desconcertar**
disconcerting *adj.* worrying/surprising: *there is a disconcerting amount of evidence against him.* □ **desconcertante**
disconnect [diskə'nekt] *v.* to undo (two things which are connected): *he disconnected two railway wagons; they disconnected the refrigerator,* they unplugged the refrigerator; *the telephone has been disconnected.* □ **desconectar**
disconnected *adj.* disjointed; with no links. □ **desconectado**
disconsolate [dis'kɔnsələt] *adj.* very sad. □ **desconsolado**
disconsolately *adv.* very sadly: *she sat disconsolately reading his letter.* □ **desconsoladamente**
discontent [diskən'tent] *n.* state of not being satisfied: *there is a lot of discontent among the office staff.* □ **descontento**
discontented *adj.* not satisfied: *he is discontented with his pay rise.* □ **descontento**
discontinue [diskən'tinju:] *v.* not to continue: *we have discontinued production of this model.* □ **suspender**
discontinuous *adj.* which stops and starts; intermittent. □ **discontinuo**
discord ['diskɔ:d] *n.* lack of agreement. □ **discordia**
discordant *adj.* **1** not in agreement: *discordant views.* □ **discordante**
2 out of harmony: *discordant music.* □ **disonante**
discotheque ['diskətek] *n.* place where people dance to recorded music. □ **discoteca**
discount ['diskaunt] *n.* percentage less than the normal price: *they are $1 each but if you buy ten, I will give you 10% discount.* □ **descuento**
discount store, shop where goods are cheaper than elsewhere. □ **tienda de descuento**
■ *v.* [dis'kaunt] not to pay any attention to (something): *they have discounted the rumours.* □ **no hacer caso de...**
discourage [dis'kʌridʒ] *v.* not to encourage; to stop (someone) doing something: *she became discouraged after she was turned down for the job.* □ **desalentar**
discouragement *n.* being discouraged; thing which stops you doing something. □ **desaliento**
discouraging *adj.* not encouraging: *we have had a very discouraging report on the future of the car industry.* □ **desalentador**
discourse ['diskɔ:s] *n.* (*formal*) talk/speech. □ **discurso**
discourteous [dis'kə:tiəs] *adj.* rude. □ **descortés**
discourteously *adv.* rudely. □ **descortésmente**
discourtesy *n.* rudeness. □ **descortesía**
discover [dis'kʌvə] *v.* to find something new: *did Columbus discover America? doctors have still not discovered a cure for the common cold; I discovered that he knew my father.* □ **descubrir**
discoverer *n.* person who finds something: *Columbus, the discoverer of America.* □ **descubridor**
discovery *n.* act of finding something new: *Lister made several important scientific discoveries; the discovery of the source of the Nile.* □ **descubrimiento**
discredit [dis'kredit] *n.* doubt/lack of belief (in someone). □ **descrédito**
■ *v.* **1** to make people doubt (something): *this theory has been discredited.* □ **desacreditar**
2 *he has been discredited,* no one believes him any more. □ **...desacreditado**
discreditable *adj.* not honourable (conduct). □ **deshonroso**
discreditably *adv.* dishonourably. □ **deshonrosamente**
discreet [dis'kri:t] *adj.* quiet; not allowing anyone to notice: *you must be discreet; he kept a discreet distance from her.* □ **discreto**
discreetly *adv.* quietly; without anyone noticing: *he discreetly left the committee to decide.* □ **discretamente**
discretion [dis'kreʃn] *n.* **1** wisdom/good sense. □ **discreción**
2 *I leave it to your discretion,* I leave it for you to decide. □ **te lo dejo a tu parecer**
discretionary *adj.* (powers) used at someone's discretion. □ **discrecional**
discrepancy [dis'krepənsi] *n.* (*pl. discrepancies*) lack of agreement: *there is a large discrepancy in these figures.* □ **discrepancia**
discriminate [dis'krimineit] *v.* to distinguish; to treat differently; to prefer (one thing to another): *this law discriminates against women; you have to discriminate between the rights of the criminal and the victim; the judge obviously discriminated in favour of the girl.* □ **discriminar**
discriminating *adj.* able to distinguish/judge: *a discriminating collector of old silver.* □ **discernidor, entendido**
discrimination [diskrimi'neiʃn] *n.* **1** judgement: *he is a man of discrimination,* he has good taste. □ **buen susto**
2 preference (for or against something): *racial discrimination,* preference for or against a race. □ **discriminación**
discursive [dis'kə:siv] *adj.* not succinct and to the point. □ **divagador**
discus ['diskəs] *n.* (*pl. discuses*) flat round disc which is thrown as a sport. □ **disco**
discuss [dis'kʌs] *v.* to talk about (a problem): *as soon as they meet, they start discussing politics.* □ **hablar de**
discussion [dis'kʌʃn] *n.* **1** talking about (a problem): *there was a lot of discussion before we finally came to a decision.* □ **análisis, examen**
2 *the question* ***under discussion,*** the problem we are talking about. □ **en examen**
disdain [dis'dein] *n.* looking down; feeling that someone/something is inferior: *the cat looked at the plate with disdain.* □ **desdén**

■ *v.* to look down on (something); to refuse to do something because it is beneath you: *he disdained to reply.* □ **desdeñar**
disdainful *adj.* superior (air). □ **desdeñoso**
disdainfully *adv.* with a superior air. □ **desdeñosamente**
disease [di'zi:z] *n.* serious illness (of animals, plants, etc.): *smallpox and tuberculosis are still serious diseases.* □ **enfermedad**
diseased *adj.* sick: *we must cut the diseased branch off the tree.* □ **enfermo**
disembark [disim'bɑ:k] *v.* to get off a ship. □ **desembarcar**
disenchanted [disin'tʃɑ:ntid] *adj.* feeling that something has not turned out as well as expected: *I am rather disenchanted with our new car,* the car does not seem as good as I had previously thought. □ **desencantado**
disenchantment *n.* feeling that something has not turned out as well as expected. □ **desencanto**
disengage [disin'geidʒ] *v.* **1** to break off: *the troops disengaged,* the troops broke off the fighting. □ **retirarse**
2 to disconnect (the gears of a car). □ **desembragar**
disentangle [disin'tæŋgl] *v.* to untie (knotted string, etc.): *can you disentangle this ball of wool for me?* □ **desenredar**
disfavour [dis'feivə] *Amer.* **disfavor** *n.* **1** shame; lack of favours. □ **desgracia**
2 *the minister fell into disfavour,* he was disgraced; *the minister incurred the king's disfavour,* he fell into disgrace with the king. □ **caer en desgracia**
disfigure [dis'figə] *v.* to make ugly: *the front of the building is disfigured by a large drainpipe.* □ **afear**
disfranchise [dis'fræntʃaiz] *v.* to remove the right to vote from (someone). □ **privar del derecho de votar**
disgorge [dis'gɔ:dʒ] *v.* **1** to pour out. □ **verter**
2 to give up (things which have been stolen). □ **restituir**
disgrace [dis'greis] *n.* shame; being out of favour with someone: *he was sent home in disgrace by the headmaster.* □ **desgracia**
to fall into disgrace (with): *the minister fell into disgrace,* he was out of favour. □ **caer en desgracia**
■ *v.* to bring shame on: *he has disgraced the school by his behaviour.* □ **deshonrar**
disgraceful *adj.* which you should be ashamed of: *the behaviour of the football crowd was disgraceful.* □ **vergonzoso**
disgracefully *adv.* in a disgraceful way: *he was disgracefully rude.* □ **vergonzosamente**
disgruntled [dis'grʌntld] *adj.* annoyed/discontented. □ **contrariado**
disguise [dis'gaiz] *n.* **1** costume, wig, etc., to make someone look like someone else: *he was wearing a policeman's uniform as a disguise.* □ **disfraz**
2 *they are detectives **in disguise**,* detectives dressed to look like something else. □ **disfrazado**
■ *v.* **1** to dress so as to look like someone else; to make (something) look/sound different: *he was disguised as a policeman; she tried to disguise her voice/her handwriting.* □ **disfrazarse**
2 *there is no disguising the fact,* you cannot hide the fact. □ **disfrazar, disimular**
disgust [dis'gʌst] *n.* strong dislike; feeling sick, very discontented: *she gave up her job in disgust.* □ **asco, indignación**
■ *v.* to make someone feel sick: *she was disgusted by the smell.* □ **producir asco**
disgusting *adj.* which makes you feel sick: *a disgusting smell; disgusting behaviour.* □ **repugnante**
dish [diʃ] *n.* (*pl. dishes*) **1** large plate (for serving food): *meat dish; vegetable dish; can I wash the dishes?,* can I do the washing up after the meal? □ **plato**
2 part of a meal; (plate of) prepared food: *there are only two meat dishes on the menu.* □ **plato**
■ *v.* **1** *he is dishing up the food,* he is serving the meal. □ **servir**
2 *they are dishing out tickets,* (*informal*) they are handing out tickets. □ **repartir**
dishcloth *n.* cloth for washing dishes. □ **estropajo, bayeta**
dishwasher *n.* machine for washing dishes. □ **lavavajillas**
dishy *adj.* (*informal*) attractive (girl). □ **mona; guapetona**
disharmony [dis'hɑ:məni] *n.* not being in agreement/in harmony. □ **disonancia**
dishearten [dis'hɑ:tn] *v.* to discourage: *he was quite disheartened by the reviews of his book.* □ **descorazonar**
disheartening *adj.* discouraging. □ **descorazonador**
dishevelled [di'ʃevəld] *adj.* uncombed (hair). □ **despeinado**
dishonest [dis'ɔnist] *adj.* not honest: *he was sacked when they discovered he was dishonest.* □ **poco íntegro/honrado**
dishonestly *adv.* not honestly; illegally: *he dishonestly took money from the till.* □ **fraudulentamente**
dishonesty *n.* lack of honesty. □ **falta de honradez**
dishonour [dis'ɔnə] *Amer.* **dishonor** *n.* lack of honour. □ **deshonor**
■ *v.* **1** to treat rudely. □ **tratar mal**
2 not to honour. □ **deshonrar**
3 *dishonoured cheque,* cheque which the bank will not pay. □ **cheque no aceptado**
dishonourable *adj.* not honourable; shameful. □ **deshonroso**
disillusion [disi'lu:ʒn] *n.* feeling of being let down/that something has not turned out as you expected. □ **desilusión**
disillusioned *adj.* feeling that something has not turned out as expected: *he was disillusioned by the reviews of his book.* □ **desilusionado**
disillusionment *n.* feeling of being let down/that something has not turned out as expected. □ **desilusión**
disincentive [disin'sentiv] *n.* something which discourages: *the low salary is a disincentive to work,* the salary does not encourage people to work. □ **freno**
disinclined [disin'klaind] *adj.* not inclined: *she is feeling disinclined to go to work today,* she does not want to go to work today. □ **renuente**
disinclination [disinkli'neiʃn] *n.* not wanting to do something: *a disinclination to work.* □ **aversión**
disinfect [disin'fekt] *v.* to remove/to prevent infection: *we had to disinfect the whole house.* □ **desinfectar**
disinfectant *n.* chemical liquid for fighting infection: *wash your mouth out with disinfectant.* □ **desinfectante**
disingenuous [disin'dʒenjuəs] *adj.* false; lacking frankness; pretending to be naive. □ **insincero**
disinherit [disin'herit] *v.* to change your will so that someone does not inherit your money when you die: *he disinherited his son.* □ **desheredar**
disintegrate [dis'intigreit] *v.* to fall to pieces: *the rocket disintegrated when it exploded.* □ **desintegrar(se)**

disintegration [disinti'greiʃn] *n.* falling to pieces. □ **desintegración**
disinter [disin'tə:] *v.* (*he disinterred*) to dig up (something) which has been buried. □ **desenterrar**
disinterested [dis'intrəstid] *adj.* not in favour of one side or the other: *he is a totally disinterested observer,* he is an impartial observer. □ **imparcial**
disinterestedness *n.* impartiality. □ **imparcialidad**
disjointed [dis'dʒɔintid] *adj.* without any links; unconnected: *disjointed style; disjointed speech.* □ **desunido; inconexo (estilo/habla)**
disk [disk] *n. see* **disc.**
dislike [dis'laik] *n.* lack of liking. □ **aversión**
to take a dislike to: *he has taken a dislike to me,* he has started to hate me. □ **me ha cogido antipatía**
■ *v.* not to like: *I dislike sleeping on a soft mattress; she dislikes his way of laughing; I don't dislike honey,* I rather like honey. □ **no gustar**
dislocate ['disləkeit] *v.* **1** to put an arm/leg, etc., out of joint: *she has dislocated her shoulder.* □ **dislocar**
2 to disorganize: *rail services have been dislocated by the strike.* □ **trastornar**
dislocation [dislə'keiʃn] *n.* **1** disorganization: *there will be some dislocation of rail services.* □ **trastorno**
2 putting an arm/leg, etc., out of joint. □ **dislocación**
dislodge [dis'lɔdʒ] *v.* to detach: *he dislodged several stones while climbing the cliff.* □ **desprender**
disloyal [dis'lɔiəl] *adj.* not loyal. □ **desleal**
disloyalty *n.* state of not being loyal: *he was accused of disloyalty to the king.* □ **deslealtad**
dismal ['dizməl] *adj.* miserable: *the dismal prospect of work in the mines; dismal weather.* □ **deprimente; mal (tiempo)**
dismally *adv.* **1** miserably. □ **tristemente**
2 *he failed his examinations dismally,* very badly. □ **lamentablemente**
dismantle [dis'mæntl] *v.* to take to pieces: *they were dismantling the car engine.* □ **desarmar, desmontar**
dismay [dis'mei] *n.* horror/consternation: *to my dismay he suddenly asked me to speak.* □ **consternación**
■ *v.* to strike with horror: *he was dismayed to find he had run out of money.* □ **espantar**
dismember [dis'membə] *v.* to cut up into parts; to take apart. □ **desmembrar**
dismiss [dis'mis] *v.* **1** to send away: *the school was dismissed early; you can dismiss that idea from your mind.* □ **alejar, descartar**
2 to remove (someone) from a job: *he was dismissed from the Police Force; the salesman was dismissed because he was rude to the customers.* □ **despedir**
3 to refuse (a request): *the judge dismissed the case.* □ **desestimar**
dismissal *n.* removal from a job: *he was threatened with instant dismissal.* □ **despido**
dismount [dis'maunt] *v.* to get off a horse/bicycle, etc. □ **desmontar**
disobey [disə'bei] *v.* not to obey: *he disobeyed the police order.* □ **desobedecer**
disobedience [disə'bi:diəns] *n.* lack of obedience. □ **desobediencia**
disobedient *adj.* not obedient. □ **desobediente**
disorder [dis'ɔ:də] *n.* **1** lack of order; untidiness. □ **desorden**
2 riot; disturbance: *the troops were brought in to prevent disorder in the streets.* □ **disturbio**
3 illness: *he has a mental disorder.* □ **trastorno**
disorderly *adj.* wild (crowd): *he was charged with being drunk and disorderly.* □ **escandaloso**
disorganize [dis'ɔ:gənaiz] *v.* to put something out of its usual order: *the rail services are disorganized.* □ **desorganizar**
disorientate [dis'ɔ:riənteit] *v.* to make (someone) lose their sense of direction; to confuse (someone). □ **desorientar**
disown [dis'oun] *v.* to refuse to acknowledge that something is yours: *he disowned his son.* □ **rechazar, repudiar**
disparage [dis'pæridʒ] *v.* to say that something is bad. □ **hablar mal de**
disparaging *adj.* critical; saying that something is bad: *he made disparaging remarks about the decoration of the house.* □ **despreciativo**
disparate ['dispərət] *adj.* varied/different. □ **dispar**
dispassionate [dis'pæʃnət] *adj.* calm and without emotion. □ **desapasionado**
dispassionately *adv.* calmly. □ **desapasionadamente**
dispatch [dis'pætʃ] *n.* (*pl. dispatches*) **1** sending. □ **despacho**
dispatch note, note saying that goods have been sent. □ **aviso, notificación de envío**
2 speed (of doing something). □ **prontitud**
3 message. □ **mensaje**
dispatch rider, motorcyclist who carries messages. □ **mensajero**
■ *v.* **1** to send: *we dispatched the goods on Friday 12th June.* □ **despachar, enviar**
2 to finish something quickly. □ **despachar**
3 to kill off. □ **despachar, matar**
dispel [dis'pel] *v.* (*he dispelled*) to clear away: *the Prime Minister's statement dispelled all fears of a rise in inflation.* □ **disipar**
dispense [dis'pens] *v.* **1** to distribute. □ **dispensar**
2 to prepare and sell medicine. □ **preparar, dispensar**
3 ***to dispense with,*** to do without: *you can dispense with your overcoat.* □ **prescindir de**
dispensary *n.* (*pl. dispensaries*) place where a chemist prepares medicines. □ **dispensario**
dispensation [dispən'seiʃn] *n.* permission not to follow a rule, etc. □ **dispensa**
dispenser *n.* automatic machine/box with a hole to allow one object to come out at a time: *these pills are sold in a dispenser.* □ **máquina automática**
dispensing *adj.* ***dispensing chemist,*** chemist who has the qualifications to prepare medicines. □ **dispensativo, farmacéutico**
disperse [dis'pə:s] *v.* to clear away: *the sun dispersed the fog; the police had to be called in to disperse the crowd; they hope to disperse the oil with detergent.* □ **dispersar**
dispirited [di'spiritid] *adj.* sad/discouraged. □ **desanimado**
displace [dis'pleis] *v.* to move something from its usual place. □ **desplazar**
displaced persons, refugees who have fled from their home lands. □ **desplazados**
displacement *n.* moving (of something); amount of water removed by a ship, (hence) the volume of the ship. □ **desplazamiento**
display [dis'plei] *n.* show/exhibition: *air display,* exhibition of flying by various aircraft; *there is a wonderful display of flowers in the public gardens; the school is putting on a gymnastic display.* □ **exposición; exhibición**
display unit, special stand for showing goods for sale. □ **exposición, escaparate**
■ *v.* to put (something) on show: *shops are displaying summer clothes in their windows; the soldier displayed great courage; notices are displayed asking people not to smoke.* □ **exhibir, exponer**
displease [dis'pli:z] *v.* not to please: *she was very dis-*

pleased with the review of her book. □ **disgustar**
displeasure [dis'pleʒə] *n.* annoyance. □ **disgusto**
dispose [dis'pouz] *v.* ***to dispose of something,*** to get rid of something: *can you dispose of all these old newspapers?* □ **deshacerse de**
disposable *adj.* which can be thrown away after use: *disposable plates/nappies.* □ **desechable**
disposable income, amount of income left after the tax has been deducted. □ **renta disponible**
disposal *n.* **1** *waste disposal unit,* machine attached to a sink which grinds up waste. □ **triturador de residuos**
2 *I am entirely at your disposal,* I am at your service; you can ask me to do anything you wish. □ **...a tu disposición**
disposed *adj. he is well disposed towards us,* he favours us. □ **está bien dispuesto...**
disposition [dispə'ziʃn] *n.* character: *he has a grumpy disposition.* □ **temperamento**
dispossess [dispə'zes] *v.* to remove possessions from (someone): *he was dispossessed of all his books.* □ **desposeer**
disproportion [disprə'pɔːʃn] *n.* being out of proportion. □ **desproporción**
disproportionate *adj.* unusual; out of proportion: *he spends a disproportionate amount of his money on food.* □ **desproporcionado**
disprove [dis'pruːv] *v.* to prove that something is wrong. □ **refutar**
dispute [dis'pjuːt] *n.* argument: *work has stopped because of a dispute over pay.* □ **disputa**
■ *v.* to argue: *I would not dispute the statement that he is mad.* □ **discutir**
disqualify [dis'kwɔlifai] *v.* (*disqualified; disqualifying*) to rule that someone is incapable of doing something/not qualified to do something: *he was disqualified from driving for a year; the athlete was disqualified because he had taken drugs.* □ **inhabilitar**
disqualification [diskwɔlifi'keiʃn] *n.* rule that someone is incapable of doing something/not qualified to do something. □ **inhabilitación**
disquiet [dis'kwaiət] *n.* worry. □ **inquietud**
disquieting *adj.* which makes you worried. □ **inquietante**
disregard [disri'gɑːd] *n.* indifference (to something); lack of worry (about something): *his total disregard for the safety of his passengers.* □ **indiferencia**
■ *v.* to take no notice of: *he totally disregarded the traffic signals.* □ **no hacer caso de**
disrepair [disri'pɛə] *n.* state of needing to be repaired. □ **mal estado**
disrepute [disri'pjuːt] *n.* bad reputation: *to bring something/someone into disrepute.* □ **desprestigio**
disreputable [dis'repjutəbl] *adj.* (street, etc.) with a bad reputation: *he is a pretty disreputable character,* he is quite a wicked person. □ **de mala fama**
disrespect [disri'spekt] *n.* lack of respect. □ **falta de respeto**
disrespectful *adj.* lacking respect; rude: *he made some disrespectful remarks about the cooking.* □ **irrespetuoso**
disrupt [dis'rʌpt] *v.* to break up/to interrupt (a meeting). □ **interrumpir**
disruption [dis'rʌpʃn] *n.* breaking up; interruption (of a meeting). □ **interrupción**
disruptive *adj.* which disrupts. □ **que trastorna**
dissatisfaction [dissætis'fækʃn] *n.* lack of satisfaction: *I want to express my total dissatisfaction with your explanation.* □ **insatisfacción**
dissatisfied [dis'sætisfaid] *adj.* not satisfied: *a dissatisfied customer.* □ **insatisfecho**
dissect [di'sekt] *v.* to cut up (a dead body/plant) in order to examine the inside. □ **disecar**
dissection *n.* cutting up (a body or plant). □ **disección**
dissemble [di'sembl] *v.* (*formal*) to hide your feelings. □ **disimular**
disseminate [dis'semineit] *v.* to spread (news) around. □ **difundir**
dissemination *n.* act of spreading news, etc., around. □ **difusión**
dissent [di'sent] *v.* not to agree: *the jury voted almost unanimously - only one juror dissented.* □ **disentir**
dissension *n.* lack of agreement. □ **disensión**
dissertation [disə'teiʃn] *n.* short (university) thesis. □ **tesis**
disservice [dis'səːvis] *n.* bad deed: *you do yourself a disservice,* you do yourself harm. □ **mal servicio, perjuicio**
dissident ['disidənt] *adj.* and *n.* (person) who does not agree with the state. □ **disidente**
dissimilar [di'similə] *adj.* not the same: *they are not dissimilar,* they are quite alike. □ **distinto**
dissipate ['disipeit] *v.* to clear away; to get rid of: *the fog will soon dissipate; he dissipated a fortune in a few years.* □ **disipar**
dissipation [disi'peiʃn] *n.* throwing away (a fortune); wild living. □ **disipación**
dissociate [di'sousieit] *v. to dissociate yourself from a question,* to say that you have nothing to do with the question. □ **declararse ajeno a**
dissolute ['disəljuːt] *adj.* depraved: undisciplined. □ **disoluto**
dissolution *n.* act of dissolving (Parliament, etc.). □ **disolución**
dissolve [di'zɔlv] *v.* **1** to make a solid substance become part of a liquid: *dissolve three spoonfuls of sugar in boiling water; these tablets dissolve in the mouth.* □ **disolver**
2 to bring to an end: *to dissolve Parliament; their marriage was dissolved.* □ **disolver**
dissuade [di'sweid] *v.* to persuade someone not to do something: *he was dissuaded from resigning.* □ **disuadir**
dissuasion *n.* persuading someone not to do something. □ **disuasión**
distance ['distəns] *n.* space from one point to another: *I can see houses far in the distance,* quite a long way away; *can you hit a target at a distance of 200 metres? long-distance race; we live within easy driving distance of the town/within walking distance of the shops.* □ **distancia**
distant *adj.* **1** far away: *a distant view of the sea.* □ **distante**
2 *he is a distant relative,* he is related to me, but not of my close family. □ **pariente lejano**
distaste [dis'teist] *n.* dislike: *his obvious distaste for the speaker's politics.* □ **aversión**
distasteful *adj.* unpleasant: *a very distasteful remark.* □ **desagradable**
distemper [dis'tempə] *n.* **1** water colour paint for walls. □ **pintura al temple**
2 sickness of dogs. □ **moquillo**
distend [dis'tend] *v.* to swell. □ **hinchar, dilatar**
distil [di'stil] *v.* (*he distilled*) to make pure water/alcohol by heating and collecting the vapour. □ **destilar**
distilled water, pure water. □ **agua destilada**
distillation *n.* act of distilling (water, alcohol, etc.). □ **destilación**

distillery *n.* factory for distilling alcohol. □ **destilería**
distinct [di'stiŋkt] *adj.* **1** separate: *try to keep the two things distinct.* □ **bien determinado, distinto**
2 clear: *there was a distinct improvement in the patient's condition.* □ **claro**
distinction [di'stiŋkʃn] *n.* **1** difference: *they make no distinction between men and women.* □ **distinción**
2 special excellence: *he had the distinction of being the first man to walk on the moon.* □ **distinción, honor**
distinctive *adj.* very noticeable; particular to one thing; which makes one thing different from others: *you can recognize the butterfly by its distinctive markings.* □ **distintivo**
distinctly *adv.* clearly: *I told him distinctly that he could not come; I distinctly heard him say, 'rubbish'.* □ **claramente**
distinguish [di'stiŋgwiʃ] *v.* **1** to see clearly; to make out (detail): *it is so dark I can hardly distinguish anything.* □ **distinguir**
2 to make a difference (between two things): *how do you distinguish between various species of deer?* □ **distinguir**
3 *he distinguished himself by his excellent knowledge of Swedish,* he made himself noticed. □ **distinguirse**
distinguishable *adj.* which can be distinguished. □ **distinguible**
distinguished *adj.* important/well known (writer/painter, etc.). □ **distinguido**
distort [di'stɔːt] *v.* to twist; to give a false impression: *he has completely distorted the meaning of my statement; the television picture is distorted.* □ **distorsionar, falsear**
distortion [di'stɔːʃn] *n.* twisting; giving a false impression. □ **distorsión, falseamiento**
distract [di'strækt] *v.* to attract away from: *a movement distracted my attention.* □ **distraer**
distraction [di'strækʃn] *n.* **1** amusement: *cricket is a pleasant Sunday afternoon distraction.* □ **distracción**
2 worry; something that distracts. □ **perturbación**
3 *he loved her to distraction,* he was wild about her. □ **...hasta volverse loco**
distraught [dis'trɔːt] *adj.* wild (with worry/grief, etc.). □ **muy turbado**
distress [di'stres] *n.* **1** great sorrow/pain: *his death caused her great distress.* □ **pena; aflicción**
2 difficulty: *when a ship is in distress it sends up rockets.* □ **en apuros**
distress signal, signal sent out by ship/aircraft in difficulties. □ **señal de socorro**
■ *v.* to make someone very sad: *the news has distressed the family greatly.* □ **apenar**
distressing *adj.* very sad; worrying. □ **doloroso**
distribute [di'stribjuːt] *v.* **1** to give to several people: *he was distributing pamphlets in the street.* □ **distribuir**
2 *we distribute Japanese cars,* we are the agents for Japanese cars. □ **ser distribuidor de**
distribution [distri'bjuːʃn] *n.* giving to several people. □ **distribución**
distributive *adj.* which distributes. □ **distributivo**
distributor [di'stribjutə] *n.* **1** company which sells goods for another (usually overseas) company. □ **distribuidor**
2 (*in a car engine*) mechanism which passes the electric spark to each sparking plug in turn. □ **delco**
district ['distrikt] *n.* area/region: *country districts; the southern districts of the town.* □ **distrito**
district nurse, nurse who visits patients at home in a particular area. □ **enfermera (visitante) de distrito**
distrust [dis'trʌst] *n.* lack of trust. □ **desconfianza**
■ *v.* not to trust: *I distrust his ability to get on with people.* □ **desconfiar**
disturb [di'stəːb] *v.* to bother/to worry (someone); to interrupt (someone): *don't disturb him when he is working; the peace of the village was disturbed by the planes from the local airbase.* □ **perturbar, molestar**
disturbance *n.* **1** noise: *he was arrested for creating a disturbance in the street.* □ **alboroto**
2 crackling noise (on radio). □ **interferencias**
3 *atmospheric disturbances,* storms. □ **perturbaciones**
disturbing *adj.* worrying: *disturbing news from the battlefield.* □ **preocupante**
disuse [dis'juːs] *n. to fall into disuse,* not to be used any more. □ **desuso**
disused ['disjuːzd] *adj.* not used: *he fell down a disused mine shaft.* □ **abandonado**
ditch [ditʃ] *n.* long trench alongside a road, for taking away water. □ **cuneta**
■ *v.* **1** to make a ditch. □ **hacer zanjas**
2 (*informal*) to abandon: *he ditched his car and walked,* he left his car by the side of the road. □ **abandonar, dejar tirado**
dither ['diðə] *n. she's all of a dither,* very agitated. □ **está nerviosísima**
■ *v.* not to be able to make up one's mind: *he's dithering about whether to go to France on holiday or not.* □ **no saber qué hacer**
ditto ['ditou] *n.* the same thing; printer's sign (") meaning that the same thing is to be repeated. □ **ídem, comillas**
ditty ['diti] *n.* (*pl. ditties*) little song. □ **cancioncilla**
diuretic [daiju'retik] *adj.* and *n.* (substance) which makes you produce more urine. □ **diurético**
divan [di'væn] *n.* low couch; bed with a solid base and no back or ends. □ **diván**
dive [daiv] *n.* **1** plunge downwards head first: *he made a beautiful dive into the pool; the aircraft went into a dive.* □ **zambullida**
2 (*informal*) bad bar/club. □ **antro**
■ *v.* (*he dived, Amer. he dove*) to plunge head first: *she dived off a rock into the sea.* □ **tirarse de cabeza**
diver *n.* person who works underwater. □ **buzo**
diving board *n.* plank at swimming pool from which people dive. □ **trampolín**
diving suit *n.* heavy suit for divers working at great depths. □ **escafandra**
diverge [dai'vəːdʒ] *v.* to split. □ **separarse**
divergence *n.* split/difference: *a considerable divergence of opinion.* □ **divergencia**
diverging *adj.* splitting: *diverging opinions,* opinions which are quite different. □ **divergente**
diverse [dai'vəːs] *adj.* varied: *very diverse costumes.* □ **diverso**
diversify *v.* to vary; to do other sorts of work: *we are booksellers, but we are diversifying into records.* □ **diversificar**
diversity *n.* great variety: *a diversity of opinions.* □ **diversidad**
diversion [dai'vəːʃn] *n.* **1** sending traffic another way: *there is a diversion because of road works.* □ **desviación, desvío**
2 amusement. □ **diversión**
3 *to create a diversion,* to do something to distract someone's attention from something you do not want him to see. □ **distraer**
divert *v.* **1** to send traffic another way: *traffic is*

being diverted because of road works. □ **desviar**
2 to amuse. □ **divertir**
3 *I am trying to divert his attention,* to distract his attention away from something I do not want him to see. □ **distraer su atención**
divest [dai'vest] *v. to divest someone of something,* (*formal*) to take something away from someone. □ **despojar a uno de algo**
divide [di'vaid] *v.* **1** to cut into parts: *divide the cake into six pieces; the country is divided by religious quarrels; we divide (up) the work among us.* □ **dividir**
2 to calculate how many of one number there are in another: *can you divide 27 by 9?* □ **dividir**
dividers *pl. n.* pair of compasses for measuring. □ **compás de puntas**
dividend ['dividend] *n.* part of profits shared out among shareholders. □ **dividendo**
divine [di'vain] *adj.* referring to God. □ **divino**
■ *v.* to predict the future; to discover hidden sources of water. □ **adivinar**
divination [divi'neiʃn] *n.* predicting what will happen in the future. □ **adivinación**
divinity [di'viniti] *n.* god; state of being a god. □ **divinidad**
division [di'viʒn] *n.* **1** splitting up into parts; calculation of how many of one number there are in another. □ **división**
long division, working out of a complicated division (such as 2,894 divided by 19) on paper. □ **división**
2 (*in Parliament*) counting of votes. □ **recuento de votos**
3 important part (of army/firm). □ **división**
divisible [di'vizəbl] *adj.* which can be divided. □ **divisible**
divisive [di'vaisiv] *adj.* which produces quarrels. □ **que crea discordia**
divorce [di'vɔːs] *n.* legal separation of husband and wife leaving each free to remarry. □ **divorcio**
■ *v.* **1** to separate (two ideas, etc.). □ **divorciar**
2 to break off a marriage legally: *they are divorced; she divorced her husband.* □ **divorciarse**
divorcee [divɔː'siː] *n.* person (usually a woman) who is divorced. □ **divorciado**
divulge [dai'vʌldʒ] *v.* to reveal (a secret). □ **revelar**
DIY [diːai'wai] *abbreviation for* do it yourself: *a DIY shop,* shop selling paint/tools, etc. □ **bricolaje**
dizzy ['dizi] *adj.* (*dizzier, dizziest*) **1** feeling that everything is spinning round: *I feel dizzy,* my head is turning; *the roundabout went so fast it made me dizzy.* □ **mareado**
2 *dizzy heights,* such great heights that they make your head turn. □ **alturas de vértigo**
dizziness *n.* feeling that everything is turning round you. □ **vértigo, mareo**
DJ ['diːdʒei] *abbreviation for* disc jockey. □ **pinchadiscos**
do [duː] *n.* (*pl. dos*) party; social gathering: *we're going to a do on Saturday night.* □ **fiesta**
■ *v.* (*he did; he has done*) **1** to work (at something); to make/to complete (something): *what have you been doing all day? have you done your homework? I'm doing my hair,* I am combing my hair; *she was doing the washing; he hasn't done the dishes; can you do today's crossword?* □ **hacer (arreglar; fregar)**
well done!, congratulations, you have worked/run, etc., well! □ **¡bien hecho!**
2 *the potatoes aren't done yet,* aren't cooked yet; *the meat is done to a turn,* the meat is well cooked. □ **...no están hechas todavía; muy hecho**
done in: *I feel done in,* (*informal*) I am tired out. □ **estoy derrengado**
3 to be satisfactory: *will this colour do? this table won't do.* □ **valer, servir**
to make do with: *we will have to make do with paper plates,* we will have to accept paper plates because there is no alternative. □ **arreglárselas**
4 to go (at a certain speed): *this car can easily do 150 kilometres per hour.* □ **hacer, alcanzar**
5 (used in negatives, questions and answers): *it doesn't matter; we didn't laugh; do you live in England? - yes, I do; but your parents don't live there, do they? - no they do not.*
6 (takes the place of another verb): *can you swim as fast as he does? he speaks French better than I do; she arrived before we did.*
7 (telling someone not to do something): *don't throw that paper away! don't run into the road.* □ **no...**
8 ***how do you do?,*** hello! □ **¿cómo está usted?**
9 (to emphasize): *why don't you work? - I do work! why didn't she tell you? - she did tell me!* □ **claro que...**
do away *v.* ***to do away with something,*** to abolish something. □ **abolir**
to do away with someone, to murder someone. □ **asesinar**
doing *n.* **1** *it takes some doing,* it is quite difficult to do. □ **lleva lo suyo**
2 *doings,* (*informal*) thing: *give me the doings.* □ **chisme**
do-it-yourself *n.* repairing/building/painting, etc., yourself, without employing a professional. □ **bricolaje**
do out *v.* to clean out (a room/a cupboard). □ **arreglar**
do up *v.* **1** to fasten: *I can't do up my zip; can you do up this parcel for me?* □ **abrochar; hacer (paquete)**
2 to renovate: *they bought an old cottage and did it up.* □ **arreglar**
do with *v.* **1** to concern: *it is nothing to do with me,* it is not my business. □ **tener que ver con**
2 *it is something to do with the new book,* it concerns/it is about the new book. □ **tiene algo que ver con**
3 *what have you done with my hat?,* where have you put my hat? □ **¿qué has hecho con...?**
do without *v.* to manage without: *can you do without a car? I can't do without a cup of tea in the morning.* □ **prescindir de**
docile ['dousail] *adj.* quiet/not aggressive: *the big dog is very docile.* □ **dócil**
dock [dɔk] *n.* **1** artificial harbour. □ **muelle**
the docks, the whole harbour: *the ship is in dock,* is tied up at the quay. □ **el puerto**
2 *my car is **in dock**,* being repaired. □ **estar en el taller**
dry dock, dock where the water is pumped out to allow repairs to be done to a ship: *the ship has been in dry dock for three months.* □ **dique seco**
3 box in a law court, where the prisoner sits: *he is in dock facing charges of assault.* □ **banquillo de los acusados**
4 wild plant with very large leaves. □ **acedera**
■ *v.* **1** to put a ship into harbour: *the liner docked at seven o'clock.* □ **atracar**
2 to link two spacecraft together in space. □ **acoplar**
3 to cut off/to remove: *they docked $2 from his wages.* □ **descontar**
docker *n.* man who works in the docks. □ **estibador**
dockyard *n.* place where ships are built. □ **astillero**

doctor ['dɔktə] *n.* (*shortened in names to Dr*) person who looks after people's health; learned person with a superior degree from a university: *I have an appointment with Dr Jones; if your back hurts you should see a doctor.* □ **doctor, médico**
■ *v.* to look after a patient/a sick animal. □ **tratar**
doctorate ['dɔktərət] *n.* higher degree from a university. □ **doctorado**
doctrine ['dɔktrin] *n.* statement of what a group of people believe. □ **doctrina**
doctrinaire [dɔktri'nɛə] *adj.* very dogmatic: *a doctrinaire socialist.* □ **doctrinario**
doctrinal [dɔk'trainl] *adj.* referring to a doctrine. □ **doctrinal**
document ['dɔkjumənt] *n.* paper with writing on it. □ **documento**
documentary [dɔkju'mentəri] *n.* (*pl. documentaries*) factual film about a real subject. □ **documental**
■ *adj.* referring to documents: *documentary evidence.* □ **documental**
documentation *n.* all the documents which refer to something. □ **documentación**
dodder ['dɔdə] *v.* to walk uncertainly/to totter. □ **andar con paso inseguro**
doddery *adj.* old and trembly. □ **chocho**
dodge [dɔdʒ] *n.* trick: *a clever dodge to avoid paying tax.* □ **maniobra; truco**
■ *v.* to avoid/to get out of the way: *he dodged the blow.* □ **esquivar**
dodgems *n. pl.* amusement at a fairground, where small electric cars are driven round and bump into each other. □ **coches de choque**
dodgy *adj.* (*dodgier, dodgiest*) unsafe. □ **marrullero**
doe [dou] *n.* female (deer/rabbit, etc.). □ **cierva, coneja, etc.**
dog [dɔg] *n.* carnivorous animal which barks, often kept as a pet: *I have to take the dog for a walk.* □ **perro**
to let sleeping dogs lie, not to disturb the existing state of affairs. □ **dejar (algo) como está**
■ *v.* (*he dogged*) *to dog someone's footsteps,* to follow someone. □ **seguir los pasos de alguien**
dog-collar *n.* **1** leather band to go round a dog's neck. □ **collar de perro**
2 white collar worn by a clergyman. □ **alzacuello de clérigo**
dog-eared *adj.* (book) with its pages bent or torn. □ **sobado, en mal estado**
dogfish *n.* huss/small white sea fish. □ **cazón**
dogged ['dɔgid] *adj.* not giving in easily: *dogged perseverance.* □ **tenaz**
doghouse *n. Amer.* (*informal*) **1** kennel. □ **perrera**
2 *he's* ***in the doghouse,*** he's in disgrace. □ **está en desgracia**
dog-tired *adj.* worn out. □ **cansadísimo**
dogsbody *n.* person who always has all the worst jobs to do. □ **burro de carga**
dogwood *n.* shrub with bright red stems. □ **cornejo**
doggerel ['dɔgərəl] *n.* bad poetry. □ **versos ramplones**
dogma ['dɔgmə] *n.* official belief. □ **dogma**
dogmatic *adj.* insistent that what you say is right. □ **dogmático**
doily ['dɔili] *n.* (*pl. doilies*) decorated paper/lace serviette to put under a cake on a plate. □ **cubrebandejas**
doldrums *n. pl.* ***in the doldrums,*** not making any progress. □ **estancado**
dole [doul] *n.* money given to people without work: *my brother is on the dole,* he is unemployed and receiving government payments. □ **subsidio de paro**
■ *v.* ***to dole out*** *soup,* to hand out bowls of soup (in a half-hearted way). □ **repartir (poca cantidad)**
doleful ['doulful] *adj.* gloomy. □ **lúgubre**
doll [dɔl] *n.* toy which looks like a baby. □ **muñeca**
dollar ['dɔlə] *n.* money used in the USA and many other countries: *this book costs four dollars ($4.00).* □ **dólar**
dollop ['dɔləp] *n.* (*informal*) large lump (of something soft): *a dollop of ice cream; a dollop of jam.* □ **porción, trozo (grande)**
dolphin ['dɔlfin] *n.* mammal like a small whale living in the sea. □ **delfín**
dolphinarium [dɔlfi'nɛəriəm] *n.* large aquarium, where people pay to watch dolphins perform tricks. □ **delfinario**
domain [də'mein] *n.* **1** area controlled by someone: *the emperor's domains.* □ **dominio**
2 area of knowledge: *in the domain of physics.* □ **esfera, dominio, campo**
dome [doum] *n.* semi-spherical roof: *the church has a large dome.* □ **cúpula**
domed *adj.* with a dome. □ **cupulado**
domestic [də'mestik] *adj.* **1** referring to the home. □ **doméstico**
domestic science, study of cooking and running a home. □ **ciencia del hogar**
domestic animals, animals which man keeps for wool/milk/meat, etc. □ **animales domésticos**
2 *domestic flights,* flights inside a country. □ **vuelos nacionales**
domesticated [də'mestikeitid] *adj.* (animal) trained to live in the house. □ **domesticado**
domesticity [dɔme'stisiti] *n.* life at home. □ **vida casera**
domiciled ['dɔmisaild] *adj.* (*formal*) living; resident: *he was domiciled at 11, Park Road.* □ **domiciliado**
dominant ['dɔminənt] *adj.* most important; supreme; commanding. □ **dominante**
dominate ['dɔmineit] *v.* **1** to rule: *big countries try to dominate smaller countries.* □ **dominar**
2 to be very obvious: *the factory chimneys dominate the landscape.* □ **dominar**
dominating *adj.* ruling; overshadowing: *the dominating presence of the superpowers.* □ **dominadora**
domineer [dɔmi'niə] *v.* to rule (someone). □ **dominar**
domineering *adj.: a domineering wife,* a wife who rules her husband. □ **dominante**
dominion [də'minjən] *n.* **1** self-governing state in the Commonwealth: *the Dominion of Canada.* □ **dominio**
2 rule (over a territory). □ **dominio**
domino ['dɔminou] *n.* (*pl. dominoes*) one of a set of small flat blocks, each divided into two sections, with up to six dots in each section: *they sat all night in the pub playing dominoes.* □ **ficha de dominó; (plural) dominó**
don [dɔn] *n.* university teacher. □ **catedrático**
■ *v.* (*he donned*) to put on (a piece of clothing). □ **ponerse**
donate [dou'neit] *v.* to give: *he donated his collection of pictures to the museum.* □ **donar**
donation [dou'neiʃn] *n.* gift: *all donations will be gratefully received,* we will accept all gifts of money. □ **donativo**
done [dʌn] *v. see* **do.**
donkey ['dɔŋki] *n.* farm animal like a small horse but with long ears. □ **burro**
donkey's years: *I haven't seen him for donkey's years,* (*informal*) I have not seen him for a long time. □ **no lo he visto desde hace siglos**
donkey jacket, thick woollen jacket with leather

patches on the shoulders, worn especially by workmen. □ **chaqueta reforzada**
donor ['dounə] *n.* person who gives. □ **donante**
blood donor, person who gives blood for blood transfusions. □ **donante de sangre**
doodle ['du:dl] *v.* to make meaningless drawings/patterns on paper. □ **hacer garabatos**
doom [du:m] *n.* **1** fate. □ **suerte; destino**
2 unhappy ending/ruin: *he met his doom.* □ **perdición**
■ *v.* to condemn (someone/something): *the whole project was doomed to failure.* □ **...condenado al fracaso**
door [dɔː] *n.* **1** barrier of wood/metal, etc., which closes an entrance: *our house has a blue door; cupboard door; oven door; shut the door please; can you leave the door open? he opened the door with his key.* □ **puerta**
front door, main door of a house. □ **puerta principal**
back door, door at the back of a house. □ **puerta de servicio, de atrás**
2 *he lives two doors down the street,* he lives two houses away. □ **vive a dos números de aquí**
doorkeeper *n.* person who is on guard at a main door. □ **portero**
doorknob *n.* round handle for opening/shutting a door. □ **pomo; tirador**
doorman *n.* (*pl. doormen*) person who is in attendance at a door (of a restaurant/hotel, etc.). □ **portero**
doormat *n.* rough carpet in front of a door. □ **felpudo**
doorstep *n.* block of stone, wood, etc. forming the base of a doorway. □ **peldaño, umbral**
doorway *n.* space filled by a door: *he stood in the doorway smoking his pipe.* □ **entrada; portal**
dope [doup] *n.* **1** (*informal*) drug. □ **droga**
2 strong glue/varnish for making models. □ **barniz**
3 (*informal*) stupid fool. □ **idiota**
dopey *adj.* (*informal*) stupid/silly. □ **atontado**
dormant ['dɔːmənt] *adj.* sleeping. □ **letárgico**
dormant plant, plant which is not growing because it is winter. □ **planta en letargo**
dormant volcano, volcano which is not erupting, but which is not extinct. □ **volcán inactivo**
dormer ['dɔːmə] *n.* ***dormer (window),*** window with a small gable roof jutting out from a sloping roof. □ **buhardilla**
dormitory ['dɔːmitri] *n.* (*pl. dormitories*) long room full of beds: *the boys sleep in a dormitory.* □ **dormitorio**
dormouse ['dɔːmaus] *n.* (*pl. dormice*) small mouse-like animal. □ **lirón**
dorsal ['dɔːsl] *adj.* (muscle/fin) which is on the back of an animal. □ **dorsal**
dose [dous] *n.* quantity of medicine: *you must take it in small doses.* □ **dosis**
■ *v.* to give (someone) medicine. □ **administrar una medicina**
dosage *n.* amount of medicine to be given. □ **dosis**
doss [dɔs] *v.* ***to doss down,*** (*informal*) to sleep on a rough bed/on the ground, etc. □ **echarse a dormir**
dosser *n.* (*informal*) tramp/vagrant. □ **vagabundo**
dosshouse *n.* (*informal*) cheap lodging for vagrants. □ **posada de mala muerte**
dossier ['dɔsiə] *n.* collection of relevant papers. □ **informe; 'dossier'**
dot [dɔt] *n.* **1** small round spot: *the Morse code is made up of dots and dashes.* □ **punto**
2 *he arrived* ***on the dot*** *of three,* exactly at three o'clock. □ **en punto**
■ *v.* (*he dotted*) **1** to mark with small spots. □ **puntear**
dotted line, line made up of small spots. □ **línea de puntos**
2 *the hillside is dotted with houses,* there are houses here and there on the hillside. □ **...salpicada de casas**
dotty *adj.* (*dottier, dottiest*) (*informal*) slightly mad. □ **chiflado**
dote [dout] *v.* ***to dote on someone,*** to be very fond of someone. □ **adorar a alguien**
dotage *n.* silly old age: *he's in his dotage.* □ **chochez**
dottle ['dɔtl] *n.* mass of unburnt tobacco at the bottom of a pipe. □ **tabaco sin quemar**
double ['dʌbl] *adj.* **1** with two parts. □ **doble**
double bed, bed for two people. □ **cama de matrimonio**
double cream, thick cream which can be whipped easily. □ **crema espesa, nata para montar**
double figures, numbers from 10 to 99: *the sales have reached double figures.* □ **de dos cifras**
2 twice as big: *I am double your age.* □ **te doblo la edad**
3 *a double whisky,* two measures of whisky. □ **güisqui doble**
4 *it takes double the time,* twice as long. □ **lleva el doble de tiempo**
5 *it is double the distance,* twice as far. □ **el doble de distancia**
■ *adv. I am seeing double,* I can see two things when there is only one there. □ **veo doble**
■ *n.* **1** ***at the double,*** at a run. □ **a paso ligero**
2 *he is my double,* he and I look exactly alike. □ **es mi doble**
3 *men's/women's/mixed* ***doubles,*** tennis matches for two men or two women or one man and one woman on each side. □ **dobles**
■ *v.* **1** to multiply by two: *think of a number and double it.* □ **doblar**
2 *he doubled back,* he turned round and came back along the same way. □ **volver sobre sus pasos**
3 *she was doubled up in pain,* was bent forwards. □ **estaba doblada por el dolor**
double-barrelled *adj.* **1** (gun) with two barrels. □ **de dos cañones**
2 (surname) with two parts linked with a hyphen. □ **apellido compuesto**
double bass *n.* very large stringed musical instrument. □ **contrabajo**
double-breasted *adj.* (jacket) which overlaps in front. □ **cruzada**
double-cross *v.* to trick someone (when he thinks that you are working on his side.). □ **traicionar**
double-crosser *n.* trickster/cheat. □ **traidor, hipócrita**
double-decker *n.* **1** bus with an upper as well as a lower deck. □ **autobús de dos pisos**
2 (*informal*) double sandwich (made with three slices of bread). □ **sandwich doble**
double-edged *adj.* **1** with two sharp edges. □ **de doble filo**
2 which has two quite different meanings. □ **de dos sentidos**
double-park *v.* to park alongside a car which is already parked at the side of the street. □ **estacionar en doble fila**
double-parking *n.* parking alongside a car which is already parked at the side of the street. □ **estacionamiento en doble fila**
double-quick *adj. you will have to do it in double-quick time,* extremely fast. □ **rapidísimamente**

doubt [daut] *n.* not being sure: *I have my doubts about his competence,* I am not sure if he is competent. □ **duda**
no doubt, of course/certainly: *no doubt you will have heard that he won the prize.* □ **indudablemente**
in doubt, uncertain: *the result of the election is in doubt.* □ **dudoso**
■ *v.* not to be sure of: *I doubt whether he will come; I don't doubt his skill.* □ **dudar**
doubtful *adj.* uncertain: *he is doubtful about being able to come with us; whether they will send any money is doubtful.* □ **dudoso**
doubtfully *adv.* hesitatingly: *'I hope they can come,' he answered doubtfully.* □ **nada convencido**
doubtless *adv.* certainly. □ **sin duda**
douche [du:ʃ] *n.* spray of water to clean part of the body. □ **ducha**
dough [dou] *n.* **1** uncooked mixture of water and flour for making bread, etc. □ **masa**
2 (*slang*) money. □ **pasta**
doughnut *n.* small round or ring-shaped cake which is cooked by frying in oil. □ **'donut'**
dour ['duə] *adj.* gloomy/silent. □ **severo**
douse [daus] *v.* to throw water on (something). □ **mojar**
dove [dʌv] *n.* **1** white domesticated pigeon. □ **paloma**
2 politician who is in favour of negotiating for peace. □ **paloma (en contraposición a halcón)**
3 [douv] *v. Amer. see* **dive.**
dovetail *v.* **1** to join (wood) together with a V-shaped joint. □ **ensamblar a cola de milano**
2 *it dovetails neatly into my timetable,* it fits my timetable very well. □ **encajar**
dowager ['dauədʒə] *n.* widow of a nobleman who has kept her title. □ **viuda de un noble**
dowdy ['daudi] *adj.* (*dowdier, dowdiest*) badly-dressed (person); dull/unfashionable (clothes). □ **desaliñado**
dowel ['dauəl] *n.* round wooden peg like a nail for attaching pieces of wood together. □ **espiga**
dowelling *n. a piece of dowelling,* a long round stick of wood from which dowels can be cut. □ **madera para espigas**
down [daun] *adv., adj.* and *prep.* **1** towards the bottom: *he went down the stairs; he tried to go up the down escalator,* the one which was going downwards; *she climbed down the ladder.* □ **abajo**
2 *he fell down,* fell to the ground. □ **se cayó al suelo**
down with *examinations!,* let's do away with examinations. □ **¡abajo con los...!**
3 at the bottom: *down below it was quite cool; he is not down here.* □ **abajo**
4 *she is down with influenza,* she has gone to bed with influenza. □ **está con gripe**
5 *inflation is down again,* inflation is lower again. □ **..ha bajado**
6 ***down under,*** (*informal*) in Australia and New Zealand. □ **en las antípodas**
■ *n.* **1** soft feathers (of a duck). □ **plumón; flojel**
2 ***the downs,*** rounded chalk hills in the South of England.
■ *v.* **1** to swallow quickly: *he downed his pint of beer in one go.* □ **beber de un trago**
2 *the workers downed tools,* they stopped work/went on strike. □ **ir a la huelga**
down-and-out *n.* tramp/person with no money who lives in the street. □ **pobre**
down-at-heel *adj.* worn/shabby (clothes). □ **gastado**
downcast *adj.* gloomy/depressed. □ **abatido**
downfall *n.* collapse/ruin: *his downfall was caused by drink; the opposition combined to bring about the Government's downfall.* □ **ruina; caída**
downgrade *v.* to reduce someone's status: *he has been downgraded in the reorganization.* □ **degradar**
downhearted *adj.* depressed/gloomy. □ **desanimado**
downhill *adv.* towards the bottom (of a hill): *the road goes downhill; from here it's downhill all the way.* □ **cuesta abajo**
down payment *n.* part of a total cost paid in advance. □ **entrada**
downpour *n.* heavy fall of rain. □ **chaparrón**
downright *adj.* complete/distinct: *it's a downright lie.* □ **manifiesto, completo**
■ *adv.* completely/distinctly: *he was downright rude to me.* □ **completamente**
downstairs *adv.* and *n.* on/to a lower, especially the ground, floor: *I am going downstairs; I will wait for you downstairs; can I show you the downstairs (rooms)?* □ **abajo**
downstream *adj.* and *adv.* towards the mouth of a river. □ **aguas abajo**
down-to-earth *adj.* straightforward/matter-of-fact (way of speaking, etc.). □ **realista; práctico**
downtown *adv.* and *n.* (in/to the) central business district of a town: *I have to go downtown; he has a downtown office.* □ **centro (de la ciudad)**
downtrodden *adj.* oppressed/badly treated. □ **oprimido, pisoteado**
downward *adj.* (movement) towards the bottom: *there is a downward trend in sales.* □ **a la baja**
downwards *adv.* towards the bottom: *he put the paper face downwards on the table.* □ **hacia abajo**
downy *adj.* covered with down/with soft feathers. □ **suave**
dowry ['dauəri] *n.* money or goods which a bride brings to her husband. □ **dote**
doyen ['dɔiən] *n.* senior member of a group. □ **decano**
dowse [daus] *v.* to look for water using a twig which jumps when near water. □ **buscar agua con vara de zahorí**
doyly ['dɔili] *n.* (*pl. doylies*) véase **doily**
doze [douz] *n.* short sleep. □ **cabezada**
■ *v.* to be half asleep. □ **dormitar**
to doze off: *he dozed off,* he went into a light sleep. □ **se quedó medio dormido**
dozen ['dʌzn] *n.* twelve: *a dozen bottles of milk; two dozen eggs; half a dozen apples,* six apples. □ **docena**
dozens of *people/times,* many people/times. □ **miles de**
Dr ['dɔktə] *abbreviation for* Doctor. □ **Dr.**
drab [dræb] *adj.* lacking bright colours; brown, grey: *the drab streets of the town.* □ **gris**
draconian [drə'kouniən] *adj.* very severe/harsh (law, etc.). □ **draconiano**
draft [drɑ:ft] *n.* **1** rough plan (of a document): *a draft treaty.* □ **borrador**
2 *Amer.* obligatory military service. □ **reclutamiento**
3 order for money to be paid by a bank. □ **libramiento, letra**
■ *v.* **1** to draw up a rough plan: *I am drafting a letter to the lawyer.* □ **hacer un borrador**
2 *Amer.* to call (someone) for service: *he was drafted into the Navy; I was drafted to attend the conference;* see also **draught.** □ **reclutar**
drag [dræg] *n.* **1** ***what a drag!,*** (*slang*) how boring! □ **¡qué rollo!**
2 (*slang*) wearing of women's clothes by a man: *he was in drag.* □ **disfrazado de mujer**
■ *v.* (*he dragged*) **1** to pull something heavy along:

he was dragging a chair behind him; she dragged her children into the shop. □ **arrastrar**
2 to hang back/to stay behind; to go slowly: *the lawsuit is dragging.* □ **demorarse**
3 *to drag a lake,* to pull a net along the bottom of a lake to try to find something. □ **dragar**
drag on *v.* to continue slowly: *the war dragged on for years.* □ **prolongarse**
drag out *v.* to pull out: *I had to drag him out of bed.* □ **sacar de la cama**
dragon ['drægən] *n.* mythological animal which breathes fire. □ **dragón**
dragonfly *n.* (*pl. dragonflies*) common insect with brilliant transparent wings which appears in summer. □ **libélula**
dragoon [drə'gu:n] *v.* to force: *he was dragooned into appearing in the play.* □ **obligar**
drain [drein] *n.* **1** pipe for carrying waste water: *the drains are blocked.* □ **alcantarilla**
2 *it's like pouring money* ***down the drain,*** (*informal*) it is a waste of money. □ **...tirar el dinero por la ventana**
3 gradual loss (of money): *it is a drain on our resources.* □ **sangría**
brain drain, emigration of professional people to work overseas for better pay. □ **fuga de cerebros**
■ *v.* to remove (a liquid): *the water will gradually drain away; we have to drain off the fluid.* □ **irse; desaguar**
drainage *n.* system of pipes for taking away waste water. □ **alcantarillado**
draining *n.* removal of excess liquid. □ **drenaje; desagüe**
draining board, sloping surface next to a sink for draining water off dishes. □ **escurreplatos**
drainpipe *n.* pipe which takes away waste water. □ **tubería de desagüe**
drake [dreik] *n.* male duck. □ **pato**
dram [dræm] *n.* small drink (of spirits). □ **trago**
drama ['drɑ:mə] *n.* **1** serious theatrical performance. □ **obra dramática (teatro)**
drama department, department which deals with plays. □ **departamento de teatro**
2 series of serious events: *the drama of the rescue of the sailors from a sinking ship.* □ **drama**
dramatic [drə'mætik] *adj.* **1** referring to drama. □ **dramático**
2 surprising; giving a shock: *it is having a dramatic effect on our sales.* □ **dramático**
dramatically *adv.* very surprisingly: *imports have risen dramatically.* □ **dramáticamente**
dramatist ['dræmətist] *n.* person who writes plays. □ **dramaturgo**
dramatization *n.* adaptation (of a novel) for the stage/for the TV. □ **dramatización**
dramatize *v.* **1** to adapt (a novel) for the stage/for the TV. □ **adaptar, dramatizar**
2 to make something seem much more dramatic than it really is. □ **dramatizar**
drank [dræŋk] *v. see* **drink.**
drape [dreip] *n. Amer.* ***drapes,*** curtains. □ **cortinas**
■ *v.* to hang (cloth) around something: *he draped a sheet round himself.* □ **cubrir**
draper ['dreipə] *n.* person who sells cloth. □ **pañero**
drapery *n.* **1** cloth goods: *drapery department.* □ **pañería**
2 thin cloth draped around someone. □ **paño, sábana**
drastic ['dræstik] *adj.* very sharp/sudden: *we had to take drastic steps to cut spending.* □ **drástico**
drastically *adv.* suddenly/sharply. □ **drásticamente**
draught [drɑ:ft] *Amer.* **draft** *n.* **1** pulling. □ **tracción**
draught horse, horse trained to pull heavy loads. □ **caballo de tiro**
beer on draught/draught beer, beer which is pumped out of a barrel, using a lever. □ **cerveza de barril**
2 mouthful/swallow: *the runners were refreshed with great draughts of beer.* □ **trago**
3 amount of a ship's bottom which is under water: *shallow-draught boat,* boat which does not go very deep into the water. □ **calado**
4 breeze (in a room): *close the door, there's a draught.* □ **corriente de aire**
5 ***draughts,*** game played with black and white counters on a board with black and white squares. □ **damas**
draughtsman ['drɑ:ftsmən] *n.* (*pl. draughtsmen*) person who draws: *he is a draughtsman working on aircraft designs; Picasso was a wonderful draughtsman.* □ **proyectista; dibujante**
draughtsmanship *n.* skill at drawing. □ **arte del dibujante**
draughty *adj.* full of breezes: *we had to sit in a cold, draughty room.* □ **lleno de corrientes de aire**
draw [drɔ:] *n.* **1** lottery: *I won a bottle of whisky in the Christmas draw.* □ **sorteo, lotería**
2 attraction: *she is the big draw at the church fête.* □ **atracción**
3 *he is* ***quick on the draw,*** he pulls out his gun and shoots quickly. □ **rápido en sacar la pistola**
4 game where neither side wins: *the result was a draw 1-1.* □ **empate**
■ *v.* (*he drew; he has drawn*) **1** to make a picture with a pen or pencil: *can you draw a picture of your house? I am no good at drawing trees.* □ **dibujar**
2 to pull: *he drew the curtains,* he opened/closed the curtains. □ **correr (las cortinas)**
3 *they drew lots to decide who would start,* they each took a piece of paper/stick, etc., from a bundle, the person taking the marked paper/stick being the one selected to go first; *she drew the winning card.* □ **echar a suertes; sacar**
to draw a blank: *he drew a blank,* he was unsuccessful. □ **fracasar, llevarse un chasco**
4 to move: *the time is drawing near; the car drew in to the side of the road; he drew up a chair to the table; the day was drawing to a close.* □ **acercarse; orillarse; acercar; anochecer**
5 not to have a winner in a game: *they drew 1-1; the match was drawn,* neither side won. □ **empatar**
6 to collect liquid: *to draw water from a well.* □ **sacar**
7 *to draw blood,* to cut someone so that they bleed. □ **hacer sangrar**
draw aside *v.* to take (someone)/to move, to one side. □ **llamar a uno a aparte**
draw back *v.* **1** *he drew back the curtains,* he opened the curtains. □ **correr**
2 *she drew back,* she moved backwards. □ **retroceder**
drawback *n.* inconvenient thing; obstacle: *lack of electricity is a considerable drawback.* □ **inconveniente**
drawbridge *n.* bridge which can be raised or lowered to give access across water. □ **puente levadizo**
drawer *n.* sliding compartment in a desk or cupboard which you open by pulling on a handle: *my desk has three drawers.* □ **cajón**
chest of drawers, piece of bedroom furniture made of several sliding compartments. □ **cómoda**
drawing *n.* picture done with pen or pencil: *here is an old drawing of our house; drawing paper.* □ **dibujo**

drawing pin, pin with a large flat head for pinning paper. □ **chincheta**
drawing board *n.* **1** large board used by designers, on which paper is laid for drawing on. □ **tablero de dibujo**
2 *it was back to the drawing board,* he had to start the project all over again. □ **volver a empezar**
drawing room *n.* sitting room; room for sitting and talking in but not eating. □ **salón; cuarto de estar**
drawl [drɔːl] *n.* slow way of speaking. □ **habla pausada**
■ *v.* to speak slowly, dragging the words. □ **hablar arrastrando las palabras**
drawn [drɔːn] *v. see* **draw.**
dray [drei] *n.* low flat lorry or cart for carrying barrels. □ **carretón**
dread [dred] *n.* great fear: *he lives in dread of the tax man.* □ **pavor**
■ *v.* to fear greatly: *I dread having to tell him he is sacked.* □ **tener pavor, horrorizarse**
dreadful *adj.* awful: *what a dreadful accident!* □ **espantoso**
dreadfully *adv.* awfully/extremely: *I am dreadfully sorry.* □ **terriblemente**
dream [driːm] *n.* thing which you think you see happening when you are asleep: *I had a strange dream last night.* □ **sueño**
■ *v.* (*he dreamed/he dreamt*) **1** to think you see things happening while you are asleep: *I dreamt I was swimming.* □ **soñar**
2 *I wouldn't dream of wearing pink socks,* I wouldn't ever think of wearing pink socks. □ **ocurrirse**
dreamer *n.* person who thinks a lot/who is out of touch with practical things. □ **soñador**
dreamily *adv.* as in a dream. □ **como si estuviera soñando**
dreamy *adj.* (*dreamier, dreamiest*) like a dream. □ **de ensueño**
dreary ['driəri] *adj.* (*drearier, dreariest*) sad/gloomy; not interesting. □ **monótono, triste**
drearily *adv.* sadly/gloomily. □ **tristemente**
dredge [dredʒ] *v.* **1** to scrape the bottom of a river or lake to remove sand or mud to find something. □ **dragar**
2 to sprinkle (with sugar, etc.). □ **espolvorear**
dredger *n.* **1** machine for removing sand or mud from the bottom of a river or lake; boat with such a machine in it. □ **draga**
2 container with holes in the top for sprinkling (sugar, etc.). □ **espolvoreador**
dregs [dregz] *n. pl.* last drops of liquid in a bottle: *he drank the dregs of the wine.* □ **posos**
drench [drentʃ] *v.* **1** to soak. □ **empapar**
2 *I was drenched when I reached home,* I was wet through. □ **empapado, calado**
dress [dres] *n.* (*pl. dresses*) **1** piece of woman's/girl's clothing, covering more or less all the body: *she was wearing a green dress.* □ **vestido**
2 special clothes: *he was in evening dress.* □ **traje**
dress rehearsal, rehearsal where the actors wear their costumes. □ **ensayo general (con todo)**
dress circle, first balcony of seats above the stalls in a theatre. □ **palcos; entresuelo**
■ *v.* **1** to put on clothes: *the bride was dressed in white; when I get up in the morning, I get dressed, and then have breakfast.* □ **vestirse**
2 to clean (a wound)/to put a bandage (on a wound). □ **limpiar; vendar**
3 to arrange a display (in a shop window). □ **decorar, arreglar**
4 to prepare (a chicken) for cooking. □ **aderezar**
dresser *n.* **1** person in theatre who helps the actors with their costumes. □ **ayudante de vestuario**
window dresser, person who arranges displays in shop windows. □ **escaparatista**
2 piece of kitchen furniture with open shelves for displaying plates and cupboards below. □ **aparador**
dressing *n.* **1** putting on clothes. □ **vestir**
dressing room, room for getting dressed, especially room where an actor puts on his costume. □ **cuarto de vestir; camerino (teatro)**
dressing gown, long robe worn over pyjamas or nightdress. □ **bata**
dressing table, bedroom table with mirrors. □ **tocador**
2 sauce (for salad). □ **aliño**
French dressing, sauce made of oil and vinegar. □ **vinagreta**
3 bandage (for a wound). □ **vendaje**
dressmaker *n.* person who makes women's clothes. □ **modista**
dressmaking *n.* making of women's clothes by hand: *she has a dressmaking business.* □ **confección; costura**
dress up *v.* to put on a costume: *the children dressed up as policemen.* □ **disfrazarse de**
dressy *adj.* very showily dressed; showy (clothes). □ **peripuesto**
drew [druː] *v. see* **draw.**
drey [drei] *n.* nest made by a squirrel. □ **nido**
dribble ['dribl] *v.* **1** to let drops of liquid run out of your mouth. □ **babear**
2 to kick a football along as you are running. □ **avanzar con el balón**
dribs and drabs ['dribzəndræbz] *n. pl.* little bits: *the money came in dribs and drabs,* a little at a time. □ **pequeñas cantidades**
drier ['draiə] *n.* = **dryer.**
drift [drift] *n.* **1** general direction. □ **sentido; dirección**
2 *I got the general drift of his argument,* I understood the general sense of his argument. □ **sentido**
3 pile of snow blown by the wind. □ **ventisquero**
4 *North Atlantic drift,* current which crosses the North Atlantic. □ **corriente**
■ *v.* **1** to let yourself move: *the boat drifted down the river.* □ **dejarse llevar por la corriente**
2 to pile up: *the snow was drifting badly.* □ **amontonarse**
drifter *n.* person with no set plan in life/person who moves aimlessly from job to job. □ **veleta, persona sin rumbo**
driftwood *n.* (*no pl.*) wood which floats and blows on to the shore. □ **madero flotante**
drill [dril] *n.* **1** machine for making holes (in wood/metal, etc.): *the dentist has a high speed drill.* □ **taladro**
pneumatic drill, machine driven by compressed air for making holes in roads. □ **martillo neumático**
2 military practice in marching and moving in time with other soldiers. □ **instrucción**
3 *what's the drill?,* (*informal*) what do we do now? □ **y ahora ¿qué hacemos?**
fire drill, practice in reaching the life boats on a ship/practice in evacuating a building in case of fire. □ **simulacro de incendio**
4 small furrow in the ground in which you sow seeds. □ **surco**
■ *v.* **1** to make holes: *they drilled three holes in the ceiling; he is drilling for oil,* he is making holes in the ground in the hope of finding oil. □ **hacer agujeros; perforar**
2 to do military practice: *the soldiers were drilling*

on the parade ground; the instructor drilled the men. □ **hacer la instrucción**

drily ['draili] *adv.* = **dryly.**

drink [driŋk] *n.* **1** liquid which you swallow: *have a drink of water; I like a hot drink before I go to bed; would you like a drink?,* are you thirsty? □ **bebida**
soft drinks, non-alcoholic drinks. □ **refrescos; bebidas no alcohólicas**
2 *he has a drink problem,* he suffers from alcoholism; *he was much the worse for drink,* he was drunk. □ **bebida**
■ *v.* (*he drank; he has drunk*) **1** to swallow liquid: *I have drunk three cups of coffee; he never drinks tea; he was drinking at the bar,* he was drinking something alcoholic at the bar. □ **beber**
2 *she doesn't drink,* she never drinks alcohol. □ **no bebe**
3 *let's **drink to** the success of the expedition,* let us raise our glasses and wish it success. □ **brindemos por el éxito...**
drinkable *adj.* nice to drink: *it is quite a drinkable wine.* □ **es un vino que entra muy bien**
drinker *n.* person who drinks (too much alcohol). □ **bebedor**
drinking *n.* action of swallowing liquid; consumption of alcohol; alcoholism. □ **beber; bebida**
drinking water, water which is safe to drink. □ **agua potable**

drip [drip] *n.* **1** small drop of water. □ **goteo**
2 (*in hospital*) device which allows liquid to drip regularly into the bloodstream of a patient. □ **'el gota a gota'**
■ *v.* (*it dripped*) **1** to fall in drops: *the rain was dripping off the trees.* □ **gotear**
2 *the tap is dripping,* drops of water are coming out of the tap which has not been turned off tightly enough. □ **el grifo está goteando**
drip-dry shirt, shirt which does not crease if it is hung to dry while it is soaking wet. □ **camisa que no precisa planchado**
dripping *n.* fat left in a pan after roasting meat. □ **pringue, grasa**

drive [draiv] *n.* **1** ride in a motor vehicle: *we went for a drive into the country.* □ **paseo en coche**
2 way in which a car is propelled or guided: *car with front-wheel drive,* car where the engine is connected directly to the front wheels; *car with left-hand drive,* car where the driver sits on the left-hand side. □ **conducción; tracción**
3 short private road leading to a house. □ **callejón particular**
4 stroke (in golf or cricket) where the ball is hit hard and far. □ **'drive'**
5 energy: *he is a man with lots of drive.* □ **energía**
6 campaign (to collect money for charity). □ **campaña**
■ *v.* (*he drove; he has driven*) **1** to make a motor vehicle travel in a certain direction: *I can swim but I can't drive; have you ever driven a bus? he was driving too fast; if you can't drive you ought to take driving lessons; I will drive you to the airport,* I will take you to the airport in my car; *in England cars drive on the left.* □ **conducir; manejar (Amér.); llevar en coche**
2 to force/to push: *he drove nails into the wood with great blows of his hammer.* □ **clavar**
3 *he was driven to it,* he was forced to do it. □ **forzar**
4 ***to drive a hard bargain:*** *she drives a hard bargain,* she is a very tough businesswoman. □ **actuar con dureza en una negociación**
5 *the pressure of work was driving her frantic,* making her become frantic. □ **poner**
drive along *v.* to ride along a road in a motor vehicle: *we were driving along the motorway when the car broke down.* □ **conducir por, ir (en coche) por**
drive at *v. what is he driving at?,* what is he trying to say? □ **insinuar**
drive away *v.* **1** to force (something/someone) to go away. □ **alejar**
2 to ride away in a motor vehicle. □ **irse en coche**
drive back *v.* **1** to push back: *the soldiers drove back the enemy.* □ **hacer retroceder**
2 to go/to come back in a motor vehicle. □ **regresar**
drive in *v.* **1** to force in: *he used a sledgehammer to drive in the nails.* □ **clavar**
2 to go in by car. □ **entrar**
drive-in cinema/restaurant, cinema/restaurant where you can drive in in a car and watch a film or eat while still sitting in the car. □ **cine con; restaurante al aire libre (desde el coche)**
drive on *v.* to continue one's journey. □ **seguir su camino**
driver *n.* person who drives (a motor vehicle): *a taxi driver; a bus driver; women drivers are a menace.* □ **conductor**
driver's licence, *Amer.* permit which allows you to drive. □ **permiso de conducción**
driving *adj.* (rain/snow) blown by the wind: *there is no sense in trying to play tennis in driving rain.* □ **(lluvia) con viento**
■ *n.* action of driving a motor vehicle. □ **conducción**
driving licence, permit which allows you to drive. □ **permiso de conducción**
driving school, school where you learn to drive. □ **autoescuela**
driving test, test taken before you can have a driving licence. □ **examen de conducir**
driving wheel, wheel which moves a part of the machinery (in a machine)/steering wheel (in a car/lorry, etc.). □ **rueda motriz**

drivel ['drivl] *n.* rubbish: *don't talk drivel.* □ **tonterías**

driven ['drivn] *v. see* **drive.**

drizzle ['drizl] *n.* thin continuous rain. □ **llovizna**
■ *v.* to rain in a thin mist: *it has been drizzling all day.* □ **lloviznar**
drizzly *adj.* (weather) where it is raining in thin mist: *another drizzly day.* □ **con llovizna**

droll [drəul] *adj.* funny in an odd way. □ **raro**

dromedary ['drɔmədəri] *n.* (*pl. dromedaries*) camel with only one hump. □ **dromedario**

drone [droun] *n.* **1** male bee. □ **zángano**
2 lazy person. □ **zángano**
3 buzz (of an insect/an engine); monotonous noise. □ **zumbido**
■ *v.* to buzz; to talk slowly and in a monotonous voice: *he was droning on about cricket.* □ **zumbar; hablar monótonamente**

drool [dru:l] *v.* **1** to slobber. □ **babear**
2 (*informal*) to show excessive pleasure about something: *she was drooling over my new car.* □ **caerse la baba**

droop [dru:p] *v.* **1** to hang down: *the flowers were drooping because they hadn't been watered; her shoulders drooped.* □ **marchitarse (flores); caer (hombros)**
2 *his spirits drooped,* he was feeling miserable. □ **decaerse**

drop [drɔp] *n.* **1** tiny quantity of liquid which falls: *a drop of water fell on my head; I will just have a drop of whisky; the doctor has given me some drops for my eyes,* liquid to be put in the eyes in small quan-

tities. □ **gota**
2 small round jewel; small round sweet. □ **pendiente; pastilla (caramelo)**
3 fall: *there's a 20 foot drop from this window to the ground; there has been a big drop in the cost of living.* □ **caída**
4 jumping by a group of people with parachutes. □ **salto**
■ *v.* (*he dropped*) **1** to fall; to let (something) fall: *he dropped the cup and broke it; prices are dropping.* □ **soltar; bajar (precios)**
2 *the wind dropped,* stopped blowing hard. □ **el viento amainó**
3 ***drop me a line*** *when you are in Paris,* (*informal*) send me a short letter when you are in Paris. □ **escríbeme unas líneas cuando...**
4 *shall I drop you at your door?,* shall I take you back and leave you at your door? □ **¿te dejo en tu casa?**
5 *he has dropped the idea of going to live in Greece,* he has given up the idea; *the whole project has been dropped,* has been stopped. □ **dejar caer; abandonar**
drop it, stop talking about it. □ **déjalo ya**
drop in *v.* to call on someone: *to drop in if you are ever in this area.* □ **dejarse caer**
drop-kick *n.* kick in football where you drop the ball to the ground and kick it as it is falling. □ **botepronto**
drop off *v.* **1** to fall off: *the peach dropped off the tree.* □ **caerse**
2 *he dropped off,* he fell asleep. □ **quedarse dormido**
drop out *v.* **1** to stop competing. □ **retirarse**
2 *he has dropped out,* he has given up his studies/has stopped living conventionally. □ **ha dejado los estudios/ha dejado de vivir...**
drop-out *n.* person who has stopped studying/stopped living conventionally: *most of his friends seem to be drop-outs.* □ **persona que no termina los estudios**
dropper *n.* glass tube for putting drops in eyes, etc. □ **cuentagotas**
droppings *n. pl.* solid waste matter from birds/animals. □ **cagada; excrementos**
dropsy ['drɔpsi] *n.* disease where liquid forms in parts of the body. □ **hidropesía**
dross [drɔs] *n.* worthless rubbish. □ **escoria**
drought [draut] *n.* time when there is no rain/when the land is dry. □ **sequía**
drove [drouv] *n.* large number (of people/animals). □ **multitud (gente); rebaño (animales)**
■ *v. see* **drive.**
drown [draun] *v.* **1** to die by being unable to breathe in water: *he fell overboard and must have drowned; six people were drowned when the boat sank.* □ **ahogarse**
2 to flood (a field). □ **anegar**
3 to cover up a noise: *the sound of the drill drowned the cries of the prisoners.* □ **ahogar**
drowse [drauz] *v.* to be half asleep: *he was drowsing after lunch in the library.* □ **dormitar**
drowsiness *n.* feeling of wanting to go to sleep. □ **somnolencia**
drowsy *adj.* sleepy: *I often feel drowsy after a good meal.* □ **soñoliento; amodorrado**
drubbing ['drʌbiŋ] *n.* beating. □ **paliza**
drudge [drʌdʒ] *n.* person who does hard/boring work. □ **esclavo del trabajo**
drudgery *n.* hard/boring work: *writing books can be sheer drudgery.* □ **trabajo penoso**
drug [drʌg] *n.* **1** medicine. □ **medicamento**
2 substance which affects the nerves, and which can be habit forming: *he takes drugs; she is a drug addict.* □ **droga**
■ *v.* (*he drugged*) **1** to give a drug (to someone). □ **drogar**
2 *his coffee had been drugged,* someone had put a drug in his coffee. □ **le han echado un narcótico en...**
druggist *n.* chemist. □ **farmacéutico**
drugstore *n. Amer.* chemist's shop and snack bar. □ **'drugstore'**
druid ['druid] *n.* priest of the old Celtic religion. □ **druida**
drum [drʌm] *n.* **1** large round percussion instrument, covered with tightly stretched material and played with a stick: *he plays the drums in the pop group.* □ **tambor**
2 large barrel; cylindrical container: *a drum of washing powder; an oil drum.* □ **tambor; bidón**
■ *v.* (*he drummed*) **1** to bang on a drum; to tap your fingers quickly on a surface: *he drummed on the table.* □ **tocar el tambor; tabalear**
2 *to drum up support,* to encourage people vigorously to give their support. □ **reunir**
3 *to drum something into someone,* to make someone learn something by constantly repeating it. □ **meterle a uno algo en la cabeza**
drummer *n.* person who plays the drums. □ **el batería**
drumstick *n.* **1** wooden stick for playing a drum. □ **baqueta; palillo**
2 lower part of a leg (of a cooked chicken/turkey, etc.). □ **muslo**
drunk [drʌŋk] *adj.* excited/incapable because of drinking alcohol: *I think he's drunk; she got drunk on gin.* □ **bebido**
■ *n.* person who is incapable because of drinking too much alcohol. □ **borracho**
drunkard *n.* person who is often drunk. □ **borracho**
drunken *adj.* referring to an excess of alcohol: *it was a very drunken party; he was lying in a drunken stupor.* □ **de borrachos**
drunkenness *n.* habit of being drunk/alcoholism. □ **embriaguez, alcoholismo**
dry [drai] *adj.* (*drier, driest*) **1** not wet: *it hasn't rained for weeks so the earth is very dry; don't sit on the chair until the paint is dry; at the end of the film there wasn't a dry eye in the house,* the film made all the audience cry. □ **seco**
2 *he only had dry bread to eat,* bread with no butter or jam. □ **pan a secas**
3 *after fifteen days in a small boat it was a relief to step on dry land,* solid land. □ **tierra firme**
4 (*of wine*) not sweet: *a dry sherry.* □ **seco**
5 (area) where alcohol is forbidden. □ **con ley seca**
6 uninteresting/boring (book). □ **aburrido**
7 *dry sense of humour,* where you make jokes without seeming to know they are funny. □ **fino sentido del humor**
■ *v.* (*dried; drying*) to stop being wet; to wipe (something) until it is dry: *hang your clothes in front of the fire to dry; can you dry the dishes for me please?* □ **secar**
dry-clean *v.* to clean clothes (with chemicals). □ **limpieza en seco**
dry-cleaner's *n.* shop where clothes are dry-cleaned. □ **tintorería**
dryer *n.* machine for drying: *a hair dryer.* □ **secador**
spin dryer, machine which dries washing by spinning it round very fast. □ **secadora centrífuga**
dry-goods store *n. Amer.* draper's shop. □ **tienda de tejidos**
dry ice *n.* solid carbon dioxide, used to produce

very cold temperatures. □ **hielo seco**
drying *n.* action of making something dry: *I'll do the drying,* I'll dry the dishes. □ **el secado**
dryly *adv.* in a sharp, sarcastic way. □ **secamente; con guasa**
dryness *n.* state of being dry. □ **sequedad**
dry out *v.* to make (something) dry: *after the rainstorm we had to dry out all our bedding.* □ **secar**
dry rot *n.* disease in wood (especially in floors) which makes the wood powdery. □ **putrefacción**
dry up *v.* **1** to stop flowing: *the rivers all dry up in the summer.* □ **secarse**
2 *he dried up in the middle of his speech,* he stopped talking and could not continue. □ **atascarse**
dual ['djuəl] *adj.* double; in a pair: *he has dual nationality,* he is a citizen of two countries. □ **doble**
dual carriageway, main road separated into two parts by a central grass bank or fence. □ **autovía**
dub [dʌb] *v.* (*he dubbed*) **1** to make someone a knight. □ **armar/hacer caballero**
2 to add a dialogue to a film in another language from the original: *it is a French film which has been dubbed in English.* □ **doblar**
dubbin ['dʌbin] *n.* type of thick oil for making boots soft and waterproof. □ **grasa para botas**
dubious ['dju:biəs] *adj.* **1** doubtful/vague; suspicious: *he made us a rather dubious offer.* □ **dudoso**
2 hesitant: *I am dubious about going to the Middle East at this time.* □ **indeciso**
dubiously *adv.* doubtfully. □ **con duda**
dubiousness *n.* doubt. □ **incertidumbre**
duchess ['dʌtʃis] *n.* (*pl. duchesses*) wife/widow of a duke. □ **duquesa**
duck [dʌk] *n.* **1** common water bird; female of this water bird; meat of this bird used as food: *wild duck; a duck's egg; roast duck.* □ **pato**
a lame duck, firm which is in financial difficulties. □ **empresa insolvente**
2 score of zero (in cricket). □ **cero**
■ *v.* **1** to lower your head quickly (to avoid hitting something): *he ducked as the cannonball whistled past his shoulder.* □ **agacharse**
2 to push (someone) under water. □ **hacer una aguadilla**
3 to avoid (an unpleasant job). □ **escaquearse**
ducking *n. he got a ducking,* he fell/was pushed into the water. □ **zambullida**
duckling *n.* baby duck. □ **patito**
duct [dʌkt] *n.* tube for carrying air/liquid, etc.: *hot-air duct; tear ducts.* □ **conducto**
ductile ['dʌktail] *adj.* (metal) which can be pulled to form thin wires. □ **dúctil**
dud [dʌd] *n.* (*informal*) failure; false coin/banknote; (shell) which will not explode: *he paid me with a dud cheque,* with a cheque which was worthless. □ **falso; obús que no estalla; sin fondos**
dudgeon ['dʌdʒən] *n.* ***in high dudgeon,*** very indignant. □ **muy enojado**
due [dju:] *adj.* **1** expected: *his plane is due to arrive at 10 o'clock; when is the baby due?,* when is the baby expected to be born? □ **tiene la llegada a...**
2 (money which is) owed: *payment is due.* □ **pagadero, que se debe**
3 just/deserved: *after due consideration, we have decided not to agree to your request.* □ **con la debida consideración...**
4 caused by: *the cracks in the wall are due to the vibrations from the traffic; the train will be late due to fog.* □ **...es debido a...**
5 ***in due course,*** subsequently: *in due course he married and had two children.* □ **a su debido tiempo**
■ *adv.* ***the plane flew due west,*** straight in a westerly direction: *his house is five miles due north of ours.* □ **derecho al...**
■ *n.* what is owed/deserved. □ **deuda**
to give him his due, *he works very hard,* to be just to him. □ **en honor a la verdad...; para ser justo con...**
harbour dues, money owed to the harbour authorities for using the harbour. □ **derechos de puerto**
duel ['djuəl] *n.* fight between two people (with swords/guns). □ **duelo**
duet [dju'et] *n.* piece of music played/sung by two people. □ **dúo**
duffel , duffle ['dʌfl] *n.* ***duffel coat,*** thick coat (often with a hood) fastened with toggles. □ **trenca**
duffel bag, tubular bag which is closed by a string. □ **bolsa de lona**
dug [dʌg] *v. see* **dig.**
duke [dju:k] *n.* highest rank of nobleman. □ **duque**
dulcet ['dʌlsit] *adj.* (voice, etc.) which sounds pleasant. □ **dulce**
dull [dʌl] *adj.* (*duller, dullest*) **1** not exciting/not interesting: *the television show was so dull it made me go to sleep.* □ **aburrido**
2 gloomy (weather): *we might as well stay at home as the weather is so dull.* □ **nublado**
3 not sharp (sound): *a dull thud as he fell to the ground.* □ **sordo**
4 not bright; gloomy (colour): *they have painted their house a dull brown.* □ **apagado**
5 rather stupid. □ **lerdo**
dullness *n.* **1** lack of excitement. □ **desinterés**
2 gloominess (of colour/weather). □ **carácter de sombrío**
3 boredom. □ **aburrimiento**
4 slowness; stupidity. □ **torpeza**
duly ['dju:li] *adv.* as you should: *he duly presented his ticket to the guard; she was asked to state her name and address, which she duly did; the invitation said 9 o'clock so we duly arrived at nine.* □ **debidamente**
dumb [dʌm] *adj.* **1** unable to speak: *he was struck dumb by the news; you should not beat poor dumb animals.* □ **mudo**
2 stupid: *get a move on, you dumb oaf!* □ **estúpido**
dumbly *adv.* silently/without saying anything. □ **en silencio**
dumbbell ['dʌmbel] *n.* bar with weights on each end used by weightlifters. □ **peso, barra con pesas**
dumbfound [dʌm'faund] *v.* to surprise/to flabbergast: *I am dumbfounded at the news,* I am astonished by the news. □ **quedarse pasmado**
dummy ['dʌmi] *n.* (*pl. dummies*) **1** plastic teat sucked by babies. □ **chupete**
2 something false: *for rifle practice we used dummy rounds of ammunition; the window was full of dummy boxes; don't put real bottles of whisky on display - just use dummies.* □ **salvas (munición); ...cajas vacías; imitaciones (botellas)**
dummy run, practice. □ **entrenamiento**
3 *tailor's dummy,* model of a person used to show clothes (in a shop window). □ **maniquí**
4 stupid fool. □ **bobo**
dump [dʌmp] *n.* **1** place to put rubbish: *throw that old mattress on the rubbish dump.* □ **vertedero**
2 *what a dump!,* what an awful place! □ **¡qué antro!**
■ *v.* **1** to put something (heavily) on the ground: *dump the sacks in the corner.* □ **descargar**
2 to throw away; to get rid of: *they took the money and dumped the safe in the woods.* □ **deshacerse de**
3 to sell surplus goods at a very cheap price (usually

overseas): *car manufacturers were accused of dumping old models.* □ **hacer 'dumping'**
dumpling ['dʌmpliŋ] *n.* small ball of dough served in stew. □ **'dumpling'**
apple dumplings, apples baked in a dough cover.
dumps [dʌmps] *n. she is* ***down in the dumps,*** (*informal*) she is miserable. □ **está baja de moral**
dumpy ['dʌmpi] *adj.* short and squat. □ **regordete**
dun [dʌn] *n.* debt collector. □ **acreedor insistente**
■ *adj.* dull brown colour. □ **pardo, bayo**
■ *v.* (*he dunned*) to pester a debtor for money. □ **apremiar**
dunce [dʌns] *n.* stupid person. □ **burro**
dune [dju:n] *n.* ***sand dunes,*** areas of grass-covered sandy ridges by the seashore. □ **duna**
dung [dʌŋ] *n.* solid waste matter (of animals): *cow dung.* □ **estiércol; boñiga**
dungarees [dʌŋgə'ri:z] *n. pl.* overalls/working clothes, usually of thick blue cloth, worn over ordinary clothes. □ **mono**
dungeon ['dʌndʒən] *n.* dark and unpleasant underground prison. □ **mazmorra**
dunk [dʌŋk] *v.* to dip (biscuit, etc.) into a liquid. □ **mojar**
dunno [də'nou] *v.* (*informal*) don't know. □ **no sé**
duodenum [dju:ou'di:nəm] *n.* part of the intestine immediately below the stomach. □ **duodeno**
duodenal *adj.* referring to the duodenum. □ **duodenal**
dupe [dju:p] *n.* person who has been tricked. □ **primo**
■ *v.* to trick (someone). □ **embaucar, engañar**
duplex ['dju:pleks] *n.* (*pl. duplexes*) *Amer.* two-family house. □ **casa para dos familias**
duplex apartment, flat with rooms on two floors. □ **un dúplex**
duplicate ['dju:plikət] *n.* and *adj.* copy/double: *this form has to be filled in duplicate; have you a duplicate key?* □ **duplicado; copia (llave)**
■ *v.* ['dju:plikeit] **1** to make a copy (of a letter, etc.). □ **duplicar, hacer una copia**
2 *you are just duplicating his work,* you are simply doing his work all over again. □ **duplicar**
duplicating *n.* action of making a copy: *a duplicating machine.* □ **reproducción en serie**
duplication [dju:pli'keiʃn] *n.* copying; repetition: *we have to avoid unnecessary duplication of effort.* □ **duplicación, copiado**
duplicator *n.* machine which makes copies of documents. □ **máquina de copias**
duplicity [dju:'plisiti] *n.* dishonesty; tricking (someone). □ **doblez, duplicidad**
durable ['djuərəbl] *adj.* which lasts/which does not wear away: *very durable shoes; this building stone is extremely durable; the conference hopes to agree on a durable peace settlement.* □ **duradero**
durability [djuərə'biliti] *n.* ability to last/not to wear out: *I doubt the durability of the agreement; a cloth of excellent durability.* □ **carácter de duradero**
duration [dju'reiʃn] *n.* period of time for which something lasts: *we are going south for the duration of the winter; he was in the Middle East for the duration of the war.* □ **duración**
duress [dju'res] *n.* force used to make someone do something: *he promised it under duress.* □ **compulsión; coacción**
during ['djuəriŋ] *prep.* for the time something lasts: *during the war we never had any butter; he went to sleep during the television show.* □ **durante**
dusk [dʌsk] *n.* twilight/period in the evening just before it gets dark. □ **crepúsculo**
dusky *adj.* (*duskier, duskiest*) dark-skinned. □ **moreno**
dust [dʌst] *n.* thin layer of dry dirt: *the table is covered with dust; wipe the dust off your shoes.* □ **polvo**
■ *v.* **1** to remove dust from something: *I must dust these books; it doesn't look as though the top of the piano has been dusted for weeks.* □ **quitar el polvo**
2 to sprinkle (sugar on a cake). □ **espolvorear**
dustbin *n.* large metal or plastic container for household rubbish. □ **cubo de la basura**
dust cover *n.* paper cover round a book. □ **sobrecubierta**
duster *n.* **1** cloth for removing dust. □ **trapo del polvo**
feather duster, brush made of feathers for removing dust. □ **plumero**
2 (*informal*) flag (on a ship). □ **bandera**
dusting *n.* **1** removing of dust. □ **limpieza**
2 sprinkling (of sugar, etc.): *there was a light dusting of snow on the street.* □ **capa**
dust jacket *n* paper cover round a book. □ **sobrecubierta**
dustman *n.* (*pl. dustmen*) person employed by a town to remove household rubbish. □ **basurero**
dustpan *n.* small wide shovel for scooping up dirt. □ **recogedor**
dust-up *n.* (*informal*) quarrel. □ **reyerta**
dusty *adj.* (*dustier, dustiest*) covered with dust: *we walked for miles along a dusty path; the room was full of piles of dusty books.* □ **polvoriento**
dusty answer, unsatisfactory reply. □ **contestación vaga**
Dutch [dʌtʃ] *adj.* referring to Holland. □ **holandés**
■ *n.* **1** language spoken in Holland. □ **holandés**
2 ***the Dutch,*** people of Holland. □ **los holandeses**
3 ***to go dutch,*** to split the expenses. □ **ir a medias**
Dutchman, Dutchwoman (*pl. Dutchmen, Dutchwomen*) man/woman from Holland. □ **holandés, holandesa**
duty ['dju:ti] *n.* (*pl. duties*) **1** what one has to do; service: *policeman have to do their duty at all times; I am on duty from 8 a.m. to noon; nurses must not all be off duty on Saturday nights.* □ **deber; estoy de servicio de 8...**
the duty chemist, the chemist's shop which is open on Sundays. □ **farmacia de guardia**
duty officer, officer who is in charge. □ **oficial de guardia**
2 money which has to be paid: *customs duty; import duty.* □ **derechos de aduana, de importación**
duty-free shop, shop at an airport/on a boat where goods can be bought free of local tax. □ **tienda libre de derechos de aduana**
dutiable *adj.* (goods) on which a customs duty must be paid. □ **sujeto al pago de derechos de aduana**
dutiful *adj.* (person) who does what he should do: *a dutiful daughter.* □ **obediente**
dutifully *adv.* as one should; submissively: *he dutifully handed over all the money to his father.* □ **cumplidamente**
duvet ['du:vei] *n.* bag stuffed with feathers, used as the only covering for a bed. □ **edredón**
dwarf [dwɔ:f] *n.* person who is much smaller than normal; variety of plant or animal which is smaller than usual: *a dwarf rose.* □ **enano**
dwarf beans, beans which form low bushes and do not climb. □ **judía enana**
■ *v.* to make something appear small: *his car was*

dwarfed by the huge lorries. □ **empequeñecer**
dwell [dwel] *v.* (*he dwelled/dwelt*) to live. □ **habitar; residir**
dwelling *n.* house. □ **residencia; domicilio**
dwell on *v.* to refer at length to (a subject). □ **explayarse en**
dwindle ['dwindl] *v.* to get less: *my savings are dwindling away rapidly.* □ **menguar**
dwindling *adj.* which is getting less: *he had to pay for it out of his dwindling savings.* □ **menguante**
dye [dai] *n.* colour (used to stain cloth). □ **tinte**
fast dye, colour which will not come out when washed. □ **tinte sólido**
■ *v.* to stain cloth (with a colour): *I have dyed the curtains blue.* □ **teñir**
dyeing *n.* staining (cloth). □ **tinte**
dying ['daiiŋ] *adj.* about to die: *the dying embers of the fire; he said a few words with his dying breath.* □ **moribundo**
dyke [daik] *n.* *see* **dike.**
dynamic [dai'næmik] *adj.* energetic/forceful (person). □ **dinámico**
dynamics *n. pl.* study of objects in movement. □ **dinámica**
dynamite ['dainəmait] *n.* high explosive. □ **dinamita**
■ *v.* to blow up with high explosive: *the engineers dynamited a tunnel through the mountain.* □ **dinamitar**
dynamo ['dainəmou] *n.* (*pl. dynamos*) small electricity generator. □ **dinamo**
dynasty ['dinəsti] *n.* (*pl. dynasties*) one family ruling a country for several generations. □ **dinastía**
dysentery ['disəntri] *n.* disease of the intestines. □ **disentería**
dyslexia [dis'leksiə] *n.* condition (of children) who have great difficulty in reading and writing. □ **dislexia**
dyslexic *adj.* (child) who has great difficulty in reading and writing. □ **disléxico**
dyspepsia [dis'pepsiə] *n.* inability to digest food properly. □ **dispepsia**
dyspeptic *adj.* unable to digest food properly. □ **dispéptico**
dystrophy ['distrəfi] *n.* *muscular dystrophy,* gradual weakening of the muscles. □ **distrofia**

E,e

E, e [iː] fifth letter of the alphabet. □ **E, e**
each [iːtʃ] *adj.* every: *each house has a number.* □ **cada**
■ *pron.* every person; everything: *they have two cars each; each of them has two cars; each of the houses has three bedrooms.* □ **cada uno**
each other, both of two people or things: *they were talking to each other; we always send each other Christmas cards; the cups fit into each other.* □ **el uno al otro, entre sí**
eager ['iːgə] *adj.* very willing to do something: *she is always eager to help.* □ **anhelante, muy deseoso**
eagerly *adv.* in an eager way: *he accepted the invitation eagerly.* □ **sin dudar**
eagerness *n.* being eager to do something. □ **anhelo**
eagle ['iːgl] *n.* large bird of prey: *there are golden eagles in the Scottish mountains.* □ **águila**
eagle-eyed *adj.* (person) who can see very clearly/who notices small details. □ **de vista de águila**
ear [iə] *n.* **1** part of the head, used for hearing. □ **oído, oreja**
middle ear, space inside the head beyond the eardrum. □ **oído medio**
inner ear, space inside the head, beyond the middle ear, which controls balance and hearing. □ **oído interno**
2 sense of hearing; sense of correct tone: *you can't play the violin if you don't have a good ear for music.* □ **tener oído**
3 *ear of corn,* head of corn seeds. □ **espiga**
earache ['iəreik] *n.* pain in the ears. □ **dolor de oídos**
eardrum *n.* tight skin inside the ear which resonates to sound waves and so allows you to hear. □ **tímpano**
earmark *v.* to reserve something (such as money) for a special purpose: *this land is earmarked for a new village hall.* □ **apartar**
earphone *n.* part of a pair of headphones which fits over one ear. □ **auricular**
earring *n.* ring attached to the ear as an ornament: *she is wearing gold earrings.* □ **pendiente**
earshot *n.* ***within earshot/out of earshot,*** near enough to be heard/too far away to be heard. □ **alcance del oído (audible/no audible)**
earl [əːl] *n.* high-ranking nobleman. □ **conde**
early ['əːli] *adv.* (*earlier, earliest*) before the proper time; at the beginning of a period of time: *the train left five minutes early; early in the afternoon; I got up early this morning; as early as the reign of King Henry VIII; can you come earlier next time?* □ **temprano, pronto**
■ *adj.* **1** which happens at the beginning of a period of time; which happens before the usual time: *in early summer; I can't leave before 4 o'clock at the earliest.* □ **al principio de, pronto**
2 *early vegetables,* vegetables which are ready in the spring. □ **verduras tempranas**
at an early date, soon. □ **en fecha próxima**
early closing day, day on which shops close in the afternoon. □ **día en que las tiendas cierran por la tarde**
earn [əːn] *v.* to be paid money for working: *he earns $50 a week; how much do you earn?* □ **ganar**
earnings ['əːniŋz] *n. pl.* amount of money earned; salary/wages: *although he earns more money, the value of his earnings has fallen through inflation.* □ **ganancias**
earnest ['əːnist] *adj.* serious: *he is a very earnest young man.* □ **serio, sincero**
■ *n.* ***in earnest,*** seriously/really. □ **en serio**
earnestly *adv.* seriously: *I earnestly hope you will be better behaved in future.* □ **seriamente**
earth [əːθ] *n.* **1** planet on which we live: *the earth is one of the planets in the solar system; the rocket came down to earth.* □ **tierra**
to come down to earth: *he came down to earth with a bump,* he stopped dreaming. □ **bajarse de las nubes**
why on earth *did you say that?,* what ever made you say that? □ **¿por qué demonios...?**
to cost the earth: *it costs the earth,* a great deal of money. □ **costar un ojo de la cara**
2 soil: *put some earth in a pot and plant your seeds.* □ **tierra**
earth wire, electric wire which connects with the ground. □ **toma de tierra**
3 fox's hole. □ **madriguera**
■ *v.* to connect electrical apparatus to the ground: *the washing machine was not properly earthed.* □ **conectar a tierra**
earthenware ['əːðnwɛə] *n.* and *adj.* (pottery) made of clay. □ **objetos de barro, de barro**
earthly *adj.* **1** *he hasn't an earthly chance,* he has no chance at all. □ **no tiene posibilidad alguna**
2 *there's no earthly reason why he shouldn't come,* of course he should come. □ **no hay ninguna razón...**
earthquake *n.* shaking of the earth caused by underground volcanic activity: *the Tokyo earthquake of 1922.* □ **terremoto**
earth up *v.* to pile earth around a growing plant: *to earth up a row of potatoes.* □ **acollar**
earthworks *n. pl.* walls of earth built as defences. □ **terraplén**
earthworm *n.* worm/small animal which looks like a very small snake and lives in earth. □ **lombriz**
earthy *adj.* (*earthier, earthiest*) *earthy humour,* coarse/rude humour. □ **grosero**
earwig ['iəwig] *n.* small insect with curved pincers on its tail. □ **tijereta**
ease [iːz] *n.* absence of difficulty: *he can do it with ease.* □ **facilidad**
■ *v.* **1** to make less painful. □ **aliviar**
2 to make easy. □ **facilitar**
ease off *v.* to become less: *the rain is easing off.* □ **moderarse**
ease up *v.* to slow down. □ **aligerarse; dejar de trabajar tanto**
easel ['iːzl] *n.* vertical frame on legs (to support a blackboard/painting, etc.). □ **caballete**
east [iːst] *n.* one of the points of the compass, the direction of the rising sun: *the sun rises in the east and sets in the west; the harbour is to the east of the mountains.* □ **este**
the Far East, countries to the east of India. □ **el Extremo Oriente**
the Middle East, countries to the east of Egypt and west of Pakistan. □ **el Oriente Medio**
the Near East, countries at the eastern end of the Mediterranean. □ **el Cercano Oriente**
■ *adj.* of the east. □ **oriental; del este**

East Anglia, eastern part of England to the north-east of London.
■ *adv.* towards the east: *the ship was heading east.* □ **hacia el este**
eastbound *adj.* going towards the east. □ **rumbo al este**
easterly *adj.* **1** *easterly wind,* wind from the east. □ **oriental; de levante**
2 towards the east: *he was heading in an easterly direction.* □ **hacia el este**
eastern *adj.* of the east: *eastern religions.* □ **oriental**
eastward *adj.* towards the east. □ **hacia el este**
eastwards *adv.* towards the east. □ **hacia el este**
Easter ['i:stə] *n.* Christian festival (in March or April). □ **Pascua; Semana Santa**
Easter Day, Sunday celebrating Christ's rising from the dead. □ **Domingo de Resurrección**
Easter egg, chocolate or sugar egg eaten at Easter. □ **huevo de Pascua**
easy ['i:zi] *adj.* (*easier, easiest*) **1** not difficult: *this sum is very easy.* □ **fácil**
it's as easy as falling off a log, (*informal*) it's very easy. □ **está chupado**
2 *the house is* ***within easy reach*** *of the station,* is conveniently close to the station. □ **...muy próxima a**
3 *my boss is very easy to get on with,* not difficult to work for. □ **es muy fácil llevarse bien con...**
■ *adv.* ***take things easy,*** to rest/to do only light work. □ **tomárselo con calma**
take it easy!, don't work too hard! □ **tómatelo con calma**
easy now!, be careful!/don't get excited! □ **¡cálmate!**
easily *adv.* without difficulty. □ **fácilmente**
easiness *n.* state of being easy/of not being difficult. □ **facilidad**
easy-chair *n.* large comfortable armchair. □ **butacón**
easy-going *adj.* (person who is) easy to get on with/not very critical. □ **de trato fácil**
eat [i:t] *v.* (*he ate: he has eaten*) **1** to chew and swallow food: *can I have something to eat? what did you eat for breakfast? I ate three eggs; the cat ate the bird; have you eaten?,* have you had anything to eat? □ **comer**
eating apple, sweet apple. □ **manzana (para comer cruda)**
2 ***to eat out of someone's hand:*** *I had him eating out of my hand,* he did everything I told him to. □ **comer de la mano de alguien**
3 *he had* ***to eat his words,*** to take back what he had said. □ **se tuvo que tragar sus palabras**
eatables *n. pl.* things to eat. □ **comestibles**
eat away *v.* (*of acid*) to corrode. □ **corroer**
eat into *v.* to reduce gradually: *inflation has eaten into my savings.* □ **comer**
eat up *v.* **1** to finish eating: *eat up your pudding!* □ **terminar de comer**
2 *car that eats up petrol,* (*informal*) car that uses a lot of petrol. □ **coche que 'chupa' mucha gasolina**
eaves [i:vz] *n. pl.* edge of a roof overhanging the wall. □ **alero**
eavesdrop *v.* (*he eavesdropped*) to listen to a conversation which you are not supposed to hear. □ **escuchar indiscretamente**
eavesdropper *n.* person who listens to a conversation which he is not supposed to hear. □ **cotilla**
ebb [eb] *n.* (tide) going down: *the ebb tide.* □ **marea menguante**
■ *v.* (*of tide*) to go down. □ **menguar**
ebony ['ebəni] *n.* black tropical wood. □ **ébano**
ebullient [i'bʌljənt] *adj.* very excited/full of life. □ **rebosante**
eccentric [ek'sentrik] *adj.* odd (person). □ **excéntrico**
eccentricity *n.* state of being odd. □ **excentricidad**
ecclesiastical [ikli:zi'æstikl] *adj.* belonging to the church. □ **eclesiástico**
echelon ['eʃəlɔn] *n.* **1** arrangement of separate things in steps, and not in a straight line. □ **escalón**
2 group of people at a certain level in an organization. □ **categoría**
echo ['ekou] *n.* (*pl. echoes*) repeated sound reverberating in a cave, etc. □ **eco**
■ *v.* **1** (*of sound*) to repeat: *the sound of footsteps echoed in the empty church.* □ **resonar**
2 *he echoed everything she said,* he repeated everything. □ **repitió todo lo que dijo**
eclair [ei'klεə] *n.* long cake made of pastry, filled with cream and covered with chocolate. □ **pepito de chocolate**
eclectic [i'klektik] *adj.* taking ideas, etc., from several different sources. □ **ecléctico**
eclipse [i'klips] *n.* phenomenon when the sun or moon disappears temporarily, because another body passes across them. □ **eclipse**
■ *v.* **1** to hide (another planet) by passing in front of it. □ **eclipsar**
2 to be more brilliant/successful than someone: *he was eclipsed by his younger brother.* □ **eclipsar**
ecology [i'kɔlədʒi] *n.* study of the relationship between plants and animals in nature. □ **ecología**
ecological [i:kə'lɔdʒikl] *adj.* referring to ecology. □ **ecológico**
ecologist *n.* person who studies ecology. □ **ecólogo**
economy [i'kɔnəmi] *n.* **1** saving (of money or resources): *fuel economy.* □ **economía**
economy pack, cheaper packet of goods. □ **lote económico**
2 way in which a country makes money; financial state of a country. □ **economía**
economic [i:kə'nɔmik] *adj.* referring to economy. □ **económico**
economical *adj.* which saves money or resources: *natural gas is the most economical source of heat.* □ **barato; económico**
economically *adv.* without waste. □ **económicamente**
economics *n.* **1** study of the finance of industry/of a country: *he is an economics lecturer.* □ **economía**
2 financial structure: *the economics of publishing baffle me.* □ **economía**
economist [i'kɔnəmist] *n.* person who specializes in the study of finance. □ **economista**
economize *v.* to save/not to waste: *I am going to economize on electricity this winter.* □ **economizar**
ecstasy ['ekstəsi] *n.* great happiness. □ **éxtasis, dicha**
ecstatic *adj.* very happy. □ **extático, dichoso**
ecumenical [i:kju:'menikl] *adj.* referring to Christian unity/concerned with joining together all Christian groups. □ **ecuménico**
eczema ['eksimə] *n.* allergic skin disease which causes itchy red spots. □ **eccema**
eddy ['edi] *n.* (*pl. eddies*) small swirl of water (in a stream). □ **remolino**
■ *v.* (*eddied; eddying*) to swirl around: *the water eddied round the stern of the ship.* □ **arremolinarse**
edge [edʒ] *n.* **1** (sharp) side of flat object: *do not put your cup so close to the edge of the table; he was leaning over the edge of the cliff; he stood the coin on its edge.* □ **filo; borde; canto**
to set someone's teeth on edge: *the violin set my teeth on edge,* made me shudder. □ **dar dentera**

on edge, nervous/jumpy. □ **tener los nervios de punta**
2 sharpened side of a knife/axe, etc. □ **filo**
3 point at the outside of something: *a house on the edge of the forest.* □ **a las afueras**
■ *v.* **1** to creep sideways: *he edged through the crowd.* □ **avanzar de lado**
2 to put along the edge: *a dress edged with silk.* □ **ribetear; orlar**
edgeways, edgewise *adv.* **1** sideways. □ **de lado**
2 *she talks so much, you can't* ***get a word in edgeways.*** □ **que no te deja meter baza**
edgy *adj.* nervous/jumpy. □ **inquieto**
edible ['edibl] *adj.* which can be safely eaten: *is this mushroom edible?* □ **comestible**
edict ['i:dikt] *n.* official order. □ **edicto**
edifice ['edifis] *n.* large building. □ **edificio**
edify ['edifai] *v.* (*formal*) to instruct and improve (someone). □ **edificar**
edit ['edit] *v.* to make notes on a text; to change a text (to make it more acceptable); to prepare a text for publication; to cut up a film/tape and stick it together in correct order to make it ready to be shown/played: *this is the edited version of the speech.* □ **preparar (libro); montar (película/cinta)**
edition [i'diʃn] *n.* **1** number of books/papers printed at the same time: *first edition,* copy of the first printing of a book. □ **edición**
2 form in which a book is published: *a paperback edition.* □ **edición**
editor *n.* **1** person who makes notes on a text/who prepares a text for publication. □ **preparador**
2 director of a newspaper or part of a newspaper: *the business editor; the sports editor.* □ **director; redactor jefe**
editorial [edi'tɔ:riəl] *adj.* referring to editors/to editing: *the editorial staff of a newspaper.* □ **editorial**
■ *n.* article written by the editor of a newspaper. **editorial**
educate ['edjukeit] *v.* to teach/to instruct (someone): *he was educated in Scotland,* he went to school in Scotland. □ **educar**
an educated person, someone who is cultivated. □ **una persona culta**
education [edju'keiʃn] *n.* (system of) teaching/being taught. □ **educación**
adult education, teaching of adults. □ **educación para adultos**
further education, teaching people who have left school. □ **educación permanente de adultos**
educational *adj.* referring to education/teaching/schools. □ **educativo**
educational film, film used for teaching. □ **película educativa**
educational publisher, publisher who produces school books. □ **editor de libros de enseñanza**
educationist *n.* person who specializes in the study of methods of teaching. □ **pedagogo**
Edwardian [ed'wɔ:djən] *adj.* referring to the time of Edward VII (1901-1910). □ **eduardiano**
eel [i:l] *n.* long thin fish like a snake. □ **anguila**
eerie ['iəri] *adj.* (*eerier, eeriest*) frightening/weird. □ **horripilante**
eerily *adv.* in a frightening way. □ **horripilantemente**
efface [i'feis] *v.* to rub out. □ **borrar**
effect [i'fekt] *n.* **1** result/influence: *he poured water on the flames but it had no effect.* □ **efecto**
to come into/to take effect: *this rule takes effect/comes into effect from November 1st,* starts to be applied. □ **entrar en vigor**
2 meaning: *he shouted 'I'll get you' or words to that effect,* words with that meaning. □ **... con esa intención**
3 ***sound effects,*** (*in theatre/film, on radio*) artificial or reproduced sounds (such as thunder, horses, creaking doors). □ **efectos sonoros**
■ *v.* to produce/to carry out: *he effected his escape through the cell window.* □ **efectuar**
effective *adj.* **1** which produces a (good) result: *a very effective burglar alarm; the description of the fire is very effective.* □ **eficaz**
2 which takes effect: *a rule effective from November 1st.* □ **vigente**
effectively *adv.* in a way which produces a good result: *the speaker effectively silenced the hecklers.* □ **eficazmente**
effectual *adj.* (*formal*) which produces the intended effect. □ **eficaz**
effeminate [i'feminət] *adj.* (*of man*) like a woman. □ **afeminado**
effervesce [efə'ves] *v.* (*of liquid*) to make bubbles giving off gas. □ **entrar en efervescencia**
effervescence *n.* bubbles in liquid; act of making bubbles. □ **efervescencia**
effervescent *adj.* which bubbles. □ **efervescente**
effete [e'fi:t] *adj.* weak/with no strength left. □ **agotado**
efficacious [efi'keiʃəs] *adj.* (medicine, etc.) which produces the correct result. □ **eficaz**
efficiency [i'fiʃənsi] *n.* **1** ability to produce the required result: *the efficiency of the English team,* ability to play well; *efficiency of a machine.* □ **eficiencia; eficacia**
2 *business efficiency,* ability to work effectively in business. □ **rendimiento**
efficient *adj.* able to work well/to produce the required result: *this electric saw is very efficient; his secretary is extremely efficient.* □ **de buen rendimiento; eficaz; eficiente**
effigy ['efidʒi] *n.* (*pl. effigies*) statue/model of someone: *the president was burnt in effigy,* a model of him was burnt as a protest. □ **efigie**
effluent ['efluənt] *n.* sewage; liquid waste (from a factory). □ **aguas residuales**
effort ['efət] *n.* use of physical energy: *he made an effort and painted the whole house.* □ **esfuerzo**
effortless *adj.* without apparently using any energy. □ **sin esfuerzo**
effrontery [i'frʌntəri] *n.* rudeness. □ **desfachatez**
effusive [i'fju:siv] *adj.* too enthusiastic (in thanks). □ **efusivo**
effusively *adv.* (to thank someone) very enthusiastically. □ **efusivamente**
e.g. [i:'dʒi:] abbreviation for *exempli gratia,* meaning for example. □ **verbigracia, por ejemplo**
egalitarian [igæli'tɛəriən] *adj.* and *n.* (person) who believes in equality for everyone. □ **igualitario**
egg [eg] *n.* **1** cell produced by a female which contains the embryo of a reptile or bird. □ **huevo**
2 hard-shelled cell, produced by a bird, especially that of a hen: *the hen laid an egg; I had a boiled egg for breakfast.* □ **huevo**
■ *v.* ***to egg someone on,*** to encourage someone to do something. □ **incitar**
eggcup *n.* small holder for a boiled egg. □ **huevera**
egg-head *n.* (*informal*) clever person. □ **'intelectual'**
eggplant *n.* aubergine/purple fruit eaten as vegetable. □ **berenjena**
eggshell *n.* shell around an egg. □ **cáscara; cascarón**

eggtimer *n.* device for timing how long an egg is boiled. □ **reloj de cocina (para huevos)**
ego ['i:gou] *n.* **1** yourself. □ **ego**
2 *it has deflated his ego,* it has made him less conceited. □ **le ha herido su ego**
egocentric [egou'sentrik] *adj.* thinking only about yourself. □ **egocéntrico**
egoism ['egouizəm] *n.* thinking about oneself. □ **egoísmo**
egoist *n.* someone who only thinks of himself. □ **egoísta**
egotism ['egoutizəm] *n.* talking only about oneself. □ **egotismo**
egotist *n.* person who only talks about himself. □ **egotista**
egregious [i'gri:dʒəs] *adv.* very bad; shocking. □ **atroz**
egret ['i:grət] *n.* type of heron with beautiful white tail feathers. □ **garceta**
Egypt ['i:dʒipt] *n.* country in North Africa. □ **Egipto**
Egyptian *adj.* referring to Egypt. □ **egipcio**
■ *n.* person from Egypt. □ **egipcio**
eiderdown ['aidədaun] *n.* bed covering made of a large bag full of feathers. □ **edredón**
eight [eit] number 8. **1** *he is eight (years old); come to see us at eight (o'clock).* □ **ocho**
2 eight people (the crew of a rowing boat). □ **(bote de a) ocho**
eighteen number 18: *he is eighteen (years old); the eighteen sixteen train,* the train which leaves at 18.16. □ **dieciocho**
the eighteen hundreds, the years between 1800 and 1899. □ **el siglo XIX**
eighteenth, 18th *adj.* referring to eighteen: *the eighteenth of May (May 18th).* □ **decimoctavo; el dieciocho de...**
the eighteenth century, period from 1700 to 1799. □ **el siglo XVIII**
eighth, 8th *adj.* and *n.* referring to eight: *the eighth of April (April 8th); Henry the Eighth (Henry VIII); half a quarter is an eighth; an eighth of the money.* □ **octavo**
the eighth century, period from 700 to 799. □ **el siglo VIII**
eightieth, 80th *adj.* referring to eighty. □ **octogésimo**
eighty number 80: *he is eighty (years old).* □ **ochenta**
eisteddfod [ai'stedfəd] *n.* Welsh literary and musical competition. □ **'eisteddfod'**
either ['aiðə, 'i:ðə] *adj.* and *pron.* **1** one or the other: *either of them will do; I don't believe either of you; either way we lose,* whatever happens. □ **uno u otro, cualquiera de los dos, ninguno de los dos**
2 both: *there are trees on either side of our house.* □ **ambos**
■ *conj.* and *adv.* **1** (showing choice): *either you come here or I go to you; either one thing or the other.* □ **o... o...**
2 (emphatic): *he isn't French and he isn't English either; you don't want to go and I don't want to either.* □ **ni tampoco**
ejaculate [i'dʒækjuleit] *v.* **1** (*formal*) to exclaim/to say (something) suddenly. □ **proferir de manera súbita**
2 (*of male*) to produce sperm. □ **eyacular**
eject [i'dʒekt] *v.* to throw out: *he was forcibly ejected from the club.* □ **echar**
ejector seat *n.* seat in an aircraft which throws the pilot out in an emergency. □ **asiento proyectable**
eke [i:k] *v. **to eke out,*** to economize (savings)/to try not to use up (resources): *he ekes out his income by selling vegetables from the garden.* □ **escatimar; suplir las deficiencias de**
elaborate [i'læbərət] *adj.* very detailed/very complicated: *she made a lot of elaborate excuses for missing the party; he was wearing an elaborate costume.* □ **rebuscado; complicado**
■ *v.* to go into details: *I will not elaborate any further on the circumstances of the crime.* □ **entrar en detalles**
elaborately *adv.* in a complicated/detailed way: *the police elaborately pieced together the clues.* □ **detalladamente**
elapse [i'læps] *v.* (*of time*) to pass: *six minutes elapsed between the alarm and the arrival of the fire engine.* □ **transcurrir**
elastic [i'læstik] *adj.* which stretches and contracts; not rigid: *the hours of work are quite elastic.* □ **elástico**
elastic band, loop of rubber for holding papers, etc., together. □ **goma**
■ *n.* piece of rubber which can stretch. □ **goma**
elasticity [ilæ'stisiti] *n.* ability to stretch. □ **elasticidad**
elated [i'leitid] *adj.* very excited and pleased: *she was elated at getting the prize.* □ **entusiasmado**
elation [i'leiʃn] *n.* feeling of excitement and pleasure. □ **entusiasmo**
elbow ['elbou] *n.* joint in the arm: *he nudged me with his elbow; don't put your elbows on the table.* □ **codo**
elbowroom *n.* space to move about. □ **espacio**
elder ['eldə] *adj.* older (person). □ **mayor**
elder statesman, statesman who is older (and wiser) than others. □ **político de más experiencia**
■ *n.* **1** older person: *you must obey your elders.* □ **los mayores**
2 common small tree with white flowers and bunches of small purple berries. □ **saúco**
elderberry *n.* **1** elder tree. □ **saúco**
2 fruit of an elder. □ **baya del saúco**
elderly *adj.* quite old: *these seats are reserved for elderly people/for the elderly; he drives an elderly Ford.* □ **mayor; muy viejo**
eldest *adj.* oldest (of a group): *he is the eldest son.* □ **el mayor**
elect [i'lekt] *v.* to choose by voting: *he was elected mayor.* □ **elegir**
■ *suffix meaning* someone who has been elected to a post, but who has not taken it up officially: *the mayor-elect.* □ **electo**
election [i'lekʃn] *n.* process of choosing by voting. □ **elección**
general election, election for the national Parliament: *presidential election.* □ **elecciones generales**
electioneering *n.* working for an election campaign. □ **campaña electoral**
elector *n.* someone who is qualified to vote in an election. □ **elector**
electoral *adj.* referring to an election. □ **electoral**
electoral roll/register, list of people who are qualified to vote in a certain area. □ **censo electoral**
electorate *n.* all the people in a country who are qualified to vote. □ **electorado**
electric [i'lektrik] *adj.* **1** moved by/worked by electricity: *electric motor; electric oven; electric wire; electric plug.* □ **eléctrico**
2 *the atmosphere was electric,* full of excitement. □ **el ambiente era electrizante**
electrical *adj.* referring to electricity: *electrical maintenance; electrical engineering.* □ **eléctrico**
electrically *adv.* by electricity: *the motor is electri-*

cally powered. □ **por electricidad**
electrician [elek'triʃn] *n.* person who works on electrical maintenance. □ **electricista**
electricity [elek'trisiti] *n.* physical current used for power: *the motor is run on electricity; the electricity supply was cut off.* □ **electricidad**
electrification [ilektrifi'keiʃn] *n.* changing to an electric source of power: *the electrification of a railway line.* □ **electrificación**
electrify [i'lektrifai] *v.* **1** to convert to an electric source of power. □ **electrificar**
2 to startle and excite. □ **electrizar**
electrocute *v.* to kill by electricity: *he was electrocuted when he touched the cable.* □ **electrocutar**
electrode *n.* rod which leads the electric current into or out of a cell. □ **electrodo**
electrolysis [ilek'trɔlisis] *n.* **1** separation of the parts of a compound liquid by passing an electric current through it. □ **electrólisis**
2 removal of unwanted hair by electric current. □ **depilación eléctrica**
electrolyte *n.* chemical solution which can be broken into parts by electrolysis. □ **electrólito**
electron *n.* basic particle in an atom. □ **electrón**
electronic [ilek'trɔnik] *adj.* using electric impulses: *electronic calculator.* □ **electrónico**
electronics *n.* (*usually with singular verb*) science of using electric impulses. □ **electrónica**
electroplate *v.* to coat (a metal, usually copper) with a thin layer of silver by means of electrolysis. □ **galvanizar**
elegant ['eligənt] *adj.* well dressed/very fashionable: *elegant women; elegant restaurant.* □ **elegant**
elegantly *adv.* fashionably: *elegantly dressed.* □ **elegantemente**
elegy ['elədʒi] *n.* (*pl. elegies*) sad poem about someone who is dead. □ **elegía**
element ['elimənt] *n.* **1** basic chemical substance: *oxygen and carbon are elements.* □ **elemento**
2 basic part (of something): *the elements of the argument.* □ **elemento**
3 natural environment: *he's in his element when he's talking about gardening.* □ **elemento**
4 ***the elements,*** bad weather (wind/rain, etc.): *to brave the elements,* to expose oneself to bad weather. □ **los elementos**
5 wire which heats in an electric heater/cooker, etc. □ **resistencia**
elementary [eli'mentri] *adj.* basic/simple: *elementary mathematics.* □ **elemental**
elephant ['elifənt] *n.* very large African or Indian animal, with a trunk and tusks. □ **elefante**
white elephant, something expensive but useless. □ **elefante blanco**
elephantine [eli'fæntain] *adj.* very large, heavy and difficult to move. □ **elefantino; pesado**
elevate ['eliveit] *v.* to raise up. □ **elevar**
elevation *n.* **1** raising. □ **elevación**
2 drawing of one side of a building. □ **alzado**
3 height (above sea-level). □ **altitud**
elevator *n.* **1** device for lifting goods (*Amer.* or people) inside a building: *he took the elevator to the ninth floor; goods elevator.* □ **ascensor; montacargas**
grain elevator, large building for hoisting and storing grain at a port or railway terminus. □ **silo, elevador de grano**
2 part of the tail of an aircraft. □ **timón de profundidad**
eleven [i'levn] number 11. **1** *he arrived at eleven (o'clock): he is eleven (years old); look at page eleven.* □ **once**
2 eleven people (as in a sports team): *the England eleven.* □ **el once**
elevenses *n.* (*informal*) snack eaten in the midmorning. □ **piscolabis de media mañana**
eleventh, 11th *adj.* referring to eleven: *the eleventh of January (January 11th).* □ **undécimo; el once de...**
at the eleventh hour, at the last minute. □ **en el último momento**
the eleventh century, period from 1000 to 1099. □ **el siglo XI**
elf [elf] *n.* (*pl. elves*) small, usually male, supernatural being. □ **elfo**
elicit [i'lisit] *v.* to obtain (information). □ **sacar**
eligible ['eligəbl] *adj.* **1** able to be chosen: *he is eligible for a pension.* □ **elegible; tiene derecho a...**
2 *eligible bachelor,* young man who has all the qualifications (especially money) to be married. □ **buen partido**
eliminate [i'limineit] *v.* **1** to remove (waste, etc.). □ **quitar**
2 to exclude (someone) after a test: *three teams were eliminated in the first round; the detectives eliminated most of the suspects.* □ **eliminar; descartar**
elimination [ilimi'neiʃn] *n.* act of eliminating. □ **eliminación**
elite [e'li:t] *n.* group of privileged people/the best people. □ **élite**
elixir [e'liksə] *n.* medicine which people imagine will cure everything. □ **elixir**
Elizabethan [elizə'bi:θən] *adj.* referring to the time of Elizabeth I (1558-1603). □ **isabelino**
elk [elk] *n.* (*pl. elk*) large European deer with flat antlers. □ **alce**
ellipse [i'lips] *n.* oval shape. □ **elipse**
ellipsis *n.* (*pl. ellipses*) absence of a word which is needed to complete the meaning of a phrase. □ **elipsis**
elliptic(al) *adj.* **1** oval. □ **elíptico**
2 difficult to understand because of a missing word or phrase. □ **elíptico**
elm [elm] *n.* large deciduous tree. □ **olmo**
Dutch elm disease, disease which kills elms. □ **enfermedad holandesa del olmo, grafiosis**
elocution [elə'kju:ʃn] *n.* way of speaking well and clearly: *he is taking lessons in elocution.* □ **elocución**
elongate ['i:lɔŋgeit] *v.* to stretch out/to make longer. □ **alargar**
elope [i'loup] *v.* to run away from home to get married. □ **fugarse para contraer matrimonio**
eloquence ['eləkwens] *n.* art of speaking well. □ **elocuencia**
eloquent *adj.* good and persuasive (speech). □ **elocuente**
else [els] *adv.* **1** otherwise: *come in or else stay out; you had better pay, or else,* or I will force you to pay. □ **de otro modo; si no**
2 other: *anyone else,* any other person; *nobody else,* no other person; *anything else,* any other thing; *something else,* some other thing: *did you speak to anyone else? would you like anything else to eat? there is something else I wanted to tell you; who else was there? what else did she say? I have forgotten everything else; there was nowhere else to put it; can't we go somewhere else/Amer. some place else?* □ **otro; más**
elsewhere *adv.* somewhere else; in other places: *if you can't find it here I should try elsewhere.* □ **en otra parte**
elucidate [i'lu:sideit] *v.* to make clear/to make easy to understand. □ **elucidar**

elude [i'lu:d] *v.* to escape/to avoid: *the escaped prisoner managed to elude the police.* □ **eludir**
elusive [i'lu:siv] *adj.* difficult to find. □ **difícil de encontrar**
emaciated [i'meisieitid] *adj.* extremely thin. □ **demacrado**
emanate ['eməneit] *v.* to come from: *the idea emanated from the managers.* □ **emanar**
emancipate [i'mænsipeit] *v.* to make (someone) free. □ **emancipar**
emancipation [imænsi'peiʃn] *n.* setting free. □ **emancipación**
embalm [im'bɑ:m] *v.* to treat (a dead body) with chemicals to prevent it from decaying. □ **embalsamar**
embankment [im'bæŋkmənt] *n.* artificial bank (along a river); road along such a bank. □ **dique**
embargo [im'bɑ:gou] *n.* (*pl. embargoes*) official prohibition (on goods/traffic/information): *the Government has put an embargo on imports from Great Britain.* □ **embargo**
■ *v.* to prohibit something officially: *the Ministry has embargoed all reports on the accident.* □ **prohibir**
embark [im'bɑ:k] *v.* **1** to go on board a ship: *the passengers embarked at Southampton.* □ **embarcar**
2 to start doing something: *we are about to embark on a completely new project.* □ **embarcarse**
embarkation [embɑ:'keiʃn] *n.* act of going on board a ship or aircraft: *port of embarkation.* □ **embarque**
embarrass [im'bærəs] *v.* to make someone feel uncomfortable (by rudeness/indecency, etc.): *I was very embarrassed by his behaviour.* □ **molestar**
embarrassment *n.* act of making someone feel uncomfortable: *his rudeness is a constant source of embarrassment to me.* □ **molestia**
embassy ['embəsi] *n.* (*pl. embassies*) home or offices of an ambassador: *the British Embassy in Moscow; the French Embassy in Washington.* □ **embajada**
embattled [im'bætld] *adj.* under attack; constantly criticized. □ **sitiado; acosado**
embed [im'bed] *v.* (*he embedded*) to fix something into a mass (of concrete/flesh, etc.): *the arrow was embedded in his leg.* □ **clavar, empotrar**
embellish [im'beliʃ] *v.* to decorate/to make beautiful. □ **embellecer**
embers ['embəz] *n. pl.* pieces of wood/coal which are red hot. □ **ascuas**
embezzle [im'bezl] *v.* to steal money which you are looking after for someone: *the accountant embezzled $1,000 out of the company's account.* □ **desfalcar**
embezzlement *n.* act of embezzling. □ **desfalco**
embezzler *n.* person who embezzles. □ **desfalcador**
embittered [im'bitəd] *adj.* (*of person*) made angry and sad (by disappointment/envy). □ **amargado**
emblem ['embləm] *n.* design which is adopted as the characteristic of a country/team/town, etc.: *the thistle is the emblem of Scotland; a pair of keys is the emblem of St Peter.* □ **emblema**
embody [im'bɔdi] *v.* (*embodied; embodying*) to show an idea in a physical form. □ **encarnar una idea**
embodiment *n.* physical expression of an idea: *the embodiment of patriotism.* □ **encarnación**
embolism ['embəlizəm] *n.* blocking of a blood vessel by a blood clot or a bubble of air. □ **embolia**
emboss [im'bɔs] *v.* to raise (a design) above a flat surface. □ **grabar en relieve**
embossed letterhead, address pressed on writing paper so that it stands above the surface. □ **dirección impresa en seco**
embrace [im'breis] *v.* **1** to hold (and kiss) someone: *the returning soldiers embraced their wives and girlfriends; they embraced before the train left.* □ **abrazar**
2 to become a convert to a belief: *he has embraced the Catholic Church.* □ **abrazar**
embrocation [embrə'keiʃn] *n.* liquid which you rub into parts of the body which are stiff. □ **linimento**
embroider [im'brɔidə] *v.* to make artistic patterns using thread, by sewing: *she embroidered a cushion for her father.* □ **bordar**
embroidery *n.* art of sewing flower designs/patterns, etc. □ **bordado**
embryo ['embriou] *n.* (*pl. embryos*) earliest state of living organisms; rudimentary idea: *all life starts from an embryo.* □ **embrión**
embryonic [embri'ɔnik] *adj.* original/in a very early state: *an embryonic plan; the project is only in its embryonic stages.* □ **embrionario**
emend [i:'mend] *v.* to change/to make correct. □ **enmendar**
emendation [i:men'deiʃn] *n.* change/correction. □ **enmienda**
emerald ['emrəld] *adj.* and *n.* green precious stone; colour of this stone. □ **esmeralda**
emerge [i'mə:dʒ] *v.* to come out from inside something: *the train finally emerged from the tunnel; after police investigation some facts slowly began to emerge.* □ **emerger, surgir**
emergent *adj. emergent nations,* countries which are slowly becoming economically independent. □ **naciente**
emergency [i'mə:dʒənsi] *n.* (*pl. emergencies*) dangerous state where decisions have to be taken quickly (such as fire/accident/breakdown of law and order): *in an emergency, you can always telephone your mother.* □ **emergencia**
state of emergency, when normal administrative processes are taken over by the police or armed forces. □ **estado de emergencia**
emergency exit, door used when a fire breaks out. □ **salida de emergencia**
emergency operation, operation carried out at short notice because the patient is seriously ill. □ **operación de emergencia**
emergency repairs, repairs carried out at short notice (as to a car which has broken down). □ **reparación de emergencia**
emeritus [i'meritəs] *adj.* (professor) who has retired but keeps his title: *the emeritus professor of French.* □ **emérito**
emery ['eməri] *n.* fine crystals used for polishing. □ **esmeril**
emery board *n.* thin stick of cardboard covered with fine crystals, used for filing fingernails. □ **lima de uñas**
emery paper *n.* sandpaper. □ **papel de lija**
emetic [i'metik] *n.* substance which makes you vomit. □ **emético**
emigrate ['emigreit] *v.* to leave a country to live in another: *he emigrated to Australia.* □ **emigrar**
emigrant *n.* person who leaves a country to live in another. □ **emigrante**
emigration [emi'greiʃn] *n.* act of leaving a country to live in another: *the population of Ireland declined because of emigration to the USA.* □ **emigración**
eminence ['eminəns] *n.* high place; high rank. □ **eminencia**
eminent ['eminənt] *adj.* very highly respected because of position or work: *an eminent professor; an eminent composer.* □ **eminente**

eminently *adv.* remarkably: *he is eminently suited to the job.* □ **eminentemente**
emir [i'mir] *n.* Muslim ruler; male descendant of Muhammad. □ **emir**
emirate *n.* rank or lands of an emir. □ **emirato**
emissary ['emisəri] *n.* person sent to negotiate on someone's behalf. □ **emisario**
emit [i'mit] *v.* (*he emitted*) to send out (a sound/ smoke, etc.) □ **emitir**
emolument [i'mɔljumənt] *n.* payment/salary. □ **emolumento**
emotion [i'mouʃn] *n.* (strong) feeling: *she spoke with a voice full of emotion.* □ **emoción**
emotional *adj.* showing emotion. □ **emocional**
emotive *adj.* which is likely to cause strong feeling. □ **emotivo**
empathy ['empəθi] *n.* being able to share the feelings of someone else, by imagining yourself as that person. □ **empatía**
emperor ['emprə] *n.* ruler of an empire. □ **emperador**
emphasize ['emfəsaiz] *v.* to stress the importance (of something): *he emphasized the need for more investment.* □ **hacer hincapié en**
emphasis ['emfəsis] *n.* stress (usually in speech): *he laid great emphasis on the need for more investment.* □ **énfasis, hincapié**
emphatic [im'fætik] *adj.* stressed: *his answer was an emphatic 'no'.* □ **enfático**
emphatically *adv.* in a forceful way: *he emphatically denied the accusation.* □ **con énfasis**
empire ['empaiə] *n.* large territories ruled by a central government: *the German Empire; the British Empire.* □ **imperio**
empirical [em'pirikl] *adj.* based on practical experiment and not on theory. □ **empírico**
emplacement [im'pleismənt] *n.* place where guns are set. □ **emplazamiento**
employ [im'plɔi] *v.* **1** to give (someone) regular work: *the factory employs forty-five technicians; he is employed as a bank clerk.* □ **emplear**
2 to use: *you must not employ too much force.* □ **emplear**
employee [emplɔi'iː] *n.* person who is employed: *each employee gets a Christmas bonus.* □ **empleado**
employer *n.* person who gives work to people and pays them. □ **empresario; empleador**
employment *n.* regular paid work. □ **empleo**
emporium [im'pɔːriəm] *n.* large shop. □ **comercio grande, emporio**
empower [im'pauə] *v.* to give (someone) the authority to do something: *he is empowered to act on my behalf.* □ **facultar**
empress ['emprəs] *n.* woman ruler of an empire; wife/widow of an emperor. □ **emperatriz**
empty ['emti] *adj.* with nothing inside: *find an empty bottle and fill it with water.* □ **vacío**
■ *n.* (*pl. empties*) thing, usually bottle, which has nothing in it: *these bottles are all empties.* □ **cascos; envases**
■ *v.* (*emptied; emptying*) to make (something) empty; to remove (the contents) from something: *can you empty this bottle? he emptied the water into the gutter.* □ **vaciar**
empty-handed *adj.* with no results; having received nothing: *they came away from the meeting empty-handed.* □ **con las manos vacías**
emu ['iːmjuː] *n.* large Australian bird which cannot fly. □ **emú**
emulate ['emjuleit] *v.* to try to do as well or better than someone. □ **emular**
emulsion [i'mʌlʃn] *n.* mixture of two liquids which do not unite completely, such as oil and water. □ **emulsión**
emulsion paint, paint made of colour added to an emulsion of oil and water. □ **pintura de emulsión**
emulsify *v.* to make into an emulsion. □ **emulsionar**
enable [i'neibl] *v.* to make it possible for someone to do something: *this enabled him to answer the question.* □ **permitir**
enamel [i'næml] *n.* **1** very hard covering of colour: *enamel paint.* □ **esmalte**
2 hard coating on the teeth. □ **esmalte**
■ *v.* (*he enamelled*) to cover with very hard colour: *enamelled bath; enamelled mug.* □ **esmaltar**
enamoured [i'næməd] *adj. I'm not enamoured of her hair style,* I don't like it very much. □ **enamorado (gustar mucho)**
encamped [in'kæmpd] *adj.* in a camp: *the enemy are encamped three miles away.* □ **acampado**
encampment *n.* large camp. □ **campamento**
encase [in'keis] *v.* to surround as if in a case. □ **encerrar**
enchanting [in'tʃɑːntiŋ] *adj.* very beautiful/magical: *an enchanting play.* □ **encantador**
encircle [in'səːkl] *v.* to surround completely: *the enemy has completely encircled the town.* □ **cercar**
enclave ['enkleiv] *n.* small group/small area completely surrounded by another quite different and larger mass: *a Welsh-speaking enclave.* □ **enclave**
enclose [in'klouz] *v.* to put an object inside something: *the sheep were enclosed in a pen; I am enclosing a bill with my letter.* □ **encerrar; adjuntar**
enclosure [in'klouʒə] *n.* **1** fenced area for keeping animals. □ **cercado**
2 paper enclosed with a letter in an envelope. □ **carta (adjunta)**
encompass [in'kʌmpəs] *v.* to surround. □ **rodear**
encore ['ɔŋkɔː] *n.* **1** calling (by the audience) for a performer to repeat a song/a piece of music. □ **¡otra!**
2 song/piece of music repeated at the request of the audience. □ **bis**
■ *v.* to call for a song, etc., to be repeated. □ **pedir un bis**
encounter [in'kauntə] *n.* **1** meeting. □ **encuentro**
2 short conflict. □ **choque**
■ *v.* to meet: *we encountered many difficulties.* □ **encontrarse con**
encourage [in'kʌridʒ] *v.* to give (someone) the confidence to do something: *I encouraged him to apply for the job.* □ **animar**
encouragement *n.* something which gives someone the confidence to do something: *I gave him a calculator as an encouragement to work harder.* □ **ánimo; estímulo**
encouraging *adj.* which encourages to do better: *our sales have doubled this year - that is very encouraging.* □ **alentador**
encroach [in'kroutʃ] *v.* to occupy space, etc., belonging to someone else: *his garage encroaches on my land.* □ **usurpar**
encrust [in'krʌst] *v.* to cover with a hard covering: *encrusted with jewels.* □ **incrustar**
encyclical [in'siklikl] *n.* solemn letter from the Pope. □ **encíclica**
encyclopaedia , encyclopedia [insaiklə'piːdiə] *n.* reference book which gives facts about things/ people/events, etc.: *look up the dates of Julius Caesar in the encyclopaedia.* □ **enciclopedia**
encyclopaedic, encyclopedic *adj.* like an encyclopaedia: *he has an encyclopaedic knowledge of tropical fish.* □ **enciclopédico**

end [end] *n.* **1** final part of something: *tie the two ends of a piece of string together; go to the end of the road and turn left.* □ **punta; final**
big end, end of the rod in a car engine which connects the piston to the camshaft. □ **cabeza de biela**
shallow end/deep end, part of a swimming pool where you can stand up in the water/where you can't touch the bottom. □ **donde no cubre/donde cubre**
to throw someone in at the deep end, to give someone a difficult job to start with. □ **dar a uno la parte más dura**
to be at a loose end, to have nothing to do. □ **estar desocupado**
2 final part of a period of time: *the end of the month; wait until the end of the record; when the concert came to an end.* □ **fin**
3 aim: *to this end,* in order to do this; *he used the letter to his own ends,* to help his plans. □ **propósito; fin**
■ *v.* to finish: *I shall end my speech by saying...; the play ends with the death of the hero; we ended up getting stopped by the police for speeding.* □ **finalizar; terminar**
ending *n.* way a story, etc., finishes: *this book has a happy ending.* □ **final**
endless *adj.* with no apparent end: *all we have are endless arguments.* □ **interminable**
endlessly *adv.* with no apparent end: *they argued endlessly about money.* □ **interminablemente**
endways *adv.* with the end first: *if the book will not fit in the shelf upright, put it in endways.* □ **de canto**
endanger [in'deindʒə] *v.* to put in danger. □ **poner en peligro**
endeavour [in'devə] *Amer.* **endeavor** *n.* (*formal*) attempt. □ **intento, empresa**
■ *v.* (*formal*) to try hard: *I will endeavour to find an answer to your problem.* □ **procurar**
endemic [en'demik] *adj.* (disease) which is often found in a particular place. □ **endémico**
endive ['endiv] *n.* vegetable of which the curly leaves are used for salads; chicory. □ **endibia; escarola**
endocrine ['endəkrain] *adj.* ***endocrine gland,*** gland which makes hormones and passes them directly into the bloodstream. □ **endocrino; glándula endocrina**
endorse [in'dɔːs] *v.* **1** to show approval. □ **aprobar**
2 *to endorse a cheque,* to sign it on the back to show it is yours. □ **endosar**
3 *his driving licence was endorsed,* had a note attached to show he had been found guilty of a traffic offence. □ **su carnet de conducir tenía una nota de inhabilitación**
endow [in'dau] *v.* **1** to give a regular income to (a school/hospital, etc.). □ **dotar**
2 ***endowed with,*** having (naturally) certain qualities: *he is endowed with a strong constitution.* □ **dotado de**
endowment *n.* **1** giving of money (to a school, etc.) to provide a regular income. □ **dotación**
2 ***endowment policy,*** type of insurance policy where a sum of money is paid to the insured person on a certain date, or to his heirs if he dies. □ **seguro de vida temporal**
endure [in'djuə] *v.* **1** to suffer: *how can you endure working in a place like this? his singing is more than I can endure.* □ **soportar**
2 to stay/to last. □ **permanecer; perdurar**
endurance *n.* ability to suffer hardship. □ **aguante**
endurance test, test of a machine/person to see if it/he works well under bad conditions. □ **prueba de resistencia**
enema ['enimə] *n.* liquid medicine put into the anus with a syringe. □ **enema**
enemy ['enəmi] *n.* (*pl. enemies*) opponent (in war): *our troops attacked the enemy; we were surrounded by enemy tanks.* □ **enemigo**
energy ['enədʒi] *n.* (*pl. energies*) force/strength: *he has enormous energy for a man of eighty-five.* □ **energía**
atomic energy, power from atomic reactions. □ **energía atómica**
energetic [enə'dʒetik] *adj.* using much force; lively: *he does very energetic exercises.* □ **enérgico**
energetically *adv.* using much force: *he opposed my arguments very energetically.* □ **enérgicamente**
enfold [in'fould] *v.* to wrap up in something. □ **envolver**
enforce [in'fɔːs] *v.* to make sure a law is obeyed: *this rule must be enforced.* □ **hacer cumplir**
enfranchise [in'fræntʃaiz] *v.* to give someone the right to vote in elections. □ **conceder derechos de sufragio**
engage [in'geidʒ] *v.* **1** to attach together (legally); to employ (new staff): *we are engaging ten more members of staff,* we are appointing them. □ **comprometerse; emplear**
2 to make parts of a machine fit into each other. □ **engranar**
3 *engage first gear,* put your car into first gear. □ **mete la primera**
4 to be occupied in doing something: *he is engaged in a long legal argument.* □ **estar ocupado**
engaged *adj.* **1** *he is engaged to my sister,* he has officially stated he is going to marry her; *they are engaged,* they are going to get married. □ **prometido**
2 busy: *he is engaged at the moment in trying to correct the fault.* □ **ocupado**
3 *the toilet is engaged,* is occupied; *the line is engaged,* the telephone line is busy. □ **ocupado**
engagement *n.* **1** appointment: *I have a business engagement tomorrow afternoon.* □ **cita**
2 statement of intention to marry: *they have announced their engagement.* □ **compromiso**
engagement ring, ring given by man to woman when they agree to marry. □ **anillo de compromiso**
engaging *adj.* charming: *an engaging smile.* □ **atractivo; encantador**
engine ['endʒin] *n.* **1** machine/large motor which produces power: *my car hasn't got a very powerful engine.* □ **motor**
2 locomotive/vehicle for pulling trains: *the train is pulled by two diesel engines.* □ **locomotora**
engined *adj.* with an engine: *single-engined aircraft,* aircraft with only one engine. □ **con motor**
engine-driver *n.* person who drives a locomotive. □ **maquinista**
engineer [endʒi'niə] *n.* **1** person who looks after technical equipment, especially engines: *telephone engineer.* □ **mecánico**
2 (*in army*) soldier who specializes in construction of bridges/defences, etc.. □ **soldado del Cuerpo de Ingenieros**
civil engineer, person (not a soldier) who specializes in construction of roads/bridges, etc. □ **ingeniero de caminos, canales y puertos**
3 *Amer.* person who drives a locomotive. □ **maquinista**
■ *v.* to arrange (something) by plotting: *he engineered his brother's election as mayor.* □ **maquinar**
engineering *n.* science/study of technical equipment: *electrical engineering; electronic engineering.* □ **ingeniería**

civil engineering, science of construction (especially of roads/bridges, etc.). □ **ingeniería (de caminos...)**
England ['iŋlənd] *n.* country forming the largest part of Great Britain. □ **Inglaterra**
English ['iŋgliʃ] *adj.* referring to England: *English weather; English countryside; I think he is English although he speaks with an American accent.* □ **inglés**
■ *n.* (*no pl.*) **1** *the English*, natives of England: *the English are fond of cricket.* □ **los ingleses**
2 language of England, the USA, Australia, and many other countries: *can you speak English? what is that in English? what's the English for 'pommes frites'?* □ **inglés**
Englishman, Englishwoman *n.* (*pl. Englishmen, Englishwomen*) person from England. □ **inglés, inglesa**
engrave [in'greiv] *v.* to cut a pattern/a letter on to a hard surface: *silver cup with his initials engraved on it.* □ **grabar**
engraver *n.* artist who engraves. □ **grabador**
engraving *n.* picture printed from an engraved plate. □ **estampa, grabado**
engrossed [in'groust] *adj.* *he is engrossed in his work*, he is very interested in it. □ **enfrascado**
engulf [in'gʌlf] *v.* to swallow up: *the house was engulfed in flames.* □ **tragar**
enhance [in'hɑːns] *v.* to increase: *the value of the painting is enhanced by its good condition.* □ **incrementar**
enigma [i'nigmə] *n.* mystery/puzzle. □ **enigma**
enigmatic [enig'mætik] *adj.* difficult to explain/difficult to understand. □ **enigmático**
enjoy [en'dʒɔi] *v.* **1** to take pleasure (in something): *I enjoy going to the races; did you enjoy the play on television last night?* □ **disfrutar**
to enjoy yourself, to have a good time/to take pleasure in something: *I am enjoying myself enormously.* □ **divertirse**
2 *he enjoys good health*, he is always well. □ **goza de buena salud**
enjoyable *adj.* pleasing: *what an enjoyable meal! we had a very enjoyable weekend.* □ **agradable**
enjoyment *n.* pleasure: *I don't want to spoil your enjoyment of the meal, but I just saw a cockroach in the kitchen.* □ **disfrute**
enlarge [in'lɑːdʒ] *v.* to make bigger: *to have a photograph enlarged.* □ **ampliar**
enlargement *n.* bigger photograph (than the original negative). □ **ampliación**
enlarger *n.* device for enlarging photographs. □ **ampliadora**
enlighten [in'laitn] *v.* to give someone a clear picture of something: *could you enlighten me as to the real reasons for the quarrel?* □ **ilustrar; aclarar**
enlightened *adj.* free of prejudice; holding approved ideas. □ **instruido, culto**
enlightenment *n.* knowledge/absence of ignorance. □ **ilustración, cultura**
enlist [in'list] *v.* **1** (*of soldier*) to join the armed forces. □ **alistarse**
2 *to enlist someone's help*, to get help from someone. □ **conseguir ayuda de alguien**
enliven [in'laivn] *v.* to make more lively. □ **avivar**
enmity ['enmiti] *n.* hatred towards someone. □ **enemistad**
enormous [i'nɔːməs] *adj.* very large: *he was knocked down by an enormous lion; we made an enormous blunder in appointing him.* □ **enorme**
enormously *adv.* very much: *I am enjoying myself enormously.* □ **enormemente**

enough [i'nʌf] *adj.* **1** sufficient; as much as is needed: *have you got enough money?* □ **suficiente**
2 *that's enough talking*, stop talking. □ **ya está bien de hablar**
■ *n.* sufficient quantity: *have you had enough to eat?; I've had enough of this*, I am fed up with this. □ **bastante**
■ *adv.* sufficiently: *it is not light enough to take pictures; you are not walking quickly enough; oddly enough, he had met her before.* □ **bastante**
enquire [iŋ'kwaiə] *v.* **1** to ask questions: *he enquired about/after Mrs Jones; she enquired about/after my health; have you enquired at the lost property office?* □ **preguntar; informarse de**
2 to conduct an official investigation: *the police are enquiring into the murder.* □ **investigar**
enquiry *n.* **1** question: *I will make an enquiry about flights to Paris; in answer to your enquiry.* □ **pregunta**
enquiries (*desk*), place (in a shop, etc.) for dealing with questions. □ **información**
2 official investigation: *Judge Smith is heading the enquiry into corruption.* □ **investigación**
enrich [in'ritʃ] *v.* to make richer. □ **enriquecer**
enrol [in'roul] *Amer.* **enroll** *v.* (*he enrolled*) to admit (new members of a party/new students): *there are only three students enrolled for my courses; he enrolled for a cookery class.* □ **inscribirse; matricularse**
enrolment *n.* action of admitting new members, students; list of all the new students: *enrolment in the college is 2% down this year.* □ **inscripción; matrícula**
en route [ɑːn'ruːt] *adv.* on the way: *he was en route to the airport when he had the accident; she stopped two nights in London en route for Berlin.* □ **camino de**
ensconced [in'skɔnst] *adj.* firmly settled. □ **asentado; instalado**
ensemble [ɑːn'sɑːmbl] *n.* group (of musicians/singers): *a wind ensemble.* □ **conjunto**
ensign ['ensain] *n.* flag used by the armed forces. □ **enseña**
enslave [in'sleiv] *v.* to make a slave of someone. □ **esclavizar**
ensue [in'sjuː] *v.* to follow: *a long period of uncertainty ensued.* □ **sobrevenir**
ensure [in'ʃuə] *v.* to make sure of: *the reviews ensured the success of the film.* □ **asegurar**
entail [in'teil] *v.* to involve/to include: *what exactly is entailed by the job? do you know what opening a shop entails?* □ **comportar**
entangle [in'tæŋgl] *v.* to be tied up (in string/bushes/problems): *he has got entangled in a deal with some bookmakers; my knitting wool has got entangled round the leg of the chair.* □ **enredar**
entanglement *n.* **1** state of being entangled. □ **enredo**
2 *barbed wire entanglement*, mass of coiled barbed wire to protect soldiers. □ **alambrada**
enter ['entə] *v.* **1** to go in/to come in: *the burglar entered the house by the back window; my son has entered the Civil Service.* □ **entrar, ingresar**
2 to write down (a name, etc.): *I have entered your name on the list for tennis; have you entered this sale in the ledger? he has entered for the examination in French.* □ **inscribir**
enteritis [entə'raitis] *n.* infection of the intestines. □ **enteritis**
enterprise ['entəpraiz] *n.* **1** new plan/adventure; ability to plan. □ **empresa**
2 method of working in business. □ **empresa**

private enterprise, business firms which are not State-owned. □ **empresa privada**
enterprising *adj.* with initiative: *an enterprising businessman.* □ **emprendedor**
entertain [entə'tein] *v.* **1** to amuse: *the King was entertained by a chorus of singers.* □ **entretener**
2 to offer someone a meal: *we are entertaining ten people tonight; we can't go out as we are entertaining tonight.* □ **tener invitados**
3 to consider (a suggestion/an idea). □ **considerar**
entertainer *n.* person/performer who entertains. □ **animador; artista**
entertaining *adj.* amusing: *what an entertaining play!* □ **entretenido, divertido**
entertainment *n.* **1** amusement: *much to the entertainment of the crowd; the only entertainment was an elderly pianist.* □ **entretenimiento; diversión**
2 hospitality. □ **hospitalidad**
entertainment allowance, money allowed for entertaining guests to meals. □ **gastos de representación**
enthralling [in'θrɔ:liŋ] *adj.* extremely interesting. □ **cautivador**
enthrone [in'θroun] *v.* to put on a throne. □ **entronizar**
enthusiasm [in'θju:ziæzm] *n.* great interest: *the critics are showing a lot of enthusiasm for his latest novel.* □ **entusiasmo**
enthuse [in'θju:z] *v.* (*informal*) to show great interest: *she is the sort who enthuses over little china ornaments.* □ **pirrarse**
enthusiast *n.* person who shows great interest in something: *my sister is a skiing enthusiast; he is a gardening enthusiast.* □ **entusiasta**
enthusiastic [inθju:zi'æstik] *adj.* showing great interest: *he was very enthusiastic about my new book; they are both enthusiastic gardeners.* □ **entusiástico**
enthusiastically *adv.* with enthusiasm: *the audience applauded enthusiastically.* □ **con entusiasmo**
entice [in'tais] *v.* to attract/to tempt: *they tried to entice the elephant into its cage.* □ **atraer**
entire [in'taiə] *adj.* whole: *the entire population of Birmingham.* □ **entero**
entirely *adv.* wholly: *I entirely agree with you.* □ **enteramente**
entirety [in'taiərəti] *n.* being whole: *he translated the book in its entirety,* completely. □ **totalidad**
entitle [in'taitl] *v.* **1** to give the right to: *this card entitles you to a 20% reduction; he is entitled to ten days' holiday a year.* □ **dar derecho a**
2 to give a title to: *a book entitled 'War and Peace'.* □ **titular**
entity ['entiti] *n.* (*pl. entities*) separate thing which exists. □ **entidad**
entomology [entə'mɔlədʒi] *n.* study of insects. □ **entomología**
entomological [entəmə'lɔdʒikl] *adj.* referring to entomology. □ **entomológico**
entomologist [entə'mɔlədʒist] *n.* person who studies insects. □ **entomólogo**
entourage [ɔntu:'rɑ:ʒ] *n.* group of people (secretaries/assistants/advisers, etc.) surrounding an important person. □ **séquito**
entrails ['entreilz] *n. pl.* insides (especially intestines) of an animal. □ **entrañas**
entrance [1] ['entrəns] *n.* (act of) going in; (door for) going in: *no entrance; he made his entrance by the back door; entrance 10p,* money paid to enter; *main entrance,* main doorway: *side entrance; back entrance.* □ **entrada**
entrance [2] [in'trɑ:ns] *v.* to bewitch. □ **embelesar**
entrancing *adj.* very attractive/beautiful. □ **fascinante**
entrant ['entrənt] *n.* person who enters for a race/a competition. □ **participante**
entreat [in'tri:t] *v.* to ask and plead: *I entreated him to write.* □ **suplicar**
entreating *adj.* pleading. □ **suplicante**
entreatingly *adv.* pleadingly: *she looked into his eyes entreatingly.* □ **suplicantemente**
entreaty *n.* plea: *he finally acted on my entreaty.* □ **súplica**
entrench [in'trentʃ] *v.* to put in trenches/to dig in. □ **atrincherar**
entrenched *adj.* holding firm opinions. □ **de ideas firmes, atrincherado**
entrepreneur [ɔntrəprə'nə:] *n.* **1** someone who directs a company and speculates commercially. □ **empresario**
2 contractor who acts as a middleman. □ **contratista**
entrepreneurial [ɔntrəprə'nə:riəl] *adj.* directorial/speculative: *an entrepreneurial decision.* □ **empresarial**
entrust [in'trʌst] *v.* to give someone the responsibility for something: *he was entrusted with the job of speaking to the chairman; the keys were entrusted to his secretary.* □ **confiar**
entry ['entri] *n.* (*pl. entries*) **1** going in: *no entry; he made his entry into the political scene; entry to the shop is by the back door.* □ **entrada**
2 written information in reference book/accounts ledger: *there is no entry under Napoleon.* □ **voz/asiento**
entwine [in'twain] *v.* to twist around. □ **enroscar**
enumerate [i'nju:məreit] *v.* to list/to make a list of: *he enumerated all the mistakes she had made.* □ **enumerar**
enunciate [i'nʌnsieit] *v.* to speak clearly. □ **pronunciar o hablar con claridad**
envelop obin'veləp] *v.* to cover/to surround with a covering. □ **envolver**
envelope ['envəloup] *n.* paper covering for sending letters: *put the bill in an envelope; seal the envelope; send a card in an unsealed envelope.* □ **sobre**
environment [in'vaiərənmənt] *n.* surroundings (in which you live): *environment is as important as heredity in forming children; delicate work is difficult in a noisy environment.* □ **medio ambiente; ambiente**
environmental [invaiərən'mentl] *adj.* which refers to the surroundings of something: *environmental studies.* □ **ambiental**
environs [in'vaiərənz] *n.* area surrounding a place: *the environs of Oxford.* □ **alrededores**
envisage [in'vizidʒ] *v.* to foresee; to plan something which may take place: *I envisage a further increase in the cost of living; no changes are envisaged for the next twelve months.* □ **prever**
envoy ['envɔi] *n.* person sent officially (by a country)/high-ranking diplomat: *the British envoy in Peking.* □ **enviado**
envy ['envi] *n.* feeling of wishing to have something which someone else has/of wanting to be or do something else: *he was green with envy.* □ **envidia**
■ *v.* (*envied; envying*) to wish to have something belonging to someone; to be unhappy because you want to be like someone else: *I envy him, he is so rich; I envy him his money; I don't envy her with a husband like that.* □ **envidiar**
enviable *adj.* which one can envy: *he has a very enviable position.* □ **envidiable**

envious *adj.* feeling envy: *he is envious of my success.* □ **envidioso**
enzyme ['enzaim] *n.* substance which can make other substances change (as in digestion). □ **enzima**
epaulette ['epəlet] *Amer.* **epaulet** *n.* decorative strip on the shoulder of a uniform. □ **charretera**
ephemeral [i'fi:mərəl] *adj.* which disappears quickly/does not last long: *an ephemeral publication.* □ **efímero**
epic ['epik] *n.* long story/poem/film, especially about war: *'Gone with the wind' is an epic of the American Civil War.* □ **novela/poema/película épica**
■ *adj.* long and difficult: *an epic struggle; the fight soon reached epic proportions.* □ **épico**
epicentre ['episentə] *n.* point on the surface of the earth which an earthquake reaches first. □ **epicentro**
epicure ['epikjuə] *n.* someone who is fond of, and knows a lot about, food. □ **epicúreo**
epidemic [epi'demik] *n.* wave of disease which affects a lot of people: *a cholera epidemic; an epidemic of measles.* □ **epidemia**
epidermis [epi'də:mis] *n.* outer layer of skin. □ **epidermis**
epiglottis [epi'glɔtis] *n.* small piece of flesh at the back of the throat which prevents food or drink going down the windpipe to the lungs. □ **epiglotis**
epigram ['epigræm] *n.* short, witty saying. □ **epigrama**
epilepsy ['epilepsi] *n.* disease which usually gives convulsive fits: *he suffers from epilepsy.* □ **epilepsia**
epileptic [epi'leptik] *adj.* referring to epilepsy: *an epileptic fit.* □ **epiléptico**
■ *n.* person who suffers from epilepsy. □ **epiléptico**
epilogue ['epilɔg] *n.* short text at the end of a longer work; short moral programme at the end of a day's television or radio programmes. □ **epílogo**
episcopal [i'piskəpl] *adj.* referring to bishops: *episcopal church,* one which has bishops. □ **episcopal**
episcopalian [ipiskə'peiliən] *adj.* and *n.* (member) of an episcopal church. □ **episcopalista**
episode ['episoud] *n.* **1** short piece of action in longer story: *the part of 'War and Peace' I like best is the episode where Natasha goes to her first ball.* □ **episodio**
2 short period (in your life). □ **episodio**
epistle [i'pisl] *n.* (*formal*) long letter. □ **epístola**
epitaph ['epitɑ:f] *n.* writing on a gravestone. □ **epitafio**
epithet ['epiθet] *n.* special name describing someone: *William I has the epithet of 'the Conqueror'.* □ **epíteto**
epitome [i'pitəmi] *n.* person who shows a particular quality very strongly: *he is the epitome of the male chauvinist.* □ **epítome**
epitomize *v.* to show (a quality) very strongly: *she epitomizes the modern businesswoman.* □ **ser la personificación de**
epoch ['i:pɔk] *n.* major period of time. □ **época**
epoch-making *adj.* very important historically: *the epoch-making discovery of the telephone.* □ **trascendental, que hace época**
equable ['ekwəbl] *adj.* calm/not easily upset: *he is a very equable person.* □ **ecuánime**
equal ['i:kwəl] *v.* (*he equalled*) to be exactly the same as/to add up to: *two plus two equals four; our turnover exactly equals that of our main rivals.* □ **ser igual**
■ *adj.* **1** exactly the same as/level with something: *equal shares for everyone.* □ **igual**
2 ***all things being equal,*** having considered everything carefully. □ **si todo sigue igual**
3 *he wasn't **equal to the task,*** he wasn't strong enough/brave enough to do it. □ **no tenía fuerzas para...**
■ *n.* someone who is on the same level as someone else: *he is better than me in geography, but in physics I'm his equal; she treats him as an equal.* □ **igual**
equality [i'kwɔliti] *n.* state of being equal: *equality of opportunity,* state where everyone has the same chance of getting a job/of doing well. □ **igualdad**
equalize ['i:kwəlaiz] *v.* to make equal; to score and make the points of both teams the same: *the score was 2-1 but Smith equalized two minutes before half-time.* □ **igualar**
equalizer *n.* goal, etc., which makes the score equal: *Smith scored the equalizer two minutes before half-time.* □ **igualada**
equally *adv.* in exactly the same way: *they are equally unpleasant to me; equally, I cannot stand them.* □ **igualmente**
equanimity [ekwə'nimiti] *n.* not getting flustered. □ **ecuanimidad**
equate [i'kweit] *v.* to see two things as equal: *he equates the modern theatre with rubbish.* □ **equiparar**
equation [i'kweiʒn] *n.* mathematical or chemical formula showing two parts which are equal: $2x + 2y = 36$ *is an equation.* □ **ecuación**
equator [i'kweitə] *n.* line around the circumference of the earth which is the same distance from the North and South Poles: *the capital of the country is on the equator.* □ **ecuador**
equatorial [ekwə'tɔ:riəl] *adj.* referring to the equator: *equatorial Africa; equatorial rain forest.* □ **ecuatorial**
equestrian [i'kwestriən] *adj.* and *n.* (person) riding on a horse. □ **ecuestre**
equidistant [i:kwi'distənt] *adj.* at an equal distance from something. □ **equidistante**
equilateral [i:kwi'lætərəl] *adj.* with sides of the same length: *an equilateral triangle.* □ **equilátero**
equilibrium [i:kwi'libriəm] *n.* state of being perfectly balanced. □ **equilibrio**
equine ['i:kwain] *adj.* referring to horses. □ **equino**
equinox ['i:kwinɔks] *n.* time of the year when the day and night are of equal length: *the spring equinox.* □ **equinoccio**
equinoctial [i:kwi'nɔkʃl] *adj.* referring to an equinox: *equinoctial tide/gale.* □ **equinoccial**
equip [i'kwip] *v.* (*he equipped*) to provide something/someone with arms/machinery/furniture, etc.: *the soldiers were equipped with machine guns; the kitchen is equipped with cooker, fridge and washing machine; they are fully equipped for camping.* □ **equipar**
well equipped, with all the arms/machinery, etc., which are thought necessary. □ **bien provisto**
equipment *n.* (*no pl.*) things which are provided to equip something: *a soldier's equipment; camping equipment; photographic equipment.* □ **equipo**
equity ['ekwiti] *n.* **1** state of justice. □ **equidad**
in equity, to be fair. □ **con imparcialidad**
2 ***equities,*** ordinary shares (in a company). □ **acciones**
equitable *adj.* fair/just. □ **equitativo**
equivalent [i'kwivələnt] *adj.* and *n.* (something) of the same value/same strength (as something): *it cost me four dollars, or the equivalent in French francs; what is the British equivalent of the Secretary of State?* □ **equivalente**
equivocate [i'kwivəkeit] *v.* to put off a decision/to change one's mind frequently. □ **aplazar una deci-**

sión; cambiar de opinión cada dos por tres

equivocal *adj.* uncertain/ambiguous: *he gave only an equivocal answer.* □ **equívoco**

era ['iərə] *n.* long period of history: *the Victorian era; how did people amuse themselves before the era of radio and television?* □ **era**

eradicate [i'rædikeit] *v.* to wipe out/to destroy completely: *doctors are trying to eradicate smallpox; this spray should eradicate all weeds.* □ **erradicar**

eradication [irædi'keiʃn] *n.* wiping out. □ **erradicación**

erase [i'reiz] *v.* to rub out writing/to remove recorded material from a tape. □ **borrar**

eraser *n. Amer.* rubber for erasing. □ **goma de borrar**

ink eraser, hand eraser for rubbing out ink. □ **goma de tinta**

erasure [i'reiʒə] *n.* place where a piece of writing has been erased. □ **borradura**

erect [i'rekt] *adj.* straight upright: *he held the spear erect.* □ **erecto**

■ *v.* to put up a mast/a building: *we will erect a monument to his memory.* □ **levantar, erigir**

erection *n.* action of putting up; thing which has been erected: *the erection of the mast took a quarter of an hour.* □ **erección**

erg [ə:g] *n.* measurement of work. □ **ergio**

ergonomics [ə:gə'nɔmiks] *n.* (*usually with singular verb*) study of conditions of work. □ **ergonomía**

ermine ['ə:min] *n.* white fur (from the winter coat of a stoat). □ **armiño**

erode [i'roud] *v.* to wear away: *water eroded the stone; stories of corruption eroded public confidence in the president.* □ **erosionar**

erosion [i'rouʒn] *n.* act of wearing away: *the rock was carved in curious shapes by the erosion of the wind; erosion of public confidence.* □ **erosión**

erogenous [i'rɔdʒənəs] *adj.* very sensitive sexually. □ **erógeno**

erotic [i'rɔtik] *adj.* strongly sexual: *erotic dances.* □ **erótico**

err [ə:] *v.* to make a mistake/to be at fault: *he erred on the right side,* his mistake was to his advantage. □ **errar**

errand ['erənd] *n.* being sent out (especially to buy something): *I'm on an errand for my mother; she always wants me to run errands for her.* □ **recado**

erratic [i'rætik] *adj.* irregular/wild: *his aim was very erratic; he is a very erratic player.* □ **irregular**

erratically *adv.* in a wild manner: *he hit the ball erratically all over the golf course.* □ **irregularmente**

erratum [i'rɑ:təm] *n.* (*pl. errata*) mistake in a printed book. □ **errata**

error ['erə] *n.* mistake: *typing error.* □ **error**

in error, by mistake. □ **por equivocación**

erroneous [i'rouniəs] *adj.* wrong: *the figures in the report are all erroneous.* □ **erróneo**

erroneously *adv.* by mistake: *they erroneously quoted last year's prices.* □ **erróneamente**

erudite ['erjudait] *adj.* learned: *the professor is a very erudite person.* □ **erudito**

erudition [erju'diʃn] *n.* learning/knowledge. □ **erudición**

erupt [i'rʌpt] *v.* to explode: *the volcano suddenly erupted.* □ **entrar en erupción**

eruption *n.* **1** explosion (of a volcano): *Pompei was buried in the eruption of Vesuvius.* □ **erupción**

2 appearance of spots on the skin. □ **erupción**

escalate ['eskəleit] *v.* to get worse/more violent; to increase steadily: *the skirmishes gradually escalated into a full-scale war; prices are escalating.* □ **intensificarse**

escalation [eskə'leiʃn] *n.* getting worse/bigger: *escalation of prices; fighting contributed to an escalation of tension in the Middle East.* □ **incremento (precios); escalada**

escalator *n.* moving stairs: *take the escalator to the second floor; dogs must be carried on the escalator.* □ **escalera mecánica**

escapade ['eskəpeid] *n.* wild act: *he got up to all sorts of escapades.* □ **aventura**

escape [i'skeip] *n.* **1** action of getting away from prison/from an awkward situation: *he made his escape by tying sheets together.* □ **fuga, huida (situación)**

2 *we had a **narrow escape** when the train hit the car,* we were almost killed. □ **escapamos por los pelos...**

escape clause, part of a contract which allows one party to avoid the obligations of the contract. □ **cláusula de excepción**

■ *v.* **1** to get away from prison/from an awkward situation: *he escaped from the cell by climbing out of the window; as the guards broke down the door he escaped through the window.* □ **escapar**

2 to avoid/to miss: *he escaped being arrested; it escaped my notice.* □ **evitar; se me pasó por alto**

3 *nothing escapes him,* he notices everything; *his name escapes me,* I cannot remember his name. □ **nada se le escapa; su nombre no me sale**

escapee [eskei'pi:] *n.* person who has escaped from prison. □ **evadido**

escapement *n.* device in a watch or clock which regulates the movement. □ **escape**

escapism *n.* avoidance of reality. □ **escapismo**

escarpment [i'skɑ:pmənt] *n.* steep slope. □ **escarpa**

escort ['eskɔ:t] *n.* person or group of people accompanying someone: *the actress has a new escort - he's the director of a film studio; the president had an escort of motorcycle riders.* □ **escolta**

■ *v.* [es'kɔ:t] to accompany (someone): *he was escorted into the court by three policemen; she was escorted out of the room.* □ **escoltar**

Eskimo ['eskimou] *n.* and *adj.* (*pl. Eskimo* or *Eskimos*) one of a people living in the north of Canada and Greenland: *Eskimos live by hunting and fishing; Eskimo art.* □ **esquimal**

esophagus [ə'sɔfəgəs] *n. Amer.* part of the throat leading from the mouth to the stomach. □ **esófago**

esoteric [isou'terik] *adj.* understood by very few people; difficult to understand: *he is interested in esoteric subjects like ancient Egyptian literature.* □ **esotérico**

espalier [i'spæliə] *n.* artificial shape of a fruit tree, with a central stem and branches attached to wires to form the shape of a ladder. □ **espaldera**

especial [i'speʃl] *adj.* particular. □ **especial, particular**

especially *adv.* particularly/very: *she is especially fond of chocolate.* □ **sobre todo, particularmente**

espionage ['espiənɑ:ʒ] *n.* spying. □ **espionaje**

industrial espionage, spying on a rival firm to try to find out trade secrets. □ **espionaje industrial**

esplanade ['espləneid] *n.* level place (along a seafront) where people can walk. □ **explanada**

espresso [i'spresou] *n.* sort of coffee made by hot water being forced through ground coffee: *espresso coffee.* □ **café exprés**

espresso bar, coffee bar which serves espresso coffee. □ **café**

esq. [es'kwaiə] *abbreviation for* esquire (very polite form of address written after man's name on envelope): *George Martin, Esq.*

essay ['esei] *n.* piece of prose writing on a particular subject: *write me an essay on political problems in South East Asia.* □ **ensayo**
essayist *n.* person who writes essays. □ **ensayista**
essence ['esəns] *n.* **1** pure extract taken from something: *vanilla essence.* □ **esencia**
2 *the essence of the argument,* the central part of the argument. □ **esencia**
essential [i'senʃl] *adj.* and *n.* (something) very important/indispensable: *it is essential that you should take out a proper insurance; it is essential for the applicant to wear a dark suit; they can hardly afford the bare essentials,* the things which are absolutely necessary. □ **esencial, imprescindible**
essentially *adv.* basically/in the most important part: *Welsh people are essentially musical; it is essentially a question of money.* □ **esencialmente**
establish [i'stæbliʃ] *v.* **1** to set up/to create: *she established a bookshop; he established a reputation as a good doctor.* □ **establecerse**
2 to show something to be true: *the police established that the witness was lying; his innocence has not yet been established; it has been established that fifty per cent of people under 30 drink alcohol.* □ **comprobar**
establishment *n.* **1** creation: *the establishment of the printing industry in the sixteenth century.* □ **creación**
2 commercial firm, etc.: *hairdressing establishment.* □ **establecimiento**
3 *the Establishment,* (small) group of people in positions of authority or influence; *his views on tanks offended the military Establishment.* □ **'establishment'**
estate [i'steit] *n.* **1** large area of land belonging to one person: *he has a house in town and a country estate.* □ **finca**
estate agent, person who arranges the sale of houses and land. □ **agente de la propiedad inmobiliaria**
housing estate, area of houses or flats built at one time. □ **bloques de viviendas**
estate car/wagon, long car, with room at the back for carrying luggage/equipment, etc. □ **ranchera**
2 property owned by someone at his death. □ **herencia**
esteem [i'sti:m] *n.* respect: *to hold someone in (high) esteem,* to respect someone (very much). □ **estima**
esteemed *adj.* respected. □ **estimado**
estimate ['estimət] *n.* calculation which shows the worth/cost/number of something: *at a rough estimate, he earns twice as much as I do; could you give me an estimate as to how much it will cost?* □ **estimación, cálculo**
■ *v.* ['estimeit] to calculate (approximately) the cost/the number, etc., of something: *the crowd was estimated at ten thousand; I estimate its value at 100 dollars.* □ **estimar**
estimation [esti'meiʃn] *n.* calculation of how much something is worth; judgement of how valuable a person is. □ **estimación; concepto**
estrange [i'streindʒ] *v.* to make unfriendly. □ **enemistar**
estuary ['estjuəri] *n.* (*pl. estuaries*) wide part of a river where the sea comes in at high tide. □ **estuario**
etc. [et'setərə] *abbreviation for* et cetera *meaning* and so on/and the others. □ **etc.; etcétera**
etceteras [et'setərəz] *n. pl.* other things. □ **otras cosas**
etch [etʃ] *v.* to engrave (on metal with acid). □ **grabar al aguafuerte**
etching *n.* picture reproduced from a metal plate which has been engraved with acid. □ **aguafuerte**
eternity [i'tə:niti] *n.* never-ending period of time: *it will take an eternity,* (*informal*) it will take a very long time. □ **eternidad**
eternal *adj.* everlasting: *eternal damnation; eternal quarrelling over money.* □ **eterno**
ether ['i:θə] *n.* very volatile liquid which burns easily and is used as an anaesthetic. □ **éter**
ethereal [i'θi:əriəl] *adj.* very light like a fairy. □ **etéreo**
ethics ['eθiks] *n. pl.* moral principles. □ **ética**
ethical *adj.* (*usually with singular verb*) morally right. □ **ético**
ethnic ['eθnik] *adj.* relating to a particular race. □ **étnico**
ethnic minority, minority of a different racial origin than that of the majority. □ **minoría étnica**
ethnology [eθ'nɔlədʒi] *n.* study of the customs of different races. □ **etnología**
ethos ['i:θɔs] *n.* beliefs or characteristics (especially of a group of people). □ **genio**
etiquette ['etiket] *n.* correct way of behaving in society. □ **buenos modales**
professional etiquette, the rules of behaviour of a particular group of people. □ **ética profesional**
etymology [eti'mɔlədʒi] *n.* (*pl. etymologies*) way in which a word has developed historically: *the etymology of the word Wednesday goes back to the name of a Scandinavian god.* □ **etimología**
etymological [etimə'lɔdʒikl] *adj.* referring to etymology. □ **etimológico**
eucalyptus [ju:kə'liptəs] *n.* evergreen tree with bluish leaves, which gives a strong-smelling oil used to treat colds. □ **eucalipto**
eucharist ['ju:kərist] *n.* Christian ceremony of taking consecrated bread and wine. □ **eucaristía**
eulogy ['ju:lədʒi] *n.* (*pl. eulogies*) (*formal*) speech or writing praising someone. □ **elogio, apología**
eulogize *v.* to praise someone strongly. □ **elogiar**
euphemism ['ju:fəmizəm] *n.* word or phrase used in place of a more offensive or unpleasant word: *'questioning' is a euphemism for 'torture'.* □ **eufemismo**
euphonium [ju:'fəuniəm] *n.* large brass wind instrument. □ **tuba**
euphoria [ju:'fɔ:riə] *n.* extreme happiness: *she was in a state of euphoria after she had won a new car.* □ **euforia**
euphoric [ju:'fɔrik] *adj.* very happy. □ **eufórico**
Europe ['juərəp] *n.* geographical area to the west of Asia and north of Africa. □ **Europa**
European [juərə'pi:ən] *adj.* and *n.* (person) from Europe. □ **europeo**
euthanasia [juθə'neiziə] *n.* killing of very sick or old persons to put them out of their misery. □ **eutanasia**
evacuate [i'vækjueit] *v.* **1** to leave a dangerous place in an emergency: *when a strong smell of gas was noticed the occupants evacuated the building; the police evacuated the entire street because of the danger of the fire spreading; during the war, families were evacuated from the towns to the countryside.* □ **evacuar**
2 to empty (the bowels). □ **evacuar**
evacuation [ivækju'eiʃn] *n.* **1** leaving a dangerous place. □ **evacuación**
2 emptying of the bowels. □ **evacuación**
evade [i'veid] *v.* to avoid: *the minister carefully evaded answering the question.* □ **eludir**
evaluate [i'væljueit] *v.* to calculate (a sum of money): *to evaluate damages after an accident.*

□ evaluar
evaluation [ivælju'eiʃn] *n.* act of calculating. □ **evaluación**
evanescent [ivə'nesənt] *adj.* (*formal*) which fades quickly. □ **evanescente**
evangelical [iːvæn'dʒelikl] *adj.* referring to certain Protestant churches and their teaching of the Bible. □ **evangélico**
evangelist [i'vændʒəlist] *n.* one of the four men who wrote the Gospels. □ **evangelista**
evaporate [i'væpəreit] *v.* **1** to turn liquid into vapour: *as it was heated, the water in the dish quickly evaporated; we evaporated the salt solution in order to produce salt crystals.* □ **evaporar, evaporarse**
2 to disappear: *his enthusiasm quickly evaporated.* □ **evaporarse**
evaporation [ivæpə'reiʃn] *n.* process of turning liquid into vapour: *the liquid in the dish was rapidly reduced by evaporation.* □ **evaporación**
evaporated *adj.* ***evaporated milk,*** milk which has been reduced in volume by evaporation, and then tinned. □ **deshidratado**
evasion [i'veiʒn] *n.* avoiding (a direct answer): *the witness answered without any evasion.* □ **evasión**
evasive [i'veisiv] *adj.* which tries to avoid: *an evasive answer; to take evasive action.* □ **evasivo**
evasively *adj.* trying to avoid a direct answer: *he answered evasively.* □ **evasivamente**
eve [iːv] *n.* night before; short time before: *on the eve of our departure,* just before we were due to leave. □ **víspera**
Christmas Eve, 24th December/day before Christmas. □ **Nochebuena**
New Year's Eve, 31st December. □ **Nochevieja**
even ['iːvn] *adj.* **1** flat/level: *the even surface of a table.* □ **plano**
2 regular: *even footsteps; he jogged along at an even pace.* □ **uniforme; regular**
3 *he is a man of very even temper,* he never gets very excited. □ **sereno**
4 equal (in a competition): *she scored 18 points, and I did the same, so we ended up even.* □ **igual, empatado**
to get even with, to try to have revenge on someone: *he cheated me, but I'll get even with him.* □ **desquitarse**
to break even: *the company is just breaking even,* it is making no profit, but no loss either. □ **cubrir gastos**
5 ***even number,*** number which can be divided by 2: *on the left side of the street all the houses have even numbers.* □ **número par**
■ *v.* **1** to flatten/to smooth something: *we must try to even the surface of the football pitch.* □ **alisar**
2 to make equal: *to even things up,* to make things equal. □ **igualar**
■ *adv.* **1** *even the biggest fruit were rotten,* not only the small but also the big fruit were rotten; *even he would understand that,* everyone should understand it easily. □ **hasta, incluso**
2 *he doesn't even like strawberries,* most people like strawberries, but he doesn't. □ **ni siquiera**
3 *that is even worse,* that is worse than before. □ **incluso**
even so, however/if you consider everything. □ **aun así**
even now, right at this minute. □ **aun ahora**
evenly *adv.* **1** in a level way: *he spread the concrete evenly on the path.* □ **uniformemente**
2 equally: *they are evenly matched,* they are equals (in competition). □ **igualmente**

evening ['iːvniŋ] *n.* late part of the day; as night falls: *this evening,* today in the evening; *I will see you tomorrow evening; the accident took place at nine o'clock in the evening; they arrived in New York on the morning of the 26th January having left London the evening before; I was talking to her all evening.* □ **tarde, noche**
evening-dress *n.* clothes worn to special occasions in the evening (long dress for women, black clothes and black or white bow tie for men). □ **vestido de noche (mujer); traje de etiqueta (hombre)**
event [i'vent] *n.* **1** happening: *I will now tell the story of the strange events which took place.* □ **acontecimiento**
happy event, birth of a child. □ **feliz acontecimiento**
in the course of events, as things turned out. □ **con el curso de los acontecimientos**
in the event of *his refusing,* if he should refuse. □ **en caso de que él se niegue**
2 result. □ **resultado**
in any event, whatever happens. □ **pase lo que pase**
at all events, in any case. □ **en todo caso**
3 sporting competition. □ **evento deportivo**
field events, jumping and throwing competitions. □ **competición atlética (sólo salto y lanzamiento)**
track events, running and hurdling. □ **competición atlética (sólo carreras y vallas)**
eventful *adj.* exciting/full of unexpected happenings: *the plane took off for what proved to be a very eventful flight.* □ **lleno de acontecimientos**
eventual [i'ventjuəl] *adj.* final: *the eventual breakup of their marriage.* □ **definitivo**
eventuality [iventju'æliti] *n.* something which might happen. □ **eventualidad**
eventually *adv.* in the end: *eventually, after a struggle, he managed to get on the bus.* □ **al fin**
ever ['evə] *adv.* **1** at any time: *nothing ever happens; did you ever meet Mr Smith? were you ever in the army?* □ **nunca; ¿...alguna vez...?**
2 *I hardly ever see her,* almost never see her. □ **apenas la veo**
3 *he started to play the trumpet louder than ever,* louder than he did before. □ **...más fuerte que nunca**
4 always: *those days have gone for ever,* those days will never come back; *I will love you for ever and ever,* always; *Scotland for ever!,* may Scotland always exist! □ **siempre**
5 ***ever since then,*** from that time onwards. □ **desde entonces**
6 *they lived happily* ***ever after,*** always. □ **...desde entonces, para siempre**
7 ***ever so,*** (*informal*) extremely; very: *I waited ever so long,* I waited for a very long time; *this puzzle is ever so difficult; he died ever so long ago,* a very long time ago. □ **muy; muchísimo**
8 (emphatic): ***what ever*** *is the matter with him?* what on earth is the matter with him? □ **¿qué diablos...?**
how ever *are you going to get across the river?,* how will it be possible for you to get across the river? □ **¿cómo demonios...?**
what ever *is it for?,* what can it be used for? □ **¿para qué sirve?**
evergreen ['evəgriːn] *adj.* (plant) which keeps its leaves all winter. □ **de hoja perenne**
■ *n.* tree which keeps its leaves all winter: *the main types of trees in the northern forests are evergreens.* □ **árbol de hoja perenne**
everlasting [evə'lɑːstiŋ] *adj.* going on for ever: *he seems to have an everlasting cold.* □ **perpetuo**
every ['evri] *adj.* **1** each; all (taken separately): *every day; the medicine has to be taken every two hours,*

at intervals of two hours; *we all meet every Christmas; every time we go for a picnic it rains; I picked six tomatoes and every one of them was rotten,* each one. □ **cada; todos**
every other day, each alternate day. □ **un día sí y otro no**
2 *I have every confidence in him,* I am very confident about him. □ **...total confianza en él**
everybody *pron.* all people: *everybody was excited; have you told everybody about it? I sent Christmas cards to everybody at the school.* □ **todo el mundo**
everyday *adj.* ordinary/very common: *it is an everyday occurrence here; everyday life in Ancient Rome.* □ **diario; cotidiano**
everyone *pron.* = **everybody.**
everything *pron.* all things: *have you got everything for the journey? after the snowstorm everything was white.* □ **todo**
everywhere *adv.* in all places: *there was broken glass everywhere; I have looked everywhere for the key.* □ **en/por todas partes**
evict [i'vikt] *v.* to put someone out of their home: *the squatters were evicted by the council.* □ **desalojar**
eviction [i'vikʃn] *n.* act of putting someone out of their home: *the council ordered the squatters' eviction.* □ **desalojo**
evidence ['evidəns] *n.* **1** traces (of crime): *there was evidence of a violent struggle.* □ **indicio**
2 written or spoken report (at a trial): *the witness gave evidence; the accused said in evidence.* □ **testimonio**
to turn Queen's evidence: *the criminal turned Queen's evidence,* the criminal gave information to the court which proved that his accomplices were guilty. □ **delatar a un cómplice**
3 ***in evidence,*** visible: *their parents were not much in evidence at the party.* □ **...no se hicieron notar mucho**
evident *adj.* obvious: *it is evident that you have been drinking.* □ **evidente**
evidently *adv.* obviously; presumably: *evidently the train has been held up somewhere.* □ **evidentemente**
evil ['i:vl] *adj.* very wicked: *he is an evil influence on the children.* □ **pernicioso**
■ *n.* wickedness; injustice: *poverty is one of the great evils of our time.* □ **mal**
evince [i'vins] *v.* (*formal*) to show a certain quality/feeling. □ **manifestar**
evoke [i'vouk] *v.* to call up (an image): *the poem evokes a picture of the English countryside.* □ **evocar**
evocative [i'vɔkətiv] *adj.* which calls up a sensation in the mind of the onlooker or reader: *a very evocative piece of music.* □ **evocador**
evolve [i'vɔlv] *v.* **1** to work out gradually (a scientific theory/a way of working): *prehistoric men gradually evolved ways of domesticating animals; after a lot of research, he evolved a theory concerning colours.* □ **desarrollar**
2 to develop (gradually): *prehistoric men gradually evolved from earlier man-like creatures.* □ **evolucionar**
evolution [i:və'lu:ʃn] *n.* gradual development: *the evolution of road transport.* □ **evolución**
the theory of evolution, theory that man and other living organisms developed gradually from earlier primitive forms of life. □ **teoría de la evolución**
ewe [ju:] *n.* female sheep. □ **oveja**
ewer ['ju:ə] *n.* large jug. □ **aguamanil**
ex- [eks] *prefix meaning* formerly; who used to be: *my ex-girl friend; the ex-secretary of the committee.* □ **ex**
exacerbate [ig'zæsəbeit] *v.* (*formal*) to make worse/more painful: *this is only going to exacerbate the problem.* □ **exacerbar**
exacerbation [igzæsə'beiʃn] *n.* making worse. □ **exacerbación**
exact [ig'zækt] *adj.* precise: *this is an exact copy; what was the exact time at which the accident took place?* □ **exacto**
■ *v.* to force something out of someone: *the hijackers exacted a ransom for their hostages.* □ **exigir**
exacting *adj.* (person) who demands a lot (of effort). □ **exigente**
exaction *n.* (*formal*) demand (for money): *the exactions of the income tax.* □ **exacción**
exactitude *n.* precision. □ **exactitud**
exactly *adv.* precisely: *he looks exactly like my brother; exactly!,* quite right. □ **exactamente**
exaggerate [ig'zædʒəreit] *v.* to make things seem larger/worse/better than they really are: *don't believe him — he always exaggerates; I am not exaggerating when I say the water came over the roof of the car.* □ **exagerar**
exaggeration [igzædʒə'reiʃn] *n.* (statement, etc.) making things seem larger/worse/better: *to say he was handsome would be something of an exaggeration; without exaggeration, the whole building simply blew away.* □ **exageración**
exalted [ig'zɔ:ltid] *adj.* in a high position: *he has a very exalted post.* □ **elevado**
examine [ig'zæmin] *v.* to inspect (to see if something is correct): to test (a student); to ask (a witness) questions: *the doctor will examine the patient; the mechanic had to examine the brakes; the customs officer will examine your luggage.* □ **examinar; reconocer; registrar**
exam [ig'zæm] *n.* (*informal*) written or spoken test: *how did you do in your exams?* □ **examen**
examination [igzæmi'neiʃn] *n.* inspection; written or spoken test: *you must pass a medical examination before you get your insurance; there is a written and an oral examination in French.* □ **examen**
examinee [igzæmi'ni:] *n.* person being tested. □ **examinando**
examiner [ig'zæminə] *n.* person who inspects or tests: *the examiners asked me questions about European history; the driving test is carried out by an official examiner.* □ **examinador**
example [ig'za:mpl] *n.* case selected to show something: *this is a good example of medieval architecture; as an example of a stupid man in charge of a large company, I can quote the case of Mr Smith.* □ **ejemplo**
to set an example, to act well, so that others may copy you: *he set an example to the staff by turning down the office heating.* □ **dar ejemplo**
to make an example of someone, to punish someone so that others will learn not to do what he did. □ **imponer a alguien un castigo ejemplar**
for example, to name one thing out of many: *he is keen on physical fitness, for example he goes running every morning.* □ **por ejemplo**
exasperate [ig'za:spəreit] *v.* to make someone furious: *I was exasperated by the delays.* □ **exasperar**
exasperation [igza:spə'reiʃn] *n.* fury: *in exasperation he was driven to biting the furniture.* □ **exasperación**
excavate ['ekskəveit] *v.* to dig (a hole in the ground): *the workers excavated a tunnel for the new railway; archaeologists are excavating the Roman villa.* □ **excavar**
excavation [ekskə'veiʃn] *n.* large hole; archaeological investigation. □ **excavación**

excavator *n.* machine for making holes in the ground. □ **excavadora**
exceed [ik'si:d] *v.* to go beyond (a limit): *you must not exceed the speed limit.* □ **exceder**
exceedingly *adv.* very: *he was exceedingly annoyed.* □ **sumamente**
excel [ik'sel] *v.* (*he excelled*) **1** to be very good (at something): *he was weak in French, but excelled at music.* □ **sobresalir**
2 *she excels herself in this novel,* she does better than she has done before. □ **se supera en esta novela**
excellence ['eksələns] *n.* very good quality: *the excellence of a meal.* □ **excelencia**
excellent *adj.* very good: *what an excellent performance!* □ **excelente**
except [ik'sept] *prep.* and *conj.* not including; other than: *you can eat anything except fish; no one saw the ghost, except old Mrs Smith; he does nothing except eat and drink,* the only thing he does is eat and drink; *all went well except that James was sick,* apart from the fact that. □ **excepto; salvo**
exception [ik'sepʃn] *n.* thing not included: *with the exception of James, we all enjoyed ourselves.* □ **excepción**
to take exception to: *he took exception to what she said,* he did not approve of what she said. □ **objetar, desaprobar**
exceptionable *adj.* not to be approved of. □ **reprobable**
exceptional *adj.* outstanding. □ **excepcional**
exceptionally *adv.* particularly: *this winter has been exceptionally mild.* □ **excepcionalmente**
excerpt ['eksə:pt] *n.* small part (of a larger piece of music or writing). □ **pasaje (música); extracto**
excess [ik'ses] *n.* **1** too much (of something). □ **exceso**
in excess, more than: *he paid in excess of a thousand dollars for it.* □ **de más**
to excess, too much/to too great a degree: *you should not drink to excess.* □ **en/con exceso**
excess baggage, more baggage than one is allowed to carry. □ **exceso de equipaje**
2 ***excesses,*** bad actions which are worse than is normally acceptable: *the general tried to control the worst excesses of his soldiers.* □ **excesos**
excessive *adj.* more than is normal: *he has an excessive love of mushrooms.* □ **excesivo**
excessively *adv.* very much: *he is excessively fond of beer.* □ **excesivamente**
exchange [iks'tʃeindʒ] *n.* **1** giving of something for another: *I gave him a knife and he gave me two books in exchange; what will you give me in exchange for this coat? he took my old car in part exchange,* he took my old car as part of the payment for the new one I was buying. □ **cambio**
exchange rate, rate at which one money is given for another: *the current exchange rate is two dollars to the pound.* □ **tipo de cambio**
foreign exchange, exchange of the money of one country for that of another. □ **divisas**
2 ***stock exchange,*** place where stocks and shares are bought and sold. □ **bolsa de valores**
3 ***telephone exchange,*** place where telephone calls are linked. □ **central telefónica**
automatic exchange, place where telephone calls are linked automatically. □ **central automática**
■ *v.* to swap/to give something for something else: *I exchanged my bicycle for a wheelbarrow.* □ **cambiar**
exchequer [eks'tʃekə] *n.* British government department dealing with public money. □ **Hacienda**
Chancellor of the Exchequer, British minister of finance. □ **ministro de Hacienda**
excise ['eksaiz] *n.* tax on certain goods. □ **impuestos indirectos**
■ *v.* to cut out. □ **extirpar**
excision *n.* cutting out. □ **extirpación**
excite [ik'sait] *v.* to arouse (someone/something); to make (someone) very emotional: *he was excited at the thought of going on holiday; don't get too excited about it; the very thought of it makes me excited.* □ **excitar; emocionar**
excitability [iksaitə'biliti] *n.* ease with which you are made very excited. □ **excitabilidad**
excitable [ik'saitəbl] *adj.* easily excited. □ **excitable**
excitement *n.* state of being excited: *there was excitement in the house as the great day drew near; what is all the excitement about?* □ **excitación**
exciting *adj.* which makes someone excited: *the most exciting news.* □ **emocionante**
exclaim [ik'skleim] *v.* to say something loudly and suddenly: *'Why, it's uncle Bill!' he exclaimed.* □ **exclamar**
exclamation [eksklə'meiʃn] *n.* shouting out. □ **exclamación**
exclamation mark, written sign (!) to show exclamation. □ **signo de exclamación**
exclude [ik'sklu:d] *v.* to shut out: *he was excluded from all the meetings.* □ **excluir**
excluding *prep.* without; other than; not including: *excluding the crew, there were twenty-three people on the aircraft.* □ **excluido**
exclusion [ik'sklu:ʒn] *n.* act of shutting out. □ **exclusión**
exclusive *adj.* **1** very select; not open to everyone: *an exclusive club,* a club which it is very difficult to join. □ **exclusivo**
2 ***exclusive right,*** right to do something which no one else is then allowed to do: *they have the exclusive right to televise the international match.* □ **derecho exclusivo**
■ *adv.* not including: *the price is exclusive of tax.* □ **excluyendo**
exclusively *adv.* solely/only: *this room is exclusively for the use of visitors.* □ **exclusivamente**
excommunicate [ekskə'mju:nikeit] *v.* to refuse communion to (a member of a church). □ **excomulgar**
excommunication [ekskəmju:ni'keiʃn] *n.* refusal of communion. □ **excomunión**
excrement ['ekskrəmənt] *n.* solid waste matter produced by the body. □ **excremento**
excrescence [ik'skresns] *n.* ugly growth/lump. □ **excrecencia**
excrete [ik'skri:t] *v.* to produce waste matter. □ **excretar**
excreta *n. pl.* (*formal*) waste matter produced by the body. □ **excrementos**
excruciating [ik'skru:ʃieitiŋ] *adj.* very painful. □ **insoportable, atroz**
excruciatingly *adv.* very painfully: *the film is excruciatingly bad.* □ **atrozmente**
excursion [ik'skə:ʃn] *n.* short pleasure trip: *we went on a one day excursion to London.* □ **excursión**
excursion ticket, special cheap ticket (on railway). □ **billete con descuento especial**
excuse [ik'skju:s] *n.* reason; apology: *his excuse for not coming is that he has a cold.* □ **excusa**
■ *v.* **1** to pardon (someone): *excuse me,* I am sorry; *my wife asks you to excuse her, but she has a cold.* □ **excusar**
2 to allow (someone) not to do something: *can I be excused from football practice today?* □ **dispensar**

3 *please may I be excused?,* please may I go to the lavatory? □ **¿puedo ir al servicio?**
excusable *adj.* which can be pardoned: *his conduct is perfectly excusable.* □ **perdonable**
ex-directory ['eksdai'rektri] *adj.* (telephone number) which is not listed in the telephone directory. □ **número que no está en la guía telefónica**
execrate ['eksikreit] *v.* (*formal*) to curse/to hate (someone). □ **execrar**
execrable *adj.* extremely bad: *we had some execrable soup.* □ **execrable**
execute ['eksikju:t] *v.* to carry out (an official order), especially to kill someone who has been condemned to death. □ **ejecutar**
execution [eksi'kju:ʃn] *n.* carrying out (of plan); legal killing of person sentenced to death: *he put the plan into execution immediately,* he carried out the plan immediately. □ **ejecución**
executioner [eksi'kjuʃənə] *n.* official who executes people who have been sentenced to death. □ **verdugo**
executive [ig'zekjutiv] *adj.* which carries out plans; which puts things into practice. □ **ejecutivo**
executive committee, committee which runs the business, etc. □ **comité ejecutivo**
■ *n.* **1** person in business who makes decisions/plans, etc. □ **ejecutivo**
2 ***the Executive,*** the part of a Government which carries out laws. □ **el Ejecutivo**
executor [ig'zekjutə] *n.* person who sees that a dead person's will is carried out. □ **albacea**
executrix [ig'zekjutriks] *n.* woman who sees that a dead person's will is carried out. □ **albacea**
exemplary [ig'zempləri] *adj.* which serves as an example: *exemplary conduct.* □ **ejemplar**
exemplify *v.* (*exemplified; exemplifying*) to show as an example. □ **ilustrar**
exempt [ig'zempt] *adj.* not forced to obey (law, etc.): *he is exempt from taxation.* □ **exento**
■ *v.* to free (someone) from having to obey a rule or law: *residents abroad are exempted from paying income tax.* □ **eximir**
exemption [ig'zempʃn] *n.* legal ruling that someone does not have to obey the law: *he has an exemption from military service.* □ **exención**
exercise ['eksəsaiz] *n.* use of physical or mental powers: *he does five minutes' physical exercise every morning; have you done your maths exercises?* □ **ejercicio**
exercise book, book for writing out work at school. □ **cuaderno**
■ *v.* **1** to make (animal) take exercise: *he exercised the dogs on the common.* □ **sacar a correr**
2 to use (power): *he exercised his right of veto.* □ **ejercer**
exert [ig'zə:t] *v.* to use (force/pressure, etc.): *she exerted her influence and got him a job.* □ **ejercer**
exertion [ig'zə:ʃn] *n.* effort: *physical exertion tires me out.* □ **esfuerzo**
exhaust [ig'zɔ:st] *n.* escape (of steam/gas). □ **escape**
exhaust (pipe), pipe in a car which carries away fumes from the engine. □ **tubo de escape**
■ *v.* to wear out; to finish: *the explorers exhausted their supplies of food; I was completely exhausted by the end of the day's shopping.* □ **agotar**
exhaustion [ig'zɔ:stʃn] *n.* state of being very tired: *the rescuers found the climbers in a state of exhaustion.* □ **agotamiento**
exhaustive *adj.* very thorough: *an exhaustive inquiry into the causes of the accident.* □ **exhaustivo**
exhaustively *adv.* thoroughly. □ **exhaustivamente**
exhibit [ig'zibit] *n.* object displayed (in court/at an exhibition). □ **prueba (juicio); objeto expuesto**
■ *v.* to display: *she was exhibiting signs of stress.* □ **mostrar**
exhibition [eksi'biʃn] *n.* display (of works of art, flowers, etc.): *an exhibition of contemporary sculpture; agricultural exhibition; scientific exhibition.* □ **exposición**
exhibitionist *n.* person who wants people to look at him and acts in a strange way for this purpose. □ **exhibicionista**
exhilarate [ig'ziləreit] *v.* to make extremely happy. □ **alegrar**
exhilarated *adj.* extremely happy. □ **alegre**
exhilarating *adj.* which makes you full of energy: *the climate is very exhilarating.* □ **estimulante**
exhilaration [igzilə'reiʃn] *n.* extreme happiness. □ **regocijo**
exhort [ig'zɔ:t] *v.* (*formal*) to urge/to encourage (someone) to do something. □ **exhortar**
exhume [ig'zju:m] *v.* to dig up (a dead person who has been buried). □ **exhumar**
exhumation [eksju'meiʃn] *n.* act of digging up a dead body which has been buried. □ **exhumación**
exigent ['egzidʒənt] *adj.* (*formal*) very urgent. □ **urgente**
exigency [ig'zidʒənsi] *n.* (*formal*) urgent need. □ **urgencia**
exile ['egzail] *n.* **1** banishment (from home country): *he went into exile.* □ **exilio**
2 person who is banished. □ **exiliado**
■ *v.* to send away: *he was exiled to a small island.* □ **exiliar**
exist [ig'zist] *v.* to live/to be: *life can exist on other planets; there is believed to exist a lost play by Shakespeare; they existed on berries and nuts for three weeks.* □ **existir**
existence *n.* life/being: *do you believe in the existence of ghosts?* □ **existencia**
existing *adj.* actual/which is present at this moment: *the existing house is the third building on the same site; he is charged under the existing regulations.* □ **existente, actual, vigente**
exit ['egzit] *n.* way out; going out: *he made his exit by the window,* he went out by the window. □ **salida**
emergency exit, door used in emergency. □ **salida de emergencia**
fire exit, door used in case of fire. □ **salida de incendios**
■ *v.* (*in a play*) to go out: *exit Mr Smith,* Mr Smith goes out. □ **salir**
exodus ['eksədəs] *n.* departure/leaving: *there was a mass exodus to the country on the first day of the holiday.* □ **éxodo**
ex officio [eksə'fiʃiou] *adv.* and *adj.* because of your position: *he's an ex officio member of the committee; the president is ex officio a member of the planning committee.* □ **de oficio**
exonerate [ig'zɔnəreit] *v.* to state that no blame should be attached to someone: *at the trial he was completely exonerated.* □ **exonerar**
exoneration [igzɔnə'reiʃn] *n.* statement that no blame is attached to someone. □ **exoneración**
exorbitant [ig'zɔ:bitənt] *adj.* very high (price). □ **exorbitante**
exorcize ['egzɔ:saiz] *v.* to drive away a devil/a ghost from a place. □ **exorcizar**
exorcism ['egzɔ:sizəm] *n.* driving away a devil/a ghost. □ **exorcismo**
exotic [ig'zɔtik] *adj.* unusual; referring to a tropical

place from a foreign place: *exotic perfume; exotic flowers.* □ **exótico**
expand [ik'spænd] *v.* to increase in size/to become larger: *the number of employees expanded; we must expand the number of shops we supply.* □ **ampliar**
expander *n.* ***chest expander,*** arrangement of springs and handles which you can use to increase the size of your chest. □ **extensor**
expanse [ik'spæns] *n.* wide extent: *the huge expanse of the ocean.* □ **extensión**
expansion [ik'spænʃn] *n.* increase in size: *the firm enjoyed a very rapid expansion in the African market.* □ **expansión**
expansive *adj.* (person) who talks freely. □ **expansivo**
expatiate [ik'speiʃieit] *v.* (*formal*) to talk at great length: *he expatiated on the beauties of the mountain scenery.* □ **explayarse**
expatriate [ik'spætriət] *n.* person who is not living in his home country. □ **expatriado**
■ *v.* to send someone outside his home country. □ **expatriar**
expect [ik'spekt] *v.* **1** to think/to hope/to assume something is going to happen: *I expect to be in Paris by five o'clock; I expect she is tired after a day at the office; he expects me to do all the housework; how do you expect me to do that? what do you expect her to say? is it going to rain? - I expect so; we're expecting visitors,* we are waiting for visitors to arrive. □ **esperar**
2 *she's expecting,* she is pregnant. □ **está en estado**
3 *she is expecting her baby in two weeks' time,* her baby is due to be born two weeks from now. □ **sale de cuentas dentro de ...**
expectancy *n.* hope. □ **expectativa**
life expectancy, number of years a person will probably live. □ **esperanza de vida**
expectant *adj.* expecting. □ **expectante**
expectant mother, pregnant woman. □ **mujer embarazada**
expectantly *adv.* hopefully: *the little boy watched the ice cream man expectantly.* □ **con expectación**
expectation [ekspek'teiʃn] *n.* hope. □ **esperanza**
expectorant [ek'spektərənt] *n.* cough medicine which makes you cough up phlegm. □ **expectorante**
expediency [ik'spi:diənsi] *n.* most simple/straightforward way of doing something. □ **conveniencia**
expedient *n.* simple way of doing something. □ **recurso**
■ *adj.* simple/straightforward. □ **conveniente**
expedite ['ekspidait] *v.* to make something happen faster: *I will do all I can to expedite the affair.* □ **acelerar**
expedition [ekspi'diʃn] *n.* journey of exploration: *to go on an expedition to the North Pole.* □ **expedición**
expeditious *adj.* prompt/rapid. □ **expeditivo**
expel [ik'spel] *v.* (*he expelled*) to throw (someone) out; to send (someone) away: *he was expelled from school for bad behaviour; to expel a country from the United Nations.* □ **expulsar**
expendable [ik'spendəbl] *adj.* **1** which cannot be used again. □ **desechable**
2 *he is expendable,* he can be sacked/left behind/killed. □ **prescindible**
expenditure [ik'spenditʃə] *n.* amount spent: *our expenditure on food is rising.* □ **gasto**
expense [ik'spens] *n.* amount of money spent: *my expenses are rising every month.* □ **gasto**
expense account, money which a businessman is allowed to spend on entertainment and personal expenses which are paid for by his firm. □ **cuenta de gastos de representación**
at someone's expense: *they had a good laugh at his expense,* they laughed at him. □ **...a su costa; a sus expensas**
expensive *adj.* which costs a lot of money: *these watches are very expensive.* □ **caro**
experience [ik'spiəriəns] *n.* something lived through; wisdom gained by living through various situations: *I have no experience of travelling in the desert; to be a car mechanic you have to have practical experience.* □ **experiencia**
■ *v.* to live through something: *have you experienced a tropical rainstorm? she was experiencing a sensation of terror.* □ **experimentar**
experienced *adj.* wise/with plenty of practice: *he is an experienced doctor.* □ **con experiencia**
experiment [ik'sperimənt] *n.* scientific test: *he was carrying out an experiment into the source of light.* □ **experimento**
■ *v.* to carry out a scientific test: *he is experimenting with a new type of car engine.* □ **experimentar**
experimental [iksperi'mentl] *adj.* used as part of a test: *experimental aircraft; the process is still at the experimental stage.* □ **experimental**
expert ['ekspə:t] *adj.* referring to someone who knows a great deal about a subject: *he will give you some expert advice.* □ **experto**
■ *n.* person who knows a great deal about a subject: *he is an expert on tropical butterflies.* □ **experto**
expertise [ekspə'ti:z] *n.* specialist knowledge. □ **pericia, competencia**
expire [ik'spaiə] *v.* **1** to come to an end: *my season ticket expires in six days' time.* □ **expirar**
2 (*formal*) to die. □ **expirar**
expiry *n.* coming to an end: *the expiry date of a ticket.* □ **expiración**
explain [ik'splein] *v.* **1** to give reasons for; to make something clear: *could you explain this calculation? no one can explain why the car ran over the cliff; she tried to explain what she meant.* □ **explicar**
2 *he tried to explain away his rude letter,* he tried to show that his letter was not meant to be rude. □ **explicar**
explanation [eksplə'neiʃn] *n.* reason for something: *what is the explanation of this sudden cold weather? he could not give any explanation for his actions.* □ **explicación**
explanatory [ik'splænətəri] *adj.* which gives reasons; which makes clear: *you must read the explanatory notes.* □ **explicativo**
expletive [ik'spli:tiv] *n.* swear word. □ **expletivo, taco**
explicable [ik'splikəbl] *adj.* which can be explained: *his reply is quite explicable in the circumstances.* □ **explicable**
explicit [ek'splisit] *adj.* straightforward/clear: *we gave him explicit instructions; she was quite explicit,* she spoke very plainly. □ **explícito**
explicitly *adv.* clearly. □ **explícitamente**
explode [ik'sploud] *v.* **1** (*of bombs, etc.*) to go off/to blow up: *at the height of the fire, the oil tanker exploded; the bomb exploded at 3 p.m.* □ **hacer explosión**
2 to make (bombs) go off: *the police exploded the bomb which was planted in a car.* □ **hacer estallar**
exploit ['eksplɔit] *n.* great/daring achievement. □ **hazaña**
■ *v.* to take (commercial) advantage of something: *to exploit the mineral resources of the North Sea; he exploited his position as manager.* □ **explotar**

exploitation [eksplɔi'teiʃn] *n.* taking advantage: *the exploitation of slave labour; the exploitation of iron ore deposits.* □ **explotación**
explore [ik'splɔ:] *v.* to investigate/to travel and discover (especially unknown lands): *they explored large areas of Africa in the nineteenth century; I am exploring the possibility of opening a bookshop.* □ **explorar**
exploration [eksplə'reiʃn] *n.* investigation (of unknown lands): *he is well known for his exploration of the deserts of Australia.* □ **exploración**
exploratory [ik'splɔrətəri] *adj.* tentative/preliminary: *we are engaged in exploratory discussions about the possibility of co-operation.* □ **exploratorio**
explorer *n.* person who explores unknown lands: *he is a polar explorer,* he has explored the Arctic/Antarctic areas. □ **explorador**
explosion [ik'splouʒn] *n.* blowing up (of bombs/oil tanks, etc.): *as the fire spread there was a series of explosions.* □ **explosión**
population explosion, rapid increase in population. □ **explosión demográfica**
explosive [ik'splousiv] *adj.* liable to blow up: *do not smoke near explosive material.* □ **explosivo**
■ *n.* material (like gunpowder) which can blow up: *an explosives factory; the car was packed with explosives.* □ **explosivo**
exponent [ik'spounənt] *n.* person who practises a certain belief/a certain art: *a leading exponent of abstract art.* □ **exponente**
export ['ekspɔ:t] *n.* goods sent to a foreign country for sale: *our exports to the Common Market have increased; we are always looking for new export markets.* □ **exportación**
export manager, person in charge of sales to foreign countries. □ **director de exportación**
■ *v.* [ik'spɔ:t] to send goods to a foreign country for sale: *we export half our production.* □ **exportar**
exporter *n.* person or company which sells goods to foreign countries. □ **exportador**
expose [ik'spouz] *v.* **1** to show: *the book exposed his ignorance of American history.* □ **poner de manifiesto**
2 to let light go on to a film. □ **exponer**
3 to reveal (a scandal): *the newspaper articles exposed corruption in the Government.* □ **revelar**
exposed *adj.* **1** open: *the house stands in a very exposed position,* the house is not sheltered from the wind. □ **expuesto, abierto**
2 *exposed film,* film which has been taken but not developed. □ **película expuesta pero sin revelar**
exposure [ik'spouʒə] *n.* **1** state of not being sheltered from cold/danger, etc.: *he died of exposure,* he died of cold/damp, etc., through not having had any shelter. □ **falta de cobijo**
2 time needed for a picture to be taken on film: *an indoor shot needs a long exposure.* □ **tiempo de exposición**
exposure meter, device for calculating the exposure for a photograph. □ **exposímetro; fotómetro**
3 revealing (of corruption, etc.). □ **descubrimiento**
4 direction in which a house faces: *a house with a southerly exposure.* □ **una casa orientada al sur**
expose [ik'spouzei] *n.* newspaper report revealing corruption/wrongdoing, etc. □ **revelar**
expostulate [ik'spɔstjuleit] *v.* (*formal*) to protest: *he expostulated with her.* □ **amonestar**
expound [ik'spaund] *v.* to explain in detail. □ **exponer**
express [ik'spres] *adj.* done on purpose: *I did it with the express intention of killing him.* □ **expreso**
■ *adj.* and *n.* rapid (train): *express train; to catch the London to Edinburgh express.* □ **expreso**
■ *v.* **1** to put into words: *I expressed myself badly,* I did not make what I wanted to say clear: *if I had to express a wish it would be to visit Japan.* □ **expresar**
2 to put into symbols: *to express a fraction in decimals.* □ **expresar**
expression [ik'spreʃn] *n.* **1** way of showing feeling: *he had a satisfied expression.* □ **expresión**
2 phrase: *to use a vulgar expression.* □ **expresión**
expressive *adj.* showing feeling: *she has a very expressive face.* □ **expresivo**
expressly *adv.* on purpose: *I expressly forbade you to see him.* □ **expresamente**
expressway *n. Amer.* fast road with few junctions. □ **autopista**
expropriate [ik'sprouprieit] *v.* (*of the state/a local authority*) to take away (property) from a private owner. □ **expropiar**
expropriation [iksproupri'eiʃn] *n.* taking of property away from a private owner. □ **expropiación**
expulsion [iks'pʌlʃn] *n.* act of being thrown out/sent away. □ **expulsión**
expurgate ['ekspəgeit] *v.* to remove rude/offensive expressions (from a book). □ **expurgar**
exquisite [ik'skwizit] *adj.* very finely made/very refined: *an exquisite meal; what an exquisite jewel!* □ **exquisito**
exserviceman [eks'sə:vismən] *n.* (*pl. exservicemen*) man who used to be a member of the armed forces. □ **ex combatiente, veterano**
extant [ik'stænt] *adj.* still in existence: *it is the only piece of clothing extant which belonged to Henry VIII.* □ **existente**
extempore [ik'stempəri] *adv.* and *adj.* without notes: *he spoke for ten minutes extempore; she made a very funny extempore speech.* □ **improvisadamente (adv.); improvisado (adj.)**
extemporize *v.* to speak without preparation/without notes. □ **improvisar**
extend [ik'stend] *v.* **1** to stretch out: *the town extends for some distance on both sides of the river.* □ **extenderse**
2 to make longer: *the bus company is extending its services to several small villages; could you extend the deadline by two weeks?* □ **extender, prolongar**
extension *n.* **1** act of extending; thing added on: *we are building an extension to our warehouse; the bank has given him an extension of two weeks to pay his debts.* □ **extensión; anexo; prórroga**
2 telephone line in an office: *call me on extension 270.* □ **extensión**
3 ***extension course,*** course of study taken by part-time students. □ **curso de divulgación**
extensive *adj.* very widespread; very vast: *he has extensive knowledge of South America; they make extensive use of the local library.* □ **extenso, amplio**
extensively *adv.* very greatly/widely: *she has read extensively about the problem; the factory was extensively damaged in the fire.* □ **extensamente, mucho**
extent [ik'stent] *n.* degree; size: *his farm covers an extent of 1,000 acres; what was the extent of the damage? to a certain extent, he is to blame.* □ **extensión; importancia**
extenuating [ik'stenjueitiŋ] *adj.* which lessens or explains a crime: *extenuating circumstances.* □ **atenuante**
exterior [ik'stiəriə] *adj.* outside: *exterior surface.*

□ **exterior**
■ *n.* outside: *the exterior of a house.* □ **exterior**

exterminate [ik'stə:mineit] *v.* to kill (large number of living things): *the disease has almost exterminated the rabbit population.* □ **exterminar**
extermination [ikstə:mi'neiʃn] *n.* act of killing (large numbers): *our target is the extermination of all mosquitoes in the area.* □ **exterminio**

external [ik'stə:nl] *adj.* of, for, from, on the outside: *external surface; medicine for external use only,* which must not be drunk or eaten; *external examiner,* examiner from outside the school or college. □ **externo**
externally *adv.* outside: *externally he is a big strong man, but inside he is just a baby.* □ **externamente**

extinct [ik'stiŋkt] *adj.* **1** *extinct volcano,* volcano which no longer erupts. □ **extinto; volcán apagado**
2 *extinct species,* species which has died out. □ **especie extinguida**
extinction [ik'stiŋkʃn] *n.* putting out (of a fire); dying out (of a species). □ **extinción**

extinguish [ik'stiŋgwiʃ] *v.* to put out (a fire). □ **extinguir**
extinguisher *n.* ***fire extinguisher,*** apparatus for putting out fires. □ **extintor**

extol [ik'stoul] *v.* (*he extolled*) (*formal*) to praise very highly. □ **ensalzar**

extort [ik'stɔ:t] *v.* to get money from someone by threats. □ **extorsionar**
extortion [ik'stɔ:ʃn] *n.* getting money from someone by threats. □ **extorsión**
extortionate *adj.* excessive (demands); very high (price). □ **exorbitante**

extra ['ekstrə] *adj.* more than normal; additional: *it will cost you an extra ten pounds.* □ **extra, más**
■ *adv.* **1** more than usual: *it will cost you ten pounds extra; extra strong string.* □ **extra**
2 in addition: *the service charge is extra.* □ **adicional**
■ *n.* **1** person (not a star) appearing in crowd scenes in a film. □ **extra**
2 something more than usual: *they charge you more for extras.* □ **extra**
■ ***extra-*** *prefix meaning* outside. □ **extra-**
extracurricular, outside the curriculum. □ **extracurricular**
extramarital, outside marriage. □ **extramatrimonial**
extraterritorial, outside the territory. □ **extraterritorial**

extract ['ekstrækt] *n.* **1** something reduced from something larger. □ **extracto**
meat extract, substance concentrated from meat. □ **concentrado de carne**
2 *extracts from a play,* short scenes from a play. □ **extracto**
■ *v.* [ik'strækt] to pull something out; to produce something: *the dentist extracted a tooth; to extract opium from poppies.* □ **extraer**
extraction [ik'strækʃn] *n.* **1** pulling out (of a tooth); production (of a product): *the extraction of oil from coal.* □ **extracción**
2 origin: *he is of French extraction,* his family originally was French. □ **origen, extracción**
extractor *n.* ***extractor fan,*** fan which sucks air out. □ **extractor**

extradite ['ekstrədait] *v.* to bring back (a criminal) to his home country for trial (by agreement with the country where he was arrested). □ **conceder la extradición, entregar**
extraditable *adj.* (crime) for which you can be extradited. □ **causante de extradición**
extradition [ekstrə'diʃn] *n.* return of a criminal to his home country. □ **extradición**

extraneous [ik'streiniəs] *adj.* not directly connected with something: *his arguments were extraneous to the case.* □ **ajeno**

extraordinary [ik'strɔ:dnri] *adj.* marvellous; quite different from everything else; strange/unusual: *what an extraordinary house; we are having extraordinary weather this year; he has an extraordinary brain.* □ **extraordinario**
extraordinarily *adv.* in a very remarkable way: *she is extraordinarily like her mother; we had an extraordinarily good meal.* □ **extraordinariamente**

extrapolate [ik'stræpəleit] *v.* to calculate something unknown on the basis of available information. □ **extrapolar**
extrapolation [ikstræpə'leiʃn] *n.* calculating something unknown on the basis of available information. □ **extrapolación**

extravagance [ik'strævəgəns] *n.* excessive expense and luxury. □ **derroche, dispendio**
extravagant *adj.* **1** (person) who spends a lot of money. □ **derrochador, dispendioso**
2 expensive and luxurious. □ **dispendioso**
extravaganza [ikstrævə'gænzə] *n.* expensive and luxurious party/show/film. □ **sarao; espectáculo extravagante; superproducción**

extreme [ik'stri:m] *adj.* **1** excessive: *in extreme old age; he holds very extreme opinions; it is an extreme case,* it is a case which is very unusual. □ **extremo**
2 *at the extreme end,* right at the end. □ **al final del todo**
■ *n.* ***to go to extremes:*** *he always goes to extremes,* he always does everything in an excessive way. □ **actuar de manera extrema**
extremely *adv.* excessively: *he is extremely small; this book is extremely expensive.* □ **extremadamente**
extremist *n.* person who has extreme views (usually about politics). □ **extremista**
extremity [ik'stremiti] *n.* (*pl. extremities*) end point: *join the two extremities of the rope together.* □ **extremidad**
the extremities, the hands and feet. □ **las extremidades**

extricate ['ekstrikeit] *v.* to get (someone) out of a difficult situation: *with some difficulty he extricated himself from the wreckage.* □ **librar**

extrovert ['ekstrəvə:t] *n.* person who is very outgoing and jolly. □ **extrovertido**

extrude [ik'stru:d] *v.* to squeeze out under pressure. □ **extrudir**

exuberance [ig'zju:bərəns] *n.* wild enthusiasm. □ **exaltación, gran entusiasmo**
exuberant *adj.* wildly enthusiastic. □ **exaltado, muy entusiasmado**

exude [ig'zju:d] *v.* to send out/to give off (a smell/a feeling) in all directions: *the plant exudes an oily liquid; he exudes self-confidence.* □ **exudar, rezumar**

exult [ig'zʌlt] *v.* to rejoice/to be glad: *he exulted over his victim,* he showed great pleasure at having a victim. □ **exultar**
exultant *adj.* full of triumph. □ **exultante**
exultantly *adv.* triumphantly. □ **exultantemente**

eye [ai] *n.* **1** part of the head, used for seeing: *she has blue eyes; keep your eyes open!,* watch out! □ **ojo**
to set eyes on something, to see something (suddenly). □ **ver (de repente)**
to catch someone's eye, to attract someone's attention: *the advertisement caught my eye; it catches the*

eye, it is very noticeable. □ **llamar la atención de alguien**
to be up to the eyes in: *I'm up to the eyes in work,* (*informal*) I have masses of work to do. □ **estar hasta arriba de**
to keep an eye on something, to guard something. □ **echar un ojo a algo**
to see eye to eye (with): *they don't see eye to eye,* they do not agree; *he doesn't see eye to eye with his father,* he does not agree with his father. □ **estar de acuerdo con...**
2 ***private eye,*** (*informal*) private detective. □ **detective**
3 small hole in a needle for passing the thread through; small loop for attaching a hook; bud on a potato through which sprouts grow. □ **ojo de la aguja; hembra de corchete; yema (patata)**
■ *v.* to look at (someone) carefully: *he eyed him up and down.* □ **mirar de pies a cabeza**
eyeball *n.* the ball of the eye. □ **globo del ojo**
eyebath *n.* small cup for covering the eye with liquid. □ **lavaojos; ojera**
eyebrow *n.* small arch of hair above the eye: *he raised his eyebrows in astonishment.* □ **ceja**
eyeful *n.* something which gets into your eye: *an eyeful of dust.* □ **algo que entra en el ojo**
to get an eyeful *of this,* (*informal*) take a look at this. □ **echar un vistazo**
eyelash *n.* hair growing round the rim of the eye. □ **pestaña**
eyelet *n.* small hole (as in a shoe, for passing the lace through). □ **ojete**
eyelid *n.* covering for the eye. □ **párpado**
eyeliner *n.* substance for drawing a dark line round the eye. □ **lápiz de ojos**
eye-opener *n.* thing which surprises you: *it was an eye-opener to me.* □ **sorpresa**
eyepiece *n.* lens at the end of a telescope through which you look. □ **ocular**
eyeshade *n.* shade attached to the head for keeping bright light out of the eyes. □ **visera**
eyeshadow *n.* substance for colouring the skin round the eye. □ **sombreador**
eyesight *n.* (*no pl.*) ability to see: *his eyesight is failing,* he can see less well. □ **vista**
eyesore *n.* something hideous/unpleasant to look at: *the whole street is an eyesore.* □ **algo que ofende a la vista**
eyestrain *n.* (*no pl.*) tiredness of the eyes. □ **vista cansada**
eyewash *n.* (*no pl.*) liquid for bathing the eyes. □ **colirio**
it's all eyewash, (*informal*) it is rubbish. □ **eso es una chorrada**
eyewitness *n.* someone who has seen something happen. □ **testigo ocular, presencial**
an eyewitness account *of the accident,* account of the accident by a person who saw it happen. □ **narración de un testigo ocular, presencial**
eyrie ['iəri] *Amer.* **aerie** *n.* nest (of an eagle); high and inaccessible house. □ **aguilera; casa en una cumbre**

F,f

F, f [ef] sixth letter of the alphabet. □ **F, f**
fable ['feibl] *n.* moral short story usually about animals, making them seem like human beings. □ **fábula**
fabric ['fæbrik] *n.***1** material: *silk and woollen fabrics are soft to the touch.* □ **tejido**
2 basic structure: *the fabric of society.* □ **tejido**
fabricate ['fæbrikeit] *v.* to invent (an untrue story); to forge (a paper). □ **inventar; falsificar**
fabrication [fæbri'keiʃn] *n.* invention: *the story is pure fabrication.* □ **invención**
faççade [fə'sɑːd] *n.* front of a large building; outward appearance which is intended to give a false impression □ **fachada; apariencia**
face [feis] *n.* **1** front part of the head: *she turned her face towards the light.* □ **cara**
face to face, talking and looking at each other. □ **cara a cara**
to make a face, to make a rude expression: *she made a face at the teacher and ran away.* □ **hacer burla**
to keep a straight face, to try not to laugh. □ **...contener la risa**
to lose face, to feel humiliated. □ **bajar la cabeza**
2 front of anything: *the face of a clock; the cliff face was impossible to climb; the cards were placed face downwards on the table.* □ **la esfera del reloj; cara (acantilado/cartas)**
on the face of it, *the suggestion seems sensible,* apparently/at first sight. □ **a primera vista**
■ *v.* **1** to put a facing/an outward covering on something. □ **poner una funda**
2 to turn your head towards: *face the front, please.* □ **cara al frente**
3 *the house faces east,* the house looks towards the east. □ **la casa está orientada al este**
to face up to something, to realize some difficulty or danger exists. □ **arrostrar**
facecloth *n.* small piece of towelling for washing the face or body. □ **manopla**
facelift *n.* **1** operation to remove wrinkles from your face. □ **estiramiento de piel**
2 *the opera house has had a complete facelift,* has been completely redecorated. □ **...un lavado completo**
face value *n.* the value stated on the face of a coin etc. □ **valor nominal**
to take something at face value, to assume that the first/obvious meaning is the correct one. □ **creer algo a pies juntillas**
facing *n.* material covering the surface of a building/the edges of a garment: *the house was made of brick with a cement facing.* □ **revestimiento (edificio); vueltas (prenda)**
facet ['fæsit] *n.* **1** one of the flat sides on a cut gem. □ **faceta**
2 aspect (of a problem). □ **faceta**
facetious [fə'siːʃəs] *adj.* funny/joking (in an offensive way). □ **jocoso**
facetiously *adv.* not seriously, in a joking way. □ **jocosamente**
facial ['feiʃl] *adj.* referring to a face: *facial expression.* □ **facial**
■ *n.* beauty treatment to make your face more beautiful. □ **tratamiento facial**
facility [fə'siliti] *n.* **1** ease/no difficulty: *he has a great facility for learning languages.* □ **facilidad**
2 ***facilities,*** equipment which can be used to do something: *room with cooking facilities,* room where you are also able to cook. □ **medios**
3 large industrial/scientific building. □ **instalaciones**
facilitate *v.* to make easy. □ **facilitar**
facsimile [fæk'simili] *n.* perfect reproduction/perfect copy. □ **facsímil**
fact [fækt] *n.* something that is true: *it's a fact that you are reading this page.* □ **hecho**
in fact/as a matter of fact, really/actually. □ **en realidad**
the facts of life, (i) basic details of the sex life of humans. □ **educación sexual básica**
(ii) *it's one of the facts of life,* it's something you can't change and must accept. □ **cosas de la vida**
faction ['fækʃn] *n.* group of people linked together in opposition to a ruler/a government. □ **facción**
factor ['fæktə] *n.* **1** number which goes exactly into another number: *2 and 4 are factors of 16.* □ **divisor**
2 something which is influential: *an important factor in our decision was the price.* □ **factor**
safety factor, the question/the problem of safety. □ **factor de seguridad**
factory ['fæktri] *n.* building where things are made: *canning factory,* place where food is sealed into tins. □ **fábrica**
factory ship, ship which freezes or cans fish which are caught by smaller fishing boats. □ **barco congelador**
factual ['fæktjuəl] *adj.* containing facts: *a factual description,* which only gives facts. □ **objetivo, real**
faculty ['fæklti] *n.* **1** special ability: *few people have the faculty of seeing in the dark.* □ **facultad**
2 division of a university: *the faculty of medicine has 600 students.* □ **facultad**
3 *Amer.* teaching staff (of a school/university/college, etc.). □ **profesorado**
fad [fæd] *n.* strange temporary mania for something: *strawberry ice cream is his latest fad.* □ **moda**
a health fad, odd diet, etc., which is supposed to improve your health. □ **manía por la salud**
faddist *n.* person who follows a fad. □ **maniático**
faddy *adj.* (*informal*) (person) who has odd likes and dislikes about food. □ **melindre**
fade [feid] *v.* to lose colour, brightness or strength: *the sun made the curtains fade in places; she is very ill and seems to be fading away; the sound of the band faded as they turned the corner.* □ **descolorarse; consumirse; desvanecerse**
faeces ['fiːsiːz] *Amer.* **feces** *n. pl. (formal)* excreta/solid waste matter from the body. □ **heces**
fag [fæg] *n.* **1** a tiring/boring work. □ **trabajo penoso**
2 (*slang*) cigarette. □ **pitillo**
■ *v.* **1** to work hard. □ **trabajar como un negro**
2 *I'm **fagged out,*** (*slang*) tired out. □ **estoy molido**
faggot ['fægət] *n.* **1** bundle of sticks for lighting a fire. □ **astillas, palos**
2 spiced meat ball. □ **albóndiga**
3 (*informal*) nasty old woman. □ **vejestoria**
Fahrenheit ['færənheit] *adj.* (scale for) measuring heat where the boiling point of water is 212° and the freezing point 32°: *the temperature outside is only twenty degrees Fahrenheit (20 °F).* □ **Fahrenheit**
fail [feil] *v.* **1** to be unsuccessful in doing something: *he has failed his examination again; the car failed to*

stop. □ **suspender (examen); fallar**
2 to grow weaker: *the light is failing so don't carry on reading.* □ **fallar**
3 not to be able to do something: *I fail to see why he has to stay in bed.* □ **no veo por qué...**
4 not to pass (a candidate) in an examination: *he was failed by the examiner.* □ **suspender**
■ *n.* ***without fail,*** certainly. □ **sin falta**
failing *n.* weakness/bad point: *with all his failings she still loves him.* □ **defectos**
■ *prep.* ***failing that,*** if that does not work: *failing that, try a hammer; failing the manager, ask for his secretary,* if the manager isn't there. □ **a falta de...**
fail-safe *adj.* (machine) made so that if anything goes wrong it will stop working and so not be dangerous. □ **autoprotectivo**
failure ['feiljə] *n.* **1** breakdown/stoppage. □ **fallo**
heart failure, dangerous condition when the heart has stopped beating. □ **paro cardiaco**
power failure, breakdown in electricity supplies. □ **corte de electricidad**
2 something which did not work out satisfactorily: *my cake was a failure, it sank in the middle; I'm a terrible failure, I can't do anything right.* □ **fracaso**
faint [feint] *adj.* **1** not clear; difficult to see or hear; weak: *we could just hear a faint noise from the cellar; the experts could read the faint writing on the old map.* □ **casi imperceptible**
I haven't the faintest idea *where he is,* I've no idea where he is. □ **...ni la más mínima idea...**
2 dizzy: *she felt faint, she felt as if she was going to lose consciousness.* □ **mareado**
■ *v.* to lose consciousness for a short time: *it was so hot several people fainted.* □ **desmayarse**
faintly *adv.* weakly: *she spoke so faintly, I could hardly hear.* □ **débilmente**
fair [fɛə] *n.* **1** group of sideshows/amusements/food stalls, etc., set up in one place for a short time. □ **verbena**
2 market for selling and advertising goods: *a trade fair; an antiques fair.* □ **feria**
■ *adj.* **1** light-coloured: *fair-haired girl; he's very fair,* he has pale skin and light-coloured hair. □ **de tez clara y pelo rubio**
2 honest/correct: *it is not fair to eat all the cake yourself.* □ **no está bien...**
3 not bad: *her work is only fair, it could be better.* □ **regular**
4 (*of weather*) dry and warm. □ **buen tiempo**
fair weather sailor/friend, person who only goes sailing in fine weather/who only acts in a friendly way when things are going well. □ **amigo que sólo está a las maduras**
fairground *n.* place in the open air where a fair is held. □ **real (de la feria)**
fairly *adv.* **1** quite/not completely: *I was fairly certain that the car would start.* □ **bastante**
2 justly/correctly: *the judge treated the prisoners fairly.* □ **con justicia**
fairness *n.* **1** light colouring. □ **lo rubio; blancura**
2 honesty/correctness: *in all fairness Bill played better than you.* □ **para ser justo con ...**
fairway *n.* part of a golf course where the grass is kept cut. □ **calle**
fairy ['fɛəri] *n.* small supernatural creature who is able to work magic: *the bad fairy waved her wand and changed the prince into a frog.* □ **hada**
fairy story/fairy tale, story about fairies/princesses/giants/ witches, etc. □ **cuento de hadas**
fairy lights, small coloured electric lights for decorating trees, etc. □ **bombillas de colores**
fairy ring, dark ring on grass, caused by a fungus. □ **cículo oscuro de hierba**
fairyland *n.* land where fairies are supposed to live. □ **país de las hadas**
faith [feiθ] *n.* **1** belief/trust: *I have no faith in the new doctor.* □ **confianza**
2 *the Christian faith,* the beliefs of the Christian church. □ **la fe cristiana**
3 *he acted* ***in good faith,*** he acted honourably, even though wrongly. □ **...de buena fe**
faithful *adj.* **1** trusting/loyal: *man's faithful friend is the dog.* □ **fiel**
2 completely correct: *a faithful account of what happened.* □ **correcto**
faithfully *adv.* **1** loyally: *the soldiers faithfully followed their general.* □ **fielmente**
2 ***yours faithfully,*** used as an ending for business letters, when addressed to no specific person. □ **le saluda atentemente...**
faithless *adj.* disloyal. □ **desleal**
fake [feik] *n.* imitation/forgery; not the real thing: *we thought the picture was by Rembrandt but it turned out to be a fake.* □ **falsificación**
■ *v.* to make an imitation of something: *he faked the chairman's signature.* □ **falsificar**
falcon ['fɔːlkən] *n.* a small bird of prey, sometimes trained to catch other birds in sport. □ **halcón**
fall [fɔːl] *n.* **1** drop/collapse: *my grandmother broke her leg in her fall off the chair; there has been a heavy fall of snow.* □ **caída**
2 (*especially Amer.*) the autumn: *in the fall the maple trees turn red.* □ **otoño**
3 ***falls,*** waterfall: *Niagara Falls.* □ **cascada; cataratas del Niágara**
4 *fall from power,* loss of a powerful position. □ **caída del poder**
■ *v.* (*he fell; he has fallen*) **1** to drop down: *he fell down the stairs; my aunt fell off her bicycle in the road.* □ **caer; caerse**
2 *night is falling,* it is beginning to get dark. □ **anochece**
3 to become less or lower: *house prices fell when they started building the motorway; the temperature is falling.* □ **descender**
4 to become: *he fell ill last Thursday; they fell in love at first sight.* □ **caer enfermo; enamorarse**
5 *I fell over the branch lying on the ground,* I caught my foot on the branch and fell down. □ **tropezar con**
6 *his face fell,* he looked sad and disappointed. □ **puso cara larga**
7 *the government fell,* was defeated. □ **el gobierno cayó**
8 *he fell from power,* he lost his powerful position. □ **perdió el poder**
fall back *v.* to retreat/to go back. □ **retroceder**
fall back on *v.* to use something which was kept as a reserve. □ **echar mano de**
fall behind *v. they had no money and fell behind with the rent,* they were late paying the rent. □ **retrasarse**
fall down *v.* to drop to the ground: *the poster fell down,* came off the wall and dropped to the ground. □ **caerse al suelo**
fallen *adj.* dropped: *fallen leaves.* □ **caído**
■ *n.* ***the fallen,*** people who have been killed in battle/in a war. □ **los caídos**
fall for *v.* **1** to fall in love with (someone). □ **chiflarse por**
2 to be tricked by (something): *don't fall for his smooth talk.* □ **caer en la trampa**

fall out *v.* **1** to drop: *his hair began to fall out when he was forty years old.* □ **caerse**
2 to have an argument: *they were business partners until they fell out.* □ **reñir**
fallout *n.* radioactive dust from a nuclear explosion. □ **lluvia radiactiva**
fall through *v.* to fail: *the plan fell through,* was dropped/not carried out. □ **fracasar; abandonarse**
fall to *v.* to start to do something (especially eat or work). □ **ponerse a**

fallacy ['fæləsi] *n.* (*pl. fallacies*) false argument; error. □ **falacia**
fallacious [fə'leiʃəs] *adj.* wrong. □ **falaz**
fallibility *n.* being capable of making mistakes. □ **falibilidad**
fallible ['fælibl] *adj.* (person) who can make a mistake. □ **falible**

fallow ['fælou] *adj.* (land) which is purposely not used for crops for a time so that it can regain its goodness: *the farmer is letting the field lie fallow this year.* □ **en barbecho**
fallow deer *n.* small deer with white spots. □ **gamo**

false [fɔ:ls] *adj.* (*falser, falsest*) **1** not true: *the prisoner's story was quite false.* □ **falso**
2 not real: *my uncle dressed up and put on a false beard.* □ **falso**
false alarm, signal for an emergency when there isn't one. □ **falsa alarma**
false teeth, artificial teeth. □ **dentadura postiza**
falsehood *n.* lie/something which is not true. □ **falsedad**
falsify *v.* (*falsified; falsifying*) to change (something) thus making it invalid: *he falsified the company accounts.* □ **falsificar**

falsetto [fɔl'setou] *n.* (*pl. falsettos*) unnaturally high voice (used by a man singing). □ **falsete**

falter ['fɔ:ltə] *v.* to move or speak hesitantly: *his voice faltered as he told the sad story of her death.* □ **quebrarse**

fame [feim] *n.* being well known: *she won fame through her scientific discoveries.* □ **fama**
famed *adj.* well known: *the town is famed for its beer.* □ **famoso**

familiar [fə'miljə] *adj.* **1** heard or seen before; well known: *the band was playing a familiar tune; his face was familiar but I couldn't remember his name.* □ **familiar**
2 *I am* ***familiar with*** *that type of machine,* I know that type of machine. □ **conozco...**
3 very informal/(too) friendly: *he started getting familiar, so she got up and walked out.* □ **empezó a tomar confianzas...**
familiarity [fəmili'æriti] *n.* **1** good knowledge of someone/something. □ **buen conocimiento**
2 excessively informal way of speaking to someone. □ **confianzas**
familiarize [fə'miljəraiz] *v.* ***to familiarize yourself with something,*** to become informed about something. □ **familiarizarse con**

family ['fæmili] *n.* (*pl. families*) **1** group of people who are closely related, especially mother, father and their children: *John is the youngest in our family; on the wall was a family photograph.* □ **familia**
family planning, birth control. □ **planificación familiar**
family tree, table of the family going back over many generations: *you can trace his family tree back to the sixteenth century.* □ **árbol genealógico**
2 group of animals/plants, etc., which are closely related: *the pea family.* □ **la familia de...**

famine ['fæmin] *n.* lack/shortage of food: *each year millions die in the famine.* □ **hambruna**
famished *adj.* (*informal*) very hungry: *I'm famished, I haven't had anything to eat since breakfast.* □ **muerto de hambre**

famous ['feiməs] *adj.* well known: *Disraeli and Gladstone were famous prime ministers; Aylesbury is famous for ducks.* □ **famoso**

fan [fæn] *n.* **1** object/machine for moving air, to make things cooler or warmer: *in the eighteenth century many ladies carried silk fans to keep them cool; fan heaters can warm up a room quickly.* □ **abanico; aparato de aire**
fan belt, loop of rubber which turns a fan to cool the engine of a car. □ **correa del ventilador**
2 passionate admirer: *he is a Liverpool fan,* a supporter of Liverpool football team. □ **admirador; hincha**
■ *v.* (*he fanned*) to make the air move: *she was fanning herself with her programme.* □ **abanicarse**
fan club *n.* organized group of admirers (of a pop star). □ **club de admiradores**
fan mail *n.* admiring letters received by a pop star, etc. □ **correspondencia de los admiradores**
fan out *v.* to spread out: *the peacock fanned out his tail feathers in the sun.* □ **abrir en abanico**

fanatic [fə'nætik] *adj.* and *n.* (person) who is madly enthusiastic about something, especially religion. □ **fanático**
fanatical *adj.* too enthusiastic: *a fanatical belief in cleanliness.* □ **fanático**

fancier ['fænsiə] *n.* person who has an interest (in a certain type of animal): *pigeon fancier,* person who breeds and races pigeons. □ **aficionado**

fancy ['fænsi] *n.* (*pl. fancies*) **1** imagination. □ **fantasía**
2 desire. □ **capricho**
to take somebody's fancy: *this tie took his fancy,* made him want it. □ **se encaprichó de esta corbata**
■ *adj.* pretty/decorated: *I'll buy a few fancy cakes, not plain ones.* □ **fino, selecto**
■ *v.* (*fancied; fancying*) **1** to imagine/to believe: *I fancy I have seen that man before.* □ **tener la impresión de que...**
2 to like/to want to have: *I think she fancies you,* (*informal*) she is attracted to you; *let him eat whatever he fancies.* □ **gustar**
fancy dress *n.* costume (worn to a party) which is supposed to represent a famous person/an animal, etc. □ **disfraz**

fanfare ['fænfɛə] *n.* piece of music played on trumpets to signal the entrance of an important person/the start of a show. □ **fanfarria**

fang [fæŋ] *n.* animal's long tooth: *the wolf leapt forwards showing its fangs.* □ **colmillo**

fanlight ['fænlait] *n.* small window over a door or a large window. □ **montante de abanico**

fantasy ['fæntəsi] *n.* (*pl. fantasies*) made-up story/not a true story. □ **fantasía**
fantastic [fæn'tæstik] *adj.* **1** strange/like in a dream. □ **fantástico**
2 (*informal*) wonderful/amazing: *we had a fantastic holiday in South America.* □ **fantástico**

far [fɑ:] *adv.* (*farther/further, farthest/furthest*) **1** a long way away/not near: *the post office is not far away; how far is it from Bonn to Berlin?; as far back as 1900.* □ **lejos; ¿qué distancia hay de...?**
as far as the eye can see, to the horizon. □ **hasta el horizonte**
as far as I know, *your mother will be here by 10 o'clock,* according to my information, your mother will be here by 10, but I may be wrong.

□ **que yo sepa...**
so far *no one has been ill,* up to now. □ **hasta ahora...**
2 much: *it's far better to play tennis than just to sit indoors,* it's much better; *he drinks far too much vodka; this is by far the best omelette I've ever eaten.* □ **mucho...**
■ *adj.* **1** distant/not near: *at the far end of the street is a baker's shop.* □ **en el otro extremo**
2 *the far side of the river,* the opposite bank to the one you are standing on. □ **al otro lado del río**
faraway *adj.* distant/remote: *for his holidays he goes to a faraway island.* □ **lejano**
far-fetched *adj.* difficult to believe: *a far-fetched story.* □ **inverosímil**
far-reaching *adj.* which has important results. □ **trascendental**
farce [fɑːs] *n.* comedy based on slapstick and ridiculous situations; absurd situation. □ **farsa**
farcical *adj.* absurd. □ **absurdo**
fare [fɛə] *n.* **1** price to be paid for a journey: *bus fares in London are quite expensive.* □ **tarifa**
return fare, fare from one place to another and back again. □ **billete de ida y vuelta**
single fare, fare from one place to another: *what is the fare from Paris to New York?* □ **billete de ida**
2 passenger in a bus/taxi. □ **viajero**
3 food. □ **comida**
■ *v.* to get on: *how did you fare in your exam?* □ **¿cómo te fue en...?**
farewell [fɛə'wel] *interjection* and *n.* (*formal*) goodbye: *they said farewell to their friends at the airport.* □ **adiós**
farinaceous [færi'neiʃəs] *adj.* made of flour. □ **farináceo**
farm [fɑːm] *n.* land used for growing crops and keeping animals: *they keep sheep on their hill farm.* □ **granja; explotación agrícola**
■ *v.* to look after a farm; to grow crops/to keep animals for sale. □ **cultivar (la tierra); criar (animales)**
farmer *n.* man who looks after a farm. □ **agricultor**
farmhouse *n.* house where the farmer and his family live. □ **casa agrícola**
farming *n.* job of looking after a farm/growing crops/keeping animals for sale. □ **agricultura; cría (de animales)**
farm out *v.* to hand over (work/child, etc.) to someone else. □ **arrendar; dejar**
farmyard *n.* space outside a farmhouse usually surrounded by farm buildings or a wall. □ **corral**
farrago [fə'rɑːgou] *n.* tangled mass. □ **fárrago**
fart [fɑːt] *n.* (*vulgar*) noise made when passing gas from the intestines through the anus. □ **pedo**
■ *v.* (*vulgar*) to make a noise by passing gas from the intestines through the anus. □ **tirarse un pedo**
farther ['fɑːðə] *adj.* and *adv.* to a greater distance; more distant: *can you throw the ball farther than I can?* □ **más lejos**
farthest ['fɑːðəst] *adj.* and *adv.* to the greatest distance; most distant: *John can throw the ball farthest.* □ **lo más lejos**
fascia ['feiʃə] *n.* long board over the windows of a shop with the name of the shop written on it. □ **rótulo**
fascinate ['fæsineit] *v.* to attract/to charm: *the older man was fascinated by her beauty.* □ **fascinar**
fascinating *adj.* attractive/very interesting: *I can't stop reading this fascinating book.* □ **fascinante**
fascination *n.* attraction/charm. □ **fascinación**
fascism ['fæʃizəm] *n.* extreme right-wing political movement. □ **fascismo**
fascist *adj.* and *n.* (person) supporting fascism. □ **fascista**
fashion ['fæʃn] *n.* **1** manner/way: *he looked at me in such a strange fashion, I felt quite frightened.* □ **manera**
after a fashion, not very well: *he answered the question after a fashion.* □ **hasta cierto punto**
2 most admired style at a particular moment: *black is in fashion again this year.* □ **moda**
fashion show, parade of models showing new styles of clothes. □ **desfile de modelos**
■ *v.* to make: *he fashioned a chair out of pieces of wood.* □ **hacer**
fashionable *adj.* in fashion: *it is not fashionable to wear a hat; Barbados is a fashionable place for a holiday.* □ **de moda**
fast [fɑːst] *adj.* and *adv.* (*faster, fastest*) **1** quick: *the fast train is leaving in two minutes; run as fast as you can to get it!* □ **rápido**
fast film, film which requires very short exposure times. □ **película de alta sensibilidad**
2 *my watch is five minutes fast,* my watch shows a time five minutes later than it really is. □ **adelantado**
3 tightly fixed: *the soldiers closed the gate and made it fast.* □ **seguro**
4 ***fast colours,*** colours in clothing which do not run when washed. □ **colores que no destiñen**
5 *fast asleep,* soundly sleeping. □ **profundamente dormido**
■ *n.* period when you stop eating. □ **ayuno**
■ *v.* to stop eating (for a time): *some people fast before going to church.* □ **ayunar**
fasten ['fɑːsn] *v.* to fix tightly: *fasten your seat belt when you drive a car; keep the windows fastened while the storm lasts.* □ **abrochar (cinturón); cerrar**
fastener *n.* device which fastens/attaches. □ **cierre; broche**
zip fastener, sliding fastener for closing openings in clothes, bags, etc. □ **cremallera**
fastidious [fæ'stidiəs] *adj.* hard to please; easily shocked. □ **exigente; quisquilloso**
fat [fæt] *adj.* (*fatter, fattest*) **1** big and round; overweight: *that fat man has such a thin wife.* □ **gordo**
2 thick: *a fat bundle of banknotes.* □ **grueso**
3 full of grease: *this meat is too fat.* □ **graso**
■ *n.* **1** grease/white layer on an animal's body under the skin: *she used bacon fat for frying the meat; you can cut the fat off if you don't like it.* □ **grasa**
2 *cooking fat,* refined oil (either vegetable or animal) used in frying, etc. □ **grasa, manteca**
fatstock *n.* (*no pl.*) cows/sheep, etc., fattened for food. □ **ganado de engorde**
fate [feit] *n.* **1** destiny; something that is certain to happen as we think it has been decided by a power beyond human control. □ **destino**
2 *the ship was wrecked but we don't know the fate of the people aboard her,* we don't know what has happened to them. □ **suerte**
fatal *adj.* **1** deadly/causing death: *the snake bite was fatal.* □ **mortal**
2 *he made the fatal mistake of saying her father was fat,* he made the terrible mistake. □ **fatal**
fatalities [fə'tælitiz] *n. pl.* deaths: *ten people were injured but there were no fatalities in the train crash.* □ **víctimas mortales**
fatally *adv.* causing death. □ **mortalmente**
fatalist *n.* person who accepts what happens, knowing that it is usually bad and cannot be avoided. □ **fatalista**

fated *adj.* destined/condemned by fate: *he seems fated never to make any money.* □ **predestinado**
fateful *adj.* (decision, etc.) important for its serious consequences in the future. □ **decisivo**
father [fɑ:ðə] *n.* **1** male parent: *father and mother.* □ **padre**
father figure, older man who is consulted for advice. □ **paternal**
2 originator: *the father of modern medicine.* □ **padre**
3 title given to a priest: *Father Murphy.* □ **padre**
■ *v.* to be the father of: *he fathered three children.* □ **tener**
father-in-law *n.* (*pl. fathers-in-law*) father of your wife or husband. □ **suegro**
fathom ['fæðəm] *n.* measure of depth of water (6 feet or 1.8 metres). □ **braza**
■ *v.* to find the meaning of (a mystery). □ **desentrañar**
fatigue [fə'ti:g] *n.* **1** tiredness: *after walking twenty miles they collapsed from fatigue.* □ **fatiga**
metal fatigue, wearing out of metal used in a construction, causing weak points. □ **fatiga del metal**
2 ***fatigues,*** cleaning duty in the army. □ **servicio de fajina**
fatten ['fætn] *v.* to make fat: *the farmer wanted to fatten the pigs ready for market.* □ **cebar; engordar**
fattening *adj.* which make you fat: *sweets and cakes are fattening foods.* □ **que engorda**
fatty *adj.* (food) which has a lot of fat in it. □ **graso**
fatuous ['fætjuəs] *adj.* stupid/silly. □ **fatuo**
faucet ['fɔ:sit] *n. Amer.* tap. □ **grifo**
fault [fɔ:lt] *n.***1** mistake: *whose fault is it?* □ **culpa**
at fault: *she's at fault,* has made a mistake. □ **culpa, falta**
2 imperfection/something which is not as it should be: *this material has a small fault in it so we can't use it.* □ **defecto**
to find fault with something, to find something wrong. □ **encontrar algún defecto**
to a fault: *he's generous to a fault,* much too generous. □ **excesivamente**
3 (*in geology*) crack in a rock formation which makes a section of rock slip down and another section rise. □ **falla**
4 (*in tennis*) error in serving. □ **falta**
■ *v.* to criticize/to find something wrong: *you cannot fault the champion's style of playing.* □ **criticar**
faultless *adj.* perfect: *a faultless performance.* □ **perfecto**
faulty *adj.* (*faultier, faultiest*) with mistakes or imperfections: *the car would not start - it had a faulty battery.* □ **erróneo; ...bateria defectuosa**
fauna ['fɔ:nə] *n.* wild animals (of an area). □ **fauna**
favour ['feivə] *Amer.* **favor** *n.* **1** friendly act/kindness: *will you do me a favour and go to the shops for me?* □ **favor**
2 support for one group/one person at the expense of others. □ **favor**
to be in favour, to be liked. □ **ser apreciado**
to be out of favour, to be disliked. □ **no ser apreciado**
3 *the score is 3-2 in his favour,* he is leading 3-2. □ **...a su favor**
4 preference/liking: *are you in favour of an early election?* □ **¿estás a favor...?**
■ *v.* **1** to like/to prefer: *my mother wants to go abroad but my father doesn't favour the idea.* □ **gustar**
2 to make things easy for someone: *the conditions favoured the home team.* □ **favorecer**
favourable ['feivrəbl] *adj.* helpful/kind: *with a favourable wind our boat should reach the port tonight; to create a favourable impression,* a good impression. □ **favorable**
favoured *adj.* preferred/liked. □ **predilecto**
the favoured few, the elite/the particularly lucky people. □ **la élite; la poca gente afortunada**
favourite *adj.* preferred/most liked: *the beech wood is my favourite place for a picnic.* □ **favorito**
■ *n.* **1** most liked thing/person. □ **favorito**
2 horse/team, etc., who most people think will win: *in the race the favourite won.* □ **favorito**
favouritism *n.* prejudice/preference for one thing/person. □ **favoritismo**
fawn [fɔ:n] *n.* young deer. □ **cervato**
■ *adj.* brownish-cream colour. □ **color de cervato**
■ *v.* ***to fawn on someone,*** to try to get someone's favour by doing everything they ask. □ **adular servilmente**
fear [fiə] *n.* terror/worry/feeling of being afraid: *fear made his hands shake; she wouldn't cross by canoe for fear of falling in the water.* □ **miedo; temor**
no fear! *I'm not going to hold the snake,* (*informal*) certainly not! □ **¡ni hablar!**
■ *v.* to be afraid: *I wanted the letter to reach him tomorrow but I fear it will not.* □ **temer**
fearful *adj.* terrible: *the room is in a fearful mess.* □ **espantoso**
fearfully *adv.* terribly/very: *let's open a window, it's fearfully hot in here.* □ **terriblemente**
fearless *adj.* with no feeling of terror. □ **intrépido**
fearlessly *adv.* not feeling afraid: *the man walked fearlessly into the lion's cage.* □ **intrépidamente**
fearsome *adj.* frightening. □ **temible**
feasible ['fi:zəbl] *adj.* **1** which can be done. □ **viable**
2 likely/probable. □ **probable**
feasibility [fi:zə'biliti] *n.* ability to be done. □ **viabilidad**
feasibility study, study to see if something can be done. □ **estudio de viabilidad**
feast [fi:st] *n.* **1** special religious day when we remember a saint or special event: *the Feast of the Passover is an important Jewish festival.* □ **festividad; fiesta**
2 very large meal: *the king expected a grand feast on his birthday.* □ **festín**
■ *v.* **1** to eat expensive food: *they feasted on strawberries.* □ **se dieron un banquete de fresas**
2 to eat a very large meal. □ **comer opíparamente**
feat [fi:t] *n.* unusual act: *a feat of daring.* □ **proeza**
feather ['feðə] *n.* one of many growths which form the covering of a bird's body: *the peacock's tail feathers were over 3 feet long.* □ **pluma**
feather bed, mattress stuffed with feathers. □ **colchón de plumas**
light as a feather, very light. □ **ligero como una pluma**
■ *v.* **1** ***to feather one's nest,*** to make a lot of money (usually fraudulently). □ **hacer su agosto**
2 to make the blade of an oar skim fast across the surface of the water. □ **alzar**
feather-brained *adj.* silly and forgetful. □ **cabeza de chorlito**
feathered *adj.* with feathers. □ **emplumado**
featherweight *n.* light weight in boxing between bantamweight and lightweight. □ **peso pluma**
feathery *adj.* light/delicate (like a feather). □ **ligero (como una pluma)**
feature ['fi:tʃə] *n.* **1** special part of the face (such as nose/mouth, etc.): *her big brown eyes are her best feature.* □ **rasgo**
2 important item in a news programme or article; important article on a special subject: *the air crash*

was the main feature in today's papers. □ **tema, artículo**
3 ***feature film,*** main long film. □ **película de largo metraje**
■ *v.* to have as the main actor/as the main subject, especially on film, TV, or in a newspaper: *the film featured Charlie Chaplin.* □ **tener como protagonista...**
February ['februəri] *n.* second month of the year: *her birthday is in February/is on February 10th.* □ **febrero**
feces ['fi:si:z] *n. pl. Amer. see* **faeces.**
feckless ['fekləs] *adj.* (person) who has no aim in life/who is incompetent. □ **inútil**
fed [fed] *v. see* **feed.**
fed up *adj.* (*informal*) bored/tired: *I'm fed up with listening to her complaints.* □ **harto**
federation [fedə'reiʃn] *n.* group of states or societies which have joined together: *two more companies have joined the Steel Federation.* □ **federación**
federal ['fedərəl] *adj.* referring to a system where a group of semi-independent states exist under a central government. □ **federal**
Federal Bureau of Investigation, United States department in charge of solving crime. □ **FBI**
fee [fi:] *n.* money paid to doctors, schools and lawyers, etc.: *the school fees have gone up and we have to pay examination fees this year too.* □ **honorarios; matrícula del colegio**
feeble ['fi:bl] *adj.* (*feebler, feeblest*) weak: *the old lady made a feeble attempt to get out of her chair.* □ **débil**
feeble-minded *adj.* of low intelligence. □ **imbécil**
feebleness *n.* weakness. □ **debilidad**
feebly *adv.* weakly. □ **débilmente**
feed [fi:d] *n.* **1** food given to animals: *cattle feed.* □ **pienso**
2 meal, especially given to babies: *the little baby has 6 feeds a day.* □ **comida**
3 means of putting material into a machine. □ **alimentación**
gravity feed, system where the material drops down into the machine. □ **alimentación por gravedad**
suction feed, system where the material is sucked into the machine. □ **alimentación por succión**
■ *v.* (*he fed*) **1** to give food (to someone/something): *the farmer fed the calves twice a day.* □ **dar de comer**
2 to eat: *sheep feed on grass.* □ **pacer; pastar**
3 to put in: *he fed information into the computer.* □ **introducir**
feedback *n.* **1** return of a signal in an electronic circuit causing a high-pitched noise. □ **realimentación**
2 information/details about something which has been done. □ **información (sobre el resultado de un proceso)**
feeder *n.* **1** feeding bottle; device for feeding material into a machine. □ **biberón (para bebé); alimentador**
2 ***feeder school,*** junior school which provides children for a senior school. □ **colegio**
feeding *adj.* giving food. □ **alimenticio**
feeding bottle, bottle used for giving milk, etc., to a baby. □ **biberón**
feel [fi:l] *n.* touch, especially with the fingers: *I can tell the jumper is made of wool by the feel of it.* □ **tacto**
■ *v.* (*he felt*) **1** to touch, especially with your fingers: *he felt in his pocket to find his car keys; when the lights went out we had to feel our way to the door; the knife felt cold; the bread feels soft.* □ **tocarse (en el bolsillo); ir a tientas**
to feel one's way: *the committee is still feeling its way,* still acting cautiously until it has more experience. □ **...anda con pies de plomo**
2 to have a feeling/sensation: *we all felt the ground shaking beneath our feet; to feel hungry/thirsty/tired/angry/hot/cold; how do you feel today? I don't feel very well; I feel a lot better.* □ **sentir; tener hambre/sed, etc.**
3 *he feels it would be unwise to mention it,* he thinks it would be unwise. □ **piensa que...**
to feel like: *I felt like shouting for joy,* I wanted to; *do you feel like a cup of tea?,* would you like a cup of tea? □ **me sentía con ganas de; apetecer**
to feel sorry for somebody, to pity somebody. □ **sentirlo**
to feel up to doing something, to feel strong enough to do it: *the garden needs to be dug but I don't feel up to it.* □ **sentirse capaz de**
feeler *n.* antenna/long part on an insect's head with which it touches. □ **antena**
to put out a feeler, to explore something/to see if something is acceptable. □ **lanzar una sonda**
feeling *n.* **1** sense of touch: *I have no feeling in that finger.* □ **sensibilidad**
2 emotion: *he spoke with great feeling.* □ **sentimiento**
3 *you've hurt his feelings,* you've made him unhappy. □ **sentimiento**
4 *I've got a feeling he won't come,* I don't think he will come. □ **presentimiento**
feet [fi:t] *n. pl. see* **foot.**
feign [fein] *v.* (*formal*) to pretend: *he feigned surprise,* he pretended to be surprised. □ **fingir**
feint [feint] *n.* pretended attack; move to confuse your opponent. □ **amago; finta**
■ *adj.* (paper) with very pale lines drawn on it. □ **papel a rayas**
■ *v.* to make a move to confuse your opponent. □ **amagar; fintar**
feline ['fi:lain] *adj.* referring to a cat; like a cat. □ **felino**
■ *n.* member of the cat family of animals. □ **felino**
fell [fel] *n.* high moorland in the North of England. □ **páramo**
■ *v.* to cut down (a tree); to knock (someone) down; *see also* **fall.** □ **talar (un árbol); derribar**
fellow ['felou] *n.* **1** man: *he's a good fellow and will always help.* □ **tipo**
2 person with whom you work or who is in the same group: *my fellow workers all agree with me; here is a fellow sufferer – she has rheumatism too.* □ **compañero**
fellowship *n.* **1** friendly feeling. □ **compañerismo**
2 group of people with similar interests. □ **asociación**
felon ['felən] *n.* criminal. □ **delincuente**
felony *n.* crime. □ **delito**
felt [felt] *n.* thick, matted material made of wool. □ **fieltro**
felt pen/felt tipped pen, pen of which the writing end is made of hard felt. □ **rotulador**
■ *v. see* **feel.**
female ['fi:meil] *adj.* **1** referring to women/girls: *I prefer female company.* □ **femenino**
2 referring to the sex which has young: *female sparrow/female kangaroo.* □ **hembra**
■ *n.* **1** (*informal*) woman/girl. □ **tía**
2 animal/insect/bird which gives birth to young; flower which produces seeds: *the zoo has one male dolphin and two females.* □ **hembra**
feminine ['femənin] *adj.* **1** belonging to a woman,

like a woman: *full of feminine charm.* □ **femenino**
2 (*in grammar*) referring to words which have a particular form to indicate the female gender: *'manageress' is the feminine of 'manager'.* □ **femenino**
femininity [femi'ninəti] *n.* womanliness; female qualities. □ **feminidad**
feminist *n.* person (usually woman) who actively supports the right of women to equal status with men. □ **feminista**

femur ['fi:mə] *n.* thigh bone. □ **fémur**

fen [fen] *n.* large area of marsh. □ **pantano**

fence [fens] *n.* **1** barrier, made of wood or wire, used to keep people or animals in or out of a place: *you need a strong wire fence around the chickens to keep the foxes out.* □ **valla; cerca**
to sit on the fence, to avoid giving a definite answer to a question. □ **no comprometerse**
2 (*slang*) person who takes stolen goods to resell them. □ **perista**
■ *v.* **1** ***to fence in/off,*** to surround with a fence: *we fenced in our garden to stop the dog getting out; that part of the garden has been fenced off to stop the children playing there.* □ **cercar**
2 to fight with swords as a sport. □ **practicar esgrima**
fencing *n.* **1** (material making up) a fence: *chainlink fencing,* strong fencing made of wires linked together. □ **materiales para cercas; alambrera**
2 sport of fighting with swords. □ **esgrima**

fend [fend] *v.* **1** ***to fend off,*** to push away: *the boxer fended off every punch.* □ **defenderse de**
2 ***to fend for yourself,*** to look after yourself. □ **valerse por uno mismo**

fender ['fendə] *n.* **1** low guard around a fireplace to stop coal or wood falling out into the room. □ **guardafuego**
2 rope mat/rubber tyre, etc., hung against the side of a boat to protect it from bumps. □ **defensas**
3 *Amer.* wing/part of a car which covers the wheel. □ **guardabarros**

fennel ['fenl] *n.* herb with a smell like aniseed. □ **hinojo**

ferment ['fə:ment] *n.* upset/agitation: *the whole town was in a ferment.* □ **agitación**
■ [fə'ment] *v.* to change by fermentation: *the liquid has fermented.* □ **fermentar**
fermentation [fə:men'teiʃn] *n.* chemical change brought about in liquids, usually leading to the production of alcohol. □ **fermentación**

fern [fə:n] *n.* type of green plant often with feathery leaves which does not have flowers or seeds. □ **helecho**

ferocious [fə'rouʃəs] *adj.* fierce/angry: *tigers are ferocious animals.* □ **feroz**
ferocity [fə'rɔsiti] *n.* fierceness. □ **ferocidad**

ferret ['ferit] *n.* small weasel-like animal half-tamed and used to drive rabbits or rats from holes. □ **hurón**
■ *v.* ***to ferret something out,*** to find out information by endless searching. □ **indagar**

ferrous ['ferəs] *adj.* containing iron. □ **ferroso**

ferry ['feri] *n.* (*pl. ferries*) **1** boat which carries goods or people to and fro across a stretch of water: *they will take the ferry from Dover to Calais.* □ **ferry; transbordador**
2 place where a boat crosses a stretch of water. □ **embarcadero**
■ *v.* (*ferried; ferrying*) **1** *to ferry someone across the water,* to take him across in a boat. □ **cruzar**
2 *the bus ferried people to and from the station,* took them back and forth. □ **transportar**
ferryman *n.* (*pl. ferrymen*) man in charge of a ferry. □ **barquero (embarcación pequeña); capitán (ferry)**

fertile ['fə:tail, *Amer.* 'fə:tl] *adj.* **1** rich enough to produce crops; (*of female*) able to produce young: *we shall be able to grow wheat on the fertile land in the valley.* □ **fértil**
2 *he has a fertile imagination,* he is very imaginative/he can imagine things very easily. □ **fecundo**
fertility [fə'tiləti] *n.* ability to produce crops or young. □ **fertilidad**
fertilization [fə:tilai'zeiʃn] *n.* the act of fertilizing something. □ **fertilización**
fertilize ['fə:tilaiz] *v.* **1** to join male and female cells together, so that a new animal/plant will be made. □ **fertilizar**
2 to spread fertilizer on the ground. □ **abonar**
fertilizer *n.* chemical or manure spread over the ground to make it richer and more able to produce crops. □ **fertilizante**

ferule ['ferul] *n.* metal cap on the end of an umbrella or stick. □ **remate, punta**

fervour ['fə:və] *Amer.* **fervor** *n.* passion. □ **fervor**
fervent *adj.* passionate. □ **ferviente**

fester ['festə] *v.* (of wound) to become bad and produce pus. □ **enconarse; supurar**

festival ['festivl] *n.* **1** religious celebration which comes at the same time each year. □ **fiesta**
harvest festival, church service to celebrate the end of the harvest. □ **fiesta de la cosecha**
2 artistic celebration/entertainment which is put on at regular intervals: *a Bach festival; the Edinburgh festival.* □ **festival**
arts festival, competitions in music, drama, painting and handicrafts, etc.. □ **festival de...**
film festival, period during which several films are shown, often competing for prizes. □ **festival de cine**
festive *adj.* happy; fit for a celebration. □ **festivo**
the festive season, Christmas. □ **las Navidades**
festivity [fe'stiviti] *n.* (*pl. festivities*) celebration. □ **festividad**

festoon [fe'stu:n] *n.* long chain of hanging decorations: *the church was decorated with festoons of flowers.* □ **guirnalda**
■ *v.* to hang with decorations. □ **festonear**

fetch [fetʃ] *v.* **1** to go and bring something back: *it's time to fetch the children from school; I'll come and fetch you from the office.* □ **recoger**
2 to be sold at a certain price: *the antique table fetched $300 in the auction.* □ **venderse**
fetch in *v.* to collect: *fetch the washing in before it rains.* □ **recoger**
fetching *adj.* attractive/pretty. □ **atractivo**
fetch up *v.* (*informal*) to arrive/to end up (in a certain place). □ **ir a parar**

fête [feit] *n.* public celebration, usually in the open air, with stalls, sideshows and competitions: *the village fête will be on June 10th this year.* □ **fiesta**
■ *v.* to celebrate (the arrival of an important person, etc.). □ **festejar**

fetid ['fi:tid] *adj.* bad-smelling (water/breath). □ **fétido**

fetish ['fetiʃ] *n.* **1** object worshipped by someone. □ **fetiche**
2 obsession. □ **obsesión**

fetter ['fetə] *v.* to chain (a prisoner). □ **poner grilletes**
fetters *n. pl.* chains. □ **grilletes**

fettle ['fetl] *n.* ***in fine fettle,*** in very good condition. □ **en buenas condiciones**

fetus ['fi:təs] *n.* *Amer.* *see* **foetus.**

feud [fju:d] *n.* bitter quarrel: *the two brothers have not*

spoken to each other for years - it is a family feud. □ **enemistad**
■ *v.* to quarrel bitterly all the time. □ **pelear**
feudal ['fju:dl] *adj. feudal system,* medieval system of holding land in return for services to an overlord or king. □ **feudal**
feudalism *n.* feudal system. □ **feudalismo**
fever ['fi:və] *n.* **1** state when the body's temperature ishigher than normal: *it is better to stay in bed until the fever has gone.* □ **fiebre**
2 *fever (pitch),* great excitement. □ **agitación**
feverish *adj.* suffering from a fever. □ **febril**
feverishly *adv.* excitedly; impatiently: *he worked feverishly to finish the job by the morning.* □ **febrilmente**
few [fju:] *adj.* and *n.* (*fewer, fewest*) **1** not many: *he has few friends; he has fewer friends than you; we made 10% fewer telephone calls than last year,* 10% less. □ **pocos**
2 *such parties are **few and far between** in this town,* rare. □ **son contadísimas...**
3 ***a few,*** some/several: *take a few photographs to show your aunts; I'll be downstairs in a few minutes.* □ **unos pocos**
4 ***a good few*** *of them are ill,* quite a lot. □ **bastantes; un buen número de**
fey [fei] *adj.* artistic (person); not interested in practical things. □ **excéntrico**
fiancé, fiancée [fi'ɔnsei] *n.* man/woman who is engaged to be married: *she introduced me to her fiancé.* □ **novio/novia**
fiasco [fi'æskou] *n.* (*pl. fiascos*) total failure: *the party was a complete fiasco.* □ **fracaso**
fib [fib] *n.* lie. □ **mentirijilla**
■ *v.* (*he fibbed*) to tell small lies. □ **decir mentirijillas**
fibre ['faibə] *Amer.* **fiber** *n.* small thread of material. □ **fibra**
coconut fibre mat, mat made of coconut hair. □ **...de fibra de coco**
fibreglass *n.* trademark for strong material made of woven threads of glass; plastic containing threads of glass. □ **fibra de vidrio**
fibrous *adj.* made of fibres. □ **fibroso**
fibula ['fibjulə] *n.* thin bone between the knee and the ankle behind the tibia. □ **peroné**
fickle ['fikl] *adj.* changeable/not steady. □ **inconstante**
fiction ['fikʃn] *n.***1** story that is not true. □ **ficción**
2 novels: *he writes both fiction and non-fiction; science fiction books are very popular.* □ **literatura**
fictitious [fik'tiʃəs] *adj.* untrue/not real: *the characters in the book are all fictitious.* □ **ficticio**
fiddle ['fidl] *n.* (*informal*) **1** cheap violin. □ **violín**
2 dishonest/illegal dealing: *he got me the tickets at half price - it must be a fiddle; he's always on the fiddle,* trying to make money illegally. □ **trampa**
■ *v.* **1** (*informal*) to play the fiddle. □ **tocar el violín**
2 to play idly with something: *I wish she would stop fiddling with her hair.* □ **juguetear con**
3 (*informal*) to handle (money) in a dishonest way: *they were caught fiddling the accounts and were sent to prison.* □ **malversar; ...amañando las cuentas y...**
fiddler *n.* (*informal*) violin player. □ **violinista**
fiddlesticks *n.* (*informal*) nonsense. □ **tonterías**
fiddly *adj.* (*informal*) small and difficult to handle: *a fiddly little screw.* □ **escurridizo**
fidelity [fi'deliti] *n.* faithfulness/accuracy (of a reproduction). □ **fidelidad**
fidget ['fidʒit] *n.* person who cannot stay still. □ **inquieto**
■ *v.* to move restlessly: *the child kept fidgeting about, he just would not sit still.* □ **enredar**
fidgety *adj.* restless. □ **inquieto**
field [fi:ld] *n.* **1** piece of cultivated land surrounded by fences or hedges: *there is wheat in that field this year.* □ **tierra**
2 large surface/area: *coal field; ice field; field of battle.* □ **campo (hielo, batalla); yacimiento (carbón)**
to have a field day, to have a busy and exciting time. □ **tener un día ajetreado**
3 piece of ground for playing games: *football field; sports field.* □ **campo**
4 special area of study: *he is doing research in the field of chemical dyes.* □ **...en el campo de...**
■ *v.* (*in cricket*) **1** to stop a ball hit by a batsman. □ **parar**
2 to be part of the side which is not batting. □ **estar de servidor**
fielder *n.* (*in cricket*) member of the side which is not batting. □ **servidor**
field glasses *n. pl.* binoculars/glasses for seeing the distance more clearly. □ **gemelos de campaña**
field marshal *n.* highest rank in the army. □ **mariscal de campo**
fieldmouse *n.* (*pl. fieldmice*) small type of country mouse. □ **ratón de campo**
fieldsman *n.* (*pl. fieldsmen*) (*in cricket*) member of the side which is not batting. □ **servidor**
fieldwork *n.* scientific research done in the open, and not in a laboratory. □ **trabajo de campo**
fiend [fi:nd] *n.* **1** devil; monster. □ **demonio**
2 *he's a fresh air fiend,* (*informal*) he's keen on having all the windows open/he likes healthy outdoor activities. □ **entusiasta**
fiendish *adj.* devilish; very cruel. □ **diabólico**
fierce ['fiəs] *adj.* **1** ferocious/angry; which will attack anything: *keep your fierce dog away from the children; fierce battle.* □ **feroz**
2 *a fierce argument,* very heated argument. □ **una discusión violenta**
fiercely *adv.* strongly and angrily: *the wind blew fiercely across the fields.* □ **fortísimamente**
fierceness *n.* violence (of a battle); heat (of a fire). □ **encarnizamiento (batalla); ardor (del fuego)**
fiery ['faiəri] *adj.* burning/full of fire; angry: *the heat from the fiery steelworks was overpowering; he has a fiery temper.* □ **ardiente**
fife [faif] *n.* small metal flute played in military bands. □ **pífano**
fifteen [fif'ti:n] number 15: (i) *he is fifteen (years old); the train is due at fifteen twenty (15.20).* □ **quince**
(ii) group of fifteen people (as in a rugby team): *the England fifteen.* □ **el quince**
the fifteen hundreds, the years between 1500 and 1599. □ **el siglo XVI**
fifteenth, 15th *adj.* referring to fifteen: *the fifteenth of May (May 15th).* □ **decimoquinto; el quince de mayo**
the fifteenth century, period from 1400 to 1499. □ **el siglo XV**
fifth, 5th [fifθ] *adj.* and *n.* referring to five: *the fifth of June (June 5th); a fifth of the sales; Henry the Fifth (Henry V).* □ **quinto; el cinco (de)**
the fifth century, period from 400 to 499. □ **el siglo V (quinto)**
fifth column, enemy sympathizers inside a country under attack. □ **quinta columna**
fifty ['fifti] number 50: *he will be fifty (years old) tomorrow.* □ **cincuenta**
in the fifties, (i) *he's in his fifties,* he's between 50 and 59 years old. □ **tiene más de cincuenta años**

(ii) between '50 and '60 in a century. □ **los años cincuenta**
fifty fifty: the silver dish cost $20 so I went fifty fifty with my brother, we each paid half of the cost. □ **...fuimos a medias**
fiftieth, 50th *adj.* referring to fifty. □ **quincuagésimo**
fig [fig] *n.* juicy sweet fruit of the fig tree. □ **higo**
fig leaf *n.* leaf of the fig tree. □ **hoja de la higuera**
fig tree *n.* tree with large leaves and small round green fruit, which grows in warm climates. □ **higuera**
fight [fait] *n.* struggle/battle; boxing match: *the fight only lasted 3 minutes.* □ **lucha; pelea**
■ *v.* (*he fought*) **1** to hit out; to struggle with someone/something: *the boys are fighting again in the playground.* □ **pelearse**
2 *to fight against disease,* to try to keep illness away. □ **luchar**
3 *to fight a case,* to defend a lawsuit. □ **negar una acusación**
to fight your way out *of a crowd,* to struggle to get out of a crowd. □ **abrirse camino**
fighter *n.* **1** person who fights. □ **luchador**
2 fast attacking aircraft. □ **caza**
fighting *n.* action of struggling with someone: *fighting broke out in the crowd.* □ **lucha; pelea**
figment ['figmənt] *n.* ***figment of the imagination,*** something which has been imagined. □ **producto de la imaginación**
figure ['figə, *Amer.* 'figjə] *n.* **1** written number (such as 28): *he earns a five figure salary/his salary is in five figures,* his salary is $10,000 or more. □ **cifra; número**
2 *he's good at figures,* he is good at arithmetic; *last year's sales figures are bad.* □ **aritmética; cifras**
3 geometric shape such as a triangle or circle; drawing/diagram in a book. □ **figura**
4 shape of a person: *in the darkness we could see a figure coming towards us; she does exercises to keep her figure slim.* □ **figura**
5 ***figure of speech,*** colourful expression used to illustrate a meaning (such as "she can swim like a fish"). □ **tropo; figura retórica**
■ *v.* **1** ***to figure something out,*** to try to understand it: *my mother is very angry but I cannot figure out why.* □ **explicarse**
that figures, that makes sense. □ **eso tiene sentido**
2 to appear: *he figures in a novel by Dickens.* □ **aparecer**
figurative ['figjurətiv] *adj.* (usage of a word) which is not the literal meaning. □ **figurado**
figurehead *n.* **1** carved wooden figure carved on the front of a ship. □ **mascarón de proa**
2 person who seems important but who has no real power. □ **testaferro**
filament ['filəmənt] *n.* thin wire (in an electric bulb). □ **filamento**
filbert ['filbət] *n.* type of hazel nut. □ **avellana**
filch [filtʃ] *v.* to steal. □ **hurtar**
file [fail] *n.* **1** metal tool used for smoothing rough surfaces. □ **lima**
2 holder for papers and documents. □ **archivador**
3 line of people: *they walked along in single file,* they walked one behind the other. □ **fila**
■ *v.* **1** to smooth a surface with a file. □ **limar**
2 to put papers away in a folder or case: *the secretary filed the letters and then locked the filing cabinet.* □ **archivar**
3 to walk in a line: *the soldiers filed past the president.* □ **desfilar**
filing cabinet *n.* box with drawers for putting files in. □ **archivo; fichero**
filings *n. pl.* small pieces of metal which are left when metal is filed smooth: *a magnet attracts iron filings.* □ **limaduras**
filial ['filiəl] *adj.* (*formal*) referring to a son or daughter. □ **filial**
filibuster ['filibʌstə] *n.* attempt to prevent a law being passed by speaking for a very long time in the debate. □ **obstruccionismo**
■ *v.* to delay the passing of a law by speaking for a very long time in the debate. □ **ser un obstruccionista**
filigree ['filigri:] *n.* very decorative ornamental work done in precious metals. □ **filigrana**
Filipino [fili'pi:nou] *adj.* and *n.* (*pl. Filipinos*) (person) from the Philippines. □ **filipino**
fill [fil] *v.* **1** to put as much as possible into something/to make full; to become full: *he filled five boxes with books; I am filled with admiration at her courage; the hall filled rapidly; she was filling her hot water bottle; her mind was filled with other thoughts.* □ **llenar**
2 *to fill a tooth,* to drill a hole in a bad tooth and fill it up with metal, etc. □ **empastar**
3 *to fill a vacancy,* to find someone to do a job. □ **cubrir una vacante**
filler *n.* material used to fill holes and cracks in walls/woodwork, etc. □ **masilla; tapaporos**
fill in *v.* **1** to fill a hole: *the gas men dug a large hole in the road and filled it in with concrete.* □ **rellenar**
2 to complete the blank spaces in a form/document: *please fill in all the details on the form,* write everything that is asked for. □ **rellenar**
3 to tell/to inform (someone): *can you fill me in on a few details?* can you tell me the details I've missed? □ **poner al corriente**
filling *n.* **1** something that fills something else up: *I have three fillings in my teeth.* □ **empaste**
2 *cake with chocolate filling,* chocolate flavoured cream in the middle of the cake. □ **relleno**
filling station *n.* place where you can buy petrol and oil. □ **estación de servicio**
fill out *v.* to write everything that is asked for on a form. □ **rellenar**
fill up *v.* **1** to fill until something is completely full; to become completely full: *she kept filling my glass up with red wine; the hall filled up rapidly; we must stop at the garage and fill the car up with petrol,* put as much petrol as possible in the car. □ **llenar**
2 *fill the form up as soon as possible,* complete the form. □ **rellenar**
fillet ['filit] *n.* good cut of meat or fish from which all the bones have been removed. □ **filete**
■ *v.* to remove the bones from a fish. □ **quitar la raspa**
fillip ['filip] *n.* sharp boost: *the publicity gave a fillip to the sales.* □ **impulso**
filly ['fili] *n.* (*pl. fillies*) young female horse. □ **potra**
film [film] *n.* **1** moving picture shown on a screen: *Walt Disney's films are worth seeing.* □ **película**
2 roll of coated plastic put in a camera and used for taking photographs or moving pictures: *colour film; black and white film; 35 mm film; X-ray film.* □ **película**
3 thin covering: *there was a film of dust on the table when we came back from our holiday.* □ **capa**
■ *v.* to take pictures of something with a cine camera. □ **filmar**
film star *n.* well known film actor or actress. □ **estrella de cine**

filmstrip *n.* strip of film with several still pictures which are projected one after the other. □ **película**
filmy *adj.* very thin/almost transparent. □ **finísimo**
filter ['filtə] *n.* **1** device/material for straining liquids or air, stopping any solids from passing through: *oil filter; water filter; air filter.* □ **filtro**
2 glass on a camera which allows only certain colours or certain strengths of light to pass through: *the sun is so bright that I'll put a sun filter over the lens.* □ **filtro**
■ *v.* **1** to pass through a filter: *the chemist filtered the liquid into the bottle.* □ **filtrar**
2 to move gradually and quietly: *the crowd filtered away and they were left alone.* □ **desperdigarse**
3 *traffic for Manchester must filter to the left,* must turn to the left. □ **dirigirse hacia**
filter lane/lights, traffic lane/lights only for cars turning. □ **para girar**
4 *to filter through/down,* to come slowly: *news is filtering through of an earthquake in China; information takes weeks to filter down to the workers on the shop floor.* □ **filtrarse**
filter paper *n.* paper used for filtering liquids. □ **papel de filtro**
filter-tip cigarettes *n. pl.* cigarettes with a filter at the mouth end. □ **con filtro**
filth [filθ] *n.* dirt. □ **suciedad**
filthy *adj.* (*filthier, filthiest*) **1** very dirty: *your hands are filthy.* □ **sucio**
2 *he has a filthy temper,* he can be very unpleasant and angry. □ **de perros**
3 obscene/not pleasant: *it was a filthy book.* □ **obsceno**
fin [fin] *n.* **1** thin limb on the body of a fish which it moves to swim. □ **aleta**
2 piece shaped in a similar way on a bomb, rocket or aircraft. □ **plano de deriva**
final ['fainl] *adj.* **1** coming at the end; last: *what was the final score in the football match? the final day of the holiday.* □ **final, último**
2 *the director's decision is final,* cannot be changed. □ **definitiva**
■ *n.* **1** last competition in a tournament between several teams or competitors. □ **la final**
Cup Final, football championship match. □ **final de copa**
2 ***finals,*** last examinations at the end of a university course, after which you get your degree. □ **exámenes finales**
finalist *n.* person taking part in the final competition. □ **finalista**
finality [fai'næliti] *n.* state of being at the end. □ **condición de último**
finalize *v.* to finish making plans for something: *we have finalized the arrangements for Saturday.* □ **finalizar**
finally *adv.* at last: *we have finally decided what to do.* □ **finalmente**
finale [fi'nɑ:li] *n.* last part of a piece of music/of a show. □ **final, escena final**
finance ['fainæns] *n.* money especially belonging to the public or to a company: *what is the state of the company's finances?,* how much money does the company have? □ **finanzas**
■ *v.* to provide money for something: *the government will finance the new power station.* □ **financiar**
financial [fi'nænʃl] *adj.* concerning money. □ **financiero**
financial year, 12 month period covered by a company's accounts: *the financial year begins in April.* □ **ejercicio económico**
financier [fi'nænsiə] *n.* person who deals with money on a large scale. □ **financiero**
finch [fintʃ] *n.* (*pl. finches*) small seed-eating bird. □ **pinzón**
find [faind] *n.* something good which you have discovered: *that old chair was a real find.* □ **hallazgo**
■ *v.* (*he found*) **1** to discover something hidden or lost: *the children found coins at the bottom of the stream; can you find my handbag for me?* □ **encontrar, buscar**
2 *to find something difficult/easy to do,* to do it with difficulty/with ease. □ **encontrar algo difícil**
3 ***to find out,*** to discover: *the police are trying to find out who murdered her; I'm going to the library to find out about water plants,* to learn. □ **descubrir; averiguar**
4 ***to find someone out,*** to discover someone is dishonest or naughty: *he used to write on walls until his mother found him out.* □ **descubrir**
5 *the jury found him guilty of the crime,* decided that he did the crime; *to find someone guilty or not guilty.* □ **declarar culpable a alguien**
6 ***to find time,*** to allow yourself a few minutes: *I must find time to write to my aunt.* □ **encontrar tiempo**
7 *it has been found that cold water helps tired feet,* it is a known fact that cold water helps tired feet. □ **se ha comprobado que...**
8 *crocodiles are found on the banks of the river Nile,* crocodiles exist on the banks of the river Nile. □ **hay**
findings *n. pl.* facts discovered/recommendations: *the findings of the tribunal.* □ **hallazgos**
fine [fain] *n.* money to be paid as a punishment for doing wrong: *he paid a $50 fine for driving too fast.* □ **multa**
■ *adj.* (*finer, finest*) **1** pure: *fine gold.* □ **puro**
2 lovely/good: *a fine fellow; there are many fine pictures in the gallery; carpets of the finest quality,* best; *I was ill yesterday, but I'm fine today.* □ **bueno, bien**
you're a fine one to talk, (*informal*) you can't criticize me, because you've done the same thing. □ **menudo eres tú**
3 (*of weather*) good; with no rain: *it will be fine today.* □ **hoy hará bueno**
4 very thin; very small: *fine powder; fine rain,* rain with very small drops; *sharpen the pencils to a very fine point.* □ **fino**
to cut it fine, to leave very little time to spare: *you're cutting it fine, you've only got one minute before the train leaves.* □ **llegar justo a tiempo**
■ *interjection* ***fine!,*** all right/agreed. □ **¡muy bien!**
■ *v.* to punish by making someone pay a fine: *he was fined $10 for a parking offence.* □ **multar**
finely *adv.* delicately/thinly/beautifully: *finely made tablecloth.* □ **primorosamente**
finery *n.* fine clothes. □ **galas; trajes vistosos**
finesse [fi'nes] *n.* skill (in dealing with awkward situations). □ **finura**
finger ['fiŋgə] *n.* **1** one of the five parts at the end of a hand, usually other than the thumb. □ **dedo**
index finger, first finger. □ **índice**
to be all fingers and thumbs, to be clumsy and unable to hold things properly. □ **manazas**
to keep your fingers crossed, to hope that something will happen as you want it. □ **cruzar los dedos**
to put your finger on something, to identify: *he's put his finger on the real cause of the problem.* □ **dar en el clavo**
to work your fingers to the bone, to work extremely hard. □ **trabajar como un negro**

to lift a finger: *he didn't lift a finger to help,* didn't make any effort to help. □ **no movió un dedo...**
to have a finger in every pie, to be involved in every plan. □ **estar metido en todo**
2 part of a glove into which a finger goes. □ **dedo**
3 something shaped like a finger. □ **dedo**
chocolate fingers/fish fingers, short sticks of biscuit covered with chocolate/of fish covered with breadcrumbs. □ **barquillo de chocolate; varitas de pescado**
■ *v.* to touch with the fingers. □ **tocar**
fingering *n.* use of the fingers when playing a musical instrument. □ **digitación**
fingernail *n.* thin horny substance which grows at the end of the fingers. □ **uña**
fingerprint *n.* mark left by the end of the finger: *the detective found fingerprints near the broken window.* □ **huella dactilar**
fingerstall *n.* cover which you put over a finger which has been hurt. □ **dedil**
fingertip *n.* the end of the finger. □ **punta/yema del dedo**
I have it at my fingertips, I know all about it. □ **lo sé al dedillo**
finicky ['finiki] *adj.* (*informal*) **1** awkward and detailed (work). □ **detallado**
2 fussy/(person) who dislikes things, especially certain types of food. □ **melindroso**
finish ['finiʃ] *n.* **1** end: *people waited to see the finish of the race.* □ **final**
2 way in which something is completed: *the table has a beautiful finish.* □ **acabado**
■ *v.* to end: *I have finished my homework; the play finished at 10.15.* □ **terminar; acabar**
finish off *v.* **1** to complete: *I am in the middle of the painting but I will finish it off tomorrow.* □ **acabar**
2 to kill: *the hunter finished off the wounded deer with his gun.* □ **rematar**
finish up *v.* **1** to end up: *we finished up in a small café.* □ **acabar**
2 to finish completely: *you must finish up your potatoes,* eat them all. □ **terminar del todo**
finish with *v.* **1** *to finish with someone,* to stop being friendly with someone. □ **romper con**
2 *to finish with something,* to need something no longer: *can I have the binoculars when you have finished with them?* □ **acabar**
finite ['fainait] *adj.* with an end/with a limit. □ **finito**
Finland ['finlənd] *n.* country in Northern Europe. □ **Finlandia**
Finn [fin] *n.* person from Finland. □ **finlandés**
Finnish *adj.* referring to Finland. □ **finlandés**
■ *n.* language spoken in Finland. □ **finlandés**
fiord ['fiɔ:d] *n.* long arm of the sea among mountains in Norway. □ **fiordo**
fir [fə:] *n.* ***fir(tree)***, evergreen tree with needle-shaped leaves. □ **abeto**
fir cone *n.* hard scaly fruit of the fir. □ **piña**
fire ['faiə] *n.* **1** something that is burning: *you warm your hands by the fire in winter; light a fire,* to start a fire burning; *to set fire to the rubbish in the garden.* □ **fuego**
to catch fire, to start burning because of something else which is in flames: *the oil tank was in flames and the nearby trees caught fire.* □ **prenderse**
on fire, burning: *your house is on fire!* □ **ardiendo**
forest fire, fire which spreads through a forest of trees. □ **incendio forestal**
bush fire, fire in the open country (in Australia or South Africa) where the fire spreads very quickly. □ **fuego abierto**
electric fire/gas fire, appliance using electricity or gas to heat a room: *we lit the gas fire because the room was cold.* □ **estufa eléctrica/de gas**
2 great enthusiasm or excitement. □ **ardor**
3 shooting of guns: *the city is under fire,* is being attacked. □ **disparo; fuego**
to cease fire, to stop shooting. □ **cesar el fuego**
■ *v.* **1** to make (something) burn. □ **prender fuego**
2 to make (someone) excited: *the scientist was fired with enthusiasm about his new discovery.* □ **exaltarse**
3 to bake/to heat: *the potter fired the vases in his kiln.* □ **cocer**
gas-fired central heating, heating where the boiler is heated by gas. □ **...a gas**
4 to shoot a gun: *the cowboy fired a revolver at the sheriff.* □ **disparar**
5 *to fire a question at someone,* to ask someone a question quickly and sharply. □ **lanzar**
fire away, ask your question. □ **¡adelante con la pregunta!**
6 to dismiss from a job: *he was fired for being late.* □ **despedir**
fire alarm *n.* bell/siren which gives warning that a fire has started. □ **alarma de incendios**
firearm *n.* any gun held in the hand. □ **arma de fuego**
fire brigade *n.* people whose job is to put out fires. □ **cuerpo de bomberos**
fire chief *n. Amer.* chief officer in a fire brigade. □ **jefe de bomberos**
fire engine *n.* vehicle used by the fire brigade to carry pumps/hoses/ladders, etc., to put out fires. □ **coche de bomberos**
fire escape *n.* stairs/ladder which can be used by people to get out of buildings on fire. □ **escalera de incendios**
fire extinguisher *n.* portable cylinder filled with chemicals or foam to put out a small fire. □ **extintor**
firefly *n.* type of insect which glows at night. □ **luciérnaga**
fireguard *n.* metal screen put in front of a fire. □ **pantalla**
firelight *n.* light given off by a fire. □ **luz de la lumbre**
firelighter *n.* block of inflammable material used to start a fire. □ **pastillas para encender**
fireman *n.* (*pl. firemen*) **1** man whose job it is to put out fires. □ **bombero**
2 man who keeps the fire burning in a furnace/a steam train. □ **fogonero**
fireplace *n.* place where a fire is lit indoors. □ **chimenea**
fireproof *adj.* which will not burn: *fireproof door/fireproof clothing.* □ **incombustible**
fireproof dish, dish which you can heat without damaging it. □ **plato a prueba de fuego**
fireside *n.* area around a fireplace in a room. □ **hogar**
firewarden *n.* person whose job it is to look out for forest fires. □ **guarda forestal**
firewood *n.* (*no pl.*) wood for making fires. □ **leña**
firework *n.* small container holding chemical powder which will sparkle or bang when lit (especially used for parties after dark): *we set off fireworks and light bonfires on November 5th.* □ **fuegos artificiales**
firm [fə:m] *n.* business/company: *my father works for a firm of architects in London.* □ **empresa**
■ *adj.* solid/fixed/strong: *as firm as a rock,* very solid. □ **firme; sólido**
■ *adv.* ***to stand firm,*** to refuse to change your mind. □ **mantenerse firme**
firmly *adv.* in a strong way: *she told them firmly to*

stop jumping around; I firmly believe that..., I am sure that... □ **con firmeza**

first [fəːst] *adj.* and *adv.* (*as a number can be written* **1st**) **1** at the beginning/coming before everything else: *he came first in the race; she lives in the first house on the right; I'll do it first thing tomorrow,* before I do anything else. □ **primero**

at first, at the beginning. □ **al principio**

the first century, the period from 1 to 99 A.D. □ **el siglo primero**

2 for the first time: *he came to England first in 1968.* □ **por primera vez**

3 in a first class seat: *he always travels first.* □ **...en primera**

■ *n.* **1** thing/person coming before everything else. □ **el primero**

2 *the car climbed the hill in first,* in first gear. □ **...en primera**

3 *he got a first in Physics,* a first-class degree. □ **sobresaliente**

4 *my birthday's on the first of August (1st August).* □ **...el uno de agosto**

first come first served, people are served in the order they arrive. □ **se atenderá en orden de llegada**

first aid *n.* help given to a person who is hurt before a doctor or ambulance arrives. □ **primeros auxilios**

first class *adj.* excellent: *we had a first class meal.* □ **de primera clase**

first class post, most expensive mail service. □ **correo urgente**

first class seat/ticket, most expensive. □ **billete de primera clase**

■ *adv. to travel first class on a train/plane,* to take the most expensive seats. □ **en primera**

first day cover *n.* special stamped envelope with the date of the first day of issue of the stamp on it. □ **sobre del día de emisión**

first floor *n.* storey above the ground floor in a building; *Amer.* ground floor. □ **primera planta**

firsthand *adj.* and *adv.* direct from the original source: *he got the information firsthand.* □ **de primera mano**

First Lady *n.* wife of the President of the USA. □ **primera dama**

firstly *adv.* to start with. □ **en primer lugar**

first night *n.* evening when a play is performed for the first time. □ **estreno**

first-rate *adj.* excellent: *a first-rate production of 'Hamlet'.* □ **de primera clase**

firth [fəːθ] *n.* (*in Scotland*) long arm of the sea. □ **estuario**

fiscal ['fiskl] *adj.* **1** referring to tax/government revenue: *the government's fiscal policy.* □ **fiscal**

2 *procurator fiscal,* (*in Scotland*) public prosecutor. □ **fiscal**

fish [fiʃ] *n.* (*pl. fish* occasionally *fishes*) **1** cold-blooded animal with fins and scales, that lives in water: *I caught six fish in the river; we bought fish and chips from the fish shop.* □ **pez; pescado**

2 ***a pretty kettle of fish,*** a poor state of affairs. □ **bonito lío**

3 *he's **like a fish out of water,*** awkward, because he feels he is not in his usual surroundings. □ **sentirse como pez fuera del agua**

4 ***to drink like a fish,*** (*informal*) to drink a lot of alcohol. □ **beber como una esponja**

■ *v.* to try to catch fish: *father goes fishing every Sunday.* □ **pescar**

to fish for compliments, to try to make someone praise you. □ **buscar elogios**

to fish something out, (*informal*) to take something out: *he fished out an old letter from the bottom of the bag.* □ **sacar**

fishbone *n.* bone in a fish. □ **espina**

fishcake *n.* round cake of fish and potato mixed together. □ **pastel de pescado**

fisherman *n.* (*pl. fishermen*) man who catches fish, either as his job or for sport. □ **pescador**

fishery *n.* (*pl. fisheries*) business of catching fish. □ **pesca**

fish-hook *n.* metal hook at the end of a line which catches in the mouth of the fish. □ **anzuelo**

fishing *n.* catching fish: *deep sea fishing,* fishing well away from the coast. □ **pesca**

fishing boat *n.* boat used for fishing. □ **barco pesquero**

fishing rod *n.* long piece of wood to which is attached the line and hook. □ **caña de pescar**

fishing tackle *n.* all the equipment used by a fisherman when going fishing. □ **aparejo de pesca**

fishmonger *n.* man who sells raw fish in a shop. □ **pescadero**

fish shop *n.* shop selling raw fish or cooked fish and chips. □ **pescadería**

fish slice *n.* flat utensil used in cooking for turning food and removing it from a frying pan. □ **paleta**

fishy *adj.* (*fishier, fishiest*) **1** like a fish: *a fishy smell.* □ **a pescado**

2 (*informal*) suspicious/odd: *his story seemed rather fishy to me.* □ **...me huele a chamusquina**

fission ['fiʃn] *n.* breaking up of something into parts. □ **fisión**

nuclear fission, breaking up of an atom in an explosion. □ **fisión nuclear**

fissure ['fiʃə] *n.* crack/split, especially in a rock or in the ground. □ **fisura**

fist [fist] *n.* tightly closed hand: *he banged on the table with his fist.* □ **puño**

fistful *n.* amount you can hold in your fist: *a fistful of pound notes.* □ **puñado**

fit [fit] *n.* **1** sudden sharp attack of illness: *he had a fit of coughing; epileptic fit; fainting fit.* □ **ataque**

2 *she had a fit when they told her the price,* was very surprised. □ **le dio un síncope...**

3 *the class was in fits of laughter,* suddenly burst into laughter which could not be controlled. □ **...ataque de risa**

4 *to do something **by fits and starts,*** at odd moments/with continual stoppages. □ **a empujones**

■ *adj.* (*fitter, fittest*) **1** right/suitable: *I've nothing fit to wear; he's so dirty he isn't fit to be seen.* □ **apropiado**

2 capable: *after being out all night she's not fit for work in the morning.* □ **en condiciones**

3 healthy: *he does exercises to keep fit.* □ **en forma**

as fit as a fiddle, perfectly healthy. □ **estoy sano como una manzana**

■ *v.* (*he fitted*) **1** to be the right size: *you need a pair of shoes that fit; this shirt doesn't fit me any more,* it is too big/too small. □ **sentar bien**

2 to put in the right place: *to fit a new washer on a tap; the cupboard fitted nicely in the corner; to do the jigsaw you must fit all the bits together.* □ **encajar**

3 to make suitable: *his years of experience fitted him for the job.* □ **capacitar**

fitful *adj.* **1** irregular. □ **vacilante**

2 *fitful sleep,* sleep when you keep waking up. □ **sueño ligero**

fit in *v.* **1** to be suitable/to match with: *she was older than the others and did not fit in the group.* □ **encajar**

2 to find room/time for something/someone: *the*

doctor didn't have enough time to fit in all his visits. □ **meter**
fitment *n.* piece of furniture which is fixed in a room. □ **mueble**
fitness *n.* health. □ **buena salud**
physical fitness, state of health of the body. □ **buenas condiciones físicas**
fit out *v.* to provide all the equipment/clothing necessary: *the shop fitted him out for school.* □ **equipar**
fitted *adj.* suitable/right; which has been made to fit. □ **apto; adecuado**
fitted sheet, sheet on a bed which is sewn with elastic so that it pulls over the mattress and stays in place. □ **sábana ajustable**
fitted carpet, wall-to-wall carpet. □ **moqueta**
fitter *n.* **1** skilled mechanic who adjusts machines and their parts. □ **ajustador**
2 person who makes sure clothes fit. □ **probador**
fitting *adj.* suitable/right: *she wrote a fitting letter to her aunt when she heard of her uncle's death.* □ **apropiado**
■ *n.* **1** action of making something fit/of trying on a new piece of clothing. □ **prueba**
fitting room, small room in a shop were you can try on clothes before you buy them. □ **probador**
2 size: *shoes are made in narrow or wide fittings.* □ **horma**
3 something which is permanently fixed in a building but which could be removed: *the bathroom has copper fittings.* □ **accesorio**
five [faiv] number 5: *he is five (years old); come to see us at five (o'clock).* □ **cinco**
fiver *n.* (*informal*) five pound note; five dollar bill. □ **billete de cinco...**
fives *n.* game in which a ball is hit off the walls of a court with the hands or a bat. □ **juego de pelota inglés**
fix [fiks] *n.* (*pl. fixes*) **1** difficult position: *he is in a fix, because he has promised to be in two places at the same time.* □ **apuro**
2 (*slang*) injection of a drug, like heroin. □ **un pico**
■ *v.* **1** to fasten/to attach: *Father fixed the name plate on to the tree with a piece of string.* □ **colocar**
2 to arrange: *the meeting is fixed for Saturday.* □ **fijar**
3 *Amer.* to make/to prepare: *can you fix me some coffee?* □ **preparar**
4 to pass a photographic plate through a liquid to stop the photographic image changing. □ **fijar**
5 to mend: *I'll fix the broken chair myself.* □ **arreglar**
fixation [fik'seiʃn] *n.* obsession about something: *she has a fixation about tall blond men,* only thinks about tall blond men. □ **fijación**
fixative ['fiksətiv] *n.* substance which fixes the colours on a painting and prevents them running. □ **fijador**
fixed *adj.* **1** attached firmly. □ **fijo**
2 arranged or agreed upon: *a fixed rule; a fixed price.* □ **fijo**
fixedly ['fiksədli] *adv.* with eyes fixed on someone: *to stare at someone fixedly.* □ **fijamente**
fixture ['fikstʃə] *n.* **1** (date for a) sports match: *the fixture list has been given to all the teams,* the programme of matches. □ **fecha fijada**
2 ***fixtures,*** objects permanently fixed in a house (like radiators): *we paid $1,000 for fixtures and fittings.* □ **instalación fija**
fix up *v.* to arrange: *it is all fixed up for the weekend,* everything has been arranged. □ **arreglar**
fizz [fiz] *n.* sound like a lot of bubbles. □ **burbujeo**
■ *v.* to bubble up. □ **burbujear**
fizzy *adj.* (*fizzier, fizziest*) bubbly: *children love fizzy drinks.* □ **efervescente**
fizzle out ['fizl'aut] *v.* (*informal*) to come to nothing/not to work. □ **resultar un fracaso**
flabbergast ['flæbəgɑːst] *v.* to amaze: *I was flabbergasted when I heard the news.* □ **pasmar**
flabby ['flæbi] *adj.* (*flabbier, flabbiest*) (person) who is soft and fat: *flabby arms/stomach.* □ **fofo**
flabbiness *n.* being soft and fat. □ **flacidez**
flaccid ['flæksid] *adj.* hanging loosely. □ **flácido**
flag [flæg] *n.* **1** piece of material with the emblem of the country/club, etc., on it: *each ship flies the flag of its own country.* □ **bandera**
2 small paper badges sold in aid of charities: *he was selling flags in aid of the Red Cross.* □ **banderita**
3 large paving stone. □ **baldosa**
4 iris/marsh plant with long flat leaves and purple flowers. □ **lirio**
■ *v.* (*he flagged*) **1** to grow tired: *we set off walking early in the morning and began to flag about 4 p.m.* □ **flaquear**
2 *to flag down a taxi,* to wave to make a taxi stop. □ **llamar a un taxi**
flag day *n.* day on which small paper flags are sold in aid of a charity. □ **día de la banderita**
flagpole *n.* tall pole on which large flags are flown. □ **asta de bandera**
flagship *n.* ship on which the admiral sails, and which therefore flies his special flag. □ **buque insignia**
flagstone *n.* large flat stone used for making pavements/floors. □ **baldosa**
flagellate ['flædʒəleit] *v.* (*formal*) to whip. □ **flagelar**
flagellation [flædʒə'leiʃn] *n.* (*formal*) whipping. □ **flagelación**
flagon ['flægən] *n.* large round container for liquids. □ **jarro**
flagrant ['fleigrənt] *adj.* (crime) which is obvious: *flagrant disobedience.* □ **flagrante**
flail [fleil] *v.* to wave (your arms) about. □ **agitar**
flair [flɛə] *n.* natural ability: *a flair for languages.* □ **don**
flak [flæk] *n.* gun fire against aircraft; sharp criticism. □ **fuego antiaéreo; crítica mordaz**
flake [fleik] *n.* **1** tiny, thin piece: *flakes of snow; flake of metal.* □ **escama; copos de nieve; viruta**
2 huss/small white sea fish. □ **galludo**
■ *v.* ***to flake off/to flake away,*** to fall off in little pieces: *paint is flaking off the door.* □ **desprenderse**
to flake out, (*slang*) to collapse with tiredness. □ **caer rendido**
flaky *adj.* (*flakier, flakiest*) in thin pieces. □ **escamoso**
flaky pastry, light pastry that breaks into thin pieces when you eat it. □ **hojaldre**
flamboyant [flæm'bɔiənt] *adj.* brightly coloured; too bright. □ **llamativo**
flame [fleim] *n.* blazing light of a fire: *the house was in flames,* was burning; *the car burst into flames,* startedto burn. □ **llama**
flameproof, flame-resistant *adj.* specially treated so that it will not catch fire or melt. □ **incombustible**
flaming *adj.* **1** in flames. □ **llameante**
2 *in a flaming temper,* furious/in a very bad mood. □ **de mala manera**
flamingo [flə'miŋgou] *n.* (*pl. flamingos*) type of water bird with very long legs and neck and often with pink feathers. □ **flamenco**

flammable ['flæməbl] *adj.* easily set on fire/inflammable. □ **inflamable**
flan [flæn] *n.* open tart: *fruit flan; cheese flan.* □ **tarta**
flange [flændʒ] *n.* rim/edge which sticks out on a pipe or wheel. □ **collarín (tubo); pestaña (rueda)**
flange coupling, joint with a rim sticking out. □ **acoplamiento de pestaña**
flank [flæŋk] *n.* side: *the farmer prodded the cow in the flanks; the guns attacked the flank of the army.* □ **costado (vaca); flanco (ejército)**
■ *v.* to be at the side of: *the president's car was flanked by police motorcyclists.* □ **flanquear**
flannel ['flænl] *n.* **1** warm woollen material. □ **franela**
flannels, flannel trousers. □ **pantalones de franela**
2 small piece of towelling for washing the face or body: *face flannel.* □ **manopla**
flannelette *n.* warm cotton material, which feels like flannel. □ **franela de algodón**
flap [flæp] *n.* **1** hinged part (which hangs down): *envelope with a gummed flap.* □ **solapa**
cat flap, small flap put in a door so that a cat can come in and out. □ **gatera**
2 (*informal*) excitement and worry: *mother gets into a flap whenever we have a party.* □ **nervios**
3 movement like that of a bird's wing. □ **aletazo**
■ *v.* (*he flapped*) to move up and down like a bird's wing: *the bird flapped its wings; the washing was flapping in the wind.* □ **aletear**
flare [flɛə] *n.* **1** device which gives a sudden blaze of light (especially as a signal): *when their boat hit the rocks they lit a flare hoping that someone would see it.* □ **bengala**
2 widening bottom part (of a skirt/of trousers). □ **vuelo (de una falda); de campana (pantalón)**
■ *v.* **1** to burn brightly. □ **fulgurar**
2 (*of a skirt/trousers*) to widen gradually. □ **acampanar**
flare up *v.* **1** to blaze suddenly: *the fire flared up.* □ **encenderse**
2 to get angry: *he flares up at the least little thing.* □ **encolerizarse**
flash [flæʃ] *n.* (*pl. flashes*) **1** short sudden burst of light or emotion: *flash of lightning; flash of temper.* □ **destello de luz; rasgo (emoción); relámpago; un ataque de furia**
news flash, short item of news. □ **avance de noticias**
in a flash, very quickly. □ **en un momento**
2 *it's just* ***a flash in the pan,*** something which will never happen again. □ **es algo que no se volverá a repetir**
3 apparatus for taking photographs in the dark: *the light was bad so I had to use a flash.* □ **flash**
■ *v.* **1** to light up quickly and suddenly: *the ship flashed a message across the water; he flashed his headlights at me.* □ **destellar**
2 to move/to pass by quickly: *his car flashed past mine.* □ **pasar como un rayo**
3 *it flashed across my mind that,* I suddenly thought that. □ **se me ocurrió una idea**
flashback *n.* scene in a film, showing what happened at an earlier date: *then there's a flashback to the night of the murder.* □ **escena retrospectiva**
flashbulb *n.* photographic light bulb which makes a short burst of light when you take a photograph. □ **bombilla de flash**
flashcube *n.* square block of four flashbulbs. □ **flash**
flashgun *n.* photographic device for holding a flashbulb. □ **disparador de flash**
flashlight *n.* hand torch/lamp. □ **linterna**
flashpoint *n.* temperature at which gas or petrol vapour will ignite; moment at which a revolution will break out. □ **punto de inflamación**
flashy *adj.* (*flashier, flashiest*) showy and bright but of poor quality. □ **llamativo; chillón**
flask [flɑːsk] *n.* (small) bottle for liquids. □ **frasco**
thermos flask/vacuum flask, insulated bottle for keeping liquids hot or cold. □ **termo**
flat [flæt] *adj.* and *adv.* (*flatter, flattest*) **1** level/smooth: *the house has a flat roof; he fell flat on his face; flat shoes,* women's shoes with low heels. □ **plano; se cayó de bruces**
flat as a pancake, very flat. □ **totalmente plano**
to fall flat: *the jokes fell flat,* nobody thought they were funny. □ **...no hicieron gracia**
flat rate, fixed charge which never changes. □ **precio fijo**
2 *a flat tyre,* a punctured tyre. □ **un pinchazo**
3 (*of drink*) no longer sparkling. □ **sin gas**
4 (*of battery*) no longer producing electricity: *the car won't start - the battery's flat.* □ **...se ha descargado**
5 (*of music*) below the correct pitch: *don't let him sing, he always sings flat.* □ **...siempre desafina**
6 definite: *I am not coming with you, and that's flat!* □ **¡es mi última palabra!**
7 *to go* ***flat out,*** as fast as you can go. □ **ir a toda pastilla**
8 *I'm flat broke,* I've no money at all. □ **estoy sin un duro**
9 *he ate the cake in five seconds flat,* in exactly five seconds. □ **...exactamente**
■ *n.* **1** place which is level. □ **superficie plana**
flat racing, horse racing on a level course, not over jumps. □ **carrera sin obstáculos**
2 *Amer.* puncture/flat tyre. □ **pinchazo**
3 accommodation made up of a set of rooms, usually on one floor, in a building containing several such groups of rooms: *block of flats.* □ **piso; bloque de pisos**
4 note in music which is a semitone lower: *E flat.* □ **bemol**
flatfish *n.* type of fish with a flattened body. □ **platija**
flatlet *n.* small flat. □ **piso pequeño**
flatly *adv.* definitely: *to refuse flatly.* □ **terminantemente**
flatten *v.* to make flat: *the corn was flattened by the rain.* □ **aplastar**
flatworm *n.* worm with a flat body. □ **platelminto**
flatter ['flætə] *v.* **1** to praise someone without meaning it. □ **adular**
2 to honour: *he was very flattered to be asked to stay with his boss.* □ **halagar**
3 ***to flatter yourself,*** to deceive yourself/to persuade yourself that something is true, when it is not. □ **engañarse**
flatterer *n.* someone who flatters. □ **adulador**
flattery *n.* insincere praise. □ **adulación**
flatulence ['flætjuləns] *n.* gas in the stomach. □ **flatulencia**
flaunt [flɔːnt] *v.* to display in a vulgar way to attract attention: *she flaunted her huge diamond ring to all the office.* □ **hacer alarde de**
flautist ['flɔːtist] *n.* person who plays the flute. □ **flautista**
flavour ['fleivə] *Amer.* **flavor** *n.* taste: *I love the flavour of fresh strawberries.* □ **sabor**
■ *v.* to add spices and seasoning in cooking: *chocolate-flavoured biscuits.* □ **condimentar; con sabor**
flavouring *n.* something added to food to give a particular taste. □ **condimento**

flaw [flɔː] *n.* fault/mistake: *a slight flaw in the material* □ **defecto**
■ *v.* to spoil. □ **estropear**
flawless *adj.* perfect. □ **sin defecto**
flax [flæks] *n.* (*no pl.*) plant used for making linen cloth □ **lino**
flaxen-haired *adj.* fair-haired. □ **rubio**
flay [flei] *v.* **1** to strip the skin off an animal. □ **desollar**
2 to beat someone harshly. □ **azotar**
flea [fliː] *n.* tiny blood-sucking insect that jumps. □ **pulga**
to send someone away with a flea in his ear, with sharp criticism. □ **echar a alguien con cajas destempladas**
flea bite *n.* **1** place where a flea has bitten. □ **picadura de pulga**
2 (*informal*) very slight bother. □ **molestia insignificante**
flea market *n.* market for secondhand goods. □ **rastro**
fleck [flek] *n.* small spot: *flecks of dust.* □ **mota; partículas de polvo**
■ *v.* to mark with spots: *blood-flecked handkerchief.* □ **motear**
fled [fled] *v. see* **flee.**
fledgling ['fledʒliŋ] *n.* small bird ready to fly from the nest. □ **volantón**
flee [fliː] *v.* (*he fled*) to run away: *I saw the snake coming closer and fled for my life.* □ **huir**
fleece [fliːs] *n.* wool of a sheep. □ **vellón**
■ *v.* (*slang*) to cheat someone and take their money. □ **pelar**
fleecy *adj.* made of fleece; covered with fleece; looking like fleece. □ **lanoso**
fleet [fliːt] *n.* **1** group of ships belonging together: *the fishing fleet left the harbour at dawn.* □ **flota**
Admiral of the Fleet, highest rank in the navy. □ **capitán general de la Armada**
2 collection of vehicles: *fleet of buses/aircraft/lorries/coaches.* □ **flota**
■ *adj.* rapid (footsteps). □ **rápido**
fleeting ['fliːtiŋ] *adj.* short and quick: *a fleeting glance; a fleeting visit.* □ **fugaz (mirada); breve (visita)**
flesh [fleʃ] *n.* **1** soft part of the body covering the bones. □ **carne**
a flesh wound, a cut which is not too deep. □ **herida superficial**
in the flesh, in reality (not on TV or in photographs). □ **en carne y hueso**
his own flesh and blood, his relations/his family. □ **los de su propia sangre**
2 soft part of a fruit: *a peach with yellow flesh.* □ **pulpa**
fleshy *adj.* (*fleshier, fleshiest*) fat/plump. □ **gordo**
flew [fluː] *v. see* **fly.**
flex [fleks] *n.* (*pl. flexes*) insulated wires for carrying electricity. □ **cable eléctrico**
■ *v.* to bend: *to flex your muscles,* to practise using them. □ **doblar; ejercitar**
flexibility [fleksi'biliti] *n.* ability to bend easily/to adapt to new circumstances. □ **flexibilidad**
flexible *adj.* **1** easy to bend. □ **flexible**
2 adaptable. □ **adaptable**
flexitime *n.* system where workers can start and stop their day's work at various times. □ **horario flexible**
flick [flik] *n.* sharp blow/tap: *at a flick of a switch the whole wall slid away.* □ **golpecito**
■ *v.* to hit lightly: *he flicked the tall grass with a stick as he walked along; she did not clean it properly, she just flicked off the dust.* □ **dar un golpecito; sacudir**
flick knife *n.* knife with a blade which can fit inside the handle and which shoots out when a spring is released. □ **navaja automática**
flick through *v.* to glance at the pages of a book very rapidly. □ **hojear rápidamente**
flicker ['flikə] *n.* **1** trembling/quivering. □ **temblor**
2 *a flicker of light,* small, trembling light. □ **parpadeo de la luz**
■ *v.* to tremble/to quiver; to burn unsteadily: *the flames flickered and then went out; we must call the engineer as the television picture keeps flickering.* □ **vacilar; llamear; ...oscilando**
flier ['flaiə] *n. see* **fly.**
flight [flait] *n.* **1** journey through the air; flying: *the flight lasts about 3 hours from London; space flight,* flight through outer space. □ **vuelo**
flight of fancy, sudden burst of imagination. □ **ilusión**
2 group of birds/aircraft flying together. □ **bandada; escuadrilla**
3 ***flight of stairs,*** group of stairs in one direction: *turn left at the top of the first flight of stairs.* □ **tramo de escaleras**
4 running away: *to put to flight,* to chase away; *to take flight,* to run away. □ **fuga**
flight deck *n.* **1** flat surface on an aircraft carrier on which aircraft land and take off. □ **cubierta de aterrizaje**
2 section at the front of a large aircraft where the pilots sit. □ **cabina**
flightless *adj.* (bird) which cannot fly. □ **incapacitado para volar**
flight lieutenant *n.* rank in the air force below squadron leader. □ **capitan**
flighty ['flaiti] *adj.* (*flightier, flightiest*) silly and empty-headed: *flighty young girl.* □ **frívolo**
flimsy ['flimzi] *adj.* (*flimsier, flimsiest*) **1** (*of material*) light and thin; poorly made: *although it was snowing she just wore a flimsy dress.* □ **ligero**
2 *a flimsy excuse,* a poor excuse. □ **una excusa pobre**
flinch [flintʃ] *v.* to move back in pain/fear: *he flinched as the doctor gave him an injection.* □ **echarse atrás**
fling [fliŋ] *n.* ***to have a fling,*** to have a wild party. □ **correrse una juerga**
■ *v.* (*he flung*) to throw wildly: *she flung her arms around his neck and kissed him; he flung the money down on the table.* □ **arrojar**
flint [flint] *n.* **1** very hard type of rock which makes sparks when struck. □ **pedernal**
2 small piece of hard substance which makes a spark to light a cigarette lighter. □ **piedra de mechero**
flip [flip] *v.* (*he flipped*) to hit lightly. □ **dar un golpecito**
to flip over, to turn over quickly. □ **darse la vuelta rápidamente**
flip flops *n. pl.* rubber sandals held on by a bar between the toes. □ **chanclas**
flip side *n.* second side of a record. □ **cara B**
flippant ['flipənt] *adj.* joking about things which should be taken seriously. □ **poco serio**
flipper ['flipə] *n.* **1** limb of a sea animal used for swimming: *seals and penguins have flippers.* □ **aleta**
2 long flat piece of rubber which you can attach to your foot to help you swim faster. □ **aleta**
flirt [flɔːt] *n.* person, especially woman, who plays at attracting the opposite sex. □ **coqueta**
■ *v.* to play at attracting people of the opposite sex

for amusement. □ **flirtear**
flirtation [flə:'teiʃn] *n.* short/brief love affair. □ **flirteo**
flirtatious *adj.* (person) who flirts a lot. □ **coqueta**
flit [flit] *n.* ***to do a moonlight flit,*** to escape quietly at night. □ **escapada a hurtadillas**
■ *v.* (*he flitted*) **1** to move quickly and quietly: *butterflies flitted past; time was flitting away,* time was passing too quickly. □ **revolotear**
2 to go away quietly without anyone noticing. □ **irse a hurtadillas**
float [flout] *n.* **1** piece of cork, plastic or feather attached to a fishing line which will float on the surface of the water. □ **flotador**
2 decorated lorry in a procession. □ **carroza**
milk float, low electric truck for delivering milk. □ **camioneta de reparto**
3 cash taken from a central supply and used for small expenses. □ **cambio**
■ *v.* **1** to lie on top of a liquid; to make something lie on the top of a liquid: *leaves were floating on the lake; the boy floated his model boat on the water.* □ **flotar**
2 *to float a company,* to start up a company by selling shares in it. □ **lanzar**
3 *to float the pound,* to let the pound sterling find its own exchange rate internationally and not fix it at a certain amount. □ **flotar**
floating *adj.* resting on the surface of a liquid. □ **flotante**
floating voter, person who is uncertain which party to vote for in an election. □ **votante indeciso**
flock [flɔk] *n.* group of similar animals together, especially sheep/goats/birds. □ **rebaño (ovejas, cabras); bandada de pájaros**
■ *v.* to move in a group: *people flocked to see the exhibition.* □ **ir en grupo**
floe [flou] *n.* large sheet of ice floating on the sea. □ **témpano de hielo**
flog [flɔg] *v.* (*he flogged*) **1** to beat hard, usually with a whip. □ **azotar**
2 (*slang*) to sell. □ **vender**
flood [flʌd] *n.* **1** large amount of water over land which is usually dry. □ **inundación**
2 large amount of anything: *flood of tears; flood of ideas; flood of complaints.* □ **torrente**
■ *v.* **1** to cover with water: *the fields by the river are flooded each winter; the washing machine flooded the kitchen floor.* □ **inundar**
2 *complaints flooded in,* came in large quantities. □ **llovieron quejas**
floodgate *n.* part of a lock/sluice/dam in a river, which can be opened or shut and which helps to control the flow of the water. □ **compuerta**
floodlight *n.* powerful light often used for lighting the outside of a building or a football pitch at night. □ **luz de foco**
■ *v.* (*floodlit*) to light with floodlights: *the Tower of London is floodlit at night.* □ **iluminar con focos**
floor [flɔ:] *n.* **1** part of a room on which you walk. □ **suelo**
2 storey/one level of rooms in a building: *my office is on the second floor.* □ **planta**
ground floor, the rooms which are level with the ground. □ **planta baja**
3 part of an assembly room where people discuss. □ **hemiciclo**
to take the floor, to start speaking in a discussion. □ **tomar la palabra**
■ *v.* **1** to knock to the ground. □ **echar al suelo**
2 to amaze and puzzle (someone): *I was floored by the examination questions.* □ **abrumar**
floorboard *n.* long piece of wood used for making wooden floors. □ **tabla de suelo**
floorcloth *n.* cloth for washing floors. □ **bayeta**
floorshow *n.* cabaret entertainment. □ **espectáculo de cabaret**
flop [flɔp] *n.* **1** (*informal*) failure: *the new play was a complete flop.* □ **fracaso**
2 movement of something falling limply. □ **desplome**
■ *v.* (*he flopped*) **1** to fall/to sit/to lie limply or heavily: *after the race the runners flopped down on the grass.* □ **desplomarse**
2 (*informal*) to fail: *the new play flopped.* □ **ser un fracaso**
floppy *adj.* which hangs limply: *a floppy hat; dog with floppy ears.* □ **colgante**
flora ['flɔ:rə] *n.* wild plants (of an area). □ **flora**
floral *adj.* referring to flowers. □ **floral**
floribunda [flɔri'bʌndə] *n.* type of rose with many small flowers. □ **tipo de rosa**
florid ['flɔrid] *adj.* red (face). □ **colorado**
florist ['flɔrist] *n.* person who sells flowers. □ **florista**
floss [flɔs] *n.* ***dental floss,*** thin thread for pulling between the teeth to remove pieces of food. □ **hilo de seda dental**
candy floss, molten sugar spun to make a fluffy mass. □ **algodón de azúcar**
flotation [flou'teiʃn] *n.* starting of a new company by selling shares in it. □ **lanzamiento**
flotilla [flə'tilə] *n.* small group of boats. □ **flotilla**
flotsam ['flɔtsəm] *n.* rubbish floating in the water. □ **restos**
flounce [flauns] *n.* border of ruffled cloth (attached to a skirt, etc.). □ **volante**
■ *v.* ***to flounce out,*** to go out of a room showing your impatience and annoyance. □ **salir enfadado**
flounder ['flaundə] *n.* common edible flat fish. □ **platija**
■ *v.* to move (in water) with difficulty: *he couldn't swim and just floundered about in the water.* □ **nadar con dificultad**
flour ['flauə] *n.* grain crushed to powder, used for making bread/cakes, etc. □ **harina**
flourmill *n.* place where grain is ground into flour. □ **molino**
flourish ['flʌriʃ] *n.* (*pl. flourishes*) **1** large movement of the arm in the air. □ **ademán**
2 large curve in handwriting: *he signed the letter with a flourish.* □ **rúbrica**
3 fanfare (of trumpets). □ **toque de trompeta**
■ *v.* **1** to grow well: *my plants flourish in the kitchen; all the children are flourishing; he has a flourishing business in secondhand books.* □ **florecer; crecer**
2 to wave something in the air: *the secretary burst in flourishing a letter in her hand.* □ **...agitando una carta...**
flout [flaut] *v.* to scorn/to disregard. □ **mofarse de**
flow [flou] *n.* movement of liquid/air, etc.: *that tap will stop the flow of water; flow of traffic/ideas/words.* □ **flujo**
■ *v.* to move along smoothly: *the river Rhone flows into the Mediterranean; tears flowed down her cheeks.* □ **fluir**
flower ['flauə] *n.* blossom of a plant: *bunch of flowers.* □ **flor**
in full flower, at its best, with its flowers open. □ **en flor**
■ *v.* to blossom: *the apple trees flowered early this year.* □ **florecer**
flowerbed *n.* part of a garden where flowers are

grown. □ **arriate; macizo**
flowerpot *n.* container to grow plants in. □ **tiesto**
flower show *n.* exhibition of flowers. □ **exposición de flores**
flowery *adj.* **1** decorated with a pattern of flowers: *flowery dress.* □ **floreado**
2 ornate: *flowery style.* □ **florido**
flown [floun] *v. see* **fly.**
flu [flu:] *n.* influenza/common illness like a bad cold often with a high temperature. □ **gripe**
fluctuate ['flʌktjueit] *v.* to move backwards and forwards/up and down: *the price of gold fluctuated all week.* □ **fluctuar**
fluctuation [flʌktju'eiʃn] *n.* movement backwards and forwards/up and down. □ **fluctuación**
flue [flu:] *n.* pipe leading to a chimney. □ **humero**
fluency ['fluənsi] *n.* ease of speaking. □ **facundia; facilidad**
fluent *adj.* able to speak easily: *I would love to be fluent in French.* □ **...hablar con soltura en...**
fluently *adv.* easily; *he speaks German fluently.* □ **con soltura**
fluff [flʌf] *n.* soft pieces of wool or hair. □ **pelusa**
fluffy *adj.* covered with soft fur: *fluffy toy.* □ **de peluche**
fluid ['flu:id] *n.* liquid; *the doctor told me to take no solids, just fluids such as soup and drinks.* □ **líquido**
■ *adj.* not settled: *the situation is still fluid,* is unstable. □ **inestable**
fluke [flu:k] *n.* (*informal*) **1** chance; lucky event: *I don't know how I passed the exam, it was a fluke.* □ **de chiripa**
2 one of the two flat parts of a whale's tail/of an anchor. □ **aleta (ballena); uña (ancla)**
3 type of flatworm. □ **trematodo**
flummox ['flʌməks] *v.* (*informal*) to confuse (someone). □ **desconcertar**
flung [flʌŋ] *v. see* **fling.**
flunk [flʌŋk] *v. Amer.* (*informal*) to fail (an examination/a candidate). □ **catear**
fluorescence [fluə'resns] *n.* ability to send out a glow of light when an electric current is applied. □ **fluorescencia**
fluorescent *adj.* giving off light. □ **fluorescente**
fluorine ['fluəri:n] *n.* (*chemical element*: F) pale yellow-green gas. □ **flúor**
fluoride ['fluəraid] *n.* compound of fluorine: *fluoride toothpaste,* toothpaste with small amount of fluoride added in order to prevent tooth decay. □ **fluoruro**
flurry ['flʌri] *n.* (*pl. flurries*) **1** hurried excitement: *I'm so excited, I'm all in a flurry.* □ **...estoy nervioso**
2 sudden small amount of snow, rain or wind. □ **nevada, chaparrón, ráfaga de viento**
flush [flʌʃ] *n.* (*pl. flushes*) **1** redness of the face. □ **rubor**
2 rush of water. □ **chorro de agua**
■ *v.* **1** to go red in the face: *flushed with excitement; flushed with success.* □ **ponerse colorado**
2 ***to flush something out,*** to drive something out of hiding. □ **descubrir**
3 *to flush a lavatory,* to wash it out by pulling or pushing a handle which makes water rush through. □ **tirar de la cadena**
■ *adj.* **1** level: *we want the light switches flush with the wall.* □ **a ras de...**
2 ***to be flush (with money),*** (*informal*) to have plenty of money to spend. □ **tener dinero a espuertas**
fluster ['flʌstə] *n.* nervous worry. □ **agitación**
■ *v.* to confuse (someone): *to be/to get flustered,* to get worried and excited; *don't get flustered, please calm down.* □ **confundir**
flute [flu:t] *n.* musical wind instrument played by blowing across a small hole at the end of a pipe. □ **flauta**
fluted *adj.* decorated with grooves or scallops. □ **estriado**
flutist *n. Amer.* person who plays the flute. □ **flautista**
flutter ['flʌtə] *n.* **1** light movement, especially of wings. □ **aleteo**
2 (*informal*) small gamble: *to have a little flutter on the football pools.* □ **apuesta**
■ *v.* **1** to move wings, etc., quickly and lightly: *the young bird fluttered to the next branch.* □ **aletear**
2 to move softly and quickly: *the leaves fluttered to the ground; my heart fluttered with excitement.* □ **revolotear; palpitar**
flux [flʌks] *n.* constant change: *foreign policy is in a state of flux.* □ **...está cambiando continuamente**
fly [flai] *n.* (*pl. flies*) **1** small insect with two wings. □ **mosca**
fly spray, spray for killing flies. □ **matamoscas**
fly fishing, sport of fishing with an imitation fly tied to the line to attract the fish. □ **pesca a mosca**
2 ***fly/flies,*** trouser front fastened by a zip or buttons: *he did up his flies.* □ **bragueta**
■ *v.* (*he flew; he has flown*) **1** to move through the air: *the birds flew away; he is flying his own plane; he was badly cut by flying glass; we're flying to Hong Kong on Tuesday; the soldiers were flown out to Germany.* □ **volar**
2 to move fast: *the dog flew at the postman; time flies by.* □ **el perro se tiró al cartero; el tiempo vuela**
to fly into a rage, to get very angry suddenly. □ **ponerse furioso**
to fly off the handle, to lose your temper. □ **perder los estribos**
to send someone flying, to knock someone over. □ **tirar a uno al suelo**
3 to put up a flag: *the ship was flying a French flag.* □ **enarbolar**
4 ***to pass*** *an exam* ***with flying colours,*** to get a very high mark. □ **aprobar un examen con sobresaliente**
flier, flyer *n.* person who pilots an aircraft. □ **aviador**
flying club *n.* society for people interested in flying aircraft. □ **club de aviación**
flying fish *n.* fish which jumps out of the water as it moves. □ **pez volador**
flying saucer *n.* unidentified flying object which people claim to see and which they think comes from another planet. □ **platillo volante**
flying squad *n.* group of policemen who arrive quickly at the scene of a crime. □ **brigada móvil**
flying start *n.* good beginning to a race/a new job, etc. □ **salida lanzada; comienzo feliz**
flying visit *n.* very short visit. □ **visita relámpago**
flyleaf *n.* blank piece of paper at the beginning and end of a book. □ **hoja de guarda**
flyover *n.* road built to pass over another. □ **paso elevado**
flypast *n.* flight of aircraft over a certain spot to celebrate something. □ **desfile de aviones**
flysheet *n.* extra roof for a small tent. □ **doble techo**
flyweight *n.* lightest category of boxer. □ **peso mosca**
flywheel *n.* large heavy wheel which turns and keeps an engine working at a steady pace. □ **volante**
foal [foul] *n.* young horse. □ **potro**
foam [foum] *n.* mass of small bubbles. □ **espuma**

foam rubber, rubber in blocks with many little holes in it, used for chair cushions, etc. □ **goma espuma**
■ *v.* to make froth: *to foam at the mouth,* to make white froth around the lips because of illness.
□ **echar espumarajos; espumajear**

fob [fɔb] *n.* little ornament attached to a watch-chain.
□ **leontina**
■ *v.* (*he fobbed*) ***to fob someone off with something,*** to deceive someone into accepting something which they don't really want: *he fobbed me off with a modern imitation when I wanted an antique clock.* □ **colocar a alguien algo**
fob watch *n.* watch which you wear in a pocket, attached to the end of a chain. □ **reloj de bolsillo**

fo'c'sle ['fouksl] *n.* front part of a ship where the crew lives. □ **castillo de proa**

focus ['foukəs] *n.* **1** (*pl. foci* ['fousai]) point where rays of light from an object meet. □ **foco**
in focus, clearly visible. □ **enfocado**
out of focus, blurred, not clear. □ **desenfocado**
2 centre of attention: *she was the focus of their interest.* □ **centro de atención**
■ *v.* to adjust so as to be able to see clearly: *this camera is difficult to focus; we must focus our attention on plans for the next meeting; all eyes focused on the Queen.* □ **enfocar; fijar; clavarse**
focal *adj.* referring to a focus. □ **focal**
focal length, distance from a lens to the focus.
□ **distancia focal**

fodder ['fɔdə] *n.* food for cows/sheep, etc., especially in winter. □ **forraje**

foe [fou] *n.* (*formal*) enemy/opponent. □ **enemigo**

foetus ['fi:təs] *Amer.* **fetus** *n.* unborn child/reptile/bird, etc., which is developing from an embryo.
□ **feto**
foetal *adj.* referring to a foetus: *in a foetal position,* curled up (like a child in the womb). □ **fetal**

fog [fɔg] *n.* thick mist through which it is difficult to see. □ **niebla**
foggy *adj.* (*foggier, foggiest*) misty: *do not drive when it is foggy.* □ **con niebla**
foghorn *n.* hooter used in fog as a warning to ships.
□ **sirena de niebla**
foglamp *n.* car lamp used in fog. □ **faro antiniebla**

foible ['fɔibl] *n.* odd way of behaving or thinking.
□ **extravagancia**

foil [fɔil] *n.* **1** thin metal sheet. □ **hoja de metal**
tin foil/cooking foil, foil used for wrapping food before cooking. □ **papel de aluminio**
2 long thin sword with a button on the end used in the sport of fencing. □ **florete**
3 person who contrasts sharply with another and so makes the other's qualities stand out. □ **contraste**
■ *v.* to defeat; to prevent someone from doing something: *the thieves were foiled in their attempt to break into the shop.* □ **desbaratar**
foiled again!, (*informal*) stopped yet again from doing something. □ **¡te han cogido otra vez!**

foist [fɔist] *v.* ***to foist something on someone,*** to force someone to accept something which they don't want. □ **encasquetar**

fold [fould] *n.* **1** small enclosure for sheep. □ **redil**
2 small crease (in paper/cloth, etc.). □ **pliegue**
■ *v.* **1** to bend something so that one part is on top of another: *she folded the letter and put it in the envelope; can you help me fold the sheets?* □ **doblar**
2 *to fold your arms,* to cross your arms across your chest. □ **cruzarse de brazos**
folder *n.* cardboard envelope for holding papers.
□ **carpeta**
folding *adj.* able to be folded: *folding chair.* □ **plegable**
fold up *v.* **1** to bend something flat to make a smaller area than before: *he folded up the newspaper.* □ **doblar**
2 (*informal*) to finish/to end: *his business folded up.*
□ **quebrar**

foliage ['fouliidʒ] *n.* leaves on a tree or plant. □ **follaje**

folio ['fouliou] *n.* **1** very large size of books. □ **folio**
2 page number. □ **número de página**

folk [fouk] *n. pl.* **1** people: *town folk and country folk.*
□ **gente**
2 *come home and meet my folk,* (*informal*) come and meet my family. □ **mi gente**
folk dance *n.* traditional dance. □ **baile popular**
folklore *n.* traditional stories and beliefs. □ **folclore**
folksong *n.* traditional song. □ **canción popular**

follicle ['fɔlikl] *n.* small hole in the skin out of which a hair grows. □ **folículo**

follow ['fɔlou] *v.* **1** to go after/to come after: *follow me and I will show you the way; to follow a road,* to continue along the road. □ **seguir**
to follow in someone's footsteps, to do the same sort of job as someone. □ **seguir los pasos**
2 to act in accordance with: *I am following my doctor's advice.* □ **seguir**
3 to understand: *I don't quite follow you.* □ **seguir**
follower *n.* supporter: *a football follower.* □ **seguidor**
following *adj.* which follows; next: *the following day,* the next day. □ **siguiente**
follow up *v.* **1** to investigate/to research (something) further. □ **seguir estudiando**
2 *I must follow up your suggestion,* act on your advice. □ **seguir**

folly ['fɔli] *n.* (*pl. follies*) silly behaviour. □ **locura**

foment [fə'ment] *v.* (*formal*) to stir up (trouble).
□ **fomentar**

fond [fɔnd] *adj.* loving: *I am fond of music,* I like music; *fond of cats/of good food.* □ **me encanta la música**
fondness *n.* liking/love: *he has a fondness for sweets.* □ **afición**

fondle ['fɔndl] *v.* to stroke lovingly. □ **acariciar**

font [fɔnt] *n.* basin holding holy water for baptism in a church. □ **pila**

food [fu:d] *n.* something eaten by people and animals or taken in by plants: *this restaurant is famous for its good food.* □ **comida**
food for thought, something that really makes you think. □ **materia de reflexión**
food poisoning, illness caused by something eaten.
□ **intoxicación alimentaria**
foodstuff *n.* something that can be eaten. □ **producto alimenticio**

fool [fu:l] *n.* **1** idiot/stupid person: *you silly fool!*
□ **tonto**
to make a fool of yourself, to behave in a silly way.
□ **hacer el ridículo**
2 type of creamed fruit dessert: *raspberry fool.*
□ **crema de...**
■ *v.* **1** to play around in a silly way: *they were fooling around instead of listening to the teacher.* □ **hacer el tonto**
2 to trick (someone): *he was fooled into giving away most of his money.* □ **engañar**

foolhardy *adj.* brave, but taking unnecessary risks.
□ **temerario**
foolish *adj.* silly/stupid. □ **tonto**
foolishness *n.* silliness/stupidity. □ **tontería**

foolproof *adj.* so simple that even an idiot could use it safely: *this is a completely foolproof method.* □ **a prueba de tontos**
foolscap ['fu:lskæp] *n.* large size of writing paper. □ **tamaño folio**
foot [fʊt] *n.* (*pl. feet*) **1** end part of the leg on which you stand: *a donkey has four feet, a man has only two.* □ **pie; pata (animal)**
on foot, walking: *we went to Jane's house on foot.* □ **a pie**
under foot, on the ground: *this grass is wet under foot.* □ **bajo los pies**
to knock someone off his feet, to push someone over (usually by accident). □ **tirar al suelo**
to get to one's feet: *he got to his feet,* he stood up. □ **se puso en pie**
to put your foot down, (i) to insist/to be firm: *I put my foot down and told him he must be home by 10 o'clock.* □ **ponerse serio**
(ii) to go faster in a car. □ **pisar a fondo**
to put your foot in it, to do or say something tactless. □ **meter la pata**
to put your feet up, to have a rest. □ **echarse**
to put your best foot forward, (i) to try hard. □ **esmerarse**
(ii) to hurry up. □ **darse prisa**
2 base/end of something: *foot of the bed; foot of the stairs; the cottage stands at the foot of the mountains.* □ **pie**
3 measure of length (=30.5 cm): *a table three feet wide.* □ **pie**
■ *v.* **1** ***to foot it,*** to walk. □ **ir a pie**
2 ***to foot the bill,*** to pay the bill. □ **pagar la cuenta**
foot and mouth disease *n.* disease of cows, etc. □ **fiebre aftosa**
football *n.* **1** game played between two teams with a ball which is kicked. □ **fútbol**
Rugby football, game played between two teams with an oval ball which can be kicked or passed by hand. □ **rugby**
2 ball used in the game of football. □ **balón**
footballer *n.* person who plays football. □ **futbolista**
footbrake *n.* brake (on a machine or car) operated by the foot. □ **freno de pedal**
foot-bridge *n.* small bridge just wide enough for people, not cars. □ **pasarela**
foothills *n. pl.* lower slopes: *the foothills of the Rockies.* □ **estribaciones**
foothold *n.* **1** place where you can put your foot when climbing. □ **apoyo para el pie**
2 ***to gain/to get a foothold in something,*** to get a small position on which you can build: *his firm has gained a foothold in the French market.* □ **lograr establecerse**
footing *n.* **1** safe place for your feet: *he slipped and lost his footing.* □ **...y perdió el equilibrio**
2 *to put things on a firm footing,* to base things firmly. □ **base**
3 *we're on a friendly footing,* we are friendly. □ **...en relaciones amistosas**
footlights *n. pl.* row of lights along the front of the stage in a theatre. □ **candilejas**
footloose *adj.* free to go anywhere; with no ties. □ **libre**
footman *n.* (*pl. footmen*) male servant. □ **criado**
footnote *n.* explanation at the bottom of a page, referring to something on the page. □ **nota a pie de página**
footpath *n.* narrow path for walkers. □ **sendero**
footplate *n.* platform in a steam engine for the driver and his helper. □ **plataforma**
footprint *n.* mark left by the foot on the ground: *we followed his footprints to see which way he had gone.* □ **huella**
footsore *adj.* (person) with feet which hurt. □ **con dolor de pies**
footstep *n.* sound of a foot touching the ground: *in the middle of the night we heard footsteps on the stairs.* □ **pisadas**
footstool *n.* small stool which supports the feet when you are sitting in a chair. □ **escabel**
footwear *n.* (*no pl.*) boots and shoes. □ **calzado**
footwork *n.* (*no pl.*) way of using your feet (especially in sports). □ **juego de piernas**
for [fɔ:] *prep.* **1** in exchange for: *he bought the vase for a pound.* □ **por**
2 in support of: *she is all for free milk for children.* □ **a favor de**
3 used for: *this drawer is for bills; what's that for? it's for writing on glass; we're having pork for lunch, what's for pudding? what did you get for Christmas?* □ **para**
4 because of: *he jumped for joy; she married him for his money.* □ **de; por**
5 in the direction of: *the train for London leaves in 20 minutes.* □ **para**
6 towards: *my love for you.* □ **por**
7 over a distance of/over a length of time: *we haven't seen a house for miles; I am going away for a fortnight.* □ **en; por**
8 as a present to; belonging to: *the postman has brought a letter for you; these flowers are for you.* □ **para**
9 in the place of: *can you write this letter for me?* □ **por**
10 with the purpose of: *to go for a walk; he had to run for the bus,* to catch the bus. □ **ir a pasear; para**
11 ***for all that,*** in spite of everything. □ **pese a todo**
12 ***as for,*** regarding: *as for the baby, he is very well.* □ **en cuanto a**
13 ***for sale,*** able to be bought: *the house is for sale.* □ **se vende**
14 ***for example,*** to name one thing out of many: *large cats, lions and tigers for example, are in that part of the zoo.* □ **por ejemplo**
15 ***for ever,*** always: *I will love you for ever.* □ **siempre**
16 ***for good,*** always: *they will stay in that house for good.* □ **para siempre**
17 ***for the most part,*** usually. □ **habitualmente**
■ *conj.* because: *I must leave for it is nearly midnight.* □ **ya que; pues**
forage ['fɔridʒ] *n.* food for horses and cattle. □ **forraje**
■ *v.* **1** to search for food/supplies. □ **buscar el forraje**
2 to rummage/to look for something. □ **hurgar**
foray ['fɔrei] *n.* sudden attack. □ **incursión**
forbade [fə'bæd] *v. see* **forbid.**
forbearance [fɔ:'bɛərəns] *n.* patience. □ **paciencia**
forbearing *adj.* patient/long-suffering. □ **paciente**
forbid [fə'bid] *v.* (*he forbade: he has forbidden*) to tell someone not to do something: *I forbade him to eat sweets in the street; smoking is forbidden in the theatre.* □ **prohibir**
forbidding *adj.* sinister/looking dangerous. □ **amenazador**
force [fɔ:s] *n.* **1** strength/power: *she was blown over by the force of the wind; the force of gravity held him down.* □ **fuerza**

in force, (i) in large numbers: *the people came in force.* □ **en masa**
(ii) operating/working: *that law is still in force and must be obeyed.* □ **en vigor**
2 organized group of people: *police force.* □ **cuerpo de policía**
the armed forces, navy, army and air force. □ **fuerzas armadas**
■ *v.* **1** to move by using strength: *they forced the door (open) with an iron bar; the soldiers forced their way into the house.* □ **forzar**
2 to compel/to make someone do something: *his mother forced him to clean his shoes.* □ **obligar**
3 to make plants grow faster/earlier than normal: *forced rhubarb; the plants have been forced in a hothouse.* □ **activar la maduración**
force back *v.* **1** to push something back very hard. □ **hacer retroceder**
2 *she forced back her tears and tried to smile,* she tried to stop crying. □ **contuvo las lágrimas**
forced *adj.* **1** compelled: *the soldiers finished a forced march of ten miles; forced landing,* quick landing of an aircraft because something is wrong. □ **marcha forzada; aterrizaje forzoso**
2 artificial/not real: *she nervously gave a small forced laugh,* she did not want to laugh. □ **forzado**
forceful *adj.* strong/powerful: *the minister made a forceful speech.* □ **enérgico**
forcemeat *n.* minced meat used as stuffing (for turkeys, etc.). □ **relleno**

forceps ['fɔːseps] *n.* (*no pl.*) pincers used by doctors in surgery. □ **fórceps**

forcible ['fɔːsibl] *adj.* done by/with force: *forcible feeding.* □ **a la fuerza**
forcibly *adv.* using force. □ **a la fuerza**

ford [fɔːd] *n.* shallow part of a river where you can cross by going through the water. □ **vado**
■ *v.* to cross a river by going through a shallow part. □ **vadear**

fore [fɔː] *n.* front part of a ship. □ **proa**
fore and aft, front and back of a ship. □ **de proa a popa**
come to the fore: *he came to the fore in 1980,* he became famous in 1980. □ **se hizo famoso...**
■ *adj.* front/before (*used mainly as a prefix in words such as **forearm, foresee***). □ **ante-; pre-**
forearm ['fɔːrɑːm] *n.* part of the arm between the hand and the elbow. □ **antebrazo**
■ *v.* to get ready for battle or a fight in good time. □ **prepararse**
foreboding [fɔː'boudiŋ] *n.* feeling that something evil will take place. □ **presentimiento**
forecast *n.* description of what will happen in the future: *we listen to the daily weather forecast.* □ **pronóstico**
■ *v.* (*he forecast*) to say what will happen in the future: *the government forecasts a rise in prices next year.* □ **pronosticar**
forecaster *n.* person who says what will happen in the future, especially concerning the weather. □ **hombre del tiempo**
forecastle ['fouksl] *n.* front part of a ship where the crew live. □ **castillo de proa**
foreclose [fɔː'klouz] *v.* to take away property because the owner cannot pay back money which he has borrowed on its security. □ **ejecutar una hipoteca**
forecourt *n.* courtyard in front of a building, especially a petrol station: *no parking on the forecourt!* □ **antepatio**
forefather *n.* ancestor. □ **antepasado**
forefinger *n.* index finger/first finger next to the thumb. □ **dedo índice**
forefront *n. to be in the forefront of a campaign,* to be one of the leaders. □ **primera línea**
forego [fɔː'gou] *v.* (*he has foregone*) to do without: *she was so busy she had to forego her lunch.* □ **renunciar a**
foregone *adj.* decided in advance: *it was a foregone conclusion that Mr Smith would win the election,* everyone knew he would win. □ **conocido de antemano; inevitable**
foreground *n.* part of a picture or scene nearest the viewer: *in the foreground are children playing and in the background is an old house.* □ **primer plano**
forehand *adj.* (*in tennis*) (stroke) played with the palm of the hand facing forwards. □ **golpe directo**
forehead ['fɔrid, 'fɔːhed] *n.* part of the head between the eyes and the hair. □ **frente**
foreleg *n.* front leg of an animal. □ **pata delantera**
foreman *n.* (*pl. foremen*) **1** (*in a factory*) workman in charge of several others. □ **capataz**
2 ***foreman of a jury,*** spokesman for the jury. □ **presidente**
foremost *adj.* and *adv.* first/chief: *Churchill was one of the foremost political leaders.* □ **principal**
first and foremost, first of all. □ **ante todo**
forenoon *n.* (*formal*) morning. □ **mañana**
forerunner *n.* somebody/something coming before another more important one: *his invention was the forerunner of the diesel engine.* □ **precursor**
foresee [fɔː'siː] *v.* (*he foresaw; he has foreseen*) to know in advance: *Marx could not have foreseen the influence of his books.* □ **prever**
foreshadow [fɔː'ʃædou] *v.* to be a sign of something which will come. □ **presagiar**
foreshore *n.* part of a beach which is covered by the sea at each high tide. □ **playa (entre pleamar y bajamar)**
foresight *n.* ability to see what will probably happen in the future; ability to plan for emergencies: *with great foresight he had taken a box of matches with him so they could light a fire.* □ **previsión**
foreskin *n.* loose skin covering the end of the penis. □ **prepucio**
forestall [fɔː'stɔːl] *v.* to anticipate/to stop someone doing something: *he forestalled my plan by leaving early.* □ **anticiparse a**
foretaste *n.* small bit of something that will be had later on. □ **degustación previa**
foretell [fɔː'tel] *v.* (*he foretold*) to predict/to say what will happen in the future: *the gypsy at the fair foretold that we would get married.* □ **predecir**
forethought *n.* thinking ahead: *she attacked him without forethought,* without thinking what the result would be. □ **premeditación**
foreword *n.* short section at the beginning of a book introducing it to the reader. □ **prefacio**

foreign ['fɔrən] *adj.* **1** not belonging to your own country: *what foreign languages can you speak?* □ **extranjero**
foreign affairs, events happening abroad: *our foreign affairs correspondent in Cairo.* □ **corresponsal en el extranjero**
the Foreign Office, British Government department which deals with overseas countries. □ **Ministerio de Asuntos Exteriores**
2 strange: *what he did was quite foreign to his nature,* it was very strange for him to do it. □ **ajeno**
3 *foreign body,* something from outside which lodges in your body. □ **cuerpo extraño**

foreigner *n.* person who does not belong to your country. □ **extranjero**

forensic [fə'rensik] *adj.* referring to the solving and punishment of crime. □ **forense**

forensic medicine, medicine concerned with crimes. □ **medicina legal**

forest ['fɔrist] *n.* large area covered with trees: *many snakes live in the rain forests of South America; deciduous forest/coniferous forest.* □ **bosque**

forester, forest ranger *n.* person whose job it is to look after a forest. □ **guarda forestal**

forestry *n.* job of looking after a forest and its trees; science of growing and maintaining forests. □ **silvicultura**

forever [fə'revə] *adv.* always. □ **siempre**

forfeit ['fɔːfit] *n.* something taken/lost as a punishment. □ **prenda; pérdida, descuento**

■ *v.* to lose (something): *he forfeited a day's pay as punishment for being late.* □ **sufrir un descuento**

forgave [fə'geiv] *v. see* **forgive.**

forge [fɔːdʒ] *n.* blacksmith's workshop where he makes horseshoes and other iron objects: *horses waited outside the village forge.* □ **herrería**

■ *v.* **1** to work metal in a forge. □ **forjar**

2 to copy something illegally: *she forged his signature at the bottom of the letter.* □ **falsificar**

3 *to forge ahead,* to go forward quickly: *the Swedish runner suddenly forged ahead of the others.* □ **adelantarse**

forged *adj.* copied illegally: *the man had a suitcase full of forged bank notes.* □ **falso**

forger *n.* person who copies something illegally. □ **falsificador**

forgery *n.* (*forgeries*) **1** making an illegal copy of something: *he was jailed for forgery.* □ **falsificación**

2 illegal copy: *the painting was a forgery, it was not by Rembrandt after all.* □ **falsificación**

forget [fə'get] *v.* (*he forgot; he has forgotten*) **1** not (to be able) to remember: *they forgot to come to tea; have you forgotten how to swim? I forgot all about my appointment.* □ **olvidar**

2 *I've forgotten my coat,* I've left my coat behind. □ **me he dejado/he perdido...**

forgetful *adj.* often unable to remember: *he is forgetful, he never remembers my birthday.* □ **olvidadizo**

forgetfulness *n.* habit of often being unable to remember things. □ **falta de memoria**

forget-me-not *n.* small blue-flowered plant. □ **nomeolvides**

forgive [fə'giv] *v.* (*he forgave: he has forgiven*) to pardon/to stop being angry with someone: *she forgave him when he said he was sorry.* □ **perdonar**

forgivable *adj.* able to be pardoned/understandable. □ **perdonable**

forgiveness *n.* pardon(ing). □ **perdón**

forgo [fɔː'gou] *v.* (*he has forgone*) to do without: *she was so busy she had to forgo her lunch.* □ **renunciar**

forgot [fə'gɔt] *v. see* **forget.**

fork [fɔːk] *n.* **1** object with a handle at one end and sharp points at the other, used for picking things up: *kitchen fork; knife and fork; garden fork.* □ **tenedor**

2 place where a branch leaves a tree trunk. □ **horcadura**

3 place where two roads split. □ **bifurcación**

■ *v.* **1** *to fork over the soil,* to turn the soil over with a fork. □ **dar vuelta a la tierra con una horca**

2 to turn off a road: *fork right for the city centre.* □ **torcer**

3 to split into two parts: *the road forks just after the church.* □ **bifurcarse**

4 *to fork out,* (*informal*) to pay for something, usually unwillingly: *father forked out $8 for the tickets.* □ **aflojar**

forked *adj.* divided into two: *the snake had a forked tongue.* □ **bífido**

forklift truck *n.* motor vehicle which can lift heavy loads on metal arms. □ **carretilla elevadora**

forlorn [fə'lɔːn] *adj.* **1** left alone and feeling sad: *the dog looked so forlorn because his master had gone away.* □ **desolado**

2 *forlorn hope,* very slight hope. □ **esperanza lejana**

form [fɔːm] *n.* **1** shape: *I have a brooch in the form of a letter A.* □ **forma**

2 paper with blank spaces for you to fill in: *when we entered England we filled in three forms for the Customs.* □ **formulario**

3 condition of an athlete/racing animal: *if the horse is on form he will win the race; the team is in good form; he has been out of form recently; he's in good form today,* he's in a good mood/he's very amusing. □ **forma**

4 structure/style of a piece of writing/a piece of music. □ **forma**

5 school class. □ **curso**

6 long wooden seat with no back. □ **banco**

7 custom/behaviour: *it is bad form to push past people.* □ **es de mala educación...**

■ *v.* **1** to shape; to take shape: *out of the clay she formed a little squirrel; an idea began to form in his mind; the soldiers formed a square,* they arranged themselves in a square. □ **modelar; tomar forma; formar**

2 to be: *bread forms the greater part of what we eat.* □ **ser, constituir**

3 to organize: *people interested in climbing formed a Climbing Club.* □ **crear**

formation [fɔː'meiʃn] *n.* **1** shaping/forming of something. □ **formación**

2 *a curious rock formation,* strange shape of rocks. □ **formación rocosa**

3 *the aircraft flew over in formation,* they kept the same distance away from each other in a pattern. □ **en formación**

formative ['fɔːmətiv] *adj.* referring to the early years of life when a person's character is being formed: *a formative period.* □ **de formación**

formal ['fɔːml] *adj.* **1** ceremonial/done according to certain rules: *the princess first met him at a formal dinner; a formal agreement,* clear written agreement. □ **formal; de etiqueta**

2 regular. □ **regular**

formality [fɔː'mæliti] *n.* (*pl. formalities*) something which has to be done to conform with the rules but which does not mean much. □ **formalidad**

formalize *v.* to make (an agreement) formal/regular. □ **formalizar**

formally *adv.* according to rules/ceremonially. □ **formalmente**

formaldehyde [fɔː'mældihaid] *n.* gas used in solution to make formalin. □ **formaldehído**

formalin *n.* solution used as a disinfectant and preservative. □ **formalina**

format ['fɔːmæt] *n.* shape/size of something: *a large-format book.* □ **formato**

former ['fɔːmə] *adj.* **1** earlier: *in former times the railway ran along the sea front but it has been removed.* □ **anterior, pasado**

2 first thing mentioned (of two): *we spend our holidays either on a farm or in the mountains but the children prefer the former,* they prefer the farm.

□ **el primero**
formerly *adv.* at an earlier time. □ **antiguamente**
formidable ['fɔ:midəbl] *adj.* frighteningly difficult; very impressive (person): *a formidable amount of work lay on my desk after the holidays.* □ **formidable**
formula ['fɔ:mjulə] *n.* (*pl. formulae*) **1** statement, usually of a scientific fact and often by means of symbols: *the chemical formula for water is H_2O; the whole world is searching for a formula for peace.* □ **fórmula**
2 *formula I race,* car race where the cars all have engines of the largest classification. □ **fórmula 1**
3 *Amer.* milky food for babies. □ **papilla**
formulate *v.* **1** to express something as a formula. □ **formular**
2 *to formulate an idea,* to express an idea clearly. □ **formular una idea**
fornicate ['fɔ:nikeit] *v.* to have sexual intercourse (when not married). □ **fornicar**
forsake [fɔ:'seik] *v.* (*he forsook; he has forsaken*) (*informal*) to leave behind. □ **dejar**
forsaken *adj.* abandoned/deserted. □ **abandonado**
forsythia [fɔ:'saiθiə] *n.* common garden shrub with yellow flowers. □ **forsitia**
fort [fɔ:t] *n.* strong building which can be defended against enemy attacks. □ **fuerte**
to hold the fort, to be in charge while someone is away: *I'm holding the fort while my friend goes to the dentist.* □ **quedarse a cargo**
forte ['fɔ:ti] *n.* particular ability: *his forte is tennis.* □ **fuerte**
forth [fɔ:θ] *adv.* (*formal*) forward: *the army went forth and attacked.* □ **hacia adelante**
back and forth, backwards and forwards: *the people ran back and forth fetching water to put out the fire.* □ **de acá para allá**
from this time forth, (*formal*) from now on. □ **de ahora en adelante**
and so forth, and so on. □ **y así sucesivamente**
forthcoming *adj.* **1** soon to appear: *there is a list of forthcoming concerts in the local newspaper.* □ **próximo**
2 (*informal*) friendly/full of information: *he was not very forthcoming about his plans.* □ **abierto**
3 available: *no money is forthcoming to pay for the building.* □ **disponible**
forthright *adj.* direct/blunt (way of speaking). □ **franco**
forthwith *adv.* immediately. □ **enseguida**
fortify ['fɔ:tifai] *v.* (*fortified; fortifying*) to make strong: *he took honey each day to fortify himself; the Romans fortified the city by building a large wall around it.* □ **fortalecerse; fortificar**
fortified wine, wine (like sherry/port) with extra alcohol added. □ **vino encabezado**
fortification [fɔ:tifi'keiʃn] *n.* **1** making strong. □ **reforzamiento**
2 ***fortifications,*** walls/towers built to defend a city. □ **fortificaciones**
fortitude ['fɔ:titju:d] *n.* strength of mind/bravery, especially when in pain: *he bore the pain of his injuries with great fortitude.* □ **entereza**
fortnight ['fɔ:tnait] *n.* two weeks. □ **quincena**
fortnightly *adj.* and *adv.* once every two weeks: *the Scientific Society holds fortnightly meetings/meets fortnightly.* □ **quincenal**
fortress ['fɔ:trəs] *n.* (*pl. fortresses*) strong building/castle. □ **fortaleza**
fortuitous [fɔ:'tjuitəs] *adj.* accidental/happening by chance: *a fortuitous meeting.* □ **fortuito**
fortuitously *adv.* by chance/accidentally. □ **fortuitamente**
fortune ['fɔ:tju:n] *n.* **1** luck/chance: *by good fortune we met someone who could help us.* □ **fortuna**
2 what will happen in the future: *the gypsy will tell your fortune by looking at your hand.* □ **destino**
3 a great deal of money: *he made a fortune out of old cars.* □ **fortuna**
fortunate ['fɔ:tʃənət] *adj.* lucky. □ **afortunado**
fortunately *adv.* by good luck. □ **afortunadamente**
fortune-teller *n.* someone who says what will happen in the future by looking at cards or lines on your hand, etc. □ **adivino**
forty ['fɔ:ti] *n.* number 40: *he is forty (years old); the six-forty train,* train at 06.40 or 18.40. □ **cuarenta**
to have forty winks, (*informal*) to have a short sleep in the daytime. □ **dar una cabezada**
the forties, (i) *she's in her forties,* she is more than forty and less than fifty years old. □ **está en los cuarenta**
(ii) between '40 and '50 in a century. □ **años cuarenta**
fortieth 40th *adj.* referring to 40: *he has passed his fortieth birthday,* he is more than 40 years old. □ **cuadragésimo**
forum ['fɔ:rəm] *n.* **1** place where matters of general interest can be discussed. □ **foro**
2 public discussion. □ **debate público**
forward ['fɔ:wəd] *adj.* **1** towards the front: *he made a forward pass with the ball.* □ **pase adelantado**
2 advanced/well ahead: *I'm forward in my work,* it is going quicker than I thought it would. □ **adelantado**
3 too confident: *she's very forward.* □ **atrevido**
■ *adv.* **1** *from that day forward,* from then on. □ **en adelante**
2 to the front: *he ran forward to meet me.* □ **hacia adelante**
to come forward, to offer help: *no one has come forward with information.* □ **responder a un llamamiento**
to look forward to something, to wait for something with pleasure. □ **esperar con ilusión...**
■ *n.* (*in football, etc.*) player in an attacking/front position: *the England forwards.* □ **delantero**
■ *v.* **1** to send on (a letter) to another address: *please forward my letters to me.* □ **remitir a nuevas señas**
2 to help something progress: *the money will help forward our plans.* □ **promover**
forward-looking *adj.* thinking ahead/dealing with the future optimistically. □ **optimista**
forwards *adv.* **1** to the front. □ **hacia adelante**
2 *they went **backwards and forwards,*** up and down/from one side to the other. □ **arriba y abajo, de un lado a otro**
fossick ['fɔsik] *v.* (*Australian*) to look for something/to search: *the customs officer was fossicking around in my suitcase.* □ **rebuscar**
fossil ['fɔsl] *n.* remains of an animal/plant left in a rock. □ **fósil**
fossil fuels, coal, oil and natural gas. □ **combustibles fósiles**
old fossil, (*informal*) elderly old-fashioned person. □ **vejestorio**
fossilized ['fɔsilaizd] *adj.* turned into a rock: *fossilized leaf.* □ **fosilizado**
foster ['fɔstə] *v.* **1** to bring up a child who is not your own. □ **criar**
2 to encourage (an idea, etc.): *he always fostered the hope of becoming director of the firm.* □ **abrigar**

foster-child *n.* (*pl. foster-children*) child brought up by parents who are not his own. □ **hijo adoptivo**
foster home *n.* family/home where a foster-child is brought up. □ **casa adoptiva**
foster-mother *n.* mother who fosters a child. □ **madre adoptiva**
foster-parents *n. pl.* parents who foster a child. □ **padres adoptivos**

fought [fɔːt] *v. see* **fight.**

foul [faul] *adj.* (*fouler, foulest*) **1** bad/dirty/unpleasant: *foul taste/air/temper/language/weather.* □ **horrible; viciado; grosero**
2 against the rules of a game: *a foul kick.* □ **una falta**
3 ***foul play,*** murder: *it may have been an accident but the police suspect foul play.* □ **asesinato**
4 ***to fall foul of someone,*** to get into trouble with someone: *the boys fell foul of the police.* □ **chocar con**
■ *n.* action against the rules of the game: *the referee blew his whistle for a foul.* □ **falta**
■ *v.* **1** to make dirty: *smoke fouled the air.* □ **ensuciar**
2 to do something against the rules of the game: *the footballer fouled his opponent.* □ **hacer una falta**
3 *the boat fouled its anchor,* its anchor got stuck in weeds, etc. □ **el ancla se encepó**
to foul something up, (*informal*) to make a mess of something; to create a problem. □ **enmarañar**

found [faund] *v.* **1** to establish/to begin (something): *the college was founded in 1720.* □ **fundar**
2 to base: *my story is founded on true life although the people are imaginary.* □ **basar**
3 to melt (metal); to make (something) out of molten metal. □ **fundir**
4 *see also* **find.**
foundation [faun'deiʃn] *n.* **1** establishing/beginning (something). □ **fundación**
2 ***foundations,*** base below ground on which a building is laid: *how deep are the foundations going to be?* □ **cimientos**
foundation stone, stone in a wall which records the start of building. □ **primera piedra**
3 organization which provides money for certain projects: *a research foundation provided money for the hospital.* □ **fundación**
4 ***foundation (cream),*** coloured cream put on the face under powder. □ **crema de base**

founder *n.* person who establishes/begins something. □ **fundador**
founder member, one of the first to establish a club, etc. □ **miembro fundador**
■ *v.* to collapse/to sink: *the boat foundered on the rocks.* □ **irse a pique**
foundling *n.* baby abandoned by its parents and found by someone else. □ **expósito**
foundry *n.* works where things are made from molten metal, etc. □ **fundición**

fount [fɔnt] *n.* set of type of one particular size and design. □ **familia de tipos**

fountain ['fauntin] *n.* jet of water in a street or garden: *there are drinking fountains on the street corners in Rome.* □ **fuente**
fountain pen *n.* pen which you can fill up with ink. □ **estilográfica**

four [fɔː] number 4: **1** *she is four (years old); they have an appointment with the doctor at four (o'clock); I have looked in all four corners of the room but cannot find the missing ring.* □ **cuatro**
2 four people (in a rowing boat): *the England four won easily.* □ **equipo de cuatro**
3 *to go **on all fours,*** to walk on hands and knees. □ **ir a gatas**
fourpart *adj.* (music) for four different voices. □ **para cuatro voces**
fourposter (bed) *n.* bed with four tall posts at each corner and curtains. □ **cama imperial con cuatro columnas y dosel**
foursome *n.* **1** activity/game played by four people. □ **partido de dobles**
2 group of four people. □ **cuarteto**
fourteen number 14: *he is fourteen (years old); the fourteen-twenty train,* train at 14.20. □ **catorce**
fourteenth, 14th *adj.* referring to fourteen *the fourteenth of July; (14th July).* □ **el catorce**
the fourteenth century, period from 1300 to 1399. □ **el siglo XIV(catorce)**
fourth, 4th *adj.* referring to four: *my daughter was fourth in the race; the fourth of August (4th August).* □ **cuarto; el cuatro de**
the fourth century, period from 300 to 399. □ **el siglo IV (cuarto)**
■ *n.* quarter: *one fourth of the people voted for him in the election.* □ **cuarta parte**

fowl [faul] *n.* (*no pl.*) domestic birds kept for food or eggs (chickens, ducks, turkeys and geese). □ **aves de corral**
wild fowl, game birds which are shot for sport. □ **aves de caza**
fowling piece *n.* gun for shooting wild fowl. □ **escopeta**

fox [fɔks] *n.* (*pl. foxes*) wild animal with reddish fur and a bushy tail. □ **zorro; raposa**
■ *v.* to puzzle/to trick: *I can do most of the crossword but I'm completely foxed by 2 across.* □ **despistar**
fox cub *n.* young fox. □ **zorrillo**
foxglove *n.* tall purple and white flower found in woods. □ **dedalera**
foxhound *n.* dog used for hunting foxes. □ **perro raposero**
foxhunting *n.* chasing foxes to catch and kill them, usually with dogs. □ **la caza del zorro**
fox terrier *n.* type of small dog. □ **fox terrier**
foxtrot *n.* type of ballroom dance. □ **fox trot**
foxy *adj.* crafty/cunning. □ **astuto**

foyer ['fɔiei] *n.* large entrance hall at the front of a hotel/theatre, etc. □ **vestíbulo**

fracas ['frækɑː] *n.* noisy disturbance. □ **gresca**

fraction ['frækʃn] *n.* **1** very small piece/amount: *I closed my eyes for a fraction of a second and he disappeared; may I have a fraction more of that cake?* □ **fracción**
2 (*in mathematics*) less than a whole number: $^1/_2$ *and* $^4/_5$ *are fractions.* □ **fracción**

fractious ['frækʃəs] *adj.* bad-tempered/crying (child). □ **malhumorado**

fracture ['fræktʃə] *n.* break (especially in bones). □ **fractura**
simple fracture, clean break of a bone. □ **fractura limpia**
compound fracture, one where the broken bone has pierced the skin. □ **fractura abierta**
■ *v.* to break (a bone): *she fractured both legs in the accident.* □ **fracturarse**

fragile ['frædʒail] *adj.* **1** easily broken/delicate: *we drank tea from fragile porcelain cups.* □ **frágil**
2 *my husband was feeling fragile after the party,* (*informal*) he was feeling weak and ill because he had drunk too much alcohol. □ **hecho polvo**
fragility [frə'dʒiliti] *n.* quality of being easily broken. □ **fragilidad**

fragment ['frægmənt] *n.* small piece. □ **fragmento**
■ *v.* [fræg'ment] to break into small pieces. □ **fragmentar**
fragmentary *adj.* in pieces/not complete. □ **fragmentario**
fragrance ['freigrəns] *n.* pleasant smell: *the fragrance of roses is wonderful.* □ **fragancia**
fragrant *adj.* perfumed/sweet-smelling. □ **fragante**
frail [freil] *adj.* weak: *Grandmother is getting old and frail.* □ **delicado**
frailty *n.* (*pl. frailties*) weakness. □ **debilidad**
frame [freim] *n.* **1** supporting structure of a building/ship/aircraft/bicycle/glasses, etc.: *the frame is of balsa wood which will then be covered with nylon.* □ **armazón; marco; montura**
frame tent, tent supported on a framework of poles. □ **estructura**
frame house, *Amer.* wooden house. □ **casa de madera**
2 bone structure of a person/animal: *the animal's frame is light and built for speed.* □ **esqueleto**
3 ***frame of mind,*** temper/mood: *don't ask him yet because he's not in the right frame of mind.* □ **estado de ánimo**
4 border of wood/metal round a picture/mirror/window: *we've painted the window frames blue.* □ **marco**
5 one picture in a length of TV or cinema film: *cut out the first ten frames and it will be better.* □ **imagen**
6 glass box for protecting young plants in a garden. □ **invernadero pequeño**
■ *v.* **1** to put into words: *he has a marvellous way of framing his sentences.* □ **elaborar**
2 to put a border around something: *to frame a picture.* □ **enmarcar**
3 (*informal*) to make an innocent person appear guilty: *I've been framed, I wasn't in town on the night of the robbery.* □ **incriminar**
frame-up *n.* (*informal*) arrangement whereby an innocent person is made to appear guilty. □ **montaje**
framework *n.* **1** structure supporting a building, etc.: *the old building had a wooden framework.* □ **estructura**
2 basis of a plan. □ **estructura**
franc [fræŋk] *n.* unit of money in France, Belgium and Switzerland, etc. □ **franco**
France [frɑːns] *n.* country in western Europe. □ **Francia**
franchise ['fræntʃaiz] *n.***1** right to vote. □ **sufragio**
2 permit to sell a company's products in a certain region/to trade using a well-known brand name. □ **licencia**
frank [fræŋk] *adj.* plain-speaking; (person) who says what they think. □ **franco**
■ *v.* to stamp a letter on a special machine: *franking machine.* □ **franquear**
frankly *adv.* speaking truthfully: *frankly I don't mind where we go for our holidays.* □ **francamente**
frankness *n.* quality of saying what you think. □ **franqueza**
frankfurter ['fræŋkfəːtə] *n.* long spiced sausage, which is boiled and sometimes eaten with a roll. □ **salchicha de Francfort**
frantic ['fræntik] *adj.* worried and wildly excited: *the drowning man made frantic efforts to reach the boat; when he didn't come back she was frantic with worry.* □ **frenético**
frantically *adv.* in an excited and worried way. □ **frenéticamente**
fraternal [frə'təːnl] *adj.* brotherly. □ **fraternal**
fraternity *n.* (*pl. fraternities*) **1** society of men with similar interests: *student fraternity, Amer.* student association for men. □ **hermandad; cofradía**
2 brotherly feeling. □ **fraternidad**
fraternize ['frætənaiz] *v.* to become friendly with someone: *it is not right for policemen to fraternize with crooks.* □ **confraternizar**
fratricide ['frætrisaid] *n.* murder of your brother. □ **fratricidio**
fraud [frɔːd] *n.* **1** (piece of) dishonesty. □ **fraude**
2 person pretending to be something he is not; thing that is not what you expect: *he said he was the company director, but he was a fraud.* □ **impostor (persona); fraude (cosa)**
fraudulence *n.* dishonesty. □ **fraudulencia**
fraudulent *adj.* dishonest: *the police accused him of fraudulent activities.* □ **fraudulento**
fraught [frɔːt] *adj.* **1** full of: *the situation is fraught with problems/with danger.* □ **cargado de**
2 (*informal*) full of anxiety: *the situation is rather fraught.* □ **tensa**
fray [frei] *n.* fight: *ready for the fray,* ready to fight. □ **combate**
■ *v.* (*of material*) to become worn/to unravel so that threads are loose: *satin frays at the edges, so stitch it soon after cutting.* □ **deshilacharse**
frazzle ['fræzl] *n.* state of exhaustion. □ **agotamiento**
freak [friːk] *n.* **1** unusual type of person/animal/plant: *the rest of the family have blond hair but he is a freak because his is black.* □ **excepción**
2 extraordinary change in something: *in hot and sunny weather there can be occasional freak storms; by a freak of fortune,* by a lucky chance. □ **inesperado**
freakish *adj.* unusual/extraordinary. □ **excepcional**
freak out *v.* (*informal*) to become very excited because of the effect of drugs. □ **colocarse; agarrarse un colocón**
freckle ['frekl] *n.* small brown mark on the skin, often caused by the sun. □ **peca**
freckled *adj.* covered in freckles. □ **pecoso**
free [friː] *adj.* (*freer, freest*) **1** not imprisoned/not tied down: *no bird likes a cage, they all want to be free.* □ **libre**
2 not occupied: *when are you free to visit us? there is a table free in the corner of the restaurant.* □ **libre**
3 not costing any money: *admission free,* it costs nothing to go in; *if you collect four labels you can have a free picture.* □ **gratis**
4 able to do what you want: *he is free to do as he likes with his money; feel free to use the telephone.* □ **libre**
to be free with something, to give something away generously: *she is very free with her money.* □ **ser generoso**
5 ***to be free from/of something,*** to be without something (usually unpleasant): *the town is free from malaria; trouble-free/germ-free,* with no trouble/no germs. □ **estar libre de**
free of duty/duty free, permitted to be brought into the country without payment of tax. □ **libre de derechos de aduana**
■ *v.* **1** to get (a person) out of prison: *the army freed all the political prisoners.* □ **liberar**
2 to release from a difficult situation: *it took two hours to free the driver from the wrecked car; the key is stuck but a few drops of oil should free it.* □ **sacar; desatascar**
freedom *n.* **1** state of being free: *the prisoners at last got their freedom,* they were set free. □ **libertad**
2 *freedom from noise,* no noise. □ **exento de ruido**
freedom of speech, ability to say what you like.

□ **libertad de expresión**
free-for-all *n.* general fight/general argument among several people. □ **refriega**
freehand *adj.* and *adv.* (drawing) drawn without the help of rulers/compasses, etc. □ **a mano alzada**
freehanded *adj.* generous. □ **generoso**
freehold *n.* and *adj.* right to own a property for as long as you want (as opposed to **leasehold** which is for a fixed length of time). □ **dominio**
free house *n.* pub which is not owned by one brewery company but can sell any make of drink that it likes. □ **bar**
freelance *adj., adv.* and *n.* independent (worker), not employed by one particular company: *freelance photographer; freelance journalist; she's a freelance; she works freelance.* □ **independiente, por su cuenta**
freeloader *n.* (*informal*) person who lives on gifts which he cadges from other people. □ **gorrón**
freely *adv.* in a frank manner/without being tied: *you can speak freely in here,* say whatever you want here. □ **libremente**
freemason *n.* member of a secret society. □ **masón**
free-range *adj.* referring to (eggs laid by) hens kept in the open, not in boxes: *free-range eggs.* □ **(huevos) de corral**
free style *n.* (*in sport*) any style; (*in swimming*) any stroke, usually crawl. □ **estilo libre**
free trade *n.* system of trade agreements between countries where goods are imported and exported free of tax. □ **libre cambio**
freeway *n. Amer.* fast motorway with few junctions. □ **autopista**
freewheel [friː'wiːl] *v.* to go along on a bicycle without pedalling. □ **andar con rueda libre**
free will *n.* **1** ability to decide for yourself. □ **libre albedrío**
2 *he did it **of his own free will**,* without being forced. □ **por voluntad propia**
freeze [friːz] *n.* **1** period of frost. □ **helada**
2 *wage freeze/price freeze,* period of standstill in wages or prices. □ **congelación de salarios/precios**
■ *v.* (*it froze; it has frozen*) **1** to change from liquid to solid because of the cold: *it is freezing outside; I expect the pond has frozen.* □ **helarse**
2 to become very cold: *my hands are freezing; light the fire, it's freezing in here.* □ **helarse**
3 to stay very still: *the deer froze when it heard the people; the smile froze on her lips.* □ **congelarse**
4 to store food at below freezing point: *how many kilos of peas have you frozen in your freezer?* □ **congelar**
5 to keep prices or wages at the present level: *the government wants to freeze prices in the shops.* □ **congelar**
6 *to freeze assets,* to prevent the owner from using or selling them. □ **congelar los activos**
freezer *n.* deep-freeze/refrigerator for freezing food and keeping it frozen. □ **congelador**
freezing point *n.* temperature at which a liquid becomes solid: *the freezing point of water is 0 °C.* □ **punto de congelación**
freight [freit] *n.* **1** transport of goods by air, sea or land: *air freight; sea freight.* □ **flete (aéreo, marítimo)**
2 goods transported. □ **cargamento**
freight train, train used for transporting goods. □ **tren de mercancías**
freight car, *Amer.* goods wagon. □ **vagón de mercancías**
freighter *n.* aircraft/ship which carries goods. □ **carguero/buque de carga**
French [frentʃ] *adj.* referring to France: *French wines are some of the best in the world.* □ **francés**
French beans, type of bean grown on low bushes and eaten when green in their pods. □ **judías verdes**
French dressing, salad dressing made of oil and vinegar. □ **vinagreta**
French fries/French fried potatoes, *Amer.* chips/long pieces of potato fried in oil. □ **patatas fritas**
French window, door made of glass usually opening on to a garden. □ **puertaventana**
to take French leave, to go away without permission. □ **despedirse a la francesa**
■ *n.* **1** language spoken in France and some other countries: *you need to speak French if you go to France or Belgium.* □ **francés**
2 ***the French,*** the people of France. □ **los franceses**
Frenchman, Frenchwoman *n.* (*pl. Frenchmen, Frenchwomen*) person from France. □ **francés, francesa**
French polish *v.* to polish (wood) with a resin polish. □ **sacar brillo a muñequilla**
frenzy ['frenzi] *n.* (*pl. frenzies*) wild excitement. □ **frenesí**
frenzied *adj.* wildly excited. □ **frenético**
frequent ['friːkwənt] *adj.* happening often; often seen: *she is a frequent visitor to our house.* □ **frecuente**
■ *v.* [fri'kwent] to go somewhere very often: *they frequent the nightclub.* □ **frecuentar**
frequency *n.* **1** rate at which something happens: *floods occur with alarming frequency in that area.* □ **frecuencia**
2 number of vibrations per second made by a radio wave: *the programme is broadcast on a frequency of 15 kilocycles.* □ **frecuencia**
frequently *adv.* often. □ **frecuentemente**
fresco ['freskou] *n.* (*pl. frescoes*) painting done on wet plaster on a wall. □ **fresco**
fresh [freʃ] *adj.* (*fresher, freshest*) **1** new/not used: *my shirt is dirty, I need a fresh one.* □ **limpio**
fresh air, open air: *I came out of the meeting to get a breath of fresh air.* □ **aire fresco**
2 recent: *fresh news; fresh cakes.* □ **noticias frescas; pasteles recién hechos**
3 not tinned or frozen: *fresh vegetables; fresh fruit.* □ **fresco**
4 *fresh wind,* quite a strong wind. □ **recio**
5 healthy-looking: *fresh complexion.* □ **de buen color**
6 *she's as **fresh as a daisy**,* she feels full of energy. □ **más fresco que una lechuga**
7 cheeky/rather rude. □ **fresco**
freshen *v.* to become/to make fresh. □ **refrescar**
fresher, freshman *n.* (*pl. freshmen*) new student in his/her first year at college. □ **estudiante de primero**
freshly *adv.* newly/recently: *freshly baked bread.* □ **recién**
freshness *n.* quality of being fresh. □ **frescura**
fresh water *n.* water in rivers or lakes. □ **agua dulce**
freshwater *adj.* referring to river or lake water, not salt water: *carp are freshwater fish.* □ **agua dulce**
fret [fret] *n.* raised metal strip crossing the neck of a guitar against which you press the strings. □ **traste**
■ *v.* (*he fretted*) to worry: *don't fret, I expect she will be safe.* □ **inquietarse**
fretful *adj.* crying and unhappy (child). □ **molesto**
fretwork ['fretwəːk] *n.* patterns in wood cut with a very fine saw. □ **calado**

fretsaw *n.* fine saw used for cutting patterns in wood. □ **segueta**
Freudian ['frɔidiən] *adj.* referring to Freud and his theories of psychoanalysis. □ **freudiano**
a Freudian slip, a mistake in speaking which seems to show your real feelings, when you are trying to hide them. □ **error freudiano**
friable ['fraiəbl] *adj.* which can be crumbled easily. □ **friable**
friar ['fraiə] *n.* member of a Christian religious order. □ **fraile**
friction ['frikʃn] *n.* **1** rubbing one thing against another. □ **fricción**
2 disagreement between two or more people: *there is always friction between the management and staff.* □ **roces**
Friday ['fraidei] *n.* fifth day of the week/day between Thursday and Saturday: *he came to see us last Friday; Mother buys fish and chips on Fridays; I'll see you next Friday.* □ **viernes**
Good Friday, Friday before Easter Sunday. □ **Viernes Santo**
fridge [fridʒ] *n.* (*informal*) refrigerator; apparatus for keeping things cold. □ **nevera**
fried [fraid] *v. see* **fry.**
friend [frend] *n.* person whom you know well and like: *I would like you to meet a friend of mine.* □ **amigo**
to make friends with someone, to get to know and like someone: *we made friends with some people we met on holiday.* □ **hacer amigos**
the Society of Friends, religious society, also called the Quakers. □ **los cuáqueros**
friendless *adj.* having no friends. □ **sin amigos**
friendliness *n.* friendly feeling. □ **amabilidad**
friendly *adj.* like a friend/kind/helpful: *don't be afraid of the dog, he's very friendly.* □ **amigable**
to be on friendly terms with someone, to be friends with someone (usually, someone important or famous). □ **llevarse bien con**
■ *n.* (*informal*) game which does not count in a tournament. □ **partido amistoso**
friendship *n.* state of being friends. □ **amistad**
fries [fraiz] *n. pl. Amer.* ***French fries,*** chips/long pieces of potato fried in oil. □ **patatas fritas**
frieze [fri:z] *n.* decorative border round the top of walls, pillars, etc. □ **friso**
frigate ['frigət] *n.* small fast-moving naval ship. □ **fragata**
fright [frait] *n.* **1** fear: *the dog barked and gave her a fright; my horse took fright at the sudden noise and galloped away.* □ **susto; mi caballo se asustó...**
2 (*informal*) awful-looking person: *she has dyed her hair green and looks a fright.* □ **adefesio**
frightful *adj.* (*informal*) terrible/awful: *we had a frightful journey.* □ **espantoso**
frightfully *adv.* (*informal*) extremely/terribly/very: *I am frightfully sorry but I must leave you now.* □ **terriblemente**
frightfulness *n.* unpleasantness. □ **desagrado**
frighten ['fraitn] *v.* to make someone afraid: *that film would frighten little children.* □ **asustar**
to frighten someone out of his wits, to terrify someone. □ **aterrorizar**
frightened *adj.* afraid/scared: *I am frightened of spiders.* □ **asustado; tengo miedo de las arañas**
frightening *adj.* causing fear. □ **espantoso**
frigid ['fridʒid] *adj.* **1** very cold/icy. □ **glacial**
2 unfriendly/not showing any warm feelings. □ **frío**
3 *frigid woman,* woman who is not interested in sex. □ **frígida**
frigidity [fri'dʒiditi] *n.* **1** great cold. □ **frialdad**
2 coldness of feelings, especially lack of interest in sex. □ **frigidez**
frill [fril] *n.* **1** piece of material gathered together and sewn on to a dress/curtains/cover, etc. □ **volante**
2 ***frills,*** unnecessary ornaments: *I want a plain meal with no frills.* □ **adornos**
frilly *adj.* (*frillier, frilliest*) with frills: *she wore a frilly petticoat.* □ **con volantes**
fringe [frindʒ] *n.* **1** hair lying over the forehead. □ **flequillo**
2 edging of material consisting of loose threads hanging down (on a shawl/dress/carpet, etc.). □ **flecos**
3 outer edge of an area: *we live on the fringe of the town.* □ **periferia**
fringe benefits, extra benefits on top of a salary (such as a free car, health insurance, etc.). □ **beneficios suplementarios**
fringe theatre, usually experimental theatre, often not using a traditional theatre building. □ **teatro experimental**
frisk [frisk] *v.* **1** *to frisk about/around,* to jump around: *lambs were frisking in the fields.* □ **brincar**
2 to search someone by running your hands over him to see what he is carrying: *police frisked the car thieves.* □ **cachear**
friskiness *n.* feeling full of life. □ **vivacidad**
frisky *adj.* (*friskier, friskiest*) lively. □ **vivaracho**
fritter ['fritə] *n.* piece of meat/fruit/vegetable dipped in a mixture of flour, egg and milk and fried: *apple fritter.* □ **...frito**
■ *v.* ***to fritter away*** *your time/your money,* to waste it. □ **desperdiciar**
frivolous ['frivələs] *adj.* silly/not serious. □ **frívolo**
frivolity *n.* (*pl. frivolities*) silliness/lack of seriousness. □ **frivolidad**
frizzle ['frizl] *v.* (*informal*) **1** (*of hair*) to be very tightly curled. □ **rizar**
2 to fry in hot fat. □ **freír**
frizzy ['frizi] *adj.* (*frizzier, frizziest*) (*informal*) tightly curled (hair). □ **ensortijado**
fro [frou] *adv.* ***to and fro,*** backwards and forwards. □ **de aquí para allá**
frock [frɔk] *n.* **1** dress/piece of female clothing covering more or less all the body: *a pretty pink frock.* □ **túnica**
2 long robe worn by monks or priests. □ **hábito**
frog [frɔg] *n.* small tailless animal which lives on both land and water: *the green frog hopped along the river bank.* □ **rana**
to have a frog in your throat, to feel you have something in your throat which stops you speaking clearly. □ **tener carraspera**
frogman *n.* (*pl. frogmen*) underwater diver. □ **hombre rana**
frogmarch *v.* to force someone (especially a prisoner) to move by carrying him by his arms (and sometimes legs). □ **arrastrar**
frogspawn *n.* (*no pl.*) transparent jelly containing frog's eggs. □ **cordón gelatinoso**
frolic ['frɔlik] *n.* happy game/party. □ **fiesta**
■ *v.* (*he frolicked*) to play happily. □ **divertirse**
from [frɔm] *prep.* **1** out of: *the walkers had a drink from the stream and then sheltered from the rain; two from five is three; he comes from South America,* he used to live there; *to pick someone out from a crowd,* to identify someone. □ **de, desde**
2 (showing where something started): *the bee moved*

from flower to flower; from Monday to Friday; I'll be in my office from 11 o'clock onwards; I have read the book from beginning to end; from now on parking is only allowed at night; it's only 6 km from here to the town. □ **de; desde**
from time to time, sometimes. □ **de vez en cuando**
3 (showing difference): *I can't tell butter from margarine; can you distinguish the blue from the purple?* □ **de**
4 sent by: *have you had a letter from Peter? tell him from me that he should have written.* □ **de**
5 because of: *he died from pneumonia.* □ **de**
6 according to: *from what I heard nobody is very happy.* □ **según lo que**
frond [frɔnd] *n.* large leaf of a fern or palm tree. □ **fronda**
front [frʌnt] *n.* **1** part which faces forward; most prominent part: *the front of the house faces the road; come up to the front of the class; the baby spilt food down his front.* □ **parte delantera**
in front of, before: *he stood in front of me in the queue.* □ **delante de**
2 *he put on a bold front,* he pretended to be confident when really he wasn't. □ **disimuló la verdad**
3 road which runs along beside the sea in a seaside town. □ **paseo marítimo**
4 line of an army nearest the enemy in battle. □ **frente**
5 (*of weather*) line separating cold and warm masses of air: *a cold front will reach the south-west by tomorrow.* □ **frente**
6 business used to hide an illegal activity: *the restaurant was a front for a gambling den.* □ **tapadera**
■ *adj.* foremost/first: *front seat; front door; front room,* room at the front of a house. □ **asientos de primera fila; puerta principal**
■ *v.* to face: *the house fronts on to the main street.* □ **dar a**
frontage ['frʌntidʒ] *n.* **1** length of a property along a road. □ **lindero**
2 land between a building and the road. □ **terreno**
frontal *adj.* of/in the front; belonging to the front: *a division of soldiers made a frontal attack.* □ **frontal**
frontier ['frʌntiə] *n.* **1** boundary line between two countries or states: *you cannot cross the frontier without a passport.* □ **frontera**
2 *the frontiers of science,* the furthest point in human knowledge. □ **las fronteras de...**
frontispiece ['frʌntispi:s] *n.* picture on the page facing the title page of a book. □ **frontispicio**
frost [frɔst] *n.* **1** weather when the temperature is below the freezing point of water: *ten degrees of frost,* ten degrees below freezing; *the flowers have been nipped by the frost,* the flowers have suffered damage from the freezing temperature. □ **bajo cero**
2 white covering on the ground/trees, etc., when the temperature is below freezing. □ **escarcha**
frostbite *n.* damage to a part of the body due to cold: *the mountaineer lost two toes through frostbite.* □ **congelación**
frostbitten *adj.* attacked by frostbite. □ **congelado**
frosted *adj.* **1** covered in frost; damaged by frost. □ **con escarcha; congelado**
2 (glass) which has a rough surface through which it is difficult to see. □ **esmerilado**
3 (cake) covered with sugar. □ **cubierto de azúcar**
frostily *adv.* coldly/in an unfriendly way. □ **con frialdad**
frosting *n.* icing on a cake. □ **glaseado**
frosty *adj.* (*frostier, frostiest*) **1** very cold; covered with frost: *it was a frosty night.* □ **cubierto de escarcha**
2 cold/unfriendly (manner): *with a frosty look.* □ **frío**
froth [frɔθ] *n.* mass of bubbles on top of a liquid. □ **espuma**
■ *v.* to have masses of bubbles: *the champagne frothed over the top of the glass.* □ **hacer espuma**
frothy *adj.* having bubbles on top. □ **espumoso**
frown [fraun] *n.* pulling down the eyebrows as a sign of anger/puzzlement, etc. □ **ceño fruncido**
■ *v.* **1** to pull down the eyebrows: *my teacher frowned when he saw my work.* □ **fruncir el ceño**
2 *to frown upon a suggestion,* to disapprove of it. □ **desaprobar**
frowzy ['frauzi] *adj.* untidy and dirty. □ **sucio y descuidado**
froze [frouz] *v. see* **freeze.**
frozen ['frouzn] *adj.* **1** very cold: *we were frozen waiting for the bus.* □ **helado**
2 at a temperature below freezing point: *frozen food,* food stored at a temperature below freezing point; *see also* **freeze.** □ **helado**
frugal ['fru:gl] *adj.* spending/costing very little money: *she is a frugal housewife; we ate a frugal meal.* □ **frugal**
fruit [fru:t] *n.* **1** (*pl.* usually *fruit*) part of a plant which contains the seeds and which is often eaten: *will you buy me some fruit at the market? fruit tree; fruit bush.* □ **fruta; árbol frutal**
dried fruit, dried currants, raisins, sultanas, apricots, etc., used mainly in cooking. □ **pasa**
fruit salad, pieces of fresh fruit mixed and served cold. □ **macedonia de frutas**
2 product (of hard work): *he lived to enjoy the fruits of his work.* □ **frutos**
■ *v.* to carry/to produce edible seed cases: *the apple trees haven't fruited this year.* □ **dar fruto**
fruitcake *n.* cake with a lot of dried fruit in it. □ **pastel de frutas**
fruiterer *n.* person who sells fruit. □ **frutero**
fruitful *adj. fruitful work,* useful work which produces good results. □ **fructífero**
fruition [fru:'iʃn] *n. my plans have **come to fruition,*** what I planned has been accomplished with good results. □ **mis planes se han realizado**
fruitless *adj.* producing no results: *fruitless efforts.* □ **infructuoso**
fruit machine *n.* gambling machine where pictures of different fruits revolve when you pull a handle. □ **máquina tragaperras**
fruity *adj.* (*fruitier, fruitiest*) **1** tasting of fruit: *a fruity wine.* □ **afrutado**
2 (*informal*) deep and tuneful (voice). □ **melodioso**
frump [frʌmp] *n.* person, usually a woman, who wears old-fashioned clothes. □ **anticuada**
frumpish *adj.* out-of-date (clothes). □ **anticuado**
frustrate [frʌ'streit] *v.* to stop (someone) from doing what he wants to do. □ **frustrar**
frustration [frʌ'streiʃn] *n.* feeling of anger and impatience when stopped from doing what you want. □ **frustración**
fry [frai] *n.* (*no pl.*) baby fish. □ **alevines**
small fry, unimportant people. □ **gente modesta**
■ *v.* (*fried; frying*) to cook in oil/fat: *fried eggs and bacon for breakfast.* □ **freír**
French fries/French fried potatoes, *Amer.* chips/long pieces of potato fried in oil. □ **patatas fritas**
frying pan *n.* shallow, open pan used for frying. □ **sartén**
to jump out of the frying pan into the fire, to go from

one difficult situation to something worse. □ **salir de Málaga y meterse en Malagón**
fuchsia ['fju:ʃə] *n.* garden plant with colourful hanging flowers. □ **fucsia**
fuddle ['fʌdl] *v.* to make someone feel hazy and stupid: *the alcohol fuddled his memory.* □ **atontar**
fudge [fʌdʒ] *n.* soft sweet made from butter, sugar and milk. □ **dulce**
■ *v.* ***to fudge the issue,*** to avoid making a decision on an issue. □ **eludir**
fuel ['fjuəl] *n.* substance (coal/gas/oil/wood, etc.) which can be burnt to make heat/to give power. □ **combustible**
to add fuel to the flames, to make matters worse. □ **echar leña al fuego**
■ *v.* (*he fuelled*) to provide fuel for. □ **abastecer de combustible**
fuelling *n.* filling up with fuel: *the aircraft must allow time for fuelling.* □ **...para repostar**
fug [fʌg] *n.* (*informal*) stuffy/hot atmosphere: *what a fug, let's open a window!* □ **cargado; ¡qué olor,...!**
fugitive ['fju:dʒətiv] *n.* and *adj.* (person) who is running away. □ **fugitivo**
fulcrum ['fulkrəm] *n.* point on which a lever rests/on which a seesaw balances. □ **fulcro**
fulfil [ful'fil] *v.* (*he fulfilled*) to complete (something) satisfactorily: *to fulfil a promise; the new machine fulfils all our requirements; have you fulfilled your duties already?* □ **cumplir (promesa); satisfacer**
fulfilment *n.* satisfactory ending: *our house is the fulfilment of our dreams,* it is just what we always wanted. □ **realización**
full [ful] *adj.* (*fuller, fullest*) **1** containing as much as possible: *the bag is full of apples; we are full of gratitude for your kindness.* □ **lleno**
full up, (i) no more room: *the hotel is full up.* □ **al completo**
(ii) *I'm full (up),* I have eaten as much as I can. □ **no puedo más**
full skirt, wide skirt made from lots of material. □ **falda amplia**
2 all; as many (as possible): *tell me the full story of your life; we need full details about your other jobs; I got full marks in my exam.* □ **completo, el máximo posible**
3 complete: *she was in the doctor's room a full hour.* □ **toda una hora**
in full flower/in full bloom, (plant) with wide open flowers. □ **en plena flor**
full meal, a meal of several courses, not just one dish. □ **una comida completa**
full fare, the price of an adult ticket: *children under 12 pay half fare, children over 12 pay full fare.* □ **billete completo**
full stop, dot (.) at the end of a sentence. □ **punto**
to come to a full stop, to stop suddenly in the middle of doing something. □ **pararse de pronto**
4 round and plump (face). □ **redondo**
full moon, moon which is completely round like a circle. □ **luna llena**
■ *n.* ***in full,*** completely/entirely: *write your name in full,* write your surname and first names too. □ **completo**
to the full, completely: *we enjoyed ourselves to the full at your party.* □ **a tope**
full back *n.* (*in Rugby/hockey*) defensive player near the goal. □ **zaguero**
full-blown *adj.* **1** (*of a flower*) wide open. □ **abierto**
2 *he is a full-blown doctor of medicine,* he has passed all his examinations and is qualified as a doctor. □ **es médico con todas las de la ley**
full-grown *adj.* adult: *he's no longer a boy, he's a full-grown man.* □ **desarrollado**
full-length *adj.* **1** from head to toe: *full-length photograph.* □ **de cuerpo entero**
2 long (story/film): *his first full-length novel.* □ **historia larga; película de largo metraje**
fullness *n.* **1** state of containing as much as possible. □ **plenitud**
2 state when all is completed. □ **plenitud**
in the fullness of time, eventually/in the end. □ **a su debido tiempo**
full-scale *adj.* complete/total: *a full-scale war.* □ **total**
full time *n.* end of a sports match: *the referee blew his whistle at full time.* □ **final del partido**
full-time *adj.* and *adv.* all the time: *he has a full-time job/he works full-time.* □ **a tiempo completo**
fully *adv.* **1** completely/entirely: *we are fully satisfied with the builder's work.* □ **totalmente**
2 *I will write more fully later,* I will write more details later. □ **...más detalladamente después**
3 *fully two hours passed,* at least two hours went by, perhaps more. □ **por lo menos**
fully-fledged *adj.* experienced/qualified: *he's a fully-fledged barrister.* □ **competente**
fulminate ['fʌlmineit] *v.* (*formal*) to protest angrily. □ **despacharse airadamente**
fulsome ['fulsəm] *adj.* excessive/too much: *fulsome praise.* □ **exagerado**
fumble ['fʌmbl] *v.* **1** to touch/to feel clumsily. □ **manosear**
2 *he fumbled in his pocket,* he felt around in his pocket. □ **revolvió en los bolsillos**
fumbling *adj.* clumsy. □ **desmañado**
fume [fju:m] *n. pl.* ***fumes,*** smoke/gas: *factory fumes; petrol fumes.* □ **humo**
■ *v.* to be angry: *he was fuming with rage.* □ **bufar de cólera**
fumigate ['fju:migeit] *v.* to clean by smoking out germs and insects: *they fumigated the room after his illness.* □ **fumigar**
fumigation [fju:mi'geiʃn] *n.* smoking out germs/insects. □ **fumigación**
fun [fʌn] *n.* amusement/pleasure: *we had fun at the seaside.* □ **diversión**
to make fun of/to poke fun at, to laugh nastily at/to mock. □ **reírse de alguien**
for fun/in fun, not seriously/as a joke. □ **en broma**
funfair *n.* group of amusements, sideshows, foodstalls, etc., collected together. □ **parque de atracciones**
function ['fʌŋkʃn] *n.* **1** job/duty: *what is the function of this machine?* □ **función**
2 gathering of people; party: *you can use the school hall for special functions.* □ **acto**
■ *v.* **1** to work: *the machine won't function properly.* □ **funcionar**
2 to serve: *it functions as a village hall and cinema.* □ **funcionar**
functional *adj.* useful but not decorative. □ **funcional**
functionary *n.* official. □ **funcionario**
fund [fʌnd] *n.* **1** sum of money set aside for a special purpose: *a fund for refugee children.* □ **fondo**
2 collection: *he has a fund of stories about the war.* □ **colección**
■ *v.* to provide money for a special purpose. □ **financiar**
fundamental [fʌndə'mentl] *adj.* basic/essential: *water is a fundamental necessity of life.* □ **fundamental**

funeral ['fju:nərəl] *n.* ceremony where a dead person is buried/cremated: *he died on Friday and the funeral will take place on Tuesday.* □ **funeral**
funereal [fju:'niəriəl] *adj.* sad and gloomy. □ **fúnebre**
fungicide ['fʌndʒisaid] *n.* chemical which kills fungus. □ **fungicida**
fungus ['fʌŋgəs] *n.* (*pl. fungi*) plant which has no green leaves or flowers and which frequently lives on other plants. □ **hongo**
funicular [fə'nikjulə] *n.* ***funicular (railway),*** railway (often held by cables) which travels up a slope. □ **funicular**
funk [fʌŋk] *n.* (*informal*) fear. □ **canguis; canguelo**
to be in a blue funk, to be terrified. □ **estar muerto de miedo**
■ *v.* (*informal*) **1** to be afraid to do something. □ **acongojarse**
2 *she funked seeing the headmaster,* she didn't see him because she was too afraid. □ **rajarse por miedo**
funnel ['fʌnl] *n.* **1** tube with a wide mouth and narrow bottom used when pouring liquids from one container into another. □ **embudo**
2 chimney on a ship from which the smoke comes. □ **chimenea**
■ *v.* (*he funnelled*) *v.* to pass through a funnel/through a narrow space. □ **verter por un embudo**
funny ['fʌni] *adj.* (*funnier, funniest*) **1** which makes people laugh: *we saw a very funny programme on television today.* □ **gracioso**
2 odd/unusual: *why are you behaving in such a funny way?* □ **raro**
3 *I feel funny,* I feel ill. □ **me siento algo raro**
funnily *adv.* oddly. □ **de una manera rara**
funny bone *n.* (*informal*) part of the elbow which hurts sharply if it is hit. □ **hueso dulce**
fur [fə:] *n.* **1** coat of an animal: *cats grow thicker fur in winter.* □ **pelaje**
fur coat, coat made of the skin of an animal. □ **abrigo de piel**
to make the fur fly, to have a violent argument. □ **armar la de Dios es Cristo**
2 deposit in kettles/water pipes, etc. □ **sarro**
■ *v.* (*it furred*) to become covered with a deposit: *our kettle is furred up.* □ **incrustar**
furry *adj.* (*furrier, furriest*) covered with fur: *a furry kitten.* □ **peludo**
furbish ['fə:biʃ] *v.* to polish/to clean. □ **bruñir**
furious ['fjuəriəs] *adj.* very angry: *a furious quarrel; furious storm; furious speed; she's furious with me for breaking her vase.* □ **furioso**
furl [fə:l] *v.* to roll up and tie securely. □ **enrollar**
furnace ['fə:nəs] *n.* **1** large brick or metal oven which can be heated to a very high temperature. □ **horno**
blast furnace, furnace where iron is heated until it melts. □ **alto horno**
2 heater which warms the water for central heating. □ **caldera**
furnish ['fə:niʃ] *v.* **1** to provide with chairs/tables, etc.: *I need to furnish the bedroom,* I need to buy beds, cupboards, carpet, curtains, etc., for the room; *furnished rooms/furnished flat,* rented place where the furniture is provided by the owner. □ **proveer; amueblar**
2 to supply: *can you furnish me with details of your previous job?* □ **proporcionar**
furnishings *n. pl.* fittings in a house. □ **accesorios**
soft furnishings, curtains, cushions, etc. □ **complementos textiles del hogar**
furniture ['fə:nitʃə] *n.* (*no pl.*) tables/chairs/cupboards/beds, etc: *furniture polish; furniture shop.* □ **muebles**
a piece of furniture, one article of furniture. □ **un mueble**
furniture remover, person who moves the contents of your old house into your new one. □ **empleado de mudanzas**
furore [fju:'rɔ:ri, fju:'rɔ:] *Amer.* **furor** *n.* outburst of anger/excitement. □ **furor**
furrier ['fʌriə] *n.* person who makes and sells fur coats, etc. □ **peletero**
furrow ['fʌrou] *n.* long groove cut in the earth by a plough. □ **surco**
■ *v.* to plough the land. □ **arar**
further ['fə:ðə] *adv.* and *adj.* **1** farther/to a greater distance/more distant: *move further back,* go backwards a bit more; *nothing was further from my mind,* I wasn't thinking of that at all. □ **más lejos**
2 additional: *we need further information.* □ **más**
without further ado *he signed the form,* without asking any more questions. □ **sin más dilación firmó...**
College of Further Education, college for people who have left school. □ **superior**
■ *v.* to advance: *to further a plan.* □ **hacer progresar**
furtherance *n.* advancing (of a plan). □ **progreso**
furthermore [fə:ðə'mɔ:] *adv.* also/in addition. □ **además**
furthermost ['fə:ðəmoust] *adj.* most distant: *to the furthermost countries in the world.* □ **más lejano**
furthest *adj.* and *adv.* to the greatest distance/most distant: *he can swim the furthest; this is the furthest north I have ever been.* □ **lo más lejos**
furtive ['fə:tiv] *adj.* secret; as if hiding something: *a furtive look.* □ **furtivo**
fury ['fjuəri] *n.* (*pl. furies*) **1** fierce anger. □ **furia**
2 *to work **like fury,*** to work very hard and fast. □ **trabajar como una furia**
furze [fə:z] *n.* gorse/prickly shrub with yellow flowers. □ **aliaga**
fuse [fju:z] *n.* **1** length of string attached to a bomb which burns slowly when lit: *light the fuse, then run away!* □ **mecha**
2 small piece of wire in an electrical circuit which melts and breaks if the circuit is overloaded and so prevents further damage. □ **fusible**
to blow a fuse, to overload the electric circuit and make the fuse break. □ **fundir un fusible**
■ *v.* **1** to break the electrical circuit: *the lights have fused.* □ **fundirse los plomos**
2 ***to fuse together,*** to join together (wires/companies, etc.). □ **fundirse**
fusebox *n.* box where the fuses are kept. □ **caja de los plomos**
fusewire *n.* specially fine wire for putting into fuses. □ **hilo de fusibles**
fuselage ['fju:zəla:ʒ] *n.* body of an aircraft. □ **fuselaje**
fusilier [fju:zə'liə] *n.* rifleman in the army. □ **fusilero**
fusillade [fju:zi'leid] *n.* rapid gunfire. □ **tiroteo**
fusion ['fju:ʒn] *n.* **1** melting together of two pieces of metal. □ **fusión**
2 joining together of two different things: *fusion of ideas; fusion of two political parties.* □ **fusión**
fuss [fʌs] *n.* (*pl. fusses*) agitated complaints about little things that do not matter: *what a lot of fuss and bother!* □ **jaleo**
to make a fuss about something, to complain at length about something unimportant. □ **montar un cirio sobre algo**
to make a fuss of someone, to pay great attention

to someone. □ **deshacerse en atenciones**
■ *v.* to be agitated; to show unnecessary care and attention about little things: *she fussed about the office, putting away papers and tidying piles of books.* □ **preocuparse por tonterías**
fussy *adj.* (*fussier, fussiest*) **1** unnecessarily careful and demanding about little things. □ **quisquilloso**
2 disliking lots of things: *she's fussy about her food.* □ **melindroso**
fusty ['fʌsti] *adj.* (*fustier, fustiest*) smelling of dampness. □ **mohoso**
futile ['fju:tail, *Amer.* 'fju:tl] *adj.* useless: *it is futile asking his permission, he always says no.* □ **inútil**
futility [fju:'tiliti] *n.* uselessness. □ **inutilidad**
future ['fju:tʃə] *n.* time which has not yet happened: *in (the) future I shall play more tennis.* □ **futuro**
in the near future, very soon. □ **en un futuro próximo**
■ *adj.* coming/not yet happened: *my future wife,* woman I'm going to marry. □ **futuro**
futuristic [fju:tʃə'ristik] *adj.* oddly modern (art). □ **futurista**
fuzz [fʌz] *n.* **1** fluffy hair. □ **pelusa**
2 ***the fuzz,*** (*slang*) the police. □ **la bofia**
fuzzy *adj.* (*fuzzier, fuzziest*) **1** fluffy and curly. □ **encrespado**
2 not clear/blurred: *a fuzzy photograph.* □ **borroso**

G,g

G, g [dʒiː] seventh letter of the alphabet. □ **G, g**
gab [gæb] *n.* (*informal*) talk/chat. □ **palique**
to have the gift of the gab: *he has the gift of the gab,* he has a talent for speaking. □ **tiene un pico de oro**
gabardine ['gæbədiːn] *n.* type of closely woven cotton material, used for making raincoats: *a gabardine raincoat.* □ **gabardina**
gabble ['gæbl] *n.* loud, unintelligible talk: *a continuous gabble could be heard from the crowd.* □ **parloteo**
■ *v.* to speak very quickly: *he gabbled out his speech; don't gabble; she gabbled on for half an hour.* □ **parlotear**
gable ['geibl] *n.* triangular upper part of a wall at the end of a roof: *there's a gable at each end of the house.* □ **hastial**
gabled *adj.* with gables: *the house has a gabled roof.* □ **...un tejado a dos aguas**
gad [gæd] *v.* (*he gadded*) ***to gad about,*** to be constantly out and about: *he's always gadding about.* □ **ir de acá para allá**
gadabout *n.* person who is always out and about. □ **trotacalles**
gadget ['gædʒit] *n.* useful machine/tool: *he had a useful gadget for removing nails from wood.* □ **artilugio**
gadgetry *n.* lots of gadgets: *he had a drawer full of gadgetry of all kinds.* □ **artilugios**
Gaelic ['geilik, *in Scotland* 'gælik] *n.* language of Scots, Manx and Irish Celts. □ **gaélico**
gaff [gæf] *n.* stick with iron hook for catching large fish. □ **garfio**
to blow the gaff, to let out a secret. □ **revelar el secreto**
gaffe [gæf] *n.* blunder; indiscreet act or remark: *she made a terrible gaffe when she remarked that her friend's hat was hideous.* □ **metedura de pata**
gaffer ['gæfə] *n.* (*informal*) **1** old man. □ **vejete**
2 boss. □ **capataz**
gag [gæg] *n.* **1** soft object such as a handkerchief put into or tied round the mouth to stop someone speaking: *they tied a gag around the prisoner's mouth.* □ **mordaza**
2 joke: *the comedian was famous for his gags.* □ **'gag'; chiste**
■ *v.* (*he gagged*) **1** to bind round the mouth; to prevent from speaking: *the victim was bound and gagged; to gag the press,* to impose censorship. □ **amordazar**
2 to retch/to choke: *the foul air made him gag.* □ **sentir náuseas**
gaga ['gɑːgɑː] *adj.* (*informal*) senile/stupid: *the old man had become a little gaga.* □ **chocho**
gaggle ['gægl] *n.* flock (of geese). □ **manada**
gaiety ['geiəti] *n.* happiness/cheerfulness: *the village fête was a scene of gaiety and merrymaking.* □ **alegría**
gaily ['geili] *adv.* happily: *he went gaily on his way.* □ **alegremente**
gain [gein] *n.* increase of possessions; profit: *the speculator made vast gains in the property market.* □ **ganancia**
■ *v.* **1** to obtain/to get: *he gained thousands of pounds; the baby gained twelve pounds in a month; she gained access to the empty house.* □ **ganar; logró entrar a la casa vacía**
to gain the upper hand, to get control: *in the argument he gained the upper hand.* □ **ganar por ventaja**
2 *the clock gains five minutes a day,* it moves five minutes ahead of the correct time in every twenty-four hours. □ **...se adelanta cinco minutos al día**
3 ***to gain on someone/something,*** to get closer to a person or thing which you are chasing: *the hounds gained on the hare.* □ **ganar terreno**
gainful *adj.* which earns money: *he has no gainful employment.* □ **lucrativo; no tiene un empleo remunerado**
gainfully *adv. gainfully employed,* doing work which earns money. □ **lucrativamente**
gainsay [gein'sei] *v.* (*he gainsaid*) (*formal*) to deny (something). □ **negar**
gait [geit] *n.* manner of walking: *the drunk walked with an unsteady gait.* □ **andares; ...con paso poco seguro**
gaiter ['geitə] *n.* covering of cloth or leather worn over the leg below the knee. □ **polaina**
gala ['gɑːlə] *n.* festive occasion: *the gala season at the Opera House.* □ **gala**
swimming gala, swimming competition. □ **competición de natación**
galaxy ['gæləksi] *n.* (*pl. galaxies*) collection of stars, found singly and in groups and clusters: *the Milky Way is a galaxy.* □ **galaxia**
galactic [gə'læktik] *adj.* belonging to a galaxy. □ **galáctico**
gale [geil] *n.* very strong wind: *the ship was hit by gales; gale force winds,* winds strong enough to be called a gale. □ **galerna**
galena [gə'liːnə] *n.* natural form of lead sulphide. □ **galena**
gall [gɔːl] *n.* **1** bile/bitter liquid produced by the liver to digest fat. □ **bilis**
2 growth produced by insects on trees, especially the oak. □ **agalla**
3 painful swelling/blister (especially on horses). □ **rozadura**
4 (*informal*) rudeness/impudence: *he had the gall to ask for more money.* □ **descaro**
■ *v.* to annoy/to humiliate: *the pupil was galled by his teacher's criticism.* □ **herir en el amor propio**
galling *adj.* humiliating; annoying: *it was a galling experience.* □ **humillante**
gall-bladder *n.* bag in the body through which bile passes. □ **vesícula biliar**
gallstone *n.* small stone-like substance which sometimes forms in the gall-bladder. □ **cálculo biliar**
gallant ['gælənt] *adj.* **1** brave/chivalrous: *the gallant soldier rode fearlessly into battle.* □ **valiente**
2 very polite towards women. □ **galante**
gallantly *adv.* in a gallant way: *he gallantly flung his cloak on the ground for the Queen to step on.* □ **galantemente**
gallantry ['gæləntri] *n.* bravery: *he won a medal for gallantry in battle.* □ **valentía**
galleon ['gæliən] *n.* large Spanish warship in the 16th century. □ **galeón**
gallery ['gæləri] *n.* (*pl. galleries*) **1** room in which pictures are often hung: *the family portraits were displayed in the picture gallery.* □ **galería; sala**
2 art museum: *the National Gallery.* □ **museo de arte**
3 shop selling pictures/antiques, etc. □ **galería de arte**

4 (*in a church/hall, etc.*) balcony which runs around part of the main hall, where people can sit; (*in a theatre/cinema*) highest rows of seats. □ **tribuna (iglesia); gallinero (teatro/cine)**
to play to the gallery, to appeal to people who have no taste. □ **actuar para la galería**
minstrels' gallery, balcony above the end of the dining hall of castles and palaces from where musicians entertained the diners. □ **galería de músicos**
5 ***shooting gallery,*** long, narrow room at one end of which is a target for shooting. □ **galería de tiro**

galley ['gæli] *n.* **1** low, flat, single-decked ship, powered by sails and rowed by slaves. □ **galera**
2 ship's kitchen: *the cook sweated in the galley below decks.* □ **cocina**
3 (*in printing*) rectangular tray which holds type. □ **galera**
galley proof *n.* proof printed on long sheets of paper. □ **galerada**

Gallic ['gælik] *adj.* French. □ **galo**
gallicism *n.* French word or phrase adopted into another language. □ **galicismo**

gallivant ['gælivænt] *v.* (*informal*) to be always out and about looking for amusement. □ **pindonguear**

gallon ['gælən] *n.* liquid measure equal to 4 quarts or 4.5 litres: *the pail holds two gallons of water.* □ **galón**

gallop ['gæləp] *n.* **1** fastest pace of a horse running with all feet off the ground in each stride: *the runaway horse went at a gallop down the hill.* □ **galope**
2 fast ride on a horse: *let's go for a gallop.* □ **a galope**
■ *v.* **1** to run/to go fast: *the winning greyhound galloped home.* □ **galopar**
2 *he galloped through his speech,* spoke it very fast. □ **pronunció su discurso muy de prisa**

gallows ['gælouz] *n.* structure on which criminals are hanged: *many highwaymen met their death on the gallows.* □ **horca**

Gallup poll ['gæləp'poul] *n.* test of public opinion on an important topic, especially of how a representative sample of the public will vote in order to forecast an election result. □ **sondeo de la opinión pública**

galore [gə'lɔː] *adv.* (*always placed after the noun*) plenty: *the greengrocer had apples galore.* □ **en abundancia**

galoshes [gə'lɔʃiz] *n. pl.* plastic/rubber shoes worn over other shoes to protect them: *a pair of galoshes.* □ **chanclo**

galumph [gə'lʌmf] *v.* (*informal*) to walk about heavily: *the elephants went galumphing about.* □ **andar con paso cansado**

galvanize ['gælvənaiz] *v.* **1** *galvanized iron,* iron coated with zinc to protect it from rust. □ **galvanizar**
2 to rouse by shock: *he was galvanized into action.* □ **sacudir**
galvanometer [gælvə'nɔmitə] *n.* instrument for measuring small electric currents. □ **galvanómetro**

gambit ['gæmbit] *n.* **1** (*in chess*) opening move whereby a player sacrifices a minor piece in order to take a major one later. □ **gambito**
2 opening move in some action: *the opening gambit of the Prime Minister was to attack the leader of the opposition.* □ **táctica**

gamble ['gæmbl] *n.* risk taken in the hope of getting good results: *as the result of a gamble he won a fortune; it's a bit of a gamble,* you can't be sure it will succeed. □ **jugada arriesgada**
■ *v.* **1** to risk money on cards or sporting results: *he gambled his fortune away at the races.* □ **jugar**
2 *don't gamble on the weather being fine tomorrow,* don't rely on it. □ **no confíes en...**
gambler *n.* person who gambles. □ **jugador**
gambling *n.* risking money; betting: *gambling was his downfall.* □ **juego**
■ *adj.* referring to gambling: *his gambling instincts were good.* □ **de jugador**

gambol ['gæmbl] *v.* (*he gambolled*) to frisk about: *the lambs were gambolling in the fields.* □ **retozar**

game [geim] *n.* **1** contest played according to rules and decided by skill, strength or luck: *would you like a game of tennis/chess? the Olympic Games take place every four years.* □ **juego; partido (tenis); partida (ajedrez)**
to play the game, to act honourably. □ **jugar limpiamente**
the game's up, we have been found out/success is now impossible. □ **se acabó**
two can play at that game, I can use the tricks you have used against me and beat you with them. □ **donde las dan las toman**
2 *so that's his little game,* now we know what his plans are. □ **conque esos son sus planes**
3 (*in tennis/bridge, etc.*) single round: *the score was two games all.* □ **juego**
4 wild animals and birds (deer, rabbits, pheasants, etc.) hunted for sport or food: *it is forbidden to shoot game in the National Parks.* □ **animales de caza**
game soup, soup made from game. □ **sopa de caza**
big game, large wild animals (lions/elephants, etc.) shot for sport. □ **caza mayor**
■ *adj.* **1** willing/courageous: *the athlete was game to try the high jump.* □ **valiente**
2 lame: *the old soldier had a game leg.* □ **lisiado**
gamekeeper *n.* person employed to breed and look after game. □ **guarda de coto**
gamely *adv.* bravely. □ **valientemente**
gamesmanship *n.* (*no pl.*) the art of winning by devious means, such as distracting your opponent. □ **maestría en juegos poco limpios**
gaming *n.* gambling: *gaming club; gaming table,* table on which gambling games are played. □ **de juego**

gamete ['gæmiːt] *n.* plant or animal which can link with another to reproduce. □ **gameto**

gamma rays ['gæmə'reiz] *n. pl.* rays of short wavelength sent out by radioactive substances. □ **rayos gamma**

gammon ['gæmən] *n.* smoked or cured ham. □ **jamón curado o ahumado**

gammy ['gæmi] *adj.* (*informal*) lame: *he has a gammy leg.* □ **pata coja**

gamut ['gæmət] *n.* **1** whole range of musical notes. □ **gama**
2 whole range or scope: *the whole gamut of crime,* every type of crime imaginable. □ **gama**

gander ['gændə] *n.* male goose. □ **ganso**

gang [gæŋ] *n.* band of people acting or going about together: *a gang of thieves; a gang of youths.* □ **banda; pandilla**
■ *v.* ***to gang up (with),*** to team up with: *the brothers ganged up against their sister.* □ **unirse a/en contra de**
to gang up on (someone), to take sides with one or more people against someone: *the rest of the class ganged up on me.* □ **confabularse contra**
gangplank *n.* long piece of wood giving access to a boat from the shore. □ **plancha**
gangster *n.* member of a gang of violent criminals.

□ **gángster**
gangway *n.* **1** (*in a theatre/cinema, etc.*) passage between rows of seats. □ **pasillo**
2 bridge from the shore to a ship. □ **pasarela**
gangling ['gæŋgliŋ] *adj.* loosely built (person); tall (person) with long arms and legs. □ **larguirucho**
ganglion ['gæŋgliən] *n.* **1** nucleus of nerves in the central nervous system. □ **ganglio**
2 small lump on a tendon. □ **inflamación**
gangrene ['gæŋgri:n] *n.* rotting of body tissue, caused by a blockage of the blood supply: *the soldier's leg had to be amputated when gangrene set in.* □ **gangrena**
gangrenous ['gæŋgrinəs] *adj.* affected by gangrene: *he had a gangrenous arm.* □ **gangrenoso**
gannet ['gænit] *n.* large white sea bird. □ **alcatraz**
gantry ['gæntri] *n.* (*pl. gantries*) metal bridge for carrying lights/a crane, etc. □ **pórtico**
gaol [dʒeil] *n.* prison: *the rioters were held in the county gaol.* □ **cárcel**
■ *v.* to put (someone) in prison: *he was gaoled for two years.* □ **encarcelar**
gaolbird *n.* person who has been sent to prison often. □ **preso reincidente**
gaoler *n.* person in charge of the prisoners in a gaol. □ **carcelero**
gap [gæp] *n.* **1** space/hole in a hedge/wall, etc.: *he climbed through a gap in the hedge; the gaps in his education were evident from his examination results.* □ **abertura; laguna**
2 gorge or pass (between mountains). □ **desfiladero**
3 space/difference. □ **vacío**
age gap, difference in age: *there was a gap of four years between the two sisters.* □ **diferencia**
generation gap, difference in years between one generation and another, often resulting in intolerance between them. □ **diferencia generacional**
gape [geip] *v.* to open your mouth wide: *he gaped at the sight of the shark.* □ **quedarse boquiabierto**
gaping *adj.* wide open: *a gaping hole appeared in the rock.* □ **grande, abierto**
garage ['gæridʒ, 'gærɑ:ʒ] *n.* **1** building for storing motor vehicles: *the car was kept in a garage next to the house.* □ **garaje**
garage sale, *Amer.* private sale of unwanted household goods (held in the garage of a house). □ **venta particular de objetos de segunda mano**
2 petrol station/place where motor vehicles are repaired: *he looked for the nearest garage when he needed petrol.* □ **gasolinera, taller**
■ *v.* to put (a vehicle) into a garage: *he garaged the car.* □ **dejar en el garaje**
garb [gɑ:b] *n.* (*no pl.*) (*formal*) clothing. □ **vestido**
garbage ['gɑ:bidʒ] *n.* refuse/rubbish. □ **basura**
garbage can, dustbin/container where you put household rubbish. □ **cubo de la basura**
garble ['gɑ:bl] *v.* to select certain items or passages from speeches/facts, etc., in order to give an unfair or malicious representation; to distort or confuse: *he gave a garbled account of the interview.* □ **desvirtuar**
garden ['gɑ:dn] *n.* piece of ground used for growing flowers, fruit, or vegetables: *the house was surrounded by garden; public gardens.* □ **jardín; huerto (hortalizas)**
garden of remembrance, garden dedicated to the memory of the dead. □ **jardín conmemorativo**
■ *v.* to look after a garden: *he gardens every weekend.* □ **trabajar en un jardín**
gardener *n.* person who looks after a garden. □ **jardinero; hortelano**
gardening *n.* looking after a garden: *she loves gardening; a gardening programme on the radio.* □ **jardinería**
gardenia [gɑ:'di:niə] *n.* shrub with fragrant white or yellow flowers. □ **gardenia**
gargantuan [gɑ:'gæntjuən] *adj.* huge/enormous: *they sat down to a gargantuan feast.* □ **pantagruélico**
gargle ['gɑ:gl] *n.* antiseptic liquid used for washing the throat: *he used a gargle for his sore throat.* □ **gargarismo**
■ *v.* to wash the throat by holding antiseptic liquid in it and breathing out at the same time: *she gargled every evening before singing.* □ **hacer gárgaras**
gargoyle ['gɑ:gɔil] *n.* water spout projecting from the gutter of a medieval building, decorated with a grotesque human or animal head. □ **gárgola**
garish ['gɛəriʃ] *adj.* bright/showy/over-decorated: *their taste in furniture was garish.* □ **chillón**
garishly *adv.* very brightly: *garishly decorated floats in a carnival procession.* □ **llamativamente**
garland ['gɑ:lənd] *n.* **1** circle of flowers or leaves worn as a decoration: *the native girls wore garlands of flowers in their hair.* □ **guirnalda**
2 decoration made of linked paper/ribbon, etc.: *the Christmas tree was hung with paper garlands.* □ **guirnalda**
■ *v.* to hang with garlands: *the May Queen was garlanded with roses and forget-me-nots.* □ **enguirnaldar**
garlic ['gɑ:lik] *n.* plant whose bulb has a strong smell and taste, used as a flavouring: *she added a clove of garlic to the stew.* □ **ajo**
garlicky *adj.* tasting/smelling of garlic. □ **aliáceo**
garment ['gɑ:mənt] *n.* article of clothing: *the bride's aunt wore a strange flowing garment.* □ **prenda**
garner ['gɑ:nə] *v.* (*formal*) to collect and store. □ **entrojar**
garnet ['gɑ:nit] *n.* semi-precious dark red stone: *her engagement ring was a garnet surrounded by pearls.* □ **granate**
garnish ['gɑ:niʃ] *v.* to decorate (especially food): *the soufflé was garnished with shrimps and parsley.* □ **aderezar**
garret ['gærət] *n.* attic room immediately under the roof of a house: *the servant slept in the garret.* □ **desván**
garrison ['gærisn] *n.* **1** troops stationed in a fortress/town, etc., in order to defend it: *the garrison was ordered to protect the inhabitants of the city against the enemy.* □ **guarnición**
2 fortress. □ **guarnición**
■ *v. to garrison a town,* to place troops on garrison duty in a town. □ **guarnecer**
garrotte [gə'rɔt] *v.* to strangle (someone) with a cord. □ **agarrotar**
garrulous ['gærjuləs] *adj.* talkative: *the garrulous old woman could be relied on for gossip.* □ **gárrulo**
garter ['gɑ:tə] *n.* band worn above or below the knee to keep a stocking or sock up. □ **liga**
Order of the Garter, highest order of English knighthood. □ **Orden de la Jarretera**
gas [gæs] *n.* (*pl. gases*) **1** chemical substance which, like air, is completely fluid and has no definite shape or volume: *some substances can become gases if the temperature is high enough; the balloon was filled with a non-flammable gas.* □ **gas**
2 substance, produced from coal or extracted naturally from the ground, which is used for cooking or heating: *I cook by gas; gas cooker; gas fire.* □ **gas**
natural gas, gas which is extracted from the earth.

□ **gas natural**
3 substance used to make you unconscious while having a tooth removed, etc. □ **anestesia**
4 *Amer.* petrol. □ **gasolina**
to step on the gas, to accelerate. □ **pisar el acelerador**
■ *v.* (*he was gassed*) to poison (someone) by making them breathe gas: *many soldiers were gassed in the First World War.* □ **asfixiar con gas**
gaseous ['gæsjəs] *adj.* referring to gas. □ **gaseoso**
gasholder *n.* large container in which gas is stored. □ **tanque de gas**
gasmask *n.* mask used as protection against poison gases. □ **careta antigás**
gasoline *n. Amer.* petrol. □ **gasolina**
gasometer [gæ'sɔmitə] *n.* large reservoir in which gas is stored. □ **gasómetro**
gas station *n. Amer.* place where you can buy petrol and oil for the car. □ **gasolinera**
gassy *adj.* full of gas/full of bubbles: *this drink's too gassy.* □ **gaseoso**
gasworks *n.* place where gas is manufactured. □ **fábrica de gas**

gash [gæʃ] *n.* (*pl. gashes*) long deep cut/wound: *the knife slipped and made a gash in his hand.* □ **corte profundo**
■ *v.* to make a long deep cut: *his arm was gashed by his opponent's sword.* □ **hacer un corte**

gasket ['gæskit] *n.* piece of thin material used to seal two parts of an engine to prevent air/gas, etc., from escaping: *the mechanic replaced the gasket.* □ **junta de culata**

gasp [gɑːsp] *n.* sharp intake of breath: *she let out a gasp when she saw the accident.* □ **resuello, grito**
to be at one's last gasp, to be at the point of death. □ **estar boqueando**
■ *v.* to struggle to breathe: *the drowning man gasped for breath; the news made me gasp.* □ **...luchaba por respirar; la noticia me dejó boquiabierto**

gasteropod ['gæstərəpɔd] *n.* type of mollusc, like a snail or limpet. □ **gasterópodo**

gastric ['gæstrik] *adj.* referring to the stomach: *she complained of gastric pains.* □ **gástrico**
gastric flu, infection of the stomach. □ **infección estomacal**
gastrectomy *n.* operation to remove the stomach. □ **gastrectomía**
gastroenteritis [gæstrouentə'raitis] *n.* illness of the stomach and intestines. □ **gastroenteritis**
gastronome ['gæstrənoum] *n.* expert on cookery. □ **gastrónomo**
gastronomic [gæstrə'nɔmik] *adj.* referring to food and drink. □ **gastronómico**

gate [geit] *n.* **1** barrier, usually made of wood or iron, closing an opening in a wall/fence, etc.: *if you leave the gate open, the sheep will get out; the city gates were closed at sunset.* □ **verja**
2 number of people who watch a football match/sports competition, etc.: *the gate was low because of the bad weather.* □ **entrada**
gatecrash *v.* to go uninvited to a party or other event. □ **colarse**
gatecrasher *n.* uninvited guest: *the gatecrashers climbed over the wall.* □ **persona que se cuela**
gate-legged table *n.* table with hinged legs which fold like a gate. □ **mesa plegable**
gatepost *n.* post to which a gate is attached by hinges. □ **pilar**
gateway *n.* gap in a wall/fence, etc., where a gate can be fitted. □ **paso**

gateau ['gætou] *n.* (*pl. gateaux*) large decorated cream cake. □ **tarta**

gather ['gæðə] *v.* **1** to bring together/to collect: *the farmer gathered in his sheep; she was gathering mushrooms; the corn was gathered into sheaves; he gathered up his papers; a crowd gathered around the speaker.* □ **recoger**
2 to gain: *the car gathered speed.* □ **ganar**
3 to understand: *I gather that you are coming.* □ **tener entendido que**
4 to pull (material) into folds by means of tiny stitches: *a gathered skirt.* □ **fruncir**
gathering *n.* **1** assembly: *there will be a gathering on the village green; a family gathering.* □ **reunión**
2 swelling with pus. □ **absceso**
■ *adj.* imminent: *a gathering storm.* □ **inminente**

gauche [gouʃ] *adj.* clumsy/tactless: *the young girl appeared rather gauche at her first dance.* □ **torpe**

gaudy ['gɔːdi] *adj.* (*gaudier, gaudiest*) too brightly coloured; showy; lacking in taste: *she had dyed hair and wore gaudy jewellery.* □ **llamativo**
gaudily *adv.* showily. □ **llamativamente**
gaudiness *n.* brightness. □ **lo llamativo**

gauge [geidʒ] *n.* **1** standard measure of width/thickness, etc. □ **calibre; medida**
2 distance between rails on a railway line: *narrow-gauge railway.* □ **ancho de vía; ferrocarril de vía estrecha**
3 instrument measuring depth/pressure, etc.: *petrol gauge; oil gauge; tyre-pressure gauge.* □ **indicador; manómetro**
■ *v.* **1** to measure exactly: *with the aid of a ruler, he gauged the length of the rod; by using a dip-stick, you can gauge the amount of oil in the tank.* □ **medir; aforar**
2 to estimate/to guess: *from the speaker's accent, we gauged that he came from the North.* □ **calcular**

gaunt [gɔːnt] *adj.* lean/haggard: *after three days without food, his face became gaunt.* □ **demacrado**

gauntlet ['gɔːntlət] *n.* strong glove with long wrist for driving, fencing, etc. □ **guante**
to fling down the gauntlet, to issue a challenge. □ **arrojar el guante**
to run the gauntlet, to go through a dangerous area. □ **jugarse el tipo**

gauze [gɔːz] *n.* thin/transparent material: *the surgeon wore a gauze mask.* □ **gasa**

gave [geiv] *v. see* **give.**

gavel ['gævl] *n.* auctioneer's or chairman's hammer: *the chairman called the meeting to order with his gavel.* □ **martillo**

gawky ['gɔːki] *adj.* (*gawkier, gawkiest*) awkward/ungainly: *the gawky lad did not know what to do with his hands.* □ **torpe**

gawp [gɔːp] *v.* (*informal*) to stare rudely. □ **fulminar con la mirada**

gay [gei] *adj.* (*gayer, gayest*) happy; full of fun: *she is always bright and gay.* □ **alegre**
■ *adj.* and *n.* (*informal*) homosexual. □ **'gay'**

gaze [geiz] *n.* intent look: *his steady gaze made her blush.* □ **mirada fija**
■ *v.* to look steadily for a long time: *he gazed out to sea.* □ **quedarse mirando fijamente**

gazebo [gə'ziːbəu] *n.* small summerhouse. □ **casita de verano**

gazelle [gə'zel] *n.* kind of antelope. □ **gacela**

gazette [gə'zet] *n.* official newspaper, giving details of public appointments, etc. □ **boletín oficial**
gazetteer [gæzə'tiə] *n.* geographical dictionary: *he looked up Namibia in the gazetteer.* □ **diccionario geográfico**

gazump [gə'zʌmp] *v.* (*of seller*) to accept a higher price for a house which someone has already agreed to buy: *he was gazumped,* he thought he was buying the house, but someone offered more money and so bought it. □ **romper el compromiso**
GB ['dʒiː'biː] *abbreviation for* Great Britain. □ **Gran Bretaña**
gear ['giə] *n.* **1** equipment: *the gas fitter kept all his gear in a canvas bag.* □ **equipo**
landing gear, undercarriage of an aircraft. □ **tren de aterrizaje**
2 (*informal*) clothing: *the pop-singer was dressed in eye-catching gear.* □ **ropa**
3 arrangement of toothed wheels, levers, etc. connecting an engine/pedals, etc., with the wheels: *the bicycle had a 3-speed gear; the driver changed down into low gear as he approached a hill.* □ **embrague, cambio, marcha**
■ *v.* to adapt/to match: *the teacher geared his lessons to the students' needs; wages are geared to the cost of living.* □ **adaptar**
gearbox *n.* casing for gears in cars, etc. □ **caja de cambios**
gearlever, gearstick *Amer.* **gearshift** *n.* handle by which the gears are changed in a car. □ **palanca del cambio**
gearwheel *n.* toothed wheel connecting with another wheel of different diameter to change the power ratio of the engine: *one of the gearwheels of the bicycle is broken.* □ **piñón**
geese [giːs] *n. pl. see* **goose.**
geezer ['giːzə] *n.* (*slang*) (old) man. □ **vejete**
Geiger counter ['gaigəkauntə] *n.* cylindrical device for detecting and recording radioactivity. □ **contador de Geiger**
geisha ['geiʃə] *n.* Japanese hostess and dancing girl. □ **geisha**
gel [dʒel] *n.* substance like a jelly. □ **gel**
gelatin(e) ['dʒelətiːn] *n.* substance obtained after stewing skin, bones, etc., and used to make jellies: *a jelly will not set properly without gelatine.* □ **gelatina**
gelatinous [dʒə'lætinəs] *adj.* like jelly. □ **gelatinoso**
gelding ['geldiŋ] *n.* castrated horse or other animal. □ **caballo castrado**
gelignite ['dʒelignait] *n.* nitroglycerine explosive: *the thieves blasted open the safe with sticks of gelignite.* □ **gelignita**
gem [dʒem] *n.* precious stone: *the necklace was set with gems.* □ **gema**
gemology [dʒe'mɔlədʒi] *n.* the science of gems. □ **gemología**
Gemini ['dʒeminai] *n.* one of the signs of the zodiac, shaped like twins. □ **Géminis**
gen [dʒen] *n.* (*slang*) information: *have you got all the gen on sailing?* □ **información**
gender ['dʒendə] *n.* grammatical classification of objects roughly corresponding to the two sexes and sexlessness: *there are three genders used in some languages — masculine, feminine and neuter.* □ **género**
gene [dʒiːn] *n.* part of a chromosome which carries characteristics transmitted by the parent: *a person's character is determined by his genes.* □ **gen**
genealogical [dʒiːniə'lɔdʒikl] *adj.* referring to genealogy: *the genealogical study of man helps us to understand his development.* □ **genealógico**
genealogist [dʒiːni'ælədʒist] *n.* person who studies genealogy. □ **genealogista**
genealogy [dʒiːni'ælədʒi] *n.* (*pl. genealogies*) study of family descent through the generations. □ **genealogía**
genera ['dʒenərə] *n. see* **genus.**
general ['dʒenrl] *adj.* completely or approximately universal; including or affecting all or nearly all parts: *there was a general air of unrest; a general election,* an election in which the whole country is involved; *the general public; general knowledge.* □ **general**
in general, as a rule: *in general, English winters are cold and wet.* □ **en general**
■ *n.* superior officer immediately below a field marshal in the army. □ **general**
generalissimo [dʒenrə'lisimou] *n.* commander-in-chief of several armed forces. □ **generalísimo**
generalization [dʒenrəlai'zeiʃn] *n.* general statement: *it is a sweeping generalization to say that all Italians are dark-haired.* □ **generalización**
generalize ['dʒenrəlaiz] *v.* to try to express something as a general notion: *it is sometimes dangerous to generalize.* □ **generalizar**
generally ['dʒenrli] *adv.* as a rule: *generally speaking, a sailor's life is a good one.* □ **generalmente**
general practitioner *n.* doctor who treats all illnesses/family doctor. □ **médico, internista**
general-purpose *adj.* serving many purposes; not specialized: *a general-purpose hammer.* □ **de uso general**
generate ['dʒenəreit] *v.* to bring into existence; to produce: *the president's visit generated much goodwill.* □ **generar**
generation [dʒenə'reiʃn] *n.* **1** bringing into existence. □ **generación**
2 all people born about the same time: *the younger generation is often misunderstood; from generation to generation.* □ **generación**
generation gap, age difference between one generation and another, often resulting in intolerance between them. □ **diferencia generacional**
3 period of time between parents and children. □ **generación**
4 members of a family born about the same time: *four generations of Smiths were at the birthday party.* □ **generación**
generator ['dʒenəreitə] *n.* apparatus for producing electricity by gas/petrol, etc. □ **generador**
generic [dʒə'nerik] *adj.* referring to a genus/group/type. □ **genérico**
generically *adv.* through a genus. □ **genéricamente**
generous ['dʒenərəs] *adj.* **1** willing to give: *she's very generous with her money; the examiner was generous in his marking.* □ **generoso**
2 large: *the lady gave a generous donation to charity; a generous helping of ice cream.* □ **generoso**
generosity [dʒenə'rɔsiti] *n.* willingness to give (money, etc.): *he is well known for his generosity.* □ **generosidad**
genesis ['dʒenəsis] *n.* (*pl. geneses*) origin/beginning. □ **génesis**
genetics [dʒə'netiks] *n.* (*usually with singular verb*) study of heredity. □ **genética**
genial ['dʒiːniəl] *adj.* cheerful/kindly: *she had a genial outlook on life.* □ **cordial**
genially *adv.* cheerfully. □ **cordialmente**
genital ['dʒenitl] *adj.* referring to the sex organs. □ **genital**
■ *n. pl.* ***genitals,*** external sex organs. □ **genitales**
genitive ['dʒenitiv] *adj.* and *n.* (*in grammar*) ***genitive (case),*** form of a word showing possession. □ **genitivo**
genius ['dʒiːniəs] *n.* (*pl. geniuses*) **1** person with very great intelligence: *he's a genius with figures.* □ **genio**
2 very great intelligence: *she has a genius for always*

saying the right thing at the right time. □ **tiene un don especial...**
3 *evil genius,* bad spirit/person with a bad influence. □ **espíritu diabólico**
genocide ['dʒenəsaid] *n.* mass killing of a race. □ **genocidio**
genre ['ʒɔŋrə] *n.* particular type (of art, etc.). □ **género**
gent [dʒent] *n.* (*informal*) gentleman. □ **caballero**
gents *n.* (*informal*) men's toilet: *he's in the gents.* □ **servicio de caballeros**
genteel [dʒen'ti:l] *adj.* too refined: *genteel manners.* □ **fino**
gentility [dʒen'tiliti] *n.* refinement (of manners). □ **finura**
gentian ['dʒenʃn] *n.* small blue alpine flower. □ **genciana**
gentile ['dʒentail] *n.* person not of Jewish race. □ **gentil**
gentle ['dʒentl] *adj.* (*gentler, gentlest*) mild/tender/soft: *a gentle touch; the gardener was gentle with the young seedlings.* □ **leve, suave**
gentleman ['dʒentlmən] *n.* (*pl. gentlemen*) **1** man of good breeding and manners: *gentlemen stand up when ladies enter the room.* □ **caballero**
2 (polite way of referring to men): *well, gentlemen, what do you think of the proposal?* □ **bien, caballeros...**
gentlemanly *adj.* like a gentleman: *gentlemanly behaviour.* □ **caballeroso**
gentleness *n.* softness/carefulness. □ **amabilidad**
gently ['dʒentli] *adv.* (*gentlier, gentliest*) softly/carefully: *handle it gently.* □ **suavemente**
gently does it!, be careful as you do it. □ **¡con cuidado!**
gentry ['dʒentri] *n.* people of high class in society, below the aristocracy. □ **alta burguesía**
gentrification [dʒentrifi'keiʃn] *n.* act of making (an area of a town) smart. □ **remodelación**
genuflect ['dʒenjuflekt] *v.* to bend the knee, especially in worship: *the nun genuflected before the altar.* □ **hacer una genuflexión**
genuine ['dʒenjuin] *adj.* authentic/true: *I have a genuine desire to be a doctor; he was genuine in his offer of help.* □ **genuino**
genuinely *adv.* truly: *she was genuinely pleased to accept the invitation.* □ **sinceramente**
genus ['dʒi:nəs] *n.* (*pl. genera*) group of animals/plants which have common characteristics, and are distinct from all other groups. □ **género**
geocentric [dʒi:əu'sentrik] *adj.* (astronomy, etc.) using the earth as the starting point when measuring distances. □ **geocéntrico**
geography [dʒi'ɔgrəfi] *n.* science of the earth's surface/form/physical features/climate, etc. □ **geografía**
geographer [dʒi'ɔgrəfə] *n.* person who studies geography. □ **geógrafo**
geographic(al) [dʒiə'græfik(l)] *adj.* referring to geography: *a geographical study of the British Isles.* □ **geográfico**
geology [dʒi'ɔlədʒi] *n.* science of the earth's crust, especially rock formations. □ **geología**
geological [dʒiə'lɔdʒikl] *adj.* referring to geology. □ **geológico**
geologist [dʒi'ɔlədʒist] *n.* person who studies geology. □ **geólogo**
geometry [dʒi'ɔmətri] *n.* mathematical science of properties and relations of lines/surfaces/solids, etc., in space. □ **geometría**
geometrical [dʒiə'metrikl] *adj.* referring to geometry: *a geometrical design,* design of lines/curves, etc. □ **geométrico**
geophysics [dʒi:əu'fiziks] *n.* study of the physical properties of the earth. □ **geofísica**
geophysicist *n.* person who studies geophysics. □ **geofísico**
Geordie ['dʒɔ:di] *adj* and *n.* (*informal*) (person) from Newcastle. □ **de Newcastle**
Georgian ['dʒɔ:dʒiən] *adj.* referring to the reigns of George I to George IV (1714-1830), or to the reign of George V (1910-1935). □ **georgiano**
geranium [dʒə'reiniəm] *n.* perennial plant with white, pink or red flowers. □ **geranio**
gerbil ['dʒə:bl] *n.* small desert rat which jumps, and is kept as a pet. □ **gerbo**
geriatrics [dʒeri'ætriks] *n.* (*usually with singular verb*) branch of medical science dealing with old age and its diseases. □ **geriatría**
geriatric *adj.* for old people: *most hospitals have a geriatric ward.* □ **geriátrico**
geriatrician [dʒeriə'triʃn] *n.* doctor specializing in geriatrics. □ **geriatra**
germ [dʒə:m] *n.* **1** portion of organism capable of developing into a new one: *wheat germ.* □ **germen**
2 micro-organism, often causing disease: *we spread germs when we sneeze.* □ **microbio**
germicide *n.* substance which kills germs. □ **germicida**
germinate *v.* (*of seeds*) to begin to grow/to sprout: *seeds germinate best when it is warm and damp.* □ **germinar**
germination [dʒə:mi'neiʃn] *n.* beginning of plant growth from a seed: *the germination of lemon pips can take several weeks.* □ **germinación**
germ warfare *n.* war fought using germs as a weapon. □ **guerra bacteriológica**
germane [dʒə:'mein] *adj.* relevant. □ **pertinente**
Germany ['dʒə:məni] *n.* European country. □ **Alemania**
German *adj.* referring to Germany. □ **alemán**
German measles, mild disease which gives a red rash and which can affect the development of an unborn child if caught by a pregnant woman. □ **rubéola**
German shepherd, *Amer.* Alsatian/large wolf-like dog used as a guard dog. □ **pastor alemán**
■ *n.* **1** person from Germany. □ **alemán**
2 language spoken in Germany, Austria and parts of Switzerland. □ **alemán**
Germanic *adj.* referring to the Germans. □ **germánico**
gerontology [dʒerɔn'tɔlədʒi] *n. problems.* □ **gerontología**
gestation [dʒe'steiʃn] *n.* period between conception and birth: *the gestation period of an elephant is two years.* □ **gestación**
gesticulate [dʒe'stikjuleit] *v.* to make expressive signs with the hands and arms: *he gesticulated wildly to attract his friend's attention.* □ **gesticular**
gesticulation [dʒestikju'leiʃn] *n.* sign with arms or hands: *the deaf and dumb man used gesticulations to make himself understood.* □ **gesticulación**
gesture ['dʒestʃə] *n.* **1** movement of limb or body, especially hands, to give an expression of feeling: *she made a gesture of despair.* □ **gesto**
2 action which expresses some positive feeling: *the government has made a gesture to the rebels.* □ **gesto**
a token gesture, small action which symbolizes feelings. □ **un detalle**
■ *v.* to make a movement to express a feeling: *he*

gestured his agreement with a nod of his head. □ **hacer un ademán**

get [get] *v.* (*he got; he has got; Amer. he has gotten*) **1** to obtain: *he got plenty of coal from the mine; the spoilt child always gets his own way.* □ **obtener**
2 to receive: *I got a letter in the post this morning; the accused got twenty years for murder.* □ **recibir; ...le echaron 20 años**
3 ***to have got,*** to possess: *they've got a large house; you've got that song on the brain,* you think of nothing else. □ **tener**
4 (*informal*) to understand: *I don't get your meaning.* □ **no llego a comprenderlo**
you've got it!, you've found the right answer/you understand correctly. □ **¡correcto!**
5 to cause to happen; to make (someone) do something: *I must get my car serviced; he got his shoes mended; I'll get him to look after you.* □ **me tienen que revisar...; le arreglaron...; haré que...**
6 ***to have got to,*** to be obliged: *you've got to come; I haven't got to agree.* □ **tener que; deber**
7 to arrive: *the train got there on time.* □ **llegar**
8 (*informal*) to start: *let's get going,* let's start now. □ **¡vamos ya!**
9 to catch: *I've got measles/a cold; the police got him a week after the murder.* □ **agarrar**
10 to become: *he's getting too old for the job.* □ **hacerse**
11 to be doing something: *she's getting dressed; they got married last week.* □ **se está vistiendo; se casaron...**

get about *v.* **1** to go from place to place: *she's still getting about at the age of ninety; he can only get about with a stick.* □ **ir de un lado para otro**
2 to be rumoured: *it soon got about that they were going to be divorced.* □ **rumorearse**

get across *v.* **1** to cross (a road): *they got across the river on ropes.* □ **atravesar**
2 to make understood: *he couldn't get the message across to his audience.* □ **hacer comprender**

get along *v.* **1** to manage: *he was getting along nicely by himself.* □ **arreglárselas**
2 ***get along with you!,*** (*informal*) go away; I don't believe you. □ **¡vamos anda!**
3 to be on friendly terms with someone: *they don't get along.* □ **llevarse bien**

get at *v.* **1** to reach: *that box on the top shelf is difficult to get at.* □ **alcanzar**
2 (*informal*) to criticize: *he is always getting at me.* □ **meterse con alguien**

get-at-able *adj.* (*informal*) easy to reach. □ **accesible**

get away *v.* to manage to go away; to escape: *they got away in a stolen car; the burglar got away with all her jewellery.* □ **conseguir marcharse**
to get away with: *he got away with it,* he wasn't found out/no one punished him for it. □ **quedar impune**

getaway *n.* escape: *they made a quick getaway: getaway car,* car used to escape in. □ **escape, fuga**

get back *v.* **1** to return: *we got back (home) at eleven o'clock.* □ **volver**
2 to recover: *they got the jewels back from the burglar.* □ **recuperar**
3 ***to get your own back on someone,*** to have your revenge. □ **vengarse**

get by *v.* **1** to pass: *no one could get by the lorry.* □ **lograr pasar**
2 (*informal*) to manage: *she can't get by on the money you give her,* it isn't enough money for her to live on. □ **arreglárselas**

get down *v.* **1** to descend: *he got down off the table.* □ **bajarse**
2 to fetch down: *can you get me down the box on the top shelf?* □ **bajar**
3 to depress; to make (someone) gloomy: *this bad weather gets me down.* □ **deprimir**
4 to make (something) be written: *get it all down on paper.* □ **anotar**
5 *to get down to some hard work,* to start to work hard. □ **ponerse a trabajar**

get in *v.* **1** to go inside (a car, etc.). □ **subir a**
2 to be elected: *he got in with a tiny majority.* □ **ser elegido**

get into *v.* **1** to go inside (a car, etc.). □ **meterse a**
2 *to get into a temper,* to become angry. □ **enfadarse**
3 *to get into trouble,* to be in a difficult situation. □ **meterse en líos**

get off *v.* **1** to come down from: *he got off his horse; they got off the bus.* □ **bajarse de**
2 *he got off lightly,* he received a light punishment. □ **recibió una pena liviana**

get on *v.* **1** to mount: *he got on his horse; they got on the bus.* □ **montarse**
2 to age: *he is getting on,* he is past middle age. □ **envejecer**
3 to succeed: *he got on so well in the company that he became a director.* □ **progresar**
4 ***to get on with someone,*** to be friendly with someone: *they don't get on,* they don't like each other. □ **llevarse bien**

get out *v.* **1** to bring out/to go out: *get out your dictionary; he got the car out of the garage; to get a book out of the library.* □ **sacar**
get out!, leave the room. □ **¡fuera!**
2 *I've got out of the habit of eating chocolates,* I don't eat chocolates any more. □ **me he quitado el hábito de...**
3 to avoid doing something: *how can I get out of paying?* □ **librarse de**

get over *v.* **1** to surmount/to overcome: *he got over his handicap.* □ **superar**
2 to recover from: *she got over her illness quickly; he'll never get over the shock.* □ **reponerse**
3 to climb over: *the burglar got over the wall.* □ **pasar por encima**

get round *v.* **1** to go round (a corner). □ **dar la vuelta a**
2 to persuade (someone) to do something: *she got round her mother by giving her flowers.* □ **persuadir**
3 to find time to do something: *I will get round to doing it next week.* □ **encontrar tiempo**

get through *v.* **1** to pass: *the bill got through the House of Commons; he got through his driving test.* □ **aprobar**
2 to manage to get in contact with someone: *he got through to the switchboard.* □ **conseguir comunicar**

get-together *n.* (*informal*) meeting. □ **reunión**

get up *v.* **1** to rise (from a sitting or lying position): *I always get up at seven o'clock,* I always get out of bed; *he fell down and couldn't get up again.* □ **levantarse**
2 to organize: *he is getting up a petition.* □ **organizar**
3 ***to get up to mischief,*** to do something wicked. □ **hacer de las suyas**

geyser ['giːzə] *n.* **1** hot spring of water. □ **géiser**
2 apparatus for heating water. □ **calentador de agua**

Ghana ['gɑːnə] *n.* West African country. □ **Ghana**
Ghanaian *adj.* and *n.* (person) from Ghana. □ **ghanés**

ghastly ['gɑːstli] *adj.* (*ghastlier, ghastliest*) horrible/

frightful: *what ghastly weather we are having!* □ **horrible**

gherkin ['gəːkin] *n.* small vegetable of the cucumber family, used for pickling. □ **pepinillo**

ghetto ['getou] *n.* (*pl. ghettoes*) area in a city where deprived people live. □ **ghetto**

ghost [goust] *n.* **1** spirit of a dead person: *Anne Boleyn's ghost is said to haunt the Tower of London.* □ **fantasma**

ghost story, story about ghosts which aims at frightening the reader. □ **cuento de fantasmas**

not the ghost of a chance, no chance at all. □ **ni la más remota posibilidad**

2 ***the Holy Ghost,*** third person of the Christian Trinity. □ **el Espíritu Santo**

3 person who writes a book for someone who then takes the credit. □ **un negro**

■ *v.* to write (book/article/speech, etc.) for someone else who then takes the credit: *many famous people have had their autobiographies ghosted.* □ **escribir por otro**

ghostly *adj.* (*ghostlier, ghostliest*) like a ghost: *the old man in his pale dressing-gown had a ghostly appearance.* □ **fantasmal**

ghost writer *n.* person who writes a book for someone else who then takes the credit. □ **un negro**

ghoul [guːl] *n.* evil ghost which haunts graves. □ **espíritu de cementerio**

ghoulish ['guːliʃ] *adj.* weird/bloodthirsty: *he read a ghoulish story of corpses rising from their graves.* □ **tremebundo**

giant ['dʒaiənt] *n.* **1** (*in fairy tales and myths*) being of human shape but of huge size: *Jack kills the giant in 'Jack and the Beanstalk'.* □ **gigante**

2 abnormally tall person, animal or plant. □ **gigante**

3 very powerful industrial organization: *a chemical giant.* □ **gigante**

4 extremely able person: *one of the giants of modern literature.* □ **gigante**

■ *adj.* very large: *a giant fig tree grew in the garden.* □ **gigante**

gibber ['dʒibə] *v.* to speak very fast and without any meaning: *he gibbered like an ape.* □ **farfullar**

gibberish ['dʒibriʃ] *n.* (*no pl.*) unintelligible speech/meaningless talk: *he spoke utter gibberish.* □ **galimatías**

gibbet ['dʒibit] *n.* gallows/structure on which criminals were hanged. □ **horca**

gibbon ['gibən] *n.* long-armed ape. □ **gibón**

gibe [dʒaib] *n.* sarcastic remark: *he replied with a gibe.* □ **pulla**

■ *v.* to jeer/to mock. □ **mofarse de**

giblets ['dʒibləts] *n. pl.* liver/heart, etc., of birds/poultry, removed before the bird is cooked. □ **menudillos**

giddy ['gidi] *adj.* (*giddier, giddiest*) dizzy; liable to spin round or stagger; feeling as if everything is spinning round: *when I stepped off the roundabout I felt giddy.* □ **mareado**

giddiness *n.* dizzy feeling: *he experienced a feeling of giddiness through lack of oxygen at the top of the mountain.* □ **mareo**

gift [gift] *n.* **1** present/something given: *on leaving he made a gift of a silver cup to the school.* □ **regalo**

gift token, card which is given as a present, and which allows the person who receives it to buy something at a shop. □ **cheque-regalo**

2 talent: *she has a gift for music.* □ **dote**

■ *v.* to give/to endow: *a thousand pounds was gifted to the College in the Principal's will.* □ **donar**

gifted *adj.* talented: *gifted children sometimes go to special schools.* □ **dotado; los niños superdotados...**

gift-wrap *v.* (*he gift-wrapped*) to wrap (something) in coloured paper to give as a present. □ **envolver como regalo**

gig [gig] *n.* **1** light carriage on two wheels. □ **calesa**

2 (*slang*) performance by popular musicians: *the group did three gigs in Glasgow.* □ **actuación**

gigantic [dʒai'gæntik] *adj.* huge/colossal: *the child built a gigantic castle of bricks.* □ **gigantesco**

giggle ['gigl] *n.* little nervous laugh: *to have a fit of the giggles,* to be unable to stop giggling. □ **risita tonta**

■ *v.* to laugh nervously/not to laugh out loud: *the girls giggled when the teacher dropped her glasses.* □ **reírse tontamente**

gild [gild] *v.* to cover with a thin layer of gold: *the cathedral spires were gilded.* □ **dorar**

gill [dʒil] *n.* liquid measure equal to a quarter of a pint (140 ml). □ **un cuarto de pinta**

gills [gilz] *n. pl.* **1** breathing organs in fish and other aquatic creatures: *a fish's gills can be seen to open and close.* □ **agallas**

2 thin vertical folds on the underside of mushrooms. □ **membrana**

gilt [gilt] *adj.* covered with a thin layer of gold: *a gilt cross.* □ **dorado**

■ *n.* young female pig. □ **cerda joven**

gilt-edged *adj.* (investment) which will not lose its value. □ **de máxima garantía**

gimcrack ['dʒimkræk] *adj.* cheap and badly made. □ **chapucero**

gimlet ['gimlət] *n.* small tool used for boring holes. □ **barrena de mano**

gimmick ['gimik] *n.* device adopted for the purpose of attracting attention or publicity. □ **truco publicitario**

gin [dʒin] *n.* **1** colourless alcoholic drink flavoured with juniper; glass of this spirit: *two gins, please.* □ **ginebra**

2 trap for catching wild animals and game: *the hare was caught in a gin.* □ **trampa**

ginger ['dʒindʒə] *n.* plant with a hot-tasting root used in cooking and medicine: *some people like ground ginger with melon.* □ **jengibre**

■ *adj.* (hair) of reddish colour: *the man with the ginger beard.* □ **rojizo**

gingerbread *n.* cake made with treacle and flavoured with ginger. □ **pan de jengibre**

ginger ale, ginger beer *n.* fizzy ginger-flavoured drink. □ **gaseosa de jengibre**

gingerly *adj.* cautious. □ **cauteloso**

■ *adv.* delicately/with caution: *she gingerly picked up the dead mouse.* □ **cautelosamente**

ginger up *v.* to stimulate/to arouse: *the director gingered up the actors in an effort to get them to do better.* □ **animar**

gingham ['giŋəm] *n.* checked cotton cloth. □ **guinga**

gingivitis [dʒindʒi'vaitis] *n.* swelling and bleeding of the gums. □ **gingivitis**

gipsy ['dʒipsi] *n.* (*pl. gipsies*) member of a wandering race: *gipsies travel about the country in caravans and never stay long in one place.* □ **gitano**

giraffe [dʒi'rɑːf] *n.* African animal with a very long neck and spotted skin. □ **jirafa**

gird [gəːd] *v.* (*formal*) to tie a belt round (something). □ **ceñir**

girder ['gəːdə] *n.* iron/steel beam used as a support: *girders are used in the construction of bridges.* □ **viga**

girdle ['gəːdl] *n.* **1** belt/sash: *the princess wore a golden girdle.* □ **cinturón**

2 corset: *with the help of a girdle she managed to look quite thin.* □ **faja**
3 *pelvic girdle,* bones around the hips supporting the lower limbs. □ **cavidad pelviana**
girl [gɜːl] *n.* female child; young woman: *girls' school.* □ **niña; chica**
girlfriend *n.* female companion (especially of a man): *he took his girlfriend out to the cinema.* □ **novia**
Girl Guides *n. pl.* social/training organization for girls: *she's joined the Girl Guides.* □ **'Girl Guides'**
girlie *adj. **girlie magazine,*** (*informal*) one with photographs of naked girls. □ **revista de desnudos**
girlish *adj.* like a young girl: *the middle-aged woman had her hair done in a girlish way.* □ **de niña; juvenil**
giro ['dʒairou] *n.* (*also **National Girobank***) banking system (in Britain run by the Post Office) in which money can be transferred directly from one account to another without writing a cheque. □ **giro postal (en Correos); transferencia bancaria**
girth [gɜːθ] *n.* **1** circumference/distance round something: *to measure the girth of a tree.* □ **circunferencia**
2 band of leather or cloth tied round the body of a horse to secure the saddle. □ **cincha**
gist [dʒist] *n.* real point of a matter; basic essentials: *the newspaper gave the gist of the Prime Minister's speech in a few lines.* □ **quid; lo esencial**
give [giv] *v.* (*he gave; he has given*) **1** to hand (something) to someone; to transfer (something) to someone: *give me another apple; he gave her a birthday present; she gave me a smack in the face; that lamp gives a poor light.* □ **dar**
2 to speak/to utter: *she gave a shriek; he gave an answer.* □ **dar; expresar**
3 to collapse; to bend: *the bridge gave under the weight of the traffic.* □ **derrumbarse; combarse**
■ *n.* **1** suppleness: *the plank hasn't enough give.* □ **flexibilidad**
2 ***give and take,*** agreement between two people/parties to make concessions. □ **toma y daca**
give away *v.* **1** to hand over (something) without asking for anything in return: *he gave all his fortune away.* □ **regalar**
2 to betray/to tell (a secret): *the spy gave himself away when he started speaking Japanese,* revealed he was a spy. □ **traicionar**
give back *v.* to return: *I must give you back the book I borrowed from you.* □ **devolver**
give in *v.* to surrender/to yield. □ **ceder**
given *adj.* **1** *she is given to crying,* she cries frequently. □ **propenso, dado**
2 particular/which has been identified: *in a given case.* □ **en un determinado caso**
3 ***given name,*** first name/Christian name. □ **nombre de pila**
give off *v.* to let out: *the fire gives off a lot of heat.* □ **desprender**
give out *v.* **1** to distribute: *he gave out the books to all the class.* □ **repartir**
2 (*informal*) to fail: *the brakes have given out.* □ **fallar**
3 to make known: *to give out notices/information.* □ **dar a conocer**
give up *v.* **1** to stop (doing something)/to abandon: *he has given up his job; he's trying to give up smoking; I give up!,* I cannot think of the answer. □ **renunciar (empleo); dejar de (fumar)**
2 *the murderer gave himself up,* surrendered to the police. □ **entregarse**
give way *v.* **1** to allow someone to go first: *give way to cars coming from the right.* □ **ceder el paso**
2 to yield; to bend; to collapse: *he refused to agree but in the end gave way; the bridge gave way under the weight of the traffic.* □ **ceder**
gizzard ['gizəd] *n.* second stomach of a bird, where its food is ground up into tiny pieces. □ **molleja**
glacé ['glæsei] *adj.* preserved in sugar: *glacé cherries.* □ **escarchado**
glacier ['glæsiə] *n.* mass of ice which slowly moves down from a mountain. □ **glaciar**
glacial ['gleiʃl] *adj.* **1** referring to ice: *the glacial period was when the northern hemisphere was mostly covered with ice.* □ **glacial**
2 very cold; without emotion: *a glacial expression.* □ **glacial**
glaciation [gleisi'eiʃn] *n.* effect of ice on rocks. □ **glaciación**
glad [glæd] *adj.* pleased/happy: *I'm glad to see you.* □ **contento**
gladden *v.* to make glad. □ **alegrar**
gladly *adv.* happily: *she gladly accepted the offer.* □ **alegremente**
gladness *n.* happiness. □ **gozo; alegría**
glade [gleid] *n.* (*formal*) clear open space in the midst of trees: *they came to a leafy glade in the middle of the forest.* □ **calvero**
gladiolus [glædi'ouləs] *n.* (*pl. gladioli*) tall garden plant with sword-shaped leaves and bright flower spikes: *a bed of gladioli.* □ **gladiolo**
glamour ['glæmə] *Amer.* **glamor** *n.* **1** magic/enchantment: *the glamour of the theatre.* □ **'glamour'**
2 outward charm/attractiveness (of a woman). □ **'glamour'**
glamorize *v.* to make something appear more appealing than it really is: *he tended to glamorize his life in the navy.* □ **idealizar**
glamorous *adj.* attractive/enchanting: *the life of a film star can be glamorous.* □ **glamoroso**
glance [glɑːns] *n.* quick look: *he gave a sideways glance.* □ **vistazo**
■ *v.* **1** to look briefly: *he glanced at the menu.* □ **echar un vistazo**
2 to glide off an object instead of striking it fully: *the ball glanced off the cricket bat.* □ **golpear con efecto**
glancing *adj.* sliding off to the side; not straight: *he struck the tree a glancing blow with his axe.* □ **oblicuo**
gland [glænd] *n.* organ of the body which produces a liquid which controls bodily changes, such as growth: *the thyroid gland.* □ **glándula**
glandular ['glændjulə] *adj.* referring to glands. □ **glandular**
glandular fever, severe illness which affects the glands. □ **fiebre glandular**
glare ['glɛə] *n.* **1** strong/fierce light: *the glare of the car's headlights dazzled me.* □ **luz deslumbradora**
2 fierce/fixed look: *the naughty boy received a glare from his teacher.* □ **mirada feroz**
■ *v.* **1** to shine too brightly: *the sun was glaring all day.* □ **brillar**
2 to look angrily: *she glared at her mother.* □ **mirar airadamente**
glaring *adj. glaring mistake,* mistake that is very obvious. □ **evidente**
glass [glɑːs] *n.* **1** substance made from sand and soda or potash, usually transparent, used for making windows, etc.: *she did not see the doors, which were made of glass.* □ **cristal**
2 vessel made of glass used especially for drinking;

contents of such a glass: *he drank a glass of wine; a wine glass,* one used especially for drinking wine. □ **vaso**
3 barometer. □ **barómetro**
4 ***looking glass,*** mirror. □ **espejo**
5 ***stained glass,*** coloured glass used frequently in the windows of a church. □ **vidriera**
glass blower *n.* someone who blows and shapes molten glass into bottles, etc. □ **soplador de vidrio**
glasses *n. pl.* spectacles: *he has to wear glasses for reading; dark glasses.* □ **gafas**
glass fibre *n.* strong material made of woven fibres of glass; plastic containing fibres of glass. □ **fibra de vidrio**
glasshouse *n.* **1** greenhouse/shelter made of glass and wood or metal, for the cultivation of plants. □ **invernadero**
people who live in glasshouses shouldn't throw stones, people who have done something wrong should beware of criticizing others. □ **el que más razones tiene para callar es el que siempre habla**
2 (*slang*) military prison. □ **la trena; presidio**
glassware *n.* (*no pl.*) articles made of glass. □ **cristalería**
glassy *adj.* **1** resembling glass. □ **vítreo**
2 dull/unseeing: *a glassy stare.* □ **vidrioso**
glaucoma [glɔːˈkoumə] *n.* disease of the eyes which can cause blindness. □ **glaucoma**
glaze [gleiz] *v.* **1** to fit with glass; to put glass in (a window): *the conservatory is to be glazed next week.* □ **poner cristales**
2 to cover with a shiny coating: *the pot was glazed before firing.* □ **vidriar**
glazier [ˈgleiziə] *n.* person whose trade is to fit glass in windows, etc. □ **cristalero**
glazing *n.* fitting with windows: *the glazing of the dolls' house was a tricky job.* □ **acristalamiento**
double glazing, windows with two sheets of glass a small distance apart, which help insulation. □ **ventana de cristal doble**
gleam [gliːm] *n.* **1** shortlived weak light: *a thin gleam of light showed under the door.* □ **destello**
2 faint/temporary show of some quality: *a gleam of hope; an occasional gleam of humour.* □ **un resquicio de esperanza; pizca de humor**
■ *v.* to shine: *the cat's eyes gleamed in the dark.* □ **brillar**
glean [gliːn] *v.* to collect (grain left after the harvest); to scrape together (news/information, etc.): *he gleaned what information he could from the garbled reports.* □ **espigar; recoger datos**
gleanings *n. pl.* odd bits of information. □ **notas; datos**
glee [gliː] *n.* joy/gaiety: *full of glee.* □ **júbilo**
gleeful *adj.* joyful. □ **jubiloso**
gleefully *adv.* happily: *the little girl ran gleefully to meet her father.* □ **con júbilo**
glen [glen] *n.* (*in Scotland*) narrow valley. □ **cañada**
glib [glib] *adj.* fluent but insincere way of speaking: *I don't trust him - he's a glib speaker.* □ **de mucha labia e insincero**
glibly *adv.* smoothly and insincerely. □ **con poca sinceridad**
glide [glaid] *n.* smooth movement. □ **deslizamiento**
■ *v.* to move smoothly: *the swan glided through the water; the ballerina was gliding across the stage.* □ **deslizarse**
glider *n.* small aircraft without an engine that relies on wind currents for propulsion. □ **planeador**
gliding *n.* sport of flying gliders: *some people practise gliding as a hobby.* □ **vuelo sin motor**
glimmer [ˈglimə] *n.* **1** feeble light: *a glimmer of light shone from the cottage window.* □ **luz tenue**
2 tiny quantity; faint/temporary show of some quality: *there was a glimmer of hope that the patient might recover,* there was a slight hope. □ **pizca; un rayo (de)**
■ *v.* to shine feebly/intermittently: *the candle glimmered through the night.* □ **rielar**
glimpse [glimps] *n.* quick/passing view: *to catch a glimpse.* □ **vislumbre**
■ *v.* to catch sight of (something): *he glimpsed his friend running through the crowd.* □ **vislumbrar**
glint [glint] *n.* flash/glitter/sparkle: *the glint of steel on steel; she had a glint in her eye.* □ **destello**
■ *v.* to flash/to glitter (like metal): *the gold cross on the steeple glinted in the sun.* □ **destellar**
glisten [ˈglisn] *v.* (*of something wet*) to shine/to sparkle: *the wet leaves glistened in the sunlight.* □ **relucir**
glitter [ˈglitə] *n.* bright light/sparkle: *the glitter of sunlight on the water.* □ **rutilancia**
■ *v.* to shine brightly/to sparkle: *her diamond rings glittered in the candlelight.* □ **rutilar**
gloat [glout] *v.* ***to gloat over,*** to take pleasure (in someone's misfortune); to look at (something) greedily: *the miser gloated over his money.* □ **recrearse con**
globe [gloub] *n.* **1** ***the globe,*** the earth. □ **el globo**
2 ball with a map of the world on it: *the geography teacher used a globe to show his pupils the continents.* □ **el globo terráqueo**
3 round object; glass ball which covers an electric light bulb. □ **globo**
globe artichoke, tall green thistle-like plant of which you eat parts of the flower head. □ **alcachofa**
global *adj.* worldwide. □ **mundial**
globetrotter *n.* tourist who travels all over the world. □ **trotamundos**
globule [ˈglɔbjuːl] *n.* small round object (such as a drop of water, etc.): *globules of water collected on the window sill.* □ **glóbulo**
globular *adj.* shaped like a globe: *the stone was globular in shape.* □ **globular**
gloom [gluːm] *n.* **1** darkness/obscurity: *the gloom of a November day.* □ **lobreguez**
2 despair/melancholy: *gloom descended on them as they waited for the bad news.* □ **abatimiento**
gloomy *adj.* (*gloomier, gloomiest*) pessimistic: *a pessimist takes a gloomy view of things; a gloomy forecast.* □ **desalentador**
glory [ˈglɔːri] *n.* (*pl. glories*) **1** fame/renown: *the glory of victory in battle.* □ **gloria**
2 magnificent sight: *the glory of the roses in full bloom.* □ **belleza**
■ *v.* (*gloried; glorying*) to glory in, to get great pleasure from/to pride oneself on: *he gloried in his success.* □ **enorgullecerse**
glorification [glɔːrifiˈkeiʃn] *n.* transforming into something more splendid. □ **glorificación**
glorify *v.* (*glorified; glorifying*) to make glorious/to transform into something more splendid: *she glorified the memory of her dead mother.* □ **glorificar**
glorious [ˈglɔːriəs] *adj.* splendid: *flowers with glorious colours; we had glorious weather for our holidays.* □ **glorioso; radiante (tiempo)**
gloss [glɔs] *n.* **1** shine on a surface; showy appearance. □ **brillo**
gloss paint, paint which is shiny when dry. □ **pintura de brillo**
2 comment about a text. □ **glosa**
■ *v.* ***to gloss over something,*** to try to hide (a mis-

take, etc.). □ **encubrir**
glossy *adj.* and *n.* (*glossier, glossiest*) *glossy magazines/glossies,* colourful, expensive magazines printed on shiny paper. □ **revista cara**
glossary ['glɔsəri] *n.* (*pl. glossaries*) short explanation of meanings of words, usually found at the end of a book. □ **glosario**
glove [glʌv] *n.* article of clothing worn on the hand: *rubber gloves; silk gloves.* □ **guante**
to handle someone with kid gloves, to deal gently with someone. □ **tratar con mucho cuidado**
hand in glove with someone, closely associated with someone: *the Foreign Secretary was hand in glove with the Prime Minister.* □ **ser uña y carne**
glove compartment, small cupboard on the dashboard of a car, in which you can put small items. □ **guantera**
glow [glou] *n.* **1** brightness/warmth: *the fire's glow.* □ **resplandor**
2 blush/bloom: *the cold air brought a glow to her cheeks.* □ **rubor**
■ *v.* to shine; to show warm colour: *he glowed with health, she was glowing with pride.* □ **rebosar de**
glowing *adj.* shining/warm: *glowing praise; glowing colours.* □ **vivo**
glow-worm *n.* female beetle which gives off a green light in the dark. □ **luciérnaga**
glower ['glauə] *v.* to frown: *the old man glowered at the frightened boy.* □ **mirar frunciendo el ceño**
glucose ['glu:kouz] *n.* natural sugar found in fruit: *glucose gives you energy.* □ **glucosa**
glue [glu:] *n.* substance which will stick things together: *she mended the broken cup with a strong glue; it's no use mending china with paper glue.* □ **pegamento**
■ *v.* **1** to stick together: *he glued the pieces together.* □ **pegar**
2 *she sat* ***glued to*** *the TV set all evening,* watching the TV without going away from it. □ **estuvo pegada a la TV**
glum [glʌm] *adj.* (*glummer, glummest*) sullen; looking dejected/miserable: *he wore a glum expression as he gave out the bad news; a glum outlook on life.* □ **sombrío**
glumly *adv.* miserably: *she sat glumly in the dentist's waiting room.* □ **tristemente**
glut [glʌt] *n.* too much of (something); supply exceeding demand: *a glut of potatoes on the market.* □ **exceso**
■ *v.* ***to be glutted (with),*** to have too much: *the markets are glutted with cheap potatoes.* □ **estar inundado**
gluten ['glu:tən] *n.* protein left when starch is removed from flour. □ **gluten**
glutinous ['glu:tinəs] *adj.* sticky. □ **pegajoso**
glutton ['glʌtn] *n.* **1** someone who eats too much: *the fat boy is a glutton.* □ **glotón**
2 person with great enthusiasm for something: *he's a glutton for hard work.* □ **entusiasta**
gluttonous *adj.* referring to overeating: *a gluttonous appetite.* □ **glotón**
glycerine ['glisəri:n] *Amer.* **glycerin** *n.* colourless, sweet liquid (used in medicines/in explosives, etc.). □ **glicerina**
gnarled [nɑ:ld] *adj.* twisted/rugged; covered with hard lumps: *the gnarled old oak tree; gnarled hands.* □ **rugoso (árbol); deforme (mano)**
gnash [næʃ] *v.* to grind (the teeth): *he gnashed his teeth in fury.* □ **hacer rechinar**
gnat [næt] *n.* small, two-winged fly/mosquito which stings: *it's irritating to be bitten by gnats.* □ **mosquito**
gnaw [nɔ:] *v.* to chew: *the dog gnawed the bone.* □ **roer**
gnome [noum] *n.* dwarf/mischievous ugly little man (in fairy stories): *young children enjoy stories about gnomes and fairies.* □ **gnomo**
the gnomes of Zurich, (*informal*) Swiss international bankers. □ **banqueros suizos**
gnu [nu:] *n.* large antelope, rather like an elk. □ **ñu**
go [gou] *n.* (*pl. goes*) **1** act of moving: *he's always on the go,* (*informal*) always moving about. □ **movimiento**
2 (*informal*) energy: *she's full of go.* □ **energía**
3 attempt/try: *he blew out the candles at one go; he had three goes, and still couldn't do it.* □ **intento**
4 *to try to make a go of it,* to try to make the business successful. □ **intentar salir adelante**
■ *v.* (*he went; he has gone*) **1** to move from one place to another; to travel: *he has gone to New York; this path goes to the church; are you going to the party? they all went across the street; he goes to school by bus; he's gone fishing; there's only ten minutes to go before the film starts.* □ **ir**
2 to work: *my watch won't go; things are not going too badly.* □ **mi reloj no funciona; ...no marchan demasiado mal**
3 to leave: *it's time for us to go.* □ **marcharse**
from the word go, from the start. □ **desde el principio**
4 to intend to do something; to be about to do something: *the tower is going to collapse; I am going to have my dinner now.* □ **ir a**
5 to fit: *the parcels are too big to go into the letter box.* □ **caber**
6 to become: *I think I am going mad; when she saw the blood she went pale.* □ **volverse, ponerse**
7 to make a noise: *the guns went bang.* □ **sonar, hacer ruido**
8 to have a certain tune/certain words: *how does the song go?* □ **¿cómo es la canción?**
9 to fail: *the brakes went as the car started down the hill.* □ **fallar**
go about *v.* **1** to try to do something/to plan how to do something: *how do you go about it?* □ **tratar, hacer**
2 (*of sailing boat*) to turn to sail in another direction. □ **virar**
3 to move around: *he goes about in a wheelchair.* □ **moverse**
go ahead *v.* to start to do something: *the director has said we can go ahead with the building plans.* □ **empezar con**
go-ahead *n.* permission to start: *the director has given us the go-ahead.* □ **vía libre**
■ *adj.* enterprising; active: *a very go-ahead firm.* □ **emprendedor**
go along with *v.* to agree with (someone). □ **estar de acuerdo con**
go back *v.* to return: *he went back to fetch his coat.* □ **volver**
go back on *v.* not to keep (a promise). □ **faltar a la palabra**
go-between *n.* person who carries messages from one person to another. □ **mensajero**
go-cart *n.* flat wooden frame with four wheels for children to play with. □ **carrito de juguete**
go down *v.* **1** to descend: *he went down the stairs.* □ **bajar**
2 to be accepted: *the suggestion went down well.* □ **caer**

go for *v.* **1** to apply for: *I'm going for the job.* □ **solicitar**
2 to like: *she doesn't go for his style of acting.* □ **gustar; no le va su estilo de...**
3 to be sold: *tomatoes are going for 30p a pound.* □ **venderse; los tomates están a...**
4 to attack: *he went for him with his fists.* □ **ir hacia**
go-getter *n.* (*informal*) energetic, ambitious person. □ **ambicioso**
go-go dancer *n.* (*informal*) person who performs an energetic (and usually erotic) dance in a night-club, etc. □ **chica 'go go'**
go in *v.* **1** to enter: *he opened the door and went in.* □ **entrar**
2 *the sun's gone in,* is hidden by clouds. □ **meterse**
go in for *v.* to enter (for a test/examination, etc.): *three candidates went in for the examination.* □ **presentarse**
going *adj.* **1** working: *the shop is being sold as a going concern.* □ **que funciona bien**
2 ***going rate,*** usual rate/current rate. □ **cambio actual**
■ *n.* **1** surface of a race track: *the going is hard.* □ **piso**
2 *do it* ***while the going is good,*** while you have the chance. □ **hazlo mientras la cosa vaya bien**
3 ***goings-on,*** unusual things which are happening. □ **tejemanejes**
go into *v.* **1** to enter: *he went into the room.* □ **entrar**
2 (*in maths*) to divide: *four goes into sixteen four times; sixty into forty won't go.* □ **dividir**
3 to examine: *we will go into the question of payment.* □ **examinar a fondo**
go-kart *n.* flat frame with four wheels and an engine, used as a small racing car. □ **'kart'**
go off *v.* **1** to explode: *the firework went off in his face.* □ **explotar**
2 to turn bad: *the meat's gone off.* □ **estropearse**
3 to dislike: *I've gone off him,* I used to like him, but now I don't. □ **dejar de gustar**
go on *v.* **1** to continue: *don't stop - go on!* □ **continuar**
2 *go on!,* (*showing disbelief*) (*informal*) I don't believe you! □ **¡venga!**
3 to happen: *what's going on here?* □ **¿qué sucede aquí?**
4 to talk all the time; to nag: *he's always going on about his cats; she goes on at her husband from morning to night.* □ **hablar**
go out *v.* **1** to leave: *she went out of the room.* □ **salir**
2 to be shut off; to die: *the lights went out; the fire's gone out.* □ **apagarse**
go out with *v.* to go to parties/the cinema, etc., with (someone of the opposite sex): *he's going out with my sister.* □ **salir con**
go round *v.* **1** to turn: *the wheels go round and round.* □ **dar vueltas**
2 to be enough: *is there enough food to go round?* □ **¿hay comida para todos?**
3 to visit: *he went round to his mother's for tea.* □ **pasarse por**
go-slow *n.* slowing down of production by the workers as a protest. □ **huelga de celo**
go under *v.* to drown; to be ruined. □ **hundirse**
go up *v.* **1** to rise: *he went up the stairs; food prices are going up.* □ **subir**
2 *the house went up in flames,* the house blazed. □ **la casa ardió**
go with *v.* to match/to fit with: *the brown curtains don't go with the blue carpet.* □ **ir con**
go without *v.* not to have: *we will have to go without sugar.* □ **pasarse sin**
goad [goud] *n.* long stick for driving cattle. □ **aguijada**
■ *v.* to urge/to drive on by annoyance: *he was goaded into battle by the jeers of the enemy.* □ **incitar**
goal [goul] *n.* **1** object of effort/ambition; aim: *his goal in life was to make a fortune.* □ **meta**
2 two posts between which a ball has to be driven to score a point in a game: *a football pitch has a goal at each end.* □ **portería**
3 points won (in football/hockey, etc.): *the winning team scored four goals.* □ **gol**
goalkeeper, goalie *n.* player who defends the goal. □ **portero**
goalmouth *n.* area just in front of the goal. □ **área de meta**
goalpost *n.* one of the two posts between which a ball is driven to score a goal. □ **poste**
goat [gout] *n.* domestic animal with horns and a beard: *people often keep goats for their milk.* □ **cabra**
to separate the sheep from the goats, to divide the good from the bad. □ **seleccionar los buenos**
to get someone's goat, (*informal*) to annoy someone. □ **sacar de quicio a alguien**
goatee [gou'tiː] *n.* small beard, like that of a goat. □ **perilla**
gob [gɔb] *n.* (*slang*) mouth: *shut your gob!,* stop talking! □ **boca**
gobble ['gɔbl] *v.* **1** to eat quickly and greedily: *he gobbled down his lunch.* □ **engullir**
2 to make a noise like a turkey: *the turkeys were gobbling in the yard.* □ **gluglutear**
gobbledegook ['gɔbldiguk] *n.* (*informal*) meaningless official/technical language. □ **jerigonza**
goblet ['gɔblət] *n.* metal or glass drinking cup without handles. □ **copa**
goblin ['gɔblin] *n.* (*in fairy stories*) mischievous ugly little man. □ **duende**
god [gɔd] *n.* **1** deity; superhuman power: *they worshipped Thor as the god of thunder.* □ **dios**
2 ***God,*** creator and ruler of the Universe, according to Christian/Jewish/Muslim, etc., belief: *God created man.* □ **Dios**
godchildren *n. pl.* children who were sponsored at baptism. □ **ahijados**
god-daughter *n.* girl who was sponsored at baptism. □ **ahijada**
goddess *n.* female god. □ **diosa**
godfather *n.* man who sponsors a child at baptism. □ **padrino**
god-fearing *adj.* sincerely religious. □ **temeroso de Dios**
godforsaken *adj.* bad/awful: *this godforsaken corner of the earth.* □ **dejado de la mano de Dios**
godliness *n.* being godly. □ **piedad**
godly *adj.* (*godlier, godliest*) holy: *the priest was a godly man.* □ **piadoso**
godmother *n.* woman who sponsors a child at baptism. □ **madrina**
godparents *n. pl.* people who sponsor a child at baptism. □ **padrinos**
godsend *n.* blessing: *the gift of money was a godsend to the bankrupt hospital.* □ **don del cielo**
godson *n.* boy who was sponsored at baptism. □ **ahijado**
goggle ['gɔgl] *v.* to stare: *the small boy goggled at the military parade.* □ **mirar con ojos desorbitados**
goggle-box *n.* (*informal*) television. □ **tele**

goggles *n. pl.* protective spectacles against dust and glare: *divers wear goggles to see under water.* □ **gafas**

goitre [gɔitə] *Amer.* **goiter** *n.* disease in which the thyroid gland in the neck swells up. □ **bocio**

gold [gould] *n.* **1** (*chemical element*: Au) precious yellow metal: *he asked to be paid in gold.* □ **oro**
2 medal made of gold (won in a sports competition): *France won three golds.* □ **medallas de oro**
■ *adj.* made of gold: *the box contained gold coins.* □ **de oro**
gold leaf, thin covering of gold: *the books were edged in gold leaf.* □ **pan de oro**
gold plate, dishes made of gold. □ **vajilla de oro**
gold-digger *n.* **1** person who digs for gold. □ **buscador de oro**
2 (*informal*) woman who marries a man for his money. □ **una interesada**
golden *adj.* made of gold; gold-coloured: *the princess had golden hair.* □ **dorado; ...pelo rubio**
a golden opportunity, a wonderful chance. □ **una oportunidad de oro**
a golden rule, a very important rule. □ **regla de oro**
golden wedding, fiftieth anniversary of marriage. □ **bodas de oro**
golden handshake, sum of money presented when you leave work. □ **generosa indemnización**
golden disc, golden record given to someone whose record has sold one million copies. □ **disco de oro**
goldfinch *n.* brightly coloured song bird. □ **jilguero**
goldfish *n.* (*no pl.*) small orange fish kept in ponds/bowls. □ **pez de colores**
goldsmith *n.* person who works in gold. □ **orfebre**

golf [gɔlf] *n.* game for two people, or two couples, where a small hard ball is struck with long-handled clubs into a series of holes, the object being to use as few strokes as possible. □ **golf**
golf club *n.* **1** wooden-/metal-headed implement for striking the golf ball. □ **palo de golf**
2 group of people who play golf, and allow others to join them on payment of a fee; clubhouse where golfers meet. □ **club de golf**
golf course *n.* piece of ground on which golf is played. □ **campo de golf**
golfer *n.* person who plays golf. □ **golfista**

golliwog ['gɔliwɔg] *n.* doll like a man with a black face and curly black hair. □ **negrito (muñeco)**

gondola ['gɔndələ] *n.* **1** boat used on the canals in Venice. □ **góndola**
2 basket/passenger compartment hanging underneath a balloon. □ **barquilla**
gondolier [gɔndə'liə] *n.* man who pushes a gondola, using a pole. □ **gondolero**

gone [gɔn] *v. see* **go.**

gong [gɔŋ] *n.* **1** metal disc with a turned rim which gives a resonant sound when struck, used especially to call people to meals: *to sound the gong.* □ **gong**
2 (*slang*) medal. □ **medalla**

gonna [gɔnə] *v.* (*slang*) going to: *I'm gonna get to the police.* □ **yo voy a, tú vas a, etc.**

goo [gu:] *n.* (*informal*) (*no pl.*) sticky stuff. □ **sustancia pegajosa**
gooey *adj.* (*informal*) sticky. □ **pegajoso**

good [gud] *adj.* (*the comparative and superlative are* ***better/best***) **1** having the right qualities/satisfactory: *the child had a good report from school; that was a good meal.* □ **bueno**
2 *did you* ***have a good time?,*** did you enjoy yourself? □ **¿te lo pasaste bien?**
3 able: *he is good at French; she is good with her hands; he's a very good footballer.* □ **bueno**
4 right/proper: *it is a good idea to think before speaking.* □ **es una buena idea...**
5 morally excellent/virtuous: *he is a good man.* □ **bueno**
6 well behaved/not troublesome: *what a good girl you are!* □ **¡qué buena chica eres!**
as good as gold, exceptionally well behaved. □ **más bueno que el pan**
7 efficient/suitable/competent: *she's not a very good secretary; she has always been a good wife to him.* □ **bueno**
8 *he was* ***as good as his word,*** he did what he said he would do. □ **cumplió su palabra**
9 ***good morning! good afternoon! good evening!*** interjections used when meeting or leaving someone in the morning, afternoon or evening. □ **¡buenos días, buenas tardes, buenas noches!**
10 valid/sound/thorough: *he had a good excuse; she has a good knowledge of the business.* □ **buena excusa; buen conocimiento**
11 not less than: *it is a good three miles to the station; she waited a good half-hour.* □ **por lo menos, más de**
12 a lot of: *a good many people; a good deal of money; he is earning good money,* he is earning a lot of money. □ **mucho/muchos**
13 ***as good as,*** practically/almost: *he as good as told me to leave; the task is as good as done.* □ **casi, prácticamente**
■ *n.* **1** ***the good,*** virtuous people: *they say the good die young.* □ **los buenos**
2 profit/advantage: *what good will it do him? it is for his own good.* □ **¿qué provecho sacará?; es por su propio bien**
to do good, to act kindly: *she went about doing good amongst the poor.* □ **hacer el bien**
3 ***for good,*** permanently/forever: *he has left the country for good.* □ **para siempre**
4 *he is* ***up to no good,*** he is acting in a suspicious manner. □ **está tramando algo malo**
5 ***goods,*** movable property: *the goods will be delivered from the warehouse.* □ **mercancías**
goods and chattels, personal movable possessions. □ **muebles y enseres**
goods train, train which carries cargo not passengers. □ **tren de mercancías**
goodbye [gud'bai] *n.* and *interjection* **1** used when leaving someone: *say goodbye to him.* □ **adiós**
2 *you can* ***say goodbye to*** *the money,* you will never get your money back. □ **ya te puedes despedir del dinero**
good-humoured *adj.* pleasant; in a happy mood. □ **de buen humor**
good-looking *adj.* handsome/pretty. □ **guapo**
good-natured *adj.* kindly/pleasant. □ **amable**
goodness *n.* virtue/kindness/generosity: *out of the goodness of her heart; thank goodness!* □ **bondad**
have the goodness to, be kind enough to. □ **tendría la amabilidad de...**
goodnight *n.* and *interjection* used when leaving someone late at night: *he said goodnight to his parents.* □ **buenas noches**
goodwill *n.* **1** kindly feeling towards a person: *peace on earth, goodwill toward men.* □ **buena voluntad**
2 good reputation of a business: *he sold the goodwill of the shop.* □ **buen nombre**
goody *n.* (*pl. goodies*) (*informal*) **1** good person: *at the end of the film, the baddies are killed by the goodies.* □ **el bueno**
2 ***goodies,*** good things/money/treasure. □ **las cosas buenas**

goody-goody *adj.* (*informal*) (person) who is too good. □ **bonachón**
goofy ['gu:fi] *adj.* (*goofier, goofiest*) (*informal*) stupid. □ **bobo**
goose [gu:s] *n.* (*pl. geese*) **1** web-footed water bird, larger than a duck. □ **ganso**
2 (*informal*) silly person: *don't be such a goose!,* don't be so stupid. □ **tonto**
gooseberry ['gu:zbri] *n.* edible green hairy fruit; bush which bears this fruit: *gooseberries need a lot of sugar; gooseberry jam.* □ **grosella, grosellero**
goose-flesh, goose-pimples *n. pl.* mass of small bumps on the skin caused by fear/by cold, etc. □ **carne de gallina**
goose-step *n.* way of marching without bending the knees: *the soldiers did the goosestep.* □ **paso de ganso**
■ *v.* (*he goosestepped*) to march without bending the knees: *the soldiers came goosestepping past.* □ **desfilar a paso de ganso**
gore [gɔ:] *n.* **1** (*formal*) blood which has thickened after coming from a wound. □ **cuajarón**
2 section of a skirt, shaped like a triangle. □ **nesga**
■ *v.* to pierce with a horn: *the bullfighter had been gored by the bull.* □ **cornear**
gory *adj.* (*gorier, goriest*) bloody. □ **sangriento**
gorge [gɔ:dʒ] *n.* narrow opening between hills. □ **garganta**
■ *v.* to eat greedily: *he gorged himself on chocolates.* □ **atracarse de**
gorgeous ['gɔ:dʒəs] *adj.* magnificent/splendid; richly coloured: *what a gorgeous cake! a gorgeous array of flowers; she wore a gorgeous purple satin cloak.* □ **magnífico**
gorgeously *adv.* splendidly: *he was gorgeously dressed in velvet robes.* □ **espléndidamente**
gorgon ['gɔ:gən] *n.* fierce woman. □ **furia**
gorilla [gə'rilə] *n.* large, powerful and ferocious African ape. □ **gorila**
gormless ['gɔ:mləs] *adj.* (*informal*) foolish/stupid: *he was so gormless that he never did anything right.* □ **estúpido**
gormlessly *adv.* stupidly: *she stood gormlessly with her mouth open.* □ **estúpidamente**
gorse [gɔ:s] *n.* prickly yellow-flowered shrub. □ **tojo**
gory ['gɔ:ri] *adj.* covered in blood. □ **ensangrentado**
gosh [gɔʃ] *interjection* showing surprise: *gosh! the water's cold.* □ **¡caramba!**
goshawk ['gɔshɔ:k] *n.* type of trained hawk. □ **azor**
gosling ['gɔzliŋ] *n.* baby goose. □ **ansarino**
gospel ['gɔspl] *n.* record of Christ's life in the books of the four evangelists: *the gospel according to St Luke.* □ **evangelio**
it's the gospel truth, it's absolutely true. □ **es una verdad como un templo**
gossamer ['gɔsəmə] *n.* **1** very fine cobweb. □ **telaraña**
2 very fine material. □ **gasa**
gossip ['gɔsip] *n.* **1** idle chat, especially about other people; news: *the story is only gossip.* □ **cotilleo**
gossip column, section in a paper which gives news about famous people and their private lives. □ **ecos de sociedad**
2 person who spreads rumours: *she's a terrible gossip.* □ **cotilla**
■ *v.* to talk idly; to spread rumours: *she was gossiping with her neighbour over the garden fence.* □ **cotillear**
got [gɔt] *v.* **1** *see* **get.**
2 ***to have got to do something,*** to be obliged/to have to do something: *I've got to go to the dentist; we've got to leave at five o'clock.* □ **tener que**
gothic ['gɔθik] *adj.* style of architecture with pointed arches used in Western Europe in 12th-16th centuries. □ **gótico**
gotta ['gɔtə] *v.* (*slang*) (have) got to: *I gotta see the manager.* □ **tengo que, tienes que, etc.**
gotten ['gɔtn] *v. Amer. see* **get.**
gouache [gu'ɑ:ʃ] *n.* kind of thick watercolour paint. □ **'gouache'**
gouge [gaudʒ] *n.* kind of chisel used in carpentry. □ **gubia**
■ *v.* to cut out: *he gouged out a hole in the block of wood.* □ **escoplear con gubia**
goulash ['gu:læʃ] *n.* Hungarian stew flavoured with paprika. □ **goulash**
gourd ['guəd] *n.* dried fruit of a climbing plant, used as a bowl. □ **calabaza**
gourmand ['guəmənd] *n.* person who eats too much. □ **glotón**
gourmet ['guəmei] *n.* connoisseur of food and wine. □ **gastrónomo**
gout [gaut] *n.* painful inflammation of the joints, especially the big toe. □ **gota**
govern ['gʌvən] *v.* **1** to rule with authority: *the President governs the country with an iron hand.* □ **gobernar**
2 to influence/to determine: *the state of his finances governs his spending.* □ **determinar**
governess *n.* (*pl. governesses*) female teacher, usually in a private household. □ **institutriz**
government ['gʌvəmənt] *n.* group of people ruling a country. □ **gobierno**
governor *n.* person who rules. □ **gobernador**
gown [gaun] *n.* **1** (*formal*) dress: *she wore a blue gown to the dance.* □ **traje largo**
2 long official robe (worn by a mayor/judge/person with a degree, etc.). □ **toga**
3 ***dressing-gown,*** long coat worn over night clothes. □ **bata**
GP ['dʒi:'pi:] *abbreviation for* general practitioner; family doctor. □ **médico general, de cabecera**
grab [græb] *n.* sudden seizing with the hands: *he made a grab for the money.* □ **agarrón**
■ *v.* (*he grabbed*) to seize: *he grabbed hold of me.* □ **agarrar**
grace [greis] *n.* **1** pleasing quality/attractiveness: *the society hostess was renowned for her grace and charm; her face was not beautiful, but her hair was her saving grace.* □ **gracia**
with good grace, with a show of willingness: *he gave in to the demands with good grace.* □ **de buena gana**
2 *he had the grace to pretend he hadn't heard the interruption,* he pretended not to hear it because it seemed to him the right thing to do. □ **tuvo la cortesía...**
3 short prayer of thanksgiving before or after a meal: *let us say grace.* □ **bendición de la mesa**
4 act of mercy; pardon from all sin: *the Grace of God.* □ **la gracia de Dios**
5 favour shown by granting a delay: *a week's grace was allowed to settle the account.* □ **gracia**
■ *v.* to honour: *she graced the meeting with her presence.* □ **honrar**
graceful *adj.* moving with ease: *she dropped a graceful curtsey.* □ **airoso**
gracefully *adv.* moving easily: *the dancer glided gracefully across the stage.* □ **con gracia**
gracefulness *n.* ease of movement. □ **gracia**

grace note *n.* note in music which need not be played, but which adds to the attraction of the piece. □ **nota de adorno**
gracious ['greiʃəs] *adj.* **1** kind/agreeable. □ **amable**
2 *gracious living,* elegant way of living. □ **vida placentera**
good gracious!, how surprising! □ **¡válgame Dios!**
graciously *adv.* kindly: *she graciously offered her hand.* □ **amablemente**
grade [greid] *n.* **1** degree/level/rank: *the boy got a good grade in maths; the soldier achieved a high grade in the tests.* □ **grado; nota (examen)**
to make the grade, to succeed. □ **tener éxito**
2 *Amer.* class (in school): *my daughter is in fifth grade.* □ **curso**
■ *v.* to arrange in grades/to sort out: *the eggs were graded according to size.* □ **clasificar**
gradation [grə'deiʃn] *n.* series of steps, passing from one level to another. □ **gradación**
grade crossing *n. Amer.* place where a railway line crosses a road. □ **paso a nivel**
gradient ['greidiənt] *n.* amount of slope in a road, railway, etc.: *a steep gradient.* □ **pendiente**
gradual ['grædjuəl] *adj.* slow/progressive: *there was a gradual decline in his health; a gradual increase in the cost of living.* □ **gradual**
gradually *adv.* little by little. □ **gradualmente**
graduate ['grædjuət] *n.* person who has obtained a degree: *she's a graduate of London University.* □ **graduado**
■ *v.* **1** to obtain a degree: *he graduated from college last year.* □ **graduarse**
2 to regulate: *income tax is graduated according to earnings.* □ **graduar**
3 to mark in a scale. □ **graduar**
a graduated measuring glass, one with quantities marked on it. □ **vaso graduado**
graduation [grædju'eiʃn] *n.* **1** obtaining a degree. □ **graduación**
graduation day, day when students are awarded their degrees. □ **día de graduación**
2 act of marking a scale. □ **graduación**
graffiti [grə'fi:ti] *n. pl.* unofficial drawings or writing on walls. □ **pintada; 'graffiti'**
graft [grɑ:ft] *n.* **1** shoot of a plant inserted into another plant from which it receives sap and of which it becomes part: *the new rose is the result of a graft.* □ **injerto**
2 (*in surgery*) piece of transplanted living tissue: *as a result of his burns he needed several skin grafts.* □ **injerto**
3 (*slang*) hard work. □ **curro pesado**
4 (*slang*) bribery; bribe. □ **mangoneo**
■ *v.* to insert (part of a plant) into another plant so that it can grow; to attach (skin, etc.) to other parts of the body: *you can graft a pear shoot on to an apple tree; they grafted new skin to cover up the scars.* □ **injertar**
grain [grein] *n.* **1** seed of a cereal: *birds love to eat grain.* □ **grano**
2 small particle of sand, gold, etc.: *a grain of salt.* □ **grano**
3 texture of particles (in stone). □ **veta**
4 lines of fibres in wood/material. □ **fibra**
it goes against the grain, it goes against natural instincts. □ **va contra natura**
gram [græm] *n.* measurement of weight, one thousandth part of a kilogram. □ **gramo**
grammar ['græmə] *n.* **1** art and science of a language; rules of the forms of words and their relationship in a language: *English grammar is not difficult to learn.* □ **gramática**
2 book which explains/teaches the rules of a language. □ **gramática**
grammar school *n.* formerly a selective secondary school (usually for boys). □ **instituto de bachillerato**
grammatical [grə'mætikl] *adj.* conforming to the rules of grammar. □ **gramatical**
grammatically *adv.* according to the rules of grammar: *it is not grammatically correct.* □ **gramaticalmente**
gramophone ['græməfoun] *n.* machine on which records are played and which is wound up with a handle. □ **gramófono**
gran [græn] *n.* (*informal*) grandmother. □ **yaya**
granary ['grænəri] *n.* (*pl. granaries*) storehouse for grain. □ **granero**
granary loaf, bread made with whole wheat grain. □ **pan integral**
grand [grænd] *adj.* (*grander, grandest*) **1** important/imposing: *the Grand Canyon.* □ **gran; grande**
2 final: *the grand sum of his achievements; the grand total of the collection was $3.50.* □ **total general**
3 conducted with solemnity: *the wedding was a very grand occasion.* □ **solemne**
4 very good: *we had a grand time.* □ **nos lo pasamos muy bien**
■ *n.* **1** grand piano. □ **piano de cola**
2 (*slang*) thousand pounds/dollars. □ **uno de los grandes; un grande**
grandad *n.* (*informal*) grandfather. □ **yayo**
grandchild *n.* (*pl. grandchildren*) child of a son or daughter. □ **nieto**
granddaughter *n.* daughter of a son or daughter. □ **nieta**
grandee [græn'di:] *n.* proud aristocrat (usually Spanish). □ **grande de España**
grandeur ['grændʒə] *n.* splendour/majesty: *the grandeur of the occasion.* □ **grandiosidad**
grandfather *n.* father of a mother or father. □ **abuelo**
grandfather clock, tall clock standing on the floor. □ **reloj de caja**
grandiloquent [græn'diləkwənt] *adj.* speaking in a pompous way. □ **grandilocuente**
grandiose ['grændious] *adj.* very splendid: *grandiose scheme for making money.* □ **grandioso**
grandma ['grænmɑ:] *n.* (*informal*) grandmother. □ **yaya**
grandmaster *n.* chessplayer of international quality. □ **gran maestro**
grandmother *n.* mother of a mother or father. □ **abuela**
grandpa ['grænpɑ:] *n.* (*informal*) grandfather. □ **yayo**
grandparents *n. pl.* parents of a mother or father. □ **abuelos**
grand piano *n.* large horizontal piano. □ **piano de cola**
grandson *n.* son of a son or daughter. □ **nieto**
grandstand *n.* building with a sloping bank of seats for spectators at a racecourse or sportsground. □ **tribuna principal**
grange [greindʒ] *n.* country house with farm buildings attached to it. □ **casa solariega, cortijo**
granite ['grænit] *n.* hard grey stone used for building. □ **granito**
granny ['græni] *n.* (*informal*) grandmother. □ **yaya; abuelita**
granny flat, part of a large house converted into a small separate flat for an old relative. □ **apartamento para...**

grant [grɑ:nt] *n.* financial aid: *the student received a grant to cover his fees.* □ **subvención; beca (estudiante)**
■ *v.* **1** to agree/to give consent: *the request was granted.* □ **otorgar**
to take something for granted, not to appreciate it any more: *his ability to do the job was taken for granted.* □ **dar por sentado**
2 to agree: *I grant you it is a difficult job,* I admit that it is difficult. □ **estar de acuerdo con**
granted *adj.* admitted/understood: *granted you have the ability, but have you the necessary drive to finish the job?* □ **está claro que...**
granulate ['grænjuleit] *v.* to form into grains: *granulated sugar.* □ **granular**
granular *adj.* containing grains; like grains. □ **granular**
granule *n.* very small particle. □ **gránulo**
grape [greip] *n.* small green or purple fruit growing in clusters on a vine, eaten as fruit or made into wine: *a bunch of grapes.* □ **uva**
grapefruit *n.* (*no pl.*) large round yellow citrus fruit. □ **pomelo**
grapevine *n.* **1** climbing plant on which grapes grow. □ **vid**
2 *I heard it **on the grapevine,*** I learnt the news by gossip/unofficially. □ **me he enterado de que...**
graph [grɑ:f] *n.* mathematical diagram/curve: *the yearly rise and fall of the company's assets were shown on a graph.* □ **gráfico**
graphic ['græfik] *adj.* **1** referring to graphs/diagrams/signs, etc. □ **gráfico**
2 vividly descriptive: *they gave a graphic account of the car crash.* □ **gráfico**
graphical *adj.* referring to graphs/diagrams/signs, etc. □ **gráfico**
graphically *adv.* **1** using graphs/diagrams/signs, etc.: *we can represent the sales figures graphically.* □ **gráficamente**
2 in a vivid/graphic way. □ **de manera gráfica**
graph paper *n.* paper with small squares for drawing graphs on. □ **papel cuadriculado**
graphite ['græfait] *n.* naturally occurring form of carbons; lead (as used in a pencil). □ **grafito**
graphology [græ'fɔlədʒi] *n.* science of discovering someone's character from handwriting. □ **grafología**
grapnel ['græpnel] *n.* small anchor with several hooks. □ **rezón**
grapple ['græpl] *v.* to wrestle/to fight: *the old lady grappled with the intruder; he grappled with the problem.* □ **luchar cuerpo a cuerpo; trató de resolver el problema**
grasp [grɑ:sp] *n.* **1** tight hold/grip: *he seized my hand in a strong grasp.* □ **apretón**
2 understanding: *he has a good grasp of the principles of English grammar.* □ **dominio**
■ *v.* **1** to seize; to grab tightly: *he grasped the hammer with both hands; he grasped at the chance of survival.* □ **agarrar; aferrarse (oportunidad)**
2 to understand: *he's unable to grasp the simplest argument.* □ **entender**
grasping *adj.* (person) who is eager to get more things. □ **avaro**
grass [grɑ:s] *n.* (*pl. grasses*) **1** green plant of which the blades or leaves and stalks are eaten by cattle, etc.: *mown and dried grass becomes hay.* □ **hierba/yerba**
not to let the grass grow under one's feet: *don't let the grass grow under your feet,* waste no time in doing something. □ **no pierdas el tiempo**
2 plant of a species related to grass (including bamboo, etc.). □ **hierba**
3 lawn/piece of ground covered with grass: *keep off the grass.* □ **césped**
4 (*slang*) police informer. □ **soplón**
5 (*slang*) marijuana. □ **hierba; maría**
■ *v.* (*slang*) to inform (the police) about a crime. □ **soplar**
grasshopper *n.* green jumping insect with long back legs. □ **saltamontes**
grassland *n.* prairie/pasture. □ **pradera, pasto**
grassroots *n. pl.* **1** ordinary members of a political party/a trade union; common people: *grassroots reaction,* reaction by the ordinary members (of a party, etc.). □ **miembros de base**
2 *to tackle a problem at grassroots (level),* at its origin. □ **abordar un problema desde su raíz**
grasssnake *n.* common snake. □ **culebra**
grasswidow *n.* wife whose husband has temporarily or permanently gone away. □ **una separada**
grasswidower *n.* husband whose wife has temporarily or permanently gone away. □ **un separado**
grassy *adj.* (*grassier, grassiest*) covered with growing grass. □ **herboso**
grate [greit] *n.* fireplace: *it is good to see a fire in the grate.* □ **chimenea**
■ *v.* **1** to reduce to small bits by rubbing on a rough surface: *grated cheese.* □ **rallar**
2 to make a noise like two rough surfaces rubbing together: *the metal grated on the stones as he opened the gate.* □ **chirriar**
3 to have an irritating effect upon: *the noise grated on my nerves.* □ **...me crispó los nervios**
grater *n.* instrument for grating cheese, etc. □ **rallador**
grating *n.* grille; framework of wooden or metal bars. □ **reja**
■ *adj. a grating sound,* an irritating sound as of the rubbing together of rough surfaces. □ **un sonido chirriante**
grateful ['greitful] *adj.* thankful: *she was grateful for his help.* □ **agradecido**
gratefully *adv.* thankfully. □ **con agradecimiento**
gratify ['grætifai] *v.* (*gratified; gratifying*) **1** to satisfy/to delight: *the Caribbean cruise gratified his desire for the sun.* □ **satisfacer**
2 to please: *she was gratified to learn that her work was appreciated.* □ **agradar**
gratification [grætifi'keiʃn] *n.* satisfaction. □ **satisfacción**
gratifying *adj.* pleasing/satisfying: *it's gratifying to know that she liked the present.* □ **gratificante**
gratis ['grætis] *adv.* free/without charge: *members of the society can get in gratis; he let me have the book gratis.* □ **gratis**
gratitude ['grætitju:d] *n.* appreciation. □ **gratitud**
gratuity [grə'tju:iti] *n.* (*pl. gratuities*) **1** present of money/tip: *the taxi driver expected a gratuity.* □ **propina**
2 sum of money given to someone on retirement. □ **gratificación**
gratuitous *adj.* unasked for; undeserved: *he gave his friend some gratuitous advice.* □ **no solicitado, no merecido**
grave [greiv] *n.* tomb/hole in the ground to put a dead body in; burial place. □ **tumba**
to have one foot in the grave, to be very near to death. □ **tener un pie en la tumba**
■ *adj.* serious/solemn: *the judge had a grave expression on his face; this is a matter of grave concern; you have made a grave mistake.* □ **grave**

gravedigger *n.* man who digs graves. □ **sepulturero**
gravely *adv.* seriously: *the headmaster looked gravely at the boy.* □ **gravemente**
gravestone *n.* memorial stone placed on a grave. □ **lápida**
graveyard *n.* cemetery/place where people are buried. □ **cementerio**

gravel ['grævl] *n.* mixture of sand and small stones: *a gravel path led to the front door.* □ **grava**

gravitate ['græviteit] *v.* to move towards: *in her second year at University she gravitated towards the arts.* □ **sentirse atraído por**
gravitation [grævi'teiʃn] *n.* force of the earth's centre which attracts and causes objects to fall to the ground if dropped: *the earth's gravitation.* □ **gravedad**

gravity ['græviti] *n.* **1** seriousness: *the gravity of the situation.* □ **gravedad**
2 weight. □ **peso**
specific gravity, density of a substance divided by the density of water. □ **peso específico**
3 force of the earth's centre which attracts and causes objects to fall to the ground if dropped: *Isaac Newton discovered the law of gravity.* □ **gravedad**

gravy ['greivi] *n.* (*no pl.*) **1** juices that drip from meat during cooking. □ **jugo**
2 brown sauce served with meat. □ **salsa**

gray [grei] *adj.* and *n.* (*usually Amer.*) = **grey.** □ **gris**

graze [greiz] *n.* slight surface wound/scratch. □ **rozadura**
■ *v.* **1** to feed on growing grass: *the cattle were grazing in the meadow.* □ **pastar; pacer**
2 to wound slightly in passing: *the flying stone grazed my cheek.* □ **rozar**
grazing *n.* pasture: *the grazing is excellent in this area.* □ **pasto**

grease [gri:s] *n.* **1** melted animal fat: *he had spots of grease on his tie.* □ **grasa**
2 oily/fatty substance: *after working on the car he was covered in grease.* □ **grasa**
■ *v.* **1** to cover/to coat with oil/fat, etc.: *the moving parts of the vehicle must be regularly greased.* □ **engrasar**
2 ***to grease someone's palm,*** (*informal*) to bribe someone. □ **untar la mano**
greasepaint *n.* make-up used by actors, etc. □ **base del maquillaje**
greaseproof paper *n.* paper which will not let oil through. □ **papel parafinado**
greasy *adj.* (*greasier, greasiest*) smeared with grease; oily: *greasy hands; greasy hair.* □ **grasiento**

great [greit] *adj.* (*greater, greatest*) **1** large/big: *he had a great deal of money.* □ **grande; ...mucho dinero**
2 extreme: *take great care.* □ **...mucho cuidado**
3 distinguished/grand: *a great occasion.* □ **una gran ocasión**
4 remarkable: *Athens is a great city; Van Gogh was a great artist.* □ **gran**
5 (*informal*) wonderful: *we had a great time at the seaside; it's great to be out in the open air.* □ **estupendo**
great-aunt *n.* aunt of a father or mother. □ **tía abuela**
Great Britain *n.* country in Northern Europe, consisting of England, Wales and Scotland. □ **Gran Bretaña**
greatcoat *n.* thick army coat. □ **capote**
great-grandchildren *n. pl.* grandchildren of a son or daughter. □ **bisnietos**
great-granddaughter *n.* granddaughter of a son or daughter. □ **bisnieta**
great-grandfather *n.* grandfather of a father or mother. □ **bisabuelo**
great-grandmother *n.* grandmother of a father or mother. □ **bisabuela**
great-grandparents *n. pl.* grandparents of a father or mother. □ **bisabuelos**
great-grandson *n.* grandson of a son or daughter. □ **bisnieto**
greatly *adv.* very much: *she was greatly concerned.* □ **muy; enormemente**
greatness *n.* remarkable ability. □ **grandeza**
great-uncle *n.* uncle of a father or mother. □ **tío abuelo**

grebe [gri:b] *n.* type of diving bird with a long neck. □ **colimbo**

Greece [gri:s] *n.* Southern European country. □ **Grecia**

greed [gri:d] *n.* too great appetite; desire for more than is necessary. □ **gula (comida); avaricia**
greedily *adv.* with great appetite: *he greedily gobbled up his food.* □ **vorazmente**
greedy *adj.* (*greedier, greediest*) always wanting (food, etc.): *he is greedy for power.* □ **glotón (comida); ...ávido de poder**

Greek [gri:k] *adj.* referring to Greece. □ **griego**
■ *n.* **1** person from Greece. □ **griego**
2 language spoken in Greece and Cyprus. □ **griego**

green [gri:n] *adj.* (*greener, greenest*) **1** of a colour like grass: *green apples.* □ **verde**
green light, light which shows you can go ahead: *his plan has been given the green light,* he has been allowed to proceed with his plan. □ **luz verde**
2 immature/gullible: *she is a bit green where high finance is concerned.* □ **está un poco verde...**
3 ***green bacon,*** plain bacon which has not been smoked. □ **panceta fresca**
■ *n.* **1** colour like that of grass: *do you see any green in her dress?* □ **verde**
2 piece of public land covered with grass: *village green.* □ **zona verde**
3 piece of land covered with smooth grass on which you can play certain games: *bowling green; putting green.* □ **'green'**
greenback *n.* (*slang*) American dollar bill. □ **un verde**
green belt *n.* area of countryside round a town, where building is prohibited. □ **cinturón verde**
greenery *n.* vegetation: *mountain greenery.* □ **vegetación**
greenfinch *n.* bird with yellow and green plumage. □ **verderón**
green fingers *n. pl.* skill in gardening: *she's got green fingers,* she's a good gardener. □ **manitas**
greenfly *n. pl.* (*greenfly* or *greenflies*) small green aphis. □ **pulgón**
greengage *n.* kind of green plum. □ **ciruela claudia**
greengrocer *n.* person who sells fruit and vegetables. □ **verdulero; frutero**
greenhouse *n.* shelter made of glass and wood or metal for cultivation of delicate plants. □ **invernadero**
greenish *adj.* rather green. □ **verdoso**
Greenland *n.* large island in the North Atlantic. □ **Groenlandia**
Green Paper *n.* official report by the government on proposals which are being studied. □ **Libro Verde**
green pound *n.* value of the pound as used in calculating the Common Market agricultural prices

and subsidies relating to the UK. □ **libra esterlina verde**
green-room *n.* room where actors can rest when they are off-stage. □ **camerino**
greens *n. pl.* (*informal*) cooked green vegetables. □ **verduras**
green thumb *n. Amer.* skill in gardening: *she has a green thumb.* □ **manitas**
greet [gri:t] *v.* to salute/to welcome: *he greeted me with open arms.* □ **saludar**
greeting *n.* reception/way of welcoming someone: *the dog gave his master a wonderful greeting.* □ **saludo**
greetings *n. pl.* good wishes: *Christmas greetings.* □ **felicitación**
gregarious [gri'gɛəriəs] *adj.* fond of company: *the child is gregarious and loves to be with other children.* □ **sociable**
gremlin ['gremlin] *n.* imaginary imp, supposed to be responsible for faults in machinery. □ **duende**
grenade [gri'neid] *n.* small bomb thrown by hand. □ **granada**
grew [gru:] *v. see* **grow.**
grey [grei] *adj.* (*greyer, greyest*) of a colour between black and white. □ **gris**
grey matter, active part of the brain; (*informal*) intelligence. □ **materia gris**
■ *n.* colour between black and white. □ **gris**
grey-haired *adj.* with grey hair (usually because of old age). □ **cano**
greyhound *n.* slender, long-legged, swift dog, often used for racing. □ **galgo**
greyish *adj.* tinged with grey. □ **grisáceo**
greylag *n.* common European wild goose. □ **ganso silvestre**
grid [grid] *n.* **1** grating/frame of spaced parallel bars. □ **reja**
2 system of numbered squares on a map: *look up the grid reference.* □ **cuadrícula**
3 national electricity supply system. □ **red**
4 ***starting grid,*** lines drawn on a track to show the start in a car/motorcycle race. □ **parrilla de salida**
griddle *n.* iron plate placed over heat for cooking flat cakes. □ **plancha**
gridiron *n.* **1** metal frame for cooking over an open fire. □ **parrilla**
2 *Amer.* football field. □ **campo de fútbol**
grief [gri:f] *n.* deep sorrow: *she was overwhelmed with grief at her daughter's death.* □ **pesar**
to come to grief, to meet with disaster. □ **fracasar**
grief-stricken *adj.* very sad. □ **afligido**
grievance ['gri:vəns] *n.* real or imagined grounds for complaint: *to air one's grievances,* to tell everyone about one's complaints. □ **motivo de queja**
grieve [gri:v] *v.* to make sad; to feel sad: *her distress grieved me.* □ **afligir**
grieve over *v.* to mourn; to feel sad because of (something): *the little girl grieved over the body of the dead bird.* □ **llorar**
grievous *adj.* severe. □ **intenso**
grievous bodily harm, severe injury to someone. □ **herido de gravedad**
griffon ['grifən] *n.* **1** type of small terrier. □ **grifón**
2 type of vulture. □ **buitre**
grill [gril] *n.* **1** part of a cooker where food is cooked under a direct source of heat: *put the bacon under the grill.* □ **'grill', gratinador**
charcoal grill, gridiron over a bed of hot charcoal. □ **parrilla de carbón vegetal**
2 restaurant where most food is cooked under a grill or on a charcoal grill. □ **asador**
3 ***mixed grill,*** collection of grilled food. □ **parrillada**
4 framework of metal/wooden bars. □ **parrilla**
■ *v.* **1** to cook under the grill: *grilled sausages.* □ **asar a la parrilla**
2 (*informal*) to interrogate/to ask searching questions. □ **acribillar a preguntas**
grille [gril] *n.* grating; frame of spaced parallel bars. □ **parrilla**
radiator grille, parallel bars in front of a radiator on a car. □ **parrilla**
grilse [grils] *n.* young salmon, which is returning to the river from the sea for the first time. □ **salmón primerizo**
grim [grim] *adj.* **1** sinister/severe: *the policeman wore a grim expression as he arrested the thief.* □ **torvo**
2 bad/gloomy: *it is a grim prospect; this is the grim truth.* □ **perspectiva sombría; ésta es la triste verdad**
3 *grim determination,* inflexible will. □ **una determinación inflexible**
grimly *adv.* tenaciously; with determination: *he hung on grimly.* □ **inflexiblemente**
grimace [gri'meis] *n.* twisted expression on the face: *he made a grimace.* □ **mueca**
■ *v.* to make a twisted expression with the face. □ **hacer muecas**
grime [graim] *n.* ingrained dirt: *the miner was covered in grime after a day's work in the pits.* □ **tizne**
grimy *adj.* (*grimier, grimiest*) dirty: *he has a grimy face.* □ **tiznado**
grin [grin] *n.* wide smile: *the small boy's mouth broke into a grin of pleasure.* □ **sonrisa de oreja a oreja**
■ *v.* (*he grinned*) to smile broadly: *he grinned sheepishly up at his teacher.* □ **sonreír irónicamente**
to grin and bear it, to put a brave face on things. □ **poner al mal tiempo buena cara**
grind [graind] *n.* boring/monotonous work. □ **trabajo pesado**
the daily grind, repetitive work to be done every day. □ **trabajo rutinario**
■ *v.* (*he ground*) **1** to reduce to small pieces by crushing between stones/teeth, etc.: *to grind corn to make flour; to grind coffee for breakfast; he ground the nuts between his teeth.* □ **moler; chascar**
2 *Amer.* to mince: *ground beef,* minced beef. □ **picar**
3 to rub surfaces together. □ **frotar**
to grind your teeth, to rub together the upper and lower jaws of the mouth, usually in anger. □ **rechinar los dientes**
to grind to a halt, to come to a standstill. □ **quedarse parado en seco**
4 to sharpen a tool/to smooth something which is rough: *jar with a ground glass stopper.* □ **afilar, pulir**
to have an axe to grind, to have a particular interest or point of view which makes your judgement biased. □ **tener algún interés personal**
grinder *n.* **1** machine for grinding: *coffee grinder.* □ **molinillo de café**
2 *Amer.* mincer. □ **picadora**
grinding *adj. grinding poverty,* terrible poverty. □ **pobreza agobiante**
grindstone *n.* stone which turns to sharpen knives, etc. □ **muela**
to keep someone's nose to the grindstone, to keep him working very hard. □ **hacer trabajar a uno como un burro**
gringo ['griŋgəu] *n.* (*informal*) (*especially in Mexico*) foreigner, usually American. □ **gringo**
grip [grip] *n.* **1** firm hold: *he held my hand in a grip of steel.* □ **asimiento, apretón**

to come to grips with, to tackle: *he came to grips with the real problem and overcame it.* □ **abordar (problema)**
to keep a grip on, to remain in control of: *he kept a grip on the situation.* □ **controlar**
2 soft bag/hold-all for carrying clothes, etc. □ **saco de ropa**
3 pin for holding your hair in place. □ **horquilla**
■ *v.* (*he gripped*) **1** to seize: *he gripped my hand; I was gripped with fear.* □ **agarrar**
2 to hold someone's attention: *the story gripped me.* □ **cautivar**
gripping *adj.* holding the attention: *gripping tale.* □ **que absorbe la atención**
gripe [graip] *v.* to moan/to complain: *he's always griping about the food.* □ **quejarse**
gripe water *n.* medicine given to babies to stop stomach pains. □ **agua de anís**
grisly ['grizli] *adj.* (*grislier, grisliest*) causing horror/dread: *the grisly remains of the slaughtered soldiers lay scattered on the ground; he told me a grisly story of the plague.* □ **espeluznante**
grist [grist] *n.* ***it's all grist to the mill,*** (*informal*) it's all useful/it all helps with the work. □ **molienda; todo se aprovecha**
gristle ['grisl] *n.* tough, whitish, flexible tissue in meat: *there is a lot of gristle on this joint.* □ **cartílago; nervios**
gristly *adj.* full of pieces of gristle. □ **cartilaginoso**
grit [grit] *n.* **1** small particles of stone/sand: *some grit in the works stopped the machinery.* □ **granos de arena**
2 (*informal*) courage: *he has grit and determination.* □ **valor**
3 ***grits,*** *Amer.* type of porridge made of maize or wheat. □ **sémola**
■ *v.* (*he gritted*) **1** to make a surface of grit; to put grit on (to prevent cars sliding on ice): *they are gritting the road outside my house.* □ **echar arena**
2 ***to grit your teeth,*** to clench your teeth together, usually in fear/determination: *he gritted his teeth for the final lap of the long race.* □ **rechinar los dientes**
gritty *adj.* containing grit. □ **arenoso**
grizzle ['grizl] *v.* (*of children*) to whimper/to cry fretfully: *the children were grizzling all day.* □ **lloriquear**
grizzled ['grizld] *adj.* with grey hair. □ **entrecano**
grizzly ['grizli] *adj.* grey; grey-haired. □ **entrecano**
■ *n.* (*pl. grizzlies*) ***grizzly (bear),*** large, fierce North American bear. □ **oso pardo**
groan [groun] *n.* deep sound expressing pain/grief/disapproval: *he gave a low groan as he regained consciousness.* □ **gemido**
■ *v.* **1** to moan deeply: *she groaned when she heard the bad news.* □ **gemir**
2 to be heavily laden: *the table was groaning with good food.* □ **estar repleto de**
grocer ['grousə] *n.* dealer in tinned foods, butter, sugar, eggs, etc., and miscellaneous domestic supplies: *we buy our cereals at the grocer's.* □ **tendero**
groceries *n. pl.* items on sale in a grocer's shop. □ **comestibles**
grocery *n.* grocer's shop. □ **tienda de ultramarinos**
grog [grɔg] *n.* drink of spirits and water. □ **grog**
groggy *adj.* unsteady: *I am feeling a bit groggy.* □ **grogui**
groin [grɔin] *n.* hollow where the legs join the body. □ **ingle**
groom [gru:m] *n.* **1** person who looks after horses. □ **mozo de cuadra**
2 bridegroom/new husband: *the bride and groom came down the aisle.* □ **novio**
■ *v.* **1** to look after/to make smart: *the horse was beautifully groomed for the show; well groomed person,* person who is smart and well-dressed. □ **almohazar; acicalar**
2 *he is being groomed to take over from his father,* he is being prepared/trained. □ **se le está preparando**
groove [gru:v] *n.* **1** channel/hollow: *the needle is stuck in a groove on the record.* □ **surco**
2 routine. □ **hábito arraigado**
to get into a groove, to be stuck in a routine. □ **no salir de la rutina**
groovy *adj.* (*groovier, grooviest*) (*slang*) fine/fashionable. □ **guay**
grope [group] *v.* **1** to feel about as if you are blind: *he groped his way along the dark corridor.* □ **andar a tientas**
2 *they were groping for a solution,* they were searching aimlessly for a solution. □ **buscar a tientas**
gross [grous] *n.* (*no pl.*) twelve dozen, 144: *I would like to order two gross of chocolate bars.* □ **gruesa**
■ *adj.* (*grosser, grossest*) **1** bloated; horribly fat: *after eating too much for years he had become gross.* □ **grueso**
2 great/excessive: *gross ignorance; gross injustice.* □ **ignorancia crasa; enorme injusticia**
3 total. □ **total**
gross weight, combined weight of container and contents: *the gross weight of the vegetables in the box is two kilos.* □ **peso bruto**
gross income, total income, before tax is deducted. □ **renta bruta**
grossly *adv.* greatly: *her experience has been grossly exaggerated.* □ **enormemente**
grotesque [grə'tesk] *adj.* outrageous/fantastic; strange and ugly: *the architecture of the house is grotesque.* □ **grotesco**
grotto ['grɔtou] *n.* (*pl. grottoes*) picturesque cave: room decorated with shells to resemble a cave. □ **gruta**
grotty ['grɔti] *adj.* (*grottier, grottiest*) (*informal*) dirty. □ **guarro**
ground [graund] *n.* **1** soil/earth: *dig the ground over before planting shrubs; the house stands on marshy ground.* □ **suelo**
2 surface of the earth: *the parachutist hit the ground at 20 miles an hour; the house was burnt to the ground.* □ **tierra**
to go to ground, to hide away. □ **esconderse**
3 area of land: *the village is built on high ground.* □ **terreno**
to stand one's ground, to maintain one's position/authority. □ **mantenerse en sus trece**
to lose ground, to become less successful/less popular. □ **perder terreno**
to have the ground cut from under your feet, to see your support suddenly removed. □ **segarle a uno la hierba bajo los pies**
to break new ground, to be the first to start a project. □ **abrir nuevos horizontes**
to get (something) off the ground, to start (something) successfully/to get (a project) going. □ **poner en marcha**
4 large area of land set aside for a particular purpose: *cricket ground; football ground.* □ **campo de...**
5 ***grounds,*** land surrounding a large house: *the castle grounds covered 50 acres.* □ **tierras**
6 ***grounds,*** reason: *have you any grounds for complaint?* □ **motivo**

7 coffee grounds, small pieces of ground coffee beans left after coffee has been made. □ **posos**
■ *v.* **1** to base: *his love of the country was grounded in his childhood there.* □ **basarse**
2 to run (a boat) on to the land. □ **varar**
3 to keep (aircraft) on the ground: *the aircraft have been grounded because of bad weather.* □ **obligar a permanecer en tierra**
4 *see also* **grind.**
grounding *n.* instruction: *he had a good grounding in mathematics.* □ **base**
groundless *adj.* without reason: *his fears were groundless.* □ **infundado**
groundnut *n.* peanut. □ **cacahuete**
groundsheet *n.* rubber/plastic cloth spread on the ground for sitting/sleeping on. □ **aislante**
groundsman *n.* (*pl. groundsmen*) person who looks after sports pitches or public or private gardens. □ **guarda**
groundswell *n.* (*no pl.*) large slow-moving waves. □ **olas de fondo**
groundwork *n.* basic work/preliminary work: *he laid the groundwork for the new treaty.* □ **preacuerdo**
groundsel ['graunsl] *n.* common weed with small yellow flowers. □ **hierba cana**
group [gru:p] *n.* **1** number of people or animals gathered close together: *a group of actors strolled onto the stage; the guests arrived in groups of two or three.* □ **grupo**
2 classification: *blood group; age group.* □ **grupo**
3 small number of people playing music together: *a jazz group.* □ **grupo**
4 several different companies linked together in the same organization: *the Shell group.* □ **grupo**
■ *v.* to form into groups: *the teacher grouped the children according to their age.* □ **agrupar**
group captain *n.* rank in the air force above wing commander. □ **coronel**
grouper *n.* large tropical sea fish, used as food. □ **mero**
group practice *n.* several doctors who share patients between them and usually work from the same offices. □ **atención médica de grupo**
grouse [graus] *n.* **1** (*pl. grouse*) reddish or black bird shot for sport and food: *we shot ten grouse yesterday.* □ **urogallo**
2 (*informal*) grumble. □ **refunfuño**
■ *v.* (*informal*) to grumble: *stop grousing about the weather!* □ **refunfuñar**
grout [graut] *v.* to fill the spaces between tiles on a floor or wall with cement. □ **echar la lechada**
grouting *n.* cement used to fill spaces between tiles. □ **lechada**
grove [grouv] *n.* small group of trees. □ **bosquecillo**
grovel ['grɔvl] *v.* (*he grovelled*) to humble yourself; to lie with your face on the ground: *the peasants grovelled in the dust as the king rode by.* □ **humillarse; los campesinos se humillaron completamente...**
grow [grou] *v.* (*he grew: he has grown*) **1** to develop/to exist as a living plant: *rice grows in the paddy fields of India; chestnut trees grow to a very large size.* □ **crecer**
2 to increase in size or height: *how your son has grown! the population is growing rapidly.* □ **crecer**
3 to become/to evolve gradually: *the girl grew more beautiful every day; he is growing old; he grew richer all the time; it's growing cold at night.* □ **ir haciéndose; ya va haciendo frío...**
4 to cultivate: *she grows roses; he has grown a moustache.* □ **cultivar; dejarse crecer (bigote)**
grower *n.* **1** person who cultivates: *he is a grower of exotic flowers.* □ **cultivador**
2 plant that grows in a specified way: *fast grower; slow grower.* □ **de crecimiento rápido/lento**
growing *adj.* getting bigger: *he's a growing lad.* □ **en crecimiento**
grown *adj.* developed to full size: *he's a grown man.* □ **crecido**
grown-up *n.* adult: *children and grown-ups.* □ **adulto**
grow out of *v.* **1** to become bigger/older (so that clothes no longer fit, etc.): *he's grown out of his jacket.* □ **no valer; no le vale la chaqueta**
2 *he'll grow out of sucking his thumb,* as he gets older he will gradually stop. □ **ya se le pasará con el tiempo...**
growth *n.* **1** development; increase in height/size: *she put on a spurt of growth at 14; the economic growth of the nation is unsatisfactory.* □ **crecimiento**
2 bump of tissue in the body. □ **tumor**
growth rate *n.* speed with which something grows. □ **índice de crecimiento**
grow up *v.* to become adult: *he grew up to be a tall strong man; what do you want to do when you're grown up?* □ **hacerse mayor**
growl [graul] *n.* sound made in the throat expressing anger: *the dog gave a low growl.* □ **gruñido**
■ *v.* to murmur angrily: *the old man growled into his beard.* □ **gruñir**
growling *n.* noise made in the throat expressing anger: *we could hear the sound of growling which came from the cage.* □ **gruñido**
grown [groun] *v. see* **grow.**
groyne [grɔin] *n.* long breakwater of stone, concrete or timber built into the sea. □ **espolón**
grub [grʌb] *n.* **1** larva of an insect; maggot/short worm which grows into an insect. □ **gusano**
2 (*slang*) food. □ **manduca**
grub's up, the meal is ready. □ **¡a comer!**
■ *v.* (*he grubbed*) to dig: *he grubbed up the old cabbage plants.* □ **cavar**
grubbiness *n.* dirty appearance. □ **desaliño**
grubby *adj.* (*grubbier, grubbiest*) dirty: *what a grubby face you have!* □ **sucio**
grudge [grʌdʒ] *n.* feeling of resentment/ill will: *after his friend had let him down he bore him a grudge for a long time.* □ **resentimiento**
■ *v.* to be unwilling to give: *I don't grudge giving up my free time to work.* □ **dar de mala gana**
grudging *adj.* reluctant. □ **reacio**
grudgingly *adv.* reluctantly: *he grudgingly gave his consent.* □ **a regañadientes**
gruel ['gruəl] *n.* thin porridge. □ **gachas**
gruelling ['gruəliŋ] *adj.* exhausting/tiring; very difficult: *a gruelling ten-mile race.* □ **agotador**
gruesome ['gru:səm] *adj.* causing horror/dread: *gruesome stories of murder.* □ **espantoso**
gruff [grʌf] *adj.* (*gruffer, gruffest*) **1** deep/rough: *a gruff voice.* □ **ronco**
2 stern: *he had a gruff manner but a kind heart.* □ **brusco**
gruffly *adv.* roughly; sternly: *he answered gruffly.* □ **rudamente**
grumble ['grʌmbl] *n.* moan/complaint: *she had a good grumble about the government.* □ **queja**
■ *v.* to complain: *he was always grumbling about the weather; she grumbled at her sister.* □ **quejarse**
grumbler *n.* someone who complains: *he's a born grumbler,* he's always complaining. □ **refunfuñador**
grumbling *adj. a grumbling appendix,* (*informal*) an appendix which hurts from time to time and which may have to be removed. □ **molesto**

grumpy ['grʌmpi] *adj.* (*grumpier, grumpiest*) bad-tempered. □ **malhumorado**
grumpily *adv.* in a bad-tempered manner: *she grumpily agreed to take the dog for a walk.* □ **de mal humor**

grunt [grʌnt] *n.* low sound, like that made by pigs: *he gave a grunt of disapproval; she gave a grunt of surprise.* □ **gruñido**
■ *v.* to make a low snorting sound: *the pigs were grunting in the pen; he grunted when he heard the unexpected news; he grunted his approval.* □ **gruñir**

guano ['gwɑːnou] *n.* (*no pl.*) manure from the dung of sea-birds. □ **guano**

guarantee [gærən'tiː] *n.* **1** legal document promising that a machine will work, etc.: *the car is still under guarantee.* □ **garantía**
2 person acting as a security: *he went guarantee for his brother's settlement of debt.* □ **fiador**
3 thing given as security: *he left a deposit as guarantee of payment.* □ **garantía**
■ *v.* to give assurance: *I can guarantee 100% success.* □ **garantizar**
guaranteed *adj.* assured: *he received a guaranteed hourly pay-rate.* □ **garantizado**
guarantor [gærən'tɔː] *n.* someone who promises to pay someone's debts. □ **garante**

guard [gɑːd] *n.* **1** watch/looking out: *to be on guard.* □ **guardia**
to keep guard, to act as sentry. □ **montar guardia**
to be on your guard, to be prepared against attack/surprise, etc. □ **estar en guardia**
to be caught off guard, to be taken unawares. □ **estar desprevenido**
2 soldier/policeman who protects someone/a building: *guard of honour,* group of soldiers acting as a ceremonial escort to the sovereign or other important person; *the President had a personal guard who went everywhere with him; armed guards are patrolling the camp.* □ **centinela; guardia**
3 ***the Guards,*** special regiments of elite soldiers. □ **guardia**
4 person in charge of a train, who gives orders to the driver. □ **jefe de tren**
5 device to prevent injury or accident: *the nursery had a guard in front of the fire.* □ **protección**
chain guard, metal strip covering a bicycle chain so that you cannot touch it. □ **cubrecadena**
■ *v.* **1** to defend/to protect; to watch (prisoners) carefully so that they cannot escape: *the sentry guarded the castle; the prisoners were closely guarded.* □ **vigilar**
2 *a closely guarded secret,* secret which is carefully kept secret. □ **un secreto guardado celosamente**
3 to be careful: *he guarded against any possible misunderstanding by putting his words in writing.* □ **guardarse**
guardian *n.* keeper/protector responsible for the upbringing of a child: *the boy's uncle acted as his legal guardian after the death of his parents.* □ **tutor**
guardianship *n.* protection: *the children were under the guardianship of their grandparents.* □ **tutela**
guardroom *n.* building at the entrance to a military camp, used as a prison. □ **cuerpo de guardia**
guardsman *n.* (*pl. guardsmen*) soldier of the Guards. □ **guardia**

guava ['gwɑːvə] *n.* orange-coloured tropical fruit. □ **guayaba**

gudgeon ['gʌdʒən] *n.* **1** small river fish. □ **gobio**
2 pin in a piston. □ **eje del pistón**
3 pin on which a hinge hangs. □ **pasador del émbolo**

guer(r)illa [gə'rilə] *n.* person (not a regular soldier) engaged in unofficial fighting. □ **guerrillero**
guerrilla warfare, kind of war waged by guerrillas. □ **guerra de guerrillas**

guess [ges] *n.* (*pl. guesses*) rough guess at the number of people present; he gave her three guesses. □ **estimación aproximada**
it is anybody's guess, no one really knows. □ **y quién lo sabe**
■ *v.* **1** to estimate: *he guessed the weight of the parcel, and he guessed right; she guessed his age.* □ **adivinar**
2 *Amer.* to think: *I guess you're right.* □ **creer**
guesswork *n.* process of guessing: *he worked out the answer by guesswork.* □ **conjetura**

guest [gest] *n.* **1** person entertained at another's house: *there were five guests for dinner.* □ **invitado**
paying guest, lodger/boarder. □ **huésped**
guest artist/guest conductor, person who is invited to play with/to conduct an orchestra. □ **artista/director invitado**
2 *hotel guest,* person staying in a hotel. □ **huésped**
guesthouse *n.* house where people pay for a bed and meals. □ **casa de huéspedes**

guffaw [gə'fɔː] *n.* loud/coarse laugh: *the man let out a guffaw of laughter.* □ **carcajada**
■ *v.* to laugh loudly: *he guffawed when he saw the clowns.* □ **reírse a carcajadas**

guide [gaid] *n.* **1** person who shows the way/who describes buildings/works of art, etc., as you see them: *I acted as their guide through the streets of London.* □ **guía**
2 indication: *her manner of dressing is a good guide to her mood; taking the old model as her guide, she designed an entirely new one.* □ **guía**
3 book of helpful advice: *he bought a guide to the district.* □ **guía**
4 member of the Girl Guides. □ **exploradora**
the Guides, the Girl Guides/social/training organization for girls. □ **the Guides**
■ *v.* to conduct/to lead: *he guided them through their course of study; we were guided by his opinions.* □ **guiar**
guided tour, tour where the tourists are led by a guide. □ **excursión con guía**
guided missile, missile which is led to the target by a controlling device. □ **misil teledirigido**
guidance *n.* advice: *he sought his teacher's guidance.* □ **asesoramiento**
guidebook *n.* book of helpful advice/information: *a guidebook to London.* □ **guía turística**
guide dog *n.* dog which is specially trained to lead a blind person. □ **perro lazarillo**
guidelines *n. pl.* advice how to proceed: *the new legislation gives the guidelines by which management and workers can reach agreement.* □ **directrices**
guiding *adj.* directing: *guiding principle.* □ **principio rector**

guild [gild] *n.* association of merchants or craftsmen. □ **gremio**
guildhall *n.* hall where a guild used to meet, now usually a town hall. □ **sede de un gremio; ayuntamiento**

guile [gail] *n.* treachery/cunning/trickery: *he used guile to outwit his opponent.* □ **engaño**
guileless *adj.* honest/straightforward. □ **cándido**

guillotine ['gilətiːn] *n.* **1** machine with a sharp blade for beheading criminals. □ **guillotina**
2 machine with a sharp blade for cutting paper. □ **guillotina**
3 arrangement to limit the length of a debate in Parliament so that a vote can be taken quickly.

□ **'guillotina'**
■ *v.* **1** to cut off (someone's head) with a guillotine. □ **guillotinar**
2 to cut (paper) with a guillotine. □ **cortar**
guilt [gilt] *n.* having committed a crime; being aware that you have committed a crime: *guilt was written all over his face,* it was obvious from his expression that he knew he had done something wrong. □ **culpabilidad, culpa**
guiltily *adv.* showing that you know you have done wrong: *he crept guiltily from the room.* □ **culpablemente**
guilty *adj.* (*guiltier, guiltiest*) blameworthy/criminal; having done wrong: *in England you are innocent until proved guilty; he has a guilty conscience.* □ **culpable**
guinea pig ['ginipig] *n.* **1** small furry animal with no tail, often kept as a pet. □ **cobaya**
2 person/animal used in a scientific experiment. □ **conejillo de Indias**
guise [gaiz] *n.* (*formal*) appearance. □ **apariencia**
guitar [gi'tɑ:] *n.* stringed musical instrument played with the fingers. □ **guitarra**
electric guitar, guitar which is connected to an amplifier. □ **...eléctrica**
guitarist *n.* person who plays a guitar. □ **guitarrista**
gulf [gʌlf] *n.* **1** area of sea partly surrounded by coast: *the Gulf of Mexico.* □ **golfo**
2 wide difference in points of view. □ **abismo**
gull [gʌl] *n.* long-winged, web-footed sea bird. □ **gaviota**
gullet ['gʌlit] *n.* food tube from the mouth to the stomach: *a small bone was lodged in the dog's gullet.* □ **esófago**
gullible ['gʌlibl] *adj.* easily taken in/ready to believe anything: *he was so gullible that he believed my lies.* □ **crédulo**
gullibility [gʌli'biliti] *n.* being easily tricked/readiness to believe anything. □ **credulidad**
gully ['gʌli] *n.* (*pl. gullies*) small ravine/water channel. □ **torrentera**
gulp [gʌlp] *n.* quick swallow: *he swallowed the drink at one gulp.* □ **trago**
■ *v.* to swallow hastily: *he gulped down the medicine in order not to taste it.* □ **tragar**
gum [gʌm] *n.* **1** sticky substance produced by some trees or manufactured artificially, used for sticking paper, wood, etc. □ **goma**
2 flesh in which the teeth are set. □ **encía**
3 (***chewing***) ***gum,*** sweet sticky substance you chew but do not swallow. □ **chicle**
■ *v.* (*he gummed*) to stick together: *the pages of the book are gummed to the spine.* □ **pegar con goma**
gumboil *n.* small sore on a gum, usually near a tooth. □ **flemón**
gumboot *n.* rubber boot. □ **botas de goma**
gumdrop *n.* type of hard sweet. □ **caramelo**
gum tree *n.* eucalyptus tree. □ **gomero**
to be up a gum tree, (*informal*) to be in a difficult spot. □ **estar en un aprieto**
gumption ['gʌmpʃn] *n.* (*no pl.*) enterprising spirit/resourcefulness; knowledge of practical things: *he showed a lot of gumption in launching his new ideas.* □ **sentido común**
gun [gʌn] *n.* weapon which uses an explosive force to send out a missile or bullet. □ **arma de fuego**
starting gun, weapon used to make a bang to start a race. □ **pistola**
grease gun, instrument for injecting a small amount of grease into a part of an engine. □ **inyector**
to stick to one's guns, to maintain one's position. □ **mantenerse firme en su posición**
to jump the gun, to start doing something before you should. □ **adelantarse**
■ *v.* (*he gunned*) **1** to shoot at: *the escaping prisoner was gunned down by the guard.* □ **matar a tiros**
2 ***to be gunning for someone,*** to be trying to attack someone. □ **andar a la caza de**
gunboat *n.* small ship carrying heavy guns. □ **lancha cañonera**
gun carriage *n.* vehicle which carries a heavy gun. □ **cureña**
gunfire *n.* firing of a gun: *the sound of gunfire could be heard far off.* □ **fuego de artillería**
gunman *n.* (*pl. gunmen*) armed robber: *three gunmen were involved in the bank raid.* □ **pistolero**
gun metal *n.* dark gray metal, made of copper, tin, lead and zinc. □ **bronce de cañón**
gunner *n.* soldier in the artillery; person who fires a gun. □ **artillero**
gunnery *n.* construction and management of large guns. □ **artillería**
gunpowder *n.* explosive substance. □ **pólvora**
gunroom *n.* **1** room where you keep sporting guns. □ **sala de armas**
2 compartment for officers in a warship. □ **sala de oficiales**
gun runner *n.* person who brings guns into a country illegally. □ **traficante de armas**
gunshot *n.* bullet from a gun: *he died of gunshot wounds.* □ **disparo**
gunsmith *n.* manufacturer of guns. □ **armero**
gunwale ['gʌnl] *n.* upper edge of ship's side. □ **borda**
gurgle ['gə:gl] *n.* bubbling sound: *the gurgle of a stream.* □ **murmullo**
■ *v.* to make a bubbling sound: *the water gurgled into the pool; the baby was gurgling in his pram.* □ **borbotear (agua); gorjear (bebé)**
gurgling *adj.* making a bubbling sound: *the little brook made a gurgling sound as it flowed over the pebbles.* □ **borboteante**
guru ['gu:ru:] *n.* notable thinker who has many disciples. □ **gurú**
gush [gʌʃ] *n.* (*pl. gushes*) sudden stream/sudden rush of liquid: *a gush of water came from the mountain spring; there was a sudden gush of blood from the wound.* □ **chorro**
■ *v.* **1** to flow heavily: *the waterfall gushed down the mountain; the oil gushed from the broken pipe.* □ **salir a borbotones**
2 to speak with effusiveness; to praise too much: *she tends to gush.* □ **hablar con excesiva efusión**
gusher *n.* oil well where the oil comes out so strongly that it does not need to be pumped. □ **pozo surtidor de petróleo**
gushing *adj.* **1** praising/talking extravagantly: *her gushing words made me writhe.* □ **efusivo**
2 rushing: *gushing water.* □ **que sale a chorros**
gusset ['gʌsit] *n.* piece of cloth shaped like a triangle, inserted in an article of clothing to make it larger. □ **escudete**
gust [gʌst] *n.* sudden violent rush of wind or rain: *a gust of wind blew his hat off.* □ **ráfaga (viento); aguacero**
■ *v.* to blow in gusts: *the wind gusted from the north.* □ **soplar a ráfagas**
gusty *adj.* (*gustier, gustiest*) windy: *it was a gusty day.* □ **ventoso**
gusto ['gʌstou] *n.* (*no pl.*) zest/enthusiasm: *everything he did, he did with gusto.* □ **placer**
gut [gʌt] *n.* **1** lower part of the intestine (especially of animals). □ **tripa**

2 ***gut reaction,*** (*informal*) natural/instinctive reaction. □ **reacción instintiva**
3 ***I hate his guts,*** (*informal*) I dislike him a lot. □ **no lo aguanto**
4 ***guts,*** (*informal*) courage: *the man's got guts; through sheer guts he reached the top of the mountain.* □ **el hombre tiene agallas; a base de coraje...**
5 material made from the intestines of animals and used for violin and tennis racket strings, etc. □ **tripa**
■ *v.* (*be gutted*) **1** to take out the internal organs of (an animal or fish): *the fish were gutted on the quayside.* □ **destripar (animal); limpiar (pescado)**
2 to remove/to destroy (the contents of something): *the house was gutted by fire; the rooms were gutted of furniture.* □ **destruir el interior de**

gutter ['gʌtə] *n.* shallow trough below the eaves of a house or at the side of a street to carry away rainwater. □ **canalón**
gutter press, newspapers which specialize in scandals. □ **prensa sensacionalista**
■ *v.* (*of a candle*) to flicker so that the molten wax runs down the side. □ **derretirse**
guttering *n.* (*no pl.*) curved metal or plastic used to make gutters: *a piece of guttering.* □ **canal**
guttersnipe *n.* dirty child, living in the poor part of a town. □ **golfillo**

guttural ['gʌtrəl] *adj.* produced in the throat: *he spoke with a guttural accent.* □ **gutural**
gutturally *adv.* spoken in the throat. □ **guturalmente**

guy [gai] *n.* **1** (*informal*) man/fellow: *he's a nice guy.* □ **tío**
2 rope: *he tightened the guys on the tent.* □ **viento**
3 figure of a man burnt on a bonfire in England on 5th November. □ **mamarracho**
■ *v.* to imitate (someone) in a funny way. □ **parodiar**
guyrope *n.* rope which holds a tent tight. □ **viento**

guzzle ['gʌzl] *v.* to eat or drink greedily. □ **engullir**
guzzler *n.* person who eats greedily. □ **tragón**

gym [dʒim] **gymnasium** [dʒim'neiziəm] *n.* hall for indoor athletics and exercises. □ **gimnasio**
gymnast ['dʒimnæst] *n.* expert in gymnastics. □ **gimnasta**
gymnastic [dʒim'næstik] *adj.* referring to gymnastics. □ **gimnástico**
gymnastics *n.* exercises on wall bars/wooden horse, etc., to help develop muscles and physical coordination. □ **gimnasia**
gymslip *n.* dark-coloured dress with no sleeves, worn by schoolgirls as part of their uniform. □ **capa**

gymkhana [dʒim'kɑːnə] *n.* competition for horse riding and racing; display of horse riding. □ **competición deportiva**

gynaecology [gainə'kɔlədʒi] *n.* study of the diseases of women's reproductive system. □ **ginecología**
gynaecologist *n.* doctor specializing in diseases of women's reproductive system. □ **ginecólogo**
gynaecological [gainəkə'lɔdʒikl] *adj.* referring to women's diseases. □ **ginecológico**

gypsum ['dʒipsəm] *n.* sulphate of lime. □ **yeso**

gypsy ['dʒipsi] *n. see* **gipsy.**

gyrate [dʒai'reit] *v.* to turn round; to move rhythmically: *the dancers gyrated to the beat of the drums.* □ **girar**
gyration [dʒai'reiʃn] *n.* circular movement. □ **giro**

gyro- ['dʒairou] *prefix meaning* revolving. □ **giro-**
gyrocompass, compass which uses a gyroscope to avoid the shock of movement. □ **brújula giroscópica**
gyroscope ['dʒairəskoup] *n.* rapidly spinning wheel mounted so that it can rotate on any axis. □ **giroscopio**
gyroscopic [dʒairə'skɔpik] *adj.* rapidly spinning. □ **giroscópico**

H,h

H, h [eitʃ] eighth letter of the alphabet. □ **H, h**
H-bomb, hydrogen bomb. □ **bomba H**
habeas corpus ['heibiəs 'kɔ:pəs] *n.* order to bring a prisoner to answer a charge in court. □ **hábeas corpus**
haberdashery ['hæbədæʃri] *n.* (*pl. haberdasheries*) shop/department selling buttons, ribbons, thread and other sewing materials. □ **mercería**
habit ['hæbit] *n.* **1** custom; regular way of doing something: *I've got into the habit of reading the paper at breakfast; she's got out of the habit of getting up early; children get into bad habits.* □ **hábito**
from force of habit, because it is something you ordinarily do: *he put three lumps of sugar into his tea from force of habit.* □ **por costumbre**
2 dress. □ **traje**
riding habit, special dress for horse riding. □ **traje de montar**
habit-forming *adj.* (drug) which you can become addicted to. □ **que envicia**
habitual [hə'bitjuəl] *adj.* regular/normal: *he has his habitual cup of tea at 6.30 in the morning.* □ **habitual**
habitually *adv.* ordinarily/in the usual way. □ **habitualmente**
habituate *v.* to accustom someone to doing something. □ **habituar**
habitat ['hæbitæt] *n.* place where a certain animal or plant is usually found: *the natural habitat of the giraffe is the plains of central Africa.* □ **hábitat**
habitation [hæbi'teiʃn] *n.* **1** place/building where someone lives: *there is no human habitation for miles around.* □ **morada**
2 *it isn't fit for habitation,* not fit to live in. □ **no es adecuado para vivir**
habitable ['hæbitəbl] *adj.* fit to live in. □ **habitable**
hack [hæk] *n.* **1** horse which is hired. □ **caballo de alquiler**
2 writer who is paid by the piece. □ **escritor a destajo**
3 (*slang*) second-rate journalist. □ **periodista de segunda**
■ *v.* to chop roughly: *he hacked the log to pieces; she was hacking away at the joint.* □ **cortar**
hacking *adj. a hacking cough,* a dry unpleasant cough. □ **tos seca**
hackles ['hæklz] *n. pl.* neck feathers (on a cock). □ **plumas del cuello**
to put someone's hackles up, to make someone annoyed. □ **encolarizar a uno**
hackney ['hækni] *n.* ***hackney carriage,*** taxi. □ **coche de alquiler**
hackneyed ['hæknid] *adj.* well-worn (phrase); (phrase) which is often used. □ **expresión estereotipada**
hacksaw ['hæksɔ:] *n.* saw for cutting metal, which has a narrow blade attached to a frame. □ **sierra para metales**
had [hæd] *v. see* **have.**
haddock ['hædək] *n.* (*pl. haddock*) white fish found in cold seas. □ **eglefino**
smoked haddock, haddock hung in smoke until it is yellow. □ **...ahumado**
haemoglobin [hi:mə'gloubin] *n.* substance in red blood cells which contains iron and carries oxygen. □ **hemoglobina**
haemophilia [hi:mə'filiə] *n.* hereditary disease in males which prevents blood from clotting. □ **hemofilia**
haemorrhage ['hemərid3] *n.* loss of large quantity of blood from a wound, usually internal. □ **hemorragia**
haemorrhoids ['hemərɔidz] *n. pl.* small swollen veins at the anus. □ **hemorroides**
haft [hɑ:ft] *n.* handle (of a knife, etc.). □ **mango**
hag [hæg] *n.* witch; ugly old woman. □ **bruja**
haggard ['hægəd] *adj.* thin/tired (face). □ **ojeroso**
haggis ['hægis] *n.* Scottish food, made of sheep's heart, liver, etc., cooked with oats in a bag. □ **plato escocés**
haggle ['hægl] *v.* to discuss the price of something to try to reduce it: *she was haggling with the fisherman over the price of a lobster.* □ **regatear**
ha-ha ['hɑ:hɑ:] *interjection* (to show that you are amused). □ **¡ja, ja!**
■ *n.* fence put at the bottom of a ditch so that it cannot spoil the view from a house. □ **foso con escarpa**
hail [heil] *n.* **1** small pieces of ice which fall like frozen rain. □ **granizo**
2 small missiles which fall: *a hail of bullets.* □ **una lluvia de balas**
3 call: *when the ship was within hail,* was near enough to be called. □ **alcance de la voz**
■ *v.* **1** to fall as small pieces of ice; to fall in small pieces: *it's hailing; stones hailed round the policemen,* stones were flying around the policemen. □ **granizar**
2 to call out to someone: *someone hailed him from the other side of the street; he hailed a taxi,* waved to a taxi to stop. □ **llamar**
3 to come from: *where does he hail from?* □ **provenir**
hailstone *n.* small piece of ice falling from the sky. □ **granizo**
hailstorm *n.* storm when small pieces of ice fall from the sky. □ **pedrisco**
hair [hɛə] *n.* **1** single long thread growing on the body of a human or animal: *there's a hair in my soup.* □ **pelo**
2 *they escaped* ***by a hair's breadth,*** they nearly didn't escape. □ **escaparon por un pelo**
3 mass of hairs growing on the head: *she's got red hair; I must have my hair cut.* □ **pelo**
to let your hair down, (*informal*) to have a good time. □ **soltarse la melena**
hairbrush *n.* special brush for keeping your hair tidy. □ **cepillo**
haircut *n.* making your hair shorter by cutting: *he needs a haircut,* his hair is too long. □ **corte de pelo**
hairdo *n.* (*pl. hairdos*) style of a woman's hair. □ **peinado**
hairdresser *n.* person who cuts/dyes/styles hair. □ **peluquero**
hairdressing *n.* cutting/dyeing/styling hair: *hairdressing salon.* □ **peluquería**
hairless *adj.* with no hair. □ **pelón**
hairnet *n.* light net worn over the hair to keep it in place. □ **redecilla**
hairpiece *n.* small wig; piece of false hair. □ **postizo**
hairpin *n.* bent piece of wire used to keep hair in place. □ **horquilla**
hairpin bend, very sharp bend, as on a mountain road. □ **curva muy cerrada**

hair-raising *adj.* frightening. □ **espeluznante**
hairspring *n.* spiral spring in a watch. □ **muelle volante**
hairstyle *n.* way of dressing/cutting, etc., the hair: *I like his new hairstyle.* □ **peinado**
hairy *adj.* **1** covered with hairs. □ **peludo**
2 (*slang*) frighteningly dangerous. □ **peligroso**
hake [heik] *n.* (*pl. hake*) common small white sea fish. □ **merluza**
halcyon ['hælsiən] *adj.* calm/beautiful (weather). □ **apacible**
hale [heil] *adj.* ***hale and hearty,*** very healthy. □ **sano; más sano que una manzana**
half [hɑːf] *n.* (*pl. halves*) **1** one of two equal parts: *he cut the apple in half.* □ **mitad**
2 *our team scored twice in the first half,* in the first part of the match. □ **...en la primera mitad**
3 *let's go **halves** over the bill,* let's each pay half of it. □ **paguemos a medias**
4 midfield player in rugby. □ **medio**
5 child's ticket which costs half the adult fare. □ **medio billete**
■ *adj.* being divided into two equal parts: *half an hour,* 30 minutes; *two and a half hours,* 150 minutes; *half price.* □ **media hora; dos horas y media; a mitad de precio**
■ *adv.* partly; not fully: *the work is half finished; it is only half as big/half as tall,* smaller by half, 50 per cent of the size. □ **...medio acabado; la mitad**
half as big again, larger by half, 150 per cent of the size. □ **una vez y media más**
half-and-half *adv.* in two equal quantities. □ **mitad y mitad**
half-back *n.* football or rugby player in defence. □ **medio**
half-baked *adj.* (plan) which has not been well thought out; stupid (person). □ **incompleto; soso (persona)**
half-breed *n.* person/animal with parents of different races. □ **mestizo**
half-brother *n.* brother who has one parent the same as you. □ **hermanastro**
half-caste *n.* person with parents of two different races. □ **mestizo**
half-closed *adj.* partly closed. □ **entreabierto**
half-cock *n.* ***to go off at half-cock:*** *it went off at half-cock,* it had a bad start. □ **hizo una salida en falso**
half-dozen *n.* six. □ **media docena**
half-dressed *adj.* partly dressed/not wearing all your clothes. □ **medio vestido**
half-empty *adj.* partly empty/not completely empty. □ **medio vacio**
half-fare *n.* fare reduced by half: *children pay half-fare.* □ **medio billete**
half-hardy *adj.* (plant) which can stand some cold but not hard frost. □ **resistente al frío**
half-hearted *adj.* lacking conviction/enthusiasm. □ **poco entusiasta**
half-heartedly *adv.* without conviction/unenthusiastically. □ **sin entusiasmo**
half-hourly *adj.* and *adv.* every thirty minutes. □ **cada media hora**
half life *n.* time taken for a substance to lose half its radioactivity. □ **período de semidesintegración**
half-mast *n. the flags are at half-mast,* the flags are flying halfway up the flagpole as a sign of mourning. □ **a media asta**
half-open *adj.* partly open/not completely open. □ **medio abierto**
halfpenny ['heipni] *n.* (*pl.* ***halfpennies*** *for the coin, **half-pence** for the price*) coin worth half a penny. □ **medio penique**
half-sister *n.* sister who has one parent the same as you. □ **hermanastra**
half-term *n.* short holiday in the middle of a school term. □ **vacaciones (en la mitad del curso)**
half-timbered *adj.* (house) made of wooden beams with brick or plaster walls between. □ **con entramado de madera**
half-time *n.* short rest in the middle of a game of football, etc. □ **decanso**
half-tone *n.* photograph reproduced by means of dots of varying sizes. □ **medio tono**
half-track *n.* vehicle driven partly by caterpillar tracks and partly by ordinary wheels. □ **semioruga**
half-volley *n.* (*in tennis*) hitting the ball just after it has bounced. □ **media volea**
halfway *adv.* in the middle of a distance or length: *halfway across the street,* in the middle of crossing a street; *halfway up the mountain.* □ **a medio camino; en mitad de**
to meet someone halfway, to compromise with someone. □ **llegar a un arreglo con uno**
halfwit *n.* idiot. □ **tonto**
half-year *n.* six months. □ **medio año**
half-yearly *adj.* and *adv.* (taking place) every six months. □ **cada medio año**
halibut ['hælibʌt] *n.* (*pl. halibut*) large white flatfish living in the sea. □ **halibut**
halitosis [hæli'tousis] *n.* bad-smelling breath. □ **halitosis**
hall [hɔːl] *n.* **1** large room; large building for public meetings: *concert hall.* □ **sala**
hall of residence, large building where students live in a college. □ **colegio mayor**
2 (***entrance***) ***hall,*** small room or passage through which you enter a house. □ **'hall'**
3 large house, usually in the country. □ **casa solariega**
hallmark ['hɔːlmɑːk] *n.* mark put on gold and silver to show that it has the correct purity. □ **contraste**
hallmarked *adj.* (silver spoon, etc.) with a hallmark stamped on it. □ **contrastado**
hallo [hə'lou] *interjection* showing a greeting: *he called hallo from the other side of the street.* □ **hola**
hallow ['hælou] *v.* to bless (something)/to declare (something) holy. □ **santificar**
hallowed ground, ground (near a church) which has been blessed. □ **campo santo**
Hallowe'en [hælou'iːn] *n.* 31st October, when witches and ghosts are said to roam about. □ **víspera de Todos los Santos**
hallucination [həluːsi'neiʃn] *n.* seeing things which are not there. □ **alucinación**
hallucinate [hə'luːsineit] *v.* to make (someone) see visions. □ **alucinar**
hallucinatory [hə'luːsinətri] *adj.* (drug) which causes hallucinations. □ **alucinante**
hallucinogen [hə'luːsinədʒən] *n.* substance which makes you see things which are not there. □ **alucinógeno**
halo ['heilou] *n.* (*pl. haloes*) glow of light (round the moon/round the head of a saint). □ **halo**
halogen ['hælədʒən] *n.* one of a group of chemical elements (including chlorine/fluorine/iodine). □ **halógeno**
halt [hɔːlt] *n.* **1** complete stop: *production came to a halt,* production stopped; *we must call a halt to these expensive parties.* □ **alto**
2 very small railway station. □ **apeadero**
■ *v.* to stop: *the new legislation is intended to halt*

the increase in traffic offences. □ **parar**
halting *adj.* hesitant. □ **vacilante**
halter ['hɔːltə] *n.* rope put round animal's neck to lead it. □ **ronzal**
halter neck dress, dress with a piece of material going round the back of the neck, leaving the arms and back bare. □ **pareo**
halve [hɑːv] *v.* **1** to divide into two equal parts. □ **partir por la mitad**
2 to reduce by half: *the travelling time has been halved.* □ **reducir a la mitad**
halves *n. pl. see* **half.**
halyard ['hæljəd] *n.* rope used to pull a flag up a pole. □ **driza**
ham [hæm] *n.* **1** salted or smoked meat from a pig's leg usually eaten cold: *ham salad; ham and eggs.* □ **jamón**
2 (*informal*) bad actor. □ **comicastro**
3 (*informal*) amateur radio operator working from home. □ **radioaficionado**
■ *v.* (*he hammed*) to act badly. □ **interpretar mal (teatro)**
ham-fisted, ham-handed *adj.* clumsy. □ **torpe**
hamburger ['hæmbɜːgə] *n.* flat cake of minced beef, cooked and eaten as a sandwich in a toasted roll. □ **hamburguesa**
hamlet ['hæmlət] *n.* small village. □ **aldea**
hammer ['hæmə] *n.* **1** heavy metal tool for knocking nails into wood/posts into the ground, etc. □ **martillo**
2 object which hits something as part of a machine: *hammers in a piano.* □ **macillo**
3 metal ball which is thrown in sporting contests. □ **martillo**
■ *v.* to bang hard, as with a hammer: *he hammered the nail into the plank; they were hammering on the door with their fists.* □ **martillar**
hammer out *v.* **1** to make (something) flat with a hammer: *to hammer out a dent.* □ **aplanar con el martillo**
2 *to hammer out an agreement,* to come to an agreement after long difficult discussions. □ **llegar a**
hammock ['hæmək] *n.* hanging bed made of a strong cloth or net. □ **hamaca**
hamper ['hæmpə] *n.* large basket. □ **canasta**
■ *v.* to stop/to hinder/to get in the way: *the search for clues was hampered by bad weather.* □ **impedir**
hamster ['hæmstə] *n.* small rodent, often kept as a pet. □ **hámster**
hamstring ['hæmstrɪŋ] *n.* tendon behind the knee. □ **tendón de la corva**
hamstrung *adj.* incapacitated; unable to do anything. □ **paralizado**
hand [hænd] *n.* **1** part of the body at the end of each arm: *he held on to the branch with both hands.* □ **mano**
2 ***to shake hands:*** *they shook hands,* they greeted each other by clasping each other's right hand. □ **darse la mano**
3 *he can* ***turn his hand to*** *anything,* he can do any sort of job. □ **poderse dedicar a cualquier cosa**
4 ***to have a hand in:*** *he had a hand in the burglary,* he helped in the burglary. □ **tener que ver en**
5 *can you* ***give*** *me* ***a hand/lend a hand*** *with the washing up?* can you help me do the washing up? □ **¿me puedes echar una mano?**
6 ***to change hands:*** *the car has changed hands twice since I sold it,* has had three owners. □ **el coche ha cambiado de manos...**
7 ***to get out of hand:*** *inflation has got out of hand,* inflation is uncontrollable. □ **la inflación se les ha escapado de las manos**
8 ***to be hand in glove with someone,*** to be someone's accomplice. □ **estar conchabado con**
9 *to lose money* ***hand over fist,*** to lose a lot of money quickly. □ **perder dinero en un abrir y cerrar de ojos**
10 workman; sailor: *his firm is very small — there is himself, his son and two hands; the ship went down with all hands,* sank with all the crew. □ **...y dos operarios; marinero**
11 *he's an* ***old hand*** *at driving steam engines,* he is very experienced. □ **es un viejo zorro...**
12 cards which have been dealt you in a game. □ **mano**
13 one of pointers on a clock or dial: *the hour hand; the minute hand.* □ **manecilla**
■ *v.* to pass (something to someone) by hand: *can you hand me the screwdriver?* □ **pasar**
handbag *n.* woman's bag for carrying money, handkerchief and other belongings. □ **bolso**
handbook *n.* book which gives instructions or information. □ **manual**
handclap *n.* ***slow handclap,*** regular slow beating of the hands to show impatience/boredom: *the audience gave the star a slow handclap.* □ **palmas**
handcuff *v.* to chain someone's wrists together: *he was handcuffed to a policeman.* □ **esposar**
handcuffs *n. pl.* metal rings linked by a chain for attaching a prisoner's hands together. □ **esposas**
handful *n.* **1** as much as you can hold in your hand: *they scattered handfuls of confetti.* □ **puñado**
2 *only a handful of people came to the meeting,* not many people. □ **sólo un puñado de gente...**
3 *he is a bit of a handful,* he is difficult to control. □ **tiene el diablo en el cuerpo**
handicap *n.* **1** physical/mental disability; something which puts you at a disadvantage: *not being able to read is a great handicap.* □ **minusvalía; 'handicap'**
2 penalty imposed on good sportsmen to make it harder for them to win. □ **'handicap'**
■ *v.* (*it handicapped*) to put at a disadvantage: *he was handicapped by his lack of money.* □ **perjudicar**
the mentally handicapped, people with a disability of the mind. □ **los deficientes mentales**
handicraft *n.* work done by hand. □ **artesanía**
handicrafts, artistic work done by hand (such as knitting/pottery, etc.). □ **objetos de artesanía**
hand in *v.* to give in by hand: *the letter was handed in by a messenger.* □ **entregar en mano**
handiwork *n.* **1** work (usually bad) done by a particular person. □ **obra**
2 *is this his handiwork?,* did he do this? □ **¿es ésta su obra?**
handkerchief ['hæŋkətʃiːf] *n.* square piece of cloth or paper for wiping your nose. □ **pañuelo**
handmade *adj.* made by hand, not by a machine: *handmade chocolates.* □ **hecho a mano**
hand on *v.* to pass on by hand. □ **pasar**
hand out *v.* to distribute. □ **repartir**
handout *n.* **1** money which is given out: *he lives on handouts from the government.* □ **ayuda**
2 sheet of paper with information printed on it which is given to people. □ **hoja informativa**
hand over *v.* to give something to someone: *hand over your money.* □ **entregar**
handrail *n.* bar which you hold on to (next to a staircase, escalator, etc.). □ **barandilla**
hand round *v.* to pass round by hand: *she handed round the cake.* □ **hacer circular**
handshake *n.* greeting when you grasp right hands. □ **apretón de manos**

handspring *n.* gymnastic exercise where you turn a somersault on your hands and land on your feet. □ **voltereta**
handstand *n. to do a handstand,* to balance on your hands with your feet in the air. □ **hacer el pino**
handwriting *n.* writing done by hand: *his handwriting is so small you can hardly read it.* □ **letra**
handwritten *adj.* written by hand; not typed or printed. □ **escrito a mano**
handy *adj.* (*handier, handiest*) **1** useful; in a convenient place: *it is a handy tool to have around; keep the salt handy when cooking.* □ **práctico (herramienta); a mano (la sal)**
2 *this will **come in handy,*** this will be useful. □ **esto vendrá bien**
handyman *n.* (*pl. handymen*) person who can do any sort of work, especially repairs in the house. □ **factótum**

handle ['hændl] *n.* part of an object which you hold in the hand: *the handle of the knife; cup handle.* □ **mango del cuchillo; asa de la taza**
■ *v.* **1** to move (goods) around (by hand). □ **manipular**
2 to deal with (something): *the director is handling the case himself.* □ **ocuparse**
3 *you must handle him very carefully,* you must treat him carefully as he is likely to be difficult. □ **tratar**
handling charge, charge which has to be paid to someone who has delivered or dealt with something. □ **cargo por manipulación**
handlebar(s) *n.* (*pl.*) bar on the front of a bicycle or motorcycle which steers the front wheel: *keep both hands on the handlebars.* □ **manillar**

handsome ['hænsəm] *adj.* **1** good-looking: *a handsome man.* □ **guapo**
2 fine/large: *we made a handsome profit.* □ **considerable**
handsomely *adv.* elegantly; generously. □ **elegantemente**

hang [hæŋ] *n.* **1** way in which something hangs/drops/falls. □ **caída**
2 ***to get the hang of something,*** (*informal*) to understand how something works. □ **cogerle el truco a algo**
3 ***not give/care a hang:*** *he doesn't give a hang,* (*informal*) he doesn't worry about it at all. □ **no le importa un bledo**
■ *v.* (*he hung*) **1** to attach/to be attached above the ground to a nail or by a string/chain, etc.: *hang your coat on the hook; he was hanging from the branch by one hand.* □ **colgar**
2 *she hung her head,* let her head droop forward. □ **bajar**
3 to stick wallpaper on a wall. □ **pegar**
4 (*he hanged*) to kill (someone) by tying a rope round his neck and suspending him off the ground: *the murderer was hanged; she hanged herself.* □ **colgar**
hang about, hang around *v.* (*informal*) to wait/to wander aimlessly in a certain place. □ **andar rondando**
hang back *v.* to stay behind the others. □ **quedarse atrás**
hang down *v.* to hang in a long piece: *her hair hangs down her back.* □ **colgar, caer**
hanger *n.* object for hanging something. □ **gancho**
coat hanger, piece of wood/plastic/metal which is placed inside a coat to hang it up. □ **percha**
hanger-on *n.* (*pl. hangers-on*) person who stays near someone in the hope of getting money or food from them. □ **gorrón**
hang glider *n.* huge kite used in hang gliding. □ **planeador**
hang gliding *n.* sport of floating through the air by hanging on to a huge kite made of a metal frame covered with plastic. □ **ala delta**
hanging *n.* carpet/tapestry which is hung on a wall as decoration. □ **colgaduras**
hangman *n.* (*pl. hangmen*) executioner who kills people by hanging them. □ **verdugo**
hangnail *n.* torn skin at the root of a fingernail. □ **padrastro**
hang on *v.* **1** to clutch (something): *he hung on to his hat.* □ **agarrarse a**
2 (*informal*) to wait: *hang on a moment,* wait a bit. □ **quedarse; esperar**
hangover *n.* **1** unpleasant effects of having drunk too much alcohol: *he has got a terrible hangover this morning.* □ **resaca**
2 something left behind from an earlier period: *it is a hangover from pre-war days.* □ **restos**
hang up *v.* to hang (something) on a hook; to replace a telephone receiver: *she hung up on me,* she replaced the receiver in the middle of my telephone call. □ **colgar**
hang-up *n.* (*pl. hang-ups*) (*slang*) something which worries you and prevents you acting normally. □ **congoja**

hangar ['hæŋə] *n.* large shed for keeping aircraft in. □ **hangar**

hank [hæŋk] *n.* wool coiled into a loose loop. □ **madeja**

hanker ['hæŋkə] *v. he is always hankering after the latest mode car,* he always wants to get the latest model car. □ **anhelar**
hankering *n.* desire. □ **anhelo**

hanky ['hæŋki] *n.* (*pl. hankies*) (*informal*) handkerchief. □ **pañuelo**

hankypanky [hæŋki'pæŋki] *n.* (*no pl.*) (*informal*) trouble/bad behaviour; trickery. □ **camelo**

haphazard [hæp'hæzəd] *adj.* done at random/unplanned. □ **fortuito**
haphazardly *adv.* at random; without any plan. □ **a la buena de Dios**

hapless ['hæpləs] *adj.* (*formal*) unfortunate/unlucky. □ **desafortunado**

happen ['hæpn] *v.* **1** to take place: *don't let it happen again! how did it happen? the accident happened at the corner of the street; what has happened to his brother?,* what is his brother doing now? what sort of job has his brother got now? *something has happened to him,* he must have had an accident. □ **suceder**
2 to take place by chance: *I happened to meet him on the way to the station; the house happened to be empty at the time.* □ **por casualidad me encontré...; dio la casualidad de que...**
happening *n.* event/something which takes place. □ **acontecimiento**

happy ['hæpi] *adj.* (*happier, happiest*) full of joy/glad: *we're happy to hear you are better; the children were happy to have an extra holiday.* □ **feliz**
Happy Christmas! Happy Birthday!, greetings said at Christmas and on a birthday. □ **¡feliz Navidad!; ¡feliz cumpleaños!**
happily *adv.* joyfully/gladly: *he lived happily in his little cottage.* □ **felizmente**
happiness *n.* joy/gladness. □ **felicidad**
happy-go-lucky *adj.* easy-going/carefree. □ **despreocupado**

hara-kiri [hærə'kiri] *n.* Japanese form of suicide. □ **haraquiri**

harangue [hə'ræŋ] *n.* loud speech. □ **arenga**
■ *v.* to make a loud speech to (someone): *he stood on a balcony and harangued the crowd for two hours.* □ **arengar**

harass ['hærəs, *Amer.* hə'ræs] *v.* to bother/to worry (someone): *she is looking harassed.* □ **agobiar**
harassment *n.* bothering/worrying; many small attacks on an enemy. □ **hostigamiento**

harbinger ['hɑːbindʒə] *n.* (*formal*) something which shows that something else is approaching: *a harbinger of summer.* □ **anuncio de la llegada de**

harbour ['hɑːbə] *Amer.* **harbor** *n.* port/safe place where ships can tie up to load or unload. □ **puerto**
■ *v.* **1** to keep: *dirty kitchens harbour disease.* □ **contener**
2 *to harbour a grudge against someone,* to have secret spiteful feelings against someone. □ **albergar**

hard [hɑːd] *adj.* **1** firm; not soft: *a hard bed; the putty has gone hard.* □ **duro**
2 *hard currency,* one which does not lose its value compared to other currencies. □ **moneda fuerte**
3 difficult: *this crossword is very hard; I find it hard to be polite to him; it was hard for her to see the children leave the house.* □ **difícil**
hard times, times when things go badly. □ **malos tiempos**
hard lines/hard luck, bad luck. □ **mala suerte**
hard labour, punishment involving difficult manual work. □ **trabajos forzosos**
4 strict/severe: *he took a hard line on cheating,* he was very strict in punishing cheating; *hard winter,* very severe winter. □ **riguroso**
5 (*of water*) containing calcium, which makes it difficult to form a lather. □ **dura**
6 strong (drink); (drug) which makes you become addicted. □ **fuerte, duro**
hard drinker, person who drinks a lot of alcohol. □ **bebedor empedernido**
■ *adv.* **1** strongly; with great energy: *hit the nail hard; they were working hard; it's raining hard.* □ **con fuerza; mucho**
2 *think hard,* think deeply. □ **pensar mucho**
3 with difficulty: *a hard-fought battle.* □ **reñido**
hard-and-fast *adj.* strict/absolute (rule). □ **rígido**
hardback *n.* book with a stiff cover. □ **en tapa dura**
hardboard *n.* artificial board made of small shreds of wood stuck together. □ **aglomerado**
hard-boiled *adj.* **1** (egg) which has been boiled until the white and yolk are set solid. □ **huevo duro**
2 (person) without much feeling/who is not easily shocked. □ **duro**
hardcore *n.* **1** packed rubble used in making paths. □ **guijo; cascajo**
2 central part (of a group): *the army is battling against the hardcore of the guerrilla movement.* □ **grueso**
■ *adj.* referring to a central group: *the hardcore prisoners,* the main group of old prisoners. □ **el grueso de los prisioneros**
harden *v.* to make hard. □ **endurecer**
hardened criminal, regular/permanent criminal. □ **habitual**
harden off *v.* to bring tender plants into the open air. □ **sacar fuera**
hard hat *n.* protective helmet worn by construction workers, etc. □ **casco**
hard-headed *adj.* practical/sensible. □ **realista**
hard-hearted *adj.* cruel. □ **insensible**
hardliner *n.* person who is very antagonistic/stern towards someone/an enemy, etc. □ **implacable**
hardly *adv.* almost not: *I hardly know him.* □ **apenas**
hardly anyone, almost no one. □ **casi nadie**
hardly ever, almost never. □ **casi nunca**
hardness *n.* being solid/hard/not soft; difficulty; strictness. □ **dureza; dificultad; severidad**
hard of hearing *adj.* (person) who is quite deaf. □ **duro de oído**
hard sell *n.* strenuous efforts to sell something. □ **método agresivo de vender**
hardship *n.* suffering caused by lack of something. □ **apuros**
hard shoulder *n.* strip along the edge of a motorway where vehicles can park if they have broken down. □ **arcén**
hard up *adj.* (*informal*) with no money. □ **(estar) sin un duro**
hardware *n.* (*no pl.*) **1** tools, pots and pans: *hardware store,* shop selling pans/hammers/nails/paint, etc. □ **artículos de ferretería**
2 physical parts/machinery of a computer. □ **'hardware'**
hard-wearing *adj.* which does not wear out easily. □ **resistente**
hardworking *adj.* (person) who works hard. □ **trabajador**
hardy *adj.* (*hardier, hardiest*) which can survive in difficult conditions: *mountain sheep are very hardy.* □ **duro**
hardy plant, plant which can stay out of doors all the year round. □ **planta resistente**

hare ['hɛə] *n.* common field mammal, like a large rabbit. □ **liebre**
harebell *n.* wild flower shaped like a little blue bell. □ **campánula**
hare-brained *adj.* mad/senseless (plan). □ **descabellado**
hare-lip *n.* split in the upper lip from birth. □ **labio leporino**

harem [hɑː'riːm] *n.* women in a Muslim household; women's quarters in a Muslim house. □ **harén**

haricot ['hærikou] *n.* ***haricot (bean),*** type of dry white bean eaten cooked. □ **judía**

hark [hɑːk] *old interjection meaning* listen. □ **¡oye!**
■ *v.* ***to hark back to something,*** to go back to a subject which was talked about earlier. □ **volver a**

harm [hɑːm] *n.* **1** damage: *a little drop of whisky doesn't do you any harm.* □ **daño**
2 *he will* ***come to harm,*** he will have an accident. □ **accidentarse**
3 ***there's no harm*** *in trying,* you might as well try. □ **no pasa nada si lo intentas**
■ *v.* to damage/to hurt; to do something bad to: *don't worry if the dog barks, he won't harm you.* □ **hacer daño**
harmful *adj.* which hurts/which causes damage. □ **perjudicial**
harmless *adj.* which causes no damage/which does not hurt. □ **inofensivo**

harmony ['hɑːməni] *n.* (*pl. harmonies*) **1** musical sounds which do not clash; agreeable effect (of music/colour, etc.). □ **armonía**
2 general agreement: *the two sides left the meeting in complete harmony.* □ **armonía**
harmonic [hɑː'mɔnik] *n.* higher note made when a note is played. □ **armónico**
harmonica [hɑː'mɔnikə] *n.* mouth organ. □ **armónica**
harmonious [hɑː'mouniəs] *adj.* (sounds) which are in agreement/which sound well together. □ **armonioso**
harmonium [hɑː'mouniəm] *n.* musical instrument

like an organ where the sound comes from air pumped through reeds. □ **armonio**
harmonize *v.* **1** to agree together. □ **estar en armonía**
2 to form chords out of the main tune of a piece of music. □ **armonizar**
harness ['hɑːnəs] *n.* (*pl. harnesses*) **1** leather straps which attach a horse to a cart. □ **arnés**
2 *he is still in harness,* he is still working. □ **está todavía en activo**
3 straps for attaching a parachute to someone; straps which have a lead attached to control a small child. □ **arnés (paracaídas); correa (niño)**
■ *v.* **1** to attach (a horse) to a cart. □ **enganchar**
2 to use (natural resources/atomic power/a waterfall, etc.) for making energy. □ **aprovechar**
harp [hɑːp] *n.* large upright musical instrument, with many strings which are plucked with the fingers. □ **arpa**
■ *v.* ***to harp on about:*** *he is always harping on about it,* he is always talking about it. □ **dar vueltas a**
harpoon [hɑː'puːn] *n.* long barbed spear used to kill whales. □ **arpón**
■ *v.* to kill (a whale) with a harpoon. □ **arponear**
harpsichord ['hɑːpsikɔːd] *n.* old musical instrument, like a piano, but with strings which are plucked mechanically. □ **clavicordio**
harrier ['hæriə] *n.* **1** dog/person who hunts hares. □ **lebrero, cazador**
2 long-distance runner. □ **corredor de fondo**
3 type of falcon. □ **halcón borní**
harrow ['hærou] *n.* large rake pulled by a tractor for breaking up heavy soil. □ **grada**
harrowing *adj.* very sad: *a harrowing story.* □ **desgarrador**
harry ['hæri] *v.* (*harries; harrying*) to bother/to worry (someone) by continual attacks. □ **fastidiar**
harsh [hɑːʃ] *adj.* (*harsher, harshest*) **1** cruel/sharp: *harsh punishment.* □ **duro**
2 rough/unpleasant: *harsh voice.* □ **bronco**
harshness *n.* cruelty/roughness. □ **rigor; aspereza**
harvest ['hɑːvist] *n.* **1** cutting/picking of ripe crops: *the apple harvest has been good.* □ **cosecha**
2 period of the year when crops are picked. □ **tiempo de la cosecha**
■ *v.* to cut/to pick ripe crops. □ **cosechar**
harvester *n.* person/machine which cuts crops. □ **cosechero (persona); cosechadora (máquina)**
has [hæz] *v. see* **have.**
has-been ['hæzbiːn] *n.* (*pl. has-beens*) (*informal*) person/thing no longer as well known/important as before. □ **vieja gloria**
hash [hæʃ] *n.* (*pl. hashes*) **1** minced meat. □ **carne picada**
to make a hash of: *he made a hash of it,* (*informal*) he did it badly. □ **se lo cargó**
2 (*informal*) hashish. □ **hachís**
■ *v.* to mince (meat, etc.). □ **picar**
hash(ed) brown potatoes, *Amer.* fried grated potatoes. □ **patatas cocidas y luego fritas**
hashish ['hæʃiʃ] *n.* hemp used as a drug. □ **hachís**
hasp [hɑːsp] *n.* metal bar which closes a door or lid by fitting over a loop which is locked with a padlock. □ **aldaba**
hassle ['hæsl] *n.* (*informal*) bother/struggle to do something: *it's too much hassle!* □ **¡qué follón!**
hassock ['hæsək] *n.* cushion for kneeling on in a church. □ **cojín**
haste [heist] *n.* speed. □ **prisa**
to make haste, to hurry up. □ **darse prisa**
hasten ['heisn] *v.* to make (something) go faster/come faster; to hurry up. □ **apremiar; acelerar**
hastily *adv.* rapidly. □ **apresuradamente**
hastiness *n.* hurry/lack of thought. □ **precipitación**
hasty *adj.* (*hastier, hastiest*) rapid and with not enough preparation. □ **precipitado**
hat [hæt] *n.* piece of clothing worn on the head: *he took his hat off when he spoke to her.* □ **sombrero**
to pass the hat round, to collect some money from people present. □ **pasar la gorra**
keep it under your hat, keep it secret. □ **manténlo en secreto**
hat trick, three goals, etc., scored by the same person in the same game. □ **marcar tres goles en un partido**
hatch [hætʃ] *n.* (*pl. hatches*) opening in a ship's deck; opening in floor or wall of an aircraft. □ **escotilla**
service hatch, small opening in a wall for passing food from a kitchen to a dining room. □ **ventanilla**
■ *v.* **1** to warm (eggs) until baby birds appear. □ **empollar**
2 *the chickens have hatched (out),* the chickens have come out of their eggs. □ **...han salido del cascarón**
3 *to hatch a plot,* to plan a plot. □ **maquinar**
4 to indicate shade in a sketch by drawing parallel lines close together. □ **sombrear**
hatchback *n.* type of car with a sloping back and a large rear door which opens upwards. □ **un tres puertas**
hatchery *n.* (*pl. hatcheries*) place where eggs are kept until they develop into young. □ **criadero**
hatchway *n.* opening in a ship's deck. □ **escotilla**
hatchet ['hætʃit] *n.* small axe. □ **destral**
to bury the hatchet, (*informal*) to make peace. □ **enterrar el hacha**
hatchet man, (*slang*) person brought into a firm to sack some of the staff. □ **contratado para despedir**
hatchet-faced, (person) with a grim pointed face. □ **de rostro afilado**
hate [heit] *n.* great dislike. □ **odio**
■ *v.* **1** to dislike intensely: *I hate cold eggs.* □ **odiar**
2 *I hate to trouble you,* I don't like troubling you. □ **siento molestarle**
hateful *adj.* horrible/unpleasant. □ **odioso**
hatred *n.* great dislike. □ **odio**
haughty ['hɔːti] *adj.* (*haughtier, haughtiest*) very proud. □ **altivo**
haughtily *adv.* proudly. □ **altivamente**
haul [hɔːl] *n.* **1** catch (of fish). □ **captura**
2 *the burglars made a good haul,* they stole a lot of valuable property. □ **botín**
3 distance travelled: *it is a good haul up this hill,* it's a long way; *a long haul flight,* flight usually between continents. □ **distancia**
■ *v.* to pull with difficulty. □ **arrastrar**
haulage *n.* moving of goods by road: *haulage contractor,* person who arranges for goods to be moved by road. □ **transporte por carretera**
haulier *n.* person who arranges for goods to be moved by road. □ **transportista por carretera**
haunch [hɔːnʃ] *n.* (*pl. haunches*) thigh and loin (of an animal): *haunch of venison; the dog was sitting on its haunches,* sitting in a squatting position. □ **pernil**
haunt [hɔːnt] *n.* place where someone goes frequently: *it is one of my favourite haunts.* □ **lugar predilecto**
■ *v.* to go to (a place) frequently; (*of ghosts*) to appear in (a place): *the house is haunted.* □ **frecuentar; aparecer en (fantasma); la casa está encantada**
have [hæv] *v.* (*I have, he has; I had, he had*) **1** (*also*

have got) to possess: *he has (got) a lot of money; she has (got) a green car.* □ **tener**
2 (*also* ***have got***) to hold: *the house has (got) no telephone.* □ **tener**
3 to take: *will you have some milk in your tea? have you had any lunch? to have a bath.* □ **tomar**
4 to play: *will you have a game of tennis?* □ **echar**
5 to get (something) done: *he is having his house painted; you ought to have your hair cut.* □ **le están pintando la casa; te deberías cortar el pelo**
6 (making the past tense of verbs): *he has eaten his meal; have you finished your work?* □ **haber; él ha comido...**
7 (showing compulsion to do something): *you will have to sing that song again; you had better say nothing.* □ **tendrás que volver a cantar...; sería mejor que no dijeras nada**
have got *v.* ***to have got to do something,*** to be obliged/to have to do something: *I've got to go to the dentist; we've got to leave at five o'clock.* □ **tener que**
have had *v. he's had it,* (*informal*) he is finished/he has missed an opportunity. □ **estar acabado, perdido**
have on *v.* **1** to be wearing: *she had nothing on.* □ **llevar puesto**
2 to be busy/occupied: *have you anything on tonight?* □ **tener algo que hacer**
3 (*informal*) to trick (someone): *they're having you on.* □ **tomar el pelo, engañar**
have out *v.* **1** *to have a tooth out,* to get a tooth removed by a dentist. □ **sacarse una muela**
2 ***to have it out with someone,*** to sort out a quarrel with someone. □ **tenerla con alguien**
have up *v.* (*informal*) to call (someone) to a court: *he has been had up for speeding.* □ **llevar a juicio**
haven ['heivn] *n.* safe port; safe place. □ **abra; refugio**
haversack ['hævəsæk] *n.* bag carried on the back. □ **mochila**
havoc ['hævək] *n.* damage: *to create havoc.* □ **estragos**
to play havoc with: *the storm has played havoc with the harvest,* done a lot of damage to the harvest. □ **...ha hecho estragos...**
haw [hɔː] *n.* small red berry on the hawthorn. □ **baya del espino**
■ *v. see* **hum.**
hawk [hɔːk] *n.* **1** bird of prey: *she has eyes like a hawk,* she has very good eyesight/notices every detail. □ **halcón**
2 person who is in favour of military attacks on an enemy/who is prepared to take a hard line in international relations. □ **halcón**
■ *v.* to sell goods from door to door. □ **vender de puerta en puerta**
hawker *n.* person who sells things from door to door. □ **vendedor de puerta en puerta**
hawser ['hɔːzə] *n.* thick rope for attaching a boat to the quay. □ **estacha**
hawthorn ['hɔːθɔːn] *n.* common hedge shrub with white flowers and red berries. □ **espino**
hay [hei] *n.* long dried grass used to feed cattle in winter. □ **heno**
to make the hay, to cut the grass in a field. □ **henificar**
to make hay while the sun shines, to enjoy yourself/to make money while you can. □ **a la ocasión la pintan calva**
hayfever *n.* running nose/eyes, etc., caused by an allergy to pollen or dust. □ **fiebre del heno**
haymaker *n.* person who is helping cut the hay. □ **henificador**
haymaking *n.* cutting of the hay. □ **henificación**
haystack *n.* bales of hay stored in a large heap built like a house. □ **almiar**
haywire *adj. he's gone haywire,* (*informal*) he's gone mad. □ **chalado**
hazard ['hæzəd] *n.* **1** risk. □ **riesgo**
2 rough ground (on a golf course). □ **obstáculo**
■ *v.* **1** to risk. □ **arriesgar**
2 *he hazarded a guess,* he made a rough guess. □ **aventurar**
hazardous *adj.* dangerous/risky. □ **arriesgado**
haze [heiz] *n.* light mist. □ **neblina**
hazily *adv.* vaguely. □ **confusamente**
hazy *adj.* (*hazier, haziest*) **1** misty. □ **nebuloso**
2 vague: *I'm a bit hazy about the details.* □ **confuso**
hazel ['heizl] *n.* tree which bears small nuts. □ **avellano**
hazel nut *n.* nut from a hazel tree. □ **avellana**
he [hiː] **1** pronoun referring to a male person or animal: *he is my father; he and I went there together.* □ **él**
2 *prefix meaning* male: *he-bear; he-goat.* □ **macho**
he-man *n.* (*pl. he-men*) strong/virile man. □ **macho**
head [hed] *n.* **1** part of the body with brain, eyes, ears, mouth, etc., which is attached to the rest of the body by the neck: *he can stand on his head; the horse won by a head,* by the length of a head; *he has a good head for business; what put that idea into your head?* □ **cabeza**
2 *it was all rather* ***over his head,*** rather more complicated than he could understand. □ **fuera de su alcance (intelectual)**
3 ***off the top of my head,*** at a guess. □ **a primera vista**
4 ***head over heels*** (i) *he rolled head over heels,* over and over. □ **dio unas volteretas**
(ii) *he fell head over heels in love,* completely in love. □ **enamorarse perdidamente**
5 top; leafy part (of a cabbage); foam (on the top of a glass of beer). □ **parte superior; hojas; espuma (cerveza)**
6 first one: *at the head of the list/of a procession.* □ **cabeza**
7 most important person: *he is the head of our export department; head gardener; head waiter.* □ **jefe**
8 top side of a coin; side of a coin with the head of a king, etc., on it. □ **cara**
9 *to play* ***heads or tails,*** to spin a coin and try to guess which side will be on top. □ **echar a cara o cruz**
10 (*no pl.*) number of animals: *thirty head of sheep.* □ **treinta cabezas...**
■ *v.* **1** to be first/to lead: *he headed the procession; she headed the delegation to Russia,* was the leader. □ **encabezar**
2 to go towards: *he is heading for London.* □ **dirigirse**
3 to hit (a ball) with your head: *he headed the ball into the net.* □ **cabecear**
headache *n.* **1** pain in the head. □ **dolor de cabeza**
2 problem which is so complicated that it might give you a pain in the head. □ **dolor de cabeza**
headboard *n.* board or panel at the top of a bed. □ **cabecera**
headdress *n.* ornamental covering for the head. □ **tocado**
header *n.* **1** dive: *he took a header into the pool.* □ **se tiró de cabeza**
2 hitting a ball with the head. □ **golpe de cabeza**

head first *adv.* with one's head first: *he dived into the pool head first.* □ **de cabeza**
head-hunter *n.* **1** member of a tribe which cuts off the heads of enemies and collects them. □ **cazador de cabezas**
2 (*informal*) person who tries to find suitably qualified candidates for important jobs. □ **cazatalentos**
heading *n.* words at the top of a text: *list all the names under the heading 'overseas visitors'.* □ **encabezamiento**
headlamp *n.* main light on the front of a car/bicycle, etc. □ **faro**
headland *n.* promontory/large hill running into the sea. □ **punta**
headlight *n.* main light on the front of a car/bicycle, etc. □ **faro**
headline *n.* words in large capitals in a newspaper. □ **titulares**
to hit the headlines, to be part of the news. □ **ser noticia**
news headlines, short summary of the main items of news on TV/radio. □ **titulares**
headlong *adj.* and *adv.* rushing/non-stop; with your head first: *he fell headlong into a ditch.* □ **de bruces**
headmaster *n.* man in charge of a school. □ **director**
headmistress *n.* (*pl. headmistresses*) woman in charge of a school. □ **directora**
head off *v.* to prevent (something) from taking place: *to head off trouble.* □ **impedir**
head-on *adj.* and *adv.* with the front; head first: *the car ran into the wall head-on.* □ **de frente**
head-on collision, collision where two cars, etc., hit each other with the front first. □ **colisión de frente**
headphones *n. pl.* apparatus for listening to radio/records, etc., which fits over your ears with a band across the top of your head: *a pair of headphones.* □ **auriculares**
headquarters *n. pl.* main offices (of an army/of a firm). □ **cuartel general; oficina central**
headrest *n.* cushion/part of a seat for leaning your head on. □ **reposacabezas**
headroom *n.* space to pass upright: *the bridge has only three metres headroom.* □ **altura libre**
headscarf *n.* (*pl. headscarves*) square piece of colourful cloth worn by women to cover their hair. □ **pañuelo de cabeza**
headset *n.* apparatus for listening to radio/records etc., which fits over your ears with a band across the top of your head. □ **auriculares**
headship *n.* position of headmaster/headmistress. □ **dirección**
headstone *n.* gravestone. □ **lápida**
headstrong *adj.* obstinate/self-willed. □ **testarudo**
headway *n.* progress/movement forward: *we are not making much headway.* □ **progreso**
headwind *n.* wind blowing in your face. □ **viento de cara**
heady *adj.* (*headier, headiest*) (drink) which is likely to make you drunk; (news) which is likely to make you excited. □ **cabezón (bebida); impresionante (noticia)**
heal [hiːl] *v.* to make (a person/a wound) become healthy; to become healthy: *his finger has healed.* □ **curar**
healing *n.* making healthy. □ **curación**
health [helθ] *n.* **1** state of the body where there is no sickness: *he enjoys good health; your health!* □ **salud**
good health!, wish said when drinking: *we will drink to the health and happiness of the bride and bridegroom.* □ **¡salud!**
health farm, clinic in the country where people who eat or drink too much go to slim. □ **clínica de adelgazamiento**
health foods, natural foods (such as yoghurt/nuts, etc.) which are good for your health. □ **comida dietética**
health service, government-run service providing medical treatment for everyone. □ **Seguridad Social**
health visitor, person who visits sick people in their homes. □ **visitador de salud**
2 general state of the body: *she's in poor health.* □ **salud**
healthy *adj.* **1** full of good health; not ill. □ **sano**
2 *healthy climate,* climate which keeps people healthy. □ **un clima sano**
heap [hiːp] *n.* **1** large pile: *a heap of dead leaves.* □ **montón**
2 *he has **heaps of** money,* lots of money. □ **...montones de dinero**
■ *v.* **1** to pile up: *he heaped his plate with strawberries.* □ **llenar**
2 *a heaped spoonful,* a very full spoonful. □ **una cucharada colmada**
hear ['hiə] *v.* (*he heard*) **1** to sense sounds by the ear; to listen to (something): *can you hear the sound of bagpipes?* □ **oír**
2 ***to hear from:*** *I heard from him only yesterday,* I received a letter from him. □ **tuve noticias de él...**
3 *have you heard that there is going to be a general election?,* have you heard the news? □ **has oído...**
4 ***to hear of:*** *he's never heard of Shakespeare,* does not know who Shakespeare was. □ **nunca ha oído hablar de...**
he won't hear of it, he will not allow it. □ **no quiere ni oír hablar de ello**
hearer *n.* person who hears. □ **oyente**
hearing *n.* **1** ability to hear: *his hearing is bad.* □ **oído**
hearing aid, small device for improving the hearing of someone who is nearly deaf. □ **audífono**
2 listening to someone: *he would not give me a hearing.* □ **no se prestara a escucharme**
3 court case: *the hearing is adjourned for a week.* □ **vista**
hearsay *n.* what you hear people are saying: *it's only hearsay,* it's only a rumour/it might not be true. □ **habladuría**
heard [həːd] *v. see* **hear.**
hearse [həːs] *n.* vehicle for carrying a coffin. □ **coche fúnebre**
heart [hɑːt] *n.* **1** organ in an animal which pumps blood round the body. □ **corazón**
heart attack, severe illness when the heart stops temporarily. □ **ataque al corazón**
heart failure, dangerous condition when the heart has stopped beating: *he died of heart failure.* □ **paro cardiaco**
2 *to learn a lesson* ***by heart,*** learn it by memory so that you can repeat it. □ **aprender de memoria**
3 centre of the emotions: *my heart sank,* I was suddenly very sad/upset. □ **corazón**
4 ***to lose one's heart to:*** *he lost his heart to the girl next door,* fell in love. □ **enamorarse**
5 ***to set one's heart on:*** *she's set her heart on a new car,* she wants a new car very much. □ **ha puesto todo su empeño...**
6 centre: *the heart of the city; at heart he is very sensitive.* □ **centro de la ciudad; en el fondo él es...**
7 courage. □ **ánimo**

8 ***his heart isn't in it,*** he has lost hope/interest. □ **no tiene puesto su ánimo...**
9 ***hearts,*** one of the four suits of playing cards: *the queen of hearts.* □ **corazones**
heartbeat *n.* sound of the heart pumping blood. □ **latido**
heart-breaking *adj.* which makes you very sad/upset. □ **desgarrador**
heart-broken *adj.* extremely sad/disappointed. □ **acongojado**
heartburn *n.* burning feeling in the chest and stomach after eating indigestible food. □ **acidez de estómago**
hearten *v.* to encourage. □ **animar**
heartfelt *adj.* sincere. □ **sentido**
heartily *adv.* vigorously; warmly: *I am heartily sick of boiled cabbage.* □ **estoy completamente harto de...**
heartless *adj.* cruel. □ **inhumano**
heart-rending *adj.* pitiful. □ **conmovedor**
heartsearching *n.* deep thought about how to deal with a problem. □ **reflexión**
heart-to-heart *adj.* earnest private (conversation). □ **muy personal**
hearty *adj.* (*heartier, heartiest*) vigorous/strong; large (meal/appetite): *he ate a hearty breakfast.* □ **abundante**

hearth [hɑːθ] *n.* base of a fireplace; a fireplace. □ **chimenea**
hearthrug *n.* small rug placed in front of a fireplace. □ **alfombrilla**

heat [hiːt] *n.* **1** great warmth: *the heat made the paint blister.* □ **calor**
in the heat of the moment, in the excitement. □ **en el acaloramiento del momento**
2 qualifying round in a competition: *he won his heat and went through to the semi-finals.* □ **eliminatoria**
dead heat, race where two competitors come in equal first. □ **empate**
■ *v.* **1** to warm to a higher temperature: *heat the soup for ten minutes.* □ **calentar**
2 *heated discussion,* discussion where people become quite angry. □ **discusión acalorada**
heater *n.* apparatus for warming. □ **calentador**
gas heater, heater which works by gas. □ **...de gas**
water heater, heater which heats water. □ **...de agua**
heating *n.* making something warm; means of heating: *the heating has gone off.* □ **calefacción**
central heating, heating system for a whole building from one source. □ **calefacción central**
heatwave *n.* period of very hot weather. □ **ola de calor**

heath [hiːθ] *n.* **1** wild country covered with low shrubs. □ **brezal**
2 heather. □ **brezo**

heathen ['hiːðn] *adj.* and *n.* (person) who is not a Christian; (person) who is not a member of any important religious group. □ **pagano**

heather ['heðə] *n.* wild plant with small purple or white bell-shaped flowers, which grows on moors and mountains. □ **brezo**

heave [hiːv] *n.* hard pull: *they gave a final heave and pulled the boat out of the water.* □ **empujón**
■ *v.* **1** to pull hard: *to heave up the anchor; to heave at a rope.* □ **levantar el ancla; halar de la cuerda**
2 (*he hove*) ***to heave to,*** to stop a ship. □ **ponerse al pairo**
3 ***to heave in sight,*** to appear. □ **aparecer**
4 (*informal*) to throw: *heave me that cushion!* □ **tirar**
5 to breathe hard: *he heaved a sigh of relief.* □ **exhalar un suspiro**

heaven ['hevn] *n.* **1** paradise/place where God and the angels live: *his soul is in heaven.* □ **cielo**
2 ***the heavens,*** the sky: *the heavens opened,* it rained very hard. □ **el cielo**
good heavens!, how surprising! □ **¡Dios mío!**
heavenly *adj.* **1** belonging to heaven: *heavenly choir of angels.* □ **celestial**
2 (*informal*) beautiful; very fine: *what heavenly perfume!* □ **divino**
heaven-sent *adj.* lucky: *a heaven-sent opportunity to make money.* □ **llovido del cielo**

heavy ['hevi] *adj.* (*heavier, heaviest*) **1** weighing a lot: *heavy luggage; a bag of potatoes is heavy.* □ **pesado**
2 *heavy meal,* meal which is very filling and indigestible. □ **comida pesada**
3 strong/great: *heavy artillery; a heavy shower of rain.* □ **artillería pesada; un fuerte chaparrón**
4 rough: *heavy sea.* □ **mar gruesa**
to make heavy weather of: he's making heavy weather of it, having difficulty in doing it. □ **las está pasando moradas...**
5 full: *a heavy timetable.* □ **un horario cargado**
6 *heavy drinker,* someone who drinks a lot of alcohol. □ **que bebe mucho**
heavily *adv.* **1** as if weighing a lot: *he fell heavily to the ground.* □ **pesadamente**
2 greatly: *he lost heavily on the horses.* □ **mucho**
3 *heavily underlined,* with thick lines written underneath. □ **muy subrayado**
4 soundly: *he slept heavily.* □ **durmió profundamente**
heaviness *n.* weight. □ **pesadez**
heavy-duty *adj.* (machine, etc.) specially made for rough work. □ **para trabajos duros**
heavy industry *n.* industry which makes large products (like steel/ships/cars, etc.). □ **industria pesada**
heavyweight *n.* heaviest category of boxer. □ **peso pesado**

Hebrew ['hiːbruː] *n.* **1** member of Jewish people living in ancient Palestine. □ **hebreo**
2 language of Jews in modern Israel. □ **hebreo**

heckle ['hekl] *v.* to call out; to interrupt a public speaker. □ **interrumpir**
heckler *n.* person who interrupts a speaker at a meeting. □ **el que interrumpe**
heckling *n.* interrupting a speaker. □ **interrupción**

hectare ['hektɑː] *n.* (measure of) area of 10,000 square metres (approximately 2.4 acres). □ **hectárea**

hectic ['hektik] *adj.* very busy/active: *the period before Christmas is always very hectic.* □ **febril**

hector ['hektə] *v.* to bully/to intimidate. □ **intimidar con bravatas**
hectoring *adj.* bullying (tone of voice). □ **con tono intimidatorio**

hedge [hedʒ] *n.* **1** screen/fence made of growing shrubs: *a beech hedge; to trim the hedge.* □ **seto**
2 protection: *it is a hedge against inflation.* □ **barrera**
■ *v.* **1** to surround with a hedge. □ **cercar con un seto**
2 to avoid answering a question. □ **contestar con evasivas**
3 *to hedge your bets,* to arrange things so that you will be protected against losing. □ **cubrirse**
hedgehog *n.* small mammal covered with prickles. □ **erizo**
hedgerow *n.* long hedge, especially by the side of a country road. □ **seto vivo**

hedonist ['hiːdənist] *n.* person who lives for pleasure. □ **hedonista**

heed [hi:d] *n.* ***to take heed of something,*** to pay attention to something. □ **consideración, atención**
■ *v.* to pay attention: *he heeded our warnings.* □ **prestar atención a**
heedless *adj.* careless/imprudent. □ **descuidado**
heedlessly *adv.* carelessly/without paying attention. □ **a la ligera**
heel [hi:l] *n.* **1** back part of the foot; back part of a sock/stocking into which the heel of the foot goes. □ **talón**
2 raised block under the back of a shoe: *soles and heels; she wears shoes with very high heels.* □ **tacón**
3 (*slang*) unpleasant person. □ **sinvergüenza**
■ *v.* **1** (*in Rugby*) to kick backward: *he heeled the ball out of the scrum.* □ **dar de tacón**
2 to put a new heel on (a shoe): *my shoes need heeling.* □ **poner tacones**
3 ***to heel over,*** (*of a ship*) to lean to one side. □ **escorarse**
hefty ['hefti] *adj.* (*heftier, heftiest*) large/strong. □ **fornido**
hegemony [hi'geməni] *n.* (*pl. hegemonies*) leadership by one country. □ **hegemonía**
heifer ['hefə] *n.* young cow. □ **novilla**
height [hait] *n.* **1** measurement of how tall or high something is: *his height is 1m 50; the height of the ceiling is 3 metres; what is the height of the town above sea level?* □ **altura**
2 highest point: *at the height of the storm; it's the height of fashion; at the height of his career.* □ **cumbre, punto máximo**
heighten *v.* to increase/to make more noticeable. □ **aumentar**
heinous ['heinəs] *adj.* wicked (crime). □ **atroz**
heir [eə] **heiress** [eə'res] *n.* person who is going to inherit money, etc., from someone else: *he is the heir to a fortune.* □ **heredero**
heirloom *n.* valuable object which has belonged to a family for years. □ **joya de familia**
held [held] *v. see* **hold.**
helicopter ['helikɔptə] *n.* type of aircraft with revolving blades on top, enabling it to take off vertically. □ **helicóptero**
helipad *n.* small marked area where a helicopter may land. □ **zona H**
heliport *n.* place where helicopters land and take off. □ **helipuerto**
helium ['hi:liəm] *n.* (*chemical element*: He) light gas which does not burn. □ **helio**
helix ['hi:liks] *n.* (*pl. helixes*) spiral shape. □ **hélice**
hell [hel] *n.* **1** place where devils live and wicked people are punished after death. □ **infierno**
2 *that machine makes a hell of a noise,* (*informal*) a very unpleasant loud noise. □ **...un ruido de mil demonios**
to give someone hell, to make life difficult for someone. □ **hacer pasar a uno las de Caín**
***what the hell** is he doing there?,* (*slang*) what on earth? □ **¿qué diablos...?**
hellish *adj.* like hell; (*informal*) unbearable. □ **infernal**
hello [hə'lou] *interjection* showing a greeting: *he said hello to me.* □ **hola**
helm [helm] *n.* wheel or handle connecting to the rudder of a ship. □ **timón**
at the helm, in charge. □ **al timón**
helmsman *n.* (*pl. helmsmen*) person who is steering a ship. □ **timonel**
helmet ['helmət] *n.* metal or plastic hat used as a protection. □ **casco**
crash helmet, helmet worn by motorcyclists, etc. □ **casco**
help [help] *n.* **1** aid/assistance: *they went to his help; I did the translation with the help of a dictionary; she called for help.* □ **ayuda**
2 person who helps: *home help.* □ **ayudante**
mother's help, person who helps a mother with housework. □ **asistenta**
■ *v.* **1** to aid (someone)/to come to someone's assistance: *I got a friend to help me move house; can you help me up the stairs?* □ **ayudar**
2 ***to help yourself,*** to serve yourself: *help yourself to pudding; the burglars helped themselves to my cigars,* they stole my cigars. □ **servirse uno mismo**
3 (*usually with negative*) to stop (doing something)/ to avoid (something): *I couldn't help laughing; he can't help it if he's deaf.* □ **no pudo dejar de reír; él no lo puede remediar si es sordo**
it can't be helped, you can't do anything to prevent it/to make it better. □ **no hay más remedio**
helper *n.* person who helps. □ **ayudante**
helpful *adj.* (person) who helps; (thing) which is useful: *this is a very helpful guide to growing roses.* □ **útil**
helping *adj.* which helps: *a helping hand.* □ **de ayuda**
■ *n.* serving/portion: *can I have a second helping of ice cream?* □ **porción**
helpless *adj.* weak/unable to help yourself. □ **desvalido**
helplessly *adv.* unable to help: *they watched helplessly as the ship sank.* □ **impotentemente**
helplessness *n.* state of being weak/of not being able to help. □ **impotencia**
help out *v.* to come to (someone's) assistance in an emergency: *I've no sugar left, can you help me out?* □ **echar una mano a uno**
helter-skelter ['heltə'skeltə] *adv.* in a confused rush: *they ran helter-skelter through the wood.* □ **atropelladamente**
■ *n.* (*in a fairground*) tower with a spiral slide round it. □ **tobogán**
hem [hem] *n.* sewn edge on a piece of cloth/a skirt/ tablecloth/handkerchief, etc. □ **dobladillo**
■ *v.* (*he hemmed*) **1** to sew a hem. □ **hacer un dobladillo**
2 ***to hem in,*** to enclose: *they were hemmed in by enemy troops on all sides.* □ **cercar**
hemline *n.* bottom edge of a dress/skirt, etc. □ **bajo**
hemisphere ['hemisfiə] *n.* half a sphere, especially half of the earth's globe. □ **hemisferio**
northern hemisphere/southern hemisphere, parts of the earth north and south of the equator. □ **hemisferio norte/sur**
hemispherical [hemi'sferikl] *adj.* shaped like half a sphere. □ **semiesférico**
hemlock ['hemlɔk] *n.* **1** common poisonous plant. □ **cicuta**
2 type of American evergreen tree. □ **pinabete**
hemoglobin [hi:mə'gloubin] *n. see* **haemoglobin.**
hemophilia [hi:mə'filiə] *n. see* **haemophilia.**
hemorrhage ['hemərid3] *n. see* **haemorrhage.**
hemorrhoids ['hemərɔidz] *n. pl. see* **haemorrhoids.**
hemp [hemp] *n.* tropical plant, which gives rough fibres for making sacks/ropes, etc., and which also provides a drug. □ **cáñamo**
hen [hen] *n.* **1** female chicken: *the hen has laid an egg.* □ **gallina**
2 female bird: *a hen grouse.* □ **hembra**
hen party, (*informal*) party for women only. □ **reunión de mujeres**

henhouse *n.* wooden hut for keeping chickens in. □ **gallinero**
henpecked *adj.* (husband) whose wife nags him continuously and tells him what to do. □ **sometido**
hence [hens] *adv.* **1** from this time: *five years hence,* in five years' time. □ **de aquí a cinco años**
2 for this reason: *hence his annoyance,* this is why he was annoyed. □ **por lo tanto; de ahí su...**
henceforth *adv.* from now on. □ **de ahora en adelante**
henchman ['hentʃmən] *n.* (*pl. henchmen*) helper/accomplice (of a criminal). □ **secuaz**
henna ['henə] *n.* red dye used to colour hair. □ **alheña**
hennaed *adj.* (hair) coloured with henna. □ **alheñado**
hepatitis [hepə'taitis] *n.* disease of the liver. □ **hepatitis**
heptagon ['heptəgən] *n.* geometrical figure with seven sides. □ **heptágono**
heptagonal [hep'tægənl] *adj.* seven-sided. □ **heptagonal**
her [hə:] pronoun referring to a female: *have you seen her? that's her over there! tell her to come in.* □ **¿la has visto?; ¡es ella, allí!; dile que entre**
■ *adj.* belonging to a female: *she has lost her bag; have you seen her brother?* □ **ha perdido su bolso**
herald ['herəld] *n.* messenger sent to announce something: *the white flowers are heralds of spring.* □ **heraldo**
■ *v.* to be a sign that something is approaching; to announce: *it heralds a new era in East-West relations.* □ **anunciar**
heraldic [he'rældik] *adj.* referring to heraldry. □ **heráldico**
heraldry *n.* study of coats of arms. □ **heráldica**
herb [hə:b] *n.* tasty or pungent plant used in cooking or as a medicine. □ **hierba**
herbaceous border [hə:'beiʃəs 'bɔ:də] *n.* flowerbed planted with flowers which sprout up again each year. □ **arriate**
herbal *adj.* containing/using herbs: *herbal remedies.* □ **herbario**
herbivore ['həαbivɔα] *n.* animal which eats plants. □ **herbívoro**
herbivorous *adj.* (animal) which eats plants. □ **herbívoro**
herd [hə:d] *n.* group of animals: *a herd of cows.* □ **rebaño**
herd instinct, tendency of people to do what others do. □ **instinto gregario**
■ *v.* to form/to make into a group: *the prisoners were herded into trucks.* □ **conducir en manada**
herdsman *n.* (*pl. herdsmen*) man who looks after a herd of cows, etc. □ **vaquero**
here ['hiə] *adv.* to/in this place: *come here please; the water came up to here.* □ **aquí; acá**
here, there and everywhere, all over the place. □ **en todas partes**
hereabouts *adv.* round about here/in this area. □ **por aquí cerca**
hereafter *adv.* from this time on. □ **de ahora en adelante**
herewith [hiə'wiθ] *adv.* with this: *I am enclosing herewith a cheque for $10.* □ **adjunto**
heredity [hi'rediti] *n.* passing on of characteristics from parent to child. □ **herencia**
hereditary *adj.* which is passed on from parent to child. □ **hereditario**
hereditary title, title (such as Lord, etc.) which is passed from father to son. □ **título hereditario**
heresy ['herəsi] *n.* (*pl. heresies*) belief which is not generally accepted/belief which is condemned by the church. □ **herejía**
heretic *n.* person who does not hold generally accepted religious beliefs. □ **hereje**
heretical [hi'retikl] *adj.* (belief) which is not generally accepted/which is condemned by the church. □ **herético**
heritage ['heritidʒ] *n.* something which is passed on from one generation to the next. □ **herencia**
hermaphrodite [hə:'mæfrədait] *n.* animal/plant which is both male and female. □ **hermafrodita**
hermetically [hə:'metikəli] *adv.* (sealed) tightly so that no air can get in. □ **herméticamente**
hermit ['hə:mit] *n.* person who lives alone and refuses to see other people. □ **ermitaño**
hermit crab, small crab which lives in empty sea shells. □ **ermitaño; paguro**
hermitage *n.* place where a hermit lives. □ **ermita**
hernia ['hə:niə] *n.* state where part of the bowel has pushed through a weak place in the wall of the abdomen. □ **hernia**
hero ['hiərou] **heroine** ['herouin] *n.* (*pl. heroes*) person who does brave deeds; main character in a book/film, etc. □ **héroe, heroína**
heroic [hi'rouik] *adj.* brave/like a hero: *heroic action against the enemy.* □ **heroico**
heroically *adv.* like a hero. □ **heroicamente**
heroism ['herouizm] *n.* bravery. □ **heroísmo**
heroin ['herouin] *n.* drug made from poppies. □ **heroína**
heron ['herən] *n.* common water bird with long legs and neck. □ **garza**
herpes ['hə:pi:z] *n.* disease which gives blisters on the skin. □ **herpes**
herring ['heriŋ] *n.* common sea fish. □ **arenque**
a red herring, a distraction/a false lead. □ **pista falsa**
herring-bone *adj.* (pattern) in a zigzag. □ **de espiga**
herring gull *n.* common large grey and white gull with a yellow beak. □ **gaviota**
hers [hə:z] *pron.* belonging to her: *this book is hers; a friend of hers.* □ **suyo (de ella)**
herself [hə:'self] pronoun referring to a female subject: *she was washing herself; she is all by herself; she wrote to me herself.* □ **se estaba lavando; ella misma**
hertz [hə:ts] *n.* (*no pl.*) standard unit of frequency of radio waves. □ **hercio**
hesitate ['heziteit] *v.* to stop for a moment; to be unable to decide: *I am hesitating about what to do next.* □ **vacilar; estoy dudando...**
hesitant *adj.* doubtful/undecided. □ **vacilante**
hesitation [hezi'teiʃn] *n.* indecision/doubt: *a moment of hesitation.* □ **vacilación**
hessian ['hesiən] *n.* rough cloth like that used for making sacks. □ **arpillera**
heterogeneous [hetərou'dʒi:njəs] *adj.* of varied sorts. □ **heterogéneo**
heterosexual [hetərou'seksjuəl] *adj.* and *n.* (person) who is attracted to people of the opposite sex. □ **heterosexual**
het up ['het'ʌp] *adj.* (*informal*) excited; anxious: *she's all het up.* □ **exaltado**
hew [hju:] *v.* to carve/to cut: *they hewed a way through the jungle.* □ **cortar; se abrieron camino a través de...**
hexagon ['heksəgən] *n.* geometrical figure with six sides. □ **hexágono**
hexagonal [hek'sægənl] *adj.* six-sided. □ **hexagonal**

hey [hei] *interjection* showing a greeting/surprise, etc. □ **¡eh!**

heyday ['heidei] *n.* period of greatest glory/success/power: *in his heyday he was the most powerful man in the country.* □ **apogeo**

hi [hai] *especially Amer. informal interjection* showing a greeting. □ **hola**

hiatus [hai'eitəs] *n.* gap/interruption. □ **hiato**

hibernate ['haibəneit] *v.* (*of animals*) to sleep during the winter. □ **hibernar**

hibernation [haibə'neiʃn] *n.* spending the winter asleep. □ **hibernación**

hiccup, hiccough ['hikʌp] *n.* repeated spasm in the throat like a small cough: *I got the hiccups after laughing so much.* □ **hipo**

■ *v.* (*he hiccupped*) to make a loud noise because of a spasm in the throat. □ **tener hipo**

hick [hik] *n. Amer.* (*informal*) stupid person from the country. □ **paleto**

hickory ['hikəri] *n.* American tree like a walnut. □ **nogal americano**

hid [hid] **hidden** ['hidn] *v. see* **hide.**

hide [haid] *n.* **1** leather; whole skin of an animal. □ **piel**

2 camouflaged place where you can sit and watch birds, etc. □ **puesto**

■ *v.* (*he hid; he has hidden*) to be out of sight; to put (a thing) somewhere so that no one can see it: *they are hiding from the police; he hid his wife's present under the bed.* □ **esconder(se)**

hide-and-seek *n.* children's game, where some hide and the others try to find them. □ **escondite**

hidebound *adj.* unwilling to change ideas/narrow-minded. □ **de miras estrechas**

hide-out *n.* secret place where you cannot be found: *the thieves had a hide-out in an old warehouse.* □ **escondite**

hiding *n.* **1** putting yourself/something out of sight: *he has gone into hiding.* □ **ha ido a esconderse**

2 (*informal*) beating/whipping. □ **tunda**

hideous ['hidiəs] *adj.* horribly ugly. □ **espantoso**

hierarchy ['haiərɑːki] *n.* (*pl. hierarchies*) arrangement in a system of ranks/grades: *he's offended the party hierarchy,* the top officials of the party. □ **jerarquía**

hierarchical [haiə'rɑːkikl] *adj.* arranged in a set system of ranks. □ **jerárquico**

hieroglyphics [haiərou'glifiks] *n. pl.* picture writing used by the Ancient Egyptians. □ **jeroglífico**

hi-fi [hai'fai] *adj.* and *n.* (*informal*) high fidelity radio/stereo (equipment). □ **de alta fidelidad**

higgledy-piggledy [higldi'pigldi] *adv.* in disorder/all over the place. □ **sin orden ni concierto**

high [hai] *adj.* (*higher, highest*) **1** going far above; tall: *how high is that tree? they built a block of offices fifteen storeys high.* □ **alto; ...¿cuánto mide ese árbol?; ...de altura**

2 great *high rank; high prices; high speed; high tide.* □ **alto; mucha (velocidad)**

high fidelity, (radio equipment) which gives excellent reproduction of sound: *high fidelity stereo set.* □ **alta fidelidad**

3 shrill (note): *she can reach the very high notes easily.* □ **nota alta**

4 (*of meat*) going rotten. □ **carne pasada**

5 main; most important: *High Street; the high seas.* □ **calle Mayor; alta mar**

6 (*informal*) influenced by drugs, etc. □ **flipado**

■ *adv.* (*higher, highest*) **1** far above: *he flew high over the houses.* □ **por encima**

2 to a great degree: *the river is running high.* □ **el río va crecido**

feelings are running high, people are getting very annoyed. □ **ánimos exaltados**

■ *n.* **1** high-pressure zone in the atmosphere. □ **zona de alta presión**

2 *prices have reached an all-time high,* the highest point they have ever reached. □ **...han alcanzado cifras nunca conocidas antes**

3 (*informal*) state of intoxication produced by a drug, etc. □ **colocón**

highball *n. Amer.* whisky and soda. □ **whisky con soda**

highbrow *adj.* and *n.* intellectual (person). □ **intelectual**

high chair *n.* small chair with very long legs for a baby to sit in to eat. □ **silla alta**

high flyer *n.* very intelligent/very ambitious person. □ **ambicioso**

high-handed *adj.* (action) done without considering other people. □ **despótico**

highland *adj.* coming from the highlands/from a mountain region: *highland cattle.* □ **de las montañas**

highlander *n.* person who lives in the highlands of Scotland. □ **montañés**

highlands *n. pl.* mountain region, especially in northern Scotland. □ **región montañosa**

highlight *n.* most interesting event: *the highlight of the evening.* □ **atracción principal**

■ *v.* to accentuate/to draw attention to: *this highlights the problems of city schools.* □ **hacer resaltar**

highly *adv.* very/greatly: *highly important; highly paid.* □ **muy importante; muy bien pagado**

highly-strung *adj.* very emotional/excitable. □ **muy tenso**

high-minded *adj.* noble/very serious. □ **de nobles sentimientos**

highness *n.* **1** being high/being above other things. □ **altura**

2 title given to princes, etc. □ **alteza**

high-pitched *adj.* sharp/shrill (sound); steep (roof). □ **agudo (sonido); empinado (tejado)**

high-powered *adj.* very powerful (engine). □ **de gran potencia**

high-rise *adj.* (building) with many floors: *a high-rise block of flats.* □ **de gran altura**

highroad *n.* main road. □ **carretera principal**

high school *n.* **1** selective secondary school (usually for girls). □ **colegio de élite**

2 *Amer.* secondary school. □ **instituto de bachillerato**

high-spirited *adj.* lively. □ **animoso**

high tea *n.* (*in North of England and Scotland*) large meal of tea, cold meat, cakes, etc., eaten in the early evening. □ **merienda-cena**

highway *n.* main road. □ **carretera principal**

highway code, official rules for people travelling on public roads. □ **código de la circulación**

highwayman *n.* (*pl. highwaymen*) person who attacked travellers and robbed them. □ **salteador de caminos**

hijack ['haidʒæk] *v.* to take control of an aircraft/a train, etc. (with the passengers on board), by threatening the pilot/driver: *the terrorists hijacked a plane.* □ **secuestrar**

hijacker *n.* person who hijacks something. □ **secuestrador**

hijacking *n.* taking control of a plane/a train, etc. by threatening the pilot/driver: *so far this year there have been six hijackings.* □ **secuestro**

hike [haik] *n.* **1** strenuous walk: *we went on a long*

hike over the hills. □ **excursión a pie**
2 *Amer.* increase (in price, etc.). □ **subida**
■ *v.* **1** to go for a strenuous walk. □ **ir de excursión**
2 *Amer.* to increase (prices, etc.). □ **subir**
hiker *n.* person who goes for long walks. □ **excursionista**
hiking *n.* walking as a relaxation: *a hiking holiday.* □ **excursionismo**

hilarious [hi'lɛəriəs] *adj.* very funny/very happy: *hilarious laughter.* □ **hilarante**
hilariously *adv.* in a very funny way. □ **alegremente**
hilarity [hi'læriti] *n.* great laughter. □ **hilaridad**

hill [hil] *n.* rise in the land, lower than a mountain: *the road went up a steep hill.* □ **colina**
hillbilly *n. Amer.* stupid person who lives in the country. □ **cateto**
hillbilly music, country style music. □ **música 'country'**
hillock *n.* little hill. □ **altozano**
hillside *n.* side of a hill. □ **ladera**
hilly *adj.* (*hillier, hilliest*) (region) with many hills. □ **montuoso**

hilt [hilt] *n.* protective shield on the handle of a sword. □ **empuñadura**
up to the hilt, totally: *it was proved up to the hilt,* proved conclusively. □ **totalmente**

him [him] *pronoun* referring to a male: *have you seen him? that's him over there; tell him to come in.* □ **¿le has visto?; es él; dile que venga**
himself [him'self] *pronoun* referring to a male subject; *he was washing himself; he is all by himself; he wrote to me himself.* □ **él mismo**

hind [haind] *n.* female deer. □ **cierva**
■ *adj.* ***hind legs,*** back legs (of an animal). □ **patas traseras**

hinder ['hində] *v.* to prevent someone from doing something: *the noise hinders my work.* □ **dificultar**
hindrance *n.* obstacle. □ **estorbo**

hindmost ['haindmoust] *adj.* furthest back. □ **postrero, último**

hindsight ['haindsait] *n.* knowing facts about an event in the past which could have been useful if they had been known at the time: *with hindsight, I see that we ought to have stopped him going.* □ **visto desde ahora**

Hindu [hin'du:] *adj.* and *n.* (person) who follows Hinduism. □ **hindú**
Hinduism ['hindu:izəm] *n.* Indian religion which has many gods and goddesses, and which practises the caste system. □ **hinduismo**

hinge [hindʒ] *n.* **1** metal bracket on which a door/a window hangs and opens: *the door creaked on its hinges.* □ **bisagra**
2 ***stamp hinge,*** small piece of gummed paper for sticking stamps into a stamp album. □ **fijasellos**
■ *v.* to centre/to depend: *everything hinges on his reply.* □ **depender**
hinged *adj.* with hinges: *a hinged lid.* □ **de bisagra**

hint [hint] *n.* **1** hidden suggestion/clue: *we gave him a hint that he ought to look for another job.* □ **indirecta**
to take a hint: *he took the hint,* he acted on the suggestion. □ **darse por aludido, coger la indirecta**
2 sign: *at the slightest hint of fog he refuses to drive.* □ **indicio**
3 ***hints,*** helpful advice: *hints on gardening.* □ **indicación**
■ *v.* to suggest/to insinuate: *they hinted that the shop might go bankrupt.* □ **dar a entender**

hinterland ['hintəlænd] *n.* area inland from a sea port/around a large town. □ **interior**

hip [hip] *n.* **1** projecting bone where the legs join the body; wide part of the body where the legs join it: *to measure someone round the hips.* □ **cadera**
2 fruit of a wild rose. □ **escaramujo**
3 ***hip, hip, hooray!,*** words used to give a cheer. □ **¡hip, hip, hurra!**
hipsters *n. pl.* trousers which only reach to the hips and not the waist. □ **pantalón de tiro corto**

hippie ['hipi] *n.* (*informal*) person who lives/dresses in a different way to the majority of people in society. □ **'hippie'**

hippopotamus [hipə'pɔtəməs] (*informal*) **hippo** ['hipou] *n.* (*pl. hippopotamuses, hippos*) very large African animal living in water and mud. □ **hipopótamo**

hire ['haiə] *n.* renting (of a car, etc.) usually for a short time. □ **alquiler**
hire purchase, system where you buy something by paying instalments until you have purchased it completely. □ **compra a plazos**
■ *v.* **1** to rent (a car, etc.). □ **alquilar**
2 *to hire new staff,* to engage new staff. □ **contratar**
to hire out: *he hires out cars,* he has cars which people can rent. □ **tiene un negocio de alquiler de coches**
hireling *n.* person who is hired to do a job. □ **contratado**

hirsute ['hə:sju:t] *adj.* covered with long hair. □ **hirsuto**

his [hiz] *adj.* **1** belonging to a male: *he has lost his keys.* □ **su, sus (de él)**
2 belonging to him: *this book is his; a friend of his telephoned me.* □ **suyo**

hiss [his] *n.* (*pl. hisses*) whistling sound like an 's', made by snakes/by gas escaping, etc.; similar sound made to show you do not like something. □ **silbido**
■ *v.* to make a whistling sound: *the snake hissed; the audience hissed the actor.* □ **silbar**

histology [hi'stɔlədʒi] *n.* science of body cells. □ **histología**

history ['histəri] *n.* **1** study of the past; story of what happened in the past: *he is writing a history of the United States.* □ **historia**
ancient history, study of what happened in ancient civilizations. □ **historia antigua**
2 ***natural history,*** study of animals and plants. □ **historia natural**
historian [hi'stɔ:riən] *n.* person who studies or writes about the past. □ **historiador**
historic [hi'stɔrik] *adj.* (event) which is so important that it will be remembered. □ **histórico**
historical *adj.* referring to history: *a historical event,* one that really happened. □ **histórico**
historical novel, novel set in the past. □ **novela histórica**
historically *adv.* as in the past. □ **históricamente**

histrionic [histri'ɔnik] *adj.* referring to acting. □ **histriónico**
histrionics *n. pl.* dramatic behaviour. □ **histrionismo**

hit [hit] *n.* **1** blow. □ **golpe**
2 *he scored three hits,* he hit the target three times. □ **diana**
3 song/play, etc. which is very popular: *hit musical.* □ **éxito**
hit parade, list of most popular songs. □ **lista de éxitos**
■ *v.* (*he hit; he has hit*) **1** to knock against; to touch (something) hard: *the car hit the lamp post; he hit the target three times; she hit him with a bottle; he hit the ball over the hedge,* he hit it so hard that it

went over the hedge. □ **golpear**
2 to affect: *the company has been badly hit by strikes.* □ **afectar**
hit and miss *adj.* erratic/careless. □ **descuidado**
hit back *v.* to defend yourself against attack. □ **devolver los golpes**
hit-man *n.* (*pl. hit-men*) person employed to kill/to hurt someone. □ **asesino a sueldo**
hit off *v.* ***to hit it off with someone,*** (*informal*) to get on well with someone: *they don't hit it off together.* □ **hacer buenas migas**
hit upon *v.* to discover. □ **dar con**
hitch [hitʃ] *n.* (*pl. hitches*) awkward delay/unexpected stoppage: *there has been a hitch in getting approval from the university; the wedding went off without a hitch.* □ **problema**
■ *v.* **1** to jerk up/to pull up: *he hitched up his trousers.* □ **subirse**
2 to get a free ride in someone's car, stopping the car by pointing your thumb: *I hitched a lift; he hitched a ride to Scotland.* □ **hacer auto-stop**
hitch-hike *v.* to get a free ride in someone's car, stopping the car by pointing your thumb. □ **hacer auto-stop**
hitch-hiker *n.* person who hitch-hikes. □ **autoestopista**
hither ['hiðə] *adv.* **1** (*formal*) to this place. □ **acá**
2 *they were running* ***hither and thither,*** all over the place. □ **de acá para allá**
hitherto *adv.* up till now. □ **hasta la fecha**
hive [haiv] *n.* **1** box in which bees make their nest. □ **colmena**
2 ***hives,*** sore red patches on the skin, usually on the face. □ **urticaria**
■ *v.* ***to hive off,*** to split off: *the sales department has been hived off to a separate office.* □ **separar**
hoard [hɔːd] *n.* mass/store (of money/food, etc.) which has been collected. □ **provisión**
■ *v.* to collect and store (money/food, etc.). □ **atesorar (dinero); acumular provisiones**
hoarder *n.* person who buys food when supplies are low. □ **acaparador**
hoarding *n.* **1** buying food, etc., when supplies are low. □ **acaparamiento**
2 fence made of rough planks. □ **valla**
3 large advertising board in the street. □ **valla publicitaria**
hoarfrost ['hɔːfrɔst] *n.* white frost which covers trees/plants, etc. □ **escarcha**
hoarse [hɔːs] *adj.* rough (voice): *I am hoarse from shouting too much.* □ **ronco**
hoarseness *n.* roughness/harshness (of voice). □ **ronquera**
hoary ['hɔːri] *adj.* (*hoarier, hoariest*) **1** (*formal*) white-haired. □ **cano**
2 (*informal*) very old (joke). □ **chiste viejo**
hoax [houks] *n.* (*pl. hoaxes*) trick: *they played a hoax on him; hoax telephone call to the police,* trick telephone call to deceive the police. □ **broma**
■ *v.* to trick/to deceive. □ **engañar**
hoaxer *n.* person who hoaxes. □ **bromista**
hob [hɔb] *n.* metal stand where a kettle can be put by the side of a fire. □ **repisa**
hobble ['hɔbl] *v.* **1** to attach the legs of a horse so that it cannot move easily. □ **trabar**
2 to walk with difficulty: *he hobbled along using a stick.* □ **cojear**
hobby ['hɔbi] *n.* (*pl. hobbies*) pastime; thing done as a relaxation: *his hobby is collecting stamps.* □ **hobby**
hobbyhorse *n.* subject which someone always talks about. □ **caballo de batalla**
hobnailed ['hɔbneild] *adj.* (boots) with large metal nails. □ **tachuelas**
hobnob ['hɔbnɔb] *v.* (*he hobnobbed*) (*informal*) to be on friendly terms (with someone important): *he hobnobs with the mayor.* □ **codearse**
hobo ['houbou] *n.* (*pl. hobos*) *Amer.* person with no home or money. □ **vagabundo**
hock [hɔk] *n.* **1** lower part of the hind leg of an animal. □ **corvejón**
2 German white wine. □ **vino del Rin**
3 ***in hock,*** (*slang*) pawned. □ **empeñado**
hockey ['hɔki] *n.* ***hockey,*** *Amer.* ***grass hockey,*** team game played on grass with long curved sticks and a hard ball. □ **hockey**
ice hockey, *Amer.* ***hockey,*** team game played on ice with long curved sticks and a small hard disk. □ **hockey sobre hielo**
hod [hɔd] *n.* **1** wooden container on the end of a pole, used by builders for carrying bricks. □ **capacho**
2 metal container for coal. □ **cubo**
hoe [hou] *n.* garden tool with a bent blade on the end of a long handle. □ **azada**
■ *v.* to take out weeds/to loosen the soil with a hoe. □ **sachar (hierbas); azadonar**
hog [hɔg] *n.* castrated male pig. □ **cerdo**
to go the whole hog, (*informal*) to do something completely. □ **llegar hasta el final**
■ *v.* (*he hogged*) **1** to eat/to drink like a pig. □ **comer como un cerdo**
2 to monopolize: *he was hogging the whole conversation.* □ **monopolizar**
hogg [hɔg] *n.* young female sheep. □ **cordera**
Hogmanay [hɔgmə'nei] *n.* Scottish festival on 31st December. □ **nochevieja**
hogshead ['hɔgzhed] *n.* **1** large barrel. □ **pipa**
2 measure of about 50 gallons. □ **aprox. 225 litros**
hoick [hɔik] *v.* (*informal*) to pull (out). □ **tirar**
hoist [hɔist] *n.* apparatus for lifting; goods lift. □ **montacargas**
■ *v.* to lift up. □ **subir**
hold [hould] *n.* **1** grip: *take hold of something; he let go his hold.* □ **asidero; agarrar**
2 influence/power: *she has a hold over him.* □ **dominio**
3 part of a ship/aircraft where cargo is carried. □ **bodega**
■ *v.* (*he held*) **1** to have in your hand, etc.: *he was holding a gun in his right hand; she held the baby in her arms; he was holding a knife between his teeth.* □ **empuñar; sostener; sujetar**
to hold tight, to take a good grip. □ **agarrar con fuerza**
2 to contain: *the bottle holds two litres; the car holds six people.* □ **tener capacidad para**
3 to make (something) take place: *to hold a meeting; the flower show will be held in the village hall.* □ **celebrar, tener lugar**
4 to keep in: *he held his breath for a minute; does this can hold water?* □ **mantener (la respiración); contener (agua)**
5 to stay: *will the good weather hold?* □ **continuar**
6 *the regulations* ***hold good*** *for all European countries,* apply in all European countries. □ **ser válido**
7 ***to hold office,*** to have a post (in a government): *he held office in the Kennedy administration.* □ **tener un puesto**
holdall *n.* large travelling bag. □ **bolsa de viaje**
hold back *v.* to keep back; not to go forward. □ **detenerse**
hold down *v.* **1** to keep (something) down. □ **sujetar**
2 *he has difficulty in holding down his job,* he is not

competent enough to do his job satisfactorily. □ **...en estar a la altura del cargo**
holder *n.* person or thing which holds. □ **poseedor**
hold forth *v.* to talk at great length. □ **hablar largamente**
holding *n.* number of shares which you own. □ **valores en cartera**
holding company, company formed to control shares in other companies. □ **'holding'**
hold off *v.* to delay; to stay away: *the rain held off all afternoon.* □ **sujetar; no llegó a llover**
hold on *v.* **1** to cling on to/to take a grip on (something): *hold on to the handle.* □ **agarrarse**
2 to wait: *you want to speak to Mr Smith? - Hold on, I'll get him for you.* □ **¡no cuelgue...!**
hold out *v.* **1** to offer: *he held out his hand.* □ **alargar**
2 to last: *supplies of food held out.* □ **durar**
3 *the garrison held out for thirty days,* they did not surrender. □ **la guarnición resistió...**
hold over *v.* to postpone (something): *the meeting has been held over until next week.* □ **aplazar**
hold up *v.* **1** to raise: *he held up his hand.* □ **levantar**
2 to support: *the awning is held up by four posts.* □ **sujetar**
3 to hinder/to delay: *we were held up in a traffic jam; the talks were held up for three days because the chief negotiator was ill.* □ **retener; interrumpir**
4 to attack and rob: *three men held up a bank.* □ **atracar**
hold-up *n.* **1** delay; breakdown: *the accident caused hold-ups on the motorway.* □ **atasco**
2 armed attack. □ **atraco**
hold with *v.* (*informal*) to accept/to agree with: *I don't hold with paying a lot for meat.* □ **estar dispuesto a**
hole [houl] *n.* **1** opening/space: *the boys looked through the hole in the fence; I've got a hole in my sock.* □ **agujero**
2 *rabbit hole,* burrow in which rabbits live. □ **madriguera**
■ *v.* **1** to make a hole in: *the ship was holed on the rocks.* □ **hacer un boquete**
2 (*in golf*) to send (the ball) into the hole. □ **meter la pelota en el hoyo**
hole up *v.* (*informal*) to hide away. □ **escaquearse**
holiday ['hɔlidei] *n.* period when you do not work: *we spend our holidays in France; how many days' holiday do you have each year? May 1st is a public holiday.* □ **vacaciones; ...días de fiesta**
■ *v.* to go on holiday: *they were holidaying in France.* □ **irse de vacaciones**
holidaymaker *n.* person on holiday. □ **veraneante**
holiness ['houlinəs] *n. see* **holy.**
Holland ['hɔlənd] *n.* country in Northern Europe. □ **Holanda**
hollow ['hɔlou] *n.* low-lying land; small depression in a flat surface. □ **tierras bajas**
■ *adj.* empty/with nothing inside: *the tree is hollow; when he tapped the wall, it made a hollow sound.* □ **hueco**
a hollow victory, a victory which is meaningless. □ **vano**
■ *v.* ***to hollow out,*** to make (something) hollow: *he hollowed out the piece of wood to make a tube.* □ **ahuecar**
holly ['hɔli] *n.* very prickly evergreen bush with red berries. □ **acebo**
hollyhock ['hɔlihɔk] *n.* common garden flower which produces very tall spikes of blossom. □ **malva real**
holocaust ['hɔləkɔːst] *n.* destruction by fire. □ **holocausto**
holster ['houlstə] *n.* leather pouch for carrying a revolver. □ **pistolera**
holy ['houli] *adj.* (*holier, holiest*) sacred (place); very pious (person). □ **sagrado, santo**
holy orders, being a priest: *he's in holy orders.* □ **órdenes sagradas; él está ordenado**
holiness *n.* being holy. □ **santidad**
his Holiness, title given to the Pope. □ **Su Santidad**
homage ['hɔmidʒ] *n.* **1** respect. □ **homenaje**
to pay homage to someone, to show someone signs of respect. □ **tener deferencia con**
2 (*formerly*) duty/service (to a feudal lord). □ **rendir homenaje a**
home [houm] *n.* **1** place where you live/place where you come from originally: *will you be at home tomorrow afternoon? my home is in Wales; Scotland is the home of porridge.* □ **casa; ...es la cuna del...**
2 ***at home,*** (*in sports*) playing on the local sports ground: *our team are playing Leeds at home.* □ **en casa**
3 house where people are looked after: *nursing home; old people's home; children's home.* □ **residencia de ancianos; orfanato**
■ *adv.* to/at the place where you live: *I will take it home with me; she gets home at six o'clock every evening.* □ **a casa**
to bring something home to someone, to make someone realize something: *seeing their mansion brought it home to me how rich they are.* □ **hacer ver claramente**
to strike home, to hit the target. □ **dar en el blanco**
■ *adj.* **1** referring to the place where you live: *what is your home address?* □ **dirección particular**
2 not foreign/internal. □ **interno**
home trade, trade inside the country. □ **comercio interior**
3 (*in sports*) referring to the local team/the local sports ground. □ **equipo de casa**
a home match, match played by the local team on their own ground. □ **partido en casa**
■ *v.* to go to a target: *the missile homed in on the enemy plane.* □ **dirigirse hacia el blanco**
Home Counties *n. pl.* the counties around London. □ **'Home Counties'**
home help *n.* person who helps an invalid, etc., with housework in the home. □ **ayuda a domicilio**
home-grown *adj.* (vegetables) grown in the garden, not bought. □ **de cosecha propia**
homeless *adj.* with nowhere to live. □ **sin hogar**
homely *adj.* (*homelier, homeliest*) **1** simple; not ostentatious. □ **sencillo**
2 plain/ugly (person). □ **feúcho**
home-made *adj.* made at home/not bought: *home-made ham.* □ **casero**
Home Office *n.* Government department which deals with internal problems of law and order in England and Wales. □ **Ministerio del Interior**
Home Secretary *n.* Minister in charge of the Home Office. □ **ministro del Interior**
homesick *adj.* unhappy because of wanting to go home: *she went to stay at her aunt's, but was homesick.* □ **nostálgico**
homesickness *n.* unhappiness caused by wanting to be at home. □ **morriña**
homestead *n.* farmhouse and the fields around it. □ **finca**
homewards *adv.* towards home. □ **hacia casa**
homework *n.* work which children take from school to be done at home in the evening. □ **deberes**
homing *adj.* ***homing pigeon,*** pigeon trained to re-

turn to the place where it is usually kept. □ **paloma mensajera**
homing device, device (on a missile) which guides it to the target. □ **mecanismo autodireccional**
homicide ['hɔmisaid] *n.* murder. □ **homicidio**
homicidal *adj.* likely to murder: *a homicidal maniac.* □ **homicida**
homily ['hɔmili] *n.* (*pl. homilies*) sermon/talk to encourage someone to be less wicked. □ **homilía**
homoeopathy [houmi'ɔpəθi] *Amer.* **homeopathy** *n.* method of curing sick people by accustoming them to very small quantities of drugs which would normally make them ill. □ **homeopatía**
homoeopath ['houmjoupæθ] *Amer.* **homeopath** *n.* doctor who practices homoeopathy. □ **homeópata**
homogeneous [hɔmou'dʒiːnjəs] *adj.* of the same sort/quality (as other things). □ **homogéneo**
homogenize [hə'mɔdʒənaiz] *v.* to mix the cream into milk: *homogenized milk.* □ **homogeneizar**
homogenization [həmɔdʒənai'zeiʃn] *n.* treatment of milk so that the cream does not separate. □ **homogeneización**
homonym ['hɔmənim] *n.* word which is spelt the same as another word with a different meaning. □ **homónimo**
homosexual [houmou'seksjuəl] *adj.* and *n.* (person) who is attracted to persons of the same sex as himself/herself. □ **homosexual**
homosexuality [houmouseksju'æliti] *n.* being attracted to persons of the same sex as yourself. □ **homosexualidad**
hone ['houn] *v.* to smooth/to sharpen (a blade). □ **afilar**
honest ['ɔnist] *adj.* truthful; not cheating or stealing. □ **honrado**
honestly *adv.* truthfully. □ **honradamente**
honesty *n.* **1** truthfulness: *he was rewarded for his honesty in returning the purse he found on the train.* □ **honradez**
2 garden flower with silvery seed cases, used as a winter decoration. □ **lunaria**
honey ['hʌni] *n.* sweet substance produced by bees. □ **miel**
honey-bee *n.* type of bee which makes honey. □ **abeja melífera**
honeycomb *n.* construction of wax cells in which bees store honey; pattern of six-sided shapes like bees' cells. □ **panal**
honeycombed *adj.* full of little holes. □ **lleno de agujeros, de rejilla**
honeydew *n.* type of melon which has green flesh. □ **melón**
honeyed *adj.* (*formal*) sweet/flattering (words). □ **meloso**
honeymoon *n.* holiday taken by man and wife immediately after their wedding. □ **luna de miel**
■ *v.* to go on a honeymoon. □ **irse de...**
honeymooners *n. pl.* people on their honeymoon. □ **recién casados**
honeysuckle *n.* common climbing plant with scented yellow and pink flowers. □ **madreselva**
honk ['hɔŋk] *n.* noise made by a goose/by a car horn. □ **graznido; bocinazo (coche)**
■ *v.* to make a noise like a goose/a car horn. □ **graznar; tocar la bocina**
honorarium [ɔnə'reəriəm] *n.* money paid to someone for work which is usually done free. □ **honorarios**
honorary ['ɔnərəri] *adj.* **1** (person) who is not paid a salary: *honorary secretary of a club.* □ **honorario**
2 given as a mark of respect: *honorary degree.* □ **de honor**
honour ['ɔnə] *Amer.* **honor** *n.* **1** self-respect. □ **honor**
2 ***on my word of honour,*** I swear that I will do it. □ **palabra de honor**
3 *he is* ***honour bound*** *to do it,* he is obliged by a sense of self-respect to do it. □ **está moralmente obligado a hacerlo**
4 title given as a mark of respect. □ **señoría**
honours list, list of titles/medals, etc. awarded to people as a mark of respect; (*in school*) list of pupils who have done well in examinations. □ **lista honorífica**
5 ***honours degree,*** university degree taken after a more difficult course of study. □ **título superior**
6 title given to a judge: *Your Honour; his Honour, Judge Smith.* □ **Su Señoría**
■ *v.* **1** to respect; to give a title/medal to (someone) as a mark of respect. □ **honrar; premiar (con una medalla)**
2 to pay (a bill); (*of a bank*) to pay (a cheque). □ **pagar, aceptar**
honourable *adj.* (person) who can be respected. □ **honorable**
honourably *adv.* in a way which you can respect. □ **honorablemente**
hooch [huːtʃ] *n.* (*slang*) alcoholic drink. □ **aguardiente**
hood [hud] *n.* **1** loose covering for the head, attached to a coat. □ **capucha**
2 folding roof on a car or pram. □ **capota**
3 *Amer.* lid covering the engine of a car. □ **capó**
4 (*slang*) gangster. □ **chorizo**
hooded *adj.* wearing a hood: *masked and hooded robbers.* □ **encapuchado**
hoodlum ['huːdləm] *n.* thug/violent hooligan. □ **matón**
hoodwink ['hudwiŋk] *v.* to trick. □ **engañar**
hoof [huːf] *n.* (*pl. hooves*) hard part of the foot of a horse, etc. □ **pezuña**
hoofed *adj.* (animal) which has hooves. □ **ungulado**
hoo-ha ['huːhɑː] *n.* (*informal*) fuss/bother: *what's all the hoo-ha about?* □ **alboroto**
hook [huk] *n.* **1** bent piece of metal used for holding or pulling, etc.: *hook and eye,* small hook and loop for fastening clothing; *the coat fastens with several hooks.* □ **gancho**
coat hook, hook for hanging coats on. □ **percha**
boat hook, pole with a bent end for pulling boats near to the shore. □ **bichero**
2 very small, bent piece of metal used for catching fish: *fish hook.* □ **anzuelo**
3 (*in boxing/cricket*) blow/stroke made with the arm bent. □ **gancho**
■ *v.* **1** to hang on a hook; to attach with a hook. □ **colgar**
2 to catch (a fish) with a hook. □ **pescar**
hooked *adj.* **1** shaped like a hook: *a hooked nose.* □ **ganchudo**
2 caught with/on a hook. □ **enganchado**
3 (*informal*) very interested in (a book, etc.). □ **enviciado**
4 addicted to (drugs): *he is hooked on heroin.* □ **enganchado**
hooker *n.* **1** (*in Rugby*) forward in the centre of the front line of the scrum, whose job is to hook the ball backwards to his own side. □ **talonador**
2 (*informal*) prostitute. □ **fulana**
hookah ['hukə] *n.* tobacco pipe where the smoke is cooled by being passed through water. □ **narguile**
hookey ['huki] *n.* *Amer.* child who avoids going to school. □ **pellero**

to play hookey, to avoid going to school. □ **hacer pellas**

hooligan ['hu:ligən] *n.* rowdy/wild person. □ **gamberro**

hooliganism *n.* wild behaviour: *football hooliganism,* rowdy behaviour of football fans. □ **gamberrismo; vandalismo**

hoop [hu:p] *n.* large ring of wood or metal. □ **aro**

hoop-la *n.* game where you have to throw hoops over little pegs. □ **juego de los anillos**

hooray [hu'rei] *interjection* showing great pleasure/excitement: *Hooray! it's my birthday.* □ **¡hurra!**

hoot [hu:t] *n.* **1** call of an owl. □ **ululato**

2 *hoots of laughter,* sound like an owl call, made when you are laughing. □ **risotadas**

3 sound made by a car horn. □ **bocinazo**

■ *v.* **1** (*of an owl*) to call: *the owls hooted in the churchyard.* □ **ulular**

2 *they hooted with laughter,* they laughed hilariously. □ **morirse de risa**

3 to sound the horn of a car: *he had to hoot several times before the pedestrians got out of the way.* □ **tocar la bocina**

hooter *n.* **1** warning siren: *a factory hooter.* □ **sirena**

2 car horn. □ **bocina**

Hoover ['hu:və] *n.* trademark for a type of vacuum cleaner. □ **aspiradora**

■ *v.* ***to hoover,*** to clean with a vacuum cleaner: *can you hoover the dining room carpet?* □ **pasar la aspiradora**

hop [hɔp] *n.* **1** little jump. □ **saltito**

to catch someone on the hop, (*informal*) catch someone unexpectedly. □ **pillar a alguien por sorpresa**

2 short flight (in a plane). □ **vuelo corto**

3 bitter fruit used in making beer; climbing plant which bears this fruit. □ **lúpulo**

■ *v.* (*he hopped*) to jump on one leg; (*of bird*) to jump with both feet together: *he hopped around the room.* □ **dar saltitos**

hopfield *n.* field where hops are grown. □ **campo de lúpulo**

hop-picker *n.* person who picks the fruit off hop plants. □ **recolector de lúpulo**

hope [houp] *n.* expectation/wanting something to happen. □ **esperanza**

what a hope!, there is no chance of it happening. □ **¡imposible que suceda!**

■ *v.* to expect that something will happen/to want something to happen: *we hope to be home by six o'clock; I hope our team wins.* □ **esperar**

hopeful *adj.* full of hope/confident; likely to happen: *the government is hopeful that a peace treaty can be signed.* □ **esperanzado**

hopefully *adv.* **1** confidently: *he is looking forward hopefully to passing his examinations.* □ **con optimismo**

2 *hopefully the weather will clear up,* let's hope/I hope the weather will clear up. □ **esperemos que...**

hopeless *adj.* **1** with no hope. □ **desesperado**

2 *hopeless case,* person who cannot be cured. □ **desahuciado**

3 *he's hopeless at chess,* he plays chess very badly. □ **es un inútil**

hopelessly *adv.* with no hope: *we're hopelessly lost,* we're completely lost. □ **sin esperanza**

hopper ['hɔpə] *n.* very large funnel for channelling loose material (like sand/corn, etc.). □ **tolva**

hopscotch ['hɔpskɔtʃ] *n.* children's game in which you hop over marked squares on the ground. □ **tejo**

horde [hɔ:d] *n.* crowd/mass. □ **horda**

horizon [hə'raizn] *n.* line where the earth seems to meet the sky: *we scanned the horizon for a sign of enemy; they could see some trees on the horizon.* □ **horizonte**

horizontal [hɔri'zɔntl] *adj.* lying flat/not upright. □ **horizontal**

horizontally *adv.* lying flat. □ **horizontalmente**

hormone ['hɔ:moun] *n.* substance produced by glands in the body, which causes various physical reactions. □ **hormona**

horn [hɔ:n] *n.* **1** hard bony growth on the head of some animals: *cow's horn; a horn drinking cup,* cup made out of horn. □ **cuerno**

2 feeler on a snail's head. □ **cuerno**

3 brass musical instrument shaped like an animal's horn: *French horn; the huntsman sounded his horn.* □ **trompa**

4 instrument on a car, etc., which makes a loud warning noise. □ **bocina**

horned *adj.* with horns. □ **con cuernos**

hornpipe *n.* vigorous dance danced by sailors. □ **baile marinero**

horny *adj.* (*hornier, horniest*) hard/rough (hands). □ **calloso**

hornbeam ['hɔ:nbi:m] *n.* common hedgerow tree. □ **carpe**

hornet ['hɔ:nit] *n.* type of large red wasp. □ **avispón**

horoscope ['hɔrəskoup] *n.* description of a person's character/forecasting of what will happen to a person in the future, based on the position of the stars when he or she was born. □ **horóscopo**

horrible ['hɔrəbl] *adj.* terrible/frightening: *it was all a horrible mistake,* a bad mistake. □ **horrible; terrible**

horribly *adv.* frighteningly/badly. □ **horriblemente**

horrid ['hɔrid] *adj.* nasty/unpleasant: *what a horrid man!* □ **antipático**

horrific [hə'rifik] *adj.* frightening/shocking: *they told horrific tales of the destruction of the town.* □ **horrendo**

horrify ['hɔrifai] *v.* to make (someone) very frightened/to shock (someone): *I am horrified by the increase in the price of petrol.* □ **horrorizar**

horror ['hɔrə] *n.* **1** terror/feeling of being very frightened: *I have a horror of spiders.* □ **horror**

horror film, film which aims to frighten the spectators. □ **película de terror**

2 ***a little horror,*** (*informal*) a very naughty child. □ **un demonio**

horror-stricken, horror-struck *adj.* very frightened. □ **horrorizado**

hors-d'oeuvre [ɔ:'də:v] *n. pl.* cold tasty food served at the beginning of a meal. □ **entremeses**

horse [hɔ:s] *n.* **1** large animal with hooves, which is used for riding or pulling vehicles. □ **caballo**

horse racing, racing of horses. □ **carreras de caballos**

2 ***a dark horse,*** someone you know nothing about and who may win: *the dark horse in the local elections is the Liberal candidate.* □ **ganador inesperado**

3 *I got it* ***straight from the horse's mouth,*** (*informal*) my information comes from a very reliable source. □ **lo sé de buena tinta**

4 apparatus made of wood over which you jump in gymnastics. □ **potro**

5 ***clothes horse,*** wooden frame used for drying clothes. □ **tendedero**

horseback *n.* ***on horseback,*** riding on a horse: *she came on horseback.* □ **a caballo**

horsebox *n.* enclosed box on wheels for transport-

ing horses from one place to another. □ **remolque**
horse-chestnut *n.* type of large tree; shiny inedible nut of this tree. □ **castaño de Indias**
horse dealer *n.* person who buys and sells horses. □ **tratante de caballos**
horsehair *n.* hair from the mane or tail of a horse, used for padding furniture: *a horsehair sofa.* □ **crin de caballo**
horseman *n.* (*pl. horsemen*) man riding a horse; man who often rides on horses: *four horsemen went riding by; he is an excellent horseman.* □ **jinete**
horseplay *n.* rough fighting/rough games. □ **juego de pelea**
horsepower *n.* unit formerly used when calculating the power of a car engine. □ **caballo**
horseradish *n.* plant with a large root used to make a sharp sauce. □ **rábano picante**
horse rider *n.* person who rides a horse. □ **caballista**
horseshoe *n.* curved metal strip nailed to the hooves of horses. □ **herradura**
horse trading *n.* arguing between parties before coming to an agreement. □ **chalaneo**
horsewoman *n.* (*pl. horsewomen*) woman riding a horse; woman who often rides on horses. □ **amazona**
horsy *adj.* **1** looking like a horse. □ **caballuno**
2 interested in horses. □ **aficionado a los caballos**
horticulture ['hɔːtikʌltʃə] *n.* science of gardening. □ **horticultura**
hose [houz] *n.* **1** long, flexible tube: *a garden hose; the firemen unrolled their hoses.* □ **manguera**
2 stockings/socks. □ **medias**
panty hose, tights/stockings and briefs in one piece. □ **'panties'**
■ *v.* to spray with water, etc., from a hose: *he hosed down his car.* □ **lavar con la manguera**
hosiery ['houzjəri] *n.* knitted pieces of clothing (especially socks/gloves, etc.). □ **calcetería**
hospice ['hɔspis] *n.* place where poor or sick people can live. □ **hospicio**
hospitable [hɔ'spitəbl] *adj.* welcoming. □ **hospitalario**
hospitably *adv.* in a welcoming way. □ **hospitalariamente**
hospitality [hɔspi'tæliti] *n.* welcome to visitors; giving visitors food, drink, bed, etc. □ **hospitalidad**
hospital ['hɔspitl] *n.* place where sick people are treated: *children's hospital; maternity hospital.* □ **hospital**
host [houst] *n.* **1** man who invites guests. □ **anfitrión**
2 hotel keeper. □ **posadero**
3 animal/plant on which other animals/plants live. □ **huésped**
4 mass of things. □ **montón**
5 *a host of reasons,* a great many reasons. □ **un montón de razones**
6 (*in church*) consecrated bread. □ **hostia**
■ *v.* to be the host (at a reception/at a conference). □ **ser el anfitrión**
hostess *n.* **1** woman who invites guests. □ **anfitriona**
2 ***air hostess,*** woman who looks after passengers on an aircraft. □ **azafata**
hostage ['hɔstidʒ] *n.* person kept prisoner until the demands of the captor are met: *the guerrillas seized three hostages.* □ **rehén**
hostel ['hɔstl] *n.* **1** building providing rooms for homeless families/students, etc. □ **albergue**
2 ***youth hostel,*** building where young walkers, etc. may stay the night cheaply. □ **albergue juvenil**
hostile ['hɔstail, *Amer.* 'hɔstl] *adj.* referring to an enemy; unfriendly: *hostile tribes.* □ **hostil**
hostility [hɔ'stiliti] *n.* **1** dislike (of a plan)/opposition (to a plan). □ **hostilidad**
2 ***hostilities,*** warfare. □ **hostilidades**
hot [hɔt] *adj.* (*hotter, hottest*) **1** very warm: *the water is boiling hot; it is very hot today.* □ **caliente**
to get into hot water, (*informal*) to get into trouble. □ **meterse en un lío**
to make things hot for someone, make life unbearable. □ **amargar la vida a uno**
2 highly spiced: *English mustard is very hot.* □ **picante**
3 very strong: *he has a hot temper.* □ **fuerte**
4 ***hot line,*** direct telephone link between heads of state. □ **teléfono rojo**
5 *he's* ***in the hot seat,*** his job involves him in awkward decisions. □ **estar en un puesto clave**
■ *v.* (*he hotted*) (*informal*) ***to hot (something) up*** (i) to warm up (cold food). □ **calentar**
(ii) *things are hotting up,* things are getting more dangerous/more exciting. □ **la situación se está caldeando**
hot air *n.* (*informal*) useless excited talk. □ **cháchara**
hotbed *n.* place where something unpleasant breeds rapidly: *hotbed of disease.* □ **foco**
hot-blooded *adj.* (person) with a violent temper. □ **apasionado**
hot dog *n.* hot sausage eaten in a roll with pickles or onions. □ **perrito caliente**
hothouse *n.* heated greenhouse. □ **invernadero**
hotplate *n.* piece of metal heated usually by electricity, used to heat food. □ **calientaplatos**
hotpot *n.* meat stew with potatoes on top. □ **estofado**
hot-tempered *adj.* (person) with a violent temper. □ **temperamental**
hot-water bottle *n.* rubber container filled with hot water which is placed in a bed to warm it. □ **bolsa de agua caliente**
hotchpotch ['hɔtʃpɔtʃ] *n.* (*informal*) mixture/jumble. □ **mezcolanza**
hotel [hou'tel] *n.* building where you can buy food and drink, and rent a room for the night. □ **hotel**
hotelier [hou'teliə] *n.* person who runs a hotel. □ **hotelero**
hound [haund] *n.* large hunting dog. □ **perro de caza, podenco**
■ *v.* to chase (someone)/to victimize (someone): *he was hounded out of the club,* he was thrown out because no one approved of him. □ **acosar**
hour ['auə] *n.* **1** period of time lasting sixty minutes: *there are twenty-four hours in the day.* □ **hora**
2 *he is paid* ***by the hour,*** he is paid money for each hour he works. □ **le pagan por horas**
3 *the hours of work are from 9 till 5,* the period during which someone works. □ **jornada**
lunch hour, time when you stop work to eat in the middle of the day. □ **la hora de comer**
4 *they took* ***hours*** *to mend the car,* a very long time. □ **les llevó horas...**
5 particular point in time: *the train leaves on the hour,* at 9, 10, etc., o'clock exactly; *why did you wake me up at this unearthly hour?,* at this inconvenient time? □ **hora**
hourly *adj.* and *adv.* every hour: *hourly news broadcast.* □ **de cada hora**
house [haus, *pl.* 'hauziz] *n.* **1** building in which people live: *he has a house in the country.* □ **casa**
2 *they* ***get on like a house on fire,*** (*informal*) they are very friendly. □ **hacen buenas migas**

3 dynasty/royal family. □ **casa real**
4 commercial firm: *a business house.* □ **casa comercial**
5 showing of a film; presentation of a play: *first house,* first showing (in an evening). □ **pase (de una película); presentación**
full house, full audience occupying all the seats. □ **lleno**
6 ***public house,*** inn/building with a licence to sell drinks. □ **bar; 'pub'**
7 *drinks are* ***on the house,*** drinks are offered free with the compliments of the innkeeper. □ **por cuenta de la casa**
8 (*in a school*) division of the school to which one group of children belongs for competitions or for boarding. □ **sección**
■ *v.* to provide accommodation for (someone/something): *the government is housing the refugees.* □ **dar alojamiento**
house-agent *n.* person who arranges the sale of houses. □ **agente inmobiliario**
house arrest *n. he is under house arrest,* he is not allowed to leave his house which is being guarded by the police. □ **arresto domiciliario**
houseboat *n.* large boat which is used as permanent accommodation. □ **casa flotante**
housebreaker *n.* burglar/person who breaks into a house to steal. □ **atracador**
housebreaking *n.* breaking into a house to steal. □ **robo**
housecoat *n.* light coat/dressing gown worn by women in the house. □ **bata**
houseful *n.* full house of people. □ **casa llena**
household *n.* family/people who live together in the same house. □ **familia, casa**
household word, saying which everybody uses. □ **dicho conocidísimo**
householder *n.* head of a family/person who owns/who is in charge of a house. □ **cabeza de familia**
housekeeper *n.* woman employed to look after a house. □ **ama de llaves**
housekeeping *n.* looking after a house. □ **gobierno de la casa**
housekeeping money, money set aside for paying food/heating, etc., in a house. □ **dinero para gastos de casa**
housemaid *n.* girl who looks after the cleaning of a house. □ **muchacha**
houseman *n.* doctor working and usually living in a hospital. □ **médico residente**
housemaster, housemistress *n.* person in charge of a house in a school. □ **bedel, bedela**
house physician *n.* doctor working and usually living in a hospital. □ **médico residente**
house plant *n.* plant which is kept in the house. □ **planta de interior**
houseroom *n.* ***I wouldn't give it houseroom,*** (*informal*) I don't like it, and wouldn't have it in my house. □ **no lo tendría en casa**
house surgeon *n.* doctor working and usually living in a hospital. □ **médico residente**
house-trained *adj.* (animal) trained not to pass excreta in the house. □ **bien enseñado**
housewarming *n.* party to celebrate moving into a new house. □ **inauguración de una casa**
housewife *n.* (*pl. housewives*) woman who spends her time looking after a house and usually has no outside work. □ **ama de casa**
housework *n.* general cleaning work in a house. □ **labores domésticas**
housing ['hauziŋ] *n.* **1** providing accommodation for people. □ **alojamiento**
housing estate, area of houses and flats built at one time. □ **urbanización**
2 covering for part of a machine. □ **bastidor**
hove [houv] *v. see* **heave.**
hovel ['hɔvl] *n.* small dirty house. □ **casucha**
hover ['hɔvə] *v.* **1** to fly/to hang in the air without moving forward: *the flies are hovering over the water of the lake.* □ **revolotear; cernerse**
2 to hang about someone: *he is always hovering around her.* □ **rondar**
hovercraft *n.* vehicle which moves over water or land on a cushion of air. □ **aerodeslizador**
how [hau] *adv.* **1** in what way/to what extent: *how are you? how big is your house? how much does it cost?* □ **cómo**
2 the means of: *tell me how to get to London from here.* □ **cómo**
3 (showing surprise): *how green the trees are!* □ **qué verdes están...**
how do you do? *interjection* showing greeting hallo. □ **¿cómo estás?**
however [hau'evə] *adv.* **1** to whatever extent: *however hard he tried, he couldn't climb the tree.* □ **por mucho que lo intentó...**
2 in spite of this: *I do not normally lend people money, however this time I will make an exception.* □ **...sin embargo...**
howl [haul] *n.* loud wail. □ **aullido**
■ *v.* to make a loud wailing noise: *the wolves are howling in the forest; the wind is howling across the fields.* □ **aullar**
howl down *v.* to stop (someone) making a speech by shouting at him. □ **abuchear (a alguien) para hacerle callar**
howler *n.* (*informal*) bad mistake. □ **error garrafal**
howling *n.* loud wailing. □ **aullido**
hub [hʌb] *n.* **1** centre of a wheel where it is connected to the axle. □ **cubo**
2 centre of activity/business. □ **centro**
hub cap *n.* metal plate covering the centre of a car wheel. □ **tapacubos**
hubbub ['hʌbʌb] *n.* confused sound of voices. □ **algarabía**
huddle ['hʌdl] *n.* ***to go into a huddle,*** to meet together to discuss something in secret. □ **reunirse**
■ *v.* to crowd together: *the sheep huddled together for warmth.* □ **apretarse unos contra otros**
hue [hju:] *n.* **1** colour. □ **tinte**
2 ***hue and cry,*** loud noise showing anger/alarm: *there was a great hue and cry at the allegations of government corruption.* □ **protesta clamorosa**
huff [hʌf] *n.* bad temper: *she's in a huff,* she's offended; *he left in a huff.* □ **rabieta**
huffy *adj.* (*informal*) bad-tempered: *he was very huffy about it.* □ **enojado**
hug [hʌg] *n.* throwing your arms round someone: *he gave her a hug.* □ **abrazo**
■ *v.* (*he hugged*) **1** to throw your arms around (someone). □ **abrazar**
2 to keep close to (something): *the ship was hugging the shore.* □ **arrimarse a**
huge [hju:dʒ] *adj.* very large/enormous. □ **enorme**
hugely *adv.* (*informal*) enormously. □ **enormemente**
hugger-mugger ['hʌgəmʌgə] *adv.* (*informal*) **1** in secret. □ **en secreto**
2 in a mess. □ **en desorden**
hulk [hʌlk] *n.* **1** rotten old ship which is no longer used for sailing. □ **casco**
2 large and clumsy thing/person. □ **armatoste**
hulking *adj.* big and awkward. □ **grande y pesado**

hull [hʌl] *n.* **1** main body of a ship. □ **casco**
2 pea or bean pod. □ **vaina**
■ *v. to hull peas,* to take peas out of their pods. □ **desvainar, pelar**
hullabaloo [hʌləbə'lu:] *n.* loud disorderly noise. □ **follón**
hullo [hə'lou] *interjection* showing a greeting: *he said hullo to me.* □ **hola**
hum [hʌm] *n.* low buzzing noise: *the hum of the engines; hum of insects.* □ **zumbido**
■ *v.* (*he hummed*) **1** to make a continual low buzzing noise: *the engine was humming.* □ **zumbar**
2 to sing the tune of a song without using the words: *he was humming an old French song.* □ **tararear**
3 (*informal*) to give off an unpleasant smell. □ **apestar**
4 ***to hum and haw,*** not to make up your mind: *he hummed and hawed about going to the party,* he hesitated. □ **titubear**
hummingbird *n.* very small brightly coloured tropical bird which hovers. □ **colibrí**
human ['hju:mən] *adj.* referring to man. □ **humano**
a human being, a person. □ **un ser humano**
human nature, general characteristics of people: *it is only human nature to want to eat well.* □ **es totalmente humano...**
■ *n.* person: *these apes do not seem at all frightened when approached by humans.* □ **persona**
humane [hju:mein] *adj.* kind/gentle. □ **humano; de buen corazón**
humanely *adv.* kindly/gently. □ **humanamente**
humanism *n.* concern with human beings rather than with religions. □ **humanismo**
humanist *n.* person who is concerned with human beings rather than with religion. □ **humanista**
humanitarian [hju:mæni'tɛəriən] *adj.* kind towards other humans. □ **humanitario**
humanity [hju:'mæniti] *n.* **1** all people. □ **humanidad; género humano**
2 great kindness. □ **humanidad**
3 ***the humanities,*** arts subjects (not sciences). □ **las humanidades**
humanly *adv. we will do everything humanly possible,* all we can. □ **humanamente**
humble ['hʌmbl] *adj.* (*humbler, humblest*) **1** modest/not proud. □ **humilde**
2 *person of humble origins,* of a very ordinary/poor family. □ **humilde**
to eat humble pie, to admit you were wrong. □ **reconocer su error**
■ *v.* to make (someone) less proud/less important. □ **humillar**
humbleness *n.* being humble. □ **humildad**
humbug ['hʌmbʌg] *n.* **1** confidence trick. □ **embuste**
2 person who tricks someone/who pretends to be something which he is not. □ **farsante**
3 kind of striped hard sweet. □ **caramelo de menta**
humdrum ['hʌmdrʌm] *adj.* dull/ordinary. □ **rutinario**
humerus ['hju:mərəs] *n.* bone in the top part of the arm. □ **húmero**
humid ['hju:mid] *adj.* damp. □ **húmedo**
humidifier *n.* machine which dampens the air (in a house). □ **humidificador**
humidity [hju:'miditi] *n.* dampness. □ **humedad**
humiliate [hju:'milieit] *v.* to make someone feel unimportant/humble/ashamed. □ **humillar**
humiliation [hju:mili'eiʃn] *n.* making someone feel unimportant/humble/ashamed. □ **humillación**
humility [hju:'militi] *n.* humbleness/being humble. □ **humildad**
hummock ['hʌmək] *n.* low hump in the ground. □ **montecillo**
humour ['hju:mə] *Amer.* **humor** *n.* **1** seeing the funny aspects of something: *the humour of the situation,* the funny side of something; *he has no sense of humour,* he is very serious and does not laugh at jokes. □ **humor**
2 general feeling/mood: *she's in a very good humour.* □ **...de buen humor**
■ *v.* to do what someone wants in order to keep them happy. □ **complacer**
humorist *n.* person who makes jokes; writer of funny stories or articles. □ **humorista**
humorous *adj.* funny/amusing. □ **humorístico**
hump [hʌmp] *n.* lump on the back; small rounded bump in the ground: *the camel has two humps.* □ **joroba**
■ *v.* (*informal*) to carry (on your shoulder): *I've been humping sacks of potatoes.* □ **cargar al hombro**
humpbacked *adj.* (person) with a hump. □ **jorobado**
humpbacked bridge, bridge with a very high arch. □ **puente de fuerte pendiente**
humus ['hju:məs] *n.* (*no pl.*) good soil made rich with decayed animal or vegetable matter. □ **humus**
hunch [hʌntʃ] *n.* (*pl. hunches*) (*informal*) feeling that something is going to happen: *I've got a hunch that he is lying.* □ **presentimiento**
■ *v.* to bend low/to crouch: *he was hunched over a pile of books.* □ **encorvarse**
hunchback *n.* person with a curved back. □ **corcovado**
hundred ['hʌndrəd] number 100: *the house is a hundred years old; he lived to be a hundred.* □ **cien**
hundreds of *people caught flu in the epidemic,* very large numbers. □ **cientos de personas**
hundredth, 100th *adj.* referring to a hundred. □ **centésimo**
hundredweight *n.* weight of 112 pounds (approximately 50 kilos). □ **quintal**
hung [hʌŋ] *v. see* **hang.**
hung parliament, one where no party has an absolute majority. □ **parlamento sin mayoría absoluta**
hung jury, *Amer.* jury which cannot reach a majority decision. □ **jurado sin mayoría**
hung over *adj.* (*informal*) feeling ill after drinking too much alcohol. □ **con resaca**
Hungary ['hʌŋgəri] *n.* country in Eastern Europe. □ **Hungría**
Hungarian [hʌŋ'gɛəriən] *adj.* referring to Hungary. □ **húngaro**
■ *n.* **1** person from Hungary. □ **húngaro**
2 language spoken in Hungary. □ **húngaro**
hunger ['hʌŋgə] *n.* wanting/needing to eat. □ **hambre**
hunger strike: *the prisoners went on hunger strike,* they refused to eat as a protest. □ **...en huelga de hambre**
hungrily *adv.* in a hungry way. □ **ansiosamente**
hungry *adj.* wanting/needing to eat: *I'm hungry; he was so hungry he ate six pieces of bread.* □ **tengo hambre; tenía tanta hambre**
hunk [hʌŋk] *n.* large rough piece of bread/cheese, etc. □ **trozo**
hunt [hʌnt] *n.* **1** chasing of wild animals for sport; group of people who meet regularly to chase wild animals, especially foxes. □ **caza**
2 search for (someone): *a police hunt for an escaped prisoner.* □ **búsqueda**
■ *v.* **1** to chase (wild animals): *he goes hunting bears.*

□ **cazar**
2 to look for (someone/something): *the police are hunting for clues.* □ **buscar**
hunt down *v.* to track (someone/an animal) and catch them. □ **acorralar**
hunter *n.* person who chases wild animals; horse used in hunting. □ **cazador**
bargain hunter, someone who is looking for bargains in shops. □ **buscador de gangas**
hunting *n.* **1** chasing wild animals: *she doesn't approve of fox hunting.* □ **caza**
2 looking for something: *we are going house-hunting,* looking for a new house. □ **...en busca de casa**
hunting ground *n.* **1** place where wild animals are often found. □ **cazadero**
2 place where things are often found: *a hunting ground for antique dealers.* □ **filón**
huntsman *n.* (*pl. huntsmen*) man who hunts wild animals; man who looks after a pack of hunting hounds. □ **cazador**
hurdle ['hə:dl] *n.* **1** moveable fence for keeping sheep in. □ **cerca**
2 small fence which has to be jumped over in a race. □ **valla**
3 obstacle: *we have got over the last hurdle before signing the agreement.* □ **traba**
hurdling *n.* running a race where you have to jump over fences. □ **carrera de vallas**
hurdy-gurdy ['hə:digə:di] *n.* (*pl. hurdy-gurdies*) machine which produces music if a handle is turned. □ **organillo**
hurl [hə:l] *v.* to throw hard: *he hurled bricks at the policeman.* □ **arrojar**
hurly-burly ['hə:libə:li] *n.* rough activity. □ **barullo**
hurrah, hurray [hu'rɑ:, hu'rei] *interjection* showing great pleasure/excitement: *hurray, the sun has come out!* □ **¡hurra!**
hurricane ['hʌrikən] *n.* violent tropical storm, especially in the West Indies. □ **huracán**
hurry ['hʌri] *n.* **1** rush: *what's the hurry?* why are you going so fast? □ **prisa**
2 *he's always **in a hurry,*** he's always rushing about. □ **siempre tiene prisa**
■ *v.* (*hurried; hurrying*) **1** to go fast: *she hurried down the corridor; hurry up, you'll be late!* □ **darse prisa**
2 to make someone go faster: *don't hurry me, I'm going as fast as I can.* □ **meter prisa**
hurried *adj.* quick/rushed: *we had a hurried breakfast.* □ **apresurado**
hurriedly *adv.* quickly: *they hurriedly packed their suitcases.* □ **a toda velocidad**
hurt [hə:t] *n.* pain. □ **dolor**
■ *v.* (*he hurt*) to give (someone) pain/to make (someone) sad: *my arm hurts; he's hurt his hand; it hurts me to have to do this,* it makes me sad to have to do this. □ **hacer daño; doler**
hurtful *adj.* which is painful to the feelings/which makes someone sad. □ **doloroso**
hurtle ['hə:tl] *v.* to move quickly/to rush dangerously: *the car hurtled down the hill.* □ **lanzarse con peligro**
husband ['hʌzbənd] *n.* man who is married to a certain woman: *he's my secretary's husband.* □ **marido**
■ *v.* (*formal*) to look after carefully/not to waste (your resources). □ **economizar**
husbandry *n.* farming. □ **agricultura**
animal husbandry, rearing of animals on a farm. □ **cría de ganado**
hush [hʌʃ] *n.* quiet: *a hush fel over the crowd.* □ **quietud**
■ *v.* to make quiet. □ **hacer callar**
hush-hush *adj.* (*informal*) secret: *he's in a hush-hush job.* □ **muy secreto**
hush money *n.* money paid to someone to stop them revealing a secret. □ **pago para callar**
hush up *v.* to suppress (a scandal): *the papers wanted to print the story, but the mayor managed to hush it up.* □ **echar tierra sobre**
husk [hʌsk] *n.* hard outside covering of a seed. □ **cáscara**
husky ['hʌski] *adj.* (*huskier, huskiest*) rough/hoarse (voice). □ **ronco**
■ *n.* (*pl. huskies*) dog which pulls sledges in the Arctic. □ **husky**
huskiness *n.* hoarseness of the voice. □ **ronquera**
huss [hʌs] *n.* dogfish/small white sea fish. □ **cazón**
hustings ['hʌstiŋz] *n. at the hustings,* during an election campaign. □ **proceso electoral**
hustle ['hʌsl] *n.* rush/violent activity. □ **ajetreo**
■ *v.* to push/to hurry (roughly): *the police hustled him away to a waiting car.* □ **empujar**
hustler *n.* person who gets things going/who hurries business along. □ **despabilado**
hut [hʌt] *n.* small rough house, usually made of wood. □ **cabaña**
hutch [hʌtʃ] *n.* (*pl. hutches*) wooden box to keep rabbits in. □ **conejera**
hyacinth ['haiəsinθ] *n.* strongly scented spring flower grown from a bulb. □ **jacinto**
hybrid ['haibrid] *adj.* and *n.* (plant/animal, etc.) produced from two different species. □ **híbrido**
hydrangea [hai'dreindʒə] *n.* garden shrub with large blue or pink flowers. □ **hortensia**
hydrant ['haidrənt] *n.* water pipe in a street to which a hose can be attached. □ **boca de riego**
fire hydrant, hydrant to which firemen can attach fire hoses. □ **boca de incendio**
hydraulic [hai'drɔ:lik] *adj.* worked by fluid: *hydraulic power; hydraulic brakes.* □ **hidráulico**
hydro ['haidrou] *n.* (*pl. hydros*) (*informal*) **1** hotel and clinic which specializes in the use of water to cure people. □ **balneario**
2 hydroelectric station. □ **central hidroeléctrica**
hydrochloric [haidrou'klɔrik] *adj.* (acid) made of hydrogen and chlorine. □ **clorhídrico**
hydroelectric [haidroui'lektrik] *adj.* referring to electricity which has been produced by water power: *a hydroelectric station.* □ **hidroeléctrico**
hydro-electricity [haidrouilek'trisiti] *n.* electricity produced by water power. □ **hidroelectricidad**
hydrofoil ['haidrəfɔil] *n.* boat which skims over the water on thin legs. □ **aerodeslizador**
hydrogen ['haidrədʒən] *n.* (*chemical element*: H) common gas which combines with oxygen to form water. □ **hidrógeno**
hydrographer [hai'drɔgrəfə] *n.* person who makes maps of the sea or sea bed. □ **hidrógrafo**
hydrolysis [hai'drɔlisis] *n.* decomposition of a chemical substance by water. □ **hidrólisis**
hydrophobia [haidrə'foubiə] *n.* rabies; fear of water (usually a symptom of rabies). □ **hidrofobia**
hydroplane ['haidrəplein] *n.* powerful flat-bottomed motorboat which skims over the surface of the water. □ **hidroavión**
hydroponics [haidrə'pɔniks] *n.* (*usually with singular verb*) science of growing plants in water, without using soil. □ **hidroponía**
hydrotherapy [haidrə'θerəpi] *n.* treatment of sick people with water. □ **hidroterapia**
hyena [hai'i:nə] *n.* fierce dog-like African animal. □ **hiena**

hygiene ['haidʒiːn] *n.* keeping clean and free of germs: *hygiene is important in hospitals.* □ **higiene**
hygienic [hai'dʒiːnik] *adj.* (which keeps) clean and free of germs. □ **higiénico**
hygrometer [hai'grɔmitə] *n.* instrument for measuring humidity. □ **higrómetro**
hymen ['haimen] *n.* thin tissue which covers the vagina of a girl who has never had sexual intercourse. □ **himen**
hymn [him] *n.* religious song. □ **himno religioso**
hymnal ['himnl] **hymn-book** *n.* book of hymns. □ **himnario**
hyper- ['haipə] *prefix* meaning to a great degree. □ **hiper**
***hyperactive*,** very active. □ **hiperactivo**
hyperbole [hai'pəːbəli] *n.* exaggerated comparison. □ **hipérbole**
hypercritical [haipə'kritikl] *adj.* extremely critical. □ **hipercrítico**
hypermarket ['haipəmɑːkit] *n.* very large supermarket. □ **hipermercado**
hypersensitive [haipə'sensitiv] *adj.* very easily offended. □ **hipersensible**
hypertension [haipə'tenʃn] *n.* very high blood pressure caused by stress. □ **hipertensión**
hyphen ['haifn] *n.* short line (-) which joins two words or separates one word into parts. □ **guión**
hyphenate *v.* to join words with a hyphen or separate one word into parts with a hyphen. □ **unir/partir con guión**
hypnosis [hip'nousis] *n.* putting someone into a trance, so that they obey your orders: *he did it under hypnosis,* while he was in a trance. □ **hipnosis**
hypnotic [hip'nɔtik] *adj.* referring to hypnosis. □ **hipnótico**
***hypnotic state*,** trance. □ **trance hipnótico**
hypnotism ['hipnətizəm] *n.* use of hypnosis as a medical process or for amusement. □ **hipnotismo**
hypnotist *n.* person who practices hypnosis. □ **hipnotizador**
hypnotize *v.* to put (someone) into a trance. □ **hipnotizar**
hypo ['haipou] *n.* substance used for fixing the picture when developing a photograph. □ **fijador**
■ *prefix* meaning under/below. □ **hipo**
hypochondria [haipə'kɔndriə] *n.* being permanently worried about your health. □ **hipocondria**
hypochondriac *n.* person who is always worried about his health. □ **hipocondriaco**
hypocrisy [hi'pɔkrəsi] *n.* pretending to be the opposite of what you really are/to feel the opposite of what you really feel. □ **hipocresía**
hypocrite ['hipəkrit] *n.* person who pretends to be/to feel the opposite of what he really is/feels. □ **hipócrita**
hypocritical [hipə'kritikl] *adj.* referring to hypocrisy. □ **hipócrita**
hypodermic [haipə'dəːmik] *adj.* ***hypodermic syringe/needle*,** medical instrument used for injections just below the surface of the skin. □ **hipodérmico**
hypotension [haipou'tenʃn] *n.* low blood pressure. □ **hipotensión**
hypotenuse [hai'pɔtənjuːz] *n.* longest side of a right-angled triangle. □ **hipotenusa**
hypothermia [haipə'θəːmiə] *n.* state where the temperature of the body is abnormally low. □ **hipotermia**
hypothesis [hai'pɔθəsis] *n.* (*pl. hypotheses*) suggestion that something is true, though without proof. □ **hipótesis**
hypothetical [haipə'θetikl] *adj.* suggested as true, but not necessarily so. □ **hipotético**
hysterectomy [histə'rektəmi] *n.* (*pl. hysterectomies*) surgical operation to remove a woman's womb. □ **histeroctomía**
hysteria *n.* nervous excitement leading to wild fits of laughing or crying. □ **histeria**
hysterical *adj.* suffering from hysteria: laughing/crying in a wild manner: *she became hysterical; hysterical laughter.* □ **histérico**
hysterically, *adv.* in an uncontrollable way: *he laughed hysterically.* □ **histéricamente**
hysterics *n. pl.* attack of hysteria: *she had hysterics when she heard her husband had had an accident.* □ **ataque histérico**

I,i

I, i [ai] ninth letter of the alphabet. □ **I, i**
to dot one's i's and cross one's t's, to be very careful about something/to settle the final details of an agreement. □ **poner los puntos sobres las íes**
I [ai] *pronoun* referring to the speaker: *he said: 'I can do it'; he and I are great friends.* □ **yo**
ibex [aibeks] *n.* mountain goat with large curved horns. □ **íbice**
ibis ['aibis] *n.* tropical water bird with long legs and a curved bill. □ **ibis**
ice [ais] *n.* **1** frozen water: *when the lakes freeze, ice forms on the surface; don't try to skate, the ice isn't thick enough yet; my hands are like ice,* very cold. □ **hielo**
to break the ice, to bring an embarrassing silence to an end: *once the ice was broken, the party went with a swing.* □ **romper el hielo**
to put on ice: *I am putting this project on ice,* I am not doing anything about it for the moment. □ **dejar para después**
2 ice cream. □ **helado**
3 ***dry ice,*** frozen carbon dioxide. □ **hielo seco**
■ *v.* **1** to cool with ice: *iced lemonade.* □ **granizar**
2 to freeze. □ **helar**
to ice up: *the wings on the plane iced up,* were covered with ice. □ **cubrirse de hielo**
3 to cover with sugar icing: *to ice a cake.* □ **glasear**
ice age *n.* geological period when parts of Europe and America were covered with ice. □ **período glacial**
ice axe *n.* axe used by mountaineers to cut footholds in ice. □ **piolet**
iceberg *n.* large floating mass of ice at sea. □ **iceberg**
the tip of the iceberg, small part of something (usually unpleasant) which makes you eventually discover the rest. □ **la punta del iceberg**
icebox *n.* (*pl. iceboxes*) **1** box containing ice to keep food or drink cool. □ **nevera**
2 *Amer.* refrigerator. □ **frigorífico**
ice-breaker *n.* boat specially strengthened to break up ice in shipping lanes. □ **rompehielos**
ice cream *n.* frozen sweet made of cream (or vegetable fat) and flavouring: *raspberry ice cream.* □ **helado**
ice cream cornet/cone, conical biscuit with ice cream in it. □ **helado de cucurucho**
ice cube *n.* small piece of ice which you put in a drink to make it cold. □ **cubito de hielo**
icefield *n.* large area of ice floating on the sea. □ **banco de hielo**
icefloe *n.* large sheet of ice floating in the sea. □ **témpano de hielo**
ice hockey *n.* form of hockey played on ice. □ **hockey sobre hielo**
icehouse *n.* house for storing ice during the summer: *it is like an icehouse in here,* it is very cold here. □ **fábrica de hielo**
icicle *n.* long hanging piece of ice formed by dripping water in cold weather. □ **carámbano**
icily *adv.* in a cold/unfriendly way: *she stared at him icily.* □ **fríamente**
iciness *n.* bitter coldness (of weather/of greeting). □ **frialdad**
icing *n.* sugar topping for a cake. □ **glaseado**
icing sugar, very fine sugar for covering cakes. □ **azúcar en polvo**
Iceland *n.* country which is an island in the North Atlantic. □ **Islandia**
Icelandic *adj.* referring to Iceland. □ **islandés**
■ *n.* **1** person from Iceland. □ **islandés**
2 language spoken in Iceland. □ **islandés**
icy *adj.* (*icier, iciest*) **1** covered with ice: *icy road.* □ **helado**
2 very cold/unwelcoming: *he gave an icy smile.* □ **glacial**
icon ['aikən] *n.* picture of Christ or a saint in the Eastern Christian church. □ **icono**
iconoclast [ai'kɔnəklæst] *n.* person who attacks beliefs which are held by many people. □ **iconoclasta**
iconoclastic [aikɔnə'klæstik] *adj.* which attacks beliefs which are held by many people. □ **iconoclasta**
I'd [aid] short for ***I would/I had/I should.***
idea [ai'diə] *n.* thought/plan in the mind: *I've had an idea,* I've just thought of a plan; *I have an idea that his father is a chemist,* I think his father is a chemist. □ **idea**
to have no idea: *I had no idea you were coming,* I did not know you were coming. □ **no tenía idea de que**
ideal [ai'diəl] *n.* **1** summit of perfection. □ **ideal**
2 *a man of ideals,* someone who has standards of perfection. □ **hombre de ideales**
■ *adj.* perfect; very suitable: *in an ideal world everyone would have as much free time as they liked; a small car is ideal for shopping.* □ **ideal**
idealism *n.* aiming at achieving an ideal. □ **idealismo**
idealist *n.* person who aims at achieving an ideal; impractical person. □ **idealista**
idealistic [aidiə'listik] *adj.* **1** too perfect. □ **ideal**
2 *his plan is rather idealistic,* his plan does not take account of how things really are. □ **idealista**
idealize *v.* to make (someone/something) seem perfect: *he idealized his teacher.* □ **idealizar**
ideally *adv.* if everything were perfect: *ideally, we ought to go together,* the ideal solution to the problem would be for us to go together. □ **idealmente, lo mejor...**
identify [ai'dentifai] *v.* (*identified; identifying*) **1** to say who someone is: *the police are trying to identify the victim of the accident; she identified him as the man who stole her purse.* □ **identificar**
2 to state that something belongs to you: *can you identify your luggage?* □ **identificar**
3 ***to identify with,*** to feel you have the same characteristics as (someone); to have a feeling of sympathy for (someone): *he has difficulty in identifying with the cause of the workers.* □ **identificarse con**
identical *adj.* exactly the same: *identical twins; our two watches are identical.* □ **idéntico**
identically *adv.* in exactly the same way: *both parents reacted identically to the news.* □ **idénticamente**
identification [aidentifi'keiʃn] *n.* saying who someone is/who something belongs to. □ **identificación**
identification parade, line of several people at a police station from whom a witness is asked to identify the criminal. □ **rueda de identificación**
identikit *n.* method of making a portrait of a criminal using pieces of photographs or drawings of different faces to form a composite picture.

□ **retrato robot**
identity *n.* (*pl. identities*) **1** who someone is: *have you any proof of identity?,* documents to prove who you are. □ **identidad**
identity card, card which shows a photograph of the holder, with the name, date of birth and other details. □ **carné de identidad**
identity parade, identification parade. □ **ronda de identificación**
a case of mistaken identity, case where someone is wrongly accused of a crime because he was mistaken for someone else. □ **...identificación errónea**
2 being the same/being identical. □ **identidad**
ideology [aidi'ɔlədʒi] *n.* (*pl. ideologies*) theory of life based on political or economic philosophy rather than religious belief: *communist ideology.* □ **ideología**
ideological [aidiə'lɔdʒikl] *adj.* referring to political or economic philosophy: *ideological quarrel between different political parties.* □ **ideológico**
idiocy ['idiəsi] *n. see* **idiot.**
idiom ['idiəm] *n.* **1** characteristic way of speaking and writing. □ **lenguaje, estilo**
2 particularly colloquial expression where the words do not have their literal meaning (such as 'to turn over a new leaf'). □ **modismo**
idiomatic [idiə'mætik] *adj.* referring to a particular way of speaking. □ **idiomático**
idiosyncrasy [idiou'siŋkrəsi] *n.* (*pl. idiosyncracies*) particular way of behaving: *one of his idiosyncrasies is that he puts salt in his coffee.* □ **idiosincrasia**
idiosyncratic [idiousiŋ'krætik] *adj.* odd/peculiar; particular to one person: *he has an idiosyncratic way of writing.* □ **idiosincrásico**
idiot ['idiət] *n.* **1** mentally deficient person. □ **idiota**
2 person who is stupid: *don't be an idiot!* □ **idiota**
idiocy *n.* stupidity. □ **idiotez**
idiotic [idi'ɔtik] *adj.* stupid: *what an idiotic thing to do!* □ **idiota**
idiotically *adv.* in a stupid way. □ **tontamente**
idle ['aidl] *adj.* **1** lazy. □ **ocioso**
bone idle, very lazy. □ **vago consumado**
2 not working: *we can't have machines lying idle.* □ **parado**
3 aimless/not worthwhile: *I went to the exhibition out of idle curiosity,* because I was curious and had nothing better to do. □ **por mera curiosidad**
■ *v.* **1** not to work; to spend time doing nothing: *we idled away the afternoon playing cards.* □ **perder**
2 *the engine was idling,* was running gently. □ **funcionando a medio gas**
idleness *n.* laziness: *he stays in bed out of sheer idleness.* □ **holgazanería**
idly *adv.* **1** lazily: *we were idly watching a game of cricket.* □ **distraídamente**
2 without being involved: *we cannot stand idly by and see our allies attacked.* □ **sin hacer nada**
idol ['aidl] *n.* **1** statue of a god. □ **ídolo**
2 favourite person. □ **ídolo**
3 star performer (who is worshipped by fans): *tennis idol.* □ **ídolo**
idolatry [ai'dɔlətri] *n.* worship of idols. □ **idolatría**
idolize *v.* to worship: *he is idolized by his fans.* □ **idolatrar**
idyll ['idil] *n.* pleasant/happy scene. □ **idilio**
idyllic [i'dilik] *adj.* pleasant/happy (in a romantic way). □ **idílico**
i.e. ['ai'i:] *abbreviation for* id est, *meaning* that is. □ **es decir**
if [if] *conj.* **1** (showing what might happen): *if it rains the ground gets wet; if he robs a bank he will be caught; if I am free I'll go for a walk; if I were free I would go for a walk.* □ **si**
2 (showing supposition): *write him a nice letter, if only to please his mother; I will try to come on Tuesday, if not, then on Wednesday.* □ **aunque sólo...**
3 (exclamation): *if only I had known!* □ **¡si lo hubiera sabido!**
4 whether: *do you know if the plane is going to be late? can I ask if you have ever been to Russia?* □ **si**
5 although: *he is a nice man, if rather absent-minded; do come and see us, even if it is a long way from your house.* □ **aunque**
6 at any time when: *if she goes out she always wears a coat.* □ **siempre que, cuando**
■ *n.* (informal) undecided question: *that is a very big if.* □ **es sumamente dudoso**
igloo ['iglu:] *n.* dome-shaped shelter built by Eskimos out of blocks of snow. □ **iglú**
igneous ['igniəs] *adj.* (rock) which was originally formed by volcanic action. □ **ígneo**
ignite [ig'nait] *v.* to set fire to; to catch fire: *the spark ignited the gas.* □ **prender fuego a**
ignition [ig'niʃn] *n.* (*in a car*) electrical device which makes the spark which fires the petrol: *he had left the ignition on,* he had left the switch turned on. □ **encendido**
ignition key, key used to switch on the ignition. □ **llave de contacto**
ignoble [ig'noubl] *adj.* (*formal*) unworthy. □ **innoble**
ignominy ['ignəmini] *n.* shame/disgrace. □ **ignominia**
ignominious [ignə'miniəs] *adj.* shameful: *he made an ignominious exit.* □ **ignominioso**
ignore [ig'nɔ:] *v.* not to notice (on purpose): *he ignored the stop sign; instead of saying 'hello' she just ignored me; the two shop assistants were chatting and simply ignored my presence.* □ **hacer caso omiso de**
ignoramus [ignə'reiməs] *n.* (*pl. ignoramuses*) person who is stupid/who knows nothing. □ **ignorante**
ignorance ['ignərəns] *n.* not knowing: *he was kept in ignorance of the real state of the company's affairs.* □ **ignorancia**
ignorance of the law is no excuse, you cannot plead you are innocent because you did not know you had broken the law. □ **la ignorancia de la ley no exime su cumplimiento**
ignorant ['ignərənt] *adj.* not knowing/stupid: *he is the most ignorant man I have ever met.* □ **ignorante**
iguana [i'gwɑ:nə] *n.* kind of tropical lizard. □ **iguana**
ilk [ilk] *n.* (*informal*) sort/type: *people of that ilk.* □ **índole**
ill [il] *adj.* (*worse, worst*) **1** sick: *eating green apples will make you ill; she's ill,* not well. □ **enfermo**
2 bad: *he suffers from constant ill health.* □ **...mala salud**
a house of ill repute, brothel. □ **...de mala reputación**
■ *n.* bad thing: *I don't wish him ill.* □ **no le deseo nada malo**
■ *adv.* **1** badly: *you mustn't speak ill of your brother.* □ **...hablar mal...**
2 *he was **ill at ease** when the policeman interviewed him,* he was awkward/nervous. □ **inquieto**
3 *we can **ill afford** the time,* we can hardly afford the time. □ **casi no tenemos tiempo**
ill-advised *adj.* not recommended: *an ill-advised decision.* □ **nada recomendable**
ill-bred *adj.* badly brought up; with bad manners. □ **mal criado**
ill-feeling *n. I hope there is no ill-feeling towards the management,* no resentment/no dislike. □ **rencor**
ill-gotten *adj.* illegally acquired: *ill-gotten gains.*

□ **ilícito**
ill-mannered *adj.* badly behaved/with bad manners/rude. □ **mal educado**
illness *n.* sickness: *the doctors havn't discovered the cause of the illness yet.* □ **enfermedad**
ill-treat *v.* to treat (animals/children) badly. □ **maltratar**
ill-will *n.* wanting something bad to happen to someone: *does he bear you any ill-will?* □ **mala voluntad**
I'll [ail] short for ***I will/I shall.***
illegal [i'li:gl] *adj.* against the law: *it is illegal to carry a gun without a permit.* □ **ilegal**
illegal immigrant, person who enters a country without permission. □ **inmigrante ilegal**
illegally *adv.* against the law: *he was trying to enter the country illegally; his car was illegally parked.* □ **ilegalmente**
illegible [i'ledʒibl] *adj.* which cannot be read: *his handwriting is quite illegible; an illegible scribble.* □ **ilegible**
illegibly *adv.* in a way which cannot be read. □ **ilegiblemente**
illegitimate [ili'dʒitəmət] *adj.* **1** (person) born of unmarried parents. □ **ilegítimo**
2 against the law. □ **ilegítimo**
illegitimacy *n.* being illegitimate. □ **ilegitimidad**
illicit [i'lisit] *adj.* against the law/illegal: *he made illicit whisky in the garden shed.* □ **ilícito**
illiteracy [i'litərəsi] *n.* inability to read and write. □ **analfabetismo**
illiteracy campaign, campaign to teach people to read and write. □ **de alfabetización**
illiterate *adj.* and *n.* (person) who cannot read or write. □ **analfabeto**
illogical [i'lɔdʒikl] *adj.* not sensible/not reasonable: *it seems illogical for him to criticize his son for smoking when he smokes so much himself.* □ **ilógico**
illogicality *n.* being illogical. □ **falta de lógica**
illuminate [i'lu:mineit] *v.* **1** to light up: *the public buildings are all illuminated.* □ **iluminar**
2 to draw coloured initials/pictures in a manuscript. □ **iluminar**
illuminating *adj.* which throws light on (a subject): *he gave an illuminating talk on Roman archaeology.* □ **instructivo**
illumination [ilu:mi'neiʃn] *n.* **1** floodlighting; decoration: *you must go to see the Christmas illuminations.* □ **iluminación**
2 coloured initial illustration in a manuscript. □ **iluminación**
illusion [i'lu:ʒn] *n.* **1** impression which is not true: *it gives an illusion of wealth.* □ **ilusión**
optical illusion, something which appears different from what it really is because the eye is being deceived. □ **ilusión óptica**
2 *he has no illusions about his job,* he does not believe his job is better/worse than it really is. □ **no tiene ilusiones...**
illusory [i'lu:zəri] *adj.* not real: *drink gives him an illusory sense of well-being.* □ **ilusorio**
illustrate ['iləstreit] *v.* **1** to add pictures to: *illustrated book/magazine; his lecture was illustrated by slides.* □ **ilustrar**
2 to give/to be an example of: *let me illustrate how the banking system works.* □ **poner un ejemplo**
illustration [ilə'streiʃn] *n.* **1** picture (which accompanies a text, etc.): *the book has thirty illustrations in black and white.* □ **ilustración**
2 example: *to give you an illustration of how mean he is.* □ **ejemplo**
illustrative ['iləstrətiv] *adj.* which illustrates/which is an example. □ **ilustrativo**
illustrator ['iləstreitə] *n.* person who draws the pictures for a book. □ **ilustrador**
illustrious [i'lʌstriəs] *adj.* very famous. □ **ilustre**
I'm [aim] short for ***I am.***
image ['imidʒ] *n.* **1** portrait/statue: *the people worshipped wooden images of their gods.* □ **imagen**
2 *he's **the spitting image** of his father,* (*informal*), he looks exactly like his father. □ **es el vivo retrato de su padre**
3 idea which other people have of a person/a company: *the scandal has ruined his public image.* □ **imagen**
4 picture produced by a lens/seen in a mirror. □ **imagen**
5 comparison/symbol used especially in poetry. □ **imagen**
imagery *n.* using comparisons/symbols (in writing) as a way of making people imagine things. □ **imágenes**
imagine [i'mædʒin] *v.* to picture (something) in your mind: *imagine yourself on a tropical island; he imagines he is a modern knight in shining armour; they are not as dark as I had imagined; I thought I heard someone shout, but I must have imagined it.* □ **imaginar(se)**
imaginable *adj.* which you can imagine: *the ball room was the biggest room imaginable.* □ **imaginable**
imaginary *adj.* false/not real. □ **imaginario**
imagination [imædʒi'neiʃn] *n.* **1** ability to picture things in your mind. □ **imaginación**
2 *don't let your imagination get the better of you,* do not dream of things and then think they are real. □ **no te dejes llevar por la imaginación**
3 *it's just his imagination,* it doesn't really exist/he's just imagining it. □ **son imaginaciones suyas**
imaginative [i'mædʒinətiv] *adj.* (artist) with a strong imagination; (drawing/poem) which shows a lot of imagination. □ **imaginativo**
imam *n.* title of various Muslim leaders; prayer leader in a mosque; scholar on Islamic law. □ **imán**
imbalance [im'bæləns] *n.* lack of balance: *there is a marked imbalance between imports and exports.* □ **desequilibrio**
imbecile ['imbəsi:l] *n.* **1** person of small mental capacity. □ **imbécil**
2 very stupid person. □ **imbécil**
imbecility *n.* being mentally deficient. □ **imbecilidad**
imbibe [im'baib] *v.* (*formal*) to drink. □ **beber**
imbue [im'bju:] *v.* (*formal*) to fill (someone/a poem, etc.) with a feeling: *imbued with a sense of doom.* □ **imbuir**
imitate ['imiteit] *v.* to copy/to do like (someone): *he is imitating his brother's hair style; he is very good at imitating the Prime Minister.* □ **imitar**
imitation [imi'teiʃn] *n.* something which is copied: *the chair is an imitation antique; imitation pearls; his imitation of the Prime Minister is extremely funny.* □ **imitación**
imitative ['imitətiv] *adj.* which copies. □ **imitativo**
imitator ['imiteitə] *n.* someone who copies. □ **imitador**
immaculate [i'mækjulət] *adj.* extremely clean/tidy: *an immaculate white shirt; her homework is always immaculate.* □ **inmaculado**
immaculately *adv.* extremely tidily: *she was immaculately dressed.* □ **inmaculadamente**
immaterial [imə'tiəriəl] *adj.* not important: *it is immaterial whether you write in French or in English;*

the age of the candidate is immaterial. □ **no hace al caso**
immature [imə'tʃuə] *adj.* not mature/not fully grown/not fully developed: *he is still rather immature for his age; the immature fruit have fallen off the apple tree.* □ **inmaduro**
immaturity *n.* not being mature. □ **inmadurez**
immeasurable [i'meʒrəbl] *adj.* which cannot be measured/very large. □ **inmensurable**
immediate [i'mi:djət] *adj.* **1** close/nearest: *my immediate neighbour,* the person sitting next to me. □ **inmediato; de al lado**
2 very soon: *in the immediate future,* very soon; *he got an immediate reply,* a reply straight away. □ **urgente**
immediately *adv.* and *conj.* straight away: *immediately after he came back; she will ring you immediately she comes in; he ate some mushrooms and immediately felt ill.* □ **inmediatamente**
immemorial [imə'mɔ:riəl] *adj.* ***from time immemorial,*** from very ancient times. □ **desde tiempo inmemorial**
immense [i'mens] *adj.* huge/very wide/enormous: *the immense plains of northern America; he earns an immense salary.* □ **inmenso**
immensely *adv.* very much: *she seems to be enjoying herself immensely.* □ **enormemente**
immensity *n.* (*pl. immensities*) vastness/huge size. □ **inmensidad**
immerse [i'mə:s] *v.* **1** to plunge (into a liquid). □ **sumergir**
2 *immersed in his work,* concentrating very hard on his work. □ **inmerso...**
immersion [i'mə:ʃn] *n.* plunging (into a liquid). □ **inmersión**
immersion heater, heater inside a water tank. □ **calentador de inmersión**
immigrate ['imigreit] *v.* to come to settle in a country: *we immigrated to Britain from Hong Kong.* □ **inmigrar**
immigrant *n.* person who comes to a country to settle. □ **inmigrante**
immigration [imi'greiʃn] *n.* settling in a new country. □ **inmigración**
immigration office, office dealing with immigrants. □ **oficina de ...**
immigration controls, restrictions placed by a country on the numbers of people allowed to enter and remain permanently in that country. □ **control de inmigración**
imminent ['iminənt] *adj.* (danger/disaster, etc.) about to happen. □ **inminente**
immobile [i'moubail] *adj.* without moving; unable to move. □ **inmóvil**
immobility [imə'biliti] *n.* state of not moving. □ **inmovilidad**
immobilization [imoubilai'zeiʃn] *n.* stopping something moving. □ **inmovilización**
immobilize [i'moubilaiz] *v.* to stop something moving: *exports were immobilized by the dock strike.* □ **inmovilizar**
immoderate [i'mɔdərət] *adj.* extravagant; not moderate. □ **inmoderado**
immoral [i'mɔrəl] *adj.* not concerned with the principles of good behaviour. □ **inmoral**
immorality [imə'ræliti] *n.* lack of morality. □ **inmoralidad**
immortal [i'mɔ:tl] *adj.* like a god; which never dies: *in the immortal words of Churchill,* in the words which will never be forgotten. □ **inmortal**
immortality [imɔ:'tæliti] *n.* being immortal/never dying. □ **inmortalidad**
immortalize [i'mɔ:təlaiz] *v.* to make (someone) be remembered forever: *she was immortalized by the poet in his poem.* □ **inmortalizar**
immovable [i'mu:vəbl] *adj.* which cannot be moved. □ **inamovible**
immune [i'mju:n] *adj.* **1** (person) who cannot catch a disease: *I seem to be immune to colds.* □ **inmune**
2 *immune to suffering,* not affected by suffering. □ **inmune a...**
immunity *n.* **1** protection (against a disease): *the injections do not give 100 per cent immunity against whooping cough.* □ **inmunidad**
2 protection against arrest. □ **inmunidad**
parliamentary/diplomatic immunity, protection of members of parliament/diplomats against being arrested. □ **inmunidad parlamentaria, etc**
immunization [imjunai'zeiʃn] *n.* giving protection against a disease. □ **inmunización**
immunize ['imjunaiz] *v.* to give protection against a disease: *children are immunized against polio.* □ **inmunizar**
immure [i'mjuə] *v.* to shut (someone) up in prison. □ **encerrar**
immutable [i'mju:təbl] *adj.* (*formal*) which cannot be changed/which does not change. □ **inmutable**
imp [imp] *n.* small devil; wicked child. □ **diablillo; trasto (niño)**
impact ['impækt] *n.* forceful shock/effect: *the impact of the collision was so great that the car was completely crushed; the new law has made a considerable impact on the sales of alcohol.* □ **impacto**
impacted [im'pæktid] *adj.* (tooth) which is stuck in the jaw and cannot grow. □ **postizo, implantado**
impair [im'pɛə] *v.* **1** to harm. □ **perjudicar**
2 *he has impaired vision,* he can't see very clearly. □ **visión deficiente**
impale [im'peil] *v.* to jab a sharp object through (someone's body): *he fell from a window and was impaled on the fence.* □ **atravesar**
impalpable [im'pælpəbl] *adj.* (*formal*) which cannot be touched. □ **impalpable**
impart [im'pɑ:t] *v.* (*formal*) to pass on/to communicate (something to someone). □ **impartir**
impartial [im'pɑ:ʃl] *adj.* not biased: *an impartial judge.* □ **imparcial**
impassable [im'pɑ:səbl] *adj.* which you cannot go through or across: *the road is impassable because of snow.* □ **intransitable**
impasse ['æmpɑ:s] *n.* deadlock/state where two sides cannot agree: *the negotiations have reached an impasse.* □ **callejón sin salida**
impassioned [im'pæʃnd] *adj.* very deeply felt/excited (speech): *he made an impassioned plea for freedom.* □ **apasionado**
impassive [im'pæsiv] *adj.* expressionless: *impassive face.* □ **impasible**
impatient [im'peiʃnt] *adj.* **1** not patient; unable to wait for something: *she gets impatient with people who read slowly.* □ **impaciente**
2 in a hurry (to do something): *he is impatient to get to the beach.* □ **está impaciente...**
impatiently *adv.* in a hurried way/not patiently: *he was walking up and down impatiently.* □ **impacientemente**
impeach [im'pi:tʃ] *v.* to charge (someone) with treason or crime against the state. □ **encausar**
impeachment *n.* accusation of treason or crime against the state. □ **acusación de alta traición**
impeccable [im'pekəbl] *adj.* perfect/perfectly correct: *he has an impeccable war record.* □ **impecable**

impecunious [impi'kju:niəs] *adj.* (*formal*) with no money. □ **sin dinero**
impede [im'pi:d] *v.* to get in the way of (something); to prevent (something) happening: *our progress was impeded by heavy falls of snow.* □ **impedir**
impedance [im'pi:dəns] *n.* resistance to an electric current. □ **impedancia**
impediment [im'pedimənt] *n.* obstacle. □ **impedimento**
speech impediment, stammer, etc., which prevents you from speaking clearly. □ **defecto del habla**
impedimenta *n. pl.* heavy, awkward, baggage or equipment. □ **impedimenta**
impel [im'pel] *v.* (*he impelled*) to push/to force: *he was impelled to call the police.* □ **impeler**
impending [im'pendiŋ] *adj.* imminent/about to happen: *impending disaster; his impending marriage.* □ **inminente**
impenetrable [im'penitrəbl] *adj.* which you cannot go through: *an impenetrable forest.* □ **impenetrable**
impenitent [im'penitənt] *adj.* not penitent/not sorry for having done something wrong. □ **impenitente**
imperative [im'perətiv] *adj.* **1** urgent/obligatory: *it is imperative that we reply to the attack.* □ **imperioso**
2 (in grammar): *verb in the imperative,* verb used as a command (such as 'come here', 'bring me my shoes'). □ **imperativo**
imperceptible [impə'septibl] *adj.* which you can hardly notice: *there was an imperceptible movement among the leaves.* □ **imperceptible**
imperceptibly *adv.* scarcely noticeably. □ **imperceptiblemente**
imperfect [im'pə:fikt] *adj.* not perfect/not complete. □ **imperfecto**
imperfection [impə'fekʃn] *n.* flaw: *the factory employs skilled people to examine the product for imperfections.* □ **imperfección**
imperial [im'piəriəl] *adj.* **1** referring to an empire. □ **imperial**
2 (weights/measures) used in the UK and the British Commonwealth: *an imperial gallon.* □ **galón inglés**
imperialism *n.* belief in the good of building an empire. □ **imperialismo**
imperialist *n.* person who builds an empire. □ **imperialista**
■ *adj.* referring to imperialism. □ **imperialista**
imperil [im'peril] *v.* (*he imperilled*) (*formal*) to put in danger. □ **poner en peligro**
imperious [im'piəriəs] *adj.* arrogant (way of giving orders). □ **autoritario**
imperiously *adv.* (giving orders) in an arrogant way. □ **autoritariamente**
impermanent [im'pə:mənənt] *adj.* not permanent/not lasting. □ **transitorio**
impermeable [im'pə:miəbl] *adj.* (rocks/membranes) which liquids cannot go through. □ **impermeable**
impersonal [im'pə:snl] *adj.* **1** without a personal touch: *the service is very impersonal,* not friendly. □ **impersonal**
2 ***impersonal verb,*** verb used without a person or object as the subject (such as 'it is snowing'). □ **impersonal**
impersonate [im'pə:sneit] *v.* to imitate (someone)/to disguise yourself as (someone): *he lived free in the hotel for several days by impersonating an Arab prince.* □ **imitar; hacerse pasar por**
impersonator *n.* person who imitates someone/who disguises himself as someone else. □ **imitador**
impertinence [im'pə:tinəns] *n.* rudeness/insolence. □ **impertinencia**
impertinent *adj.* rude/insolent. □ **impertinente**
imperturbable [impə'tə:bəbl] *adj.* calm. □ **imperturbable**
imperturbably *adv.* calmly: *the barman imperturbably went on serving drinks while the gunmen attacked the hotel.* □ **sin perturbarse**
impervious [im'pə:viəs] *adj.* **1** (rocks) which water cannot go through. □ **impermeable**
2 *he is impervious to reason,* you can't persuade him to change his mind. □ **no atiende a razones**
impetigo [impi'taigou] *n.* contagious disease of the skin (especially in children). □ **impétigo**
impetuous [im'petjuəs] *adj.* thoughtless/hasty (act); (person) who rushes to do something without thinking. □ **impetuoso**
impetuosity [impetju'ɔsiti] *n.* rushing to do something without thinking. □ **impetuosidad**
impetuously [im'petjuəsli] *adv.* without thinking: *he impetuously left home to join the navy.* □ **impetuosamente**
impetus ['impətəs] *n.* (*pl. impetuses*) movement forward: *advertising has given sales an added impetus; the car moved forward under the impetus of the bump from the car behind.* □ **ímpetu**
impinge [im'pindʒ] *v.* to affect: *how does this impinge on our relations with Canada?* □ **afectar a**
implacable [im'plækəbl] *adj.* who/which cannot be satisfied. □ **implacable**
implacably *adv.* in an implacable way: *he is implacably opposed to the marriage.* □ **implacablemente**
implant [im'plɑ:nt] *v.* to fix (something) in deeply: *to implant an idea in someone's mind.* □ **implantar**
implement ['implimənt] *n.* tool/instrument: *garden implements,* spade/ fork/rake, etc.; *writing implements.* □ **utensilio; apero; útil**
■ *v.* to put into action: *the government has implemented the recommendations of the committee.* □ **poner en práctica**
implementation [implimən'teiʃn] *n.* putting into effect. □ **puesta en práctica**
implicate ['implikeit] *v.* to suggest that someone was connected with something: *he was implicated in the murder.* □ **implicar**
implication [impli'keiʃn] *n.* **1** suggestion (that someone is connected with a crime): *I deny the implication.* □ **complicidad**
2 thing which is implied. □ **implicación**
3 *he said John took after his father, and* ***by implication,*** *that he was mad,* he hinted that he was mad. □ **de manera implícita**
implicit [im'plisit] *adj.***1** which is not defin suggested: *the threat was implicit in his remarks.* □ **implícito**
2 *implicit faith,* faith without questioning. □ **fe ciega**
implicitly *adv.* without questioning: *he believes implicitly everything I say.* □ **implícitamente**
implore [im'plɔ:] *v.* to beg (someone to do something). □ **suplicar**
imply [im'plai] *v.* (*implied; implying*) **1** to suggest: *he seems to be implying that we have made him lose money.* □ **dar a entender**
2 *implied agreement,* agreement which is not stated, but understood. □ **acuerdo tácito**
impolite [impə'lait] *adj.* rude/not polite. □ **descortés**
impolitic [im'pɔlitik] *adj.* (*formal*) not wise. □ **imprudente**
imponderables [im'pɔndrəblz] *n. pl.* things whose

importance you cannot easily calculate. □ **imponderables**

import ['impɔːt] *n.* **1** *imports,* goods which are brought into a country. □ **importaciones**
import duty, tax paid on goods brought into a country. □ **derechos de importación**
import controls, rules limiting goods which can be brought into a country. □ **restricciones a la importación**
2 (*formal*) meaning (of words): *no one grasped the full import of his speech.* □ **significado**
■ *v.* to bring goods into a country: *they have to import most of their oil from the Middle East.* □ **importar**
importer [im'pɔːtə] *n.* **1** person who brings goods into a country: *a car importer.* □ **importador**
2 country which has to import certain goods: *Britain is an importer of cotton.* □ **importador**

importance [im'pɔːtns] *n.* seriousness/serious effect/influence: *the importance of the meeting is that it is the first time the two sides have really met; the discovery of the knife was of vital importance in solving the murder mystery; what is the importance of the British steel industry in the national economy? she doesn't realize the importance of this examination.* □ **importancia**
important *adj.* **1** serious/with a serious effect/which matters a great deal: *how important is it for you to get to London tomorrow? an important announcement from the Prime Minister's office.* □ **importante**
2 with great influence/holding an influential position: *an important civil servant.* □ **importante**
importantly *adv.* seriously/with a serious effect. □ **en tono serio**

importune [im'pɔːtjuːn] *v.* (*formal*) to pester/to bother (someone). □ **importunar**
importunate [im'pɔːtjunət] *adj.* pestering/bothering: *the tourists were surrounded by a crowd of importunate beggars.* □ **importuno**

impose [im'pouz] *v.* **1** to inflict: *the government has imposed a tax on whisky; we must impose conditions on the sale of the building.* □ **imponer**
2 *I don't want to impose on you,* I don't want to give you trouble. □ **no quiero imponerme a ti**
3 *he doesn't like being imposed upon,* he doesn't like people who take advantage of him. □ **...que la gente se aproveche de él**
imposing *adj.* grand/solemn: *the ruined castle is an imposing sight.* □ **imponente**
imposition [impə'ziʃn] *n.* **1** making people pay a tax; laying down (of conditions). □ **imposición**
2 taking advantage (of someone). □ **abuso**
3 unfair duty; punishment (in school): *counting all these bricks is a real imposition.* □ **castigo**

impossible [im'pɔsibl] *adj.* **1** which cannot be done: *this crossword puzzle is impossible; it's impossible to find a taxi when it's raining.* □ **imposible**
2 awkward: *he's an impossible person,* he's very difficult/awkward to deal with. □ **insufrible; inaguantable**
impossibility *n.* being impossible/not being able to be done. □ **imposibilidad**

impostor [im'pɔstə] *n.* person who pretends to be someone else. □ **impostor**
imposture [im'pɔstʃə] *n.* pretending to be someone else. □ **impostura**

impotence ['impətəns] *n.* **1** lack of strength. □ **impotencia**
2 (*of man*) inability to have sexual intercourse, and so inability to have children. □ **impotencia**
impotent *adj.* **1** weak. □ **impotente**
2 (*of man*) unable to have sexual intercourse. □ **impotente**

impound [im'paund] *v.* to take something away and put it in a safe place: *the customs have impounded all the goods I was trying to import.* □ **confiscar**

impoverish [im'pɔvəriʃ] *v.* to make poor. □ **empobrecer**

impracticable [im'præktikəbl] *adj.* (plan) which cannot work; (road) which cannot be used: *it would be impracticable to try to cross the river by raft.* □ **imposible**

impractical [im'præktikl] *adj.* (plan) which is not easy to put into practice; (person) who is not good at doing things with his hands. □ **poco práctico**

imprecation [impri'keiʃn] *n.* oath/curse. □ **imprecación**

imprecise [impri'sais] *adj.* not precise/not accurate. □ **impreciso**

impregnable [im'pregnəbl] *adj.* (castle) which cannot be captured. □ **inexpugnable**

impregnate ['impregneit] *v.* **1** to soak (with something): *a cloth impregnated with antiseptic.* □ **impregnar**
2 to make pregnant. □ **empreñar**

impresario [impri'sɑːriou] *n.* (*pl. impresarios*) person who organizes concerts and operas. □ **empresario musical**

impress [im'pres] *v.* **1** to make (someone) admire/respect something/ someone: *the size of the room impresses the visitors; I'm impressed by him,* I have formed a good opinion of his qualities; *she was not impressed,* she formed a bad opinion (of him). □ **impresionar**
2 to make someone understand: *I must impress upon you the importance of being punctual.* □ **hacer comprender**
3 to stamp (a pattern on something). □ **estampar**
impression [im'preʃn] *n.* **1** effect on someone's mind: *he made a good impression,* people have formed a good opinion of him; *her table manners made a bad impression; first impressions are very important,* the immediate opinion you form of someone when you meet for the first time is very important. □ **impresión**
2 imitation/copying of how someone talks/behaves: *she does impressions of the Prime Minister.* □ **imitación**
3 mark (of a pattern): *impression of a horse's hooves in the mud.* □ **huella**
4 printing (of a book): *this book has reached its fourth impression,* has been reprinted three times. □ **impresión**
impressionable *adj.* (person) who is easily influenced (by others). □ **impresionable**
impressionism *n.* art movement where painters tried to convey an impression of reality, in particular of light. □ **impresionismo**
impressionist *adj.* and *n.* referring to impressionism: *an impressionist painter; the impressionists,* impressionist painters. □ **impresionista**
impressionistic [impreʃə'nistik] *adj.* rough/sketchy: *he gave a rather impressionistic description of the party.* □ **impresionista**
impressive [im'presiv] *adj.* which commands respect: *his piano technique is very impressive.* □ **imponente, excelente**

imprimatur [impri'mɑːtə] *n.* official permission to print a book. □ **imprimátur**

imprint ['imprint] *n.* **1** mark made by something

pressed down: *the imprint of a horse's hooves in the mud.* □ **huella**
2 name of publishing firm printed in a book. □ **sello editorial**
■ *v.* to stamp/to mark: *the date is imprinted in my memory.* □ **imprimir; tengo la fecha grabada...**
imprison [im'prizn] *v.* to put/to keep in prison. □ **encarcelar**
imprisonment *n.* putting/keeping in prison: *he was sentenced to six years' imprisonment.* □ **prisión**
improbable [im'prɔbəbl] *adj.* not probable; unlikely. □ **improbable**
impromptu [im'prɔmptju:] *adj.* and *adv.* without any rehearsal or practice: *he made an impromptu speech; he spoke impromptu for ten minutes.* □ **improvisado; de improviso**
improper [im'prɔpə] *adj.* **1** rude. □ **indecoroso**
2 (word) used in a wrong way. □ **inexacta**
improperly *adv.* **1** *improperly dressed,* (soldier) whose uniform is not correct. □ **sin decoro**
2 (word which is used) wrongly. □ **incorrectamente**
impropriety [imprə'praiəti] *n.* being improper; improper action. □ **falta de propiedad**
improve [im'pru:v] *v.* to make/to get better: *he has improved the look of his house by painting it white; she scored 2 - can you improve on/upon her score?,* can you do better? *the patient has improved considerably,* has got a lot better. □ **mejorar; superar**
improvement *n.* **1** something which makes/is better: *my new car is an improvement on the old one.* □ **mejora**
2 *she was very ill but is now showing signs of improvement,* signs of getting better: *they have made many improvements to the house.* □ **mejoría, mejora**
improvident [im'prɔvidənt] *adj.* (person) who spends too much money. □ **despilfarrador**
improvise ['imprəvaiz] *v.* **1** to do something without preparation: *when he asked me why I was late, I had to improvise an excuse,* to make up an excuse. □ **improvisar**
2 *to improvise on a theme by Bach,* to compose and play a piece of music based on a tune by Bach (without having prepared it before). □ **improvisar**
3 to make something, using whatever happens to be available: *they improvised a shelter from branches and blankets; an improvised workshop,* a room which is not really a workshop, but which is used as one. □ **improvisar**
improvisation [imprəvai'zeiʃn] *n.* making something without any preparation. □ **improvisación**
imprudent [im'pru:dənt] *adj.* careless/not prudent. □ **imprudente**
impudent ['impjudənt] *adj.* rude/cheeky. □ **descarado**
impudence *n.* rudeness/cheekiness: *he had the impudence to ask for more money.* □ **descaro**
impudently *adv.* rudely/cheekily. □ **descaradamente**
impugn [im'pju:n] *v.* (*formal*) to attack (someone's character/the truth of a statement). □ **impugnar**
impulse ['impʌls] *n.* **1** shock (which makes something move/work): *an electric impulse makes the doors open.* □ **impulso**
2 sudden feeling/decision. □ **impulso**
impulse buying/buying on impulse, buying things because you suddenly see them, not because you really need them. □ **compra impulsiva**
impulsive [im'pʌlsiv] *adj.* acting on a sudden decision/without thinking. □ **impulsivo**
impunity [im'pju:niti] *n.* ***with impunity,*** without risking punishment. □ **impunidad**
impure [im'pjuə] *adj.* not pure. □ **impuro**
impurities *n. pl.* dirt making something not pure: *there are impurities in the water.* □ **impurezas**
impute [im'pju:t] *v.* to attribute something to someone; to say that something is caused by someone/something: *he imputed John's behaviour to his being drunk.* □ **imputar**
imputation *n.* saying that someone is at fault. □ **imputación**
in [in] *prep.* and *adv.* **1** (showing place): *in Japan; in Russia; in the bathroom; in bed; in the distance; I think the manager is in,* is in his office; *is your mother in?,* is your mother at home? □ **en; dentro; en casa**
2 (showing time): *in autumn; in the evening; in 1963; in January; in the past; she will be here in half an hour; he finished the crossword puzzle in ten minutes; strawberries are in,* they are in season. □ **en; es la temporada de...**
day in, day out, every day. □ **día tras día**
3 *long skirts are in this year,* they are fashionable. □ **...están de moda**
4 ***one in ten,*** one out of ten: *one in ten children wears glasses.* □ **uno de cada diez**
5 (showing state): *she's dressed in pink; he ran outside in his pyjamas; to speak in public; she's in a hurry; the child was in tears; write a letter in German; the dictionary is in alphabetical order; the kings are listed in chronological order.* □ **viste de rosa; tiene prisa; ...en alemán**
6 *she's **all in,*** (*informal*) she is tired out. □ **está agotada**
7 ***all in*** *price,* price which includes everything. □ **todo incluido**
■ *n.* ***the ins and outs,*** the intricate details. □ **los pormenores**
■ *adj.* (*informal*) fashionable: *it's the in thing to do.* □ **es lo que se lleva**
in for *adv.* ***to be in for (something),*** to be about to get: *we're in for some rain; he's in for a nasty shock.* □ **parece que...; está expuesto a**
in on *adv.* ***to be in on*** (*a secret*), to know a secret. □ **estar al tanto de**
to let someone in on *a secret,* to tell someone a secret. □ **hacer partícipe**
inability [inə'biliti] *n.* being unable/lack of ability: *his inability to write.* □ **incapacidad**
inaccessible [inək'sesibl] *adj.* impossible to reach: *the farm is often inaccessible in winter.* □ **inaccesible**
inaccurate [in'ækjurət] *adj.* not exact; not accurate: *he couldn't find it because he was given inaccurate information.* □ **inexacto**
inaccuracy *n.* (*pl. inaccuracies*) **1** not being exact; lack of accuracy. □ **inexactitud**
2 *the book is full of inaccuracies,* pieces of incorrect information. □ **...lleno de errores**
inactive [in'æktiv] *adj.* not active/not doing anything: *the volcano has been inactive for many years.* □ **inactivo**
inaction *n.* lack of action; doing nothing. □ **inacción, omisión**
inactivity [inæk'tiviti] *n.* lack of activity; doing nothing: *he is bored through inactivity.* □ **inactividad**
inadequate [in'ædikwət] *adj.* **1** not enough; insufficient: *she failed the examination because of inadequate preparation.* □ **insuficiente**
2 *he felt inadequate,* not competent enough. □ **...poco preparado**
inadequately *adv.* not enough; insufficiently: *the meat was inadequately cooked.* □ **insuficientemente**
inadmissible [inəd'misəbl] *adj.* (evidence) not allowed to be presented in a court. □ **inadmisible**

inadvertent [inəd'və:tənt] *adj.* said/done by mistake, not on purpose: *he let slip an inadvertent remark.* □ **involuntario**
inadvertently *adv.* by mistake: *she inadvertently picked up my parcel instead of her own.* □ **involuntariamente**

inadvisable [inəd'vaizəbl] *adj.* unwise/not recommended: *there is a gale coming, so it would be inadvisable to set off by boat.* □ **poco aconsejable**

inalienable [in'eiljənəbl] *adj.* (*formal*) which cannot be taken away or refused: *inalienable right to a fair trial.* □ **inalienable**

inane [i'nein] *adj.* stupid: *he made several inane remarks.* □ **inane**

inanimate [in'ænimət] *adj.* not alive: *a pebble is an inanimate object.* □ **inanimado**

inapplicable [inə'plikəbl] *adj.* unsuitable/which does not apply: (on a form) *Mr/Mrs/Miss – delete whichever is inapplicable.* □ **inaplicable**

inappropriate [inə'proupriət] *adj.* not appropriate/not suitable/not fitting the circumstances. □ **inapropiado**

inaptitude [in'æptitju:d] *n.* unsuitableness; lack of ability: *his inaptitude for his job made him lose it.* □ **ineptitud**

inarticulate [inɑ:'tikjulət] *adj.* **1** not speaking clearly: *when asked to make a speech he suddenly became inarticulate.* □ **inarticulado**
2 unable to speak: *he was inarticulate with rage.* □ **mudo**

inartistic [inɑ:'tistik] *adj.* not artistic; not concerned with the arts. □ **sin arte**

inattentive [inə'tentiv] *adj.* not paying attention/not attentive. □ **desatento, distraído**
inattention *n.* not paying attention. □ **falta de atención**

inaudible [in'ɔ:dibl] *adj.* which cannot be heard: *she spoke in an inaudible whisper.* □ **inaudible**
inaudibly *adv.* so quietly that it cannot be heard: *he mumbled a few words inaudibly.* □ **de modo inaudible**

inaugurate [in'ɔ:gjureit] *v.* to swear in (a new president); to open officially (a new building/a festival/a new air route). □ **tomar posesión (de un cargo); inaugurar**
inaugural *adj. an inaugural address,* speech given at an opening ceremony; *inaugural flight,* first flight of an aircraft along a new route. □ **inaugural; (discurso) de apertura; primer (vuelo)**
inauguration [inɔ:gju'reiʃn] *n.* swearing in of a new official, especially a president; official opening of a new building/a festival/a new air route. □ **toma de posesión; inauguración**

inauspicious [inɔ:'spiʃəs] *adj.* **1** unlucky/not auspicious: *the meeting got off to an inauspicious start.* □ **poco propicio**
2 *inauspicious weather,* bad weather. □ **tiempo desfavorable**

inborn ['inbɔ:n] *adj.* (feelings/ideas) which a person has had since birth: *his inborn politeness.* □ **innato**

inbred ['inbred] *adj.* (feelings/ideas) which a person has had since a very young age: *his inbred politeness.* □ **de siempre**

Inc. [in'kɔ:pəreitid] *Amer. short for* incorporated. □ **constituido en sociedad**

incalculable [in'kælkjuləbl] *adj.* which cannot be calculated/so large that it cannot be measured: *the speech did incalculable damage among his supporters,* very great damage. □ **incalculable**

incandescent [inkæn'desnt] *adj.* which burns with a very bright light. □ **incandescente**
incandescence *n.* very bright light. □ **incandescencia**

incantation [inkən'teiʃn] *n.* magic words. □ **conjuro**

incapable [in'keipəbl] *adj.* **1** not able: *he was incapable of any movement; drunk and incapable,* so drunk that you cannot stand up. □ **incapaz**
2 not capable; not competent: *the manager must be dismissed - he is quite incapable.* □ **incompetente**
incapability [inkeipə'biliti] *n.* incompetence/not being capable: *he was dismissed for incapability.* □ **incompetencia**

incapacity [inkə'pæsiti] *n.* lack of strength/ability to do something. □ **incapacidad**
incapacitate *v.* to make (someone) unable to do something: *he was incapacitated by illness.* □ **incapacitar**

incarcerate [in'kɑ:səreit] *v.* (*formal*) to put/to keep in prison. □ **encarcelar**
incarceration [inkɑ:sə'reiʃn] *n.* putting/keeping in prison. □ **encarcelamiento**

incarnate [in'kɑ:nət] *adj.* in human form: *he is wickedness incarnate.* □ **encarnado**
incarnation [inkɑ:'neiʃn] *n.* appearance in human form. □ **encarnación**

incautious [in'kɔ:ʃəs] *adj.* not prudent. □ **imprudente**

incendiary [in'sendjəri] *adj.* which causes fire: *incendiary bomb.* □ **incendiario**
■ *n.* **1** bomb which causes fire. □ **bomba incendiaria**
2 person who sets fire to buildings. □ **incendiario**

incense ['insens] *n.* spice powder which when burnt gives a strong smell. □ **incienso**
■ *v.* [in'sens] to make (someone) annoyed: *he was incensed by the newspaper reports.* □ **sulfurar**

incentive [in'sentiv] *n.* something which encourages: *the workers do not work hard because they lack incentives.* □ **incentivo**
incentive bonus, extra money paid when production is increased. □ **prima**

inception [in'sepʃn] *n.* beginning: *the scheme was doomed to failure from its inception.* □ **principio**

incessant [in'sesnt] *adj.* unceasing/continuous: *the incessant noise of the machines makes people nervous.* □ **incesante**

incest ['insest] *n.* sexual intercourse with a close member of the family (such as brother/father/daughter, etc.). □ **incesto**
incestuous [in'sestjuəs] *adj.* referring to incest: *incestuous relationship.* □ **incestuoso**

inch [intʃ] *n.* (*pl. inches*) small measure of length (= 2.54 cm.): *the fog was so thick you couldn't see an inch in front of you.* □ **pulgada**
give him an inch and he'll take a mile, if you allow a small concession he will take more than you allow. □ **dale la mano y te cogerá el brazo**
■ *v.* to go (slowly): *he inched slowly up the wall.* □ **avanzar poco a poco**

incident ['insidənt] *n.* **1** minor happening. □ **incidente**
2 (usually violent) action/disturbance: *the meeting went off without incident; there were three incidents involving the troops and police over the weekend,* three armed attacks involving troops and police. □ **incidente**
incidence *n.* rate: *high incidence of accidents; low incidence of deaths from tuberculosis.* □ **incidencia**
incidental [insi'dentl] *adj.* happening in connection with something else, but forming an unimportant part; subsidiary. □ **secundario**
incidental music *to a film,* background music which accompanies the film. □ **música de fondo**
incidental expenses, secondary expenses. □ **gastos secundarios**

incidentally *adv.* by the way: *incidentally, I met your mother yesterday.* □ **a próposito, por cierto**
incinerate [in'sinəreit] *v.* to destroy by burning. □ **incinerar**
incinerator *n.* furnace for burning rubbish. □ **incinerador**
incipient [in'sipiənt] *adj.* (*formal*) beginning/coming: *an incipient cold,* a cold which is about to start. □ **incipiente**
incision [in'siʒn] *n.* cut. □ **incisión**
incisive [in'saisiv] *adj.* sharp/cutting: *incisive remark.* □ **incisivo**
incisively *adv.* sharply: *the report criticizes the government incisively.* □ **incisivamente**
incisor [in'saizə] *n.* sharp front tooth for cutting. □ **incisivo**
incite [in'sait] *v.* to encourage (someone to crime): *his speech was intended to incite the crowds to attack the police.* □ **incitar**
incitement *n.* encouragement (to crime): *he was accused of incitement to revolt.* □ **incitación**
incivility [insi'viliti] *n.* (*formal*) rudeness. □ **descortesía**
inclement *adj.* (*formal*) (*of weather*) bad. □ **inclemente**
incline ['inklain] *n.* slope: *the road climbs a 10° incline/at an incline of 1 in 10.* □ **pendiente**
■ *v.* **1** to slope: *the plank is inclined at an angle of 45°.* □ **inclinar**
2 to encourage (someone) to do something: *the information inclines me to take the first course of action.* □ **inducir**
3 to tend: *he inclines to fatness.* □ **ser propenso**
4 to bend/to bow: *he inclined his head.* □ **inclinar**
inclination [inkl'neiʃn] *n.* **1** (angle of) slope. □ **inclinación**
2 slight bow (of the head). □ **inclinación**
3 tendency: *she has an inclination to lose her temper.* □ **propensión**
inclined *adj.* **1** sloping: *run the ball down an inclined plane.* □ **inclinado**
2 likely (to do something): *he is inclined to get angry if someone contradicts him; she is inclined to put on weight easily.* □ **propenso**
include [in'klu:d] *v.* to count (someone/something) along with others: *we were sixteen for dinner including the children; up to and including the 31st December; did you include Aunt Mabel among the people you have invited?* □ **incluir**
inclusion [in'klu:ʒn] *n.* counting someone/something in among others: *they voted against the inclusion of clause 3.* □ **inclusión**
inclusive *adj.* **1** which counts everything: *from the 30th December to 6th January inclusive.* □ **incluido**
2 *inclusive price,* price which covers everything. □ **precio total**
incognito [inkɔg'ni:tou] *adv.* and *n.* **1** *to travel incognito,* to travel under a false name. □ **incógnito; viajar de incógnito**
2 *he had difficulty preserving his incognito,* he had difficulty preventing people from finding out who he really was. □ **...para guardar el incógnito**
incoherent [inkou'hiərənt] *adj.* not coherent; not linked; which does not make sense: *an incoherent speech.* □ **incoherente**
incoherently *adv.* not in a coherent way; in a way which does not make sense: *they found him muttering incoherently about being attacked by swans.* □ **de modo incoherente**
income ['iŋkʌm] *n.* revenue/money which you receive. □ **ingresos**
income tax, tax on income. □ **impuesto sobre la renta**
unearned income, income from investments/rents, etc. □ **renta del capital mobiliario/inmobiliario**
incoming ['inkʌmiŋ] *adj.* which is arriving/coming in: *the incoming tide.* □ **entrante**
the incoming president, the president who has been elected but who has not taken office. □ **el presidente entrante**
incoming calls, telephone calls received. □ **llamadas recibidas**
■ *n. pl.* ***incomings,*** money which is coming in/revenue. □ **ingresos**
incommunicado [inkəmju:ni'kɑ:dou] *adv.* not allowed to see or write to any person: *he was held incommunicado for five days before the consul was allowed to see him.* □ **incomunicado**
incomparable [in'kɔmprəbl] *adj.* which cannot be compared to anything else: *she has an incomparable voice.* □ **incomparable**
incomparably *adv.* vastly; so much that it cannot be compared: *the new car is incomparably smoother than the old one.* □ **incomparablemente**
incompatible [inkəm'pætibl] *adj.* which cannot live/work/fit together: *they're quite incompatible,* they can't get along together; *his evidence is incompatible with that of the police,* does not agree. □ **incompatible**
incompatibility [inkəmpætə'biliti] *n.* inability to live/work/fit together: *the marriage broke up because of their incompatibility.* □ **incompatibilidad**
incompetent [in'kɔmpitənt] *adj.* not good at doing something/not competent/not capable: *he should be sacked, he is so incompetent.* □ **incompetente**
incompetence *n.* lack of competence/not being capable: *he was sacked for incompetence.* □ **incompetencia**
incomplete [inkəm'pli:t] *adj.* not complete/not finished. □ **incompleto**
incomprehensible [inkɔmpri'hensibl] *adj.* which cannot be understood: *the report about the computer is quite incomprehensible.* □ **incomprensible**
inconceivable [inkən'si:vəbl] *adj.* which cannot be imagined: *it is inconceivable that they set sail without any fresh water on board.* □ **inconcebible**
inconclusive [inkən'klu:siv] *adj.* not final; without a definite result: *the evidence against him was inconclusive,* not clear enough to show that he was guilty. □ **no concluyente**
inconclusively *adv.* vaguely/not finally; without a definite result: *the book finishes rather inconclusively.* □ **de manera no concluyente**
incongruous [in'kɔŋgruəs] *adj.* which does not fit with the rest; which seems out of place: *he looked rather incongruous on the beach in his raincoat; an incongruous remark,* which doesn't fit in with the rest of the conversation. □ **incongruente**
incongruity *n.* being out of place. □ **incongruencia**
inconsequential [inkɔnsi'kwenʃl] *adj.* not of any importance. □ **sin trascendencia**
inconsiderable [inkən'sidərəbl] *adj.* small: *a not inconsiderable sum of money,* a large sum of money. □ **insignificante**
inconsiderate [inkən'sidərət] *adj.* not thinking of other people: *he made some inconsiderate remarks about the guests.* □ **desconsiderado**
inconsiderately *adv.* not thinking about other people: *he has behaved very inconsiderately to his mother.* □ **desconsideradamente**
inconsistent [inkən'sistənt] *adj.* **1** which does not

follow/which contradicts: *the minister's statement is inconsistent with official policy.* □ **contradictorio**
2 (person) who changes his mind frequently/who acts differently: *he was inconsistent in his replies to the journalists; he played an inconsistent game of golf.* □ **inconsecuente**
inconsistency *n.* (*pl. inconsistencies*) lack of consecutive thought. □ **inconsecuencia**
inconsolable [inkən'souləbl] *adj.* (person) who cannot be consoled/comforted: *after the death of her cat she was inconsolable.* □ **inconsolable**
inconspicuous [inkən'spikjuəs] *adj.* not very noticeable. □ **discreto**
inconspicuously *adv.* not noticeably/without being noticed: *he tried to creep away as inconspicuously as possible.* □ **discretamente**
inconstant [in'kɔnstənt] *adj.* (*formal*) not constant (especially in love). □ **inconstante; voluble (relaciones amorosas)**
inconstancy *n.* (*pl. inconstancies*) lack of constancy (especially in love). □ **inconstancia; volubilidad (relaciones amorosas)**
incontinent [in'kɔntinənt] *adj.* unable to control your bladder, so that you pass water without being able to stop it. □ **incontinente**
incontrovertible [inkɔntrə'vəːtəbl] *adj.* (fact) with which you must agree. □ **incontrovertible**
inconvenience [inkən'viːniəns] *n.* **1** awkwardness. □ **inconveniencia**
2 *I am putting you to a lot of inconvenience,* I am giving you a lot of trouble. □ **te estoy causando muchas molestias**
■ *v.* to bother (someone): *does my cigar smoke inconvenience you?* □ **incomodar**
inconvenient *adj.* awkward; not handy: *he came at an inconvenient time; could you come at 5.30 if it is not too inconvenient?,* if it suits you? □ **incómodo**
inconveniently *adv.* awkwardly: *the visitors came inconveniently early.* □ **inoportunamente**
incorporate [in'kɔːpəreit] *v.* **1** to bring into one main part: *the additions have been incorporated into the main text.* □ **incorporar**
2 to form an official body: *the incorporated society of translators.* □ **constituir oficialmente**
3 *Amer.* to form a large firm: *Smith Chemicals Incorporated.* □ **constituir una sociedad**
incorrect [inkə'rekt] *adj.* not correct/false. □ **incorrecto**
incorrectly *adv.* wrongly/falsely: *he filled up his income tax form incorrectly.* □ **incorrectamente**
incorrigible [in'kɔridʒəbl] *adj.* (person) who cannot be corrected/changed: *he is an incorrigible liar,* he cannot be cured of his habit of lying. □ **incorregible**
incorruptible [inkə'rʌptəbl] *adj.* (person) who cannot be corrupted/be persuaded to behave dishonestly. □ **incorruptible**
increase ['inkriːs] *n.* **1** growth/expansion: *the increase in the cost of living; she asked for an increase,* for a rise in salary. □ **aumento**
2 *crime is* ***on the increase,*** the crime rate is getting higher. □ **aumentando**
■ *v.* to rise/to grow/to expand: *sales are increasing; we are trying to increase our production; the price of this washing machine has been increased by 10 per cent.* □ **aumentar**
increasing *adj.* growing. □ **creciente**
increasingly *adv.* more and more: *it is becoming increasingly difficult to find cheap accommodation; he is becoming increasingly deaf.* □ **cada vez más**
incredible [in'kredibl] *adj.* which it is difficult to believe: *he told us the story of his incredible adventures.* □ **increíble**
incredibly *adv.* unbelievably: *incredibly, no one was killed in the accident.* □ **increíblemente**
incredulous [in'kredjuləs] *adj.* (person) who does not believe. □ **incrédulo**
incredulity [inkrə'djuːliti] *n.* lack of belief. □ **incredulidad**
incredulously *adv.* as if you do not believe: *he smiled incredulously when we told him the price.* □ **incrédulamente**
increment ['inkrimənt] *n.* regular automatic addition (to salary): *his salary rises by annual increments.* □ **incremento**
incremental [inkri'mentl] *adj.* referring to regular automatic increases: *there is an incremental scale of salaries.* □ **de incremento**
incriminate [in'krimineit] *v.* to show that (someone) took part in a crime, etc.: *his statement to the police incriminated his brother.* □ **incriminar**
incriminating *adj.* which shows that someone took part in a crime: *the police seized some incriminating letters.* □ **que incrimina**
incubate ['inkjubeit] *v.* to keep (eggs) warm until they hatch; to have (the germs of a disease) in your body: *the farmer incubated dozens of eggs.* □ **incubar**
incubation [inkju'beiʃn] *n.* keeping eggs warm until they hatch. □ **incubación**
incubation period, period during which a disease develops in your body. □ **período de incubación**
incubator *n.* warm box in which eggs are kept until they hatch; sterilized receptacle for keeping very small babies in until they are strong. □ **empollador (huevos); incubadora**
incubus ['iŋkjubəs] *n.* (*pl. incubuses*) problem which causes great worry. □ **incordio**
inculcate ['inkʌlkeit] *v.* (*formal*) to fix (ideas, etc.) in the mind of a young person. □ **inculcar**
incumbent [in'kʌmbənt] *n.* person who holds a post, especially priest in charge of a parish: *the incumbent of St Mary's is near retirement.* □ **titular; párroco**
■ *adj. it is incumbent on you to deal with mail,* (*formal*) it is your responsibility to deal with mail. □ **te incumbe a ti...**
incumbency *n.* period when someone holds a post/when a priest is in charge of a parish. □ **período de titularidad**
incur [in'kəː] *v.* (*he incurred*) to run (a risk); to be liable (to be blamed); to bring on yourself: *he incurred the wrath of the manager,* he made the manager very angry; *they incurred considerable damages,* they had to pay considerable damages; *he has incurred debts of over $1,000,* he has accumulated debts. □ **incurrir en**
incurable [in'kjuərəbl] *adj.* which cannot be made better: *the disease is incurable; he is incurable.* □ **incurable**
incurably *adv.* in a way which cannot be made better: *she is incurably lazy.* □ **incurablemente**
incurious [in'kjuəriəs] *adj.* not curious/not showing any curiosity. □ **sin curiosidad**
incursion [in'kəːʃn] *n.* movement into something; attack on something: *his incursion into the antique business,*his first attempt to start trading in antiques; *the enemy has made several incursions behind our lines; the children made incursions into the refrigerator,* they raided the refrigerator. □ **incursión**
indebted [in'detid] *adj.* owing something to someone: *I am indebted to you for this piece of information.* □ **en deuda**

indebtedness *n.* extent to which you owe someone something. □ **endeudamiento**

indecent [in'di:snt] *adj.* not decent; rude: *indecent film.* □ **indecente**
indecency *n.* being indecent: *he committed an act of indecency.* □ **indecencia**
indecently *adv.* **1** not decently; rudely; in a way which shocks. □ **indecentemente**
2 *he is indecently rich,* so rich that it is embarrassing. □ **insultantemente**

indecipherable [indi'saifrəbl] *adj.* (writing/message) that cannot be read/understood. □ **indescifrable**

indecision [indi'siʒn] *n.* (state of) not being able to decide; hesitating: *he is in a permanent state of indecision.* □ **indecisión**
indecisive [indi'saisiv] *adj.* (battle, etc.) without a positive result; which/who cannot decide anything: *the debate in parliament was indecisive.* □ **no decisivo; indeciso**

indecorous [in'dekərəs] *adj.* (*formal*) slightly rude. □ **incorrecto**

indeed [in'di:d] *adv.* **1** really/truly: *he is very grateful indeed for your help; thank you very much indeed for your kind letter; it is indeed nothing short of a miracle that so many people escaped.* □ **verdaderamente**
2 in fact: *she is not rich, indeed she relies on charity; he is quite young, indeed he is younger than I am.* □ **en realidad**
3 *interjection* meaning really! □ **¿de verdad?**
indeed not!, of course not! □ **¡por supuesto que no!**

indefatigable [indi'fætigəbl] *adj.* tireless/who cannot be tired out: *his indefatigable research into the causes of cancer.* □ **infatigable**
indefatigably *adv.* tirelessly. □ **infatigablemente**

indefensible [indi'fensibl] *adj.* which cannot be defended/excused: *his conduct is indefensible.* □ **indefendible**

indefinable [indi'fainəbl] *adj.* which cannot be defined/explained: *there was an indefinable sense of gloom about the house.* □ **indefinible**

indefinite [in'definit] *adj.* vague; not definite: *he will be held in prison for an indefinite period,* not a stated period. □ **indefinido**
indefinite article, 'a' (*as opposed to the definite article* 'the'). □ **artículo indeterminado**
indefinitely *adv.* for an unknown period of time/for an indefinite period: *we have had to postpone the meeting indefinitely.* □ **indefinidamente**

indelible [in'delibl] *adj.* which cannot be rubbed out: *indelible pencil; indelible ink.* □ **indeleble**
indelibly *adv.* permanently: *the picture of the accident is indelibly printed on my memory.* □ **indeleblemente**

indelicate [in'delikət] *adj.* rude/not polite. □ **poco delicado**

indemnify [in'demnifai] *v.* (*indemnified; indemnifying*) to pay (someone) for damage: *the insurance company will indemnify you for any loss.* □ **indemnizar**
indemnity *n.* (*pl. indemnities*) **1** payment (for loss/damage). □ **indemnización**
2 guarantee (of payment) against loss/damage. □ **indemnidad**

indent [in'dent] *v.* **1** (*in printing, etc.*) to start a line several spaces in from the left-hand margin: *the second line of each entry in this dictionary is indented.* □ **sangrar**
2 (*in commerce*) to put in an order for (something): *he has indented for six pads of typing paper.* □ **hacer un pedido**
indentation [iden'teiʃn] *n.* inward cut along an edge; deep bay/inlet on a coastline. □ **muesca; entrante**
indented *adj.* with a jagged edge: *heavily indented coastline,* coastline with deep bays and inlets. □ **mellado; con entrantes**

indentures [in'dentʃəz] *n. pl.* contract by which a person is apprenticed to a master craftsman. □ **contrato de aprendizaje**

independent [indi'pendənt] *adj.* **1** free/not ruled by anyone else; not needing/not relying on anyone else: *the country became independent on January 1st.* □ **independiente**
2 *he is of independent means,* he has enough income from investments to live on. □ **vive de las rentas**
3 *he's standing for parliament as an independent/as an independent candidate,* as a candidate of no political party. □ **...como independiente**
4 ***independent school,*** private school, not run by the state. □ **colegio privado**
independence *n.* freedom; not needing/not relying on anyone else: *the country attained independence on January 1st; his independence of thought shows in his book.* □ **independencia**
independently *adv.* freely; separately. □ **independientemente**

indescribable [indi'skraibəbl] *adj.* which cannot be described: *indescribable scenes of excitement.* □ **indescriptible**
indescribably *adv.* in a way which cannot be described: *the book is indescribably boring.* □ **de manera indescriptible**

indestructible [indi'strʌktəbl] *adj.* which cannot be destroyed. □ **indestructible**

indeterminable [indi'tə:minəbl] *adj.* (question, etc.) which cannot be decided/solved. □ **indeterminable**

indeterminate [indi'tə:minət] *adj.* vague/not precise: *an indeterminate quantity of poison.* □ **indeterminado**

index ['indeks] *n.* (*pl. indexes* or, *indices*) **1** ***index (finger),*** first finger (next to the thumb). □ **índice**
2 classified list (showing the contents/references, etc.) in a book: *there is no index in the back of the book; index of authors,* alphabetical list of authors. □ **índice**
card index, filing system based on small cards. □ **sistema de fichas**
3 ***cost of living index,*** regular government statistics which show the rises and falls in the cost of living. □ **índice del coste de la vida**
■ *v.* **1** to write an index for (a book). □ **poner un índice a un libro**
2 to relate (pensions) to the cost of living index. □ **ajustar**
indexer *n.* person who specializes in compiling indexes. □ **catalogador**
indexing *n.* **1** relating something to the cost of living index. □ **indización**
2 compiling of an index. □ **catalogación**
index-linked *adj.* calculated according to the cost of living index: *our pensions are index-linked,* they rise or fall in proportion to the changes in the cost of living index. □ **ligado al índice...**

India ['indjə] *n.* large country in Asia. □ **India**
Indian *adj.* referring to India; referring to the indigenous people of America. □ **indio**
in Indian file, in line/one behind the other. □ **en fila india**
Indian ink, black ink which cannot be removed by washing. □ **tinta china**
Indian summer, period of hot weather in early autumn. □ **veranillo de San Martín**

■ *n.* **1** person from India. □ **indio**
2 member of one of the indigenous tribes of America. □ **indio**
Indian Ocean *n.* large ocean south of India, separating Africa and Australia. □ **Océano Indico**
indicate ['indikeit] *v.* to show/to point out: *a fall in the barometric pressure indicates a change in the weather; the manager has indicated that no bonus will be paid this year.* □ **indicar**
indication [indi'keiʃn] *n.* sign/pointer: *there's no indication of a rise in the cost of living.* □ **indicación**
indicative [in'dikətiv] *adj.* **1** typical/which shows: *this letter is indicative of his dislike of children.* □ **típico**
2 (tense of a verb) which shows that the action actually took place/is taking place: *'he went' is past indicative of 'to go'.* □ **indicativo**
indicator *n.* **1** thing which indicates; flashing light (on a car, etc.) which shows which way you intend to turn. □ **indicador**
2 large board which shows details (of train times, etc.): *the arrivals indicator.* □ **panel de información**
indict [in'dait] *v.* to accuse (someone) of a crime: *he was indicted for drug smuggling.* □ **acusar**
indictable *adj.* (offence) which you can be charged with. □ **procesable**
indictment [in'daitmənt] *n.* detailed accusation: *the clerk of the court read out the indictment.* □ **acusación**
indifferent [in'difrənt] *adj.* **1** not caring; not interested: *he is indifferent to the suffering of others,* he does not mind how much other people suffer. □ **indiferente**
2 ordinary/mediocre; not special: *we had indifferent weather on holiday,* not very good weather; *he produced a very indifferent score,* not a very good score. □ **regular; pobre**
indifference *n.* lack of interest: *I cannot understand his total indifference to good food.* □ **indiferencia**
indifferently *adv.* **1** not bothering. □ **indiferentemente**
2 in a mediocre way. □ **mediocremente**
indigenous [in'didʒənəs] *adj.* which has always lived (in a place): *the indigenous population was driven out by the invaders; what are the commonest indigenous plants in Scotland?* □ **indígena, autóctono**
indigent ['indidʒənt] *adj.* (*formal*) very poor. □ **indigente**
indigestion [indi'dʒestʃn] *n.* not being able to digest food; pain caused when the body is unable to digest food: *he suffers from indigestion; indigestion tablets,* tablets to cure indigestion. □ **indigestión**
indigestible *adj.* which cannot be digested; which causes pain because the body cannot digest it: *all we had to eat was a piece of indigestible meat.* □ **indigestible**
indignant [in'dignənt] *adj.* feeling offended/angry: *he was indignant when he heard of the increased prices; her attitude makes me indignant.* □ **indignado**
indignantly *adv.* angrily; with a sharp feeling of offence: *he indignantly refused my offer of money.* □ **con indignación**
indignation [indig'neiʃn] *n.* feeling of being offended: *she expressed her indignation in a letter to the headmaster.* □ **indignación**
indignity [in'digniti] *n.* (*pl. indignities*) rudeness/offence to dignity: *she had to suffer the indignity of being dragged out of bed by the police.* □ **indignidad**
indigo ['indigou] *n.* blue dye; blue colour (of clothes such as jeans). □ **índigo; añil**
indirect [indi'rekt, indai'rekt] *adj.* **1** not direct/oblique: *his article was an indirect attack on the Prime Minister.* □ **indirecto**
indirect taxation, tax added to the price of goods and not paid directly to the government. □ **impuestos indirectos**
2 ***indirect speech,*** reporting what someone has said: *'he said he would come' is indirect speech for 'he said "I will come"'.* □ **estilo indirecto**
indirectly *adv.* not directly. □ **indirectamente**
indiscreet [indi'skri:t] *adj.* revealing/not discreet: *he made some indiscreet remarks about his host's money problems.* □ **indiscreto**
indiscretion [indi'skreʃn] *n.* **1** lack of discretion/being careless about what you do or say. □ **indiscreción**
2 doing something careless. □ **descuido**
3 *she was criticized for some youthful indiscretions,* love affairs. □ **...por algunos deslices de juventud**
indiscriminate [indi'skrimənət] *adj.* widespread/not selective: *farmers are criticized for their indiscriminate use of pesticides.* □ **indiscriminado**
indiscriminately *adv.* **1** in every direction: *he hit out indiscriminately at everyone near him.* □ **indiscriminadamente**
2 without selecting/without choosing. □ **sin distinción**
indispensable [indi'spensəbl] *adj.* which you cannot do without: *for mountain climbing, a good pair of boots is indispensable.* □ **indispensable**
indisposed [indi'spouzd] *adj.* **1** slightly ill. □ **indispuesto**
2 unwilling. □ **poco dispuesto**
indisposition [indispə'ziʃn] *n.* **1** slight illness. □ **indisposición**
2 unwillingness. □ **poca disposición**
indisputable [indi'spju:təbl] *adj.* which cannot be argued with: *it is an indisputable fact that he is related to the Prime Minister.* □ **indiscutible**
indisputably *adv.* certainly: *she is indisputably the prettiest of his four daughters.* □ **sin duda alguna**
indissoluble [indi'sɔljubl] *adj.* which cannot be destroyed/dissolved. □ **indisoluble**
indistinct [indi'stiŋkt] *adj.* vague/unclear. □ **indistinto**
indistinctly *adv.* vaguely/unclearly: *I could hear indistinctly the sound of voices.* □ **indistintamente**
indistinguishable [indi'stiŋgwiʃəbl] *adj.* which cannot be told apart: *this forged note is indistinguishable from the real thing.* □ **indistinguible**
individual [indi'vidjuəl] *n.* **1** single person: *each individual has to have his own passport; I am here as a private individual,* not in an official capacity. □ **individuo**
2 (*informal*) person: *he's a nasty individual.* □ **tipo**
■ *adj.* **1** single: *the police examined each individual clue.* □ **individual**
2 belonging to a particular person: *he has a very individual way of dressing.* □ **personal**
3 for one person: *individual meat pie,* small pie for one person. □ **individual**
individualist *n.* person who emphasizes that he is unique and not a member of a group. □ **individualista**
individuality [individju'æliti] *n.* quality which makes each person different from all others. □ **individualidad**
individually *adv.* singly/as a single person: *can you ask each of them individually what they thought of the holiday?* □ **individualmente**
indivisible [indi'vizəbl] *adj.* which cannot be divided/separated. □ **indivisible**

indivisibly *adv.* in a way which prevents it being divided/separated. □ **indivisiblemente**
indoctrinate [in'dɔktrineit] *v.* to teach (someone), especially political ideas: *the prisoners were indoctrinated by the soldiers in the prisoner of war camp; he was indoctrinated with ideas of anarchy and total revolution.* □ **adoctrinar**
indoctrination [indɔktri'neiʃn] *n.* teaching someone, especially political ideas. □ **adoctrinamiento**
indolence ['indələns] *n.* laziness. □ **indolencia**
indolent *adj.* lazy. □ **indolente**
indomitable [in'dɔmitəbl] *adj.* which cannot be overcome: *the indomitable spirit of the defenders.* □ **indómito**
indoor ['indɔ:] *adj.* done/found inside a building: *his house has an indoor swimming pool; indoor plants.* □ **interior**
indoors [in'dɔ:z] *adv.* inside a building: *I think you had better stay indoors until your cough clears up; they were playing tennis, but they must have gone back indoors.* □ **en casa, dentro**
indubitable [in'dju:bitəbl] *adj.* which cannot be doubted. □ **indudable**
indubitably *adv.* certainly/definitely. □ **indudablemente**
induce [in'dju:s] *v.* **1** to persuade (someone) to do something: *I cannot think what induced him to take up yoga; the doctor tried to induce her to take a holiday.* □ **inducir**
2 to provoke (something)/to make (something) happen: *the programme induces sleep,* makes you go to sleep; *the delivery was induced,* doctors made the birth of the baby happen artificially. □ **inducir, provocar**
inducement *n.* something which helps persuade you to do something: *as an added inducement he offered me a 10 per cent rise in salary; the condition of the offices is no inducement to stay.* □ **aliciente**
induction [in'dʌkʃn] *n.* **1** entry of a person into a new job. □ **incorporación**
induction course, training course for people who have recently started their jobs. □ **cursillo de preparación**
2 creation of electricity in an object by placing it near a magnet or near something which is electrically charged. □ **inducción**
indulge [in'dʌldʒ] *v.* **1** to spoil (someone). □ **mimar**
2 to give way (to something enjoyable): *he likes to indulge in a small cigar; will you indulge?,* would you like a drink? *she indulges in a little gambling from time to time.* □ **recrearse, darse gusto**
indulgence *n.* softness/great generosity (towards someone). □ **indulgencia**
indulgent *adj.* kind/soft; too generous: *he gave an indulgent smile.* □ **indulgente**
indulgently *adv.* kindly; too generously. □ **indulgentemente**
industry ['indəstri] *n.* (*pl. industries*) **1** all manufacturing processes: *the leather industry; the British car industry.* □ **industria**
heavy industry, industry making large products (steel/cars/aircraft, etc.). □ **industria pesada**
light industry, industry making small products (watches/ball bearings, etc.). □ **industria ligera**
2 hard work/steady work. □ **trabajo pesado/largo**
industrial [in'dʌstriəl] *adj.* referring to manufacturing work: *industrial unrest; industrial injuries.* □ **industrial; laboral; de trabajo**
industrial disputes, disagreements between management and workers. □ **desacuerdos laborales**
industrial action, strike or protest by workers. □ **conflicto laboral**
industrial estate, group of factories built together. □ **polígono industrial**
industrialist *n.* owner/director of a factory. □ **industrial**
industrialization [indʌstriəlai'zeiʃn] *n.* changing of a society from agricultural to industrial by encouraging the setting up of industries. □ **industrialización**
industrialize [in'dʌstriəlaiz] *v.* to create industry (where there was none before). □ **industrializar**
the industrialized countries, countries whose economies depend on industry and not agriculture. □ **los países industrializados**
industrious *adj.* (person) who works steadily and hard. □ **trabajador**
inebriate [i'ni:briət] *adj.* (*formal*) (person) who is often drunk. □ **ebrio**
inebriated *adj.* drunk. □ **embriagado**
inedible [in'edibl] *adj.* which you cannot eat: *the food in this hotel is absolutely inedible.* □ **incomible**
ineffable [in'efəbl] *adj.* (*formal*) so wonderful that it cannot be properly described. □ **inefable**
ineffective [ini'fektiv] *adj.* which does not have any effect: *the laws against drugs have been quite ineffective.* □ **ineficaz**
ineffectual [ini'fektjuəl] *adj.* (attempt) which is unsuccessful; (person) who is weak/incapable of asserting his authority. □ **inútil**
inefficient [ini'fiʃnt] *adj.* not efficient; not competent: *the industry is plagued with inefficient salesmen.* □ **incompetente**
inefficiency *n.* incompetence/lack of efficiency. □ **ineficacia**
inelegant [in'eligənt] *adj.* not elegant. □ **inelegante**
ineligible [in'elidʒəbl] *adj.* (person) who is not qualified to do something: *he is ineligible to vote because he is a foreigner.* □ **que no tiene derecho a**
inept [in'ept] *adj.* (*inepter, ineptest*) stupid (remark); incapable (person). □ **inoportuno (observación); inepto (persona)**
ineptitude *n.* stupidity/silliness; being unable to do something. □ **ineptitud**
inequality [ini'kwɔliti] *n.* (*pl. inequalities*) lack of equality: *inequality of opportunity.* □ **desigualdad**
inequitable [in'ekwitəbl] *adj.* unjust/not fair. □ **injusto**
ineradicable [ini'rædikəbl] *adj.* which cannot be eradicated/removed. □ **que no se puede erradicar**
inert [i'nə:t] *adj.* unmoving. □ **inerte**
inert gas, gas which does not react with other substances. □ **gas inerte**
inertia [i'nə:ʃə] *n.* **1** lack of motion in a body. □ **inercia**
2 continuous movement of a body, unless checked by a force. □ **inercia**
3 laziness: *he did not act because of simple inertia.* □ **pereza**
inertia selling, method of selling goods through the post where it is assumed that the person who receives them wants to buy them if he does not return them. □ **venta por inercia**
inescapable [ini'skeipəbl] *adj.* which you cannot avoid: *it is an inescapable fact.* □ **ineludible**
inessential [ini'senʃl] *adj.* and *n.* (thing) which is not absolutely necessary: *he wastes his time on inessentials.* □ **no esencial**
inestimable [in'estiməbl] *adj.* which cannot be estimated/calculated. □ **inestimable**
inevitable [in'evitəbl] *adj.* which cannot be avoided: *the inevitable result of his letter was that he was*

sacked. □ **inevitable**
inevitably *adv.* of course: *inevitably he quarrelled with his mother-in-law.* □ **evidentemente**
inexact [inig'zækt] *adj.* not exact/not correct. □ **inexacto**
inexactitude *n.* error. □ **inexactitud**
inexcusable [inik'skju:zəbl] *adj.* which cannot be excused/forgiven: *his absence from the meeting is quite inexcusable.* □ **inexcusable**
inexhaustible [inig'zɔ:stəbl] *adj.* which cannot be used up: *he has an inexhaustible supply of jokes; almost inexhaustible mineral resources.* □ **inagotable**
inexorable [in'eksərəbl] *adj.* which cannot be changed/influenced. □ **inexorable**
inexpensive [inik'spensiv] *adj.* cheap/not expensive. □ **económico**
inexperienced [inik'spiəriənst] *adj.* with no experience/lacking experience: *to the inexperienced eye this forged banknote looks just like the real ones.* □ **sin experiencia**
inexpert [in'ekspə:t] *adj.* not expert/not skilled. □ **inexperto**
inexplicable [inik'splikəbl] *adj.* which cannot be explained. □ **inexplicable**
inexplicably *adv.* in a way which cannot be explained. □ **inexplicablemente**
inexpressible [inik'spresibl] *adj.* which cannot be expressed in words. □ **inexpresable**
inextricable [ineks'trikəbl] *adj.* which you cannot get out of: *he has got himself into an inextricable muddle with the income tax.* □ **inextricable**
inextricably *adv.* in a way which cannot be disentangled. □ **inextricablemente**
infallible [in'fæləbl] *adj.* always correct/true: *his judgement is infallible; I'm not infallible,* I make mistakes sometimes. □ **infalible**
infallibility [infæli'biliti] *n.* being always right/never making mistakes. □ **infalibilidad**
infallibly *adv.* unfailingly/always: *he is infallibly late.* □ **indefectiblemente**
infamous ['infəməs] *adj.* very wicked (person/action): *their treatment of prisoners was infamous.* □ **infame**
infant ['infənt] *n.* young child: *infant school.* □ **niño; preescolar**
infant prodigy, small child who is exceptionally good at something, such as music/chess, etc. □ **niño prodigio**
infancy *n.* young childhood: *in his infancy he was looked after by his grandmother.* □ **primera infancia**
infanticide [in'fæntisaid] *n.* killing of a baby. □ **infanticidio**
infantile ['infəntail] *adj.* referring to a small child; childish. □ **infantil**
infantry ['infəntri] *n.* (*pl. infantries*) section of an army which fights on foot: *an infantry regiment; the infantry attacked at dawn.* □ **infantería**
infatuated [in'fætjueitid] *adj.* mad about/wildly in love with: *he has become infatuated with a girl of nineteen.* □ **chiflado**
infatuation [infætju'eiʃn] *n.* blind love for someone. □ **gran enamoramiento**
infect [in'fekt] *v.* to make diseased: *infected finger; his wound became infected,* was diseased. □ **infectar**
infection *n.* **1** making diseased. □ **contagio**
2 disease which spreads: *she caught a virus infection.* □ **infección**
infectious *adj.* **1** (disease) which is catching/which can be passed from one person to another: *measles is a common infectious disease.* □ **contagioso**
2 *his laughter was infectious,* when he started laughing everyone laughed too. □ **contagioso**
infer [in'fə:] *v.* (*he inferred*) **1** to deduce: *one can infer from his statement that he had ordered the attack himself.* □ **inferir**
2 to imply/to hint: *are you inferring that the policeman took bribes?* □ **dar a entender**
inference ['infərəns] *n.* conclusion/deduction. □ **inferencia**
inferior [in'fiəriə] *adj.* not as good: *his second novel is inferior to the first.* □ **inferior**
■ *n.* person of a lower rank/subordinate: *he is hopeless at talking to his inferiors.* □ **subordinado**
inferiority [infiəri'ɔriti] *n.* **1** state of being not as good as someone else. □ **inferioridad**
2 *he has an* ***inferiority complex,*** he is obsessed with the idea that he is not as good as others. □ **...complejo de inferioridad**
infernal [in'fə:nl] *adj.* (*informal*) like in hell/hellish: *infernal row,* terrible noise. □ **infernal; endemoniado**
infernally *adv. it's infernally hot today,* (*informal*) it is extremely hot today. □ **de mil demonios**
inferno [in'fə:nou] *n.* (*pl. infernos*) blaze of fire: *the burning warehouse rapidly became a raging inferno.* □ **infierno**
infertile [in'fə:tail, *Amer.* in'fə:tl] *adj.* not fertile/not capable of having young; (land) which is not rich enough to produce crops. □ **estéril**
infertility [infə'tiliti] *n.* being unable to have young. □ **esterilidad**
infest [in'fest] *v.* (*of pest*) to cover/to swarm over in large numbers: *the cat is infested with fleas; the plant is infested with small black flies.* □ **infestar**
infestation *n.* being covered with pests. □ **infestación**
infidel ['infidəl] *n.* person who is opposed to Christianity. □ **infiel**
infidelity [infi'deliti] *n.* (*pl. infidelities*) being unfaithful. □ **infidelidad**
infighting ['infaitiŋ] *n.* bitter argument between members of a group. □ **lucha intestina**
infiltrate ['infiltreit] *v.* to enter (a political group) secretly: *the secret police had infiltrated the anarchist group.* □ **infiltrarse**
infiltration [infil'treiʃn] *n.* sneaking into a political group: *the infiltration of the group by members of the police.* □ **infiltración**
infiltrator ['infiltreitə] *n.* person who infiltrates. □ **un infiltrado**
infinite ['infinət] *adj.* endless/with no end: *he has infinite patience; they take infinite trouble with the Christmas decorations.* □ **infinito**
infinitely *adv.* completely; much more: *it is infinitely preferable to go on holiday in the summer than in November.* □ **infinitamente**
infinitesimal [infini'tesiml] *adj.* tiny/microscopic: *he added an infinitesimal quantity of gunpowder.* □ **infinitesimal**
infinitive [in'finitiv] *adj.* and *n. verb in the infinitive,* form of the verb used with other verbs and with 'to' (such as 'he could ride'; 'she wants to sing'): *'to ride' is an infinitive.* □ **infinitivo**
infinity *n.* never-ending space: *the horizon stretched away to infinity; parallel lines meet in infinity,* never meet. □ **infinito**
infirm [in'fə:m] *adj.* (*infirmer, infirmest*) sick/weak person: *hospital for elderly infirm patients.* □ **enfermo**
infirmary *n.* (*pl. infirmaries*) **1** hospital. □ **hospital**
2 sickbay in a factory or school. □ **enfermería**

infirmity *n.* (*pl. infirmities*) physical weakness. □ **debilidad**

inflame [in'fleim] *v.* **1** (*formal*) to make violent: *the sight of her inflamed his passion.* □ **inflamar**
2 *the wound has become inflamed,* red and swollen. □ **...se ha inflamado**
inflammable [in'flæməbl] *adj.* which catches fire easily: *petrol is a highly inflammable substance.* □ **inflamable**
inflammation [inflə'meiʃn] *n.* irritation; infection: *inflammation of the lungs,* illness where the lungs are infected. □ **inflamación**
inflammatory [in'flæmətəri] *adj.* (speech) which makes people behave violently. □ **incendiario**

inflate [in'fleit] *v.* **1** to blow up (balloon/tyre): *the balloon is fully inflated.* □ **inflar**
2 *inflated prices,* prices which have been artificially increased. □ **precios excesivos**
inflatable *adj.* which can be blown up: *an inflatable dinghy.* □ **inflable**
inflation [in'fleiʃn] *n.* economic state where prices and wages are rising fast to keep pace with each other: *inflation is currently running at 10 per cent; the rate of inflation is under 10 per cent.* □ **inflación**
inflationary *adj.* (policy) which tends to increase inflation. □ **inflacionista**

inflect [in'flekt] *v.* (*of a word*) to change its ending (e.g. when used in the plural). □ **declinar**

inflexible [in'fleksəbl] *adj.* which cannot be bent/altered; (person) who cannot be persuaded to change his mind. □ **inflexible**
inflexibility [infleksi'biliti] *n.* not being able to bend/to adapt. □ **inflexibilidad**
inflexibly *adv.* in an unbending way. □ **inflexiblemente**

inflict [in'flikt] *v.* **1** *the bombers inflicted heavy punishment on the town,* caused heavy damage. □ **infligir**
2 *I don't want to inflict myself on you,* I don't want to force myself on you. □ **...imponerme a ti**
infliction [in'flikʃn] *n.* causing (of damage). □ **castigo**

inflow ['inflou] *n.* flowing in: *the inflow of money.* □ **afluencia**

influence ['influəns] *n.* ability to make someone/something change; effect on others: *the head of the police force wields a great deal of influence with the government; the changes in the climate have had considerable influence on the agriculture of the country; the architecture of the church shows Italian influence.* □ **influencia**
■ *v.* to make (someone/something) change: *the speech of the Prime Minister certainly influenced the voters; his writing was influenced by his brother.* □ **influir**
influential [influ'enʃl] *adj.* so powerful as to cause change; having an effect on others: *she is one of the most influential writers of this century; if you want to get your visa quickly you need influential friends in the passport office.* □ **influyente**

influenza [influ'enzə] *n.* virus disease like a bad cold, with a high temperature. □ **gripe**

influx ['inflʌks] *n.* (*pl. influxes*) entry (of a crowd of people): *the recent influx of refugees.* □ **entrada**

inform [in'fɔ:m] *v.* **1** to tell officially; to give details: *I must inform you that your car has been stolen; keep me informed of any new developments in the case.* □ **informar**
2 *he informed against his former colleagues,* he told the police that they had taken part in a crime. □ **delató a sus...**
informant *n.* person who passes on information/who gives details. □ **informante**
information [infə'meiʃn] *n.* details/knowledge: *I'm trying to get some information about flights to Moscow.* □ **información**
information bureau, office where one can ask for details about something. □ **oficina de información**
information ministry, government department which controls the official reporting of news. □ **ministerio de información**
informative [in'fɔ:mətiv] *adj.* which tells you a lot/which conveys a lot of detailed information. □ **informativo**
informed *adj.* up-to-date/reliable: *I got this from an informed source.* □ **informado**
informer *n.* person who informs against his criminal accomplices. □ **delator**

informal [in'fɔ:ml] *adj.* not formal/relaxed; not following any rules; not official: *we are just having an informal talk; an informal dinner party.* □ **informal; amistoso; poco ceremonioso**
informally *adv.* not formally/unofficially. □ **sin ceremonia**
informality [infɔ:'mæliti] *n.* lack of any special ceremony. □ **ausencia de ceremonia**

infra-red [infrə'red] *adj.* (heat rays) which are invisible and longer than visible red heat rays: *an infra-red lamp; infra-red grill.* □ **infrarrojo**

infrastructure ['infrəstrʌktʃə] *n.* basic structure; supporting framework: *the party organization has a solid infrastructure throughout the country.* □ **infraestructura**

infrequent [in'fri:kwənt] *adj.* not frequent; not happening very often: *we only have a very infrequent train service.* □ **poco frecuente**
infrequently *adv.* not very often/not frequently. □ **raramente**

infringe [in'frindʒ] *v.* to break (a law): *this book infringes the law of copyright.* □ **infringir**
infringement *n.* breaking of a law: *infringement of parking regulations.* □ **infracción**

infuriate [in'fjuərieit] *v.* to make (someone) furious: *what infuriates me is that the train is never on time.* □ **enfurecer**

infuse [in'fju:z] *v.* to pour hot water (on tea/lime flowers) to make a drink. □ **hacer una infusión**
infusion [in'fju:ʒn] *n.* drink made by pouring hot water on dried leaves. □ **infusión**

ingenious [in'dʒi:niəs] *adj.* very clever (device/person): *he had made an ingenious contraption for opening the door automatically.* □ **ingenioso**
ingenuity [indʒə'nju:iti] *n.* cleverness/skill in inventing new techniques. □ **ingenio**

ingenuous [in'dʒenjuəs] *adj.* naive/innocent; lacking experience. □ **ingenuo**

inglenook ['iŋgəlnuk] *n.* seat at the side of a very large fireplace. □ **rincón de la chimenea**

ingot ['iŋgət] *n.* bar (of gold, etc.). □ **lingote**

ingrained ['ingreind] *adj.* **1** fixed: *ingrained dirt,* dirt which has been ground into the skin and which is difficult to get off. □ **incrustado**
2 *ingrained prejudice,* prejudice which is fixed in someone's mind and which cannot be removed. □ **prejuicio profundamente arraigado**

ingratiate [in'greiʃieit] *v. he ingratiated himself with the headmaster,* he made the headmaster like him. □ **congraciarse con**
ingratiating *adj.* which will help you worm your way into someone's favour: *he gave an ingratiating smile.* □ **congraciador**

ingratitude [in'grætitju:d] *n.* lack of gratitude; not being grateful. □ **ingratitud**
ingredient [in'gri:diənt] *n.* **1** substance which goes to make something: *the ingredients for a cake; list of ingredients for a recipe.* □ **ingrediente**
2 *there were all the ingredients for a disaster,* everything was there which could contribute to a disaster. □ **...ingredientes...**
ingrowing ['ingrouiŋ] *adj.* (toenail) which grows into the flesh. □ **uñero**
inhabit [in'hæbit] *v.* to live (in a house/on an island etc.): *is the island inhabited?* □ **habitar**
inhabitable *adj.* (place) which can be lived in. □ **habitable**
inhabitant *n.* person who lives in a place: *the inhabitants of the village dislike tourists.* □ **habitante**
inhale [in'heil] *v.* to draw into the lungs when breathing: *do you inhale when you smoke?* □ **inhalar**
inhalant *n.* medicine which has to be inhaled. □ **medicamento que se inhala**
inhaler *n.* device which makes a vapour which has to be inhaled. □ **inhalador**
inherent [in'hiərənt] *adj.* natural/inborn: *this is an inherent defect in this type of car.* □ **inherente**
inherently *adv.* naturally: *he is just inherently awkward.* □ **inherentemente**
inherit [in'herit] *v.* **1** to take over (money, etc.) from a person who has died; to have (characteristics) passed on from a parent: *when his father died he inherited all his estate; he has inherited his love of travelling from his mother.* □ **heredar**
2 to take over (from a predecessor): *the committee has inherited many problems; he inherited the filing system.* □ **heredar**
inheritance *n.* money/goods which you receive on the death of someone. □ **herencia**
inhibit [in'hibit] *v.* to restrain (someone) from doing something: *he felt inhibited because his wife was there,* he could not let himself go. □ **inhibir**
inhibition [inhi'biʃn] *n.* something which prevents you from expressing yourself freely/from letting yourself go: *get rid of your inhibitions.* □ **inhibición**
inhospitable [inhɔ'spitəbl] *adj.* not welcoming. □ **inhóspito**
inhuman [in'hju:mən] *adj.* not human; savage/brutal. □ **inhumano**
inhumanity [inhju:'mæniti] *n.* cruelty; barbarity. □ **inhumanidad**
inhumanly *adv.* savagely/brutally. □ **inhumanamente**
inimical [i'nimikl] *adj.* (*formal*) unfriendly. □ **hostil**
inimitable [i'nimitəbl] *adj.* which cannot be imitated: *his inimitable style of telling jokes.* □ **inimitable**
iniquitous [i'nikwitəs] *adj.* (*formal*) wicked. □ **inicuo**
iniquity *n.* wickedness. □ **iniquidad**
initial [i'niʃl] *adj.* first: *their initial meeting.* □ **inicial**
■ *n.* ***initials,*** first letters (of name): *his initials are S.O.B.* □ **iniciales**
■ *v.* (*he initialled*) to write your initials (on a document) to show you have read and approved it: *he initialled the minutes of the meeting.* □ **firmar con las iniciales**
initially *adv.* in the first place/at the beginning. □ **inicialmente**
initiate [i'niʃieit] *v.* **1** to start (something) going: *he initiated the discussions between the two parties.* □ **iniciar**
2 to introduce (someone) into a secret society; to show (someone) the basic information about something: *he was initiated into the sect.* □ **iniciar**
initiation [iniʃi'eiʃn] *n.* introduction to a secret society: *initiation ceremony.* □ **iniciación**
initiative [i'niʃjətiv] *n.* **1** decision to get something going; ability to decide. □ **iniciativa**
2 *he did it **on his own initiative,*** he took the decision to do it all by himself. □ **...por iniciativa propia**
3 *you have **to take the initiative,*** you have to take the first step (without waiting for someone else to tell you what to do). □ **...que tomar la iniciativa**
initiator *n.* person who starts (a project). □ **promotor**
inject [in'dʒekt] *v.* **1** to pump a liquid into (something/someone) under pressure: *he injected the patients with a tranquillizer,* he gave them an injection using a hypodermic syringe. □ **inyectar**
2 *she tried to inject some life into the club,* she tried to force the club to become more lively. □ **intentó infundir...**
injection *n.* act of pumping a liquid into someone/something under pressure: *you will have to have a tetanus injection,* an injection against tetanus. □ **inyección**
fuel-injection system, type of car engine where fuel is pumped into the cylinders under pressure. □ **...de inyección**
injudicious [indʒu:'diʃəs] *adj.* (*formal*) unwise. □ **poco juicioso**
injunction [in'dʒʌŋkʃn] *n.* **1** order (by a court) preventing someone from doing something: *he obtained a temporary injunction against a rival firm,* an order preventing the rival from acting for a time. □ **entredicho**
2 instruction. □ **precepto**
injure ['indʒə] *v.* **1** to hurt/to wound: *he was injured in a car accident.* □ **herir**
the injured party, the party in a court case who has been offended. □ **la parte ofendida**
2 *an injured tone of voice,* a tone of voice showing that you have been offended. □ **un tono ofendido**
injured *n. pl.* people who have been wounded: *ambulances carried the injured to the nearest hospital.* □ **los heridos**
injury *n.* hurt/wound: *he died from his injuries; you will do yourself an injury,* you will hurt yourself. □ **herida**
injustice [in'dʒʌstis] *n.* lack of justice; not being fair: *the injustice of the arrangement shocks me; you do him an injustice,* you are not fair to him. □ **injusticia**
ink [iŋk] *n.* liquid for writing with a pen: *he signed his name in red ink.* □ **tinta**
invisible ink, ink which cannot be seen until the paper is heated. □ **tinta simpática**
■ *v.* **1** to write with a pen and ink; to cover with ink. □ **pasar a tinta**
2 *he inked in the diagram,* he drew the diagram in ink over the pencil lines. □ **pasó a tinta el diagrama**
ink pad *n.* pad of cloth soaked in ink used for inking date stamps, etc. □ **tampón**
inkwell *n.* pot to put ink in. □ **tintero**
inky *adj.* **1** (black) like ink. □ **negruzco; entintado**
2 covered with ink. □ **lleno de tinta**
inkling ['iŋkliŋ] *n.* suspicion/idea: *he never had an inkling that he was going to get the prize.* □ **sospecha**
inlaid [in'leid] *v. see* **inlay.**
inland ['inlænd] *adj.* and *adv.* (to/of) the interior of a country: *they used to live by the sea, but they have moved inland.* □ **interior (adj.); tierra adentro (adv.)**
the Inland Revenue, government department dealing with tax. □ **Hacienda**
in-laws ['inlɔ:z] *n. pl.* (*informal*) parents related to you by marriage: *he is going to spend the weekend*

with his in-laws, with his wife's parents. □ **parientes políticos; suegros**
inlay [in'lei] *v.* (*he inlaid*) to insert small pieces of stone/wood/metal in a surface to create a pattern: *the table is inlaid with ivory.* □ **incrustrar**
inlet ['inlət] *n.* **1** small branch of water off a large stretch of water. □ **brazo**
2 ***inlet pipe,*** pipe for introducing a liquid into something. □ **tubo de entrada**
inmate ['inmeit] *n.* resident (of a house); person living in a home for old people/in a prison. □ **residente; recluso (en prisión)**
inmost ['inmoust] *adj.* furthest inside: *his inmost thoughts.* □ **íntimo**
inn [in] *n.* small hotel; public house. □ **posada**
innkeeper *n.* person who runs a public house. □ **posadero**
innards ['inədz] *n. pl.* (*informal*) intestines; inside workings: *he was poking about in the innards of the car.* □ **tripas**
innate [i'neit] *adj.* inborn/natural: *innate sense of decency.* □ **innato**
inner ['inə] *adj.* inside: *inner room,* room leading off another room. □ **interior**
inner tube, light tube containing air inside a tyre. □ **cámara**
inner sole, soft flat lining inside a shoe. □ **plantilla**
inner ear, space inside the head, beyond the middle ear, which controls balance and hearing. □ **oído interno**
innermost *adj.* furthest inside: *his innermost thoughts.* □ **íntimo**
innings ['iniŋz] *n.* (*pl. innings*) **1** (*in cricket*) turn to bat. □ **turno**
2 *he's had a good innings,* he's been a long time at his job/he's lived a long time. □ **ha tenido una larga vida**
innocent ['inəsnt] *adj.* **1** not guilty: *you are innocent until you are proved guilty.* □ **inocente**
2 *she has such an innocent air,* she looks so pure and good. □ **...aire inocente**
innocence *n.* lack of guilt: *he went to prison still proclaiming his innocence.* □ **inocencia**
innocently *adv.* in a way which shows lack of experience/knowledge: *'why is the teacher so red in the face?', the boy asked innocently.* □ **inocentemente**
innocuous [i'nɔkjuəs] *adj.* inoffensive/harmless: *the medicine is quite innocuous.* □ **inocuo**
innovate ['inəveit] *v.* to introduce changes/new methods. □ **innovar**
innovation [inə'veiʃn] *n.* invention which is new; change (in doing something): *his shop layout is quite an innovation.* □ **innovación**
innovative ['inəveitiv] *adj.* which breaks new ground/which changes everything. □ **innovador**
innovator *n.* person who introduces changes. □ **innovador**
innuendo [inju'endou] *n.* (*pl. innuendoes*) remark which suggests criticism: *he made several sly innuendoes against the Prime Minister.* □ **indirecta**
innumerable [i'nju:mərəbl] *adj.* countless/which cannot be counted: *Finland is a country of innumerable lakes.* □ **innumerable**
inoculate [i'nɔkjuleit] *v.* to prevent someone catching a disease by injecting him with a virus (so that the body can set up defences against it): *to inoculate a child against measles.* □ **inocular**
inoculation [inɔkju'leiʃn] *n.* injection to stop you catching a disease. □ **inoculación**
inoffensive [inə'fensiv] *adj.* mild/harmless. □ **inofensivo**
inoperable [in'ɔprəbl] *adj.* (disease) which is so bad that it cannot be operated on. □ **inoperable**
inoperative [in'ɔprətiv] *adj.* which is not in operation/which is not working. □ **inoperante**
inopportune [in'ɔpətju:n] *adj.* awkward/badly timed: *he came in at an inopportune moment,* just at the wrong time. □ **inoportuno**
inordinate [in'ɔ:dinət] *adj.* excessive: *he has an inordinate passion for chocolate.* □ **desmesurado**
inordinately *adv.* excessively. □ **inmoderadamente**
inorganic [inɔ:'gænik] *adj.* not relating to living organisms. □ **inorgánico**
inorganic chemistry, chemistry dealing with substances which are not organic. □ **química inorgánica**
input ['input] *n.* electric current put into an apparatus; data/information fed into a computer. □ **energía de entrada; 'input' (en ordenador)**
inquest ['iŋkwest] *n.* legal inquiry into a death. □ **encuesta postmortem**
inquire [iŋ'kwaiə] *v.* **1** to ask questions: *have you inquired at the lost property office? I inquired about his health.* □ **preguntar**
2 to conduct an official investigation: *the police are inquiring into the payments he made to the mayor.* □ **indagar**
inquiring *adj.* interested in finding out information: *he has an inquiring mind.* □ **curioso**
inquiringly *adv.* in a questioning way: *he glanced inquiringly at her.* □ **inquisitivamente**
inquiry *n.* (*pl. inquiries*) **1** formal investigation: *the government is holding an inquiry into the sales of guns abroad.* □ **investigación**
2 question: *he is making inquiries about his missing uncle; in answer to your inquiry.* □ **pregunta**
inquisition [iŋkwi'ziʃn] *n.* asking very thorough questions, usually using threats or force. □ **inquisición**
inquisitor [iŋ'kwizitə] *n.* person who asks very thorough questions. □ **persona inquisitiva**
inquisitive [iŋ'kwizətiv] *adj.* curious/asking questions. □ **inquisitivo**
inquisitively *adv.* curiously/inquiringly: *the cat peered inquisitively into the hole.* □ **inquisitivamente**
inquisitiveness *n.* curiosity/desire to find out about something. □ **curiosidad**
inroads ['inroudz] *n. pl.* ***to make inroads into something,*** to use up a large quantity of something: *the children made inroads into our supply of jam.* □ **incursión**
inrush ['inrʌʃ] *n.* sudden quick movement inwards: *there was an inrush of shoppers when the doors of the store were opened.* □ **afluencia**
insane [in'sein] *adj.* mad: *he became insane; she has an insane desire to climb Mount Everest.* □ **loco**
the insane, mad people. □ **los locos**
insanely *adv.* madly: *he is insanely jealous.* □ **locamente**
insanity [in'sæniti] *n.* madness. □ **locura; insania**
insanitary [in'sænitəri] *adj.* not clean/not hygienic: *the kitchen of the restaurant is quite insanitary.* □ **insalubre**
insatiable [in'seiʃəbl] *adj.* which cannot be satisfied: *his insatiable desire for power.* □ **insaciable**
inscribe [in'skraib] *v.* to write (officially) (in a book/on a stone): *on his gravestone is inscribed only his surname.* □ **grabar, inscribir**
inscription [in'skripʃn] *n.* official writing: *inscription on a gravestone; can you read the inscription on this coin?* □ **inscripción**
inscrutable [in'skru:təbl] *adj.* mysterious/which you cannot understand. □ **inescrutable**

insect ['insekt] *n.* small six-legged animal with a body in three parts: *ants, beetles and flies are insects, but spiders are not.* □ **insecto**
insecticide [in'sektisaid] *n.* liquid/powder which kills insects. □ **insecticida**
insectivorous [insek'tivərəs] *adj.* (bird, etc.) which eats insects. □ **insectívoro**
insecure [insi'kjuə] *adj.* **1** not safe; wobbly/not firmly fixed. □ **inseguro**
2 *he's feeling insecure,* he feels unsafe. □ **se siente inseguro**
insecurity *n.* feeling of not being safe. □ **inseguridad**
insemination [insemi'neiʃn] *n.* ***artificial insemination,*** introduction of sperm from a male into a female by a doctor or veterinary surgeon. □ **inseminación**
insensible [in'sensəbl] *adj.* **1** not conscious. □ **sin conocimiento**
2 with no feeling. □ **insensible**
3 gradual (change). □ **imperceptible**
insensitive [in'sensitiv] *adj.* not sensitive. □ **insensible**
insensitivity *n.* lack of sensitivity/lack of awareness of how other people feel. □ **insensibilidad**
inseparable [in'seprəbl] *adj.* which cannot be separated: *they are inseparable,* they are always together. □ **inseparable**
insert ['insəːt] *n.* something which is put in. □ **cosa insertada**
■ *v.* to put (something) in: *he inserted the key into the lock.* □ **introducir**
insertion [in'səːʃn] *n.* act of putting something in; something which is put in. □ **inserción**
inset ['inset] *n.* small piece which is fixed/put into something larger. □ **recuadro**
■ *adj.* with something fixed into it: *the ring was inset with diamonds.* □ **engastado**
inshore [in'ʃɔː] *adj.* and *adv.* near a coast: *inshore fishing; the boat was fishing inshore.* □ **cercano a la costa, de bajura**
inside [in said] *n.* **1** inner part (of something): *I know his house from the outside but what is the inside like? the inside of this orange is rotten.* □ **¿...pero cómo es por dentro?**
2 *I've got a pain in my* ***insides,*** I've got stomach ache. □ **...en la tripa**
3 ***inside out,*** with the inner part facing outwards: *he put his pyjamas on inside out.* □ **al revés**
4 ***to turn inside out:*** *the burglars turned the room inside out,* they made a mess of the room. □ **...registraron la habitación de arriba abajo**
5 *they know London* ***inside out,*** they know London very well. □ **...a fondo**
6 *inside left/right,* (*in games*) forward players next to the wings. □ **interior izquierda/derecha**
■ *adj.* **1** indoors; which is in the interior: *inside wall,* wall in the interior of a house. □ **interior**
2 (secret) known only to people working inside a certain organization: *he must have got some inside information.* □ **...información confidencial**
3 *it's an inside job,* crime committed with the help of someone working inside the bank, etc., which is being robbed. □ **es un trabajo de alguien de dentro, de la casa**
■ *adv.* to/in the interior: *come inside if it starts to rain; the weather was so bad we just sat inside and watched television.* □ **dentro**
■ *prep.* **1** to/in the interior of something: *he was sitting inside the car; the cat went inside the chicken cage.* □ **dentro de**
2 within: *inside three hours,* in less than three hours; *he finished the job inside a week.* □ **en**
insider *n.* person who works inside an organization and therefore knows secret information. □ **persona enterada**
insidious [in'sidiəs] *adj.* quietly treacherous; working secretly to do harm: *the insidious attack of a disease.* □ **insidioso**
insidiously *adv.* quietly and dangerously. □ **insidiosamente**
insight ['insait] *n.* **1** clear thought: *he is a scholar of great insight.* □ **perspicacia, visión**
2 deep knowledge; good look into something: *it is not often you can get an insight into the workings of a secret society.* □ **buen conocimiento**
insignia [in'signiə] *n. pl.* badges/chains/crowns, etc., which symbolize an office: *the mayor's insignia.* □ **insignias**
insignificant [insig'nifikənt] *adj.* unimportant: *he is an insignificant little man.* □ **insignificante**
insincere [insin'siə] *adj.* not sincere; false. □ **poco sincero**
insincerity *n.* lack of sincerity. □ **falta de sinceridad**
insinuate [in'sinjueit] *v.* **1** to suggest (by dropping hints): *he insinuated that the director was planning to divorce his wife.* □ **insinuar**
2 *he insinuated himself into her good books,* he gradually worked himself into the position of being her favourite. □ **congraciarse**
insinuation [insinju'eiʃn] *n.* (usually cruel) hint/suggestion. □ **insinuación**
insipid [in'sipid] *adj.* watery/not strong; with no flavour/no excitement: *this tea is a bit insipid; the play has an insipid plot.* □ **insípido**
insipidity *n.* lack of excitement/flavour. □ **insipidez**
insist [in'sist] *v.* to state firmly (that something should be done): *I insist on seeing the manager; she insisted that she had paid for the coat; I insist that you should see a doctor; it was only because he insisted that we finally got seats.* □ **insistir**
insistence *n.* firm demands. □ **insistencia**
insistent *adj.* demanding firmly: *the club was closed because of the insistent demands from the neighbours.* □ **insistente**
insistently *adv.* in a way which demands attention: *the baby birds called insistently for food.* □ **insistentemente**
insole ['insoul] *n.* soft pad which you put inside a shoe to make it more comfortable or fit better. □ **plantilla**
insolent ['insələnt] *adj.* rude. □ **insolente**
insolence *n.* rudeness. □ **insolencia**
insolently *adv.* rudely. □ **insolentemente**
insoluble [in'sɔljubl] *adj.* **1** (substance) which will not dissolve, usually in water. □ **insoluble**
2 (problem) which cannot be solved. □ **insoluble**
insolubility [insɔlju'biliti] *n.* inability (of a chemical) to dissolve. □ **insolubilidad**
insolvent [in'sɔlvənt] *adj. he became insolvent,* he went bankrupt/was unable to pay his debts. □ **insolvente**
insolvency *n.* bankruptcy; inability to pay debts. □ **insolvencia**
insomnia [in'sɔmniə] *n.* chronic inability to sleep: *he suffers from insomnia.* □ **insomnio**
insomniac *n.* person who suffers from insomnia. □ **insomne**
inspect [in'spekt] *v.* to examine closely: *I must inspect your luggage; the official inspected the shop's scales; the general inspected the soldiers on parade.* □ **inspeccionar**

inspection [in'spekʃn] *n.* examining something closely: *the soldiers were lined up for the general's inspection; during their inspection the police found several clues to the crime.* □ **inspección**
inspector *n.* senior official who examines. □ **inspector**
school inspector, official of the department of education who examines the teaching in schools. □ **inspector de enseñanza**
police inspector, officer in the police force. □ **inspector de policía**
inspectorate *n.* all inspectors (in a certain area) taken as a group. □ **cuerpo de inspectores**
inspire [in'spaiə] *v.* to make (someone) feel a certain sensation: *his poems are inspired by his native mountains; he does not inspire confidence; the talk inspired me to take up yoga.* □ **inspirar**
inspiration [inspi'reiʃn] *n.* **1** sudden urge to write (poems)/to compose (music), etc.: *his inspiration comes from the sound of the sea.* □ **inspiración**
2 sudden good idea. □ **inspiración**
instability [instə'biliti] *n.* lack of stability; not being steady. □ **inestabilidad**
install [in'stɔ:l] *v.* to put (a person into a job/a machine into a workshop): *he was installed as head of the university; we have just installed a new drilling machine; he has installed himself in my chair.* □ **poner/instalar**
installation [instə'leiʃn] *n.* **1** putting (a machine in place): *the installation of the boilers took three days.* □ **instalación**
2 group of machines which have been put in place: *bombers attacked the oil installations.* □ **...instalaciones petrolíferas**
instalment [in'stɔ:lmənt] *Amer.* **installment** *n.* part (of something which is being delivered in parts); regular payment (of part of a total sum): *you pay $10 down, and twelve monthly instalments of $5; I am paying for it by instalments; have you read the latest instalment of his memoirs?* □ **plazo**
installment plan, *Amer.* hire purchase/system where you buy something by paying instalments until you have purchased it completely. □ **compra a plazos**
instance ['instəns] *n.* example/case: *if you take as an instance the number of attacks there have been recently on old women.* □ **ejemplo**
for instance, as an example: *he's accident prone – for instance he has broken his leg twice in the last year.* □ **por ejemplo**
■ *v.* to give an example: *he instanced the case of he old lady who had no telephone.* □ **poner como ejemplo**
instant ['instənt] *n.* moment/second: *come here this instant,* come here immediately. □ **instante**
■ *adj.* immediate: *instant solution to every problem.* □ **inmediato**
instant coffee, coffee powder to which you add hot water to make coffee rapidly. □ **café instantáneo**
instantaneous [instən'teiniəs] *adj.* immediate: *death must have been instantaneous,* must have taken place immediately. □ **instantáneo**
instantly *adv.* straight away/immediately. □ **instantáneamente**
instead [in'sted] *adv.* **1** ***instead of,*** in the place of/rather than: *he'll go instead of me; instead of trying to fight back he ran away; would you like an orange instead of that apple?* □ **en vez de**
2 *if she can't go, can I go instead?,* in place of her. □ **...en su lugar**
instep ['instep] *n.* arched part of a foot. □ **empeine**
instigate ['instigeit] *v.* to provoke/to start (something): *his action instigated the government inquiry.* □ **instigar**
instigation [insti'geiʃn] *n.* suggestion: *I am doing this work at his instigation.* □ **instigación**
instigator *n.* person who stirs up trouble/who provokes action. □ **instigador**
instil [in'stil] *v.* (*he instilled*) to put (an idea, etc.) into someone's mind gradually. □ **inculcar**
instinct ['instiŋkt] *n.* feeling/ability for doing something which you have from birth and have not learnt: *he did it by instinct; instinct told him not to reveal the secret.* □ **instinto**
instinctive [in'stiŋktiv] *adj.* natural/inborn (reaction): *cats seem to have an instinctive fear of water.* □ **instintivo**
instinctively *adv.* because of a natural impulse: *she instinctively stepped back and so missed being killed.* □ **instintivamente**
institute ['institju:t] *n.* **1** organization set up for a purpose: *research institute; institute for the blind.* □ **instituto**
2 building which houses an organization set up for a particular purpose. □ **instituto**
■ *v.* **1** to set up/to start. □ **instituir**
2 *they are instituting proceedings against him,* they are going to prosecute him. □ **van a entablar...**
institution [insti'tju:ʃn] *n.* **1** setting up (of an organization). □ **institución**
2 organization/society set up for a purpose: *educational institution.* □ **institución educativa**
3 permanent feature; longstanding custom: *afternoon tea is an English institution.* □ **institución**
institutional *adj.* referring to an institution: *institutional buying,* buying of shares by insurance companies, etc. □ **institucional**
institutionalize *v.* to make (something) into an institution. □ **institucionalizar**
instruct [in'strʌkt] *v.* **1** to teach: *he was instructing me in the art of bricklaying.* □ **instruir**
2 to order: *I instructed the soldiers to proceed south for two miles.* □ **mandar**
3 to give orders to (a solicitor) to start legal proceedings. □ **dar instrucciones a**
instruction [in'strʌkʃn] *n.* **1** teaching: *a course of instruction,* series of lessons. □ **enseñanza**
2 ***instructions,*** orders; indication of how something is to be used: *he gave me no instructions; she gave me full instructions how to reach her house; are there any instructions with this sewing machine?* □ **instrucciones**
instructions booklet, booklet showing how a piece of machinery should be used. □ **manual de instrucciones**
instructive *adj.* which teaches: *the book was very instructive.* □ **instructivo**
instructor *n.* teacher (especially of sport): *swimming instructor; driving instructor.* □ **instructor**
instrument ['instrumənt] *n.* **1** piece of equipment: *surgical instruments; he was hit on the head with a blunt instrument,* with something blunt. □ **instrumento**
2 *she pulled the instrument out of the wall,* pulled out the telephone. □ **...el aparato**
3 ***musical instrument,*** device which is blown/hit/plucked, etc., to make a musical note: *the instruments of an orchestra.* □ **instrumento**
wind instruments, instruments which are played by blowing. □ **instrumentos de viento**
stringed instruments, instruments with strings which make different notes when rubbed or plucked. □ **...de cuerda**

instrumental [instru'mentl] *adj.* **1** *he was instrumental in getting the government subsidy,* he was responsible/played an important role in getting the subsidy. □ **contribuyó a...**
2 referring to a musical instrument: *instrumental music,* music played on instruments, not sung. □ **instrumental**
instrumentalist *n.* person who plays a musical instrument. □ **instrumentalista**
insubordinate [insə'bɔːdinət] *adj.* unruly; not obeying orders. □ **insubordinado**
insubordination [insəbɔːdi'neiʃn] *n.* not obeying orders. □ **insubordinación**
insubstantial [insəb'stænʃl] *adj.* not substantial/not solid. □ **insubstancial**
insufferable [in'sʌfrəbl] *adj.* intolerable/which you cannot bear. □ **insufrible**
insufferably *adv.* intolerably: *he is insufferably pompous.* □ **insufriblemente**
insufficient [insə'fiʃnt] *adj.* not sufficient/not enough: *he had insufficient time to finish the examination.* □ **insuficiente**
insufficiently *adv.* not enough: *she failed because she was insufficiently prepared for her test.* □ **insuficientemente**
insular ['insjulə] *adj.* **1** referring to an island. □ **insular**
2 narrow-minded. □ **estrecho de miras**
3 *he is too insular in his approach,* too restricted. □ **es demasiado estrecho de miras...**
insularity [insju'læriti] *n.* prejudice/narrowness of opinions. □ **estrechez de miras**
insulate ['insjuleit] *v.* to cover so as to prevent heat/electricity/sound escaping: *the electric cable was not insulated properly; you must insulate your hot water tank.* □ **aislar**
insulation [insju'leiʃn] *n.* **1** covering to prevent heat/electricity/sound escaping. □ **aislamiento**
2 material which prevents heat/electricity/sound escaping. □ **aislante**
insulator ['insjuleitə] *n.* material/device which prevents electricity escaping. □ **aislante**
insulin ['insjulin] *n.* hormone which regulates the use of sugar by the body, and is used to treat diabetes. □ **insulina**
insult ['insʌlt] *n.* rude word said to or about a person. □ **insulto**
■ *v.* to say rude things about (someone): *I have never been so insulted in my life.* □ **insultar**
insulting *adj.* rude: *insulting remarks.* □ **insultante**
insuperable [in'sjuːprəbl] *adj.* which cannot be overcome: *insuperable difficulties.* □ **insuperable**
insupportable [insə'pɔːtəbl] *adj* unbearable/which cannot be borne. □ **insoportable**
insure [in'ʃuə] *v.* to agree with a company that if you pay them a regular sum, they will compensate you for loss or damage to property or persons: *is your car properly insured? I am insured for $200,000; it was lucky he had insured his luggage before he left.* □ **asegurar**
insurance *n.* agreement with a company by which you are paid compensation for loss or damage in return for regular payments of money: *he took out an insurance against burglary.* □ **seguro**
insurance policy, document with the details of an insurance. □ **póliza de seguros**
insurance broker, person who arranges an insurance. □ **agente de seguros**
life insurance, insurance against someone's death. □ **seguro de vida**
National Insurance, government-run insurance which provides for state medical care, unemployment payments, etc. □ **Seguridad Social**
insurer *n.* person/company which insures. □ **asegurador**
insurgent [in'səːdʒənt] *adj.* and *n.* (person) in a state of revolt. □ **insurgente**
insurmountable [insə'mauntəbl] *adj.* which cannot be overcome. □ **insuperable**
insurrection [insə'rekʃn] *n.* uprising/revolution. □ **insurrección**
intact [in'tækt] *adj.* in one piece/not broken: *the china survived the journey intact.* □ **intacto**
intake ['inteik] *n.* **1** *fuel intake,* quantity of fuel taken in; *calorie intake,* quantity of calories taken into the body. □ **consumo; ingesta**
2 *an intake of new recruits,* group of new people taken in by an organization. □ **una entrada de**
intangible [in'tændʒəbl] *adj.* which cannot be touched/which cannot be assessed. □ **intangible**
integral ['intigrəl] *adj.* forming (part of) a whole: *this is an integral part of the apparatus.* □ **integrante**
integer ['intidʒə] *n.* whole number (not a fraction). □ **número entero**
integrate ['intigreit] *v.* to link to form a whole; to make (people) full members of society: *the new arrivals have integrated into the population.* □ **integrar(se)**
integration [inti'greiʃn] *n.* bringing parts together to form a whole; making people full members of society. □ **integración**
integrity [in'tegriti] *n.* honesty. □ **integridad**
intellect ['intəlekt] *n.* ability to think or reason; brainpower: *the human intellect.* □ **entendimiento**
intellectual [intə'lektjuəl] *adj.* referring to the brain; good at using the brain: *intellectual work.* □ **intelectual**
■ *n.* person who believes that brainpower is very important/who uses his brain to make a living. □ **intelectual**
intellectually *adv.* referring to intelligence: *he is intellectually inferior to her,* he is not as clever as she is. □ **intelectualmente**
intelligence [in'telidʒəns] *n.* **1** quickness of understanding/mental ability. □ **inteligencia**
intelligence test, test to calculate how clever you are. □ **test de inteligencia**
intelligence quotient, number showing how clever you are compared to others. □ **cociente intelectual**
2 secret information. □ **información secreta**
3 *he works in intelligence,* he is in the secret service. □ **servicio de información**
intelligent *adj.* clever/mentally able: *she is very intelligent.* □ **inteligente**
intelligentsia [inteli'dʒensiə] *n.* intellectual class of society. □ **los intelectuales**
intelligible [in'telidʒəbl] *adj.* which can be understood: *the message was hardly intelligible.* □ **inteligible**
intemperate [in'temprət] *adj.* wild/not moderate: *an intemperate outburst.* □ **inmoderado**
intend [in'tend] *v.* to plan to do something/to mean: *I intend to leave the office early today; she intends to study biology; the result was not what was intended.* □ **tener la intención de; pretender**
intense [in'tens] *adj.* (*intenser, intensest*) **1** very strong/vigorous (action): *she has an intense dislike of snakes; he felt an intense feeling of disappointment.* □ **intenso**
2 *he is a very intense young man,* he is extremely serious. □ **es un joven muy serio**
intensely *adv.* strongly: *I dislike cigarette smoke in-*

tensely. □ **muchísimo**

intensify *v.* to grow/to make stronger. □ **intensificar(se)**

intensity *n.* strength/violence (of pain). □ **intensidad**

intensive *adj.* very concentrated: *the government has launched an intensive campaign against teenage violence; we carried out an intensive search of the archives.* □ **intensivo, intenso**

intensive care unit, section of a hospital dealing with seriously ill patients who need a lot of attention. □ **unidad de vigilancia intensiva (U.V.I.)**

intensively *adv.* very strongly. □ **intensivamente**

intent [in'tent] *adj.* determined/absorbed: *he is intent on going to France; she was intent on doing well.* □ **resuelto**

■ *n.* ***with intent to*** *defraud,* with the aim of deceiving. □ **propósito**

to all intents and purposes, virtually/in nearly every way. □ **prácticamente**

intently *adv.* fixedly: *the cat was gazing intently at the goldfish.* □ **atentamente**

intention [in'tenʃn] *n.* **1** aim: *my intention was to sail to the Mediterranean.* □ **intención**

2 *he did it with the best of intentions,* he wanted to do something good, although the result was bad. □ **...con la mejor de las intenciones**

intentional *adj.* on purpose: *was his rudeness intentional?* □ **deliberado**

intentionally *adv.* on purpose: *he was intentionally late.* □ **deliberadamente**

inter [in'tə:] *v.* (*he interred*) (*formal*) to bury. □ **enterrar**

interact [intər'ækt] *v.* to have an effect on each other: *the two chemicals interact.* □ **actuar recíprocamente**

interaction [intər'ækʃn] *n.* effect of two things on each other. □ **interacción**

intercede [intə'si:d] *v.* to plead; to make an appeal: *he interceded with the minister on behalf of the prisoners.* □ **interceder**

intercession [intə'seʃn] *n.* pleading (on behalf of someone). □ **intercesión**

intercept [intə'sept] *v.* to stop (something) as it is passing: *the ball was intercepted by one of the forwards; his messages were intercepted by the enemy.* □ **interceptar**

interception [intə'sepʃn] *n.* stopping (of something which is passing). □ **interceptación**

interceptor *n.* person/aircraft which intercepts. □ **interceptor**

interchange ['intətʃeindʒ] *n.* **1** exchange (of ideas). □ **intercambio**

2 large road junction where motorways cross. □ **cruce**

interchangeable [intə'tʃeindʒəbl] *adj.* which can be substituted for each other: *the two lids are interchangeable.* □ **intercambiable**

intercom ['intəkɔm] *n.* device for speaking to people over a short distance: *the pilot talked to the passengers on/over the intercom.* □ **intercomunicador, interfono**

intercontinental [intəkɔnti'nentl] *adj.* from one continent to another: *intercontinental air services.* □ **intercontinental**

intercourse ['intəkɔ:s] *n.* **1** reproductive act between a male and a female. □ **cópula**

2 communication between people. □ **relaciones**

interdict ['intədikt] *n.* (*formal*) forbidding (something). □ **interdicto**

interest ['intrəst] *n.* **1** percentage return on investment; percentage payable on a loan: *the bank account gives a 5 per cent interest; we have to pay 12 per cent interest on the mortgage; the company has offered me an interest-free loan.* □ **interés**

2 financial share: *he has a substantial interest in the company.* □ **participación**

3 particular attention: *he takes a special interest in his grandchildren.* □ **interés**

4 thing which you pay attention to: *his main interests are old churches and castles.* □ **interés**

5 advantage: *it is against our best interests,* it will not benefit us; *is it in our interest to let him join the group?,* will it help us/will we get any advantage? □ **provecho**

in the interest of *public safety,* because of/for reasons of public safety. □ **en beneficio de...**

■ *v.* **1** to attract someone's attention: *the architecture of the building interested him enormously; he is particularly interested in modern music.* □ **interesar**

2 *can I interest you in some tickets for the theatre?,* can I persuade you to buy some tickets? □ **¿le interesan...?**

interesting *adj.* which attracts attention: *an interesting article in the newspaper; an interesting report on juvenile crime.* □ **interesante**

interface ['intəfeis] *n.* area where two different systems meet and interact. □ **superficie de contacto**

interfere [intə'fiə] *v.* **1** to meddle/to get involved: *don't interfere with the electric wiring system; try not to interfere in their quarrel; he doesn't like people interfering in his business affairs.* □ **interferir; intervenir; entrometerse (asuntos)**

2 to affect the reception of radio/TV programmes. □ **producir interferencias**

interference *n.* **1** involvement/meddling: *I don't like interference in my private life.* □ **intromisión**

2 noise which affects radio/TV programmes (caused by aircraft/lightning, etc.). □ **interferencia**

interim ['intərim] *adj.* and *n.* ***interim report,*** report given halfway through an investigation. □ **ínterin; provisional**

in the interim, meanwhile/in the time between a proposal and a final decision. □ **en el ínterin**

interior [in'tiəriə] *adj.* and *n.* inner part (of a building/car): *interior walls; the interior of the house is all painted white.* □ **interior**

ministry of interior, ministry dealing with affairs inside a country, in particular the police. □ **ministerio del interior**

interject [intə'dʒekt] *v.* to make a sudden exclamation. □ **exclamar**

interjection [intə'dʒekʃn] *n.* exclamation; word used to show surprise. □ **interjección**

interleave [intə'li:v] *v.* to put (something) between the pages of a book. □ **intercalar**

interlock ['intəlɔk] *v.* to fit together: *a jigsaw is made of hundreds of interlocking pieces.* □ **encajar**

interlocutor [intə'lɔkjutə] *n.* person who speaks to someone else. □ **interlocutor**

interloper ['intəloupə] *n.* person who comes in/who intrudes. □ **intruso**

interlude ['intəlu:d] *n.* quiet time between two lively periods; rest period between parts of a performance: *the orchestra will play during the interlude.* □ **intermedio**

intermarry [intə'mæri] *v.* (*intermarried; intermarrying*) to marry within the same family group. □ **casarse entre consanguíneos**

intermediary [intə'mi:djəri] *adj.* and *n.* (*pl. intermediaries*) (person) who goes between two others/who acts as messenger. □ **intermediario**

intermediate [intə'mi:djət] *adj.* halfway between

two extremes: *lessons are graded according to whether they are 'elementary', 'intermediate' or 'advanced'; he occupies an intermediate position between the left and right wings of the party.* □ **intermedio**

interminable [in'tə:minəbl] *adj.* never-ending: *he made an interminable speech,* a very long (and boring) speech. □ **interminable**

interminably *adv.* without coming to an end. □ **interminablemente**

intermingle [intə'miŋgl] *v.* to mix together. □ **entremezclar**

intermission [intə'miʃn] *n.* **1** interval (in a play/film/concert). □ **descanso**

2 ***without intermission,*** without a break/without stopping. □ **sin descanso**

intermittent [intə'mitənt] *adj.* which takes place from time to time: *intermittent showers of rain.* □ **intermitente**

intermittently *adv.* (taking place) from time to time/on and off. □ **a intervalos**

intern ['intə:n] *n.* junior doctor who works and lives in a hospital. □ **interno**

■ *v.* to put (prisoners) in a prison without trial. □ **internar**

internee [intə:'ni:] *n.* prisoner in a detention camp who has not been tried. □ **interno**

internment *n.* putting prisoners in a prison or camp without trial. □ **internamiento**

internal [in'tə:nl] *adj.* inside: *internal angles of a triangle; the internal affairs of a country.* □ **interno**

internal memo, note circulated only to people inside an organization. □ **informe interno**

internal telephone, private telephone inside a building. □ **teléfono interno**

internal combustion engine, engine in which the fuel is burnt inside a closed space (as in the cylinders in a car engine). □ **motor de explosión**

internally *adv.* inside: *not to be taken internally,* (ointment, etc.) which must be put on the skin and not swallowed. □ **internamente**

international [intə'næʃnl] *adj.* between countries: *international trade; international telephone call.* □ **internacional**

■ *n.* **1** sportsman who has played for his country's team against another country. □ **internacional**

2 game/sporting competition between two countries. □ **internacional**

internecine [intə'ni:sain] *adj* (*formal*) (two things) which destroy each other. □ **recíprocamente destructivos**

interphone ['intəfoun] *n.* short-distance internal telephone (as in a private house). □ **interfono**

interplanetary [intə'plænətri] *adj.* (travel, etc.) between planets. □ **interplanetario**

interplay ['intəplei] *n.* reaction between two forces. □ **interacción**

interpolate [in'tə:pəleit] *v.* to add words in between others. □ **interpolar**

interpolation [intə:pə'leiʃn] *n.* adding of words between existing words in a text. □ **interpolación**

interpose ['intəpouz] *v.* to place in between. □ **interponer**

interpret [in'tə:prit] *v.* **1** to explain (something) to someone who does not understand: *can you interpret the meaning of these signs?* □ **interpretar**

2 to translate aloud what is spoken from one language into another: *he is going to interpret for the Finnish delegation.* □ **traducir (oralmente)**

interpretation [intə:pri'teiʃn] *n.* **1** meaning: *I put quite a different interpretation on his remarks.* □ **interpretación**

2 translating aloud from one language to another. □ **traducción oral, interpretación**

interpreter *n.* person who translates aloud from one language to another: *a Russian interpreter.* □ **intérprete**

interregnum [intə'regnəm] *n.* period between the reigns of successive kings; period of inactivity after one boss has left and before his successor has arrived. □ **interregno**

interrelated [intəri'leitid] *adj.* (several things) which are related. □ **interrelacionado**

interrogate [in'terəgeit] *v.* to question severely: *the police interrogated the prisoners.* □ **interrogar**

interrogation [interə'geiʃn] *n.* severe questioning (of a prisoner). □ **interrogatorio**

interrogative [intə'rɔgətiv] *adj.* and *n.* questioning: *the phrase 'he sat down' becomes 'did he sit down?' when it is put into the interrogative.* □ **interrogativo**

interrogative pronoun, pronoun which asks a question: *'who', 'which', 'what', are interrogative pronouns.* □ **pronombre interrogativo**

interrogator [in'terəgeitə] *n.* person who questions (a prisoner) closely: *police interrogator.* □ **interrogador policial**

interrupt [intə'rʌpt] *v.* to break into (someone's speech); to stop (something) continuing: *I was just starting to tell my story when I was interrupted by the telephone; train services have been interrupted by the derailment.* □ **interrumpir**

interruption [intə'rʌpʃn] *n.* something which breaks into a speech/which stops something continuing: *he spoke for twenty minutes in spite of numerous interruptions; there has been an interruption in the bus service,* a break in the usual schedule. □ **interrupción**

intersect [intə'sekt] *v.* to cut across; to cut across (each other): *there are traffic lights at the corner where the main roads intersect.* □ **cruzar(se)**

intersection [intə'sekʃn] *n.* place where lines cut across each other; crossroads. □ **intersección**

intersperse [intə'spə:s] *v.* to scatter: *the speech was interspersed with loud applause.* □ **esparcir; el discurso quedó salpicado con...**

interstellar [intə'stelə] *adj.* (space, etc.) between stars. □ **interestelar**

interstice [in'tə:stis] *n.* small space in between other things. □ **intersticio**

intertwine [intə'twain] *v.* to twist together; to be twisted together. □ **entrelazar**

interval ['intəvl] *n.* **1** period/gap (between two points/between two acts in a play): *there are two intervals during the play; luckily there were some bright intervals between the showers.* □ **intervalo; entreacto (en teatro)**

2 *we only meet* ***at intervals,*** from time to time; *the buses run at half-hourly intervals,* every 30 minutes. □ **de tarde en tarde; intervalo**

intervene [intə'vi:n] *v.* **1** to come/to arrive in between: *then the war intervened; he tried to intervene in the quarrel,* he tried to enter the quarrel to stop it. □ **surgir; intervenir**

2 *in the intervening period,* during the period in between. □ **en el período intermedio**

intervention [intə'venʃn] *n.* coming between; entry into something: *his intervention in the dispute was badly timed; the intervention of the army in the civil war.* □ **intervención**

interview ['intəvju:] *n.* **1** discussion (on radio/TV/in the newspaper) between an important or interesting person and a journalist: *he gave an interview to the*

local reporter, he allowed the reporter to ask him questions. □ **entrevista**
2 questioning (by one or more people) of a person applying for a job: *I have written hundreds of job applications but I have only been asked to one interview.* □ **entrevista**
■ *v.* **1** to ask (a famous/interesting person) questions in order to show his answers publicly: *he interviewed the Prime Minister.* □ **entrevistar**
2 to ask questions of a person applying for a job: *we have interviewed ten people and have not found anyone who is suitable.* □ **entrevistar**
interviewee [intəvju:'i:] *n.* person who is being/who is going to be interviewed. □ **el entrevistado**
interviewer *n.* person who asks the questions at an interview. □ **entrevistador**
interweave [intə'wi:v] *v.* (*he interwove; he has interwoven*) to weave/to bind together. □ **entretejer**
intestate [in'testeit] *adj.* not having made a will: *she died intestate.* □ **intestado**
intestine [in'testin] *n.* long tube in the body through which food passes from the stomach to the anus. □ **intestino**
intestinal *adj.* referring to the intestine. □ **intestinal**
intimate ['intimət] *adj.* **1** very close: *an intimate friend; are you on intimate terms with the headmaster?* □ **íntimo**
2 *he has an intimate knowledge of Russian stamps,* he knows all the details about them. □ **profundo**
3 sexual (relationship). □ **relación íntima**
■ *n.* close friend. □ **íntimo**
■ *v.* to suggest: *he intimated that it would be better if we stayed at home.* □ **insinuar**
intimacy *n.* close relationship (with someone). □ **intimidad**
intimately *adv.* closely: *I know him intimately.* □ **íntimamente**
intimation [inti'meiʃn] *n.* suggestion. □ **insinuación**
intimidate [in'timideit] *v.* to frighten (someone) by threats. □ **intimidar**
intimidating *adj.* frightening. □ **intimidante**
intimidation [intimi'deiʃn] *n.* frightening by threats. □ **intimidación**
into ['intu] *prep.* **1** (movement) towards the inside: *he went into the house; she fell into the swimming pool; it fell into the hands of the enemy; the bad weather continued into August.* □ **en**
2 so as to become; to develop as: *she changed the prince into a frog; he burst into tears.* □ **en**
3 dividing: *four into three won't go.* □ **cuatro dividido por...**
intolerable [in'tɔlərəbl] *adj.* which you cannot bear: *he suffered intolerable pain.* □ **intolerable**
intolerably *adv.* unbearably. □ **intolerablemente**
intolerant [in'tɔlərənt] *adj.* (person) who cannot bear people with different ideas from his own: *he is intolerant of people who do not agree with his point of view.* □ **intolerante**
intolerance *n.* not accepting other people's points of view: *religious intolerance,* hostility towards other religions. □ **intolerancia**
intonation [intə'neiʃn] *n.* stress (in speech or singing). □ **entonación**
intone [in'toun] *v.* to recite (psalms, etc.) in a singing voice. □ **salmodiar**
intoxicate [in'tɔksikeit] *v.* to make drunk. □ **embriagar**
intoxicating *adj.* **1** which makes you drunk: *intoxicating drink,* alcoholic drink. □ **embriagador; alcohólica**
2 *intoxicating news,* exciting news. □ **noticias de gran interés**
intoxication [intɔksi'keiʃn] *n.* drunkenness: *he was in a state of intoxication.* □ **borrachera**
intractable [in'træktəbl] *adj.* very difficult to deal with; (problem) which is impossible to solve. □ **intratable; insoluble**
intransigent [in'trænsidʒənt] *adj.* firm; obstinate/not shifting your position/not changing your mind. □ **intransigente**
intransigence *n.* firmness/being obstinate. □ **intransigencia**
intransitive [in'trænsitiv] *adj.* (verb) which has no object (such as 'he went', 'she came'). □ **intransitivo**
intravenous [intrə'vi:nəs] *adj.* (injection) made into a vein. □ **intravenoso**
intrepid [in'trepid] *adj.* fearless/very brave. □ **intrépido**
intricate ['intrikət] *adj.* very complicated; made of many different parts. □ **intrincado**
intricacy *n.* (*pl. intricacies*) complexity. □ **complejidad**
intrigue [in'tri:g] *n.* secret plot. □ **intriga**
■ *v.* **1** to plot: *he was intriguing against the government.* □ **intrigar**
2 to make someone interested: *I was intrigued to learn that he had got married.* □ **despertar la curiosidad de**
intrinsic [in'trinzik] *adj.* forming a basic part of something: *it is an object of no intrinsic beauty, although it is very valuable,* it is not in itself very beautiful. □ **intrínseco**
intrinsically *adv.* basically. □ **intrínsecamente**
introduce [intrə'dju:s] *v.* **1** to present (someone) to another person/to people who did not know him previously: *may I introduce my new assistant? she introduced him to her father.* □ **presentar**
2 to announce (a TV/radio programme, etc.). □ **presentar**
3 to make (something) go in; to bring (something) in: *to introduce a motion for debate,* to present a subject for discussion. □ **introducir; presentar**
introduction [intrə'dʌkʃn] *n.* **1** act of presenting something; thing which presents something. □ **presentación**
2 making someone known to another person/to people who did not know him previously: *as I know everyone here, let me make the introductions.* □ **presentación**
3 piece at the beginning of a book which explains the rest of the book. □ **prólogo**
4 *'An Introduction to Electrical Engineering',* an elementary book about electrical engineering. □ **introducción**
introductory *adj.* (words) which introduce something: *the Chairman made a few introductory remarks.* □ **introductorio**
introductory offer, offer of a new range of goods at a specially low price. □ **oferta de lanzamiento**
introspective [intrə'spektiv] *adj.* inward-looking; thinking a lot about yourself. □ **introspectivo**
introspection [intrə'spekʃn] *n.* looking inwards at yourself. □ **introspección**
introvert ['intrəvə:t] *n.* quiet person who thinks mainly about himself. □ **introvertido**
intrude [in'tru:d] *v.* to enter where you are not wanted: *I don't want to intrude; am I intruding?* □ **entrometerse; ¿molesto?**
intruder *n.* someone who has come in where he is not wanted; burglar. □ **intruso**
intrusion [in'tru:ʒn] *n.* coming in where you are not wanted: *pardon this intrusion,* excuse me for inter-

rupting. □ **intrusión; entremetimiento**
intrusive [in'tru:siv] *adj.* unwanted. □ **intruso**
intuition [intju'iʃn] *n.* **1** thinking of something/knowing something naturally without it being explained. □ **intuición**
2 *a flash of intuition,* a sudden bright idea. □ **un golpe de intuición**
intuitive [in'tjuitiv] *adj.* based on intuition: *he has an intuitive sense of danger.* □ **intuitivo**
inundate ['inʌndeit] *v.* to flood: *we have been inundated with requests for help.* □ **inundar**
inundation [inʌn'deiʃn] *n.* flood. □ **inundación**
inure [in'juə] *v.* (*formal*) to accustom to something unpleasant: *he is inured to fatigue.* □ **habituarse**
invade [in'veid] *v.* to attack and enter (a country) with an army: *the enemy has invaded the eastern provinces; the invading forces.* □ **invadir**
invader *n.* person who enters a country with an army. □ **invasor**
invalid ['invəlid] *adj.* and *n.* sick/disabled (person). □ **inválido**
invalid carriage, small vehicle for one disabled person. □ **coche de inválido**
■ *v.* ['invəli:d] to make (someone) retire because of ill health: *he was invalided out of the army.* □ **dar de baja por invalidez**
■ *adj.* not valid/not legal: *this makes the contract invalid; my passport is invalid.* □ **nulo (contrato); caducado (pasaporte)**
invalidate [in'vælideit] *v.* to make (something) invalid: *this invalidates the agreement; his will was invalidated by the court.* □ **invalidar**
invaluable [in'væljuəbl] *adj.* extremely valuable: *his help has been invaluable.* □ **inestimable**
invariable [in'vɛəriəbl] *adj.* always the same/not changing. □ **invariable**
invariably *adv.* always: *the librarian is invariably helpful.* □ **invariablemente**
invasion [in'veiʒn] *n.* attacking and entering a country with armed forces: *airborne invasion; the invasion of Italy.* □ **invasión**
invective [in'vektiv] *n.* insulting speech/abuse: *the political debate ended in a torrent of invective.* □ **invectiva**
inveigh [in'vei] *v.* ***to inveigh against something,*** (*formal*) to speak violently against something. □ **lanzar invectivas contra**
inveigle [in'veigl] *v.* to trick (someone) into doing something: *he was inveigled into selling his house.* □ **embaucar**
invent [in'vent] *v.* to create (a new process/new machine); to think up (an excuse): *he invented a machine for peeling potatoes; who invented the telephone?* □ **inventar**
invention [in'venʃn] *n.* **1** creation (of new process/new machine): *the world has not been the same since the invention of the atom bomb.* □ **invento**
2 new machine: *have you seen his latest invention?* □ **invento**
inventive *adj.* creative: *she has an inventive mind.* □ **inventivo**
inventiveness *n.* ability to invent. □ **inventiva**
inventor *n.* person who invents new processes/new machines. □ **inventor**
inventory ['invəntri] *n.* (*pl. inventories*) **1** list (of contents of a house, etc.). □ **inventario**
2 *Amer.* list of stock. □ **inventario**
inverse ['invə:s] *adj.* and *n.* **1** opposite/contrary: *no, the inverse is true,* no, the opposite is true. □ **inverso; lo contrario**
2 *output is **in inverse proportion to** the number of workers,* the more workers there are, the lower is the output. □ **inverso**
inversion [in'və:ʃn] *n.* turning something round in a contrary way: *'so did I' is an example of inversion of verb and subject.* □ **inversión**
invert [in'və:t] *v.* to turn something upside down/back to front. □ **invertir**
inverted commas, printing sign ("") which indicates speech: *to open (")/to close (") the inverted commas; single/double inverted commas ('/").* □ **comillas**
invertebrate [in'və:tibreit] *adj.* and *n.* (animal) without a backbone: *worms are invertebrates.* □ **invertebrado**
invest [in'vest] *v.* to put (money) into savings/property, etc., so that it will increase in value: *he is investing his money in a savings account; she invested in property; we are investing in a new car,* we are buying a new car. □ **invertir**
investiture [in'vestitʃə] *n.* ceremony where someone is given a medal/where someone is installed in office. □ **investidura**
investment *n.* money placed so that it will increase in value: *gold coins are a good investment.* □ **inversión**
investor *n.* person who puts money into savings or property or shares. □ **inversionista**
investigate [in'vestigeit] *v.* to study/to examine: *the police are investigating the disappearance of the money; scientists are investigating the mysterious light in the sky.* □ **investigar**
investigation [investi'geiʃn] *n.* examination: *as a result of police investigations six people were arrested; a scientific investigation into the origins of the explosion.* □ **investigación**
investigator *n.* detective; person who investigates. □ **investigador**
inveterate [in'vetərət] *adj.* obstinate/hardened: *he's an inveterate smoker,* he is a heavy smoker. □ **empedernido**
invidious [in'vidiəs] *adj.* which is likely to offend people unreasonably: *he has put himself into an invidious position.* □ **odioso**
invigilate [in'vidʒileit] *v.* to supervise an examination. □ **vigilar**
invigilator *n.* supervisor of an examination. □ **vigilante**
invigorate [in'vigəreit] *v.* to make strong/vigorous; to make (someone) feel livelier: *invigorating sea air.* □ **vigorizar**
invincible [in'vinsəbl] *adj.* which cannot be defeated: *the invincible World Cup champions.* □ **invencible**
invincibility [invinsə'biliti] *n.* state of being unbeatable. □ **invencibilidad**
invisible [in'vizəbl] *adj.* which cannot be seen: *a cloud of invisible gas.* □ **invisible**
invisibility [invizə'biliti] *n.* not being able to be seen. □ **invisibilidad**
invite [in'vait] *v.* **1** to ask (someone) to do something: *I invited him to come in; shall we invite him to the party?* □ **invitar**
2 *to invite comments from the audience,* to ask the audience to comment. □ **invitar a que haga comentarios**
invitation [invi'teiʃn] *n.* asking (someone to do something): *we sent him an invitation to the party; he has had an invitation to speak at the dinner.* □ **invitación**
inviting *adj.* attractive: *the meal looks very inviting.* □ **atrayente**

invocation [invə'keiʃn] *n.* (*formal*) calling on someone for help/support. □ **invocación**
invoice ['invɔis] *n.* note sent to ask for payment for services or goods: *we still have not paid this invoice.* □ **factura**
■ *v.* to send a note asking for payment for services or goods: *he was invoiced for goods which he did not order.* □ **facturar**
invoicing *n.* sending of an invoice. □ **facturación**
invoke [in'vouk] *v.* to call on (someone) for help/support: *he invoked clause 4 of the contract.* □ **invocar**
involuntary [in'vɔləntri] *adj.* not voluntary/not willingly done. □ **involuntario**
involuntarily *adv.* not willingly: *he was involuntarily involved in the fight.* □ **sin querer**
involve [in'vɔlv] *v.* **1** to bring (someone/something) into (a dispute/a scheme): *three cars were involved in the crash; he got involved in a dispute over the garden fence; he has been involved with the police on several occasions; she is involved in a scheme for teaching adults to read.* □ **implicar; intervenir**
2 to make necessary: *going on holiday always involves a lot of expense and bother.* □ **traer consigo**
involved *adj.* intricate/complicated (style of writing): *a very involved sentence.* □ **enrevesado**
involvement *n.* contact/collaboration: *I think he regrets his involvement in the affair.* □ **participación**
invulnerable [in'vʌlnərəbl] *adj.* which cannot be successfully attacked: *they built the castle in an invulnerable position on the cliff.* □ **invulnerable**
inward ['inwəd] *adj.* on/to the inside: *inward-looking,* facing towards the inside. □ **interior; hacia dentro**
inwardly *adv.* on the inside: *he was inwardly afraid of the interview.* □ **en su interior**
inwards *adv.* towards the inside: *turn the edges of the sheet inwards towards the centre.* □ **hacia dentro**
iodine ['aiədi:n] *n.* (*chemical element*: I) substance which is used in solution as a disinfectant. □ **yodo**
ion ['aiən] *n.* atom with an electric charge. □ **ion**
ionize *v.* to produce ions; to become ions. □ **ionizar**
ionosphere [ai'ɔnəsfiə] *n.* part of the atmosphere surrounding the earth which reflects radio waves back to earth. □ **ionosfera**
iota [ai'outə] *n.* very small piece. □ **ápice**
IOU [aiou'ju:] *n.* paper promising that you will pay back money which you have borrowed. □ **un pagaré**
IQ ['ai'kju:] *abbreviation for* intelligence quotient: *he has a very low IQ,* his intelligence is lower than that of people of his age. □ **cociente intelectual**
Iran [i'rɑ:n] *n.* large country in the Middle East. □ **Irán**
Iranian [i'reinjən] *adj.* referring to Iran. □ **iranio, iraní**
■ *n.* person from Iran. □ **iraní**
Iraq [i'rɑ:k] *n.* large country in the Middle East. □ **Iraq**
Iraqi [i'rɑ:ki] *adj.* referring to Iraq. □ **iraquí**
■ *n.* (*pl. Iraqis*) person from Iraq. □ **iraquí**
irascible [i'ræsibl] *adj.* easily becoming angry. □ **irascible**
ire ['aiə] *n.* (*formal*) anger. □ **ira**
irate *adj.* very angry. □ **airado**
Ireland ['aiələnd] *n.* large island to the west of Britain. □ **Irlanda**
iridescent [iri'desnt] *adj.* with changing / shimmering colours. □ **iridescente**
iris ['aiəris] *n.* (*pl. irises*) **1** marsh or garden plant with tall flat leaves and usually purple flowers. □ **lirio**
2 part of the eye which is coloured. □ **iris**
Irish ['aiəriʃ] *adj.* referring to Ireland. □ **irlandés**
■ *n.* **1** language spoken in parts of Southern Ireland. □ **irlandés**
2 ***the Irish,*** people from Ireland. □ **los irlandeses**
Irishman, Irishwoman *n.* (*pl. Irishmen, Irishwomen*) person from Ireland. □ **irlandés, irlandesa**
irk [ə:k] *v.* to annoy/to bother. □ **fastidiar**
irksome *adj.* annoying/bothersome. □ **fastidioso**
iron ['aiən] *n.* and *adj.* (*chemical element*: Fe) **1** common grey metal which can be made into a magnet: *iron railings.* □ **hierro**
iron ore, iron in its natural state. □ **mineral de hierro**
pig iron, lumps of unrefined iron. □ **arrabio**
cast iron, (i) iron which has been melted and cast into a shape: *cast iron frying pan.* □ **hierro colado**
(ii) *cast iron excuse,* very good excuse. □ **excusa perfecta**
wrought iron, iron which has been twisted or beaten into a shape when it was hot. □ **hierro forjado**
corrugated iron, sheets of wavy metal used for roofs. □ **chapa ondulada**
Iron Age, period when man first used iron. □ **Edad de Hierro**
2 electric household instrument for smoothing the creases from clothes. □ **plancha**
steam iron, iron into which you pour water which makes steam and dampens the cloth to be pressed. □ **plancha de vapor**
3 *he spent three years in irons,* he was imprisoned for three years with iron chains round his ankles. □ **pasó tres años con grilletes**
4 metal frame to support a weak leg. □ **aparato ortopédico**
5 golf club with a metal head. □ **hierro**
■ *v.* to press cloth with an iron: *I have been ironing shirts all day.* □ **planchar**
to iron out *a problem/a difficulty,* to sort out a problem/difficulty. □ **allanar**
Iron Curtain *n.* **1** border between Communist countries in Eastern Europe and non-communist Western Europe. □ **Telón de Acero**
2 *to trade **behind the Iron Curtain,*** to trade with Communist countries of Eastern Europe. □ **el Telón de Acero**
the Iron Curtain countries, Communist countries of Eastern Europe. □ **los países del Telón de Acero**
ironing *n.* **1** pressing clothes with an electric iron. □ **planchado**
2 clothes which need pressing: *I have piles of ironing waiting to be done.* □ **plancha**
ironing board *n.* high, narrow table used for ironing clothes. □ **tabla de planchar**
ironmonger *n.* person who runs a hardware shop, selling tools, paint, pans, etc. □ **ferretero**
ironwork *n.* (decorative) locks/handles/gates, etc., made of iron. □ **carpintería metálica**
ironworks *n.* (*no pl.*) factory which produces iron. □ **fundición de hierro**
irony ['aiərəni] *n.* (*pl. ironies*) **1** way of referring to something where you say the opposite of what you mean: *there was a touch of irony in his voice.* □ **ironía**
2 quality of happening at the wrong moment, as if deliberately planned: *the irony of it is that after having nursed him she then fell ill herself,* the curious turn of events. □ **lo irónico de...**
ironic, ironical [ai'rɔnik(l)] *adj.* mocking/slightly funny: *ironical smile.* □ **irónico**

ironically *adv.* in a mocking way: *ironically enough, the result was the same.* □ **irónicamente**
irradiate [i'reidieit] *v.* (*of heat/light/rays*) to shine on (something). □ **irradiar**
irrational [i'ræʃnl] *adj.* not rational/not sensible/against common-sense: *an irrational decision.* □ **irracional**
irreconcilable [irekən'sailəbl] *adj.* which cannot be made to agree: *irreconcilable hatred; the two brothers are irreconcilable.* □ **irreconciliable**
irredeemable [iri'di:məbl] *adj.* (loss) which cannot be made good; (pledge) which cannot be redeemed. □ **irredimible**
irrefutable [iri'fju:təbl] *adj.* (argument) which cannot be disproved. □ **irrefutable**
irregular [i'regjulə] *adj.* **1** not regular; not level; not happening at the same time: *irregular heartbeat; irregular paving stones; the trains run at irregular intervals.* □ **irregular**
2 not according to the rules: *borrowing so much money from your firm is highly irregular.* □ **irregular**
irregular verb, verb which has forms which do not fit the usual patterns of grammar (such as *I go, I went, I have gone*). □ **verbo irregular**
■ *n. pl.* ***irregulars,*** soldiers who do not form part of the regular army. □ **soldados no regulares**
irregularity [iregju'læriti] *n.* (*pl. irregularities*) something which goes against the rules/the law: *we are investigating irregularities in the accounts.* □ **irregularidad**
irregularly *adv.* not regularly: *his heart was beating irregularly.* □ **de forma irregular**
irrelevant [i'reləvənt] *adj.* not relevant/which has no connection to the subject: *whether she is pretty or not is quite irrelevant as far as her job is concerned.* □ **no hace al caso**
irrelevance *n.* having no connection with the subject. □ **falta de pertinencia**
irreligious [iri'lidʒəs] *adj.* not religious; not showing respect for religion. □ **irreligioso**
irreparable [i'reprəbl] *adj.* which cannot be repaired: *the vandals did irreparable damage to the church.* □ **irreparable**
irreparably *adv.* in a way which cannot be repaired: *the roof was irreparably damaged by fire.* □ **irreparablemente**
irreplaceable [iri'pleisəbl] *adj.* which cannot be replaced; (something) for which there is no substitute: *those vases which were stolen were quite irreplaceable.* □ **irreemplazable**
irrepressible [iri'presəbl] *adj.* which cannot be held back: *an irrepressible laugh.* □ **irrefrenable**
irreproachable [iri'proutʃəbl] *adj.* perfect/which cannot be criticized: *his conduct has been irreproachable.* □ **irreprochable**
irresistible [iri'zistəbl] *adj.* which cannot be resisted; which you cannot help accepting: *she had an irresistible urge to throw a tomato at the speaker.* □ **irresistible**
irresolute [i'rezəlu:t] *adj.* undecided; (person) who hesitates/cannot decide. □ **irresoluto**
irresolutely *adv.* not knowing what to do: *he stood irresolutely on the empty station platform.* □ **de manera indecisa**
irrespective of [iri'spektiv 'ɔv] *prep. irrespective of the time,* no matter what time it is/taking no account of the time. □ **con independencia de**
irresponsible [iri'spɔnsəbl] *adj.* wild/senseless; not responsible. □ **irresponsable**
irresponsibly *adv.* with no sense of responsibility: *he has behaved irresponsibly with the club's money.* □ **irresponsablemente**
irretrievable [iri'tri:vəbl] *adj.* which cannot be found again. □ **irrecuperable**
irretrievably *adv. the game was irretrievably lost,* there was no hope of winning the game. □ **irreparablemente**
irreverent [i'revrənt] *adj.* not serious; disrespectful. □ **irreverente**
irreverently *adv.* not in a serious way; disrespectfully. □ **de modo irreverente**
irreversible [iri'və:səbl] *adj.* (decision) which cannot be altered. □ **irrevocable**
irrevocable [i'revəkəbl] *adj.* which cannot be changed: *an irrevocable decision.* □ **irrevocable**
irrigate ['irigeit] *v.* **1** to water (land) by using canals and pumps: *the farmers irrigate their fields with water from the river.* □ **regar**
2 to wash (a wound) with a flow of water. □ **irrigar**
irrigation [iri'geiʃn] *n.* watering of fields (by using canals and pumps): *the irrigation system in the area.* □ **riego**
irritate ['iriteit] *v.* **1** to annoy: *he was irritated by constant telephone calls.* □ **irritar**
2 to prickle/to burn: *an irritating rash.* □ **que escuece**
irritable ['iritəbl] *adj.* easily annoyed: *he gets irritable when his meals are late.* □ **irritable**
irritably *adv.* in a bad-tempered way. □ **de mal talante**
irritant *n.* something which annoys/causes a burning feeling. □ **agente irritante**
irritating *adj.* which annoys: *she has such an irritating laugh.* □ **irritante**
irritation [iri'teiʃn] *n.* annoyance; something which annoys/which causes a burning feeling. □ **irritación**
irruption [i'rʌpʃn] *n.* sudden appearance: *the irruption of several noisy guests into the party.* □ **irrupción**
is [iz] *v. see* **be.**
Islam ['izlæm] *n.* religion of the Muslims. □ **Islam**
Islamic *adj.* referring to Islam. □ **islámico**
island ['ailənd] *n.* piece of land entirely surrounded by water. □ **isla**
traffic island, small raised piece of pavement in the centre of the road where pedestrians can safely stand. □ **isleta**
islander *n.* person who lives on an island. □ **isleño**
isle [ail] *n.* island: *the British Isles.* □ **isla**
the Isle of Man, island in the Irish Sea, between England and Ireland. □ **la isla de Man**
islet *n.* small island. □ **islote**
isn't ['iznt] *v. short for* is not.
isobar ['aisouba:] *n.* line on a weather map showing places of equal barometric pressure. □ **isobara**
isolate ['aisəleit] *v.* **1** to put (something/someone) in a place alone: *we have to isolate the fever victims.* □ **aislar**
2 to separate (a chemical) substance from a compound. □ **aislar**
isolated *adj. an isolated farm house,* one with no other houses nearby; *an isolated attack,* a single attack, not repeated. □ **aislado**
isolation [aisə'leiʃn] *n.* cutting off from communication with other people. □ **aislamiento**
isolation hospital, hospital for people suffering from dangerous diseases. □ **hospital de contagiosos**
a policy of isolation, government policy of cutting communications with other countries. □ **una política de aislamiento**
isolationism *n.* policy of not communicating with

other countries. □ **aislacionismo**

isolationist *n.* person who advocates a policy of international isolation. □ **aislacionista**

isosceles [ai'sɔsili:z] *adj.* ***isosceles triangle,*** triangle with two sides the same length. □ **isósceles**

isotherm ['aisouθə:m] *n.* line on a weather map showing places with equal temperatures. □ **isoterma**

isotope ['aisətoup] *n.* one of two or more forms of a chemical element which have atoms which are chemically similar but with different atomic weights. □ **isótopo**

Israel ['izreil] *n.* country in the Near East, bordering on the Mediterranean. □ **Israel**

Israeli [iz'reili] *adj.* referring to Israel. □ **israelí**

■ *n.* (*pl. Israelis*) person from Israel. □ **israelí**

issue ['iʃu:] *n.* **1** result: *we are awaiting the issue of the debate.* □ **resultado**

2 problem: *I don't want to confuse the issue,* I don't want to mix everything up. □ **cuestión; asunto**

3 *he tried to make an issue of it,* he wanted to have a big discussion about it. □ **...hacer de un asunto tema de discusión**

the point at issue, the question which is being discussed. □ **...en cuestión**

4 *that is where we **take issue with** him,* where we disagree with him. □ **ahí es donde estamos en desacuerdo**

5 publication (of a book); putting on sale (new stamps); putting into circulation (new coins/notes); giving out (of uniforms/official permits, etc.). □ **publicación; emisión**

6 one copy of a newspaper or magazine: *I noted in last week's issue; in your issue of December 4th.* □ **número**

■ *v.* **1** to come out: *smoke was issuing from the windows.* □ **salir**

2 to put on sale (new stamps); to publish (books); to put (new banknotes) into circulation; to give out/to hand out (uniforms/official permits, etc.). □ **poner en circulación; publicar; emitir**

isthmus ['isməs] *n.* (*pl. isthmuses*) narrow piece of land connecting two larger pieces of land: *the Panama Isthmus.* □ **istmo**

it [it] *pronoun* referring to a thing **1** (standing in the place of thing just mentioned): *he grabbed an apple and took a bite out of it; I put my hat down somewhere and now I've lost it; where's my hat? - it's on the chair; let the dog in and give it something to eat.* □ **él, ella, ello; lo, la; le**

2 (referring to nothing in particular): *the worst of it is that he has no money left; they have had a bad time of it; who is it? - it's George; it's raining; it's Tuesday today; it's getting cold; it's absolute nonsense making arrangements like that.* □ **(–)**

now you're for it, (*informal*) now you are going to be in trouble. □ **ahora te vas a enterar**

italic [i'tælik] *adj.* and *n.* sloping (letter): *this is printed in italics.* □ **cursiva**

italicize [i'tælisaiz] *v.* to print in italics. □ **imprimir en letra cursiva**

Italy ['itəli] *n.* country in Southern Europe. □ **Italia**

Italian *adj.* referring to Italy. □ **italiano**

■ *n.* **1** person from Italy. □ **italiano**

2 language spoken in Italy. □ **italiano**

itch [itʃ] *n.* (*pl. itches*) tickling sensation: *I've got an itch.* □ **comezón**

■ *v.* **1** to tickle: *my nose is itching.* □ **picar**

2 *he's itching to get going,* he's very eager to get going. □ **tiene muchas ganas de...**

itching *n.* tickling sensation. □ **picor**

itchy *adj.* **1** tickly; making you feel you want to scratch. □ **que pica**

2 *he's getting **itchy feet,*** he wants to change jobs/ to travel. □ **es un culo de mal asiento**

item ['aitəm] *n.* thing (in a list): *how many items are there on the agenda?,* how many subjects are to be discussed? □ **ítem, punto**

items of clothing, pieces of clothing. □ **artículo**

news items, separate pieces of news on a news programme. □ **sueltos**

itemize *v.* to make a detailed list: *the missing articles are itemized on a separate sheet.* □ **detallar**

itinerary [i'tinərəri] *n.* (*pl. itineraries*) route; list of places to be visited on a tour: *we've drawn up our itinerary for our holiday in Scotland.* □ **itinerario**

itinerant *adj.* wandering/travelling. □ **ambulante**

itinerant musician, musician who travels from place to place. □ **músico ambulante**

its [its] *adj.* belonging to a thing/to it: *is the dog on its lead? here's the kettle, but where is its lid?* □ **su**

it's [its] *short for* it is/it has.

itself [it'self] *pronoun* referring to a thing/to it **1** (referring to an object): *a house standing all by itself; the dog has hurt itself.* □ **él/ella/ello mismo**

2 (for emphasis): *the wire is intact, so there must be something wrong with the television itself.* □ **mismo**

I've [aiv] *short for* I have.

ivory ['aivəri] *adj.* and *n.* (made of) whitish substance from an elephant's tusk: *ivory statue.* □ **marfil**

ivory tower, imaginary place where an intellectual can keep away from contact with the everyday world. □ **torre de marfil**

ivy ['aivi] *n.* (*pl. ivies*) evergreen plant which climbs up walls and trees. □ **hiedra**

J,j

J, j [dʒei] tenth letter of the alphabet. □ **J, j**
jab [dʒæb] *n.* **1** sharp blow (often with a pointed object): *she gave him a jab in the arm.* □ **pinchazo**
2 (*informal*) injection: *the doctor gave him a jab against typhoid/a typhoid jab.* □ **pinchazo**
■ *v.* (*he jabbed*) to poke firmly (especially with a pointed object): *he was jabbing (at) the blackboard with his pencil.* □ **señalar**
jabber ['dʒæbə] *n.* quick, indistinct talk: *all they could hear was a jabber of voices.* □ **algarabía**
■ *v.* to speak quickly and indistinctly: *he was jabbering away in French.* □ **chapurrear**
jack [dʒæk] *n.* **1** instrument for raising a heavy object (especially a motor vehicle): *always keep the jack in the boot of the car.* □ **gato**
2 (*in playing cards*) the card between the queen and the ten: *jack of hearts.* □ **sota; valet**
3 male of certain mammals: *jack hare.* □ **macho**
4 (*at bowls*) small white ball for players to aim at. □ **boliche**
5 flag. □ **pabellón (bandera de proa)**
the Union Jack, flag of the United Kingdom. □ **la bandera del Reino Unido**
jackboot *n.* high military boot. □ **bolta alta**
jackbooted *adj.* wearing jackboots: *jackbooted soldiers.* □ **...con botas altas**
jack-in-the-box *n.* box from which a toy figure springs up when the lid is opened. □ **caja sorpresa**
jack-knife *n.* (*pl. jack-knives*) type of large folding knife. □ **navaja**
■ *v.* (*of vehicle pulling a trailer*) to fold in half in an accident: *the lorry jack-knifed in the crash.* □ **colear, doblarse**
jack-of-all-trades *n.* person who is reasonably good at a large number of jobs. □ **factótum; manitas**
jack up *v.* **1** to raise with a jack: *he jacked up his car to change the wheel.* □ **levantar con el gato**
2 (*informal*) to raise (artificially): *they jacked up the profit by adding in other items.* □ **inflar**
jackal ['dʒækl] *n.* type of wild dog, which feeds chiefly on dead flesh. □ **chacal**
jackdaw ['dʒækdɔ:] *n.* type of small crow. □ **chova; grajilla**
jacket ['dʒækit] *n.* **1** short coat. □ **chaqueta**
2 outer casing or covering; loose paper cover for a book. □ **forro**
3 skin (of vegetable): *potatoes in their jackets,* cooked in their skins. □ **piel**
jacketed *adj.* with a jacket. □ **forrado**
jackpot ['dʒækpɔt] *n. to win the jackpot,* to win a high prize in a lottery/to enjoy particular success in something. □ **premio gordo**
Jacobean [dʒækəu'bi:ən] *adj.* referring to the time of James I (1601-1625). □ **de la época de Jacobo I**
Jacobite ['dʒækəbait] *adj.* and *n.* (person) who supported James II or his descendants in exile. □ **jacobita**
jade [dʒeid] *n.* hard, usually green, precious stone. □ **jade**
jade-green *adj.* of the bluish-green colour of jade. □ **verde jade**
jaded ['dʒeidəd] *adj.* worn out/tired. □ **reventado**
jag [dʒæg] *n.* (*slang*) drinking session: *they went on the jag.* □ **se fueron de juerga**
jagged ['dʒægid] *adj.* with an irregular, rough and usually spiky edge. □ **dentado; mellado**
jaguar ['dʒægjuə] *n.* type of large wild cat of Central and South America, related to the leopard. □ **jaguar**
jail [dʒeil] *n.* prison: *the rioters were held in the county jail.* □ **cárcel**
■ *v.* to put (someone) in prison: *he was jailed for two years.* □ **encarcelar**
jailbird *n.* person who has been sent to prison often. □ **preso reincidente**
jailer *n.* person who guards prisoners in a jail. □ **carcelero**
jalopy [dʒə'lɔpi] *n.* (*pl. jalopies*) (*informal*) old car. □ **cacharro**
jam [dʒæm] *n.* **1** stoppage/blockage caused by too many things in too small a space: *traffic jam.* □ **atasco**
2 (*informal*) difficult situation: *can he get himself out of the jam?* □ **aprieto**
3 sweet food made by boiling together fruit, sugar, etc.: *strawberry jam; he was eating a slice of bread and jam.* □ **mermelada; confitura**
money for jam, money very easily earned. □ **dinero fácil**
■ *v.* (*he jammed*) **1** (*of machine, etc.*) to stop/to stick so that it cannot move: *the brake has jammed; the hinges got jammed; he jammed on the brakes; he jammed his finger in the door.* □ **agarrotarse; se pilló los dedos...**
2 to crowd/to force into a small space: *they all jammed into the car; she jammed all her clothes into the bag.* □ **apretujarse (en un coche); meter hasta arriba (ropa)**
3 to make a radio broadcast impossible to understand by broadcasting noise on the same wavelength. □ **causar interferencia en**
jamming *n.* making a radio broadcast impossible to understand. □ **interferencia**
Jamaica [dʒə'meikə] *n.* island country in the Caribbean. □ **Jamaica**
Jamaican *adj.* referring to Jamaica. □ **jamaicano**
■ *n.* person from Jamaica. □ **jamaicano**
jamb [dʒæm] *n.* side post of a door, etc. □ **jamba**
jamboree [dʒæmbə'ri:] *n.* large meeting (especially of Scouts); big festival/party, etc. □ **'jamboree' (en los Scouts); fiesta**
jangle ['dʒæŋgl] *n.* harsh clanging noise: *there was a jangle of bells from the old steeple.* □ **cencerreo; hubo un repique de campanas...**
■ *v.* **1** to make a harsh clanging noise. □ **hacer sonar**
2 to disturb/to irritate (the nerves). □ **sacar de quicio**
janitor ['dʒænitə] *n.* caretaker, especially in a school or college. □ **conserje**
January ['dʒænjuəri] *n.* first month of the year: *my birthday is on January 6th.* □ **enero**
Japan [dʒə'pæn] *n.* country in the Far East. □ **Japón**
Japanese *adj.* referring to Japan. □ **japonés**
■ *n.* **1** (*no pl.*) person from Japan. □ **japonés**
2 language spoken in Japan. □ **japonés**
jar [dʒɑ:] *n.* container for jam, etc., often of glass and usually cylindrical: *a jar of jam; jam jar,* special jar for putting jam in. □ **tarro**

■ *v.* (*he jarred*) **1** to make a nasty/unpleasant sound: *the noise of the engine jarred on his ears.* □ **chirriar**
2 *to jar on someone's nerves,* to annoy. □ **ponerle a uno los nervios de punta**
3 to bump/to give a shock to. □ **chocar contra**
4 (*of colours, etc.*) to shock/to look unpleasant. □ **chocar**

jargon ['dʒɑːgən] *n.* special form of language used by a trade/profession or particular group of people: *the article is difficult to understand because it's full of scientific jargon.* □ **jerga**

jasmine ['dʒæzmin] *n.* shrub with sweet-smelling white or yellow flowers. □ **jazmín**

jasper ['dʒæspə] *n.* coloured quartz. □ **jaspe**

jaundice ['dʒɔːndis] *n.* sickness which makes the skin turn yellow, due to a disorder of the liver or bile. □ **ictericia**
jaundiced *adj.* **1** suffering from jaundice. □ **ictérico**
2 miserable/dispirited; envious; resentful: *to take a jaundiced view of things.* □ **amargado**

jaunt [dʒɔːnt] *n.* short excursion: *they went for a jaunt in their new car.* □ **fueron a dar una vuelta...**
jaunting car *n.* (*in Ireland*) light two-wheeled carriage. □ **tílburi irlandés**

jaunty ['dʒɔːnti] *adj.* cheerful/lively: *he wore his hat at a jaunty angle.* □ **garboso**
jauntily *adv.* cheerfully. □ **con desenvoltura**
jauntiness *n.* lively manner. □ **garbo**

javelin ['dʒævlin] *n.* type of long spear used in battle or in sport. □ **jabalina**

jaw [dʒɔː] *n.* **1** two hinged bones which allow the mouth to open and shut: *top jaw, upper jaw/bottom jaw, lower jaw,* bones in which the teeth are fixed. □ **mandíbula**
2 ***jaws,*** two parts of a tool which grip: *the jaws of a vice.* □ **garras, dientes**
■ *v.* (*informal*) to talk (too much). □ **hablar por los codos**
jawbone *n.* one of the two bones forming a jaw. □ **maxilar; quijada**

jay [dʒei] *n.* brightly coloured bird of the crow family. □ **arrendajo**
jaywalker *n.* pedestrian who does not take care when crossing the street. □ **peatón suicida**
jaywalking *n.* crossing a street without taking care. □ **cruce imprudente**

jazz [dʒæz] *n.* type of music with strong rhythm, originally played by American negroes. □ **jazz**
jazz up *v.* (*informal*) to make bright/attractive. □ **animar**

jealous ['dʒeləs] *adj.* feeling sorrow/anger because you want something someone else has got: *they're jealous of my long holidays.* □ **celoso; envidioso**
jealously *adv.* in a jealous way. □ **celosamente**
jealousy *n.* jealous feeling. □ **celos; envidia**

jeans [dʒiːnz] *n. pl.* (often blue) trousers made of a type of strong cotton. □ **vaqueros**

jeep [dʒiːp] *n.* trademark for a type of strongly built vehicle used for travelling over rough ground. □ **'jeep'**

jeer ['dʒiə] *n.* mocking/laughing in a nasty way: *the jeers of the crowd.* □ **abucheo**
■ *v.* to mock/to laugh at (someone) in a nasty way: *the crowd jeered when the player was sent off the field; they jeered at him.* □ **abuchear**

Jehovah [dʒi'həuvə] *n.* the God of Israel. □ **Jehová**

jell [dʒel] *v.* **1** (*of liquid*) to become a jelly: *the jam has begun to jell.* □ **cuajar**
2 (*of plan*) to become definite. □ **cuajar**
jelly ['dʒeli] *n.* (*pl. jellies*) **1** semi-solid substance, especially a type of sweet food made of gelatine/water/fruit flavouring, etc. □ **gelatina**
2 type of jam made of fruit juice boiled with sugar. □ **jalea**
jellied ['dʒelid] *adj.* cooked/preserved in a jelly: *jellied eels.* □ **en conserva**
jellybean *n. Amer.* sweet of coloured jelly shaped like a bean. □ **judía, pastilla**
jellyfish *n.* sea creature with jelly-like body. □ **medusa**
jelly roll *n. Amer.* swiss roll. □ **brazo de gitano**

jemmy ['dʒemi] *n.* (*pl. jemmies*) flat iron bar with a curved end, used by burglars to open doors or windows. □ **palanqueta**

jenny ['dʒeni] *n.* female donkey. □ **burra**

jeopardize ['dʒepədaiz] *v.* to put in danger/at risk: *the plans were jeopardized by his careless action.* □ **poner en peligro**
jeopardy ['dʒepədi] *n.* danger/risk: *all our plans were put in jeopardy.* □ **peligro**

jeremiad [dʒeri'maiəd] *n.* (*formal*) long complaining statement about your problems. □ **jeremiada**

jerk [dʒəːk] *n.* **1** sudden uneven movement; sharp pull. □ **tirón**
2 *Amer.* (*slang*) stupid person. □ **necio**
■ *v.* to make a sudden movement; to pull sharply: *she jerked the paper out of the box.* □ **sacar bruscamente**
jerkily *adv.* with an abrupt/sudden movement. □ **de un tirón**
jerky *adj.* abrupt/sudden. □ **espasmódico**

jerkin ['dʒəiːkin] *n.* short coat with no sleeves. □ **jubón; coleto sin mangas**

jerrican ['dʒerikæn] *n.* large metal container for water/petrol, etc. □ **bidón**

jerry-builder ['dʒeribildə] *n.* person who builds cheap, poorly constructed, buildings. □ **chapucero**
jerry-built *adj.* (building) which is cheaply built. □ **chapuza**

jersey ['dʒəːzi] *n.* **1** close-fitting upper garment, usually of wool or other warm material; special shirt of a football team, etc. □ **jersey; camiseta (equipo de fútbol)**
2 ***jersey (cloth),*** type of loosely woven, usually woollen, cloth. □ **tejido de punto**

jest [dʒest] *n.* joke; something done or said for amusement only: *spoken in jest.* □ **broma**
jester *n.* person who plays jokes, especially someone employed to do this at a royal court. □ **bufón**

jet [dʒet] *n.* **1** type of black mineral which can be highly polished. □ **azabache**
jet black, very black. □ **negro azabache**
2 long narrow spray of liquid or gas. □ **chorro**
3 opening to allow gas to escape: *gas jet.* □ **llama; mechero de gas**
4 jet-propelled aircraft: *he flies his own jet.* □ **reactor**
jet lag, tiredness felt by travellers who fly by jet across time zones. □ **cansancio por desfase horario**
jet set, wealthy people who frequently travel by jet. □ **'jet set'**
■ *v.* (*he jetted*) (*informal*) to travel by jet. □ **volar en reactor**
jet engine *n.* engine which is propelled by a jet. □ **reactor**
jet-propelled *adj.* pushed forward by a backward movement of jets of gas. □ **de propulsión a chorro**
jet propulsion *n.* being propelled forward by a backward movement of jets of gas. □ **propulsión a chorro**

jetsam ['dʒetsəm] *n.* things which have been thrown into the water from a boat. □ **echazón**
jettison ['dʒetizn] *v.* to throw (unwanted things) out from a ship/balloon, etc., to lighten it. □ **echar por la borda**
jetty ['dʒeti] *n.* (*pl. jetties*) wall built into the sea/into a river, where boats can tie up. □ **malecón; espigón**
Jew [dʒuː] *n.* person descended from the Hebrews of ancient Palestine. □ **judío**
Jewish *adj.* referring to Jews. □ **judío**
jewel ['dʒuəl] *n.* **1** precious stone. □ **piedra preciosa**
2 ornament, usually to be worn, made from precious stones and/or precious metals, or of imitation stones. □ **joya**
jeweller *n.* person who makes/sells jewellery. □ **joyero**
jewellery *n.* ornaments to be worn, made of precious stones/metals. □ **joyas; alhajas**
jib [dʒib] *n.* **1** triangular sail in the front of a boat. □ **foque**
2 projecting arm of a crane. □ **pescante; aguilón**
■ *v.* (*he jibbed*) **1** (*of horse*) to refuse (a fence etc.) □ **plantarse**
2 to refuse to do something: *he jibbed at having to go to town twice in one day.* □ **rehusar**
jibe [dʒaib] *n.* and *v.* *see* **gibe.**
jiffy ['dʒifi] *n.* (*informal*) very short time: *I'll be ready in a jiffy.* □ **santiamén**
jig [dʒig] *n.* **1** type of fast lively dance; music for this dance. □ **giga**
2 instrument for guiding a tool and holding the material being worked on. □ **guía**
■ *v.* (*he jigged*) to jump up and down; to move about jerkily. □ **dar saltitos**
jigger *n.* **1** small insect which lives in sand. □ **nigua**
2 measure for serving alcohol. □ **medida**
jigsaw *n.* **1** type of saw with very fine blade for cutting out shapes. □ **sierra de vaivén**
2 ***jigsaw (puzzle),*** puzzle of irregularly shaped pieces of wood/cardboard which when fitted together form a picture. □ **rompecabezas**
jiggle ['dʒigl] *v.* (*informal*) to move rapidly/nervously: *she was jiggling about in her chair.* □ **zangolotearse**
jilt [dʒilt] *v.* to (encourage and then) reject (a lover). □ **dejar plantado**
jingle ['dʒiŋgl] *n.* **1** sound made by small pieces of metal knocking together. □ **cascabeleo**
2 verse with a very simple rhyme and/or rhythm. □ **copla**
publicity jingle, catchy tune advertising a product. □ **anuncio comercial cantado**
■ *v.* to make a tinkling sound (like pieces of metal): *the keys were jingling about in the box; he jingled the keys round his fingers.* □ **tintinear**
jinks [dʒiŋks] *n. pl.* ***high jinks,*** wild amusement. □ **jolgorio**
jinx [dʒinks] *n.* (*pl. jinxes*) (*informal*) bad luck. □ **mala potra**
jitters ['dʒitəz] *n. pl.* ***to have the jitters,*** to be (unnecessarily) nervous/flustered. □ **entrar el canguelo**
jittery *adj.* nervous/flustered. □ **inquieto**
jive [dʒaiv] *n.* type of fast rhythmic dance; music for this dance. □ **'swing'**
■ *v.* to dance to jive music. □ **bailar el 'swing'**
job [dʒɔb] *n.* **1** piece of work. □ **trabajo**
to make a good job of something, to do it well. □ **hacer un buen trabajo**
it's a good job that, (*informal*) it's lucky that. □ **menos mal que...**
to give something up as a bad job, to stop making useless efforts to do something. □ **abandonar un cometido por inútil**
just the job, (*informal*) exactly what is needed. □ **es justo lo que necesitaba**
odd jobs, pieces of work, especially in the house: *odd job man,* person who does odd jobs. □ **tareas de casa**
2 difficult task: *I had a job to eat my meal,* it was difficult. □ **tarea ingrata**
3 position in employment: *he knows his job.* □ **...su cometido**
to be out of a job, to be unemployed. □ **estar parado**
jobs for the boys, giving of employment to your supporters, etc. □ **trabajo para los chicos**
4 (*informal*) crime, especially a theft: *an inside job.* □ **trabajo**
jobber *n.* person who buys and sells shares on behalf of someone else. □ **corredor de bolsa**
jobbing *adj.* (*of a workman*) (person) who is paid by the individual task: *jobbing gardener.* □ **a destajo**
job centre *n.* government offices which show vacant jobs which are available. □ **oficina de empleo**
jobless *adj.* with no job. □ **parado**
■ *n.* ***the jobless,*** people who have no jobs. □ **los parados**
job lot *n.* group of miscellaneous items sold together. □ **lote**
jockey ['dʒɔki] *n.* person who rides horses in races. □ **'jockey'; yóquey**
■ *v.* ***to jockey for position,*** to try to improve your position, especially by cheating or trickery. □ **maniobrar**
jocular ['dʒɔkjulə] *adj.* good humoured; treating things as a joke. □ **guasón**
jocularity [dʒɔkju'læriti] *n.* good humour. □ **jocosidad**
jocularly *adv.* in a joking way. □ **chistosamente**
jocund *adj.* (*formal*) cheerful. □ **jocundo**
jodhpurs ['dʒɔdpəz] *n. pl.* special trousers for horse riding which are narrow below the knee. □ **pantalones de montar**
jog [dʒɔg] *n.* **1** rather slow pace. □ **trote corto**
2 light blow, especially from the elbow. □ **codazo**
■ *v.* (*he jogged*) **1** to move at a steady, but rather slow pace: *we are jogging along,* we are progressing but not very quickly. □ **avanzar poco a poco**
2 to run at an easy pace, especially for exercise. □ **hacer 'jogging'**
3 to shake/to push lightly: *he jogged my elbow.* □ **darle en el codo a uno suavemente**
4 ***to jog someone's memory:*** *it jogged his memory,* it made him remember. □ **le refrescó la memoria**
jogger *n.* person who jogs as a form of exercise. □ **'jogger'**
jogging *n.* running at an easy pace for exercise. □ **'jogging'**
jogtrot *n.* rather slow, easy pace: *they moved along at a jogtrot.* □ **a trote corto**
join [dʒɔin] *n.* place/line where two things come together. □ **juntura**
■ *v.* **1** to come together/to be united; to bring together: *the two roads join a mile ahead; join the two pieces of string together.* □ **juntar, juntarse**
2 to (meet and) go along with; to do something together: *will you join us for a cup of coffee? my wife joins with me in thanking you for your good wishes.* □ **unirse a**
to join forces, to do something by combined effort. □ **aliarse, unir fuerzas**
3 to become a member of: *to join the tennis club/*

the Labour Party. □ **hacerse socio de un club; ingresar en un partido**
joiner *n.* person who constructs things from wood, especially furniture and house fittings. □ **carpintero; ebanista**
joinery *n.* joiner's trade. □ **carpintería**
join in *v.* to take part. □ **tomar parte en**
join up *v.* to become a member of the armed forces. □ **alistarse**
joint [dʒɔint] *n.* **1** (place where) two or more pieces are attached, especially in building or carpentry. □ **junta (metal); ensambladura (madera)**
2 place where bones come together, allowing movement: *elbow joint.* □ **articulación**
out of joint, dislocated. □ **dislocado**
3 large piece of meat, especially for roasting. □ **corte para asar; un cuarto**
4 (*informal*) low class night club or gambling den. □ **garito**
5 (*slang*) cigarette containing marijuana. □ **porro**
■ *v.* **1** to cut up (a chicken, etc.) into pieces. □ **descuartizar**
2 to provide with joints. □ **ensamblar**
■ *adj.* together/combined; shared by two or more. □ **en común**
joint account, bank account shared by two people. □ **cuenta corriente conjunta**
joint author, author who writes a book with another. □ **coautor**
joint statement, made by two or more people or groups. □ **declaración conjunta**
jointed *adj.* having joints. □ **articulado**
jointly *adv.* together; by combined effort. □ **conjuntamente**
joist [dʒɔist] *n.* beam which supports a ceiling or floorboards. □ **vigueta**
joke [dʒouk] *n.* something said or done for amusement, to cause laughter. □ **chiste**
practical joke, action which makes someone uncomfortable for the amusement of others. □ **broma pesada**
■ *v.* to tell or make jokes; to say or do something for amusement or to make it seem less important: *she's always joking; he joked about his illness; I was only joking,* I did not mean it seriously. □ **bromear**
joker *n.* **1** person who jokes. □ **bromista**
2 extra card in a pack used as a bonus in certain games. □ **comodín**
jokingly *adv.* in a joking way. □ **en broma**
jolly ['dʒɔli] *adj.* merry/happy. □ **jovial**
■ *adv.* (*informal*) very: *I'm jolly glad I came; it was jolly cold yesterday.* □ **me alegro mucho...; hizo bastante frío ayer**
■ *v.* (*jollied; jolliying*) ***to jolly someone along,*** (*informal*) to encourage someone by keeping him happy. □ **animar**
jollification [dʒɔlifi'keiʃn] *n.* enjoyment/being jolly. □ **alegría**
jollity *n.* merriness. □ **jolgorio**
jolt [dʒoult] *n.* abrupt shake/shock; violent jerk. □ **sacudida**
■ *v.* **1** to move with a jumping movement: *the car jolted along.* □ **traquetear**
2 to push/to shake abruptly. □ **dar un empujón**
3 to give a sudden shock to: *the accident jolted her out of her easy way of life.* □ **hizo que saliera bruscamente...**
joss stick ['dʒɔsstik] *n.* oriental stick with incense painted on it, which burns slowly giving off a pleasant smell. □ **pebete perfumado**
jostle ['dʒɔsl] *v.* to push/to bump (especially with the elbows); to push your way (through a crowd, etc.): *they were jostling their way to the other side of the hall.* □ **abrirse paso a codazos**
jot [dʒɔt] *n.* very small amount: *I don't care a jot.* □ **pizca; no me importa un bledo**
■ *v.* (*he jotted*) ***to jot something down,*** to make (quick) notes about something. □ **apuntar**
jotter *n.* small pad of paper for making notes. □ **bloc**
jottings *n. pl.* (random) notes. □ **apuntes**
joule [dʒu:l] *n.* standard unit of work and energy. □ **julio**
journal ['dʒə:nl] *n.* **1** diary. □ **diario**
2 periodical, especially on a learned subject. □ **revista especializada**
3 book for recording each day's business. □ **diario**
journalese [dʒə:nə'li:z] *n.* style of language used by bad journalists. □ **estilo periodístico malo**
journalism ['dʒə:nəlizəm] *n.* profession of writing for newspapers or periodicals. □ **periodismo**
journalist *n.* person who writes for newspapers or periodicals. □ **periodista**
journey ['dʒə:ni] *n.* **1** long trip: *he went on a journey across Russia.* □ **viaje**
2 long distance travelled: *it's two days' journey from here.* □ **son dos días de viaje**
■ *v.* (*formal*) to make a long trip. □ **viajar**
jovial ['dʒouviəl] *adj.* good-humoured/merry. □ **jovial**
joviality [dʒouvi'æliti] *n.* good humour. □ **jovialidad**
jovially *adv.* in a merry way. □ **jovialmente**
jowl [dʒaul] *n.* jaw/cheek. □ **mandíbula/carrillo**
cheek by jowl, very close together. □ **cara a cara**
joy [dʒɔi] *n.* (cause of) very great happiness. □ **alegría**
joyful *adj.* very happy. □ **alegre**
joyfully *adv.* very happily. □ **alegremente**
joyless *adj.* very sad: *owing to the bad news the outing was a joyless occasion.* □ **sin alegría**
joyride *n.* excursion for pleasure, especially in a stolen car. □ **paseo en coche (sin permiso del dueño)**
joystick *n.* rod which controls the movements of an aircraft. □ **palanca de mando**
jubilant ['dʒu:bilənt] *adj.* full of happiness/triumph. □ **jubiloso**
jubilantly *adv.* triumphantly. □ **jubilosamente**
jubilation [dʒu:bi'leiʃn] *n.* great happiness/triumph. □ **júbilo**
jubilee ['dʒu:bili:] *n.* (celebration of the) anniversary of an important event. □ **aniversario**
silver/golden/diamond jubilee, celebration twenty-five/fifty/sixty years after an event took place. □ **de plata/oro/diamantes**
Judaism ['dʒu:deiizm] *n.* religion of the Jews. □ **judaísmo**
judder ['dʒʌdə] *v.* (*usually of a machine*) to shake. □ **vibrar**
judge [dʒʌdʒ] *n.* **1** person appointed to make decisions, especially in a higher court of law. □ **juez**
2 person who decides which is the best entry in a competition, etc. □ **juez**
3 person with good judgement: *he's a good judge of character; you are the best judge of that.* □ **árbitro**
■ *v.* **1** to make decisions in a court of law/competition, etc. □ **juzgar (ley); arbitrar (deporte)**
2 to have as your opinion; to estimate: *I judge him to be the best.* □ **considerar**
judgement *n.* **1** making a decision. □ **juicio**
2 sentence of a court; legal decision. □ **fallo; sentencia**
3 ability to see things clearly/to make good decisions: *to have good judgement; I did it against my*

better judgement, although I felt it was not the right thing to do. □ **criterio**

judicial [dʒuːˈdiʃl] *adj.* referring to a legal process/to a court of law: *judicial inquiry.* □ **judicial**

judicature [ˈdʒuːdikətʃə] *n.* all the judges in a country. □ **judicatura**

judicially *adv.* legally. □ **judicialmente**

judiciary [dʒuːˈdiʃəri] *n.* all the judges in a country. □ **poder judicial**

judicious *adj.* based on/having good judgement: *a judicious choice.* □ **juicioso**

judiciously *adv.* in a well judged way. □ **juiciosamente**

judo [ˈdʒuːdou] *n.* (*no pl.*) form of Japanese wrestling. □ **judo**

jug [dʒʌg] *n.* **1** container with a handle, used for pouring liquids: *milk jug.* □ **jarra**

2 (*slang*) jail. □ **talego**

jugged hare *n.* hare soaked in wine and cooked slowly. □ **civet de liebre**

juggernaut [ˈdʒʌgənɔːt] *n.* **1** overpowering force to which people sacrifice themselves. □ **fuerza inexorable**

2 (*informal*) very large lorry. □ **camión articulado**

juggle [ˈdʒʌgl] *v.* **1** to throw several objects in the air and keep them there. □ **hacer juegos malabares**

2 to change things around very quickly, especially in order to deceive: *they juggled with the figures in order to prove their case.* □ **escamotear**

juggler *n.* person who juggles. □ **malabarista**

jugular [ˈdʒʌgjuːlə] *n.* main vein in the neck. □ **yugular**

juice [dʒuːs] *n.* **1** liquid from fruit/vegetables/meat, etc.: *lemon juice.* □ **zumo (fruta); jugo (carne)**

to stew in your own juice, to suffer the consequences of your own mistakes. □ **pagar los propios errores**

2 (*informal*) petrol; electricity. □ **gasolina; electricidad**

juiciness *n.* state of being full of juice. □ **jugosidad**

juicy *adj.* full of juice: *a juicy orange.* □ **jugoso**

juju [ˈdʒuːdʒuː] *n.* African magic charm. □ **grisgrís**

jujube [ˈdʒuːdʒuːb] *n.* type of soft sweet. □ **pastilla de azufaifa**

jukebox [ˈdʒuːkbɔks] *n.* coin-operated record-playing machine. □ **máquina de discos**

julep [ˈdʒuːləp] *n. Amer.* drink made of alcohol and water, usually with a mint flavour. □ **julepe**

July [dʒuˈlai] *n.* seventh month of the year: *my birthday is in July/is on July 5th.* □ **julio**

jumble [ˈdʒʌmbl] *n.* mixture/confusion. □ **revoltijo**

jumble sale, sale of second-hand goods, usually for charity. □ **venta benéfica**

■ *v.* to mix; to confuse. □ **mezclar**

jumbo [ˈdʒʌmbou] *n.* (*pl. jumbos*) **1** child's name for an elephant. □ **elefante**

2 anything very large. □ **coloso**

3 *jumbo jet,* very large aircraft holding several hundred people. □ **jumbo**

jump [dʒʌmp] *n.* **1** leap (in the air). □ **salto**

long jump/high jump, (*in sports*) competition to see how far/how high you can leap. □ **salto de longitud/de altura**

2 sudden movement: *he gave a jump when the door banged.* □ **salto**

3 (*in sports*) obstacle to be jumped over: *the horse cleared the third jump* □ **obstáculo**

■ *v.* **1** to move suddenly, especially upwards: *he jumped up in the air.* □ **saltar**

prices jumped, they rose suddenly. □ **los precios subieron**

2 to move by jumping: *to jump down from the wall; to jump over the stream.* □ **bajar de un salto; salvar la corriente**

3 to make a sudden movement, especially from some emotion: *to jump for joy; the banging of the door made me jump,* frightened me. □ **saltar de alegría**

4 ***to jump the gun,*** to begin before your turn/before the correct time. □ **salir antes de tiempo**

5 ***to jump the queue,*** to go ahead of your turn. □ **colarse**

jumped-up *adj.* (person) who has been promoted faster than his qualities merit: *a jumped-up office boy.* □ **trepador**

jumper *n.* **1** person who jumps. □ **saltador**

2 warm knitted upper garment. □ **jersey**

jump jet *n.* aircraft which can take off vertically. □ **avión de despegue vertical**

jump lead *n.* cable which allows two car batteries to be connected to help a car to start. □ **cables de batería**

jump rope *n. Amer.* skipping rope. □ **comba**

jumpy *adj.* (*informal*) nervous; excited. □ **asustadizo**

junction [ˈdʒʌŋkʃn] *n.* joining (place), especially of railway lines/roads. □ **cruce (carretera); empalme (vía férrea)**

juncture [ˈdʒʌŋktʃə] *n.* (*formal*) point in time. □ **coyuntura**

at this juncture, at this point in the situation. □ **en esta coyuntura**

June [dʒuːn] *n.* sixth month of the year: *his birthday is in June/is on June 15th.* □ **junio**

jungle [ˈdʒʌŋgl] *n.* **1** thick impassable tropical forest. □ **selva; jungla**

2 confused mass; place or circumstances where progress is difficult: *jungle of little huts.* □ **maraña; poblacho**

blackboard jungle, schools with uncontrollable pupils. □ **colegio de salvajes**

junior [ˈdʒuːniə] *adj.* **1** younger: *J. Smith Junior,* son of J. Smith Senior. □ **joven; juvenil; hijo**

2 for younger children: *junior sports.* □ **deportes para los pequeños**

junior school, school for children from 7 to 11 years old. □ **escuela de enseñanza primaria**

3 lower in rank: *junior officers.* □ **subalterno**

■ *n.* **1** person who is younger/lower in rank: *he is my junior by five years.* □ **le llevo cinco años**

2 *Amer.* third-year student. □ **estudiante de tercer año**

juniper [ˈdʒuːnipə] *n.* type of shrub with evergreen leaves and dark berries, used as flavouring for gin. □ **enebro**

junk [dʒʌŋk] *n.* **1** type of large Chinese sailing boat. □ **junco**

2 useless articles/rubbish: *junk heap.* □ **porquería**

3 (inferior) second-hand goods: *junk shop.* □ **chamarilería**

4 (*slang*) drugs, especially heroin. □ **droga, caballo (heroína)**

junkie *n.* (*slang*) drug addict. □ **'yonqui'; drogata**

junket [ˈdʒʌŋkit] *n.* **1** sweet food made of curdled milk. □ **dulce de leche cuajada**

2 feast/celebration. □ **fiesta**

3 pleasure trip made by an official at public expense. □ **excursión con fondos públicos**

■ *v.* to have a celebration, especially by eating and drinking: *after the conference they all went junketing.* □ **festejar**

junta [ˈdʒʌntə] *n.* group of soldiers who seize power and rule a country. □ **junta militar**

jurisdiction [dʒuəris'dikʃn] *n.* (legal) power. □ **jurisdicción**

jurisprudence [dʒuəris'pru:dəns] *n.* study of the law. □ **jurisprudencia**

jury ['dʒuəri] *n.* (*pl. juries*) **1** group of citizens sworn to decide a verdict on the strength of evidence in a court of law. □ **jurado**
2 group of judges in a competition, etc. □ **jurado**
juror, juryman *n.* (*pl. jurymen*) member of a jury. □ **miembro del jurado**

just [dʒʌst] *adj.* showing no favour; true/correct: *just treatment; just anger.* □ **justo**
■ *adv.* **1** exactly; very nearly/almost: *just by the door; not just yet; just how many?* □ **justo en la puerta; ahora mismo no; ¿cuántos exactamente?**
it's just about ready, almost ready. □ **está casi listo**
that's just it, that is exactly the problem. □ **eso es precisamente**
2 (used to indicate the immediate past or future): *he's just arrived; I'm just going; the book is just out,* recently published. □ **acaba de llegar; ya voy**
3 only: *just a minute! just once; just listen; we're just good friends.* □ **¡un momento!; sólo**
4 ***just now,*** (i) at the present moment: *he's very busy just now.* □ **...en este momento**
(ii) a short time ago: *I saw him just now.* □ **le he visto hace un momento**
5 ***just as,*** (i) exactly when: *I got it just as I was leaving.* □ **precisamente cuando**
(ii) exactly in the manner that: *it is just as good as it seems.* □ **es exactamente tan bueno como parece**
justly *adv.* fairly; with justice: *he was justly treated; she was justly famous,* she deserved to be famous. □ **con justicia; justamente**
justness *n.* fairness. □ **equidad**

justice ['dʒʌstis] *n.* **1** quality of being fair: *there's no justice.* □ **justicia**
to do justice to: *he did justice to the meal,* he ate it with the enjoyment it deserved. □ **hizo los debidos honores a la comida**
to do justice to someone/to do someone justice: *the portrait doesn't do her justice,* it is not a good likeness. □ **...no la favorece**
2 ***to bring someone to justice,*** to bring legal proceedings against him. □ **llevar a uno ante los tribunales**
3 (*especially as title*) judge/magistrate: *Mr Justice Simmons; Justice of the Peace.* □ **el magistrado Sr...; juez de paz**

justify ['dʒʌstifai] *v.* (*justified; justifying*) to show that something is fair/to prove that something is right: *to justify one's actions; his aims were justified by the results.* □ **justificar**
justifiable *adj.* which can be justified. □ **justificable**
justification [dʒʌstifi'keiʃn] *n.* reason which shows that something is fair. □ **justificación**

jut [dʒʌt] *v.* (*it jutted*) to stick out, usually horizontally: *the plank was jutting out from the wall.* □ **sobresalir**

jute [dʒu:t] *n.* fibre of plants used for making sacks, etc. □ **yute**

juvenile ['dʒu:vənail] *adj.* of/for young people: *juvenile books.* □ **juvenil**
juvenile delinquent, young person who is guilty of a crime. □ **delincuente juvenil**
■ *n.* young person. □ **joven**

juxtapose [dʒʌkstə'pouz] *v.* to place side by side/very close together. □ **yuxtaponer**
juxtaposition [dʒʌkstəpə'ziʃn] *n.* being side by side/very close together. □ **yuxtaposición**

K,k

K, k [kei] eleventh letter of the alphabet. □ **K, k**
kale [keil] *n.* (*no pl.*) type of cabbage with wrinkled leaves: *a field of kale.* □ **col rizada**
kaleidoscope [kə'laidəskoup] *n.* toy made of a tube with mirrors which reflect small pieces of coloured glass and make patterns which can be seen through a viewer. □ **calidoscopio**
kaleidoscopic [kəlaidə'skɔpik] *adj.* like a kaleidoscope, with bright changing colours; frequently changing. □ **calidoscópico**
kangaroo [kæŋgə'ru:] *n.* Australian animal, which carries its young in a pouch. □ **canguro**
kangaroo court, illegal court set up by terrorists/strikers, etc., to judge one of their members. □ **tribunal ilegal**
kaolin ['keiəlin] *n.* fine white clay, used for making porcelain, and sometimes in medicine. □ **caolín**
kapok ['keipɔk] *n.* kind of cotton wool, used for stuffing cushions, etc. □ **miraguano**
kaput [kə'put] *adj.* (*informal*) finished; broken. □ **'kaput'**
karat ['kærət] *n. Amer.* measure of purity of gold: *18-karat gold.* □ **quilate**
karate [kə'rɑ:ti] *n.* Japanese style of fighting, where you hit with the side of the hand. □ **karate**
kayak ['kaiæk] *n.* **1** Eskimo canoe, covered with sealskins □ **kayac**
2 small canoe with a narrow opening for the canoeist. □ **kayac**
kebab [ki'bæb] *n.* small cubes of meat grilled on a skewer. □ **'kebab'; brocheta**
kedgeree [kedʒə'ri:] *n.* spicy mixture of rice, fish and eggs. □ **'kedgeree'**
keel [ki:l] *n.* lowest timber in a ship, on which the framework is built. □ **quilla**
on an even keel, stable/steady. □ **en equilibrio**
■ *v.* ***to keel over,*** to fall over: *one blow from the champion made his opponent keel over.* □ **desplomarse**
keen [ki:n] *adj.* (*keener, keenest*) **1** eager/willing: *he was keen to win the race.* □ **estaba deseoso de...**
to be keen on: *he's keen on rowing,* very enthusiastic about rowing. □ **es muy aficionado al remo**
2 sharp: *his knife had a keen blade.* □ **afilado**
3 sensitive/acute: *she has a keen sense of smell; he has a keen ear for a wrong note.* □ **...olfato sensible; ...oído fino**
4 *keen prices,* (*informal*) very competitive prices. □ **precios ajustados**
keenly *adv.* sharply: *he was keenly disappointed.* □ **profundamente**
keep [ki:p] *n.* **1** central tower/strongest part of a castle. □ **torre del homenaje**
2 maintenance. □ **subsistencia**
to earn one's keep: *she doesn't earn her keep,* she doesn't earn enough money to pay for her food and lodging. □ **...el sustento**
3 ***for keeps,*** (*informal*) for ever: *the ring was hers for keeps.* □ **para siempre**
■ *v.* (*he kept*) **1** to continue to have/to possess: *he's kept my watch; can I keep the receipt?* □ **quedarse con**
2 to continue to do something: *the watch will keep going even under water; he kept running to avoid the police.* □ **continuar**
3 to pay regard to: *he kept his promise; she kept to her word; you must keep your appointment.* □ **mantener**
4 to own/to manage: *he kept bees; the farmer keeps cattle.* □ **dedicarse a la cría de**
5 to maintain: *the road was badly kept.* □ **conservar**
6 ***to keep open house:*** *she keeps open house,* everyone is welcome at her house. □ **tiene la casa abierta a todos**
7 to support financially: *she has her aged parents to keep.* □ **mantener**
8 to have for sale: *we always keep bread in stock.* □ **tener a la venta**
9 to detain/to restrain: *the prisoner was kept in jail; don't let me keep you.* □ **mantener**
10 to conceal: *keep this information to yourself; she keeps nothing from me.* □ **guardar**
11 to reserve: *I'll keep a place for you.* □ **guardar**
12 to prevent: *the noise of the traffic kept him from sleeping.* □ **no dejar**
13 to remain. □ **quedar(se)**
14 *let's* ***keep in touch,*** we mustn't lose contact with each other. □ **no perdamos el contacto**
15 ***to keep (someone) company:*** *she kept him company,* she stayed with him. □ **le hizo compañía**
16 *to keep a diary,* to write notes every day about what you have done. □ **llevar un diario**
17 to continue to stay in good condition: *raspberries don't keep,* go rotten quickly. □ **conservarse**
keeper *n.* **1** person in charge of animals in a zoo; person in charge of a museum. □ **guarda (zoo); conservador (museo)**
2 fruit which stays in good condition for a long time. □ **fruta que se conserva bien**
keeping *n.* **1** custody: *she gave her jewels to the bank manager for safe keeping.* □ **custodia**
2 ***in keeping with,*** in harmony with: *the carpets are in keeping with the rest of the furnishings.* □ **de acuerdo con**
keep in with *v.* to stay on friendly terms with (someone): *it's useful to keep in with the manager.* □ **llevarse bien**
keep on *v.* **1** to continue to do something: *although the policeman shouted at him to stop he just kept on running.* □ **seguir**
2 (*informal*) to criticize without stopping: *she keeps on at me about painting the kitchen,* she tells me all the time that I should paint the kitchen. □ **dar la vara**
keepsake *n.* memento; thing kept to remind you of the giver. □ **recuerdo**
keep up *v.* to continue: *keep up the good work! she kept up her studies; to keep up appearances.* □ **continuar; mantener las apariencias**
keep up with *v.* **1** to keep yourself informed about: *he kept up with the latest events.* □ **mantenerse al tanto**
2 to go forward at the same pace: *the runners couldn't keep up with the leaders in the race; his salary did not keep up with the cost of living.* □ **seguir el paso**
3 *we try* ***to keep up with the times,*** we try to keep our outlook up-to-date. □ **mantenerse al día**
4 ***to keep up with the Jones's,*** to try to maintain the same social level as your neighbours. □ **no querer ser menos**

keg [keg] *n.* small barrel, often containing beer. □ **barrilete**
kelp [kelp] *n.* (*no pl.*) kind of large seaweed. □ **varec, alga**
kelvin ['kelvin] *n.* standard unit of temperature. □ **kelvin**
ken [ken] *n.* knowledge. □ **saber**
beyond our ken, out of our normal range of knowledge. □ **ser incomprensible para uno**
■ *v.* (*he kenned*) (*in Scotland*) to know. □ **saber**
kennel ['kenl] *n.* shelter for a dog. □ **perrera**
kennels, place where dogs can be left when their owners go away/where dogs are bred. □ **hotel de perros/criadero**
■ *v.* (*he kennelled*) to keep in a kennel: *the dog was kennelled in the yard.* □ **encerrar el perro**
Kenya ['kenjə] *n.* country in Eastern Africa. □ **Kenia**
Kenyan *adj.* referring to Kenya. □ **keniata**
■ *n.* person from Kenya. □ **keniata**
kept [kept] *v. see* **keep.**
kerb [kə:b] *n.* stone edging to a pavement/path. □ **bordillo**
kerchief ['kə:tʃ'if] *n.* large square scarf worn over your head. □ **pañuelo**
kernel ['kə:nl] *n.* **1** softer part inside the hard shell of a nut. □ **almendra**
2 essential part/centre: *the kernel of the matter.* □ **el meollo de la cuestión**
kerosene ['kerəsi:n] *n.* paraffin. □ **queroseno**
kestrel ['kestrəl] *n.* type of small falcon. □ **cernícalo**
ketch [ketʃ] *n.* (*pl. ketches*) two-masted sailing boat. □ **queche**
ketchup ['ketʃəp] *n.* sauce made from tomatoes and spices. □ **'ketchup'**
kettle ['ketl] *n.* metal container, with a lid and a spout, used for boiling water. □ **hervidor**
a pretty kettle of fish, an awkward state of affairs. □ **bonito lío**
kettle-drum *n.* large drum with a round bottom. □ **timbal**
key [ki:] *n.* **1** piece of metal, usually iron or brass, for turning locks: *I've lost the key to the front door.* □ **llave**
2 solution/explanation: *the key to the crossword puzzle was printed beside it; the key to the symbols on a map.* □ **solución; clave**
3 *he's the keyman,* the most important man; *she was the key witness in the trial.* □ **hombre clave**
4 system of musical notes related to each other: *he sang the song in a lower key; the concerto was in the key of A major.* □ **tono**
5 part of a piano/flute/typewriter, etc., which you press down to make the instrument work. □ **tecla**
6 seed case, shaped like a key: *sycamore key.* □ **vaina**
■ *v.* to link to/to make suitable for: *the factory is keyed to the production of military equipment.* □ **estar acondicionado**
keyboard *n.* set of keys on a piano, etc.: *I need a typewriter with a French keyboard,* with letters, numbers, accents, etc., arranged in the French manner. □ **teclado**
keyed up *adj.* nervous/tense (before an examination/a battle, etc.). □ **excitado**
keyhole *n.* hole in a lock into which a key is put. □ **ojo de la cerradura**
keynote *n.* **1** dominating musical note. □ **nota tónica**
2 main theme in a speech. □ **tema central**
keynote speech, main speech (at a conference). □ **discurso principal**
key ring *n.* ring for carrying several keys together. □ **llavero**
key stone *n.* central supporting block of stone or brick in an arch; important idea on which everything else is based. □ **clave; piedra angular**
khaki ['kɑ:ki] *adj.* and *n.* dull yellow-brown (colour); the colour of soldiers' uniforms. □ **caqui**
kibbutz [ki'bu:ts] *n.* (*pl. kibbutzim*) farming settlement in Israel. □ **kibutz**
kibosh ['kaibɔʃ] *n.* ***to put the kibosh on something,*** (*informal*) to stop something happening. □ **acabar con algo de una vez**
kick [kik] *n.* **1** blow with the foot: *he gave the man a savage kick.* □ **patada**
2 (*informal*) thrill/excitement: *I get a kick out of watching our local team win.* □ **alegría, emoción**
3 *he did it* ***for kicks,*** to give himself a thrill. □ **me lo paso bomba viendo a...**
■ *v.* to strike with the foot: *the angry footballer kicked the referee; kicking and screaming, he was dragged away.* □ **dar una patada**
kickback *n.* (*slang*) bribe/illegal commission paid to someone who helps a business deal. □ **mordida; unto**
kick off *v.* to start a game of football: *they kicked off at 2.30.* □ **empezar**
kick-off *n.* start (of a football game): *the kick-off is at 2.30.* □ **inicio del juego**
kick up *v.* (*informal*) to make (a fuss/a row). □ **armar un lío**
kid [kid] *n.* **1** young goat. □ **cabrito**
2 (*informal*) child. □ **chaval**
■ *v.* (*he kidded*) (*informal*) **1** to make (someone) believe something that is not true: *he kidded his teacher that he'd been ill.* □ **meter una trola**
2 *I'm only kidding,* I don't mean it. □ **lo digo en broma**
no kidding?, is it really true? □ **¿en serio?**
kiddy *n.* (*pl. kiddies*) (*informal*) child. □ **chaval**
kidnap ['kidnæp] *v.* (*he kidnapped*) to steal (a child); to carry (a person) off by force illegally: *the millionaire's daughter was kidnapped last week.* □ **secuestrar**
kidnapper *n.* person who kidnaps. □ **secuestrador**
kidnapping *n.* carrying off a person by force: *there have been three kidnappings in this town.* □ **secuestro**
kidney ['kidni] *n.* one of a pair of organs in animals that extract impurities from the blood. □ **riñón**
kidney bean, type of bean with reddish seeds. □ **alubia pinta**
kidney machine, device by which a patient's blood can be purified when his kidneys do not function properly. □ **riñón artificial**
kill [kil] *n.* putting an animal to death for sport. □ **matar**
to be in at the kill, to be there at the end of the competition. □ **llegar a la final**
■ *v.* **1** to put to death; to make (someone/an animal/a plant) die: *St George killed the dragon; the frost has killed the tomato plants.* □ **matar**
2 *he was killing himself with laughter,* he was laughing very heartily. □ **se moría de risa**
3 ***to kill time,*** to fill in time/to make time pass more quickly. □ **matar el tiempo**
4 ***to kill two birds with one stone,*** to get two successful results from one action. □ **matar dos pájaros de un tiro**
5 *my feet are killing me,* (*informal*) my feet hurt. □ **me están matando**
killer *n.* person who kills: *the killer struck twice in one week.* □ **asesino**

killer whale, medium-sized black and white carnivorous whale. □ **orca**
killing *n.* putting to death: *the killing of elephants is a crime.* □ **matanza**
kill-joy *n.* someone who spreads gloom on a happy occasion. □ **aguafiestas**
kill off *v.* to get rid of (a pest, etc.) by killing: *the locusts were killed off by a new chemical.* □ **exterminar**
kiln [kiln] *n.* oven for baking pottery or bricks: *the clay pots were fired in a kiln.* □ **horno**
kilo ['ki:lou] *n.* (*pl. kilos*) kilogram. □ **kilo**
kilocycle ['kiləsaikl] *n.* one thousand cycles as a frequency of radio waves. □ **kilociclo**
kilogram ['kiləgræm] *n.* standard unit of weight, equal to one thousand grams. □ **kilogramo**
kilohertz ['kilouhə:ts] *n.* one thousand hertz. □ **kilohercio**
kilometre [ki'lɔmi:tə] *Amer.* **kilometer** *n.* one thousand metres. □ **kilómetro**
kilowatt ['kiləwɔt] *n.* one thousand watts. □ **kilovatio**
kilt [kilt] *n.* pleated skirt, usually of tartan cloth, worn by men in Scotland, and also by women. □ **falda escocesa**
kilted ['kiltid] *adj.* wearing a kilt. □ **vestido con falda...**
kimono [ki'mounou] *n.* (*pl. kimonos*) long, loose robe worn by Japanese women. □ **quimono**
kin [kin] *n. her son was her next of kin,* her son was her nearest relative. □ **...pariente más próximo**
kind [kaind] *n.* **1** type/variety: *what kind of animal is that? a beetle is a kind of insect; there are all kinds of reasons why I don't like it.* □ **clase**
2 ***it's nothing of the kind,*** not at all true. □ **nada de eso**
3 ***payment in kind,*** payment in goods or natural produce, not in money. □ **pago en especie**
4 *I feel* ***kind of*** *sorry,* (*informal*) rather sorry. □ **en cierto modo lo sentí**
■ *adj.* amiable/thoughtful; friendly/thinking of others: *it's so kind of you to come.* □ **amable**
kind-hearted *adj.* thoughtful about other people: *she was a kind-hearted old lady.* □ **de buen corazón**
kindly *adj.* and *adv.* (*kindlier, kindliest*) **1** thoughtful/pleasant; in a thoughtful/pleasant way: *his kindly neighbour did his shopping when he was ill.* □ **bondadoso**
2 ***to take kindly to:*** *she did not take kindly to dogs,* she did not like dogs. □ **no aceptaba gustosa los perros**
3 *kindly shut the door,* will you please shut the door. □ **puede hacer el favor de cerrar...**
kindness *n.* being kind: *he showed great kindness to others.* □ **amabilidad**
kindergarten ['kindəgɑ:tn] *n.* school for very young children. □ **jardín de infancia**
kindle ['kindl] *v.* to make a fire; to catch fire: *he kindled a fire on the campsite; the wood kindled easily.* □ **encender(se)**
kindling *n.* (*no pl.*) small pieces of wood used to start a fire. □ **astillas**
kinetic [kai'netik] *adj.* produced by moving; (energy) which a body has in motion. □ **cinético**
king [kiŋ] *n.* **1** male sovereign or hereditary ruler of a country. □ **rey**
2 main piece in chess/draughts; (*in cards*) card following the queen: *the king of hearts.* □ **rey**
kingcup *n.* large buttercup. □ **botón de oro**
kingdom *n.* **1** land ruled over by a king: *the kingdom of Scotland is joined to that of England.* □ **reino**
2 part of the world of nature: *the animal kingdom.* □ **el reino animal**
kingfisher *n.* small bird with brilliant blue feathers that dives for fish. □ **martín pescador**
kingpin *n.* central bolt; central person in an organization. □ **perno real; persona clave**
king-size(d) *adj.* very large: *king-sized bed; he smokes king-sized cigarettes.* □ **grande; cama de tamaño extra; cigarrillos extralargo**
kink [kiŋk] *n.* **1** knot/twist in a length of cord, wire or rope. □ **retorcimiento, nudo**
2 peculiar mental state. □ **manía**
kinky *adj.* (*kinkier, kinkiest*) (*slang*) odd/peculiar. □ **raro**
kinship ['kinʃip] *n.* family relationship. □ **parentesco**
kiosk ['ki:ɔsk] *n.* small outdoor cabin for the sale of newspapers/sweets, etc.; telephone booth. □ **quiosco**
kip [kip] *n.* (*slang*) short sleep: *to have a quiet kip.* □ **sueñecito**
■ *v.* (*he kipped*) (*slang*) to sleep: *where can I kip down for the night?* □ **dormir**
kipper ['kipə] *n.* split smoked herring. □ **arenque ahumado**
kirk [kə:k] *n.* (*in Scotland*) church. □ **iglesia**
kiss [kis] *n.* (*pl. kisses*) touching someone/something with the lips: *as she left, she gave her mother a kiss; she blew him a kiss,* sent him a kiss from a distance. □ **beso**
■ *v.* to touch with the lips: *they kissed each other goodbye; let's kiss and be friends.* □ **besar**
kit [kit] *n.* **1** clothes and personal equipment, usually packed for travelling: *the tennis player took his kit everywhere he went; the tool kit is in the back of the car.* □ **equipo; caja de las herramientas**
first aid kit, supplies for the emergency treatment of injuries. □ **botiquín**
2 box containing pieces which can be put together to make a model/a piece of furniture, etc.: *a model aircraft kit; he built the table from a kit.* □ **'kit'**
kitbag *n.* round bag for carrying a soldier's clothes and equipment. □ **saco**
kit out *v.* (*he kitted out*) to supply with clothes and equipment: *the soldier was fully kitted out for the battle.* □ **equipar**
kitchen ['kitʃn] *n.* room in which food is cooked. □ **cocina**
kitchenette *n.* very small kitchen. □ **cocina pequeña**
kitchen garden *n.* fruit and vegetable plot in a garden, usually near the kitchen. □ **huerto**
kite [kait] *n.* **1** large bird of prey of the falcon family. □ **milano**
2 toy made of light wood and paper or cloth which is flown in a strong wind on the end of a string: *to fly a kite.* □ **cometa**
3 ***to fly a kite:*** *he's just flying a kite,* he's putting forward an idea to see how people react to it. □ **ha lanzado una idea para sondear la opinión**
kith [kiθ] *n.* ***kith and kin,*** friends and relatives. □ **amigos y parientes**
kitsch [kitʃ] *n.* (*no pl.*) lack of artistic taste; tasteless artistic production. □ **'kitsch'**
kitten ['kitn] *n.* young cat. □ **gatito**
to have kittens, (*informal*) to be afraid/nervous. □ **morirse del susto**
kittenish *adj.* playful/like a kitten. □ **juguetón**
kitty ['kiti] *n.* (*pl. kitties*) joint fund: *the friends put their combined earnings into a kitty.* □ **fondo común**
kiwi ['ki:wi:] *n.* non-flying bird, native of New Zealand. □ **kiwi**
Kleenex ['kli:neks] *n.* (*pl. Kleenexes*) trademark for a type of paper handkerchief. □ **kleenex**

kleptomania [kleptə'meiniə] *n.* irresistible tendency to steal what you have enough money to buy. □ **cleptomanía**
kleptomaniac *n.* person who cannot stop stealing: *the kleptomaniac had stolen more than a hundred items from one shop.* □ **cleptómano**
knack [næk] *n.* talent/ability: *he has the knack of always saying the right thing.* □ **habilidad**
knacker ['nækə] *n.* person who buys and kills useless horses. □ **tratante y jifero**
knackered *adj.* (*informal*) worn out. □ **rendido**
knapsack ['næpsæk] *n.* canvas or leather bag carried on the back. □ **mochila**
knave [neiv] *n.* (*in playing cards*) jack/card between the ten and the queen: *the knave of hearts.* □ **sota, jota**
knead [ni:d] *v.* to press (clay/flour and water) into a dough with the hands: *the baker kneaded the dough before placing the loaves in the oven.* □ **amasar**
knee [ni:] *n.* joint between your thigh and lower leg: *he went down on his knees; she was sitting on his knee,* sitting on his thighs. □ **rodilla**
kneecap *n.* bone in front of the knee. □ **rótula**
■ *v.* to punish (someone) by shooting his kneecap off. □ **disparar en las rodillas**
knee-deep *adj.* up to the knees: *she waded knee-deep into the water.* □ **hasta las rodillas**
kneel [ni:l] *v.* (*he knelt*) to go on your knees: *he knelt at the high altar; they were all kneeling in church.* □ **arrodillarse**
kneel down *v.* to go down on your knees. □ **ponerse de rodillas**
kneeler *n.* hard cushion for kneeling on in church. □ **cojín**
knell [nel] *n.* (*formal*) sound of a bell, rung at a solemn ceremony such as a funeral. □ **tañido fúnebre**
knelt [nelt] *v. see* **kneel.**
knew [nju:] *v. see* **know.**
knickers ['nikəz] *n. pl.* undergarment worn by a woman or girl on the lower part of the body. □ **bragas**
knick-knack ['niknæk] *n.* small/light article; trinket: *the box on her dressing table was full of rings, brooches, and other knick-knacks.* □ **baratija**
knife [naif] *n.* (*pl. knives*) cutting blade with a sharpened edge fixed into a handle: *the robbers attacked with knives and axes.* □ **cuchillo**
to have your knife into someone, to try to hurt/to behave nastily towards someone. □ **tener inquina contra alguien**
■ *v.* to stab with a knife: *the victim was knifed in the back by the murderer.* □ **apuñalar**
knight [nait] *n.* **1** man honoured by a king for personal merit or services to his country (and taking the title *Sir*). □ **caballero**
2 (*in medieval times*) brave soldier often devoted to the service of a lady: *the black knight fought the white knight for the hand of the princess.* □ **caballero**
3 one of the pieces in a chess set, usually with a horse's head. □ **caballo**
■ *v.* to make someone a knight: *Sir Francis Drake was knighted by Queen Elizabeth I.* □ **armar caballero**
knighthood *n.* title of knight. □ **título de caballero/de 'Sir'**
knit [nit] *v.* **1** (*he knitted*) to make (a garment) out of wool, etc., by linking two threads together with the aid of two long needles: *her jacket was knitted in bright red wool; will you knit me two pullovers?* □ **hacer punto**
to knit one's brows, to frown. □ **fruncir el ceño**
2 (*it knit*) (*of broken bone*) to join together again: *the bones have knit quite rapidly.* □ **el hueso se soldó**
knitting *n.* woollen garment which is in the process of being made: *she left her knitting lying on the chair.* □ **labor de punto**
knitting machine *n.* machine for knitting. □ **tricotosa**
knitting needle *n.* long needle for knitting: *you need three knitting needles to knit socks.* □ **aguja de hacer punto**
knitwear *n.* knitted woollen garments. □ **géneros de punto**
knives [naivz] *n. see* **knife.**
knob [nɔb] *n.* **1** rounded bump; round lump: *a knob of butter.* □ **una nuez de mantequilla**
2 round handle of door/drawer: *the door knob was made of brass.* □ **pomo (puerta); tirador (cajón)**
knobbly *adj.* bumpy; covered with knobs: *the surface of the wooden chest was knobbly and rough.* □ **nudoso**
knock [nɔk] *n.* sharp blow; sound of a sharp blow: *he's had a knock on the head; there was a loud knock at the door.* □ **golpe**
■ *v.* **1** to strike with a hard blow: *the boxer was knocked against the ropes.* □ **golpear**
2 *he knocked on the door,* hit the door with his knuckles to call attention. □ **llamó a la puerta**
3 (*informal*) to criticize: *he's always knocking the management.* □ **criticar duramente**
knock about *v.* **1** to drift aimlessly: *he knocked about the world for two years before settling down.* □ **vagabundear**
2 (*of car engine*) to make a sharp noise because of misfiring. □ **fallar**
3 ***to knock (someone) about,*** to beat (someone): *his wife had been badly knocked about.* □ **maltratar**
knock back *v.* (*informal*) to swallow quickly: *he knocked back three whiskies before lunch.* □ **beber de un trago**
knock down *v.* **1** to hit (someone/something) to the ground: *the old lady was knocked down by a car.* □ **atropellar**
2 to sell (an item) at an auction to a purchaser: *the antique vase was knocked down to the lady in the corner.* □ **adjudicar**
knock-down *adj.* very low (price). □ **de precio de saldo**
knocker *n.* iron or brass knob or ring hinged to a door which can be struck against it to call attention. □ **aldaba**
knocking *n.* series of sharp blows; noise made by an engine which is misfiring: *she heard the sound of knocking on the other side of the wall.* □ **golpeteo**
knock-kneed *adj.* having knees that turn inwards and may touch each other when walking. □ **patizambo**
knock off *v.* **1** to hit (something) so that it falls off: *the cat knocked the vase off the table.* □ **tirar**
2 *he knocked off work at 4.30,* (*informal*) he stopped working at 4.30. □ **terminar**
3 *the vendor knocked $10 off the price of the car,* he reduced the price of the car by $10. □ **rebajar**
knock out *v.* to hit (someone) so hard that he loses consciousness. □ **noquear**
knockout *n.* **1** hitting someone so hard that he loses consciousness: *he won by a knockout.* □ **K.O.**
2 ***knockout competition,*** contest where several teams compete against each other and are eliminated in turn. □ **eliminatoria**
knock up *v.* **1** to waken. □ **despertar**
2 to make very tired. □ **derrengar**

knoll [nɔl] *n.* small hill. □ **montículo**

knot [nɔt] *n.* **1** looping the ends of string/rope, etc., and fastening them together: *he tied a firm knot at the end of the string.* □ **nudo**

2 *knots of people,* small groups of people. □ **corrillos de gente**

3 ***to tie yourself in knots,*** to get into difficulties. □ **meterse en líos**

4 hard round place in a piece of wood where a branch used to join it. □ **nudo**

5 measurement by which a ship's/an aircraft's speed is calculated (= one nautical mile per hour): *the ship was travelling at 15 knots.* □ **nudo**

■ *v.* (*he knotted*) to tie in a knot: *the string was knotted in three places.* □ **anudar**

knotty *adj. a knotty problem,* a difficult problem. □ **espinoso**

know [nou] *n.* ***to be in the know,*** to be well informed about something which is not generally known. □ **estar informado**

■ *v.* (*he knew; he has known*) **1** to have in your mind because of learning or experience: *he doesn't know how to change a car wheel; do you know your eight times table? he didn't know that she was married.* □ **saber**

2 *do you know French and German?,* do you speak French and German? □ **¿sabes francés y...?**

3 to recognize: *I knew him at once for my long lost brother; I always know an American when I see one.* □ **reconocer**

not know someone from Adam: *I don't know him from Adam,* I don't recognize him at all. □ **no lo conozco ni por asomo**

4 to be acquainted with: *I know him by sight; she knew him by name; he knows France very well.* □ **conocer**

5 to have personal experience of: *I know what it is like to have a tooth out.* □ **saber; yo sé lo que...**

6 ***to know better than:*** *he knew better than to contradict his father,* he was wise enough not to contradict his father. □ **fue lo suficientemente listo como para no....**

7 ***to know your own mind,*** to be clear and firm in your views. □ **saber lo que uno quiere**

know-all *n.* person who claims he knows everything. □ **sabelotodo**

know-how *n.* (*informal*) knowledge about how something is made/is done. □ **conocimientos técnicos**

knowing *adj.* **1** understanding; having knowledge. □ **instruido**

2 *he threw* ***a knowing glance*** *at his friend,* a glance which showed that he knew the secret. □ **...una mirada de complicidad**

knowingly *adv.* deliberately: *I have never knowingly hurt anyone.* □ **a sabiendas**

knowledge ['nɔlidʒ] *n.* **1** what someone knows: *he had no knowledge of Greek.* □ **conocimiento**

2 what is generally known: *human knowledge.* □ **conocimiento humano**

knowledgeable *adj.* (person) who knows a lot about something: *the science teacher was knowledgeable on his subject.* □ **entendido**

know of *v.* to be aware of: *they knew of the dangers of mountaineering.* □ **tener conocimiento de**

knuckle ['nʌkl] *n.* **1** finger joint. □ **nudillo**

near the knuckle, verging on the indecent. □ **rayando en la indecencia**

2 (*on an animal*) joint on the leg (especially when used as food): *a knuckle of pork.* □ **codillo**

knuckle down *v.* to apply yourself seriously to work: *he knuckled down to revision before the examinations.* □ **hincar los codos**

knuckle duster *n.* metal instrument worn on the knuckles, either as a protection or as a weapon. □ **manopla**

knuckle under *v.* to give in/to submit. □ **pasar por el aro**

koala [kou'ɑːlə] *n.* ***koala (bear),*** small Australian animal which carries its young in a pouch and lives in trees. □ **coala**

kookaburra ['kukəbʌrə] *n.* large Australian kingfisher. □ **martín cazador**

Koran [kɔː'rɑːn] *n.* sacred book containing the Prophet Muhammad's oral revelations. □ **Corán**

Koranic *adj.* of the Koran. □ **coránico**

Korea [kə'riə] *n.* country in Asia. □ **Corea**

Korean *adj.* referring to Korea. □ **coreano**

■ *n.* **1** person from Korea. □ **coreano**

2 language spoken in Korea. □ **coreano**

kosher ['kouʃə] *adj.* (food) prepared according to Jewish law. □ **permitido por la religión judía**

kosher restaurant/butcher, restaurant/butcher preparing food according to Jewish law. □ **para judíos**

kowtow [kau'tau] *v.* to show great respect. □ **saludar humildemente**

kraal [krɑl] *n.* (*in South Africa*) village with a fence round it. □ **craal**

Kremlin ['kremlin] *n.* the Russian government. □ **Kremlin**

kudos ['kjuːdɔs] *n.* glory/renown: *he gained kudos by coming first in the examination.* □ **celebridad; ganó muchos puntos...**

Kuwait [ku'weit] *n.* Arab country in the Middle East. □ **Kuwait**

Kuwaiti *adj.* and *n.* (*pl. Kuwaitis*) (person) from Kuwait. □ **kuwaití**

L,l

L, l [el] twelfth letter of the alphabet. □ **L, l**
L plates, white signs with a red L on them, attached to the front and rear of a car, etc., to show that the driver is a learner. □ **placa L**
lab [læb] *n. short for* **laboratory.** □ **laboratorio**
label ['leibl] *n.* **1** piece of paper/card, etc., attached to something to indicate price/contents/name/address, etc. □ **etiqueta**
2 name under which something is generally known: *record under the Decca label.* □ **disco en el sello de...**
■ *v.* (*he labelled*) **1** to put a label on: *they labelled the parcel.* □ **etiquetar**
2 to name/to describe: *he was labelled as a Communist.* □ **tachar de**
labial ['leibiəl] *adj.* referring to the lips. □ **labial**
laboratory [lə'bɔrətri, *Amer.* 'læbrətɔ:ri] *n.* place where scientific experiments/research are carried out. □ **laboratorio**
laborious [lə'bɔ:riəs] *adj.* **1** involving a great deal of work: *laborious task.* □ **laborioso; una tarea penosa**
2 showing signs of effort: *laborious style.* □ **estilo elaborado**
labour ['leibə] *Amer.* **labor** *n.* **1** (hard) work. □ **trabajo**
hard labour, prison sentence involving heavy manual work. □ **trabajos forzados**
2 workers/the workforce: *skilled labour.* □ **mano de obra cualificada**
3 ***Labour/the Labour Party,*** socialist political party linked with the trade unions and concerned with the welfare of workers. □ **Partido Laborista**
4 (pains of) childbirth: *labour pains; she went into labour.* □ **dolores del parto; se puso de parto**
■ *v.* **1** to work (hard). □ **trabajar (duro)**
2 ***to labour under a delusion,*** to have a (persistently) wrong impression. □ **estar equivocado**
3 ***to labour the point,*** to argue/to discuss something too long. □ **insistir en un punto**
4 (*of car engine, etc.*) to work with difficulty. □ **funcionar a duras penas**
laboured *adj.* **1** (*of style*) heavy/clumsy. □ **recargado**
2 (*of breathing*) heavy/difficult. □ **fatigoso**
labourer *n.* person who does heavy manual work. □ **trabajador**
labour-saving *adj.* (*of machine/gadget*) which lessens work. □ **que ahorra trabajo**
labrador ['læbrədɔ:] *n.* type of large dog, usually black or yellow. □ **retriever de Labrador**
laburnum [lə'bə:nəm] *n.* tree with bright yellow flowers and poisonous seeds in pods. □ **codeso**
labyrinth ['læbirinθ] *n.* maze; place where it is difficult to find your way about (because of numerous complications): *the house was a labyrinth of corridors; there was a labyrinth of rules and regulations.* □ **laberinto**
lace [leis] *n.* **1** thin strip of material for tying up a shoe, etc. □ **cordón**
2 decorative cloth like a net made into open patterns by weaving threads together: *lace handkerchief.* □ **encaje**
■ *v.* **1** to tie with a lace. □ **atar**
2 to pour a little alcohol into (another liquid): *milk laced with rum.* □ **echar**
lacerate ['læsəreit] *v.* (*formal*) to wound/to tear (flesh). □ **lacerar**
laceration [læsə'reiʃn] *n.* tearing; place where flesh has been torn. □ **laceración**
lachrymose ['lækrimous] *adj.* (*formal*) (person) who tends to cry. □ **lacrimoso**
lack [læk] *n.* not having something: *the plants died through lack of rain.* □ **falta**
■ *v.* not to have (enough of) something: *they lacked food; the reservoir lacked water; he lacks a sense of humour.* □ **faltar; les falta comida**
lacking *adj.* not enough/without: *water was lacking; she's lacking in willpower.* □ **carente; había escasez de agua; le falta...**
lackadaisical [lækə'deizikl] *adj.* not showing any vigour/any enthusiasm. □ **apático**
lacklustre ['læklʌstə] *Amer.* **lackluster** *adj.* dull/not brilliant: *the government's lacklustre performance.* □ **poco brillante**
laconic [lə'kɔnik] *adj.* using few words: *laconic style.* □ **lacónico**
laconically *adv.* using few words. □ **lacónicamente**
lacquer ['lækə] *n.* **1** type of hard shiny varnish/paint, often used on metals. □ **laca**
2 spray for keeping your hair in place. □ **laca**
■ *v.* to coat with lacquer. □ **laquear**
lacrosse [lə'krɔs] *n.* team game played with a ball and a curved stick with a net at the end. □ **lacrosse**
lacy ['leisi] *adj.* (*lacier, laciest*) like lace; made of a network of fine threads. □ **de encaje**
lad [læd] *n.* (*informal*) boy; young man. □ **chaval**
ladder ['lædə] *n.* **1** object made of horizontal bars between two uprights, used for climbing to higher or lower places. □ **escalera de mano**
2 long hole in a stocking. □ **carrera**
■ *v.* (*of stocking, etc.*) to get ladders: *these tights ladder easily.* □ **hacerse una carrera**
laden ['leidn] *adj.* carrying a (heavy) load; (*of ship*) containing a cargo. □ **cargado**
lading *n.* **1** loading of ships. □ **cargamento**
2 cargo. □ **carga**
ladle ['leidl] *n.* large deep spoon for serving soup, etc. □ **cacillo**
■ *v.* to serve with a ladle: *he's ladling out the soup.* □ **servir (con cacillo)**
to ladle out: *she ladled out compliments,* gave them in large quantities. □ **repartió cumplidos a todos**
lady ['leidi] *n.* (*pl. ladies*) **1** woman, especially one of high social standing or with good manners: *she's a real lady; a lady doctor.* □ **señora; es toda una señora; doctora**
2 ***Lady,*** (*as title*) feminine equivalent of Lord; title of wife or sometimes daughter of a peer; title of wife of a knight or baronet. □ **Lady**
3 ***Our Lady,*** the Virgin Mary. □ **Nuestra Señora**
ladies *n.* (*informal*) women's toilet: *she's in the ladies.* □ **servicio de señoras**
ladybird *Amer.* **ladybug** *n.* type of small beetle, usually red with black spots or black with reddish spots. □ **mariquita**
ladykiller *n.* (*informal*) man who is attractive to women. □ **guaperas**
ladylike *adj.* well-mannered/polite (as a lady should be). □ **fino**
ladyship *n.* (used as a form of address or to refer formally to a titled lady): *Your Ladyship; Her Ladyship.* □ **su señoría**
lag [læg] *n.* **1** (*in time*) space/interval, especially be-

tween two parts of an event, etc.: *there was a long time lag between his appearances.* □ **intervalo**
2 ***jet lag,*** tiredness felt by travellers who fly by jet across time zones. □ **cansancio por desfase horario**
3 (*slang*) person who has been put in prison: *old lag.* □ **presidiario**
■ *v.* (*he lagged*) **1** to go/fall/be behind: *he was lagging behind the others.* □ **rezagarse**
2 to cover (a heating appliance, pipes, etc.) to prevent heat loss or to prevent freezing. □ **revestir**
laggard ['lægə] *n.* person who is behind the others. □ **rezagado**
lagging *n.* material for wrapping round pipes. □ **revestimiento**
lager ['lɑ:gə] *n.* type of light fizzy beer. □ **cerveza tipo Pilsen**
lagoon [lə'gu:n] *n.* area of sea water almost completely surrounded by land, especially by a coral island. □ **albufera**
laid [leid] *v. see* **lay.**
lain [lein] *v. see* **lie.**
lair [lεə] *n.* resting place of a wild animal. □ **guarida**
laird ['lεəd] *n.* (*in Scotland*) owner of a country estate. □ **terrateniente**
laity ['leiiti] *n.* people who have not been trained as priests or have not had other expert training. □ **seglares**
lake [leik] *n.* **1** (large) inland stretch of water. □ **lago**
2 type of reddish dye. □ **laca**
lama ['lɑ:mə] *n.* Buddhist priest, especially in Tibet. □ **lama**
lamb [læm] *n.* **1** young sheep. □ **cordero**
2 flesh of sheep used as food: *roast lamb.* □ **cordero**
lambing ['læmiŋ] *n.* giving birth to lambs: *the lambing season.* □ **parición; paridera**
lambswool *n* (*no pl.*) very soft wool. □ **lana de cordero**
lambast [læm'beist] *v.* to criticize (someone) sharply. □ **criticar con dureza**
lame [leim] *adj.* (*lamer, lamest*) **1** unable to walk properly: *he became lame as a result of an accident.* □ **cojo; lisiado**
2 weak/unsatisfactory: *lame excuse.* □ **una excusa poco convincente**
■ *v.* to injure someone so that he cannot walk properly: *she was lamed by the accident.* □ **lisiar**
lame duck *n.* person/company in difficulties and having to rely on outside support. □ **inútil (persona); empresa deficitaria**
lamely *adv.* weakly. □ **con poca convicción**
lameness *n.* being lame. □ **cojera**
lamé ['lɑmei] *n.* cloth with gold or silver threads. □ **lamé**
lament [lə'ment] *n.* **1** song/music for mourning. □ **endecha**
2 expression of grief; complaint: *their lament was that they couldn't escape.* □ **lamento**
■ *v.* to be very sad, especially about the death of someone: *he was long lamented; he lamented the loss of his car.* □ **llorar; lamentar**
lamentable ['læməntəbl] *adj.* very bad: *your writing is lamentable.* □ **lamentable**
lamentably *adv.* very badly. □ **lamentablemente**
lamentation [læmən'teiʃn] *n.* expression of great sorrow. □ **lamentación**
laminated ['læmineitid] *adj.* **1** formed in thin layers: *laminated glass.* □ **laminado**
2 covered with a thin layer of plastic: *laminated book jacket.* □ **sobrecubierta plastificada**
lamp [læmp] *n.* object which produces light: *table lamp; gas lamp.* □ **lámpara**
lamplight *n.* light from a lamp: *by lamplight.* □ **luz de la lámpara**
lamp-post *n.* large post which holds a street lamp. □ **poste de alumbrado**
lampshade *n.* (decorative) cover to put over a lamp. □ **pantalla**
lampoon [læm'pu:n] *n.* writing which makes someone seem ridiculous. □ **libelo**
■ *v.* to ridicule (someone) in writing. □ **satirizar**
lance [lɑ:ns] *n.* type of long spear. □ **lanza**
■ *v.* to cut (a wound/an abscess, etc.) with a lancet. □ **abrir con lanceta**
lance-corporal *n.* (*in the army*) non-commissioned officer below the rank of corporal. □ **cabo (interino)**
lancet *n.* **1** pointed two-edged surgical knife. □ **lanceta**
2 tall thin pointed window. □ **ventana ojival**
land [lænd] *n.* **1** solid part of the earth's surface: *on land; to come to land.* □ **tierra**
2 earth/soil: *cultivating the land.* □ **tierra**
to go back to the land, to go back to being a farmer again. □ **volver a vivir de la tierra**
3 country: *children of many lands.* □ **país**
4 part of a country owned by someone: *he has land(s) in Wales.* □ **tierras**
■ *v.* **1** to come to land; to bring to land: *the plane landed smoothly; the ship landed in the bay; the pilot landed the plane safely.* □ **aterrizar (avión); fondear (barco)**
to land on one's feet: *he always lands on his feet,* he enjoys easy success/doesn't meet with many difficulties. □ **siempre sale adelante**
2 to bring a fish out of water and on to the land: *they landed a big catch of herring.* □ **sacar (del agua)**
3 *they landed a large prize,* they won it. □ **consiguieron un gran premio**
4 *he landed a good job,* he obtained a good job. □ **consiguió un buen trabajo**
5 to give/to deal: *he landed him a blow in the eye.* □ **asestar**
6 to arrive/to reach: *we landed (up) in London unexpectedly; they landed in jail.* □ **ir a parar**
landed *adj.* owning land: *the landed gentry.* □ **terrateniente**
landfall *n.* seeing land for the first time from sea or air: *their first landfall was in Florida.* □ **recalada (mar); vista de tierra (aire)**
landing *n.* **1** (*especially of aircraft*) touching land: *good landing; crash landing.* □ **aterrizaje**
landing gear, wheels on which an aircraft lands. □ **tren de aterrizaje**
2 space at the top of a flight of stairs. □ **rellano**
landing-net *n.* net at the end of a long pole, used for taking fish out of water. □ **salabardo; redeña**
landing stage *n.* (floating) platform where passengers can leave boats. □ **desembarcadero flotante**
landlady *n.* **1** woman from whom you rent a house/room, etc. □ **casera (casa); patrona (habitación)**
2 woman who keeps a hotel, etc. □ **hostelera**
landlocked *n.* (sea/harbour) surrounded by land. □ **rodeado de tierra**
landlord *n.* **1** a man from whom you rent a house/room, etc. □ **casero; patrón**
2 man who keeps a hotel, etc. □ **hostelero**
landlubber *n.* (*informal*) person who is not used to going on ships. □ **marinero de agua dulce; hombre de tierra**
landmark *n.* **1** object on land which you can see easily, especially one used by ships to find out their position. □ **marca de tierra**

2 outstanding/significant event, etc.: *this invention was a landmark in the history of shipbuilding.* □ **hito**
landowner *n.* person who owns a country estate. □ **terrateniente**
landscape ['lændskeip] *n.* **1** scenery/appearance of the countryside: *beautiful mountain landscape.* □ **paisaje**
2 painting of a country scene: *landscape by Constable.* □ **un paisaje de Constable**
■ *v.* to improve (a garden) by creating small hills/lakes, planting trees, etc. □ **hacer paisajismo (jardines)**
landscape gardener *n.* person who designs the layout of large gardens/pieces of land. □ **jardinero paisajista**
landslide *n.* **1** slipping of large amounts of earth, etc., down a hillside. □ **desprendimiento de tierras**
2 overwhelming event, especially an electoral victory in which one party is totally defeated: *a landslide victory; the result was a landslide for the opposition.* □ **triunfo aplastante**
landwards *adv.* towards the land. □ **hacia tierra**
lane [lein] *n.* **1** narrow road, often in the country. □ **camino**
2 way/road/course for traffic, usually in a particular direction: *four-lane motorway.* □ **carril**
turning lane, part of a road marked for traffic which is going to turn. □ **carril para girar**
shipping lanes, routes in narrow sea channels where ships pass frequently. □ **rutas**
bus lane, part of a road where only buses may drive. □ **carril bus**
language ['læŋgwidʒ] *n.* **1** way of speaking of a country/a group of people: *the French language.* □ **lengua; idioma**
language laboratory, room with earphones and tape recorders where students can study foreign languages. □ **laboratorio de idiomas**
2 way of speaking/writing: *his language is very clear; literary language.* □ **lenguaje**
bad language, swearing. □ **palabrotas**
3 human speech. □ **lenguaje**
4 means of communication: *sign language; the language of birds.* □ **lenguaje**
languid ['læŋgwid] *adj.* slow-moving/lacking energy: *she gave a languid wave; languid summer hours; languid style.* □ **lánguido**
languidly *adv.* lazily. □ **lánguidamente**
languish ['læŋgwiʃ] *v.* to become weak/depressed/ill, often because of sorrow. □ **languidecer**
languor ['læŋgə] *n.* **1** lack of energy. □ **languidez**
2 tender emotional mood. □ **languidez**
languorous *adj.* slow-moving/lazy. □ **lánguido**
lank [læŋk] *adj.* (*lanker, lankest*) **1** (*of hair*) straight/dull/lifeless. □ **lacio**
2 (*of person*) thin/drooping. □ **escuálido**
lanky *adj.* tall/thin/awkward (person). □ **larguirucho**
lanolin ['lænəlin] *n.* fat from sheep's wool used in skin creams. □ **lanolina**
lantern ['læntən] *n.* lamp with a covering to protect it which can be carried in the hand. □ **linterna**
lanyard ['lænjəd] *n.* string worn around your neck or shoulder with a whistle, etc., on it. □ **cordón (al cuello)**
lap [læp] *n.* **1** your body from waist to knees, when you are in a sitting position: *she took the baby on her lap.* □ **regazo**
in the lap of luxury, in great luxury. □ **rodeado de lujo**
2 circuit/round (of a racecourse): *they ran four laps,* they ran round the course four times. □ **vuelta (de una pista)**
■ *v.* (*he lapped*) **1** (*of animal*) to drink with the tongue: *the cat lapped up the milk.* □ **beber a lengüetadas**
2 to take in greedily: *she lapped up the gossip.* □ **absorber con avidez; se tragaba todo el cotilleo**
3 (*of waves, etc.*) to wash against (the shore/the edge of something). □ **bañar**
4 to go so fast that you are a whole lap ahead of another competitor: *he lapped the slowest runners.* □ **sacar una vuelta**
lapdog *n.* small pet dog. □ **perro faldero**
lapel [lə'pel] *n.* part of collar of coat, etc., which folds back. □ **solapa**
lapidary ['læpidəri] *adj.* referring to stones (especially precious stones). □ **lapidario**
lapis lazuli [læpis'læzju:lai] *n* bright blue stone. □ **lapislázuli**
lapse [læps] *n.* **1** failure to do something (properly): *lapse from duty.* □ **fallo**
2 interval of time, especially when something does not take place: *there was a lapse of three months between the two meetings.* □ **lapso**
■ *v.* **1** to fail/to cease to do something: *they lapsed from duty.* □ **fallar; faltaron a su deber**
2 to cease to be valid: *he let his membership lapse.* □ **caducar**
3 to fall into a lower/less active state: *they lapsed into silence/into apathy.* □ **caer**
lapwing ['læpwiŋ] *n.* bird found in fields and moors. □ **avefría**
larceny ['lɑ:sni] *n.* crime of stealing. □ **latrocinio**
larch [lɑ:tʃ] *n.* (*pl. larches*) cone-bearing tree which loses its leaves in winter. □ **alerce**
lard [lɑ:d] *n.* melted down pig fat used in cooking. □ **manteca de cerdo**
lardy cake *n.* type of bread, made with fat and covered with sticky sugar. □ **mantecada**
larder ['lɑ:də] *n.* cupboard for storing food. □ **despensa**
large [lɑ:dʒ] *adj.* (*larger, largest*) **1** (very) big: *large box; large sum; large fortune.* □ **grande**
2 ***at large,*** (i) free/not imprisoned: *a prisoner is still at large.* □ **en libertad**
(ii) in general: *the public at large.* □ **en general**
largely *adv.* mostly/for the most part: *the inhabitants were largely Christians.* □ **en su mayor parte**
largesse [lɑ:'dʒes] *n.* generous gift of money. □ **dádiva**
largo ['lɑ:gəN] *adv.* and *n.* (piece of music) which is played slowly. □ **largo**
lariat ['læriət] *n.* lasso. □ **lazo**
lark [lɑ:k] *n.* **1** bird which sings and flies high in the sky. □ **alondra**
2 (*informal*) piece of fun/joke. □ **broma**
3 *they did it* ***for a lark,*** for amusement. □ **lo hicieron como una gracia**
■ *v.* ***to lark*** (***about***), (*informal*) to fool around/to play jokes: *they're always larking about.* □ **bromear**
larva ['lɑ:və] *n.* (*pl. larvae*) insect at an early stage of its development, different in form from the adult: *a caterpillar is the larva of a butterfly.* □ **larva**
larynx ['lærinks] *n.* (*pl. larynxes*) upper part of the windpipe, where sounds are made by the voice. □ **laringe**
laryngitis [lærin'dʒaitis] *n.* inflammation of the larynx causing a sore throat. □ **laringitis**
lasagne [læ'zæŋi] *n.* type of pasta which is made of flat strips. □ **lasaña**

lascivious [lə'siviəs] *adj.* full of sexual desire. □ **lascivo**

laser ['leizə] *n.* instrument which produces highly concentrated beams of light: *laser beam.* □ **láser**

lash [læʃ] *n.* (*pl. lashes*) **1** stroke of whip; beating with a whip. □ **latigazo**
2 flexible part of a whip. □ **tralla**
3 eyelash/short fine hair on the edge of the eyelid: *long lashes.* □ **pestaña**
■ *v.* **1** to beat with a whip: *she lashed her horse.* □ **azotar; fustigó al caballo**
2 to make a movement like beating with a whip: *the rain lashed against the windows.* □ **la lluvía azotaba los cristales**
3 *he lashed himself into a fury,* he worked himself into a rage. □ **se puso furioso**
4 to join/to fasten/to tie down tightly with rope/string, etc. □ **atar; amarrar**
lashing *n.* **1** whipping. □ **flagelación**
2 tying/binding with rope, etc. □ **atadura; ligadura**
lashings *n.pl.* (*informal*) plenty: *lashings of cream.* □ **un montón**
lash out *v.* **1** *to lash out at someone,* to become (unexpectedly) very angry at/to try to hit someone. □ **arremeter contra**
2 (*informal*) to become (unexpectedly) very extravagant and spend a large sum of money: *he lashed out on an expensive meal.* □ **gastar; se pagó una comida bien cara**

lass [læs] **lassie** ['læsi] *n.* (*in the north of England and Scotland*) (*informal*) girl; young woman. □ **zagala**

lassitude ['læsitju:d] *n.* (*formal*) tiredness, especially if causing inactivity. □ **lasitud**

lasso [lə'su:] *n.* (*pl. lassoes*) rope with looped end for catching horses/cattle, etc. □ **lazo**
■ *v.* to catch (animals) with a lasso. □ **lazar**

last [lɑ:st] *adj.* **1** placed/coming at the end (of a list/line/period of time): *she was the last to arrive.* □ **último**
last thing at night, at the very end of the day. □ **al final del día**
last but one, the one before the final/end one. □ **penúltimo**
last but not least, at the end of a list, but not because it is the least important. □ **el último en orden pero no en importancia**
***the last word** in hats,* the very latest fashion. □ **el último grito en sombreros**
2 *he's the last person I would want to go on holiday with,* he's the most unlikely person. □ **es la última persona con quien iría...**
3 most recent/belonging to the previous group, etc.: *last Monday; last week; the last group left early.* □ **el pasado lunes; el último grupo...**
■ *n.* **1** shape on which a shoe is made or repaired. □ **horma**
2 final thing(s)/period/sight, etc.: *that's the last of the raspberries; that was the last I saw of him.* □ **último**
3 ***at (long) last,*** in the end/after a long time. □ **por último**
4 ***to the last,*** till the very end. □ **hasta el final**
■ *adv.* **1** at the end: *he came last.* □ **en último lugar**
2 most recently: *when I last saw her.* □ **por última vez**
■ *v.* to continue (to exist); to remain in good condition: *supplies won't last out; raspberries don't last; the good weather won't last.* □ **durar**
lasting *adj.* which continues for a long time: *lasting friendship.* □ **duradero**
lastly *adv.* at the end/finally: *lastly I want to thank all my friends.* □ **finalmente**

latch [lætʃ] *n.* (*pl. latches*) fastening for a door, etc. consisting of a small bar which fits into a catch: *the door is on the latch,* is held shut by a latch but is not locked. □ **picaporte**
■ *v.* **1** to close with a latch. □ **cerrar con picaporte**
2 ***to latch on to something,*** (*informal*) to seize/to take up: *they latched on to the idea.* □ **agarrar; cogieron la idea**
latchkey *n.* key for a front door. □ **llave de la puerta de la calle**
latchkey child, child who has a key to the house and lets himself in when he comes home from school because both parents are at work. □ **niño con llave de casa**

late [leit] *adj.* (*later, latest*) **1** at a time after that decided or intended: *the train is ten minutes late; he's very late in arriving; it's rather late to change your mind.* □ **tarde**
2 at/towards the end of a period of time: *it was late afternoon when she finally arrived.* □ **a última hora**
3 at/towards/past the end of a season: *late potatoes; late frost.* □ **tardío**
4 last/most recent: *his latest book; is there any later news?* □ **último; de última hora**
5 (*formal*) referring to someone who has died or is no longer in a certain position: *my late father; the late chairman.* □ **mi difunto padre; el anterior presidente**
■ *adv.* (*later, latest*) **1** after the appointed time: *to arrive late; better late than never.* □ **tarde**
2 after a certain time: *to stay up/to go to bed late; very late at night; a month later; later on in the morning.* □ **tarde**
latecomer *n.* person who arrives after others or after the appointed time: *latecomers will not be admitted until the interval.* □ **un tardón**
lately *adv.* in recent times; during recent days, weeks, etc.: *he's been acting very strangely lately; have you seen her lately?* □ **últimamente**
lateness *n.* being late: *your lateness is becoming a problem; the lateness of the hour.* □ **retraso; lo avanzado de la hora**

latent ['leitənt] *adj.* present but not developed/hidden: *latent talent.* □ **latente**

lateral ['lætərəl] *adj.* referring to the side. □ **lateral**
lateral fin, fin on the side of a fish's body. □ **aleta lateral**
lateral thinking, solving problems by unusual ideas. □ **pensamiento lateral, original**
laterally *adv.* towards the side. □ **lateralmente**

latex ['leiteks] *n.* milky juice from a rubber tree. □ **látex**

lath [lɑ:θ] *n.* narrow thin strip of wood, etc. □ **listón**

lathe [leið] *n.* machine for holding and turning wood/metal, etc., so that it can be shaped. □ **torno**

lather ['læðə] *n.* **1** mass of (soap) bubbles. □ **espuma**
2 (*especially on horse*) frothy sweat. □ **sudor**
to get in a lather, to get upset/flustered. □ **excitarse**
■ *v.* **1** to make (something) form a lather; to form a lather: *this shampoo lathers easily.* □ **hacer espuma**
2 to cover with lather: *the barber lathered his chin.* □ **enjabonar**

Latin ['lætin] *n.* **1** language formerly spoken by the Romans. □ **latín**
2 person from Italy, Spain, Portugal or South America. □ **latino**
■ *adj.* **1** referring to the language of ancient Rome. □ **latino**
2 referring to Italy, Spain, Portugal and South

America. □ **latino**
Latin America, countries in South America where Spanish or Portuguese is spoken. □ **Latinoamérica**

latitude ['lætitju:d] *n.* **1** breadth of view/tolerance/scope: *they were allowed considerable latitude in their behaviour.* □ **amplitud; se les daba bastante libertad...**
2 position on the earth's surface measured in degrees north or south of the equator: *lines of latitude; in northern latitudes,* in areas north of the equator. □ **latitud**

latrine [lə'tri:n] *n.* lavatory in a military camp or prison. □ **letrina**

latter ['lætə] *adj.* **1** second (-mentioned) of two: *of France and Spain, I prefer the latter as a holiday destination,* I prefer Spain. □ **segundo; la última**
2 recent; of the final part/period: *during the latter half of June; the latter part of the book.* □ **último**
latterly *adv.* recently: *latterly he's been in Paris.* □ **últimamente**

lattice ['lætis] *n.* pattern (of pieces of wood in a fence, etc.) made of crisscross diagonal lines. □ **celosía**
lattice window, window with small panes and lead frames forming a crisscross pattern. □ **ventana de celosía**

laudable ['lɔ:dəbl] *adj.* worthy of praise: *laudable effort.* □ **laudable, loable**
laudably *adv.* in a praiseworthy way. □ **laudablemente**

laudanum ['lɔ:dnəm] *n.* opium in alcohol, used as a sedative. □ **láudano**

laugh [lɑ:f] *n.* **1** sound/movement made to express amusement/happiness, etc.: *she said it with a laugh.* □ **risa**
2 *to do something* ***for a laugh,*** to do it for amusement only/as a joke. □ **hacer algo para divertirse**
■ *v.* **1** to make sounds which express amusement/happiness: *they all laughed heartily.* □ **reír(se)**
to laugh up one's sleeve, to laugh secretly. □ **reír para su capote**
2 to make fun of: *they laughed at him.* □ **reírse de**
3 ***to laugh away/off:*** *he laughed the matter off,* he treated it as a joke; *they laughed his fears away,* dismissed them with laughter. □ **tomar a risa**
laughable *adj.* only worth laughing at; ridiculous. □ **irrisorio**
laughing gas *n.* gas which makes you laugh when you breathe it, used especially by dentists as an anaesthetic. □ **gas hilarante**
laughing stock *n.* (main) object of laughter; person whom everyone makes fun of: *he's the laughing stock of the school.* □ **hazmerreír**
laughter *n.* (sound/act of) laughing: *laughter was heard upstairs; they all burst into laughter.* □ **risa; todos soltaron la carcajada**

launch [lɔ:ntʃ] *n.* (*pl. launches*) **1** type of small motor boat. □ **lancha**
2 act of launching (boat/rocket, etc.). □ **botadura (barco); lanzamiento (cohete)**
■ *v.* **1** to put (a boat/ship) into the water, especially for the first time. □ **botar**
2 to send off (a rocket into the air). □ **lanzar**
3 to give (something/someone) a start: *they launched an attack on the enemy; the book was launched with considerable fuss.* □ **lanzar**
launching pad *n.* starting platform for a rocket, etc. □ **plataforma de lanzamiento**
launch out *v.* to start doing something expensive or ambitious. □ **emprender**

laundry ['lɔ:ndri] *n.* (*pl. laundries*) **1** place where clothes/sheets, etc., are washed. □ **lavandería**
2 clothes/sheets, etc. for washing, or which have been washed. □ **colada**
launder *v.* to wash clothes. □ **lavar**
laund(e)rette ['lɔ:ndret] **laundromat** ['lɔ:ndrəmæt] *n.* shop with coin-operated washing machines for public use. □ **lavandería**

laureate ['lɔ:riət] *n.* person who has been awarded a prize. □ **laureado**
Poet Laureate, leading poet who is asked to write commemorative verse for special occasions. □ **poeta laureado**

laurel ['lɔrəl] *n.* tree with smooth shiny evergreen leaves. □ **laurel**
to rest on your laurels, to enjoy your past success, without trying to gain more. □ **dormirse en los laureles**

lav [læv] *n.* (*informal*) lavatory. □ **lavabo**

lava ['lɑ:və] *n.* hot liquid matter flowing from a volcano which becomes solid when it cools. □ **lava**

lavatory ['lævətri] *n.* (*pl. lavatories*) **1** small room for getting rid of waste matter from the body, usually with a flushing bowl. □ **servicio**
2 bowl with a seat and a flushing system, for getting rid of waste matter from the body. □ **retrete**

lavender ['lævində] *n.* **1** plant with sweet-smelling bluish-purple flowers. □ **espliego**
2 bluish-purple colour. □ **azul lavanda**

lavish ['læviʃ] *adj.* **1** generous/ample: *lavish helpings.* □ **abundante**
2 extravagant/over-generous: *lavish expenditure; he isn't lavish with his praise.* □ **desmesurado**
■ *v.* to give (over-)generously: *he lavished too much money on his daughter.* □ **no escatimar gastos**

law [lɔ:] *n.* **1** body of rules by which a country is governed and the people controlled: *criminal law; law and order; to study law.* □ **ley; derecho penal**
2 rule by which a country is governed: *there's a law against it.* □ **ley**
3 rule/controlling force: *the laws of physics.* □ **ley**
4 *her word is law,* she is always obeyed. □ **lo que dice va a misa**
5 ***to lay down the law,*** to state something in a dogmatic way. □ **decir algo de manera autoritaria**
6 ***to be a law unto yourself,*** to do exactly what you want, regardless of rules or of anyone else. □ **hacer lo que le da la gana a uno**
7 process of upholding the rules of a country: *to go to law; court of law.* □ **recurrir a la justicia**
law-abiding *adj.* obeying the law: *law-abiding citizens.* □ **observante de la ley**
lawful *adj.* according to law/legal: *lawful wife.* □ **legal; esposa legítima**
lawfully *adv.* in a lawful way. □ **lícitamente**
lawless *adj.* wild/uncivilized; paying no attention to law. □ **ingobernable**
lawsuit *n.* legal case: *to bring a lawsuit against someone.* □ **pleito**
lawyer *n.* person who has studied law and can advise people on legal matters. □ **abogado**

lawn [lɔ:n] *n.* **1** (area of) short grass in a garden. □ **césped**
2 very fine cotton material. □ **linón**
lawnmower *n.* machine for cutting grass. □ **cortacésped**

lax [læks] *adj.* (*laxer, laxest*) loose; not rigid: *lax morals; his discipline is very lax.* □ **laxo**
laxative *adj.* and *n.* (substance) which helps to open the bowels. □ **laxante**
laxity, laxness *n.* being loose/not being rigid: *the laxity of the authorities led to unrest.* □ **laxitud**

lay [lei] *adj.* **1** (someone) who is not trained as a priest: *lay preacher.* □ **seglar, laico**
2 not belonging to a profession or specialization: *lay opinions are not usually as reliable as professional ones.* □ **profano**
■ *v.* (*he laid*) **1** to place/to put, often in a horizontal position: *he laid the book (down) on the desk; she laid her head on the pillow; they have laid all the facts of the case before me.* □ **poner; colocar**
2 to place in the right position: *to lay a carpet/to lay bricks.* □ **poner**
3 to cause to settle/to subside: *lay the dust by sprinkling water on the floor.* □ **asentar el polvo**
4 (*of bird*) to produce (an egg): *the hens aren't laying.* □ **poner**
5 to make (a bet). □ **hacer (una apuesta)**
6 to set/to place dishes, etc. on (a table): *lay the table for three.* □ **poner la mesa**
7 to set (a trap/a scene): *the scene is laid in Paris.* □ **situar**
8 *see also* **lie.**
layabout *n.* (*informal*) person who does no work and wanders about idly. □ **vagabundo**
lay aside, lay by *v.* to put away for future use: *please lay these aside for me.* □ **poner a un lado**
layby *n.* place at the side of a road where vehicles can park □ **área de aparcamiento**
lay down *v.* **1** to put down/to give up: *lay down one's arms.* □ **deponer**
2 to state clearly in writing: *it is all laid down in the rule book.* □ **formular**
layer *n.* **1** (horizontal) thickness of something: *layer of cement.* □ **capa**
2 *this hen is a good layer,* produces many eggs. □ **ponedora**
lay in *v.* to make a store/to store up: *they laid in a stock of sugar.* □ **almacenar**
lay into *v.* (*informal*) to attack/to hit (someone). □ **dar una paliza a (alguien)**
layman *n.* (*pl. laymen*) person who does not belong to a particular profession or specialization: *to the layman these calculations may seem complicated.* □ **lego**
lay off *v.* **1** to dismiss (workers) temporarily. □ **despedir temporalmente**
2 (*informal*) to stop: *lay off (hitting him)!* □ **dejar de**
lay-off *n.* temporary dismissal from work. □ **despido temporal**
lay on *v.* to put on/in; to provide: *water is laid on; they laid on a large supper.* □ **servir**
lay out *v.* **1** to place in an orderly way, especially on a table, etc.: *they laid out the presents on the table.* □ **colocar**
2 to make a design for (a garden/a book, etc.). □ **trazar, maquetar**
3 to spend (money): *they laid out $30 to buy the chair.* □ **desembolsar**
layout *n.* design, especially of a garden/a book. □ **trazado, maquetación**
lay up *v.* **1** to store (away): *the car was laid up for the winter; to lay up trouble for yourself.* □ **encerrar en el garaje; acumular**
2 ***to be laid up,*** to be ill in bed. □ **guardar cama**
layette [lei'et] *n.* clothes for a new-born baby. □ **canastilla**
lazy ['leizi] *adj.* (*lazier, laziest*) not wanting to do any work: *lazy boy.* □ **vago; perezoso**
lazy day, one on which you do very little. □ **día ocioso**
laze *v.* to do nothing or very little: *they lazed about all day.* □ **hacer el vago**
lazily *adv.* in a lazy way. □ **perezosamente**
laziness *n.* (*no pl.*) being lazy. □ **pereza**
lazybones *n.* (*informal*) person who does not like work/who does nothing. □ **gandul**
leach [li:tʃ] *v.* to remove a substance from soil, etc., by passing water through it. □ **lixiviar**
lead[1] [led] *n.* **1** (*chemical element*: Pb) heavy soft bluish-grey metal. □ **plomo**
2 weight at the end of a rope, used for measuring the depth of water. □ **sonda**
3 writing part of a pencil: *sharpen the lead.* □ **mina**
leaden ['ledn] *adj.* of/like lead. □ **plúmbeo; plomizo**
leaden sky, dull grey sky. □ **cielo plomizo**
lead[2] [li:d] *n.* **1** front position/first action: *to follow someone's lead; to go into the lead/to take the lead.* □ **seguir el ejemplo de alguien; ponerse en cabeza**
to be in the lead, to be first/in the front (of a race). □ **ir en cabeza**
2 (*in cards*) right to play first: *to have the lead.* □ **mano; ser mano**
3 strap to keep a dog in control: *dogs must be kept on a lead.* □ **correa**
4 electric wire, etc., which joins an appliance to its source of power. □ **cable**
5 (actor who plays a) main role: *he played the lead in 'Hamlet'.* □ **papel principal**
6 amount by which one is ahead: *they had a lead of 4 hours/of 2 kilometres.* □ **ventaja**
■ *v.* (*he led*) **1** to go/to be ahead/to show the way: *he's leading the group; she led us to the cottage; they were led into bad habits by their friends.* □ **conducir, llevar**
2 to be the first/to have the most important place: *their horse is leading in the race; at one time Britain led the world in industry.* □ **encabezar; liderar**
3 to make (something) have; to have: *she leads a dull life.* □ **llevar**
4 *it led me to think she was lying,* made me think. □ **me llevó a pensar...**
5 *he leads her a dog's life,* makes her life miserable. □ **le hace llevar una vida de perros**
6 to be at the head of/to direct: *he led his men into battle; he leads his team very well.* □ **dirigir**
7 (*in cards*) to play as first card; to play first: *to lead the queen.* □ **salir con**
8 to go in a particular direction: *this road leads to Dublin; their discovery led to improvements; this will lead to nothing.* □ **llevar**
leader ['li:də] *n.* **1** person who manages/directs others: *he is the leader of the group; she's a born leader.* □ **líder**
2 main article in a newspaper. □ **artículo de fondo**
3 chief player, especially of the violin, in an orchestra. □ **primer violín**
leadership *n.* state or quality of being the person who manages/directs others: *qualities of leadership; much was achieved under his leadership.* □ **liderazgo**
leading *adj.* which leads; most important. □ **conductor; sobresaliente**
leading article, main article in a newspaper, giving views on topics of current interest. □ **editorial**
leading aircraftman/seaman, junior rank in the air force/in the navy. □ **aviador/marinero de primera**
leading lady/man, actress/actor taking the main role. □ **primer actor; primera actriz**
leading question, question which is worded in order to get a particular answer. □ **pregunta que sugiere la respuesta**
lead on *v.* **1** to go ahead, so that others will follow. □ **ir delante**

2 *they led him on,* encouraged him to go on, especially to do something stupid. □ **le empujaron a hacerlo**
lead up to *v.* to prepare the way for something (in conversation): *she knew he was leading up to a proposal of marriage.* □ **preparar el terreno para**
leaf [li:f] *n.* (*pl. leaves*) **1** flat, usually green, part of a plant, growing from a stem or branch. □ **hoja**
2 *the trees are **in leaf,*** have leaves. □ **los árboles tienen hojas**
3 sheet of paper forming two pages of a book: *the leaves are torn.* □ **hoja**
to turn over a new leaf, to change your ways/to try to improve. □ **hacer borrón y cuenta nueva**
to take a leaf out of someone's book, to follow someone's example. □ **tomar ejemplo de alguien**
4 flat folding part (of a table). □ **tablero abatible**
5 very thin sheet of metal, etc.: *gold leaf.* □ **hoja; pan de oro**
■ *v. **to leaf through** the pages of a book,* to turn them over rapidly without reading. □ **hojear**
leaflet *n.* sheet of paper, often folded, giving information as an advertisement: *have you any leaflets on holidays in Greece?* □ **folleto**
leafy *adj.* (*leafier, leafiest*) covered with leaves. □ **frondoso**
league [li:g] *n.* **1** group joined together for some purpose. □ **liga**
2 *he was **in league with** them,* was co-operating/working with them against someone else. □ **estaba aliado con ellos**
3 association of sports clubs which play against each other: *football league.* □ **liga**
■ *v.* to join together/to form a group for a particular purpose. □ **aliarse**
leak [li:k] *n.* **1** hole through which liquid/gas, etc., can escape or enter: *there's a leak in the pipe/the flour bag.* □ **fuga**
to spring a leak: *the ship sprang a leak,* got a hole. □ **se abrió una vía de agua en el barco**
2 escape of information: *there was a leak of government secrets.* □ **filtración**
■ *v.* **1** (*of liquid/gas, etc.*) to flow away/to escape: *there's water leaking out.* □ **salirse**
2 (*of container*) to allow liquid/gas, etc., to escape or enter: *the pipe/the bag/the boat/my shoe is leaking.* □ **escaparse (gas); perder (líquido); dejar entrar el agua**
3 to allow information to escape: *they leaked the decision to the press,* they passed on the secret information. □ **filtrar**
leakage *n.* amount of liquid, etc., which has escaped: *leakage from a pipe.* □ **gotera; escape**
leaky *adj.* (*leakier, leakiest*) which leaks: *a leaky boat.* **perforado; que hace agua (barca)**
lean [li:n] *adj.* (*leaner, leanest*) **1** thin/with little flesh. □ **enjuto**
2 (*of meat*) with little fat. □ **magro**
3 poor/unproductive: *lean years.* □ **años de vacas flacas**
■ *n.* meat with little fat. □ **carne magra**
■ *v.* (*he leaned/he leant*) **1** to support (yourself/something) on: *to lean your elbows on the table; to lean against the wall; lean the ladder against the wall.* □ **apoyarse (en la mesa/contra la pared)**
2 *he leant heavily on his family,* looked to them for support. □ **dependía mucho de su familia**
3 to stand/to be in a position at an angle: *leaning forward; the post is leaning towards the gate.* □ **inclinarse**
4 to have a tendency towards: *he leans towards Communism.* □ **inclinarse**
leaning *n.* tendency towards/interest in: *he has leanings towards Communism.* □ **inclinación**
leanness *n.* being thin. □ **delgadez**
lean over *v.* to bend (in a particular direction): *he leant over to speak to her.* □ **inclinarse (hacia delante)**
to lean over backwards (to): *he leant over backwards to help her,* made every effort to help. □ **no escatimó esfuerzos para ayudarla**
lean-to *n.* (small) building with a sloping roof supported against the wall of a larger building. □ **cobertizo**
leap [li:p] *n.* **1** jump: *the dog made a leap in the air.* □ **salto**
2 upward/forward movement: *his discovery was a great leap forward.* □ **paso**
3 *to advance **by leaps and bounds,*** to make rapid progress. □ **avanzar a pasos agigantados**
4 ***leap in the dark,*** action where you are unsure of the consequences. □ **salto en el vacío**
■ *v.* (*he leaped/leapt*) **1** to jump: *he leapt to his feet; you'll have to leap* (*over*) *the ditch.* □ **cayó de pie en su salto**
2 to rise suddenly: *the flames leapt in the air.* □ **elevarse de repente**
leap at *v.* to seize/to accept eagerly: *they leapt at the offer.* □ **no dejar escapar**
leapfrog *n.* game in which one person jumps over the bent back of another. □ **pídola**
■ *v.* (*he leapfrogged*) to jump over the bent back of someone. □ **saltar por encima de**
leap year *n.* every fourth year, in which February has 29 days. □ **año bisiesto**
learn [lə:n] *v.* (*he learned/learnt*) **1** to gain knowledge of something/of how to do something: *learn your lessons; he's only learning; they're learning to swim.* □ **aprender**
2 to hear (news, etc.): *yesterday I learned that they were leaving.* □ **enterarse**
learned ['lə:nid] *adj.* **1** having much knowledge: *the learned professions.* □ **instruido**
2 for people who have great knowledge of a particular subject: *learned journal.* □ **revista especializada**
learner *n.* person who is learning: *she's a quick learner.* □ **estudiante**
learner driver, person who is learning to drive. □ **alumno de autoescuela**
learning *n.* **1** gaining knowledge of something/of how to do something. □ **aprendizaje**
2 great study/knowledge: *man of learning.* □ **cultura, saber**
lease [li:s] *n.* **1** letting/renting of a building/piece of land etc., for a specified period: *to have a flat on a long lease.* □ **arrendamiento**
2 *it's given him **a new lease of life,*** it's made him want to make a fresh start/to live more fully. □ **dar nuevas fuerzas a uno**
■ *v.* to take/to give/to hold on a lease: *he leased the shop to his brother; his brother leased the shop from him.* □ **arrendar**
leasehold *n.* (holding of) property on a lease. □ **arrendamiento**
■ *adj.* held on a lease. □ **arrendado**
leash [li:ʃ] *n.* (*pl. leashes*) strap/cord to keep a dog in control. □ **correa**
least [li:st] *adj.* and *n.* (of) the smallest/most unimportant (amount): *that's the least of my worries; he hadn't the least fear of it.* □ **menor; lo que menos...; el más mínimo**

at least you'll have something to eat. □ **al menos...**
not in the least, not at all: *it doesn't matter in the least.* □ **en absoluto, nada**
■ *adv.* in the smallest way: *he deserves it least of all; the least rich of them.* □ **menos**

leather ['leðə] *n.* skin of certain animals, prepared and used to make shoes/bags, etc. □ **cuero**
leathery *adj.* (tough) like leather. □ **correoso**

leave [li:v] *n.* **1** permission: *without asking anybody's leave.* □ **permiso**
2 time off; permission to be away: *three months' leave; absent without leave.* □ **permiso**
3 ***to take leave of someone,*** to say goodbye to. □ **despedirse de alguien**
4 *have you taken leave of your senses?,* have you become quite mad? □ **¿has perdido la cabeza?**
■ *v.* (*he left*) **1** to go away (from): *he left yesterday; she left the house.* □ **marcharse**
2 to allow to remain behind/to forget to take: *he left his toothbrush in the hotel; he left the room in a muddle.* □ **dejar, dejarse**
3 ***leave me alone,*** don't pester me. □ **déjame en paz**
4 ***leave it to me,*** let me deal with it. □ **déjamelo a mí**
5 *she left the cooking until the morning of the party,* did not do it until then. □ **dejar**
6 to abandon: *he left his wife.* □ **dejar**
7 to give (to someone) in your will: *he left all his money to his family; she left me $100.* □ **dejar**
8 to have at the time of one's death: *he leaves a widow (and three daughters).* □ **dejar**
leave behind *v.* to forget to take (something) with you: *he left his glasses behind.* □ **dejarse; se dejó las gafas**
leave off *v.* to stop: *where did we leave off? you'll have to leave off smoking.* □ **parar; dejar de (fumar)**
leave out *v.* to forget/to omit: *he left his son out of his will; you left out the most important part of the story.* □ **dejar fuera (testamento); omitir**
leaving *n.* going away: *there was general dismay at his leaving.* □ **partida**
leavings *n. pl.* what is left over, especially food. □ **sobras**

leaven ['levn] *n.* substance which causes a dough to rise; something which causes a change. □ **levadura**

Lebanon ['lebənən] *n.* country at the Eastern end of the Mediterranean. □ **Líbano**
Lebanese [lebə'ni:z] *adj.* referring to the Lebanon. □ **libanés**
■ *n.* (*pl. Lebanese*) person from the Lebanon. □ **libanés**

lecher ['letʃə] *n.* man who frequently indulges in sex. □ **libertino**
lecherous *adj.* (person) who indulges in sex. □ **lascivo**

lectern ['lektən] *n.* stand with a sloping surface on which you can put a book/papers, etc., from which you are going to read aloud in public. □ **atril**

lecture ['lektʃə] *n.* **1** talk, especially to students or other group of people on a particular subject: *she gave a lecture on Greek architecture.* □ **conferencia**
2 (long) scolding: *their father gave them a lecture on their bad behaviour.* □ **reprimenda**
■ *v.* to give a lecture (to): *he lectured (them) on politics; she's always lecturing her children.* □ **dar una conferencia; sermonear**
lecturer *n.* **1** person who gives a talk on a particular subject: *the lecturer brought some slides with him.* □ **conferenciante**
2 teacher in a university or college: *lecturer in economics.* □ **profesor; profesor de economía**

led [led] *v. see* **lead²**.

ledge [ledʒ] *n.* flat (narrow) part which sticks out from a cliff or building: *they walked along the narrow ledge; there's a ledge outside the window.* □ **saliente (acantilado); antepecho (ventana)**

ledger ['ledʒə] *n.* book in which accounts are kept. □ **libro mayor**

lee [li:] *n.* side of a ship sheltered from the wind: *lee side of a ship.* □ **sotavento**
lee shore, shore towards which the wind is blowing. □ **costa de sotavento**
leeward *adj., adv.* and *n.* (side of a ship) sheltered from the wind. □ **a sotavento (adj., adv.); banda de sotavento (n.)**
leeway *n.* **1** time which has been lost. □ **tiempo perdido**
to make up leeway, to make up for lost time/opportunity. □ **recuperar lo perdido**
2 extra time/extra space: *have you left enough leeway to catch the train?* □ **margen; margen de tiempo**

leech [li:tʃ] *n.* (*pl. leeches*) type of worm which sucks blood. □ **sanguijuela**

leek [li:k] *n.* type of vegetable related to the onion, with white bulb and long green leaves. □ **puerro**

leer ['liə] *n.* nasty sideways look, often expressing sexual desire: *he said it with a leer.* □ **mirada de reojo lasciva**
■ *v.* to look with a leer: *he leered at her.* □ **mirar de reojo con lascivia**

lees [li:z] *n.pl.* sediment left at the bottom of a wine bottle, etc. □ **poso**

left [left] *n.* **1** side of the body which normally has the weaker hand: *on my left; on/to the left.* □ **izquierda**
2 left hand/fist: *the boxer hit his opponent with his left.* □ **izquierdo (puño); izquierda (mano)**
3 (*in politics*) group/policy supporting the rights of the workers: *he is on the left of the party; the proposal was rejected by the left.* □ **izquierda**
■ *adj.* **1** of/on the side of the body which normally has the weaker hand: *left hand; left side; left bank,* bank of a river, etc., on your left when facing downstream. □ **izquierdo**
2 of the left (in politics). □ **de la izquierda**
■ *adv.* on/to the left: *turn left at the crossroads.* □ **a la izquierda**
■ *see also* **leave.**
left-handed *adj.* using the left hand more than the right. □ **zurdo**
leftist *adj.* and *n.* (person) who is on the left of the socialist party. □ **izquierdista**
left-luggage office *n.* place in a station, etc., where suitcases, etc., can be left and collected later for a fee. □ **consigna**
leftovers *n.pl.* what is not used, especially food which has not been eaten. □ **sobras**
left-wing *adj.* politically on the left: *left-wing members of the party.* □ **izquierdista**
left-winger *n.* person who is on the left politically. □ **izquierdista**

leg [leg] *n.* **1** part of the body on which a person or animal walks. □ **pierna (persona); pata (animal)**
to be on one's last legs, to be almost exhausted. □ **estar en las últimas**
to give someone a leg up, to help him to climb to a higher position. □ **ayudarle a uno a subir**
to pull someone's leg, to joke by telling him something untrue. □ **tomarle a uno el pelo**
2 leg of an animal for food: *leg of lamb.* □ **pierna**
3 part of a garment which covers the leg: *trouser leg.* □ **pernera**

4 part which supports: *table leg; chair leg.* □ **pata**
5 section of a race/journey: *he overtook his opponent in the first leg.* □ **etapa**
legged [legd, 'legid] *suffix meaning* with legs: *four-legged animal; three-legged table.* □ **de... patas**
leggings *n.pl.* thick leather/canvas covering for the lower leg. □ **polainas**
legless *adj.* without any legs. □ **sin piernas; sin patas**
leg-pull *n.* (*informal*) hoax. □ **tomadura de pelo**
leggy *adj.* with long legs. □ **patilargo**

legacy ['legəsi] *n.* (*pl. legacies*) what is left to a person (after someone's death): *he was left a legacy by his aunt; his ill health was a legacy of his life in the tropics.* □ **legado**
legatee [legə'ti:] *n.* person who receives a legacy. □ **legatario**

legal ['li:gl] *adj.* **1** in accordance with/obeying the law: *it's not legal to park your car here.* □ **legal; no es lícito...**
legal tender, money which must legally be accepted if you give it in payment. □ **moneda de curso legal**
2 referring to the (processes of the) law: *legal proceedings; to get a legal opinion; legal document.* □ **jurídico**
legalistic [ligə'listik] *adj.* too concerned with the law: *a legalistic approach to the problem.* □ **legalista**
legality [li'gæliti] *n.* being allowed by law: *the legality of the evidence was in doubt.* □ **legalidad**
legalize *v.* to authorize (something) by law. □ **legalizar**
legally *adv.* in accordance with the law: *legally responsible.* □ **legalmente**

legate ['legət] *n.* official envoy (from the Pope). □ **legado**
legation [li'geiʃn] *n.* group of officials who represent their government in a foreign country; building where a group of official representatives abroad live or work. □ **legación**

legend ['ledʒənd] *n.* **1** story from the past which may not be based on fact: *the legend of St George and the dragon.* □ **leyenda**
2 *he was a legend in his own lifetime,* he was very famous even before he died. □ **fue una leyenda en vida**
legendary *adj.* referring to a legend. □ **legendario**

legible ['ledʒibl] *adj.* clear/able to be read (easily): *legible handwriting.* □ **legible**
legibility [ledʒi'biliti] *n.* being easily read. □ **legibilidad**
legibly *adv.* in a legible way. □ **legiblemente**

legion ['li:dʒən] *n.* **1** division of an army. □ **legión**
2 association/body, especially of soldiers. □ **legión**
the Foreign Legion, private army, organized by France, which serves overseas. □ **la Legión Extranjera**
3 very large number. □ **legión**

legislate ['ledʒisleit] *v.* to make laws. □ **legislar**
to legislate for: *you can't legislate for good weather,* it cannot be arranged deliberately. □ **ordenar, dictar**
legislation [ledʒi'sleiʃn] *n.* (making of) laws: *there is some new legislation which forbids it.* □ **legislación**
legislative ['ledʒislətiv] *adj.* referring to laws/law-making: *legislative assembly.* □ **legislativo; asamblea legislativa**
legislature ['ledʒislətʃə] *n.* law-making body. □ **legislatura**

legitimacy [li'dʒitiməsi] *n.* being in accordance with the law. □ **legitimidad**
legitimate *adj.* **1** legal/lawful. □ **legítimo**
legitimate child, child born to married parents. □ **hijo legítimo**
2 reasonable/justifiable: *legitimate excuse.* □ **válido; una excusa válida**
legitimately *adv.* in accordance with the laws. □ **legítimamente**
legitimize *v.* to make (something) lawful. □ **legitimar**

legume ['legju:m] *n.* plant (like a pea or bean) which has seeds in pods. □ **legumbre**
leguminous [le'gju:minəs] *adj.* (plant) which has seeds in pods. □ **leguminoso**

leisure ['leʒə] *n.* time free to do what you want: *to have leisure for reading; leisure time; in my leisure moments,* when I am not working. □ **ocio**
at one's leisure: *examine it at your leisure,* when there is an opportunity/without hurry. □ **...en tus ratos libres; tiempo libre**
leisure pursuits, pastimes. □ **pasatiempos**
leisured *adj.* having plenty of leisure. □ **desocupado**
leisured classes, people who do not need to work to earn money. □ **clases acomodadas**
leisurely *adj.* without hurry: *at a leisurely pace.* □ **sin prisa; a un ritmo pausado**

leitmotiv ['laitməuti:f] *n.* theme which reappears and which shows a special feeling/state. □ **leitmotiv**

lemon ['lemən] *n.* **1** pale yellow sour-tasting fruit; tree which bears such fruit. □ **limón; limonero**
lemon squash, drink made from lemons and sugar, etc. □ **zumo de limón**
lemon curd, type of cream made with eggs and lemons, used to spread on bread. □ **crema de limón**
2 *she was wearing a lemon(-coloured) scarf,* a pale yellow scarf. □ **llevaba un pañuelo amarillo limón**
lemonade [lemə'neid] *n.* usually fizzy lemon-flavoured drink. □ **limonada**

lemur ['li:mə] *n.* monkey-like animal with a long nose and tail. □ **lémur**

lend [lend] *v.* (*he lent*) **1** to give (something to someone) for a certain period of time: *will you lend me your book for a day or two?* □ **prestar**
2 to give/to contribute (to): *the lights lend a brighter look to the garden.* □ **dar**
3 ***to lend someone a hand,*** to help someone: *can you lend me a hand with the washing?* □ **echar una mano**
4 ***to lend itself to:*** *the shed lends itself to being used as a studio,* it is suitable for use as a studio. □ **puede utilizarse, se presta para**
lender *n.* person who lends (money). □ **prestamista**
lending library *n.* section of a library from which books may be taken away for a time. □ **biblioteca de préstamo**

length [leŋθ] *n.* **1** measurement of how long something is from end to end: *it's 2 metres in length.* □ **longitud**
2 *he won the race by a length,* by the length of a horse/man/boat, etc.. □ **ganó la carrera por un cuerpo**
3 *she swam two lengths of the pool,* up and down the pool. □ **nadó dos largos de la piscina**
4 *throughout* ***the length and breadth of*** *the country,* all over the country. □ **a lo largo y ancho del país**
5 piece of a particular length: *a dress length of cloth; a length of rope.* □ **trozo**
6 being long. □ **condición de largo**
7 *a stay of some length,* quite a long stay. □ **una larga estancia**
8 *award for length of service,* for long service. □ **regalo por los muchos años de servicio**
9 ***at length,*** (i) at last: *at length they reached Rome.* □ **finalmente**

(ii) for a long time: *he spoke at (some) length.* □ **habló largo y tendido**
10 *to go to great lengths,* to make great efforts. □ **hacer un gran esfuerzo**
lengthen *v.* to make/to become longer: *she lengthened the skirt; his face lengthened.* □ **alargar(se)**
lengthily *adv.* for a long time/at length. □ **largamente**
lengthiness *n.* being long. □ **prolijidad**
lengthways, lengthwise *adv.* along the length/along the longest side: *measure it lengthways.* □ **longitudinalmente, a lo largo**
lengthy *adj.* (very) long: *lengthy speech.* □ **largo; un discurso prolijo**
leniency ['li:njənsi] *n.* being merciful/not being strict. □ **indulgencia**
lenient *adj.* showing mercy/not strict or severe: *the judge was often considered too lenient.* □ **indulgente**
leniently *adv.* in a lenient way. □ **con indulgencia**
lens [lenz] *n.* (*pl. lenses*) **1** piece of glass/plastic, etc., curved so as to cause light rays to join or spread out, and used in spectacles/telescopes/cameras, etc. □ **lente**
2 part of the eye. □ **cristalino**
3 *contact lens,* small piece of plastic, etc., worn on the eyeball to help you to see. □ **lentilla**
lent [lent] *v. see* **lend.**
Lent [lent] *n.* (*in the Christian church*) period before Easter when many Christians eat less/give up some luxury. □ **Cuaresma**
Lenten *adj.* referring to Lent. □ **cuaresmal**
lentil ['lentl] *n.* small round dried seed used as food: *lentil soup.* □ **lenteja**
Leo ['liou] *n.* one of the signs of the zodiac, shaped like a lion. □ **Leo**
leonine ['li:əunain] *adj.* referring to a lion. □ **leonino**
leopard ['lepəd] *n.* large spotted animal of the cat family. □ **leopardo**
leotard ['liətɑ:d] *n.* skin-tight one-piece costume worn by ballet dancers, etc. □ **leotardo**
leper ['lepə] *n.* person who has leprosy. □ **leproso**
leprosy *n.* serious infectious skin disease which slowly destroys flesh and nerves. □ **lepra**
leprechaun ['leprəkɔ:n] *n.* (*in Ireland*) wicked little elf. □ **duendecillo**
lesbian ['lezbiən] *adj.* and *n.* (woman) who is sexually attracted to other women. □ **lesbiana**
lesion ['li:ʒn] *n.* wound; change in body tissue. □ **lesión**
less [les] *adj.* and *n.* (of a) smaller quantity/size/value: *of less value; a sum less than $1; less bread; in less than an hour; at less than cost price.* □ **menos**
■ *prep.* minus/with a certain amount taken away: *purchase price less 10%.* □ **menos**
■ *adv.* in a smaller amount/to a smaller degree: *she's trying to eat less; he is less well known than James; I'm less afraid of it now.* □ **menos**
lessen *v.* to make (something) become less; to reduce. □ **reducir**
lesser *adj.* smaller: *the lesser of two evils.* □ **menor**
lessee [le'si:] *n.* person who holds a lease/who pays rent. □ **arrendatario**
lessor [le'sɔ:] *n.* person who gives a lease/who receives rent. □ **arrendador**
lesson ['lesn] *n.* **1** period of time in school, etc., during which you are taught something: *during the French lesson; to take driving lessons.* □ **clase**
2 means by which you learn: *that was a hard lesson; let that be a lesson to you.* □ **lección**
3 *he's learnt his lesson,* he is wiser. □ **ha aprendido la lección**
to teach someone a lesson, to make someone wiser/to punish someone. □ **darle a uno una lección**
4 piece of the Bible which is read in church. □ **lectura**
lest [lest] *conj.* **1** (*formal*) in order to avoid: *he wore a coat lest he catch cold.* □ **para que no**
2 for fear of: *they were terrified lest they should be caught.* □ **por miedo a que**
let [let] *v.* (*he was letting; he let*) **1** to permit/to allow: *let me do it; when can you let me have it? let him hear your story.* □ **permitir**
2 to give for a period of time in return for money: *house to let; they let boats at the pier.* □ **alquilar**
■ *v.* (showing command/suggestion): *let's hurry; don't let's start yet; let them all come.* □ **démonos prisa; no empecemos aún; que vengan todos**
■ *n.* (*informal*) period of lease of a property: *flats available for short lets.* □ **arriendo**
let down *v.* **1** to take down/to lower: *she let down the hem of her dress.* □ **bajar; le bajó el dobladillo al vestido**
2 to fail to help/to disappoint: *I won't let you down.* □ **fallar**
letdown *n.* disappointment: *after all the publicity the actual performance was a letdown.* □ **decepción**
let go *v.* **1** to lose hold: *don't let go of the handle.* □ **soltar**
2 to allow (someone) to leave: *the police questioned them for an hour and then let them go.* □ **dejar ir(se)**
let in *v.* **1** to allow to come in: *let him in; these shoes are letting in water.* □ **dejar entrar/pasar**
2 *I didn't know what I was letting myself in for,* what I was going to have to do. □ **...lo que tenía que hacer**
let off *v.* **1** to make (a gun/rocket, etc.) fire. □ **disparar (una pistola); tirar (un cohete)**
2 *to let someone off,* not to punish/not to charge someone after all. □ **dejar libre**
let on *v.* (*informal*) to say/to tell: *don't let on that I was there.* □ **que no se te escape que estaba allí**
let out *v.* **1** to allow to go out/to escape: *they let the animals out by mistake; she let out a yell.* □ **dejar salir; se le escapó un grito**
2 to give for a period of time in return for money: *they let out boats.* □ **alquilar**
3 to make (a garment, etc.) wider. □ **ensanchar**
let out *n.* way of avoiding doing something which you ought to do. □ **escaqueo**
let up *v.* to stop/to become less: *the rain hasn't let up all day.* **disminuir; no ha dejado de llover en todo el día**
lethal ['li:θl] *adj.* deadly/causing death: *lethal weapon.* □ **letal**
lethargy ['leθədʒi] *n.* (feeling of) unwillingness to do anything. □ **letargo**
lethargic [lə'θɑ:dʒik] *adj.* feeling/appearing unwilling to do anything: *in a lethargic manner.* □ **letárgico**
let's [lets] *short for* let us.
letter ['letə] *n.* **1** written/printed symbol representing a sound of speech: *the letter L.* □ **letra**
2 *to carry out something **to the letter,*** to the last detail. □ **al pie de la letra**
3 piece of writing sent from one person/organization to another to pass on information: *they sent him a letter of thanks.* □ **carta**
4 *letters,* learning, especially in literature, etc.: *man of letters.* □ **letras**
■ *v.* to mark with letters: *lettered book cover.* □ **estampar con letras**
letterbox *n.* box where letters are posted; hole in a door through which letters are delivered. □ **buzón**

letterhead *n.* printed heading on writing paper. □ **membrete**
lettering *n.* **1** writing letters. □ **rotulación**
2 letters in an inscription, etc.: *the lettering on the stone.* □ **inscripción**
letterpress *n.* method of printing using metal letters. □ **impresión tipográfica**
lettuce ['letis] *n.* green vegetable whose leaves are often used in salads. □ **lechuga**
leucocyte ['lju:kəusait] *n.* white blood cell. □ **leucocito**
leukaemia [lu:'ki:miə] *Amer.* **leukemia** *n.* serious, often fatal, illness, which increases the white cells in the blood. □ **leucemia**
levee ['levi] *n. Amer.* embankment built along the bank of a river which is liable to flood. □ **malecón**
level ['levl] *n.* **1** flat/horizontal position. □ **nivel**
on the level, (i) in a flat position. □ **a nivel**
(ii) (*informal*) straight/honest. □ **honrado**
2 position in relation to height and depth; position on a scale/in a list: *at sea level; room on a level with the garden; discussions at managerial level,* among managers. □ **nivel; a la altura del**
3 instrument for testing whether something is level or not: *spirit level.* □ **nivel**
■ *adj.* **1** flat/even/horizontal: *a level surface.* □ **a nivel**
2 at the same level as: *level with the water.* □ **al nivel de**
3 calm/even: *keep a level head.* □ **sereno**
4 ***to do one's level best,*** (*informal*) one's very best. □ **esforzarse al máximo**
■ *v.* (*he levelled*) **1** to make/to become level: *the road levels* (*out*) *at the top of the hill; the ground was levelled for building; they levelled the house to the ground,* they destroyed it completely. □ **nivelar; arrasar**
2 to point/to aim: *he levelled his gun at the doorman; accusations were levelled at him.* □ **apuntar (arma); dirigir**
level crossing *n.* place where a road crosses a railway line without a bridge or tunnel. **paso a nivel**
level-headed *adj.* calm/able to act sensibly. □ **sensato**
lever ['li:və] *n.* instrument such as a bar which helps to raise a heavy object, or to move part of a machine etc.. □ **palanca**
gear lever, handle in a car which changes the gears. □ **palanca de cambio**
■ *v.* to move with a lever: *they levered up the heavy weight.* □ **levantar con una palanca**
leverage *n.* **1** force of a lever. □ **fuerza de la palanca**
2 influence which you can use to reach your aims. □ **influencia**
leveret ['levrət] *n.* young hare. □ **lebrato**
leviathan [li'vaiəθən] *n.* huge powerful monster or machine. □ **leviatán**
levitate ['leviteit] *v.* (*of person/heavy body*) to rise into the air. □ **levitar**
levitation [levi'teiʃn] *n.* rising into the air. □ **levitación**
levity ['leviti] *n.* disrespectful way of considering serious things. □ **ligereza**
levy ['levi] *n.* (*pl. levies*) **1** demand for/collection of (a tax/a number of soldiers). □ **exacción, recaudación (impuestos); leva (soldados)**
2 tax/number of soldiers (which has been collected). □ **recaudación (impuestos); reclutamiento (soldados)**
■ *v.* to demand/to collect (a tax/a number of soldiers). □ **recaudar (impuestos); reclutar (soldados)**
lewd [lu:d] *adj.* indecent/rude. □ **depravado**
lexicon ['leksikən] *n.* dictionary. □ **léxico**
lexicography [leksi'kɔgrəfi] *n.* writing of dictionaries. □ **lexicografía**
lexicographer *n.* person who writes dictionaries. □ **lexicógrafo**
liable ['laiəbl] *adj.* **1** (legally) responsible. □ **responsable**
2 *he is liable for their debts,* he has to pay their debts. □ **responsable de sus deudas**
3 obliged/bound to get: *liable to pay a fine; liable for military service.* □ **sujeto; expuesto**
4 apt (to)/likely (to): *this car is liable to overturn; difficulties are liable to occur.* □ **propenso; probable**
liability [laiə'biliti] *n.* (*pl. liabilities*) **1** (legal) responsibility: *he has no liability for the crimes of others.* □ **responsabilidad**
2 obligation: *liability to pay income tax.* □ **deber**
3 *he couldn't meet his liabilities,* he couldn't pay his debts. □ **no pudo pagar sus deudas**
4 tendency to something: *liability to catch disease.* □ **tendencia**
5 *he's a liability,* (*informal*) he causes problems. □ **estorbo**
liaison [li'eizən] *n.* joining/relationship/connection. □ **unión**
liaise *v.* to join with others, especially for discussion: *you'll have to liaise with your colleagues.* □ **juntarse con**
liar ['laiə] *n.* person who tells lies. □ **mentiroso**
lib [lib] *n.* (*informal*) *short for* liberation: *women's lib.* □ **liberación**
libel ['laibl] *n.* untrue statement(s) in writing, damaging to someone's character: *he was accused of libel.* □ **libelo**
■ *v.* (*he libelled*) to damage someone's character in writing. □ **difamar (por escrito)**
libellous *adj.* (writing) which damages someone's character. □ **difamatorio**
liberal ['librəl] *adj.* **1** wide in views/meaning, etc.: *liberal ideas; a liberal interpretation of a rule.* □ **liberal; amplio**
2 ample/generous: *he made liberal provision for his family,* left them plenty of money: *a liberal offer; liberal with one's money.* □ **generoso**
3 ***Liberal,*** (*in politics*) having views/policies based on freedom of individuals, democratic reform, etc. □ **liberal**
■ *n.* ***Liberal,*** (*in politics*) member or supporter of a Liberal party or policy. □ **liberal**
liberalism *n.* (*in politics*) liberal views/policies. □ **liberalismo**
liberality [libə'ræliti] *n.* **1** being open-minded. □ **amplitud de ideas**
2 generosity. □ **liberalidad**
liberally *adv.* in a generous way. □ **liberalmente**
liberate ['libəreit] *v.* to set/to make free: *the city was liberated from the enemy.* □ **liberar**
liberation [libə'reiʃn] *n.* setting free. □ **liberación**
liberator *n.* person who sets someone free. □ **libertador**
libertine ['libəti:n] *n.* man who is sexually immoral. □ **libertino**
liberty ['libəti] *n.* (*pl. liberties*) freedom. □ **libertad**
to be at liberty, to be free/not in captivity: *you are at liberty to leave when you like.* □ **estar en/tener libertad**
to take the liberty of doing something, do it without knowing whether it is allowed or not. □ **tomarse la libertad de hacer algo**
to take liberties, to do something without permission. □ **permitirse libertades**

to take liberties with something/someone, to treat something/someone too familiarly. □ **tomarse (muchas) libertades con**

libido [li'bi:dəu] *n.* (*pl. libidos*) sexual urge. □ **libido**

Libra ['li:brə] *n.* one of the signs of the zodiac, shaped like a pair of scales. □ **Libra**

library ['laibrəri] *n.* (*pl. libraries*) **1** place where books are stored (to be read/borrowed/consulted): *the new public library.* □ **biblioteca**
2 collection of books: *is it in the library?* □ **biblioteca**
record library, collection of records available for borrowing. □ **fonoteca**
librarian [lai'brɛəriən] *n.* person who works in a library/who is in charge of a library. □ **bibliotecario**

libretto [li'bretou] *n.* (pl. *librettos*) words of an opera. □ **libreto**
librettist *n.* person who writes a libretto. □ **libretista**

Libya ['libjə] *n.* Arab country in North Africa. □ **Libia**
Libyan *adj.* referring to Libya. □ **libio**
■ *n.* person from Libya. □ **libio**

lice [lais] *n.pl. see* **louse.**

licence ['laisəns] *Amer.* **license** *n.* **1** (document giving) official permission to have/to do something: *television licence; driving licence.* □ **licencia; permiso de conducción**
2 freedom, especially when used too much or wrongly: *he was given too much licence.* □ **libertad**
3 *poetic licence,* use of language in poetry which would not be acceptable in prose. □ **licencia poética**

license ['laisəns] *n. Amer. see* **licence**
■ *v.* to give official permission to. □ **autorizar**
licensed grocer, one allowed by law to sell alcoholic drink. □ **expendedor (de bebidas alcohólicas)**
licensee [laisən'si:] *n.* holder of a licence, especially landlord of a public house. □ **titular de una licencia**

licentious [lai'senʃəs] *adj.* indulging in sex or other pleasures beyond what is normally permitted: *licentious behaviour.* □ **licencioso**
licentiousness *n.* excessive indulgence in sex. □ **libertinaje**

lichen ['laikən] *n.* type of flat grey/yellow/green plant which grows on stones or on other plants. □ **liquen**

lick [lik] *n.* **1** stroke with the tongue: *he had a lick at his lollipop.* □ **lamido**
2 thin coating: *lick of paint.* □ **mano (de pintura)**
3 (*informal*) speed: *rushing along at a great lick.* □ **a todo gas**
4 ***to have a lick and a promise,*** (*informal*) to have a quick wash. □ **lavarse a toda mecha**
■ *v.* **1** to taste/to stroke with the tongue: *to lick a lollipop; the cat licked its kitten.* □ **lamer**
to lick someone's boots, to behave very humbly towards him to gain favour. □ **hacer la pelota a alguien**
to lick into shape, (i) to train (a person) into proper ways. □ **moldear**
(ii) to put (something) into good order. □ **arreglar**
2 to beat/to hit. □ **dar una paliza**
3 to defeat (in a game): *they licked us at tennis.* □ **ganar**
licking *n.* **1** stroking with the tongue. □ **lamido**
2 beating: *he got a good licking for that.* □ **paliza**
3 defeat. □ **victoria**

licorice ['likəris] *n. Amer. see* **liquorice.**

lid [lid] *n.* **1** covering for a container, often with a handle: *pot lid.* □ **tapadera**
that's put the lid on it, (*informal*) that's more than enough. □ **esto ya es el colmo**
2 eyelid/covering of the eye. □ **párpado**

lido ['li:dəu] *n.* (*pl. lidos*) swimming pool and terraces round it. □ **piscina con terrazas**

lie [lai] *n.* **1** statement which is not true: *to tell lies; it's a pack of lies.* □ **mentira**
2 position/direction in which something is situated. □ **posición; dirección**
the lie of the land, state of affairs. □ **el estado de las cosas**
■ *v.* **1** (*he lied; he was lying*) to say something which is not true: *you're lying.* □ **mentir**
2 (*he lay; he was lying; he has lain*) to be in a horizontal position: *he was lying on the couch; the book is lying on the table; he lay dead on the ground.* □ **estar echado**
3 *the snow didn't lie,* melted quickly. □ **la nieve no cuajó**
4 to be: *time lies heavy on her hands; the problem lies with him.* □ **estar; el tiempo no pasa en balde para ella**
see how the land lies, see what the condition/position of something is. □ **mira a ver cómo están las cosas**
lie down *v.* **1** to put yourself in a horizontal position: *he lay down on the couch.* □ **tumbarse**
2 ***to take lying down:*** *they won't take that lying down,* they won't accept it without protest. □ **no lo aceptarán sin rechistar**
lie-down *n.* (*informal*) putting yourself in a horizontal position for a short rest: *I'm going to have a little lie-down.* □ **voy a echarme un rato**
lie in *v.* to stay in bed longer than usual. □ **quedarse en la cama**
lie-in *n.* ***to have a lie-in,*** (*informal*) to stay in bed longer than usual. □ **quedarse un rato más en la cama**

lien ['liən] *n.* legal right to take and hold someone else's goods until a debt is paid. □ **derecho de retención**

lieu [lju:] *n.* ***in lieu of,*** instead of: *we haven't any blue washbasins in stock, so we have sent a green one in lieu.* □ **en lugar de**

lieutenant [lef'tenənt, *Amer.* lu:'tenənt] *n.* **1** rank in the armed services below a higher rank (*in the Army below* captain, *in the Navy below* lieutenant-commander). □ **teniente**
lieutenant-colonel, rank in the army below colonel. □ **teniente coronel**
lieutenant-commander, rank in the navy below commander. □ **capitán de corbeta**
flight lieutenant, rank in the air force below squadron leader. □ **capitán**
2 henchman: *the gang leader and his lieutenants.* □ **secuaz**

life [laif] *n.* (*pl. lives*) **1** state of being alive: *a matter of life and death; she saved my life.* □ **vida**
life insurance, insurance paid if you die. □ **seguro de vida**
2 ***to run for your life,*** as fast as you can. □ **¡sálvese quien pueda!**
3 ***I can't for the life of me*** *understand,* I can't understand at all. □ **por mucho que quiera no lo entenderé**
4 ***not on your life,*** not under any circumstances. □ **¡ni hablar!**
5 liveliness/energy: *he doesn't have much life in him.* □ **vida**
6 living things: *animal life; is there life on Mars?* □ **vida**
7 (length of) time you are alive: *his whole life was*

spent in China. □ **vida**
life imprisonment, imprisonment for the rest of your life. □ **cadena perpetua**
8 *in early life,* when he was a child. □ **en su infancia**
9 account/story of someone's life: *he's writing a life of Dickens.* □ **vida, biografía**
lifebelt *n.* cork-filled ring to keep a person afloat. □ **cinturón salvavidas**
lifeboat *n.* boat used to rescue people at sea. □ **bote salvavidas**
life cycle *n.* life of an animal/plant through various stages. □ **ciclo vital**
lifeguard *n.* person who rescues people who get into difficulties while swimming. □ **socorrista**
life jacket *n.* cork-filled coat to keep a person afloat. □ **chaleco salvavidas**
lifeless *adj.* **1** not alive: *his lifeless body lay where it fell.* □ **sin vida**
2 not lively: *what a lifeless party!* □ **sin animación**
lifelike *adj.* (*of a picture, etc.*) looking like the real person/thing. □ **que parece vivo**
lifelong *adj.* lasting your whole life: *lifelong friendship.* □ **de toda la vida**
life preserver *n.* **1** short stick, used in self-defence. □ **cachiporra**
2 *Amer.* lifebelt/ring to keep a person afloat. □ **salvavidas**
life-saving *n.* rescuing people from drowning. □ **salvamento**
life-size(d) *adj.* (statue/painting, etc.) which is the same size as the real thing or person. □ **de tamaño natural**
lifetime *n.* time when you are alive: *in his lifetime; once in a lifetime.* □ **vida**
it's the chance of a lifetime, the best chance you are ever likely to get. □ **es la ocasión de tu vida**

lift [lift] *n.* **1** (act of) raising. □ **levantamiento**
to give someone a lift up, help them to climb. □ **echar una mano a alguien (para subir)**
2 ride in a car: *can I give you a lift to the station?* □ **llevar en coche**
3 mechanical device for carrying people or goods from one floor of a building to another: *goods lift; the lift holds ten people.* □ **ascensor; montacargas**
ski lift, device to take skiers to the top of a ski slope. □ **remonte; telesilla**
■ *v.* **1** to raise (to a higher position): *lift your head; he lifted the book off the table.* □ **levantar**
2 to pick up (out of the ground): *to lift potatoes.* □ **coger**
3 to take away/to remove: *to lift a ban.* □ **levantar**
4 (*informal*) to steal: *their radio got lifted.* □ **mangar**
5 to rise: *the fog lifted at last.* □ **disiparse**
lift-off *n.* vertical take-off of a space rocket. □ **despegue**

ligament ['ligəmənt] *n.* tough tissue which holds bones together. □ **ligamento**

ligature ['ligətʃuə] *n.* thread used for tying in surgical operations. □ **ligadura**

light [lait] *n.* **1** brightness which allows you to see: *light of the sun; electric light; don't stand in my light,* between me and the source of light. □ **luz**
2 object which gives light: *a light above the door; rear light of a car.* □ **luz; luz trasera de un coche**
3 ***in the light of*** *what he said,* in consideration of it. □ **a la luz de**
4 ***to throw light on something,*** make it clearer. □ **arrojar luz sobre algo**
5 ***to come to light,*** be discovered. □ **ser descubierto**
6 appearance/aspect: *that put him in a good light.* □ **aspecto**
7 means of making a cigarette, etc., catch fire: *have you got a light?* □ **fuego**
8 ***lights,*** (i) lungs of certain animals used as food. □ **bofes**
(ii) traffic lights. □ **semáforos**
■ *v.* (*he lit*) **1** to put fire to: *light the fire/the candle; the fire won't light.* □ **encender**
2 to give light to: *the room is lit by electricity; the moon lit up the battlefield.* □ **iluminar**
3 to become bright with pleasure: *her face lit up.* □ **iluminarse**
4 ***to light on,*** to come across/to find. □ **encontrar**
■ *adj.* (*lighter, lightest*) **1** having a lot of light, allowing you to see well: *a light room; it's hardly light yet.* □ **iluminado**
2 of a pale colour: *light blue dress; light hair.* □ **claro; pelo rubio**
3 not heavy: *light weight; light work; light punishment.* □ **ligero**
4 *she's a light sleeper,* wakens easily. □ **tiene el sueño ligero**
5 not serious: *light comedy; light reading.* □ **ligero**
to make light of, to treat as unimportant. □ **restar importancia a**
■ *adv.* with little luggage: *I always travel light.* □ **ligero de equipaje**
lighten *v.* **1** to make lighter/not so dark: *she had her hair lightened.* □ **aclarar**
2 to make lighter/not so heavy: *to lighten the load.* □ **aligerar**
lighter *n.* **1** small instrument for making cigarettes, etc., burn. □ **mechero**
2 boat used for loading other boats. □ **gabarra**
light-fingered *adj.* (person) who is likely to steal. □ **ligero de dedos**
light-headed *adj.* dizzy/feeling excited. □ **aturdido**
light-hearted *adj.* cheerful/without a care. □ **despreocupado**
light heavyweight *n.* weight in boxing between middleweight and heavyweight. □ **peso semipesado**
lighthouse *n.* tall building containing a light to guide ships. □ **faro**
lighting-up time *n.* time at which street lamps and car lights have to be switched on. □ **hora del alumbrado**
lightly *adv.* in a light way: *lightly dressed,* wearing thin clothes. □ **ligeramente**
to get off lightly, with little or no punishment. □ **salir bien librado de**
lightness *n.* state/quality of being light. □ **ligereza**
lightship *n.* ship which carries a large light, acting as a floating lighthouse. □ **buque faro**
lightweight *n.* **1** weight in boxing between featherweight and welterweight. □ **peso ligero**
2 person without much influence. □ **persona de poca influencia**
■ *adj.* **1** light: *lightweight trousers.* □ **ligero**
2 not very influential/important. □ **de poca entidad**
light year *n.* distance travelled by light during one year (about six million million miles). □ **año luz**

lightning ['laitniŋ] *n.* flash of electricity in the sky, followed by thunder: *struck by lightning.* □ **relámpago; rayo**
lightning conductor, rod for carrying a lightning charge straight to the ground to prevent damage to buildings, etc. □ **pararrayos**
■ *adj.* extremely fast. □ **relámpago**
lightning strike, industrial strike taking place without warning. □ **huelga relámpago**

like [laik] *adj.* (nearly) the same/similar: *of like minds.* □ **semejante; de similar parecer**

■ *prep.* in the same way as/the same as/similar to: *he's like his father; it doesn't look like her; what's the weather like? it costs something like $10; he stood like a statue; to drink like a fish; to run like mad.* □ **como**
to feel like: *I feel like some chocolate,* I would like to eat some chocolate. □ **me apetece chocolate**
■ *n.* something similar: *I never saw the like; he and his like.* □ **semejanza; semejante**
■ *adv.* ***(as) like as not/like enough,*** probably. □ **probablemente**
■ *conj.* as: *do it like I do.* □ **como; hazlo como yo**
■ *v.* **1** to have pleasant feelings about: *do you like butter? how do you like him?* □ **gustar**
2 to desire/to want: *I'd like to see them; take as much as you like; what would you like? do as you like.* □ **gustar**
likeable *adj.* pleasant. □ **agradable**
likelihood *n.* probability: *in all likelihood.* □ **probabilidad**
likely *adj.* **1** probable: *it's very likely to happen; he's not likely to win.* □ **probable**
2 suitable (for)/apt (to): *conditions likely to cause an accident; the likeliest place for camping.* □ **apropiado**
■ *adv.* probably: *most likely; as likely as not.* □ **probablemente; a lo mejor**
not likely!, certainly not. □ **¡claro que no!**
liken ['laikən] *v.* to compare, by showing how one thing is similar to another. □ **comparar**
likeness *n.* something which looks like someone/something: *these portraits are a good likeness.* □ **parecido; estos retratos están muy conseguidos**
likes *n. pl.* **1** *likes and dislikes,* things you like and don't like. □ **gustos**
2 *the likes of me,* (*informal*) people like me. □ **personas como yo**
likewise *adv.* **1** in the same way: *likewise they brought their own cutlery.* □ **del mismo modo**
2 similarly/the same: *to do likewise.* □ **asimismo; hacer lo mismo**
liking *n.* pleasant feeling towards someone; fondness for someone/something: *I've taken a liking to him; is the food to your liking?,* do you like it? □ **cariño; gusto**
lilac ['lailək] *n.* **1** tree with large (pale) purple or white flowers. □ **lila**
2 pale purple colour. □ **color lila**
lilliputian [lili'pju:ʃn] *adj.* very small. □ **liliputiense**
lilt [lilt] *n.* song/way of speaking with a light well-marked rhythm. □ **canción, cadencia**
■ *v.* to sing/to play a tune with a light well-marked rhythm. □ **cantar melodiosamente**
lily ['lili] *n.* (*pl. lilies*) one of many types of often white flowers which grow from bulbs. □ **lirio; azucena**
lily-of-the-valley *n.* spring plant with small white flowers growing in clusters. □ **lirio de la pradera**
lima bean ['li:mə'bi:n] *n.* broad bean; type of vegetable of which the fat green seeds are eaten. □ **haba de Lima**
limb [lim] *n.* **1** leg/arm/wing: *danger to life and limb,* danger that you may be hurt. □ **miembro**
2 (main) branch of a tree. □ **rama**
3 *he's **out on a limb,*** in a difficult/exposed situation. □ **está en una situación peligrosa**
limber ['limbə] *v.* ***to limber up,*** to do exercises to warm your muscles before taking part in a sporting contest. □ **desentumecer los músculos**
limbo ['limbou] *n.* **1** position of not being accepted or rejected; being halfway between two stages: *the plan is in limbo.* □ **limbo; el plan está olvidado**
2 ***limbo dancing,*** type of West Indian dance where the dancer bends his body backwards parallel to the floor to pass under a horizontal bar. □ **'limbo'**
lime [laim] *n.* **1** white substance containing calcium, used in making cement. □ **cal**
2 small yellowish-green tropical fruit like a lemon; tree which bears such fruit. □ **lima (fruta); limero (árbol)**
3 northern deciduous tree with smooth leaves and yellowish flowers. □ **tilo**
lime green *adj.* and *n.* green colour of lime. □ **verde lima**
limelight *n.* attention/publicity: *he's in the limelight.* □ **candelero**
limestone *n.* light-coloured stone containing calcium. □ **piedra caliza**
limerick ['limərik] *n.* type of amusing five-line poem. □ **quintilla jocosa**
limit ['limit] *n.* furthest point/extent; boundary; end (beyond which you cannot go): *age limit; speed limit; within certain limits.* □ **límite**
that's the limit, (*informal*) too much. □ **es el colmo**
■ *v.* to put a limit on/to keep within limits; not to allow (something) to go beyond a certain point. □ **limitar**
limited (liability) company, company in which the members only have to pay debts up to the amount of capital they have put in. □ **sociedad (de responsabilidad) limitada**
limitation [limi'teiʃn] *n.* **1** act of limiting. □ **limitación**
2 something which stops you going further: *he knows his limitations,* he knows that he is not able/not physically fit to do something. □ **limitación**
limousine [limə'zi:n] *n.* large luxurious car. □ **limusina**
limp [limp] *n.* way of walking unevenly: *she has a bad limp; he walks with a limp.* □ **cojera**
■ *v.* to walk with an uneven step: *after the accident he limped badly.* □ **cojear**
■ *adj.* (*limper, limpest*) without stiffness/soft; without energy: *limp hand; book in a limp binding,* in a soft/paper cover. □ **flojo; blando**
limply *adv.* in a soft way. □ **flojamente**
limpness *n.* softness; lacking stiffness/energy. □ **flojedad**
limpet ['limpit] *n.* type of cone-shaped shellfish which clings to rocks. □ **lapa**
limpid ['limpid] *adj.* clear: *limpid water.* □ **límpido**
limpidity *n.* (*formal*) being clear/transparent. □ **limpidez**
linchpin ['lintʃpin] *n.* **1** pin which goes through an axle to hold a wheel on. □ **pezonera**
2 very important person/piece of machinery. □ **persona indispensable; pieza clave**
linctus ['liŋktəs] *n.* cough syrup. □ **jarabe para la tos**
line [lain] *n.* **1** (long) narrow mark/shape: *to draw a straight line; lines on your forehead.* □ **línea; arrugas de la frente**
to draw the line at, to stop short of/not to do. □ **no ir más allá de**
to be on the right lines, to be doing things the right way. □ **ir por buen camino**
2 long wire/cord: *fishing line.* □ **cable; cuerda; sedal (pesca)**
3 ***hard lines,*** bad luck. □ **es mala suerte**
4 ***telephone line,*** cable along which telephone messages are sent: *the line's bad,* it is difficult to make out what someone is saying; *crossed line,* two tele-

phone conversations which intermingle by error. □ **cable de teléfono; línea**
5 row of people/cars/words, etc.: *to stand in line; a long line of buses; a line of poetry.* □ **línea; una fila; un verso**
6 ***to drop someone a line,*** (*informal*) to send a short letter. □ **mandar unas letras**
7 *Amer.* queue/row of people waiting to buy something/to get on a bus, etc. □ **cola**
8 tracks on which trains run. □ **vías**
9 shipping/air company. □ **línea**
10 sequence of ancestors/descendants: *descended in direct line from Henry VIII.* □ **línea**
11 ***lines,*** shape/outline: *I like the lines of that car.* □ **línea**
12 direction; method; course of action: *in the line of fire; line of argument; to take a firm line; to take a hard line,* to be aggressive/not to weaken in any way. □ **línea; curso; tomar una actitud firme**
13 type of work/goods: *that's more in his line; they have a good line in coloured sheets.* □ **gama**
■ *v.* **1** to put lines on: *a face lined with worry; lined paper.* □ **rayar; una cara llena de preocupación; papel rayado**
2 to form a line (along the edge of): *tree-lined avenue; troops lined the streets.* □ **alinear**
3 to put a layer of material inside: *to line a dress; fur-lined boots.* □ **forrar**
lineaments *n. pl.* outline of the face/features. □ **facciones**
linear ['liniə] *adj.* referring to lines/to length: *linear measurements.* □ **lineal**
liner *n.* **1** something used for lining. □ **forro**
bin liner, plastic bag for putting inside a dustbin. □ **bolsa del cubo de la basura**
2 large passenger ship. □ **transatlántico**
linesman *n.* (*pl. linesmen*) person who stays on the sideline in a game to see if the ball goes over the line. □ **juez de línea**
line up *v.* to form a line/a queue. **alinearse**
line-up *n.* row/list of people. □ **fila**
lining *n.* layer of material inside something: *coat with a fur lining.* □ **forro**
linen ['linin] *n.* **1** cloth made from flax: *linen sheets.* □ **lino**
2 (*household*) *linen,* sheets/pillowcases/tablecloths, etc. □ **ropa blanca**
3 underwear. □ **ropa interior**
don't wash your dirty linen in public, do not tell shameful personal secrets. □ **los trapos sucios se lavan en casa**
ling [liŋ] *n.* heather. □ **brezo**
linger ['liŋgə] *v.* **1** to wait/to remain/to stay longer than necessary/expected: *to linger over a meal; an odd suspicion lingers in his mind.* □ **demorar(se); tardar; ...persistía en su mente**
2 (*of sick person*) to remain alive. □ **sobrevivir**
lingerie ['lænʒəri] *n.* women's underwear. □ **lencería**
lingo ['liŋgou] *n.* (*pl. lingoes*) (*slang*) language: *I can't speak the lingo, so don't ask me to translate.* □ **idioma**
linguist ['liŋgwist] *n.* **1** person who knows foreign languages well. □ **políglota**
2 person who studies linguistics. □ **lingüista**
linguistic [liŋ'gwistik] *adj.* **1** referring to language(s). □ **lingüístico**
2 referring to the science of language. □ **lingüístico**
linguistics *n.* science of language. □ **lingüística**
liniment ['linimənt] *n.* oily substance which you rub on the skin to lessen pains. □ **linimento**
link [liŋk] *n.* ring which forms part of a chain. □ **eslabón**
2 something which connects two parts: *the marriage formed a link between the two families; air link; the island has a telephone link to the mainland.* □ **vínculo (familia); enlace**
■ *v.* to join: *with linked arms; the facts are closely linked; they linked up with their associates in Rome.* □ **unir(se)**
linkman *n.* (*pl. linkmen*) person who speaks between parts of TV programmes. □ **presentador, locutor de continuidad**
links [liŋks] *n.pl.* golf course. □ **campo de golf**
linnet ['linit] *n.* type of small singing bird. □ **pardillo**
lino ['lainou] *n.* (*informal*) linoleum/hard smooth floor covering. □ **linóleo**
linocut ['lainoukʌt] *n.* design printed from a block of linoleum which has been cut into a pattern. □ **grabado en linóleo**
linoleum [li'nouliəm] *n.* hard smooth floor covering. □ **linóleo**
linseed ['linsi:d] *n.* seed of flax: *linseed oil.* □ **linaza**
lint [lint] *n.* soft cloth used for putting on wounds. □ **hilas**
lintel ['lintl] *n.* piece of wood/stone over a door or window. □ **dintel**
lion ['laiən] *n.* large wild animal of the cat family, the male of which has a long mane. □ **león**
the lion's share, the biggest part. □ **la parte del león**
lioness *n.* female lion. □ **leona**
lionize *v.* to treat (someone) as very important. □ **agasajar en desmesura**
lip [lip] *n.* **1** one of two fleshy parts round the outside of the mouth. □ **labio**
to keep a stiff upper lip, not to show emotion in time of trouble. □ **poner a mal tiempo buena cara**
to smack one's lips over, to express great enjoyment of. □ **relamerse los labios**
2 (*slang*) cheek/rudeness: *none of your lip.* □ **pasada; no te pases**
3 edge of a bowl/cup, etc. □ **borde**
lip-read *v.* (*he lip-read*) (*of a deaf person*) to follow speech by watching the movements of the lips of the person speaking. □ **leer los labios**
lip service *n. to pay lip service to something,* to give a false impression of respecting/obeying something. □ **jarabe de pico**
lipstick *n.* (stick of) substance for colouring the lips. □ **barra de labios**
liquefy ['likwifai] *v.* (*liquefied; liquefying*) to become liquid; to make (something) become liquid. □ **licuar(se)**
liquefaction [likwi'fækʃn] *n.* making/becoming liquid. □ **licuefacción**
liqueur [li'kə:] *n.* strong sweet alcoholic drink. □ **licor**
liquid ['likwid] *n.* substance which flows easily like water, and which is neither a gas nor a solid. □ **líquido**
■ *adj.* **1** which is neither gas nor solid, and which flows easily. □ **líquido**
2 (*of assets, etc.*) able to be changed easily into cash. □ **líquido**
3 (*of sounds*) pure/clear: *liquid tones.* □ **claro**
liquidate *v.* **1** to close (a company) which cannot pay its debts; to pay (a debt). □ **liquidar**
2 (*informal*) to kill. □ **liquidar**
liquidation [likwi'deiʃn] *n.* closing of a company which cannot pay its debts: *the company is in liquidation.* □ **liquidación**
liquidity [li'kwiditi] *n.* (*in finance*) being able to change assets into cash. □ **liquidez**

liquidizer ['likwidaizə] *n.* machine which reduces food to liquid form. □ **licuadora**
liquor ['likə] *n.* **1** alcoholic drink. □ **licor**
2 liquid produced in cooking something. □ **jugo**
liquorice ['likəris] *Amer.* **licorice** *n.* black substance from the root of a plant, used in medicine and in sweets. □ **regaliz**
lira ['liːrə] *n.* unit of money used in Italy. □ **lira**
lisp [lisp] *n.* speech defect in which 's' is pronounced as 'th'. □ **ceceo**
■ *v.* to speak with a lisp. □ **cecear**
lissom ['lisəm] *adj.* lithe/supple. □ **ágil**
list [list] *n.* **1** number of items written/spoken one after another: *shopping list; alphabetical list; wine list,* names of wines available in a restaurant; *to be on the sick list,* to be reported sick. □ **lista; carta de vinos**
to be on the danger list, to be dangerously ill. □ **estar gravemente enfermo**
2 leaning to one side: *the ship developed a 10 degree list.* □ **inclinación**
■ *v.* **1** to place in a list: *he is not listed,* he is not on the list. □ **colocar en una lista**
2 *I list him among my friends,* consider him to be one of them. □ **le cuento entre mis amigos**
3 (*of ship*) to lean over to one side. □ **escorarse**
listen ['lisn] *v.* to pay attention in order to hear: *listen to the music; just listen to me.* □ **escuchar**
listener *n.* person who listens. □ **oyente**
listless ['listləs] *adj.* (feeling) dull, without interest or energy. □ **desganado**
listlessly *adv.* in a way which shows lack of interest. □ **con desgana**
listlessness *n.* lack of interest/energy. □ **desgana**
lit [lit] *v. see* **light.**
litany ['litəni] *n.* (*litanies*) form of prayer with repeated responses, used in churches. □ **letanía**
liter ['liːtə] *n. Amer.* litre/measurement for liquids. □ **litro**
literacy ['litərəsi] *n.* ability to read and write. □ **capacidad de leer y escribir**
literal *adj.* keeping to the exact meaning of the original words: *literal translation.* □ **literal**
literally *adv.* in a literal way: *translate it literally;* (to emphasize) *his eyes were literally popping out of his head.* □ **literalmente**
literary *adj.* referring to literature. □ **literario**
literate ['litərət] *adj.* **1** able to read and write. □ **que sabe leer y escribir**
2 well educated, especially in literary subjects. □ **letrado**
literature ['litritʃə] *n.* **1** books/writing, especially novels, poetry, drama, biography, etc. □ **literatura**
2 what has been written on a particular subject. □ **bibliografía**
3 written information about something: *get me all the literature about washing machines.* □ **información (escrita)**
lithe [laið] *adj.* supple/bending easily: *lithe body.* □ **flexible**
lithograph ['liθəgrɑːf] *n.* painting/drawing, etc., reproduced by lithography. □ **litografía**
■ *v.* to print by lithography. □ **litografiar**
lithographic [liθə'græfik] *adj.* of lithography. □ **litográfico**
lithography [li'θɔgrəfi] *n.* method of printing using oil and ink on a flat surface such as a stone/a sheet of metal, etc. □ **litografía**
litigate ['litigeit] *v.* to go to law; to bring a lawsuit against someone. □ **litigar**
litigant *n.* person involved in a lawsuit. □ **litigante**
litigation [liti'geiʃn] *n.* **1** bringing a lawsuit against someone. □ **litigio**
2 lawsuit. □ **pleito**
litigious [li'tidʒəs] *adj.* ready to go to law/ready to argue. □ **litigioso**
litmus ['litməs] *n.* blue substance which is turned red by an acid and back to blue by an alkali. □ **tornasol**
litmus paper *n.* paper containing litmus used to test for acids and alkalis. □ **papel de tornasol**
litre ['liːtə] *Amer.* **liter** *n.* measurement for liquids (almost 2 pints): *a litre of wine.* □ **litro**
litter ['litə] *n.* **1** rubbish left on streets, etc.: *don't throw litter; litter bin.* □ **desperdicios**
2 (*in former times*) stretcher/bed on which a person was carried. □ **camilla**
3 bedding of straw, etc., for animals. □ **cama de paja**
4 (*of animals*) group of young born at one time: *a litter of pigs.* □ **camada**
■ *v.* **1** to drop rubbish about: *the place was littered with papers.* □ **ensuciar**
2 (*of animals*) to produce young. □ **parir**
little ['litl] *adj.* (*less/least*) **1** small: *little finger.* □ **pequeño; el dedo meñique**
2 *his little sister,* his younger sister. □ **su hermana menor**
3 ***a little,*** small amount of: *he has a little money in the bank.* □ **un poco**
4 not much: *he has little money; she eats very little bread.* □ **poco**
■ *n.* small amount: *give me a little; I see very little of him these days.* □ **poco**
little by little, gradually. □ **poco a poco**
■ *adv.* **1** (by) a small amount: *little more than an hour ago.* □ **poco**
2 *I see him very little,* not very often. □ **poco**
3 *he little thought he would win,* he had no idea that he would win. □ **ni se imaginaba que ganaría**
liturgy ['litədʒi] *n.* form of public service in church. □ **liturgia**
liturgical [li'təːdʒikl] *adj.* referring to liturgy. □ **litúrgico**
live *adj.* laiv] **1** in a living state: *live animals.* □ **vivo**
2 *a real live filmstar,* an actual filmstar. □ **una estrella de verdad**
3 burning: *live coals.* □ **encendido; ascuas**
4 (*of broadcast, etc.*) not recorded: *the boxing match is being televised live.* □ **en directo**
5 carrying an electric circuit: *live wire.* □ **con corriente**
6 *he's* ***a real live wire,*** (*informal*) very lively and energetic. □ **es puro nervio**
■ *v.* **1** to be alive/to have life: *he won't live through the winter; they lived in the 18th century.* □ **vivir**
live and let live, be tolerant. □ **vive y deja vivir**
2 to have your (place of) residence: *he lives in Paris with his grandparents; this house isn't fit to live in.* □ **vivir**
3 to lead a certain type of life: *he lives in style.* □ **llevar una vida; se da buena vida**
to live up to: *she lives up to her reputation,* she always acts in the way people expect of her. □ **actúa conforme a su reputación**
to live it up, (*informal*) to lead a life of wild parties, etc. □ **llevar una vida de juerga**
4 ***to live on,*** to get food/money, etc., from: *they live on vegetables; you can't live on your capital these days.* □ **vivir de**
live down *v.* to cause (a disgrace) to be forgotten: *he's trying to live down the scandal; he'll never live it down,* it will never be forgotten. □ **olvidar**

live in *v.* to live in the building where you work: *all the hotel staff live in.* □ **vivir en el lugar de trabajo**
livelihood ['laivlihud] *n.* (way of getting) your means of living. □ **sustento**
liveliness ['laivlinəs] *n.* being lively. □ **viveza**
lively *adj.* bright/wide-awake/(very) active: *lively conversation; to take a lively interest.* □ **vivo, animado**
liven ['laivn] *v.* to make lively: *liven up the conversation.* □ **animar**
livestock ['laivstɔk] *n.* animals kept on a farm. □ **ganado**
living ['liviŋ] *adj.* alive: *I didn't meet a living soul.* □ **vivo; ...ni un alma**
■ *n.* **1** (way of) life: *standard of living.* □ **forma/nivel de vida**
2 means of subsistence: *earn one's living; he writes for a living.* □ **ganarse la vida; se gana la vida escribiendo**
3 ***the living,*** people who are alive: *I wonder if he's still in the land of the living,* if he's still alive. □ **los vivos**
living room *n.* room in a house for general use. □ **cuarto de estar**
liver ['livə] *n.* organ in the lower part of the body which helps the digestion by producing bile; animal's liver used as food: *liver pâté; liver sausage.* □ **hígado**
liverish *adj.* feeling rather sick and unwell; irritable. □ **pachucho; irritable**
livery ['livri] *n.* **1** special clothing of a group of servants/of an organization. □ **librea**
2 care of horses for payment. □ **cuidado**
livery stable, place where horses may be looked after and may also be hired. □ **cuadra de caballos de alquiler**
livid ['livid] *adj.* **1** of the dark grey colour of lead. □ **plomizo**
2 ***livid with rage,*** furiously angry. □ **lívido**
lizard ['lizəd] *n.* type of reptile with four legs and scales. □ **lagarto; lagartija**
llama ['lɑːmə] *n.* thick-haired camel-like animal found in South America. □ **llama**
load [loud] *n.* **1** heavy object(s) which have to be carried. □ **carga**
2 (*on vehicle*) what has to be/what is being transported. □ **carga**
3 amount of material transported: *order another load of gravel.* □ **carga**
4 amount of power carried by an electric circuit. □ **carga**
5 something which is difficult to bear. □ **carga**
a load off someone's mind, feeling much less worried. □ **me he quitado un peso de encima**
6 (*informal*) plenty/lots: *we've loads of time.* □ **montón**
■ *v.* **1** to put (especially something heavy) into/on to: *load the van carefully; load the cases on.* □ **cargar**
2 to put ammunition into (a gun)/to put film into (a camera). □ **cargar**
3 to give large quantities of something to: *they loaded him with presents.* □ **llenar**
loaded *adj.* **1** (*informal*) having a lot of money: *she's loaded.* □ **forrado**
2 ***loaded question,*** question which is worded in such a way so as to trap the person who answers. □ **pregunta capciosa**
loaf [louf] *n.* (*pl. loaves*) **1** (large) piece of bread baked separately. □ **barra**
meat loaf, spiced minced meat baked in the oven in a long oblong shape. □ **rollo de carne picada**
2 (*slang*) head: *use your loaf,* use your brains. □ **tarro; mollera**
■ *v.* to wander about/to waste time doing nothing: *he loafs about all day.* □ **holgazanear**
loafer *n.* **1** person who does nothing all day. □ **holgazán**
2 *Amer.* light casual shoe with no laces. □ **mocasín**
loam [loum] *n.* fertile soil which crumbles easily. □ **marga**
loan [loun] *n.* **1** lending of something: *can I have the loan of your bike?,* can I borrow it? *they only have it on loan.* □ **préstamo**
2 something lent (especially a sum of money from a bank): *to raise a loan.* □ **préstamo**
■ *v.* to lend. □ **prestar**
loath [louθ] *adj.* very unwilling: *I'm very loath to leave.* □ **reacio**
loathe [louð] *v.* to hate very much: *I just loathe him; I loathe doing it.* □ **aborrecer**
loathing *n.* feeling of hate/disgust (against). □ **aborrecimiento**
loathsome *adj.* disgusting/horrible. □ **asqueroso**
lob [lɔb] *v.* (*he lobbed*) to throw slowly in a high curve: *the terrorist lobbed a grenade into the bus.* □ **volear, lanzar**
lobby ['lɔbi] *n.* (*lobbies*) **1** entrance hall/corridor. □ **hall**
2 corridor where members of Parliament go to vote. □ **'lobby'**
3 hall in the House of Commons used especially for interviews with members of the public. □ **'lobby'**
■ *v.* (*lobbied; lobbying*) to try to influence (someone) (especially in order to get a bill through Parliament). □ **cabildear**
lobe [loub] *n.* **1** lower curved part of the ear. □ **lóbulo**
2 division of the lungs/brain/liver, etc. □ **lóbulo**
lobster ['lɔbstə] *n.* shellfish with a long body, two large claws, and eight legs, used as food. □ **langosta**
local ['loukl] *adj.* referring to a place/district: *local government.* □ **local**
local shops, those near at hand. □ **tiendas del barrio**
local anaesthetic, which numbs a particular area of the body. □ **anestesia local**
■ *n.* **1** person who lives in a district, especially the district where you live: *there are more tourists here than locals.* □ **vecino; persona del barrio**
2 (*informal*) nearest public house: *we're going round to the local for a drink.* □ **bar de al lado**
locale [lou'kɑːl] *n.* place where something takes place. □ **local**
locality [lou'kæliti] *n.* area/district. □ **localidad**
localize ['loukəlaiz] *v.* to set in a particular place; to be confined to a particular area. □ **ubicar**
locally *adv.* in the (same) district: *he's well known locally.* □ **localmente; es muy conocido por aquí**
locate [lou'keit] *v.* **1** to find (the position of): *to locate a leak (in a pipe).* □ **localizar**
2 ***to be located,*** to be in a particular position: *the house is located in the centre of the village.* □ **estar situado**
location [lou'keiʃn] *n.* **1** finding the position of something. □ **localización**
2 place/position: *this is an excellent location for the office.* □ **sitio**
3 place where filming takes place in a real setting, not in a studio: *filmed on location.* □ **exteriores**
loch [lɔk] *n.* lake in Scotland. □ **lago**
lock [lɔk] *n.* **1** device for closing a door/container, etc., by means of a key. □ **cerradura**
to put something under lock and key, to shut it in firmly. □ **encerrar algo bajo llave**

2 part in a gun by which it is fired. □ **cierre**
lock, stock and barrel, (everything) all together. □ **por completo**
3 amount by which the wheels of a car are able to turn: *turn full lock.* □ **ángulo de giro; dobla toda la dirección**
4 section of a canal/river with barriers which can be opened or closed to control the flow of water, thus allowing boats to move up or down to different levels. □ **esclusa**
5 piece of hair: *she kept a lock of his hair in an envelope.* □ **mechón**
■ *v.* **1** to close (a door/a box, etc.) with a key: *lock the door behind you; to lock someone up in a room.* □ **cerrar con llave**
2 to fix/to become fixed in certain position: *the wheels locked.* □ **bloquear(se)**
locker *n.* small cupboard for personal belongings which you can close with a key. □ **armario personal**
locker room, room in a sports stadium where players change and leave their clothes in lockers. □ **vestuario**
lock-keeper *n.* person who looks after a lock in a canal/river. □ **esclusero**
lock out *v.* to prevent (someone) from going in: *he came back late and found himself locked out; he locked himself out of his room,* he closed the door and left his key inside. □ **cerrar la puerta a**
lockout *n.* industrial dispute in which employees are kept out of the factory until they agree to certain terms. □ **cierre patronal**
locksmith *n.* person who makes/repairs locks. □ **cerrajero**
lock up *v.* **1** to close (a building) by locking doors. □ **cerrar**
2 to keep (a person/thing) inside by locking doors, etc. □ **encerrar**
lockup *n.* **1** prison (cell). □ **calabozo**
2 ***lockup garage/shop,*** garage/shop which can be locked and which is not part of the owner's house. □ **garaje/almacén exterior**
locket ['lɔkit] *n.* small ornamental case to hold a picture/lock of hair, etc., worn round the neck. □ **medallón; guardapelo**
locomotive [loukə'moutiv] *adj.* referring to movement/moving: *locomotive force.* □ **locomotor; fuerza locomotriz**
■ *n.* engine of a train. □ **locomotora**
locomotion *n.* (power of) movement. □ **locomoción**
locum (tenens) ['loukəm('tenenz)] *n.* person who does the work of a doctor/clergyman, while the latter is away. □ **suplente**
locust ['loukəst] *n.* type of insect, like a large grasshopper, which destroys crops. □ **langosta**
lode [loud] *n.* vein of metal ore. □ **filón**
lodestar *n.* pole star. □ **estrella polar**
lodestone *n.* magnetic iron ore. □ **piedra imán**
lodge [lɔdʒ] *n.* **1** small house at the gates of a large building. □ **casa del guarda**
2 house in the country used for shooting parties. □ **pabellón de caza**
3 (meeting place for a) group of freemasons, etc. □ **logia**
4 home of beavers. □ **madriguera**
■ *v.* **1** to rent a room: *she lodges with Mrs Smith.* □ **hospedarse**
2 to be/to remain: *the bullet lodged in his neck.* □ **alojar**
3 (*formal*) to make/to place: *to lodge a complaint with the authorities.* □ **presentar**
lodger *n.* person who rents a room. □ **inquilino**
lodging *n.* **1** (giving of) rooms to rent: *a night's lodging.* □ **alojamiento en alquiler**
2 ***lodgings,*** rented rooms. □ **habitaciones en alquiler**
loess ['louəs] *n.* type of yellow powdery earth found in China, North America, etc. □ **loess**
loft [lɔft] *n.* **1** top part of a house immediately under the roof. □ **desván**
2 ***organ loft,*** gallery for an organ in a church, etc. □ **triforio del órgano**
3 ***hay loft,*** top part of a barn used for storing hay. □ **pajar**
lofty ['lɔfti] *adj.* (*loftier, loftiest*) **1** (*formal*) very high: *a lofty tower.* □ **elevado**
2 arrogant/proud: *lofty manner.* □ **altivo**
loftiness *n.* **1** (*formal*) height. □ **elevación**
2 pride. □ **altivez**
log [lɔg] *n.* **1** thick piece of a tree trunk/large branch. □ **tronco**
to sleep like a log, very soundly. □ **dormir como un tronco**
as easy as falling off a log, very easy. □ **es cosa de coser y cantar**
2 device for calculating the speed of a ship. □ **corredera**
3 daily detailed record of speed/position/happenings, especially on a ship. □ **cuaderno de bitácora**
4 short for ***logarithm.*** □ **logaritmo**
■ *v.* (*he logged*) **1** to write down details of something which has happened (in a logbook). □ **anotar en el cuaderno de bitácora**
2 to cover a distance/to spend time: *they logged 30 kilometres of the journey; he has logged over 100 hours flying.* □ **recorrer**
logbook *n.* **1** (*on ship, etc.*) book with record of a journey. □ **cuaderno de bitácora**
2 official record book showing details of the owners of a car. □ **documentación**
loganberry ['ləugənberi] *n.* (*pl. loganberries*) type of soft fruit, a cross between a blackberry and a raspberry. □ **frambuesa americana**
logarithm ['lɔgəriðm] *n.* one of a set of numbers listed in such a way as to help with calculations by adding and subtracting instead of multiplying and dividing. □ **logaritmo**
loggerheads ['lɔgəhedz] *n.* ***to be at loggerheads*** (***with someone***), to quarrel constantly/never to agree with someone. □ **estar enfrentado (con alguien)**
loggia ['lɔdʒiə] *n.* (*in southern Europe*) covered gallery which is open on one side. □ **logia**
logic ['lɔdʒik] *n.* science of reasoning; power of reasoning clearly. □ **lógica**
logical *adj.* **1** clearly reasoned: *logical argument.* □ **lógico**
2 (*of person*) able to reason clearly. □ **lógico**
logically *adv.* in a logical way/according to logic; in a reasonable way. □ **lógicamente**
logistics [lɔ'dʒistiks] *n.* organization of the movement of supplies/people, etc. □ **logística**
logo ['ləugou] *n.* (*pl. logos*) symbol/design used by a company to identify its products. □ **logotipo**
loin [lɔin] *n.* **1** (meat from the) back of an animal: *loin of pork.* □ **lomo**
2 ***loins,*** part of the body between the hips. □ **'riñones'**
loincloth *n.* long cloth wrapped round the hips in hot countries. □ **taparrabo**
loiter ['lɔitə] *v.* to wander about slowly/aimlessly; to stand about: *no loitering.* □ **vagar**
loiterer *n.* person who wanders/who is standing about. □ **vagabundo**
loll [lɔl] *v.* **1** to sit/stand/lie in a lazy way: *to loll in*

an armchair. □ **repantigarse; repanchigarse en un sillón**
2 (*of tongue*) to hang out. □ **colgar**
lollipop ['lɔlipɔp] *n.* sweet on the end of a stick. □ **chupa-chup; pirulí**
lolly ['lɔli] *n.* (*pl. lollies*) **1** (*informal*) lollipop. □ **chupa; pirulí**
ice lolly, lump of flavoured ice on the end of a stick. □ **polo**
2 (*slang*) (*no pl.*) money. □ **guita**
lone [loun] *adj.* alone; lonely: *a lone rider.* □ **solitario**
lone wolf, person who likes to be alone. □ **solitario; lobo estepario**
lonely *adj.* **1** with few or no people: *lonely place.* □ **solitario**
2 feeling sad because of being alone: *to feel lonely.* □ **sentirse solo**
loneliness *n.* being alone; feeling sad because you are alone. □ **soledad**
loner *n.* person who prefers to work alone. □ **solitario**
lonesome *adj.* lonely/sad because of being alone. □ **triste (por estar solo)**
long [lɔŋg] *adj.* (*longer, longest*) **1** measured in space from end to end; not short: *how long is the rope? it's 10 metres long; she has long legs; it's a long way to London.* □ **largo; de larga**
2 measured in time: *how long are the holidays? that job will take three days at the longest; they stayed for a long time.* □ **¿cuánto tiempo...?; a lo sumo; largo tiempo**
■ *adv.* **1** for a long time: *has he been here long? he wasn't long in finishing; I won't be long; I have long realized that he is a fool; I couldn't wait any longer; she died long ago.* □ **largo tiempo; mucho tiempo**
2 ***all night long,*** for the whole night. □ **toda la noche**
3 ***as long as,*** while: *as long as I live.* □ **mientras**
4 ***so/as long as,*** provided that: *you can come so long as you don't disturb me.* □ **con tal que**
■ *n.* long time: *it won't take long.* □ **mucho tiempo**
before long, in a short time. □ **pronto**
for long, for a long time. □ **por mucho tiempo**
■ *v.* ***to long (for), to want very much:*** *they longed to be back home; I'm longing for a cold drink.* □ **anhelar**
long-distance *adj.* **1** (*in sport*) (race) run between two places which are far apart: *long-distance runner.* □ **de larga distancia; corredor de fondo**
2 (telephone call) made over a long distance: *long-distance call.* □ **de larga distancia**
longhand *n.* ordinary writing (not shorthand). □ **escritura normal**
longing *n.* great desire. □ **anhelo**
long johns *n. pl.* (*informal*) long underpants. □ **calzones largos**
long-playing *adj.* (record) which plays for about 20 minutes. □ **de larga duración, LP**
longshoreman *n.* (*pl. longshoremen*) *Amer.* person who works at a port, loading or unloading ships. □ **estibador**
long-sighted *adj.* able to see things at a distance more clearly than things which are close. □ **présbita**
longstanding *adj.* which has been made some time before: *longstanding arrangement.* □ **antiguo**
long-suffering *adj.* patient/tolerating much: *his long-suffering mother.* □ **sufrido**
long-term *adj.* lasting/planned to last for a long time: *long-term projects.* □ **a largo plazo**
long wave *n.* radio wave longer than 1,000 metres: *a long wave transmitter.* □ **onda larga**
long-winded *adj.* (person) who talks too much in a boring way; (talk) which lasts too long. □ **prolijo**
longevity [lɔn'dʒeviti] *n.* very long life. □ **longevidad**
longitude ['lɔndʒitju:d] *n.* position on the earth's surface measured in degrees east or west of an imaginary line running through Greenwich, London. □ **longitud**
longitudinal *adj.* which runs lengthwise. □ **longitudinal**
loo [lu:] *n.* (*informal*) lavatory. □ **retrete**
loofah ['lu:fə] *n.* type of long sponge, made from a dried plantpod. □ **esponja vegetal**
look [luk] *n.* **1** turning your eyes (often quickly) to see something: *have a look; they had a look round the town.* □ **mirada; vistazo**
2 search: *have a look for them under the bed.* □ **búscalos debajo de la cama**
3 appearance; the way something/someone seems: *to judge by looks; I don't like the look of it; they have a foreign look.* □ **aspecto**
4 ***looks,*** beauty/pleasing personal appearance: *good looks; he has both looks and charm.* □ **belleza**
■ *v.* **1** to make efforts to see: *look at these houses; look out of the window; look* (*and see*) *what time it is.* □ **mirar**
look here!, I object. □ **¡mira!**
2 to stare at: *he looked me straight in the face.* □ **mirar**
3 *they looked him up and down,* stared carefully at him. □ **le miraron de arriba abajo**
4 to seem/to have the appearance of: *he looks ill; things look bad; what does he look like? she looks the part,* looks right for the job; *it looks like rain.* □ **parecer**
look after *v.* to take care of: *they looked after us well; look after yourself.* □ **cuidar**
look ahead *v.* to make plans for the future. □ **mirar al futuro**
lookalike *n.* (*informal*) person who looks like someone else (especially someone famous). □ **sosia**
look at *v.* to make efforts to see/to examine/to consider: *look at your watch; look at the results; he wouldn't look at my plan.* □ **mirar; examinar; considerar**
look back *v.* **1** to turn round to see behind you. □ **mirar hacia atrás**
2 *after that they never looked back,* they were very successful. □ **después de aquello progresaron**
look back on *v.* to think about something in the past. □ **rememorar**
look down *v.* ***to look down on someone/to look down your nose at someone,*** to think you are better than someone. □ **mirar por encima del hombro**
looker-on *n.* (*pl. lookers-on*) person who is watching (without taking part). □ **espectador**
look for *v.* to try to find: *he looked for the money.* □ **buscar**
look forward *v.* to think about (something) in the future (usually with pleasure): *we're looking forward to seeing you.* □ **esperar**
look in *v.* (*informal*) to visit someone briefly: *I'll look in* (*on you*) *tomorrow.* □ **hacer una visitilla**
look-in *n.* (*informal*) chance/opportunity (to share in something): *they won't get a look-in.* □ **ocasión**
looking glass *n.* mirror. □ **espejo**
look into *v.* to examine/to find out about: *I'll look into the matter soon.* □ **ocuparse de**
look on *v.* **1** to watch without taking part: *they're only looking on.* □ **mirar**
2 to consider/to think of something as: *they looked on the conference as a holiday.* □ **tomarse**

look out *v.* **1** to have a view towards: *the kitchen looks out on to the garden.* □ **dar**
2 to keep looking in order to find: *look out for mushrooms on your walk; I'll look out for you at the party.* □ **buscar**
3 ***look out!,*** be careful. □ **¡cuidado!**
lookout *n.* **1** place from which you can see what is happening. □ **atalaya; mirador**
2 careful attention: *keep a sharp lookout; to be on the lookout for.* □ **estáte ojo avizor; estar al acecho de**
3 future hope: *it's a poor lookout for them.* □ **expectativa**
4 affair: *that's his lookout,* he must deal with it himself. □ **asunto**
5 person who watches: *they stationed lookouts all round the camp.* □ **vigilante**
look over *v.* to examine. □ **revisar**
look round *v.* **1** to turn to see behind you. □ **volver la cabeza**
2 to examine all of a place: *they looked round the house.* □ **inspeccionar**
look through *v.* **1** to examine the whole of something (often quickly): *he looked through the papers.* □ **echar un vistazo**
2 to pretend not to see: *she just looked (straight) through me.* □ **fingir no ver**
look to *v.* **1** to expect (help) from: *they looked to me to do it.* □ **contar con**
2 (*formal*) to take care of: *you must look to your profits.* □ **cuidar**
look up *v.* **1** to turn your eyes in an upward direction: *he looked up from his book.* □ **levantar los ojos**
2 to get better: *things are looking up.* □ **mejorar**
3 to try to find (something) in a reference book, etc.: *look up a word in the dictionary/a number in the telephone book.* □ **buscar**
4 to get in contact with: *look me up when you're in town.* □ **venir a ver**
look up to *v.* to consider with respect/admiration: *he always looked up to his elder brother.* □ **apreciar**
loom [luːm] *n.* machine on which cloth is woven. □ **telar**
■ *v.* (*of something large and often threatening*) to appear, to come into sight (gradually): *the car loomed up out of the fog; these events loomed large in his memory.* □ **surgir (de forma amenazadora)**
loony ['luːni] *adj.* and *n.* (*loonier, looniest*) (*informal*) mad (person). □ **chiflado; zumbado**
loop [luːp] *n.* **1** curve formed by a piece of thread/ribbon, etc. which crosses over itself. □ **lazo**
2 something of this shape: *the road forms a loop.* □ **la carretera forma un lazo**
■ *v.* **1** to make a loop/loops: *loop the thread over.* □ **hacer un lazo**
2 *loop back the curtain,* to tie it back with a cord, etc. □ **recoger, sujetar**
3 ***to loop the loop,*** (*of aircraft*) to fly in a complete circle vertically, turning upside down at the top. □ **hacer el rizo**
loophole *n.* **1** narrow hole in a wall for shooting through. □ **aspillera**
2 means of escape/of avoiding: *a loophole in the income tax regulations.* □ **escapatoria**
loose [luːs] *adj.* (*looser, loosest*) **1** not (fully) attached/not fixed: *loose rope; parts of the machine were loose; the horse is loose.* □ **flojo; suelto**
to be at a loose end, to have nothing special to do. □ **estar sin nada en que ocuparse**
2 not tight: *loose knot; loose sheets.* □ **flojo; suelto**
3 with pieces separated: *loose earth.* □ **desmenuzado; tierra poco firme**
4 ***loose change,*** money in coins only. □ **dinero suelto**
5 not very exact/not following the original closely: *loose translation.* □ **traducción libre**
6 of doubtful morality: *loose living.* □ **vida disoluta**
■ *v.* to make (something) become untied/to let (something) go. □ **soltar**
■ *adv.* not tightly: *the screw came loose.* □ **flojo**
loosebox *n.* (*pl. looseboxes*) stable where a horse can move about. □ **cuadra**
loosely *adv.* **1** not tightly: *the knot was loosely tied.* □ **sin apretar**
2 in an inexact way: *loosely translated.* □ **de manera poco exacta**
looseleaf *adj.* (book) of which the pages can be removed and replaced. □ **de hojas sueltas**
loosen *v.* to make (something) less tight: *he loosened his grip.* □ **aflojar**
to loosen someone's tongue, force them to talk. □ **soltarle la lengua**
loot [luːt] *n.* **1** things which have been taken: *the burglars made off with the loot.* □ **botín**
2 (*slang*) money. □ **pasta**
■ *v.* to steal. □ **saquear**
looter *n.* person who steals (especially from shops during a riot). □ **saqueador**
lop [lɔp] *v.* (*he lopped*) to cut off (especially tree branches). □ **podar**
lope [loup] *n.* running with long slow strides. □ **zancada**
■ *v.* to run with long (slow) strides: *to lope along.* □ **correr a zancadas**
lop-eared ['lɔpiəd] *adj.* (rabbit) with drooping ears. □ **de orejas gachas**
lop-sided [lɔp'saidid] *adj.* with one side larger/lower/heavier than the other. □ **desproporcionado**
loquacious [lɔ'kweiʃəs] *adj.* (person) who talks a lot/too much. □ **locuaz**
loquaciousness, loquacity [lɔ'kwæsiti] *n.* talking too much. □ **locuacidad**
lord [lɔːd] *n.* **1** nobleman/ruler: *lords and ladies.* □ **señor**
2 (*as title*) title for certain peers: *Lord Rosebery.* □ **lord**
3 ***the Lord,*** Jesus Christ: *in the year of our Lord.* □ **el Señor**
4 title for men in certain positions (such as bishops/judges, etc.): *Lord Mayor.* □ **ilustrísima (obispos); señoría (jueces)**
5 expression of surprise/shock: *Good Lord!* □ **¡Dios mío!**
■ *v.* ***to lord it over someone,*** to behave as if you are their superior. □ **enseñorearse ante alguien**
lordliness *n.* **1** nobility. □ **señorío**
2 pride. □ **altivez**
lordly *adj.* **1** referring to the nobility. □ **señorial**
2 proud/arrogant: *in a lordly manner.* □ **arrogante**
lordship *n.* (used as a form of address or to refer formally to a lord): *Your Lordship; His Lordship.* □ **señoría; su señoría**
lore [lɔː] *n.* (*no pl.*) traditional beliefs and knowledge: *Indian medical lore.* □ **saber popular; la medicina popular india**
lorry ['lɔri] (*pl. lorries*) large motor vehicle for carrying goods. □ **camión**
lorry driver *n.* person who drives a lorry. □ **camionero**
lose [luːz] *v.* (*he lost*) **1** to stop having/owning (something): *she lost her gloves,* did not know where they were; *he lost an arm in the war; to lose your reputation; to lose strength,* become weaker.

□ **perder**
2 ***to lose sight of:*** *they lost sight of it,* could no longer see it. □ **lo perdieron de vista**
3 *that joke was lost on him,* he did not understand it. □ **no cogió el chiste**
4 to fail to get/to win: *they lost the match by 3 goals; they lost their case in the law courts.* □ **perder**
5 to cause the loss of: *lack of ammunition lost them the battle.* □ **hacer perder**
6 ***to get lost/to lose your way,*** to be/become unable to find the way to where you are going: *they got lost on the way back.* □ **perderse**
get lost!, (*slang*) go away! □ **¡esfúmate!**
7 to become less: *these shares will lose in value.* □ **perder**
8 *to lose weight,* to become lighter. □ **perder peso**
9 (*of clock/watch*) to become/to go slow: *that clock loses 10 minutes a day.* □ **atrasarse**
loser *n.* person who does not win: *I'm the loser in that bargain; he's a bad loser,* behaves badly when he loses a game. □ **perdedor**
losing *adj.* which loses: *losing side.* □ **perdedor**
lost [lɔst] *adj.* **1** which has been lost: *is that your lost ball?* □ **perdido**
to give something up for lost, have no hope of ever having it again. □ **dar algo por perdido**
2 *he looks lost,* looks as if he doesn't know where he is/what he should do. □ **parece perdido**
3 *she's lost in her book,* she is reading it so attentively that she doesn't notice anything else. □ **está enfrascada en...**
lost property office *n.* place where articles which people have left on trains/buses, etc., are stored, and where they can be claimed by the loser. □ **oficina de objetos perdidos**

loss [lɔs] *n.* (*pl. losses*) **1** no longer having something: *loss of blood; without loss of time,* without wasting any time; *they suffered a terrible loss.* □ **pérdida**
2 thing/amount which you no longer have: *profit and loss.* □ **pérdida**
3 *they sold it* ***at a loss,*** for less than they paid for it. □ **con pérdida**
4 *he's* ***not much loss,*** not much missed. □ **no se le echa mucho de menos**
5 *that's* ***a dead loss,*** (*informal*) no use at all. □ **es una birria**
6 ***to be at a loss*** *what to do,* not to know what to do; *I'm at a loss for words,* can't think what to say. □ **no saber lo que hacer**
loss leader *n.* article which is sold cheaply to attract customers. □ **artículo de reclamo**

lost [lɔst] *v. see* **lose.**

lot [lɔt] *n.* **1** ***a lot (of)/lots (of),*** (*informal*) a large amount/number (of): *we've lots of time; what a lot of apples! lots of cheese; I've seen quite a lot of him lately,* seen him many times; *he knows quite a lot about you; times have changed a lot; that's a lot better.* □ **cantidad; mucho**
2 ***the lot,*** everything: *that's the lot; the whole lot of them.* □ **todo; eso es todo; todos ellos**
3 set of things (for selling); thing/group of things together offered at an auction sale: *to buy in large lots; lot 22 is a Chinese vase.* □ **lote**
4 ***bad lot,*** wicked person. □ **mal tipo**
5 *especially Amer.* piece of land. □ **parcela**
parking lot, place where cars can be parked. □ **aparcamiento**
6 fate/fortune: *it fell to my lot to decide; to envy someone else's lot.* □ **fortuna; suerte**
7 ***to draw lots,*** to decide something by taking pieces of paper from a box/throwing dice, etc. □ **echar a suertes**

loth [louθ] *adj.* very unwilling: *I'm very loth to leave.* □ **reacio**

lotion ['louʃn] *n.* liquid used to soothe/to soften/to heal the skin. □ **loción**

lottery ['lɔtri] *n.* (*pl. lotteries*) game of chance in which tickets are sold with prizes given for certain numbers. □ **lotería**

loud [laud] *adj.* **1** having a sound which is (too) easily heard: *a loud noise; in a loud voice.* □ **alto; fuerte**
2 (*of colours, etc.*) too striking/showy. □ **chillón**
■ *adv.* in a way which is easily heard: *those who shout loudest; he said it out loud,* in a voice which could be easily heard. □ **en voz alta**
loudly *adv.* **1** in a way which is easily heard: *he was complaining loudly about the service.* □ **en voz alta**
2 *she was loudly dressed,* in bright/clashing colours. □ **llevaba un vestido de color llamativo**
loud-mouthed *adj.* talking in a way which is too easily heard. □ **gritón**
loudness *n.* being (too) easily heard. □ **fuerza (voz, ruido)**
loudspeaker *n.* device for making sounds louder; part of a radio, etc., which allows sound to be heard. □ **altavoz**

lounge [laundʒ] *n.* **1** room for sitting in, such as in a hotel, etc. □ **salón; sala**
2 ***lounge*** (***bar***), more comfortable/more expensive bar in a hotel, etc. □ **salón**
3 sitting around doing nothing or very little. □ **haraganería**
■ *v.* to sit/to lie doing nothing or very little: *they lounged about all day.* □ **haraganear; siempre están echados a la bartola**

louring ['lauəriŋ] *adj.* gloomy/threatening(-looking): *louring sky.* □ **encapotado**

louse [laus] *n.* (*pl. lice*) small insect which lives on human and animal bodies: *infested with lice.* □ **piojo**
lousy ['lauzi] *adj.* (*lousier, lousiest*) **1** covered with lice. □ **piojoso**
2 (*informal*) horrible/unfair: *a lousy trick.* □ **una cochinada**

lout [laut] *n.* awkward/rude/ill-mannered person: *he's a lazy lout.* □ **patán**
loutish *adj.* awkward/rude/ill-mannered. □ **grosero**

louvre ['lu:və] *Amer.* **louver** *n.* sloping wooden strips in a frame which overlap and only allow some light to enter: *louvre doors.* □ **puertas de lamas**

love [lʌv] *n.* **1** great liking/respect for someone/something: *love of your country/your friends.* □ **amor**
2 *to do something* ***for the love of it,*** without looking for profit. □ **hacer algo por amor al arte**
3 *give my love to your parents,* send them friendly greetings. □ **dales recuerdos a tus padres**
4 *it* ***can't be had for love or money,*** not at all/by any means. □ **...por nada del mundo**
5 ***there's no love lost between them,*** they hate each other. □ **se odian**
6 great liking/passion for someone, especially strong sexual feeling towards someone: *to be in love/to fall in love with someone.* □ **estar enamorado; enamorarse de alguien**
7 ***to make love*** (***to someone***), have sexual intercourse with. □ **hacer el amor**
love story, one about sexual love. □ **historia de amor**
love affair, (often short) sexual relationship. □ **aventura amorosa**
8 person whom you love: *my love.* □ **mi amor**
9 (*informal*) form of address, especially to a woman

or child: *that's right, love.* □ **cariño**
10 (*in tennis, etc.*) score of nothing: 30-love. □ **cero**
■ *v.* **1** to have strong feelings of affection for: *he loves his family.* □ **querer**
2 to have great liking/passion, especially strong sexual feelings for (someone). □ **querer**
3 to like very much: *I just love cream cakes.* □ **me encanta...**
lovable *adj.* pleasant/easy to love: *a lovable puppy.* □ **encantador**
lovebird *n.* budgerigar. □ **periquito**
loveliness *n.* being very attractive. □ **encanto**
lovely *adj.* **1** beautiful: *isn't she lovely? a lovely dress.* □ **encantador**
2 (*informal*) very pleasant: *it's been lovely seeing you again.* □ **ha sido un placer...**
lover *n.* **1** person (especially a man) who is in love. □ **amante, enamorado**
2 person who loves (something): *lover of sport; nature lover.* □ **amante**
loving *adj.* affectionate/showing love. □ **cariñoso**
lovingly *adv.* in a loving way. □ **cariñosamente**
lovesick *adj.* unhappy because of being in love. □ **herido de amor**
low [lou] *adj.* (*lower, lowest*) **1** at/near/towards the bottom of something; in a position below (others): *lower jaw; low ceiling; the lowest price; low speed; low note; low voice,* one which is not easily heard. □ **bajo**
2 coarse/mean; inferior: *the lower animals; that was a low trick.* □ **animales inferiores; una mala jugada**
3 feeling depressed/ill, etc.: *he's in low spirits; she's very low today.* □ **está desanimado**
■ *adv.* in a low direction/way/position: *to aim low; the lowest-paid workers.* □ **apuntar abajo; ...peor pagados**
to lie low, to keep hidden. □ **permanecer escondido**
to run low: *supplies are running low,* are becoming scarce. □ **escasean las...**
■ *n.* **1** low-pressure zone in the atmosphere, bringing bad weather. □ **zona de bajas presiones**
2 *sales are at an all-time low,* the lowest point ever. □ **...en su punto más bajo**
■ *v.* to make a sound like a cow. □ **mujir**
lowbrow *adj.* and *n.* (person) with few/no intellectual interests: *lowbrow tastes.* □ **poco culto**
lowdown *adj.* mean/bad/to be despised: *a lowdown trick.* □ **vil**
■ *n.* ***to give someone the lowdown (on something),*** (*informal*) the details (especially confidential). □ **...detalles confidenciales**
lower *v.* **1** to make (something) reach a position further down: *lower the boats into the water; they lowered their prices; lower your voice,* speak more quietly. □ **bajar**
2 ***to lower yourself (so far as to),*** to do something of which you should be ashamed. □ **rebajarse**
low-grade *adj.* of poor quality: *low-grade petrol.* □ **de baja calidad**
lowland *adj.* coming from a low-lying region. □ **de tierras bajas**
lowlands *n. pl.* low-lying region. □ **tierras bajas**
lowly ['louli] *adj.* humble/modest; not high: *of lowly rank.* □ **humilde**
low-lying *adj.* (region) which is at a low altitude/ almost at sea level. □ **bajo**
lowering ['lauəriŋ] *adj.* gloomy/threatening (-looking): *lowering sky.* □ **amenazador; cielo encapotado**
loyal ['lɔiəl] *adj.* faithful/supporting (someone/something): *he's a loyal friend; loyal to one's country.* □ **leal**
loyalist *n.* person who is loyal. □ **leal**
loyally *adv.* in a faithful way. □ **lealmente**
loyalty *n.* being faithful. □ **lealtad**
lozenge ['lɔzindʒ] *n.* **1** diamond shape (especially as used in heraldry). □ **losange, rombo**
2 sweet; medicine tablet. □ **pastilla**
Ltd ['limitid] *short for* limited: *John Smith Ltd.* □ **limitado**
lubricate ['lu:brikeit] *v.* to make (something) run smoothly with oil or grease: *well lubricated engine.* □ **lubricar**
lubricant *adj.* and *n.* (substance) which makes something run smoothly. □ **lubricante**
lubrication [lu:bri'keiʃn] *n.* covering with oil or grease. □ **lubricación**
lucerne [lu'sə:n] *n.* plant like clover used as fodder for cattle. □ **alfalfa**
lucid ['lu:sid] *adj.* **1** clear/easily understood: *lucid style.* □ **claro**
2 able to think clearly: *the madman had lucid intervals.* □ **lúcido**
lucidity [lu:'siditi] *n.* being clear. □ **lucidez**
lucidly *adv.* in a clear way. □ **lúcidamente**
luck [lʌk] *n.* **1** chance/fortune: *good/bad luck; better luck next time.* □ **suerte**
hard luck!, I'm sorry you are unlucky. □ **¡mala suerte!**
as luck would have it, as it happened. □ **la suerte quiso que...**
to be down on your luck, have bad luck. □ **tener una mala racha**
2 good fortune: *to be in luck; stroke of luck.* □ **suerte**
to be out of luck, have bad luck. □ **estar de mala suerte**
luckily *adv.* by good fortune. □ **afortunadamente**
lucky *adj.* (*luckier, luckiest*) **1** having good fortune/ success: *he's a lucky man.* □ **afortunado**
2 having good fortune associated with it: *lucky day; 13's my lucky number; at a lucky moment; lucky charm.* □ **de suerte; oportuno**
lucrative ['lu:krətiv] *adj.* bringing in (much) money/ profit: *lucrative piece of business.* □ **lucrativo**
ludicrous ['lu:dikrəs] *adj.* causing laughter; ridiculous. □ **absurdo**
ludicrously *adv.* in a ludicrous way. □ **de manera absurda**
ludo ['lu:dəu] *n.* children's game, played on a board with dice and counters. □ **parchís**
luff [lʌf] *v.* to sail towards the wind. □ **orzar**
lug [lʌg] *n.* small projecting piece on the side of a jar, etc., for carrying it or for attaching something to it. □ **asa**
■ *v.* (*he lugged*) to pull (something heavy) along. □ **arrastrar**
lughole *n.* (*slang*) ear. □ **oreja**
luggage ['lʌgidʒ] *n.* (*no pl.*) suitcases/bags, etc., for carrying your belongings when travelling. □ **equipaje**
luggage rack, space for bags, etc., above seats in a train, etc. □ **redecilla**
lugubrious [lə'gu:briəs] *adj.* very miserable/mournful. □ **lúgubre**
lukewarm ['lu:kwɔ:m] *adj.* **1** slightly warm, but not hot: *lukewarm water.* □ **tibio**
2 without enthusiasm: *lukewarm support.* □ **poco entusiasta**
lull [lʌl] *n.* quiet(er)/calm(er) interval: *there was a lull between the two battles.* □ **intervalo, tregua**
■ *v.* to make calmer/to soothe: *to lull the baby to sleep; they lulled his fears.* □ **arrullar (bebé); aquietar (el miedo)**

lullaby ['lʌləbai] *n.* (*pl. lullabies*) song/piece of music designed to make a child sleep. □ **nana**
lumbago [lʌm'beigou] *n.* pain in the lower part of the back. □ **lumbago**
lumbar ['lʌmbə] *adj.* referring to the lower part of the back: *the lumbar region.* □ **lumbar**
lumber ['lʌmbə] *n.* **1** old articles which are not in use at the moment; junk. □ **trastos viejos**
lumber room, room in which you keep boxes/unwanted articles. □ **trastero**
2 *Amer.* wood which has been cut. □ **maderos**
■ *v.* **1** to fill (a room, etc.) (with junk). □ **amontonar**
2 (*informal*) to give (someone) things he doesn't really want: *they lumbered him with all their old books.* □ **cargar**
3 to move with a slow heavy step/pace: *to lumber along.* □ **moverse pesadamente**
lumberjack *n.* person who cuts down trees. □ **leñador**
lumber jacket *n.* short thick working coat. □ **pelliza corta**
luminous ['lu:minəs] *adj.* giving out light (in the dark): *watch with a luminous dial.* □ **luminoso**
lump [lʌmp] *n.* **1** (often shapeless) mass of something: *lump of clay.* □ **trozo; una pella de arcilla**
sugar lump, solid cube of sugar. □ **terrón de azúcar**
2 *there are lumps in the porridge,* solid parts. □ **hay grumos en...**
3 ***lump sum,*** money (paid) in one amount/not divided up. □ **suma total**
4 swelling on the body. □ **bulto**
5 (*informal*) heavy, clumsy person: *she's a great fat lump.* □ **pesado**
■ *v.* **1** ***to lump together,*** to put together in one place/in one group. □ **amontonar**
2 ***if he doesn't like it he can lump it/he'll have to lump it,*** (*informal*) he'll just have to tolerate it. □ **...se tendrá que aguantar**
lumpy *adj.* (*lumpier, lumpiest*) having solid parts: *lumpy porridge.* □ **grumoso**
lunacy ['lu:nəsi] *n.* madness. □ **locura**
lunatic *adj.* and *n.* mad (person). □ **lunático**
lunar ['lu:nə] *adj.* referring to the moon: *lunar month.* □ **lunar**
lunch [lʌntʃ] *n.* (*pl. lunches*) midday meal: *to have lunch.* □ **almuerzo**
■ *v.* (*formal*) to have the midday meal. □ **almorzar**
luncheon ['lʌntʃən] *n.* (*formal*) midday meal. □ **almuerzo**
luncheon meat, tinned meat loaf. □ **fiambre; embutido**
luncheon voucher, ticket given to an employee to buy food with. □ **vale de comida**
lunchtime *n.* period when the midday meal is usually eaten: *I met her yesterday lunchtime.* □ **hora de almorzar**
lung [lʌŋ] *n.* one of two organs in the chest, with which you breathe. □ **pulmón**
iron lung, machine which allows a person to breathe if his lungs are not working properly. □ **pulmón de acero**
lunge [lʌndʒ] *n.* sudden forward movement. □ **arremetida**
■ *v.* to make a sudden movement forward. □ **arremeter**
lupin ['lu:pin] *n.* garden flower with tall flower spikes. □ **lupino**
lurch [lə:tʃ] *n.* (*pl. lurches*) **1** sudden (unsteady) movement. □ **sacudida**
2 ***to leave someone in the lurch,*** (*informal*) to leave them/fail them in time of trouble or crisis. □ **dejar a uno en la estacada**
■ *v.* to move with a sudden movement. □ **sacudir**
lurcher *n.* dog used to retrieve game. □ **perro cobrador**
lure ['ljuə] *n.* **1** small object used to attract fish, etc., in order to catch them. □ **cebo**
2 something which traps/attracts: *the lure of the sea.* □ **el encanto del mar**
■ *v.* to attract, especially into something bad: *he was lured away from his duties.* □ **apartar a uno de**
lurid ['ljuərid] *adj.* **1** (light, etc.) which glows in an unpleasant sinister way: *lurid colours.* □ **misterioso, siniestro**
2 (*of book/film*) sensational/meant to shock: *he told the story in lurid detail.* □ **...con detalles espeluznantes**
lurk [lə:k] *v.* to hide/to remain hidden: *the animal lurked behind the trees; lurking suspicion.* □ **estar al acecho**
luscious ['lʌʃəs] *adj.* rich/good to taste. □ **suculento**
lush [lʌʃ] *adj.* (*lusher, lushest*) (plants) growing thickly/richly. □ **exuberante**
■ *n.* (*slang*) drunkard. □ **borrachuzo**
lust [lʌst] *n.* **1** strong sexual desire. □ **lascivia**
2 great desire for something: *a lust for money.* □ **codicia de dinero**
■ *v.* ***to lust after,*** to have a great desire for. □ **codiciar**
lustre ['lʌstə] *Amer.* **luster** *n.* shine/brilliance: *lustre of pearls; lustre of city life.* □ **lustre**
lustrous *adj.* brilliant. □ **lustroso**
lusty ['lʌsti] *adj.* (*lustier, lustiest*) strong/healthy. □ **lozano**
lustiness *n.* great strength/health. □ **lozanía**
lute [lu:t] *n.* old stringed musical instrument played like a guitar. □ **laúd**
luv [lʌv] *n.* (*informal*) (form of address): *that's right, luv.* □ **amorcito**
luxuriance [lʌg'ʒu:riəns] *n.* great quantity/abundance. □ **exuberancia**
luxuriant *adj.* growing abundantly: *luxuriant greenery.* □ **exuberante**
luxuriantly *adv.* in a luxuriant way. □ **exuberantemente**
luxuriate *v.* to enjoy freely/to laze happily: *to luxuriate in idleness; to luxuriate in a hot bath.* □ **deleitarse**
luxury ['lʌkʃəri] *n.* (*pl. luxuries*) **1** great comfort: *to live in luxury.* □ **lujo**
2 something which is pleasant to have but not necessary: *a second car is just a luxury.* □ **lujo**
luxurious [lʌg'ʒuriəs] *adj.* very comfortable; very expensive: *a luxurious fur coat; luxurious couch; luxurious way of life.* □ **lujoso**
luxuriously *adv.* in a comfortable/expensive way. □ **de manera lujosa**
luxuriousness *n.* being comfortable/expensive. □ **lujo**
lych-gate ['litʃgeit] *n.* gate with a roof at the entrance to a churchyard. □ **puerta con sotechado**
lying ['laiiŋ] *v. see* **lie.**
lymph [limf] *n.* liquid found in animal tissues. □ **linfa**
lymphatic [lim'fætik] *adj.* referring to lymph. □ **linfático**
lynch [linʃ] *v.* (*of a mob*) to kill (someone) without a trial (especially by hanging): *the murderer was nearly lynched by the crowd.* □ **linchar**
lynx [liŋks] *n.* (*pl. lynxes*) spotted short-tailed animal

of the cat family. □ **lince**

lynx-eyed *adj.* with very good eyesight. □ **con vista de lince**

lyre ['laiə] *n.* old harp-like stringed musical instrument. □ **lira**

lyric ['lirik] *adj.* and *n.* **1** (poem, etc.) concerned with feeling. □ **lírico**

2 (poem, etc.) intended to be sung. □ **letra de canción**

lyrical *adj.* **1** (poem) using suitable language to express feelings: *lyrical description.* □ **lírico**

2 (*informal*) eager/enthusiastic: *he got quite lyrical about the new tractor.* □ **entusiasmado**

lyricism ['lirisizəm] *n.* quality of a poem which expresses feelings. □ **lirismo**

lyricist *n.* person who writes the words of a song. □ **letrista**

lyrics *n.pl.* words of a song. □ **letra**

M,m

M, m [em] thirteenth letter of the alphabet. □ **M, m**
ma [mɑː] *n.* (*informal*) mother. □ **mamá**
mac [mæk] *n.* (*informal*) raincoat: *don't forget to take your macs with you.* □ **impermeable**
macabre [mə'kɑːbr] *adj.* causing horror; gruesome. □ **macabro**
macadam [mə'kædəm] *n.* road surface made of small pieces of broken stone. □ **macadán**
macadamized *adj.* covered with macadam. □ **pavimentado con macadán**
macaroni [mækə'rouni] *n.* Italian food, made of short thick tubes of flour paste. □ **macarrones**
macaroon [mækə'ruːn] *n.* small sweet almond biscuit. □ **almendrado**
macaw [mə'kɔː] *n.* type of South American parrot with brightly coloured feathers. □ **guacamayo**
mace [meis] *n.* **1** heavy bar of wood/metal used in ceremonies to symbolize authority. □ **maza**
2 spice made from the outside part of a nutmeg. □ **macís**
macerate ['mæsəreit] *v.* to soak in a liquid until soft. □ **macerar**
Mach (number) ['mæk(nʌmbə)] *n.* figure showing the speed of supersonic aircraft in relation to the speed of sound: *at Mach one,* at the speed of sound. □ **Mach**
machete [mə'tʃeti] *n.* jungle knife used in South America. □ **machete**
machination [mæki'neiʃn] *n.* plot. □ **maquinación**
machine [mə'ʃiːn] *n.* **1** device in which power from a motor drives wheels /gears, etc.: *washing machine; sewing machine.* □ **máquina**
2 *he fell off his machine at the corner,* his motor cycle. □ **se cayó de la moto...**
3 organization: *the Communist party machine.* □ **organización, aparato**
■ *v.* to make/to shape with a machine; to sew with a sewing machine. □ **trabajar a máquina; coser a máquina**
machine gun *n.* gun which automatically fires many bullets one after the other. □ **ametralladora**
machinery *n.* (*no pl.*) **1** mechanism; collection of all the working parts of machines; machines: *the shed was full of machinery.* □ **maquinaria**
2 organization: *the local government machinery; have we the machinery for putting this proposal into practice?* □ **organización, mecanismos**
machine tools *n. pl.* tools operated by a motor and used to shape metal/wood, etc. □ **máquinas herramienta**
machining *n.* process of working with a machine. □ **trabajo de máquina**
machinist *n.* person who works a machine, especially a sewing machine. □ **maquinista**
mackerel ['mækrəl] *n.* common sea fish. □ **caballa**
mackintosh ['mækintɔʃ] *n.* raincoat. □ **impermeable**
macramé [mə'krɑːmei] *n.* (*no pl.*) knotted string articles. □ **macramé**
macro- ['mækrou] *prefix meaning* very large/covering a wide area. □ **macro-**
macrobiotic [mækroubai'ɔtik] *adj.* referring to a diet of cereals/vegetables, etc., said to make you healthy. □ **macrobiótico**
mad [mæd] *adj.* (*madder, maddest*) **1** not sane; wild/silly: *he's raving mad; he went mad,* he became insane; *you're driving me mad.* □ **loco**
like mad, (*informal*) very fast, hard, etc.: *they ran like mad; he shook the bottle like mad,* very violently. □ **como un loco**
2 *he's mad with/at you,* he is angry with you. □ **está furioso contigo**
3 very enthusiastic: *she's mad about pop-stars,* wildly interested in pop-stars. □ **loco; está loca por...**
4 ***mad dog,*** dog suffering from rabies. □ **perro rabioso**
madden *v.* to make mad; to exasperate/to annoy: *maddened with pain.* □ **enloquecer**
maddening *adj.* exasperating. □ **enloquecedor**
madhouse *n. this place is like a madhouse,* full of noise and people rushing about. □ **manicomio**
madly *adv.* like a madman; wildly: *he drove madly around in circles; she's madly in love.* □ **locamente**
madman *n.* (*pl. madmen*) lunatic: *he drove like a madman,* he drove very fast/furiously. **loco**
madness *n.* illness of the brain; lunacy: *to try to cross the desert with no water is just sheer madness.* □ **locura**
madam ['mædəm] *n.* formal way of addressing a woman; (on a formal letter to a woman) *Dear Madam.* □ **señora**
made [meid] *v. see* **make.**
madeira [mə'diərə] *n.* **1** sweet dessert wine. □ **madeira**
2 ***madeira cake,*** type of sponge cake. □ **pastel de madeira**
madonna [mə'dɔnə] *n.* (picture/statue of) the Virgin Mary. □ **madona**
madrigal ['mædrigl] *n.* group song popular in the sixteenth and seventeenth centuries. □ **madrigal**
maestro ['maistrou] *n.* (*pl. maestros*) (*informal*) musical genius; conductor. □ **maestro**
mafia ['mæfiə] *n.* secret (Italian) organization dealing in crime. □ **mafia**
magazine [mægə'ziːn] *n.* **1** (illustrated) paper which appears at regular intervals: *a monthly magazine.* □ **revista**
2 radio/TV programme made up from various items on the same theme, broadcast regularly. □ **revista**
3 box containing ammunition/film which clips on to a gun/a camera. □ **cargador (fusil); cartucho (cámara)**
slide magazine, box to keep photographic slides in. □ **carro de diapositivas**
4 room/building used as a store for explosives. □ **polvorín**
magenta [mə'dʒentə] *n.* and *adj.* (of a) dark red-purple colour. □ **magenta**
maggot ['mægət] *n.* white grub (of a bluebottle) which lives in rotting meat. □ **cresa**
magic ['mædʒik] *n.* spells/conjuring tricks, etc., which do not appear to follow normal scientific rules. □ **magia**
as if by magic, suddenly/from nowhere: *as if by magic a birthday cake appeared from the kitchen.* □ **por arte de magia**
black magic, evil spells designed to harm people. □ **magia negra**
■ *adj.* enchanted: *a magic castle.* □ **encantado**
magical *adj.* produced by magic: fairy-like. □ **mágico**

magically *adv*. by magic. □ **por arte de magia**

magician [mə'dʒiʃn] *n*. wizard/conjuror. □ **mago**

magisterial [mædʒi'stiəriəl] *adj*. with an air of authority. □ **autoritario**

magisterially *adv*. in a commanding way. □ **de forma autoritaria**

magistrate ['mædʒistreit] *n*. judge in a minor court. □ **magistrado**

magnanimous [mæg'næniməs] *adj*. very generous. □ **magnánimo**

magnanimity [mægnə'nimiti] *n*. great generosity. □ **magnanimidad**

magnate ['mægneit] *n*. important businessman: *an oil magnate; a shipping magnate*. □ **magnate**

magnesium [mæg'ni:ziəm] *n*. (*chemical element*: Mg) metal which burns with a brilliant white light. □ **magnesio**

magnesia [mæg'ni:ziə] *n*. white powder made from magnesium used in medicines. □ **magnesia**

magnet ['mægnət] *n*. something which attracts, especially a metal object which attracts iron and steel and points roughly north and south when suspended. □ **imán**

magnetic [mæg'netik] *adj*. **1** having a power of attraction. □ **magnético**

magnetic field, area around a magnet which is under its influence. □ **campo magnético**

magnetic mine, floating bomb which is attracted to a passing ship. □ **mina magnética**

magnetic pole/magnetic north, the point to which the needle of a compass points. □ **polo magnético**

magnetic tape, plastic tape for recording music/information, etc.. □ **cinta magnética**

2 *she has a magnetic personality*, she attracts people. □ **tiene una personalidad magnética**

magnetically *adv*. by a magnet. □ **magnéticamente**

magnetism ['mægnətizəm] *n*. **1** study of magnets. □ **magnetismo**

2 personal power of attraction. □ **magnetismo**

magnetize *v*. to make (a piece of metal) into a magnet. □ **imantar**

magneto [mæg'ni:tou] *n*. (*pl. magnetos*) device in a car engine which produces electricity and ignites the petrol. □ **magneto**

magnificent [mæg'nifisnt] *adj*. very fine/splendid/very luxurious. □ **magnífico**

magnificence *n*. splendour/luxury. □ **magnificencia**

magnify ['mægnifai] *v*. (*he magnified; he was magnifying*) to make (something) appear larger. □ **aumentar**

magnifying glass, lens which makes small objects appear larger. □ **lupa**

magnification [mægnifi'keiʃn] *n*. making something appear larger; degree to which things appear larger. □ **aumento**

magnitude ['mægnitju:d] *n*. size; (*of stars*) brightness: *the magnitude of the task before us*. □ **magnitud**

magnolia [mæg'nouliə] *n*. **1** large tree with huge white flowers. □ **magnolia**

2 very pale pink colour. □ **color magnolia**

magnum ['mægnəm] *n*. very large bottle (of wine, especially champagne). □ **botella de dos litros**

magpie ['mægpai] *n*. common large black and white bird. □ **urraca**

maharajah [ma:hə'ra:dʒə] *n*. Indian prince. □ **maharajá**

maharani [ma:hə'ra:ni:] *n*. Indian princess. □ **maharani**

mahatma [mə'hætmə] *n* (*in India*) title given to a holy man. □ **mahatma**

mahogany [mə'hɔgəni] *n*. dark wood used for making furniture. □ **caoba**

maid [meid] *n*. female servant (especially in a hotel). □ **doncella; camarera (hotel)**

old maid, middle-aged unmarried woman. □ **solterona**

maiden *n*. (*formal*) unmarried girl/woman. □ **doncella**

■ *adj*. unmarried (woman): *maiden lady; maiden aunt*, unmarried aunt. □ **soltera**

maiden name, surname of a woman before she is married. □ **nombre de soltera**

maiden speech, first speech of a member of parliament. □ **primer discurso**

maiden voyage/flight, first voyage of a new ship/of a new aircraft. □ **primera travesía; primer vuelo**

maidenhair *n*. type of fern. □ **culandrillo**

mail [meil] *n*. **1** letters delivered: *have you opened the mail yet?* □ **correspondencia**

2 postal services: *send it by registered mail*. □ **correo**

mail order, ordering and buying something by post: *I bought it by mail order; a mail order catalogue*. □ **pedido postal**

3 ***chain mail***, type of armour made of small interlocking metal rings; *a coat of mail*. □ **cota de mallas**

■ *v*. to send by the postal services: *I have mailed him $600*. □ **mandar por correo**

mailbag *n*. large canvas bag for carrying mail. □ **saca postal**

mailbox *n*. *Amer*. **1** box for posting letters. □ **buzón**

2 box where letters are put by the mailman to be collected by the householder. □ **buzón**

mailman *n*. (*pl. mailmen*) *Amer*. man who delivers letters. □ **cartero**

maim [meim] *v*. to wound; to make lame. □ **mutilar**

main [mein] *n*. **1** ***with might and main***, (*formal*) with all your strength. □ **con todas sus fuerzas**

2 ***in the main***, generally speaking. □ **por lo general**

3 central pipe for distributing water/gas, etc.: *a water main burst in the High Street; a gas main*. □ **cañería (agua); conducto (gas)**

4 ***the mains***, electric power: *the vacuum cleaner was plugged into the mains*. □ **la red (eléctrica)**

■ *adj*. most important: *the main thing is to keep on working; main crop; main road*. □ **principal**

to have an eye to the main chance, to watch out for the best way of making money/of improving your position. □ **estar a la expectativa**

mainland ['meinlənd] *n*. large solid mass of land: *the mainland of Asia*. □ **territorio continental**

mainly *adv*. mostly/in a very important way: *the farm is mainly given over to growing vegetables*. □ **principalmente**

mainspring *n*. **1** central spring of a watch. □ **muelle real**

2 most important force which makes you do something. □ **causa principal**

mainstay *n*. principal support. □ **soporte principal**

mainstream *n*. most important trend in a form of art: *mainstream jazz*. □ **corriente principal**

maintain [mein'tein] *v*. **1** to keep (order); to keep (doing something): *he maintained a strict silence*. □ **mantener**

2 to keep something working: *to maintain an army; to maintain a car*. □ **mantener**

3 to state/to assert: *he maintains that he never went near the sea at all*. □ **mantener**

maintenance ['meintnəns] *n*. **1** keeping: *the maintenance of law and order*. □ **mantenimiento**

2 upkeep: *car maintenance*. □ **mantenimiento**

maisonette [meizə'net] *n.* flat on two floors. □ **dúplex**
maize [meiz] *n.* tall cereal crop. □ **maíz**
majesty ['mædʒəsti] *n.* (*pl. majesties*) **1** greatness: *the majesty of the great cathedral.* □ **majestad**
2 form of address to a King or Queen: *Your Majesty; His Majesty.* □ **Su Majestad**
majestic [mə'dʒestik] *adj.* grand/stately. □ **majestuoso**
majestically *adv.* grandly. □ **majestuosamente**
major ['meidʒə] *n.* **1** army officer above a captain. □ **comandante**
2 (*formal*) legally adult person. □ **mayor de edad**
■ *adj.* **1** bigger; more important: *the major part of the work,* most of the work. □ **mayor**
major road, main road. □ **carretera principal**
2 musical key where there are semitones between the third and fourth, and between the seventh and eighth notes: *symphony in F major.* □ **mayor**
■ *v.* to specialize in a subject as an undergraduate: *she is majoring in French.* □ **especializarse**
majordomo *n.* chief servant in a large house. □ **mayordomo**
majorette [meidʒə'ret] *n.* girl bandleader or marcher. □ **'majorette'**
major-general *n.* senior army officer below a lieutenant-general. □ **general de división**
majority [mə'dʒɔriti] *n.* (*pl. majorities*) **1** larger part: *the majority of the holidaymakers reached home safely; the non-smokers are in the majority,* there are more non-smokers than smokers. □ **mayoría**
2 larger number of voters: *the government has a majority of one,* has one more member of parliament than the opposition. □ **mayoría**
3 legally adult age. □ **mayoría de edad**
make [meik] *n.* **1** brand; country of origin (of an object): *an Italian make of car; I would only buy a well-known make of washing machine.* □ **marca**
2 *he's* ***on the make,*** (*informal*) all he wants to do is to make money. □ **sólo trata de hacer dinero**
■ *v.* (*he made*) **1** to prepare; to do: to construct: *to make the tea; he's making a rocking chair; they made a fuss.* □ **hacer**
2 *to make the beds,* to tidy the beds after they have been slept in. □ **hacer las camas**
3 to earn: *I make $50 a week; how much do you make selling ice cream?* □ **ganar**
4 to add up to; to score: *three and three make six; he made seven runs.* □ **hacer**
5 to cause (someone) to be: *to make someone happy; the smell of cooking makes me hungry; it makes me tired just to watch them working; he made himself comfortable.* □ **hacer; dar (hambre ...); ponerse**
6 to force (someone) to do something: *I made him clean his shoes; he was made to do the work all over again; I don't know what made him do it.* □ **hacer**
make away with *v.* ***to make away with something,*** to remove something/to make something disappear. □ **hacer desaparecer**
make-believe *n.* pretending/believing something is true when it is not. □ **simulación**
make do *v.* ***to make do with something,*** to put up with something/to use something even if it is not suitable: *I lost my toothpaste, so I had to make do with soap.* □ **arreglárselas con**
make for *v.* to aim; to go towards: *he is making for London; the design makes for easy cleaning.* □ **dirigirse hacia; el diseño facilita la limpieza**
make of *v.* to consider: *what do you make of it?,* what do you think of it? *I don't know what to make of it.* □ **pensar**
make off with *v.* ***to make off with something,*** to run away with something/to steal something. □ **arramblar con**
make out *v.* **1** to draw up (a list); to write (a cheque): *who do I make the cheque out to?,* what name do I put on the cheque? □ **hacer (una lista); extender (un cheque)**
2 to distinguish/to see properly: *I can't make out the details because of the bad light.* □ **vislumbrar**
3 to assert/to maintain: *the climate isn't as bad as you make out/as you make it out to be.* □ **mantener**
4 (*informal*) to succeed: *she's making out very well.* □ **irle bien a uno**
make over *v.* to transfer. □ **traspasar**
maker *n.* person who makes something: *cabinet maker.* □ **fabricante**
makeshift *adj.* and *n.* (something) used temporarily in place of something else: *a makeshift tent.* □ **solución temporal; una tienda improvisada**
make up *v.* **1** to complete/to fill up. □ **completar**
to make up one's mind: *I can't make up my mind,* I can't decide. □ **no puedo decidirme**
to make up for lost time, to do something specially quickly. □ **recuperar en poco tiempo**
2 to put lipstick/powder, etc., on your face. □ **maquillar(se)**
3 to invent: *he made up the whole story.* □ **inventar**
4 to become friends again: *after the argument they soon made it up.* □ **hacer las paces**
5 ***to make it up to someone,*** to compensate someone for something lost/damaged, etc. □ **compensar**
make-up *n.* **1** composition: *what is the make-up of the new government?* □ **composición**
2 character: *it is a defect in his make-up.* □ **carácter**
3 lipstick/cream/powder, etc., used to beautify your face. □ **maquillaje**
makeweight *n.* small quantity added to make up the weight of something. □ **complemento de peso**
maladjusted [mælə'dʒʌstid] *adj.* (person) who does not fit into society. □ **inadaptado**
maladroit [mælə'drɔit] *adj.* (*formal*) clumsy. □ **torpe**
malaise [mæ'leiz] *n.* (*formal*) awkward feeling; slight sickness. □ **malestar**
malaria [mə'lɛəriə] *n.* tropical fever caused by a parasite carried by mosquitoes. □ **malaria**
Malaysia [mə'leiʒə] *n.* country in south-east Asia. □ **Malasia**
Malaysian *adj.* referring to Malaysia. □ **malasio**
■ *n.* person from Malaysia. □ **malasio**
male [meil] *adj.* **1** referring to men/boys: *the village has a male voice choir.* □ **varonil; masculino**
2 referring to the sex which fertilizes eggs produced by females: *a male spider.* □ **macho**
■ *n.* **1** man/boy. □ **varón**
2 animal/insect which does not give birth to offspring: *the male has much brighter feathers than the female.* □ **macho**
malevolence [mə'levəlns] *n.* (*formal*) ill-will; desire to hurt others. □ **malevolencia**
malevolent *adj.* wishing (someone) ill. □ **malévolo**
malformation [mælfɔː'meiʃn] *n.* being wrongly shaped/badly formed. □ **malformación**
malformed *adj.* badly formed/shaped. □ **malhecho**
malfunction [mæl'fʌŋkʃn] *n.* bad/incorrect working (of a machine/of the heart, etc.). □ **mal funcionamiento**
■ *v.* to work badly. □ **funcionar mal**
malice ['mælis] *n.* unfriendly feelings: *he did it out of malice,* he did it to be spiteful. □ **maldad, rencor**
malicious [mə'liʃəs] *adj.* wicked/intentionally spite-

ful; wanting to hurt others: *he spread malicious rumours.* □ **malvado**
maliciously *adv.* spitefully. □ **con maldad**
malign [mə'lain] *v.* to say bad things about someone: *he has been much maligned,* people have criticized him a lot. □ **difamar**
malignancy [mə'lignənsi] *n.* being malignant. □ **malignidad**
malignant *adj.* **1** wishing harm to someone. □ **malvado**
2 likely to prove fatal: *a malignant tumour.* □ **maligno**
malinger [mə'liŋgə] *v.* to pretend to be ill (to avoid work). □ **fingirse enfermo**
malingerer *n.* person who pretends to be ill. □ **enfermo fingido**
mallard ['mælɑːd] *n.* common wild duck. □ **lavanco**
malleable ['mæliəbl] *adj.* soft/which can be moulded into shape. □ **maleable**
mallet ['mælit] *n.* large wooden hammer. □ **mazo**
mallow ['mælou] *n.* common wild flower growing in marshy ground. □ **malva**
malnutrition [mælnjuː'triʃn] *n.* lack of enough good food: *the children suffered from malnutrition.* □ **desnutrición**
malodorous [mæl'oudərəs] *adj.* (*formal*) which smells bad. □ **hediondo**
malpractice [mæl'præktis] *n.* illegal use of your position/authority to gain money. □ **procedimientos ilegales**
malt [mɔːlt] *n.* grain which has been prepared for making beer or whisky by being allowed to sprout and then dried: *malt whisky.* □ **malta**
malted *adj.* tasting of malt: *malted milk.* □ **malteado**
Malta ['mɔːltə] *n.* island country in the Mediterranean. □ **Malta**
Maltese *adj.* referring to Malta. □ **maltés**
Maltese cross, type of cross with each arm of equal length, and spreading out from the central point. □ **cruz de Malta**
■ *n.* **1** language spoken in Malta. □ **maltés**
2 (*pl. Maltese*) person from Malta. □ **maltés**
maltreat [mæl'triːt] *v.* to treat someone badly. □ **maltratar**
maltreatment *n.* rough treatment. □ **maltrato**
mammal ['mæml] *n.* type of animal which gives birth to live young and suckles them with milk. □ **mamífero**
man [mæn] *n.* (*pl. men*) **1** human being: *man is superior to all other mammals; men have only existed for a very short period when compared with fish.* □ **hombre**
2 person. □ **hombre**
the man in the street, the ordinary citizen. □ **el hombre de la calle**
no man's land, land between two armies which belongs to neither side. □ **tierra de nadie**
3 male human adult: *an old man; he bore pain like a man; she dressed like a man.* □ **hombre**
4 husband: *they lived together as man and wife for many years.* □ **marido**
5 servant; ordinary soldier; member of a sports team. □ **sirviente; soldado; jugador**
6 piece (in chess, etc.). □ **pieza**
■ *v.* (*he manned*) to provide with men: *we need someone to man this stall,* to serve behind this stall; *six soldiers manned the gun.* □ **encargarse**
man-eater *n.* animal which eats people. □ **antropófago**
man-eating *adj.* (animal) which eats people: *a man-eating tiger.* □ **antropófago**
manfully *adv.* like a man; in a strong/forceful way. □ **virilmente**
manhandle *v.* **1** to move (something large and heavy) by hand: *they manhandled the piano down the stairs.* □ **trasladar a mano**
2 to handle someone roughly: *the youths were manhandled by the police.* □ **maltratar**
manhole *n.* hole in the road or pavement through which you go down into the sewers/into a coal store, etc. □ **tapa de alcantarilla; trampilla (carbón)**
manhood *n.* (*no pl.*) state of being an adult male. □ **hombría**
mankind [mæn'kaind] *n.* (*no pl.*) the human race. □ **humanidad**
manliness *n.* virility/male characteristics. □ **virilidad**
manly *adj.* (*manlier, manliest*) virile/with strong male features; brave. □ **varonil**
man-made *adj.* (artificial) material, etc.: *man-made fibres.* □ **artificial**
mannish *adj.* (woman) who looks/dresses like a man. □ **hombruna**
manpower *n.* work force/number of workmen: *there is a manpower shortage.* □ **mano de obra**
manslaughter *n.* killing someone without intending to do so: *he was charged with murder, but found guilty of manslaughter.* □ **homicidio involuntario**
manacle ['mænəkl] *n.* one of two steel rings connected by a chain, which attach the wrists of a prisoner together. □ **esposa**
■ *v.* to attach (a prisoner's) wrists together. □ **esposar**
manage ['mænidʒ] *v.* **1** to direct: *she manages the south-east area of our operations.* □ **dirigir**
2 to arrange to do something; to succeed in doing something: *can you manage to be there on time? I didn't manage to get the lid off; he managed to lift the box; can she manage all by herself?,* can she cope/can she do the work all by herself? □ **arreglárselas, lograr**
manageable *adj.* which can be managed/directed. □ **dirigible**
management *n.* **1** handling of (a tool); directing (of work). □ **manejo, dirección**
2 group of people who direct workers: *I am going to complain to the management about the food in the canteen; the shop is under new management,* has a new owner/manager. □ **dirección**
manager *n.* **1** head of a department in a commercial firm: *sales manager; export manager; production manager.* □ **director, jefe**
2 person who manages/directs; director of a theatre; organizer of a sports team/singer, etc.; person who runs a shop. □ **gerente (teatro); 'manager'; apoderado**
manageress [mænidʒə'res] *n.* (*pl. manageresses*) woman who runs a shop. □ **encargada**
managerial [mænə'dʒiəriəl] *adj.* referring to a manager: *managerial skills; discussions at managerial level,* discussions among managers. □ **directivo**
managing director *n.* overall director of a firm. □ **director gerente**
mandarin ['mændərin] *n.* **1** small orange with a soft easily peeled skin. □ **mandarina**
2 important government official: *Whitehall mandarins.* □ **mandarín**
3 ***Mandarin,*** principal form of the Chinese language. □ **mandarín**
mandate ['mændeit] *n.* power given to a person to act on behalf of someone else: *the government has*

a mandate from the people to cut taxes, people approved of the plan to cut taxes when they voted for the government. □ **mandato**
mandatory ['mændətəri] *adj.* obligatory; compulsory. □ **obligatorio**
mandible ['mændibl] *n.* lower jawbone (of birds/insects, etc.). □ **mandíbula**
mandoline ['mændəlin] *n.* stringed instrument like a small guitar. □ **mandolina**
mane [mein] *n.* long hair on neck of a lion or horse; long untidy hair. □ **melena (león); crin (caballo)**
maneuver [mə'nu:və] *n.* and *v. Amer. see* **manoeuvre.**
manganese ['mæŋgəni:z] *n.* (*Chemical element:* Mn) grey metal. □ **manganeso**
mange [meindʒ] *n.* disease of the skin of animals, which makes the hair fall out. □ **sarna**
mangy *adj.* dirty/diseased: *a mangy dog.* □ **sarnoso**
mangel-wurzel ['mæŋglwə:zl] *n.* beet used as food for cattle. □ **remolacha forrajera**
manger ['meindʒə] *n.* box for food for horses/cows, etc. □ **pesebre**
mangle ['mæŋgl] *n.* device with rollers for squeezing the water out of clothes. □ **escurridor**
■ *v.* **1** to squeeze water out of clothes by passing them through a mangle. □ **escurrir**
2 to tear; to chop up; to mess up. □ **destrozar**
mango ['mæŋgou] *n.* (*pl. mangoes*) large yellow tropical fruit with a big stone. □ **mango**
mangrove ['mæŋgrouv] *n.* kind of tropical tree growing in wet areas: *a mangrove swamp.* □ **mangle; manglar**
mania ['meiniə] *n.* madness/exaggerated passion: *he has a mania for old cars,* he is very keen on old cars. □ **manía**
maniac *n.* mad person. □ **maniaco**
manic ['mænik] *adj.* referring to mania. □ **maniaco**
manicure ['mænikjuə] *n.* looking after the hands: *to have a manicure,* to have your hands cleaned and nails trimmed. □ **manicura**
■ *v.* to look after the hands: *she was manicuring her nails,* she was cutting/filing/polishing her nails. □ **hacerse la manicura**
manicure set *n.* small box or bag with scissors/nail file, etc. □ **estuche de manicura**
manicurist *n.* person who looks after people's hands. □ **manicuro**
manifest ['mænifest] *adj.* (*formal*) obvious/plain to see: *his manifest alcoholism.* □ **manifiesto**
■ *n.* list of goods in a shipment. □ **manifiesto**
■ *v.* to appear/to show: *the disease manifested itself in the form of big red spots.* □ **manifestarse**
manifestation [mænife'steiʃn] *n.* appearance. □ **manifestación**
manifestly *adv.* (*formal*) obviously. □ **manifiestamente**
manifesto [mæni'festou] *n.* (*pl. manifestos*) programme of action outlined by a political party: *the Communist Party manifesto.* □ **manifiesto**
manifold ['mænifould] *adj.* (*formal*) of varying sorts: *it appears in manifold forms.* □ **múltiple**
■ *n.* ***exhaust manifold,*** tubes of an exhaust pipe of a car. □ **tubo de escape**
manilla [mə'nilə] *n.* thick brown paper (used for envelopes). □ **papel manila**
manipulate [mə'nipjuleit] *v.* **1** to handle: *to manipulate a piece of machinery.* □ **manipular**
2 *to manipulate the accounts,* to falsify accounts to make them seem more profitable. □ **manipular las cuentas**
manipulation [mənipju'leiʃn] *n.* handling (of machinery); falsification (of accounts). □ **manipulación**
manna ['mænə] *n.* unexpected help/food. □ **maná**
mannequin ['mænikin] *n.* model/person or dummy who wears clothes to show them to possible buyers. □ **maniquí**
manner ['mænə] *n.* **1** way of behaving/acting. □ **manera; modo**
2 *the doctor has a good* ***bedside manner,*** he is very kind with a sick patient. □ **el médico tiene un trato muy atento**
3 ***manners,*** way of acting in public: *table manners; bad manners; it is bad manners to put your knife in your mouth.* □ **modales**
4 sort. □ **clase**
all manner of things, all sorts of things. □ **toda clase de cosas**
in a manner of speaking, in a sort of way. □ **por decirlo así**
mannered *adj.* full of mannerisms. □ **amanerado**
mannerism *n.* affected way of acting/odd way of doing something. □ **amaneramiento**
manoeuvre [mə'nu:və] *Amer.* **maneuver** *n.* **1** action of moving something: *turning a car round in a narrow street is a tricky manoeuvre.* □ **maniobra**
2 ***manoeuvres,*** military exercises: *they are on manoeuvres,* they are out on an exercise. □ **maniobras**
■ *v.* **1** to move something heavy/awkward: *he manoeuvred the piano into the dining room.* □ **meter con dificultad**
2 *he manoeuvred himself into a position of authority,* he worked his way into a position of authority. □ **fue abriéndose paso**
manoeuvrable *adj.* which can be manoeuvred/moved: *it is big but easily manoeuvrable.* **maniobrable; ...pero fácil de manejar**
manor ['mænə] *n.* (land surrounding) a country house. □ **señorío**
manor house, country house. □ **casa solariega**
manse [mæns] *n.* (*in Scotland*) church minister's house. □ **casa de un pastor protestante**
mansion ['mænʃən] *n.* very large private house. □ **mansión**
mansions, large block of flats. □ **bloque de pisos**
mantelpiece ['mæntlpi:s] *n.* shelf above a fireplace. □ **repisa de la chimenea**
mantle ['mæntl] *n.* **1** cloak. □ **manto**
2 gauze cover for a gas lamp. □ **camisa incandescente**
manual ['mænjuəl] *adj.* **1** done by hand: *manual labour.* □ **manual**
2 (model of a car) where the gears are changed by hand. □ **de cambio manual**
■ *n.* book of instructions: *car repair manual.* □ **manual**
manually *adv.* by hand. □ **a mano**
manufacture [mænju'fæktʃə] *n.* making of a commercially produced product: *the tea service is of British manufacture.* □ **manufactura**
■ *v.* to make products commercially: *the factory manufactures most of the cloth in the area.* □ **manufacturar**
manufacturing town, industrial town. □ **ciudad industrial**
manufacturer *n.* person/company producing industrial products. □ **fabricante**
manure [mə'njuə] *n.* dung of animals used as a fertilizer on land: *horse manure.* □ **estiércol**
manure heap, heap of dung and straw kept at a farm for spreading on fields. □ **estercolero**
■ *v.* to spread manure on land: *well manured vegetable plot.* □ **estercolar**

manuscript ['mænjuskript] *adj.* and *n.* (document/novel/poem) written by hand or typed, etc., but not printed. □ **manuscrito**
Manx [mæŋks] *adj.* and *n.* (person, etc.) from the Isle of Man. □ **(habitante, etc.) de la isla de Man**
many ['meni] *adj.* and *n.* **1** (*the comparative and superlative are **more/most***) great number: *there are many old churches in the city; many of us knew him as a boy; so many people asked for tickets that there were not enough seats to go round; he ate twice as many apples as you; how many people have been to the exhibition?* □ **muchos**
2 ***a good many** prisoners,* quite a large number. □ **un buen número de**
3 *I've been there **many a time**,* often. □ **...muchas veces**
4 ***many a** soldier felt the urge to desert,* a large number of soldiers. □ **muchos soldados...**
map [mæp] *n.* diagram of a town/country as if seen from above: *a map of the moon.* □ **mapa**
physical map, diagram showing mountains/rivers, etc.. □ **mapa físico**
political map, diagram showing the borders of countries/administrative districts, etc. □ **mapa político**
street map, diagram showing streets with their names. □ **plano**
■ *v.* (*he mapped*) **1** to draw a diagram (of a town or country): *he mapped the west coast of Africa.* □ **trazar el mapa de**
2 ***to map out** a route,* to plan a journey in advance; *he has it all mapped out,* he has planned everything in advance. □ **proyectar**
mapping *n.* art of making maps. □ **cartografía**
mapping pen, pen with a very fine nib. □ **plumilla**
maple ['meipl] *n.* northern tree, whose sap is sweet. □ **arce**
maple sugar/maple syrup, sugar/syrup made from the sap of the maple tree. □ **azúcar/jarabe de arce**
mar [mɑː] *v.* (*he marred*) to spoil: *the open air festival was only marred by the bad weather.* □ **estropear; ...quedó deslucido por el mal tiempo**
marathon ['mærəθən] *n.* long distance race. □ **maratón**
a marathon debate, debate which lasts a long time. □ **un debate maratoniano**
maraud [mə'rɔːd] *v.* to raid (a town). □ **saquear**
marauder *n.* person who raids: *the farm was attacked by marauders.* □ **saqueador**
marauding *adj.* (person) who raids: *marauding soldiers.* □ **que saquea**
marble ['mɑːbl] *n.* **1** very hard type of limestone which can be brilliantly polished: *marble steps; marble statue.* □ **mármol**
2 small glass ball for playing with: *the children were playing marbles.* □ **canica**
marbled *adj.* with streaks of different colours. □ **jaspeado**
March [mɑːtʃ] *n.* third month of the year: *his birthday is in March/is on March 6th.* □ **marzo**
march [mɑːtʃ] *n.* **1** military walking in step. □ **marcha**
march past, ceremonial parade of soldiers. □ **desfile**
quick march, rapid walking pace. □ **paso rápido**
route march, long training march. □ **marcha**
slow march, slow walking pace. □ **paso lento**
2 music for marching: *the band played a slow march.* □ **marcha**
3 progress/advance of time/events: *the inevitable march of the seasons.* □ **paso**
■ *v.* **1** to walk in step: *the soldiers marched off the parade ground; the regiment marched past in quick time,* the regiment paraded; *the police marched him off to prison,* removed him quickly to prison. □ **desfilar**
quick march!, order to walk at a rapid pace. □ **¡paso rápido!**
2 to walk quickly and purposefully: *he marched into the office and sat down.* □ **caminar con aire marcial**
mare ['meə] *n.* female horse. □ **yegua**
mare's nest, discovery which turns out to be useless. □ **parto de los montes**
mare's tails, thin wispy clouds showing a change in the weather. □ **cirro**
margarine [mɑːdʒə'riːn] *n.* mixture of animal or vegetable fat which is used instead of butter. □ **margarina**
marge [mɑːdʒ] *n.* (*informal*) margarine. □ **margarina**
margin ['mɑːdʒin] *n.* **1** edge/border (of a page): *when you write, leave a wide margin; put the corrections in the margin.* □ **margen**
2 extra space/time: *leave a margin for error,* allow extra space/time in case you have made a mistake in your calculations; *this does not leave us much margin,* we have not much space/time to spare. □ **margen**
safety margin, space/time left to allow for safety. □ **margen de seguridad**
3 profit/money received which is more than money paid. □ **margen de beneficio**
marginal *adj.* **1** in a margin: *marginal corrections.* □ **al margen**
2 ***marginal seat,*** parliamentary seat where there is very little difference in the votes of the opposing parties. □ **escaño por poco margen**
3 slight: *there has been a marginal improvement in his condition.* □ **ligero**
marguerite [mɑːgə'riːt] *n.* common large white daisy. □ **margarita**
marigold ['mærigould] *n.* common garden plant with yellow flowers. □ **caléndula**
marijuana [mæri'hwɑːnə] *n.* drug made from hemp. □ **marihuana**
marina [mə'riːnə] *n.* harbour for yachts/motor boats, etc. □ **puerto deportivo**
marinade [mæri'neid] *n.* mixture of wine and herbs, etc., in which meat or fish is soaked before cooking. □ **marinada**
■ *v.* to soak (meat or fish) in a mixture of wine and herbs. □ **marinar**
marine [mə'riːn] *adj.* referring to the sea: *marine life; marine fishing; marine insurance.* □ **marino**
■ *n.* **1** ***the merchant marine,*** the merchant navy. □ **la marina mercante**
2 soldier serving on a ship. □ **marino**
mariner ['mærinə] *n.* sailor. □ **marinero**
marionette [mæriə'net] *n.* string puppet. □ **marioneta**
marital ['mæritl] *adj.* referring to marriage: *they have marital problems.* □ **marital**
maritime ['mæritaim] *adj.* referring to the sea: *a maritime power.* □ **marítimo**
marjoram ['mɑːdʒərəm] *n.* common herb used as flavouring. □ **mejorana**
mark [mɑːk] *n.* **1** spot/stain; something which can be seen: *I can't get the ink marks off your shirt; there were marks of small feet on the earth.* □ **mancha**
2 target. □ **objetivo**
wide of the mark, far from correct. □ **lejos del objetivo**
3 sign: *as a mark of respect.* □ **señal**

punctuation mark, printing sign (such as full stop/comma, etc.). □ **signo de puntuación**
4 number of points given to a student: *he got good marks in French; you'll get a bad mark for being late.* □ **nota**
5 starting line in a race. □ **línea de salida**
on your marks, get ready at your places. □ **a sus puestos**
6 line indicating a point reached: *high-water mark; the fund has reached the $2,000 mark.* □ **nivel de agua; ...ha alcanzado el punto de...**
7 unit of money in Germany. □ **marco**
■ *v.* **1** to make a sign on (something): *he marked the tree with a red cross.* □ **marcar**
2 to correct and give points: *the teacher marked our homework.* □ **calificar**
3 *to mark time,* to march on one spot/to stay in one place/not to advance: *exports seem to be marking time.* □ **estancarse**
4 to follow closely an opposing player (in football/rugby, etc.). □ **marcar**
mark down *v.* to lower the price of (something). □ **rebajar**
marked *adj.* obvious/noticeable: *a marked improvement.* □ **acusado**
a marked man, man who has been selected by the enemy as a probable target. □ **objetivo**
markedly ['mɑ:kidli] *adv.* obviously. □ **notablemente**
marker *n.* thing which marks; person who notes the scores in a competition, etc. □ **marcador**
marker buoy, buoy used to indicate a dangerous spot. □ **boya**
marking *n.* **1** making marks. □ **marca**
marking ink, black ink which will not wash off. □ **tinta indeleble**
2 *markings,* spots/stripes, etc. on a bird or animal: *you can tell the difference between the species by their distinctive wing markings.* □ **manchas**
3 correcting (exercises/homework, etc.): *the maths teacher had a lot of marking to do.* □ **calificación**
mark out *v.* to indicate the boundaries of (a land); to select. □ **delimitar; seleccionar**
marksman *n.* (*pl. marksmen*) person who shoots well. □ **tirador**
marksmanship *n.* ability to shoot well. □ **puntería**
mark up *v.* to increase the price of something. □ **subir los precios**
mark-up *n.* amount added to the cost price to give the selling price. □ **margen de beneficio**
market ['mɑ:kit] *n.* **1** selling of produce (from stalls); place where produce is sold (from stalls): *market place; covered market; cattle market.* □ **mercado**
market day, special day when a market is held. □ **día de mercado**
2 sale: *a new product has come on to the market; his house is on the market at $20,000.* □ **venta**
3 place where something is required/could be sold; need for a product: *Europe is our biggest market; there is no market for black soap.* □ **mercado**
market research, examination of the possible sales of a product before it is launched. □ **análisis de mercado**
the Common Market, the European Economic Community. □ **el Mercado Común**
black market, illegal selling at high prices: *I bought some butter on the black market.* □ **mercado negro**
■ *v.* to sell products: *the firm markets six different ranges of kitchen furniture.* □ **comercializar**
marketable *adj.* which can be sold easily. □ **comercial**
market garden *n.* small farm growing vegetables/fruit for sale in a nearby town. □ **huerto**
market gardener *n.* person who runs a market garden. □ **hortelano**
marketing *n.* selling techniques (publicity/packaging, etc.) for a product. □ **mercadotecnia**
marmalade ['mɑ:məleid] *n.* jam made from oranges/lemons or grapefruit. □ **mermelada**
marmoset [mɑ:mə'zet] *n.* small American monkey. □ **tití**
marmot ['mɑ:mət] *n.* small burrowing animal. □ **marmota**
maroon [mə'ru:n] *adj.* and *n.* deep purple red (colour). □ **castaño**
■ *n.* firework used as a distress signal by ships. □ **bengala**
■ *v.* to abandon in an awkward place: *they were marooned on a small island; the tide came up and marooned the children on some rocks.* □ **dejar abandonado/aislado**
marquee [mɑ:'ki:] *n.* very large tent. □ **carpa**
marquetry ['mɑ:kətri] *n.* (making) patterns on the surface of wood with inlaid pieces of different-coloured wood or ivory. □ **marquetería**
marriage ['mæridʒ] *n.* **1** state of being legally joined as husband and wife: *their marriage lasted only three years; they are related by marriage,* they are relatives because members of their families are married; *marriage certificate/marriage lines; marriage licence.* □ **matrimonio**
2 ceremony of being married: *they had a very simple marriage.* □ **boda**
marriageable *adj.* suitable to become married: *a marriageable age.* □ **casadero**
marrow ['mærou] *n.* **1** soft interior of bones. □ **médula**
2 large green vegetable growing on a creeping plant. □ **calabacín**
marry ['mæri] *v.* **1** to make (two people) husband and wife: *the priest married them in a chapel; he's marrying his daughter to the son of the innkeeper.* □ **casar**
2 to become married to someone: *I'm marrying the girl next door; they married in December; she married into a family of schoolteachers,* most of her husband's family are schoolteachers. □ **casarse**
married *adj.* joined as husband or wife: *is she married? they got married last Saturday; what's her married name?,* what name did she take when she got married? **casado**
marsh [mɑ:ʃ] *n.* wet/swampy land. □ **marjal, marisma**
marsh marigold, common yellow flower growing in marshes. □ **calta**
marsh mallow, common pink flower growing in marshes. □ **malvavisco**
marshmallow *n.* soft and sticky white or pink sweet. □ **dulce de merengue**
marshy *adj.* swampy/wet (land). □ **pantanoso**
marshal ['mɑ:ʃl] *n.* **1** very high-ranking military officer. □ **mariscal**
Marshal of the Royal Air Force, highest rank in the Royal Air Force. □ **capitán general de las Fuerzas Aéreas**
2 organizer (of a race/a show). □ **maestro de ceremonias**
■ *v.* (*he marshalled*) to set out (facts) in order; to organize (a race/a show). □ **poner en orden (hechos); organizar**
marshalling yard *n.* railway yard where wagons are sorted out into trains. □ **zona de clasificación**

marsupial [mɑːˈsuːpiəl] *adj.* and *n.* (animal) which carries its young in a pouch. □ **marsupial**
mart [mɑːt] *n.* market. □ **mercado**
marten [ˈmɑːtən] *n.* small wild flesh-eating animal like a weasel. □ **marta**
martial [ˈmɑːʃl] *adj.* referring to war. □ **marcial**
martial arts, oriental fighting techniques using swords/sticks, etc. □ **artes marciales**
martial law, maintenance of law by the army instead of the police: *martial law has been declared in six towns.* □ **ley marcial**
martial music, marches played by military bands. □ **música militar**
martin [ˈmɑːtən] *n.* small dark bird similar to a swallow. □ **avión**
martinet [mɑːtiˈnet] *n.* very strict person. □ **un sargento**
martini [mɑːˈtiːni] *n.* drink made of gin/vodka and vermouth. □ **martini**
martyr [ˈmɑːtə] *n.* **1** person killed because of his religious beliefs: *the Christian martyrs.* □ **mártir**
2 *she is a martyr to migraine,* she suffers a lot from migraine. □ **es víctima de...**
■ *v.* to kill (someone) for their religious beliefs. □ **martirizar**
martyrdom *n.* death for your beliefs: *he suffered martyrdom at the hands of the Romans.* □ **martirio**
marvel [ˈmɑːvl] *n.* object of wonder: *one of the marvels of modern technology; it's a marvel he's still alive.* □ **maravilla**
■ *v.* (*he marvelled*) to show wonder/surprise at something: *I still marvel at the builders of the Egyptian pyramids.* □ **maravillarse**
marvellous *adj.* wonderful/amazing. □ **maravilloso**
marvellously *adv.* wonderfully/amazingly. □ **maravillosamente**
marzipan [ˈmɑːzipæn] *n.* paste made from almonds, used for making sweets or covering cakes. □ **mazapán**
mascara [mæˈskɑːrə] *n.* black liquid/paste for making eyelashes dark. □ **rimel**
mascot [ˈmæskət] *n.* object/animal which brings good luck: *this toy car is my lucky mascot.* □ **mascota**
masculine [ˈmæskjulin] *adj.* **1** male/manly. □ **masculino**
2 (*in grammar*) referring to words which have a particular form to indicate the male gender. □ **masculino**
masculinity [mæskjuˈliniti] *n.* manliness. □ **masculinidad**
maser [ˈmeizə] *n.* device which produces highly concentrated electric force. □ **máser**
mash [mæʃ] *n.* **1** mixture of things crushed together. □ **amasijo**
2 (*informal*) mashed potatoes: *sausage and mash.* □ **puré de patatas**
■ *v.* to crush (something) into a paste: *to mash potatoes; mashed potatoes.* □ **hacer un puré de**
masher *n.* device for crushing. □ **trituradora**
potato masher, kitchen implement for mashing potatoes. □ **pasapurés**
mask [mɑːsk] *n.* covering to disguise/to protect the face: *a surgeon's mask; the bank robbers wore black masks; for the carnival he wore a mask like a pig.* □ **máscara**
■ *v.* to cover up/to hide: *it only serves to mask the real state of the company's finances.* □ **enmascarar**
masked *adj.* wearing a mask: *a masked robber.* □ **enmascarado**
masochist [ˈmæsəkist] *n.* person who enjoys being hurt. □ **masoquista**
masochism *n.* enjoyment at being hurt. □ **masoquismo**
mason [ˈmeisn] *n.* **1** person who builds with stone. □ **albañil**
2 member of a secret society of freemasons. □ **masón**
masonic [məˈsɔnik] *adj.* referring to freemasons: *masonic lodge.* □ **masónico**
masonry [ˈmeisnri] *n.* art of building with stone; large stones in a building. □ **mampostería; albañilería**
masquerade [mɑːskəˈreid] *n.* **1** dance/party where people wear masks. □ **baile de máscaras**
2 pretence/hiding of the truth. □ **enmascaramiento**
■ *v.* to pretend to be somebody: *he masqueraded as a government inspector.* □ **hacerse pasar por**
mass [mæs] *n.* **1** Catholic communion service: *music for mass.* □ **misa**
high mass, mass with full ceremony. □ **misa mayor**
low mass, mass without ceremony. □ **misa rezada**
2 *Mozart's **Requiem Mass,*** music for a mass for the dead composed by Mozart. □ **misa de réquiem**
3 (*in physics*) solid body: *water displaced by a mass.* □ **masa**
4 (*in physics*) weight of a body. □ **masa**
5 large number/large quantity: *a mass of people; a mass of dead leaves; he was a mass of bruises,* covered with bruises; *mass murderer,* killer of a large number of people; *mass meeting,* meeting of a lot of people. □ **montón; masas**
mass media, means of communicating (TV/radio/newspapers) which reach a large number of people. □ **medios de comunicación**
mass production, production of a large number of products. □ **producción en serie**
6 ***the masses,*** the common people. □ **las masas**
■ *v.* to group together into a mass: *clouds were massing on the horizon.* □ **concentrarse**
massacre [ˈmæsəkə] *n.* killing of a lot of people/animals. □ **matanza**
■ *v.* to kill a lot of people/animals. □ **matar**
massage [ˈmæsɑːʒ] *n.* rubbing of the body to relieve pain or to reduce weight. □ **masaje**
■ *v.* to rub (someone's body) to relieve pain or to reduce weight. □ **dar un masaje**
masseur [mæˈsəː] *n.* man who massages. □ **masajista**
masseuse [mæˈsəːz] *n.* woman who massages. □ **masajista**
massive [ˈmæsiv] *adv.* very large: *a massive blood transfusion; massive loans from the bank; a massive silver cup.* □ **enorme, macizo**
mast [mɑːst] *n.* **1** tall pole on a ship to carry the sails. □ **mástil**
2 tall metal construction to carry an aerial: *wireless mast.* □ **torre**
3 (*no pl.*) seeds of beech/oak, etc., trees. □ **hayuco (haya); bellota (roble)**
mastectomy [mæˈstektəmi] *n.* operation to remove a breast. □ **mastectomía**
master [ˈmɑːstə] *n.* **1** person in control: *I'm my own master,* I work for myself/on my own; *master of a ship; the dog ran around looking for its master.* □ **amo; patrón de un barco**
2 male teacher: *the French master.* □ **profesor**
Master of Science, (person with a) second degree in science from a university. □ **'master'**
3 head of a college. □ **director**
4 skilled person: *he is master of his craft; an old master,* painting by a great painter of the past; *he*

is a past master at smuggling goods through the Customs, he is very clever at smuggling. □ **maestro**
■ *adj.* controlling. □ **maestro**
master bedroom, main bedroom. □ **dormitorio principal**
master key, main key. □ **llave maestra**
master switch, switch which controls all other switches. □ **interruptor diferencial**
master tape, main tape from which copies are made. □ **'master'**
■ *v.* to become skilled at (something); to gain control of (something): *he mastered the rules of the game very quickly.* □ **dominar**
master-at-arms *n.* (*in the navy*) petty officer in charge of small arms and discipline. □ **sargento de marina**
masterful *adj.* commanding/like a commander. □ **dominante**
masterfully *adv.* in a commanding way. □ **de forma dominante**
masterly *adj.* clever; like an expert: *he served drinks in a masterly way.* □ **magistral**
mastermind *n.* very clever person. □ **cerebro**
■ *v.* to be the brains behind (a plan): *he masterminded the whole burglary.* □ **ser el cerebro de**
masterpiece *n.* very fine painting/book/piece of music, etc. □ **obra maestra**
masterstroke *n.* very clever action. □ **golpe maestro**
mastery *n.* control over someone; complete understanding of a subject; great skill at a game. □ **dominio**

masticate ['mæstikeit] *v.* (*formal*) to chew. □ **masticar**
mastication [mæsti'keiʃn] *n.* chewing. □ **masticación**

mastiff ['mæstif] *n.* large fierce breed of dog. □ **mastín**

mastoid ['mæstɔid] *n.* **1** bone just behind the ear. □ **mastoides**
2 ***mastoids,*** (*informal*) inflammation of the mastoid. □ **mastoiditis**

mat [mæt] *n.* **1** small piece of carpet/woven straw, etc., used as a floor covering: *straw mat; wipe your shoes on the mat.* □ **estera; felpudo**
bath mat, small carpet to step on to when getting out of a bath. □ **alfombrilla del cuarto de baño**
2 small piece of cloth/wood/glass put under a plate on a table: *table mat/place mat.* □ **mantel individual**
matted *adj.* stuck together (like a mat): *matted hair.* □ **enmarañado**
matting *n.* (material for making) large mats. □ **material para hacer esteras**
coconut matting, floor covering made from coconut fibres. □ **estera de fibra de coco**

match [mætʃ] *n.* **1** someone/something equal: *he has met his match.* □ **pareja**
2 *this shirt and tie are a good match,* they go well together. □ **...hacen juego**
3 game: *football match; tennis match.* □ **partido**
test match, international cricket match. □ **partido internacional**
4 small piece of wood/cardboard with a chemical tip which lights when rubbed against a rough surface: *a box of matches; he lit/struck a match.* □ **cerilla**
5 marriage. □ **matrimonio**
■ *v.* **1** to be equal to: *the two boxers are evenly matched,* they are equal in strength. □ **ser igual a**
2 to fit/to go with: *I want some gloves to match this hat.* □ **ir con**
matchbox *n.* small box containing matches. □ **caja de cerillas**
matching *adj.* which fit/go together: *matching hat and gloves.* □ **a juego**
matchless *adj.* which cannot be equalled: *she has a matchless complexion.* □ **sin igual**
matchmaker *n.* person who arranges a marriage. □ **casamentero**
matchstick, *Amer.* **matchstalk** *n.* stick of wood forming a match. □ **palo de la cerilla**
matchstick men, sketches of people drawn with single lines for each limb. □ **monigotes de palo**
matchwood *n.* small pieces of wood: *the ship was smashed to matchwood.* □ **astillas**

mate [meit] *n.* **1** one of a pair of animals; husband or wife: *the female bird sits on the eggs while her mate fetches food.* □ **macho/hembra**
2 (*informal*) friend/companion: *look here, mate!* □ **amigo**
3 helper: *a plumber's mate.* □ **ayudante**
4 (*in merchant navy*) officer. □ **oficial**
5 (*in chess*) a position where the king cannot move, and the game ends. □ **mate**
■ *v.* **1** (*of animals*) to breed: *the birds are mating; the mating season.* □ **aparear**
2 (*in chess*) to put your opponent's king in a position from which he cannot escape. □ **dar jaque mate**

material [mə'tiəriəl] *n.* **1** something which can be used for making something: *construction materials; raw materials.* □ **material**
2 useful implements. □ **material**
writing materials, pens/pencils/ink/paper, etc. □ **artículos de escritorio**
3 cloth: *I have got some beautiful material to make a skirt.* □ **tela**
4 subject matter/notes: *he's gathering material for a book on the theatre.* □ **material**
■ *adj.* **1** referring to physical things: *he is only interested in material things; have you enough for your material needs?* □ **material**
2 important: *it is of material importance; does it make any material difference?* □ **es de suma importancia; ¿...una diferencia tan enorme?**
materialism *n.* interest only in physical things/belief that only physical things are important. □ **materialismo**
materialist *n.* person who believes in materialism. □ **materialista**
materialize *v.* to become real/to appear: *the promised increase in salary never materialized.* □ **materializar**
materially *adv.* greatly/noticeably: *this evidence has materially altered the case.* □ **notablemente**

maternal [mə'tə:nl] *adj.* referring to a mother: *maternal instincts; maternal grandfather,* father of your mother. □ **maternal**
maternally *adv.* like a mother. □ **maternalmente**
maternity *n.* becoming a mother; giving birth. □ **maternidad**
maternity hospital, hospital specializing in births. □ **maternidad**
maternity leave, paid leave from a job while you are having a baby. □ **permiso por maternidad**
maternity wear, clothes worn by pregnant women. □ **vestidos de embarazada**

mathematics [mæθə'mætiks] *n.* science of numbers and measurements: *he is studying mathematics.* □ **matemáticas**
mathematical *adj.* referring to mathematics. □ **matemático**
mathematically *adv.* by mathematics: *it is all cal-*

culated mathematically. □ **matemáticamente**
mathematician [mæθimə'tiʃn] *n.* expert at mathematics. □ **matemático**
maths, *Amer.* **math** *n.* (*informal*) mathematics. □ **matemáticas**
matinée ['mætinei] *n.* afternoon performance of a play or film. □ **función de tarde, primera sesión**
matins ['mætinz] *n. pl.* prayers said in the morning. □ **maitines**
matriarch ['meitriɑ:k] *n.* woman who leads a family/a group. □ **matriarca**
matriarchal [meitri'ɑ:kl] *adj.* referring to a matriarch: *a matriarchal society,* society where women rule families. □ **matriarcal**
matricide ['mætrisaid] *n.* murder of your mother. □ **matricidio**
matriculate [mə'trikjuleit] *v.* to pass an examination which allows you to join a university; to become a member of a university. □ **aprobar el examen de selectividad; entrar en la universidad**
matriculation [mətrikju'leiʃn] *n.* joining a university after passing an examination; examination which you need to pass in order to join a university. □ **matrícula; selectividad**
matrimony ['mætriməni] *n.* state of being married. □ **matrimonio**
matrimonial [mætri'mouniəl] *adj.* referring to marriage. □ **matrimonial**
matrix ['meitriks] *n.* plan/pattern from which copies are made. □ **matriz**
matron ['meitrən] *n.* **1** (*formerly*) senior nursing officer in charge of a hospital. □ **enfermera jefa**
2 woman (usually a nurse) who looks after children in a boarding school. □ **cuidadora**
3 middle-aged married woman. □ **matrona**
matt [mæt] *adj.* dull/not shiny: *a matt photograph; matt black paint.* □ **mate**
matter ['mætə] *n.* **1** substance/material: *vegetable matter; decaying matter.* □ **materia**
2 thing/business: *it's a matter for the police; that's quite another matter,* that's something quite different. □ **asunto**
3 problem: *what's the matter? he walked around as if nothing was the matter; something's the matter with the engine,* something has gone wrong with the engine. □ **¿qué pasa?; algo le pasa al motor**
4 ***no matter what*** *book,* any book; *at no matter what time of day,* at any time of day. □ **cualquier**
no matter how *urgent,* however urgent it might be. □ **por muy urgente que sea**
■ *v.* to be important: *it doesn't matter; it matters a lot if you are late; what does it matter if he's always late?,* is it really important if he's always late? □ **importar**
matter-of-fact *adj.* practical. □ **prosaico, práctico**
mattress ['mætrəs] *n.* thick, soft part of a bed made of a canvas case with various fillings: *a straw mattress.* □ **colchón**
sprung mattress, mattress with springs inside. □ **colchón de muelles**
mature [mə'tjuə] *adj.* ripe; older; reasonable/adult (attitude). □ **maduro**
mature student, student who is older than normal. □ **estudiante maduro**
■ *v.* to ripen: *the wine has to mature for five years in a barrel.* □ **madurar**
maturity *n.* ripeness/readiness. □ **madurez**
maudlin ['mɔ:dlin] *adj.* weeping/silly through drink: *they were singing maudlin songs.* □ **llorón**
maul [mɔ:l] *v.* **1** to attack: *he was mauled by a tiger.* □ **herir de gravedad**
2 *our team was mauled,* was badly beaten. □ **a nuestro equipo lo vapulearon**
maunder ['mɔ:ndə] *v.* to mumble disconnected phrases. □ **divagar**
Maundy Thursday ['mɔ:ndi'θə:zdi] *n.* Thursday before Easter Sunday. □ **Jueves Santo**
mausoleum [mɔ:zə'liəm] *n.* imposing burial building. □ **mausoleo**
mauve [mouv] *adj.* and *n.* light pinkish purple (colour). □ **malva**
maverick ['mævərik] *n.* **1** *Amer.* animal which has not been branded and which is running loose. □ **animal sin marcar**
2 person who does not fit in to the usual pattern: *maverick politician,* who is not tied to his party's views. □ **rebelde; disidente**
mawkish ['mɔ:kiʃ] *adj.* silly/sentimental. □ **sensiblero**
maxim ['mæksim] *n.* wise saying: *it's a maxim of mine – 'never trust someone who brings you a present'.* □ **máxima**
maximum ['mæksiməm] *adj.* and *n.* greatest possible (number/amount): *this requires the maximum of effort; the maximum speed of a car.* □ **máximo**
at the maximum, at most: *at the maximum, you need work three hours a week.* □ **como máximo**
maximize ['mæksimaiz] *v.* to make as large as possible. □ **aumentar al máximo**
May [mei] *n.* **1** fifth month of the year: *his birthday is in May/is on May 15th.* □ **mayo**
May Day, May 1st. □ **primero de mayo**
2 ***may,*** hawthorn/wild shrub growing in hedges and flowering in May. □ **espino**
mayday *n.* international distress signal: *we sent out a mayday call.* □ **S.O.S**
maypole *n.* tall pole around which people dance on the first of May. □ **mayo**
may [mei] *v.* (*he might*) **1** (*used with other verbs to mean*) it is possible: *he may miss the train; he might be waiting; you might have left it on the train,* perhaps you left it on the train. □ **poder**
2 *we* ***might as well*** *turn off the music,* it would be better if we turned off the music. □ **podríamos también quitar la música**
3 *he might have done something to help,* he ought to have done something/it would have been better if he had done something to help. □ **podría haber ayudado en algo**
4 ***much good may it do you!,*** I hope it does you a lot of good (though I doubt if it will). □ **más vale que te vaya bien**
5 (*used with other verbs to mean*) it is allowed: *you may sit down if you want to; might I ask you a question?* □ **puede sentarse si lo desea; ¿puedo hacerle...?**
maybe *adv.* perhaps: *maybe he's had an accident.* □ **tal vez**
maybe not, possibly not. □ **tal vez no**
mayhem ['meihem] *n.* wild confusion: *it created mayhem among the crowds.* □ **pánico**
mayonnaise [meiə'neiz] *n.* cream sauce made with egg yolks and oil. □ **mayonesa**
mayor ['mɛə] *n.* elected leader of a town: *he is mayor of Brighton.* □ **alcalde**
mayoress ['mɛəres] *n.* wife of a mayor. □ **alcaldesa**
maze [meiz] *n.* network of puzzling paths in which you can get lost: *he was soon lost in a maze of corridors.* □ **laberinto**
me [mi:] *pron.* referring to the speaker: *give it to me; can you hear me? come along with me; he is younger than me.* □ **me; (after prep.) mí**
meadow ['medou] *n.* large green field. □ **prado**

meagre ['mi:gə] *Amer.* **meager** *adj.* **1** scanty/few: *he existed on meagre rations.* □ **escaso**
2 thin. □ **magro**
meagreness *n.* small amount: *meagreness of information.* □ **escasez**

meal [mi:l] *n.* **1** food taken at a sitting: *we eat our evening meal at 8 o'clock; you should take some exercise after a heavy meal; they had a light meal of bread and cheese.* □ **comida**
2 coarse flour. □ **harina**
mealtime *n.* time when you usually eat. □ **hora de la comida**
mealy *adj.* floury: *mealy potatoes.* □ **harinoso**
mealy-mouthed *adj.* not straightforward; (person) who doesn't say what he thinks. □ **camandulero**

mean [mi:n] *n.* **1** middle; average; middle point between two extremes: *you have to find the mean between the fastest and slowest times.* □ **promedio**
2 ***means,*** way/method of doing something: *can he find the means to do it? is there any means of getting there tonight? we have to do it by some means or other.* □ **medios**
by no means, not at all. □ **de ninguna manera**
by all means, certainly. □ **claro que sí**
3 ***means,*** money/resources: *it's beyond my means,* it's too expensive for me; *has he the means to run two cars?* □ **está fuera del alcance de mis medios**
means test, inquiry into the amount of money earned by someone in order to calculate how much state benefit he should receive. □ **estimación de renta**
■ *adj.* **1** average/middle: *what is the mean result after six tests?* □ **resultado medio**
2 miserable/low: *he has no mean opinion of himself,* he thinks a lot of himself. □ **bajo**
3 *what a mean trick,* what an unkind trick. □ **qué jugarreta**
4 miserly: *he's very mean with his money; they're so mean that they won't buy their little girl new clothes.* □ **tacaño**
■ *v.* (*he meant*) **1** to intend: *he didn't mean to do it; does she really mean to climb Everest? the shot was meant for you.* □ **tener la intención de**
to mean well: *he means well,* he has good intentions. □ **tener buenas intenciones**
2 *do you mean my Uncle Richard?,* are you talking about my Uncle Richard? □ **¿te refieres a...?**
3 *he said he would run away, and he meant it,* he was serious; *do you really mean it when you say they are all mad?* □ **dijo que se escaparía, y lo hizo; lo dices de verdad...**
4 to signify/to show: *a red light means you have to stop; what does the word 'transitory' mean? does the name Andrew Beard mean anything to you?* □ **significar**
meaning *n.* signification: *what's the meaning of these red marks? if you want to know the meaning of the word look it up in a dictionary.* □ **significado**
■ *adj.* significant: *she gave him a meaning look.* □ **significativo**
meaningful *adj.* **1** full of meaning; significant. □ **que tiene sentido**
2 *meaningful discussions,* discussions which lead to some agreement. □ **discusiones provechosas**
meaningfully *adv.* significantly. □ **con significado**
meaningless *adj.* not signifying anything: *this phrase is quite meaningless.* □ **sin sentido**
meanly *adv.* poorly: *meanly clothed.* □ **humildemente**
meanness *n.* miserliness; dislike of sharing things/of spending money. □ **tacañería**
mean-spirited *adj.* sly/unpleasant. □ **malicioso**

meander [mi'ændə] *n.* bend in a river. □ **meandro**
■ *v.* to wind/to wander about: *the river meandered across the plain.* □ **serpentear**
meandering *adj.* wandering/very winding (path). □ **serpenteante**

meant [ment] *v. see* **mean.**

meantime ['mi:ntaim] *n.* ***in the meantime,*** while: *the film only starts at four o'clock, in the meantime let's have an ice cream,* while we are waiting. □ **mientras tanto**
■ *adv.* during this time. □ **mientras tanto**

meanwhile ['mi:nwail] *adv.* during this time: *meanwhile, the police were closing in.* □ **entretanto**

measles ['mi:zlz] *n.* children's disease which gives you a red rash. □ **sarampión**
German measles, mild disease which gives a red rash and which can affect an unborn child if caught by a pregnant woman. □ **rubéola**
measly *adj.* (*informal*) miserable/small: *they gave us a measly spoonful of potatoes.* □ **ínfima**

measure ['meʒə] *n.* **1** quantity; size of something: *cubic measure.* □ **medida**
2 *he has his clothes* ***made to measure,*** made specially to fit his measurements. □ **a la medida**
3 unit for showing the size/quantity of something: *an amp is a measure of electrical current.* □ **medida**
4 thing for showing the size/quantity of something; small metal cup: *pour out a measure of whisky.* □ **medida**
tape measure, long tape with centimetres/inches marked on it. □ **metro (cinta métrica)**
5 action: *as a precautionary measure,* as a precaution; *the police will take measures to combat violence.* □ **medida**
6 seam/layer of coal. □ **yacimiento**
7 plan of a new law/a bill: *the government has proposed a new measure concerning working hours.* □ **medida**
■ *v.* to be of a certain size/length/quantity, etc.; to find out the length/quantity of (something): *the carpet measures 3 metres by 2; apparatus for measuring the speed of an aircraft; a barometer measures atmospheric pressure; he was measured for a suit,* a tailor took his measurements. □ **medir**
to measure one's length: *he measured his length on the floor,* he fell down flat on the floor. □ **dio de bruces contra el suelo**
measurable *adj.* which can be measured. □ **medible**
measured *adj.* regular: *he walked with measured tread,* in a slow and stately way. □ **moderado**
measureless *adj.* so large that it cannot be measured. □ **inconmensurable**
measurement *n.* **1** finding out the size/length/quantity of something: *the measurement of very fine particles.* □ **medición**
2 quantity/size, etc., found out when you measure: *I will have to take your measurements; what are the measurements of the room?* □ **medida**
measuring *n.* finding out the size/length/quantity of something. □ **medición**
measuring glass/jug, glass jar with quantities marked on it by lines. □ **probeta**
measuring tape, long tape with centimetres/inches marked on it. □ **metro**

meat [mi:t] *n.* flesh of an animal which is eaten: *can I have some more meat?* □ **carne**
meat ball *n.* minced meat rolled into a ball and cooked. □ **albóndiga**
meaty *adj.* **1** with a lot of meat: *a meaty hamburger.*

□ **carnoso**
2 with a lot of details/information: *a meaty article on African economics.* □ **detallado**

mechanic [mi'kænik] *n.* person who works on engines: *a car mechanic.* □ **mecánico**
mechanical *adj.* referring to a machine: *mechanical engineering; mechanical gestures,* gestures done automatically as if you were a machine. □ **mecánico**
mechanically *adv.* by machine; like a machine; automatically: *machine which opens letters mechanically; he just repeated the same words mechanically over and over again.* □ **mecánicamente**
mechanics *n.* **1** the study of force and power. □ **mecánica**
2 the study of machines. □ **mecánica**
3 way in which something is going to work: *he explained the mechanics of the new payment system.* □ **mecanismo**
mechanism ['mekənizəm] *n.* **1** working parts (of a machine): *the mechanism of a watch.* □ **mecanismo**
2 way in which something works: *what is the mechanism for transferring money abroad?* □ **mecanismo**
mechanization [mekənai'zeiʃn] *n.* introduction of machines to take the place of manual labour. □ **mecanización**
mechanize ['mekənaiz] *v.* to introduce machines in place of manual labour. □ **mecanizar**

medal ['medl] *n.* metal disc, usually attached to a ribbon, made to commemorate an important occasion or battle: *the soldier had several rows of medals; he was awarded a medal for bravery.* □ **medalla**
gold/silver/bronze medals, medals for first/second/third place in competitions: *she won two gold medals in the Olympics.* □ **medalla de oro/plata/bronce**
medallion [mi'dæljən] *n.* large medal. □ **medallón**
medallist *n.* person who has won a medal in a sports competition, etc.: *an Olympic gold medallist.* □ **el medalla de oro/plata/bronce**

meddle ['medl] *v.* to interfere with someone else's affairs: *don't meddle in my affairs.* □ **entrometerse en**
meddler *n.* person who likes to interfere. □ **entrometido**
meddling *n.* interfering in someone else's affairs: *no meddling with the gas taps!* □ **intromisión; ¡no tocar...!**
■ *adj.* (person) who is always interfering: *that meddling fool.* □ **entrometido**

media ['mi:diə] *n. pl.* **1** means of communicating information. □ **medios de comunicación**
the (mass) media, newspapers/TV/radio, etc.. □ **los medios de comunicación**
media resources centre, centre for communicating information by television/films/tapes, etc. □ **centro de comunicaciones**
2 *see also* **medium.**

mediate ['mi:dieit] *v.* to intervene/to try to bring peace between two opponents: *the United Nations is trying to mediate in the dispute between the two countries.* □ **mediar**
mediation [mi:di'eiʃn] *n.* attempt to make two opponents agree. □ **mediación**
mediator *n.* person who tries to make two opponents agree. □ **mediador**

medical ['medikl] *adj.* referring to the study of disease: *the medical profession,* all doctors; *medical student.* □ **médico**
medical officer of health, person responsible for the health services of a town, etc. □ **concejal de sanidad**
■ *n.* (*informal*) examination of the body by a doctor: *I am having a medical tomorrow; he wanted to join the Navy but failed his medical.* □ **reconocimiento médico**
medically *adv.* in a medical way: *medically speaking, there is nothing the matter with him.* □ **desde un punto de vista médico**
medicated *adj.* with a medicine added: *a medicated shampoo.* □ **medicinal**

medicine ['medsin] *n.* **1** study of disease, ill health and its cure: *he is going to study medicine.* □ **medicina**
2 liquid/powder/pill taken to cure an illness: *cough medicine; I have to take the medicine three times a day.* □ **medicina**
medicine chest, cupboard for keeping medicines in. □ **botiquín**
medicinal [me'disinl] *adj.* used to treat an illness: *I keep a bottle of brandy for medicinal purposes,* to use as a medicine. □ **medicinal**
medicinally *adv.* as a medicine. □ **medicinalmente**

medieval [medi'i:vl] *adj.* referring to the Middle Ages: *a medieval church.* □ **medieval**

mediocre [mi:di'oukə] *adj.* ordinary; not good or bad. □ **mediocre**
mediocrity [mi:di'ɔkriti] *n.* **1** not being good or bad; ordinariness. □ **mediocridad**
2 very ordinary person with no special talents. □ **mediocre**

meditate ['mediteit] *v.* to think deeply about something: *I am meditating a plan; he is meditating on human wickedness.* □ **meditar**
meditation [medi'teiʃn] *n.* long and deep thought (often of a religious nature). □ **meditación**
meditative *adj.* thoughtful. □ **meditativo**

medium ['mi:diəm] *adj.* middle/average: *he is of medium height; a medium-sized car.* □ **medio**
■ *n.* (*pl. media/mediums*) **1** middle point. □ **medio**
a happy medium, a compromise. □ **término medio**
2 type of paint used by an artist: *he works best in the medium of watercolours.* □ **medio**
3 means of doing something/of communicating something: *his face was soon well known through the medium of television.* □ **medio**
4 person who thinks the spirits of dead people can talk through him/her. □ **médium**

medlar ['medlə] *n.* fruit like a brown apple; tree which bears this fruit. □ **níspero**

medley ['medli] *n.* mixture. □ **mezcolanza; popurrí (música)**

meek [mi:k] *adj.* quiet/humble. □ **manso**
meekly *adv.* quietly/humbly: *he accepted his punishment meekly.* □ **sumisamente**
meekness *n.* quietness/humility. □ **mansedumbre**

meet [mi:t] *n.* gathering of huntsmen. □ **partida de caza**
■ *v.* (*he met*) **1** to come together: *they met on the stairs; I'll meet you at the station; we'll arrange to meet somewhere before we go to the theatre.* □ **encontrarse**
2 to become acquainted with someone: *haven't I met you before?; we have already met,* we know each other already. □ **conocerse**
3 to satisfy: *this ought to meet all our requirements.* □ **satisfacer**
4 *he can't meet his bills,* he hasn't enough money to pay his bills. □ **no puede hacer frente a sus facturas**
meeting *n.* **1** coming together: *we must arrange a meeting; it was a coincidence, our meeting like that.* □ **encuentro**

2 group of people who meet for a special purpose. □ **reunión**
annual general meeting, yearly assembly of all the members of a club/society/of all the shareholders in a company. □ **reunión anual**
election meeting, gathering of people where a political candidate can speak. □ **mitin**
meet with *v.* **1** to find/to come up against: *we met with a lot of problems; he met with an accident.* □ **encontrarse con**
2 *Amer.* to come together (with another person): *I met with him for lunch.* □ **reunirse con**
mega- ['megə] *prefix meaning* **1** very large. □ **mega**
2 one million. □ **mega**
megacycle ['megəsaikl] *n.* frequency of radio waves of one million cycles per second. □ **megaciclo**
megalith ['megəliθ] *n.* huge stone set up by prehistoric man. □ **megalito**
megalomania [megələ'meiniə] *n.* mad belief that you are more important/more powerful than you really are. □ **megalomanía**
megaphone ['megəfoun] *n.* metal trumpet which makes the voice sound louder. □ **megáfono**
megaton ['megətʌn] *n.* force of an explosion equal to the force produced by exploding one million tons of TNT. □ **megatón**
melancholy ['melənkəli] *n.* great sadness. □ **melancolía**
■ *adj.* very sad: *I have to tell her the melancholy news.* □ **tristísimo**
melancholic [melən'kɔlik] *adj.* very sad. □ **melancólico**
mellow ['melou] *adj.* ripe (fruit); (wine) which has matured; soft/rich (voice); calm and relaxed (older person). □ **maduro; añejo; melosa**
■ *v.* to grow ripe/to mature; to become soft/rich: *he has mellowed,* he is much less angry/unpleasant than he used to be. □ **madurar**
mellowness *n.* ripeness/maturity. □ **madurez**
melodrama ['melədrɑːmə] *n.* extremely exciting but badly written play which emphasizes violently alternating passions. □ **melodrama**
melodramatic [melədrə'mætik] *adj.* arousing violent emotions: *a melodramatic description of the attack.* □ **melodramático**
melody ['melədi] *n.* tune: *he played a beautiful Irish melody.* □ **melodía**
melodic [mi'lɔdik] *adj.* referring to tunes. □ **melódico**
melodious [mə'loudiəs] *adj.* tuneful; pleasant to listen to. □ **melodioso**
melodiously *adv.* in a tuneful way. □ **melodiosamente**
melon ['melən] *n.* large round fruit of a creeping plant. □ **melón**
water melon, very large type of melon with red flesh and black seeds. □ **sandía**
melt [melt] *v.* **1** to change from solid to liquid by heating: *the butter has melted in the sun; melt the wax in a metal dish.* □ **derretir, derretirse**
2 ***to melt away:*** *the mob of rioters melted away when the police appeared,* they disappeared. □ **...se disolvieron cuando...**
3 ***to melt down*** *scrap metal,* to heat it and make it into blocks so that it can be used again. □ **fundir**
4 *my heart melted at the sight of the little puppies,* became softened/less angry. □ **ablandarse**
melting point *n.* temperature at which a solid becomes liquid: *what is the melting point of iron?* □ **punto de fusión**
melting pot *n.* **1** pot in which metals can be melted. □ **crisol**
2 place where people of different origins come to live together. □ **zona de aluvión**
member ['membə] *n.* **1** person who belongs to a group: *a member of a club; members of the party; a woman member of the audience.* □ **miembro**
Member of Parliament, person elected to the lower house of a parliament. □ **diputado**
2 limb on a human body. □ **miembro**
membership *n.* **1** belonging to a group. □ **pertenencia**
membership card, card which shows you belong (to a club/party). □ **carné de socio**
2 all the members of a group: *we will have to ask the membership to vote on the proposal.* □ **miembros**
membrane ['membrein] *n.* thin layer of tissue in the body. □ **membrana**
memento [mə'mentou] *n.* thing kept to remind you of something; a souvenir: *a memento of our holiday in Greece.* □ **recuerdo**
memo ['memou] *n.* note/short message between people working in the same organization: *send a memo to the accounts department.* □ **memorándum**
memo pad, pad of paper for writing short notes. □ **bloc de notas**
memoir ['memwɑː] *n.* **1** ***memoirs,*** written account of what you can remember of your life: *he is writing his memoirs,* his autobiography. □ **memorias**
2 short official/scientific note. □ **reseña**
memorandum [memə'rændəm] *n.* (*pl. memoranda*) note/short message: *we have had a memorandum from the accounts department.* □ **memorándum**
memory ['meməri] *n.* **1** ability to remember: *he has a wonderful memory for faces; I have no memory for names; he recited the poem from memory; if my memory serves me right, his house has a red door,* if I can remember it correctly. □ **memoria**
2 what you remember: *childhood memories of a fishing village.* □ **recuerdo**
3 ***in memory of*** *our dead parents,* to remind us of our dead parents. □ **en memoria de...**
memorable *adj.* which you cannot forget/very striking: *he made a memorable speech.* □ **memorable**
memorial [mi'mɔːriəl] *adj.* which reminds you of something/someone. □ **conmemorativo**
a memorial service, a church service to remember someone who has died. □ **funeral**
■ *n.* monument to remind you of something/someone: *war memorial.* □ **monumento conmemorativo**
memorize *v.* to learn (something) by heart: *the spy memorized the code.* **memorizar**
men [men] *n. pl. see* **man.**
menace ['menəs] *n.* **1** threat; bad thing: *big lorries are a menace; the oil spillage is a menace to our beaches.* □ **amenaza**
2 *that child's a menace,* very naughty. □ **ese niño es un demonio**
■ *v.* **1** to threaten. □ **amenazar**
2 *menacing clouds,* clouds which threaten to bring rain. □ **nubes que amenazan lluvia**
menagerie [mi'nædʒəri] *n.* small zoo; collection of more or less wild animals. □ **zoo (pequeño)**
mend [mend] *n.* **1** place where clothing has been repaired: *he has mends in his socks.* □ **remiendo**
2 *she's* ***on the mend,*** (*informal*) she is getting better. □ **va mejorando**
■ *v.* **1** to repair; to be repaired: *can you mend a puncture? he's mending the exhaust pipe.* □ **arreglar**
2 *her fractured leg is mending,* is getting better. □ **...va mejorando**
mending *n.* **1** repairing. □ **arreglo**

2 clothes which need repairing: *there is a pile of mending on the table.* □ **ropa para remendar**
mendacity [men'dæsiti] *n.* (*formal*) telling lies. □ **mendacidad**
mendacious [men'deiʃəs] *adj.* not truthful. □ **mendaz**
menfolk ['menfouk] *n. pl.* all the men (in a family/group, etc.). □ **hombres**
menial ['mi:niəl] *adj.* low; badly paid: *menial tasks,* dirty jobs which a servant might do. □ **bajo; servil**
meningitis [menin'dʒaitis] *n.* inflammation of the membrane covering the brain. □ **meningitis**
menopause ['menəpɔ:z] *n.* period of life (around the age of 50) when women become no longer capable of bearing children. □ **menopausia**
male menopause, difficult period in a man's life (around the age of 50). □ **menopausia masculina**
menstruate ['menstrueit] *v.* (*of women*) to lose blood through the vagina at regular periods. □ **menstruar**
menstrual *adj.* referring to the regular monthly loss of blood through the vagina: *the menstrual cycle.* □ **menstrual**
menstruation [menstru'eiʃn] *n.* monthly loss of blood through the vagina. □ **menstruación**
menswear ['menzwεə] *n.* (*no pl.*) clothes for men. □ **ropa de caballero**
mental ['mentl] *adj.* **1** referring to the mind: *mental arithmetic,* calculations done in the head. □ **mental**
mental age, way of showing the development of a person's mind, by expressing it as the age at which such development is normal: *he is 25, with a mental age of 11.* □ **edad mental**
mental hospital, hospital for those who suffer from illnesses of the mind. □ **hospital psiquiátrico**
2 *she's a bit mental,* (*informal*) she's a bit mad. □ **está de los nervios**
mentality [men'tæliti] *n.* **1** mental power. □ **mentalidad**
2 way of thinking which is typical of someone/of a group: *can you understand the mentality of football hooligans?* □ **mentalidad**
mentally *adv.* concerning the brain: *I did the calculation mentally.* □ **mentalmente**
mentally defective, well below normal intelligence. □ **deficiente mental**
mention ['menʃn] *n.* reference to something: *there is no mention of the accident in the newspaper.* □ **mención**
■ *v.* **1** to refer to (something): *he never mentioned his wife's illness; do you want me to mention it to him?* □ **mencionar**
2 *there were lions and elephants in the circus,* ***not to mention*** *the seals,* not forgetting/as well as the seals. □ **sin olvidar a las focas**
mentor ['mentɔ:] *n.* (*formal*) person who teaches/helps another (younger) person. □ **mentor**
menu ['menju:] *n.* list of food available in a restaurant: *fish isn't on the menu.* □ **menú**
meow [mi:'au] *Amer.* = **miaow.**
mercantile ['mə:kəntail] *adj.* referring to commerce. □ **mercantil**
mercenary ['mə:sənəri] *adj.* (person) who is interested in money: *her mercenary instincts.* □ **materialista**
■ *n.* person who serves foreigners as a soldier for money: *the base was attacked by mercenaries.* □ **mercenario**
merchant ['mə:tʃənt] *n.* businessman; person who buys and sells: *wine merchant; he's a tobacco merchant.* □ **comerciante**
merchant navy, commercial ships of a country. □ **marina mercante**
merchant seaman, seaman in the merchant navy. □ **marino mercante**
merchandise *n.* goods for sale: *there is a lot of merchandise in the shops for Christmas.* □ **género**
■ *v.* to sell (goods) by wide and varied advertising. □ **comercializar**
merchantman *n.* (*pl. merchantmen*) commercial ship. □ **buque mercante**
mercury ['mə:kjəri] *n.* (*chemical element*: Hg) liquid metal used in thermometers/barometers, etc. □ **mercurio**
mercurial [mə:'kjuəriəl] *adj.* (person) whose temper changes frequently. □ **voluble**
mercy ['mə:si] *n.* **1** compassion/pity; kindness towards unfortunate people; desire not to punish/harm someone: *he had mercy on the poor woman.* □ **misericordia**
to leave someone to the tender mercies of: *he was left to the tender mercies of the police,* he was left for the police to deal with (harshly). □ **le dejaron en las manos poco compasivas...**
2 gift (of fate). □ **merced**
3 *we must be thankful for small mercies,* we must be grateful that everything has turned out fairly well so far. □ **siempre hay algo por lo que estar agradecido**
merciful *adj.* (person) who forgives/who is kind. □ **clemente**
mercifully *adv.* thankfully; in a forgiving/kindly way: *his oral examination was mercifully short.* □ **compasivamente**
merciless *adj.* harsh/cruel. □ **despiadado**
mercilessly *adv.* harshly/cruelly. □ **despiadadamente**
mercilessness *n.* lack of pity; hardness (of character). □ **falta de compasión**
mere ['miə] *n.* small lake. □ **lagunilla**
■ *adj.* simply/only: *he's a mere boy,* only a boy; *for the sake of a mere $2,000,* for the sake of a small sum like $2,000; *the mere sight of grass makes me sneeze,* just the sight/simply the sight of grass makes me sneeze. □ **mero; no es más que**
merely *adv.* only/simply: *instead of answering he merely smiled; I merely asked for an ice cream.* □ **meramente**
meretricious [meri'triʃəs] *adj.* showy and cheap. □ **de oropel**
merge [mə:dʒ] *v.* to join together: *the two lines merged; the transport company will merge with a property company.* □ **fusionarse**
merger *n.* amalgamation/joining of two companies. □ **fusión**
meridian [mə'ridiən] *n.* imaginary line drawn from the North Pole to the South Pole. □ **meridiano**
the Greenwich meridian, a line passing through Greenwich (near London) from which longitude is calculated. □ **el meridiano de...**
meringue [mə'ræŋ] *n.* sweet baked dessert made of egg whites and sugar. □ **merengue**
merino [mə'ri:nou] *n.* type of long-haired sheep. □ **merina**
merit ['merit] *n.* value/quality/excellence: *the proposals will be judged on their merits; a novel of considerable merit; is there any merit in the proposal to reduce tax? to go into the merits of a plan,* to examine the good and bad points of a plan. □ **mérito**
■ *v.* to be worthy of/to deserve (something): *the book merits careful study.* □ **merecerse**

meritorious [meri'tɔːriəs] *adj.* (*formal*) which is valuable/which should be rewarded. □ **meritorio**
mermaid ['məːmeid] *n.* mythical creature, half woman and half fish. □ **sirena**
merry ['meri] *adj.* **1** happy: *Merry Christmas!* □ **feliz**
to make merry, to have a good time. □ **divertirse**
the more the merrier, the more there are the happier everything is. □ **cuantos más mejor**
2 (*informal*) slightly drunk. □ **alegre**
merrily *adv.* happily. □ **felizmente**
merriment *n.* fun. □ **diversión**
merry-go-round *n.* roundabout with wooden horses, etc., in a funfair. □ **caballitos**
merrymaker *n.* person who is enjoying himself. □ **juerguista**
merrymaking *n.* festivity/celebration. □ **fiestas**
mesh [meʃ] *n.* space between the threads of a net: *fine mesh; coarse mesh.* □ **malla**
■ *v.* (*of a cogwheel*) to link together with another toothed wheel. □ **engranar**
mesmerize ['mezməraiz] *v.* to hypnotize: *the little boy was mesmerized by the toy shop window.* □ **quedarse boquiabierto**
mess [mes] *n.* **1** dirt; disorder/confusion: *the builders made a mess all over the floor; everything's in a mess; he's got himself into a mess; the company is in a financial mess.* □ **porquería; lío, follón**
to make a mess of: *they made a mess of the repair job,* they did the repair job very badly. □ **hicieron una chapuza de...**
2 group of soldiers/sailors who eat together; room where they eat. □ **rancho; comedor**
the officers' mess, the building where officers eat and sleep. □ **residencia de oficiales**
■ *v.* **1** (*informal*) to dirty: *she has messed up her new dress.* □ **ensuciarse**
2 (*informal*) to ruin/to spoil: *they messed up the party.* □ **echar a perder**
3 to eat together. □ **compartir la mesa**
mess about *v.* **1** to spend your spare time doing something: *he likes messing about in boats.* □ **entretenerse con**
2 to waste time: *stop messing about, and get on with your work.* □ **perder el tiempo**
3 ***to mess someone about,*** (*informal*) to disrupt someone's way of life/to treat someone badly. □ **fastidiar a uno**
messy *adj.* dirty; disorderly: *changing the oil in a car can be a messy job.* □ **sucio**
message ['mesidʒ] *n.* news/information sent to someone: *your boss has left a message for you.* □ **mensaje**
to get the message: *he got the message,* (*informal*) he understood. □ **lo cogió**
messenger *n.* person who brings a message: *an office messenger.* □ **mensajero**
Messrs ['mesəz] *n. used formally as plural of* Mr: *Messrs Smith, Jones and Company.* □ **Sres.**
met [met] *v. see* **meet.**
metabolism [me'tæbəlizəm] *n.* processes by which plants and animals use food to create energy: *the excessive use of the drug has upset his metabolism.* □ **metabolismo**
metabolic [metə'bɔlik] *adj.* referring to metabolism. □ **metabólico**
metacarpus [metə'kɑːpəs] *n.* bones of the hand. □ **metacarpo**
metal ['metl] *n.* usually solid mineral substance which can conduct heat and electricity: *gold, iron and mercury are all metals; a metal coffee pot; he has a metal pin in his hip joint.* □ **metal**
metalled *adj.* (road) covered with small stones set in tar. □ **pavimentado**
metallic [mə'tælik] *adj.* referring to metal: *metallic sheen,* shine such as you get on polished metal; *my car is metallic blue.* □ **metálico; metalizado**
metallurgist [me'tælədʒist] *n.* person who studies metals. □ **metalúrgico**
metallurgy [me'tælədʒi] *n.* study of metals. □ **metalurgia**
metalwork *n.* making things with metal; pieces of metal made into a construction/a work of art. □ **metalistería**
metamorphosis [metə'mɔːfəsis] *n.* (*pl. metamorphoses*) change, especially an insect's change of form: *the caterpillar in the chrysalis underwent a metamorphosis and turned into a butterfly.* □ **metamorfosis**
metamorphose [metə'mɔːfouz] *v.* to change from one state to another. □ **metamorfosearse**
metaphor ['metəfə] *n.* way of describing something by suggesting it has the properties of something else (such as 'the sea thundered against the rocks'; 'the housewife slaved all day in the kitchen'). □ **metáfora**
metaphorical [metə'fɔrikl] *adj.* like a metaphor: *think of a metaphorical use of the word 'sun'.* □ **metafórico**
metaphorically *adv.* used as a metaphor. □ **metafóricamente**
metaphysics [metə'fiziks] *n.* philosophical study of truth/knowledge/existence, etc. □ **metafísica**
metaphysical *adj.* referring to metaphysics. □ **metafísico**
metatarsus [metə'tɑːsəs] *n.* bones in the foot. □ **metatarso**
mete out ['miːt'aut] *v.* to give (punishment). □ **infligir un castigo**
meteor ['miːtiə] *n.* small object which flashes through space and shines brightly as it burns up on entering the earth's atmosphere. □ **meteoro**
meteoric [miːti'ɔrik] *adj.* like a meteor/very rapid: *a meteoric rise to fame.* □ **meteórico**
meteorite ['miːtiərait] *n.* lump of rock/iron which falls to earth from space. □ **meteorito**
meteorology [miːtiə'rɔlədʒi] *n.* study of climate and weather. □ **meteorología**
meteorological [miːtiərə'lɔdʒikl] *adj.* referring to the climate and weather: *the government meteorological office; a meteorological station,* research station which notes weather conditions. □ **meteorológico**
meteorologist [miːtiə'rɔlədʒist] *n.* person who studies climate and weather. □ **meteorólogo**
meter ['miːtə] *n.* **1** device for counting how much time/water/gas, etc., has been used: *to read the electricity meter; the taxi will cost at least $2 according to the meter.* □ **contador**
parking meter, device into which you put money to pay for parking. □ **parquímetro**
2 *Amer.* metre. □ **metro**
■ *v.* to count by a meter: *in some countries water consumption is metered.* □ **medir**
methane ['miːθein] *n.* colourless gas, which easily catches fire and is found naturally in the ground. □ **metano**
method ['meθəd] *n.* **1** way of doing something: *what's your method for avoiding paying tax? describe the method of making carbon dioxide.* □ **método**
2 well-organized way of doing something: *there's method in his way of tackling problems.* □ **método**
methodical [mi'θɔdikl] *adj.* ordered/regulated: *he works in a very methodical way.* □ **metódico**

methodically *adv.* in a well-organized way: *the police methodically checked all the owners of green cars.* □ **metódicamente**
methylated spirits ['meθileitid'spirits] (*informal*) **meths** [meθs] *n.* alcohol coloured purple, used for lighting or heating. □ **alcohol de quemar**
meticulous [mi'tikjuləs] *adj.* attentive to detail: *he is very meticulous about cleaning his shoes/about paying his debts.* □ **meticuloso**
meticulously *adv.* carefully/paying attention to details: *her office is meticulously clean.* □ **meticulosamente**
metre ['miːtə] *Amer.* **meter** *n.* **1** standard measurement of length (approximately 39.4 inches): *there are one hundred centimetres in a metre; the room is four metres by three; it occupies twelve square metres.* □ **metro**
2 regular rhythm in poetry. □ **metro**
metric ['metrik] *adj.* **1** referring to metre as a measurement. □ **métrico**
the metric system, system of measurement based on metres, litres, etc. □ **sistema métrico**
2 referring to metre as rhythm. □ **métrico**
metrical *adj.* (poem) written in a regular rhythm. □ **métrico**
metricate ['metrikeit] *v.* to express in metres/centimetres, etc. □ **expresar en metros**
metrication [metri'keiʃn] *n.* changing of a measuring system to the metric system. □ **cambio al sistema métrico**
metronome ['metrənoum] *n.* device which beats time regularly, and which you can use when practising/playing music. □ **metrónomo**
metropolis [mə'trɔpəlis] *n.* large capital city. □ **metrópoli**
metropolitan [metrə'pɔlitən] *adj.* referring to a large capital city: *metropolitan police force.* □ **metropolitano**
■ *n.* chief bishop in the Orthodox Church. □ **metropolitano**
mettle ['metl] *n.* **1** vigour/strength of character (of a person). □ **genio**
2 *this will* ***put him on his mettle,*** it will make him try to do his best. □ **esto le picará el amor propio**
mettlesome *adj.* (*formal*) vigorous/active. □ **fogoso**
mew [mjuː] *n.* soft noise which a cat makes. □ **maullido**
■ *v.* to make a soft noise like a cat. □ **maullar**
mews [mjuːz] *n.* **1** row of former stables or garages converted into houses: *a mews house; a mews flat; they live in a mews.* □ **callejón**
2 stables. □ **caballerizas**
Mexico ['meksikou] *n.* country in central America. □ **Méjico; México**
Mexican *adj.* referring to Mexico. □ **mejicano**
■ *n.* person from Mexico. □ **mejicano**
mezzanine ['metsəniːn] *n.* floor between the ground floor and the first floor. □ **entresuelo**
mezzo-soprano ['metsousə'prɑːnou] *n.* singer or voice lower in pitch than a soprano. □ **mezzo-soprano**
miaow [miː'au] *Amer.* **meow** *n.* call of a cat. □ **miau**
■ *v.* to call like a cat. □ **maullar**
miasma [mi'æzmə] *n.* unpleasant/poisonous air. □ **miasma**
mica ['maikə] *n.* type of rock which splits into thin glittering layers. □ **mica**
mice [mais] *n. pl. see* **mouse.**
Michaelmas daisy ['mikəlməs'deizi] *n.* common autumn garden flower. □ **áster silvestre**
micro- ['maikrou] *prefix meaning* **1** very small. □ **micro**
2 one millionth: *a microsecond.* □ **una millonésima de segundo**
microbe ['maikroub] *n.* germ; tiny living organism. □ **microbio**
microcosm ['maikrəkɔzəm] *n.* miniature version of something: *the population of the school is a microcosm of the population of the whole town.* □ **microcosmos**
microfiche ['maikrəfiːʃ] *n.* index card made of microfilms. □ **microficha**
microfilm ['maikrəfilm] *n.* film on which something is photographed in very small scale: *the newspaper is now available on microfilm.* □ **microfilme**
microfilm reader, apparatus with an enlarger and a display screen for reading microfilms. □ **lectora de microfilmes**
■ *v.* to make a very small-scale photograph: *the spy microfilmed the papers.* □ **microfilmar**
micron ['maikrɔn] *n.* one millionth of a metre. □ **micra**
microphone ['maikrəfoun] *n.* apparatus for capturing sound and passing it to a loudspeaker or recording apparatus: *the speaker shouted into the microphone.* □ **micrófono**
microscope ['maikrəskoup] *n.* apparatus which enlarges things which are very small: *he examined the specks of dust through a microscope.* □ **microscopio**
microscopic [maikrə'skɔpik] *adj.* so small as to be visible only through a microscope. □ **microscópico**
microwave ['maikrəweiv] *n.* very short electric wave. □ **microonda**
microwave oven, small oven which cooks very rapidly using short electric waves. □ **horno de microondas**
mid- [mid] *prefix meaning* middle: *the planes collided in mid-air; we will be going on holiday in mid-June.* □ **en medio de, a mitad de**
midday *n.* twelve o'clock noon. □ **mediodía**
midland *adj.* and *n.* (referring to the) central part of England. □ **región central**
the Midlands, the central part of England. □ **las Midlands**
midnight *n.* twelve o'clock at night. □ **medianoche**
midriff *n.* **1** front part of the body above the waist and below the chest. □ **diafragma**
2 *he caught a blow in the midriff,* he was hit in the stomach. □ **...en la boca del estómago**
midshipman *n.* (*pl. midshipmen*) trainee officer in the Royal Navy. □ **guardia marina**
midst *n.* **1** middle: *in the midst of all the commotion; I am in the midst of answering correspondence.* □ **medio**
2 *there is a spy in our midst,* among us. □ **...entre nosotros**
midstream *n.* middle part of a river. □ **medio del río**
midsummer *n.* middle of the summer. □ **pleno verano**
Midsummer's Day, June 24th. □ **día de San Juan**
midway *adv.* half-way: *the police station is midway between the post office and the Town Hall.* □ **a mitad de camino**
Midwest *n.* central part of the United States. □ **medio oeste**
midwinter *n.* middle of the winter. □ **pleno invierno**
middle ['midl] *adj.* in the centre; half-way between two things. □ **medio**
middle sized, neither big nor small. □ **tamaño medio**
middle class, professional class (between the upper class and the lower/working class): *he lives in a*

middle-class district. □ **clase media**
the Middle Ages, historical period between the Dark Ages and the Renaissance (about 1000 to 1500 AD). □ **la Edad Media**
■ *n.* **1** centre; central point: *he was standing in the middle of the room; the explosion took place in the middle of the afternoon; he woke up in the middle of the night; I am in the middle of doing the washing up.* □ **medio**
2 waistline: *the water came up to my middle.* □ **cintura**
middle-aged *adj.* not young and not old (between 40 and 60 years of age): *a middle-aged man.* □ **de mediana edad**
middleman *n.* (*pl. middlemen*) businessman who buys from one source to sell to another. □ **intermediario**
middle-of-the-road *adj.* centre/moderate (politics). □ **centrista**
middleweight *n.* weight in boxing between welterweight and light heavyweight. □ **peso medio**
middling *adj.* neither good nor bad; not very large or small: *the exam results were bad to middling; there are no large potatoes, but plenty of middling ones.* □ **regular; mediano**
midge [midʒ] *n.* small stinging flying insect. □ **mosquito**
midget ['midʒit] *n.* very small person. □ **canijo**
midget submarine, submarine which can only carry one or two people. □ **submarino de bolsillo**
midwife ['midwaif] *n.* (*pl. midwives*) person (usually a woman) trained to help deliver a baby. □ **comadrona**
midwifery ['midwifri] *n.* work of helping deliver babies. □ **partería**
might [mait] *v. see* **may.**
■ *n.* force/strength: *he hit the post with all his might; the might of the Roman army.* □ **fuerza, poderío**
mighty *adj.* **1** strong. □ **potente**
2 great: *a mighty king; a mighty army.* □ **poderoso**
3 *you're in a mighty hurry,* (*informal*) you are very impatient. □ **andas volado**
mightily *adv.* greatly. □ **poderosamente**
migraine ['mi:grein] *n.* recurrent very bad headache. □ **jaqueca**
migrate [mai'greit] *v.* to move from one place to another with the seasons: *swallows migrate south in winter.* □ **migrar**
migrant ['maigrənt] *adj.* and *n.* (bird) which moves from one place to another with the seasons; (workman) who moves from one job to another or from one country to another. □ **migratorio (ave); emigrante (trabajador)**
migration [mai'greiʃn] *n.* movement of birds from one country to another. □ **migración**
migratory ['maigrətəri] *adj.* referring to migration: *migratory birds.* □ **migratorio**
mike [maik] *n.* (*informal*) microphone. □ **micro**
mild [maild] *adj.* **1** soft/not severe: *mild punishment; mild form of measles.* □ **suave**
2 not harsh (weather): *a mild winter; it's very mild today.* □ **templado**
3 not strong/powerful: *mild mustard; mild shampoo.* □ **suave**
mildly *adj.* **1** softly/kindly. □ **suavemente**
2 *he's a bit of a fool,* ***to put it mildly,*** not to say anything ruder. □ **para decirlo suavemente**
mildness *n.* kindness/softness; warmness (of winter weather). □ **suavidad**
mildew ['mildju:] *n.* powdery fungus on plants/paper/leather, etc.: *the grapes have got mildew.* □ **mildiu**
■ *v.* to become covered with mildew: *my shoes are all mildewed.* □ **enmohecer**
mile [mail] *n.* **1** measure of length (1,760 yards/1.61 kilometres): *to walk miles; the car was travelling at 60 miles an hour.* □ **milla**
2 ***miles of*** *string,* (*informal*) very long piece of string. □ **metros de**
3 *it's* ***miles*** *too big,* much too big; *he missed it by miles,* by a wide margin. □ **es grandísimo; no acertó por mucho**
mileage *n.* **1** distance travelled in miles: *car with a low mileage,* car which has not travelled as much as is normal. □ **distancia en millas; kilometraje**
mileage allowance, money paid to someone to repay him for using a private car on business. □ **kilometraje**
2 ***to get a lot of mileage out of something,*** (*informal*) to gain benefit from. □ **sacarle el jugo a algo**
to make a lot of mileage out of something, to use something to your advantage. □ **sacar en provecho de uno**
mileometer [mai'lɔmitə] *n.* dial showing number of miles travelled. □ **cuentamillas, cuentakilómetros**
milestone *n.* **1** stone showing distance in miles. □ **mojón; hito**
2 *a milestone in his career,* an important point in his career. □ **un hito/jalón en su carrera**
militant ['militənt] *adj.* and *n.* (person) who supports a policy of violence; (person) who is very active in supporting a cause/a political party: *he's a militant communist; a militant supporter of women's lib; the militants were out protesting in the streets.* □ **militante**
militancy *n.* activity/vigour (in supporting a political party/a cause). □ **militancia**
military ['militri] *adj.* referring to the army: *military service; military camp.* □ **militar**
■ *n.* ***the military,*** the army. □ **los militares**
militarism *n.* belief in the use of the army to solve political problems. □ **militarismo**
militaristic *adj.* believing that the army should be used to solve political problems. □ **militarista**
militate *v.* to work actively (against): *this militates against his being chosen as a candidate.* □ **militar**
militia [mi'liʃə] *n.* emergency army; police force organized like an army. □ **milicia**
milk [milk] *n.* white liquid produced by female mammals for feeding their young, especially the milk produced by cows: *have you drunk your milk? can I have a glass of milk?* □ **leche**
milk chocolate, pale brown chocolate (flavoured with milk). □ **chocolate con leche**
milk shake, milk mixed with flavouring and ice cream. □ **batido**
milk teeth, first set of teeth produced by a child. □ **dientes de leche**
■ *v.* **1** to take the milk from (an animal): *to milk the cows.* □ **ordeñar**
2 to get all the money from (someone). □ **exprimir**
milker *n.* **1** person who milks. □ **ordeñador**
2 *good milker,* cow which produces a lot of milk. □ **buena vaca lechera**
milking *n.* taking milk from a cow. □ **ordeño**
milking machine, machine which milks cows automatically. □ **ordeñadora mecánica**
milkman *n.* (*pl. milkmen*) person who delivers the milk to houses each morning. □ **lechero**
milky *adj.* tasting like milk; cloudy like milk; containing milk. □ **lácteo**

the Milky Way, luminous band in the night sky composed of many stars. □ **la Vía Láctea**

mill [mil] *n.* **1** machine for grinding corn into flour; building which contains such a machine. □ **molino**
to be/go through the mill, (*informal*) (i) *he's been through the mill,* he has been fully trained. □ **se le ha entrenado rigurosamente**
(ii) he has suffered a great deal. □ **las ha pasado canutas**
2 small instrument for grinding: *pepper mill.* □ **molinillo**
3 large factory: *steel mill; cotton mill.* □ **fábrica**
■ *v.* **1** to grind (corn, etc.). □ **moler**
2 to put vertical lines around the edge of a coin: *the coin has a milled edge.* □ **acordonar**

mill about, mill around *v.* to move in various directions: *the crowd was milling about all over the square.* □ **moverse por todas partes**

miller *n.* man who runs a flour mill. □ **molinero**

millpond *n.* **1** water dammed to provide power for a watermill. □ **alberca del molino**
2 *the sea was like a millpond,* was perfectly calm. □ **el mar estaba como una balsa**

millstone *n.* **1** large grooved stone used to grind corn. □ **piedra de molino**
2 great obstacle which causes trouble. □ **carga pesada**

millenium [mi'leniəm] *n.* **1** period of a thousand years. □ **milenio**
2 period of great happiness. □ **edad de oro**

millet ['milit] *n.* grain used for food. □ **mijo**

milli- ['mili] *prefix meaning* one thousandth. □ **mili-**

milligram ['miligræm] *n.* one thousandth of a gram. □ **miligramo**

millimetre ['milimi:tə] *Amer.* **millimeter** *n.* one thousandth of a metre. □ **milímetro**

milliner ['milinə] *n.* person who makes/sells women's hats. □ **sombrerero**

millinery *n.* hats and ribbons. □ **sombrerería de señoras**

million ['miljən] number 1,000,000/one thousand thousands. □ **millón**

millionaire [miljə'nɛə] *n.* person who has more than a million pounds: *dollar millionaire,* person who has more than a million dollars. □ **millonario**

millionth, 1,000,000th *adj.* referring to a million. □ **millonésimo**
■ *n.* one of a million parts: *a millionth of a second.* □ **una millonésima de segundo**

millipede ['milipi:d] *n.* small creeping animal with a large number of legs. □ **ciempiés**

mime [maim] *n.* **1** actor who does not speak, but conveys a story/emotions through gesture. □ **mimo**
2 gesture used to convey a story/emotions. □ **mímica**
3 story conveyed by gestures. □ **pantomima**
■ *v.* to convey a story/emotion through gesture: *he mimed the story of Red Riding Hood.* □ **representar mímicamente**

mimic ['mimik] *n.* person who imitates. □ **mimo**
■ *v.* (*he mimicked*) to imitate. □ **imitar**

mimicry *n.* imitation of something/someone; imitation of one animal by another. □ **imitación (de algo/alguien); mimetismo (animales)**

mimosa [mi'mouzə] *n.* semi-tropical tree with yellow, scented flowers. □ **mimosa**

minaret [minə'ret] *n.* tower attached to a mosque. □ **minarete**

mince [mins] *n.* meat which has been ground up into very small pieces. □ **carne picada**
■ *v.* **1** to grind up (meat/vegetables) until they are in very small pieces: *minced beef.* □ **picar**
2 *not to mince matters/one's words,* to be straightforward: *he didn't mince his words,* he said what he had to say in a straightforward way. □ **no andarse con rodeos**
3 *to mince along,* to walk along in a very affected manner, taking small steps. □ **andar a paso corto**

mincemeat *n.* mixture of apples, spices, dried fruit, etc.. □ **relleno**
to make mincemeat out of: he made mincemeat out of his opponents, he defeated them completely. □ **les hizo picadillo a sus oponentes**

mince pie *n.* small pie filled with mincemeat and eaten at Christmas. □ **pastel**

mincer *n.* machine for grinding up meat, etc.: *put the meat through the mincer.* □ **picadora**

mincing *adj.* affected (way of walking). □ **remilgado**
mincing machine, machine for grinding up meat. □ **picadora**

mind [maind] *n.* **1** power of thinking; memory. □ **mente; memoria**
2 *bear him in mind,* remember him. □ **tenle presente**
3 *to bring/call to mind: it calls to mind a speech I once heard,* it reminds me of a speech. □ **me trae a la memoria...**
4 *to make up your mind about something,* to decide what to do about something. □ **decidirse**
5 *to be in two minds (about): I'm in two minds about going,* I can't decide whether to go or not. □ **no sé a qué carta quedarme**
6 *I have a good mind to do it myself,* I would very much like to do it myself. □ **tengo ganas de hacerlo yo mismo**
7 *to change one's mind: he's changed his mind twice already,* he has changed his decision/his point of view. □ **ya ha cambiado de parecer dos veces**
8 *what do you have in mind?,* what are you thinking of?. □ **¿en qué piensas?**
9 *to have something on one's mind: I think he's got something on his mind,* he is worried about something. □ **creo que le ocurre algo**
10 *to take someone's mind off something: we must try to take her mind off the subject,* try to stop her thinking about the subject. □ **...quitarle esa idea de la cabeza**
11 *I don't think he's in his right mind,* I think he is mad. □ **...muy bien de la cabeza**
12 *state of mind,* general opinion/mood/feeling: *she's in a very gloomy state of mind.* □ **estado de ánimo**
■ *v.* **1** to be careful about: *mind the step; mind you don't fall; mind you get back by 10 o'clock.* □ **tener cuidado con**
2 to bother about/to be busy about. □ **entrometerse**
mind your own business, don't interfere in my affairs. □ **no te metas en lo que no te importa**
never mind, don't bother/don't worry. □ **no importa**
3 to object to/to be annoyed by: *he doesn't mind criticism; she won't mind if you are late.* □ **importar**
would you mind shutting the door?, would you be so good as to shut the door? □ **¿le importaría cerrar la puerta?**
I wouldn't mind a cup of tea, I would rather like a cup of tea. □ **tomaría una taza de té**
4 to look after: *to mind the house; she's minding the children while I am shopping.* □ **cuidar**

minded *adj.* **1** interested (in doing something). □ **dispuesto**
2 *he is very commercially minded,* he is a keen businessman. □ **tiene una mentalidad comercial**

mindful *adj.* remembering/thinking of: *always mindful of the needs of others.* □ **atento**
mindless *adj.* without thinking/stupid. □ **despreocupado**
mind reader *n.* person who seems to be able to guess what someone else is thinking. □ **adivinador del pensamiento**

mine [main] *n.* **1** deep hole in the ground for digging out minerals: *coal mine; bauxite mine.* □ **mina**
2 *he is **a mine of information**,* he is full of information/he knows a lot about something. □ **es una mina de...**
3 explosive device which is planted underground or underwater: *the truck ran over a mine and was blown up.* □ **mina**
■ *v.* **1** to excavate/to dig for minerals: *they mine coal here.* □ **extraer**
2 to plant mines underground or under water: *the entrance to the harbour has been mined.* □ **minar**
■ *pron.* belonging to me: *that hat is mine; he's a friend of mine,* one of my friends. □ **mío**
minefield *n.* area of land/sea full of mines. □ **campo de minas**
minelayer *n.* ship which specializes in planting mines under water. □ **minador**
minelaying *n.* placing of mines under water. □ **minado**
miner *n.* person who works in a mine. □ **minero**
miner's lamp, special lamp which gives warning of poisonous gas in a mine. □ **lámpara**
minesweeper *n.* ship which specializes in removing mines placed under water by the enemy. □ **dragaminas**
mining *n.* **1** action of extracting minerals: *a gold mining town; coal mining is an important industry.* □ **minería**
2 placing mines underground or under water. □ **minado**

mineral ['minrəl] *adj.* and *n.* (non-living substance) which is extracted from the earth: *mineral deposits.* □ **mineral**
mineral water, (i) water from a spring. □ **agua mineral**
(ii) non-alcoholic fizzy drink. □ **agua mineral con gas**
mineral rights, permission to dig out minerals. □ **derechos mineros**
mineralogist [minə'rælədʒist] *n.* scientist who studies minerals. □ **mineralogista**
mineralogy *n.* study of minerals. □ **mineralogía**

minestrone [mini'strouni] *n.* type of Italian vegetable soup. □ **minestrone**

mingle ['miŋgl] *v.* to mix: *the police mingled with the crowd.* □ **mezclarse**

mingy ['mindʒi] *adj.* (*informal*) mean; not generous (with money, etc.). □ **tacaño**

mini ['mini] *n.* **1** trade name for a very small British car. □ **mini**
2 very short skirt. □ **mini**
■ *adj.* and *prefix* very small: *a mini-report; a mini-demonstration.* □ **mini**
minibus *n.* small bus holding about twelve people. □ **microbús**
miniskirt *n.* very short skirt. □ **minifalda**
miniskirted *adj.* wearing a very short skirt: *mini-skirted majorettes.* □ **en/con minifalda**

miniature ['minitʃə] *n.* very small model/portrait/painting: *the Houses of Parliament in miniature.* □ **miniatura**
■ *adj.* very small: *miniature locomotive; miniature submarine.* □ **de miniatura**

minim ['minim] *n.* note in music lasting for two crotchets or half as long as a semibreve. □ **blanca**

minimum ['miniməm] *adj.* and *n.* smallest possible (quantity): *with the minimum of fuss; a minimum amount of noise; to reduce expenses to the minimum.* □ **mínimo**
minimal *adj.* smallest possible: *contact between the two sides of the family is minimal.* □ **mínimo**
minimize *v.* to reduce to the smallest amount; to make (something) seem very small: *to minimize the danger of fire; to minimize expenditure.* □ **reducir al mínimo**

minion ['minjən] *n.* low-grade assistant (who flatters his boss). □ **pelota**

minister ['ministə] *n.* **1** member of a government in charge of a department: *the Minister of Defence.* □ **ministro**
2 protestant clergyman. □ **ministro**
■ *v.* ***to minister to*** *someone's needs,* to look after someone/to take care of someone. □ **atender las necesidades de...**
ministerial [mini'stiəriəl] *adj.* referring to a government minister: *he held ministerial office,* he was a minister; *the ministerial correspondence.* □ **ministerial**
ministering *adj.* (angel) who looks after the needs of people. □ **ángel de la guarda**
ministration [mini'streiʃn] *n.* care given by a priest. □ **ministerio**
ministry *n.* **1** government: *the Labour Ministry of 1945.* □ **gobierno**
2 government department; offices of a government department: *the Ministry of Defence.* □ **ministerio**
3 work of a priest/priesthood: *he is studying for the ministry.* □ **sacerdocio**

mink [miŋk] *n.* small (originally Arctic) animal whose fur is very valuable: *a mink coat; mink farm,* farm where these animals are reared. □ **visón**

minnow ['minou] *n.* small freshwater fish. □ **carpín**

minor ['mainə] *adj.* **1** small/unimportant: *he played a minor part in the revolution; a minor operation on his elbow; the play is only of minor interest.* □ **menor**
Asia Minor, Turkey. □ **Asia Menor**
2 musical key where there are semitones between the second and third, and between the fifth and sixth notes: *a symphony in B minor.* □ **menor**
■ *n.* young person under the age of 18. □ **menor**
minority [mai'nɔriti] *n.* **1** quantity less than half of a total: *the men are in the minority,* there are more women than men; *the government is in a minority of two,* has two Members of Parliament less than the total of the other parties. □ **minoría**
a minority government, with fewer members of parliament than the opposition. □ **gobierno minoritario**
2 period when a person is less than 18 years old. □ **menor de edad**

minster ['minstə] *n.* (*usually in names*) large/important church. □ **catedral**

mint [mint] *n.* **1** factory where coins are made. □ **casa de la moneda**
2 *it's **in mint condition**,* it is perfect/exactly as when it was made. □ **está como nuevo**
3 *it must cost **a mint of money**,* (*informal*) a great deal of money. □ **...un montón de dinero**
4 common herb used as flavouring: *mint tea; mint sauce.* □ **menta**
5 small white sweet tasting of peppermint. □ **pastilla de menta**
■ *v.* to make money. □ **acuñar**

minus ['mainəs] *prep.* **1** less: *ten minus three equals*

seven (10 − 3 = 7). □ **menos**
2 *he came minus his wife,* (*informal*) without his wife. □ **...sin su esposa**
■ *n.* **1** sign (−) meaning less: *the temperature was minus 10 degrees (−10°).* □ **...10 grados bajo cero**
2 *he got a minus for bad behaviour,* he got a bad mark. □ **...una mala nota...**

minute ['minit] *n.* **1** one sixtieth part of an hour or of a degree in an angle: *there are sixty minutes in an hour; ten minutes past three,* 3.10; five minutes to four, 3.55. □ **minuto**
minute hand, long hand on watch or clock. □ **minutero**
minute steak, thin slice of beef which can be cooked quickly. □ **filete fino**
2 very short space of time: *wait a minute; just a minute; I'll not be more than a couple of minutes; he'll be here any minute now,* any time now. □ **momento**
3 note of what is said at a meeting: *the minutes of the previous meeting.* □ **acta**

minute [mai'nju:t] *adj.* very small: *a minute speck of dust; he examines everything in the minutest detail.* □ **diminuto**
minutely [mai'nju:tli] *adv.* in great detail. □ **minuciosamente**
minuteness *n.* very small size. □ **minuciosidad**

minutiae [mi'nju:ʃii:] *n. pl.* very small details. □ **minucias**

miracle ['mirəkl] *n.* something marvellous which happens apparently by the power of God; very wonderful happening: *it's a miracle he's still alive.* □ **milagro**
miraculous [mi'rækjuləs] *adj.* wonderful; inexplicable: *a miraculous cure.* □ **milagroso**
miraculously *adv.* wonderfully / inexplicably: *miraculously, no one was injured in the crash.* □ **milagrosamente**

mirage ['mirɑ:ʒ] *n.* imaginary image caused by heat (such as water and palm trees seen in a desert). □ **espejismo**

mire ['maiə] *n.* (*formal*) muddy place; mud. □ **fango**

mirror ['mirə] *n.* glass backed by metal which reflects an image: *she looked at her face in the mirror.* □ **espejo**
driving mirror/rear-view mirror, mirror inside a car which enables the driver to see what is behind without turning his head. □ **retrovisor**
mirror image, exact copy, but reversed as in a mirror. □ **imagen especular**
■ *v.* to reflect as in a mirror: *the trees are mirrored in the water of the lake.* □ **reflejarse**

mirth [mə:θ] *n.* (*formal*) gaiety/happiness. □ **regocijo**

mis- [mis] *prefix meaning* wrongly. □ **mal-**

misadventure [misəd'ventʃə] *n.* unlucky accident: *death by misadventure.* □ **desgracia**

misanthrope ['mizənθroup] **misanthropist** [mi'zænθrəpist] *n.* person who dislikes the human race. □ **misántropo**
misanthropic [mizən'θrɔpik] *adj.* (person) who dislikes the human race. □ **misantrópico**
misanthropy [mi'zænθrəpi] *n.* dislike of the human race. □ **misantropía**

misapply [misə'plai] *v.* to use (something) wrongly. □ **usar indebidamente**

misapprehend [misæpri'hend] *v.* not to understand. □ **no comprender**
misapprehension [misæpri'henʃən] *n.* not understanding: *he's labouring under a misapprehension,* he doesn't understand the situation correctly. □ **mala comprensión**

misappropriate [misə'prouprieit] *v.* to use (public money) for your own purposes. □ **malversar**
misappropriation [misəproupri'eiʃn] *n.* using public money for your own purposes: *misappropriation of funds.* □ **malversación**

misbehave [misbi'heiv] *v.* to act badly/to behave badly. □ **portarse mal**
misbehaviour *n.* bad behaviour. □ **mala conducta**

miscalculate [mis'kælkjuleit] *v.* to calculate wrongly: *the waiter miscalculated when he was adding up the bill; we miscalculated the time it would take to get to the station.* □ **calcular mal**
miscalculation [miskælkju'leiʃn] *n.* mistake in calculating: *it was a bad miscalculation to suppose that he wouldn't ask for his money back.* □ **error de cálculo**

miscarry [mis'kæri] *v.* **1** to go wrong: *the scheme miscarried.* □ **resultar mal**
2 to produce a baby which is not sufficiently developed to live: *there is a danger she might miscarry.* □ **abortar**
miscarriage ['miskæridʒ] *n.* **1** failure (of a scheme). □ **fracaso**
miscarriage of justice, wrong decision by a court. □ **error judicial**
2 loss of a baby during pregnancy: *after the accident she had a miscarriage.* □ **aborto**

miscast [mis'kɑ:st] *v.* (*he miscast*) to put (an actor/actress) into a part which is unsuitable. □ **dar un papel poco apropiado**

miscellaneous [misə'leiniəs] *adj.* varied/mixed: *we are selling a lot of miscellaneous pieces of furniture.* □ **variado**
miscellany [mi'seləni] *n.* collection of varied things (usually varied pieces of writing). □ **miscelánea**

mischance [mis'tʃɑ:ns] *n.* (*formal*) bad luck. □ **infortunio**

mischief ['mistʃif] *n.* **1** bad behaviour/bad action: *they mean mischief,* they are intending to do damage/to wreck. □ **mal; daño**
to make mischief, to make trouble/to make two people angry with each other. □ **sembrar la discordia**
2 *the little boy is always getting into mischief,* he's always doing something naughty. □ **...haciendo travesuras**
mischief-maker *n.* person who tries to start trouble. □ **liante**
mischievous ['mistʃivəs] *adj.* wicked/naughty. □ **travieso**
mischievousness *n.* tendency to cause trouble. □ **malicia**

misconception [miskən'sepʃən] *n.* mistaken idea. □ **idea falsa**

misconduct [mis'kɔndʌkt] *n.* bad conduct/bad behaviour. □ **mala conducta**
professional misconduct, behaviour which is not acceptable in a member of a profession. □ **negligencia profesional**

misconstrue [miskən'stru:] *v.* not to understand: *he misconstrued my meaning.* □ **entender mal**
misconstruction [miskən'strʌkʃn] *n.* wrong interpretation of an action. □ **mala interpretación**

miscount [mis'kaunt] *v.* to count wrongly. □ **contar mal**

miscreant ['miskriənt] *n.* wicked person/criminal. □ **bellaco**

miscue [mis'kju:] *v.* to make a bad stroke at billiards. □ **pifiar**

misdeed [mis'di:d] *n.* wicked action. □ **fechoría**

misdemeanour [misdi'miːnə] *Amer.* **misdemeanor** *n.* unlawful act: *he was found guilty of a misdemeanour.* □ **delito**
misdirect [misdai'rekt] *v.* to give wrong directions: *the judge misdirected the jury,* the judge gave the jury incorrect advice. □ **dirigir erradamente**
miser ['maizə] *n.* person who hoards money and refuses to spend it. □ **avaro**
miserliness *n.* dislike of spending money. □ **tacañería**
miserly *adj.* not wanting to spend money. □ **tacaño**
miserable ['mizrəbl] *adj.* **1** sad/unhappy: *she was miserable when he didn't write to her.* □ **desdichado**
2 *what miserable weather!,* what awful/bad/unpleasant weather! □ **¡qué tiempo más horrible!**
3 *he earns a miserable salary,* a very low salary. □ **...un salario miserable**
miserably *adv.* sadly/unhappily. □ **miserablemente**
misery ['mizəri] *n.* **1** sadness; suffering: *her life was sheer misery,* was very unhappy. □ **aflicción; miseria**
2 *we ought to put the dog out of its misery,* we ought to kill the dog because it is in pain. □ **poner fin a su sufrimiento**
3 ***to put someone out of his misery,*** to tell someone the result/not to keep someone waiting any longer. □ **satisfacer por fin a uno**
misfire [mis'faiə] *v.* **1** not to fire properly: *the gun misfired.* □ **fallar**
2 *the car engine is misfiring,* is not igniting the petrol at the right time. □ **le falla el encendido al coche**
3 *his great plan misfired,* went wrong. □ **...salió mal**
misfit ['misfit] *n.* person who does not fit in with a group/fit into society. □ **inadaptado**
misfortune [mis'fɔːtjuːn] *n.* bad luck: *it was his misfortune to be stopped by the inspector when he had left his ticket at home.* □ **mala suerte**
misgiving [mis'giviŋ] *n.* doubt/fear: *I have considerable misgivings about the success of the plan; he agreed, but not without misgivings.* □ **recelo**
misguided [mis'gaidid] *adj.* badly advised; wrongly judged; foolish: *in a misguided attempt to smuggle books into Spain.* □ **mal orientado, descaminado**
mishap ['mishæp] *n.* accident: *the journey went off without mishap.* □ **percance**
misinform [misin'fɔːm] *v.* to give (someone) wrong information: *I was misinformed.* □ **informar mal**
misinterpret [misin'təːprit] *v.* to interpret wrongly; not to understand correctly. □ **malinterpretar**
misinterpretation [misintəːpri'teiʃn] *n.* wrong interpretation; misunderstanding. □ **mala interpretación**
misjudge [mis'dʒʌdʒ] *v.* to judge wrongly; to form a wrong opinion about (someone/something): *I misjudged her capabilities.* □ **juzgar mal**
mislay [mis'lei] *v.* (*he mislaid*) to put (something) down and not to remember where you have put it: *I have mislaid my car keys.* □ **extraviar**
mislead [mis'liːd] *v.* (*he misled*) to give (someone) wrong information/to make (someone) make a mistake: *I think I misled you when I said you would be paid at the end of the week.* □ **equivocar**
misleading *adj.* wrong/erroneous; likely to cause you to make a mistake. □ **engañoso**
mismanage [mis'mænidʒ] *v.* to manage wrongly/badly: *the school had been badly mismanaged for some time.* □ **administrar mal**
mismanagement *n.* bad management. □ **mala administración**
misnomer [mis'noumə] *n.* wrong name/wrong term. □ **nombre equivocado**
misogynist [mi'sɔdʒinist] *n.* man who dislikes women. □ **misógino**
misplace [mis'pleis] *v.* to put in the wrong place: *a misplaced stress in a word; misplaced confidence.* □ **colocar mal**
misprint ['misprint] *n.* error in printing. □ **errata**
mispronounce [misprə'nauns] *v.* to pronounce wrongly. □ **pronunciar mal**
mispronunciation [misprənʌnsi'eiʃn] *n.* pronouncing wrongly. □ **mala pronunciación**
misquote [mis'kwout] *v.* to quote wrongly/incorrectly. □ **citar mal**
misquotation [miskwou'teiʃn] *n.* incorrect quotation. □ **cita errónea**
misread [mis'riːd] *v.* (*he misread*) to read wrongly; to make a mistake when reading: *I must have misread the telegram.* □ **leer mal**
misrepresent [misrepri'zent] *v.* to show (something) wrongly; to distort (facts): *I have been misrepresented,* someone has distorted what I said. □ **representar mal; tergiversar**
misrepresentation [misreprizen'teiʃn] *n.* distortion of what someone said or wrote. □ **tergiversación**
miss [mis] *n.* **1** failure to hit: *he scored two hits and three misses.* □ **fallo**
2 *I think we'll* ***give it a miss,*** we will not do it/not go to see it. □ **...prescindimos de ello**
3 title of unmarried woman: *Miss Jones.* □ **señorita**
4 title given to schoolmistress/used to call a waitress, etc.: *please, miss!* □ **señorita**
■ *v.* **1** not to hit/see, etc.: *she missed the target; he was aiming at the rabbit but missed it by miles; we missed the house in the dark; she ran, but missed the bus; I read the paper twice, but I missed the article about you; you missed a very good concert; you didn't miss much,* there wasn't much to see/the performance was not very good. □ **errar (el tiro); perder**
2 *he just missed being killed,* he was very nearly killed. □ **se salvó por poco**
3 to regret the absence of someone/something: *do you miss your cat? I miss those long evening walks we used to take; they'll miss you if you go to work somewhere else.* □ **echar de menos; extrañar**
missing *adj.* absent/lost; stolen: *two sailors were drowned and another is missing; the police found the missing jewels.* □ **desaparecido**
missal ['misl] *n.* book containing the text of the Catholic mass and other prayers. □ **misal**
missel ['misl] *n.* ***missel thrush,*** type of woodland thrush. □ **cagaaceite**
misshapen [mis'ʃeipn] *adj.* deformed/oddly shaped. □ **deforme**
missile ['misail, *Amer.* 'misl] *n.* **1** weapon which is thrown: *the rioters threw stones and other missiles.* □ **arma arrojadiza**
2 explosive rocket which can be guided to its target. □ **misil**
mission ['miʃn] *n.* **1** aim/purpose for which someone is sent: *his mission is to rescue the climbers on the mountain; her mission in life is to help orphans,* her calling/her chosen task. □ **misión**
2 house/office of a missionary: *guerrillas attacked a Christian mission.* □ **misión**
3 group of people sent somewhere with a particular aim: *a United Nations peace mission; we are sending a trade mission to Japan.* □ **misión**
missionary ['miʃənri] *adj.* and *n.* (person) whose duty is to try to convert people to his religion: *a Christian missionary; a missionary society.* □ **misional (adj.); misionero (n.)**

missive ['misiv] *n.* (*formal*) letter. □ **misiva**
misspell [mis'spel] *v.* (*he misspelled/misspelt*) to spell wrongly: *my name is misspelt.* □ **deletrear mal**
misspelling *n.* spelling mistake. □ **falta de ortografía**
misstatement [mis'steitmənt] *n.* wrong statement of facts. □ **declaración errónea**
missus ['misiz] *n.* (*informal*) wife. □ **la parienta**
mist [mist] *n.* thin fog/haze: *the mist came down over the mountains.* □ **neblina**
■ *v.* **1** to get covered with fog: *the mountains misted over.* □ **cubrir de niebla**
2 *the rear window has misted up,* is covered with condensation. □ **...se ha empañado**
misty *adj.* **1** full of mist: *a misty valley; it is quite a misty morning.* □ **brumoso; neblinoso**
2 vague: *I have a misty recollection of it.* □ **vago**
mistake [mi'steik] *n.* error; wrong action: *I made a mistake; he did it by mistake.* □ **equivocación**
■ *v.* (*he mistook; he is mistaken*) **1** to understand (something) wrongly. □ **equivocarse**
2 to assume (someone) is someone else: *I mistook you for your brother.* □ **tomar por**
mistaken *adj.* wrong: *he is mistaken in thinking Dr Smith is your brother; if I am not mistaken, Dr Smith is his father; she has a mistaken belief in the magic power of her cat.* □ **equivocado**
a case of mistaken identity, where someone is thought to be someone else. □ **identidad errónea**
mistakenly *adv.* by mistake/in error: *he mistakenly accused the old man of lying.* □ **por equivocación**
mister ['mistə] *n.* (*informal*) title given to a man: *hey, mister can you tell me the time?* □ **caballero**
mistime [mi'staim] *v.* to choose the wrong time/an inconvenient time to do something: *he mistimed his arrival at the party.* □ **llegar a deshora**
mistletoe ['misltou] *n.* parasitic plant which grows on oaks or apple trees, and which is used as a Christmas decoration. □ **muérdago**
mistook [mi'stuk] *v. see* **mistake.**
mistress ['mistrəs] *n.* **1** woman in charge/who employs: *she's her own mistress,* she is independent. □ **encargada, jefa**
2 *the maths mistress,* the woman who teaches maths. □ **la señorita de...**
3 woman who has a sexual relationship with a man without being married to him. □ **amante**
mistrust [mi'strʌst] *n.* wariness/lack of trust. □ **desconfianza**
■ *v.* not to trust (someone)/to be doubtful about (someone): *I mistrust him.* □ **desconfiar**
misunderstand [misundə'stænd] *v.* (*he misunderstood*) not to understand: *I must have misunderstood the instructions.* □ **comprender mal**
misunderstanding *n.* wrong understanding/disagreement: *the whole quarrel is due to a misunderstanding.* □ **malentendido**
misuse [mis'juːs] *n.* wrong use. □ **mal uso**
■ *v.* [mis'juːz] to use (something) in a wrong way; to treat (someone) badly. □ **emplear mal (algo); maltratar a (alguien)**
mite [mait] *n.* **1** very small child: *poor little mite.* □ **chiquillo**
2 very small creature like a spider, living in stale food. □ **acárido**
miter ['maitə] *n. Amer.* = **mitre.**
mitigate ['mitigeit] *v.* to make (a crime) less serious. □ **mitigar**
mitigation [miti'geiʃn] *n.* making less serious: *in mitigation of his offence, he pleaded that at the time he was under the influence of drugs.* □ **mitigación**
mitre ['maitə] *Amer.* **miter** *n.* **1** hat worn by bishops and archbishops. □ **mitra**
2 (*in woodwork*) type of sloping joint/sloping edge. □ **inglete**
mitred *adj.* sloping (joint/edge). □ **a inglete**
mitt [mit] **mitten** ['mitn] *n.* glove without separate fingers, especially a glove to wash with or to hold hot dishes with: *an oven mitt.* □ **manopla**
mix [miks] *n.* blend/mingling of several things: *an odd mix of two sorts of coffee.* □ **mezcla**
■ *v.* to blend/to mingle: *mix all the ingredients together in a bowl; if you mix blue and yellow together you get green; I don't usually mix with people at the office.* □ **mezclar**
mixed *adj.* **1** made up of different things put together: *a pound of mixed chocolates.* □ **mezclado**
mixed marriage, marriage between two people of different races. □ **matrimonio exogámico**
mixed doubles, (*in tennis*) doubles match where a man and woman play against another man and woman. □ **dobles mixtos**
mixed school, school with both boys and girls/coeducational school. □ **escuela mixta**
2 *I have very mixed feelings about the project,* in some ways I am for it and in others I am against it. □ **...sentimientos contradictorios...**
3 *it's **a mixed blessing,*** in some ways it is a good thing, but in others it is not. □ **es una buena suerte a medias**
mixer *n.* **1** machine for mixing: *a food mixer; an electric mixer; a cement mixer.* □ **mezcladora; batidora; hormigonera**
2 person who fits in well with other people: *he is a very good mixer.* □ **persona sociable**
mixture ['mikstʃə] *n.* blend; mingling together: *the walls are painted a mixture of blue and red; she spoke a mixture of Russian and Greek; the doctor gave me an unpleasant mixture to drink; cough mixture,* liquid medicine to cure a cough; *it tastes like cough mixture,* it tastes awful. □ **mezcla; jarabe**
mix up *v.* **1** to confuse: *I always mix him up with his brother,* I always think he is his brother. □ **confundir**
2 to involve: *he got mixed up in a plot to kill the president.* □ **verse implicado**
3 *the speaker got all mixed up,* he got confused/lost his notes. □ **...se armó un lío**
mix-up *n.* (*informal*) confusion: *there was some sort of mix-up over the entrance tickets.* □ **lío**
mnemonic [ni'mɔnik] *adj.* and *n.* (rhyme) which helps you to remember certain facts. □ **nemotécnico**
moan [moun] *n.* **1** low groan: *moans of the dying soldiers.* □ **gemido**
2 general complaint: *a moan about the office toilets.* □ **queja**
■ *v.* **1** to make a low groan: *the sick man moaned.* □ **gemir**
2 to complain: *she is always moaning about her salary.* □ **quejarse**
moat [mout] *n.* wide ditch with water in it, surrounding a castle/old house. □ **foso**
moated *adj.* with a moat: *a moated farmhouse.* □ **rodeado con un foso**
mob [mɔb] *n.* crowd of unruly people: *the mob surrounded the parliament building.* □ **turba**
■ *v.* (*they mobbed*) to surround in a wild crowd: *the demonstrators mobbed the police; the film stars were mobbed by their fans.* □ **acosar**
mobile ['moubail, *Amer.* 'moubl] *adj.* which can move: *he is not very mobile,* he can't walk easily; *mobile library,* library in a van which travels

around from place to place; *mobile bookshop.* □ **móvil; biblioteca ambulante**
■ *n.* artistic creation using pieces of metal/paper, etc., which when hung up can move. □ **móvil**
mobility [mou'biliti] *n.* ability to move. □ **movilidad**
mobilization [moubilai'zeiʃn] *n.* grouping of people together (especially to join the armed forces): *the government ordered a general mobilization.* □ **movilización**
mobilize ['moubilaiz] *v.* to group (people) together (especially to join the armed forces): *all able-bodied men have been mobilized; he is mobilizing his supporters.* □ **movilizar**
moccasins ['mɔkəsinz] *n. pl.* soft leather shoes. □ **mocasines**
mock [mɔk] *adj.* false/imitation. □ **simulado**
mock examinations, trial examinations carried out before the real ones. □ **simulacro de examen**
■ *v.* to laugh at (someone/something): *he mocked the pictures in the exhibition; she mocked his accent.* □ **burlarse de**
mockery *n.* **1** laughing at: *an object of mockery.* □ **burla**
2 something which is only a bad imitation: *a mockery of a trial.* □ **burla**
mocking *adj.* and *n.* laughing at (someone/something): *a mocking laugh.* □ **burlón**
mockingbird *n.* bird from the southern United States which imitates the song of other birds. □ **sinsonte**
mockingly *adv.* in a sarcastic way. □ **burlonamente**
mock-up *n.* scale model of a new product for testing purposes, etc. □ **maqueta**
mode [moud] *n.* way (of doing something): *a mode of life.* □ **modo; una manera de vivir**
modal *adj.* and *n.* (verb) which is used with other verbs, and not alone (such as *can, must,* etc.). □ **modal**
model ['mɔdl] *n.* and *adj.* **1** small-scale copy of something: *model train; model aeroplane.* □ **tren/avión de miniatura**
2 something which you can take as a perfect example to be copied: *it is a model of its kind; model town; take this as your model.* □ **modelo**
3 *artist's model,* person whose job is to sit while an artist draws pictures of him/her. □ **modelo**
4 person whose job is to wear new clothes to show them to customers. □ **modelo**
5 style of a car, etc., produced in a particular period: *this is last year's model; this is the latest model in freezers; it's a pre-war model.* □ **modelo**
■ *v.* (*he modelled*) **1** to make a model; to make shapes (of clay): *modelling clay,* special clay for sculpture. □ **modelar**
2 *he modelled his way of walking on that of his father,* he imitated his father's way. □ **seguir el modelo de**
3 to wear (new clothes) to show to customers. □ **pasar modelos**
moderate ['mɔdərət] *adj.* and *n.* **1** not excessive; middling: *a moderate-sized room; prices here are quite moderate.* □ **moderado**
2 (person) without a violent political bias: *a moderate party; a group of moderates.* □ **moderado**
■ *v.* to diminish/to make less strong: *please moderate your language; the union members moderated their pay claim; the storm moderated.* □ **moderar**
moderately *adv.* quite/not excessively: *the play was moderately successful.* □ **moderadamente**
moderation [mɔdə'reiʃn] *n.* not an excessive use; calming down: *moderation of language; he smokes, but only in moderation.* □ **moderación**
moderator *n.* **1** chairman of a church meeting. □ **el que preside un acto en la iglesia**
2 examiner from outside the school/college, etc., who checks that examination standards are high enough. □ **miembro de un tribunal**
modern ['mɔdən] *adj.* of the present day; not ancient: *modern furniture; a modern house; modern languages,* languages which are spoken today. □ **moderno**
modernity [mə'də:niti] *n.* being modern. □ **modernidad**
modernize *v.* to make modern; to renovate: *he has bought an old house and is modernizing it.* □ **modernizar**
modest ['mɔdist] *adj.* **1** not boasting: *he is very modest about his success.* □ **modesto**
2 not demanding/not excessive: *he made a modest proposal; he has a modest income; they live in a modest flat,* which does not look expensive. □ **humilde; modesto**
modesty *n.* **1** not being boastful. □ **modestia**
2 not being excessive/demanding: *the modesty of our requirements.* □ **moderación**
modicum ['mɔdikəm] *n.* small quantity: *if he only had a modicum of intelligence.* □ **pizca**
modify ['mɔdifai] *v.* **1** to change/to alter (something) to fit a different use: *the design of the engine was modified.* □ **modificar**
2 to reduce: *he modified his demands.* □ **rebajar**
modification [mɔdifi'keiʃn] *n.* change: *a modification to the design.* □ **modificación**
modish ['moudiʃ] *adj.* fashionable. □ **de moda**
modulate ['mɔdjuleit] *v.* to change the pitch of a note/a musical key. □ **modular**
modulation [mɔdju'leiʃn] *n.* change of pitch: *frequency modulation.* □ **modulación**
module ['mɔdju:l] *n.* section of a larger combination. □ **módulo**
lunar module, section of a spacecraft which lands on the moon. □ **módulo lunar**
modular *adj.* made of various modules. □ **modular**
mohair ['mouhεə] *n.* very soft wool from a type of goat: *a mohair coat.* □ **mohair**
moist [mɔist] *adj.* slightly wet/damp: *the climate is warm and moist; rub the table with a moist cloth.* □ **húmedo**
moisten ['mɔisn] *v.* to make moist: *to moisten a cloth.* □ **humedecer**
moistness *n.* being moist. □ **humedad**
moisture ['mɔistʃə] *n.* slight wetness: *he squeezed all the moisture out of the cloth; moisture condensed on the bathroom mirror.* □ **humedad; empañamiento (espejo)**
moisturizer ['mɔistʃəraizə] *n.* cream which makes the skin softer. □ **crema hidratante**
moisturizing *adj.* (cream) which makes the skin softer. □ **hidratante**
molar ['moulə] *n.* large back tooth used for grinding food. □ **molar**
molasses [mə'læsiz] *n.* thick black raw syrup removed from unrefined sugar. □ **melaza**
mold [mould] *Amer.* = **mould.**
mole [moul] *n.* **1** small black mammal which lives underground. □ **topo**
2 small dark spot on the skin. □ **lunar**
3 (*informal*) member of a secret service organisation who is in the pay of the enemy. □ **topo**
4 stone jetty/pier used as a breakwater. □ **malecón**
5 standard measurement of the amount of a sub-

stance. □ **mol**

molehill *n.* little heap of earth pushed up by a mole. □ **topera**

to make a mountain out of a molehill, to make a great deal of fuss about something which is really trivial. □ **hacer una montaña de un grano de arena**

moleskin *n.* skin of a mole used for making clothes: *a moleskin waistcoat.* □ **molesquín**

molecule ['mɔlikju:l] *n.* smallest unit into which a substance is divided. □ **molécula**

molecular [mə'lekjulə] *adj.* referring to molecules. □ **molecular**

molecular weight, mass of one molecule of a substance compared to that of one atom of carbon. □ **peso molecular**

molest [mə'lest] *v.* to attack/to beat (someone). □ **meterse con (alguien)**

mollify ['mɔlifai] *v.* to lessen the anger of (someone). □ **aplacar**

mollusc ['mɔlʌsk] *Amer.* **mollusk** *n.* animal with no backbone, but usually with a shell (such as snails/oysters, etc.). □ **molusco**

mollycoddle ['mɔlikɔdl] *v.* to spoil (someone)/to treat (someone) too softly. □ **mimar**

molt [moult] *Amer.* = **moult.**

molten ['moultən] *adj.* not solid; melted: *molten lava.* □ **fundido; lava líquida**

moment ['moumənt] *n.* **1** very short space of time: *wait a moment, please.* □ **momento**

2 *I am expecting him to arrive* ***at any moment,*** very soon. □ **...en cualquier momento**

3 ***at the moment,*** just now. □ **ahora mismo**

4 ***for the moment,*** for the time being. □ **por el momento**

5 *we've heard of it only* ***this moment,*** just recently. □ **...ahora mismo**

6 importance: *the document is of great moment.* □ **...de gran importancia**

momentarily *adv.* for a short space of time: *the pilot was momentarily unconscious.* □ **momentáneamente**

momentary *adj.* shortlived/passing: *a momentary feeling of sickness.* □ **momentáneo**

momentous [mə'mentəs] *adj.* very important: *a momentous decision.* □ **trascendental**

momentum [mə'mentəm] *n.* impetus; movement forwards: *the international peace movement is gaining momentum/losing momentum,* progressing faster/slower. □ **ímpetu**

monarch ['mɔnək] *n.* king or queen; ruler. □ **monarca**

monarchic(al) [mə'nɑ:kik(l)] *adj.* referring to a monarchy. □ **monárquico**

monarchist ['mɔnəkist] *n.* supporter of a monarchy. □ **monárquico**

monarchy ['mɔnəki] *n.* system of government with a hereditary ruler such as a king or queen. □ **monarquía**

monastery ['mɔnəstri] *n.* group of buildings where monks live. □ **monasterio**

monastic [mə'næstik] *adj.* referring to a monastery/to monks: *monastic life.* □ **monástico**

Monday ['mʌndi] *n.* first day of the week/day between Sunday and Tuesday: *we don't work on Mondays; I saw her last Monday.* □ **lunes**

monetary ['mʌnitəri] *adj.* referring to money or currency: *a monetary system.* □ **monetario**

monetarist *n.* person who believes that inflation can be checked by reducing the amount of money available in the economy. □ **monetarista**

money ['mʌni] *n.* coins or notes which are used for buying and selling: *how much money have you got on you?; we were offered our money back,* a refund of what we had already paid; *we ran out of money,* we had no money left. □ **dinero**

to come into money, to inherit money. □ **heredar dinero**

moneybox *n.* box that can be locked and in which you can keep money. □ **hucha**

moneyed *adj.* rich: *the moneyed classes.* □ **adinerado**

moneylender *n.* person who lends money. □ **prestamista**

money order *n.* order for passing money from one person to another via the post office. □ **giro postal**

money-spinner *n.* (*informal*) book/record, etc., which sells very well. □ **mina**

mongol ['mɔŋgəl] *adj.* and *n.* (person) born with mongolism. □ **mongólico**

mongolism *n.* defect in a person from birth, of which the symptoms are slanting eyes, flattened skull and low intelligence. □ **mongolismo**

mongoose ['mɔŋgu:s] *n.* small tropical mammal which kills snakes. □ **mangosta**

mongrel ['mʌŋgrəl] *adj.* and *n.* not pure-bred (dog)/(dog) of mixed breeds. □ **chucho; perro cruzado**

monitor ['mɔnitə] *n.* **1** person who watches/surveys the progress of something. □ **monitor**

2 senior pupil (in a school) who has a particular duty to perform. □ **veterano**

3 apparatus for checking the progress of something, especially a small television screen in a television studio. □ **monitor**

■ *v.* to check/to survey (the progress of something): *to monitor the flight of a rocket; to monitor foreign broadcasts.* □ **comprobar, vigilar**

a monitoring station, radio station specially for listening to foreign broadcasts and obtaining information from them. □ **servicio de escucha**

monk [mʌŋk] *n.* man who is a member of a religious group and lives in a monastery. □ **monje**

monkey ['mʌŋki] *n.* **1** usually tropical mammal which looks rather like a man, but which normally has a tail: *monkeys walk on four legs.* □ **mono**

2 *you little monkey!,* (*informal*) you naughty little child! □ **¡diablillo!**

monkey nut, peanut. □ **cacahuete**

monkey puzzle tree, type of tropical pine tree with spiky branches. □ **araucaria**

monkey wrench, large spanner with an adjustable grip. □ **llave inglesa**

■ *v.* ***to monkey about,*** (*informal*) to play/to mess around: *don't go monkeying about with my paints.* □ **enredar con**

mono ['mɔnou] *prefix meaning* single. □ **mono**

■ *n.* and *adj.* not stereophonic; (machine/record) which reproduces sound through a single channel: *a mono record; this record is available in both stereo and mono.* □ **mono**

monochrome ['mɔnəkroum] *adj.* and *n.* (in a) single colour, usually black on white. □ **monocromo**

monocle ['mɔnəkl] *n.* eye glass/single lens worn to correct sight. □ **monóculo**

monogamy [mə'nɔgəmi] *n.* system of marriage to one person at a time. □ **monogamia**

monogamous *adj.* (marriage) to one husband or one wife. □ **monógamo**

monogram ['mɔnəgræm] *n.* design based on the initials of your name. □ **monograma**

monogrammed *adj.* with your initials on it: *monogrammed briefcase/pyjamas.* □ **con las iniciales**

monograph ['mɔnəgrɑ:f] *n.* short book about a specialized subject. □ **monografía**

monolith ['mɔnəliθ] *n.* single standing stone. □ **monolito**
monolithic [mɔnə'liθik] *adj.* solid/heavy; changeless. □ **monolítico**
monologue ['mɔnəlɔg] *n.* long speech written for one actor who is alone on the stage. □ **monólogo**
monomania [mɔnə'meiniə] *n.* mania about a single thing. □ **monomanía**
mononucleosis [mɔnənju:kli'ousis] *n. Amer.* glandular fever. □ **mononucleosis**
monophonic [mɔnə'fɔnik] *adj.* not stereophonic; (record) with sound coming from a single channel. □ **monofónico**
monopoly [mə'nɔpəli] *n.* system where one person or company supplies all needs in one area without any competition: *a sugar monopoly; they have the monopoly of electrical parts.* □ **monopolio**
monopolization [mənɔpəlai'zeiʃn] *n.* creating of a monopoly. □ **monopolización**
monopolize [mə'nɔpəlaiz] *v.* **1** to create a monopoly. □ **monopolizar**
2 *he monopolized the discussion,* he did all the talking and didn't let anyone else speak. □ **monopolizó...**
monorail ['mɔnəreil] *n.* train which runs on a single rail. □ **monocarril**
monosyllable ['mɔnəsiləbl] *n.* word which only has one syllable (such as 'dog', 'cat'). □ **monosílabo**
monosyllabic [mɔnəsi'læbik] *adj.* (word) with only one syllable; (conversation) using only monosyllables. □ **monosílabo**
monotonous [mə'nɔtənəs] *adj.* not varied/not changing/boring: *a monotonous tone of voice.* □ **monótono**
monotonously *adv.* in a monotonous way/in a boring way: *he spoke monotonously for half an hour.* □ **de manera monótona**
monotony *n.* lack of variety. □ **monotonía**
monoxide [mə'nɔksaid] *n.* chemical compound containing one atom of oxygen: *carbon monoxide.* □ **monóxido**
monsoon [mɔn'su:n] *n.* **1** season of wind and rain in the tropics. □ **monzones**
2 wind blowing in the Indian Ocean. □ **monzón**
monster ['mɔnstə] *n.* **1** horrible/strange creature: *film about monsters from outer space.* □ **monstruo**
2 very large and terrifying animal or thing. □ **monstruo**
3 cruel/wicked person. □ **monstruo**
■ *adj.* very large: *a monster box of chocolates.* □ **enorme**
monstrosity [mɔn'strɔsiti] *n.* horrible/strange/ugly thing: *the new theatre is a monstrosity.* □ **monstruosidad**
monstrous ['mɔnstrəs] *adj.* huge/ugly/horrible. □ **monstruoso**
montage [mɔn'tɑ:ʒ] *n.* picture/piece of music, etc., made of several items brought together; action of putting several items together to make a picture/piece of music, etc. □ **montaje**
month [mʌnθ] *n.* one of the twelve periods which form a year: *what day of the month is it? February is the shortest month; I'm going on holiday next month; a month today, I shall be sitting on the beach,* in exactly one month's time from today. □ **mes**
monthly *adj.* and *adv.* occurring every month: *you have to pay by monthly instalments.* □ **mensual, mensualmente**
■ *n.* magazine which appears each month. □ **revista mensual**
monument ['mɔnjumənt] *n.* **1** stone/building/statue, etc., erected in memory of someone who is dead: *a monument to the dead of two world wars.* □ **monumento**
2 building which is very old: *the castle is scheduled as an ancient monument.* □ **monumento**
monumental [mɔnju'mentl] *adj.* **1** very large: *a monumental work; a monumental mistake.* □ **monumental**
2 referring to a monument. □ **monumental**
monumental mason, person who makes gravestones. □ **marmolista**
moo [mu:] *n.* sound made by a cow: *I heard a loud moo.* □ **mugido**
■ *v.* to make a sound like a cow. □ **mugir**
mood [mu:d] *n.* **1** general feeling: *he's in a bad mood; she's in a good mood; what is the general mood of the meeting?* □ **humor**
2 bad temper: *he's in one of his moods.* □ **mal humor**
moodiness *n.* gloomy feeling; quick change from good to bad temper. □ **humor cambiadizo**
moody *adj.* often gloomy/often bad-tempered; changing quickly from good to bad temper. □ **malhumorado**
moon [mu:n] *n.* **1** satellite which travels round a planet, especially one which travels round the earth each month and shines with reflected light from the sun: *the rocket landed on the moon.* □ **luna**
2 *it only happens* ***once in a blue moon,*** very rarely. □ **...de Pascuas a Ramos**
moonbeam *n.* ray of light from the moon. □ **rayo de luna**
moonlight *n.* light from the moon: *everything looked white in the moonlight.* □ **luz de luna**
moonlighting *n.* doing a second job (usually in the evening) apart from your regular work. □ **pluriempleo**
moonlit *adj.* lit by light from the moon. □ **iluminado por la luna**
moonstone *n.* semi-precious stone with a white shine. □ **adularia**
moor ['muə, mɔ:] *n.* uncultivated land covered with low shrubs. □ **páramo**
■ *v.* to attach (a boat) to a quayside/to a buoy: *the ship is moored near the entrance to the harbour.* □ **amarrar**
moorhen *n.* common water bird. □ **polla de agua**
mooring *n.* **1** action of attaching a boat: *mooring ropes.* □ **amarre**
2 ***moorings,*** place where a ship is moored; ropes, etc., used to moor a ship. □ **amarradero**
moorland *n.* area of uncultivated land covered with low shrubs. □ **páramo**
moose [mu:s] *n.* (*no pl.*) American elk. □ **alce de América**
moot [mu:t] *adj.* ***a moot point,*** a question which is open to discussion. □ **discutible**
■ *v.* to raise (a question/a suggestion): *someone mooted the possibility of forming another company.* □ **plantear**
mop [mɔp] *n.* **1** brush for washing floors with a head made of soft string or foam rubber. □ **fregona**
2 *he's got a great mop of hair,* his hair is long and untidy. □ **...una buena pelambrera**
■ *v.* (*he mopped*) **1** to wash a floor, using a mop. □ **fregar el suelo**
2 to wipe: *he was mopping his brow with his handkerchief.* □ **secar**
mop up *v.* **1** to clear up (liquid) using a mop: *we had to mop up the water which covered the kitchen floor.* □ **recoger con la fregona**
2 to clear up (pockets of resistance by groups of enemy soldiers): *mopping-up operations.* □ **limpiar**

mope [moup] *v.* to be miserable/gloomy: *he spends all day moping about.* □ **estar abatido**
moped ['mouped] *n.* two-wheeled cycle with a low-powered motor. □ **ciclomotor**
moraine [mə'rein] *n.* heap of gravel, etc., left by a glacier. □ **morena/morrena**
moral ['mɔrəl] *adj.* **1** referring to right and wrong in human behaviour: *a moral issue.* □ **moral**
2 referring to good human behaviour: *a decline in moral standards.* □ **moral**
3 *we gave him moral support,* we encouraged him but did not do anything to help him. □ **...apoyo moral**
■ *n.* lesson to be drawn from a story: *the moral of the story is not to take gifts from strangers.* □ **moraleja**
morals, personal character and way of behaving. □ **moralidad**
moralist *n.* person who criticizes low moral standards. □ **moralista**
morality [mə'ræliti] *n.* correct way of behaving; sense of moral standards. □ **moralidad**
moralize ['mɔrəlaiz] *v.* to draw a lesson from a story or something which has happened. □ **moralizar**
morally *adv.* according to correct human behaviour: *he is morally bound to refuse the gift.* □ **moralmente**
morale [mə'rɑːl] *n.* feeling of confidence: *what's the morale of the troops like?* □ **moral**
morass [mə'ræs] *n.* **1** deep swamp/marsh. □ **pantano**
2 mass of things which prevent any progress: *the case is bogged down in a morass of international regulations.* □ **embrollo**
moratorium [mɔrə'tɔːriəm] *n.* temporary ban on some activity (strikes/nuclear testing, etc.). □ **moratoria**
morbid ['mɔːbid] *adj.* **1** interested in death/unpleasant things: *it's his morbid curiosity.* □ **morboso**
2 connected with disease. □ **mórbido**
morbidity [mɔː'biditi] *n.* sickly interest in death/unpleasant things. □ **lo malsano**
mordant ['mɔːdənt] *adj.* (*formal*) cruel (sarcasm). □ **mordaz**
more [mɔː] *adj.* extra/additional: *can I have some more coffee? I need ten more men.* □ **más**
■ *n.* extra/additional amount: *that's more than I need; is there any more of this jam?* □ **más**
■ *adv.* **1** additionally/to a larger extent: *he was more surprised than annoyed.* □ **más**
2 (forming comparative) *she is more intelligent than her brother.* □ **más**
3 *he doesn't write to me **any more,*** he no longer writes to me. □ **ya no me escribe**
4 *she has **more or less** retired,* approximately/practically. □ **...más o menos...**
moreover [mɔː'rouvə] *adv.* besides; in addition. □ **además**
morgue [mɔːg] *n.* building where dead bodies are kept for identification. □ **instituto anatómico forense**
moribund ['mɔribʌnd] *adj.* dying; going out of existence. □ **moribundo**
morning ['mɔːniŋ] *n.* early part of the day, before 12 noon: *in the morning; tomorrow morning we will go to town; I woke up at 4 in the morning,* at 4 a.m.; *the morning train,* the train which leaves every morning. □ **mañana**
morocco [mə'rɔkou] *n.* fine soft leather. □ **tafilete**
moron ['mɔːrɔn] *n.* **1** adult with the intelligence of a child. □ **retrasado mental**
2 stupid person. □ **idiota**
moronic [mə'rɔnik] *adj.* stupid. □ **idiota**
morose [mə'rous] *adj.* gloomy and bad-tempered. □ **hosco**
morphia ['mɔːfiə] **morphine** ['mɔːfiːn] *n.* drug which kills pain and makes you go to sleep. □ **morfina**
morphology [mɔː'fɔlədʒi] *n.* study of the way in which words change in the plural, or according to gender or conjugation. □ **morfología**
morris ['mɔris] *n.* ***morris dance,*** old English dance, danced by a group of men in white clothes with bells on their legs and arms. □ **morris**
Morse code [mɔːs'koud] *n.* system of dots and dashes for sending messages. □ **alfabeto Morse**
morsel ['mɔːsl] *n.* small piece of food: *a tasty morsel.* □ **pedazo**
mortal ['mɔːtl] *adj.* **1** causing death: *he was struck by a mortal blow.* □ **mortal**
2 *my mortal enemy,* deadly enemy. □ **mi enemigo mortal**
3 referring to the body: *mortal remains,* corpse. □ **restos mortales**
■ *n.* human being: *the king is just an ordinary mortal like everyone else.* □ **mortal**
mortality [mɔː'tæliti] *n.* **1** human state. □ **mortalidad**
2 number of deaths (as a percentage of population): *the infant mortality rate.* □ **índice de mortalidad infantil**
mortally *adv.* so as to cause death: *he was mortally wounded in the battle.* □ **mortalmente**
mortar ['mɔːtə] *n.* **1** cement mixture for holding together bricks or stones when building. □ **mortero**
2 bowl for crushing things in with a pestle. □ **mortero**
3 short cannon. □ **mortero**
mortar-board *n.* black cap with a square top worn at ceremonies by people who have university degrees. □ **birrete**
mortgage ['mɔːgidʒ] *n.* agreement whereby someone lends you money on the security of a property; money lent to you on the security of your property: *I have bought my house with a $10,000 mortgage; I repay my mortgage in monthly instalments.* □ **hipoteca**
second mortgage, further loan obtained on a property which is already mortgaged. □ **segunda hipoteca**
■ *v.* to give (your house or flat) as security for a loan: *my house is mortgaged.* □ **hipotecar**
mortgagee [mɔːgi'dʒiː] *n.* person who loans money on mortgage. □ **acreedor hipotecario**
mortgagor [mɔːgi'dʒɔː] *n.* person who borrows money on a mortgage. □ **deudor hipotecario**
mortice ['mɔːtis] *n.* hole cut in the end of a piece of wood into which another piece fits to form a joint. □ **muesca**
mortician [mɔː'tiʃn] *n. Amer.* undertaker. □ **empresario de pompas fúnebres**
mortify ['mɔːtifai] *v.* to humiliate (someone). □ **mortificar**
mortification [mɔːtifi'keiʃn] *n.* feeling of shame/humiliation. □ **mortificación**
mortise ['mɔːtis] *n.* hole cut in the end of a piece of wood into which another piece fits to form a joint. □ **muesca**
mortuary ['mɔːtjuəri] *n.* place where dead bodies are kept before burial. □ **tanatorio**
mosaic [mə'zeiik] *n.* tiny pieces of coloured stone

stuck to a wall or floor in patterns: *a Roman mosaic floor; the mosaics in the interior of a Greek church.* □ **mosaico**
Moslem ['mɔzləm] *adj.* and *n.* Muslim/(person) who is a follower of the religion of the prophet Mohammed. □ **musulmán**
mosque [mɔsk] *n.* religious building for Moslems. □ **mezquita**
mosquito [məs'ki:tou] *n.* (*pl. mosquitoes*) small flying insect which sucks blood: *in the tropics mosquitoes can cause malaria.* □ **mosquito**
mosquito net, thin net spread over a bed to prevent mosquitoes biting you at night. □ **mosquitero**
moss [mɔs] *n.* primitive green plant growing in compact low clumps on the ground or on stone walls. □ **musgo**
mossy *adj.* covered with moss. □ **musgoso**
most [moust] *adj.* the largest number/largest quantity of something: *most people have breakfast at eight o'clock; most children like watching television.* □ **la mayoría de**
■ *n.* **1** the largest number/largest quantity: *most of the work has been done.* □ **la mayor parte de**
2 *you must **make the most of it,*** you must get as much profit/value from it as possible. □ **...sacar el máximo partido de ello**
■ *adv.* to the largest extent: **1** (forming superlative): *the most intelligent child in the class.* □ **más**
2 (intensive): *I find it most annoying that there is no mail before ten o'clock; most probably the postmen are on strike.* □ **muy**
mostly *adv.* in most cases/most often. □ **casi siempre**
motel [mou'tel] *n.* hotel specially for car drivers where there is a car-parking space for every room. □ **motel**
moth [mɔθ] *n.* flying insect with large wings like a butterfly, but flying mainly at night. □ **mariposa nocturna**
clothes moth, type of moth whose caterpillars eat clothes. □ **polilla**
mothballs *n. pl.* **1** small white balls of a chemical substance which you put among clothes to keep moths away. □ **bola de naftalina**
2 *the ship has been **put in mothballs,*** has been retired from active service and specially protected so that it can be brought out again if needed in the future. □ **pusieron el barco a buen recaudo**
motheaten *adj.* full of holes made by moths; old and decrepit. □ **apolillado**
mother ['mʌðə] *n.* female parent: *he still lives with his mother, although he's over thirty; unmarried mother.* □ **madre**
mother country, country where you or your ancestors were born. □ **madre patria**
mother tongue, first language a child speaks. □ **lengua materna**
Mother Superior, woman head of a religious community. □ **madre superiora**
■ *v.* **1** to give birth to (someone). □ **dar a luz**
2 to look after (someone) very attentively. □ **cuidar como una madre**
motherhood *n.* being a mother. □ **maternidad**
mother-in-law *n.* (*pl. mothers-in-law*) mother of your wife or husband. □ **suegra**
motherless *adj.* with no mother. □ **huérfano de madre**
motherly *adj.* maternal/like a mother. □ **maternal**
mother of pearl *n.* shiny substance found on the inside of oyster shells. □ **madreperla; nácar**
motif [mou'ti:f] *n.* distinctive repeating pattern in a design/in a piece of music. □ **motivo**
motion ['mouʃn] *n.* **1** movement/act of moving: *the car is in motion,* is moving. □ **movimiento**
2 gesture/movement. □ **gesto**
to go through the motions: *he went through the motions,* he did something for the sake of appearances, but really did not believe in it. □ **actuar para salvar las apariencias**
3 proposal which is to be put to the vote (at a meeting): *to propose a motion.* □ **moción**
to second a motion, to support the person who has first proposed the motion. □ **apoyar una moción**
■ *v.* to make a gesture: *the policeman motioned him to pull in to the side of the road.* □ **indicar con la mano**
motionless *adj.* still/not moving. □ **inmóvil**
motive ['moutiv] *n.* reason which makes you do something: *what can their motive be for refusing to cooperate?* □ **motivo**
■ *adj.* which makes something move: *motive power.* □ **fuerza motriz**
motivate ['moutiveit] *v.* to make (someone) do something; to encourage (someone) to do something: *the children in the class are highly motivated,* are all eager to study. □ **motivar**
motivation [mouti'veiʃn] *n.* reason for doing something/encouragement to do something: *they don't work well because they lack motivation.* □ **motivación**
motley ['mɔtli] *adj.* varied; of varied sorts or colours: *a motley collection of soldiers.* □ **variado; multicolor**
motor ['moutə] *n.* **1** machine which causes motion; engine: *the motor in a car; the train has an electric motor; the pump is driven by a diesel motor.* □ **motor**
2 car. □ **coche**
motor show, show where new models of cars are shown to the public. □ **salón del automóvil**
■ *v.* to go travelling in a car. □ **viajar en coche**
motorbike *n.* (*informal*) motorcycle/two-wheeled cycle powered by a motor. □ **moto**
motorboat *n.* small boat with a motor. □ **motora**
motorcade *n. Amer.* offical procession of cars. □ **desfile de automóviles**
motorcar *n.* car. □ **coche**
motorcycle *n.* two-wheeled cycle powered by a motor. □ **moto, motocicleta**
motorcyclist *n.* person riding a motorcycle. □ **motorista**
motoring *n.* driving of a car: *school of motoring,* driving school. □ **automovilismo**
motorist *n.* driver of a car. □ **automovilista**
motorize *v.* to provide (something) with an engine; to equip (someone) with motor transport. □ **motorizar**
motorway *n.* special road for high-speed traffic with very few exit and entry points: *we went up to Birmingham on the motorway.* □ **autopista**
mottled ['mɔtld] *adj.* spotted with different colours. □ **moteado, de varios colores**
motto ['mɔtou] *n.* **1** short phrase which is used to sum up the attitude of a family/group, etc.: *'Be prepared' is the Boy Scouts' motto.* □ **lema**
2 amusing phrase on a piece of paper inside a Christmas cracker. □ **texto divertido**
mould [mould] *Amer.* **mold** *n.* **1** soft earth. □ **tierra vegetal**
leaf mould, soft earth formed from dead leaves. □ **mantillo**
2 hollow shape into which a liquid is poured, so that when the liquid becomes hard it takes that

shape: *the statue is cast in a mould; jelly mould,* shape for making jelly/blancmange, etc. □ **molde**
3 greyish powdery fungus which grows on food, etc.: *the cheese was covered with mould.* □ **moho**
■ *v.* to shape (something): *he moulded the clay into the form of a girl's head.* □ **moldear**
moulder *n.* person who moulds. □ **moldeador**
■ *v.* to rot away: *a mouldering ruin.* □ **desmoronarse**
mouldiness *n.* being mouldy/rotten. □ **enmohecimiento**
moulding *n.* something which has been moulded: *plaster mouldings on the ceiling.* □ **moldeado**
mouldy *adj.* rotten/covered with mould: *mouldy cheese; this bread has gone mouldy,* has become covered with mould. □ **enmohecido**

moult [moult] *Amer.* **molt** *v.* to lose feathers/fur: *the birds are moulting.* □ **mudar**

mound [maund] *n.* small heap/hill: *a mound of rubbish.* □ **montón**

mount [maunt] *n.* **1** (*usually in names*) mountain: *Mount Vernon.* □ **monte**
2 cardboard frame for a picture: *photograph mount.* □ **borde; marco**
3 horse/donkey, etc., on which a rider sits. □ **montura**
■ *v.* **1** to climb on to (something); to rise: *to mount a ladder; to mount a horse; the car mounted the pavement; expenses are mounting.* □ **subir a; montar**
mounted police, police on horseback. □ **policía montada**
2 ***to mount guard over something,*** to stand on guard to protect something. □ **montar la guardia**
3 to set (something) in a cardboard frame: *to mount a picture.* □ **poner un marco a (algo)**
4 *to mount diamonds,* to set diamonds in a metal ring/brooch, etc. □ **engastar diamantes**
5 to organize: *to mount an exhibition/an expedition.* □ **montar**
mount up *v.* to rise/to increase: *our expenses are rapidly mounting up.* □ **elevarse a**

mountain ['mauntn] *n.* **1** very high land: *the mountains of Wales; Everest is the highest mountain in the world; mountain sheep,* sheep which are specially bred to live on mountains. □ **montaña**
mountain ash, common northern tree with red berries. □ **serbal**
2 large amount: *there's mountains of work to be done.* □ **hay montañas de...**
butter mountain, large quantity of butter stockpiled by governments because of overproduction. □ **excedentes de mantequilla**
mountaineer [mauntə'niə] *n.* person who climbs mountains for pleasure. □ **montañero**
mountaineering *n.* climbing of mountains as a sport. □ **montañismo**
mountainous *adj.* (area) full of mountains; very high (waves). □ **montañoso; enorme**

mourn [mɔ:n] *v.* to regret/to weep: *we are mourning his death.* □ **llorar la muerte de**
mourner *n.* person who regrets/weeps, especially for someone who has died: *the mourners,* people attending a funeral. □ **doliente**
mournful *adj.* very sad: *he spoke in a mournful voice; she sang a mournful song; a mournful expression.* □ **lúgubre**
mournfully *adv.* in a very sad way. □ **afligidamente**
mourning *n.* **1** period of time when one regrets the death of a relative or friend.□ **duelo**
2 dark clothes worn as a mark of respect for someone who has died: *she is in mourning.* □ **luto**

mouse [maus] *n.* (*pl. mice*) small rodent with long tail, often living in houses. □ **ratón**
mousehole *n.* small hole in which mice live. □ **ratonera**
mouser *n. the cat is a good mouser,* is good at catching mice. □ **cazador de ratones**
mousetrap *n.* trap for catching mice. □ **ratonera**
mousetrap cheese, (*informal*) strong/old/inferior cheese. □ **queso barato**
mousy *adj.* **1** small and insignificant (person). □ **alfeñique**
2 brownish-grey (colour). □ **pardusco**

mousse [mu:s] *n.* light food made of beaten up eggs, cream and flavouring: *strawberry mousse; salmon mousse.* □ **'mousse'**

moustache [mə'stɑ:ʃ] *Amer.* **mustache** ['mʌstæʃ] *n.* hair grown on the upper lip. □ **bigote**

mouth [mauθ] *n.* **1** part of the head through which you take in food and drink and through which you speak: *don't speak with your mouth full; he was sleeping with his mouth open.* □ **boca**
2 wide entrance: *mouth of a cave; mouth of a tunnel.* □ **entrada**
3 *mouth of a river,* place where a river enters the sea. □ **desembocadura de un río**
■ *v.* [mauð] to move the mouth as if speaking, without making any sound; to speak without being heard. □ **esbozar con los labios**
mouthful *n.* **1** quantity of something contained in the mouth: *he took a mouthful of soup.* □ **bocanada**
2 (*informal*) complicated word/phrase. □ **galimatías**
mouthorgan *n.* small musical instrument played by blowing, with a series of small valves giving different notes: *to play the mouthorgan.* □ **armónica**
mouthpiece *n.* **1** part of a musical instrument which goes into the mouth. □ **boquilla**
2 person who speaks on behalf of someone: *he's only the mouthpiece of the party.* □ **portavoz**
mouthwash *n.* antiseptic solution for cleaning the inside of the mouth. □ **enjuague**
mouthwatering *adj.* very delicious. □ **que hace la boca agua**

move [mu:v] *n.* **1** action of moving; movement: *he is always on the move.* □ **movimiento; no para ni un momento**
2 ***get a move on!,*** hurry up. □ **¡muévete!**
3 *we must* ***make a move,*** (*informal*) we must leave. □ **es hora de irnos**
4 movement (of a piece in chess): *who has the first move? whose move is it?* □ **jugada; ¿quién sale?; ¿a quién le toca mover?**
5 *what's the next move?,* what do we have to do next? □ **¿y ahora qué hacemos?**
6 changing of place of residence. □ **mudanza**
■ *v.* **1** to change the position (of something); to change your position: *move the chairs away from the table; a tiger was moving in the bushes; the general moved two divisions up to the front; don't move!,* stand still! □ **cambiar (las sillas); moverse; adelantar**
2 *we must be moving,* (*informal*) we must leave. □ **hemos de irnos**
3 to leave one place to go to live in another: *they moved to Edinburgh from London.* □ **trasladarse**
4 to change the feelings of (someone): *the song moved me to tears.* □ **hacer (llorar, reír, etc.) a alguien**
5 to propose (a motion in a debate). □ **proponer**
movable, moveable *adj.* which can be moved: *is the seat movable?* □ **movible**
move about *v.* **1** to change something from one place to another: *he is always moving his books about.* □ **cambiar de sitio**

2 to wander about: *the soldiers were moving about in the streets.* □ **ir y venir**
move away *v.* to change to another place further away; to change (something) to a position further away: *the ship moved away from the quay; they moved the pigsty away from the house; we are moving away from London,* we are changing our house from London to another town. □ **alejarse, irse**
move back *v.* **1** to go backwards; to change (something) to a place further back. □ **retroceder, retrasar**
2 to return to a previous place. □ **volver**
move forward *v.* to go forward; to change (something) to a place further forward. □ **avanzar**
move in *v.* to settle with furniture in a new house. □ **instalarse**
movement *n.* **1** action of changing position/of not being still: *we saw a movement in the trees; the doctors knew he was alive because of a slight movement of his eyelids; an upward movement in prices.* □ **movimiento**
2 mechanism (of a clock). □ **mecanismo**
3 main part of a large piece of music. □ **movimiento**
4 group of people working towards a certain aim: *the labour movement; a movement for sexual equality.* □ **movimiento**
move off *v.* to go away: *the train moved off,* began to leave. □ **ponerse en camino, salir**
move on *v.* to go forward; to make (someone) go forward: *the police moved the demonstrators on.* □ **hacer circular**
mover *n.* **1** person who moves furniture from one house to another. □ **empleado de mudanzas**
2 person who proposes a motion in a debate. □ **autor**
movie *n. Amer.* cinema film. □ **película**
moving *adj.* **1** which changes position/which is not still: *don't jump off a moving bus.* □ **móvil; en marcha**
moving staircase, escalator. □ **escalera mecánica**
2 which affects your feelings: *a moving letter; the book ends with a moving description of the death of the heroine.* □ **conmovedor**
mow [mou] *v.* (*he has mown*) to cut (grass): *he is mowing the lawn.* □ **segar**
mow down *v.* to kill/to slaughter: *the attackers were mown down by the defenders' fire.* □ **barrer**
mower *n.* **1** person who cuts grass. □ **segador**
2 machine which cuts grass: *motor mower,* lawnmower powered by an engine. □ **cortacésped**
Mr ['mistə] *n.* title given to a man: *Mr Jones.* □ **Sr.**
Mrs ['misiz] *n.* title given to a married woman: *Mrs Jones.* □ **Sra.**
Ms [məz, miz] *n.* title given to any woman (married or unmarried): *Ms Jones.* □ **Srta.**
much [mʌtʃ] *adj.* a lot of: *with much love; how much bread? how much does it cost? I never carry much money in my pocket; he eats too much meat.* □ **mucho; ¿cuánto pan?; come demasiada carne**
■ *adv.* **1** (the comparative and superlative are *more/most*) to a great extent/very: *she's feeling much better; it's much less cold today; does it matter very much?* □ **mucho**
2 *the shop is much the most expensive in town,* by far the most expensive. □ **la tienda es con mucho la más...**
3 ***it's a bit much!,*** (*informal*) it's quite unreasonable! □ **¡te has pasado!**
4 ***much to my amazement,*** to my great surprise. □ **para mi gran sorpresa**
■ *n.* **1** a lot: *much of the work has been finished.* □ **gran parte**
2 *do you see much of one another?,* do you meet very often? □ **¿os veis mucho?**
3 ***not up to much:*** *it isn't up to much,* (*informal*) it isn't very good. □ **no vale mucho**
muck [mʌk] *n.* dirt; manure: *what's all this muck on the floor?* □ **porquería**
■ *v.* **1** ***to muck out*** *a stable,* to clean a stable. □ **limpiar**
2 ***to muck about*** *with electricity,* (*informal*) to play about with electricity. □ **juguetear**
3 ***to muck up*** *a recording,* (*informal*) to ruin a recording. □ **echar a perder**
4 *you must all* ***muck in*** *together,* (*informal*) you must all cooperate in the work. □ **...arrimar el hombro**
mucky *adj.* dirty; covered with muck. □ **asqueroso**
mucus ['mju:kəs] *n.* shiny substance which coats the inside of organs of the body. □ **mucosidad**
mucous *adj.* referring to mucus. □ **mucoso**
mud [mʌd] *n.* very wet earth: *we were up to our knees in mud; the tractor got stuck in the mud.* □ **barro**
muddy *adj.* full of mud: *a muddy path; muddy shoes; I have got my boots all muddy.* □ **lleno de barro**
■ *v.* to put mud on something. □ **embarrar**
to muddy the waters, to stir up trouble/confusion. □ **crear follón**
mudflap *n.* flap hanging behind the wheel of a car to prevent mud and water being splashed. □ **guardabarros de goma**
mudguard *n.* strip of metal over the wheel on a bicycle to stop mud and water being splashed. □ **guardabarros**
mud slinging *n.* insults. □ **calumnias**
muddle ['mʌdl] *n.* confusion/mixture: *my papers are in a muddle; there's been a muddle over the plane tickets.* □ **lío**
■ *v.* to confuse/to mix up: *he was rather muddled over his facts; the agency got the tickets muddled.* □ **confundir**
muddleheaded *adj.* confused. □ **liado**
muddle through *v.* to get through one's business/to succeed in a muddled way. □ **salir del paso**
muesli ['mju:zli] *n.* breakfast food made of flakes of cereal/dried fruit/brown sugar, etc., eaten with milk. □ **muesli**
muezzin [mu:'ezin] *n.* the official of a mosque who calls the faithful to prayer from the minaret. □ **almuecín**
muff [mʌf] *n.* warm covering for a particular part of the body, especially the hands: *ear muffs.* □ **manoplas, orejeras**
■ *v.* to do (something) badly. □ **hacer algo mal**
muffin ['mʌfin] *n.* small round cake eaten warm with butter. □ **mollete**
muffle ['mʌfl] *v.* **1** to wrap up in clothes: *he was muffled up because of the cold.* □ **abrigarse**
2 to deaden (a loud noise): *a muffled sound of gunfire.* □ **amortiguar**
muffler *n.* **1** long scarf. □ **bufanda**
2 *Amer.* silencer (on car exhaust). □ **silenciador**
Mufti ['mʌfti] *n.* a Muslim legal expert and adviser on the law of the Koran. □ **muftí**
mufti *n.* ***in mufti,*** (*informal*) in civilian clothes; not in uniform. □ **vestido de paisano**
mug [mʌg] *n.* **1** large glass/cup with a handle: *beer mug; a mug of tea.* □ **jarra (cerveza); tazón (té)**
2 (*informal*) stupid person/person who is easily taken in. □ **primo**
3 (*informal*) face: *an ugly mug.* □ **careto**
■ *v.* (*he mugged*) **1** ***to mug up*** *a subject,* (*informal*)

to study a subject very hard at the last minute just before an examination. □ **pegarse un atracón al final**
2 to attack and rob (in the street): *he was mugged on the way home.* □ **asaltar**
mugger *n.* person who attacks and robs someone in the street. □ **asaltante**
mugging *n.* robbery with violence (in the street). □ **asalto**
muggy ['mʌgi] *adj.* (*informal*) warm and wet (weather). □ **bochornoso**
mulatto [mjuː'lætou] *n.* person of mixed Negro and white race. □ **mulato**
mulberry ['mʌlbəri] *n.* **1** tree with soft purple fruit: *silk worms live on mulberry trees.* □ **morera**
2 fruit of the mulberry. □ **mora**
mulch [mʌltʃ] *n.* covering of manure/rotten leaves, etc., spread on the ground to improve the soil. □ **pajote**
■ *v.* to spread manure/rotten leaves, etc., on the ground round plants. □ **cubrir con pajote**
mulct [mʌlkt] *v.* to take money away from someone: *to mulct the profits from a company.* □ **desplumar**
mule [mjuːl] *n.* animal which is a hybrid between a donkey and a horse; obstinate person. □ **mula**
muleteer [mjulə'tiə] *n.* person who drives mules carrying loads. □ **mulero**
mulish *adj.* obstinate/difficult to deal with. □ **terco**
mull [mʌl] *v.* to heat (wine) with spices/sugar, etc. □ **calentar**
mull over *v.* to ponder/to think about (something). □ **reflexionar sobre**
mullet ['mʌlit] *n.* type of small sea fish. □ **mújol**
mullion ['mʌljən] *n.* vertical (wooden/metal) bar between panes of glass in a window. □ **parteluz**
multi- ['mʌlti] *prefix meaning* many. □ **multi—**
multicoloured ['mʌltikʌləd] *adj.* with many colours. □ **multicolor**
multifarious [mʌlti'fɛəriəs] *adj.* very varied/in many different types. □ **diverso**
multinational [mʌlti'næʃnl] *adj.* and *n.* (company) which operates in several different countries. □ **multinacional**
multiple ['mʌltipl] *adj.* many/repeated: *multiple injuries/copies.* □ **múltiple**
multiple store, company with many shops in several towns. □ **cadena de tiendas**
■ *n.* **1** number which contains another number several times exactly: *27 is a multiple of 9.* □ **múltiplo**
2 repeated groups of the same number of something: *the packets are sold in multiples of five,* you can buy five, ten, fifteen packets (but not three, four, nine, etc.). □ **múltiplo**
multiplication [mʌltipli'keiʃn] *n.* action of multiplying. □ **multiplicación**
multiplication sign, ×, sign used to show that numbers are to be multiplied. □ **signo de la multiplicación**
multiplication tables, lists of figures to learn by heart how each number is multiplied. □ **tabla de la multiplicación**
multiplicity [mʌlti'plisiti] *n.* vast and varied mass: *a multiplicity of different methods of teaching languages.* □ **multiplicidad**
multiply ['mʌltiplai] *v.* **1** to calculate the sum of several numbers repeated a stated number of times: *three multiplied by three is nine; multiply 240 by 23.* □ **multiplicar**
2 to increase in number: *rabbits multiply rapidly.* □ **multiplicarse**

multiracial [mʌlti'reiʃl] *adj.* (society) whose members come from various races. □ **multirracial**
multistorey ['mʌltistɔːri] *adj.* with many storeys: *a multistorey car park.* □ **de varios pisos**
multitude ['mʌltitjuːd] *n.* great number/crowd. □ **multitud**
multitudinous [mʌlti'tjuːdinəs] *adj.* in very large numbers. □ **multitudinario**
mum [mʌm] *adj.* silent: *he kept mum,* he didn't say a word. □ **chitón; se mantuvo callado**
■ *n.* (*informal*) mother: *my mum has gone shopping.* □ **mamá**
mumble ['mʌmbl] *n.* speech which you can't understand because it is indistinct: *he spoke in a mumble.* □ **refunfuño, palabras entre dientes**
■ *v.* not to speak distinctly: *he mumbled a few words of thanks.* □ **hablar entre dientes**
mumbo-jumbo [mʌmbou'dʒʌmbou] *n.* nonsense/meaningless talk. □ **guirigay**
mummy ['mʌmi] *n.* **1** (*informal*) mother: *my mummy has gone shopping.* □ **mamá**
2 corpse preserved with ointments and bandages as in Ancient Egypt. □ **momia**
mummify *v.* to preserve in a perfect state (something which has died). □ **momificar**
mumps [mʌmps] *n.* infectious illness with swelling on either side of the neck: *he's caught mumps; she's got mumps; he's in bed with mumps.* □ **paperas**
munch [mʌntʃ] *v.* to chew (something crisp or dry) with large regular movements of the jaws: *he munched a biscuit; she was munching an apple.* □ **mascar**
mundane [mʌn'dein] *adj.* ordinary: *he's only interested in mundane matters.* □ **mundano, cotidiano**
municipal [mjuː'nisipl] *adj.* referring to a town: *municipal gardens,* park which belongs to a town; *municipal buildings,* town hall. □ **municipal**
municipality [mjuːnisi'pæliti] *n.* self-governing town. □ **municipio**
munificence [mjuː'nifisns] *n.* (*formal*) great generosity. □ **munificencia**
munificent *adj.* (*formal*) extremely generous. □ **munificente**
munitions [mjuː'niʃnz] *n. pl.* weapons and ammunition: *a munitions factory.* □ **municiones**
mural ['mjuərəl] *adj.* referring to walls. □ **mural**
■ *n.* painting on a wall: *the restaurant is decorated with murals.* □ **mural**
murder ['məːdə] *n.* **1** killing of someone illegally: *he was accused of murder.* □ **asesinato**
2 (*informal*) something awful or unpleasant: *the first day of the sales was sheer murder.* □ **algo espantoso**
■ *v.* **1** to kill (someone) illegally: *she murdered her husband.* □ **asesinar**
2 (*informal*) to ruin (a song) by singing it badly. □ **interpretar desastrosamente**
murderer *n.* person who has committed murder. □ **asesino**
murderess ['məːdrəs] *n.* woman who has committed murder. □ **asesina**
murderous ['məːdərəs] *adj.* likely to kill. □ **asesino**
murky ['məːki] *adj.* dark/gloomy (water): *in the murky waters of the Atlantic.* □ **lóbrego**
murkiness *n.* being dark/gloomy: *the divers couldn't see because of the murkiness of the water.* □ **lobreguez**
murmur ['məːmə] *n.* low whisper of voices/low sound: *a murmur of approval; the murmur of flies.* □ **murmullo**
■ *v.* to speak in a low voice; to complain in a low

voice. □ **murmurar**
murmuring *n.* **1** speaking in a low voice. □ **murmurante**
2 ***murmurings,*** grumblings/complaints. □ **quejas**
muscle ['mʌsl] *n.* spring-like parts of the body which allow the limbs to move: *he has strong thigh muscles; he's flexing his muscles,* he's preparing to fight/to do something great. □ **músculo**
■ *v.* ***to muscle in on something,*** (*informal*) to push yourself forward to take part in something which is organized by someone else. □ **hacer ganas y participar**
muscular ['mʌskjulə] *adj.* **1** referring to muscles. □ **muscular**
2 *she has very muscular legs,* she has strong muscles in her legs. □ **...piernas muy musculosas**
muse [mju:z] *n.* (*formal*) goddess who inspires poets, musicians, etc. □ **musa**
■ *v.* to think deeply; to daydream. □ **meditar; soñar despierto**
museum [mju:'ziəm] *n.* building in which a collection of valuable or rare objects are put on show permanently: *railway museum; museum of country life; war museum.* □ **museo**
mush [mʌʃ] *n.* soft half-liquid mess: *the potatoes have turned into a mush.* □ **masa blanda**
mushy *adj.* soft and partly liquid: *mushy potatoes.* □ **blando**
mushroom ['mʌʃru:m] *n.* edible white fungus: *to pick mushrooms; mushroom omelette.* □ **seta; champiñón**
■ *v.* to spring up rapidly. □ **crecer como hongos**
music ['mju:zik] *n.* sounds made by playing instruments or singing: *music was coming from the windows of the restaurant; do you like classical music? she's having music lessons.* □ **música**
musical *adj.* **1** referring to music: *musical instrument.* □ **musical**
2 *she's very musical,* she likes music/she plays music a lot. □ **es muy aficionada a la música**
musical chairs, (i) game where people try to sit on chairs when the music stops, one chair being removed each time. □ **juego de las sillas vacías**
(ii) (*informal*) continual movement from office to office/from job to job. □ **de la Ceca a la Meca**
■ *n.* play with songs and popular music: *there's a new musical on in town.* □ **comedia musical**
music-box *n.* small box with a clockwork motor which plays a tune when the box is opened. □ **caja de música**
music hall *n.* theatre specializing in variety shows. □ **teatro de variedades**
musician [mju:'ziʃn] *n.* person who plays music professionally/skillfully. □ **músico**
musk [mʌsk] *n.* perfume obtained from glands of a deer. □ **almizcle**
musk-rat *n.* musquash/American water rat with fine fur. □ **ratón almizclero**
musk-rose *n.* old-fashioned scented rose. □ **rosa almizcleña**
musky *adj.* with a smell like musk. □ **almizclero**
Muslim ['muzlim] *adj.* and *n.* Moslem/(person) who is a follower of the religion of the prophet Mohammed. □ **musulmán**
muslin ['mʌzlin] *n.* very fine thin cotton cloth. □ **muselina**
musquash ['mʌskwɔʃ] *n.* American water rat with fine fur. □ **rata almizclera**
muss [mʌs] *v. Amer.* (*informal*) to ruffle (hair, etc.). □ **despeinar**
mussel ['mʌsl] *n.* mollusc with a dark blue shell, whose soft parts can be eaten. □ **mejillón**
must [mʌst] *v.* **1** *used with other verbs to mean* it is necessary: *you must hurry up; we must not be late.* □ **deber; tener que**
2 (*used with verbs to mean*) it is probable: *I must have made a mistake; it must be the doctor/it must be them,* it cannot be anyone else. □ **debe de**
■ *n.* **1** (*informal*) something which is very necessary: *it's an absolute must.* □ **es de absoluta necesidad**
2 grape juice. □ **mosto**
mustache ['mʌstæʃ] *n. Amer.* = **moustache.** □ **bigote**
mustang ['mʌstæŋ] *n.* wild American horse. □ **mustang**
mustard ['mʌstəd] *n.* **1** sharp-tasting yellow powder made from crushed seeds; paste made from this powder: *do you want some mustard with your meat?* □ **mostaza**
mustard yellow, bright yellow. □ **amarillo mostaza**
2 plant whose seeds make mustard powder. □ **mostaza**
mustard and cress, seedlings of the mustard plant, together with seedlings of cress, eaten as a salad. □ **mostaza y berros**
muster ['mʌstə] *n.* gathering; parade and inspection of soldiers. □ **revista**
to pass muster, to be acceptable. □ **ser aceptable**
■ *v.* to gather together: *he mustered all his courage; the soldiers have orders to muster at 8 a.m.* □ **reunir; formar...**
musty ['mʌsti] *adj.* smelling damp/rotten/stale; smelling old: *some musty old books; the room smelled musty.* □ **mohoso**
mustiness *n.* rotten/stale smell. □ **olor a cerrado**
mutate [mju:'teit] *v.* to change genetically. □ **sufrir una mutación**
mutant *n.* animal/plant which has changed genetically. □ **mutante**
mutation [mju:'teiʃn] *n.* genetic change. □ **mutación**
mute [mju:t] *adj.* **1** silent/dumb (person). □ **mudo**
2 (letter) which is not pronounced: *the 'h' is mute in words like 'honour' and 'honest'.* □ **muda**
■ *n.* **1** person who cannot speak/who is dumb. □ **mudo**
deaf mute, person who cannot hear or speak. □ **sordomudo**
2 attachment used to soften the sound of a musical instrument. □ **sordina**
mutilate ['mju:tileit] *v.* to cut off a limb/an ear, etc., from (someone); to damage. □ **mutilar**
mutilation [mju:ti'leiʃn] *n.* loss of a limb; great damage. □ **mutilación**
mutiny ['mju:tini] *n.* uprising, especially of soldiers/sailors, etc., against the orders of their officers: *the mutiny on the 'Bounty'.* □ **motín**
■ *v.* to refuse to carry out orders/to rise up against officers: *the troops mutinied because of bad food.* □ **amotinarse**
mutineer [mjuti'niə] *n.* person who mutinies. □ **amotinado**
mutinous ['mju:tinəs] *adj.* likely to mutiny/rebellious. □ **rebelde**
mutter ['mʌtə] *n.* low indistinct way of speaking. □ **murmullo**
■ *v.* to mumble/to speak in a low and indistinct voice. □ **murmurar**
muttering *n.* **1** speaking indistinctly. □ **refunfuño**
2 *there were mutterings at the back of the room,* people were complaining in low voices. □ **murmurando**

mutton ['mʌtn] *n.* meat of a sheep: *a leg of mutton.* □ **carne de cordero**

mutual ['mju:tjuəl] *adj.* felt/done by two people to each other; between two people; belonging to two people: *our mutual friend,* the friend of both of us; *by mutual consent,* with the agreement of both parties. □ **mutuo**

mutually *adv.* to two people; by two people: *the contract has to be mutually agreed.* □ **mutuamente**

muzzle ['mʌzl] *n.* **1** nose of an animal. □ **morro**

2 straps placed round the mouth of a dog to prevent it biting. □ **bozal**

3 mouth of a gun. □ **boca**

■ *v.* **1** to tie up the mouth of (a dog) to prevent it biting. □ **abozalar**

2 *to muzzle the press,* to stop newspapers from printing what they want. □ **amordazar**

muzzy ['mʌzi] *adj.* (*informal*) dizzy/in a daze. □ **atontado**

my [mai] *adj.* belonging to me: *I've broken my arm; have you seen my new hat?* □ **mi**

myopia [mai'oupiə] *n.* short-sightedness/not being able to see things which are far away. □ **miopía**

myopic [mai'ɔpik] *adj.* short-sighted. □ **miope**

myriad ['miriəd] *n.* (*formal*) very large number: *myriads of flies.* □ **millones de moscas**

■ *adj.* very many. □ **innumerables**

myrrh [mə:] *n.* sweet-smelling resin used to make incense etc. □ **mirra**

myrtle ['mə:tl] *n.* evergreen plant with scented flowers. □ **mirto**

myself [mai'self] *pronoun* referring to me: **1** *I've hurt myself; I bought the hat as a present but I have decided to keep it for myself; I saw it myself.* □ **yo mismo**

2 *I did it all* ***by myself,*** on my own. □ **lo hice yo solo**

mystery ['mistri] *n.* something which cannot be explained; state of not being able to be explained: *it's a mystery how the burglar got into the house.* □ **misterio**

mysterious [mi'stiəriəs] *adj.* secret/which cannot be explained: *a mysterious message.* □ **misterioso**

mysteriously *adv.* secretly/in a way which cannot be explained. □ **misteriosamente**

mystic ['mistik] *n.* person who attempts to make contact with God through prayer/meditation, etc. □ **místico**

■ *adj.* in contact with God. □ **místico**

mystical *adj.* in contact with God by some process which cannot be understood. □ **místico**

mysticism ['mistisizəm] *n.* religion based on attempts to contact God by processes which cannot be understood. □ **misticismo**

mystify ['mistifai] *v.* to puzzle/to bewilder: *she was quite mystified by the mysterious message.* □ **dejar perplejo**

mystification [mistifi'keiʃn] *n.* puzzle; bewilderment. □ **perplejidad**

mystique [mi'sti:k] *n.* mysterious atmosphere about a person or thing. □ **aire misterioso**

myth [miθ] *n.* **1** ancient folk story about gods: *the Greek myths.* □ **mito**

2 untrue, but commonly held notion: *there are a lot of myths about the drinking of wine.* □ **mito**

mythical *adj.* **1** referring to ancient tales of gods: *a mermaid is a mythical animal.* □ **mítico**

2 untrue/not existing: *he invented a mythical uncle in South America.* □ **imaginario**

mythological [miθə'lɔdʒikl] *adj.* referring to mythology. □ **mitológico**

mythology [mi'θɔlədʒi] *n.* study of myths; ancient folk stories from a particular source: *Greek mythology.* □ **mitología**

myxomatosis [miksəmə'tousis] *n.* fatal disease of rabbits. □ **mixomatosis**

N,n

N, n [en] fourteenth letter of the alphabet. □ **N, n**
nth *adj.* **1** of a very great number: *for the nth time.* □ **por enésima vez**
2 *all the rules were observed* ***to the nth degree,*** to a very great extent. □ **...al máximo**
nab [næb] *v.* (*he nabbed*) **1** (*informal*) to snatch/to pull away (something) suddenly; /to steal: *the gang nabbed the firm's wages packets.* □ **mangar**
2 (*informal*) to catch in the act/to pounce on: *they were nabbed by the police.* □ **echar el guante**
nag [næg] *n.* (*informal*) horse: *our old nag.* □ **penco; jamelgo**
■ *v.* (*he nagged*) to say the same thing again and again/to criticize without seeming to stop: *he was nagged by his wife to stop smoking.* □ **dar la vara**
nagging *adj.* persistent/never stopping: *a nagging pain.* □ **continuo**
nail [neil] *n.* **1** hard covering at the ends of fingers and toes. □ **uña**
nail file, small file for smoothing nails. □ **lima para las uñas**
nail scissors, curved scissors for cutting nails. □ **tijeras para las uñas**
2 small metal spike with a pointed end, used to hold things together: *the picture was hung up on a nail.* □ **clavo**
hard as nails, very strong/tough. □ **más duro que una piedra**
to hit the nail on the head, (*informal*) to make an accurate judgement/to say the right answer. □ **dar en el clavo**
to pay on the nail, (*informal*) to pay immediately/promptly/on the spot. □ **pagar a tocateja**
■ *v.* to attach with nails: *he nailed the pieces of wood together.* □ **clavar**
to nail down *a carpet,* to attach it to the floor with nails. □ **sujetar con clavos**
naive [nai'iːv] *adj.* inexperienced and innocent: *he asked a naive question,* question which showed he knew nothing about the subject. □ **ingenuo**
naively *adv.* in a naive way. □ **ingenuamente**
naivety *n.* being naive. □ **ingenuidad**
naked ['neikid] *adj.* **1** with no clothes on; with no covering: *the children were running around naked; a naked flame,* flame with no protective shield. □ **desnudo**
2 *invisible to the* ***naked eye,*** which can only be seen using a telescope/microscope. □ **...a simple vista**
nakedness *n.* not wearing clothes. □ **desnudez**
name [neim] *n.* **1** title/word which you use to call people/things: *what's the name of that river?* □ **nombre**
Christian name/first name, particular name given to someone as a child. □ **nombre**
2 *he has* ***put his name down*** *to join the sports club,* he has applied to join; *they* ***put forward his name*** *as candidate for the election.* □ **inscribirse, presentar**
3 ***to call somebody names:*** *the child called the teacher names,* insulted her. □ **poner verde, insultar**
4 ***in name only,*** using a name which is not really correct: *the island is British in name only; a wife in name only.* □ **sólo de nombre**
5 *poor service gives the firm a bad name,* a bad reputation. □ **...una mala reputación**
to make a name for oneself: *the nuclear scientist made a name for himself,* he acquired a high reputation. □ **hacerse un nombre**
■ *v.* **1** to call by a name; to give a name to: *the son was named after his father; he was named the winner; can you name five towns in Germany?* □ **nombrar**
2 to specify. □ **fijar**
3 *he asked her to name the day,* to fix the date for her wedding. □ **...que fijara el día**
nameless *adj.* with no name; (word/name) not to be used because of disgust or in order to remain anonymous: *he was struck by a nameless fear; the words were spoken by someone who shall remain nameless.* □ **anónimo**
namely *adv.* that is to say: *the winners of the semifinals, namely Smith and Jones, go forward to the finals.* □ **a saber**
namesake *n.* person with the same name as another. □ **tocayo**
nan [næn] **nana** ['nænə] *n.* child's name for grandmother. □ **yaya**
nanny ['næni] *n.* **1** nurse paid to look after children in their own home: *the nanny supervised the children's bath time.* □ **niñera**
2 ***nanny goat,*** female goat. □ **cabra**
nap [næp] *n.* **1** short sleep: *an afternoon nap.* □ **sueñecito**
2 raised surface of cloth, such as velvet. □ **lanilla**
3 card game. □ **napolitana**
■ *v.* to sleep for a short time. □ **dormitar**
to catch someone napping, to find someone off guard. □ **coger desprevenido a alguien**
napalm ['neipɑːm] *n.* inflammable substance used in incendiary bombs. □ **napalm**
nape [neip] *n.* back of the neck: *dressmakers measure length from the nape of the neck.* □ **cogote**
naphtha ['næfθə] *n.* oil derived from coal/petroleum, used to light fires/clean clothes, etc. □ **nafta**
naphthalene *n.* strong-smelling white chemical used to make mothballs. □ **naftalina**
napkin ['næpkin] *n.* **1** small, square cloth used to protect clothes and wipe your mouth at mealtimes. □ **servilleta**
2 (*formal*) nappy. □ **pañal**
nappy ['næpi] *n.* towel used to cover a baby's bottom. □ **pañal**
narcissus [nɑː'sisəs] *n.* (*pl. narcissi* [nɑː'sisai]) white flower similar to a daffodil grown from a bulb. □ **narciso**
narcotic *adj.* and *n.* (substance) which can make you feel sleepy or become unconscious: *opium is a drug which produces narcotic effects; it's a narcotic sometimes used by doctors.* □ **narcótico**
narcotics squad, *Amer.* police department dealing with drug offences. □ **brigada antidroga**
nark [nɑːk] *v.* (*slang*) to annoy. □ **fastidiar**
narrate [nə'reit] *v.* to write/to speak about events; to tell (a story): *the details of the air-crash were later narrated by the survivors.* □ **narrar**
narration *n.* speaking/writing about events. □ **narración**
narrative ['nærətiv] *n.* what is actually written or told: *the narrative was read by the author.* □ **narración**
■ *adj.* describing events which took place: *a narrative account.* □ **narrativo**
narrator [nə'reitə] *n.* person who gives an actual

account; person who reads a story: *the narrator's vivid account made it easy for us to imagine what had happened.* □ **narrador**

narrow ['nærou] *adj.* **1** not wide: *a narrow lane.* □ **estrecho**

2 ***a narrow squeak/a narrow escape,*** escape at the last minute from an awkward or dangerous situation. □ **escapada por los pelos**

3 *the government had a narrow majority,* they won by a very small margin of votes. □ **...una mayoría escasa**

■ *v.* to restrict/to make smaller; to make less wide; to become smaller: *the number of suspects had been narrowed down to two; she narrowed her eyes in the strong sunlight; the road narrows suddenly.* □ **estrechar**

narrowly *adv.* nearly/only just: *the government narrowly avoided defeat.* □ **por muy poco**

narrow-minded *adj.* not capable of seeing many points of view/not tolerant. □ **de miras estrechas**

nasal ['neizl] *adj.* spoken as if through the nose: *his accent sounds nasal.* □ **nasal**

nasally *adv.* through the nose: *a cold makes you speak nasally.* □ **nasalmente**

nasturtium [nə'stəːʃəm] *n.* creeping plant with large orange or yellow flowers. □ **capuchina**

nasty ['nɑːsti] *adj.* **1** unpleasant/disagreeable: *a nasty smell; nasty weather.* □ **asqueroso**

2 *a nasty corner,* a dangerous corner. □ **una esquina peligrosa**

3 ***to turn nasty,*** to become hostile/unfriendly. □ **volverse antipático**

4 ***a nasty piece of work,*** (*informal*) unpleasant person who could harm you. □ **persona desagradable y amenazadora**

5 *it came as a nasty blow,* a bad surprise. □ **...una sorpresa desagradable**

nation ['neiʃn] *n.* people of a particular British nation; people of all nations. □ **nación**

national *adj.* belonging to the people of a particular country: *national treasures; national costume.* □ **nacional**

■ *n.* person of a particular country: *he's a German national.* □ **nacional**

nationalism *n.* feeling of pride in one's nation; desire for independence for a country: *the spirit of nationalism could hinder the formation of a united Europe.* □ **nacionalismo**

nationalist *n.* person who supports nationalism. □ **nacionalista**

nationality *n.* citizenship of a country: *he acquired French nationality.* □ **nacionalidad**

nationalization *n.* conversion of private industries to ownership by the state: *nationalization of the gas industry.* □ **nacionalización**

nationalize *v.* to put (a private industry) under central government ownership and control: *the power industries have been nationalized.* □ **nacionalizar**

nationwide *adj.* all over the country: *a nationwide search.* □ **por todo el país**

native [nei'tiv] *n.* **1** person born in a particular country: *a native of Belgium.* □ **nativo**

2 uncivilized original inhabitant: *the explorers were attacked by natives.* □ **indígena**

3 plant/animal which originally comes from a particular country: *the tiger is a native of India.* □ **el tigre es originario de...**

■ *adj.* **1** natural; (qualities) with which a person is born. □ **innato**

2 unaltered/undeveloped: *diamonds are found in their native state in South Africa.* □ **natural**

3 belonging to those born in a country: *native customs; his native language is Welsh.* □ **costumbres del país; lengua materna**

4 (plant/animal) which originally comes from a certain country: *oak trees are native to northern Europe.* □ **originario**

nativity [nə'tiviti] *n.* birth, especially that of Jesus Christ. □ **natividad**

nativity play, play describing the events surrounding the birth of Jesus Christ. □ **auto del nacimiento**

natter ['nætə] *n. to have a natter,* (*informal*) to have a friendly informal conversation/chat. □ **charla**

■ *v.* (*informal*) to have a friendly informal chat. □ **estar de charleta**

natty ['næti] *adj.* **1** smart/tidy (personal appearance). □ **elegante**

2 cleverly designed (gadget). □ **ingenioso**

natural ['nætʃrəl] *adj.* **1** based on inner knowledge or instinct; not learnt: *self-defence is a natural instinct.* □ **natural**

2 normal/not artificial: *a small child's behaviour is usually natural; death from natural causes.* □ **natural**

3 not surprising/not unexpected: *it's natural that very old people should get deaf.* □ **natural**

4 dealing with (the study of) nature: *natural history; natural science; natural gas,* gas which is found in the earth. □ **natural**

5 (*in music*) (note) which is neither sharp nor flat. □ **nota natural**

■ *n.* person who is naturally suitable for a job/a part in a play, etc. □ **persona dotada**

naturalism *n.* (*in art/literature*) showing things as they really are. □ **naturalismo**

naturalist *n.* **1** person who studies animals or plants. □ **naturalista**

2 artist/writer who shows things as they really are. □ **naturalista**

naturalization [nætʃərəlai'zeiʃn] *n.* acquiring the citizenship of a country other than that in which you were born: *he had lived in England for several years before he applied for naturalization.* □ **naturalización**

naturalize ['nætʃərəlaiz] *v.* **1** to introduce (a plant or animal) into another country: *grey squirrels have become naturalized in England.* □ **aclimatar**

2 to let cultivated plants become wild: *daffodils are smaller when they have become naturalized.* □ **aclimatarse**

3 to grant (someone) citizenship of a country other than that in which he was born: *a naturalized American.* □ **naturalizar**

naturally ['nætʃrəli] *adv.* **1** in a natural/unstudied way: *she behaved quite naturally even after she had discovered the body of her husband in the bath.* □ **con naturalidad**

2 as you would expect/of course: *naturally the beginner was beaten by the champion.* □ **naturalmente**

nature ['neitʃə] *n.* **1** character (of a person/thing/animal): *it's not in his nature to be unkind; an animal may be aggressive by nature.* □ **naturaleza; no es propio de él ser...**

human nature, attitudes and behaviour which are typical of human beings. □ **naturaleza humana**

2 kind/class (of thing): *something of that nature happened.* □ **clase**

3 world of plants and animals: *the laws of nature,* what happens in the world of plants and animals; *nature study,* the study of plant or animal life in a junior school. □ **naturaleza**

naturism *n.* belief in the physical and mental advantages of going about naked. □ **naturismo**

naturist *n.* nudist/person who believes in the physical and mental advantages of going about naked. □ **naturista**
naught [nɔːt] *n.* (*formal*) nothing. □ **nada**
naughty [nɔːti] *adj.* bad/disobedient (child): *the naughty little boy had upset all the drinks.* □ **travieso**
naughtily *adv.* wickedly: *the little boy naughtily snatched the sweets.* □ **traviesamente**
naughtiness *n.* wickedness: *naughtiness will be punished.* □ **mala conducta**
nausea ['nɔːziə] *n.* feeling of sickness/of extreme dislike: *he suffers from nausea every time he goes on a ship.* □ **náusea**
nauseate *v.* to make (someone) loathe/dislike very much: *he was nauseated by the corruption in the government.* □ **dar náuseas a**
nauseating *adj.* horrible/which makes you sick: *the heap of rubbish was a nauseating sight.* □ **nauseabundo**
nauseous *adj.* which makes you feel sick. □ **nauseabundo**
nautical ['nɔːtikl] *adj.* referring to ships, sailing and boating. □ **náutico**
nautical mile, measure of length at sea (2,025 yards or 1.85 kilometres). □ **milla marina**
naval ['neivl] *adj.* referring to ships and especially to a navy: *naval warfare; naval officer; a naval engagement,* battle at sea. □ **naval; guerra en el mar; oficial de marina**
naval base, port for warships. □ **base naval**
naval college, establishment for training naval officers. □ **escuela naval**
nave [neiv] *n.* main part of a church: *the nave of the cathedral extends from the west door to the chancel.* □ **nave central**
navel ['neivl] *n.* small hollow in the middle of your stomach where the umbilical cord was attached. □ **ombligo**
navel orange, large seedless orange with a small hollow at the top. □ **naranja navel**
navigate ['nævigeit] *v.* to guide/to steer a ship or aircraft; to tell the driver of a car, etc., which way to go: *explorers navigate unknown waters.* □ **navegar**
navigability [nævigə'biliti] *n.* being navigable. □ **navegabilidad**
navigable *adj.* **1** steerable/seaworthy: *the ship was navigable at all times.* □ **navegable**
2 (river) deep enough for ships to sail in it: *the river Thames is navigable for some distance up stream.* □ **navegable**
navigation [nævi'geiʃn] *n.* guiding/steering a ship/an aircraft along a certain course. □ **navegación**
inland navigation, travel by boat along rivers or canals. □ **navegación interior**
navigator ['nævigeitə] *n.* person who guides/steers a ship or an aircraft; person who tells the driver of a car which way to go. □ **navegante**
navvy ['nævi] *n.* labourer/person employed for digging or excavating: *navvies dug out the foundations of the building.* □ **peón**
navy ['neivi] *n.* **1** all a country's warships together with the crews: *the Royal Navy.* □ **marina; armada**
2 ***the Merchant Navy,*** all ships of a country which carry cargo. □ **marina mercante**
■ *adj.* and *n.* ***navy (blue),*** dark blue. □ **azul marino**
neap [niːp] *n.* ***neap tide,*** tide which does not rise or fall very much, midway between the spring tides. □ **marea muerta**
Neapolitan [niə'pɔlitən] *adj.* referring to Naples, a town in southern Italy. □ **napolitano**
Neapolitan ice cream, ice cream made of layers of different colours and flavours. □ **helado al corte**
near ['niə] *adv.* close/at only a little distance in space or time: *the shops were near at hand; the bus station was nearer than the railway station; their wedding anniversary is quite near.* □ **cerca**
■ *prep.* close by (an object); not far away in time: *bring your chair near the fire; phone me again nearer the day when you want to see me; he was near his end,* approaching death. □ **cerca de**
■ *adj.* **1** *near relations,* closest relations. □ **relaciones estrechas**
2 *near side,* side closest to the kerb (in a car). □ **lado del bordillo**
3 ***a near miss,*** a narrow escape. □ **un fallo por poco**
■ *v.* to draw near to/to approach: *the motorist was nearing his destination; nearing your goal,* about to achieve your aim. □ **acercarse**
nearby *adj.* which is situated close by: *the nearby house was for sale.* □ **cercano**
near by *adv.* close by: *their friends lived near by.* □ **cerca**
nearly *adv.* **1** almost: *the war lasted nearly ten years; she's nearly a hundred years old.* □ **casi**
2 closely: *the two girls nearly resemble each other.* □ **mucho**
3 ***not nearly*** *accurate enough,* far from accurate. □ **no es ni mucho menos exacto**
nearness *n.* closeness. □ **proximidad**
near-sighted *adj.* short-sighted/only able to see clearly things which are near. □ **corto de vista**
neat [niːt] *adj.* **1** tidy/clean: *she always looks neat and tidy; the girl's room was neat.* □ **limpio**
2 with no water added: *he was drinking neat gin; I'll take my whisky neat.* □ **solo**
3 apt/precise (words): *a neat turn of phrase.* □ **apropiado**
4 skilful/well handled: *the darn was the neatest repair she'd ever seen.* □ **hábil**
neatly *adv.* in a tidy/clean way: *neatly dressed people; a neatly turned compliment.* □ **pulcramente**
neatness *n.* **1** tidy/clean appearance: *neatness is required in sewing.* □ **pulcritud**
2 *neatness of expression,* clearness. □ **claridad de expresión**
nebula ['nebjulə] *n.* (*pl. nebulae*) cloud of dust in space which shines like a star at night. □ **nebulosa**
nebulous ['nebjuləs] *adj.* vague: *his plans are rather nebulous at the moment.* □ **nebuloso**
necessary ['nesəsəri] *n.* what is essential/what must be done: *to do the necessary; we can't do without the necessaries of life.* □ **lo necesario; lo imprescindible**
the necessary, (*informal*) the required amount of money. □ **lo necesario**
■ *adj.* essential/which cannot be avoided: *it's necessary to pay tax by a certain date; he helped more than was strictly necessary; all the necessary arrangements have been made.* □ **necesario**
necessarily [nesə'serəli] *adv.* in an unavoidable way: *taking the train isn't necessarily dearer than the bus,* it can be cheaper. □ **necesariamente**
necessitate [ni'sesiteit] *v.* to make essential/to compel: *the injury necessitated a change of plans; a lower income necessitates a cut in living standards.* □ **necesitar**
necessitous *adj.* (*formal*) poor/needy. □ **necesitado**
necessity *n.* **1** need/compulsion: *there's no necessity for you to come; a case of absolute necessity.* □ **necesidad**
2 absolutely essential thing: *some people don't have*

the bare necessities for living; a car is a necessity for a travelling salesman. □ **indispensable**

neck [nek] *n.* **1** part of the body connecting the head to the shoulders: *I can't turn my head because of a stiff neck; to break your neck.* □ **cuello**
2 ***to be up to your neck in work,*** (*informal*) have a lot of work to do. □ **estar hasta el cuello de trabajo**
3 ***to breathe down someone's neck,*** to watch someone very closely/to follow close behind someone. □ **seguirle la pista a alguien**
4 ***to win by a neck,*** win a race by a very short distance. □ **ganar por una cabeza**
5 ***to finish neck and neck,*** to be equal winners. □ **acabar parejos**
6 ***a pain in the neck,*** (*informal*) a troublesome/awkward person/thing. □ **un rollazo**
7 ***to save your neck,*** escape hanging/punishment. □ **salvar el cuello**
8 ***to get it in the neck,*** (*informal*) to be severely criticized. □ **cargársela**
9 ***to stick your neck out,*** (*informal*) take a chance/to be asking for trouble. □ **buscársela**
10 narrow passage leading to a wider area: *the neck of a bottle; an isthmus is a narrow neck of land.* □ **cuello**
11 ***in this neck of the woods,*** (*informal*) in this part of the world. □ **por estos andurriales**
12 part of a garment which goes round your neck: *the neck of a pullover; jumper with a V neck.* □ **cuello**
13 part of an animal eaten as food: *best end of neck,* joint of lamb consisting of the ribs nearest the neck. □ **cuello; chuletas de aguja**
necklace *n.* string of stones/pearls, etc. worn round the neck. □ **collar**
necktie *n. especially Amer.* band of material worn round the neck and tied in front with a knot. □ **corbata**

necromancy ['nekrəmænsi] *n.* art of black magic/of predicting the future by speaking to the dead. □ **nigromancia**

nectar ['nektə] *n.* **1** sweet substance produced by flowers: *bees are attracted by the nectar in plants.* □ **néctar**
2 any extremely pleasant drink: *water tastes like nectar to a traveller in the desert.* □ **néctar**

nectarine ['nektəri:n] *n.* fruit like a peach with a smooth skin. □ **nectarina**

neé [nei] *adj.* with the maiden name of: *Mrs Smith, neé Taylor.* □ **de soltera**

need [ni:d] *n.* **1** what is necessary: *if need be/if there's a need; what need is there? there's no need to say that.* □ **necesidad**
2 ***in need of,*** requiring something: *to be in need of food; not in need of help.* □ **tener necesidad de**
3 time of difficulty/poverty: *to help people in need.* □ **...que está necesitada**
a friend in need is a friend indeed, someone who helps you when you are in difficulties is a real friend. □ **en la adversidad se conoce a los amigos**
■ *v.* to be necessary/to be required: *this needs explaining; it needs a lot of patience; we needed to check the bill; we shall need money for our holiday; need he go? you needn't wait; I need hardly tell you; he needn't go, need he?* □ **necesitar**
needless *adj.* unnecessary/not called for: *needless presents; needless to say.* □ **innecesario**
needs *n. pl.* actual requirements: *my needs are few; nurses see to patients' needs.* □ **necesidades**
to fit your needs, to fulfil your requirements. □ **satisfacer las necesidades**
■ *adv.* (*used only with the word* must): *if needs must, if it has to be done.* □ **si se ha de hacer**
needy *adj.* in need of/requiring help or food: *needy people.* □ **necesitado**

needle ['ni:dl] *n.* **1** thin metal/plastic/wooden tool with a sharp point at one end: *knitting needle; sewing needle.* □ **aguja**
it's like looking for a needle in a haystack, it's a hopeless task. □ **es como buscar una aguja en un pajar**
2 ***hypodermic needle,*** needle used for injections. □ **aguja hipodérmica**
3 ***gramophone needle,*** the small pointed jewel which touches a record as it turns. □ **aguja de tocadiscos**
4 ***compass needle,*** the indicator on the dial of a compass. □ **aguja imantada**
5 leaf of a pine tree: *pine needles.* □ **aguja de pino**
■ *v.* to irritate/to provoke (someone): *when needled he lost his temper.* □ **pinchar**
needlewoman *n. good needlewoman,* woman who is good at sewing. □ **costurera**
needlework *n.* sewing done with needle and thread. □ **labor de aguja**

nefarious [ni'fɛəriəs] *adj.* (*formal*) very wicked. □ **infame**

negate [ni'geit] *v.* to oppose/to cancel out (something): *we shall have to negate his statement; theories may be negated by the discovery of more facts.* □ **negar**
negation [ni'geiʃn] *n.* what is cancelled out/negated: *the war saw the negation of all his aims.* □ **negación**
negative ['negətiv] *n.* **1** reply indicating no: *he answered in the negative; two negatives make an affirmative.* □ **negativa**
2 reverse image of a photograph: *to take a print from a negative.* □ **negativo**
3 one of the terminals in a battery: *you must be able to tell the negative from the positive before you connect up the wires.* □ **negativo**
■ *adj.* **1** meaning no; showing opposition/refusal: *a negative vote.* □ **un voto negativo**
2 without good/positive qualities: *negative virtues; the results of the tests were negative.* □ **negativo**
3 minus; less than zero. □ **negativo**
■ *v.* to contradict/to oppose (something). □ **rechazar**
negatively *adv.* in a way which suggests opposition: *the bored child responded negatively.* □ **negativamente**

neglect [ni'glekt] *n.* disregard/lack of care or attention: *the child was put in a home because of his parents' neglect.* □ **negligencia**
■ *v.* **1** to fail to look after/to fail to maintain: *we shouldn't neglect this opportunity.* □ **no cumplir con**
2 to omit to do something which should be done: *he neglected to pay the telephone bill.* □ **dejar de**
neglected *adj.* not looked after: *the gardens look neglected.* □ **descuidado**
neglectful *adj.* ***to be neglectful of,*** to forget about. □ **olvidadizo**
negligence ['neglidʒəns] *n.* absence of proper care and attention: *negligence causes accidents.* □ **negligencia**
negligent *adj.* not giving proper care and attention. □ **negligente**
negligible *adj.* not significant/not worth regarding: *the effects of the fire were negligible.* □ **insignificante**

negotiate [ni'gousieit] *v.* **1** to discuss so as to make an agreement with someone: *the countries negotiated before signing a peace treaty.* □ **negociar**
2 to make a financial arrangement: *a sale was ne-*

gotiated; we shall negotiate payments by cheque. □ **negociar**
3 to overcome an obstacle/difficulty: *to negotiate a bend in the road.* □ **salvar**
negotiable [ni'gousiəbl] *adj.* **1** which can be overcome: *difficulties may be negotiable.* □ **negociable**
2 *this cheque is not negotiable,* is not exchangeable for cash. □ **negociable**
negotiation [nigousi'eiʃn] *n.* discussing/arranging by discussion: *wages may be fixed by negotiation.* □ **negociación**
negotiator *n.* person who discusses to try to reach an agreement: *each dispute requires a negotiator.* □ **negociador**

negro ['ni:grou] **negress** ['ni:grəs] *adj.* and *n.* member of a dark-skinned race of people originating in Africa: *West African negroes; the negro race; negro people are noted for their height.* □ **negro; negra**
negroid *adj.* having the characteristics of negroes: *negroid features.* □ **negroide**

neigh [nei] *n.* sound made by a horse: *from the stable came a welcoming neigh.* □ **relincho**
■ *v.* to make a sound like a horse: *the pony was neighing at the approach of its owner.* □ **relinchar**

neighbour ['neibə] *Amer.* **neighbor** *n.* **1** person who lives in a nearby house/road/country: *our next-door neighbours; our nearest neighbours; our neighbours across the English channel.* □ **vecino**
2 closest person: *my neighbour at the dinner table.* □ **vecino**
neighbourhood *n.* **1** district and its people: *the neighbourhood was fairly friendly.* □ **vecindad**
2 (used as an adjective): *your friendly neighbourhood grocer,* (*informal*) your local grocer. □ **el tendero del barrio**
3 ***in the neighbourhood of,*** around/near to (in space or amount): *we live in the neighbourhood of London; the sum was in the neighbourhood of $10.* □ **en los alrededores de; cerca de**
neighbouring *adj.* next to each other: *Buda and Pest are neighbouring towns.* □ **vecino**
neighbourly *adj.* in a friendly/helpful way: *acting in a neighbourly fashion when help was needed.* □ **de buen vecino**

neither ['naiðə, 'ni:ðə] *adv.* and *conj.* not either: *he will neither eat nor drink; he doesn't like curry and neither do I; neither does it seem that he was innocent.* □ **ni; ni comerá ni beberá**
■ *adj.* and *pron.* not either of two things or persons: *neither person can tell you; neither guess is right; neither is a pleasant person; neither of them knows the truth.* □ **ninguno de los dos (adj.); ninguno (pro.)**

neo- ['niou] *prefix meaning* new. □ **neo**

neolithic *adj.* belonging to the late Stone Age: *neolithic man had weapons of polished stone.* □ **neolítico**

neon ['niɔn] *n.* (*chemical element*: Ne) colourless gas often used in tubes to make illuminated signs: *neon signs.* □ **neón**

nephew ['nefju:] *n.* son of your brother or sister: *the nephews ran their uncle's business.* □ **sobrino**

nepotism ['nepətizm] *n.* giving members of your family jobs for which they are not necessarily qualified. □ **nepotismo**

nerve [nə:v] *n.* **1** one of many thin threads forming part of the body's system for conveying messages to and from the brain: *when nerves are damaged paralysis may result.* □ **nervio**
to be in a state of nerves, in a tense/anxious state. □ **estar muy nervioso**
to get on someone's nerves, to irritate/annoy someone. □ **crisparle los nervios a uno**
2 courage/confidence: *to lose one's nerve for heights.* □ **valor; amilanarse por la altura**
3 ***to have a nerve,*** (*informal*) to be cheeky/rude/over-confident: *he's got a nerve; he had the nerve to tell me I was late.* □ **tiene un morro; tuvo el valor de decirme...**
4 ***to strain every nerve,*** to make tremendous efforts. □ **hacer todo lo posible**
■ *v.* to summon up strength/confidence: *he nerved himself to enter the room.* □ **armarse de valor**
nervelessness *n.* a lack of energy/limpness. □ **falta de nervio**
nerve-racking *adj.* disturbing: *the nerve-racking sound of guns.* □ **crispante**
nervous *adj.* **1** ***the nervous system*** *of the body,* the pattern of nerve fibres. □ **nervioso**
nervous breakdown, physical and mental collapse caused by worry. □ **depresión nerviosa**
2 timid/easily disturbed/easily upset: *she was nervous before taking her driving test.* □ **nervioso; miedoso**
nervously *adv.* in a worried/frightened way: *he laughed nervously at our jokes.* □ **con miedo**
nervy *adj.* (*informal*) not relaxed/irritable. □ **nervioso**

nest [nest] *n.* **1** place built by birds to lay their eggs: *an eagle's nest.* □ **nido**
to feather your nest, to make a lot of money (usually fraudulently). □ **hacer su agosto**
2 hiding place/collecting place for people or animals: *a nest of robbers; a wasps' nest; an ants' nest.* □ **una cueva de ladrones; avispero; hormiguero**
3 ***nest of tables,*** tables of different sizes fitting under each other. □ **mesas nido**
■ *v.* (*of birds*) to build a nest: *birds nest in trees; birds nest only at certain times of year; the nesting season.* □ **anidar**
nest egg *n.* investment/money put aside for future use. □ **ahorrillos**

nestle ['nesl] *v.* **1** to settle down comfortably: *the cat was nestling into the cushions.* □ **arrellanarse**
2 to have close and loving contact: *the baby nestled in its mother's arms.* □ **acurrucarse**
nestling ['nesliŋ] *n.* small bird not yet ready to leave the nest: *the nestlings had to learn to fly.* □ **polluelo**

net [net] *n.* piece of material loosely woven so that it has a regular pattern of holes, and can be made up into different articles: *net curtains; fishing net; tennis net.* □ **red**
■ *v.* (*he netted*) **1** to catch in a net: *the fish were netted at sea; he netted a salmon.* □ **coger (con red)**
2 to make a true profit: *to net a big profit,* to make a lot of money; *he netted three hundred dollars,* he made three hundred dollars profit. □ **ganar neto**
■ *adj.* (price/weight) left after taking away the weight of the container/the tax paid, etc.: *net profit,* actual gain after expenses have been paid; *net weight,* true weight without the wrappings. □ **neto**
netball *n.* team game (usually played by women) where the ball has to be thrown so that it goes through a ring placed high up at the end of the court. □ **'netball'**
netting *n.* material made of string/wire loosely woven into a regular pattern of holes: *wire netting.* □ **red**
network *n.* interconnecting system: *the railway network; there's a network of radio stations which covers the country.* □ **red**

nether ['neðə] *adj.* (*formal*) lower. □ **inferior**
nether regions, bottom part. □ **el infierno**
nethermost *adj.* lowest. □ **más profundo**

Netherlands ['neðələndz] *n.* Holland/flat, low-lying country in Northern Europe. □ **Países Bajos**

nettle ['netl] *n.* ***(stinging) nettle,*** weed with stinging leaves. □ **ortiga**

■ *v.* to anger/to irritate: *the criticism nettled him; he became nettled by the questions and answered back sharply.* □ **hacer rabiar**

nettle-rash *n.* skin rash caused by an allergy. □ **urticaria**

neural ['njurəl] *adj.* referring to nerves. □ **neural**

neuralgia *n.* nerve pains in the face or head. □ **neuralgia**

neurologist [nju'rɔlədʒist] *n.* person who studies the nervous system. □ **neurólogo**

neurology *n.* study of the body's nervous system. □ **neurología**

neurosis [nju'rousis] *n.* (*pl. neuroses*) mental illness caused by a nervous disorder: *some people's strange behaviour is directly due to their neuroses; fear of cats may be a neurosis.* □ **neurosis**

neurotic [nju'rɔtik] *adj.* unbalanced (behaviour): *neurotic fears are often illogical.* □ **neurótico**

neuter ['nju:tə] *adj.* (*in grammar*) not having a masculine or feminine gender: *the Latin language has neuter nouns.* □ **neutro**

■ *v.* to make incapable of breeding/to castrate: *to neuter a cat; to have your cat neutered.* □ **castrar**

neutral *adj.* **1** not favouring or supporting either side in a dispute: *Switzerland is a neutral country.* □ **neutral**

2 not having a distinctive colour: *grey is a neutral colour.* □ **neutro**

3 *the car is in neutral,* not in gear. □ **...en punto muerto**

neutrality [nju'træliti] *n.* being uncommitted/neutral; not taking sides: *some countries pursue a policy of armed neutrality.* □ **neutralidad**

neutralize ['nju:trəlaiz] *v.* to cancel out by using an opposite: *acids may be neutralized by alkalis.* □ **neutralizar**

neutron *n.* basic particle with no electric charge. □ **neutrón**

never ['nevə] *adv.* **1** not ever/not at any time: *I shall never forget; I never go there.* □ **nunca**

2 (*for emphasis*) not: *I never expected him; he never said a word about it.* □ **jamás**

3 (*exclamation of surprise*) surely not: *well, I never!,* how surprising! □ **¡no me digas!**

never-ending *adj.* which does not stop. □ **sin fin**

nevermore *adv.* (*formal*) not any more: *doomed nevermore to see his homeland.* □ **nunca más**

never-never *n.* (*informal*) hire-purchase system: *to buy something on the never-never.* □ **compra a plazos**

nevertheless [nevəθə'les] *adv.* despite all that; all the same: *he fell down but nevertheless decided to continue in the race.* □ **sin embargo**

never-to-be-forgotten *adj.* memorable. □ **inolvidable**

new [nju:] *adj.* **1** completely different/not thought of before/not met before: *new ideas; to break new ground; new and original designs.* □ **nuevo**

2 changed/different: *it's made a new man of me.* □ **nuevo**

3 fresh/unused: *take a new piece of paper.* □ **nuevo**

to turn over a new leaf, become better/start again. □ **mejorar**

4 most recent: *new arrivals in a country; new boys in the school; new potatoes.* □ **nuevo**

the new moon, moon when it is a thin crescent. □ **luna nueva**

5 just bought/just acquired: *have you seen his new car? she introduced me to her new boyfriend.* □ **nuevo**

6 (used when naming newly discovered territories or towns after known ones): *New England; New Zealand; New York; New South Wales.* □ **Nueva/Nuevo**

newborn *adj.* just born: *newborn baby.* □ **recién nacido**

newcomer *n.* person who has just come to an area. □ **recién llegado**

new-laid *adj.* (*of eggs*) freshly laid/just laid. □ **recién puesto**

newly *adv.* most recently: *newly born babies; newly elected members of Parliament.* □ **recién**

newly-weds, people who have just got married. □ **recién casados**

newness *n.* being recent/fresh; not having been used: *the material was stiff with newness.* □ **carácter de nuevo, no estrenado**

news [nju:z] *n.* spoken or written information about events: *the nine o'clock news on television; the rescue was good news.* □ **noticias**

it's in the news, it is of topical interest. □ **está de actualidad**

to break the news to someone, to tell someone bad/unwelcome news. □ **dar una noticia a alguien**

no news is good news, the absence of bad news means things may be going well. □ **las malas noticias llegan las primeras**

newsagent *n.* person who runs a shop which sells newspapers. □ **vendedor de periódicos**

newscaster *n.* person who reads the news on television. □ **locutor**

news flash *n.* short news item. □ **noticia de alcance**

newsletter *n.* printed sheet giving news to members of a church/club, etc.: *the parish newsletter.* □ **hoja informativa**

newsman *n.* (*pl. newsmen*) journalist. □ **periodista**

newspaper *n.* daily/weekly paper containing information and news. □ **periódico**

newsprint *n.* paper for printing newspapers and magazines. □ **papel de prensa**

newsreel *n.* short film about current events shown in a cinema. □ **noticiario documental**

news vendor *n.* person who sells newspapers in the street. □ **vendedor de periódicos**

newsworthy *adj.* (events) worth recording/mentioning in papers or on television. □ **de interés periodístico**

newt [nju:t] *n.* small, lizard-like animal which can live either in or out of water. □ **tritón**

newton ['njutən] *n.* standard measurement of force. □ **newton**

next [nekst] *adj.* **1** (*of time/sequence*) coming after: *the next day; the next size in shoes.* □ **próximo (día); el siguiente número**

2 (*of place*) closest to/nearest: *the next room.* □ **la habitación de al lado**

3 *she lives **next door,*** in the house/flat next to yours. □ **...en la casa de al lado**

■ *adv.* **1** coming after in place/time: *he sat next to her; what shall we do next? when you are next in Edinburgh; next came his brother.* □ **al lado de; ¿y ahora...?; próximamente**

2 ***what next!,*** what other amazing or absurd things can we expect? □ **¿y ahora qué?**

3 *it costs **next to nothing,*** it costs very little. □ **apenas cuesta nada**

■ *n.* **1** person who follows: *next please!; her next was a boy,* the following child she had was a boy.

□ **el siguiente**
2 *the week after next,* not the next week but the following one. □ **en una semana a partir de la que entra**
next-door *adj.* living next door: *the next-door neighbours.* □ **de al lado**
nib [nib] *n.* pointed writing end of a pen. □ **punta**
nibble ['nibl] *n.* bite/very small amount eaten: *a nibble of cheese; the fish had a nibble at the bait.* □ **mordisco**
■ *v.* to take very small, cautious bites: *the sheep were nibbling the grass; the fish had nibbled the bait; the invalid nibbled his food.* □ **mordisquear**
nibble away *v.* to remove gradually/in little pieces: *inflation is nibbling away at my savings.* □ **comer poco a poco**
nice [nais] *adj.* **1** generally pleasant: *a nice day; a nice sleep; nice holidays.* □ **buen/bueno**
2 (used ironically): *a nice mess we're in! a nice way to behave!* □ **bonito**
3 precise; subtle; skilful: *a nice distinction; a nice hand at pastry,* good at pastry-making; *a nice judgement in the legal case.* □ **acertado**
nice-looking *adj.* pretty/pleasant to look at. □ **bonito**
nicely *adv.* in a satisfactory/good manner: *the patient's getting on nicely; the work's progressing nicely.* □ **bien**
niceness *n.* quality of being agreeable. □ **amabilidad**
nicety *n.* fine/exact detail: *the niceties of the ceremony were observed.* □ **detalles**
niche [niːʃ] *n.* hollow in a wall or pillar to put a statue/vase/decoration in. □ **hornacina**
to find your niche in life/to find a niche for yourself, to find a completely satisfying role/job. □ **encontrar un hueco**
nick [nik] *n.* **1** small dent/notch (usually to mark a place): *the nick in the cloth indicated where the cut had to be made.* □ **muesca; la marca en la tela...**
in the nick of time, (*informal*) at exactly the right moment/just in time. □ **al pelo**
2 (*slang*) prison. □ **trullo**
3 ***to be in good nick,*** (*slang*) to be in good form. □ **estar en forma**
■ *v.* **1** to make a small notch/cut. □ **hacer muescas**
2 (*slang*) to steal: *the burglar nicked the silver.* □ **mangar**
3 (*slang*) to catch: *the police nicked the whole gang.* □ **trincar**
nickel ['nikl] *n.* **1** (*chemical element*: Ni) silver-coloured metal: *a nickel alloy.* □ **níquel**
2 *Amer.* coin worth 5 cents. □ **níquel**
■ *v.* (*he nickelled*) to coat with nickel: *nickelled silverware.* □ **niquelar**
nickname ['nikneim] *n.* abbreviated or pet name: *Mr Stephenson's nickname was 'Rocket'.* □ **apodo**
■ *v.* to give (someone) a nickname: *Mr White was nicknamed 'Chalky'.* □ **apodar**
nicotine ['nikətiːn] *n.* poisonous brown liquid obtained from tobacco: *the nicotine in cigarettes is harmful; nicotine-stained fingers,* yellow-stained smoker's fingers. □ **nicotina**
niece [niːs] *n.* daughter of your brother or sister: *nephews and nieces are near relations; the aunt and niece looked alike.* □ **sobrina**
nifty ['nifti] *adj.* (*informal*) quick and agile; clever (gadget). □ **listo**
Nigeria [nai'dʒiəriə] *n.* large country in West Africa. □ **Nigeria**
Nigerian *adj.* referring to Nigeria. □ **nigeriano**
■ *n.* person who comes from Nigeria. □ **nigeriano**
niggardly ['nigədli] *adj.* mean; very small in amount: *a niggardly person; he donated a niggardly sum to charity.* □ **tacaño; ...una miserable cantidad...**
niggle ['nigl] *v.* to be fussy about relatively unimportant details. □ **preocuparse por pequeñeces**
to be niggled by someone, to be annoyed/upset by someone's spiteful or petty criticism. □ **molestarse**
niggling *adj.* unimportant/insignificant: *the discussion was ruined by concern for niggling details.* □ **de poca monta**
night [nait] *n.* last part of each day; period of darkness from sunset to sunrise: *night succeeds day; late at night.* □ **noche**
last night, yesterday after dark: *tonight we'll go out, since we stayed in last night.* □ **anoche**
the first night, the official opening performance of a play or entertainment. □ **estreno**
a night out, an evening spent outside the home. □ **una noche fuera**
nightcap *n.* bed-time drink. □ **bebida antes de acostarse**
nightclothes *n. pl.* clothes worn in bed. □ **ropa de dormir**
nightclub *n.* club only open at night. □ **sala de fiestas**
nightdress *n.* dress worn by women and girls in bed. □ **camisón**
nightie *n.* (*informal*) nightdress. □ **camisón**
nightingale *n.* small brown singing bird. □ **ruiseñor**
nightlight *n.* small dim light or candle left burning at night. □ **lamparilla**
nightly *adv.* every night: *twice nightly performances; take the pills nightly for a week.* □ **cada noche**
nightmare *n.* **1** vivid frightening dream. □ **pesadilla**
2 horrible event: *the passengers had a nightmare ride as the train went out of control.* □ **pesadilla**
nightmarish *adj.* vividly frightening. □ **de pesadilla**
nightshade *n.* (any of) a family of plants related to the potato and including some poisonous plants. □ **hierba mora**
deadly nightshade, poisonous plant of the potato family with small black berries. □ **belladona**
night-time *n.* period of night: *a night-time flight,* flight during the hours of darkness. □ **noche**
nil [nil] *n.* nothing/zero: *the score was one goal to nil/one - nil.* □ **cero**
nimble ['nimbl] *adj.* agile/fast-moving; physically fit and alert: *dancers need nimble feet; the old lady was still very nimble.* □ **vivo**
nimbly *adv.* in an expert way: *she sewed nimbly while talking.* □ **ágilmente**
nincompoop ['ninkəmpuːp] *n.* silly person/fool. □ **lelo; memo**
nine [nain] number 9: *nine sheep; he's nine* (*years old*); *come to see us at nine* (*o'clock*). □ **nueve**
nine times out of ten, in most cases. □ **el noventa por ciento de las veces**
dressed up to the nines, (*informal*) wearing your most elaborate clothes. □ **de punta en blanco**
possession is nine tenths of the law, it is easy to claim ownership of something which is already in your possession. □ **la posesión es prácticamente tuya**
ninepins *n. pl.* skittles. □ **juego de bolos**
to go down like ninepins: *they went down like ninepins,* they fell down/caught the disease very easily. □ **cayeron como moscas**
nineteen number 19: *he is nineteen* (*years old*); *the nineteen sixteen train,* the train which leaves at 19.16. □ **diecinueve/diez y nueve**

the nineteen hundreds, the years after 1900. □ **en los años de 1900**
nineteenth, 19th *adj.* referring to nineteen: *the nineteenth of January (January 19th).* □ **decimonoveno; el diecinueve**
the nineteenth century, period from 1800 to 1899. □ **el siglo diecinueve**
the nineteenth hole, (*informal*) the bar in a golf club. □ **el bar del club**
ninetieth 90th *adj.* referring to ninety: *his ninetieth birthday.* □ **nonagésimo; su noventa cumpleaños**
ninety number 90: *he's ninety (years old).* □ **noventa**
in the nineties, (i) *she's in her nineties,* she is between 90 and 99 years old. □ **está en los noventa**
(ii) between '90 and '99 in a century. □ **decenio de los años 90**
ninth, 9th *adj.* referring to nine: *the ninth of May (May 9th); the ninth day of the holiday.* □ **noveno; el nueve de**
the ninth century, period from 800 to 899. □ **el siglo nueve**
nip [nip] *n.* **1** small amount of alcohol: *a nip of whisky.* □ **traguito**
2 short sharp bite/pinch: *the dog got in a nip at his heels.* □ **mordisco**
a nip in the air, a sudden/sharp burst of cold weather. □ **un frío repentino**
■ *v.* (*he nipped*) **1** to bite/to pinch sharply or suddenly: *the crab nipped his fingers.* □ **pellizcar**
2 (*informal*) to go out very quickly/for a short time: *the thief nipped out quickly; I'll nip round to the shop.* □ **pirarse**
nipper *n.* (*informal*) small child. □ **chiquillo**
nippy *adj.* (*informal*) agile/fast-moving. □ **rápido**
nipple ['nipl] *n.* **1** small projection on the tip of a breast from which, in females, the mother's milk comes. □ **pezón**
2 projection/bump on a surface: *a nipple formed on blown glass.* □ **protuberancia**
3 small hole in a machine for greasing. □ **pezón de engrase**
nit [nit] *n.* **1** egg of a flea. □ **liendre**
2 (*slang*) idiot. □ **imbécil**
nit-picking *n:* (*informal*) petty criticism/finding small faults to criticise. □ **quisquilloso**
nitwit *n.* (*informal*) idiot. □ **imbécil**
nitrogen ['naitrədʒən] *n.* (*chemical element:* N) gas which makes up four-fifths of the atmosphere. □ **nitrógeno**
nitrate *n.* combination of nitrogen and oxygen: *nitrates are used as soil fertilizers.* □ **nitrato**
nitric acid *n.* acid containing nitrogen. □ **ácido nítrico**
nitrous *adj.* containing nitrogen: *nitrous oxide is known as laughing gas.* □ **nitroso**
nitty-gritty [niti'griti] *n.* (*informal*) basic details (of an argument). □ **el quid (de la cuestión)**
no [nou] *n.* and *adv.* showing the negative/opposite of yes: *I won't take no for an answer; two noes don't make a yes.* □ **no**
the noes have it, most people have voted against what was proposed. □ **hay mayoría de votos en contra**
■ *adj.* none of/not any of: *there's no butter left; no reply was given; it's no distance,* not at all far/a very short distance away; *no surrender.* □ **no**
it's no joke, not funny but serious. □ **en serio**
no admission, entrance not allowed. □ **no se permite la entrada**
no way, (*informal*) certainly not. □ **ni hablar**
■ *adv.* not; not at all: *I'm no better than he is; he is no longer there.* □ **no**
no sooner said than done, something was done immediately. □ **dicho y hecho**
to be no more: *he's no more,* he is dead. □ **está muerto**
nobble ['nɔbl] *v.* (*informal*) to give drugs to (a horse) to prevent it running well in a race; to try to influence (someone). □ **drogar; sobornar (a alguien)**
noble ['noubl] *n.* person of high rank by title or birth: *the nobles paid their taxes to the king.* □ **noble**
■ *adj.* of high rank/dignified; worthy of praise/splendid: *the rescue was a noble deed; the play featured families of noble birth.* □ **noble**
nobility [nə'biliti] *n.* **1** titled members of society/the aristocracy. □ **nobleza**
2 high-mindedness. □ **hidalguía**
nobleman *n.* (*pl. noblemen*) noble. □ **noble**
noble-mindedness *n.* high-mindedness/worthy thoughts. □ **nobleza**
nobly *adv.* in a noble fashion/heroically: *she coped nobly in the emergency.* □ **noblemente**
nobody ['noubədi] *n.* ***a nobody,*** a person of no importance. □ **un don nadie**
■ *pron.* no one/no person: *nobody is perfect; there's nobody there; I saw nobody.* □ **nadie**
nocturnal [nɔk'tə:nl] *adj.* referring to the night; (animals which are) most active at night: *owls are nocturnal birds.* □ **nocturno**
nocturne ['nɔktə:n] *n.* painting/piece of music conveying a feeling of night. □ **escena nocturna (pintura); nocturno (música)**
nod [nɔd] *n.* **1** forward movement of the head as a greeting/as a sign of agreement: *he gave me a nod.* □ **saludo con la cabeza, asentimiento**
2 *it went through **on the nod,*** (*informal*) it was agreed without any discussion. □ **quedó aprobado sin discusión**
■ *v.* (*he nodded*) to show agreement/to give permission/to greet by a forward movement of the head: *she nodded/she nodded her head; he nodded agreement.* □ **asentir con la cabeza**
to nod off, to fall asleep. □ **quedarse dormido**
a nodding acquaintance, someone you know only slightly. □ **un conocido de vista**
node [noud] *n.* **1** place where leaves grow from a plant's stem. □ **nudo**
2 knob on a root/branch/human joint: *rheumatic nodes appear on stiff joints.* □ **nodo**
nodal *adj.* central/at the point where lines meet. □ **nodal**
nodule ['nɔdju:l] *n.* small node. □ **nódulo**
Noel [nou'el] *n.* Christmas. □ **Navidad**
noise [nɔiz] *n.* loud (usually unpleasant) sound: *don't make so much noise!* □ **ruido**
to make a noise about something, to make a fuss/to complain. □ **quejarse mucho de**
a big noise, (*informal*) an important person. □ **un pez gordo**
■ *v. **to noise abroad,*** to make public/to spread the news. □ **divulgar**
noiseless *adj.* without any sound: *if only aircraft were noiseless!* □ **silencioso**
noiselessly *adv.* in a silent way: *the thief crept away noiselessly.* □ **silenciosamente**
noisily *adv.* in a noisy/loud way: *he burst in noisily.* □ **ruidosamente**
noisy *adj.* loud: *noisy behaviour is not tolerated.* □ **ruidoso**
nomad ['noumæd] *adj.* and *n.* (member) of a wandering tribe with no fixed home: *a desert nomad takes his tent with him; nomad tribes.* □ **nómada**

nomadic [nou'mædik] *adj.* not staying in one place/travelling: *pop groups are almost nomadic.* □ **nómada**
no-man's-land ['noumænzlænd] *n.* territory between two armies which belongs to neither side. □ **tierra de nadie**
nomenclature [nə'menklətʃə] *n.* (*formal*) system of naming: *medical nomenclature; botanical nomenclature is based on Latin.* □ **nomenclatura**
nominal ['nɔminl] *adj.* **1** referring to names: *the nominal roll of electors.* □ **nominal**
2 in name rather than in fact. □ **sólo de nombre**
3 *a nominal fee was charged,* a very small amount of money/a token payment. □ **se cobró una suma simbólica**
nominally *adv.* in name rather than in fact: *he is nominally in charge.* □ **nominalmente**
nominate ['nɔmineit] *v.* to name/to propose: *he was nominated as chairman; seven election candidates were nominated.* □ **designar**
nominations [nɔmi'neiʃnz] *n. pl.* proposed/suggested names: *the list of nominations was closed,* no more names were allowed to be proposed. □ **candidaturas**
nominee [nɔmi'niː] *n.* person who is nominated. □ **candidato**
non- [nɔn] *prefix meaning* not/the opposite. □ **no, in-**
nonagenarian [nɔnədʒə'nriən] *adj.* and *n.* (person) who is between 90 and 99 years old. □ **nonagenario**
non-aggression [nɔnə'greʃn] *n.* agreement not to engage in war: *a non-aggression pact was signed.* □ **no agresión**
non-alcoholic [nɔnælkə'hɔlik] *adj.* not intoxicating/not containing alcohol: *soft drinks are non-alcoholic.* □ **sin alcohol**
non-aligned [nɔnə'laind] *adj.* (country) which is not linked to a large and powerful bloc of countries: *non-aligned nations.* □ **no alineado**
non-alignment *n.* policy of not linking to one of the powerful blocs of countries. □ **neutralismo**
nonchalant ['nɔnʃələnt] *adj.* casual/unexcited. □ **indiferente**
nonchalance *n.* being calm/unmoved: *the accused assumed an air of nonchalance in court.* □ **indiferencia, aplomo**
nonchalantly *adv.* in a calm way: *he strolled nonchalantly through the excited crowd.* □ **con aplomo**
non-combatant [nɔn'kɔmbətənt] *adj.* and *n.* (person) who does not fight: civilian/priest, etc., attached to an army. □ **no combatiente**
non-commissioned [nɔnkə'miʃnd] *adj.* ***non-commissioned officer,*** soldier of a lower rank than a commissioned officer. □ **suboficial**
non-committal [nɔnkə'mitl] *adj.* not favouring a definite course of action/not agreeing with either side in an argument: *his non-committal replies provoked further questions.* □ **que no se compromete a nada**
nonconformist [nɔnkən'fɔːmist] *n.* person who does not act in the same way as most people/who does not hold the views of the established church. □ **inconformista**
■ *adj.* not conforming to the established church/generally not in agreement with conventional viewpoints: *he was criticized for his nonconformist behaviour.* □ **disidente**
nondescript ['nɔndiskript] *adj.* very ordinary/without individual qualities. □ **mediocre**
none [nʌn] *pron.* **1** not any (of): *none of this concerns me; a little money is better than none at all.* □ **nada**
none of your cheek! don't be rude. □ **¡no seas grosero!**
2 no person/no one: *none of them left.* □ **ninguno**
■ *adv.* (*used with* ***the*** *and comparative or* ***too***) not at all: *the salary is none too good; he was none the worse for his fall.* □ **el sueldo no es nada bueno; no estaba peor por...**
nonentity [nɔ'nentiti] *n.* person of no importance. □ **nulidad**
nonexistent [nɔnig'zistənt] *adj.* not having any existence in fact/not real: *nonexistent fears and worries.* □ **inexistente**
non-fiction ['nɔnfikʃn] *n.* (*no pl.*) books which are not fiction/which are factual: *the non-fiction section of the library includes books on travel and cookery.* □ **ensayo**
non-iron [nɔn'aiən] *adj.* not needing ironing: *a non-iron shirt.* □ **que no necesita plancha**
non-payment [nɔn'peimənt] *n.* failing to pay what is due: *he was expelled from the club for non-payment of his subscription.* □ **falta de pago**
non-plussed [nɔn'plʌst] *adj.* puzzled/confused. □ **anonadado**
non-refundable [nɔnri'fʌndəbl] *adj.* which will not be refunded: *non-refundable deposit.* □ **no reembolsable**
non-resident [nɔn'rezidənt] *adj.* and *n.* (person) not living in/not staying very long in a place: *the hotel doesn't cater for non-residents.* □ **no residente**
a non-resident's work permit, permit which allows someone from another country to work. □ **permiso de trabajo para extranjeros**
non-returnable [nɔnri'təːnəbl] *adj.* not to be given/taken back: *used or damaged goods are non-returnable.* □ **que no se cambia**
non-returnable bottle, bottle on which there is no deposit and which the manufacturers do not want back. □ **casco no retornable**
nonsense ['nɔnsəns] *n.* foolish ideas/ridiculous behaviour: *don't talk nonsense! nonsense - I'm quite right.* □ **tonterías**
no nonsense!, behave properly! □ **¡pórtate bien!**
nonsensical [nɔn'sensikl] *adj.* absurd: *nonsensical dreams of power and riches.* □ **disparatado**
non sequitur [nɔn'sekwitə] *n.* phrase/word which does not follow logically from what has gone before; conclusion drawn incorrectly from the evidence. □ **conclusión errónea**
non-skid [nɔn'skid] *adj.* which prevents skidding: *non-skid road surfaces.* □ **antideslizante**
non-smoker ['nɔnsmoukə] *n.* **1** person who does not smoke: *these seats are for non-smokers only.* □ **no fumador**
2 place where smoking is not allowed: *the railway compartment was a non-smoker.* □ **departamento de no fumadores**
non-smoking *adj.* where smoking is not allowed: *non-smoking area.* □ **donde está prohibido fumar**
non-starter [nɔn'stɑːtə] *n.* **1** horse which is not ready to start at the beginning of a race. □ **caballo retirado**
2 project/plan which is never going to be accepted. □ **nonato**
non-stick ['nɔnstik] *adj.* covered with a substance which prevents food from sticking when cooking: *a non-stick frying pan.* □ **antiadherente**
non-stop ['nɔnstɔp] *adj.* not stopping/travelling directly from point of departure to terminus: *non-stop train.* □ **directo, sin paradas**
■ *adv.* ceaselessly/without stopping: *the train goes*

from London to Glasgow non-stop; she talks non-stop. □ **directamente; sin parar**
non-union [nɔn'juːniən] *adj.* not belonging to a union: *non-union labour.* □ **no sindicado**
non-violence [nɔn'vaiələns] *n.* absence of physical violence/of aggression: *a policy of non-violence.* □ **no violencia**
noodles ['nuːdlz] *n. pl.* strips of paste for cooking. □ **fideos (redondos); tallarines (planos)**
nook [nuk] *n.* small hiding place. □ **escondrijo**
in every nook and cranny, in every little hole and corner. □ **en cada esquina**
noon [nuːn] *n.* midday/12 o'clock: *the sun is hottest at noon.* □ **mediodía**
noonday *n. **the noonday sun,*** the sun at noon. □ **el sol de mediodía**
no one ['nouwʌn] *pron.* no person: *there's no one there; no one came.* □ **nadie**
noose [nuːs] *n.* rope knotted to form a loop which can be tightened by pulling. □ **nudo**
nor [nɔː] *conj.* **1** (*usually followed by verb then subject*) not either/and not: *nor was this all; nor does it seem true.* □ **tampoco**
2 ***neither... nor,*** not one... and not the other: *neither he nor you must go.* □ **ni... ni...**
norm [nɔːm] *n.* **1** normal/standard pattern: *conforming to the norm of human behaviour.* □ **norma**
2 *temperature above the norm,* above normal/above average. □ **...por encima de lo normal**
normal ['nɔːml] *adj.* usual/regular/expected: *wet weather is normal in winter.* □ **normal**
normality *n.* being normal/not having unusual features: *the end of the war saw a return to normality.* □ **normalidad**
normally *adv.* in the usual way: *I'm normally here at six.* □ **normalmente**
north [nɔːθ] *n.* one of the points of the compass, the direction to the right of the equator when you are facing the setting sun: *the north of England; snow from the north.* □ **norte**
■ *adv.* towards the north: *to travel north; to face north.* □ **al norte**
■ *adj.* referring to the north: *the north coast; the North Sea; the North Pole; North America.* □ **norte; (del) Norte**
north wind, wind which blows from the north. □ **viento del norte**
northbound *adj.* going towards the north. □ **que se dirige hacia el norte**
north-east *n.* direction half-way between east and north: *the north-east of the country.* □ **nordeste**
north-eastern *adj.* referring to the north-east: *the north-eastern railway.* □ **del nordeste**
northerly ['nɔːðəli] *adj.* and *n.* in/to/from the north; (wind) from the north: *in a northerly direction.* □ **al/del norte**
northern *adj.* referring to the north: *northern latitudes; Northern Ireland.* □ **del norte; del Norte**
northerner *n.* person who lives in/comes from the north. □ **norteño**
northward *adj.* towards the north. □ **hacia el norte**
northwards *adv.* towards the north: *the train sped northwards.* □ **hacia el norte**
north-west *n.* direction half-way between west and north: *people of the north-west.* □ **noroeste**
north-western *adj.* referring to the north-west: *north-western valleys.* □ **del noroeste**
Norway ['nɔːwei] *n.* country in Scandinavia. □ **Noruega**
Norwegian [nɔː'wiːdʒən] *adj.* referring to Norway. □ **noruego**
■ *n.* **1** person from Norway. □ **noruego**
2 language spoken in Norway. □ **noruego**
nose [nouz] *n.* **1** part of the face used for breathing in air and smelling: *he has a red nose; dogs have damp noses.* □ **nariz**
2 ***as plain as the nose on your face,*** very obvious. □ **claro como el agua**
3 ***to speak through your nose,*** speak as if your nose is blocked. □ **hablar nasalmente**
4 ***to pay through the nose (for),*** (*informal*) to pay far too much (for). □ **pagar un dineral**
5 *I did it* ***under his very nose,*** did it right in front of him but he didn't notice. □ **lo hice delante de sus narices**
6 ***to poke your nose into,*** to interfere unasked. □ **meter las narices donde no te llaman**
7 ***to cut off your nose to spite your face,*** to do something when you are angry which in fact harms you. □ **vengarse con perjuicio para sí mismo**
8 ***follow your nose,*** go straight on. □ **seguir recto**
9 ***to keep someone's nose to the grindstone,*** to make someone work hard all the time. □ **hacer trabajar a alguien como una bestia de carga**
10 ***to look down your nose at someone,*** to regard someone else as inferior. □ **mirar por encima del hombro**
11 ***to turn up your nose at something,*** to reject something as not good enough. □ **despreciar**
12 good sense of smell: *the dog has a nose for rabbits.* □ **olfato**
13 *that policeman has a good nose for crime,* an instinct for detecting that a crime has been committed. □ **...tiene buen olfato para...**
14 front end of a vehicle: *Concorde's nose is very pointed; the cars were parked nose to tail.* □ **morro**
■ *v.* **1** to discover by smell: *the dog nosed out the pheasants.* □ **olfatear**
2 (*informal*) to detect/to discover: *the facts were nosed out.* □ **descubrir**
3 to push in: *the boat nosed its way into the harbour.* □ **abrirse paso hacia**
nose about, nose around *v.* to look/to search around: *he was nosing about all day,* being inquisitive/searching about. □ **curiosear; husmear**
nosebag *n.* bag containing food hung around an animal's neck: *the horse munched food from its nosebag.* □ **morral; cebadera (del caballo)**
nosebleed *n.* flow of blood from the nose: *to have a nosebleed.* □ **hemorragia nasal**
nose cone *n.* round pointed part at the top of a rocket. □ **morro**
nosedive *n.* steep downward dive of an aircraft: *as the engine cut out the aircraft went into a nosedive.* □ **caída en picado**
■ *v.* to dive down steeply front first: *the aircraft nosedived and crash-landed.* □ **caer en picado**
nosegay *n.* small bunch of flowers. □ **ramillete**
nosey, nosy *adj.* (*informal*) curious/interested in the affairs of other people: *our nosy neighbour peered out at our visitors.* □ **fisgón**
a nosy parker, very inquisitive person. □ **metomentodo**
nosh [nɔʃ] *n.* (*slang*) food. □ **papeo**
nostalgia [nɔ'stældʒiə] *n.* longing for/sentimental recollection of the past: *overcome with nostalgia for his homeland; she remembered her childhood with nostalgia.* □ **nostalgia**
nostalgic *adj.* encouraging nostalgia: *a nostalgic song.* □ **nostálgico**
nostril ['nɔstrl] *n.* one of the two holes in the nose to admit air and smells. □ **ventana de la nariz**

not [nɔt] *adv.* **1** (used with verbs to make the action negative; short form **n't**): *he will not come/he won't come; she is not there/she isn't there; you understand, don't you?* □ **no**
2 (used to make negative words/phrases/sentences): *not at all; I think not,* I don't think so; *good or not, it's done; why not? not negotiable; not knowing; not included.* □ **no**
3 (providing emphasis by a form of contrast): *not one but many; not yours but mine.* □ **no**
4 (used to show the opposite): *not a few,* many; *not too well,* badly; *not sorry to leave,* glad to leave; *not without reason,* with good reason. □ **no**
not half *adv.* (*informal*) extremely: *I wasn't half glad to see him; was he angry? - not half!* □ **muy mucho**
notable ['noutəbl] *adj.* worth noticing; large: *a notable quantity of stolen goods; notable scientists conducted advanced research.* □ **notable**
■ *n.* important person. □ **notable**
notability [noutə'biliti] *n.* **1** being important. □ **notabilidad**
2 notable/important person: *notabilities from various countries attended the conference.* □ **personaje**
notably *adv.* significantly/particularly: *a task notably well done; notably absent from the meeting.* □ **notablemente**
notary (public) ['noutəri ('pʌblik)] *n.* person who has authority to see that legal documents are correctly written and who witnesses their signing. □ **notario**
notation [nou'teiʃn] *n.* system of symbols used to show notes in music/to show mathematical signs. □ **notación**
notch [nɔtʃ] *n.* small cut (usually V-shaped) used to mark/to record: *he made notches on the door to show how the children had grown; fit the shelves into the notches.* □ **muesca**
■ *v.* **1** to mark with notches: *he notched the wood with a saw.* □ **hacer una muesca en**
2 *he notched up more victories,* he added to his total of victories. □ **apuntarse**
note [nout] *n.* **1** musical sound: *he can't sing a note.* □ **nota**
2 written sign which indicates a musical sound. □ **nota**
3 key on a piano, etc.: *to play only the black notes.* □ **tecla**
to strike the right note, to play the correct note/to provide the appropriate tone/atmosphere/words in a particular situation. □ **dar en el clavo; acertar**
4 very short letter; very brief written/printed document: *he made notes for his speech; make a note of that.* □ **tomó notas para su...**
5 banknote/piece of paper money: *a five pound note.* □ **billete de banco**
6 notice/attention/importance: *worthy of note; a historian of note.* □ **digno de atención; un historiador notable**
to take note of, to pay attention to/to be aware of. □ **fijarse**
7 indication: *a note of despair came into her voice.* □ **nota**
■ *v.* **1** to write down: *he noted the event in his diary.* □ **anotar**
2 to pay attention to: *his reluctance was noted; I shall note his behaviour.* □ **tenerse en cuenta**
notebook *n.* book in which you write notes. □ **cuaderno**
notecase *n.* wallet or container for banknotes. □ **billetero**
noted *adj.* famous/well-known: *a noted musician.* □ **célebre**
notepaper *n.* writing paper for letters. □ **papel de cartas**
noteworthy *adj.* deserving attention: *a noteworthy deed.* □ **digno de mención**
nothing ['nʌθiŋ] *n.* **1** not anything: *nothing could be simpler; nothing of any importance happened.* □ **nada**
to say nothing about, to keep silent about. □ **no decir nada...**
there's nothing in it, no truth in it. □ **es falso**
to make something out of nothing, to exaggerate something. □ **exagerar**
nothing doing!, (*informal*) I refuse. □ **¡ni hablar!**
to get something for nothing, get something free. □ **sacar algo gratis**
there's nothing else for it, there's no alternative. □ **no hay más remedio que**
to think nothing of it, make it seem easy: *he thinks nothing of cycling to work every day.* □ **tener por fácil; para él no tiene importancia ...**
to have nothing to do with, not to associate with/not to become involved in. □ **no tener nada que ver con**
it's nothing to do with *you,* not your concern. □ **no tener nada que ver con**
to come to nothing, be unsuccessful. □ **quedar en nada**
2 (*used with an adj. following*) not anything: *nothing new appeared; there was nothing more to be said; nothing much happened.* □ **nada nuevo...; nada más...**
3 (used as a comparison/to suggest something inferior): *that's nothing to what I saw.* □ **eso no es nada comparado con lo que yo...**
■ *adv.* in no way/not at all: *nothing like as grand.* □ **en absoluto**
nothing daunted, not intimidated. □ **sin inmutarse**
nothingness *n.* void/nothing at all. □ **nada**
notice ['noutis] *n.* **1** advance information/warning: *he had to leave with only ten minutes' notice; wait until further notice; it was all done at short notice; he had to give a week's notice before he resigned.* □ **aviso**
notice to quit, legal document telling someone to leave premises. □ **aviso de desalojo**
2 attention/awareness: *he never takes any notice when I speak; babies soon sit up and take notice.* □ **interés; nunca presta atención...**
3 written account/announcement; written information: *notices are displayed on the staff notice board.* □ **aviso**
4 review: *good notices in the press help to sell more tickets for the show.* □ **reseña; crítica**
■ *v.* to pay attention to: *she noticed the stain; it's nice to be noticed.* □ **darse cuenta de**
noticeable *adj.* easily seen: *the change in her appearance was most noticeable; the stain isn't very noticeable.* □ **notable; no se nota mucho**
noticeboard *n.* flat piece of wood, etc., on a wall, on which notices can be pinned. □ **tablón de anuncios**
notify ['noutifai] *v.* to announce/to declare/to advise/to inform: *the parents were notified as soon as their child was found; we shall notify them of our intentions; to notify the police about a burglary.* □ **avisar, notificar**
notifiable *adj.* which has to be notified to the authorities. □ **de declaración obligatoria**
notification [noutifi'keiʃn] *n.* formal information: *I require written notification of your intentions; advance notification is essential.* □ **notificación**

notion ['nouʃn] *n.* **1** vague awareness/idea/thought: *he had little notion of what had been said; she has no notion of loyalty; I originally had no notion of attending.* □ **noción**
2 ***notions,*** *Amer.* shop or department selling buttons/thread/ribbons, etc. □ **mercería**
notional *adj.* vague but assumed to be correct: *put down a notional sum for expenses.* □ **aproximado**
notorious [nou'tɔ:riəs] *adj.* well known (usually for doing something bad): *a notorious gambler; a notorious record for crime.* □ **famoso**
notoriety [noutə'raiəti] *n.* bad/unfavourable reputation: *the gangster achieved notoriety.* □ **mala fama**
notoriously *adv.* unfavourably significant: *the climbers were notoriously ill equipped; notoriously cruel deeds.* □ **manifiestamente**
notwithstanding [nɔtwiθ'stændiŋ] *prep.* (*formal*) despite: *he went out notwithstanding my instructions not to.* □ **a pesar de**
■ *adv.* all the same/anyway. □ **sin embargo**
nougat ['nu:gɑ:] *n.* type of white sweet made with nuts, honey and egg whites. □ **turrón**
nought [nɔ:t] *n.* zero/nothing; the sign 0: *nought has no value as a mathematical sign.* □ **cero**
to come to nought, be unsuccessful. □ **fracasar**
noughts and crosses, game for two players where each puts a cross or a nought in one of nine squares in turn, the object being to be the first to make a line of three noughts or three crosses. □ **tres en raya**
noun [naun] *n.* word used as a name of a person or thing. □ **nombre**
nourish ['nʌriʃ] *v.* **1** to provide (something) with food so that it will grow: *plants are nourished by salts in the soil.* □ **alimentar**
2 to keep alive (ideas/feelings): *nourishing hopes for the future.* □ **abrigar; abrigando esperanzas...**
nourishing *adj.* providing nourishment: *nourishing food.* □ **nutritivo**
nourishment *n.* food which enables plants/animals to grow: *proteins provide us with most nourishment.* □ **alimento**
nova ['nouvə] *n.* star which suddenly becomes much brighter and then fades away. □ **nova**
novel ['nɔvl] *n.* long fictional story in the form of a book: *Charles Dickens wrote many novels.* □ **novela**
■ *adj.* new/original: *he has some novel ideas about food.* □ **nuevo**
novelette [nɔvə'let] *n.* short novel with no literary merit. □ **novela sin valor**
novelist *n.* person who writes novels. □ **novelista**
novelty *n.* **1** new/original thing: *cars were a novelty in 1900.* □ **novedad**
2 small/unusual toy or trinket. □ **novedad**
3 newness: *I am attracted by the novelty of the idea.* □ **originalidad**
November [nə'vembə] *n.* eleventh month of the year: *today is November 5th; her birthday is on November 15th/is in November.* □ **noviembre**
novice ['nɔvis] *n.* **1** beginner/someone who is inexperienced: *I am a novice at hang-gliding.* □ **novato**
2 person who is intending to join a religious order but who has not yet taken the vows. □ **novicio**
now [nau] *adv.* **1** at this moment: *I can see him coming now; now or never; now that I know.* □ **ahora**
2 immediately/beginning from this time: *he won't be long now; it's going to begin now.* □ **ahora**
3 in the immediate past: *it happened just now.* □ **ahora**
4 (*when relating events*) then/next/by that time: *now it happened that; all was now ready.* □ **entonces**
now and then, from time to time. □ **de cuando en cuando**
■ *interjection showing* warning/criticism: *now, that was silly enough but this is worse; come on now! now then! well now!* □ **vamos (que); no es para tanto**
■ *conj.* as a result of/since: *now I'm older I see things differently; now you've reminded me.* □ **ahora que**
■ *n.* this time; the present time: *in a week from now; he should have arrived by now; until now/up to now.* □ **dentro de una semana; debería haber llegado ya; hasta ahora**
nowadays ['nauədeiz] *adv.* at the present day/in these modern times: *everything is different nowadays; nowadays everyone watches television.* □ **hoy en día**
nowhere ['nouwεə] *adv.* not in/at/to any place: *she was nowhere to be seen.* □ **por ninguna parte**
nowhere near *completion,* far from being finished. □ **ni mucho menos está acabado**
to get nowhere: *I got nowhere,* I was totally unsuccessful in what I was trying to do. □ **no conseguí nada**
noxious ['nɔkʃəs] *adj.* unpleasant/harmful: *noxious gas; noxious exhaust fumes of cars.* □ **nocivo**
nozzle ['nɔzl] *n.* special fitting at the end of a pipe or hose for controlling what comes out: *by adjusting the nozzle you can get either a spray or a jet of water.* □ **boquilla**
nth [enθ] *adj.* **1** of a very great number: *for the nth time.* □ **por enésima vez**
2 *all the rules were observed* ***to the nth degree,*** to a very great extent. □ **...al máximo**
nuance ['nju:ɑ:ns] *n.* shade of meaning. □ **matiz**
nub [nʌb] *n.* central point: *the nub of the matter.* □ **el quid de la cuestión**
nubile ['nju:bail] *adj.* (*of a young woman*) very attractive physically. □ **atractiva**
nucleus ['nju:kliəs] *n.* **1** vital central part around which things collect: *each living cell has a nucleus; a few rare books formed the nucleus of his collection.* □ **núcleo**
2 central part of an atom. □ **núcleo**
nuclear *adj.* concerned with/belonging to a nucleus, especially of an atom. □ **nuclear**
nuclear reactor, device for producing energy. □ **reactor nuclear**
nuclear power, power from atomic energy. □ **energía nuclear**
nuclear submarine, driven by nuclear power. □ **submarino atómico**
nude [nju:d] *n.* **1** person without clothes/naked person. □ **desnudo**
2 ***in the nude,*** naked. □ **desnudo**
■ *adj.* naked/bare: *statues of nude figures; nude bathing is allowed on some beaches.* □ **desnudo**
nudism *n.* belief in the physical and mental advantages of going about naked. □ **nudismo**
nudist *n.* person who believes in going about naked. □ **nudista**
nudist colony, club/camp for those who wish to go about naked. □ **colonia de nudistas**
nudity *n.* not wearing any clothes/nakedness. □ **desnudez**
nudge [nʌdʒ] *n.* slight push/prod with the elbow to attract someone's attention: *a quick nudge woke him up in time; he gave me a nudge.* □ **codazo**
■ *v.* to attract someone's attention, usually by pushing with the elbow: *he nudged me when it was my turn.* □ **dar un codazo a**
nugatory ['nju:gətri] *adj.* (*formal*) worthless; useless. □ **insignificante**
nugget ['nʌgit] *n.* lump of gold in its natural state.

□ **pepita**
nugget of information, piece of useful information. □ **una noticia valiosa**
nuisance ['nju:sns] *n.* something/someone annoying or disagreeable: *that child's a nuisance; what a nuisance, I've forgotten my key!* □ **fastidio**
public nuisance, action which bothers other people in such a way as to be against the law. □ **perjuicio público**
null [nʌl] *adj.* without significance/cancelled out. □ **nulo**
null and void, no longer valid/having lost its previous importance. □ **nulo y sin valor**
nullify *v.* to cancel out/to make invalid: *the old contract was nullified by the new one; marriages can be nullified.* □ **anular**
nullity *n.* nothingness/something that is null. □ **nulidad**
numb [nʌm] *adj.* without feeling or sensation/unable to move: *his fingers were numb with cold; numb with fear.* □ **entumecido; petrificado de miedo**
■ *v.* to make incapable of movement or feeling: *the victim was numbed with shock; anaesthetic numbs the brain.* □ **paralizar**
numbness *n.* having no feeling or sensation/being incapable of action: *she suffered from numbness of the legs.* □ **parálisis**
numbskull *n.* (*informal*) stupid person. □ **lelo**
number ['nʌmbə] *n.* **1** name of a figure; total of objects or persons: *the number four; five in number; one of their number,* one of them: *a car with a registration number 840 PQ.* □ **número**
to take care of number one, (*informal*) to look after yourself/your own interests. □ **mirar por uno**
2 ***numbers,*** many in quantity: *large numbers of people have complained; outvoted by sheer weight of numbers.* □ **grandes cantidades; ...por una cantidad ingente**
3 (*in grammar*) term indicating whether a noun is singular or plural: *learn the gender of a noun and the number.* □ **número**
4 copy of a periodical/a song/a piece of played music: *back numbers of magazines are kept in libraries; try that new number on the piano.* □ **número**
back number, something which is out of date. □ **número atrasado**
his number's up, (*informal*) he's dying. □ **le llegó la hora**
■ *v.* **1** to count/to include among/to total: *I number him among my friends; the crowd numbered several thousand.* □ **contar**
his days are numbered, he hasn't much time to live. □ **sus días están contados**
2 to put a number/figure on: *the rooms are numbered one to ten.* □ **numerar**
numberless *adj.* which cannot be counted: *numberless days to wait; numberless hordes of attackers.* □ **innumerable**
numeral ['nju:mərəl] *n.* actual sign representing a number: *the numerals on the clock face were clearly seen.* □ **número**
Roman numerals, I, II, III, IV, etc. □ **números romanos**
numeracy *n.* ability to calculate mathematically/ability to work out sums. □ **capacidad para el cálculo**
numerate ['nju:mərət] *adj.* able to calculate mathematically: *he's a wonderful writer, but barely numerate.* □ **calculador numérico**
numerical [nju:'merikl] *adj.* referring to number: *in numerical order.* □ **numérico**
numerically *adv.* by/in number: *numerically superior to the opposing army.* □ **numéricamente**
numerous ['nju:mərəs] *adj.* many/a lot of: *numerous people thronged the streets; numerous friends and acquaintances.* □ **numeroso**
numismatics [nju:miz'mætiks] *n.* study of coins. □ **numismática**
numismatist [nju:'mizmətist] *n.* person who collects/studies coins. □ **numismático**
nun [nʌn] *n.* woman who is a member of a religious order living in a separate community or convent. □ **monja**
nunlike *adj.* very calm/good/restrained: *a nunlike expression on her face.* □ **monjil**
nunnery *n.* convent/community where nuns live. □ **convento de monjas**
nuptial ['nʌpʃl] *adj.* (*formal*) referring to marriage/wedding ceremonies: *nuptial vows.* □ **nupcial**
nuptials *n. pl.* wedding: *after the nuptials came the party.* □ **nupcias**
nurse [nə:s] *n.* (usually female) person trained and employed to look after the sick: *a male nurse.* □ **enfermera, enfermero**
night nurse, nurse who is on duty at night. □ **enfermera de noche**
■ *v.* **1** to look after sick people: *his wife nursed him back to health.* □ **cuidar**
2 to look after: *she's nursing a cold; to nurse tender plants; to nurse a constituency,* to look after the needs of electors in the hope that they will vote for you at the next election. □ **tratar de curar; cuidar; cultivar**
3 to think about/to ponder over: *he's nursing a grievance.* □ **estar dándole vueltas a**
4 to hold close: *to nurse a child on your lap; he nursed his foot in agony.* □ **mecer**
nursemaid *n.* young woman who is paid to look after children. □ **niñera**
nursery *n.* **1** room/building where babies or young children are looked after. □ **cuarto de los niños**
day nursery, place where babies are looked after during the day time. □ **guardería infantil**
nursery rhyme, little poem telling a simple story told or sung to young children. □ **canción infantil**
nursery school, school for very young children. □ **jardín de infancia**
2 place where people are brought up or trained: *this university has been a nursery for many politicians.* □ **cantera**
nursery slopes, gentle slopes where you can learn to ski. □ **pistas de aprendizaje**
3 place where young plants are grown: *tree nursery.* □ **vivero**
nurseryman *n.* (*pl. nurserymen*) man who looks after young plants. □ **encargado del vivero**
nursing *adj.* (person) who nurses/looks after. □ **enfermero**
nursing mother, mother who breast-feeds her baby. □ **lactante**
nursing staff, hospital nurses. □ **personal de enfermería**
nursing home, small (usually private) hospital. □ **clínica**
■ *n.* profession of looking after the sick: *she chose nursing as a career.* □ **enfermería**
nurture ['nə:tʃə] *v.* (*formal*) to protect and bring up carefully. □ **criar**
nut [nʌt] *n.* **1** fruit with an edible centre inside a hard shell: *hazel nut; to crack nuts,* to open the shells to get at the edible centres. □ **nuez; avellana**
a tough nut to crack, (*informal*) a hard person/a dif-

ficult problem. □ **un hueso duro de roer**
2 small metal ring used for tightening a bolt: *wing nut,* nut with two projecting pieces for turning; *nuts and bolts.* □ **tuerca**
3 (*informal*) head. □ **tarro**
off one's nut, mad; insane. □ **faltarle a uno un tornillo**
4 ***nuts about,*** (*informal*) very keen on/enthusiastic about: *she's nuts about chocolates.* □ **se vuelve loca por...**
5 small lump: *nut of butter.* □ **nuez de mantequilla**
■ *v.* ***to go nutting,*** to gather nuts. □ **ir a recoger...**
nutcase *n.* (*informal*) mad person. □ **pirado**
nutcrackers *n. pl.* pincers for cracking nuts. □ **cascanueces**
nutmeg *n.* seed of a tropical tree, used as a spice. □ **nuez moscada**
nutshell *n.* hard outside covering of a nut: *crack the nuts and throw away the nutshells.* □ **cáscara**
in a nutshell, with all the important details given as briefly as possible. □ **en pocas palabras**
nutty *adj.* **1** tasting of/full of nuts: *nutty chocolate bars; nutty flavour.* □ **...con nueces; que sabe a nueces**
2 (*informal*) crazy/very enthusiastic: *she's quite nutty about her boss; nutty on pop music.* □ **loco**
nutriment ['nju:trimənt] *n.* something which nourishes. □ **alimento nutritivo**
nutrient *adj.* and *n.* (food) which feeds/nourishes: *glucose is a nutrient.* □ **nutriente, nutritivo**
nutrition [nju:'triʃn] *n.* giving/receiving of nourishment: *milk is a baby's main source of nutrition.* □ **nutrición**
nutritious [nju:'triʃəs] *adj.* nourishing/providing food which is necessary for growth: *a diet must be balanced and nutritious.* □ **nutritivo**
nutritive ['nju:trətiv] *n.* food which is necessary for growth: *water is not sufficient as a nutritive for the body.* □ **alimento**
■ *adj.* providing food/nourishment: *milk and cheese are nutritive foods.* □ **nutritivo**
nuzzle ['nʌzl] *v.* to press the nose up to/to snuggle up to: *the pony nuzzled my hand; the puppy was nuzzling up to its mother.* □ **acariciar con el hocico**
nylon ['nailɔn] *n.* very tough synthetic material: *a nylon rope; rope made of nylon has tremendous strength.* □ **nailon**
nylons *n. pl.* women's stockings. □ **medias**
nymph [nimf] *n.* **1** young girl; minor goddess. □ **ninfa**
2 young insect, especially young dragonfly. □ **crisálida**
nymphet *n.* sexually desirable young girl. □ **joven atractiva**
nymphomania [nimfə'meiniə] *n.* (*in woman*) uncontrollably strong sexual desire. □ **ninfomanía**
nymphomaniac *n.* woman who has uncontrollable sexual desires. □ **ninfómana**

O,o

O, o [ou] **1** fifteenth letter of the alphabet. □ **O, o**
2 zero/nothing. □ **cero**
oaf [ouf] *n.* stupid/clumsy/unfeeling person: *you great oaf!* □ **zoquete**
oafish *adj.* like an oaf. □ **lerdo**
oak [ouk] *n.* type of large deciduous tree; wood of this tree: *an oak table.* □ **roble**
oak apple *n.* round growth on oak trees caused by an insect. □ **agalla**
oakum ['oukəm] *n.* (*no pl.*) loose pieces of old rope formerly used for stuffing into the seams of wooden ships. □ **estopa**
oar [ɔ:] *n.* long pole with a flat end, used for moving a boat along. □ **remo**
to stick your oar in, (*informal*) to interfere. □ **meter baza en**
oarlock *n. Amer.* rowlock/metal support for an oar. □ **escálamo**
oarsman *n.* (*pl. oarsmen*) person who rows a boat. □ **remero**
oasis [ou'eisis] *n.* (*pl. oases*) **1** place in the desert with water, where plants grow. □ **oasis**
2 place which is pleasantly different from its surroundings: *their house is an oasis of calm.* □ **oasis**
oasthouse ['ousthaus] *n.* building for drying hops. □ **secadero para el lúpulo**
oatcake ['outkeik] *n.* dry biscuit made of oats. □ **torta de avena**
oath [ouθ] *n.* **1** swearing that you are telling the truth: *he said it on oath; to take an oath.* □ **juramento**
2 promise. □ **juramento**
to swear an oath of allegiance, to promise to be faithful. □ **jurar bandera (en el ejército)**
3 swear word: *his conversation is just a string of oaths.* □ **palabrota**
oatmeal ['outmi:l] *n.* coarse flour made from oats. □ **harina de avena**
oats [outs] *n. pl.* cereal plant whose grain is used as food. □ **avena**
to sow one's wild oats: *he sowed his wild oats,* behaved in a very free and unruly way. □ **la corrió bien**
obdurate ['ɔbdjurət] *adj.* stubborn/unyielding/unmoving: *obdurate behaviour.* □ **obstinado**
obduracy *n.* being obdurate. □ **obstinación**
obedience [ə'bi:diəns] *n.* being obedient. □ **obediencia**
obedient *adj.* (person) who does what he is told to do: *obedient child; obedient to the rules.* □ **obediente**
obediently *adv.* in an obedient way. □ **obedientemente**
obelisk ['ɔbəlisk] *n.* four-sided pillar which becomes narrower towards the top. □ **obelisco**
obese [ə'bi:s] *adj.* very fat. □ **obeso**
obesity [ə'bi:siti] *n.* being very fat. □ **obesidad**
obey [ə'bei] *v.* to do what you are told to do (by someone): *he never obeyed his father; you must obey the rules.* □ **obedecer**
obituary [ə'bitjuəri] *n.* written report of someone's death, usually with details of his life. □ **necrología**
obituary column, part of a newspaper which gives reports of deaths. □ **necrológicas**
object ['ɔbdʒekt] *n.* **1** thing. □ **objeto**
object lesson, (i) lesson using an object as a teaching aid. □ **lección práctica**
(ii) something which makes a course of action very clear; *that was an object lesson in how not to run a business.* □ **ejemplo**
2 aim; thing aimed at/purpose: *with this object in mind.* □ **propósito**
3 person/thing to which feeling, etc., is directed: *he was an object of pity.* □ **objeto; él daba lástima**
4 (*in grammar*) noun/pronoun, etc., which follows directly from a verb or preposition: *in 'the dog chased the cat', the word 'cat' is the object of the verb 'chased'.* □ **complemento**
■ *v.* [əb'dʒekt] to refuse to agree to; to express unwillingness towards/disapproval of: *I object to that; he objects to waiting so long.* □ **oponerse**
objection [əb'dʒekʃn] *n.* act of objecting; reason against: *I have no objection to it; to raise an objection; I see no objection to it.* □ **objeción**
objectionable *adj.* **1** causing disapproval: *objectionable course of action.* □ **censurable**
2 (*especially of person*) very unpleasant. □ **molesto**
objective [əb'dʒektiv] *adj.* **1** (*in grammar*) referring to the object: *objective case.* □ **objetivo**
2 referring to the external world. □ **objetivo**
3 considering matters from a general viewpoint and not just your own. □ **objetivo**
■ *n.* **1** aim/object in view: *that's our next objective.* □ **objetivo**
2 lens in a microscope which is nearest to the object being examined. □ **objetivo**
objectively *adv.* in an objective way/without being influenced by your own feelings: *to consider a problem objectively.* □ **objetivamente**
objector *n.* person who objects. □ **objetante**
conscientious objector, person who refuses to join the armed forces because he feels war is wrong. □ **objetor de conciencia**
oblige [ə'blaidʒ] *v.* **1** to make (someone) feel it is their duty to do something: *you're obliged to come; he felt obliged to apologize for his son's behaviour.* □ **obligar**
2 to force (someone) to do something: *he was obliged to leave the country.* □ **obligar**
3 to do something useful for/helpful to (someone): *to oblige a friend; can you oblige me with a light?* □ **hacer un favor**
4 ***to be obliged to someone,*** to owe them gratitude: *I'm most obliged to you.* □ **estarle muy agradecido a uno**
obligate ['ɔbligeit] *v.* to oblige. □ **obligar**
obligation [ɔbli'geiʃn] *n.* **1** duty; legal bond. □ **obligación**
to be under an obligation: *you are under no obligation to buy,* you are not forced to buy. □ **estar obligado**
2 *he couldn't meet his obligations,* he couldn't pay his debts. □ **no pudo cumplir con sus obligaciones**
3 duty to be grateful: *to put someone under an obligation.* □ **obligarle a uno a hacer algo**
obligatory [ə'bligətəri] *adj.* necessary according to rules or laws: *a licence is obligatory.* □ **obligatorio**
obliging *adj.* ready to help. □ **servicial**
obligingly *adv.* in an obliging way. □ **atentamente**
oblique [ə'bli:k] *adj.* **1** at a slant. □ **oblicuo**
oblique angle, angle which is not a right angle. □ **ángulo oblicuo**
2 from the side; not direct: *oblique view; oblique*

reference. □ **oblicuo, indirecto**
obliquely *adv.* in an oblique way. □ **indirectamente**
obliterate [ə'blitəreit] *v.* to wipe out/to destroy: *the picture was obliterated by the ink; the whole village was obliterated in the war.* □ **borrar, destruir**
obliteration [əblitə'reiʃn] *n.* act of obliterating; being obliterated. □ **borradura; eliminación**
oblivion [ə'bliviən] *n.* forgetting totally; being completely forgotten: *state of oblivion; to sink into oblivion.* □ **olvido**
oblivious *adj.* forgetful/unaware: *he is quite oblivious of what is going on.* □ **olvidadizo**
oblong ['ɔblɔŋ] *n.* and *adj.* (referring to a) rectangular shape with two pairs of equal sides, one pair being longer than the other. □ **rectángulo (n.); rectangular (adj.)**
obnoxious [ɔb'nɔkʃəs] *adj.* very unpleasant/offensive. □ **odioso**
oboe ['oubou] *n.* high-pitched musical instrument of the woodwind family. □ **oboe**
oboist *n.* person who plays the oboe. □ **oboísta**
obscene [ɔb'si:n] *adj.* offending moral standards/sensitive feelings; indecent. □ **obsceno**
obscenity [ɔb'seniti] *n.* **1** state or quality of being obscene. □ **obscenidad**
2 obscene word: *he let out a string of obscenities.* □ **grosería**
obscure [əb'skjuə] *adj.* **1** (*of place*) dark/gloomy: *obscure corner.* □ **oscuro**
2 not clear: *obscure argument.* □ **oscuro**
3 not well-known: *obscure poet.* □ **desconocido**
■ *v.* to hide, especially by covering: *clouds obscured the sun.* □ **oscurecer**
obscurely *adv.* in an obscure way. □ **oscuramente**
obscurity *n.* being obscure: *he was rescued from obscurity by the exhibition.* □ **oscuridad**
obsequious [əb'si:kwiəs] *adj.* too humble; showing too much respect for/obedience to (someone): *obsequious manner.* □ **servil**
obsequiously *adv.* in an obsequious way. □ **servilmente**
obsequiousness *n.* being obsequious. □ **servilismo**
observe [əb'zə:v] *v.* **1** to follow/to obey (a law/rule/custom). □ **observar**
2 to watch/to look (at): *to observe the moon.* □ **observar**
3 to notice: *I observed a dark stain on the paper.* □ **notar**
4 to remark/to note: *'in fact', he observed, 'it's never stopped raining.'* □ **decir**
observance *n.* (act of) observing: *observance of the rules; religious observance.* □ **observancia**
observant *adj.* noticing (many details): *he is very observant.* □ **observador**
observation [ɔbzə'veiʃn] *n.* **1** (act of) observing. □ **observación**
to escape observation, to avoid being noticed. □ **pasar inadvertido**
to put someone under observation, to keep a detailed watch, as for symptoms of a disease. □ **poner en observación**
2 calculation of position of a ship: *take an observation.* □ **observación**
3 remark: *he made an observation about the current situation.* □ **observación**
observatory *n.* place from which stars and planets can be watched. □ **observatorio**
observer *n.* person who attends and watches (especially without taking part). □ **observador**
obsess [ɔb'ses] *v.* to fill someone's thoughts: *he was obsessed with the idea.* □ **obsesionar(se)**
obsession [əb'seʃn] *n.* idea/subject which fills your mind constantly. □ **obsesión**
obsessive *adj.* caused by an obsession: *he has an obsessive interest in bees.* □ **obsesivo**
obsolete ['ɔbsəli:t] *adj.* no longer in general use: *obsolete word; obsolete custom.* □ **obsoleto**
obsolescent [ɔbsə'lesənt] *adj.* going out of use/out of fashion. □ **algo anticuado**
obstacle ['ɔbstəkl] *n.* something which is in the way/which prevents progress: *his poor sight was an obstacle to success.* □ **obstáculo**
obstacle race *n.* race in which various things have to be passed through/over/under, etc. □ **carrera de obstáculos**
obstetric [ɔb'stetrik] *adj.* referring to obstetrics or childbirth. □ **obstétrico**
obstetrician *n.* doctor who specializes in obstetrics. □ **tocólogo**
obstetrics *n.* branch of medicine dealing with childbirth. □ **obstetricia**
obstinate ['ɔbstinət] *adj.* **1** sticking to your opinion/course of action, etc. against all arguments: *as obstinate as a mule.* □ **obstinado; más terco que una mula**
2 which will not go away: *obstinate pain.* □ **persistente**
obstinacy *n.* being obstinate. □ **obstinación**
obstreperous [ɔb'strepərəs] *adj.* behaving in an uncontrolled/wild/loud way. □ **estrepitoso**
obstruct [əb'strʌkt] *v.* to get in the way of (something); to prevent/to hinder the progress of (something): *to obstruct a view; to obstruct the traffic.* □ **obstruir**
obstruction [əb'strʌkʃn] *n.* **1** act of obstructing. □ **obstrucción**
2 something which gets in the way: *there's an obstruction in the pipe; the accident was caused by an obstruction on the line.* □ **atasco, obstrucción**
obstructive *adj.* which causes/aims to cause an obstruction: *an obstructive attitude.* □ **que obstruye**
obtain [əb'tein] *v.* **1** to get: *aluminium is obtained from bauxite.* □ **obtener**
2 to exist as a rule: *this obtains in a majority of cases.* □ **prevalecer**
obtainable *adj.* which can be obtained. □ **obtenible**
obtrude [əb'tru:d] *v.* (*formal*) to come/to put in the way; to form an obstacle: *to obtrude oneself on someone.* □ **imponer(se)**
obtrusion [əb'tru:ʒn] *n.* **1** (act of) obtruding. □ **entrometimiento**
2 something which is in the way. □ **intrusión**
obtrusive *adj.* (something) which sticks out/which is in the way. □ **que sobresale**
obtuse [əb'tju:s] *adj.* **1** stupid/dull (person). □ **obtuso**
2 ***obtuse angle,*** angle of between 90° and 180°. □ **ángulo obtuso**
obverse ['ɔbvə:s] *n.* side of a coin with the head on it/the main side of a coin. □ **anverso**
obviate ['ɔbvieit] *v.* to avoid/to get round: *the difficulty could be obviated.* □ **obviar**
obvious ['ɔbviəs] *adj.* clear; easily seen/easily noticed: *obvious fact; that's the obvious thing to do.* □ **obvio**
obviously *adv.* in an obvious way/clearly: *she's obviously wrong.* □ **obviamente**
obviousness *n.* being obvious. □ **obviedad**
occasion [ə'keiʒn] *n.* **1** something which causes something else: *if the occasion arises; I have no occasion for complaint.* □ **ocasión**
2 (time of a) happening: *on several occasions; on the occasion of her marriage.* □ **ocasión**

3 special event: *their party was quite an occasion.* □ **acontecimiento**
■ *v.* to cause to happen. □ **ocasionar**
occasional *adj.* happening now and then/not often: *occasional showers; occasional visitors.* □ **ocasional**
occasionally *adv.* sometimes/not often: *they went out only occasionally.* □ **de vez en cuando**
Occident ['ɔksidənt] *n.* (*formal*) the west; the western world. □ **occidente**
occidental [ɔksi'dentl] *adj.* referring to the Occident. □ **occidental**
occult ['ɔkʌlt] *adj.* and *n.* (referring to the) supernatural; magic: *he is interested in the occult.* □ **oculto**
occupy ['ɔkjupai] *v.* **1** to fill/to take up (space or time): *the exhibition occupies most of the hall; the work occupied much of his time.* □ **ocupar**
2 to take/to have possession of: *the firm occupied the building for two years.* □ **ocupar**
3 to take possession and remain in control of: *the army occupied the radio station.* □ **ocupar**
4 to give work/activity to: *he was fully occupied with looking after the shop and the children at the same time; these problems continued to occupy her mind.* □ **ocupar**
occupant *n.* person who occupies a place/who is in a certain seat. □ **ocupante**
occupation [ɔkju'peiʃn] *n.* **1** (act of) occupying; being occupied: *to be in occupation; army of occupation; the occupation lasted two years.* □ **ocupación**
2 job/position/employment: *what's his occupation?* □ **ocupación**
occupational *adj.* referring to an occupation: *occupational risks.* □ **profesional**
occupational therapy, treating sick people by encouraging them to do special activities. □ **terapia ocupacional**
occupier *n.* person who lives in (a house): *the occupier is responsible for repairs.* □ **inquilino**
occur [ə'kəː] *v.* (*it occurred*) **1** to take place/to happen: *when the opportunity occurs.* □ **ocurrir; cuando se presente la oportunidad**
2 to come into your thoughts: *it occurs to me that.* □ **ocurrir; se me ocurre que**
3 to be (found): *these plants occur only occasionally in Africa.* □ **encontrarse**
occurrence [ə'kʌrəns] *n.* happening: *an everyday occurrence.* □ **acontecimiento**
ocean ['ouʃn] *n.* large expanse of sea surrounding the land masses of the earth; a part of this sea: *Pacific Ocean; ocean currents.* □ **océano**
oceanic [ouʃi'ænik] *adj.* referring to the ocean. □ **oceánico**
oceanography *n.* [ouʃə'nɔgrəfi] study of the sea. □ **oceanografía**
ocelot ['ɔsilɔt] *n.* leopard-like animal found in Central and South America. □ **ocelote**
ochre ['oukə] *Amer.* **ocher** *n.* yellow/red natural material used for colouring; dull yellow colour. □ **ocre**
o'clock [ə'klɔk] *adv. phrase used with the numbers meaning* the exact hour: *at six o'clock; the six o'clock train.* □ **a las seis (en punto)**
octagon ['ɔktəgən] *n.* geometrical figure with eight sides. □ **octógono**
octagonal *adj.* eight-sided. □ **octogonal**
octane ['ɔktein] *n.* ***octane number/octane rating,*** number given to types of petrol to indicate their quality: *high-octane petrol.* □ **octano**
octave ['ɔkteiv] *n.* (*in music*) space between the first and last notes of an eight-note scale. □ **octava**
octet [ɔk'tet] *n.* group of eight people, especially musicians; piece of music for such a group. □ **octeto**
October [ɔk'toubə] *n.* tenth month of the year: *in October; on October 6th.* □ **octubre**
octogenarian [ɔktədʒə'nɛəriən] *adj.* and *n.* (person) who is between 80 and 89 years old. □ **octogenario**
octopus ['ɔktəpəs] *n.* sea animal with a beak and eight arms. □ **pulpo**
ocular ['ɔkjulə] *adj.* referring to the eyes/to sight. □ **ocular**
oculist *n.* doctor who specializes in care of the eyes. □ **oculista**
odd [ɔd] *adj.* **1** (number) which cannot be divided exactly by two: *3, 5, and 7 are odd numbers.* □ **impar**
2 approximately/a little more than: *$6 odd; 100 odd sheep.* □ **6 dólares y pico; unas 100 ovejas**
3 occasional; referring to various individual things/items: *odd jobs; at odd moments; he writes the odd story for magazines.* □ **pequeños arreglos; en los ratos perdidos; él escribe alguna que otra historia...**
odd lots, (*in an auction*) groups of different items for sale. □ **lotes sueltos**
4 referring to a member of a set or pair, when separated from the rest: *an odd glove; two odd socks,* socks which do not match. □ **sin pareja**
5 strange/peculiar: *how odd; he's very odd.* □ **qué raro; es muy raro**
oddity *n.* **1** being odd. □ **rareza**
2 odd thing/person: *what an oddity!* □ **¡qué rareza!**
oddly *adv.* in an odd way; for odd reasons: *he has been behaving rather oddly.* □ **extrañamente**
oddly enough, *they haven't told us,* it is curious but they haven't told us. □ **por extraño que parezca...**
oddments *n. pl.* bits and pieces; items left over. □ **cosillas**
odds *n. pl.* **1** difference between the amount which has been bet and the amount to be won: *odds of 10 to 1.* □ **10 contra 1**
2 more than an equal chance: *the odds are against it; to fight against great odds.* □ **tiene muchas probabilidades de perder; luchar contra algo abrumador**
3 difference: *what's the odds?* □ **¿qué más da?**
it makes no odds, it doesn't make any difference. □ **da igual**
4 ***to be at odds with someone,*** to quarrel constantly. □ **estar peleado con uno**
5 ***odds and ends,*** bits and pieces. □ **chismes**
ode [oud] *n.* long poem often addressed to a person or thing: *'Ode to a Nightingale'.* □ **oda**
odious ['oudiəs] *adj.* hateful/horrible. □ **odioso**
odiousness *n.* being odious. □ **lo odioso**
odium *n.* great unpopularity/hatred. □ **odio**
odometer [ou'dɔmitə] *n.* device for measuring the distance a vehicle travels. □ **odómetro**
odour ['oudə] *Amer.* **odor** *n.* **1** scent/smell: *strange odour.* □ **olor**
2 ***to be in good/bad odour with someone,*** to be in/out of favour with someone. □ **caer en gracia/desgracia**
odorous *adj.* with a strong scent. □ **oloroso**
odourless *adj.* without any smell: *odourless gas.* □ **inodoro**
Oedipus complex ['iːdipəs'kɔmpleks] *n.* feeling (in a man) of hatred for his father and love for his mother. □ **complejo de Edipo**
oesophagus [ə'sɔfəgəs] *Amer.* **esophagus** *n.* part of the throat down which food passes from the mouth to the stomach. □ **esófago**
of [ɔv] *prep.* **1** belonging to/connected with: *Albert Smith, son of John Smith; she's the widow of a doctor; he's a friend of mine; 1st of June; it's no business*

of yours; doctor of medicine. □ **de**
2 being a part/a quantity: *two of us; how much do you want of it? there are six of them; a pint of milk; a box of matches.* □ **de**
3 (who/which) is: *the town of Bath; a child of ten; that fool of a sergeant.* □ **de**
4 by/from: *free of illness; south of the border; made of wool; the works of Shakespeare; of necessity; he died of his wounds; that's very kind of you.* □ **de**
5 about/concerning: *well, what of it?* □ **bien, ¿y qué?**
6 (after superlative): *the best of men; he likes these best of all.* □ **los mejores hombres del mundo; estos son los que más le gustan**

off [ɔf] *adv.* **1** away (from something): *I'm off to London; a house a kilometre off; off we go; they're off,* they've started running. □ **a; nos vamos; han salido**
2 *a day off,* a day away from work. □ **un día libre**
3 not on: *take your shoes off; the lights are off.* □ **quítate los zapatos; ...están apagadas**
4 *the deal is off,* has been cancelled. □ **el trato se ha roto**
5 *chicken is off,* (*in restaurant*) not available. □ **ya no queda pollo**
6 no longer fresh: *that meat's gone off.* □ **esa carne se ha estropeado**
7 ***well/badly off,*** having plenty/not enough (money). □ **bien/mal de dinero**
8 *he's* ***better off*** *where he is,* he's in a better position. □ **está mucho mejor donde está**
9 ***right/straight off,*** immediately. □ **al momento**
10 ***on and off,*** sometimes/from time to time. □ **de vez en cuando**
11 (*with verbs*) completely: *to go off to sleep; to finish off your work.* □ **irse de una vez a dormir; terminar de una vez...**
■ *prep.* **1** (away) from: *take it off the table; he fell off his horse; the door is off its hinges; 2% off the price; a day off work.* □ **de; fuera de; un día libre**
2 at some/a certain distance from: *the ship was moored off Dover; a few miles off the coast; a house just off the main road.* □ **...a la altura de; ...de la costa; ...justo al lado de**
3 branching from: *side street off the main road.* □ **calle lateral que sale de la carretera...**
4 disliking/not wanting: *he's off his food.* □ **detesta la comida**
■ *adj.* away; not on. □ **a**
off day, one on which you are less successful. □ **un día malo**
off season, less busy season. □ **temporada baja**
off side, (*in a car*) the furthest from the side of the road; *see also* **offside.** □ **lado izquierdo (en España porque conducimos por la derecha)**
off-chance *n.* slight possibility: *they went to the cinema on the off-chance that there were still some empty seats.* □ **posibilidad remota**
off-colour *adj.* not well: *he's a bit off-colour today.* □ **paliducho**
offhand *adv.* and *adj.* **1** without preparation/without thinking carefully: *do you know offhand what are the times of trains to London?* □ **sin pensarlo**
2 rude/without courtesy: *offhand manner.* □ **brusco**
off-licence *n.* (shop, etc., which has) a licence to sell alcholic drinks to be taken away. □ **bodega**
off-peak *adj.* away from the busiest/most used times: *off-peak electricity,* electricity which is cheaper during the night. □ **de menor consumo (electricidad); de menos tráfico**
off-putting *adj.* (*informal*) causing (mild) annoyance. □ **molesto**
offset [ɔfset] *n.* method of printing from a plate to a rubber surface and then to paper: *offset lithography.* □ **offset**
■ *v.* [ɔf'set] (*he offset*) to balance one thing against another: *they offset their loss against future profits.* □ **compensar**
offshoot ['ɔfʃu:t] *n.* small side shoot of a plant; anything which branches from something else: *the firm is just an offshoot of a larger company.* □ **retoño (planta); ramificación**
offshore *adj.* (away) from/at a distance from the shore: *offshore wind; offshore island.* □ **de la costa; ...cercana a la costa**
offside [ɔf'said] *adv.* (*in football*) between the ball and the opposing team's goal: *the player was offside.* □ **fuera de juego**
■ *adj.* referring to the side of a car nearest to the middle of the road: *my offside front headlight was smashed.* □ **lado izquierdo**
offspring ['ɔfspriŋ] *n.* (*no pl.*) child; young (of an animal). □ **vástago**
offstage *adv.* and *adj.* not on the stage/unseen by the audience. □ **entre bastidores**

offal ['ɔfl] *n.* internal organs (heart etc.) of animals, used as food. □ **asaduras**

offence [ə'fens] *n.* **1** state of offending; being offended: *to take offence* (*at something*)*; to give offence; I meant no offence.* □ **ofensa**
2 crime; (act of) offending (especially against a law): *minor offence; that's an offence against the traffic regulations.* □ **falta; infracción**
offend [ə'fend] *v.* to be/to go against (the law/opinions/wishes/feelings): *their behaviour offended the others; the pattern offends the eye; it offends our sense of justice; she's much too easily offended.* □ **ofender**
offender *n.* person who offends (especially against a law): *young offenders.* □ **infractor; delincuente**
offensive *adj.* **1** which is unpleasant: *to be offensive to someone; offensive manner; offensive smell.* □ **ofensivo; detestable; repugnante**
2 (*in army*) which is used in an attack: *offensive weapons; offensive strategy.* □ **armas ofensivas**
■ *n.* (military) attack. □ **ofensiva**
to take the offensive, to be the first to attack. □ **tomar la ofensiva**
to go on the offensive, to start to attack. □ **empezar a atacar**
offensively *adv.* in an offensive way. □ **ofensivamente**

offer ['ɔfə] *n.* (act of) indicating that you will do/give something; what is offered: *that's the best offer I can make; offers of help.* □ **oferta**
on offer, offered. □ **en venta**
special offer, goods which are put on sale at a reduced price. □ **oferta especial**
■ *v.* **1** to say/to indicate that you will do/give something: *they offered us a meal; they offered to go with us; how much will you offer for it?; to offer resistance.* □ **ofrecer**
2 to make/to express: *to offer a remark/an opinion.* □ **hacer (observación); manifestar (opinión)**
offering *n.* what is offered. □ **oferta**

office ['ɔfis] *n.* **1** room/building where business or professional activity is carried out: *head office; he's working in his office; lawyer's office; office manager.* □ **oficina**
doctor's office, *Amer.* room where a doctor sees his patients. □ **consulta/consultorio**
office boy, young man who carries out unskilled tasks in an office. □ **botones**
2 position/function: *he has the office of secretary;*

office-holder; the government is in office; he held office under two presidents, he was a member of their governments. □ **tiene el puesto de...; funcionario; el gobierno que está en el poder**
3 (*especially in titles*) organization: *Office of Fair Trading; International Labour Office.* □ **oficina**
4 help/services: *through the good offices of the mayor.* □ **oficio**
officer *n.* **1** person who holds an official position: *the officers of the society,* the Chairman, the Secretary, the Treasurer, etc. □ **cargo**
2 person who holds one of the commissioned ranks in the armed forces, etc.: *the officers' mess.* □ **oficial**
3 ***police officer,*** policeman: *officer, can you tell me how to get to Piccadilly Circus?* □ **agente de policía**
official [ə'fiʃl] *adj.* of/for/from an organization which is recognized by a government, etc.: *official news; official car; in his official capacity.* □ **oficial**
■ *n.* person holding a recognized position: *an official from the Ministry; a railway official.* □ **funcionario**
officialese *n.* (*informal*) clumsy language used by administrative organizations. □ **lenguaje burocrático**
officially *adv.* in an official way: *officially appointed.* □ **oficialmente**
officiate [ə'fiʃieit] *v.* **1** (*of clergyman*) to perform a religious ceremony. □ **oficiar**
2 to act as chairman, etc.: *he had to officiate at the meeting.* □ **ejercer las funciones de**
officious *adj.* too ready to interfere or to offer help: *officious behaviour.* □ **entrometido**
officiously *adv.* in an officious way. □ **entrometidamente**
officiousness *n.* being officious. □ **entrometimiento**
offing ['ɔfiŋ] *n.* ***in the offing,*** available soon: *there may be a job for you in the offing.* □ **en perspectiva**
often ['ɔfn] *adv.* many times; in many instances: *how often have you been here?* □ **a menudo**
every so often, now and then. □ **alguna que otra vez**
as often as not, usually. □ **habitualmente**
oftentimes *adv. Amer.* often. □ **a menudo**
ogre ['ougə] *n.* cruel giant who eats human beings; cruel terrifying person. □ **ogro**
oh [ou] *interjection* expressing surprise, shock/calling attention to something: *oh look!* □ **¡oh!**
ohm [oum] *n.* standard measure of electrical resistance. □ **ohmio**
oil [ɔil] *n.* **1** thick smooth-running liquid of various kinds (used in cooking/heating/engineering/painting): *olive oil; to paint in oils.* □ **aceite**
2 liquid found mainly underground and used to produce power: *mineral oil; oil well; the oil industry.* □ **aceite mineral; petróleo**
■ *v.* to put oil on/in (especially to make a machine run more smoothly): *you should oil the hinges of the door.* □ **engrasar**
to oil the wheels, to help to make things run more smoothly. □ **hacerlo más llevadero**
well-oiled, (*informal*) rather drunk. □ **algo borracho**
oil-bearing *adj.* (rocks, etc.) which contain oil. □ **petrolífero**
oilfield *n.* area where oil is found. □ **campo/yacimiento petrolífero**
oilrig *n.* structure for drilling for oil. □ **plataforma petrolífera**
oilskin(s) *n.* (clothing of) material made waterproof with oil. □ **hule**
oilslick *n.* thin covering of oil on the surface of the sea. □ **mancha de petróleo**
oiltanker *n.* large ship/large lorry for carrying oil. □ **petrolero**
oily *adj.* **1** like oil; covered with oil. □ **aceitoso**
2 (*of manner*) too smooth and pleasant; insincere. □ **zalamero**
ointment ['ɔintmənt] *n.* smooth healing or soothing substance spread on the skin. □ **ungüento**
OK, okay [ou'kei] (*informal*) *interjection* and *adj.* all right: *OK, let's go, I'm feeling OK now.* □ **está bien; vale; OK**
■ *n.* sign of approval: *give the OK to something.* □ **aprobación**
■ *v.* to give a sign of approval to: *their plans were OK'd/okayed by the boss.* □ **dar el visto bueno a**
old [ould] *adj.* **1** having great age: *to grow old; old man; old buildings; old and young.* □ **viejo; antiguo**
old wives' tale, belief based on tradition rather than on fact. □ **cuento de viejas**
2 having been in use for a long time: *old clothes.* □ **ropas viejas**
3 being of a particular age: *how old are you?; three years old; he's old enough to work.* □ **¿cuántos años tienes?; tengo tres años; es lo suficientemente mayor como para...**
4 having been in a certain state/having been done for a long time: *old friend; that's an old trick.* □ **viejo**
5 former: *old boy of the school.* □ **antiguo**
6 term showing vagueness/affection/disrespect, etc.: *any old thing.* □ **cualquier cosa**
the old man, (*informal*) boss/headmaster/father. □ **el viejo**
old woman, fussy man. □ **una vieja**
old-fashioned *adj.* not in fashion; out of date. □ **anticuado; pasado de moda**
oldie *n.* (*informal*) old-fashioned/out of date thing (especially record). □ **un clásico**
oldish *adj.* rather old. □ **algo viejo**
old maid *n.* older woman who has never married. □ **una solterona**
old timer *n.* former worker/soldier, etc. □ **un veterano**
olfactory [ɔ'fəktəri] *adj.* (*formal*) referring to the sense of smell. □ **olfativo**
oligarchy ['ɔligɑ:ki] *n.* (country with a) government by a few powerful people. □ **oligarquía**
olive ['ɔliv] *n.* **1** small black or green fruit which produces oil and is used as food; tree which bears this fruit: *olive oil.* □ **aceituna, oliva; olivo (árbol)**
to hold out the olive branch, sign of peace. □ **ofrecer la paz**
2 ***olive*** (***green***), dull green colour of unripe olives. □ **verde oliva**
Olympic [ə'limpik] *adj.* and *n.* referring to the Olympic Games: *an Olympic runner.* □ **olímpico**
the Olympic Games/the Olympics, international athletic competition held every four years. □ **Olimpiada; Juegos Olímpicos**
Olympiad *n.* major international sporting competition: *the chess Olympiad.* □ **Olimpiada**
ombudsman ['ɔmbədzmən] *n.* official who investigates complaints by members of the public against government departments. □ **defensor del pueblo**
omelette ['ɔmlət] *Amer.* **omelet** *n.* egg mixture cooked (in butter) often with savoury substances added: *a ham omelette.* □ **tortilla**
omen ['oumən] *n.* something (considered as) giving an indication of the future: *to take something as a good omen.* □ **augurio**
ominous ['ɔminəs] *adj.* threatening bad results: *ominous warning.* □ **inquietante**

ominously *adv.* in an ominous way. □ **de manera inquietante**
omit [ə'mit] *v.* (*he omitted*) **1** to leave out: *the results were omitted from the report.* □ **omitir**
2 not to do something: *they omitted to tell us.* □ **olvidarse de**
omission [ə'miʃn] *n.* **1** act of omitting. □ **omisión**
2 thing omitted. □ **cosa omitida**
omnibus ['ɔmnibəs] *adj.* (including several items) all together: *omnibus edition of the writer's works.* □ **completo**
omnipotence [ɔm'nipətəns] *n.* quality of being all-powerful. □ **omnipotencia**
omnipotent *adj.* all-powerful. □ **omnipotente**
omnivorous [ɔm'nivərəs] *adj.* **1** eating everything; (animal) which eats both plants and other animals. □ **omnívoro**
2 *she's an omnivorous reader,* she reads everything she can find. □ **que lee todo lo que encuentra**
on [ɔn] *prep.* **1** touching the top/outer surface of something: *on the table; to step on something; on the high seas; on the wall; on the ceiling.* □ **en**
2 in/at: *on the train; on shore; on page 4; on the right.* □ **en**
3 with: *have you any money on you?* □ **¿tienes dinero encima?**
4 belonging to/a member of: *on the staff; on the committee.* □ **es miembro del personal/de la comisión**
5 indicating a means of moving: *on foot; on horseback.* □ **a pie; a caballo**
6 engaged in: *on business; on holiday; he's on the telephone to Paris; they are on strike.* □ **de negocios/vacaciones; está al teléfono; están en huelga**
7 from/by: *to have something on good authority; on pain of death; on the cheap; to live on a small income.* □ **so pena de muerte; a bajo precio; vivir de una renta pequeña**
8 (indicating a time): *on Sundays; on a hot day; on April 15th; on my arrival.* □ **los domingos; en un día cálido; el 15 de abril; al llegar yo**
9 ***on application,*** when you apply. □ **al hacer la petición**
10 ***on sale,*** for sale. □ **en venta**
11 approximately: *just on a year ago.* □ **hace un año más o menos**
12 because of: *to congratulate someone on his success.* □ **por**
13 about/concerning: *a book on Wales.* □ **sobre**
14 towards/against: *to have pity on someone; an attack on someone; the police have nothing on him,* have no proof of an offence against him. □ **tener lástima de; un ataque contra alguien**
15 (*informal*) paid by: *the drinks are on me.* □ **...corren de mi cuenta**
16 (as a bet): *to put $10 on a horse,* to bet $10 that the horse will win. □ **apostar a/por un caballo**
17 following: *war on war.* □ **guerra tras guerra**
■ *adv.* **1** in position: *put the kettle on; the actors are on,* on stage. □ **pon agua a calentar; los actores ya han salido; en escena**
it's just not on, (*informal*) cannot be allowed. □ **eso no se hace**
2 in action; open: *the gas is on; you've left the light on; to turn the engine on.* □ **...abierto; ...encendida; ...en marcha**
3 happening: *what's on at the theatre? have you anything on this evening?* □ **¿qué representan en el teatro?; ¿tienes algún compromiso...?**
4 being worn: *put your shoes on; he had nothing on, he was naked.* □ **ponte los zapatos**
5 (in a) continuing (way): *they worked on for another hour.* □ **siguieron trabajando otra hora más**
6 (indicating passing of time): *later on; from that time on; well on in years.* □ **más tarde; a partir de entonces; entrado en años**
7 ***to be on at:*** *he's always on at me,* (*informal*) scolding/criticizing. □ **siempre se está metiendo conmigo**
8 ***on and off,*** not continuously/with breaks in between. □ **de vez en cuando**
on and on, without stopping. □ **sin cesar**
9 ***to have someone on,*** (*informal*) to tell something untrue as a joke. □ **tomar el pelo**
once [wɔns] *adv.* **1** for one time: *once only; once a week.* □ **una vez**
once and for all, completely/in order to finish. □ **de una vez por todas**
2 at all/ever: *if you once stop you'll find it hard to start again.* □ **alguna vez**
3 at a (particular) time in the past: *I knew him once; once when I was going home; once upon a time.* □ **una vez; hace siglos**
4 ***at once,*** (i) immediately: *do it at once!* □ **en seguida**
(ii) at the same time: *don't all speak at once!* □ **al mismo tiempo**
■ *conj.* as soon as: *once mother finds out; once I'm on holiday.* □ **una vez que**
once-over *n.* (*informal*) quick examination: *give the engine the once-over.* □ **vistazo**
oncoming ['ɔnkʌmiŋ] *adj.* coming towards you: *give way to the oncoming traffic.* □ **que viene**
one [wʌn] number 1. **1** first number: *he is one year old; twenty-one; a hundred and one; the typist has left out a one.* □ **uno**
look after number one, (*informal*) look after yourself first. □ **cuidarse uno**
2 single unit in quantity or number: *there's only one left.* □ **sólo queda uno**
last but one, the item before the last. □ **penúltimo**
3 ***to have a quick one,*** (*informal*) a quick drink. □ **echar un trago**
4 *she hit him one with the bottle,* hit him a blow. □ **le dio uno con...**
■ *adj.* **1** single (example of): *that's one way to do it.* □ **esa es una manera...**
2 the only: *that's the one way to do it.* □ **esa es la única manera...**
3 the same: *it's all one to me.* □ **me es lo mismo**
■ *pron.* **1** thing/person indicated: *this one; which one do you want? she's the one who helped him.* □ **éste; ¿cuál quieres?; ella es la que le ayudó**
2 example of a type: *the green ones.* □ **los verdes**
■ *indefinite adj.* (on) a certain: *one stormy night.* □ **uno**
■ *indefinite pron.* **1** (*pl. some/any*) an example of something: *I've no pen on me - have you got one? one of the boys will help you; one after the other; we treat him like one of the family,* like a member of it. □ **uno**
2 ***I for one*** *shall come,* for example. □ **por ejemplo, por lo menos**
3 (*formal*) anyone/an indefinite person: *one just can't do that sort of thing; it's enough to kill one; to cut one's finger.* □ **uno**
the Evil One, the Devil. □ **el demonio**
one-armed bandit *n.* gambling machine worked by a handle.□ **máquina tragaperras**
one-horse town *n.* (*informal*) small town where very little happens. □ **un poblacho/pueblucho**
one-legged ['wʌn'legid] *adj.* with only one leg.

□ **con una sola pierna**
one-night stand *n.* performance (of a play/of a show) for one night only. □ **una única actuación**
one-off *adj.* done/made once only: *a one-off offer.* □ **una única y definitiva oferta**
oneself *pronoun* referring to a person as an indefinite subject: *to wash oneself; to talk to oneself; one must do it oneself.* □ **uno mismo**
one-sided *adj.* treating or giving justice to one side only: *one-sided argument.* □ **unilateral**
one-time *adj.* former: *a one-time actor.* □ **antiguo**
one-track mind *n.* mind which concentrates on one thing at a time. □ **mente incapaz de abarcar más de un tema a la vez**
one-upmanship *n.* art of putting yourself at an advantage over others. □ **habilidad para superar a otros**
one-way *adj.* for traffic in one direction only: *one-way street.* □ **de dirección única**
one-way ticket, ticket for a single journey only. □ **de ida**
onerous ['ɔnərəs] *adj.* causing much (tiring) effort: *onerous task.* □ **oneroso**
onion ['ʌnjən] *n.* vegetable whose round white bulb has a very strong smell and is used as food: *onions make you cry; onion soup.* □ **cebolla**
onlooker ['ɔnlukə] *n.* person who watches. □ **espectador; mirón**
only ['ounli] *adj.* (the) single/(the) one without any others: *his only hope; you're the only one who can help.* □ **único**
■ *adv.* **1** and not anyone/anything else: *I've only got three; staff only; I only touched it.* □ **sólo; solamente**
2 as recently as: *only yesterday.* □ **ayer mismo**
only too, very: *I'm only too pleased to help.* □ **encantado de**
if only, expressing a strong wish/desire: *if only I had known.* □ **ojalá**
■ *conj.* but: *it's a lovely dress only it's rather expensive.* □ **sólo que**
onrush ['ɔnrʌʃ] *n.* rushing in/on. □ **oleada**
onset ['ɔnset] *n.* beginning (of an attack, etc.) □ **comienzo**
onslaught ['ɔnslɔːt] *n.* sudden severe attack: *the defenders faced repeated onslaughts from the attackers.* □ **embestida violenta**
onus ['ounəs] *n.* responsibility (for a difficult task): *the onus is on you to do it.* □ **responsabilidad; le incumbe a usted hacerlo**
onward ['ɔnwəd] *adj.* forward: *the onward march of the army.* □ **hacia adelante**
■ *adv.* (*also* **onwards**) forward: *marching onward; from this day onwards.* □ **hacia adelante; desde hoy en adelante**
ooze [uːz] *n.* slimy mud. □ **cieno**
■ *v.* **1** to flow slowly and gently: *oil oozed out of the nozzle.* □ **rezumar**
2 *courage oozed out of him,* disappeared slowly but surely. □ **le faltaba el valor**
opacity [ə'pæsiti] *n.* state of being opaque. □ **opacidad**
opal ['oupl] *n.* semi-precious stone with varied or changing colours. □ **ópalo**
opaque [ou'peik] *adj.* which you cannot see through: *opaque paper; opaque glass.* □ **opaco**
open ['oupn] *adj.* **1** not closed: *open box; the door is wide open.* □ **abierto**
2 which you can enter: *open to the public; are the pubs open on Sundays?* □ **abierto**
3 without limits: *the open air; the open sea; an open view.* □ **al aire libre; mar abierto; vista despejada**
4 without protection from something: *open to all the winds; open to criticism.* □ **abierto**
5 ready to accept/to be accepted: *open to suggestions; the job's still open; there are two courses open to us.* □ **abierto a sugerencias; el puesto está todavía vacante; quedan dos posibilidades**
6 with no attempt (being made) to hide something: *open secret; open administration.* □ **secreto a voces; administración transparente**
to be open with someone, to speak frankly. □ **abrirse a uno**
7 with space between the parts: *open weave cloth.* □ **calado**
8 with no fixed idea(s)/conditions: *to keep an open mind.* □ **tener la mente abierta**
9 without restrictions: *open competition; open prison,* where there are fewer restrictions than in a normal prison. □ **abierto**
■ *v.* **1** to (cause to) become open: *to open the door; the door opened; he opened his mail; to open a path through the forest.* □ **abrir, abrirse**
2 to start (up)/to set going: *to open a shop/an account/a game.* □ **abrir**
3 to have an exit on to: *the door opens on to the garden.* □ **dar**
■ *n.* unlimited area outdoors: *the feîe will be held in the open.* □ **al aire libre**
open-air *adj.* outdoor/not held in a building: *an open-air exhibition.* □ **al aire libre**
opencast *adj.* (mine) dug on the surface of the ground. □ **a cielo abierto**
opener *n.* device for opening something: *can opener/tin opener; bottle opener.* □ **abrelatas; abrebotellas**
opening *n.* **1** act of opening: *the opening of an exhibition; opening hours.* □ **apertura; inauguración; horario de trabajo**
2 beginning: *opening of a speech.* □ **comienzo**
3 place where something opens: *opening in a fence.* □ **abertura, grieta**
4 opportunity: *there may be an opening for you in the firm.* □ **oportunidad**
■ *adj.* which opens: *opening sentence.* □ **de apertura**
openly *adv.* in an open way: *he openly denied that he had been there.* □ **abiertamente**
openness *n.* quality of being open. □ **franqueza**
open out *v.* to open (fully); to spread out widely: *open out the map; the view opens out as you go down the valley.* □ **desplegar**
open up *v.* **1** to open (completely): *cutting down the trees has opened up the view.* □ **abrir**
2 to bring into use: *to open up new country; to open up a new shop.* □ **abrir**
opera ['ɔprə] *n.* **1** dramatic performance with music, in which the words are partly or wholly sung: *to perform one of Mozart's operas.* □ **ópera**
2 company which performs operas: *the Vienna Opera.* □ **ópera**
opera glasses *n. pl.* small binoculars for looking at performers on the stage. □ **gemelos de teatro**
opera house *n.* theatre in which opera is performed. □ **teatro de la ópera**
operatic [ɔpə'rætik] *adj.* of/like/for opera. □ **operístico**
operetta [ɔpə'retə] *n.* opera with a light-hearted story in which some of the words are spoken. □ **opereta**
operate ['ɔpəreit] *v.* **1** to act: *his firm operates from London.* □ **operar**

2 to (cause to) work: *the machine operates on oil.* □ **funcionar**
3 *to operate on a patient,* to treat a patient by cutting open the body in some way; *operating theatre; she's being operated on tomorrow.* □ **operar a un paciente; quirófano**
operable ['ɔpərəbl] *adj.* which can be operated on: *her cancer is operable.* □ **operable**
operation [ɔpə'reiʃn] *n.* (act of) operating; being operated on: *she had an operation for appendicitis; military operation.* □ **operación**
to come into operation: *the new law came into operation last year,* began to be applied. □ **...entró en vigor...**
operational *adj.* **1** referring to the working of something: *operational research.* □ **operacional**
2 ready for use: *the machinery is now operational.* □ **en condiciones de servicio**
operative ['ɔpərətiv] *adj.* in operation: *the law is now operative.* □ **operativo; la ley ya está en vigor**
■ *n.* worker, especially one who operates a machine, etc. □ **operario**
operator ['ɔpəreitə] *n.* **1** person who works instruments, etc.: *telephone operator; radio operator.* □ **operador; telefonista; radiotelegrafista**
2 person who carries things out or organizes things: *tour operator.* □ **agente de viajes**
3 *he's a smart operator,* (*informal*) he's a clever businessman. □ **es un negociante listo**
ophthalmic [ɔf'θælmik] *adj.* referring to (the medical treatment of) the eye: *ophthalmic surgeon.* □ **oftálmico**
ophthalmologist [ɔfθæl'mɔlədʒist] *n.* doctor who specializes in diseases of the eye. □ **oftalmólogo**
opinion [ə'pinjən] *n.* **1** what a person thinks/feels about something: *what's your opinion on this/about the situation? to ask someone's opinion; he has a low opinion of his boss.* □ **opinión**
2 what people think/feel about something: *it's a matter of opinion; public opinion.* □ **sobre eso hay diferentes pareceres; opinión pública**
3 view; piece of (usually expert) advice: *to ask for a second opinion,* to ask another specialist to advise. □ **opinión**
opinionated *adj.* (person) with rigid opinions/who thinks he is always right. □ **testarudo**
opium ['oupiəm] *n.* drug which puts you to sleep made from a type of poppy: *opium poppy; opium addict* □ **opio**
opossum [ə'pɔsəm] *n.* small North American animal which carries its young in a pouch. □ **oposum**
opponent [ə'pounənt] *n.* person/group which is against you: *he managed to defeat all his opponents.* □ **oponente**
opportune ['ɔpətju:n] *adj.* coming (by chance) at the right time: *his arrival was very opportune; at an opportune moment.* □ **oportuno**
opportunely *adv.* in an opportune way; at the right time. □ **oportunamente**
opportunist *n.* person who takes advantage of opportunities, especially for himself at the expense of others. □ **oportunista**
opportunity [ɔpə'tju:niti] *n.* chance/circumstances which allow you to do something: *when the opportunity arises; that'll give you an opportunity to finish.* □ **oportunidad**
oppose [ə'pouz] *v.* to act against (someone/something); to try to prevent: *he opposed his boss at the meeting; to oppose a motion,* to be/to speak against a motion. □ **oponerse**
opposed *adj.* **1** against: *the newspapers are opposed to the government.* □ **opuesto**
2 in contrast to: *beer as opposed to wine.* □ **en comparación con**
opposite ['ɔpəzit] *adj.* **1** facing: *their house is just opposite; on opposite pages.* □ **enfrente, enfrentado**
2 at/in/towards the other side of something: *in the opposite direction; on the opposite side of the street.* □ **en sentido contrario; al otro lado de la calle**
3 belonging to a completely different type/position: *the opposite sex; opposite poles of a magnet.* □ **el otro sexo; polos opuestos de...**
■ *n.* something which is completely different: *that's the opposite of what he said; what's the opposite of 'magnify'?* □ **opuesto**
■ *prep.* **1** in an opposite position to: *opposite the house.* □ **enfrente de la casa**
2 *she played opposite him in 'Hamlet',* she was the leading lady when he played Hamlet. □ **...el otro papel principal...**
opposition [ɔpə'ziʃn] *n.* **1** (act of) opposing: *the army didn't meet with any opposition; in opposition to public opinion.* □ **oposición**
2 (*especially in politics*) the party/group which opposes the government: *spokesman for the Opposition; the leader of the Opposition.* □ **la oposición**
3 rivalry: *to set up a shop in opposition to someone.* □ **competencia**
oppress [ə'pres] *v.* **1** to cause to suffer, especially by harsh rule. □ **oprimir**
2 to cause depression/sadness in: *oppressed by the dull atmosphere.* □ **agobiar**
oppression [ə'preʃn] *n.* (act of) oppressing; being oppressed. □ **opresión**
oppressive *adj.* oppressing: *oppressive measures; oppressive atmosphere.* □ **opresivo**
oppressiveness *n.* state of being oppressive. □ **opresión**
oppressor *n.* person who oppresses. □ **opresor**
opprobrium [ə'proubriəm] *n.* (*formal*) disgrace; (cause of) strong disapproval. □ **oprobio**
opt [ɔpt] *v.* to decide (in favour of): *they opted for more holiday instead of more pay.* □ **optar por**
opt out *v.* to decide not to (take part): *they opted out of the competition.* □ **decidir abandonar**
optical ['ɔptikl] *adj.* referring to the eyes/to the eyesight; referring to optics: *optical illusion; optical instruments.* □ **óptico**
optic *adj.* referring to the eye/to sight: *optic nerve.* □ **óptico**
optician [ɔp'tiʃn] *n.* person who prescribes/makes/sells spectacles or contact lenses, etc. □ **óptico**
optics *n.* science of light. □ **óptica**
optimism ['ɔptimizəm] *n.* belief that everything is as good as it can be/will work out for the best; confident/cheerful attitude. □ **optimismo**
optimist ['ɔptimist] *n.* person who believes everything will work out for the best. □ **optimista**
optimistic [ɔpti'mistik] *adj.* feeling that everything will work out for the best; giving cause for optimism: *optimistic attitude; the signs are optimistic.* □ **optimista**
optimistically *adv.* in an optimistic way. □ **con optimismo**
optimum ['ɔptiməm] *n.* best way: *to use the opportunity to the optimum.* □ **óptimo**
■ *adj.* best: *to race under optimum conditions.* □ **...condiciones óptimas**
option ['ɔpʃn] *n.* **1** choice/alternative possibility: *you have no option.* □ **elección**
2 opportunity to buy/sell something within a cer-

tain time or at a certain price: *they have it on option.* □ **opción**
optional *adj.* which may or may not be chosen: *a car radio is an optional extra.* □ **optativo**
optometrist [ɔp'tɔmətrist] *n. Amer.* optician. □ **optometrista**
opulence ['ɔpjuləns] *n.* being rich/luxurious. □ **opulencia**
opulent *adj.* rich/luxurious/splendid. □ **opulento**
opulently *adv.* in an opulent way. □ **opulentamente**
opus ['oupəs] *n.* **1** piece of music. □ **opus**
2 any large work of art. □ **obra**
or [ɔ:] *conj.* **1** *indicating* the opposite/the alternative/the other (possibility): *you can go or you can stay; he can't read or write; either fish or meat.* □ **o**
2 *indicating* approximation: *3 or 4; $5 or so.* □ **o**
3 ***or (else)***, if not: *wear a coat or (else) you will catch cold; do what you're told to do, or else,* or you will be punished. □ **si no**
oracle ['ɔrəkl] *n.* **1** (*in Ancient Greece*) place where the gods answered questions about the future; person who answered questions about the future. □ **oráculo**
2 very wise and knowing person. □ **oráculo**
oral ['ɔ:rl] *adj.* **1** by speaking: *oral examination.* □ **oral**
2 taken by the mouth: *oral contraceptive; oral vaccine.* □ **oral**
■ *n.* examination where you answer questions by speaking: *he failed his French orals.* □ **examen oral**
orally *adv.* **1** in/by speech. □ **oralmente**
2 by the mouth. □ **por vía oral**
orange ['ɔrindʒ] *n.* usually sweet citrus fruit, reddish yellow when ripe; tree which bears this fruit. □ **naranja**
■ *adj.* and *n.* colour of an orange. □ **anaranjado**
orangeade [ɔrindʒ'eid] *n.* fizzy orange-flavoured drink. □ **naranjada**
orang-utang [ərænu:'tæŋ] *n.* type of large ape found in South-East Asia. □ **orangután**
oration [ə'reiʃn] *n.* (formal) speech: *funeral oration.* □ **oración**
orator *n.* person who is able to speak forcefully and persuasively to large numbers of people; person making a speech. □ **orador**
oratorical [ɔrə'tɔrikl] *adj.* full of eloquence: *oratorical style.* □ **oratorio; estilo retórico**
oratory ['ɔrətəri] *n.* **1** eloquent/forceful public speaking. □ **oratoria**
2 private chapel. □ **oratorio**
oratorio [ɔrə'tɔ:riou] *n.* piece of music for orchestra, choir and soloists, often telling a religious story. □ **oratorio**
orb [ɔ:b] *n.* **1** spherical object (such as a planet or an eyeball). □ **esfera; globo del ojo**
2 ornamental globe with a cross on top used by a king as a symbol of state power. □ **orbe**
orbit ['ɔ:bit] *n.* **1** curved track (of an object moving through space): *the earth's orbit; to put a satellite into orbit round the moon.* □ **órbita**
2 extent of influence: *within his orbit.* □ **órbita**
■ *v.* to (cause to) move in an orbit round something: *to orbit round the moon/to orbit the moon.* □ **estar en órbita**
orchard ['ɔ:tʃəd] *n.* (enclosed) field with fruit trees. □ **huerto**
orchestra [ɔ:'kestrə] *n.* **1** large group of musicians who play together. □ **orquesta**
2 part of a theatre, usually next to the stage, where the musicians sit. □ **lugar de la orquesta**
orchestra stalls, seats very close to where the orchestra sits. □ **patio de butacas; platea**
orchestral [ɔ:'kestrəl] *adj.* referring to an orchestra. □ **orquestal**
orchestrate ['ɔ:kistreit] *v.* **1** to arrange (a piece of music) for an orchestra. □ **orquestar**
2 to organize (a demonstration, etc.). □ **orquestar**
orchestration [ɔ:ki'streiʃn] *n.* (act of) orchestrating; being orchestrated. □ **orquestación**
orchid ['ɔ:kid] **orchis** ['ɔ:kis] *n.* type of flowering plant with showy flowers divided into three parts of which the middle one is shaped like a cup. □ **orquídea**
ordain [ɔ:'dein] *v.* **1** to make (someone) a priest/a clergyman in a formal ceremony. □ **ordenar**
2 (*formal*) to order/to command (that something be done): *the king ordained a pardon for all prisoners; ordained by fate.* □ **ordenar**
ordeal [ɔ:'di:l] *n.* painful test of strength/courage; difficult period: *they went through a terrible ordeal.* □ **prueba muy dura**
order ['ɔ:də] *n.* **1** command/demand that something should be done: *he gave an order; I have orders to do it.* □ **orden**
2 obeying of rules or laws without unrest or violence: *law and order.* □ **orden**
3 demand/request for goods from a customer; goods supplied to a customer: *a large order from Japan; your order is now ready; these cups are made to order.* □ **pedido**
4 *that's* ***a tall order,*** (*informal*) a lot to ask. □ **eso es mucho pedir**
5 organization of items in succession: *to arrange books in alphabetical order; in order of seniority; the books have got out of order.* □ **orden**
6 good/correct arrangement: *is your passport in order? is it in order for me to ask a question?,* may I ask/is it the correct procedure? □ **orden, ¿puedo...?**
out of order, not working: *the lift is out of order.* □ **no funciona**
7 arrangement of an army: *in battle order.* □ **en orden de combate**
8 rules for an assembly/meeting. □ **procedimiento**
9 ***to call to order:*** *the chairman called the meeting to order,* (i) intervened to stop a disorderly discussion. □ **llamar al orden**
(ii) *Amer.* started the meeting. □ **empezar**
10 organization of monks/priests, etc.: *Benedictine Order; he's in holy orders,* he is a priest. □ **orden**
11 organization of knighthood; group of people to whom a certain honour has been given: *Order of Merit.* □ **orden**
12 type/kind/classification/rank: *workmanship of the highest order.* □ **orden**
the lower orders, the lower classes. □ **la clase baja**
13 paper which authorizes the transfer of money: *banker's order; postal order.* □ **orden bancaria; giro postal**
14 ***in order to/that,*** so that/for the purpose of: *in order to arrive in time; in order that they may succeed.* □ **para; con el fin de**
■ *v.* **1** to command/to demand/to say (that something should be done): *he ordered them to leave; don't order me about; the doctor ordered three weeks' rest.* □ **ordenar**
2 to demand/to request (goods/services, etc.): *they ordered 20 kilos of sugar; please order me a taxi.* □ **pedir**
3 to arrange/to put in order: *to order your affairs.* □ **ordenar**
orderliness ['ɔ:dəlinəs] *n.* **1** being in good order/tidiness. □ **orden**

2 being quiet/being orderly. □ **proceder metódico**
orderly *adj.* **1** in good order; tidy or well-arranged: *orderly way of life.* □ **en orden; una vida ordenada**
2 well-behaved: *orderly crowd.* □ **disciplinado**
■ *n.* person whose duty it is to carry out routine tasks (in a hospital or in the armed services): *he's on orderly duty; a medical orderly.* □ **está de servicio; enfermero**
ordinal ['ɔːdinl] *n.* and *adj.* (referring to a) number indicating the position in a series: *1, 2, and 20 are cardinal numbers, 1st, 2nd and 20th are all ordinals/ ordinal numbers.* □ **ordinal**
ordinance ['ɔːdinəns] *n.* laws/rule made by an authority. □ **ordenanza**
ordinary ['ɔːdnri] *adj.* normal/not unusual; typical of its class/not having any special characteristics: *they live in a very ordinary house; he's just an ordinary little man; ordinary way of life.* □ **corriente**
out of the ordinary, extraordinary. □ **fuera de lo común**
ordinarily *adv.* in the usual way/usually. □ **de ordinario**
ordination [ɔːdi'neiʃn] *n.* (act/ceremony of) ordaining someone as a priest. □ **ordenación**
ordnance ['ɔːdnəns] *n.* **1** heavy guns. □ **artillería**
2 (government department dealing with) military supplies. □ **servicio de material de guerra**
ordnance survey *n.* government department which produces detailed maps. □ **servicio oficial de topografía**
ore [ɔː] *n.* material found in the earth from which metals are obtained. □ **mena**
organ ['ɔːgən] *n.* **1** part of the body with a special function: *organs of speech.* □ **órgano**
2 periodical which gives the views of a group/of an organization: *organ of the Labour Party.* □ **órgano**
3 musical instrument with keyboard(s) and many pipes through which air is pumped to make a sound. □ **órgano**
organic [ɔː'gænik] *adj.* **1** referring to an organ/to organs *organic disease.* □ **orgánico**
2 referring to living things. □ **orgánico**
organic chemistry, concerned with carbon compounds. □ **química orgánica**
organic farming, using only natural fertilizers. □ **agricultura natural**
3 having an organized structure: *organic system.* □ **sistema orgánico**
organically [ɔː'gænikli] *adv.* in an organic way: *organically grown vegetables.* □ **orgánicamente**
organism ['ɔːgənizm] *n.* living being. □ **organismo**
organist *n.* person who plays the organ. □ **organista**
organization *n.* **1** (act of) arranging; being arranged: *good organization.* □ **organización**
2 organized group or institution: *youth organization; a government organization.* □ **organización**
organize ['ɔːgənaiz] *v.* to arrange/to put into a special form of order; to put into good order: *the factory is organized in small units; your work could be better organized.* □ **organizar**
organizer *n.* person who arranges things: *area organizer; he's a good organizer.* □ **organizador**
orgasm ['ɔːgæzm] *n.* climax of sexual excitement. □ **orgasmo**
orgy ['ɔːdʒi] *n.* uncontrolled indulgence in drinking/ dancing; uncontrolled state or activity: *orgy of colour; drunken orgy.* □ **orgía**
orient ['ɔːriənt] *n.* ***the Orient,*** the East/Eastern countries. □ **oriente**
■ *v.* to put in a certain direction; to find the position of something. □ **orientar**
oriental [ɔːri'entl] *adj.* referring to the Orient: *oriental carpets.* □ **oriental**
■ *n.* person from the Orient. □ **oriental**
orientate ['ɔriənteit] *v.* to put in a certain direction; to find the position of something: *I haven't been able to orientate myself yet,* find out where I am/ get used to my surroundings. □ **orientar**
orientation [ɔːriən'teiʃn] *n.* (act of) orientating/putting in a certain position/direction. □ **orientación**
orienteering *n.* sport of finding your way across country by means of maps and compasses. □ **exploración**
orifice ['ɔrifis] *n.* (*formal*) hole/opening. □ **orificio**
origin ['ɔridʒin] *n.* beginning/root; where something/ someone comes from: *country of origin.* □ **origen**
original [ə'ridʒinl] *adj.* **1** from its beginning(s); from earliest times: *original inhabitants; original meaning of a word.* □ **original**
2 new/different; created for the first time/not a copy: *original work of art.* □ **original**
3 showing ideas not based on those of other people: *original style; original thinker.* □ **original**
■ *n.* **1** something from which other things are copied/translated, etc.: *is that picture an original?; to read a French novel in the original,* in French. □ **original**
2 an unusual person. □ **original**
originality [ɔridʒi'næliti] *n.* **1** being original/new/ different. □ **originalidad**
2 ability to create something which has never been done before. □ **originalidad**
originally *adv.* **1** in an original way. □ **con originalidad**
2 at or from the beginning: *originally they came from Sussex.* □ **originalmente**
originate [ə'ridʒineit] *v.* **1** to bring into existence for the first time: *they originated the plan.* □ **crear**
2 to begin/to have its beginning: *the revolt originated in the hilly districts.* □ **originarse**
originator *n.* person who originates. □ **creador**
oriole ['ɔːriəl] *n.* bird with black and yellow feathers. □ **oropéndola**
ornament ['ɔːnəmənt] *n.* thing(s) used as decoration: *the ribbon is only there for ornament; there are two ornaments on the shelf.* □ **adorno**
■ *v.* ['ɔːnəment] to decorate/to help to make more beautiful. □ **adornar**
ornamental [ɔːnə'mentl] *adj.* acting as an ornament; being pretty rather than useful: *that's purely ornamental.* □ **ornamental; decorativo**
ornate [ɔː'neit] *adj.* having (too) much ornament. □ **adornado, recargado**
ornery ['ɔːəri] *adj. Amer.* (*informal*) bad-tempered. □ **desagradable**
ornithology [ɔːni'θɔlədʒi] *n.* study of birds. □ **ornitología**
ornithological *adj.* referring to ornithology. □ **ornitológico**
ornithologist [ɔːni'θɔlədʒist] *n.* person who studies birds. □ **ornitólogo**
orphan ['ɔːfn] *n.* child who has no parents. □ **huérfano**
■ *v.* to cause to be an orphan: *he was orphaned at an early age,* his parents died when he was very young. □ **dejar huérfano**
orphanage ['ɔːfənidʒ] *n.* home where orphans are looked after. □ **orfanato**
orthodox ['ɔːθədɔks] *adj.* holding the generally accepted beliefs of a religion/a philosophy, etc.: *orthodox views; an orthodox Communist; orthodox*

Jews, Jews who observe traditional practices very strictly. □ **ortodoxo**
the Orthodox Church, the Christian Church of Eastern Europe. □ **la Iglesia Ortodoxa**
orthodoxy *n.* being orthodox. □ **ortodoxia**
orthography [ɔːˈθɔgrəfi] *n.* (correct) spelling. □ **ortografía**
orthographical *adj.* referring to orthography. □ **ortográfico**
orthopaedic [ɔːθəˈpiːdik] *adj.* referring to diseases and deformities of bones (especially in children): *orthopaedic surgery.* □ **ortopédico**
orthopaedics *n.* branch of medicine dealing with bones, etc. □ **ortopedia**
oscillate [ˈɔsileit] *v.* to swing from one side to the other. □ **oscilar**
oscillation *n.* (act of) oscillating. □ **oscilación**
osier [ˈouziə] *n.* type of willow tree whose branches are used to make baskets/furniture, etc. □ **mimbrera**
osmosis [ɔzˈmousis] *n.* movement of liquid into another liquid through the porous walls of a container. □ **ósmosis**
osprey [ˈɔspri] *n.* large bird of prey which eats fish. □ **águila pescadora**
ossify [ˈɔsifai] *v.* **1** to make into bone/like bone; to make rigid. □ **osificar**
2 *the bureaucracy has become ossified,* has become opposed to any change. □ **...se ha osificado**
ostensible [ɔˈstensibl] *adj.* which shows on the surface; which is meant to seem real: *that is the ostensible reason for his resignation.* □ **aparente**
ostensibly *adv.* seemingly: *ostensibly he went to Paris but in fact he stayed in London.* □ **aparentemente**
ostentatious [ɔstenˈteiʃəs] *adj.* showy/aiming to impress. □ **ostentoso**
ostentation *n.* showing off in a luxurious way which is intended to impress. □ **ostentación**
osteoarthritis [ɔstiouɑːˈθraitis] *n.* painful disease of the joints. □ **osteoartritis**
osteopath [ˈɔstiəpæθ] *n.* person who treats diseases of the bones and muscles by moving or massaging the patient's limbs. □ **osteópata**
ostracism [ˈɔstrəsizəm] *n.* being cut off from a group/from society. □ **ostracismo**
ostracize [ˈɔstrəsaiz] *v.* to force/to keep (someone) out of a group: *after the trial he was ostracized by his workmates.* □ **condenar al ostracismo**
ostrich [ˈɔstritʃ] *n.* large, fast-running, flightless bird found in Africa. □ **avestruz**
other [ˈʌðə] *adj.* **1** different/not the one already mentioned/not the same: *the other boys are at home; other people say; all other things being equal.* □ **otro**
2 second of two: *one pencil is red and and the other is blue.* □ **el otro**
every other week, every second week. □ **cada dos semanas**
3 (expressing a vague/approximate idea): *some hotel or other.* □ **un hotel u otro**
the other day, a day or two ago. □ **el otro día**
■ *pron.* **1** different person/different thing: *I don't like these apples, aren't there any others? the happiness of others; no one other than the minister arrived.* □ **otros; nadie más que el ministro...**
2 (used to contrast two things or groups): *one after the other; some stayed while others left.* □ **uno tras otro**
■ *adv.* **1** ***other than that*** *I have no idea,* apart from that. □ **aparte de eso**
2 *they couldn't have done* ***other than*** *they did,* anything different. □ **... otra cosa que la que hicieron**
otherwise *adv.* **1** in a different manner/situation: *otherwise we should have had to leave; she could scarcely have done otherwise; otherwise engaged.* □ **de otra manera**
2 in other respects: *otherwise he is just the same.* □ **por lo demás**
3 if not/or else: *leave now otherwise you will be late.* □ **si no; de lo contrario**
otherworldly *adj.* (person) who is not interested in material things/who is vague and impractical. □ **despegado del mundo**
otter [ˈɔtə] *n.* fish-eating mammal with webbed feet living mainly by rivers. □ **nutria**
ottoman [ˈɔtəmən] *n.* box for storing goods with a padded seat on top. □ **otomana**
ought [ɔːt] *v.* (past tense: *he ought to have*) *used with other verbs* **1** (expressing duty or obligation): *you really ought to go,* it is your duty to go; *I thought I ought to tell you.* □ **deber**
2 (expressing something which is vaguely desirable): *you ought to hear that concert; you ought to have seen them! you oughtn't to eat so many cakes.* □ **deber**
3 (expressing something which is probable): *that horse ought to win; you ought to get there by lunchtime,* you will probably get there. □ **ese caballo tiene más posibilidades de ganar; debes/deberías de estar allí...**
ounce [auns] *n.* measure of weight (28 grams). □ **onza**
our [ˈauə] *adj.* belonging to us: *our house; our child; one of our books.* □ **nuestro**
ours [ˈauəz] *pron.* thing(s)/person(s) belonging to us: *that book is ours; is that her boy? - no, he's ours; a friend of ours.* □ **el nuestro**
ourselves [auəˈselvz] *pron. referring to the subject* we **1** (emphatic): *we did it ourselves; we ourselves are to blame.* □ **nosotros mismos**
2 (reflexive): *we can help ourselves.* □ **nosotros mismos**
oust [aust] *v.* to force someone to leave a place/position (often by taking his place): *the Prime Minister was ousted in a military coup.* □ **expulsar, destituir**
out [aut] *adv.* **1** not in (a building, etc.): *John is out; out of town; a long way out (of the town).* □ **fuera**
2 *the men are out,* on strike. □ **...en huelga**
3 away from the starting point (of something): *out at sea; out there; the tide is out.* □ **mar adentro; por allí; es marea baja**
4 (*in a direction*) away from the inside/from the starting point: *to go out; he's out in the fields; the voyage out; hang out the washing; he pulled out a revolver.* □ **salir; ...fuera; ...de ida; sacó...**
5 having appeared/become known: *the hawthorn is out,* in flower; *her book is just out; the secret is out.* □ **el espino está en flor; su libro acaba de salir**
6 *he said it out loud,* so that it could be heard; *I told her straight out.* □ **...en voz alta; se lo dije sin rodeos**
7 not in the right position/state: *she's put her shoulder out (of joint),* bones are in the wrong position. □ **se le ha salido el hombro**
8 ***out of practice,*** not having done enough practice. □ **desentrenado**
9 *the Conservatives are out,* have lost power. □ **...están fuera del poder**
10 *they're out of the competition,* have been beaten/disqualified. □ **fuera de...**
11 *he is 62 not out,* (in cricket) he has scored 62 and has not been bowled/caught, etc. □ **ha puntuado 62**

a favor y ninguno en contra
12 mistaken: *you're out in your calculations; I am $5 out,* I have $5 too much/too little; *I wasn't so far out,* not so far wrong. □ **equivocado; me faltan $5; no andaba tan descaminado**
13 (*of fire, etc.*) no longer burning; (*of hairstyle, etc.*) no longer fashionable: *short skirts are out.* □ **el fuego está apagado; la minifalda ya no está de moda**
14 finished; having reached the end: *to hear someone out; before the week is out.* □ **escuchar hasta el final a alguien; antes de que termine la semana**
■ *n. to know* ***the ins and outs of,*** to know something in all its details. □ **conocer todos los pormenores de**
out-and-out *adj.* and *adv.* complete(ly)/total(ly): *out-and-out liar.* □ **empedernido**
outback *n.* (*especially in Australia*) area(s) away from centres of population. □ **llanura desértica**
outbid *v.* (*he outbid*) (*at auction*) to bid a higher sum than (someone). □ **sobrepujar**
outboard *adj.* (engine) which is attached to the outside of a boat. □ **fuera borda**
outbreak *n.* sudden occurrence of an illness or unrest. □ **erupción, estallido**
outbuildings *n. pl.* buildings standing apart from the main building. □ **edificios anexos**
outburst *n.* sudden display of (violent) emotion: *outburst of rage/laughter.* □ **arrebato de ira; una carcajada**
outcast *n.* and *adj.* (person who has been) rejected by/driven away from a society or a group. □ **proscrito**
outcome *n.* result: *the outcome of their discussions.* □ **resultado**
outcry *n.* loud protest from a number of people: *the council's decision caused a public outcry.* □ **protesta ruidosa**
outdated *adj.* old-fashioned. □ **anticuado**
outdo *v.* (*he outdid; he has outdone*) to do better than: *she outdid all her classmates.* □ **aventajar**
outdoor *adj.* in the open air: *an outdoor swimming pool.* □ **al aire libre**
outdoors *adv.* and *n.* (in/to) the open air. □ **fuera (adv.); aire libre (n.)**
outer *adj.* further out; on the outside; beyond the limits: *the outer harbour; in an outer room; outer surface.* □ **exterior**
outer space, space beyond the earth's atmosphere. □ **espacio exterior**
outermost *adj.* furthest out: *the outermost islands.* □ **más alejado**
outfit *n.* **1** set of equipment needed for a particular purpose: *first-aid outfit.* □ **equipo**
2 set of clothing: *nurse's outfit.* □ **uniforme de enfermera**
3 (*informal*) organization: *that new outfit in the High Street.* □ **sociedad**
outfitter *n.* supplier of (especially men's) clothing. □ **proveedor textil**
outgoing *adj.* **1** going out: *outgoing tide.* □ **saliente**
2 *outgoing president,* president who is approaching the end of his term of office. □ **saliente**
3 open/lively: *an outgoing personality.* □ **sociable**
outgoings *n. pl.* money spent. □ **gastos**
outgrow *v.* (*he outgrew; he has outgrown*) to grow too big for (clothes); to leave behind as one grows up: *to outgrow an illness/an interest, etc.* □ **crecer más que, perder al crecer**
outhouse *n.* building standing apart from the main building. □ **edificio anexo**
outing *n.* trip, usually for pleasure: *an outing to the seaside.* □ **salida**
outlandish *adj.* strange/different from the usual: *outlandish customs.* □ **extravagante**
outlast *v.* to live longer than: *he outlasted all his colleagues.* □ **sobrevivir a**
outlaw *n.* person who has been outlawed. □ **proscrito**
■ *v.* to declare (someone) to be beyond (the protection of) the law. □ **proscribir**
outlay *n.* expenditure: *capital outlay.* □ **desembolso**
outlet *n.* **1** means by which something can escape: *outlet pipe; outlet for your energies.* □ **desagüe; modo/salida para emplear tus energías**
2 place where something can be sold or distributed: *they have outlets for their goods in all large towns.* □ **punto de venta**
outline *n.* line showing the outer edge(s) of something; broad description without much detail: *draw the outline of a horse; the outline of a plan.* □ **contorno; bosquejo**
■ *v.* to make a broad description: *he outlined his plan.* □ **resumir**
outlive *v.* to live longer than: *he outlived all his friends.* □ **sobrevivir a**
outlook *n.* view from a building/of the world/of the future: *outlook from a house; his outlook on life; the outlook is none too promising.* □ **vista (desde la casa); visión (de la vida); las perspectivas no son...**
outlying *adj.* away from the centre or the main part: *outlying districts.* □ **remoto; las afueras (de una ciudad)**
outmanoeuvre *Amer.* **outmaneuver** *v.* to beat someone by acting/working more cleverly. □ **ser mejor estratega que**
outmoded *adj.* old-fashioned. □ **pasado de moda**
outnumber *v.* to be greater in number than: *they outnumbered the enemy by ten to one.* □ **exceder en número**
out of *prep.* **1** outside of; away from: *out of the window; out of season; to put something out of your mind; you must be out of your mind,* be mad: *he turned them out of the house.* □ **fuera de**
2 from: *drink out of a glass; one out of every ten.* □ **bebida de un vaso; uno de cada diez**
3 made from: *made out of a few old planks.* □ **hecho de**
4 because of: *out of courtesy.* □ **por**
5 no longer having: *a million people are out of work; we are out of tea.* □ **sin**
6 ***out of print,*** (*of books*) with no printed copies left. □ **agotado**
out of date *adj.* **1** no longer in fashion. □ **anticuado**
2 no longer valid: *your passport is out of date.* □ **caducado**
out of the way *adj.* **1** very far from the centre. □ **apartado**
2 unusual/extraordinary: *that is not an out of the way price for a good coat.* □ **inasequible**
outpatient *n.* person who attends a hospital without staying overnight. □ **paciente externo**
outpost *n.* small garrison of soldiers in a distant part of an occupied territory: *an outpost of the empire.* □ **puesto de avanzada**
outpourings *n. pl.* flood (of complaints/of emotional speech). □ **efusiones**
output *n.* amount which a firm/machine/person produces. □ **producción**
outrider ['autraidə] *n.* guard on a motorcycle or horse, riding beside a car/carriage in a procession. □ **escolta**

outright ['autrait] *adv.* and *adj.* **1** complete(ly); all at once: *to buy something outright; outright sale.* □ **en el acto (adv.); completo (adj.)**
2 straight out/without pretending: *to laugh at someone outright.* □ **abiertamente**
outset ['autset] *n.* beginning: *at/from the outset.* □ **al/desde el principio**
outshine [aut'ʃain] *v.* (*he outshone*) to do much better than someone else: *she outshone the rest of the class.* □ **brillar más que**
outside [aut'said] *n.* **1** outer surface (of something); what is beyond the outer surface/edge of something: *open the door from the outside; the address is on the outside of the parcel.* □ **exterior**
2 ***at the outside,*** at the most: *$10 at the outside.* □ **como mucho**
■ *adj.* **1** on the outer surface: *outside walls.* □ **exterior**
2 the most (possible): *an outside estimate.* □ **una estimación por lo alto**
3 from the outside/from another group, etc.: *outside workers.* □ **externo**
■ *adv.* and *prep.* beyond the outer surface/edge of (something): *I left the dog outside; outside the house; he came in from outside.* □ **afuera/fuera**
outsider *n.* **1** person who does not belong to a group, etc. □ **forastero**
2 horse which is not expected to win, and does not have high bets placed on it. □ **caballo no favorito**
outsize ['autsaiz] *n.* and *adj.* (of) a size which is larger than the normal or usual range: *outsize clothes.* □ **talla muy grande (n.); de talla (adj.)**
outskirts ['autskə:ts] *n. pl.* outer edges of a town, etc. □ **afueras**
outsmart [aut'smɑ:t] *v.* to trick (someone) by being cleverer. □ **ser más listo que**
outspoken [aut'spoukən] *adj.* speaking (too) frankly. □ **franco**
outstanding [aut'stændiŋ] *adj.* **1** excellent; of unusual quality/very high standard, etc.: *outstanding feature; outstanding talent.* □ **destacado**
2 not yet fulfilled/completed: *outstanding payments; there are still three bills outstanding.* □ **deudas por pagar; quedan tres cuentas pendientes**
outstandingly *adv.* to an outstanding degree: *he is outstandingly talented.* □ **excepcionalmente**
outstay [aut'stei] *v.* to stay longer than: *don't outstay your welcome.* □ **quedarse más tiempo que**
out to *adj.* trying to/aiming for: *she's out to beat her rivals.* □ **está decidida a...**
outvote [aut'vout] *v.* to defeat by having more votes than: *they were outvoted by the opposition parties.* □ **vencer en una elección**
outward ['autwəd] *adj.* and *adv.* **1** towards the outside; away from the centre or starting point: *outward voyage; outward bound.* □ **hacia fuera (adv.); viaje de ida; con rumbo hacia**
2 on the outside: *outward appearances.* □ **las apariencias que nos rodean**
outwardly *adv.* (appearing) on the outside: *outwardly he didn't seem frightened.* □ **aparentemente**
outwards *adv.* towards the outside. □ **hacia fuera**
outweigh [aut'wei] *v.* to be more important than something: *the problem of security outweighs all other problems.* □ **pesar más que**
outwit [aut'wit] *v.* (*he outwitted*) to trick (someone) by being cleverer: *he outwitted his pursuers by taking a different route.* □ **ser más listo que**
outrage ['autreidʒ] *n.* offence; vigorous attack (especially against moral standards): *their treatment of the children was an outrage.* □ **ultraje, agravio**
■ *v.* to shock/to be a cause of moral indignation to: *he was outraged by their behaviour.* □ **ultrajar, agraviar**
outrageous [aut'reidʒəs] *adj.* causing (moral) indignation/shock: *outrageous behaviour/prices.* □ **ultrajante, escandaloso**
outrageously *adv.* in an outrageous way. □ **de una manera escandalosa**
ova ['ouvə] *n. pl. see* **ovum.**
oval ['ouvl] *n.* and *adj.* (of) a long rounded shape: egg-shape(d): *an oval plate.* □ **oval**
ovary ['ouvəri] *n.* one of the two organs of a female mammal in which eggs are produced. □ **ovario**
ovation [ə'veiʃn] *n.* great applause: *the conductor received a standing ovation,* the audience stood up to applaud him. □ **ovación**
oven ['ʌvn] *n.* enclosed box which can be heated for cooking/for baking pottery, etc.: *bread baked in the oven.* □ **horno**
ovenware *n.* (*no pl.*) dishes which can be put in a hot oven. □ **platos termorresistentes**
over ['ouvə] *prep.* **1** on the top (surface) of: *to spread a cloth over the table.* □ **sobre**
2 higher than: *he was bent over his work; over the door; jutting out over the street; with water over her ankles.* □ **por encima de**
3 across/on to the other side (of something): *to throw something over the wall; a bridge over the river.* □ **por encima de (la pared); sobre (el río)**
4 from the top of: *he threw it over the cliff; she fell over the edge.* □ **lo tiró por...; se cayó encima del...**
5 on the other/on the far side of: *over the border; he lives over the road.* □ **al otro lado de**
6 everywhere in: *all over the town; the whole world over.* □ **por toda la ciudad; por todo el mundo**
7 during: *over the last three years; over dinner.* □ **durante**
8 more than: *over $50; over 5 (years old); over and above that.* □ **más de; además de eso**
9 better than: *to have an advantage over someone.* □ **sobre**
10 about: *they quarrelled over the money in the will; two dogs were fighting over a bone.* □ **por**
■ *adv.* **1** in all parts of (something): *to be dusty all over; he read the letter over.* □ **estar cubierto de polvo; leyó la carta hasta el final**
2 repeatedly: *to do it (all) over again; ten times over; over and over again.* □ **una y otra vez**
3 above the top of (something): *to jump over; the milk boiled over.* □ **cruzar de un salto; la leche se salió**
4 downwards from a previous vertical position: *to lean over; it fell over; to knock something over.* □ **inclinarse; se cayó; tirar algo**
5 into another position: *to bend (something) over; please turn over,* turn the page; *he folded it over.* □ **doblar algo, pasar**
6 to the other side of something: *to cross over; over there.* □ **cruzar; por allá**
7 more/higher in number: *children of 12 and over,* who are 12 years old or older; *there are reductions for groups of 30 and over,* with 30 or more members. □ **chicos de 12 años para arriba; ...de 30 y más**
8 in excess/left behind: *keep what was left over; I have two cards over; the question is left over until the next meeting.* □ **me quedan dos cartas; ...se pospone hasta el...**
9 past/finished: *the danger is over; it's all over; when the war was over; the party's over.* □ **el peligro ha terminado; se acabó; cuando terminó la guerra**

10 *prefix meaning* too (much): *overexcited.* □ **sobreexcitado**
■ *n.* one of the sections of a cricket match, during which one bowler bowls six times. □ **serie**
overall *adj.* **1** covering; taking in all aspects: *overall view.* □ **global; visión de conjunto**
2 *overall length,* length from end to end. □ **longitud total**
■ *n.* **1** light coat worn by women at work. □ **bata**
2 ***overalls,*** man's one-piece suit worn to protect the other clothes. □ **mono**
overawe [ouvə'ɔ:] *v.* to frighten: *he was overawed by the panel of examiners.* □ **intimidar**
overbalance *v.* to (cause to) lose balance. □ **hacer perder el equilibrio**
overbearing *adj.* trying to dominate others: *overbearing manner.* □ **autoritario**
overboard *adv.* into the water from the edge of a ship, etc: *he fell overboard.* □ **por la borda**
overcast *adj.* (*of sky*) heavy/dull/cloudy. □ **cubierto**
overcharge *v.* to charge too much for something. □ **cobrar de más**
overcoat *n.* (full-length) coat for outdoor wear. □ **abrigo**
overcome *v.* **1** (*he overcame; he has overcome*) to gain victory over (an enemy/a problem/an emotion). □ **vencer; superar**
2 *the firemen were overcome by the smoke,* became ill because of the smoke. □ **el humo pudo con los bomberos**
3 *he was overcome by grief,* helpless with grief. □ **vencido por el dolor**
overcrowded *adj.* (*of building/place/vehicle*) containing too many people/animals, etc. □ **atestado de gente**
overdo *v.* (*he overdid; he has overdone*) **1** to do too much; to exaggerate: *she always overdoes things.* □ **exagerar**
2 to cook too much: *the roast is overdone.* □ **...está demasiado hecho**
overdose *n.* too large a dose (of a drug): *she died of an overdose of sleeping tablets.* □ **sobredosis**
overdraft *n.* amount by which a bank account is overdrawn; amount which the bank allows you to borrow. □ **descubierto**
overdraw *v.* (*he overdrew; he has overdrawn*) to take out money (from a bank account) when there is no money there. □ **girar en descubierto**
overeat *v.* (*he overate; he has overeaten*) to eat too much. □ **atracarse a comer**
overeating *n.* eating too much. □ **atracón**
overestimate *v.* to estimate too much; to think something is larger than it is. □ **sobrestimar**
overexposed *adj.* (film) which has been exposed too much. □ **con exceso de exposición**
overfed *adj.* given too much to eat. □ **sobrealimentado**
overflow *v.* **1** to flow over the top: *he filled the glass until it overflowed; the river has overflowed its banks.* □ **derramarse; desbordarse**
2 to occupy greater space: *the meeting overflowed into the next room.* □ **desbordarse hasta**
■ *n.* **1** liquid which has overflowed. □ **desbordamiento**
2 pipe to catch overflowing liquid. □ **cañería de desagüe**
3 amount or number which will not fit a given space: *we shall need the small hall to take the overflow from the meeting.* □ **exceso**
overgrown *adj.* covered (with plants, etc.): *the garden is overgrown with weeds.* □ **cubierto de hierba**
overhanging *adj.* which juts out over. □ **sobresaliente**
overhaul [ouvə'hɔ:l] *v.* **1** to examine carefully, repairing where necessary: *the engine was overhauled before they left.* □ **revisar**
2 to overtake (another ship). □ **alcanzar a un buque**
■ *n.* ['ouvəhɔ:l] (act of) overhauling: *the engine needs a complete overhaul.* □ **revisión**
overhead *adv.* above: *aircraft flying overhead.* □ **por encima de la cabeza**
■ *adj.* **1** above: *overhead cable.* □ **cable aéreo**
2 ***overhead expenses,*** general expenses incurred by a business as a whole, such as salaries/heating/rent, etc. □ **gastos generales**
overheads *n. pl.* overhead expenses. □ **gastos generales**
overhear [ouvə'hi:ə] *v.* (*he overheard*) to hear accidentally (often what you are not meant to hear). □ **oír por casualidad**
overheat *v.* to heat too much: *the engine is overheating.* □ **recalentar(se)**
overjoyed *adj.* very happy. □ **lleno de alegría**
overland *adv.* and *adj.* by land: *to travel overland; overland route.* □ **por tierra**
overlap *v.* (*it overlapped*) to cover the same area/time as a section of something: *their holidays overlapped.* □ **traslapar**
■ *n.* amount by which something overlaps. □ **superposición**
overleaf *adv.* on the other side of a page. □ **a la vuelta**
overload *v.* to put too heavy a load on: *to overload a car/machine, etc.* □ **sobrecargar**
overlook *v.* **1** not to notice: *I overlooked the fact.* □ **no advertir**
2 to pretend not to notice; to pay no attention to: *we will overlook your rudeness for once.* □ **pasar por alto**
3 to look out on to: *the kitchen window overlooks the garden.* □ **tener vistas a**
overly *adv.* (*used in North of England, Scotland and America*) too much: *it's not overly good.* □ **excesivamente**
overmuch *adv.* too much. □ **demasiado**
overnight *adv.* **1** until morning: *they stayed overnight; will the food keep overnight?* □ **por una noche**
2 *conditions became worse almost overnight,* very rapidly. □ **...de la noche a la mañana**
■ *adj.* for the night: *overnight bag; an overnight stay.* □ **neceser; estancia de una noche**
overnight train, train which travels through the night. □ **tren nocturno**
overpass *n.* road which crosses over the top of another road. □ **paso elevado**
overplay *v.* ***to overplay your hand,*** to attempt (to gain) too much in negotiations. □ **aspirar demasiado**
overpower *v.* to gain control of (by force): *the criminal was overpowered by the police.* □ **sujetar y tener quieto**
overpowering *adv.* very strong: *an overpowering smell.* □ **irresistible**
overproduction *n.* excess production. □ **superproducción**
overrate *v.* to estimate/to value (something) higher than it is: *his powers of leadership are vastly overrated.* □ **sobrestimar**
overreach *v.* ***to overreach yourself,*** to go too far (and fail in what you are trying to do). □ **ir demasiado lejos**
overreact *v.* to react very violently. □ **reaccionar violentamente**

override *v.* (*he overrode; he has overridden*) **1** to pay no attention to (an order, etc.). □ **no hacer caso de**
2 to be more important than other things: *that is the overriding consideration.* □ **primordial**
overrider *n.* rubber pad fixed to the bumper of a car. □ **parachoques de goma**
overrule *v.* to rule/to order against: *they were overruled by the majority vote; the judge overruled the decision of the lower court.* □ **rechazar**
overrun *v.* (*he overran; he has overrun*) **1** to go into/to attack all parts of: *the invading army overran the whole country; the house was overrun by mice.* □ **invadir**
2 to continue beyond (a time limit): *the broadcast overran its time.* □ **rebasar**
overseas *adv.* and *adj.* across the sea: *overseas sales staff; his parents live overseas.* □ **en el extranjero**
overseer *n.* person who supervises other people at work. □ **supervisor**
overshadow *v.* to hide/to make less conspicuous by greater brilliance: *he was overshadowed by his father's reputation.* □ **eclipsar**
overshoes *n. pl.* rubber/plastic shoes worn over ordinary shoes to protect them. □ **chanclo**
overshoot *v.* (*he overshot*) to go beyond a natural stopping place: *the aircraft overshot the runway.* □ **llegar más allá de**
to overshoot the mark, to go beyond what you were aiming for. □ **pasarse de la raya**
oversight *n.* not doing something because of forgetfulness/not noticing: *his lack of reply was just an oversight; he failed to reply through an oversight.* □ **descuido**
oversleep *v.* (*he overslept; he has overslept*) to sleep longer than you meant to: *he overslept and missed the train.* □ **quedarse dormido más de lo previsto**
overspend *v.* (*he overspent*) to spend more than you should; *he has overspent his budget.* □ **gastar más de**
overstate *v.* to state too strongly/with too much detail: *he damaged his case by overstating it.* □ **exagerar**
overstatement *n.* act of overstating; what is overstated: *that was a gross overstatement of the facts.* □ **exageración**
overstep *v.* (*he overstepped*) to go further than you ought to: *to overstep the mark.* □ **pasarse de la raya**
overstuffed *adj.* well padded (sofa). □ **relleno**
oversubscribed *adj. the issue of shares was oversubscribed,* more people applied for shares than there were shares available. □ **se pidieron más acciones de las que había**
overtake *v.* (*he overtook; he has overtaken*) to reach (and go past) (someone ahead of you); to pass (another car) which is going more slowly than you: *he was overtaken by disaster; no overtaking on corners.* □ **adelantar**
overtax *v.* **1** to demand too much tax from: *this country is grossly overtaxed.* □ **exigir demasiados impuestos**
2 *he overtaxed his strength,* he did more than he was physically capable of. □ **exigirse demasiado**
overthrow *v.* (*he overthrew; he has overthrown*) to defeat: *the government was overthrown in a coup; his plans were overthrown by the committee.* □ **derrocar, rechazar**
overtime *n.* **1** time worked beyond normal working hours. □ **horas extraordinarias**
2 money paid for working beyond normal hours: *you will get your overtime at the end of the month.* □ **pago de horas extraordinarias**
■ *adv.* beyond normal hours: *to work overtime.* □ **trabajar horas extraordinarias**
overtones *n. pl.* suggestion of something different from the general content: *there were overtones of suspicion in the conversation.* □ **insinuación**
overturn [ouvə'tə:n] *v.* to (cause to) fall over/to turn upside down: *the car was overturned in the accident.* □ **volcar**
overview *n.* general view (of a subject). □ **visión general**
overweening [ouvə'wi:niŋ] *adj. overweening pride,* excessive pride of an arrogant person. □ **orgullo desmesurado**
overweight [ouvə'weit] *adj.* too heavy: *have you always been overweight? the parcel is two kilos overweight.* □ **con sobrepeso**
overwhelm [ouvə'welm] *v.* **1** to conquer (completely). □ **vencer**
2 ***to be overwhelmed with*** *work,* to have more work than you can do. □ **estar agobiado de trabajo**
overwhelming *adj.* enormous; greater than all others: *they won by an overwhelming majority.* □ **abrumador**
overwork [ouvə'wə:k] *n.* too much work: *he'll kill himself with overwork.* □ **exceso de trabajo**
■ *v.* to (cause to) work too hard: *he has been overworking lately; he's grossly overworked.* □ **trabajar demasiado; está agotado de trabajar tanto**
overwrought [ouvə'rɔ:t] *adj.* very agitated/under a lot of stress. □ **sobrexcitado**
overt [ou'və:t] *adj.* open/not hidden: *overt criticism.* □ **abierto; crítica pública**
overture ['ouvətʃə] *n.* **1** (short) piece of music played at the beginning of an opera/concert, etc. □ **obertura**
2 ***to make overtures to someone,*** to try to begin a conversation/negotiations with someone. □ **hacer una propuesta a alguien**
ovoid ['ouvɔid] *adj.* shaped like an egg. □ **ovoide**
ovum ['ouvəm] *n.* (*pl. ova*) female egg which can develop inside the mother's body when fertilized. □ **óvulo**
ovulate ['ɔvjuleit] *v.* to produce female eggs. □ **ovular**
owe [ou] *v.* **1** to be obliged; to be due to pay (someone): *how much do I owe you for the petrol? we owe you a return visit.* □ **deber**
2 to have something because of (someone/something): *I owe him my life; he owes a great deal to his family.* □ **deber**
owing to *prep.* because of: *owing to bad weather.* □ **debido a**
owl [aul] *n.* bird of prey which is mainly active at night. □ **lechuza; búho**
own [oun] *v.* **1** to have/to possess: *I don't own a car; who owns this land?* □ **poseer; tener**
2 to recognize as belonging to you: *a dog that no one will own.* □ **aceptar como propio**
3 to admit; to say that something is true: *he owned that he believed in ghosts.* □ **reconocer**
4 ***to own up to something,*** (*informal*) to admit/to say that you have done something wrong: *he owned up to his mistake; she owned up to having stolen the money.* □ **confesar**
■ *adj.* belonging to yourself (alone): *her own money; the house is our own; he has his own warehouse.* □ **propio**
■ *n.* **1** *my own/his own,* mine/his: *I have money of my own; for reasons of his own.* □ **lo mío/lo suyo; tengo dinero mío; por motivos personales**
to come into your own, to have the success which

you deserve. □ **conseguir lo que uno se merece**
to get your own back, (*informal*) have your revenge. □ **desquitarse**
to hold your own, to remain firm against some threat. □ **mantenerse firme**
2 ***on your own,*** alone/by yourself: *he did it on his own; I'm on my own today.* □ **él solo; hoy estoy solo**
owner *n.* person who owns: *who's the owner of the house? cars are parked at owners' risk.* □ **dueño**
ownership *n.* state of owning: *the cafe is under new ownership.* □ **propiedad; nuevo propietario (el café)**
ox [ɔks] *n.* (*pl. oxen*) **1** large animal of the cow family. □ **toro**
2 castrated bull. □ **buey**
oxtail *n.* tail of the ox used as food: *oxtail soup.* □ **rabo de toro**
oxide ['ɔksaid] *n.* chemical compound of oxygen. □ **óxido**
oxidation [ɔksi'deiʃn] *n.* act of oxidizing. □ **oxidación**
oxidize ['ɔksidaiz] *v.* to (cause to) combine with oxygen. □ **oxidar**
oxyacetylene [ɔksiə'setiliːn] *n.* and *adj.* (referring to a) mixture of oxygen and acetylene: *oxyacetylene lamp.* □ **oxiacetileno; oxiacetilénico**
oxygen ['ɔksidʒən] *n.* (*chemical element*: O) gas which forms part of the earth's atmosphere and is essential for plant and animal life. □ **oxígeno**
oyster ['ɔistə] *n.* type of double-shelled shellfish highly valued as food. □ **ostra**
oyster bed, part of the sea floor where oysters are found. □ **criadero de ostras**
oystercatcher *n.* common black and white bird which lives on the seashore. □ **ostrero**
ozone ['ouzoun] *n.* **1** type of oxygen. □ **ozono**
2 (*informal*) refreshing sea air. □ **aire fresco**

P,p

P, p [piː] sixteenth letter of the alphabet. □ **P, p**
pace [peis] *n.* **1** stride/step; distance covered by one step: *the treasure is buried six paces north of the tree.* □ **paso**
2 speed. □ **paso**
at a good pace, quite quickly. □ **a buen paso**
to keep pace with: *I can't keep pace with him,* keep up with him. □ **no le puedo seguir el paso**
to set the pace, (*of a runner*) to decide how fast a race should be run/to lead in a race. □ **marcar el ritmo**
■ *v.* **1** to walk: *he paced up and down outside the door.* □ **pasearse**
2 to measure by walking: *they paced out thirty yards.* □ **medir a pasos**
3 to set the pace (for a runner, etc.). □ **marcar el ritmo**
pacemaker *n.* **1** runner who sets the pace in a race; person who runs alongside a runner to encourage him to run faster. □ **liebre**
2 electric device which makes heartbeats regular. □ **marcapasos**
pachyderm ['pækidəːm] *n.* animal with a thick skin (such as an elephant). □ **paquidermo**
pacify ['pæsifai] *v.* to calm. □ **tranquilizar**
pacific [pə'sifik] *adj.* peaceful/calm. □ **pacífico**
Pacific Ocean, ocean separating America from Asia and Australasia. □ **Océano Pacífico**
pacification [pæsifi'keiʃn] *n.* calming (of people in revolt). □ **pacificación**
pacifier ['pæsifaiə] *n. Amer.* dummy/plastic teat sucked by babies. □ **chupete**
pacifism *n.* opposition to war. □ **pacifismo**
pacifist *n.* person who believes international disputes should not be settled by war. □ **pacifista**
pack [pæk] *n.* **1** bundle of things: *pack of cards; it's a pack of lies.* □ **baraja de cartas; sarta de mentiras**
2 rucksack/bag carried on the back. □ **mochila**
3 group of animals/people: *pack of wolves/thieves.* □ **manada de lobos; pandilla de ladrones**
the pack, the forwards in a rugby team. □ **el 'pack'**
4 articles put in a box for selling: *economy pack.* □ **lote**
5 ***face pack,*** cream which is spread on your face and left on it for a time to clean the skin. □ **mascarilla**
6 ***ice pack,*** bag of ice placed on the forehead to cure a headache, etc. □ **bolsa de hielo**
■ *v.* **1** to put things in order in a case/box: *she's busy packing,* busy putting things in suitcases; *the plates are packed in straw.* □ **embalar**
2 to squeeze many things into a small area: *packed like sardines; the trains are packed with holidaymakers; they managed to pack eleven people into the car.* □ **como sardinas en lata; los trenes están abarrotados...; consiguieron meter once...**
3 *they packed the children off to their grandparents',* they sent them away. □ **les endilgaron los niños...**
package *n.* **1** bundle of things/parcel: *the postman has brought this package.* □ **paquete**
2 ***package deal,*** deal where everything is agreed and paid for in advance. □ **acuerdo global**
3 ***package tour,*** tour which is organized and paid for in advance. □ **viaje con todo pagado**
■ *v.* to wrap/to present (goods) in an attractive way. □ **envolver**
packaging *n.* wrapping of goods in an attractive way. □ **envoltorio**
packer *n.* person who packs goods. □ **empaquetador**
packet *n.* small parcel; small box: *packet of cigarettes.* □ **paquete**
pack ice *n.* mass of ice covering the sea. □ **banco de hielo**
packing *n.* **1** putting things into containers. □ **embalaje**
packing case, special wooden box for packing goods (especially for transport). □ **cajón de embalaje**
2 material used to protect goods which are being packed. □ **embalaje**
pack up *v.* to put things away (before closing a shop/before leaving a place). □ **recoger**
pact [pækt] *n.* agreement/treaty. □ **pacto**
pad [pæd] *n.* **1** soft part under the feet of some animals; soft protective cushion. □ **almohadilla**
2 (*in cricket*) protective guard for the batsman's leg. □ **espinillera**
3 set of sheets of paper lightly attached: *pad of notepaper; writing pad; note pad.* □ **taco**
4 ***launching pad,*** area from which a rocket is launched. □ **plataforma de lanzamiento**
5 (*slang*) room/flat. □ **cuarto**
■ *v.* (*he padded*) **1** to soften (something hard) by using soft material: *padded chair.* □ **acolchar; silla acolchada**
2 ***to pad out*** *a speech/an article,* to make a speech/an article longer by inserting irrelevant material. □ **meter paja en**
3 to walk about softly: *the tiger padded across the cage.* □ **andar a pasos quedos**
padding *n.* **1** irrelevant words added to a speech or article to make it longer. □ **paja**
2 soft material used to make cushions, etc. □ **borra**
paddle ['pædl] *n.* **1** short oar used to propel a canoe. □ **canalete**
2 round bat used in table tennis. □ **paleta**
3 walk in shallow water: *let's go for a paddle in the pool.* □ **mojarse los pies**
■ *v.* **1** to make a boat move forward using a paddle. □ **remar con canalete**
2 to walk about in very shallow water. □ **andar mojándose los pies**
paddle steamer *n.* old type of boat driven by large wheels on either side, each wheel having horizontal blades to push against the water. □ **buque de ruedas de paletas**
paddle wheel *n.* wheel on a paddle steamer. □ **rueda de paletas**
paddling pool *n.* small shallow pool for little children. □ **piscina para niños**
paddock ['pædək] *n.* small field for horses. □ **'paddock'**
paddy field ['pædifiːld] *n.* field where rice is grown. □ **arrozal**
padlock ['pædlɔk] *n.* small portable lock with a hook which can be unlocked and twisted to pass through a ring to lock a gate/a box, etc. □ **candado**
■ *v.* to lock with a padlock: *the gates were chained and padlocked.* □ **cerrar con candado**
paean ['piːən] *n.* (*formal*) great song praising someone. □ **himno de alegría**

paediatrician [piːdiə'triʃn] *n.* doctor who specializes in treating children's diseases. □ **pediatra**
paediatrics [piːdi'ætriks] *n.* science of treatment of children's diseases. □ **pediatría**
pagan ['peign] *adj.* and *n.* (person) who does not believe in one of the established religions; (person) who is not a Christian. □ **pagano**
page [peidʒ] *n.* **1** one of the sides of a sheet of paper in a book or magazine: *this book has 456 pages; turn to page 54.* □ **página**
2 messenger boy in a hotel. □ **botones**
3 small boy who accompanies the bride at a wedding. □ **paje**
■ *v.* to call (someone) over a loudspeaker in a hotel: *can you page Mr Smith for me?* □ **buscar a uno diciendo su nombre**
pageant ['pædʒənt] *n.* grand display of people in costume. □ **desfile**
pageantry *n.* grand ceremonies where people wear showy costumes. □ **ceremonias con boato**
paginate ['pædʒineit] *v.* to number the pages in a book. □ **paginar**
pagoda [pə'goudə] *n.* tall tower made of several storeys, found in the Far East. □ **pagoda**
paid [peid] *v. see* **pay.**
pail [peil] *n.* bucket. □ **cubo**
pain [pein] *n.* **1** sensation of being hurt: *I've got pains in my back,* my back hurts. □ **dolor**
2 ***to take great pains over something/to do something,*** to take great care. □ **hacer grandes esfuerzos**
3 ***on pain of death,*** at the risk of being sentenced to death. □ **so pena de muerte**
■ *v.* to hurt: *it pains me to have to tell you this.* □ **doler**
pained *adj.* sad/sorrowful (expression). □ **apenado**
painful *adj.* which hurts: *he's had a painful operation.* □ **doloroso**
painfully *adv.* in a way which hurts: *he walked painfully across the room.* □ **penosamente**
painless *adj.* which does not hurt. □ **indoloro**
painkiller *n.* drug which stops part of your body hurting. □ **calmante**
painkilling *adj.* (drug) which stops part of your body hurting. □ **calmante**
painstaking *adj.* careful/well-done (work). □ **esmerado**
paint [peint] *n.* liquid in various colours used to colour something: *I gave the ceiling two coats of paint; don't sit down - the paint is still wet.* □ **pintura**
box of paints, box with blocks of colour which are mixed with water to make pictures. □ **caja de pinturas**
■ *v.* **1** to cover with colour: *he painted the front door blue.* □ **pintar**
2 to make a picture (of someone/something): *he painted the portrait of his mother; she painted the village church.* □ **pintar**
painter *n.* **1** person who paints pictures: *Rembrandt was a famous Dutch painter.* □ **pintor**
2 person who paints houses/cars, etc. □ **pintor**
3 rope for tying up a boat. □ **amarra**
painting *n.* **1** making pictures: *he's studying painting; she's taken up oil painting.* □ **pintura**
2 picture: *do you like this painting of Venice?* □ **cuadro**
paintwork *n.* (*no pl.*) painted surfaces (doors/windows, etc.). □ **pintura**
pair ['pɛə] *n.* **1** two things taken together; two people: *a pair of shoes; they're a happy pair,* the two of them are happy together. □ **par**
2 two things joined together to make one: *a pair of scissors/of trousers/of binoculars.* □ **unas tijeras; unos pantalones; unos gemelos**
■ *v.* **1** to join together in twos: *the dancers paired off.* □ **emparejar**
2 to mate. □ **aparearse**
pajamas [pə'dʒɑːməz] *n. pl. Amer.* pyjamas/light shirt and trousers worn in bed. □ **pijama**
Pakistan [pæki'stɑːn] *n.* Muslim country in Asia. □ **Paquistán**
Pakistani *adj.* referring to Pakistan. □ **paquistaní**
■ *n.* person from Pakistan. □ **paquistaní**
pal [pæl] *n.* (*informal*) friend. □ **amiguete**
palace ['pæləs] *n.* large building where a king/queen/president, etc., lives. □ **palacio**
palate ['pælət] *n.* top part of the inside of the mouth. □ **paladar**
palatable *adj.* nice to eat/tasting good. □ **sabroso**
palatial [pə'leiʃl] *adj.* magnificent/like a palace. □ **suntuoso**
palaver [pə'lɑːvə] *n.* (*informal*) fuss/bother. □ **follón**
pale [peil] *adj.* light-coloured: *he turned pale at the sight of blood; she's wearing a pale green dress.* □ **pálido**
■ *n. he's* ***beyond the pale,*** he does things which are not acceptable in society. □ **está al margen de la sociedad**
■ *v.* **1** to lose colour; to become light. □ **palidecer**
2 to become less important: *it pales into insignificance beside the statement from the Prime Minister.* □ **resulta insignificante al lado de la declaración...**
paleness *n.* light colour. □ **palidez**
paleolithic [pæliou'liθik] *adj.* referring to the early part of the Stone Age. □ **paleolítico**
paleontology [pæliən'tɔlədʒi] *n.* study of fossils. □ **paleontología**
Palestine ['pælistain] *n.* area at the eastern end of the Mediterranean, now forming Israel and Jordan. □ **Palestina**
Palestinian [pæli'stiniən] *adj.* and *n.* (person) from Palestine. □ **palestino**
palette ['pælət] *n.* flat board on which an artist mixes his colours. □ **paleta**
palette knife, long flat knife with a rounded end, used for mixing paint, etc. □ **espátula**
palindrome ['pælindroum] *n.* word or phrase which is spelt the same backwards as forwards (such as 'madam I'm Adam'). □ **palíndromo**
paling(s) ['peiliŋ(z)] **palisade** [pæli'seid] *n.* fence made of pointed pieces of wood. □ **empalizada**
pall [pɔːl] *n.* **1** (*formal*) thick layer (of smoke). □ **capa de humo**
2 cloth put over a coffin. □ **paño mortuorio**
■ *v.* to become less interesting. □ **dejar de gustar**
pallbearer *n.* person who walks beside a coffin in a funeral procession. □ **portador del féretro**
pallet ['pælit] *n.* **1** flat platform on which goods can be stacked and moved from place to place. □ **paleta**
2 straw-filled mattress. □ **jergón**
palliate ['pælieit] *v.* to try to reduce (a vice/pain); to cover up (a mistake). □ **paliar**
palliative ['pæliətiv] *adj.* and *n.* (something) which reduces pain. □ **paliativo**
pallid ['pælid] *adj.* pale (face). □ **pálido**
pallor ['pælə] *n.* paleness (of face). □ **palidez**
palm [pɑːm] *n.* **1** soft inside surface of your hand: *he held the egg carefully in the palm of his hand.* □ **palma**
2 tall tropical tree with long leaves at the top: *date palm; coconut palm.* □ **palmera**
palmist *n.* person who tells what will happen to you in the future by looking at the lines in the palm of

your hand. □ **quiromántico**
palmistry *n.* telling what will happen in the future from the lines of the hand. □ **quiromancia**
palm off *v.* (*informal*) to give (something bad) to someone without his knowing: *he palmed the rotten bananas off on to me.* □ **colar algo a uno**
Palm Sunday *n.* Sunday before Easter Sunday, when Christ's last entry to Jerusalem is remembered. □ **Domingo de Ramos**
palpable ['pælpəbl] *adj.* which can be felt/which can be easily seen. □ **palpable**
palpitate ['pælpiteit] *v.* to beat very quickly. □ **palpitar**
palpitations [pælpi'teiʃnz] *n. pl.* rapid beating of the heart. □ **palpitaciones**
paltry ['pɔ:ltri] *adj.* insignificant. □ **ínfimo**
pampas ['pæmpəs] *n.* grass-covered plains in South America. □ **pampa**
pampas grass, type of tall grass grown in gardens as an ornamental plant. □ **cortadera argentina**
pamper ['pæmpə] *v.* to spoil (a child/a dog) by giving them too much food/by treating them too well. □ **mimar**
pamphlet ['pæmflət] *n.* small book with only a few pages, which is not bound with a hard cover. □ **folleto**
pan- [pæn] *prefix meaning* over a wide area. □ **pan-**
pan-American, covering the whole of America. □ **panamericano**
pan [pæn] *n.* **1** metal kitchen cooking container with a handle: *frying pan; put the potatoes into a pan of boiling water.* □ **cazo; sartén (para freír)**
2 metal dish. □ **cacerola**
■ *v.* (*he panned*) **1** to move a camera sideways to take in a wider view. □ **tomar una vista panorámica**
2 (*informal*) to criticize: *the critics panned the film.* □ **poner de vuelta y media**
3 *to pan for gold,* to sift mud in a stream, hoping to find pieces of gold in it. □ **lavar con batea**
pancake ['pæŋkeik] *n.* thin soft flat cake made of flour, milk, eggs, etc. □ **tortita**
pan out *v.* (*informal*) to turn out/to succeed. □ **salir bien**
panacea [pænə'si:ə] *n.* something which cures everything/which solves every problem. □ **panacea**
panache [pə'næʃ] *n.* showy way of doing things. □ **brío**
panchromatic [pænkrə'mætik] *adj.* (film) which is sensitive to all colours. □ **pancromático**
pancreas ['pæŋkriəs] *n.* gland which produces insulin, and also a liquid which helps digest food. □ **páncreas**
panda ['pændə] *n.* ***(giant) panda,*** large black and white Chinese animal. □ **panda**
Panda car, police car which patrols the streets. □ **coche patrulla**
pandemic [pæn'demik] *adj.* (disease) which occurs over the whole world/over a large area. □ **pandémico**
pandemonium [pændi'mouniəm] *n.* great uproar and confusion. □ **pandemónium, jaleo**
pander ['pændə] *v.* to give in to; to satisfy: *this film panders to the lowest taste of the cinema public.* □ **complacer**
pane [pein] *n.* sheet of glass (in a window, etc.). □ **cristal**
panegyric [pæni'dʒirik] *n.* (*formal*) speech in praise of someone. □ **panegírico**
panel ['pænl] *n.* **1** flat surface which is higher/lower/thicker, etc., than the rest of the surface: *panel of a door.* □ **panel**
instrument panel, range of dials on an aircraft or in a car. □ **cuadro de mandos**
2 section of different coloured material in a dress. □ **paño**
3 group of people who answer questions/who judge a competition; group of doctors in the same practice. □ **jurado; cuadro médico**
■ *v.* (*he pannelled*) to cover with sheets of wood: *a pannelled dining room,* room with walls covered with wooden panels. □ **revestir**
panel game *n.* game (on radio/TV) where a group of people answer questions/guess answers, etc. □ **concurso de preguntas y respuestas**
panelling *n.* sheets of wood used to cover walls, etc. □ **revestimiento**
panellist *n.* member of a panel answering questions/judging a competition. □ **concursante; miembro del jurado**
pang [pæŋ] *n.* sudden sharp pain: *pangs of hunger.* □ **punzada**
panic ['pænik] *n.* terror/fright: *there was a moment of panic as the audience realized that the theatre was on fire.* □ **pánico**
■ *v.* (*he panicked*) to become frightened: *don't be panicked into selling your house; the soldiers panicked when faced by the wild crowd of students.* □ **entrarle a uno pánico**
panic-stricken *adj.* wild with fright. □ **preso de pánico**
panicky *adj.* likely to panic. □ **asustadizo**
pannier ['pæniə] *n.* bag carried on the side of a bicycle. □ **cartera**
panoply ['pænəpli] *n.* fine show/grand display of costume, etc. □ **panoplia**
panorama [pænə'rɑ:mə] *n.* wide expanse of landscape. □ **panorama**
panoramic [pænə'ræmik] *adj.* wide: *a panoramic view.* □ **panorámico**
pansy ['pænzi] *n.* **1** small multicoloured garden flower. □ **pensamiento**
2 (*informal*) effeminate man. □ **marica**
pant [pænt] *v.* to breathe fast: *he was panting for breath at the top of the stairs.* □ **jadear**
pantheism ['pænθiizəm] *n.* belief that God and the universe are one and the same; worship of many gods. □ **panteísmo**
panther ['pænθə] *n.* large black leopard. □ **pantera**
panties ['pæntiz] *n.* (*informal*) women's brief undergarment worn on the lower part of the body. □ **bragas**
pantograph ['pæntəgrɑ:f] *n.* metal frame on the roof of an electric locomotive which rises to touch an overhead electric wire to pick up electricity. □ **pantógrafo**
pantomime ['pæntəmaim] *n.* Christmas theatrical entertainment on a traditional fairy-tale subject. □ **pantomima**
pantry ['pæntri] *n.* cool cupboard or room for keeping food in. □ **despensa**
pants [pænts] *n. pl.* **1** (*informal*) brief undergarment worn on the lower part of the body: *he rushed out of the bedroom wearing only his pants.* □ **calzoncillos**
2 (*informal*) trousers: *I've spilt soup all over my pants.* □ **pantalones**
panty hose ['pænti'houz] *n. pl.* tights/women's one-piece garment of stockings and briefs covering the lower part of the body and legs. □ **'panties'**
papacy ['peipəsi] *n.* position of the Pope. □ **papado**
papal *adj.* referring to the Pope. □ **papal**
paper ['peipə] *n.* **1** thin material made from rags/wood pulp, etc., used for printing/writing, etc.:

writing paper; wrapping paper; cigarette paper. □ **papel**
2 sheet of paper: *I threw out a lot of old papers.* □ **papel**
3 ***examination paper,*** written questions/written answers in an examination. □ **preguntas y respuestas de un examen**
4 newspaper: *has the paper been delivered? the story was in all the Sunday papers.* □ **periódico**
5 scientific/learned article. □ **artículo (por escrito); comunicación (para ser leída)**
■ *v.* to cover (the walls of a room) with paper. □ **empapelar**
paperback *n.* book with a paper cover. □ **libro en rústica**
paper boy *n.* boy who delivers newspapers to houses. □ **repartidor de periódicos**
paperchase *n.* game where people follow a trail of bits of paper. □ **caza de papelitos**
paperclip *n.* piece of bent wire for holding pieces of paper together. □ **clip**
paperknife *n.* (*pl. paperknives*) long knife for cutting paper (especially for opening envelopes). □ **abrecartas**
paper round *n.* group of streets/houses where one paper boy delivers newspapers. □ **zona de reparto**
paperweight *n.* block of glass/metal used to put on papers to prevent them from being blown away. □ **pisapapeles**
papier-mâché [pæpiei'mæʃei] *n.* mixture of wet paper, used to make models, etc. □ **cartón piedra**
paprika ['pæprikə] *n.* red spice made from powdered sweet peppers. □ **paprika, pimentón**
papyrus [pə'pairəs] *n.* reed growing in the Middle East, used by the ancient Egyptians to make a type of paper. □ **papiro**
par [pɑ:] *n.* **1** equal level. □ **par**
to be on a par with someone, to be equal to someone. □ **estar en pie de igualdad con**
2 *to buy shares at par,* at their face value. □ **comprar acciones a la par**
3 (*in golf*) number of strokes usually needed to hit the ball into the hole. □ **par**
4 *I'm feeling a bit **below par**,* I am not feeling very well. □ **me siento algo indispuesto**
parable [pærəbl] *n.* usually religious story with a moral. □ **parábola**
parabola [pə'ræbələ] *n.* curve like the path of an object which is thrown into the air and comes down again. □ **parábola**
parabolic [pærə'bɔlik] *adj.* referring to a parabola: *a parabolic curve.* □ **parabólico**
parachute ['pærəʃu:t] *n.* large piece of thin material shaped like an umbrella, with cords and a harness attached, which allows you to float down safely from an aircraft: *they dropped supplies by parachute; a parachute landing.* □ **paracaídas**
■ *v.* to jump from an aircraft with a parachute: *the pilot parachuted to safety.* □ **saltar con paracaídas**
parachutist *n.* person who jumps regularly with a parachute. □ **paracaidista**
parade [pə reid] *n.* **1** military display/march past. □ **desfile**
parade ground, square area on a military camp where parades are held. □ **plaza de armas**
2 series of bands/decorated cars, etc., passing in a street. □ **cabalgata**
3 ***fashion parade,*** display of new clothes by models. □ **desfile de modelos**
4 wide street (where people like to walk up and down). □ **paseo**
■ *v.* to march past in ordered lines: *the army paraded before the general; the scouts paraded before going to church.* □ **desfilar**
paradise ['pærədais] *n.* ideal place where good people are supposed to live after death; any beautiful place. □ **paraíso**
paradox ['pærədɔks] *n.* something which appears to contradict itself but may really be true. □ **paradoja**
paradoxical [pærə'dɔksikl] *adj.* contradictory: *it seems paradoxical, but the more people we have working in the office, the less work gets done.* □ **paradójico**
paraffin ['pærəfin] *n.* thin oil for lamps/heaters, etc.. □ **parafina**
liquid paraffin, refined oil taken as a medicine. □ **aceite de parafina**
paraffin wax, solid white substance used for making candles. □ **parafina**
paragon ['pærəgən] *n.* perfect model (of virtue, etc.). □ **dechado**
paragraph ['pærəgrɑ:f] *n.* section of several lines of prose, usually starting with a short blank space at the beginning of a new line. □ **párrafo**
parakeet [pærə'ki:t] *n.* kind of small tropical parrot. □ **periquito**
parallel ['pærəlel] *adj.* **1** (lines) which are side by side and remain the same distance apart without ever touching: *railway lines run parallel.* □ **paralelo**
2 similar: *it is a parallel case to that which we are working on.* □ **paralelo**
■ *n.* **1** geometrical line which runs parallel to another. □ **paralela**
2 line running round the globe from east to west parallel to the equator: *the city is on the 49th parallel.* □ **paralelo**
3 closely similar situation; something which can be compared: *there is a parallel between his case and ours; he drew a parallel between the two battles.* □ **caso parejo; estableció un paralelo entre....**
■ *v.* to be similar to: *his way of dealing with the problem parallels mine exactly.* □ **ser paralelo**
parallelogram [pærə'leləgræm] *n.* four-sided figure where each side is parallel to the one opposite. □ **paralelogramo**
paralyse ['pærəlaiz] *Amer.* **paralyze** *v.* to make unable to move: *after the accident he was paralysed in both legs; the country was paralysed by a series of strikes.* □ **paralizar**
paralysis [pə'ræləsis] *n.* being unable to move. □ **parálisis**
paralytic [pærə'litik] *adj.* **1** unable to move. □ **paralítico**
2 (*slang*) very drunk. □ **como una cuba**
parameter [pə'ræmitə] *n.* figure which shows the upper or lower level of some expected result: *pay settlement within the parameters laid down by the government.* □ **parámetro**
paramilitary [pærə'milətri] *adj.* organized in the same way as the army, but not a part of it: *paramilitary groups.* □ **paramilitar**
paramount ['pærəmaunt] *adj.* extreme/supreme: *it's of paramount importance.* □ **supremo; es de extrema importancia**
paranoia [pærə'nɔiə] *n.* type of mental disease where you feel extremely important or that everyone is against you. □ **paranoia**
paranoiac *adj.* and *n.* (person) who suffers from paranoia. □ **paranoico**
paranoid *adj.* and *n.* **1** (person) suffering from paranoia. □ **paranoico**

2 *he's absolutely paranoid about noise,* (*informal*) he becomes mad when he hears noise. □ **se vuelve loco...**

parapet ['pærəpet] *n.* small wall at the edge of a ledge/bridge, etc. □ **pretil**

paraphernalia [pærəfə'neiliə] *n.* (*no pl.*) mass of bits and pieces; equipment. □ **trastos**

paraphrase ['pærəfreiz] *n.* writing which repeats something in different words. □ **paráfrasis**

■ *v.* to repeat what someone has said or written, using different words. □ **parafrasear**

paraplegia [pærə'pli:dʒə] *n.* paralysis of the legs and lower part of the body. □ **paraplejía**

paraplegic *adj.* and *n.* (person) who suffers from paraplegia. □ **parapléjico**

parasite ['pærəsait] *n.* animal/plant which lives on other animals or plants; person who does no useful work. □ **parásito**

parasitic [pærə'sitik] *adj.* (insect, etc.) which lives off others. □ **parásito**

parasol ['pærəsɔl] *n.* light umbrella to keep off the rays of the sun. □ **parasol**

paratrooper ['pærətru:pə] *n.* soldier who is a parachutist. □ **paracaidista**

paratroops *n. pl.* soldiers who are parachutists. □ **paracaidistas**

parboil ['pɑ:bɔil] *v.* to half-cook (food) in boiling water. □ **sancochar**

parcel ['pɑ:sl] *n.* **1** package (to be sent by post, etc.). □ **paquete**

2 small area of land. □ **parcela**

■ *v.* (*he parcelled*) to wrap and tie (something) up to send: *he parcelled up three lots of books.* □ **empaquetar**

parcel out *v.* to divide up between several people. □ **repartir**

parch [pɑ:tʃ] *v.* to dry: *parched desert; my throat is parched.* □ **secar; desierto reseco; tengo la garganta reseca**

parchment ['pɑ:tʃmənt] *n.* skins of animals which have been treated and which can be used for writing on; fine quality yellowish paper. □ **pergamino**

pardon ['pɑ:dn] *n.* **1** forgiveness. □ **perdón**

I beg your pardon, excuse me. □ **usted perdone/discúlpeme**

2 freeing someone from prison or from punishment. □ **indultar**

■ *v.* **1** to forgive: *pardon me, but aren't you Mr Smith?* □ **perdóneme...**

2 to allow (someone) to leave prison; not to punish (someone). □ **poner en libertad; perdonar**

pardonable *adj.* which can be excused: *it was a pardonable mistake.* □ **perdonable**

pare ['pɛə] *v.* to cut off the skin/peel (of a fruit/vegetable, etc.); to cut back (expenses). □ **mondar (fruta); reducir (gastos)**

parent ['pɛərənt] *n.* father or mother. □ **padre/madre**

parent organization, organization which rules another. □ **matriz**

parentage *n.* origin. □ **ascendencia**

parental [pə'rentl] *adj.* referring to parents: *parental responsibility.* □ **de los padres**

parenthesis [pə'renθəsis] *n.* (*pl. parentheses*) **1** phrase in the middle of a sentence which is placed in brackets or between dashes. □ **paréntesis**

in parenthesis, I might add that he is not British, as a piece of additional information. □ **dicho sea de paso, yo...**

2 (round) bracket: *the next two words are in parenthesis.* □ **entre paréntesis**

pariah [pə'raiə] *n.* person who is thrown out by civilized society. □ **paria**

parish ['pæriʃ] *n.* **1** administrative area round a church and under the care of a clergyman. □ **parroquia**

2 (*in England*) administrative district in a county. □ **municipio**

parishioner [pə'riʃənə] *n.* person who lives in or belongs to a parish. □ **feligrés**

parity ['pæriti] *n.* equality. □ **paridad**

park [pɑ:k] *n.* **1** open public place usually with grass and trees: *the park in the centre of the town.* □ **parque**

national park, large area of countryside kept in a natural state. □ **parque nacional**

2 ***car park,*** place where cars can be left temporarily. □ **aparcamiento**

■ *v.* to leave one's car in a particular place. □ **aparcar**

no parking, don't leave your car here. □ **prohibido aparcar**

parking meter, device into which you put money to pay for parking. □ **parquímetro**

parking lot, *Amer.* place where cars can be left temporarily. □ **aparcamiento**

parka ['pɑ:kə] *n.* warm jacket with a hood. □ **anorak**

parlance ['pɑ:ləns] *n.* (*formal*) way of speaking. □ **lenguaje**

parley ['pɑ:li] *n.* discussion between enemies with a view to agreeing peace terms. □ **negociaciones**

■ *v.* to discuss peace terms with an enemy. □ **parlamentar**

parliament ['pɑ:ləmənt] *n.* group of elected representatives who vote the laws of a country. □ **parlamento**

parliamentarian [pɑ:ləmən'tɛəriən] *n.* member of a parliament. □ **parlamentario**

parliamentary [pɑ:lə'mentəri] *adj.* referring to parliament: *parliamentary elections.* □ **parlamentario**

parlour ['pɑ:lə] *Amer.* **parlor** *n.* ***beauty parlour,*** place where women can have their hair done and their faces made up. □ **salón de belleza**

parochial [pə'roukiəl] *adj.* **1** referring to a parish: *the parochial council.* □ **parroquial; el consejo municipal**

2 restricted (views); narrow-minded (person). □ **estrecho de miras**

parody ['pærədi] *n.* imitation in order to make fun of someone/something. □ **parodia**

■ *v.* to imitate in order to make fun. □ **parodiar**

parole [pə'roul] *n. prisoner on parole,* prisoner let out of prison before the end of his sentence on condition that he behaves well. □ **libertad condicional**

■ *v.* to let a prisoner out of prison on condition that he behaves well. □ **poner en libertad condicional**

paroxysm ['pærəksizəm] *n.* wild fit (of anger, etc.). □ **paroxismo**

parquet ['pɑ:kei] *n.* small wooden blocks used to make a floor: *parquet flooring.* □ **parqué**

parricide ['pærisaid] *n.* murder of your own father; person who kills his father. □ **parricida**

parrot ['pærət] *n.* colourful tropical bird with a large curved beak which can be taught to say words. □ **loro**

parrot-fashion *adv.* (repeating words) without really understanding them: *they repeated the phrases parrot-fashion.* □ **como un loro**

parry ['pæri] *v.* to prevent (a blow) from hitting you. □ **esquivar**

parse [pɑ:z] *v.* to describe the grammatical function of each word in a sentence. □ **analizar gramaticalmente**

parsimony ['pɑːsimənі] *n.* (*formal*) miserliness. □ **avaricia**
parsimonious [pɑːsi'mouniəs] *adj.* miserly. □ **avaro**
parsley ['pɑːsli] *n.* kind of green herb used in cooking. □ **perejil**
parsnip ['pɑːsnip] *n.* vegetable with a long white edible root. □ **chirivía**
parson ['pɑːsn] *n.* clergyman in charge of a parish in the Church of England. □ **párroco**
parsonage *n.* house of a parson. □ **casa del párroco**
part [pɑːt] *n.* **1** piece/bit of something: *parts of the book are good; we live in the south part of London; spare parts of an engine,* replacement pieces of an engine. □ **parte; repuestos**
2 ***parts of speech,*** types of word according to usage (noun/verb, etc.). □ **partes de la oración**
3 *I agree with you* ***in part,*** not completely. □ **...en parte**
4 role: *he played an important part in the film; she played an important part in capturing the burglar.* □ **papel**
to take part in something, to be active in something. □ **tomar parte en algo**
5 ***for my part,*** as far as I am concerned. □ **por mi parte**
■ *adv.* not entirely: *the potatoes are only part-cooked.* □ **...cocidas en parte**
■ *v.* **1** to separate: *he parts his hair on the right hand side.* □ **dividir; se hace la raya...**
2 ***to part company:*** *we parted company,* we left each other. □ **separarse**
3 *they parted the best of friends,* they separated the best of friends. □ **separar**
4 *he doesn't like parting with money,* spending/giving away money. □ **...gastar**
parting *n.* **1** separation in the hair. □ **separación; raya del pelo**
2 leaving: *I gave him some parting instructions,* as he left I gave him some instructions. □ **despedida**
partly *adv.* not entirely: *the house is partly built.* □ **en parte**
part-time *adj.* and *adv.* not for the whole working day: *she has a part-time job; he works part-time as a bus-driver.* □ **de/a media jornada (adj.); media jornada (adv.)**
partial ['pɑːʃl] *adj.* **1** biased/with a liking for: *I am partial to a glass of wine.* □ **aficionado (a)**
2 not complete: *a partial success.* □ **parcial**
partiality [pɑːʃi'æliti] *n.* strong bias in favour of: *the judge's partiality towards the prisoner.* □ **parcialidad**
partially *adv.* **1** in a biased way. □ **con parcialidad**
2 not completely: *a partially completed building.* □ **en parte**
participate [pɑː'tisipeit] *v.* to take part: *we participated in the international exhibition.* □ **participar**
participant *n.* person who participates. □ **participante**
participation [pɑːtisi'peiʃn] *n.* taking part in something. □ **participación**
participatory *adj.* in which you participate. □ **participativo**
participle ['pɑːtisipl] *n.* part of a verb, used either to form compound tenses or as an adjective or noun: *'eating' and 'eaten' are the participles of the verb 'eat'.* □ **participio**
particle ['pɑːtikl] *n.* very small piece; minor part of speech: *a particle of dust.* □ **partícula**
particoloured ['pɑːtikʌləd] *Amer.* **particolored** *adj.* with one part in one colour, and the other part in another. □ **abigarrado**
particular [pə'tikjulə] *adj.* **1** special; referring to one thing or person: *I don't like that particular restaurant.* □ **concreto, determinado**
in particular, as a special point. □ **especialmente**
2 fussy: *he is very particular about his food.* □ **exigente**
■ *n.* detail: *the police took all the particulars of the stolen car.* □ **detalle**
particularly *adv.* specially: *I particularly wanted you to come.* □ **particularmente, especialmente**
partisan [pɑːti'zæn] *n.* **1** person who strongly supports a certain point of view. □ **partidario**
partisan speech, speech biased in favour of a certain point of view. □ **discurso parcial**
2 guerrilla fighting against an army which has occupied his country. □ **de partisanos**
partition [pɑː'tiʃn] *n.* thin wall splitting a large room into two: *there's a glass partition between the offices.* □ **tabique**
■ *v.* to divide (by means of a partition): *the room has been partitioned off into three small offices.* □ **separar con un tabique**
partner ['pɑːtnə] *n.* **1** person who has a part share in a business. □ **socio**
2 person who plays/dances with someone: *my partner in the tennis doubles; she's looking for a partner for the next dance.* □ **pareja**
partnership *n.* business association between two or more people where the risks and profits are shared: *the three brothers went into partnership.* □ **asociación**
partridge ['pɑːtridʒ] *n.* large brown and grey bird, shot for sport and food. □ **perdiz**
party ['pɑːti] *n.* **1** enjoyable meeting of several people on invitation: *we're having a dinner party tomorrow; can you come to my birthday party?* □ **fiesta; ...una cena mañana**
2 group of people: *a party of tourists; the rescue party set off up the mountain.* □ **grupo; equipo**
3 person involved (especially in legal matters): *was he a party to the theft? she's the guilty party.* □ **parte**
third party, third person, in addition to the two principal people involved. □ **tercero**
third-party insurance, insurance againt injuring someone not named in the insurance policy. □ **seguro de daños a terceros**
4 ***party line,*** a shared telephone line. □ **línea colectiva (para varios abonados)**
5 ***party wall,*** wall which forms part of two houses. □ **pared medianera**
6 ***(political) party,*** official group of people with the same political ideas: *the Democratic Party; the Communist Party; a party conference.* □ **partido**
to follow the party line, to do/to say exactly what the party's policy lays down. □ **seguir la línea del partido**
pass [pɑːs] *n.* **1** lower area between two mountain peaks. □ **puerto**
2 (*in football, etc.*) moving the ball to another player. □ **pase**
3 acceptance at an examination: *he got a pass in English.* □ **aprobado**
4 bus/train season ticket; permit to get in or out. □ **pase**
■ *v.* **1** to go past: *on the way to the Post Office you pass the church on your left; I passed him in the corridor; time seems to pass very slowly; I passed him on his bicycle,* I overtook him. □ **pasar**
2 to move (something) towards someone: *can you pass me the sugar? he passed the ball to the goalkeeper.* □ **pasar**
3 to get through (an examination/inspection): *he*

passed his final examination; the car was passed by an inspector. □ **pasar**
4 *the meeting passed a motion,* they voted by a majority for a motion. □ **...aprobó la moción**
5 ***to pass comments,*** to make comments. □ **hacer comentarios**
6 ***to pass water,*** to urinate/to let waste water out of the body. □ **orinar**
passable *adj.* fairly good. □ **pasable**
passably *adv.* fairly well. □ **bastante bien**
passage ['pæsidʒ] *n.***1** corridor: *he ran down the passage towards the exit.* □ **pasillo**
2 section of a text: *did you read the passage in his speech where he talks about inflation?* □ **pasaje**
3 *sea passage,* journey by sea. □ **travesía**
passbook *n.* book which records how much money you put in or take out of your savings account in a bank or with a building society. □ **libreta de ahorros**
passenger ['pæsindʒə] *n.* traveller (in a vehicle): *my car can take four passengers.* □ **pasajero**
passer-by [pɑːsə'bai] *n.* (*pl. passers-by*) person who is walking past. □ **transeúnte**
pass for *v.* to be thought to be: *she could pass for an Englishwoman any day.* □ **pasar por**
passing *adj.* **1** not permanent: *a passing phase.* □ **pasajero**
2 which is going past: *he was knocked down by a passing car.* □ **...por un coche que pasaba**
pass off *v.* **1** to take place: *the meeting passed off without any incident.* □ **celebrarse**
2 *he passed himself off as a German general,* he pretended to be. □ **hacerse pasar**
pass out *v.* (*informal*) to faint. □ **desmayarse**
pass over *v.* **1** to go past above: *the planes pass directly over our house.* □ **pasar por encima**
2 *to pass someone over for promotion,* to miss someone who should have been promoted. □ **saltarse**
passover ['pɑːsouvə] *n.* Jewish festival which celebrates the freeing of the Jews from captivity in Egypt. □ **pascua de los hebreos**
passport *n.* official document allowed you to pass from one country to another. □ **pasaporte**
password *n.* secret word which you say to go past a guard. □ **contraseña**
passion ['pæʃn] *n.* violent emotion/enthusiasm: *he has a passion for cleaning his car; he smashed all the plates in a fit of passion.* □ **pasión**
passionate *adj.* violently emotional. □ **apasionado**
passionately *adv.* violently: *he is passionately fond of chocolates.* □ **apasionadamente**
passive ['pæsiv] *adj.* not resisting; which allows things to happen. □ **pasivo**
passive resistance, resisting (the police, etc.) by refusing to obey orders but not using violence. □ **resistencia pasiva**
passive verb, verb which shows that the subject is being acted upon (such as 'the picture was taken by my father'). □ **voz pasiva**
passively *adv.* not offering any resistance/not doing anything positive. □ **pasivamente**
passivity [pə'siviti] *n.* being passive. □ **pasividad**
past [pɑːst] *adj.* **1** (time) which has gone by: *the past hour.* □ **pasado**
2 *she is a past president of the society,* she used to be president. □ **fue presidenta**
■ *n.* time which has gone by: *forget about the past; he told me all about his past.* □ **pasado**
■ *prep.* after; beyond: *it's past your bedtime; twenty past two,* 2.20: *go past the Post Office; he walked past without stopping.* □ **por delante de, más allá de; ya es hora de ir a la cama**
past master *n.* expert: *he's a past master at opening safes.* □ **maestro**
pasta ['pæstə] *n. pl.* Italian food made of flour and water, such as spaghetti/macaroni, etc. □ **pasta**
paste [peist] *n.* **1** thin glue, usually made of flour and water. □ **masa**
2 soft substance: *mix the ingredients to a smooth paste; shrimp paste,* soft mixture made of shrimps. □ **pasta**
■ *v.* to glue (paper, etc.). □ **pegar**
pastel ['pæstl] *n.* **1** coloured crayon like chalk. □ **pastel**
pastel colours, soft, light shades. □ **colores pastel**
2 picture done with coloured crayons like chalk. □ **pintura al pastel**
pasteurize ['pɑːstʃəraiz] *v.* to kill the germs in (milk) by heating it. □ **pasteurizar**
pasteurization [pɑːstʃərai'zeiʃn] *n.* action of pasteurizing. □ **pasteurización**
pastiche [pæ'stiːʃ] *n.* poem/piece of music, etc. which is a deliberate imitation of the style of another artist. □ **pastiche**
pastille ['pæstl] *n.* small sweet made of fruit-flavoured jelly. □ **pastilla**
pastime ['pɑːstaim] *n.* hobby/way of passing your spare time. □ **pasatiempo**
pastor ['pɑːstə] *n.* clergyman. □ **pastor**
pastoral *adj.* **1** referring to shepherds. □ **pastoril**
2 referring to moral guidance: *the pastoral duties of a teacher.* □ **pastoral**
pastry ['peistri] *n.* **1** paste made of flour, fat and water which is used to make pies, etc.: *he was rolling out the pastry.* □ **masa**
2 cooked pie crust. □ **pastel**
3 ***pastries,*** sweet cakes made of pastry filled with cream/fruit, etc. □ **pasteles**
pasture ['pɑːstʃə] *n.* grassy area where cows and sheep can graze. □ **pasto**
■ *v.* to put (cows and sheep) to graze. □ **pastar**
pasty ['peisti] *adj.* white (face). □ **pálido**
■ *n.* pastry folded round a filling, usually of meat and vegetables. □ **empanada**
pat [pæt] *n.* **1** light hit. □ **golpecito**
a pat on the back, praise. □ **una palmadita en la espalda**
2 small piece of butter. □ **un pedacito de mantequilla**
■ *v.* (*he patted*) to give (someone/something) a light hit: *she patted his arm.* □ **dar palmaditas**
patch [pætʃ] *n.* **1** small piece of material used for covering up holes: *he has leather patches on the elbows of his jacket.* □ **remiendo**
not a patch on: *she isn't a patch on her sister,* (*informal*) she is nothing like as good as her sister. □ **no tiene ni punto de comparación con...**
2 small area: *a patch of blue sky; a vegetable patch.* □ **trozo; un bancal de hortalizas**
■ *v.* **1** to repair by attaching a piece of material over a hole. □ **remendar**
2 *the mechanic managed to patch up the engine,* managed to repair it more or less. □ **arreglar un poco...**
patchwork *n.* small pieces of material sewn together in patterns: *patchwork quilt.* □ **labor de retazos; centón**
patchy *adj.* in small areas; not the same all through: *patchy fog.* □ **desigual**
paté ['pætei] *n.* paste made of cooked meat or fish finely minced. □ **paté**
patent ['peitənt] *n.* official confirmation that you have invented something and have the right to

make it commercially: *he took out a patent for a new potato peeler.* □ **patente**
■ *adj.* **1** covered by an official patent. □ **patentado**
patent medicine, medicine made under a trade name by one company. □ **específico**
2 ***patent leather,*** extremely shiny leather. □ **charol**
3 obvious: *his story was a patent lie.* □ **palmario**
■ *v.* to obtain a patent: *he has patented his invention.* □ **patentar**
patentee [peitən'tiː] *n.* person who has obtained a patent. □ **titular de una patente**
patently *adv.* obviously/clearly: *the whole idea is patently absurd.* □ **claramente**

paternity [pə'təːniti] *n.* being a father. □ **paternidad**
paternal *adj.* referring to a father; like a father: *my paternal grandfather,* my father's father. □ **paternal**
paternalistic [pətəːnə'listik] *adj.* overpowering (way of ruling a country/of managing a company). □ **paternalista**

path [pɑːθ] *n.* **1** narrow way for walking/cycling, etc: *the path goes across the field with the cows in it; the explorers cut a path through the jungle.* □ **camino**
2 way in which something moves: *the moon's path; the house stands directly on the path of the new road.* □ **el recorrido de la luna; ...camino de la nueva carretera**
pathway *n.* track for walking along. □ **sendero, camino**

pathetic [pə'θetik] *adj.* which makes you feel pity or contempt: *a pathetic scene in the snow; he made a pathetic attempt to score a goal.* □ **patético**
pathetically *adv.* in a pathetic way. □ **patéticamente**

pathogen ['pæθədʒən] *n.* germ which causes a disease. □ **agente patógeno**

pathology [pə'θɔlədʒi] *n.* study of disease. □ **patología**
pathological [pæθə'lɔdʒikl] *adj.* **1** referring to pathology: *a pathological case,* a case caused by disease. □ **patológico**
2 caused by mental or physical disease: *a pathological killer.* □ **un asesino patológico**
3 unhealthy: *a pathological interest in crime.* □ **patológico**
pathologist [pə'θɔlədʒist] *n.* doctor specializing in the study of disease; doctor who examines dead bodies to discover the cause of death. □ **patólogo**

pathos ['peiθɔs] *n.* something which makes you feel pity. □ **patetismo**

patience ['peiʃns] *n.* **1** being able to wait for a long time; being able not to lose your temper. □ **paciencia**
2 card game for one person. □ **solitario**
patient *adj.* **1** (person) who can wait for a long time/who remains calm/who doesn't lose his temper: *you have to be patient if you are at the end of a long queue.* □ **paciente**
2 careful/painstaking: *the crime was solved after days of patient investigation by the police.* □ **paciente**
■ *n.* person who is in hospital or being treated by a doctor/dentist, etc. □ **paciente**
patiently *adv.* calmly: *the crowd waited patiently in the rain for two hours.* □ **pacientemente**

patina ['pætinə] *n.* green sheen on old bronze objects; shine on old wooden furniture, etc. □ **pátina**

patio ['pætiou] *n.* paved area outside a house for sitting or eating: *we were sitting on the patio.* □ **patio**

patisserie [pə'tiːsəri] *n.* shop selling continental style cakes and pastries. □ **pastelería**

patois ['pætwɑː] *n.* dialect spoken in a small area. □ **dialecto**

patrial ['peitriəl] *n.* person who has the right to live in a country because one of his parents or grandparents was born in that country. □ **un oriundo**

patriarch ['peitriɑːk] *n.* **1** bishop/high dignitary of an Eastern church. □ **patriarca**
2 old man whom you respect. □ **patriarca**
patriarchal *adj.* referring to a patriarch: *a patriarchal society,* one which is controlled by men. □ **patriarcal**

patrician [pə'triʃn] *adj.* and *n.* (referring to an) aristocrat. □ **patricio**

patricide ['pætrisaid] *n.* murder of your own father; person who kills his father. □ **parricidio**

patrimony ['pætriməni] *n.* inheritance/property which has been passed from father to son for generations. □ **patrimonio**

patriot ['peitriət] *n.* person who fights for/who is proud of his country. □ **patriota**
patriotic [pætri'ɔtik] *adj.* proud of your country; willing to fight for your country. □ **patriótico, patriota**
patriotism ['peitriətizəm] *n.* pride in your country. □ **patriotismo**

patrol [pə'troul] *n.* **1** keeping guard by walking or driving up and down: *soldiers on patrol.* □ **patrulla**
2 group of people keeping guard: *a police patrol.* □ **una patrulla de policía**
patrol car, police car which drives up and down the streets. □ **coche patrulla**
■ *v.* (*he patrolled*) to keep guard by walking or driving up and down: *the police patrolled the streets of the town.* □ **patrullar**
patrolman *n.* (*pl. patrolmen*) *especially Amer.* policeman. □ **policía**

patron ['peitrən] *n.* **1** person who protects or supports someone/something. □ **protector, mecenas**
patron saint, saint who is believed to protect a special group of people. □ **santo patrón**
2 regular customer (of a shop); person who goes regularly to the theatre. □ **cliente habitual**
patronage ['pætrənidʒ] *n.* giving support/encouragement (to an artist, etc.). □ **mecenazgo**
patronize ['pætrənaiz] *v.* **1** to support/to encourage (an artist, etc.). □ **patrocinar**
2 to act in a condescending way (to someone). □ **tratar con condescendencia**
3 to go regularly (to a shop/public house/theatre). □ **ser cliente asiduo de**
patronizing *adj.* condescending; (tone) which makes someone feel inferior. □ **protector**

patter ['pætə] *n.* **1** soft repeated tapping noise: *patter of falling rain; patter of children's feet.* □ **repiqueteo (lluvia); pasos ligeros**
2 rapid talk by a conjuror/salesman/trickster to distract attention from what he is really doing. □ **parloteo**
■ *v.* to make a soft repeated tapping noise: *the rain pattered on the tin roof.* □ **repiquetear**

pattern ['pætən] *n.* **1** model/example which you should copy. □ **modelo**
dressmaking pattern, paper which shows how to cut out cloth to make a piece of clothing. □ **patrón**
knitting pattern, instructions on how to knit (a garment). □ **instrucciones**
2 design of repeated lines/pictures, etc: *the wallpaper has a pink flowered pattern; a check pattern.* □ **dibujo**
patterned *adj.* with a repeated design: *patterned wallpaper/carpet,* not plain. □ **estampado**

patty ['pæti] *n.* small pie. □ **empanadilla**

paucity ['pɔːsiti] *n.* (*formal*) small number/too little (of something). □ **escasez**

paunch [pɔːntʃ] *n.* fat stomach. □ **barriga**
pauper ['pɔːpə] *n.* poor person. □ **pobre**
pause [pɔːz] *n.* short stop in work, etc.: *there was a pause in the conversation.* □ **pausa**
■ *v.* to stop doing something for a short time: *we will pause now for a short coffee break.* □ **hacer una pausa**
pave [peiv] *v.* to cover (a road/path, etc.) with a hard surface: *a paved courtyard.* □ **pavimentar**
to pave the way for something, to prepare the way: *this defeat paves the way for a general election.* □ **preparar el camino para**
pavement *n.* **1** hard path at the side of a road. □ **acera**
2 *Amer.* hard road surface. □ **calzada**
paving stone *n.* large flat stone slab used for making paths/courtyards, etc. □ **losa**
pavilion [pə'viljən] *n.* **1** small building for sportsmen to rest in between games: *tennis pavilion; cricket pavilion.* □ **vestuario**
2 building for an exhibition: *the British pavilion at the World Fair.* □ **pabellón**
paw [pɔː] *n.* hairy foot of an animal with claws. □ **garra**
■ *v.* **1** to tap with a paw/hand, etc.: *the cat pawed the cushion; the horse pawed the ground with its front hoofs.* □ **dar zarpazos (gato, león); tocar con la pata (caballo)**
2 *stop pawing me,* (*informal*) stop fondling me. □ **¡las manos quietas!**
pawn [pɔːn] *n.* **1** smallest piece on the chessboard. □ **peón**
2 person used by someone more powerful: *we are just the pawns of the big companies.* □ **peón**
3 ***in pawn,*** (object) left in exchange for money which has been borrowed. □ **empeñado**
■ *v.* to leave (an object) in exchange for borrowing money (which you claim back when the money is repaid): *he pawned his watch for $20.* □ **empeñar**
pawnbroker *n.* person who lends money in exchange for valuables left with him. □ **prestamista**
pay [pei] *n.* wages/salary: *holidays with pay.* □ **sueldo**
■ *v.* (*he paid*) **1** to give money for something: *did he pay for all those watches he took away? I paid $20 for this painting; she paid him $1 to wash her car.* □ **pagar**
2 to be worth while: *it pays to be strict with children; it pays to read the instructions carefully.* □ **compensar**
3 to suffer punishment: *he paid for his mistake.* □ **pagar**
4 *to pay a visit/a call,* to make a visit/a call. □ **hacer**
5 to make/to show: *to pay attention to something; to pay someone a compliment.* □ **prestar atención**
payable *adj.* which must be paid: *the bill is payable in thirty days' time.* □ **pagadero**
pay-as-you-earn *n.* system of collecting income tax direct from salaries. □ **retención en fuente**
pay back *v.* **1** to return money to someone. □ **reembolsar**
2 ***to pay someone back,*** to get your revenge on someone. □ **hacérselas pagar a uno**
pay bed *n.* bed in a public hospital for which you pay. □ **habitación privada**
paycheck *n. Amer.* salary payment. □ **paga**
payee *n.* person who receives money. □ **beneficiario**
paymaster *n.* officer who pays soldiers. □ **habilitado**
payment *n.* giving money for something: *on payment of $2 you get a membership card.* □ **pago**
pay off *v.* **1** to remove (a debt) by paying the money owed. □ **saldar**
2 (*informal*) to be successful: *the scheme paid off in the end.* □ **merecer la pena**
pay out *v.* **1** to give money to someone: *he had to pay out hundreds of pounds.* □ **desembolsar**
2 to unroll a rope. □ **desenrollar**
payroll *n.* list of people who receive wages: *he's on the payroll,* he works for us. □ **nómina**
pay up *v.* to pay what you owe: *he paid up quickly when we sent three men round for the money.* □ **liquidar**
pea [piː] *n.* climbing plant of which the round green seeds are eaten as vegetables: *frozen peas.* □ **guisante**
sweet peas, plant of the pea family grown for its scented flowers. □ **guisantes de olor**
peace [piːs] *n.* **1** state of not being at war: *the countries signed a peace treaty.* □ **paz**
2 calm/quiet: *the peace of a country village; now they have caught the burglar, we can all sleep in peace.* □ **paz**
peaceable *adj.* liking peace; not quarrelsome. □ **pacífico**
peaceably *adv.* calmly/without quarrelling. □ **de modo pacífico**
peaceful *adj.* **1** calm: *the peaceful waters of the lake.* □ **pacífico**
2 liking peace: *peaceful coexistence,* living side by side without making war. □ **pacífico**
peacefully *adv.* **1** calmly. □ **pacíficamente**
2 without making war. □ **pacíficamente**
peacemaker *n.* person who tries to bring about peace. □ **pacificador**
peach [piːtʃ] *n.* sweet fruit, with a large stone and velvety skin. □ **melocotón**
peach (tree), tree which bears peaches. □ **melocotonero**
■ *v.* ***to peach on someone,*** (*informal*) to inform (the police) about someone. □ **delatar**
peacock ['piːkɔk] **peahen** [piː'hen] *n.* **1** large bird, of which the cock has a huge tail with brilliant blue and green feathers. □ **pavo real**
2 type of brown butterfly with round purple spots. □ **pavón**
peak [piːk] *n.* **1** top of a mountain: *snow-covered peaks.* □ **cumbre**
2 highest point: *output has reached its peak.* □ **pico**
peak period, period of the day when most electricity is used/when most traffic is on the roads, etc. □ **horas de mayor consumo/tráfico**
3 front part of a cap which juts out. □ **visera**
■ *v.* to reach a high point: *the runner ran hard but peaked too early.* □ **llegar al tope**
peaked *adj.* (cap) with a peak. □ **con visera**
peaky *adj.* looking ill. □ **paliducho**
peal [piːl] *n.* **1** set of bells of different sizes; sound of bells ringing: *they rang peals of bells to celebrate the victory.* □ **repique**
2 loud reverberating noise: *a peal of thunder; peals of laughter.* □ **estallido**
■ *v.* **1** to ring a peal of bells. □ **repicar**
2 (*of thunder*) to roll/to make a loud noise. □ **retumbar**
peanut ['piːnʌt] *n.* **1** nut which grows in the ground in pods like a pea. □ **cacahuete**
peanut butter, paste made from crushed peanuts. □ **manteca de cacahuete**
2 ***peanuts,*** very little money. □ **miseria**
pear ['pɛə] *n.* elongated fruit with one end fatter than the other. □ **pera**

pear (tree), tree which bears pears. □ **peral**
pear-shaped *adj.* shaped like a pear. □ **en forma de pera**
pearl [pɜːl] *n.* precious round white gem formed inside an oyster: *pearl necklace; a string of pearls.* □ **perla**
pearl barley, barley grains which have been rolled until they are shaped like pearls. □ **cebada perlada**
pearl-diver *n.* person who dives to the bottom of the sea to look for oysters with pearls in them. □ **pescador de perlas**
pearly *adj.* shiny like a pearl. □ **nacarado**
peasant ['pezənt] *n.* farm labourer living in a backward region. □ **campesino**
peat [piːt] *n.* decayed vegetable matter cut out of a bog and used as fuel or in gardening. □ **turba**
pebble ['pebl] *n.* small round stone. □ **guijarro**
pebble-dash *n.* covering for outside walls of houses, where small stones are stuck into wet cement. □ **enfoscado (con guijarros)**
peccadillo [pekə'dilou] *n.* (*pl. peccadilloes*) (*formal*) slight error/fault. □ **peccata minuta**
peck [pek] *n.* **1** bite with a bird's beak. □ **picotazo**
2 little kiss. □ **besito**
■ *v.* **1** to bite with a beak: *the hens pecked at the corn.* □ **picotear**
pecking order, unwritten order of importance of people in a firm/office, etc. □ **escalafón particular**
2 (*informal*) to give (someone) a little kiss. □ **dar un besito**
pecker *n.* ***keep your pecker up,*** (*slang*) keep cheerful/optimistic. □ **ánimo**
peckish *adj. I feel a bit peckish,* (*informal*) a bit hungry. □ **tengo gazuza**
pectin ['pektin] *n.* jelly-like substance in fruit which helps jam to set hard. □ **pectina**
pectoral ['pektərəl] *adj.* (*formal*) referring to the chest. □ **pectoral**
pectoral cross, cross worn by a priest round the neck. □ **pectoral**
peculate ['pekjuleit] *v.* (*formal*) to embezzle money. □ **desfalcar**
peculation [pekju'leiʃn] *n.* embezzlement. □ **desfalco**
peculiar [pi'kjuːljə] *adj.* **1** odd/strange: *what a peculiar smell!* □ **raro**
2 belonging to one particular place or person: *rhyming slang is peculiar to London.* □ **peculiar**
peculiarity *n.* being peculiar; strange feature/detail which stands out. □ **peculiaridad**
peculiarly *adv.* oddly/strangely: *this is a peculiarly interesting case; she's behaving rather peculiarly.* □ **singularmente**
pecuniary [pi'kjuːnjəri] *adj.* referring to money: *he's in pecuniary difficulties,* he is short of money. □ **pecuniario**
pedagogical [pedə'gɔdʒikl] *adj.* referring to teaching. □ **pedagógico**
pedal ['pedl] *n.* lever worked by your foot: *bicycle pedal; piano pedal.* □ **pedal**
brake pedal, pedal which works a brake. □ **pedal de freno**
pedal bin, rubbish bin with a lid which is worked by a pedal. □ **cubo de la basura de pedal**
■ *v.* (*he pedalled*) to make a bicycle go by pushing on the pedals: *he was pedalling furiously up the hill.* □ **pedalear**
pedant ['pedənt] *n.* person who pays too much attention to small details or who likes to show off his knowledge. □ **pedante**
pedantic [pi'dæntik] *adj.* which pays too much attention to detail/shows off knowledge. □ **pedante**
pedantry ['pedəntri] *n.* showing off knowledge/paying too much attention to details. □ **pedantería**
peddle ['pedl] *v.* to go about trying to sell something: *he was caught peddling drugs.* □ **andar vendiendo**
peddler *n.* **1** person who sells dangerous drugs. □ **camello**
2 *Amer.* person who goes about trying to sell small articles. □ **vendedor ambulante**
pedestal ['pedistl] *n.* base (for a statue). □ **pedestal**
pedestrian [pə'destriən] *n.* person who goes about on foot. □ **peatón**
pedestrian crossing, specially indicated place where pedestrians can cross a road. □ **paso de peatones**
pedestrian precinct, street or group of streets closed to traffic so that people can walk about freely. □ **zona peatonal**
■ *adj.* heavy/unimaginative: *rather pedestrian playing by the orchestra.* □ **pedestre**
pediatrician [piːdiə'triʃn] *n.* doctor who specializes in treating children's diseases. □ **pediatra**
pediatrics [piːdi'ætriks] *n.* science of treatment of children's diseases. □ **pediatría**
pedigree ['pedigriː] *n.* table of ancestors of a person/animal. □ **pedigrí**
pedigree bull, bull with a certificate showing it is pure bred. □ **toro de raza**
pedlar ['pedlə] *n.* person who goes about trying to sell small articles. □ **buhonero**
pee [piː] *n.* (*informal*) **1** waste water from the body. □ **pis**
2 passing waste water from the body: *I must have a pee.* □ **tengo que hacer pis**
■ *v.* (*informal*) to pass waste water from the body: *the dog has peed all over the carpet.* □ **mear**
peek [piːk] *n.* (*informal*) quick look. □ **mirada rápida**
■ *v.* (*informal*) to look at something quickly. □ **echar una mirada rápida**
peel [piːl] *n.* outer skin of a fruit, etc.: *apple peel.* □ **monda**
■ *v.* **1** to take the outer skin off a fruit/off a vegetable. □ **mondar**
2 to come off in layers: *the paint is peeling off the window frame.* □ **desconcharse**
peeler *n.* special instrument for peeling vegetables: *potato peeler.* □ **peladora; pelapatatas**
peelings *n. pl.* bits of skin from vegetables: *they fed the pigs on potato peelings.* □ **mondaduras**
peep [piːp] *n.* short/quick look: *he took a peep at the pictures.* □ **mirada furtiva**
■ *v.* to look at something quickly and secretly: *we peeped round the corner.* □ **echar una mirada furtiva**
peephole *n.* small hole in a door which you can look through to see who is outside. □ **mirilla**
peer ['piə] *n.* **1** member of the nobility. □ **par**
2 person of the same rank/class as another. □ **igual**
peer group, group of people of equal (social) status. □ **clase social**
■ *v.* to look at something hard when you cannot see very well: *we were peering through the fog, trying to read the names of the streets.* □ **mirar entornando los ojos**
peeved [piːvd] *adj.* (*informal*) annoyed/bothered. □ **irritado**
peevish *adj.* bad-tempered/complaining. □ **quejica**
peewit ['piːwit] *n.* lapwing/bird found in fields and moors. □ **avefría**
peg [peg] *n.* small wooden or metal stake/pin. □ **pinza**
tent peg, stake used to hold the ropes of a tent. □ **estaca**

hat peg, piece of wood/metal attached to a wall and used to hang hats on. □ **percha**
to buy *clothes* ***off the peg,*** ready made. □ **...de confección**
■ *v.* (*he pegged*) **1** to attach with a peg. □ **enclavijar**
2 to hold stable: *price increases have been pegged at 2%.* □ **estabilizar**

pejorative [pəˈdʒɔrətiv] *adj.* disapproving/showing that you feel something is bad: *a pejorative use of the word 'doll'.* □ **peyorativo**

pelican [ˈpelikən] *n.* large white water bird, with a pouch under its beak in which it keeps the fish it has caught. □ **pelícano**
pelican crossing, pedestrian crossing with traffic lights worked by the pedestrians. □ **paso de peatones**

pellet [ˈpelit] *n.* **1** small ball: *he made bread pellets and flicked them at the teacher.* □ **bolita**
2 small lead ball, used in shotguns. □ **perdigón**

pell-mell [pelˈmel] *adv.* in disorder. □ **en tropel**

pelmet [ˈpelmit] *n.* decorative strip of wood/cloth, etc., over a window which hides the curtain fittings. □ **galería**

pelt [pelt] *n.* skin of an animal with fur on it. □ **pellejo**
■ *v.* **1** to fling things at someone: *he was pelted with tomatoes.* □ **tirar**
2 *the rain was pelting down,* pouring down. □ **llovía a cántaros**

pelvis [ˈpelvis] *n.* bones in the lower part of the body forming the hips. □ **pelvis**
pelvic *adj.* referring to the pelvis. □ **pélvico**

pen [pen] *n.* **1** small fenced area for sheep. □ **redil**
submarine pen, shelter where submarines can hide in wartime. □ **refugio de submarinos**
2 writing instrument using ink: *ballpoint pen; felt-tip pen.* □ **bolígrafo; rotulador**
pen name, name used by a writer which is not his own. □ **seudónimo**
pen friend, person overseas whom you have never met, but with whom you exchange letters. □ **amigo con quien uno se cartea**
■ *v.* (*he penned*) **1** to enclose (sheep) in a pen. □ **encerrar**
2 to write with a pen. □ **escribir**

penal [ˈpi:nl] *adj.* referring to a legal punishment: *the penal system,* the system of punishments relating to various crimes. □ **penal**
penalize *v.* to punish: *the footballer was penalized for a foul.* □ **penalizar**
penalty [ˈpenəlti] *n.* **1** punishment: *the death penalty.* □ **castigo; la pena de muerte**
2 punishment in sport, especially a kick at goal awarded to the opposite side in football. □ **penalty**
3 disadvantages: *one of the penalties of old age.* □ **penalidad**

penance [ˈpenəns] *n.* punishment which a person accepts to make amends for a sin. □ **penitencia**

pence [pens] *n. pl. of* penny: *the book costs seventy-five pence (75p).* □ **penique**

pencil [ˈpensl] *n.* instrument for writing, made of wood with a graphite centre: *the letter was written in pencil.* □ **lápiz**
■ *v.* (*he pencilled*) to write with a pencil: *a pencilled note.* □ **escribir a lápiz**
pencil sharpener *n.* instrument for sharpening pencils to a point. □ **sacapuntas**

pendant [ˈpendənt] *n.* ornament which hangs from a chain round the neck. □ **colgante**

pending [ˈpendiŋ] *adj.* and *prep.* **1** waiting. □ **pendiente**
the pending tray, tray for papers and letters which are waiting to be dealt with. □ **asuntos pendientes**
2 *the war is continuing, pending the outcome of the peace negotiations,* while the two sides wait for the outcome. □ **en espera de**

pendulum [ˈpendjuləm] *n.* weight on the end of a rod or chain which swings from side to side, such as that which makes a clock work. □ **péndulo**
pendulous *adj.* which hangs down heavily. □ **colgante**

penetrate [ˈpenitreit] *v.* to enter (with difficulty): *the guerrillas managed to penetrate the camp's defences.* □ **penetrar en**
penetrating *adj.* deep/searching (look); very profound (questions). □ **penetrante**
penetration [peniˈtreiʃn] *n.* **1** getting into something. □ **penetración**
2 deep understanding. □ **discernimiento**

penguin [ˈpeŋgwin] *n.* Antarctic bird which swims well but cannot fly. □ **pingüino**

penicillin [peniˈsilin] *n.* substance made from a mould, used to kill bacteria. □ **penicilina**

peninsula [pəˈninsjulə] *n.* large piece of land jutting into the sea. □ **península**
peninsular *adj.* referring to a peninsula. □ **peninsular**

penis [ˈpi:nis] *n.* part of the male body used for urinating and for sexual intercourse. □ **pene**

penitent [ˈpenitənt] *adj.* and *n.* (person) who is sorry for having done something wrong. □ **penitente**
penitential [peniˈtenʃl] *adj.* referring to penance. □ **penitencial**
penitentiary [peniˈtenʃəri] *n. Amer.* prison. □ **penitenciaría**

penknife [ˈpennaif] *n.* (*pl. penknives*) small folding pocket knife. □ **navaja**

penny [ˈpeni] *n.* (*pl. pennies* = coins; *pence* = price) small coin (the smallest unit in some currencies); (*in Britain*) one hundredth part of a pound. □ **centavo/céntimo; penique (en Gran Bretaña)**
pennies, several of these coins. □ **peniques**
pence, price in several pennies: *it costs sixty pence (60p).* □ **peniques**
the penny's dropped, he's understood at last. □ **caer por fin (en la cuenta)**
penniless *adj.* with no money. □ **sin un duro**

pension [ˈpenʃn] *n.* money paid regularly to someone who has retired from work/to a widow, etc. □ **pensión**
old age pension, money paid regularly by the state to people over a certain age. □ **subsidio de vejez**
■ *v.* ***to pension someone off,*** to make someone stop working and live on a pension. □ **jubilar**
pensionable *adj.* (person) who has the right to have a pension; (job) which gives you the right to have a pension. □ **con derecho a pensión**
pensioner *n.* person who gets a pension: *old age pensioner.* □ **pensionista**

pensive [ˈpensiv] *adj.* thoughtful. □ **pensativo**
pensively *adv.* thoughtfully. □ **pensativamente**

pent [pent] *adj. pent-up emotions,* violent emotions which are repressed. □ **emociones reprimidas**

pentagon [ˈpentəgən] *n.* geometrical figure with five sides. □ **pentágono**
pentagonal [penˈtægənl] *adj.* five-sided. □ **pentagonal**

pentathlon [penˈtæθlən] *n.* athletic competition where competitors have to compete in five different sports. □ **pentatlón**

penthouse [ˈpenthaus] *n.* top-floor flat in a block of flats or hotel. □ **ático**

penultimate [pe'nʌltimət] *adj.* next to last: *Y is the penultimate letter of the alphabet.* □ **penúltimo**
penumbra [pi'nʌmbrə] *n.* edge of a shadow where only part of the light is cut off. □ **penumbra**
penury ['penjuri] *n.* (*formal*) **1** extreme poverty. □ **penuria**
2 great lack. □ **escasez**
penurious [pi'njuəriəs] *adj.* very poor. □ **pobrísimo**
peony ['piəni] *n.* perennial summer flower with large scented flowerheads. □ **peonía**
people ['pi:pl] *n.* **1** (*pl.*) human beings: *how many people are there in the room? thousands of people have been to the exhibition.* □ **personas, gente**
country people, persons who live in the country. □ **la gente del campo**
2 citizens (of a town or country): *the Russian people; the peoples of Africa; government by the people; a people's democracy.* □ **el pueblo ruso; los pueblos de África; una democracia popular**
■ *v.* to fill with people: *the land was peopled by several tribes.* □ **poblar**
pep [pep] *n.* (*informal*) vigour. □ **energía**
pep pill, medicine taken to make you more lively and active. □ **píldora estimulante**
pep talk, talk designed to encourage people to work hard/to win a match, etc. □ **palabras de ánimo**
■ *v.* ***to pep someone up,*** (*informal*) to make someone more lively and active. □ **animar**
pepper ['pepə] *n.* **1** sharp spice used in cooking. □ **pimienta**
2 green or red fruit used as a vegetable. □ **pimiento**
■ *v.* to sprinkle/to throw at: *the enemy was peppered with bullets; the speaker was peppered with questions.* □ **acribillar**
peppercorn *n.* dried seed of pepper. □ **grano de pimienta**
peppercorn rent, nominal/very low rent. □ **alquiler mínimo, simbólico**
peppermill *n.* small grinder used for grinding peppercorns. □ **molinillo de pimienta**
peppermint *n.* **1** common plant with a sharp mint flavour: *peppermint-flavoured chewing gum.* □ **menta**
2 sweet flavoured with peppermint: *he was sucking a peppermint.* □ **caramelo de menta**
peppery *adj.* **1** (soup, etc.) with too much pepper in it. □ **picante**
2 very easily angered: *a peppery old man.* □ **enojadizo**
peptic ['peptik] *adj.* referring to the digestive system. □ **péptico**
peptic ulcer, ulcer in the stomach. □ **úlcera péptica**
per [pə:] *prep.* **1** out of: *ten per thousand,* ten out of every thousand. □ **por**
2 in: *sixty kilometres per hour,* sixty kilometres in every hour; *two thousand revolutions per minute.* □ **por**
3 for: *it costs 10p per kilo; he earns $10 per hour.* □ **cuesta 10p el kilo; gana $10 la hora**
per head: *the consumption is 25 litres per head,* each person consumes 25 litres. □ **...por cabeza**
per annum, in each year: *the salary is $6,000 per annum ($6,000 p.a.).* □ **al año**
per capita, for each person. □ **per cápita**
perambulator *n.* (*formal*) *n.* pram/carriage for a baby. **cochecito de niño**
perceive *v.* to notice through the senses; to become aware of. □ **percibir**
perceptible [pə'septibl] *adj.* which can be seen/heard/smelled, etc.: *a hardly perceptible glow.* □ **perceptible**
perceptibly *adv.* noticeably. □ **perceptiblemente**
perception [pə'sepʃn] *n.* ability to notice. □ **percepción**
perceptive *adj.* acute; able to notice quickly. □ **perceptivo**
per cent [pə'sent] *adv.* and *n.* cent (5%); *fifty per cent (50%) of the electors voted,* half the electors. □ **por ciento**
percentage [pə'sentidʒ] *n.* proportion shown as part of a hundred: *what is the percentage of fatal accidents?,* how many accidents are fatal out of every hundred accidents? *three-quarters expressed as a percentage is 75%.* □ **porcentaje**
percentile [pə'sentail] *n.* one of a hundred equal groups into which a large number can be divided. □ **percentil**
perch [pə:tʃ] *n.* **1** branch/ledge on which a bird can sit. □ **percha**
2 type of freshwater fish. □ **perca**
■ *v.* to sit on a perch; to be set in a high place: *the owl was perched on the chimney; the house is perched on top of a cliff.* □ **posarse en**
percolate ['pə:kəleit] *v.* to filter (through): *the news percolated through; the coffee is percolating,* is in the process of filtering. □ **filtrarse**
percolator *n.* coffee pot where the water boils up and filters through coffee. □ **cafetera de filtro**
percussion [pə'kʌʃn] *n.* **1** action of hitting together. □ **percusión**
percussion instruments, musical instruments which are hit (drums/triangles, etc.). □ **...de percusión**
percussion cap, piece of paper with a small amount of explosive powder which explodes when hit. □ **cabo fulminante**
2 ***the percussion,*** section of an orchestra with percussion instruments. □ **percusión**
peregrine ['perigrin] *n.* type of falcon. □ **halcón peregrino**
peremptory [pə'remptəri] *adj.* abrupt (tone)/curt (refusal). □ **perentorio**
perennial [pə'reniəl] *adj.* which continues from year to year: *it's a perennial problem.* □ **perenne**
■ *n.* plant which flowers every year without needing to be sown again. □ **planta vivaz, perenne**
perennially *adv.* always. □ **perennemente**
perfect ['pə:fikt] *adj.* **1** without any mistakes/flaws: *his English is perfect; a perfect circle.* □ **perfecto**
2 total: *he is a perfect stranger.* □ **(me es) completamente desconocido**
3 ***perfect (tense),*** past tense of a verb which shows that the action has been completed. □ **tiempo perfecto**
■ *v.* [pə'fekt] to make perfect: *he has come to England to perfect his English; he's perfecting his new invention.* □ **perfeccionar**
perfection [pə'fekʃn] *n.* state of being perfect. □ **perfección**
perfectionist *n.* person who insists that perfection is possible/that everything has to be perfect. □ **perfeccionista**
perfectly ['pə:fiktli] *adv.* completely. □ **perfectamente**
perforate ['pə:fəreit] *v.* to make a hole/to pierce. □ **perforar**
perforation [pə:fə'reiʃn] *n.* **1** action of making a hole. □ **perforación**
2 small hole: *perforations in a sheet of stamps,* small holes that allow you to tear off each stamp. □ **agujero; trepado**
perform [pə'fɔ:m] *v.* **1** to carry out an action: *they*

performed feats of bravery; our rugby team performed very well, played very well. □ **realizar**
2 to act in public: *the conjuror has performed in many European cities.* □ **actuar**
performance *n.* **1** working of a machine; action of a sportsman: *the performance of the engine has been bad; the football team's remarkable performance last Saturday.* □ **funcionamiento (máquina); actuación (deportista)**
2 public show: *there is no performance this evening because the star is ill.* □ **representación**
performer *n.* person who gives a public show. □ **actor, artista**
perfume ['pəːfjuːm] *n.* **1** pleasant smell: *the perfume of roses.* □ **perfume**
2 liquid scent: *a bottle of perfume.* □ **perfume**
■ *v.* [pə'fjuːm] **1** to give a pleasant smell to (something): *garden perfumed with roses.* □ **perfumar**
2 to pour perfume on: *a perfumed handkerchief.* □ **un pañuelo perfumado**
perfunctory [pə'fʌŋktəri] *adj.* rapid and superficial: *a perfunctory glance.* □ **somero**
perhaps [pə'hæps] *adv.* possibly/maybe: *perhaps he will come.* □ **quizás/quizá, tal vez**
peril ['perəl] *n.* great danger: *the perils of the sea.* □ **peligro**
perilous *adj.* very dangerous. □ **peligroso**
perimeter [pə'rimitə] *n.* outside line round an enclosed area: *the perimeter of a circle.* □ **perímetro**
perimeter fence, fence surrounding a field/camp, etc. □ **cercado**
period ['piəriəd] *n.* **1** length of time: *for a short period; in the pre-war period.* □ **período**
period furniture, antique furniture from a certain time. □ **muebles de época**
period piece, piece of antique furniture, etc. □ **mueble clásico**
2 class time in a school: *the maths period; we have four periods of maths per week.* □ **clase**
3 full stop/dot (.) used in writing to mark the end of a sentence: *he's a fool, period,* (*figuratively, informal*) he's a fool and that's all. □ **punto**
4 regular monthly flow of blood from a woman's vagina. □ **período**
periodic [piːri'ɔdik] *adj.* repeated after a regular length of time: *she is in one of her periodic fits of efficiency.* □ **periódico**
periodic table, list of chemical elements arranged in order of their atomic numbers. □ **tabla periódica**
periodical *adj.* periodic; repeated after a regular length of time: *a periodical check.* □ **periódico**
■ *n.* magazine which appears regularly. □ **semanario; publicación periódica**
periodically *adv.* from time to time. □ **periódicamente**
peripatetic [peripə'tetik] *adj.* (person) who wanders from place to place: *peripatetic violin teacher,* teacher who goes from school to school teaching children to play the violin. □ **ambulante**
periphery [pə'rifəri] *n.* edge: *on the periphery of the jungle area.* □ **periferia**
peripheral *adj.* minor/not very important. □ **periférico**
periscope ['periskoup] *n.* long tube with mirrors which allows someone in a submerged submarine to look above the surface of the water. □ **periscopio**
perish ['periʃ] *v.* **1** (*formal*) to die. □ **perecer**
2 to rot: *the rubber has perished.* □ **estropearse**
3 *I'm perished,* (*informal*) I'm cold. □ **estoy helado**
perishable *adj.* (food) which can go bad easily. □ **perecedero**
perishables, goods (especially fruit/vegetables) which go bad quite quickly. □ **artículos perecederos**
peritonitis [peritə'naitis] *n.* inflammation of the lining of the abdomen. □ **peritonitis**
periwinkle ['periwiŋkl] *n.* **1** small creeping plant with blue flowers. □ **vincapervinca**
2 edible snail which lives in salt water. □ **bígaro**
perjure ['pəːdʒə] *v.* ***to perjure yourself,*** to tell lies in a court of law when you have sworn to tell the truth. □ **perjurar**
perjurer *n.* person who has committed perjury. □ **perjuro**
perjury *n.* crime of telling lies in court when you have sworn to tell the truth. □ **perjurio**
perk [pəːk] *v.* ***to perk up,*** to become more alert/more interested. □ **entonarse**
■ *n. pl.* ***perks,*** (*informal*) valuable extras which you are given by your employer in addition to your salary: *one of the perks of the job is a monthly trip to Paris.* □ **atenciones**
perky *adj.* (*informal*) lively/interested. □ **despabilado**
perm [pəːm] *n.* (*informal*) **1** curls or a wave put into your hair artificially: *she's just had a perm.* □ **permanente**
2 combination of football teams on a football pools coupon. □ **múltiple**
■ *v.* (*informal*) **1** to put a wave or curls into someone's hair: *I've had my hair permed.* □ **me han hecho la permanente**
2 to select several football teams in various combinations on a football pools coupon. □ **hacer una múltiple**
permanent ['pəːmənənt] *adj.* lasting for ever/supposed to last for ever: *have you a permanent address in London?* □ **permanente**
permanency *n.* state of being permanent. □ **permanencia**
permanently *adv.* always. □ **permanentemente**
permanganate [pə'mæŋgəneit] *n.* salt containing manganese. □ **permanganato**
permanganate of potash, dark purple crystals used for disinfecting. □ **...de potasio**
permeate ['pəːmieit] *v.* to filter; to spread right through. □ **impregnar**
permeability [pəːmiə'biliti] *n.* being permeable. □ **permeabilidad**
permeable *adj.* which lets liquid pass through. □ **permeable**
permissible [pə'misəbl] *adj.* which can be allowed. □ **permisible**
permission [pə'miʃn] *n.* freedom which you are given to do something: *you have my permission to leave the room; he left the school without permission.* □ **permiso**
permissive [pə'misiv] *adj.* free; allowing many things to be done which formerly were not allowed: *permissive society.* □ **permisivo; sociedad tolerante**
permit ['pəːmit] *n.* paper which allows you to do something: *he has a permit to use the library.* □ **permiso**
■ *v.* [pə'mit] (*he permitted*) to allow: *he was permitted to leave the prison to visit his wife; smoking is not permitted in the theatre.* □ **permitir**
permutation [pəːmjuː'teiʃn] *n.* grouping of several items together in varied combinations; combination of various items in a different order. □ **permutación**
pernicious [pə'niʃəs] *adj.* harmful/evil. □ **pernicioso**
pernickety [pə'nikəti] *adj.* (*informal*) very fussy: *he*

is pernickety about his food. □ **quisquilloso; es muy exigente con la comida**
peroxide [pə'rɔksaid] *n.* chemical used for bleaching hair or killing germs. □ **peróxido**
perpendicular [pə:pən'dikjulə] *adj.* and *n.* (line) standing vertically/at right angles to a base. □ **perpendicular**
perpetrate ['pə:pitreit] *v.* (*formal*) to commit (a crime). □ **perpetrar**
perpetual [pə'petjuəl] *adj.* continuous/without any end: *she's in a perpetual state of worry.* □ **perpetuo**
perpetually *adv.* always: *they're perpetually borrowing money.* □ **perpetuamente**
perpetuate *v.* to make (something) continue for ever. □ **perpetuar**
perpetuity [pə:pi'tju:iti] *n.* ***in perpetuity,*** (*formal*) for ever/ without any end. □ **en perpetuidad**
perplex [pə'pleks] *v.* to confuse/to puzzle (someone): *I was perplexed by the curious letter.* □ **dejar perplejo**
perplexity *n.* bewilderment/puzzled state. □ **perplejidad**
perquisite ['pə:kwizit] *n.* (*formal*) valuable extra which is given to you by your employer in addition to your salary. □ **atención**
perry ['peri] *n.* alcoholic drink made from fermented pear juice. □ **licor de pera**
persecute ['pə:sikju:t] *v.* to torment/to treat cruelly: *people are still persecuted because of their religious beliefs.* □ **perseguir**
persecution [pə:si'kju:ʃn] *n.* relentless killing (because of religious beliefs). □ **persecución**
persecution mania, mental disease where you feel that everyone is against you. □ **manía persecutoria**
persecutor ['pə:sikju:tə] *n.* person who persecutes. □ **perseguidor**
persevere [pə:si'viə] *v.* to continue doing something (in spite of obstacles): *he persevered with building the bookshelf.* □ **perseverar**
perseverance *n.* act of persevering. □ **perseverancia**
persist [pə'sist] *v.* to continue doing something (in spite of obstacles); to continue to exist: *he persisted in trying to find the lost children; fog will persist for most of the day.* □ **persistir**
persistence *n.* obstinacy; refusal to stop doing something. □ **persistencia**
persistent *adj.* continual: *persistent rumours.* □ **persistente**
person ['pə:sn] *n.* **1** human being: *a third person joined the discussion.* □ **persona**
2 *the President appeared **in person,*** the President appeared himself. □ **en persona**
3 (*in grammar*) one of the three forms of verbs or pronouns which indicate who the speaker is: *first person,* I or we; *second person,* you; *third person,* he, she, it, they. □ **persona**
personable *adj.* attractive/good-looking/having a pleasant character. □ **bien parecido**
personage *n.* important person. □ **personaje**
personal *adj.* **1** referring to a person: *a letter marked 'personal',* addressed so that you and no one else may open it; *personal liberty; he has his own personal jet.* □ **personal**
2 rude: *he made some very personal remarks about my father.* □ **...unos comentarios muy fuertes...**
3 ***personal pronoun,*** (*in grammar*) pronoun which refers to someone, such as 'I', 'he', 'she', etc. □ **pronombre personal**
personality [pə:sə'næliti] *n.* **1** character: *he has a strong personality.* □ **personalidad**
2 famous person: *a TV personality.* □ **figura**
personalized *adj.* with your name or initials printed on it: *personalized briefcase.* □ **grabado con las iniciales de uno**
personally *adv.* **1** from your own point of view: *personally, I am tired out.* □ **personalmente**
2 in person: *the mayor spoke to me personally.* □ **en persona**
3 as an insult: *don't take it personally,* don't think it was meant to be rude about you. □ **como una alusión personal**
personification [pəsɔnifi'keiʃn] *n.* good example of an abstract quality in a person: *he is the personification of good humour.* □ **personificación**
personify [pə'sɔnifai] *v.* to be a good example of: *she personifies the romantic spirit.* □ **personificar**
personnel [pə:sə'nel] *n.* staff/people employed by a company. □ **personal**
naval personnel, seamen. □ **marinería**
personnel manager, manager who looks after pay/ sick leave/administration, etc., for all the staff. □ **jefe de personal**
perspective [pə'spektiv] *n.* **1** (*in art*) way of drawing objects/scenes, so that they appear to have depth or distance. □ **perspectiva**
2 way of looking at something. □ **perspectiva**
3 *we have to put their offer **in perspective,*** we have to consider the offer in relation to everything else. □ **en contexto**
perspex ['pə:speks] *n.* trademark for a type of tough clear plastic. □ **plexiglás**
perspicacious [pə:spi'keiʃəs] *adj.* (person) who understands clearly. □ **perspicaz**
perspicacity [pə:spi'kæsiti] *n.* clearness of understanding. □ **perspicacia**
perspicuity [pə:spi'kju:iti] *n.* clearness of expression. □ **claridad**
perspire [pə'spaiə] *v.* to sweat: *he was perspiring heavily as he dug the garden in the sun.* □ **transpirar**
perspiration [pə:spə'reiʃn] *n.* sweat. □ **sudor**
persuade [pə'sweid] *v.* to get someone to do what you want by explaining or pleading: *can you persuade your brother to come to the office? the police persuaded her not to jump off the bridge.* □ **persuadir**
persuasion [pə'sweiʒn] *n.* **1** act of persuading. □ **persuasión**
2 firm (usually religious) belief: *he is of the Christian persuasion.* □ **creencia religiosa**
persuasive [pə'sweisiv] *adj.* that persuades: *he's very persuasive,* he is good at convincing people to do what he wants. □ **persuasivo; convincente**
pert [pə:t] *adj.* cheeky. □ **impertinente**
pertain [pə'tein] *v.* (*formal*) to be relevant. □ **ser propio de**
pertinacious [pə:ti'neiʃəs] *adj.* obstinate. □ **pertinaz**
pertinacity [pə:ti'næsiti] *n.* obstinateness/stubbornness. □ **pertinacia**
pertinent ['pə:tinənt] *adj.* relevant: *he made several pertinent remarks,* remarks which were to the point. □ **pertinente**
perturb [pə'tə:b] *v.* to make (someone) anxious. □ **perturbar, inquietar**
perturbation [pə:tə'beiʃn] *n.* anxiety/bother. □ **perturbación, inquietud**
Peru [pə'ru:] *n.* country in South America. □ **Perú**
Peruvian *adj.* referring to Peru. □ **peruano**
■ *n.* person from Peru. □ **peruano**
peruse [pə'ru:z] *v.* (*formal*) to read carefully. □ **leer atentamente**
perusal *n.* reading: *after a careful perusal of the documents.* □ **lectura atenta**

pervade [pə'veid] *v.* to spread everywhere: *a smell of boiled fish pervades the house.* □ **invadir, impregnar**
pervasive [pə'veisiv] *adj.* penetrating: *a pervasive smell.* □ **penetrante**
pervasiveness *n.* penetrating everywhere. □ **capacidad de penetración**
perverse [pə'və:s] *adj.* obstinately awkward; continuing to do something even if it is wrong. □ **obstinado**
perversely *adv.* in an obstinate way: *he perversely kept saying we were going in the wrong direction.* □ **obstinadamente**
perverseness *n.* contrariness: *the perverseness of the weather.* □ **adversidad**
perversion [pə'və:ʃn] *n.* corruption (of someone to do something evil). □ **perversión**
pervert *n.* person who commits unnatural sexual acts. □ **pervertido**
■ *v.* [pə'və:t] **1** to corrupt (someone) to do evil. □ **pervertir**
2 *to pervert the course of justice,* to influence a court so that justice is not done. □ **desvirtuar**
pessimism ['pesimizəm] *n.* belief that only bad things will happen. □ **pesimismo**
pessimist ['pesimist] *n.* person who believes that only bad things will happen. □ **pesimista**
pessimistic [pesi'mistik] *adj.* gloomy/believing that only bad things will happen: *a pessimistic view of the economy.* □ **pesimista**
pessimistically *adv.* gloomily. □ **con pesimismo**
pest [pest] *n.* **1** troublesome animal, often an insect: *flies are a pest in summer.* □ **plaga**
2 (*informal*) person who annoys: *he's a real pest.* □ **es un pelmazo**
pester *v.* to bother someone: *he is always pestering me to lend him money.* □ **molestar**
pesticide ['pestisaid] *n.* poison to kill insects, etc.: *he sprayed his cabbages with pesticide.* □ **plaguicida**
pestilence ['pestiləns] *n.* (*formal*) plague/disease. □ **pestilencia**
pestilential [pesti'lenʃl] *adj.* like a plague/very unpleasant. □ **pestilente**
pestle ['pesl] *n.* round-headed heavy tool for crushing things in a bowl. □ **mano**
pet [pet] *n.* animal kept in the home to give pleasure: *we keep a lot of pets: a cat, two budgerigars and several hamsters.* □ **animal doméstico**
pet shop, shop which sells puppies/budgerigars, etc. □ **pajarería**
■ *adj.* **1** favourite: *it's his pet subject.* □ **preferido**
pet name, special name given to someone you are fond of. □ **nombre cariñoso**
2 tame (animal): *he has a pet snake.* □ **domesticado**
■ *v.* (*he petted*) to caress/to fondle. □ **acariciar**
petal ['petl] *n.* one of several colourful leaf-like parts of a flower: *rose petals.* □ **pétalo**
petard [pə'tɑ:d] *n.* ***to be hoist with your own petard,*** (*formal*) to be caught in a trap which you have set for someone else. □ **petardo; caer en su propia trampa**
peter ['pi:tə] *v.* ***to peter out,*** to come to an end/to fade away: *the path petered out among the sand dunes.* □ **morir, desaparecer**
petite [pə'ti:t] *adj.* (*of woman*) small and dainty. □ **chiquita**
petit four [pəti'fuə] *n.* small fancy cake or biscuit eaten at parties, etc. □ **tipo de pastita de té**
petition [pə'tiʃn] *n.* **1** official request (often signed by many people): *they got up a petition to stop the council widening the street.* □ **petición**
2 legal request: *she filed a petition for divorce,* she asked the court to grant her a divorce. □ **...demanda de divorcio**
■ *v.* to ask (someone) for something/to make an official request: *they petitioned the mayor to prevent the old houses being demolished.* □ **solicitar**
petrel ['petrəl] *n.* type of sea bird which flies long distances. □ **petrel**
petrify ['petrifai] *v.* **1** to turn to stone. □ **petrificar**
2 to strike (someone) still with fear: *they were petrified,* terror-stricken. □ **petrificar**
petrochemical [petrou'kemikl] *adj.* and *n.* (chemical) produced from petroleum or natural gas: *the petrochemical industry.* □ **petroquímico**
petrodollar [petrou'dɔlə] *n.* dollar which is earned by a country selling oil. □ **petrodólar**
petrol ['petrəl] *n.* inflammable liquid produced from petroleum and used as a fuel to drive motor engines, etc.: *I almost ran out of petrol.* □ **gasolina**
petrol station, garage which sells petrol (but may not do repairs). □ **estación de servicio**
petroleum [pə'trouliəm] *n.* raw mineral oil (from the earth). □ **petróleo**
petroleum products, substances (like petrol/plastics, etc.) which are made from petroleum. □ **productos petrolíferos**
petticoat ['petikout] *n.* piece of women's underwear/light skirt worn under another skirt. □ **enaguas**
petty ['peti] *adj.* **1** insignificant/unimportant. □ **pequeño**
petty cash, small amounts of cash (in an office). □ **fondo para gastos menores**
petty officer, non-commissioned officer in the Royal Navy. □ **contramaestre**
2 with a narrow point of view: *don't be so petty,* don't be so small-minded. □ **no seas tan mezquino**
pettiness *n.* **1** unimportance. □ **pequeñez**
2 narrowness of outlook. □ **mezquindad**
petulant ['petjulənt] *adj.* irritable/bad-tempered. □ **de mal humor**
petulance *n.* irritability. □ **malhumor**
petunia [pi'tju:niə] *n.* common summer garden flower. □ **petunia**
pew [pju:] *n.* long bench seat in a church. □ **banco de iglesia**
take a pew, (*informal*) sit down. □ **tome asiento**
pewter ['pju:tə] *n.* alloy, usually a mixture of tin and lead, used for making mugs/plates, etc. □ **peltre**
pH [pi:'eitʃ] *n.* ***pH factor,*** measurement of how much acid there is (in the soil, etc.). □ **factor pH**
phallus ['fæləs] *n.* (*formal*) penis in erection. □ **falo**
phallic *adj.* referring to an erect penis. □ **fálico**
phallic symbol, something which resembles a penis, and is taken to symbolize male sex. □ **símbolo fálico**
phantom ['fæntəm] *n.* ghost. □ **fantasma**
pharmaceutical [fɑ:mə'sju:tikl] *adj.* referring to medicines. □ **farmacéutico**
pharmacist ['fɑ:məsist] *n.* person who makes and sells medicines. □ **farmacéutico**
pharmacopoeia [fɑ:məkə'pi:ə] *n.* collection of drugs; book which lists drugs. □ **farmacopea**
pharmacy *n.* study of medicines; shop which makes and sells medicines. □ **farmacia**
pharynx ['færiŋks] *n.* space at the back of the nose. □ **faringe**
pharyngitis [færin'dʒaitis] *n.* inflammation of the pharynx. □ **faringitis**
phase [feiz] *n.* period; stage in development of something: *the phase of the moon; the baby has reached an awkward phase.* □ **fase**
■ *v.* ***to phase in/out,*** to introduce/to remove gradually: *we are phasing out the old models of type-*

writers. □ **introducir/eliminar poco a poco**

pheasant ['fezənt] *n.* large bright-coloured bird with a long tail, shot for sport and food. □ **faisán**

phenomenon [fe'nɔminən] *n.* (*pl. phenomena*) **1** something which happens/occurs naturally; especially remarkable thing/remarkable happening: *hot springs are a natural phenomenon.* □ **fenómeno**
2 *he is a phenomenon on the trumpet,* (*informal*) he plays the trumpet remarkably well. □ **es un fenómeno con la trompeta**

phenomenal *adj.* remarkable: *she's got a phenomenal memory.* □ **fenomenal**

phial ['fail] *n.* (*formal*) small bottle. □ **frasco**

philanthropy [fi'lænθrəpi] *n.* love of/caring for human beings, shown especially by giving money to charity. □ **filantropía**

philanthropic [filən'θrɔpik] *adj.* kind (towards human beings). □ **filantrópico**

philanthropist [fi'lænθrəpist] *n.* person who is kind to human beings. □ **filántropo**

philately [fi'lætəli] *n.* stamp collecting. □ **filatelia**

philatelist *n.* person who studies or collects stamps. □ **filatelista**

-phile [fail] *suffix meaning* (person) who likes. □ **-filo**
Francophile, person who likes the French. □ **francófilo**

philharmonic [filɑ:'mɔnik] *adj.* liking music (used in names of orchestras/concert halls, etc.). □ **filarmónica**

Philippines ['filipi:nz] *n.* country made of several islands in the Pacific Ocean. □ **Filipinas**

philistine ['filistain] *adj.* and *n.* (person) who is unsympathetic to the arts. □ **filisteo**

philology [fi'lɔlədʒi] *n.* study of (the history of) language. □ **filología**

philological [filə'lɔdʒikl] *adj.* referring to the study of language. □ **filológico**

philologist [fi'lɔlədʒist] *n.* person who studies language. □ **filólogo**

philosophy [fi'lɔsəfi] *n.* study of the meaning of human existence; study of the methods and limits of human knowledge; general way of thinking: *he has a simple philosophy of life,* way of living. □ **filosofía**

philosopher *n.* person who studies the meaning of human existence. □ **filósofo**

philosophical [filə'sɔfikl] *adj.* **1** thoughtful; calm. □ **filosófico, reflexivo**
2 referring to the study of the meaning of human existence. □ **filosófico**

philosophically *adv.* thoughtfully; calmly: *he accepted being sacked very philosophically.* □ **filosóficamente**

phlebitis [fli'baitis] *n.* inflammation of a vein. □ **flebitis**

phlegm [flem] *n.* **1** slimy substance in the throat, etc., when you have a cold. □ **flema**
2 calmness. □ **flema**

phlegmatic [fleg'mætik] *adj.* calm/not easily annoyed. □ **flemático**

phlox [flɔks] *n.* common perennial flower. □ **flox**

-phobe [foub] *suffix meaning* (person) who does not like. □ **-fobo**
xenophobe, person who dislikes foreigners. □ **xenófobo**

phobia ['foubiə] *n.* abnormal terror/hatred of something. □ **fobia**

phone [foun] *n.* telephone/device for speaking to someone over a distance using electric current running along wires, or by radio: *he put the phone down; what's his phone number?* □ **teléfono**
to be on the phone, (i) *he's been on the phone for twenty minutes,* has been talking to someone by telephone.□ **ha estado al teléfono...**
(ii) *are you on the phone?,* do you have a telephone? □ **¿tienes teléfono?**
■ *v.* to call (someone) by telephone: *I want to phone New York; I'll phone you in the morning; he phoned back at six o'clock,* he replied by telephone. □ **telefonear**

phone book *n.* book which lists people's names, addresses and phone numbers. □ **guía telefónica**

phone box *n.* small cabin for a public telephone. □ **cabina telefónica**

phonetic [fə'netik] *adj.* referring to spoken sounds: *the phonetic alphabet.* □ **fonético; el alfabeto fonético**
■ *n. pl.* ***phonetics,*** (i) study of sounds of a language. □ **fonética**
(ii) signs which indicate sounds: *the way each word should be spoken is indicated by phonetics.* □ **símbolos fonéticos**

phonetically *adv.* using phonetics. □ **fonéticamente**

phoney, phony ['founi] *adj.* (*informal*) false. □ **falso**

phonograph ['founəgrɑ:f] *n. Amer.* gramophone/machine on which records are played. □ **fonógrafo**

phosphate ['fɔsfeit] *n.* chemical compound containing phosphorus, often used as a fertilizer. □ **fosfato**

phosphorescence *n.* ability to shine in the dark after being exposed to light: *the phosphorescence on the waves at night.* □ **fosforescencia**

phosphorescent [fɔsfə'resnt] *adj.* which shines in the dark after being exposed to light. □ **fosforescente**

phosphorus ['fɔsfərəs] *n.* (*chemical element*: P) poisonous yellow substance which shines in the dark. □ **fósforo**

photo ['foutou] *n.* (*informal*) photograph: *look at our holiday photos.* □ **foto**

photocopy ['foutoukɔpi] *n.* copy (of a document) made by photographing it: *he took a photocopy of the letter.* □ **fotocopia**
■ *v.* to copy (something) photographically and make a print of it. □ **fotocopiar**

photocopier *n.* machine which takes photocopies. □ **fotocopiadora**

photoelectric [foutoui'lektrik] *adj.* referring to electricity controlled by light. □ **fotoeléctrico**
photoelectric cell, cell which converts light into electricity or which operates a machine when a beam of light is broken. □ **célula fotoeléctrica**

photo finish ['foutoufiniʃ] *n.* very close end of a race when a photograph is used to decide who is the winner: *he won in a photo finish.* □ **foto 'finish'**

photogenic [foutou'dʒi:nik] *adj.* (person) who looks well in photographs. □ **fotogénico**

photograph ['foutəgrɑ:f] *n.* picture taken by a camera by means of exposing sensitive film to light: *a black and white photograph; to take someone's photograph; photograph album.* □ **fotografía**
■ *v.* to take a picture with a camera: *a hidden camera photographed the bank robbers.* □ **hacer una fotografía**

photographer [fə'tɔgrəfə] *n.* person who takes photographs. □ **fotógrafo**

photographic [foutou'græfik] *adj.* referring to photography. □ **fotográfico**
photographic library, library of photographs. □ **biblioteca fotográfica**
photographic memory, ability to remember things in exact detail. □ **memoria fotográfica**

photography [fə'tɔgrəfi] *n.* (art of) taking pictures on sensitive film with a camera. □ **fotografía**

photostat ['foutoustæt] *n.* trademark for a type of photographic copy. □ **fotostato**
■ *v.* (*he photostatted*) to make a photographic copy. □ **hacer una copia fotostática**

phrase [freiz] *n.* **1** expression; short sentence; group of words taken together: *he kept repeating the phrase 'must find a horse'.* □ **frase**
phrase book, book of translations of common expressions. □ **diccionario de expresiones**
2 group of notes in a piece of music. □ **frase**
■ *v.* to express/to word (a sentence, etc.): *he could have phrased it more politely.* □ **expresar**
phraseology [freizi'ɔlədʒi] *n.* way of expressing something; choice of words and phrases. □ **fraseología**

phrenology [fre'nɔlədʒi] *n.* study of the outside shape of the skull. □ **frenología**

physical ['fizikl] *adj.* **1** referring to matter/energy, etc.. □ **físico**
physical geography, study of rocks and earth, etc. □ **geografía física**
physical chemistry, study of chemical substances. □ **fisicoquímica**
2 referring to the human body. □ **físico**
physical exercise, exercise of the body. □ **ejercicio físico**
physically *adv.* referring to the body or to the laws of nature: *physically handicapped people; he is physically very fit; it is physically impossible to get the car through that archway.* □ **físicamente**

physician [fi'ziʃn] *n.* doctor. □ **médico**

physics ['fiziks] *n.* study of matter/energy, etc. □ **física**
physicist ['fizisist] *n.* person who studies physics. □ **físico**

physiognomy [fizi'ɔnəmi] *n.* human face. □ **fisonomía**

physiology [fizi'ɔlədʒi] *n.* study of the way in which living things work. □ **fisiología**
physiologist *n.* person who studies physiology. □ **fisiólogo**

physiotherapy [fiziou'θerəpi] *n.* treatment of an illness, pain, etc., by exercise or rubbing. □ **fisioterapia**
physiotherapist *n.* person who practices physiotherapy. □ **fisioterapeuta**

physique [fi'zi:k] *n.* shape of a person's body: *he has a splendid physique.* □ **físico**

pi [pai] *n.* letter of the Greek alphabet (π), symbolizing the quantity 3.14159, which is used to calculate the circumference of a circle from a known radius. □ **pi**

piano ['pjænou] *n.* musical instrument with many black and white keys which makes notes by striking wires with hammers. □ **piano**
grand piano, large piano with horizontal wires. □ **piano de cola**
pianist ['piənist] *n.* person who plays the piano. □ **pianista**
pianoforte ['pjænoufɔ:ti] *n.* (*formal*) piano. □ **piano**
pianola [piə'noulə] *n.* trademark for a piano which plays music automatically from a reel of paper with holes in it which activates the keys and hammers. □ **pianola**

piazza [pi'ætsə] *n.* Italian square, often surrounded by arcades. □ **plaza**

picaresque [pikə'resk] *adj.* fancifully romantic (story). □ **picaresco**

piccalilli [pikə'lili] *n.* pickle made of vegetables, such as cauliflower, onions, etc., in a mustard sauce. □ **verduras con salsa picante**

piccolo ['pikəlou] *n.* small wind instrument, like a little flute. □ **flautín**

pick [pik] *n.***1** heavy tool (for breaking hard ground/concrete, etc.) with a long handle and a curved metal bar with pointed ends. □ **pico**
2 select group. □ **lo más escogido**
the pick of the bunch, the best. □ **lo mejor**
take your pick, choose which one you want. □ **escoja el que quiera**
■ *v.* **1** to break up (hard ground/concrete, etc.) with a pick. □ **picar**
2 to remove small pieces of something with your fingers/with a pointed tool; to clean the inside of your nose with your fingers: *she picked the bits of wool off his suit; he was picking his teeth with a matchstick; he was picking his nose.* □ **quitarse, hurgarse, mondarse**
3 to eat very daintily and without any appetite: *she was picking at her food.* □ **picotear**
4 to choose: *the team leader picked his group of men; hand-picked group of police,* carefully selected; *he picked his way through the heaps of rubbish.* □ **seleccionar**
5 to collect ripe fruit from a tree/to cut flowers: *we picked a basketful of apples; she picked a bunch of grapes/a bunch of roses.* □ **coger**
6 to open (a lock) with a piece of wire: *the burglar picked the lock very quickly.* □ **abrir con ganzúa**
7 to steal something from (someone's pocket): *my pocket has been picked.* □ **robar**
8 ***to pick someone's brains,*** to ask him for ideas on how you should act/to obtain information which you can use. □ **explotar los conocimientos de alguien**
pickaxe, *Amer.* **pickax** *n.* pick/tool for breaking hard ground. □ **piocha**
pick on *v.* to select someone as a target for criticism/for bullying: *why do you always pick on children who are smaller than you?* □ **meterse con**
pick out *v.* to select/to choose. □ **elegir**
pickpocket *n.* person who steals things from people's pockets. □ **carterista**
pick up *v.* **1** to take (something) which is on the ground: *he picked up the books which had fallen on the floor.* □ **recoger**
2 to learn (a language, etc.) unsystematically: *I was never taught to type - I just picked it up.* □ **aprender a la buena de Dios**
3 to give (someone) a lift in a car; (*of a bus*) to take (passengers) on board; (*of police*) to arrest/to take to a police station; to start an acquaintanceship with (someone) by chance: *I picked up a hitchhiker; he picked up a girl in a coffee bar.* □ **llevar (en coche, autobús, a la comisaría); empezar una amistad**
4 to get stronger: *he was ill, but he is picking up now.* □ **mejorar**
5 *the car picked up speed,* went faster. □ **el coche tomó velocidad**
pick-up *n.* **1** (*informal*) person who has been picked up. □ **persona recogida, llevada...**
2 needle and arm of a record player. □ **brazo**
3 light van with an open back. □ **furgoneta**

picket ['pikit] *n.* **1** guard. □ **guarda**
2 striking workman/union official who stands at the entrance to a factory to try to prevent other workmen from going to work. □ **piquete**
picket line, line of pickets preventing other workmen going to work. □ **piquetes**
■ *v.* to post strikers at the entrance of a factory to try to prevent workers going to work. □ **formar piquetes**

pickle ['pikl] *n.* vegetables preserved in spicy vinegar: *a jar of pickles.* □ **encurtido**
■ *v.* to preserve vegetables in spicy vinegar: *pickled onions; pickled cucumbers.* □ **encurtir; cebollitas/pepinillos en vinagre**
picnic ['piknik] *n.* excursion with a meal eaten in the open air: *they went on a picnic; we had a picnic in the woods.* □ **merienda campestre**
■ *v.* (*he picnicked*) to eat a picnic: *we were picnicking by the side of the road.* □ **merendar en el campo**
picnicker *n.* person who goes on a picnic. □ **excursionista**
pictorial [pik'tɔːriəl] *adj.* referring to pictures: *pictorial representation,* representation by pictures. □ **pictórico, con imágenes**
picture ['piktʃə] *n.* **1** painting/drawing, etc., of something: *he has bought a picture by Rembrandt.* □ **cuadro**
2 *she's **the picture of** health,* looks very healthy. □ **imagen**
3 *I'll **put** you **in the picture,*** (*informal*) I'll tell you all the relevant details. □ **te voy a poner al corriente**
4 image (on a TV screen, etc.): *the picture has gone blurred.* □ **imagen**
5 ***the pictures,*** cinema: *what's on at the pictures?* □ **el cine**
■ *v.* to imagine: *picture him standing in the middle of the road in his pyjamas.* □ **imaginar**
picturesque [piktʃə'resk] *adj.* which would make a good picture; very artistic: *a picturesque scene in a Greek market.* □ **pintoresco**
piddle ['pidl] *v.* (*informal*) to let out waste water from the body. □ **hacer pipí**
piddling *adj.* (*informal*) very small. □ **de poca monta**
pidgin ['pidʒin] *n.* ***pidgin (English),*** simplified form of English used in the Far East. □ **'pidgin English'**
pie [pai] *n.* cooked dish, usually of pastry with a filling of meat or fruit: *chicken pie; plum pie.* □ **empanada, pastel**
cottage pie/shepherd's pie, dish of minced meat covered with mashed potato. □ **plato de carne picada con puré de patatas**
pie in the sky, unattainable ideal. □ **castillos en el aire**
pie-chart *n.* diagram shaped like a circle with different segments to indicate how something is divided up. □ **diagrama en círculo**
pie-eyed *adj.* **1** with eyes wide open. □ **con ojos como platos**
2 (*informal*) drunk. □ **borracho**
piebald ['paibɔːld] *adj.* (horse) with black and white patches. □ **pío**
piece [piːs] *n.* **1** small part/bit (of something): *can I have a piece of cake? I need three pieces of paper; the watch came to pieces in my hand; the mechanic took the engine to pieces; I want to give you a piece of advice.* □ **pedazo, trozo**
to give somebody a piece of one's mind: *she gave him a piece of her mind,* she criticized him sharply. □ **le dijo cuatro verdades**
to go to pieces: *he went completely to pieces,* he lost control of himself/had a nervous breakdown. □ **se vino abajo**
2 short composition in music: *he played three pieces by Chopin.* □ **pieza**
3 one of the figures used in chess, but not usually a pawn. □ **pieza**
4 gun. □ **pieza (de artillería)**
fowling piece, gun for shooting wild birds. □ **escopeta**
■ *v.* ***to piece together,*** to join separate parts together: *the police are trying to piece together the various clues.* □ **juntar**
piecemeal *adv.* in bits; a bit at a time; separately. □ **por partes**
piecework *n.* work for which you are paid by the amount of work done and not by the hour. □ **trabajo a destajo**
pied [paid] *adj.* having two colours, usually black and white. □ **de dos colores**
pier ['piə] *n.* **1** long construction going out into the sea, used as a landing place for ships. □ **muelle**
2 pillar (of a bridge). □ **pilar**
pierce ['piəs] *v.* to make a hole: *the bullet pierced the car door; she has had her ears pierced,* she has had holes made in her lobes so that she can wear earrings. □ **perforar**
piercing *adj.* very loud, shrill (cry); very sharp/severe (cold or wind). □ **penetrante**
piety ['paiəti] *n.* **1** being pious. □ **piedad**
2 great respect for religion. □ **devoción**
pig [pig] *n.* **1** farm animal (often pink) which gives pork/bacon, etc.; various wild species of this animal; (*informal*) dirty/greedy person. □ **cerdo**
2 large block of metal. □ **lingote**
pig iron, iron in rough moulded blocks. □ **arrabio, hierro en lingotes**
piggyback *n., adj.* and *adv.* carrying someone on your back with his arms round your neck: *give me a piggyback* (*ride*). □ **a cuestas**
piggybank *n.* child's money box in the shape of a pig. □ **hucha**
pig-headed *adj.* (*informal*) obstinate. □ **testarudo**
piglet *n.* little pig. □ **cochinillo**
pigskin *n.* leather made from the skin of a pig. □ **piel de cerdo**
pigsty *n.* shed where pigs are kept. □ **pocilga**
pigtail *n.* hair hanging down in a plait at the back of the head. □ **trenza**
pigeon ['pidʒn] *n.* common greyish bird, sometimes shot as vermin. □ **paloma, pichón**
pigeonhole *n.* small square space in a series of shelves divided by partitions, used for filing papers/letters, etc. □ **casilla**
■ *v.* **1** to file letters/papers, etc. (often as the best way to forget them). □ **archivar**
2 to put (someone/something) into a particular category. □ **clasificar**
pigment ['pigmənt] *n.* colouring matter. □ **pigmento**
pigmentation [pigmən'teiʃn] *n.* colouring of the skin. □ **pigmentación**
pigmy ['pigmi] *n. see* **pygmy.**
pike [paik] *n.* (*no pl.*) large ferocious freshwater fish. □ **lucio**
pilchard ['piltʃəd] *n.* small fish similar to a herring. □ **sardina**
pile [pail] *n.* **1** heap: *pile of old books.* □ **pila**
2 ***to make one's pile:*** *he's made his pile,* (*informal*) his fortune. □ **ha hecho un montón de pasta**
3 *I've got **piles of** work to do,* a lot of work. □ **tengo un montón de cosas que hacer**
4 large stake/concrete shaft driven into the earth to provide a foundation. □ **estaca**
5 thickness of tufts of wool in a carpet. □ **pelo**
6 ***piles,*** haemorrhoids/small painful swellings around or in the anus. □ **almorranas**
■ *v.* ***to pile (up),*** to heap up: *the snow piled up by the side of the house; pile the logs neatly.* □ **amontonar(se)**
piledriver *n.* machine for forcing piles into the earth. □ **martinete**
pile-up *n.* series of cars or lorries which have

smashed into each other (usually on a motorway). □ **accidente en cadena**

pilfer ['pilfə] *v.* to steal (small objects). □ **mangar**

pilferer *n.* person who steals small amounts of money or objects of little value. □ **chorizo**

pilfering *n.* stealing small objects or amounts of money. □ **hurto**

pilgrim ['pilgrim] *n.* person who goes to visit a holy place. □ **peregrino**

pilgrimage *n.* journey to visit a holy place/a famous place: *they went on a pilgrimage; he made a pilgrimage to the house where he was born.* □ **peregrinación**

pill [pil] *n.* small round tablet of medicine. □ **píldora**

the pill, (*informal*) contraceptive tablet. □ **la píldora**

to be on the pill: *she's on the pill,* she takes contraceptive tablets. □ **está tomando la píldora**

pillbox *n.* **1** round box for pills. □ **cajita para píldoras**

2 concrete shelter for a small gun. □ **fortín; nido de ametralladoras**

pillage ['pilidʒ] *n.* plundering by soldiers. □ **saqueo**

■ *v.* (*of soldiers*) to plunder/to steal goods (from a captured town, etc.). □ **saquear**

pillar ['pilə] *n.* **1** column: *a row of pillars dividing the church.* □ **pilar**

2 *a pillar of the church,* a fervent churchgoer. □ **un pilar de...**

pillar box *n.* round red metal container into which you can put letters which will then be collected by the post office and sent to their destination. □ **buzón**

pillar-box red, bright red. □ **rojo fuerte**

pillion ['piljən] *n.* seat for a passenger on a motorcycle: *pillion seat; pillion passenger; she was riding pillion.* □ **asiento trasero**

pillow ['pilou] *n.* bag full of soft material which you put your head on in bed. □ **almohada**

pillowcase, pillowslip *n.* cloth bag to cover a pillow with. □ **funda de la almohada**

pilot ['pailət] *n.* **1** person who guides ships into harbour or through dangerous channels. □ **práctico**

pilot scheme, small scheme used as a test before starting a full-scale scheme. □ **plan piloto**

2 person who flies an aircraft. □ **piloto**

3 ***pilot light,*** small gas light on a cooker/water, heater, etc., from which the main gas jets are lit. □ **llama piloto**

■ *v.* **1** to guide: *he piloted the ship between the rocks.* □ **guiar; practicar**

2 to fly an aircraft: *he's piloting his own plane.* □ **pilotar**

pilot officer *n.* lowest rank of officer in the air force. □ **alférez de aviación**

pimento [pi'mentou] *Amer.* **pimiento** [pimi'entou] *n.* green or red fruit with a hot spicy taste used as a vegetable. □ **pimiento picante**

pimple ['pimpl] *n.* small bump on the surface of the skin. □ **grano**

pimply *adj.* covered with pimples. □ **lleno de granos**

pin [pin] *n.* **1** small sharp metal stick with a round head, used for attaching clothes/papers, etc., together. □ **alfiler**

safety pin, type of bent pin where the sharp point is held by a metal shield. □ **imperdible**

pins and needles, prickling feeling in your hand or foot after it has been numb for a time. □ **hormigueo**

2 blunt wooden or metal bolt used for fastening things together. □ **perno**

■ *v.* (*he pinned*) **1** to attach with a pin: *the notice was pinned to the wall/was pinned up on the board.* □ **pinchar**

2 *I am trying to pin him down,* to get him to say what he really thinks/to get him to make his mind up. □ **hacer que alguien concrete**

3 to hold fast: *the car pinned him to the wall.* □ **clavar, inmovilizar**

pinball *n.* table game where a ball has to be rolled into holes. □ **billar americano**

pincushion *n.* round pad in which you can stick pins. □ **acerico**

pin money *n.* (*informal*) money earned by a woman for part-time work. □ **ingreso complementario**

pinpoint *v.* to indicate exactly: *he pinpointed the source of the gas leak.* □ **señalar**

pinprick *n.* something which is slightly annoying. □ **puya**

pinstripe *n.* dark cloth with a very thin white line in it: *pinstripe suit.* □ **traje a rayas**

pin-up *n.* (*informal*) (photograph of a) pretty girl which you can pin up on a wall. □ **'pinup'**

pinafore ['pinəfɔː] *n.* apron worn to cover a dress. □ **delantal**

pincers ['pinsəz] *n. pl.* **1** ***pincers/pair of pincers,*** tool, shaped like scissors, with two curved pieces of metal which you use for holding something tight. □ **tenazas**

2 claws of a crab/of a lobster. □ **pinzas**

pinch [pintʃ] *n.* **1** squeezing tightly/nipping between finger and thumb: *he gave me a pinch.* □ **pellizco**

at a pinch, if really necessary: *I can translate Italian at a pinch.* □ **en caso de necesidad**

to feel the pinch, to be in difficulty because of lack of money. □ **pasar apuros**

2 small quantity of something held between finger and thumb: *a pinch of salt.* □ **una pizca de sal**

■ *v.* **1** to squeeze tightly, using the finger and thumb: *he pinched me.* □ **pellizcar**

2 to hold tight and hurt: *these shoes pinch.* □ **apretar**

3 (*informal*) to steal: *he pinched some chocolate from the sweetshop.* □ **guindar**

4 (*slang*) to arrest. □ **pescar**

pine [pain] *n.* type of evergreen tree; wood from a pine tree: *a pine forest; a pine chest of drawers.* □ **pino; madera de pino**

pine needle, thin leaf of a pine tree. □ **aguja de pino**

■ *v.* to waste away (because you want something): *the dog is pining for its master.* □ **suspirar por**

pineapple ['painæpl] *n.* kind of large tropical fruit, shaped like a pine cone with stiff prickly leaves on top. □ **piña**

pine cone *n.* fruit of a pine tree. □ **piña**

pinewood *n.* a wood of pine trees. □ **madera de pino**

ping [piŋ] *n.* noise made when a small metal bell/a glass, etc., is hit. □ **tintín**

ping pong ['piŋpɔŋ] *n.* (*informal*) table tennis. □ **ping pong**

pinion ['pinjən] *n.* **1** large outer feather on a bird's wing. □ **remera**

2 toothed wheel or cogwheel. □ **piñón**

■ *v.* to tie up (someone's arms) tightly. □ **maniatar**

pink [piŋk] *adj.* and *n.* (colour) like pale red or flesh colour: *a pink rose; her hat is a dark shade of pink.* □ **rosa**

■ *n.* scented garden flower like a small carnation. □ **clavellina**

■ *v.* (*of an engine*) to make a knocking noise when misfiring. □ **picar**

pinking shears *n. pl.* large scissors used by dressmakers, which give a zigzag edge to a cut. □ **tijeras dentadas**

pinnacle ['pinəkl] *n.* topmost point (of a pointed rock); tall, thin stone spire or tower. □ **pináculo**
pint [paint] *n.* liquid measure (= .568 of a litre or 1/8 of a gallon): *a pint of milk.* □ **pinta**
pioneer [paiə'niə] *n.* person who is among the first to try to do something/who is the first to explore/settle in a new land: *a pioneer in the field of nuclear physics.* □ **pionero; explorador; colonizador**
■ *v.* to be first to do something: *he pioneered a new way of treating cancer.* □ **abrir nuevos caminos**
pious ['paiəs] *adj.* showing great respect for religion. □ **piadoso**
pip [pip] *n.* **1** small seed in certain fruit: *apple pip; orange pip.* □ **pepita**
2 star on the shoulder showing an officer's rank. □ **estrella**
3 short high pitched call used on radio to show a time signal. □ **pitido**
pipe [paip] *n.* **1** tube: *water pipe; gas pipe.* □ **conducto**
2 instrument for smoking tobacco: *he's given up cigarettes and now smokes a pipe.* □ **pipa**
pipe cleaner, wire covered with material for cleaning the tube inside a pipe. □ **limpiapipas**
3 thin metal flute. □ **flautín**
the pipes, bagpipes. □ **las gaitas**
■ *v.* to send water/gas, etc., along a pipe. □ **conducir por cañerías**
piped music, recorded music played continuously (in a restaurant, etc.). □ **música enlatada**
pipe down *v.* (*informal*) to stop talking. □ **cerrar el pico**
pipeline *n.* very large tube for carrying oil/natural gas, etc., over long distances. □ **tubería; oleoducto/gasoducto**
it's in the pipeline, it's being worked on/it's on the way. □ **se está tramitando**
piper *n.* person who plays the bagpipes. □ **gaitero**
pipe up *v.* (*informal*) to start talking. □ **empezar a hablar**
piping *n.* **1** collection of tubes; section of metal tube: *a piece of copper piping.* □ **tuberías**
2 decoration like white tubes on a cake/on a dress. □ **adornos (pastel)/ ribete (vestido)**
■ *adv.* ***piping hot,*** extremely hot. □ **muy caliente**
pipette [pi'pet] *n.* thin glass measuring tube used in laboratories. □ **pipeta**
piquant ['pi:kənt] *adj.* nice sharp (flavour); pleasantly interesting/amusing. □ **picante**
pique [pi:k] *n.* resentment/annoyance: *a fit of pique.* □ **pique; un ataque de resentimiento**
■ *v.* **1** to make (someone) resentful. □ **herir**
2 to arouse someone's curiosity. □ **picarle a alguien la curiosidad**
piranha [pi'rɑ:nə] *n.* small tropical fish which attacks animals, including man. □ **piraña**
pirate ['paiərət] *n.* **1** robber (especially at sea). □ **pirata**
2 person who takes money from someone else. □ **ladrón**
pirate radio, illegal radio station. □ **radio pirata**
■ *v. to pirate books,* to publish books which are copied from those of another publisher without having the right to do so; *a pirated edition.* □ **piratear; una edición pirata**
piracy *n.* robbery (at sea); illegal publishing of books. □ **piratería**
piratical [pai'rætikl] *adj.* referring to a pirate. □ **pirata**
pirouette [piru'et] *n.* spinning round on one foot when dancing. □ **pirueta**
■ *v.* to spin round on one foot. □ **hacer piruetas**
Pisces ['paisi:z] *n.* one of the signs of the zodiac, shaped like fish. □ **piscis**
piss [pis] *n.* (*informal* and *vulgar*) **1** waste water from the body. □ **pis**
2 passing waste water from the body: *to have a piss.* □ **meada**
■ *v.* (*informal* and *vulgar*) to pass waste water from the body. □ **mear**
pistachio [pi'stæʃiou] *n.* small green tropical nut. □ **pistacho**
pistil ['pistil] *n.* female part of a flower, which produces seeds. □ **pistilo**
pistol ['pistl] *n.* small gun which is held in the hand. □ **pistola**
starting pistol, pistol used to start a race. □ **pistola**
piston ['pistn] *n.* (*in an engine*) metal disc which moves up and down in a cylinder. □ **pistón**
piston rod, rod which is attached to a piston and which drives other parts of the engine. □ **vástago del émbolo**
pit [pit] *n.* **1** deep, dark hole in the ground. □ **hoyo**
gravel pit, large hole dug to extract gravel. □ **gravera**
2 coalmine: *he went to work in the pit at the age of sixteen.* □ **mina**
3 (*at car races*) place where the cars are inspected and repaired. □ **box**
4 back part of the ground floor of a theatre. □ **patio de butacas**
5 depths of your stomach. □ **boca del estómago**
6 *Amer.* stone of some fruit: *a cherry pit.* □ **hueso**
■ *v.* (*he pitted*) **1** to try against: *he pitted his strength against the fighter; he was pitted against the champion,* he was set to fight the champion. □ **poner a prueba**
2 to take the stone out of a fruit: *pitted dates.* □ **deshuesar**
3 to mark with a hole: *face pitted by smallpox.* □ **picar; cara picada de viruela**
pithead *n.* entrance to a coalmine shaft. □ **bocamina**
pithead ballot, vote taken as miners go to work. □ **votación al ir a la mina**
pitch [pitʃ] *n.* **1** black substance which comes from tar and is used for waterproofing boats/roofs, etc. □ **brea**
2 level of tone in music. □ **tono**
3 ground on which a game is played: *football pitch.* □ **campo de fútbol**
4 height (of anger/of excitement). □ **nivel**
5 angle of a sloping roof. □ **grado de inclinación**
■ *v.* **1** to put up (a tent): *we pitched camp at the foot of the mountain.* □ **armar**
2 to throw (a ball). □ **lanzar**
3 to set the level of a musical tone. □ **entonar**
4 to rock with the front and back going up and down: *the ship pitched heavily in the gale.* □ **cabecear**
pitch-black, pitch dark *adj.* very black; very dark. □ **negro como el carbón, oscuro como la boca del lobo**
pitched *adj.* ***pitched battle,*** battle fought on a selected piece of ground; fierce argument. □ **batalla campal**
pitcher ['pitʃə] *n.* **1** large earthenware jug. □ **cántaro, jarro**
2 person who pitches a ball. □ **lanzador**
pitchfork *n.* large fork for moving bales of hay. □ **horca**

■ *v.* to put (someone) suddenly into an awkward position. □ **poner a alguien en una situación comprometida**

pitfall ['pitfɔːl] *n.* trap/danger. □ **trampa**

pith [piθ] *n.* **1** soft part in the centre of a plant stem; soft white stuff under the skin of a lemon/an orange, etc. □ **médula; piel interna (blanca)**
2 important part: *the pith of the argument.* □ **el meollo de la cuestión**
pithy *adj.* **1** (wood) with a soft centre. □ **meduloso**
2 concise; full of serious meaning. □ **sustancial**

pittance ['pitns] *n.* low wage: *he works for a pittance.* □ **miseria**

pitterpatter ['pitəpætə] *n.* series of small sounds: *the pitterpatter of rain on the roof.* □ **golpeteo suave y continuo**

pituitary [pi'tjuitri] *adj.* ***pituitary gland,*** gland in the brain which produces hormones which control the development and function of the body. □ **pituitario**

pity ['piti] *n.* feeling of sympathy for someone who is unfortunate: *he took pity on the little boy.* □ **compasión**
what a pity!, how sorry I am! □ **¡qué pena!**
■ *v.* to feel sympathy for (someone): *I pity his poor wife.* □ **compadecerse de**
piteous ['pitiəs] **pitiable** *adj.* which deserves pity: *a piteous cry for help.* □ **patético**
pitiful *adj.* **1** deserving sympathy; sad: *he's in a pitiful state.* □ **lastimoso**
2 inadequate: *his speech was pitiful.* □ **lamentable**
pitifully *adv.* in a way which deserves sympathy: *they are pitifully short of medical supplies.* □ **lamentablemente**
pitiless *adj.* showing no pity. □ **despiadado**

pivot ['pivət] *n.* point on which something turns: *the whole machine rotates on a pivot.* □ **eje**
■ *v.* to turn on a point; to depend on something. □ **girar; depender**
pivotal *adj.* of great importance. □ **fundamental**

pixie ['piksi] *n.* small fairy. □ **duende**

pizza ['piːtsə] *n.* Italian savoury dish, consisting of a flat round piece of dough cooked with tomatoes, onions, etc., on top. □ **pizza**

placard ['plækɑːd] *n.* poster. □ **cartel**
■ *v.* to stick posters up. □ **pegar carteles**

placate [plə'keit] *v.* to calm (someone); to make (someone) less angry. □ **apaciguar**

place [pleis] *n.* **1** location/spot: *there were books all over the place; why did you put the vase in a different place? this is the place where I lost my purse.* □ **lugar**
2 house/home: *come back to my place for coffee.* □ **casa**
3 open area: *market place.* □ **plaza**
4 name of a smart street in a town. □ **calle**
5 set position: *is this anybody's place?; I changed places with Mrs Smith,* we exchanged seats. □ **sitio**
out of place, not in the right position. □ **fuera de su sitio**
to take place, to happen/to be held: *the ceremony will take place tomorrow.* □ **tener lugar**
6 rank (in a series): *he's in first place,* he is winning; *the first three places were taken by the German runners.* □ **lugar**
in the first place, first of all. □ **en primer lugar**
7 job: *he's got a place as a doorman.* □ **empleo**
■ *v.* **1** to put: *place your hands flat on the table.* □ **colocar**
2 to give (an order): *he placed an order for six chairs.* □ **hacer (un pedido)**
3 to put in a set position: *he was placed third in the relay race.* □ **poner**
4 to remember who someone is: *I can't place him.* □ **situar**

placebo [plə'siːbou] *n.* harmless substance given to a patient instead of a drug to make the patient believe that he is receiving treatment. □ **placebo**

placenta [plə'sentə] *n.* tissue in the womb which nourishes the unborn baby. □ **placenta**

placid ['plæsid] *adj.* calm. □ **plácido**
placidity [plə'siditi] *n.* calmness. □ **placidez**
placidly *adv.* calmly. □ **plácidamente**

plagiarism ['pleidʒərizəm] *n.* copying what someone else has written. □ **plagio**
plagiarist *n.* author who copies the work of someone else. □ **plagiario**
plagiarize *v.* to copy the work of another author. □ **plagiar**

plague [pleig] *n.* **1** fatal infectious disease transmitted by fleas from rats: *bubonic plague.* □ **peste**
2 great quantity of pests: *a plague of ladybirds.* □ **plaga**
■ *v.* to annoy/to bother (someone): *we were plagued with constant interruptions.* □ **plagar**

plaice [pleis] *n.* (*no pl.*) common flat sea fish. □ **platija**

plaid [plæd] *n.* (*in Scotland*) tartan cloth. □ **tartán**

plain [plein] *adj.* **1** obvious/easy to understand: *it's plain that he's incompetent.* □ **evidente**
2 simple/uncomplicated: *plain country cooking; plain truth.* □ **cocina sencilla; la pura verdad**
3 not pretty: *she's quite plain compared to her sister.* □ **no tiene atractivo comparada con...**
4 ***plain chocolate,*** dark chocolate, usually more bitter than milk chocolate. □ **chocolate puro**
5 ***plain flour,*** white flour with no baking powder in it. □ **harina pura**
■ *n.* large flat area of country. □ **llanura**
plainclothes *n. pl.* ordinary/everyday clothes (not uniform). □ **de paisano**
plainclothes detective, detective not in uniform. □ **...vestido de paisano**
plainly *adv.* **1** obviously. □ **evidentemente**
2 simply. □ **sencillamente**
plainness *n.* **1** clearness. □ **claridad**
2 simpleness. □ **sencillez**
plain-spoken *adj.* (person) who speaks in a straightforward way. □ **franco**

plaintiff ['pleintif] *n.* person who starts a legal action against someone else. □ **demandante**

plaintive ['pleintiv] *adj.* sad: *a plaintive cry.* □ **lastimero**

plait [plæt] *n.* (hair/wool, etc.) with three strands woven into a long rope. □ **trenza**
■ *v.* to weave hair, etc., to form a plait. □ **trenzar**

plan [plæn] *n.* **1** scheme: *we have drawn up a plan for changing our hours of work.* □ **plan**
to go according to plan: *the change went according to plan,* as we had intended. □ **...según el plan**
2 drawing of the way something is to be built or constructed: *the architect's plan for a new office building; a plan of a new type of car engine.* □ **plano**
3 map of streets: *town plan.* □ **plano**
■ *v.* (*he planned*) **1** to draw up a scheme to construct something: *he planned the kitchen himself.* □ **hacer un plan**
2 to scheme/to propose to do something: *we're planning to go on holiday in August.* □ **planear**
planner *n.* person who draws up schemes. □ **planificador**
town planner, person who designs how a town should develop. □ **urbanista**
planning *n.* making plans. □ **planificación**

town planning, general design of the way in which a town should develop. □ **planificación urbanística**
family planning, decision by parents on how many children to have. □ **planificación familiar**
plane [plein] *n.* **1** flat surface: *horizontal plane; inclined plane.* □ **plano**
2 aircraft: *three enemy planes were shot down.* □ **avión**
3 tool for smoothing wood. □ **cepillo**
4 type of tree often grown in towns, of which bark comes off in large pieces. □ **plátano**
■ *adj.* level/flat. □ **plano**
■ *v.* to smooth (wood) flat with a plane. □ **cepillar**
planet ['plænit] *n.* body which revolves round a star, especially round the sun: *the earth is one of the planets.* □ **planeta**
planetarium [plæni'tɛəriəm] *n.* domed building in which you sit and watch as pictures of the stars are projected against the ceiling. □ **planetario**
planetary ['plænitri] *adj.* referring to the planets. □ **planetario**
plank [plæŋk] *n.* **1** long flat piece of wood used in building. □ **tablón**
2 proposal in a political programme. □ **punto de un programa (político)**
planking *n.* series of planks. □ **entablado**
plankton ['plæŋktn] *n.* tiny organisms living in the sea. □ **plancton**
plant [plɑːnt] *n.* **1** thing which grows in the ground, is usually green, and cannot move from one place to another: *plants usually have roots, stems, leaves and flowers; a tomato plant; a plant pot.* □ **planta**
2 factory: *a chemical plant.* □ **una planta química**
3 machinery: *to install new plant.* □ **maquinaria**
■ *v.* to put (a plant) into the ground; to put in a special position: *I've planted three rows of cabbages; they planted a bomb under his car.* □ **plantar**
plantation [plɑːn'teiʃn] *n.* **1** area of trees specially planted. □ **plantación**
2 tropical estate growing a particular crop: *tobacco plantation.* □ **plantación de tabaco**
planter *n.* **1** person in charge of a plantation: *a tea planter; a rubber planter.* □ **plantador**
2 decorative container to hold plants in pots. □ **macetero**
plantain ['plæntin] *n.* common weed. □ **llantén**
plaque [plæk] *n.* **1** decorative plate hung on a wall; stone/metal/earthenware plate with an inscription: *the mayor unveiled a plaque in memory of the famous writer.* □ **placa**
2 deposit which forms on the teeth. □ **placa**
plasma ['plæzmə] *n.* liquid part of blood. □ **plasma**
plaster ['plɑːstə] *n.* **1** mixture of fine sand and lime which when mixed with water is used for covering walls of houses: *a plaster ceiling.* □ **yeso; un techo de escayola**
2 white powder which, when mixed with water, is used to make moulds/to make coverings to hold broken arms and legs in place: *he's had his leg in plaster for four weeks.* □ **escayola, yeso**
3 ***sticking plaster,*** adhesive cloth tape used for holding bandages in place/for covering small wounds. □ **esparadrapo**
■ *v.* to cover with plaster; to cover as if with plaster: *he plastered the wall; the wall was plastered with election posters.* □ **enlucir (la pared); tenía la pared cubierta...**
plaster-cast *n.* **1** block of plaster put round a broken leg, etc. □ **escayola**
2 mould made by covering something with plaster. □ **molde**
3 copy of a statue made in plaster. □ **vaciado en yeso**
plasterer *n.* person who covers walls with plaster. □ **yesero**
plastic ['plæstik] *n.* artificial substance, which can be moulded into any shape: *plastic glasses; plastic spoon; it's not real wood, it's only plastic.* □ **plástico**
plastic bomb, explosive material which can be moulded in the hand. □ **bomba de plástico**
■ *adj.* soft/pliable. □ **maleable**
plastic surgery, operation to replace damaged skin or to improve someone's appearance. □ **cirugía plástica**
plate [pleit] *n.* **1** thin flat sheet of metal/glass, etc: *plate glass window.* □ **chapa, lámina; ventana de vidrio cilindrado**
number plate, metal plate at front and back of a car with the registration number on it. □ **matrícula**
2 flat dish for putting food on: *cake plate; a plate of scones; pass your dirty plates to the end of the table.* □ **plato**
3 dishes made of gold or silver: *they ate off gold plate.* □ **vajilla de oro**
4 thin layer of gold/silver on a less precious metal; objects made of this: *the teapot is silver plate.* □ **bañado en oro**
5 book illustration on shiny paper. □ **lámina**
6 plastic sheet with false teeth attached which fits into your mouth. □ **dentadura postiza**
■ *v.* to cover with a thin layer of gold or silver: *they are not real silver, only plated.* □ **bañar**
plateful *n.* quantity held by a plate: *he helped himself to a plateful of meat.* □ **plato**
platelayer *n.* railway worker who sets the rails in place/who repairs rails. □ **asentador de vías**
plateau ['plætou] *n.* (*pl. plateaux*) high flat area of land. □ **meseta**
platelet ['pleitlət] *n.* small cell in the blood which helps blood to clot. □ **plaqueta**
platform ['plætfɔːm] *n.* **1** raised floor space for speakers in a hall: *the leaders of the union sat on the platform.* □ **plataforma**
2 raised pavement by the side of the rails in a railway station so that passengers can get on and off trains easily: *the train is leaving from platform number 5.* □ **andén**
3 proposals put forward by the leaders of a political party before an election. □ **plataforma electoral**
platinum ['plætinəm] *n.* (*chemical element*: Pt) rare light-coloured precious metal. □ **platino**
platinum blonde, woman with silvery blonde hair. □ **rubia platino**
platitude ['plætitjuːd] *n.* ordinary saying, especially one which the speaker thinks is very important. □ **tópico**
platoon [plə'tuːn] *n.* small group of soldiers/part of a company. □ **pelotón**
platter ['plætə] *n.* large serving plate. □ **fuente**
platypus ['plætipəs] *n.* Australian mammal which lays eggs. □ **ornitorrinco**
plaudits ['plɔːdits] *n. pl.* applause. □ **aplausos**
plausible ['plɔːzibl] *adj.* which sounds as though it is correct when it often is not: *his explanation of the accident was very plausible.* □ **plausible**
plausibility [plɔːzi'biliti] *n.* possibility that something is correct. □ **plausibilidad**
play [plei] *n.* **1** way of amusing yourself; sport: *we saw some very interesting play in the chess tournament; play begins at 1 o'clock,* the game (of football, etc.) begins. □ **juego; partido**
it's child's play, it's very easy. □ **es un juego de niños**

2 theatrical performance; script of a theatrical performance: *the author of the play is French; the play starts at 6 o'clock; a book of Shakespeare's plays.* □ **obra/representación teatral**
3 freedom to move: *the screw is not tight enough, it allows too much play.* □ **holgura**
■ *v.* **1** to amuse yourself/to pass the time in a pleasant way: *the children were playing in the park; he was playing with his dog.* □ **jugar**
2 to take part in a game: *he plays football for the school; they were playing cricket; can you play chess?* □ **jugar**
3 to perform on a musical instrument: *he plays the violin; to play a record on a record player.* □ **tocar (un instrumento); poner (un disco)**
4 to act a part in a theatrical performance: *who's playing Hamlet?* □ **hacer el papel de**
5 to aim: *the firemen played their hoses on the flames.* □ **apuntar**
6 to let a fish which has been caught on a hook swim until it is tired and can easily be landed. □ **cansar**
play at *v.* **1** to do something wrong: *what are you playing at?* □ **jugar; ¿a qué juegas?**
2 (*of children*) to pretend to be: *the children were playing at doctors and nurses.* □ **...estaban jugando a los médicos**
play back *v.* to listen to something which you have just recorded on tape. □ **volver a poner (algo grabado)**
playboy *n.* rich man who spends his time amusing himself rather than working. □ **'playboy'**
play down *v.* to minimize/to make something seem less important: *he played down the seriousness of the accident.* □ **quitar importancia**
player *n.* person who plays: *a tennis player; a trumpet player.* □ **jugador**
playful *adj.* liking to play: *a playful puppy.* □ **juguetón**
playground *n.* area, especially round school buildings, where children can play. □ **patio del recreo**
playgroup *n.* group of small children who play together under supervision. □ **grupo que juega**
playing card *n.* one of a set of fifty-two cards, marked in four designs (clubs, hearts, diamonds, spades), used for playing various games. □ **carta**
playing field *n.* area of grass where sports can be played. □ **campo de deportes**
play-pen *n.* type of cage in which babies can be left to play safely. □ **parque, corral**
plaything *n.* toy. □ **juguete**
playtime *n.* time in nursery school when children can play. □ **recreo**
play up *v.* (*informal*) to make trouble: *the engine is playing up.* □ **dar guerra**
playwright *n.* person who writes plays. □ **dramaturgo**
plea [pliː] *n.* **1** answer to a charge in court: *the prisoner entered a plea of not guilty.* □ **alegato; ...se declaró inocente**
2 (*formal*) request: *all my pleas for more money have been turned down.* □ **petición**
3 excuse: *his plea was that he did not have enough money to pay.* □ **disculpa**
plead [pliːd] *v.* **1** to answer a charge in a law court: *the prisoner pleaded not guilty.* □ **declararse**
2 to give an excuse: *she pleaded illness and didn't come.* □ **alegar**
3 to try to change someone's mind by asking again and again: *he pleaded with her to let him see her again.* □ **implorar**
pleasant ['pleznt] *adj.* agreeable/which pleases: *pleasant weather; he wrote me a very pleasant letter.* □ **agradable**
pleasantly *adv.* in a pleasant way: *we passed the afternoon very pleasantly.* □ **de manera agradable**
pleasantry *n.* joke; pleasant remark. □ **chiste; ocurrencia agradable**
please [pliːz] *v.* **1** to make someone happy/satisfied: *he's hard to please; I'm pleased with my new car.* □ **agradar; es difícil de agradar; estoy contento con...**
please yourself, do as you like. □ **...como Ud. quiera**
2 (*polite expression after an order or request, meaning* if you would like): *close the door, please; please go away.* □ **por favor**
pleasing *adj.* which pleases: *he has a very pleasing expression.* □ **agradable**
pleasurable ['pleʒərəbl] *adj.* pleasant. □ **grato**
pleasure ['pleʒə] *n.* amusement/happiness: *I will do it with pleasure,* very willingly; *pleasure trip; it gives me great pleasure to be here today; he takes great pleasure in teasing his wife.* □ **placer**
pleat [pliːt] *n.* vertical fold (in a skirt, etc.). □ **pliegue**
■ *v.* to iron vertical folds: *a pleated skirt.* □ **plisar; una falda plisada**
plebiscite ['plebisit] *n.* general vote by the inhabitants of a country on an important issue: *they are holding a plebiscite on the new constitution.* □ **plebiscito**
plebs [plebz] *n. pl.* (*informal*) ordinary people. □ **la plebe**
plebeian [pli'biːən] *adj.* common/ordinary; of the working class. □ **plebeyo**
plectrum ['plektrəm] *n.* small stick for plucking the strings of a guitar, etc. □ **plectro, púa**
pledge [pledʒ] *n.* **1** object given to the lender when borrowing money, and which will be returned to the borrower when the money is paid back. □ **garantía, prenda**
2 promise: *I am under a pledge of secrecy.* □ **he prometido guardarlo en secreto**
to take the pledge, to swear never to drink alcohol again. □ **hacer promesa de abstenerse de beber alcohol**
■ *v.* **1** to give (something) as a pledge when borrowing money. □ **dar en prenda**
2 to promise: *to pledge support.* □ **prometer**
3 to drink (a toast). □ **brindar por**
plenary ['pliːnəri] *adj.* complete. □ **plenario**
plenary session, session of a conference where all the delegates meet together. □ **sesión plenaria**
plenipotentiary [plenipə'tenʃəri] *adj.* and *n.* (person) who has full powers to act on behalf of his country. □ **plenipotenciario**
plenteous ['plentiəs] *adj.* (*formal*) more than enough. □ **abundante**
plenty ['plenti] *n.* large quantity: *you've got plenty of time; he has plenty of money.* □ **mucho**
plentiful *adj.* abundant; in large quantities: *a plentiful supply of food.* □ **abundante**
plethora ['pleθərə] *n.* (*formal*) too many: *a plethora of questions.* □ **plétora**
pleurisy ['pluərəsi] *n.* disease of the membrane covering the lungs. □ **pleuresía**
pliable ['plaiəbl] **pliant** ['plaiənt] *adj.* which can be bent easily; (person) who can be easily persuaded. □ **plegable (cosa); flexible (persona)**
pliers ['plaiəz] *n. pl.* ***pliers/pair of pliers,*** tool shaped like scissors for pinching, twisting or cutting wire. □ **alicates**
plight [plait] *n.* bad state. □ **condición inquietante**

plimsolls ['plimsəlz] *n. pl.* canvas shoes worn when doing gymnastics. □ **zapatillas de deporte**
plinth [plinθ] *n.* pedestal on which a statue stands. □ **plinto**
plod [plɔd] *v.* (*he plodded*) to walk heavily: *he was plodding along the muddy path.* □ **andar con paso pesado**
plodder *n.* person who works steadily but rather slowly. □ **que anda pesadamente**
plonk [plɔŋk] *n.* (*informal*) **1** dull sound. □ **ruido sordo**
2 inferior wine. □ **vino peleón**
■ *v.* (*informal*) to put (something) down heavily: *the waitress just plonked the bottle down on the table; he plonked himself down next to me.* □ **dejar caer**
plop [plɔp] *n.* noise made by a stone falling into water. □ **plaf**
■ *v.* (*it plopped*) to make a noise like a stone falling into water. □ **hacer plaf**
plot [plɔt] *n.* **1** small area of land for building/for growing vegetables, etc. □ **parcela**
2 basic story of a book/play/film: *the plot concerns twin brothers who marry twin sisters.* □ **argumento**
3 wicked plan: *a plot to kill the Prime Minister.* □ **conspiración**
■ *v.* (*he plotted*) **1** to mark on a map; to draw a graph: *he plotted the course of the aircraft; the graph plots the rise in inflation.* □ **señalar**
2 to draw up a wicked plan: *they were plotting to overthrow the government.* □ **urdir**
plough [plau] *Amer.* **plow** *n.* **1** farm machine for turning over soil. □ **arado**
2 ***snow plough,*** machine like a tractor with a large blade in front, used for clearing snow from streets/railway lines, etc. □ **máquina quitanieves**
■ *v.* **1** to turn over the soil: *a newly ploughed field.* □ **arar**
2 to work slowly: *he ploughed through masses of documents.* □ **trabajar paso a paso**
plough back *v.* to invest (profits) back in a business. □ **reinvertir**
ploughman *n.* (*pl. ploughmen*) farm worker who drives a plough. □ **labrador**
ploughman's lunch, bread, cheese and pickles. □ **almuerzo**
plover ['plʌvə] *n.* type of wading bird (found in fields and moors). □ **chorlito**
plow [plau] *n.* and *v. Amer. see* **plough.**
ploy [plɔi] *n.* clever trick. □ **truco**
pluck [plʌk] *n.* courage. □ **agallas**
■ *v.* **1** to pull out feathers or eyebrows. □ **desplumar (un ave); depilarse (cejas)**
2 to pick (flowers, etc.). □ **coger**
3 to pull and release the strings of a guitar to make a sound. □ **puntear**
pluck up *v.* ***to pluck up courage,*** to get ready to face a danger. □ **armarse de valor**
plucky *adj.* brave. □ **valeroso**
plug [plʌg] *n.* **1** disc which covers a hole, especially the hole for waste water in a bath/sink, etc.: *to pull the plug,* to release the flushing mechanism in a toilet. □ **tapón**
2 device with pins which go into a series of small holes in an electric socket, and which then allow the current to pass through: *a three-pin plug.* □ **enchufe**
sparking plug, (*in a car*) device which passes the electric spark through the petrol vapour. □ **bujía**
3 (*informal*) piece of publicity: *a plug for a new car.* □ **cuña publicitaria**
4 piece of tobacco which you chew. □ **andullo**
■ *v.* (*he plugged*) **1** to block up a hole: *we managed to plug the hole in the ship's side.* □ **taponar**
2 (*informal*) to publicize: *they are plugging a new sort of soap.* □ **hacer publicidad**
plughole *n.* hole in a bath/washbasin through which the dirty water runs away. □ **desagüe**
plug in *v.* to push an electric plug into a socket: *the television wouldn't work, but then we discovered it wasn't plugged in.* □ **enchufar**
plum [plʌm] *n.* gold, red or purple fruit with a smooth skin and a large stone. □ **ciruela**
plum (tree), tree which bears plums. □ **ciruelo**
plum pudding, rich boiled fruit pudding, usually eaten at Christmas. □ **budín de pasas**
plum job, (*informal*) very good job. □ **un chollo de trabajo**
plumage ['plu:midʒ] *n.* feathers on a bird: *the male is in winter plumage.* □ **plumaje**
plumb [plʌm] *adj.* straight; vertical. □ **a plomo**
■ *n.* lead weight for testing if something is straight. □ **plomada**
■ *v.* to measure the depth of the sea by using a plumbline. □ **sondar**
■ *adv.* **1** exactly. □ **exactamente**
plumb in the middle, right in the middle. □ **justo en el medio**
2 *Amer.* completely: *you're plumb crazy.* □ **completamente**
plumber *n.* person who installs water pipes, etc. □ **fontanero**
plumbing *n.* system of water pipes in a house. □ **fontanería**
plumbline *n.* rope with a weight on the end, dropped over the side from a ship to find how deep the water is or held beside a wall to see if it is vertical. □ **sonda, plomada**
plume [plu:m] *n.* tall feather (worn in a hat, etc.); tall column of smoke. □ **pluma; penacho de humo**
plummet ['plʌmit] *v.* to fall sharply: *he missed his footing and plummeted towards the ground.* □ **caer en picado**
plummy ['plʌmi] *adj.* rich/full (voice). □ **pastoso**
plump [plʌmp] *adj.* fat and tender; round fat (person). □ **regordete**
■ *v.* **1** ***to plump up*** *the cushions,* to shake squashed cushions until they are fat. □ **sacudir los cojines**
2 ***to plump for,*** (*informal*) to decide on: *we've plumped for a holiday in Spain.* □ **decidirse**
plumpness *n.* fatness. □ **gordura**
plunder ['plʌndə] *n.* booty/goods seized, especially in war. □ **botín**
■ *v.* to seize goods by force: *the soldiers plundered the town.* □ **saquear**
plunge [plʌndʒ] *n.* dive. □ **zambullida**
to take the plunge: *he took the plunge,* he suddenly decided to do something. □ **aventurarse a**
■ *v.* **1** to dive deeply; to throw yourself into: *he plunged into the sea.* □ **zambullirse**
2 *the room was plunged in darkness,* suddenly went dark. □ **...se quedó a oscuras**
plunger *n.* **1** device which goes up and down in a cylinder. □ **émbolo**
2 handle with a soft rubber head, for clearing blocked pipes by suction. □ **desatascador**
plural ['pluərəl] *adj.* and *n.* (*in grammar*) form of a word showing more than one: *'we' and 'they' are plural pronouns; 'boxes' is the plural of 'box'.* □ **plural**
plus [plʌs] *prep.* in addition to: *three plus four equals seven* ($3 + 4 = 7$): *the hot weather plus the long*

walk made him tired. □ **más**
■ *adj.* and *n.* **1** sign (+) meaning more than zero: *a temperature of plus twenty degrees; the temperature was forty degrees plus.* □ **sobre cero**
2 (*informal*) favourable sign: *if he can cook, that's a big plus in his favour.* □ **punto**
plush [plʌʃ] *n.* soft pile cloth for furnishings, etc. □ **felpa**
■ *adj.* (*informal*) luxurious. □ **lujoso**
plutocrat ['plu:təkræt] *n.* person who is very rich. □ **plutócrata**
plutocracy [plu:'tɔkrəsi] *n.* government by the very rich. □ **plutocracia**
plutonium [plu:'touniəm] *n.* (*chemical element*: Pu) radioactive substance, used to produce nuclear power. □ **plutonio**
ply [plai] *n.* **1** thickness of wood in plywood. □ **chapa**
2 strand of wool. □ **cabo**
3-ply wool, wool with three strands. □ **lana de tres cabos**
■ *v.* **1** to go backwards and forwards: *the ferry plies between England and France.* □ **ir y venir**
2 to force something on (someone): *to ply someone with questions; they plied her with drink.* □ **acosar**
plywood *n.* sheet made of several thin sheets of wood stuck together. □ **contrachapado**
p.m. [pi:'em] *adv.* in the afternoon/after midday: *I'm catching the 6 p.m. train.* □ **abrev. de *post meridiem*, de la tarde/noche**
pneumatic [nju:'mætik] *adj.* driven by compressed air: *pneumatic drill.* □ **neumático**
pneumonia [nju:'mouniə] *n.* illness caused by inflammation of the lungs. □ **neumonía**
poach [poutʃ] *v.* **1** to cook eggs (without their shells)/fish, etc., in gently boiling water: *poached eggs on toast.* □ **escalfar (huevos); hervir (pescado)**
2 to shoot/to catch game illegally. □ **cazar furtivamente**
poacher *n.* person who catches game illegally. □ **cazador furtivo**
pocket ['pɔkit] *n.* **1** small bag attached to the inside of a coat/ trousers, etc., for holding a handkerchief/money/keys, etc.: *I've looked in my trouser pockets but I can't find the key.* □ **bolsillo**
pocket calculator/pocket dictionary, small calculator/dictionary which you can keep in your pocket. □ **...de bolsillo**
pocket money, money given each week to a child to spend as he pleases. □ **dinero de bolsillo**
2 ***to be in pocket,*** to make money. □ **hacer dinero**
to be out of pocket, to lose money: *after the party I was $15 out of pocket.* □ **perder dinero**
3 hole with a small bag at each corner and side of a billiard table. □ **tronera**
4 small patch/small group of people in a certain place: *pockets of frost; the army has surrendered, but there are still pockets of resistance.* □ **placa de hielo; ...focos de resistencia**
■ *v.* **1** to put in your pocket: *the waiter pocketed the change.* □ **meterse en el bolsillo**
2 to send (a billiard ball) into one of the small bags at the corners and sides of the table. □ **meter**
pocketful *n.* amount contained in a pocket: *I've got a pocketful of small coins.* □ **tengo el bolsillo lleno de...**
pod [pɔd] *n.* long case in which peas/beans, etc., are formed: *the pea pods are swelling.* □ **vaina**
podgy ['pɔdʒi] *adj.* (*informal*) fat: *podgy fingers.* □ **gordinflón**
podium ['poudiəm] *n.* raised platform (for winning sportsmen/orchestral conductors, etc., to stand on). □ **podio**
poem ['pouim] *n.* piece of writing, in a particular rhythm, and often with lines of a regular length which rhyme. □ **poema**
poet *n.* person who writes poems. □ **poeta**
poetic(al) [pou'etik(l)] *adj.* referring to poetry; imaginative/rhythmic (as in a poem). □ **poético**
poetry ['pouətri] *n.* writing of poems; poems taken as a type of literature: *English poetry of the nineteenth century.* □ **poesía**
pogrom ['pɔgrəm] *n.* official persecution/massacre (especially of Jews). □ **pogromo**
poignant ['pɔinjənt] *adj.* moving/sad (thought). □ **conmovedor, patético**
poignancy *n.* sadness: *the poignancy of the situation,* the way in which the situation moves you to sadness. □ **patetismo**
poignantly *adv.* sadly/in a way which moves you to sadness. □ **patéticamente**
poinsettia [pɔin'setiə] *n.* plant with large green leaves, turning red at the top, used as a Christmas decoration. □ **flor de pascuas**
point [pɔint] *n.* **1** sharp end: *point of a needle; to sharpen a pencil to a point.* □ **punta**
2 dot. □ **punto**
decimal point, dot used to indicate the division between units and decimals (such as 3.25). □ **coma**
3 place/spot: *point of departure.* □ **punto**
point of no return, place where you can only go on and not go back. □ **punto en el que uno no puede volverse atrás**
4 reason/purpose: *what's the point of all these lights? I see no point in overspending; there's no point in trying to phone him — he's gone away.* □ **razón**
5 meaning/argument: *he made several good points in his speech.* □ **observación, cuestión**
6 *can we **get back to the point?**,* please let us return to the question we were discussing. □ **volvamos a la cuestión**
7 specific time: *at that point in the conversation the lights went out.* □ **momento**
8 *I was **on the point of** telephoning,* I was just about to telephone. □ **estaba a punto de...**
9 headland/large area of land jutting into the sea. □ **punta**
10 mark in games or competitions; mark on a scale: *he scored six points; the freezing point of water.* □ **punto**
11 movable rails which allow trains to cross from one line to another. □ **aguja**
12 electric socket. □ **enchufe**
■ *v.* **1** to aim (a gun/your finger) at someone/something: *he pointed at the shadow on the wall.* □ **apuntar**
2 to sharpen to a point. □ **sacar punta a**
3 to fill the spaces in between bricks with mortar. □ **llaguear**
point-blank *adj.* and *adv.* **1** at very close range: *the robber shot him point-blank/at point-blank range.* □ **a quemarropa**
2 sharply/directly: *he refused the invitation point-blank.* □ **categóricamente**
pointed *adj.* **1** with a sharp end: *a pointed stick.* □ **puntiagudo**
2 obviously unfriendly (remark). □ **agresivo**
pointedly *adv.* **1** which attacks. □ **agresivamente**
2 *she pointedly refused to shake hands,* she showed her displeasure by refusing to shake hands. □ **se negó intencionadamente...**
pointer *n.* **1** dog which is trained to point out game

with its nose. □ **perro de muestra**
2 arrow/rod which points. □ **indicador; manecilla (reloj); fiel (balanza)**
pointless *adj.* **1** meaningless. □ **sin sentido**
2 *it's pointless looking for your ring in the dark,* it is useless. □ **es inútil buscar...**
point out *v.* to indicate/to show: *he pointed out the faults in the translation.* □ **señalar**
poise [pɔiz] *n.* balance/graceful way of holding your head or of standing upright. □ **porte**
■ *v.* **1** to balance: *the rock is poised on the edge of the cliff.* □ **estar suspendido**
2 *we're poised to attack,* we are all ready to attack. □ **estamos listos para...**
poison ['pɔizn] *n.* substance which kills or makes you very ill if it is swallowed or if it gets into the bloodstream: *rat poison; he took poison to avoid being caught by the police.* □ **veneno**
■ *v.* to kill with poison: *he was poisoned by his wife.* □ **envenenar**
poisoner *n.* person who poisons. □ **envenenador**
poisoning *n.* killing by poison. □ **envenenamiento**
food poisoning, severe illness caused by eating bad food. □ **intoxicación alimenticia**
poisonous *adj.* which can kill or harm with poison: *poisonous berries; poisonous snake.* □ **venenoso**
poke [pouk] *v.* **1** to push with your finger/with a stick: *he poked his finger into the hole; she poked the fire.* □ **meter el dedo/un palo; atizar (el fuego)**
2 *the doctor poked his head round the door,* put his head round the door. □ **el médico asomó la cabeza...**
3 ***to poke about,*** to search. □ **fisgonear**
4 ***to poke one's nose into:*** *he's always poking his nose into other people's affairs,* interfering in other people's business. □ **siempre está metiendo las narices donde no le llaman**
poker *n.* **1** long metal rod for stirring up a fire. □ **atizador**
2 game of cards in which the players gamble. □ **póker/póquer**
poky ['pouki] *adj.* (*informal*) cramped/small (room). □ **cuchitril**
Poland ['poulənd] *n.* country in Eastern Europe. □ **Polonia**
polar ['poulə] *adj.* referring to the North/South Poles: *polar bear.* □ **polar; oso polar**
polarize ['pouləraiz] *v.* **1** to be attracted as if to a magnet. □ **polarizar**
2 *interest has polarized around the two main political parties,* has centred/gathered around. □ **el interés se ha polarizado...**
polarization [poulərai'zeiʃn] *n.* attraction around two opposite poles; division into main groups. □ **polarización**
pole [poul] *n.* **1** one of the points at each end of the earth's axis: *the North Pole.* □ **polo; el Polo Norte**
2 one of the two opposing ends of a magnet. □ **polo**
3 *they are **poles apart,*** they are very different/they will never come to an agreement. □ **son polos opuestos**
4 long wooden/metal rod: *tent pole; telephone pole,* pole carrying telephone wires. □ **palo; palo de la tienda**
pole vaulting, sport where you have to jump over a high bar with the help of a long pole. □ **salto con pértiga**
5 ***Pole,*** person from Poland. □ **polaco**
pole star *n.* star which appears to be near to the North Pole. □ **estrella polar**
polemic [pə'lemik] *n.* argument/attack on someone's views. □ **polémica**
police [pə'li:s] *n.* (*usually pl.*) group of people who keep law and order in a country: *a police constable; police station; the police are looking for him.* □ **policía**
■ *v.* to keep law and order: *they don't have enough men to police the streets.* □ **mantener el orden**
policeman, policewoman *n.* (*pl. policemen, policewomen*) member of the police. □ **policía**
policy ['pɔlisi] *n.* **1** way of acting: *my policy is never to lend money; foreign policy,* government's general way of dealing with other countries. □ **política**
2 written agreement with an insurance company. □ **póliza de seguros**
poliomyelitis [poulioumaiə'laitis] (*informal*) **polio** *n.* disease of the nerves in the spinal cord, sometimes causing paralysis. □ **poliomielitis, polio**
polish ['pɔliʃ] *n.* **1** shiny surface: *a table with a high polish.* □ **brillo; una mesa con mucho brillo**
2 rubbing to make something shiny: *I'll just give the table a polish.* □ **voy a sacar brillo a la mesa**
3 substance used to make things shiny: *floor polish; shoe polish.* □ **cera (muebles, suelo); betún (zapatos)**
■ *v.* to rub (something) to make it shiny: *he polished the car.* □ **sacar brillo**
polished *adj.* **1** shiny: *a highly polished floor.* □ **pulido, brillante**
2 made perfect by practice: *a polished performance on the violin.* □ **brillante**
3 polite (manners). □ **refinado**
polish off *v.* to finish off (a job) quickly/to eat (a meal) quickly. □ **liquidar (un trabajo); zampar (una comida)**
polish up *v.* (*informal*) to improve: *polish up your German.* □ **perfeccionar**
Polish ['pouliʃ] *adj.* referring to Poland. □ **polaco**
■ *n.* language spoken in Poland. □ **polaco**
polite [pə'lait] *adj.* not rude; courteous: *he wasn't very polite to me over the phone.* □ **cortés**
politely *adv.* courteously; in a well mannered way: *he politely refused another drink.* □ **cortésmente**
politeness *n.* good manners. □ **cortesía**
politics ['pɔlitiks] *n.* **1** study of how to govern a country. □ **política**
party politics, interest in or working for government by a certain political party. □ **política de partido**
2 *he had decided to go for a career in politics,* to work as a professional politician. □ **...dedicarse a la política**
politic *adj.* wise/careful: *he found it politic to say nothing.* □ **prudente**
political [pə'litikl] *adj.* referring to government/party politics: *political party,* organized group of people who believe in one particular method of ruling a country. □ **político**
politically *adv. he is on the left wing politically,* as far as politics are concerned. □ **políticamente**
politician [pɔli'tiʃn] *n.* person who works in politics, especially a member of parliament. □ **político**
poll [poul] *n.* **1** vote/voting: *the poll closes at eight o'clock; the country goes to the polls next week,* will vote in a general election. □ **votación**
2 number of votes: *a very heavy poll.* □ **un elevado porcentaje de votos**
3 ***opinion poll,*** questioning of a sample group of people to guess at the views of the whole population on a question. □ **sondeo de opinión**
■ *v.* **1** to vote. □ **votar**
2 to get a number of votes in an election: *the loser only polled 23 votes.* □ **obtener**

polling *n.* voting; elections: *polling day.* □ **día de elecciones**
polling station, place where you vote in an election. □ **colegio electoral**
pollen ['pɔln] *n.* usually yellow powder in flowers which fertilizes them. □ **polen**
pollen count, number showing the amount of pollen in the air (which can cause hayfever). □ **índice de polen**
pollinate ['pɔlineit] *v.* to fertilize with pollen. □ **polinizar**
pollination [pɔli'neiʃn] *n.* fertilizing with pollen. □ **polinización**
pollute [pə'lu:t] *v.* to make dirty: *the air is polluted with fumes from the factory.* □ **contaminar**
pollution [pə'lu:ʃn] *n.* dirt; making dirty: *the pollution of the atmosphere.* □ **contaminación**
polo ['poulou] *n.* **1** ball game in which the two teams ride on ponies. □ **polo**
water polo, ball game played by two teams in the water. □ **waterpolo**
2 *polo neck pullover,* pullover with a high rolled neck. □ **jersey de cuello vuelto**
poltergeist ['pɔltəgaist] *n.* type of ghost which knocks things over/makes loud sounds, etc. □ **duende**
poly- ['pɔli] *prefix meaning* several. □ **poli-**
polyanthus [pɔli'ænθəs] *n.* common garden flower, like a primrose with a large flower head. □ **prímula**
polyester [pɔli'estə] *n.* type of synthetic fibre used in clothing. □ **poliéster**
polygamy [pə'ligəmi] *n.* custom of having several wives at the same time. □ **poligamia**
polygamist *n.* man with several wives. □ **polígamo**
polygamous *adj.* referring to polygamy. □ **polígamo**
polyglot ['pɔliglɔt] *adj.* and *n.* (person) who speaks several languages; (dictionary, etc.) written in several languages. □ **políglota**
polygon ['pɔligən] *n.* geometrical figure with many sides. □ **polígono**
polygonal [pə'ligənl] *adj.* with many sides. □ **poligonal**
polymer ['pɔlimə] *n.* chemical compound whose molecule is made of several single similar molecules. □ **polímero**
polyp ['pɔlip] *n.* **1** small primitive animal shaped like a tube and living in water. □ **pólipo**
2 growth inside the human body. □ **pólipo**
polystyrene [pɔli'stairi:n] *n.* light plastic used as a heat insulator or as packing material. □ **poliestireno**
polysyllable ['pɔlisiləbl] *n.* word with several syllables. □ **polisílabo**
polysyllabic [pɔlisi'læbik] *adj.* (word) with several syllables. □ **polisilábico**
polytechnic [pɔli'teknik] *n.* educational establishment for school-leavers, giving degrees, especially in technical subjects. □ **politécnico**
polythene ['pɔliθi:n] *n.* type of almost transparent plastic used in thin sheets: *polythene bag.* □ **polietileno**
polyunsaturated [pɔliʌn'sætjureitid] *adj.* (fat) which does not form cholesterol in the blood. □ **poliinsaturada**
polyurethane [pɔli'juəriθein] *n.* type of plastic used in paints. □ **poliuretano**
pomegranate ['pɔmigrænit] *n.* tropical fruit with red flesh and many seeds. □ **granada**
pommel ['pɔml] *n.* high front part of a saddle. □ **perilla**
pomp [pɔmp] *n.* splendid ceremony. □ **pompa**
pompous *adj.* very solemn/too dignified. □ **pomposo**
pompom ['pɔmpɔm] *n.* small tufted ball of wool worn as an ornament on a hat, etc. □ **borla**
ponce [pɔns] *n.* (*slang*) man who lives off the money earned by prostitutes. □ **chulo**
poncho ['pɔnʃou] *n.* type of cloak made of a single large piece of material, with a hole in the centre for your head. □ **poncho**
pond [pɔnd] *n.* small lake: *village pond; duck pond.* □ **estanque**
ponder ['pɔndə] *v.* to think deeply: *he pondered (over) the question for a long time.* □ **meditar**
ponderous *adj.* very heavy and slow-moving. □ **laborioso**
pong [pɔŋ] *n.* (*slang*) unpleasant smell: *what a pong of fish!* □ **pestazo**
■ *v.* (*slang*) to make an unpleasant smell: *the whole house pongs of fish.* □ **apestar**
pontiff ['pɔntif] *n.* the Pope. □ **pontífice**
pontifical [pɔn'tifikl] *adj.* referring to the Pope. □ **pontificio**
pontificate [pɔn'tifikeit] *v.* to speak/to write in a pompous way. □ **pontificar**
pontoon [pɔn'tu:n] *n.* **1** boat used to support a floating temporary bridge. □ **pontón**
a pontoon bridge, bridge built on pontoons. □ **puente de pontones**
2 card game. □ **veintiuna**
pony ['pouni] *n.* small horse. □ **poni**
pony-trekking, holiday sport riding ponies across country. □ **excursión con ponis**
poodle ['pu:dl] *n.* type of curly-haired dog, usually clipped in a curious way. □ **caniche**
pool [pu:l] *n.* **1** small lake. □ **charca**
2 area of water or other liquid: *a pool of blood on the floor.* □ **charco**
3 ***swimming pool,*** enclosed tank of water for swimming. □ **piscina**
4 common supply of money/food, etc., for a group of people: *we all contributed to the pool.* □ **fondo**
5 *typing pool,* group of typists working for several departments. □ **servicio de mecanografía**
6 ***football pools,*** system of gambling where you have to forecast the results of football matches. □ **quinielas**
7 *Amer.* game similar to snooker. □ **billar de casino**
■ *v.* to group together: *we pooled our resources.* □ **reunir**
poolroom *n. Amer.* public room where you can play pool. □ **sala de billar**
poor ['puə, pɔ:] *adj.* **1** having little or no money: *a poor man; to give your money to the poor.* □ **pobre, malo**
2 not very good: *poor soil; he's in poor health; poor quality.* □ **pobre, malo**
poorly *adv.* **1** in quite a bad way: *he played very poorly.* □ **mal**
2 without money: *she was poorly dressed.* □ **pobre**
■ *adj.* ill: *she's looking quite poorly.* □ **enfermo, mal**
poorness *n.* bad quality. □ **mala calidad**
pop [pɔp] *n.* **1** noise like a cork coming out of a bottle: *the bottle went off pop.* □ **pum**
2 (*informal*) father. □ **papá**
3 (*informal*) popular song: *top of the pops,* song which is most popular at the moment. □ **pop**
4 (*informal*) fizzy drink: *a bottle of pop.* □ **una gaseosa**
■ *v.* (*he popped*) **1** to make a pop: *the corks popped.* □ **saltar**

2 (*informal*) to go quickly: *I'll just pop round the corner; he popped over to the baker's.* □ **acercarse**
3 to put quickly: *she popped the cake into the oven.* □ **meter rápidamente**
■ *adj.* popular: *pop music; a pop singer.* □ **pop**
popcorn *n.* sweet corn which has been heated until it bursts. □ **palomita de maíz**
pop-gun *n.* toy gun which makes a pop. □ **pistola de pistones**
Pope [poup] *n.* the head of the Roman Catholic Church. □ **Papa**
poplar ['pɔplə] *n.* common tree which often grows in a tall and slender form. □ **álamo**
poplin ['pɔplin] *n.* strong cotton cloth used for making shirts. □ **popelín**
poppy ['pɔpi] *n.* common flower, red when wild, but other colours in the garden. □ **amapola**
populace ['pɔpjuləs] *n.* ordinary people. □ **populacho**
popular ['pɔpjulə] *adj.* **1** referring to the ordinary people: *a popular uprising; popular belief/error,* belief/error held by most people. □ **popular**
2 liked by a lot of people: *the film has been very popular; green is a popular colour this year.* □ **popular**
popularity [pɔpju'læriti] *n.* being liked by a lot of people. □ **popularidad**
popularize ['pɔpjuləraiz] *v.* to make something understood/liked by a lot of people. □ **popularizar**
popularly *adv.* generally; by most people: *it is popularly believed that he was murdered.* □ **popularmente**
populate ['pɔpjuleit] *v.* to put people to live in a place: *the island was populated by pirates; thickly populated area.* □ **poblar**
population [pɔpju'leiʃn] *n.* number of people who live in a place: *what's the population of Paris? the population of the village has declined; the whole population turned out to cheer.* □ **población**
populous ['pɔpjuləs] *adj.* thickly populated (district of a town). □ **populoso**
porcelain ['pɔːslin] *n.* fine china: *a porcelain teacup.* □ **porcelana**
porch [pɔːtʃ] *n.* shelter over a doorway. □ **porche**
porcupine ['pɔːkjupain] *n.* American/African rodent with long sharp spikes covering its body. □ **puerco espín**
pore [pɔː] *n.* small hole in the skin through which sweat passes. □ **poro**
■ *v.* ***to pore over*** *a book,* to look at it very closely. □ **escudriñar**
pork [pɔːk] *n.* meat from a pig: *pork chop; roast pork.* □ **cerdo (carne)**
pornography [pɔː'nɔgrəfi] *n.* films/books/art which deal with sex in an indecent way. □ **pornografía**
porn [pɔːn] *n.* (*informal*) pornography: *hard/soft porn,* extremely indecent/less indecent pornographic material. □ **porno**
pornographic [pɔːnə'græfik] *adj.* (book, etc.) which deals with sex in an indecent way. □ **pornográfico**
porous ['pɔːrəs] *adj.* (solid) which allows liquid to pass through. □ **poroso**
porpoise ['pɔːpəs] *n.* large sea mammal which tends to swim in groups. □ **marsopa**
porridge ['pɔridʒ] *n.* oatmeal cooked in water. □ **gachas de avena**
port [pɔːt] *n.* **1** harbour. □ **puerto**
home port, harbour at which a ship is based. □ **puerto de matrícula**
2 town with a harbour. □ **puerto**
3 left side (when looking forward on board a ship/aircraft). □ **babor**
4 dark red sweet wine from Portugal. □ **oporto**
portable ['pɔːtəbl] *adj.* which can be carried: *portable typewriter.* □ **portátil**
portal ['pɔːtl] *n.* imposing entrance. □ **pórtico**
portcullis [pɔːt'kʌlis] *n.* gate which was dropped to close the entrance to a medieval castle. □ **rastrillo**
portent ['pɔːtənt] *n.* (*formal*) warning (that something unpleasant is going to happen). □ **augurio**
portentous [pɔː'tentəs] *adj.* important/significant; warning that something unpleasant is going to happen. □ **portentoso; de mal augurio**
porter ['pɔːtə] *n.* **1** person who carries luggage for travellers. □ **mozo de estación**
2 doorkeeper (in a hotel). □ **portero**
portfolio [pɔːt'fouliou] *n.* **1** large (cardboard) case for carrying paintings, etc. □ **cartera**
2 collection of shares owned by someone. □ **cartera de acciones**
3 minister's job in government: *he has accepted the portfolio of Foreign Affairs.* □ **cartera**
porthole ['pɔːthoul] *n.* round window in the side of a ship. □ **portilla**
portico ['pɔːtikou] *n.* roof supported by columns forming a porch in front of the entrance to a building. □ **pórtico**
portion ['pɔːʃn] *n.* **1** part: *a portion of the profit has to be paid in tax.* □ **parte**
2 serving of food: *he got a large portion of potatoes.* □ **ración**
■ *v.* ***to portion something out,*** to share out. □ **dividir**
portly ['pɔːtli] *adj.* rather fat. □ **gordito**
portrait ['pɔːtreit] *n.* painting/photograph of a person. □ **retratismo**
portraiture ['pɔːtrətʃə] *n.* art of painting portraits. □ **retratismo**
portray [pɔː'trei] *v.* to paint/to describe a scene or a person. □ **retratar**
portrayal *n.* painting; description of a scene or person. □ **retrato**
Portugal ['pɔːtjugl] *n.* country in Southern Europe. □ **Portugal**
Portuguese [pɔːtju'giːz] *adj.* referring to Portugal. □ **portugués**
■ *n.* **1** person from Portugal. □ **portugués**
2 language spoken in Portugal. □ **portugués**
pose [pouz] *n.* **1** way of standing/sitting: *he was sitting in a rather stiff pose.* □ **postura**
2 way of behaving which is just a pretence: *he looks intellectual, but it's just a pose.* □ **pose**
■ *v.* **1** to stand/to sit still while someone paints/photographs you. □ **posar**
2 to pretend to be: *he posed as an Italian prince.* □ **dárselas de**
3 *to pose a problem,* to set a problem: *how to get there when there is no bus service poses something of a problem.* □ **plantear un problema**
poser *n.* (*informal*) difficult question. □ **pregunta peliaguda**
poseur [pou'zəː] *n.* person who behaves in a false way. □ **presumido**
posh [pɔʃ] *adj.* (*informal*) very smart: *he speaks with a posh accent; it's a very posh hotel.* □ **afectado (acento); elegante (hotel)**
position [pə'ziʃn] *n.* **1** way of standing/sitting: *he was found in a sitting position.* □ **posición**
2 place: *are all the soldiers in position? put yourself in my position; what's his position in the class? she's in a very awkward position.* □ **posición**
3 job: *she got a position as a secretary.* □ **empleo**
■ *v.* to place: *he carefully positioned himself near the door.* □ **situar**
positive ['pɔzitiv] *adj.* **1** meaning yes: *he gave a posi-*

tive reply; the tests were positive. □ **positivo**
2 certain: *it's a positive fact.* □ **cierto**
3 sure/convinced: *a positive tone of voice; I'm positive that is the man I saw running away.* □ **convencido**
4 plus; more than zero. □ **positivo**
■ *n.* **1** photograph printed from a negative, where the light and dark appear as they are in nature. □ **positivo**
2 one of the terminals in a battery: *make sure you can tell the negative from the positive before you connect up the battery.* □ **polo positivo**
positively *adv.* absolutely: *it's positively revolting.* □ **rotundamente**
posse ['pɔsi] *n.* group of armed men/police. □ **pelotón**
possess [pə'zes] *v.* **1** to own: *he possesses vast estates in the north of the country.* □ **poseer**
2 to occupy someone's mind: *what possessed him to ask for more money?,* what gave him the stupid idea of asking for more money? □ **dominar la mente de alguien**
possession [pə'zeʃn] *n.* **1** ownership: *to take possession of a house.* □ **posesión**
2 *to buy a house with vacant possession,* a house which is empty, and which you can occupy immediately. □ **comprar una casa sin inquilinos**
3 thing you own: *all his possessions were thrown out into the street.* □ **posesión**
possessive *adj.* **1** (*in grammar*) (word) which indicates possession: *'mine' is a possessive pronoun.* □ **posesivo**
2 (person) who treats another person as if he owns him: *she is very possessive about her son.* □ **posesivo**
possessor *n.* owner. □ **poseedor**
possible ['pɔsibl] *adj.* **1** which can happen: *it's a possible source of an accident; give me as much time as possible; as far away as possible.* □ **posible**
2 likely: *it's possible that the train has been held up by fog.* □ **probable**
possibility [pɔsi'biliti] *n.* **1** chance; being likely: *there's a possibility that he may leave.* □ **posibilidad**
2 *the plan has possibilities,* may well work. □ **el plan promete**
possibly *adv.* **1** which may happen: *he can't possibly eat all those sausages.* □ **posiblemente**
2 perhaps: *possibly the train will be late.* □ **quizá**
post [poust] *n.* **1** wooden/concrete stake fixed in the ground: *fencing post; gate post.* □ **poste**
2 place where a sentry is on duty. □ **puesto**
3 job/position: *he has applied for a post in the town hall.* □ **puesto**
4 small settlement far from civilization: *a trading post.* □ **enclave**
5 ***the last post,*** bugle call to commemorate the dead. □ **toque de ánimas**
6 mail; letters, etc., sent by mail: *has the post arrived? send it by post; can you put this letter in the post for me?* □ **correo**
■ *v.* **1** to send (someone) on duty: *he was posted to a town in the north of the country.* □ **destinar**
2 to send (a letter) by mail: *the letter was posted last week.* □ **mandar por correo**
keep him posted *as to what happens,* keep him informed. □ **manténle al tanto de lo que pasa**
postage *n.* payment for sending a letter by mail: *what's the postage for a postcard to Australia?* □ **franqueo**
postage stamp, piece of paper which you buy and stick on a letter, etc., to pay for it to be sent to its destination. □ **sello**
postal *adj.* referring to the post: *postal service.* □ **postal**
postal ballot, where people send their votes by post. □ **voto por correo**
postal order, order to pay money, which can be bought and cashed at a post office. □ **giro postal**
postbox *n.* box in a wall into which you can put letters, which will then be collected by the post office and sent to their destination. □ **buzón**
postcard *n.* card (sometimes with a picture) which you send through the post. □ **postal**
postcode *n.* system of letters or numbers to indicate the town or street where someone lives, so as to make the sorting of letters more rapid. □ **código postal**
poster *n.* large notice stuck up on a wall, etc.; large picture/advertisement stuck on a wall. □ **cartel**
poste restante [poust'restɑ:nt] *n.* service where letters can be addressed to someone at a post office where he can collect them. □ **lista de correos**
post-haste *adv.* very fast. □ **a toda prisa**
postman *n.* (*pl. postmen*) person who delivers letters to houses. □ **cartero**
postmark *n.* mark put on a letter with a rubber stamp to show when it was sent off. □ **matasellos**
■ *v.* to stamp (a letter) with a postmark. □ **matar**
postmaster, postmistress *n.* person in charge of a post office. □ **jefe de estafeta**
post office *n.* **1** building where mail is received/stamps sold, etc. □ **estafeta, oficina de correos**
2 organization which runs the postal services: *he has retired after fifty years with the post office.* □ **Correos**
post- [poust] *prefix meaning* later than/after. □ **post-**
postdate *v.* to put a date (on a cheque) which is later than the day on which you actually write it. □ **posfechar**
postgraduate *n.* person who has a first degree from a university and who is studying for a further degree. □ **postgraduado**
posthumous ['pɔstjuməs] *adj.* after death: *a posthumous award for bravery.* □ **póstumo**
posthumously *adv.* after death: *he was awarded the medal posthumously.* □ **póstumamente**
post mortem [poust'mɔ:təm] *n.* **1** examination of a dead person to find out the cause of death. □ **autopsia**
2 *to conduct a post mortem on the election results,* to examine them to try to discover why people voted as they did. □ **hacer un análisis de...**
postnatal *adj.* referring to the time after the birth of a child. □ **posnatal**
postpone [pəs'poun] *v.* to put off until later: *he postponed the meeting until next week.* □ **aplazar**
postponement *n.* putting off until later. □ **aplazamiento**
postscript *n.* additional note at the end of a letter. □ **posdata**
postwar *adj.* referring to the period after the war. □ **de la posguerra**
posterior [pɔ'stiəriə] *n.* behind/buttocks. □ **trasero**
posterity [pɔ'steriti] *n.* generations which will follow. □ **posteridad**
postulate ['pɔstjuleit] *v.* to suppose (that something is true). □ **suponer**
posture ['pɔstʃə] *n.* way of sitting/standing, etc. □ **postura**
■ *v.* to take up a particular position for effect. □ **adoptar una postura**
posy ['pouzi] *n.* small bunch of flowers. □ **ramillete**

pot [pɔt] *n.* **1** container made of glass or clay: *pot of jam, plant pot.* □ **olla, puchero; tarro de mermelada; tiesto; maceta**
2 *he has **pots of money,*** (*informal*) lots of money. □ **...montones de pasta**
3 ***to go to pot,*** (*informal*) to become ruined/useless. □ **estropearse**
4 (*slang*) marijuana. □ **maría**
■ *v.* (*he potted*) **1** to put in a pot: *to pot flowers.* □ **poner en maceta**
2 *to pot a ball,* (*in billiards*) to send a ball into one of the small bags at the side and corners of the table. □ **entronerar una bola**
pot-hole *n.* **1** hole in rock worn away by water. □ **marmita de gigante**
2 hole in a road surface. □ **socavón**
pot-holer *n.* person who climbs down pot-holes as a sport. □ **espeleólogo**
pot-holing *n.* sport of climbing inside pot-holes. □ **espeleología**
potluck *n.* ***to take potluck,*** to take whatever comes, with no possibility of choice. □ **lo que haya**
potshot *n.* ***to take a potshot at someone,*** (*informal*) to try to shoot them without aiming properly. □ **tiro sin apuntar**
potted *adj.* **1** condensed: *a potted biography.* □ **condensado**
2 put in a pot: *potted meat; potted shrimps.* □ **en conserva**
potting shed *n.* small building in a garden where you put plants in pots. □ **cobertizo**
potash ['pɔtæʃ] *n.* potassium salts. □ **potasa**
potassium [pə'tæsiəm] *n.* (*chemical element*: K) light white metallic substance. □ **potasio**
potato [pə'teitou] *n.* (*pl. potatoes*) common vegetable, formed under the soil: *boiled potatoes; potatoes in their jackets,* cooked without being peeled. □ **patata**
sweet potato, yam/root of a tropical plant, eaten as a vegetable. □ **batata**
potency ['poutənsi] *n.* strength. □ **potencia**
potent *adj.* strong: *a very potent argument; a potent drink.* □ **potente; una razón poderosa; una bebida fuerte**
potentate ['poutənteit] *n.* Eastern ruler. □ **potentado**
potential [pə'tenʃl] *adj.* possible: *he's a potential murderer,* he could become a murderer. □ **potencial**
■ *n.* **1** possibility of developing into something valuable: *she has considerable potential.* □ **potencial**
2 (*in physics*) electrical property which governs the flow of an electric charge. □ **potencial**
potentially *adv.* possibly. □ **en potencia**
potentiometer *n.* instrument for measuring differences in electrical potential. □ **potenciómetro**
potion ['pouʃn] *n.* liquid mixture to make you sleep, etc. □ **poción**
potter ['pɔtə] *n.* person who makes pots out of clay. □ **alfarero**
■ *v.* ***to potter about,*** not to do anything in particular/to do little jobs. □ **no hacer nada en particular**
pottery *n.* **1** potter's workshop. □ **alfarería**
2 pots; articles made of clay, earthenware. □ **cerámica**
potty ['pɔti] *n.* (*informal*) child's chamberpot. □ **orinal**
■ *adj.* (*informal*) mad. □ **chalado**
pouch [pautʃ] *n.* **1** small bag for carrying coins/ammunition, etc. □ **bolsa (monedas); cartuchera (munición)**
2 bag in the skin in front of some marsupials (such as the kangaroo), where the young live and grow for some time after birth. □ **bolsa**
poultice ['poultis] *n.* hot wet dressing put on a wound. □ **cataplasma**
■ *v.* to dress (a wound) with a poultice. □ **poner una cataplasma**
poultry ['poultri] *n.* common farm birds which are reared for eggs or to be eaten, such as ducks/hens, etc. □ **aves de corral**
poulterer ['poultərə] *n.* shopkeeper who specializes in selling poultry. □ **pollero**
pounce [pauns] *v.* to jump (on something): *the cat pounced on the pigeon; he always pounces on any mistake I make.* □ **saltar**
pound [paund] *n.* **1** measure of weight (= approximately 0.45 kilogram): *a pound of sugar; he weighs 120 pounds (120 lb).* □ **libra**
2 standard unit of money in Great Britain and several other countries: *this coat costs ten pounds ($10); a pound note; a five-pound note.* □ **libra**
3 place where stray animals or illegally parked cars are put. □ **depósito**
■ *v.* **1** to smash into little pieces; to hit hard: *the sea pounded against the wrecked tanker; he pounded on the table with his fist.* □ **golpear**
2 *he pounded up the stairs,* he ran heavily up the stairs. □ **con fuertes pisadas**
3 to beat fast: *my heart was pounding.* □ **latir a toda velocidad**
poundage ['paundidʒ] *n.* rate charged for each pound. □ **tasa de tanto por libra**
pour [pɔː] *v.* **1** to flow out/down: *oil poured out of the hole in the pipe; smoke was pouring out of the window; the rain was pouring down; the people poured out of the hall.* □ **derramarse (aceite); salir a raudales (humo); diluviar**
2 to transfer liquid from one container to another: *he poured the oil into a smaller drum; she poured out three glasses of beer; can you pour me another cup of tea?* □ **echó el aceite...; sirvió tres...; me puedes servir...**
pout [paut] *n.* sulky expression where the lips stick out. □ **puchero**
■ *v.* to make a sulky expression with the lips. □ **hacer pucheros**
poverty ['pɔvəti] *n.* **1** being poor: *he lives in poverty.* □ **pobreza**
2 *below the **poverty line,*** with less than the smallest income necessary to provide the minimum necessities to live. □ **umbral de pobreza**
powder ['paudə] *n.* very fine dry grains (like flour): *they crushed the blocks of chalk to powder; talcum powder.* □ **polvo**
(face) powder, scented flour-like substance for putting on the face. □ **polvos para la cara**
powder compact, small box containing face powder. □ **polvera**
powder room, place in a public building where women may go to the toilet, wash, etc. □ **tocador**
■ *v.* to put on powder: *she was powdering her face.* □ **empolvarse**
powdery *adj.* fine/like powder: *powdery snow.* □ **en polvo**
power ['pauə] *n.* **1** strength: *the power of an engine.* □ **potencia**
2 ability: *power of speech.* □ **habilidad**
3 driving force: *electric power; power cut; the mill is worked by water power.* □ **fuerza eléctrica; corte de corriente; energía hidráulica**
power pack, portable source of electricity. □ **fuente de alimentación**

power point, wall plug which supplies electricity. □ **punto de luz**
4 (*in mathematics*) number of times a number is multiplied by itself: *two to the power of three* (2^3). □ **potencia**
5 (*in physics*) strength of a lens. □ **potencia**
6 political/social strength (of a person/a group): *he has considerable bargaining power.* □ **poder**
black power, moral strength of black people in their fight for civil rights. □ **'black power'**
7 political control: *he came to power in 1953; the Conservatives are in power.* □ **poder**
powerful *adj.* very strong: *a powerful drug.* □ **potente, fuerte**
powerless *adj.* unable to do anything: *he's powerless to act.* □ **impotente**
power station, *Amer.* **power plant** *n.* works where electricity is produced: *nuclear power station.* □ **central eléctrica**
powwow ['pauwau] *n.* meeting to discuss some problem. □ **conferencia**
practicable ['præktikəbl] *adj.* which can be done/which can be put into practice: *his plan is hardly practicable.* □ **realizable**
practicability [præktikə'biliti] *n.* ability to be put into practice. □ **practicabilidad**
practical ['præktikl] *adj.* interested in practice/action rather than ideas; referring to practice rather than theory: *he has a practical turn of mind; a practical suggestion; he can put his skill at carpentry to practical use.* □ **práctico**
practical joke, trick played on someone to make other people laugh. □ **broma pesada**
■ *n.* (*informal*) examination/test to show how well someone can work in practice. □ **examen práctico**
practicality *n.* way in which something works in practice. □ **carácter práctico**
practically *adv.* **1** in practice: *but practically this will just not work.* □ **en la práctica**
2 almost: *we've had practically no rain for weeks.* □ **prácticamente**
practice ['præktis] *n.* **1** actual application: *it's a good idea, but will it work in practice?* □ **práctica**
2 *the practice of medicine,* working as a doctor. □ **el ejercicio de la medicina**
3 habit: *I make a practice of telephoning my mother every day.* □ **tengo por costumbre telefonear...**
4 repeated exercise: *music practice; target practice; with practice, you should be able to play the piano quite well; he's out of practice.* □ **ejercicios (en el piano); no está en forma**
5 the business of a doctor/dentist/lawyer: *he has a thriving practice; he has a country practice.* □ **consulta (médico); bufete (abogado)**
6 ***practices,*** ways of doing things: *barbaric practices.* □ **prácticas**
■ *v. Amer. see* **practise.**
practise ['præktis] *Amer.* **practice** *v.* **1** to put something into practice. □ **practicar, poner en práctica**
to practise what you preach, to do as you tell others to do. □ **predicar con el ejemplo**
2 to do repeated exercises: *he practises on the piano/in the gym for two hours a day.* □ **hacer ejercicios**
3 to carry on a job as a doctor or lawyer. □ **ejercer de**
practised *adj.* skilled. □ **experto**
practitioner [præk'tiʃənə] *n.* doctor. □ **médico**
general practitioner, doctor who treats all patients/all illnesses. □ **médico (de medicina general)**
pragmatic [præg'mætik] *adj.* dealing with fact/practical matters, not concerned with theory. □ **pragmático**
pragmatically *adv.* in a pragmatic, not theoretical, way. □ **de forma pragmática**
prairie ['prɛəri] *n.* ***the prairies,*** grass-covered plains in North America. □ **pradera**
praise [preiz] *n.* admiration/expression of approval: *in praise of older women; I have nothing but praise for her courage.* □ **elogio**
■ *v.* to express strong approval: *the judges praised all the entries in the competition.* □ **elogiar**
praiseworthy *adj.* which should be praised. □ **digno de elogio**
pram [præm] *n.* (*informal*) small carriage in which you can push a baby. □ **cochecito de niño**
prance [prɑːns] *v.* to jump about/to move lightly. □ **hacer cabriolas**
prank [præŋk] *n.* trick. □ **broma**
prawn [prɔːn] *n.* shellfish like a large shrimp. □ **langostino**
pray [prei] *v.* **1** to speak to God; to ask God something; to ask someone for something: *they are praying for fine weather to finish the harvest; to pray for someone,* to speak to God on behalf of someone. □ **rezar**
2 ***pray be seated,*** (*formal*) please sit down. □ **le ruego tome asiento**
prayer *n.* act of speaking to God; a request: *he said his prayers.* □ **oración**
pre- [pri] *prefix meaning* before: *the pre-Christian era; the pre-holiday rush; it happened pre-1914.* □ **pre-**
preach [priːtʃ] *v.* **1** to give a sermon in church. □ **predicar**
2 to recommend/to advise; to give moral advice: *he is always preaching about the dangers of alcohol.* □ **aconsejar**
preacher *n.* person who gives a sermon. □ **predicador**
preamble [priː'æmbl] *n.* introduction/remarks at the beginning (of a speech/treaty, etc.). □ **preámbulo**
precarious [pri'kɛəriəs] *adj.* likely to fall; uncertain: *he makes a precarious living selling matches.* □ **precario**
precariously *adv.* unsafely: *he was clinging precariously to a chimney.* □ **precariamente**
precaution [pri'kɔːʃn] *n.* care taken in advance (to avoid something unpleasant): *he took the precaution of locking all the doors and windows.* □ **precaución**
precautionary *adj.* (measures) taken to avoid something unpleasant. □ **preventivo**
precede [pri'siːd] *v.* to take place before: *the rain was preceded by high winds.* □ **preceder**
precedence ['presidəns] *n.* ***to take precedence over someone/something,*** to go before/to be more important than. □ **precedencia**
precedent ['presidənt] *n.* something which has happened before, and which can be a guide as to what should be done: *to create/to set a precedent; there's no precedent for this.* □ **precedente**
preceding [pri'siːdiŋ] *adj.* before: *the preceding day; the preceding twenty-four hours were crucial.* □ **precedente, anterior**
precept ['priːsept] *n.* command; guiding rule. □ **precepto**
precinct ['priːsiŋkt] *n.* area surrounded by a wall; administrative district of a town: *within the precincts of the embassy,* inside the embassy grounds. □ **recinto**
shopping precinct/pedestrian precinct, area of a

town which is closed to traffic. □ **zona comercial/ peatonal**
precious ['preʃəs] *adj.* worth a lot of money; of great value: *precious stones.* □ **precioso**
precipice ['presipis] *n.* high cliff (not usually near the sea). □ **precipicio**
precipitous [pri'sipitəs] *adj.* very steep. □ **escarpado**
precipitate [pri'sipitət] *n.* chemical substance which settles at the bottom of a liquid. □ **precipitado**
■ *v.* [pri'sipiteit] **1** to make something happen suddenly: *his decision precipitated a crisis.* □ **precipitar**
2 to settle at the bottom of a liquid. □ **precipitarse**
■ *adj.* rushed/hurried: *precipitate action.* □ **precipitado**
precipitation *n.* **1** (*formal*) great hurry. □ **precipitación**
2 quantity of rain/snow, etc., which falls on a certain place. □ **precipitación**
précis ['preisi] *n.* (*pl. précis*) summary of the main points of a text. □ **resumen**
precise [pri'sais] *adj.* **1** exact: *at the precise moment when I was going to phone.* □ **preciso**
2 careful: *he's very precise about checking his quotations.* □ **meticuloso**
precisely *adv.* **1** exactly: *I'll meet you at ten o'clock precisely.* □ **exactamente**
2 in a careful way. □ **con precisión**
precision [pri'siʒn] *n.* accuracy. □ **precisión**
precision instruments, instruments which measure something precisely. □ **instrumentos de precisión**
preclude [pri'klu:d] *v.* to prevent: *the crisis precluded any decision being taken.* □ **imposibilitar**
precocious [pri'kouʃəs] *adj.* (child) who is surprisingly advanced for his age. □ **precoz**
precociously *adv.* in a precocious way. □ **precozmente**
precociousness, precocity [pri'kɔsiti] *n.* being advanced for your age. □ **precocidad**
preconceive [pri:kən'si:v] *v.* to have an idea or belief from the beginning/before something starts: *preconceived idea.* □ **preconcebir**
preconception [pri:kən'sepʃn] *n.* preconceived idea. □ **idea preconcebida**
precursor [pri'kə:sə] *n.* thing which leads to an invention/person who goes in advance: *it's one of the precursors of the telephone.* □ **precursor**
precursory *adj.* which is in advance. □ **precursor**
predate ['pri:deit] *v.* to come before in date: *it predates the reign of King Henry VIII.* □ **preceder**
predator ['predətə] *n.* animal which lives by eating other animals. □ **predador**
predatory *adj.* (animal) which eats other animals; (person) who lives off other people. □ **depredador; gorrón (persona)**
predecease [pri:di'si:s] *v.* (*formal*) to die before (someone). □ **morir antes que**
predecessor ['pri:disesə] *n.* person who has held the same job, etc., before you. □ **predecesor, antecesor**
predestine [pri:'destin] *v.* to decide the fate of (someone) in advance. □ **predestinar**
predestination [pri:desti'neiʃn] *n.* being predestined. □ **predestinación**
predetermine [pri:di'tə:min] *v.* to decide in advance. □ **predeterminar**
predicament [pri'dikəmənt] *n.* troubles/difficult situation: *she's in an awkward predicament.* □ **apuro**
predict [pri'dikt] *v.* to foretell/to tell in advance what will happen. □ **predecir**
predictable *adj.* which could be predicted. □ **fácil de predecir; previsible**
predictably *adv.* in a way which could have been predicted. □ **previsiblemente**
prediction [pri'dikʃn] *n.* foretelling: *the old man's prediction came true.* □ **predicción**
predilection [pri:di'lekʃn] *n.* liking/preference. □ **predilección**
predispose [pri:di'spouz] *v.* to make (someone) favour something in advance: *the good reports predisposed him in my favour.* □ **predisponer**
predisposition [pri:dispə'ziʃn] *n.* being predisposed. □ **predisposición**
predominate [pri'dɔmineit] *v.* to be bigger/stronger/more numerous. □ **predominar**
predominant [pri'dɔminənt] *adj.* most striking/obvious: *his predominant characteristic.* □ **predominante**
pre-eminent [pri:'eminənt] *adj.* excellent/much better than everything else. □ **preeminente**
pre-empt [pri:'empt] *v.* **1** to get an advantage by doing something before anyone else. □ **adelantarse**
2 *to pre-empt someone's decision,* to act as if someone had decided, but before the decision is taken. □ **adelantarse a una decisión**
pre-emptive *adj.* which gains an advantage by acting before anyone else: *a pre-emptive air attack.* □ **en primer lugar, por adelantado**
preen [pri:n] *v.* (*of bird*) to smooth its feathers. □ **arreglarse las plumas con el pico**
to preen yourself, to smarten yourself up. □ **arreglarse**
to preen yourself on something, to congratulate yourself. □ **enorgullecerse de**
prefabricated [pri:'fæbrikeitid] *adj.* built in advance; (house) built out of pieces which are assembled on the site. □ **prefabricado**
prefabrication *n.* building in advance. □ **prefabricación**
preface ['prefəs] *n.* piece written (usually by the author) to introduce a book. □ **prólogo, prefacio**
■ *v.* to say/to write something as an introduction: *he prefaced his remarks with a quotation from Shakespeare.* □ **prologar**
prefatory ['prefətri] *adj.* which acts as a preface. □ **preliminar**
prefect ['pri:fekt] *n.* **1** school pupil chosen to be in charge of others. □ **prefecto**
2 high official. □ **prefecto**
prefer [pri'fə:] *v.* (*he preferred*) to like (to do) something better than something else: *I would prefer to stay indoors and watch television; which do you prefer — chocolate or vanilla ice-cream?* □ **preferir**
preferable ['prefrəbl] *adj.* which you would prefer: *it would be preferable if you could bring your bicycle.* □ **preferible**
preferably *adv.* if possible: *I like travelling, preferably alone.* □ **preferiblemente**
preference ['prefrəns] *n.* liking for one thing more than another: *he has a strong preference for sticky cakes.* □ **preferencia**
preferential [prefə'renʃl] *adj.* showing that you prefer one thing more than another: *he got preferential treatment when he said that he was the manager's son.* □ **preferente**
preferment [pri'fə:mənt] *n.* promotion to a more important post. □ **ascenso**
prefix ['pri:fiks] *n.* word put in front of another: *many words start with the prefix 'anti-'.* □ **prefijo**
■ *v.* to put some word in front of another/to preface: *I will prefix my statement with a short poem.* □ **poner a manera de prefijo**

pregnancy ['pregnənsi] *n.* state of being pregnant/of carrying an unborn child. □ **embarazo**
pregnancy test, test to see if a woman is pregnant. □ **prueba del embarazo**
pregnant *adj.* **1** carrying an unborn child. □ **embarazada**
2 *pregnant pause,* pause while everyone waits for something to happen/for someone to say something. □ **silencio en espera de algo**
prehensile [pri:'hensail] *adj.* which can grasp/hold on to something: *some monkeys have prehensile tails.* □ **prensil**
prehistory [pri:'histəri] *n.* time before written history. □ **prehistoria**
prehistorian [pri:hi'stɔ:riən] *n.* person who specializes in the study of prehistory. □ **prehistoriador**
prehistoric [pri:hi'stɔrik] *adj.* belonging to prehistory: *prehistoric man.* □ **prehistórico**
prejudge [pri:'dʒʌdʒ] *v.* to judge something without hearing the facts of the case. □ **prejuzgar**
prejudice ['predʒədis] *n.* (usually unjust) feeling against someone: *he has a strong prejudice against people with red hair; racial prejudice,* antagonism towards people because they are of a different race. □ **prejuicio**
■ *v.* **1** to make (someone) unfriendly towards someone else: *he was prejudiced against her from the start.* □ **predisponer**
2 to harm: *his action has prejudiced his chances of promotion.* □ **perjudicar**
prejudicial [predʒu'diʃl] *adj.* which might be damaging. □ **perjudicial**
prelate ['prelət] *n.* person of high rank in a church (bishop/abbot, etc.). □ **prelado**
preliminary [pri'liminəri] *adj.* which goes before. □ **preliminar**
preliminaries *n. pl.* things which have to be done before something can take place. □ **preliminares, preparativos**
prelims ['pri:limz] *n. pl.* (*informal*) **1** first few pages of a book (including title page/contents list, etc.) before the text starts. □ **páginas de introducción**
2 first examinations (at a university). □ **exámenes preliminares**
prelude ['prelju:d] *n.* something (especially piece of music) which introduces something more important; short piece of music on one theme. □ **preludio**
premature [premə'tjuə] *adj.* which happens before the right time. □ **prematuro**
premature baby, baby born less than nine months after conception. □ **bebé prematuro**
prematurely *adv.* before the right time. □ **prematuramente**
premeditate [pri:'mediteit] *v.* to think over/to plan in advance: *a premeditated crime.* □ **premeditar**
premeditation [pri:medi'teiʃn] *n.* planning in advance. □ **premeditación**
premier ['premiə] *n.* Prime Minister. □ **primer ministro; 'premier'**
■ *adj.* first/most important. □ **principal**
première ['premiεə] *n.* first performance of a film/play, etc. □ **estreno**
premise ['premis] *n.* statement which is the basis for reasoning. □ **premisa**
premises ['premisiz] *n. pl.* building and land around it: *on the premises,* in the building; *off the premises,* away from the building; *food may not be consumed on the premises.* □ **en el local; fuera del local**
premiss ['premis] *n.* statement which is the basis for reasoning. □ **premisa**
premium ['pri:miəm] *n.* **1** annual amount paid for an insurance policy. □ **prima**
2 *at a premium,* scarce, and therefore valuable: *during the drought water was at a premium.* □ **difícil de conseguir**
3 bonus. □ **gratificación**
premium offer, specially attractive price. □ **oferta**
premolar [pri:'moulə] *n.* tooth between the canines and the molars. □ **premolar**
premonition [premə'niʃn] *n.* feeling that something is going to happen. □ **premonición**
premonitory [pri'mɔnitri] *adj.* warning (sign). □ **premonitorio**
prenatal [pri:'neitl] *adj.* referring to the time before the birth of a child. □ **prenatal**
preoccupation [pri:ɔkju'peiʃn] *n.* only thinking about one thing: *his preoccupation with golf.* □ **preocupación**
preoccupied *adj.* thinking only about one thing; worried. □ **preocupado**
preoccupy *v.* to make (someone) think about only one thing and worry about it. □ **preocupar**
prep [prep] *n.* (*informal*) **1** homework. □ **deberes**
2 *prep school,* private school for children up to the age of 13. □ **colegio privado**
prepare [pri'pεə] *v.* to get ready: *prepare to die at dawn; he is preparing the way for negotiations.* □ **preparar(se)**
preparation [prepə'reiʃn] *n.* **1** getting ready: *this dish hardly needs any preparation; he made hurried preparations to leave the country.* □ **preparación**
2 substance which has been mixed: *a preparation to remove stains.* □ **preparado**
preparatory [pri'pærətri] *adj.* ***preparatory school,*** private school for children up to the age of 13. □ **preparatorio**
preparatory to our departure, before we leave. □ **en preparación de**
prepared *adj.* ready: *be prepared to leave very quickly.* □ **preparado**
prepay ['pri:pei] *v.* (*he prepaid*) to pay in advance: *prepaid telegram,* telegram where the answer has been paid for in advance. □ **pagar por adelantado**
preponderance [pri'pɔndərəns] *n.* larger number: *the audience contained a preponderance of middle-aged ladies.* □ **preponderancia**
preposition [prepə'ziʃn] *n.* word which is used with a noun/pronoun to show how it is linked to another word: *'near' and 'down' are prepositions in the phrases 'his house is near the sea' and 'he ran down the stairs'.* □ **preposición**
prepossessing [pri:pə'zesiŋ] *adj.* pleasant. □ **agradable**
preposterous [pri:'pɔstərəs] *adj.* silly/absurd: *a preposterous hair style.* □ **ridículo**
prerequisite [pri:'rekwizit] *n.* something which you must have before you can do something. □ **requisito previo**
prerogative [pri'rɔgətiv] *n.* privilege belonging to one person or group: *it is father's prerogative to get up late on Saturday mornings.* □ **prerrogativa**
prescient ['presiənt] *adj.* (*formal*) (person) who can tell what is likely to take place in the future. □ **presciente**
prescribe [pri'skraib] *v.* to order something to be done; to tell someone to use something: *this book has been prescribed for the examination; the doctor prescribed some medicine.* □ **prescribir; recomendar (libro); recetar (medicina)**
prescription [pri'skripʃn] *n.* paper on which a doc-

tor has written out particulars of the medicine to be taken by the patient □ **receta**

presence ['prezns] *n.* **1** being present: *in the presence of the mayor.* □ **presencia**

2 ***presence of mind,*** sense/calmness; ability to act quickly: *when the riots broke out he kept his presence of mind.* □ **presencia de ánimo**

3 *stage presence,* impressive appearance/way of acting on the stage. □ **presencia, tablas**

present ['preznt] *adj.* **1** being at the place/at the time: *he was present when the old man died.* □ **presente**

2 being here now: *the present state of affairs.* □ **el estado actual de la cuestión**

3 *in the present case,* in the case we are studying now. □ **en el caso presente**

4 ***present (tense),*** (*in grammar*) (tense) which describes what is happening now. □ **presente**

■ *n.* **1** at the time we are in now: *up until the present.* □ **presente**

at present, now. □ **actualmente**

2 gift: *a birthday present.* □ **regalo, presente**

■ *v.* [pri'zent] **1** to give: *he presented him with a silver watch.* □ **regalar**

2 to put on (a play): *he will be presenting 'Hamlet' in the autumn.* □ **representar**

3 to introduce (someone into society/an artist to the audience). □ **presentar**

4 *he presented himself at the manager's office,* he appeared. □ **presentarse**

presentable [pri'zentəbl] *adj.* (person) who is suitable to appear in company: *her father is really quite presentable.* □ **presentable**

presentation [prezən'teiʃn] *n.* act of giving: *presentation of prizes at the end of a sports day.* □ **presentación**

present-day *adj.* modern: *present-day standards.* □ **actual**

presently *adv.* **1** soon. □ **luego, inmediatamente**

2 *Amer.* (and *in Scotland*) now. □ **ahora, actualmente**

presentiment [pri'zentimənt] *n.* feeling that something unpleasant will soon happen. □ **presentimiento**

preserve [pri'zə:v] *n.* **1** place where game/fish, etc., are protected so that they can be killed for sport. □ **coto**

2 ***preserves,*** jam/pickles, etc. □ **conservas**

■ *v.* **1** (*formal*) to keep/to protect: *God preserve me from my friends.* □ **proteger**

2 to treat (food) so that it keeps for a long time: *preserved fruit.* □ **conservar**

3 *she's well preserved for her age,* she looks a lot younger than she is. □ **se conserva muy bien...**

preservation [prezə'veiʃn] *n.* protecting. □ **preservación**

preservative [pri'zə:vətiv] *n.* substance used to make food keep/to stop food from going bad. □ **conservante**

preserving pan *n.* very large pan for making jam/chutney, etc. □ **cazuela**

preside [pri'zaid] *v.* **1** to sit at the head of the table. □ **presidir**

2 *to preside at a meeting,* to be the chairman of a meeting. □ **presidir una reunión**

presidency ['prezidnsi] *n.* job of president. □ **presidencia**

president ['prezidənt] *n.* head of a republic; chief member of a club; (*especially Amer.*) head of a business firm: *President Kennedy; the French President/the President of France.* □ **presidente**

presidential [prezi'denʃl] *adj.* referring to a president: *the presidential palace; presidential election.* □ **presidencial**

presidium [pri'sidiəm] *n.* ruling committee (in a communist country). □ **presidium**

press [pres] *n.* **1** machine which squeezes: *a hydraulic press; a trouser press.* □ **prensa**

2 ***printing press,*** machine for printing books/newspapers, etc. □ **prensa; máquina impresora**

3 newspapers and magazines taken as a whole: *the British press has reported that an earthquake has taken place in Iceland; press conference; members of the press,* journalists. □ **prensa**

freedom of the press, freedom of newspapers to print whatever they like. □ **libertad de prensa**

4 *press of people,* crowd. □ **multitud de gente**

■ *v.* **1** to push down; to push against; to squeeze: *press the top button if you want a cup of coffee.* □ **prensar; apretar; pulsar**

2 *to press a pair of trousers,* to remove the creases with an iron; *your skirt needs pressing.* □ **planchar**

3 to force (someone): *he's pressing me for an answer.* □ **presionar**

4 ***to press on/to press forward,*** to continue/to go ahead. □ **seguir adelante**

pressed *adj.* **1** *I'm* ***pressed for time,*** I haven't much time. □ **tengo poco tiempo**

2 *I'd be hard pressed to think of an answer,* if I were asked I would find it difficult to give an answer. □ **me sería muy difícil...**

pressing *adj.* urgent: *a pressing engagement.* □ **apremiante**

press-up *n.* exercise where you lie flat on the floor and push yourself up with your hands. □ **flexión**

pressure ['preʃə] *n.* **1** act of squeezing/pushing down. □ **presión**

to bring pressure to bear, to try to influence something. □ **ejercer presión sobre algo**

to put pressure on someone to do something, to try to force someone to do something. □ **ejercer presión sobre alguien**

2 force of something pushing down/moving/being heavy, etc.: *check the tyre pressure.* □ **presión**

3 ***atmospheric pressure,*** force of the air: *a low-pressure zone,* area where the atmospheric pressure is low. □ **presión atmosférica**

4 ***blood pressure,*** force with which the blood is driven round the body. □ **tensión arterial**

5 stress: *the work is being done under great pressure; he had to resign because of pressure of work.* □ **tensión**

pressure cooker *n.* type of saucepan with a tight-fitting lid, which cooks food rapidly under pressure. □ **olla a presión**

pressure group *n.* group of people who try to influence the government, etc. □ **grupo de presión**

pressurize *v.* to put under pressure; to try to force (someone) to do something. □ **presurizar**

pressurized cabin, cabin of an aircraft where the atmospheric pressure is controlled. □ **cabina presurizada**

prestige [pre'sti:ʒ] *n.* admiration aroused by someone because of rank or qualifications or job. □ **prestigio**

prestigious [pre'stidʒəs] *adj.* which brings prestige: *a prestigious address,* address in a part of the town where everyone wants to live. □ **prestigioso**

presume [pri'zju:m] *v.* **1** to suppose/to assume: *I presume there's someone in the shop; I presume you all know why this meeting has been called.* □ **presumir; suponer**

2 to take the liberty of doing something: *he pre-*

sumed to call the headmaster by his Christian name. □ **permitirse**
presumably *adv.* probably; as you would expect. □ **probablemente**
presumption [pri'zʌmpʃn] *n.* **1** something which is assumed to be true. □ **presunción**
2 rudeness. □ **insolencia**
presumptuous [pri'zʌmptjuəs] *adj.* rude/bold. □ **atrevido; presuntuoso**
presuppose [pri:sə'pouz] *v.* to assume in advance (that certain conditions are met). □ **presuponer**
pretend [pri'tend] *v.* **1** to make believe so as to deceive someone: *he pretended to be a gas inspector; the children were pretending to be doctors and nurses.* □ **fingir**
2 to be bold enough to claim: *I wouldn't pretend to know as much about the business as you do.* □ **pretender**
pretence [pri'tens] *Amer.* **pretense** *n.* **1** making believe: *a pretence of friendship.* □ **pretensión**
2 *to obtain money **by false pretences**,* by pretending to be something you are not. □ **...fraudulentamente**
pretender *n.* someone who has (false) claims to something, usually person who claims to be king. □ **pretendiente**
pretension [pri'tenʃn] *n.* claim: *she has pretensions to artistic fame,* she thinks she is a famous artist. □ **pretensión**
pretentious [pri'tenʃəs] *adj.* very showy; claiming to be more important than you are. □ **presumido; pretencioso**
pretext ['pri:tekst] *n.* excuse: *he tried to borrow money on the pretext that his wallet had been stolen.* □ **pretexto**
pretty ['priti] *adj.* **1** pleasant to look at; attractive: *he has two pretty daughters; it is said to be the prettiest village in England.* □ **bonito**
2 *you've got us into **a pretty mess**,* a terrible mess. □ **...en un bonito lío**
■ *adv.* (*informal*) quite: *she's pretty much the same as she was last week; we had a pretty good evening.* □ **bastante**
prettily *adv.* daintily. □ **lindamente; con gracia**
prettiness *n.* attractiveness/pleasantness. □ **lo bonito; lindeza**
pretzel ['pretsəl] *n.* hard biscuit flavoured with salt, made in the shape of a knot. □ **'pretzel'**
prevail [pri'veil] *v.* (*formal*) **1** ***to prevail upon,*** to persuade: *he was prevailed upon to act as chairman; can I prevail on you to push the car?* □ **persuadir**
2 to be usual/common: *calm prevails.* □ **reina la calma**
prevailing *adj.* usual/common: *prevailing winds.* □ **vientos dominantes**
prevalence ['prevələns] *n.* being widespread. □ **condición de generalizado**
prevalent *adj.* widespread: *heart disease is prevalent among westerners.* □ **muy frecuente**
prevaricate [pri'værikeit] *v.* (*formal*) to try not to tell the truth. □ **evitar la verdad**
prevarication [priværi'keiʃn] *n.* attempt not to tell the truth; lie. □ **evasivas**
prevent [pri'vent] *v.* to stop (something) happening; to stop (someone) doing something: *I was prevented from coming by the floods; we must try to prevent the public knowing about this.* □ **impedir**
prevention [pri'venʃn] *n.* stopping something happening: *the prevention of accidents.* □ **prevención**
preventive [pri'ventiv] *adj.* which stops something happening. □ **preventivo**
preventive medicine, science which tries to stop diseases occurring. □ **medicina preventiva**
preview ['pri:vju:] *n.* showing of a film/an exhibition, etc., before it is open to the general public. □ **visionado privado (filme); presentación privada (exposición)**
previous ['pri:viəs] *adj.* **1** former: *my previous job; the previous day,* the day before. □ **previo**
2 *he had a previous engagement,* he had already agreed to go somewhere else. □ **...un compromiso anterior**
■ *adv.* before: *previous to my departure.* □ **antes**
previously *adv.* before: *previously he was the manager of a record shop.* □ **anteriormente**
pre-war ['pri:wɔ:] *adj.* and *adv.* existing/happening before a war: *pre-war Britain.* □ **de preguerra**
prey [prei] *n.* animal eaten by another. □ **presa**
birds of prey, birds which eat other birds/animals. □ **aves de presa/rapiña**
■ *v.* **1** ***to prey on/upon,*** to attack animals and eat them. □ **atacar, devorar**
2 *something is preying on his mind,* something in particular is worrying him. □ **algo le está preocupando mucho**
price [prais] *n.* **1** quantity of money which has to be paid for something: *the price of meat is going up; I wouldn't go to Mr Smith's shop – his prices are too high; what's the price of that table?* □ **precio**
at a price, if you are willing to pay a lot: *you can still get asparagus in the winter, but only at a price* □ **pero a qué precio**
2 that which one must lose or suffer in order to gain something: *being recognized by people in the street is the price you have to pay for being a television star.* □ **precio**
■ *v.* to give (something) a price: *it won't sell because it's too highly priced.* □ **preciar**
to price out of: *he's priced himself out of the market,* he charges so much that no one will buy his goods. □ **pasarse con el precio (de venta)**
priceless *adj.* **1** extremely valuable. □ **de incalculable valor**
2 very funny (joke). □ **divertidísimo**
pricey *adj.* (*informal*) expensive. □ **carito**
prick [prik] *n.* pain caused by something sharp: *I felt a slight prick in my shoulder.* □ **pinchazo**
■ *v.* **1** to jab with something sharp; to make small holes in (something): *she pricked her finger on the needle.* □ **pinchar**
2 ***to prick up your ears,*** to listen attentively. □ **aguzar el oído**
3 ***to prick out*** *seedlings,* to plant small seedlings in the open ground after they have been grown in boxes. □ **trasplantar**
prickle *n.* thorn/sharp point (on a plant/hedgehog, etc.): *be careful, the rose is covered with prickles.* □ **espina**
prickly *adj.* **1** covered with prickles. □ **espinoso**
2 (person) who takes offence easily. □ **susceptible**
pride [praid] *n.* **1** pleasure in your own abilities/achievements/possessions. □ **orgullo**
to take pride in something, to be proud of something. □ **estar orgulloso de**
2 very high opinion of yourself. □ **soberbia**
3 group of lions. □ **grupo de leones**
■ *v.* ***to pride yourself on something,*** to be extremely proud of something you have done: *he prides himself on getting to the office early every morning.* □ **enorgullecerse**
priest [pri:st] *n.* person who has been ordained to serve God/to interpret the wishes of God/to carry

out formal religious duties. □ **cura**
parish priest, priest who is in charge of a parish. □ **cura párroco**
priesthood *n.* job of being a priest. □ **sacerdocio**
prig [prig] *n.* very moral and conceited person. □ **mojigato**
priggish *adj.* very moral and conceited. □ **gazmoño**
prim [prim] *adj.* very correct/unbending: *she is very prim and proper.* □ **formal; (viste) muy decorosamente**
prima ballerina [pri:məbælə'ri:nə] *n.* leading woman dancer in a ballet company. □ **primera bailarina**
prima donna [pri:mə'dɔnə] *n.* leading woman singer in opera; person who is conceited and liable to outbursts of emotion. □ **prima donna**
prima facie [praimə'feiʃi] *adv.* and *adj.* based on what seems right at first sight. □ **a primera vista**
primary ['praiməri] *adj.* basic. □ **primario**
primary colours, basic colours (red, yellow and blue) which go to make up all the other colours. □ **colores primarios**
primary election, *Amer.* first election to choose a candidate to represent a political party in a main election. □ **primarias**
primary product, raw material. □ **producto primario**
primary school, school for small children (up to the age of eleven). □ **escuela primaria**
■ *n. Amer.* first election to choose a candidate to represent a political party in a main election. □ **primarias**
primarily *adv.* mainly/mostly. □ **ante todo**
primate ['praimət] *n.* **1** leading bishop. □ **primado**
2 ***the primates,*** members of the highest level of mammals (apes, human beings, etc.). □ **los primates**
prime [praim] *adj.* **1** most important: *Prime Minister.* □ **principal; primer ministro**
2 of best quality: *prime beef.* □ **de primera clase**
3 ***prime number,*** number (such as 2, 5, 11, etc.) which can only be divided by itself or by 1. □ **número primo**
■ *n* period when you are at your best: *he's in his prime; she's a bit past her prime.* □ **flor de la vida, época mejor**
■ *v.* **1** to get (something) prepared. □ **preparar**
2 *to prime wood/metal,* to give wood/metal a first coat of special paint, before giving the top coats. □ **dar la primera mano de...**
3 to put water into a water pump/oil into a machine so as to start it working. □ **cebar**
4 to give (someone) information in advance. □ **informar a uno de antemano**
primer *n.* **1** special paint to cover an unpainted surface. □ **primera mano**
2 elementary text book. □ **cartilla; manual elemental**
primeval [prai'mi:vl] *adj.* referring to the prehistoric period: *the primeval forests.* □ **primitivo**
primitive ['primitiv] *adj.* **1** referring to very early/prehistoric times: *primitive man; a primitive form of elephant.* □ **primitivo**
2 rough/crude: *toilet facilities at the campsite are a bit primitive.* □ **primitivo**
primrose ['primrouz] *n.* wild spring flower, with small pale yellow flowers. □ **primavera**
primula ['primjulə] *n.* garden flower, like a primrose, but with many colours. □ **oreja de oso**
prince [prins] *n.* son of a king; male ruler of a small state; male member of a royal family. □ **príncipe**
princess *n.* daughter of a king; female member of a royal family; female ruler of a small state. □ **princesa**
principal ['prinsipl] *adj.* main/most important: *the principal subjects in the school timetable.* □ **principal**
■ *n.* **1** head (of a school/a college); main actor (in a play). □ **director (colegio); primera figura (obra)**
2 money on which interest is paid/capital which has been invested. □ **principal**
principality [prinsi'pæliti] *n.* land ruled by a prince. □ **principado**
principally *adv.* mainly. □ **principalmente**
principle ['prinsipl] *n.* **1** law/general rule: *the business is run on the principle that the customer is always right.* □ **principio**
2 *we agree* ***in principle,*** in a general way, though some details need to be changed. □ **...en principio**
3 personal sense of truth: *he is a man of high principles.* □ **...de nobles principios**
4 *I refused to answer the letter* ***on principle,*** because I believed it was wrong to do so. □ **por principio**
print [print] *n.* **1** mark made on something; *see also* **footprint/fingerprint.** □ **marca, señal**
2 letters printed on a page: *if you can't see well you should try to read books with large print.* □ **letras de imprenta**
3 *the book is still* ***in print/is out of print,*** is (not) available. □ **el libro está todavía disponible/está agotado**
4 ***the small print,*** conditions on a contract, usually written in very small letters. □ **la letra pequeña**
5 picture which has been printed; photograph which has been reproduced on paper; cloth with a design printed on it. □ **copia (foto); estampado (tela)**
■ *v.* **1** to mark letters on paper by a machine: *to print a book/a newspaper.* □ **imprimir**
2 to write capital letters or letters which are not joined together: *please print your name and address on the top of the form.* □ **escribir con mayúsculas**
3 to reproduce a photograph/pattern, etc.: *printed cotton.* □ **estampado**
printer *n.* **1** person who prints books/newspapers, etc. □ **impresor**
2 machine which prints automatically: *computer printer.* □ **impresora**
printing *n.* art of printing books/newspapers, etc.: *the invention of printing,* invention of movable metal letters allowing books to be printed. □ **imprenta**
printing press, machine which prints books, etc. □ **imprenta**
print-out *n.* printed information from a computer. □ **salida impresa**
prior ['praiə] *adj.* and *adv.* **1** before; previous: *prior engagement.* □ **anterior**
2 coming first (in importance): *I have a prior claim.* □ **...una petición preferente**
3 ***prior to*** *your departure,* before you leave. □ **antes de su salida**
■ *n.* male head of a priory. □ **prior**
prioress *n.* woman head of a priory. □ **priora**
priority [prai'ɔriti] *n.* **1** right to be first: *the fire engine has priority in heavy traffic; this case has priority over all the others.* □ **prioridad**
2 thing which has to be done first: *painting the house is a top priority this spring.* □ **...lo primero esta primavera**
priory ['praiəri] *n.* building where monks or nuns live. □ **priorato**
prise [praiz] *v. to prise something up,* to lift it up with the help of a lever; *to prise something out,* to pull something out using a lever; *they prised open the*

cellar door; she prised the lid off the box. □ **levantar algo con una palanca; abrir**

prism ['prizəm] *n.* glass block usually with a triangular cross-section, which splits white light up into the colours of the rainbow. □ **prisma**

prismatic [priz'mætik] *adj.* referring to a prism. □ **prismático**

prison ['prizn] *n.* place where people are kept by law after they have been found guilty of a crime: *he was sent to prison for ten years; she's in prison.* □ **cárcel**

prisoner *n.* person who is in prison. □ **preso**

prisoner of war, soldier/airman, etc., who has been captured by the enemy. □ **prisionero de guerra**

pristine ['pristi:n] *adj.* (*formal*) fresh; unspoilt. □ **prístino**

private ['praivət] *adj.* **1** belonging to one person, not to everyone: *a private house; a private conversation; private road; his private life,* his personal life as opposed to his official public life. □ **privado**

private means, personal income from investments. □ **renta**

private parts, sex organs. □ **partes pudendas**

private eye, detective employed by an ordinary person. □ **detective**

2 belonging to certain people, but not to the state or the general public: *private medicine; private enterprise.* □ **medicina privada; empresa privada**

private view, preview of an exhibition for certain invited guests. □ **inauguración privada**

■ *n.* **1** being away from other people: *can I speak to you in private?,* not in front of other people. □ **privado**

2 ordinary soldier of the lowest rank: *Private Thomas.* □ **soldado raso**

privacy ['privəsi] *n.* being away from other people: *I can never get any privacy.* □ **intimidad**

privation [prai'veiʃn] *n.* lack of money/food, etc. □ **privación**

privet ['privit] *n.* common shrub, used for garden hedges. □ **aligustre**

privilege ['privilidʒ] *n.* favour/right granted to some people but not to everyone. □ **privilegio**

privileged *adj.* having a privilege: *you should feel privileged to be here.* □ **privilegiado**

privy ['privi] *adj.* ***to be privy to*** *a secret,* (*formal*) to know the details of a secret. □ **estar al tanto de**

■ *n.* (*informal*) rough toilet outside a house. □ **retrete**

prize [praiz] *n.* money or object given to a winner: *the prize for the top scorer is $10; we are holding a raffle with several very good prizes.* □ **premio**

prize pig, pig which has won a prize in a show. □ **premiado**

■ *v.* **1** to value: *I prize his friendship very highly.* □ **valorar**

2 ***to prize something up,*** *Amer.* to lift it up with the help of a lever. *See also* **prise.** □ **levantar con una palanca**

to prize something out, to pull something out using a lever. □ **sacar con una palanca**

pro [prou] *prefix meaning* in favour of: *they're very pro-British.* □ **pro-**

■ *n.* **1** ***pros and cons*** *of a case,* arguments for and against it. □ **pros y contras**

2 (*informal*) professional sportsman/actor, etc. □ **profesional**

probable ['prɔbəbl] *adj.* likely: *it's probable that the ship was sunk by a very large wave.* □ **probable**

probability [prɔbə'biliti] *n.* likelihood. □ **probabilidad**

probably *adv.* likely: *they are probably going to be late because of the fog.* □ **probablemente**

probate ['proubeit] *n.* proving in law that a document (especially a will) is valid. □ **legalización**

probation [prə'beiʃn] *n.* **1** period when someone is being tested: *you will have three months' probation when you start your job.* □ **período de prueba**

2 period when a criminal is supervised instead of being put in prison: *he was put on probation.* □ **en libertad condicional**

probation officer, official who looks after prisoners on probation. □ **agente judicial de vigilancia**

probationary *adj.* (period) when someone is being tested: *the first three months in the job is a probationary period.* □ **de prueba**

probationer *n.* criminal who is on probation. □ **delincuente en libertad condicional**

probe [proub] *n.* **1** instrument used by doctors to examine wounds. □ **sonda**

2 thorough investigation. □ **exploración (en medicina); investigación**

3 ***space probe,*** spacecraft sent into space for scientific purposes. □ **sonda espacial**

■ *v.* to examine (something) deeply: *the surgeon probed into the wound; the police are probing the corruption racket.* □ **hacer una exploración (médico); investigar (policía)**

problem ['prɔbləm] *n.* something which is difficult to solve: *housing problem; the problem of unemployment; he's trying to solve a maths problem.* □ **problema**

problematic(al) [prɔblə'mætik(l)] *adj.* doubtful; likely to cause a problem. □ **problemático**

proboscis [prou'bɔsis] *n.* long sucking tube coming from the head of an animal (such as the trunk of an elephant/the sting of a mosquito). □ **probóscide**

proceed [prə'si:d] *v.* to continue/to go further: *before we proceed to the next item on the agenda; I was proceeding along the street at 30 miles per hour.* □ **seguir**

procedure [prə'si:dʒə] *n.* way in which something ought to be carried out: *what's the correct procedure for asking for an overdraft?* □ **procedimiento**

proceed against *v.* to start a lawsuit against (someone). □ **proceder contra**

proceedings *n. pl.* report of what takes place at a meeting. □ **acta**

proceeds ['prousi:dz] *n. pl.* money which you receive when you sell something: *he sold his car and bought a horse with the proceeds.* □ **ganancias**

process ['prouses] *n.* **1** method of making something: *building a motorway can be a very long process; this glass is made using a totally new process.* □ **proceso**

2 ***in the process,*** while doing something: *he climbed in through a bedroom window and was arrested in the process.* □ **in fraganti**

3 ***in process of*** *construction,* which is still being constructed. □ **en curso de**

■ *v.* **1** to make manufactured goods using raw materials. □ **transformar**

processed cheese, cheese which has been treated so that it will keep for a long time. □ **queso preparado**

2 to prepare (figures) for a computer; to sort out (information). □ **procesar (información)**

3 (*informal*) to walk in a procession. □ **desfilar**

processing *n.* treating raw materials; sorting out information: *data processing.* □ **transformación; procesamiento**

procession [prə'seʃn] *n.* group of people marching (with a band, etc.) in line (through the streets): *a*

funeral procession. □ **procesión (funeral); desfile (grupo musical)**
proclaim [prə'kleim] *v.* to state officially and in public. □ **proclamar**
proclamation [prɔklə'meiʃn] *n.* official public statement. □ **proclamación**
proclivity [prə'kliviti] *n.* (*formal*) tendency. □ **propensión**
procrastinate [prou'kræstineit] *v.* (*formal*) to delay/to put something off until later. □ **aplazar**
procrastination [prəkræsti'neiʃn] *n.* delaying/putting off. □ **aplazamiento**
procreate ['proukrieit] *v.* (*formal*) to produce (young). □ **procrear**
procure [prə'kjuə] *v.* (*formal*) to obtain: *really good cheese is difficult to procure.* □ **conseguir**
procurable *adj.* which can be obtained. □ **asequible**
procurator ['prɔkjureitə] *n.* ***procurator fiscal,*** (*in Scotland*) public prosecutor. □ **fiscal**
prod [prɔd] *n.* **1** poke. □ **pinchazo**
2 *give him a prod,* nudge him/try to get him to act. □ **dale un meneo**
■ *v.* (*he prodded*) to poke with a finger/stick, etc.: *he prodded the pig to see if it was fat.* □ **meter el dedo**
prodigal ['prɔdigl] *adj.* wasteful; (person) who spends a lot. □ **pródigo**
prodigally *adv.* wastefully. □ **pródigamente**
prodigy ['prɔdidʒi] *n.* remarkable person or thing: *musical prodigy,* young child who plays a musical instrument very well. □ **prodigio**
prodigious [prə'didʒəs] *adj.* remarkable/enormous. □ **prodigioso**
prodigiously *adv.* remarkably/enormously. □ **prodigiosamente**
produce ['prɔdju:s] *n.* something grown on the land: *farm produce; garden produce.* □ **productos agrícolas**
■ *v.* [prə'dju:s] **1** to bring out: *he produced his driving licence.* □ **mostrar**
2 to make/to manufacture: *the electric current produced a spark; we are producing a new sort of toothpaste.* □ **producir**
3 to put on (a play/a film). □ **presentar**
4 to yield: *the garden produces enough vegetables for us to live on.* □ **producir**
producer [prə'dju:sə] *n.* **1** person who puts on a play/a film. □ **director de escena; productor**
2 person/country which makes/grows something: *the world's most important producer of rubber.* □ **productor**
product ['prɔdʌkt] *n.* **1** thing which is manufactured/produced: *steel products.* □ **producto**
2 result: *the product of years of ill treatment.* □ **resultado**
3 (*in mathematics*) result of multiplying two numbers. □ **producto**
production [prə'dʌkʃn] *n.* **1** manufacturing: *our production of cars has fallen.* □ **producción**
2 putting on a play/film: *a new production of 'Hamlet'.* □ **producción**
productive [prə'dʌktiv] *adj.* which produces: *the garden has been very productive; I think the meeting was productive.* □ **productivo**
productivity [prɔdʌk'tiviti] *n.* rate of output/of production (in a factory). □ **productividad**
productivity bonus, bonus paid for increased output □ **comisiones por productividad**
profane [prə'fein] *adj.* not religious; blasphemous. □ **profano**
profanity [prə'fæniti] *n.* rudeness: swearing/blasphemy. □ **lo profano; blasfemia**
profess [prə'fes] *v.* to declare: *I don't profess to be an expert in computers.* □ **pretender**
professed *adj.* declared. □ **declarado**
professedly [prə'fesidli] *adv.* openly. □ **abiertamente**
profession [prə'feʃn] *n.* **1** work which needs special training/skill/knowledge: *he is a doctor by profession.* □ **profesión**
2 *the legal/medical profession,* all lawyers/doctors taken together. □ **la profesión médica; la abogacía**
3 declaration (of belief in something). □ **profesión de fe**
professional *adj.* referring to a profession; expert: *he is only an amateur gardener but his work is really professional.* □ **profesional**
a professional footballer, footballer who is paid to play. □ **profesional**
■ *n.* **1** expert: *you ought to ask a professional.* □ **profesional**
2 sportsman who is paid to play: *she used to be an amateur, but now she has turned professional.* □ **profesional**
professionalism *n.* **1** expertise/skill. □ **profesionalidad**
2 being a professional sportsman. □ **profesionalismo**
professionally *adv.* in a professional way: *he is my brother, but he is acting for me professionally.* □ **de modo profesional**
professor *n.* **1** chief teacher in a subject at a university: *the professor of engineering; Professor Smith.* □ **catedrático**
2 teacher of music/art, etc. □ **profesor**
professorship *n.* position of professor at a university. □ **cátedra**
proficient [prə'fiʃnt] *adj.* very capable (of doing something). □ **capaz**
proficiency *n.* skill in doing something: *cycling proficiency; his proficiency in mathematics.* □ **habilidad; pericia**
profile ['proufail] *n.* **1** view of someone's head from the side. □ **perfil**
to maintain a low profile, to be quiet/unobtrusive. □ **no llamar la atención**
2 short biography/description of a famous person (in a newspaper). □ **perfil**
profit ['prɔfit] *n.* money gained: *we sold the car and made a profit of $100,* we sold the car for $100 more than we paid for it; *we sold it at a profit,* we made money by selling it. □ **ganancia**
profit margin, percentage of money gained against money paid out. □ **margen de beneficio**
■ *v.* to gain: *he profited by the illness of the director.* □ **beneficiarse**
profitability [prɔfitə'biliti] *n.* ability of something to produce a profit. □ **rentabilidad**
profitable ['prɔfitəbl] *adj.* likely to produce a profit. □ **rentable**
profitably *adv.* at a profit. □ **rentablemente**
profiteer [prɔfi'tiə] *n.* person who makes too much profit. □ **especulador**
■ *v.* to make too much profit. □ **lucrarse; logrear**
profiteering *n.* making too much profit. □ **ganancias excesivas**
profligate ['prɔfligət] *adj.* and *n.* (*formal*) (person) who is very extravagant/who leads a wild life. □ **despilfarrador, libertino**
profligacy ['prɔfligəsi] *n.* extravagance/spending money wildly. □ **despilfarro**

proforma [prouˈfɔːmə] *adj.* and *n.* (invoice) sent asking the purchaser to pay in advance. □ **(factura) pro forma**

profound [prəˈfaund] *adj.* very serious/very deep (understanding/thought): *profound sympathy.* □ **profundo**

profoundly *adv.* extremely: *I am profoundly sorry.* □ **profundamente**

profundity [prəˈfʌnditi] *n.* depth (of thought or understanding). □ **profundidad**

profuse [prəˈfjuːs] *adj.* abundant/ excessive. □ **profuso**

profusely *adv.* excessively/too much: *he thanked her profusely.* □ **con profusión**

profusion [prəˈfjuːʒn] *n.* very large quantity: *a profusion of flowers.* □ **profusión**

progeny [ˈprɔdʒəni] *n.* (*no pl.*) (*formal*) children/ offspring. □ **progenie**

progesterone [prouˈdʒestəroun] *n.* hormone which stops women ovulating, and helps the uterus in the first stages of pregnancy. □ **progesterona**

prognosticate [prɔgˈnɔstikeit] *v.* (*formal*) to foretell. □ **pronosticar**

prognosis [prɔgˈnousis] *n.* forecast. □ **pronóstico**

programme [ˈprougræm] *Amer.* **program** [ˈprougrəm] *n.* **1** list of items in an entertainment: *a theatre programme; what is on the programme this afternoon?,* what are we doing this afternoon? □ **programa**

2 show/item on TV or radio: *a comedy programme; a quiz programme.* □ **programa**

3 (*always:* ***program***) instructions given to a computer. □ **programa**

■ *v.* **1** to arrange shows on TV/radio. □ **programar**

2 (*always:* ***to program***) to give instructions to a computer. □ **programar**

programmer *n.* **1** person who arranges shows on TV/radio. □ **programador**

2 person who programs a computer. □ **programador**

progress [ˈprougres] *n.* movement forwards: *we are making progress; work is now in progress on the new dam; they are making slow progress with the new road.* □ **progreso**

progress report, report showing how much progress is being made. □ **informe sobre la marcha de los trabajos**

■ *v.* [prəˈgres] to advance: *how are you progressing with your work? is the work progressing satisfactorily?* □ **progresar**

progression [prəˈgreʃn] *n.* advance/movement forwards. □ **progresión**

progressive *adj.* **1** (movement) in stages. □ **progresivo**

2 advanced (ideas). □ **progresista**

progressively *adv.* by stages: *his illness got progressively worse.* □ **progresivamente**

prohibit [prəˈhibit] *v.* to forbid: *smoking is prohibited in the cinema.* □ **prohibir**

prohibition [prouhiˈbiʃn] *n.* forbidding (especially the sale of alcohol). □ **prohibición**

prohibitive [prəˈhibitiv] *adj. prohibitive price,* price which is so high that you cannot pay it. □ **prohibitivo**

project [ˈprɔdʒekt] *n.* **1** plan: *a building project; a project for a new housing development.* □ **proyecto**

2 work planned by students on their own: *he is working on a project about life in medieval Europe.* □ **proyecto**

■ *v.* [prəˈdʒekt] **1** to plan: *the projected town hall; his projected tour of Eastern Europe.* □ **proyectar**

2 to throw (a picture on a screen). □ **proyectar**

projectile [prəˈdʒektail] *n.* something which is thrown/shot: *his car was hit by several projectiles.* □ **proyectil**

projecting *adj.* sticking/jutting/standing out: *he hit his head against a projecting beam.* □ **saliente**

projection *n.* **1** something planned/forecast: *our projection of sales over the next three years.* □ **nuestras perspectivas de...**

2 (*in geography*) picture of the shape of the earth on a flat surface. □ **planisferio**

3 something which stands/sticks out. □ **saliente**

4 action of projecting a picture on a screen. □ **proyección**

projector *n.* apparatus for throwing pictures on a screen: *cine projector; slide projector.* □ **proyector**

prolapse [ˈproulæps] *n.* state where an organ in the body moves out of place. □ **prolapso**

proletariat [prouliˈtɛəriət] *n.* working class. □ **proletariado**

proletarian [prouliˈtɛəriən] *adj.* and *n.* (member) of the working class. □ **proletario**

prolific [prəˈlifik] *adj.* producing many children; very productive: *a prolific writer of pop songs.* □ **prolífico**

prolix [ˈprouliks] *adj.* (*formal*) long-winded/using too many words. □ **prolijo**

prologue [ˈproulɔg] *n.* piece spoken as the introduction of a play or poem; preliminary section in a book. □ **prólogo**

prolong [prəˈlɔŋ] *v.* to lengthen. □ **prolongar**

prolongation [proulɔŋˈgeiʃn] *n.* lengthening. □ **prolongación**

promenade [prɔməˈnɑːd] (*informal*) **prom** *n.* **1** terrace along the seashore where you can walk. □ **paseo marítimo**

promenade deck, (*on a ship*) deck where passengers can stroll about. □ **cubierta de paseo**

2 ***prom concerts/the proms,*** inexpensive concerts of classical music where part of the audience stands and can walk about. □ **conciertos populares**

prominence [ˈprɔminəns] *n.* **1** standing out; something which stands out. □ **prominencia**

2 fame: *to give someone prominence,* to make someone appear famous. □ **importancia**

prominent *adj.* **1** standing out/easily seen: *she has a very prominent scar on her cheek.* □ **prominente**

2 famous: *a prominent musician; he played a prominent part in the Russian Revolution.* □ **destacado**

prominently *adv.* so as to be easily seen. □ **destacadamente**

promiscuous [prəˈmiskjuəs] *adj.* (person) who does not prefer one thing to another, especially who has sexual relations with many people. □ **promiscuo**

promiscuity [prɔmiˈskjuːiti] *n.* having sexual relations with many people. □ **promiscuidad**

promise [ˈprɔmis] *n.* **1** word you give to say that you will definitely do something: *he broke his promise that he would not see her again.* □ **promesa**

2 *to show great promise,* to make people feel that you will do well in the future. □ **prometer mucho**

■ *v.* **1** to give your word that you will definitely do something: *he promised to telephone as soon as he got home.* □ **prometer**

2 to show signs of what may happen in the future: *the discussion promised to be quite bitter.* □ **...prometía ser bastante...**

promising *adj.* (person) who is likely to succeed. □ **prometedor**

promissory [ˈprɔmisəri] *adj.* ***promissory note,*** note in which you promise to pay someone money on a certain date. □ **promisorio; pagaré (nota)**

promontory ['prɔməntəri] *n.* piece of land jutting out into the sea. □ **promontorio**
promote [prə'mout] *v.* **1** to give (someone) a better job: *he was promoted to be branch manager.* □ **ascender**
2 to advertise: *we are promoting a new detergent.* □ **promocionar**
3 to encourage: *to promote international understanding.* □ **fomentar**
promotion [prə'mouʃn] *n.* **1** advancement to a better job. □ **ascenso**
2 advertising (a new product). □ **promoción**
promotional *adj.* (material) used in advertising. □ **de promoción**
prompt [prɔmpt] *adj.* done at once; quick/rapid: *a prompt reply.* □ **pronto; una respuesta rápida**
■ *v.* **1** to suggest to (someone) that he should do something: *the article prompted me to enquire about air fares to Paris; he didn't need any prompting,* he did it of his own free will. □ **mover a uno (a hacer algo)**
2 to tell an actor words which he has forgotten. □ **apuntar**
prompter *n.* person who prompts an actor. □ **apuntador**
promptly *adv.* immediately; rapidly: *he's always paid his bills promptly.* □ **con prontitud**
promptness *n.* quickness. □ **prontitud**
promulgate ['prɔmlgeit] *v.* (*formal*) to make (a law) known to the public. □ **promulgar**
prone [proun] *adj.* **1** (lying) flat. □ **prono; boca abajo**
2 likely: *he is prone to lose his temper; she's accident prone,* she often has accidents. □ **propenso a...**
prong [prɔŋ] *n.* one of the sharp points of a fork; point of an attack. □ **diente (de tenedor); punta (de ataque)**
pronged *adj.* with prongs: *a three pronged fork; a two-pronged attack.* □ **de tres puntas**
pronoun ['prounaun] *n.* (*in grammar*) a word which stands in place of a noun (such as 'he', 'me', 'mine', 'who', etc.). □ **pronombre**
pronounce [prə'nauns] *v.* **1** to speak a series of sounds which form a word: *how do you pronounce l-a-u-g-h?* □ **pronunciar**
2 to declare in a formal way. □ **declarar**
pronounced *adj.* noticeable: *he has a pronounced Scottish accent; there was a pronounced smell of onions.* □ **pronunciado**
pronouncement *n.* official/formal statement. □ **declaración**
pronunciation [prənʌnsi'eiʃn] *n.* way of pronouncing words: *he speaks German fluently, but his pronunciation is poor.* □ **pronunciación**
proof [pru:f] *n.* **1** something which proves/which shows that something is true: *the police have proof that he was not at home that night.* □ **prueba**
2 percentage of alcohol in a drink: *that whisky is 40° proof.* □ **graduación**
3 test sheet of printing which has to be corrected by the author before the book can be produced; copy of a photograph/lithograph, etc., for the artist to examine to see if it is acceptable. □ **prueba; galerada**
■ *adj.* safe against/not affected by: *heat-proof paint,* paint which is not affected by heat; *the town is proof against attack.* □ **resistente, a prueba de**
prop [prɔp] *n.* **1** support; stick which holds something up. □ **puntal**
2 *props,* articles used in the production of a play/film. □ **accesorios**
■ *v.* (*he propped*) to support: *the roof was propped up with posts; he propped the door open with a stick.* □ **apuntalar**
propaganda [prɔpə'gændə] *n.* spreading of (frequently false) political ideas. □ **propaganda política**
propagandist *n.* person who spreads political ideas. □ **propagandista**
propagate ['prɔpəgeit] *v.* **1** to make (new plants) by sowing seed/taking cuttings. □ **propagar**
2 to spread (ideas). □ **propagar**
propagation [prɔpə'geiʃn] *n.* making of new plants; spreading of ideas. □ **propagación**
propagator *n.* small glass-covered box for growing new plants. □ **propagador**
propane ['proupein] *n.* colourless gas used for heating and cooking. □ **propano**
propel [prə'pel] *v.* (*he propelled*) to send forward: *the car is propelled by electricity; the model plane is propelled by an elastic band.* □ **propulsar**
propeller *n.* mechanism with blades which turns rapidly to drive boats and aircraft. □ **hélice**
propensity [prə'pensiti] *n.* (*formal*) tendency/leaning: *he has a propensity for stealing things in shops.* □ **propensión**
proper ['prɔpə] *adj.* **1** right: *he didn't put the book back in the proper place; is this the proper way to eat oysters? seven o'clock in the morning is hardly the proper time to drink whisky.* □ **apropiado**
2 *we're giving the office a proper cleaning,* a thorough cleaning. □ **...una limpieza a fondo**
3 ***proper noun,*** (*in grammar*) noun which is a name of a person/a country, etc. (such as 'Russia', 'Anne', 'Hamlet'). □ **nombre propio**
4 very correct. □ **exacto**
5 *she's very* ***prim and proper,*** very conventional/very respectable. □ **muy formal**
6 itself exactly: *this has nothing to do with the lawsuit proper; the text proper starts on page 23.* □ **propiamente dicho**
properly *adv.* **1** rightly/correctly: *he quite properly called the police; they did not connect the water taps properly.* □ **bien; como es debido**
2 thoroughly. □ **completamente**
property ['prɔpəti] *n.* **1** thing which belongs to someone. □ **propiedad**
lost property, personal possessions which have been left behind on trains, etc. □ **objetos perdidos**
2 building or buildings: *he has a large property in the north,* a large estate; *residential property is getting more expensive; he bought a pre-war property,* a house built before 1939. □ **propiedad; compró un inmueble de antes...**
3 ***properties,*** articles used in the production of a play/film. □ **accesorios**
property man, person responsible for all the articles used in a play/film. □ **encargado de los accesorios**
4 quality: *this new type of glass has several interesting properties.* □ **propiedad**
prophecy ['prɔfəsi] *n.* foretelling what will happen in the future: *prophecies of doom.* □ **profecía**
prophesy ['prɔfisai] *v.* to foretell what will happen in the future: *he prophesied the coming of a new leader.* □ **profetizar**
prophet ['prɔfit] *n.* person who foretells what will happen; religious leader. □ **profeta**
prophetic [prə'fetik] *adj.* which is like a prophecy. □ **profético**
prophylaxis [prɔfi'læksis] *n.* prevention of a disease. □ **profilaxis**
prophylactic [prɔfi'læktik] *adj.* and *n.* (substance) which prevents disease. □ **profiláctico**
propitiate [prə'piʃieit] *v.* (*formal*) to appease/to

make someone less angry. □ **aplacar**
propitiation [prəpiʃi'eiʃn] *n.* act of appeasing. □ **aplacamiento**
propitiatory [prə'piʃiətəri] *adj.* which tries to appease/to make less angry: *a propitiatory gesture.* □ **propiciatorio**
propitious [prə'piʃəs] *adj.* favourable. □ **propicio**
proportion [prə'pɔːʃn] *n.* **1** part (of a total): *only a small proportion of the electors voted; divide up the proceeds in equal proportions.* □ **proporción**
2 relationship between a part and a total: *what's the proportion of sand to cement in this concrete?* □ **proporción**
3 *you have* ***to keep a sense of proportion,*** keep a feeling of the right measure. □ **...el sentido de la medida**
4 ***in/out of proportion,*** (not) in the right amount; (not) sensibly: *the expense is out of all proportion to the income.* □ **en proporción con; el gasto está desproporcionado con...**
5 *the proportions of a building or room,* the relative height/length, etc. □ **dimensiones**
proportional *adj.* which is directly related. □ **proporcional**
proportional representation, system of voting where the votes cast for each party are more or less accurately reflected in the number of seats each party has in parliament. □ **representación proporcional**
proportionally *adv.* in proportion. □ **proporcionalmente**
proportionate *adj.* in proportion. □ **proporcionado**
propose [prə'pouz] *v.* **1** to suggest/to make a suggestion: *I propose we all go to bed; what do you propose to do now? to propose a toast/a motion,* to speak formally suggesting a toast or a motion; *he proposed Mrs Smith for the position of treasurer.* □ **proponer**
2 ***to propose to someone,*** to ask someone to marry you. □ **pedir la mano**
proposal *n.* **1** suggestion/something which is suggested: *can I make a proposal?* □ **propuesta**
2 asking someone to marry you. □ **petición de mano**
proposer *n.* person who proposes (a motion). □ **ponente**
proposition [prɔpə'ziʃn] *n.* **1** something which has been proposed: *I have a proposition to make to you.* □ **proposición**
2 *a tough proposition,* problem which is difficult to solve. □ **un asunto difícil de resolver**
propound [prə'paund] *v.* (*formal*) to put forward (an idea). □ **proponer**
proprietor [prə'praiətə] *n.* owner: *he's the proprietor of the local restaurant.* □ **propietario**
proprietary [prə'praiətri] *adj.* **1** referring to a proprietor. □ **propietario**
2 ***proprietary medicine,*** medicine which is sold under a brand name and manufactured by a particular company. □ **medicamento registrado**
propriety [prə'praiəti] *n.* decency; good behaviour. □ **decencia**
propulsion [prə'pʌlʃn] *n.* moving forward: *jet propulsion,* being moved forward by jets. □ **propulsión**
pro rata [prou'rɑːtə] *adv.* and *adj.* in proportion: *the fee is $10 per hour – periods of less than one hour will be charged pro rata.* □ **a prorrata, proporcionalmente**
prorogue [prou'roug] *v.* to end a session of parliament. □ **levantar**
prosaic [prə'zeiik] *adj.* ordinary; not poetic; rather dull. □ **prosaico**
prosaically *adv.* in a dull way/not poetically. □ **prosaicamente**
proscenium [prə'siːniəm] *n.* part of a stage in a theatre which sticks out beyond the curtain. □ **proscenio**
proscenium arch, arch above the front part of a stage in a theatre. □ **embocadura**
proscribe [prou'skraib] *v.* (*formal*) to forbid by law. □ **proscribir**
prose [prouz] *n.* writing which is not in verse. □ **prosa**
prosy *adj.* verbose/wordy. □ **prosaico; tedioso**
prosecute ['prɔsikjuːt] *v.* to bring (someone) to court to answer a charge: *he was prosecuted for dangerous driving.* □ **procesar**
prosecution [prɔsi'kjuːʃn] *n.* **1** court case against someone. □ **procesamiento, causa**
2 people who have accused someone of a crime in a court: *a witness for the prosecution.* □ **parte acusadora**
prosecutor ['prɔsikjuːtə] *n.* person who prosecutes. □ **demandante**
public prosecutor, government lawyer who accuses a criminal in a law court on behalf of the state. □ **acusador público**
prosody ['prɔsədi] *n.* rules of writing poetry. □ **prosodia**
prospect ['prɔspekt] *n.* **1** view. □ **vista**
2 ***to have something in prospect,*** to expect something to happen. □ **tener algo en perspectiva**
3 *there's no prospect of an end to the strike,* the strike is not expected to end soon. □ **no hay perspectivas de...**
4 *pl.* ***prospects,*** future possibilities: *the prospects for this year's harvest are excellent; he has a job with very good prospects.* □ **perspectivas**
■ *v.* [prə'spekt] to search (a land for minerals). □ **hacer una prospección**
prospective [prə'spektiv] *adj.* in view/possible: *a prospective client.* □ **posible**
prospector *n.* person who searches for minerals. □ **prospector**
prospectus [prə'spektəs] *n.* paper giving information about something in the hope of attracting clients/customers. □ **folleto**
prosper ['prɔspə] *v.* to succeed; to become rich. □ **prosperar**
prosperity [prɔ'speriti] *n.* being rich. □ **prosperidad**
prosperous ['prɔspərəs] *adj.* wealthy/rich. □ **próspero**
prostate ['prɔsteit] *n.* gland round the bladder in men. □ **próstata**
prostitute ['prɔstitjuːt] *n.* person who receives money for sexual intercourse. □ **prostituta**
■ *v.* ***to prostitute your talents,*** to use your talents in a low/unworthy way. □ **prostituir tu talento**
prostitution [prɔsti'tjuːʃn] *n.* offering sexual intercourse for payment. □ **prostitución**
prostrate ['prɔstreit] *adj.* (lying) flat. □ **boca abajo**
■ *v.* **1** ***to prostrate oneself before someone,*** to fall down in front of someone (as a mark of respect, fear, etc.). □ **prosternarse**
2 *he was prostrated by an attack of malaria,* he had to stay lying down. □ **quedó postrado por...**
prostration *n.* lying down/falling down in front of someone. □ **postración**
protagonist [prə'tægənist] *n.* main character in a play/book, etc.: leader of one side in a conflict. □ **protagonista**
protect [prə'tekt] *v.* to defend against attack; to shield against dirt/germs, etc.: *he was protected by*

a steel helmet; the town was protected by a high wall. □ **proteger**
protection [prə'tekʃn] *n.* **1** shelter: *this raincoat is no protection against heavy rain.* □ **protección**
2 defence: *the President was under the protection of the army.* □ **protección**
protective *adj.* which protects: *you must wear protective clothing when you go down a mine.* □ **protector**
protector *n.* person/thing which protects. □ **protector**
protégé ['prɔteʒei] *n.* person (usually young) who is supported in work with money or advice by someone else. □ **protegido**
protein ['prouti:n] *n.* one of the elements in food which is necessary to keep the human body working properly. □ **proteína**
protest ['proutest] *n.* **1** statement that you object or disapprove: *they made a protest against unemployment.* □ **protesta**
2 *I will do it, but only* ***under protest,*** only if I make it clear that I object. □ **lo haré, pero que conste mi desacuerdo**
3 *they went on strike* ***in protest*** *against low wages,* to show that they objected to low wages. □ **...como protesta por los bajos salarios**
protest march, march in procession to show that you protest against something. □ **marcha de protesta**
■ *v.* **1** to object/to raise a violent objection: *they protested against the plans/Amer. they protested the plans.* □ **protestar**
2 to state solemnly: *he protested his innocence.* □ **declarar**
Protestant ['prɔtistənt] *adj.* and *n.* (member) of a Christian church which is not part of the Roman Catholic Church. □ **protestante**
protestation [prɔti'steiʃn] *n.* violent statement of protest. □ **protesta enérgica**
protocol ['proutəkɔl] *n.* correct (diplomatic) behaviour. □ **protocolo**
proton ['proutɔn] *n.* nucleus of a hydrogen atom, found in all atoms. □ **protón**
protoplasm ['proutəplæzəm] *n.* basic jelly-like substance in all matter. □ **protoplasma**
prototype ['proutətaip] *n.* first model of a new machine. □ **prototipo**
protracted [prə'træktid] *adj.* very lengthy. □ **prolongado**
protractor *n.* semicircular device, used for measuring angles in geometry. □ **transportador**
protrude [prə'tru:d] *v.* to stick out: *he has protruding teeth.* □ **sobresalir**
protuberance [prə'tju:bərəns] *n.* bump/swelling. □ **protuberancia**
protuberant *adj.* which swells outwards. □ **protuberante**
proud [praud] *adj.* full of pride; thinking a lot of yourself/of something belonging to you: *he is very proud of his cooking; she is proud of her children; he is too proud to go into an ordinary pub,* he thinks too much of himself. □ **orgulloso**
■ *adv.* ***to do someone proud:*** *he did himself proud,* (*informal*) he gave himself a large meal. □ **se dio un homenaje**
proudly *adv.* with pride; with great satisfaction: *proudly he showed off his new car.* □ **orgullosamente**
prove [pru:v] *v.* **1** to demonstrate that something is right: *the police proved he was not at home that night; it's difficult to prove that there is life on other planets.* □ **demostrar**
2 to turn out: *the news proved to be true; the weather proved to be even worse than they expected.* □ **demostrarse, resultar**
proven [prouvn] *adj.* **1** which has been shown to be right: *she's a lawyer of proven ability.* □ **probado**
2 ***not proven,*** (*in Scotland*) decision to release a prisoner because his guilt cannot be proved or disproved. □ **absuelto por falta de pruebas**
provenance ['prɔvənəns] *n.* (*formal*) origin. □ **procedencia**
proverb ['prɔvə:b] *n.* saying which has a moral/which teaches you something (such as 'many hands make light work'). □ **proverbio**
proverbial [prə'və:biəl] *adj.* well known: *his generosity is proverbial.* □ **proverbial**
provide [prə'vaid] *v.* **1** to supply: *he provided us with a car; the hosts are providing the drink.* □ **suministrar**
2 *he has to provide for five children,* earn enough to feed and clothe them. □ **tiene que mantener a...**
3 to take care of: *these expenses are provided for in the accounts.* □ **estipular**
provided that, providing *conj.* on condition that: *I will come provided that someone pays for me/providing someone pays for me.* □ **con tal que**
providence ['prɔvidəns] *n.* (lucky) fate. □ **providencia**
provident *adj.* careful to think about the future and keep money/stores for use in time of need. □ **previsor**
providential [prɔvi'denʃl] *adj.* lucky. □ **providencial**
province ['prɔvins] *n.* **1** large administrative division of a country. □ **provincia**
the provinces, country districts. □ **las provincias**
2 area of knowledge; area of responsibility. □ **esfera**
provincial [prə'vinʃl] *adj.* **1** referring to a province/to the provinces. □ **provincial**
2 *they're rather provincial,* narrow-minded/not very civilized. □ **son algo provincianos**
provision [prə'viʒn] *n.* **1** thing that is provided. □ **provisión**
to make provision for something, to see that something is allowed for in the future. □ **atender a las necesidades de...**
2 *pl.* ***provisions,*** food. □ **provisiones**
3 condition in a document: *one of the provisions of the treaty.* □ **disposición**
■ *v.* to stock up with food. □ **abastecer**
provisional *adj.* temporary. □ **provisional**
provisionally *adv.* temporarily. □ **provisionalmente**
proviso [prə'vaizou] *n.* condition. □ **condición**
provoke [prə'vouk] *v.* **1** to incite (someone) to do something violent: *the crowd was provoked by the actions of the referee; don't provoke me,* don't make me angry. □ **provocar**
2 to make (a reaction) start. □ **provocar.**
provocation [prɔvə'keiʃn] *n.* action of provoking. □ **provocación**
provocative [prə'vɔkətiv] *adj.* likely to provoke a violent response. □ **provocativo**
prow [prau] *n.* front end of a ship. □ **proa**
prowess ['praues] *n.* (*formal*) skill. □ **habilidad**
prowl [praul] *n.* ***to be on the prowl,*** to be creeping about. □ **ronda**
■ *v.* to creep about quietly: *tigers were prowling round the camp.* □ **merodear**
prowler *n.* person who creeps about, especially a burglar. □ **merodeador**
proximity [prɔk'simiti] *n.* closeness. □ **proximidad**

in close proximity to something, very close to something. □ **muy cerca de**
proxy ['prɔksi] *n.* **1** document giving someone the power to act/to vote on your behalf: *to vote by proxy.* □ **poder; votar por poderes**
2 person who acts/votes on your behalf. □ **representante, apoderado**
prude [pru:d] *n.* person who has very strict moral principles and who is easily shocked. □ **mojigato**
prudery, prudishness *n.* state of having very strict principles. □ **mojigatería**
prudish *adj.* with strict principles and easily shocked. □ **mojigato**
prudence ['pru:dns] *n.* great care/caution. □ **prudencia**
prudent *adj.* very careful/very cautious. □ **prudente**
prune [pru:n] *n.* dried plum. □ **ciruela pasa**
■ *v.* to cut branches off a tree; to cut back a tree/shrub (to keep it in good shape or to encourage it to produce flowers); to cut back (expenditure, etc.); to cut out (parts of a book, etc.). □ **podar (árbol); reducir gastos; mutilar (un texto)**
pry [prai] *v.* **1** to look inquisitively into something: *she is always prying into my affairs.* □ **fisgar**
2 *Amer.* to lift open with a lever; to prise/to prize: *they pried open the cellar door.* □ **abrir con una palanca**
PS [pi:'es] *short for* post scriptum, additional note at the end of a letter. □ **P.D. (postdata)**
psalm [sɑ:m] *n.* religious song from the Book of Psalms in the Bible. □ **salmo**
psephology [se'fɔlədʒi] *n.* study of elections/voting patterns and opinion polls of voters. □ **estudio de cuestiones electorales**
psephologist *n.* person who specializes in psephology. □ **experto en elecciones**
pseudo- ['sju:dou] *prefix meaning* false/pretending: *pseudo-intellectuals.* □ **pseudo-**
pseudonym ['sju:dənim] *n.* false/invented name: *he writes under a pseudonym.* □ **seudónimo**
psychedelic [saikə'delik] *adj.* so full of bright moving colours that you become hallucinated. □ **psicodélico**
psychiatry [sai'kaiətri] *n.* study of mental disease. □ **psiquiatría**
psychiatric [saiki'ætrik] *adj.* referring to psychiatry: *a psychiatric ward in a hospital.* □ **psiquiátrico**
psychiatrist [sai'kaiətrist] *n.* person who studies and treats mental disease. □ **psiquiatra**
psychic ['saikik] *adj.* and *n.* (person) in contact with supernatural forces. □ **psíquico**
psychoanalysis [saikouə'næləsis] *n.* treatment of mental disorder by discussion. □ **psicoanálisis**
psychoanalyst [saikou'ænəlist] *n.* person who treats patients by psychoanalysis. □ **psicoanalista**
psychology [sai'kɔlədʒi] *n.* study of the human mind. □ **psicología**
psychological [saikə'lɔdʒikl] *adj.* referring to psychology. □ **psicológico**
psychologically *adv.* mentally. □ **psicológicamente**
psychologist [sai'kɔlədʒist] *n.* person who studies the human mind. □ **psicólogo**
psychopath ['saikəpæθ] *n.* dangerous, mentally unstable criminal. □ **psicópata**
psychopathic [saikə'pæθik] *adj.* mentally unstable in a dangerous way. □ **psicopático**
psychosis [sai'kousis] *n.* (*pl. psychoses*) mental illness which changes the patient's personality. □ **psicosis**
psychosomatic [saikousə'mætik] *adj.* (physical illness) created by a mental state. □ **psicosomático**
pub [pʌb] *n.* (*informal*) public house/inn: *to go on a pub crawl,* to go from inn to inn having a drink in each. □ **'pub'**
puberty ['pju:bəti] *n.* period of adolescence when a person becomes sexually mature. □ **pubertad**
pubic ['pju:bik] *adj.* referring to the area around the sexual organs. □ **púbico**
public ['pʌblik] *adj.* **1** referring to the people in general: *public library; he made a public announcement.* □ **público**
public holiday, holiday for everyone. □ **fiesta**
public house, inn/place where you can buy and drink alcohol. □ **bar**
2 ***public school,*** (*in Britain*) private fee-paying school which is not part of the state system; (*in the USA*) a state school. □ **colegio privado (G.B.); colegio público (Amér.)**
■ *n.* people in general: *the British public.* □ **los ingleses**
in public, in the open; in front of everyone. □ **en público**
publican *n.* person who runs a public house. □ **tabernero**
publication [pʌbli'keiʃn] *n.* **1** making public/publishing: *the publication of a newspaper.* □ **publicación**
2 book/paper which has been published: *a new publication on archaeology.* □ **publicación**
publicist ['pʌblisist] *n.* person who attracts people's attention to a product. □ **publicista**
publicity [pʌb'lisiti] *n.* advertising; attracting people's attention to a product. □ **publicidad**
publicize *v.* to attract people's attention to a product/to make publicity for a product: *we are publicizing a brand of petrol.* □ **anunciar**
publicly *adv.* in public: *he publicly attacked the government.* □ **públicamente**
public relations *n.* maintaining good relations between an organization and the public. □ **relaciones públicas**
public-spirited *adj.* (person) who acts energetically for the good of the community. □ **lleno de civismo**
publish ['pʌbliʃ] *v.* to make publicly known; to bring out a book/newspaper for sale. □ **editar, publicar**
publisher *n.* person who produces books/newspapers for sale. □ **editor**
publishing *n.* producing books/newspapers for sale. □ **publicación**
publishing house, firm which publishes books. □ **editorial, casa editora**
puce [pju:s] *adj.* dark purplish red. □ **de color castaño rojizo**
puck [pʌk] *n.* small disc which is hit in ice hockey. □ **disco**
pucker ['pʌkə] *n.* wrinkle/fold. □ **frunce**
■ *v.* to wrinkle (your brow). □ **fruncir (el ceño)**
pudding ['pudiŋ] *n.* **1** dessert/sweet course at the end of the meal: *what's for pudding?* □ **postre**
2 sweet food which has been cooked or boiled. □ **budín**
rice pudding, dish made with rice, sugar and milk. □ **budín de arroz (arroz con leche)**
Christmas pudding, boiled food like a cake made with flour, eggs, dried fruit, etc., eaten at Christmas. □ **pastel de Navidad**
3 ***black pudding,*** sausage made with blood. □ **morcilla**
puddle ['pʌdl] *n.* small pool of water (such as one left after rain). □ **charco**
puerile ['pjuərail] *adj.* childish/stupid. □ **pueril**
puff [pʌf] *n.* **1** small breath: *puff of air; puff of smoke.*

□ **soplo de aire; bocanada de humo**
2 ***powder puff,*** light pad for powdering the skin. □ **borla de polvos**
3 ***puff pastry,*** light sort of pastry. □ **hojaldre**
■ *v.* to blow: *he was puffing as he ran up the hill.* □ **jadear**
puffed (out) *adj.* (*informal*) out of breath. □ **sin aliento**
puffy *adj.* swollen (face). □ **hinchado**
puffin ['pʌfin] *n.* black and white bird with a large coloured beak, living near the sea. □ **frailecillo**
pugilist ['pju:dʒilist] *n.* (*formal*) fighter/boxer. □ **púgil**
pugnacious [pʌg'neiʃəs] *adj.* (*formal*) (person) who likes fighting; quarrelsome. □ **belicoso**
pugnacity [pʌg'næsiti] *n.* liking fighting. □ **belicosidad**
puisne ['pju:ni] *adj.* (judge) who is junior to other judges in the supreme court. □ **juez asesor**
puke [pju:k] *v.* ***to puke (up),*** (*informal*) to vomit. □ **vomitar**
pukka ['pʌkə] *adj.* (*informal*) real. □ **auténtico**
pule [pju:l] *v.* (*of children*) to wail/to whimper. □ **lloriquear**
pull [pul] *n.* **1** act of dragging/moving something towards you: *give it a big pull.* □ **tirón**
2 influence: *the pull of earth's gravity; he has a lot of pull,* (*informal*) he is influential. □ **atracción**
3 handle (which has to be pulled): *door pull/bell pull.* □ **tirador**
■ *v.* **1** to move (something) by dragging; to move (something) towards you: *the horse was pulling the cart; he pulled the bundle of papers out of his pocket.* □ **tirar**
2 *he pulled a face,* he made a grimace. □ **hacer un gesto**
3 to strain: *I have pulled a muscle in my back.* □ **tener un tirón**
pull down *v.* **1** to bring (something) down by pulling: *to pull down the branch of a tree.* □ **echar abajo**
2 *they pulled down the old town hall,* demolished it. □ **derribar**
pull in *v.* to drive close to the side of the road (and stop): *we pulled in to let the ambulance go past.* □ **retirarse**
pull off *v.* **1** to take off (a piece of clothing/a handle, etc.) by pulling. □ **quitarse**
2 (*informal*) to succeed in doing (something): *he pulled it off; the gang pulled off a daring bank robbery.* □ **lograr**
pull round, pull through *v.* to recover from an illness. □ **recuperarse**
pull together *v.* ***to pull oneself together:*** *he pulled himself together,* he became calmer/he controlled his emotions. □ **serenarse**
pull up *v.* **1** to stop (in a vehicle): *we pulled up at the traffic lights.* □ **pararse**
2 to raise by pulling. □ **levantar tirando**
3 *he'll have* ***to pull his socks up,*** (*informal*) he'll have to do better/try harder. □ **tendrá que espabilar**
pullet ['pulit] *n.* young chicken. □ **pollo**
pulley ['puli] *n.* apparatus for lifting heavy weights with a grooved wheel round which a rope runs. □ **polea**
pullman ['pulmən] *n.* **1** luxurious railway carriage. □ **pullman**
2 *Amer.* sleeping car (on a train). □ **coche-cama**
pullover ['pulouvə] *n.* piece of clothing made of wool covering the top part of the body and which you pull on over your head. □ **jersey**
pulmonary ['pʌlmənri] *adj.* referring to the lungs: *pulmonary diseases.* □ **pulmonar**
pulp [pʌlp] *n.* squashy mass. □ **pulpa**
wood pulp, soft mixture of wood and water which is used for making paper. □ **pulpa de madera**
■ *v.* to crush to a squashy mass. □ **reducir a pulpa**
pulpit ['pulpit] *n.* enclosed platform in a church where the priest preaches. □ **púlpito**
pulsar ['pʌlsə] *n.* invisible star which sends out radio signals. □ **púlsar**
pulse [pʌls] *n.* **1** regular beat of the heart. □ **pulso**
to feel/take someone's pulse: *he took your pulse,* he felt the beating of your heart with his fingers placed on your wrist. □ **le tomó el pulso**
2 dried seed of peas/beans. □ **semillas de legumbres**
pulsate [pʌl'seit] *v.* to throb regularly. □ **latir**
pulsation [pʌl'seiʃn] *n.* regular throbbing. □ **pulsación**
pulverize ['pʌlvəraiz] *v.* to crush to powder. □ **pulverizar**
pulverization [pʌlvərai'zeiʃn] *n.* crushing to powder. □ **pulverización**
pumice (stone) ['pʌmis('stoun)] *n.* block of light grey porous lava used for rubbing stains off your skin. □ **piedra pómez**
pummel ['pʌml] *v.* (*he pummelled*) to hit someone with many blows. □ **aporrear**
pump [pʌmp] *n.* **1** machine for forcing liquids or air: *bicycle pump,* device for blowing up the tyres of a bicycle. □ **bomba**
petrol pump, machine for putting petrol into a car. □ **surtidor de gasolina**
wind pump, device for forcing water up out of the ground, which is driven by the wind. □ **bomba de viento**
2 soft dancing shoe. □ **zapatilla**
■ *v.* **1** to force (liquid/air) with a pump: *they pumped the water out of the boat; he pumped up the tyres of his bicycle.* □ **bombear (líquido); inflar (neumático)**
2 ***to pump someone,*** (*informal*) to ask someone searching questions. □ **sonsacar**
pumpkin ['pʌmpkin] *n.* large round orange-coloured vegetable. □ **calabaza**
pun [pʌn] *n.* play with words of different meanings. □ **juego de palabras**
■ *v.* (*he punned*) to play with words of different meanings. □ **hacer un juego de palabras sobre**
punch [pʌntʃ] *n.* **1** blow with the fist: *he gave him a punch in the face.* □ **puñetazo**
punch line, last sentence of a story/joke which gives the point or which makes you laugh. □ **gracia**
2 metal tool for making holes. □ **punzón**
3 drink made of wine or spirits and spices. □ **ponche**
■ *v.* **1** to hit (someone) with your fist: *he punched him in the chest.* □ **dar un puñetazo**
2 to make holes in (something) with a punch: *the ticket collector punched the tickets.* □ **picar**
punch bowl *n.* **1** bowl for mixing wine and spices to make punch. □ **ponchera**
2 small valley surrounded by hills. □ **vega**
punch-drunk *adj.* suffering from brain damage from being punched on the head too often. □ **grogui**
punch-up *n.* (*informal*) fight. □ **pelea**
punctilious [pʌŋk'tiliəs] *adj.* attentive to detail/extremely fussy. □ **puntilloso**
punctual ['pʌŋktjuəl] *adj.* on time: *she's always very punctual.* □ **puntual**
punctuality [pʌŋktju'æliti] *n.* being on time/never being late. □ **puntualidad**
punctually *adv.* on time: *he arrived punctually at eight o'clock.* □ **puntualmente**

punctuate ['pʌŋktjueit] *v.* **1** to split a sentence using punctuation marks. □ **puntuar**
2 to interrupt: *his speech was punctuated by applause.* □ **interrumpir**
punctuation [pʌŋktju'eiʃn] *n.* splitting of a sentence using punctuation marks. □ **puntuación**
punctuation marks, signs used in writing (such as full stop, comma, dash) to show how a sentence is split up. □ **signos de puntuación**
puncture ['pʌŋktʃə] *n.* hole in a tyre; very small hole: *we had to change the wheel because we had a puncture.* □ **pinchazo**
■ *v.* to make a small hole in (something). □ **perforar**
pundit ['pʌndit] *n.* expert (especially in political matters). □ **autoridad**
pungent ['pʌndʒənt] *adj.* sharp (smell); sarcastic (comment). □ **acre (olor); mordaz (comentario)**
punish ['pʌniʃ] *v.* to make someone suffer because of a crime: *he was punished for stealing a ruler.* □ **castigar**
punishing race, very long and hard race. □ **carrera muy dura**
punishable *adj.* (offence) for which you can be punished. □ **castigable**
punishment *n.* treatment given to someone to make them suffer for a crime: *the punishment for stealing is six months in prison.* □ **castigo**
punk [pʌŋk] *n.* (*informal*) **1** wild hooligan. □ **'punk'**
2 follower of punk rock. □ **'punk'**
■ *adj.* (*informal*) bad/inferior. □ **malucho**
punk rock *n.* loud music played by people wearing outrageous costumes, etc. □ **música rockera punki**
punnet ['pʌnit] *n.* small box made of plastic or thin pieces of wood for holding strawberries, etc. □ **canastilla**
punt [pʌnt] *n.* long flat-bottomed boat, propelled with a pole. □ **batea**
■ *v.* to push a punt with a pole: *to go punting.* □ **impulsar con percha**
punter *n.* **1** person who gambles, especially on horseraces. □ **jugador**
2 person who pushes a punt along with a pole. □ **que lleva una batea**
puny ['pju:ni] *adj.* weak/feeble; very small. □ **debilucho**
pup [pʌp] *n.* young of certain animals, especially young dog. □ **cachorro**
pup tent, small ridge tent. □ **tienda de campaña canadiense**
pupa ['pju:pə] *n.* (*pl. pupae*) resting period in the life of an insect when it is changing from a grub/caterpillar to a butterfly/beetle, etc. □ **crisálida**
pupate [pju:'peit] *v.* (*of caterpillar*) to turn into a pupa. □ **convertirse en crisálida**
pupil ['pju:pil] *n.* **1** child at a school; person learning from a teacher. □ **alumno**
2 hole in the central part of the eye, through which the light passes. □ **pupila**
puppet ['pʌpit] *n.* doll which moves and which is used to give a performance. □ **títere**
glove puppet, puppet worn on your hand like a glove. □ **marioneta**
puppet state, country controlled by another country. □ **país títere**
string puppet, puppet moved with strings. □ **marioneta**
puppeteer [pʌpi'tiə] *n.* man who gives a performance using puppets. □ **titiritero**
puppy ['pʌpi] *n.* young dog. □ **cachorrillo**
puppy fat, fatness in young children and adolescents. □ **gordura**
purchase ['pə:tʃəs] *n.* **1** something bought. □ **compra**
2 grip/ability to lift something by using a lever: *I can't get any purchase on it.* □ **agarre**
■ *v.* to buy. □ **comprar**
purchasing power, amount that can be bought: *the purchasing power of the pound has fallen over the last five years.* □ **poder adquisitivo**
purchaser *n.* person who buys something. □ **comprador**
pure ['pjuə] *adj.* **1** very clean; not mixed with other things: *pure gold; pure spring water.* □ **puro**
2 *meeting him was pure chance,* complete chance. □ **...fue por pura casualidad**
purely *adv.* only; completely: *this book is purely and simply rubbish,* is complete rubbish. □ **puramente**
pureé ['pjuərei] *n.* semi-liquid pulp (of a vegetable/fruit): *tomato pureé.* □ **puré**
purgatory ['pə:gətri] *n.* place where you suffer temporarily after death; (place of) suffering. □ **purgatorio**
purge [pə:dʒ] *n.* **1** medicine which clears the bowels. □ **purga**
2 removal of political opponents: *the president ordered a purge of the civil service and army.* □ **purga, depuración**
■ *v.* to clear out (waste matter); to remove (political opponents): *he purged the army.* □ **purgar (desperdicio); depurar (oponente)**
purgative ['pə:gətiv] *adj.* and *n.* (medicine) which clears the bowels. □ **purgante**
purify ['pjuərifai] *v.* to clean/to make pure. □ **purificar**
purification [pjuərifi'keiʃn] *n.* making pure. □ **purificación**
purist ['pjuərist] *n.* person who insists on everything being done in the correct way. □ **purista**
purity *n.* being pure/absolutely clean. □ **pureza**
puritan ['pjuəritən] *n.* person who is very strict morally. □ **puritano**
puritanical [pjuəri'tænikl] *adj.* very strict concerning morals. □ **puritano**
purl [pə:l] *v.* to knit putting your needle into the back of the loop. □ **hacer punto del revés**
purple ['pə:pl] *adj.* and *n.* dark reddish-blue. □ **morado, violeta**
purport [pə:'pɔ:t] *n.* (*formal*) meaning. □ **sentido**
■ *v.* **1** (*formal*) to mean. □ **significar**
2 *the new aircraft are purported to be for defensive purposes only,* are supposed to be. □ **...pretenden ser para...**
purpose ['pə:pəs] *n.* **1** aim/plan; use: *what's the purpose of this yellow wire? what's the purpose in going there by train when we could go by car?* □ **propósito**
2 *he did it **on purpose,*** according to what he had planned/intentionally. □ **lo hizo a propósito**
purposeful *adj.* intentional; (person) with set aims. □ **decidido, intencionado**
purposely *adv.* on purpose/intentionally. □ **adrede**
purr [pə:] *n.* **1** noise made by a cat when pleased. □ **ronroneo**
2 low noise made by a powerful engine. □ **zumbido**
■ *v.* **1** (*of cat*) to make a noise to show pleasure: *the cat is purring.* □ **ronronear**
2 (*of engine*) to make a low noise: *the car purred along the motorway.* □ **zumbar**
purse [pə:s] *n.* **1** small bag for carrying money. □ **monedero**
2 *Amer.* handbag. □ **bolso**
■ *v. **to purse your lips,*** to pinch/to press your lips

together to show you are displeased. □ **apretar los labios**

purser *n.* officer on a ship who deals with the money, supplies and the passengers' accommodation. □ **contador de navío**

pursue [pə'sju:] *v.* **1** to chase (someone/something). □ **perseguir**

2 to continue to do something: *he pursued his studies.* □ **proseguir**

pursuer *n.* person who is chasing someone. □ **perseguidor**

pursuit [pə'sju:t] *n.* **1** chase: *he was running away with the policeman in pursuit,* with the policeman following him. □ **persecución**

in pursuit of *happiness,* looking for happiness. □ **búsqueda de la felicidad**

2 (*formal*) career/occupation: *a man of scholarly pursuits.* □ **ocupación**

purveyor [pə'veiə] *n.* person who supplies goods. □ **proveedor**

pus [pʌs] *n.* yellowish liquid which gathers in infected wounds/spots, etc. □ **pus**

push [puʃ] *n.* **1** act of pressing something so that it moves away from you: *he gave the car a push.* □ **empujón**

2 energy. □ **empuje**

3 *she's got a lot of push,* (*informal*) she's very determined to do well/to get a good job. □ **tiene mucho empuje**

4 ***at a push,*** (*informal*) if necessary/if the worst comes to the worst. □ **en un momento de apuro**

5 ***to give someone the push,*** (*informal*) to dismiss someone from a job. □ **poner de patitas en la calle a alguien**

■ *v.* **1** to press: *push the button to close the doors; the crowd was pushing and shoving to get into the bus; they had to push the car to get it to start; the policeman pushed his way through the crowd.* □ **pulsar (botón); empujar (gentío, el coche); abrirse camino (la policía)**

2 *I am* ***pushed for time,*** I haven't much time to spare. □ **ando escaso de tiempo**

3 (*slang*) to sell (drugs) illegally. □ **camellear**

pushbike *n.* (*informal*) bicycle. □ **bici**

push button *n.* switch which is operated by pushing. □ **pulsador, botón**

pushchair *n.* light folding carriage for pushing a child in. □ **silla**

pusher *n.* (*slang*) person who sells drugs illegally. □ **camello**

pushing *adj.* ambitious; eager to get what you want. □ **ambicioso**

push off *v.* (*informal*) to get going; to start a journey: *push off!,* go away! □ **ponerse en marcha**

pushover *n.* (*informal*) easy task; person who is easily influenced. □ **cosa chupada; persona fácil de convencer**

push-up *n. Amer.* press-up/exercise where you lie flat on the floor and push yourself up with your hands. □ **flexión**

pushy *adj.* (*informal*) wanting to succeed/ambitious. □ **ambicioso**

pusillanimous [pju:si'lænimәs] *adj.* (*formal*) timid/afraid. □ **pusilánime**

puss [pus] **pussy** ['pusi] **pussycat** ['pusikæt] *n.* familiar words for a cat. □ **minino**

put [put] *v.* (*he put; he is putting*) **1** to place: *to put something on the table; I've put some milk in your tea.* □ **poner**

to stay put: *I'm staying put,* (*informal*) I'm staying where I am/I have no intention of moving. □ **me quedo donde estoy**

2 to express in words: *to put it bluntly, you're an idiot; can I put a question to the speaker? if you put it like that, it sounds quite unpleasant.* □ **para ser claro, eres idiota; ¿puedo hacer una pregunta?; dicho así...**

3 to estimate: *the police put the crowd at more than 10,000.* □ **calcular**

4 ***to put a stop to something,*** to stop it. □ **poner freno a algo**

5 (*of ships*) to sail: *to put out to sea; to put into harbour.* □ **hacerse a la mar; entrar de arribada**

put across *v.* to explain (something) in a convincing way. □ **transmitir**

put away *v.* to clear (things) away: *put the clothes away in the cupboard; put your books away.* □ **guardar**

put back *v.* to place (something) where it was before: *put all the papers back in the files.* □ **volver a poner**

to put the clock back, to turn the hands of the clock backwards: *is it today we put the clocks back?* □ **retrasar**

put by *v.* to save: *I have a little money put by.* □ **ahorrar**

put down *v.* **1** to place at a lower level/on the ground: *put that book down!* □ **poner algo en el suelo**

2 to let passengers get off: *the bus put me down at the corner.* □ **dejar**

3 to note: *put it down on my account.* □ **anotar**

4 to kill a sick animal: *we had to have our dog put down.* □ **sacrificar**

5 ***to put your foot down,*** (i) to be very strict/firm. □ **ser firme**

(ii) (*in a car*) to go faster. □ **apretar el acelerador**

put in *v.* **1** to place inside: *put the letter in the envelope.* □ **meter**

2 *he put in three hour's work,* he worked for three hours. □ **echó tres horas de trabajo**

3 *to put in for a job,* to apply. □ **solicitar**

put off *v.* **1** to delay: *the party was put off until the following week.* □ **aplazar**

2 to frighten/to embarrass someone so that they can't do something: *I can't concentrate because you are putting me off.* □ **intimidar, molestar**

3 *his stories about the hospital put me off my food,* made me feel so sick that I couldn't eat. □ **quitar las ganas**

put on *v.* **1** to place: *to put the kettle on,* to place it on the stove in order to boil water; *to put a record on.* □ **poner**

2 to dress: *put your gloves on; he put on his shoes.* □ **ponerse**

3 to switch on: *put on the light; he put on the heating.* □ **encender**

4 to add. □ **añadir**

5 *he's* ***put on weight,*** he's got fatter. □ **engordar**

put out *v.* **1** to place outside: *to put out the washing; before you leave, put the cat out.* □ **tender (la ropa); sacar (el gato)**

2 to stretch out: *he put out his hand; the little boy put his tongue out at the policeman.* □ **sacar**

3 to switch off: *put all the lights out.* □ **apagar**

4 ***to be put out,*** (*informal*) to be annoyed. □ **estar cabreado**

5 *I don't want to put you out,* to give you any trouble. □ **no quiero crearte problemas**

put up *v.* **1** to fix upright: *to put up a picture; to put up new curtains.* □ **colocar**

2 *they're putting up a new shopping centre,* they're building. □ **están construyendo un nuevo...**

3 to raise: *put your hands up; they've put up the price of petrol again.* □ **levantar (las manos); subir (el precio)**
4 to offer: *he put up a great fight.* □ **ofrecer**
5 to find a place for someone to sleep: *can you put me up for the night?* □ **alojar**
6 ***to put up with someone/something,*** to accept someone/something, even if they are unpleasant/noisy, etc: *people living near the airport have to put up with aircraft noise.* □ **aguantar**
7 ***to put someone up to something,*** to encourage someone to do something. □ **animar**
put-upon *adj.* forced to do something unpleasant. □ **compelido**

putative ['pju:tətiv] *adj.* (formal) *the putative author,* the person who is supposed to be the author. □ **putativo**

putrefy ['pju:trifai] *v.* to rot. □ **pudrir/podrir**
putrefaction [pjutri'fækʃn] *n.* rotting. □ **putrefacción**
putrid *adj.* rotten; smelling rotten. □ **pútrido**

putt [pʌt] *n.* short shot (on a green) in golf. □ **'putt'**
■ *v.* to hit a short shot in golf. □ **patear**

putter ['pʌtə] *v.* ***to putter around,*** *Amer.* not to do anything in particular/to do little jobs here and there. □ **ocuparse en fruslerías**

putty ['pʌti] *n.* soft substance which hardens after a time, used especially for sealing the glass in windows. □ **masilla**

puzzle ['pʌzl] *n.* **1** problem; something which is difficult to solve: *it's a puzzle to me why she doesn't sell the house.* □ **enigma**
2 game where you have to solve a problem: *crossword puzzle; jigsaw puzzle.* □ **crucigrama; rompecabezas**
■ *v.* to perplex/to mystify; to be a problem: *it puzzles me why she doesn't sell the house; he spent hours puzzling over his maths homework.* □ **desconcertar; romperse la cabeza**
puzzling *adj.* which does not make sense/which is a problem. □ **enigmático**

pygmy ['pigmi] *adj.* and *n.* (type of animal) which is smaller than normal; very short (person). □ **enano**

pyjamas [pi'dʒɑ:məz] *n. pl.* light shirt and trousers worn in bed. □ **pijama**

pylon ['pailən] *n.* tall metal tower for carrying electric cables. □ **torre metálica**

pyramid ['pirəmid] *n.* shape with a square base and four sides rising to meet at a point. □ **pirámide**

pyre ['paiə] *n.* ceremonial fire: *funeral pyre,* pile on which a dead body is cremated. □ **pira**

pyrites [pai'raiti:z] *n.* yellowish chemical substance containing a metal: *iron pyrites.* □ **pirita**

pyromaniac [pairou'meiniæk] *n.* person who sets fire to buildings/who is mad about fire. □ **pirómano**

pyrotechnics [pairou'tekniks] *n. pl.* science of fireworks. □ **pirotecnia**

python ['paiθn] *n.* large snake which kills its prey by crushing. □ **pitón**

Q,q

Q, q [kju:] seventeenth letter of the alphabet. □ **Q, q**
quack [kwæk] *n.* **1** sound made by a duck. □ **graznido**
2 (*informal*) unqualified doctor. □ **curandero**
■ *v.* to make a noise like a duck. □ **graznar**
quad [kwɔd] *n.* (*informal*) quadrangle. □ **cuadrilátero**
quadrangle ['kwɔdræŋgl] *n.* open square surrounded by buildings (in a school/college). □ **patio**
quadrant ['kwɔdrənt] *n.* **1** quarter of a circle. □ **cuadrante**
2 instrument used for measuring angles. □ **cuadrante**
quadraphonic [kwɔdrə'fɔnik] *adj.* (sound) which is reproduced through four loudspeakers. □ **cuadrofónico**
quadrilateral [kwɔdri'lætərəl] *adj.* and *n.* (shape) with four sides. □ **cuadrilátero**
quadruped ['kwɔdruped] *n.* animal with four legs. □ **cuadrúpedo**
quadruple [kwɔ'drupl] *v.* to multiply four times: *the population has quadrupled in the last ten years.* □ **cuadruplicar**
quadruplets ['kwɔdruplets] *n. pl.* four babies born at almost the same time to the same mother. □ **cuatrillizos**
quadruplicate [kwɔ'dru:plikət] *n.* ***in quadruplicate,*** in four copies. □ **por cuadruplicado**
quads [kwɔdz] *n. pl.* (*informal*) quadruplets. □ **cuatrillizos**
quagmire ['kwɔgmaiə] *n.* bog/area of dangerous marsh □ **ciénaga**
quail [kweil] *n.* small game bird. □ **codorniz**
■ *v.* to shrink back in fear; to shudder: *he quailed at the thought of speaking to the commanding officer.* □ **acobardarse**
quaint [kweint] *adj.* picturesque/oddly old-fashioned: *he has some rather quaint ideas.* □ **curioso**
quake [kweik] *n.* (*informal*) earthquake. □ **temblor**
■ *v.* to shake (with fear/cold). □ **temblar**
Quaker *n.* (*informal*) member of a Christian religious society, known as the Society of Friends. □ **cuáquero**
qualify ['kwɔlifai] *v.* **1** to study for and obtain a diploma which allows you to do a certain type of work: *he has qualified as a doctor; a qualified pilot.* □ **graduarse, licenciarse; piloto con título**
2 to modify; to attach conditions: *he only gave a qualified acceptance.* □ **aceptación con reservas**
qualification [kwɔlifi'keiʃn] *n.* **1** proof that you have studied for and obtained a diploma: *what are his qualifications?,* what sort of diploma does he have? □ **título**
2 modification/condition which limits: *we accepted the proposal without qualification,* without imposing any conditions. □ **reservas**
quality ['kwɔliti] *n.* **1** worth: *good quality cloth; this soap is of very poor quality.* □ **calidad**
2 characteristics: *he has many good qualities.* □ **cualidades**
qualitative *adj.* referring to quality. □ **cualitativo**
qualm [kwɑ:m] *n.* feeling of guilt/worry: *he had no qualms about taking some days extra holiday,* he wasn't worried/he didn't have a bad conscience. □ **escrúpulo**
quandary ['kwɔndri] *n.* puzzle/problem: *I'm in a quandary,* I am puzzled/I don't know what to do. □ **dilema**
quango ['kwəŋgou] *n.* large national body (such as a government commission which investigates a special problem) where the directors are appointed by the government, but without direct government control. □ **organización nacional cuasiautónoma del gobierno (acrónimo)**
quantify ['kwɔntifai] *v.* to calculate in quantities/in amounts: *can you quantify the effect of raising the tax rate?* □ **cuantificar**
quantifiable *adj.* which can be quantified: *the value of the property damaged in the earthquake is hardly quantifiable.* □ **cuantificable**
quantity ['kwɔntiti] *n.* amount: *a quantity of waste paper,* a lot; *I need only a small quantity of money.* □ **cantidad**
an unknown quantity, something/someone you know nothing about. □ **una incógnita**
quantity surveyor, person who estimates how much material is required for a building. □ **aparejador**
quantitative *adj.* referring to quantity. □ **cuantitativo**
quantum ['kwɔntəm] *n.* ***quantum theory,*** theory in physics that energy exists in fixed amounts. □ **teoría cuántica/de los cuantos**
quarantine ['kwɔrənti:n] *n.* period of time when an animal/a person (usually coming from another country) has to be kept apart to avoid the risk of passing on disease: *he has been in quarantine for ten days.* □ **cuarentena**
■ *v.* to put (someone/an animal) in quarantine. □ **poner en cuarentena**
quarrel ['kwɔrəl] *n.* argument: *to get into a quarrel with someone.* □ **riña**
to pick a quarrel with someone, to start an argument. □ **tener una pelea con**
■ *v.* (*he quarrelled*) to argue: *he was quarrelling with his wife over the colour of the new carpet.* □ **discutir**
quarrelling *n.* arguments. □ **disputas**
quarrelsome *adj.* argumentative/often getting into quarrels. □ **pendenciero**
quarry ['kwɔri] *n.* **1** place where stone, etc., is dug out of the ground. □ **cantera**
2 animal which is being hunted; person/thing which is being looked for. □ **presa**
■ *v.* to dig (stone) out of the ground. □ **extraer**
quart [kwɔ:t] *n.* measure of liquid (= 2 pints, approximately one litre). □ **cuarto de galón**
quarter ['kwɔ:tə] *n.* **1** one of four parts: *the bottle is only a quarter full; cut the cake into quarters.* □ **un cuarto**
2 period of three months: *he paid a quarter's rent; he pays the rent every quarter.* □ **trimestre**
3 period of fifteen minutes: *it's a quarter to six/a quarter past ten.* □ **cuarto**
4 area: *letters of complaint came from all quarters; the poor quarters of a town; he got no help from that quarter,* from that area. □ **barrio, zona**
5 accommodation for people in the armed forces: *he has very comfortable quarters.* □ **cuartel**
6 25 cent coin. □ **cuarto de dólar**
■ *v.* **1** to cut into four equal parts. □ **partir en cuartos**
2 to place (soldiers) in lodgings: *the battalion was*

quartered in a little village. □ **acuartelar**
quarter day *n.* day which marks the beginning of a three month period for accounting purposes. □ **primer día a efectos contables**
quarter-final *n. (in sport)* one of four matches in a competition, the winners of which go into the semi-finals. □ **cuartos de final**
quarter-finalist *n.* team/player in a quarter-final. □ **cuartofinalista**
quarterlight *n.* small, usually triangular, window in a car. □ **derivabrisas/cortavientos**
quarterly *adj., adv.* and *n.* **1** (magazine) which appears every three months. □ **publicación trimestral**
2 *quarterly payment,* payment every three months. □ **pago trimestral**
quartet(te) [kwɔː'tet] *n.* **1** four people. □ **grupo de cuatro**
2 four musicians playing together. □ **cuarteto**
3 piece of music for four musicians. □ **cuarteto**
quarto ['kwɔːtou] *adj.* and *n.* size of paper one quarter of a standard sheet. □ **cuarto**
quartz [kwɔːts] *n.* hard crystalline mineral, used for making watches because of its very regular vibrations: *quartz watch.* □ **cuarzo**
quash [kwɔʃ] *v.* to annul (a legal sentence). □ **anular**
quasi- ['kweizai] *prefix meaning* almost: *quasi-independent.* □ **cuasi-**
quatrain ['kwɔtrein] *n.* stanza of poetry with four lines. □ **cuarteta**
quaver ['kweivə] *n.* **1** musical note lasting half as long as a crotchet. □ **corchea**
2 tremble (in the voice). □ **temblor**
■ *v.* to tremble: *his voice quavered with emotion.* □ **temblar**
quavering *adj.* trembling (voice). □ **voz trémula**
quay [kiː] *n.* stone jetty/place where ships tie up to load or unload. □ **muelle**
quayside *n. at the quayside,* next to the quay. □ **muelle**
queasy ['kwiːzi] *adj.* ill: *I'm feeling queasy after the rough ride in the hovercraft.* □ **mareado**
queen [kwiːn] *n.* **1** wife of a king; woman ruler of a country. □ **reina**
queen mother, mother of a king or queen who is the widow of a king. □ **reina madre**
2 (*at cards*) the card between the jack and the king: *the queen of spades.* □ **reina; caballo (en las cartas españolas)**
3 important piece in chess. □ **reina**
4 *queen ant/bee,* leading ant/bee in a colony. □ **reina**
5 the best/the most perfect: *beauty queen; carnival queen; this island is the queen of the Pacific islands.* □ **reina; esta isla es la perla de...**
6 (*slang*) male homosexual. □ **reinona**
queer ['kwiə] *adj.* **1** odd/strange: *there is a queer smell; what a queer look!* □ **raro**
2 *adj.* and *n.* (*slang*) homosexual. □ **maricón**
3 ill: *I felt very queer after the rough ride in the hovercraft.* □ **mareado**
■ *v.* to make something go wrong. □ **estropear**
to queer someone's pitch, to upset someone's plans. □ **estropear los proyectos de alguien**
queerness *n.* strangeness/oddness. □ **rareza**
quell [kwel] *v.* to calm (a riot); to hold back (your feelings). □ **sofocar (un disturbio); dominar (tus sentimientos)**
quench [kwentʃ] *v.* ***to quench your thirst,*** to have a drink. □ **apagar la sed**
thirst-quenching drink, a drink which satisfies your thirst. □ **que apaga la sed**
querulous ['kwerjuləs] *adj.* bad-tempered/peevish; always complaining. □ **quejumbroso**
query ['kwiəri] *n.* **1** question: *we've had several queries about our advertisement.* □ **pregunta**
2 question mark/sign (?) which shows that a question is being asked. □ **signo de interrogación**
■ *v.* to doubt whether something is true; to ask a question: *I queried the figures on the bank statement.* □ **poner en duda**
quest [kwest] *n.* (*formal*) search: *they went on holiday in quest of fine weather.* □ **en busca de**
question ['kwestʃn] *n.* **1** sentence which requires an answer: *we asked him a question; he refused to answer our questions.* □ **pregunta**
question mark, sign (?) which shows that a question is being asked. □ **signo de interrogación**
2 problem: *the human rights question.* □ **cuestión**
3 matter: *he brought up the question of overtime payments; it's all a question of time.* □ **tema; es una cuestión de tiempo**
it's out of the question, it's unthinkable. □ **ni hablar de eso**
■ *v.* **1** to ask someone questions: *the police questioned the prisoner.* □ **preguntar**
2 to doubt: *I question whether we should leave tomorrow.* □ **preguntarse**
questionable *adj.* doubtful. □ **discutible**
questioner *n.* person who asks questions. □ **interrogador**
questionnaire [kwestʃən'nɛə] *n.* printed list of questions given to people to answer. □ **cuestionario**
queue [kjuː] *n.* line of people/cars, etc., waiting one behind the other for something: *people were standing in queues for bread.* □ **cola**
to jump the queue, to go in front of people standing in a queue/not to wait your turn. □ **colarse**
■ *v.* to form a queue: *we had to queue for two hours to get the tickets; queue here for taxis.* □ **hacer cola**
quibble ['kwibl] *n.* argument about details. □ **sutileza**
■ *v.* to argue about details/to argue over the meaning of words. □ **ser quisquilloso**
quibbler *n.* person who argues about details. □ **quisquilloso**
quiche [kiːʃ] *n.* open tart with a filling of eggs/meat/vegetables, etc. □ **'quiche'**
quick [kwik] *adj.* **1** fast/rapid: *which is the quickest way to the post office? I had a quick snack.* □ **rápido**
2 *she has a quick temper,* she loses her temper easily. □ **irascible**
3 *he has a quick ear for music,* a sharp/acute ear. □ **tiene un oído fino...**
■ *n.* **1** live flesh (especially flesh around fingernails/toenails). □ **carne viva**
2 *he **cut** me **to the quick** with that unkind remark,* he hurt my feelings deeply. □ **me hirió en lo vivo**
quick-acting *adj.* (medicine) which takes effect rapidly. □ **de acción rápida**
quicken *v.* **1** to make (something) go faster: *he quickened his step.* □ **acelerar**
2 to stimulate (appetite). □ **estimular**
quickie *n.* (*informal*) something rapid; a quick drink/question, etc. □ **uno rápido/una rápida (trago, pregunta, etc.)**
quicklime *n.* lime/white substance containing calcium used in making cement. □ **cal viva**
quickly *adv.* rapidly: *he finished his meal quickly.* □ **rápidamente**
quicksand *n.* dangerous area of soft sand where you can sink in easily. □ **arena movediza**
quicksilver *n.* mercury. □ **mercurio**

quick-tempered *adj.* (person) who loses his temper easily. □ **irascible**
quick-witted *adj.* intelligent (person)/(person) who understands quickly. □ **de mente rápida**
quid [kwid] *n.* **1** (*slang*) pound (in money): *it'll cost you five quid.* □ **pavo**
2 lump of chewing tobacco. □ **mascada**
quiescent [kwai'esnt] *adj.* (*formal*) calm. □ **en reposo**
quiescence *n.* calmness. □ **reposo**
quiet ['kwaiət] *n.* **1** absence of noise; calm/tranquillity: *the quiet of the autumn evening was shattered by the noise of the motorbikes.* □ **tranquilidad**
2 *to do something* ***on the quiet,*** in secret. □ **...a hurtadillas**
■ *adj.* **1** calm/making no noise: *to keep quiet; tell the children to be quiet.* □ **en silencio; diles que se callen**
2 simple: *a quiet wedding,* with few guests. □ **sencillo**
3 *quiet colour scheme,* where the colours aren't bright. □ **poco llamativo**
■ *v.* to calm; to stop (someone) being noisy. □ **tranquilizar**
quieten *v.* to calm; to stop (someone) being noisy: *after a time they quietened down.* □ **hacer callar**
quietly *adv.* **1** without making any noise. □ **sin hacer ruido**
2 secretly. □ **silenciosamente**
quietness *n.* calm/tranquillity. □ **tranquilidad**
quiff [kwif] *n.* hair combed upwards and backwards from a man's forehead. □ **copete**
quill [kwil] *n.* long feather (formerly used as a pen). □ **pluma**
quilt [kwilt] *n.* padded cover for a bed. □ **colcha**
■ *v.* to sew a pad between two layers of cloth: *a quilted jacket.* □ **acolchar**
quince [kwins] *n.* hard fruit used for making jelly; tree producing this fruit. □ **membrillo**
quinine ['kwini:n] *n.* drug made from the bark of a tropical tree, used to treat malaria. □ **quinina**
quintessence [kwin'tesns] *n.* essential part (of something); perfect example. □ **quintaesencia**
quintet(te) [kwin'tet] *n.* **1** group of five musicians playing together. □ **quinteto**
2 piece of music for five musicians. □ **quinteto**
quintuple ['kwintjupl] *v.* to multiply five times: *the population has quintupled in the last fifteen years.* □ **quintuplicar**
quins [kwinz] *n. pl.* (*informal*) quintuplets. □ **quintillizos**
quintuplets *n. pl.* five babies born at almost the same time to the same mother. □ **quintillizos**
quip [kwip] *n.* joke/clever remark. □ **chiste/ocurrencia**
■ *v.* (*he quipped*) to make a joke/a clever remark. □ **hacer un chiste/comentario ocurrente**
quire ['kwaiə] *n.* 24 sheets of paper. □ **mano**
quirk [kwə:k] *n.* oddity/strange event: *a quirk of fate.* □ **rareza**
quit [kwit] *v.* (*he quit/he quitted*) **1** (*informal*) to leave: *he quit the room; to quit your job,* to resign. □ **dejar**
2 *she's been given* ***notice to quit,*** she has been told she must leave her house/flat. □ **...para que desalojara la casa**
3 *Amer.* (*informal*) to stop: *quit making that noise!* □ **dejar de**
quits *adj.* ***to be quits,*** to be equal. □ **estar en paz**
quite [kwait] *adv.* **1** completely: *I quite understand; that's quite enough arguing; he's quite right.* □ **por completo**
2 fairly/relatively: *his book is quite interesting; she isn't quite so good a tennis player as he is.* □ **bastante**
quite a few, several. □ **unos cuantos**
quiver ['kwivə] *n.* **1** tremor/slight shake: *a quiver of his eyelids.* □ **temblor; parpadeo**
2 holder for arrows. □ **carcaj**
■ *v.* to tremble: *he quivered like a leaf.* □ **temblar**
quixotic [kwik'sɔtik] *adj.* strange/impractical (person). □ **quijotesco**
quiz [kwiz] *n.* series of questions; TV/radio programme where people are asked questions. □ **concurso de preguntas**
■ *v.* (*he quizzed*) to ask (someone) questions. □ **hacer preguntas**
quizmaster *n.* person who asks the questions in a TV/radio quiz. □ **presentador de concurso**
quizzical ['kwizikl] *adj.* amused: *a quizzical smile.* □ **burlón**
quoin [kɔin] *n.* block of stone making a corner of a building. □ **piedra angular**
quoit [kɔit] *n.* large ring used in a game to throw over pegs: *to play quoits.* □ **tejo**
quorum ['kwɔ:rəm] *n.* number of people who have to be present to make a vote valid: *do we have a quorum?* □ **quórum**
quota ['kwoutə] *n.* fixed amount of goods which can be supplied; fixed number: *we have received our quota of new cars; I've had my quota of arguments today,* I've had enough arguments. □ **cuota**
quote [kwout] *n.* **1** passage quoted: *it's a quote from the Bible.* □ **cita**
2 estimate. □ **cálculo estimado**
3 ***quotes,*** (*informal*) inverted commas (" "). □ **comillas**
■ *v.* **1** to repeat a number (as a reference); to repeat a text of an author: *please quote reference number X8; he can quote whole passages of Shakespeare; he quoted one of the Common Market regulations; can I quote you?,* can I repeat what you have said? □ **citar**
2 to indicate the beginning of a quotation (when speaking): *the President is reported to have said and I quote 'I cannot stand this fool of a Prime Minister' unquote.* □ **...comienza la cita '...' fin de la cita**
3 to give an estimate for work to be done: *can you quote me a price for two tons of cement?* □ **presupuestar**
quotation [kwou'teiʃn] *n.* **1** passage quoted: *a quotation from Shakespeare.* □ **cita**
2 estimate: *his quotation was much lower than anyone else's.* □ **presupuesto**
3 ***quotation marks,*** inverted commas (" "). □ **comillas**
quotient ['kwouʃnt] *n.* result when one number is divided by another. □ **cociente**

R,r

R, r [ɑː] eighteenth letter of the alphabet. □ **R, r**
the three Rs, basic subjects in primary school (reading, writing, arithmetic). □ **lectura, escritura y aritmética**
rabbi ['ræbai] *n.* Jewish priest. □ **rabino**
rabbinical [rə'binikl] *adj.* referring to a rabbi. □ **rabínico**
rabbit ['ræbit] *n.* common wild grey animal with long ears and short white tail which lives in burrows: *rabbit hole.* □ **conejo**
■ *v.* (*informal*) to talk at great length: *she was rabbiting on about cooking.* □ **no parar de hablar**
rabble ['ræbl] *n.* crowd/unruly mass of people. □ **el populacho**
rabid ['ræbid] *adj.* **1** suffering from rabies: *a rabid dog.* □ **rabioso**
2 wild/fanatic. □ **furioso**
rabies ['reibiːz] *n.* hydrophobia/frequently fatal disease communicated mainly by dogs and foxes. □ **rabia**
raccoon [rə'kuːn] *n.* type of small North American flesh-eating wild animal. □ **mapache**
race [reis] *n.* **1** competition to see who is the fastest: *to run a race; horse races; a long-distance race.* □ **carrera**
2 rush of water in a narrow channel. □ **corriente**
3 group of human beings with similar physical characteristics. □ **raza**
race relations, relations between different racial groups in the same country. □ **interraciales**
4 species/breed of plant/animal, etc. □ **raza**
■ *v.* **1** to run/to drive, etc., to see who is the fastest: *I'll race you to that tree.* □ **echar una carrera**
2 to go very fast: *his pulse was racing.* □ **ir deprisa; su pulso latía a ritmo acelerado**
racecourse *n.* grassy track where horse races are run. □ **pista de carreras; hipódromo**
racehorse *n.* horse specially bred and trained to run in races. □ **caballo de carreras**
racer *n.* **1** person who is running in a race. □ **corredor**
2 special bicycle/car for racing. □ **bicicleta/coche de carreras**
racetrack *n.* grassy track where horse races are run. □ **pista de carreras**
racial ['reiʃl] *adj.* referring to race: *racial characteristics.* □ **racial**
racial discrimination/prejudice, discrimination/prejudice against someone because of race. □ **discriminación/prejuicio racial**
racialism *n.* prejudice against a group of people because of their race. □ **racismo**
racialist *adj.* and *n.* (person) who treats someone differently because of race. □ **racista**
racing *n.* competitions to see who is fastest: *horse/motor racing; a racing car.* □ **carreras**
racism *n.* prejudice against a group of people because of their race. □ **racismo**
racist *adj.* and *n.* (person) who treats someone differently because of race. □ **racista**
racy *adj.* vigorous (style of writing). □ **vigoroso**
rack [ræk] *n.* **1** frame to hold things (such as letters/pieces of toast). □ **estante, soporte**
luggage rack, shelf in a train to hold luggage. □ **redecilla**
roof rack, grid attached to the roof of a car for carrying luggage. □ **baca**
2 *to go to rack and ruin,* to become dilapidated. □ **arruinarse**
■ *v.* **1** *to rack your brains,* to think very hard. □ **devanarse los sesos**
2 to cause pain: *he was racked with arthritis; a racking cough.* □ **sufrir mucho**
rack and pinion *n.* toothed wheel which connects with a toothed bar to drive a machine (especially a mountain railway) forward. □ **engranaje de cremallera y piñón**
rack railway *n.* railway with engines driven by a toothed wheel connecting with a central toothed rail. □ **tren de cremallera**
racket ['rækit] *n.* **1** instrument made of a light frame with tight strings across it, used for hitting the ball in tennis, squash and badminton: *a tennis racket.* □ **raqueta**
2 (*informal*) loud noise. □ **barullo**
3 (*informal*) illegal profit-making deal. □ **chanchullo**
racketeer [rəki'tiə] *n.* swindler; gangster. □ **timador**
racquet ['rækit] *n.* tennis/squash/badminton racket. □ **raqueta**
radar ['reidɑː] *n.* system by which you can detect objects (such as enemy aircraft) and judge their position by sending radio signals to them which are reflected back as dots on a small screen. □ **radar**
radiate ['reidieit] *v.* to send out/to give off (rays/heat); to spread out (from a central point). □ **irradiar**
radial *adj.* which spreads out from a central point: (tyre) with grooves which give a better grip of the road surface. □ **radial**
radiance *n.* brightness. □ **resplandor**
radiant *adj.* bright (smile); (heat) which radiates. □ **radiante**
radiantly *adv.* brilliantly (happy). □ **brillantemente**
radiation [reidi'eiʃn] *n.* sending out/giving off (rays, heat): *nuclear radiation.* □ **radiación**
radiator ['reidieitə] *n.* **1** water-filled metal panel for heating. □ **radiador**
2 water-filled metal panel for cooling a car engine. □ **radiador**
radical ['rædikl] *adj.* **1** thorough/complete: *to make a radical change.* □ **radical**
2 *a radical difference,* basic difference. □ **radical**
3 ***radical party,*** a party which believes in the necessity of making great changes in the system of running a country. □ **partido radical**
■ *n.* member of a radical party. □ **un radical**
radically *adv.* completely/basically. □ **radicalmente**
radio ['reidiou] *n.* system for sending out/receiving messages using atmospheric waves; apparatus which sends out/receives messages using atmospheric waves: *we received a message by radio; radio programme; radio announcer; switch on the radio; did you hear the programme on the radio about whales?* □ **radio**
■ *v.* to send a message using a radio: *they radioed for help.* □ **radiar**
radioactive [reidiou'æktiv] *adj.* (substance) which gives off harmful radiation through the breaking up of its atoms. □ **radiactivo**
radioactivity [reidiouæk'tiviti] *n.* giving off of harmful radiation due to the breaking up of atoms. □ **radiactividad**

radiographer [reidi'ɔgrəfə] *n.* person who takes X-ray photographs. □ **radiólogo**
radiology [reidi'ɔlədʒi] *n.* science of X-rays and their use in medicine. □ **radiología**
radiotelephone *n.* long distance telephone (from a ship) which uses radio. □ **radioteléfono**
radiotherapy [reidiou'θerəpi] *n.* use of X-rays to treat disease. □ **radioterapia**
radish ['rædiʃ] *n.* small red root vegetable, eaten raw. □ **rábano**
radium ['reidiəm] *n.* (*chemical element*: a) radioactive metal used in treating cancer. □ **radio**
radius ['reidiəs] *n.* (*pl. radii* ['reidii]) **1** distance from the centre of a circle to the circumference: *within a radius of ten kilometres from the house,* the area around the house up to ten kilometres away. □ **radio**
2 one of the two bones in the lower part of the arm. □ **radio**
raffia ['ræfiə] *n.* (*no pl.*) strips from a palm leaf used to make baskets, etc. □ **rafia**
raffish ['ræfiʃ] *adj.* vulgar and showy; rather disreputable. □ **chulesco**
raffle ['ræfl] *n.* lottery where you buy a numbered ticket in the hope of winning a prize. □ **rifa**
■ *v.* to offer (a prize) for a lottery: *they raffled a car to raise money for the sports club.* □ **rifar**
raft [rɑːft] *n.* flat boat made of pieces of wood/logs tied together. □ **balsa**
rafter ['rɑːftə] *n.* sloping beam which holds up a roof. □ **viga**
rag [ræg] *n.* **1** piece of torn cloth. □ **harapo**
2 *they were dressed **in rags,*** they wore old, torn clothes □ **...en harapos/andrajos**
3 ***the rag trade,*** (*informal*) dressmaking trade. □ **la industria de la moda**
4 (*informal*) newspaper: *the local rag.* □ **periodicucho**
■ *v.* (*he ragged*) to play jokes on (someone): *he was ragged by the other boys.* □ **gastar bromas a**
rag-day *n.* day when students dress up to collect money for charity. □ **día de colecta benéfica**
ragged ['rəgid] *adj.* **1** torn. □ **hecho jirones**
2 ***ragged edge,*** uneven edge. □ **mellado**
3 (person) wearing rags. □ **andrajoso**
rage [reidʒ] *n.* violent anger: *he flew into a rage.* □ **furia; se puso furioso**
to be all the rage: *it's all the rage,* (*informal*) very fashionable. □ **es el último grito**
■ *v.* to be violently angry/to be violent: *the storm/the battle raged.* □ **encarnizarse**
raglan ['ræglən] *n.* style of coat where the sleeves continue straight to the collar, with no seam on the shoulder. □ **ranglan**
raid [reid] *n.* **1** sudden attack: *air raid; a raid into enemy territory.* □ **ataque repentino**
2 *the police made several raids on nightclubs,* made several surprise visits. □ **...varias redadas...**
■ *v.* to make a sudden attack/a sudden visit: *the police raided the gang's headquarters.* □ **hacer una redada**
raider *n.* person who takes part in a raid. □ **invasor**
rail [reil] *n.* **1** bar of wood/metal (in a fence, etc.): *he leant over the rail and looked down.* □ **barandilla**
2 ***rails,*** metal bars along which trains run. □ **raíles**
the live rail, rail which conducts electricity for electric trains. □ **raíl con corriente**
3 railway. □ **vía férrea, ferrocarril**
4 *I came **by rail,*** on a train. □ **vine en tren**
■ *v.* ***to rail against something,*** to speak violently against something. □ **arremeter contra**
railings *n. pl.* fence made of bars of metal: *he peered through the railings into the park.* □ **verja**
railroad *n. Amer.* railway. □ **vía ferrea, ferrocarril**
■ *v.* (*informal*) to force: *the bill was railroaded through parliament; he was railroaded into voting for the bill.* □ **hacer votar apresuradamente**
railway *n.* track with two metal rails along which trains run; train system of a country: *railway station; the French railways.* □ **vía férrea; ferrocarril; estación (de ferrocarril)**
railwayman *n.* (*pl. railwaymen*) man who works on the railways. □ **ferroviario**
rain [rein] *n.* water falling from clouds in drops: *the rain has flattened the wheat; we've had no rain for days.* □ **lluvia**
■ *v.* to fall in drops of water: *it's starting to rain; it was raining hard.* □ **llover**
rainbow *n.* coloured arch which appears in the sky when the sun's light falls on rain. □ **arco iris**
rain check *n. Amer.* **1** agreement to have/to do something later. □ **promesa**
2 *I'll **take a rain check** on that,* I'll not accept your offer now, but I will take it up again later. □ **aceptaré**
raincoat *n.* waterproof coat worn over other clothes to keep the rain out. □ **gabardina**
raindrop *n.* drop of rain. □ **gota de lluvia**
rainfall *n.* amount of rain which falls in a certain place over a certain period: *annual rainfall.* □ **precipitación**
rain forest *n.* thick, lush tropical jungle where it rains frequently. □ **selva tropical, pluvisilva**
rainwater *n.* water which has fallen as rain, and has been collected: *rainwater barrel.* □ **agua de lluvia**
rainy *adj.* with a lot of rain: *a rainy day; the rainy season.* □ **lluvioso**
raise [reiz] *n. Amer.* increase in salary: *I asked for a raise.* □ **aumento (de sueldo)**
■ *v.* **1** to lift; to make (something) higher: *he raised his arm; they raised a statue to the heroes of the revolution; don't raise your voice; I'm going to raise your salary.* □ **levantar; subir (sueldo)**
2 to bring up (a subject) for discussion: *he raised the question of unemployment pay; she raised a series of objections.* □ **plantear**
3 to rear (animals/a family). □ **criar**
4 to collect: *how can we raise the money to pay for the new building? they raised an army of ten thousand men.* □ **conseguir (dinero); reclutar (un ejército)**
raisin ['reizn] *n.* dried grape. □ **pasa**
rake [reik] *n.* **1** tool with a long handle and bent metal teeth, used for smoothing earth/for gathering fallen leaves, etc. □ **rastrillo**
2 immoral man. □ **crápula**
■ *v.* to smooth/to gather (using a rake): *he was raking up the dead leaves; he raked together about $1,000,* gathered together. □ **recoger con el rastrillo; reunir**
rake-off *n.* (*informal*) illegal payment paid as a commission. □ **comisión ilegal**
rake up *v. to rake up an old argument,* to start talking about it again. □ **sacar a relucir (un tema del pasado)**
rakish *adj.* (hat) worn at a slant/tilted sideways. □ **inclinado**
rally ['ræli] *n.* **1** gathering of members of a group/association/political party. □ **reunión**
2 car competition where cars have to cross difficult country in a certain time. □ **'rally'**

3 return to strength (of someone who is ill). □ **recuperación**
4 long series of shots in tennis. □ **peloteo**
■ *v.* **1** to gather together: *the president rallied his supporters.* □ **reunir**
2 to recover (temporarily) from an illness/a setback. □ **recuperarse**
ram [ræm] *n.* **1** male sheep. □ **carnero**
2 heavy machine for pressing down hard. □ **martillo pilón**
■ *v.* (*he rammed*) **1** to batter something down hard: *they rammed the posts into the ground.* □ **clavar**
2 to hit another ship/car, etc., hard: *the police car rammed the bank robbers' van.* □ **chocar con**
Ramadan ['ræmədæn] *n.* ninth month of the Muslim year, when Muslims fast between sunrise and sunset. □ **ramadán**
ramble ['ræmbl] *n.* walk for pleasure in the country. □ **paseo por el campo**
■ *v.* **1** to go for a walk. □ **pasear**
2 to talk on and on in a confused way. □ **divagar**
rambler *n.* **1** person who goes for walks in the country. □ **excursionista**
2 type of rose which climbs. □ **rosal trepador**
rambling *adj.* **1** confused (speech). □ **enmarañado**
2 (house) which is old and full of rooms and corridors. □ **laberíntico**
ramekin ['ræməkin] *n.* small dish for baking food in an oven; food cooked in this way. □ **cazuelilla**
ramification [ræmifi'keiʃn] *n.* part of a large complicated system: *the ramifications of the income tax law.* □ **ramificación**
ramp [ræmp] *n.* slightly sloping surface, joining two different levels; slight hump in a road surface. □ **rampa**
rampage [ræm'peidʒ] *n.* ***to go on the rampage,*** to go about breaking things/creating disorder. □ **andar destrozándolo todo**
■ *v.* ***to rampage about,*** to create disorder. □ **desmadrarse**
rampant ['ræmpənt] *adj.* (crime) which is widespread and uncontrollable: *rampant corruption.* □ **desenfrenada**
rampart ['ræmpɑːt] *n.* defensive wall: *the castle ramparts.* □ **muralla**
ramshackle ['ræmʃækl] *adj.* dilapidated/falling to pieces. □ **desvencijado**
ran [ræn] *v. see* **run.**
ranch [rɑːntʃ] *n.* (*in America*) farm where horses or cattle are reared. □ **rancho**
rancher *n.* person who owns/runs a ranch. □ **ranchero**
rancid ['rænsid] *adj.* bad/stale (butter). □ **rancio**
rancour ['rəŋkə] *Amer.* **rancor** *n.* bitterness/dislike. □ **rencor**
rancorous *adj.* bitter/hateful. □ **rencoroso**
random ['rændəm] *adj.* and *n.* done aimlessly/without any planning: *he spoke at random; a random shot.* □ **fortuito; habló sin pensar; una bala perdida**
a random sample, a sample for testing taken without any selection. □ **muestra aleatoria**
randy ['rændi] *adj.* eager to have sexual intercourse. □ **cachondo**
rang [ræŋ] *v. see* **ring.**
range [reindʒ] *n.* **1** series (of buildings/mountains) in line. □ **grupo (de edificios); cordillera (de montañas)**
2 large open pasture. □ **dehesa**
free-range hens, chickens which are allowed to run about in fields. □ **gallinas de corral**
3 choice/series (of colours, etc.): *a wide range of curtain materials.* □ **gama**
4 distance which a shell/bullet can reach; distance which an aircraft can fly without refuelling; distance for which you can see/hear: *the ship was within range,* was near enough for our guns to hit it. □ **alcance (bala); autonomía (avión); campo visual/auditivo**
5 old-fashioned kitchen stove which burns wood or coal. □ **cocina económica**
■ *v.* to spread/to vary: *his research ranges over several fields of study; the temperature ranges from minus ten to plus thirty degrees; prices ranging from $2 to $200.* □ **extender; oscilar; ir desde...**
rangefinder *n.* device (on a gun/camera) for calculating the distance of an object. □ **telémetro**
rangy *adj.* with long legs. □ **patilargo**
rank [ræŋk] *n.* **1** row of soldiers. □ **fila**
2 ***other/the ranks,*** ordinary soldiers. □ **soldados rasos**
to rise from the ranks, to rise from the rank of an ordinary soldier to that of an officer. □ **ascender en graduación**
the rank and file, ordinary people. □ **la gente del montón**
3 position in society/in the army: *he reached the rank of captain; people in the top ranks of society.* □ **posición (social); rango (de capitán)**
4 ***taxi rank,*** place where taxis wait in line. □ **parada de taxis**
■ *v.* to classify/to be classified in order of importance: *he ranks among the top sixteen tennis players in the world; where do you rank him among international golfers?* □ **clasificar; contarse entre**
■ *adj.* **1** (plants) which grow luxuriantly: *rank nettles.* □ **exuberante**
2 complete/total: *a rank outsider.* □ **rematado**
3 with an unpleasant smell. □ **maloliente**
rankle ['ræŋkl] *v.* to cause bitterness: *his success still rankles with me.* □ **fastidiar**
ransack ['rænsæk] *v.* to search/to turn over (a room to find something): *the burglars ransacked the bedroom in search of jewellery.* □ **registrar**
ransom ['rænsəm] *n.* payment asked for before a hostage is set free: *they took his daughter hostage and asked for a ransom of $10,000; armed men held him to ransom.* □ **rescate**
■ *v.* to pay a ransom: *he ransomed his daughter for $10,000.* □ **rescatar**
rant [rænt] *v.* to declaim/to shout violently. □ **vociferar**
rap [ræp] *n.* tap; sharp blow: *a rap on the door.* □ **golpecito**
to take the rap, (*informal*) to accept responsibility. □ **pagar el pato**
■ *v.* (*he rapped*) to tap/to give a sharp blow. □ **golpear**
rapacious [rə'peiʃəs] *adj.* greedy. □ **codicioso**
rapacity [rə'pæsiti] *n.* greed. □ **codicia**
rape [reip] *n.* **1** act of having sexual intercourse with a woman against her will. □ **violación**
2 type of vegetable with yellow flowers, whose seeds are used to produce oil. □ **colza, aceite de colza**
■ *v.* to commit rape upon (a person). □ **violar**
rapist *n.* person who rapes someone. □ **violador**
rapid ['ræpid] *adj.* fast: *rapid steps.* □ **rápido**
■ *n. pl.* ***rapids,*** place where a river runs fast over boulders and down a steep slope. □ **rápidos**
rapidity [rə'piditi] *n.* speed. □ **rapidez**
rapidly *adv.* fast. □ **rápidamente**

rapier ['reipiə] *n.* long, thin sword for thrusting. □ **estoque**
rapport [ræ'pɔ:] *n.* understanding/close link. □ **compenetración**
rapt [ræpt] *adj. with rapt attention,* very attentively. □ **absorto; con atención fija**
rapture ['ræptʃə] *n.* delight. □ **éxtasis**
to go into raptures: *she went into raptures over the new car,* she was delighted by the new car. □ **se extasió con...**
rapturous *adj.* excited and delighted (applause, etc.). □ **entusiasta**
rapturously *adv.* delightedly. □ **con entusiasmo**
rare [rɛə] *adj.* **1** very unusual: *a rare species of monkey; a rare stamp; a rare occurrence.* □ **raro**
2 (meat) which is very lightly cooked. □ **poco hecha**
rarely *adv.* hardly ever: *it occurs very rarely.* □ **raras veces, raramente**
rarefied ['rɛərifaid] *adj.* (air) which is not very dense. □ **enrarecido**
rarity *n.* **1** uncommonness: *a stamp of great rarity.* □ **rareza**
2 a rare object: *this stamp is a great rarity.* □ **rareza**
rarebit ['rɛəbit] *n.* ***Welsh rarebit,*** cooked cheese on toast. □ **pan tostado con queso derretido**
raring ['rɛəriŋ] *adj. he's raring to go,* (*informal*) eager to go. □ **deseoso**
rascal ['rɑ:skəl] *n.* naughty person/child. □ **tunante**
rash [ræʃ] *n.* red area/red spots on the skin. □ **erupción cutánea**
heat rash, spots caused by hot weather. □ **sarpullido**
■ *adj.* not cautious/thoughtless: *rash action,* action done without thinking. □ **precipitado**
rashly *adv.* without thinking: *he rashly offered to fight the champion.* □ **sin reflexionar**
rashness *n.* being rash/acting rashly. □ **precipitación**
rasher ['ræʃə] *n.* slice (of bacon). □ **loncha**
rasp [rɑ:sp] *n.* rough metal file used for smoothing surfaces. □ **escofina**
■ *v.* to make a grating noise: *a rasping voice.* □ **raspar; voz áspera**
raspberry ['rɑ:zbri] *n.* **1** common red soft fruit growing on tall canes; bush which bears this fruit. □ **frambuesa**
2 (*informal*) rude noise made with the mouth to show derision. □ **sonido despectivo**
rat [ræt] *n.* **1** common grey rodent, living in cellars/sewers/on ships. □ **rata**
2 sly unpleasant person. □ **rata**
■ *v.* (*he ratted*) **1** to hunt rats: *they went ratting.* □ **cazar ratas**
2 (*informal*) to go back on a promise/to betray: *they ratted on us.* □ **incumplir una promesa; ser un chaquetero**
rat race *n.* competition for success in the business world. □ **una lucha constante (por subir)**
ratchet(wheel) ['rætʃət('wi:l)] *n.* wheel with teeth and a catch to prevent it from turning backwards. □ **rueda de trinquete**
rate [reit] *n.* **1** number expressed as a proportion of one quantity to another. □ **proporción**
birth rate/death rate, number of births/deaths per 1,000 of population. □ **índice/tasa de natalidad/mortalidad**
2 frequency at which something is done/level of cost (as compared to a previous level): *rate of growth; what's the rate of interest on the loan? interest rates have increased by 2%.* □ **índice/tasa de crecimiento**
3 speed: *the car went past at a tremendous rate; he spends money at a terrific rate.* □ **velocidad**
4 ***first rate,*** very good. □ **de primera clase**
second rate, rather bad. □ **de segunda clase**
5 ***at any rate,*** in any case. □ **de cualquier modo**
6 ***rates,*** local taxes on property. □ **impuestos municipales**
water rate, water tax. □ **canon sobre el agua**
■ *v.* to value: *he's rated among the top sixteen tennis players.* □ **considerar**
rateable *adj. rateable value,* value of a house as calculated for local taxes. □ **valor catastral**
ratepayer *n.* person who pays local taxes. □ **contribuyente**
rating *n.* **1** valuing. □ **valoración**
2 ***TV ratings,*** comparative estimates of audiences for competing TV shows. □ **datos de audiencia**
3 ***naval rating,*** ordinary seaman. □ **marinero**
rather ['rɑ:ðə] *adv.* **1** relatively/quite: *it's rather cold today; her dress is rather a pretty shade of green.* □ **bastante**
2 (used with ***would*** to show preference): *I'd rather stay at home,* I would prefer to stay at home; *I'd rather not,* I would prefer not to; *he'd rather we didn't mention it,* he would prefer us not to mention it. □ **mejor me quedo en casa; preferiría que...**
3 ***rather than,*** in preference to: *rather than wait for a bus in the rain, I decided to take a taxi.* □ **antes que**
ratify ['rætifai] *v.* to approve (a treaty) officially. □ **ratificar**
ratification [rætifi'keiʃn] *n.* official approval. □ **ratificación**
ratio ['reiʃiou] *n.* proportion: *what's the ratio of pupils to teachers/the pupil-teacher ratio? you add sugar in the ratio of 100 grams to one litre of liquid.* □ **proporción**
ration ['ræʃn] *n.* amount of food/supplies allowed: *he's already eaten his ration of sugar.* □ **ración**
■ *v.* to allow only a certain amount of food/supplies: *petrol is going to be rationed; they are rationed to two litres of petrol per week.* □ **racionar**
rationing *n.* allowing only a certain amount of food/supplies: *the government had to introduce petrol rationing.* □ **racionamiento**
rational ['ræʃənl] *adj.* reasonable/based on reason: *a rational argument.* □ **racional**
rationale [ræʃə'nɑ:l] *n.* set of reasons which are the basis of a system/of a series of actions. □ **fundamento**
rationalization [ræʃnəlai'zeiʃn] *n.* act of rationalizing. □ **racionalización**
rationalize [ræʃnə'laiz] *v.* **1** to find a reason for usually unreasonable actions. □ **racionalizar**
2 to streamline/to modernize (old-fashioned production methods). □ **reorganizar en forma racional**
rationally *adv.* based on reason. □ **racionalmente**
rattan [rə'tæn] *n.* tropical cane, used to make furniture, etc.: *a rattan chair.* □ **rotén**
rattle ['rætl] *n.* **1** child's/football fan's (wooden) instrument which makes a loud repeated noise. □ **carraca**
2 repeated clattering noise: *the rattle of an old car; rattle of a chain.* □ **traqueteo**
■ *v.* **1** to make a repeated clattering noise: *he rattled his keys in his pocket; the windows rattled at the explosion.* □ **hacer sonar (llaves); golpetear (ventana)**
2 (*informal*) to worry/to upset: *he never gets rattled.* □ **ponerse nervioso**
rattle off *v.* (*informal*) to speak rapidly: *he rattled off a series of numbers.* □ **decir a toda pastilla**

rattlesnake *n.* American poisonous snake which makes a rattling noise with its tail. □ **serpiente de cascabel**
raucous ['rɔ:kəs] *adj.* rough/hoarse (cough/cry). □ **ronco**
ravage ['rævidʒ] *v.* to devastate/to ruin (a town, etc.). □ **asolar**
rave [reiv] *v.* **1** to be wildly mad: *he's raving.* □ **desvariar**
2 (*informal*) to be fanatical about something: *they raved about the new pop group.* □ **pirrarse por**
raven ['reivn] *n.* large black bird of the crow family. □ **cuervo**
ravenous ['rævənəs] *adj.* very hungry. □ **hambriento**
ravenously *adv.* (to eat) as if you are very hungry. □ **vorazmente**
ravine [rə'vi:n] *n.* deep narrow valley. □ **hondonada**
ravioli [rævi'ouli] *n.* Italian dish of small pasta squares filled with a meat stuffing. □ **ravioli**
ravish ['ræviʃ] *v.* **1** to steal by force. □ **arrebatar**
2 to enchant. □ **encantar**
ravishing *adj.* very beautiful/very delightful. □ **encantador**
raw [rɔ:] *adj.* **1** uncooked: *raw meat; she eats only raw vegetables.* □ **crudo**
2 basic/untreated: *raw materials; raw silk.* □ **materias primas; seda cruda**
raw recruits, new soldiers who have not been trained. □ **nuevos reclutas**
3 cold and damp (weather). □ **frío y húmedo**
4 ***a raw deal,*** bad/unfair treatment. □ **tratamiento injusto**
5 exposed/sensitive: *her arm is raw where she scraped it against the wall.* □ **en carne viva**
to touch a raw nerve, to touch a sensitive spot. □ **tocar un punto sensible**
■ *n.* **1** sensitive spot: *to touch someone on the raw.* □ **punto sensible**
2 wild state: *nature in the raw.* □ **en estado salvaje**
ray [rei] *n.* **1** beam of light/heat; small quantity (of hope). □ **rayo**
X-rays, rays which go through the soft tissue, and allow the bones and organs in the body to be photographed. □ **rayos X**
2 large, flat, sometimes edible, sea fish. □ **raya**
rayon ['reiɔn] *n.* trade name for artificial silk. □ **rayón**
raze [reiz] *v.* ***to raze*** *a castle* ***to the ground,*** to demolish it completely. □ **arrasar**
razor ['reizə] *n.* instrument with a very sharp blade for removing hair: *electric razor; a razor blade.* □ **maquinilla de afeitar; hoja de afeitar**
razor-sharp *adj.* extremely sharp (blade/mind, etc.). □ **afiladísimo (hoja); agudísimo (mente)**
razzmatazz ['ræzmətæz] *n.* (*informal*) energetic publicizing (of an election campaign). □ **publicidad machacona**
re [ri:] *prep.* concerning: *re your last letter.* □ **con referencia a**
re- [ri:] *prefix meaning* again: *to re-read; to revisit; remarriage; to remarry.* □ **re- (volver a)**
reach [ri:tʃ] *n.* **1** distance you can travel easily; distance you can stretch out your hand: *the village is within easy reach of London; our house is within reach of the station; the medicine cupboard should be out of the children's reach.* □ **alcance, radio**
2 straight section of a river. □ **tramo recto**
■ *v.* **1** to stretch out: *he reached out and grabbed the hammer; can you reach the top of the cupboard?* □ **alcanzar; alargó la mano y...**
2 to arrive at: *we reached home at 10 o'clock; what time are we supposed to reach Paris? your letter never reached me.* □ **llegar**
3 to come to (an agreement): *they reached agreement on all the points under discussion.* □ **llegar a (un acuerdo)**
react [ri'ækt] *v.* **1** to do/to say something in reply to words or an action: *when they heard the news, the ministers reacted quickly; they reacted to the news of the attack.* □ **reaccionar**
2 *teenagers* ***react against*** *their teachers,* show their opposition to. □ **los adolescentes reaccionan....**
3 *acids react with metals,* change their chemical composition. □ **reaccionar**
reaction [ri'ækʃn] *n.* act of reacting; something done/said in reply: *a chemical reaction; reaction against strict discipline; what was his reaction?,* what did he say/do? □ **reacción**
reactionary *adj.* and *n.* (person) who is opposed to any political change/to any reforms. □ **reaccionario**
reactivate *v.* to make (something) work again. □ **reactivar**
reactor *n.* device for producing atomic energy: *nuclear reactor.* □ **reactor**
read [ri:d] *n.* (*informal*) looking at and understanding printed words: *I was having a quiet read when the telephone rang.* □ **lectura**
■ *v.* (*he read/he has read*) **1** to look at and understand written words; to speak aloud words which are written: *I'm reading a book about archaeology; he read his poems out loud; he read the children a story; I can't read the thermometer,* I can't see what temperature it shows. □ **leer**
to read between the lines, to understand a hidden meaning which is not immediately apparent. □ **leer entre líneas**
2 to study at university: *he's reading physics.* □ **hacer la carrera de**
3 to interpret: *to read someone's palm,* to interpret the lines on a hand as indications of what will happen in the future. □ **leer**
readable *adj.* **1** legible/which can be read: *the writing is so faint it's hardly readable.* □ **legible**
2 *a very readable story,* one which is a pleasure to read. □ **...que merece la pena leerse**
reader *n.* **1** person who reads: *the magazine has over 10,000 regular readers.* □ **lector**
2 senior teacher at a university. □ **profesor titular**
3 school book to help children read (in their own language or a foreign language). □ **libro de lectura**
reading *n.* **1** act of looking at and understanding printed words: *I'm not very fond of reading.* □ **lectura**
2 *he gave poetry readings,* he read poems in public. □ **...recitales de poesía**
3 interpretation: *my reading of his letter is that he wants us to pay more.* □ **interpretación**
reading room *n.* room (in a library) specially for reading. □ **sala de lectura**
readdress [ri:ə'dres] *v.* to put another address on an envelope/parcel. □ **poner señas nuevas**
readjust [riə'dʒʌst] *v.* to adjust again; to put back to the original position. □ **reajustar**
ready ['redi] *adj.* **1** prepared: *I'm ready to go; he's always ready to lend money.* □ **listo, preparado**
2 fit to be used: *is the car ready yet? the tea's ready.* □ **listo**
3 quick/rapid: *he has a ready reply to anything,* he always has an answer. □ **rápido**
4 ***ready cash,*** cash which is immediately available. □ **(dinero) líquido disponible**

readily *adv.* willingly. □ **de buena gana**
readiness *n.* willingness. □ **buena disposición**
to hold something in readiness, to keep something ready for use. □ **tener listo**
ready-cooked *adj.* (food) which has been cooked in advance. □ **listo para comer**
ready-made, ready-to-wear *adj.* (clothes) which are made by mass production, to fit any person of a certain size. □ **(ropa) de confección**
reagent [ri eidʒnt] *n.* substance used in a chemical reaction. □ **reactivo**
real [ril] *adj.* **1** true/not imitation; (something) which exists: *the watch is real gold; he's been a real friend to me.* □ **verdadero, auténtico**
2 ***real estate,*** (*especially Amer.*) land or buildings which are bought or sold. □ **bienes inmuebles**
3 ***real tennis,*** medieval form of tennis played with a hard ball in a court with high walls. □ **tenis medieval**
realism *n.* **1** facing facts/accepting life as it is. □ **realismo**
2 showing things (in writing/painting) as they really are. □ **realismo**
realist *n.* **1** artist/writer who shows things as they really are. □ **realista**
2 person who accepts life as it really is, and doesn't idealize it. □ **realista**
realistic [riə'listik] *adj.* **1** which looks as if it is real: *the painting is very realistic.* □ **realista**
2 accepting life as it really is: *let's be realistic - we can't hope to sell the house for $100,000.* □ **seamos realistas...**
reality [ri'æliti] *n.* what is real/not imaginary. □ **realidad**
really *adv.* truly: *is it really true? he really meant what he said.* □ **realmente**
realign [riə'lain] *v.* to set in a new direction; to set in a new group: *the party has realigned itself with the socialists.* □ **realinear**
realize ['riəlaiz] *v.* **1** to come to understand clearly: *he gradually realized that he was becoming deaf.* □ **darse cuenta**
2 to sell property for money: *he realized $10,000 by selling his wife's jewels.* □ **obtener**
3 to make real; to make (something) come true: *he realized his ambition when he met the Prime Minister.* □ **hacer realidad**
realization [riəlai'zeiʃn] *n.* **1** gradual understanding. □ **comprensión**
2 conversion of property into money. □ **realización**
3 carrying out of a plan. □ **realización**
realm [relm] *n.* **1** kingdom. □ **reino**
2 general area: *the realms of fantasy.* □ **esfera**
realtor ['riəltə] *n. Amer.* estate agent/person who arranges the sale of property. □ **agente de la propiedad (inmobiliaria)**
ream [ri:m] *n.* **1** 480 sheets of paper. □ **resma**
2 ***reams,*** very large quantity (of paper): *he wrote reams of notes.* □ **montones**
reanimate [ri'ænimeit] *v.* to bring back to life. □ **reanimar**
reap [ri:p] *v.* **1** to harvest (corn, etc.). □ **cosechar**
2 *he reaped the benefit of his hard work,* he benefited from it. □ **recogió los beneficios...**
reaper *n.* person/machine which harvests corn. □ **cosechador/a**
reappear [riə'piə] *v.* to appear again. □ **reaparecer**
reappearance *n.* second appearance. □ **reaparición**
rear ['riə] *n.* back part: *the rear of an army; he came in the rear of the procession.* □ **parte posterior; retaguardia (ejército)**
to bring up the rear: *the police brought up the rear,* marched behind. □ **...cerraba la marcha**
■ *adj.* back: *rear seat; (in a car) rear window.* □ **trasero**
rear-view mirror, mirror in a car so that you can see what is behind you without turning round. □ **espejo retrovisor**
■ *v.* **1** to breed/to raise: *she reared four healthy sons; they rear pigs.* □ **criar**
2 (*of horse, etc.*) to stand up on its back legs. □ **encabritarse**
rear-admiral *n.* high-ranking naval officer (beneath vice-admiral). □ **contraalmirante**
rearguard *n.* **1** soldiers defending the back part of an army. □ **retaguardia**
2 *they fought* ***a rearguard action,*** they defended themselves against someone who was winning. □ **combatieron para cubrir la retirada**
rearm [ri'ɑ:m] *v.* to arm/to stock up with weapons again. □ **rearmarse**
rearmament [ri'ɑ:məmənt] *n.* arming again. □ **rearme**
rearrange [riə'reinʒ] *v.* to arrange again. □ **volver a arreglar**
reason ['ri:zn] *n.* **1** cause/explanation for why something happens: *they sacked him without giving a reason; what was the reason for the delay?* □ **razón**
2 power of thought; common-sense: *he wouldn't listen to reason.* □ **no se avenía a razones**
■ *v.* **1** to think/to plan carefully and logically. □ **razonar**
2 ***to reason with someone,*** to try to calm someone/to make someone change his mind. □ **hacer entrar en razones**
reasonable *adj.* **1** not extravagant/moderate: *their demands were quite reasonable; a very reasonable price.* □ **razonable**
2 sensible: *you must be reasonable.* □ **razonable**
reasoning *n.* putting your mind to use: *I don't follow your reasoning,* I can't see how you reached this conclusion. □ **razonamiento**
reassemble [riə'sembl] *v.* **1** to put back together. □ **volver a juntar**
2 to gather together again: *the school reassembles after the summer holidays.* □ **reunirse, reanudarse**
reassure [riə'ʃuə] *v.* to calm (someone)/to make (someone) less afraid/less doubtful: *you must try to reassure her about the operation.* □ **tranquilizar**
rebate ['ri:beit] *n.* reduction in the amount of money which should be paid; money which is returned to the person who paid it: *you get a 10% rebate for early payment,* if you pay early, you pay only 90% of the bill. □ **descuento**
rebel ['rebəl] *n.* person who fights against the government/against the person in charge: *rebel taxpayers; rebels have attacked the president's house.* □ **rebelde**
■ *v.* (*he rebelled*) to fight (against): *the people rebelled against the president; she is rebelling against parental authority.* □ **rebelarse**
rebellion [ri'beljən] *n.* revolt/fight against the government/against authority. □ **rebelión**
rebellious [ri'beliəs] *adj.* fighting against the government/against authority. □ **rebelde**
rebound ['ri:baund] *n.* bouncing back: *he caught the ball on the rebound.* □ **rebote**
■ *v.* [ri:'baund] to bounce back: *the ball rebounded off the goalpost.* □ **rebotar**
rebuff [ri'bʌf] *n.* refusal: *he met with a rebuff.*

□ **negativa**
■ *v.* to refuse: *he was rebuffed.* □ **rechazar**
rebuild [riː'bild] *v.* (*he rebuilt*) to build again. □ **reconstruir**
rebuke [ri'bjuːk] *n.* (*formal*) blame/reproof. □ **reproche**
■ *v.* to blame/to scold. □ **reprender**
rebut [ri'bʌt] *v.* (*he rebutted*) to reject/to disprove (an argument). □ **rebatir**
recalcitrant [ri'kælsitrənt] *adj.* (*formal*) difficult/disobedient. □ **recalcitrante**
recall [ri'kɔːl] *n.* **1** calling back. □ **llamar**
2 *it's gone **beyond recall,*** gone and cannot be called back. □ **se ha ido y pertenece al pasado**
■ *v.* **1** to call/to summon back (an ambassador/defective cars). □ **retirar**
2 to remember: *I don't recall ever meeting him before.* □ **recordar**
recant [ri'kænt] *v.* to admit that your former beliefs were wrong. □ **retractarse**
recapitulate [riːkə'pitjuleit] (*informal*) **recap** ['rikæp] *v.* to repeat the main points of an argument: *let me just recap the main details.* □ **recapitular**
recapitulation, (*informal*) **recap** *n.* repeating the main points: *can you give me a recap of what has been said so far?* □ **recapitulación**
recapture [riː'kæptʃə] *n.* catching again (an escaped prisoner). □ **nueva detención**
■ *v.* to catch again (an escaped prisoner). □ **volver a capturar**
recast [riː'kɑːst] *v.* **1** to make again: *they had to recast the bell.* □ **refundir**
2 *to recast a statement,* to write a statement again in a different way. □ **dar nueva forma**
recede [ri'siːd] *v.* to go away/to retreat: *the mountains receded into the distance.* □ **retroceder**
receding *adj.* **1** ***receding forehead,*** forehead which slopes backwards. □ **frente huidiza**
2 ***receding hair,*** hair which begins to disappear from the front of the forehead. □ **entradas**
receipt [ri'siːt] *n.* **1** receiving. □ **recepción**
***on receipt of** the letter,* when you receive the letter. □ **al recibo de la carta**
2 paper showing that you have paid/that you have received something: *keep the receipt, because you will need it if you want to claim back your clothes.* □ **recibo**
3 ***receipts,*** money taken in a business. □ **recaudación, ingresos**
receive [ri'siːv] *v.* **1** to get something which has been sent: *he received a parcel for his birthday.* □ **recibir**
2 *he was **on the receiving end of** a lot of criticism,* (*informal*) he had to suffer a lot of criticism. □ **fue el que se llevó todos los palos**
3 to greet/to welcome; to entertain: *he was received with open arms.* □ **recibir**
receiver *n.* **1** person who accepts stolen goods. □ **perista**
2 official put in charge of a bankrupt company. □ **síndico**
3 part of a telephone which you can lift and listen to: *he lifted the receiver.* □ **auricular**
4 part of a radio which receives broadcast programmes. □ **receptor**
recent ['riːsənt] *adj.* which took place not very long ago: *a recent film; in the Prime Minister's recent speech.* □ **reciente**
recently *adv.* not long ago/only a short time ago. □ **recientemente**
receptacle [ri'septəkl] *n.* container. □ **receptáculo**
reception [ri'sepʃn] *n.* **1** welcome: *the football team had a great reception when they returned home.* □ **recepción**
2 (*in a hotel*) desk where you check in. □ **recepción**
3 big party held to welcome special guests: *wedding reception.* □ **recepción**
4 quality of sound of a radio/TV broadcast: *the reception is very bad.* □ **recepción**
receptionist *n.* person in a hotel/doctor's office, etc., who meets visitors and answers the telephone. □ **recepcionista (hotel); enfermera (consulta)**
receptive *adj.* eager to take in new ideas. □ **receptivo**
recess [ri'ses] *n.* **1** alcove/part of the wall of a room which is set back. □ **hueco**
2 official holiday of the law courts or parliament: *parliament is in recess; the summer recess.* □ **período de vacaciones**
3 (*Amer.* and *in Scotland*) recreation period at school. □ **recreo**
4 *deep in the recesses of my mind,* far back in my mind. □ **en lo más recóndito de mi mente**
recession [ri'seʃn] *n.* collapse of world economy/of trade. □ **recesión**
recidivist [rə'sidivist] *n.* hardened criminal/person who commits a crime regularly. □ **reincidente**
recipe ['resipi] *n.* **1** instructions for cooking something: *I am trying a new recipe for marmalade.* □ **receta de cocina**
2 effective way to do something: *it's a recipe for success,* it's bound to lead to success. □ **receta**
recipient [ri'sipiənt] *n.* person who receives. □ **destinatario**
reciprocate [ri'siprəkeit] *v.* to do the same thing in return: *he sent me a Christmas card and I reciprocated.* □ **corresponder**
reciprocal *adj.* mutual. □ **recíproco**
a reciprocal trade agreement, agreement on two-way trade between countries. □ **un acuerdo comercial recíproco**
reciprocity [resi'prɔsiti] *n.* principle that if one country buys goods from another, the second country will reciprocate. □ **reciprocidad**
recite [re'sait] *v.* to speak (verse, etc.) aloud in public: *he recited the whole of the first act of 'Hamlet'.* □ **recitar**
recital *n.* **1** speaking in public something which has been written: *a poetry recital.* □ **recital**
2 performance of music by one or a few musicians: *a recital of music by Bach/a Bach recital.* □ **recital**
recitation [resi'teiʃn] *n.* something recited from memory. □ **recitado**
recitative [resitə'tiːv] *n.* (*in an opera*) speech sung in a rhythmic way. □ **recitativo**
reckless ['rekləs] *adj.* foolish/rash/not thinking of others: *reckless driving.* □ **imprudente**
recklessly *adv.* foolishly/rashly: *he recklessly spent all the money he had inherited.* □ **a la buena de Dios**
recklessness *n.* foolishness/rashness. □ **imprudencia; atolondramiento**
reckon ['rekn] *v.* **1** to calculate/to estimate: *I reckon the cost at $1,000; I reckon it cost him $1,000.* □ **calcular**
2 to think: *do you still reckon they'll come?* □ **pensar**
3 ***to reckon on something,*** to count on something/to depend on something: *I'm reckoning on making a profit.* □ **contar con**
4 ***to reckon with,*** to have to deal with. □ **ajustar cuentas con**
5 *he's a man **to be reckoned with,*** he is powerful. □ **...con el que hay que contar**

reckoning *n.* calculation. □ **cálculo**
day of reckoning, time when you have to pay for your mistakes. □ **día del juicio final**
reclaim [ri'kleim] *v.* to make (useless land) fit for use; to take back (land) from the sea. □ **roturar (tierra); ganar (tierra) al mar**
reclamation [reklə'meiʃn] *n.* reclaiming (of land). □ **roturación**
recline [ri'klain] *v.* to lie back: *she was reclining on a sofa.* □ **reclinarse**
recluse [ri'klu:s] *n.* person who lives alone and hidden away. □ **solitario**
recognize ['rekəgnaiz] *v.* **1** to know (someone/something) because you have seen him/it before: *I recognized him by the way he walked; she recognized him as the man who had stolen her purse; the police recognized the handwriting on the cheque.* □ **reconocer**
2 to admit: *he recognized his mistake.* □ **reconocer**
3 to admit the value of (something): *the government recognized his services.* □ **reconocer**
4 *to recognize a government,* to accept that a new government is the legal authority in a country. □ **reconocer un gobierno**
recognition [rekəg'niʃn] *n.* recognizing. □ **reconocimiento**
to change beyond all recognition, to change so much so as to be impossible to recognize. □ **ha llegado a ser irreconocible**
recognizable [rekəg'naizəbl] *adj.* which can be recognized. □ **reconocible**
recognizance [re'kɔgnizəns] *n.* money given as a pledge to a court that someone will obey the conditions laid down by the court. □ **fianza**
recoil ['ri:kɔil] *n.* sudden movement backwards of a gun when it is fired. □ **culatazo**
■ *v.* to move backwards suddenly/to shrink back from something unpleasant. □ **retroceder**
recollect [rekə'lekt] *v.* to remember: *as far as I can recollect, the post office is just past the supermarket.* □ **recordar**
recollection [rekə'lekʃn] *n.* remembering. □ **recuerdo**
recommend [rekə'mend] *v.* **1** to advise someone to do something: *the doctor recommended that he should take a rest; I wouldn't recommend you to buy that dictionary.* □ **recomendar**
2 to praise (something/someone): *the waiter recommended the roast beef.* □ **recomendar**
3 *she has two qualities to recommend her,* which make her useful/pleasant. □ **hablar en favor de**
recommendation [rekəmen'deiʃn] *n.* **1** advice. □ **recomendación**
2 praise; something which is in your favour. □ **recomendación**
recompense ['rekəmpens] *n.* payment for someth time lost, etc. □ **recompensa**
■ *v.* to pay someone for something done/for time lost, etc. □ **recompensar**
reconcile ['rekənsail] *v.* **1** to make two enemies become friendly. □ **reconciliar**
2 *I've reconciled myself to a long wait,* I must accept that I will have a long wait. □ **me he resignado...**
3 to make (two accounts/statements) agree. □ **conciliar**
reconciliation [rekənsili'eiʃn] *n.* the bringing together of two enemies, so that they become friends; making two accounts/statements agree. □ **reconciliación**
recondite [ri'kɔndait] *adj.* (*formal*) obscure (information). □ **oscuro**
recondition [rikən'diʃn] *n.* to overhaul thoroughly: *reconditioned engine.* □ **motor revisado**
reconnaissance [ri'kɔnisns] *n.* survey of land for military information: *reconnaissance aircraft.* □ **reconocimiento**
reconnoitre [rekə'nɔitə] *Amer.* **reconnoiter** *v.* to make a survey to get information/to make a reconnaissance. □ **reconocer**
reconsider [ri:kən'sidə] *v.* to think over again: *the judge reconsidered his verdict.* □ **reconsiderar**
reconstruct [ri:kən'strʌkt] *v.* **1** to build again. □ **reconstruir**
2 *the police reconstructed the crime,* worked out how the crime must have been committed. □ **la policía reconstruyó...**
record ['rekɔ:d] *n.* **1** report of something which has happened. □ **informe**
2 *he is **on record** as saying,* he is accurately reported as saying. □ **consta que**
3 *she spoke **off the record**,* in private/what she said is not to be made public. □ **...'off the record'; oficiosamente**
4 note/written account: *record of attendance.* □ **registro de asistencias**
5 flat plastic disc on which sound is fixed by a recording instrument: *long-playing record; a new record of Beethoven's 5th Symphony.* □ **disco**
6 description of someone's past career: *he has a criminal record.* □ **antecedentes, historial**
7 sporting achievement which is better than any other: *he holds the world speed record; he broke the world record for the 100 metres,* he did better than the previous record; *she set up a new record.* □ **marca; récord**
at record speed, very fast. □ **a una velocidad increíble**
■ *v.* [ri'kɔ:d] **1** to report; to make a note: *I want my statement to be recorded in the minutes.* □ **constar**
recorded delivery, postal service where you must sign a receipt to show you have received a parcel/a letter, etc. □ **carta/paquete certificado**
2 to fix sound on a plastic disc or tape: *he recorded the song of several rare birds; she's recorded six songs by Schubert.* □ **grabar**
record-breaking *adj.* which breaks records: *his record-breaking performance in the 100 metres.* □ **que ha batido el récord**
recorder [ri'kɔ:də] *n.* **1** judge in certain courts. □ **juez municipal**
2 instrument which records: *tape recorder.* □ **grabadora**
3 wooden flute held forwards when played. □ **flauta**
recording *n.* **1** act of fixing sounds on tape/on disc: *recording session; recording studio.* □ **grabación**
2 music/speech which has been recorded: *let me play you this new recording of Beethoven's 5th Symphony.* □ **grabación**
record-player *n.* machine for playing back music/speech, etc., from a record. □ **tocadiscos**
recount ['ri:kaunt] *n.* counting votes again (when the result is very close). □ **repetir el escrutino**
■ *v.* [ri'kaunt] **1** to tell (a story). □ **relatar**
2 to count again. □ **volver a contar**
recoup [ri'ku:p] *v.* *to recoup your losses,* to get back money which you have lost. □ **resarcirse (de una pérdida)**
recourse [ri'kɔ:s] *n.* *to have recourse to something,* to use something in an emergency. □ **recurso; recurrir a algo**

recover [ri'kʌvə] *v.* **1** to get back (something which has been stolen/lost): *the police recovered most of the stolen jewels.* □ **recuperar**
2 to get well again after an illness: *he's recovering from his operation; she caught pneumonia and never recovered.* □ **recuperarse**
3 to get over: *when he had recovered from his astonishment.* □ **recuperarse**
4 to put a new cover (on a chair). □ **tapizar**
recoverable *adj.* which can be got back. □ **recuperable**
recovery *n.* **1** getting back (stolen property). □ **recuperación**
2 getting well again: *he is well on the way to recovery.* □ **restablecimiento**
3 return to good condition: *he was losing 5 - 0, but made a marvellous recovery; the country has made a remarkable economic recovery.* □ **recuperación**

recreation [rekri'eiʃn] *n.* pleasant occupation for your spare time: *his main recreation is gardening.* □ **esparcimiento**
recreation ground, public sports ground. □ **polideportivo**

recrimination [rikrimi'neiʃn] *n.* accusation made by someone who is accused. □ **recriminación**
recriminatory [ri'kriminətri] *adj.* (remarks) which accuse someone. □ **recriminatorio**

recrudescence [ri:kru:'desəns] *n.* (*formal*) breaking out again (of a disease). □ **recrudecimiento**

recruit [ri'kru:t] *n.* new soldier; new member of a club, etc. □ **recluta (ejército); nuevo socio (club)**
■ *v.* to encourage (someone) to join the army/a club, etc. □ **reclutar (ejército); hacerse socio (club)**
recruitment *n.* encouraging people to join the army/a club, etc. □ **reclutamiento; inscripción**

rectal ['rektəl] *adj.* referring to the rectum: *rectal thermometer,* thermometer which is inserted into the rectum. □ **rectal**

rectangle ['rektæŋgl] *n.* four-sided shape with right angles and two sets of opposite and equal sides. □ **rectángulo**
rectangular [rek'tæŋgjulə] *adj.* like a rectangle. □ **rectangular**

rectify ['rektifai] *v.* to correct/to make right. □ **rectificar**
rectifiable *adj.* which can be corrected. □ **rectificable**

rectitude ['rektitju:d] *n.* (especially moral) correctness. □ **rectitud**

recto ['rektou] *n.* right/main side (of a piece of paper, page of a book, etc.). □ **recto**

rector ['rektə] *n.* **1** priest in charge of a parish. □ **párroco**
2 official representative of the students at a Scottish university. □ **delegado estudiantil**
3 (*in Scotland*) head of a school/college/university. □ **rector**
rectory *n.* house of a rector. □ **casa del cura**

rectum ['rektəm] *n.* lower part of the intestine, leading to the anus. □ **recto**

recumbent [ri'kʌmbənt] *adj.* (*formal*) lying down. □ **recostado**

recuperate [ri'kju:pəreit] *v.* to recover/to get better after an illness or a loss. □ **recuperar(se)**
recuperation [rikju:pə'reiʃn] *n.* getting better. □ **recuperación**

recur [ri'kə:] *v.* (*it recurred*) to happen again. □ **repetirse**
recurrence [ri'kʌrəns] *n.* reappearance/happening again: *he had a recurrence of his old illness.* □ **reaparición; reproducción (enfermedad)**
recurrent [ri'kʌrənt] **recurring** [ri'kə:riŋ] *adj.* **1** which happens again: *recurrent/recurring bouts of fever.* □ **repetido**
2 ***recurring,*** (decimal figure) which is repeated for ever: *six point three three recurring (6.3333).* □ **periódico**

recycle [ri:'saikl] *v.* to process waste material so that it can be used again: *recycled waste paper,* which is used to make paper once more. □ **reciclar**

red [red] *adj.* and *n.* **1** (colour) like blood or fire: *he has red hair; their house is painted red.* □ **rojo**
2 *it makes him **see red,*** (*informal*) get very angry. □ **le saca de quicio**
3 ***to be in the red,*** (*informal*) to be in debt. □ **estar en números rojos**
4 ***red tape,*** official rules which stop you doing something quickly. □ **papeleo**
5 ***a red herring,*** false track/something which leads you away from the main problem. □ **un pretexto (para desviar la atención)**
6 ***the Reds,*** (*informal*) the Communists. □ **los rojos**
red-brick *adj.* ***red-brick university,*** British university built in the nineteenth century. □ **universidad del siglo pasado**
Red Cross *n.* international organization which cares for the sick and injured, and also organizes relief work. □ **la Cruz Roja**
red currant *n.* common red soft fruit growing in small clusters; the bush which bears this fruit. □ **grosella roja**
redden *v.* to turn red/to blush. □ **enrojecer**
reddish *adj.* rather red. □ **rojizo**
red-handed *adj. they caught him red-handed,* as he was committing a crime. □ **...con las manos en la masa**
red-letter day *n.* very special day. □ **día señalado**
redwood *n.* type of very tall coniferous tree growing on the west coast of North America. □ **secoya**

redecorate [ri:'dekəreit] *v.* to decorate/to paint again. □ **redecorar, pintar de nuevo**

redeem [ri'di:m] *v.* **1** to buy back (something which you have pledged to borrow money); to pay off (a debt). □ **desempeñar; amortizar (una deuda)**
2 to compensate: *his faults are redeemed by his pleasant personality.* □ **expiar**
3 to save from sin. □ **redimir**
Redeemer *n.* Jesus Christ. □ **Redentor**
redeeming *adj.* which compensates: *his one redeeming quality.* □ **que compensa**
redemption [ri'dempʃn] *n.* **1** payment of a debt. □ **amortización**
2 being saved from sin. □ **redención**

redeploy [ri:di'plɔi] *v.* to move (workers/soldiers) from one place to another. □ **recolocar (trabajadores); redesplegar (soldados)**

redouble [ri:'dʌbl] *v. to redouble your efforts,* to try even harder. □ **redoblar esfuerzos**

redoubtable [ri'dautəbl] *adj.* formidable/bold. □ **temible**

redound [ri'daund] *v. it will redound to your credit,* (*formal*) will make you more admired. □ **redundar**

redress [ri'dres] *n.* compensation done to make up for something wrong. □ **reparación**
■ *v.* to correct/to compensate/to repair. □ **corregir, reparar**
to redress the balance, to make things equal again. □ **restablecer**

reduce [ri'dju:s] *v.* **1** to make smaller/lower: *to reduce speed; the temperature has been reduced; the strike has reduced output by half.* □ **reducir**
to reduce someone to the ranks, to punish an officer

by making him an ordinary soldier. □ **degradar**
2 *she's trying* ***to reduce weight***/(*informal*) ***to reduce,*** to get thinner. □ **adelgazar**
3 to force: *he was reduced to begging for money in the street; his opponents were reduced to silence.* □ **obligar**
reduction [ri'dʌkʃn] *n.* lowering (of price/speed/standards). □ **reducción**
redundant [ri'dʌndənt] *adj.* **1** more than necessary. □ **superfluo**
2 *he was made redundant,* he lost his job because he was not needed any more. □ **se quedó sin empleo**
redundancy *n.* losing a job because you are no longer needed. □ **desempleo**
reed [ri:d] *n.* **1** marsh plant with tall stem. □ **caña, junco**
2 part of a wind instrument which vibrates to make a note. □ **lengüeta**
reedy *adj.* **1** high-pitched (voice). □ **aflautada, atiplada**
2 (marsh) which is full of reeds. □ **lleno de juncos**
reef [ri:f] *n.* **1** ridge of rock in the sea: *coral reefs.* □ **arrecife**
2 ***reef knot,*** type of flat knot which does not come undone easily. □ **nudo de rizo**
■ *v.* ***to reef a sail,*** to reduce the size of a sail by rolling part of it up. □ **arrizar las velas**
reefer *n.* **1** sailor's short coat. □ **chubasquero**
2 (*slang*) marijuana cigarette. □ **porro**
reek [ri:k] *n.* strong smell. □ **tufo**
■ *v.* to smell strongly: *the whole place reeked of onions.* □ **apestar**
reel [ri:l] *n.* **1** spool for winding thread/string/film round: *the reel on a fishing rod; a reel of cotton; a cotton reel.* □ **carrete**
2 vigorous Scottish dance. □ **'reel'**
■ *v.* **1** to wind round a reel: *he reeled in his line.* □ **recoger, enrollar**
2 to quote at length: *he reeled off masses of figures.* □ **recitar de un tirón**
3 to stagger. □ **tambalearse**
reelect [ri:i'lekt] *v.* to elect again. □ **reelegir**
reelection [ri:i'lekʃn] *n.* being elected again. □ **reelección**
reenter [ri:'entə] *v.* to enter again. □ **volver a entrar**
reentry [ri:'entri] *n.* entering again: *the spacecraft made a successful reentry into the earth's atmosphere.* □ **nueva entrada**
ref [ref] *n.* (*informal*) (*in sports*) referee. □ **árbitro**
refectory [ri'fektəri] *n.* eating hall (in a school, etc.). □ **comedor**
refectory table, long narrow dining table. □ **mesa de comedor**
refer [ri'fə:] *v.* (*he referred*) **1** to mention: *are you referring to me?* □ **referirse**
2 to look into something for information: *he referred to his notebook/his dictionary.* □ **recurrir**
3 to pass (a problem) to someone else to decide: *the case was referred to the Supreme Court.* □ **remitir**
4 to tell (someone) to see somebody else: *he was referred to the sales department.* □ **mandar**
referee [refə'ri:] *n.* **1** (*in sports*) person who sees that the game is played according to the rules/who judges between two sides: *football referee; the referee stopped the fight.* □ **árbitro**
2 person who gives a report on your character. □ **que da referencias**
■ *v.* to act as a referee in a sports match. □ **arbitrar**
reference ['refrəns] *n.* **1** mention: *there's no reference to the court case in the paper; he kept making references to his uncle.* □ **referencia**
2 direction for further information. □ **referencia**
page reference, note indicating which page to look at. □ **referencia, nota**
reference book, book (such as dictionary/encyclopedia) where you can look up information. □ **libro de consulta**
reference library, library of reference books. □ **biblioteca de consulta**
3 report on someone's character, etc.: *he was given a very good reference from his last job.* □ **referencias**
referral [ri'fə:rl] *n.* act of referring. □ **envío, remisión**
referendum [refə'rendəm] *n.* (*pl. referenda/referendums*) vote by all the people of a country to decide a problem of national importance. □ **referéndum**
refill ['ri:fil] *n.* container with a fresh quantity of liquid/ink, etc.: *I need a refill for my pen; would you like a refill?,* another drink. □ **recambio; otro/a**
■ *v.* [ri:'fil] to fill again. □ **rellenar**
refine [ri'fain] *v.* to make better/more pure: *refined gold.* □ **refinar**
refined *adj.* pure; elegant: *refined taste.* □ **refinado**
refinement *n.* **1** elegance. □ **refinamiento**
2 improvement: *the new car has several refinements.* □ **mejora**
refinery *n.* factory where something is refined: *sugar refinery; oil refinery.* □ **refinería**
refit ['ri:fit] *n.* repairs (to a ship): *she's in harbour for a refit.* □ **embonada, reparación**
■ *v.* [ri:'fit] (*he refitted*) to repair (a ship). □ **calafatear, embonar**
reflate [ri:'fleit] *v.* to stimulate (an economy which has previously been deflated). □ **reactivar**
reflation [ri:'fleiʃn] *n.* action of stimulating a deflated economy. □ **reactivación**
reflect [ri'flekt] *v.* **1** to send back (light/heat/an image): *the light is reflected by the mirror on to the wall; he could see his face reflected in the water.* □ **reflejar**
2 to think back into the past/to ponder: *she reflected that she had never been very lucky.* □ **reflexionar**
3 ***to reflect on someone,*** to be a criticism of someone. □ **desacreditar**
reflection, reflexion [ri'flekʃn] *n.* **1** sending back of light/heat; reflected image: *the cat was looking at her reflection in the mirror.* □ **reflejo**
2 thought. □ **reflexión**
on reflection, on thinking more about it. □ **pensándolo bien**
3 criticism: *it's no reflection on you, if your brother has been sent to prison.* □ **crítica**
reflector *n.* apparatus which reflects. □ **reflector**
reflex ['ri:fleks] *n.* automatic action/instinctive response: *a soldier's reflexes have to be very sharp.* □ **reflejo**
■ *adj.* **1** which is automatic. □ **reflejo**
reflex action, action which is done instinctively. □ **acto reflejo**
2 which returns as a reflection. □ **reflejo**
reflex camera, camera where the picture is reflected from the lens to the viewfinder exactly as it will appear on the photograph. □ **cámara réflex**
reflex angle, angle of more than 180°. □ **ángulo mayor de 180°, cónvaco**
reflexive [ri'fleksiv] *adj.* (*in grammar*) verb or pronoun which refers back to the subject; (as in *'he killed himself'*). □ **reflexivo**
refloat [ri:'flout] *v.* to float again (a ship which has gone aground). □ **poner de nuevo a flote**

reform [ri'fɔ:m] *n.* improving/improvement: *the reform of the educational system; social reforms.* □ **reforma**
■ *v.* **1** to correct/to improve: *she reformed the educational system.* □ **reformar**
2 to become good/to stop committing crime. □ **reformarse**
reformation [refə'meiʃn] *n.* act of reforming. □ **reforma**
the Reformation, religious movement in sixteenth century Europe which brought about the creation of the Protestant churches. □ **la Reforma**
reformatory [ri'fɔ:mətri] *n.* type of prison school where young criminals are sent in the hope that they will be reformed. □ **reformatorio**
reformer *n.* person who tries to improve (a system). □ **reformador**
refraction [ri'frækʃn] *n.* bending of light as it goes from one substance to another (such as into water). □ **refracción**
refractory [ri'fræktəri] *adj.* difficult/disobedient. □ **difícil, rebelde**
refrain [ri'frein] *n.* chorus which is repeated after each section of a song or poem. □ **estribillo**
■ *v.* not to do something: *he refrained from making any comment.* □ **abstenerse**
refresh [ri'freʃ] *v.* **1** to make fresh again; to make less tired: *he had a drink of water to refresh himself; she woke up refreshed after a good night's sleep.* □ **refrescar**
2 *let me* ***refresh your memory,*** help you to remember something which you seem to have forgotten. □ **déjame refrescarte la memoria**
refresher course *n.* lessons which bring your knowledge of your job up to date. □ **cursillo de perfeccionamiento**
refreshing *adj.* **1** which refreshes: *a refreshing shower of rain.* □ **refrescante**
2 new and invigorating: *the new man is a refreshing change from the old headmaster.* □ **estimulante**
refreshment *n.* food and drink: *after the talk light refreshments will be served.* □ **refrigerio, refacción**
refreshment room, room at a railway station where food and drink are served. □ **cantina**
refrigerator [ri'fridʒəreitə] *n.* cooling cupboard for keeping things (especially food) cold: *take the milk out of the refrigerator.* □ **frigorífico, nevera**
refrigerated *adj.* kept cold. □ **refrigerado**
refrigeration [rifridʒə'reiʃn] *n.* keeping things cold. □ **refrigeración**
refuel [ri:'fjuəl] *v.* to put more fuel into (a ship/plane/car, etc.). □ **repostar; echar gasolina (en coche)**
refuge ['refju:dʒ] *n.* place to hide/to shelter: *they took refuge in a mountain hut.* □ **refugio**
refugee [refju:'dʒi:] *n.* person who has been driven out of his own country and needs shelter: *political refugee,* person who has left his country for political reasons; *as the fighting broke out thousands of refugees crossed the border.* □ **refugiado**
refund ['ri:fʌnd] *n.* repayment of money: *this shirt doesn't fit: can I have a refund?* □ **reembolso**
■ *v.* [ri'fʌnd] to pay back (money): *if you are not satisfied your money will be refunded.* □ **reembolsar**
refurbish [ri'fə:biʃ] *v.* to polish up again. □ **restaurar**
refuse ['refju:s] *n.* rubbish: *refuse dump.* □ **desperdicios; basurero**
■ *v.* [ri'fju:z] **1** to say that you do not accept/that you will not do something: *they refused my offer of a lift home; he refuses to say anything.* □ **rechazar; negarse a**
2 not to give someone permission: *he was refused permission to leave the country.* □ **denegar**
refusal [ri'fju:zl] *n.* **1** saying no: *my suggestion met with a flat refusal,* it was refused completely. □ **negativa**
2 ***(the) first refusal,*** the first choice of buying something. □ **primera opción**
refute [ri'fju:t] *v.* to prove that something is wrong. □ **refutar**
refutation [refju:'teiʃn] *n.* proof that something is wrong. □ **refutación**
regain [ri:'gein] *v.* to get back: *he regained consciousness only six days after the accident.* □ **recobrar**
regal ['ri:gl] *adj.* referring to a king/queen; royal. □ **regio**
regalia [ri'geiliə] *n.* robes/crown, etc., worn by a king/queen/mayor, etc. □ **atributos**
regale [ri'geil] *v.* to entertain: *she regaled us with stories about the office where she works.* □ **agasajar**
regard [ri'gɑ:d] *n.* **1** concern: *he has no regard for other people's feelings.* □ **consideración**
with regard to *your application,* concerning your application. □ **con respecto a**
2 esteem: *I have a high regard for her intelligence.* □ **respeto; tengo un buen concepto...**
3 ***regards,*** best wishes: *please give my kind regards to your mother.* □ **recuerdos**
■ *v.* **1** to consider: *I regard him as an idiot; the police are regarding the fire as a case of arson.* □ **considerar**
2 ***as regards*** *your last letter,* concerning your letter. □ **en cuanto a**
regarding *prep.* concerning: *the police are making investigations regarding the disappearance of the jewels.* □ **por lo que se refiere a**
regardless *adj.* **1** paying no attention to. □ **sin hacer caso de**
regardless of expense, not bothering about the expense. □ **sin pensar para nada en lo que cuesta**
2 *carry on regardless,* carry on in spite of everything. □ **adelante, pase lo que pase**
regatta [ri'gætə] *n.* series of boat races (for either yachts or rowing boats). □ **regata**
regenerate [ri'dʒenəreit] *v.* to start up again. □ **regenerar**
regeneration [ridʒenə'reiʃn] *n.* growing again/starting again. □ **regeneración**
regent ['ri:dʒənt] *n.* person who rules in place of a king or queen. □ **regente**
regency *n.* period when a regent is ruling. □ **regencia**
reggae ['regei] *n.* type of West Indian music. □ **'reggae'**
régime [re'ʒi:m] *n.* system of government/administration: *a military régime has come to power.* □ **régimen**
regiment ['redʒimənt] *n.* group of soldiers, usually commanded by a colonel or lieutenant-colonel: *an infantry regiment.* □ **regimiento**
regimental [redʒi'mentl] *adj.* belonging to a regiment. □ **de regimiento**
regimentation [redʒimen'teiʃn] *n.* very strict discipline. □ **organización estricta**
region ['ri:dʒən] *n.* **1** area: *the London region,* area around London. □ **región**
2 *the car costs* ***in the region of*** *$10,000,* about $10,000. □ **alrededor de**
regional *adj.* referring to a region: *regional differences in accent.* □ **regional**
register ['redʒistə] *n.* **1** list (of names): *school register; register of voters.* □ **lista**
2 range of notes covered by a voice/a musical

instrument. □ **registro**
3 ***cash register,*** device which records sales/money taken in a shop. □ **caja registradora**
4 (*in printing*) fitting of several printing plates in such a way that various colours correspond exactly on the paper. □ **registro**
5 level of language (such as formal/colloquial, etc.). □ **registro**
■ *v.* **1** to write a name officially in a list: *are you registered as a voter? to register a child's birth; to register at a hotel,* to write your name and address when you arrive at the hotel. □ **registrar(se)**
2 to put into someone's special care: *to register a parcel; we sent the letter by registered mail.* □ **facturar (un paquete); ...por correo certificado**
3 to record: *the thermometer registered a temperature of* $-10°$. □ **registrar**
4 *it didn't register with her,* she did not seem to be impressed. □ **no parece que le haya impresionado**
registered *adj.* which has been officially recorded: *registered letter; registered trade mark.* □ **carta certificada; marca registrada**
registrar ['redʒistrɑː] *n.* **1** person who keeps official records; person who keeps the records of a university: *registrar of births, marriages and deaths.* □ **registrador; archivero (universidad); secretario del registro civil**
2 specialist doctor in training. □ **(médico) especialista en prácticas**
registration [redʒi'streiʃn] *n.* act of registering. □ **inscripción**
registration plate, number plate of a car. □ **matrícula**
registration number, official number of a car. □ **serie y número de bastidor**
registry ['redʒistri] *n.* place where official records are kept. □ **registro**
registry office, office where records of births, marriages and deaths are kept/place where you can be married in a civil ceremony. □ **registro civil**
regress [ri'gres] *v.* to go back to an earlier, and usually worse, condition. □ **retroceder**
regression *n.* going back. □ **retroceso**
regressive *adj.* which regresses. □ **regresivo**
regret [ri'gret] *n.* sorrow: *much to my regret the house had been sold,* I was very sorry. □ **pena, pesar**
■ *v.* (*he regretted*) to be sorry that something has happened: *I regret to have to tell you that your father is seriously ill.* □ **sentir**
regretful *adj.* sorry/sad. □ **pesaroso**
regretfully *adv.* sadly. □ **con pesar**
regrettable *adj.* which must be regretted: *a regrettable incident.* □ **lamentable**
regular ['regjulə] *adj.* **1** habitual/done at the same time each day: *he is as regular as clockwork; this is my regular time for going to bed; you must have regular meals.* □ **regular**
2 usual/ordinary: *is this your regular seat? regular size packet.* □ **habitual; normal**
3 ***regular army,*** permanent, professional army. □ **ejército regular**
regular officer, professional officer. □ **oficial**
4 ***regular verb,*** (*in grammar*) verb which has no unusual parts. □ **verbo regular**
■ *n.* **1** (*informal*) customer who always shops in a particular shop/who always drinks in a certain bar, etc. □ **cliente habitual**
2 professional soldier. □ **regular**
regularity [regju'læriti] *n.* being regular. □ **regularidad**
regularize ['regjuləraiz] *v.* to make legal. □ **regularizar**
regulate ['regjuleit] *v.* to adjust (a machine) so that it works regularly: *to regulate a clock; to regulate the supply of coal to the power station.* □ **regular**
regulation [regju'leiʃn] *n.* rule. □ **regulación**
regulator *n.* person/instrument which regulates a machine. □ **regulador**
regurgitate [ri'gəːdʒiteit] *v.* (*formal*) to spout out (food which has already been swallowed/information which has already been digested). □ **regurgitar**
rehabilitate [riːhə'biliteit] *v.* to train (a disabled person/an ex-prisoner, etc.) to lead a normal life and fit into society. □ **rehabilitar**
rehabilitation [riːhəbili'teiʃn] *n.* training people to lead a normal life and fit into society. □ **rehabilitación**
rehash ['riːhæʃ] *n.* something produced again in more or less the same form as before. □ **repetición**
■ *v.* [riː'hæʃ] to bring out (an old story/book etc.) in more or less the same form as before. □ **volver a sacar**
rehearse [ri'həːs] *v.* to practise (a play/a concert, etc.) before a public performance. □ **ensayar**
rehearsal [ri'həːsəl] *n.* practice of a play/concert, etc., before a public performance. □ **ensayo**
dress rehearsal, last rehearsal of a play, etc., when everyone is in costume. □ **ensayo general**
reign [rein] *n.* period when a king/queen/emperor rules: *during the reign of Henry VIII.* □ **reinado**
reign of terror, period when law and order have broken down. □ **régimen de terror**
■ *v.* to rule: *chaos reigned during the bus strike.* □ **reinar**
reimburse [riːim'bəːs] *v.* to pay (someone) back the money he has spent. □ **reembolsar**
rein [rein] *n.* strap which controls a horse. □ **rienda**
to keep someone on a tight rein, under strict control. □ **atar corto a alguien**
■ *v.* ***to rein in,*** to pull on the reins to control (a horse). □ **refrenar**
reincarnation [riːinkɑː'neiʃn] *n.* survival of a person's soul which is born again in another body after death. □ **reencarnación**
reindeer ['reindiə] *n.* type of deer which lives in the Arctic. □ **reno**
reinforce [riːin'fɔːs] *v.* to strengthen/to consolidate. □ **reforzar**
reinforced concrete, concrete strengthened with metal rods. □ **hormigón armado**
reinforcement *n.* **1** act of reinforcing. □ **refuerzo**
2 ***reinforcements,*** new soldiers to support others already fighting. □ **refuerzos**
reinstate [riːin'steit] *v.* to put (someone) back into a post which he used to hold. □ **restituir**
reinstatement *n.* putting someone back into a post. □ **reintegración**
reiterate [riː'itəreit] *v.* to repeat. □ **reiterar**
reiteration [riːitə'reiʃn] *n.* repetition. □ **reiteración**
reject ['riːdʒekt] *n.* thing which has been thrown away as not satisfactory. □ **desecho**
rejects, substandard goods sold at a reduced price. □ **productos defectuosos**
■ *v.* [ri'dʒekt] to refuse to accept (something); to throw (something) away as not satisfactory. □ **rechazar**
rejection [ri'dʒekʃn] *n.* refusal. □ **rechazo**
rejoice [ri'dʒɔis] *v.* to be very happy. □ **alegrarse; regocijarse**
rejoicing *n.* great happiness. □ **regocijo**

rejoicings, celebrations. □ **fiestas**
rejoin [ri'dʒɔin] *v.* to join again. □ **reunirse con**
rejoinder *n.* (*formal*) reply. □ **réplica**
rejuvenation [ridʒuːvə'neiʃn] *n.* increase in vitality/becoming temporarily young again. □ **rejuvenecimiento**
rekindle [riː'kindl] *v.* to light again. □ **volver a encender**
relapse [ri'læps] *n.* becoming ill again (after a temporary improvement); getting back into old bad habits. □ **recaída (en mala salud); reincidencia (malas costumbres)**
■ *v.* to become ill again; to get back into old bad habits. □ **recaer (en mala salud); reincidir (malas costumbres)**
relate [ri'leit] *v.* **1** to tell (a story). □ **relatar**
2 to connect two things: *I find it difficult to relate the two aims.* □ **relacionar**
related *adj.* **1** linked. □ **relacionado**
2 belonging to the same family: *we are related; he's related to me by marriage.* □ **emparentado**
relation [ri'leiʃn] *n.* **1** story. □ **relato**
2 linking/links (between two things): *relations between the two countries have got worse.* □ **relación**
public relations, maintaining good connections with the public, especially to put across a point of view/to publicize a product. □ **relaciones públicas**
3 member of a family: *all our relations came together for grandfather's birthday.* □ **familiar**
relationship *n.* link/connection; being related. □ **relación**
relative ['relətiv] *n.* person who is related to someone/a member of a family: *she wouldn't speak to any of her relatives.* □ **pariente, familiar**
■ *adj.* **1** which is compared to something: *the relative performance of two different models of car; their relative poverty,* their poverty compared with really wealthy people or with the wealth they used to have. □ **relativo**
2 ***relative pronoun,*** (*in grammar*) pronoun (such as 'who' and 'which') which connects two clauses. □ **pronombre relativo**
relatively *adv.* comparatively/more or less: *she is relatively happy; he's relatively satisfied with the results.* □ **relativamente**
relativity [relə'tiviti] *n.* (*in physics*) relationship between objects and time and speed. □ **relatividad**
relax [ri'læks] *v.* **1** to slacken/to decrease tension; to make less strict: *the president has relaxed the censorship; the headmaster relaxed the rules about smoking in school.* □ **relajar**
2 to rest from work: *I like to relax in the evening with a good book and a glass of beer.* □ **descansar**
relaxation [riːlæk'seiʃn] *n.* **1** slackening of a rule, etc. □ **relajamiento**
2 rest: *you must take more relaxation.* □ **descanso**
relaxed *adj.* (*informal*) happy/not upset: *he was quite relaxed about it.* □ **tranquilo**
relay ['riːlei] *n.* **1** shift of people working: *they worked in relays to clear the wreckage.* □ **relevo**
2 ***relay race,*** running race by teams in which one runner passes a baton to another who then runs on. □ **carrera de relevos**
■ *v.* [ri'lei] to pass on a message; to pass on a TV/radio broadcast through a relay station. □ **transmitir**
relay station *n.* transmitting station which receives signals from a main transmitter and broadcasts them further. □ **estación repetidora**
release [ri'liːs] *n.* **1** setting free: *the order came for the release of the prisoner.* □ **puesta en libertad**
2 new record/piece of information which is made public: *this week's releases; a government press release.* □ **puesta en venta (de un disco); comunicado de prensa**
■ *v.* **1** to set free: *the prisoners were released.* □ **poner en libertad**
2 to make available to the public: *the government has released details of the trade deal.* □ **dar a conocer**
relegate ['religeit] *v.* to put into a worse position: *the team was relegated,* moved down from one football division to a lower one. □ **relegar; el equipo descendió**
relegation [reli'geiʃn] *n.* moving into a worse position. □ **relegación**
relent [ri'lent] *v.* to change your mind about a strict decision you have taken/to be less strict: *he refused to let her go to the cinema, but after a while he relented.* □ **ablandarse**
relentless *adj.* pitiless. □ **despiadado**
relentlessly *adv.* with no pity. □ **despiadadamente**
relevant ['relivənt] *adj.* which relates/has to do with something being spoken of: *pass me all the relevant documents.* □ **pertinente**
relevance *n.* being relevant: *this information has no relevance to our problem.* □ **aplicabilidad**
reliable [ri'laiəbl] *adj.* which can be relied on/which can be trusted: *they're a very reliable firm; he's an extremely reliable goalkeeper.* □ **fiable, serio (empresa); seguro (portero)**
reliably *adv.* in a way which can be trusted: *I am reliably informed that he is dead.* □ **sé de fuente fidedigna que...**
reliability [rilaiə'biliti] *n.* being reliable: *what I look for in a car is reliability.* □ **seguridad, fiabilidad**
reliant *adj.* which relies on something. □ **confiado**
reliance *n.* trust/confidence. □ **confianza**
relic ['relik] *n.* object which has been left over from the past; holy remains (such as the bones of a saint): *relics of the Roman period.* □ **reliquia; vestigios**
relict *n.* (*formal*) widow. □ **viuda**
relief [ri'liːf] *n.* **1** reducing pain/tension: *she breathed a sigh of relief when the examination was over.* □ **alivio**
2 help: *international relief work.* □ **socorro**
famine relief fund, money collected to help victims of a famine. □ **fondo de socorro contra el hambre**
3 someone/something who takes over from someone else: *a relief nurse; they sent a relief train when the first train broke down.* □ **de relevo**
4 carving in which the details of design stand out. □ **relieve**
relief map, map where mountains are drawn so that an impression of height is given. □ **mapa en relieve**
relieve [ri'liːv] *v.* **1** to reduce (pain/tension): *I was relieved to hear that no one was hurt in the accident.* □ **aliviar**
to relieve yourself, to urinate or defecate. □ **hacer uno sus necesidades**
2 to help: *they set up a fund to relieve the victims of the flood.* □ **socorrer**
3 to take over from (someone): *I have come to relieve you – you can go to bed now.* □ **relevar**
4 to remove a weight from (someone): *let me relieve you of your coat; the robbers relieved him of all his money.* □ **quitar (el abrigo, el dinero a alguien)**
religion [ri'lidʒən] *n.* belief in gods or in one God; system of worship: *the Christian religion.* □ **religión**
religious *adj.* referring to religion. □ **religioso**
religiously *adv.* regularly/at a fixed time of day: *he religiously washes his car every Saturday morning.* □ **religiosamente**

relinquish [ri'liŋkwiʃ] *v.* (*formal*) to leave/to let go: *he relinquished control of the company.* □ **renunciar a**
relish ['reliʃ] *n.* **1** seasoning/flavour; spicy pickles/spicy sauce. □ **picante; aliño**
2 enjoyment: *he told the story with great relish.* □ **fruición**
■ *v.* **1** to enjoy: *he relished every moment of the play.* □ **disfrutar con**
2 *I don't much relish the idea of having to dig the garden,* I am not very enthusiastic. □ **no me entusiasma la idea de...**
relocate [ri:lə'keit] *v.* to set in a new location: *to relocate offices.* □ **trasladar**
relocation [rilə'keiʃn] *n.* setting (offices) in a new location. □ **traslado**
reluctant [ri'lʌktənt] *adj.* not eager/not willing: *I'm reluctant to say yes.* □ **reacio**
reluctantly *adv.* not willingly: *he paid the bill reluctantly.* □ **de mala gana**
reluctance *n.* lack of eagerness. □ **desgana**
rely [ri'lai] *v.* to trust: *I am relying on you to keep me informed; the blind man relied on his dog to guide him.* □ **confiar**
remain [ri'mein] *v.* **1** to stay: *he remained seated, while everyone else stood up; the weather will remain cold for the next few days; after the attack only three houses remained undamaged.* □ **quedarse**
2 ***it remains to be seen,*** we will see in due course. □ **está por ver**
remainder *n.* **1** what is left over: *he spent the remainder of his life in a wheelchair.* □ **el resto**
2 ***remainders,*** books which are sold off cheaply. □ **restos de edición**
■ *v.* to sell off (new books) cheaply. □ **saldar**
remains *n. pl.* **1** dead body. □ **restos mortales**
2 things left over/left behind: *after the fire the remains of the house had to be pulled down; we will eat the remains of the chicken for supper.* □ **restos (de la casa); sobras (de comida)**
remand [ri'mɑ:nd] *v.* to order (a prisoner) to appear at a later hearing of a trial when more evidence will be produced: *he was remanded in custody for two weeks.* □ **mantener bajo custodia**
remand home, place where young criminals can be kept while awaiting trial. □ **reformatorio de menores**
remark [ri'mɑ:k] *n.* comment/observation: *he made a few remarks; they passed remarks about his hair style,* made rude comments. □ **observación; comentario**
■ *v.* to notice/to comment: *I remarked on it several times,* I commented on it. □ **advertir**
remarkable *adj.* unusual/which you might comment on: *a remarkable production of a play.* □ **extraordinario**
remarkably *adv.* unusually: *the weather is remarkably warm for the time of the year.* □ **extraordinariamente**
remedy ['remədi] *n.* something which may cure: *what's your favourite remedy for a cold?* □ **remedio**
■ *v.* to make (something) better/to put (something) right. □ **remediar**
remedial [ri'mi:diəl] *adj.* which cures/which makes something better. □ **curativo; remediador**
remedial class, class of special instruction (as in English or maths) for students who are weak in a subject. □ **clases de recuperación**
remember [ri'membə] *v.* **1** to call back into your mind (something which you have seen/read/heard, etc., before): *I can't remember where I put my book; do you remember the evening we spent by the sea? I don't remember having been to this restaurant before; I'll always remember what my grandfather told me before he died.* □ **acordarse de; recordar**
2 to send good wishes to someone: *remember me to your mother.* □ **dar recuerdos de uno**
3 *he remembered me in his will,* he left me something in his will. □ **me tuvo presente en su testamento**
remembrance *n.* memory: *in remembrance of the soldiers who died.* □ **memoria**
remind [ri'maind] *v.* to make (someone) remember something: *remind me to phone my wife; he reminds me of his father.* □ **recordar**
reminder *n.* something (such as a letter) which reminds you of something: *my library book was overdue, so they sent me a reminder.* □ **recordatorio**
reminiscence [remi'nisəns] *n.* memory of something from the past: *he wrote down his reminiscences of life in the Far East.* □ **recuerdo**
reminisce [remi'nis] *v.* to talk about memories of the past. □ **contar los recuerdos**
reminiscent *adj.* which reminds you of the past: *it is reminiscent of a Greek church.* □ **evocador**
remiss [ri'mis] *adj.* careless: *it was remiss of me to forget.* □ **negligente**
remission [ri'miʃn] *n.* pardon (for your sins); cutting short a prison sentence. □ **perdón (pecado); remisión**
remit ['ri:mit] *n.* orders; area of responsibility. □ **órdenes; responsabilidad**
■ *v.* (*he remitted*) **1** to pardon (sins); to cut short (a prison sentence). □ **perdonar (pecado); rebajar (la pena)**
2 to send (money). □ **remitir**
remittance *n.* sending money; money which is sent. □ **giro**
remnant ['remnənt] *n.* piece/quantity left over: *a few remnants of cloth; the remnants of the army struggled back to their camp.* □ **resto; unos retales (de tela); el resto del ejército...**
remonstrate ['remənstreit] *v.* to protest against something: *I remonstrated with him about his bad habits.* □ **amonestar**
remorse [ri'mɔ:s] *n.* regret about something wicked which you have done. □ **remordimiento**
remorseless *adj.* pitiless/cruel. □ **sin remordimiento**
remorselessly *adv.* cruelly. □ **despiadadamente**
remote [ri'mout] *adj.* **1** distant: *a remote country; a remote possibility.* □ **remoto**
remote control, control (of a model plane, etc.) by radio signals. □ **control remoto**
2 *he hasn't the remotest chance of winning,* the slightest chance. □ **no tiene ni la más remota posibilidad...**
remotely *adv.* distantly: *we are remotely related.* □ **remotamente**
remount [ri:'maunt] *v.* to get back on to (a horse/bicycle, etc.). □ **volver a montar**
remove [ri'mu:v] *n.* grade: *one remove from,* one grade up/down from. □ **grado**
■ *v.* **1** to take away: *he removed my name from the list; they removed the chairs to make room for the dancers.* □ **quitar**
2 to dismiss (someone) from a job: *they're trying to remove the mayor.* □ **destituir**
removable *adj.* which can be removed. □ **trasladable**
removal *n.* moving of a home. □ **mudanza**
removal van, van in which your furniture is moved from one house to another. □ **camión de mudanzas**
remover *n.* **1** person who moves furniture from one house to another. □ **empresario/mozo de mudanzas**

2 something which removes: *paint remover,* liquid which removes old paint. □ **quita...**

remunerate [ri'mju:nəreit] *v.* (*formal*) to pay (someone). □ **remunerar**

remuneration [rimju:nə'reiʃn] *n.* payment. □ **remuneración**

remunerative [ri'mju:nərətiv] *adj.* well paid. □ **remunerativo**

renaissance [re'neisəns] *n.* rebirth/starting again: *a renaissance of interest in spiritualism.* □ **renacimiento**

the Renaissance, artistic movement in late medieval Europe based on a renewal of interest in the Greek and Roman civilizations. □ **el Renacimiento**

renal ['ri:nl] *adj.* referring to the kidneys. □ **renal**

render ['rendə] *v.* **1** to give (back). □ **dar, devolver**

to render an account, to send in a bill. □ **pasar factura**

2 to translate. □ **traducir**

3 ***to render (down),*** to melt (fat). □ **derretir**

4 to cover (a wall) with a coating of cement. □ **enlucir**

5 to make (someone) be: *he was rendered speechless by their attacks.* □ **dejar; le dejaron sin habla...**

rendering *n.* translation; performance (of a song, etc.): *his rendering of the song reduced us to tears.* □ **interpretación**

rendezvous ['rɔndeivu:] *n.* meeting place; meeting: *we have a rendezvous here at 8 o'clock.* □ **lugar de una cita; cita**

■ *v.* (*he rendezvoused*) to arrange to meet: *they rendezvoused at 10 o'clock.* □ **citarse**

rendition [ren'diʃn] *n.* performance (of a song, etc.). □ **interpretación**

renegade ['renigeid] *adj.* and *n.* (person) who gives up a faith/a belief to adopt another; (person) who leaves one group to join another: *a renegade Socialist.* □ **renegado**

renege [ri'neig] *v. to renege on an undertaking,* not to do something which you had promised to do. □ **incumplir**

renew [ri'nju:] *v.* to start again; to replace (something old) with something new: *he had to renew his driving licence; we must renew our subscription to the paper.* □ **renovar**

renewal *n.* act of renewing: *renewal of a licence.* □ **renovación**

rennet ['renit] *n.* substance which when added to milk makes it curdle and so form cheese. □ **cuajo**

renounce [ri'nauns] *v.* to give up officially: *she renounced her claim to the jewels.* □ **renunciar**

renouncement *n.* act of renouncing. □ **renuncia**

renovate ['renəveit] *v.* to make (something) like new: *they are renovating an old house.* □ **renovar**

renovation [renə'veiʃn] *n.* making something like new. □ **renovación**

renown [ri'naun] *n.* fame. □ **renombre**

renowned *adj.* famous for something: *he's renowned for his paintings of street scenes.* □ **célebre**

rent [rent] *n.* **1** money paid for the hire of a flat/house/office, etc.: *the rent of the house is $60 per month.* □ **alquiler**

2 tear/slit (in cloth). □ **rasgón**

■ *v.* **1** to pay money to hire (a house/flat, etc.): *we rent this office from my father.* □ **alquilar**

2 to hire out (a house/flat, etc.) for money: *we rented our house to an American family for the summer.* □ **alquilar**

rental *n.* rent/money paid to hire a room/flat/office, etc. □ **alquiler**

renunciation [rinʌnsi'eiʃn] *n.* giving up/renouncing of a claim. □ **renuncia**

reopen [ri:'oupən] *v.* to open again: *we must try to reopen negotiations; the shop has closed for repairs; it will reopen on March 1st.* □ **volver a abrir**

reorganize [ri:'ɔ:gənaiz] *v.* to organize in a new way. □ **reorganizar**

reorganization [riɔ:gənai'zeiʃn] *n.* act of reorganizing: *the reorganization of the office.* □ **reorganización**

reorientate [ri'ɔ:riənteit] *v.* to set (something) in another direction. □ **dar nueva orientación a**

rep [rep] *n.* (*informal*) **1** travelling salesman. □ **representante**

2 repertory theatre. □ **teatro de repertorio**

repaid [ri:'peid] *v. see* **repay.**

repair [ri'pɛə] *n.* **1** mending: *road repairs; the car broke down and so we had to carry out emergency repairs.* □ **reparación**

2 condition: *to be in a good state of repair/in good repair.* □ **estado; estar en buen/mal estado**

■ *v.* to mend: *I left my shoes to be repaired.* □ **arreglar**

repairer *n.* person who mends. □ **reparador**

repairable *adj.* which can be mended. □ **reparable**

reparation [repə'reiʃn] *n.* something/money which makes up for a wrong. □ **compensación (económica)**

repartee [repɑ:'ti:] *n.* series of witty answers in a conversation. □ **salidas agudas**

repatriate [ri:'pætrieit] *v.* to bring/to send (someone) back to their home country. □ **repatriar**

repatriation [ripætri'eiʃn] *n.* bringing/sending back to the home country. □ **repatriación**

repay [ri:'pei] *v.* (*he repaid*) **1** to pay back: *you don't need to repay the money immediately; how can I repay you for your kindness?* □ **devolver el dinero; pagar**

2 to be worth: *it repays close examination,* it's worth examining carefully. □ **merecer la pena**

repayment *n.* paying back: *repayment of loan.* □ **devolución**

repeal [ri'pi:l] *n.* abolition of a law, so that it is no longer valid. □ **revocación**

■ *v.* to do away with a law. □ **revocar**

repeat [ri'pi:t] *n.* and *adj.* performance which is repeated: *there will be a repeat/a repeat showing of the film tomorrow night.* □ **repetición**

■ *v.* to say/to do (something) again: *could you repeat what you have just said? he repeated the piece of music all over again.* □ **repetir**

repeatedly [ri'pi:tidli] *adv.* over and over again: *he banged on the table repeatedly with a hammer.* □ **repetidamente**

repeater *n.* old pocket watch which rings the hours; gun which can fire several times without being reloaded. □ **reloj de repetición; arma de repetición**

repel [ri'pel] *v.* (*he repelled*) **1** to drive back (an attack). □ **repeler**

2 to disgust/to be so unpleasant that you drive people away. □ **repugnar**

repelling *adj.* disgusting. □ **repugnante**

repellent *adj.* and *n.* (thing) which drives away/which repels: *his breath is really repellent.* □ **repelente**

insect repellent, spray which keeps insects away. □ **producto contra los insectos**

repent [ri'pent] *v.* to be very sorry for something: *he repented his action.* □ **arrepentirse de**

repentance *n.* great regret. □ **arrepentimiento**

repercussion [ripə:'kʌʃn] *n.* result/effect: *the letter*

in the newspaper had wide repercussions, had a surprisingly far-reaching effect. □ **repercusión**
repertoire ['repətwɑː] *n.* works which someone can play/sing by heart; works which a theatre company has ready for performance: *he has a wonderful repertoire of Russian songs.* □ **repertorio**
repertory ['repətri] *n.* **1** ***repertory theatre,*** theatre with a permanent group of actors who play a series of plays, changing them at regular intervals. □ **teatro de repertorio**
2 store (of information/stories, etc.). □ **repertorio, fuente**
repetition [repi'tiʃn] *n.* something which is repeated: *I don't want a repetition of the disgraceful scene last night* □ **repetición**
repetitive [ri'petitiv] *adj.* which repeats itself too frequently. □ **repetitivo**
replace [riː'pleis] *v.* **1** to put (something) back in place: *please replace the books where you found them.* □ **volver a poner**
2 to put (something) in place of something else: *we want to replace our oil heating with gas; he is getting old — we will have to replace him.* □ **sustituir**
replacement *n.* **1** putting something back; replacing something with something else. □ **sustitución**
2 something which is used to replace. □ **recambio**
replacement parts, spare parts (of an engine) used to replace something which has worn out. □ **repuestos**
replay ['riːplei] *n.* **1** football match which is played again because the first match was a draw. □ **repetición de un encuentro**
2 ***action replay,*** section of a sporting event which is shown again on TV at a slower speed, so that the action can be appreciated. □ **repetición**
replenish [ri'pleniʃ] *v.* to fill up again with something: *to replenish supplies.* □ **reponer (las existencias)**
replete [ri'pliːt] *adj.* (*formal*) full and satisfied. □ **repleto**
replica ['replikə] *n.* exact copy of a painting/old aircraft, etc. □ **réplica**
reply [ri'plai] *n.* answer: *what was his reply?* □ **contestación**
■ *v.* to answer: *I wrote to him three weeks ago, but he hasn't replied.* □ **contestar**
report [ri'pɔːt] *n.* **1** description/story of what has happened: *the paper had a long report on the trial.* □ **informe**
2 comments by teachers on a child's progress in school; comments by a commission on a problem: *he's had a very good report this term; a government report on the increase in crime.* □ **informe**
3 explosion: *the gun went off with a loud report.* □ **estampido**
■ *v.* **1** to write a description of what happened: *he reported on his visit to Russia.* □ **escribir un informe/crónica**
2 *you must report the burglary to the police,* give them the details. □ **debes denunciar el robo...**
3 to make a complaint about someone: *I will report you to the headmaster.* □ **dar parte de alguien a**
4 to present yourself officially: *report to the office; he reported for work.* □ **presentarse**
5 *he reports directly to the director,* he is responsible to the director. □ **da cuenta directamente...**
reporter *n.* journalist who writes articles for a newspaper on events. □ **reportero**
repose [ri'pouz] *n.* (*formal*) calm/resting. □ **reposo**
■ *v.* (*formal*) to rest. □ **reposar**
repository [ri'pɔzitri] *n.* warehouse where you can store furniture; store (of information, etc.). □ **guardamuebles; fuente**
reprehensible [repri'hensibl] *adj.* which can be criticized. □ **reprensible**
represent [repri'zent] *v.* **1** to mean/to show: *this symbol represents the site of a battle.* □ **representar**
2 to speak on behalf of (someone/a group of people): *he represents the teachers' union.* □ **hablar en nombre de**
3 to sell goods on behalf of (someone): *he represents two soap firms.* □ **representar**
representation [reprizen'teiʃn] *n.* **1** being represented. □ **representación**
proportional representation, system of voting where the votes cast for each party are more or less accurately reflected in the number of seats each party has in parliament. □ **representación proporcional**
2 ***to make representations about something,*** to protest about something. □ **presentar una petición sobre algo; quejarse por algo**
representative [repri'zentətiv] *adj.* typical: *this is a representative sample of our work.* □ **representativo**
■ *n.* person who represents; travelling salesman; (*in the United States*) member of the lower house of Congress: *the House of Representatives.* □ **representante; el Congreso**
repress [ri'pres] *v.* to keep down/to control. □ **reprimir**
repressed *adj.* kept under strict control. □ **reprimido**
repression [ri'preʃn] *n.* keeping under control. □ **represión**
repressive *adj.* severe/sharp. □ **represivo**
reprieve [ri'priːv] *n.* pardon given to a prisoner: *he was sentenced to death, but the president granted him a reprieve.* □ **indulto**
■ *v.* to pardon: *he was sentenced to death and then reprieved.* □ **indultar**
reprimand ['reprimɑːnd] *n.* severe rebuke. □ **reprimenda**
■ *v.* to criticize someone severely: *he was officially reprimanded for his bad behaviour.* □ **reprender**
reprint ['riːprint] *n.* book which has been printed again. □ **reimpresión**
■ *v.* to print a book again. □ **reimprimir**
reprisal [ri'praizl] *n.* punishment of people (often at random) in revenge for something: *the men of the village were shot as a reprisal for the assassination of the general.* □ **represalia**
reproach [ri'proutʃ] *n.* **1** something which is a disgrace: *these slums are a reproach to the town council.* □ **deshonra**
2 *his conduct was* ***beyond reproach,*** blameless. □ **...era impecable**
3 rebuke: *he heaped reproaches on his staff.* □ **reproche**
■ *v.* to blame (someone) for something: *I reproached him with/for being late.* □ **reprochar**
reproachful *adj.* which blames: *she gave him a reproachful look.* □ **de reproche**
reprobate ['reprəbeit] *n.* wicked person: *he's an old reprobate.* □ **réprobo; malvado**
reproduce [riːprə'djuːs] *v.* **1** to copy: *can this picture be reproduced?* □ **reproducir**
2 to produce young. □ **reproducir**
reproduction [riːprə'dʌkʃən] *n.* **1** copy (of a painting, etc.): *the reproduction is bad on this record,* the quality of the sound is bad. □ **reproducción**
2 production of young. □ **reproducción**

reproductive *adj.* (organs) which produce young. □ **reproductor**
reprographics [riprou'græfiks] *n. pl.* pictures which are reproduced in a book. □ **reprografía**
reproof [ri'pru:f] *n.* (*formal*) blame/criticism. □ **censura**
reprove [ri'pru:v] *v.* (*formal*) to criticize/to blame (someone). □ **censurar**
reproving *adj.* criticizing: *a reproving look.* □ **censurador**
reptile ['reptail] *n.* cold-blooded animal which lays eggs and is covered with scales. □ **reptil**
reptilian [rep'tiliən] *adj.* like a reptile. □ **reptil**
republic [ri'pʌblik] *n.* system of government where there may be elected representatives or where the head of state is an elected or nominated president. □ **república**
republican *adj.* and *n.* referring to a republic; (supporter) of a republic. □ **republicano**
repudiate [ri'pju:dieit] *v.* to reject/to refuse to accept. □ **repudiar**
repudiation [ripju:di'eiʃn] *n.* rejection. □ **repudio**
repugnant [ri'pʌgnənt] *adj.* unpleasant/nasty. □ **repugnante**
repugnance *n.* feeling of distaste/dislike: *she couldn't overcome her repugnance of spiders.* □ **repugnancia**
repulse [ri'pʌls] *v.* to push back. □ **repeler**
repulsion [ri'pʌlʃn] *n.* feeling of dislike/distaste. □ **repulsión**
repulsive *adj.* unpleasant/nasty. □ **repulsivo**
repulsively *adv.* horribly. □ **repulsivamente**
repute [ri'pju:t] *n.* reputation/general opinion: *I only know her by repute,* I have never met her, but I know what people think of her. □ **reputación**
reputable ['repjutəbl] *adj.* well thought of/with a good reputation: *a reputable firm of solicitors.* □ **acreditado**
reputation [repju'teiʃn] *n.* general opinion (of someone): *he has a very good reputation as a children's doctor; he has the reputation of being always drunk.* □ **reputación**
reputed [ri'pju:tid] *adj.* supposed: *the picture is reputed to be by Rembrandt.* □ **supuesto; se atribuye el cuadro a...**
reputedly [ri'pju:tidli] *adv.* according to most people: *he is reputedly the best heart specialist in the country.* □ **según dicen**
request [ri'kwest] *n.* **1** asking/demand: *they are coming here at my request; his request was granted.* □ **petición**
2 *further instructions are available* ***on request,*** if you ask for them. □ **a petición del interesado...**
3 ***request stop,*** bus stop where buses stop only if you signal to them. □ **parada discrecional**
■ *v.* to ask/to demand politely: *as you requested, I am sending a catalogue.* □ **solicitar**
requiem ['rekwiəm] *n.* mass for the dead; music to be sung at a mass for the dead. □ **réquiem**
require [ri'kwaiə] *v.* **1** to demand/to request: *you are required to appear at the court on Monday.* □ **requerir; exigir**
2 to need: *if you want to go to Russia you'll require a visa; do you require anything more?* □ **necesitar**
requirement *n.* what is needed: *one of the requirements for the job is a good knowledge of Arabic.* □ **requisito**
requisition [rekwi'ziʃn] *n.* official order (for something). □ **requisitoria**
■ *v.* to demand/to order that something should be handed over; to demand and take supplies (for an army); to order supplies (for a school). □ **requerir; hacer un pedido (para el colegio)**
requisite ['rekwizit] *adj.* and *n.* (thing) which is necessary. □ **requisito**
toilet requisites, soap/brushes, etc. □ **artículos de baño**
rerun ['ri:rʌn] *n.* second showing of a film on TV. □ **reestreno**
rescind [ri'sind] *v.* to annul/to cancel (a law). □ **rescindir**
rescue ['reskju:] *n.* saving: *rescue of people trapped on a mountain.* □ **rescate**
rescue squad, group of people who are going to save someone. □ **expedición de rescate**
■ *v.* to save: *the firemen rescued ten people from the burning house.* □ **rescatar**
research [ri'sə:tʃ] *n.* scientific study/trying to find out facts: *after years of research they still had not found a cure for the common cold; research team; research worker.* □ **investigación**
■ *v.* to study/to try to find out facts: *he is researching into the cause of the common cold.* □ **investigar**
researcher *n.* person who researches. □ **investigador**
resemble [ri'zembl] *v.* to be similar to: *he resembles his brother.* □ **parecerse a**
resemblance *n.* looking like someone: *there is a strong family resemblance between the brothers.* □ **parecido**
resent [ri'zent] *v.* to feel annoyed at a real or imaginary injury: *I think your mother resents my being here.* □ **tomar a mal**
resentful *adj.* annoyed. □ **resentido**
resentment *n.* annoyance: *there is some resentment because he's had a salary increase.* □ **resentimiento**
reserve [ri'zə:v] *n.* **1** quantity kept back for future special use: *reserves of money; Britain's gold reserves; I'm keeping this bottle of wine in reserve.* □ **reserva**
2 (*in sport*) extra player. □ **reserva**
3 ***reserves,*** part-time troops kept to help the regular army if necessary. □ **reservistas**
4 ***nature reserve,*** area of land where animals and vegetation are protected. □ **reserva natural**
5 shyness; not speaking openly. □ **reserva**
6 (*at an auction*) price which an item must reach before the owner will allow it to be sold. □ **base mínima (en un remate)**
■ *v.* to keep back for a special use; to book (a seat/a table): *I'm reserving this seat for a friend.* □ **reservar**
reservation [rezə'veiʃn] *n.* **1** booking (of a seat/table): *have you a reservation?* □ **reserva**
2 doubts: *I agreed to the plan, but with reservations; he accepted without any reservation.* □ **reserva**
3 national park; area where indigenous tribes live: *Indian reservation.* □ **reserva**
reserved *adj.* **1** booked: *are these seats reserved?* □ **reservado**
2 shy; (person) who does not speak openly. □ **reservado**
reservist [ri'zə:vist] *n.* part-time soldier who is a member of the army reserves. □ **reservista**
reservoir ['rezəvwɑ:] *n.* **1** large (usually artificial) lake where water is kept for pumping to a town. □ **embalse**
2 container (for storing liquids); mass (of information/facts) which can be used if necessary. □ **depósito**
reshuffle [ri:'ʃʌfl] *n.* reorganization (of ministers in

a government) □ **crisis de gobierno**
■ *v.* **1** to shuffle again: *he reshuffled the cards.* □ **volver a barajar**
2 to reorganize (the ministers in a government). □ **reorganizar**

reside [ri'zaid] *v.* (*formal*) to live/to have a house: *he resides in the country.* □ **residir**
residence ['rezidəns] *n.* **1** place where you live: *the mayor's residence.* □ **residencia**
2 act of living in a place: *is he in residence?,* is he living here now? □ **residencia**
3 ***hall of residence,*** block of flats where students live. □ **residencia de estudiantes**
resident ['rezidənt] *adj.* living permanently in a place: *he's the resident engineer; he was resident in London for several years.* □ **residente; el ingeniero fijo**
■ *n.* person who lives in a place: *she's a resident of Paris.* □ **residente**
residential [rezi'denʃl] *adj.* (part of a town) with houses rather than shops or factories. □ **residencial**

residue ['rezidju:] *n.* what is left over: *pour the residue into a glass jar.* □ **residuo**
residual [re'zidjuəl] *adj.* remaining. □ **residual**

resign [ri'zain] *v.* **1** to give up a job: *he resigned and bought a farm.* □ **dimitir**
2 ***to resign yourself to doing something,*** to accept that you will have to do it. □ **resignarse a**
resignation [rezig'neiʃn] *n.* **1** giving up a job: *he tendered/handed in his resignation,* he resigned. □ **dimisión**
2 acceptance that something has to happen. □ **resignación**
resigned *adj.* accepting that something has to happen: *she was resigned to spending the rest of her life alone.* □ **resignado**
resignedly [ri'zainidli] *adv.* patiently/calmly/without complaining. □ **con resignación**

resilient [ri'ziliənt] *adj.* (material) which easily returns to its original shape (after being crushed); (person) who is strong/able to recover easily from a blow. □ **elástico (material); resistente (persona)**
resilience *n.* ability to recover easily after a blow. □ **elasticidad; resistencia**

resin ['rezin] *n.* sticky sap, especially from pine trees. □ **resina**

resist [ri'zist] *v.* **1** to oppose/not to give in to (something): *the castle resisted the attacks of the enemy; I resisted the temptation to have another cake.* □ **resistir**
2 *she couldn't resist telling the headmaster what she thought of him,* she couldn't stop herself. □ **no pudo resistir decirle...**
resistance *n.* **1** opposition/fight against something: *the town surrendered and offered no resistance.* □ **resistencia**
resistance movement, movement of ordinary people against an invader. □ **movimiento de resistencia**
2 *he took* ***the line of least resistance,*** he did it the easiest way. □ **siguió la ley del mínimo esfuerzo**
3 (*in physics*) force which opposes something; ability not to conduct electricity/heat, etc. □ **resistencia**
resistor *n.* device which increases the resistance to an electric current/which prevents a current from flowing. □ **reóstato**

resit [ri:'sit] *v.* to take (an examination) again (after failing the first time). □ **examinarse por segunda vez**

resolute ['rezəlu:t] *adj.* determined/having made up your mind. □ **resuelto**
resolution [rezə'lu:ʃn] *n.* **1** decision reached at a meeting; proposal to be decided at a meeting: *the resolution was passed unanimously.* □ **resolución**
2 determination (to do something)/strength of character. □ **decisión**
3 solving (of a problem). □ **resolución**
4 splitting up into chemical parts. □ **separación**

resolve [ri'zɔlv] *n.* determination (to do something). □ **decisión**
■ *v.* **1** to decide to do something: *the meeting resolved to write to the Prime Minister.* □ **decidir**
2 to solve (a problem). □ **resolver**
3 to split up into chemical parts. □ **descomponer**

resonant ['rezənənt] *adj.* which sounds/rings/echoes loudly: *he has a resonant voice.* □ **resonante**
resonance *n.* deep loud ringing tone. □ **resonancia**

resort [ri'zɔ:t] *n.* **1** place where people go on holidays: *holiday resort; seaside resort; we went to a little resort in the Swiss mountains.* □ **lugar de veraneo**
2 ***as a last resort/in the last resort,*** when everything else fails: *he tried all the keys in the house to open the cupboard door, and as a last resort used a piece of bent wire.* □ **como último recurso**
■ *v.* to use something (in a difficult situation/when everything else has failed): *in the end he resorted to violence.* □ **recurrir**

resound [ri'zaund] *v.* to make a loud, echoing, deep noise. □ **resonar**
resounding *adj.* great/total: *it was a resounding success.* □ **clamoroso**

resource [ri'sɔ:s] *n.* source of supply for what is needed/used: *a country's natural resources,* minerals/oil/trees, etc.. □ **recurso**
resource centre, area in a school which provides books/equipment for school work. □ **centro didáctico**
to leave someone to his own resources: *he was left to his own resources,* he was left to look after himself. □ **fuerzas, recursos**
resourceful *adj.* good at looking after yourself/at dealing with problems. □ **despabilado**

respect [ri'spekt] *n.* **1** admiration/regard: *I hold him in respect; you must show him proper respect.* □ **respeto**
2 *please give your father my respects,* best wishes. □ **...mis respetos a tu padre**
3 concern/detail. □ **respecto**
in respect to *your complaint,* concerning. □ **con respecto a...**
in some respects, in some ways. □ **en algunos aspectos**
■ *v.* **1** to admire/to honour (someone). □ **respetar**
2 to pay attention to (something): *we will respect his desire for secrecy.* □ **respetar**
respectability [rispektə'biliti] *n.* being respectable. □ **respetabilidad**
respectable [ri'spektəbl] *adj.* **1** proper/worthy of respect: *a very respectable family doctor.* □ **respetable**
2 quite large/fairly large: *he earns a respectable salary.* □ **respetable**
respectably *adv.* properly: *he was very respectably dressed.* □ **respetablemente**
respectful *adj.* full of respect: *a respectful bow.* □ **respetuoso**
respectfully *adv.* showing respect. □ **respetuosamente**
respective *adj.* referring to each one separately: *after dinner we went to our respective bedrooms; their respective ages are thirty, twenty-eight and twenty-two.* □ **respectivo**
respectively *adv.* referring to each one separately:

they are thirty, twenty-eight and twenty-two years old respectively. □ **respectivamente**
respiration [respi'reiʃn] *n.* breathing in of air. □ **respiración**
to give someone artificial respiration, to force someone (who is almost dead from drowning) to breathe. □ **respiración artificial**
respite ['respait] *n.* rest: *he worked for days without respite,* without stopping. □ **respiro; tregua**
resplendent [ri'splendənt] *adj.* very splendid. □ **resplandeciente**
respond [ri'spɔnd] *v.* to reply/to react: *he responded to treatment,* he began to get better; *when we first made the suggestion they responded very angrily.* □ **responder**
respondent *n.* defendant in a law suit, especially in a divorce case. □ **demandado**
response *n.* **1** answer: *in response to your request; we've had no response to our advertisement.* □ **respuesta**
2 reply made by the congregation to the priest in a church service. □ **contestación**
responsibility [rispɔnsi'biliti] *n.* **1** being responsible: *position of responsibility,* position where decisions have to be taken; *he has taken on a lot of responsibility,* he has agreed to be responsible for many things. □ **responsabilidad**
2 thing which you are responsible for: *locking the door is the caretaker's responsibility.* □ **responsabilidad**
responsible *adj.* **1** causing: *the fire was responsible for damage amounting to millions of dollars.* □ **responsable**
2 taking decisions for something/directing something: *Jones is responsible for all our sales in Europe.* □ **responsable**
3 *responsible to someone,* being under the authority of someone who expects you to carry out the work well: *he is responsible to the manager for running the department.* □ **responsable**
4 trustworthy: *she is a very responsible person.* □ **responsable**
5 *responsible position,* post where decisions have to be taken. □ **cargo de responsabilidad**
responsive *adj.* (person) who reacts quickly/who shows sympathy. □ **sensible**
responsiveness *n.* sensitivity. □ **sensibilidad**
rest [rest] *n.* **1** sleep/calm state: *he had a good night's rest.* □ **descanso**
to set someone's mind at rest, to calm someone's worries. □ **tranquilizar a alguien**
2 stop. □ **parada**
to come to rest: *the car came to rest at the bottom of the hill,* stopped moving. □ **detenerse**
3 (*in music*) short break between notes. □ **pausa**
4 support. □ **apoyo**
arm rest, part of a chair which you put your arms on. □ **brazo**
head rest, cushion to support your head (usually attached to a seat in a car). □ **apoyacabezas**
5 remains/what is left over: *what are the rest of you going to do? he poured the rest of his tea down the sink.* □ **resto**
■ *v.* **1** to sleep/to be calm: *she's resting.* □ **descansar**
2 to make (something) be calm: *sit down and rest your poor legs.* □ **descansar**
3 ***to let the matter rest,*** not to deal with the problem any more. □ **dejar estar**
restful *adj.* calm/which makes you feel calm. □ **descansado**
restless *adj.* **1** always on the move. □ **inquieto**
2 *the patient had a restless night,* was not able to sleep properly. □ **...noche intranquila**
restlessness *n.* agitation/constant movement. □ **inquietud**
restroom *n. Amer.* toilet/lavatory. □ **lavabos**
restaurant ['restrɔnt] *n.* place where you can buy a meal. □ **restaurante**
self-service restaurant, where you serve yourself. □ **autoservicio**
restaurant car, carriage on a train where you can have a meal. □ **coche restaurante**
restitution [resti'tju:ʃn] *n.* compensation/paying back. □ **restitución; indemnización**
restive ['restiv] *adv.* nervous/agitated. □ **intranquilo**
restiveness *n.* agitation. □ **intranquilidad**
restore [ris'tɔ:] *v.* **1** to give back: *the stolen jewels were restored to their owners.* □ **restituir**
2 to repair/to make (something) new again: *to restore an old house/a painting.* □ **restaurar**
restoration [restə'reiʃn] *n.* **1** giving back. □ **devolución**
2 repairing something/making something look like new again. □ **restauración**
restorative [ri'stɔrətiv] *adj.* and *n.* (medicine) which makes you stronger. □ **reconstituyente**
restorer *n.* person who restores old paintings, etc.. □ **restaurador**
hair restorer, liquid which is supposed to make your hair grow again. □ **crecepelo**
restrain [ri'strein] *v.* **1** to hold back. □ **frenar**
to restrain someone from doing something, to prevent/to try and stop. □ **impedir**
2 *I had difficulty in restraining myself,* in keeping myself under control. □ **encontré difícil contenerme**
restrained *adj.* controlled/calm. □ **comedido**
restraint *n.* control: *with great restraint,* without losing your temper; *lack of restraint,* (excessive) freedom. □ **restricción**
wage restraint, keeping wage increases under control. □ **moderación salarial**
restrict [ri'strikt] *v.* to limit: *you are restricted to three gallons of petrol.* □ **restringir**
restricted *adj.* limited. □ **restringido**
restricted area, (i) area where cars must obey a speed limit. □ **zona de velocidad limitada**
(ii) area where only certain people are allowed. □ **zona de acceso restringido**
restriction [ri'strikʃn] *n.* limitation: *speed restrictions.* □ **limitación de velocidad**
restrictive *adj.* which restricts/limits. □ **restrictivo**
result [ri'zʌlt] *n.* **1** something which happens because of something; outcome: *the result of all our efforts was that a committee will study the problem; he complained several times, but with no result.* □ **resultado**
2 score (in a game); marks (in an exam). □ **resultado**
■ *v.* to happen because of something which has been done; to produce as an effect: *the riots resulted from an increase in the price of bread; the road works resulted in a traffic jam.* □ **derivarse de (agitación); tener como resultado (las obras)**
resume [ri'zju:m] *v.* to start again after an interruption: *the meeting will resume in 15 minutes' time; the men resumed work yesterday.* □ **reanudar(se)**
resumption [ri'zʌmpʃn] *n.* starting again: *resumption of work/of negotiations.* □ **reanudación**
résumé ['rezu:mei] *n.* short summing up of the main points: *a résume of a long newspaper article.* □ **resumen**
resurface [ri:'sə:fəs] *v.* **1** to put a new surface (on a

road). □ **rehacer el firme**
2 to reappear on the surface. □ **volver a salir a la superficie**

resurgent [ri'sə:dʒənt] *adj.* which is rising again/becoming more powerful again. □ **renaciente**
resurgence *n.* reappearance/rising again. □ **resurgimiento**

resurrect [rezə'rekt] *v.* to bring back to use; to start up again: *they've resurrected a medieval play.* □ **resucitar**
resurrection [rezə'rekʃn] *n.* bringing back to life. □ **resurrección**

resuscitate [ri'sʌsiteit] *v.* to bring (someone who is almost dead) back to life. □ **resucitar**
resuscitation [risʌsi'teiʃn] *n.* bringing back to life. □ **resurrección**

retail ['ri:teil] *n.* selling small quantities of goods to an ordinary person (not to a shopkeeper who will sell them again): *what is the difference between the retail and wholesale price?* □ **venta al por menor**
retail outlet, shop which sells goods direct to the customer. □ **comercio minorista**
■ *v.* 1 to sell goods direct to customers who will not sell them again: *this clock retails at $20,* is sold at $20. □ **vender**
2 to pass on (gossip). □ **repetir (cotilleo)**
retailer *n.* shopkeeper who sells goods to users. □ **minorista**

retain [ri'tein] *v.* 1 to keep: *he managed to retain control of the car on the icy road.* □ **mantener**
2 *to retain a lawyer to act for you,* to agree with a lawyer that he will act for you (and to pay him in advance). □ **contratar a un abogado...**
retaining wall, wall which holds back a mass of earth/the water in a reservoir, etc. □ **muro de contención**
retainer *n.* 1 money paid in advance to someone for work he will do later. □ **anticipo**
2 (old) servant. □ **criado**

retaliate [ri'tælieit] *v.* to hit back/to attack (someone) in revenge: *after he refused to pay his telephone bill, the post office retaliated by cutting off his telephone.* □ **tomar represalias**
retaliation [ritæli'eiʃn] *n.* ***in retaliation,*** as a reprisal for something. □ **represalia**

retard [ri'tɑ:d] *v.* to make slow/to keep something late. □ **retardar; retrasar**
retarded *adj.* mentally slower than someone of the same age. □ **retrasado**

retch [retʃ] *v.* to have spasms in the throat as if you were about to vomit. □ **náusea**

retention [ri'tenʃn] *n.* keeping/holding. □ **retención**
retentive *adj.* (memory) which retains well. □ **retentivo**

rethink [ri:'θiŋk] *v.* to think again/to reconsider: *we must rethink our foreign policy.* □ **repensar**

reticent ['retisənt] *adj.* uncommunicative/not willing to talk about something. □ **reservado**
reticence *n.* unwillingness to talk. □ **reserva**

retina ['retinə] *n.* back part of the eye which is sensitive to light. □ **retina**

retinue ['retinju:] *n.* group of people following an important person. □ **séquito; comitiva**

retire [ri'taiə] *v.* 1 to stop work (and take a pension); to make (someone) stop work (and take a pension): *most men retire when they are sixty-five; the retiring age for women is sixty; he was retired early.* □ **jubilarse**
2 to go away into a place by yourself: *she is a retiring sort of person,* quiet and reserved. □ **retirarse**
3 *he retired to bed/he retired for the night,* he went to bed. □ **se fue a dormir/acostarse**
retirement *n.* 1 act of retiring from work. □ **jubilación**
2 period of life when you are retired: *is your father enjoying his retirement?* □ **retiro; jubilación**

retort [ri'tɔ:t] *n.* 1 sharp reply. □ **réplica**
2 glass bottle with a long, thin bent neck used for distilling. □ **retorta**
■ *v.* to reply sharply: *'don't be so silly', he retorted.* □ **replicar**

retouch [ri:'tʌtʃ] *v.* to improve (a picture/a photograph) by adding or removing lines by hand. □ **retocar**

retrace [ri:'treis] *v.* 1 to go back to the origins of something. □ **remontarse a**
2 *he retraced his steps,* went back over the same path again. □ **volvió sobre sus pasos**

retract [ri'trækt] *v.* to pull back; to withdraw (something said): *the pilot retracted the undercarriage; he retracted his accusation.* □ **retirar**
retractable *adj.* (undercarriage of a plane) which folds up into the body of the plane. □ **retráctil**
retraction [ri'trækʃn] *n.* pulling back; folding up. □ **retracción**

retread ['ri:tred] *n.* tyre which has had its surface renewed: *I have only got one new tyre - the other three are retreads.* □ **recauchutado**
■ *v.* to renew the surface of a tyre. □ **recauchutar**

retreat [ri'tri:t] *n.* 1 withdrawing from a battle: *the retreat of the French army from Moscow.* □ **retirada**
2 quiet place: *he has a little retreat in the country.* □ **refugio**
3 period of calm meditation (in a religious establishment). □ **retiro**
■ *v.* to withdraw from a battle: *the enemy retreated into the mountains.* □ **retirarse**

retrench [ri'trentʃ] *v.* to economize/to cut back on expenditure. □ **ahorrar**
retrenchment *n.* reduction of expenditure. □ **ahorro**

retrial [ri:'traiəl] *n.* second trial: *the judge ordered a retrial,* ordered the case to be heard again. □ **nuevo juicio**

retribution [retri'bju:ʃn] *n.* punishment. □ **castigo justo**

retrieve [ri'tri:v] *v.* to get back (something) which was lost; to bring back (something): *the police retrieved the revolver from the lake; I must retrieve my umbrella from the cloakroom.* □ **recuperar**
retrieval *n.* getting back. □ **recuperación**
retrieval system, system (in a catalogue/in a computer program) to allow information to be retrieved. □ **sistema de recuperación (de datos)**
retriever *n.* type of dog trained to fetch birds which have been shot. □ **perro cobrador**

retroactive [retrou'æktiv] *adj.* which takes effect from a time in the past: *a pay increase retroactive to last April,* which takes effect from last April. □ **retroactivo**

retrograde ['retrəgreid] *adj.* 1 backward. □ **retrógrado**
2 *it would be a retrograde step,* it would make things worse than they were before. □ **...un paso hacia atrás**

retrospect ['retrəspekt] *n.* ***in retrospect,*** when you look back: *if you consider his career in retrospect.* □ **retrospectivamente**
retrospective [retrə'spektiv] *adj.* and *n.* which looks back on past events; (exhibition) of works of

art covering the whole career of an artist. □ **retrospectivo/a**

return [ri'tə:n] *n.* **1** going back/coming back: *on my return home,* when I got back home. □ **vuelta; regreso**

return ticket, ticket which allows you to go to one place and come back: *I want two returns to London,* two return tickets. □ **billete de ida y vuelta**

many happy returns of the day, best wishes for a happy birthday. □ **feliz cumpleaños**

by return of post, by the next post service back. □ **a vuelta de correo**

2 profit/income from money invested: *does the savings bank give you a good return on capital?* □ **interés; rédito**

3 sending back. □ **devolución**

4 *to sell something on sale or return,* the wholesaler will take it back if the retailer cannot sell it. □ **en depósito**

5 ***income-tax return,*** statement of income, etc., to the tax office. □ **declaración de la renta**

6 (*in tennis, etc.*) sending back of a ball. □ **resto (en tenis)**

7 ***return match,*** match played between two teams who have played each other recently. □ **encuentro de vuelta**

■ *v.* **1** to come back/to go back: *they returned from holiday last week; the strikers have returned to work.* □ **volver**

2 to give back/to send back: *he borrowed a saucepan and never returned it.* □ **devolver**

3 to elect someone to parliament: *he was returned with a large majority.* □ **elegir**

returning officer *n.* official who is responsible for an election in a constituency. □ **escrutador**

reunion [ri:'ju:niən] *n.* meeting of people who have not met for a long time: *a reunion of old soldiers.* □ **reunión**

reunite [ri:ju:'nait] *v.* to join two things together again. □ **reunir; juntar**

rev [rev] *n.* (*informal*) *short for* revolution: *the engine was turning at 4,000 revs a minute.* □ **revolución**

■ *v.* (*he revved*) (*informal*) to make a car engine go quickly while the car is standing still: *he was revving up his engine.* □ **pegar acelerones con el coche parado**

revalue [ri:'vælju:] *v.* to value again (usually at a higher value). □ **revalorizar**

revaluation [rivælju'eiʃn] *n.* revaluing/recalculating the value. □ **revaloración**

revamp [ri:'væmp] *v.* (*informal*) to improve the appearance of (something which is slightly old-fashioned). □ **renovar**

reveal [ri'vi:l] *v.* to show (something) which was hidden: *he revealed the identity of the masked raider; the curtains opened, revealing a bare stage with two chairs.* □ **revelar**

revealing dress, dress which shows a woman's figure very clearly. □ **vestido transparente**

revelation [revə'leiʃn] *n.* surprise: *the book came as a revelation to me,* was an unexpected surprise. □ **revelación**

reveille [ri'væli] *n.* (*in the army*) signal to soldiers to get up in the morning. □ **diana**

revel ['revəl] *n.* ***revels,*** merrymaking/happy celebrations. □ **juerga**

■ *v.* (*he revelled*) to take delight; to have a happy time: *he revels in long arguments.* □ **deleitarse con**

reveller *n.* person who is celebrating. □ **juerguista**

revelry *n.* celebration. □ **juerga; jarana**

revenge [ri'venʒ] *n.* action to harm someone in return for harm he has caused you: *I'll get/have my revenge on you; he took his revenge; they burnt down the farmhouse in revenge for the farmer's cruelty.* □ **venganza**

■ *v.* to harm (someone) in return for harm he has caused you: *he revenged the murder of his mother; she revenged herself on her sister.* □ **vengarse de**

revengeful *adj.* wanting revenge. □ **vengativo**

revenue ['revənju:] *n.* money which is received; taxes which a government receives. □ **renta; rentas públicas; ingresos del erario**

reverberate [ri'və:bəreit] *v.* to echo/to ring out loudly in an echo: *the sound of the cannon reverberated round the hills.* □ **reverberar**

reverberation [rivə:bə'reiʃn] *n.* echoing. □ **reverberación**

revere [ri'viə] *v.* to worship/to respect someone very highly. □ **reverenciar/venerar**

reverence ['revrəns] *n.* **1** great respect. □ **reverencia**

2 bow (as a mark of respect). □ **inclinación de la cabeza**

reverend *adj.* **1** worthy of respect. □ **reverendo**

2 title given to priests: *the Reverend Albert Smith.* □ **reverendo**

reverent *adj.* showing respect. □ **reverente**

reverently *adv.* very respectfully. □ **reverentemente**

reverie ['revəri] *n.* daydream. □ **ensueño**

reversal [ri'və:səl] *n.* **1** change to something opposite. □ **cambio completo**

2 *a reversal of fortune,* bad luck. □ **revés**

reverse [ri'və:s] *adj.* **1** opposite. □ **opuesto**

2 *say the alphabet in reverse order,* say 'z - y - x - w - v', etc. □ **...al revés**

■ *n.* **1** the opposite: *the truth is quite the reverse,* just the opposite (of what has been said); *are you too cold? - quite the reverse.* □ **lo contrario**

2 gear of a car which makes you go backwards: *he put the car into reverse.* □ **marcha atrás**

3 defeat (in battle): *the enemy suffered a series of reverses.* □ **revés**

■ *v.* **1** to do the opposite; to make a car go backwards: *he reversed into the garage.* □ **cambiar por completo; dar marcha atrás**

to reverse the charges, (*on the phone*) to ask the person you are calling to pay for the call. □ **llamar a cobro revertido**

2 to change a decision to the opposite: *the judge reversed the sentence which had been passed on the prisoner; the director reversed his decision.* □ **revocar**

reversible *adj.* (cloth/coat) which can be worn with either side out. □ **reversible**

revert [ri'və:t] *v.* **1** to go back/to come back to: *he tried speaking in French, but soon reverted to English; the property reverted to its original owner.* □ **volver a**

to revert to type, to go back to an original state. □ **volver a su estado primitivo**

2 *to revert to a subject,* to start talking about the subject again. □ **volver al tema**

reversion [ri'və:ʃn] *n.* return to an original state/to an original owner. □ **reversión**

review [ri'vju:] *n.* **1** written opinion of a book/play/film, etc.: *he writes the film reviews in our local paper.* □ **crítica; reseña**

2 magazine which contains articles about new books/films/plays, etc. □ **revista**

3 general examination: *he gave a review of the firm's progress over the past few years.* □ **repaso general**

to come under review: *the organization of the club has come under review recently,* people have been

examining it critically. □ **...la han examinado críticamente**
4 general inspection of soldiers/naval vessels, etc. □ **revista**
■ *v.* **1** to write your opinion of (a book/play/film, etc.): *the book has been well reviewed.* □ **reseñar; criticar**
2 to inspect (soldiers/naval vessels, etc.). □ **pasar revista**
3 to consider generally: *he reviewed the firm's progress over the past few years.* □ **analizar**
reviewer *n.* person who writes opinions of books/plays/films, etc. □ **crítico**

revile [ri'vail] *v.* (*formal*) to insult; to criticize sharply. □ **injuriar**

revise [ri'vaiz] *v.* **1** to read/to study a lesson again: *you must revise your geography as your exam is tomorrow.* □ **repasar**
2 to correct/to change: *a revised draft of the club rules; the editors spent years revising the encyclopedia; to revise your opinion,* to alter your opinion. □ **modificar; corregir**
revision [ri'viʒən] *n.* act of revising. □ **revisión**
revisionism *n.* revising the original pure concept (of a political movement, especially communism). □ **revisionismo**

revive [ri'vaiv] *v.* to come back/to bring back to life again: *business is reviving after the war; the theatre is reviving a nineteenth century comedy.* □ **reanimar**
revival *n.* bringing back to life: *a revival of interest in archery.* □ **restablecimiento**
religious revival, period of new interest in religion. □ **despertar religioso**
revivalist *n.* person who leads a religious revival. □ **evangelista**

revoke [ri'vouk] *v.* to cancel: *your licence has been revoked.* □ **revocar; han suspendido tu permiso**

revolt [ri'voult] *n.* uprising against authority: *the workers are in revolt.* □ **rebelión**
■ *v.* **1** to rise up against authority: *the people revolted against the taxes imposed by the government.* □ **rebelarse**
2 to disgust: *he was revolted by what he saw in the kitchen.* □ **repugnar**
revolting *adj.* disgusting/which makes you feel ill: *a revolting mess of food.* □ **repugnante**

revolution [revə'lu:ʃn] *n.* **1** rotation/turning around a central point: *the earth completes a revolution round the sun; the engine was turning at 1,000 revolutions per minute.* □ **revolución; giro**
2 uprising against a government: *the Russian Revolution.* □ **revolución**
revolutionary *adj.* **1** aiming to change things completely; very new: *a revolutionary new toothpaste.* □ **revolucionario**
2 referring to a political revolution. □ **revolucionario**
■ *n.* person who takes part in an uprising against a government: *the revolutionaries were sentenced to be shot.* □ **revolucionario**
revolutionize *v.* to change completely: *the computer has completely revolutionized the printing of newspapers.* □ **revolucionar**

revolve [ri'vɔlv] *v.* **1** to turn round: *the wheel revolves round its axle.* □ **girar**
2 to be centred on: *the problem revolves around the weak foundations.* □ **girar en torno a**
revolver *n.* small hand gun with a cartridge chamber which turns after each shot is fired. □ **revólver**
revolving *adj.* which turns round: *revolving doors.* □ **puertas giratorias**

revue [ri'vju:] *n.* stage show with satirical sketches/songs, etc. □ **revista**

revulsion [ri'vʌlʃn] *n.* (*formal*) disgust: *she stepped back from the corpse in revulsion.* □ **repulsión**

reward [ri'wɔ:d] *n.* money/present given to someone as a prize or for information: *she gave him $1 as a reward for finding her purse; the bank is offering $500 reward for information about the robber.* □ **recompensa**
■ *v.* to give (someone) money/a present as a prize or for giving information: *the boy did some shopping for the old lady and she rewarded him with a slice of cake.* □ **recompensar; ...y ella le premió con...**
rewarding *adj.* which gives moral satisfaction: *a rewarding task.* □ **que compensa**

rhapsody ['ræpsədi] *n.* **1** poetry/music/song showing great excitement/passion. □ **rapsodia**
2 ***to go into rhapsodies:*** *he went into rhapsodies over the car he had seen,* he praised it extravagantly. □ **se deshizo en elogios...**
rhapsodize *v.* to praise extravagantly: *she rhapsodized over their new house.* □ **estar entusiasmado**

rheostat ['riəstæt] *n.* device for making lights fade by cutting down the flow of electric current gradually. □ **reóstato**

rhesus ['ri:səs] *adj.* ***rhesus monkey,*** small monkey, often used in laboratories for scientific research. □ **macaco de la India**
rhesus factor, substance in the blood (or absent from it) which can affect new-born babies and people having blood transfusions. □ **factor rhesus (Rh)**
rhesus positive, having a rhesus factor. □ **Rh positivo**
rhesus negative, with no rhesus factor. □ **Rh negativo**

rhetoric ['retərik] *n.* art of speaking forcefully and eloquently. □ **retórica**
rhetorical [ri'tɔrikl] *adj.* referring to rhetoric. □ **retórico**
a rhetorical question, question to which you do not expect an answer. □ **una pregunta retórica**

rheumatism ['ru:mətizəm] *n.* disease causing pains in the joints or muscles. □ **reumatismo**
rheumatic [ru:'mætik] *adj.* referring to rheumatism: *a rheumatic knee.* □ **reumático**
rheumatic fever, serious disease of children and young people where your joints swell. □ **fiebre reumática**
rheumatoid arthritis *n.* continuing disease of the joints where they become stiff, swollen and painful. □ **artritis reumatoide**

rhinestone ['rainstoun] *n.* imitation colourless precious stone. □ **piedra falsa**

rhinoceros [rai'nɔsərəs] (*informal*) **rhino** *n.* huge Asiatic or African animal with a thick skin and one or two horns on its head. □ **rinoceronte**

rhododendron [roudə'dendrən] *n.* large evergreen shrub with clusters of huge colourful flowers. □ **rododendro**

rhombus ['rɔmbəs] *n.* shape with four equal sides but with no right angles. □ **rombo**
rhomboid *adj.* shaped like a rhombus/diamond-shaped. □ **romboidal**
■ *n.* four-sided shape with opposite sides equal in length and no right angles. □ **romboide**

rhubarb ['ru:bɑ:b] *n.* garden plant with large poisonous leaves, whose stalks are cooked as a dessert. □ **ruibarbo**

rhyme [raim] *n.* **1** sameness of sounds between two words (used in poetry): *can you think of a rhyme*

for 'gold'? □ **rima**
2 little piece of poetry. □ **poesía**
nursery rhyme, (often nonsensical) piece of poetry for children. □ **poesía infantil**
■ *v.* to have the same sound: *'gold' rhymes with 'cold'; 'cough' and 'though' don't rhyme.* □ **rimar**
rhyming slang, slang devised in London, where words are replaced by words or phrases which rhyme with them (such as 'apples and pears' = 'stairs'). □ **jerga con rima**

rhythm ['riðəm] *n.* regular beat in music/poetry, etc.: *they danced to the rhythm of the accordion.* □ **ritmo**
rhythmic ['riðmik] *adj.* with a regular beat. □ **rítmico**

rib [rib] *n.* **1** one of several bones forming a cage across the chest. □ **costilla**
2 piece of meat with the rib attached to it. □ **costilla**
spare ribs, cooked pork ribs in a savoury sauce. □ **costillas en adobo/adobadas**
3 one of the spokes of an umbrella. □ **varilla**
4 thicker part in a leaf. □ **nervio**
5 thicker line of stitches in knitting. □ **cordoncillo**

ribald ['ribəld] *adj.* rude (song/joke). □ **verde; chiste verde**

ribbon ['ribn] *n.* long flat thin piece of material for tying or decoration: *she tied her hair with pink ribbon.* □ **cinta**
typewriter ribbon, flat piece of material covered with ink, which is struck by the letters in a typewriter. □ **cinta de máquina de escribir**
ribbon development, building of lines of houses along the side of a road stretching into the countryside. □ **urbanización**

rice [rais] *n.* common tropical cereal, grown in wet ground or water. □ **arroz**
brown rice, rice which still has its outer covering. □ **arroz integral**
rice paper, very thin paper which you can eat and which is used in cooking. □ **papel de arroz**
rice pudding, dessert made of rice, milk and sugar. □ **arroz con leche**

rich [ritʃ] *adj.* **1** having a great deal of money: *rich people; he's very rich.* □ **rico**
2 (food) with a lot of cream/fat/eggs, etc. in it: *a rich cake; the food was so rich it made me sick.* □ **sabroso; la comida tenía tanta grasaza que.../era tan empalagosa que...**
3 deep and resonant (voice); dark (colour): *a rich purple.* □ **sonora (voz); intenso (color)**
4 fertile (soil). □ **rico**
5 with many resources: *the land is rich in mineral deposits; a region which is rich in Roman remains.* □ **rico**
■ *n.* ***the rich,*** rich people. □ **los ricos**
riches ['ritʃiz] *n.* wealth: *riches didn't make him any happier.* □ **riqueza/riquezas**
richly *adv.* **1** splendidly: *a dress richly decorated with diamonds.* □ **suntuosamente**
2 *you **richly deserve** it,* you deserve it very much. □ **te lo tienes bien merecido**
richness *n.* wealth; being rich. □ **riqueza**

rick [rik] *n.* large pile of straw or hay built like a house. □ **almiar**

rickets ['rikits] *n.* disease of children (caused by lack of vitamins) where bones become bent. □ **raquitismo**
rickety *adj.* wobbly (chair). □ **tambaleante**

ricochet ['rikəʃei] *v.* (*it ricocheted*) to bounce off a surface at an angle: *the stone ricocheted off the wall and broke the windscreen of my car; the ball ricocheted off the post into the goal.* □ **rebotar**

rid [rid] *v.* (*he rid*) to clear away: *I wanted to rid the town of corruption.* □ **librar**
to get rid of something, to dispose of something/to throw something away: *I can't get rid of this cold; he's trying to get rid of his old car.* □ **deshacerse de alguien/algo**
riddance *n.* ***good riddance,*** I am glad to get rid of it. □ **¡en buena hora me libré!**

riddle ['ridl] *n.* **1** guessing game where you have to guess the answer to a deliberately puzzling question: *tell me a riddle.* □ **acertijo**
2 puzzle: *he is trying to solve the riddle of how the cat got up the chimney.* □ **enigma**
3 large sieve for separating soil from stones. □ **criba**
■ *v.* ***to riddle** someone **with** bullets,* to shoot someone many times. □ **acribillar a balazos**
riddled with *adj.* full of: *the book is riddled with mistakes; the door was riddled with holes.* □ **repleto de**

ride [raid] *n.* trip/journey on horseback/on a bicycle/ in a car, etc.: *we're going for a ride in the car; do you want to go for a ride on the train? it is only a short bus ride from our house.* □ **viaje; paseo (a caballo); vuelta (en bicicleta, coche)**
to take someone for a ride, (*slang*) (i) to trick someone: *he was taken for a ride.* □ **le timaron**
(ii) to murder someone. □ **le dieron el paseo**
■ *v.* (*he rode; he has ridden*) **1** to go for a trip on horseback/on a bicycle/in a car, etc.: *have you ever ridden a camel? he can't ride a bike.* □ **montar (a caballo; en bicicleta); ir en coche**
2 *the ships rode at anchor,* they floated. □ **los barcos estaban fondeados**
3 ***to ride out:*** *the ships rode out the storm,* they remained at anchor during the storm. □ **...capearon el temporal**
rider *n.* **1** person who rides: *a horse and rider.* □ **jinete**
2 additional clause to a contract. □ **cláusula adicional**
riderless *adj.* (horse) with no rider. □ **sin jinete**
riding *n.* sport of going on horseback. □ **equitación**
riding school, school where you learn to ride a horse. □ **picadero; escuela hípica**
riding boots, long boots worn when riding. □ **botas de montar**

ridge [ridʒ] *n.* long narrow raised part: *a mountain ridge; the ridge of a roof; the plough turned the field into ridges and furrows.* □ **cadena (de montañas); caballete; caballones**
ridge tent, tent made of two sloping sides and a horizontal pole. □ **tienda de campaña canadiense**
ridge pole, pole along the top of a tent. □ **caballete**

ridicule ['ridikju:l] *n.* mocking/laughing at someone. □ **irrisión**
to hold someone up to ridicule, to laugh at someone. □ **poner en ridículo**
■ *v.* to laugh at (someone/something): *she ridiculed his little hat.* □ **mofarse de**
ridiculous *adj.* silly/which can be laughed at: *he was wearing a ridiculous hat.* □ **ridículo**
ridiculously *adv.* **1** in a silly way: *his trousers are ridiculously long.* □ **ridículamente**
2 *she answered the exam in a ridiculously short time,* amazingly short. □ **...en un tiempo ridículo**
ridiculousness *n.* silliness. □ **ridiculez**

rife [raif] *adj.* common: *violence is rife in the old part of the town.* □ **corriente**

riffraff ['rifræf] *n.* (*no pl.*) worthless ordinary people. □ **gentuza**

rifle ['raifl] *n.* hand gun with a long barrel with spiral

grooves inside. □ **rifle**
■ *v.* **1** to search and to steal: *the burglars had rifled the cupboards.* □ **saquear**
2 to make spiral grooves inside a gun barrel. □ **rayar**
rift [rift] *n.* split/crack: *a rift in the clouds; a rift in the leadership of the party.* □ **grieta; un claro en las nubes; una escisión en la dirección**
rig [rig] *n.* **1** metal construction for drilling for minerals: *an oil rig.* □ **torre de perforación**
2 (*informal*) set of clothes. □ **vestimenta**
■ *v.* (*he rigged*) **1** to fit out a ship with sails. □ **aparejar**
2 to arrange a dishonest result: *the election was rigged.* □ **amañar**
rigging *n.* ropes on a ship. □ **aparejo**
rig up *v.* to arrange/to construct (something) quickly: *they rigged up a pump to reduce the water in the boat.* □ **improvisar**
right [rait] *adj.* **1** good/honest: *it's only right that he should get the prize.* □ **bueno**
2 correct: *he gave the right answer to the question; is your watch right? is that the right time? he thinks he's always right; you say the answer is 23, he says it is 25, you can't both be right; is this the right train for London? put the box the right side up; the book isn't in the right place.* □ **correcto**
quite right!, perfectly correct! □ **¡perfecto!**
3 ***to get on the right side of someone,*** to make someone like you. □ **hacer a semejanza de alguien**
4 *she's* ***on the right side of*** *forty,* (*informal*) she is less than forty years old. □ **no llegará a los cuarenta**
5 ***right angle,*** angle of 90° (as in each corner of a square): *the two roads meet at right angles,* they cross each other at exactly the same angle. □ **ángulo recto**
6 straight/in order: *things will come right in the end; everything is all right.* □ **bien**
7 *is he* ***in his right mind?,*** is he sane? □ **¿está en su sano juicio?**
8 *she's* ***all right*** *again now,* she's better. □ **ahora se siente mejor**
9 not left; referring to the hand which most people use for writing: *my right arm is longer than the left; in England you are not supposed to drive on the right side of the road.* □ **derecho**
■ *n.* **1** what is correct/good: *the rights and the wrongs of the case.* □ **bien; lo bueno y lo malo...**
2 legal title to something: *he has a right to be heard; there is no right of appeal; she has no right to be here at all,* she should not be here. □ **derecho**
civil rights, legal entitlements of every citizen. □ **derechos civiles**
3 ***by rights*** *he ought to be in prison,* if things were done properly. □ **en justicia debería estar en prisión**
4 the right-hand side/the right-hand direction: *turn to the right; keep to the right.* □ **la derecha**
5 ***the right,*** political parties which are conservative. □ **la derecha**
■ *adv.* **1** straight: *keep right on to the end of the road.* □ **siga derecho hasta el final de la carretera**
2 immediately: *he phoned the police right away.* □ **en seguida**
3 completely: *right at the bottom of the bag; right in the middle of the fight; go right along to the end of the corridor.* □ **justo, del todo**
4 correctly: *if I remember right; nothing seems to be going right.* □ **bien**
5 ***it serves you right,*** you deserved it. □ **te lo mereces**
6 to the right-hand side: *turn right at the traffic lights; he looked right and left before crossing the street.* □ **a la derecha**
■ *v.* **1** to correct: *to right a wrong.* □ **corregir; deshacer un entuerto**
2 to put back straight: *the boat righted itself,* it almost capsized, but returned to the correct position. □ **enderezar**
3 *the machine will right itself,* will correct its own mistakes. □ **la máquina se corrige sola**
■ *interjection* **1** agreed/OK: *right, let's go!* □ **¡bien!**
2 do you understand: *from now on, you take orders from me, right?* □ **..., ¿de acuerdo?**
right-angled *adj.* with a 90° angle: *a right-angled bend.* □ **en ángulo recto**
righteous ['raitʃəs] *adj.* virtuous/very good. □ **recto**
righteousness ['raitʃəsnəs] *n.* virtue/goodness. □ **rectitud**
rightful *adj.* legally correct: *the rightful owner of the house.* □ **légitimo**
right-hand *adj.* referring to the right hand: *on the right-hand side of the street; the jam is in the top right-hand cupboard.* □ **de la derecha**
one's right-hand man, one's most useful helper: *the boss's right-hand man.* □ **la mano derecha del jefe**
right-handed *adj.* (person) who uses the right hand for writing/cutting, etc. □ **diestro**
rightly *adv.* **1** correctly: *if I remember rightly.* □ **bien**
2 *I can't rightly say,* I am not very sure. □ **no lo puedo decir con seguridad**
right-minded *adj.* (person) who has correct ideas/who thinks like most people think. □ **cabal**
rightness *n.* correctness. □ **exactitud**
right of way *n.* **1** right to walk over someone else's property: *this path is a public right of way.* □ **servidumbre de paso**
2 right (of one vehicle) to go first at a crossroads. □ **prioridad de paso**
right-wing *adj.* belonging to the conservative political parties: *a right-wing politician.* □ **de derechas**
right-winger *n.* person who is on the right politically. □ **derechista**
rigid ['ridʒid] *adj.* stiff/unbending: *a rigid code of conduct.* □ **rígido**
rigidly *adv.* stiffly: *the soldiers stood rigidly to attention.* □ **rígidamente**
rigidity [ri'dʒiditi] *n.* stiffness/lack of flexibility. □ **rigidez**
rigmarole ['rigməroul] *n.* long incoherent speech/meaningless jumble of words. □ **galimatías**
rigour ['rigə] *Amer.* **rigor** *n.* severity (of the law, etc.); harshness (of the climate). □ **rigor**
rigorous *adj.* very strict. □ **riguroso**
rigorously *adv.* strictly. □ **rigurosamente**
rile [rail] *v.* (*informal*) to annoy. □ **sulfurar**
rill [ril] *n.* small stream. □ **riachuelo**
rim [rim] *n.* edge of a wheel/of a cup; frame of spectacles. □ **llanta (rueda); borde (taza); montura (gafas)**
rimless *adj.* (spectacles) with no frame. □ **sin aros**
rime [raim] *n.* white frost. □ **escarcha**
rind [raind] *n.* skin on fruit/meat, etc. □ **piel, cáscara**
ring [riŋ] *n.* **1** circular piece of metal/wood, etc., with a hole in the centre: *she wore a gold ring on her finger.* □ **anillo**
serviette ring, ring for keeping a serviette in. □ **servilletero**
2 anything shaped like a circle: *they were sitting in a ring.* □ **corro, círculo, anillo**
3 ***to run rings around someone,*** (*informal*) to do

things better than someone. □ **dar quince y raya a uno**
4 group of people (usually criminals): *the heroin ring.* □ **banda**
5 centre of a circus where performances take place; square place where a boxing/wrestling match takes place. □ **pista (circo); cuadrilátero (boxeo)**
6 sound of a bell: *there was a ring at the door.* □ **toque de timbre**
7 call on the telephone: *I'll give you a ring tomorrow.* □ **telefonazo**
■ *v.* (*he rang; he has rung*) **1** to make a sound of a bell: *he rang at the door; the doorbell rang twice; she rang for the waiter; all the alarm bells were ringing.* □ **llamar; llamó a la puerta; el timbre sonó dos veces**
it rings a bell, (*informal*) it reminds me of something. □ **me suena a algo**
2 *my ears are ringing,* there is a sound like that of bells in my ears. □ **me zumban los oídos**
3 to telephone: *I rang him when he was in bed.* □ **llamar por teléfono**
to ring someone up, to call someone on the telephone. □ **llamar por teléfono**
to ring off, to stop the telephone call/to put down the receiver: *when I tried to explain he just rang off.* □ **colgar**
■ *v.* (*he ringed*) **1** to put a ring on the leg of a bird for marking purposes: *we ringed thirty geese.* □ **anillar**
2 to mark with a circle: *he ringed the names in red pencil.* □ **rodear con un círculo**
ringleader *n.* chief of a gang or group/person who organizes a crime. □ **cabecilla**
ringlet *n.* long curl (of hair). □ **rizo**
ringmaster *n.* master of ceremonies in a circus. □ **maestro de ceremonias**
ring road *n.* bypass/road which goes round a town. □ **carretera de circunvalación**
ringside *adj.* by the side of a ring: *we watched the circus from ringside seats.* □ **primera fila**
ringworm *n.* disease of the skin which causes round red patches. □ **tiña**

rink [riŋk] *n.* place where you can roller-skate or skate on ice; ice for skating: *ice rink; skating rink.* □ **pista de patinaje**

rinse [rins] *n.* **1** putting soapy washing/soapy hair through clean water to remove the soap: *give your hair a rinse; she had a blue rinse,* she had rinsed her hair with liquid containing a blue dye. □ **aclarado**
2 liquid for rinsing hair which contains colouring. □ **reflejo**
■ *v.* to put something soapy/dirty into clean water to remove the soap/the dirt: *rinse out the empty bottles.* □ **aclarar**

riot ['raiət] *n.* **1** disorder among crowds of people: *the government ordered a curfew to prevent the riots in the streets.* □ **disturbio**
to run riot, to become disordered/to get out of control: *the crowd ran riot; price increases are running riot.* □ **desmandarse**
2 mass (of sounds/colours). □ **derroche**
■ *v.* to take part in a riot/to get out of control: *the crowd rioted in the square.* □ **amotinarse**
rioter *n.* person who takes part in a riot: *rioters threw stones at the police.* □ **manifestante**
rioting *n.* riots/outbreaks of civil disorder. □ **disturbios**
riotous *adj.* wild/out of control. □ **alborotado**
riot police *n.* police specially equipped to deal with rioters. □ **policía antidisturbios**

rip [rip] *n.* tear (in cloth): *there's a rip in my coat.* □ **desgarrón**
■ *v.* (*he ripped*) to tear: *he ripped his trousers on the barbed wire.* □ **desgarrar**
to let rip, (*informal*) to allow something to go freely. □ **soltar**
ripcord *n.* cord you pull to make a parachute open. □ **cabo de desgarre**
rip off *v.* **1** to tear off. □ **quitar de un tirón**
2 ***to rip someone off,*** (*slang*) to cheat someone/to make someone pay too much. □ **clavar**
rip-off *n.* (*slang*) bad deal/something which costs too much. □ **timo**

riparian [ri'pɛriən] *adj.* (*formal*) referring to the banks of a river. □ **ribereño**

ripe [raip] *adj.* **1** ready to eat/to be harvested: *ripe cherries; the cheese is not quite ripe yet.* □ **maduro**
2 *he lived to* ***a ripe old age,*** until he was very old. □ **edad muy avanzada**
3 ***the time is ripe for something,*** it is the right time to do something. □ **ha llegado el momento de...**
ripen *v.* to become ripe: *the apples are ripening well; the corn won't ripen because the weather's too cold.* □ **madurar**
ripeness *n.* readiness; state of being ripe. □ **madurez**

riposte [ri'pɔst] *n.* quick, sharp reply. □ **respuesta aguda**
■ *v.* to make a quick, sharp reply. □ **responder con viveza**

ripple ['ripl] *n.* little wave: *the boat made ripples as it glided over the water.* □ **onda; rizo**
■ *v.* to make little waves: *the wind rippled the surface of the lake.* □ **rizar**

rise [raiz] *n.* movement upwards; slope upwards: *a gentle rise in the road; a rise in the cost of living.* □ **elevación**
2 increase in salary: *he asked for a rise.* □ **aumento**
3 ***to give rise to something,*** to start something off: *his frequent absences gave rise to rumours that he was ill.* □ **dar pie a**
■ *v.* (*he rose; he has risen*) **1** to move upwards; to get up: *the sun rises in the east; he rose at ten o'clock; the road rises gradually for three miles; prices have risen sharply this year.* □ **levantarse (el sol, de la cama); subir (carretera, precios)**
2 to stop meeting: *the court rose at three o'clock.* □ **levantarse (la sesión)**
3 (*of a river*) to start: *the river rises in the eastern mountains.* □ **nacer**
4 ***to rise in revolt/to rise against someone,*** to riot/to rebel. □ **levantarse contra**
riser *n.* ***early riser,*** person who gets up early in the morning. □ **madrugador**
rising *adj.* which is moving upwards/which is increasing: *the rising cost of living.* □ **creciente; en ascenso**
the rising generation, the new generation which will follow this one. □ **la nueva generación**
■ *prep. she is rising forty,* she is nearly forty. □ **ya raya en los cuarenta**
■ *n.* **1** movement upwards: *the rising and falling of the ship with the tide.* □ **subida**
2 rebellion/revolt: *there was a rising against the government.* □ **levantamiento**

risk [risk] *n.* **1** possible harm; dangerous chance: *he takes terrible risks when he rides his motorbike.* □ **riesgo**
2 *they* ***run the risk of*** *being caught,* they may well be caught. □ **corren el riesgo de...**
■ *v.* to chance/to do something which may possibly harm: *I'll risk going out without a raincoat; he's risk-*

ing his life up there on the roof. □ **arriesgar(se)**
risky *adj.* dangerous/which may cause harm. □ **arriesgado**

risotto [ri'sɔtou] *n.* Italian dish of cooked rice with meat/fish/vegetables in it. □ **arroz (con carne, pescado, verdura, etc)**

risqué ['ri:skei] *adj.* slightly indecent. □ **verde, de color subido**

rissole ['risoul] *n.* ball of meat/fish, etc. which is fried. □ **croqueta**

rite [rait] *n.* religious ceremony. □ **rito**
last rites, communion for someone who is dying. □ **extremaunción**
ritual ['ritjuəl] *adj.* and *n.* (referring to) a religious ceremony: *a ritual blessing of candles.* □ **ritual**

rival ['raivl] *n.* and *adj.* (person) who competes: *he's my rival for the prize; a rival company won the contract.* □ **rival**
■ *v.* (*he rivalled*) to compete with someone; to be of similar quality. □ **rivalizar**
rivalry *n.* competition. □ **rivalidad**

river ['rivə] *n.* large stream of water which goes into another stream, or into the sea: *river bank.* □ **río; orilla del río**
riverside *adj.* on the banks of a river: *a riverside inn.* □ **junto al río**

rivet ['rivit] *n.* nail which fastens metal plates together. □ **remache**
■ *v.* **1** to fasten metal plates together. □ **remachar**
2 to attract someone's attention: *a riveting performance.* □ **cautivador**

road [roud] *n.* **1** path for cars and other vehicles; way of getting somewhere: *you must drive on the left-hand side of the road.* □ **carretera**
road sense, care in avoiding danger when driving. □ **conducción prudente**
2 *the road to success,* the path which leads to success. □ **el camino de la gloria**
3 *he is out* ***on the road*** *all week,* he travels from place to place (as a travelling salesman/worker). □ **en la carretera**
4 ***roads,*** part of the sea near a port where ships can lie at anchor. □ **rada**
roadblock *n.* barrier put across a road by the police. □ **control**
roadhog *n.* (*informal*) fast dangerous driver. □ **loco de la carretera**
road-mender *n.* person who repairs the road surface. □ **peón caminero**
roadside *n.* by the side of a road: *a roadside cafe.* □ **(café) de carretera**
roadstead *n.* part of the sea near a port where ships can lie at anchor. □ **rada**
roadway *n.* main surface of a road. □ **calzada**
roadworks *n. pl.* repairs to a road. □ **obras (de carretera)**
roadworthy *adj.* in a fit state to be driven on a road. □ **en condiciones para circular**

roam [roum] *v.* to wander. □ **vagar por**

roan [roun] *adj.* and *n.* (horse) with grey hairs in its coat. □ **rosillo**

roar [rɔ:] *n.* loud, deep call; loud shouting: *the lion gave a roar; the roars of the crowd; he burst into roars of laughter.* □ **rugido**
■ *v.* to make a loud call: *the lions roared; the crowd roared its approval.* □ **rugir**
roaring *adj.* wild: *it was a roaring success; he was roaring drunk.* □ **clamoroso (éxito); totalmente (borracho)**
■ *n.* sound of loud, deep calls: *the roaring of the lions.* □ **rugido**

roast [roust] *n.* meat which has been/which will be cooked in an oven: *a roast of beef; our Sunday roast.* □ **asado**
■ *v.* to cook over a fire/in an oven: *to roast a chicken.* □ **asar**
■ *adj.* which has been roasted: *roast beef and potatoes.* □ **asado; rosbif y patatas**
roasting *adj.* (chicken) which is ready to be roasted. □ **para asar**

rob [rɔb] *v.* (*he robbed*) to steal from someone: *the bandits went about robbing travellers of their money.* □ **robar**
robber *n.* person who steals money from someone. □ **ladrón**
robbery *n.* stealing. □ **robo**

robe [roub] *n.* long, loose dress (for men or women); *Amer.* dressing gown. □ **bata**

robin ['rɔbin] *n.* common small brown bird with a red breast. □ **petirrojo**
round robin, letter of complaint signed by many people. □ **escrito de protesta con muchas firmas**

robot ['roubɔt] *n.* machine which works like a man; (*in science fiction*) machine which looks a little like a man and which can act like one. □ **robot**

robust [rə'bʌst] *adj.* strong/vigorous. □ **robusto**

rock [rɔk] *n.* **1** stone/the solid part of the earth's surface: *the house is built on solid rock; he's studying the rock formations of the island.* □ **roca**
2 large piece of stone: *the earthquake made rocks fall down from the mountain; the ship ran on to the rocks.* □ **peñasco; escollo (en el mar)**
rock plant, alpine plant/plant which grows among rocks. □ **planta rupestre**
3 ***whisky on the rocks,*** (*informal*) whisky with ice. □ **...con hielo**
4 sweet shaped like a stick, often with the name of a town printed in it: *a stick of rock; Brighton rock.* □ **pirulí**
5 music with a strong rhythm. □ **rock**
■ *v.* to sway from side to side; to make (something) sway from side to side: *the house rocked during the earthquake; he rocked his daughter on his knee; the waves rocked the boat.* □ **vibrar (la casa); mecer (a un niño); zarandear (el barco)**
to rock the boat: *don't rock the boat,* (*informal*) don't disturb what has been arranged/don't change the way things work. □ **mejor dejarlo como está**
rock bottom *n.* the lowest point: *prices have reached rock bottom.* □ **fondo; los precios están por los suelos**
rock cake *n.* small cake with currants in it. □ **pasta de pasas**
rocker *n.* **1** semicircular wooden piece which a rocking chair stands on. □ **arco**
2 *Amer.* rocking chair. □ **mecedora**
3 type of electric switch which rocks. □ **interruptor**
rockery *n.* garden planted around a collection of rocks. □ **jardincito rocoso**
rocking *adj.* swaying. □ **balanceo**
rocking-horse, child's wooden horse on rockers. □ **caballito de balancín**
rocking-chair, chair which rocks backwards and forwards on rockers. □ **mecedora**
rocky *adj.* **1** full of rocks: *a rocky cliff.* □ **rocoso**
2 (*informal*) wobbly: *this chair is a bit rocky.* □ **poco firme**

rocket ['rɔkit] *n.* **1** type of firework which, when lit, flies up into the sky; spacecraft; type of bomb which is shot through space at an enemy. □ **cohete**
2 engine driven by burning gas, which powers a spacecraft or bomb. □ **cohete**
3 (*informal*) sharp criticism: *he's had a rocket from*

the boss; the boss gave him a rocket. □ **rapapolvo**
■ *v.* to shoot upwards very fast: *prices are rocketing.* □ **subir vertiginosamente**
rod [rɔd] *n.* **1** long stick. □ **barra**
2 ***fishing rod,*** long stick with a line attached, used for fishing. □ **caña de pescar**
rode [roud] *v. see* **ride.**
rodent ['roudənt] *n.* type of animal which chews and gnaws (such as a mouse/rat, etc.). □ **roedor**
rodeo [rou'deiou] *n.* display of skill by cowboys. □ **rodeo**
roe [rou] *n.* **1** fish eggs. □ **hueva**
2 type of small deer. □ **corzo**
roebuck *n.* male roe deer. □ **corzo**
roentgen ['rʌntjən] *adj.* referring to X-rays. □ **de rayos X**
roger ['rɔdʒə] *interjection* and *signal meaning* message received and understood. □ **¡recibido!**
rogue [roug] *adj.* and *n.* **1** wicked/dishonest person. □ **canalla**
2 ***a rogue elephant,*** (i) elephant driven out of the herd by the other elephants. □ **elefante solitario**
(ii) person who does not behave in the same way as others. □ **pícaro**
roguish *adj.* wicked/dishonest. □ **granuja**
role [roul] *n.* part played by someone (in a play or in real life). □ **papel**
roll [roul] *n.* **1** something which has been turned over and over to make a tube: *a roll of paper; a roll of carpet; a toilet roll.* □ **rollo**
swiss roll/*Amer.* ***jelly roll,*** cake rolled up with jam or cream in it. □ **brazo de gitano**
sausage roll, small pastry with a sausage inside. □ **empanadilla de salchicha**
2 very small loaf: *a roll and butter.* □ **panecillo**
3 list of names. □ **lista**
roll of honour, list of prizewinners/list of soldiers who have died during a war. □ **lista de honor**
4 movement from side to side: *the ship made a sudden roll.* □ **el buque se balanceó de repente**
■ *v.* **1** to make a tube out of something flat: *he rolled up the carpet.* □ **enrollar**
2 to flatten by using a roller: *to roll a lawn.* □ **apisonar con rodillo**
3 to make (something) move forward by turning it over and over: *he rolled the ball across the table; the tears rolled down her cheeks.* □ **hacer rodar**
4 *he's rolling in money,* (*informal*) he has a great deal of money. □ **nada en la abundancia**
5 to rock from side to side: *the ship rolled in the storm.* □ **balancearse**
6 ***to roll one's r's:*** *he rolls his r's,* when speaking the letter 'r', he makes the tip of his tongue vibrate. □ **pronunciar fuerte las erres**
7 to make a low rumbling noise: *the thunder rolled.* □ **retumbar**
rollcall *n.* calling names from a list: *there were three people missing at the rollcall.* □ **pasar lista**
roller *n.* **1** round object which rolls: *ink roller; lawn roller.* □ **rodillo**
steam roller, machine for flattening new road surfaces. □ **apisonadora**
2 large wave in the sea. □ **ola grande**
3 ***roller towel,*** continuous towel hanging on a horizontal bar. □ **toalla de rodillo**
4 plastic tube used for rolling your hair into curls. □ **rulo**
roller coaster *n. Amer.* fairground railway which goes up and down steep slopes. □ **montaña rusa**
roller-skate *n.* ***roller-skates,*** devices with wheels which you strap to your feet so as to glide along fast. □ **patín de ruedas**
■ *v.* to glide on roller-skates. □ **patinar**
rolling *adj.* ***rolling countryside,*** country which is a mass of small hills. □ **ondulado**
rolling pin, wooden roller with handles, for flattening pastry. □ **rodillo**
rolling stock, carriages/wagons/engines used on a railway. □ **material rodante**
Roman ['roumən] *adj.* referring to Rome. □ **romano**
Roman candle, type of firework giving a brilliant fountain of light. □ **candela romana**
Roman numerals, numbers written in the Roman style (I, II, III, IV, etc.). □ **números romanos**
Roman Catholic *adj.* and *n.* (person) belonging to the Christian church of which the Pope is the head. □ **católico romano**
romance [rə'mæns] *n.* **1** ***romance language,*** language which has derived direct from Latin. □ **romance**
2 love affair. □ **aventura sentimental**
3 love story. □ **novela romántica**
4 story remote from daily life. □ **de aventuras**
■ *v.* to invent/to make up a story. □ **fantasear**
romantic [rə'mæntik] *adj.* **1** full of mystery and romance. □ **romántico**
romantic novel, novel about a love story. □ **novela romántica**
2 (literary/artistic style) which is very imaginative/based on personal emotions. □ **romántico**
romanticize *v.* to turn (something) into a romantic story. □ **hacer romántico**
Romanesque [roumə'nesk] *adj.* and *n.* architectural style with round arches and vaults found in Europe in the early Middle Ages. □ **románico**
Romania [ru:'meiniə] *n.* country in Eastern Europe. □ **Rumania**
Romanian *adj.* referring to Romania. □ **rumano**
■ *n.* **1** person from Romania. □ **rumano**
2 language spoken in Romania. □ **rumano**
Romany ['roumәni] *n.* **1** gipsy. □ **gitano**
2 language spoken by gipsies. □ **caló**
romp [rɔmp] *n.* energetic children's game. □ **retozo**
■ *v.* to play about energetically. □ **retozar**
to romp home: *the horse romped home,* won easily. □ **el caballo ganó como quiso**
rompers *n.* one-piece suit for a baby. □ **mono**
roof [ru:f] *n.* **1** covering over a building: *pigeons were sitting on the roof of the house; the roof is letting in water.* □ **tejado**
2 top of the inside of the mouth: *I burnt the roof of my mouth with the hot soup.* □ **cielo de la boca**
3 top of a car/bus/lorry, etc.. □ **techo**
sunshine roof, roof which you can open in fine weather. □ **techo corredizo**
roof rack, grid fixed to the roof of a car for carrying luggage. □ **baca**
■ *v.* to put a roof on (a building): *the house is roofed with sheets of corrugated iron.* □ **tejar; poner techo de**
rook [ruk] *n.* **1** large black bird of the crow family which lives in large groups. □ **grajo**
2 (*in chess*) piece shaped like a castle. □ **torre**
■ *v.* (*slang*) to cheat. □ **timar**
rookery *n.* place where rooks nest. □ **colonia de grajos**
rookie ['ruki] *n.* (*informal*) new recruit in the armed forces/in the police. □ **novato**
room [ru:m] *n.* **1** one of the divisions inside a house: *living room; sitting room; play room; furnished rooms to let; our flat has five rooms, a kitchen and a bathroom; I have reserved a single room with bath,* room (in a hotel) for one person. □ **habitación**

2 space: *this table takes up a lot of room; can you make room for me?,* squeeze up to give me space to sit down? □ **sitio**
3 *there's room for improvement,* things could be improved. □ **esto se puede mejorar aún**
■ *v.* to live in furnished rooms. □ **alojarse**
rooming-house *n. Amer.* house with furnished rooms to let. □ **casa de huéspedes**
room-mate *n.* person with whom you share a room. □ **compañero de cuarto**
roomy *adj.* spacious: *the car has a very roomy boot.* □ **amplio**
roost [ru:st] *n.* perch for a bird. □ **percha**
to rule the roost, to be in charge/the boss. □ **llevar la voz cantante**
■ *v.* to perch: *the pigeons have come home to roost.* □ **recogerse**
rooster *n.* cockerel. □ **gallo**
root [ru:t] *n.* **1** part of a plant which goes down into the ground, and which takes nourishment from the soil; part of a hair/a tooth which goes down into the skin: *she pulled his hair out by the roots.* □ **raíz**
to take root, to start to grow. □ **echar raíces**
to put down roots, to begin to feel at home in a place. □ **echar raíces en un sitio**
2 source: *money is the root of all evil; what's the root cause of the problem?* □ **raíz; el origen...**
3 (*in language*) word which is a base for other words. □ **raíz**
4 ***square root,*** number which if multiplied by itself gives the number you have: *three is the square root of nine.* □ **raíz cuadrada**
cube root, number which if multiplied by itself twice gives the number you have: *three is the cube root of twenty seven.* □ **raíz cúbica**
■ *v.* **1** to put down/to make roots: *the cutting rooted in sand; deeply rooted fear,* fear which is very strongly felt. □ **echar raíces, arraigar**
2 to dig up/to look for something: *pigs were rooting about in the mud.* □ **hozar**
3 ***to root for*** *a team, Amer.* to cheer a team on. □ **animar**
root crop *n.* crop which is grown for its edible roots (such as carrots, turnips, etc.). □ **cultivo de tubérculos**
root up, root out *v.* to pull up (a plant) by its roots; to remove something completely. □ **arrancar**
rope [roup] *n.* thick string/thick cord: *they pulled on a rope to lift the crate.* □ **cuerda**
to know the ropes, (*informal*) to know all about (the conditions, rules, etc.)/how to go about doing something. □ **se lo sabe al dedillo**
■ *v.* to tie together with a rope: *the climbers were roped together.* □ **amarrar; los escaladores estaban encordados**
to rope off, to stop people going into a place by putting a rope around it. □ **acordonar**
ropy *adj.* (*informal*) of bad quality; not healthy. □ **deteriorado**
rosary ['rouzəri] *n.* string of beads used when saying prayers. □ **rosario**
rose [rouz] *n.* **1** scented flower which grows on a prickly bush: *a rose bud; a rose bush.* □ **rosa; capullo de rosa; rosal**
2 pink colour. □ **rosa**
3 piece of metal/plastic with many holes in it, which is attached to the spout of a watering can, so that the water comes out in a spray. □ **alcachofa, difusor**
■ *v. see* **rise.**
rose window *n.* large round decorated window found usually in the west wall of a church. □ **rosetón**
rosy *adj.* **1** bright pink. □ **rosado**
2 very favourable: *the future doesn't look too rosy.* □ **halagüeño**
rosé [rou'sei] *n.* pink wine. □ **vino rosado**
rosemary ['rouzməri] *n.* common herb with scented evergreen leaves. □ **romero**
rosette [rə'zet] *n.* ribbon bunched to look like a flower, used as a decoration or as a badge. □ **escarapela**
rosin ['rɔzin] *n.* solid resin used to rub a violin bow. □ **colofonia**
roster ['rɔstə] *n.* list of duties which have to be done and the people who have to do them. □ **lista**
rostrum ['rɔstrəm] *n.* raised stand for a speaker. □ **tribuna**
rot [rɔt] *n.* decay. □ **putrefacción**
dry rot, decay in house timbers caused by a fungus. □ **pudrimiento**
the rot has set in, things are beginning to go badly. □ **esto está empezando a estropearse**
■ *v.* (*it rotted*) to decay; to go bad: *rotting leaves; the fence has just rotted away.* □ **pudrir(se); hojas podridas**
rotten *adj.* decayed: *a bag of rotten apples.* □ **podrido**
feel rotten, (*informal*) (i) to feel ill, tired, unhappy. □ **me encuentro fatal**
(ii) to feel ashamed. □ **me siento avergonzado**
rotter *n.* (*informal*) bad person. □ **sinvergüenza**
rota ['routə] *n.* list of duties which have to be done in turn and the people who have to do them. □ **lista**
rotate [rou'teit] *v.* to turn round: *the wheel rotates round an axle.* □ **hacer girar**
rotary ['routəri] *adj.* **1** which turns/rotates. □ **rotatorio**
2 *rotary printing press,* one where the paper passes round large rollers. □ **rotativa**
rotation [rou'teiʃn] *n.* turning/taking turns. □ **rotación**
rotation of crops, growing different crops in turn. □ **rotación de cultivos**
rotor *n.* piece of machinery which rotates; the blades of a helicopter. □ **rotor; las paletas de un helicóptero**
rote [rout] *n.* learning by heart: *rote learning.* □ **de memoria**
rotund [rə'tʌnd] *adj.* round/fat. □ **gordo; rechoncho**
rotunda *n.* circular building with a dome. □ **rotonda**
rouble ['ru:bl] *n.* unit of money in the Soviet Union. □ **rublo**
rouge [ru:ʒ] *n.* pink cream/powder which you put on your face to give yourself more colour. □ **colorete**
rough [ruf] *adj.* **1** not smooth; bumpy; uneven: *rough surface of a brick; rough road; the sea's rough; we had a rough crossing.* □ **áspero (ladrillo); lleno de baches (carretera); embravecido (mar); dura (travesía)**
2 harsh: *a rough game of rugby.* □ **violento**
to give someone a rough time, treat someone badly. □ **hacérselas pasar canutas a alguien**
3 unfinished; approximate: *rough translation; rough drawing; he made a rough guess.* □ **no muy exacto (traducción); bosquejo; hizo un cálculo aproximado**
■ *n.* **1** area of long grass on a golf course. □ **'rough'**
2 unfinished design: *here are the roughs for the new magazine.* □ **boceto**
3 hooligan: *he was attacked by a gang of roughs.* □ **gamberro**
■ *adv.* **1** brutally/harshly: *to play rough.* □ **duro**

2 *to sleep rough,* without a proper bed. □ **dormir en el suelo (en la casa)/al raso (en el campo)**
■ *v. **to rough out** a plan,* to make a rough design. □ **bosquejar un plan**
to rough it, to live uncomfortably. □ **pasar apuros**
to rough someone up, to beat/to attack someone. □ **dar una paliza a**
roughage *n.* coarse stuff, such as bran you eat to help digestion. □ **forraje (animales); fibra (persona)**
rough and ready *adj.* approximate; not beautifully finished. □ **tosco**
roughen *v.* to make/to become rough. □ **poner áspero/tosco**
roughness *n.* being rough. □ **aspereza**
roughshod *adj. **to ride roughshod over** someone's feelings,* to pay no attention to/to trample on someone's feelings. □ **hacer caso omiso de/tratar a uno sin miramientos**
roulette [ruːˈlet] *n.* game of chance where bets are made on the number of a box where a small ball will stop in a rotating wheel. □ **ruleta**
Russian roulette, game played with a revolver containing a single bullet which is spun round and then fired at the player's head. □ **ruleta rusa**
round [raund] *adj.* **1** circular/shaped like a circle: *a round table; a round carpet.* □ **redondo**
2 ***round trip,*** trip to a destination and back. □ **de ida y vuelta**
round trip ticket, return ticket. □ **billete de ida y vuelta**
3 exact (number): *a round dozen.* □ **una docena exacta**
■ *n.* **1** circle. □ **círculo; esfera**
2 *round of toast,* piece(s) of toast from one slice of bread. □ **una tostada**
3 *round of sandwiches,* sandwiches from two slices of bread. □ **unos 'sandwiches'**
4 regular route: *a continual round of parties; the postman's round; a newspaper round,* number of houses where a boy regularly delivers newspapers. □ **recorrido**
a round of golf, going round all the holes in a golf course. □ **todos los hoyos**
5 part of a contest/of a boxing match: *he was knocked out in the third round; our team won, and moves to the next round of the championship.* □ **'round' (boxeo); vuelta (campeonato)**
6 *round of drinks,* series of drinks bought by one person: *it's my turn to buy a round.* □ **ronda**
7 *round of applause,* burst of clapping. □ **salva de aplausos**
8 one bullet; one shell: *they fired twenty rounds at the enemy camp.* □ **tiro**
■ *adv.* **1** in a circle: *the wheel went round and round.* □ **la rueda dio vueltas y vueltas**
2 completely. □ **totalmente**
all year round, during the whole year. □ **todo el año**
3 surrounding: *the garden has a wall which goes right round.* □ **...está rodeado por un muro**
to look round, (i) to look around. □ **miró alrededor suyo**
(ii) to turn the head (to see). □ **miró detrás de sí**
4 from one to another. □ **de uno a otro**
to hand round: *he handed round the cups of tea,* he handed a cup to each person. □ **pasar; repartir**
5 *is there enough cake **to go round?**,* enough for everybody. □ **¿...para todos?**
6 *why don't you **come round** for a drink?,* come to my house. □ **¿por qué no te pasas por casa a tomar una copa?**
■ *prep.* in a circle: *they sat round the table; we went round the museum,* visited it completely; *the wall goes right round the garden; the earth revolves round the sun.* □ **alrededor de**
■ *v.* **1** to make round: *to round the corners of a piece of wood.* □ **redondear**
2 to go round: *the ship rounded the cape.* □ **doblar**
3 ***to round on someone,*** to attack someone. □ **rodear a alguien (con la idea de atacar)**
4 ***to round up*** *sheep,* to gather sheep together. □ **reunir**
5 to make a whole number: *to round a number up,* to make the nearest whole number above (such as 2.8 = 3, 189 = 200, etc.). □ **redondear**
roundabout *n.* **1** place where several roads meet and the traffic moves in a circle. □ **glorieta**
2 type of children's amusement in a park, a heavy wooden wheel which you push to turn round and then sit on; (*in a fair*) a revolving machine (with wooden horses) on which you can ride. □ **tíovivo**
■ *adj.* not straight: *we took a roundabout way to get here.* □ **indirecto; un rodeo**
rounded *adj.* with smooth/round corners or edges. □ **redondeado**
rounders *n.* team game played with a bat and ball, where the batsman has to run round the pitch to score. □ **(juego parecido al béisbol)**
roundly *adv.* sharply/critically; totally: *the team was roundly beaten.* □ **rotundamente**
rouse [rauz] *v.* to wake (someone) who is sleeping; to get (someone) to act: *she roused him to action.* □ **despertar**
rousing *adj.* loud/exciting: *a rousing song; three rousing cheers.* □ **emocionante**
roustabout [ˈraustəbaut] *n.* labourer on an oil rig. □ **peón**
rout [raut] *n.* complete defeat (of an army). □ **derrota total**
■ *v.* **1** to defeat completely: *the enemy was routed.* □ **derrotar**
2 to search. □ **hurgar**
to rout someone out, to pull someone out from where he is hidden. □ **hacer salir**
route [ruːt] *n.* way to be followed to get to a destination: *bus route,* normal way which a bus follows; *he took a roundabout route to get to the church.* □ **ruta**
route march, training march by soldiers. □ **marcha de entrenamiento**
■ *v.* to send (someone) along a route: *the bus has been routed down the high street.* □ **mandar; el autobús pasa ahora por...**
routine [ruːˈtiːn] *n.* normal/regular way of doing things. □ **rutina**
daily routine, things which you do every day. □ **la rutina cotidiana**
■ *adj.* normal/everyday: *routine investigation.* □ **rutinario**
roving [ˈrouviŋ] *adj.* wandering. □ **errante**
roving instincts, tendency to travel a great deal. □ **instinto andariego**
row [rou] *n.* **1** line (of chairs, etc.): *all the staff stood in a row; we were sitting in the front row.* □ **fila**
2 short trip in a rowing boat: *let's go for a row.* □ **paseo en barca**
■ *v.* to make a boat go forward by using oars: *he can't row; we rowed the boat across the lake.* □ **remar**
rower *n.* person who rows. □ **remero**
rowing *n.* making a boat move by the use of oars: *I'm very fond of rowing.* □ **me encanta remar**

rowing boat, small boat for rowing. □ **bote/barca de remos**
row [rau] *n.* **1** loud noise: *the engine is making a terrible row.* □ **ruido**
2 sharp argument: *I had a row with the boss.* □ **bronca**
rowan ['rouən] *n.* mountain ash/common tree with red berries. □ **serbal**
rowdy ['raudi] *adj.* making a great deal of noise: *a rowdy party.* □ **ruidoso**
■ *n.* rough person, who makes a lot of noise. □ **camorrista**
rowlock ['rɔlək] *n.* metal support for oars. □ **escálamo**
royal ['rɔiəl] *adj.* **1** referring to a king or queen: *the royal palace.* □ **real**
the Royal Family, family of a king or queen. □ **la familia real**
2 ***royal blue,*** bright dark blue. □ **azul de cobalto**
3 *he gave us* ***a right royal welcome,*** a splendid welcome. □ **nos recibió como a reyes**
■ *n.* ***the Royals,*** (*informal*) members of the Royal Family. □ **la familia real**
royalist *n.* person who is a political supporter of a king. □ **monárquico**
royally *adv.* splendidly/with great pomp. □ **regiamente**
royalty *n.* **1** state of being royal; members of a king's family. □ **realeza**
2 money paid to the author of a book/an actor in a film, etc., as a percentage of the receipts of sale. □ **derechos (de autor, etc.)**
rub [rʌb] *v.* (*he rubbed*) to move something across the surface of something else: *he was rubbing his hands together; rub the table with a cloth.* □ **frotar**
rubbing *n.* action of rubbing: *the rubbing of the wheel wore away the stone.* □ **frotamiento**
rubbing alcohol, *Amer.* pure alcohol used as an antiseptic. □ **alcohol (para uso externo)**
rub down *v.* to rub (someone/a horse) vigorously. □ **secar frotando (persona); almohazar (caballo)**
rub in *v.* to make (a cream) enter the skin by rubbing. □ **darse (una crema)**
to rub it in, (*informal*) to keep reminding someone of a fault, failure, etc.: *I know I made a mistake, but you needn't rub it in.* □ **¡no machaques!**
rub out *v.* to remove (a pencil mark) with rubber. □ **borrar**
rub up *v.* ***to rub someone up the wrong way,*** (*informal*) to make someone irritable. □ **sacar de quicio a alguien**
rubber ['rʌbə] *n.* **1** elastic material made from the sap of a tree: *rubber tyres; rubber dinghy.* □ **caucho; neumáticos; lancha neumática**
rubber plant, type of indoor plant with thick shiny green leaves. □ **ficus**
2 ***rubbers,*** *Amer.* rubber/plastic shoes worn over ordinary shoes to protect them. □ **chanclos de goma**
3 number of games of bridge. □ **rubber**
4 piece of rubber used for removing pencil marks. □ **goma**
rubber stamp *n.* stamp made of rubber, with words or figures cut on it, which is used for stamping documents. □ **tampón; sello de caucho**
■ *v.* to agree to something automatically without examining it. □ **aprobar maquinalmente**
rubbery *adj.* flexible and strong like rubber. □ **parecido a la goma**
rubbish ['rʌbiʃ] *n.* (*no pl.*) **1** waste/things which are to be thrown away: *rubbish bin; rubbish dump.* □ **basura; vertedero**
2 nonsense: *don't talk rubbish.* □ **no digas tonterías**
rubble ['rʌbl] *n.* small stones/broken bricks, etc. used in constructing paths, etc. □ **escombros**
rubicund ['ru:bikənd] *adj.* (*formal*) red (face). □ **rubicundo**
rubric ['ru:brik] *n.* written instructions; written heading to a piece of writing. □ **preceptos; encabezamiento**
ruby ['ru:bi] *n.* red precious stone. □ **rubí**
■ *adj.* dark red. □ **color de rubí**
rucksack ['rʌksæk] *n.* bag carried on the back of a walker. □ **mochila**
ructions ['rʌkʃənz] *n. pl.* (*informal*) argument/angry scene: *if you're late there'll be ructions.* □ **si llegas tarde se va a armar gorda**
rudder ['rʌdə] *n.* flat plate at the stern of a boat/on the tail of an aircraft, used for steering. □ **timón**
ruddy ['rʌdi] *adj.* **1** red/fire-coloured. □ **rojizo**
2 (*slang*) awful: *he's a ruddy liar!* □ **condenado**
rude [ru:d] *adj.* **1** impolite; obscene: *he was rude to the customers; they made rude drawings on the wall.* □ **grosero**
2 sudden: *it came as a rude shock to him.* □ **repentino**
3 rough/primitive: *he built a rude shelter out of branches.* □ **tosco**
rudely *adv.* not politely: *he rudely refused to move when his mother asked him to shut the door.* □ **con descortesía**
rudeness *n.* being rude. □ **grosería; descortesía**
rudiments ['ru:dimənts] *n.* simple/elementary facts: *he knows the rudiments of physics.* □ **rudimentos; se sabe las primeras nociones de...**
rudimentary [ru:di'mentəri] *adj.* basic; not fully developed. □ **rudimentario**
rue [ru:] *n.* bitter herb. □ **ruda**
■ *v.* to regret: *I rue the day I ever met him.* □ **lamentar**
rueful *adj.* sorry/regretful. □ **arrepentido**
ruff [rʌf] *n.* **1** wide collar of ruffed lace. □ **gorguera**
2 bird with a ring of coloured feathers round its neck. □ **collarín**
ruffian ['rʌfiən] *n.* hooligan/violent person. □ **rufián**
ruffle ['rʌfl] *n.* material/lace gathered into a bunch and used as decoration on clothes/curtains, etc. □ **volante**
■ *v.* **1** to disturb (feathers/water/someone's hair): *the wind ruffled the bird's feathers.* □ **encrespar (plumas); rizar (agua); despeinar (pelo)**
2 *he's never ruffled,* (*informal*) he never gets flustered. □ **nunca se aturulla**
rug [rʌg] *n.* **1** small carpet. □ **alfombrilla**
2 thick blanket, especially one used for travelling. □ **manta de viaje**
Rugby ['rʌgbi] *n.* type of football played with an oval ball, which can be passed from hand to hand as well as being kicked. □ **'rugby'**
rugged ['rʌgid] *adj.* **1** rough/uneven: *rugged mountain scenery; rugged face.* □ **accidentado (montañas); de rasgos fuertes (cara)**
2 strict; sturdy: *rugged independence.* □ **vigoroso**
rugger ['rʌgə] *n.* (*informal*) Rugby. □ **'rugby'**
ruin ['ru:in] *n.* **1** wreck; complete loss of all your money: *the business is going to ruin; ruin stared him in the face,* it was very likely he would lose all his money. □ **ruina**
2 ***ruins,*** remains of collapsed buildings: *the castle is in ruins; after the earthquake, the rescue-workers searched the ruins for survivors.* □ **ruinas**
■ *v.* **1** to wreck/to spoil completely: *the bad weather*

has ruined the harvest; his bad manners have ruined his chances of promotion. □ **arruinar**
2 to bring to financial collapse: *the fall in the exchange rate ruined him.* □ **arruinar**
ruination [rui'neiʃn] *n.* act of ruining: *his daughter will be the ruination of him,* she will ruin him by spending too much. □ **ruina**
ruined *adj.* in ruins: *a ruined castle.* □ **en ruinas**
ruinous *adj.* so expensive as to cause ruin. □ **ruinoso**
ruinously *adv.* extremely (expensive). **extremadamente caro**
rule [ru:l] *n.* **1** general way of conduct: *I make it a rule never to smoke cigarettes before breakfast.* □ **regla; norma**
as a (general) rule, *I get to work at 9 o'clock,* usually. □ **por regla general...**
2 strict order of the way to behave: *you must play according to the rules of the game.* □ **regla**
work to rule, (in industry) working only according to the rules laid down in the union agreement. □ **hacer huelga de celo**
3 government: *the country is under the rule of the army; under Napoleon's rule, France became a great power.* □ **el país está bajo el mando...; bajo el dominio de Napoleón,...**
4 wood/metal rod with measurements on it, used in carpentry, etc. □ **regla**
■ *v.* **1** to govern/to control: *the president rules very strictly.* □ **mandar**
2 to give an official/legal decision: *the court ruled that the evidence could not be accepted.* □ **disponer**
3 to draw a straight line using a ruler. □ **trazar**
ruled paper, paper with lines on it. □ **papel rayado**
ruler *n.* **1** person who governs: *the ruler of an African state.* □ **gobernante**
2 strip of wood/plastic with measurements marked on it, used for drawing straight lines. □ **regla**
ruling *adj.* which governs: *ruling passion.* □ **pasión dominante**
ruling party, party which forms the government. □ **el partido en el poder**
■ *n.* legal decision: *the judge gave a ruling in favour of the defendant.* □ **fallo, sentencia**
rule out *v.* to leave something out/not to consider something: *we have ruled out going for a walk because of the weather; the police have not ruled out murder,* they consider it may be murder. □ **descartar algo**
rum [rʌm] *n.* alcoholic drink made from the juice of sugar cane. □ **ron**
■ *adj.* (*informal*) odd/strange. □ **raro**
rumble ['rʌmbl] *n.* low rolling noise: *the rumble of thunder in the distance.* □ **retumbo**
■ *v.* to make a low rolling noise: *lorries rumbled past all night.* □ **rodar**
ruminate ['ru:mineit] *v.* **1** to chew over food which has already been swallowed once (as a cow does). □ **rumiar**
2 to think over a problem. □ **rumiar**
ruminant ['ru:minənt] *adj.* and *n.* animal (like a cow) which chews its cud. □ **rumiante**
rumination [ru:mi'neiʃn] *n.* deep thought. □ **reflexión**
rummage ['rʌmidʒ] *n.* **1** searching about for something: *I was having a rummage around and found this old book.* □ **estaba hurgando y...**
2 old junk. □ **objetos diversos**
rummage sale, sale of unwanted objects for a charity. □ **venta benéfica**
■ *v.* to search about for something: *he rummaged around in the back of the cupboard.* □ **revolverlo todo**
rummy ['rʌmi] *n.* card game where each player tries to collect sets of similar cards or several cards in sequence. □ **'rummy'**
rumour ['ru:mə] *Amer.* **rumor** *n.* story passed on from one person to another without necessarily being true: *there were rumours that the government might resign; rumour has it that he's already been married twice.* □ **rumor**
rumoured *adj. it's rumoured that he has been married before,* people say. □ **se dice que...**
rump [rʌmp] *n.* back part of an animal. □ **ancas; cuarto trasero (para comer)**
rump steak, steak cut from the rump. □ **filete**
rumple ['rʌmpl] *v.* to crush/to dishevel: *his hair was rumpled.* □ **arrugar; estaba despeinado**
rumpus ['rʌmpəs] *n.* noisy disorder. □ **jaleo**
to kick up a rumpus, to make a fuss. □ **armó una bronca**
run [rʌn] *n.* **1** act of going quickly on foot. □ **carrera**
2 *a prisoner **on the run,*** running away from prison. (*see also (6) below*). □ **un preso fugado**
3 ***to break into a run,*** to start to run: *the soldiers broke into a run.* □ **...empezaron a correr**
4 ***to go for a run,*** (i) to take some exercise by running. □ **ponerse a correr**
(ii) to go for a short ride in a car. □ **dar una vuelta en coche**
5 period: *he's had a run of bad luck.* □ **lleva una racha de mala suerte**
6 *he ate nothing for three days **on the run,*** for three consecutive days. □ **...durante tres días seguidos**
7 access to: *he has the run of the house,* he can go anywhere in the house. □ **tiene acceso a...**
8 track for running, etc.: *ski run.* □ **pista**
9 caged area where chickens are kept. □ **gallinero**
10 point made in cricket: *he scored ten runs.* □ **...diez puntos**
11 ladder/long hole in a stocking. □ **carrera**
12 excessive demand: *there's been a run on sugar.* □ **...una gran demanda de azúcar**
13 *a run on the pound,* sudden selling of the pound on foreign exchanges. □ **un asedio sobre la...**
■ *v.* (*he ran; he has run*) **1** to go very quickly on foot; to race: *he ran upstairs; the dog ran across the road; he is running in the 100 metres race.* □ **correr**
2 to travel (fast): *the yacht was running before the wind; the trains are not running today because of fog.* □ **navegar (yate); circular (tren)**
3 to work: *he left the engine of the car running; you can run this razor off the mains,* you can work it by plugging it into the electric system. □ **estar en marcha**
4 to amount to: *his expenses run to over $50 a week.* □ **ascender**
5 *they want to charge $50 but I can't run to that,* can't afford that. □ **...no me lo puedo permitir**
6 to go: *an idea keeps running through my head; the main street runs north and south through the town; the film runs for two hours.* □ **me da vueltas una idea...; la calle va de norte a sur...; la película dura...**
7 to direct: *he runs his own business.* □ **llevar**
8 to own and drive (a car): *he runs two Rolls-Royces; I can't afford to run a car; this car is very economical to run.* □ **tener; es muy poco el mantenimiento de este coche**
9 to drive: *I'll run you down to the station,* I'll drive you in my car. □ **llevar en coche**
10 *to run a bath,* to fill a bath with water. □ **llenar la bañera**

11 *he's running for president, Amer.* he is a candidate for the office of president. □ **se presenta a las elecciones**
12 (*of liquid*) to flow: *his nose is running,* liquid is coming from his nose (because he has a cold). □ **correr, fluir**
13 *this colour won't run,* will not come out if put in water. □ **...no se correrá**
run across *v.* **1** to cross quickly on foot: *he ran across the road.* □ **cruzar corriendo**
2 to find/to meet by chance. □ **toparse con**
run along *v.* to go alongside: *the road runs along the river.* □ **correr a lo largo de**
run away *v.* to escape: *he ran away from prison.* □ **escaparse**
runaway *n.* person who has escaped. □ **fugitivo**
■ *adj. runaway success,* great success. □ **éxito arrollador**
run down *v.* **1** to go down quickly on foot: *the boys ran down the escalator.* □ **bajar corriendo**
2 *the clock is running down,* it needs to be wound up. □ **el reloj está parado**
3 to criticize (someone): *he is always running his brother down.* □ **hablar mal de**
4 to reduce: *to run down stocks.* □ **reducir**
5 to knock down (with a vehicle): *he was run down by a bus.* □ **atropellar**
6 ***to be run down,*** to feel unwell/tired. □ **no estar bien de salud**
rundown *adj.* delapidated/not looked after: *a rundown old car.* □ **ruinoso**
■ *n.* summary: *give me a rundown of the sales figures.* □ **resumen**
run in *v.* **1** to work (a new engine) slowly until it works properly. □ **hacer el rodaje**
2 (*informal*) to arrest (someone). □ **detener**
runner *n.* **1** person who is running (in a race). □ **corredor**
2 shoot of a plant which makes roots where it touches the soil: *a strawberry runner.* □ **estolón**
runner bean, type of climbing bean. □ **judía escarlata**
3 sharp blade of a skate/a sledge. □ **cuchilla**
4 narrow carpet. □ **alfombra de pasillo**
runner up *n.* (*pl. runners up*) person who comes after the winners in a race. □ **subcampeón**
running *adj.* **1** which runs: *running water.* □ **agua corriente**
running commentary, commentary on an action while the action is taking place. □ **...en directo**
running total, total which is carried from one column of figures to the next. □ **subtotal, suma y sigue**
2 used in running: *running shorts.* □ **pantalón de deporte**
3 one after another: *he went without food for three days running.* □ **...seguidos**
■ *n.* **1** race. □ **el correr**
2 *he is in the running for the job,* he may get the job. □ **tiene posibilidades de...**
3 working: *the running of the trains; smooth running of a hotel.* □ **circulación de trenes; funcionamiento de un hotel**
run-of-the-mill *adj.* ordinary. □ **corriente y moliente**
run off *v.* **1** to escape/to flee: *he ran off with the boss's daughter.* □ **escaparse**
2 *to run off several photocopies,* to make several photocopies. □ **hacer**
run out *v.* to go short: *we are running out of petrol.* □ **acabarse**
run over *v.* **1** to look at (something) quickly. □ **mirar por encima**
2 to knock (someone) down: *he was run over by a bus.* □ **atropellar**
run up *v.* **1** to go up quickly on foot: *they ran up the stairs.* □ **subir corriendo**
2 to come closer quickly on foot: *the police came running up.* □ **acudir corriendo**
3 ***to run up against something,*** (i) to find something by chance. □ **darse de bruces con**
(ii) to find your way blocked by something. □ **tropezar con dificultades**
4 to sew (something) quickly: *she ran me up this dress in a couple of hours.* □ **coser en un santiamén**
runway *n.* track on which aircraft land. □ **pista de aterrizaje**
rung [rʌŋ] *n.* one of the bars on a ladder. □ **escalón**
■ *v. see* **ring.**
runny ['rʌni] *adj.* **1** liquid: *runny honey; I like eggs cooked with the yolk still runny.* □ **líquido**
2 *he's got a runny nose,* his nose is running (because he has a cold). □ **le moquea la nariz**
rupture ['rʌptʃə] *n.* **1** break (in negotiations); burst/break (of part of the body): *rupture of a blood vessel.* □ **ruptura (negociaciones); rotura (vaso sanguíneo)**
2 hernia/state where part of the bowel pushes through a weak place in the abdominal wall. □ **hernia**
■ *v.* **1** to break off (negotiations). □ **romper**
2 to burst through. □ **quebrarse**
3 *he ruptured himself lifting a heavy box,* the strain caused a hernia. □ **se hernió levantando...**
rural ['ruərəl] *adj.* referring to the countryside: *a rural scene.* □ **rural**
ruse ['ru:z] *n.* clever trick. □ **ardid**
rush [rʌʃ] *n.* **1** type of wild grass growing in water. □ **junco**
2 fast movement. □ **movimiento rápido**
3 *there was a general rush for the doors,* everyone tried to get to the doors. □ **...desbandada general hacia la puerta**
4 ***rush hour,*** time of day when traffic is bad/when trains are full. □ **hora punta**
5 ***rushes,*** first prints of a film, before it has been edited. □ **copión**
■ *v.* **1** to go forward fast: *he rushed into the room; she was rushed to hospital.* □ **entró muy deprisa; la llevaron a toda prisa**
2 *don't rush me,* don't keep on hurrying me. □ **no me metas prisa**
3 to attack suddenly: *the police rushed the gangsters' headquarters.* □ **tomar al asalto**
rusk [rʌsk] *n.* hard biscuit given to babies to suck. □ **chusco; tostada**
russet ['rʌsit] *n.* type of sweet brown apple. □ **variedad de manzana**
■ *adj.* and *n.* reddish-brown (colour). □ **color bermejo**
Russia ['rʌʃə] *n.* large country in Eastern Europe and Asia, part of the Soviet Union. □ **Rusia**
Russian *adj.* referring to Russia. □ **ruso**
■ *n.* **1** person from Russia. □ **ruso**
2 language spoken in Russia. □ **ruso**
rust [rʌst] *n.* **1** red formation on iron or steel which is left in damp air. □ **óxido; herrumbre**
2 red fungus disease of plants. □ **roya**
■ *v.* to get rusty: *don't leave the hammer outside – it will rust.* □ **oxidarse**
rust proof *adj.* (metal) which will not rust. □ **inoxidable**
rusty *adj.* **1** covered with rust: *he injured himself on a rusty nail.* □ **oxidado**

2 not in practice; (person) who lacks practice: *my German is rusty.* □ **tengo que practicar más el...**
rustic ['rʌstik] *adj.* rough/of country style: *a rustic seat.* □ **rústico**
■ *n.* rough peasant. □ **palurdo**
rustle ['rʌsl] *n.* noise of dry leaves/silk, etc. rubbing together. □ **susurro (hojas); frufrú (seda); crujido (papel)**
■ *v.* **1** to make a soft crackling noise: *he rustled his papers; the dead leaves rustled underfoot.* □ **hacer crujir (papel); susurrar (hojas)**
2 to steal cattle. □ **robar ganado**
rustle up *v.* (*informal*) to get (something) ready quickly: *can you rustle up a meal for ten people?* □ **preparar, improvisar**
rustling *n.* stealing (of cows). □ **robo de ganado**
rut [rʌt] *n.* long deep track made in soft earth by a wheel. □ **rodada**
to get into a rut, to start to lead a dull life with no excitement or career prospects. □ **hacerse esclavo de la rutina**
rutted *adj.* (path) full of ruts. □ **lleno de rodadas**
rutabaga ['ru:təbɑ:gə] *n. Amer.* swede. □ **nabo sueco**
ruthless ['ru:θləs] *adj.* pitiless/cruel. □ **despiadado**
ruthlessly *adv.* cruelly. □ **despiadadamente**
ruthlessness *n.* cruelty. □ **falta de piedad**
rye [rai] *n.* **1** type of dark brown cereal: *rye bread.* □ **centeno**
2 American whisky made from rye. □ **whisky de centeno**

S,s

S, s [es] nineteenth letter of the alphabet. □ **S, s**
Sabbath ['sæbəθ] *n.* seventh day of the week; a religious day of rest; (*for Christians*) Sunday; (*for Jews*) Saturday: *the Jews keep the Sabbath as a Holy day.* □ **domingo (crist.); sábado (judíos)**
sabbatical [sə'bætikl] *n.* and *adj.* (leave) granted to teachers, etc., for study and travel after a period of work: *he takes a sabbatical every four years; sabbatical leave; sabbatical year.* □ **sabático**
sable ['seibl] *n.* small brown-furred arctic animal; fur from this animal: *a sable coat; sable paintbrushes.* □ **marta cibelina**
sabotage ['sæbətɑːʒ] *n.* malicious/deliberate destruction: *the derailment of the train was the result of an act of sabotage.* □ **sabotaje**
■ *v.* to destroy/to render useless: *the manager's plan was sabotaged by the workers.* □ **sabotear**
saboteur [sæbə'təː] *n.* person who commits sabotage. □ **saboteador**
sabre ['seibə] *Amer.* **saber** *n.* sword with curved blade. □ **sable**
sac [sæk] *n.* bag-like part of an animal or plant. □ **saco**
saccharin ['sækərin] *n.* extremely sweet substance used as a substitute for sugar. □ **sacarina**
saccharine *adj.* too sweet/very sickly. □ **empalagoso**
sachet ['sæʃei] *n.* **1** small bag. □ **bolsita**
2 *sachet of shampoo,* small plastic bag containing enough shampoo for one washing. □ **bolsita de champú**
sack [sæk] *n.* **1** large bag made of strong rough cloth: *the coal merchant delivered twenty sacks of coal.* □ **saco**
2 (*informal*) dismissal. □ **despido**
to give someone the sack, to dismiss someone from a job. □ **despedir a uno**
to get the sack/to be given the sack, to be dismissed from a job: *he got the sack last week and can't find another job.* □ **ser despedido**
■ *v.* **1** to plunder: *the town was sacked by the invading army.* □ **saquear**
2 (*informal*) to dismiss (someone) from a job: *he was sacked for incompetence.* □ **le echaron (del trabajo) por...**
sacking *n.* **1** coarse material from which sacks are made; old sacks: *the tramp lay in a barn on a bed of sacking.* □ **arpillera**
2 plunder: *the sacking of the castle took place immediately after the battle.* □ **saqueo**
3 (*informal*) dismissal: *the sacking of the manager caused a strike.* □ **despido**
sackcloth *n.* coarse fabric. □ **arpillera**
sackcloth and ashes, (i) clothes worn at times of penitence. □ **hábito de penitencia**
(ii) symbol of repentance. □ **sayal**
sacrament ['sækrəmənt] *n.* **1** Christian religious ceremony: *the sacrament of marriage.* □ **sacramento**
2 the consecrated bread (and wine) taken at Communion: *he received the Last Sacraments on his deathbed.* □ **Eucaristía; recibió los últimos sacramentos...**
sacred ['seikrəd] *adj.* **1** associated with religion: *the Sacred Writings of the Prophets; sacred music,* music written on a religious theme. □ **sagrado**
2 holy: *the chapel was sacred to the memory of Saint Francis.* □ **consagrado**
3 respected: *nothing was sacred to him.* □ **sagrado**
sacredness *n.* holiness/sacred character. □ **lo sagrado; santidad**
sacrifice ['sækrifais] *n.* **1** killing of animal/person as offering to a god: *human sacrifice.* □ **sacrificio**
2 animal killed as an offering to god: *the High Priest offered a lamb as a sacrifice at the altar.* □ **sacrificio**
3 something given up at personal cost in order to achieve something else: *he succeeded in business at the sacrifice of his health; you will gain nothing by the sacrifice of your principles.* □ **sacrificio**
■ *v.* **1** to offer as a sacrifice. □ **sacrificar**
2 to give up/to devote: *she sacrificed her whole life to the care of the sick.* □ **sacrificar**
sacrificial [sækri'fiʃl] *adj.* as a sacrifice: *they made a sacrificial offering.* □ **como sacrificio**
sacrilege ['sækrilidʒ] *n.* using something sacred in a disrespectful way: *some people consider it a sacrilege to hold dances in a church.* □ **sacrilegio**
sacrilegious [sækri'lidʒəs] *adj.* referring to sacrilege. □ **sacrílego**
sacristy ['sækristi] *n.* room in a church where vestments/vessels, etc., are kept. □ **sacristía**
sacristan *n.* person who looks after a church, especially the vestments/holy vessels, etc. □ **sacristán**
sacrosanct ['sækrousæŋkt] *adj.* very sacred/protected by religious respect: *his sacrosanct glass of sherry in the evening.* □ **sacrosanto**
sad [sæd] *adj.* unhappy/sorrowful: *the news of her friend's death made her feel very sad; he had a sad expression.* □ **triste**
sadly *adv.* unhappily: *sadly I can't come to your wedding; she walked sadly away.* □ **tristemente**
sadden *v.* to make unhappy: *it saddened him to hear of his friend's distress.* □ **entristecer**
saddle ['sædl] *n.* **1** rider's seat on a bicycle/on the back of a horse: *she jumped into the saddle and rode away.* □ **silla**
2 ridge between two mountains. □ **puerto; paso**
3 *saddle of lamb,* joint of meat from the back of a sheep. □ **silla**
■ *v.* **1** to put a saddle on (a horse, etc.): *the huntsman saddled and bridled his horse.* □ **ensillar**
2 to burden (someone) with a task or responsibility: *the prefect was saddled with the responsibility of keeping order when the teacher was away.* □ **cargar**
saddlebag *n.* bag attached to a bicycle; one of a pair of bags on a horse. □ **alforja**
saddler *n.* maker of saddles and other equipment for horses. □ **guarnicionero**
sadism ['seidizəm] *n.* pleasure derived from being cruel or watching cruelty. □ **sadismo**
sadist ['seidist] *n.* person who delights in sadism. □ **sádico**
sadistic [sə'distik] *adj.* referring to sadism: *he gained sadistic pleasure from seeing prisoners tortured.* □ **sádico**
safari [sə'fɑːri] *n.* hunting expedition in Africa: *he killed three wild boar while on safari in Kenya.* □ **safari**
safari park, park where large wild animals run free, and visitors can look at them from their cars. □ **safari 'park'**
safe [seif] *n.* **1** fire-proof and burglar-proof box for

valuables: *she kept her diamond rings in a safe at her bank.* □ **caja fuerte**
2 ventilated cupboard for food: *the meat safe was in the larder.* □ **fresquera**
■ *adj.* **1** uninjured: *the little girl was found safe and sound two miles from her home.* □ **sano y salvo**
2 secure/out of danger: *the baby lay safe in his mother's arms; she kept her money in a safe place; is it safe to leave him alone.* □ **seguro**
to be on the safe side, to take precautions against risks: *they arrived half an hour early at the station, just to be on the safe side.* □ **...para mayor seguridad**
it's safe to say, it may be said without risk of exaggeration. □ **se puede decir con confianza**
3 certain/to be relied upon: *he always uses safe methods.* □ **seguro**
safe-conduct *n.* paper which allows someone to go through enemy territory. □ **salvoconducto**
safeguard ['seifgɑːd] *n.* protection: *as a safeguard against influenza, he had an injection.* □ **salvaguardia**
■ *v.* to guard/to protect: *he wanted to safeguard his good reputation by avoiding publicity.* □ **salvaguardar**
safely *adv.* without any danger; without being harmed. □ **sin peligro**
safety ['seifti] *n.* freedom from danger or risk. □ **seguridad**
there's safety in numbers, a large group of people is less likely to be attacked. □ **cuantos más, menos peligro**
road safety, care to be taken by pedestrians and drivers. □ **seguridad vial**
safety belt, belt worn by someone riding in a car/in an aircraft as protection in case of accident. □ **cinturón de seguridad**
safety catch, lock which stops a gun being fired by accident. □ **seguro**
safety curtain, fireproof barrier between the stage and the auditorium in a theatre. □ **telón de seguridad**
safety pin, pin whose point is protected by a guard. □ **imperdible**
safety valve, valve in steam-boiler, which lets out excess pressure automatically. □ **válvula de seguridad**

saffron ['sæfrən] *n.* orange-coloured powder made from crocus flowers, from which colouring and flavouring are obtained. □ **azafrán**
■ *adj.* orange-coloured: *Buddhist monks wear saffron robes.* □ **color azafrán**

sag [sæg] *v.* (*he sagged*) to sink/to bend (in the middle) under weight or pressure: *the wooden bridge sagged under the weight of the tank.* □ **hundirse**

saga ['sɑːgə] *n.* **1** story of heroic achievement or adventure: *the explorer told the saga of his journey to the Antarctic.* □ **epopeya**
2 series of books telling the history of a family: *The Forsyte Saga.* □ **saga**

sagacious [sə'geiʃəs] *adj.* (*formal*) wise/shrewd. □ **sagaz**
sagaciously *adv.* wisely. □ **sagazmente**
sagacity [sə'gæsiti] *n.* exceptional intelligence/wisdom. □ **sagacidad**

sage [seidʒ] *n.* **1** aromatic herb used in cookery: *sage and onion stuffing.* □ **salvia**
sage green, greyish green colour. □ **verde salvia**
2 very wise man. □ **sabio**
■ *adj.* wise/discreet. □ **sensato**

Sagittarius [sædʒi'tɛəriəs] *n.* one of the signs of the zodiac, shaped like an archer. □ **Sagitario**

sago ['seigou] *n.* kind of white powder used as food: *sago pudding.* □ **sagú**
sago palm, palm tree whose pith yields sago. □ **palmera de sagú**

said [sed] *v. see* **say.**

sail [seil] *n.* **1** piece of canvas/nylon, etc., attached to the mast of a boat to catch the wind: *when the wind dropped the sails flapped idly.* □ **vela**
to set sail, to start a voyage. □ **hacerse a la mar**
2 trip in a boat: *to go for a sail.* □ **dar un paseo en barco**
3 arm of a windmill which turns with the wind: *a windmill has four sails.* □ **aspa**
■ *v.* **1** to travel on water. □ **navegar**
2 *the ship sails at 4 o'clock,* it leaves the port. □ **zarpar**
3 to travel in a sailing boat: *she was the first woman to sail alone across the Atlantic.* □ **navegar; ...en cruzar el Atlántico**
to sail close to the wind, (i) to sail nearly against the wind. □ **bolinear**
(ii) to come very near to breaking the law: *by informing on his colleagues he was sailing very close to the wind.* □ **estar a punto de infringir una ley**
4 to control (a sailing boat): *a catamaran is difficult to sail; children were sailing their boats on the pond.* □ **gobernar; manejar**
5 to glide in the air: *the clouds sailed across a blue sky.* □ **deslizarse**
sailboat *n. Amer.* yacht/sailing boat. □ **barco de vela**
sailcloth *n.* canvas for making sails. □ **lona**
sailing *adj.* (ship) which uses sails: *sailing boat; sailing ship.* □ **velero**
■ *n.* **1** journey by ship. □ **navegación**
2 *we have a night sailing to France,* our booking is for a night ferry. □ **tenemos una travesía nocturna...**
plain sailing, straightforward progress, with no problems: *the work has been difficult, but from now on it should be plain sailing.* □ **es cosa de coser y cantar**
sailor ['seilə] *n.* seaman/person who sails: *the boy wanted to join the navy and become a sailor.* □ **marinero**
to be a good/bad sailor, person who is liable/not liable to seasickness: *he dreaded the Atlantic crossing as he was a very bad sailor.* □ **...porque se mareaba**

saint [seint] *n.* (*abbreviated with names to* **St**) person recognised by the Christian church as having led an exceptionally holy life, and canonized after death: *St Christopher is the patron saint of travellers,* he is supposed to protect travellers. □ **santo**
saintliness *n.* holiness/piety. □ **santidad**
saintly *adj.* holy: *her saintly manner set her apart from others.* □ **santo**

sake [seik] *n.* **1** ***for the sake of; for someone's/something's sake,*** out of consideration for/in the interest of: *for the sake of peace and quiet she allowed her children to switch on the television; for goodness' sake remember your manners! please do it for my sake.* □ **por; en consideración a**
2 *let's get together* ***for old time's sake,*** to remember what it was like in the old days. □ **...por los viejos tiempos**

salacious [sə'leiʃəs] *adj.* erotic/obscene. □ **salaz**
salaciousness, salacity [sə'læsiti] *n.* being salacious. □ **salacidad**

salad ['sæləd] *n.* cold dish of various cooked or raw

vegetables; cold meat served with a dressing and lettuce: *ham salad; tomato salad; rice salad; a plate of salad.* □ **ensalada**
salad cream, type of sauce made of eggs/oil/vinegar, etc., used on salad. □ **mayonesa**
salad dressing, mixture of oil/vinegar, etc., used on salad. □ **aliño**
fruit salad, various fresh fruit chopped up and served mixed together. □ **macedonia de frutas**

salami [sə'lɑːmi] *n.* salty Italian sausage, eaten cold. □ **salami**

salary ['sæləri] *n.* fixed payment made to an employee, usually every month: *salary cheque.* □ **salario, sueldo**
salaried *adj.* (person) who is paid a salary: *the salaried staff; the advertised job is a salaried one.* □ **asalariado**

sale [seil] *n.* **1** exchange of something for money: *this house is for sale; goods are on sale in the market; a sale has been agreed.* □ **venta**
2 goods sold at reduced/special prices for a short period of time: *sale of slightly soiled goods; shoppers pour into London for the January sales.* □ **rebajas**
3 organized selling of goods. □ **venta**
jumble sale, selling of unwanted household goods. □ **rastrillo**
sale of work, selling of handmade goods. □ **venta de objetos de artesanía**
4 ***sales,*** money received in a business: *our sales have risen by 10%.* □ **ventas**
saleable *adj.* fit for sale. □ **vendible**
saleroom *n.* room in which an auction is carried out. □ **sala de subastas**
sales girl *n.* girl in a shop who sells goods to customers. □ **dependienta**
salesman *n.* (*pl. salesmen*) **1** person who sells a producer's goods to a shop: *in his job as a travelling salesman he went all over the country.* □ **representante**
2 man in a shop who sells goods to customers. □ **vendedor**
salesmanship *n.* the art of selling: *by sheer salesmanship he persuaded me to buy some useless gadgets.* □ **arte de vender**
saleswoman *n.* (*pl. saleswomen*) woman in a shop who sells goods to customers. □ **vendedora**

salient ['seiliənt] *n.* projecting part of a fortification/of a line of battle. □ **saliente**
■ *adj.* prominent/conspicuous/most important: *he picked the salient points in the argument.* □ **sobresaliente**

saline ['seilain] *adj.* containing salt: *a saline solution.* □ **salino**

saliva [sə'laivə] *n.* liquid formed in the mouth to help digestion: *saliva dripped from the dog's mouth.* □ **saliva**
salivary *adj.* ***salivary gland,*** gland which produces saliva. □ **salival**
salivate *v.* to make saliva. □ **salivar**

sallow ['sælou] *adj.* sickly yellow colour: *sallow complexion.* □ **cetrino; tez cetrina**

sally ['sæli] *n.* **1** sudden rush (of soldiers) out of a defended position: *the defenders made a sally from the camp.* □ **salida**
2 witticism: *the Prime Minister's speech contained many sallies against the Opposition.* □ **agudezas**
■ *v.* to go out: *she put on her raincoat and sallied out/forth into the rain.* □ **salir a**

salmon ['sæmən] *n.* (*no pl.*) large pink-fleshed fish: *salmon fishing is particularly good in Scotland.* □ **salmón**
■ *adj.* coloured orange-pink: *she wore a salmon (pink) dress.* □ **de color salmón**
salmon trout *n.* type of large sea trout with pink flesh. □ **trucha asalmonada**

salon ['sælɔn] *n.* hairdresser's/dressmaker's business; room/building housing a hairdresser's or dressmaker's: *he runs a beauty salon.* □ **salón**

saloon [sə'luːn] *n.* **1** large lounge in a ship. □ **salón**
2 comfortable bar in a public house. □ **salón interior**
3 *Amer.* public bar. □ **bar**
4 ***saloon (car),*** covered car. □ **berlina**

salt [sɔːlt] *n.* **1** white substance used to season and preserve food; (*in chemistry*) combination of a metal with an acid: *salt is an essential ingredient in any savoury dish.* □ **sal**
to take something with a pinch of salt, (*informal*) not to believe something completely. □ **admitir algo con reservas**
2 ***old salt,*** (*informal*) experienced sailor. □ **lobo de mar**
■ *adj.* containing salt; cured/preserved/seasoned with salt: *salt pork; salt water.* □ **salado**
■ *v.* to add salt to: *I forgot to salt the potatoes; in snowy weather streets are often salted.* □ **salar**
salt away *v.* to put (something) aside for the future: *he has a few thousand pounds salted away in the bank.* □ **ahorrar**
salt cellar *n.* small pot containing salt, usually with holes in the top so that it can be sprinkled on food. □ **salero**
salt-free *adj.* without salt. □ **sin sal**
saltpetre, *Amer.* **saltpeter** *n.* potassium nitrate/powder used to make gunpowder. □ **nitro**
salty *adj.* containing salt: *this drink has a salty taste.* □ **salado**

salubrious [sə'luːbriəs] *adj.* (*formal*) healthy: *mountain air is said to be salubrious.* □ **salubre**
salubrity *n.* healthiness. □ **salubridad**

saluki [sə'luːki] *n.* breed of hound. □ **'saluqui'**

salute [sə'luːt] *n.* gesture expressing respect/homage/recognition: *the soldier gave a salute as his commanding officer passed by; a salute of 21 guns was fired.* □ **saludo**
to take the salute, to stand on a dais and be saluted by soldiers on parade: *the Queen took the salute at the parade.* □ **recibir el saludo**
■ *v.* to give a salute: *the sailors saluted the captain of the ship as he came on board.* □ **hacer un saludo**
salutary ['sæljutəri] *adj.* useful/helpful; which has a good effect: *a salutary warning.* □ **útil**
salutation [sælju'teiʃn] *n.* words spoken/written in praise of someone. □ **salutación**

salvage ['sælvidʒ] *n.* **1** payment made for saving a ship/its cargo from loss by wreck: *salvage money.* □ **derechos de salvamento**
2 objects saved (from a boat/fire, etc.). □ **objetos salvados**
■ *v.* to save (from wreck/fire, etc.): *various treasures were salvaged from the wrecked ship by divers.* □ **salvar**

salvation [sæl'veiʃn] *n.* saving of the soul from sin; saving of a person from evil. □ **salvación**
Salvation Army *n.* religious organization run on military lines which specializes in missionary and welfare work among poorer people. □ **Ejército de Salvación**

salve [sælv] *n.* healing ointment. □ **ungüento**
lip salve, ointment which prevents lips cracking in cold weather. □ **protector; cacao**
■ *v. to do something **to salve your conscience,*** be-

cause your conscience tells you to do it. □ **tranquilizar la conciencia**

salver ['sælvə] *n.* large flat plate (usually made of silver). □ **bandeja**

salvo ['sælvou] *n.* **1** simultaneous discharge of several guns in a battle at sea or as a salute: *the naval squadron fired a salvo.* □ **salva**
2 round of applause: *a salvo of applause greeted the conductor when he stepped on to the rostrum.* □ **salva de aplausos**

Samaritan [sə'mæritən] *n.* person who helps someone who is in trouble. □ **samaritano**

same [seim] *adj.* identical; monotonous/unchanging: *it's the same old story; she got very bored with having to do the same work day after day; she wore the very same dress as she was wearing last year.* □ **mismo**
it's all the same to me, I don't mind: *it's all the same to me whether you accept or refuse.* □ **me da igual**
■ *pron.* the identical thing: *I'd do the same again; we all stay the same.* □ **lo mismo**
■ *adv.* ***all the same/just the same,*** (*informal*) nevertheless: *although it's a nice day, all the same I don't feel like going out.* □ **me es igual**
sameness *n.* **1** being the same. □ **igualdad**
2 monotony: *the sameness of the scenery bored me.* □ **monotonía**

samovar ['sæmouvɑ:] *n.* type of urn used in Russia for boiling water for tea. □ **samovar**

sampan ['sæmpæn] *n.* small Chinese boat. □ **sampán**

samphire ['sæmfaiə] *n.* type of fern which grows near the sea. □ **hinojo marino**

sample ['sɑ:mpl] *n.* specimen: *she brought some samples of curtain material home; is this a fair sample of your work?* □ **muestra**
■ *v.* to test/to try: *she sampled six different wines before choosing one to buy.* □ **probar/catar**
sampler *n.* decorated tapestry panel (usually with letters, numbers and simple pictures) made to show skill in sewing stitches. □ **dechado**

samurai ['sæmurai] *n.* medieval Japanese warrior. □ **samurai**

sanatorium [sænə'tɔ:riəm] *n.* hospital for the treatment of invalids, especially people suffering from tuberculosis. □ **sanatorio**

sanctify ['sæŋktifai] *v.* to consecrate/to make holy. □ **santificar**
sanctimonious [sæŋkti'mouniəs] *adj.* pretending to be holy: *from his sanctimonious expression it was hard to believe he had committed the crime.* □ **santurrón**
sanctity ['sæŋktiti] *n.* holiness of life/saintliness: *the sanctity of marriage.* □ **santidad**

sanction ['sæŋkʃn] *n.* **1** law/decree: *the contract contained some binding sanctions.* □ **sanción**
2 penalty: *sanctions were imposed by the government when the company broke its pay policy.* □ **sanción**
■ *v.* **1** to approve: *the chairman signed an agreement sanctioning a new salary scale.* □ **autorizar**
2 to permit: *the policeman was sanctioned to arrest the man.* □ **autorizar**

sanctuary ['sæŋktjuəri] *n.* **1** holy place: *Jerusalem is full of famous sanctuaries.* □ **santuario**
2 part of a church where the high altar is placed. □ **sagrario**
3 place for the protection of wild animals or birds. □ **reserva**
4 refuge: *he sought sanctuary in a foreign embassy.* □ **asilo**

sanctum ['sæŋktəm] *n.* **1** holy place. □ **lugar sagrado**
2 private room. □ **habitación privada**
the inner sanctum, the most private/secret office. □ **sanctasanctórun**

sand [sænd] *n.* **1** mass of tiny fragments of worn-down rock found on seashores/river beds/deserts, etc.: *children love to play in the sand/to build sand castles.* □ **arena**
2 beach/seashore: *they raced their motorcycles across the sand.* □ **playa de arena**
■ *v.* **1** to rub smooth with sandpaper. □ **lijar**
2 to spread sand (on icy roads). □ **enarenar**
sandbag *n.* bag filled with sand and used as a defence/as ballast: *soldiers in the trenches were protected by sandbags.* □ **saco de arena**
sandbank *n.* ridge of sand in sea or river: *the boat ran aground on a sandbank.* □ **banco de arena**
sand blast *v.* to clean (the exterior of a building) by directing a powerful jet of sand on to it. □ **limpiar con chorro de arena**
sander *n.* machine/person who sands. □ **pulidora (máquina); pulidor (persona)**
sandpaper *n.* paper with a coating of sand for smoothing. □ **lija**
■ *v.* to rub smooth with sandpaper: *he had to sandpaper the walls before he could paint them.* □ **lijar**
sandpiper *n.* small bird with a long bill which lives on beaches. □ **lavandera**
sands *n. pl.* seashore: *they raced across the sands.* □ **playa de arena**
sandstone *n.* rock made of compressed sand. □ **arenisca**
sandy *adj.* like sand; made of sand: *sandy beaches; she has sandy-coloured hair.* □ **arenoso**

sandal ['sændl] *n.* light open shoe worn in the summer. □ **sandalia**
sandalwood *n.* **1** tropical tree; fragrant wood from this tree. □ **sándalo**
2 scent from this tree: *sandalwood soap.* □ **sándalo**

sandwich ['sændwitʃ] *n.* two slices of bread with sweet or savoury filling: *he ordered a round of ham sandwiches.* □ **'sandwich'**
■ *v.* to insert (something) between two others: *his speech had to be sandwiched between the chairman's and the secretary's; in the train she found herself sandwiched between two very fat ladies.* □ **insertar, colocar entre**
sandwich board *n.* pair of boards worn over the shoulders in the street to advertise something. □ **carteles de hombre anuncio**
sandwich course *n.* course where students spend time working in a factory between periods of study at a college. □ **curso práctico intercalado**
sandwich man *n.* man who carries a sandwich board. □ **hombre anuncio**

sane [sein] *adj.* reasonable; not mad: *she had a very sane approach to the problem.* □ **sensato/cuerdo**
sanely *adv.* in a reasonable way: *he treated the matter sanely.* □ **con sensatez**
sanity ['sæniti] *n.* being sane: *despite prolonged torture he kept his sanity.* □ **cordura**

sang [sæŋ] *v. see* **sing.**

sanguinary ['sæŋgwinəri] *adj.* delighting in bloodshed or killing. □ **sanguinario**

sanguine ['sæŋgwin] *adj.* confident/optimistic: *he has a sanguine outlook on life.* □ **optimista**

sanitation [sæni'teiʃn] *n.* hygiene/conditions affecting health: *lack of adequate sanitation can lead to the spreading of disease.* □ **saneamiento**
sanitary ['sænitəri] *adj.* referring to sanitation/hygiene: *the sanitary conditions in the shanty towns are very bad.* □ **sanitario**
sanitary towel, pad of absorbent material worn by

women to absorb blood lost during menstruation. □ **compresa**

sank [sæŋk] *v. see* **sink.**

sap [sæp] *n.* **1** juice circulating in plants and trees: *sap rises in trees in the spring.* □ **savia**
2 (*in warfare*) digging a tunnel to get near to the enemy. □ **zapar**
■ *v.* (*he sapped*) **1** to weaken/to drain away: *his energy had been sapped by constant illness.* □ **minar**
2 to undermine/to make insecure by removing foundations: *the pounding of the waves had sapped the cliffs and made them dangerous.* □ **socavar**
sapper *n.* soldier in the Royal Engineers. □ **zapador**

sapling ['sæpliŋ] *n.* young tree. □ **árbol joven**

sapphire ['sæfaiə] *n.* blue precious stone: *her ring consisted of a sapphire surrounded by diamonds.* □ **zafiro**
■ *adj.* clear blue (colour). □ **de color zafiro**

saraband ['særəbænd] *n.* slow Spanish dance. □ **zarabanda**

sarcasm ['sɑːkæzəm] *n.* making sharp unpleasant remarks. □ **sarcasmo**
sarcastic [sɑː'kæstik] *adj.* scornful: *she was disliked for her sarcastic comments.* □ **sarcástico**
sarcastically *adv.* scornfully: *she replied sarcastically that she would rather die than go out with him.* □ **con sarcasmo**

sarcoma [sɑː'koumə] *n.* kind of malignant tumour. □ **sarcoma**

sarcophagus [sə'kɔfəgəs] *n.* stone coffin often decorated with sculpture. □ **sarcófago**

sardine [sɑː'diːn] *n.* **1** small fish of the herring family: *a tin of sardines.* □ **sardina**
2 *the passengers were* ***packed in like sardines,*** very tightly. □ **...como sardinas en lata**

sardonic [sɑː'dɔnik] *adj.* scornful/cynical: *sardonic laughter.* □ **sardónico**

sari ['sɑːri] *n.* long piece of cloth worn by Indian women. □ **sari**

sarong [sə'rɔŋ] *n.* cloth worn wrapped round the lower part of the body by both men and women in parts of south-east Asia. □ **'sarong'**

sartorial [sɑː'tɔːriəl] *adj.* (*formal*) referring to men's clothes. □ **de sastre, en el vestir**

sash [sæʃ] *n.* **1** ornamental scarf: *she wore a sash of blue silk around her waist.* □ **fajín**
2 wooden frame holding panes of glass. □ **marco**
sash cord *n.* rope in a sash window which allows the frames to slide up and down smoothly. □ **cuerda de ventana**
sash window *n.* window made of panes of glass set in two frames which slide up and down. □ **ventana de guillotina**

Sassenach ['sæsənæk] *n.* (*in Scotland*) Englishman. □ **inglés**

sat [sæt] *v. see* **sit.**

Satan ['seitən] *n.* the devil. □ **Satán/Satanás**
satanic [sə'tænik] *adj.* diabolical/like the devil. □ **satánico**

satchel ['sætʃəl] *n.* small leather/canvas bag worn on the shoulders: *children carry their schoolbooks in satchels.* □ **cartera**

satellite ['sætəlait] *n.* **1** heavenly body which goes round a planet: *the moon is a satellite of the earth.* □ **satélite**
2 artificial body which was launched from and which goes round the earth: *television pictures can now be transmitted round the world by satellite.* □ **satélite**
a satellite photograph, photograph taken by a satellite. □ **una foto de satélite**
satellite state *n.* country controlled by a more powerful one. □ **país satélite**
satellite town *n.* small town dependent on a larger town near by. □ **ciudad satélite**

satiate ['seiʃieit] *v.* to satisfy totally/to fill to overflowing: *the feast satiated the diners.* □ **saciar**

satin ['sætin] *n.* silk fabric with a glossy surface: *her wedding dress was of white satin.* □ **raso**
■ *adj.* made of satin: *the page-boy wore satin trousers.* □ **de raso**

satire ['sætaiə] *n.* **1** attacking someone in speech/writing by making them seem ridiculous. □ **sátira**
2 humorously critical piece of writing. □ **sátira**
satiric, satirical [sə'tirikl] *adj.* humorously critical: *in his essay the writer takes a satirical look at politicians.* □ **satírico**
satirically *adv.* in a humorously critical way. □ **satíricamente**
satirist ['sætirist] *n.* writer of satires. □ **escritor satírico**
satirize ['sætiraiz] *v.* to attack (something) in a more or less amusing way: *in his pictures Hogarth satirized life in eighteenth century England.* □ **satirizar**

satisfaction [sætis'fækʃn] *n.* **1** payment of debt; compensation (for damage). □ **liquidación (de una deuda); compensación económica**
2 good feeling; sense of comfort/happiness: *they heard the good news with great satisfaction; he had the satisfaction of being able to prove he was right.* □ **satisfacción**
satisfactory *adj.* causing satisfaction; quite good: *the negotiations were brought to a satisfactory conclusion.* □ **satisfactorio**
satisfactorily *adv.* in a satisfactory way; quite well: *he managed to carry out the task satisfactorily.* □ **satisfactoriamente**

satisfy ['sætisfai] *v.* **1** to comply with/to fulfil: *the competitor's work satisfied the requirements of the judges.* □ **satisfacer**
2 to show adequate proof: *he satisfied the immigration official as to his nationality.* □ **convencer**
3 to make (someone) content/pleased: *their performance always satisfies me; to satisfy your curiosity.* □ **satisfacer**
4 to be sure/to ascertain: *I have satisfied myself that all is well.* □ **asegurarse**
satisfying *adj.* which satisfies: *it was a satisfying experience for them to see their son win the school prize.* □ **satisfactorio**

satsuma [sæt'suːmə] *n.* type of small sweet seedless orange. □ **'satsuma'**

saturate ['sætʃureit] *v.* **1** to make very wet: *his clothes were saturated after walking in the rain.* □ **empapar**
2 *saturated with information,* full of information. □ **saturado de información**
saturation [sætʃu'reiʃn] *n.* complete filling. □ **saturación**
saturation point, (i) point at which a substance cannot take in any more liquid. □ **punto de saturación** (ii) *the market has reached saturation point,* no more goods can be sold. □ **punto de saturación**

Saturday ['sætədei] *n.* sixth day of the week; day between Friday and Sunday: *we go to the pub on Saturdays; I saw her last Saturday; I'll see you on Saturday.* □ **sábado**

saturnine ['sætənain] *adj.* gloomy: *his saturnine character.* □ **saturnino**

sauce [sɔːs] *n.* **1** liquid poured over food: *mint sauce; apple sauce; chocolate sauce.* □ **salsa**

2 (*informal*) impertinence: *I don't want any of your sauce!* □ **¡eres un fresco!**
sauce-boat *n.* vessel in which sauce is served. □ **salsera**
saucepan *n.* metal pan with a long handle used for boiling. □ **cazo**
saucily *adv.* (*informal*) cheekily. □ **con frescura**
sauciness *n.* (*informal*) impudence. □ **frescura**
saucy *adj.* (*informal*) cheeky. □ **fresco**
saucer ['sɔːsə] *n.* shallow dish placed under a cup: *cup and saucer.* □ **platillo**
flying saucer, object shaped like a saucer which people say they have seen in the sky. □ **platillo volante**
Saudi Arabia ['saudiə'reibiə] *n.* country in the Middle East. □ **Arabia Saudita**
Saudi, Saudi Arabian *adj.* and *n.* (person) from Saudi Arabia. □ **saudí/saudita**
sauerkraut ['sauəkraut] *n.* German dish of pickled cabbage. □ **chucrut**
sauna ['sɔːnə] *n.* **1** very hot steam bath: *a sauna bath.* □ **sauna**
2 room where you can have a sauna bath. □ **sauna**
saunter ['sɔːntə] *n.* stroll/leisurely walk: *shall we go for a saunter in the garden?* □ **paseo tranquilo**
■ *v.* to walk in a leisurely way/to stroll: *they sauntered down the street.* □ **pasearse tranquilamente**
sausage ['sɔsidʒ] *n.* tube of edible skin full of minced and seasoned pork or other meat: *a string of sausages; sausage and mash,* sausages served with mashed potatoes. □ **salchicha**
sausage-meat *n.* meat and breadcrumbs minced and seasoned. □ **carne de salchicha**
sausage roll *n.* small piece of sausage cooked in pastry. □ **empanadilla de salchicha**
sauté ['soutei] *adj.* fried in a little fat: *sauté potatoes.* □ **salteado**
■ *v.* (*he sautéed*) to fry in a little fat: *sautéed potatoes.* □ **saltear**
savage ['sævidʒ] *adj.* **1** uncivilized/primitive: *the savage life of early settlers.* □ **salvaje**
2 fierce/ferocious: *one of the most savage wild animals is the bear.* □ **feroz**
■ *n.* wild/uncivilized human being: *they rushed at me like savages.* □ **salvaje**
■ *v.* to attack with teeth: *the burglar was savaged by the guard dogs.* □ **atacar con ferocidad**
savagery *n.* ferocity: *the savagery of the enemy's attack took them by surprise.* □ **salvajismo**
save [seiv] *v.* **1** to rescue from misfortune: *he saved her from drowning; he saved my life,* he prevented me from being killed. □ **salvar**
2 to keep for future use/to reserve: *she saved up all her pocket money; he saved his strength for the final effort.* □ **ahorrar (dinero); reservar (energías)**
3 to make an economy/not to spend: *if I buy a second-hand car it will save me hundreds of pounds; he delivered the parcel by hand to save the postage.* □ **ahorrar(se)**
4 (*in sport*) to prevent opponents from scoring: *the goalkeeper saved three goals.* □ **salvar**
5 to gain: *in order to save time he travelled by air.* □ **ahorrar (tiempo)**
6 to avoid: *to save him the trouble, I took the message myself.* □ **evitar (molestias)**
■ *prep.* and *conj.* except: *everyone wanted to go save only me; all the dresses save three were sold at reduced prices.* □ **excepto; salvo**
saver *n.* person who saves money. □ **ahorrador**
saving *n.* economy: *the new rates represent a saving of six per cent.* □ **ahorro**
■ *adj.* redeeming: *although he can be bad-tempered, he has the saving grace of a sense of humour.* □ **que le salva**
saving clause *n.* reservation clause in a contract/agreement, etc. □ **cláusula de salvaguardia**
savings *n.* money saved: *the old lady's entire savings amounted to only $200.* □ **ahorros**
savings bank *n.* bank which gives interest on small deposits of money. □ **caja de ahorros**
saveloy ['sævəlɔi] *n.* highly-seasoned dried sausage. □ **salchicha seca muy sazonada**
saviour ['seivjə] *Amer.* **savior** *n.* person who saves. □ **salvador**
our Saviour, Jesus Christ. □ **el Salvador**
savour ['seivə] *Amer.* **savor** *n.* **1** characteristic taste. □ **sabor**
2 suspicion/hint: *his remarks had a savour of bitterness.* □ **regusto**
■ *v.* **1** to appreciate (food and wine): *he savoured the aroma of the coffee.* □ **saborear**
2 ***to savour of,*** to suggest: *the offer savours of bribery.* □ **oler a**
savouriness *n.* appetizing taste or smell: *the savouriness of the soup appealed to him.* □ **buen sabor**
savoury *adj.* **1** appetizing: *a savoury stew.* □ **apetitoso**
2 salty/not sweet: *she preferred savoury dishes.* □ **salado**
■ *n.* food served at the beginning or end of a meal to stimulate your appetite or help your digestion: *cocktail savouries.* □ **entradas (al principio); digestivo (al final)**
savoy [sə'vɔi] *n.* type of curly winter cabbage. □ **berza de Saboya**
saw [sɔː] *n.* steel tool with a blade with a serrated edge, used for cutting wood/metal etc.: *power saw; circular saw.* □ **sierra**
■ *v.* (*he sawed; he has sawn*) **1** to cut (wood, etc.) with a saw: *he cut down the tree and sawed the branches into logs; I'll saw that wood for you; the tree was sawn in two.* □ **serrar**
2 *see also* **see.**
sawdust *n.* powder produced from sawing wood. □ **serrín**
sawmill *n.* power-driven mill which saws wood mechanically. □ **aserradero**
saxophone ['sæksəfoun] *n.* brass musical instrument with keys. □ **saxofón**
saxophonist [sæk'sɔfənist] *n.* saxophone player. □ **saxofonista**
say [sei] *n.* right to decide: *her husband had no say in choosing the dining room carpet.* □ **voz y voto**
■ *v.* (*he said: he has said*) **1** to speak: *he only said a few words; the judge asked the prisoner if he had anything to say.* □ **decir**
2 to put in writing: *his letter says he will arrive on Saturday; the timetable says there are no trains on Sundays.* □ **decir**
3 to give (an opinion); to put an idea into words: *she said she was tired; I suggested he ought to lie down, but he said not; he is said to be rich,* people say he is rich. □ **decir**
4 to suggest: *choose a number — let's say sixteen; you may have to pay a lot, say, more than $20.* □ **digamos, por ejemplo**
saying *n.* proverb/phrase which is often used: *an old country saying.* □ **dicho; refrán**
as the saying goes, according to the proverb. □ **como dice el refrán**
scab [skæb] *n.* **1** dry rough crust formed over a wound when it is healing. □ **costra**

2 (*informal*) workman who refuses to take part in a strike. □ **esquirol**

scabbard ['skæbəd] *n.* sheath/holder for a dagger or sword. □ **vaina**

scabious ['skeibiəs] *n.* perennial plant with pincushion-shaped flowers. □ **escabiosa**

scaffold ['skæfəld] *n.* platform on which executions take place: *Mary Queen of Scots was blindfolded on the scaffold before she was beheaded.* □ **patíbulo**

scaffolding *n.* structure of poles and planks providing workmen with a platform to stand on while building or repairing a house, etc.: *when the cathedral was being cleaned it was completely covered in scaffolding.* □ **andamio**

scald [skɔːld] *n.* burn caused by boiling liquid. □ **escaldadura**

■ *v.* to injure with hot liquid or steam: *she scalded herself when she dropped the tea-pot.* □ **escaldar**

scalding *n.* being burnt by a hot liquid. □ **escaldado**

■ *adj.* very hot: *she burnt her tongue on the scalding tea.* □ **hirviente**

scale [skeil] *n.* **1** thin horny plate protecting the skin of fish and snakes. □ **escama**

2 hard deposit stuck to a surface: *scale on teeth; the inside of the boiler was covered in scale.* □ **sarro (dientes); incrustaciones (caldera)**

3 arrangement of musical notes in order: *the scale of C major; the minor scale.* □ **escala**

4 graded system: *she was on a fixed salary scale.* □ **escala**

sliding scale, system of payment which increases according to various factors. □ **escala móvil**

5 relative measurements of a small object which are exactly similar to those of a larger object: *the model village is built on a scale of one centimetre to one metre; a map with a scale of one inch to the mile; a scale model.* □ **escala**

■ *v.* **1** to remove scales: *the fisherman scaled the fish before gutting them.* □ **quitar las escamas**

2 to remove deposit from teeth: *the dentist scaled and polished her teeth.* □ **quitar el sarro**

3 ***to scale off,*** to drop off in thin layers: *the paint scaled off the walls.* □ **desconcharse**

4 to climb up/to climb over: *the prisoner scaled the high walls using a rope; the climbers scaled the mountain.* □ **escalar**

5 ***to scale up/down,*** to increase/to reduce proportionally: *salaries were scaled up when the business did well.* □ **aumentar/reducir proporcionalmente**

scales *n. pl.* instrument for weighing: (*a pair of*) *scales,* weighing machine; *the boxer tipped/turned the scales at 14 stone; she weighed the ingredients out on her kitchen scales.* □ **báscula; peso**

scallion ['skæliən] *n.* type of young onion eaten raw in salad. □ **cebollino**

scallop ['skɔləp] *n.* **1** type of shellfish with a semicircular ridged shell. □ **vieira**

2 ornamental edging of material in small semicircles. □ **festón**

scalp [skælp] *n.* skin and hair on the top of the head: *the hairdresser massaged her scalp.* □ **cuero cabelludo**

■ *v.* **1** to cut off someone's scalp. □ **cortar la cabellera**

2 (*informal*) to sell tickets at a very high price. □ **dedicarse a la reventa**

scalper *n.* (*informal*) person who sells tickets at a very high price. □ **revendedor**

scalpel ['skælpl] *n.* small surgical knife. □ **escalpelo**

scamp [skæmp] *n.* rascal: *although the boy looked angelic, he was a little scamp.* □ **diablillo**

■ *v.* to do (something) in an unsatisfactory way: *he scamped the building of the shed.* □ **chapucear**

scamper ['skæmpə] *n.* run/gallop: *the dog went for a scamper across the fields.* □ **carrera rápida**

■ *v.* to run fast: *at the sound of the gun the deer scampered into the forest; don't scamper off before I've talked to you.* □ **correr a toda prisa**

scampi ['skæmpi] *n.* large prawns: *fried scampi.* □ **gambas**

scan [skæn] *v.* (*he scanned*) **1** to test the rhythm of a line of poetry: *this poem doesn't scan.* □ **rimar, escandiar**

2 to look intently all over: *he scanned the horizon with his telescope; I anxiously scanned her face; we scanned the newspapers for news from abroad.* □ **explorar con la vista (horizonte); examinar (la cara); hacer un recorrido por (noticias)**

3 to pass a radar beam over an area. □ **barrer**

■ *n.* action of passing a radar beam over an area. □ **barrido**

scanner *n.* machine for carrying out scanning by radar. □ **antena direccional giratoria**

scandal ['skændl] *n.* **1** unkind gossip: *she spread scandal about her neighbours.* □ **chismes**

2 something that produces a general feeling of anger: *it's a scandal that nothing is done for old people.* □ **es una vergüenza que...**

scandalize *v.* to shock: *her way of life scandalized the neighbours.* □ **escandalizar**

scandalized *adj.* shocked: *she was scandalized to hear what the vicar had done.* □ **escandalizado**

scandalmonger *n.* person who spreads gossip. □ **difamador; chismoso**

scandalous *adj.* shameful: *it's scandalous how much they charge for petrol.* □ **escandaloso**

scandalously *adv.* terribly. □ **escandalosamente**

Scandinavia [skændi'neiviə] *n.* group of countries (including Norway, Sweden, Denmark and Iceland) in north east Europe. □ **Escandinavia**

Scandinavian *n.* and *adj.* (person) from Scandinavia. □ **escandinavo**

scansion ['skænʃn] *n.* art of scanning poetry. □ **escansión**

scant [skænt] *adj.* hardly enough: *he had scant regard for her opinion.* □ **escaso**

scantily *adj. scantily dressed,* with very few clothes on. □ **insuficientemente; vestido muy ligeramente**

scantiness *n.* lack; smallness: *the scantiness of their resources was evident from the poor conditions in which they lived.* □ **escasez**

scanty *adj.* small; not sufficient: *he had only a scanty knowledge of engineering.* □ **escaso**

scapegoat ['skeipgout] *n.* person who carries the blame for someone else: *after the leak of secret information the government was looking for a scapegoat.* □ **cabeza de turco; chivo expiatorio**

scapula ['skæpjulə] *n.* shoulder blade. □ **escápula**

scar [skɑː] *n.* mark left after a wound has healed: *her operation left a scar on her arm.* □ **cicatriz**

■ *v.* (*he scarred*) **1** to wound (someone) causing a permanent mark: *he scarred the other man's cheek with the point of his sword.* □ **dejar una cicatriz en**

2 to leave a mark on someone's mind: *the terrible experience scarred her for life.* □ **marcar**

scarce [skεəs] *adj.* insufficient for the demand/hard to find: *when potatoes were scarce many people starved; good craftsmen are growing scarce these days.* □ **escaso**

to make oneself scarce, (*informal*) to disappear/to keep out of the way: *when their father was in a bad temper the children made themselves scarce.*

□ **escaquearse**
scarcely *adv.* hardly/only just: *she could scarcely speak as she had a very sore throat; you'll scarcely believe it; I scarcely know what to say.* □ **apenas**
scarcity *n.* lack/insufficiency: *the hard winter brought a scarcity of food.* □ **escasez**

scare [skɛə] *n.* **1** fright/terror: *when he saw the ghost it gave him a terrible scare.* □ **susto**
2 *a rabies scare,* frightening rumour that a rabies epidemic is about to occur. □ **rumores alarmistas de una epidemia de...**
3 ***to raise a scare,*** to spread alarm. □ **alarmar**
■ *v.* **1** to frighten: *you scared me when you screamed.* □ **asustar**
2 to be alarmed: *I don't scare easily; she was nearly scared out of her mind.* □ **alarmarse**
scared *adj.* frightened: *he had a scared look.* □ **asustado**
scarecrow *n.* figure looking like a man set up in a field to frighten off birds. □ **espantapájaros**
scaremonger *n.* one who likes to alarm others. □ **alarmista**
scaremongering *n.* spreading of alarm. □ **el sembrar la alarma**
scary *adj.* frightening: *I find this book of ghost stories rather scary.* □ **que da miedo**

scarf [skɑːf] *n.* (*pl. scarves*) long strip or square of material worn round the neck to keep you warm: *silk scarf; the boys wore their school scarves.* □ **bufanda**

scarlet ['skɑːlət] *adj.* brilliant red colour: *she was so embarrassed that she blushed scarlet.* □ **escarlata**
scarlet fever *n.* infectious disease producing a bright red rash. □ **escarlatina**

scathing ['skeiðiŋ] *adj.* very critical: *the pupil was upset when his teacher made scathing remarks about his work.* □ **mordaz**

scatter ['skætə] *v.* **1** to throw here and there: *he scattered the contents of his briefcase on the floor; the farmer is scattering seed in the field.* □ **esparcir**
2 to go/to run in all directions: *when they heard a bomb had been planted nearby the crowd scattered.* □ **dispersarse**
scatterbrain *n.* person who doesn't use his brains: *she is such a scatterbrain that she never remembers where she has put anything.* □ **cabeza de chorlito**
scattered *adj.* spread out: *the population was scattered thinly over the country.* □ **disperso**
scatty *adj.* (*informal*) stupid. □ **atolondrado**

scavenger ['skævindʒə] *n.* **1** animal which feeds on other dead animals: *scavengers pulled at the dead buffalo.* □ **carroñero**
2 person who looks for useful things among rubbish. □ **basurero**
scavenge *v.* to look for useful things among rubbish. □ **rebuscar en la basura**

scenario [si'nɑːriou] *n.* written version of a play with details of characters/scenes, etc.: *the producer studied the scenario carefully.* □ **guión**

scene [siːn] *n.* **1** subdivision of an act in a play: *Act 1, Scene 2; the scene is set in a forest; the balcony scene in 'Romeo and Juliet'.* □ **escena**
2 *she worked hard* ***behind the scenes,*** without being obvious/without many people knowing. □ **...entre bastidores**
3 place in which events actually occur: *the police were swiftly at the scene of the crime; the war reporter wanted to reach the scene of operations; five minutes after the accident an ambulance appeared on the scene.* □ **escenario (del crimen); teatro (de operaciones); lugar (del accidente)**
4 view/surroundings: *a change of scene will do you good; she watched the changing scene from the window of her train.* □ **aires; paisaje**
5 display of temper: *the small boy made a scene when his mother refused to give him any more sweets; family scenes,* family quarrels. □ **escena; bronca**
6 ***it's not my scene,*** (*informal*) it doesn't interest me/it is not the sort of thing I usually do. □ **esto no me va**
scenery *n.* **1** painted cloth backgrounds and other props used in a theatre to make the stage resemble the supposed scene of action: *the scenery in the first act was limited to a series of white pillars.* □ **decorado**
2 view of the countryside: *the scenery in the Lake District; mountain scenery.* □ **paisaje**
scenic *adj.* referring to scenery. □ **escénico; del paisaje**
scenic railway, miniature railway running through artificial picturesque scenery at a fair. □ **tren de recreo**
scenic route, road running through beautiful countryside. □ **ruta turística**

scent [sent] *n.* pleasant smell: *the scent of flowers/of new mown hay.* □ **perfume**
2 characteristic smell: *foxes have a strong scent.* □ **olor**
on the scent, following a trail: *the detective was on the murderer's scent very quickly.* □ **en la pista**
to put off the scent, deceive by false information: *they told the policeman that the man he was looking for had left, and so put him off the scent.* □ **despistar**
3 perfume: *he gave her a bottle of scent.* □ **perfume**
4 sense of smell. □ **olfato**
■ *v.* **1** to find out by smelling: *the dog scented the fox.* □ **olfatear**
2 to begin to suspect: *he scented danger as soon as he opened the door.* □ **sospechar**
3 to make fragrant: *the roses scented the June evening.* □ **perfumar**

sceptic ['skeptik] *Amer.* **skeptic** *n.* **1** person who doubts the truth of religion: *he is a sceptic where religion is concerned.* □ **escéptico**
2 person who always doubts the truth of what he is told: *he was known to be a sceptic and therefore hard to convince.* □ **escéptico**
sceptical *adj.* doubtful/(person) who doubts: *he was sceptical about the value of the debate.* □ **escéptico**
sceptically *adv.* doubtfully/distrustfully: *he asked his daughter sceptically whether she would be returning home after the party.* □ **escépticamente**
scepticism *n.* doubt/uncertainty: *his scepticism caused him to be wary of new ideas.* □ **escepticismo**

sceptre ['septə] *Amer.* **scepter** *n.* gold stick covered with precious stones which is carried by a king or queen. □ **cetro**

schedule ['ʃedjuːl, *Amer.* 'skedʒuːl] *n.* **1** timetable: *airlines operate different schedules in winter and summer; the summer schedule is now in operation.* □ **horario**
2 programme/list of events: *the Prime Minister asked to see his schedule for the following week; the mayor had a very heavy schedule of engagements.* □ **programa**
3 plan: *everything went according to schedule; the work was finished on schedule/ahead of schedule.* □ **plan;...a su debido tiempo/antes de lo debido**
4 appendix to a document: *there were several schedules attached to the formal contract.* □ **apéndice**
■ *v.* **1** to list officially: *the house is scheduled as a*

place of historical interest. □ **catalogar**
2 to plan something for a particular time: *I have scheduled you to speak at 3.30; the plane is scheduled to make three stops.* □ **fijar la hora de**
scheduled service, regular (bus/train, etc.) service. □ **servicio regular**
scheme [ski:m] *n.* **1** plan/arrangement: *the colour scheme of this room is most attractive; he has thought up a good scheme for making money; they have put forward a scheme to open the canal again.* □ **disposición; combinación (de colores); plan (para hacer dinero); proyecto (canal)**
2 plot: *a shady scheme.* □ **treta**
■ *v.* to plot: *they schemed together to rob the bank; he was scheming to alter his mother's will.* □ **tramar**
schemer *n.* person who plots. □ **intrigante**
scheming *adj.* (person) who plots. □ **intrigante**
scherzo ['skɛətsou] *n.* lively section of a longer piece of music. □ **'scherzo'**
schism [skizəm] *n.* division of a religious community into factions. □ **cisma**
schismatic [skiz'mætik] *adj.* tending to break away: *a schismatic faction.* □ **cismático**
schist [ʃist] *n.* rock which splits into thin layers. □ **esquisto**
schizophrenia [skitsou'fri:niə] *n.* mental illness where thoughts, feelings and actions are all disconnected. □ **esquizofrenia**
schizophrenic [skitsou'frenik] *adj.* referring to schizophrenia. □ **esquizofrénico**
schmaltz [ʃmɔlts] *n.* too much sentimentality (in writing/music, etc.). □ **sensiblería**
schnitzel ['ʃnitzl] *n.* thin flat piece of veal fried in breadcrumbs. □ **filete empanado**
scholar ['skɔlə] *n.* **1** person who studies: *at the age of 90 he was still an avid scholar.* □ **estudiante**
2 learned person: *he's a noted scholar in the field of ancient history.* □ **erudito**
3 student at school or university who has all or part of his fee paid by someone. □ **becario**
scholarly *adj.* learned/seeking to learn: *he has a very scholarly approach to his work.* □ **erudito**
scholarship *n.* **1** profound learning: *the professor was known for his scholarship.* □ **erudición**
2 money given to a student to help pay for the cost of his study: *he won a scholarship to Oxford.* □ **beca**
scholastic [skɔ'læstik] *adj.* referring to schools or teaching: *the scholastic year starts in September.* □ **escolar**
school [sku:l] *n.* **1** place for teaching (usually children): *primary school; secondary school; boarding school; he has missed school through illness this week; I went to school in Scotland.* □ **escuela; colegio**
art school, college where art is taught. □ **Escuela de Bellas Artes**
evening school, classes (usually for adults) held in the evening. □ **clases nocturnas**
medical school, department of a university which teaches medicine. □ **Facultad de Medicina**
2 followers of a philosopher/artist, etc: *the school of Raphael; the Venetian school.* □ **escuela**
3 large group of fish or sea animals: *a school of porpoises.* □ **banco**
■ *v.* to teach/to train: *they schooled him in the art of self-defence; he schooled himself to control his temper.* □ **instruir**
schoolbook *n.* book used in school. □ **libro de texto**
schoolboy, schoolgirl *n.* child who goes to school. □ **escolar**
schoolchildren *n. pl.* children who go to school. □ **escolares**
schooling *n.* education at school level: *she received her schooling in a convent.* □ **enseñanza**
schoolmaster, schoolmistress *n.* person who teaches in a school. □ **profesor, profesora**
schoolmastering *n.* the profession of teacher: *he became interested in schoolmastering when he was a boy.* □ **enseñanza**
schoolteacher *n.* person who teaches in a school. □ **profesor**
schooner ['sku:nə] *n.* **1** sailing ship with two or more masts and sails running lengthwise down the ship. □ **goleta**
2 tall glass for sherry. □ **copa**
sciatica [sai'ætikə] *n.* pain in the back and legs. □ **ciática**
sciatic nerve *n.* nerve in the top part of the back of the legs. □ **nervio ciático**
science ['saiəns] *n.* **1** knowledge obtained from observation and arranged into a system: *political science; natural sciences.* □ **ciencia**
2 study based on observation and experiment (such as chemistry/biology, etc.): *he decided to study sciences rather than arts at University; she has a science degree.* □ **ciencia**
science fiction *n.* stories on the subject of space travel/life in the future. □ **ciencia ficción**
scientific [saiən'tifik] *adj.* referring to science: *scientific instruments; he carried out various scientific experiments.* □ **científico**
scientifically *adv.* according to scientific experiment: *his theory was proved to be scientifically inaccurate.* □ **científicamente**
scientist ['saiəntist] *n.* person who studies science. □ **científico**
scintillate ['sintileit] *v.* to sparkle. □ **centellear**
scintillating *adj.* sparkling: *her scintillating conversation held everyone spellbound.* □ **brillante**
scintillation [sinti'leiʃn] *n.* wit/sparkle. □ **brillantez**
scion ['saiən] *n.* piece of a plant which is grafted on to another; young member of a noble family. □ **esqueje; vástago (noble)**
scissors ['sizəz] *n. pl.* ***(a pair of) scissors,*** instrument for cutting fabric/paper etc. constructed of two blades with handles for thumb and fingers: *she took her scissors to cut her hair; I need a pair of scissors; have you seen my nail scissors?* □ **tijeras**
sclerosis [sklə'rousis] *n.* hardening of soft tissue: *sclerosis of the arteries.* □ **esclerosis**
multiple sclerosis, gradual disease where hardening of tissue causes general paralysis. □ **esclerosis múltiple**
scoff [skɔf] *v.* **1** ***to scoff at,*** to make fun of in a nasty way: *he scoffed at danger; she scoffed at his clumsiness.* □ **burlarse de**
2 (*informal*) to eat greedily: *who's scoffed all the cake?* □ **zamparse**
scoffing *adj.* mocking. □ **burlón**
scoffingly *adv.* mockingly. □ **burlonamente**
scold [skould] *v.* to speak to (someone) angrily: *his mother scolded him for rolling in the mud.* □ **reprender**
scolding *n.* rebuke: *he received a scolding for his bad behaviour.* □ **reprensión**
scone [skɔn] *n.* small soft cake usually eaten with cream and jam. □ **bollo**
scoop [sku:p] *n.* **1** short-handled shovel/spoon: *he put the grain into sacks using a scoop.* □ **paleta**
ice cream scoop, round spoon for serving ice cream. □ **pinzas**
2 portion of ice cream: *cone with two scoops of ice*

cream. □ **bola**
3 piece of news which is published in one newspaper before any other: *the story of the spy was a scoop for the paper.* □ **primicia**
■ *v.* **1** to lift, using a scoop: *he scooped the spilt sugar into a bowl.* □ **recoger**
to scoop out the inside, to remove the inside of something with a spoon. □ **sacar con cuchara**
2 to obtain against competition: *by betting on an outsider which won the race he scooped all the prize money.* □ **ganar contra todo pronóstico**
to scoop the pool, to win all the money. □ **ganar un pleno**
3 *to scoop a newspaper,* to print a news item before another paper does. □ **adelantarse con una exclusiva**

scooter ['sku:tə] *n.* **1** child's two-wheeled vehicle with footboard and a long steering handle, pushed along with one foot. □ **patinete**
2 ***motor scooter,*** motorized two-wheel bicycle with a curving shield in front and a platform for the feet. □ **'scúter'**

scope [skoup] *n.* **1** reach of observation/action: *this problem is outside my scope; he wanted to extend the scope of his work; there is ample scope for improvement.* □ **alcance; campo**
2 opportunity: *he was given full scope to make any necessary changes.* □ **le dieron carta blanca...**

scorch [skɔ:tʃ] *v.* to burn slightly/to brown: *the hot iron scorched my shirt; grass scorched by the sun.* □ **quemar**
scorched-earth policy, tactics in war where all the resources are destroyed before retreating and giving up territory to the enemy. □ **política de tierra quemada**
scorcher *n.* (*informal*) very hot day. □ **día abrasador**
scorching *adj.* very hot/which scorches: *scorching heat.* □ **calor abrasador**

score [skɔ:] *n.* **1** scratch (in paint, etc.) □ **raya**
2 debt. □ **cuenta**
to settle an old score, to get your own back on someone after a long delay. □ **desquitarse con uno**
3 number of points made in a game: *the score is one all,* each side has made one goal; *what's the score?,* what is the result so far? □ **resultado**
to keep the score, to write down the number of points made. □ **apuntar los tantos**
to know the score, (*informal*) to know all the facts of the case. □ **se lo sabe al dedillo**
4 piece of music written out showing the parts for each instrument or voice: *orchestral score.* □ **partitura**
5 twenty. □ **veintena**
three score years and ten, seventy. □ **setenta años**
***scores of** times/questions,* many times/many questions. □ **muchísimas veces/preguntas por docenas**
6 question/matter: *you need have no worry on that score.* □ **asunto**
■ *v.* **1** to scratch: *score the surface with a knife before putting on the glue.* □ **rayar**
2 to make a point in a game: *he scored ten; our team scored two goals before half-time.* □ **marcar un tanto**
3 to write down the score in a game. □ **llevar el tanteo**
4 to write out (a piece of music) with parts for each instrument or voice: *the concerto is scored for two violins.* □ **orquestar**
scoreboard *n.* large board showing the score in a cricket match/tennis match, etc. □ **marcador**
scorer *n.* person who makes a point in a game; person who writes down the scores in a game. □ **marcador; tanteador**
score off *v.* to make points against someone in a conversation. □ **apuntarse un tanto**
score out *v.* to cross out. □ **tachar**

scorn [skɔ:n] *n.* feeling of looking down/disrespect: *she turned down his offer with scorn.* □ **desprecio**
■ *v.* to look down on/not to respect: *he scorned all offers of help.* □ **despreciar**
scornful *adj.* looking down: *a scornful smile.* □ **desdeñoso**

Scorpio ['skɔ:piou] *n.* one of the signs of the zodiac, shaped like a scorpion. □ **Escorpión**

scorpion ['skɔ:piən] *n.* poisonous tropical insect which stings with a long curved tail. □ **escorpión**

Scotch [skɔtʃ] *adj.* (*not used of people; **Scottish** is preferred as adj. in Scotland*) referring to Scotland. □ **escocés**
Scotch broth, soup made with mutton and barley. □ **sopa escocesa**
Scotch eggs, hard boiled eggs covered with sausage meat and fried. □ **huevos escoceses**
■ *n.* (*not used of people*) **1** whisky/alcoholic drink distilled from barley; a glass of this drink: *a small Scotch.* □ **whisky (escocés)**
2 trademark for a type of transparent sticky tape. □ **papel celo**
■ *v.* ***to scotch** a rumour,* to try to stop a rumour. □ **desmentir**

scot-free [skɔt'fri:] *adj.* ***to get off scot-free,*** without being punished. □ **impune**

Scotland ['skɔtlənd] *n.* country to the north of England, forming part of Great Britain. □ **Escocia**
Scot *n.* person from Scotland. □ **escocés**
Scots *adj.* referring to Scotland. □ **escocés**
■ *n.* form of English spoken in Scotland. □ **escocés**
Scotsman, Scotswoman *n.* (*pl. Scotsmen, Scotswomen*) person from Scotland. □ **escocés, escocesa**
Scottish *adj.* referring to Scotland. □ **escocés**

scoundrel ['skaundrəl] *n.* wicked person. □ **canalla**

scour ['skauə] *v.* **1** to clean by scrubbing with a hard material: *to scour a saucepan.* □ **fregar**
scouring powder, rough powder for cleaning pans. □ **arena de fregar**
2 to search everywhere: *the police scoured the countryside looking for the escaped prisoners.* □ **dar una batida**
scourer *n.* pad of steel wool for cleaning pans. □ **estropajo**

scourge [skə:dʒ] *n.* something which causes suffering: *malaria used to be the scourge of tropical countries.* □ **azote**
■ *v.* to cause suffering. □ **azotar**

scout [skaut] *n.* **1** person sent out to look for information: *the commander sent scouts ahead to try to locate the enemy camp.* □ **explorador**
2 boy who belongs to the Boy Scouts' Association. □ **scout**
the Scouts, the Boy Scouts' Association. □ **los scouts**
■ *v.* ***to scout around for something,*** to search for something: *I have been scouting around for Christmas presents.* □ **buscar**
scoutmaster *n.* leader of a group of scouts. □ **'scouter'**

scowl [skaul] *n.* angry look made by wrinkling the forehead: *a scowl on his face.* □ **mirada con el ceño fruncido**
■ *v.* to make a threatening/unpleasant expression by wrinkling the forehead: *he scowled when he was arrested.* □ **fruncir el ceño**

scraggy ['skrægi] *adj.* thin and bony: *a scraggy neck.* □ **flaco**

scramble ['skræmbl] *n.* **1** rush: *there was a scramble for bargains at the sales.* □ **carrera**
2 cross-country motorcycle race. □ **carrera de motocross**
■ *v.* **1** to hurry along on hands and knees: *they scrambled up a mountain.* □ **trepar; subir gateando**
2 to try to get somewhere by pushing: *the crowd scrambled to get into the bomb shelter.* □ **abrirse paso**
3 ***scrambled eggs,*** eggs mixed together and stirred as they are cooked in butter. □ **huevos revueltos**
4 to mix up a radio signal/telephone link, so that it cannot be understood without an apparatus for unmixing it. □ **distorsionar**
scrambler *n.* machine for scrambling radio signals. □ **distorsionador**
scrambler telephone, telephone which automatically mixes up the message. □ **distorsionador**

scrap [skræp] *n.* **1** small piece: *scraps of paper; he overheard scraps of conversation; there isn't a scrap of evidence against him.* □ **pedazo; retazo; ápice**
2 ***scraps,*** bits of waste food/waste material. □ **sobras (comida); desperdicios (material)**
scrap heap, heap of rubbish. □ **montón de chatarra**
scrap metal, waste metal: *the car was sold for scrap,* as waste metal. □ **chatarra**
3 fight: *he got into a scrap.* □ **se metió en una pelea**
■ *v.* (*he scrapped*) **1** to throw away as waste: *the car had to be scrapped.* □ **desguazar**
2 to give up (plans): *the government scrapped their plans for the school system.* □ **desechar**
3 to fight: *the children were always scrapping in the street.* □ **pelear**
scrapbook *n.* large book with blank pages for sticking photographs/newspaper cuttings, etc., into. □ **álbum de recortes**
scrappy *adj.* made of bits and pieces: *a scrappy game,* very disconnected, with the side not playing as a team. □ **hecho de retazos; inconexo**

scrape [skreip] *n.* **1** mark made by something hard being pulled across a surface: *I have a scrape on one of the doors of the car.* □ **arañazo**
2 awkward situation/trouble: *he keeps on getting into scrapes.* □ **lío**
3 very thin layer of butter/dripping spread on bread. □ **capita de mantequilla/chorrito sobre el pan**
■ *v.* to scratch with a hard object being pulled across a surface: *to scrape the old paint off a door; he scraped the car along the wall; she fell off her bike and scraped her knee.* □ **raspar**
scraper *n.* instrument for scraping. □ **rascador**
scrape together *v.* to collect with difficulty: *he managed to scrape together enough money to pay for the car.* □ **arañar**
scrape through *v.* to get through (an examination) with difficulty. □ **aprobar por los pelos**

scratch [skrætʃ] *n.* **1** long slight wound/mark made by a sharp point: *a scratch on the polished table; she had scratches on her face from crawling through the hedge; after the car crash, the driver got out without a scratch.* □ **rasguño**
2 sound of a sharp point being pulled across a surface. □ **chirrido**
3 act of scratching a part of the body which itches: *the monkey gave his head a good scratch.* □ **arañazo**
4 ***to start from scratch,*** to start at the beginning/with no previous preparation. □ **empezar desde cero**
5 ***to come up to scratch,*** to satisfy. □ **ser tan bueno como siempre**
6 *he wasn't* ***up to scratch,*** wasn't very good. □ **no estuvo a la altura de las circunstancias**
■ *adj.* **1** ***scratch team,*** team of players brought together at the last minute. □ **equipo de circunstancias**
2 ***scratch player,*** player who starts with no handicap. □ **jugador que no recibe ventaja**
■ *v.* **1** to make a long wound/mark with a sharp pointed instrument: *she scratched her initials on the window with a diamond ring; they scratched the top of the piano as they were carrying it upstairs; she scratched her hands on the rose bush.* □ **rasguñar**
to scratch the surface, to deal with only the first part of the problem and not to get down to the real basic details. □ **no profundizar**
2 to make a sound by pulling a sharp point across a surface. □ **hacer un chirrido**
3 to rub with your fingernails (a part of the body which itches): *he scratched his head; can you scratch my back for me?* □ **rascar(se)**
4 (*of competitor*) to cross your name off the list of entrants for a race: *he scratched at the last minute because his engine blew up.* □ **borrarse**
scratchy *adj.* which makes a scratching noise. □ **chirriante**

scrawl [skrɔːl] *n.* bad/careless handwriting: *I can't read his scrawl.* □ **garabato**
■ *v.* to write badly/carelessly. □ **hacer garabatos**

scrawny ['skrɔːni] *adj.* thin and bony. □ **escuálido**

scream [skriːm] *n.* **1** loud/piercing cry: *the screams of the victims could be heard through the noise of the fire.* □ **chillido**
2 *screams of laughter,* loud/piercing laughter. □ **grandes carcajadas**
3 (*informal*) something/person who is very funny: *the play was a scream.* □ **divertidísimo**
■ *v.* **1** to make loud/piercing cries: *she screamed when the masked man appeared at the window.* □ **chillar**
2 *the audience screamed with laughter,* laughed uproariously. □ **...se rió a carcajadas**
screamingly *adv. screamingly funny,* extremely funny. □ **de morirse de risa**

scree [skriː] *n.* loose stones on a mountainside. □ **guijarros**

screech [skriːtʃ] *n.* piercing cry (of an animal). □ **chillido**
■ *v.* to make a piercing cry: *the monkeys were screeching all night.* □ **chillar**

screed [skriːd] *n.* very long document. □ **escrito largo y pesado**

screen [skriːn] *n.* **1** something which acts as protection against draught/fire/noise, etc.: *fire screen; the row of trees acts as a screen.* □ **pantalla**
2 flat white surface for projecting films/slides. □ **pantalla**
television screen, the glass front of a TV set where the picture appears. □ **pantalla de televisión**
the small screen, television. □ **la pequeña pantalla**
3 device like a large sieve for sifting sand/gravel into varying sizes. □ **criba**
■ *v.* **1** to protect from draught/fire/noise, etc.: *the house was screened by rows of thick bushes.* □ **proteger**
2 to show on a film/TV screen: *the first time the film has been screened.* □ **proyectar**
3 to question/to examine people to find out if they have a disease/if they have committed a crime. □ **investigar**
4 to sift (sand/gravel) into varying sizes. □ **cribar**
screenplay *n.* scenario/story written ready to be

used for making a film. □ **guión cinematográfico**
screenwriter *n.* person who writes screenplays. □ **guionista**

screw [skru:] *n.* **1** metal pin with a groove winding up from the point to the head, so that when twisted it goes into a hard surface: *he undid the screws and the table legs fell off.* □ **tornillo**
2 propeller. □ **hélice**
3 act of turning a screw with a screwdriver: *give it another screw.* □ **vuelta**
4 small piece of twisted paper with something in it: *a screw of salt.* □ **papelina**
5 twisting motion of a ball. □ **efecto**
6 (*slang*) pay/wages. □ **paga**
7 (*slang*) prison warder. □ **carcelero**
■ *v.* **1** to attach with screws: *they screwed down the lid of the box; to screw a notice on to the door.* □ **atornillar**
2 to attach by twisting: *screw the top back on the jar.* □ **apretar**
his head's screwed on the right way, (*informal*) he's very sensible. □ **es muy sensato**
3 to twist: *he screwed up the paper into a little ball.* □ **hizo una bola de papel**
screwdriver *n.* tool with a long handle and small flat end which is used for turning screws. □ **destornillador**
screw-top jar *n.* jar with a top which screws on and off. □ **tarro de rosca**
screwy *adj.* (*informal*) mad. □ **chiflado**

scribble ['skribl] *n.* **1** (child's) meaningless marks: *he can't write his name, but he made a scribble on the Christmas card.* □ **garabato**
2 bad writing: *I can't read her scribble.* □ **garabato**
■ *v.* **1** to make meaningless marks: *the little boy scribbled all over the tablecloth.* □ **hacer garabatos**
2 to write badly/hurriedly: *she scribbled a note to her husband.* □ **escribir deprisa**

scrimmage ['skrimidʒ] *n.* wild struggle (in a game of Rugby/at the door of a shop when the sales start). □ **melée abierta (rugby); arrebatiña**

scrip [skrip] *n.* (*no pl.*) new shares issued by a company instead of paying a dividend. □ **acciones gratuitas**

script [skript] *n.* **1** style of handwriting: *letter written in italic script.* □ **letra**
2 something written by hand/manuscript; handwritten answer to an examination. □ **manuscrito**
3 written version of words which are spoken in a film/play. □ **guión**

scripture ['skriptʃə] *n.* holy writing; the Bible. □ **Escrituras**

scroll [skroul] *n.* roll of paper with writing on it. □ **rollo de escritura**

scrotum ['skroutəm] *n.* bag containing the testicles. □ **escroto**

scrounge [skraundʒ] *v.* to try to get (something) from someone without paying for it: *he was scrounging for a free meal; he scrounged a free meal off my father.* □ **gorronear**
scrounger *n.* person who scrounges. □ **gorrón**

scrub [skrʌb] *n.* **1** (area of land covered by) small bushes: *scrub land.* □ **matorral; monte bajo**
2 action of cleaning with a stiff brush: *these shirts need a good scrub to get them clean.* □ **fregado**
■ *v.* (*he scrubbed*) **1** to clean by rubbing with a stiff brush: *he was scrubbing the floor with soap and water.* □ **fregar**
2 *to scrub a tape,* (*informal*) to remove what is recorded on it. □ **borrar**
scrub that, forget about that. □ **olvídalo**
scrubbing-brush *n.* stiff brush with no handle, for scrubbing floors, etc. □ **cepillo duro**

scruff [skrʌf] *n.* skin at the back of the neck: *the cat picked up her kitten by the scruff of the neck.* □ **pescuezo**
scruffy *adj.* untidy/dirty. □ **desaliñado**

scrum [skrʌm] *n.* **1** (*in Rugby football*) groups of forwards from both sides pushing against each other to get the ball. □ **melée**
2 struggling crowd: *what a scrum to get on to the train!* □ **lucha**

scrumptious ['skrʌmʃəs] *adj.* (*informal*) very good to eat. □ **de rechupete**

scruple ['skru:pl] *n.* doubt about whether something is right which stops you from doing it: *he had no scruples about borrowing money and never returning it.* □ **escrúpulo**
■ *v.* to have doubts about doing something: *he didn't scruple to tell lies to the police.* □ **tener escrúpulos**
scrupulous ['skru:pjuləs] *adj.* very careful: *she is scrupulous over details.* □ **escrupuloso**
scrupulously *adv.* carefully: *scrupulously clean kitchen.* □ **escrupulosamente**

scrutinize ['skru:tinaiz] *v.* to examine very carefully. □ **escudriñar**
scrutiny *n.* careful examination/very close look at something. □ **escrutinio**

scuba ['sku:bə] *n.* underwater breathing apparatus: *a scuba diver.* □ **escafandra autónoma**

scuff [skʌf] *v.* to scrape the outside surface/the soles (of shoes) when walking. □ **rozar; arrastrar**

scuffle ['skʌfl] *n.* small fight: *scuffles broke out in the crowd.* □ **riña**
■ *v.* to fight: *the demonstrators scuffled with the police.* □ **pelearse**

scull [skʌl] *n.* one of two short oars used by a single rower. □ **espadilla**
■ *v.* to row a boat with two oars: *he sculled up the river.* □ **remar**

scullery ['skʌləri] *n.* small room at the back of a kitchen, used for washing up. □ **'office'**

sculpt [skʌlpt] *v.* to carve (figures, etc.) out of wood/metal/stone, etc. □ **esculpir**
sculptor ['skʌlptə] *n.* person who makes figures/artistic constructions out of wood/metal/stone, etc. □ **escultor**
sculpture ['skʌlptʃə] *n.* **1** art of making figures out of wood/metal/stone etc. □ **escultura**
2 figure made by a sculptor: *a sculpture by Michaelangelo.* □ **escultura**

scum [skʌm] *n.* **1** thick dirty foam layer on the surface of a liquid. □ **espuma**
2 people of the worst type; worthless person. □ **escoria de la sociedad**

scupper ['skʌpə] *n.* hole in the side of the ship to let water run off. □ **imbornal**
■ *v.* **1** to sink (a ship) intentionally by opening holes in the bottom to let water in. □ **abrir los imbornales de**
2 (*informal*) to bring to an end: *this has scuppered our plans.* □ **acabar con**

scurf [skə:f] *n.* dandruff/bits of dead skin in the hair. □ **caspa**

scurrilous ['skʌriləs] *adj.* very insulting/rude: *scurrilous article about the Prime Minister.* □ **injurioso**
scurrility [skʌ'riliti] *n.* rude words. □ **carácter injurioso**

scurry ['skʌri] *v.* to run fast, taking short steps: *the mice scurried towards their hole.* □ **ir a toda prisa**

scurvy ['skə:vi] *n.* disease caused by lack of fruit and vegetables. □ **escorbuto**
scuttle ['skʌtl] *n.* type of bucket for keeping coal in the house. □ **cubo del carbón**
■ *v.* **1** (*of the crew*) to sink (a ship) intentionally by opening holes in the bottom to allow water to come in. □ **barrenar**
2 ***to scuttle off,*** to run away fast. □ **escabullirse**
scythe [saið] *n.* tool with a wide blade on the end of a long handle, used for cutting grass. □ **guadaña**
■ *v.* to cut (grass) with a scythe. □ **segar con guadaña**
sea [si:] *n.* **1** area of salt water: *most of the globe is covered by sea; the Mediterranean Sea; the North Sea.* □ **mar**
2 salt water: *we went swimming in the sea; the ship put out to sea.* □ **mar**
3 *he's completely* ***at sea,*** (*informal*) he doesn't understand what is happening. □ **está que no se aclara**
4 mass: *there was a sea of faces staring up at the speaker.* □ **había una multitud de caras...**
sea anemone *n.* primitive sea animal which looks like a flower. □ **anémona**
sea bird *n.* bird which lives by the sea: *gulls and other sea birds.* □ **ave marina**
seaboard *n.* country by the edge of the sea: *Canada's Atlantic seaboard.* □ **litoral**
sea breeze *n.* light wind blowing inland from the sea. □ **brisa marina**
sea coast *n.* land along the edge of the sea. □ **costa**
seafarer *n.* person who travels/works on the sea. □ **marinero/marino**
seafood *n.* fish and shellfish which can be eaten. □ **pescado (fish); marisco (shellfish)**
sea front *n.* road running along the edge of the sea at a resort town. □ **paseo marítimo**
seagull *n.* type of usually white sea bird. □ **gaviota**
sea horse *n.* small black fish which looks like a horse. □ **caballito de mar**
sea legs *n. he's got his sea legs,* he is used to travelling by sea and isn't seasick. □ **está acostumbrado a viajar en barco**
sealion *n.* large type of seal. □ **león marino**
seaman *n.* (*pl. seamen*) sailor; person who travels/works on the sea. □ **marinero**
seamanship *n.* art of sailing a ship. □ **marinería**
sea plane *n.* plane with floats which can land on the sea. □ **hidroavión**
seaport *n.* port on the sea. □ **puerto de mar**
sea shell *n.* shell of a shellfish which lives in the sea. □ **concha marina**
seashore *n.* land along the edge of the sea. □ **orilla del mar**
seasick *adj.* ill because of the motion of a ship. □ **mareado**
seasickness *n.* illness caused by the movement of a ship. □ **mareo**
seaside *n.* land by the side of the sea: *I do like to be beside the seaside; a seaside holiday.* □ **costa; unas vacaciones en la playa**
sea urchin *n.* type of small spiny sea animal. □ **erizo de mar**
seaweed *n.* plant which grows in the sea. □ **alga**
seaworthy *adj.* (boat) which is fit to go to sea. □ **en condiciones de navegar**
seal [si:l] *n.* **1** large animal living mainly in the sea, with flippers for swimming. □ **foca**
2 piece of hard red wax with a design stamped on it, used for showing that a document has been officially approved or for attaching an envelope/parcel so that it cannot be opened secretly. □ **sello**
3 metal stamp with a design, used for sealing with wax. □ **sello**
4 tight fit (of a bottle): *this jar has a bad seal,* the lid doesn't fit tightly. □ **precinto; plomo**
■ *v.* **1** to attach and stamp a piece of hard wax to show that a document has been officially approved/to prevent an envelope being opened. □ **lacrar**
2 to close tightly so that something cannot be opened. □ **precintar**
3 *he sealed the envelope,* licked it and stuck down the flap. □ **cerró el sobre**
4 *the jar has sealed,* the lid has been attached tightly. □ **se ha cerrado bien...**
5 *to seal an agreement/a bargain,* to agree on the terms. □ **cerrar un trato**
sealing-wax *n.* hard red wax used for making official seals. □ **lacre**
seal off *v.* to close off so as to prevent anyone getting inside: *when dangerous gas escaped from the factory, the police sealed off the whole area.* □ **aislar**
sealskin *n.* skin of a seal: *a sealskin coat.* □ **piel de foca**
seam [si:m] *n.* **1** line where two pieces of cloth are sewn together/where two pieces of metal are welded together. □ **costura (tela); junta (metal)**
2 layer (of coal, etc.). □ **filón; veta**
seamless *adj.* (stockings, etc.) with no seam. □ **sin costura**
seamy *adj.* ***the seamy side*** *of life,* the unpleasant parts of life. □ **el lado sórdido de...**
séance ['seiɑ:ns] *n.* meeting where people try to get in touch with the spirits of dead people. □ **sesión de espiritismo**
sear ['siə] *v.* to burn severely: *searing heat.* □ **abrasar**
search [sə:tʃ] *n.* trying to find something: *we're starting a search for father's watch; he wandered around the town in search of a bed for the night; police search,* inspection of a house, etc. by the police looking for stolen goods/bombs, etc.. □ **busca; búsqueda; registro**
search party, group of people sent to look for someone: *they sent search parties into the mountains to look for the lost climbers.* □ **grupo de salvamento**
search warrant, official permit to carry out a search. □ **orden de registro**
■ *v.* **1** to examine carefully: *he was searched by the customs officials.* □ **registrar**
2 to try to find: *they've searched the woods for the lost boy; scientists are still searching for a cure for cancer.* □ **buscar**
searching *adj.* very careful (examination): *he asked some searching questions.* □ **agudo**
searchlight *n.* powerful light used to try to see things, especially aircraft, at night. □ **reflector**
search warrant *n.* document signed by a magistrate which allows the police to search private premises. □ **orden de registro**
season ['si:zn] *n.* **1** one of four parts into which a year is divided: *spring, summer, autumn and winter are the four seasons.* □ **estación**
2 any period of the year when something usually takes place: *the holiday season; the cricket season.* □ **temporada**
3 *raspberries are* ***in season,*** are ripe at this time of year. □ **es la temporada de...**
season ticket, ticket which is valid for a long period. □ **billete de abono**
■ *v.* **1** to add spices to food: *soup seasoned with pepper.* □ **sazonar**

2 to dry (wood) until it is ready to be used: *seasoned timber.* □ **curar**
seasonable *adj.* which fits the season: *seasonable weather.* □ **propio de la estación**
seasonal *adj.* which only lasts for a season: *seasonal work,* work for the (summer) season only. □ **estacional; de temporada**
seasoning *n.* spices which are added to food. □ **condimento**

seat [si:t] *n.* **1** something you sit on: *a garden seat; front seat of a car; I want two seats for the concert tomorrow night.* □ **asiento; quiero dos localidades para...**
please take a seat, sit down. □ **tome asiento...**
2 ***parliamentary seat,*** constituency. □ **escaño**
3 part of a chair on which you sit: *the chair has a straw seat.* □ **asiento**
4 part of a pair of trousers which covers the buttocks: *he's torn the seat of his trousers.* □ **culo**
5 *seat of government,* place where the government is carried on. □ **sede**
6 ***country seat,*** large house in the country. □ **finca; casa solariega**
7 way of sitting on a horse: *she has a good seat,* she rides a horse well. □ **monta bien**
■ *v.* **1** to make someone sit down. □ **sentarse**
please be seated, sit down. □ **siéntate**
2 to have room for people to sit down: *this table seats eight people.* □ **tener capacidad para**
seat belt *n.* belt worn by someone riding in a car/in an aircraft as protection in case of accident. □ **cinturón de seguridad**
seating *n.* giving seats to people. □ **distribución de asientos**
seating plan, chart showing where people are to sit at a formal dinner. □ **distribución de asientos**
seating capacity, number of seats available: *the hall has a seating capacity of two hundred.* □ **aforo**

secateurs [sekə'tə:z] *n. pl.* ***(pair of) secateurs,*** very strong scissors used in gardening. □ **tijeras de podar**

secede [si'si:d] *v.* (*formal*) to break away: *one state seceded from the federation.* □ **secesionarse**
secession [si'seʃn] *n.* act of seceding. □ **secesión**

secluded [si'klu:did] *adj.* (place) which is quiet/away from crowds. □ **retirado**
seclusion [si'klu:ʒn] *n.* quiet/solitude. □ **retiro**

second ['sekənd] (*as a number can be written* **2nd**) *n.***1** sixtieth part of a minute: *the bomb will go off in ten seconds.* □ **segundo**
second hand, long fast-moving hand on a watch. □ **segundero**
2 *I'll be back* ***in a second,*** very quickly. □ **...en un segundo**
3 sixtieth part of a degree. □ **segundo**
4 person/thing which comes after the first: *the American was first, the British runner came second; Charles the Second* (*Charles II*); *the second of January* (*2nd January*). □ **en segundo lugar; Carlos Segundo; el dos de enero**
5 person who helps a boxer/wrestler. □ **segundo**
6 ***seconds,*** articles which are not perfect and are sold cheaply: *these glasses are seconds.* □ **...de segunda clase**
7 second gear: *the car climbed the hill easily in second.* □ **segunda**
■ *adj.* **1** coming next after the first: *February is the second month of the year; we live on the second floor; this is the second tallest building in the world; the second largest house in the street.* □ **segundo**
second class, ordinary type of railway carriage, etc., which is not as luxurious or expensive as first class: *I always travel second class.* □ **segunda (clase)**
second gear, gear in a car after the first: *go down the hill in second gear.* □ **segunda**
second in command, person directly under the commanding officer/managing director, etc.. □ **segundo en mando**
the second century, period from 100 AD to 199. □ **el siglo segundo**
2 ***every second day,*** every other day/on alternate days. □ **un día sí y otro no**
■ *v.* **1** to support: *he seconded the motion; she was ably seconded by her brother.* □ **secundar**
2 to transfer from one job to another for a period of time: *he was seconded to the Australian police force.* □ **trasladar temporalmente**
secondary ['sekəndri] *adj.* **1** second in importance/in position: *the question of money is of secondary importance,* is not as important as something else. □ **secundario**
secondary picketing, picketing of a factory, etc., by people who do not work there. □ **acción de piquetes de fuera**
2 ***secondary education/secondary school,*** education/school for children of about 11 years of age and older. □ **enseñanza secundaria; instituto de bachillerato**
secondarily *adv.* in second place in importance. □ **en segundo lugar (en importancia)**
second childhood *n.* period in old age when old people seem to act like children: *he's in his second childhood.* □ **segunda niñez**
seconder *n.* person who supports a motion. □ **que apoya una moción**
secondhand *adj.* and *adv.* **1** not new/used: *a secondhand car; I bought it off him secondhand,* it was not new when I bought it. □ **de segunda mano**
secondhand shop, shop selling used goods. □ **compraventa**
2 *I heard the news at secondhand,* not from the original source of the news. □ **...de segunda mano**
secondly *adv.* in second place. □ **en segundo lugar**
secondment [si'kɔndmənt] *n.* being transferred for a period of time to another job: *he is on secondment from the Ministry of Defence.* □ **traslado temporal**
second nature *n. it is second nature to him,* he does it quite naturally/it is a habit with him. □ **es natural en él**
second-rate *adj.* not of good quality. □ **de segunda categoría**
second thoughts *n. pl. he had second thoughts about signing the contract,* he changed his mind about it. □ **se lo pensó dos veces...**
second wind *n. he got his second wind,* he could breathe again easily after having lost his breath while taking exercise. □ **resuello; recobró el resuello**

secrecy ['si:krəsi] *n.* keeping something secret: *the government's plans are surrounded in secrecy.* □ **secreto**

secret ['si:krət] *adj.* hidden from other people; not known: *a secret hiding place; he tried to keep the news secret.* □ **secreto**
■ *n.* **1** something which is not known/which is kept hidden: *the secret of his business success.* □ **secreto**
2 *can you* ***keep a secret?,*** can you not tell anyone a secret? □ **¿puedes guardar un secreto?**
3 *he left the town* ***in secret,*** without anyone knowing. □ **...en secreto**
secretive *adj.* liking to keep things secret: *he is very secretive about his money.* □ **reservado**
secretly *adv.* in secret/without anyone knowing: *they were secretly married.* □ **secretamente**

secretary ['sekrətəri] *n.* **1** person who writes letters/files documents, etc., for someone. □ **secretario**
2 person who deals with correspondence/arranges meetings, etc., in a club/society. □ **secretario**
3 minister in a government: *Secretary of State.* □ **ministro**
4 official in a government office/in an embassy. □ **secretario**
first secretary, assistant to an ambassador. □ **primer secretario**
permanent secretary, main civil servant in a ministry. □ **secretario perpetuo**
secretarial [sekrə'tɛəriəl] *adj.* referring to a secretary: *secretarial duties.* □ **...de secretario**
secretariat *n.* group of officials who administer a large office: *the United Nations secretariat.* □ **secretaría**
secrete [si'kri:t] *v.* **1** to hide: *the documents were secreted in the boot of the car.* □ **esconder**
2 to produce a liquid: *the glands secrete saliva.* □ **segregar**
secretion [si'kri:ʃn] *n.* liquid produced by an organ/a plant. □ **secreción**
sect [sekt] *n.* religious group. □ **secta**
sectarian [sek'tɛəriən] *adj.* referring to a religious group: *sectarian violence,* violence between different religious groups. □ **sectario**
section ['sekʃn] *n.* **1** cutting. □ **sección**
Caesarean section, Caesarean operation. □ **cesárea**
2 part: *a large section of the population; the wind section of an orchestra.* □ **parte**
3 picture of something showing what it is like when cut through: *a section through a tooth showing the hard exterior and the nerves inside.* □ **sección**
4 part of something which, when joined to other parts, goes to make up a whole: *this bookcase is made in sections.* □ **parte**
sectional *adj.* **1** (diagram) showing a section through something. □ **en sección**
2 (built) in sections. □ **(fabricado) por partes**
sector ['sektə] *n.* **1** section of a circle between two lines drawn from the centre to the circumference. □ **sector**
2 part: *a sector of the community; the business sector.* □ **sector**
the private sector, the part of industry which is privately owned. □ **el sector privado**
the public sector, the nationalized industries and the civil service. □ **el sector público**
secular ['sekjulə] *adj.* not religious/not connected with religion. □ **seglar**
secure [si'kju:ə] *adj.* **1** safe: *to make a camp secure against attack.* □ **seguro**
2 firmly fixed: *is the ladder secure?* □ **seguro**
3 *a secure job,* where you can't be sacked. □ **un empleo seguro**
4 confident: *secure in the knowledge that his mother would give him more money.* □ **seguro**
■ *v.* **1** to make firm/to fasten: *he secured the windows and bolted the door.* □ **cerrar, asegurar**
2 to obtain: *I've secured the services of a waiter; he has secured himself a job in the Civil Service.* □ **conseguir**
securely *adv.* firmly: *the door is securely shut.* □ **firmemente**
security *n.* **1** safety: *they raced back to the security of the castle.* □ **seguridad**
2 protection against criminals/against hardship: *airport security,* measures to protect aircraft against hijackers. □ **seguridad**
social security, government help to poor/old people. □ **seguridad social**
the security forces *were in evidence in the streets,* the police/the army. □ **las fuerzas de seguridad...**
3 thing given to someone who has lent you money and which is returned when the loan is paid back: *he lent me $20 and kept my watch as security; I borrowed $10,000 on the security of my house; we lend money at high interest without security.* □ **fianza**
4 ***government securities,*** papers showing that the government will pay back money which people have lent it. □ **bonos/obligaciones del Estado**
sedan [si'dæn] *n. Amer.* covered family car. □ **turismo; sedán**
sedan-chair *n.* seat in a box carried on long poles by bearers. □ **silla de manos**
sedate [si'deit] *adj.* serious/dignified. □ **sosegado**
■ *v.* to give (a patient) sedatives. □ **sedar**
sedately *adv.* in a calm/serious way. □ **tranquilamente**
sedative ['sedətiv] *n.* medicine which makes you calm/which makes you go to sleep. □ **sedante**
sedation [si'deiʃn] *n.* giving medicine to calm a patient: *the patient is under sedation.* □ **sedación**
sedentary ['sedəntri] *adj.* always sitting down: *a sedentary job in an office.* □ **sedentario**
sediment ['sedimənt] *n.* solid which forms at the bottom of a liquid. □ **sedimento**
sedimentary [sedi'mentəri] *adj.* (rocks) which were formed from mud deposited at the bottom of the sea. □ **sedimentario**
sedition [sə'diʃn] *n.* encouraging people to rebel against the government. □ **sedición**
seditious *adj.* which encourages people to rebel: *a seditious poster.* □ **sedicioso**
seduce [si'dju:s] *v.* **1** to persuade (someone) to do something which is perhaps wrong: *he was seduced from his university career by an offer of money.* □ **seducir**
2 to persuade (someone) to have sexual intercourse. □ **seducir**
seducer *n.* person who seduces someone. □ **seductor**
seduction [si'dʌkʃn] *n.* act of seducing. □ **seducción**
seductive [si'dʌktiv] *adj.* attractive. □ **seductor**
see [si:] *n.* area over which a bishop rules: *the see of Canterbury.* □ **sede**
■ *v.* (*he saw: he has seen*) **1** to sense with your eyes: *can you see that tree over there? cats can see in the dark; there was water as far as the eye could see; I can see a bicycle coming down the street.* □ **ver**
2 to accompany: *I'll see you to the door; the policeman saw an old lady across the street; do you want me to see you home?* □ **acompañar**
3 to understand: *I don't see the point of spending so much money; do you see what I mean? I see!,* I understand. □ **ver, entender**
4 to examine: *let me see what's the matter with the brakes.* □ **ver**
5 to make sure: *he saw to it that everything was ready; can you see that he doesn't get out of bed?* □ **asegurarse**
6 to visit/to meet: *we see a lot of my uncle because he lives near; see you on Thursday! see you soon!; have you seen the doctor about your cold?* □ **ir a ver; ¡te veo el jueves!; ¡hasta luego!; ¿has visto al médico...?**
7 to go to a performance (of a play/film, etc.): *have you seen the new film?* □ **ir a ver**
seeing *n.* action of sensing with the eyes: *it's well worth seeing.* □ **vale la pena verlo**
seeing is believing, you will believe something only

if you see it. □ **ver para creer**
seeing that he is still ill, since he is ill. □ **puesto que...**
see through *v.* **1** to understand someone's plans to trick you: *I saw through his little plan.* □ **calar a uno**
2 to work on something until it is finished. □ **llevar a cabo**
see-through *adj.* transparent: *a see-through blouse.* □ **transparente**
see to *v.* to busy yourself about something: *see to it that there is enough petrol in the tank; can you see to the invitations?* □ **ocuparse de**
seed [si:d] *n.* **1** part of a plant which appears after the flowers and which when planted produces a new plant: *to sow seeds.* □ **semilla**
to go/run to seed, (i) *the cabbages have gone/have run to seed,* they have produced flowers and seeds and are therefore useless. □ **...han granado**
(ii) *he's gone to seed,* he's become lazy/he's got worse. □ **ha ido a menos**
2 tennis player who has been selected as one of the best players in a tournament (before the tournament starts). □ **preseleccionado**
the top seed/number one seed, person selected as the best player in a tournament. □ **el número uno**
■ *v.* **1** to produce seeds: *these plants seeded themselves,* they have grown from seed which fell on the ground from other plants. □ **granar**
2 to select the best players in a tennis tournament and arrange them so that they do not play each other until the later rounds. □ **preseleccionar**
seedbed *n.* special area of fine soil where you can sow seeds. □ **semillero**
seedling *n.* very young plant. □ **plantón**
seedsman *n.* (*pl. seedsmen*) person who specializes in growing and selling seeds. □ **vendedor de semillas**
seedy *adj.* worn-out (clothes); sick (person): *seedy-looking,* in bad shape. □ **raído (ropa); pachucho (persona); desaseado**
seek [si:k] *v.* (*he sought*) **1** to look for: *they sought shelter in a mountain hut.* □ **buscar**
2 to ask for: *he sought my advice.* □ **solicitar**
seem [si:m] *v.* to appear: *he seems to like his new job; they seem to be enjoying themselves; it seems they got lost in the fog; it seems like yesterday,* you would think it happened yesterday. □ **parecer**
seeming *adj.* not real, though appearing to be: *the seeming disaster turned out to be a stroke of luck.* □ **aparente**
seemingly *adj.* apparently: *a seemingly innocent smile.* □ **aparentemente**
seemly *adj.* decent/correct. □ **decoroso**
seen [si:n] *v. see* **see.**
seep [si:p] *v.* (*of a liquid*) to pass through a narrow opening: *water seeped in through a crack in the side of the boat; petrol seeped out of the cracked tank.* □ **filtrarse**
seepage *n.* act of seeping; liquid which has seeped. □ **filtración**
seesaw ['si:sɔ:] *n.* children's toy made of a plank with seats at each end, and balanced in the middle, so that when one end goes up the other goes down. □ **subibaja**
■ *v.* to go up and down: *petrol prices seem to have seesawed all year.* □ **oscilar**
seethe [si:ð] *v.* **1** to be very angry: *he was seething with anger.* □ **indignarse muchísimo**
2 to move about like boiling water: *the crowd seethed around the police station.* □ **borbotear**
segment ['segmənt] *n.* **1** part of a circle. □ **segmento**
2 *a segment of an orange,* one of the separate pieces inside an orange. □ **un gajo de naranja**
segmented [seg'mentid] *adj.* with segments. □ **segmentado**
segregate ['segrigeit] *v.* to divide one group from another. □ **segregar**
segregation [segri'geiʃn] *n.* division of one group from another. □ **segregación**
racial segregation, splitting of a population into groups according to race or colour. □ **segregación racial**
seismic ['saizmik] *adj.* referring to earthquakes. □ **sísmico**
seismograph *n.* instrument for recording earthquakes. □ **sismógrafo**
seismology [saiz'mɔlədʒi] *n.* study of earthquakes. □ **sismología**
seize [si:z] *v.* **1** to grab/to hold tight: *he seized a large stick.* □ **agarrar**
2 to confiscate/to take by force: *the police seized a large quantity of drugs at the airport.* □ **incautarse de**
seize up *v.* (*of an engine*) to stop working/to become blocked. □ **griparse**
seizure ['si:ʒə] *n.* **1** confiscation of goods by the police. □ **incautación**
2 stroke/illness caused by lack of blood to the brain. □ **ataque**
seldom ['seldəm] *adv.* rarely/not often: *I seldom go to the theatre.* □ **rara vez**
select [si'lekt] *v.* to choose: *he was selected to play in the English team; she selected six ripe apples from the basket.* □ **seleccionar**
■ *adj.* **1** of top quality: *select wines.* □ **vinos selectos**
2 *select club,* club which only lets in certain people. □ **club selecto**
3 *a select area of the town,* a smart area. □ **zona elegante de una ciudad**
selection [si'lekʃn] *n.* **1** choice: *they made a selection of French wines,* they selected some French wines. □ **selección**
2 things chosen: *we stock a good selection of English cheeses.* □ **surtido**
selective *adj.* which chooses: *you have to be selective,* you have to choose carefully. □ **selectivo**
selector *n.* person who chooses players to play in a football team/cricket team, etc. □ **seleccionador**
self [self] *n.* (*pl. selves*) **1** your own person or character. □ **uno mismo**
2 *he's quite his old self again,* he is back to normal. □ **vuelve a ser el mismo de antes**
3 ***pay self,*** (*on cheques*) pay the person who has signed the cheque. □ **al firmante**
self-addressed *adj.* (envelope) on which you have written your own address. □ **con la dirección de uno mismo**
self-assertive *adj.* (person) who makes others do what he wants. □ **enérgico**
self-assurance *n.* being sure you are capable of doing something. □ **con confianza en sí mismo**
self-assured *adj.* sure you are capable of doing something. □ **seguro de sí mismo**
self-catering *n.* doing the cooking for yourself. □ **autosuficiente en la cocina**
self-catering holiday, one where you rent a house, but cook your own meals. □ **vacaciones con derecho a cocina**
self-centred *adj.* (person) who only thinks of himself. □ **egocéntrico**
self-confidence *n.* being sure that you are capable of doing something: *he lacks self-confidence,* he is not sure of himself. □ **confianza en sí mismo**

self-confident *adj.* sure you are capable of doing something. □ **seguro de sí mismo**
self-conscious *adj.* embarrassed because you feel you have certain faults. □ **cohibido**
self-consciously *adv.* with embarrassment: *she self-consciously stood up to make a speech of welcome.* □ **cohibidamente**
self-contained *adj.* (flat) which has its own kitchen/bathroom, etc., and does not share these facilities with other flats in the same building. □ **independiente**
self-control *n.* keeping your feelings under control: *he exercised an enormous amount of self-control when the boy was rude to him.* □ **autodominio**
self-defeating *adj.* (plan) which works in such a way that it defeats its own purpose. □ **contraproducente**
self-defence *n.* protecting yourself: *he only used the knife in self-defence.* □ **defensa propia**
self-denial *n.* refusing to give yourself something/going without something which you would like. □ **abnegación**
self-determination *n.* choosing your own political future: *each country has the right of self-determination.* □ **autodeterminación**
self-drive car *n.* car which you can rent and drive yourself. □ **coche de alquiler (sin chófer)**
self-educated *adj.* (person) who has taught himself everything he knows and who has not been to school. □ **autodidacta**
self-effacing *adj.* (person) who tries to be inconspicuous/who does not want people to notice him. □ **modesto; humilde**
self-employed *adj.* (person) who works for himself, and is not paid a salary by someone else. □ **autónomo**
self-esteem *n.* pride in yourself. □ **amor propio**
self-evident *adj.* obvious. □ **evidente**
self-explanatory *adj.* obvious; which explains itself. □ **que se explica por sí mismo**
self-governing *adj.* (country) which governs itself. □ **autónomo**
self-important *adj.* (person) who feels he is very important when he really is not. □ **vanidoso**
self-indulgent *adj.* (person) who gives himself everything he wants. □ **inmoderado**
selfish *adj.* only interested in yourself/doing something only for yourself. □ **egoísta**
selfishly *adv.* (done) only for yourself. □ **de modo egoísta**
selfishness *n.* thinking only of yourself. □ **egoísmo**
selfless *adj.* not selfish; thinking only of others. □ **desinteresado**
self-made man *n.* person who has become rich entirely through his own efforts. □ **hombre hecho a sí mismo**
self-pity *n.* pity for yourself. □ **compasión de sí mismo**
self-portrait *n.* painting which an artist has made of himself. □ **autorretrato**
self-possessed *adj.* calm; not bothered. □ **dueño de sí mismo**
self-raising flour *n.* flour which contains baking powder to make cakes rise. □ **harina de fuerza**
self-reliant *adj.* independent/relying only on yourself. □ **seguro de sí mismo**
self-respect *n.* pride in yourself/concern that you have a good character and work well. □ **dignidad; pundonor**
self-sacrifice *n.* giving up something which you would like, so that others may enjoy it. □ **renuncia; sacrificio de sí mismo**
self-satisfied *adj.* contented with what you have done: *a self-satisfied smile.* □ **complaciente**
self-service *n.* and *adj.* (shop) where you take things yourself from the counters and pay at a cash desk: *self-service restaurant.* □ **autoservicio**
self-service garage, where you put the petrol into your car yourself. □ **gasolinera autoservicio**
self-sufficiency *n.* producing enough food for all your needs. □ **autosuficiencia**
self-sufficient *adj.* (person) who produces enough food for all his needs: *the country is self-sufficient in oil,* produces enough oil for all needs. □ **autosuficiente**
self-taught *adj.* (person) who has taught himself a certain skill. □ **autodidacta**
self-willed *adj.* obstinate/always wanting to have your own way. □ **terco**
sell [sel] *n.* act of selling. □ **venta**
hard sell, forceful selling of a product. □ **venta difícil**
■ *v.* (*he sold; he has sold*) to give goods to someone in exchange for money: *he sold me the chair for $10; these biscuits are selling well; a tin of coffee sells for $1.* □ **vender**
seller *n.* **1** person who sells. □ **vendedor**
2 *this record is a good seller,* it sells well. □ **...se vende bien**
sell off *v.* to sell (something) cheaply to get rid of it: *he's selling off his old stock.* □ **está liquidando/saldando...**
sell out *v.* to sell so many things that you have none left: *we've sold out of sugar.* □ **liquidar todas las existencias**
sell-out *n.* show/play etc. where all the tickets have been sold. □ **lleno**
sell up *v.* to sell a business: *he sold up and retired to the country.* □ **vender el negocio**
sellotape ['selәteip] *n.* trade name for a type of transparent sticky tape. □ **papel celo**
selvedge ['selvidʒ] *n.* edge of a piece of cloth which does not fray. □ **orillo**
semaphore ['semәfɔː] *n.* way of signalling using two arms (and flags) in different positions for each letter. □ **semáforo**
semblance ['semblәns] *n.* appearance: *he gave a semblance of enjoying himself,* he pretended. □ **semblante**
semen ['siːmәn] *n.* liquid in which male sperm floats. □ **semen**
semester [sә'mestә] *n. Amer.* term in a school year which only has two terms. □ **semestre**
semi ['semi] *n.* (*informal*) semi-detached house. □ **casa adosada**
semi- ['semi] *prefix meaning* half. □ **semi-**
semi-breve *n.* long note in music, lasting two minims. □ **semibreve**
semicircle *n.* half a circle. □ **semicírculo**
semi-circular *adj.* like a half circle in shape. □ **semicircular**
semi-colon *n.* punctuation mark (;) showing a pause. □ **punto y coma**
semiconductor *n.* material (such as silicon) which is partly able to conduct electricity. □ **semiconductor**
semi-conscious *adj.* half conscious. □ **semiconsciente**
semi-detached *adj.* (house) which is joined to another similar house on one side, but is not joined on the other. □ **adosada**
semi-final *n.* one of two matches in a competition,

the winners of which go into the final game. □ **semifinal**
semi-finalist *n.* team/player in a semi-final. □ **semifinalista**
semi-official *adj.* not quite official. □ **semioficial**
semi-precious stone *n.* stone which is quite valuable, but not in the same class as diamonds/rubies/sapphires, etc. □ **piedra semipreciosa**
semi-quaver *n.* note in music lasting half as long as a quaver. □ **semicorchea**
semitone *n.* (*in music*) half a tone on the scale. □ **semitono**

seminal ['seminl] *adj.* which acts as the starting point for something new: *his seminal work on nuclear physics.* □ **original y de gran influencia**

seminar ['seminɑː] *n.* class given to a small group of students who meet to discuss a problem with a teacher. □ **seminario**

seminary ['seminəri] *n.* college for priests. □ **seminario**

Semitic [sə'mitik] *adj.* referring to a group of races including Jews and Arabs: *the Semitic peoples.* □ **semítico**

semolina [semə'liːnə] *n.* hard crushed wheat, used to make spaghetti and milk puddings. □ **sémola**

senate ['senət] *n.* **1** upper house of parliament in some countries. □ **senado**
2 main committee which governs a university. □ **junta de gobierno**
senator *n.* member of the upper house of parliament. □ **senador**

send [send] *v.* (*he sent; he has sent*) **1** to tell (someone) to go somewhere; to make (something) go from one place to another: *I sent the children out to buy some flowers; we sent a parcel of presents to my mother; he sent the books flying with a blow of his fist,* made them fly all over the place. □ **enviar; mandar**
2 to give (someone) a sensation: *the noise of the drill sends shivers down my spine; his constant talking will send me mad.* □ **producir; volver**
3 to put out: *as the seed starts to grow, it sends out roots and a shoot.* □ **echar**
4 *this music sends me,* (*informal*) makes me excited. □ **me hace vibrar**
send away *v.* **1** to make (someone/something) go away: *the doctor came to visit her, but she sent him away.* □ **despedir**
2 ***to send away for,*** to write asking someone to send something to you: *he sent away for information about holidays in Russia.* □ **requerir**
send back *v.* to return. □ **devolver**
send down *v.* to dismiss (a student) from a university. □ **expulsar**
sender *n.* person who sends. □ **remitente**
send for *v.* to pass a message to someone asking them to come: *when he became ill, his wife sent for the doctor.* □ **hacer llamar**
send off *v.* **1** to make (someone/something) go off: *he sent off messengers into the forest.* □ **mandar**
2 to post: *I sent this letter off yesterday.* □ **echar al correo**
to send off for, to write asking someone to send something to you: *I sent off for information about holidays in Russia.* □ **pedí información...**
3 to tell (a player) to leave the football field because of bad conduct: *one of the forwards was sent off in the first half.* □ **expulsar**
send-off *n.* party to say goodbye to someone leaving on a long journey. □ **despedida**
send out *v.* to make (someone/something) go out: *they sent out a search party.* □ **enviar**
send up *v.* **1** to make (someone/something) go up: *they sent up a balloon; the bad weather has sent up the price of vegetables.* □ **lanzar (globo); hacer subir (precios)**
2 ***to send someone up,*** (*informal*) to make fun of someone. □ **cachondearse de alguien**

senile ['siːnail] *adj.* old and mentally weak. □ **senil**
senility [sə'niliti] *n.* mental weakness in old age. □ **senilidad**

senior ['siːnjə] *adj.* **1** older: *he is my senior by two years/he is two years' senior to me; J. Smith Senior,* father of J. Smith Junior. □ **me saca/lleva dos años; padre**
senior school, school for older children. □ **instituto de bachillerato**
senior citizen, old person living on a pension. □ **jubilado; pensionista**
2 more important: *senior rank; senior minister in the government.* □ **superior**
■ *n.* **1** older person. □ **el de mayor edad**
the seniors, the older children in a school. □ **los mayores**
2 *Amer.* fourth-year student. □ **estudiantes de C.O.U.**
seniority [siːni'ɔriti] *n.* being senior. □ **antigüedad**

sensation [sen'seiʃn] *n.* **1** feeling: *I had a curious sensation of floating in the air.* □ **sensación**
2 great excitement: *the new book has created quite a sensation.* □ **sensación**
sensational *adj.* very exciting: *a sensational win by our team.* □ **sensacional**

sense [sens] *n.* **1** one of the five ways in which you notice something: *the five senses; he's lost all sense of smell.* □ **sentido**
sixth sense, intuition/ability to feel that something has taken place/will take place, without using any of the five senses. □ **el sexto sentido**
2 feeling: *he has a good sense of direction; we felt a sense of loss; she has no sense of humour.* □ **sentido**
3 ***senses,*** power of reasoning. □ **juicio**
to take leave of one's senses: *has he taken leave of his senses?,* has he gone mad? □ **¿ha perdido el juicio?**
to come to one's senses: *he came to his senses,* he became reasonable. □ **recobró el juicio**
4 meaning: *can you make any sense of this message?,* can you see what the message means?; *I'm using the word 'engine' in the sense of 'locomotive'.* □ **sentido**
to make sense: *the letter doesn't make sense,* it is meaningless. □ **...no tiene sentido**
5 reasonableness/good judgement: *he had the sense to keep his mouth shut; he talks sense.* □ **buen juicio**
■ *v.* to feel: *I sense that things are going to be difficult.* □ **sentir**
senseless *adj.* **1** stupid: *a senseless murder.* □ **sin sentido**
2 unconscious: *he was knocked senseless by the blow.* □ **inconsciente**
senselessness *n.* stupidity. □ **insensatez**

sensible ['sensibl] *adj.* **1** reasonable/well judged: *he made several very sensible suggestions.* □ **sensato**
2 (person) who has commonsense. □ **persona sensata**
3 *sensible walking shoes,* strong, but not fashionable, walking shoes. □ **zapatos prácticos**
sensibility [sensi'biliti] *n.* being capable of delicate feeling. □ **sensibilidad**
sensibly *adv.* reasonably/with good judgement: *he spoke very sensibly about the proposal.* □ **con sensatez**

sensitive ['sensitiv] *adj.* **1** able to feel keenly/sharply: *he is sensitive to criticism; the lens is sensitive to light.* □ **sensible**
2 *don't touch his arm – it is still sensitive,* it hurts at the slightest touch. □ **...todavía está muy sensible**
sensitivity [sensi'tiviti] **sensitiveness** *n.* being sensitive. □ **sensibilidad**
sensitize *v.* to make sensitive (to light, etc.): *sensitized paper.* □ **sensibilizar**
sensor ['sensə] *n.* apparatus which detects something by sense of heat/light/smell of smoke, etc. □ **sensor**
sensory *adj.* referring to the senses. □ **sensorio**
sensory nerve, nerve which carries impulses to the brain. □ **nervio sensitivo**
sensual ['sensjuəl] *adj.* referring to pleasures of the body, not of the mind: *sensual pleasures.* □ **sensual**
sensuality *n.* experience of pleasures of the body; giving of physical pleasure. □ **sensualidad**
sensuous ['sensjuəs] *adj.* which gives pleasure to the senses: *the sensuous softness of velvet.* □ **sensual**
sent [sent] *v. see* **send.**
sentence ['sentəns] *n.* **1** words put together to form a complete separate statement, usually ending with a full stop: *translate this sentence into French.* □ **oración**
2 decision of a judge which gives the details of punishment: *death sentence; a prison sentence.* □ **sentencia**
■ *v.* to condemn (someone) to a certain punishment: *she was sentenced to ten years in prison.* □ **sentenciar**
sententious [sen'tenʃs] *adj.* too full of moral sense. □ **sentencioso**
sentiment ['sentimənt] *n.* **1** show of feeling. □ **sentimiento**
2 ***sentiments,*** opinions: *those are my sentiments,* that's my opinion. □ **éste es mi sentir**
sentimental [senti'mentəl] *adj.* full of emotion/full of feeling: *I have a sentimental attachment to the house, because I spent my childhood here.* □ **sentimental**
sentimentality [sentimən'tæliti] *n.* playing on the emotions (in literature/music). □ **sentimentalismo**
sentimentally *adv.* by feeling: *he's sentimentally attached to that old watch.* □ **sentimentalmente**
sentry ['sentri] *n.* soldier on duty at a gate, etc. □ **centinela**
sentry-box *n.* wooden shelter for a sentry. □ **garita**
sepal ['sepəl] *n.* green leaf under the petals of a flower. □ **sépalo**
separate ['seprət] *adj.* detached; not together: *I'm sending the book in a separate parcel; can we have two separate bills please?* □ **separado**
■ *v.* ['sepəreit] **1** to detach/to divide: *to separate the larger stones from the sand; the family got separated in the struggle to get on the train; the search party separated and searched in different directions.* □ **separar**
2 *his parents have decided to separate,* to live apart. □ **separarse**
separation [sepə'reiʃn] *n.* dividing/living apart. □ **separación**
separatism ['sepərətizəm] *n.* political ideal of separating from a large country. □ **separatismo**
separatist *adj.* and *n.* (person) who wants his region to separate from a large country. □ **separatista**
sepia ['si:piə] *n.* brown colour. □ **color sepia**
sepsis ['sepsis] *n.* being septic. □ **sepsia**
September [sep'tembə] *n.* ninth month of the year: *he will be six years old in September; she was born on September 22nd.* □ **septiembre/setiembre**
septet [sep'tet] *n.* group of seven musicians; piece of music for seven instruments. □ **septeto**
septic ['septik] *adj.* (wound) which has gone bad/become poisoned: *his finger turned septic; she has a septic finger.* □ **séptico**
septic tank, large hole near a house for collecting sewage. □ **fosa séptica**
septicaemia [septi'si:miə] *n.* poisoning of the blood. □ **septicemia**
septuagenarian [septjuədʒə'nɛəriən] *n.* person who is between seventy and eighty years old. □ **septuagenario**
sepulchre ['sepəlkə] *Amer.* **sepulcher** *n.* tomb. □ **sepulcro**
sepulchral [se'pʌlkrəl] *adj.* **1** referring to a sepulchre. □ **sepulcral**
2 *sepulchral voice,* very deep gloomy voice. □ **voz de ultratumba**
sequel ['si:kwəl] *n.* **1** continuation of a story/play, etc. □ **continuación**
2 result: *the court case had an unfortunate sequel.* □ **consecuencia**
sequence ['si:kwəns] *n.* **1** series of things happening; series of numbers which follow each other: *the sequence of events,* order in which the events took place. □ **sucesión; orden**
2 scene in a film. □ **secuencia**
sequin ['si:kwin] *n.* small round shiny metal ornament, stitched to clothing. □ **lentejuela**
sequoia [si'kwɔiə] *n.* very tall coniferous tree growing on the west coast of America. □ **secoya**
serenade [serə'neid] *n.* love song. □ **serenata**
■ *v.* to sing a love song to (someone). □ **dar una serenata**
serene [sə'ri:n] *adj.* calm; not worried. □ **sereno**
serenity [sə'reniti] *n.* calmness; lack of worry. □ **serenidad**
serge [sə:dʒ] *n.* type of thick cloth. □ **sarga**
sergeant ['sɑ:dʒənt] *n.* senior non-commissioned officer in the army/the police. □ **sargento**
sergeant-major *n.* rank in the army above sergeant. □ **sargento mayor**
serial ['siəriəl] *adj.* ***serial number,*** number of a series: *each bank note has a serial number printed on it.* □ **serial; número de serie**
■ *n.* story/TV play which is told in several instalments. □ **serial**
series ['siəri:z] *n.* (*no pl.*) **1** group of things which come one after the other in a set order: *a series of numbers.* □ **serie**
2 group of things: *he wrote a series of letters to the paper.* □ **serie**
serious ['siəriəs] *adj.* **1** not humorous: *a serious story; serious newspaper; I'm being serious,* I'm not joking. □ **serio**
2 important/bad: *serious mistake; serious injury.* □ **grave**
seriously *adv.* **1** not humorously: *he takes this very seriously,* he thinks it is important. □ **seriamente**
2 badly: *she's seriously ill.* □ **gravemente**
seriousness *n.* importance: *the seriousness of the crime.* □ **gravedad**
sermon ['sə:mən] *n.* serious speech made in church. □ **sermón**
serpent ['sə:pənt] *n.* snake. □ **serpiente**
serpentine *adj.* like a snake; winding. □ **sinuoso**
serrated [sə'reitid] *adj.* toothed (blade); with a zigzag edge: *the cloth has a serrated edge.* □ **dentado**
serum ['siərəm] *n.* yellow liquid in the blood, which

can be injected into someone's body to fight disease. □ **suero**

serve [sə:v] *v.* **1** to help at table: *let me serve the potatoes; serve yourself; lunch is now being served; this recipe will serve six people,* will make enough food for six people. □ **servir**

2 to work for: *he served his country loyally for forty years; he served in the armed forces for six years.* □ **servir**

3 to be useful: *this rock will serve as a table.* □ **servir**

4 to deal with (a customer): *are you being served? the bus serves the outlying villages.* □ **atender (cliente); hacer el servicio (bus)**

5 to undergo punishment: *he has served six years of his prison sentence.* □ **cumplir**

6 to start a game of tennis by hitting the ball first. □ **servir**

7 ***it serves you right,*** you deserve the punishment you have got. □ **te lo has buscado**

servant *n.* **1** person who is paid to work in the house. □ **sirviente**

2 ***civil servant,*** government employee. □ **funcionario del Estado**

server *n.* **1** person who serves at table. □ **camarero**

2 large flat knife for serving food; spoon and fork for serving fish or salad. □ **pala (pescado); cubierto (ensalada)**

service ['sə:vis] *n.* **1** working for someone: *he got a medal for his services to the community; military service,* period which you spend in the army/navy/air force. □ **servicio**

service flat, flat where cleaning, etc., is provided. □ **piso con servicio (de criada, portero, etc.,)**

2 *the car needs its first service/a 10,000 kilometre service,* needs to be examined by the garage. □ **rodaje**

3 *service charge,* charge added to a bill for the work carried out; *is the service included?,* does the bill include a tip for the waiter? □ **servicio**

4 group of people working together. □ **personal**

civil service, all the government employees: *he has a job in the civil service.* □ **los funcionarios**

the foreign service, people who represent their country abroad. □ **el cuerpo diplomático**

the services, the army, navy and air force. □ **las fuerzas armadas**

5 providing basic essentials which people require. □ **servicio**

the essential services, provision of water/electricity/sewers, etc.. □ **servicios de infraestructura**

bus service, regularly passing bus: *the service on this route is supposed to be every ten minutes.* □ **servicio de autobuses**

6 regular religious ceremony: *church service.* □ **servicios religiosos**

7 act of starting a game of tennis by hitting the ball first. □ **servicio**

8 *tea service/dinner service,* set of china for use at tea/dinner. □ **juego de té; servicio de mesa**

■ *v.* to do any repairs which need doing to (a car, etc.): *you have to have your car serviced regularly.* □ **revisar**

serviceable *adj.* practical; which will be useful. □ **servible, práctico**

serviceman *n.* (*pl. servicemen*) member of the army/navy/air force. □ **militar**

service-station *n.* garage which sells petrol/oil, etc. □ **gasolinera/estación de servicio**

serviette [sə:vi'et] *n.* square of cloth or soft paper used to wipe your mouth at table. □ **servilleta**

serviette-ring *n.* ring for putting your serviette into so that no one else will use it. □ **servilletero**

servile ['sə:vail] *adj.* like a slave. □ **servil**

servility [sə:'viliti] *n.* acting like a slave. □ **servilismo**

servitude ['sə:vitju:d] *n.* slavery. □ **servidumbre**

session ['seʃn] *n.* **1** meeting of a committee/parliament, etc.. □ **sesión**

2 *the council is now* ***in session,*** is in the process of meeting. □ **...está reunido**

3 meeting to study/to practise: *a practice session on the football field.* □ **sesión**

set [set] *n.* **1** group of things which go together: *a set of glasses; I need a new set of sparking plugs; tea set,* pieces of china with the same pattern which are used tea. □ **juego**

2 apparatus: *television set.* □ **aparato**

3 one of the main parts of a tennis match. □ **set**

4 group of people: *he goes around with the tennis set,* the group who like playing tennis. □ **grupo; la gente del tenis**

5 scenery on a stage. □ **decorados (teatro); plató (cine)**

6 position/direction: *the set of her head; set of a saw's teeth,* way in which the teeth of a saw are bent. □ **forma**

7 arranging of hair: *to have a shampoo and set.* □ **lavar y marcar**

8 *onion set,* very small onion which is planted and then grows into a large one. □ **cebollitas para sembrar**

9 burrow of a badger. □ **tejonera**

■ *v.* (*he set; he has set*) **1** to put/to place: *to set the table,* put the knives and forks/glasses, etc. on the table; *to set sentries round the camp; to set a diamond in a ring.* □ **poner/colocar**

2 to arrange/to fix a machine: *I set my alarm for six o'clock; the bomb was set to go off at 10.15; he set a trap for rabbits.* □ **poner en hora; armar (trampa)**

3 to arrange in place: *to have your hair set; the doctor set her broken arm.* □ **marcar (pelo); reducir (hueso)**

4 *her arm has now set,* has mended in place. □ **su brazo ha vuelto a su sitio**

5 to give work to: *the teacher set us four maths questions; this book has been set for the exam,* we will be questioned on this book in the exam; *they were set the task of beating a score of 400 in under two hours; they set him to work weeding the garden.* □ **poner**

6 to make: *he was set free; they set fire to the house.* □ **le pusieron en libertad; prender**

7 to become solid: *the jelly has set; the jam still wouldn't set although we had cooked it for three hours; don't walk on the cement, it hasn't set yet.* □ **cuajar (gelatina, mermelada); fraguar (cemento)**

8 (*of sun/stars*) to go down: *the sun is setting in the west.* □ **ponerse**

9 to write music to go with words: *the poem was set to music by Stravinsky.* □ **poner música a un texto**

10 to place scenery on a stage; to put the action of a story in a certain period: *the scene is set for the death of the hero; the novel is set in South America; the action of the play is set at the end of the 19th century.* □ **situar**

11 to arrange letters in rows for printing: *the book is set by hand.* □ **componer**

■ *adj.* **1** fixed; which cannot be changed: *set smile; set price; meals are at certain set times.* □ **fijo**

2 ready: *they were all set to go for a walk.* □ **preparado**
'on your marks, get set, go!' words used to start a race. □ **preparados, listos, ya!**
set about *v.* to start doing something: *I don't know how to set about building a boat.* □ **emprender**
set aside *v.* **1** to put to one side/to reject: *his proposal was set aside.* □ **apartar/rechazar**
2 to keep to one side (for future use): *this money has been set aside for building the new church hall.* □ **apartar**
set back *v.* **1** to make late: *the bad weather has set back the harvest by three weeks.* □ **retrasar**
2 *it set me back $10,* (*informal*) it cost me $10. □ **me salió por diez dólares**
setback *n.* holding back progress: *the theft of the plans was a serious setback.* □ **revés**
set down *v.* **1** to write down on paper. □ **poner por escrito**
2 to let passengers get off: *the bus set down three old ladies at the corner of the street.* □ **dejar bajar**
set in *v.* to start: *winter is setting in; gangrene has set in.* □ **empezar**
set off *v.* **1** to start: *we're setting off on a shopping trip* □ **emprender**
2 to light (fireworks); to make (a bomb) explode; to start (a reaction). □ **lanzar; hacer estallar; ponerse a**
3 to show up: *the black dress sets off her red hair.* □ **acentuar**
set out *v.* **1** to put out: *the items for sale are set out on the table; the sales figures are set out in columns.* □ **disponer**
2 to start: *the explorers set out from their camp.* □ **partir**
set-square *n.* instrument to help you draw lines, shaped like a right angled triangle. □ **escuadra**
setting *n.* **1** action of setting. □ **colocación**
2 background for a story; frame in which a diamond is fixed. □ **escenario (historia); engaste**
3 ***place setting,*** set of knives/forks/spoons, etc., for one person. □ **servicio**
set to *v.* to get to work: *they set to, and soon built a log hut.* □ **poner manos a la obra**
set-to *n.* (*informal*) argument; fight. □ **pelea**
set up *v.* to build; to establish: *he set up in business as a plumber; they set up house in a disused barn.* □ **establecerse**
set-up *n.* (*informal*) arrangement; organization: *the whole set-up seems quite inefficient.* □ **tinglado**
set upon *v.* to attack: *he was set upon by three men.* □ **agredir**

settee [sə'ti:] *n.* sofa; long comfortable seat for several people. □ **canapé**

setter ['setə] *n.* type of hunting dog trained to point out game by standing still. □ **setter**

settle ['setl] *n.* long wooden bench with a back. □ **banco**
■ *v.* **1** to arrange/to agree: *he settled his affairs and left the country; we settled the date for the Christmas party; it's all settled,* it has all been agreed; *we settled it among ourselves,* we arranged it without anyone else interfering; *have you settled the price yet? we've settled on dark green as the colour for the carpet; I'll settle up later,* pay the bill. □ **arreglar (asuntos); fijar (fecha)**
2 to place in a comfortable position; to rest: *the birds settled down for the night; has he settled down in his new job?; the snow is settling,* is staying on the ground without melting. □ **posarse (pájaro); adaptarse (nuevo empleo)**
3 *the house slowly settled on its foundations,* slowly sank. □ **asentarse**
4 to go to live in a new country: *they settled in Canada.* □ **fijar su residencia**
5 *the mud settled at the bottom of the jar,* fell to the bottom. □ **posarse**
6 to pass (money/property) to someone by a legal process: *he settled $10,000 on his daughter when she got married.* □ **dar en dote**
settled *adj.* fixed/unchanging: *settled weather; a settled policy.* □ **estable**
settlement *n.* **1** payment (of a bill); agreement in a dispute: *please find enclosed $5 in settlement of your invoice.* □ **liquidación**
2 place where a group of people has settled: *there were settlements all along the river.* □ **asentamiento**
settler *n.* person who goes to settle in a new country: *English settlers were farming in Australia.* □ **colono**

seven ['sevn] number 7: *she is seven* (*years old*); *come for dinner at seven* (*o'clock*). □ **siete**
seventeen number 17: *he is seventeen* (*years old*); *the seventeen sixteen train,* the train which leaves at 17.16. □ **diecisiete**
the seventeen hundreds, the years between 1700 and 1799. □ **el siglo XVIII**
seventeenth, 17th *adj.* referring to seventeen: *the seventeenth of June (17th June).* □ **decimoséptimo; el 17 de junio**
the seventeenth century, period from 1600 to 1699. □ **el siglo diecisiete**
seventh, 7th *adj.* referring to seven: *the seventh of December (7th December); Edward the Seventh* (*Edward VII*). □ **séptimo; el siete de diciembre; Eduardo VII (séptimo)**
the seventh century, period from 600 to 699. □ **el siglo séptimo**
seventieth, 70th *adj.* referring to seventy. □ **septuagésimo**
seventy number 70: *he is seventy* (*years old*). □ **setenta**
in the seventies, (i) *she is in her seventies,* she is more than seventy years old but less than eighty. □ **tiene más de setenta**
(ii) between '60 and '80 in a century. □ **en la década de los setenta**

sever ['sevə] *v.* to cut off: *his arm was severed in accident; the storm has severed all communications with the island; the government has severed diplomatic relations with the invading country.* □ **cortar (brazo, comunicaciones); romper (relaciones)**
severance *n.* cutting off. □ **corte**
severance pay, money paid as compensation to someone who is losing a job. □ **indemnización por despido**

several ['sevrəl] *adj.* and *pron.* more than a few, but not very many: *I have seen him several times in the pub; several of us are going.* □ **varios; algunos**

severe [sə'viə] *adj.* **1** very strict: *severe punishment.* □ **severo**
2 very bad: *he's got severe bronchitis; a severe winter,* one which is very cold. □ **grave; riguroso**
severely *adv.* **1** strictly: *he was severely punished.* □ **con severidad**
2 badly: *she was severely wounded in the war.* □ **gravemente**
severity [sə'veriti] *n.* **1** harshness/strictness. □ **severidad**
2 sharpness (of cold); badness (of weather). □ **intensidad (frio); inclemencia (del tiempo)**

sew [sou] *v.* (*he has sewn*) to attach/to mend by using

a needle and thread; to make (with a needle and thread): *to sew on a button; to sew up the edge of a dress.* □ **coser**
sewing *n.* **1** action of attaching/mending with needle and thread: *sewing cotton; sewing needle.* □ **de coser**
2 work which someone is in the process of sewing: *she left her sewing on the table.* □ **labor (de costura)**
sewing machine *n.* machine which sews. □ **máquina de coser**
sewer ['suə] *n.* large tube in the ground used for taking away waste and dirty water from houses. □ **alcantarilla**
sewage ['su:idʒ] *n.* waste and dirty water. □ **aguas residuales**
sewage works/sewage farm, place where waste is collected and treated to kill germs. □ **estación depuradora**
sex [seks] *n.* **1** one of two groups (male and female) into which animals and plants can be divided: *please state on the form your name, age and sex.* □ **sexo**
sex appeal, attractiveness to members of the other sex. □ **'sex-appeal', atractivo sexual**
2 *to have sex with someone,* to have sexual intercourse. □ **tener relaciones sexuales con alguien**
■ *v. to sex chickens,* to tell whether chickens are male or female. □ **'sexar'**
sexist *adj.* and *n.* (person) who is biased against one of the sexes. □ **'sexista'**
sexual ['seksjuəl] *adj.* referring to sex. □ **sexual**
sexual intercourse, reproductive act between a male and a female. □ **coito**
sexy *adj.* sexually attractive. □ **'sexy'**
sextant ['sekstənt] *n.* instrument for calculating the position of a ship by referring to the stars. □ **sextante**
sextet [seks'tet] *n.* **1** group of six musicians playing together. □ **sexteto**
2 piece of music for six musicians. □ **sexteto**
sexton ['sekstən] *n.* man who works in a church/rings the bells/digs graves, etc. □ **sacristán**
shabby ['ʃæbi] *adj.* poor/worn out: *shabby clothes; shabby furniture.* □ **viejo**
shabbily *adv.* poorly: *shabbily dressed.* □ **andrajosamente vestido**
shabbiness *n.* poor condition (of clothes/furniture). □ **pobreza**
shack [ʃæk] *n.* rough wooden hut. □ **choza**
■ *v.* ***to shack up with someone,*** (*slang*) to go to live with someone. □ **ir a vivir con alguien**
shackle ['ʃækl] *n.* ***shackles,*** chains (for attaching a prisoner). □ **grilletes**
■ *v.* to attach with a chain: *the prisoners were shackled to the walls of the cell.* □ **encadenar**
shade [ʃeid] *n.* **1** dark place which is not in the sunlight: *he was sitting in the shade; we had tea in the shade of an old beech tree.* □ **sombra**
to put someone in the shade, to make them seem less important/hardworking, etc.: *he works 18 hours a day — he puts me in the shade.* □ **hacer sombra a alguien**
2 dark part of a picture. □ **sombra**
3 cover put on a lamp. □ **pantalla**
4 type of colour; slight difference: *a beautiful shade of blue; shades of meaning.* □ **una tonalidad de azul; matices de significado**
5 little bit: *the dress could be a shade longer.* □ **poquitín**
■ *v.* **1** to protect from sunlight: *the garden is shaded by some old apple trees.* □ **proteger contra el sol**
2 to make a picture darker. □ **sombrear**
3 to change from one colour to another gradually: *the blue shades off into green.* □ **degradarse**
shadiness *n.* being shady. □ **lo umbroso**
shading *n.* action of making shade; making part of a picture darker. □ **sombreado**
shady *adj.* **1** full of shade: *a shady garden.* □ **sombreado**
2 dishonest/disreputable: *a shady deal.* □ **turbio**
shadow ['ʃædou] *n.* **1** shade made by an object in light: *the shadow of a man; the attackers hid in the shadows.* □ **sombra**
2 small amount: *there isn't the shadow of a doubt that he is guilty.* □ **...sombra de duda...**
3 person who is following someone. □ **sombra; policía**
4 opposition in parliament which parallels the government. □ **la oposición**
the shadow cabinet, senior members of the opposition who parallel the government: *the shadow minister of health,* the member of the opposition who studies the problems of health and may be minister of health if his party forms a government. □ **gobierno en la sombra**
■ *v.* to follow (someone): *he was shadowed by two secret agents.* □ **seguir y vigilar**
shadowy *adj.* vague/indistinct: *a shadowy form appeared in the mist.* □ **poco claro**
shaft [ʃɑ:ft] *n.* **1** long stick which is the main part of an arrow/a javelin, etc.; long pole in front of a cart to which a horse is attached. □ **astil (flecha); vara (carro)**
2 ray of light. □ **rayo de luz**
3 rod which turns in an engine. □ **eje; árbol**
4 pillar. □ **fuste**
5 deep hole in the ground: *mine shaft.* □ **pozo**
6 ***lift shaft,*** hole down the centre of a building in which a lift moves up and down. □ **hueco del ascensor**
shaggy ['ʃægi] *adj.* with long hair: *shaggy dog; shaggy carpet.* □ **peludo; lanudo (perro)**
shaggy dog story, very long story with an unexpectedly silly ending. □ **chiste largo e idiota**
shake [ʃeik] *n.* **1** act of moving from side to side or up and down: *give your watch a good shake to get it started.* □ **sacudida**
2 *he has got the shakes,* he is trembling. □ **está temblando de miedo; tiene escalofríos**
3 drink made by mixing milk and flavouring: *milk shake.* □ **batido**
■ *v.* (*he shook: he has shaken*) **1** to move from side to side or up and down: *he shook his watch to see if it would go; during the earthquake the building shook; he shook his head,* moved his head from side to side to indicate 'no'; *to shake your fist at someone,* to threaten them by waving your fist. □ **sacudir; temblar (edificio)**
2 ***to shake hands with someone,*** to hold each other's hand in sign of greeting. □ **dar la mano**
3 *he was shaking all over,* trembling. □ **estaba temblando**
4 *he was badly shaken by the news,* very upset/disturbed. □ **quedó conmocionado por...**
shake down *v.* to settle down (after a period of uncertainty). □ **instalarse**
shaking *adj.* trembling: *a shaking voice.* □ **tembloroso**
shake off *v.* to get rid of something unpleasant: *he has managed to shake off his cold; he shook off the police car which was following him.* □ **quitarse de encima**

shake-up *n.* (*informal*) total change: *there has been a shake-up in the central office.* □ **reorganización**
shaky *adj.* **1** wobbly; trembling: *shaky hand.* □ **tembloroso**
2 *my maths is a bit shaky,* not very reliable. □ **...poco sólido**
shale [ʃeil] *n.* type of rock which splits into soft thin pieces. □ **esquisto**
shall [ʃæl] *v.* used with ***I*** and ***we*** to form future and requests (negative: ***shan't;*** past: ***should***) **1** (suggestion/request): *shall I shut the door? shall we sit down?* □ **¿cierro la puerta?**
2 (emphasis in the future): *you will not go to the party — yes I shall!* □ **...sí, ¡iré!**
3 (future): *we shall leave for France on Tuesday; I shan't say anything.* (note: except for **1** ***shall*** is gradually being replaced by ***will***); see also **should.** □ **saldremos...; no diré...**
shallot [ʃə'lɔt] *n.* type of small onion which grows in clusters. □ **chalote**
shallow ['ʃælou] *adj.* **1** not deep: *the river was shallow so we could easily touch the bottom; the shallow end of a swimming pool; shallow dish.* □ **poco profundo**
2 *he has a shallow mind,* he thinks superficially. □ **superficial**
■ *n.* ***shallows,*** water which is not deep: *the boat ran aground in the shallows.* □ **bajío**
shallowness *n.* being shallow. □ **poca profundidad**
sham [ʃæm] *adj.* false: *sham diamonds.* □ **falso**
■ *n.* something which is false: *they didn't really fight — it was all a sham.* □ **engaño**
■ *v.* (*he shammed*) to pretend: *he is not asleep — he is only shamming.* □ **fingir**
shamble ['ʃæmbl] *v.* ***to shamble along,*** to wander along dragging your feet. □ **ir arrastrando los pies**
shambles ['ʃæmblz] *n.* disorder/mess: *the burglars left the place in a shambles.* □ **ruina**
shame [ʃeim] *n.* **1** feeling caused by being guilty/being ashamed: *she covered her face in shame.* □ **vergüenza**
to put someone/something to shame, to make someone feel ashamed; to show something to be inferior: *your beautiful house puts mine to shame.* □ **hacer avergonzarse a alguien**
2 ***what a shame,*** what a pity/how sad: ***it's a shame*** *it rained on her wedding day.* □ **¡qué lástima!**
■ *v.* to make someone ashamed so that he does something: *she shamed him into giving her mother a present.* □ **avergonzar a alguien para que haga algo**
shamefaced *adj.* embarrassed/ashamed. □ **avergonzado**
shamefacedly *adv.* in embarrassment. □ **con vergüenza**
shameful *adj.* scandalous/disgraceful. □ **vergonzoso**
shameless *adj.* without shame: *shameless exploitation of poor workers.* □ **descarado**
shampoo [ʃæm'pu:] *n.* liquid soap for washing your hair/a carpet, etc. □ **champú**
■ *v.* to wash (your hair/the carpet, etc.) with a shampoo. □ **lavar con champú**
shamrock ['ʃæmrɔk] *n.* small clover-like plant with leaves which are split into three parts. □ **trébol**
shandy ['ʃændi] *n.* mixture of beer and lemonade. □ **clara; 'shandy'**
shan't [ʃɑ:nt] *v. see* **shall.**
shanty ['ʃænti] *n.* **1** rough wooden hut. □ **chabola**
shanty town, group of huts belonging to poor people. □ **barrio de chabolas**
2 *sea shanty,* old song sung by sailors. □ **saloma**
shape [ʃeip] *n.* **1** form: *a birthday cake in the shape of an engine; this pullover is beginning to lose its shape,* beginning to stretch. □ **forma**
to take shape: *the picture is taking shape,* is beginning to look like something. □ **...a tomar forma**
to knock into shape: *he has written the first draft of the play but it still has to be knocked into shape,* to be polished and finished. □ **...darle forma**
in any shape or form, of any sort: *I have not had a holiday in any shape or form for two years.* □ **de ninguna clase**
2 mould for making a jelly. □ **molde**
■ *v.* **1** to form/to make into a shape: *the baker shaped the dough into a figure eight.* □ **dar forma a**
2 *business is shaping well,* is turning out well. □ **resultando bien**
shapeless *adj.* with no definite shape: *she was wearing a shapeless green coat.* □ **sin forma definida**
shapely *adj.* with an attractive shape: *shapely legs.* □ **bien proporcionado**
share ['ʃɛə] *n.* **1** part which belongs to someone: *he has a share of the profits.* □ **parte**
2 *he wants me* ***to go shares with*** *him,* to split the cost/the profit, etc., with him. □ **...que vaya a medias con él**
3 contribution which each person makes: *I have done my share of hard work; has he paid his share?* □ **parte**
4 one of the parts into which a company's capital is divided: *he has bought 50% of the shares of the company; oil/gold shares,* shares in oil/gold companies. □ **acción**
■ *v.* **1** to divide up among several people: *we have to share the cake among six of us.* □ **compartir**
2 to allow someone to use something which you also use: *let the little girl share your toys; we share a bathroom with the flat next door.* □ **compartir**
3 to have something in common: *they share a liking for sticky cakes.* □ **compartir**
shareholder *n.* person who owns shares in a company. □ **accionista**
shareholding *n.* group of shares in a company owned by one person. □ **paquete de acciones**
shark [ʃɑ:k] *n.* **1** large dangerous fish which can kill a man. □ **tiburón**
2 (*informal*) crook/swindler. □ **tiburón (en la Bolsa); estafador**
sharp [ʃɑ:p] *adj.* **1** with a fine cutting edge: *be careful with that knife — it's very sharp; I don't like walking in my bare feet on these sharp stones.* □ **afilado**
2 very cutting/harsh: *a sharp frost; he wrote a very sharp letter to the income tax; she has a sharp tongue,* she often says cruel things. □ **fuerte helada; ...una carta contundente; ...lengua mordaz**
3 with a very acute angle: *a sharp corner; the car made a sharp turn.* □ **esquina cerrada; ...giro brusco**
4 bitter: *sharp apple.* □ **ácido**
5 clever/intelligent: *this little boy is very sharp.* □ **agudo**
6 with a highly developed sense: *the dog has very sharp hearing.* □ **fino**
7 high-pitched (sound): *a sharp cry.* □ **agudo**
8 (*in music*) (note) which is slightly higher than the correct pitch: *a sharp note on the piano.* □ **agudo**
9 clear: *the photograph is very sharp.* □ **nítido**
■ *n.* note in music which is a semitone higher: *F sharp.* □ **sostenido**
■ *adv.* **1** acutely: *the road turns sharp left.* □ **repentinamente**
2 exactly: *we will leave at ten o'clock sharp.* □ **justo**
3 (*in music*) higher than the correct pitch: *he always sings sharp.* □ **siempre da un agudo**

sharpen *v.* to make sharp: *to sharpen a pencil.* □ **afilar**
sharpener *n. pencil sharpener,* small instrument for sharpening pencils. □ **sacapuntas**
sharply *adv.* **1** acutely: *the road turns sharply to the left.* □ **bruscamente**
2 completely: *the party is sharply divided over its foreign policy.* □ **claramente**
3 harshly: *he answered her very sharply.* □ **abruptamente**
sharpness *n.* being sharp. □ **lo afilado**
sharp practice *n.* dishonest activity. □ **prácticas ilícitas**
sharpshooter *n.* soldier who is trained to shoot very accurately. □ **tirador de primera**
sharp-witted *adj.* clever. □ **listo**
shatter ['ʃætə] *v.* **1** to break into little pieces: *the stone shattered the windscreen.* □ **hacer añicos**
2 *he was shattered by the news,* overwhelmed/extremely upset. □ **quedó destrozado por...**
shave [ʃeiv] *n.* act of cutting off the hair on your face with a razor: *I haven't had a shave for two days.* □ **afeitado**
a close shave, a near miss: *that was a close shave – you missed the old lady by inches.* □ **de milagro, por los pelos**
■ *v.* **1** to cut off the hair on your face: *he cut himself while shaving.* □ **afeitar**
2 to slice off very thin pieces. □ **cortar en rodajas finas**
shaven *adj.* shaved. □ **afeitado**
clean-shaven, with no beard or moustache. □ **sin barba ni bigote**
shaver *n.* razor; machine for shaving: *an electric shaver.* □ **maquinilla de afeitar**
shaving *n.* **1** act of cutting off hair. □ **afeitado**
shaving cream, cream which you put on your face before shaving. □ **crema de afeitar**
2 ***shavings,*** small thin slices of wood made by a plane. □ **virutas**
shawl [ʃɔ:l] *n.* large square of warm material for wrapping round your shoulders/your head. □ **chal**
she [ʃi:] **1** *pron.* referring to a female person: *she's my sister; she and I went to the church together.* □ **ella**
2 *prefix meaning* female: *she-wolf.* □ **loba**
sheaf [ʃi:f] *n.* (*pl. sheaves*) bundle of corn/of papers. □ **gavilla (trigo); fajo (papeles)**
shear ['ʃiə] *v.* (*he has sheared/shorn*) to cut off: *to shear sheep,* cut the wool off sheep; *the plane sheared through the trees as it crashed.* □ **esquilar; rapar**
shearer *n.* person who cuts the wool off sheep. □ **esquilador**
shears *n.* cutting tool like large scissors: *a pair of shears.* □ **tijeras**
sheath [ʃi:θ] *n.* holder (for a knife, etc.). □ **funda**
sheath-knife, knife which is kept in a sheath attached to a belt. □ **cuchillo de funda**
sheathe [ʃi:ð] *v.* to put a knife back into its holder. □ **envainar**
sheaves [ʃi:vz] *n. see* **sheaf.**
shed [ʃed] *n.* wooden building to keep things in: *garden shed; bicycle shed.* □ **cobertizo**
customs shed, large hall where customs officials inspect cargo. □ **sala de aduana**
■ *v.* **1** to lose (leaves); to lose/to take off (clothes). □ **dejar caer (hojas); quitarse (ropa)**
2 to let flow: *no tears were shed when he left,* no one was upset; *the lamp shed a dim light in the corner of the room.* □ **verter; saltarse (lágrimas)**
3 ***to shed blood,*** to wound. □ **derramar**
4 *can you* ***shed*** *some* ***light on*** *the problem?,* can you help us solve the problem? □ **puedes arrojar luz...?**
sheen [ʃi:n] *n.* brilliant shining surface. □ **lustre**
sheep [ʃi:p] *n.* (*no pl.*) farm animal, reared for wool or for meat: *a flock of sheep; twenty sheep.* □ **oveja/ovejas**
sheep dip *n.* bath of disinfectant into which sheep are put to kill parasites. □ **baño desinfectante**
sheepdog *n.* type of dog specially trained for herding sheep. □ **perro pastor**
sheepish *adj.* ashamed/embarrassed. □ **vergonzoso**
sheepishly *adv.* with an embarrassed air. □ **tímidamente**
sheepskin *n.* the skin of a sheep with the wool attached: *a sheepskin coat; a sheepskin rug.* □ **piel vuelta; zamarra**
sheer ['ʃiə] *adj.* **1** complete/total: *it's sheer nonsense; it's a sheer waste of time.* □ **puro; mero**
2 very steep: *sheer cliffs.* □ **escarpado**
3 very thin: *sheer nylon tights.* □ **fino**
■ *adv.* straight up or down: *the cliff rose sheer above their heads.* □ **verticalmente**
■ *v.* to swerve to avoid something: *the ship came close to the quay and then sheered away.* □ **desviarse**
sheet [ʃi:t] *n.* **1** large piece of thin cloth which is put on a bed. □ **sábana**
2 large flat piece: *sheet of glass; sheet of metal; sheet of paper; if there isn't enough room for your answer write on the back of the sheet.* □ **plancha; chapa de metal; hoja de papel**
sheet lightning, lightning which appears as a sheet and not as a single flash. □ **fucilazo**
3 rope for attaching a sail. □ **escota**
sheet-anchor *n.* large anchor used if a ship is in difficulties. □ **ancla de la esperanza**
sheikh [ʃeik] *n.* Arab leader. □ **jeque**
sheikhdom ['ʃeikdəm] *n.* country ruled by a sheikh. □ **dominio de un jeque**
shelf [ʃelf] *n.* (*pl. shelves*) **1** plank attached to a wall/in a cupboard on which things can be put: *bookshelf; shelves in a bookcase; a shelf full of pots of jam.* □ **estante**
to be left on the shelf, to be left behind/forgotten about; not to get married (when all your friends are married). □ **quedarse para vestir santos**
shelf life, length of time a packet of food can be kept in a shop before it goes bad. □ **vida de un producto alimenticio**
2 a narrow ledge of rock. □ **cama de roca**
shell [ʃel] *n.* **1** hard outside of some animals: *the tortoise/the snail went back into its shell.* □ **concha**
2 hard outside of an egg/a nut. □ **cáscara**
3 shape/exterior of a building: *only the shell of the building was left after the fire.* □ **revestimiento**
4 metal tube full of explosive fired from a gun. □ **proyectil**
■ *v.* **1** to take (peas) out of their pods/(a hardboiled egg) out of its shell, etc. □ **desenvainar (guisantes); quitar la cáscara a**
2 to bombard with shells: *the town was shelled by the enemy.* □ **bombardear**
shellfish *n.* (*no pl.*) sea animal with a shell (such as a crab/mussel, etc.). □ **crustáceo**
shell out *v.* (*informal*) to pay money. □ **aflojar (la pasta)**
shellac ['ʃelæk] *n.* resin used to make varnish. □ **laca**
shelter ['ʃeltə] *n.* place where you can go for protection: *they took shelter from the rain in a doorway; keep your new bicycle under shelter.* □ **refugio**
bus shelter, small roofed construction to protect

people waiting at a bus stop. □ **marquesina del autobús**
bomb shelter, concrete construction underground where you can take shelter from air attack. □ **refugio**
■ *v.* to give (someone) protection; to take shelter: *the sheep sheltered close to the hedge; they sheltered from the storm.* □ **proteger; refugiarse**
sheltered *adj.* protected from wind/cold/unpleasant happenings: *a sheltered garden; they lead a very sheltered life.* □ **un jardín abrigado; llevan una vida muelle**
shelve [ʃelv] *v.* **1** to put off discussing a problem: *my request for more money has been shelved.* □ **dar carpetazo a**
2 to slope down: *the beach shelves gently.* □ **descender**
■ *n. pl. see* **shelf.**
shelving *n.* set of shelves. □ **estantería**
shepherd [ˈʃepəd] *n.* man who looks after sheep. □ **pastor**
shepherd's pie, minced meat cooked with mashed potatoes on top. □ **pastel de carne y puré de patatas**
■ *v.* to guide: *the teacher shepherded the group of children into the museum.* □ **guiar**
shepherdess *n.* woman who looks after sheep. □ **pastora**
sherbet [ˈʃɜːbət] *n.* **1** fizzy powder/fizzy drink. □ **gaseosa**
2 *Amer.* water ice. □ **sorbete**
sheriff [ˈʃerif] *n.* **1** *Amer.* county police officer. □ **'sheriff'**
2 (*in England*) ceremonial chief official in a county. □ **gobernador civil**
3 (*in Scotland*) chief judge of a district. □ **presidente del tribunal**
sherry [ˈʃeri] *n.* type of strong wine, originally from Spain. □ **jerez**
shield [ʃiːld] *n.* **1** large protective plate carried by riot police/knights in armour, etc. □ **escudo**
2 protection against something dangerous. □ **escudo, protección**
■ *v.* to protect: *she shielded her eyes against the sun.* □ **proteger**
shift [ʃift] *n.* **1** change of place/of direction: *a shift in the country's foreign policy; a shift in the wind direction.* □ **cambio**
2 group of workers who work for a period and whose place is then taken by another group: *shift work; they worked in shifts; he is on the night shift,* in the group which works at night. □ **turno; ...por turnos**
3 loose dress. □ **vestido suelto**
■ *v.* **1** to change position/direction; to move: *the wind has shifted; to shift the furniture around in a room; can you shift your car – it is blocking the entrance to my garage.* □ **cambiar; cambiar de sitio (coche)**
2 ***to shift for yourself,*** to look after yourself. □ **arreglárselas solo**
shiftiness *n.* dishonest look. □ **aspecto de falso**
shiftless *adj.* lazy. □ **holgazán**
shifty *adj.* looking dishonest: *he has shifty eyes.* □ **falso; no mira nunca a los ojos**
shilly-shally [ˈʃiliˈʃæli] *v.* to hesitate. □ **titubear**
shimmer [ˈʃimə] *v.* to quiver with light: *the water shimmered in the sunshine.* □ **rielar; relucir**
shin [ʃin] *n.* **1** front of the bottom part of your leg. □ **espinilla**
2 *shin of beef,* meat from the bottom part of the front legs of cattle. □ **jarrete/corvejón**
■ *v.* (*he shinned*) ***to shin up*** *a tree,* to climb up. □ **trepar**
shindy [ˈʃindi] *n.* (*informal*) row; noisy party. □ **ruido estrepitoso; fiesta a tope**
shine [ʃain] *n.* **1** brightness: *his boots have a brilliant shine; the shine in her eyes.* □ **brillo**
2 act of polishing: *you ought to give your shoes a shine.* □ **...sacar brillo a tus zapatos**
■ *v.* (*he shone*) **1** to glint brightly: *the sun was shining; her face shone with joy; he polished the table until it shone.* □ **brillar**
2 to be brilliant: *he doesn't shine in conversation.* □ **brillar**
3 to polish: *he was shining his boots.* □ **limpiar**
shining *adj.* brilliant: *a shining new coin; he is a shining example of a successful businessman.* □ **reluciente (moneda); notable (ejemplo)**
shiny *adj.* bright/polished: *a shiny table.* □ **brillante**
shingle [ʃiŋgl] *n.* **1** mass of small stones: *a shingle beach; the boats were pulled up on the shingle.* □ **guijarros**
2 flat piece of wood/asbestos nailed on a wall or roof as a covering. □ **ripia**
3 ***shingles,*** painful rash caused by an infectious disease related to chickenpox. □ **herpes**
shingly *adj.* covered with small stones. □ **guijarroso**
ship [ʃip] *n.* large boat for carrying goods/passengers: *to go on board ship; cargo ship; passenger ship; we went round the Mediterranean on a cargo ship; she's a fine ship.* □ **buque; barco**
■ *v.* (*he shipped*) **1** to put/to take on board a ship: *she is shipping wood for Italy; she shipped a lot of water in the storm.* □ **embarcar**
2 to send goods (by post, etc. not necessarily on a ship): *we are shipping the flowers by air; they will ship furniture to any part of the country for you.* □ **transportar por vía marítima**
shipbuilder *n.* person who builds ships. □ **ingeniero naval; constructor naval**
shipbuilding *n.* building of ships: *the shipbuilding industry.* □ **construcción naval**
shipmate *n.* sailor on the same ship as you. □ **compañero/camarada de a bordo**
shipment *n.* **1** sending: *the shipment of explosives by post is prohibited.* □ **envío**
2 quantity of goods shipped: *we are waiting for a shipment of wood from Norway.* □ **envío**
shipowner *n.* person who owns a ship. □ **armador; naviero**
shipper *n.* person who sends goods. □ **consignador; expedidor**
shipping *n.* **1** sending of goods. □ **envío por mar**
shipping company, which specializes in the sending of goods. □ **compañía naviera**
2 (group of) ships: *they attacked the enemy shipping.* □ **flota**
shipping lanes, tracks across the sea which are regularly used by ships. □ **rutas comerciales**
shipshape *adj.* neat/tidy. □ **en buen orden**
shipwreck *n.* wrecking of a ship. □ **naufragio**
shipwrecked *adj.* (person) involved in a shipwreck: *they were shipwrecked on a desert island; the shipwrecked sailors were rescued by a lifeboat.* □ **naufragado**
shipyard *n.* works where ships are built. □ **astillero**
shire [ˈʃaiə] *n.* county. □ **condado**
shire horse, large powerful horse used for farm work. □ **percherón**
shirk [ʃɜːk] *v.* to try not to do something/not to work. □ **eludir**

shirker *n.* person who avoids doing his work. □ **holgazán**
shirt [ʃɜːt] *n.* piece of light clothing worn on the top part of the body. □ **camisa**
keep your shirt on!, (*informal*) keep calm/don't lose your temper. □ **¡mantén la cabeza fría!**
shirtsleeves *n. he was in his shirtsleeves,* he was wearing no jacket. □ **en mangas de camisa**
shit [ʃit] *v.* (*vulgar*) **1** excreta/solid waste matter from the body. □ **mierda**
2 dirt. □ **porquería**
■ *v.* (*vulgar*) to pass solid waste matter from the body. □ **cagar**
shiver ['ʃivə] *n.* tremble (with cold/fear): *the howl of the wolves sent shivers up my spine.* □ **temblor, escalofrío**
■ *v.* **1** to tremble (with cold/fear/fever): *she was shivering after waiting half an hour for the bus.* □ **temblar**
2 to break into tiny pieces. □ **hacer añicos**
shivery *adj. to feel shivery,* to tremble (especially with fever). □ **tener escalofríos**
shoal [ʃoul] *n.* **1** (also *shoals*) bank of sand under the water. □ **banco de arena**
2 group of fish swimming about. □ **banco de peces**
shock [ʃɔk] *n.* **1** untidy mass of hair: *he has a shock of red hair.* □ **greñas**
2 sudden surprise: *it gave me a shock to see him there, because I thought he was dead.* □ **impresión**
3 mental/physical collapse (after a blow/a sudden surprise): *he was in a state of shock.* □ **shock**
4 *electric shock,* sudden painful passing of electric current through the body: *when she touched the cooker it gave her a shock.* □ **descarga**
electric shock treatment, medical treatment of mental illness using electric shocks. □ **electrochoque**
5 great blow: *the shock waves from an explosion.* □ **onda expansiva**
shock absorbers, part of a car/aircraft which reduces the effect of bumps. □ **amortiguadores**
■ *v.* to give (someone) a sudden (unpleasant) surprise: *she's easily shocked,* she is upset by rude/indecent things; *I was shocked to hear of his death.* □ **conmocionar**
shocking *adj.* upsetting/unpleasant. □ **horrible**
shockingly *adv.* in an unpleasant/upsetting way. □ **horriblemente**
shock-proof *adj.* (watch, etc.) which is not affected by shocks. □ **a prueba de choques**
shock troops *n.* soldiers specially trained to attack violently. □ **fuerzas de choque**
shod [ʃɔd] *adj.* wearing shoes. □ **calzado**
shoddy ['ʃɔdi] *adj.* **1** badly made: *shoddy goods.* □ **de mala calidad**
2 low/nasty: *he played a shoddy trick on the old woman.* □ **jugarreta**
shoddiness *n.* bad quality. □ **baja calidad**
shoe [ʃuː] *n.* **1** article of clothing which you wear on your feet both inside and outside the house, not covering your ankles: *he put his shoes on; take off your shoes.* □ **zapato**
2 *I'd hate **to be in his shoes**,* to be in his place/to be in the situation he is in. □ **...estar en su pellejo**
3 ring of metal nailed under a horse's hoof. □ **herradura**
4 *brake shoes,* curved metal blocks which tighten round a wheel. □ **zapatas**
■ *v. to shoe a horse,* to attach metal horseshoes to its hooves. □ **herrar**
shoehorn *n.* curved piece of plastic/metal which you put into the heel of a shoe to make it easier to put on. □ **calzador**
shoelace *n.* lace for tying up shoes. □ **cordón**
shoemaker *n.* person who makes and mends shoes. □ **zapatero**
shoestring *n. Amer.* lace for tying up shoes. □ **cordón**
on a shoestring, with only a little money: *he started his business on a shoestring.* □ **con cuatro (perras) gordas**
shone [ʃɔn] *v. see* **shine.**
shoo [ʃuː] *interjection meaning* go away (*used to frighten away birds, etc*). □ **¡fuera!**
■ *v. to shoo away,* to frighten away birds/small children etc.: *the teacher shooed the children out of the classroom.* □ **espantar (animales); mandar a otra parte (niños)**
shook [ʃuk] *v. see* **shake.**
shoot [ʃuːt] *n.* **1** new growth on a plant: *the branch has sent out three little shoots.* □ **brote**
2 slide for goods/rubbish, etc.: *a rubbish shoot.* □ **vertedero**
3 expedition to kill wild animals with guns. □ **partida de caza**
4 land where game can be shot. □ **coto**
5 *the whole shoot,* (*informal*) everything. □ **toda la pesca**
■ *v.* (*he shot*) **1** to fire a bullet from a gun/an arrow from a bow; to kill (someone/an animal) with a bullet or an arrow: *he shot three rabbits; the police shot blanks at the crowd of demonstrators.* □ **disparar; mató tres conejos**
2 to hunt with a gun: *we go shooting every weekend in the winter.* □ **ir de caza**
3 to rush/to go fast: *he shot up the stairs; our car shot ahead of the others.* □ **salir disparado**
to shoot the rapids, to race through rapids in a light boat. □ **salvar los rápidos**
4 to send out new growths: *the bulbs are shooting.* □ **brotar**
5 to kick a ball hard; to score (a goal). □ **chutar**
6 to make (a film): *the film was shot in Italy.* □ **rodar**
shoot down *v.* to make (an aircraft) crash by hitting it with a shell: *we shot down three enemy aircraft.* □ **derribar**
shooting *n.* action of shooting with a gun: *a shooting match.* □ **tiros; prueba de tiro al blanco**
shooting stick, walking stick with a handle which unfolds to make a seat. □ **bastón taburete**
■ *adj.* which goes very fast. □ **a toda velocidad**
shooting star, meteor/star which travels fast across the sky. □ **estrella fugaz**
shoot up *v.* to go up fast: *prices are shooting up; flames shot up into the sky.* □ **dispararse**
shop [ʃɔp] *n.* **1** place where you can buy goods: *grocer's shop; furniture shop; shop window.* □ **tienda**
shop assistant, person who serves in a shop. □ **dependiente**
2 *she left her clothes **all over the shop**,* (*informal*) scattered everywhere. □ **...por todas partes**
3 workshop/place where goods are made. □ **taller**
closed shop, works where all the workers have to belong to a single union. □ **coto cerrado**
to talk shop, to talk about your job/about your office. □ **hablar de asuntos profesionales**
■ *v.* (*he shopped*) **1** to buy things in a shop: *we have been shopping; they were shopping for Christmas presents.* □ **ir de compras**
to shop around, to go to various shops and compare prices before buying what you want. □ **comparar precios**
2 *to shop someone,* (*slang*) to report someone to the

police. □ **delatar a uno**
shopfloor *n.* working area in a factory: *the workers on the shopfloor.* □ **nave**
shopkeeper *n.* person who runs a shop. □ **tendero**
shoplifter *n.* person who steals things from a shop. □ **mechero**
shoplifting *n.* stealing from a shop. □ **ratería**
shopper *n.* person who buys goods from a shop. □ **comprador**
shopping *n.* **1** goods which you have bought in a shop: *they came back laden with shopping; put the shopping on the table.* □ **compra(s)**
2 action of buying things in a shop: *shopping basket.* □ **cesta de la compra**
shopping centre, group of shops specially built as a unit. □ **centro comercial**
shop-soiled *adj.* made dirty by being on display in a shop. □ **deteriorado**
shop steward *n.* elected union representative in a factory/office, etc. □ **enlace sindical**
shopwalker *n.* person who supervises a department in a shop. □ **jefe de sección**

shore [ʃɔː] *n.* **1** land at the edge of the sea or a lake; beach: *we walked along the shore; these plants are found on the shores of the Mediterranean.* □ **orilla**
2 prop/piece of wood used to hold up something which might fall down. □ **puntal**
■ *v.* to hold up (something) which might fall down: *to shore up a ceiling; troops were sent in to shore up the government.* □ **apuntalar**

shorn [ʃɔːn] *adj.* **1** cut off. □ **cortado de raíz**
2 *to be shorn of something,* to lack something. *see also* **shear.** □ **estar desprovisto de**

short [ʃɔːt] *adj.* **1** not long: *a short walk; a short piece of rope.* □ **corto**
2 *Co. is short for Company,* is the abbreviated form of Company; *his name is Robert, but he is called Bob for short.* □ **abreviatura**
3 not long in time/not lasting a long time: *a short conversation; a short time ago; he had a short sleep on the train.* □ **conversación breve; hace poco tiempo; durmió un rato...**
4 not tall: *he is shorter than his brother.* □ **bajo**
5 rude: *he was very short with the customer; he has a short temper,* he gets angry easily. □ **brusco**
6 not enough/not as much as is needed: *we are short of sugar; when we added up the money, we found we were $2 short,* we had $2 less than we should; *one of our forwards was sent off, so we had to play with one man short.* □ **escaso de; de menos**
short weight, not quite as much in weight as supposed: *he always gives short weight.* □ **peso insuficiente**
7 *if you can't afford to pay, you'll have* ***to go short,*** to do without. □ **...que pasarte sin ello**
8 *he is rather* ***short of breath,*** he is panting. □ **se ha quedado sin aliento**
9 light/crumbly (pastry). □ **quebradizo**
■ *n.* **1** short film. □ **cortometraje**
2 short circuit. **3** *pl.* ***shorts,*** trousers not going below the knee: *football shorts; you are not allowed into the restaurant in shorts.* □ **cortocircuito; pantalón corto**
■ *adv.* **1** abruptly: *to stop short.* □ **en seco**
2 not far enough: *to fall short of the target.* □ **corto**
3 *I don't know what we can do with these papers,* ***short of*** *burning them,* unless we burn them. □ **...a menos que los quememos**
■ *v.* to short-circuit/to make an electric current jump between two wires and so put the electrical system out of action. □ **poner en cortocircuito**
shortage *n.* lack: *a shortage of bread,* not enough bread; *a water shortage; there is no shortage of drink in their house.* □ **escasez**
shortbread *n.* thick sweet crumbly biscuit. □ **especie de torta**
shortcake *n.* **1** thick sweet crumbly biscuit. □ **especie de torta**
2 *Amer.* cake with fruit and cream. □ **torta de frutas**
short-circuit *n.* jump of electric current between two points, missing out part of the normal circuit. □ **cortocircuito**
■ *v.* **1** to make a short-circuit: *the car seems to be short-circuiting.* □ **hacer cortocircuito**
2 to get through difficulties by taking a short cut: *to short-circuit administrative delays.* □ **tomar un atajo**
shortcoming *n.* fault/defect: *he has many shortcomings.* □ **defecto**
short cut *n.* way which is shorter than usual; quicker way of reaching your destination: *there are no short cuts to becoming a doctor.* □ **atajo**
shorten *v.* to make shorter: *to shorten a piece of rope; the days are shortening.* □ **acortar**
shortening *n. Amer.* lard/cooking fat. □ **manteca**
shortfall *n.* amount which is missing to make up an expected total. □ **déficit**
shorthand *n.* way of writing fast by using a system of signs: *the secretary took the letters down in shorthand; he kept shorthand notes of the meeting.* □ **taquigrafía**
shorthand typist, typist who can take shorthand. □ **taquígrafo**
short-handed *adj.* with not enough workers: *we are rather short-handed today.* □ **falto de personal**
shorthorn *n.* type of cattle with short horns. □ **vaca (para carne) 'shorthorn'**
short list *n.* list of some of the people who have applied for a job, and who have been chosen to come for an interview. □ **preseleccionados**
short-list *v.* to make a short list of candidates for a job; to put someone's name on a short list: *I've been short-listed for the job.* □ **preseleccionar**
shortlived *adj.* which does not last long: *shortlived pleasure; his happiness was shortlived.* □ **efímero**
shortly *adv.* **1** soon: *we will be leaving shortly.* □ **en breve**
2 abruptly/rudely: *he answered very shortly.* □ **secamente**
shortness *n.* **1** state of being short: *shortness of breath; shortness of a journey.* □ **cortedad; falta de aliento; poca duración de un viaje**
2 rudeness. □ **sequedad**
short order *n. Amer.* order given for something to be cooked on the spot (such as ham and eggs). □ **plato rápido**
short-sighted *adj.* **1** (person) who only can see clearly things that are near. □ **miope**
2 not paying attention to what may happen in the future: *it is very short-sighted of you not to save any money.* □ **es muy imprudente por tu parte...**
short-sightedness *n.* **1** only seeing clearly objects which are near. □ **miopía**
2 not paying attention to what may happen in the future. □ **falta de previsión**
short-sleeved *adj.* (shirt, etc.) with short sleeves. □ **de manga corta**
short-staffed *adj.* with not enough workers: *we are rather shortstaffed at the moment, so service is slow.* □ **falto de personal**
short-tempered *adj.* (person) who easily gets angry. □ **de genio vivo**

short-term *adj.* not lasting long: *a short-term improvement in the financial situation; a short-term loan.* □ **a corto plazo**
short time *n.* shorter working hours than usual: *the factory was put on short time because of lack of spare parts.* □ **jornada reducida**
short wave *n.* radio wave about 50 metres long: *a short wave transmitter.* □ **onda corta**
shot [ʃɔt] *adj.* (silk) which changes colour according to the light. □ **tornasolado**
■ *n.* **1** (*no pl.*) small pellets/bullets fired from a gun: *he was peppered with shot.* □ **perdigones/balas**
2 large heavy ball thrown in a competition. □ **peso**
to put the shot, throw the weight in a competition. □ **lanzamiento de peso**
3 act of shooting; the sound of shooting: *the police fired two shots; I heard a shot.* □ **disparo**
4 *he answered my letter **like a shot,*** very rapidly. □ **de inmediato**
5 person who shoots: *he's a first-class shot.* □ **tirador**
6 attempt: *let me have a shot at it,* let me try to do it. □ **intento; déjame probar suerte**
7 (*slang*) injection. □ **pico/chute (de heroína)**
8 (*slang*) small drink of alcohol. □ **copa/trago**
9 (*informal*) photograph. *see also* **shoot.** □ **foto**
shotgun *n.* gun which fires small pellets. □ **escopeta**
should [ʃud] *v. used to show certain moods.* **1** ought: she did not like chocolate; I shouldn't say anything. □ **;...no debería decir nada**
2 must: *why should I be the one to go?,* why must I be the one? □ **¿por qué debo ser yo...?**
3 *who should we meet but my aunt,* what a surprise we had when we met my aunt; *what should happen but he fell of the chair,* what a surprise that he then fell off the chair. □ **con quién íbamos a encontrarnos sino con mi tía; qué sorprendente que se cayera de...**
4 (tentative suggestion): *should I try telephoning again?* □ **¿lo intento de nuevo?**
5 (future after ***that***): *it is strange that he should want to go to France; I suggest that we should ask the Mayor to attend.* **...que quisiera ir a Francia; sugiero que le pidamos al...**
shoulder ['ʃouldə] *n.* **1** part of the body at the top of the arm/between the top of the arm and the neck: *the policeman tapped him on the shoulder; he carried his spade over his shoulder.* □ **hombro**
2 part of a piece of clothing between the top of the arm and the neck: *a coat with wide shoulders.* □ **hombro**
3 top part of the front leg of a sheep: *a shoulder of lamb.* □ **paletilla**
4 ***hard shoulder,*** reinforced side part of a road: *parking is not allowed on the hard shoulder of a motorway.* □ **arcén**
■ *v.* **1** to put on your shoulder: *the soldiers shouldered their rifles.* □ **echar al hombro**
2 *he shouldered the extra responsibility,* he took on the responsibility. □ **cargó con...**
3 to push with your shoulder: *he shouldered his way through the crowd.* □ **abrirse paso con los hombros**
shoulder bag *n.* bag which can be carried over the shoulder. □ **bolso de bandolera**
shoulderblade *n.* large flat bone in the shoulder. □ **omóplato**
shout [ʃaut] *n.* loud cry: *the announcement was greeted with shouts of joy.* □ **grito**
■ *v.* to make a loud cry: *they shouted for help; he shouted himself hoarse,* shouted so loudly that he became hoarse. □ **gritar**
to shout someone down, to shout so loudly that someone cannot speak. □ **callar a voces**
shouting *n.* loud cries: *shouting broke out at the back of the hall.* □ **gritos**
shove [ʃʌv] *n.* (*informal*) sharp push: *give it a shove.* □ **empujón**
■ *v.* (*informal*) to give a push: *I had to shove the boxes out of the way; just shove it in the oven,* just put it in. □ **dar empujones**
shovel ['ʃʌvl] *n.* wide spade. □ **pala**
mechanical shovel, type of tractor with a wide scoop on the front used for picking up and lifting. □ **excavadora**
■ *v.* (*he shovelled*) to lift up with a shovel: *they were shovelling sand into the lorry.* □ **echar con la pala**
shovelful *n.* contents of a shovel: *just one shovelful of sand.* □ **palada**
show [ʃou] *n.* **1** exhibition/display: *flower show; fashion show; agricultural show.* □ **exposición**
show house, house which is built to show what similar houses can look like. □ **casa/piso piloto**
2 performance. □ **actuación**
show business, actors/actresses/producers, etc. (considered as a group); the entertainment world. **mundo del espectáculo**
3 pretence: *he made a show of friendship,* he pretended he was a friend. □ **alarde**
4 (*informal*) affair/business: *he is trying to run the whole show single-handed.* □ **cotarro**
■ *v.* (*he has shown*) **1** to make (something) seen; to allow someone to see (something); to be seen: *let me show you my stamp collection; your wallet is showing out of your pocket; I am showing my roses at the flower show.* □ **enseñar; mostrar**
2 to indicate: *my watch shows the date as well as the time; the firm is showing a profit.* □ **indicar**
3 to point out/to direct: *could you show me the way to the station? he showed me how the engine worked; the guide showed us round the castle.* □ **indicar (camino); enseñar (motor); llevar por (castillo)**
4 to prove/to demonstrate: *it just shows that I was right; his car is beginning to show its age,* to prove how old it is. □ **demostrar**
showcase *n.* cupboard with a glass front/box with a glass top for putting things on show in a shop or museum. □ **vitrina**
showdown *n.* final argument which will solve a crisis. □ **momento decisivo**
showiness *n.* being showy/being too bright. □ **ostentación**
show-jumper *n.* horse which is specially trained for show-jumping. □ **caballo de saltos**
show-jumping *n.* riding competition where horses have to jump over different obstacles in a short time. □ **concurso hípico**
showman *n.* (*pl. showmen*) person who puts on shows (such as circuses, etc.). □ **empresario de espectáculos**
showmanship *n.* art of putting on attractive shows. □ **talento organizativo**
show off *v.* **1** to display (something) to great effect. □ **hacer gala de**
2 to try to make people look at you by doing something which will attract their attention: *she is always showing off at parties.* □ **presumir**
show-off *n.* (*informal*) person who tries to attract people's attention. □ **fardón; fantasmón**
showpiece *n.* important item in an exhibition. □ **obra maestra**
showroom *n.* room where goods are shown to customers. □ **sala de exposición**
show up *v.* **1** to reveal/to show someone's/some-

thing's faults: *their beautiful house shows ours up.* □ **poner en evidencia (los defectos)**
2 to stand out: *the picture shows up very well against the dark wall.* □ **destacar**
3 (*informal*) to arrive: *we had invited six people but none of them showed up.* □ **aparecer**
showy *adj.* too bright (colours); too ostentatious. □ **llamativo**
shower ['ʃauə] *n.* **1** light fall of rain/small stones, etc.: *in April we often have showers; a shower of leaves fell to the ground.* □ **chaparrón**
2 spray device in a bathroom for washing your whole body: *we have fixed up a shower over the bath.* □ **ducha**
3 bath taken in a spray of water from above: *after the football match we had a shower.* □ **ducha**
4 *Amer.* party where presents are given to a girl about to get married. □ **fiesta de regalos**
■ *v.* **1** to pour/to fall in a quantity: *the speaker was showered with questions.* □ **le llovieron**
2 to wash under a spray. □ **lavar**
shower bath *n.* **1** spray device in a bathroom for washing your whole body. □ **ducha**
2 bath taken in a spray of water. □ **ducha**
showerproof *adj.* (raincoat) which can protect against light rain. □ **impermeable**
shower room *n.* room with a shower bath in it. □ **ducha**
showery *adj.* with many showers: *showery weather.* □ **lluvioso**
shrank [ʃræŋk] *v. see* **shrink.**
shrapnel ['ʃræpnl] *n.* (*no pl.*) pieces of metal from an exploded shell or bomb, etc.: *a piece of shrapnel.* □ **metralla**
shred [ʃred] *n.* **1** long strip torn off something: *her skirt was torn to shreds on the barbed wire.* □ **jirón**
2 small piece: *there isn't a shred of evidence against him.* □ **trozo; no hay ni chispa de verdad...**
■ *v.* (*he shredded*) to tear into long strips; to cut into very thin strips: *to shred paper; shredded carrots.* □ **hacer trizas**
shredder *n.* machine for tearing waste paper into long strips; device for cutting vegetables into long thin strips. □ **trituradora**
shrew [ʃru:] *n.* **1** type of animal like a mouse with a long nose. □ **musaraña**
2 unpleasant bad-tempered woman who is always criticizing. □ **arpía; fiera**
shrewish *adj.* bad-tempered (woman). □ **regañona**
shrewd [ʃru:d] *adj.* clever/wise: *a shrewd businessman.* □ **sagaz**
2 *I've got a shrewd idea that,* I believe (and I am quite likely to be right) that. □ **se me ocurre que...**
shrewdly *adv.* wisely. □ **sagazmente**
shrewdness *n.* cleverness/wisdom. □ **sagacidad**
shriek [ʃri:k] *n.* loud high-pitched cry: *shrieks of laughter.* □ **chillido**
■ *v.* to make a loud high-pitched cry: *the girls ran shrieking out of the room as the two men started fighting; they were shrieking with laughter.* □ **chillar**
shrill [ʃril] *adj.* high-pitched: *a shrill whistle.* □ **agudo; estridente**
shrimp [ʃrimp] *n.* small shellfish with a long tail. □ **camarón**
shrimping *n.* fishing for shrimps: *to go shrimping; a shrimping net.* □ **ir a pescar camarones**
shrine [ʃrain] *n.* tomb/chapel where a saint is buried. □ **sepulcro, santuario**
shrink [ʃriŋk] *v.* (*he shrank; he has shrunk*) **1** to make/to get smaller: *my pullover has shrunk in the wash; our savings have shrunk away to nothing.* □ **encoger**
2 to move back. □ **echarse atrás**
to shrink from doing something, to be unwilling to do something. □ **ser reacio a hacer algo**
shrinkage *n.* action of becoming smaller; amount by which something becomes smaller: *you must make the pullover too big to allow for shrinkage when it is washed.* □ **encogimiento**
shrivel ['ʃrivl] *v.* (*it shrivelled*) to make/to become dry and wrinkled: *the heat has shrivelled the leaves; these apples have shrivelled up,* become wrinkled. □ **arrugar(se)**
shroud [ʃraud] *n.* **1** long cloth covering a dead body. □ **mortaja**
2 ***shrouds,*** ropes from a mast to the sides of a ship. □ **obenques**
■ *v.* to cover up: *the whole affair is shrouded in mystery; mist shrouded the mountain tops.* □ **envolver**
Shrove Tuesday ['ʃrouv'tju:zdei] *n.* the Tuesday before Lent. □ **martes de carnaval**
shrub [ʃrʌb] *n.* small bush. □ **arbusto**
shrubbery *n.* part of a garden planted with shrubs. □ **plantío de arbustos**
shrug [ʃrʌg] *n.* raising the shoulders to show you are not interested: *he gave a shrug of his shoulders and walked away.* □ **encogimiento de hombros**
■ *v.* (*he shrugged*) ***to shrug your shoulders,*** to raise your shoulders to show you are not interested. □ **encogerse de hombros**
shrug off *v.* to treat (something) as if it is not a cause of worry. □ **no dejarse impresionar**
shrunk [ʃrʌŋk] *v. see* **shrink.**
shrunken ['ʃrʌŋkən] *adj.* wrinkled; dried up: *shrunken features.* □ **apergaminado**
shudder ['ʃʌdə] *n.* big tremble of horror: *a shudder ran through her body.* □ **estremecimiento**
■ *v.* to tremble violently with horror. □ **estremecerse**
shuffle ['ʃʌfl] *v.* **1** to walk dragging your feet: *he shuffled up to the door; the queue shuffled slowly along the pavement.* □ **arrastrar los pies**
2 to mix (playing cards). □ **barajar**
shun [ʃʌn] *v.* (*he shunned*) to avoid: *he shuns other people.* □ **evitar**
shunt [ʃʌnt] *v.* to move (a train) into a siding; to move (someone) backwards and forwards. □ **cambiar de vía; mandar a uno de acá para allá**
shunting yard *n.* area of railway lines where wagons are kept/sorted into trains. □ **estación de maniobras**
shush [ʃuʃ] (*informal*) *interjection meaning* be quiet. □ **¡chitón!**
shut [ʃʌt] *v.* (*he shut; he has shut*) **1** to close: *can you shut the window? shut your eyes; he must learn to keep his mouth shut,* not to tell secrets. □ **cerrar**
2 to lock up (something) so that it cannot escape: *they shut the bull in the farm yard.* □ **encerrar**
3 to close for business: *the shops are shut on Sundays; the pubs shut at 3 o'clock.* □ **cerrar**
shut down *v.* to make (a factory) stop working: *the strike shut down the steel works.* □ **cerrar**
shutdown *n.* closure of a factory. □ **cierre**
shuteye *n.* (*informal*) sleep: *let's have a bit of shuteye.* □ **sueñecito**
shut in *v.* to lock inside; to surround: *the garden is shut in by high walls.* □ **cercar**
shut off *v.* to switch off (an engine/the water supply, etc.). □ **parar (motor); cortar (agua)**
shut out *v.* **1** to block: *the trees shut out the view.* □ **impedir ver**

2 to lock (someone) outside: *he was shut out when the door banged.* □ **negar la entrada**

shutter *n.* **1** folding wooden/metal cover which covers a window: *the shutters are closed.* □ **contraventana**

2 (*in camera*) part which opens and closes very rapidly to allow the light to go on to the film. □ **obturador**

shut up *v.* **1** to close: *to shut up shop,* to close a shop for business completely. □ **cerrar**

2 (*informal*) to be quiet; to make (someone) be quiet: *shut up! I can't hear the music; can't someone shut that dog up?* □ **callar**

shuttle ['ʃʌtl] *n.* part of a loom which carries the thread from side to side between the vertical threads. □ **lanzadera**

shuttle diplomacy, in which a leader goes backwards and forwards from one country to another to try to reach agreement. □ **giras diplomáticas**

shuttle service, bus/aircraft, etc., which goes backwards and forwards between two places. □ **servicio regular (entre dos puntos)**

■ *v.* to go backwards and forwards; to send (someone) backwards and forwards: *he was shuttled from one doctor to another.* □ **ir de acá para allá**

shuttlecock *n.* small light object with feathers stuck in it, which is hit in badminton. □ **volante**

shy [ʃai] *adj.* timid/afraid to do something: *he's hiding behind the door because he's shy.* □ **tímido**

to fight shy of doing something, to prefer not to do something. □ **procurar evitar**

■ *n.* throwing (of a ball). □ **tiro/pase**

coconut shy, game at fairs where you try to knock down a coconut with a hard ball. □ **tiro al blanco (con pelotas)**

■ *v.* **1** to throw: *the boys were shying stones at the windows.* □ **tirar**

2 to jump with fear: *the horse shied and threw off the rider.* □ **espantarse**

shyly *adv.* timidly: *she shyly offered a bunch of flowers to the teacher.* □ **tímidamente**

shyness *n.* being timid. □ **timidez**

sick [sik] *adj.* **1** ill/not well: *she's sick in bed.* □ **enfermo**

sick leave, time off work because of illness. □ **baja por enfermedad**

2 vomiting; feeling ready to vomit: *he ate too many cakes and felt sick; she was sick all over the car,* she vomited. □ **con ganas de vomitar**

3 showing disgust/dislike: *I'm sick of hearing complaints all day long; I'm sick and tired of having to look after all these children.* □ **estar harto de**

sickbay *n.* **1** hospital ward (on a ship). □ **enfermería**

2 small hospital attached to a factory/school, etc. □ **enfermería**

sicken *v.* to become ill. □ **ponerse enfermo**

sickening *adj.* which makes you sick: *his head hit the wall with a sickening thud.* □ **nauseabundo**

sickly *adj.* **1** not well; weak: *sickly child/plant.* □ **enfermizo**

2 *he gave a sickly smile,* a weak smile. □ **...sonrisa forzada**

sickness *n.* **1** illness: *there is a lot of sickness about at this time of year.* □ **enfermedad**

sickness benefit, payment made by the government to someone who is ill and cannot work. □ **subsidio de enfermedad**

2 feeling of vomiting. □ **ganas de vomitar**

air sickness/car sickness, feeling of nausea felt in an aircraft/car. □ **mareo**

sick pay *n.* wages paid to someone who is ill and cannot work. □ **subsidio de enfermedad**

sickle ['sikl] *n.* tool with a semi-circular blade, used for cutting corn. □ **hoz**

side [said] *n.* **1** edge; area near the edge: *on the side of the road; the north side of the field; he jumped over the stream to get to the other side.* □ **lado**

2 one of four parts which (with the top and bottom) make a box; wall (of a house): *tip the box on its side; the house has a garden on one side only.* □ **lado**

3 part of the body between the hips and the shoulder. □ **costado**

4 *he stood by my side,* next to me. □ **...a mi lado**

5 *they stood **side by side**,* next to each other. □ **...uno al lado del otro**

6 surface: *only write on one side of the piece of paper; he put the tablecloth on the table with the wrong side up.* □ **cara (de la hoja); lado (del mantel)**

the other side of the picture, the opposite story. □ **la otra cara de...**

7 slope (of a mountain); surface/part: *his house is on the side of the hill; we live on the sunny side of the street,* the part of the street which gets the most sun. □ **ladera; acera**

8 *always **look on the bright side of things**,* always take an optimistic view. □ **...en el lado bonito...**

9 team: *the English side has been chosen for the international match.* □ **equipo**

10 group holding a particular point of view: *I am on the side of the small businessman; whose side are you on?* □ **lado**

to take sides: *they took sides,* they decided to support one party or another in a quarrel. □ **tomaron partido por**

11 family connection: *he is Welsh on his mother's side,* his mother's family is Welsh. □ **...por parte de su madre**

■ *adj.* **1** secondary/less important: *a side road.* □ **secundario**

2 at the side (not the front or back): *side entrance/side door.* □ **lateral; accesorio**

■ *v.* ***to side with someone,*** to support someone in an argument. □ **tomar partido por uno**

sideboard *n.* **1** piece of dining room furniture for holding plates, a type of table with a cupboard beneath. □ **aparador**

2 ***sideboards,*** whiskers down the side of your face. □ **patillas**

sideburns *n. Amer.* whiskers down the side of your face. □ **patillas**

sidecar *n.* small seating compartment for one passenger attached to the side of a motorcycle. □ **sidecar**

side effects *n.* secondary and unexpected effects (of a drug). □ **efectos secundarios**

sidelight *n.* **1** unusual information: *this diary throws some sidelights on life in seventeenth century Scotland.* □ **información inusual**

2 small light on the front of a car: *he drove with only his sidelights on.* □ **luz de posición**

sideline *n.* **1** business which is extra to your normal work: *he is a bank manager but he sells antiques as a sideline.* □ **actividad suplementaria**

2 *pl.* ***sidelines,*** lines at the edge of a football pitch, etc. □ **líneas de banda**

to sit on the sidelines, not to take part in something. □ **ver los toros desde la barrera**

sidelong *adj.* from one side: *a sidelong glance.* □ **de soslayo**

sideshow *n.* small show/stall with a game of skill (at a fair, etc.). □ **caseta**

sidestep *v.* (*he sidestepped*) to avoid: *he is expert at sidestepping difficult questions.* □ **esquivar**
sidetrack *v.* to get someone's attention away from the main problem: *he was going to talk about money but got sidetracked.* □ **apartarse del asunto principal**
sidewalk *n. Amer.* pavement, path at the side of a road where pedestrians can walk. □ **acera**
sideways *adv.* to the side; with the side in front: *crabs walk sideways; if you look at him sideways you will see just how thin he is.* □ **de lado**
siding *n.* minor railway line where trains are kept until needed. □ **vía muerta**
sidle ['saidl] *v.* to walk sideways, not directly forwards: *he sidled up to me and asked for money.* □ **acercarse furtivamente**
siege [si:dʒ] *n.* act of surrounding an enemy town with an army to make it surrender: *to lay siege to a town.* □ **sitio; cerco**
sienna [si'enə] *n.* ***burnt sienna,*** reddish-brown colour. □ **siena**
raw sienna, yellowish-brown colour. □ **siena crudo**
siesta [si'estə] *n.* afternoon rest: *don't disturb mother, she's having a siesta.* □ **siesta**
sieve [siv] *n.* kitchen utensil with very small holes for passing liquid through to hold back lumps/for sorting out large pieces in a powder. □ **colador**
■ *v.* to pass (a liquid/a powder) through a sieve to sort out large lumps: *to sieve flour.* □ **colar (líquido); cerner (polvo)**
sift [sift] *v.* **1** to put through a sieve: *sift the flour before making pastry.* □ **cerner**
2 to examine carefully: *the police sifted through masses of evidence.* □ **escudriñar**
sifter *n.* container with small holes in the lid for sprinkling sugar or flour. □ **cernedor**
sigh [sai] *n.* deep breath, showing sadness/relief, etc.: *she heaved a sigh of relief.* □ **suspiro**
■ *v.* to breathe deeply showing sadness, relief, etc.: *she sighed when her mother told her she must stay indoors.* □ **suspirar**
sight [sait] *n.* **1** one of the five senses, the ability to see: *my father has lost his sight.* □ **vista**
2 glimpse: *to catch sight of someone; I cannot bear the sight of worms.* □ **divisar a alguien; ...la visión de gusanos**
to shoot at sight, as soon as you see the target. □ **disparar a la primera de cambio**
love at first sight, when two people meet for the first time and fall in love. □ **un flechazo**
3 range of vision: *the mountains came into sight; they waved until the ship was out of sight.* □ **las montañas...a la vista; el barco...fuera de nuestra vista**
4 spectacle; something you ought to see: *he went round the town to see the sights; the derelict houses are a sad sight.* □ **vista**
5 something funny/odd: *you look a sight in that strange hat.* □ **raro**
6 part of a gun through which you look to take aim. □ **mira/alza**
7 ***a sight more,*** (*informal*) a lot more: *it's a sight more useful than sitting at home doing nothing.* □ **mucho más**
■ *v.* **1** to see for the first time: *we sighted land on January 2nd.* □ **divisar**
2 to aim a gun. □ **apuntar**
sightless *adj.* blind. □ **ciego**
sightseeing *n.* visiting the sights of a town: *a sightseeing tour; we are going sightseeing.* □ **visita de puntos de interés**
sightseer *n.* tourist/person seeing the sights. □ **turista, excursionista**
sign [sain] *n.* **1** movement (of hand/head, etc.) which means something: *he made a sign with his hand and everyone stopped talking.* □ **seña**
2 mark: *plus sign* (+); *take-away sign* (−). □ **signo**
3 indication/something which suggests that something may happen: *is there any sign of the snow stopping? I take that remark as a sign that he's pleased.* □ **indicio**
4 trace/marks: *there is no sign of any car having been this way.* □ **marca**
5 advertising board; panel showing the name of a shop; panel showing directions on a road: *pub sign; neon sign; go to the first roundabout and follow the signs marked 'town centre'.* □ **cartel; letrero**
6 *the signs of the Zodiac,* twelve astrological symbols referring to different stars/to different parts of the year. □ **los signos del...**
■ *v.* **1** to write your signature at the end of a letter or on a document, etc.: *I forgot to sign the cheque.* □ **firmar**
2 to make a movement which has a meaning: *he signed to us to come.* □ **hacer una seña**
signboard *n.* panel with a sign. □ **cartel**
sign off *v.* to end a radio broadcast. □ **acabar el programa**
sign on *v.* to join the armed services for a period; to start work: *he has signed on for seven years; my boy has signed on at the factory.* □ **alistarse (ejército); firmar un contrato, entrar**
signpost *n.* post with a sign showing directions to a place. □ **señal de tráfico**
■ *v.* to indicate a direction with signs: *the road is badly signposted.* □ **señalizar**
sign up *v.* **1** to join the armed services for a period: *he signed up for seven years.* □ **alistarse**
2 *he was signed up by the football club,* he signed a contract to play only for them. □ **fichó por...**
signal ['signl] *n.* **1** movement of the hand/head, etc., which tells someone to do something: *they gave the signal for the competitors to start.* □ **señal**
2 lights/mechanical flags, etc., used to tell someone to do something: *the signal was against us, so the train stopped,* it told us to stop. □ **señal**
traffic signals, coloured lights which regulate the flow of traffic in a road. □ **semáforos**
3 sound heard on a radio receiver: *the signal is weak.* □ **señal**
■ *adj.* remarkable: *a signal success; a signal failure.* □ **notable**
■ *v.* (*he signalled*) to make signs to tell someone to do something: *the policeman signalled to the driver to stop; she didn't signal that she was turning right,* she did not use her indicator to show that she was turning. □ **hacer una señal; indicar**
signal box *n.* building by the side of the railway where the signalman controls the signals. □ **garita de señales**
signally *adv.* remarkably: *he has been signally unsuccessful.* □ **notablemente**
signalman *n.* (*pl. signalmen*) person who controls railway signals. □ **guardagujas**
signature ['signətʃə] *n.* **1** name which has been signed: *I can't make out the signature at the end of the letter.* □ **firma**
2 group of pages of a book (usually 32 or 64) which are folded out of one sheet of paper. □ **pliego**
3 ***signature tune,*** tune which is used regularly at the beginning or end of a broadcast to identify the broadcast. □ **sintonía**
signet ['signit] *n.* seal (for sealing with wax). □ **sello**
signet ring, ring worn on the little finger with a de-

sign carved on to it to use as a seal. □ **anillo de sello**

signify ['signifai] *v.* **1** to mean: *it doesn't signify that they accept.* □ **significar**
2 to show: *they signified their pleasure by applauding.* □ **mostrar**
that signifies, that makes sense. □ **eso cuadra**
3 to be of importance: *it does not signify much.* □ **tener importancia**
significance *n.* **1** meaning. □ **significado**
2 importance: *I don't attach much significance to the colour of the ink he uses.* □ **importancia**
significant *adj.* which is important/which has a lot of meaning: *a significant proportion of the voters refused to vote; I think it is particularly significant that he didn't go to his son's wedding.* □ **significativo**
significantly *adv.* with a lot of meaning: *she smiled significantly as she opened the bedroom door.* □ **de modo significativo**

silage ['sailidʒ] *n.* green crops fermented in a silo and used to feed animals. □ **forraje ensilado**

silence ['sailəns] *n.* **1** lack of noise: *the crowd stood in silence for hours; it was impossible to get silence in the meeting; the chairman called for silence.* □ **silencio**
2 not saying anything: *she sat in silence for the whole meeting; his silence is assumed to mean that he disagrees.* □ **silencio**
■ *v.* **1** to make (someone) stop talking: *the government has methods of silencing its critics.* □ **hacer callar**
2 to stop (something) making a noise. □ **silenciar**
silencer *n.* **1** apparatus to stop the noise of the exhaust of a car. □ **silenciador**
2 apparatus attached to a gun to stop the noise of it being fired. □ **silenciador**
silent *adj.* quiet. □ **silencioso**
to keep silent, to say nothing: *he knew what was happening but kept silent.* □ **guardar silencio**
silently *adv.* making no noise: *the cat silently crossed the room.* □ **en silencio**

silhouette [silu:'et] *n.* black outline of someone's head in profile. □ **silueta**
■ *v.* to stand out in profile: *the trees were silhouetted against the evening sky.* □ **destacarse contra**

silica ['silikə] *n.* mineral compound of silicon. □ **sílice**
silica gel *n.* hard crystals used to keep things dry in humid conditions. □ **gel de sílice**

silicon ['silikən] *n.* (*chemical element*: Si) common element which is not a metal, and which is usually found in compounds. □ **silicio**
silicon chip, small piece of silicon used in transistors and very small electronic devices. □ **chip de silicio**

silicone ['silikoun] *n.* chemical substance used in making oils. □ **silicona**

silicosis [sili'kousis] *n.* disease of the lungs caused by breathing in dust. □ **silicosis**

silk [silk] *n.* **1** thread which is produced by a caterpillar; cloth woven from this thread: *a silk tie.* □ **seda**
2 ***to take silk,*** to be accepted as a leading barrister. □ **tomar la toga**
silken *adj.* soft and shiny: *silken hair.* □ **sedoso**
silkscreen printing *n.* printing by forcing colours through a taut piece of cloth. □ **serigrafía**
silkworm *n.* caterpillar which produces silk. □ **gusano de seda**
silky *adj.* soft and shiny: *silky fur.* □ **sedoso**

sill [sil] *n.* ledge beneath a window/a door. □ **alféizar**

silly ['sili] *adj.* stupid/idiotic: *what a silly question; that was a silly thing to do.* □ **tonto**
silliness *n.* being silly. □ **estupidez**

silo ['sailou] *n.* **1** large tower for storing grain/for storing green crops (as food for animals). □ **silo**
2 deep hole in the ground in which rockets are kept. □ **lanzador subterráneo**

silt [silt] *n.* fine mud washed down by a river. □ **cieno**
■ *v.* ***to silt up,*** to fill with silt: *the harbour is gradually silting up.* □ **enarenarse**

silver ['silvə] *n.* **1** (*chemical element*: Ag) precious white metal: *silver spoons; a silver teapot.* □ **plata**
2 *don't forget to polish the silver,* the silver cutlery. □ **...la plata**
3 ***silver wedding,*** anniversary of 25 years of marriage. □ **bodas de plata**
4 ***silver paper,*** sheet of thin shiny metal which looks like silver, used for wrapping food in. □ **papel de plata/estaño**
5 coins made of white metal: *instead of giving me notes, he gave me all the change in silver.* □ **suelto**
6 light shining colour like silver: *silver waves in the moonlight.* □ **de plata**
silver birch *n.* common northern tree with white bark. □ **abedul**
silverside *n.* good quality beef, cut from the back part of the animal. □ **carne del lomo alto**
silversmith *n.* craftsman who makes things in silver. □ **platero**
silverware *n.* (*no pl.*) articles made of silver. □ **vajilla de plata**
silvery *adj.* **1** shiny like silver: *the silvery light of the moon.* □ **plateado**
2 light ringing (sound): *a silvery laugh.* □ **argentino**

similar ['similə] *adj.* same/very alike: *he drives a similar car to mine.* □ **similar**
similarly *adv.* in the same way. □ **del mismo modo**
similarity *n.* sameness/likeness: *is there any similarity between him and his brother?* □ **similitud**

simile ['simili] *n.* comparison using 'like' or 'as' ('as small as a mouse'; 'don't stand there with your mouth open like a fish'). □ **símil**

simmer ['simə] *v.* **1** to boil gently: *the soup has to be simmered for two hours.* □ **cocer a fuego lento**
2 *revolt was simmering among the army officers,* was preparing. □ **...se estaba cociendo...**
3 ***to simmer down,*** to become calmer: *he was furious, but simmered down after a while.* □ **calmarse**

simper ['simpə] *v.* to make a silly affected smile. □ **sonreír afectadamente**

simple ['simpl] *adj.* **1** not complicated; not difficult; easy: *the answer is quite simple; a simple crossword puzzle.* □ **sencillo**
2 *he's a bit simple,* (*informal*) not very intelligent. □ **es un poco simple**
3 ***simple interest,*** interest calculated as a percentage per annum on the original sum without adding each year's interest to the capital. □ **interés simple**
4 plain/ordinary: *we're having just a simple meal; he's just a simple farmer.* □ **sencillo**
simpleton *n.* person who is not very intelligent. □ **simplón**
simplicity [sim'plisiti] *n.* state of being simple. □ **sencillez**
it's simplicity itself, it is extremely easy. □ **es de lo más sencillo**
simplification [simplifi'keiʃn] *n.* making simple. □ **simplificación**
simplify ['simplifai] *v.* to make (something) simple. □ **simplificar**
simply *adv.* **1** without complication: *he spoke simply and directly.* □ **sencillamente**

2 absolutely: *you simply must come to see our new house.* □ **terminantemente**
3 purely/only: *he did it simply to see if you would laugh.* □ **simplemente**
simulate ['simjuleit] *v.* **1** to pretend. □ **simular**
2 *simulated crash,* crash which has been arranged with models for testing purposes. □ **simulacro de accidente**
simulation [simju'leiʃn] *n.* pretence. □ **simulación**
simulator ['simjuleitə] *n.* machine which allows a learner to experience simulated conditions (as in a car/aircraft, etc.). □ **simulador**
simultaneous [siməl'teiniəs] *adj.* happening at the same time. □ **simultáneo**
simultaneously *adv.* at the same time. □ **simultáneamente**
sin [sin] *n.* wicked deed; action which goes against the rules of religion. □ **pecado**
to live in sin, to live together without being married. □ **vivir en el pecado**
■ *v.* (*he sinned*) to do something wicked/wrong. □ **pecar**
sinful *adj.* wicked (person/action). □ **pecaminoso**
sinner *n.* person who has done something wicked. □ **pecador**
since [sins] *adv.* from then onwards: *he was rude to my mother and she hasn't spoken to him since; she married a doctor and has been interested in medicine ever since.* □ **desde entonces**
■ *prep.* from a certain time: *he has been up since 7 o'clock; since when have you been working for the railway?* □ **desde**
■ *conj.* **1** from a certain time: *since he arrived things have gone from bad to worse.* □ **desde**
2 because: *I can't take him with me since he's ill.* □ **puesto que**
sincere [sin'siə] *adj.* very honest/open: *he's sincere in his promise to work better.* □ **sincero**
sincerely *adv.* really/truly: *he sincerely believes that the earth is flat.* □ **sinceramente**
yours sincerely, greeting written at the end of a letter. □ **le saluda atentamente**
sincerity [sin'seriti] *n.* honesty: *in all sincerity,* very sincerely. □ **sinceridad**
sine [sain] *n.* (*in mathematics*) ratio between the length of one of the shorter sides opposite an acute angle to that of the hypotenuse in a right-angled triangle. □ **seno**
sinecure ['sainikjuə] *n.* job for which you get paid but which does not involve much work. □ **sinecura; canonjía**
sinew ['sinju:] *n.* strong cord which joins a muscle to a bone. □ **tendón**
sinewy *adj.* very strong. □ **vigoroso**
sing [siŋ] *v.* (*he sang; he has sung*) **1** to make music with your mouth: *he sang as he worked; can you sing that song again?* □ **cantar**
2 *my ears are singing,* are buzzing. □ **me están zumbando los oídos**
singer *n.* person who sings. □ **cantante**
singsong *adj. singsong voice,* with a rising and falling tone; *he told the story in a singsong voice,* half singing. □ **cantarina**
■ *n.* singing party: *let's have a singsong round the piano.* □ **vamos a echar unas coplillas...**
singe [sindʒ] *v.* to burn slightly: *she singed her hair by bending over the gas stove.* □ **chamuscar**
single ['siŋgl] *adj.* **1** alone/one by itself: *it was raining hard and there wasn't a single bus in sight; I haven't seen a single newspaper for months.* □ **solo**
2 for one person: *single bed; single room.* □ **individual**
3 unmarried. □ **soltero**
4 *single ticket,* ticket for one journey. □ **billete de ida**
■ *n.* **1** tennis game played between two people: *the men's singles.* □ **individuales**
2 ticket for one journey: *I want a single to London.* □ **billete de ida**
3 (*in cricket*) one run. □ **golpe de un tanto**
4 small record of pop music with only one piece of music on each side. □ **single**
■ *v.* ***to single someone/something out,*** to select: *he was singled out by the judges.* □ **escoger**
singlebreasted *adj.* (coat) which does not fold over widely in the front to button. □ **recto; sin cruzar**
singledecker *n.* bus with only one deck. □ **autobús de un piso**
singlehanded *adj.* all by yourself: *she sailed round the world singlehanded.* □ **en solitario; sin ayuda**
singleness *n.* **1** being unmarried. □ **soltería**
2 *singleness of purpose,* having only one aim. □ **con un solo propósito**
singly *adv.* one by one. □ **uno a uno**
singlet ['siŋglət] *n.* man's (sleeveless) undergarment for the top part of the body. □ **camiseta**
singular ['siŋgjulə] *adj.* and *n.* referring to one person/thing: *singular noun; verb in the first person singular.* □ **singular**
■ *adj.* **1** odd/peculiar: *what a singular man!* □ **singular**
2 remarkable: *singular devotion to duty.* □ **singular**
singularity [siŋgju'læriti] *n.* oddness/peculiarity. □ **singularidad**
singularly *adv.* **1** strangely. □ **extrañamente**
2 particularly. □ **singularmente**
sinister ['sinistə] *adj.* looking evil; which promises evil: *a sinister occurrence.* □ **siniestro**
sink [siŋk] *n.* basin for washing in a kitchen. □ **fregadero**
to pour something down the sink, throw something liquid away. □ **...por el fregadero**
■ *v.* (*he sank; he has sunk*) **1** to go to the bottom of water/mud, etc.; to send to the bottom of water: *the boat sank in the middle of the river; he sank into the mud up to his knees; we sank three enemy submarines.* □ **hundir(se)**
2 to fix in the mind: *the real meaning of the letter is only just beginning to sink in,* to be realized; *I told him he had to work harder, but it just hasn't sunk in,* he doesn't realize it is important. □ **entenderse, incorporar**
3 to go down: *he sank into an armchair; she sank to the floor in a heap; the sun was sinking in the west.* □ **arrellanarse (sillón); doblarse (al suelo); ponerse (el sol)**
4 *his heart sank,* he became dispirited. □ **se le cayó el alma a los pies**
5 *the pound is sinking,* is going down in value. □ **...se está hundiendo**
6 to make (a well): *they sank a thirty metre well.* □ **perforar**
7 ***to sink your teeth into something,*** to bite. □ **meterle el diente a algo**
8 to invest: *to sink money into a business.* □ **meter dinero**
Sino- ['sainou] *prefix meaning* Chinese: *a Sino-British treaty.* □ **sino-**
sinuous ['sinjuəs] *adj.* winding. □ **sinuoso**
sinuosity [sinju'ɔsiti] *n.* **1** being sinuous. □ **sinuosidad**

2 bend (in a pipe or road). □ **codo (cañería); curva (carretera)**

sinus ['sainəs] *n.* hole in the bones of the head connected with the nose and air passages: *sinus trouble; sinus infection.* □ **seno**

sinusitis [sainə'saitis] *n.* infection of the sinuses. □ **sinusitis**

sip [sip] *n.* small quantity of liquid: *he took a sip of tea.* □ **sorbo**

■ *v.* (*he sipped*) to drink taking only a small quantity at a time: *she sipped her coffee because it was so hot.* □ **sorber**

siphon ['saifn] *n.* **1** device for making fizzy water: *a soda siphon.* □ **sifón**

2 bent tube to allow you to take liquid from one container to another placed at a lower level. □ **sifón**

■ *v.* **1** to remove (liquid) by using a siphon: *he siphoned off the petrol from the tank of my car.* □ **sacar con sifón**

2 to remove money from one source illegally: *funds were siphoned into the secretary's bank account.* □ **malversar**

sir [sə:] *n.* **1** respectful way of addressing a man (usually an older or more important man): *please sit down, sir; would you like to order your lunch, sir?* □ **señor**

2 title given to a knight or baronet (always used with the first name and sometimes with the surname as well): *Sir John Smith; please take a seat, Sir John.* □ **sir**

3 way of addressing a man in a formal letter: *Dear Sir.* □ **Muy señor mío:**

sire ['saiə] *n.* **1** male horse which is a father: *this foal's sire is our black stallion.* □ **semental**

2 ***Sire,*** way of addressing a king. □ **Majestad**

■ *v.* (*of a horse*) to be father of: *he has sired six foals.* □ **engendrar**

siren ['sairn] *n.* loud warning signal which wails. □ **sirena**

sirloin ['sə:lɔin] *n.* best cut of beef from the back of the animal. □ **solomillo**

sister ['sistə] *n.* **1** female child whose parents are the same as yours: *she's my sister.* □ **hermana**

2 senior nurse. □ **enfermera**

3 nun; title given to nuns: *Sister Josephine.* □ **hermana**

■ *adj.* similar/identical. □ **gemelo**

sister ship, ship of the same design. □ **barco gemelo**

sister-in-law *n.* (*pl. sisters-in-law*) wife of your brother; sister of your husband or wife. □ **cuñada**

sisterly *adj.* like a sister. □ **como una hermana**

sit [sit] *v.* (*he sat*) **1** to be seated; to rest in a seated position with your behind on a chair/on the ground, etc.: *she was sitting on the floor; he's sitting at the typewriter; the birds sat on the telephone lines.* □ **sentarse**

2 *to sit for your portrait,* to pose (not necessarily in a seated position). □ **posar**

3 *she sat her baby on the cushion,* made him sit. □ **sentó al niño...**

4 to be in session/to meet: *Parliament is sitting.* □ **celebrar una sesión**

5 to be a member of: *he sits in Parliament for the Oxford constituency; she sits on three committees.* □ **ser diputado/miembro**

6 *the hen is sitting,* is hatching her eggs. □ **...está empollando**

7 to take (an examination): *she failed and had to sit the examination again.* □ **presentarse**

sit back *v.* to be seated and lean backwards: *sit back and enjoy the film.* □ **recostarse**

sit down *v.* to take a seat: *the speaker ended his speech and the audience stayed sitting down; please sit down.* □ **sentarse**

sit-down *adj.* **1** ***sit-down meal,*** meal where you sit at a table. □ **comida a la mesa/sentados**

2 ***sit-down strike,*** strike where workers do not move from their place of work. □ **huelga de brazos caídos**

sit-in *n.* occupation of the place of work by workers/students, etc. □ **sentada**

sitter *n.* person who sits/poses for a painter. □ **modelo**

baby-sitter, person who looks after a child when its parents are out. □ **canguro**

sit tight *v.* to stay where you are/to refuse to move. □ **quedarse quieto**

sitting *n.* **1** act of sitting; session: *he ate three chickens at one sitting.* □ **de una sentada**

2 *first sitting for lunch,* the first group of people who can be accommodated in the restaurant. □ **primer turno...**

sitting-room *n.* room where you can relax in comfortable chairs. □ **cuarto de estar**

sit up *v.* **1** to straighten yourself on your chair. □ **ponerse derecho**

2 *this will make him sit up,* will surprise him. □ **...le va a sorprender**

3 to stay up/not to go to bed. □ **quedarse levantado**

site [sait] *n.* **1** place where a building/town is situated: *his house occupies a ten-acre site in the middle of the town; they selected a spectacular site for the new capital of the country; building site/demolition site,* place where a building is being constructed/being demolished. □ **solar (casa); emplazamiento (capital)**

2 place where an event took place: *the site of a battle.* □ **escenario; lugar**

■ *v.* to place (a building/town) on a particular piece of land. □ **situar**

situate ['sitjueit] *v.* to place: *the house is situated on the south side of the town.* □ **situar**

situation [sitju'eiʃn] *n.* **1** place where a building is: *the town hall has an impressive situation.* □ **ubicación**

2 state of affairs: *we're in rather an awkward situation; this has put him in an embarrassing situation; in the teaching situation,* when you are teaching; *we are in a no money situation,* we have no money. □ **situación**

3 job: *situations vacant,* list of vacancies in jobs. □ **ofertas de trabajo**

six [siks] number 6: *he is six* (*years old*); *come and see me at six* (*o'clock*). □ **seis**

at sixes and sevens, (*informal*) very disorganized; confused; undecided. □ **hecho un lío**

sixteen number 16: *she is sixteen* (*years old*); *the sixteen twenty train,* the train leaving at 16.20. □ **dieciséis**

the sixteen hundreds, the years between 1600 and 1699. □ **el siglo diecisiete**

sixteenth, 16th *adj.* referring to sixteen: *the sixteenth of August* (6th August). □ **decimosexto; el dieciséis de agosto**

the sixteenth century, period from 1500 to 1599. □ **el siglo dieciséis**

sixth, 6th *adj.* and *n.* referring to six: *the sixth of June* (*6th June*); *Edward the Sixth* (*Edward VI*); *a sixth of the pupils were ill.* □ **sexto**

the sixth century, period from 500 to 599. □ **el siglo sexto**

sixth form, top class in a secondary school. □ **COU**

sixtieth, 60th *adj.* referring to sixty. □ **sexagésimo**
sixty *adj.* and *n.* number 60. □ **sesenta**
in the sixties, (i) *she's in her sixties,* she is aged between 60 and 69. □ **tiene más de sesenta años**
(ii) between '60 and '70 in a century. □ **en la década de los sesenta**
size [saiz] *n.* **1** largeness of something: *one of our onions is the size of a tennis ball; he has a garage about the size of a normal house.* □ **tamaño**
2 measurements: *what's the size of the swimming pool? I take size 8 in shoes; what size shirts does he wear?* □ **dimensiones (piscina); yo calzo el número...; talla (camisa)**
3 type of pastelike glue. □ **cola**
■ *v.* ***to size someone up,*** to judge someone's capabilities. □ **hacerse un juicio de alguien**
sizeable *adj.* quite large. □ **considerable**
sizzle [sizl] *v.* **1** to make a hissing sound when frying: *the sausages were sizzling in the pan.* □ **chisporrotear**
2 *a sizzling shot into the goal,* one that went very fast. □ **un disparo fulminante...**
3 *a sizzling day,* a very hot day. □ **un día sofocante**
skate [skeit] *n.* **1** large flat fish with white flesh. □ **raya**
2 sharp blade worn under boots for sliding on ice: *he put on his skates.* □ **cuchillas**
■ *v.* **1** to slide on ice wearing skates: *we went skating on the pond; skating competition; skating rink.* □ **patinar sobre hielo**
2 ***to skate over/round something,*** not to mention something which could be embarrassing. □ **evitar hablar de**
skateboard *n.* board with two pairs of wheels which you stand on to glide about. □ **monopatín**
skater *n.* person who goes skating. □ **patinador**
skedaddle [ski'dædl] *v.* (*informal*) to go quickly. □ **salir pitando**
skein [skein] *n.* length of wool loosely wound round and round into a loop. □ **madeja**
skeleton ['skelitn] *n.* **1** bones inside a body: *medical students have to study the skeleton.* □ **esqueleto**
a skeleton in the cupboard, a secret that a family or person is trying to keep hidden. □ **vergüenza de la familia**
2 ***skeleton staff,*** few staff left to carry on essential work while the others are away. □ **plantilla mínima**
3 *the buses operated a* ***skeleton service*** *on Christmas Day,* minimal/basic service. □ **...servicios mínimos el día de...**
4 ***skeleton key,*** key which will fit any lock in a building. □ **llave maestra**
5 rough outline: *this is the skeleton of the plan.* □ **esbozo**
skeletal *adj.* like a skeleton. □ **esquelético**
skeptic ['skeptik] *n. Amer. see* **sceptic.** □ **escéptico**
sketch [sketʃ] *n.* **1** rough drawing: *he made a sketch to show what the house would look like.* □ **esbozo**
2 short amusing play. □ **'sketch'**
■ *v.* to make a rough drawing/a rough plan of: *he was sketching the castle; she sketched out the plan of the sales campaign.* □ **bosquejar**
sketch-book *n.* book of drawing paper for sketching. □ **bloc de apuntes**
sketching *n.* rough drawing. □ **apunte**
sketch-map *n.* roughly drawn map. □ **mapa esbozado**
sketchpad *n.* pad of paper for sketching. □ **bloc de apuntes**
sketchy *adj.* rough/incomplete: *he has only a sketchy knowledge of the history of London.* □ **superficial**
skewbald ['skju:bɔ:ld] *adj.* (horse) with patches of white with another colour, but not black. □ **pintado**
skewer ['skjuə] *n.* long thin metal rod for putting through pieces of meat when cooking. □ **pincho**
■ *v.* to stick a long metal rod through (something). □ **espetar**
ski [ski:] *n.* long flat narrow piece of wood, etc., which you attach under your boot for walking on snow. □ **esquí**
water skis, similar pieces of wood for gliding over water. □ **esquís acuáticos**
■ *v.* to travel on skis: *they skied down the mountain; to go skiing,* to travel on skis as a sport; *a skiing holiday.* □ **esquiar**
water skiing, sliding over water on skis as a sport. □ **esquí acuático**
skiboots *n. pl.* special boots for skiing. □ **botas de esquiar**
skier *n.* person travelling on skis. □ **esquiador**
ski jump *n.* slope with a sudden drop at the bottom to allow a skier to jump high in the air. □ **saltos de esquí**
ski lift *n.* device to take skiers to the top of a slope. □ **remonte**
skid [skid] *n.* **1** sliding sideways: *the car went into a skid and crashed.* □ **patinazo; derrape**
2 plank for sliding heavy objects along. □ **rampa**
■ *v.* (*he skidded*) to slide sideways in a vehicle with the wheels not gripping the surface: *he skidded round the corner.* □ **derrapar**
skiff [skif] *n.* light rowing boat. □ **esquife**
skill [skil] *n.* cleverness/ability to do something: *her skill at the piano; all the skill of the surgeon couldn't save his life.* □ **destreza**
skilful *adj.* clever/very able: *a skilful surgeon.* □ **diestro; hábil**
skilled *adj.* having/requiring a particular skill: *skilled workman,* one who has had particular training; *making buttonholes is a skilled job.* □ **cualificado; especializado**
skillet ['skilit] *n. Amer.* frying pan. □ **sartén**
skim [skim] *v.* (*he skimmed*) **1** to remove things floating on the surface of a liquid. □ **espumar**
skimmed milk, milk from which the cream has been removed. □ **leche desnatada**
2 to dash over the surface of something. □ **pasar casi tocando**
3 *to skim through a book,* to read a book quickly. □ **echar una ojeada**
skimp [skimp] *v.* **1** to do a job badly: *the work has been skimped.* □ **hacer una chapuza**
2 not to give enough: *they have skimped our rations; they skimp on food,* they don't spend much money on food. □ **escatimar**
skimpy *adj.* insufficient (meal); tight/short (clothes). **escaso**
skin [skin] *n.* **1** outer surface of an animal's body: *he scraped the skin off his knee; the hunter was dressed in animal skins.* □ **piel**
by the skin of one's teeth: *they won the match by the skin of their teeth,* they only just won. □ **...por los pelos**
2 outer surface: *the skin of a banana; a skin formed on the hot milk as it cooled.* □ **piel (plátano); nata (leche)**
■ *v.* (*he skinned*) to remove the skin of: *to skin a rabbit.* □ **desollar**
skin-deep *adj.* on the surface/superficial: *his politeness is only skin-deep.* □ **epidérmico**

skindiver *n.* person who dives and swims underwater with breathing apparatus but without special clothing. □ **submarinista sin traje**
skindiving *n.* sport of swimming underwater with breathing apparatus but without special clothing. □ **submarinismo sin traje**
skinflint *n.* miser/person who does not like giving/spending money. □ **roñoso**
skinny *adj.* (*informal*) thin. □ **flaco**
skip [skip] *n.* **1** act of skipping: *she ran off with a skip and a jump.* □ **brinco**
2 large metal container for builder's rubbish. □ **contenedor de escombros**
■ *v.* (*he skipped*) **1** to jump over a rope; to run along half hopping and half jumping. □ **saltar a la comba**
2 to miss out (part of a book): *you can skip the chapter on European geography.* □ **saltarse**
skipping rope *n.* child's rope which you jump over as it turns. □ **comba; cuerda de saltar**
skipper ['skipə] *n.* captain (of a ship/of a team). □ **patrón**
■ *v.* to be the captain of (a team). □ **capitanear**
skirmish ['skə:miʃ] *n.* slight battle between opposite sides. □ **escaramuza**
skirt [skə:t] *n.* **1** piece of woman's clothing covering the lower part of the body from the waist to the knees or ankles. □ **falda**
2 *the skirt of a dress,* the lower part of a dress. □ **falda**
■ *v.* **1** to go round/to avoid going through: *the path skirts the village.* □ **rodear**
2 *the minister carefully skirted around some of the difficult questions of policy,* avoid discussing them. □ **...evitó entrar en...**
skirting board *n.* decorative board running along the bottom edge of a wall in a room. □ **rodapié**
skit [skit] *n.* play/story which makes fun of someone/something: *the play is a skit on life in the suburbs.* □ **parodia**
skittle ['skitl] *n.* wooden object shaped like a bottle which you have to try to knock down with a ball: *to have a game of skittles.* □ **bolo; juego de bolos**
skive [skaiv] *v.* (*informal*) to avoid working. □ **hacerse el remolón**
skiver *n.* (*informal*) person who avoids work. □ **vago redomado**
skulk [skʌlk] *v.* **1** to hide away (because you are planning something wicked). □ **procurar no ser visto**
2 to creep about mysteriously. □ **acechar sin ser visto**
skull [skʌl] *n.* bony part of the head. □ **cráneo**
skullcap *n.* small round hat which fits tight on the head. □ **casquete; solideo**
skunk [skʌŋk] *n.* American mammal with black and white fur, which produces a foul smell. □ **mofeta**
sky [skai] *n.* area above the earth which is blue during the day, and where the moon and stars appear at night: *he looked up at the sky and said he thought it would stay fine; red sky at night – shepherd's delight,* if the sky is red at sunset, it will be a fine day tomorrow; *there is a patch of blue sky in between the clouds; the sky is clear,* there are no clouds. □ **cielo**
sky-blue *adj.* and *n.* bright light blue (colour). □ **azul celeste**
sky-high *adv.* as high as the sky. □ **hasta las nubes**
to blow something sky-high, to blow something up with a powerful explosive. □ **volar algo en mil pedazos**
skylark *n.* small singing bird which sings as it flies upwards. □ **alondra**
■ *v.* to play wild games. □ **jaranear**
skylight *n.* window in a roof or ceiling. □ **tragaluz**
skyline *n.* horizon; shape of distant tall buildings silhouetted against the sky: *the New York skyline.* □ **línea del horizonte**
skyscraper *n.* very tall building. □ **rascacielos**
slab [slæb] *n.* thick flat rectangular block: *a slab of marble; a slab of cake.* □ **losa de mármol; porción de pastel**
slack [slæk] *adj.* **1** not taut/not tight: *the rope is slack; the knot is too slack.* □ **flojo**
2 not busy: *business is rather slack at the moment; November is always a slack month for us.* □ **flojo**
3 lazy; not working well: *he is slack at his work.* □ **perezoso**
■ *n.* **1** looseness; loose part of a rope. □ **flojedad; parte floja**
to take up the slack (*in a rope*), to tighten. □ **tensar la cuerda**
2 very small pieces of coal. □ **cisco**
3 ***slacks,*** trousers. □ **pantalones**
■ *v.* ***to slack (off),*** to be lazy/to do less work: *work tends to slack off at Christmas.* □ **flojear**
slacken *v.* **1** to loosen: *to slacken a rope/a screw.* □ **aflojar**
2 ***to slacken off,*** to work less. □ **flojear**
slacker *n.* person who doesn't work hard. □ **vago**
slackly *adv.* **1** loosely. □ **flojamente**
2 lazily. □ **con pereza**
slackness *n.* state of being slack. □ **flojedad**
slag [slæg] *n.* waste material left after metal has been extracted from ore: *slag heap,* mountain of slag left near a metal works or coalmine. □ **escoria**
slain [slein] *v. see* **slay.**
slake [sleik] *v.* **1** *to slake your thirst,* to drink to remove your thirst. □ **aplacar/apagar la sed**
2 to mix lime with water. □ **apagar la cal**
slalom ['slɑ:ləm] *n.* test in skiing, where you have to ski fast between a series of posts. □ **'slalom'**
slam [slæm] *n.* **1** banging of a door: *the door closed with a slam.* □ **portazo**
2 ***grand slam,*** winning all the games in a competition. □ **gran 'slam'**
■ *v.* (*he slammed*) **1** to bang: *he slammed the door shut; she slammed the book down on the table.* □ **golpear; cerró dando un portazo; cerró el libro de un golpe**
2 (*informal*) to criticize: *the critics slammed the new film.* □ **poner a parir**
slander ['slɑ:ndə] *n.* untrue things said about a person which hurt his reputation; crime of saying such things. □ **difamación**
■ *v.* to say untrue things about a person. □ **difamar**
slanderous *adj.* (statement) which is slander. □ **calumnioso; difamatorio**
slang [slæŋ] *n.* words or phrases used by certain groups of people in popular speech which are not used in correct or written language. □ **argot; jerga**
slanging match *n.* bitter argument where two people call each other rude names. □ **...y se pusieron a parir**
slant [slɑ:nt] *n.* **1** slope. □ **pendiente**
2 ***on the slant,*** sloping. □ **inclinado**
3 *the pipe goes into the wall* ***at a slant,*** at an angle (not straight). □ **inclinado**
4 point of view: *this gives a new slant to the problem.* □ **perspectiva**
■ *v.* **1** to slope: *the plank slants from right to left.* □ **estar inclinado**

2 to show news or information in a particular way: *the news items were slanted to show the country's economy in a favourable light.* □ **estar sesgado**
slanting *adj.* sloping. □ **inclinado**
slantwise *adv.* at an angle; on a slope. □ **con inclinación**
slap [slæp] *n.* smack with your hand flat: *a slap in the face.* □ **bofetada**
■ *v.* (*he slapped*) **1** to hit with your hand flat: *to slap someone's face.* □ **abofetear**
2 to bring (something) down flat on to a surface: *he slapped the fish down on the table.* □ **tirar**
to slap down: *she was slapped down by the chairman,* was told off sharply. □ **el presidente la apabulló...**
■ *adv.* ***to run slap into*** *the wall,* right into the wall. □ **dar de lleno contra**
slapdash *adj.* careless: *slapdash work.* □ **descuidado**
slapstick *adj.* and *n.* rough (comedy) which depends on physical jokes like pouring water down someone's trousers. □ **payasadas**
slap-up *adj.* (*informal*) good and expensive (meal). □ **banquetazo**
slash [slæʃ] *n.* long cut. □ **cuchillada**
■ *v.* **1** to make a long cut: *he slashed the curtains with a knife.* □ **rajar**
2 to shorten: *his speech was slashed from forty minutes to ten.* □ **acortar**
3 to reduce the price of something drastically. □ **abaratar mucho**
slat [slæt] *n.* thin flat piece of wood. □ **tablilla**
slatted *adj.* made of slats. □ **entablado**
slate [sleit] *n.* **1** black stone which splits into thin sheets; piece of this stone used as a roof covering or for writing on: *a slate roof; the wind blew several slates off the roof.* □ **pizarra**
to start a clean slate, to start again (without any faults held against you). □ **hacer borrón y cuenta nueva**
2 *Amer.* group of candidates in an election. □ **lista de candidatos**
■ *v.* (*informal*) to criticize (a play/a book, etc.). □ **vapulear**
slate grey *adj.* and *n.* very dark blue-grey (colour). □ **gris pizarra**
slaughter ['slɔ:tə] *n.* **1** killing of animals for meat. □ **matanza**
2 killing of people (in war). □ **matanza**
■ *v.* **1** to kill (animals) for meat. □ **sacrificar**
2 to kill (many people) in war. □ **matar**
slaughterhouse *n.* place where animals are killed for meat. □ **matadero**
slave [sleiv] *n.* person who belongs to and works for someone. □ **esclavo**
■ *v.* to work hard: *I have been slaving away all day at the washing.* □ **estar esclavizado**
slave driver *n.* (*informal*) employer who makes his workers work very hard. □ **negrero**
slavery *n.* state of being a slave; buying and selling slaves. □ **esclavitud**
slavish *adj.* exact (imitation) without any imagination. □ **servil**
slavishly *adv.* (to obey rules) exactly without exercising any imagination. □ **servilmente**
slaver ['sleivə] *n.* liquid which dribbles out of your mouth. □ **baba**
■ *v.* to dribble/to let liquid trickle out of your mouth. □ **babear**
slay [slei] *v.* (*formal*) (*he slew, he has slain*) to kill. □ **matar**
sleazy ['sli:zi] *adj.* (*informal*) dirty/disreputable. □ **asqueroso**
sled [sled] *n.* small vehicle with runners for sliding over the snow. □ **trineo**
sledge [sledʒ] *n.* small vehicle with runners for sliding over the snow. □ **trineo**
■ *v.* ***to go sledging,*** to play at sliding on the snow on a sledge. □ **deslizarse en trineo**
sledge-hammer *n.* very large heavy hammer. □ **almádena**
sleek [sli:k] *adj.* smooth/shiny; well-kept: *sleek hair.* □ **liso y brillante**
■ *v.* to smooth down (hair) with oil. □ **alisar**
sleekness *n.* smoothness/shininess (of hair). □ **lisura y brillantez**
sleep [sli:p] *n.* **1** state of resting naturally and unconsciously: *to get a good night's sleep; he had a short sleep in the middle of the afternoon.* □ **sueño**
to go/to get to sleep, to start sleeping: *she went to sleep in front of the television; I went to bed late, but couldn't get to sleep.* □ **ir a dormir**
to send someone to sleep, to make someone go to sleep (from boredom/by hypnosis). □ **dormir a alguien**
to put *an animal* ***to sleep,*** to kill. □ **sacrificar un animal**
2 *my foot has gone to sleep,* has become numb. □ **se me ha dormido el pie**
■ *v.* (*he slept*) **1** to be in a state of natural rest and unconsciousness: *don't disturb him — he is sleeping.* □ **dormir**
2 ***to sleep like a log,*** very soundly. □ **dormir como un lirón**
3 ***I'll sleep on it,*** I will make a decision on the problem in the morning. □ **lo consultaré con la almohada**
4 ***to sleep off*** *the effects of the party,* to get rid of the effects by sleeping: *if he's drunk, he'll go to bed and sleep it off.* □ **dormirla**
5 ***to sleep with someone,*** to have sexual intercourse with someone. □ **acostarse con**
6 to have enough beds for: *we can sleep six people in our house.* □ **tener camas para**
sleeper *n.* **1** person who is asleep. □ **persona dormida**
2 *he is a light sleeper,* he wakes easily. □ **tiene el sueño ligero**
3 wooden bar which rails are attached to. □ **traviesa**
4 sleeping car. □ **coche-cama**
5 overnight train with sleeping cars: *I will catch the sleeper to Scotland.* □ **...coche-cama a Escocia**
sleepily *adv.* in a sleepy way. □ **soñolientamente**
sleepiness *n.* state of feeling ready to go to sleep. □ **somnolencia**
sleeping *adj.* asleep. □ **dormido**
sleeping partner, partner who does not take an active interest in the business. □ **socio comanditario**
■ *n.* state of being asleep. □ **sueño**
sleeping bag, quilted bag for sleeping in a tent, etc.. □ **saco de dormir**
sleeping car, carriage on a train with beds where passengers can sleep. □ **coche-cama**
sleeping pill, medicine which makes you go to sleep. □ **pastilla para dormir**
sleeping sickness, tropical disease which affects the nervous system. □ **enfermedad del sueño**
sleepless *adj.* with no sleep: *a sleepless night.* □ **en blanco**
sleeplessness *n.* having no sleep; not being able to get to sleep. □ **insomnio**
sleepwalk *v.* to walk about when you are asleep. □ **caminar sonámbulo**
sleepwalker *n.* person who walks about when he

is asleep. □ **sonámbulo**
sleepy *adj.* **1** half asleep; ready to go to sleep. □ **soñoliento**
2 *sleepy little town,* town where nothing very exciting ever happens. □ **ciudad muerta**
sleet [sli:t] *n.* mixture of snow and rain. □ **aguanieve**
■ *v. it is sleeting,* snow and rain are falling together. □ **está cayendo aguanieve**
sleeve [sli:v] *n.* **1** part of clothing which covers your arm: *I've torn the sleeve of my coat.* □ **manga**
to keep something up your sleeve, to have a plan which you are keeping secret. □ **guardarse algo en la manga**
2 cover for a piece of machinery. □ **funda**
3 square cardboard cover for a gramophone record. □ **funda**
sleigh [slei] *n.* large sledge pulled by horses or reindeer, etc. □ **trineo**
sleight [slait] *n.* ***sleight of hand,*** quickness of a conjurer's movements when performing a card trick: *it is all done by sleight of hand.* □ **juego de manos**
slender ['slendə] *n.* **1** very thin/slim: *a slender young tree.* □ **fino**
2 not strong; not large: *our slender resources; we have only slender hopes of finding the lost climbers alive.* □ **...escasos recursos; ...ligeras esperanzas**
slenderness *n.* state of being slender. □ **escasez; ligereza**
slept [slept] *v. see* **sleep.**
sleuth [slu:θ] *n.* (*informal*) detective. □ **sabueso**
slew [slu:] *v.* **1** to turn/to twist: *the car slewed round and hit a tree.* □ **girar**
2 *see* **slay.**
slice [slais] *n.* **1** thin piece cut off something: *a slice of bread; a slice of tomato; don't cut the slices of ham too thick.* □ **rebanada de pan; trozo de tomate; loncha de jamón**
2 *fish slice,* flat broad knife for serving fish. □ **pala del pescado**
3 (*in games*) stroke which makes the ball spin towards the right. □ **efecto**
■ *v.* **1** to cut into slices: *he sliced the bread very thinly.* □ **cortar en rodajas; rebanadas, etc.**
2 to cut sharply: *they sliced through the jungle with their machetes.* □ **adentrarse**
3 to hit a ball on an angle so that it spins towards the right. □ **dar efecto**
slicer *n.* machine for slicing meat/bread, etc. □ **picadora (carne); rebanadora (pan)**
slick [slik] *adj.* clever (in a way which tricks people). □ **listillo**
■ *n.* ***oil slick,*** layer of oil which has spilled on the sea from a tanker or oil rig. □ **mancha de aceite**
slid [slid] *v. see* **slide.**
slide [slaid] *n.* **1** action of slipping on a smooth surface: *to go for a slide.* □ **deslizamiento**
2 slippery surface (on ice); slippery metal slope for children to slide down. □ **resbaladero (hielo); tobogán**
3 thin glass plate to put under a microscope. □ **portaobjeto**
4 plastic transparent photograph which can be projected on a screen. □ **diapositiva**
5 clip which slips into the hair to hold it in place. □ **pasador**
■ *v.* (*he slid*) **1** to move smoothly: *the door slides easily open; the children were sliding on the ice.* □ **deslizarse**
2 ***to let things slide,*** to allow things to become worse/not to care if things get worse. □ **dejar que se pudra algo**
slide-rule *n.* device for calculating, made of a ruler marked with numbers and a central part which slides sideways. □ **regla de cálculo**
slight [slait] *adj.* **1** thin/slender (person). □ **delgado, esbelto**
2 not very large; not very important: *a slight pain; a slight frost; they were never in the slightest danger.* □ **ligero**
■ *n.* insult: *I take his remarks as a personal slight.* □ **desaire**
■ *v.* to insult/to be rude to (someone). □ **ofender**
slightingly *adv.* rudely/insultingly. □ **despreciativamente**
slightly *adv.* not very much: *he is slightly better; I only know him slightly.* □ **ligeramente**
slim [slim] *adj.* **1** thin/slender/not fat: *he has lost weight and now looks quite slim.* □ **delgado**
2 small: *there is only a slim chance of recovery.* □ **pequeño**
■ *v.* (*he slimmed*) to diet in order to become thin. □ **adelgazar**
slime [slaim] *n.* thin mud; dirty, sticky liquid: *the rocks are covered with slime.* □ **limo**
slimy *adj.* unpleasantly muddy/slippery/sticky. □ **viscoso**
sling [sliŋ] *n.* **1** device for throwing a stone. □ **honda**
2 carrying strap; bandage tied round your neck to hold steady your wounded arm: *a rifle sling; he has his arm in a sling.* □ **portafusil; cabestrillo (brazo herido)**
3 apparatus made of ropes and pulleys for hoisting and carrying goods. □ **eslinga**
■ *v.* (*he slung*) **1** to throw: *he slung the bundle over his shoulder.* □ **echar**
2 to hold up/to hang by a sling. □ **colgar**
slingshot *n. Amer.* catapult/strong elastic band on a forked stick, used for throwing stones. □ **tirachinas**
slink [sliŋk] *v.* (*he slunk*) to creep about furtively: *he slunk away into the bushes.* □ **escabullirse**
slinky *adj.* smooth (shape); tight smooth (clothes). □ **esbelto (figura); provocativo (ropa)**
slip [slip] *n.* **1** action of sliding by mistake. □ **desliz**
2 mistake: *I made a slip when I was writing the cheque.* □ **equivocación**
a slip of the tongue, a mistake in speaking. □ **lapsus linguae**
3 ***to give someone the slip,*** to escape from someone. □ **dar esquinazo a uno**
4 ***pillow slip,*** cotton or nylon bag to cover a pillow. □ **funda de almohada**
5 small piece of paper. □ **trozo de papel**
6 petticoat. □ **combinación**
7 ***slips,*** long smooth slope on which ships are built. □ **gradas**
8 mixture of clay and water which is used in pottery. □ **barbotina**
■ *v.* (*he slipped*) **1** to slide by mistake: *she slipped over on the ice,* fell down. □ **resbalarse**
2 to go quietly: *he slipped into the back of the church; the smugglers' boat slipped out of the harbour.* □ **introducirse/salir sin hacer ruido**
3 to miss/not to connect: *the clutch is slipping.* □ **el embrague patina**
4 *it slipped my memory,* I forgot it. □ **me falló la memoria**
5 ***slipped disc,*** painful state where one of the cushioning discs in the spine has become displaced. □ **hernia discal**
slipper *n.* light comfortable shoe worn indoors. □ **zapatilla**

slippery *adj.* **1** so smooth that one can easily slip on it: *be careful – the pavement is very slippery.* □ **resbaladizo**
2 *he's a slippery customer,* he cannot be trusted. □ **no fiable**
slip road *n.* road which leads on to a motorway. □ **carril de acceso**
slipshod *adj.* badly carried out (work); careless (dress). □ **chapucero (trabajo); descuidado (vestido)**
slipstream *n.* air blown backwards by an aircraft engine; point just behind a fast moving vehicle. □ **estela**
slip up *v.* (*informal*) to make a mistake. □ **meter la pata**
slip-up *n.* (*informal*) mistake. □ **metedura de pata**
slipway *n.* smooth slope on which ships are built or repaired. □ **grada**
slit [slit] *n.* long cut; narrow opening: *put the card into the slit.* □ **hendidura**
■ *v.* (*he slit*) to make a long cut with a knife: *he slit open the envelope.* □ **cortar**
slither ['sliðə] *v.* to slide about in various directions. □ **ir rodando**
sliver ['slivə] *n.* thin piece of wood or meat. □ **astilla (madera); trocito (carne)**
slobber ['slɔbə] *v.* to dribble saliva from your mouth. □ **babear**
sloe [slou] *n.* bitter wild fruit like a plum; tree which bears this fruit. □ **endrina; endrino (árbol)**
slog [slɔg] *n.* difficult work; difficult walk: *it is a long hard slog to get to the top of the mountain.* □ **cuesta mucho trabajo...**
■ *v.* (*he slogged*) to work hard at something difficult: *he was slogging away at his homework.* □ **sudar tinta**
slogger *n.* person who works hard. □ **trabajador nato**
slogan ['slougn] *n.* phrase used in publicity for a product/for a political party, etc. □ **eslogan**
slop [slɔp] *v.* (*he slopped*) to spill: *the tea was slopping into the saucer; she slopped her coffee all over the floor.* □ **derramar(se)**
sloppily *adv.* untidily. □ **descuidadamente**
sloppy *adj.* **1** untidy; badly done (work). □ **descuidado; chapucero (trabajo)**
2 stupidly sentimental. □ **sensiblero**
slops *n. pl.* **1** liquid food given to people who are too ill to eat. □ **caldo**
2 waste food given to pigs. □ **bazofia**
3 liquid refuse. □ **agua sucia**
slope [sloup] *n.* slanting surface; angle of a slanting surface: *the path goes down a steep slope; his house is built on the lower slopes of the mountain.* □ **cuesta; pendiente**
■ *v.* to slant upwards or downwards: *the road slopes steeply down into the village.* □ **ascender/descender**
slope off *v.* (*informal*) to creep away quietly. □ **largarse**
slosh [slɔʃ] *v.* **1** to splash. □ **salpicar**
2 (*informal*) to hit. □ **zurrar**
sloshed *adj.* (*informal*) drunk. □ **borracho**
slot [slɔt] *n.* narrow opening (for putting a coin into): *put two coins into the slot.* □ **ranura**
slot machine, machine which (when you put a coin into the slot) will give chocolate/cigarettes/drinks, etc., automatically. □ **máquina automática**
■ *v.* (*he slotted*) ***to slot into,*** to fit into (a slot): *the lid slots into the back of the box.* □ **encajar**
sloth [slouθ] *n.* **1** (*formal*) laziness. □ **indolencia**
2 slow-moving South American mammal, like a bear. □ **oso bezudo**
slothful *adj.* (*formal*) lazy. □ **indolente**
slouch [slautʃ] *v.* to stand/to sit in a bad position/ with bent shoulders. □ **estar/ir encogido**
to slouch along, to walk along bending forwards. □ **andar encogido**
slouch hat *n.* hat with a wide brim which can be turned down. □ **sombrero de ala flexible**
slough [slʌf] *n.* **1** old skin of a snake. □ **camisa**
2 marshy place. □ **ciénaga**
■ *v.* (*of a snake*) to lose its skin. □ **mudar la piel**
slovenly ['slʌvənli] *adj.* untidy; careless (work). □ **dejado; chapucero**
slow [slou] *adj.* **1** not fast: *the car was travelling at a very slow speed; we were slow in deciding where to go on holiday; slow train,* train which stops at each station. □ **lento**
2 *to be slow,* (*of clock, etc.*) to show a time which is earlier than the correct time: *my watch is five minutes slow.* □ **atrasarse**
3 not quick to learn. □ **lento**
4 *he's a bit* ***slow on the uptake,*** (*informal*) he does not understand things quickly. □ **es un poco lento...**
■ *adv.* not fast. □ **lento**
to go slow, (i) to advance less quickly. □ **ir despacio** (ii) to protest by working slowly. □ **trabajar a ritmo lento**
■ *v.* ***to slow down,*** to go more slowly; to make (something) go more slowly: *the car slowed down as it came to the crossing.* □ **reducir la marcha**
slowcoach *n.* person who goes slower than others. □ **tardón**
slowly *adv.* in a slow way: *he walked slowly across the field.* □ **lentamente**
slow motion *n.* (*in films*) action which appears to take place very slowly because the film speed has been slowed down. □ **cámara lenta**
slow-worm *n.* snake-like lizard. □ **lución**
sludge [slʌdʒ] *n.* wet mud; wet refuse. □ **fango**
slug [slʌg] *n.* **1** common garden animal like a snail with no shell. □ **babosa**
2 small metal pellet. □ **posta, trozo de metal**
■ *v.* (*he slugged*) (*informal*) to hit (someone) a heavy blow. □ **dar un tortazo**
sluggish *adj.* lazy/slow-moving. □ **lento**
sluggishly *adv.* in a slow way: *the river flowed sluggishly past.* □ **lentamente**
sluice [slu:s] *n.* **1** channel for taking water round a dam; gate which allows water to enter this channel. □ **canal; compuerta**
2 *to give your car a sluice down,* wash it with buckets of water. □ **darle un agua**
■ *v.* to wash (something) with lots of water: *they sluiced out the stables.* □ **limpiar con agua**
sluice gate *n.* gate which allows water to enter the sluice channel. □ **compuerta**
slum [slm] *n.* poor, rundown area of a town. □ **barrio bajo**
slumber ['slʌmbə] *n.* gentle sleep. □ **sueño ligero**
■ *v.* to sleep gently. □ **dormitar**
slumberwear *n.* (*no pl.*) clothes (pyjamas/nightdress, etc.) worn to go to bed. □ **ropa de dormir**
slump [slʌmp] *n.* collapse (of prices); economic collapse (of a country). □ **desplome**
■ *v.* **1** to fall suddenly: *prices slumped overnight.* □ **desplomarse**
2 *he sat slumped in his chair,* half lying in his chair. □ **se dejó caer pesadamente...**
slung [slʌŋ] *v. see* **sling.**
slunk [slʌŋk] *v. see* **slink.**
slur [slə:] *n.* **1** insult: *to cast a slur on someone's good*

name, to insult someone. □ **calumnia**
2 playing several notes without a break between them; mark on a musical score to show that notes should be played without a break. □ **ligado**
■ *v.* (*he slurred*) **1** to speak words indistinctly. □ **hablar entre dientes**
2 (*in music*) to play several notes without a break between them. □ **ligar**

slurp [slə:p] *v.* (*informal*) to drink noisily. □ **sorber**

slush [slʌʃ] *n.* **1** half-melted snow. □ **nieve medio derretida**
2 sentimentality. □ **sensiblería**
slush fund *n.* (*informal*) money kept for the purposes of bribery. □ **fondo de reptiles**
slushy *adj.* **1** covered with half-melted snow. □ **cubierto por nieve a medio derretir**
2 very sentimental: *a slushy story.* □ **sentimentaloide**

slut [slʌt] *n.* (*informal*) dirty woman. □ **marrana**

sly [slai] *adj.* **1** cunning (person). □ **astuto**
2 *he did it **on the sly,*** without anyone knowing. □ **...a hurtadillas**
slyly *adv.* cunningly. □ **astutamente**
slyness *n.* being cunning. □ **astucia**

smack [smæk] *n.* **1** blow with the flat of the hand: *I'll give him a smack in the eye.* □ **tortazo**
2 ***fishing smack,*** small fishing boat. □ **queche**
3 loud kiss. □ **beso sonoro**
4 particular taste: *there is a smack of onion about it.* □ **saborcillo**
■ *v.* **1** to hit (someone): *I'll smack his face.* □ **abofetear**
2 *she smacked her lips,* made a loud noise (as if hungry). □ **hizo un chasquido con...**
3 to smell/to taste. □ **saber**
to smack of: *that smacks of bribery,* it sounds as though bribery is involved. □ **eso huele a...**
■ *adv.* (*informal*) straight/directly: *the car ran smack into the wall; the telephone rang smack in the middle of the dinner party.* □ **justo en**

small [smɔ:l] *adj.* **1** not large; little: *he has a small car; she's smaller than her husband.* □ **pequeño**
2 delicate/soft (voice). □ **voz débil**
3 not imposing: *he has a small electrical business; he has won a small sum of money on the football pools; he is quite successful in a small way.* □ **pequeño**
4 petty/thinking only of trivial things: *he has a small mind.* □ **mezquino**
■ *n.* **1** *the small of the back,* the lower part of the back. □ **la región lumbar**
2 ***smalls,*** (*informal*) underwear. □ **paños menores**
■ *adv.* in little bits: *cut the meat up small.* □ **en trocitos**
smallholding *n.* very small farm. □ **granja pequeña**
small hours *n.* period just after midnight: *they stayed up into the small hours of the morning.* □ **altas horas (de la noche)**
small-minded *adj.* thinking only of yourself/of trivial things. □ **mezquino**
smallpox *n.* dangerous infectious disease causing a rash which leaves marks on the skin. □ **viruela**

smart [smɑ:t] *n.* sharp pain (from a wound). □ **punzada**
■ *v.* to hurt/to feel as if burning: *my eyes are smarting from the smoke.* □ **escocer**
■ *adj.* **1** sharp (blow). □ **golpe seco**
2 rapid/efficient: *to walk at a sharp pace.* □ **paso vivo**
3 clever: *he gave a very smart answer to the question.* □ **listo**
4 well-dressed; elegant. □ **elegante**
to make yourself smart, to dress well. □ **ponerse guapo**
smarten *v.* ***to smarten yourself up,*** to make yourself look smart. □ **acicalarse**

smash [smæʃ] *n.* **1** crash (of a car): *three people were killed in the smash on the motorway.* □ **choque**
2 financial collapse. □ **quiebra**
3 powerful shot (in tennis). □ **smash**
■ *v.* **1** to break (something) to pieces: *the police smashed down the door; they smashed open the safe.* □ **...echó abajo la puerta; reventaron la caja**
2 to hit something hard: *the plane smashed into a wireless mast.* □ **chocar**
3 to hit (a ball) hard: *he smashed the ball into the net.* □ **golpear**
smash-and-grab raid *n.* burglary done by breaking a shop window and stealing as much as you can get hold of. □ **robo relámpago**
smash hit *n.* play/film, etc., which is very successful. □ **exitazo**
smashing *adj.* (*informal*) very good/fantastic. □ **'chachi'**

smattering ['smætriŋ] *n.* small knowledge: *he has a smattering of French.* □ **nociones**

smear ['smiə] *n.* **1** dirty mark; something smeared. □ **mancha**
smear test, test for cancer of the womb. □ **una citología**
2 insult. □ **calumnia**
smear campaign, campaign to discredit someone by spreading gossip about his private life. □ **campaña de desprestigio**
■ *v.* **1** to make dirty marks. □ **manchar**
2 to spread (something greasy): *he smeared butter on his bread; they smeared glue on the teacher's chair.* □ **untar**

smell [smel] *n.* **1** one of the five senses, felt through the nose: *dogs have a keen sense of smell.* □ **olfato**
2 something which you can sense through the nose: *there is a smell of roses in the dining room; I don't like the smell of onions.* □ **olor**
3 something unpleasant which you can sense through the nose: *what a smell!* □ **¡qué olor!**
■ *v.* (*he smelled/smelt*) **1** to notice (something) by the nose: *I can smell smoke.* □ **oler**
2 to sniff in order to sense the smell: *she smelled the roses; the dog was smelling around the lamppost.* □ **oler; olfatear (perro)**
3 to give off a smell: *the roast meat smells very good; the house smells damp.* □ **oler; huele a humedad**
smelly *adj.* which gives off an unpleasant smell: *smelly feet.* □ **maloliente; te huelen los pies**

smelt [smelt] *n.* small edible fish. □ **eperlano**
■ *v.* **1** to produce metal by melting ore: *to smelt iron.* □ **fundir**
2 *see also* **smell.**
smelter *n.* works where metal is extracted from ore. □ **fundición**
smelting *n.* production of metal by heating ore with coke and limestone. □ **fundición**

smile [smail] *n.* expression of pleasure with the mouth turned up at the corners: *she gave a bright smile; he had a broad smile on his face.* □ **sonrisa**
■ *v.* to make an expression of happiness by turning up the corners of the mouth: *she smiled at the doctor.* □ **sonreír**

smirk [smə:k] *n.* unpleasant superior smile. □ **sonrisa afectada**
■ *v.* to give an unpleasant superior smile. □ **sonreír afectadamente**

smith [smiθ] *n.* person who works in metal. □ **herrero**

smithy ['smiði] *n.* workshop where a blacksmith works □ **herrería**
smithereens [smiðə'ri:nz] *n.* very small bits: *the plate was smashed to smithereens.* □ **añicos**
smock [smɔk] *n.* long loose overall worn over clothes to protect them. □ **bata**
smocking *n.* embroidery on gathered material. □ **adorno**
smog [smɔg] *n.* mixture of fog and exhaust fumes of cars. □ **contaminación con niebla**
smoke [smouk] *n.* **1** vapour and gas given off when something burns: *I can smell smoke; smoke billowed out of the burning house.* □ **humo**
2 action of smoking a cigarette: *would you like a smoke?* □ **...echar un cigarro?**
■ *v.* **1** to send out clouds of vapour and gas: *the ruins of the house were still smoking two days after the fire; the chimney smokes,* the smoke of the fire comes out into the room instead of going up the chimney. □ **humear**
2 to cure (bacon/fish, etc.) by hanging in wood smoke: *smoked ham; smoked trout.* □ **ahumar; trucha ahumada**
3 to suck in smoke from a burning cigarette/pipe, etc.: *he only smokes cigars; he was smoking a pipe.* □ **fumar**
smokeless *adj.* which makes no smoke: *smokeless fuel.* □ **sin humo**
smokeless zone, area where you are not allowed to make any smoke. □ **zona de no fumadores**
smoker *n.* **1** person who smokes cigarettes, etc.: *he's a pipe smoker.* □ **fumador**
2 railway carriage where you can smoke. □ **de fumadores**
smokescreen *n.* thick smoke made so that the enemy cannot see; anything which is deliberately used to hide what is going on. □ **cortina de humo**
smoky *adj.* full of cigarette smoke: *a smoky room.* □ **lleno de humo**
smooth [smu:ð] *adj.* **1** (surface) with no bumps/no roughness: *as smooth as glass.* □ **liso**
2 with no bumps/jolts: *a smooth landing.* □ **suave**
3 with no hair: *a smooth chin.* □ **imberbe**
4 too pleasant (person): *he's a very smooth character.* □ **afable**
■ *v.* to make smooth: *she smoothed down the sheets on the bed.* □ **alisar**
to smooth the way for something, to make it easy. □ **preparar el terreno**
to smooth things over, to settle an argument. □ **limar asperezas**
smoothly *adv.* **1** with no bumps. □ **suavemente**
2 with no hitch: *the ceremony went off very smoothly.* □ **...sobre ruedas**
3 too agreeably: *he smoothly suggested we should go for a walk.* □ **afablemente**
smother ['smʌðə] *v.* **1** to stifle and kill (someone): *he was smothered on the orders of the Emperor.* □ **asfixiar**
2 to cover: *a cake smothered in cream,* covered with cream. □ **cubrir**
smoulder ['smouldə] *Amer.* **smolder** *v.* to burn slowly. □ **arder sin llama**
smudge [smʌdʒ] *n.* dirty (ink) stain. □ **borrón (en papel); mancha (en la ropa)**
■ *v.* to make a mark, such as by rubbing ink which is not dry. □ **emborronar**
smudgy *adj.* (paper) with a dirty mark on it. □ **emborronado**
smug [smʌg] *adj.* self-satisfied. □ **pagado de sí mismo**
smugly *adv.* in a way which shows you are pleased with yourself. □ **con aire de suficiencia**
smuggle ['smʌgl] *v.* to take (goods) past the customs without declaring them for duty; to take (something) into or out of a prison without the warders seeing: *he smuggled all his gold out of the country.* □ **pasar de contrabando**
smuggler *n.* person who smuggles goods. □ **contrabandista**
smut [smʌt] *n.* **1** small black mark: *you have got a smut on your nose.* □ **mota**
2 indecent stories. □ **obscenidades**
smutty *adj.* indecent: *he told some smutty jokes.* □ **...chistes verdes**
snack [snæk] *n.* light meal: *we'll have a snack on the way to the meeting.* □ **bocadillo; piscolabis**
snackbar *n.* restaurant where you can have a light meal, usually sitting at a counter. □ **cafetería; bar**
snag [snæg] *n.* **1** obstacle; something which prevents you from doing something: *we have run into a snag; the snag is that the car won't start.* □ **pega**
2 sharp point; place where a piece of clothing has been caught on a sharp point. □ **objeto punzante; enganchón**
■ *v.* (*he snagged*) to catch and tear (your clothes) on a sharp point. □ **engancharse**
snail [sneil] *n.* **1** common slimy animal with a shell. □ **caracol**
2 *to creep along **at a snail's pace,*** extremely slowly. □ **ir a paso de tortuga**
snake [sneik] *n.* long, sometimes poisonous, reptile which wriggles along the ground. □ **serpiente**
■ *v.* to wriggle like a snake. □ **serpentear**
snap [snæp] *n.* **1** sudden dry noise: *I heard the snap of a twig.* □ **chasquido**
2 ***cold snap,*** sudden spell of cold weather. □ **ola de frío**
3 type of brittle biscuit: *a ginger snap.* □ **galleta**
4 photograph: *let me show you our holiday snaps.* □ **foto**
5 kind of card game where you say 'snap' if you play the same card as your opponent. □ **juego de naipes**
■ *adj.* taken hurriedly: *a snap decision; a snap election.* □ **instantánea**
■ *v.* (*he snapped*) **1** to try to bite: *the dog was snapping at my ankles.* □ **mordisquear**
2 to speak sharply: *'shut up', he snapped.* □ **decir con brusquedad**
3 to break sharply; to make a dry noise (in breaking): *a twig snapped.* □ **partirse**
to snap your fingers, to make a click by rubbing your fingers together. □ **castañetear los dedos**
4 to take a photograph of someone. □ **hacer una foto**
5 ***to snap up a bargain,*** to buy a bargain quickly. □ **agarrar una ganga**
6 ***to snap out of it,*** (*informal*) to get out of a state of depression. □ **animarse**
snapdragon *n.* common garden plant (antirrhinum) whose flowers open like a dragon's mouth when squeezed. □ **dragón**
snap fastener *n.* fastening for clothes, made of two two small metal studs which fit into each other. □ **automático**
snappy *adj.* **1** irritable/short-tempered. □ **temperamental**
2 ***make it snappy!,*** (*informal*) do it quickly. □ **a toda pastilla**
snapshot *n.* informal photograph taken quickly. □ **foto, instantánea**

snare ['snɛə] *n.* trap for catching animals made with a noose which is pulled tight. □ **lazo/trampa**
■ *v.* to catch with a snare. □ **cazar con lazo/trampa**

snarl [snɑ:l] *n.* angry growl. □ **gruñido**
■ *v.* **1** to growl angrily: *the dog snarled when we tried to take away its bone.* □ **gruñir**
2 to make tangled: *the rope was snarled round the tree stump; the traffic has become all snarled up.* □ **enmarañar**
snarl-up *n.* (*informal*) traffic jam. □ **tapón; atasco**

snatch [snætʃ] *n.* **1** grabbing something. □ **robo**
2 short piece: *a snatch of a song; to work in snatches.* □ **fragmento; trabajar a ratos**
■ *v.* to grab (something) rapidly: *he snatched the money out of my hand; they snatched the old lady's handbag; I managed to snatch a meal between interviews.* **arrebatar; ...para comer algo a toda prisa entre...**

sneak [sni:k] *n.* (*informal*) person who tells tales about someone. □ **chivato**
■ *v.* **1** to creep without being seen: *he sneaked up behind the policeman; they sneaked away before they could be arrested.* □ **escabullirse**
2 (*informal*) to report that someone has done something wrong: *he sneaked on me to the teacher.* □ **chivarse**
sneakers *n. pl. Amer.* soft sports shoes with rubber soles. □ **zapatillas**
sneaking *adj.* **1** secret. □ **furtivo**
2 *I have a sneaking regard for this criminal,* I admire him in secret. □ **oculto**
sneaky *adj.* (*informal*) deceitful/not open. □ **vil**

sneer ['sniə] *n.* sarcastic smile; unpleasant smile: *he looked at her with a sneer.* □ **sonrisa burlona**
■ *v.* to give someone a sarcastic smile to show contempt; to speak in a contemptuous way: *he sneered at our little old car; 'I'll make you sorry for this', he sneered.* □ **mofarse**

sneeze [sni:z] *n.* sudden blowing out of air through your mouth and nose because of irritation in your nose: *he gave a loud sneeze.* □ **estornudo**
■ *v.* to blow air suddenly through your mouth because of irritation in your nose: *the smell of flowers makes me sneeze;* (*informal*) *he had a sudden sneezing fit.* □ **estornudar**
it's not to be sneezed at, (*informal*) you should not refuse it/despise it. □ **no es de despreciar**

snick [snik] *n.* **1** small cut (with a knife). □ **muesca; corte**
2 (*in cricket*) sharp stroke. □ **golpe (con el borde del bate)**
■ *v.* to hit (a ball) a sharp glancing blow. □ **golpear**

snide [snaid] *adj.* (*informal*) unpleasant/envious (remark): *he keeps making snide comments about me.* □ **despreciativo**

sniff [snif] *n.* short intake of air through the nose: *she gave a sniff.* □ **inhalación**
■ *v.* to take in air rapidly through the nose: *the dog was sniffing at the cupboard door; he sniffed and said he could smell burning.* □ **husmear, aspirar**
it's not to be sniffed at, (*informal*) you should not refuse it/despise it. □ **no es de despreciar**
sniffle *n.* slight cold in the head. □ **resfriado**
■ *v.* to keep on sniffing because of a cold. □ **sorberse los mocos**

snigger ['snigə] *v.* to laugh quietly at something in an unpleasant way. □ **reír disimuladamente**
sniggering *n.* hidden laughter. □ **risita**

snip [snip] *n.* **1** piece which has been cut off. □ **recorte**
2 (*informal*) bargain: *it's a snip at that price.* □ **ganga**
■ *v.* (*he snipped*) to cut with scissors: *he snipped off all her hair.* □ **cortar a tijeretazos**
snippet *n.* little bit (of cloth, etc.): *I overheard snippets of conversation.* □ **retal (tela); ...fragmentos de una conversación**

snipe [snaip] *n.* large marsh bird with a long beak. □ **agachadiza**
■ *v.* ***to snipe at someone,*** to shoot at someone from a hiding place/to make continuous criticism of someone. □ **disparar desde un escondite; estar siempre criticando**
sniper *n.* soldier who is hidden and shoots at the enemy: *sniper fire,* shooting by snipers. □ **francotirador**

snitch [snitʃ] *v.* (*informal*) to steal. □ **afanar**

snivel ['snivl] *v.* (*he snivelled*) **1** to have a runny nose. □ **moquear**
2 to cry and complain. □ **lloriquear**

snob [snɔb] *n.* person who likes people who are of a higher social class than himself. □ **esnob**
intellectual snob, person who looks down on those who are not as well educated as he feels he is himself. □ **esnob intelectual**
snobbery, snobbishness *n.* state of being a snob. □ **esnobismo**
snobbish *adj.* referring to a snob. □ **esnob/esnobista**

snooker ['snu:kə] *n.* game like billiards played on a table with twenty two balls of various colours. □ **'snooker', billar**

snoop [snu:p] *v.* to creep about investigating something secretly. □ **fisgonear**
snooper *n.* person who spies on someone secretly. □ **fisgón**

snooty ['snu:ti] *adj.* (*informal*) superior (air/expression). □ **creído**
snootily *adv.* in a superior way. □ **con aires de superioridad**

snooze [snu:z] *n.* short sleep: *I am going to have a snooze.* □ **sueñecito**
■ *v.* to sleep lightly for a short time: *he was snoozing in his chair.* □ **echar una cabezada/siestecita**

snore [snɔ:] *n.* loud noise in the throat made by breathing air when you are asleep. □ **ronquido**
■ *v.* to make a loud noise by breathing air when asleep. □ **roncar**
snoring *n.* making a noise through the nose when asleep: *his snoring kept everyone awake.* □ **ronquido**

snorkel ['snɔ:kl] *n.* tube which goes from the mouth or mask of an underwater swimmer to the surface to allow him to breathe in air. □ **'esnórquel'**

snort [snɔ:t] *n.* noise made by blowing air out through the nose: *he gave a snort.* □ **bufido**
■ *v.* to make a loud noise blowing air out through the nose: *the horse snorted; he snorted in anger.* □ **bufar**

snot [snɔt] *n.* (*informal*) waste liquid in the nose. □ **moco**

snout [snaut] *n.* nose of an animal (especially a pig). □ **hocico**

snow [snou] *n.* water vapour which freezes and falls in light white flakes: *a fall of snow; ten centimetres of snow had fallen overnight; snow flurries.* □ **nieve**
■ *v.* **1** to fall in flakes of snow: *it is starting to snow.* □ **nevar**
2 *we were* ***snowed up*** *for ten days,* trapped in the house by heavy snow. □ **estuvimos atrapados por la nieve...**
3 *I am* ***snowed under*** *with work,* overwhelmed with

work. □ **estoy agobiado de...**
snowball *n.* ball of snow which children throw. □ **bola de nieve**
■ *v.* **1** to throw snowballs: *they went out snowballing.* □ **lanzar bolas de nieve**
2 to get bigger and bigger: *our debts have snowballed.* □ **aumentar sin parar**
snow-blindness *n.* painful lack of sight caused by the brightness of snow. □ **ceguera causada por la nieve**
snowbound *adj.* trapped by snow. □ **atrapado por la nieve**
snow-capped *adj.* (mountain) with its summit covered with snow. □ **coronado de nieve**
snowdrift *n.* heap of snow which has been piled up by the wind. □ **ventisquero**
snowdrop *n.* small spring bulb with little white flowers. □ **campanilla blanca**
snowfall *n.* amount of snow which has fallen: *a light snowfall; the heavy snowfall blocked most roads.* □ **nevada**
snowflake *n.* flake of snow. □ **copo de nieve**
snowline *n.* point on a high mountain above which there is always snow. □ **límite de nieves perpetuas**
snowman *n.* figure of a man made out of large balls of snow piled on top of each other. □ **muñeco de nieve**
snowmobile ['snouməbi:l] *n.* vehicle with caterpillar tracks specially designed for driving on snow. □ **coche oruga**
snow plough *Amer.* **snow plow** *n.* heavy vehicle with a huge plough on the front for clearing snow off roads/railways, etc. □ **quitanieves**
snowshoes *n. pl.* frames shaped like tennis rackets, with a light web, which are tied under the feet for walking on snow. □ **raquetas de nieve**
snowstorm *n.* storm which brings snow. □ **tormenta de nieve**
snow white *adj.* pure white. □ **níveo**
snowy *adj.* covered with snow; white like snow: *the snowy mountain wastes; a snowy white shirt.* □ **de mucha nieve; blanco como la nieve**

snub [snʌb] *n.* insult; insulting refusal to speak to someone. □ **desaire**
■ *v.* (*he snubbed*) to insult (someone) by refusing to speak to him/by not paying any attention to him. □ **desairar**
■ *adj.* ***snub nose,*** small nose which is turned up at the end. □ **nariz respingona**

snuff [snʌf] *n.* powdered tobacco which is sniffed into the nose. □ **rapé**
■ *v.* to put out a candle. □ **despabilar, apagar**

snuffle ['snʌfl] *v.* to sniff noisily: *the pig was snuffling about in the shed.* □ **resollar**

snug [snʌg] *adj.* warm and comfortable: *snug armchair; he was lying snug in bed.* □ **cómodo y calentito**
snuggle *v.* to curl yourself up to be warm; to curl up close to someone for warmth: *she snuggled up to him.* □ **acurrucarse**

so [sou] *adv.* **1** to such an extent: *it is so cold that the river has frozen; he is not so feeble as he looks; I am not so sure; we enjoyed ourselves so much that we will be going back there on holiday next year.* □ **tan**
2 in this way: *it so happened that the train was late that day; put the cake mixture into the pan so.* □ **así**
3 true/correct: *I think so,* I think it is true; *I'm afraid so; is that so?* □ **así**
4 in the same way: *she says it is going to rain, and I think so too; he was late and so was I.* □ **también**
5 ***or so,*** approximately: *I waited an hour or so in the rain; we had two hundred or so letters.* □ **o así**
6 ***and so on,*** and in a similar way; etcetera. □ **y así sucesivamente**
7 *he talked for hours about the history of the school,* ***and so on (and so forth),*** and other similar things. □ **...y así todo el rato**
■ *conj.* **1** therefore: *it was raining, so we did not go out; so that is why you were late.* □ **por tanto**
2 for the purpose of: *cyclists should wear orange jackets so that drivers can see them easily; we ran to the station so as not to miss the train.* □ **para que**
so-and-so *n.* **1** somebody (whom you do not want to name): *so-and-so will call for the parcel.* □ **fulanito**
2 (*informal*) naughty person: *the little so-and-so – he has picked all our flowers and sold them to the lady next door.* □ **golfo**
so-called *adj.* wrongly called: *he is a so-called retired director,* he calls himself one, but is not one really. □ **llamado**
so-so *adj.* and *adv.* (*informal*) not very well: *I am feeling so-so; how did you get on in the competition? – so-so.* □ **así así**

soak [souk] *n.* state of being very wet: *I like to lie in the bath and have a good soak.* □ **empapado; ...pegarme un buen baño**
■ *v.* to put (something) to lie in a liquid; to get/to make very wet: *soak the dried peas in water overnight; we got soaked in the thunderstorm; the stains will come out if you put the cloth to soak in hot water.* □ **poner en remojo**
soaking *n.* action of being soaked: *we got a soaking in the storm.* □ **nos calamos con la tormenta**
■ *adj.* and *adv.* wet through: *his coat is soaking (wet).* □ **empapado**
soak up *v.* to absorb (a liquid): *the dry cloth has soaked up all the milk.* □ **absorber**

soap [soup] *n.* material made of oil and fat used for washing: *a bar of soap; soap powder/soap flakes.* □ **jabón**
■ *v.* to wash with soap: *soap yourself all over.* □ **enjabonar**
soapbox *n.* box on which a speaker stands to talk to a meeting outdoors. □ **tribuna improvisada**
soap opera *n.* trite serial story on television. □ **culebrón; telenovela**
soapsuds *n. pl.* foam made from soap. □ **espuma**
soapy *adj.* full of soap; covered with soap: *soapy water.* □ **jabonoso**

soar [sɔ:] *v.* **1** to fly high into the air; (*of bird*) to glide without beating its wings: *the skier soared into the air; eagles were soaring round the mountain peak.* □ **elevarse**
2 to rise rapidly: *prices have soared,* have gone upwards rapidly. □ **dispararse**
soaring *adj.* which is flying high; (prices) which are rising rapidly. □ **altísimo; disparado (precio)**

sob [sɔb] *n.* short breath like a hiccup when crying: *she managed to tell her story through her sobs.* □ **sollozo**
■ *v.* (*he sobbed*) to weep, taking short breaths like hiccups. □ **sollozar**

sober ['soubə] *adj.* **1** not drunk. □ **sobrio**
2 serious: *a sober discussion.* □ **serio**
3 dark (colour). □ **sobrio**
■ *v.* ***to sober up,*** to get over your drunkenness. □ **quitarse la borrachera**
soberly *adv.* seriously. □ **seriamente**
soberness, sobriety [sə'braiiti] *n.* being sober. □ **sobriedad**

soccer ['sɔkə] *n.* football/game played between two

sides of eleven players who can only kick or head the ball. □ **fútbol**

sociable ['souʃəbl] *adj.* friendly/liking the company of other people. □ **sociable**
sociability [souʃə'biliti] *n.* state of being sociable. □ **sociabilidad**

social ['souʃl] *adj.* **1** referring to society: *social problems.* □ **social**
social science, study of the problems of society. □ **ciencias sociales**
social security, money/help provided by the government to people who need it. □ **seguridad social**
social worker, one who works to help families in need. □ **asistente social**
the social system, the way society is organized. □ **el sistema social**
2 living in groups: *ants are social insects.* □ **social**
3 *social evening,* evening party for a group of people. □ **velada**
■ *n.* party: *we're holding a social for the old people tomorrow evening.* □ **velada**
socialism *n.* political system where the state owns and runs the wealth of the country; belief that all property should belong to the state and that every citizen is equal. □ **socialismo**
socialist *adj.* and *n.* (person) who believes in socialism; (policies) which follow the principles of socialism. □ **socialista**
socialize *v.* to organize (a country) along the principles of socialism. □ **socializar**

society [sə'saiiti] *n.* **1** way in which people are organized; a group of people who live in the same way: *Western society.* □ **sociedad**
2 group/club/association of people with the same interests: *society for protection of ancient monuments.* □ **sociedad**
3 top class of people: *high society; a society hostess.* □ **alta sociedad**
sociology [sousi'ɔlədʒi] *n.* study of society and how people live in society. □ **sociología**
sociological [sousiə'lɔdʒikl] *adj.* referring to society and the way in which society changes. □ **sociológico**
sociologist [sousi'ɔlədʒist] *n.* person who studies society and how people live in it. □ **sociólogo**

sock [sɔk] *n.* **1** woollen covering for the foot and lower part of the leg. □ **calcetín**
ankle socks, short socks which cover the ankles. □ **calcetines**
knee socks, socks which go up to the knee. □ **medias**
2 *you'll have* ***to pull your socks up,*** (*informal*) try to do better. □ **tendrás que esforzarte**
■ *v.* (*informal*) to hit: *he socked him on the jaw.* □ **sacudir**

socket ['sɔkit] *n.* **1** hole or holes into which something is fitted. □ **hueco**
2 *his eyes nearly popped out of their sockets,* he was very surprised. □ **...se salieron de las órbitas**
3 *electric socket,* one which a bulb/plug can be fitted into. □ **enchufe**

soda ['soudə] *n.* compound of sodium. □ **sosa**
baking soda/bicarbonate of soda, white powder used in baking or as a medicine. □ **bicarbonato sódico**
ice cream soda, sweet fizzy drink mixed with ice cream. □ **soda con helado**
soda (water), water made fizzy by putting gas into it. □ **soda; agua de Seltz**
soda fountain *n.* bar where sweet drinks and ice cream are served. □ **bar de bebidas refrescantes**

sodden ['sɔdn] *adj.* very wet. □ **empapado**

sodium ['soudiəm] *n.* (*chemical element*: Na) white soft metal, which can catch fire, and is usually found in combination with other substances. □ **sodio**

sofa ['soufə] *n.* long soft seat with a soft back for several people. □ **sofá**

soft [sɔft] *adj.* **1** not hard: *soft cushion; the seats in the car are too soft.* □ **blando**
2 quiet: *he spoke in a soft voice.* □ **suave**
3 not strict: *she's too soft with the boys in the class; he has a soft heart.* □ **blando**
4 (*informal*) stupid: *she's a bit soft in the head; don't be soft.* □ **bobo**
5 ***soft water,*** water with little calcium in it. □ **agua fina**
6 ***soft drink,*** drink which is not alcoholic. □ **bebida refrescante**
7 ***soft drugs,*** drugs which are not addictive. □ **drogas blandas**
soft-boiled *adj.* (egg) which has not been boiled very much, so that the yolk is still runny. □ **pasado por agua**
soften *v.* to make/to become soft. □ **ablandar**
to soften someone up, to make someone weak before attacking or before asking for a favour. □ **debilitar al enemigo; ablandar el corazón a alguien**
softener *n.* ***water softener,*** apparatus for making hard water soft. □ **descalcificador**
soft fruit *n. pl.* small fruit (like raspberries/strawberries, etc.) which go bad quickly. □ **fruta delicada**
soft-hearted *adj.* not strict/too kind. □ **bondadoso**
softly *adv.* **1** in a soft way. □ **suavemente**
2 *to tread softly,* walk without making any noise. □ **andar sin hacer ruido**
softness *n.* state of being soft. □ **blandura; suavidad**
soft soap *n.* (*informal*) flattery. □ **coba**
software *n.* computer programs (as opposed to the machines). □ **'software'**

soggy ['sɔgi] *adj.* wet and soft. □ **empapado**

soil [sɔil] *n.* earth: *garden soil; poor soil needs a fertilizer.* □ **suelo**
■ *v.* to make dirty. □ **ensuciar**

sojourn ['sʌdʒən] *n.* (*formal*) stay. □ **estancia**
■ *v.* (*formal*) to stay. □ **residir**

solace ['sɔləs] *n.* (*formal*) comfort. □ **consuelo**

solar ['soulə] *adj.* referring to the sun. □ **solar**
solar heating, heating system run by light from the sun. □ **calefacción solar**
the solar system, series of planets orbiting the sun. □ **el sistema solar**
solar plexus, (i) group of nerves behind the bottom of the lungs and the stomach. □ **plexo solar**
(ii) (*informal*) the lower part of the body where the stomach is: *he was hit in the solar plexus.* □ **vientre**

sold [sould] *v. see* **sell.**

solder ['souldə] *n.* soft metal used to join metal surfaces together when it is melted. □ **soldadura**
■ *v.* to join (metal surfaces together) with solder. □ **soldar**
soldering iron *n.* tool which is heated to apply solder to metal surfaces. □ **soldador**

soldier ['souldʒə] *n.* member of the army: *soldiers are on guard at the president's palace.* □ **soldado; militar**
■ *v.* **1** to be on military service. □ **servir como soldado**
2 to continue doing a hard job: *we are soldiering on,* (*informal*) pressing on with the work. □ **seguir adelante con el trabajo**

sole [soul] *n.* **1** underside of the foot; bottom part of a shoe. □ **suela**
2 flat sea fish. □ **lenguado**
■ *v.* to put a new sole (on a shoe): *these shoes need soling.* □ **poner suelas**

■ *adj.* **1** only: *the sole survivors of the crash.* □ **único**
2 *he has the sole right to,* he is the only person allowed to. □ **exclusivo**
solely *adv.* only: *the club is open solely to members and their families.* □ **únicamente**
solemn ['sɔləm] *adj.* **1** special and religious (ceremony): *it is your solemn duty to defend the country.* □ **solemne**
2 very serious: *his expression was solemn.* □ **solemne**
solemnity [sə'lemniti] *n.* being solemn: *the solemnity of the occasion.* □ **solemnidad**
solemnization [sɔləmnai'zeiʃn] *n.* celebration (of a marriage/of a religious ceremony). □ **celebración**
solemnize ['sɔləmnaiz] *v.* to celebrate/to perform (a marriage/a religious ceremony). □ **celebrar**
solemnly *adv.* in a solemn way: *he solemnly laid a wreath on the tomb.* □ **solemnemente**
solenoid ['sɔlənoid] *n.* coiled wire which produces a magnetic field when an electric current passes through it. □ **solenoide**
solfa [sɔl'fɑː] *n.* system of indicating tones in music by syllables (*doh-ray-me*, etc.). □ **solfeo**
solicit [sə'lisit] *v.* to ask for something: *to solicit advice.* □ **solicitar**
solicitation [səlisi'teiʃn] *n.* asking for something. □ **solicitación**
solicitor *n.* lawyer who gives advice to people on legal problems. □ **abogado**
solicitous *adj.* worried/anxious about something: *he was most solicitous about my mother's health.* □ **solícito**
solicitude *n.* anxiety/worry about something. □ **solicitud**
solid ['sɔlid] *adj.* **1** not liquid: *the bucket of water has frozen solid; the baby has started to eat solid food.* □ **sólido**
2 not hollow: *a solid ball.* □ **macizo**
3 made all of one material: *the table is made of solid oak; solid silver candlesticks.* □ **macizo**
4 *he slept for eight hours solid,* without stopping. □ **...de un tirón**
5 trustworthy: *a very solid firm; he's very solid.* □ **sólida (empresa); firme (persona)**
■ *n.* **1** solid substance: *he's so ill he can't eat solids.* □ **alimentos sólidos**
2 three-dimensional shape: *a cube is a solid.* □ **sólido**
solidarity [sɔli'dæriti] *n.* common interest with someone: *they went on strike out of solidarity with the other workers.* □ **solidaridad**
solidify *v.* to become solid; to make (something) become solid: *the molten lava solidified to form rock.* □ **solidificar**
solidity [sə'liditi] *n.* being solid. □ **solidez**
solidly *adv.* completely: *they voted solidly for the motion.* □ **unánimemente**
solid-state *adj.* (TV set, etc.) which uses transistors and not valves. □ **de estado sólido**
soliloquy [sə'liləkwi] *n.* speech spoken by a character alone on the stage. □ **soliloquio**
solitaire [sɔli'tɛə] *n.* **1** game for one person, made of balls which have to be moved from hole to hole removing them one at a time. □ **solitario**
2 single diamond (in a ring, etc.). □ **solitario**
solitary ['sɔlitri] *adj.* **1** single/sole: *not a solitary soldier was left on the battlefield.* □ **único; solo**
2 lonely: *a solitary mountain hut.* □ **solitario**
solitary confinement, imprisonment alone in a cell. □ **incomunicación**
solitude *n.* being alone. □ **soledad**
solo ['soulou] *n.* piece of music for one person: *a violin solo.* □ **solo**
■ *adj.* carried out by one person: *a solo crossing of the Atlantic.* □ **a solas**
soloist *n.* musician who plays a solo. □ **solista**
solstice ['sɔlstis] *n.* ***summer solstice,*** time when the days are longest (June 21st). □ **solsticio de verano**
winter solstice, time when the days are shortest (December 21st). □ **solsticio de invierno**
soluble ['sɔljubl] *adj.* **1** which can be dissolved: *salt is soluble in water.* □ **soluble**
2 (problem) which can be solved. □ **que se puede resolver**
solubility [sɔlju'biliti] *n.* ability to be dissolved. □ **solubilidad**
solution [sə'luːʃn] *n.* **1** liquid in which something has been dissolved: *a salt solution; a weak salt solution,* solution with not much salt in it. □ **solución**
2 act of solving a problem; the answer to a problem: *the solution to this week's crossword is on page 3.* □ **solución**
solve [sɔlv] *v.* to find the answer to (a problem): *the government is trying to solve the housing shortage; have you solved the maths problems yet?* □ **resolver**
solvency ['sɔlvənsi] *n.* state of having enough money to pay your debts. □ **solvencia**
solvent *adj.* having enough money to pay your debts. □ **solvente**
■ *n.* liquid which dissolves another substance. □ **disolvente**
sombre ['sɔmbə] *Amer.* **somber** *adj.* dark and gloomy. □ **sombrío**
sombrero [səm'brɛərou] *n.* hat with a wide brim worn in South America. □ **sombrero de ala ancha**
some [sʌm] *adj.* **1** not a particular one: *I will see you some day next week; we will have to find some other way of solving the problem; I will write some sort of reply to his letter.* □ **algún**
2 certain: *some days it's so hot I don't go out; some people don't like milk; some houses are too cold to be comfortable.* □ **algunos días...; algunas personas...; algunas casas...**
3 several/a few; a little: *you must eat some oranges; there are some people in the queue already; if your throat is dry you should drink some water.* □ **...que comer naranjas; ya hay gente...; ...debes beber agua/un poco de agua**
4 wonderful: *that was some dinner!; some help you are!,* you are not much help. □ **¡aquello sí que fue cenar!**
■ *pron.* several out of a group; part of a whole: *some of our neighbours are pleasant people; some of these apples are rotten; if you like sweets, take some more; some of the time I have nothing to do.* □ **algunos**
■ *adv.* approximately: *the film lasts some 50 or 60 minutes; there were some 20 or 30 people in the hall.* □ **unos**
somebody ['sʌmbədi] *pron.* a particular unknown person: *somebody's knocking at the door; somebody has stolen my purse.* □ **alguien**
somehow ['sʌmhau] *adv.* **1** in one way or another: *somehow, we have to get to London by 4 o'clock.* □ **de algún modo**
2 for no particular reason: *somehow we have never got on well together.* □ **por alguna razón**
someone ['sʌmwɔn] *pron.* a particular unknown person: *someone has eaten my sandwiches.* □ **alguien**
some place ['sʌmpleis] *adv. Amer.* (*informal*) in an unknown place: *you will have to try some place else.* □ **en otra parte**
something ['sʌmθiŋ] *pron.* **1** a particular unknown thing: *something has gone wrong with the engine;*

can I have something to eat? □ **algo**
2 thing which is possibly important: *there is something in what you say; it is something that no one got hurt.* □ **algo**
3 (replacing a forgotten detail): *the 4 something train,* the train which leaves at some time after 4 o'clock; *what's his name? Peter something (or other), isn't it?* □ **el tren de las 4 y algo; ...Pedro o algo así**
sometime ['sʌmtaim] *adv.* at a particular unknown time: *it happened sometime last year; we will try to meet again sometime soon.* □ **sucedió el año pasado; ...en algún momento pronto**
sometimes ['sʌmtaimz] *adv.* from time to time/at times: *sometimes the car goes well, sometimes it just doesn't go at all; sometimes I think he's mad.* □ **unas veces el coche..., otras veces...; a veces pienso que...**
somewhat ['sʌmwɔt] *adv.* rather: *he was somewhat surprised to get a letter from me.* □ **algo**
somewhere ['sʌmwɛə] *adv.* at some particular unknown place: *I left my hat somewhere in the church; somewhere or other there must be a chemist's shop in the town; I would go somewhere else if I were you.* □ **en alguna parte**
somersault ['sʌməsɔ:lt] *n.* rolling over, with your head underneath and feet over your head: *he turned three somersaults one after the other.* □ **salto mortal**
■ *v.* to do a somersault/to roll over: *the car somersaulted into the ditch.* □ **dar una vuelta de campana (coche); dar un salto mortal (persona)**
somnambulism [sɔm'næmbjulizəm] *n.* walking in your sleep. □ **sonambulismo**
somnambulist *n.* person who walks when asleep. □ **sonámbulo**
somnolence ['sɔmnələns] *n.* (*formal*) being sleepy/sleepiness. □ **somnolencia**
somnolent *adj.* sleepy. □ **soñoliento**
son [sʌn] *n.* male child: *my son is called Simon; he has two sons and a daughter.* □ **hijo**
son-in-law *n.* (*pl. sons-in-law*) husband of your daughter. □ **yerno**
sonar ['sounɑ:] *n.* device for finding underwater objects by using sound waves. □ **sonar**
sonata [sə'nɑ:tə] *n.* piece of music in three or four movements for a solo instrument, usually with an accompaniment on the piano or with an orchestra. □ **sonata**
song [sɔŋ] *n.* **1** singing: *he burst into song; the bird song woke me up.* □ **canción**
2 words and music to be sung: *a pop song; a folk song; they sang rude songs in the coach.* □ **canción**
3 *to buy something* ***for a song,*** for very little money. □ **...por cuatro cuartos**
4 *he made a great* ***song and dance*** *about it,* (*informal*) a great fuss. □ **armó un follón**
songbird *n.* bird which sings particularly well. □ **pájaro cantor**
songster *n.* person or bird that sings. □ **cantor**
sonic ['sɔnik] *adj.* referring to sound waves. □ **sónico**
sonic boom, bang made by an aircraft travelling faster than the speed of sound. □ **estampido sónico**
sonnet ['sɔnit] *n.* poem with fourteen lines with a fixed rhyming pattern. □ **soneto**
sonorous ['sɔnərəs] *adj.* which makes a loud ringing noise. □ **sonoro**
soon [su:n] *adv.* **1** in a very short time: *we'll be home again soon; it was soon after midnight; I want to see you as soon as possible.* □ **pronto**
2 ***sooner or later,*** at some time to come: *sooner or later someone will realize what has happened.* □ **más pronto o más tarde**
3 ***no sooner*** *had I sat down* ***than*** *the telephone rang,* as soon as I had sat down. □ **no había hecho nada más que sentarme cuando el teléfono...**
4 willingly: *I would as soon stay as go away.* □ **más me gustaría quedarme que...**
5 *I* ***would sooner*** *stay than go away,* I would rather stay. □ **mejor me quedo...**
soot [sut] *n.* black carbon dust which collects in chimneys. □ **hollín**
sooty *adj.* black; covered with soot. □ **cubierto de hollín**
soothe [su:ð] *v.* to calm: *a cup of tea will soothe your nerves; this cold bandage will soothe the pain.* □ **apaciguar**
sop [sɔp] *n.* something given as a bribe to make someone keep quiet. □ **regalo; atención**
■ *v.* (*he sopped*) to soak up (a liquid). □ **absorber**
sopping *adj.* ***sopping wet,*** soaked. □ **empapado**
soppy *adj.* (*informal*) silly and sentimental. □ **sensiblero**
sophistication [səfisti'keiʃn] *n.* **1** cultured way of life. □ **sofisticación**
2 advanced ideas behind the construction of a machine. □ **complejidad**
sophisticated *adj.* **1** cultured: *a sophisticated person.* □ **sofisticado**
2 complicated/advanced: *the new car engine is very sophisticated.* □ **complejo**
sophomore ['sɔfəmɔ:] *n. Amer.* second-year student. □ **estudiante de segundo (año)**
soporific [sɔpə'rifik] *adj.* and *n.* (medicine) which makes you go to sleep. □ **soporífico (adj.); somnífero (n.)**
soprano [sə'prɑ:nou] *n.* high-pitched singing voice; woman or boy with such a voice. □ **soprano**
sorbet ['sɔ:bei] *n.* water ice. □ **sorbete**
sorcery ['sɔ:səri] *n.* witchcraft/magic. □ **brujería**
sorcerer *n.* wizard/man who makes magic. □ **brujo**
sorceress *n.* witch/woman who makes magic. □ **bruja**
sordid ['sɔ:did] *adj.* unpleasant/dirty: *a sordid crime; tell me all the sordid details.* □ **sórdido**
sore [sɔ:] *adj.* **1** painful/which hurts: *a sore foot; I've got a sore throat.* □ **un pie malo; tengo dolor de garganta**
2 (*informal*) upset/annoyed: *he is sore because no one gave him a present.* □ **molesto**
■ *n.* painful spot on the skin. □ **llaga**
sorely *adv.* very much: *he is sorely in need of money.* □ **muchísimo**
sorority [sə'rɔriti] *n. Amer.* student society for women. □ **asociación femenina de estudiantes**
sorrel ['sɔrəl] *n.* **1** common sour-tasting plant used to make soup. □ **acedera**
2 horse which is a reddish brown colour. □ **alazán**
sorrow ['sɔrou] *n.* sadness: *to my great sorrow, I can't accept your invitation.* □ **pesar; muy a mi pesar,...**
sorrowful *adj.* very sad. □ **pesaroso**
sorrowfully *adv.* sadly: *he sorrowfully went away from the house for the last time.* □ **con pesar**
sorry *adj.* **1** regretting something: *I'm sorry I'm so late; we're sorry you can't come; I'm sorry, but I just do not agree.* □ **siento llegar tarde; sentimos...; lo siento, pero...**
2 feeling pity/sympathy for someone: *I feel sorry for him; he is feeling rather sorry for himself,* rather miserable. □ **lo siento por él; se siente desgraciado**
3 pitiful: *he is in a sorry state.* □ **lastimoso**
sort [sɔ:t] *n.* **1** type/variety: *three sorts of pudding; he's a strange sort of man; what sort of day is it going to be?* □ **clase**

2 *he's a good sort,* he's a pleasant type of person. □ **es un buen tipo**
3 ***something of the sort,*** something like that. □ **algo por el estilo**
4 ***sort of,*** (i) *I'm feeling sort of tired,* (*informal*) rather tired. □ **...algo cansado**
(ii) *she sort of simply stopped eating,* more or less stopped eating. □ **de algún modo dejó de comer**
5 *we had a meal* ***of sorts,*** not a very good meal. □ **no se podía llamar una comida**
6 *he is feeling* ***out of sorts*** *today,* slightly unwell. □ **...algo indispuesto hoy**
■ *v.* to arrange in different groups: *you must sort out the books into alphabetical order; have you sorted out the bad apples from the good ones? they sort the letters at the post office.* □ **ordenar (libros); separar (manzanas); clasificar (cartas)**
sorter *n.* person who arranges things in different groups, especially person who sorts letters in a post office. □ **clasificador**
sorting *n.* action of arranging in groups. □ **clasificación**
sorting office, department of a post office where letters are grouped according to their addresses. □ **sala de batalla**

sortie ['sɔːtiː] *n.* **1** sudden attack; bombing raid (by aircraft). □ **salida**
2 sudden excursion into an unpleasant area. □ **salida**

soufflé ['suːflei] *n.* light cooked dish, made from beaten up eggs. □ **'soufflé'**

sought [sɔːt] *v. see* **seek.**
sought after *adj.* which people want: *these old chairs are very much sought after.* □ **buscado**

soul [soul] *n.* **1** the spirit in a person (as opposed to the body): *when you die your soul will go to heaven.* □ **alma**
2 central character: *he was* ***the life and soul of the party,*** made the party go well. □ **alma**
3 *she is the soul of honour,* a fine example of honour. □ **es la personificación del honor**
4 person: *the ship sank with all souls; she is a dear old soul; we walked for miles without meeting a living soul.* □ **alma**
soul-destroying *adj.* (work) which is very dull, or does not allow you to use your mind. □ **de lo más aburrido**
soulful *adj.* with a lot of feeling: *a soulful expression.* □ **conmovedor**
soulless *adj.* (work) which is very dull. □ **mecánico; monótono**
soul music *n.* popular music played by black musicians, which conveys deep feelings. □ **música 'soul'**
soul-searching *n.* examination of your own motives/conscience: *after much soul-searching he decided to accept the offer.* □ **examen introspectivo**

sound [saund] *n.* **1** noise: *the sound of music coming from an open window; the sound of waves breaking on rocks.* □ **sonido**
2 ***sound wave,*** wave in the air which carries sound. □ **onda sonora**
3 *the plane broke through the* ***sound barrier,*** went faster than the speed of sound. □ **...barrera del sonido**
4 *I don't like the sound of it,* I am not very pleased by it. □ **no me huele bien**
5 stretch of sea water. □ **brazo de mar**
■ *v.* **1** to make a noise: *they sounded the alarm; he sounded his horn; the letter 'b' is not sounded in 'doubt'.* □ **tocar, sonar**
2 ***to sound like,*** to be similar in sound to something; to have the effect of being: *this piece of music sounds like Mozart; that sounds like his car now,* I think I can hear his car; *your idea sounds like a good one.* □ **sonar a**
3 *the thunder sounds a long way off,* it seems from the noise that the thunder is a long way off. □ **...suena a lo lejos**
4 ***to sound someone out,*** to talk to someone to try to find out his opinion. □ **sondear a alguien**
5 to measure the depth of water. □ **sondar**
■ *adj.* **1** healthy/not rotten: *he's sound in wind and limb,* very healthy; *this wood is still sound; are the foundations sound? our financial position is very sound.* □ **está en forma; esta madera está todavía bien/en buenas condiciones**
2 reasonable/trustworthy: *his judgement is always sound.* □ **bien fundado**
3 thorough/deep: *he fell into a sound sleep; we gave them a sound beating.* □ **...profundo sueño; ...buena paliza**
sound effects *n. pl.* noises made in a play/film, etc., which imitate real sounds (such as thunder/gunfire, etc.). □ **efectos sonoros**
sounding *n.* **1** making of noise: *the sounding of the horn.* □ **sonido**
2 investigation: *sounding out of public opinion.* □ **sondeo**
3 measuring the depth of water. □ **sondeo**
4 *I will take soundings tomorrow,* I will ask people's opinion tomorrow. □ **haré un sondeo...**
soundless *adj.* which does not make any noise. □ **silencioso**
soundlessly *adv.* not making any noise. □ **silenciosamente**
soundly *adv.* thoroughly/deeply: *he slept soundly right through the battle; we beat them soundly.* □ **profundamente (dormir); bien (pegar)**
soundness *n.* being sound: *the soundness of the foundations.* □ **solidez**
sound off *v.* (*informal*) to start talking loudly about something: *he sounded off about pollution of the atmosphere.* □ **poner el grito en el cielo**
soundproof *adj.* made so that sound cannot get through: *a soundproof room.* □ **insonorizado**
■ *v.* to make (a building) soundproof: *the rooms in the hotel by the airport have all been soundproofed.* □ **insonorizar**
soundtrack *n.* part of a film where the sound is recorded: *this record is made from the soundtrack of the film.* □ **banda sonora**

soup [suːp] *n.* **1** liquid dish usually eaten at the beginning of a meal: *vegetable soup; leek soup.* □ **sopa**
soup plate, special plate for eating soup. □ **plato sopero**
2 *now we're* ***in the soup,*** (*informal*) in real trouble. □ **ahora sí que estamos hasta el cuello**
soup up *v.* (*informal*) to increase the power of an engine: *he has a souped-up Ford.* □ **preparar**

sour ['sauə] *adj.* **1** not sweet: *these oranges are very sour.* □ **ácido**
2 *sour milk,* milk which has gone bad; *the milk has turned sour.* □ **leche cortada**
3 bad tempered/unpleasant (person): *she gave a sour grimace.* □ **desabrido**
4 ***it's just sour grapes,*** (*informal*) he is saying those unpleasant things because he is envious. □ **es pura envidia**
■ *v.* to make bad: *this has soured relations between the two countries for years.* □ **agriar**

sourly *adv.* in a bad-tempered way: *he smiled sourly.* □ **agriamente**

source [sɔːs] *n.* place of origin/place where something starts or comes from: *the source of the river Thames; this is the source of all our problems.* □ **nacimiento (río); origen (problema)**

souse [saus] *v.* **1** to soak in water. □ **empapar**
2 to pickle herrings in salt water: *soused herrings.* □ **escabechar; ...en escabeche**

south [sauθ] *n.* one of the points of the compass; (*in areas north of the equator*) the direction of the sun at midday: *the harbour is to the south of the town; the south of the country is covered with snow.* □ **sur**
■ *adj.* of the south: *South America.* □ **América del Sur**
■ *adv.* towards the south: *the ship was heading south; birds fly south in winter.* □ **hacia el sur**
southbound *adj.* going towards the south. □ **con rumbo al sur**
south-east *adj., adv.* and *n.* direction between south and east: *the south east of the country; south east Spain.* □ **sudeste**
south-easterly, south-eastern *adj.* referring to the south-east. □ **sudoriental**
southerly [ˈsʌðəli] *adj.* **1** *southerly wind,* wind from the south. □ **viento del sur**
2 *he was heading in a southerly direction,* towards the south. □ **...en dirección al sur**
southern [ˈsʌðən] *adj.* referring to the south: *the southern United States.* □ **del sur**
southerner [ˈsʌðənə] *n.* person who lives in the south. □ **habitante del sur; meridional**
southward *adj.* towards the south. □ **hacia el sur**
southwards *adv.* towards the south. □ **hacia el sur**
south-west *adj., adv.* and *n.* direction between south and west: *rocks to the south west of Ireland; south west Scotland.* □ **sudoeste**
south-westerly south-western *adj.* referring to the south-west. □ **sudoccidental**

souvenir [suːvəˈniə] *n.* something which reminds you of a place/an event: *a souvenir of Spain; a souvenir of our Spanish holiday.* □ **recuerdo**

sou'wester [sauˈwestə] *n.* waterproof sailor's hat. □ **sueste**

sovereign [ˈsɔvrin] *n.* **1** ruler/king or queen. □ **soberano**
2 British gold coin. □ **soberano**
■ *adj.* **1** powerful: *a sovereign remedy.* □ **potente, eficaz**
2 self-governing: *a sovereign state.* □ **un estado soberano**
sovereignty *n.* high power; self-government. □ **soberanía**

Soviet Union [ˈsouviətˈjuːnjən] *n.* large country in Europe and Asia made up of Russia and other republics. □ **la Unión Soviética**
Soviet *adj.* and *n.* **1** (person) from the Soviet Union/from Russia. □ **soviético**
2 council/committee in a Communist country. □ **soviet**

sow [sau] *n.* female pig. □ **cerda**
■ *v.* (*he sowed; he has sown*) to put seed into earth so that it grows: *to sow cabbages; I have sown this field with barley.* □ **sembrar**
sower [ˈsouə] *n.* person who sows seed. □ **sembrador**

soy [sɔi] **soya** [ˈsɔjə] *n.* sort of tropical bean which is very nutritious: *soya bean.* □ **soja**
soy(a) sauce, salty Chinese sauce made from soya beans. □ **salsa de soja**

spa [spɑː] *n.* place where mineral water comes out of the ground naturally and where people go to drink or bathe in the water because of its medicinal properties. □ **balneario**

space [speis] *n.* **1** place; empty area between two objects/on a sheet of paper, etc.: *I will park my car in that space over there; write your name and address in the space at the top of the form; your desk takes up a lot of space.* □ **espacio**
2 short period of time: *he got dressed, had breakfast and drove to work, all in the space of fifteen minutes.* □ **espacio**
3 area beyond the earth's atmosphere: *space flight; space station.* □ **vuelo/estación espacial**
■ *v.* ***to space out,*** to time (things) at intervals; to place (things) with gaps between them: *he will space out his visits; garden with trees neatly spaced out across the lawn.* □ **espaciar**
spacecraft *n.* rocket in which astronauts travel in space. □ **nave espacial**
spaceman *n.* (*pl. spacemen*) person who travels in space. □ **astronauta**
spacesaving *adj.* (piece of furniture, etc.) which is compact or which folds, and so saves space. □ **que economiza espacio**
spaceship *n.* rocket in which astronauts travel in space. □ **nave espacial**
spacesuit *n.* special clothes worn by spacemen. □ **traje espacial**
spacing *n.* action of putting gaps between something: *type this letter with double spacing,* with two spaces between the lines. □ **espaciamiento**
spacious [ˈspeiʃəs] *adj.* very large/with lots of space: *a spacious house.* □ **espacioso**
spaciousness [ˈspeiʃəsnəs] *n.* state of being large/having a lot of space. □ **espaciosidad**

spade [speid] *n.* **1** garden tool with a sharp blade for digging holes in the ground. □ **pala**
2 *to do the* ***spade work,*** the preliminary work for a new project. □ **hacer el trabajo preliminar**
3 ***to call a spade a spade,*** to say what you think without trying to hide your opinions. □ **llamar al pan pan y al vino vino**
4 one of the four suits in a pack of cards: *the ten of spades.* □ **espadas**

spaghetti [spəˈgeti] *n.* Italian food formed of long strings of pasta. □ **espaguetis**

Spain [spein] *n.* country in south west Europe. □ **España**

span [spæn] *n.* **1** width (of wings/an arch, etc.): *wing span of 10 metres.* □ **envergadura, luz**
2 arch of a bridge: *the bridge across the river has four spans.* □ **ojo; el puente ... cuatro ojos**
3 length of time: *within a span of twelve months; time span; life span.* □ **en un lapso de doce meses**
■ *v.* (*he spanned*) to stretch across: *the bridge spans the river; his term as Prime Minister spanned three decades.* □ **extenderse sobre (puente); durar (mandato)**

Spaniard [ˈspænjəd] *n.* person from Spain. □ **español**

spaniel [ˈspænjəl] *n.* type of dog with large hanging ears. □ **perro de aguas**

Spanish [ˈspæniʃ] *adj.* referring to Spain. □ **español**
■ *n.* language spoken in Spain and some Latin American countries. □ **español**

spank [spæŋk] *v.* to smack on the behind. □ **azote**
spanking *adj.* (*informal*) fast: *he drove along at a spanking pace.* □ **paso veloz**
■ *n.* series of smacks on the behind. □ **azotaina**

spanner [ˈspænə] *n.* metal tool with an opening which fits round a nut so that it can be twisted to loosen or tighten. □ **llave**

to throw a spanner in the works, to bring things to a state of confusion. □ **armar la de Dios es Cristo**

spar [spɑː] *n.* ship's mast or a wooden beam for holding the sails. □ **palo**

■ *v.* (*he sparred*) to practise boxing: *sparring match; sparring partner.* □ **entrenarse en el boxeo; combate con 'sparring'; 'sparring'**

spare ['spɛə] *adj.* not used/extra: *what do you do in your spare time? spare time activities; we can put you up for the night in our spare bedroom.* □ **libre; ...habitación para invitados**

spare parts, replacement parts for a machine. □ **recambios**

spare wheel, wheel carried to replace one that has a puncture. □ **rueda de repuesto**

■ *n.* something extra/replacement: *when you buy a new car, always check if spares are easy to get.* □ **recambio**

■ *v.* **1** to do without: *I can't spare anyone to help you.* □ **pasarse sin**

2 to give up; not to need: *I can't spare the time; can you spare me a few minutes? have you any clothes you can spare for the raffle? can you spare a cup of tea?* □ **...perder el tiempo; ¿...dedicar unos minutos?; ¿tienes una taza de té?**

3 ***to spare someone's life,*** not to kill someone whom you have defeated; to have mercy on someone. □ **perdonar la vida a uno**

4 *he was spared the embarrassment,* they saved him from being embarrassed. □ **le salvaron de...**

5 *spare me the details,* don't give me all the details. □ **ahórrate los detalles**

sparing *adj.* ***to be sparing with something,*** to economize: *be sparing with the butter – it is all we have got.* □ **parco (en palabras); no te pongas mucha...**

sparingly *adv.* using little: *go sparingly with the jam; you need to water the plants sparingly in winter.* □ **con moderación**

spark [spɑːk] *n.* little flash of fire/of electricity: *sparks from the blaze set fire to the shed; he hasn't a spark of enthusiasm.* □ **chispa**

■ *v.* **1** to send out sparks/to make electric sparks: *the engine is not sparking properly,* the sparking plugs are not working. □ **chispear; ...no enciende bien**

2 *his speech sparked off a violent argument,* started an argument. □ **...provocó una discusión violenta**

sparking plug *Amer.* **spark plug** *n.* (*in a car engine*) device which produces a spark which ignites petrol vapour. □ **bujía**

sparkle ['spɑːkl] *n.* bright shiny light; small spark. □ **destello**

■ *v.* **1** to glitter/to shine brightly: *her eyes sparkled when she saw the fur coat.* □ **destellar**

2 *he sparkles in conversation,* he speaks brilliantly/wittily. □ **anima muchísimo la...**

3 ***sparkling wine,*** wine which bubbles. □ **vino espumoso**

sparkler *n.* type of firework which sends out sparks. □ **bengala**

sparrow ['spærou] *n.* common small brown and grey bird. □ **gorrión**

sparrowhawk *n.* common small hawk. □ **gavilán**

sparse [spɑːs] *adj.* not thick; thinly spread: *a few sparse trees.* □ **disperso**

sparsely *adv.* with few (things); thinly: *sparsely populated area; a sparsely attended meeting.* □ **escasamente**

spartan ['spɑːtən] *adj.* harsh/hard; simple; uncomfortable: *you get used to a spartan way of life in the army.* □ **espartano**

spasm ['spæzəm] *n.* **1** sudden uncontrollable pulling of the muscles. □ **espasmo**

2 sudden fit (of work): *he works in spasms.* □ **a rachas**

spasmodic [spæz'mɔdik] *adj.* coming in spasms/from time to time: *spasmodic fits of tidiness.* □ **espasmódico**

spasmodically *adv.* from time to time. □ **a rachas**

spastic ['spæstik] *adj.* and *n.* (person) who has suffered from brain damage which causes partial paralysis. □ **espástico**

spat [spæt] *v. see* **spit.**

spate [speit] *n.* **1** *river in spate,* in flood. □ **avenida; crecida**

2 *a sudden spate of orders,* sudden rush. □ **un torrente de...**

spatial ['speiʃəl] *adj.* referring to space. □ **espacial**

spatter ['spætə] *v.* to splash (someone) with little spots of liquid: *spattered with mud/blood.* □ **salpicar**

spatula ['spætjulə] *n.* **1** wide flat blunt flexible knife. □ **espátula**

2 piece of flat wood used by a doctor to hold down your tongue while he is examining your throat. □ **depresor**

spawn [spɔːn] *n.* eggs (of a fish/frog, etc.). □ **freza; hueva**

mushroom spawn, material like seeds from which mushrooms grow. □ **semillas**

■ *v.* to produce eggs. □ **frezar; desovar**

speak [spiːk] *v.* (*he spoke; he has spoken*) **1** to say words and phrases: *he walked past me without speaking; she was speaking to the policeman about the street lights; I know him to speak to,* I know him enough to get into conversation with him. □ **hablar**

2 to talk in public: *he is speaking at a meeting tomorrow night.* □ **hablar**

3 to be able to say things in a foreign language: *can you speak Russian?* □ **hablar**

speaker *n.* **1** person who speaks: *he is an amusing speaker,* he makes amusing speeches; *the speaker tonight is the chief of the traffic police.* □ **conversador; conferenciante**

2 *the Speaker of the House of Commons,* (*in Parliament*) the chairman. □ **presidente**

3 loudspeaker/device which allows the sound from a radio, etc., to be heard. □ **altavoz**

speak for *v.* to plead on someone's behalf: *I am speaking for those people who are opposed to the plan; let him speak for himself,* fight his own case. □ **hablar en nombre de**

speaking *n.* **1** action of talking: *I don't like speaking in public.* □ **no me gusta hablar en público**

2 ***on speaking terms,*** willing to talk and be polite to another, especially after a quarrel: *He and his father are not on speaking terms.* □ **acercamiento; no nos hablamos**

speak up *v.* **1** to speak more loudly: *can you speak up as we can't hear you at the back of the hall?* □ **hablar alto**

2 ***to speak up for someone,*** to support someone's point of view. □ **intervenir en favor de**

spear ['spiə] *n.* long pointed throwing weapon. □ **lanza**

■ *v.* to jab (something) with a spear: *he speared three fish.* □ **traspasar (algo) con una lanza**

spearhead *n.* front part of a force of attackers. □ **punta de lanza**

■ *v.* to be in the front of an attacking force: *the tanks spearheaded the attack; he spearheaded the new sales drive in South America.* □ **encabezar**

spearmint *n.* common type of mint, often used in chewing gum. □ **menta verde**
special ['speʃəl] *adj.* **1** particular/referring to one particular thing: *I've made a special study of bees; a special knife for pruning trees.* □ **especial**
2 extraordinary/rare/unusual: *it is a very special occasion; there is nothing special about my car.* □ **especial**
■ *n.* **1** particular edition of a newspaper: *the late night special.* □ **edición extraordinaria**
2 particular dish on a menu: *today's special is roast beef.* □ **plato del día**
specialist *n.* person who has studied something very deeply: *a brain specialist; a specialist in European history.* □ **especialista**
speciality [speʃi'æliti] *n.* particular interest; subject which you have studied/something you are known for: *the restaurant's speciality is roast beef; his speciality is imitations of the Prime Minister.* □ **especialidad**
specialization [speʃəlai'zeiʃn] *n.* act of specializing; thing you specialize in. □ **especialización**
specialize ['speʃəlaiz] *v.* ***to specialize in something,*** to study something in particular; to produce something in particular. □ **especializarse**
specially *adv.* particularly; unusually: *the discussion is specially important; the weather has been specially fine.* □ **especialmente**
species ['spi:ʃiz] *n.* (*no pl.*) **1** group of animals/plants which are closely similar, and which can breed together: *a European species of moth.* □ **especie**
2 (*informal*) sort: *it looks like a species of old bicycle bell.* □ **clase de**
specie *n. pl.* (*formal*) coins: *to be paid in specie.* □ **en metálico**
specify ['spesifai] *v.* to state clearly what is required: *I specified a heavy carpet material.* □ **especificar**
specific [spe'sifik] *adj.* particular/precise (details): *what is the specific aim of your group? does this machine have any specific purpose?* □ **específico**
specifically *adv.* particularly: *I specifically told you not to open that door; I specifically asked for the ceiling to be painted brown.* □ **específicamente**
specification [spesifi'keiʃn] *n.* detailed plan/information: *what are the specifications of the new car?* □ **especificaciones**
specific gravity *n.* density of a substance divided by the density of water. □ **peso específico**
specimen ['spesimən] *n.* **1** sample of something which is selected for study or exhibition: *he has several specimens of rare gold coins in his collection.* □ **ejemplar; modelo**
2 sample/example: *can you give me a specimen of your handwriting? I would like to see a specimen of your work before we employ you.* □ **muestra**
specious ['spi:ʃəs] *adj.* not really as good/as true as it seems: *a specious argument.* □ **especioso, engañoso**
speck [spek] *n.* tiny spot: *the sheet was covered with little specks of black; the boat was a speck on the horizon.* □ **mota**
speckle *n.* small (usually brown) spot. □ **punto; mota**
speckled *adj.* covered with spots: *speckled egg.* □ **moteado**
specs [speks] *n. pl.* (*informal*) glasses. □ **gafas**
spectacle ['spektəkl] *n.* **1** show: *changing the guard is an impressive spectacle; don't make a spectacle of yourself.* □ **espectáculo**
2 ***spectacles,*** glasses worn in front of your eyes to correct defects in your sight: *he wears thick spectacles.* □ **gafas**
spectacular [spek'tækjulə] *adj.* impressive (show/display). □ **espectacular**
spectator *n.* person who watches a show/a football match, etc. □ **espectador**
spectre ['spektə] *Amer.* **specter** *n.* **1** ghost. □ **espectro**
2 fear: *the spectre of unemployment.* □ **fantasma**
spectrum ['spektrəm] *n.* range (of colours, etc.). □ **gama, espectro**
speculate ['spekjuleit] *v.* **1** ***to speculate about something,*** to make guesses about something. □ **especular**
2 to gamble by buying things whose value you hope will rise. □ **especular**
speculation [spekju'leiʃn] *n.* **1** guesswork/guesses made about something. □ **especulación**
2 gambling by buying things whose value you hope will rise. □ **especulación**
speculative ['spekjulətiv] *adj.* **1** made by guessing. □ **especulativo**
2 gambling. □ **especulativo**
3 ***a speculative share,*** one whose future price is quite uncertain. □ **una acción especulativa**
speculator ['spekjuleitə] *n.* person who buys goods in the hope of reselling them again at a profit: *a property speculator.* □ **especulador**
sped [sped] *v. see* **speed.**
speech [spi:tʃ] *n.* **1** ability to talk: *he lost the power of speech.* □ **habla**
2 spoken language. □ **habla**
the parts of speech, different groups of words (nouns/verbs, etc.) which are used in a similar way in language. □ **las partes de la oración**
3 talk given in public: *he made a short speech.* □ **discurso**
speech day, day when children are given prizes at school for good work, etc. □ **día de reparto de premios**
speechless *adj.* incapable of saying anything. □ **mudo**
speed [spi:d] *n.* **1** quickness of movement: *the car was travelling at a speed of 25 miles an hour; the train began to pick up speed,* to go faster; *the engine is working at full speed.* □ **velocidad**
2 rate of movement: *the car was going at a very slow speed.* □ **velocidad**
■ *v.* **1** (*he sped; he has sped*) to go fast: *he sped round the corner and hid.* □ **ir a toda prisa**
2 *we must **speed up** the work,* make the work go faster. □ **activar**
3 (*he speeded*) *the police stopped him for speeding,* for going faster than the legal speed. □ **exceso de velocidad**
speedboat *n.* racing motor boat. □ **lancha rápida**
speedometer [spi:'dəmitə] *n.* dial which shows you how fast you are travelling. □ **velocímetro**
speedway *n.* racing track for motor cycles. □ **circuito**
speedy *adj.* very fast. □ **veloz**
speleology [spi:li'ələdʒi] *n.* pot-holing; climbing down into caves or holes in the ground. □ **espeleología**
speleologist *n.* person who climbs in or explores caves and holes in the ground. □ **espeleólogo**
spell [spel] *n.* **1** magic curse; words which may have a magic effect: *the witch cast a spell over the princess.* □ **hechizo**
2 period: *a spell of cold weather; a cold spell; I did two spells of duty last week.* □ **ola de frío; hice dos servicios...**
■ *v.* (*he spelt*) **1** to say aloud/to write correctly the letters which form a word: *d-o-g spells 'dog'; how*

do you spell your name? □ **deletrear; escribir**
to spell something out, (i) to read something with difficulty. □ **leer algo con dificultad**
(ii) to explain something very clearly. □ **explicar algo de forma clara**
2 to mean: *that spells disaster.* □ **significar**
spellbound *adj.* bewitched/enchanted: *the audience watched the ballet spellbound.* □ **hechizado/embelesado**
spelling *n.* way in which a word is spelt; writing words correctly: *his spelling is weak.* □ **ortografía**
spend [spend] *v.* (*he spent*) **1** to pay money in exchange for something: *I spent $3 on a pair of socks; we spent $10 on rail fares.* □ **gastar**
2 to pass (time): *we spent our holidays in France; he spent two hours mending his car.* □ **pasar**
3 ***to spend yourself,*** to tire yourself out. □ **agotarse**
spending *n.* action of using money to buy something. □ **gasto**
spending power, amount which can be bought with a sum of money: *the spending power of the dollar.* □ **poder adquisitivo**
spendthrift *adj.* and *n.* (person) who spends money fast. □ **derrochador**
spent [spent] *adj.* used: *a spent cartridge; see also* **spend.** □ **usado**
sperm [spə:m] *n.* **1** male fluid which fertilizes the eggs of a female. □ **esperma**
2 ***sperm whale,*** type of large whale which provides oil. □ **cachalote**
spew [spju:] *v.* ***to spew (out),*** (*informal*) to vomit; to pour out: *the machine was spewing out meaningless figures.* □ **vomitar; echar fuera**
sphere ['sfiə] *n.* **1** object which is perfectly round. □ **esfera**
2 area (of influence); society: *he moves in very distinguished spheres; is this within your sphere of responsibility?* □ **esfera**
spherical ['sferikl] *adj.* shaped like a sphere/perfectly round. □ **esférico**
sphinx [sfinks] *n.* legendary animal in Egypt with the head of a woman and the body of a lion; large stone monument of this animal. □ **esfinge**
spice [spais] *n.* **1** flavouring made from seeds/leaves of plants, etc.: *add some spices to the soup; Indian food usually contains a lot of spices.* □ **especia**
2 something which excites interest: *this will add some spice to the story.* □ **picante**
■ *v.* to add spices to (a dish): *spiced meat; this meat dish is highly spiced.* □ **condimentar**
spiciness *n.* state of being spicy. □ **lo picante**
spicy *adj.* **1** with a lot of spices: *spicy food gives me indigestion.* □ **picante**
2 rather rude (story). □ **picante**
spick and span ['spikən'spæn] *adj.* very clean/tidy. □ **impecablemente limpio**
spider ['spaidə] *n.* eight-legged animal, which makes a web and eats flies. □ **araña**
spider's-web *n.* web made by a spider. □ **telaraña**
spidery *adj.* thin and scrawling (handwriting). □ **de patas de mosca, garabateada**
spiel [spi:l] *n.* (*informal*) long flow of talk aimed at persuading someone to buy something or to believe something. □ **rollo**
spigot ['spigət] *n.* tap (in a barrel). □ **espita**
spike [spaik] *n.* **1** long sharp point: *spikes along the top of railings.* □ **pica**
2 ***spikes,*** sharp points in the soles of running shoes. □ **clavos**
spiky *adj.* standing up in sharp points. □ **puntiagudo**
spill [spil] *n.* **1** fall: *the horserider took a spill at the second fence,* fell off his horse. □ **caída**
2 long thin piece of wood for lighting cigarettes/candles, etc. □ **pajuela**
■ *v.* (*he spilled/spilt*) to pour (liquid) out of a container by mistake: *I have spilled some milk on the carpet; considerable amounts of oil are spilling from the wrecked tanker.* □ **derramar**
spillage *n.* action of spilling; amount of something which has been spilt: *oil spillage.* **derramamiento; mancha de petróleo**
spin [spin] *n.* **1** action of turning round and round: *the car went into a spin.* □ **vuelta**
2 *he got* ***into a flat spin,*** (*informal*) got into a state of confusion. □ **estaba totalmente despistado**
3 *he gave the ball some spin,* hit it so that it turned round and round in the air. □ **le dio efecto al balón**
4 short fast trip: *we went for a spin in the car.* □ **vuelta**
■ *v.* (*he spun*) **1** to turn round and round very fast: *the car spun round twice and crashed into the wall.* □ **dar vueltas**
2 ***to spin a coin,*** to throw it up into the air and catch it, so as to decide which side plays first, etc.. □ **echar a cara o cruz**
3 *to spin a ball,* make it turn as it goes through the air. □ **dar efecto a un balón**
4 to twist (raw wool/cotton, etc.) to form a strong thread: *the spider spins a web,* produces thin silky threads to make a web. □ **hilar; la araña teje...**
spin drier *n.* machine for drying washing by turning it round very fast. □ **secadora centrífuga**
spin-dry *v.* to dry (washing) in a spin-drier. □ **centrifugar**
spinner *n.* person who spins thread. □ **hilandero**
spinneret [spinə'ret] *n.* part of the spider which spins the threads to make a web. □ **pezón hilador**
spinning wheel *n.* apparatus for twisting and winding wool. □ **rueca**
spin-off *n.* secondary result; useful by-product. □ **subproducto**
spin out *v.* (*informal*) to make (something) last a long time. □ **prolongar**
spina bifida [spainə'bifidə] *n.* condition from birth, where the spine is badly formed allowing the membrane covering the spinal cord to protrude. □ **espina bífida**
spinach ['spinitʃ] *n.* common green-leaved vegetable. □ **espinaca**
spindle ['spindl] *n.* **1** pin used for twisting thread in a spinning machine. □ **huso**
2 central pin round which something turns. □ **eje**
spindrift ['spindrift] *n.* foam/spray which is blown from breaking waves. □ **rocío del mar**
spine [spain] *n.* **1** backbone; series of connecting bones which forms the back of a skeleton. □ **columna vertebral**
2 back of a book. □ **lomo**
3 prickle (on a cactus/hedgehog, etc.). □ **espina**
spinal *n.* referring to the spine: *spinal injury.* □ **espinal**
spinal column, the spine. □ **columna vertebral**
spinal cord, group of nerves running down the inside of the spine. □ **médula espinal**
spineless *adj.* (person) who is weak and indecisive. □ **débil de carácter**
spiny *adj.* covered with prickles. □ **espinoso**
spinnaker ['spinəkə] *n.* large balloon-like sail on the front of a racing yacht. □ **'espináquer'**
spinney ['spini] *n.* small wood. □ **soto**

spinster ['spinstə] *n.* unmarried woman (usually middle-aged). □ **solterona**
spiral ['spaiərəl] *n.* **1** something which is twisted round and round like a spring: *the spring is in the form of a spiral.* □ **espiral**
2 anything which turns round and round getting higher or lower all the time: *the wages spiral; an inflationary spiral.* □ **espiral**
■ *adj.* twisted round and round like a spring: *spiral staircase.* □ **espiral; escalera de caracol**
■ *v.* (*he spiralled*) to go round and round and rise at the same time: *inflation is spiralling.* □ **dar vueltas en espiral; la inflación se dispara**
spire ['spaiə] *n.* tall pointed construction on top of a church tower, etc. □ **aguja**
spirit ['spirit] *n.* **1** soul: *his spirit is still with us.* □ **espíritu**
2 *she is with us **in spirit,*** even if she is not present she will be thinking of us at this moment. □ **en espíritu**
3 ghost: *he was attacked by evil spirits.* □ **espíritu**
the Holy Spirit, the third person of the Christian Trinity. □ **el Espíritu Santo**
4 energetic way of doing something: *that's the spirit,* that's the right way to do it. □ **espíritu**
5 *he lacks spirit,* he's not bold enough. □ **le falta valor**
6 *to enter into the spirit of the thing,* to join in in a lively way. □ **meterse en el espíritu de algo**
7 *she is rather low in spirits,* feeling gloomy; *they kept up their spirits by singing songs,* kept their morale high. □ **está baja de moral**
8 real meaning (not always expressed in words): *the spirit of the law/the spirit of Christmas.* □ **espíritu**
9 alcohol. □ **alcohol**
surgical spirit, pure alcohol used for rubbing on the skin, etc. □ **alcohol de 96 (grados)**
10 *spirits,* strong alcoholic drink (whisky/gin, etc.). □ **bebidas alcohólicas**
■ *v.* ***to spirit something away,*** to remove something as if by magic: *he was spirited away by the secret police.* □ **hacer desaparecer**
spirited *adj.* very vigorous: *a spirited defence.* □ **enérgico**
spirit level *n.* tool for testing if a surface is level using a glass tube containing an airbubble. □ **nivel (de burbuja)**
spiritual *adj.* referring to the spirit; dealing with the soul. □ **espiritual**
■ *n.* religious song sung by black people in the southern United States. □ **espiritual**
spiritualism *n.* belief that you can communicate with the spirits of dead people. □ **espiritismo**
spiritualist *n.* person who tries to communicate with the spirits of dead people. □ **espiritista**
spit [spit] *n.* **1** long metal rod passed through meat which turns so that the meat is evenly cooked. □ **asador**
2 long thin stretch of land going out into the sea. □ **punta; banco de arena**
3 liquid formed in the mouth: *put some spit on the cloth to polish the mirror.* □ **escupitajo**
4 ***spit and polish,*** excessive cleaning. □ **preocupación exagerada por la limpieza**
5 *he is **the (dead) spit and image of** his father,* (*informal*) he looks exactly like his father. □ **es el vivo retrato...**
■ *v.* **1** (*he spitted*) to put meat on a spit to roast. □ **ensartar**
2 (*he spat*) to send liquid out of the mouth: *he coughed and spat into his handkerchief; the baby spat out all his spinach.* □ **escupir**
3 *he is **the spitting image of** his father,* (*informal*) he looks exactly like his father. □ **es el vivo retrato...**
4 to send sparks out; to rain slightly: *it is not raining properly, just spitting.* □ **chisporrotear**
spittle ['spitl] *n.* saliva. □ **salivazo**
spittoon [spi'tu:n] *n.* dish for spitting into. □ **escupidera**
spite [spait] *n.* **1** bad feeling against someone/desire to hurt someone: *he did it out of spite.* □ **rencor**
2 ***in spite of something,*** without bothering about: *he did it in spite of the fact that he had been told not to; we are going for a long walk in spite of the rain.* □ **a pesar de algo**
■ *v.* to try to annoy: *he just does it to spite me.* □ **fastidiar**
spiteful *adj.* full of bad feeling/wishing to hurt someone: *a spiteful letter.* □ **rencoroso**
spitefully *adv.* nastily/in a way which you hope will hurt. □ **rencorosamente**
spitefulness *n.* desire to hurt someone. □ **malevolencia**
splash [splæʃ] *n.* **1** noisy throwing of liquid; sound of liquid being thrown noisily: *the splash of waves on the rocks; he fell into the lake with a great splash.* □ **chapoteo**
2 mark made by dirty liquid being scattered. □ **salpicadura**
3 bright patch of colour. □ **mancha**
4 short spurt (of soda water). □ **chorrito**
5 sudden show: *to make a splash.* □ **causar sensación**
■ *v.* **1** (*of liquid*) to make a noise while hitting (a solid): *the waves splashed against the rocks; the children splashed in the puddles; the drowning man was splashing in the water.* □ **chapotear**
2 to send dirty liquid on to: *the car splashed me with mud; his shirt was splashed with oil.* □ **salpicar**
3 to display: *the news was splashed across the front page of the newspaper.* □ **poner, mostrar**
splash down *v.* (*of space capsule*) to land in the sea. □ **amerizar**
splash-down *n.* landing (of a spacecraft) in the sea. □ **amerizaje**
splash out *v.* (*informal*) to spend a lot of money: *he splashed out and bought a new car.* □ **derrochar**
spleen [spli:n] *n.* organ near the stomach which keeps the blood in good condition. □ **bazo**
splendid ['splendid] *adj.* magnificent/wonderful: *what a splendid meal! we had a splendid holiday in Sweden.* □ **estupendo**
splendidly *adv.* wonderfully/extremely well. □ **estupendamente**
splendour *Amer.* **splendor** *n.* magnificence. □ **esplendor**
splice [splais] *n.* joint which links two pieces of rope. □ **empalme**
■ *v.* to join (two pieces of rope) by twisting the threads together; to join (two pieces of film) together. □ **empalmar**
splicer *n.* device for joining pieces of film together. □ **empalmadora**
splint [splint] *n.* stiff bar tied to a broken leg, etc., to keep it straight: *he has his arm in splints.* □ **tablilla; ...brazo entablillado**
splinter ['splintə] *n.* small pointed piece (of wood/metal): *I have a splinter in my finger.* □ **astilla**
splinter group, group of people who have separated from a main group. □ **grupo disidente**
■ *v.* to split into thin pointed pieces. □ **astillar**
split [split] *n.* **1** thin crack; sharp break: *there is a*

split in this piece of wood. □ **raja**
2 *a split has developed in the committee of the party,* there is a disagreement between two sections. □ **una escisión...**
3 ***splits,*** gymnastic exercise where you sit on the floor with one leg stretched out in front, and the other behind you: *to do the splits.* □ **'ecart'; despatarrarse**
4 ***banana split,*** dessert of bananas, cream, ice cream and nuts. □ **'banana split'**
■ *v.* (*he split*) **1** to divide (something) into parts; to make (something) divide/crack: *to split a log; let's split the profits; my trousers split when I bent down; the committee has split into three groups.* □ **partir (leño; beneficios); rajarse (pantalones); escindirse (comité)**
2 *my head is splitting,* (*informal*) I have a bad headache. □ **la cabeza me estalla**
3 ***to split on someone,*** (*informal*) to tell tales about someone. □ **chivarse**
■ *adj.* **1** which has been cracked. □ **partido**
split peas, dried peas broken in half. □ **guisantes abiertos**
2 ***in a split second,*** very fast. □ **en menos de un segundo**
3 *to have* ***a split personality,*** to have two ways of behaving which are quite different in varying circumstances. □ **tener un desdoblamiento de la personalidad**
split-level *adj.* (room, etc.) with part of the floor higher than the rest. □ **a dos niveles**
split up *v.* to divide: *the search party split up into groups.* □ **dividirse**
splodge [splɔdʒ] **splotch** [splotʃ] *n.* dirty mark; oddly shaped spot of colour. □ **mancha**
splurge [splə:dʒ] *v.* (*informal*) to spend money extravagantly: *we splurged on a new colour TV.* □ **derrochar**
splutter ['splʌtə] *v.* to spit when speaking; to speak rapidly. □ **hablar chisporroteando; farfullar**
spoil [spɔil] *v.* (*he spoilt/spoiled*) **1** to ruin/to make bad: *the bad weather spoilt our holiday.* □ **estropear**
2 *the meat has spoilt,* gone rotten. □ **...se ha echado a perder**
3 *to spoil a child,* to treat a child so leniently that it ruins his character. □ **mimar**
■ *n.* **1** ***spoils,*** booty, goods taken by soldiers from a defeated enemy. □ **botín**
2 ***spoils,*** rubbish from a mine. □ **escombros**
spoil for *v.* to be eager for: *he is spoiling for a fight.* □ **tener ganas de**
spoilsport *n.* person who spoils other people's enjoyment. □ **aguafiestas**
spoilt *adj.* badly brought up (child). □ **mimado**
spoke [spouk] *n.* one of the rods running from the axle of a wheel to the rim: *a bicycle wheel has wire spokes.* □ **radio**
to put a spoke in someone's wheel, to stop someone from doing what they had planned to do. □ **poner trabas a alguien**
■ *v. see also* **speak.**
spokeshave *n.* tool with a curved blade for smoothing something round. □ **raedera**
spoken ['spoukn] *v. see* **speak.**
spokesman ['spouksmən] *n.* (*pl. spokesmen*) person who speaks on behalf of someone: *the government spokesman on defence; a spokesman for the university said that there was no crisis.* □ **portavoz**
sponge [spʌnʒ] *n.* **1** soft skeleton of a sea animal/block of plastic full of small holes, which soaks up water and is used for washing. □ **esponja**
to throw up/in the sponge, (*informal*) to give in; to admit you are beaten. □ **tirar la toalla**
2 act of washing with a sponge: *give the table a sponge.* □ **pasa la esponja por la mesa**
3 ***sponge cake,*** light soft cake. □ **bizcocho esponjoso**
■ *v.* **1** to wash with a sponge: *I am going to sponge down the car.* □ **pasar una esponja**
2 ***to sponge on someone,*** (*informal*) to live by begging for money from someone. □ **vivir a costa de alguien; gorronear**
spongebag *n.* small plastic bag for carrying washing things (toothbrush/soap, etc.). □ **bolsa de aseo**
sponger *n.* person who doesn't work but gets money by begging for it from friends. □ **gorrón**
spongy *adj.* soft and full of holes: *spongy tissue.* □ **esponjoso**
sponsor ['spɔnsə] *n.* **1** person who helps someone/something by taking responsibility: *sponsor of a new bill in parliament.* □ **patrocinador**
2 person or firm who pays for a television show/opera performance/cricket match, etc., as a form of advertisement. □ **patrocinador**
3 person who pays money to a charity if someone else walks, swims, runs, a certain distance, etc. □ **patrocinador**
■ *v.* **1** to be responsible for (a bill in parliament); to pay for (a television show/a cricket match, etc.). □ **patrocinar**
sponsored walk, walk where a sponsor agrees to pay money to charity according to the distance covered by a certain walker. □ **marcha apadrinada**
2 *to sponsor a child at baptism,* (*of god-parent*) to promise to help the child lead a Christian life. □ **apadrinar**
sponsorship *n.* action of sponsoring something. □ **patrocinio**
spontaneous [spɔn'teiniəs] *adj.* which happens freely/which is not forced: *a spontaneous reaction from the audience.* □ **espontáneo**
spontaneously *adv.* in a spontaneous/natural way. □ **espontáneamente**
spontaneity [spɔntə'niəti] *n.* acting in a natural way. □ **espontaneidad**
spoof [spu:f] *n.* (*informal*) hoax/amusing imitation: *a spoof letter from the Prime Minister.* □ **trampa; carta apócrifa**
spook [spu:k] *n.* ghost. □ **espectro**
spooky *adj.* (*informal*) frightening; (place) which is likely to be haunted. □ **horripilante**
spool [spu:l] *n.* cylinder round which something is wound: *a spool of tape.* □ **carrete; bobina (cinta)**
spoon [spu:n] *n.* eating utensil with a small bowl and a long handle: *soup spoon; coffee spoon.* □ **cuchara**
wooden spoon, (i) spoon made of wood. □ **cuchara de madera**
(ii) silly prize given to someone who is last in a competition. □ **premio de consolación**
■ *v.* ***to spoon something up/into,*** to lift something up/to put something in with a spoon. □ **sacar/meter con cuchara**
spoonfeed *v.* to give a baby food with a spoon; to teach people by giving them answers to questions and not allowing them to work by themselves; to provide everything for (someone) so that they need do nothing to help themselves. □ **dar de comer con cuchara a (un niño); dárselo masticado a alguien**
spoonful *n.* amount contained in a spoon: *I take two spoonfuls of sugar in my tea.* □ **cucharada**
spoor ['spuə)] *n.* (*no. pl.*) tracks left by an animal. □ **rastro**
sporadic [spə'rædik] *adj.* which happens at irregular

intervals: *sporadic gunfire.* □ **esporádico**
sporadically *adv.* happening at irregular intervals: *gunfire could be heard sporadically.* □ **esporádicamente**
spore [spɔː] *n.* plant cell which reproduces without requiring to be fertilized. □ **espora**
sporran ['spɔrən] *n.* leather bag worn by Scotsmen in front of the kilt. □ **'sporran'**
sport [spɔːt] *n.* **1** game (such as football/hockey/tennis, etc.); games in general: *outdoor sports; winter sports; indoor sports; sports ground/sports field; sports equipment.* □ **deporte**
sports day, day when school teams compete for prizes. □ **día de competiciones deportivas**
sports car, light fast open car. □ **(coche) deportivo**
sports jacket/sports coat, man's tweed jacket. □ **chaqueta de sport**
blood sports, hunting animals as a sport. □ **caza**
2 *he's a good sport,* (*informal*) a pleasant person always willing to help. □ **es una bellísima persona**
■ *v.* to wear: *he was sporting a flower in his buttonhole.* □ **llevar puesto**
sporting *adj.* **1** (person) who plays according to the rules/who is pleasant and willing to help. □ **deportivo; caballeroso**
2 *you've got* ***a sporting chance*** *of winning,* you have quite a good chance. □ **buenas posibilidades de ganar**
sportsman *n.* (*pl. sportsmen*) **1** person who takes part in a sport: *Olympic sportsman.* □ **deportista**
2 person who plays properly. □ **caballero**
sportsmanlike *adj.* (playing a game) in a proper way/according to the rules; not cheating. □ **caballeroso**
sportsmanship *n.* quality of being a good sportsman/of not cheating. □ **deportividad**
sportswear *n.* (*no pl.*) clothes worn to play sports. □ **ropa de deporte**
sportswoman *n.* (*pl. sportswomen*) woman who takes part in a sport. □ **deportista**
sporty *adj.* too interested in sport; interested in sport and in nothing else. □ **obseso de los deportes**
spot [spɔt] *n.* **1** place: *this is the spot where the accident took place; I know a quiet little spot for a picnic.* □ **lugar**
on the spot, (i) *you must always be on the spot,* on duty/at your post. □ **...en tu puesto**
(ii) *do it on the spot,* immediately; *he was killed on the spot,* straight away. □ **hazlo ya; en el acto**
to put someone on the spot/to be in a spot, (*informal*) in a difficult position. □ **poner a alguien entre la espada y la pared**
2 small inflamed bump on the skin: *his face is covered with red spots.* □ **grano**
3 usually round coloured mark: *a tie with green spots; you have some spots of mud on your coat; leopards and other animals with spots.* □ **lunar (en la corbata); mancha (de barro); pinta (animal)**
4 ***to knock spots off someone/something,*** (*informal*) to defeat someone easily; to be much better: *this car knocks spots off the old model.* □ **meter una paliza; este coche deja muy atrás...**
5 small amount; a little: (*informal*) *would you like a spot of food/a spot of whisky?; we are having a spot of bother with the heating.* □ **poquitín**
6 *spots of rain,* widely spaced rain drops. □ **gotas de lluvia**
7 spotlight/bright light which only shines on one spot. □ **foco**
■ *v.* (*he spotted*) **1** to mark with a spot: *the walls were spotted with ink; a green spotted tie.* □ **manchar (pared); motear (corbata)**
2 *it's spotting with rain,* drops are falling here and there. □ **está chispeando**
3 to notice: *I've spotted three mistakes in your work.* □ **detectar**
4 *did you spot the winner?,* did you guess who was going to win? □ **¿has adivinado el ganador?**
spot check *n.* surprise check (on items at random). □ **comprobación en el acto**
spotless *adj.* very clean. □ **limpísimo; inmaculado**
spotlessly *adj. spotlessly clean,* extremely clean. □ **limpísimo**
spotlight *n.* bright light which shines on one small area. □ **foco**
■ *v.* to highlight/to draw attention to something. □ **poner de relieve**
spot-on *adj.* (*informal*) absolutely correct. □ **justo**
spotter *n.* person who notes things. □ **observador**
bird spotter, person who sees and notes different species of birds. □ **ornitólogo**
train spotter, person who watches trains and notes the types of engines. □ **aficionado a los trenes**
spotty *adj.* covered with pimples. □ **lleno de granos**
spouse ['spauz] *n.* (*formal*) husband or wife. □ **esposo/a**
spout [spaut] *n.* tube for pouring liquid out of a kettle, etc.; tube for sending waste water/rainwater away from the wall of a building. □ **pitorro (vasija); caño (aguas); canalón (agua de lluvia)**
up the spout, (*informal*) lost/ruined/wasted. □ **con la soga al cuello**
■ *v.* **1** to come out in a jet: *water spouted out of the burst pipe; steam was spouting out of the kettle.* □ **salir a chorro**
2 (*informal*) to speak continuously: *he went spouting on about pollution for hours.* □ **rajar**
sprain [sprein] *n.* twist of a joint. □ **torcedura; esguince**
■ *v.* to twist (a joint): *I've sprained my ankle.* □ **torcerse**
sprang [spræŋ] *v. see* **spring.**
sprat [spræt] *n.* very small herring-like fish. □ **sardineta**
sprawl [sprɔːl] *n.* irregular spread: *the ugly sprawl of the factories over the countryside.* □ **dispersión**
urban sprawl, spread of buildings over the countryside. □ **urbanización caótica**
■ *v.* **1** to lie with arms and legs spread out: *he was sprawled in an armchair; the body lay sprawled on the carpet.* □ **arrellanarse, extenderse**
2 to spread out in an irregular way: *the new suburbs sprawl for miles over the countryside.* □ **extenderse**
spray [sprei] *n.* **1** branch with flowers on it: *a spray of peach blossom.* □ **ramita**
2 liquid in the form of tiny drops/in a mist: *the wind blew the spray from the sea; a spray of perfume.* □ **espuma (del mar); una rociada de perfume**
3 apparatus/machine for sending out a mist of liquid: *put a fine spray on the watering can.* □ **pulverizador**
■ *v.* to send out liquid in a fine mist: *to spray apple trees with insecticide; to spray paint on a door; he was sprayed with paint when he went too close to the workmen.* □ **rociar**
sprayer *n.* machine for spraying: *paint-sprayer.* □ **pulverizador; atomizador**
spray gun *n.* tool shaped like a pistol with a small container attached (used for spraying paint/insecticide, etc.). □ **pistola**
spread [spred] *n.* **1** wide expanse; width: *the spread*

of a bird's wings. □ **extensión; envergadura de las alas...**
2 act of sending out over a wide area: *the spread of disease; the spread of knowledge.* □ **propagación**
3 (*informal*) feast: *what a spread!*, what a lot to eat! □ **banquetazo**
4 soft paste for putting on bread, etc.: *cheese spread.* □ **pasta**
5 *double-page spread,* text which runs over two facing pages in a book or newspaper. □ **a doble página**
■ *v.* (*he spread*) **1** to send out/to go out over a wide area: *the soldiers spread out across the fields; the salesman spread out his goods on the counter; she spread a cloth over the tables; the disease spread rapidly; the fire has spread to the house next door.* □ **desplegarse; extender**
2 to space out over a period of time: *the payments are spread over six months.* □ **espaciar**
3 to cover bread, etc., with something: *spread the butter thinly; spread the glue over all the paper.* □ **extender**
4 *margarine spreads easily,* it is easy to spread. □ **...se extiende con facilidad**
spreadeagled *adj.* lying flat with arms and legs stretched out. □ **con piernas y brazos extendidos**
spree [spriː] *n.* **1** happy time. □ **juerga**
2 *to go on a spending spree,* to have a happy time spending money. □ **tirar la casa por la ventana**
sprig [sprig] *n.* small branch. □ **ramita**
sprightly ['spraitli] *adj.* light and vigorous: *sprightly footsteps.* □ **vivo**
spring [spriŋ] *n.* **1** small stream of water coming out of the ground. □ **manantial**
2 season of the year following winter when plants begin to grow and put out leaves: *in spring; spring flowers.* □ **primavera**
spring onion, thin white onion plant eaten raw in salads. □ **cebolleta**
3 leap in the air. □ **salto; brinco**
4 coiled wire which returns to its original shape after being stretched or compressed; strong bent metal plates which allow a vehicle to ride over bumps: *this mattress has no springs.* □ **ballestas (vehículo); muelle (colchón)**
spring clip, clip which closes with a spring. □ **resorte**
spring balance, device for weighing made of a large spring which stretches when weight is attached to it. □ **peso de muellle**
5 bounciness: *he walked along with a spring in his step; this bed has no spring left in it.* □ **elasticidad; andaba con paso ligero; ...no le queda ni un muelle**
■ *v.* (*he sprang; he has sprung*) **1** to leap/to bounce: *he sprang out of bed; the lid sprang open; the lid sprang back shut,* shut again suddenly. □ **saltar**
2 to set off/to make something happen suddenly: *to spring a surprise on someone; he sprang the question on me.* □ **coger a uno de improviso; espetar (una pregunta)**
3 to come from: *where did you spring from? his interest in Germany springs from the fact that his mother is German.* □ **salir; su interés por Alemania le viene de...**
4 ***to spring a leak,*** to start taking in water through a crack. □ **hacer agua**
springboard *n.* long flexible board used to give an impetus to a diver or jumper. □ **trampolín**
springbok ['spriŋbɔk] *n.* type of African deer. □ **gacela**
spring-clean *v.* to clean thoroughly after the winter: *I must spring-clean my bedroom.* □ **hacer limpieza general**
spring-cleaning *n.* thorough cleaning after the winter. □ **limpieza general**
spring fever *n. Amer.* feeling of mad excitement at the coming of spring. □ **desasosiego primaveral**
springiness *n.* being springy. □ **elasticidad**
springlike *adj.* (weather) which is mild like in spring. □ **primaveral**
spring tide *n.* tide which rises and falls very sharply, and occurs at the new and full moon. □ **marea viva**
springtime *n.* spring/the season after winter: *in the springtime.* □ **primavera**
springy *adj.* flexible; (board) which bends: (carpet/grass) which is very soft. □ **elástico**
sprinkle ['spriŋkl] *v.* to scatter water/sand etc. □ **rociar; salpicar**
sprinkler *n.* device for sprinkling: *to put the sprinkler on the lawn,* to water the lawn with a sprinkler. □ **regadera**
sprinkler system, system of automatic fire control which sprinkles water on a fire and is set off by rising heat. □ **sistema de aspersión automática**
sprinkling *n.* **1** action of scattering water/sand, etc. □ **aspersión; rociada**
2 small quantities: *a sprinkling of snow fell during the night.* □ **un poco de; algo de**
sprint [sprint] *n.* fast short running race. □ **(e)sprint**
■ *v.* to run very fast over a short distance. □ **esprintar**
sprinter *n.* runner who specializes in sprint races. □ **(e)sprínter**
sprocket ['sprɔkit] *n.* small tooth on a wheel. □ **diente**
sprocket-wheel, toothed wheel which connects with a chain. □ **rueda dentada**
sprout [sprout] *n.* young shoot of a plant. □ **brote**
Brussels sprouts, edible shoots from a type of cabbage. □ **coles de Bruselas**
■ *v.* to send out shoots/horns: *the potatoes are sprouting; the young deer is sprouting horns.* □ **brotar (plantas); echar/salir (cuernos)**
spruce [spruːs] *n.* type of fir tree. □ **picea**
■ *adj.* smart. □ **elegante**
■ *v.* ***to spruce yourself up,*** to make yourself neat. □ **arreglarse**
sprung [sprʌŋ] *v. see* **spring.**
spry [sprai] *adj.* (old person) who is vigorous and active. □ **ágil**
spud [spʌd] *n.* (*informal*) potato. □ **patata**
spun [spʌn] *v. see* **spin.**
spur [spəː] *n.* **1** metal point attached to the heels of a rider's boots which pricks a horse to make it go faster. □ **espuela**
to win your spurs, to show for the first time how good you are. □ **demostrar lo que vale uno**
2 low hill running from a higher range of mountains; road leading off a main road; railway line leading off a main line. □ **estribación (montaña); carretera secundaria; vía muerta/ramal corto (tren)**
3 impetus/stimulus. □ **acicate**
on the spur of the moment, without planning in advance: *we decided to go to Scotland on the spur of the moment.* □ **sin pensarlo dos veces**
■ *v.* (*he spurred*) to urge on: *he spurred on his horse; the manager spurred on his team to greater efforts.* □ **espolear**
spurious ['spjuəriəs] *adj.* false: *a spurious claim.* □ **espurio**
spuriousness *n.* falseness. □ **lo espurio**

spurn [spɜːn] *v.* to reject (an offer) scornfully. □ **desdeñar**
spurt [spɜːt] *n.* **1** jet of liquid: *a sudden spurt of water from the burst pipe.* □ **chorro**
2 sudden effort: *he put on a final spurt and won the race.* □ **último esfuerzo**
■ *v.* **1** ***to spurt out,*** to come out in a jet: *oil spurted out from the pipe.* □ **salir a chorros**
2 to run fast suddenly: *he spurted ahead.* □ **acelerar**
sputter ['spʌtə] *v.* to spit/to send out sparks or fat: *the logs sputtered in the fire.* □ **chisporrotear**
sputum ['spjuːtəm] *n.* spittle/saliva which is spat out of the mouth. □ **esputo**
spy [spai] *n.* person who is paid to try to find out what the enemy/a criminal gang/a rival firm is planning to do. □ **espía**
■ *v.* to see: *I spied six horsemen in the distance.* □ **divisar**
to spy on someone, to try, in secret, to find out what someone is doing. □ **espiar**
spying *n.* action of trying to find out an enemy's plans. □ **espionaje**
squab [skwɔb] *n.* small pigeon. □ **pichón**
squabble ['skwɔbl] *n.* quarrel/argument: *there was a squabble over who should pay the bill.* □ **disputa**
■ *v.* to argue: *they are squabbling over/about pay.* □ **pelearse**
squad [skwɔd] *n.* **1** small group of soldiers. □ **pelotón**
firing squad, group of soldiers who shoot someone who has been condemned to death. □ **pelotón de ejecución**
2 small group of workmen/police: *the council sent a squad of workmen to clear the fallen tree.* □ **brigada**
squad car, police car on patrol. □ **coche-patrulla**
squadron ['skwɔdrən] *n.* group of soldiers on horseback; group of aircraft; group of naval ships. □ **escuadrón (a caballo); escuadrilla/escuadrón (aviones); escuadra (buques)**
squadron leader, rank in the air force above flight lieutenant. □ **comandante**
squalid ['skwɔlid] *adj.* sordid/unpleasant/dirty. □ **miserable; sórdido**
squalor *n.* dirt; dirty state. □ **mugre; asquerosidad**
squall [skwɔːl] *n.* sudden gust of wind. □ **ráfaga; racha**
■ *v.* to cry loudly: *a squalling baby.* □ **chillar**
squally *adj.* accompanied by gusts of wind: *squally showers.* □ **(que viene) a ráfagas**
squander ['skwɔndə] *v.* to waste (money/energy). □ **despilfarrar**
square ['skwɛə] *n.* **1** shape with four equal sides and four right angles: *a chess board is divided into black and white squares.* □ **cuadrado**
back to square one, (*informal*) we'll have to start planning again from the beginning. □ **y vuelta a empezar**
2 open area in a town, surrounded by high buildings: *Trafalgar Square; Red Square; the band was playing in the square.* □ **plaza**
3 instrument for drawing right angles: *set-square.* □ **escuadra**
4 a number multiplied by itself: *100 is the square of 10.* □ **cuadrado**
■ *adj.* **1** shaped like a square: *a square table; this piece of paper isn't square.* □ **cuadrado**
2 ***square corner,*** corner with a right angle. □ **en ángulo recto**
3 fair/straightforward: *I want to get things square.* □ **claro; ...dejar las cosas bien claras**
a square deal, honest treatment. □ **trato equitativo**
a square meal, a good filling meal. □ **una comida importante**
4 straight: *with square shoulders,* not stooping. □ **derecho**
5 multiplied by itself. □ **cuadrado**
square metre, area of one metre multiplied by one metre. □ **metro cuadrado**
square root, number which when multiplied by itself produces the number you have: *10 is the square root of 100.* □ **raíz cuadrada**
■ *adv.* **1** in a level/straight way: *the table was standing square against the wall.* □ **en ángulo recto con**
2 directly: *he punched him square on the nose.* □ **justo**
■ *v.* **1** to make (a round stone, etc.) square. □ **labrar a escuadra**
squared paper, paper with squares drawn on it (for making graphs, etc.). □ **papel cuadriculado**
2 to balance (accounts); to pay (someone) what is owed; to pay (someone) a bribe: *I'll square the doorman.* □ **cuadrar; hacer arqueo; liquidar; untar la mano; sobornar**
3 *his story doesn't square with that of the policeman,* does not agree. □ **...no cuadra con...**
4 to multiply (something) by itself: *100 is 10 squared.* □ **al cuadrado**
5 to straighten (your shoulders). □ **sacar el pecho; enderezarse**
6 ***to square up to:*** *he squared up to his attacker,* faced him ready to defend himself. □ **le hizo frente a su...**
squarely *adv.* in a straightforward way: *he looked me squarely in the eye.* □ **firmemente**
squash [skwɔʃ] *n.* **1** crowded mass of people: *what a squash in the underground!* □ **montón de gente**
2 concentrated juice of a fruit to which water has been added: *a glass of orange squash; a bottle of orange squash,* concentrated orange juice. □ **zumo**
3 fast game played with rackets in a court with high walls. □ **'squash'**
4 vegetable like a marrow/pumpkin, etc. □ **calabaza**
■ *v.* **1** to crush: *he sat on his hat and squashed it flat; a hundred people squashed into the little room; we are rather squashed in here.* □ **aplastar**
2 to stop (a revolt) by force; to stop (someone) speaking by being rude to them. □ **aplastar**
squash court *n.* court for playing squash. □ **cancha**
squashy *adj.* soft and wet: *these pears have gone squashy.* □ **blanducho**
squat [skwɔt] *n.* **1** action of occupying an empty house without the permission of the owner. □ **ocupación ilegal de una vivienda**
2 empty house which is suitable for squatting in. □ **vivienda vacía**
■ *v.* (*he squatted*) **1** to crouch down, sitting on your heels: *the campers were squatting around the fire.* □ **ponerse en cuclillas**
2 to occupy an empty house without the permission of the owner. □ **ocupar ilegalmente una vivienda**
■ *adj.* short and thick: *a squat building; his mother is a short, squat woman.* □ **achaparrado**
squatter *n.* person who occupies an empty house without the permission of the owner. □ **ocupante ilegal**
squaw [skwɔː] *n.* American Indian woman. □ **india norteamericana**
squawk [skwɔːk] *n.* short harsh cry: *the chicken gave a squawk and ran away.* □ **graznido**
■ *v.* to make short harsh cries: *the hens started squawking when they saw the fox.* □ **graznar**
squeak [skwiːk] *n.* little high-pitched cry (like that

of a mouse); high-pitched sound (like a rusty hinge). □ **chillido**

■ *v.* to make a high-pitched sound: *the mice squeaked; we must oil the garden gate because it squeaks.* □ **chillar (ratón); chirriar (puerta)**

squeaky *adj.* (gate) which makes squeaks. □ **chirriante**

squeal [skwi:l] *n.* long loud high-pitched cry: *a squeal of pain; a squeal of brakes.* □ **chillido (dolor); chirrido (frenos)**

■ *v.* to make long loud high-pitched cries: *the children ran squealing out of the room; the police car squealed as it turned the corner/the police car squealed round the corner.* □ **chillar (niños); chirriar (coche)**

squeamish ['skwi:miʃ] *adj.* easily made sick/easily shocked: *he is too squeamish to be a doctor.* □ **remilgado**

squeamishness *n.* state of being easily made sick/easily shocked. □ **remilgos**

squeegee ['skwi:dʒi:] *n.* implement for cleaning floors, made of a wad of sponge which is attached to a hinged plate. □ **fregona/enceradora de esponja**

squeeze [skwi:z] *n.* **1** pressure; crushing: *he gave her hand a squeeze.* □ **apretón**

2 *it was **a tight squeeze,*** there was a crowd of people crushed together. □ **estar muy apretados**

3 *credit squeeze,* restriction on credit. □ **restricción crediticia**

4 *a squeeze of lemon,* a few drops of lemon juice. □ **unas gotas de limón**

■ *v.* **1** to crush/to force/to press: *he squeezed her hand; she squeezed a few drops of lemon juice on her pancake; he has squeezed as much money as he can out of the bank.* □ **apretar (mano); exprimir (limón); sacar (dinero)**

2 to push together; to push to get into/through a small space: *they all squeezed into the little car; can you squeeze in another passenger?* □ **meterse en (coche)**

squeezer *n.* device which squeezes. □ **exprimidor**

a lemon squeezer, device for pressing citrus fruit to get the juice. □ **exprimelimones**

squeeze up *v.* to crush together to make room for someone else. □ **apretujarse**

squelch [skweltʃ] *n.* noise made by a wet sticky substance. □ **chapaleo; chapoteo**

■ *v.* to make a wet sucking noise: *he squelched through the mud.* □ **chapalear; chapotear**

squib [skwib] *n.* small firework which bangs. □ **buscapiés**

damp squib, something exciting/new which doesn't work properly. □ **un fallo**

squid [skwid] *n.* sea animal like a small octopus. □ **calamar**

squiggle ['skwigl] *n.* illegible curly handwriting. □ **garabato**

■ *v.* to make curly marks. □ **hacer garabatos**

squint [skwint] *n.* **1** state where your two eyes look in different directions: *he has a bad squint.* □ **estrabismo**

2 (*informal*) look: *take a squint at these jewels.* □ **vistazo; echa un vistazo...**

■ *v.* **1** to have eyes which look in different directions: *he squints.* □ **bizquear**

2 to half-close your eyes to look at a bright light. □ **mirar con los ojos entrecerrados**

squire ['skwaiə] *n.* gentleman living in the country, often the owner of a large house. □ **propietario; terrateniente**

squirm [skwə:m] *v.* **1** to wriggle about: *he squirmed in his chair.* □ **retorcerse**

2 *it makes me squirm,* it makes me very embarrassed. □ **me pone violento**

squirrel ['skwirəl] *n.* common small mammal with a large bushy tail, living in trees. □ **ardilla**

squirt [skwə:t] *n.* sharp jet of liquid: *put a squirt of soda water in my drink.* □ **chorrito**

■ *v.* to send out a sharp jet of liquid: *water was squirting all over the place from the burst pipes.* □ **salir a chorros**

St [snt] *short form of* Saint: *St George.* □ **San**

stab [stæb] *n.* wound made with a sharp knife: *a stab wound.* □ **puñalada; navajazo**

stab in the back, attack on someone to whom you are thought to be loyal. □ **puñalada por la espalda**

to have a stab at something, (*informal*) to try to do something. □ **probar a hacer algo**

■ *v.* (*he stabbed*) to wound with a sharp knife. □ **apuñalar**

to stab someone in the back, to attack someone who thinks you are his friend. □ **apuñalar a alguien por la espalda**

stable ['steibl] *n.* **1** compartment for keeping a horse. □ **cuadra**

2 ***stables,*** place where horses are kept for breeding/racing, etc. □ **caballeriza**

■ *v.* to keep a horse in a stable. □ **estabular**

■ *adj.* **1** solid; steady/not wobbly: *that bench doesn't look very stable; prices have kept stable for several months.* □ **estable**

2 (*in chemistry*) (compound) which does not change or decompose easily. □ **estable**

stability [stə'biliti] *n.* steadiness: *stability of relations between two countries.* □ **estabilidad**

stabilization [steibilai'zeiʃn] *n.* making stable. □ **estabilización**

stabilize ['steibilaiz] *v.* to make steady: *we are trying to stabilize prices.* □ **estabilizar**

stabilizer *n.* fin attached to the hull of a ship to prevent rolling; small wheels attached to the back wheel of a child's bicycle to allow the child to learn to ride without falling off. □ **estabilizador**

staccato [stə'ka:tou] *adj.* sharp (noise): *a staccato burst of gunfire.* □ **'staccato'; el repiqueteo de...**

stack [stæk] *n.* **1** heap: *stack of coins; stack of hay;* (*informal*) *he's got stacks of money.* □ **montón de monedas; almiar (heno)**

2 brick pillar housing a chimney. □ **cañón de chimenea**

3 inner part of a library where books are kept without being open to the public. □ **estanterías interiores**

■ *v.* **1** to pile up: *he was stacking up wood.* □ **amontonar**

2 (*of aircraft*) to circle round waiting in turn for permission to land at a busy airport: *we were stacking for forty minutes before we could get down to land.* □ **dar vueltas**

stadium ['steidiəm] *n.* large building for sports: *football stadium.* □ **estadio**

staff [sta:f] *n.* **1** long thick stick. □ **bastón; tranca**

2 people working in a school/college/firm: *we employ a staff of 25; cleaning staff; kitchen staff; teaching staff.* □ **personal docente; plantilla**

staff room, room for teachers in a school. □ **sala de profesores**

3 officers who help the commander organize a military force: *a staff officer.* □ **Estado Mayor; oficial del Estado Mayor**

the general staff, officers who work at headquarters. □ **el Estado Mayor**

■ *v.* to provide employees for a firm, etc.: *the firm is staffed with lunatics.* □ **proveer de personal**
stag [stæg] *n.* male deer. □ **ciervo**
stag party, party for men only. □ **(fiesta de) despedida de soltero, reunión de hombres**
stag-beetle *n.* large black beetle with horns. □ **ciervo volante**
stage [steidʒ] *n.* **1** platform (on which a play is acted, etc.). □ **escenario**
stage directions, notes in the script of a play showing what the actors have to do. □ **acotaciones**
stage whisper, loud whisper which everyone can hear. □ **aparte**
to go on the stage, to become an actor/to take up the theatre as a career. □ **hacerse actor/actriz**
2 period/phase: *the stages in the development of modern English; the baby has reached the crawling stage,* the period when he can crawl but not walk. □ **etapa; fase**
3 each of the parts of a rocket. □ **cuerpo**
4 ***landing stage,*** wooden platform for boats to tie up to. □ **desembarcadero**
5 part of a journey: *to travel by easy stages; fare stage,* point on a bus route where the fare increases. □ **etapa; sección**
■ *v.* **1** to put on/to arrange (a performance of a play, etc.): *we are staging an exhibition of paintings by school children.* □ **organizar**
2 to make/to organize: *the general staged a coup; the old singer tried to stage a comeback.* □ **dar (un golpe); efectuar (vuelta)**
stagecoach *n.* old-fashioned horsedrawn passenger coach which ran regularly along certain routes. □ **diligencia**
stagecraft *n.* art of the theatre. □ **arte escénico**
stagehand *n.* person who moves scenery/prepares the stage (in a theatre). □ **tramoyista**
stage-manage *v.* to arrange/to organize (a performance); to plan (a trick/a coup): *the whole thing was stage-managed in advance.* □ **dirigir la tramoya; preparar (algo de antemano)**
stage manager *n.* person who organizes a performance of a play/opera, etc. □ **director de escena; regidor (en TV)**
staging *n.* **1** putting on (of a play). □ **puesta en escena**
2 racks for storing: *metal staging.* □ **andamiaje**
stagger ['stægə] *v.* **1** to walk unsteadily: *they staggered down the street arm in arm; the boxer staggered to his feet,* got up unsteadily. □ **tambalearse**
2 to astonish: *I was staggered to hear the price.* □ **asombrar**
3 to arrange things so that they do not coincide exactly: *payments are staggered over a period of six months.* □ **escalonar**
staggered holidays, holidays arranged so that not everyone is away on holiday at the same time. □ **vacaciones escalonadas**
staggering *adj.* astonishing: *a staggering loss.* □ **asombroso**
stagnant ['stægnənt] *adj.* **1** (water) which does not flow/which is not pure enough to drink: *a stagnant pond.* □ **estancado; aguas estancadas**
2 (business) which does not make increased sales. □ **estancado**
stagflation [stæg'fleiʃn] *n.* period when the economy stagnates but inflation increases. □ **estanflación**
stagnate [stæg'neit] *v.* to stay static; not to advance. □ **estancarse**
stagnation [stæg'neiʃn] *n.* state of not advancing/not increasing sales: *the economy is in a period of stagnation.* □ **estancamiento**
staid [steid] *adj.* serious/not adventurous. □ **formal**
stain [stein] *n.* **1** dirty mark which is difficult to remove: *I can't get the stains off the tablecloth.* □ **mancha**
2 *he hasn't a stain on his character,* he is absolutely blameless. □ **...sin una sola mancha en su reputación**
3 liquid used to change the colour of wood: *the table was painted with a dark oak stain.* □ **nogalina**
■ *v.* **1** to make a dirty mark on something: *his reputation has been stained by this bribery affair; ink-stained fingers.* □ **manchar; dedos manchados de...**
2 to change the colour (of wood, etc.): *we will have the floor stained dark brown.* □ **teñir; dar una mano de nogalina (a la tarima)**
stained glass, coloured glass for windows (especially in church). □ **vidrio de color; vidriera (iglesia)**
stainless *adj.* without any stain. □ **inmaculado**
stainless steel, steel which contains nickel and chromium so that it does not rust in contact with air or water. □ **acero inoxidable**
stair ['stɛə] *n.* **1** step (on a staircase): *she sat on the bottom stair and cried.* □ **peldaño; escalón**
2 (***flight of***) ***stairs,*** series of steps leading from one floor of a building to the next: *he ran up the stairs; she fell down the stairs.* □ **tramo de escalera; subió las escaleras; se cayó por las...**
staircarpet *n.* long narrow piece of carpet for covering stairs. □ **alfombra de escalera**
staircase *n.* set of steps leading from one floor of a building to the next (usually with a handrail). □ **escalera**
stair rod *n.* metal rod which keeps a staircarpet in place. □ **varilla**
stake [steik] *n.* **1** strong pointed stick: *to drive a stake into the ground; to tie tomato plants to stakes.* □ **estaca; rodrigón (para tomates, etc.)**
2 money which is gambled: *they played cards for high stakes,* for large amounts of money. □ **apuesta; ...posturas altas**
3 *he has a stake in the company,* he has invested some money in the company, hoping to make a profit. □ **...intereses en la compañía**
at stake, which may be lost; at risk: *the future of the car industry is at stake; we must act quickly, there are lives at stake.* □ **en juego; en peligro**
■ *v.* **1** to put a stick in the ground: *to stake tomatoes,* to put a stick in to hold up tomato plants. □ **poner estacas; rodrigar tomates**
2 *to stake a claim,* to suggest that you hold the right to own something. □ **hacer una reclamación**
3 to bet (money, etc.): *he staked $20 on the game; he staked his reputation on the case.* □ **apostar (dinero); puso en juego su reputación**
stalactite ['stæləktait] *n.* long point of limestone hanging from the ceiling of a cave, formed by mineral deposits from dripping water. □ **estalactita**
stalagmite ['stæləgmait] *n.* long point of limestone rising from the floor of a cave formed by mineral deposits from dripping water. □ **estalagmita**
stale [steil] *adj.* **1** no longer fresh: *stale bread; stale air.* □ **rancio; pan duro; aire viciado**
stale joke, one that has been repeated many times. □ **chiste muy viejo**
2 ***to go stale,*** to become bored/tired so that you cannot work well. □ **atocinarse**
stalemate *n.* **1** (*in chess*) position where a player cannot move without being checkmated. □ **ahogado**

2 situation where neither side will compromise: *the negotiations have reached a stalemate.* □ **punto muerto**
staleness *n.* being stale. □ **ranciedad**
stalk [stɔ:k] *n.* **1** thin stem of a plant: *cut the flowers with long stalks.* □ **tallo**
2 small part of the stem which attaches a fruit to the plant: *stalk of an apple.* □ **rabillo**
■ *v.* **1** to try to get close enough to an animal to shoot it. □ **cazar al acecho**
2 to march along in a proud way: *he stalked out of the room.* □ **andar con paso majestuoso**
stalker *n.* person who stalks animals. □ **cazador al acecho**
stall [stɔ:l] *n.* **1** compartment for one animal in a stable, etc.: *the cows have gone into their stalls.* □ **pesebre**
2 ***stalls,*** seats in church for the choir and priests; seats on the ground floor (in a theatre/cinema). □ **sillas de coro (iglesia); butacas (cine/teatro)**
3 table with goods laid out for sale; small moveable shop: *he has a vegetable stall in the market; newspaper stall.* □ **puesto; tenderete; quiosco de periódicos**
■ *v.* **1** (*of a car engine*) to stop unintentionally: *he stalled the engine at the crossroads; the engine stalled.* □ **calarse**
2 (*of an aircraft*) to go so slowly that it falls suddenly. □ **perder velocidad**
3 to put off making a decision: *he has been stalling by pretending to be ill.* □ **buscar evasivas**
stallholder *n.* person who runs a stall in a market. □ **dueño de un puesto**
stallion ['stæljən] *n.* male horse, especially one kept for breeding. □ **semental**
stalwart ['stɔlwət] *adj.* strong/vigorous/brave. □ **robusto**
■ *n.* a strong/vigorous/brave person. □ **partidario leal; tipo fuerte**
stamen ['steimən] *n.* one of the thin spikes in the centre of a flower which carry the pollen. □ **estambre**
stamina ['stæminə] *n.* ability to do something hard for a long time: *he can work all day and night – he has wonderful stamina.* □ **resistencia**
stammer ['stæmə] *n.* unintentional repetition of sounds when speaking: *he has a bad stammer.* □ **tartamudeo**
■ *v.* to repeat sounds when speaking: *he can't help stammering; 'p-p-put that g-g-gun d-d-down', he stammered; he stammered out his reply,* he replied very nervously, muddling his words. □ **tartamudear**
stammerer *n.* person who stammers. □ **tartamudo**
stamp [stæmp] *n.* **1** banging your foot on the ground. □ **zapatazo**
2 object for making a mark on something. □ **sello**
date stamp, device with moveable figures which form the date for stamping. □ **fechador**
rubber stamp, device with rubber figures or letters which you use for marking. □ **sello**
3 device for cutting out a design. □ **plantilla**
4 small piece of gummed paper for sticking on an envelope/parcel, etc., to pay for it to be sent by mail: *postage stamp; stamp machine,* machine which sells stamps automatically; *stamp collector; stamp album.* □ **sello**
5 any small piece of gummed paper used to show you have made a payment: *insurance stamp.* □ **timbre; póliza de seguros**
trading stamp, stamp given with purchases instead of a discount. □ **cupón**
6 mark made by a rubber stamp: *a customs stamp.* □ **sello**
■ *v.* **1** to bang your foot hard on the ground: *they stamped their feet to keep warm; he stamped out of the room; she stamped down the stairs; he threw the flower on the ground and stamped on it.* □ **golpear con los pies; salió de estampida**
2 to make a mark on something: *this parcel is stamped 'Fragile'; did they stamp your passport?* □ **sellar**
3 to stick a (paper) stamp on (something). □ **pegar**
a stamped addressed envelope, envelope with your own name, address and a stamp, which you enclose in a letter so that the person you are writing to can reply. □ **sobre con sello y dirección**
stamping *n.* action of banging your feet/of marking something with a stamp. □ **pataleo (con pies); sellado**
stamping ground, (*informal*) place where you often are/would like to be. □ **lugar preferido**
stamp out *v.* to stop/to eradicate: *to stamp out corruption; to stamp out a disease.* □ **acabar con**
stampede [stæm'pi:d] *n.* mad rush (of animals/people): *there was a stampede to get to the doors.* □ **espantada; estampida**
■ *v.* to rush madly: *the herd of cattle stampeded; the crowd stampeded across the square.* □ **desbandarse**
stance [stɑns] *n.* **1** way of standing. □ **postura**
2 attitude/position. □ **postura**
stanch [stɑ:ntʃ] *v.* to stop blood flowing: *to stanch someone's wound.* □ **restañar**
stanchion ['stæntʃn] *n.* vertical post/bar which holds something up. □ **montante**
stand [stænd] *n.* **1** position: *to take a firm stand.* □ **posición; adoptar una actitud firme**
to make a stand, to resist. □ **oponer resistencia**
2 support; thing which holds something up; flat base: *the electric drill is fixed to a stand; put the teapot on the stand; hat stand,* device with hooks for hanging hats. □ **pie; soporte; perchero**
3 arrangement of shelves/posters, etc., at an exhibition. □ **pabellón; 'stand'**
4 ***stands,*** series of seats for spectators at a football match. □ **tribuna**
5 ***witness stand,*** *Amer.* place where a witness gives evidence in court. □ **estrado**
6 ***taxi stand,*** place where taxis wait. □ **parada de taxis**
■ *v.* (*he stood*) **1** to be/to place in an upright position: *after the earthquake only three houses were left standing; the church stands on the top of a hill; stand the book up on its end; stand the ladder against the wall; the bookcase was standing in the middle of the room; she stood the vase of flowers in the middle of the table.* □ **quedar en pie; estar; poner derecho; colocar**
2 to be on your feet/not to be sitting down: *I am so tired I can hardly stand; she stood in the doorway and waved; don't just stand there watching – come and help.* □ **tenerse de pie; se quedó en la puerta y...**
3 to stay/to remain: *the contract stands,* is valid. □ **...sigue en vigor**
4 ***to stand in need of something,*** to need something. □ **necesitar**
5 *I don't stand to lose anything,* I am not likely to lose anything. □ **no tengo nada que perder**
6 to bear/to accept: *I can't stand all this noise.* □ **soportar; no soporto/aguanto todo...**
7 to put your name forward in an election: *he stood*

for Parliament; she is standing as a Labour candidate in the local elections. □ **presentarse**
8 to pay for: *I'll stand the next round of drinks.* □ **invitar**
stand aside *v.* to step to one side: *he stood aside in favour of the other candidate,* withdrew from the election. □ **ponerse a un lado; se retiró...**
stand back *v.* to step backwards; to be behind: *the house stands back from the road,* is not directly on the road/is separated from the road by some ground. □ **echarse atrás; la casa está retranqueada...**
stand by *v.* **1** to be ready: *stand by for action!* □ **estar preparado**
2 to stand at one side without taking part in the action: *he stood by and didn't do anything to help.* □ **quedarse al margen**
3 to support/to be faithful: *I stand by what I said; will he stand by his promise? his wife stood by him during all the investigation.* □ **cumplir; apoyar**
standby *n.* **1** something which is ready to go into action if necessary: *a standby crew; standby plane; a good standby,* something which it is good to have at hand in case of need. □ **de reserva**
2 waiting: *he is on standby,* he is waiting to see if he is needed. □ **está en lista de espera**
standby ticket, (*at an airport*) cheap ticket which allows you to wait to see if there are any empty places. □ **billete de lista de espera**
stand down *v. to stand down in favour of someone,* withdraw from an election to let someone else win. □ **retirarse en favor de**
stand for *v.* **1** to mean: *what do the letters B.R. stand for?* □ **significar**
2 to accept/to allow: *I won't stand for any rudeness.* □ **tolerar**
stand in *v.* to take someone's place: *I am standing in for Mr Smith because he is ill.* □ **suplir**
stand-in *n.* person who takes someone's place. □ **suplente**
standing *n.* **1** being on your feet. □ **de/en pie**
standing room, room for people to stand, not to sit. □ **sólo hay sitio de pie**
2 social position: *he is a person of some standing in the Labour party.* □ **posición; es una persona de cierta categoría...**
3 length of time: *he is a friend of long standing.* □ **es un amigo de hace tiempo**
■ *adj.* **1** upright/not lying or sitting. □ **derecho**
2 permanent. ***a standing joke,*** it is something we always laugh about. □ **chiste eterno**
standing order, permanent order to send something or pay something regularly. □ **pedido regular**
standoffish *adj.* (person) who is cold/who does not make friends. □ **reservado; endiosado**
standoffishness *n.* unfriendliness. □ **reserva; endiosamiento**
stand out *v.* to be obvious: *it stands out a mile,* (*informal*) it is very noticeable. □ **ser evidente, destacar**
stand over *v.* ***to stand over someone,*** to be just behind someone and supervise what he is doing. □ **estar sobre alguien**
standpipe *n.* upright pipe connected to the water main in the street, with a tap which allows water to be taken off when the supply to houses has been cut. □ **columna de alimentación**
standpoint *n.* point of view/position from which you look at a problem: *look at the problem from the standpoint of the old-age pensioner.* □ **punto de vista**
standstill *n.* state of being stopped: *the car came to a standstill against the fence; all production was brought to a standstill by the strike.* □ **parada; el coche se paró**
stand up *v.* **1** to get to your feet: *when she came into the room the children stood up.* □ **ponerse de pie**
2 ***stand up straight!,*** hold yourself straight. □ **¡ponte derecho!**
3 ***to stand up for something,*** to defend/to support. □ **salir en defensa de**
4 ***to stand up to someone,*** to resist/to fight. □ **resistir**
5 ***to stand someone up,*** (*informal*) not to meet someone at a rendezvous: *he stood me up.* □ **dar plantón**
stand-up *adj.* ***a stand-up buffet,*** buffet where you eat standing up. □ **tomado de pie**
stand-up fight, real fight where people come to blows. □ **riña a puñetazos**
standard ['stændəd] *n.* **1** model with which something is compared: *a high standard of living; official standard for testing cars.* □ **nivel (de vida); norma (oficial)**
2 excellent quality which is set as a target: *he expects a high standard of honesty; this material is not up to standard.* □ **nivel**
3 large flag. □ **estandarte**
4 ***lamp standard,*** tall pole with a light on top for lighting a street. □ **poste de farola**
5 tree/bush grown with a tall trunk: *I will grow this pear as a standard.* □ **árbol de tronco derecho**
■ *adj.* **1** normal/usual: *he takes a standard size in shoes; this is our standard model,* ordinary model without any extra items. □ **normal; estándar**
the standard authors, the classical authors/authors everyone usually reads. □ **los clásicos**
standard pronunciation, pronunciation which is generally used. □ **pronunciación normal**
2 on a tall pole. □ **en un poste, de pie**
standard lamp, lamp in a room on a tall pole. □ **lámpara de pie**
standard rose, rose grown with a tall trunk. □ **manzano/rosal derecho**
3 which is taken as a measure: *standard time.* □ **hora oficial**
standardization [stændədai'zeiʃn] *n.* setting of a standard; making sure that everything conforms to a standard: *standardization of egg sizes/of yachting rules.* □ **estandarización, normalización**
standardize ['stændədaiz] *v.* to make everything conform to a standard: *we are trying to standardize road signs throughout Europe.* □ **normalizar; estandarizar**
stank [stæŋk] *v. see* **stink.**
stanza ['stænzə] *n.* section of a poem made up of a series of lines: *the poem is dividied into seven-line stanzas.* □ **estrofa**
staphylococcus [stæfilə'kɔkəs] *n.* (*pl. staphylococci*) type of bacteria which causes infection in the blood. □ **estafilococo**
staple ['steipl] *n.* piece of strong bent wire used to hold things in place; small wire clip for attaching papers together by being passed through them and then bent over. □ **armella; grapa (papeles)**
■ *adj.* **1** main product of a country/town. etc.: *coffee is a staple product of some South American countries.* □ **básico**
2 main part of what you eat: *rice is a staple diet in the Far East.* □ **básico**
■ *v.* to attach with a staple: *he stapled the pages together.* □ **grapar**
stapler *n.* small instrument for attaching papers together with staples. □ **grapadora**

star *n.* [stɑː] **1** body in the sky like a very distant sun which shines at night: *the stars come out as the sun goes down.* □ **estrella**
2 the sign of the zodiac which marks your birth: *your stars,* your horoscope. □ **signo del zodiaco**
3 *you can thank your lucky stars you were not caught by the police,* (*informal*) you must consider yourself very lucky. □ **ya puedes dar (las) gracias a Dios que...**
4 shape with several regular points: *biscuit shaped like a star; a white star on the top of the Christmas tree.* □ **estrella**
5 asterisk/mark in writing or printing to draw attention to something. □ **asterisco**
five-star hotel, hotel which is so good that the guide book has marked it with five stars. □ **hotel de cinco estrellas**
6 actor/actress who is very well known to the public: *film star; a star role in the new film.* □ **estrella de cine; un papel destacado...**
■ *v.* (*he starred*) **1** to play an important part in a film: *he has starred in six westerns.* □ **protagonizar; ser protagonista**
2 to have a famous actor playing: *a film starring Jane Smith as Queen Elizabeth.* □ **con la estrella...**
3 to mark with a star. □ **señalar con un asterisco**
stardom *n.* being a film star: *he rose to stardom with his part in 'The Third Man'.* □ **estrellato**
starfish *n.* sea animal shaped like a star. □ **estrella de mar**
starless *adj.* (night) when no stars are visible. □ **sin estrellas**
starlet *n.* young film actress. □ **actriz principiante**
starlight *n.* light from the stars. □ **luz de las estrellas**
starlit *adj.* (night) lit by the light of the stars. □ **iluminado por las estrellas**
starry *adj.* covered with stars. □ **estrellado**
starry-eyed *adj.* wildly hopeful. □ **soñador**

starboard ['stɑːbəd] *n.* and *adj.* right side of a ship when facing forwards. □ **estribor**

starch [stɑːtʃ] *n.* **1** white energy-giving carbohydrate in bread/potatoes/rice, etc. □ **almidón**
2 white powder mixed with water to make (cloth) stiff. □ **almidón**
■ *v.* to make cloth stiff with starch: *starched collar; a starched tablecloth.* □ **almidonar**
starchy *adj.* **1** full of starch: *if you are getting fat, you should avoid starchy food.* □ **feculento**
2 very formal (manner). □ **estirado**

stare ['stɛə] *n.* fixed look from the eyes: *he gave me a blank stare.* □ **mirada fija**
■ *v.* to look at someone/something with a fixed gaze: *he stared in horror at the fire; it is rude to stare at people; what are you staring at?,* why are you looking at me in that way? □ **mirar fijamente**
to stare one in the face, (i) *it's staring you in the face,* it is very obvious. □ **salta a la vista**
(ii) *disaster stared them in the face,* it seemed that they were going to meet with disaster imminently. □ **parecía inminente...**
staring *adj.* and *adv.* with a fixed look: *wild staring eyes.* □ **que mira fijamente**
stark staring mad, totally mad. □ **está loco de remate**

stark [stɑːk] *adj.* **1** total/pure: *stark nonsense.* □ **absoluto; auténtica tontería**
2 bare: *stark landscape.* □ **desolado**
■ *adv.* completely: *he was stark naked.* □ **completamente**
stark staring mad, completely mad. □ **loco de remate**

starling ['stɑːliŋ] *n.* common dark bird with a green sheen to its feathers. □ **estornino**

start [stɑːt] *n.* **1** beginning: *from start to finish.* □ **principio**
to make a fresh start, to begin again. □ **empezar de nuevo**
to make an early start, set off on a journey early. □ **salir temprano**
for a start, in the first place: *she's no use as a typist – for a start she's too slow.* □ **para empezar**
2 *to give someone two metres' start,* to place him at the beginning of a race two metres in front of you; *we will never catch them since they have two hours' start,* since they left two hours before us. □ **ventaja**
3 sudden jump/sudden movement: *he woke up with a start; you gave me a start,* made me jump. □ **sobresalto; susto**
4 *it only works* ***by fits and starts,*** odd moments. □ **a trompicones**
■ *v.* **1** to begin: *let us start by testing your eyes; he started in business with only $100; we must start to get ready otherwise we'll miss the train; he started eating his sandwiches; have you started your lunch? they started back at two o'clock,* began to return; *he started off at a fast pace,* began to go. □ **empezar; comenzar; iniciar**
2 to begin to work; to make (something) begin to work: *the engine/the car won't start; I can't start the engine.* □ **arrancar**
3 to set (something) going: *the sparks started a fire; the headmaster will start the race.* □ **iniciar**
4 to jump (in surprise): *you made me start.* □ **sobresaltarse**
starter *n.* **1** person or animal who starts: *there are six starters in the race.* □ **corredor**
2 person who gives the signal for the start of a race. □ **juez de salida**
3 (*informal*) first course in a meal: *what do you want as a starter/for starters?* □ **¿qué quiere para empezar?**
4 machine which starts a car engine. □ **motor de arranque**
starting *n.* beginning (of a race, etc.). □ **salida**
starting pistol, pistol fired to start a race. □ **pistola**
starting point, point from which everything begins. □ **punto de partida**
start off, start out *v.* to begin to do/to go: *he started off at a fast pace; they started out as a TV repair business, but were soon selling TV sets as well.* □ **partir; empezar (negocio)**
start up *v.* to make (an engine, etc.) begin to work: *he has started up a grocery business; the drivers are starting up their engines.* □ **poner; arrancar**

startle ['stɑːtl] *v.* to make (someone) jump in surprise: *he was startled by a noise downstairs.* □ **asustar**
startling *adj.* remarkable/surprising: *a startling resemblance to his father.* □ **asombroso**

starve [stɑːv] *v.***1** not to give enough food to (someone); to die from lack of food: *he starved to death.* □ **pasar/morirse de hambre**
I'm starving, (*informal*) I am very hungry. □ **me estoy muriendo de hambre**
2 *we are starved of information,* we are not given enough information. □ **nos falta información**
starvation *n.* lack of food: *he died of starvation.* □ **hambre, inanición**
starvation wages, such small wages that you have not enough money to buy food. □ **salarios de hambre**

stash [stæʃ] *v. to stash food/money away,* (*informal*) to store food/money in a safe place: *he must have got thousands of pounds stashed away somewhere.* □ **ir acumulando**

state [steit] *n.* **1** condition: *the house isn't in a very good state; his state of health is getting worse; he got into a terrible state,* (*informal*) very angry. □ **estado**
2 government of a nation. □ **estado**
head of state, chief person in a country. □ **jefe de estado**
state-owned, owned by the country/government (not privately owned). □ **estatal**
police state, country where the police are all-powerful. □ **estado policiaco**
Welfare State, state which looks after the health and wellbeing of its citizens. □ **estado del bienestar**
3 independent country: *the oil-producing states; one of the states in Western Africa.* □ **estado**
4 one of the semi-independent parts of a federal country: *United States of America; the State of New York; the state capital.* □ **estado**
5 *they live **in state**,* with great show; *he travelled in state,* very comfortably, with an escort, etc. □ **lujosamente; con lujo/gran pompa**
■ *adj.* belonging to/run by/given by the government: *he has a state pension; state schools.* □ **del estado, público**
■ *v.* to say clearly/to claim: *he stated that he had never been to Paris; the policeman asked her to state her name and address.* □ **declarar**
stated *adj.* fixed/regulated: *the car park is closed on stated days.* □ **indicado**
stateless *adj.* (person) who is not a citizen of any state. □ **apátrida**
stately *adj.* noble/dignified: *a stately procession.* □ **majestuoso**
stately home, palace/castle belonging to a lord, etc. □ **casa solariega**
statement *n.* declaration clearly written or spoken: *he made a statement to the police; the government issued an official statement.* □ **declaración**
bank statement, paper from the bank showing how much money you have in your account. □ **extracto de cuenta**
States *n. pl.* ***the States,*** (*informal*) the United States of America: *we are going to the States for Christmas.* □ **Estados Unidos**
stateside *adj.* and *adv. Amer.* in/to the United States of America. □ **en/a/hacia Estados Unidos**
statesman *n.* (*pl. statesmen*) person who is or was a member of a government. □ **estadista**
statesmanlike *adj.* like a statesman: *he acted in a very statemanlike way.* □ **propio de un estadista**
statesmanship *n.* skill in government of a country. □ **arte de gobernar**

static ['stætik] *adj.* not moving. □ **estático**
static electricity, electricity which stays in one place (in a car/a pullover). □ **electricidad estática**
■ *n.* electrical interference in the air which disturbs a radio signal. □ **parásitos**

station ['steiʃn] *n.* **1** place where trains stop to pick up and put down passengers: *railway station; underground station; can you tell me the way to the station?* □ **estación**
coach station/bus station, place where coaches/buses begin or end their journeys. □ **estación de autocares/autobuses**
2 central building for some sort of service: *police station; life-boat station; fire station.* □ **comisaría; puesto de bomberos**
service station, garage which sells petrol. □ **estación de servicio; gasolinera**
3 ***power station,*** factory making electricity. □ **central eléctrica**
4 *radio station/TV station,* broadcasting headquarters with its own frequency. □ **emisora**
5 position in society: *she has ideas above her station.* □ **posición social**
6 *sheep station,* large sheep farm in Australia. □ **dehesa de ovejas**
■ *v.* to place (someone) at a spot: *we stationed guards at all street corners; our regiment is stationed in Scotland; he stationed himself on a windowsill so that he could see the procession.* □ **estacionar; destinar**
stationary *adj.* not moving: *a stationary car; the train ran into the back of a stationary goods train.* □ **estacionario; inmóvil**
stationmaster *n.* man in charge of a railway station. □ **jefe de estación**
station wagon *n.* long car with a part at the back for carrying goods. □ **break**

stationer ['steiʃənə] *n.* person who sells paper/pens/ink, etc. □ **dueño de una papelería**
stationery *n.* materials for writing, such as paper/pens/ink, etc. □ **efectos de escritorio**

statistics [stə'tistiks] *n. pl.* **1** study of facts given in the form of figures. □ **estadística**
2 facts in the form of figures: *here are the government statistics for 1976.* □ **estadísticas**
statistical *adj.* referring to figures: *statistical analysis.* □ **estadístico**
statistician [stætis'tiʃn] *n.* person who studies/analyses statistics. □ **estadístico**

statue ['stætju:] *n.* figure of a person carved in stone/made of metal, etc. □ **estatua**
statuary *n.* collection of statues. □ **estatuas**
statuesque [stætju'esk] *adj.* (woman) who is beautiful but large and dignified. □ **escultural**
statuette [stætju'et] *n.* small statue. □ **estatuilla**

stature ['stætʃə] *n.* **1** height: *he was small in stature.* □ **estatura**
2 importance: *this book has increased his stature among academics.* □ **valor**

status ['steitəs] *n.* (*no pl.*) **1** legal position: *he has no official status; his status as a British citizen.* □ **condición**
2 importance/position in the eyes of other people: *social status.* □ **posición social**
status symbol, object (like an expensive car) which may make other people think more highly of you. □ **signo externo de prestigio**
status quo ['steitəs'kwou] *n.* (*no pl.*) state of things as they are at the moment: *we must try to preserve the status quo.* □ **statu quo**

statute ['stætju:t] *n.* **1** law. □ **ley; estatuto**
2 *it has been put in the **statute book**,* it is a written law of the country. □ **código civil/penal**
statutory ['stætjutri] *adj.* legal; officially imposed: *a statutory holiday.* □ **estatutario; obligatorio**

staunch [stɔ:ntʃ] *adj.* firm (friend). □ **leal**
■ *v.* to stop (a flow of blood): *he tried to staunch the wound with his handkerchief.* □ **restañar**
staunchly *adv.* firmly: *he staunchly denied the accusation.* □ **firmemente**

stave [steiv] *n.* **1** curved piece of wood which forms part of a barrel. □ **duela**
2 set of five lines on which music is written. □ **pentagrama**
■ *v.* **1** (*he stove in*) ***to stave in,*** to batter a hole in a boat/a barrel. □ **desfondar**
2 ***to stave off,*** to hold off/to prevent: *to stave off*

the pangs of hunger, to have something to eat to satisfy your hunger for a short while. □ **rechazar, contener**

stay [stei] *n.* **1** time which you spend in a place: *I am only here for a short stay.* □ **estancia**
2 ***stay of execution,*** delay ordered by a judge in carrying out a sentence. □ **aplazamiento**
3 strong rope which holds a mast upright on a ship. □ **estay**
■ *v.* to stop in a place: *I shall stay at home tomorrow; we will stay two nights in Edinburgh; he has to stay in bed; will you stay for dinner?* □ **quedarse**
to stay put: *he is staying put,* he is staying where he is/he has no intention of moving. □ **quedarse en el mismo sitio**
stay-at-home *n.* person who does not like going out to visit people. □ **casero**
stay away *v.* to keep away/not to come. □ **ausentarse**
stayer *n.* person/horse who can run long distances without tiring. □ **persona/caballo resistente**
stay in *v.* to stay at home. □ **quedarse en casa**
stay out *v.* not to come home. □ **no volver a casa**
stay up *v.* not to go to bed. □ **quedarse levantado**

stead [sted] *n.* **1** *it stood him in good stead,* it was very useful to him. □ **le fue útil**
2 *I shall act* ***in your stead,*** in place of you. □ **en tu lugar**

steadfast ['stedfɑːst] *adj.* firm/constant. □ **firme; resuelto**
steadfastly *adv.* firmly/constantly: *he steadfastly refused to see a doctor.* □ **firmemente**

steady ['stedi] *adj.* **1** firm/not wobbling: *a steady hand; keep the boat steady,* don't allow it to rock. □ **firme**
2 continuing regularly: *a steady downpour of rain; a steady pace; he kept up a steady seventy miles per hour.* □ **constante; regular**
3 (person) who is not easily upset. □ **sereno**
■ *n.* (*informal*) boyfriend/girlfriend whom you go out with regularly. □ **ligue**
■ *interjection* ***steady on!,*** be careful. □ **¡cuidado!**
■ *v.* **1** to make/to keep firm: *he steadied the boat with his hand; you need a drink to steady your nerves.* □ **mantener firme**
2 *prices are steadying,* not fluctuating. □ **se están estabilizando**
steadily *adv.* **1** firmly: *he held the glass steadily in his hand.* □ **con firmeza**
2 regularly/continuously: *his health was steadily getting worse; he's been working steadily at his painting for three days.* □ **constantemente**
steadiness *n.* **1** firmness/stability. □ **firmeza**
2 regularity. □ **regularidad**

steak [steik] *n.* **1** thick slice of beef cut from the best part of the animal: *fillet steak.* □ **filete**
2 thick slice of fish: *a salmon steak.* □ **rodaja**
steakhouse *n.* restaurant serving steak and other grilled food. □ **restaurante**

steal [stiːl] *v.* (*he stole; he has stolen*) **1** to take (something which does not belong to you): *the burglars stole three silver cups from the house.* □ **robar**
2 ***to steal a glance at someone,*** to look at someone quickly and secretly. □ **mirar de soslayo a uno**
3 ***to steal a march on someone,*** to do something stealthily before they can do it. □ **ganar a alguien por la mano**
4 to creep about: *she stole into the kitchen and opened the refrigerator.* □ **deslizarse en**

stealth [stelθ] *n.* ***by stealth,*** in a secret way/without anyone knowing. □ **secreto; a escondidas**
stealthily *adv.* secretly/furtively. □ **a hurtadillas**
stealthy *adj.* secret; without anyone knowing or seeing. □ **secreto**

steam [stiːm] *n.* **1** vapour which comes off hot water/from warm breath: *steam was coming out of the kettle; steam formed on the car windows.* □ **vapor**
steam engine, engine which runs on steam pressure. □ **máquina de vapor**
steam radio, (*informal*) old-fashioned radio (as opposed to television). □ **una patata de radio**
2 *in the days of steam,* when railways used steam locomotives. □ **antiguamente**
3 ***to let off steam,*** (*informal*) (i) to use up your excess energy. □ **desfogarse**
(ii) to explode with anger. □ **explotar**
■ *v.* **1** to cook by steam: *a steamed pudding.* □ **cocer al vapor**
2 *to steam open a letter,* to hold an envelope in the steam of a kettle to melt the glue; *to steam a stamp off an envelope.* □ **abrir un sobre...; despegar un sello con vapor**
3 to send out steam: *the water is steaming; a steaming bowl of soup.* □ **echar vapor**
4 to move by steam power: *the old engine steamed out of the station; the ship was steaming at ten knots.* □ **avanzar**
5 to be covered by a mist: *the kitchen windows have steamed up.* □ **empañarse**
6 ***to get all steamed up about something,*** (*informal*) to get very annoyed. □ **cabrearse**
steamboat *n.* boat powered by steam. □ **vapor**
steamer *n.* **1** large passenger ship (powered by steam). □ **vapor**
2 type of pan with holes in the bottom which is placed over boiling water for steaming vegetables/puddings, etc. □ **olla para cocer al vapor**
steamroller *n.* vehicle with a very heavy roller for flattening newly laid road surfaces. □ **apisonadora**
steamship *n.* large passenger ship (powered by steam). □ **vapor**
steamy *adj.* full of steam: *a steamy kitchen.* □ **lleno de vapor**

steel [stiːl] *n.* **1** hard flexible metal made from iron and carbon: *steel cutlery; steel plating.* □ **acero**
steel band, West Indian band which plays music on steel drums of varying sizes. □ **banda de bidoneros**
2 bar of rough steel for sharpening knives. □ **chaira**
■ *v.* ***to steel yourself to do something,*** to get up enough courage to do something. □ **armarse de valor**
steel wool *n.* very fine steel wire used in wads for cleaning metal pans. □ **esponjilla de níquel**
steelworks *n.* factory which produces steel. □ **acería**
steely *adj.* sharp or hard like steel: *a steely glance.* □ **de acero, duro**

steep [stiːp] *adj.* **1** which rises or falls sharply: *steep hill; steep climb; a steep increase in prices.* □ **escarpado; desmesurado**
2 (*informal*) excessive: *that's a bit steep!* □ **te has pasado**
■ *v.* **1** to soak in a liquid for a long time. □ **dejar en remojo**
2 *place* ***steeped in*** *history,* full of history. □ **saturado de historia**
steepen *v.* to become steeper. □ **volverse más empinado**
steeply *adv.* (rising) sharply: *steeply rising prices; the road rises steeply for three miles.* □ **en ascenso vertiginoso**

steeply graded test, which becomes rapidly more difficult. □ **prueba de menor a mayor dificultad**

steeple ['sti:pl] *n.* church tower with the top rising to a point. □ **aguja**

steeplechase *n.* race (for horses or people) run over open country and over fences, hedges, etc. □ **carrera de obstáculos**

steeplejack *n.* person who climbs towers/factory chimneys, etc., to do repairs. □ **que trabaja en las alturas**

steer ['stiə] *n.* young bull raised for meat. □ **novillo**
■ *v.* to guide/to make (a vehicle) go in a certain direction: *he steered the car into a ditch; she steered the boat into the middle of the lake.* □ **conducir**

to steer clear of something, to avoid something. □ **evitar cualquier contacto**

steering *n.* mechanism in a car which steers it: *the steering is stiff.* □ **dirección**

power-assisted steering, steering in a large and heavy car which is helped by power from the engine. □ **dirección asistida**

steering column, metal tube to which the steering wheel is attached. □ **columna de dirección**

steering committee, small committee which does detailed work on the agenda for a large committee meeting. □ **comité directivo**

steering wheel, wheel which is turned by the driver to alter the direction of a car. □ **volante**

stellar ['stelə] *adj.* referring to stars. □ **estelar**

stem [stem] *n.* **1** long stalk on which flowers and leaves grow: *the stem of a plant; cut the roses with long stems.* □ **tallo**
2 thin part of a wine glass/of a tobacco pipe. □ **pie, cañón**
3 basic part of a word to which endings or prefixes are added: *'act' is the stem for 'action' and 'reactor'.* □ **radical, raíz**
4 ***from stem to stern,*** from the bows to the stern of a boat. □ **de proa a popa**
■ *v.* (*he stemmed*) **1** ***to stem from something,*** to result from something: *it all stems from his dislike of women.* □ **derivarse**
2 to stop/to prevent: *the doctors tried to stem the flow of blood.* □ **detener**

stench [stentʃ] *n.* strong unpleasant smell. □ **hedor**

stencil ['stensl] *n.* **1** sheet of cardboard or metal with a pattern or letters cut out of it, so that if it is placed on a surface and colour is passed over it, the pattern will appear on the surface; a pattern/letters/numbers, etc., which are painted in this way. □ **plantilla, estarcido**
2 sheet of waxed paper used for making large numbers of copies. □ **cliché**
■ *v.* (*he stencilled*) **1** to mark with a stencil: *the words 'this side up' must be stencilled on each box.* □ **estarcir**
2 to make a copy of (a document) using a stencil: *we received a stencilled letter from the income tax office.* □ **multicopiar**

stengun ['stengʌn] *n.* small machine gun. □ **metralleta**

stenographer [stə'nɔgrəfə] *n.* person who can write down fast in shorthand what someone says. □ **estenógrafo**

stenography [stə'nɔgrəfi] *n.* shorthand. □ **estenografía**

stentorian [sten'tɔ:riən] *adj.* (*formal*) very loud (voice). □ **estentóreo**

step [step] *n.* **1** single movement of the foot when walking/running; distance covered by this movement: *he took two steps forward.* □ **paso**

step by step, little by little: *step by step we are solving our problems.* □ **paso a paso**
2 sound made by moving a foot forward: *I thought I heard a step.* □ **paso**
3 regular movement of the feet: *the soldiers marched in step.* □ **paso**

to keep in step, to move at the same pace as everyone else: *soldiers have to keep in step when marching; wages are not keeping in step with prices.* □ **llevar el paso; mantener el ritmo**

out of step, not moving at the same pace as everyone else. □ **sin llevar el paso**
4 action: *he took steps to cut back expenses; if the situation becomes critical we will take the necessary steps to correct it; the first step is to get accurate figures,* first thing to do. □ **medida**
5 stair (on a staircase); flat rung (on a ladder). □ **peldaño**

a flight of steps *led down to the lawn,* a series of steps. □ **escalera**

(***a pair of***) ***steps,*** ladder with two parts hinged at the top, which can stand solidly without leaning against anything. □ **escalera de tijera**
■ *v.* (*he stepped*) to make a movement with a foot: *he stepped into the boat; she stepped aside to let the cow go past; step inside the shop and I will show you some new chairs; he got off the bus and stepped heavily on my foot.* □ **dar un paso/varios pasos**

to step on the brakes, to push the brake pedal hard. □ **pisar el freno a fondo**

step in *v.* to involve yourself/to interfere: *the strike was going to take place until the minister stepped in.* □ **intervenir**

stepladder *n.* pair of steps/hinged ladder which can stand solidly without leaning against anything. □ **escalera de tijera**

stepping-stone *n.* **1** one of a series of stones in a stream which allow you to cross it. □ **piedra para cruzar un río**
2 *a stepping-stone to success,* a means of becoming successful. □ **trampolín**

step up *v.* to increase: *we have stepped up production.* □ **aumentar**

step- [step] *prefix* showing a family relationship which is through a parent who has remarried. □ **-astro**

stepbrother *n.* male child of your stepfather or stepmother. □ **hermanastro**

stepchild *n.* child of your wife/husband. □ **hijastro/hijastra**

stepdaughter *n.* daughter of your wife/husband by another marriage. □ **hijastra**

stepfather *n.* husband of your mother who is not your father. □ **padrastro**

stepmother *n.* wife of your father, who is not your mother. □ **madrastra**

stepsister *n.* female child of your stepfather or stepmother. □ **hermanastra**

stepson *n.* son of your wife/husband by another marriage. □ **hijastro**

steppe [step] *n.* wide grass-covered plain in Russia and Asia. □ **estepa**

stereo- ['steriou] *prefix* referring to something which has two dimensions. □ **estereo-**

stereo ['steriou] *n.* and *adj.* (machine, etc.) which reproduces sound through two different channels and loudspeakers: *a stereo record; stereo broadcast; stereo record-player; this record is available in both stereo and mono; my radio cannot get broadcasts in* *stereo.* □ **estereofónico**

stereophonic [steriou'fɔnik] *adj.* referring to sound which comes from two places at once: *a stereophonic recording.* □ **estereofónico**

stereoscope ['steriouskoup] *n.* apparatus which shows a picture which appears to have depth and be three-dimensional. □ **estereoscopio**

stereoscopic [steriə'skɔpik] *adj.* referring to seeing a picture in three dimensions: *stereoscopic vision,* ability to see the same object with both eyes, and so judge solidity and distance. □ **estereoscópico**

stereotype ['steriətaip] *n.* pattern for certain types of person: *he's the stereotype of an Englishman; he doesn't fit the stereotype of the civil servant.* □ **estereotipo**

stereotyped *adj.* fitting certain rigid patterns: *the play is full of stereotyped characters.* □ **estereotipado**

sterile ['sterail] *adj.* **1** not capable of bearing fruit/children, etc. □ **estéril**

2 so pure that no germs/bacteria can grow: *sterile soil.* □ **estéril**

sterility [ste'riliti] *n.* inability to grow fruit/to produce children or ideas. □ **esterilidad**

sterilization [sterilai'zeiʃn] *n.* action of sterilizing. □ **esterilización**

sterilize ['sterilaiz] *v.* **1** to make (someone) incapable of producing children. □ **esterilizar**

2 to make so clean that bacteria/germs cannot grow: *the surgeon's equipment must be carefully sterilized.* □ **esterilizar**

sterilizer *n.* apparatus for sterilizing surgical equipment/bottles for fruit, etc. □ **esterilizador**

sterling ['stə:liŋ] *adj.* of a certain standard/of good quality: *he has given sterling service.* □ **excelente**

sterling silver, silver of a certain high purity. □ **plata de ley**

■ *n.* standard measure of British currency: *one pound sterling; sterling has risen against the dollar,* the value of the British pound has increased. □ **esterlina**

stern [stə:n] *adj.* harsh/strict: *stern discipline.* □ **severo**

■ *n.* rear part of a ship: *the ship broke in two, and the stern sank.* □ **popa**

sternly *adv.* strictly. □ **severamente**

sternness *n.* strictness. □ **severidad**

sternwheeler *n.* large pleasure ship (on American rivers) with a paddle wheel at the stern. □ **barco de recreo**

sternum ['stə:nəm] *n.* central bone on the chest. □ **esternón**

steroid ['stiərɔid] *n.* one of a group of natural substances in plants and animals, including hormones. □ **esteroide**

stethoscope ['steθəskoup] *n.* doctor's instrument for listening to a patient's chest. □ **estetoscopio**

stevedore ['sti:vədɔ:] *n.* person who works at a port, unloading or loading ships. □ **estibador**

stew [stju:] *n.* dish of meat and vegetables cooked together for a long time. □ **estofado**

■ *v.* to cook for a long time in liquid: *stewed apples.* □ **cocer en compota**

steward ['stjuəd] *n.* **1** man who serves meals or drinks on a ship/aircraft/in a club, etc. □ **auxiliar de vuelo**

2 person who organizes a meeting; person who looks after a farm or estate for the owner. □ **organizador; mayoral**

3 ***shop steward,*** elected union representative in a factory/office, etc. □ **representante sindical**

stewardess *n.* woman who looks after passengers on a ship or aircraft. □ **azafata**

stick [stik] *n.* **1** piece of wood: *we want some small sticks to light a fire.* □ **palo**

(***walking***) ***stick,*** strong piece of wood with a handle used as a support when walking: *he has to walk on two sticks.* □ **bastón**

hockey stick, stick with a curved end, used in playing hockey. □ **'stick'**

2 long piece: *stick of celery; stick of rhubarb; stick of gelignite.* □ **rama, tallo**

■ *v.* (*he stuck*) **1** to jab or push (something sharp) into something: *she stuck a drawing pin into the door; he stuck a needle into his finger; stick the letter in your pocket/in a drawer.* □ **meter, introducir**

2 to glue; to attach: *he stuck the stamp on the envelope; I can't get this envelope to stick; he tried to stick the cup together with glue; the jam has stuck to the bottom of the pan,* has burnt in cooking. □ **pegar(se)**

3 to stay: *stick close to me and you won't get lost.* □ **quedarse**

stick to the facts, keep to the facts. □ **atenerse a los hechos**

4 to be fixed/not to be able to move: *the car is stuck in a snowdrift; his thumb is stuck in a pipe; the lift has stuck; the door seems to have stuck.* □ **atascarse, pararse**

5 (*informal*) to bear/to accept: *I can't stick people who moan all the time.* □ **soportar**

stick at *v.* **1** ***to stick at nothing,*** to be ruthless/to do anything to achieve your aim. □ **no detenerse ante nada**

2 to stay: *he stuck at his post for hours.* □ **permanecer**

sticker *n.* small piece of paper or plastic with a pattern/motto, etc., which you can stick on a surface as a decoration. □ **pegatina**

election sticker, paper showing the name of a candidate or a party slogan which is stuck up at election time. □ **pegatina electoral**

stickiness *n.* state of being sticky. □ **pegajosidad**

sticking plaster *n.* strip of cloth which can be stuck to the skin to cover a cut. □ **esparadrapo**

stick-in-the-mud *n.* (*informal*) person who will not accept new ideas/who will not change his way of working. □ **chapado a la antigua**

stick-on *adj.* which sticks on to a surface: *a stick-on label.* □ **adhesivo**

stick out *v.* **1** to push out; to be further out than usual: *he stuck his tongue out at the teacher; the gun was sticking out of his pocket.* □ **sacar, sobresalir**

2 to be easily seen: *his red hair sticks out a mile.* □ **verse**

stick up *v.* **1** to put up (a notice, etc.): *he stuck up a poster.* □ **fijar, poner**

stick them up!, put your hands up (to show you surrender). □ **¡arriba las manos!**

2 ***to stick up for someone,*** (*informal*) to defend someone. □ **dar la cara por alguien**

sticky *adj.* **1** covered with glue; which sticks easily: *there is something sticky on the table; a sticky label.* □ **pegajoso**

2 (*informal*) difficult/awkward: *he's rather sticky about these things; a sticky problem.* □ **quisquilloso; peliagudo**

to come to a sticky end: *he came to a sticky end,* he died/was put in prison/was ruined, etc. □ **acabar mal**

stickleback ['stiklbæk] *n.* common small freshwater fish with spines along its back. □ **picón**
stickler ['stiklə] *n.* someone who attaches great importance to something: *he is a stickler for punctuality/for details.* □ **persona quisquillosa**
stiff [stif] *adj.* **1** which cannot be bent or moved easily: *stiff hinges; stiff knee; the lid of this jar is stiff; after the game of tennis I was stiff for two days; stiff brush,* with hard bristles; *stiff collar,* with a lot of starch in it. □ **rígido; duro; tieso; agarrotado**
frozen stiff, so cold that it has become solid. □ **duro (por el frío)**
bored stiff, so bored that you can't move. □ **aburrido como una ostra**
2 solid/thick: *the paint has gone stiff; mix the ingredients to a stiff paste.* □ **duro; espeso**
3 *stiff breeze,* strong breeze. □ **fuerte**
4 difficult/hard: *stiff examination; the police want stiffer penalties for football hooligans.* □ **difícil; duro**
5 *stiff whisky,* large whisky with not much water added. □ **seco**
6 unfriendly/unsociable. □ **poco amistoso/sociable**
stiffen *v.* **1** to become stiff; to make stiff: *my twisted knee has now stiffened.* □ **ponerse rígido; agarrotarse**
2 to become cautious or unfriendly: *the dog stiffened when he heard a sound outside.* □ **ponerse alerta**
3 *the wind is stiffening,* becoming stronger. □ **hacerse más fuerte**
4 *the general's remarks stiffened the resistance among the soldiers,* made it stronger. □ **reforzar**
stiffly *adv.* **1** in a stiff way: *he walked stiffly across the room.* □ **con rigidez**
2 *he bowed stiffly,* in a cold or unfriendly way. □ **fríamente**
stiff-necked *adj.* obstinate. □ **terco**
stiffness *n.* being stiff: *there is still some stiffness in my knee when I stand up.* □ **agarrotamiento, entumecimiento**
stifle ['staifl] *v.* **1** to prevent (someone) from breathing: *he was stifled by the smoke.* □ **sofocar**
2 to hold back: *she stifled a yawn.* □ **reprimir**
stifling *adj.* suffocating; extremely hot. □ **sofocante**
stigma ['stigmə] *n.* **1** disgrace; feeling of shame: *social stigma; there is no stigma attached to being poor.* □ **estigma**
2 top of the centre of a flower which receives pollen to make seeds. □ **estigma**
stigmatize ['stigmətaiz] *v.* to give a bad name to (something). □ **estigmatizar**
stile [stail] *n.* steps to get over a wall or fence, which stop animals getting out. □ **escalera**
stiletto [sti'letou] *n.* **1** long thin dagger. □ **estilete**
2 ***stiletto heels,*** high thin heels on women's shoes. □ **tacones de aguja**
still [stil] *n.* **1** apparatus for producing alcohol. □ **alambique**
2 one picture from a moving film. □ **fotograma**
■ *adj.* **1** calm/motionless: *the surface of the lake was absolutely still; you can't expect a child to sit still for hours.* □ **quieto**
2 *still lemonade,* not fizzy. □ **sin gas**
3 ***still life,*** picture of flowers or objects, not people or animals. □ **bodegón**
■ *adv.* **1** up until this/that moment: *he came at ten o'clock and he's still talking about his garden; I've still got some money left.* □ **todavía**
2 even: *still more people came; I don't want to see them, still less go to their house.* □ **aún**
3 however: *it wasn't very hot but still it didn't rain.* □ **sin embargo**
stillborn *adj.* (child) which is born dead; (idea) which is never put into practice. □ **mortinato; malogrado**
stillness *n.* calm: *the stillness of the evening air.* □ **quietud**
stilt [stilt] *n. house built on stilts,* on poles to raise it above the ground. □ **pilotes**
pair of stilts, two poles with foot rests to enable you to walk high in the air. □ **zancos**
stilted *adj.* (style of writing) which is very formal/not natural. □ **afectado**
stimulate ['stimjuleit] *v.* **1** to excite/to encourage: *to stimulate production.* □ **estimular**
2 *what you need is stimulating exercise,* exercise which will make you feel more active. □ **estimulante**
stimulant *n.* drug or medicine which makes you more active. □ **estimulante**
stimulation [stimju'leiʃn] *n.* being stimulated. □ **estimulación**
stimulus *n.* (*pl. stimuli* ['stimjulai]) thing that encourages further activity: *it acts as a stimulus to trade.* □ **estímulo**
sting [stiŋ] *n.* **1** tiny needle in the tail of an insect/leaf of a plant which injects poison. □ **aguijón**
2 wound made by an insect or plant: *wasp sting; nettle sting; a bee can give you a nasty sting.* □ **picadura**
3 burning feeling: *the sting of lemon juice on my cut finger.* □ **escozor**
■ *v.* (*it stung*) **1** to wound with a sting: *I have been stung by a wasp; he has got stung by the nettles.* □ **picar, pinchar**
2 to have a burning feeling: *my eyes are stinging; the gas makes your eyes sting.* □ **escocer**
3 to hurt (someone) so that he reacts: *the letter stung him into action.* □ **pinchar**
4 (*informal*) to ask for money: *he stung me for $10.* □ **dar un sablazo**
stinging nettle *n.* common wild plant which causes a rash. □ **ortiga**
stingray *n.* large flat fish with a sting in its tail. □ **pastinaca**
stingy ['stindʒi] *adj.* (*informal*) mean; not free with money. □ **tacaño**
stinginess *n.* meanness. □ **tacañería**
stink [stiŋk] *n.* unpleasant smell. □ **hedor**
to create a stink about something, (*informal*) to object to something vigorously. □ **oponerse**
■ *v.* (*he stank; he has stunk*) to make an unpleasant smell: *this meat stinks; he comes home late, stinking of whisky.* □ **apestar**
stint [stint] *n.* **1** amount of work: *I have just done a five-week stint down a coal mine; he has done his stint,* his share of the work. □ **tarea**
2 ***without stint,*** in large quantities/with no restriction. □ **sin límite**
■ *v.* to give a very small amount: *don't stint yourself,* go on, take a lot. □ **no cojas tan poco**
stipend ['staipend] *n.* salary of a priest or a magistrate. □ **estipendio**
stipendiary [stai'pendjəri] *adj.* (magistrate) who is paid. □ **remunerado**
stipple ['stipl] *v.* to colour with small dots. □ **puntear**
stipulate ['stipjuleit] *v.* to insist; to make a condition: *the contract stipulates a payment in advance; the owner must stipulate that the tenant shall keep the house in good condition.* □ **estipular**
stipulation [stipju'leiʃn] *n.* condition (in a contract). □ **estipulación, condición**
stir [stəː] *n.***1** mixing up a liquid: *give your tea a stir.* □ **movimiento, agitación**

2 fuss/agitation: *his departure created a stir.* □ **agitación**
■ *v.* (*he stirred*) **1** to mix up a liquid: *stir your coffee; he stirred the paint with a stick.* □ **remover**
2 to cause fuss/agitation: *he was stirred to pity/to take action.* □ **provocar, mover**
3 to move: *the sleeping man stirred; I shall not stir out of the house.* □ **moverse**
stirring *adj.* exciting: *we live in stirring times; the minister made a stirring speech.* □ **agitado; animado**
stir up *v.* to cause (trouble): *she's always stirring up trouble in the office; the tribesmen were stirred up by their leaders,* were led to react violently. □ **provocar; espolear**
stirrup ['stirəp] *n.* metal loop hanging from the saddle into which the rider puts his foot. □ **estribo**
stirrup cup, drink taken on horseback before setting off on a ride. □ **espuela**
stitch [stitʃ] *n.* **1** small loop of cotton or wool made with a needle in sewing or knitting. □ **puntada**
to drop a stitch, lose the wool from the needle when knitting. □ **salirse el punto**
2 (*informal*) clothes: *I haven't got a stitch to wear,* I have no clothes which I could wear (to the party, etc.). □ **ropa**
3 small loop of thread used by a surgeon to attach a wound together: *he had to have three stitches in his head.* □ **punto**
4 sharp pain in the side of the body which comes after you have been running: *she had to drop out of the race because she got a stitch.* □ **punzada**
5 *he was* ***in stitches,*** (*informal*) laughing uproariously. □ **desternillándose de risa**
■ *v.* to attach with a needle and thread: *to stitch a patch on a sleeve; the surgeon stitched up the wound.* □ **coser**
stoat [stout] *n.* small brown flesh-eating animal. □ **armiño**
stock [stɔk] *n.* **1** plant on which other plants are grafted: *roses are grafted on to wild rose stock.* □ **patrón**
2 race/family: *he comes of British stock.* □ **raza, linaje, origen**
3 handle of a rifle. □ **culata**
4 ***stocks,*** yard where ships are built: *we have three ships on the stocks,* being built. □ **grada, astilleros**
5 quantity of things for use; quantities of goods for sale: *we have laid in a stock of firewood; our stock of beer seems to be running low; we haven't any sugar left in stock; this book is out of stock at the moment.* □ **reserva, existencias**
to take stock, to count what you have in stock. □ **hacer inventario**
to take stock of the situation, to examine and see what should be done. □ **examinar**
6 farm animals (cattle/sheep, etc.). □ **ganado**
fat stock, animals reared for meat. □ **ganado de carne**
7 liquid made from boiling bones, etc., in water, used as a base for soups and sauces. □ **caldo, fondo**
8 common scented garden flower. □ **alhelí**
9 capital invested in a business: *stocks and shares.* □ **títulos**
government stocks, loans made to the state. □ **deuda pública**
stock market, buying and selling of shares. □ **bolsa de valores**
stock exchange, building in which shares are bought and sold. □ **bolsa**
■ *v.* **1** to keep goods for sale: *we are a grocery so we don't stock paintbrushes.* □ **tener (a la venta)**
2 to provide goods/animals/plants, etc.: *well-stocked garden/larder/farm.* □ **surtir**
■ *adj.* **1** usual. □ **normal**
stock size, normal size. □ **tamaño normal**
2 *stock argument,* one which is frequently used. □ **argumento clásico**
stockbroker *n.* person who deals in shares in the stock exchange. □ **corredor de bolsa**
stockcar *n.* old ordinary car adapted for brutal racing: *stockcar racing.* □ **'stockcar'**
stockist *n.* person/shop which stocks a certain brand of goods. □ **distribuidor**
stockman *n.* (*pl. stockmen*) man who looks after farm animals. □ **ganadero**
stockpile *n.* supplies kept in reserve (in case of an emergency). □ **reservar**
■ *v.* to collect supplies in case of emergency: *the power stations are stockpiling coal.* □ **acumular**
stockpot *n.* large pot for making soup. □ **olla grande**
stock-still *adv.* without moving: *he stood stock-still and listened.* □ **sin moverse**
stocktaking *n.* counting of goods in stock at the end of a period. □ **inventario**
stocky *adj.* short and strong (person). □ **rechoncho**
stockade [stɔ'keid] *n.* strong fence made of thick upright poles. □ **estacada**
stocking ['stɔkiŋ] *n.* **1** long light piece of clothing to cover your leg and foot: *nylon stockings; she wears woollen stockings in winter.* □ **media**
2 *he measures 1m 50* ***in his stocking feet,*** without his shoes on. □ **descalzo**
stodge [stɔdʒ] *n.* heavy filling food (such as puddings). □ **comida pesada**
stodgy *adj.* heavy (food); dull (book): *a stodgy diet.* □ **pesado**
stoic ['stouik] *n.* person who accepts problems or pain without complaining. □ **estoico**
stoical *adj.* referring to a stoic: *a stoical acceptance of his fate.* □ **estoico**
stoicism ['stouisizəm] *n.* accepting your fate without complaining. □ **estoicismo**
stoke [stouk] *v.* to put fuel in (a furnace): *to stoke (up) the boiler.* □ **alimentar**
stoker *n.* person who stokes a furnace. □ **fogonero**
stole [stoul] *n.* wide light scarf worn around the shoulders. □ **estola**
■ *v. see* **steal.**
stolen ['stoulən] *v. see* **steal.**
stolid ['stɔlid] *adj.* slow and heavy; not excitable. □ **impasible**
stolidly *adv.* slowly and calmly. □ **impasiblemente**
stomach ['stʌmək] *n.* **1** bag inside the body in which food is digested. □ **estómago**
stomach ache, pain in the stomach. □ **dolor de estómago**
2 part of the body lower than the chest: *he hit him in the stomach; he crawled on his stomach,* lying flat on the ground. □ **estómago**
3 desire/courage: *he has no stomach for a fight.* □ **valor**
■ *v.* to put up with/to tolerate: *I can't stomach these quarrels any longer.* □ **soportar**
stone [stoun] *n.* **1** small piece of rock: *the beach was covered with stones; don't throw stones at the windows.* □ **piedra**
2 *it's only* ***a stone's throw*** *away,* it is not very far away. □ **a tiro de piedra**
3 piece of rock which has been cut for building, etc.: *the church is built of stone and flint; a stone quarry; a stone castle; a stone fireplace; the statue*

was carved out of solid stone. □ **piedra**
Stone Age, prehistoric period when men made tools out of stone. □ **Edad de Piedra**
precious stone, rare type of mineral which is very valuable. □ **piedra preciosa**
4 hard seed inside some types of fruit: *cherry stone; date stone.* □ **hueso**
5 hard piece of mineral which forms inside the body (in the kidneys, etc.) and causes pain. □ **piedra, cálculo**
6 measure of weight (= 14 pounds or 6.35 kilograms). □ **(unidad de peso)**
■ *adv.* completely: *stone dead; stone deaf.* □ **totalmente**
stone broke, *Amer.* with no money. □ **sin blanca**
■ *v.* **1** *to stone someone to death,* to throw stones at someone and kill him. □ **matar a pedradas**
2 to take the stones out of fruit: *stoned dates.* □ **deshuesar**
stonecrop *n.* type of plant which grows among stones. □ **uva de gato**
stoned *adj.* (*slang*) **1** drunk. □ **borracho**
2 drugged. □ **drogado**
stonemason *n.* person who cuts and builds with stone. □ **cantero**
stonewall *v.* to speak for a long time without answering the question: *when asked about the government's intentions, the minister stonewalled.* □ **salirse por la tangente**
stoneware *n.* (*no pl.*) grey pottery made of rough clay. □ **gres**
stonily *adv.* with no feeling: *he stared stonily at her.* □ **fríamente**
stony *adj.* **1** covered with stones: *stony ground.* □ **pedregoso**
2 hard; with no feeling: *stony look; stony silence.* □ **duro; frío**
3 ***stony broke,*** (*informal*) with no money. □ **sin blanca**

stood [stud] *v. see* **stand.**

stooge [stuːdʒ] *n.* (*informal*) **1** person who does what he is told to do. □ **sumiso; secuaz**
2 the stupid one of a pair of comedians. □ **comparsa**
■ *v.* ***to stooge about,*** (*informal*) to wander about waiting to be told what to do. □ **estar a la espera de órdenes**

stool [stuːl] *n.* **1** seat with no back. □ **taburete**
to fall between two stools, (i) to miss each of two targets. □ **no conseguir ni lo uno ni lo otro**
(ii) not to take up either of two opportunities. □ **no aprovechar ni lo uno ni lo otro**
2 lump of waste matter passed from the bowels. □ **deposición**

stoop [stuːp] *n.* bending forward: *he walks with a stoop.* □ **encorvamiento**
■ *v.* **1** to bend forward: *he had to stoop to get through the door.* □ **agacharse, encorvarse**
2 *he stoops,* he has a permanently bent back. □ **está encorvado**
3 to allow yourself to do something which you feel is beneath you: *I wouldn't stoop to begging even if I had no money.* □ **rebajarse**

stop [stɔp] *n.* **1** act of not moving/not doing something: *to put a stop to something; we made several stops on the journey; the car came to a stop against a brick wall; all work on the house came to a stop when the builder could not pay the wages.* □ **parada; detención**
2 place where a bus, etc., usually stops to pick up or put down passengers: *bus stop; request stop.* □ **parada**
3 ***full stop,*** round dot (.) showing the end of a sentence. □ **punto**
4 block which prevents something closing: *door stop.* □ **tope**
5 knob on an organ which switches on a different set of pipes; set of pipes on an organ which produce a particular sound. □ **registro**
6 ***to pull out all the stops,*** to do everything possible. □ **tocar todas las teclas**
■ *v.* (*he stopped*) **1** to make (something which is moving) come to a halt; to come to a halt: *the policeman stopped the traffic to let the children cross the road; the car failed to stop at the red light; fast trains don't stop at small stations; stop that man, he's stolen my wallet.* □ **parar; pararse**
2 to make (something) cease working/cease doing something; to cease working/doing something: *the clock has stopped at ten to three; can't you stop them making that noise? it's stopped raining; the rain has stopped; he spoke for two hours without stopping.* □ **pararse; impedir; dejar de...**
stop it!, that's enough! □ **¡basta!**
3 to stay in a place: *we stopped for a few days at my parents' house; we are travelling round France, stopping each night in small hotels.* □ **quedarse**
4 to block: *the pipe has got stopped up.* □ **atascarse**
to stop a gap, to fill a gap. □ **llenar un hueco**
5 to cut off (supply); to prevent (money being paid): *to stop the supply of electricity; to stop a cheque,* to tell the bank not to pay a cheque which you have written; *to stop someone's wages,* not to pay someone. □ **cortar; no autorizar; no pagar**
stop by *v.* (*informal*) to visit someone for a short time. □ **pasar por**
stopcock *n.* tap which stops the supply of water to a house/through a pipe. □ **llave de paso**
stopgap *n.* and *adj.* something which is used temporarily while waiting for something more suitable to turn up: *a stopgap solution to the problem.* □ **recurso provisional**
stop off *v.* to make a stop on a long journey: *we will stop off in Paris on the way to Moscow.* □ **hacer escala**
stop over *v.* to make an overnight stop on a long journey. □ **hacer noche**
stopover *n.* overnight stop on a long journey. □ **noche de escala**
stoppage *n.* action of stopping/blocking: *stoppage of work; a stoppage in a pipe.* □ **interrupción; obstrucción**
stopper *n.* piece of glass/cork, etc., which fits the mouth of a jar, etc., to close it. □ **tapón**
stop press *n.* and *adj.* last piece of news added to a newspaper before it is printed. □ **noticia de última hora**
stop watch *n.* watch which can be started and stopped by pressing a button, used for timing races. □ **cronómetro**

store [stɔː] *n.* **1** supply of food, etc., kept for later use: *our stores are running low; we have laid in a store of drink for Christmas.* □ **reservas**
2 *there's a surprise* ***in store*** *for you,* waiting for you. □ **te espera...**
3 ***to set great store by something,*** think that something is very important. □ **conceder mucha importancia**
4 place in which goods are kept: *out furniture has been put in store.* □ **almacén**
5 shop: *the village stores.* □ **tienda**
■ *v.* **1** to keep (something) for future use: *we store our firewood in the shed; how much food have you*

stored away? □ **almacenar, guardar**
2 to put (something) in a warehouse: *we have stored our furniture while we are looking for somewhere to live.* □ **almacenar**
storage *n.* act of keeping/putting in store: *storage charges.* □ **almacenamiento**
storage heaters, electric heaters where the electricity warms bricks which then store the heat and release it gradually. □ **acumuladores**
storehouse *n.* place where something is stored: *he is a storehouse of information about local history.* □ **depósito, mina**
storekeeper *n.* shopkeeper. □ **tendero**
storeroom *n.* room where something is stored. □ **despensa, almacén**
storey ['stɔːri] *Amer.* **story** *n.* whole floor in a building: *a seventy-storey skyscraper.* □ **planta**
stork [stɔːk] *n.* large, usually white, bird with long legs and long beak. □ **cigüeña**
storm [stɔːm] *n.* **1** period of bad weather with wind: *thunderstorm; snowstorm; the storm blew for three days.* □ **tormenta**
a storm in a teacup, lot of fuss for no good reason. □ **tormenta en un vaso de agua**
2 *storm of applause,* loud burst of clapping and cheering. □ **salva de aplausos**
3 ***to take*** *a town* ***by storm,*** (i) to attack a town suddenly and capture it. □ **por sorpresa, por asalto** (ii) to become suddenly very popular in a town. □ **ganarse rápidamente**
storm troops, soldiers who are specially trained to attack and capture. □ **tropas de asalto**
■ *v.* **1** to be violently angry: *he stormed about the office shouting at the secretaries.* □ **andar enfurecido**
2 to attack and capture: *the castle was stormed.* □ **tomar por asalto**
stormy *adj.* **1** referring to a storm: *stormy weather.* □ **tormentoso**
2 *stormy seas,* with high waves raised by the wind. □ **con temporal**
3 *stormy discussion,* violent argument. □ **acalorado, tempestuoso**
story ['stɔːri] *n.* **1** tale of what has happened: *tell the policeman your story.* □ **historia**
it's a long story, it is very complicated. □ **es una larga historia**
2 piece of fiction: *a detective story; a short story; read me a bedtime story.* □ **historia, cuento**
3 (*informal*) lie: *you shouldn't tell stories.* □ **cuento, mentira**
4 *Amer. see also* **storey.**
storyline *n.* plot of a novel/film, etc. □ **trama**
storyteller *n.* **1** person who tells a story. □ **narrador**
2 (*informal*) person who tells lies. □ **cuentista**
stout [staut] *adj.* **1** fat: *a stout old gentleman; she is getting a bit stout.* □ **grueso**
2 strong/thick: *stout walking shoes.* □ **fuerte**
3 brave: *he has a stout heart; they put up a stout resistance.* □ **fuerte, firme**
■ *n.* strong dark beer. □ **cerveza fuerte**
stout-hearted *adj.* brave. □ **valiente**
stoutly *adv.* **1** vigorously: *he stoutly denied the charges brought against him; they defended themselves stoutly.* □ **enérgicamente**
2 solidly/strongly: *these walls are stoutly built.* □ **sólidamente**
stoutness *n.* being fat. □ **gordura**
stove [stouv] *n.* machine for heating or cooking: *electric stove; gas stove.* □ **estufa, hornillo**
stovepipe *n.* metal chimney which carries the smoke from a wood- or coal-burning stove. □ **tubo**
stow [stou] *v.* to put away; to pack: *all the luggage was stowed in the boot of the car.* □ **guardar**
stow away *v.* **1** to pack: *I have stowed away all my gear.* □ **guardar**
2 to travel secretly on a ship/aircraft without paying the fare. □ **viajar de polizón**
stowaway *n.* person who travels secretly without paying the fare. □ **polizón**
straddle ['strædl] *v.* **1** to stand with legs apart, and your feet on either side of (something): *he straddled the little stream.* □ **estar a horcajadas**
2 *the town straddles the main road,* is built on both sides of it. □ **estar situado a ambos lados de**
straggle ['strægl] *v.* to hang/to walk in an untidy way: *his hair straggled down over his face; the soldiers straggled behind the retreating guns.* □ **rezagarse, desparramarse**
straggler *n.* person who walks well behind the main group of people. □ **rezagado**
straggly *adj.* which grows untidily: *a straggly hedge.* □ **desordenado**
straight [streit] *adj.* **1** not curved: *a straight line; the road ran in a straight line for several miles.* □ **recto**
2 *straight hair,* not curly. □ **liso**
3 honest/frank: *I want a straight answer,* don't tell me lies; *he wasn't completely straight with me,* he didn't tell me the complete truth. □ **sincero, franco**
4 simple/not complicated. □ **sencillo**
a straight fight, an election where there are only two candidates. □ **de dos candidatos**
a straight whisky, a glass of whisky with no water or ice added. □ **seco**
5 not crooked/tidy: *your tie isn't straight; put your room straight.* □ **bien puesto; en orden**
6 *I must try* ***to get things straight*** *with the income tax,* to arrange things. □ **arreglar**
7 ***to keep a straight face,*** to stop yourself smiling. □ **ponerse serio**
■ *n.* ***the straight,*** part of a racecourse (usually near the finish) which is not curved. □ **recta**
■ *adv.* **1** in a straight line: *he can't shoot straight; keep straight on until you come to a crossroads; he drove straight through the cornfield.* □ **en línea recta**
2 immediately: *I'll come straight back; he came straight here after he heard the news.* □ **inmediatamente**
3 directly: *he drank the milk straight from the bottle; she looked him straight in the face; he told them straight out that they were idiots.* □ **directamente**
4 honestly: *they are not playing straight.* □ **limpiamente**
to go straight, (*informal*) to lead an honest life after having been a criminal. □ **reformarse**
straight away *adv.* immediately/at once. □ **inmediatamente**
straighten *v.* to make/to become straight: *to straighten your tie; the soldiers were slouching about, but straightened up when the general came in.* □ **poner bien; ponerse derecho**
straightforward *adj.* frank/honest: *a straightforward reply.* □ **sincero**
straightforwardly *adv.* in an honest way. □ **sinceramente**
straight off *adv.* at once: *he gave the answer straight off.* □ **al momento**
straight out *adv.* directly: *he said straight out what he thought of the headmaster.* □ **directamente**
strain [strein] *n.* **1** act of pulling tight; tension: *the strain was too much for the rope; the wall collapsed under the strain; we have several ropes to take the strain,* to hold back something which is pulling

hard. □ **tensión**
2 hurt caused by pulling a muscle too hard. □ **tirón**
3 stress; mental/physical tension: *she can't stand the strain of bringing up six children; he has had to take some days off because of strain of overwork.* □ **tensión**
4 way of speaking: *he went on in the same strain for several minutes.* □ **tono**
5 breed: *a new strain of virus; a hardy strain of tomatoes.* □ **cepa**
6 quality or defect which is inherited: *a fatal strain of weakness in his character.* □ **vena**
7 tune: *strains of music came through the open window.* □ **sonidos**
■ *v.* **1** to pull/to work too hard: *he strained his leg and had to retire from the competition; he strained his eyes by reading at night.* □ **forzar demasiado**
2 to make a great effort: *he strained to hear what they were whispering; they strained to grab the branch of the tree.* □ **hacer un esfuerzo**
3 *you strain my patience,* you make me nearly lose patience. □ **agotar**
4 to pass a liquid through a sieve: *to strain the vegetables,* pour off the water in which they were cooked. □ **escurrir**
strained *adj.* **1** which has been pulled/worked too hard: *he retired from the game with a strained tendon.* □ **forzado, con un tirón**
2 tense/unfriendly: *a strained conversation; relations between the two countries are strained.* □ **tenso**
strainer *n.* type of sieve for separating liquids from solids. □ **escurridor**

straits [streits] *n. pl.* **1** narrow piece of sea water between two masses of land: *the Straits of Gibraltar.* □ **estrecho**
2 money difficulties: *they are in dire straits.* □ **estrechez**
straitened *adj.* ***to be in straitened circumstances,*** not to have enough money to live on. □ **pasar apuros de dinero**
straitjacket *n.* **1** strong coat whose sleeves are tied behind the back to prevent a mad person from attacking people. □ **camisa de fuerza**
2 something which prevents you from acting freely. □ **camisa de fuerza**
straitlaced *adj.* with very strict ideas about correct moral behaviour. □ **mojigato**

strand [strænd] *n.* **1** long piece of hair/thread, etc. □ **mechón, trenza**
2 (*formal*) shore. □ **costa**
■ *v.* to leave your ship on the shore: *they stranded the ship and walked inland to look for help.* □ **varar**
stranded *adj.* alone and helpless: *people were stranded on the island by the storm; the car broke down and left us stranded.* □ **dejado tirado**

strange [streinʒ] *adj.* **1** odd/bizarre: *a strange sound came from the car engine; his behaviour was very strange.* □ **extraño**
2 which you have never seen/heard, etc., before: *a strange country; we went to a Japanese restaurant and had several strange sorts of fish.* □ **extraño, desconocido**
strangely *adv.* oddly/curiously: *his face is strangely familiar; strangely enough he does not know how to drive.* □ **extrañamente**
strangeness *n.* oddness; novelty. □ **novedad**
stranger *n.* **1** person whom you do not know: *a stranger came into the bar; don't accept lifts from strangers; you're quite a stranger,* I haven't seen you for a long time. □ **extraño**
2 *he is a stranger to the town,* he does not know the town well. □ **forastero**

strangle ['stræŋgl] *v.* to kill (someone) by pressing on his throat so that he cannot breathe: *he was strangled with a piece of rope.* □ **estrangular**
stranglehold *n.* control which prevents you doing what you want to do: *they have a stranglehold over the country's economy.* □ **dominio absoluto**
strangulation [stræŋgju'leiʃn] *n.* being strangled: *he died from strangulation.* □ **estrangulamiento**

strap [stræp] *n.* long flat piece of leather or material for attaching something: *his case was held together with a leather strap; watch strap.* □ **correa**
■ *v.* (*he strapped*) **1** to attach with a strap: *the luggage was strapped on to the roof of the car.* □ **atar con una correa**
2 to wrap a bandage tightly round a wound. □ **vendar**
3 to hit (someone) with a leather strap. □ **azotar**
strap hanging *n.* travelling standing in a crowded bus, underground train, etc., holding on to one of the straps hanging from the roof. □ **viajar de pie agarrado a la correa**
strapless *adj.* with no straps: *strapless bra.* □ **sin tirantes**
strapping *adj.* big/strong (young man or girl). □ **robusto**

strata ['strɑːtə] *n. see* **stratum.**

stratagem ['strætədʒəm] *n.* clever plan to trick an enemy. □ **estratagema**

strategic, strategical [strə'tiːdʒik(l)] *adj.* referring to strategy: *a strategic advance.* □ **estratégico**
strategic position, position which gives an advantage over the enemy. □ **posición estratégica**
strategically *adv.* according to strategy: *the enemy is strategically placed on the hills overlooking the road.* □ **estratégicamente**
strategist ['strætədʒist] *n.* officer who plans military attacks. □ **estratega**
strategy ['strætədʒi] *n.* planning of war/of an action: *a master of strategy.* □ **estrategia**

stratify ['strætifai] *v.* to form layers; to be arranged in layers: *a stratified society.* □ **estratificar**
stratification [strætifi'keiʃn] *n.* forming layers; arranging in layers. □ **estratificación**

stratosphere ['strætəsfiə] *n.* upper layer of the earth's atmosphere. □ **estratosfera**

stratum ['strɑːtəm] *n.* (*pl. strata* ['strɑːtə]) **1** layer: *several strata of rock.* □ **estrato**
2 *they come from different social strata,* social backgrounds. □ **estrato**

stratus ['strɑːtəs] *n. stratus clouds,* low flat clouds. □ **estrato**

straw [strɔː] *n.* **1** dry stalks of plants like corn: *a heap of straw; a straw hat; straw mattress.* □ **paja**
2 one single dry stalk of a plant; thin plastic tube for sucking liquid: *he was drinking orange juice through a straw.* □ **paja**
that's the last straw, (*informal*) that is all I can stand/as much as I can take. □ **esto es el colmo**
straw poll, random questioning to test the general opinion of the public/of a group: *he conducted a straw poll of the office staff.* □ **sondeo**
strawberry *n.* common red summer fruit growing on low plants: *a strawberry plant; strawberry jam.* □ **fresa**

stray [strei] *adj.* and *n.* (animal, etc.) which is wandering away from home: *stray dog; she takes in strays.* □ **perdido, abandonado**
■ *adj.* **1** wandering off course: *he was killed by a stray bullet,* one that did not hit its target. □ **perdido**

2 *a few stray weeds growing in the lawn,* scattered weeds. □ **disperso**
■ *v.* **1** to wander: *the sheep strayed over the hill.* □ **perderse, vagar**
2 *his thoughts strayed to his summer holidays,* he thought about his holidays when he should have been thinking of something else. □ **perderse, vagar**
streak [stri:k] *n.* **1** band/line (of colour); flash (of light): *a streak of green in the material covering the chairs.* □ **franja**
2 *he raced past* ***like a streak of lightning,*** very fast. □ **como un rayo**
3 quality of character: *there is a streak of cowardice in him; she has a mean streak.* □ **vena**
■ *v.* **1** to rush: *the cars came streaking round the corner.* □ **ir a toda velocidad**
2 (*informal*) to run about with no clothes on. □ **correr desnudo en público**
streaker *n* (*informal*) person who runs about with no clothes on. □ **el que corre desnudo en público**
streaky *adj.* **1** with smudges of colour or dirt. □ **veteado**
2 ***streaky bacon,*** bacon with fat and lean streaks. □ **entreverado**
stream [stri:m] *n.* **1** small flow of water; a small river: *he drank from a mountain stream.* □ **riachuelo**
2 continuous flow: *streams of cars headed for the beaches; he let out a stream of abuse; I can't turn right across the stream of traffic.* □ **oleada; riada**
3 current: *to swim against the stream.* □ **corriente**
4 ***to come on stream,*** to start to be produced/to function: *when our new processing plant comes on stream.* □ **entrar en funcionamiento**
■ *v.* to flow: *tears streamed down her face; cars were streaming over the bridge; people streamed into the tent.* □ **correr**
streamer *n.* long thin flag; long paper decorations put up at Christmas, etc. □ **pendón; colgaduras**
streaming *adj.* dripping (wet): *he was streaming with sweat; I've got a streaming cold,* which makes my nose run. □ **que gotea**
streamline *v.* **1** to design a car/plane/boat, etc., so that it can move easily through water or air: *the streamlined hull of a yacht.* □ **...con línea aerodinámica**
2 to make more efficient; to modernize. □ **modernizar**
street [stri:t] *n.* **1** road in a town, with houses or shops on each side: *street lighting; Oxford Street.* □ **calle**
the High Street, main shopping street in a town. □ **calle mayor**
2 ***the man in the street,*** the ordinary citizen. □ **el hombre de la calle**
3 ***at street level,*** on the same level as the street. □ **al nivel de la calle**
4 *they are* ***streets ahead of*** *us,* (*informal*) much more advanced than we are. □ **nos llevan mucha delantera**
5 ***up one's street:*** *it is right up my street,* (*informal*) it is something I am very interested in/something I know a lot about. □ **es lo mío**
streetcar *n. Amer.* tram. □ **tranvía**
strength [streŋθ] *n.* **1** being strong: *strength of character; he doesn't know his own strength,* how strong he really is. □ **fuerza**
2 *strength of a solution,* ratio of the substance dissolved to the quantity of liquid. □ **proporción**
3 numbers. □ **número**
4 *they turned up* ***in full strength,*** all together/none of them was missing. □ **completos**
5 number of people employed: *is he on the strength?,* is he part of the regular workforce? □ **efectivos**
6 ***on the strength of*** *his letter,* because of his letter. □ **basándose en**
strengthen *v.* to make stronger: *we will have to strengthen this wall.* □ **reforzar**
strenuous ['strenjuəs] *adj.* **1** energetic: *strenuous exercise; he leads a very strenuous life.* □ **activo, intenso**
2 *to offer strenuous opposition,* to oppose something vigorously. □ **fuerte, enérgica**
strenuously *adv.* vigorously. □ **enérgicamente**
strenuousness *n.* being strenuous. □ **energía**
streptococcus [streptə'kɔkəs] *n.* (*pl. streptococci* [streptə'kɔkai]) type of bacteria which causes infections, such as a sore throat. □ **estreptococo**
streptomycin [streptə'maisin] *n.* type of antibiotic. □ **estreptomicina**
stress [stres] *n.* **1** force; pressure: *to calculate the stress of a roof on the walls.* □ **carga**
2 nervous strain: *he couldn't stand the stress of modern life.* □ **estrés**
3 emphasis: *the stress in 'London' falls on the first syllable.* □ **acento tónico**
to lay stress on something, to emphasize it. □ **hacer hincapié en algo**
■ *v.* to emphasize: *I must stress again that no one really knows what happened; he stressed the importance of hygiene in hospitals; in the word 'present' meaning 'a gift', it is the first syllable which is stressed.* □ **subrayar**
stretch [stretʃ] *n.* **1** act of being pulled out. □ **alargamiento**
by no stretch of the imagination *could you say he was handsome,* it is impossible to say that he is handsome. □ **ni haciendo un esfuerzo de imaginación**
2 act of putting out your arms and legs as far as they will go: *the cat got up and had a good stretch.* □ **estiramiento**
3 long piece (of road); long period (of time); (*slang*) time spent in prison: *after all those bumps it is pleasant to find a level stretch of road; for long stretches no one said anything.* □ **recta; período**
4 *she cried for hours* ***at a stretch,*** for hour after hour. □ **sin parar**
■ *v.* **1** to pull out (something elastic): *the wire was stretched between two poles; the work has stretched our resources to the full.* □ **estirar**
2 to pull out (something) too far: *you have stretched the neck of your pullover by pulling it over your head; my pullover has stretched,* become too big. □ **dar de sí**
3 to be able to be pulled out: *this sheet of rubber will stretch in any direction; don't worry if your gloves are tight — they will stretch.* □ **estirarse; ensancharse**
4 to put out your arms or legs as far as they will go: *he stretched out his hand and took a book from the shelf; the cat got up from the chair and stretched; she lay stretched out on the floor.* □ **alargar; estirarse**
to stretch one's legs: *I am going for a walk to stretch my legs,* to have some exercise after sitting down for some time. □ **estirar las piernas**
5 to be enough: *will the money stretch to pay for both of us?* □ **dar**
6 to lie for a great distance: *two thousand years ago forests stretched over Southern England; the empty sea stretched as far as the eye could see in every direction.* □ **extenderse**
7 ***to stretch a point/to stretch the rules,*** to make a concession: *we'll stretch a point and let you go home*

early today. □ **hacer una excepción**

stretcher *n.* portable bed with handles at each end for carrying sick people: *he was carried away on a stretcher.* □ **camilla**

stretcher bearer, person who lifts one end of a stretcher. □ **camillero**

strew [struː] *v.* (*he has strewn*) to scatter: *the floor was strewn with pieces of paper; bodies lay strewn all over the ground.* □ **salpicar**

stricken ['strikn] *adj.* hit/struck by disease/emotion, etc.: *the children were terror-stricken; the whole family was stricken with hay fever.* □ **afectado; aquejado**

strict [strikt] *adj.* **1** exact: *in the strict sense of the word,* in its precise meaning. □ **estricto**

2 *strict orders,* orders which must be obeyed: *he was under strict instructions to let no one in without a ticket.* □ **órdenes estrictas**

3 severe/harsh; (person) who insists that rules are obeyed: *strict discipline; you have to be strict with small children; she was brought up by a very strict aunt.* □ **estricto**

strictly *adv.* **1** exactly/precisely: *strictly speaking.* □ **estrictamente**

2 in a way which must be obeyed: *the carrying of firearms is strictly forbidden.* □ **estrictamente**

3 harshly; according to strict rules: *he was brought up very strictly.* □ **estrictamente**

strictness *n.* being strict. □ **severidad, exactitud**

stricture ['striktʃə] *n.* criticism/words of blame. □ **crítica**

stride [straid] *n.* long step with your legs: *he takes great strides.* □ **zancada**

to make great strides *in mathematics,* to make a lot of progress. □ **hacer grandes avances**

to take something/it in one's own stride: *he takes it all in his stride,* it does not worry him/he does it without too much effort. □ **tomarse algo con calma**

■ *v.* (*he strode*) to take long steps: *he strode away; she strode into the shop and asked to see the manager.* □ **dar zancadas**

strident ['straidənt] *adj.* unpleasantly loud/harsh/high (sound). □ **estridente**

strife [straif] *n.* fighting; trouble between people: *industrial strife.* □ **pelea; conflicto laboral**

strike [straik] *n.* **1** stopping of work by workers (because of disagreement with management): *the technicians' strike has lasted two weeks; the office staff came out on strike; they went on strike for higher pay.* □ **huelga**

2 *air strike,* rapid attack from the air. □ **ataque aéreo**

3 *oil strike,* discovery of oil. □ **descubrimiento de petróleo**

■ *v.* (*he struck*) **1** to hit: *he struck the policeman with a bottle; the car ran out of control and struck a tree; the ship sank after it struck a mine; he must have died when his head struck the pavement; the tree was struck by lightning.* □ **golpear; chocar con**

2 *to strike a match/to strike a light,* to light a match. □ **encender**

3 ***to strike a coin/a medal,*** to make a coin/a medal: *only two hundred medals were struck.* □ **acuñar**

4 ***to strike a bargain,*** to agree/to make a bargain. □ **cerrar un trato**

5 *to be struck down with flu,* to have a sudden attack of flu. □ **tener gripe, un ataque de gripe**

6 *she was struck with terror,* suddenly overcome with terror. □ **ser presa del terror**

7 to make an impression on (someone): *I was struck by what he said; how did she strike you?; he strikes me as being quite efficient,* it seems to me that he is quite efficient; *what struck me was the awful waste of money,* what surprised me. □ **impresionar; causar impresión**

8 to discover: *we have struck oil; as they dug deeper they struck a coal seam.* □ **descubrir**

9 to lower (a flag); to pack up (a tent): *we struck camp in the morning and headed for home.* □ **arriar; desmontar**

10 to ring (a note): *he struck G sharp; the clock struck seven,* rang seven times. □ **tocar**

11 to go in a certain direction: *they struck across the desert; he struck out for the shore,* he set off to swim to the shore. □ **atravesar; ponerse en camino**

12 to stop working because of disagreement or in protest: *the staff are striking for higher wages.* □ **ponerse en huelga**

strikebound *adj.* not able to move because of a strike. □ **paralizado por la huelga**

strikebreaker *n.* worker who continues to work when his colleagues are on strike. □ **esquirol**

strike off *v.* **1** to remove by force. □ **quitar de golpe**

2 *he was struck off the list,* his name was removed because he had done something wrong. □ **tachar de**

strike pay *n.* wages paid to striking workers by their union. □ **subsidio de huelga**

striker *n.* **1** person who goes on strike. □ **huelguista**

2 football player whose job is to score goals. □ **delantero**

strike up *v.* **1** to start playing a piece of music: *just as he started to say something, the band struck up.* □ **empezar a tocar**

2 ***to strike up an acquaintance with someone,*** to start getting to know someone. □ **iniciar una relación**

striking *adj.* remarkable: *he has a striking resemblance to his father.* □ **notable**

strikingly *adv.* remarkably: *she is strikingly beautiful.* □ **notablemente**

string [striŋ] *n.* **1** thin rope for tying things together: *the parcel was tied up with string; a ball of string.* □ **cuerda**

with no strings attached, (*informal*) with no hidden conditions: *there are no strings attached to this offer.* □ **sin condiciones**

to pull strings, (*informal*) to try to obtain something through influential friends. □ **mover los hilos**

2 series of things tied together: *a string of pearls; a string of onions; he let out a long string of curses.* □ **sarta**

3 thin wire in a musical instrument: *piano string; violin string.* □ **cuerda**

the strings, part of an orchestra playing stringed instruments. □ **sección de cuerda**

4 tough thread (in a bean pod). □ **hebra**

■ *v.* (*he strung*) **1** to tie together in a series: *to string pearls.* □ **ensartar**

2 to put a string in (a musical instrument). □ **poner una cuerda**

3 ***highly strung,*** easily excitable; very nervous: *she is highly strung and can't take shocks.* □ **muy nervioso**

string along *v.* to go along in a line behind someone. □ **ir detrás**

to string someone along, to make someone promises to get him to co-operate. □ **prometer algo a alguien**

string bag *n.* shopping bag made of a net of knotted string. □ **bolsa de red**

string bean *n. Amer.* runner bean. □ **judía de enrame**

stringed *adj.* (musical instrument) with strings.

□ **de cuerda**
string up *v.* to hang up with a string: *flags were strung up across the street.* □ **colgar con cuerda**
to string someone up, (*informal*) to hang someone. □ **colgar a alguien**
string vest *n.* vest made of cotton woven like a net. □ **camiseta de malla**
stringy *adj.* (meat or vegetables) with tough threads. □ **fibroso, correoso**
stringent ['strindʒənt] *adj.* strict/severe: *the government has introduced stringent controls over public spending.* □ **estricto**
stringency *n.* being strict/severe. □ **rigor**
strip [strip] *n.* long narrow piece: *a strip of paper; a strip of land along the side of the road.* □ **tira, franja**
strip cartoon/comic strip, cartoon story made of a series of small drawings side by side. □ **tira, historieta**
■ *v.* (*he stripped*) **1** to make naked; to take off your clothes: *the doctor asked him to strip; he stripped off his shirt.* □ **desnudarse**
2 to remove (something): *the birds have stripped all the cherries off the tree; he was stripped of all his government posts and sent to prison; you should strip the old paint off the door before you start painting it; the house was completely stripped,* everything was taken out of it. □ **quitar; despojar; vaciar**
strip down *v.* to take to pieces: *to strip down a car engine.* □ **desmontar**
strip lighting *n.* type of lighting using a long round tube. □ **alumbrado con tubos**
stripper *n.* **1** liquid for removing old paint; sharp tool for stripping off old paint or old wallpaper. □ **decapante; espátula**
2 woman who performs a striptease. □ **la que hace 'striptease'**
striptease *n.* type of entertainment where (a woman) takes her clothes off piece by piece. □ **'striptease'**
stripe [straip] *n.* **1** long strip of colour: *he has a shirt with red white and blue stripes; zebras have black and white stripes.* □ **raya**
2 strip of coloured cloth sewn to a uniform to show a certain rank in the army. □ **galón**
striped *adj.* with stripes: *I like striped shirts.* □ **de rayas**
stripy *adj.* covered with many stripes. □ **con muchas rayas**
stripling ['stripliŋ] *n.* very young man. □ **mozalbete**
strive [straiv] *v.* (*he strove: he has striven*) to try very hard: *he strove to finish his work on time.* □ **esforzarse**
strobe [stroub] *n.* light which flashes on and off very rapidly. □ **luz intermitente**
stroboscope *n.* illuminated figures on a turntable, which enable you to tell if it is turning at the correct speed; device which makes lights flash on and off (on a dance floor). □ **estroboscopio**
strode [stroud] *v. see* **stride.**
stroke [strouk] *n.* **1** gentle touch. □ **toque**
2 line made by a pen/brush, etc. □ **trazo**
oblique stroke, printing sign (/) used to show an alternative (as in 'men and/or women'). □ **barra**
3 blow: *he killed him with one stroke of his sword.* □ **golpe**
4 illness/paralysis caused by damage to part of the brain: *he died from a stroke.* □ **ataque, apoplejía**
5 one movement: *with a stroke of his paddle he sent the canoe away from the bank; he crossed the swimming pool in six strokes.* □ **golpe, brazada**
6 *he hasn't done a stroke of work,* no work at all. □ **mi golpe**
7 *he had a stroke of good fortune,* a piece of luck. □ **golpe**
8 particular style of swimming: *breast stroke.* □ **estilo**
9 one ring of a clock's bell: *on the stroke of nine,* at exactly nine o'clock. □ **al dar las...**
10 rower seated in the stern who gives the time for all the others in a boat. □ **primer remero**
■ *v.* **1** to run your hand gently over: *he stroked her face; to stroke a cat.* □ **acariciar**
2 to set the time for the other rowers in a boat: *he stroked his crew to victory.* □ **guiar como primer remero**
stroll [stroul] *n.* short leisurely walk: *let's go for a stroll in the park.* □ **paseo**
■ *v.* to walk slowly along. □ **pasear**
stroller *n.* **1** person who strolls. □ **paseante**
2 light pram for babies. □ **cochecito**
strong [strɔŋ] *adj.* **1** powerful: *strong wind; are you strong enough to lift that table?; she isn't very strong,* she is rather weak. □ **fuerte**
2 large (in numbers): *a strong contingent of police.* □ **fuerte**
3 *our party is thirty strong,* there are thirty of us. □ **somos treinta**
4 with a powerful smell/noise, etc.: *he has a strong voice; I don't like strong cheese; there is a strong smell of onions; strong light.* □ **fuerte**
strong drink, alcohol. □ **fuerte**
■ *adv. it's still **going strong,*** (*informal*) still working very well after a long time. □ **sigue marchando bien**
strong box *n.* small safe for keeping jewels. □ **caja fuerte pequeña**
stronghold *n.* fortress; place which is difficult to capture. □ **fortaleza**
strongly *adv.* **1** powerfully: *the room smelt strongly of cheese.* □ **fuertemente, mucho**
2 *a strongly-worded reply,* very forceful. □ **muy enérgico**
3 *I don't feel very strongly about it,* I do not have any particular opinion about it. □ **no tengo ideas firmes sobre...**
strong man *n.* powerful man: *he is the strong man in the new government.* □ **hombre fuerte**
strong-minded *adj.* with very clear ideas. □ **resuelto, de ideas muy claras**
strong point *n.* area in which you are an expert: *maths isn't my strong point.* □ **punto fuerte**
strongroom *n.* room with thick walls and door where a bank keeps money/jewels, etc. □ **cámara acorazada**
strontium ['strɔntiəm] *n.* (*chemical element*: Sr) white radioactive metal. □ **estroncio**
stroppy ['strɔpi] *adj.* (*informal*) angry/obstinate: *he got stroppy when the policeman started to talk to him.* □ **enfurecido/terco**
strove [strouv] *v. see* **strive.**
struck [strʌk] *v. see* **strike.**
structure ['strʌktʃə] *n.* **1** way in which things are put together: *the structure of society; bone structure of a mammal.* □ **estructura**
2 building: *a solid structure of concrete blocks.* □ **estructura**
■ *v.* to arrange in a certain way: *the organization is structured in such a way that no one can find out what is happening.* □ **estructurar**
structural *adj.* referring to a structure. □ **estructural**
structural defects, defects in construction. □ **estructurales**
struggle ['strʌgl] *n.* bitter fight: *a struggle for survi-*

val; he didn't give in without a struggle; it's a struggle to exist on my salary. □ **lucha**
■ *v.* **1** to fight violently: *he struggled to succeed; they struggle to have enough to live on.* □ **luchar**
2 *he struggled to his feet,* he made a great effort and got up on his feet; *we struggled for miles through the thick forest,* moved ahead with great difficulty. □ **con gran esfuerzo**
struggling *adj.* (person) who has difficulty in getting enough money to live on: *a struggling artist.* □ **que lucha por la vida**
strum [strʌm] *v.* (*he strummed*) to play (a piano/guitar) in an informal way. □ **tocar**
strung [strʌŋ] *v. see* **string.**
strut [strʌt] *n.* **1** support: *struts between girders.* □ **soporte**
2 proud and important-looking way of walking. □ **pavoneo**
■ *v.* (*he strutted*) to walk in a proud and important way: *now he has got some money he struts about looking as if he owned the place.* □ **pavonearse**
strychnine ['strikni:n] *n.* type of bitter poison. □ **estricnina**
stub [stʌb] *n.* **1** small piece left after something has been used: *stub of a pencil; cigarette stub.* □ **cabo; colilla**
2 piece of paper left after a cheque or a ticket has been torn out of a book. □ **matriz**
■ *v.* (*he stubbed*) **1** *to stub your toe against a rock,* to hurt your toe by hitting it against a rock. □ **darse con**
2 *to stub out a cigarette,* to put out a cigarette by pressing the stub against something. □ **apagar**
stubby *adj.* short and fat (fingers). □ **rechoncho**
stubble ['stʌbl] *n.* **1** short stems left after corn has been cut. □ **rastrojo**
2 short hairs which grow if a man does not shave for several days: *he has two days' growth of stubble.* □ **barba de días**
stubbly *adj.* covered with short bristles. □ **con pelos, hirsuto**
stubborn ['stʌbən] *adj.* **1** obstinate; (person) who will only do what he wants to do. □ **terco**
2 (something) which will not do what you want it to do: *stubborn nail,* nail which will not go in or come out; *stubborn engine,* engine which will not start. □ **rebelde**
stubbornly *adv.* obstinately: *he stubbornly refused to apologize.* □ **tercamente**
stubbornness *n.* being stubborn. □ **terquedad**
stucco ['stʌkou] *n.* plaster put on walls and painted; plaster used to make moulded decorations in buildings. □ **estuco**
stuck [stʌk] *v. see* **stick.**
stuck-up *adj.* (*informal*) supercilious/proud. □ **engreído**
stud [stʌd] *n.* **1** nail with a large head: *carpet studs,* nails for hammering down a carpet. □ **tachón**
2 *studs in a road,* metal markers which show a pedestrian crossing, etc. □ **chinchetas**
3 type of button with two heads for passing through two holes to fasten a shirt: *collar stud.* □ **gemelo, botón**
press stud, stud which is in two parts which clip together when pressed. □ **automático**
4 horses which are kept for breeding; farm where horses are kept for breeding. □ **semental; cuadra**
stud book, register of pedigree horses, etc. □ **registro genealógico**
■ *v.* (*he studded*) to cover with nails. □ **tachonar**
studded *adj.* covered (with nails/stars, etc.): *sky studded with stars; field studded with bales of corn.* □ **salpicado**
student ['stju:dənt] *n.* person who is studying at college or university: *medical student; student organization.* □ **estudiante**
studio ['stju:diou] *n.* **1** place where artists paint/where photographers take photographs. □ **estudio**
2 place where films/broadcasts/recordings are made: *TV studios; a studio broadcast,* broadcast not made outside/in the open air/in a concert hall, etc. □ **estudio**
3 very small flat. □ **estudio**
studious ['stju:diəs] *adj.* **1** showing careful study: *his glasses give him a studious look.* □ **detenido, atento**
2 careful: *studious politeness.* □ **cuidadoso**
studiously *adv.* carefully: *he studiously avoided mentioning money.* □ **cuidadosamente**
study ['stʌdi] *n.* **1** act of examining something carefully to learn more about it: *his study of fossil birds; she made a study of Chinese customs.* □ **estudio**
2 *he has finished his studies,* has finished his course at university, etc. □ **estudios**
3 room in which someone works/studies: *the headmaster's study.* □ **estudio**
4 piece of music which aims to improve the players' technique; work of art in which new ideas are practised: *a study in green and blue; study in F major.* □ **estudio**
5 *when she heard the news, her face was a real study,* it was instructive/amusing to watch her expression. □ **poema**
■ *v.* **1** to examine (something) in detail to learn more about it: *he is studying the effects of pollution.* □ **estudiar**
2 to follow a course at college or university: *he is studying chemistry; don't disturb her - she's studying for her examinations.* □ **estudiar**
studied *adj.* done very carefully; done on purpose: *with studied indifference.* □ **estudiado**
stuff [stʌf] *n.* **1** material of which something is made: *it's made of some hard blue stuff; there's some sticky stuff on the chair.* □ **material**
2 (*informal*) equipment/belongings: *have you brought your climbing stuff? she left her stuff in my bedroom.* □ **cosas**
3 *come on,* ***do your stuff,*** do what you have to do. □ **haz lo que tienes que hacer**
4 ***that's the stuff!,*** that's it! □ **¡eso es!**
5 ***stuff and nonsense!,*** rubbish! □ **¡tonterías!**
6 cloth. □ **tela**
■ *v.* **1** to fill (something) very full: *he stuffed the papers into his pockets; we all stuffed ourselves full of pudding; they tried to stuff ten people into an office which only holds four.* □ **llenar; meter a la fuerza**
2 to block (a hole): *my nose is all stuffed up.* □ **taponar**
3 to fill the skin of a dead animal with material to make it look lifelike: *a stuffed owl.* □ **disecar**
4 to put a savoury mixture into (a chicken/turkey, etc.) before cooking: *chicken stuffed with onions.* □ **rellenar**
5 ***you can stuff it,*** (*slang*) I don't want to have anything to do with your plan. □ **allá tú**
6 ***get stuffed!,*** (*slang*) stop bothering me!; *the headmaster can go and get stuffed!* □ **irse a paseo**
stuffing *n.* **1** savoury mixture put inside a chicken/turkey, etc., before cooking. □ **relleno**
2 material used to fill cushions/chair seats, etc. □ **relleno**
stuffy ['stʌfi] *adj.* **1** (room) full of bad air from lack

of ventilation: *can you open a window - the room is so stuffy.* □ **cargado**
2 prudish; old-fashioned: *our boss is a bit stuffy.* □ **pomposo; a la antigua**
stuffiness *n.* being stuffy. □ **mala ventilación; envaramiento**
stultify ['stʌltifai] *v.* (*formal*) to make (someone) stupid. □ **poner en ridículo**
stumble ['stʌmbl] *n.* tripping over; awkward step. □ **tropezón**
■ *v.* **1** to trip over something; to walk awkwardly: *he stumbled over the tree root; she stumbled into the police station.* □ **tropezar**
2 ***to stumble across something,*** to find something by chance. □ **tropezar con algo**
stumbling block *n.* something which prevents you doing something: *the biggest stumbling block is that no one here speaks Russian.* □ **escollo, pega**
stump [stʌmp] *n.* **1** short piece left after something has been finished or cut down: *stump of a tree/tree stump; stump of a pencil.* □ **tocón; cabo**
2 one of the three sticks placed in the ground as a target in cricket: *stumps were drawn,* the game of cricket came to an end (temporarily). □ **estaca**
■ *v.* **1** ***to stump along,*** to walk along heavily; *he stumped into the room.* □ **andar renqueando**
2 (*informal*) to puzzle: *this question stumped me completely/had me completely stumped.* □ **dejar perplejo**
3 (*in cricket*) to put a batsman out by touching the stumps with the ball when he is not in the hitting area. □ **expulsar a un bateador**
stump up *v.* (*informal*) to pay up. □ **apoquinar**
stumpy *adj.* (*informal*) short and squat. □ **rechoncho**
stun [stʌn] *v.* (*he stunned*) to knock out; to shock completely: *he was stunned by the force of the explosion; the news of his death stunned the family.* □ **aturdir; pasmar**
stunning *adj.* extraordinary/marvellous. □ **extraordinario; que aturde**
stung [stʌŋ] *v. see* **sting.**
stunk [stʌŋk] *v. see* **stink.**
stunt [stʌnt] *n.* trick; dangerous action done to attract attention. □ **truco; maniobra peligrosa**
■ *v.* to shorten/to prevent (something) from growing: *stunted trees.* □ **atrofiar**
stunt man *n.* (*pl. stunt men*) person who carries out dangerous actions in films in place of the film star. □ **doble, especialista**
stupefy ['stju:pifai] *v.* **1** to make stupid: *he was stupefied with drugs.* □ **atontar**
2 to astonish: *I was stupefied when he asked me to speak.* □ **dejar estupefacto**
stupefaction [stjupi'fækʃn] *n.* astonishment. □ **estupefacción**
stupendous [stju'pendəs] *adj.* extraordinary/magnificent. □ **estupendo, prodigioso**
stupid ['stju:pid] *adj.* **1** not very intelligent; with no sense: *don't be stupid – you can't hit a policeman and not expect to be arrested.* □ **estúpido**
2 dull; with a dull mind: *drugs had made him stupid.* □ **atontado**
stupidity [stju'piditi] *n.* being stupid. □ **estupidez**
stupor ['stju:pə] *n.* being in a daze; being half senseless: *he lay in a drunken stupor on the floor.* □ **estupor**
sturdy ['stə:di] *adj.* strong and vigorous: *she has two sturdy sons; our team put up some sturdy opposition.* □ **fuerte, robusto; enérgico**
sturdily *adv.* in a sturdy way. □ **con fuerza**
sturdiness *n.* being sturdy. □ **fuerza, energía**
sturgeon ['stə:dʒən] *n.* large edible fish whose eggs are caviare. □ **esturión**
stutter ['stʌtə] *n.* speech defect where you repeat the same sounds: *he has a bad stutter.* □ **tartamudeo**
■ *v.* to repeat the same sounds when speaking: *he stutters when he speaks in public.* □ **tartamudear**
sty [stai] *n.* shed in which a pig lives. *see also* **stye.** □ **pocilga**
stye, sty [stai] *n.* infected pimple near the eye. □ **orzuelo**
style [stail] *n.* **1** way/manner of doing something: *his style of writing; he answered in a very humorous style.* □ **estilo**
2 *they live* ***in style,*** very grandly. □ **a lo grande**
3 fashion: *the latest style in hats; he was dressed in the style of the 1920's.* □ **estilo**
4 elegance: *she has no style.* □ **estilo**
■ *v.* **1** to name: *he styles himself 'the Emperor'.* □ **dar el nombre**
2 to give a certain style to (hair, etc.). □ **peinar/vestir a la moda**
stylish *adj.* elegant/fashionable. □ **con estilo, elegante**
stylishness *n.* fashion/elegance. □ **estilo, elegancia**
stylist *n.* person who gives (a) style to something. □ **estilista**
hair stylist, hairdresser. □ **peluquero**
stylistics [stai'listiks] *n.* study of style of writing. □ **estilística**
stylization [stailai'zeiʃn] *n.* showing something in a stylized way. □ **estilización**
stylize *v.* to show (something) according to a fixed pattern/not in a natural way: *the road sign shows a stylized railway engine.* □ **estilizar**
stylus ['stailəs] *n.* needle of a record player. □ **aguja**
stymie ['staimi] *v.* to block (someone's plan): *the whole plan was stymied by the opposition of the staff.* □ **bloquear**
styptic ['stiptik] *adj.* which stops bleeding. □ **estríptico, astringente**
styptic pencil, small stick of white substance which stops bleeding from cuts made while shaving, etc. □ **lápiz astringente**
suave [swɑ:v] *adj.* extremely polite with very smooth manners (but often with an unpleasant character). □ **afable**
suavity *n.* being extremely polite. □ **afabilidad**
sub [sʌb] *n.* (*informal*) **1** subsidy; money lent to someone until he gets his wages: *can you let me have a sub until Friday?* □ **subsidio, anticipo**
2 subscription: *you haven't paid your sub yet.* □ **subscripción**
3 subeditor. □ **corrector**
4 submarine: *the radar has picked up an enemy sub.* □ **submarino**
■ *v.* (*he subbed*) (*informal*) **1** to subedit. □ **corregir**
2 to act as a substitute: *he's subbing for me.* □ **suplir**
3 *prefix* ***sub-,*** below/under. □ **sub-**
subaltern ['sʌbəltən] *n.* junior army officer. □ **subalterno**
subaqua [sʌb'ækwə] *adj.* referring to underwater sports (such as skindiving): *subaqua club.* □ **subacuático**
subcommittee ['sʌbkəmiti:] *n.* small committee which is part of a large committee: *the finance subcommittee.* □ **subcomisión**
subconscious [sʌb'kɔnʃəs] *adj.* (idea or feeling) which you have in your mind without being aware of it: *his subconscious dislike of children.*

□ **subconsciente**
■ *n.* part of your mind which has ideas or feelings without your being aware of them: *deep down in his subconscious he really hates animals.* □ **subconsciente**
subconsciously *adv.* in a subconscious way. □ **de manera subconsciente**
subcontinent [sʌb'kɔntinənt] *n.* mass of land which is part of a continent: *the Indian subcontinent.* □ **subcontinente**
subcontract [sʌb'kɔntrækt] *n.* agreement between a main supplier or contractor and another small firm who will do part of the work which the contractor has agreed to do. □ **subcontrato**
■ *v.* [sʌbkən'trækt] to agree with a smaller firm that they will do part of the work which you have agreed to do: *the electrical work has been subcontracted to a local firm.* □ **subcontratar**
subcontractor *n.* person or company who does work for a contractor. □ **subcontratista**
subcutaneous [sʌbkju'teiniəs] *adj.* (*formal*) under the skin. □ **subcutáneo**
subdivide [sʌbdi'vaid] *v.* to divide something which has already been divided: *the company is divided into three main divisions and these are subdivided into departments.* □ **subdividir**
subdivision *n.* **1** division of something into smaller units. □ **subdivisión**
2 *Amer.* land which has been divided up into plots for houses. □ **subdivisión, organización**
subdue [sʌb'dju:] *v.* **1** to overcome/to conquer: *the invaders subdued the resistance of the population; she managed to subdue her fears of snakes.* □ **vencer**
2 to make quiet; to make less bright: *he seemed very subdued after he had seen the headmaster.* □ **calmar**
subdued *adj.* **1** overcome/beaten. □ **sometido**
2 *subdued light,* low light. □ **luz suave**
subdued colours, (i) dull colours. □ **colores apagados** (ii) pastel shades. □ **tonos pastel**
subedit [sʌb'edit] *v.* to correct (what someone has written) before it is printed. □ **corregir**
subeditor *n.* person who subedits. □ **corrector**
subheading ['sʌbhediŋ] *n.* secondary heading. □ **subtítulo**
subject ['sʌbdʒikt] *n.* **1** person who belongs to a country: *I am a British subject; the king spoke to his subjects,* to his people. □ **súbdito**
2 word which shows the person or thing which does an action, etc.: *in the phrase 'the frog jumped into the water', the word 'frog' is the subject of the verb 'to jump'.* □ **sujeto**
3 thing which is being discussed: *the subject of the book is the history of India; she is giving a talk on the subject of 'women's place in society'; his life story has been the subject of a film and two books; let's change the subject,* let us talk about something different. □ **tema**
4 something which is being studied: *I have to study five subjects – English, maths, science, history and geography; what subject does Mr Smith teach?* □ **asignatura**
■ *adj.* **1** belonging to; under the power of (a king): *subject nations.* □ **súbdito**
2 likely to be ruled by/to suffer from: *prices are subject to sudden increases; she is subject to hay fever.* □ **sujeto; aquejado**
3 depending on: *subject to agreement by the management; subject to contract,* depending on the contract being signed. □ **sujeto a**
■ *v.* [sʌb'dʒekt] to make (something) undergo something unpleasant: *he subjected his students to a series of tests; he was subjected to torture.* □ **someter**
subjection [sʌb'dʒekʃn] *n.* state of being subjected to something: *his total subjection to the influence of his wife; the mass of the people are in a state of subjection.* □ **sometimiento**
subjective [sʌb'dʒektiv] *adj.* seen from your own point of view: *this is only my personal subjective opinion.* □ **subjetivo**
sub judice [sʌb'dʒu:disi] *adv.* being considered in a court of law (and therefore not to be mentioned in the press): *the case is still sub judice.* □ **sub judice**
subjunctive [sʌb'dʒʌŋktiv] *adj.* and *n.* (referring to) a form of a verb used to show doubt/desire, etc.: *in the phrase 'if only he were taller' 'were' is the subjunctive form; the verb is in the subjunctive.* □ **subjuntivo**
sublease [sʌb'li:s] *n.* lease of a building which is already leased. □ **subarriendo**
■ *v.* to sublet. □ **subarrendar**
sublet [sʌb'let] *v.* to lease (a building/room) which you yourself rent: *the flat I rent is too large so I want to sublet part of it.* □ **subarrendar**
sublieutenant [sʌblef'tenənt] *n.* junior officer in the navy below the rank of lieutenant. □ **alférez de navío**
sublimate ['sʌblimeit] *v.* (*formal*) to channel (crude energy/emotion) into an activity which is accepted in society. □ **sublimar**
sublime [sə'blaim] *adj.* grand/wonderful: *a sublime panorama of snow-capped mountains; his sublime indifference to what other people think.* □ **sublime**
sublimely *adv.* wonderfully. □ **de manera sublime**
subliminal [sʌb'liminl] *adj.* below the consciousness of the senses. □ **subliminal**
subliminal advertising, advertising by flashing pictures on a TV screen for such a short time that you are not aware of them, but their message has nevertheless entered your subconscious. □ **publicidad subliminal**
submachine gun [sʌbmə'ʃi:ngʌn] *n.* light machine gun. □ **metralleta**
submarine [sʌbmə'ri:n] *adj.* which lives/takes place under the water: *submarine life; submarine exploration.* □ **submarino**
■ *n.* ship which travels mostly under the water. □ **submarino**
submariner [sʌb'mærinə] *n.* member of the crew of a submarine. □ **marino de submarino**
submerge [sʌb'mə:dʒ] *v.* to go/to be under the surface of the water: *the submarine submerged; the ship hit a submerged rock.* □ **sumergirse**
submergence, submersion [sʌb'mə:ʃn] *n.* state of being submerged. □ **sumersión**
submission [sʌb'miʃn] *n.* **1** state of giving in/giving way: *he beat his servants into submission.* □ **sumisión**
2 evidence/documents/opinion submitted to someone: *a submission to an investigating committee.* □ **testimonio**
in my submission, in my opinion. □ **a mi juicio**
submissive [sʌb'misiv] *adj.* meek/(person) who gives in easily: *you are too submissive - you should fight back.* □ **sumiso**
submissiveness *n.* meekness. □ **sumisión**
submit *v.* (*he submitted*) **1** to give way; to yield: *the people had to submit to the will of the dictator.* □ **someterse**
2 to give (evidence/documents/opinion) for someone to examine: *to submit your luggage to customs inspection; he submitted the relevant documents to the court of enquiry; I submit that the prisoner is*

guilty, my opinion is that he is guilty. □ **presentar; opinar**

subnormal [sʌbˈnɔːml] *adj.* less than normal; below normal standard. □ **subnormal**

subordinate [səˈbɔːdnət] *adj.* and *n.* (person) who is under the control of someone else: *he has difficulty in talking to his subordinates; the query was dealt with by a subordinate official.* □ **subordinado**
subordinate clause, phrase in a sentence which cannot stand alone, and which is dependent on another clause: *in the sentence 'he ate the apple which his mother had left on the table', 'he ate the apple' is the main clause and 'which his mother had left on the table' is the subordinate.* □ **oración subordinada**
■ *v.* to put something in a less important position; to consider something is less important: *you must learn to subordinate your wishes to the needs of the family.* □ **subordinar**

subpoena [sʌbˈpiːnə] *n.* order to come to a court. □ **citación**
■ *v.* to order (someone) to come to a court: *he was subpoenaed to appear in court on January 21st.* □ **citar**

subscribe [sʌbˈskraib] *v.* **1** to give money (to a charity): *he subscribed $10 to the present for the retiring secretary.* □ **contribuir con**
2 to pay for a series of issues of a magazine/for a series of tickets to concerts, etc.: *I subscribe to three French magazines,* I have paid in advance for three magazines which I receive regularly. □ **suscribirse, estar suscrito**
3 *to subscribe to an opinion,* to agree with an opinion. □ **suscribir**
subscriber *n.* person who subscribes to a charity/ to a magazine; person who has a telephone. □ **suscriptor; abonado**
subscriber trunk dialling, telephone system where you can dial direct long distance or international numbers without asking the operator to do so for you. □ **llamada directa**
subscription [sʌbˈskripʃn] *n.* **1** money paid to a charity: *they are asking for subscriptions for the old people's home.* □ **contribución**
2 money paid to a magazine/to a club to give you a series of issues/a year's membership: *to take out a subscription to a magazine,* to pay for the first time your subscription to a magazine. □ **suscripción**

subsequent [ˈsʌbsikwənt] *adj.* which follows later: *at a subsequent meeting,* at a later meeting. □ **ulterior**
subsequently *adv.* later: *subsequently she found out he was already married.* □ **después, ulteriormente**

subservient [səbˈsəːviənt] *adj.* weak/always giving in to someone. □ **servil**
subservience *n.* weak attitude. □ **servilismo**

subside [sʌbˈsaid] *v.* **1** to sink down: *the ground subsided; the flood waters have subsided.* □ **ceder, hundirse, bajar**
2 to become less violent: *his anger subsided after a time.* □ **ceder**
subsidence [sʌbˈsaidəns] *n.* sinking down (of the ground). □ **hundimiento**

subsidiary [sʌbˈsidjəri] *adj.* and *n.* (something which is) less important. □ **subsidiario**
subsidiary company/a subsidiary, company which is controlled by another. □ **filial**

subsidy [ˈsʌbsidi] *n.* money given to help pay for something unprofitable/for a cultural activity: *the car industry received large government subsidies.* □ **subvención**
subsidize [ˈsʌbsidaiz] *v.* to help by giving money: *the state subsidizes several important firms; the opera performance is subsidized by a television company; the profits on this soap powder help to subsidize the loss on other products.* □ **subvencionar**

subsist [sʌbˈsist] *v.* to exist (with difficulty). □ **subsistir**
subsistence [sʌbˈsistəns] *n.* **1** existence; survival with very little money or food: *means of subsistence,* way of surviving. □ **subsistencia**
2 *they* ***live at subsistence level,*** they have only just enough to live on. □ **al nivel de subsistencia**

subsoil [ˈsʌbsɔil] *n.* layer of soil under the topsoil which is on the surface. □ **subsuelo**

substance [ˈsʌbstəns] *n.* **1** matter/material of which things can be made: *polythene is a man-made substance.* □ **sustancia**
2 basis (of an argument/report): *there is no substance in the rumour that the minister is going to resign.* □ **fundamento**
to lend substance to: *this lends substance to the rumour,* makes it seem more likely to be true. □ **dar solidez a**
3 ***a man of substance,*** a wealthy man. □ **de fortuna**
substantial [sʌbˈstænʃl] *adj.* **1** large/important: *substantial differences.* □ **sustancial**
2 large/solid: *he lives in a substantial house; a substantial meal.* □ **amplio; de fundamento**
substantially *adv.* mostly/mainly: *his success is substantially due to his own efforts.* □ **sustancialmente**
substantiate [sʌbˈstænʃieit] *v.* to justify; to make (something) seem true: *this evidence substantiates his claim that he had nothing to do with the crime.* □ **justificar**

substandard [sʌbˈstændəd] *adj.* second-rate; below the normal standard. □ **inferior, de segunda**

substantive [ˈsʌbstəntiv] *n.* noun. □ **sustantivo**

substation [ˈsʌbsteiʃn] *n.* small local electricity station. □ **subestación**

substitute [ˈsʌbstitjuːt] *n.* person/thing taking the place of someone/something else: *if the goalkeeper is ill, we must find a substitute; people use sugar substitutes to try to lose weight.* □ **sustituto**
■ *v.* to put in the place of (someone/something): *he substituted an identical bag for the one he had just stolen; is anyone substituting for the doctor while he is away?* □ **sustituir**
substitution [sʌbstiˈtjuːʃn] *n.* replacing something by something else. □ **sustitución**

substratum [sʌbˈstrɑːtəm] *n.* (*pl. substrata*) lower layer of rock/soil. □ **sustrato**

subtenant [sʌbˈtenənt] *n.* person to whom a flat/ house has been sublet. □ **subarrendatario**

subterfuge [ˈsʌbtəfjuːdʒ] *n.* trick; clever plot. □ **subterfugio**

subterranean [sʌbtəˈreiniən] *adj.* under the ground: *a subterranean river.* □ **subterráneo**

subtitle [ˈsʌbtaitl] *n.* **1** secondary title on a book. □ **subtítulo**
2 ***subtitles,*** translation of the dialogue of a foreign film which is shown on the bottom of the screen. □ **subtítulos**
■ *v.* **1** to give a secondary title to (something). □ **subtitular**
2 to show the translation of the dialogue of (a foreign film): *the film is subtitled in English.* □ **subtitular**

subtle [ˈsʌtl] *adj.* **1** difficult to explain; very delicate (scent): *a subtle distinction; a subtle taste of lemon.* □ **sutil**
2 cunning: *a subtle trick.* □ **ingenioso, astuto**
subtlety [ˈsʌtlti] *n.* something which is difficult to

explain/to describe: *the subtleties of the English language.* □ **sutileza**
subtract [sʌb'trækt] *v.* to take away (one number from another): *subtract 24 from 86 and you get 62.* □ **sustraer, restar**
subtraction [sʌb'trækʃn] *n.* taking away a number from another. □ **sustracción**
suburb ['sʌbə:b] *n.* residential area on the outskirts of a town: *a suburb of New York.* □ **suburbio**
the suburbs, all the area round a town where most people live. □ **los suburbios**
suburban [sə'bə:bən] *adj.* referring to the suburbs. □ **suburbano**
suburban trains, trains which go from the town centre to the suburbs. □ **trenes suburbanos**
suburbia [sə'bə:biə] *n.* (*informal*) the suburbs. □ **los suburbios**
subvention [sʌb'venʃn] *n.* subsidy: *a state subvention.* □ **subvención**
subversion [sʌb'və:ʃn] *n.* destroying the authority of a government, etc. □ **subversión**
subversive [sʌb'və:siv] *adj.* which tries to destroy the power of a government: *a subversive newspaper.* □ **subversivo**
subvert [sʌb'və:t] *v.* to try to destroy the authority of (the government). □ **subvertir**
subway ['sʌbwei] *n.* **1** underground passage. □ **paso subterráneo**
2 *Amer.* underground railway system: *the New York subway; to take the subway.* □ **metro**
subzero [sʌb'ziərou] *adj.* below zero degrees: *subzero temperatures.* □ **bajo cero**
succeed [sək'si:d] *v.* **1** to follow on; to take the place of: *Mr Smith was succeeded by Mrs Jones as treasurer; each succeeding day,* each day which followed. □ **suceder**
2 to do well; to do what you have been trying to do: *he succeeded in opening the door; how to succeed in business.* □ **lograr; tener éxito**
success [sək'ses] *n.* **1** doing what you have been trying to do: *his success in the tennis tournament; I have tried to get a job but with no success so far.* □ **éxito**
2 something/somebody who does well: *the film was a great success; he was a success in the part of Hamlet.* □ **éxito**
successful *adj.* which succeeds: *a successful party; the restaurant wasn't successful and has closed.* □ **que tiene éxito, satisfactorio**
succession [sək'seʃn] *n.* **1** series: *a succession of accidents,* one accident after another. □ **sucesión**
2 *in rapid succession,* one coming quickly after another. □ **en rápida sucesión**
3 *for three years* ***in succession,*** for three years in a row. □ **consecutivos**
4 right to take someone's place; act of taking someone's place. □ **sucesión**
successive [sək'sesiv] *adj.* one after the other: *we went to Greece on three successive holidays.* □ **sucesivo, seguido**
successively *adv.* one after the other: *he was successively secretary, treasurer, and then president.* □ **sucesivamente**
successor *n.* person who takes someone's place: *we must appoint a successor to Mr Jones who has retired.* □ **sucesor**
succinct [sək'siŋkt] *adj.* concise/not using many words: *a succinct report.* □ **sucinto**
succinctly *adv.* without using many words: *write your report as succinctly as possible.* □ **sucintamente**
succour ['sʌkə] *Amer.* **succor** *n.* (*formal*) help. □ **socorro**
■ *v.* (*formal*) to help. □ **socorrer**
succulent ['səkjulənt] *adj.* juicy/full of juice: *a succulent steak.* □ **suculento**
■ *n.* type of plant with thick fleshy leaves and stems (like a cactus). □ **planta carnosa**
succumb [sə'kʌm] *v.* to give in to/to yield: *he succumbed to his injuries,* he died from his injuries. □ **sucumbir**
such [sʌtʃ] *adj.* **1** like/similar: *people such as you; such people as doctors need years of training; there is no such thing as a plastic saucepan.* □ **como; tal cosa**
2 so large/so great: *there was such a crowd; he's such a slow worker; people can't afford to live in such big houses; such was his excitement that he couldn't get to sleep.* □ **tanto, tan**
3 of this type: *do it in such a way that you don't make any noise; I'll take such action as seems necessary.* □ **de manera que; las medidas que**
■ *pron.* thing/person of a certain kind: *I don't read novels as such.* □ **como esa**
as such, *the machine is not much use,* in itself/as a machine it is not very useful. □ **como tal**
such as it is, although it is not very good: *you can try to use your influence, such as it is.* □ **si, se puede llamar así**
such-and-such *pron.* a particular/a certain: *he wants to meet me on such-and-such a day.* □ **tal o cual**
suchlike *adj.* and *pron.* similar (people/things): *I don't like spiders and suchlike animals.* □ **parecido**
suck [sʌk] *n.* action of drawing in liquid through the mouth: *he gave the lollipop a suck.* □ **chupada**
■ *v.* **1** to pull (liquid) into your mouth: *he sucked the milk up through a straw; he was sucking a lollipop,* licking it hard. □ **sorber; chupar**
2 to pull in (something) by suction: *the vacuum cleaner sucks in dust; the birds were sucked into the jet engine.* □ **absorber**
sucker *n.* **1** shoot which sprouts from a stock, not from the grafted plant. □ **chupón**
2 something which sticks on to a surface by suction: *the octopus has suckers on its arms; the hook has a sucker to attach it to the wall.* □ **ventosa**
3 (*informal*) person who is easily tricked. □ **primo**
suckle *v.* to give (a child) milk from the breast: *she was suckling her baby.* □ **amamantar, dar el pecho**
suck up to *v.* ***to suck up to someone,*** (*informal*) to try to make someone like you (by giving presents/making compliments, etc.): *she's always sucking up to the teacher.* □ **hacer la pelota**
suction ['sʌkʃən] *n.* action of sucking in air/liquid, so that something will be pulled in/will stick to a surface because of the vacuum created. □ **succión, aspiración**
suction pad, small concave pad which will stick to a surface if pressed hard. □ **almohadilla succionadora, ventosa**
suction pump, pump which sucks up liquid when air is pulled out of it. □ **bomba aspirante**
sudden ['sʌdn] *adj.* which happens rapidly/unexpectedly: *a sudden shower of rain; there is a sudden turn in the road.* □ **repentino**
all of a sudden, suddenly. □ **de repente**
suddenly *adv.* rapidly/unexpectedly. □ **de repente**
suddenness *n.* being rapid/unexpected: *the revolution took place with astonishing suddenness.* □ **carácter de repentino**

suds [sʌdz] *n. pl.* ***soap suds,*** foam made with soap. □ **espuma de jabón**
sue [su:] *v.* to take (someone) to court/to start a lawsuit against (someone): *he is suing the company for damages.* □ **demandar**
suede [sweid] *n.* soft leather with a rough/furry surface: *blue suede shoes.* □ **ante**
suet ['suit] *n.* hard fat from an animal, used in cooking: *suet pudding.* □ **sebo**
suffer ['sʌfə] *v.* **1** to feel pain; to be in a difficult situation: *he suffers from constant headaches; the fruit trees have suffered in the frost; his bad back makes him suffer; she suffers from not being able to drive a car; because he's lazy, his work suffers.* □ **sufrir, ser dañado**
2 to put up with: *he doesn't suffer fools gladly,* he can't stand silly people. □ **soportar**
3 to undergo: *to suffer a change.* □ **experimentar**
sufferance *n. he is only here* ***on sufferance,*** we allow him to be here but we don't really want him. □ **por tolerancia**
sufferer *n.* person who suffers: *sufferers from rheumatism.* □ **persona aquejada de...**
fellow sufferer, someone who has the same disease as you. □ **compañero de sufrimientos**
suffering *n.* feeling pain: *the doctor tried to lessen the patient's suffering.* □ **sufrimiento**
suffice [sə'fais] *v.* (*formal*) to be enough: *that will suffice.* □ **bastar**
suffice it to say that *nothing happened,* I need only say that in the end nothing happened. □ **baste decir que...**
sufficiency [sə'fiʃənsi] *n.* enough supplies: *there is a sufficiency of sugar.* □ **cantidad suficiente**
sufficient [sə'fiʃənt] *adj.* enough: *will two chickens be sufficient for ten people?* □ **suficiente**
sufficiently *adv.* enough: *everyone has eaten sufficiently.* □ **suficientemente**
suffix ['sʌfiks] *n.* part added after a word to make another word: *to make a personal noun from a verb you usually add the suffix '-er' – such as, 'walk'/ 'walker'.* □ **sufijo**
suffocate ['sʌfəkeit] *v.* not to be able to breathe; to kill/to die by stopping breathing: *the baby suffocated under the pillow; it's suffocating in here,* so hot that it is difficult to breathe. □ **asfixiarse; calor sofocante**
suffocation [sʌfə'keiʃn] *n.* not being able to breathe: *she died from suffocation.* □ **asfixia**
suffrage ['sʌfridʒ] *n.* right to vote in elections: *we have universal suffrage,* in our country everyone (over a certain age) can vote. □ **sufragio**
sugar ['ʃugə] *n.* sweet substance made from the juice of a sugar cane or from sugar beet: *granulated sugar; castor sugar; sugar bowl.* □ **azúcar**
■ *v.* to put sugar into: *have you sugared my tea?* □ **echar azúcar en**
to sugar the pill, to make some unpleasant news more acceptable. □ **dorar la píldora**
sugar beet *n.* plant with a large root which when crushed gives sugar. □ **remolacha azucarera**
sugar cane *n.* tropical plant whose stalks when crushed give sugar and rum. □ **caña de azúcar**
sugar-coated *adj.* covered with a coating of hard sugar: *sugar-coated almonds.* □ **garrapiñado**
sugar daddy *n.* old man who entertains young girls, and gives them presents. □ **amigo viejo**
sugary *adj.* with too much sugar in it. □ **azucarado**
suggest [sə'dʒest] *v.* **1** to propose (an idea): *I suggest we all go for a walk; he suggested we should ask a lawyer.* □ **sugerir**
2 to hint/to insinuate: *are you suggesting I'm not telling the truth?* □ **sugerir**
suggestible *adj.* (person) who can easily be influenced. □ **sugestionable**
suggestion *n.* proposal: *he made several suggestions but no one agreed with them; it was my suggestion that we should all go for a walk.* □ **sugerencia**
suggestive *adj.* **1** which suggests: *suggestive of corruption,* which suggests that corruption has taken place. □ **que sugiere**
2 which gives an impression of indecency: *a suggestive remark.* □ **que sugiere**
suicide ['suisaid] *n.* **1** killing yourself: *to commit suicide; attempted suicide.* □ **suicidio**
2 *it would be suicide to try to beat the champion team,* it would be certain defeat. □ **suicidio**
3 person who has killed himself. □ **suicida**
suicidal [sui'saidl] *adj.* referring to suicide: *she has suicidal tendencies,* she has tried to commit suicide. □ **suicida**
suit [su:t] *n.* **1** two or three pieces of clothing made of the same cloth (jacket/waistcoat and trousers or skirt): *he was wearing a dark grey suit; she had a tweed suit.* □ **traje**
2 lawsuit/court case. □ **pleito**
3 one of the four groups with the same symbol in a pack of cards. □ **palo**
4 ***to follow suit,*** to do what someone else has done: *he dived into the water and we all followed suit.* □ **seguir el ejemplo**
■ *v.* **1** to fit together: *they are suited to each other.* □ **adaptarse**
2 to be completely acceptable/convenient: *that suits me fine; I'll do it when it suits me.* □ **ir bien**
suit yourself, do what you want. □ **haz lo que quieras**
3 to fit someone's appearance: *that hat suits you; green suits you because it matches your eyes.* □ **sentar bien a**
suitability [su:tə'biliti] *n.* being suitable. □ **conveniencia**
suitable ['su:təbl] *adj.* convenient; (something) which fits: *a black tie is most suitable to wear to a funeral; the most suitable date to meet would be next Saturday.* □ **conveniente**
suitably *adv.* in a convenient/fitting way: *they threw him out of the restaurant because he wasn't suitably dressed.* □ **convenientemente**
suitcase *n.* box with a handle for carrying clothes in when you are travelling. □ **maleta**
suitor *n.* person who wants to marry a certain girl. □ **pretendiente**
suite [swi:t] *n.* **1** series of rooms/pieces of furniture which make a set: *a suite of rooms.* □ **suite**
bathroom suite, bath, washbasin and lavatory. □ **cuarto de baño completo**
dining room suite, set of chairs, tables and sideboard. □ **comedor completo**
2 group of people accompanying a king, queen or other important person. □ **séquito**
3 several short pieces of music which are played together as a group. □ **suite**
4 ***en suite,*** attached: *bedroom with bathroom en suite,* bedroom with a door leading into a private bathroom. □ **al lado**
sulfa ['sʌlfə] *n. Amer. see* **sulpha.**
sulfur ['sʌlfə] *n. Amer. see* **sulphur.**
sulk [sʌlk] *n.* being grumpy/annoyed in silence: *he had a fit of the sulks.* □ **enfado**
■ *v.* to show you are annoyed by not saying any-

thing: *he sat sulking in the corner.* □ **poner cara larga**
sulky *adj.* bad-tempered/grumpy. □ **malhumorado**
sullen ['sʌln] *adj.* silently angry; unpleasant: *his sullen face.* □ **hosco**
sullenly *adv.* in a sullen way: *he sat sullenly refusing to say anything.* □ **hoscamente**
sully ['sʌli] *v.* (*formal*) to dirty (someone's reputation). □ **manchar**
sulpha ['sʌlfə] *Amer.* **sulfa** *n. sulpha drug,* sulphonamide. □ **sulfamida**
sulphur ['sʌlfə] *Amer.* **sulfur** *n.* (*chemical element:* S) solid substance, usually found as a yellow powder. □ **azufre**
sulphate *n.* salt formed from sulphuric acid: *copper sulphate.* □ **sulfato**
sulphide *n.* combination of sulphur with another substance. □ **sulfuro**
sulphonamide *n.* drug used against bacteria. □ **sulfamida**
sulphuric acid [sʌl'fjuərik'æsid] *n.* very strong acid containing sulphur. □ **ácido sufúrico**
sulphurous ['sʌlfərəs] *adj.* like sulphur. □ **sulfuroso**
sultan ['sʌltən] *n.* Muslim prince. □ **sultán**
sultana [sʌl'tɑːnə] *n.* **1** wife of a sultan. □ **sultana**
2 type of seedless raisin. □ **pasa de Esmirna**
sultry ['sʌltri] *adj.* **1** hot/heavy (weather). □ **bochornoso**
2 (woman/beauty) strongly attractive to men. □ **provocativa**
sum [sʌm] *n.* **1** total of numbers added together: *the sum of 8 and 4 is 12.* □ **suma**
the sum total, the total of several sums added together. □ **la suma total**
2 quantity of money: *he spent large sums (of money) on racehorses.* □ **suma**
3 arithmetic problem: *he tried to do the sum in his head; complicated long-division sums.* □ **suma**
■ *v.* (*he summed up*) **1** ***to sum up,*** to make a summary/to tell briefly what has happened: *the judge summed up the case,* made a summary of all the evidence. □ **resumir; recapitular**
2 *I summed up the situation,* I made a quick judgement of the situation. □ **resumir**
summarize ['sʌməraiz] *v.* to make a brief account of something which is long: *can you summarize the story of War and Peace?* □ **resumir**
summary *n.* short account of what has happened; short version of something which is longer: *a summary of the debate in Parliament.* □ **resumen**
■ *adj.* **1** brief: *a summary report on what took place.* □ **resumido**
2 done quickly without wasting too much time: *summary justice.* □ **justicia sumarísima**
summarily *adv.* quickly: *the prisoners were summarily executed.* □ **sumariamente**
summing-up *n.* the summary of evidence made by a judge at the end of a trial. □ **resumen**
summer ['sʌmə] *n.* season of the year following spring, when plants begin to make fruit; the warmest season: *summer clothes; these birds are summer visitors,* they visit the country to nest in the summer. □ **verano**
summer holidays, main/longest holidays during a school year. □ **vacaciones de verano**
summer school, classes held at a school/university during the summer holiday. □ **escuela de verano**
summerhouse *n.* small wooden house in a garden where you can sit in the summer. □ **cenador**
summertime *n.* the summer season: *in summertime everyone goes for picnics.* □ **verano**
summer time *n.* system of altering the clocks during the summer to take advantage of the longer period of daylight: *summer time starts in March and ends in October.* □ **hora de verano**
summery *adj.* like the summer. □ **veraniego**
summit ['sʌmit] *n.* **1** top (of a mountain). □ **cima; cumbre**
2 ***summit (meeting),*** meeting of heads of government to discuss international problems. □ **cumbre**
summitry *n.* (*informal*) diplomacy carried on at summit meetings. □ **encuentros a alto nivel**
summon ['sʌmən] *v.* **1** to call: *he summoned a meeting; he was summoned to appear in court.* □ **convocar**
2 *to summon up enough courage,* to get together all your courage to do something. □ **armarse de valor**
summons *n.* **1** official demand to go to see someone: *I have had a summons to go to see the headmaster.* □ **requerimiento**
2 official legal order to appear in court. □ **citación judicial**
■ *v.* to order (someone) to appear in court: *he was summonsed for driving offences.* □ **citar ante la justicia**
sump [sʌmp] *n.* **1** part of a car engine containing the oil. □ **cárter**
2 pit in which water collects. □ **sumidero**
sumptuous ['sʌmtʃuəs] *adj.* very luxurious/splendid. □ **suntuoso**
sun [sʌn] *n.* **1** very hot body around which the earth revolves and which provides heat and daylight: *everything looks happier when the sun is shining; the sun rises in the east and sets in the west.* □ **sol**
2 light from the sun: *let's sit in the sun.* □ **sol**
■ *v.* (*he sunned*) ***to sun yourself,*** to sit in the sun: *the lizard was sunning itself on the wall.* □ **tomar el sol**
sunbathe *v.* to lie in the sun to get your body brown. □ **tomar el sol**
sunbather *n.* person who is sunbathing. □ **persona que toma el sol**
sunbathing *n.* lying in the sun in order to get brown. □ **baños de sol**
sunbeam *n.* ray of sunlight. □ **rayo de sol**
sunburn *n.* painful inflammation of the skin caused by being in the sun for too long. □ **quemadura**
sunburnt *adj.* made brown or red by the sun. □ **quemado**
sundeck *n.* top deck of a passenger ship where people can sit in the sun. □ **cubierta de sol**
sundial *n.* round clock face with a central pointer whose shadow points to the time when the sun shines on it. □ **reloj de sol**
sundown *n.* moment when the sun goes down. □ **puesta de sol**
sundrenched *adj.* (always) very sunny. □ **inundado de sol**
sunflower *n.* very large yellow flower on a tall stem. □ **girasol**
sunflower oil, oil made from the seeds of a sunflower. □ **aceite de girasol**
sunglasses *n.* dark glasses to protect your eyes from the sun. □ **gafas de sol**
sunlamp *n.* lamp which gives off ultraviolet rays like the sun, used to give a suntan indoors. □ **lámpara ultravioleta**
sunless *adj.* with no sun. □ **sin sol**
sunlight *n.* light from the sun: *flowers open in the sunlight.* □ **luz solar, diurna**
sunlit *adj.* lit by the sun. □ **iluminado por el sol**

sunny *adj.* **1** full of sunlight: *a sunny day; the sunny side of the street.* □ **soleado**
2 *a sunny character,* a happy character. □ **un carácter risueño**
3 ***sunny side up,*** *Amer.* (*informal*) (egg) fried without being turned over to cook both sides. □ **frito sólo por un lado**
sunrise *n.* time at which the sun rises: *he was up at sunrise.* □ **salida del sol**
sunroof *n.* part of a roof of a car which slides open. □ **techo corredizo**
sunset *n.* time when the sun goes down behind the horizon; colourful sky as the sun goes down: *a beautiful sunset; after sunset the lamps were lit.* □ **puesta del sol**
sunshade *n.* light bright-coloured umbrella to protect from the sun. □ **sombrilla**
sunshine *n.* light from the sun: *sitting in the sunshine; the sunshine hurts your eyes.* □ **sol; luz del sol**
sunshine roof *n.* part of a roof of a car which slides open. □ **techo corredizo**
sunspot *n.* dark spot which appears on the surface of the sun. □ **mancha solar**
sunstroke *n.* illness caused by being too much in the sunlight: *she got sunstroke.* □ **insolación**
suntan *n.* brown colour of the skin caused by the sun. □ **bronceado; moreno**
suntan oil/cream, oil/cream used to protect the skin from the effects of the sun. □ **bronceador**
suntanned *adj.* with a skin made brown by the sun: *suntanned face.* □ **moreno**
suntrap *n.* very sunny place. □ **solana**
sun-up *n.* sunrise. □ **salida del sol**
sundae ['sʌndi] *n.* dessert of ice cream, cream and fruit. □ **helado con frutas**
Sunday ['sʌndi] *n.* last day of the week (a holiday in most countries); day between Saturday and Monday: *I'll see you next Sunday; he came on Sunday; the shops are shut on Sundays.* □ **domingo**
in his Sunday best, in his best clothes. □ **hecho un pincel**
sundry ['sʌndri] *adj.* various: *sundry items.* □ **varios**
■ *n.* **1** ***all and sundry,*** everyone. □ **todos y cada uno**
2 ***sundries,*** various small articles/small items on a list. □ **artículos diversos**
sung [sʌŋ] *v. see* **sing.**
sunk [sʌŋk] *adj.* ruined/lost: *we're sunk without a map. see also* **sink.** □ **perdido**
sunken *adj.* **1** which is beneath the surface: *sunken rocks.* □ **hundido**
a sunken ship, ship which has sunk. □ **un barco hundido**
2 lower than the surrounding area: *sunken garden; sunken cheeks.* □ **jardín a desnivel; mejillas hundidas**
super ['su:pə] *adj.* (*informal*) wonderful. □ **estupendo**
■ *n.* (*informal*) **1** police superintendent. □ **el súper**
2 extra actor. □ **figurante**
■ *prefix meaning* more/greater/of better quality. □ **super-**
superabundance [su:pərə'bʌndəns] *n.* great abundance; very large quantity. □ **superabundancia**
superabundant *adj.* very abundant/in very large quantities: *superabundant energy.* □ **superabundante**
superannuated [su:pə'rænjueitid] *adj.* too old to work properly; old-fashioned. □ **jubilado**
superannuation [su:pərænju'eiʃn] *n.* **1** retirement of workers when they reach a certain age. □ **jubilación**
2 pension paid to someone who has retired. □ **jubilación**
superannuation fund, money collected to pay pensions. □ **fondo de jubilación**
superb [su:'pə:b] *adj.* marvellous/wonderful. □ **soberbio**
superbly *adv.* wonderfully: *the meal was superbly cooked.* □ **soberbiamente**
supercharged ['su:pətʃɑ:dʒd] *adj.* (motor/person) with much increased energy. □ **sobrealimentado**
supercharger *n.* apparatus on a car engine for increasing the power. □ **sobrealimentador**
supercilious [su:pə'siliəs] *adj.* looking down on others; considering others as inferior. □ **arrogante**
superciliousness *n.* being supercilious. □ **arrogancia**
superficial [su:pə'fiʃl] *adj.* **1** touching only the top surface; not going deeply beneath the surface: *superficial wound; he gave it a superficial inspection.* □ **superficial**
2 *he has a superficial mind,* he does not think about things very seriously or deeply. □ **superficial**
superficially *adv.* in a superficial way. □ **superficialmente**
superfine [su:pə'fain] *adj.* very fine. □ **extrafino**
superfluous [su:'pə:fluəs] *adj.* which is more than is needed. □ **superfluo**
superfluity [su:pə'flu:iti] *n.* being superfluous/more than is needed; excess: *a superfluity of talk and not enough action.* □ **superfluidad**
superhighway [su:pə'haiwei] *n. Amer.* important motorway. □ **autopista**
superhuman [su:pə'hju:mən] *adj.* more than is normal in human beings: *a superhuman effort.* □ **sobrehumano**
superimpose [su:pərim'pouz] *v.* to place on top of something: *the picture of the prime minister was superimposed on a photograph of a flock of sheep.* □ **sobreponer**
superintend [su:pərin'tend] *v.* to be in charge: *he superintended the loading of the lorry.* □ **supervisar**
superintendent *n.* **1** person in charge: *the superintendent of the hospital.* □ **inspector**
2 senior police officer. □ **comisario**
superior [su:'piəriə] *adj.* **1** of better quality; of a larger quality: *to be superior in numbers; superior quality meat.* □ **superior**
2 higher in rank: *a superior officer.* □ **superior**
3 thinking yourself to be better than others: *he gave a superior smile.* □ **superior**
■ *n.* **1** person of higher rank: *do not contradict your superiors.* □ **superior**
2 leader of a religious community: *Mother Superior.* □ **madre superiora**
superiority [su:piəri'ɔriti] *n.* being superior: *their superiority in weapons.* □ **superioridad**
superlative [su:'pə:lətiv] *adj.* of the best quality: *she's a superlative tennis player; his work is absolutely superlative.* □ **extraordinario**
■ *n.* form of an adjective or adverb showing the highest level of comparison: *'best' 'silliest' and 'most stupidly' are the superlatives of 'good', 'silly' and 'stupidly'.* □ **superlativo**
superlatively *adv.* extremely well: *she played superlatively.* □ **extremadamente bien**
superman ['su:pəmæn] *n.* man who has superhuman strength, power or ability. □ **superhombre**
supermarket ['su:pəmɑ:kit] *n.* large store selling mainly food, where you serve yourself. □ **supermercado**
supernatural [su:pə'nætʃərəl] *adj.* and *n.* (things) which happen not in accordance with the laws of nature: *supernatural occurrence.* □ **sobrenatural**
supernova ['su:pənouvə] *n.* large star which ex-

plodes and suddenly appears in the sky. □ **supernova**
supernumerary ['su:pə'nju:mərəri] *adj.* and *n.* (person) who is in addition to the usual number of people. □ **supernumerario**
superpower ['su:pəpauə] *n.* extremely powerful country (such as the United States or the Soviet Union). □ **superpotencia**
supersede [su:pə'si:d] *v.* to take the place of (something which is older or less efficient). □ **sustituir**
supersonic [su:pə'sɔnik] *adj.* faster than the speed of sound: *a supersonic aircraft.* □ **supersónico**
superstition [su:pə'stiʃn] *n.* belief in magic and the supernatural: *it's an old superstition that black cats are lucky.* □ **superstición**
superstitious [su:pə'stiʃəs] *adj.* believing in magic and the supernatural: *he is superstitious – he never walks under a ladder.* □ **supersticioso**
superstructure ['su:pəstrʌktʃə] *n.* top structure of a ship; structure built on top of something else. □ **superestructura**
supertanker ['su:pətæŋkə] *n.* very large oil tanker. □ **superpetrolero**
supervene [su:pə'vi:n] *v.* to happen so that things are changed: *complications supervened and the agreement had to be altered.* □ **sobrevenir**
supervise ['su:pəvaiz] *v.* to watch over work, etc., to see that it is well done: *to supervise the laying of the drains.* □ **supervisar**
supervision [su:pə'viʒn] *n.* watching over something to see that it is well done/that there is no disturbance, etc.: *the demonstration went off under police supervision.* □ **supervisión**
supervisor ['su:pəvaizə] *n.* person who supervises. □ **supervisor**
supervisory [su:pə'vaizəri] *adj.* as a supervisor: *I serve in a supervisory capacity.* □ **de supervisor**
superwoman ['su:pəwumən] *n.* woman who has superhuman strength/power/ability. □ **supermujer**
supine ['su:pain] *adj.* (*formal*) **1** lying flat on your back. □ **supino**
2 uninterested/lazy. □ **indolente**
supper ['sʌpə] *n.* evening meal: *to have supper.* □ **cena**
suppertime *n.* time for supper: *the most interesting TV programmes are always at suppertime.* □ **hora de cenar**
supplant [sə'plɑ:nt] *v.* to take (someone's) place by cunning manoeuvres. □ **suplantar**
supple ['sʌpl] *adj.* flexible/which bends easily: *a supple stick; supple limbs.* □ **flexible**
suppleness *n.* being supple: *it's lost all its suppleness.* □ **flexibilidad**
supply ['sʌpli] *adv.* in a flexible way. □ **flexiblemente**
supplement ['sʌplimənt] *n.* **1** something which is in addition: *a supplement to his normal diet of potatoes and fish.* □ **suplemento**
2 *the paper has produced a special supplement on the Common Market,* an additional separate part. □ **suplemento**
■ *v.* ['sʌpliment] to add to: *he supplements his income by writing for the local paper.* □ **complementar**
supplementary [sʌpli'mentri] *adj.* in addition: *supplementary payments.* □ **adicional**
supplementary benefits, payments from the Government to people who have very low incomes. □ **pensión suplementaria**
supplication [sʌpli'keiʃn] *n.* (*formal*) begging for help. □ **súplica**
supply [sə'plai] *n.* **1** providing something which is needed: *the supply of electricity to industry; supply routes to guerrilla forces.* □ **suministro**
2 stock of something which has been provided: *we've laid in a supply of food for the winter.* □ **provisiones**
3 *eggs are* ***in short supply,*** there are not many eggs available. □ **hay escasez de huevos**
4 ***supplies,*** food, etc., which has been stocked/which is going to be provided: *supplies of eggs are running low; the army is dropping supplies to the villages cut off by snow.* □ **provisiones**
■ *adj.* ***supply teacher,*** teacher who replaces a permanent teacher who is away. □ **sustituto**
■ *v.* **1** to provide (something) which is necessary: *to supply food to starving villagers; bread is supplied by the local baker.* □ **suministrar**
2 to provide (something) to someone: *the village is supplied with water from the lake; to supply someone with food/with information.* □ **suministrar**
3 to satisfy: *it supplies an urgent need.* □ **satisfacer**
■ *adv.* ['sʌpli] *see also* **supple.**
supplier [sə'plaiə] *n.* person/shop/country which supplies: *the main supplier of oil to the USA.* □ **proveedor**
support [sə'pɔ:t] *n.* **1** something which holds up something: *he was hanging without any visible means of support; the bridge is held up by three supports; you should tie your tomato plants to supports or they will fall down.* □ **apoyo**
2 moral/financial encouragement: *we are demonstrating in support of our wage claim; collection in support of a charity.* □ **apoyo**
■ *v.* **1** to hold up: *the bridge is supported by three pillars.* □ **apoyarse**
2 to provide/to earn money so that someone can live: *he supports his wife and three children.* □ **mantener**
3 to encourage/to agree with: *I support the idea that we should open an office in Paris; we support our local football team.* □ **apoyar**
4 *please support the blind,* give some money to help the blind. □ **ayudar**
supporter *n.* person who encourages a plan/a football team, etc. □ **partidario; hincha (fútbol)**
supporting cast *n.* group of actors who play the minor parts in a play. □ **actores en papeles secundarios**
suppose [sə'pouz] *v.* **1** to assume something to be correct (even if it is not): *let's suppose you're my boss.* □ **suponer**
2 to think; to believe: *I suppose they know about the meeting; I suppose he will be late as usual; he is supposed to be an excellent doctor,* people say he is; *I don't suppose they will come; I supposed he was ill,* I assumed that he was ill. □ **suponer; creer**
3 what happens if?: *suppose it stays wet? suppose you got knocked down by an ambulance?* □ **y si?**
supposedly [sə'pouzidli] *adv.* as it is assumed: *he is supposedly coming here next week.* □ **según cabe suponer**
supposing *conj.* what happens if?: *supposing he came back and found us here?* □ **supónte que**
supposition [sʌpə'ziʃn] *n.* something which is assumed; guess: *his supposition turned out to be correct.* □ **suposición**
suppository [sə'pɔzitəri] *n.* soft tablet of medicinal material which is put into the anus or vagina, and which melts there. □ **supositorio**
suppress [sə'pres] *v.* **1** to crush; to stop (a revol-

ution): *the revolt was suppressed with the use of tanks.* □ **suprimir; sofocar**
2 to forbid the publication of (something): *his book was suppressed; the government tried to suppress the unemployment figures.* □ **prohibir; ocultar**
3 to hide (feelings): *to suppress a laugh.* □ **contener**
suppression [sə'preʃn] *n.* act of suppressing (a revolution/information, etc.). □ **represión; ocultación**
suppressor *n.* machine which prevents an electric appliance from interfering with radio/TV signals. □ **dispositivo antiparasitario**
supranational [suːprə'næʃnl] *adj.* over/beyond several nations and their interests. □ **supranacional**
supreme [su'priːm] *adj.* **1** highest: *supreme court.* □ **supremo**
2 *supreme indifference,* total indifference. □ **suma indiferencia**
supremely *adv.* totally/completely. □ **en grado sumo**
supremacy [su'preməsi] *n.* highest power: *his supremacy over all his rivals.* □ **supremacía**
supremo [su'priːmou] *n.* (*informal*) person in charge of many organizations; officer in charge of several armies. □ **jefe supremo**
surcharge ['səːtʃɑːdʒ] *n.* extra charge: *there is a 10% surcharge on heavy parcels.* □ **recargo**
■ *v.* [səː'tʃɑːdʒ] to charge an extra amount. □ **cobrar con recargo**
sure [ʃɔː, 'ʃuːə] *adj.* **1** without any doubt; certain: *I'm sure he'll come; I'm sure of it,* certain that it is true/that it will happen; *are you sure you haven't lost the key? it's sure to be cold; make sure you're there early; he made sure everyone was there on time.* □ **seguro**
for sure, for certain. □ **claro; seguro**
2 reliable: *it is a sure way to make money; the affair is in sure hands.* □ **seguro**
3 ***sure of yourself,*** confident: *he's far too sure of himself.* □ **seguro de uno mismo**
■ *adv.* **1** certainly: *sure enough, he arrived on time.* □ **efectivamente**
2 ***sure!,*** *Amer.* certainly: *it sure was cold!.* □ **¡sí que hacía frío!**
sure-fire *adj. Amer.* (*informal*) absolutely certain: *it's a sure-fire winner.* □ **totalmente seguro**
sure-footed *adj.* able to walk on slippery rocks/narrow ledges without slipping. □ **de pie firme**
surely *adv.* **1** carefully: *slowly but surely.* □ **con paso seguro**
2 naturally/of course: *surely you don't expect him to go out in all this snow?* □ **seguramente**
sureness *n.* being sure. □ **certeza**
surety *n.* **1** person who takes the responsibility that someone will do something: *to stand surety for someone.* □ **fiador**
2 money paid as a guarantee that someone will appear in court. □ **fianza**
surf [səːf] *n.* line of breaking waves along a shore; foam from breaking waves. □ **rompiente**
■ *v.* to ride on breaking waves on a board. □ **hacer surf**
surfboard *n.* board which you stand on to ride on breaking waves. □ **tabla**
surfboat *n.* light boat for riding on surf. □ **bote para rompientes**
surfer *n.* person who rides on waves. □ **'surfista'**
surfing, surf-riding *n.* riding on breaking waves as a sport. □ **hacer 'surfing'**
surface ['səːfəs] *n.* top layer; outside of something: *the earth's surface; a surface wound,* one that does not go deep; *flies flew over the surface of the lake; on the surface everything seemed calm.* □ **superficie**
■ *v.* **1** to come up from under the water/to appear on the top of the water: *the submarine surfaced.* □ **salir a la superficie**
2 to cover (a road, etc.) with a hard substance: *the walls were surfaced with marble.* □ **echar firme; revistieron las...**
surface mail *n.* post which travels by van/train/ship, etc., and not by air. □ **correo por vía terrestre o marítima**
surfeit ['səːfit] *n.* too much: *he had a surfeit of rich food.* □ **hartura**
surge [səːdʒ] *n.* **1** rising up of water into waves: *the surge of the sea round the wreck.* □ **oleaje**
2 sudden increase: *a surge of enthusiasm.* □ **arranque**
■ *v.* **1** to rise up: *the sea surged round the wreck.* □ **agitarse**
2 *the crowd surged forward towards the palace,* moved forward in a mass. □ **...avanzó...**
surgeon ['səːdʒən] *n.* doctor who carries out operations. □ **cirujano**
dental surgeon, dentist. □ **odontólogo**
house surgeon, young surgeon in a hospital. □ **cirujano interno**
surgery *n.* **1** treatment of disease or wounds by cutting open part of the body. □ **cirugía**
dental surgery, treatment of rotten teeth by drilling and filling. □ **odontología**
plastic surgery, replacement of burnt flesh or skin by whole skin from another part of the body. □ **cirugía plástica**
2 doctor's/dentist's consulting room. □ **consultorio**
3 consultation given by a member of parliament to any of his constituents: *the MP holds a surgery each week.* □ **gabinete de consulta**
surgical ['səːdʒikl] *adj.* referring to surgery. □ **quirúrgico**
surgical appliances, straps/rods, etc., worn to correct a defect in the bones or muscles. □ **accesorios quirúrgicos**
surgical spirit, pure alcohol used to rub on the skin. □ **alcohol de 90**
surly ['səːli] *adj.* grumpy/sullen. □ **hosco**
surliness *n.* being bad-tempered. □ **hosquedad**
surmise [sə'maiz] *n.* guess/supposition. □ **conjetura**
■ *v.* to guess: *as I surmised, the meeting went off badly,* as I foresaw. □ **conjeturar**
surmount [səː'maunt] *v.* **1** to overcome (an obstacle). □ **superar**
2 to be on top: *the pillar was surmounted by a golden ball.* □ **coronar**
surname ['səːneim] *n.* family name: *I know he's called James but what's his surname?* □ **apellido**
surpass [sə'pɑːs] *v.* **1** to do better than. □ **superar**
2 *he surpassed himself,* he did even better/even worse than expected. □ **se superó a sí mismo**
surplice ['səːpləs] *n.* long white robe worn by priests/choirboys, etc. □ **sobrepelliz**
surplus ['səːpləs] *adj.* and *n.* extra (stock); (material) left over: *after paying our debts we have a surplus of $100; surplus goods; surplus stock.* □ **excedente**
surprise [sə'praiz] *n.* shock caused by something which is unexpected: *let's give him a surprise; much to my surprise, they elected me chairman.* □ **sorpresa**
to take by surprise: *it took me by surprise,* I did not expect it to happen. □ **me cogió por sorpresa**
■ *v.* **1** to give (someone) a surprise/an unexpected shock: *I was surprised to hear he was in prison; I shouldn't be surprised if it snows,* it would not surprise me. □ **sorprender**

2 to catch (someone) unexpectedly: *the police surprised the burglars climbing in through the window.* □ **sorprender**
surprising *adj.* astonishing/unusual. □ **sorprendente**
surprisingly *adv.* in an unusual way: *it's surprisingly warm for January.* □ **de modo sorprendente**

surrealism [sə'riəlizəm] *n.* 20th century art movement in which an artist depicts realistic objects in an unreal environment, emphasizing the meaning he sees beyond reality. □ **surrealismo**
surrealist *adj.* and *n.* (artist) following the principles of surrealism. □ **surrealista**
surrealistic *adj.* very strange/totally unreal. □ **surrealista**

surrender [sə'rendə] *n.* **1** giving in (to an enemy): *the commander discussed the terms for the surrender of his forces.* □ **rendición**
2 giving up (of goods); giving up (of an insurance policy). □ **cesión; rescate**
surrender value, amount of money you will receive if you end an insurance before the normal completion date. □ **valor de rescate**
■ *v.* **1** to give in to (an enemy): *the soldiers surrendered in thousands; the city refused to surrender; the escaped prisoner surrendered to the police.* □ **rendirse**
2 to give up (a ticket/insurance policy, etc.). □ **ceder; rescatar**

surreptitious [sʌrəp'tiʃəs] *adj.* done in secret: *he took a surreptitious peep at the answers.* □ **subrepticio**
surreptitiously *adv.* in secret: *he surreptitiously had a glass of whisky while no one was looking.* □ **subrepticiamente**

surround [sə'raund] *n.* border; edge; bare floor space round a carpet: *have you polished the surrounds?* □ **borde**
■ *v.* to be/to come all round (something): *the town is surrounded by high stone walls; he's always surrounded by a crowd of young girls.* □ **rodear**
surrounding *adj.* which surrounds: *the surrounding countryside.* □ **circundante**
surroundings *n. pl.* area around a place: *he found himself in unfamiliar surroundings.* □ **cercanías; entorno**

surtax ['sə:tæks] *n.* extra tax on high incomes. □ **impuesto adicional**

surveillance [sə:'veiləns] *n.* strict watch: *the house was under police surveillance for some weeks,* was carefully watched. □ **vigilancia**

survey ['sə:vei] *n.* **1** general account: *a general survey of English literature.* □ **panorama**
2 careful examination of a building to see if it is in good condition. □ **inspección**
3 taking measurements of land heights/distances/roads/buildings, etc., to produce accurate plans or maps: *aerial survey.* □ **medición**
■ *v.* [sə'vei] **1** to look at/to talk about (something) in a general way: *he surveyed the scene from the windows of his house; in his talk he surveyed the development of the social services.* □ **contemplar; referirse**
2 to make a survey of (a building). □ **inspeccionar**
3 to measure land in order to produce an accurate plan or map. □ **levantar un plano**
surveyor *n.* person who surveys buildings or measures land. □ **topógrafo**

survive [sə'vaiv] *v.* **1** to continue to live after an accident, etc.: *only one of the passengers survived; he survived the crash.* □ **sobrevivir**
2 to live longer than (someone): *he survived his brother.* □ **sobrevivir**
survival *n.* continuing to live. □ **supervivencia**
survival of the fittest, theory that only the best adapted animals or plants survive and develop, while less well adapted species die out. □ **selección natural**
survivor *n.* person who survives: *there were no survivors,* everyone was killed in the accident. □ **superviviente**

susceptible [sə'septibl] *adj.* **1** *susceptible of proof,* which can be proved. □ **susceptible**
2 *he is susceptible to a disease,* he is likely to catch it. □ **es propenso a ...**
3 easily upset: *she is very susceptible.* □ **susceptible**
susceptibility [səseptə'biliti] *n.* being susceptible: *you must try to avoid hurting her susceptibilities.* □ **susceptibilidad**

suspect ['sʌspekt] *adj.* and *n.* **1** (person) who is thought to have committed a crime: *the police have arrested three suspects for questioning.* □ **sospechoso**
2 *a suspect tin of salmon,* one which might be poisonous. □ **sospechoso**
■ *v.* [sə'spekt] **1** to think that (someone) may have committed a crime: *he is suspected of murder.* □ **sospechar**
2 to guess/to think: *I suspect he was right.* □ **sospechar**

suspend [sə'spend] *v.* **1** to hang: *the lamp is suspended from the ceiling on a chain.* □ **suspender**
2 to stop for a time: *the court suspended its hearings; the bus service has been suspended.* □ **suspender**
3 to take (something) away as a punishment: *his driving licence was suspended for 12 months.* □ **retirar**
4 *the headmaster has suspended three pupils,* has refused to allow them to come to school. □ **echar de clase**
suspenders *n. pl.* **1** elastic straps to hold up stockings or socks. □ **ligas**
2 *Amer.* braces/straps going over your shoulders to hold up your trousers. □ **tirantes**
suspense *n.* impatient wait for something to happen or for a decision to be reached: *he was kept in suspense for several hours.* □ **suspense**
suspension *n.* **1** act of suspending: *suspension of a bus service/of a driving licence.* □ **suspensión; retirada**
suspension bridge, one which hangs by ropes/chains, etc., from tall towers. □ **puente colgante**
2 system of springs, etc., in a car which attaches the chassis to the axles and lessens the effects of bumps in the road: *the car has a very poor suspension.* □ **suspensión**

suspicion [sə'spiʃn] *n.* **1** feeling that something is wrong or that someone has committed a crime: *I have my suspicions about him,* I don't trust him; *to look on someone with suspicion,* not to trust someone; *he was arrested on suspicion of murder; don't make any telephone calls — we don't want to arouse his suspicions,* to make him suspect that something is wrong. □ **sospecha**
2 guess; general feeling: *I have a suspicion it's going to rain.* □ **sospecha**
3 slight hint: *a suspicion of annoyance in his voice.* □ **pizca**
suspicious *adj.* **1** which can be suspected: *a suspicious character; that parcel looks suspicious.* □ **sospechoso**
2 *I am suspicious about her,* I suspect that she may have committed a crime, etc. □ **sospecho de ella**
suspiciously *adv.* **1** in a suspicious way: *he was act-*

ing very suspiciously near the silver shop; it looks suspiciously like measles, I suspect it is measles. □ **sospechosamente**
2 as if you suspect something: *he examined the parcel suspiciously.* □ **con recelo**

sustain [sə'stein] *v.* **1** to keep (something) going: *the singer sustained a high note.* □ **sostener**
2 to suffer: *he sustained an injury to his leg.* □ **sufrir**
3 to support: *these pillars will sustain quite heavy weights.* □ **soportar**
sustained *adj.* which continues for a long time: *sustained effort; sustained applause.* □ **sostenido; prolongado**
sustaining *adj.* which will support or nourish: *a good thick sustaining soup.* □ **nutritivo**

sustenance ['sʌstənəns] *n.* **1** food. □ **sustento**
2 ***means of sustenance,*** way of keeping alive or keeping strong. □ **medios de subsistencia**

suture ['suːtʃə] *n.* thread used for stitching wounds together; stitching (of a wound); stitch made to hold a wound together. □ **sutura**

swab [swɔb] *n.* **1** cloth for wiping floors clear of water. □ **bayeta**
2 piece of material (like cottonwool) used for cleaning a wound or for taking samples of infection for analysis. □ **torunda; tapón**
3 sample of infection taken for analysis. □ **muestra**
■ *v.* (*he swabbed*) to clean a floor with a swab: *they were swabbing down the decks of the ship.* □ **fregar**

swag [swæg] *n.* (*informal*) stolen goods (especially jewellery/silver, etc.). □ **botín**

swagger ['swægə] *n.* proud way of walking. □ **contoneo**
■ *v.* to walk in a proud way, swinging your body: *he swaggered into the restaurant.* □ **contonearse**

swallow ['swɔlou] *n.* **1** mouthful of liquid which you drink in one movement. □ **trago**
2 common fast-flying bird with long wings and tail. □ **golondrina**
■ *v.* **1** to make (food/liquid) pass down your throat from your mouth to the stomach: *I have swallowed a fly; he swallowed his dinner and went out,* ate his dinner quickly. □ **tragar**
2 *she swallowed and tried to answer the question,* made a nervous movement as if she was swallowing food. □ **tragar saliva**
3 *the policeman seemed to swallow the story,* to accept the story as true. □ **...tragarse la historia**
swallow up *v.* to make (something) disappear: *his salary increase is swallowed up by the increased electricity bills.* □ **consumir**

swam [swæm] *v. see* **swim.**

swamp [swɔmp] *n.* area of wet soft land. □ **pantano**
■ *v.* **1** to fill (a boat) with water: *the boat was swamped by a large wave.* □ **llenar de agua**
2 *the office is swamped with telephone calls,* has so many calls that it cannot cope. □ **la oficina está inundada...**

swan [swɔn] *n.* large white water bird, with a long curved neck. □ **cisne**
■ *v.* (*he swanned*) (*informal*) to travel about: *he went swanning around the Far East for two years.* □ **irse de viaje**
swan song *n.* last performance by an artist (especially a singer); last work by a writer. □ **el canto del cisne**

swank [swæŋk] *n.* (*informal*) showing off; showing that you think a lot of yourself. □ **'farde'**
■ *v.* (*informal*) to show off; to show that you think a lot of yourself. □ **fardar**
swanky *adj.* (*informal*) pretentious; (acting) in a way which shows that you think a lot of yourself. □ **'fardón'**

swap, swop [swɔp] *n.* (*informal*) **1** exchange: *we did a swap,* we exchanged (cars/houses, etc.); *I got this chair as a swap for my bicycle.* □ **intercambio**
2 ***swaps,*** stamps/coins, etc., which a collector has ready to exchange for others. □ **(sellos/monedas) repetidos**
■ *v.* (*he swapped/swopped*) (*informal*) to exchange: *instead of going on holiday we swapped houses; to swap places with someone; I'll swap my bicycle for that armchair of yours.* □ **intercambiar (casas); cambiar (una bici por un sillón)**

swarm [swɔːm] *n.* large group of insects, etc., flying about together: *a swarm of bees; a swarm of photographers.* □ **enjambre (abejas, avispas, etc.); nube de fotógrafos**
■ *v.* **1** to move about in a large group: *the bees are swarming,* moving to find a new place to live. □ **pulular**
2 *the place is swarming with police,* there are police everywhere. □ **...está repleto de policías**
3 to climb using your hands and feet like a monkey: *he swarmed up a rope.* □ **trepar**

swarthy ['swɔːði] *adj.* with a dark complexion. □ **moreno**

swashbuckling ['swɔʃbʌkliŋ] *adj.* daring; living dangerously: *a swashbuckling hero.* □ **valentón**

swastika ['swɔstikə] *n.* ancient sign, shaped like a cross with each arm bent at right angles, used as a symbol by the German Nazi Party. □ **esvástica**

swat [swɔt] *n.* flat disc on a handle for killing flies, etc. □ **palmeta, matamoscas**
■ *v.* (*he swatted*) to squash (a fly etc.). □ **aplastar**
swatter *n.* flat disc on a handle for killing flies, etc. □ **palmeta, matamoscas**

swathe [sweið] *v.* to wrap up: *his head was swathed in bandages.* □ **envolver**

sway [swei] *n.* power. □ **poder**
under his sway, under his influence. □ **bajo su dominio**
■ *v.* **1** to move from side to side; to make (something) move from side to side: *the trees were swaying in the wind.* □ **balancearse**
2 to influence: *his speeches swayed public opinion.* □ **influir en**

swear ['swɛə] *v.* (*he swore; he has sworn*) **1** to promise solemnly: *he swore to avenge his father; he swore that he would work better in the future.* □ **jurar**
2 to make (someone) take an oath: *the witness was sworn in,* made to swear that he would tell the truth; *to swear someone to secrecy,* make someone swear not to tell the secret. □ **hacer jurar; hacer prometer a alguien...**
3 *I could have sworn he was there,* I was sure he was there. □ **hubiera jurado que...**
4 to curse: *he swore at the strikers; he was kicking and swearing when the police tried to arrest him.* □ **decir palabrotas**
5 ***to swear by something,*** to believe completely or enthusiastically in something: *he swears by cold showers,* (*informal*) thinks they do you a lot of good. □ **para él no hay nada como una buena ducha fría**
swear word *n.* word used as a curse or to show annoyance. □ **palabrota**

sweat [swet] *n.* drops of liquid which come through your skin when you are hot: *the sweat trickled down his brow.* □ **sudor**
to break out in a cold sweat, to get very nervous or worried. □ **estar apurado**

■ *v.* **1** to perspire/to produce drops of liquid through the skin: *the hot room made me sweat.* □ **sudar**
2 *here I am, sweating away at my work,* working very hard. □ **...sudando la gota gorda**
3 *we'll just have* ***to sweat it out,*** keep on with it, even if it is unpleasant/difficult. □ **tendremos que aguantar el chaparrón**
sweat band *n.* band of towelling worn round your head or wrist to stop sweat trickling down. □ **muñequera; cinta**
sweated *adj.* ***sweated labour,*** hard work which is very badly paid. □ **muy mal pagado**
sweater *n.* pullover with long sleeves. □ **suéter**
sweatshirt *n.* light cotton shirt with no collar or buttons, but with long sleeves. □ **sudadera**
sweaty *adj.* damp with sweat. □ **sudoroso**
Sweden ['swi:dn] *n.* country in northern Europe. □ **Suecia**
Swede *n.* **1** person from Sweden. □ **sueco**
2 ***swede,*** type of root vegetable like a yellow turnip. □ **colinabo**
Swedish *adj.* referring to Sweden. □ **sueco**
■ *n.* language spoken in Sweden. □ **sueco**
sweep [swi:p] *n.* **1** act of sweeping (with a brush); act of swinging (a sword or your hand): *he made a wide sweep with his arm; to give a room a good sweep.* □ **barrido (con una escoba)**
to make a clean sweep, to clear something away completely or to win completely: *the new owner had made a clean sweep of all the staff; the party made a clean sweep at the local elections.* □ **hacer tabla rasa de**
2 wide stretch: *the broad sweep of a river/of a lawn.* □ **extensión**
3 person who cleans chimneys. □ **deshollinador**
4 sweepstake: *he won the office sweep.* □ **lotería; porra**
■ *v.* (*he swept*) **1** to clean with a brush: *to sweep a chimney.* □ **barrer; deshollinar (chimenea)**
to sweep the board: *the party swept the board in the local elections,* won completely. □ **el partido barrió...**
2 to clear up (dust/snow, etc.) with a brush: *to sweep dead leaves into a pile; he swept up the dead leaves,* brushed them into a pile. □ **quitar (polvo/nieve); barrer (hojas)**
3 to make a wide movement: *he made a great sweeping movement with his arm; he swept the horizon with his telescope.* □ **hizo un movimiento muy amplio...; examinaba toda la extensión del horizonte...**
4 to move rapidly; to carry (something) along rapidly: *the flood waters swept through the town; the water swept away part of the railway line; the opera singer swept into the director's office; the guerillas swept down from the mountains; the mountains sweep down to the sea; he was swept to power by a massive vote; he was swept out of office by a massi ve vote.* □ **mover/pasar/llevarse bruscamente**
sweeper *n.* person/machine that sweeps: *road sweeper; carpet sweeper.* □ **barrendero; limpia-alfombras**
sweeping *adj.* **1** wide-ranging/far-reaching: *sweeping changes.* □ **amplio; cambio radical**
2 *sweeping statement,* statement which is partly true but too general. □ **declaración demasiado general**
sweepstake *n.* form of gambling on a horserace where the holders of the winning tickets take all the money which has been bet. □ **'sweepstake'**
sweet [swi:t] *adj.* **1** tasting like sugar; not sour: *lemons are not at all sweet; I don't like sweet food.* □ **dulce**
2 *he has* ***a sweet tooth,*** he likes eating sweet things. □ **le gusta el dulce**
3 pleasant; fragrant: *sweet-smelling flowers; the sweet smell of success; sweet breath; sweet music; sweet-tempered; a sweet little puppy.* □ **flores fragantes; el dulce sabor del éxito**
sweet pea, pea with scented flowers. □ **guisante de olor; dulce**
4 *revenge is sweet,* it is pleasant to be able to take your revenge. □ **la venganza es un placer**
■ *n.* **1** piece of sweet food, made with sugar or chocolate: *a bag of sweets; eating sweets is bad for your teeth.* □ **caramelo**
2 sweet course at the end of a meal: *what's for sweet?* □ **postre**
sweetbread *n.* pancreas of an animal eaten as food. □ **mollejas**
sweet corn *n.* maize, eaten as food. □ **maíz dulce**
sweeten *v.* **1** to make sweet: *to sweeten a cup of coffee; to sweeten the air.* □ **endulzar**
2 (*informal*) to give (someone) a bribe to make sure he is favourable to you. □ **untar**
sweetener *n.* **1** thing or material which sweetens. □ **edulcorante**
artificial sweetener, one which does not contain sugar. □ **edulcorante artificial**
2 (*informal*) bribe. □ **astilla**
sweetening *n.* act of making sweet; substance which makes something sweet. □ **endulzamiento; edulcorante**
sweetheart *n.* darling; boy or girl friend. □ **cariño; novio/novia**
sweetie *n.* (*informal*) **1** sweet. □ **caramelito**
2 darling. □ **cariñito**
sweetly *adv.* **1** in a sweet way: *to sing sweetly; she very sweetly offered to lend me money.* □ **dulcemente**
2 *the engine is running sweetly,* smoothly. □ **...con suavidad**
sweetness *n.* being sweet. □ **dulzura**
all is sweetness and light, everything is working very smoothly (though it may not last long). □ **todo va como la seda**
sweet potato *n.* yam/type of edible tropical root. □ **batata**
sweetshop *n.* shop which sells sweets and chocolates. □ **confitería**
sweet william *n.* type of common scented garden flower. □ **minutisa**
swell [swel] *n.* **1** rising movement of the sea: *a heavy swell was running.* □ **marejada**
2 increasing loudness: *the swell of a church organ.* □ **crescendo**
■ *adj. Amer.* fine: *a swell meal.* □ **de primera**
■ *v.* (*it has swollen/swelled*) **1** to increase: *the crowd swelled to over 10,000; some late arrivals came to swell the party.* □ **sobrepasar (cifra); engrosar (número de invitados)**
2 ***to swell (up),*** to become larger/to increase in size: *after the wasp sting, his arm swelled up.* □ **hincharse**
3 ***to swell (out),*** to become or to make fully rounded: *the wind swelled the sails.* □ **inflar**
swelling *n.* part of the body which has swollen up: *she has a swelling on her knee.* □ **hinchazón**
swelter ['sweltə] *v.* to be very hot: *we were sweltering in the heat.* □ **abrasarse**
sweltering *adj.* very hot: *a sweltering day; it's sweltering in here.* □ **sofocante**
swept [swept] *v. see* **sweep.**

swerve [swɜːv] *n.* movement to the side: *the car made a sharp swerve and mounted the pavement.* □ **viraje**
■ *v.* to move to one side: *the car swerved to avoid the cyclist; the cyclist swerved out into the middle of the road.* □ **hacerse a un lado**

swift [swift] *adj.* fast: *a swift reply; he took swift action.* □ **rápido**
■ *n.* fast-flying bird like a swallow but with shorter wings and tail. □ **vencejo; avión**
swiftly *adv.* fast: *he moved swiftly to avoid a fight.* □ **rápidamente**
swiftness *n.* rapidity. □ **rapidez**

swig [swig] *n.* (*informal*) large mouthful of liquid: *he took a swig at the bottle.* □ **lingotazo**
■ *v.* (*he swigged*) (*informal*) to drink in large mouthfuls: *he was swigging a pint of beer.* □ **beber a grandes tragos**

swill [swil] *n.* **1** washing a floor with a lot of water. □ **(dar) un agua**
2 food for pigs. □ **bazofia**
■ *v.* **1** to wash a floor with a lot of water: *he swilled out the stables.* □ **dar un agua**
2 (*informal*) to drink a lot of alcohol. □ **soplar**

swim [swim] *n.* **1** act of moving in the water using arms/legs/flippers, etc.: *we went for a swim yesterday.* □ **baño**
2 *he's in the swim of things,* he's up to date/he knows what's going on. □ **está al tanto de las cosas**
■ *v.* (*he swam; he has swum*) **1** to move in water using arms, legs, flippers, etc.: *he swam across the river; penguins swim very well; can you swim?* □ **nadar**
2 to cross (a river, etc.) by using your arms and legs to move in the water: *he has swum the English Channel three times.* □ **cruzar a nado**
3 to be covered with liquid: *the meat was swimming in gravy; the room was swimming in blood.* □ **estar nadando**
4 to seem to turn: *my head is swimming with all these figures; the room swam before his eyes.* □ **dar vueltas**
swimmer *n.* person who swims. □ **nadador**
swimming *n.* action of moving in water: *he's taking swimming lessons.* □ **natación**
swimming trunks, shorts worn for swimming. □ **pantalón de baño; bañador**
swimming bath *n.* large public pool for swimming. □ **piscina**
swimmingly *adv.* (*informal*) very well: *everything went swimmingly.* □ **a pedir de boca**
swimming pool *n.* pool for swimming: *we have a swimming pool in the garden.* □ **piscina**
swimsuit *n.* bathing costume. □ **traje de baño; bañador**

swindle ['swindl] *n.* trick to get money from someone. □ **timo**
■ *v.* to get money from (someone) by a trick: *he was swindled out of $100.* □ **timar**
swindler *n.* person who swindles someone. □ **timador**

swine [swain] *n.* (*no pl.*) **1** pig. □ **cerdo**
2 (*informal*) unpleasant person. □ **cerdo**
swine fever *n.* infectious disease of pigs. □ **peste porcina**

swing [swiŋ] *n.* **1** movement from side to side or forwards and backwards: *the swing of a pendulum.* □ **balanceo; oscilación (péndulo)**
2 *the election results have shown a swing to the government,* a movement of voters to vote for the government. □ **...un viraje hacia el gobierno**
3 ***to go with a swing,*** (i) to have a regular beat: *the music goes with a swing.* □ **tener un ritmo marcado**
(ii) *the party went with a swing,* went very well. □ **...de maravilla**
4 *the party was* ***in full swing*** *when the police arrived,* was running well. □ **...en pleno apogeo...**
5 ***to get into the swing of things,*** to work at the same rhythm/in the same spirit as everyone else. □ **ahora que le has cogido el tranquillo a...**
6 seat on the end of two ropes which you can sit on and swing backwards and forwards. □ **columpio**
■ *v.* (*he swung*) **1** to move from side to side or forwards and backwards: *the voters have swung away from the government; the girl was swinging on a swing; the monkey was swinging from a branch; the door swung open.* □ **desplazarse; columpiarse; balancearse**
2 to make (something) turn round; to turn round: *he swung the car to the left; she swung round in her chair; the car swung round and went into the ditch on the opposite side of the road.* □ **hacer girar**
3 to move in a rhythmic way with a regular motion: *he swung off down the street.* □ **moverse rítmicamente**
4 *the troops swung into action,* moved smoothly into action; *the rider swung into the saddle.* □ **...entraron sigilosamente en acción**
swing bridge *n.* bridge which can be made to turn to allow ships to pass underneath. □ **puente giratorio**
swing door *n.* door which is not attached with a catch, and which opens when you push it. □ **puerta de batiente**
swinging *n.* action of moving backwards and forwards. □ **oscilación; balanceo**
■ *adj.* **1** moving backwards and forwards. □ **oscilante**
2 (*informal*) lively; fashionably modern: *swinging London.* □ **movido; marchoso**

swingeing ['swindʒiŋ] *adj.* harsh (tax); severe (cuts): *to impose a swingeing duty on imports; swingeing cuts in public services.* □ **severísimo**

swipe [swaip] *n.* (*informal*) sweeping hit/blow: *he took a swipe at the ball; she gave him a swipe round the ear.* □ **golpetazo; tortazo**
■ *v.* **1** (*informal*) to hit (someone) with a sweeping blow: *she swiped him across the face; he swiped the ball over the heads of the crowd.* □ **dar un tortazo**
2 (*slang*) to steal: *who's swiped my pen?* □ **mangar; afanar**

swirl [swɜːl] *n.* whirling/twisting movement. □ **remolino**
■ *v.* to move with a whirling/twisting motion: *water swirled round the rocks; her dress swirled out as she danced.* □ **arremolinarse**

swish [swiʃ] *n.* soft rustle (of a dress/of dead leaves); whistle (of a stick). □ **crujido; chasquido (de un palo)**
■ *v.* **1** to make a whistling noise with a whip-stick. □ **hacer chasquear**
2 *the cat swished its tail from side to side,* moved it from side to side. □ **el gato meneó la cola...**

Swiss [swis] *adj.* **1** referring to Switzerland. □ **suizo**
2 ***swiss roll,*** type of cake made of a thin layer of cake rolled up with cream or jam as a filling. □ **brazo de gitano**
■ *n.* person from Switzerland. □ **suizo**
the Swiss, the people of Switzerland. □ **los suizos**

switch [switʃ] *n.* **1** apparatus for starting or stopping an electric current: *a light switch.* □ **interruptor**
2 sudden change: *there was a complete switch of emphasis; a foreign policy switch.* □ **cambio**
3 whip made of a thin stick. □ **fusta**
■ *v.* to send (a train, etc.) in a different direction;

to do something quite different: *to switch the train into a siding; we used to have coal fires, but now we have switched to gas; the army switched over to the offensive,* changed tactics to start attacking. □ **cambiar de vía (tren); cambiar (a otra cosa)**
switchback *n.* **1** fairground railway which goes up and down steep slopes. □ **montaña rusa**
2 road or railway which goes up and down hills. □ **carretera en zigzag**
switchboard *n.* central telephone office in a building where calls can be transferred to different rooms. □ **centralita**
switch off *v.* **1** to stop an electric current: *switch off the radio; to switch the washing machine off.* □ **apagar**
2 *he's switched off,* (*informal*) he has stopped listening to what you are saying. □ **ha desconectado**
switch on *v.* **1** to start an electric current flowing: *to switch on the light/to switch the light on.* □ **encender**
2 *she's switched on,* (*informal*) she is up to date/knows all that is happening. □ **está a la última**
Switzerland ['switsələnd] *n.* country in Europe to the south of Germany and to the east of France. □ **Suiza**
swivel ['swivl] *n.* joint between two parts which enables either part to turn without the other. □ **eslabón giratorio**
■ *v.* (*he swivelled*) to turn around; to pivot: *he swivelled round in his chair.* □ **girar**
swivel chair *n.* chair which pivots, so that the seat can turn while the legs stay stationary. □ **silla giratoria**
swizzle ['swizl] *n.* (*informal*) swindle/trick. □ **timo**
swizzle-stick *n.* small stick put into a glass of fizzy drink to make it less fizzy. □ **varilla de cóctel**
swollen ['swoulən] *adj.* blown up; increased in size: *swollen river; she has a swollen ankle. see also* **swell.** □ **río crecido; tiene un tobillo inchado**
swollen-headed, (person) who has a high opinion of himself. □ **creído; engreído**
swoop [swu:p] *n.* coming rapidly down from a height to attack; sudden attack: *the police made a swoop and arrested several demonstrators.* □ **ataque en picado; la policía hizo una redada...**
at one fell swoop, in a sudden move/all at once. □ **de un solo golpe**
■ *v.* to come down rapidly to attack; to attack suddenly: *the eagle swooped on the rabbit; the planes swooped down over the presidential palace; the police swooped on the terrorists.* □ **lanzarse sobre (águila); atacar en picado (avión); hacer una redada (policía)**
swop [swɔp] *n.* and *v. see* **swap.**
sword [sɔ:d] *n.* weapon with a long sharp blade held by a handle. □ **espada**
to cross swords with someone, to get into an argument with someone. □ **habérselas con uno**
swordfish *n.* fish with a long pointed upper jaw like a sword. □ **pez espada**
swordsman *n.* (*pl. swordsmen*) person who fights well with a sword. □ **espadachín**
swordstick *n.* walking stick which is hollow and contains a long sharp blade. □ **bastón de estoque**
swore [swɔ:] *v. see* **swear.**
sworn [swɔ:n] *adj. sworn enemies,* total enemies. *see also* **swear.** □ **enemigos implacables**
swot [swɔt] *n.* (*slang*) **1** hard school work. □ **montón de deberes**
2 person who studies hard. □ **empollón**
■ *v.* (*he swotted*) (*slang*) to study hard. □ **empollar**
to swot something up, learn the facts of a subject quickly. □ **aprender rápido y al dedillo**
swum [swʌm] *v. see* **swim.**
swung [swʌŋ] *v. see* **swing.**
sycamore ['sikəmɔ:] *n.* common deciduous tree with very large leaves. □ **sicomoro**
sycophant ['sikəfænt] *n.* person who flatters someone in power. □ **adulador**
sycophantic [sikə'fæntik] *adj.* which flatters excessively. □ **adulatorio**
syllable ['siləbl] *n.* unit of sound which forms a whole word or part of a word: *'sound' has only one syllable while 'railway' has two; let me explain in words of one syllable,* as simply as possible. □ **sílaba; de manera sencilla**
syllabic [si'læbik] *adj.* referring to a syllable. □ **silábico**
syllabub ['siləbʌb] *n.* sweet food made of cream whipped with wine. □ **batido**
syllabus ['siləbəs] *n.* list of subjects to be studied: *chemistry is not on the primary school syllabus.* □ **plan de estudios**
symbiosis [simbi'ousis] *n.* state where two living organisms live close together and depend on each other to a certain extent. □ **simbiosis**
symbol ['simbl] *n.* sign/letter/picture/object which represents something/which is a short way of indicating something: *the letter P is a symbol for a parking sign; C is the chemical symbol for carbon; Yy is the symbol for division; the dove is the symbol for peace; the revolutionaries considered the state prison as the symbol of dictatorship.* □ **símbolo**
symbolic [sim'bɔlik] *adj.* which acts as a symbol. □ **simbólico**
symbolically *adv.* using something as a symbol. □ **simbólicamente**
symbolism *n.* **1** movement in literature and art which used symbols to express emotion, etc. □ **simbolismo**
2 using symbols to express emotion, etc. □ **simbolismo**
symbolize ['simbəlaiz] *v.* to represent (something) as a symbol: *the dove symbolizes peace; the artist has symbolized international friendship by showing a series of hands clasped.* □ **simbolizar**
symmetry ['simətri] *n.* state where two sides of something are exactly similar: *the symmetry of a classical building.* □ **simetría**
symmetrical [si'metrikl] *adj.* referring to symmetry: *the building is not symmetrical,* the left part is not exactly the same as the right. □ **simétrico**
sympathy ['simpəθi] *n.* **1** feeling of pity or sorrow because someone else has problems: *to write a letter of sympathy to someone whose father has died.* □ **compasión; escribir una carta de condolencia...**
2 common feeling; sharing ideas: *I am totally in sympathy with your political opinions; the engineers went on strike and the office staff went on strike in sympathy,* to show that they approved of the engineers' action; *his sympathies lie with the workers,* he supports the workers. □ **comparto totalmente tus opiniones...; ...en solidaridad; él simpatiza con los...**
sympathize *v.* **1** to show sympathy to someone in trouble: *I sympathized with him over his problems with his son.* □ **entender**
2 to approve; to agree with: *I sympathize with your point of view.* □ **compartir**
sympathizer *n.* person who sympathizes with someone's political views. □ **simpatizante**
sympathetic [simpə'θetik] *adj.* showing sympathy:

he was very sympathetic when I told him my story. □ **comprensivo**

sympathetically *adv.* in a way which shows sympathy: *he listened sympathetically when I told my story.* □ **comprensivamente**

symphony ['simfəni] *n.* piece of music in several parts for a full orchestra. □ **sinfonía**

symphonic [sim'fɔnik] *adj.* referring to a symphony. □ **sinfónico**

symposium [sim'pouziəm] *n.* (*pl. symposia*) organized meeting to discuss a specific subject; collection of articles written on a specific subject. □ **simposio**

symptom ['simptəm] *n.* something which shows visibly that feelings exist/that changes are taking place: *the swelling is a symptom of mumps; absenteeism is a general symptom of lack of interest in the work.* □ **síntoma**

symptomatic [simptə'mætik] *adj.* which shows visibly that changes are taking place or that feelings exist: *it's symptomatic of the state of the economy.* □ **sintomático**

synagogue ['sinəgɔg] *n.* building where Jews worship. □ **sinagoga**

synchromesh ['siŋkrəmeʃ] *n.* type of gear system used in modern cars, where the gears revolve at the same speeds before being engaged. □ **cambio sincronizado**

synchronize ['siŋkrənaiz] *v.* to adjust (watches) to the same time; to arrange (things) so that they happen at the same time. □ **sincronizar**

synchronization [siŋkrənai'zeiʃn] *n.* action of synchronizing. □ **sincronización**

syncopate ['siŋkəpeit] *v.* (*in music*) to stress (a beat) which would not regularly be stressed and so change the rhythm: *syncopated beat.* □ **sincopar**

syndicate ['sindikət] *n.* group of people or companies working together to make money. □ **consorcio**

■ *v.* to produce (an article/a cartoon) which is then sold to a series of newspapers: *syndicated column; his column is syndicated in sixteen papers.* □ **publicar en varios periódicos**

syndrome ['sindroum] *n.* **1** series of symptoms which show an illness. □ **síndrome**

2 symptoms which show a general feeling/way of approaching a problem, etc. □ **síndrome**

synod ['sinəd] *n.* meeting of religious leaders. □ **sínodo**

synonym ['sinənim] *n.* word which means the same thing as another word: *'angry' and 'annoyed' are synonyms.* □ **sinónimo**

synonymous [si'nɔniməs] *adj.* which has the same meaning: *'angry' is synonymous with 'annoyed'; 'cramp' is synonymous with 'acute discomfort'.* □ **sinónimo**

synopsis [si'nɔpsis] *n.* (*pl. synopses*) summary (of main points made in a book or article). □ **sinopsis**

syntax ['sintæks] *n.* grammatical rules for putting words together into sentences. □ **sintaxis**

synthesis ['sinθəsis] *n.* (*pl. syntheses*) bringing several parts together to form a whole. □ **síntesis**

synthesize ['sinθəsaiz] *v.* to combine (several things) together to make a whole. □ **sintetizar**

synthetic [sin'θetik] *n.* artificial/man-made material. □ **sintético**

■ *adj.* artificial; made in such a way that it looks natural: *synthetic rubber; synthetic cream.* □ **sintético**

syphilis ['sifilis] *n.* serious disease transmitted by sexual intercourse or inherited. □ **sífilis**

Syria ['siriə] *n.* country in the Middle East. □ **Siria**

Syrian *adj.* and *n.* (person) from Syria. □ **sirio**

syringe [si'rindʒ] *n.* tube with a piston or rubber bulb so that liquids can be sucked into it then squeezed out, as in giving injections. □ **jeringuilla**

garden syringe, instrument for spraying trees with insecticide, etc. □ **fumigador**

■ *v.* to clean by blowing liquid with a syringe. □ **jeringar**

syrup ['sirəp] *n.* thick sweet liquid; thin golden juice from sugar. □ **sirope, almíbar**

syrupy *adj.* like syrup; very sweet. □ **almibarado**

system ['sistəm] *n.* **1** arrangement of things which work together: *the road system; the digestive system; the nervous system.* □ **sistema**

2 way of organizing things to work together: *the education system; the system of government departments.* □ **sistema**

3 method. □ **sistema**

4 body: *cold water is a shock to the system.* □ **organismo**

systematic [sistə'mætik] *adj.* orderly/methodical: *a systematic search.* □ **sistemático**

systematically *adv.* in a methodical way: *the burglars went through each room systematically.* □ **sistemáticamente**

systematize ['sistəmətaiz] *v.* to organize into a system. □ **sistematizar**

systemic [sis'temik] *adj.* which affects the whole system: *systemic insecticides.* □ **sistémico**

systems analysis *n.* use of a computer to forecast needs, etc., by analysing the way in which a system is actually operating. □ **análisis de sistemas**

systems analyst *n.* person who specializes in systems analysis. □ **analista de sistemas**

T,t

T, t [ti:] **1** twentieth letter of the alphabet. □ **T, t**
T-bone steak, type of beef steak with a bone shaped like a T in it. □ **chuletón**
T-junction, junction in the shape of a T where one road joins another at right angles. □ **cruce en T**
T shirt, light cotton shirt with no buttons or collar and short sleeves. □ **camiseta**
T square, device shaped like a T for drawing right angles. □ **doble escuadra**
2 *it suits him **to a T,*** (*informal*) it suits him perfectly. □ **le sienta divino**
3 ***to dot one's i's and cross one's t's,*** to settle the final details (of an agreement)/to be very careful about something. □ **poner los puntos sobre las íes**
ta [tɑ] *interjection* (*informal*) thank you. □ **gracias**
tab [tæb] *n.* **1** small loop of cloth for hanging up a coat/for pulling open a box. □ **presilla**
2 little coloured marker attached to cards in an index so that they can be found easily. □ **uñero**
to keep tabs on someone, (*informal*) to keep watch on someone. □ **echar un ojo a alguien**
to pick up the tab, (*informal*) to pay the bill. □ **soltar la tela**
tabby (cat) ['tæbi(kæt)] *n.* (*pl. tabbies*) striped black, brown, and grey cat. □ **gato atigrado**
tabernacle ['tæbənækl] *n.* **1** place of worship. □ **tabernáculo**
2 ornamental box for keeping consecrated bread and wine in. □ **sagrario**
table ['teibl] *n.* **1** piece of furniture with a flat top and legs, used for eating at/for working at, etc.: *dining room table.* □ **mesa**
to set the table, to get the table ready for a meal. □ **poner la mesa**
to clear the table, to remove dirty plates/knives, etc. after a meal. □ **quitar la mesa**
table knife, knife used for eating at table (and not for cutting in the kitchen). □ **cuchillo de mesa**
2 *the family was sitting at table,* was eating a meal. □ **...a la mesa**
3 ***to turn the tables on someone,*** to put yourself in a superior position, where before you were in an inferior one. □ **cambiar las tornas**
4 printed list of figures/facts: *the postal charges are set out in a table.* □ **tabla**
multiplication tables, lists of figures to learn by heart how each number is multiplied ('once two is two, two twos are four, three twos are six', etc.): *he can't remember his seven times table.* □ **tablas de multiplicar**
table of contents, list of contents of a book. □ **índice de materias**
■ *v.* to suggest (items for discussion by a committee): *to table an amendment to a proposal.* □ **presentar**
tablecloth *n.* cloth for covering a table during a meal. □ **mantel**
tableland *n.* high flat land. □ **meseta; páramo**
table linen *n.* cloth items used on a table (such as tablecloths/serviettes, etc.). □ **mantelería**
table manners *n. pl.* polite way of eating according to the rules of society. □ **modales de mesa**
table mat *n.* mat for protecting the surface of a table. □ **salvamanteles**
tablespoon *n.* large spoon for serving food at table. □ **cucharón**
tablespoonful *n.* quantity held in a tablespoon: *add two tablespoonfuls of sugar.* □ **cucharada**
table tennis *n.* game played on a large table with a net across the centre, using small round bats and a very light white ball. □ **tenis de mesa; ping-pong**
tableau ['tæblou] *n.* (*pl. tableaux*) scene where actors represent a historic occasion, etc., without moving. □ **cuadro**
table d'hôte ['tɑ:blədout] *n.* menu which has a restricted number of dishes at a reduced price. □ **menú**
tablet ['tæblət] *n.* **1** small round pill of medicine. □ **tableta**
2 flat stone with an inscription on it in memory of someone. □ **lápida**
3 bar (of soap/chocolate). □ **pastilla (jabón); tableta (chocolate)**
tabloid ['tæblɔid] *n.* popular newspaper with a small page size, usually with a large proportion of pictures. □ **tabloide**
taboo [tə'bu:] *adj.* forbidden (by religion/by custom): *don't mention his name here — it's taboo.* □ **tabú**
■ *n.* (religious) custom which forbids something. □ **tabú**
tabular ['tæbjulə] *adj.* arranged in a table: *the figures are given in tabular form.* □ **tabular**
tabulate ['tæbjuleit] *v.* to arrange (figures) in a table. □ **tabular**
tabulation *n.* arrangement (of figures) in a table. □ **tabulación**
tabulator *n.* device on a typewriter which allows the typist to make columns automatically. □ **tabulador**
tachograph ['tækəgrɑ:f] *n.* machine placed in the cab of a lorry which records details of the mileage and time spent on a journey. □ **tacógrafo**
tacit ['tæsit] *adj.* (agreement, etc.) which is understood, but not actually given. □ **tácito**
tacitly *adv.* (agreement given) without speaking, but nevertheless understood. □ **tácitamente**
taciturn *adj.* (someone) who does not say much. □ **taciturno**
taciturnity [tæsi'tə:niti] *n.* silence/not saying much. □ **taciturnidad**
tack [tæk] *n.* **1** small nail (with a large head): *carpet tacks,* tacks for nailing down a carpet. □ **tachuela**
to get down to brass tacks, (*informal*) to talk real business/to get down to discussing the real problem. □ **ir al grano**
2 (*in sewing*) light stitch to hold cloth in place and which can be taken out later. □ **hilván**
3 diagonal movement of a ship so that it is sailing against the wind. □ **virar por avante**
4 *you're **on the right tack,*** you're doing the right thing. □ **vas bien encaminado**
5 saddle and equipment for horse-riding. □ **aparejo**
■ *v.* **1** to nail (something) using tacks: *to tack down a carpet.* □ **clavar tachuelas**
2 to make a light temporary stitch: *I've tacked the hem of the skirt.* □ **hilvanar**
3 to change direction so that you are sailing into the wind: *they were tacking up the river,* they sailed in a zigzag way up the river against the wind. □ **cambiar de bordada**
tackle ['tækl] *n.* **1** equipment for doing something: *are you taking your fishing tackle on holiday?* □ **aparejo**

2 ***block and tackle,*** arrangement of ropes, pulleys and hooks for lifting heavy weights. □ **aparejo**
3 (*in football, etc.*) trying to get possession of the ball from an opposing player; (*in Rugby*) grabbing an opposing player so that he falls to the ground and releases the ball. □ **acoso (fútbol); placaje (rugby)**
■ *v.* **1** to grab (someone/something): *to tackle a burglar.* □ **agarrar**
2 *to tackle a problem,* to try to deal with it. □ **abordar un problema**
3 (*in football, etc.*) to try to get possession of the ball from an opposing player; (*in Rugby*) to grab (an opposing player) so that he falls to the ground. □ **acosar (fútbol); placar (rugby)**
tackler *n.* person who tackles. □ **defensa**
tacky ['tæki] *adj.* (*tackier, tackiest*) sticky. □ **pegajoso**
tact [tækt] *n.* care in your relationships with people so that you do not offend them: *you must exercise tact in dealing with temperamental office staff.* □ **tacto**
tactful *adj.* using tact: *he gave a tactful reply.* □ **llena de tacto**
tactfully *adv.* in a tactful way: *she tactfully refused the invitation.* □ **con tacto**
tactless *adj.* lacking tact/unintentionally offensive: *what a tactless thing to say!* □ **falto de tacto**
tactlessly *adv.* in a tactless way: *he tactlessly asked his girl friend to a party to meet his first wife.* □ **con poco tacto**
tactic ['tæktik] *n.* (*often pl.*) way of doing something so as to be at an advantage: *to use delaying tactics,* to delay in order to put yourself at an advantage. □ **táctica**
military tactics, way of placing troops/guns, etc., so as to be in a better position than the enemy. □ **táctica militar**
tactical *adj.* **1** referring to tactics. □ **táctico**
a tactical error, a mistake in planning. □ **error táctico**
2 which is used in a limited area: *tactical nuclear weapon.* □ **táctico**
tactician [tæk'tiʃn] *n.* person who is an expert at tactics. □ **táctico**
tactile ['tæktail] *adj.* which is sensitive to touch; referring to the sense of touch. □ **táctil**
tadpole ['tædpoul] *n.* baby frog/toad in its first stage after hatching. □ **renacuajo**
taffeta ['tæfitə] *n.* thin shiny stiff cloth. □ **tafetán**
taffrail ['tæfreil] *n.* guard rail round the stern of a ship. □ **coronamiento**
tag [tæg] *n.* **1** small loop of cloth; metal piece at the end of a shoelace. □ **pingajo (tela); herrete (cordón)**
2 label: *the price tag is still on your coat.* □ **etiqueta**
3 old common quotation: *'plus ça change,' as the old French tag goes.* □ **dicho**
4 children's game where you have to try to touch another child who then chases the others in turn. □ **tula**
■ *v.* (*he tagged*) ***to tag on to someone,*** (*informal*) to stay close to someone. □ **pegarse**
to tag along behind, to follow closely. □ **seguir de cerca**
tail [teil] *n.* **1** part of an animal at the rear of its body, usually sticking out at the back: *a bird's tail; the fish swims with its tail; the dog was wagging its tail.* □ **rabo; cola**
2 *he went away* ***with his tail between his legs,*** defeated. □ **...con el rabo entre las piernas**
3 ***to turn tail:*** *they turned tail and fled,* they ran away. □ **huir**
4 back part of a long coat/ of a shirt, etc.: *he was wearing tails,* wearing evening-dress. □ **faldón; llevaba frac**
5 back part (of a line); back (of a car): *the tail end of a queue; the cars were standing nose to tail.* □ **final de la cola; parte trasera (coche)**
6 ***tails,*** reverse side of a coin/the side of a coin without the head of a king, etc., on it. □ **cruz**
7 (*informal*) detective who is following someone closely. □ **sabueso**
■ *v.* **1** to take the stems off (gooseberries, etc.). □ **quitar el rabo a**
2 to follow (someone) closely: *the detective was tailing the criminal.* □ **seguir de cerca**
tail away *v.* to die away/to fade away. □ **ir apagándose**
tailback *n.* long line of cars held up by an accident, etc. □ **cola de coches**
tailboard, tailgate *n.* hinged board at the back of a lorry which can be let down to load or unload the contents. □ **plataforma**
tail coat *n.* man's black evening jacket with a long tail at the back. □ **frac**
tailless *adj.* (animal) with no tail. □ **sin rabo**
taillight *n.* rear light (of a car, etc.). □ **piloto**
tail off *v.* to die away/to fade away: *her speech tailed off as she saw the soldiers enter the hall.* □ **ir apagándose**
tailplane *n.* flat wings on the tail of an aicraft. □ **plano de cola**
tail wind *n.* wind blowing behind an aircraft, and therefore making it go faster. □ **viento de cola**
tailor ['teilə] *n.* person who makes outer clothes (suits/coats, etc.) usually for men. □ **sastre**
■ *v.* **1** to make clothes which fit: *a well-tailored suit.* □ **hacer a la medida; un traje bien cortado**
2 to make (something) fit particular circumstances: *the insurance plan is tailored to suit the individual's needs.* □ **adaptar**
tailor-made *adj.* made to fit: *tailor-made suit; tailor-made plan.* □ **hecho a la medida**
taint [teint] *n.* slight trace of evil/of corruption. □ **tacha (de corrupción)**
■ *v.* to infect/to corrupt. □ **corromper**
tainted food, food which has become rotten (by touching other rotten food). □ **comida echada a perder**
take [teik] *n.* **1** one scene of a film which has been filmed. □ **toma**
2 money taken in a shop/in a business: *he wants a share of the take.* □ **ingresos**
■ *v.* (*he took; he has taken*) **1** to hold/to grasp/to carry: *to take someone on your back; he took the book from the shelf; can you take this parcel to the post office?* □ **tomar; coger**
2 to remove/to steal: *someone's taken my pen; the thief took some silver candlesticks.* □ **coger**
3 to buy/to rent/to occupy: *these seats are taken; we took a house in Wales for the holidays; to take a newspaper,* to have a newspaper delivered to your house regularly. □ **coger; suscribirse a un periódico**
take a seat, sit down. □ **tome asiento**
to take the chair, to act as chairman (at a meeting). □ **presidir**
4 to win (a prize): *he took first prize in the flower show.* □ **llevarse**
5 to be a candidate for (an examination): *she's taking her university entrance exam this year; he took his driving test three times before he passed.* □ **presentarse a (un examen)**
6 to eat/to drink (regularly): *he's taking food again;*

do you take sugar in your tea? □ **tomar**
7 to make (a photograph): *he took a picture of me in the rowing boat.* □ **tomar, hacer**
8 to accept: *he won't take any responsibility; he took the news badly; she refused to take any money; take my advice,* do as I suggest. □ **tomar; sigue mi consejo**
take it from me, believe what I say. □ **hazme caso**
9 *she's taking legal advice,* she is consulting a lawyer. □ **se lo lleva un abogado**
10 to need: *it took three men to lift the piano; we took two days/it took us two days to get to London; it won't take long; it takes courage to be a soldier; I take size 15 in shirts.* □ **se necesitaron tres hombres...; nos llevó dos días; no nos llevará tiempo...**
11 to lead: *they took the first turning on the right; he took me to meet his mother; can you take me to the station?,* can you drive me to the station? □ **tomar; llevar**
12 to hold: *this car can take four passengers; this meter only takes 10p coins.* □ **admitir**
13 to do (a certain action): *to take a walk/a bath/a holiday.* □ **dar un paseo; tomar un baño/unas vacaciones**
to take a decision, to decide. □ **tomar una decisión**
14 to stand/to put up with: *I can't take his continual talking; I can't take any more of this,* I've had enough. □ **aguantar**
15 to be successful/to have effect: *the kidney transplant has taken,* has been successful. □ **ser un éxito**
16 *the cuttings have taken,* have sprouted roots. □ **han agarrado los esquejes**
take after *v.* to be like (a parent): *he takes after his father.* □ **parecerse**
take away *v.* **1** to remove: *the police took the gun away from him; he was taken away in an ambulance.* □ **quitar, llevar**
2 to subtract: *ten take away four leaves six.* □ **a 10 le quitas 4...**
takeaway *n.* and *adj.* (*informal*) (shop where you can buy) hot food to eat elsewhere: *a Chinese takeaway; we'll have a takeaway meal.* □ **para llevar**
take back *v.* **1** to return: *the shoes don't fit, so I'll take them back to the shop.* □ **devolver**
2 *will you take back these shoes?,* will you accept them? □ **¿puedo devolver...?**
3 *I take it all back,* I withdraw what I said and apologise for having said it. □ **lo retiro todo**
take down *v.* **1** to lower (something which is hanging): *he took his gun down from the wall.* □ **bajar**
2 to write down what someone says: *take this letter down; the policeman took down the evidence.* □ **anotar**
3 to demolish: *to take down some old houses.* □ **demoler**
take-home pay *n.* amount of money you actually receive out of your wages, after tax, etc., has been deducted. □ **salario neto**
take in *v.* **1** to accept/to bring inside: *she takes in lodgers; the boat's taking in water.* □ **alojar (huéspedes); el barco hace agua**
2 to include. □ **incluir**
3 to trick: *he was taken in by the man's easy way of talking.* □ **embaucar**
taken with *adj.* (*informal*) attracted by: *we're very taken with the idea of a holiday in Greece.* □ **nos atrae la idea de...**
take off *v.* **1** to remove: *he took off all his clothes/he took all his clothes off.* □ **quitarse**
2 to fly into the air: *the flight to Paris took off ten minutes late.* □ **despegar**
3 (*informal*) to imitate: *he takes off the headmaster.* □ **imitar**
take-off *n.* **1** departure (of an aircraft). □ **despegue**
2 (*informal*) imitation. □ **parodia**
take on *v.* **1** to agree to do (some work): *he had taken on three more jobs; he's taken on more than he can handle.* □ **aceptar**
2 to agree to employ (someone): *I'll take you on for one month's trial period.* □ **contratar**
3 to fight; to play against: *he took on the entire workforce.* □ **luchar contra**
4 to make a scene: *don't take on so!* □ **montar un número**
take out *v.* **1** to pull something out: *he took an apple out of his pocket; the dentist had to take out two of my teeth/to take two of my teeth out.* □ **sacar**
2 to invite (someone) to go out: *he's taking me out to dinner.* □ **sacar**
3 *to take out an insurance policy on something,* to start to insure something. □ **sacarse una póliza de...**
4 ***to take it out on someone,*** to make someone suffer to help relieve your own feelings: *if you're angry, don't take it out on the children.* □ **pagarlas con**
5 *the heat takes it out of me,* makes me very tired. □ **el calor me agota**
take over *v.* **1** to buy (a business): *our firm was taken over last year.* □ **absorber**
2 to start to do something in place of someone else: *I'll take over from you now; he took over from our headmaster last year.* □ **sustituir**
takeover *n.* buying of a business. □ **adquisición**
takeover bid, offer to buy a business. □ **OPA (oferta pública de adquisición)**
taker *n.* person who wants to buy: *are there any takers?,* does anyone want to buy? □ **comprador**
take to *v.* **1** to start to do something to help you out of a bad situation: *he caught flu and took to his bed; the runaway prisoner took to the woods,* went into the woods to hide; *she took to drink,* started to drink alcohol regularly. □ **...y guardó cama; ...se dirigió hacia el bosque; se dio a la bebida**
2 to start to like (someone): *he took to me very quickly.* □ **tomar cariño**
take up *v.* **1** to pick up: *they took up the carpets; the bus stopped to take up passengers.* □ **recoger**
2 *they've taken up the road,* removed the road surface. □ **han levantado la calzada**
3 to occupy space: *this chair takes up a lot of room; it takes up too much of my time.* □ **ocupar**
4 to start to do (a sport/a craft): *he's taken up tennis/painting.* □ **iniciarse en**
5 *to take up an idea/a case,* to start to work on an idea/to start to discuss a case. □ **empezar a trabajar en**
6 to make shorter: *to take up the hem of a skirt.* □ **acortar**
7 ***to take someone up on something,*** (*informal*) to accept a suggestion which someone has made. □ **seguir**
takings *n. pl.* money received in a shop/in a business: *the gunman went off with the day's takings.* □ **recaudación**
talc [tælk] *n.* smooth soft mineral used to make powder to put on the body; powder made from this mineral: *he sprinkled some talc on his hands.* □ **talco**
talcum powder *n.* powder made from talc. □ **polvos de talco**
tale [teil] *n.* **1** story: *tales of mystery.* □ **cuento**
old wives' tale, superstitious belief. □ **cuento de viejas**
2 *he's been telling tales (out of school),* telling lies/

informing on someone. □ **ha estado contando chismes/chivándose**

talent ['tælənt] *n.* **1** natural gift/ability: *he has a great talent as an artist; she has a talent for remembering people's names.* □ **talento**
2 people with natural ability: *the local talent,* local people who can sing/dance, etc. □ **talento**
talent contest, contest to find new singers/comedians, etc. □ **concurso de talentos**
talented *adj.* very gifted: *a talented musician.* □ **de talento**

talisman ['tælizmən] *n.* object kept because it supposedly brings good luck. □ **talismán**

talk [tɔːk] *n.* **1** spoken words: *there's talk of a general election.* □ **habla**
idle talk, gossip. □ **habladurías**
double talk, saying one thing and thinking the opposite. □ **lo contrario de lo que se piensa**
2 conversation: *we had a talk to discuss our problems; if you want to borrow money, have a talk with your bank manager.* □ **conversación**
3 lecture/informal speech: *he's going to give us a talk on Roman history.* □ **charla**
■ *v.* **1** to speak: *the baby's learning to talk; we were talking French; does he know what he's talking about? he's going to talk to the headmaster about his son's results; she's talking of opening a bookshop.* □ **hablar a (alguien)/de (algo)**
now you're talking, (*informal*) that is a good idea. □ **eso es hablar**
2 to gossip: *don't go out with her so often, people are talking.* □ **hablar**
3 to give information (usually unwillingly): *we have ways of making you talk.* □ **hablar**
talkative *adj.* (person) who likes to chat/to gossip. □ **hablador**
talk down *v.* **1** to speak in a condescending way/in an exaggeratedly simple way (to someone). □ **abrumar con palabras**
2 to give instructions over the radio to a pilot for landing his aircraft when visibility is bad. □ **dirigir el aterrizaje**
talker *n.* **1** person who talks. □ **hablador**
2 *she's a great talker,* she likes to talk. □ **es una gran conversadora**
talking *n.* speech; conversation: *no talking, please; he did all the talking,* the others said nothing. □ **conversación; ¡silencio, por favor!**
talking-point *n.* something people argue about. □ **tema de conversación**
talking-shop *n.* place where things are discussed but no action is ever taken. □ **mentidero**
talking-to *n.* (*informal*) scolding: *I gave them a good talking-to.* □ **bronca**
talk into *v. we talked him into paying for lunch,* we persuaded him. □ **convencer**
talk over *v.* **1** *I talked him over,* I persuaded him to change his mind. □ **convencer**
2 *come and talk it over,* come and discuss it. □ **ven y lo hablamos**
talk round *v.* **1** *I talked him round,* I persuaded him to change his mind. □ **llegar a convencer**
2 *we just talked round the subject,* we never discussed the main problem. □ **no llegamos a entrar en harina**

tall [tɔːl] *adj.* (*taller, tallest*) **1** high: *a tall man; he is six feet tall; how tall are you? a tall building/tree.* □ **alto**
2 (*informal*) unbelievable: *a tall story.* □ **increíble; un cuento chino**
3 *that's **a tall order,*** command which is extremely difficult to carry out. □ **ésa es una orden peliaguda**
tallboy *n.* type of tall chest of drawers. □ **cómoda alta**

tallow ['tælou] *n.* fat from animals, used to make candles. □ **sebo**

tally ['tæli] *n.* (*pl. tallies*) note/account: *keep a tally of how much you spend.* □ **lleva la cuenta de lo que gastas**
■ *v.* (*tallied; tallying*) to agree: *his notes don't tally with mine.* □ **cuadrar**

talon ['tælən] *n.* claw (of an eagle, etc.). □ **garra**

tamarisk ['tæmərisk] *n.* shrub with feathery evergreen leaves, which is often grown near the sea. □ **tamarisco**

tambourine [tæmbə'riːn] *n.* small drum with metal pieces loosely attached to the rim, so that they jangle when it is beaten. □ **pandereta**

tame [teim] *adj.* (*tamer, tamest*) **1** (animal) which is not wild/which can be approached by human beings: *a tame lion.* □ **domesticado**
2 *our tame tax expert,* (*informal*) the tax expert whom we call on regularly for advice. □ **habitual**
3 *the film was rather tame,* not very exciting. □ **la película era más bien sosa**
■ *v.* to make (an animal) tame; to make safe: *he tames lions; to tame the forces of a volcano.* □ **domar**
tamely *adv.* humbly: *his wife told him to resign and he tamely did what she said.* □ **sumisamente**
tameness *n.* being tame. □ **mansedumbre**
tamer *n.* person who tames wild animals: *a lion tamer.* □ **domador**

tam-o'-shanter [tæmə'ʃæntə] *n.* flat Scottish cap, like a beret. □ **boina escocesa**

tamp [tæmp] *v.* to press down. □ **apisonar**

tamper ['tæmpə] *v. **to tamper with something,*** to meddle with something/to try to stop something working: *someone has been tampering with the lock on the safe.* □ **manosear; alguien ha estado tratando de forzar...**

tampon ['tæmpɔn] *n.* pad of cotton wool used to soak up blood, etc. □ **tapón; tampón**

tan [tæn] *n.* and *adj.* brownish yellow (colour): *tan shoes; light tan shoe polish.* □ **marrón**
■ *n.* brown colour of the skin after sitting in the sun: *she came back from holiday with a beautiful tan.* □ **moreno; bronceado**
■ *v.* (*he tanned*) **1** to treat (animal skins) to make leather. □ **curtir**
2 to get brown by sitting in the sun: *dark-haired people tan easily; his face was tanned by the sun.* □ **ponerse moreno**
tanner *n.* person who makes animal skins into leather. □ **curtidor**
tannery *n.* (*pl. tanneries*) factory where skins are made into leather. □ **curtiduría**

tandem ['tændəm] *n.* bicycle for two people. □ **tándem**
in tandem, in pairs together: *we run the two businesses in tandem.* □ **en tándem; a la par**

tang [tæŋ] *n.* sharp smell/taste: *the tang of the sea; the tang of oranges.* □ **olor/sabor penetrante**
tangy *adj.* with a sharp taste/smell. □ **de olor/sabor penetrante**

tangent ['tændʒənt] *n.* line which touches a curve without cutting through it. □ **tangente**
to go off at a tangent, to change direction/to follow another line of thought. □ **salirse por la tangente**
tangential [tæn'dʒenʃl] *adj.* referring to a tangent. □ **tangencial**

tangerine [tændʒə'riːn] *n.* small orange with soft skin which peels easily. □ **mandarina; clementina**

tangible ['tændʒəbl] *adj.* which can be touched; real: *there's a tangible difference between the two cloths; there is no tangible evidence that he was involved in the crime.* □ **tangible**

tangibly *adv.* in a real/definite way. □ **tangiblemente**

tangle ['tæŋgl] *n.* **1** mix of threads/string/hair: *this string has got into a tangle.* □ **maraña**

2 *his business is all* ***in a tangle,*** all mixed up. □ **...enmarañado**

■ *v.* **1** to mix things together in knots: *tangled hair.* □ **enredar; pelo enredado**

2 *he's got tangled up in some affair with Mr Smith,* mixed up in a confusing way. □ **se ha metido en un lío con...**

tango ['tæŋgou] *n.* (*pl. tangos*) dance where you glide sideways. □ **tango**

tank [tæŋk] *n.* **1** large (metal) container for liquids: *water tank; petrol tank; I've a tank full of petrol so we won't need to stop.* □ **depósito**

2 ***tank wagon,*** railway wagon for carrying liquids. □ **vagón cisterna**

3 armoured vehicle with caterpillar tracks and a powerful gun. □ **tanque**

tanker *n.* **1** special ship for carrying liquids (especially oil): *oil tanker.* □ **petrolero**

2 special lorry for carrying liquids: *a petrol tanker; a tanker driver.* □ **camión cisterna**

tank up *v.* (*informal*) to drink a lot. □ **chupar**

tankard ['tæŋkəd] *n.* large metal mug for drinking beer. □ **jarra**

tannin ['tænin] *n.* red-brown liquid (found in the bark of trees/in tea) which is used to make leather. □ **tanino**

tannic *adj.* ***tannic acid,*** tannin. □ **tánico**

tantalize ['tæntəlaiz] *v.* to tease (someone) by offering him something which he can't have: *a tantalizing smell of roast chicken.* □ **tentar; un tentador olor...**

tantalizingly *adv.* in a tantalizing way: *we were tantalizingly close to reaching the top of the mountain, but we had to turn back.* □ **de modo tentador**

tantamount ['tæntəmaunt] *adj.* equivalent/equal: *that is tantamount to saying 'no'; their offer is tantamount to an insult.* □ **equivalente a**

tantrum ['tæntrəm] *n.* attack of bad temper: *the little girl got into a tantrum and kicked the furniture.* □ **rabieta**

tap [tæp] *n.* **1** apparatus with a twisting knob and a valve which, when you turn it, allows liquid to come out of a pipe/a container: *water tap; the tap on a barrel; turn off the tap, the bath's full; I can hear a tap dripping; tap water,* water which comes from the mains and not from a well. □ **grifo**

on tap, readily available: *we have a consultant on tap to give us the latest information.* □ **a mano**

2 slight blow: *a tap on the door; I didn't hurt him, I just gave him a little tap.* □ **golpecito**

■ *v.* (*he tapped*) **1** to run liquid out of (a barrel) by fixing a tap: *to tap a barrel.* □ **espitar**

2 *to tap a rubber tree,* to cut a ring round the stem of the tree so that the sap flows down and drips from a small spout. □ **sangrar un árbol**

3 to attach a secret listening device to (a telephone): *my phone's been tapped.* □ **pinchar**

4 to start to exploit (something new): *Canada's reserves of coal have hardly been tapped yet; we're aiming to tap new markets with this product.* □ **explotar (reservas); abrir (nuevos mercados)**

5 to hit lightly: *he tapped twice on the door; to tap your feet in time to the music; music which sets your feet tapping.* □ **golpear suavemente**

tap dance *n.* dance done by beating time to the music with metal-soled shoes. □ **zapateado**

tap dancer *n.* dancer who specializes in tap dancing. □ **bailarín (de zapateado)**

tap dancing *n.* dancing with special shoes with metal soles, so that the dancer beats time to the music. □ **zapateado**

tapping *n.* action of opening new sources of power/of running liquid out of a container/of listening to telephone conversations/of hitting something lightly: *the tapping of a barrel/of new sources of energy; phone tapping,* listening secretly to telephone conversations through a device attached to the line. □ **espitaje de un barril; explotación de una nueva fuente de energía**

tap root *n.* main root (of a tree) which goes straight down into the soil. □ **raíz primaria**

tape [teip] *n.* **1** long thin flat strip (of cloth/plastic, etc.). □ **cinta**

insulating tape, sticky tape for wrapping round electrical connections. □ **cinta aislante**

magnetic tape, sensitive plastic tape for recording: *to record a piece of music on tape.* □ **cinta (magnetofónica)**

measuring tape, long strip marked in centimetres/inches, etc. for measuring. □ **cinta métrica**

sticky tape, glued plastic strip for sticking pieces of paper together, etc. □ **cinta adhesiva**

2 long string held across the finishing line of a race. □ **cinta**

■ *v.* **1** to attach with a tape: *I've taped up the parcel.* □ **atar con cinta**

2 to record (something) on magnetic tape: *he taped the concert last night.* □ **grabar**

3 ***to have someone taped:*** *I've got him taped,* (*informal*) I know exactly what he's like/I understand him completely. □ **le tengo calado**

4 ***we've got it all taped,*** everything is under control/we know how to do it perfectly. □ **lo tenemos todo bien organizado**

tape deck *n.* apparatus which plays tape and records on tape, but does not have its own amplifier or loudspeakers. □ **pletina/platina**

tape measure *n.* long strip of cloth/metal marked in centimetres/inches, etc., used for measuring. □ **cinta métrica**

tape-record *v.* to record (something) on tape: *I've tape-recorded the concert.* □ **grabar**

tape-recorder *n.* apparatus which records on tape and plays back these tapes. □ **grabadora**

tapeworm *n.* long flatworm which lives in the intestines of man and other animals. □ **tenia; solitaria**

taper ['teipə] *n.* long thin candle, made of a wick covered with a thin layer of wax. □ **vela**

■ *v.* to make (something) become thinner at the end; to become thinner at the end: *the stick tapers off to a point.* □ **estrecharse**

tapestry ['tæpistri] *n.* (*pl. tapestries*) thick woven cloth with a picture or design, usually hung on walls or used to cover chairs. □ **tapiz**

tapioca [tæpi'oukə] *n.* white starchy powder which comes from a tropical plant and is used to make puddings. □ **tapioca**

tapir ['teipə] *n.* South American animal like a pig with a short trunk. □ **tapir**

tappet ['tæpit] *n.* small projecting piece which opens or closes a valve by tapping on it. □ **alzaválvulas**

tar [tɑː] *n.* black oily substance which comes from

coal and is used for covering roads: *tar sprayer.* □ **alquitrán**
■ *v.* (*he tarred*) to cover with tar: *tarred roads.* □ **alquitranar**
tarred paper, thick brown waterproof paper with an inner layer of tar. □ **papel alquitranado**
to tar and feather someone, to cover someone with hot tar and feathers as a punishment. □ **emplumar**
to be tarred with the same brush, to have the same weaknesses/to make the same mistakes (as someone). □ **estar cortados por el mismo patrón**

tarantula [tæ'ræntjulə] *n.* large mildly poisonous tropical spider. □ **tarántula**

tardy ['tɑːdi] *adj.* (*tardier, tardiest*) (*formal*) late. □ **tardío**

tare [tεə] *n.* **1** allowance made for the weight of the lorry, etc., in calculating transport costs. □ **tara**
2 weed. □ **vicia**

target ['tɑːgit] *n.* something which you aim at: *to hit the target; we have set ourselves a target of $600; the Prime Minister is a marvellous target for cartoonists.* □ **blanco; objetivo**
target language, language which you are learning/ into which you are translating. □ **lengua objeto de estudio/traducción**
target practice, practising at shooting at a target. □ **tiro al blanco**

tariff ['tærif] *n.* **1** tax to be paid for importing goods: *to lift tariff barriers,* to reduce import taxes. □ **arancel**
2 list of prices (in a restaurant/hotel/bar, etc.). □ **lista de precios**

tarmac ['tɑːmæk] *n.* **1** trademark for a hard surface of a road made of tar mixed with small stones. □ **alquitranado**
2 runway of an airport. □ **pista de aterrizaje**
tarmacked *adj.* covered with tarmac. □ **alquitranado**

tarn [tɑːn] *n.* small lake in mountains. □ **laguna**

tarnish ['tɑːniʃ] *v.* (*of metal*) to become discoloured; to ruin: *the silver has become tarnished; the scandal tarnished his reputation.* □ **perder su brillo (metal); empañar (reputación)**

tarot ['tærou] *n.* set of cards specially designed for use in telling fortunes. □ **tarot**

tarpaulin [tɑː'pɔːlin] *n.* large waterproof cloth. □ **lona alquitranada**

tarragon ['tærəgən] *n.* common herb used in cooking. □ **estragón**

tarry ['tæri] *v.* (*he tarried*) to stay behind. □ **quedarse atrás**

tarsus ['tɑːsəs] *n.* set of bones in the ankle. □ **tarso**

tart [tɑːt] *n.* **1** small pastry dish filled with sweet food: *jam tart; apple tart.* □ **pastelillo**
2 (*slang*) prostitute. □ **fulana**
■ *adj.* **1** bitter (taste). □ **ácido**
2 sharp (answer). □ **respuesta cáustica**
■ *v.* ***to tart yourself up,*** (*informal*) to make yourself look very smart. □ **acicalarse**
tartly *adv.* sharply. □ **ásperamente**
tartness *n.* sourness (of taste). □ **acidez**

tartan ['tɑːtən] *n.* and *adj.* (cloth) woven into a special pattern for one of the Scottish clans; distinctive pattern in such a cloth: *the MacDonald tartan; a tartan skirt.* □ **tartán**

tartar ['tɑːtə] *n.* **1** hard substance which forms on teeth. □ **sarro**
2 ***cream of tartar,*** white powder used in cooking and in medicine. □ **crémor tártaro**
3 (*informal*) fierce person. □ **arpía**

tartare sauce [tɑːtɑː'sɔːs] *n.* mayonnaise containing finely chopped pieces of vegetables. □ **salsa tártara**

task [tɑːsk] *n.* **1** work which has to be done: *to set someone a task; to carry out a task.* □ **tarea**
2 ***to take someone to task*** *for doing something,* to criticize someone. □ **llamar a uno a capítulo**
task force *n.* special group (especially of soldiers) chosen to carry out a hard task. □ **fuerza de choque**
taskmaster *n.* person who sets a hard task. □ **capataz**

tassel ['tæsl] *n.* group of threads tied together at one end to form a ball, with the other ends hanging free. □ **borla**
tasselled *adj.* with tassels. □ **adornado con borlas**

taste [teist] *n.* **1** sense by which you can tell differences of flavour between things you eat. □ **gusto**
taste buds, cells on the tongue which enable you to tell differences in flavour. □ **papilas del gusto**
2 flavour of food or drink: *it has a taste of onions; this ice cream has no taste at all.* □ **sabor**
3 very small quantity (of food/drink): *I'll just have a taste of cheese.* □ **pizca**
4 *he's had a taste of prison,* he has been in prison once. □ **ya ha tenido una experiencia en la cárcel**
5 liking (for something): *he has an expensive taste in cars,* he likes expensive cars. □ **tiene un gusto caro**
6 *good/bad taste,* ability/inability to judge what is fine/beautiful/refined: *he has an appalling taste in socks; she has a fine taste for music; it's very bad taste to refer so rudely to her mother who has just died.* □ **gusto**
■ *v.* **1** to sense the flavour of (something): *can you taste the garlic in this soup?* □ **notar**
2 to have a flavour: *this soup tastes of garlic; sea water tastes salty.* □ **saber**
3 to try (something): *have you tasted the new wine? would you like to taste this cake?* □ **probar**
4 *the zoo animals have never tasted freedom,* have never experienced freedom. □ **probar**
tasteful *adj.* showing good taste: *tasteful flower decorations.* □ **de buen gusto**
tastefully *adv.* in good taste: *the room is tastefully decorated in pink and white.* □ **con buen gusto**
tasteless *adj.* **1** with no particular flavour: *the ice cream is quite tasteless.* □ **insípido**
2 showing bad taste: *tasteless furniture.* □ **de mal gusto**
taster *n.* person whose job is to taste food to test its quality: *a tea-taster.* □ **catador**
tasty *adj.* (*tastier, tastiest*) with a particular pleasant flavour: *a tasty meal.* □ **sabroso**

tat [tæt] *n.* (*no pl.*) (*informal*) untidiness; shabby/ cheap things. *see also* **tit.** □ **basuras**

ta-ta [tə'tɑː] *interjection* (*informal*) goodbye. □ **hasta luego; ¡chao!**

tatters ['tætəz] *n.* ***in tatters,*** (i) torn (clothes). □ **en harapos**
(ii) (person) wearing old torn clothes. □ **andrajoso**
tattered ['tætəd] *adj.* torn and old. □ **andrajoso**

tatting ['tætiŋ] *n.* type of lace made by hand. □ **(trabajo de) encaje**

tattle ['tætl] *v.* (*formal*) to gossip. □ **chismorrear**

tattoo [tə'tuː] *n.* **1** military parade in the evening. □ **desfile**
2 rapid beating (of drums): *to beat a tattoo.* □ **tamborileo**
3 decoration on your skin made by pricking it with a needle and putting colour into the wound: *he had a tattoo of an anchor on his arm.* □ **tatuaje**
■ *v.* to make decorations on someone's skin by

pricking it and putting colour into the wound: *he had an anchor tattooed on his arm.* □ **tatuar**

tatty ['tæti] *adj.* (*tattier, tattiest*) untidy/not well looked after/shabby. □ **desaseado**

taught [tɔ:t] *v. see* **teach.**

taunt [tɔ:nt] *n.* sarcastic jeering: *he had to suffer the taunts of the other children.* □ **mofa; pulla**

■ *v.* to jeer at (someone) sarcastically: *they taunted him with his stutter.* □ **mofarse de**

Taurus ['tɔ:rəs] *n.* one of the signs of the zodiac, shaped like a bull. □ **Tauro**

taut [tɔ:t] *adj.* stretched tight: *to pull a rope taut.* □ **tenso; tirante**

tauten *v.* to make tight; to become tight: *the rope tautened.* □ **tensar**

tautology [tɔ:'tɔlədʒi] *n.* unnecessary use in a phrase of different words which mean the same thing. □ **tautología**

tautological *adj.* using tautology. □ **tautológico**

tavern ['tævən] *n.* inn/public house. □ **posada/taberna (bar)**

tawdry ['tɔ:dri] *adj.* cheap and in bad taste. □ **de oropel**

tawny ['tɔ:ni] *adj.* orange brown. □ **rojizo oscuro**

tax [tæks] *n.* (*pl. taxes*) **1** money taken by the state from incomes/sales, etc., which pays for government services: *income tax; sales tax; there is a 10% tax on petrol; his income is tax free,* he does not have to pay any tax on it. □ **impuesto**

2 burden: *it's a severe tax on our resources,* it strains our resources. □ **carga**

■ *v.* **1** to put a tax on (something/someone): *incomes are taxed at 35%; the company is taxed on its profits.* □ **gravar**

2 to strain: *it will tax our resources to feed sixty people.* □ **exigir un esfuerzo excesivo a**

3 (*formal*) to accuse: *I taxed him with being late.* □ **acusar**

taxable *adj.* which can be taxed: *taxable income.* □ **renta imponible**

taxation [tæk'seiʃn] *n.* **1** (system of) imposing taxes: *our taxation is the highest in Europe.* □ **impuestos**

2 money raised from taxes: *the government has promised to reduce taxation.* □ **impuestos**

taxman *n.* (*pl. taxmen*) (*informal*) civil servant who deals with tax (usually income tax). □ **funcionario de Hacienda**

taxpayer *n.* person who pays taxes. □ **contribuyente**

taxi ['tæksi] *n.* (*also* ***taxicab***) car which can be hired: *he called a taxi; they took a taxi to the station.* □ **taxi**

taxi rank, place marked in the street where taxis can wait. □ **parada de taxis**

■ *v.* (*of an aircraft*) to go along the ground before take-off or after landing: *the plane taxied to a stop.* □ **rodar por la pista**

taximeter *n.* machine fitted inside a taxi which shows the price for the journey. □ **taxímetro**

taxidermy ['tæksidə:mi] *n.* art of stuffing the skins of dead animals so that they look lifelike. □ **taxidermia**

taxidermist *n.* person who stuffs the skins of dead animals so that they look lifelike. □ **taxidermista**

taxonomy [tæk'sɔnəmi] *n.* scientific classification (especially of plants and animals). □ **taxonomía**

TB ['ti:'bi:] *abbreviation for* tuberculosis. □ **tuberculosis**

tea [ti:] *n.* **1** dried leaves of a tropical plant which are used to make a common drink: *he bought a pound of tea; put two spoonfuls of tea into the pot.* □ **té**

2 drink made by pouring boiling water on to dried leaves of the tea plant: *a cup of tea; would you like some more tea?* □ **té**

3 any hot drink made in a similar way. □ **infusión**

lime tea, made with the dried flowers of the lime tree. □ **té de lima**

4 afternoon meal: *what are we having for tea? I invited Mrs Smith round for tea.* □ **merienda**

tea service/tea set, plates/cups/saucers, etc., used at tea. □ **juego de té**

high tea, large meal eaten in the early evening in the North of England and Scotland. □ **merienda-cena**

teabag *n.* small paper bag full of tea which is put into the pot instead of loose tea. □ **bolsita de té**

tea break *n.* rest period at work, when you can drink tea. □ **descanso para el té**

teacake *n.* type of bun with raisins in it, usually eaten hot with butter. □ **bollito**

tea-chest *n.* light wooden packing case in which tea is shipped. □ **caja para el té**

teacloth *n.* cloth for drying dishes. □ **paño de cocina**

tea cosy *n.* cover for putting over a teapot to keep it warm. □ **cubretetera**

teacup *n.* large cup for tea. □ **taza de té**

tealeaf *n.* (*pl. tealeaves*) small piece of tea left in the cup after you have drunk the tea. □ **poso**

tea party *n.* party (held in the afternoon or early evening) when you drink tea, eat cakes, etc. □ **fiesta**

teapot *n.* special pot with a handle and spout for making tea in. □ **tetera**

tearoom, teashop *n.* small restaurant which serves mainly tea and light meals. □ **salón de té**

teaspoon *n.* small spoon for stirring tea. □ **cucharilla**

teaspoonful *n.* quantity contained in a teaspoon: *add a teaspoonful of mustard to the sauce.* □ **cucharadita**

teatime *n.* time when you have tea (about 4 o'clock in the afternoon). □ **hora del té**

tea towel *n.* cloth for drying dishes. □ **trapo de cocina**

tea trolley *n.* small table on wheels from which you can serve food. □ **carrito del té**

teach [ti:tʃ] *v.* (*he taught*) **1** to give (someone) information; to give lessons (in a school); to show (someone) how to do something: *he taught me maths; she teaches handicapped children how to swim; he taught himself Greek,* he learnt Greek by himself without a teacher. □ **enseñar**

2 *she wants to teach,* to take up a career as a teacher. □ **quiere dedicarse a la enseñanza**

3 *that'll teach him to be so rude,* (*informal*) he is being punished for being rude. □ **eso le enseñará a...**

teacher *n.* person who teaches: *a music teacher.* □ **profesor**

teach-in *n.* (*informal*) informal discussion on a topic. □ **seminario**

teaching *n.* **1** action of giving knowledge/giving lessons: *the teaching profession,* teachers as a group; *he's going in for teaching,* he's going to be a teacher. □ **enseñanza; docencia**

2 political or moral ideas/philosophy: *according to the teachings of Marx.* □ **enseñanzas**

teak [ti:k] *n.* large tropical tree; hard tropical wood which does not warp, and is used for making furniture, etc. □ **teca; madera de teca**

teal [ti:l] *n.* small type of wild duck. □ **cerceta**

team [ti:m] *n.* **1** group of people playing together/working together: *football team; we have a small design team working on the project.* □ **equipo**

team spirit, good feeling of those who play or work well together as a team. □ **espíritu de equipo**
2 group of animals working together: *team of horses; a dog team pulling a sledge.* □ **tiro de caballos/perros; yunta de bueyes**
■ *v.* ***to team up with someone,*** to join someone to work together: *three of us have teamed up to open a bookshop.* □ **asociarse**
teamster *n. Amer.* lorry driver. □ **camionero**
teamwork *n.* ability to work together as a group; working together as a group. □ **trabajo en equipo**

tear¹ ['tiə] *n.* **1** drop of water formed in the eyes when you cry: *tears ran down her cheeks.* □ **lágrima**
2 ***to burst into tears:*** *he burst into tears when he heard the news,* suddenly started to cry. □ **echarse a llorar**
3 *she ran out of the office* ***in tears,*** crying. □ **...llorando**
tearful *adj.* sad/crying: *she waved a tearful farewell.* □ **lloroso**
tearfully *adv.* sadly/crying: *he tearfully waved goodbye.* □ **llorando**
tear-gas *n.* gas which makes you cry, used to control crowds of rioters. □ **gas lacrimógeno**
tear-stained *adj.* (face) with the marks of tears. □ **manchado de lágrimas**

tear² ['tɛə] *n.* **1** hole torn in a piece of cloth: *I have a tear in my trousers.* □ **roto; desgarrón**
2 ***wear and tear,*** normal usage (of a house/car, etc.) which wears something away: *you have to pay for the wear and tear of the car which you've hired; he couldn't stand the wear and tear of life in the city.* □ **desgaste**
■ *v.* (*he tore: he has torn*) **1** to make a hole in (something) by pulling: *he tore his trousers on the barbed wire; I've torn a button off my coat.* □ **romper**
2 *this cloth tears easily,* it can easily have holes made in it by pulling. □ **...se rasga con facilidad**
3 *we were torn between staying at home and going to the theatre,* we couldn't decide which to do. □ **estábamos indecisos...**
4 *he was tearing his hair in exasperation,* pulling his hair out. □ **se tiraba de los pelos...**
5 ***that's torn it,*** (*informal*) that has ruined what we were planning/that has spoilt everything. □ **se lo ha cargado**
6 to pull to pieces: *I tore up the letter; the policeman tore down the poster; to tear a page out of a book; they tore down the old houses; they tore up the road,* dug up the road surface. □ **romper (carta, cartel, página); derribar (casa)**
7 *he can't tear himself away from the television,* he won't leave the television. □ **no puede despegarse de...**
8 (*informal*) to go fast: *he tore along the passage; the car tore across the traffic lights; she tore down the road on her motorbike.* □ **ir a toda velocidad**
tearaway *n.* wild young hooligan. □ **macarra**

tease [ti:z] *n.* person who annoys/irritates people on purpose. □ **bromista**
■ *v.* **1** to annoy (someone)/to irritate (someone) on purpose: *he teases all the girls; they teased him about his big ears.* □ **fastidiar**
2 to disentangle threads (with a comb); to brush (cloth) to make it soft. □ **cardar**
teaser *n.* (*informal*) problem which is difficult to solve/question which is difficult to answer. □ **rompecabezas**

teasel ['ti:zl] *n.* tall plant with prickly flower heads. □ **cardencha**

teat [ti:t] *n.* **1** projection on a cow's udder through which milk passes. □ **teta**
2 rubber cap put on a baby's feeding bottle through which the baby sucks milk. □ **tetina**

technical ['teknikl] *adj.* **1** referring to a particular industry/practical work, etc. □ **técnico**
a technical term, term used by specialists. □ **un término técnico**
technical subjects, subjects which teach practical skills (such as woodwork, engineering, etc.). □ **temas técnicos**
technical training, training in a practical skill. □ **formación técnica**
2 referring to a fixed interpretation of the rules: *the champion was beaten on a technical knockout,* the referee stopped the fight because the champion was too hurt to continue. □ **técnico**
technically *adv.* **1** in a technical way: *this machine is technically advanced.* □ **técnicamente**
2 strictly speaking: *technically, I'm supposed to be at work, but I've taken the day off.* □ **en teoría**
technicality [tekni'kæliti] *n.* **1** technical detail: *he spent hours explaining the technicalities of the new engine.* □ **cosa técnica**
2 strict interpretation of rules/of laws: *he was found guilty on a technicality.* □ **punto técnico**
technician [tek'niʃn] *n.* person who is specialized in industrial or scientific work: *a laboratory technician; the technicians are trying to repair the aircraft.* □ **técnico**
technique [tek'ni:k] *n.* skilled way of doing something: *the peasants were learning new techniques of farming/new farming techniques; his technique is to look away when it is his turn to buy a round of drinks.* □ **técnica**
technocrat ['teknəkræt] *n.* person with particular technical/organizational skills, brought in to run a country/an organization. □ **tecnócrata**
technology [tek'nɔlədʒi] *n.* (*pl. technologies*) knowledge/study of new industrial or scientific skills: *modern technology has made life easier for most people.* □ **tecnología**
technological [teknə'lɔdʒikl] *adj.* referring to technology: *a supersonic aircraft is a great technological achievement.* □ **tecnológico**

teddy (bear) ['tedi ('bɛə)] *n.* (*pl. teddies*) child's toy bear. □ **osito de peluche**

tedious ['ti:diəs] *adj.* boring. □ **tedioso**
tediously *adv.* in a boring way. □ **aburridamente**
tediousness, tedium ['ti:diəm] *n.* boredom/being boring: *he sang to relieve the tedium of the long wait.* □ **tedio**

tee [ti:] *n.* spot on a golf course where the ball is placed before you hit it. □ **'tee'**
■ *v.* ***to tee off,*** to hit the ball from a tee. □ **golpear desde el 'tee'**

teem [ti:m] *v.* **1** to be full of/covered with something: *the place is teeming with ants/with policemen; the teeming crowds.* □ **pulular; atestado de gente**
2 *it's teeming down,* (*informal*) it's pouring down (with rain). □ **llueve a placer**

teens [ti:nz] *n. pl.* age between 13 and 19: *she's in her teens.* □ **quinceañeros**
teenage ['ti:neidʒ] *adj.* adolescent; referring to someone aged between 13 and 19: *a teenage murderer.* □ **adolescente**
teenager *n.* person aged between 13 and 19. □ **joven; adolescente**

teeny(-weeny) ['ti:ni'(wi:ni)] *adj.* (*informal*) very small. □ **chiquitito**

tee-shirt ['ti:ʃə:t] *n.* light cotton shirt with no buttons or collar and short sleeves. □ **camiseta**

teeter ['tiːtə] *v.* to wobble: *to teeter on the edge of a precipice.* □ **balancearse**
teeter-totter *n. Amer.* seesaw/toy made of a plank with seats at each end, and balanced in the middle so that when one end goes up the other goes down. □ **balancín**
teeth [tiːθ] *n. see* **tooth.**
teethe [tiːð] *v.* to grow your first teeth: *the baby is crying because she's teething.* □ **echar los dientes**
teething troubles *n.* problems which develop when a baby grows its first teeth/when anything is in its first stages: *we've had some teething troubles with the new machinery.* □ **problemas de dentición/rodaje**
teetotal [tiː'toutl] *adj.* **1** (person) who never drinks any alcohol. □ **abstemio**
2 *a strictly teetotal party,* where no alcohol is served. □ **una fiesta sin alcohol**
teetotaller *n.* person who never drinks any alcohol. □ **abstemio**
tele- ['teli] *prefix meaning* over a distance. □ **tele-**
telecast ['telikɑːst] *n.* TV broadcast. □ **transmisión deportiva**
telecommunications [telikəmjuːni'keiʃnz] *n. pl.* system of passing messages over a great distance (such as telephone/radio, etc.). □ **telecomunicaciones**
telegram ['teligræm] *n.* message sent by telegraph: *there were two telegrams on his desk.* □ **telegrama**
telegraph ['teligrɑːf] *n.* system of sending messages along wires. □ **telegrafía**
telegraph line, the wire along which telegraph messages are sent. □ **línea telegráfica**
telegraph pole, pole which holds up a telegraph line. □ **poste telegráfico**
bush telegraph, (*informal*) passing information by gossip. □ **radio macuto**
■ *v.* to send (a message) along wires: *he telegraphed to say he was ill.* □ **telegrafiar**
telegrapher [tə'legrəfə] *n.* person who sends messages by telegraph. □ **telegrafista**
telegraphic [teli'græfik] *adj.* referring to telegraph. □ **telegráfico**
telegraphic address, short form of an address used on telegrams. □ **dirección telegráfica**
telegraphist [tə'legrəfist] *n.* person who sends messages by telegraph. □ **telegrafista**
telegraphy *n.* sending messages by telegraph. □ **telegrafía**
telepathy [tə'lepəθi] *n.* sending feelings/sympathy/mental images from one person to another without the use of the senses. □ **telepatía**
telepathic [teli'pæθik] *adj.* referring to telepathy: *a telepathic communication.* □ **telepático**
telephone ['telifoun] *n.* device/system for speaking to someone over a distance using electric current running along wires, or by radio: *he lifted the telephone and dialled 999; she's on the telephone all day,* speaking into the telephone; *I tried to contact you by telephone; they're not on the telephone,* they haven't got a telephone; *what's his telephone number?; telephone directory.* □ **teléfono**
telephone box, outdoor booth with a public telephone in it. □ **cabina telefónica**
■ *v.* to speak to (someone) by telephone: *have you telephoned the police? how much does it cost to telephone Canada?* □ **llamar por teléfono**
telephonic [teli'fɔnik] *adj.* referring to the telephone. □ **telefónico**
telephonist [tə'lefənist] *n.* person who connects telephone calls in a central exchange. □ **telefonista**
telephoto lens [teli'foutou'lenz] *n.* lens for a camera which gives a large picture of something which is at a distance. □ **teleobjetivo**
teleprinter ['teliprintə] *n.* apparatus like a typewriter which sends out and receives messages by telegraph, and which prints them when they are received. □ **teletipo**
telescope ['teliskoup] *n.* tube with a series of lenses for looking at very distant objects: *he looked at the moon through a powerful telescope.* □ **telescopio**
radio telescope, apparatus which detects radio signals from stars and follows their movements. □ **radiotelescopio**
■ *v.* to push together, so that one piece slides into another; to crush together: *the first two coaches of the train were telescoped together.* □ **hacer encastrar**
telescopic [teli'skɔpik] *adj.* **1** referring to a telescope: *telescopic sights (of a rifle).* □ **telescópico**
2 which slide together like a telescope: *a stand with telescopic legs.* □ **telescópico**
teletypewriter [teli'taipraitə] *n. Amer.* teleprinter. □ **teleimpresora**
television [teli'viʒn] *n.* system for sending pictures by radio waves: *they're linked up by television; I saw the film on television; we've bought a colour television; he watches television every night.* □ **televisión**
television (set), apparatus for showing pictures sent by radio waves. □ **televisor**
televise ['telivaiz] *v.* to broadcast (something) by television: *the show is televised in colour; the boxing match is being televised live,* shown direct/not recorded and broadcast later. □ **televisar**
telex ['teleks] *n.* (*pl. telexes*) system of sending messages by teleprinter; message sent by teleprinter: *this telex has just come in; can you send a telex reminding them about their order?* □ **télex**
■ *v.* to send a message to (someone), using the teleprinter: *he telexed his office.* □ **poner un télex**
tell [tel] *v.* (*he told*) **1** to say: *is he telling the truth?* □ **decir**
2 to pass on information: *they told me what had happened; she told him a long story; he told her about his family; tell me when it's time to start.* □ **contar**
3 to give instructions: *I told him not to touch the wet paint; can you tell me how to get to the post office? he told the audience to sit down.* □ **decir**
4 to make out the difference between two things; to notice a quality: *you can't tell her from her twin sister; you can tell he's annoyed by the way his ears go red.* □ **distinguir**
5 to have an effect: *his age told in the end,* finally he lost because he was older than the other competitors. □ **tener efecto**
6 to count (money/votes). □ **contar**
all told, altogether: *there are ten of them all told.* □ **...en total**
teller ['telə] *n.* person who counts votes; clerk in a bank who counts money and pays it out to customers. □ **escrutador; cajero (en un banco)**
telling *adj.* which has an effect: *a telling blow; a telling statement.* □ **contundente**
tell off *v.* (*informal*) to reprimand/to criticize (someone): *I got told off for walking on the grass.* □ **echar una bronca**
tell on *v.* ***to tell on someone,*** (*informal*) to let out a secret about someone: *someone must have told on us.* □ **dar un chivatazo**
telltale *n.* person who gives away a secret. □ **soplón**
■ *adj.* something which gives away a secret: *telltale signs of a fatal illness.* □ **revelador**
telly ['teli] *n.* (*informal*) television: *I saw it on the telly; switch off the telly.* □ **tele**

temerity [tə'meriti] *n.* audacity; daring to do something. □ **temeridad**

temp [temp] *n.* (*informal*) *short for* temporary secretary. □ **'secre' por horas**

temper ['tempə] *n.* **1** usually calm state of mind. □ **temple**
to lose one's temper: *he lost his temper,* he became very angry. □ **perdió la paciencia**
to keep one's temper: *she kept her temper,* she stayed calm and did not get angry. □ **no se alteró; se contuvo**
2 state of mind: *he's in a bad temper/a vile temper; she's in a good temper just now.* □ **está de buen/mal humor**
3 fit of anger: *he's in a temper; she flew into a temper.* □ **se puso de mal genio**
4 hardness of a metal due to heating: *the temper of steel.* □ **temple**
■ *v.* **1** to harden (steel). □ **templar**
2 to moderate/to make less strong: *to temper a passion.* □ **templar**

tempera ['tempərə] *n.* type of thick paint which can be diluted with water. □ **pintura al temple**

temperament ['temprəmənt] *n.* state of mind; nature of a person. □ **temperamento**
temperamental [temprə'mentl] *adj.* (person) likely to change his state of mind frequently; likely to get easily excited or depressed: *she's very temperamental.* □ **temperamental**

temperance ['temprəns] *n.* **1** being moderate/controlled. □ **templanza**
2 not drinking alcohol. □ **abstinencia**
the temperance movement, group of people who try to persuade others not to drink alcohol. □ **campaña antialcohólica**

temperate ['temprət] *adj.* moderate/sober (language/habits). □ **moderado**
temperate climate, neither extremely hot nor cold. □ **clima templado**

temperature ['temprətʃə] *n.* **1** amount of heat measured in degrees: *what is the temperature of boiling water? the temperature outside was −20° Celsius.* □ **temperatura**
2 state where the temperature of the body is higher than it should be: *she has a temperature; she's in bed with a temperature.* □ **fiebre**

tempest ['tempist] *n.* storm. □ **tempestad**
tempestuous [tem'pestjuəs] *adj.* **1** violently stormy/very wild: *tempestuous waves; a tempestuous meeting.* □ **tempestuoso**
2 *tempestuous applause,* very enthusiastic applause. □ **aplauso cerrado**

template ['templeit] *n.* thin sheet, used as a pattern for cutting pieces of wood/metal, etc., to an exact shape. □ **plantilla**

temple ['templ] *n.* **1** flat part of the front of the head on each side of the forehead. □ **sien**
2 building for worship (not usually Christian or Muslim). □ **templo**

tempo ['tempou] *n.* (*pl. tempos/tempi*) rhythm; beat (of music, etc.): *the regular tempo of the band; the tempo of modern life.* □ **tempo**

temporal ['temprəl] *adj.* **1** referring to the temple/the flat part of the side of the head near the forehead. □ **temporal**
2 referring to this world/not eternal/not spiritual. □ **temporal**
3 referring to time. □ **temporal**
temporal clause, clause relating to time. □ **oración temporal**

temporary ['temprəri] *adj.* which only lasts a short time/which is meant to last a short time: *a temporary improvement; a temporary post as lecturer.* □ **transitoria (mejoría); interino (trabajo)**
temporarily ['temprərəli] *adv.* for a short time: *we are temporarily out of stock of sugar.* □ **temporalmente**

temporize *v.* to try to gain time: *he was asked to appear in court but he temporized.* □ **tratar de ganar tiempo**

tempt [temt] *v.* **1** to attract (someone); to try to persuade (someone) to do something: *a tempting plate of sweets; a tempting smell; he was tempted by the bribe.* □ **tentar**
2 *I am tempted to accept,* I think I will accept. □ **estoy tentado de...**
3 *to tempt providence,* to take a great risk. □ **tentar a Dios**
temptation [tem'teiʃn] *n.* state of being tempted; thing which attracts you: *she fell victim to temptation; the temptation to kick him is very strong; not many people can resist the temptation of money.* □ **tentación**
tempter, temptress *n.* person who tempts. □ **tentador**
tempting *adj.* attractive: *a tempting offer.* □ **tentador**

ten [ten] *n.* number 10: *she is ten (years old); come and see me at ten (o'clock); ten to one,* ten minutes before one o'clock. □ **diez**
ten to one *he finds out,* (*informal*) I bet you he will find out/he's very likely to find out. □ **te apuesto lo que quieras que...**

tenable ['tenəbl] *adj.* **1** which can be held. □ **sostenible**
2 *his theory isn't tenable,* cannot be supported. □ **...defendible**

tenacious [ti'neiʃəs] *adj.* which holds on to something tightly; obstinate; determined. □ **tenaz**
tenacity [tə'næsiti] *n.* holding to something too tightly. □ **tenacidad**

tenant ['tenənt] *n.* person who rents a room/flat/house/land, etc., from someone: *to buy a house with a sitting tenant,* with someone living in it and paying rent. □ **inquilino**
tenancy *n.* period during which a tenant rents a property. □ **inquilinato**

tench [tentʃ] *n.* (*pl. tench*) type of small fish. □ **tenca**

tend [tend] *v.* **1** to look after: *to tend the sick; to tend the flowers.* □ **atender**
2 to be likely (to do something): *noise tends to make him angry; he tends to forget what he has just said; this paper tends to go yellow.* □ **tender**
3 to lean (in a certain direction): *he tends towards the view that an election will be held in the autumn.* □ **inclinarse**
tendency *n.* being likely to do something: *men in his family have a tendency to go bald.* □ **tendencia**
tendentious [ten'denʃəs] *adj.* (book/article/speech) which puts over a strong point of view which is not generally approved. □ **tendencioso**

tender ['tendə] *n.* **1** boat which brings supplies to a large ship; wagon carrying coal behind a coal-burning locomotive. □ **bote de servicio; ténder (vagón)**
2 offer to do work at a certain price: *we are asking for tenders to paint the outside of the town hall.* □ **oferta**
3 ***legal tender,*** coins/notes which are legally acceptable when offered in payment. □ **de curso legal**
■ *adj.* **1** soft/delicate. □ **frágil**

tender meat, which can be chewed/cut easily. □ **carne tierna**
2 *tender plants*, which cannot stand frost. □ **plantas sensibles (al frío)**
3 *child of tender years*, very young child. □ **niño de tierna edad**
4 *with a tender heart*, very affectionate/very loving. □ **...un corazón sensible**
5 painful: *the swelling is tender to the touch*. □ **sensible**
6 *you've touched him on* ***a tender spot***, (*informal*) you have mentioned something which he is very touchy about. □ **...un tema muy espinoso**
■ *v.* 1 (*formal*) to offer: *please tender the correct fare; I wish to tender my resignation*. □ **presentar**
2 to offer to do work at a certain price: *two firms have tendered for the job of painting the town hall*. □ **ofertar**
tenderhearted *adj.* kind. □ **tierno de corazón**
tenderize *v.* to make (meat) tender. □ **ablandar**
tenderly *adv.* gently; with kindness. □ **con ternura**
tenderloin ['tendəlɔin] *n.* piece of tender beef or pork from the side of the backbone. □ **filete**
tenderness *n.* being tender. □ **ternura**
tendon ['tendən] *n.* strong cord of tissue attaching a muscle to a bone. □ **tendón**
tendril ['tendrəl] *n.* thin curling part with which a plant clings to a support. □ **zarcillo**
tenement ['tenəmənt] *n.* 1 large (often dilapidated) building which is divided into flats. □ **casa de pisos**
2 (*in Scotland*) building which is rented as flats. □ **casa de pisos alquilados**
tenet ['tenet] *n.* basic principle/belief. □ **principio**
tenfold ['tenfould] *adv.* ten times as much: *the profits have increased tenfold*. □ **diez veces**
tenner ['tenə] *n.* (*informal*) ten pound note. □ **billete de diez libras**
tennis ['tenis] *n.* game for two players or two pairs of players who use rackets to hit a ball backwards and forwards over a net: *tennis ball; tennis tournament*. □ **tenis**
tennis court, specially marked ground for playing tennis. □ **pista de tenis**
tennis elbow, painful condition of the elbow joint caused by strain. □ **sinovitis del codo**
tenon ['tenən] *n.* small projection from the end of a piece of wood which fits into a corresponding hole in another piece to form a joint. □ **espiga**
tenor ['tenə] *n.* 1 man who sings with the highest normal male voice: *an operatic tenor*. □ **tenor**
2 highest male voice; musical instrument with a high pitch: *a tenor saxophone*. □ **tenor**
3 (*formal*) general meaning: *what's the tenor of his letter?* □ **tenor**
4 (*formal*) general way: *the even tenor of life in the village*. □ **curso**
tense [tens] *n.* form of a verb which shows when the action takes place: *the past tense of 'to go' is 'went'; in English the future tense is formed with the word 'will'*. □ **tiempo**
■ *adj.* 1 stretched tight. □ **tenso**
2 nervous and anxious: *a tense moment; I was tense before the interview*. □ **tenso**
■ *v.* to make/to become tense. □ **tensar**
tensely *adv.* in a tense way. □ **con tensión**
tenseness *n.* being tense. □ **tirantez; tensión**
tensile ['tensail] *adj.* referring to tension. □ **extensible, tensor**
tensile strength, force needed to stretch something until it breaks. □ **resistencia a la tensión**
tension ['tenʃn] *n.* 1 tightness; being stretched; (*in knitting*) tightness of the stitches calculated on the number of stitches or rows per centimetre. □ **tensión**
2 nervous anxiety: *tension along the border between the two states; there is tension between the two sisters*, a strained relationship. □ **tensión**
3 electric power: *high-tension cables*. □ **tensión**
tent [tent] *n.* small canvas shelter held up by poles and attached to the ground with pegs and ropes. □ **tienda de campaña**
to pitch a tent, to put up a tent. □ **montar una tienda**
oxygen tent, shelter put up over a sick person's bed to allow oxygen to be pumped in. □ **tienda de oxígeno**
tentacle ['tentəkl] *n.* long arm with suckers (such as that of an octopus). □ **tentáculo**
tentative ['tentətiv] *adj.* uncertain; done as a trial: *a tentative proposal*, made to find out what the response is. □ **de tanteo, provisional**
tentatively *adv.* in an uncertain way. □ **con indecisión, provisionalmente**
tenterhooks ['tentəhu:ks] *n. pl.* ***to be on tenterhooks***, to be impatiently waiting/to be anxious and uncertain. □ **estar sobre ascuas**
to keep someone on tenterhooks, to keep someone in a state of uncertainty. □ **tener a alguien sobre ascuas**
tenth, 10th [tenθ] *adj.* and *n.* 1 referring to ten: *the tenth of July* (10th July). □ **décimo**
2 *you only do a tenth of the work he does*, a very small part in comparison. □ **...una décima parte del trabajo...**
the tenth century, period from 900 to 999. □ **el siglo diez**
tenuous ['tenjuəs] *adj.* thin; not strong: *a tenuous connection*. □ **tenue**
tenuousness *n.* being tenuous. □ **tenuidad**
tenure ['tenjə] *n.* 1 right to hold property/to have employment; holding of a property or employment: *during his tenure of office*. □ **posesión; ejercicio**
2 right to hold a job permanently: *does he have tenure of his job as librarian?* □ **puesto a perpetuidad**
tepee ['ti:pi:] *n.* cone-shaped tent of North American Indians. □ **tipi**
tepid ['tepid] *adj.* slightly warm: *tepid water*. □ **tibio**
tercentenary [tə:sen'ti:nəri] *n.* (*pl. tercentenaries*) anniversary of 300 years (since an event/the birth/death of someone, etc.): *this year is the tercentenary of the founding of the university*. □ **tricentenario**
term [tə:m] *n.* 1 length of time: *during his term of office as President; he was sentenced to a term of imprisonment; long-term advantages*. □ **mandato (presidente); condena (de prisión); a largo plazo (ventaja)**
in the long term/in the short term, for a long period from now/for a short period from now. □ **a largo/corto plazo**
2 end of a period of time: *she was approaching her term*, nearly at the end of her pregnancy. □ **plazo; ...al término (de su embarazo)**
3 part of a school/university year: *the summer term; during his last term at school*. □ **trimestre**
4 conditions: *what are the terms of the agreement? under the terms of the agreement we can sell our goods in Italy; I wouldn't do it on any terms*, I would never do it. □ **condiciones**
to come to terms with, (i) to accept it as inevitable: *he managed to come to terms with his illness*. □ **aceptar**
(ii) *they came to terms*, they reached agreement. □ **llegaron a un acuerdo**

terms of reference, areas which a committee/an inspector has to examine or discuss. □ **mandato**
terms of payment, way in which a payment shall be made. □ **condiciones de pago**
5 relationship: *we're on good/bad terms with him,* we have a friendly/unfriendly relationship; *they're on the best of terms; they're no longer on speaking terms with the vicar.* □ **se llevan de maravilla; ya no se hablan con el...**
6 particular word: *it's a scientific term used in atomic physics; he spoke in disparaging terms about me; how dare you speak to me in such terms?* □ **término**
7 ***in terms of*** *health/**in** health **terms,*** regarding health; *I'm thinking in terms of weekly payments,* my idea is that the payments should be made each week. □ **por lo que se refiere a...; estoy pensando en pagos...**
■ *v.* to call: *I would term it disgraceful.* □ **llamar**

terminal ['tɜːminl] *adj.* **1** at the end: *terminal shoot,* shoot at the end of a branch. □ **brote terminal**
2 referring to a school term: *terminal exams.* □ **exámenes trimestrales**
3 in the last period of life: *terminal cancer; terminal case,* patient who is soon going to die. □ **terminal**
■ *n.* **1** building at an airport where passengers arrive or leave: *your plane leaves from Terminal No. 1.* □ **terminal**
2 terminus. □ **término**
air terminal, building in the centre of a town where coaches arrive from an airport. □ **terminal aérea**
3 *electric terminal,* one of the connecting points in an electric circuit: *connect the brown wire to the terminal marked +.* □ **borne; terminal**
4 apparatus which can be used for putting information into and getting information from a distant computer (to which it is linked by cable). □ **terminal**
terminate ['tɜːmineit] *v.* to finish/to bring (something) to an end: *to terminate an agreement; the meeting terminated at 3 o'clock.* □ **concluir (un acuerdo); terminar (a una hora)**
termination [tɜːmi'neiʃn] *n.* bringing to an end: *the termination of the meeting.* □ **terminación**

terminology [tɜːmi'nɔlədʒi] *n.* special words or phrases used in a particular science: *I don't understand medical terminology.* □ **terminología**
terminological [tɜiːminə'lɔdʒikl] *adj.* referring to terminology. □ **terminológico**

terminus ['tɜːminəs] *n.* (*pl. termini* ['tɜːminai]) station at the end of a railway line; station at the end of a journey for a bus or a coach. □ **término**

termite ['tɜːmait] *n.* destructive white insect, rather like an ant, which lives in tropical countries. □ **termita**

tern [tɜːn] *n.* white sea bird similar to a gull. □ **golondrina de mar**

terrace ['terəs] *n.* **1** flat area which is raised above another area: *the french windows open on to the terrace; the rice fields are laid out in terraces up the side of the hill.* □ **terraza**
2 row of houses connected together and built in a similar style. □ **hilera de casas adosadas**
3 ***the terraces,*** rows of wide steps on which the spectators stand (at a football stadium). □ **gradas**
■ *v.* **1** to make a flat raised area: *the hillsides are terraced to make a series of small fields.* □ **aterrizar**
2 ***terraced houses,*** connected houses built all in a similar style. □ **casas adosadas**

terracotta [terə'kɔtə] *n.* red clay used to make small statues; a statue made of red clay: *a Greek terracotta.* □ **terracota**

terrain [tə'rein] *n.* area of country: *the soldiers had to cross a rocky terrain.* □ **terreno**

terrapin ['terəpin] *n.* type of small American turtle. □ **tortuga de agua dulce**

terrestrial [tə'restriəl] *adj.* referring to the earth. □ **terrestre**

terrible ['teribl] *adj.* **1** awful/which makes you very frightened: *a terrible sight met his eyes; he had a terrible accident.* □ **terrible**
2 (*informal*) very bad: *what a terrible meal!* □ **horrible**
terribly *adv.* **1** frighteningly: *it is terribly dangerous.* □ **terriblemente**
2 (*informal*) very: *he is terribly intelligent; these chocolates are terribly expensive.* □ **...inteligentísimo; ...carísimos**

terrier ['teriə] *n.* small dog (originally used in hunting). □ **terrier**

terrific [tə'rifik] *adj.* (*informal*) awful/wonderful: *there was a terrific bang; she's a terrific swimmer.* □ **tremendo**
terrifically *adv.* (*informal*) wonderfully/awfully. □ **tremendamente**
terrify ['terifai] *v.* to frighten completely: *he was terrified that he might lose his job; she's terrified of snakes.* □ **aterrorizar**
terrifying *adj.* frightening: *a terrifying film.* □ **aterrador**

terrine [tə'riːn] *n.* type of pâtè. □ **tarrina de paté**

territory ['teritri] *n.* (*pl. territories*) **1** land which belongs to a country; large stretch of land: *we are in enemy territory.* □ **territorio**
2 area which an animal/bird, etc. considers as its own. □ **territorio**
3 area visited by a travelling salesman: *his territory covers Scotland and the North of England.* □ **zona**
territorial [teri'tɔːriəl] *adj.* referring to territory. □ **territorial**
territorial waters, area of sea round a country which that country controls. □ **aguas territoriales**

terror ['terə] *n.* **1** extreme fear: *the children ran out of the burning school in terror.* □ **terror**
2 thing which causes fear: *the great lorries are the terror of the village.* □ **terror**
3 (*informal*) naughty/uncontrollable person: *he's a little terror.* □ **un niño terrible**
4 *she's a terror for punctuality,* she insists on everyone being punctual. □ **es una maniática de...**
terrorism *n.* policy of using violence in a political cause. □ **terrorismo**
terrorist *adj.* and *n.* (person) who practises terrorism: *terrorists have hijacked the aircraft; terrorist bombs have killed three people.* □ **terrorista**
terrorize *v.* to frighten (someone) very much: *the small shopkeepers were terrorized by gangs of teenagers.* □ **aterrorizar**
terror-stricken, terror-struck *adj.* extremely frightened. □ **aterrorizado**

terry ['teri] *n.* type of cloth where uncut loops stand above the surface: *terry cloth; terry towelling.* □ **felpa**

terse [tɜːs] *adj.* concise/short; using few words: *a terse statement.* □ **sucinto**
tersely *adv.* briefly/concisely: *when asked for his opinion, the police chief said tersely: 'no comment'.* □ **sucintamente**

tertiary ['tɜːʃəri] *adj.* referring to a third stage, especially to the level of education after the secondary: *a tertiary college.* □ **tercero, terciario, superior**

Terylene ['terili:n] *n.* trademark for a type of manmade thread; cloth made of this thread. □ **'terylene'**
tessellated ['tesəleitid] *adj.* covered with mosaic. □ **con teselas**
test [test] *n.* **1** examination to see if something works well/is reliable/if someone is healthy: *they carried out fuel consumption tests,* tests to see how much fuel was used; *blood tests/urine tests; the doctor carried out a test for anaemia,* to see if the patient had anaemia. □ **prueba**
test pilot, pilot who flies a new aircraft to see if it works well. □ **piloto de prueba**
2 short written or practical examination to see if someone knows information/knows how to do something: *we're having a maths test this morning.* □ **prueba**
intelligence test/aptitude test, test to show how intelligent/how capable you are. □ **prueba**
driving test, to see if you can drive a car: *I'm taking my driving test tomorrow; he failed his driving test three times.* □ **examen de conducir**
3 ***to put something/someone to the test,*** to try something/someone out to see if they can stand up to certain conditions. □ **poner algo/alguien a prueba**
4 international cricket match. □ **partido internacional**
■ *v.* **1** to examine (something) to see if it is working well; to examine (someone) to see if he is healthy: *to test a new car; I have to have my eyes tested.* □ **examinar; probar (un coche); graduar (la vista)**
2 to give (someone) a short examination: *the teacher tested him in geography/tested his French.* □ **hacer una prueba**
test case *n.* court case where the decision sets a precedent for other similar cases to follow. □ **juicio que hace jurisprudencia**
test-drive *v. to test-drive a car,* to drive a new car before you buy it to see if it works well. □ **probar**
test match *n.* international cricket match. □ **encuentro internacional**
test tube *n.* small round-bottomed glass tube used in a laboratory for making chemical tests. □ **tubo de ensayo**
test-tube baby, baby born through artificial insemination. □ **niño probeta**
testament ['testəmənt] *n.* **1** ***last will and testament,*** document written by a person before death to indicate what should happen to his property after he dies. □ **testamento**
2 ***Old Testament/New Testament,*** the two main sections of the Bible. □ **Nuevo/Antiguo Testamento**
testate ['testeit] *adj.* (person who has died) leaving a will. □ **testado**
testicle ['testikl] *n.* one of two male glands which produce sperm. □ **testículo**
testify ['testifai] *v.* to give evidence that something is true: *he testified that he had seen the bank robbers drive off in a blue car; I can testify to the truth of that statement.* □ **atestiguar**
testimonial [testi'mouniəl] *n.* **1** statement showing what you know of a person's qualities: *a written testimonial of good character.* □ **referencias; una carta de recomendación**
2 something done for a person/given to a person to show appreciation. □ **testimonio de aprecio, gratitud...**
a testimonial dinner, dinner organized to give a present to someone. □ **una cena en homenaje a...**
testimony ['testiməni] *n.* evidence that something is true: *his testimony in court was proved to be false.* □ **testimonio**
testis ['testis] *n.* (*pl. testes* ['testi:z]) one of two male glands which produce sperm. □ **testículo**
testy ['testi] *adj.* irritable; easily made angry. □ **malhumorado**
testily *adv.* irritably/angrily. □ **de mal humor**
tetanus ['tetənəs] *n.* serious disease caused by infection in a wound, which can make especially the jaw muscles stiffen. □ **tétanos**
tetchy ['tetʃi] *adj.* (*tetchier, tetchiest*) badtempered. □ **irritable**
tetchily *adv.* in a badtempered way. □ **malhumoradamente**
tête-á-tête [teitɑ:'teit] *n.* private conversation between two people. □ **conversación privada**
tether ['teðə] *n.* **1** rope which attaches an animal to a post. □ **ronzal; soga**
2 *he's **at the end of his tether,*** he can't stand any more/he has lost all patience. □ **está harto**
■ *v.* to attach (an animal) to a post with a rope. □ **atar**
tetrahedron [tetrə'hi:drən] *n.* solid shape with four sides, each of which is a triangle. □ **tetraedro**
text [tekst] *n.* **1** main written part of a book (not the notes or pictures, etc.). □ **texto**
2 original words of a speech: *the text of the President's speech is being translated into Russian.* □ **texto**
3 quotation from the Bible used as a moral guide. □ **pasaje**
textbook *n.* book which students read for information about the subject they are studying. □ **libro de texto**
textual *adj.* referring to a text: *textual differences,* differences between various versions of a book. □ **textual**
textile ['tekstail] *adj.* and *n.* (referring to) cloth: *textile industry; a textile factory; a factory making textiles.* □ **textil**
texture ['tekstʃə] *n.* quality of something which can be felt: *the soft texture of wool; bread with a gritty texture.* □ **textura**
textured *adj.* with a certain feel: *rough-textured surface.* □ **con textura...**
Thailand ['tailænd] *n.* country in south-east Asia. □ **Tailandia**
Thai *adj.* referring to Thailand. □ **tailandés**
■ *n.* **1** person from Thailand. □ **tailandés**
2 language spoken in Thailand. □ **tailandés**
than [ðæn, ðən] *conj.* and *prep.* (used to introduce the second part of comparisons): *I have less than you; he knows me better than anyone; there are more than twenty people in the room; if there are less than twenty people there's no point in holding the meeting; no sooner had we arrived than the music started.* □ **que**
thank [θæŋk] *v.* **1** to show gratitude to (someone): *he thanked the family for their help; she thanked them for coming to see her.* □ **dar las gracias a**
2 *you have only yourself to thank for the mess you're in,* you are the only person responsible for the mess. □ **tú eres el único que tiene la culpa**
thankful *adj.* showing gratitude; glad because an anxiety has gone: *I'm thankful that no one was killed.* □ **agradecido; me alegro que nadie...**
thankfully *adv.* showing relief that an anxiety has gone: *after the interview he closed the door thankfully.* □ **con alivio**
thankless *adj.* (work) for which no one will thank you; difficult/hopeless (task): *it's a thankless task, trying to persuade people to pay their taxes.* □ **ingrato**

thanks *n. pl.* **1** words which show you are grateful: *please give him our thanks for his help; to pass a vote of thanks to Mr Smith,* to thank Mr Smith officially in the minutes of the meeting. □ **gracias**
2 *have another chocolate – **thanks,*** thank you. □ **gracias**
no, thanks, no, thank you. □ **no, gracias**
3 ***thanks to,*** as a result of: *thanks to your help we arrived at the station on time; thanks to the strike, no trains were running.* □ **gracias a**
thanksgiving *n.* (religious) festival where thanks are shown to God. □ **acción de gracias**
Thanksgiving American and Canadian festival when thanks are given for a safe harvest. □ **día de Acción de Gracias**
thank you *interjection showing* gratitude: *thank you for the present; thank you for coming to see me;* (*informal*) *let's say a big thank-you to Miss Smith for playing the piano.* □ **gracias**
thank-you letter, letter in which you thank someone for something. □ **carta de agradecimiento**

that [ðæt] *adj.* and *pron.* (*pl. those* [ðouz]) *used to indicate* something further away (*as opposed to* **this**): *that book is the one I meant, not this one; give the parcel to that tall man standing by the door; what happened to those people who lived next door to you?* □ **ese; esa; eso**
■ *pron.* (linking a subject or object to a verb): *the house that is next to the post office; where is the letter that he sent you? during all the years that he was living next to us; where is the box that the glasses were packed in?* □ **que**
■ *adv.* (*informal*) to such an extent; so much: *the little boy is only that high; I knew they were going to be early, but not that early; it isn't as interesting as all that,* not so very interesting. □ **...es sólo así de alto; ...pero no tan temprano**
■ *conj.* (introducing a clause): *he didn't know that we were late; I'm glad that you were able to come; I said that we would think about their offer; it's not that he needs the money,* the point is not that he needs the money; *come closer so that I can whisper in your ear; he is sitting all by himself in the garden so that everyone can see he's annoyed; it was so delicious that I ate it all.* □ **que**

thatch [θætʃ] *n.* reeds/straw, etc., used to make a roof. □ **paja**
■ *v.* to cover a house with a roof of reeds/straw, etc.: *a thatched cottage.* □ **techar con paja**
thatcher *n.* person who thatches houses. □ **techador**

thaw [θɔː] *n.* warm weather (which results in the melting of snow/ice): *a thaw set in; when the thaw comes the rivers flood.* □ **deshielo**
■ *v.* **1** to melt; to unfreeze (something) which is frozen: *the snow is thawing on the pavements; the warm weather will thaw the ice; he tried to thaw the frozen pipes with a candle; leave the frozen turkey for 24 hours to thaw.* □ **deshelar**
2 *after a few drinks he began to thaw,* to get less unfriendly/less shy. □ **...a cobrar confianza**

the [ðə] (*before a vowel or when stressed* [ðiː]). *definite article.* **1** (referring to a particular person or thing): *the man with the red nose; where is the parcel? the hills of Scotland.* □ **el, la, los, las, lo**
2 (referring to something in general): *the Russians are lively people; he's caught the measles; nurses are looking after the injured.* □ **el, lo, los, la, las**
3 (stressed): *he's the top surgeon in England; it is the shop for furniture.* □ **es el mejor...; es la tienda**
■ *adv.* (in comparisons): *it will be all the easier; the less you spend the more you save; it's the best plan; the sooner you do it the better.* □ **más fácil; cuanto menos gastes, más...; es el mejor plan**

theatre ['θiətə] *Amer.* **theater** *n.* **1** building in which plays are performed: *we're going to the theatre tonight.* □ **teatro**
2 *Amer.* cinema. □ **cine**
3 art of acting/of producing plays; business of putting on plays: *the British theatre since 1930; he's going in for the theatre.* □ **teatro**
4 collection of plays. □ **teatro**
5 place where important events happen: *theatre of war.* □ **teatro**
6 ***operating theatre,*** room in a hospital where operations take place. □ **quirófano**
theatregoer *n.* person who goes to the theatre. □ **aficionado al teatro**
theatrical [θi'ætrikl] *adj.* **1** referring to the theatre: *theatrical performance; theatrical company.* □ **teatral**
2 very dramatic/not acting naturally: *with a theatrical gesture, he flung the book out of the window.* □ **teatral**
theatricals *n. pl. amateur theatricals,* performances of a play by amateurs. □ **teatro de aficionados**

theft [θeft] *n.* stealing: *he was accused of theft.* □ **robo**

their ['ðɛə] *adj.* belonging to them: *is this their house? everyone should carry their own luggage.* □ **su, sus**

theirs ['ðɛəz] *pron.* belonging to them: *which house is theirs? she's a friend of theirs.* □ **el suyo, la suya, los suyos, las suyas**

them [ðem] *pron.* referring to persons/things which are objects of a verb: *I like them; have you seen them? tell them to come in.* □ **los, las; les; (después de prep.) ellos, ellas**
themselves [ðem'selvz] *pron.* **1** referring to a plural subject: *cats clean themselves very carefully; they're working for themselves;* (stressed) *they themselves told me.* □ **ellos mismos, ellas mismas; se; (después de prep.) sí mismos/mismas**
2 *the children did it all **by themselves,*** without any help from anyone else. □ **ellos solos lo hicieron; ellos mismos me lo dijeron**

theme [θiːm] *n.* **1** subject (of book/article): *we're holding a discussion on the theme of 'man in society'.* □ **tema**
2 main tune in a piece of music: *theme and variations.* □ **tema**
theme tune/theme song, catchy tune/song played several times in a film or TV serial which makes the audience recognize it: *the theme tune from 'The Third Man'.* □ **tema musical**
thematic [θi'mætik] *adj.* referring to a theme. □ **temático**

then [ðen] *adv.* **1** at that time: *he did it then and there.* □ **entonces**
now and then, from time to time. □ **de vez en cuando**
2 afterwards: *we sat down, and then started to talk; where did you go then?* □ **luego**
3 also/in any case: *I haven't the time to do it, but then it's nothing to do with me.* □ **en cualquier caso**
4 therefore; the result is: *if you don't like fish then you'll have to eat meat; then you knew all the time that the money had been stolen?* □ **entonces**
■ *n.* that time: *until then; before then; ever since then.* □ **hasta entonces; antes; a partir de entonces**
■ *adj.* existing at that time: *the then Prime Minister.* □ **el entonces primer...**

thence [ðens] *adv.* (*formal*) **1** from that place; from there: *he went to France, and thence to Germany.* □ **de allí**
2 so/therefore. □ **por consiguiente**

thenceforth *adv.* (*formal*) from that time onwards. □ **desde entonces**
theodolite [θi'ɔdəlait] *n.* device for measuring angles when surveying land. □ **teodolito**
theology [θi'ɔlədʒi] *n.* study of belief in God; study of God and God's relations with man. □ **teología**
theologian [θiə'loudʒiən] *n.* person who specializes in the study of God/in the interpretation of religion. □ **teólogo**
theological [θiə'lɔdʒikl] *adj.* referring to theology. □ **teológico**
theological college, college where people study to become priests. □ **seminario**
theorem ['θi:ərəm] *n.* something which has to be proved in mathematics. □ **teorema**
theory ['θiəri] *n.* (*pl. theories*) **1** explanation of something which has not been proved but which you believe is right: *the theory of evolution; the police have a theory that the murderer was Italian.* □ **teoría**
2 statement of general principles (which may not apply in practice). □ **teoría**
3 ***in theory,*** if you follow general principles: *his plan seems ideal in theory, but will it work in practice?* □ **en teoría...**
theoretical [θiə'retikl] *adj.* referring to a theory; not proved in practice: *the car has a theoretical top speed of 200 miles per hour.* □ **teórico**
theoretically *adv.* in theory, but not in practice: *theoretically the house belongs to his mother.* □ **teóricamente**
theoretician [θiərə'tiʃn] *n.* person who forms (political) theories: *a leading socialist theoretician.* □ **teórico**
theorize ['θiəraiz] *v.* to make up a theory about something. □ **teorizar**
therapy ['θerəpi] *n.* treatment of illness (especially without using medicine). □ **terapia**
group therapy, treatment by getting patients together in groups to discuss their problems. □ **terapia de grupo**
occupational therapy, curing by getting patients to do things. □ **terapia ocupacional**
speech therapy, treatment of difficulty in speaking. □ **logopedia**
therapeutic [θerə'pju:tik] *adj.* which may cure. □ **terapéutico**
therapist *n.* person who applies therapy. □ **terapeuta**
there ['ðεə] *adv.* **1** in that place/to that place: *is the burglar still there? I'll go there at 10 o'clock; there it is on the top shelf!* □ **allí; allá; ahí**
2 *there she goes again,* (*informal*) that is her doing it again. □ **ahí va de nuevo**
■ *interjection* (showing various feelings): *there, there, don't cry; there, what did I tell you! I'll go to the party all by myself, so there!* □ **ya, ya, no llores; ¡vaya, qué te dije!; ¡...a la fiesta yo solo, pero vamos!**
■ *pron.* (used as subject of a clause usually with the verb ***to be,*** when the real subject follows the verb): *there's a big car coming up the hill; there's a page missing in this book; there weren't very many people at the meeting; was there anything to drink? there appears to be a mistake; there followed a long silence.* □ **hay un coche...; no había mucha gente...**
thereabouts [ðεərə'bauts] *adv.* in that area/approximately: *it's near the church or somewhere thereabouts; we lost $250 or thereabouts.* □ **por ahí**
thereafter [ðεər'α:ftə] *adv.* after that: *always thereafter he was scared of spiders.* □ **después de eso**
thereby [ðεə'bai] *adv.* (*formal*) by doing this. □ **por eso**
therefore ['ðεəfɔ:] *adv.* consequently; for this reason: *there is a lot of snow, therefore the trains are late; the children are growing up and therefore don't need so much attention.* □ **por tanto**
thereupon [ðεərə'pɔn] *adv.* (*formal*) immediately after that: *thereupon he was arrested by the police.* □ **en eso**
therm [θə:m] *n.* measure of heat, used for measuring gas in Britain. □ **termia**
thermal *adj.* referring to heat. □ **termal**
thermal baths, baths of natural hot water. □ **termas**
thermal current, current of warm air/water. □ **corriente térmica**
■ *n.* current of warm air: *the glider soared upwards on a thermal.* □ **corriente de aire caliente**
thermionic [θə:mi'ɔnik] *adj.* (radio valve) made of a vacuum tube containing heated electrodes. □ **termiónico**
thermodynamics [θə:moudai'næmiks] *n.* study of heat and its relationship to power. □ **termodinámica**
thermometer [θə:'mɔmitə] *n.* instrument for measuring the temperature. □ **termómetro**
thermonuclear [θə:mou'nju:kliə] *adj.* referring to the high temperature caused by atomic fusion: *thermonuclear device.* □ **termonuclear**
thermoplastic [θəi:mə'plæstik] *adj.* and *n.* (material) which becomes soft when heated and hard when cold. □ **termoplástico**
Thermos (flask) ['θə:məs'flα:sk] *n.* trademark for a type of vacuum flask: *we took a Thermos of coffee.* □ **termo**
thermostat ['θə:məstæt] *n.* instrument which controls the temperature by setting off heating or cooling devices. □ **termostato**
thermostatically *adv.* (controlled) by a thermostat. □ **por un termostato**
thesaurus [θə'sɔ:rəs] *n.* (*pl. thesauruses*) book with words collected according to their similar meanings, and not in alphabetical order. □ **diccionario de ideas afines**
these [ði:z] *adj.* and *pron. see* **this.**
thesis ['θi:sis] *n.* (*pl. theses* ['θi:si:z]) **1** long piece of written research done for a higher university degree. □ **tesis**
2 particular point of view. □ **tesis**
thews [θju:z] *n. pl.* strength. □ **músculos**
they [ðei] *pron.* **1** (referring to several persons or things): *where are the plates? - they are in the cupboard; they all went to the restaurant for a meal.* □ **ellos**
2 (referring to people in general): *they say it's going to rain; they tell me you're married; nobody here will admit they are to blame,* that one of them is to blame. □ **(ellos); dicen...**
thick [θik] *adj.* (*thicker, thickest*) **1** fat/not thin/with a large distance between the two surfaces: *a thick plank; thick slices of bread; the wall is a metre thick; orange with a thick skin.* □ **grueso; ...tiene un metro de espesor**
2 with a large diameter: *a thick stick; thick string.* □ **gordo**
3 dense/packed close together: *thick forest; thick mist; thick grass.* □ **espeso**
4 (liquid) which does not flow easily: *thick syrup; thick paint; thick soup.* □ **espeso**
5 not clear: *thick voice.* □ **voz poco clara**
6 ***that's a bit thick,*** (*informal*) that's very unreasonable. □ **no hay derecho**
7 (*informal*) stupid: *she's a bit thick.* □ **lerdo**

■ *n.* **1** the middle part: *he was there in the thick of the battle.* □ **en mitad de**
2 *to stick to someone* ***through thick and thin,*** through times of difficulty as well as through easy times. □ **apoyar a uno contra viento y marea**
■ *adv.* in a thick layer: *you're spreading butter too thick; he cut the bread thick.* □ **estás poniendo mucha mantequilla; ...el pan muy ancho**
to lay it on thick, to praise someone excessively. □ **exagerar**
thick and fast, rapidly and heavily. □ **a golpetazos**
thicken *v.* **1** to make thick/to become thick: *the fog is thickening; to thicken soup by adding flour.* □ **espesar**
2 *the plot is thickening,* it is becoming very complicated. □ **...se está enmarañando**
thicket ['θikit] *n.* small wood of trees and bushes growing wild close together. □ **matorral**
thickly *adv.* **1** in a thick way: *the snow lay thickly; she was thickly dressed for the cold weather; sow the seeds thickly; the grass is growing thickly.* □ **espesamente; nevaba muchísimo**
2 *he spoke thickly,* in an unclear voice. □ **...con voz poco clara**
thickness *n.* being thick; distance between sides: *the thickness of a wall; thickness of the fog; to mix the soup to a rich thickness.* □ **espesor**
thickset *adj.* **1** *thickset hedge,* planted with bushes close together. □ **denso**
2 short stocky (person). □ **rechoncho**
thick-skinned *adj.* **1** (orange) with a thick skin. □ **de piel gruesa**
2 (*of person*) insensitive/not easily hurt. □ **duro**
thief [θi:f] *n.* (*pl. thieves*) person who steals: *thieves broke into the shop last night.* □ **ladrón**
thieve *v.* to steal. □ **robar**
thieving *n.* act of stealing: *thieving by the public is a problem in self-service shops.* □ **robo**
thigh [θai] *n.* thick top part of the leg between the knee and the hip. □ **muslo**
thimble ['θimbl] *n.* small metal/plastic, etc., cover worn to protect the end of your finger when sewing. □ **dedal**
thimbleful *n.* (*informal*) very small quantity (of liquid). □ **unas gotas**
thin [θin] *adj.* (*thinner, thinnest*) **1** not thick/with only a small distance between the two surfaces: *a thin slice of bread; a thin sheet of paper; orange with a thin skin.* □ **delgado; naranja de piel fina**
2 not fat: *his legs are very thin;* (*informal*) *she is as thin as a rake.* □ **delgado; ...más delgada que un fideo**
3 with a small diameter: *thin string; a thin bamboo stick.* □ **cuerda fina; un palo fino de bambú**
4 not very dense/not close together: *thin hair.* □ **pelo ralo**
5 very watery (liquid): *thin soup; add water until the paint is quite thin.* □ **sopa aguada; ...la pintura está clara**
■ *adv.* in a thin way: *you've cut the bread too thin; spread the paint thin.* □ **...en trozos muy delgados; pon poca pintura**
■ *v.* (*he thinned*) **1** to become thin: *his face has thinned down.* □ **adelgazar**
2 to make liquid thin: *to thin the soup/paint by adding water.* □ **aguar**
3 to make less dense; to become less dense: *to thin* (*out*) *seedlings until they are 10 cm apart; the crowd thinned; his hair is thinning.* □ **aclarar(se)**
thinly *adv.* **1** in a thin way: *she's thinly dressed for the winter; sow the seeds thinly; thinly populated.* □ **ligeramente**
2 *thinly veiled allusion,* allusion which is easy to see. □ **alusión apenas disimulada**
thinness *n.* being thin. □ **delgadez**
thinnings *n.* small plants which are removed to allow others more space. □ **vamos a entresacar plantas...**
thin-skinned *adj.* **1** with a thin skin: *these oranges are thin-skinned.* □ **de piel fina**
2 sensitive/easily hurt. □ **sensible**
thing [θiŋ] *n.* **1** object: *what's that thing for?; get out the dinner things,* plates/knives/forks, etc. □ **cosa**
2 (*informal*) person/animal: *his mother's such a nice old thing; what a sweet little thing!* □ **cosa**
3 clothes/equipment: *I haven't got a thing to wear; bring your tennis things; I'll pack our things into the back of the car.* □ **...nada que ponerme; ...equipo de tenis; pondré nuestras cosas...**
4 item; unspecified subject; something referred to: *you mustn't take things so seriously; that's just the thing I wanted; how are things going?; it's just one thing after another,* one problem after another. □ **cosa**
5 ***it's a good thing*** *you came with us,* it's lucky. □ **está muy bien...**
6 *first thing in the morning/last thing at night,* as soon as you get up/just before you go to bed. □ **lo primero...**
7 (*informal*) mania: *she's got a thing about pink curtains.* □ **tiene una fijación con...**
8 *he wants to do his own thing,* (*informal*) to do what he really feels like doing. □ **sólo quiere hacer lo que le viene en gana**
thingamajig ['θiŋəmədʒig] **thingummy** ['θiŋəmi] *n.* (*informal*) some object/person whose name you have forgotten: *pass me the thingamajig to open the bottle.* □ **chisme (cosa); ese tío**
think [θiŋk] *n.* time when you have thoughts/when you consider plans in your mind: *to have a quiet think; we'll all have to have a think about this.* □ **reflexionar; tendremos que pensar sobre esto**
you've got another think coming, (*informal*) you'll have to change your ideas, as this one won't work. □ **otra idea, ésta no vale**
■ *v.* (*he thought*) **1** to use your mind: *he did it without thinking; think before you say anything; I'd think twice before I went into the lion's cage,* consider very deeply whether it is safe; *what do you think we ought to do?* □ **pensar**
to think aloud, to speak your thoughts as they come into your mind. □ **pensar en voz alta**
2 to believe; to have as your opinion: *I think she's pretty; everyone thought he was mad; I thought it was all over; they are thought to be in France; she doesn't think him very attractive.* □ **creer**
3 to expect: *I didn't think the train would be as late as this.* □ **creer**
4 to plan: *he thought he would go to work in Canada.* □ **creer**
to think again, to change your mind. □ **pensar dos veces**
think big!, (*informal*) only consider large-scale projects. □ **¡piensa a lo grande!**
think about *v.* **1** to consider (something) in your mind: *he has so much to think about that he doesn't know where to start; what are you thinking about?* □ **pensar en**
2 to plan something: *he's thinking about going to work in Canada.* □ **está pensando en...**
3 to have an opinion: *what do you think about the new wage offer?* □ **pensar sobre**
think back *v.* to remember: *if you think back to what*

happened last week. □ **recordar**
thinker *n.* person who thinks. □ **pensador**
great thinker, philosopher. □ **filósofo**
thinking *n.* reasoning. □ **pensamiento**
to my way of thinking, *this is nonsense,* my opinion is that it is nonsense. □ **según mi modo de ver...**
think of *v.* **1** to consider (something) in your mind: *don't think of the price; think of what would happen if your father became ill.* □ **pensar en**
2 to plan something: *he's thinking of going to work in Canada; have you thought of seeing a doctor about your stiff knee?* □ **está pensando en ir a...; has pensado en ver...**
3 to remember: *I haven't time to think of everything.* □ **recordar**
4 to have an opinion: *what do you think of my new tie? he thinks a great deal of himself,* considers he is very intelligent/smart, etc.; *I told him what I thought of him,* I criticized him. □ **pensar**
to think highly of, to have a high opinion of. □ **tener en gran estima a**
to think nothing of: *she thinks nothing of working 12 hours a day,* she finds it easy. □ **encuentra normal trabajar...**
think nothing of it, don't bother to thank me for it. □ **ni hablar**
to think better of it: *he was going to go to France, but thought better of it,* changed his mind. □ **...pero se lo pensó mejor**
think out *v.* to consider carefully all the details: *the plans need to be properly thought out; a carefully thought-out reply.* □ **...hay que pensárselo bien**
think over *v.* to consider (something) seriously: *think it over, and give me your answer tomorrow.* □ **pensar bien**
think tank *n.* group of experts who advise the government on matters of general policy. □ **grupo de asesores**
think through *v.* to consider carefully all the details. □ **considerar detalladamente**
think up *v.* to invent: *he thought up an idea for making a plane that will fly backwards; the government has thought up a plan for helping rural areas.* □ **idear**
third, 3rd [θəːd] *n.* and *adj.* **1** referring to three: *the third of April* (*3rd April*); *a third of the books; George the Third* (*George III*). □ **tercero; el 3 de abril; un tercio de los libros; Jorge III**
third person, pronoun or part of a verb referring to a person or thing who is being mentioned: *'he', 'she', and 'they' are third person pronouns.* □ **tercera persona**
third party insurance, insurance which covers someone not named in it. □ **seguro a terceros**
the Third World, countries with no strong connections to the superpowers. □ **el Tercer Mundo**
2 *the car went up the hill* ***in third,*** in third gear. □ **...en tercera**
third-rate *adj.* very bad: *a third-rate provincial hotel.* □ **de tercera**
thirst [θəːst] *n.* wanting to drink; desire: *to quench your thirst; his thirst for knowledge/for power.* □ **sed**
■ *v.* to desire: *they're thirsting for blood/for revenge.* □ **estar sediento**
thirsty *adj.* (*thirstier, thirstiest*) **1** wanting to drink: *I'm thirsty, give me a glass of water.* □ **sediento; tengo sed...**
2 *thirsty work,* hard/hot work which makes you thirsty. □ **trabajo duro/que da sed**
thirstily *adv.* in a thirsty way. □ **con avidez**
thirteen [θəːˈtiːn] number 13: *she is thirteen* (*years old*); *the thirteen ten train,* train which leaves at 13.10. □ **trece**
the thirteen hundreds, years between 1300 and 1399. □ **el siglo catorce**
thirteenth, 13th *adj.* referring to thirteen: *the thirteenth of August* (*13th August*). □ **decimotercero; el trece de agosto**
the thirteenth century, period from 1200 to 1299. □ **el siglo trece**
thirty [ˈθəːti] number 30: *she's over thirty* (*years old*). □ **treinta**
in the thirties, (i) *she's in her thirties,* she is more than thirty years old but less than forty. □ **tiene más de treinta años**
(ii) between '30 and '40 in a century. □ **la década de los treinta**
thirtieth, 30th *adj.* referring to thirty: *the thirtieth of June* (*30th June*). □ **trigésimo, treinta**
this [ðis] *adj.* and *pron.* (*pl. these* [ðiːz]) *used to indicate* something near (*as opposed to* **that**) **1** *this is the book I meant, not that one; this is Mr Martin; where did these parcels come from? this is odd; this is where I live.* □ **este; esta; esto**
2 ***this morning/this evening,*** today in the morning/evening: *they're coming to see us this evening; the letter came this morning.* □ **esta mañana/tarde**
■ *adv.* (*informal*) to such an extent: *he's only this high,* quite small; *I didn't expect you to be this late,* as late as this. □ **es sólo así de alto; ...llegar tan tarde**
thistle [ˈθisl] *n.* large prickly weed with purple flowers. □ **cardo**
thistledown *n.* soft white feathery substance attached to thistle seeds, which allows them to be blown by the wind. □ **vilano**
thither [ˈðiðə] *adv.* (*formal*) to that place. □ **allá**
thong [θɔŋ] *n.* thin leather strap used for tying. □ **correa**
thorax [ˈθɔːræks] *n.* part of the body between the neck and the abdomen; chest (of an animal/a person); part of an insect's body to which the wings and legs are attached. □ **tórax**
thoracic [θɔːˈræsik] *adj.* referring to a thorax. □ **torácico**
thorn [θɔːn] *n.* **1** spike (of a prickly plant). □ **espina**
2 *he's* ***a thorn in*** *our* ***flesh,*** a constant annoyance. □ **es como una paja en el ojo**
thorny *adj.* (*thornier, thorniest*) **1** covered with thorns. □ **espinoso**
2 *thorny problem,* which is difficult to solve. □ **problema peliagudo**
thorough [ˈθʌrə] *adj.* **1** very careful/detailed: *a thorough search; a thorough investigation; he's a very thorough worker.* □ **minucioso**
2 complete: *it's a thorough mess; he's a thorough idiot.* □ **completo**
thoroughbred *adj.* and *n.* pure bred (horse). □ **de pura sangre (adj.); pura sangre (n.)**
thoroughfare *n.* way through which the public can go: *public thoroughfare; the main thoroughfare of the town is the High Street.* □ **vía pública**
thoroughgoing *adj.* complete: *a thoroughgoing idiot.* □ **perfecto; auténtico**
thoroughly *adv.* completely/totally: *I'm thoroughly fed up with this weather; our team was thoroughly beaten.* □ **totalmente**
thoroughness *n.* completeness: *the thoroughness of the inspection.* □ **minuciosidad**
those [ðouz] *adj.* and *pron. see* **that.**
though [ðou] *conj.* although; in spite of the fact that: *though he's small, he can hit hard; even though it was raining we still went out for a walk; strange though it may seem,* although it may seem strange.

□ **aunque**
as though, as if: *it looks as though he's gone.* □ **como si**
■ *adv.* in spite of this: *the film was too long, I enjoyed it, though.* □ **sin embargo**

thought [θɔːt] *n.* **1** action of thinking: *is he capable of rational thought? the mere thought of it makes me sick; what a gloomy thought! he was lost in thought,* thinking so hard that you could not attract his attention. □ **pensamiento**
2 considering in your mind: *after much thought,* after considering (the plan) for a long time. □ **después de pensarlo mucho**
on second thoughts, *I've decided to stay at home,* having considered everything a second time. □ **pensándolo bien...**
3 plan: *he's had thoughts of going to work in Canada; I had no thought of hurting you.* □ **intención**
4 regard: *he has no thought for other people's feelings.* □ **consideración**
■ *v. see* **think.**
thoughtful *adj.* **1** thinking hard: *you're looking thoughtful.* □ **pensativo**
2 considerate to other people: *he's always thoughtful of others; how thoughtful of you to remember my birthday.* □ **considerado; ¡qué detalle acordarte de mi cumpleaños!**
3 showing deep thought: *a thoughtful article on the new archbishop.* □ **concienzudo**
thoughtfulness *n.* being thoughtful. □ **consideración**
thoughtless *adj.* without thinking; not thinking about: *it was very thoughtless of you to leave your mother standing in the rain.* □ **desconsiderado**
thoughtlessness *n.* being thoughtless. □ **desconsideración**
thought reader *n.* person who claims to be able to say what someone else is thinking. □ **adivino de pensamientos**

thousand ['θauzənd] number 1,000: *the book has more than a thousand pages; I paid two thousand pounds for it; thousands of people were made homeless in the floods.* □ **mil; miles de personas...**
thousandth, 1000th *adj.* referring to thousand. □ **milésimo**
■ *n.* one of a thousand parts: *a milligram is a thousandth of a gram.* □ **milésimo**

thrall [θrɔːl] *n.* ***in thrall,*** (*formal*) in slavery. □ **esclavo; en esclavitud**

thrash [θræʃ] *v.* **1** to beat (with a stick). □ **golpear**
2 to beat (another team) decisively. □ **dar una paliza**
thrash about *v.* to move/to wave your arms and legs violently: *they were thrashing about in the mud.* □ **revolcarse**
thrashing *n.* **1** beating: *he got a thrashing from his father.* □ **paliza**
2 *our team had a thrashing last Saturday,* were beaten decisively. □ **le dieron una paliza a nuestro equipo...**
thrash out *v.* to discuss in detail: *to thrash out a problem; the details will be thrashed out at the next meeting.* □ **discutir largamente**

thread [θred] *n.* **1** long thin piece of cotton/silk, etc.: *I want some strong thread to sew on a button; cloth with gold threads woven into it.* □ **hilo**
2 ***to hang by a thread:*** *his life hangs by a thread,* he is very likely to die. □ **su vida pende de un hilo**
3 ***to lose the thread of*** *a conversation,* to forget what the conversation is about. □ **perder el hilo de una conversación**
4 spiral ridge going round a screw/a bolt or inside a nut: *a screw with a left-handed thread,* which you have to turn to the left to tighten. □ **rosca**
■ *v.* **1** to put a piece of cotton, etc., through the eye of a needle: *the light is so bad I can't thread the needle.* □ **enhebrar**
2 to put (beads, etc.) on a string: *to thread pearls.* □ **ensartar**
3 *to thread your way through a crowd,* to squeeze through a crowd carefully. □ **deslizarse entre la multitud**
threadbare *adj.* worn out (clothes). □ **raído**
threadlike *adj.* long and thin like a thread. □ **filiforme**
threadworm *n.* long thin worm which lives in human intestines. □ **lombriz intestinal**

threat [θret] *n.* warning that something unpleasant will happen or will be done: *his threat to sack all the staff; there's a threat of rain in the air; he was kept in prison under threat of execution; the cold weather poses a threat to the harvest.* □ **amenaza**
threaten *v.* to warn that something unpleasant will be done/that some action will be taken: *he threatened to call the police; the burglar threatened him with a gun; a new economic crisis is threatening,* is possibly going to take place. □ **amenazar**
threateningly *adv.* menacingly. □ **de modo amenazador**

three [θriː] number 3. **1** *he is three* (*years old*); *the three fifteen train,* which leaves at 3.15; *it's three o'clock.* □ **tres; tiene tres años**
2 *they arrived* ***in threes,*** in groups of three at a time. □ **llegaron de tres en tres**
three-act *adj.* (play) with three acts. □ **de tres actos**
three-cornered *adj.* with three corners. □ **triangular**
three-cornered fight, election where there are three candidates. □ **lucha entre tres candidatos**
three-dimensional *adj.* (picture) which has depth as well as length and breadth. □ **tridimensional**
threefold *adv.* three times as much: *costs have risen threefold.* □ **tres veces**
three-piece *adj.* with three parts: *three-piece suit,* suit with jacket, trousers and waistcoat; *three-piece suite,* set of living room furniture consisting of a sofa and two armchairs. □ **de tres piezas; terno; tresillo**
three-ply *adj.* (wool) with three threads twisted together; (plywood) made of three layers stuck together. □ **de tres hebras (lana); de tres capas (madera)**
three-point turn *n.* turning a car in a narrow street in three movements. □ **cambio de sentido en tres movimientos**
three-quarter *adj.* referring to three fourths of a whole: *a three-quarter length dress.* □ **tres cuartos**
■ *n.* **1** ***three-quarters*** (*6*), three fourths of a whole: *they drank three-quarters of a bottle; three-quarters of an hour,* 45 minutes. □ **tres cuartos**
2 (*in Rugby*) one of the fast attacking players behind the forwards. □ **tres cuartos**
■ *adv.* ***three-quarters,*** three fourths: *the room was three-quarters full; a bottle three-quarters empty.* □ **tres cuartas partes**
threesome *n.* group of three people, especially three players playing a game. □ **grupo de tres**

thresh [θreʃ] *v.* to beat (corn) so that the grain falls out. □ **trillar**
threshing machine, machine which threshes corn automatically. □ **trilladora**

threshold ['θreʃould] *n.* **1** wooden or stone bar across the floor of a doorway: *to cross the threshold.*

□ **umbral**
2 edge/beginning: *we are on the threshold of a new discovery.* □ **umbral**
3 limit: *threshold of pain,* point at which pain becomes unbearable; *he has a very low boredom threshold,* he gets bored very easily. □ **límite de tolerancia del dolor**

threw [θru:] *v. see* **throw.**

thrice [θrais] *adv.* three times. □ **tres veces**

thrift [θrift] *n.* **1** saving (money) by wise use and restricting spending. □ **economía**
2 type of seashore plant with small tufts of pink flowers. □ **césped de Olimpo**
thrifty *adj.* (*thriftier, thriftiest*) careful with money. □ **ahorrativo**

thrill [θril] *n.* (shudder of) excitement: *the thrill of sliding down a slope on a sledge; it gave me a thrill to see her win the prize.* □ **estremecimiento**
■ *v.* to give (someone) a shudder of excitement; to be excited: *the crowd was thrilled by the tightrope walker; they thrilled to the sound of the bagpipes.* □ **electrizar, estremecer**
thriller *n.* exciting novel/film, etc. (usually about crime). □ **novela/película de suspense**
thrilling *adj.* very exciting: *it was thrilling to watch the ski-jumping championships; a thrilling race.* □ **emocionante**

thrive [θraiv] *v.* (*he thrived/throve*) **1** to grow well/to be strong: *these plants thrive in chalky soil; all our family are thriving; a thriving business.* □ **desarrollarse bien**
2 *he thrives on solving problems,* he enjoys/gets excitement from solving problems. □ **disfruta solucionando problemas**

throat [θrout] *n.* **1** front part of your neck below the chin: *he grabbed me by the throat; she was found dead with her throat cut.* □ **cuello**
2 pipe running from the back of your mouth down the inside of your neck: *I've got a sore throat; a lump of meat got stuck in his throat.* □ **garganta**
to clear your throat, to give a short cough. □ **carraspear**
to ram/force something down somebody's throat: *he's always ramming figures down my throat,* (*informal*) making me think of figures. □ **siempre me está machacando con números**
throaty *adj.* (*throatier, throatiest*) ***throaty voice,*** low, rough-sounding voice. □ **gutural**
throaty cough, cough which shows that your throat is infected. □ **tos de garganta**

throb [θrɔb] *n.* beating (of heart/machine). □ **latido (corazón); vibración (máquina)**
■ *v.* (*he throbbed*) **1** to beat regularly: *her heart was throbbing with excitement; a throbbing engine.* □ **latir (corazón); vibrar (motor)**
2 *my finger is throbbing,* has a regular pain. □ **siento pinchazos en el dedo**

throes [θrouz] *n. pl. death throes,* great suffering just before death. □ **agonía**
in the throes, in the middle: *we're in the throes of buying a new house; the country was in the throes of a general election.* □ **en medio de, inmerso**

thrombosis [θrɔm'bousis] *n.* clot in a blood vessel, especially in the heart. □ **trombosis**

throne [θroun] *n.* ceremonial chair for a king/queen, etc. □ **trono**
the throne, the position of king: *a claimant to the throne of France.* □ **el trono**

throng [θrɔŋ] *n.* great crowd of people: *throngs of shoppers tried to get on to the bus.* □ **multitud**
■ *v.* to crowd together: *the street was thronged with people; people thronged into the cinema.* □ **atestar**

throttle ['θrɔtl] *n.* valve on a pipe which allows variable quantities of steam/petrol, etc., to pass into an engine: *to open up the throttle,* to make the engine go faster. □ **válvula de admisión; acelerar**
■ *v.* **1** to strangle (someone) by squeezing the neck, and preventing them breathing. □ **estrangular**
2 ***to throttle down,*** to reduce the supply of petrol to an engine, making it go more slowly. □ **reducir la velocidad**

through [θru:] *prep.* **1** crossing something inside it/going in at one side and coming out at the other: *to go through a door; to look through a window; water flows through a pipe.* □ **a través de**
2 during: *all through his life; halfway through the film the lights went on; I am halfway through this book.* □ **durante; a mitad de**
3 *Amer.* up to and including: *Monday through Friday,* from Monday to Friday inclusively. □ **de lunes a viernes**
4 by means of: *to send a letter through the post; I heard of it through my sister.* □ **por**
5 because of: *he is absent through illness; it all happened through his forgetting to write the letter.* □ **a causa de**
■ *adv.* **1** from one side to another: *the water poured through; the crowd wouldn't let the police through.* □ **el agua caló completamente; ...no dejará pasar a la policía**
2 completely: *I'm wet through.* □ **completamente**
3 to the finish: *we must see the plan through,* see that it is completed. □ **...el plan acabado**
4 in contact by telephone: *I am trying to get through to Holland; can you put me through to the manager?* □ **...hablar con Holanda; ¿puedes ponerme con...?**
■ *adj.* **1** which goes from one side to the other without stopping: *a through carriage to Rome,* a carriage on a train which will continue to Rome, although the rest of the train does not go as far. □ **directo**
through traffic, traffic going through a town without stopping. □ **tráfico directo**
2 finished/completed: *I'm through with her,* (*informal*) I've broken off our friendship; *can you pass me the newspaper when you're through with it?,* when you have finished reading it. □ **he roto con ella; ...cuando lo hayas terminado**
through and through *adv.* completely. □ **hasta la médula**
throughout [θru:'aut] *prep.* in every part; at all times: from beginning to end: *roads are blocked by snow throughout the whole of the region; we have had no heating throughout the whole winter; he snored throughout the whole lecture.* □ **por todas partes; todo el tiempo**
■ *adv.* everywhere; at all times: *the house has been furnished throughout with antiques.* □ **por todas partes**
throughput ['θru:put] *n.* amount of work done/of goods produced in a certain time. □ **rendimiento**
throughway *n. Amer.* motorway/high-speed road with few junctions. □ **autopista**

throve [θrouv] *v. see* **thrive.**

throw [θrou] *n.* **1** sending something through the air: *his throw fell short; she is in hospital after a throw from a horse.* □ **tiro; derribo (de caballo)**
2 distance something is sent through the air: *the athlete made a record-breaking throw.* □ **lanzamiento**
3 *they live* ***a stone's throw away,*** quite close. □ **...a tiro de piedra**

■ *v.* (*he threw; he has thrown*) **1** to send (something) through the air: *how far can you throw this ball? he threw a stone through the window; the car hit a lamp post and the driver was thrown out; she threw the letter into the fire.* □ **echar; lanzar; tirar**
2 *can you **throw** any **light on** the problem?*, make the problem clearer. □ **puedes arrojar...**
3 to make (a pot) with clay (on a wheel). □ **tornear**
4 (*informal*) to hold (a party): *he's throwing a party for five hundred guests.* □ **dar (una fiesta)**
5 (*informal*) to surprise/to confuse: *the phone call threw him.* □ **desconcertar**
throw away *v.* **1** to get rid of (something) which you no longer need: *he threw away his skis after he broke his leg.* □ **tirar**
2 to waste: *she threw away the chance to be a film star.* □ **desperdiciar**
throwaway *adj.* which can be got rid of: *throwaway paper plates.* □ **desechable**
a throwaway line, joke said so quickly that it seems that the speaker did not want anyone to hear it. □ **chiste rápido**
throwback *n.* animal which shows characteristics of distant ancestors; something which shows a connection with the past: *his pipe is a throwback to his days in the Navy.* □ **recuerdo, salto atrás**
throw in *v.* **1** to add: *when making soup you should always throw in a few herbs; he sold me the car and threw in the roof rack for the same price,* added it for no extra money. □ **añadir**
2 (*in football*) to throw the ball back into play. □ **sacar de banda**
throw-in *n.* (*in football*) throwing the ball back into play from the touch line. □ **saque de banda**
throw off *v.* to get rid (of something): *I've had a cold for weeks and just can't throw it off.* □ **quitarse**
throw out *v.* **1** to put (something/someone) outside using force: *he was thrown out of the restaurant/the club.* □ **echar, expulsar**
2 to send out: *the fire throws out a considerable amount of heat.* □ **despedir**
3 to reject: *the committee threw out the proposal.* □ **rechazar**
throw up *v.* **1** to send up into the air: *he threw the ball up into the tree.* □ **lanzar**
2 to vomit: *the dog has thrown up all over the kitchen floor.* □ **vomitar**
3 to give up/to abandon: *he's thrown everything up and gone to live in Scotland; she threw up her job.* □ **dejar, abandonar**

thru [θru:] *prep., adv.* and *adj. Amer.* (*informal*) = **through.**
thruway *n. Amer.* = **throughway.**

thrush [θrʌʃ] *n.* (*pl. thrushes*) **1** common brown bird with a speckled breast. □ **tordo**
2 infectious throat disease in children. □ **afta**

thrust [θrʌst] *n.* **1** push; force which pushes: *the thrust of the rocket's engines.* □ **empuje**
2 stab with a sword or dagger. □ **estocada**
■ *v.* (*he thrust*) **1** to push energetically: *they thrust a piece of paper into his hand; he walked along with his hands thrust into his trouser pockets; the soldiers thrust their way through the crowd.* □ **meter**
2 ***to thrust yourself on someone,*** to force someone to accept you as a guest/companion, etc. □ **imponerse, pegarse**

thud [θʌd] *n.* dull noise: *the rock landed on the roof of the car with a thud.* □ **ruido sordo**
■ *v.* (*he thudded*) to make a dull noise: *he thudded into the wall; the heavy envelope thudded on to the doormat.* □ **hacer un ruido sordo, golpear**

thug [θʌg] *n.* ruffian/violent person. □ **gamberro, canalla**

thumb [θʌm] *n.* **1** short thick finger which is placed apart from the other four fingers on each hand. □ **pulgar**
2 *his fingers are **all thumbs,*** he is awkward with his hands. □ **es un manazas**
3 *it's a useful **rule of thumb,*** (i) a useful way of calculating approximately. □ **cálculo a ojo**
(ii) a practical way of approaching a problem. □ **sistema práctico**
4 ***to be under someone's thumb,*** to be dominated by someone. □ **estar dominado por...**
5 ***thumbs up*** (***sign***), (*informal*) gesture to show that everything is all right. □ **bien, resultado positivo**
6 ***to give someone the thumbs up,*** to show that all is right/that you have won, etc. □ **indicar un resultado positivo**
7 ***thumbs down*** (***sign***), (*informal*) gesture to show that something has gone wrong. □ **mal, resultado negativo**
8 ***to give something the thumbs down,*** to refuse to allow something to happen. □ **no autorizar**
9 part of a glove into which the thumb goes. □ **dedo**
■ *v.* **1** *to thumb through a book,* to flick through the pages using your thumb. □ **hojear**
a well-thumbed book, one which has been used often. □ **manoseado**
2 *to thumb a lift,* to get a lift from a passing car by making a sign with your thumb. □ **hacer autoestop**
thumbnail *n.* nail on a thumb. □ **uña del pulgar**
thumbnail sketch, rapid, very small sketch/description. □ **breve**
thumb-index *n.* series of notches cut in the edges of the pages of a dictionary/encyclopedia so that you can easily see where a new letter/chapter starts. □ **uñeros**
■ *v.* to give a book a thumb-index: *a thumb-indexed copy of the Bible.* □ **poner uñeros**
thumbscrew *n.* machine for torturing, which squeezes the victim's thumb. □ **empulgueras**
thumbtack *n. Amer.* drawing pin/pin with a large flat head for pinning paper. □ **chincheta**

thump [θʌmp] *n.* **1** dull noise. □ **ruido sordo**
2 punch; heavy blow with the fist. □ **puñetazo**
■ *v.* **1** to hit with the fist: *he thumped the table.* □ **dar un puñetazo**
2 to make a dull noise: *his heart thumped.* □ **latir con fuerza**
thumping *adj.* (*informal*) very large: *he was elected with a thumping majority.* □ **enorme**

thunder ['θʌndə] *n.* **1** rumbling noise in the air caused by lightning: *a clap of thunder.* □ **trueno**
to steal someone's thunder, to take the credit for something someone has done/to do something remarkable so that no one notices what another person has done. □ **robar el mérito**
2 loud rumbling noise: *a thunder of applause.* □ **estruendo**
■ *v.* **1** to make a rumbling noise: *it's thundering,* there is a rumbling noise caused by lightning; *the train thundered through the station; the rain thundered on the metal roof.* □ **tronar; retumbar**
2 to speak loudly: *'get out!', he thundered.* □ **tronar**
thunderbolt *n.* **1** flash of lightning and thunder: *he was struck down by a thunderbolt.* □ **rayo**
2 sudden (unpleasant) surprise. □ **bomba**
thunderclap *n.* sudden noise of thunder. □ **trueno**
thundercloud *n.* large black cloud which will bring

thunder and lightning. □ **nube tormentosa**
thundering *adj.* (*informal*) very big/terrible: *he was in a thundering rage.* □ **tremendo**
thunderous *adj.* very loud (applause). □ **estruendoso**
thunderstorm *n.* rainstorm with thunder and lightning. □ **tormenta**
thunderstruck *adj.* astonished. □ **asombrado**
thundery *adj.* (weather) when thunder is likely. □ **tormentoso**

Thursday ['θə:zdei] *n.* fourth day of the week/day between Wednesday and Friday: *I saw her last Thursday; he doesn't go to work on Thursdays.* □ **jueves**

thus [ðʌs] *adv.* (*formal*) **1** in this way: *to open the lock you put the key in the hole and turn it thus.* □ **así**
2 and so: *thus it happened that they quarreled; thus, if you want to get a good job you should study more.* □ **así**

thwack [θwæk] *n.* sound made when hitting something hard. □ **golpe**
■ *v.* to hit (something) hard. □ **golpear**

thwart [θwɔ:t] *n.* seat for a rower in a boat. □ **bancada**
■ *v.* to prevent (someone) doing something: *he was thwarted in his attempt; the attempted coup was thwarted.* □ **frustrar**

thyme [taim] *n.* common herb used as flavouring. □ **tomillo**

thyroid (gland) ['θairɔid('glænd)] *n.* gland in the neck which influences the growth, etc., of the body. □ **tiroides**
thyroidectomy *n.* operation to remove the thyroid gland. □ **tiroidectomía**

tiara [ti'ɑ:rə] *n.* headpiece with jewels, like a small crown. □ **diadema**

tibia ['tibiə] *n.* one of the two large bones between the knee and the ankle. □ **tibia**

tic [tik] *n.* twitch of the muscles which cannot be controlled: *a nervous tic.* □ **tic**

tick [tik] *n.* **1** (*informal*) very short moment: *wait a tick; I'll be with you in two ticks.* □ **momento, segundo**
2 mark on paper to indicate that something is correct: *to put a tick against someone's name,* to indicate that he is present. □ **señal, marca**
3 small insect or similar creature which lives on the skin of birds and animals. □ **garrapata**
4 (*informal*) credit: *to buy something on tick.* □ **crédito**
5 small click made by a clock/watch, etc. □ **tictac**
■ *v.* **1** to mark with a tick: *he ticked the names on the list; please tick the items you require.* □ **marcar**
2 to make a small clicking noise: *the clock was ticking; the bomb was ticking.* □ **hacer tictac**
3 *to try to find out what makes someone tick,* (*informal*) what is the reason for his behaviour. □ **la razón de su comportamiento**
tick away *v.* (*of time*) to pass: *the minutes were ticking away.* □ **pasar**
ticker *n.* (*informal*) **1** watch. □ **reloj**
2 heart. □ **corazón**
tickertape *n.* long paper tape which carries information printed automatically by telegraph. □ **cinta perforada**
tick off *v.* **1** to mark with a tick: *he ticked off the names on his list.* □ **marcar**
2 (*informal*) to reprimand (someone): *the policeman ticked him off for riding without any lights.* □ **echar una bronca**
tick over *v.* (*of car engine*) to run gently while the car is stationary. □ **funcionar al ralentí**

ticket ['tikit] *n.* **1** piece of paper/card allowing you to travel; piece of paper which allows you to go into a theatre/cinema, etc.; piece of paper showing a price/information; piece of paper which you are given when you leave a coat in a cloakroom: *theatre ticket; cloakroom ticket; can I have a return ticket to London? ticket collector; he's lost his plane tickets; the price on the ticket is $6.* □ **billete, entrada, etiqueta**
parking ticket, piece of paper showing that you have parked illegally and must pay a fine. □ **tique**
2 ***master's ticket,*** licence held by the captain of a ship which shows he is qualified. □ **título del capitán**
3 *Amer.* list of candidates sponsored by a political party. □ **lista**
■ *v.* to stick a ticket on (something for sale). □ **poner etiquetas**

ticking ['tikiŋ] *n.* thick cloth for covering mattresses, etc. □ **terliz**

tickle ['tikl] *n.* irritation which makes you laugh/cough: *I have a tickle at the back of my throat.* □ **picor**
■ *v.* **1** to irritate mildly a part of someone's body in order to make him laugh: *they tickled the soles of his feet; the feather tickled his nose.* □ **hacer cosquillas**
2 *he was **tickled pink** to get the invitation,* (*informal*) very pleased and amused. □ **encantar**
3 to itch/to be irritated: *my back tickles.* □ **picar**
ticklish *adj.* **1** (person) who is easily made to laugh by tickling. □ **cosquilloso**
2 (*informal*) difficult (problem). □ **peliagudo**
tickly *adj.* irritated so as to make you want to scratch: *my foot is all tickly.* □ **con picor, irritado**

tic-tac-toe [tiktæk'tou] *n.* *Amer.* noughts and crosses/game for two players where each puts a cross or a nought in one of nine squares, the object being to make a line of noughts or crosses first. □ **tres en raya**

tidbit ['tidbit] *n.* *Amer.* *see* **titbit.**

tiddler ['tidlə] *n.* (*informal*) very small fish. □ **pececillo**

tiddly ['tidli] *adj.* (*informal*) rather drunk. □ **borracho**
tiddly-winks *n.* game where small discs have to be flicked into a little cup. □ **pulga**

tide [taid] *n.* **1** regular rising and falling movement of the sea: *high tide is at 7 o'clock.* □ **marea**
2 movement (of public opinion, etc.): *the tide of public opinion is running strongly against the president.* □ **corriente**
to swim against the tide, to go against what most people think. □ **ir contra corriente**
■ *v.* ***to tide someone over,*** to help him get past a difficult period: *we have enough sugar to tide us over until the shops open again.* □ **ayudar a salir de un apuro**
tidal *adj.* referring to the tide. □ **de la marea**
tidal wave, huge wave in the sea. □ **ola de gran tamaño**
tidal stretch of the river, part of the river near its mouth where the movement of the tides is noticeable. □ **estuario**
tidemark *n.* **1** mark showing the top limit of a tide. □ **línea de la marea**
2 (*informal*) dirty line round a bath showing where the water reached to; line (as on your neck) showing which part of the body has been washed and which has not. □ **línea de suciedad**

tideway *n.* current caused by the tide running in a tidal stretch of a river. □ **canal de marea**
tidings ['taidiŋz] *n. pl.* (*formal*) news. □ **noticias**
tidy ['taidi] *adj.* (*tidier, tidiest*) **1** neat/in good order: *he keeps his books tidy; make yourself tidy.* □ **limpio; ordenado**
2 (*informal*) quite large: *it will cost a tidy sum of money.* □ **bonito**
■ *n.* small container for putting things in to keep them tidy. □ **recipiente, caja**
■ *v.* to make (something) neat: *he was tidying his room.* □ **ordenar, limpiar**
tidily *adv.* in a tidy way. □ **bien, en orden**
tidiness *n.* being tidy. □ **orden, limpieza**
tidy up *v.* to make (something) completely tidy; to remove (a mess): *can't you tidy up all those papers? we must tidy everything up before the visitors arrive.* □ **ordenar, arreglar**
tie [tai] *n.* **1** something which attaches/which restricts: *to attach a plant to a stick with a plastic tie; the ties of friendship; she finds her children a tie,* finds that they prevent her from doing what she wants. □ **cuerda; vínculo; atadura**
2 band of cloth which is worn knotted round the neck under the shirt collar: *a bow tie; old school tie,* particular tie which shows which school you went to. □ **corbata**
3 linking mark in music to show that several notes are to be played as one long note. □ **ligado**
4 equal score in a competition/election: *there was a tie for second place,* two people were equal second; *the result was a tie, so a second vote had to be taken.* □ **empate**
5 ***cup tie,*** football match as a result of which one team is eliminated from a championship. □ **partido de copa**
■ *v.* **1** to attach/to fasten: *the parcel is tied with string; the horse was tied to a fence; the burglars tied his hands behind his back.* □ **atar**
2 *she's tied to her work,* can never get away from it. □ **atar**
3 to knot: *tie your shoelaces; to tie a knot in a piece of string.* □ **atar, hacer un nudo**
4 to come equal in a competition: *the two runners tied for second place.* □ **empatar**
tie-breaker *n.* (*in tennis*) game to decide the winner of a set, played when the score is 6-6. □ **'tie-breaker'**
tied *adj.* attached. □ **atado, vinculado**
tied house, public house which belongs to a brewery. □ **bar**
tied cottage, cottage belonging to a farmer who rents it to his farmworkers. □ **casa agrícola alquilada**
tie down *v.* to attach (to the ground). □ **atar**
to tie someone down, to make him accept certain conditions. □ **atar, someter**
tie-on *adj.* ***tie-on label,*** label with a string attached so that it can be tied. □ **etiqueta para atar**
tiepin *n.* pin for attaching a tie. □ **alfiler de corbata**
tie up *v.* **1** to attach/to fasten: *to tie up a parcel; the ship was tied up at the quay; that dog ought to be tied up.* □ **atar, amarrar**
2 to keep motionless. □ **inmovilizar**
3 *this is tying up a large sum of money,* keeping it so that it cannot be used for other purposes. □ **inmovilizar**
4 ***to be tied up:*** *I'm rather tied up at the moment,* (*informal*) rather busy. □ **estar liado**
tie-up *n.* link/connection: *we have a tie-up with a firm in the States.* □ **relación, enlace**
tier ['tiə] *n.* one of a series of steps, usually a row of seats in a theatre: *the seats rise in tiers; a wedding cake with four tiers/a four-tier wedding cake,* made of four separate cakes balanced one on top of the other. □ **piso, grada, fila**
tiered *adj.* with tiers: *tiered seats.* □ **en grada**
tiff [tif] *n.* small argument/quarrel. □ **riña**
tiffin ['tifin] *n.* (*in India, etc.*) lunch. □ **almuerzo**
tiger ['taigə] *n.* large striped cat-like wild animal. □ **tigre**
tiger lily, lily with spotted orange flowers. □ **variedad de lirio**
paper tiger, something which seems fierce but is really harmless. □ **tigre de papel**
tigress *n.* female tiger. □ **tigresa**
tight [tait] *adj.* (*tighter, tightest*) **1** which fits (too) closely: *the jar has a tight lid; this dress is too tight, I can't bend down; he was wearing very tight trousers; these shoes are too tight.* □ **prieto, ajustado**
2 closely packed together: *it's a tight fit/a tight squeeze.* □ **apretado**
3 *I have a very tight schedule,* my timetable allows no spare time. □ **apretado**
4 stretched taut: *is the string tight? pull the cover tight.* □ **tenso**
5 (*informal*) difficult to get: *money is tight these days.* □ **difícil**
6 (*informal*) drunk. □ **borracho**
■ *adv.* **1** closely/firmly: *shut the door tight; to hold someone tight; she held the money tight in her hand; hold tight - we're turning a corner; screw the lid on tight.* □ **bien, con fuerza, herméticamente**
2 closely packed: *the boxes fit tight into each other.* □ **justo**
3 ***to sit tight,*** (*informal*) to stay where you are. □ **quedarse en el sitio, quieto**
tighten *v.* to make/to become tight: *to tighten a nut; to tighten the lid on a jar.* □ **apretar**
to tighten one's belt, (*informal*) to try to live on less money: *if the economy gets worse, we shall have to tighten our belts.* □ **apretarse el cinturón**
tightfisted *adj.* (*informal*) mean/not generous. □ **tacaño**
tightfitting *adj.* which fits tightly: *tightfitting trousers.* □ **ajustado**
tightly *adv.* closely/in a tight way: *he screwed the lid on tightly; she held tightly on to the rail.* □ **bien, herméticamente, justo**
tightrope *n.* rope stretched between two poles on which someone can walk/can perform tricks: *he crossed the river on a tightrope; a tightrope walker.* □ **cuerda floja**
tights *n. pl.* close-fitting piece of clothing worn by girls, women, dancers, etc., on the legs and lower part of the body. □ **leotardos, mallas**
tile [tail] *n.* flat piece of baked clay used to cover floors/walls/roofs. □ **teja, baldosa, azulejo**
carpet tiles, square pieces of carpet which can be laid on a floor like tiles. □ **losetas**
■ *v.* to cover a roof/a floor/a wall with tiles: *a tiled floor.* □ **tejar, embaldosar, alicatar**
till [til] *n.* cash drawer for keeping money in a shop. □ **caja**
■ *v.* to cultivate (land). □ **labrar**
■ *prep.* until/up to (a time): *I won't be home till very late; from morning till night.* □ **hasta**
■ *conj.* up to/until: *the performance cannot start till everyone is sitting down.* □ **hasta que**
tiller ['tilə] *n.* handle which is attached to a rudder and so steers a boat. □ **caña del timón**
tilt [tilt] *n.* **1** slope/slant. □ **inclinación**
2 ***at full tilt,*** at full speed: *he ran full tilt into a wall.*

□ **a toda velocidad**
■ *v.* to slope; to place at a slope: *he tilted his chair back; the yacht tilted over and sank.* □ **inclinar(se)**

timber ['timbə] *n.* **1** cut wood ready for building: *timber merchant,* person who sells timber. □ **madera**
2 growing trees which could be cut down and used for building. □ **árboles para madera**
3 large beam/plank used in building a house/a ship. □ **cuaderna**
timbered *adj.* (house) made of wooden beams. □ **con estructura de madera**
timberyard *n.* place where cut wood is sold. □ **serrería**

timbre ['tæmbə] *n.* quality of sound (of a voice or musical instrument). □ **timbre**

time [taim] *n.* **1** existence for a period (such as years/centuries, etc.). □ **tiempo**
time alone will tell, the result will only become apparent later. □ **sólo el tiempo lo dirá**
to have time (on your hands), to have a leisure period with nothing to do: *I've no time to stand here talking; have you time for a cup of tea? you've plenty of time.* □ **tener tiempo**
there's no time to be lost, we must hurry. □ **no hay tiempo que perder**
to make up for lost time, to do things rapidly because time has been wasted. □ **recuperar el tiempo perdido**
2 period between two happenings: *in a short time; to take a long time over something; I haven't seen him for a long time; in three weeks' time,* three weeks from now. □ **tiempo, plazo, intervalo**
all the time, continuously. □ **todo el tiempo**
3 particular period: *this house will last our time,* will last as long as we live. □ **tiempo, época**
to do time, (*informal*) to serve a prison sentence. □ **cumplir una condena**
full time/part time, working a full day's work/half a day's work. □ **dedicación completa/parcial**
4 ***times,*** age/period: *in Roman times/in former times.* □ **época**
5 *he's* ***behind the times,*** out of date. □ **anticuado**
6 particular point at which something took place: *I was away at the time,* when it happened; *at the present time,* now; *at any given time; he may arrive at any time.* □ **en ese momento; ahora...**
by the time *I got there,* when I got there. □ **cuando**
from time to time/at times, occasionally. □ **de vez en cuando**
for the time being, temporarily. □ **por el momento**
7 point expressed in hours and minutes: *the time is exactly ten past six; what's the time? what time do you make it?* □ **hora**
Greenwich Mean Time, internationally accepted correct time system. □ **hora del meridiano de Greenwich**
8 hour at which something usually happens: *when is closing time? dinner time; is it time to go to bed?* □ **hora**
9 ***on time,*** (i) *the train arrived on time,* at the right time. □ **a tiempo**
(ii) *he's always on time,* punctual. □ **puntual**
10 *we were* ***in time*** *to see the beginning of the film,* we were early enough. □ **a tiempo**
11 (pleasant/bad) period: *we had a good time at the party; he had a rough time in hospital.* □ **pasarlo bien/mal**
12 one of several occasions: *I've seen the film three times; next time, bring your swimming things; this box is four times as big as that one.* □ **vez**
13 ***times,*** multiplied by: *six times four is twenty-four; he doesn't know his seven times table,* the list of numbers multiplied by seven. □ **por; tabla del siete**
14 rhythm: *he beat time to the music with his foot; he tried to keep time with the rest of the band; the soldiers marched in time.* □ **compás**
■ *v.* **1** to choose the right moment: *he timed his remarks very well.* □ **elegir el momento**
2 to calculate the time something takes: *you run round the course and I'll time you.* □ **calcular, cronometrar**
time bomb *n.* bomb with a clock attached, which sets off the bomb at a particular moment. □ **bomba de relojería**
time-honoured *adj.* (custom) which has been observed for a long time, and therefore is respected. □ **consagrado**
timekeeper *n.* **1** person who times a race. □ **cronometrador**
2 *a good timekeeper,* person who is always on time/watch which always shows the correct time. □ **puntual**
timekeeping *n.* being on time. □ **puntualidad**
timelag *n.* delay. □ **retraso**
timeless *adj.* permanent: *timeless beauty.* □ **eterno**
time limit *n.* period during which something should be done: *to set a time limit for payment.* □ **límite temporal, plazo**
timeliness *n.* being timely. □ **oportunidad**
timely *adj.* which happens at the right moment: *a timely warning.* □ **oportuno**
timepiece *n.* old-fashioned watch or clock. □ **reloj antiguo**
timer *n.* person/device which times. □ **cronometrador/cronómetro**
egg timer, device which times how long an egg boils. □ **reloj de cocina**
timeserver *n.* person who changes his opinions to match those of people in power. □ **chaquetero**
time-signal *n.* accurate radio signal showing the exact time. □ **señal horaria**
time-switch *n.* switch which can be set to start a machine/to stop a light, etc., at a particular time. □ **temporizador**
timetable *n.* list which shows the times of trains/aircraft/classes in school/appointments: *have you the latest train timetable? there are two English lessons on the timetable today; we have to keep to a strict timetable of appointments.* □ **horario**
■ *v.* to draw up a list of times; to appear on a list of times: *I have two appointments timetabled for ten o'clock.* □ **fijar, programar**
time-work *n.* work which is paid for at a rate of money for a particular time. □ **trabajo por horas**
time zone *n.* zone on the earth in which a certain uniform time is kept. □ **huso horario**
timing *n.* **1** the action of recording the time (of a race). □ **cronometraje**
2 controlling the time at which something happens. □ **coordinación, control**
3 (*in a car engine*) rate at which the spark coincides with the flow of petrol. □ **reglaje**

timid ['timid] *adj.* afraid/frightened. □ **tímido, asustadizo**
timidity [ti'miditi] *n.* being timid. □ **timidez**
timidly ['timidli] *adv.* in a frightened way. □ **tímidamente**
timorous ['timərəs] *adv.* very frightened. □ **asustadizo**

timpani ['timpəni] *n. pl.* group of kettledrums in an orchestra. □ **timbales**

timpanist *n.* person who plays the timpani. □ **timbalero**
tin [tin] *n.* **1** (*chemical element*: Sn) silvery metal. □ **estaño**
2 metal covered with a thin layer of tin: *a tin box; a tin whistle.* □ **hojalata**
3 (usually round) metal box for keeping food in: *a tin of peas; a sardine tin.* □ **lata**
cake tin, tin for baking or keeping cakes in. □ **lata, molde**
■ *v.* (*he tinned*) to preserve (food) by packing it in a tin: *tinned peas; tinned sardines.* □ **enlatar**
tinfoil *n.* thin metal sheet used especially to wrap food up. □ **papel de aluminio**
tinny ['tini] *adj. to sound tinny/to make a tinny sound,* make a weak metallic sound (not ringing like a bell). □ **metálico**
a tinny car, a car which rattles. □ **que traquetea**
tin opener *n.* device for opening tins. □ **abrelatas**
tin plate ['tinpleit] *n.* thin sheet of iron covered with tin. □ **hojalata**
tinpot *adj.* (*informal*) not of good quality. □ **regular, malo**
tin tack *n.* nail with a large head used to nail down carpets, etc. □ **tachuela**
tincture ['tiŋktʃə] *n.* medicine dissolved in alcohol. □ **tintura**
tinder ['tində] *n.* very dry material for starting a fire. □ **yesca**
tine [tain] *n.* prong of a fork. □ **punta**
tinge [tindʒ] *n.* slight colour/taste, etc., of something: *green with an orange tinge.* □ **tinte, matiz**
■ *v.* to give a slight colour/taste to (something): *orange tinged with green; laughter tinged with sadness.* □ **teñir**
tingle ['tiŋgl] *n.* sharp prickling feeling. □ **escozor**
■ *v.* **1** to have a sharp prickling feeling: *the cold wind makes my ears tingle.* □ **escocer**
2 *tingling with excitement,* very excited. □ **muy excitado**
tinker [tiŋkə] *n.* mender of saucepans who travels from place to place. □ **calderero ambulante**
■ *v.* ***to tinker with something,*** to try (often in a clumsy way) to make something work better: *he was tinkering with the car engine; the government is tinkering with the economy.* □ **tratar de arreglar, pelearse con**
to tinker about, to do odd jobs at random. □ **picotear, hacer trabajillos**
tinkle ['tiŋkl] *n.* ringing (like a little bell): *tinkle of coins.* □ **tintineo**
■ *v.* to make a little ringing noise: *when you open the shop door a little bell tinkles.* □ **sonar, tintinear**
tinsel ['tinsl] *n.* thin strips of glittering metal used for decorating Christmas trees, etc. □ **cintas de oropel**
tint [tint] *n.* slight shade of colour: *a blue tint.* □ **matiz**
■ *v.* to give a slight shade of colour. □ **matizar**
tinted glass, glass which has a slight shade of brown/blue, etc. □ **de color**
tiny ['taini] *adj.* (*tinier, tiniest*) very small: *give me just a tiny bit of cheese/a tiny drop of wine.* □ **muy pequeño, trocito, pizca**
tip [tip] *n.* **1** pointed end: *she could touch it with the tips of her fingers; walking stick with a metal tip; filter-tip cigarette.* □ **punta**
I have it/it's on the tip of my tongue, I am going to remember it in a moment. □ **en la punta de la lengua**
the tip of the iceberg, small part of something (usually unpleasant) which makes you eventually discover the rest. □ **la punta del iceberg**
2 money given to a waiter, etc. to show thanks for his services: *I gave him a $1 tip; is the tip included in the bill?* □ **propina**
3 piece of helpful information: *racing tips,* suggestions as to which horses are likely to win; *if you take my tip, you won't go to that shop again,* if you take my advice; *here's a useful tip on how to clean carpets.* □ **consejo, información**
4 ***rubbish tip,*** public place where rubbish can be dumped. □ **vertedero**
■ *v.* (*he tipped*) **1** to put a tip on (something): *a metal-tipped stick.* □ **poner una contera**
2 to make (something) slope/lean. □ **inclinar, ladear**
3 to pour out/to empty (something): *he picked up the box and tipped a pile of coins on to the table.* □ **verter**
4 to throw away rubbish. □ **volcar, tirar**
5 to give (a waiter, etc.) a small gift of money: *I tipped him $1 to let us in to the party without an invitation.* □ **dar propina**
6 to give (someone) a piece of helpful information. □ **dar una información**
to tip someone off/to tip someone the wink, (*informal*) to warn someone: *someone must have tipped the gangsters off that the police were watching the house.* □ **advertir, avisar**
7 to forecast confidently that someone will do something: *the horse is tipped to win the race; he's tipped to become the next president.* □ **dar una información confidencial**
tip-off *n.* (*informal*) piece of useful information; warning. □ **información, aviso**
tip over *v.* to lean and fall over; to make (something) lean so far that it falls over: *he tipped over the bottle; the bottle tipped over and milk poured on to the table.* □ **volcar(se)**
tipster *n.* person who gives advice on which horse is likely to win a race. □ **pronosticador**
tiptoe *n.* ***on tiptoe,*** quietly on the tips of your toes: *he came up the stairs on tiptoe.* □ **de puntillas**
■ *v.* to walk quietly on the tips of your toes: *he tiptoed up the stairs.* □ **andar de puntillas**
tiptop *adj.* (*informal*) excellent. □ **de primera**
tip up *v.* **1** to turn (something) over so that the contents fall out. □ **volcar**
2 to swing on a hinge: *chair which tips up.* □ **levantarse**
tip-up *adj.* (chair/lorry) which tips up. □ **volquete**
tipple ['tipl] *n.* (*informal*) drink. □ **copa**
■ *v.* (*informal*) to drink alcohol regularly. □ **empinar el codo**
tipsy ['tipsi] *adj.* (*tipsier, tipsiest*) (*informal*) rather drunk. □ **borracho**
tipsy cake/pudding, cake soaked in sherry, etc., and served with custard. □ **tarta emborrachada**
tirade [tai'reid] *n.* long angry speech. □ **diatriba**
tire [taiə] *n. Amer. see* **tyre.**
■ *v.* **1** to become/to make weary; to need a rest after physical exercise: *we walked so fast that we tired him out; she tires easily.* □ **cansar(se)**
2 to lose interest in doing something: *I never tire of hearing his storie.* □ **cansarse**
tired *adj.* **1** feeling sleepy/in need of rest: *I was so tired I went to bed early.* □ **cansado**
2 ***tired of something,*** bored with something/having no patience with something: *I'm tired of his continual complaints; I'm tired of having to do all the work.* □ **cansado**
tiredness *n.* feeling in need of rest. □ **cansancio**
tireless *adj.* full of energy/never needing to rest: *thanks to your tireless efforts.* □ **incansable**
tiresome *adj.* annoying/bothering: *he's a tiresome*

man. □ **pesado**
tiring *adj.* which makes you tired: *a tiring journey through the snow.* □ **que cansa, agotador**
tiro ['tairou] *n.* (*pl. tiros*) complete beginner/person with no experience. □ **principiante, novato**
tissue ['tiʃuː] *n.* **1** group of cells which make up a part of an animal or plant: *nervous tissue; leaf tissue.* □ **tejido**
2 thin cloth. □ **tisú**
3 soft paper handkerchief: *a box of tissues.* □ **pañuelo de papel**
4 *tissue of lies,* a mass of lies. □ **sarta de mentiras**
tissue paper *n.* thin soft paper used for wrapping delicate objects. □ **papel de seda**
tit [tit] *n.* **1** type of common small bird: *blue tit.* □ **paro**
2 (*slang*) teat; breast. □ **teta**
3 ***tit for tat,*** paying back a blow with another blow. □ **golpe por golpe**
titanic [tai'tænik] *n.* very large. □ **titánico**
titbit ['titbit] *Amer.* **tidbit** *n.* special little piece (of food/of information). □ **bocado exquisito, noticia especial**
tithe [taið] *n.* produce which used to be paid to the church. □ **diezmo**
tithebarn *n.* barn in which tithes were kept. □ **granero para los diezmos**
titillate ['titileit] *v.* to excite. □ **excitar**
titivate ['titiveit] *v.* ***to titivate (yourself),*** (*informal*) to make yourself look smart. □ **acicalarse**
title ['taitl] *n.* **1** name of a book/play/film, etc.: *the title of his second novel is 'Back to the beginning'.* □ **título**
title page, page at the beginning of a book, where the title is written in large letters. □ **portada**
title role, part in a play/film which gives the name to the play/film: *he played the title role in 'Hamlet'.* □ **papel principal (que da el título)**
credit titles, words at the beginning of a film showing who is the director, etc. □ **títulos de crédito**
2 word (usually put in front of a name) to indicate an honour/a qualification: *he now has the title 'Dr'; he assumed the title of Emperor.* □ **título**
3 (*in sport*) position of champion: *they are fighting for the title of world heavyweight champion; a world title fight.* □ **título**
4 right to own (property). □ **título de propiedad**
title deed, paper showing that you are the owner of a property. □ **título de propiedad**
titled *adj.* with a title (such as Lord, Sir, etc.) to show that you are a nobleman. □ **con título**
titration [tai'treiʃn] *n.* method of analysis of the concentration of a chemical solution. □ **titulación**
titter ['titə] *n.* little laugh. □ **risita, sonrisa**
■ *v.* to give a little laugh: *the audience tittered when the actor forgot his lines.* □ **sonreír**
tittle tattle ['titl'tætl] *n.* (*informal*) gossip. □ **chismorreo**
titular ['titjulə] *adj.* holding a title but without direct power: *the titular head of state.* □ **titular**
tiz [tiz] **tizzy** ['tizi] *n.* (*informal*) bother/nervous state: *she got into a tizzy about having to go to court.* □ **estado de nervios**
TNT ['tiːen'tiː] *n.* common high explosive. □ **TNT**
to [tuː] *prep.* **1** (showing direction or position): *he went to France; I'm going to the grocer's; the road to London; move to the right; it's slightly to the east of the town.* □ **a**
2 (showing time): *from day to day; it's ten to six,* ten minutes before six o'clock. □ **a; seis menos diez**
3 (showing person who receives something): *give it to me; she threw the ball to her sister; pass the sugar to your father; you must be kind to animals; to drink to someone's health.* □ **a**
4 (showing relationship): *is this the key to the box? he is heir to his uncle's estate; she is secretary to the managing director.* □ **de**
5 concerning: *what did he say to my suggestion?* □ **sobre**
there's nothing to it, there's no difficulty in doing it. □ **no hay problema**
6 (showing ratio): *they lost by six goals to four; the exchange rate is two dollars to the pound; pressure of two kilograms to the square centimetre.* □ **a, por**
7 (showing comparison): *I prefer butter to margarine.* □ **a**
■ *adv.* **1** *he came to,* he regained consciousness. □ **volvió en sí**
2 *he pulled the door to,* he pulled it until it was almost shut. □ **entornó la puerta**
■ (*forming infinitive*) **1** (after verbs): *he bent down to tie up his shoelaces; they came to help us; he attempted to run away; she told me to shut the door.* □ **para; trató de escapar**
2 (after adjectives): *I'm glad he is able to do it; are these apples good to eat?* □ **de, para**
3 (after nouns): *he made no attempt to run away; it was a sight to make you want to cry.* □ **de, dan ganas de llorar**
4 (when the verb is a subject): *to refuse the invitation would have been too rude.* □ **rechazar la invitación...**
to and fro *adv.* backwards and forwards: *the guards walked to and fro in front of the palace.* □ **de acá para allá**
toad [toud] *n.* amphibian like a large frog, which lives mostly on land. □ **sapo**
toad in the hole, sausages cooked in a dish of batter. □ **plato de salchichas**
toadstool *n.* fungus shaped like a mushroom, but usually not edible, and sometimes poisonous. □ **seta**
toady *n.* (*pl. toadies*) person who flatters someone (in the hope of getting something in return). □ **adulador**
■ *v.* (*toadied; toadying*) to flatter (someone). □ **adular**
toast [toust] *n.* **1** slices of bread which have been grilled brown: *a piece of toast; poached eggs on toast.* □ **tostada**
2 taking a drink and wishing someone success: *let's drink a toast to your future happiness; the toast is 'good health to all of us'.* □ **copa con brindis**
■ *v.* **1** to grill (bread, etc.) until it is brown; to warm: *toasted scones; toasted cheese; he was toasting his feet in front of the fire.* □ **tostar, gratinar**
2 to drink and wish someone success: *they toasted her health in wine.* □ **brindar**
toaster *n.* electric device for toasting bread. □ **tostadora**
toastmaster *n.* person (at a banquet) who calls on people to speak and announces the toasts. □ **maestro de ceremonias**
toastrack *n.* device for holding slices of toast. □ **portatostadas**
tobacco [tə'bækou] *n.* (dried leaves of a) plant used for smoking in cigarettes/cigars and in pipes: *a tobacco plant; he grows tobacco in his back garden; a packet of pipe tobacco.* □ **tabaco**
tobacconist *n.* person who sells tobacco/cigarettes, etc.: *I must go to the tobacconist's to get some more cigarettes.* □ **estanquero, estanco**

toboggan [tə'bɔgən] *n.* long sledge curved upwards at the front. □ **tobogán**
■ *v.* to slide on a toboggan: *to go tobogganing.* □ **deslizarse por un tobogán**

toby jug ['toubi 'dʒʌg] *n.* small mug made in the shape of a head. □ **jarra de cerveza en forma de cabeza**

toccata [tɔ'kɑːtə] *n.* piece of music for the organ or piano. □ **tocata**

today [tə'dei] *adv.* and *n.* **1** this present day: *he said he would see me today; today's his wedding day; we'll meet again today week/a week today,* in exactly seven days' time. □ **hoy**
2 this present time: *today's children are tomorrow's adults; life today is much more comfortable than it was fifty years ago.* □ **hoy, actualmente**

toddle ['tɔdl] *v.* **1** to walk unsteadily: *the baby is just starting to toddle.* □ **andar inseguro**
2 *I must toddle,* (*informal*) I must go. □ **tengo que irme**
toddler *n.* child who is just learning to walk. □ **niño que empieza a andar**

toddy ['tɔdi] *n.* (*pl. toddies*) alcohol and hot water and sugar. □ **ponche**

to-do [tə'duː] *n.* (*informal*) excitement/confusion/bother: *he made a great to-do about having lost his umbrella; what a to-do!* □ **jaleo**

toe [tou] *n.* **1** one of the five parts like fingers at the end of your foot: *the baby was sucking his toes; big toe/little toe,* the largest/smallest of the five toes; *he trod on my toe.* □ **dedo del pie**
on one's toes, ready for action; alert: *he keeps you on your toes.* □ **alerta**
2 end part of a shoe/a sock: *toe cap,* hard end to a shoe. □ **punta**
■ *v.* ***to toe the line,*** to do what you are told to do/to do what everyone else does. □ **hacer lo que está mandado**
toehold *n.* grip with the toes; small foothold. □ **punto de apoyo**
toenail *n.* nail at the end of a toe.□ **uña del pie**

toffee ['tɔfi] *n.* sticky sweet made with sugar and butter. □ **toffee**
toffee apple, apple covered with toffee (usually sold on a short stick to eat out of doors). □ **manzana con caramelo**
for toffee, (*informal*) at all: *he can't do it for toffee.* □ **en absoluto**
toffee-nosed *adj.* (*informal*) supercilious. □ **presumido**

together [tə'geðə] *adv.* **1** in a group/all at the same time: *we'll go to the police station all three of us together; we must stay together or we'll get lost; I'll pay for everything together.* □ **juntos**
2 *we must **get together** again soon,* meet. □ **reunirse**
3 into contact one with another: *to stick the pieces together; to bring two rivals together; tie the ends of the rope together; add all these numbers together.* □ **juntar, reunir, sumar**

toggle ['tɔgl] *n.* short piece of wood attached to a coat with string, used in place of a button; small clasp used for attaching a scarf. □ **alamar**

togs [tɔgz] *n. pl.* (*informal*) clothes. □ **ropa**

toil [tɔil] *n.* hard work. □ **trabajo duro**
■ *v.* **1** to work hard. □ **trabajar duro**
2 *he toiled up the mountain,* climbed the mountain with great difficulty. □ **subió con gran esfuerzo**

toilet ['tɔilət] *n.* **1** washing and dressing: *she seems to be taking a long time over her toilet.* □ **aseo, arreglo**
2 bowl with a seat on which you sit to pass waste matter from the body; room with this bowl in it: *to go to the toilet; where's the ladies' toilet? none of the toilets seem to work.* □ **retrete, servicios**
toilet paper, soft paper for wiping your anus after getting rid of waste matter. □ **papel higiénico**
toilet roll, a roll of toilet paper. □ **rollo de papel higiénico**
toilet water, scented water. □ **agua de colonia**
toiletries *n. pl.* facecloths/soap/perfume, etc., used in washing. □ **artículos de aseo**

token ['toukən] *n.* **1** something visible which is a mark/sign (of respect, etc.): *please accept this gift as a token of my friendship; a 24 hour truce was called as a token of respect for the dead.* □ **prueba, señal**
by the same token, in a similar way. □ **análogamente**
2 *a token strike,* short strike which stands as a symbol of grievances; *to make a token payment,* a small symbolic payment. □ **simbólico**
the token woman, only woman (on a committee, etc.) who feels she is there to please the women's liberation movement. □ **con presencia simbólica**
3 piece of paper/card/plastic which is used to replace money: *book/flower/record token,* card which can only be exchanged for books/flowers/records. □ **vale**

told [tould] *v. see* **tell.**

tolerate ['tɔləreit] *v.* **1** to suffer (noise, etc.) without complaining: *I can't tolerate this unruly behaviour.* □ **tolerar**
2 to allow (something which you do not agree with): *opposition parties are not tolerated.* □ **permitir**
tolerable ['tɔlərəbl] *adj.* **1** bearable: *the noise is hardly tolerable.* □ **tolerable**
2 fairly good: *it was a tolerable meal.* □ **aceptable**
tolerably *adv.* in a fairly good way: *a tolerably good film,* quite a good film. □ **aceptablemente**
tolerance *n.* **1** putting up with (unpleasantness, etc.); allowing (something which you do not agree with) to exist: *the government has shown tolerance to the opposition parties.* □ **tolerancia**
2 amount by which a measurement can vary from what is specified on a plan: *to allow for a tolerance of 2 cm.* □ **tolerancia**
3 ability to stand the effect of a drug/a poison. □ **tolerancia**
tolerant *adj.* (person) who tolerates: *a tolerant man.* □ **tolerante**
toleration [tɔlə'reiʃn] *n.* allowing (something which you do not agree with) to exist: *religious toleration.* □ **tolerancia**

toll [toul] *n.* **1** payment for using a road/a bridge/a ferry. □ **peaje**
a toll bridge, one where a toll is paid. □ **puente de peaje**
2 loss/damage: *the fighting took a heavy toll of the defence forces,* many of them were killed; *the high death toll on the roads.* □ **precio, víctimas**
■ *v.* to ring (a bell) solemnly as for a funeral: *the bells were tolling for the dead; the church bell tolled midnight,* rang in a gloomy way. □ **tocar**
toll call *n. Amer.* long-distance telephone call. □ **conferencia**
toll free *adv. Amer.* without having to pay the charge for a long-distance call: *call this number toll free.* □ **gratis**

tom(cat) ['tɔm(kæt)] *n.* male cat. □ **gato (macho)**

tomahawk ['tæməhɔːk] *n.* light North American Indian axe. □ **tomahawk**

tomato [tə'mɑːtou; *Amer.* tə'meitou] *n.* (*pl. tomatoes*) red fruit growing on annual plants and used in

salads; the plant which bears tomatoes. □ **tomate**
tomato sauce, sauce made with tomatoes. □ **salsa de tomate**

tomb [tu:m] *n.* large grave (usually with an underground vault in which to put a dead person). □ **tumba**
tombstone *n.* large stone placed on a grave with the name of the dead person written on it. □ **lápida**

tombola [tɔm'boulə] *n.* game where people buy numbered tickets and one or more tickets win prizes. □ **tómbola**

tomboy ['tɔmbɔi] *n.* girl who plays rough games like a boy. □ **chicazo**

tome [toum] *n.* (*formal*) large book. □ **libro grande, tomo**

tomfool ['tɔmfu:l] *adj.* (*informal*) idiotic: *some tomfool idea of his.* □ **estúpido**
tomfoolery *n.* stupid behaviour. □ **estupidez**

tommy gun ['tɔmigʌn] *n.* small machine gun. □ **ametralladora pequeña**

tomorrow [tə'mɔrou] *adv.* and *n.***1** the day which follows today: *tomorrow morning/evening; can you meet me tomorrow lunchtime? tomorrow is my birthday.* □ **mañana**
2 the future: *tomorrow's world will be a safer place.* □ **el mañana**

tomtom ['tɔmtɔm] *n.* small drum beaten with your hands. □ **tantán**

ton [tʌn] *n.* **1** weight equal to 2,240 pounds: *a ton of cement.* □ **tonelada**
metric ton, 1,000 kilograms. □ **tonelada métrica**
2 space in a ship equivalent to 100 cubic feet: *a 60,000 ton tanker.* □ **tonelada**
3 ***tons,*** (*informal*) lots: *there was tons of food left over after the party; he's bought tons of jam.* □ **toneladas**
4 ***to do a ton,*** (*slang*) to go at 100 miles per hour. □ **ir a 100 millas por hora**
tonnage *n.* **1** space in a ship measured in tons. □ **tonelaje**
2 total number of ships in a navy/belonging to a company, calculated by adding together their individual sizes. □ **tonelaje**
tonne [tʌn] *n.* metric ton, equal to 1,000 kilograms. □ **tonelada métrica**

tone [toun] *n.* **1** quality of sound of music/voice: *the soft tones of a lute; the harsh tones of a brass band; the tone is bad on this transistor.* □ **tono**
2 (*in music*) difference between two notes which have one note between them on the piano. □ **tono**
3 way of speaking/writing which shows a particular emotion: *she spoke in a gentle tone; I don't like your tone of voice; I don't like the tone of his letter.* □ **tono**
4 shade of colour. □ **tono**
5 strength of the body and muscles. □ **tono**
6 general quality of appearance: *the general tone of the district has gone down; by giving grants to repaint houses, the council has improved the general tone of the neighbourhood.* □ **tono, nivel**
■ *v.* to fit in well/to harmonize: *the chairs tone (in) with the curtains.* □ **armonizar**
tonal ['tounl] *adj.* referring to tone. □ **tonal**
tonality [tə'næliti] *n.* quality of tone (in the colours of a painting/in a piece of music). □ **tonalidad**
tone-deaf *adj.* not able to recognize differences in musical pitch. □ **con mal oído**
tone down *v.* to reduce (something) excessive: *he toned down some of the criticisms in the report.* □ **suavizar**
tone up *v.* to make fitter: *you ought to do exercises every day to tone yourself up.* □ **coger tono, mejorar la forma física**

tongs [tɔŋs] *n. pl.* (***pair of***) ***tongs,*** instrument for picking things up, with small claws on the ends of two arms. □ **tenazas, pinzas**
sugar tongs, tongs for picking up lumps of sugar. □ **pinzas**

tongue [tʌŋ] *n.* **1** long, movable piece of muscular flesh in the mouth, which is used for tasting and speaking: *to stick your tongue out at someone.* □ **lengua**
2 *he said it* ***with his tongue in his cheek,*** he did not really mean it seriously. □ **irónicamente**
3 ***to hold one's tongue,*** to remain silent. □ **morderse la lengua, callarse**
4 piece of movable flesh in an animal's mouth, used as food: *a plate of cold tongue.* □ **lengua**
5 language: *his mother tongue is English,* his first language. □ **lengua materna**
6 *tongue in a shoe,* loose piece of leather under the laces. □ **lengüeta**
7 *tongues of flame/a tongue of land,* long, thin flames/piece of land. □ **lengua**
tongue-tied *adj.* so shy as to be unable to say anything. □ **mudo (por timidez)**
tonguetwister *n.* phrase (like *red lorry, yellow lorry*) which is difficult to say quickly. □ **trabalenguas**

tonic ['tɔnik] *adj.* **1** referring to a musical tone. □ **tónico**
tonic solfa, system of writing the tones in music using syllables (*doh-ray-me,* etc.). □ **solfeo tónico**
2 referring to physical strength/wellbeing: *the tonic qualities of vitamin C.* □ **tónico**
■ *n.* **1** note which sets the key to a scale of music. □ **tónica**
2 anything (such as medicine) which strengthens the body. □ **tónico**
3 *the news acted like a tonic on him,* made him more energetic. □ **tónico**
4 ***tonic*** (***water***), fizzy drink containing quinine. □ **(agua) tónica**

tonight [tə'nait] *adv.* and *n.* the night of the present day: *tonight we are having a party; can you phone me at 11 o'clock tonight?* □ **esta noche**

tonnage ['tʌnidʒ] *n. see* **ton.**

tonne [tʌn] *n. see* **ton.**

tonsil ['tɔnsl] *n.* one of two soft lumps of flesh at the back of your throat. □ **amígdala**
tonsillectomy *n.* operation to remove the tonsils. □ **amigdalectomía**
tonsillitis [tɔnsi'laitis] *n.* painful infection of the tonsils. □ **amigdalitis**

tonsure ['tɔnʃə] *n.* shaving off all or part of the hair of people becoming monks; part of the head which has been shaved. □ **tonsura**

too [tu:] *adv.* **1** more than necessary: *he has too much money; she's too thin, she should eat more; it's too wet to go for a walk; don't buy shoes which are too small or they will hurt your feet.* □ **demasiado**
2 as well: *she had some cake, and I had some too; he, too, is French.* □ **también**
3 (*informal*) very: *he's not too happy about his salary.* □ **muy**
too bad!, it's a shame! □ **¡qué pena!**

took [tuk] *v. see* **take.**

tool [tu:l] *n.* **1** hand instrument for doing work (such as hammer/spade, etc.): *gardening tools; a set of tools.* □ **herramienta**
2 *the prime minister is just the tool of the army,* is used by the army to keep power. □ **instrumento**

■ *v.* to decorate using a tool: *a finely tooled silver cup.* □ **labrar**

toot [tu:t] *n.* short sound made by a horn. □ **bocinazo**
■ *v.* to blow a horn sharply. □ **tocar**

tooth [tu:θ] *n.* (*pl. teeth*) **1** one of a set of bony structures in the mouth, used by animals for chewing and biting. □ **diente, muela**
milk teeth, first set of teeth grown by a baby, and replaced by permanent teeth as a child. □ **dientes de leche**
false teeth, set of plastic teeth to replace teeth which have been taken out. □ **dentadura postiza**
2 *I had* ***to have a tooth out,*** to have a tooth removed. □ **tengo que sacarme un diente/una muela**
3 ***in the teeth of*** *all opposition/the gale,* running against opposition/into a gale. □ **pese a**
4 *he's getting* ***long in the tooth,*** old. □ **de muchos años**
5 ***armed to the teeth,*** fully armed. □ **armado hasta los dientes**
6 part of a saw/of a comb/of a cogwheel shaped like a tooth: *some of the teeth of the saw are blunt.* □ **diente**
toothache ['tu:θeik] *n.* pain in a tooth. □ **dolor de muelas**
toothbrush *n.* small brush with a long handle used for cleaning your teeth. □ **cepillo de dientes**
toothcomb *n.* **1** comb with teeth set close together. □ **peine fino**
2 *to go through something* ***with a (fine) toothcomb,*** to inspect something very carefully. □ **examinar minuciosamente**
toothed *adj.* with teeth. □ **con dientes**
toothed wheel, cogwheel. □ **rueda dentada**
toothless *adj.* with no teeth. □ **desdentado**
toothpaste *n.* paste used with a toothbrush for cleaning your teeth: *a tube of toothpaste.* □ **pasta de dientes**
toothpick *n.* small pointed piece of wood/metal, etc., for pushing between the teeth to remove pieces of food. □ **palillo, mondadientes**
toothy *adj.* showing a lot of teeth: *a toothy grin.* □ **enseñando los dientes**

top [tɔp] *n.* **1** highest point: *the top of a mountain; the bird was sitting on the top of a tree; we searched the house from top to bottom, but found nothing; a cake with a cherry on top.* □ **parte superior, encima de, arriba**
on top of *everything else,* in addition to everything else. □ **encima de**
2 flat upper surface; lid: *the top of a desk; to lift the top off a box; put the top back on that jar.* □ **tapa**
3 *Amer.* roof (of a car). □ **techo**
4 highest/most important place: *look at the top of the page; he sat at the top end of the table; our team is at the top of the first division.* □ **parte superior**
5 *big top,* large circus tent. □ **carpa**
6 ***at the top of his voice,*** as loud as possible. □ **a voz en grito**
7 *the car went up the hill* ***in top,*** in the highest gear. □ **directa**
8 child's toy which spins when twisted sharply. □ **peonza**
■ *adj.* **1** highest: *the top floor of the building; top coat of paint; top gear.* □ **último; directa**
2 most important: *the top man in the team; the top boy in the class.* □ **más importante**
■ *v.* (*he topped*) **1** to cut the top off: *to top and tail gooseberries.* □ **quitar el rabo y las hojas...**
2 to put something on top: *the cake was topped with cherries.* □ **coronar, rematar**
3 to go higher: *his salary has topped $10,000.* □ **superar**
to top it all, (*informal*) in addition to everything else. □ **encima de todo**
top dog *n.* (*slang*) winner. □ **ganador**
top hat *n.* man's tall black hat. □ **sombrero de copa**
top-heavy *adj.* unstable because the top part is heavier than the bottom. □ **inestable**
topping out *n.* ceremony to mark the completion of the main work on a new building. □ **celebración al cubrir aguas**
topless *adj.* (*of woman*) wearing nothing on the top part of the body. □ **'topless'**
top-level *adj.* (talks) involving important people: *to hold top-level discussions.* □ **de alto nivel**
topmost *adj.* highest: *the topmost branches of the tree.* □ **más alto**
topper *n.* (*informal*) top hat. □ **sombrero de copa**
top secret *adj.* very secret: *top secret documents.* □ **muy confidencial**
topside *n.* best quality beef for roasting. □ **lomo**
topsoil *n.* layer of good light soil on the surface (of a field, etc.). □ **tierra, primera capa**
top up *v.* to fill completely (something which is half empty): *to top up the petrol tank; to top up someone's glass.* □ **llenar del todo**

topaz ['toupæz] *n.* type of yellow semi-precious stone. □ **topacio**

topee, topi ['toupi] *n.* helmet worn in hot countries to protect your head from the sun. □ **salacot**

topiary ['toupjəri] *n.* art of cutting bushes into odd shapes for ornament. □ **corte decorativo**

topic ['tɔpik] *n.* subject (for discussion/of a conversation). □ **tema**
topical *adj.* which is of interest at the present time: *a very topical subject; the subject is of topical interest.* □ **de actualidad**
topicality *n.* being topical. □ **actualidad**

topography [tə'pɔgrəfi] *n.* description of land mentioning rivers, mountains, roads, buildings, etc. □ **topografía**
topographical [tɔpə'græfikl] *adj.* which describes land. □ **topográfico**

topology [tə'pɔlədʒi] *n.* study of the properties of geometrical shapes which remain the same even when the shapes change. □ **topología**

topple (over) ['tɔpl'ouvə] *v.* to make (something) fall down/to fall down: *the chimney toppled over in the storm; the government was toppled by an army coup.* □ **derribar**

topsy-turvy ['tɔpsi'tə:vi] *adj.* and *adv.* upside down/in confusion. □ **pata arriba**

tor [tɔ:] *n.* rocky hill. □ **peñasco, risco**

torch [tɔ:tʃ] *n.* (*pl. torches*) **1** portable electric light which you can hold in your hand: *the policeman shone his torch into the cellar.* □ **linterna**
2 flaming piece of wood. □ **antorcha**
torchlight *n.* light from a flaming torch. □ **luz de antorcha**
a torchlight procession, procession of people at night carrying flaming torches. □ **con antorchas**

tore [tɔ:] *v. see* **tear.**

torment ['tɔ:mənt] *n.* extreme pain: *he suffered torments of agony from his tooth; she's in torment,* in great pain. □ **tormento, suplicio**
■ *v.* to make (someone) suffer: *he was tormented by strange dreams/by pangs of hunger.* □ **atormentar**
tormentor *n.* person who makes someone suffer. □ **atormentador**

torn [tɔ:n] *v. see* **tear.**

tornado [tɔː'neidou] *n.* (*pl. tornadoes*) violent whirlwind. □ **tornado**
torpedo [tɔː'piːdou] *n.* (*pl. torpedoes*) self-propelled missile which travels through the water: *the submarine launched a torpedo,* sent one off; *a torpedo attack.* □ **torpedo**
■ *v.* to sink (a ship) using a torpedo; to ruin (someone's plans). □ **torpedear**
torpid ['tɔːpid] *adj.* half asleep with heat; dull; sluggish. □ **adormilado; apático**
torpor *n.* being half asleep/sluggish. □ **sopor, apatía**
torque [tɔːk] *n.* mechanical force to make something rotate. □ **momento de torsión**
torrent ['tɔrənt] *n.* **1** fast rushing stream: *the rain turned the little stream into a torrent.* □ **torrente**
2 fast flow: *the rain fell in torrents; torrents of abuse.* □ **a mares; oleadas**
torrential [tə'renʃəl] *adj.* like a torrent: *a torrential rainstorm.* □ **torrencial**
torrid ['tɔrid] *adj.* **1** very hot. □ **tórrido**
2 intense (passion). □ **desaforado**
torsion ['tɔːʃn] *n.* being twisted; strain caused by twisting. □ **torsión**
torso ['tɔːsou] *n.* (*pl. torsos*) body (excluding the head arms and legs). □ **torso**
tort [tɔːt] *n.* act which is the subject of a civil action in court. □ **agravio**
tortoise ['tɔːtəs] *n.* reptile covered with a hard domed shell, which moves very slowly and can live to a great age. □ **tortuga**
tortoiseshell *adj.* and *n.* speckled brown material (from the shell of a tortoise) used for making combs/frames for glasses, etc.: *glasses with tortoiseshell frames.* □ **carey, concha**
a tortoiseshell cat, brown, yellow and black cat. □ **gato jaspeado, atigrado**
tortoiseshell butterfly, common brown and red butterfly. □ **mariposa jaspeada**
tortuous ['tɔːtjuəs] *adj.* which twists and turns: *tortuous path; tortuous argument.* □ **tortuoso**
torture ['tɔːtʃə] *n.* pain inflicted on someone as a punishment or to make them reveal a secret: *the prisoners were subjected to torture.* □ **tortura**
■ *v.* to inflict torture on someone: *the prisoners were tortured before being executed.* □ **torturar**
torturer *n.* person who tortures. □ **torturador**
Tory ['tɔːri] *adj.* and *n.* (*pl. Tories*) (member) of the Conservative party. □ **'tory', conservador**
toss [tɔs] *n.* (*pl. tosses*) **1** action of throwing something into the air. □ **lanzamiento**
the toss of a coin, throwing a coin up to see which side is on top when it comes down: *the English team won the toss,* they guessed correctly which side of the coin came down on top. □ **a cara o cruz**
to argue the toss, to argue about someone's final decision. □ **discutir la decisión final**
2 *toss of the head,* sharp disdainful movement of the head. □ **gesto desdeñoso**
■ *v.* **1** to throw (something) into the air: *he tossed the ball to me; the bull tossed him into the air.* □ **lanzar**
to toss a coin, to throw a coin to see which side is on top when it comes down: *let's toss for it,* the person who guesses right, starts to play first/has first choice. □ **echar a cara o cruz**
2 to move about: *the waves tossed the boat about; he tossed about in bed trying to get to sleep.* □ **sacudir; dar vueltas**
3 *she tossed her head,* made a sharp disdainful movement of her head. □ **hacer un gesto desdeñoso**
toss up *v.* to toss a coin. □ **echar a cara o cruz**
toss-up *n. it's a toss-up which one will win,* (*informal*) you can't tell which one will win. □ **no se sabe...**
tot [tɔt] *n.* **1** little child: *the tiny tots.* □ **niño pequeño**
2 (*informal*) small glass of alcohol. □ **copa, trago**
■ *v.* (*he totted*) ***to tot up,*** to add up: *I'm just totting up the bill to see if it is right; his expenses tot up to more than $100.* □ **sumar; ascender**
total ['toutl] *adj.* and *n.* complete/whole (amount): *the total sum; the book was a total failure; the plane was a total wreck; what is the total we have to pay? the total is at the bottom of the bill.* □ **total**
■ *v.* (*he totalled*) to add up: *I am just totalling all the amounts which you owe; his debts total over $1,000.* □ **sumar; ascender**
totality [tou'tæliti] *n.* whole amount. □ **totalidad**
totally *adv.* completely: *the house was totally demolished; he was totally ruined.* □ **totalmente**
totalitarian [toutæli'tɛəriən] *adj.* (state) governed by a single party/group which refuses to allow the existence of any opposition. □ **totalitario**
totalizator ['toutəlaizeitə] *n.* machine which calculates the amount to be paid to people who bet on a winning horse. □ **totalizadora, sumadora**
tote [tout] *n.* ***the tote,*** (*informal*) totalizator/machine which calculates the amount to be paid to people who bet on a winning horse. □ **sumadora**
■ *v. Amer.* to carry. □ **llevar**
tote-bag *n.* large carrying bag. □ **bolsa**
totem pole ['toutəmpoul] *n.* tall carved pole on which North American Indians carve figures of gods. □ **tótem**
totter ['tɔtə] *v.* to walk unsteadily/to wobble: *he tottered down the steps.* □ **andar tambaleándose**
tottery *adj.* wobbly/likely to fall: *he's getting a bit tottery.* □ **tambaleante**
toucan ['tuːkæn] *n.* American tropical bird with huge coloured beak. □ **tucán**
touch [tʌtʃ] *n.* (*pl. touches*) **1** sense by which you feel something: *this cloth is rough to the touch; he felt his way by touch.* □ **tacto**
2 way of bringing your fingers into contact with something: *she has a very soft touch; his delicate touch when playing the piano.* □ **toque**
3 *she's lost her touch,* she isn't as successful as she was. □ **toque, maestría**
4 slight tap: *I felt a touch on my shoulder.* □ **golpecito**
5 slight stroke (of a paintbrush): *to add a few touches of green.* □ **toque**
to put the finishing touches to something, to finish it off. □ **dar los últimos toques**
6 contact: *I'll be in touch with you next week; he is rather out of touch now he lives in the country.* □ **contacto**
to lose touch: *we've lost touch with him,* have stopped exchanging letters with him. □ **perder el contacto**
7 slight taste/trace: *a touch of garlic in the soup; he spoke with a touch of an Irish accent.* □ **toque**
8 (*in football*) part of the field outside the playing area: *to kick the ball into touch.* □ **fuera de banda**
■ *v.* **1** to feel (with the fingers); to come into contact: *the policeman touched me on the shoulder; don't touch the cement, it isn't dry yet; he's so small, his feet don't touch the floor when he sits on a chair; I wouldn't touch it,* I wouldn't have anything to do with it; *don't touch my things,* don't interfere with them/don't move them. □ **tocar**
2 *to touch on a subject,* to refer to a subject. □ **tocar**
3 to eat or drink: *I never touch coffee.* □ **probar, tomar**

4 to affect the emotions of (someone): *she was touched to see that he had sent her a birthday card; she has a touching innocence.* □ **conmover, emocionar**
5 to reach the same level as (someone): *no one in the school can touch her in maths.* □ **igualar**
6 (*informal*) to ask (someone) for a loan: *he touched me for $5.* □ **pedir, sablear**
touch and go *n. it was touch and go whether we would catch the train,* it was doubtful if we would catch the train. □ **dudoso, aventurado**
touch down *v.* **1** (*of plane*) to land. □ **aterrizar**
2 (*in Rugby*) to score a try. □ **anotarse**
touchdown *n.* **1** landing (of a plane). □ **aterrizaje**
2 (*in Rugby*) scoring a try. □ **anotación**
touchiness *n.* being susceptible/easily offended. □ **susceptibilidad**
touching *adj.* which affects the emotions: *a touching scene.* □ **conmovedor**
■ *prep.* concerning/about: *touching the problem which you mentioned yesterday.* □ **en cuanto a**
touch line *n.* white line along one side of a football pitch □ **línea de banda**
touch off *v.* to set off (an explosion, etc.): *it touched off a violent reaction.* □ **desencadenar**
touchpaper *n.* chemically treated paper used as a fuse to light a firework. □ **papel nitrado**
touchstone *n.* something used as a standard to test other things against. □ **piedra de toque**
touch type *v.* to type without looking at the keys on the typewriter. □ **escribir a máquina a ciegas**
touch up *v.* to add little strokes of paint to improve the appearance of something. □ **retocar**
touchy *adj.* (*informal*) highly susceptible/easily offended: *he's very touchy about his wig.* □ **susceptible**
tough [tʌf] *adj.* (*tougher, toughest*) **1** hard; difficult to chew/to cut/to break: *tough meat; tough wood.* □ **duro**
as tough as old boots, (*informal*) (i) extremely tough. □ **duro como una piedra**
(ii) unable to feel pity, sympathy, etc. □ **duro, insensible**
2 strong/hardy: *tough mountain people; tough soldiers who have been trained to deal with emergencies.* □ **duro**
3 difficult: *we're up against some tough opposition.* □ **duro**
to get tough with someone, to deal roughly/harshly with someone. □ **tratar con dureza a alguien**
4 ***tough luck!,*** (*informal*) hard luck! it's a pity! □ **¡mala suerte!**
that's tough, that's unfortunate. □ **¡qué mala suerte!**
■ *n.* (*informal*) rough criminal: *a band of young toughs.* □ **delincuente**
toughen *v.* to make tough: *you ought to go mountain-climbing in winter - that would toughen you up.* □ **endurecer**
toughened glass, specially strengthened glass. □ **vidrio templado**
toughness *n.* being tough. □ **dureza**
toupee ['tu:pei] *n.* small wig. □ **postizo**
tour ['tuə] *n.* **1** journey which goes round various places and returns to its starting point: *guided tour of a castle; to go on a tour of southern Europe.* □ **visita, viaje**
package tour, one which has been totally organized in advance. □ **viaje organizado**
2 *tour of inspection,* visit (to a factory, etc.) to inspect. □ **visita de inspección**
3 *the theatre company is* ***on tour*** *in the Far East,* it puts on plays in different towns. □ **gira**
■ *v.* to visit; to go on a tour: *we were touring in France; they toured the factory.* □ **visitar, ir de viaje**
touring company, theatre company which goes from one town to another in the provinces. □ **compañía que hace giras**
tourism *n.* business of providing lodging and entertainment for tourists. □ **turismo**
tourist *adj.* and *n.* person who goes on holiday to visit places. □ **turista**
tourist centre, town which is used as a base by tourists. □ **centro turístico**
tourist class, type of seating in an aircraft which is cheaper than first class. □ **clase turista**
tour de force [tu:ədə'fɔ:s] *n.* act showing remarkable skill. □ **'tour de force', hazaña**
tournament ['tuənəmənt] *n.* sporting competition which involves many games which eliminate competitors: *tennis tournament; to play in a chess tournament.* □ **torneo**
tourniquet ['tuənikei] *n.* tight bandage put round an arm or leg to stop bleeding from a wound. □ **torniquete**
tousle ['tauzl] *v.* to make (hair) untidy. □ **despeinar**
tout [taut] *n.* **1** person who tries to sell something to people he meets. □ **vendedor pesado**
ticket tout, person who sells tickets (to a football match, etc.) at high prices to people in the street. □ **revendedor**
2 person who tries to persuade people to vote/to buy things in a shop/to stay in a hotel. □ **gancho**
■ *v.* to try to persuade people to vote/to buy things/ to stay in a hotel: *he's touting for customers; he touted his new invention round several factories.* □ **buscar clientes**
tow [tou] *n.* **1** pulling a car/a ship behind you: *to take a ship in tow; can I give you a tow to a garage?* □ **remolcar**
2 *he always has his family* ***in tow,*** dragging behind him. □ **a cuestas**
3 short, coarse pieces of flax. □ **estopa**
■ *v.* to pull (a car/a ship) which cannot move by itself: *the car was towing a caravan; tug towing a string of barges.* □ **remolcar**
tow-line, tow-rope *n.* rope which attaches a car/a ship to something being towed. □ **sirga, remolque**
towpath *n.* path along the bank of a river/canal (along which horses used to walk to tow barges). □ **camino de sirga**
towards [tə'wɔ:dz] *prep.* **1** in the direction of: *he ran towards the gate; the car was going towards London.* □ **hacia**
2 to (a person/a country, etc.): *her feelings towards me; his kindness towards his parents.* □ **hacia, para con**
3 as part payment for: *he gives me $5 a week towards the cost of his food.* □ **en pago de**
4 near (a time): *it was towards nightfall that he returned home; can we meet towards the end of next week?* □ **hacia**
towel ['tauəl] *n.* piece of soft absorbent cloth for drying: *he dried his hair with a towel.* □ **toalla**
to throw in the towel, to give up/not to continue a contest. □ **tirar la toalla**
■ *v.* (*he towelled*) to rub dry with a towel. □ **secar con toalla**
towelling *n.* type of rough soft cloth used for making towels. □ **felpa**
tower ['tauə] *n.* **1** tall building: *church tower.* □ **torre**
control tower, tall airport building containing the control room. □ **torre de control**

2 *he's a tower of strength,* very strong and sympathetic person. □ **un fenómeno de fuerza**
■ *v.* to rise very high: *the office block towers above the other houses in the street; he towers above other men of his generation.* □ **elevarse sobre**
towering *adj.* very tall; very great: *a towering cliff; he was in a towering rage.* □ **altísimo; enorme**
town [taun] *n.* place where people live and work, with houses, shops, offices and factories (as opposed to the country). □ **ciudad**
the town council, elected committee which runs a town. □ **ayuntamiento (corporación)**
town hall, offices of the committee which runs a town. □ **ayuntamiento (edificio)**
town planning, science of planning the development of a town. □ **urbanismo**
town planner, person who plans the development of a town. □ **urbanista**
to go to town over something, (*informal*) to spend a lot of money on something. □ **tirar la casa por la ventana**
to paint the town red, (*informal*) to have a wild party in the town. □ **correrse una juerga en la ciudad**
town house *n.* **1** house in a town. □ **casa urbana**
2 house built in a row of similar houses all touching each other, with small gardens. □ **casa unifamiliar adosada**
townsfolk *n. pl.* people who live in a town. □ **gente de la ciudad**
township *n.* **1** (*in US and Canada*) small town and the administrative area round it. □ **municipio y término municipal**
2 (*in South Africa*) area where black people live near a large town. □ **'township', barrio negro**
townsman, townswoman *n.* (*pl. townsmen, townswomen*) person who lives in a town. □ **habitante de la ciudad**
townspeople *n. pl.* people who live in a town. □ **gente de la ciudad**
toxaemia [tɔk'siːmiə] *Amer.* **toxemia** *n.* blood poisoning. □ **toxemia**
toxic ['tɔksik] *adj.* poisonous: *toxic gases.* □ **tóxico**
toxicity *n.* being toxic. □ **toxicidad**
toxicologist [tɔksi'kɔlədʒist] *n.* scientist who studies poisons. □ **toxicólogo**
toxicology [tɔksi'kɔlədʒi] *n.* scientific study of poisons. □ **toxicología**
toxin *n.* poisonous substance. □ **toxina**
toy [tɔi] *adj.* and *n.* thing which children play with: *he's playing with his toys; toy soldier; toy car.* □ **juguete**
■ *v.* **1** ***to toy with*** *your food,* to eat it reluctantly. □ **comer de mala gana**
2 *I'm toying with the idea of going to France,* I am turning the idea over in my mind. □ **estoy jugando con la idea**
toyshop *n.* shop which sells toys. □ **juguetería**
trace [treis] *n.* **1** ***traces,*** set of tracks/footprints left by an animal. □ **huellas, rastro**
2 small amount: *there's no trace of any alcohol in the blood; just a trace of onion in the soup.* □ **indicio, pizca**
3 *he's vanished* ***without a trace,*** leaving nothing behind to show where he has gone. □ **sin dejar huella**
4 ***traces,*** straps by which a horse is attached to a carriage. □ **tirantes**
to kick over the traces, to rebel (against authority). □ **rebelarse, desmandarse**
■ *v.* **1** to follow the tracks left by (something); to try to find where (someone/something) is: *the police have traced her to New York; I can trace my family tree back to William the Conqueror; I can't trace your letter in my files.* □ **seguir la pista; encontrar**
2 to copy (something), by placing a piece of thin transparent paper over a picture/a map and drawing on it. □ **calcar**
traceable *adj.* which can be traced. □ **que se puede seguir**
trace element *n.* chemical element of which a tiny amount is needed by a plant or animal to grow properly. □ **oligoelemento**
tracer *n.* type of bullet/shell which leaves a visible stream of sparks/smoke as it flies. □ **bala trazadora**
tracery *n.* delicate stone patterns holding the glass in a church window. □ **tracería**
tracing *n.* drawing done by tracing: *a tracing of a map.* □ **trazado**
tracing paper, thin transparent paper for tracing drawings. □ **papel de calco**
trachea [træ'kiːə] *n.* windpipe. □ **tráquea**
tracheotomy [træki'ɔtəmi] *n.* operation to make a hole in the windpipe from the outside of the neck. □ **traqueotomía**
track ['træk] *n.* **1** footprints of animal/marks of wheels, etc.: *there are elephant tracks here; to follow in someone's tracks.* □ **rastro, huellas**
on somebody's track: *the police are on his track,* they are following him. □ **siguiendo la pista**
to keep track of *expenditure,* to keep an account/to keep oneself informed of the expenditure. □ **vigilar, controlar**
to lose track of something, not to know where it is any longer. □ **perder la pista**
to make tracks for home, to set off for home. □ **irse**
2 path: *we followed a cart track through the wood.* □ **sendero**
on the wrong track, working wrongly/making a wrong assumption. □ **por mal camino, pista falsa**
3 course for racing: *cycle track.* □ **pista**
track events, running competitions in an athletics tournament. □ **atletismo**
track suit, type of warm two-piece suit worn by sportsmen when practising. □ **chándal**
track shoes, running shoes with spikes in the soles. □ **zapatillas de correr**
4 *he has a good* ***track record,*** he has been very successful in the past. □ **historial**
5 line of rails: *to lay a new stretch of track; the locomotive left the track.* □ **vía**
single-track railway, on which trains go up and down the same rails with passing places at intervals. □ **ferrocarril de vía única**
to have a one-track mind, (*informal*) to give all one's attention to one subject. □ **concentrarse demasiado en algo, idea fija**
6 endless belt on which a caterpillar tractor/tank, etc., runs. □ **oruga**
7 part of a magnetic tape on which something can be recorded: *four-track tape.* □ **pista**
8 one song on a record containing several popular songs. □ **corte**
■ *v.* to follow an animal; to follow a moving performer with a camera. □ **seguir el rastro; seguir**
track down *v.* to follow and catch (an animal/a criminal): *he was tracked down to his parent's home.* □ **localizar, capturar**
tracker *n.* animal/person who follows tracks: *police tracker dog.* □ **perseguidor**
trackless *adj.* with no paths. □ **sin caminos**
tract [trækt] *n.* **1** wide stretch of countryside. □ **terreno, zona**

2 short (religious) pamphlet. □ **opúsculo, octavilla**
3 system of organs in the body which are linked together: *the digestive tract.* □ **aparato**
tractable ['træktəbl] *adj.* which can be tamed/made to do what is necessary. □ **dócil**
tractability [træktə'biliti] *n.* being tractable. □ **docilidad**
traction ['trækʃn] *n.* **1** pulling force. □ **tracción**
traction engine, large steam-driven engine which used to be used for pulling heavy loads. □ **locomotora de tracción**
2 pulling (a broken leg, etc.) up with pulleys (in hospital): *his leg is in traction.* □ **tracción**
tractor ['træktə] *n.* farm vehicle with large back wheels for pulling a plough, etc. □ **tractor**
trad [træd] *adj.* (*informal*) traditional. □ **tradicional**
trade [treid] *n.* **1** business; buying and selling: *foreign trade; competition is good for trade; an increase in trade between Common Market countries; the book trade; the tourist trade.* □ **comercio, sector**
2 people who buy and sell a particular type of goods/who work in a particular industry: *he's well known in the trade.* □ **sector, ramo**
trade price, special price to another dealer in the same business. □ **precio al revendedor**
3 job: *he's an electrician by trade.* □ **oficio**
■ *v.* **1** to carry on a business: *he made a fortune trading in cotton; he trades under the name 'Easyfit Shoes'.* □ **comerciar**
2 ***to trade something for something,*** to exchange. □ **cambiar**
trade in *v.* to exchange an old car, etc. as part payment for a new one: *I want to trade this car in.* □ **entregar como parte del pago**
trade-in *n.* exchange of an old car, etc., for a newer one: *what will you give me for this car as a trade-in?* □ **entrega como parte del pago**
trademark, trade name *n.* particular name, sign, etc., which has been registered by a producer and which cannot be copied by other manufacturers. □ **marca de fábrica**
trade on *v.* to exploit/to profit from: *he is trading on the reputation of his father.* □ **beneficiarse de**
trader *n.* person who does business. □ **comerciante, negociante**
tradesman *n.* (*pl. tradesmen*) person who runs a shop. □ **comerciante (tienda)**
tradespeople *n. pl.* shopkeepers. □ **comerciantes, vendedores**
trade union, trades union *n.* organization which groups together workers from similar industries to represent them in wage bargaining with employers. □ **sindicato**
trade unionist *n.* member of a trade union. □ **sindicalista**
tradewind *n.* tropical wind blowing towards the equator. □ **viento alisio**
trading *n.* business. □ **comercio, negocio**
trading estate *n.* group of factories built together. □ **polígono industrial**
tradition [træ'diʃn] *n.* customs/habits/stories which are passed from generation to generation: *according to local tradition, Queen Elizabeth once stayed in this inn.* □ **tradición**
traditional *adj.* referring to tradition: *a traditional recipe,* which has been passed from generation to generation. □ **tradicional**
traffic ['træfik] *n.* **1** movement of vehicles, especially cars/lorries/buses, etc., on the roads: *heavy traffic; the traffic came to a halt when the lights were red.* □ **tráfico**
traffic jam, blockage of traffic on a road. □ **embotellamiento**
traffic circle, *Amer.* roundabout/place where several roads meet, and traffic has to turn in a circle. □ **encrucijada**
air traffic, aircraft flying. □ **tráfico aéreo**
2 illegal international business: *the drugs traffic; traffic in drugs.* □ **tráfico**
■ *v.* (*he trafficked*) *to traffic in drugs,* to deal in drugs illegally: *drug trafficking.* □ **traficar**
trafficator *n.* light on a car which flashes to show that the car is about to turn. □ **intermitente**
traffic lights *n.* red, green and amber lights which regulate the movement of traffic: *you must stop when the traffic lights are red; turn right at the next set of traffic lights.* □ **semáforo**
traffic warden *n.* person who controls traffic, especially the parking of cars. □ **guardia de tráfico**
trafficker *n.* person who traffics (in drugs, etc.). □ **traficante**
tragedy ['trædʒədi] *n.* (*pl. tragedies*) **1** play/film/story with a sad story. □ **tragedia**
2 *personal tragedy,* unhappy events (usually a death in your family). □ **tragedia personal/familiar**
tragedian [trə'dʒiːdiən] *n.* person who acts in tragedies. □ **actor trágico**
tragic *adj.* very sad: *the tragic death of his father.* □ **trágico**
tragically *adv.* very sadly. □ **trágicamente**
trail [treil] *n.* **1** tracks left by an animal: *to follow an elephant's trail.* □ **rastro**
2 path: *the trail led through the bushes.* □ **camino, sendero**
3 something which stretches a long way behind: *the plane left a trail of smoke; the horse raced off leaving a trail of dust.* □ **estela**
■ *v.* **1** to let (something) drag behind you: *your scarf is trailing in the mud; the children trailed behind their teacher.* □ **quedarse atrás**
2 to follow the tracks of (an animal/a person): *the police trailed him across town.* □ **seguir el rastro**
3 ***trailing plant,*** one which hangs or creeps along the ground. □ **planta trepadora/rastrera**
trailer *n.* **1** goods vehicle pulled behind a car. □ **remolque**
2 caravan. □ **caravana**
3 short film showing parts of a full-length film as an advertisement. □ **tráiler**
train [trein] *n.* **1** series of coaches or wagons pulled by a railway engine: *the train to Edinburgh leaves from platform 3; I go to work by train; to catch/to miss a train.* □ **tren**
train ferry, boat which carries a train across water from one country to another. □ **transbordador de trenes**
2 series of events; line of animals carrying goods; retinue (of an important person): *a camel train.* □ **serie; fila; séquito**
3 *a train of thought,* series of thoughts which follow on one from another. □ **hilo**
4 long fuse (to light an explosive). □ **mecha**
5 part of a dress which hangs down on to the ground at the back. □ **cola**
■ *v.* **1** to teach (someone/an animal) to do something; to learn how to do something: *to train a dog to carry a newspaper; he's training to be a pilot.* □ **entrenar**
2 *to train a plant up a stick,* to attach a plant so that it will climb upwards. □ **guiar**

3 to practise (for a sport): *he's training for the 100 metres race.* □ **entrenarse**
4 to point (a rifle/a telescope) at something. □ **apuntar**
trainee [trei'niː] *n.* person who is being taught something: *a trainee pilot.* □ **aprendiz; en prácticas**
trainer *n.* **1** person who trains animals/sportsmen. □ **entrenador**
2 small aircraft in which you learn to fly. □ **avión de adiestramiento**
training *n.* action of being taught/of practising: *his military training has proved useful.* □ **entrenamiento; capacitación**
in training, (i) practising (for a sport): *the team has to go to bed early when they're in training.* □ **entrenando**
(ii) fit; in good physical condition. □ **en buena forma**
traipse [treips] *v.* (*informal*) to walk about in a heavy/tired way: *they traipsed for hours around the shops.* □ **dar vueltas, andar**
trait [trei(t)] *n.* particular point of someone's character: *one of his most attractive traits is his calmness.* □ **rasgo**
traitor ['treitə] *n.* person who sides with the enemy/who gives away secrets to the enemy. □ **traidor**
trajectory [trə'dʒektri] *n.* (*pl. trajectories*) curved course taken by something which has been thrown through the air: *the trajectory of a rocket.* □ **trayectoria**
tram [træm] *n.* form of public transport, consisting of carriages running on rails laid in the street. □ **tranvía**
tramcar *n.* single carriage of a tram. □ **vagón de tranvía**
tramlines *n. pl.* **1** rails along which a tram runs. □ **líneas/vías de tranvía**
2 two parallel side lines on a tennis court. □ **líneas laterales**
tramway *n.* rails, etc., on which trams run. □ **vía de tranvía**
trammel ['træml] *n.* **1** type of fishing net. □ **trasmallo**
2 something which prevents you from doing something. □ **traba**
■ *v.* (*he trammelled*) (*formal*) to stop someone doing something. □ **poner trabas; impedir**
tramp [træmp] *n.* **1** noise of feet hitting the ground heavily: *the tramp of the soldiers marching past.* □ **ruido de pisadas**
2 long energetic walk: *they went for a tramp across the moors.* □ **caminata**
3 person who has nowhere to live and walks from place to place begging for food or money. □ **vagabundo**
■ *v.* **1** to walk heavily: *the soldiers tramped over the bridge; they tramped up and down the platform in the snow; he tramped the streets for hours looking for somewhere to spend the night.* □ **andar con paso pesado**
2 to trample on (something): *to tramp the grapes,* to crush grapes by stepping on them to extract the juice. □ **pisar**
tramp steamer *n.* cargo boat which goes from port to port, but not on a regular route. □ **buque mercante sin línea fija**
trample ['træmpl] *v.* to crush (by walking): *the crowd trampled on the flowers; several people were trampled underfoot in the panic.* □ **pisotear**
trampoline ['træmpəliːn] *n.* frame with a large sheet of elastic material on which you can bounce/perform exercises, etc. □ **trampolín**
trance [trɑːns] *n.* state when you are not fully conscious, and do not notice what is going on: *he walked about the room in a trance.* □ **trance**
tranny ['træni] *n.* (*pl. trannies*) (*informal*) transistor radio. □ **transistor**
tranquil ['træŋkwil] *adj.* calm/peaceful: *the tranquil waters of a lake.* □ **tranquilo**
tranquillity [træŋ'kwiliti] *n.* calm. □ **tranquilidad**
tranquillize ['træŋkwilaiz] *v.* to make (someone) calm (by giving drugs). □ **tranquilizar**
tranquillizer *n.* drug which makes a person calm. □ **tranquilizante**
trans- [trænz] *prefix meaning* through/across. □ **trans-**
transact [træn'zækt] *v.* to carry out (a piece of business). □ **hacer una transacción/operación**
transaction *n.* business: *a cash transaction,* piece of business which is paid for in cash. □ **transacción**
transactions, report of what takes place at a meeting of a learned/scientific society. □ **actas, memorias**
transatlantic [trænzət'læntik] *adj.* across the Atlantic; from the other side of the Atlantic: *a transatlantic flight.* □ **transatlántico**
transatlantic treaty, one which involves countries on both sides of the Atlantic. □ **tratado transatlántico**
transcend [træn'send] *v.* to go better/further than something: *spiritual peace which transcends all earthly worries.* □ **trascender**
transcendental [trænsən'dentəl] *adj.* which rises above the level of ordinary thought or reasoning. □ **trascendental**
transcontinental [trænzkɔnti'nentl] *adj.* across a continent. □ **transcontinental**
transcribe [træn'skraib] *v.* to write out the text (of something which is heard); to write out in full (what has been written down in shorthand); to rewrite a piece of music for another instrument than the one for which it was originally written. □ **transcribir**
transcript ['trænskript] *n.* written text of what was said (on the radio/at a trial, etc.). □ **transcripción**
transept ['trænsept] *n.* one of the two branches at right angles to the nave and choir in a cross-shaped church. □ **transepto**
transfer ['trænsfə] *n.* **1** movement of something/someone to a new place: *transfer of money to another account; she doesn't like the department she works in, so she has asked for a transfer; to put a footballer on the transfer list,* on the list of players whom the team would agree to see move to another team. □ **transferencia, traslado, traspaso**
2 design which can be stuck on to a surface. □ **transferencia, reporte**
■ *v.* (*he transferred*) to move (something/someone) to another place: *the passengers transferred from the plane to a bus; to transfer a sum of money to your account.* □ **transbordar, transferir, trasladar**
transferable [trænz'fəːrəbl] *adj.* which can be transferred: *this ticket is not transferable,* can only be used by the person to whom it was issued/whose name is on it. □ **transferible**
transfigure [trænz'figə] *v.* to change for the better the appearance of something/someone: *her face was transfigured with happiness.* □ **transfigurar**
transfix [trænz'fiks] *v.* to prevent (someone) from moving (by giving a shock): *he was transfixed with astonishment.* □ **paralizar**
transform [trænz'fɔːm] *v.* to change completely.

□ **transformar**
transformation [trænzfə'meiʃn] *n.* complete change of appearance. □ **transformación**
transformer [trænz'fɔ:mə] *n.* apparatus for changing the voltage of an alternating electric current. □ **transformador**
transfuse [trænz'fju:z] *v.* to move liquid from one container to another. □ **trasvasar**
transfusion [trænz'fju:ʒn] *n. blood transfusion,* giving someone else's blood to a sick patient who needs it. □ **transfusión**
transgress [trænz'gres] *v.* (*formal*) to go against a rule. □ **transgredir**
tranship [træns'ʃip] *v.* (*he transhipped*) to move (goods) from one ship or lorry to another. □ **transbordar**
transience ['trænziəns] *n.* state of not being permanent. □ **transitoriedad**
transient ['trænziənt] *adj.* which will not last. □ **transitorio**
transients, Amer. people who stay in a hotel for a short time. □ **clientes de paso**
transistor [træn'zistə] *n.* **1** device made of semi-conductors which can increase an electric current. □ **transistor**
2 ***transistor (radio),*** small pocket radio which uses transistors. □ **transistor**
transistorize *v.* to put transistors into (something). □ **poner transistores en**
transit ['trænzit] *n.* **1** movement of passengers/goods (on the way to another destination): *passengers in transit.* □ **tránsito**
transit lounge, waiting room in an airport where you wait for another flight which connects with the one you have just arrived on. □ **sala de tránsito**
2 moving of a planet across the face of the sun or other planet. □ **tránsito**
transition [træn'ziʃn] *n.* movement between one state and another: *transition of power from one government to another.* □ **transición**
transitional *adj.* referring to transition. □ **de transición, transitorio**
transitional government, temporary government between two different constitutions. □ **gobierno de transición**
transitive ['trænzitiv] *adj. transitive verb,* one which has an object; *in the phrase 'he climbed the ladder', the verb 'climb' is transitive.* □ **transitivo**
transitory ['trænzitri] *adj.* which does not last for long. □ **transitorio**
translate [trænz'leit] *v.* to put (something) which is said/written in one language into another: *he asked me to translate the letter into Japanese; the book was translated from the German.* □ **traducir**
translation [trænz'leiʃn] *n.* text of something which has been translated; the action of translating: *there is a new translation of Cervantes; I have read this Chinese novel in a French translation; she is an expert in simultaneous translation,* in translating into another language what a speaker is saying. □ **traducción**
translator *n.* person who translates. □ **traductor**
transliterate [trænz'litəreit] *v.* to put foreign words into the letters of a different alphabet: *how do you transliterate the name of the Chinese Prime Minister?* □ **transliterar**
translucent [trænz'lu:snt] *adj.* which light can pass through, but which you cannot see through: *translucent glass.* □ **translúcido**
transmit [trænz'mit] *v.* (*he transmitted*) **1** to pass (from one person to another): *he was found guilty of transmitting secrets to the enemy; the disease is transmitted by dirty food.* □ **transmitir**
2 to send out by radio/TV: *the broadcast is being transmitted live.* □ **transmitir**
transmission [trænz'miʃn] *n.* **1** passing (of disease) from one person to another. □ **transmisión**
2 sending out by radio/TV; a radio/TV broadcast: *this transmission is coming to you live from the Olympic Games.* □ **transmisión**
3 (*in a car*) series of moving parts which pass the power from the engine to the wheels. □ **transmisión**
transmitter *n.* ***radio/television transmitter,*** apparatus for sending out radio/TV signals. □ **transmisor**
transmute [trænz'mju:t] *v.* to make (something) change its shape or substance. □ **transmutar**
transom ['trænsəm] *n.* cross beam in a window; beam across the top of a door. □ **travesaño, dintel**
transparency [træns'pærənsi] *n.* (*pl. transparencies*) **1** being transparent. □ **transparencia**
2 photograph which is printed on transparent film so that it can be projected on to a screen. □ **diapositiva**
transparent *adj.* **1** which you can see through: *transparent curtains.* □ **transparente**
2 obvious: *it was a transparent lie.* □ **transparente, patente**
transpire [træn'spaiə] *v.* **1** to happen: *this is his account of what transpired.* □ **ocurrir**
2 to pass moisture through the surface of the skin/of a leaf, etc. □ **transpirar**
transplant ['trɑ:nsplɑ:nt] *n.* **1** act of taking an organ from one person and grafting it into someone else's body: *a kidney transplant.* □ **trasplante**
2 small plant which is moved to another place to grow. □ **trasplante**
■ *v.* **1** to graft (an organ) into someone's body: *to transplant a kidney.* □ **trasplantar**
2 to plant (small plants) in another place where they will grow permanently. □ **trasplantar**
transport ['trænspɔ:t] *n.* **1** movement of goods/people; means of moving goods/people: *rail transport; have you any transport for getting home?* □ **transporte, medio de transporte**
public transport system, system of buses/trams/underground trains for moving the public. □ **transporte público**
transport café, restaurant where lorry-drivers, etc., eat. □ **restaurante de camioneros**
2 ship/aircraft which carries goods or soldiers. □ **barco/avión de transporte**
3 great emotion: *transports of joy.* □ **arrebato**
■ *v.* **1** to move (goods/people) from one place to another. □ **transportar**
2 *to be transported with joy,* to be very happy. □ **arrebatar**
transportable *adj.* which can be moved from one place to another. □ **transportable**
transportation [trænspɔ:'teiʃn] *n.* movement of goods/people; means of moving goods/people. □ **transporte**
transporter [træn'spɔ:tə] *n.* large lorry for carrying several cars. □ **transportador de automóviles**
transporter bridge, platform which is suspended from a bridge and moves across a river on cables, carrying cars, etc. □ **puente transbordador**
transpose [træn'spouz] *v.* to make (two things) change places: *when he wrote 'conutry' he transposed two letters.* □ **transponer, cambiar de sitio**
transship [træns'ʃip] *v.* (*he transshipped*) to move (goods) from one ship or lorry to another. □ **transbordar**

transuranic [trænzju'rænik] *adj.* (element) which has atoms heavier than those of uranium. □ **transuránico**

transverse ['trænzvɜ:s] *adj.* which lies across: *one of the transverse beams in the ceiling.* □ **transverso, transversal**

transvestite [trænz'vestait] *n.* person who wants to wear the clothes of the opposite sex. □ **travestido**
transvestism [trænz'vestizəm] *n.* desire to wear the clothes of the opposite sex. □ **travestismo**

trap [træp] *n.* **1** device to catch an animal; plan to catch someone/to take someone by surprise: *to set a trap to catch a rabbit.* □ **trampa**
police radar trap, device to catch a motorist who is driving too fast. □ **detector de velocidad con radar**
2 gate which allows a greyhound to start to run in a race. □ **jaula**
3 ***trap door,*** door in a floor/in a ceiling. □ **trampa**
4 bend in a waste pipe which is filled with water, and so stops unpleasant smells coming back up the pipe from a sewer. □ **sifón**
5 (*slang*) mouth: *shut your trap!; keep your trap shut,* stop talking/don't say anything. □ **pico; ¡cierra el pico!**
■ *v.* (*he trapped*) to catch: *several people were trapped in the burning building; the police trapped the burglars in the bank; he earns his living by trapping rats.* □ **atrapar**
trapper *n.* person who catches wild animals for their fur. □ **trampero**

trapeze [træ'pi:z] *n.* bar which hangs from ropes, and which acrobats use in a circus. □ **trapecio**

trapezium [træ'pi:ziəm] *n.* (*in geometry*) four-sided shape, where two of the sides are parallel. □ **trapecio**
trapezoid ['træpizɔid] *n.* (*in geometry*) four-sided shape, where none of the sides is parallel. □ **trapezoide**

trappings ['træpiŋz] *n. pl.* ornaments/clothes/decorations which are suitable for a particular occasion. □ **adornos, galas**

trash [træʃ] *n.* (*no pl.*) rubbish: *that magazine is just trash.* □ **basura**
trash-can *n. Amer.* dustbin/container where you put household rubbish. □ **cubo de la basura**
trashy *adj.* very bad/completely worthless. □ **malo**

trauma ['trɔ:mə] *n.* **1** sharp shock/unpleasant experience which affects your mental outlook: *the traumas of modern city life.* □ **trauma**
2 injury. □ **trauma**
traumatic [trɔ:'mætik] *adj.* which gives a sharp and unpleasant shock: *their divorce was a traumatic experience.* □ **traumático**

travel ['trævl] *n.* moving from one country to another/from one place to another: *he is still on his travels,* on a long journey. □ **viaje**
■ *v.* (*he travelled*) **1** to move from one country to another/from one place to another: *they are travelling in France; what was the distance travelled by the bullet before it hit him?* □ **viajar; recorrer**
2 to be a sales representative (in an area): *he travels the west part of the country.* □ **ser viajante por**
travel agency *n.* office which arranges tickets/hotel reservations, etc., for you when you are making a journey. □ **agencia de viajes**
travel agent *n.* person who runs a travel agency. □ **encargado de agencia de viajes**
travelator *n.* moving belt which you stand on to move from one point to another (such as in an airport). □ **cinta transportadora**
traveller *n.* **1** person who is travelling from one place to another. □ **viajero**
traveller's cheques, international currency cheques which you can buy at your bank and which can then be cashed in a foreign country. □ **cheques de viajero**
2 (***commercial***) ***traveller,*** sales representative of a business firm who visits clients to persuade them to buy stock. □ **viajante de comercio**

traverse ['trævɜ:s] *n.* **1** crossing. □ **travesía**
2 thing which crosses another. □ **travesaño**
3 (*in mountaineering*) crossing of a dangerous flat rock face. □ **travesía**
■ *v.* to cross. □ **atravesar, cruzar**

travesty ['trævəsti] *n.* (*pl. travesties*) parody; ridiculous copy/poor imitation: *it's a travesty of the truth.* □ **parodia**
■ *v.* (*travestied; travestying*) to imitate (something) in a ridiculous way. □ **parodiar**

trawl [trɔ:l] *n.* long net shaped like a bag, pulled at sea by a trawler. □ **red de arrastre**
■ *v.* to fish with a long bag-shaped net. □ **pescar al arrastre**
trawler *n.* fishing boat which uses a trawl to catch fish. □ **arrastrero**

tray [trei] *n.* **1** flat board for carrying glasses/cups and saucers, etc. □ **bandeja**
2 flat open box/basket for papers. □ **bandeja**
in tray/out tray, box for papers waiting to be dealt with/for papers which have been dealt with. □ **asuntos pendientes/resueltos**

treachery ['tretʃəri] *n.* act of betraying/being a traitor to your friends, etc. □ **traición**
treacherous *adj.* **1** likely to betray. □ **traicionero**
2 dangerous: *treacherous sand; treacherous road surface.* □ **traicionero**

treacle ['tri:kl] *n.* thick dark-brown syrup produced when sugar is refined. □ **melaza**
treacly *adj.* thick and sticky like treacle. □ **meloso**

tread [tred] *n.* **1** way of walking: *the solemn tread of the policeman.* □ **paso**
2 sound of a footstep. □ **paso**
3 part of a step (on stairs/an escalator) on which you put your foot. □ **huella**
4 surface of a tyre marked with a pattern of lines: *the tyre has lost its tread; the tread has been worn down.* □ **dibujo**
■ *v.* (*he trod: he has trodden*) **1** to walk: *tread softly, we don't want them to wake up.* □ **andar, pisar**
2 to trample on/to crush with your feet: *to tread the grapes; he trod on my toe.* □ **pisar**
to tread water, to keep afloat in water by moving your legs up and down. □ **mantenerse a flote**
treadle ['tredl] *n.* foot pedal which makes a machine turn. □ **pedal**
treadmill *n.* device turned by people/animals as they walk around a circular path or inside a large wheel. □ **rueda de molino movida por...**

treason ['tri:zn] *n.* betraying your country/giving your country's secrets to the enemy. □ **traición**
treasonable *adj.* which can be considered as treason. □ **traicionero**

treasure ['treʒə] *n.* **1** store of money/jewels/gold, etc. □ **tesoro**
treasure hunt, children's game where you follow clues from place to place until you find a prize. □ **búsqueda del tesoro**
treasure trove, buried treasure found by accident which then becomes the property of the state. □ **tesoro hallado**
2 thing which is highly valued. □ **tesoro**
■ *v.* to value (something) very highly: *the burglar*

stole my treasured collection of photographs. □ **valorar en mucho**
treasurer *n.* person who looks after the finances of a club, etc. □ **tesorero**
treasury *n.* (*pl. treasuries*) **1** place where treasure is kept. □ **tesoro**
2 government department which deals with the nation's money. □ **Ministerio de Hacienda**
treat [tri:t] *n.* **1** special meal/outing, etc., which should give pleasure: *we're going out to the theatre as a special treat.* □ **ocasión especial, festín**
2 *that's a treat in store for you,* that will be a special surprise for you. □ **sorpresa especial**
3 *this is my treat,* I am paying the bill. □ **yo pago la cuenta**
■ *v.* **1** to deal with: *the customer was badly treated by the bank; I treat it all as a joke,* I deal with it as if it were a joke; *to treat a subject artistically/humorously,* to write about a subject in an artistic/humorous way. □ **tratar**
2 to give (someone) a special meal/outing, etc., as a surprise gift: *I'll treat you all to an ice cream; he treated himself to a holiday in Italy.* □ **invitar por sorpresa, regalarse**
3 to look after (a sick person): *after the accident he was treated for shock; you ought to have your hand treated by a doctor.* □ **tratar**
4 to pass (a substance) through a certain process: *the metal is specially treated to withstand extreme heat.* □ **tratar**
5 (*formal*) to negotiate: *to treat with the enemy.* □ **negociar**
treatment *n.* **1** way of dealing with something: *the treatment of prisoners in jail; harsh treatment.* □ **trato, tratamiento**
2 way of looking after a sick person: *this is the new treatment for burns; she is in hospital for treatment to her back.* □ **tratamiento**
treatise ['tri:tiz] *n.* long learned piece of writing on a subject: *a treatise on anatomy.* □ **tratado**
treaty ['tri:ti] *n.* (*pl. treaties*) **1** agreement between two or more countries: *international treaty on the law of the sea; they signed a treaty of mutual friendship.* □ **tratado**
2 agreement between private people: *to sell a house by private treaty,* in private, not using an estate agent. □ **acuerdo**
treble ['trebl] *n.* **1** voice which sings high-pitched notes: *she sings treble.* □ **voz de tiple**
2 something three times as large; three points: *he scored a treble.* □ **triple**
■ *adj.* **1** three times as large: *a treble portion of ice cream.* □ **triple**
treble chance, possible way of winning the football pools, where you try to forecast the matches which will be drawn. □ **pronóstico**
2 high (voice/note). □ **de tiple**
a treble guitar, type of guitar which has the highest range of notes. □ **guitarra aguda**
treble clef, sign in music showing that the notes are in a high pitch. □ **clave de sol**
■ *adv.* three times as much: *a small car does treble the number of miles per gallon.* □ **triple, tres veces**
■ *v.* to increase by three times: *salaries have trebled over the last few years.* □ **triplicar(se)**
trebly *adv.* three times as much. □ **tres veces**
tree [tri:] *n.* **1** large plant with a wooden stem and branches: *a fir tree; an apple tree.* □ **árbol**
2 ***family tree,*** diagram showing the development of a family over a long period of time. □ **árbol genealógico**
treecreeper *n.* small bird which creeps up the trunk of trees, looking for insects. □ **trepador**
treeless *adj.* with no trees. □ **sin árboles**
treen *n.* (*no pl.*) small spoons/rings, etc., made of wood. □ **objetos pequeños de madera**
treetop *n.* top of a tree: *the monkeys were chattering in the treetops.* □ **copa**
trefoil ['tri:fɔil] *n.* design/leaf shaped in three equal parts like that of clover. □ **trifolio, trébol**
trek [trek] *n.* long and difficult journey: *it's quite a trek to reach their house.* □ **odisea**
■ *v.* (*he trekked*) to make a long and difficult journey. □ **hacer un viaje largo y difícil**
trellis ['trelis] *n.* (*pl. trellises*) openwork fence made of thin pieces of wood in a crisscross pattern. □ **enrejado**
tremble ['trembl] *n.* shaking/shuddering: *a tremble in his voice; I'm all of a tremble,* shaking all over with excitement. □ **temblor**
■ *v.* **1** to shake/to quiver: *his voice trembled; her hand trembled; the earthquake made the houses tremble.* □ **temblar**
2 to be very worried: *I tremble to think what her father's going to say.* □ **temblar**
trembly *adj.* shaky/doddery. □ **tembloroso**
tremendous [tri'mendəs] *adj.* enormous/very large: *it was a tremendous success; a tremendous clap of thunder.* □ **tremendo**
tremendously *adv.* greatly. □ **tremendamente**
tremor ['tremə] *n.* shaking. □ **temblor**
earth tremor, slight earthquake. □ **temblor de tierra**
tremulous ['tremjuləs] *adj.* shaking/quivering: *a tremulous voice.* □ **trémulo**
trench [trentʃ] *n.* (*pl. trenches*) long narrow ditch in the ground: *the soldiers sat in their trenches.* □ **trinchera**
■ *v.* to dig a long narrow ditch. □ **hacer una trinchera**
trench coat *n.* waterproof coat with a belt. □ **trinchera**
trenchant ['trentʃənt] *adj.* sharp/biting (remark); vigorous (style). □ **mordaz; enérgico**
trend [trend] *n.* general tendency: *the trend nowadays is to a formal style of dress; the upward trend of prices.* □ **tendencia**
trend-setter *n.* person who sets the fashion. □ **el que dicta la moda**
trendy *adj.* (*informal*) (*trendier, trendiest) following fashion: trendy restaurant,* which is particularly fashionable. □ **de moda**
■ *n.* (*pl. trendies*) (*informal*) person who follows fashion. □ **el que sigue la moda**
trepan [tri'pæn] **trephine** [tri'fi:n] *n.* saw for cutting out round pieces of bone. □ **trépano**
■ *v.* (*he trepanned*) to cut a round piece of bone (especially out of the skull). □ **trepanar**
trepidation [trepi'deiʃn] *n.* anxiety: *he waited in fear and trepidation for his exam results.* □ **inquietud, turbación**
trespass ['trespəs] *v.* to go into someone's property without permission: *you're trespassing on private property.* □ **entrar sin permiso, invadir**
to trespass on someone's preserves, to deal with affairs which someone regards as his private affairs. □ **meterse en los asuntos de...**
trespasser *n.* person who trespasses on private property: *trespassers will be prosecuted.* □ **intruso**
tresses ['tresiz] *n. pl.* long hair. □ **melena**
trestle ['tresl] *n.* pair of folding legs which can be used to hold up a table. □ **caballete**

trestle table, table made of planks resting on folding legs. □ **mesa de caballete**

trews [tru:z] *n. pl.* close-fitting trousers made of tartan cloth. □ **pantalones escoceses**

tri- [trai] *prefix meaning* three. □ **tri-**

trial ['traiəl] *n.* **1** court case to judge a criminal: *a murder trial.* □ **juicio, proceso**

to stand trial, to be tried in court. □ **ser procesado**

2 test: *to go for a trial run in a new car; sheepdog trials,* competition to select the best sheepdogs. □ **prueba, concurso**

on trial, being tested to see if it is acceptable: *you can have the machine on two weeks' trial,* you can test it for two weeks before you make up your mind if you want to buy it. □ **a prueba**

3 *a process of **trial and error,*** process of testing and rejecting various things until you find the one which suits you. □ **eliminación**

4 game played to test the skills of players before they are selected for a team. □ **preselección**

5 motorcycle competition held on rough ground. □ **trial**

triangle ['traiæŋgl] *n.* **1** geometrical shape with three sides and three angles. □ **triángulo**

eternal triangle, situation where two people are both in love with a third person. □ **triángulo**

2 musical instrument made of a piece of metal bent into the shape of a triangle. □ **triángulo**

triangular [trai'æŋgjulə] *adj.* shaped like a triangle. □ **triangular**

tribe [traib] *n.* **1** group of people ruled by a chief: *an African tribe.* □ **tribu**

2 (*informal*) large family/group: *a tribe of little children.* □ **tribu**

tribal *adj.* referring to a tribe: *tribal customs.* □ **tribal**

tribesman *n.* (*pl. tribesmen*) member of a tribe. □ **miembro de una tribu**

tribulation [tribju'leiʃn] *n.* (*formal*) great misery. □ **tribulación**

tribunal [trai'bju:nl] *n.* court/official committee which judges special problems or writes a report on a special problem: *rent tribunal,* court which decides if a rent is fair or excessive. □ **tribunal**

tribute ['tribju:t] *n.* **1** money paid to a conqueror by people who have been conquered. □ **tributo**

2 words/gifts, etc., to show thanks/praise. □ **ofrenda**

to pay tribute to: *he paid tribute to the mayor's great qualities,* he praised the mayor's great qualities. □ **rendir tributo/homenaje**

floral tributes, flowers given to an important person/flowers sent to a funeral. □ **ofrenda floral**

tributary *adj.* (person) who pays tribute. □ **tributario**

■ *n.* river which flows into a larger river: *a tributary of the Thames.* □ **afluente**

trice [trais] *n. **in a trice,*** very rapidly. □ **en un santiamén**

trick [trik] *n.* **1** clever action which can deceive/confuse someone: *he played a trick on his teacher; what a rotten trick!* □ **truco**

card tricks/conjuring tricks, clever games with cards/with hats, handkerchiefs, etc., to amuse an audience. □ **juegos de manos**

tricks of the trade, (*informal*) clever dealings which are associated with a certain trade. □ **trucos del negocio**

that should do the trick, (*informal*) should do what is wanted/should make it work. □ **eso servirá**

not/never miss a trick, (*informal*) to know everything that is going on. □ **no perderse una**

2 (*in card games*) points won at the end of a round. □ **tantos**

3 odd way of doing something: *she has a trick of pretending to be ill whenever you ask her to do something.* □ **costumbre**

■ *adj.* which deceives: *trick photography.* □ **trucado**

a trick question, one which is intended to catch people out. □ **pregunta con trampa**

a trick pencil, one which for example bends instead of writing. □ **lápiz de broma**

■ *v.* to deceive/to confuse: *he was tricked out of his money,* cheated so that he lost his money. □ **timar, estafar**

to trick someone into doing something, to deceive someone so that he does something which he did not intend to do. □ **embaucar**

trickery *n.* act of deceiving. □ **engaño**

trickster *n.* person who tricks. □ **timador, embaucador**

confidence trickster, person who cheats someone out of his money by some fraudulent scheme which seems to be honest. □ **timador que se gana la confianza**

tricky *adj.* (*trickier, trickiest*) **1** difficult/awkward: *a tricky situation; it's a tricky thing to set up a time bomb.* □ **difícil, peliagudo**

2 (*informal*) sly/deceitful/untrustworthy. □ **poco de fiar**

trickle ['trikl] *n.* small flow of water. □ **chorrito, hilo**

trickle charger, device which charges a car battery slowly. □ **cargador lento**

■ *v.* to flow in a small quantity: *honey trickled down his chin; people trickled into the waiting room.* □ **gotear, entrar poco a poco**

tricolour ['trikələ] *n.* flag with three bands of colour, especially the national flag of France. □ **tricolor**

tricycle ['traisikl] *n.* three-wheeled pedal vehicle like a bicycle with two back wheels. □ **triciclo**

trident ['traidənt] *n.* spear with three prongs. □ **tridente**

tried [traid] *v. see* **try.**

triennial [trai'eniəl] *adj.* happening every three years. □ **trienal**

trier ['traiə] *n.* person who tries. □ **el que prueba**

trifle ['traifl] *n.* **1** small insignificant thing. □ **fruslería**

2 small amount: *she's a trifle younger than her husband; he's a trifle fatter than the last time I saw him.* □ **poquito**

3 pudding made of cake/biscuits/jelly/jam/sherry and cream. □ **'trifle'**

■ *v.* to play with/not to treat something seriously: *he's not in a mood to be trifled with,* he is annoyed and must be taken seriously. □ **jugar con**

trifling *adj.* slight/very small: *a trifling accident.* □ **sin importancia**

trigger ['trigə] *n.* small metal lever on a gun which you pull to fire it. □ **gatillo**

■ *v. **to trigger off,*** to start a series of things happening: *the fire triggered off a series of explosions.* □ **desencadenar**

trigger-happy *adj.* ready to shoot/ready to act quickly without thinking. □ **preparado para disparar/actuar**

trigonometry [trigə'nɔmitri] *n.* science which deals with the relationships between the sides and angles of triangles. □ **trigonometría**

trilateral ['trailætrəl] *adj.* with three people/groups taking part. □ **trilateral**

trilby ['trilbi] *n.* (*pl. trilbies*) type of man's hat. □ **sombrero flexible**

trill [tril] *n.* **1** warbling song (like a bird): *trills of laughter.* □ **trino**
2 (*in music*) two notes rapidly repeated. □ **trino**
■ *v.* to warble/to sing like a bird. □ **trinar**

trillion ['triljən] *n.* **1** one million million millions. □ **trillón**
2 *especially Amer.* one million millions. □ **billón**

trilogy ['trilədʒi] *n.* (*pl. trilogies*) novel/play, etc., in three separate related parts. □ **trilogía**

trim [trim] *n.* **1** neatness: *everything was in good trim.* □ **orden, estado**
2 cutting (of hair/bush, etc.): *the hedge needs a trim; I'm going to the barber's for a trim.* □ **corte, recorte**
3 decoration: *the car has grey upholstery with a blue trim.* □ **adorno**
■ *adj.* (*trimmer, trimmest*) neat: *a trim figure; he keeps his garden very trim.* □ **cuidado, arreglado**
■ *v.* (*he trimmed*) **1** to cut (something) so that it is tidy: *to trim a beard; he was trimming the hedge with a pair of shears; to trim the edges of a lawn.* □ **recortar**
2 to cut back: *to trim expenses.* □ **recortar**
3 to ornament/to decorate: *dressed trimmed with lace.* □ **adornar**
4 (*on a sailing boat*) to put sails into the best position. □ **orientar**
5 to change your political opinions to fit the current popular trend. □ **cambiar de modo oportunista**
trimmer *n.* person/device that trims. □ **cortador/cortadora**
hedge trimmer, electric cutter for hedges. □ **cortadora eléctrica**
trimming *n.* **1** ornament added to decorate something: *dress with fur trimmings.* □ **adornos**
2 *roast pork* ***with all the trimmings,*** with the usual sauces and vegetables. □ **guarnición**
3 ***trimmings,*** pieces cut off (a hedge, etc.) when it is being trimmed. □ **recortes**

trimaran ['traimərӕn] *n.* yacht with three parallel hulls. □ **trimarán**

trinity ['triniti] *n.* **1** group of three. □ **trinidad**
2 ***the Trinity,*** the three persons in the Christian God – the Father, Son and Holy Ghost. □ **Trinidad**

trinket ['triŋkit] *n.* cheap ornament. □ **baratija**

trio ['triou] *n.* **1** piece of music for three instruments. □ **trío**
2 three musicians; a group of three people: *a trio of Japanese businessmen.* □ **trío**

trip [trip] *n.* **1** journey: *we're going for a trip up the Thames; he's on a business trip to Canada.* □ **viaje, excursión**
day trip, journey lasting one day. □ **excursión de un día**
2 (*slang*) trance caused by drugs. □ **viaje**
■ *v.* (*he tripped*) **1** ***to trip along,*** to go along with light footsteps. □ **andar con paso ligero**
2 to catch your foot so that you stagger and fall: *he tripped over the doorstep.* □ **tropezar**
tripmeter *n.* dial on a car dashboard which shows how far you go on one particular journey. □ **cuentakilómetros parcial**
tripper *n.* person on a short (usually one day) trip. □ **viajero, excursionista**
trip up *v.* **1** ***to trip someone up,*** to make someone fall down: *the boys put a piece of string across the path to trip up the postman.* □ **hacer caer**
2 to force (someone) to make a mistake: *the children asked a trick question to try to trip the teacher up.* □ **pillar**
trip wire *n.* wire stretched low above the ground, which, when you touch it, sets off a gun/camera, etc. □ **alambre disparador**

tripartite [trai'pɑːtait] *adj.* with three parts; (agreement) between three countries. □ **tripartito**

tripe [traip] *n.* **1** part of a cow's/sheep's stomach used as food. □ **tripa, callos**
2 (***a load of***) ***tripe,*** (*informal*) rubbish/nonsense. □ **tontería**

triple ['tripl] *adj.* made of three parts; three times as big. □ **triple**
■ *v.* to become three times as large; to make (something) three times as large: *the production of cars has tripled.* □ **triplicar(se)**
triplet *n.* **1** (*in music*) three notes played quickly together. □ **tresillo**
2 one of three children born to the same mother at approximately the same time. □ **trillizo**
triplicate *n.* ***in triplicate,*** in three copies. □ **triplicado**

tripod ['traipɔd] *n.* stand with three legs. □ **trípode**

triptych ['triptik] *n.* religious picture formed of three parts, often placed on or above an altar. □ **tríptico**

trite [trait] *adj.* very ordinary/unexciting (remark). □ **trivial**

triumph ['traiəmf] *n.* **1** great victory: *one of the army's greatest triumphs.* □ **triunfo**
2 celebration of a victory: *to ride in triumph,* to ride in procession after a victory. □ **triunfo**
■ *v.* ***to triumph over someone,*** to win a victory over someone; to show that you are very glad that you won a victory. □ **vencer; congratularse**
triumphal [trai'ʌmfl] *adj.* referring to triumph. □ **triunfal**
triumphal arch, archway set up to celebrate a victory. □ **arco triunfal**
triumphant *adj.* victorious: *the triumphant army.* □ **triunfante**
triumphantly *adv.* in victory: *he triumphantly showed his prize to his parents.* □ **triunfalmente**

triumvirate [trai'ʌmvirət] *n.* group of three people who rule/manage something. □ **triunvirato**

trivet ['trivət] *n.* **1** small three-legged stand for a kettle. □ **trébede**
2 metal stand for putting inside a pan to stop food sticking to the bottom. □ **trébede**

trivial ['triviəl] *adj.* not important; ordinary: *even the most trivial incident may be important to the police.* □ **trivial**
trivia *n. pl.* unimportant details. □ **trivialidades**
triviality [trivi'ӕliti] *n.* being unimportant; unimportant detail. □ **trivialidad**

trod [trɔd] **trodden** ['trɔdn] *v. see* **tread.**

troglodyte ['trɔglədait] *n.* person who lives in a cave. □ **troglodita**

troika ['trɔikə] *n.* **1** Russian carriage pulled by three horses. □ **troica**
2 three people holding power together (usually in Communist countries). □ **troica**

Trojan ['troudʒn] *n.* ***to work like a Trojan,*** to work very hard. □ **troyano; como un negro**

troll [troul] *n.* (*in Scandinavia*) bad-tempered dwarf. □ **gnomo**

trolley ['trɔli] *n.* wheeled cart for carrying luggage (such as at an airport); wheeled cart for pushing round a supermarket; small wheeled table for putting food on. □ **carrito**
sweet trolley, trolley with a selection of desserts in a restaurant. □ **carro de los postres**
trolley-bus *n.* bus which works on electricity taken from overhead wires by contact poles. □ **trolebús**

trombone [trɔm'boun] *n.* brass wind instrument

with a sliding tube. □ **trombón**
trombonist *n.* person who plays the trombone. □ **trombón**
troop [tru:p] *n.* **1** group of people: *a troop of horsemen; a troop of little children.* □ **grupo**
2 group of boy scouts. □ **grupo**
3 ***troops,*** soldiers: *British troops went into the attack.* □ **tropas**
troop ship/troop train, ship/train which carries soldiers. □ **de transporte de tropas**
■ *v.* to move in a large group: *people began to troop into the meeting; they all trooped off to the cinema.* □ **moverse en grupo**
trooper *n.* **1** cavalry soldier. □ **soldado de caballería**
2 *Amer.* policeman from a state police force. □ **policía**
trooping *n.* ***trooping the colour,*** military parade with the regimental flag. □ **desfile ante la bandera**
trophy ['troufi] *n.* (*pl. trophies*) **1** prize given for winning a competition. □ **trofeo**
2 something taken from the enemy and kept as a prize. □ **trofeo**
tropic ['trɔpik] *n.* **1** ***Tropic of Cancer/of Capricorn,*** two imaginary lines running round the earth, parallel to the equator, and about 23° north/south of it. □ **trópico**
2 ***the tropics,*** the hot areas of the world lying between these two imaginary lines. □ **los trópicos**
tropical *adj.* very hot; (plant, etc.) growing in the tropics. □ **tropical**
trot ['trɔt] *n.* running with short regular steps: *he went for a trot round the football field; the soldiers broke into a trot,* started to run. □ **trote**
to keep someone on the trot, (*informal*) to make someone work continuously/do all the work. □ **no dejar parar**
on the trot: *they won four games on the trot,* (*informal*) one after the other. □ **seguidos**
■ *v.* (*he trotted*) **1** to run with short regular steps. □ **trotar**
2 ***to trot out*** *the same old excuse,* (*informal*) to produce the same excuse again. □ **poner**
trotter *n.* pig's foot cooked for food. □ **pie de cerdo**
trouble ['trʌbl] *n.* **1** misfortune: *his troubles are over now.* □ **apuro, desgracia**
2 problem/difficult situation: *she has money troubles; the trouble is that the car won't start.* □ **problema**
to ask for trouble: *it's just asking for trouble,* that type of behaviour will simply cause problems for you. □ **buscar problemas**
to be in trouble: *he's in trouble with the police,* has been accused by the police of a crime. □ **tener problemas**
to get someone into trouble, (i) to make someone be accused of doing something wrong. □ **meter en un lío**
(ii) to make someone pregnant. □ **embarazar**
3 care which is put into an action: *he took the trouble to write; it's no trouble; he doesn't give me any trouble.* □ **molestia**
4 illness; mechanical defect: *she has heart trouble; the car dropped out of the race with engine trouble.* □ **problemas, trastornos**
5 riots/disturbances: *were you in the country at the time of the troubles?* □ **disturbios**
■ *v.* **1** to worry (someone): *he isn't troubled by the problem.* □ **preocupar**
2 to create problems for (someone); to bother (someone): *I'm sorry to trouble you, but could you tell me the way to the post office? I won't trouble you with all the details.* □ **molestar**
3 to bother (to do something): *don't trouble to change your dress; he didn't trouble to write.* □ **molestarse en**
troublemaker *n.* person who creates problems/who stirs up unrest. □ **perturbador**
trouble-shooter *n.* person whose job is to sort out problems (in a business/in international affairs). □ **el que arregla problemas/mediador**
troublesome *adj.* causing trouble: *his cough has become quite troublesome.* □ **molesto**
troublespot *n.* area where trouble is likely to occur. □ **ámbito difícil**
trough [trɔf] *n.* **1** large container for animal food or drink: *the pigs were at the trough.* □ **pesebre, comedero**
horse trough/water trough, container for water for horses to drink. □ **abrevadero**
2 low-pressure area in the atmosphere; low part of the sea between two waves. □ **bajas presiones, depresión**
trounce [trauns] *v.* to beat (someone) soundly. □ **pegar**
troupe [tru:p] *n.* company (of actors/circus clowns, etc.). □ **compañía, 'troupe'**
trouper *n.* old member of a troupe. □ **miembro de una compañía**
trousers ['trauzəz] *n. pl.* (***pair of***) ***trousers,*** outer clothes which cover the legs and the lower part of the body. □ **pantalones**
trousseau ['tru:sou] *n.* clothes and linen collected by the bride before her wedding. □ **ajuar**
trout [traut] *n.* (*no pl.*) type of edible freshwater fish. □ **trucha**
salmon trout, large sea trout with pink flesh like that of a salmon. □ **trucha asalmonada**
trove [trouv] *adj. see* **treasure.**
trowel ['trauəl] *n.* **1** small hand spade used in gardening. □ **paleta**
2 tool with a flat blade used for spreading mortar between bricks. □ **llana**
truant ['tru:ənt] *adj.* and *n.* (child) who is absent from school without permission. □ **que hace novillos**
to play truant, not to go to school. □ **hacer novillos**
truancy ['tru:ənsi] *n.* being away from school without permission. □ **novillos**
truce [tru:s] *n.* period when two armies/enemies, etc., agree to stop fighting temporarily. □ **tregua**
truck [trʌk] *n.* **1** open railway wagon for carrying goods. □ **vagón, vagoneta**
2 heavy lorry. □ **camión**
3 small hand cart. □ **carretilla**
4 ***to have no truck with something,*** not to have anything to do with something. □ **no tener que ver con...**
5 *Amer.* fruit and vegetables grown for sale in a town market: *truck farming; truck farmer.* □ **fruta y hortalizas para el mercado**
truck driver *Amer.* **trucker** *n.* lorry driver. □ **camionero**
trucking *n. Amer.* transport of goods by lorry. □ **transporte en camión**
truckload *n.* amount carried in a truck: *two truckloads of sand.* □ **camión**
truckle bed ['trʌkl 'bed] *n.* low bed which can be pushed under another bed in daytime. □ **cama baja (nido)**
truculence ['trkjuləns] *n.* threatening attitude. □ **agresividad**
truculent *adj.* threatening/fierce; eager to quarrel. □ **agresivo**

trudge [trʌdʒ] *v.* to walk heavily. □ **andar con dificultad**

true [tru:] *adj.* (*truer, truest*) **1** correct: *that's true; what he says is true.* □ **verdad, cierto**
2 real: *a true friend; he's not a true Scotsman.* □ **auténtico, verdadero**
3 correctly adjusted: *the cog wheel is not quite true.* □ **ajustado**
true north, north towards the north pole, and not the magnetic north. □ **norte geográfico**
4 faithful: *he promised to be true to her.* □ **fiel**
■ *adv.* **1** correctly. □ **correctamente**
to come true: *the forecast came true,* what was forecasted really happened. □ **cumplirse**
2 *she didn't sing true,* was out of tune. □ **desafinado**
3 *the wheel wasn't running true,* wasn't turning straight. □ **bien, recto**
■ *n.* ***out of true,*** not quite straight/not correctly adjusted. □ **desajustado**
truly *adv.* really: *she was truly sorry; he's really and truly pleased,* he really is completely happy. □ **verdaderamente**
yours truly, ending of a letter which is slightly formal. □ **atentamente**

truffle ['trʌfl] *n.* **1** type of round black edible fungus found under the earth. □ **trufa**
2 soft chocolate-covered sweet (usually flavoured with rum). □ **trufa**

trug [trʌg] *n.* long shallow basket for picking flowers. □ **cesta**

truism ['tru:izəm] *n.* saying which is quite obviously true and therefore need not be said. □ **obviedad**

trump [trʌmp] *n.* (*in card games*) suit which is chosen as being of higher value than the other suits: *hearts are trumps.* □ **triunfo**
trump card, advantage which is kept ready for use to win an argument/a competition: *he played his trump card.* □ **baza**
to turn/come up trumps, (*informal*) to be very generous, especially unexpectedly. □ **tener un ataque de generosidad**
■ *v.* **1** *to trump a card,* to play a card of the suit which is trumps, and so win. □ **jugar un triunfo**
2 ***to trump up,*** to invent: *he was arrested on a trumped-up charge of possessing drugs.* □ **inventar**

trumpet ['trʌmpit] *n.* brass musical instrument with three keys. □ **trompeta**
to blow your own trumpet, (*informal*) to praise what you yourself have done. □ **darse bombo**
■ *v.* **1** to play the trumpet. □ **tocar la trompeta**
2 to make a loud noise: *he trumpeted his victory all over the place.* □ **anunciar con estrépito**
3 (*of elephant*) to call. □ **barritar**
trumpeter *n.* person who plays the trumpet. □ **trompetista**

truncated [trʌn'keitid] *adj.* cut off; shortened. □ **truncado**

truncheon ['trʌntʃn] *n.* short, heavy stick used by policemen. □ **porra**

trundle ['trʌndl] *v.* to roll/to push along something which is heavy: *he trundled the barrel along the pavement.* □ **hacer rodar/empujar**

trunk [trʌŋk] *n.* **1** main stem (of a tree); body (of a person). □ **tronco**
2 long nose (of an elephant). □ **trompa**
3 large box for sending clothes, etc., in: *I'm packing my trunk.* □ **baúl**
4 *Amer.* boot/luggage compartment at the back of a car. □ **maletero**
5 ***trunks,*** men's shorts for swimming. □ **bañador (masculino)**
trunk call *n.* long-distance telephone call. □ **conferencia**
trunk road *n.* main road. □ **carretera nacional**

truss [trʌs] *n.* (*pl. trusses*) **1** bundle of straw. □ **haz**
2 beam holding up a bridge/a roof. □ **cuchillo**
3 belt to support a hernia. □ **braguero**
■ *v.* **1** to tie up (straw) into bundles. □ **atar en haces**
2 to tie up (a chicken) ready for the oven; to tie up (a prisoner). □ **atar**

trust [trʌst] *n.* **1** confidence that something is correct/is good/will work well, etc.: *to take something on trust,* without examining it to see if it is all right; *I don't place any trust in what I read in newspapers.* □ **confianza**
2 hope: *he put his trust in the judge's common-sense.* □ **esperanza**
3 responsibility: *he has a position of trust in the bank.* □ **confianza**
4 passing of goods/money to someone who will look after it: *her money is held in trust for her daughter; to set up a family trust,* to put the family money in the hands of a group of people who will administer it. □ **depósito, fideicomiso**
5 group of business companies which combine to avoid competing with each other. □ **'trust'**
■ *v.* **1** to be sure of (someone); to have confidence in (someone): *I wouldn't trust him with my money; can she be trusted to keep a secret?; trust him to be late,* (*informal*) as usual, he is late. □ **confiar**
2 to hope: *I trust you've got over your cold; I trust you will all come to the party.* □ **confiar, esperar**
trustee [trʌs'ti:] *n.* person who has charge of money on trust for someone; person who administers a family trust/who directs a charity, etc. □ **fideicomisario, administrador**
trustful, trusting *adj.* full of confidence (in someone). □ **confiado**
trustworthiness *n.* being depended upon. □ **honradez**
trustworthy *adj.* which can be depended upon. □ **digno de confianza**
trusty ['trʌsti] *n.* (*pl. trusties*) prisoner who is given certain responsibilites because he can be trusted. □ **preso con privilegios**
■ *adj.* which can be depended upon. □ **digno de confianza**

truth [tru:θ] *n.* something which is true; true story: *to tell the truth; there's some truth in what he says; the truth of the matter is that he is mad.* □ **verdad**
to tell someone a few home truths, to tell someone what you think of them/to criticize someone's behaviour/character. □ **decir unas verdades**
truthful *adj.* (person) who always tells the truth. □ **veraz**
truthfully *adv.* in a truthful way. □ **verazmente**

try [trai] *n.* (*pl. tries*) **1** attempt (to do something): *she's going to have a try at flying a plane; he did it first try.* □ **intento**
2 goal scored in Rugby by touching the ball down behind the opposing goal line: *to score a try; to convert a try.* □ **ensayo**
■ *v.* (*tried; trying*) **1** to test: *try my beef stew; have you tried the new toothpaste yet?* □ **probar**
2 to attempt: *he tried to climb over the wall; the police tried to keep the two gangs apart.* □ **intentar**
3 to make (something) suffer: *this tiny print tries my eyes.* □ **cansar**
4 to judge (a case/a person) in court: *he was tried in the Central Court and found guilty.* □ **juzgar**
trying *adj.* difficult to put up with: *trying times; little children can be very trying.* □ **difícil, molesto**

try on *v. to try on a pair of new shoes,* to put shoes on to see if they fit. □ **probarse**
to try it on with someone, (*informal*) to act boldly to see if someone will accept your behaviour. □ **tratar de engañar**
try out *v.* to test (something): *he's trying out his new car.* □ **probar**
tsetse ['tsetsi] *n.* ***tsetse*** (***fly***), type of African fly which transmits disease by biting. □ **tsé-tsé**
tub [tʌb] *n.* **1** round (wooden) container: *to plant trees in tubs.* □ **tina, barreño**
ice cream tub, small, round cardboard box of ice cream. □ **tarrina**
2 bath. □ **bañera**
tubby *adj.* (*informal*) fat. □ **gordo**
tuba ['tju:bə] *n.* large bass brass instrument. □ **tuba**
tube [tju:b] *n.* **1** long pipe for carrying liquids or gas: *to syphon petrol out of a car using a plastic tube.* □ **tubo**
inner tube, rubber pipe for air inside a tyre. □ **cámara**
2 long pipe (in the body). □ **trompa**
bronchial tubes, tubes leading to the lungs. □ **bronquios**
3 soft pipe with a screw top which contains paste, etc.: *a tube of tooth paste; a tube of glue.* □ **tubo**
4 (*especially in London*) the underground railway system: *I go to work by tube/on the tube; take the tube to Oxford Circus.* □ **metro**
5 ***television tube,*** glass bulb in a television set which projects the picture on the screen. □ **tubo**
tubeless *adj.* (tyre) with no inner tube. □ **sin cámara**
tubing *n.* tubes made of metal/plastic, etc.: *a length of rubber tubing.* □ **tubería**
tubular ['tju:bjulə] *adj.* like a tube. □ **tubular**
tubular bells, pieces of metal tubing of varying lengths which when hung up and hit with a hammer give different notes. □ **carillón**
tuber ['tju:bə] *n.* thick piece of root which can be planted to make a new plant grow: *potato tubers.* □ **tubérculo**
tuberous *adj.* (root) which produces tubers. □ **tuberoso**
tuberculosis [tjubə:kju'lousis] *n.* disease of the lungs. □ **tuberculosis**
tubercular [tju'bə:kjulə] *adj.* suffering from tuberculosis. □ **tuberculoso**
tuberculin-tested [tju'bə:kjulin'testid] *adj.* (milk/cow) which has been tested to show that it is free from tuberculosis. □ **con la prueba de la tuberculina**
tuck [tʌk] *n.* **1** little fold/pleat in a piece of cloth: *to take a tuck in,* to make a little stitched fold (to improve the fit of a piece of clothing). □ **pliegue, alforza**
2 (*informal*) cakes/sweets, etc., eaten by schoolchildren: *tuck shop,* shop in a school selling sweets/cakes, etc. □ **chucherías**
■ *v.* **1** to fold (a blanket) around you and push the ends underneath you: *to tuck a rug round someone/under someone's knees.* □ **remeter**
2 to fold cloth into little pleats. □ **alforzar**
tucker *n.* (*in Australia*) (*informal*) food. □ **comida**
tuck in *v.* **1** to push the edge of a piece of cloth underneath someone to keep them warm: *to tuck the bedclothes in.* □ **arropar, remeter**
2 (*informal*) to eat a large quantity of food: *they tucked in to a big meal.* □ **zampar**
tuck in!, start eating! □ **¡empieza a comer!**
tuck-in *n.* (*slang*) big meal. □ **comilona**
tuck up *v.* to push the edge of the bedclothes around (someone) to keep them warm: *to tuck someone up in bed; the little girl was snugly tucked up in bed.* □ **arropar, remeter**
Tuesday ['tju:zdei] *n.* second day of the week/day between Monday and Wednesday: *I don't go to work on Tuesdays; I saw her last Tuesday; I'll see you on Tuesday.* □ **martes**
tuft [tʌft] *n.* small bunch of grass/hair, etc. □ **mechón**
tug [tʌg] *n.* **1** sudden pull: *the dentist gave a good tug and the tooth came out.* □ **tirón**
2 powerful boat used for towing barges/ships which have run aground, ships which are entering port, etc. □ **remolcador**
■ *v.* (*he tugged*) to pull hard: *the dog was tugging at the leash; she was tugging the sack along behind her.* □ **tirar de**
tugboat *n.* powerful boat used for towing barges/ships which have run aground, ships which are entering port, etc. □ **remolcador**
tug-of-war *n.* **1** competition where two teams pull against each other on a strong rope. □ **sogatira**
2 bitter struggle where two sides win alternately. □ **lucha enconada**
tuition [tju'iʃn] *n.* teaching (especially to one student): *driving tuition.* □ **enseñanza**
tulip ['tju:lip] *n.* common spring bulb with brilliant flowers shaped like cups. □ **tulipán**
tulip tree *n.* large evergreen tree, with big shiny leaves and large white flowers. □ **tulipero**
tulle [tju:l] *n.* thin silk/artificial material like a veil. □ **tul**
tumble ['tʌmbl] *n.* fall: *he took a tumble as the horse jumped over the fence.* □ **caída**
■ *v.* **1** to fall down: *the house came tumbling down; rocks tumbled down the mountainside.* □ **caer, derrumbarse**
2 to come down in confusion: *he tumbled into bed after a long day at the office; six little children tumbled out of the car; a tumbled heap of dirty clothes.* □ **caer, salir atropelladamente**
tumbledown *adj.* (house) which is falling down/coming to pieces. □ **que se viene abajo**
tumbler *n.* round, straight glass for drinking. □ **vaso recto**
tumbler dryer *n.* machine which dries washing. □ **secadora**
tumble to *v.* (*informal*) to understand: *he suddenly tumbled to the idea.* □ **caer en**
tummy ['tʌmi] *n.* (*pl. tummies*) (*informal*) stomach. □ **barriga**
tummyache *n.* (*informal*) pain in the stomach. □ **dolor de barriga**
tumour ['tju:mə] *Amer.* **tumor** *n.* abnormal growth in or on the body: *brain tumour; stomach tumour.* □ **tumor**
tumult ['tju:mʌlt] *n.* loud, excited noise (of a crowd). □ **tumulto**
tumultuous [tju'mʌltjuəs] *adj.* noisy/excited: *he had a tumultuous reception from the crowd.* □ **tumultuoso**
tumulus ['tju:mjuləs] *n.* mound of earth covering an ancient tomb. □ **túmulo**
tun [tʌn] *n.* large barrel (for wine/beer). □ **cuba**
tuna ['tju:nə] *n.* (*pl. tuna*) large sea fish (used for food). □ **atún**
tundra ['tʌndrə] *n.* Arctic plain with no trees. □ **tundra**
tune [tju:n] *n.* **1** series of musical notes which make a recognizable melody: *he was whistling a tune from a musical; to play a tune on the mouth-organ.* □ **aire, melodía**

to change one's tune: *he's changed his tune,* he has changed his way of thinking. □ **cambiar de forma de pensar**
to the tune of: *you have a bill to the tune of $100,* (*informal*) of at least $100. □ **de al menos...**
2 correct musical tone: *the piano is out of tune; please all try to sing in tune.* □ **tono; desafinado; entonados**
to be in tune with: *his ideas are in tune with those of his group,* are similar to those of the other people. □ **concordar con**
■ *v.* **1** to adjust (a musical instrument) so that it has the correct tone: *to tune a piano.* □ **afinar**
2 to adjust (an engine) so that it works more efficiently. □ **poner a punto**
tuneful *adj.* full of catchy tunes. □ **melodioso**
tune in *v.* to adjust a radio to a particular station: *he was tuned in to Radio London.* □ **sintonizar**
tuner *n. piano tuner,* person who tunes pianos. □ **afinador**
tune up *v.* **1** to adjust instruments before playing: *the orchestra is tuning up.* □ **afinar los instrumentos**
2 *to tune up an engine,* adjust it so that it works more efficiently. □ **poner a punto**
tuning fork *n.* metal fork which gives a correct note when it is hit, used for tuning musical instruments and giving the correct pitch to singers. □ **diapasón**

tungsten ['tʌŋstən] *n.* (*chemical element*: W) hard grey metal used to make steel and electric light filaments. □ **tungsteno**

tunic ['tju:nik] *n.* **1** loose top garment. □ **túnica**
2 short jacket worn by soldiers/policemen, etc. □ **guerrera**

Tunisia [tju:'niziə] *n.* Arab country in North Africa. □ **Túnez**
Tunisian *adj.* and *n.* (person) from Tunisia. □ **tunecino**

tunnel ['tʌnl] *n.* long hole in the ground: *the road goes through the mountain in a long tunnel.* □ **túnel**
■ *v.* (*he tunnelled*) to make a long passage under the ground: *the prisoners escaped by tunnelling under the wall; engineers are trying to tunnel through the mountain.* □ **hacer un túnel**

tunny ['tʌni] *n.* (*pl. tunny*) tuna/large edible sea fish. □ **atún**

turban ['tə:bən] *n.* long piece of cloth wrapped round the head to cover the hair. □ **turbante**

turbid ['tə:bid] *adj.* muddy (water). □ **turbio**

turbine ['tə:bain] *n.* engine driven by the force of water/steam, etc., which turns a wheel with blades: *gas turbine engine.* □ **turbina**

turbo-jet ['tə:bou'dʒet] *n.* aircraft jet engine driven by a turbine; aircraft powered by this engine. □ **turborreactor**
turbo-prop ['tə:bou'prɔp] *n.* aircraft jet and propeller engine driven by a turbine; aircraft powered by this engine. □ **turbopropulsor**

turbot ['tə:bət] *n.* large flat edible sea fish. □ **rodaballo**

turbulent ['tə:bjulənt] *adj.* **1** disturbed/violently moving (water/air). □ **turbulento**
2 likely to riot: *a turbulent crowd of football supporters.* □ **turbulento**
turbulence *n.* disturbance in the air causing an aircraft to rock suddenly; disturbance in water. □ **turbulencia**

tureen [tju'ri:n] *n.* large bowl for serving soup. □ **sopera**

turf [tə:f] *n.* **1** stretch of grassy lawn. □ **césped**
2 (*pl. turves* [tə:vz]) piece of grass and soil which can be planted to form a lawn; (*in Ireland*) block of peat for burning. □ **césped; turba**
3 ***the turf,*** the world of horse racing. □ **las carreras de caballos**
■ *v.* **1** to make a lawn by putting turves on the ground. □ **cubrir con césped**
2 ***to turf someone out,*** (*informal*) to throw someone out. □ **echar**

turgid ['tə:dʒid] *adj.* swollen; grand-sounding, meaningless (words). □ **turgente; ampuloso**

Turkey ['tə:ki] *n.* **1** country in the Middle East. □ **Turquía**
2 ***turkey,*** large domestic bird, often eaten at Christmas. □ **pavo**
Turk *n.* person from Turkey. □ **turco**
Turkish *adj.* referring to Turkey. □ **turco**
Turkish bath, steam bath after which you plunge into cold water. □ **baño turco**
Turkish delight, sweet jelly (sometimes with nuts in it), eaten in lumps. □ **dulces**
■ *n.* language spoken in Turkey. □ **turco**

turmeric ['tə:mərik] *n.* yellow spice, used for making pickles, etc. □ **cúrcuma**

turmoil ['tə:mɔil] *n.* wild disorder. □ **alboroto**

turn [tə:n] *n.* **1** circular movement (of a wheel, etc.): *give the screw two turns.* □ **vuelta**
to a turn: *the meat is done to a turn,* properly cooked all through. □ **en su punto**
2 change of direction: *the car made a sudden turn to the right; the mountain road makes several sharp turns.* □ **giro**
to take a turn for the better/worse: *the patient has taken a turn for the better,* has suddenly started to get better. □ **mejorar/empeorar**
on the turn, about to turn or change. □ **a punto de girar/cambiar**
at the turn of the century, about 1900. □ **al comienzo/final de siglo**
3 sudden attack (of illness): *she had one of her turns yesterday and was taken to hospital.* □ **ataque**
4 *it gave me quite a turn to see him when I thought he had been killed,* it gave me a shock. □ **impresión, vuelco**
5 chance to do something in order: *it's your turn to throw the dice; the children went up in turn to be examined by the doctor; let me go first - it's my turn, not yours.* □ **turno**
to take turns: *they took it in turns to carry the box/ they took turns to carry the box/they carried the box in turn,* they each carried it for part of the way and then passed it to the next person. □ **turnarse**
6 way of speaking/thinking/acting: *he has a beautiful turn of phrase; the car has a good turn of speed.* □ **forma de hablar; mucha velocidad**
7 ***to do someone a good turn,*** to do something to help them. □ **prestar ayuda**
8 performance (in a variety show): *a comedy turn.* □ **número**
■ *v.* **1** to go round/to make (something) go round in a circle: *to turn a wheel; to turn a doorknob; to turn the key in the lock; the wheels turned round very slowly; the hands of the clock slowly turned; he turned over and over in bed; the boat turned upside down; the door turns on a pair of hinges.* □ **girar**
2 to change direction: *turn right at the next crossroads; the road turned to the left; the wind has turned to the north; the tide has turned,* has started to rise/ fall; *his luck turned,* changed. □ **girar, cambiar**
3 to change (into something else): *tadpoles turn into frogs; his face turned white; the grass turned brown the leaves are beginning to turn,* to change to brown;

we're turning this field into a tennis court. □ **ponerse, cambiar, transformar**
4 *the milk's turned,* has gone sour. □ **se ha cortado**
5 to aim: *he turned his gun on the policeman.* □ **apuntar**
6 ***to turn someone's head,*** to make someone very proud/vain. □ **subirse a la cabeza**
to turn someone's stomach, to make someone feel sick. □ **revolver el estómago**
7 to shape a round piece of wood by carving it on a lathe: *to turn a chair leg.* □ **tornear**
8 to pass a particular point in time: *it's turned seven,* it is past seven o'clock; *he's turned fifty,* he's more than fifty years old. □ **pasar de**
turn aside *v.* to move to one side. □ **apartar**
turn away *v.* **1** to move away: *he turned away so as not to look at the dead body.* □ **apartarse**
2 to send (someone) away: *the theatre's full, we're turning people away.* □ **rechazar**
turn back *v.* **1** to turn and go back in the opposite direction. □ **dar la vuelta**
2 to send (someone) back: *the frontier guards turned back the refugees.* □ **rechazar**
turncoat *n.* person who switches from one opinion to another. □ **chaquetero**
turn down *v.* **1** to refuse: *I was offered the job but I turned it down.* □ **rechazar**
2 to reduce: *turn down the gas under the kettle; turn down the music,* reduce the sound. □ **bajar**
3 *to turn down a sheet/a bed,* to fold back the sheet on a bed, so that the pillow is uncovered. □ **abrir**
turner *n.* person who makes chair legs, etc., on a lathe. □ **tornero**
turn in *v.* **1** to hand back (equipment) to someone in authority. □ **devolver**
2 (*informal*) to go to bed: *it's time for me to turn in.* □ **acostarse**
turning *n.* **1** action of moving in a circle/of changing direction. □ **vuelta, giro**
2 point where a road leaves another road: *take the third turning on the left.* □ **bocacalle**
turning point *n.* important/decisive moment: *a turning point in his career; turning point in the history of international relations.* □ **momento decisivo**
turn off *v.* **1** to switch off: *turn off the gas; turn the light off.* □ **apagar, cerrar**
2 to change direction away from a straight line: *he turned off the main road.* □ **desviarse**
turn on *v.* **1** to switch on: *turn the light on; turn on the gas.* □ **encender, abrir**
2 to attack: *the dogs turned on the postman.* □ **volverse contra**
turn out *v.* **1** to throw (someone) out: *he was turned out of the club.* □ **expulsar**
2 to clear out: *she turned out the garden shed.* □ **vaciar**
3 to produce: *the factory turns out 200 washing machines a day.* □ **producir**
4 to switch off: *he turned out the light and went to bed.* □ **apagar**
5 to happen: *it turned out that he knew my sister; everything turned out all right in the end.* □ **resultar**
6 to come out in a crowd: *crowds of people turned out to see the decorations.* □ **asistir en masa**
7 ***well turned out,*** well dressed. □ **bien arreglado**
turnout *n.* crowd of people who turn out: *there was a poor turnout to see the cricket match because of the rain.* □ **asistencia**
turn over *v.* **1** to move (the page of a book) so that you can read the next one. □ **pasar la página**
2 *he's promised* ***to turn over a new leaf,*** to be better behaved. □ **corregirse**
3 to think about: *I'm turning over a plan in my mind.* □ **dar vueltas a**
4 to roll over: *the lorry turned over.* □ **volcar**
5 (*of engine*) to run gently. □ **funcionar con suavidad**
6 to have sales (of a certain amount): *we turn over $500 a week.* □ **facturar**
7 *to turn someone over to the police,* to hand a criminal to the police. □ **entregar**
turnover *n.* **1** ***apple turnover,*** type of pie made with pastry turned over pieces of apple. □ **tarta de manzana**
2 change (in staff): *there's been a rapid turnover of staff.* □ **cambio**
3 amount of sales: *a turnover of $500 a week.* □ **facturación**
turnpike *n. Amer.* motorway with tolls. □ **autopista de peaje**
turnstile *n.* gate which turns round on a pivot, allowing only one person to go through at a time. □ **torniquete**
turntable *n.* **1** flat part of a record player which turns with the record on it. □ **plato**
2 flat turning platform with rails on it, to enable railway locomotives to go off in a different direction. □ **plataforma giratoria**
turn up *v.* **1** to arrive: *half the guests didn't turn up; he finally turned up in Edinburgh.* □ **aparecer**
2 *the lost jewels turned up in France,* were found in France. □ **...aparecieron en Francia**
3 to increase: *turn up the gas under the kettle; turn up the sound.* □ **subir**
4 to roll up: *he turned up his sleeves.* □ **arremangarse**
5 *he turned up his collar to protect himself from the wind,* unrolled his collar. □ **se subió el cuello...**
turnup *n.* folded part at the bottom of each leg of a pair of trousers. □ **vuelta**
turnip ['tə:nip] *n.* common vegetable, with a round white root. □ **nabo**
turpentine ['tə:pəntain] *n.* oil which comes from fir trees, used for removing or thinning paint. □ **trementina**
turps [tə:ps] *n.* (*informal*) turpentine. □ **trementina**
turpitude ['təi:pitju:d] *n.* (*formal*) wickedness. □ **bajeza**
turquoise ['tə:kwɔiz] *n.* green-blue precious stone. □ **turquesa**
■ *adj.* green-blue (colour). □ **azul turquesa**
turret ['tʌrit] *n.* small tower; small armoured construction housing a gun (on a ship/tank, etc.). □ **torreón; torreta (en barco/carro, etc.)**
turreted *n.* with turrets. □ **con torreones/torretas**
turtle ['tə:tl] *n.* sea reptile with a hard shell like a tortoise. □ **tortuga**
to turn turtle, to capsize. □ **dar una vuelta de campana (coche); zozobrar (barco)**
turtledove *n.* type of wild pigeon with a soft, cooing call. □ **tórtola**
turtleneck pullover *n.* pullover with a high rolled neck. □ **...de cuello de cisne**
turves [tə:vz] *n. see* **turf.**
tusk [tʌsk] *n.* long tooth coming far out from the mouth of some animals (such as elephants/walruses, etc.). □ **colmillo**
tusker *n.* (*informal*) elephant. □ **elefante**
tussle ['tʌsl] *n.* fight/argument: *to have a tussle with the income tax.* □ **agarrada**
■ *v.* to fight/to struggle. □ **pelearse**
tussock ['tʌsək] *n.* large tuft of grass. □ **mata de hierba**
tutor ['tju:tə] *n.* teacher (especially one who teaches

one student or small groups of students): *private tutor.* □ **preceptor; profesor particular**
■ *v.* to teach (a small group of students). □ **dar una clase particular a**
tutorial [tju'tɔ:riəl] *n.* discussion meeting between a tutor and students. □ **clase; tutoría**
tut-tut [tʌt'tʌt] *n.* sound made to show you disapprove. □ **sonido de desaprobación**
■ *v.* (*he tut-tutted*) to make disapproving sounds. □ **desaprobar**
tutu ['tu:tu:] *n.* girl ballet dancer's short stiff skirt. □ **tutú**
tuxedo [tʌk'si:dou] *n.* (*pl. tuxedos*) *Amer.* dinner jacket. □ **esmoquin**
TV [ti:'vi:] *n.* **1** television: *I saw it on TV; a TV programme.* □ **TV**
2 television set: *we've bought a colour TV.* □ **televisor**
twaddle ['twɔdl] *n.* (*informal*) rubbish/nonsense: *don't talk twaddle.* □ **chorradas**
twang [twæŋ] *n.* **1** sound made, such as when a guitar string is pulled and released. □ **punteado**
2 *nasal twang,* accent made by speaking through the nose. □ **gangueo**
■ *v.* to make a twang: *he was twanging his guitar.* □ **puntear**
tweak [twi:k] *n.* sharp pull. □ **pellizco**
■ *v.* to pull suddenly. □ **pellizcar**
twee [twi:] *adj.* (*informal*) small, delicate and sentimental. □ **delicaducho**
tweed [twi:d] *n.* **1** rough woollen cloth made of strands of different colours: *a tweed jacket.* □ **tweed**
2 *she was wearing tweeds,* a suit made of tweed. □ **...un traje de tweed**
tweet [twi:t] *n.* little sound made by a small bird. □ **pío**
■ *v.* to make a little sound like a bird. □ **piar**
tweeter *n.* loudspeaker which reproduces high sounds. □ **altavoz para agudos**
tweezers ['twi:zəz] *n. pl.* (***pair of***) ***tweezers,*** small pincers used for pulling out hair/for picking up delicate objects. □ **pinzas**
twelve [twelv] number 12: *he is twelve* (*years old*); *come for a drink at twelve* (*o'clock*); *the twelve twenty train,* train which leaves at 12.20. □ **doce**
twelfth, 12th [twelfθ] *adj.* referring to twelve: *the twelfth of March* (*12th March*). □ **duodécimo; el 12 de marzo**
the twelfth century, period from 1100 to 1199. □ **el siglo doce**
twenty ['twenti] number 20: *she's twenty* (*years old*); *the twenty forty train,* train which leaves at 20.40. □ **veinte**
in the twenties, (i) *she's in her twenties,* she is over twenty but under thirty years old. □ **en la veintena**
(ii) between '20 and '30 in a century. □ **en los años veinte**
twentieth, 20th *adj.* referring to twenty: *the twentieth of June* (*20th June*). □ **vigésimo**
the twentieth century, period from 1900 to 1999. □ **el siglo veinte**
twerp [twə:p] *n.* (*slang*) silly idiot. □ **capullo**
twice [twais] *adv.* two times; double: *twice two is four; he's twice my age,* two times as old as I am; *twice as much money; this book is twice as big as that one/is twice the size of that one.* □ **dos veces**
twiddle ['twidl] *v.* to turn/to twist with no particular aim: *he was twiddling the knobs on the radio.* □ **juguetear con**
to twiddle your thumbs, holding your hands together, to turn your thumbs round and round as a sign of not having anything to do. □ **estar mano sobre mano**
twig [twig] *n.* little branch. □ **ramita**
■ *v.* (*he twigged*) (*informal*) to understand. □ **caer en la cuenta de**
twilight ['twailait] *n.* (period of) weak light between night and sunrise or between sunset and night: *I could just make out the shape of the ruins in the twilight.* □ **crepúsculo**
twill [twil] *n.* thick cloth woven in diagonal lines. □ **tela cruzada**
twin [twin] *adj.* and *n.* (child) born at approximately the same time as another to the same mother: *my twin brother.* □ **gemelo**
identical twins, two children born at the same time from the same egg, who look very similar. □ **gemelos homólogos**
■ *adj.* made of two similar parts: *twin beds; twin-engined aircraft.* □ **camas gemelas; bimotor**
■ *v.* (*he twinned*) to join (a town) to a similar town in another country for exchange visits and to encourage international understanding: *our town is twinned with one in Germany and another in France.* □ **hermanar**
twine [twain] *n.* thick, rough string. □ **bramante**
■ *v.* to twist round and round: *the ivy twined round the tree.* □ **enroscarse**
twinge [twindʒ] *n.* short sharp pain: *I had a sudden twinge in my back.* □ **punzada**
twinkle ['twiŋkl] *n.* little flicker of light. □ **centelleo**
with a twinkle in his eye, with his eyes shining with amusement. □ **le brillaban los ojos**
■ *v.* **1** to glitter: *the stars were twinkling in the sky; a twinkling light.* □ **centellear**
2 (*of eyes*) to shine (with amusement/wickedness, etc.). □ **brillar**
twinkling *n.* little flicker. □ **centelleante**
in the twinkling of an eye, very fast. □ **en un abrir y cerrar de ojos**
twirl [twə:l] *n.* **1** spinning movement: *the twirl of the dancer's skirt.* □ **giro**
2 spiral shape: *he was drawing twirls in his notebook.* □ **rasgo, espiral**
■ *v.* **1** to spin round: *the cowboy twirled the rope round.* □ **dar vueltas a**
2 to twist in your fingers: *he twirled his pencil.* □ **dar vueltas con los dedos**
twist [twist] *n.* **1** something which has been twisted: *a twist of hair.* □ **mecha; trenza**
a twist of paper, small container made of a piece of paper with its end twisted. □ **cucurucho**
2 something which twists: *the mountain road has many twists and turns.* □ **vuelta**
3 act of twisting: *give the bottle top a sharp twist.* □ **torsión**
4 *this has added a new twist to the story,* an unexpected change. □ **...un nuevo giro**
■ *v.* **1** to turn round and round: *to twist threads together to make a string; the road twists and turns.* □ **trenzar (una cuerda); dar vueltas y vueltas (carretera)**
2 to wind (something) round something: *he twisted the rope twice round the post.* □ **atar**
3 to bend in the wrong way: *the metal roof was twisted by the wind; she tripped and twisted her ankle,* sprained her ankle. □ **alabear; torcerse**
to twist someone's arm, (*informal*) to persuade someone to do what you want. □ **hacer entrar en razones a alguien**
4 to change the meaning of: *the newspaper report twisted my words out of context.* □ **tergiversar**

twister *n.* (*slang*) **1** dishonest person. □ **tramposo**
2 *Amer.* whirlwind. □ **huracán**

twit [twit] *n.* (*slang*) silly idiot. □ **lelo**
■ *v.* (*he twitted*) to make fun of (someone). □ **tomar el pelo a**

twitch [twitʃ] *n.* (*pl. twitches*) sudden jerk/sudden movement: *he gave the rope a twitch.* □ **tirón**
■ *v.* to jerk suddenly/to make a sudden movement: *his hands twitched; he twitched the rope.* □ **crispar (las manos); tirar bruscamente de (la cuerda)**

twitter ['twitə] *n.* **1** little calls made by birds. □ **gorjeo**
2 *she was **all of a twitter**,* very excited. □ **estaba nerviosísima**
■ *v.* to make little sounds (like birds). □ **gorjear**

two [tu:] number 2: *his son is two (years old); he didn't get home until two (o'clock).* □ **dos**
one or two, a few: *there were only one or two people at the show.* □ **uno o dos**
to put two and two together, to come to a conclusion by comparing various facts. □ **atar cabos**
to be in two minds about something, not to be able to decide. □ **estar indeciso**
two-bit *adj. Amer.* (*informal*) cheap; second-rate. □ **de poca monta**
two-faced *adj.* deceitful. □ **falso**
twofold *adv.* twice as much. □ **doble**
two-legged [tu:'legid] *adj.* with two legs. □ **de dos piernas/patas**
twopenny ['tʌpni] *adj.* costing two pence. □ **de dos peniques**
two-piece *adj.* made of two pieces. □ **de dos piezas**
two-piece suit, suit made of a jacket and skirt/trousers. □ **traje (de dos piezas)**
two-ply *adj.* made of two threads/two pieces: *two-ply wool.* □ **de dos cabos/capas**
two-seater *n.* car/aircraft with only two seats. □ **de dos plazas**
twosome *n.* two people (playing a game); game for two people. □ **partido de dos**
two-stroke *adj.* (engine) with two pistons. □ **de dos tiempos**
two-stroke fuel, fuel for small engines. □ **gasolina con mezcla**
two-time *v.* (*informal*) to be unfaithful (to a girlfriend/boyfriend). □ **pegársela con otro/otra**
two-timer *n.* (*informal*) unfaithful person. □ **infiel**
two-tone *adj.* coloured with two tones of the same colour: *two-tone telephone.* □ **bicolor**
two-way *adj.* going in two directions: *two-way radio; two-way traffic.* □ **transmisor-receptor; de doble sentido (circulación)**

tycoon [tai'ku:n] *n.* wealthy businessman. □ **magnate**

tying ['taiiŋ] *v. see* **tie.**

tympanum [tim'pɑ:nəm] *n.* (*formal*) eardrum. □ **tímpano**

type [taip] *n.* **1** sort/kind: *there are two types of seat material — cloth and plastic; a new type of early potato.* □ **tipo**
2 example: *he's a real northern type,* a good example of a northerner. □ **tipo**
3 small pieces of metal with letters moulded on them, used for printing; collection of pieces of metal for printing: *the book is in type.* □ **tipo**
■ *v.* to write with a typewriter: *he's learning to type; he spends all day typing letters; he types his letters himself.* □ **escribir a máquina**
typecast *v.* (*he typecast*) to give an actor the same sort of part all the time: *she doesn't want to be typecast as a dull spinster.* □ **encasillar**
typescript *n.* document typed on a typewriter. □ **mecanograma**
typesetter *n.* person who sets manuscripts in type ready for printing. □ **cajista**
typewriter *n.* machine which prints letters on a piece of paper when you press the keys. □ **máquina de escribir**
typewritten *adj.* (document) which has been written with a typewriter. □ **escrito a máquina**
typing *n.* **1** action of writing letters with a typewriter: *his typing is very bad.* □ **mecanografía**
typing pool, group of typists who work for several departments in a company. □ **servicio de mecanógrafas**
typing paper, special paper for typewriters. □ **papel para...**
2 action of classifying into types. □ **clasificación**
blood typing, classification of blood into a certain group. □ **determinación del grupo sanguíneo**
typist *n.* person whose job is to type letters on a typewriter. □ **mecanógrafo**
typographic(al) [taipə'græfik(l)] *adj.* referring to typography. □ **tipográfico**
typography [tai'pɔgrəfi] *n.* art of arranging material for printing/of designing a printed page. □ **tipografía**

typhoid ['taifɔid] *adj.* and *n.* ***typhoid (fever),*** serious disease caused by infected food or drink. □ **fiebre tifoidea**

typhoon [tai'fu:n] *n.* tropical storm (in the Far East). □ **tifón**

typhus ['taifəs] *n.* serious fever, where the virus is carried by lice. □ **tifus**

typical ['tipikl] *adj.* **1** obviously belonging to a particular group: *he's a typical Scot.* □ **típico**
2 *that's typical of him,* that's exactly what he always does. □ **es típico de él**
typically *adv.* in a typical way. □ **típicamente**
typify *v.* to be an excellent example of: *this typifies his attitude to his work.* □ **tipificar**

tyranny ['tirəni] *n.* (*pl. tyrannies*) cruel rule by undemocratic government/ruler. □ **tiranía**
tyrannical [ti'rænikl] **tyrannous** ['tirənəs] *adj.* cruel. □ **tiránico**
tyrannize *v.* to rule (someone) in a cruel way. □ **tiranizar**
tyrant ['tairənt] *n.* cruel, undemocratic ruler. □ **tirano**

tyre ['taiə] *Amer.* **tire** *n.* thick rubber cover round a wheel: *you ought to check the pressure in your tyres; he's got a flat tyre,* the tyre has a hole in it so that the air has come out. □ **neumático**

tyro ['tairou] *n.* (*pl. tyros*) complete beginner; person with no experience: *I'm a complete tyro at gardening.* □ **principiante**

U,u

U, u [juː] twenty-first letter of the alphabet. □ **U, u**
U-turn, (i) turn made by a car in a road so that it faces in the opposite direction. □ **viraje en U**
(ii) *the government has done a U-turn,* has changed its policy completely. □ **...ha dado un giro de 180 grados**
it is not U to say 'serviette', (*informal*) it is not polite in upper class style. □ **es de macarras decir...**
U-boat *n.* German submarine. □ **submarino (alemán)**
ubiquitous [ju'bikwitəs] *adj.* (something) which is/which seems to be everywhere. □ **ubicuo**
ubiquity *n.* being everywhere. □ **ubicuidad**
udder ['ʌdə] *n.* bag producing milk which hangs under the body of a cow or goat. □ **ubre**
UFO [juːef'ou] *n. abbreviation for* unidentified flying object. □ **ovni**
ugh [əː] *interjection* showing a feeling that something is unpleasant: *Ugh! a spider dropped on my hat.* □ **¡uf!**
ugly ['ʌgli] *adj.* (*uglier, ugliest*) **1** not pleasant to look at: *she is fat and ugly; they live in an ugly little house.* □ **feo**
2 dangerous: *he's in an ugly mood.* □ **...humor de perros**
ugliness *n.* being ugly. □ **fealdad**
UHF [juːeitʃ'ef] *abbreviation for* ultra high frequency. □ **UHF**
UHT [juːeitʃ'tiː] *adj. abbreivation for* ultra heat treated. □ **UHT (uperizado)**
UK [juː'kei] *abbreviation for* United Kingdom: *we come from the UK; the UK minister of Defence.* □ **Reino Unido**
ukulele [juːkə'leili] *n.* very small guitar. □ **ukelele**
ulcer ['ʌlsə] *n.* sore on the inside or outside of the body: *he has a stomach ulcer.* □ **úlcera**
ulcerate *v.* to cover with ulcers; to become covered with ulcers. □ **ulcerar**
ulcerous *adj.* covered with ulcers. □ **ulceroso**
ulna ['ʌlnə] *n.* one of the two bones on the lower part of the arm. □ **cúbito**
ulterior [ʌl'tiəriə] *adj.* hidden/secret: *he must have an ulterior motive for acting in this way.* □ **oculto**
ultimate ['ʌltimət] *adj.* final: *the ultimate decision is with the referee.* □ **definitivo**
ultimately *adv.* finally. □ **finalmente**
ultimatum [ʌlti'meitəm] *n.* final message sent to an opponent stating that unless demands are met by a certain time, violent action (usually war or a strike) will start. □ **ultimátum**
ultra- ['ʌltrə] *prefix meaning* extremely/very; beyond: *ultra high frequency; ultra-sonic; ultra-fashionable; ultra-sensitive; you have to be ultra-careful.* □ **ultra-**
ultramarine [ʌltrəmə'riːn] *adj.* and *n.* (colour) of deep sea blue. □ **azul de ultramar**
ultraviolet [ʌltrə'vaiələt] *adj.* (light rays) which are beyond the violet of the spectrum and which tan the skin: *a sunlamp has an ultraviolet bulb.* □ **ultravioleta**
umbel ['ʌmbl] *n.* flower head made of many single flowers on long stalks. □ **umbela**
umber ['ʌmbə] *adj.* and *n.* brown (colour) like earth. □ **ocre**
umbilical [ʌm'bilikl] *adj.* ***umbilical cord,*** tube joining the mother to her baby before birth, and through which nourishment passes. □ **umbilical**
umbrage ['ʌmbridʒ] *n.* ***to take umbrage at something,*** to feel insulted by something. □ **resentimiento; ofenderse por**
umbrella [ʌm'brelə] *n.* round shade of folded cloth which is opened on a frame and held over your head to keep off the rain. □ **paraguas**
beach umbrella, large colourful parasol used to keep off the sun on a beach. □ **sombrilla**
umbrella organization, large organization which covers several smaller ones. □ **organización general**
umpire ['ʌmpaiə] *n.* person who acts as a judge in cricket/tennis/baseball, etc., to see if the game is played according to the rules. □ **árbitro**
■ *v.* to act as an umpire: *he umpired a game of cricket.* □ **arbitrar**
umpteen [ʌm'tiːn] *adj.* and *n.* (*informal*) very large number: *I telephoned her umpteen times but her telephone was always out of order.* □ **no sé cuantas veces**
umpteenth *adj.* (*informal*) referring to umpteen: *that is the umpteenth glass he has broken since he started working here.* □ **enésimo**
un- [ʌn] *prefix meaning* not; the opposite: *unpleasant; to undo a belt; it's very un-English to like garlic.* □ **in-; des-; no; nada; poco; sin; anti-**
'un [ʌn] *pron.* (*informal*) one: *the little 'uns.* □ **los pequeñajos**
UN ['juː'en] *abbreviation for* United Nations. □ **ONU**
unabated [ʌnə'beitid] *adj.* with no loss of vigour: *the storm continued unabated.* □ **sin perder fuerza**
unable [ʌn'eibl] *adj.* not able: *he was quite unable to speak; she is unable to attend.* □ **incapaz**
unabridged [ʌnə'bridʒd] *adj.* (text) which has not been shortened. □ **íntegro**
unacceptable [ʌnək'septəbl] *adj.* which cannot be accepted: *he made several unacceptable demands.* □ **inaceptable**
unaccompanied [ʌnə'kʌmpnid] *adj.* alone; (musical instrument) without any accompaniment: *sonata for unaccompanied violin.* □ **solo**
unaccountable [ʌnə'kauntəbl] *adj.* which cannot be explained. □ **inexplicable**
unaccountably *adv.* without explanation: *he was unaccountably late.* □ **inexplicablemente**
unaccounted for *adj.* lost, with no explanation for the loss. □ **que falta; no hay noticias de**
unaccustomed [ʌnə'kʌstəmd] *adj.* not accustomed: *unaccustomed as I am to receiving gifts.* □ **desacostumbrado**
unacquainted [ʌnə'kweintid] *adj. to be unacquainted with the works of Shakespeare,* not to know the works of Shakespeare. □ **desconozco las obras...**
unadopted [ʌnə'dɔptid] *adj.* (road) which it is not the duty of the local council to keep in good repair. □ **fuera de la competencia, no mantenido**
unadulterated [ʌnə'dʌltəreitid] *adj.* pure; with nothing added. □ **sin mezcla**
unaffected [ʌnə'fektid] *adj.* sincere/natural: *unaffected happiness.* □ **verdadero, sincero**
unaided [ʌn'eidid] *adj.* without help: *she can walk a few steps unaided.* □ **solo**
unalloyed [ʌnə'lɔid] *adj.* pure. □ **puro**
unalterable [ʌn'ɔltrəbl] *adj.* which cannot be altered. □ **inalterable**
unaltered *adj.* which has not changed. □ **inalterado**

unambiguous [ʌnæm'bigjuəs] *adj.* clear/not ambiguous. □ **inequívoco**
unanimous [ju'næniməs] *adj.* where everyone agrees: *a unanimous vote.* □ **unánime**
unanimously *adv.* all agreeing together. □ **por unanimidad**
unanimity [junə'nimiti] *n.* being unanimous. □ **unanimidad**
unannounced [ʌnə'naunsd] *adj.* without being announced. □ **sin ser anunciado**
unanswerable [ʌn'ɑːnsərəbl] *adj.* which cannot be answered. □ **incontestable**
unappetizing [ʌn'æpitaiziŋ] *adj.* which does not make you want to eat/which takes away your appetite. □ **poco apetecible**
unapproachable [ʌnə'proutʃəbl] *adj.* (person) who is difficult to talk to/very formal; (place) which cannot be approached easily. □ **inaccesible**
unarmed [ʌn'ɑːmd] *adj.* with no weapons: *an unarmed policeman.* □ **desarmado**
unashamed [ʌnə'ʃeimd] *adj.* not ashamed. □ **desvergonzado**
unasked [ʌn'ɑːskd] *adj.* without being asked: *he stopped to help us unasked.* □ **de motu proprio**
unassuming [ʌnə'sjuːmiŋ] *adj.* quiet/modest. □ **sin pretensiones**
unattached [ʌnə'tætʃd] *adj.* not attached; not married. □ **suelto; soltero (persona)**
unattainable [ʌnə'teinəbl] *adj.* which cannot be reached. □ **inalcanzable**
unattended [ʌnə'tendid] *adj.* alone; not looked after: *do not leave your luggage unattended.* □ **desatendido**
unattractive [ʌnə'træktiv] *adj.* not attractive. □ **poco atractivo**
unauthorised [ʌn'ɔːθəraizd] *adj.* which is not permitted. □ **no autorizado**
unavoidable [ʌnə'vɔidəbl] *adj.* which cannot be avoided. □ **inevitable**
unaware [ʌnə'wɛə] *adj.* not knowing/not aware: *he was unaware of the fact that she was unhappy.* □ **inconsciente**
unawares *adv.* without noticing. □ **desprevenido**
to catch someone unawares, by surprise. □ **...desprevenido**
unbalanced [ʌn'bælənst] *adj.* erratic/slightly mad. □ **desequilibrado**
unbearable [ʌn'bɛərəbl] *adj.* which cannot be borne. □ **insoportable**
unbearably *adv.* so much that you cannot bear it: *it is unbearably hot in this room.* □ **hace un calor inaguantable en...**
unbeatable [ʌn'biːtəbl] *adj.* which cannot be beaten: *an unbeatable performance.* □ **insuperable**
unbeaten *adj.* which has not been beaten: *an unbeaten record.* □ **no superado**
unbeknown [ʌnbi'noun] *adj. unbeknown to anyone,* (*informal*) without anyone knowing. □ **sin saberlo nadie**
unbelievable [ʌnbi'liːvəbl] *adj.* incredible/which you cannot believe. □ **increíble**
unbelievably *adv.* incredibly/amazingly. □ **increíblemente**
unbend [ʌn'bend] *v.* (*he unbent*) to stop being stiff and start behaving naturally: *after a few drinks he unbent.* □ **hacerse más afable**
unbending *adj.* inflexible/harsh (rule). □ **inflexible**
unbiased [ʌn'baiəsd] *adj.* impartial/not biased: *I want someone to give me an unbiased opinion.* □ **no sesgado**
unbleached [ʌn'bliːtʃt] *adj.* (cloth, etc.) which has not been bleached. □ **sin blanquear**
unblock [ʌn'blɔk] *v.* to take a blockage away from (something). □ **desbloquear**
unbolt [ʌn'boult] *v.* to pull back the bolt on (a door). □ **desatrancar**
unbosom [ʌn'buzəm] *v. she unbosomed herself to her teacher,* she told all her private thoughts and troubles. □ **desahogarse**
unbounded [ʌn'baundid] *adj.* with no limits: *he has unbounded enthusiasm.* □ **ilimitado**
unbreakable [ʌn'breikəbl] *adj.* which cannot be broken. □ **irrompible**
unbridled [ʌn'braidld] *adj.* (passion) which is not controlled. □ **desenfrenado**
unbroken [ʌn'broukn] *adj.* **1** which has not been broken: *an unbroken record.* □ **intacto; un récord imbatido**
2 *unbroken case of wine,* case which has not been opened. □ **...sin empezar**
unburden [ʌn'bəːdn] *v.* ***to unburden yourself,*** to tell (someone) all your troubles/secrets. □ **abrirse**
unbusinesslike [ʌn'biznəslaik] *adj.* not efficient; not businesslike. □ **poco práctico**
unbutton [ʌn'bʌtn] *v.* to undo the buttons on: *he unbuttoned his shirt.* □ **desabrochar**
uncalled for [ʌn'kɔːldfɔː] *adj.* not necessary; not deserved: *these remarks are quite uncalled for.* □ **gratuito**
uncanny [ʌn'kæni] *adj.* mysterious/which seems unnatural: *he has an uncanny resemblance to his dead brother.* □ **extraordinario**
uncared for [ʌn'kɛədfɔː] *adj.* not looked after: *his flat has an uncared for look.* □ **descuidado**
unceasing [ʌn'siːsiŋ] *adj.* ceaseless; without any stopping: *the unceasing vigilance of the police.* □ **incesante**
unceremonious [ʌnseri'mouniəs] *adj.* not dignified; not polite. □ **descortés**
unceremoniously *adv.* in an undignified way: *he was unceremoniously thrown out of the meeting.* □ **sin miramientos**
uncertain [ʌn'səːtən] *adj.* **1** not certain/not sure: *he was uncertain whether to go or stay at home; I am uncertain about my itinerary.* □ **incierto**
2 which cannot be forecast: *uncertain weather.* □ **imprevisible**
uncertainty *n.* being uncertain; lack of certainty. □ **incertidumbre**
unchallenged [ʌn'tʃælənʒd] *adj.* without a challenge. □ **incontestado**
to let something pass unchallenged, to let something be said or written without questioning it. □ **dejar pasar algo por alto**
unchangeable [ʌn'tʃeinʒəbl] *adj.* which cannot be changed. □ **inmutable**
uncharitable [ʌn'tʃæritəbl] *adj.* unkind. □ **poco caritativo**
unchecked [ʌn'tʃekt] *adj.* with no check. □ **no comprobado**
uncivilized [ʌn'sivilaizd] *adj.* not civilized; barbarous. □ **incivilizado**
unclaimed ['unkleimd] *adj.* which has not been claimed: *unclaimed baggage,* cases, etc., which have been left in a left-luggage office and not been taken back by their owners. □ **sin reclamar**
unclassified [ʌn'klæsifaid] *adj.* not classified/not secret. □ **sin clasificar**
uncle ['ʌŋkl] *n.* brother of your father or mother; husband of your aunt. □ **tío**
unclean [ʌn'kliːn] *adj.* dirty. □ **sucio**
uncluttered [ʌn'klʌtəd] *adj.* tidy. □ **limpio**
uncoil [ʌn'kɔil] *v.* to unwind. □ **desenrollar**

uncomfortable [ʌn'kʌmftəbl] *adj.* **1** not comfortable: *an uncomfortable bed.* □ **incómodo**
2 embarrassed; ill at ease: *she felt uncomfortable as he talked to her about getting married.* □ **incómodo**

uncommitted [ʌnkə'mitid] *adj.* with no strong beliefs; (country) which has not decided which group to support; (voter) who has not decided which way to vote. □ **no comprometido**

uncommon [ʌn'kɔmən] *adj.* (*uncommoner, uncommonest*) strange/odd; rare: *an uncommon wild flower.* □ **poco común**
uncommonly *adv.* very: *this meal is uncommonly good.* □ **extraordinariamente**

uncommunicative [ʌnkə'mju:nikətiv] *adj.* silent/not talkative. □ **poco comunicativo**

uncomplimentary [ʌnkɔmpli'mentri] *adj.* not complimentary. □ **despectivo; poco halagüeño**

uncompromising [ʌn'kɔmprəmaiziŋ] *adj.* unwilling to give in or to change ideas. □ **intransigente**

unconcealed [ʌnkən'si:ld] *adj.* open; not hidden. □ **no disimulado**

unconcerned [ʌnkən'sə:nd] *adj.* not worried/not bothered by something. □ **despreocupado**

unconditional [ʌnkən'diʃnl] *adj.* without any conditions: *unconditional surrender; unconditional acceptance of an offer.* □ **incondicional; rendición sin condiciones**
unconditionally *adv.* without insisting on conditions: *he accepted the offer unconditionally.* □ **incondicionalmente**

unconnected [ʌnkə'nektid] *adj.* with no connection: *the two events are quite unconnected.* □ **desconectado**

unconscious [ʌn'kɔnʃəs] *adj.* **1** not conscious: *after the operation he was unconscious for two days.* □ **inconsciente; sin sentido**
2 not aware: *she was quite unconscious of the hatred she inspired.* □ **no se daba cuenta del...**
■ *n.* ***the unconscious,*** deep level of the mind, with thoughts or feelings of which you are not conscious. □ **el inconsciente**
unconscionable [ʌn'kɔnʃnəbl] *adj.* (*informal*) unreasonable/excessive: *she spends an unconscionable time getting dressed.* □ **desmedido**
unconsciously *adv.* in an unconscious way. □ **inconscientemente**

uncontrollable [ʌnkən'trouləbl] *adj.* which cannot be controlled: *uncontrollable fit of laughing.* □ **incontrolable; un ataque incontenible de risa**

unconventional [ʌnkən'venʃnl] *adj.* not usual: *she was wearing a very unconventional dress.* □ **poco convencional**

uncooked [ʌn'kukd] *adj.* not cooked: *a bowl of uncooked rice.* □ **sin cocer**

uncooperative [ʌnkou'ɔpərətiv] *adj.* unhelpful/not cooperative. □ **nada servicial**

uncork [ʌn'kɔ:k] *v.* to take the cork out of (a bottle). □ **descorchar**

uncorrected [ʌnkə'rektid] *adj.* which has not been corrected. □ **sin corregir**

uncorroborated [ʌnkə'rɔbəreitid] *adj.* (evidence) which has not been confirmed. □ **sin corroborar**

uncouple [ʌn'kʌpl] *v.* to detach (things) which are attached. □ **desacoplar; desenganchar**

uncouth [ʌn'ku:θ] *adj.* rude/badly brought up. □ **grosero**

uncover [ʌn'kʌvə] *v.* to take the cover off; to find: *the police uncovered a store of stolen guns.* □ **descubrir**

uncrossed [ʌn'krɔsd] *adj.* (cheque) which has not been crossed. □ **sin cruzar**

uncrushable [ʌn'krʌʃəbl] *adj.* (material) which does not make creases if it is crushed. □ **que no se arruga**

unction ['ʌŋkʃn] *n.* putting oil on a person in a religious ceremony. □ **unción**
unctuous ['ʌŋktʃuəs] *adj.* extremely and unpleasantly polite. □ **afectadamente fervoroso**

uncultivated [ʌn'kʌltiveitid] *adj.* (land) which has not been cultivated. □ **yermo; incultivado**

uncut [ʌn'kʌt] *adj.* which has not been cut; (film) which has not been censored; (book) with pages still joined together at the edges. □ **sin cortar**

undamaged [ʌn'dæmidʒd] *adj.* not damaged. □ **indemne**

undaunted [ʌn'dɔ:ntid] *adj.* bold/with no fear. □ **impertérrito, intrépido**

undecided [ʌndi'saidid] *adj.* (person) who has not made up his mind: *we are still undecided whether to reply to the letter or not.* □ **indeciso (persona); no hemos decidido todavía...**

undefended [ʌndi'fendid] *adj.* not defended; (divorce case) which the defendant does not defend. □ **indefenso; ganado (por no comparecer el demandado)**

undemocratic [ʌndemə'krætik] *adj.* not democratic. □ **nada democrático**

undeniable [ʌndi'naiəbl] *adj.* which cannot be denied/which is quite clearly true. □ **innegable**

under ['ʌndə] *prep.* **1** in a place which is directly below: *he hid under the table; the coin rolled under the piano.* □ **bajo**
under water, below the surface of the water: *he can swim under water.* □ **bajo el agua**
2 less than: *she is under thirty; he is under age; it was sold for under $100; he ran the mile in under four minutes.* □ **menos de; él es menor**
3 being ruled/managed/commanded by someone: *the department is under the manager; he served under a Russian general.* □ **bajo las órdenes de**
4 in; because of: *under the circumstances; he is under no obligation to buy; under the terms of the agreement.* □ **en ningún caso; no tiene obligación de; en los términos...**
5 in a state of: *under treatment,* being treated. □ **en**
under repair, being repaired. □ **en reparación**
under lock and key, locked up. □ **bajo llave**
under control, being controlled. □ **bajo control**
■ *adv.* in a lower place. □ **debajo**
to go under, (i) to drown. □ **ahogarse**
(ii) to fail/to go bankrupt. □ **sucumbir/arruinarse**
down under, (*informal*) in Australia and New Zealand. □ **en/de Australia...**
■ *adj.* lower/bottom: *the under surface of a box.* □ **inferior**
■ ***under-,*** *prefix meaning* less important; not enough: *under-secretary; under-gardener; the meat is undercooked.* □ **subsecretario; ayudante de jardinero; la carne está poco hecha**
under-age, younger than the minimum age. □ **menor**

underachieve [ʌndəə'tʃi:v] *v.* to do less well than expected. □ **rendir menos**
underachiever *n.* student who does not do as well as expected. □ **estudiante vago**

underarm ['ʌndeɑ:m] *adv.* (thrown) with the hand kept lower than the shoulder: *he threw the ball underarm.* □ **sobaco; axila**

undercarriage ['ʌndəkæridʒ] *n.* the wheels and their supports on an aircraft. □ **tren de aterrizaje**

undercharge [ʌndə'tʃɑ:dʒ] *v.* to charge less than you

should: *he undercharged me by $10.* □ **cobrar de menos**
underclothes ['ʌndəklouðz] *n. pl.* clothes worn next to your skin, under other clothes: *he walked around the house in his underclothes.* □ **ropa interior**
undercoat ['ʌndəkout] *n.* first coat of paint. □ **primera mano**
undercover ['ʌndəkʌvə] *adj.* secret. □ **secreto**
an undercover agent, spy. □ **agente secreto**
undercurrent ['ʌndəkʌrənt] *n.* **1** current of water under the surface. □ **corriente submarina**
2 hidden feelings: *an undercurrent of anger.* □ **un odio oculto**
undercut ['ʌndəkʌt] *v.* (*he undercut*) to sell more cheaply than (someone). □ **vender más barato que**
underdeveloped [ʌndədi'veləpd] *adj.* not developed; not industrially advanced: *she is underdeveloped for her age; underdeveloped countries.* □ **subdesarrollado**
underdog ['ʌndədɔg] *n.* person who is inferior to someone stronger/who always loses. □ **desvalido/perdedor**
underdone ['ʌndədʌn] *adj.* not cooked enough; not too cooked. □ **poco hecho**
underestimate [ʌndə'estimət] *n.* estimate which is less than the real quantity: *we thought it would cost about $10 per person, but this was an underestimate.* □ **infravaloración**
■ *v.* to estimate at less than the real quantity: *the government underestimated the strength of public support.* □ **infravalorar**
underexposed [ʌndəik'spouzd] *adj.* (film) which has not been exposed sufficiently. □ **subexpuesto**
underfed [ʌndə'fed] *adj.* with not enough to eat. □ **desnutrido**
underfelt ['ʌndəfelt] *n.* soft material put on the floorboards beneath a carpet. □ **arpillera**
underfoot [ʌndə'fut] *adv.* under the feet: *the ground was very soft underfoot.* □ **debajo de los pies**
undergarment ['ʌndəgɑ:mənt] *n.* piece of clothing worn next to the skin, under other clothes. □ **prenda interior**
undergo [ʌndə'gou] *v.* (*he underwent; he has undergone*) to suffer/to experience: *he underwent a full medical examination.* □ **sufrir**
undergraduate [ʌndə'grædjuət] *n.* student at university who has not yet passed the final examination for a first degree. □ **estudiante universitario**
underground [ʌndə'graund] *adv.* **1** under the ground: *the cables went underground for several metres.* □ **bajo tierra**
2 in hiding: *he went underground for several weeks while the police were looking for him.* □ **clandestinamente**
■ *adj.* **1** under the ground: *an underground passageway; underground storeroom.* □ **subterráneo**
2 secret; against the ruling authorities: *underground opponents; underground writers.* □ **clandestino**
■ *n.* **1** city railway which runs beneath the ground: *he took the underground to get to his office.* □ **metro**
2 secret organization. □ **organización clandestina**
undergrowth ['ʌndəgrouθ] *n.* bushes which grow thickly together under trees. □ **maleza**
underhand(ed) [ʌndə'hænd(id)] *adj.* cunning; deceitful. □ **engañoso**
underlay ['ʌndəlei] *n.* material (such as felt) for putting under a carpet; *see also* **underlie.** □ **arpillera**
underlie [ʌndə'lai] *v.* (*it underlay; it has underlain*) to be underneath; to be the basic/hidden cause (of something): *the underlying cause of his failure.* □ **subyacer; ser la base de**
underline ['ʌndəlain] *v.* to write a line under (a word); to emphasize: *this underlines the importance of the treaty.* □ **subrayar**
underling ['ʌndəliŋ] *n.* person who works for someone else. □ **subordinado**
undermanned [ʌndə'mænd] *adj.* with not enough staff. □ **sin el debido personal**
undermentioned [ʌndə'menʃənd] *adj.* mentioned lower down on the page. □ **abajo citado**
undermine [ʌndə'main] *v.* to weaken: *his health was undermined by the climate.* □ **minar**
underneath [ʌndə'ni:θ] *prep.* under/beneath: *she wore a long woollen cardigan underneath her jacket; he was sheltering underneath a chestnut tree.* □ **debajo de**
■ *adv.* under: *he was wearing a thin shirt with nothing underneath.* □ **debajo**
■ *n.* the bottom part: *the underneath of this plate is wet.* □ **fondo**
undernourished [ʌndə'nʌriʃt] *adj.* not having enough to eat. □ **desnutrido**
underpaid [ʌndə'peid] *adj.* not paid enough. □ **mal pagado**
underpants ['ʌndəpænts] *n. pl.* men's undergarment for the lower part of the body. □ **calzoncillos**
underpass ['ʌndəpɑ:s] *n.* (*pl. underpasses*) place where a road goes under another road. □ **paso inferior**
underprivileged [ʌndə'privilidʒd] *adj.* not having the same opportunities as other people. □ **no privilegiado**
underrate [ʌndə'reit] *v.* to value (something) less than you ought: *I underrated his speed as a swimmer.* □ **subestimar**
underseal ['ʌndəsi:l] *n.* protective paint to stop the underneath of a car rusting. □ **capa anticorrosión**
■ *v.* to paint the underneath of a car with protective paint. □ **dar una capa de pintura anticorrosión**
undersell [ʌndə'sel] *v.* (*he undersold*) to sell more cheaply than (someone). □ **vender más barato que**
undershirt ['ʌndəʃə:t] *n. Amer.* light undergarment for the top half of the body. □ **camiseta**
underside ['ʌndəsaid] *n.* side which is underneath. □ **envés**
undersigned ['ʌndəsaind] *n.* ***the undersigned,*** person who has signed a letter. □ **el abajo firmante**
undersized ['ʌndəsaizd] *adj.* smaller than normal. □ **de tamaño menor**
underslung ['ʌndəslʌŋ] *adj.* (car chassis) which hangs below the axles. □ **colgante**
understaffed [ʌndə'stɑ:fd] *adj.* with not enough staff. □ **corto de personal**
understand [ʌndə'stænd] *v.* (*he understood*) **1** to know; to see the meaning of something: *do you understand this problem? he doesn't understand French.* □ **comprender; entender**
2 to be an expert in something: *he understands finance; I just don't understand horses.* □ **saber de**
3 to think/to have an impression: *I understood he was leaving for Africa; am I to understand that you are dissatisfied?* □ **tener entendido**
4 to take something for granted, even if it is not written or spoken: *it was understood that the payments were to be made in dollars; in the phrase 'going away?' the words 'are you' are understood.* □ **sobrentender**
5 to know why (something is done) and accept it: *if you don't want to come, I shall quite understand.* □ **comprender**
understandable *adj.* which can be understood. □ **comprensible**

understandably *adv.* in a way which can be understood: *he was understandably annoyed when the stone broke his window.* □ **comprensiblemente**
understanding *n.* **1** ability to understand. □ **comprensión**
2 sympathy for another person's problems: *he showed no understanding towards his children.* □ **comprensión**
3 private agreement: *they came to an understanding; you can have a party in the house on the understanding that you don't make any noise.* □ **entendimiento**
■ *adj.* sympathetic: *an understanding mother.* □ **comprensivo**
understate [ʌndə'steit] *v.* to make something seem less important than it really is: *he understates the seriousness of the problem.* □ **subestimar**
understatement *n.* statement which does not tell the facts forcefully enough: *to say that he was worried was an understatement - he was frantic.* □ **declaración insuficiente; eufemismo**
understood [ʌndə'stud] *v. see* **understand.**
understudy ['ʌndəstʌdi] *n.* (*pl. understudies*) actor who learns a part in the play so as to be able to act it if the main actor is ill. □ **suplente**
■ *v.* (*understudied, understudying*) to learn a part in a play so as to be able to act it if the main actor is ill. □ **aprender un papel para poder suplir a**
undertake [ʌndə'teik] *v.* (*he undertook; he has undertaken*) to promise to do (something); to accept to do (something): *he undertook to deliver the goods the following morning.* □ **comprometerse a**
undertaker *n.* person who organizes funerals. □ **encargado de pompas fúnebres**
undertaking *n.* **1** business: *a commercial undertaking.* □ **empresa**
2 promise: *he gave me an undertaking that he would not be late.* □ **promesa**
3 job: *building a new railway is quite an undertaking,* is a very difficult job. □ **tarea**
undertone ['ʌndətoun] *n.* **1** ***in an undertone,*** in a quiet voice. □ **voz baja**
2 hidden feeling: *undertones of war.* □ **aires de guerra**
undertow ['ʌndətou] *n.* strong current under the surface of water, which flows in a different direction to that on the surface. □ **resaca**
undervalue [ʌndə'væljuː] *v.* to value at less than the true rate. □ **infravalorar**
underwater [ʌndə'wɔːtə] *adj.* below the surface of the water: *underwater swimming.* □ **submarino**
underwear ['ʌndəwɛə] *n.* (*no pl.*) clothes worn next to your skin under other clothes: *he ran into the street in his underwear.* □ **ropa interior**
underweight [ʌndə'weit] *adj.* which weighs less than usual. □ **de peso insuficiente**
underwent [ʌndə'went] *v. see* **undergo.**
underworld ['ʌndəwəːld] *n.* criminal world: *an underworld killing,* murder of a criminal by other criminals. □ **hampa; bajos fondos**
underwrite [ʌndə'rait] *v.* (*he underwrote; he has underwritten*) to insure (especially ships); to accept responsibility for (something). □ **asegurar**
underwriter ['ʌndəraitə] *n.* person who insures (especially ships). □ **asegurador**
undeserved [ʌndi'zəːvd] *adj.* not deserved. □ **inmerecido**
undesirable [ʌndi'zaiərəbl] *adj.* not wanted; not pleasant. □ **indeseable**
■ *n.* person who is not wanted/who is considered a bad influence. □ **un indeseable**
undetected [ʌndi'tektid] *adj.* not noticed. □ **no descubierto**
undetectable *adj.* which cannot be detected. □ **que no se puede descubrir**
undeveloped [ʌndi'veləpt] *adj.* which has not been developed. □ **subdesarrollado**
undid [ʌn'did] *v. see* **undo.**
undies ['ʌndiz] *n. pl.* (*informal*) (women's) underwear. □ **paños menores**
undignified [ʌn'dignifaid] *adj.* not dignified: *there was an undignified rush for the bar.* □ **indecoroso**
undiluted [ʌndai'ljuːtid] *adj.* without any water added. □ **puro**
undischarged [ʌndis'tʃɑːʒd] *adj.* **1** *undischarged debt,* which has not been paid. □ **impagado**
2 *undischarged bankrupt,* person who is still legally a bankrupt. □ **insolvente**
undistinguished [ʌndis'tiŋgwiʃt] *adj.* ordinary. □ **mediocre**
undivided [ʌndi'vaidid] *adj.* complete/not split: *to give something your undivided attention.* □ **entero; todo**
undo [ʌn'duː] *v.* (*he undid; he has undone*) **1** to untie a knot; to unbutton: *he undid his tie; she undid her overcoat; to undo a parcel.* □ **deshacer; desatar (nudo/corbata); desabrochar (botón/abrigo); desenvolver (paquete)**
2 to ruin: *to undo all the good which has been done.* □ **arruinar**
undoing *n.* ruin: *drink will be his undoing.* □ **ruina**
undone *adj.* **1** unfastened: *the string came undone; your shoelace is undone.* □ **desatado**
2 not complete: *he left some of his work undone.* □ **sin hacer**
undoubted [ʌn'dautid] *adj.* certain: *his play is an undoubted success.* □ **indudable**
undoubtedly *adv.* certainly. □ **indudablemente**
undreamt of [ʌn'dremtɔv] *adj.* which no one can imagine. □ **inimaginable**
undress [ʌn'dres] *v.* to take off (usually all your) clothes: *he undressed and got into bed.* □ **desnudarse**
undressed *adj.* not wearing clothes. □ **desnudo**
undrinkable [ʌn'driŋkəbl] *adj.* (liquid) which is so unpleasant/so polluted that you cannot drink it. □ **imbebible/no potable**
undue ['ʌndjuː] *adj.* excessive/too much: *undue optimism; with undue haste,* too fast. □ **excesivo**
unduly [ʌn'djuːli] *adv.* excessively/too much: *she seems unduly nervous.* □ **excesivamente**
undulate ['ʌndjuleit] *v.* to rise and fall like waves: *undulating countryside.* □ **ondular**
undulation [ʌndju'leiʃn] *n.* rise or fall (of land, etc.). □ **ondulación**
undying [ʌn'daiiŋ] *adj.* which lasts for ever: *his undying hatred.* □ **imperecedero**
unearned ['ʌnəːnd] *adj.* ***unearned income,*** income from investments/rents, etc. □ **renta del capital**
unearth [ʌn'əːθ] *v.* to dig up; to discover. □ **desenterrar**
unearthly *adj.* **1** supernatural: *an unearthly light.* □ **sobrenatural**
2 *why did you ask me to get up at this unearthly hour?,* (*informal*) at this very early time. □ **...a esta hora tan intempestiva**
uneasy [ʌn'iːzi] *adj.* (*uneasier, uneasiest*) worried: *he is uneasy about his future.* □ **inquieto**
uneasiness *n.* worry/anxiety. □ **inquietud**
uneatable [ʌn'iːtəbl] *adj.* (food) which is so unpleasant that you cannot eat it. □ **incomible**
uneconomic(al) [ʌniːkə'nɔmik(l)] *adj.* which is not

economic/which does not make a profit. □ **antieconómico**
uneducated [ʌn'edjukeitid] *adj.* not educated; (person) who has not been well brought up; (way of speaking) which is not refined. □ **inculto**
unemployed [ʌnim'plɔid] *adj.* without any permanent work. □ **parado**
the unemployed, people with no jobs. □ **los parados**
unemployment [ʌnim'plɔimənt] *n.* lack of jobs: *a high level of unemployment.* □ **paro**
unending [ʌn'endiŋ] *adj.* ceaseless/with no end: *an unending stream of traffic.* □ **interminable**
unenlightened [ʌnin'laitənd] *adj.* lacking knowledge. □ **ignorante**
unenviable [ʌn'enviəbl] *adj.* which no one would envy. □ **poco envidiable**
unequal [ʌn'i:kwəl] *adj.* **1** not equal: *unequal distribution of wealth.* □ **desigual**
2 *he was unequal to the task,* he was not good/strong enough to perform the task. □ **no estaba a la altura de la tarea**
unequalled *adj.* which has no equal. □ **sin igual**
unequivocal [ʌni'kwivəkl] *adj.* clear; easily understood; which cannot be misunderstood: *an unequivocal order.* □ **inequívoco**
unerring [ʌn'ə:riŋ] *adj.* faultless/making no mistake: *he has an unerring knack of saying the right thing.* □ **infalible**
unethical [ʌn'eθikl] *adj.* (conduct) which does not follow the usual rules of a profession. □ **poco ético**
uneven [ʌn'i:vn] *adj.* **1** bumpy/not flat: *the uneven surface of the road.* □ **desigual**
2 odd (numbers). □ **impar**
uneventful [ʌni'ventfəl] *adj.* without any particularly exciting incidents: *an uneventful journey.* □ **sin incidentes**
unexceptionable [ʌnik'sepʃənəbl] *adj.* very satisfactory. □ **intachable**
unexceptional [ʌnik'sepʃnəl] *adj.* ordinary. □ **corriente**
unexpected [ʌnik'spektid] *adj.* which was not expected: *an unexpected letter.* □ **inesperado**
unexplored [ʌnik'splɔ:d] *adj.* which has never been explored. □ **inexplorado**
unexposed [ʌnik'spouzd] *adj.* (film) which has not been used. □ **no expuesto**
unexpurgated [ʌn'ekspə:geitid] *adj.* (book, etc.) which has not had offensive parts removed. □ **sin expurgar, íntegro**
unfailing [ʌn'feiliŋ] *adj.* which never fails: *with unfailing regularity.* □ **infalible**
unfailingly *adv.* without fail. □ **infaliblemente**
unfair [ʌn'fɛə] *adj.* not fair: *this tax system is unfair to married men.* □ **injusto**
unfair competition, commercial competition from a firm which has special advantages which you do not have. □ **competencia desleal**
unfaithful [ʌn'feiθfəl] *adj.* not faithful (to your husband or wife). □ **infiel**
unfamiliar [ʌnfə'miliə] *adj.* not familiar. □ **desconocido**
unfasten [ʌn'fɑ:sn] *v.* to undo (something which is fastened). □ **desatar**
unfavourable [ʌn'feivrəbl] *adj.* not favourable: *an unfavourable review of a play.* □ **desfavorable**
unfeeling [ʌn'fi:liŋ] *adj.* insensitive; not sympathetic to someone. □ **insensible**
unfit [ʌn'fit] *adj.* **1** (person) who is not fit/not in good physical condition. □ **no apto**
2 not suitable: *food which is unfit for human consumption.* □ **impropio**
unflinchingly [ʌn'flintʃiŋli] *adv.* bravely. □ **intrépidamente**
unfold [ʌn'fould] *v.* **1** to spread out (a newspaper). □ **desplegar**
2 *the story unfolded,* the story became clear/was told. □ **la historia se reveló**
unforeseen [ʌnfɔ:'si:n] *adj.* not foreseen/not anticipated: *a number of unforeseen problems.* □ **imprevisto**
unforgettable [ʌnfə'getəbl] *adj.* which cannot be forgotten. □ **inolvidable**
unfortunate [ʌn'fɔ:tʃənət] *adj.* **1** unlucky: *he has been unfortunate with his new car - it is always breaking down.* □ **desafortunado**
2 sad; to be regretted: *it is unfortunate that you have never met him.* □ **es una pena que...**
unfortunately *adv.* sadly: *unfortunately I cannot attend the meeting,* it is a pity, but I cannot attend. □ **desafortunadamente, por desgracia**
unfounded [ʌn'faundid] *adj.* without any basis in truth: *an unfounded accusation.* □ **infundado**
unfreeze [ʌn'fri:z] *v.* (*he unfroze; he has unfrozen*) to warm (something) so that it stops being frozen. □ **descongelar**
unfrequented [ʌnfri'kwentid] *adj.* (place) where few people go. □ **poco frecuentado**
unfriendly [ʌn'frendli] *adj.* (*unfriendlier, unfriendliest*) not like a friend: *his attitude is quite unfriendly.* □ **poco amistoso**
unfurl [ʌn'fə:l] *v.* to unroll (a flag). □ **desplegar**
unfurnished [ʌn'fə:niʃt] *adj.* (house) with no furniture in it. □ **desamueblado**
ungainly [ʌn'geinli] *adj.* (*ungainlier, ungainliest*) awkward/clumsy (way of walking). □ **desgarbado/torpe**
ungetatable [ʌnget'ætəbl] *adj.* which you cannot reach easily. □ **inaccesible**
ungodly *adj.* (*ungodlier, ungodliest*) **1** wicked unpleasant/inconvenient. □ **malvado**
2 *why did you have to call me at such an ungodly hour?,* (*informal*) at such an inconvenient time. □ **...a una hora tan intempestiva**
ungracious [ʌn'greiʃəs] *adj.* not gracious/not polite. □ **descortés**
ungrateful [ʌn'greitfəl] *adj.* not grateful. □ **desagradecido**
unguarded [ʌn'gɑ:did] *adj.* careless. □ **descuidado**
in an unguarded moment, without thinking about the consequences. □ **en un momento de descuido**
ungulate ['ʌngjuleit] *n.* animal with hooves. □ **ungulado**
unhappy [ʌn'hæpi] *adj.* (*unhappier, unhappiest*) sad: *she looks unhappy.* □ **desgraciado**
unhappily *adv.* sadly/unfortunately. □ **desgraciadamente**
unharmed [ʌn'hɑ:md] *adj.* safe. □ **ileso**
unhealthy [ʌn'helθi] *adj.* (*unhealthier, unhealthiest*) **1** not healthy: *an unhealthy climate; he has an unhealthy complexion.* □ **insalubre (clima); enfermizo (aspecto)**
2 unnatural: *he is taking an unhealthy interest in my business.* □ **ilógico**
unheard of [ʌn'hə:dɔv] *adj.* strange/odd: *it is quite unheard of for him to get up before nine o'clock.* □ **inaudito**
unhelpful [ʌn'helpfəl] *adj.* not helpful. □ **poco servicial**
unheralded [ʌn'herəldid] *adj.* not announced/publicized beforehand. □ **sin aviso**
unhinged [ʌn'hindʒd] *adj.* mad: *his mind is unhinged; she is unhinged.* □ **desquiciado**

unholy [ʌn'houli] *adj.* (*unholier, unholiest*) (*informal*) unpleasant: *they were making an unholy row.* □ **infernal**

unhook [ʌn'huk] *v.* to take (something) off a hook; to unfasten (something) which is attached with hooks. □ **desenganchar**

unhoped for [ʌn'houptfɔː] *adj.* unexpected. □ **inesperado**

unhurt [ʌn'həːt] *adj.* not hurt; safe and sound: *all the passengers escaped unhurt.* □ **ileso**

unicorn ['juːnikɔːn] *n.* mythological animal like a horse, but with a single long, straight horn. □ **unicornio**

unidentified [ʌnai'dentifaid] *adj.* which has not been identified: *the guerrillas belong to an unidentified political group.* □ **no identificado**

unidentified flying object, mysterious object in the sky which cannot be identified. □ **objeto volador no identificado**

unification [junifi'keiʃn] *n.* act of unifying; joining together into one: *the unification of a country.* □ **unificación**

uniform ['juːnifɔːm] *n.* specially designed clothing worn by all members of a group: *army uniform; school uniform; she was wearing the uniform of the Red Cross.* □ **uniforme**

■ *adj.* all the same; never changing: *the buses are all painted a uniform colour; washing machines are all made to a uniform size.* □ **uniforme**

uniformity [juni'fɔmiti] *n.* being all exactly the same: *we are trying to bring some uniformity into the various systems used in different countries.* □ **uniformidad**

unify ['juːnifai] *v.* (*unified; unifying*) to join together into one: *he has unified the country.* □ **unificar**

unilateral [juni'lætərəl] *adj.* on one side only; done by one side only: *unilateral decision.* □ **unilateral**

unilaterally *adv.* (done) by one side only: *they decided unilaterally to break the agreement.* □ **unilateralmente**

unimpaired [ʌnim'peəd] *adj.* not damaged. □ **intacto**

unimpeachable [ʌnim'piːtʃəbl] *adj.* which can be trusted completely. □ **irrecusable**

unimportant [ʌnim'pɔtənt] *adj.* not important. □ **sin importancia**

uninformed [ʌnin'fɔːmd] *adj.* without full knowledge: *uninformed opinion.* □ **mal informado; opinión desinformada**

uninhabitable [ʌnin'hæbitəbl] *adj.* which cannot be lived in: *the house is quite uninhabitable.* □ **inhabitable**

uninhabited *adj.* not lived in: *an uninhabited island.* □ **deshabitado; una isla desierta**

uninhibited [ʌnin'hibitid] *adj.* free; not bound by the customs of society. □ **desinhibido**

uninitiated [ʌni'niʃieitid] *n.* ***the uninitiated,*** people who are not experts. □ **no iniciado**

unintelligible [ʌnin'telidʒəbl] *adj.* which cannot be understood: *the radio signal was so faint that it was unintelligible.* □ **ininteligible**

uninterrupted [ʌnintə'rʌptid] *adj.* with no breaks; continuous: *an uninterrupted flow of conversation.* □ **ininterrumpido**

uninvited [ʌnin'vaitid] *adj.* without an invitation: *they came to the party uninvited; an uninvited guest.* □ **sin invitación**

uninviting *adj.* not very attractive. □ **poco atractivo**

union ['juːniən] *n.* **1** being joined together; countries or states which are joined together: *the Soviet Union.* □ **unión; la Unión Soviética**

2 (*formal*) marriage: *their union was blessed with three children.* □ **unión**

3 group of people working in the same type of industry joined together for mutual protection: *a trade union; the shipworkers' union; to join a union.* □ **sindicato**

unionist *n.* member of a trade union. □ **sindicalista**

unionize *v.* to form a trade union: *the factory is completely unionized,* all the workers are represented by trade unions. □ **sindicar**

Union Jack *n.* national flag of the United Kingdom. □ **bandera británica**

unique [ju'niːk] *adj.* so special that there is nothing similar to it: *a unique collection of coins; his unique gift for getting on with people.* □ **único**

uniquely *adv.* in a special or unique way. □ **singularmente**

unisex ['juːniseks] *adj.* which can be used by both men and women: *unisex clothes; unisex hairdresser's.* □ **unisex**

unison ['juːnisn] *n.* **1** *they sang in unison,* they sang the same note all together; *to shout in unison.* □ **unisonancia; cantaron al unísono; gritar a la vez**

2 ***in unison,*** in total agreement. □ **al unísono**

unit ['juːnit] *n.* **1** one part (of a larger whole). □ **unidad**

kitchen unit, one cupboard/one set of shelves, etc., which can be matched with others to form a whole kitchen. □ **elemento de cocina**

wall unit, one which is attached to a wall. □ **elemento de pared**

2 one part (of an army): *a tank unit; an army unit; units of enemy paratroopers.* □ **unidad**

3 standard measurement by which something is counted: *the decibel is a unit of measurement of sound; electricity consumption is calculated in units.* □ **unidad**

4 one single part of a group investment. □ **unidad**

unit trust, company which invests its members' money in a varied range of investments, each member buying one or more units. □ **empresa de inversión mobiliaria**

5 number one: *the number fifteen contains one ten and five units.* □ **unidad**

unitary *adj.* referring to a unit. □ **unitario**

unite [juː'nait] *v.* to join together as a whole: *his action has united all his family against him; the two groups have united to present a joint proposal.* □ **unir**

the United Kingdom, England, Wales, Scotland and Northern Ireland. □ **el Reino Unido**

the United States (of America), a federal union of states, especially that of (north) America. □ **los Estados Unidos**

the United Nations, an international organization of states that was formed to promote international cooperation and security. □ **las Naciones Unidas**

unity ['juːniti] *n.* state of being one whole: *the desire for unity of the Christian church.* □ **unidad**

univalve ['juːnivælv] *n.* animal (such a smail) with a single shell. □ **univalvo**

universe ['juːnivəːs] *n.* all that exists, including the earth, the planets and the stars. □ **universo**

universal [juni'vəːsəl] *adj.* which is everywhere; which affects everyone: *he is a universal favourite; there was universal disappointment when the champion failed to beat his opponent.* □ **universal; general**

universal joint, mechanical joint made so that each of two connected rods can move in any direction. □ **junta universal**

universally *adv.* everywhere; by everyone: *it is uni-*

versally accepted that smoking is a cause of cancer. □ **universalmente; generalmente**

university [juni'vəːsiti] *n.* (*pl. universities*) place of high learning, where degrees are given to successful students, and a wide range of specialized subjects are taught: *he went to university in France.* □ **universidad**

a university town, town with a university built near or in it. □ **ciudad universitaria**

unjust [ʌn'dʒʌst] *adj.* not fair. □ **injusto**

unjustified [ʌn'dʒʌstifaid] *adj.* which is not justified. □ **injustificado**

unkempt [ʌn'kemt] *adj.* dishevelled/untidy. □ **desaliñado**

unkind [ʌn'kaind] *adj.* harsh/cruel: *you mustn't be unkind to animals.* □ **severo; no debes ser cruel con los animales**

unkindly *adv.* in a cruel way. □ **cruelmente**

unknown ['ʌnnoun] *adj.* not known: *an unknown painter; unknown to the police, he was planning to escape.* □ **desconocido**

unladen ['ʌnleidn] *adj.* without a load. □ **vacío**

unladylike [ʌn'leidilaik] *adj.* (behaviour) which is not like that of a lady. □ **impropio de una señora**

unlawful [ʌn'lɔːfəl] *adj.* against the law. □ **ilegal**

unleash [ʌn'liːʃ] *v.* to unfasten the leash (of a dog); to set free/to set loose: *his action unleashed the fury of the crowd.* □ **soltar (perro); dejar en libertad; su acción desató la furia de la multitud**

unleavened [ʌn'levənd] *adj.* (bread) made without yeast. □ **ácimo**

unless [ʌn'les] *conj.* **1** if ... not: *unless you start at once, you'll be late,* if you do not start at once. □ **a menos que**

2 except if: *the fête will be held in the garden unless it rains,* except if it rains. □ **a no ser que**

unlike ['ʌnlaik] *adj.* and *prep.* **1** not similar (to); different (from): *they are totally unlike in their habits; he is quite unlike his father.* □ **distinto**

2 *it is unlike him to be rude,* he is not usually rude. □ **no es habitual en él ser grosero**

unlikely [ʌn'laikli] *adj.* **1** improbable: *he is unlikely to come; it is unlikely that he will come, as he is in bed with influenza.* □ **improbable**

2 *an unlikely story,* story which is probably not true. □ **una historia inverosímil**

unlimited [ʌn'limitid] *adj.* with no limits: *he seems to have an unlimited supply of money.* □ **ilimitado**

unload [ʌn'loud] *v.* to remove a load from a vehicle: *to unload a lorry/a ship/an aircraft; they unloaded the crates from the lorry.* □ **descargar**

unloaded *adj.* with no bullets in it: *he threatened the bank staff with an unloaded gun.* □ **descargado**

unlock [ʌn'lɔk] *v.* to open (something) which was locked: *he unlocked the door.* □ **abrir (con llave)**

unlooked for [ʌn'lukdfɔː] *adj.* not expected. □ **imprevisto**

unlucky [ʌn'lʌki] *adj.* **1** (*unluckier, unluckiest*) not lucky: *he is unlucky.* □ **desafortunado**

2 *it is unlucky to walk under a ladder,* it brings bad luck. □ **trae mala suerte pasar por debajo una escalera**

unluckily *adv.* unfortunately: *unluckily for him a policeman happened to be passing by.* □ **desafortunadamente**

unmanageable [ʌn'mænidʒəbl] *adj.* (person/animal) who is difficult to control. □ **poco dócil**

unmanned ['ʌnmænd] *adj.* without a crew/without any staff: *an unmanned spacecraft.* □ **sin tripulación/personal**

unmarried ['ʌnmærid] *adj.* not married. □ **soltero**

unmarried mother, woman who has a child but is not married. □ **madre soltera**

unmask [ʌn'mɑːsk] *v.* to remove a mask; to show (someone) as they really are: *the trickster was unmasked by the police.* □ **desenmascarar**

unmentionable [ʌn'menʃnəbl] *adj.* which you must not talk about because it is so indecent/unpleasant, etc. □ **que no se debe mencionar**

unmistakeable [ʌnmis'teikəbl] *adj.* which is easily recognized/which cannot be mistaken: *she was showing unmistakeable signs of becoming mad.* □ **inconfundible**

unmitigated [ʌn'mitigeitid] *adj.* total/complete: *an unmitigated disaster.* □ **absoluto**

unmoved [ʌn'muːvd] *adj.* not touched/not affected: *the magistrate was unmoved by her plea.* □ **impasible**

unmusical [ʌn'mjuːzikl] *adj.* not interested in music; not able to play a musical instrument. □ **poco aficionado a la música; sin oído para la música**

unnatural [ʌn'nætʃərəl] *adj.* which is not natural; which does not follow the usual pattern. □ **no natural**

unnecessary [ʌn'nesəsəri] *adj.* which is not necessary: *to avoid unnecessary delays.* □ **innecesario**

unnecessarily *adv.* uselessly; for no good reason: *I would not want to disturb you unnecessarily.* □ **sin necesidad**

unnerve [ʌn'nəːv] *v.* to make (someone) lose his nerve/his courage: *the champion was unnerved by the insults of his opponent.* □ **acobardar**

unnoticed [ʌn'noutisd] *adj.* not noticed: *it passed unnoticed,* it happened without anyone noticing it. □ **inadvertido; pasar desapercibido**

unnumbered [ʌn'nʌmbəd] *adj.* with no numbers; which cannot be counted. □ **sin numerar; innumerable**

unobservant [ʌnəb'zəːvənt] *adj.* not observant; (person) who does not notice things. □ **poco observador; distraído**

unobstructed [ʌnəb'strʌktid] *adj.* with nothing in the way: *an unobstructed view of the stage.* □ **despejado**

unobtainable [ʌnəb'teinəbl] *adj.* which cannot be obtained. □ **agotado**

unobtrusive [ʌnəb'truːsiv] *adj.* not obvious; not easily noticed. □ **discreto**

unoccupied [ʌn'ɔkjupaid] *adj.* not occupied; empty: *she left her seat unoccupied for two minutes.* □ **desocupado**

unofficial [ʌnə'fiʃl] *adj.* not official. □ **extraoficial**

unofficial strike, strike which has not been officially approved by a union. □ **huelga no autorizada**

unopposed [ʌnə'pouzd] *adj.* **1** with no opposition. □ **sin oposición**

2 *the candidate was returned unopposed,* was elected because he was the only candidate. □ **el candidato fue elegido sin oposición**

unorthodox [ʌn'ɔːθədɔks] *adj.* not usual: *he has an unorthodox way of playing billiards,* an unusual way. □ **poco ortodoxo**

unpack [ʌn'pæk] *v.* to take (things) out of containers in which they were transported: *they unpacked the china and found most of it was broken; I must go to my room and unpack (my suitcase).* □ **desempaquetar; deshacer (maleta)**

unpaid ['ʌnpeid] *adj.* not paid: *he is an unpaid gardener at the old people's home.* □ **no retribuido**

unpalatable [ʌn'pælətəbl] *adj.* not pleasant to the taste; unpleasant (fact). □ **desagradable**

unparalleled [ʌn'pærəleld] *adj.* with no parallel or no equal: *an unparalleled explosion.* □ **sin par**

unpardonable [ʌn'pɑːdnəbl] *adj.* which cannot be excused: *unpardonable rudeness.* □ **imperdonable**
unpatriotic [ʌnpætri'ɔtik] *adj.* not patriotic. □ **no patriótico**
unperson ['ʌnpəːsən] *n.* person who is treated as if he did not exist (because of opposition to the government). □ **persona a la que se le hace el vacío**
unpick [ʌn'pik] *v.* to remove (stitches): *to unpick a seam.* □ **descoser**
unplaced [ʌn'pleist] *adj.* (horse) which is not one of the first three in a race. □ **no colocado**
unpleasant [ʌn'plezənt] *adj.* **1** not pleasing: *an unpleasant smell.* □ **desagradable**
2 *an unpleasant old man,* nasty old man. □ **un viejo asqueroso**
unpleasantness *n.* argument/disagreement: *'come along quietly', said the policeman, 'we don't want any unpleasantness'.* □ **disgusto**
unpopular [ʌn'pɔpjulə] *adj.* not popular: *the government is more unpopular than it was.* □ **impopular**
unpopularity [ʌnpɔpju'læriti] *n.* being unpopular. □ **impopularidad**
unprecedented [ʌn'presidentid] *adj.* which has never happened before: *there was an unprecedented demand for tickets to the concert.* □ **sin precedentes**
unprejudiced [ʌn'predʒudist] *adj.* fair; not prejudiced. □ **imparcial**
unpremeditated [ʌnpri'mediteitid] *adj.* which has not been planned: *an unpremeditated attack.* □ **impremeditado**
unprepared [ʌnpri'pɛəd] *adj.* not ready: *the attack caught the enemy unprepared.* □ **desprevenido**
unprepossessing [ʌnpripə'zesiŋ] *adj.* not very attractive. □ **poco atractivo**
unpretentious [ʌnpri'tenʃəs] *adj.* modest/not showing off. □ **nada pretencioso**
unprincipled [ʌn'prinsipld] *adj.* without any moral standards. □ **sin principios**
unprintable [ʌn'printəbl] *adj.* (words) so rude that you could not print them: *when the policeman stopped him for speeding he said something unprintable.* □ **intranscribible**
unproductive [ʌnprə'dʌktiv] *adj.* (discussion) which does not produce any result; (land) which does not produce any crops. □ **infructuoso (discusión); improductivo (tierra)**
unprofessional [ʌnprə'feʃnəl] *adj.* (conduct) which is not of the sort you would expect from a member of the profession: *the solicitor was charged with unprofessional conduct.* □ **contrario a la ética profesional**
unprofitable [ʌn'prɔfitəbl] *adj.* which does not make a profit; which is useless: *an unprofitable discussion.* □ **de poco provecho**
unpronounceable [ʌnprə'naunsəbl] *adj.* (name) which is difficult to say. □ **impronunciable**
unprotected [ʌnprə'tektid] *adj.* with no protection. □ **desprotegido**
unprovoked [ʌnprə'voukt] *adj.* (action) which was not provoked: *an unprovoked attack.* □ **sin provocación**
unqualified [ʌn'kwɔlifaid] *adj.* **1** (person) who has not passed the examinations to qualify for a profession: *an unqualified doctor.* □ **sin título**
2 total/complete: *it was an unqualified success.* □ **fue un éxito total**
unquestionable [ʌn'kweʃtʃənəbl] *adj.* which is certain/not doubtful. □ **indiscutible**
unquestionably *adv.* certainly. □ **indiscutiblemente**
unquestioning *adj.* without doubting: *unquestioning obedience.* □ **incondicional**
unquote ['ʌnkwout] *v.* to indicate the end of a quotation (when speaking): *the President is reported to have said: quote 'I cannot stand this fool of a Prime Minister' unquote.* □ **fin de la cita**
unravel [ʌn'rævl] *v.* (*he unravelled*) to disentangle (something which is knotted); to solve (a mystery). □ **desenmarañar**
unreal [ʌn'riəl] *adj.* not real; imaginary. □ **irreal**
unreasonable [ʌn'riːznəbl] *adj.* not reasonable/too large: *he made some unreasonable demands; the price is quite unreasonable.* □ **poco razonable**
unrecognizable [ʌnrekəg'naizəbl] *adj.* which cannot be recognized. □ **irreconocible**
unrecorded [ʌnri'kɔːdid] *adj.* not recorded. □ **sin grabar; no registrado**
unrefined [ʌnri'faind] *adj.* (sugar/oil) which has not been refined. □ **sin refinar**
unrelated [ʌnri'leitid] *adj.* not related/with no connection: *he spoke on several unrelated subjects.* □ **inconexo**
unreliable [ʌnri'laiəbl] *adj.* which cannot be relied on: *the bus service is quite unreliable.* □ **poco fiable**
unrelieved [ʌnri'liːvd] *adj.* not lessened: *a story of unrelieved gloom.* □ **absoluto**
unremitting [ʌnri'mitiŋ] *adj.* never ceasing: *unremitting hard work.* □ **incesante**
unrequited [ʌnri'kwaitid] *adj.* (love) which is not returned. □ **no correspondido**
unreserved [ʌnri'zəːvd] *adj.* not reserved: *unreserved seats.* □ **sin reservar**
unreservedly [ʌnri'zəːvidli] *adv.* definitely: *I can recommend this hotel unreservedly.* □ **sin reservas**
unrest [ʌn'rest] *n.* **1** being restless/dissatisfied. □ **malestar**
2 *political unrest/industrial unrest,* agitation to get political/industrial change. □ **agitación**
unrivalled [ʌn'raivəld] *adj.* with no equal: *he has an unrivalled knowledge of local history.* □ **sin par**
unroll [ʌn'roul] *v.* to undo (something which is rolled up): *he unrolled a large map.* □ **desenrollar**
unruffled [ʌn'rʌfld] *adj.* calm/not anxious. □ **tranquilo**
unruly [ʌn'ruːli] *adj.* (*unrulier, unruliest*) wild/with no discipline: *a group of unruly youths attacked a bus conductor.* □ **salvaje/indisciplinado**
unsafe [ʌn'seif] *adj.* (*unsafer, unsafest*) dangerous. □ **peligroso**
unsaid [ʌn'sed] *adj. better leave it unsaid,* better not to say it. □ **sin decir; será mejor no decirlo**
unsalted ['ʌnsɔltid] *adj.* (butter, etc.) with no salt. □ **sin sal**
unsatisfactory [ʌnsætis'fæktri] *adj.* not satisfactory. □ **insatisfactorio**
unsatisfied [ʌn'sætisfaid] *adj.* not satisfied: *several unsatisfied customers brought their television sets back to the shop.* □ **insatisfecho**
unsavoury [ʌn'seivəri] *Amer.* **unsavory** *adj.* unpleasant/disgusting: *an unsavoury reputation.* □ **repugnante**
unscathed [ʌn'skeiðd] *adj.* not harmed. □ **ileso**
unscientific [ʌnsaiən'tifik] *adj.* not scientific. □ **poco científico**
unscramble [ʌn'skræmbl] *v.* to put back in order: *try to unscramble this mess.* □ **desembrollar**
unscrew [ʌn'skruː] *v.* to open by twisting a screw or a screw lid anticlockwise: *he unscrewed the shelf from the wall,* he removed the shelf by taking out the screws. □ **desatornillar**
unscripted [ʌn'skriptid] *adj.* (broadcast) made without a script. □ **sin guión**

unscrupulous [ʌn'skru:pjuləs] *adj.* not worrying too much about honesty. □ **sin escrúpulos**
unsealed [ʌn'si:ld] *adj.* (envelope, etc.) which has not been sealed. □ **sin sellar**
unseat [ʌn'si:t] *v.* to make (someone) fall off a horse; to remove (a Member of Parliament) at an election: *he was unseated in the last General Election.* □ **derribar; perdió su escaño...**
unseen ['ʌnsi:n] *adj.* and *n.* **1** not seen/invisible; (piece of writing) which you have not seen before, and which you have to translate in an examination. □ **invisible; inédito**
2 *to buy something* ***sight unseen,*** without having been able to examine it first. □ **comprar algo a primera vista**
unselfish [ʌn'selfiʃ] *adj.* not selfish/thinking of others before yourself. □ **desinteresado/altruista**
unsettle [ʌn'setl] *v.* to upset: *she was unsettled by the constant changes in the office.* □ **perturbar; estaba molesta por...**
unsettled *adj.* (weather) which changes often. □ **variable**
unsightly [ʌn'saitli] *adj.* ugly: *unsightly heaps of rotting food.* □ **desagradable a la vista**
unsigned [ʌn'saind] *adj.* not signed. □ **sin firmar**
unskilled ['ʌnskild] *adj.* (worker) who has no particular skill. □ **no especializado**
unsociable [ʌn'souʃəbl] *adj.* not friendly; not wishing to make friends. □ **insociable**
unsocial [ʌn'souʃəl] *adj. to work unsocial hours,* hours of work which mean that you are rarely free at the same time as others. □ **trabajar fuera de las horas normales**
unsolicited [ʌnsə'lisitid] *adj.* which has not been asked for. □ **no solicitado**
unsolved ['ʌnsɔlvd] *adj.* (problem) which has not been solved. □ **sin resolver**
unsophisticated [ʌnsə'fistikeitid] *adj.* simple; not sophisticated: *he is an unsophisticated sort of man; a relatively unsophisticated type of aircraft.* □ **sencillo**
unsound ['ʌnsaund] *adj.* **1** ***of unsound mind,*** mad. □ **tarado; sonado**
2 *his reasoning is unsound,* is not based on fact or logic. □ **su razonamiento es poco sólido**
unsparing [ʌn'spɛəriŋ] *adj.* generous; not reluctant: *she was unsparing in her efforts to help.* □ **pródigo**
unspeakable [ʌn'spi:kəbl] *adj.* extremely unpleasant. □ **incalificable**
unspoilt ['ʌnspɔilt] *adj.* (countryside) which has not been spoilt. □ **virgen**
unstable [ʌn'steibl] *adj.* **1** not stable; changeable: *an unstable government,* which is likely to fall at any moment. □ **inestable**
2 *he is quite unstable,* dangerously mad. □ **está bastante desequilibrado**
unsteady [ʌn'stedi] *adj.* (*unsteadier, unsteadiest*) not steady; wobbly. □ **poco firme**
unstick [ʌn'stik] *v.* (*he unstuck*) **1** to remove something which is stuck on: *to unstick the stamps from envelopes.* □ **despegar**
2 *their plans came badly unstuck,* went badly wrong. □ **sus planes se vinieron abajo**
unstoppable [ʌn'stɔpəbl] *adj.* which cannot be stopped. □ **imparable**
unstuck [ʌn'stʌk] *adj.* not stuck together. □ **despegado**
to come unstuck: *the plan came unstuck,* (*informal*) it failed. □ **el plan se fue al garete**
unsuccessful [ʌnsək'sesfəl] *adj.* not successful: *an unsuccessful attempt to climb Mount Everest.* □ **sin éxito; un fallido intento de...**
unsuitable [ʌn'su:təbl] *adj.* not suitable. □ **inadecuado**
unsure [ʌn'ʃuə] *adj.* **1** not sure. □ **inseguro**
2 *he is very unsure of himself,* he lacks self-confidence. □ **inseguro**
unsuspected [ʌnsəs'pektid] *adj.* which is not suspected to exist: *an unsuspected danger.* □ **insospechado**
unsuspecting *adj.* (person) who does not realize something/that a danger is imminent. □ **confiado**
unswerving [ʌn'swə:viŋ] *adj.* (loyalty) which does not change. □ **inquebrantable**
unsympathetic [ʌnsimpə'θetik] *adj.* not sympathetic: *he is not unsympathetic to the request,* he sympathizes with the request. □ **no favorable**
untapped [ʌn'tæpt] *adj.* not previously used: *an untapped source of money/of oil.* □ **sin explotar**
untenable [ʌn'tenəbl] *adj.* (position/theory) which cannot be defended. □ **insostenible**
unthinkable [ʌn'θiŋkəbl] *adj.* which cannot be considered or thought of: *it is unthinkable that there should not be a children's pantomime at Christmas.* □ **inconcebible**
unthinking [ʌn'θiŋkiŋ] *adj.* done without thinking. □ **irreflexivo**
untidy [ʌn'taidi] *adj.* (*untidier, untidiest*) not tidy/in disorder: *untidy rooms.* □ **desordenado**
untidiness *n.* being untidy. □ **desorden**
untie [ʌn'tai] *v.* (*untied; untying*) to unfasten (something which is tied with a knot): *he was untying a parcel; my shoelace has come untied,* has become unfastened. □ **desatar**
until [ʌn'til] *prep.* and *conj.* **1** up to (a certain time): *he worked here until last month; she cannot come until after dinner; wait until we are all ready; he won't come until you apologize.* □ **hasta; hasta que**
2 up to (a certain place): *don't get off the bus until the post office.* □ **hasta**
untimely [ʌn'taimli] *adj.* **1** which happened too soon: *his untimely death.* □ **prematuro**
2 which is not suitable: *she made some untimely comments about his lateness.* □ **inoportuno**
unto ['ʌntu] *prep.* (*formal*) *see* **to.**
untold [ʌn'tould] *adj.* very large; so large that it cannot be counted: *untold riches; the storm did untold damage.* □ **incalculable**
untouchable [ʌn'tʌtʃəbl] *adj.* which cannot be touched. □ **intocable**
■ *n.* person from the lowest caste in India. □ **intocable**
untoward [ʌntə'wɔ:d] *adj.* unlucky/inconvenient: *nothing untoward took place,* everything went off well. □ **inconveniente**
untried [ʌn'traid] *adj.* which has not been tested. □ **no probado**
untrue [ʌn'tru:] *adj.* wrong/not true: *it is untrue to say that he is rich.* □ **falso**
untrustworthy [ʌn'trʌstwə:ði] *adj.* (person) who cannot be trusted. □ **poco fiable**
untruthful [ʌn'tru:θfəl] *adj.* (person) who does not tell the truth; (statement) which is wrong. □ **mentiroso; falso**
unusable [ʌn'ju:zəbl] *adj.* which cannot be used. □ **inutilizable**
unused [ʌn'ju:zd] *adj.* **1** new/clean; which has not been used. □ **sin usar**
2 not accustomed: *he is unused to speaking in public.* □ **no acostumbrado**
unusual [ʌn'ju:ʒuəl] *adj.* strange/extraordinary: *an*

unusual number of tourists; there is nothing unusual about that. □ **inusual**

unusually *adv.* strangely/extraordinarily: *it was unusually cold for June.* □ **inusualmente**

unvarnished [ʌn'vɑːniʃt] *adj.* **1** with no varnish. □ **sin barnizar**

2 ***the unvarnished truth,*** the plain/simple truth. □ **la pura verdad**

unveil [ʌn'veil] *v.* to uncover (a new statue/a new plan, etc.): *the mayor unveiled a plaque to mark the author's birthplace; the minister unveiled a plan to encourage the construction of new factories.* □ **descubrir (estatua); revelar (plan)**

unversed in [ʌn'vəːst in] *adj.* with no experience in. □ **poco ducho en**

unwanted *adj.* which is not wanted. □ **no deseado**

unwarranted [ʌn'wɔrəntid] *adj.* which is not justified. □ **injustificado**

unwary [ʌn'wɛəri] *adj.* (person) who does not take care. □ **despreocupado**

unwell [ʌn'wel] *adj.* sick/ill. □ **malo**

unwholesome [ʌn'houlsəm] *adj.* not healthy/which might harm. □ **nocivo**

unwieldy [ʌn'wiːldi] *adj.* large and awkward: *an unwieldy parcel.* □ **poco manejable**

unwilling [ʌn'wiliŋ] *adj.* reluctant; not willing. □ **(estar) poco dispuesto**

unwind [ʌn'waind] *v.* (*he unwound*) **1** to undo (something which has been wound): *to unwind a ball of string.* □ **desenrollar**

2 (*informal*) to relax: *to unwind after a hard day at the office.* □ **relajarse**

unwise [ʌn'waiz] *adj.* rash/imprudent; not wise. □ **imprudente**

unwittingly [ʌn'witiŋli] *adv.* without intending to; not intentionally: *he unwittingly told her the secret.* □ **sin querer**

unwonted *adj.* not usual: *she greeted him with unwonted warmth.* □ **insólito**

unworkable [ʌn'wəːkəbl] *adj.* (plan) which will not work in practice. □ **inviable**

unworthy [ʌn'wəːði] *adj.* (*unworthier, unworthiest*) **1** which does not deserve (something): *the plan is unworthy of serious consideration.* □ **...no merece una consideración...**

2 *this work is unworthy of you,* it is not as good as we might expect from you. □ **...indigno de ti**

unwound [ʌn'waund] *v. see* **unwind.**

unwrap [ʌn'ræp] *v.* (*he unwrapped*) to take the wrapping off: *she was unwrapping a parcel.* □ **desenvolver**

unwritten [ʌn'ritən] *adj. unwritten law,* custom which has grown up over a period of time but which is not written down. □ **no escrito**

unzip [ʌn'zip] *v.* (*he unzipped*) to undo a zip fastener: *he unzipped his jacket.* □ **bajar la cremallera**

up [ʌp] *adv.* **1** towards a higher place: *to go up; to climb right up to the top; the water came halfway up.* □ **hacia/para arriba**

hands up!, lift your hands into the air to show you surrender. □ **¡manos arriba!**

2 in a higher place: *what is the cat doing up there?* □ **¿...ahí arriba?**

this side up, this side must be on top. □ **arriba**

3 to an important town; towards the north: *they have come up to town from the country; they went up to Scotland for a holiday.* □ **bajar/subir a**

4 to a higher level: *the temperature has gone up; prices have shot up.* □ **dispararse**

5 to the end; completely: *eat up your dinner; to screw up the top of the jar; they tied him up with string.* □ **acábate la cena; del todo; bien**

6 not in bed: *he got up at ten o'clock; she stayed up all night.* □ **levantado**

7 close to: *he parked his car right up against mine; he came up to me in the street.* □ **aparcó su coche muy cerca del mío; se me acercó...**

■ *prep.* **1** towards a higher part of (something): *she was climbing up a ladder; he went up the stairs on his hands and knees.* □ **arriba**

2 along: *go up the street for 100 yards and then turn left.* □ **sigue por...**

3 *to sail up the river,* towards the source of the river. □ **navegar río arriba**

4 *he walked **up and down** the platform,* backwards and forwards. □ **...de un lado a otro del andén**

■ *adj.* **1** which is going up: *he tried to go down the up escalator.* □ **ascendente; ...por la escalera mecánica de subida**

2 which is in a higher position: *the sun is up; wait until the moon is up; this year's sales are up.* □ **alto**

3 *when the new building is up,* has been completely built. □ **cuando el edificio esté acabado**

4 *the roads are all up,* all being dug up for repairs. □ **las carreteras están en obras**

5 not in bed: *is he up yet? why is your little girl still up at eleven o'clock?* □ **levantado**

6 finished: *your time is up,* you have to stop now; *his leave is up,* he has to go back to the army. □ **terminado**

7 ***what's up** with you?,* what is the matter with you? □ **¿qué te pasa?**

■ *n. the **ups and downs** of business,* the good and bad periods. □ **altibajos**

■ *v.* (*he upped*) **1** to raise: *they upped all their prices by 10%.* □ **subir**

2 (*informal*) to get up suddenly: *he upped and left her.* □ **levantarse**

up-and-coming [ʌpən'kʌmiŋ] *adj.* (person) who looks as though he might succeed: *an up-and-coming young lawyer.* □ **un joven y prometedor abogado**

up-and-up ['ʌpənʌp] *n.* ***to be on the up-and-up,*** to be doing well. □ **ir cada vez mejor**

up for *prep.* **1** ready for: *he is up for trial on Tuesday,* he will be tried. □ **listo para**

2 *her house is **up for sale,*** is on sale. □ **su casa está en venta**

up to *prep.* **1** as many as: *the car will hold up to six passengers.* □ **hasta**

2 capable enough to do something: *she is not really up to her job; it is an interesting assignment but is he up to it?* □ **apto**

3 (showing responsibility): *it's up to you to try to get your money back.* □ **depende de ti**

4 doing: *what is he up to now?* □ **¿qué hace ahora?**

up to date *adj.* and *adv.* modern/using the most recent information, etc.: *have you an up to date railway timetable? you must keep your information up to date.* □ **al día**

upbraid [ʌp'breid] *v.* (*formal*) to scold. □ **reprender**

upbringing ['ʌpbriŋiŋ] *n.* education; training of a child. □ **educación**

update [ʌp'deit] *v.* to revise (something) so that it is more up to date. □ **poner al día**

upend [ʌp'end] *v.* to stand (something) on its end. □ **volver de arriba abajo**

upgrade [ʌp'greid] *v.* to put (someone) into a more important job; to improve the quality of (something). □ **ascender; mejorar**

upheaval [ʌp'hiːvəl] *n.* great change/disturbance: *there has been a great upheaval in that firm.* □ **convulsión**

uphill ['ʌphil] *adj.* going upwards; difficult: *it was an*

uphill task to teach him maths. □ **ascendente; fue una tarea ardua...**
■ *adv.* upwards: *drive uphill for six miles.* □ **cuesta arriba**
uphold [ʌp'hould] *v.* (*he upheld*) to support; to say that a decision is right: *the verdict was upheld in the court of appeal.* □ **apoyar; confirmar**
upholster [ʌp'houlstə] *v.* to cover (chairs etc.) with padded seats and covers. □ **tapizar**
upholsterer *n.* person who covers or fits padded seats on furniture. □ **tapicero**
upholstery *n.* **1** covering chairs, etc., with padded seats and covers. □ **tapicería**
2 covers for chairs; padded seats and cushions. □ **relleno**
upkeep ['ʌpki:p] *n.* (cost of) keeping a house/a car, etc., in good order. □ **(gastos de) mantenimiento**
upland ['ʌplənd] *n.* mountainous area (of a country). □ **meseta**
uplift ['ʌplift] *n.* **1** something which gives a feeling of happiness or goodness: *moral uplift.* □ **edificación**
2 raising: *an uplift in the exchange rate.* □ **subida**
■ *v.* to lift up/to raise. □ **levantar**
upon [ʌ'pɔn] *prep.* (*formal*) **1** on. □ **en; sobre**
2 *they fought battle upon battle,* one battle after another. □ **lucharon batalla tras batalla**
3 at the time: *upon the third stroke of midnight.* □ **sobre**
upper ['ʌpə] *adj.* **1** higher: *the upper storeys of the building caught fire; he broke his upper jaw.* □ **superior**
2 further up: *the upper reaches of a river.* □ **alto**
3 more important; of higher rank. □ **superior**
the upper classes, the nobility. □ **la clase alta**
the upper forms, (*in a school*) forms with older pupils. □ **clases superiores**
4 ***to get/have the upper hand,*** to have or to win an advantage over. □ **llevar ventaja**
■ *n.* top part of a shoe: *the upper has come away from the sole.* □ **pala**
uppermost *adj.* **1** highest: *his office is on the uppermost floor of the building.* □ **más alto**
2 furthest up: *the uppermost reaches of a river.* □ **más alto**
3 most important. □ **primordial**
■ *adv. what is uppermost in their minds is money,* the subject they think about most. □ **lo que más les importa es el dinero**
uppity *adj.* (*informal*) feeling superior to other people: *she's getting uppity.* □ **engreído**
upright ['ʌprait] *adj.* **1** vertical: *upright freezer; hold the stick upright; he kept himself upright by holding on to the wall.* □ **vertical**
2 very honest: *upright character.* □ **honrado**
■ *n.* **1** vertical post: *the ball bounced off one of the uprights of the goal.* □ **poste**
2 piano with the strings and body vertical. □ **vertical**
uprising ['ʌpraiziŋ] *n.* revolt (against authority). □ **sublevación**
uproar ['ʌprɔ:] *n.* loud noise/disturbance: *the meeting ended in uproar.* □ **alboroto**
uproarious [ʌp'rɔ:riəs] *adj.* noisy: *uproarious laughter.* □ **escandaloso**
uproot [ʌp'ru:t] *v.* **1** to dig up (a plant) with its roots: *the wind uprooted two large trees.* □ **arrancar**
2 to make (a family) move to a totally new area. □ **desplazar, obligar a emigrar**
upset ['ʌpset] *n.* **1** complete change for the worse: *this has caused an upset in the government's plans.* □ **revés**
2 great worry/cause of unhappiness. □ **malestar**
3 slight illness: *he is off work with a stomach upset.* □ **indisposición**
■ *v.* (*he upset*) **1** to knock over; to fall over: *he upset a pile of plates; the boat upset and they all fell into the water.* □ **volcar**
2 to change completely (for the worse): *the weather has upset all our holiday plans.* □ **desbaratar**
3 to make (someone) worried/unhappy: *she is easily upset.* □ **preocuparse**
4 to make slightly ill: *the food seems to have upset my stomach.* □ **indisponer**
■ *adj.* **1** very worried/unhappy/anxious: *he gets upset at the slightest criticism; she was very upset when her daughter stayed out all night.* □ **preocupado**
2 made ill: *an upset stomach.* □ **indispuesto**
upshot ['ʌpʃɔt] *n.* result: *the upshot was that we decided to stay at home.* □ **resultado**
upside down ['ʌpsaid'daun] *adv.* **1** with the top turned to the bottom: *hold the bottle upside down.* □ **al revés**
2 *the burglars turned the bedroom upside down,* made a mess of it. □ **los ladrones dejaron el dormitorio patas arriba**
upstage [ʌp'steidʒ] *adv.* at the back of the stage. □ **en el fondo del escenario**
■ *v.* **1** to move nearer the front of the stage than (someone). □ **atraer la atención del público**
2 to take attention away from (someone who feels he ought to have it). □ **eclipsar a alguien**
upstairs [ʌp'stεəz] *adv.* towards the upper part of a house: *he went upstairs.* □ **arriba**
■ *adj.* on the upper floors of a house: *an upstairs bedroom.* □ **de arriba**
■ *n.* the upper floors of a house: *the ground floor is large, but the upstairs is tiny.* □ **piso superior**
upstanding [ʌp'stændiŋ] *adj.* strong; honest: *a fine upstanding young man.* □ **robusto/honrado; un buen mozo**
upstart ['ʌpstɑ:t] *n.* person who claims to be more important or capable than he really is. □ **presuntuoso**
upstream ['pstri:m] *adv.* and *adj.* (moving) towards the source of a river, against the flow of the current. □ **aguas arriba**
uptake ['ʌpteik] *n.* ***to be slow/quick on the uptake,*** slow/quick to understand. □ **ser duro de mollera/ ser rápido de comprensión**
uptight ['ʌptait] *adj.* (*informal*) nervous and annoyed. □ **tenso**
upturn ['ʌptə:n] *n.* movement upwards (in sales, etc.). □ **mejora; alza**
upward ['ʌpwəd] *adj.* moving towards a higher level: *the upward movement of prices.* □ **alcista**
upwards *adv.* **1** towards a higher level: *the kite flew upwards.* □ **hacia arriba**
2 on the top: *put the picture down face upwards.* □ **pon la fotografía boca arriba**
3 more: *upwards of fifty students were arrested; we accept children of ten years old and upwards.* □ **más de cincuenta...; ...de diez años para arriba**
uranium [ju'reiniəm] *n.* (*chemical element*: U) radioactive metal used in producing atomic energy. □ **uranio**
urban ['ə:bən] *adj.* **1** referring to towns: *urban problems; urban development.* □ **urbano**
2 living in towns: *urban guerillas.* □ **guerrilla urbana**
urbanization *n.* act of urbanizing. □ **urbanización**
urbanize *v.* to make (an area) into a town; to make (something/someone from the country) become accustomed to the town. □ **urbanizar**

urbane [ɜːˈbein] *adj.* very polite. □ **cortés**
urchin [ˈɜːtʃin] *n.* dirty little boy. □ **golfillo**
sea urchin, small sea creature with a round shell covered with spikes. □ **erizo de mar**
ureter [juːˈriːtə] *n.* tube taking urine from the kidneys to the bladder. □ **uréter**
urethra [juːˈriːθrə] *n.* tube taking urine from the bladder out of the body. □ **uretra**
urge [ɜːdʒ] *n.* strong desire: *I have an urge to eat chocolate; she felt an overwhelming urge to kick him.* □ **impulso; vivo deseo**
■ *v.* **1** to encourage; to push (someone) to do something: *to urge someone to greater efforts.* □ **instar/animar a uno a hacer algo**
2 to suggest strongly: *the doctor urged that his patient should be sent to hospital; the police urged drivers to go slowly.* □ **recomendar encarecidamente**
urgency [ˈɜːdʒənsi] *n.* being urgent; need for something to be done quickly: *it is a matter of great urgency; what's the urgency?,* why are you all hurrying? □ **urgencia**
urgent *adj.* which needs to be done quickly: *could you reply immediately - the matter is urgent; to give urgent consideration to a question; an urgent telephone call.* □ **urgente**
urgently *adv.* quickly/immediately: *doctors are urgently needed at the scene of the disaster.* □ **urgentemente**
urine [ˈjuərin] *n.* liquid waste matter from the body. □ **orina**
urinal [juəˈrainəl] *n.* place where men can pass waste liquid from the body; bowl to catch waste liquid passed from the body. □ **urinario; orinal**
urinary [ˈjuərinəri] *adj.* referring to urine. □ **urinario**
urinary tube, one used to pass urine. □ **conducto urinario**
urinate *v.* to pass waste liquid from the body: *the dog urinated against the lamp post.* □ **orinar**
urn [ɜːn] *n.* very large vase. □ **urna**
tea urn, large metal container with a tap, in which large quantities of tea can be made. □ **tetera**
us [ʌs] *pron.* **1** *referring to* we: *did he see us? there are three of us and only two of you; give us your money; it wasn't us.* □ **nosotros; nos**
2 (*informal*) *referring to* I: *let us/let's have a go,* let me have a go. □ **yo; me**
US [ˈjuˈes] **USA** [juesˈei] *abbreviation for* United States (of America): *he's going to the US on business.* □ **EE. UU.; Estados Unidos (de América)**
use [juːs] *n.* **1** being used; way in which something is used: *can you find a use for this piece of wood? make good use of your time; the tin of food is all ready for use; this car has been in constant use for ten years.* □ **uso**
2 ability to be used: *he has lost the use of his right hand; a one-room flat with use of the kitchen and bathroom downstairs.* □ **uso**
3 usefulness: *what is the use of making plans? it's no use discussing what we should do; can I be of any use to you?* □ **¿de qué sirve hacer planes?; no merece la pena discutir...; ¿puedo ser útil...?**
■ *v.* **1** to put to a purpose: *someone has used my knife to open a tin of sardines; he used the money to buy a greenhouse; we may have to use force to get our money back; can you use your influence?* □ **usar**
2 to take advantage of (someone): *they're just using you.* □ **utilizar**
3 to do something regularly in the past: *we used to go to the seaside on holiday every year; she used not to smoke at all/she did not use to smoke; didn't there use to be/usen't there to be a man in the office called Jack?,* (*informal*) wasn't there at one time? □ **solíamos ir...; no fumaba...**
usable [ˈjuːzəbl] *adj.* which can be used. □ **utilizable**
usage [ˈjuːsidʒ] *n.* **1** custom; way of doing things. □ **uso**
2 way of using a word: *it's common usage in the north of the country.* □ **uso**
used [juːzd] *adj.* **1** not new; which has been put to a purpose: *used cars; it is hardly used; a pile of used paper plates.* □ **usado**
2 accustomed: *I am used to getting up early.* □ **acostumbrado**
3 *you will **get used to** the work in time,* will become accustomed to the work. □ **te acostumbrarás**
useful [ˈjuːsfəl] *adj.* that helps: *a useful book; he is very useful in the garden; she made herself useful in the office,* she did helpful things. □ **útil**
usefully *adv.* in a helpful way. □ **útilmente**
usefulness *n.* being useful: *this pen has outlived its usefulness,* is no longer working well. □ **utilidad**
useless [ˈjuːsləs] *adj.* **1** which does not help: *a useless piece of advice.* □ **inútil**
2 *she is quite useless,* (*informal*) of no help at all. □ **es una inútil**
uselessness *n.* being useless. □ **inutilidad**
user [ˈjuːzə] *n.* person who uses: *road user,* person who drives on the road. □ **usuario**
use up *v.* to finish: *he has used up all the paint.* □ **agotar**
usher [ˈʌʃə] *n.* person who shows people to their seats (in a theatre/in a church). □ **acomodador**
■ *v.* **1** *to usher someone in/out,* to bring (someone) in/out. □ **hacer pasar/salir a**
2 *the assassination ushered in a period of unrest,* started/was the beginning. □ **el asesinato anunció...**
usherette [ʌʃəˈret] *n.* girl who shows people their seats in a cinema. □ **acomodadora**
USSR [juesesˈɑː] *abbreviation for* Union of Soviet Socialist Republics. □ **URSS**
usual [ˈjuːʒuəl] *adj.* ordinary; which happens often: *let's meet at the usual time; it's usual for the customer to make a payment in advance; winter came earlier than usual; as usual it rained on my birthday.* □ **usual; normal**
usually *adv.* mostly/ordinarily: *he usually gets home at 7 o'clock.* □ **normalmente**
usurer [ˈjuːzjurə] *n.* person who lends money for high interest. □ **usurero**
usury *n.* lending money for high interest. □ **usura**
usurp [juːˈzɜːp] *v.* to take the place of (someone) illegally: *to usurp the throne; to usurp someone's rights.* □ **usurpar**
usurper *n.* person who usurps (a throne). □ **usurpador**
utensil [juːˈtensl] *n.* tool/pan/knife, etc., used for housework or in the kitchen. □ **utensilio**
uterus [ˈjuːtərəs] *n.* part of a female body where an unborn baby is carried. □ **útero**
uterine [ˈjuːtərain] *adj.* referring to the uterus. □ **uterino**
utility [juːˈtiliti] *n.* (*pl. utilities*) **1** usefulness. □ **utilidad**
utility van, small van for carrying goods. □ **furgoneta**
utility room, room in a house where you put the washing machine/freezer, etc. □ **'office'**
2 *utilities,* essential public services (such as electricity/gas/water, etc.). □ **servicios públicos**
utilitarian [juːtiliˈtɛəriən] *adj.* referring to practical use, not decoration. □ **utilitario**

utilizable [juːti'laizəbl] *adj.* which can be used. □ **utilizable**
utilization [juːtilai'zeiʃn] *n.* making use of something. □ **utilización**
utilize ['juːtilaiz] *v.* to use; to make use of something (for profit): *to utilize fully all your resources.* □ **utilizar**
utmost ['ʌtmoust] *adj.* **1** greatest that can be: *to take the utmost care.* □ **máximo**
to the utmost, as far as is humanly possible. □ **hasta más no poder**
2 furthest: *to the utmost ends of the earth.* □ **más lejano**
utopia [ju'toupiə] *n.* imaginary perfect world. □ **utopía**
utopian *adj.* very perfect (ideas). □ **utópico**
utter ['ʌtə] *adj.* complete/total: *he is an utter fool; an utter failure.* □ **completo**
■ *v.* to speak; to make a sound: *he uttered a feeble cry.* □ **pronunciar**
utterance *n.* something spoken. □ **expresión**
utterly *adv.* completely: *the book has been utterly forgotten.* □ **totalmente**
uttermost *adj.* **1** greatest that can be: *it is of the uttermost importance.* □ **es de la máxima importancia**
2 furthest: *to the uttermost ends of the earth.* □ **más lejano**
uvula ['juːvjulə] *n.* small lump of flesh hanging down at the back of the mouth. □ **campanilla**
uxorious [ʌk'sɔːriəs] *adj.* (man) who is very fond of his wife. □ **muy enamorado de su mujer**

V,v

V, v [vi:] twenty-second letter of the alphabet. □ **V, v**
V-neck pullover, one with a neckline shaped like a V. □ **jersey de cuello de pico**
V sign, sign made with two fingers raised in the air (either meaning victory or showing extreme rudeness). □ **signo de victoria**

v. ['vɜ:səs] *prep.* against. *see* **versus.** □ **contra**

vac [væk] *n.* (*informal*) vacation. □ **vacaciones**

vacancy ['veikənsi] *n.* (*pl. vacancies*) **1** being vacant. □ **lo vacante**
2 empty place/room/job: *we have vacancies for typists and cleaners; we have no vacancies for the month of August,* no vacant rooms. □ **vacante**
vacant *adj.* **1** empty/not occupied: *there are two vacant seats in the front row.* □ **libre**
2 *to sell a house with **vacant possession,*** with no one living in it. □ **...sin inquilino**
3 ***situations vacant,*** jobs which need to be filled. □ **ofertas de empleo**
4 *vacant expression,* with no interest/liveliness. □ **expresión alelada**
vacantly *adv.* with a vacant expression: *he stared vacantly into space.* □ **distraídamente**
vacate [və'keit] *v.* to leave/to make (something) empty: *to vacate the premises; he vacated his office.* □ **dejar vacante**
vacation [və'keiʃn] *n.* **1** holiday (especially in universities and law courts). □ **vacaciones**
2 act of vacating (an office, etc.). □ **vacante**
■ *v. Amer.* to go on holiday: *they're vacationing in Canada.* □ **ir/tomar las vacaciones**

vaccinate ['væksineit] *v.* to put a small quantity of disease-producing virus into (someone), so that his body will react against it and thus protect him from catching the disease: *to vaccinate someone against smallpox.* □ **vacunar**
vaccination [væksi'neiʃn] *n.* act of vaccinating: *have you had your smallpox vaccination?* □ **vacunación**
vaccine ['væksi:n] *n.* substance which contains the virus of a disease which when put into someone, gives protection against the disease: *smallpox vaccine.* □ **vacuna**

vacillate ['væsileit] *v.* to waver/to hesitate: *he was vacillating,* he was not sure what to do. □ **vacilar**
vacillation [væsi'leiʃn] *n.* hesitation/wavering. □ **vacilación**

vacuous ['vækjuəs] *adj.* **1** with no meaning/sense. □ **vacuo; vacío**
2 *vacuous expression,* silly/vacant expression. □ **expresión perdida**
vacuity [və'kjuiti] **vacuousness** *n.* emptiness of meaning/silliness. □ **vacuidad**

vacuum ['vækjuəm] *n.* **1** space from which all matter, including air, has been removed: *no animal can live in a vacuum.* □ **vacío**
vacuum-packed, (food) packed in a vacuum, so that no air can enter the package. □ **envasado al vacío**
2 *his resignation has created a vacuum,* an empty space which must be filled. □ **...un vacío**
■ *v.* (*informal*) to clean with a vacuum cleaner: *he's vacuumed the whole house from top to bottom.* □ **pasar la aspiradora**
vacuum cleaner *n.* cleaning machine which sucks up dust. □ **aspiradora**
vacuum flask *n.* bottle with double walls which keeps liquids warm or cold. □ **termo**

vagabond ['vægəbɔnd] *adj.* and *n.* (person) who wanders about/who has no home. □ **vagabundo**

vagaries ['veigəriz] *n. pl.* oddities/strange behaviour: *the vagaries of the London transport system.* □ **irregularidades**

vagina [və'dʒainə] *n.* tube in a female mammal connecting the uterus to the vulva and through which a baby is born. □ **vagina**
vaginal *adj.* referring to the vagina. □ **vaginal**

vagrant ['veigrənt] *adj.* and *n.* (tramp/person) who wanders from place to place with no home or work. □ **vagabundo**
vagrancy *n.* being a vagrant. □ **vagabundeo**

vague [veig] *adj.* (*vaguer, vaguest*) not clear/not precise: *a vague idea.* □ **vago**
I haven't the vaguest idea, I have no idea at all. □ **...ni la más vaga idea**
vaguely *adv.* more or less; in a vague way: *he pointed vaguely in the direction of the police station.* □ **vagamente**
vagueness *n.* lack of precision: *there's a vagueness about the details of the plan.* □ **vaguedad**

vain [vein] *adj.* (*vainer, vainest*) **1** useless; meaningless: *vain hopes; vain gestures.* □ **vano**
2 very proud of your appearance: *he's so vain that he keeps on looking in the mirror.* □ **vanidoso**
3 ***in vain,*** without any success/result: *we waited in vain for a bus; it was in vain that we tried to get the hotel to provide some food.* □ **en vano**
vainly *adv.* with no success/with no result: *we vainly tried to telephone the police.* □ **vanamente**

valance ['væləns] *n.* short frilled curtain. □ **bambalinón**

vale [veil] *n.* (*used in names of places*) valley. □ **valle**

valence ['veiləns] **valency** ['veilənsi] *n.* (*in chemistry*) power of an atom to combine. □ **valencia**

valentine ['væləntain] *n.* **1** person chosen as a loved one on February 14th (St Valentine's Day): *will you be my valentine?* □ **novio**
2 (usually unsigned) card sent to someone you love on February 14th. □ **tarjeta del día de San Valentín**

valerian [və'liəriən] *n.* type of wild plant with pink flowers. □ **valeriana**

valet ['vælei, 'vælit] *n.* male servant who looks after his master's clothes. □ **ayuda de cámara**
valet service, cleaning service in a hotel. □ **servicio de limpieza**

valetudinarian [vælitju:di'neəriən] *n.* person who likes to feel he is an invalid. □ **valetudinario**

valiant ['væliənt] *adj.* brave. □ **valiente**
valiantly *adv.* bravely. □ **valientemente**

valid ['vælid] *adj.* **1** which is acceptable because it is logical: *he has a valid excuse.* □ **válido**
2 which can be lawfully used: *this ticket is valid for three months; he has a valid passport.* □ **válido; vigente (pasaporte)**
validate *v.* to make valid: *to validate a maths course,* to make it acceptable to the education authorities. □ **validar**
validity [və'liditi] *n.* **1** legal force: *what is the validity of this passport?* □ **validez; vigencia**
2 truth: *can we check the validity of his excuse?* □ **validez**

valley ['væli] *n.* long stretch of low land through

which a river runs: *the valley of the Mississippi; the Thames Valley.* □ **valle**
valour ['vælə] *Amer.* **valor** *n.* bravery. □ **valor**
value ['vælju:] *n.* **1** worth (in money or esteem): *what is the value of this silver spoon? these presents are of no value; to get value for money,* to get a good bargain; *at $5 it is very good value,* it is well worth the price; *the burglars took several items of sentimental value,* not worth much inRmoney, but important because of personal attachment to them. □ **valor**
2 usefulness: *a good telescope is of great value to an astronomer.* □ **valor**
■ *v.* **1** to put a price in money on (an object): *I want to have this silver valued for insurance purposes; it was valued at $20,000.* □ **valorar**
2 to set a high value on (something): *if you value your daughter's life, give me $10,000.* □ **estimar (algo) en mucho**
valuable *adj.* worth a lot of money; very useful: *a valuable painting; I have found this compass very valuable when out walking.* □ **valioso**
■ *n. **valuables,*** jewellery/silver, etc., of great value. □ **objetos de valor**
valuation [vælju'eiʃn] *n.* estimate of the worth of something; act of estimating the worth of something. □ **valoración**
value added tax *n.* tax imposed on the value of goods or services. □ **impuesto sobre el valor añadido**
valueless *adj.* worthless/with no value. □ **sin valor**
valuer *n.* person who estimates the value of property. □ **tasador**
valve [vælv] *n.* **1** mechanical device which allows air/liquid to pass through in one direction only: *a bicycle tyre has a valve to prevent the air escaping.* □ **válvula**
safety valve, valve which allows gas/steam, etc., to escape if the pressure is too great. □ **válvula de seguridad**
2 flap in a tube in the body which allows air/blood, etc., to circulate in one direction only: *heart valve.* □ **válvula**
3 part of a radio/TV set which controls the flow of electricity. □ **lámpara**
4 single shell (of a shellfish). □ **valva**
valvular ['vælvjulə] *adj.* referring to a valve in the heart. □ **valvular**
vamp [væmp] *n.* front part of the upper of a shoe or boot. □ **empeine**
vampire ['væmpaiə] *n.* person who supposedly sucks blood from his victims. □ **vampiro**
vampire bat *n.* type of small bat which sucks blood from animals. □ **vampiro**
van [væn] *n.* **1** small vehicle for carrying goods by road or rail: *a bread van.* □ **furgoneta**
guard's van, wagon at the end of a train where the guard rides. □ **furgón de cola**
2 ***in the van,*** in the front (of a movement/of an attack). □ **a la vanguardia**
vandal ['vændl] *n.* person who destroys property for the pleasure of destruction. □ **vándalo**
vandalism *n.* meaningless destruction of property. □ **vandalismo**
vandalize *v.* to smash (something) up for no reason at all: *a vandalized telephone kiosk.* □ **destrozar**
vane [vein] *n.* one of the blades on a water wheel/on a pump/weathercock, etc. □ **aspa; pala**
vanguard ['væŋgɑ:d] *n.* front part of an army. □ **vanguardia**
in the vanguard, in the front (of a movement). □ **a la vanguardia**
vanilla [və'nilə] *n.* scented substance coming from the seed pods of a tropical plant: *vanilla flavouring; vanilla ice cream.* □ **vainilla**
vanish ['væniʃ] *v.* **1** to disappear/to go out of sight: *the speeding car vanished round the corner.* □ **desaparecer**
2 *he's just vanished into thin air,* disappeared completely. □ **se acaba de esfumar**
vanishing cream *n.* scented cream rubbed into the skin to make it soft. □ **crema de día**
vanishing point *n.* **1** point in a drawing where the horizontal lines seem to meet at eye level. □ **punto de fuga**
2 *his enthusiasm has dwindled to vanishing point,* has disappeared completely. □ **...hasta esfumarse**
vanity ['væniti] *n.* (*pl. vanities*) **1** pride/feeling that you are more handsome than you really are. □ **vanidad**
2 uselessness. □ **inutilidad**
vanity case *n.* small bag for carrying makeup/powder, etc. □ **neceser**
vanquish ['væŋkwiʃ] *v.* to defeat. □ **vencer**
vantage point ['vɑ:ntidʒpɔint] *n.* place from which you can see well. □ **posición ventajosa**
vapid ['væpid] *adj.* dull (conversation). □ **insulsa**
vaporize ['veipəraiz] *v.* to turn into vapour: *the petrol vaporized rapidly.* □ **vaporizarse**
vaporization *n.* changing into vapour. □ **vaporización**
vaporizer *n.* machine which turns liquids (especially water) into vapour. □ **vaporizador**
vapour, *Amer.* **vapor** *n.* gas form of a liquid, usually caused by heating: *water vapour.* □ **vapor**
vapour trail, line of white vapour left in the sky by an aircraft. □ **estela de humo**
variability [vɛəriə'biliti] *n.* being variable. □ **variabilidad**
variable ['vɛəriəbl] *adj.* which varies/changes all the time: *variable weather.* □ **variable**
■ *n.* something which varies: *the variable in the problem is the temperature of the solution.* □ **variable**
variance *n. **to be at variance,*** to disagree: *experts are at variance over the date; these results are at variance with the data.* □ **estar en desacuerdo**
variant *adj.* and *n.* (version/spelling, etc.) which is slightly different: *this is a local variant of the old rhyme 'Three Blind Mice'.* □ **variante**
variation [vɛəri'eiʃn] *n.* **1** act of varying: *there may be a variation of heart beat.* □ **variación**
2 amount by which something varies: *in Canada there are great variations of temperature between summer and winter.* □ **variación**
3 ***variations,*** pieces of music which repeat the same theme but written in a different fashion: *variations on the tune 'Greensleeves'.* □ **variaciones**
varicose vein ['værikous'vein] *n.* swollen vein, especially in the leg. □ **variz**
variegated ['vɛərigeitid] *adj.* (plant which is) striped/marked in contrasting colours: *variegated ivy.* □ **jaspeado**
variegation [vɛəri'geiʃn] *n.* irregular marking in contrasting colours. □ **abigarramiento**
variety [və'raiəti] *n.* (*pl. varieties*) **1** being of different sorts: *I read books on a variety of subjects; the work in the office has a lot of variety; for a variety of reasons,* for several different reasons. □ **variedad**
2 different type (of plant): *which variety of apple do you prefer — Granny Smith or Golden Delicious?*

□ **variedad**
3 ***variety show,*** entertainment which includes several different types of performers (such as singers/conjurors/ventriloquists, etc.). □ **revista**
various ['vɛəriəs] *adj.* different/several: *we've met on various occasions; there are various ways of getting to London from here.* □ **varios, diversos**
variously *adv.* in different ways. □ **de diverso modo**
varnish ['vɑːniʃ] *n.* **1** liquid which when painted on something gives it a shiny surface: *a pot of nail varnish.* □ **barniz**
2 shiny surface made by painting with varnish: *someone has scratched the varnish on the table.* □ **barniz**
■ *v.* **1** to paint with a liquid varnish; to give a shiny surface to something: *a varnished table.* □ **barnizar**
2 to cover up (a mistake/disagreement). □ **tapar**
vary ['vɛəri] *v.* (*varied; varying*) **1** to make different; to become different: *you ought to vary your diet,* eat different sorts of food; *his temperature hasn't varied; his opinions vary from day to day,* they change continually. □ **variar**
2 to have different views: *experts vary on this point.* □ **diferir**
varied *adj.* of various kinds/different: *you should eat a more varied diet; we have a varied response to our questionnaire.* □ **variado**
vascular ['væskjulə] *adj.* referring to veins, etc., which carry blood or sap. □ **vascular**
vase [vɑːz] *n.* container for putting flowers in: *a flower vase; a vase of flowers.* □ **jarrón**
vasectomy [və'sektəmi] *n.* (*pl. vasectomies*) operation on a man to cut the tubes through which sperm flows and so to make him sterile. □ **vasectomía**
vassal ['væsl] *n.* servant; country which is under the rule of another country. □ **vasallo**
vast [vɑːst] *adj.* (*vaster, vastest*) very large: *he spends vast sums of money on food.* □ **vasto; inmenso**
vastly *adv.* very much. □ **enormemente**
vastness *n.* large size. □ **inmensidad**
vat [væt] *n.* large container for liquids (especially wine). □ **cuba**
VAT [væt, viːei'tiː] *abbreviation for* **value added tax,** government tax on goods or services. □ **I.V.A.**
vatman *n.* (*pl. vatmen*) (*informal*) government inspector dealing with VAT. □ **inspector de hacienda**
vault [vɔːlt] *n.* **1** arched stone ceiling. □ **bóveda**
2 underground room (for keeping things safe): *the bank vaults.* □ **cámara acorazada**
3 underground room for burying people. □ **panteón**
4 high jump. □ **salto**
the pole vault, leap over a high bar, using a pole to swing you up. □ **salto con pértiga**
■ *v.* to jump over something by putting one hand on it to steady yourself: *he vaulted over the gate.* □ **saltar**
vaulted *adj.* with a stone arch. □ **abovedado**
vaunt [vɔːnt] *v.* to boast about (something): *his much vaunted new invention,* the one he has boasted about so much. □ **jactarse de**
VD ['viː'diː] *abbreviation for* venereal disease. □ **enfermedad venérea**
veal [viːl] *n.* meat from a calf. □ **ternera (carne)**
vector ['vektə] *n.* (*in mathematics*) something which has both direction and size. □ **vector**
veer ['viə] *v.* **1** to turn: *the ship veered away; the wind has veered to the west.* □ **virar**
2 *the government's policy has veered right round,* is now the opposite of what it was. □ **...ha virado a lo opuesto**
veg [vedʒ] *n.* (*no pl.*) (*informal*) (cooked) vegetable(s): *can I have some more veg?* □ **verdura**
vegan ['viːgən] *adj.* and *n.* (person) who only eats plant products (vegetables and fruit). □ **vegeteriano**
vegetable ['vedʒitəbl] *adj.* and *n.* **1** (referring to) plants: *vegetable oil.* □ **vegetal**
the vegetable kingdom, all plant life. □ **el reino vegetal**
2 plant grown for food, not usually sweet: *vegetable garden; plate of meat and two vegetables,* two types of cooked vegetables. □ **hortaliza; verdura**
3 person who is more or less incapable of movement or thought. □ **un vegetal**
vegetarian [vedʒi'tɛəriən] *adj.* and *n.* (person) who does not eat meat; (restaurant) which does not serve meat. □ **vegetariano**
vegetate *v.* to live like a vegetable, not moving or doing anything. □ **vegetar**
vegetation [vedʒi'teiʃn] *n.* plants: *he is studying the vegetation of Northern Europe.* □ **vegetación**
vehemence ['viəməns] *n.* forceful way (of saying what you think). □ **vehemencia**
vehement ['viəmənt] *adj.* forceful. □ **vehemente**
vehemently *adv.* in a forceful way: *he vehemently denied having stolen the watch.* □ **vehementemente**
vehicle ['viəkl] *n.* **1** machine on wheels which travels along the road; rocket which travels in space: *motor vehicle.* □ **vehículo**
commercial vehicle, one which carries goods. □ **vehículo comercial**
2 way of expressing something: *the cinema as a vehicle for revolutionary propaganda,* as a means of spreading. □ **vehículo**
vehicular [vi'ikjulə] *adj.* referring to vehicles: *vehicular traffic.* □ **de vehículos; circulación rodada**
veil [veil] *n.* light cloth which can cover a woman's head or face: *a hat with a dark veil.* □ **velo**
to draw a veil over something, not to mention something which is wrong/unpleasant. □ **correr un tupido velo sobre algo**
to take the veil, to become a nun. □ **tomar el velo**
■ *v.* **1** to cover with a veil: *all the women were veiled.* □ **cubrir con un velo**
2 *veiled threats,* half-hidden threats. □ **amenazas veladas**
vein [vein] *n.* **1** small tube in the body along which blood runs to the heart. □ **vena**
2 thin line on the leaf of a plant. □ **vena**
3 thin layer of a mineral in a rock. □ **filón**
4 mood: *when he is in a poetic vein,* when he is feeling poetic. □ **cuando le da la vena poética**
veined *adj.* covered with veins. □ **con venas; veteado**
veldt [velt] *n.* grass-covered plain in South Africa. □ **sabana**
vellum ['veləm] *n.* **1** good quality writing paper. □ **papel vitela**
2 skin of an animal made very thin and used for binding books or writing on. □ **vitela**
velocity [və'lɔsiti] *n.* (*pl. velocities*) speed. □ **velocidad**
velour [və'luə] *n.* thick, soft cloth with a soft surface like velvet. □ **velludillo**
velvet ['velvət] *adj.* and *n.* **1** cloth (made from silk, etc.) with a soft surface of cut threads: *velvet jacket.* □ **terciopelo**
2 *velvet lawn,* soft and smoothly cut like velvet. □ **cortado al ras**
velveteen *n.* velvet made of cotton. □ **pana**

velvety *adj.* with a soft surface like velvet: *velvety moss.* □ **aterciopelado**
venal ['viːnəl] *adj.* (person) who will take a bribe; (act) which is dishonest/which is done for a bribe. □ **venal**
vendetta [ven'detə] *n.* private quarrel between families sometimes lasting for generations. □ **'vendetta'**
vending ['vendiŋ] *n.* selling. □ **venta**
vending machine, machine which provides cigarettes/chocolate, etc., when money is put into a slot. □ **máquina expendedora**
vendor ['vendə] *n.* person who sells: *the vendor of a house; a peanut vendor.* □ **vendedor**
veneer [və'niə] *n.* **1** thin layer of expensive wood glued to the surface of ordinary wood: *the table has a mahogany veneer.* □ **chapeado**
2 thin layer of politeness/knowledge which covers a person's bad qualities: *a veneer of respectability.* □ **apariencia**
■ *v.* to cover (wood) with a veneer. □ **chapear**
venerate ['venəreit] *v.* to respect greatly: *the headmaster is venerated by the boys.* □ **venerar**
venerable *adj.* very old and likely to be respected: *a venerable old priest.* □ **venerable**
veneration [venə'reiʃn] *n.* respect. □ **veneración**
to hold somone in veneration, to respect someone greatly. □ **tener veneración por alguien**
venereal [və'niəriəl] *adj.* *venereal disease,* disease transmitted during sexual intercourse. □ **venéreo**
venetian blind [və'niːʃn'blaind] *n.* blind to shut out light, made of horizontal strips of plastic/wood, etc., which can be opened or shut, or raised and lowered by pulling a string. □ **persiana veneciana**
vengeance ['vendʒəns] *n.* **1** harm caused to someone in return for harm they have caused you: *to take vengeance on someone.* □ **venganza**
2 *it is snowing with a vengeance,* (*informal*) very strongly. □ **nieva a rabiar**
venial ['viːniəl] *adj.* slight (mistake); (sin) which can be excused. □ **venial**
venison ['venizn] *n.* meat from a deer. □ **carne de venado**
venom ['venəm] *n.* **1** poison (from a snake, etc.). □ **veneno**
2 bitter hatred. □ **odio a muerte**
venomous *adj.* **1** poisonous: *not all snakes are venomous.* □ **venenoso**
2 bitterly spiteful: *she wrote a venomous letter.* □ **venenoso**
venous ['viːnəs] *adj.* referring to veins (in the body). □ **venoso**
vent [vent] *n.* **1** hole through which air/gas can escape: *an air vent; vent of a volcano.* □ **abertura (aire); chimenea (volcán)**
2 slit in the back of a coat: *jacket with a centre vent/with two side vents.* □ **raja**
3 *to give vent to your anger,* to let your anger explode. □ **desahogarse, descargar**
■ *v. he vented his anger on her,* he made her the target of his anger. □ **descargó su ira con ella**
ventilate ['ventileit] *v.* **1** to allow fresh air to come into: *to ventilate a room; a well-ventilated room.* □ **ventilar**
2 to discuss (a question) in the open: *a subject which should be ventilated in public.* □ **ventilar**
ventilation [venti'leiʃn] *n.* **1** bringing in fresh air. □ **ventilación**
ventilation shaft, tube which allows fresh air to go down into a coal mine. □ **pozo de ventilación**
2 public discussion (of something): *ventilation of a question.* □ **discusión**
ventilator ['ventileitə] *n.* opening which allows fresh air to come in; machine which pumps in fresh air. □ **ventilador**
ventral ['ventrəl] *adj.* (*formal*) referring to the abdomen. □ **ventral**
ventricle ['ventrikl] *n.* space in the heart which fills up with blood and then pumps it out into the arteries. □ **ventrículo**
ventriloquist [ven'triləkwist] *n.* person who can make his voice appear to come from a puppet. □ **ventrílocuo**
ventriloquism *n.* act of being a ventriloquist. □ **ventriloquia**
venture ['ventʃə] *n.* commercial deal which involves risk: *a business venture; it is a totally new venture, selling kits to make your own refrigerator.* □ **aventura**
■ *v.* to dare/to be bold enough to do something dangerous: *he ventured to ask his boss for a rise; the explorers ventured into the jungle; old people rarely venture out of doors when the pavements are icy.* □ **aventurarse**
venturesome *adj.* (person) who dares to take a risk. □ **aventurero**
venue ['venju] *n.* agreed place where something will take place: *we must decide on the venue for the next meeting.* □ **lugar de reunión**
veracious [və'reiʃəs] *adj.* truthful. □ **veraz**
veracity [və'ræsiti] *n.* truth: *we will investigate the veracity of your claim.* □ **veracidad**
veranda(h) [və'rændə] *n.* covered terrace along the side of a house with no outside wall: *let's have our coffee on the verandah.* □ **mirador; galería**
verb [vəːb] *n.* part of speech/a word which shows how someone or something acts/is/feels: *in the sentence 'he tripped and hurt his hand', 'tripped' and 'hurt' are verbs.* □ **verbo**
verbal *adj.* **1** referring to a verb. □ **verbal**
2 spoken. □ **verbal**
verbal agreement, one which is not written down. □ **acuerdo verbal**
verbally *adv.* in spoken words: *he agreed verbally.* □ **verbalmente**
verbatim [vəː'beitim] *adj.* and *adv.* word for word; in exactly the same words: *a verbatim report; he told me what was said verbatim.* □ **literal; al pie de la letra**
verbena [vəː'biːnə] *n.* type of scented herb, used to make soap or in hot drinks. □ **verbena**
verbiage ['vəːbiidʒ] *n.* lot of useless words: *cut out all the verbiage.* □ **verborrea**
verbose [və'bous] *adj.* using more words than necessary: *a very verbose report.* □ **prolijo**
verbosity [və'bɔsiti] *n.* being verbose. □ **verborrea**
verdant ['vəːdənt] *adj.* (*formal*) green (grass). □ **verde**
verdict ['vəːdikt] *n.* **1** judgement/decision by a judge or jury: *the verdict of the court is that you are guilty.* □ **veredicto**
2 opinion: *the general verdict was that the film was a disaster.* □ **opinión**
verdigris ['vəːdigris] *n.* green discolouring of copper, etc., through contact with damp. □ **verdín; cardenillo**
verge [vəːdʒ] *n.* **1** edge; grass strip along the side of a road: *do not park on the grass verges.* □ **borde; arcén**
2 *he is* ***on the verge of*** *a collapse,* he is near to collapsing; *she was on the verge of tears,* nearly crying. □ **al borde de; a punto de**
■ *v.* ***to verge on,*** to be near to: *it verges on madness*

to try to use an umbrella as a parachute; his attitude verges on hysteria; the carpet is green verging on grey. □ **rayar en**

verger ['vɜːdʒə] *n.* man who looks after a church. □ **sacristán**

verify ['verifai] *v.* (*verified; verifying*) to check/to see if a statement is correct: *the police will verify your statement.* □ **verificar**

verifiable [veri'faiəbl] *adj.* which can be verified. □ **verificable**

verification [verifi'keiʃn] *n.* checking that something is correct. □ **verificación**

verisimilitude [verisi'militjuːd] *n.* appearance of being true. □ **verosimilitud**

veritable ['veritəbl] *adj.* true/real. □ **verdadero**

vermicelli [vɜːmi'seli] *n.* type of very thin spaghetti. □ **fideos**

vermilion [və'miliən] *adj.* and *n.* bright red (colour). □ **bermellón**

vermin ['vɜːmin] *n.* unwanted animals or birds which are pests, such as rats, fleas, pigeons, etc. □ **bichos**

verminous *adj.* covered with fleas. □ **lleno de pulgas**

vermouth ['vɜːməθ] *n.* type of wine flavoured with herbs, usually drunk before a meal. □ **vermú**

vernacular [və'nækjulə] *adj.* and *n.* (referring to) the ordinary spoken language of a country or region: *the invaders could not speak the vernacular.* □ **vernáculo (adj.); lengua vernácula (n.)**

vernal ['vɜːnl] *adj.* (*formal*) referring to the spring. □ **primaveral**

verruca [və'ruːkə] *n.* wart/small hard growth on the skin. □ **verruga**

versatile ['vɜːsətail] *adj.* (person/machine) able to do various things equally well: *a versatile musician,* one who can play many different instruments. □ **versátil**

versatility [vɜːsə'tiliti] *n.* ability to do various things with equal skill. □ **versatilidad**

verse [vɜːs] *n.* **1** group of lines of poetry which form a part of a poem: *the poem has six four-line verses.* □ **estrofa**

2 poetry; lines of writing with a rhythm and sometimes rhyme: *he writes in verse; a verse drama.* □ **poesía; escribe en verso**

3 one line of a poem. □ **verso**

4 short (numbered) sentence from the Bible. □ **versículo**

to give chapter and verse for something, to quote exactly the origin of a statement. □ **citar con pelos y señales**

versed *adj.* ***well versed in something,*** knowing a lot about something/being well skilled in something. □ **versado**

versification [vɜːsifi'keiʃn] *n.* making of poetry; way in which a poem is written. □ **versificación**

versify ['vɜːsifai] *v.* (*versified; versifying*) to write (usually bad) poetry. □ **versificar**

version ['vɜːʃn] *n.* **1** story of what happened as seen from a particular point of view: *now let's hear the policeman's version of the accident; a new version of the Greek myths.* □ **versión**

2 translation: *an English version of Hindu legends.* □ **versión**

3 model (of car, etc.): *this is the most expensive version available.* □ **modelo**

verso ['vɜːsou] *n.* (*pl. versos*) left side/back (of a piece of paper/a page of a book, etc.). □ **verso**

versus ['vɜːsəs] *prep.* (*usually written **v.***) against: (in a civil court case) *Jones v. Smith;* (in sport) *England v. France.* □ **contra**

vertebra ['vɜːtibrə] *n.* (*pl. vertebrae*) one of the bones which form the spine. □ **vértebra**

vertebrate ['vɜːtibrət] *adj.* and *n.* (animal) which has a backbone. □ **vertebrado**

vertex ['vɜːteks] *n.* (*pl. vertices*) top; angle at the top of a triangle. □ **vértice**

vertical ['vɜːtikl] *adj.* upright. □ **vertical**

■ *n.* **1** upright line (in geometry). □ **vertical**

2 *this wall is **out of the vertical,*** it is leaning. □ **desplomado**

vertically *adv.* straight up/down: *the cliff rises vertically for 200 metres.* □ **verticalmente**

vertigo ['vɜːtigou] *n.* dizziness caused by heights: *he gets vertigo if he climbs up a ladder.* □ **vértigo**

verve [vɜːv] *n.* enthusiasm/feeling of liveliness. □ **entusiasmo/brío**

very ['veri] *adv.* **1** to a high degree: *it's very hot in here; she's very tall; I don't think this meat is very good; it's very much the same; at the very latest.* □ **muy**

2 exactly: *it's the very same,* exactly the same. □ **es lo mismo**

3 *the very first man to fly,* absolutely the first. □ **el primer hombre...**

■ *adj.* **1** exactly the same/exactly the right (person): *it's the very thing you need; he's the very man I'm looking for; those were his very words; at the very beginning of the book,* right at the beginning of the book. □ **exactamente...**

2 *the very thought of jumping with a parachute makes me shudder,* the mere thought/only to think of jumping. □ **sólo pensar que...**

vesicle ['vezikl] *n.* small hollow in the body (usually filled with liquid). □ **vesícula; ampolla**

vespers ['vespəz] *n.* church service in the evening. □ **vísperas**

vessel ['vesl] *n.* **1** container (for a liquid): *put the wine in an earthenware vessel.* □ **recipiente**

blood vessel, tube which carries blood round the body. □ **vaso sanguíneo**

2 ship. □ **buque**

vest [vest] *n.* **1** light undergarment for the top half of the body. □ **camiseta**

2 *Amer.* waistcoat. □ **chaleco**

vested *adj. the right is vested in the management,* the management holds the right. □ **concedido**

vested interest, pressure on someone not to make changes, because it is in their interest to keep the present system. □ **derechos adquiridos**

vestibule ['vestibjuːl] *n.* entrance hall. □ **vestíbulo**

vestige ['vestidʒ] *n.* trace: *are there any vestiges of life on Mars? there was not a vestige of truth in what he said.* □ **vestigio, indicio**

vestigial [ves'tidʒəl] *adj.* which exists as a vestige: *a vestigial tail,* a trace of a tail which an animal's remote ancestors may have had. □ **una cola rudimentaria**

vestments ['vestmənts] *n. pl.* clergyman's robes. □ **vestiduras litúrgicas**

vestry ['vestri] *n.* (*pl. vestries*) clergyman's room in a church. □ **sacristía**

vet [vet] *n.* (*informal*) doctor who specializes in treating sick animals. □ **veterinario**

■ *v.* (*he vetted*) to examine carefully: *the application has to be vetted by the police.* □ **someter a una investigación**

vetch [vetʃ] *n.* (*pl. vetches*) type of wild pea. □ **arveja**

veteran ['vetrən] *n.* **1** person who has given long service: *a veteran of three expeditions to the North Pole.* □ **veterano**

2 old/retired soldier. □ **veterano**

3 *Amer.* person (not necessarily old) who has served

in the armed services. □ **excombatiente**
■ *adj.* old; experienced: *he's a veteran mountain climber.* □ **veterano**
veteran car, car made before 1916. □ **coche antiguo**
veterinary ['vetrinri] *adj.* referring to the treatment of sick animals. □ **veterinario**
veterinary surgeon, doctor who specializes in treating sick animals. □ **veterinario**
veterinarian [vetəri'nɛəriən] *n. Amer.* veterinary surgeon. □ **veterinario**
veto ['vi:tou] *n.* (*pl. vetoes*) power to forbid something: *he has a veto; the chairman exercised his power of veto,* he forbade the proposed action. □ **veto**
■ *v.* to forbid: *he vetoed the whole project.* □ **vetar**
vex [veks] *v.* to annoy. □ **molestar**
vexation [vek'seiʃn] *n.* annoyance. □ **molestia**
vexatious [vek'seiʃəs] *adj.* annoying. □ **molesto**
vexed *adj.* **1** annoyed. □ **enfadado**
2 *a vexed question,* question which is often discussed but which has not been solved. □ **una cuestión controvertida**
VHF [vi:eitʃ'ef] *abbreviation for* very high frequency. □ **VHF**
via ['vaiə] *prep.* (travelling) through: *to go to Washington via New York; I sent him a message via the milkman,* the milkman passed on the message to him. □ **vía; por**
viable ['vaiəbl] *adj.* **1** able to work in practice: *is solar energy a really viable proposition?* □ **viable**
2 (*of new born young*) sufficiently developed to survive. □ **que sale adelante**
viaduct ['vaiədʌkt] *n.* long bridge carrying a road/railway/canal over a wide valley. □ **viaducto**
vial ['vaiəl] *n.* small glass bottle. □ **frasco**
viands ['vaiəndz] *n. pl.* (*formal*) food. □ **viandas**
vibrate [vai'breit] *v.* to shudder/to shake: *the house vibrated with the noise of the party; the air was vibrating with excitement before the match.* □ **vibrar**
vibrant ['vaibrənt] *adj.* full (of energy). □ **vibrante**
vibration [vai'breiʃn] *n.* act of vibrating; rapid movement: *the vibrations of the surface of a drum.* □ **vibración**
viburnum [vai'bə:nəm] *n.* common shrub with pink or white flowers. □ **viburno**
vicar ['vikə] *n.* clergyman in charge of a parish. □ **vicario**
vicarage ['vikridʒ] *n.* vicar's house. □ **vicaría**
vicarious [vi'kɛəriəs] *adj.* felt through imagining what another person feels: *to experience vicarious pleasure,* to have pleasure because you imagine how someone is enjoying something. □ **experimentado por otro**
vice [vais] *n.* **1** sexual wickedness/immorality: *a den of vice.* □ **vicio; un templo del vicio**
the vice squad, police department dealing with prostitution, etc. □ **brigada contra el vicio**
2 great wickedness. □ **vicio**
3 bad habit: *he doesn't smoke or drink, so has none of the usual vices.* □ **vicio**
4 tool with jaws that screw tight to hold something: *hold the block of wood tight in a vice before you start drilling holes in it; the policeman held his arm like a vice.* □ **torno de banco**
vice-like *adj.* like a vice: *a vice-like grip.* □ **atenazador**
vice- [vais] *prefix meaning* deputy; second in rank: *vice-chairman; vice-president.* □ **vice-**
vice-chancellor [vais'tʃɑ:nsələ] *n.* executive head of a university. □ **rector**
viceroy ['vaisrɔi] *n.* person who represents a king or queen. □ **virrey**
viceregal [vais'ri:gl] *adj.* referring to a viceroy. □ **virreinal**
vice versa [vais'və:sə] *adv.* the other way round: *when he's well she's ill and vice versa,* and when she's well he's ill. □ **viceversa**
vicinity [vi'siniti] *n.* (*pl. vicinities*) area around something. □ **vecindad**
in the vicinity, near by: *his office is in the vicinity of the law courts.* □ **al lado de**
vicious ['viʃəs] *adj.* **1** wicked: *a vicious attack on an old lady; vicious criticism in the press.* □ **malvado**
2 ***vicious circle,*** interlocking chain of bad circumstances from which it is impossible to escape: *you can only get a job if you already have experience, but you can only get experience by having a job – it's a vicious circle.* □ **círculo vicioso**
viciously *adv.* in a wicked/spiteful way. □ **con maldad**
vicissitude [vi'sisitju:d] *n.* (*formal*) variation in luck. □ **vicisitud**
the vicissitudes of life, the ups and downs of life. □ **las vicisitudes de la vida**
victim ['viktim] *n.* person who suffers an attack/an accident: *she was the victim of a brutal attack; victims of the disaster were rushed to hospital.* □ **víctima**
victimization [viktimai'zeiʃn] *n.* picking on someone as a victim; harsh treatment of an individual. □ **persecución**
victimize ['viktimaiz] *v.* to choose (someone) as a victim; to treat someone more harshly than others: *I've been victimized.* □ **tomar como víctima**
victor ['viktə] *n.* person who wins (a game/a battle). □ **vencedor**
Victorian [vik'tɔ:riən] *adj.* referring to the reign of Queen Victoria (1837-1901). □ **victoriano**
victorious [vik'tɔ:riəs] *adj.* (person/general) who has won a game/a battle. □ **victorioso**
victory ['viktri] *n.* win: *their victory over the Scottish team; Wellington's victory at Waterloo.* □ **victoria**
victual ['vitl] *n.* ***victuals,*** (*formal*) food. □ **vituallas**
■ *v.* to supply (a ship/an army) with food. □ **avituallar**
victualler ['vitlə] *n.* *licensed victualler,* innkeeper/person who serves food and drink. □ **proveedor**
video ['vidiou] *adj.* and *n.* (system) which shows pictures on a television screen. □ **vídeo**
videocassette *n.* small cassette containing a videotape. □ **videocasete**
video-recorder *n.* machine which records television pictures on tape, so that they can be played back later. □ **vídeo; magnetoscopio**
videotape *n.* magnetic tape which can record pictures and sound for playing back through a television set. □ **cinta de vídeo**
■ *v.* to record (pictures/film, etc.) on magnetic tape. □ **hacer un vídeo de**
vie [vai] *v.* ***to vie with someone,*** to rival/to try to beat someone. □ **rivalizar con**
view [vju:] *n.* **1** scene (which you can see from a certain place): *the view from my window/from the top of a hill; window with a view over the harbour; front view of a building; this is a side view of our new car.* □ **vista**
2 sight; action of looking at something: *the pictures are on view in the art gallery; range of view,* width of the scene you can see; *you can get a good view of the race from this corner.* □ **vista**

3 opinion: *in my view, the government ought to act; he holds right wing/left wing views; I share your view of the mayor,* I agree with your opinion; *he takes a dim view of people who are late,* he disapproves of them. □ **comparto tu punto de vista...**
point of view, way of looking at things. □ **el punto de vista...**
4 ***in view of,*** when you consider: *in view of the weather, we decided to stay indoors,* because of the weather. □ **en vista de; considerando**
5 *we are taking advice* ***with a view to*** *selling the house,* because we are planning to sell. □ **...con vistas a vender la casa**
6 *what/who do you* ***have in view?,*** what are you planning to do/who are you going to appoint? □ **¿a la vista?**
■ *v.* **1** to look at (something)/to consider: *I don't view the problem in that light,* I don't think about it in that way. □ **ver**
2 to watch television. □ **ver la tele**
the viewing public, people who watch television. □ **los televidentes**
viewer *n.* **1** person who watches television. □ **televidente**
2 small device for looking at colour slides. □ **visionador**
viewfinder *n.* small window in a camera which you look through when taking a picture, and which shows the exact picture you are about to take. □ **visor**
viewpoint *n.* way of looking at things/of considering things: *look at it from the viewpoint of the consumer.* □ **punto de vista**
vigil ['vidʒil] *n.* keeping awake/on guard all night. □ **vigilia**
vigilance *n.* being watchful/on guard. □ **vigilancia**
vigilant *adj.* watchful/on guard. □ **vigilante**
vigilante [vidʒi'lænti] *n.* person who tries to enforce law and order, especially when the police find it impossible to do so: *a group of vigilantes; a vigilante group.* □ **vigilante**
vigour ['vigə] *Amer.* **vigor** *n.* energy. □ **vigor**
vigorous *adj.* energetic/very active; strong. □ **vigoroso**
vigorously *adv.* energetically: *he argued vigorously with the policemen who were trying to arrest him.* □ **vigorosamente**
vile [vail] *adj.* (*viler, vilest*) extremely unpleasant/bad: *he was in a vile temper.* □ **asqueroso; estaba de un humor de perros**
vilify ['vilifai] *v.* (*vilified; vilifying*) to say extremely bad things about (someone). □ **vilipendiar**
vilification [vilifi'keiʃn] *n.* saying bad things about someone (to try to influence people against him): *a campaign of vilification.* □ **vilipendio**
villa ['vilə] *n.* **1** large country (or seaside) house (usually in a warm country like Spain, California, etc.). □ **casa de campo**
2 suburban house. □ **chalé**
village ['vilidʒ] *n.* small group of houses (usually with a church) in the country: *a village shop; the village pub; village school.* □ **pueblo; aldea**
villager *n.* person who lives in a village. □ **vecino; aldeano**
villain ['vilən] *n.* wicked person. □ **malvado**
the villain of the piece, the person who is causing all the trouble. □ **el malo de la película**
villainous *adj.* wicked. □ **malvado**
villainy *n.* wickedness. □ **maldad**
vim [vim] *n.* (*informal*) energy. □ **empuje**
vinaigrette [vinei'gret] *n.* sauce made of oil and vinegar. □ **vinagreta**
vindicate ['vindikeit] *v.* to justify; to show that someone was right: *his theory was vindicated.* □ **justificar**
vindication [vindi'keiʃn] *n.* **1** proving that you were right: *it's a complete vindication of my theory,* it proves that my theory has been right all along. □ **justificación**
2 *in vindication of my theory,* to prove that my theory is right. □ **en defensa de...**
vindictive [vin'diktiv] *adj.* wanting to take revenge; spiteful. □ **vengativo**
vindictively *adv.* spitefully: *he vindictively took away the old lady's television set.* □ **en venganza**
vindictiveness *n.* spite; desire to take revenge. □ **deseo de venganza**
vine [vain] *n.* **1** climbing plant which bears grapes: *to grow a vine up a wall; vine-growing areas of Germany.* □ **vid**
2 climbing plant. □ **parra**
vinegar ['vinigə] *n.* liquid made from sour wine/cider/beer, etc., used in cooking and for preserving food: *onions pickled in vinegar.* □ **vinagre**
vinegary *adj.* (wine, etc.) tasting like vinegar; bad-tempered (person). □ **avinagrado**
vineyard ['vinjəd] *n.* field of vines for producing wine: *the vineyards of France.* □ **viña; viñedo**
vino ['vi:nou] *n.* (*slang*) cheap wine. □ **vino peleón**
vintage ['vintidʒ] *n.* **1** collecting of grapes to make wine; grapes which are collected. □ **vendimia**
2 fine wine made in a particular year: *this is a bottle of the 1973 vintage.* □ **cosecha**
vintage wine/vintage port, fine/expensive old wine/port. □ **vino/oporto de crianza**
3 year of make: *what vintage is your car?* □ **año**
a vintage car, one made between 1917 and 1930. □ **coche de época**
4 high quality: *a vintage year for American films; a vintage Marx Brothers film.* □ **una temporada excelente...; un filme clásico...**
vinyl ['vainl] *n.* type of plastic sheet which looks like leather/tiles etc.: *vinyl shoes; vinyl wallpaper.* □ **vinilo**
viola [vai'oulə] *n.* **1** small pansy-like garden flower. □ **violeta**
2 stringed instrument slightly larger than a violin. □ **viola**
violate ['vaiəleit] *v.* **1** to break/to go against (the law/a treaty): *to violate human rights.* □ **violar**
2 (*formal*) to rape. □ **violar**
violation [vaiə'leiʃn] *n.* act of violating: *to act in violation of an internatioal agreement,* against the terms of the agreement. □ **violación**
violence ['vaiələns] *n.* **1** force/strength: *the violence of his anger/of the waves.* □ **violencia**
2 rough action: *robbery with violence; they committed acts of violence.* □ **violencia**
violent *adj.* **1** strong: *violent storm; violent burst of anger.* □ **violento**
2 rough: *he died a violent death; a violent game of Rugby.* □ **violento**
violently *adv.* strongly; roughly. □ **violentamente**
violet ['vaiələt] *n.* and *adj.* **1** small wild plant with bluish purple flowers. □ **violeta**
2 bluish purple (colour): *he was wearing violet socks.* □ **violeta**
violin [vaiə'lin] *n.* stringed musical instrument played with a bow. □ **violín**
violinist *n.* person who plays the violin. □ **violinista**

violoncello [vaiəlin'tʃelou] *n.* (*formal*) cello. □ **violonchelo**
VIP [vi:ai'pi:] *abbreviation for* very important person: *he got VIP treatment,* he was treated as if he was a very important person. □ **VIP**
viper ['vaipə] *n.* adder/poisonous snake. □ **víbora**
viral ['vairəl] *adj.* referring to a virus. □ **vírico**
virgin ['və:dʒin] *n.* **1** person who has never had sexual intercourse. □ **virgen**
2 ***the Virgin*** (***Mary***), the mother of Jesus Christ. □ **la Virgen**
■ *adj.* pure/untouched: *virgin land/forest.* □ **virgen**
virginal *adj.* pure like a virgin. □ **virginal**
virginity [və:'dʒiniti] *n.* being a virgin: *to lose your virginity,* to have sexual intercourse for the first time. □ **virginidad**
virginia creeper [və:'dʒiniə'kri:pə] *n.* common climbing plant which grows on walls, with leaves which turn bright red in autumn. □ **viña loca**
Virgo ['və:gou] *n.* one of the signs of the zodiac, shaped like a girl. □ **Virgo**
virile ['virail] *adj.* manly; masculine. □ **viril**
virility [vir'iliti] *n.* being virile; strength; manliness. □ **virilidad**
virology [vai'rɔlədʒi] *n.* study of viruses. □ **virología**
virtual ['və:tjuəl] *adj.* almost, if not in fact: *he lives in virtual imprisonment; he is the virtual head of the firm.* □ **virtual; prácticamente vive en prisión; verdadero**
virtually *adv.* almost: *there's virtually nothing left in the fridge.* □ **prácticamente**
virtue ['və:tju:] *n.* **1** particular goodness (of someone's character); good quality: *he is a man of many virtues; obedience is a virtue in a soldier.* □ **virtud**
2 special quality: *the main virtue of the scheme is that it is cheap.* □ **virtud**
3 ***by virtue of,*** because of: *by virtue of his position he can spend money as he likes.* □ **en virtud de**
virtuous *adj.* very good/very honest. □ **virtuoso**
virtuously *adv.* in a virtuous way. □ **virtuosamente**
virtuoso [və:tju'ouzou] *n.* (*pl. virtuosos, virtuosi*) person who is skilled in an art, especially who can play a musical instrument extremely well. □ **virtuoso**
virtuosity [və:tju'ɔsiti] *n.* ability to play a musical instrument/sing, etc., extremely well. □ **virtuosismo**
virulence ['virjuləns] *n.* (*of a disease*) great strength (causing great danger). □ **virulencia**
virulent *adj.* very bad (attack of disease); very harsh (attack). □ **virulento**
virus ['vairəs] *n.* (*pl. viruses*) germ which is smaller than bacteria and which causes colds/pneumonia, etc.: *virus pneumonia; virus infection.* □ **virus**
visa ['vi:zə] *n.* special mark on a passport/special paper allowing you to enter a country: *tourist visa; a 30-day visa,* visa which allows you to stay in a country for 30 days. □ **visado**
vis-à-vis [vizə'vi:] *prep.* **1** in relation to: *what is your opinion vis-à-vis the increase in the cost of living?* □ **respecto a**
2 compared with: *what is our inflation rate vis-à-vis that in the States?* □ **en comparación con**
viscera ['visərə] *n. pl.* organs inside the body, especially the intestines. □ **vísceras**
viscosity [vis'kɔsiti] *n.* state of being viscous. □ **viscosidad**
viscose ['viskouz] *n.* man-made silk material, made from viscous cellulose. □ **viscoso**
viscous ['viskəs] *adj.* thick/sticky (liquid). □ **viscoso**
viscount ['vaikaunt] *n.* title of a nobleman below an earl. □ **vizconde**
vise [vais] *n. Amer.* tool with jaws that screw tight to hold something: *fix the block of wood tight in the vise before you start drilling holes in it; the detective gripped his arm like a vise.* □ **torno de banco**
viselike *adj. Amer.* tight, as in a vise. □ **muy apretado**
visible ['vizibl] *adj.* which can be seen: *there was nothing visible; are there any visible signs of an attack?* □ **visible**
visibility [vizi'biliti] *n.* ability to be seen clearly: *good visibility,* ability for things to be seen at long distances because the air is clear; *poor visibility made landing the aircraft difficult.* □ **visibilidad**
visibly *adv.* obviously; in a way which can be seen: *she was visibly annoyed.* □ **visiblemente**
vision ['viʒn] *n.* **1** ability to see. □ **visión**
field of vision, range from one side to another over which you can see clearly: *the deer moved into my field of vision.* □ **campo visual**
2 ability to look and plan ahead: *a man of vision.* □ **un hombre con mucha vista**
3 something which you imagine: *he has visions of himself as Prime Minister,* he imagines he will be Prime Minister one day. □ **se ve a sí mismo como...**
4 ghost; strange sight. □ **visión**
visionary *adj.* idealistic/impracticable (plan). □ **visionario**
■ *n.* person whose plans are idealistic and may be impracticable. □ **visionario**
visit ['vizit] *n.* short stay in someone's house/in a town/country, etc.: *they are on a visit to Germany; we'll pay a visit to the new supermarket; let's pay your mother a visit.* □ **visita**
■ *v.* to stay a short time (in someone's house/in a town/country etc.): *I must visit my brother who is in hospital; he was taken ill while visiting the factory,* while inspecting the factory. □ **visitar**
visiting hours, times when you can visit patients in hospital. □ **horas de visita**
the visiting team, the opposing team who has come to play on our home ground. □ **el equipo visitante**
visitation [vizi'teiʃn] *n.* **1** trouble which is thought to be sent as a divine punishment. □ **castigo bíblico**
2 official visit: *I've had a visitation from the police.* □ **visita**
visitor ['vizitə] *n.* person who visits: *how many visitors are staying in the hotel at the moment?* □ **visitante**
summer visitor, person/bird which only comes to this country in the summer. □ **turista**
prison visitor, private person who regularly spends time visiting prisoners and talking to them. □ **visitante de prisiones**
visor ['vaizə] *n.* moveable part of a helmet, which drops down to protect the face; folding shield above the windscreen which protects the driver of a car from bright sunshine. □ **visera**
vista ['vistə] *n.* **1** wide view: *a vista over the valley.* □ **vista**
2 *this opens up new vistas for us,* gives us new ideas. □ **...nuevas perspectivas para nosotros**
visual ['vizjuəl] *adj.* referring to what can be seen. □ **visual**
visual arts, painting/sculpture, etc. (as opposed to music). □ **artes visuales**
visual aids, slides/films and apparatus for projecting them on to a screen as part of teaching a subject. □ **medios visuales**
visualize ['vizjuəlaiz] *v.* to picture/to see (something) in your mind: *I find it difficult to visualize*

what the house will look like when it is built. □ **imaginarse**
vital ['vaitl] *adj.* **1** very important: *it's vital that supplies of oil should be kept in reserve; the question is of vital importance.* □ **vital**
2 vigorous/energetic: *he's a very vital person.* □ **vital**
vitally *adv.* in a very important way: *it's vitally important that you should be there.* □ **de vital importancia**
vitality [vai'tæliti] *n.* great energy: *he's full of vitality.* □ **vitalidad**
vital statistics *n.* **1** official statistics concerning populations, births, deaths, etc. □ **estadísticas demográficas**
2 (*informal*) measurements of bust, waist and hips of a woman. □ **medidas**
vitamin ['vitəmin] *n.* chemical substance occurring in food which is important for the development or health of the human body: *Vitamin C is found in orange juice; eggs contain Vitamin D; I take three vitamin tablets every day.* □ **vitamina**
vitaminized ['vitəminaizd] *adj.* with vitamins added: *vitaminized orange juice.* □ **vitaminado**
vitiate ['viʃieit] *v.* to make bad/to make weak. □ **viciar**
vitreous ['vitriəs] *adj.* like glass: *vitreous enamel; vitreous rocks.* □ **vítreo**
vitrify ['vitrifai] *v.* (*vitrified; vitrifying*) to make into glass; to become like glass. □ **vitrificar**
vitriol ['vitriəl] *n.* sulphuric acid. □ **vitriolo**
vitriolic [vitri'ɔlik] *adj.* very violent/very rude (attack). □ **virulento**
vituperation [vitjupə'reiʃn] *n.* (*formal*) abuse; insulting words. □ **vituperación**
vituperative *adj.* (*formal*) insulting/abusive. □ **vituperador**
viva ['vaivə] *n.* oral examination: *he passed in the written exam, but failed the viva.* □ **examen oral**
vivacious [vi'veiʃəs] *adj.* full of life/full of excitement. □ **vivaz**
vivaciousness, vivacity *n.* being vivacious. □ **vivacidad**
vivid ['vivid] *adj.* **1** very bright (light/colour): *a vivid flash; she was wearing a vivid green dress.* □ **intenso, vivo**
2 *he has a vivid imagination,* he imagines things in a lifelike way/he imagines things too much. □ **vivo**
3 *vivid description,* very lifelike description. □ **descripción gráfica**
vividly *adj.* **1** very brightly. □ **vivamente**
2 in a very lifelike way. □ **de modo pintoresco**
vividness *n.* **1** brightness: *the vividness of the sunset.* □ **intensidad**
2 being lifelike: *the vividness of his description.* □ **viveza**
viviparous [vi'vipərəs] *adj.* (animal) which produces live young (that is, which does not lay eggs). □ **vivíparo**
vivisection [vivi'sekʃən] *n.* operating on a live animal for the purpose of scientific research. □ **vivisección**
vixen ['viksn] *n.* female fox. □ **zorra; raposa**
viz. [viz *or* 'neimli] *adv.* namely: *we grow three types of fruit, viz. apples, pears and plums.* □ **verbigracia**
vocabulary [və'kæbjuləri] *n.* (*pl. vocabularies*) **1** words used by a person or group of persons: *he has the vocabulary of a child of eight; to read a newspaper you need a vocabulary of 10,000 words.* □ **vocabulario**
2 printed list of words: *there is a vocabulary of difficult words at the back of the book.* □ **vocabulario**
vocal ['voukl] *adj.* **1** referring to the voice. □ **vocal**
vocal cords, muscles in the throat which produce sounds. □ **cuerdas vocales**
2 *very vocal opposition to the plans,* very loud/insistent opposition. □ **oposición ruidosa...**
■ *n. pl.* ***vocals,*** popular songs performed with a group. □ **canciones populares**
vocalist *n.* singer. □ **vocalista**
vocalize *v.* to make a sound with your voice. □ **vocalizar**
vocally *adv.* in a loud way. □ **ruidosamente**
vocation [və'keiʃn] *n.* job which you feel you have been called to do/for which you have a special talent: *he followed his vocation and became a missionary; she's missed her vocation,* she should be in another job for which she is better suited. □ **vocación**
vocational *adj.* referring to a vocation. □ **vocacional**
vocational training, training for a particular job. □ **formación profesional**
vociferate [və'sifəreit] *v.* (*formal*) to shout protests against something. □ **vociferar**
vociferous *adj.* loud/shouting: *vociferous protests.* □ **vocinglero; protestas ruidosas**
vociferously *adv.* loudly: *they protested vociferously.* □ **a gritos**
vodka ['vɔdkə] *n.* Russian or Polish alcoholic drink made from grain. □ **vodka**
vogue [voug] *n.* fashion; popularity: *the vogue for floppy hats; short skirts are in vogue again; there was a vogue for bright red cars, but it seems to have passed.* □ **moda**
voice [vɔis] *n.* **1** sounds made by a person speaking or singing: *I couldn't recognize your voice over the phone; she's lost her voice,* she can't speak (because of a cold); *she spoke for a few minutes in a low voice,* quietly; *don't raise your voice,* don't talk so loud. □ **voz**
2 opinion: *the voice of the people.* □ **voz del pueblo**
3 ***active voice/passive voice,*** forms of a verb which show whether the subject is doing something or having something done to him (such as *'he hit the ball'* and *'he was hit by the ball'*). □ **voz activa/pasiva**
■ *v.* to express (an opinion). □ **expresar; hacerse eco de**
voiceless *adj.* silent; with no voice. □ **mudo, sin voz**
void [vɔid] *adj.* **1** empty: *the moon is apparently void of life.* □ **vacío**
2 *the contract is* ***null and void,*** is not valid. □ **nulo; sin fuerza legal**
■ *n.* emptiness: *the earth is spinning in a black void.* □ **vacío**
■ *v.* to empty. □ **vaciar**
volatile ['vɔlətail] *adj.* **1** (liquid) which can easily change into vapour. □ **volátil**
2 (person) who changes his mind/his mood frequently. □ **volátil**
vol-au-vent [vɔlou'vɔn] *n.* small pastry case with savoury mixture inside: *mushroom vol-au-vents.* □ **'vol-au-vent'**
volcano [vɔl'keinou] *n.* (*pl. volcanoes*) mountain with an opening on the top through which lava, ash and gas can come: *the volcano is erupting.* □ **volcán**
an extinct volcano, one which no longer erupts. □ **un volcán apagado**
volcanic [vɔl'kænik] *adj.* referring to volcanoes: *volcanic ash.* □ **volcánico**
volcanic rocks, rocks which originally came from lava. □ **rocas volcánicas**

vole [voul] *n.* small animal, resembling a rat or mouse. □ **ratón de campo**
volition [və'liʃn] *n.* (*formal*) **1** wish/will. □ **volición**
2 *he did it **of his own volition,*** he did it because he wanted to and not because he was told to do it. □ **...por voluntad propia**
volley ['vɔli] *n.* **1** series of shots/missiles which are fired/thrown at the same time: *the speaker was greeted with a volley of rotten eggs/of jeers.* □ **descarga; salva**
2 (*in tennis*) hitting the ball before it touches the ground. □ **volea**
■ *v.* **1** to fire several shots/throw several missiles at the same time. □ **lanzar una descarga**
2 (*in tennis*) to hit the ball before it touches the ground. □ **volear**
volleyball *n.* team game in which a large ball is thrown across a high net, and must not touch the ground. □ **balonvolea**
volt [vɔlt] *n.* standard unit of electric potential: *a two-volt battery.* □ **voltio**
voltage *n.* amount of electric force: *high-voltage cable.* □ **voltaje**
volte face ['vɔlt'fæs] *n.* sudden unexpected change of opinion. □ **cambio súbito de opinión**
voluble ['vɔljubl] *n.* (person) who speaks easily with a lot of words. □ **locuaz**
volubility [vɔlju'biliti] *n.* use of a lot of words. □ **locuacidad**
volubly *adj.* with a lot of words. □ **de modo locuaz**
volume ['vɔlju:m] *n.* **1** book (especially one book of a series): *volume 3 of the encyclopaedia.* □ **volumen**
2 space taken up by something: *how do you calculate the volume of a cube? what is the volume of this reservoir?* □ **volumen**
3 amount: *we don't do a large volume of business.* □ **volumen**
4 loudness: *turn down the volume of the radio, I want to make a phone call.* □ **volumen**
voluminous [və'lju:minəs] *adj.* large; taking up a lot of space: *a voluminous report on the country's economic situation.* □ **voluminoso**
volunteer [vɔlən'tiə] *n.* **1** person who offers to do something without being told to do it: *I want three men to cross that river - any volunteers?* □ **voluntario**
2 soldier who has joined the army of his own free will. □ **voluntario**
■ *v.* **1** to offer to do something; to join the armed services of your own free will: *she volunteered for the job of looking after the baby; he volunteered for the army.* □ **ofrecerse (voluntario)**
2 *to volunteer information,* to give information without being forced. □ **ofrecer voluntariamente**
voluntary ['vɔləntri] *adj.* **1** done of your own free will: *he made a voluntary confession to the police.* □ **voluntario**
2 done for no payment: *voluntary service.* □ **servicio voluntario**
voluntary organization, charity/organization which is organized by voluntary help and not subsidized by the government. □ **organización de voluntarios**
■ *n.* ***organ voluntary,*** solo piece of music played on the organ during or at the beginning or end of a church service. □ **solo de órgano**
voluntarily *adv.* freely: *he voluntarily confessed to the crime.* □ **voluntariamente**
voluptuous [və'lʌptjuəs] *adj.* absorbed in/evoking sensual pleasure. □ **voluptuoso**
vomit ['vɔmit] *n.* food brought up through the mouth when you are sick. □ **vómito**
■ *v.* to bring up food through your mouth when you are sick. □ **vomitar**
voodoo ['vu:du:] *n.* witchcraft practised in the West Indies. □ **vudú**
voracious [və'reiʃəs] *adj.* **1** greedy; wanting to eat a lot: *voracious appetite.* □ **voraz**
2 ***voracious reader,*** person who reads a lot. □ **lector voraz**
voraciousness, voracity [vɔ'ræsiti] *n.* being voracious. □ **voracidad**
vortex ['vɔ:teks] *n.* (*pl. vortices*) matter which is turning round and round very fast. □ **vórtice**
votary ['voutri] *n.* (*pl. votaries*) (*formal*) person who worships/who admires something fervently: *a votary of physical fitness.* □ **devoto**
vote [vout] *n.* **1** expressing your opinion by marking a paper/by holding up your hand/by speaking: *my vote goes to the suggestion made by Mr Smith; he cast his vote in favour of Mr Smith's proposal.* □ **voto**
2 action of voting: *if we can't agree, the various proposals must be put to the vote; the opposition proposed a vote of censure on the government,* a vote criticizing the government; *the vote went against the government.* □ **votación**
3 right to vote in an election/to vote on a proposal: *only members of the club have a vote; anyone over the age of 18 has the vote.* □ **derecho de voto**
■ *v.* **1** to express an opinion by marking a paper/by holding up your hand/by speaking: *this area votes solidly for the socialist party; I vote that we hold the picnic next Sunday; did you vote for Mr Smith?* □ **votar**
2 *he was voted on to the committee,* he was elected a member of the committee; *he was voted off the committee,* he was not re-elected a member of the committee. □ **elegir/no elegir**
voter *n.* person who votes/who has the right to vote. □ **votante**
floating voter, person who has not decided which party to vote for in an election. □ **votante indeciso**
votive ['voutiv] *adj.* (offering) given to fulfil a promise made to a god or to a saint. □ **votivo**
vouch [vautʃ] *v.* ***to vouch for something,*** to guarantee something: *I can vouch for his honesty; we will vouch for the truth of the newspaper report.* □ **atestiguar**
voucher *n.* paper which guarantees payment. □ **documento justificativo**
gift voucher, ticket bought from a shop, which you give as a present, and which can be used to buy articles in the shop. □ **cheque-regalo**
luncheon voucher, ticket (given by your employer) which can be exchanged for food in a restaurant. □ **vale de comida**
vouchsafe [vautʃ'seif] *v.* (*formal*) to ensure/to guarantee (that someone has the right to do something). □ **otorgar**
vow [vau] *n.* solemn promise (especially one sworn to God): *he made a vow to give up smoking.* □ **promesa**
■ *v.* to make a solemn promise: *she vowed she would never lose her temper; he vowed revenge,* he swore he would have his revenge. □ **prometer; jurar**
vowel ['vauəl] *n.* sound made without using the teeth, tongue or lips; one of five letters (a, e, i, o, u) which represent these sounds. □ **vocal**
vowel sound, sound made in this way. □ **sonido vocálico**
voyage ['vɔiidʒ] *n.* long journey (especially by sea): *a voyage to Australia; a voyage of discovery.*

□ **viaje por mar**
■ *v.* to make a long journey (by sea). □ **viajar por mar**
voyager *n.* person who makes a long journey by sea. □ **viajero**
vulcanize ['vʌlkənaiz] *v.* to treat rubber with sulphur so that it is made stronger, harder and more elastic. □ **vulcanizar**
vulcanization *n.* process of vulcanizing. □ **vulcanización**
vulcanology [vʌlkə'nɔlədʒi] *n.* study of volcanoes. □ **vulcanología**
vulgar ['vʌlgə] *adj.* **1** rude/indecent: *vulgar words; he's very vulgar when he loses his temper.* □ **vulgar**
2 not in good taste: *vulgar ostentation.* □ **de mal gusto**
3 ***vulgar fraction,*** fraction written as one number above and another below a line (such as 3/4). □ **fracción común**
vulgarization *n.* making common/popular. □ **vulgarización**
vulgarly *adv.* in a rude/indecent way. □ **vulgarmente**
vulgarity [vʌl'gæriti] *n.* rudeness; lack of good taste. □ **vulgaridad**
vulnerable ['vʌlnərəbl] *adj.* which can be easily attacked/easily hurt: *he is in a very vulnerable position.* □ **vulnerable**
vulnerability [vʌlnərə'biliti] *n.* being vulnerable. □ **vulnerabilidad**
vulture ['vʌltʃə] *n.* large tropical bird that eats mainly dead flesh. □ **buitre**
vulva ['vʌlvə] *n.* part of female body around the opening of the vagina. □ **vulva**

W,w

W, w ['dʌblju:] twenty-third letter of the alphabet. □ **W, w**
wad [wɔd] *n.* **1** thick piece of soft material: *wads of cotton wool were packed around the cups to stop them from breaking.* □ **bola de algodón**
2 thick pile of banknotes/papers. □ **fajo (billetes); lío de papeles**
3 (*informal*) thick sandwich. □ **'sandwich' gigante**
■ *v.* (*he wadded*) to stuff/to press into a wad. □ **rellenar**
wadding *n.* thick, soft material used for lining a coat/quilting/stuffing. □ **relleno**
waddle ['wɔdl] *v.* to walk swaying from side to side like a duck. □ **andar como un pato**
wade [weid] *v.* **1** to walk through deep water or mud: *the horses easily waded across the river.* □ **vadear**
2 ***to wade through*** *a book,* to find a book difficult to read. □ **leer con dificultad**
3 ***to wade into*** *a pile of work,* to start dealing with a pile of work vigorously. □ **ponerse a trabajar con ganas**
wader *n.* **1** bird which spends most of its time in shallow water or mud. □ **ave zancuda**
2 ***waders,*** long waterproof boots worn by fishermen. □ **botas altas de goma**
wafer ['weifə] *n.* **1** thin sweet biscuit eaten with ice cream. □ **barquillo**
2 thin disc of bread eaten at communion or mass in Church. □ **hostia**
waffle ['wɔfl] *n.* **1** type of crisp cake cooked in an iron mould and eaten with syrup. □ **tipo de barquillo**
2 unnecessary or muddled speaking/writing. □ **perorata**
■ *v.* to talk too much without saying anything clearly: *what is he waffling on about?* □ **perorar**
waffle-iron *n.* iron mould used for making waffles. □ **molde**
waft [wɔft] *n.* gentle smell. □ **olorcillo**
■ *v.* to carry (something) gently through the air: *the wind wafted the perfume of roses in through the windows.* □ **llevar**
wag [wæg] *n.* **1** movement from side to side or up and down: *the dog knocked over the vase with one wag of its tail.* □ **meneo**
2 *he's a bit of a wag,* (*informal*) he likes making jokes/facetious remarks. □ **es un poco bromista**
■ *v.* (*he wagged*) **1** to move from side to side or up and down: *the dog was wagging its tail.* □ **menear**
2 *that'll* ***set*** *people's* ***tongues wagging,*** that will give them something to talk about to their friends. □ **eso les dará que hablar**
wage [weidʒ] *n.* (*also* ***wages***) weekly payment given for work done: *he earns a good wage at the steel works.* □ **salario**
wage freeze, period of standstill in wages. □ **congelación de los salarios**
■ *v.* ***to wage war,*** to fight a war: *the police are waging a war on crime.* □ **librar una batalla**
wage-earner *n.* person who works for wages. □ **asalariado**
wager ['weidʒə] *n.* bet/money which you promise to pay if something you expect to happen does not take place. □ **apuesta**
■ *v.* to bet. □ **apostar**
waggle ['wægl] *v.* to move from side to side: *my front tooth is loose, I can waggle it easily.* □ **menear**
wagon, waggon ['wægn] *n.* **1** four-wheeled vehicle pulled by horses and used for carrying heavy loads. □ **carreta; carro**
2 railway truck: *goods wagon.* □ **furgón**
3 ***to be on the wagon,*** (*informal*) to drink only non-alcoholic drinks. □ **no beber**
wag(g)oner *n.* person who drives a wagon. □ **carretero**
wagtail ['wægteil] *n.* small bird which wags its tail up and down as it walks. □ **aguzanieves**
waif [weif] *n.* homeless child or animal. □ **niño/ animal abandonado**
waifs and strays, homeless abandoned children or animals. □ **niños/animales abandonados**
wail [weil] *n.* high-pitched sad cry: *the wail of the police sirens.* □ **lamento**
■ *v.* to make a high-pitched mournful cry: *the sirens wailed to warn people that a prisoner had escaped.* □ **lamentarse; las sirenas sonaron...**
wainscot ['weinzkət] *n.* wood panelling covering the lower part of a wall in a house. □ **zócalo**
waist [weist] *n.* narrow part of the body between the chest and the hips: *my daughter has a very slim waist.* □ **cintura**
waistcoat ['weiskout] *n.* short close-fitting sleeveless garment which goes over a shirt and under a jacket. □ **chaleco**
waistline *n.* **1** measurement around the waist. □ **talle**
2 *I can't eat cream cakes as I'm watching my waistline,* I am trying to slim. □ **cuidar la línea**
wait [weit] *n.* act of staying until something happens or someone arrives: *we had a long wait for the next train.* □ **espera**
to lie in wait, to hide waiting for someone to pass by in order to attack him. □ **acechar**
■ *v.* **1** to stay somewhere until something happens or someone/something arrives: *we're waiting for the bus; don't keep your father waiting! wait and see, you'll know the answer tomorrow.* □ **esperar**
to wait up: *when I'm late home my mother always waits up for me,* she doesn't go to bed until I'm home. □ **...se queda levantada hasta...**
2 ***to wait on someone,*** to serve food to someone at table. □ **servir**
waiter *n.* man who serves food to people in a restaurant. □ **camarero**
head waiter, person in charge of all the other waiters. □ **jefe de camareros**
dumb waiter, (i) small table (usually with wheels) for keeping food on. □ **carrito**
(ii) lift for carrying food from one floor to another. □ **montaplatos**
waiting *n.* act of staying until something happens or someone arrives. □ **espera**
no waiting, cars are not allowed to stop here. □ **prohibido detenerse**
waiting-room, room where travellers wait for their trains/buses, etc./where patients wait to see a doctor, etc.. □ **sala de espera**
waiting list, list of people waiting to see someone or do something: *there is a long waiting list for new houses.* □ **lista de espera**

waitress *n.* woman who serves food to people in a restaurant. □ **camarera**
waive [weiv] *v.* to give up (a right/a claim): *the king waived his right to three deer from the forest each year.* □ **renunciar a**
waiver *n.* giving up (of a right/claim). □ **renuncia**
wake [weik] *n.* **1** waves left by a boat, etc., moving through water: *our canoe was caught in the wake of the ferry boat.* □ **estela**
in the wake of someone/something, immediately behind: *relief workers arrived in the wake of the earthquake.* □ **inmediatamente después de**
2 staying up all night with a dead body before the funeral. □ **velatorio**
■ *v.* (*he woke; he has woken*) to stop (someone) sleeping; to stop sleeping: *my alarm clock usually wakes me, but today I woke before it started to ring.* □ **despertar(se)**
wakeful *adj.* **1** not at all sleepy/not able to go to sleep. □ **despierto**
2 *I had several wakeful nights,* nights when I couldn't sleep properly. □ **...noches en blanco**
waken *v.* to stop (someone) sleeping: *go and waken John now! I wakened early this morning.* □ **despertar(se)**
wakes *n. pl.* holiday for industrial workers in the North of England. □ **fiesta anual**
wake up *v.* **1** to stop sleeping: *I woke up at 6 o'clock.* □ **despertarse**
2 ***to wake up to something,*** to realize: *he's just woken up to the fact that we owe him money.* □ **darse cuenta**
waking *adj.* not asleep: *during his waking hours,* when he was not asleep. □ **...horas en que uno está despierto**
Wales [weilz] *n.* country which is part of Great Britain and lies to the west of England. □ **Gales; el País de Gales**
walk [wɔːk] *n.* **1** journey on foot: *we are going for a walk after dinner; the castle is about an hour's walk from here; will you take the dog for a walk now?* □ **paseo**
2 way of walking: *I recognized him by his walk.* □ **manera de andar**
3 wide path in a park or garden. □ **paseo**
4 ***walk of life,*** social position or occupation: *people from all walks of life spend their holidays here.* □ **posición/condición social**
■ *v.* **1** to move along on the feet at a normal speed: *I'll walk to the bus stop with you; can your baby walk yet?* □ **andar**
2 to accompany (someone/an animal) on foot: *he's gone out to walk the dog; I'll walk you to the bus stop.* □ **pasear a (perro); acompañar a (persona)**
walkabout *n.* walk among a crowd by an important person. □ **recorrido**
walker *n.* person who walks, or who is fond of walking: *the mountains in summer are ideal for walkers.* □ **paseante**
walkie-talkie *n.* portable two-way radio-telephone. □ **transmisor-receptor portátil**
walk in *v.* to enter: *please walk in!* □ **entrar**
walking *n.* act of walking: *I like walking.* □ **andar**
■ *adj.* (article) used when walking: *walking stick; walking shoes.* □ **bastón; zapatos (para andar)**
walk into *v.* **1** to enter: *he walked into the museum.* □ **entrar**
2 to hit by accident: *I turned round and walked straight into the door.* □ **tropezar con**
walk off *v.* **1** to go away: *she walked off angrily.* □ **marcharse**
2 *she walked off with all the prizes,* she won all the prizes. □ **se llevó todos...**
3 *the thief walked off with all the silver,* stole the silver. □ **el ladrón se llevó...**
4 *to walk off your dinner,* to go for a walk after a big dinner to help you digest it. □ **bajar la comida dando un paseo**
walk on *v.* **1** to continue walking. □ **seguir andando**
2 to have a non-speaking part in a play. □ **hacer de comparsa**
walk-on *adj.* (part) in a play where the actor doesn't have to speak. □ **de comparsa**
walk out *v.* **1** to go out of somewhere. □ **salir**
2 to leave angrily. □ **marcharse enfadado**
3 to go on strike: *when the shop steward was dismissed the entire workforce walked out.* □ **declararse en huelga**
4 ***to walk out on someone,*** to leave someone suddenly. □ **dar plantón**
walkout *n.* strike of workers. □ **huelga**
walk over *v.* **1** to walk across: *he walked over the hills to the next town.* □ **ir por**
2 ***to walk over to someone,*** to cross (a room) to see someone/to go up to someone. □ **pasar a ver**
walkover *n.* (*informal*) easy victory: *in the election it was a walkover for our candidate.* □ **paseo militar**
walk up *v.* **1** to climb (on foot): *we walked up the hill to the castle.* □ **subir a pie**
2 ***to walk up (to someone),*** to approach/to go to speak (to someone). □ **acercarse a uno**
walkway *n.* passage/path where you can walk. □ **camino**
wall [wɔːl] *n.* **1** structure of brick/stone, etc., forming the side of a room/building, or the boundary of a piece of land: *James is building a brick wall at the bottom of the garden; on the lounge walls were dozens of paintings.* □ **pared (en casa); tapia/muro (fuera de casa)**
wall clock, clock fixed to a wall. □ **reloj de pared**
wall painting, mural/large painting on a wall. □ **pintura mural**
2 ***to go to the wall,*** to be defeated. □ **fracasar**
3 *he sends me* ***up the wall,*** (*informal*) he makes me furious. □ **me pone furioso**
walled *adj.* with walls: *a walled garden.* □ **tapiado**
wallflower *n.* **1** garden flower with a sweet scent. □ **alhelí**
2 (*at a dance*) (*informal*) woman who is not asked to dance and is left sitting alone. □ **no comerse una rosca (bailando)**
wall in *v.* to surround with walls: *I like open air – I don't like the feeling of being walled in.* □ **tapiar**
wallpaper *n.* decorative paper which is stuck on the walls of a room. □ **papel pintado**
■ *v.* to stick paper on the walls (of a room). □ **empapelar**
wall-to-wall *adj.* (carpet) which covers all the floor space of a room. □ **moqueta**
wall up *v.* to close/to block with a wall: *the old doorway was walled up.* □ **tabicar**
wallaby ['wɔləbi] *n.* (*pl. wallabies*) Australian animal like a small kangaroo. □ **ualabí**
wallet ['wɔlit] *n.* small leather case used for holding banknotes in a pocket. □ **cartera**
wallop ['wɔləp] *n.* (*informal*) **1** hard blow: *she slipped and fell with a wallop.* □ **golpazo**
2 beer. □ **cerveza**
■ *v.* (*informal*) to hit hard: *his father walloped him when he came home late.* □ **pegar una tunda**
walloping *adj.* (*informal*) huge: *a walloping great elephant came towards us.* □ **enorme**
wallow ['wɔlou] *n.* mud hollow where animals can

roll. □ **revolcadero**
■ *v.* **1** (*of animals*) to roll delightedly around in mud. □ **revolcarse**
2 to take too much pleasure in: *to wallow in emotion; to wallow in tears.* □ **rebosar de alegría; nadar en lágrimas**

walnut ['wɔlnʌt] *n.* **1** hard round nut with a wrinkled shell. □ **nuez**
2 tree on which walnuts grow. □ **nogal**
3 wood from a walnut tree, often used in making furniture. □ **nogal**

walrus ['wɔlrʌs] *n.* (*pl. walruses*) Arctic animal like a large seal with two long tusks pointing downwards. □ **morsa**
walrus moustache, moustache whose long ends point downwards. □ **bigote caído**

waltz [wɔls] *n.* (*pl. waltzes*) **1** dance in which a man and woman turn around together as they move forwards. □ **vals**
2 music suitable for such a dance. □ **vals**
■ *v.* **1** to dance together. □ **bailar el vals**
2 (*informal*) to walk smoothly/happily: *she came waltzing in with a bunch of flowers.* □ **ir/venir dando saltos (de alegría)**

wan [wɔn] *adj.* pale/looking ill: *she is feeling better but her face still looks pale and wan; a wan light glimmered in the distance.* □ **macilento**

wand [wɔnd] *n.* slim stick carried by magicians or fairies: *the fairy waved her wand and the apple turned to gold.* □ **varita**

wander ['wɔndə] *v.* **1** to walk about with no special purpose or direction: *let's wander around the old town this morning.* □ **vagar por**
2 ***to wander off,*** to walk away from the correct path: *keep to the footpath and don't wander off on your own!* □ **salirse de**
3 to go away from the subject when talking: *her mind was on other things and she kept wandering from the subject of the lesson.* □ **salirse del tema**
4 *his mind is wandering,* he is not following the subject because of illness or old age. □ **está fallando, perdida**
wanderer *n.* person who wanders. □ **vagabundo; hombre errante**
wanderlust *n.* passion for going off on journeys and adventures: *we can't keep our dog at home, he's got the wanderlust.* □ **pasión por escaparse**

wane [wein] *n.* **1** *the moon is* ***on the wane,*** appears to be getting smaller. □ **menguante**
2 *his influence is* ***on the wane,*** is diminishing. □ **está menguando su...**
■ *v.* to appear smaller/to decrease: *the moon is waning; the power of the emperor is waning.* □ **menguar**

wangle ['wæŋgl] *n.* (*informal*) trick/something dishonestly obtained: *the whole thing is a wangle.* □ **chanchullo**
■ *v.* (*informal*) to get (something) by a trick: *he wangled a week's holiday out of the boss.* □ **agenciarse**
wangler *n.* (*informal*) person who gets things by a trick. □ **chanchullero**

want [wɔnt] *n.* **1** state of being without: *for want of something better,* as something better is not available; *he died for want of the right medicine,* because he did not have the right medicine; *for want of a better name,* because I can't think of a better way to describe it. □ **falta**
2 desire/wish: *a long-felt want to see the world.* □ **deseo**
■ *v.* **1** to wish/to desire/to long for: *he wants a bicycle for his birthday; how much do you want for your car?,* how much money are you asking for as a price? □ **querer**
2 to need/to require: *we haven't enough space – we want a bigger house; your hair wants cutting; this work wants plenty of patience.* □ **necesitar**
3 to look for (someone) to ask him questions: *he is wanted by the police in connection with the murder.* □ **requerir**
wanted *adj.* **1** desired/needed: *I've brought the wanted papers with me.* □ **anhelado**
2 searched for by the police, usually because of a crime: *he can't return to France because he's a wanted man.* □ **buscado**
wanting *adj.* **1** needing. □ **necesitado**
2 having very little of something: *he is a little wanting in intelligence.* □ **falto de**

wanton ['wɔntn] *adj.* wild/undisciplined: *after the battle the wanton destruction of the town began.* □ **desenfrenado**

war [wɔː] *n.* **1** fighting carried on between two or more nations: *in 1814 Britain was at war with France/Britain and France were at war; millions died in the war in Vietnam; World War Two started in 1939.* □ **guerra**
civil war, war between two parties in one country. □ **guerra civil**
he's been in the wars, (*informal*) he looks as though he has had a fight. □ **como si viniera de la guerra**
2 fight/battle: *war against crime; war against poverty.* □ **guerra**
war of words, bitter argument (usually between countries). □ **guerra de palabras**
war-cry *n.* loud shouts given when going into battle. □ **grito de guerra**
war-dance *n.* dance before the start of a battle. □ **danza guerrera**
warfare *n.* fighting a war; type of war: *chemical warfare; jungle warfare.* □ **guerra**
warhead *n.* top of a missile which is full of explosives: *nuclear warhead.* □ **cabeza nuclear**
warhorse *n.* **1** heavy, strong horse formerly used for carrying soldiers into battle. □ **caballo de guerra**
2 old soldier/politician who has seen many battles. □ **veterano**
warlike *adj.* for war; like war. □ **belicoso; guerrero**
warmonger *n.* person who wants to start a war. □ **belicista**
warpaint *n.* bright colour put on the face and body before battle to make the enemy afraid. □ **pinturas de guerra**
warpath *n.* ***to be on the warpath,*** (*informal*) to be angry and looking for a fight. □ **estar buscando pelea**
warring *adj.* at war: *warring nations.* □ **en guerra**
warship *n.* armed fighting ship. □ **buque de guerra**
wartime *n.* time when there is a war: *you can't expect to buy luxuries in wartime.* □ **tiempo de guerra**

warble ['wɔːbl] *n.* trembling song (of a bird). □ **trino**
■ *v.* to sing with a trembling note: *a thrush is warbling in the apple tree.* □ **trinar**
warbler *n.* type of bird which sings with a trembling note. □ **curruca**

ward [wɔːd] *n.* **1** young person in the care of someone other than his parents: *on his father's death he became the ward of his aunt.* □ **pupilo**
ward of court, child who is under the protection of the court. □ **persona bajo la protección del tribunal**
2 large room in a hospital with many beds: *emergency ward; surgical ward; children's ward.* □ **sala**
3 part of a town for election purposes: *Mr Brown is the councillor for the Northern Ward of the town.*

□ **distrito**
■ *v. **to ward off,*** to keep away: *I take whisky to ward off colds.* □ **prevenir**
warden *n.* **1** person in charge of an institution/old people's home/students' hostel, etc. □ **director (institución); portero**
2 person who looks after a park or forest. □ **guarda**
traffic warden, person who controls the parking of cars, etc., in a town. □ **guardia de tráfico**
warder, wardress *n.* prison officer/person who guards prisoners. □ **celador**
wardrobe ['wɔːdroub] *n.* **1** large cupboard in which clothes may be hung up. □ **armario**
2 a person's clothes: *she has a magnificent wardrobe of 200 dresses.* □ **vestuario**
3 costumes in a theatre. □ **vestuario**
wardrobe mistress, woman in charge of the costumes in a theatre. □ **guardarropa**
wardroom [wɔːdrum] *n.* general living-room of officers on a warship. □ **cámara de oficiales**
ware ['wɛə] *n.* **1** (*no pl.*) goods made of a certain material (usually pottery). □ **loza**
earthenware, pottery. □ **cerámica**
ovenware, dishes that can go in the oven without breaking. □ **plato termorresistente**
silverware, things made of silver. □ **plata**
2 *pl. **wares,*** things that have been made and are for sale: *merchants spread their wares on the pavement.* □ **artículos**
warehouse ['wɛəhaus] *n.* large building for storing goods. □ **almacén**
■ *v.* to store (goods) in a large building. □ **almacenar**
warehouseman *n.* (*pl. warehousemen*) person who works in a warehouse. □ **almacenero**
warm [wɔːm] *adj.* (*warmer, warmest*) **1** quite hot/pleasantly hot: *it's cold outside but it's nice and warm by the fire; keep warm by jumping up and down; it's warm work chopping wood.* □ **caliente; templado**
2 *you're getting warm,* (*in a game*) you're near the right answer. □ **caliente, caliente**
3 kind and friendly: *the people gave us a warm welcome; she has a warm heart.* □ **...una acogida calurosa; ...corazón afectuoso**
■ *n.* state of being/keeping warm; warm place: *I'm not going out today, I'm staying in the warm; come and have a warm by the fire.* □ **...me quedo al calorcito; ven a calentarte...**
■ *v.* to make hot or hotter: *while you warm yourself by the fire, I'll make some soup.* □ **calentar**
to warm to someone, to feel more and more friendly towards someone. □ **tomarle simpatía a alguien**
warm-blooded *adj.* (*of birds and mammals*) having warm blood. □ **de sangre caliente**
warm-hearted *adj.* friendly and welcoming. □ **afectuoso**
warming pan *n.* metal container in which hot coals were put and which was used to warm beds. □ **calentador (de cama)**
warmly *adv.* in a warm way: *she's warmly dressed; they thanked him warmly for his help.* □ **calurosamente**
warmth *n.* **1** heat/state of being warm: *the baby lay close to its mother for warmth.* □ **calor**
2 enthusiasm: *the warmth of his welcome; the warmth of his greeting.* □ **calor**
warm up *v.* **1** to heat/to make warm again: *to warm up some soup.* □ **calentar/recalentar**
2 to exercise before a game/a contest. □ **calentar**
warn [wɔːn] *v.* **1** to tell of possible danger: *I must warn the children not to go in the forest; we were warned against going into the sea because of sharks.* □ **advertir**
2 *the children were warned off the railway line,* were told not to go near it; *I've been warned off alcohol,* I have been advised not to drink alcohol. □ **advertir**
warning *n.* **1** notice of danger: *the police car sounded its horn as a warning; have you read the warning on the bottle of medicine?* □ **advertencia, aviso**
2 ***without warning,*** suddenly: *without warning he started to take off his clothes; the car drove straight into the road without warning,* without giving any signal. □ **sin previo aviso; sin avisar**
■ *adj.* which tells of danger: *he had pains in the chest which were warning signs that something was wrong.* □ **de aviso**
warp [wɔːp] *n.* **1** twisting out of shape of a piece of wood. □ **alabeo**
2 threads running lengthwise in a length of material. □ **urdimbre**
3 heavy rope used for moving boats along. □ **estacha; espía**
■ *v.* **1** to twist out of shape: *snow and rain have warped the wood; teak is a hard wood which doesn't warp.* □ **alabear**
2 to make (mind/character) evil: *the punishments in this schools must have been invented by someone with a warped mind.* □ **pervertir**
3 (*of boats*) to move by pulling on a rope. □ **espiar; atoar**
warped *adj.* twisted. □ **retorcido**
warrant ['wɔrənt] *n.* **1** written official paper permitting someone to do something: *the police had a warrant to search the house; the company gave me a warrant for payment.* □ **autorización legal; orden**
2 ***warrant officer,*** highest rank in the army for non-commissioned officers. □ **brigada**
■ *v.* **1** to guarantee/to promise: *it won't happen again, I warrant you.* □ **asegurar**
2 to justify/to deserve: *no crime can warrant such a terrible punishment.* □ **justificar**
warranty *n.* guarantee/legal document promising that a machine will work, etc.: *my watch has a 12-month warranty with it.* □ **garantía**
warren ['wɔrn] *n.* piece of land under which hundreds of rabbits have made their homes. □ **conejal**
warrior ['wɔriə] *n.* person who fights in a war. □ **guerrero**
wart [wɔːt] *n.* small, hard, dark lump on the skin. □ **verruga**
warts and all, with all faults shown. □ **con todas sus imperfecciones**
warthog *n.* type of wild African pig. □ **jabalí verrugoso**
wary ['wɛəri] *adj.* (*warier, wariest*) careful/cautious: *it is sometimes better to be wary of strangers.* □ **cauteloso**
warily *adv.* cautiously/looking around all the time. □ **precavidamente**
wariness ['wɛərinəs] *n.* cautiousness/taking care and watching all the time. □ **cautela**
was [wɔz] *v. see* **be.**
wash [wɔʃ] *n.* (*pl. washes*) **1** act of cleaning with water or another liquid: *I must have a quick wash before I go out; I'll put the sheets in the wash tomorrow.* □ **lavado**
2 *it will all **come out in the wash,*** (*informal*) it will all be made clear in due course. □ **todo se arreglará**

3 clothes which are being washed. □ **colada**
4 movement of the sea or water: *you can hear the wash of the waves against the shore.* □ **murmullo**
5 *don't go too near the ship or you'll be caught in its wash,* the waves it leaves behind it. □ **...en su estela**
6 thin mixture of liquid. □ **aguachirle**
colour wash, thin pale mixture of paint and water. □ **mano/capa de color**
mouthwash, antiseptic liquid mixture for cleaning the inside of the mouth. □ **enjuague antiséptico**
■ *v.* **1** to clean with water or another liquid: *wash your hands before dinner! I'll wash the dirty clothes today.* □ **lavar(se)**
2 to be able to be washed: *this material won't wash - it must be dry-cleaned.* □ **ser lavable**
3 (*of water/ sea/lakes/rivers*) to flow past/to touch: *the waves were washing the top of the steps.* □ **bañar**
4 *to be washed overboard,* to be swept off the deck of a ship by a wave. □ **arrebatar**
wash away *v.* to remove by water: *the sea will wash away our footprints.* □ **limpiar**
washable *adj.* able to be washed. □ **lavable**
washbasin *n.* fixed container, with taps, for holding water for washing the hands and face. □ **lavabo**
washbowl *n.* bowl for holding water, but not fixed and with no taps. □ **palangana**
washcloth *n. Amer.* flannel/cloth used for washing yourself. □ **manopla**
washday *n.* day when the clothes are washed. □ **día de la colada**
wash down *v.* **1** to clean with a lot of water: *to wash down the deck of a ship.* □ **lavar; barrer la cubierta**
2 *to wash down the medicine with a drink of water,* to help the medicine go down by means of a drink to follow. □ **tragar**
washdown *n.* quick wash all over: *I'll give the car a washdown before we leave.* □ **(pegar) un lavado**
washer *n.* **1** person who washes. □ **lavador**
2 steel or rubber ring under a bolt or nut; rubber ring inside a tap which prevents water escaping when the tap is turned off. □ **arandela**
3 machine for washing. □ **lavadora**
4 ***windscreen washer,*** attachment on a car which squirts water on to the windscreen so that the glass can be kept clean. □ **lavaparabrisas**
washerwoman *n.* (*pl. washerwomen*) woman who washes clothes for other people. □ **lavandera**
washing *n.* **1** act of cleaning with water. □ **lavado**
2 clothes which are to be washed/which have just been washed: *the washing dried quickly in the wind.* □ **colada**
washing day *n.* day when a great many clothes are washed. □ **día de la colada**
washing machine *n.* machine for washing clothes. □ **lavadora**
washing-up *n.* washing of cups/plates/knives and forks, etc., after a meal. □ **fregado de los platos**
washing-up machine *n.* machine for washing plates/cups/knives and forks, etc., after a meal. □ **lavavajillas**
washing-up bowl *n.* bowl or container in which the plates/cups/knives and forks, etc., are washed after a meal. □ **pila**
washleather *n.* piece of soft leather used for cleaning windows. □ **gamuza**
wash off *v.* to clean away with water: *the mark on the table will wash off with soap and water.* □ **quitarse (con agua y...)**
wash out *v.* **1** to clean/to be cleaned with water: *the ink stain won't wash out; will you wash out a few shirts for me?* □ **la mancha ... no saldrá; ¿me puedes lavar unas camisas?**
2 *I feel completely washed out,* I feel tired and have no energy. □ **estoy agotado**
3 *the game was washed out,* could not be played because of rain. □ **...se tuvo que cancelar por la lluvia**
washout *n.* (*informal*) **1** useless person: *he's a washout.* □ **desastre**
2 something that has failed: *the carnival was a washout as few people came to it.* □ **fracaso**
washroom *n.* room where you can wash your hands and use the toilet. □ **servicios**
washstand *n.* **1** table on which a washbowl and jug of water used to stand in a bedroom. □ **palanganero**
2 *Amer.* fixed bowl, with taps, for holding water for washing the hands and face. □ **lavabo**
wash up *v.* **1** to clean with water the cups/plates/knives and forks, etc., used during a meal. □ **fregar los platos**
2 *Amer.* to wash yourself. □ **lavarse**
3 (*of the sea*) to throw on to the shore: *after the storm lots of pieces of wood were washed up on the beach.* □ **...fueron arrojados a la playa**

wasp [wɔsp] *n.* striped insect, like a bee, which can sting but which does not make honey: *wasps' nest.* □ **avispa**
wasp waist, (woman's) very slim waist. □ **cintura/talle de avispa**
waspish *adj.* irritable/quick-tempered. □ **enojadizo**

waste [weist] *n.* **1** wild/uncultivated land: *the desert wastes.* □ **yermo/baldío**
2 unnecessary use: *waste of time; waste of money.* □ **pérdida de tiempo/dinero**
3 rubbish: *put the waste in the dustbin; radioactive waste.* □ **desperdicios; desechos**
waste pipe, pipe which takes dirty water from a sink to the drains. □ **desagüe**
waste disposal unit, machine attached to a kitchen sink which grinds up and washes away kitchen rubbish. □ **triturador de basuras**
■ *v.* **1** to use more than necessary/to use badly: *I've wasted hours waiting for buses; he wastes his money on cigarettes.* □ **malgastar**
waste not, want not, don't throw anything away, you may need it later. □ **todo vale**
2 to become thin/to lose weight: *my grandfather is wasting away through illness.* □ **quedarse en los huesos**
■ *adj.* **1** (*of land*) uncultivated/not used for any particular purpose: *waste land; waste ground.* □ **erial**
to lay waste, to destroy the crops and houses in an area, especially in time of war. □ **asolar**
2 old and useless. □ **desechado**
waste paper basket, small container where useless papers can be put. □ **papelera**
wastage *n.* **1** loss: *we lose many workers through natural wastage,* many workers leave to go to other jobs or stop working altogether. □ **pérdidas; reconversión**
2 amount lost by waste. □ **lo malgastado**
wasted *adj.* lost by waste. □ **malgastado**
wasteful *adj.* extravagant/which wastes a lot: *it's a wasteful use of electricity to leave the light on all day.* □ **derrochador**
wastefully *adv.* in an extravagant way. □ **con derroche**
waster *n.* **1** person/thing which wastes a lot: *television is a real time-waster.* □ **una pérdida de tiempo**
2 person who is useless and idle. □ **inútil**

wastrel *n.* person who is useless and idle. □ **inútil; perdido**

watch [wɔtʃ] *n.* (*pl. watches*) **1** act of looking at someone/something; observation: *I'm keeping a watch on the saucepan of milk; the soldiers are on the watch for strangers.* □ **observación, vigilancia**
2 group of people who guarded a town or village at night. □ **vigilantes**
3 period of duty for sailors on a ship: *the first watch is from 8 p.m. to midnight.* □ **guardia**
4 small clock worn on the arm or carried in a pocket. □ **reloj**
a digital watch, a watch which shows the time in numbers (10.27) rather than on a circular dial. □ **reloj digital**
■ *v.* **1** to look at/to observe: *did you watch television last night?* □ **observar; ver (la televisión)**
2 to be careful. □ **tener cuidado con**
watch it!, (*informal*) don't do what you're thinking of doing. □ **¡cuidado!**
watch committee *n.* group of people in a town or village who make sure that people and houses are safe at night. □ **comisión de vigilancia**
watchdog *n.* **1** dog which guards a house or other buildings. □ **perro guardián**
2 person/committee which examines public spending/public morals, etc. □ **comisión de seguimiento**
watcher *n.* person who watches/observes: *bird-watcher.* □ **observador**
watchful *adj.* very careful. □ **atento; alerta**
watchfully *adv.* very carefully. □ **vigilantemente**
watching *n.* act of looking/observing: *my hobby is bird-watching,* I like watching birds. □ **observación**
watchmaker *n.* person who makes and mends clocks and watches. □ **relojero**
watchman *n.* (*pl. watchmen*) person who guards a building, usually when it is empty: *night watchman.* □ **vigilante**
watch out *v.* to be careful: *watch out! the road is icy.* □ **tener cuidado**
to watch out for something, to be careful to avoid it. □ **tener cuidado con**
watch tower *n.* tower from the top of which you can see if the enemy is coming. □ **atalaya**
watchword *n.* slogan/password. □ **santo y seña; contraseña**

water ['wɔːtə] *n.* **1** compound of hydrogen and oxygen; liquid that is in rain/rivers/lakes and the sea: *may I have a glass of water? the hotel has hot and cold water in each bedroom.* □ **agua**
drinking water, water that is safe to drink. □ **agua potable**
hot water bottle, rubber or stone bottle filled with hot water and used to warm a bed. □ **bolsa/botella del agua caliente**
by water, on a boat: *coal comes here by water.* □ **en barco**
to be under water, to be covered by water: *our garden was under water for a month last winter.* □ **estar inundado**
2 *to have water laid on to a house,* to have pipes put from the main water supply to the house. □ **meter el agua**
3 *high water/low water,* highest/lowest point that the sea or river reaches each day. □ **marea alta/baja**
to keep your head above water, (i) to swim with your head out of the water. □ **mantener la cabeza fuera del agua**
(ii) to be able to keep out of difficulties: *we have too much work, but so far we're keeping our heads above water.* □ **ir apañándose**
4 ***to pass water,*** to urinate. □ **orinar**
5 ***waters,*** large amount of water in a lake/sea: *the still waters of the lake.* □ **aguas**
to take the waters, to drink the mineral water which springs out of the ground in certain places. □ **tomar las aguas**
6 ***water on the brain,*** (*informal*) illness where liquid forms on the brain, causing mental deficiency. □ **hidrocefalia**
7 mixture of water with other substances: *soda water; toilet water.* □ **agua de soda**
8 (*of diamonds/precious stones*) brilliance. □ **aguas**
of the first water, of the finest quality. □ **de primera categoría**
■ *v.* **1** to give water to: *I shall water the plants tonight; the farmer watered his horse at the river.* □ **regar (plantas); abrevar (caballo)**
2 to add water to (wine or spirits). □ **aguar**
3 (*of eyes/mouth*) to fill with water: *smoke makes my eyes water.* □ **llorar**
4 (*of boats*) to take in supplies of drinking water. □ **abastecer de agua**
water biscuit *n.* thin hard biscuit eaten with cheese. □ **galleta**
water-boatman *n.* insect which skims across the surface of lakes/rivers, etc. □ **garapito; chinche de agua**
waterbrash *n.* bitter liquid which comes up from the stomach into the mouth. □ **acidez**
water cannon *n.* machine for sending strong jets of water (for dispersing rioters, etc.). □ **cañón de agua**
water closet *n.* (*formal*) lavatory/bowl which you sit on to pass the waste substances from the body, which are then washed by water down a pipe and away from the building. □ **'wáter'**
watercolour *n.* **1** paint used by artists which is mixed with water, not oil. □ **acuarela**
2 picture painted in watercolours. □ **acuarela**
watercourse *n.* path of a stream/river. □ **cauce**
watercress *n.* creeping plant grown in water and eaten in salads. □ **berro**
watered silk *n.* silk with wavy markings in it. □ **seda tornasolada**
waterfall *n.* fall of a river, etc., from a high level over the edge of a cliff. □ **catarata**
waterfowl *n. pl.* birds which like to live around ponds and lakes (such as ducks/geese, etc.). □ **aves acuáticas**
waterfront *n.* bank of a river/shore of the sea and the buildings along it. □ **orilla**
water ice *n.* type of light ice cream made of water and flavouring. □ **sorbete**
watering *n.* **1** act of giving water to something. □ **riego**
2 ***watering down,*** dilution (of wine or spirits) by adding water. □ **aguado**
3 filling of the eyes with water. □ **ojos llorosos**
watering-can *n.* container with a long spout used for giving water to plants, etc. □ **regadera**
waterless *adj.* without water. □ **sin agua**
waterlevel *n.* level of water: *the waterlevel in the reservoir is getting low.* □ **nivel de agua**
waterline *n.* line where the water reaches on the hull of a ship: *the shell hit the ship below the waterline.* □ **línea de flotación**
waterlogged *adj.* very wet/full of water: *the field is waterlogged so the cattle can't go into it.* □ **anegado**
water-main *n.* principal pipe carrying water underground along a road, and into buildings. □ **cañería principal**

watermark *n.* **1** faint design put in paper to show who made it: *those postage stamps have a crown as a watermark.* □ **filigrana**
2 mark showing where the tide reaches: *the high and low watermarks are shown on the map.* □ **marca del nivel del agua**
water-melon *n.* large, juicy fruit with red flesh which can be eaten. □ **sandía**
water-mill *n.* mill driven by the power of water running over a large wheel. □ **molino de agua**
water pistol *n.* toy gun which squirts water when the trigger is pressed. □ **pistola de agua**
water-polo *n.* ball game played in water between two teams. □ **waterpolo**
water-power *n.* power/energy of running water, used to drive machines: *a water-mill uses water-power.* □ **energía hidráulica**
waterproof *adj.* which will not let water through: *waterproof hat; waterproof boots.* □ **impermeable**
■ *n.* coat which will not let water through. □ **impermeable**
■ *v.* to make (something) waterproof. □ **impermeabilizar**
watershed *n.* **1** high ground separating different rivers and the streams that run into them. □ **línea divisoria de las aguas; cuenca**
2 point where the situation changes permanently: *a watershed in industrial relations.* □ **giro**
waterside *n.* bank of a river/lake/sea; houses which front a river/lake/sea. □ **orilla**
water-skiing *n.* sport of gliding along the surface of water standing on a pair of skis and pulled by a fast boat. □ **esquí acuático**
water softener *n.* chemical/device for removing the hardness in water. □ **descalcificador**
watersplash *n.* place where a shallow stream flows over a road. □ **lugar encharcado**
waterspout *n.* **1** pipe carrying rainwater away from a roof. □ **canalón**
2 tornado at sea when the water rises in a high column. □ **tromba marina**
water supply *n.* system of pipes/tanks, etc., bringing water to people's homes; amount of water in the system: *the village water supply dried up during the long hot summer.* □ **abastecimiento de agua**
water table *n.* natural level of water below ground. □ **capa freática**
watertight *adj.* **1** so tightly fitting that water cannot get in or out. □ **hermético**
2 so strong that it cannot be disproved: *a watertight argument; a watertight excuse.* □ **un argumento aplastante; una excusa perfecta**
water tower *n.* tower holding a large tank of water. □ **depósito de agua**
waterway *n.* canal or deep river along which boats can easily travel: *holidays on the English waterways.* □ **vía navegable**
waterweed *n.* weed which grows in water. □ **planta acuática**
waterwheel *n.* wheel which is turned by water and so makes a machine work. □ **rueda hidráulica**
waterworks *n.* **1** buildings from which water is piped to houses and factories. □ **abastecimiento de aguas**
2 ***to turn on the waterworks,*** (*informal*) to cry. □ **echarse a llorar**
3 *there is something wrong with my waterworks,* there is something wrong with my urinary system (bladder/kidneys, etc.). □ **trastorno urinario**
watery *adj.* which has a lot of water: *watery soup; watery eyes.* □ **aguado**

watt [wɔt] *n.* standard unit of electrical power: *most of our lights have 100 watt bulbs.* □ **vatio**
wattage ['wɔtidʒ] *n.* amount of electricity in watts. □ **potencia en vatios**
wattle ['wɔtl] *n.* **1** woven twigs/laths used to make light walls. □ **zarzo**
wattle and daub, type of medieval building material consisting of woven strips of wood covered with mud. □ **zarzos y esteras**
2 type of Australian tree. □ **acacia**
3 fold of red skin hanging under the throat of some birds (such as turkeys). □ **barba; moco (del pavo)**
wave [weiv] *n.* **1** ridge on the surface of the sea: *the big waves hit the rocks.* □ **ola**
2 up-and-down movement by which sound, heat, light, etc. is carried or spread: *radio waves.* □ **onda; ondas de radio**
3 *she gave me a wave as she went past,* she moved her hand up and down as a greeting. □ **me saludó con la mano...**
4 ridge on the surface: *he has a nice wave in his hair.* □ **ondulación; ...onda en el pelo**
permanent wave, treatment which makes hair wave and curl. □ **permanente**
5 sudden feeling (usually affecting many people): *wave of emotion; wave of despair; wave of anger.* □ **oleada**
■ *v.* **1** to move up and down: *the washing is waving in the wind; he waved his handkerchief as the train left.* □ **agitar**
to wave to someone, to signal to someone with the hand. □ **hacer señas**
to wave someone aside, to dismiss someone with a movement of the hand. □ **hacer una señal a uno para que se aparte**
to wave someone on, to tell someone to go on by a movement of the hand. □ **hacer señales a uno para que siga**
2 to have/to make ridges on the surface: *my hair waves naturally.* □ **ondular(se)**
waveband *n.* group of wavelengths which are close together. □ **banda de ondas**
waved *adj.* (*of hair*) treated to look wavy. □ **ondulado**
wavelength *n.* **1** distance between similar points on radio waves: *on what wavelength do you get local news?* □ **longitud de onda**
2 *they're **not on the same wavelength,*** (*informal*) they don't understand each other at all. □ **no están en la misma onda**
wavy *adj.* which goes up and down: *they painted a wavy line along the side of the car; her hair is long and wavy.* □ **ondulado**
waver ['weivə] *v.* **1** to tremble/to move from side to side: *the flame wavered each time the door opened; he was so sad that his voice wavered.* □ **vacilar (luz); temblar (voz)**
2 to hesitate: *I'm wavering - I don't know whether to go or not.* □ **dudar**
waverer *n.* someone who is uncertain and hesitates. □ **indeciso**
wavering *adj.* trembling/hesitant. □ **vacilante**
wax [wæks] *n.* **1** solid substance made by bees to build the cells of their honeycomb. □ **cera**
2 solid substance similar to this: *wax candles; paraffin wax; wax in the ears.* □ **cera**
■ *v.* **1** to put polish on (furniture, etc.). □ **encerar**
2 to grow bigger: *the moon waxes and wanes each month,* grows larger and smaller each month. □ **crecer**
waxwing *n.* small bird with bright marks on its

wings. □ **ampelis**

waxworks *n.* exhibition of wax models of famous people. □ **museo de cera**

waxy *adj.* **1** like wax. □ **ceroso**

2 *waxy potatoes,* yellowish potatoes. □ **patatas amarillentas**

way [wei] *n.* **1** road/path: *the soldiers cut a way through the trees; my friend lives across the way.* □ **camino**

***to make your way** through a crowd,* to push through a crowd. □ **abrirse camino...**

way in, entrance/door through which you go in. □ **entrada**

way out, exit/door through which you go out. □ **salida**

by the way, incidentally/in passing: *by the way, what are you doing for the holidays?* □ **a propósito**

by way of, (i) via: *the plane goes to Sydney by way of Singapore.* □ **vía**

(ii) as a sort of: *the dog barked by way of a warning.* □ **como si**

2 right direction/right road: *which is the way to the station? I lost my way in the town; you lead the way and I'll follow; she's holding the book the wrong way up so she can't be reading it.* □ **dirección; camino; ...el libro al revés...**

***to go out of your way** to help someone,* to make a special effort to help someone. □ **hacer un esfuerzo**

3 particular direction: *which way is the wind blowing? on the way to school I met a friend; he didn't want to speak to me, he looked the other way.* □ **dirección**

one-way street, street where the traffic can only move in one direction. □ **calle de una única dirección**

4 method/means/manner: *grandmother showed me the way to make bread; he smiled in a friendly way.* □ **forma**

to get one's own way: *she always gets her own way,* she gets what she wants. □ **...se sale con la suya**

to have a way with: *uncle has a way with little children,* uncle knows how to amuse and please children. □ **tener mano con**

***to find a way out of** a difficulty,* to find a solution to a problem. □ **encontrar una salida a...**

5 *I know all his little ways,* I know all the odd little things he does. □ **...todas sus triquiñuelas**

6 distance (from one place to another): *it's a long way from New York to New Orleans; I'll go part of the way home with you but I haven't time to go the whole way; I've got a long way to go before I've finished the dress,* I've many more hours of work until the dress is finished. □ **distancia; me queda mucho hasta que...**

7 *he'll **go a long way,*** he will be very successful. □ **llegará lejos**

8 space in which someone wants to move: *please get out of my way! he was standing in my way again; your father is angry, so keep out of his way.* □ **camino**

9 state/condition: *he's in a bad way after his fall.* □ **estado**

in the ordinary way, usually. □ **como de costumbre**

out of the way, unusual. □ **fuera de lo común**

in many ways, in lots of aspects/points. □ **en muchos aspectos**

in no way, not at all. □ **en absoluto**

10 progress/movement forwards: *the flood is making way fast.* □ **está avanzando**

to be under way: *the ship is under way,* the ship is moving. □ **...está navegando**

to get under way: *we must get the work under way,* we must start doing the work. □ **...poner manos a la obra**

to make your way in the world, to be successful. □ **abrirse camino en la vida**

to pay your way, to pay for yourself. □ **pagar su parte**

■ *adv.* (*informal*) away/far: *it happened way back in 1950; way up in the hills.* □ **allá en...**

waybill *n.* list of goods/passengers carried. □ **hoja de ruta**

wayfarer *n.* (*formal*) traveller. □ **viajero**

waylay [wei'lei] *v.* (*he waylaid*) to wait for (someone) in order to attack/to ambush. □ **aguardar emboscado**

way out *adj.* (*slang*) strange/unusual. □ **insólito**

wayside *adj.* and *n.* (referring to the) side of the road: *the children picked flowers from the wayside.* □ **al borde del camino**

wayward *adj.* (child) who wants to do what he wants. □ **desobediente**

waywardness *n.* being difficult; uncontrollable. □ **desobediencia**

WC ['dʌblju'siː] *n. short for* water closet; bowl which you sit on to pass waste matter from the body, which is then washed by water away from the building. □ **WC**

we [wiː] *pron.* **1** referring to people who are speaking/to the person speaking and others: *we are reading our books; here we are! we English like a large breakfast.* □ **nosotros**

2 (*informal*) you: *are we feeling hungry?* □ **¿qué, tenemos hambre?**

weak [wiːk] *adj.* (*weaker, weakest*) **1** not strong in body or in character: *after his illness he felt very weak; Bill is a weak person — he never speaks up for himself.* □ **débil**

2 (*of a liquid*) watery/not strong: *this tea is terrible, it's far too weak.* □ **flojo**

3 not good at: *he's weak at maths.* □ **flojo**

4 ***weak verb,*** (*in grammar*) verb which forms its past tense using a suffix (such as 'help', 'helped'). □ **regular**

weaken *v.* to make/to become weak. □ **debilitar(se)**

weakening *n.* becoming weak. □ **debilitamiento**

weak-kneed *adj.* soft/timid/cowardly. □ **sin carácter**

weakling *n.* weak person. □ **enfermizo; delicado**

weakly *adv.* not strongly/feebly. □ **débilmente**

weak-minded *adj.* not strong in character. □ **mentecato**

weakness *n.* (*pl. weaknesses*) **1** being weak. □ **debilidad**

2 *I have a weakness for cream cakes,* (*informal*) I especially like cream cakes. □ **tengo debilidad por...**

weal [wiːl] *n.* raised mark left on the skin by a blow from a whip or a stick. □ **verdugón**

wealth [welθ] *n.* **1** riches: *his wealth is famous.* □ **riqueza**

2 large amount: *the guidebook gives us a wealth of information about the town.* □ **abundancia, mucho**

wealthy *adj.* and *n.* (*wealthier, wealthiest*) very rich (people): *the wealthy seem to get richer and richer.* □ **rico**

wean [wiːn] *v.* to make (a baby) start to eat solid food after only drinking milk. □ **destetar**

to wean someone off something/away from something, to get someone to drop a (bad) habit. □ **hacer que alguien deje de... (fumar, drogarse, etc.)**

weapon ['wepən] *n.* object with which you fight: *he*

used a broken bottle as a weapon. □ **arma**
weaponry *n.* (*no pl.*) weapons. □ **armamento**
wear ['wɛə] *n.* **1** act of carrying on your body as a piece of clothing: *a long dress is more suitable for evening wear; the trousers are strong enough to stand normal wear and tear,* normal use. □ **uso; ...para traje de noche**
2 clothes: *the men's wear department is on the first floor, the children's wear on the second.* □ **ropa**
3 damage through much use: *there are signs of wear on the tyres.* □ **desgaste**
4 ability to stand much use: *leather boots will stand hard wear; don't throw that jacket away – it has plenty of wear left in it.* □ **uso**
■ *v.* (*he wore: he has worn*) **1** to carry on your body as a piece of clothing: *I'm wearing a brown coat and shoes today; she showed us the ring she was wearing.* □ **llevar**
2 to become damaged through much use: *the car tyres are worn; I have worn a hole in my trousers.* □ **desgastarse (neumáticos); hacer un agujero (pantalón)**
3 to stand up to much use/to last a long time: *woollen cloth wears well.* □ **...dura mucho**
4 to have on your face: *he wore a sad expression.* □ **tener**
5 (*informal*) to accept/to put up with something: *the boss won't wear it,* will never accept this suggestion. □ **tragar**
wearable *adj.* able to be worn. □ **ponible**
wear away *v.* to disappear/to make (something) disappear by rubbing or much use: *the sea is wearing away the cliffs; the pattern on the plates has worn away through daily use.* □ **desgastar(se)**
wearer *n.* person who wears clothes. □ **el/la que lleva algo puesto**
wearing *adj.* tiring: *listening to lectures on the economy can be very wearing.* □ **cansado**
wear off *v.* to disappear gradually/to make (something) disappear: *the writing on the wall has worn off; my earache is gradually wearing off.* □ **borrarse (escritura); desaparecer (dolor)**
wear on *v. as the evening wore on,* as time passed in the evening. □ **pasar lentamente**
wear out *v.* **1** to become useless through much use; to make (something) become useless through much use: *the boys wear out four pairs of shoes each year.* □ **gastar**
2 ***to wear yourself out/to be worn out,*** to become tired through doing a lot: *after a good game of football I'm worn out.* □ **acabar agotado**
weary ['wi:ri] *adj.* (*wearier, weariest*) very tired/tiring: *I'm longing to sit down and rest my weary legs; are you weary of waiting for buses? a weary wait at the bus stop.* □ **cansado**
■ *v.* to become tired/to make tired: *we soon wearied of their company; long car journeys weary him.* □ **cansar(se)**
wearily *adv.* in a tired way. □ **cansadamente**
weariness *n.* tiredness. □ **cansancio**
wearisome *adj.* tiring/boring. □ **cansado/aburrido**
weasel ['wi:zl] *n.* small animal with a long thin body and short legs, which kills and eats rabbits, etc. □ **comadreja**
weather ['weðə] *n.* state of the air and atmosphere at a certain time: *what's the weather like today? mild weather; the weather will be cold for the time of year; thundery weather.* □ **tiempo**
in all weathers, in every sort of weather. □ **con cualquier tiempo**
to make heavy weather of a job, to have unnecessary difficulty in doing the job. □ **complicar un trabajo**
to be/to feel under the weather, to feel miserable/unwell. □ **sentirse desgraciado**
■ *v.* **1** (*of sea/frost/wind, etc.*) to wear down (rocks, etc.): *the waves have weathered the rocks and made them smooth.* □ **desgastar, erosionar**
2 to season (planks of wood)/to make (wood) suitable for use by leaving it outside for several years. □ **curar**
3 *to weather a storm,* to survive a storm; *the government safely weathered the crisis,* survived the crisis. □ **...superó la crisis**
weather-beaten *adj.* **1** marked by the weather. □ **deteriorado por la intemperie**
2 (*of face*) tanned/made brown by the wind, rain and sun: *the weather-beaten faces of the fishermen.* □ **curtido**
weather boarding *n.* overlapping boards of wood used for covering the sides of a building to protect them against bad weather. □ **tablazón**
weather bureau, weather centre *n.* office where the weather is forecast. □ **servicio meteorológico**
weathercock *n.* weather vane in the shape of a cock which turns around to show the direction of the wind. □ **veleta**
weather forecast, weather report *n.* description of the weather about to come in the next few hours or days: *here is the weather forecast for the weekend.* □ **previsión meteorológica**
weatherman *n.* (*pl. weathermen*) (*informal*) expert who describes the coming weather, usually on TV or radio. □ **hombre del tiempo**
weatherproof *adj.* able to keep out the wind and the rain. □ **a prueba de mal tiempo**
weather strip (ping) *n.* strip of plastic foam/of metal which is attached to the inside of a window frame to prevent draughts. □ **burlete**
weather vane *n.* metal shape on a high building which turns round to show the direction of the wind. □ **veleta**
weave [wi:v] *n.* pattern of cloth; way in which cloth has been woven: *material with a loose weave.* □ **tejido**
■ *v.* (*he wove: he has woven*) **1** to make cloth by winding threads in and out. □ **tejer**
2 to make (something) by a similar method: *you can weave baskets from twigs.* □ **tejer**
3 to twist and turn: *he was weaving his way to the front of the crowd.* □ **abrirse paso entre la gente**
weaver *n.* person who weaves. □ **tejedor**
weaving *n.* action of making cloth by winding threads in and out: *you can learn weaving at evening classes.* □ **tejeduría**
to get weaving, (*informal*) to start work. □ **poner manos a la obra**
web [web] *n.* **1** something that is woven: *a web of material.* □ **tejido**
2 *spider's web,* net spun by spiders. □ **tela de araña**
3 skin between the toes of a water bird, etc. □ **membrana**
webbed *adj.* with skin between the toes: *ducks have webbed feet.* □ **palmeado**
webbing *n.* strong tape used in upholstery. □ **lona**
webfooted *adj.* with webbed feet. □ **palmípedo**
wed [wed] *v.* (*he wedded*) **1** (*formal*) to marry/to become husband and wife. □ **casarse con**
2 *to be wedded to an idea,* to be firmly attached to an idea. □ **estar aferrado a una idea**
wedding *n.* marriage ceremony: *Brian and Sylvia are having a big wedding in church.* □ **boda**
silver/golden wedding, anniversary of 25/50 years of

marriage. □ **bodas de plata/oro**
wedding breakfast, meal eaten after the wedding ceremony. □ **banquete nupcial**
wedding cake, special cake made for a wedding. □ **tarta nupcial**
wedding ring, ring which the man gives the woman (and sometimes the woman gives to the man) during the wedding ceremony. □ **alianza**
wedlock *n.* state of being married. □ **matrimonio**

wedge [wedʒ] *n.* **1** V-shaped piece of wood/metal, used for splitting wood: *the woodcutter drove wedges into one side of the tree trunk.* □ **cuña**
it's the thin end of the wedge, small beginning which will bring greater changes later: *the manager has brought one son into the firm, but that's just the thin end of the wedge as he has three more sons to come.* □ **es un primer paso**
2 V-shaped piece: *wedge of cake.* □ **porción**
■ *v.* **1** to split with a wedge. □ **partir con cuña**
2 to fix firmly with a wedge: *we wedged the door open with a thick newspaper.* □ **dejar abierta la puerta poniéndole una cuña**
3 to become tightly fixed: *I sat wedged between two fat women on the bus.* □ **quedar apretujado**

Wednesday ['wenzdi, 'wedənzdei] *n.* third day of the week/day between Tuesday and Thursday: *shops are closed on Wednesdays; I saw her last Wednesday.* □ **miércoles**

wee [wiː] *adj.* (*in Scotland*) very small: *a wee mouse looked out of its hole.* □ **minúsculo**
■ *n.* (*child's word*) (*also* **wee-wee**) urine. □ **pis**
■ *v.* (*child's word*) (*also* **wee-wee**) to urinate. □ **hacer pis**

weed [wiːd] *n.* plant that you do not want in a garden: *the front garden is full of weeds.* □ **hierbajo, mala hierba**
■ *v.* **1** to pull out unwanted plants from: *I spent hours weeding the front garden yesterday.* □ **limpiar de malas hierbas**
2 ***to weed out,*** to remove: *the examination weeded out the weaker candidates.* □ **eliminar**
weedkiller *n.* chemical which kills unwanted plants. □ **herbicida**
weedy *adj.* **1** covered with weeds: *a weedy piece of ground.* □ **cubierto de malas hierbas**
2 thin and weak (person). □ **enclenque**

week [wiːk] *n.* **1** period of seven days: *there are 52 weeks in a year; what day of the week is it? my aunt always visits us once a week; a week from now,* this day next week. □ **semana**
yesterday week, a week ago yesterday. □ **ayer hizo una semana**
2 part of a seven day period: *a working week; he works a 35 hour week,* he works 35 hours every week. □ **...a la semana**
weekday *n.* any day of the week except Sunday (and sometimes Saturday). □ **día laborable**
weekend *n.* period from Friday evening or Saturday morning until Sunday evening: *we're going to spend the weekend at my mother's.* □ **fin de semana**
weekly *adv.* and *adj.* once a week: *you have to pay six weekly instalments; I pay the baker weekly.* □ **semanal; semanalmente**
■ *n.* magazine published once a week. □ **semanario**

weeny ['wiːni] *adj.* (*informal*) very small. □ **chiquito**

weep [wiːp] *v.* (*he wept*) to cry: *she wept bitterly at the news of his death; I'm so happy I could weep for joy.* □ **llorar**
weeping *adj.* **1** crying: *a weeping child.* □ **llorón**
2 (*of tree*) with branches hanging down: *weeping willow.* □ **sauce llorón**

weevil ['wiːvl] *n.* type of beetle which eats plants, grain, etc. □ **gorgojo**

weft [weft] *n.* threads going across a length of material. □ **trama**

weigh [wei] *v.* **1** to measure how heavy something is: *please would you weigh this fish for me?* □ **pesar**
2 to have a certain heaviness: *the fish weighs 1 kilo.* □ **pesar**
3 *time weighs heavily on his hands,* he has nothing to do. □ **está ocioso a todas horas**
4 ***to weigh anchor,*** to lift the anchor of a ship in order to sail away. □ **levar anclas**
weighbridge *n.* large machine for weighing heavy lorries and their goods. □ **báscula**
weigh down *v.* to press down: *the branches of the tree are weighed down with apples.* □ **doblarse**
weigh in *v.* (*of boxers/jockeys*) to be weighed before a fight or race. □ **pesarse**
weigh up *v.* (*informal*) **1** to guess rightly what someone/something is like: *the new secretary soon weighed up her boss.* □ **calar**
2 *to weigh up the pros and cons,* to examine all the arguments for and against. □ **sopesar los pros y contras**

weight [weit] *n.* **1** heaviness (of something): *the weight of the fish is 1 kilo; what's your weight?* □ **peso**
2 *I'm trying **to put on/to lose weight,*** I'm trying to get fatter/thinner. □ **...perder/ganar peso**
3 ***to pull your weight,*** to do your best. □ **esforzarse**
4 piece of metal used to measure the exact heaviness of something else: *we have a set of weights which we use in the kitchen.* □ **pesa**
5 something heavy: *if you lift heavy weights you may hurt your back; put a weight on top of the letters.* □ **peso**
a weight off someone's mind: *that's a weight off my mind!,* I no longer need to worry about that. □ **me he quitado un peso de encima**
6 importance: *whatever he says carries weight with the town council.* □ **peso**
to throw your weight about, (*informal*) to use your authority in an arrogant way. □ **darse importancia**
■ *v.* **1** to attach a weight to (something): *he weighted the fishing line with lead pellets.* □ **poner peso**
2 to add (a quantity) to a sum to produce a certain result: *the questions are weighted against competitors from Scotland.* □ **cargar**
weighting *n.* additional salary paid to someone to compensate for living in an expensive area: *a London weighting.* □ **aumento por coste de vida**
weightlessness *n.* state of having no weight: *astronauts are used to the feeling of weightlessness in space.* □ **ingravidez**
weightlifter *n.* person who lifts heavy weights as a sport. □ **halterófilo; levantador de pesos**
weightlifting *n.* sport of lifting heavy weights. □ **halterofilia**
weighty *adj.* **1** heavy. □ **pesado**
2 important (problem, etc.). □ **de peso**

weir ['wiə] *n.* **1** small dam/wall built across a river to control the flow of water. □ **presa**
2 fence across a lake or river to trap fish. □ **encañizada**

weird ['wiəd] *adj.* (*weirder, weirdest*) strange/odd: *walking into the old house I had a weird feeling that someone was watching me.* □ **extraño**
weirdly *adv.* in a strange way. □ **extrañamente**
weirdo ['wiədou] *n.* strange/odd person; person who behaves in a strange way. □ **tipo raro**

welcome ['welkəm] *n.* greeting/reception: *they gave us a warm welcome; the news received a cold welcome,* the news was not received gladly. □ **bienvenida**
■ *v.* **1** to greet (someone) as he arrives: *my friends welcomed me at the door.* □ **dar la bienvenida**
2 to hear (news) happily: *I welcome the news of his election to Parliament.* □ **alegrarse por**
■ *adj.* **1** pleasing/received with pleasure: *the Browns made us most welcome in their home; the sunshine of the Caribbean was a welcome change from the winter here.* □ **los Brown nos recibieron con los brazos abiertos...; el sol...fue un cambio grato...**
2 willingly permitted: *you're welcome to try out our new machine.* □ **puede perfectamente...**
3 *Amer.* (*informal*) (*as a reply to* ***thank you***) *you're welcome!,* it was a pleasure to do it. □ **de nada**

weld [weld] *n.* joint made by joining two pieces of metal together by first heating, then pressing. □ **soldadura**
■ *v.* to join (two pieces of metal) together by first heating, then pressing. □ **soldar**
welder *n.* **1** person who welds metal. □ **soldador**
2 machine which welds metal. □ **soldadora**
welding *n.* process of joining two pieces of metal together: *oxyacetylene welding.* □ **soldadura**

welfare ['welfɛə] *n.* happiness/comfort/freedom from want: *old people need others to see to their welfare.* □ **bienestar**
Welfare State, state which looks after the health and wellbeing of its citizens. □ **Estado del bienestar**
child welfare, health and wellbeing of children. □ **bienestar de los niños**

well [wel] *n.* **1** deep hole at the bottom of which is water or oil: *thousands of oil wells are pumping out oil in Saudi Arabia.* □ **pozo**
2 deep hole; space in the centre of a building where the staircase or lift is. □ **hueco de la escalera/del ascensor**
3 low part of a courtroom where clerks, etc., sit. □ **estrado**
■ *v.* ***to well up,*** to start to flow: *tears welled up in her eyes.* □ **manar; se le llenaron los ojos de lágrimas**
■ *adv.* (*better/best*) **1** in a good way/properly: *are you working well? I'm doing as well as I can; can you speak Russian well? I speak it fairly well but I speak Polish better.* □ **bien**
to do well, to prosper: *the business is small but it's doing well.* □ **ir bien**
to go well, (i) to be successful/to have good results: *I hope all goes well with your work/I hope your work goes well.* □ **ir bien**
(ii) to fit/to suit: *those shoes will go well with your new dress.* □ **ir bien**
to speak well of someone/something, to praise/to say nice things about: *your teacher spoke well of you.* □ **hablar bien**
2 to a large degree: *well after 7 o'clock,* a long time after 7 o'clock; *it's well worth trying to see an opera at La Scala,* it is really worth the effort. □ **bien pasadas las 7; merece la pena intentar...**
pretty well *all the family,* almost all the family. □ **casi toda la familia**
to be well up in *a subject,* to know a lot about the subject. □ **dominar un tema**
3 lucky/desirable: *it would be as well to write him a letter,* it would be desirable. □ **no estaría de más que le escribiéramos...**
all's well that ends well, if the result is fine then everything is fine. □ **todo lo que bien empieza bien acaba**
4 *it was* ***just as well*** *you were at home when the strangers arrived,* it was lucky. □ **menos mal que estabas en casa...**
5 *you* ***may well*** *be right,* you probably are right. □ **puede que tengas razón**
6 ***may as well:*** *you might just as well have stayed at home for you haven't helped at all,* it would have been the same if you had stayed at home. □ **habría dado igual que te hubieras quedado...**
7 ***to wish someone well,*** to wish them good luck. □ **desear lo mejor**
8 ***as well,*** also/too: *please can I bring John as well? can I have a cake as well as a biscuit?* □ **también**
■ *adj.* healthy and in good condition: *she's looking very well today; he isn't very well.* □ **muy bien**
■ *interjection* **1** (starting a sentence and meaning nothing in particular): *well, as I was saying...; well then, we must go now.* □ **bien, bueno...**
2 (showing surprise): *well, well, well! I can't believe it!* □ **bueno, bueno**
well-advised *adj.* wise: *you would be well-advised to take an umbrella.* □ **sensato**
well-behaved *adj.* good/having good manners: *the children were very well-behaved when the visitors came.* □ **bien educado**
wellbeing *n.* health and happiness. □ **bienestar**
well-bred *adj.* polite/well educated. □ **bien educado**
well-earned *adj.* which has been deserved: *he had a well-earned rest.* □ **merecido**
well-heeled *adj.* (*informal*) rich. □ **montado en el dólar**
well-informed *adj.* knowing a lot about a subject: *a well-informed guide told us the history of the castle.* □ **bien informado**
well-known *adj.* famous/known by many people: *it's a well-known fact that the Dead Sea is very salty.* □ **muy conocido**
well-mannered *adj.* polite/with good manners. □ **de buenos modales**
well-meaning *adj.* (person) who does something with good intentions. □ **bienintencionado**
wellnigh *adv.* (*formal*) almost. □ **casi**
well-off *adj.* (*informal*) rich: *you need to be well-off to have a Rolls Royce.* □ **adinerado**
well-oiled *adj.* (*slang*) drunk. □ **borracho**
well-read *adj.* having read many books and therefore knowing a lot. □ **versado**
well-spoken *adj.* speaking with a good accent/speaking well. □ **bienhablado**
well-to-do *adj.* rich. □ **acaudalado**
well-wisher *n.* person who is friendly towards another. □ **amistoso**
well-worn *adj.* used a lot: *well-worn pair of shoes; well-worn argument.* □ **desgastado**

wellington boots ['weliŋtən'bu:ts] **wellingtons** ['weliŋtənz], (*informal*) **wellies** ['weliz] *n. pl.* rubber waterproof boots. □ **botas de goma**

Welsh [welʃ] *adj.* referring to Wales: *Welsh butter is delicious.* □ **galés**
Welsh rarebit, toasted cheese on bread. □ **pan con queso tostado**
■ *n.* **1** *pl.* ***the Welsh,*** the people of Wales. □ **los galeses**
2 language spoken in Wales. □ **galés**
■ *v.* ***to welsh,*** to leave without paying your debts. □ **irse sin pagar**
to welsh on someone, to break a promise made to someone. □ **no cumplir con**
Welshman, Welshwoman *n.* person from Wales. □ **galés, galesa**

welt [welt] *n.* **1** leather edging for attaching the upper

part of a shoe to the sole. □ **vira**
2 strong edge to a piece of knitting. □ **ribete**
3 weal/mark made on the skin by a blow. □ **verdugón**

welter ['weltə] *n.* confused mass: *the conference ended in a welter of contradictory statements.* □ **confusión**
welterweight *n.* medium weight in boxing between middleweight and lightweight. □ **peso 'welter'**

wench [wenʃ] *n.* (*pl.* *wenches*) (*formal*) young woman. □ **mozuela**

wend [wend] *v.* ***to wend your way,*** to go: *we were wending our way home after the party.* □ **encaminarse a**

went [went] *v. see* **go.**

wept [wept] *v. see* **weep.**

were [wəː] *v. see* **be.**

west [west] *n.* **1** one of the points of the compass, the direction in which the sun sets: *the sun rises in the east and sets in the west.* □ **oeste**
west wind, wind coming from the west. □ **viento del oste**
2 ***the West,*** the non-communist world. □ **el Oeste**
■ *adv.* towards the west: *I drove west towards California.* □ **hacia el oeste**
to go west: *that's another cup gone west!,* (*informal*) that's another cup broken. □ **¡otra copa rota!**
westbound *adj.* going towards the west. □ **con rumbo al oeste**
West End *n.* the fashionable part of London, where the main shopping area is found. □ **West End**
West Indian *adj.* referring to the West Indies. □ **de las Antillas**
■ *n.* person from the West Indies. □ **antillano**
West Indies [west'indiz] *n.* Caribbean islands between North and South America. □ **Antillas**
westerly *adj.* **1** from the west: *a westerly wind.* □ **del oeste**
2 towards the west: *in a westerly direction.* □ **hacia el oeste**
western *adj.* of the west: *Western Europe.* □ **occidental**
■ *n.* novel/film about cowboys and Indians in the USA. □ **novela/película del oeste**
westerner *n.* person who lives in the west. □ **occidental**
westernize *v.* to make more European or American. □ **occidentalizar**
westward *adj.* towards the west. □ **hacia el oeste**
westwards *adv.* towards the west. □ **hacia el oeste**

wet [wet] *adj.* (*wetter, wettest*) **1** covered or soaked with water or other liquid: *the grass is wet after the rain; the ink is still wet on the paper.* □ **húmedo**
2 *I hadn't an umbrella and I'm* ***wet through/soaking wet,*** all my clothes are very wet. □ **...estoy calado**
3 *he's* ***a wet blanket,*** (*informal*) he spoils any fun. □ **es un cenizo**
4 rainy: *February is a wet month.* □ **lluvioso**
5 *he's a bit wet,* (*informal*) he's a dull/uninteresting/weak person. □ **es un poco soso**
■ *n.* rain: *don't go out in the wet if you're not well.* □ **lluvia**
■ *v.* (*he wetted*) to dampen with water: *I'll wet a cloth and clean the marks off.* □ **humedecer**
wetness *n.* being wet. □ **humedad**
wetsuit *n.* suit worn by divers which keeps the body warm with a layer of warm water. □ **traje isotérmico**
wetting *n.* soaking/getting wet: *I got a wetting in the storm yesterday.* □ **remojo; me calé ayer...**

wether ['weðə] *n.* young castrated sheep. □ **carnero castrado**

whack [wæk] *n.* **1** hard, noisy blow. □ **porrazo**
2 *let's* ***have a whack at it!,*** (*informal*) let's try to do it. □ **probemos**
■ *v.* **1** to hit hard, making a loud noise: *his father whacked him with a slipper; he whacked the ball into the lake.* □ **sacudir, pegar**
2 to defeat (in a match): *we whacked the other team in the hockey match.* □ **pegar una paliza a**
whacked *adj.* **1** beaten. □ **zurrado**
2 (*informal*) worn out/tired: *I'm whacked, I must sit down.* □ **estoy para el arrastre**
whacking *adj.* (*informal*) huge: *a whacking great lorry.* □ **colosal**
■ *n.* beating. □ **zurra**

whale [weil] *n.* **1** huge sea mammal. □ **ballena**
2 *we had* ***a whale of a time,*** (*informal*) we enjoyed ourselves very much. □ **nos lo pasamos 'chupi'**
whaleboat *n.* boat used when hunting whales. □ **ballenero**
whalebone *n.* thin bone taken from the jaws of whales and formerly used in corsets. □ **ballena**
whaler *n.* **1** boat used when hunting whales. □ **ballenero**
2 person who hunts whales. □ **ballenero**
whaling *n.* hunting of whales. □ **pesca de ballenas**

wharf [wɔːf] *n.* (*pl. wharfs/wharves*) place in a dock where a ship can tie up and load or unload. □ **muelle (cerrado)**
wharfinger *n.* person who is in charge of a wharf. □ **representante del armador en el muelle**

what [wɔt] *adj.* **1** that which: *he bought a house with what money he had left,* the small amount of money he had left. □ **el poco**
2 (*asking a question*) which?: *what time is it? what sort of person is he?; what good is this to us?,* what is the use of this? □ **¿qué?**
3 (*showing surprise*) how much/how great/how strange: *what an idea! what a lot of biscuits you've eaten!* □ **¡qué idea!; ¡qué cantidad de...!**
■ *pron.* **1** that which: *I saw what was in the box; what I like most is swimming.* □ **lo que**
come what may, *we won't sell the house,* whatever happens we won't sell it. □ **pase lo que pase...**
2 (*asking a question*) which thing or things: *what's that? what are you doing here? what's his name?; what is the German for table?,* what is the German word meaning table? □ **¿qué?**
what's the use of *learning Latin?,* why learn Latin? □ **¿para qué sirve aprender...?**
what about *stopping for lunch now?,* do you think we should stop for lunch now? □ **¿qué tal si...?**
what did you say/(not polite) ***what?,*** I didn't hear what you said, please say it again. □ **¿qué has dicho?/¿qué?**
what if?, what will happen if: *what if she doesn't come?* □ **¿qué pasa si...?**
to know what's what, to know what the situation is and what to do. □ **saber lo que uno se trae entre manos**
■ *interjection* (showing surprise): *what! can't you come?* □ **¿qué?, ¿no puedes venir?**
what's-it/what-d'you-call-it *n.* (*informal*) something the name of which you have forgotten for the moment: *have you got the what's-it for making holes in metal?* □ **chisme**
whatever [wɔ'tevə] *pron.* **1** anything at all: *you can eat whatever you like.* □ **todo lo que; lo que**
2 *I'll buy it whatever it costs,* no matter what price

it is. □ **...no importa lo que cueste**
■ *adj.* **1** (*strong form of* **what**) *I'll come at whatever time you say.* □ **...a la hora que digas**
2 any ...at all: *have there been any letters? – none whatever; is there any hope whatever? – no, nothing whatever can help him now.* □ **nada en absoluto**
what for *pron.* **1** why: *We're going to London - What for?* □ **¿para qué?**
2 what is the purpose of: *what's that light over the door for?* □ **¿para qué sirve...?**
3 ***to give someone what for,*** (*informal*) to be angry with someone. □ **reñir a uno**
whatnot *n.* **1** a vague thing. □ **cualquier cosa**
2 wooden stand with shelves for small books and ornaments. □ **estantería**
whatsoever [wɔtsou'evə] *adj.* and *pron.* (*strong form of* **whatever**): *there are no tickets whatsoever left for the match,* none at all. □ **en absoluto**
wheat [wi:t] *n.* cereal plant: *farmers grow wheat and send it to the mill to be made into flour.* □ **trigo**
wheatmeal *n.* brown flour containing most of the grain. □ **harina integral**
wheatsheaf *n.* large bundle of stalks of wheat bound together. □ **gavilla**
wheedle ['wi:dl] *v.* to ask someone for something in a particularly nice, flattering way: *I wheedled some money out of him.* □ **engatusar**
wheel [wi:l] *n.* **1** circular frame which turns around a central axis (as a support for cars/trains/bicycles, etc.): *a bicycle has two wheels and a car usually has four.* □ **rueda**
2 any similar circular object: *steering wheel,* wheel which the driver of a car holds and turns to follow the road; *to take the wheel,* to drive the car.
□ **rueda; volante**
potter's wheel, horizontal disc on which a potter throws the clay to make pottery. □ **torno de alfarero**
■ *v.* **1** to push along (something) that has wheels: *he wheeled his bicycle through the door.* □ **hacer rodar**
2 to turn around suddenly: *the teacher wheeled round and faced the class.* □ **volverse**
3 (*in army*) to change direction. □ **dar media vuelta**
left wheel!, turn left! □ **¡vuelta a la izquierda!**
4 to circle: *the seabirds were wheeling above the fishing boats.* □ **dar vueltas**
5 ***to wheel and deal,*** to negotiate to obtain concessions in business. □ **trapichear**
wheelbarrow *n.* small handcart used by builders and gardeners, which has one wheel in front, and is held by two handles behind. □ **carretilla**
wheelbase *n.* distance between the front and rear axles of a car/lorry, etc. □ **batalla**
wheelchair *n.* chair on wheels used by people who cannot walk. □ **silla de ruedas**
wheelwright *n.* man who makes wheels. □ **carretero**
wheeze [wi:z] *v.* to breathe noisily and with difficulty: *I've had bronchitis and I'm still wheezing a lot.*
□ **resollar**
whelk [welk] *n.* type of edible sea snail. □ **buccino**
whelp [welp] *n.* young of a dog. □ **cachorro**
■ *v.* to give birth to a young dog. □ **parir**
when [wen] *adv.* (*asking a question*) at what time: *when does the train leave? since when have you been living in Paris? until when are you staying here?*
□ **cuándo**
■ *conj.* **1** at the time that: *when I was young; I'll leave when the programme finishes; one day when I was all alone.* □ **cuando**
2 if: *hold my hand when necessary; when you meet a car, get off your bike!* □ **cuando**
whenever [we'nevə] *adv.* at any time that: *come whenever you like; I go there whenever I can.*
□ **siempre que**
whence [wens] *adv.* (*formal*) from where. □ **de donde**
where ['wɛə] *adv.* (*asking a question*) in/at/to what place? *where am I? where did the mouse go? where do you come from?* □ **dónde**
■ *adv.* (showing place): *I shall stay where I am; he still lives in the house where he was born; that's where he keeps his money.* □ **donde**
whereabouts ['wɛərəbauts] *n. pl.* place where someone/something is: *nobody knows his whereabouts since last Christmas.* □ **paradero**
■ *adv.* in what place? *I left it in the bedroom – Whereabouts in the bedroom? – On the bed.* □ **¿dónde?**
whereas [wɛər'æz] *conj.* on the other hand/while/in contrast with the fact that: *I only speak English whereas my brother speaks five languages.* □ **mientras que**
wherefore *conj.* and *adv.* (*formal*) why. □ **por lo que**
wherever [wɛər'evə] *adv.* in every place: *wherever I go I meet interesting people.* □ **dondequiera que**
whereupon [wɛərə'pɔn] *conj.* at that point/after that: *he sat down, whereupon all the audience clapped.* □ **a lo que**
wherewithal *n.* (*formal*) necessary money: *I haven't the wherewithal to buy the car yet.* □ **recursos**
wherry ['weri] *n.* (*pl. wherries*) small rowing boat.
□ **esquife**
whet [wet] *v.* (*he whetted*) **1** to sharpen: *the butcher was whetting his knive before cutting the meat.*
□ **afilar**
2 ***to whet your appetite,*** to make you more interested in something by giving you a little taste of it.
□ **despertar el apetito**
whetstone *n.* stone used to sharpen knives, etc.
□ **amoladera; piedra de afilar**
whether ['weðə] *conj.* **1** if: *I don't know whether it is true; it depends on whether we have enough money or not.* □ **si**
2 either: *whether by day or by night.* □ **sea de día o de noche**
whey [wei] *n.* liquid left when milk is made into cheese. □ **suero**
which [witʃ] *adj.* what (person/thing): *which dress shall I wear? which one is your brother? in which hand do you hold your pen?* □ **qué; cuál**
■ *pron.* **1** (*asking a question*) what person/what thing: *which have you chosen? which of you ate the cake? I don't mind which,* it doesn't matter what one I have. □ **cuál; ... el que sea**
2 (*only used with things not persons*) that/the thing that: *the house which is on the corner is empty; the house which I can see on the corner is empty; he can read well, which is a good thing; the sailor told me many stories, all of which were true.* □ **que; el/la/lo cual**
3 (with a preposition such as *from, with, after, to*): *the house of which we were speaking is now empty; after which he went out; the car in which we were travelling was stolen.* □ **de la que; de lo cual; en el que**
whichever *pron.* and *adj.* **1** anything that: *take whichever book you like!* □ **cualquier(a) el ... que**
2 (*strong form of* **which**) *whichever method you use, it will be expensive,* no matter which. □ **cualquier**
whiff [wif] *n.* slight smell: *a whiff of cigars.* □ **olorcillo**
while [wail] *n.* **1** length of time: *a little while; a short while ago.* □ **un ratito; hace un rato**

quite a while/a good while, a fairly long time: *I've been waiting for you quite a while.* □ **bastante rato**
once in a while, from time to time. □ **de vez en cuando**
2 ***to be worth while,*** to be worth doing: *it's worth while having two keys in case you lose one.* □ **merecer la pena**
3 *if you will paint the house for me I'll* ***make it worth your while,*** I'll pay you well. □ **...te recompensaré**
■ *v.* ***to while away*** *the time,* to make the time pass while you are waiting for something. □ **pasar el tiempo**
■ *conj.* **1** during/as long as: *while I was making the dinner John was cleaning the house; you will always have a home while I'm alive.* □ **mientras**
2 although: *while I understand your opinion I still don't agree with it.* □ **aunque**
3 whereas/in contrast with: *I like coffee while you like tea.* □ **mientras que**
whilst [wailst] *conj.* while. □ **mientras**
whim [wim] *n.* sudden wish or desire. □ **capricho; antojo**
whimsical ['wimzikl] *adj.* odd/fanciful. □ **caprichoso**
whimsy *n.* strange/fanciful idea. □ **capricho**
whimper ['wimpə] *n.* sad/weak cry. □ **gimoteo**
■ *v.* (*of small dogs*) to cry weakly: *the dog held up its hurt paw and whimpered.* □ **gimotear**
whine [wain] *n.* complaint/moan. □ **quejido**
■ *v.* to moan/to complain in a long high voice: *the dog can't be left or he will whine for hours; I don't like whining children.* □ **lloriquear**
whinge [windʒ] *v.* (*informal*) to complain in a whining way. □ **llorar**
whinny ['wini] *n.* (*pl. whinnies*) sound which a horse makes when pleased. □ **relincho**
■ *v.* (*of a horse*) to make a happy sound. □ **relinchar**
whip [wip] *n.* **1** long, thin piece of leather fixed to a handle and used for hitting animals: *horse whip; riding whip.* □ **látigo**
2 ***party whip,*** member of parliament whose job it is to keep order among members of his party.
□ **'whip', coordinador**
3 instructions given by a party whip. □ **(dar) un toque**
4 *he issued* ***a three-line whip,*** the strictest instructions. □ **dio un toque en serio (de atención) para que fueran a votar a la sala**
5 sweet pudding. □ **batido instantáneo**
instant whip, sweet milk pudding made quickly by adding milk to a packet of powder. □ **batido instantáneo**
■ *v.* (*he whipped*) **1** to hit with a whip: *the driver whipped the horses to make them go faster.* □ **dar latigazos a**
2 to beat sharply: *the rain whipped our faces as we walked; meringues are made from whipped egg whites.* □ **azotar**
3 (*informal*) to move quickly: *she whipped behind the door so that no one could see her.* □ **escabullirse**
4 ***to whip out:*** *the cowboy whipped out a gun,* pulled a gun out quickly. □ **...de repente sacó un revólver**
whiphand *n.* ***to have the whiphand,*** to have the advantage. □ **aventajar**
whiplash *n.* piece of thin leather which is part of a whip. □ **tralla**
whip off *v.* to move quickly; to remove quickly: *he whipped off before I could stop him; the man whipped off his hat.* □ **irse rápidamente; quitarse a toda prisa (sombrero)**
whippersnapper *n.* boy/young man who is too sure of himself. □ **mequetrefe**
whipping *n.* beating. □ **azotamiento**
whip round *v.* to turn round quickly. □ **volverse de repente**
whip-round *n.* ***to have a whip-round,*** (*informal*) to ask everyone to give some money: *we had a whip-round in the office for Tom's wedding present.* □ **colecta**
whip up *v.* to encourage/to make (something) increase. □ **avivar**
whippet ['wipit] *n.* breed of small thin dog trained for racing. □ **lebrel**
whirl [wəːl] *n.* **1** rapid turning movement. □ **giro; remolino**
2 giddy/dizzy feeling: *my head's in a whirl.* □ **me da vueltas la cabeza**
■ *v.* **1** to turn round quickly/to spin: *the sails of the windmill whirled in the wind; whirling dancers.* □ **dar vueltas**
2 to move quickly: *we whirled down the hill on our bicycles; the train whirled us off to the South.* □ **bajamos corriendo...; el tren nos llevó en un santiamén a...**
whirligig *n.* something which turns round rapidly (like a top). □ **molinete**
whirlpool *n.* water which turns rapidly round and round. □ **remolino**
whirlwind *n.* **1** wind blowing round and round in a circle. □ **manga de viento**
2 confused rush: *a whirlwind of parties.* □ **torbellino**
whirlwind engagement, very rapid engagement before marriage. □ **compromiso a lo loco**
whirr [wəː] *Amer.* **whir** *n.* noise of something spinning round quickly: *whirr of a sewing-machine; whirr of a helicopter.]*□ **runrún**
■ *v.* to make a spinning noise. □ **runrunear**
whisk [wisk] *n.* **1** swift movement: *with a whisk of his tail.* □ **movimiento rápido; coletazo**
2 light brush for removing dust. □ **plumero**
3 kitchen utensil used for beating eggs/cream, etc.: *egg whisk.* □ **batidor**
■ *v.* **1** to move quickly: *the cows whisked their tails.*
□ **sacudir (la cola)**
2 *the teacher whisked the book away before I could open it,* removed it quickly. □ **el profesor se llevó rápidamente...**
3 to beat (eggs/cream) very quickly. □ **batir**
whisker ['wiskə] *n.* **1** long stiff hair at the side of an animal's mouth: *the cat cleans its whiskers after each meal.* □ **bigote(s)**
2 ***whiskers,*** moustache and beard on the side of a man's face. □ **patillas**
whiskery *adj.* covered with whiskers. □ **con patillas**
whisky ['wiski] *n.* (*pl. whiskies*) **1** alcoholic drink (usually made in Scotland), distilled from grain: *Scotch whisky.* □ **whisky**
2 glass of this drink: *he drank a whisky and soda.*
□ **whisky**
whiskey ['wiski] *n.* whisky (made in Ireland or North America). □ **whisky irlandés o americano**
whisper ['wispə] *n.* **1** quiet sound/words quietly spoken: *in the church she spoke in a whisper.* □ **susurro**
2 rumour: *there have been whispers that the director is leaving soon.* □ **rumor**
■ *v.* **1** to speak very quietly: *she whispered to me so that the others wouldn't hear.* □ **susurrar**
2 to make a very quiet sound: *the wind whispered in the trees.* □ **susurrar**
whist [wist] *n.* card game for four people. □ **'whist'**
whist drive, competition of several games of whist

played at the same time in a large room. □ **certamen de 'whist'**

whistle ['wisl] *n.* **1** simple wind instrument played by blowing. □ **pito**

penny whistle/tin whistle, cheap metal flute played mainly in country or folk music. □ **silbato**

2 small pipe which gives a loud shrill noise when blown: *referee's whistle; policeman's whistle; train whistle; the guard blew his whistle.* □ **pito**

3 musical sound made by almost closing the lips and blowing air through the small hole: *you can hear the happy whistle of the postman as he comes to the door.* □ **silbido**

■ *v.* **1** to blow through the lips and make a musical or shrill sound: *he was whistling the latest pop song; my dog comes when I whistle for him.* □ **silbar**

you can whistle for it, (*informal*) you will never get it. □ **puedes esperar sentado**

2 to make a shrill sound: *the train whistled as it came under the bridge; a bullet whistled past my ear.* □ **pitar (tren); silbar (bala)**

whistlestop tour *n. Amer.* election tour where a candidate stops for a brief period in many different towns. □ **gira electoral**

whit [wit] *n.* very small amount. □ **pizca**

not a whit more, nothing more. □ **ni pizca**

Whit [wit] *adj.* referring to Whitsun/Christian festival taking place seven Sundays after Easter: *Whit Sunday; the Whit weekend.* □ **Pentecostés**

white [wait] *adj.* (*whiter, whitest*) colour of snow/very light colour: *the pages of the book are white; he was so frightened that his face went as white as a sheet/as a ghost; I prefer white wine to red wine.* □ **blanco**

white coffee, coffee with milk. □ **(café) con leche**

white Christmas, Christmas with snow on the ground. □ **Navidades blancas**

■ *n.* **1** colour of snow/very light colour: *the dazzling white of the snow.* □ **blanco**

2 person whose skin is not black, brown, yellow or red. □ **blanco**

3 ***white of an egg,*** part of the egg which is not yellow. □ **clara del huevo**

4 ***white of the eye,*** white part of the eye. □ **blanco del ojo**

white ant *n.* termite/white insect, which looks like an ant, and lives in tropical countries. □ **comején; hormiga blanca**

whitebait *n. (pl. whitebait)* small young fish eaten fried. □ **chanquetes; morralla**

whitecollar worker *n.* office worker. □ **administrativo**

white elephant *n.* something which is big and expensive but useless to the owner. □ **elefante blanco**

white-haired *adj.* with white hair: *most people become white-haired as they grow older.* □ **con/de pelo blanco**

Whitehall *n.* (*informal*) British Civil Service: *it is rumoured in Whitehall that government spending will increase.* □ **Whitehall**

Whitehall mandarins, top civil servants. □ **altos funcionarios de Whitehall**

white heat *n.* very high temperature, when white light is produced by heated metal. □ **rojo blanco**

white lie *n.* innocent lie: *I had to tell a white lie, so as not to hurt her feelings.* □ **mentira piadosa**

whiten *v.* to make white: *I must whiten my tennis shoes before the match.* □ **blanquear**

whitener *n.* white liquid for making shoes, etc., white. □ **blanqueador**

White Paper *n.* government report on a problem. □ **Libro Blanco**

white sale *n.* sale of sheets/pillowcases, etc. □ **venta de ropa de cama**

white slave *n.* white girl captured and sent abroad as a prostitute. □ **chica para trata de blancas**

white spirit *n.* turpentine substitute used for cleaning paint-brushes, etc. □ **aguarrás**

whitewash *n.* **1** mixture of water and lime used for painting the walls of houses. □ **cal, lechada de cal**

2 attempt to cover up mistakes. □ **disculpa**

■ *v.* **1** to paint with a mixture of water and lime: *we'll whitewash the cottage this spring.* □ **encalar**

2 to attempt to cover up (mistakes): *the company has lost a lot of money but they are trying to whitewash the directors.* □ **disculpar**

whitewood *n.* unpainted soft wood, such as pine. □ **madera natural**

whither ['wiðə] *adv.* (*formal*) to which place. □ **¿a dónde?**

whiting ['waitiŋ] *n.* (*no pl.*) type of small sea fish. □ **pescadilla**

whitlow ['witlou] *n.* infected spot near a nail. □ **panadizo**

Whitsun ['witsən] *n.* Christian festival on the seventh Sunday after Easter. □ **Pentecostés**

whittle ['witl] *v.* **1** to shape (a piece of wood) by cutting off small pieces with a knife: *he whittled the piece of wood to make a dog's head.* □ **tallar**

2 ***to whittle something away/down,*** to make something gradually smaller: *our savings have been whittled away over the years; they managed to whittle down their debts.* □ **reducir poco a poco**

whiz [wiz] *v.* (*he whizzed*) to move very fast: *cars were whizzing along the motorway.* □ **pasar como un rayo**

whiz-kid *n.* (*informal*) brilliant young businessman. □ **prodigio**

who [huː] (***who*** is the subject form, ***whom*** is the object form: *who is standing outside? whom can you see outside?* In everyday speech ***who*** is used in both cases: *who can you see outside? who are you going home with?*) *pron.* **1** (*asking a question*) which person/which people? *who is at the door? who found it?* □ **¿quién?**

2 the person/people that: *the friend who visited us yesterday lives by the church; those who have no money can't see the film.* □ **que**

whodunit [huː'dʌnit] *n.* (*informal*) detective story. □ **novela policíaca**

whoever *pron.* **1** anyone who/no matter who: *whoever finds the money may keep it.* □ **quienquiera que, el que**

2 (*strong form of* **who**): *stop ringing the bell, whoever you are!* □ **¡...quienquiera que sea!**

whoa [wəu] *interjection* used to tell a horse to stand still. □ **¡so!**

whole [houl] *adj.* complete/all (of something); not broken/not damaged: *whole families were killed in the war; I've walked the whole length of the street but can't find the house; she stayed in bed a whole week; he ate the whole cake,* he ate all the cake; *he ate the cake whole,* he put it all in his mouth at once and ate it, without cutting it up. □ **entero, todo**

■ *n.* all: *the whole of the class.* □ **la clase entera**

as a whole, altogether/generally. □ **en conjunto**

on the whole, for the most part: *it's a good idea on the whole.* □ **en general**

wholehearted *adj.* complete/total: *he has my wholehearted support.* □ **sincero; ...completo apoyo**

wholeheartedly *adv.* completely/totally. □ **incondicionalmente**

wholemeal *n.* brown flour containing all parts of the grain. □ **harina integral**
whole number *n.* number which is complete, and not a fraction. □ **número entero**
wholesale *n.* and *adj.* **1** sale of goods in large quantities to shops which then sell them to people in small quantities: *the wholesale price of vegetables is far less than the retail price.* □ **al por mayor**
2 in large quantities/on a large scale: *wholesale destruction of old parts of the town.* □ **destrucción general...**
wholesaler *n.* person who buys and sells goods in large quantities. □ **mayorista**
wholly *adv.* completely/altogether: *I wholly agree with you.* □ **totalmente**
wholesome ['houlsəm] *adj.* healthy/good: *wholesome food,* food that is good for your health; *wholesome air.* □ **sano; aire puro**
whom [hu:m] *pron.* (*see also* **who**) **1** (*formal*) (*object in questions*) which person/which persons: *whom did you visit yesterday? about whom were you speaking?* □ **¿a quién?**
2 (*object in statements*) the person/persons that: *the girl whom I like is sitting over there; the people with whom she came have now left.* □ **a quien; la chica que me gusta...; las personas con las que ella vino...**
whoop [wu:p] *n.* loud cry: *he gave a whoop of joy.* □ **alarido**
whoopee *interjection showing* excitement. □ **¡hurra!** ***to make whoopee,*** to enjoy yourself noisily. □ **pasarlo en grande**
whooping cough ['hu:piŋkɔf] *n.* children's illness which causes coughing and loud noises when the child tries to breathe. □ **tos ferina**
whoops *interjection showing* surprise: *whoops, I nearly dropped the plates.* □ **¡epa!**
whopper ['wɔpə] *n.* (*informal*) very large thing. □ **cosa enorme**
whopping *adj.* (*informal*) very large. □ **grandísimo**
whore ['hɔ:] *n.* (*formal*) prostitute. □ **puta**
whorl [wə:l] *n.* coiled/spiral shape. □ **espiral**
whose [hu:z] *pron.* **1** (*asking a question*) of which person/persons: *whose house is that? whose books are these?* □ **de quién/de quiénes**
2 belonging to which person/persons: *the people whose cars are in the way must move them; my son, whose books are famous, lives in South Africa.* □ **cuyo/cuyos**
why [wai] *adv.* (*asking a question*) for what reason: *why did you phone me? why don't you go for a walk?* □ **por qué**
■ *n.* the reason: *it's snowing, that's why I didn't come by car; you're coming on Saturday or I'll want to know why.* □ **el porqué**
■ *interjection* (showing surprise): *why, look, it's David! why of course I recognised you!* □ **¡vaya!**
wick [wik] *n.* length of string in the middle of a candle/piece of material in an oil lamp which is lit and burns slowly. □ **mecha**
wicked ['wikid] *adj.* very bad/very nasty: *the wicked king put all good citizens into prison.* □ **malvado**
wickedly *adv.* in a naughty/nasty way. □ **con mala intención**
wickedness *n.* evil; being nasty. □ **maldad**
wicker ['wikə] *n.* (*no pl.*) thin twigs used to make chairs or baskets. □ **mimbre**
wickerwork *n.* (*no pl.*) things made of thin twigs woven together. □ **artículos de mimbre**
wicket ['wikit] *n.* **1** small gate/door set in or next to a larger one (as in a castle gate or city wall). □ **portillo**
2 *Amer.* position on the counter in a post office/bank, etc. □ **ventanilla**
3 (*in cricket*) set of three sticks put in the ground and used as the target; the ground between two sets of these sticks: *the bowler hit the wicket with his first ball.* □ **palos**
4 *it's a slow/fast wicket,* where the ball moves slowly/fast on the ground. □ **es un campo lento/rápido**
5 ***a sticky wicket,*** (*informal*) an awkward/difficult situation. □ **una situación apurada**
wicket-keeper *n.* (*in cricket*) player standing behind the wicket to stop the balls that the batsman does not hit. □ **guardameta**
wide [waid] *adj.* (*wider, widest*) **1** stretching far from side to side: *a wide river; a wide road.* □ **ancho**
2 measurement from side to side: *how wide is the river? it's ten metres wide here.* □ **¿cuánto tiene de ancho...?**
3 enormous: *she has a wide knowledge of astronomy; he left home and went out into the wide, wide world; the college offers a wide range of courses.* □ **extenso**
■ *adv.* **1** greatly/a long way apart/far: *the child opened his eyes wide; the door stood wide open.* □ **completamente (ojos); de par en par (puerta)**
2 *the bomb fell wide of the target,* missed the target. □ **...no dio en el blanco**
wide-angle *adj.* (lens) which takes in a wider area than an ordinary lens. □ **gran angular**
wide awake *adj.* very much awake/not at all sleepy. □ **completamente despierto**
widely *adv.* **1** greatly: *the explorer has travelled widely.* □ **extensamente**
2 *Hemingway's books are widely read,* many people read his books. □ **...muy leídos**
3 *the professor is a widely-read man,* he has read many books on many subjects. □ **...que ha leído mucho**
widen *v.* to make larger/to become wide: *the hole in the road was widening; you can widen your knowledge by reading more.* □ **ensanchar**
wide-ranging *adj.* (discussion) which covers a wide field of subjects. □ **amplia**
widespread *adj.* far/over a large area: *the fire did widespread damage.* □ **extendido**
widgeon ['widʒn] *n.* (*no pl.*) type of small wild duck. □ **ánade silbón**
widow ['widou] *n.* woman whose husband has died. □ **viuda**
grass widow, woman whose husband is away from home on business. □ **esposa sola**
widowed *adj.* (woman) who has become a widow; (man) who has become a widower: *he lives with his widowed mother.* □ **viuda/viudo**
widower *n.* man whose wife has died. □ **viudo**
grass widower, man whose wife is away from home on business. □ **marido solo**
widowhood *n.* being a widow. □ **viudez**
width [widθ] *n.* **1** measurement from side to side: *what is the width of the material? it's 150 cms in width.* □ **anchura**
2 piece of material (cut right across a roll): *a width of silk/of wallpaper.* □ **corte**
wield ['wi:ld] *v.* **1** to hold (something), usually by the handle, and use it: *the soldier wielded an axe above his head.* □ **empuñar**
2 to use/to control: *her mother wields a great influence over her; the minister wields all the real power.* □ **ejercer**

wiener ['wi:nə] *n. Amer.* frankfurter. □ **salchicha de Fráncfort**
wife [waif] *n.* (*pl. wives*) woman to whom a man is married. □ **esposa**
wifely *adj.* of a wife. □ **de esposa**
wig [wig] *n.* false hair worn on the head: *the actress had a dozen different wigs of all colours.* □ **peluca**
wiggle ['wigl] *v.* (*informal*) to move slightly up and down or from side to side: *the boy wiggled his tooth until it came out.* □ **menear**
wiggly *adj.* (*informal*) wavy; (line) which goes up and down. □ **sinuoso**
wigwam ['wigwæm] *n.* cone-shaped tent of the North American Indians. □ **'wigwam'**
wild [waild] *adj.* (*wilder, wildest*) **1** not tame/free to live naturally: *wild animals.* □ **salvaje**
wild life, birds/plants/animals living free, untouched by man. □ **fauna y flora**
2 (plant) which is not a garden plant: *wild flowers cover the mountains in springtime.* □ **planta silvestre**
3 stormy/rough: *it was a wild night when the wind blew and the rain beat down.* □ **de tormenta**
4 savage/angry: *don't touch the cat – it's a wild one and will bite.* □ **fiera**
wild beast, savage, fierce animal. □ **fiera**
to be wild with someone, (*informal*) to be angry with someone. □ **estar furioso con**
to be wild with *excitement,* to be over-excited. □ **estar loco de entusiasmo**
to be wild about, (*informal*) to be very enthusiastic about: *she's wild about horses.* □ **se vuelve loca por los caballos**
5 rough/uncivilized: *the wild country; he leads a wild life, sleeping anywhere, doing anything.* □ **tierra virgen; lleva una vida de crápula**
6 rash/reckless/badly aimed: *he had the wild idea of swimming down the Amazon; I didn't know the answer but I made a wild guess at it.* □ **tuvo la descabellada idea...; ...una conjetura extravagante**
■ *n.* ***in the wild,*** in country which is uninhabited and where animals can live freely. □ **en estado natural**
wildcat *adj.* risky/reckless: *a wildcat scheme.* □ **descabellado**
wildcat strike, unofficial strike/strike of workers without the union's permission. □ **huelga salvaje**
wilderness ['wildənəs] *n.* uncultivated/uninhabited country; desert. □ **región sin cultivar/habitar; desierto**
wildfire *n.* ***to spread like wildfire,*** to spread very quickly: *the news spread like wildfire.* □ **propagarse como la pólvora**
wildfowl *n. pl.* wild birds shot for sport (such as ducks and geese). □ **aves de caza**
wild goose chase *n.* hopeless search for something. □ **búsqueda inútil**
wildlife *n.* (*no pl.*) wild animals. □ **fauna**
wildlife park, park where wild animals (such as lions, zebras) are allowed to run wild. □ **parque de animales salvajes**
wildly *adv.* **1** in a wild way: *the dog attacked the man wildly.* □ **furiosamente**
2 *what he wrote is wildly inaccurate,* completely wrong. □ **...no tiene ni pies ni cabeza**
wiles [wailz] *n. pl.* clever tricks. □ **tretas**
wilful ['wilfəl] *adj.* **1** (person) determined to do what he wants: *he's a wilful child – he doesn't do what I tell him.* □ **terco**
2 done on purpose. □ **deliberado**
wilful murder, murder which has been planned. □ **...premeditado**
wilfully *adv.* intentionally/on purpose. □ **deliberadamente**
will [wil] *n.* **1** strength of mind and character: *he has a strong will; she has a will of her own.* □ **voluntad**
to work with a will, to work very hard and earnestly. □ **trabajar con ilusión**
2 wish: *my son bought a motorbike against my will.* □ **voluntad**
of one's own free will: *I signed the paper of my own free will,* I was not forced to sign it. □ **...por mi propia voluntad**
at will: *we leave the window open and the cat comes and goes at will,* as she wishes. □ **...entra y sale a su antojo**
3 written instructions of someone as to what should happen to his belongings when he dies: *have you made your will yet? I've left the house to my son in my will.* □ **testamento**
■ *v.* **1** to suggest strongly to someone else by power of mind: *while watching the match I was willing my team to win.* □ **desear**
2 to leave your belongings after death to others by writing down your wishes: *my father has willed all his property to my mother.* □ **legar**
■ *v.* (used with an infinitive): (present: ***he will;*** past and conditional: ***he would; will not/would not*** contract to ***won't/wouldn't***). **1** to wish: *stop that noise – I won't have it!* □ **¡...no quiero oírlo!**
2 (polite form of asking someone to do something): *would you please sit down?/won't you sit down?/take a seat, will you?* □ **¿le importaría sentarse?**
3 to be certain to happen: *accidents will happen; I forgot your birthday – you would! the cat will keep eating the dog's food; she would come home at 6 o'clock and her dinner would always be ready.* □ **se producirán accidentes**
4 to guess the identity: *would this be your cousin?* □ **¿será éste tu primo?**
■ *verb forming future tense.* **1** (showing something happening in the future): *you will get a letter tomorrow; he won't be coming on Saturday; you will remember, won't you? you won't forget, will you? if you invite him he'll come; if you invited him he would come.* □ **mañana recibirás una carta**
2 (command in the future): *you'll arrive at 2 o'clock and you will be on time!* □ **vas a llegar a las 2 y...**
3 (showing a condition): *he would come if he could; if she were still alive, she would be a hundred years old today.* □ **vendría si pudiera; ...hoy tendría cien años**
willing *adj.* wanting to do something/eager to help: *I need a few willing people to help move the car; are you willing to help?* □ **dispuesto**
■ *n.* eagerness to help: *to show willing,* to show you are ready to help. □ **buena disposición; buena voluntad**
willingly *adv.* eagerly. □ **de buena gana**
willingness *n.* eagerness. □ **buena voluntad**
willpower *n.* strength of will: *I haven't the willpower to give up smoking.* □ **fuerza de voluntad**
willies ['wiliz] *n. pl. it gives me the willies,* (*informal*) it makes me scared. □ **canguis; me da canguis**
willow ['wilou] *n.* tree with thin supple branches often found along river banks. □ **sauce**
willowherb *n.* common weed with tall spikes of pink flowers. □ **adelfa**
willow pattern *n.* china with a blue and white Chinese design on it. □ **plato de estilo chino**
willowy *adj.* tall and slender. □ **esbelto**
willy-nilly [wili'nili] *adv.* whether you want to or not:

he had to go along with the crowd, willy-nilly. □ **quiera o no quiera**

wilt [wilt] *n.* disease of plants which makes them droop. □ **marchitamiento**

■ *v.* to become weak and droop: *she was wilting after walking in the hot sun; plants wilt if they haven't enough water.* □ **languidecer (persona); marchitarse**

wily ['waili] *adj.* (*wilier, wiliest*) crafty/full of tricks: *make sure he pays you the money first, as he's a wily old fellow.* □ **astuto**

wimple ['wimpl] *n.* linen covering worn by nuns over their heads. □ **griñón**

win [win] *n.* action of beating someone in a competition/game: *in the last four games our team has had three wins and one draw.* □ **victoria**

■ *v.* (*he won*) **1** to defeat someone in a contest/race, etc.; to be first in a race/competition, etc.: *our team won at home; my horse won the race easily.* □ **ganar**

2 to gain/to get: *his roses won him a gold medal in the Flower Show; I won a holiday in the lottery; to win someone's love.* □ **valer a alguien (medalla); ganar (vacaciones); enamorar a uno**

win back *v.* to get back/to regain. □ **reconquistar**

winner *n.* **1** person who has won a race/a prize, etc.: *the winner of the 100 metres was a German.* □ **vencedor**

2 (*informal*) thing which is certain to be successful: *his play is a real winner.* □ **éxito**

winning *adj.* **1** which wins: *winning ticket; winning team.* □ **ganador**

2 attractive: *a winning smile.* □ **encantador**

■ *n.* **1** victory: *the winning of the race is the driver's aim.* □ **victoria**

winning post, post which marks the end of the race. □ **meta**

2 ***winnings,*** money, etc., which has been won at a game of chance. □ **premio**

win over *v.* to persuade: *his election speech won over many voters.* □ **atraer**

win through *v.* to succeed in the end after many difficulties. □ **triunfar por fin**

wince [wins] *n.* movement which shows you feel pain. □ **mueca de dolor**

■ *v* to show signs of pain, especially by moving the face: *she winced as the needle went into her arm.* □ **hacer una mueca de dolor**

winceyette [winsi'et] *n.* soft cotton material, often used for babies' clothes. □ **franela**

winch [wintʃ] *n.* (*pl. winches*) device which pulls things up by winding a rope around a drum. □ **torno**

■ *v.* to pull up/to lift by using a winch. □ **izar por medio de un torno**

wind[1] [wind] *n.* **1** moving air: *there's a light westerly wind today; in high winds boats look for a harbour,* in very strong winds. □ **viento**

head wind, wind blowing straight towards the face. □ **viento de cara**

in the teeth of the wind, against the wind. □ **contra el viento**

to go like the wind, (*informal*) to run quickly: *my new car goes like the wind.* □ **ir como el rayo**

to get/to have the wind up, (*informal*) to be frightened. □ **tener el miedo metido en el cuerpo**

to put the wind up someone, (*informal*) to frighten someone. □ **meter a uno el miedo en el cuerpo**

to sail close to the wind, (i) to sail a boat almost directly into the wind. □ **bolinear; ceñir**

(ii) to be very near to being dishonest or rude: *the comedian sailed a bit close to the wind with some of his jokes.* □ **estar a punto de pasarse**

to take the wind out of someone's sails, to spoil someone's plans, usually by doing what he was going to do. □ **tomar la delantera**

2 breath: *I had to stop running until I got my wind back.* □ **resuello**

to get your second wind, to get enough breath again after being tired, to be able to make a second effort. □ **recobrar el resuello**

3 smell or scent, when hunting: *the dog got wind of the rabbit and rushed after it.* □ **rastro**

***to get wind of** a plan,* to hear a rumour about a plan. □ **enterarse**

4 gas in the stomach: *cucumbers give me the wind.* □ **gases**

5 woodwind instruments in an orchestra: *the strings start the melody, followed by the wind.* □ **los instrumentos de viento**

■ *v.* **1** to make (someone) breathless, especially by hitting him in the chest: *his head hit me and completely winded me.* □ **dejar a uno sin aliento**

2 to smell or scent when hunting. □ **olfatear**

windbag *n.* (*informal*) person who talks too much. □ **charlatán**

windbreak *n.* fence/hedge which shelters something against the wind: *a line of trees is a good windbreak.* □ **protección contra el viento**

windburn *n.* inflammation of the skin caused by cold wind. □ **irritación cutánea**

windcheater, *Amer.* **windbreaker** *n.* short jacket, often with a hood, to keep out the wind. □ **cazadora**

windfall *n.* **1** fruit which has been blown to the ground from a fruit tree. □ **fruta caída**

2 unexpected good fortune: *I've had a sudden windfall — my aunt has given me $1,000.* □ **golpe de suerte; bonanza**

wind gauge *n.* instrument for measuring the force of the wind. □ **anemómetro**

windmill *n.* mill driven by sails pushed around by the wind. □ **molino de viento**

windpipe *n.* pipe leading from the nose and mouth to the lungs. □ **tráquea**

windscreen, *Amer.* **windshield** *n.* glass window in the front of a car/lorry, etc. □ **parabrisas**

windsock *n.* tube of material at the end of a tall pole, which shows the direction of the wind at an airfield. □ **manga (de viento)**

windswept *adj.* blown by strong winds: *windswept hair; windswept countryside.* □ **despeinada (persona); azotado por el viento (campo)**

windward *adj.* and *n.* (side of a ship) from which the wind blows: *it's cold on the windward side of the ship.* □ **de barlovento**

windy *adj.* **1** having much wind: *the washing dries well on a windy day.* □ **de mucho viento; ventoso**

2 (*informal*) cowardly. □ **acobardado**

wind[2] [waind] *n.* bend/twist/turn: *I have given the clock a few winds,* I have turned the key a few times. □ **vuelta**

■ *v.* (*he wound*) **1** to turn: *the road winds up the hill; the procession wound through the streets of the town.* □ **serpentear (carretera); dar vueltas a (procesión)**

2 to roll up/to roll round: *I'm winding the wool into a ball; the nurse wound a bandage round his arm.* □ **enrollar; hacer un ovillo de lana; vendar**

3 *to wind a watch/a clock,* to turn a key until the spring is tight: *you need to wind this watch every day.* □ **dar cuerda**

winding *adj.* turning/twisting: *a winding road.* □ **tortuoso**

■ *n.* action of turning/rolling: *winding the wool takes a long time.* □ **devanado**
wind up *v.* **1** to roll up: *I'm winding up the wool into a ball.* □ **devanar; ovillar**
2 to tighten a spring on a watch/clockwork toy, etc.: *have you wound up the clock today?* □ **dar cuerda**
3 to finish: *he wound up his speech with a story about his childhood; I wound up one bank account, but kept the other open.* □ **terminar**
4 *the company is being wound up,* being put into liquidation. □ **están liquidando la compañía**
5 ***to be all wound up,*** (*informal*) to be nervous/tense. □ **estar nervioso**

windlass ['windləs] *n.* (*pl. windlasses*) hand winch for pulling something up by winding a rope round a drum. □ **cabrestante**

window ['windou] *n.* opening in a wall/door, etc. filled with glass: *look out of the window! it is dangerous to lean out of car windows.* □ **ventana**
stained-glass window, window made of small pieces of coloured glass, found especially in churches. □ **vidriera**
window box *n.* long box for plants kept in the open air, on the outside ledge of a window. □ **jardinera**
window dressing *n.* art of displaying goods in an artistic way in a shop window; putting on a display to hide the real state of affairs. □ **decoración de escaparates**
windowledge, windowsill *n.* ledge/flat piece of wood, etc., inside and outside a window: *there is a row of plants on each windowsill.* □ **alféizar**
window-pane *n.* single piece of glass, used as part of a whole window. □ **cristal**
window shopping *n.* looking at goods in shop windows without buying them. □ **mirar escaparates**

wine [wain] *n.* **1** alcoholic drink made from the juice of grapes: *dry wine; sweet wine; Burgundy is an important wine-producing region.* □ **vino**
wine list, list of wines which are available at a restaurant. □ **carta de vinos**
2 alcoholic drink made from the juice of fruit or flowers: *rhubarb wine; elderberry wine.* □ **vino de ruibarbo; de saúco**
■ *v.* ***to wine and dine someone,*** to take someone out for dinner and drinks. □ **invitar a cenar/comer fuera**
wine cellar *n.* cool room underground where wine is kept. □ **bodega**
wineglass *n.* glass used for drinking wine. □ **copa; vaso para vino**
wine-growing *n.* growing of vines to produce wine. □ **vinicultura**
wine merchant *n.* person who sells wines and spirits in a shop. □ **bodeguero**
wine waiter *n.* person in charge of serving the wines in a restaurant. □ **'sommelier'**

wing [wiŋ] *n.* **1** one of the two limbs which a bird/butterfly, etc., uses to fly: *the blackbird flapped its wings and flew off.* □ **ala**
to take someone under your wing, to protect/to look after. □ **tomar a uno bajo su protección**
2 one of the two flat projecting parts on an aircraft. □ **ala**
3 side part of a large building which leads off the main part: *the west wing of the house is open to the public.* □ **ala**
4 part of a car body which covers the wheel. □ **aleta**
5 part of an army which stretches to one side; part of a political party which has a certain tendency: *the left wing of the army was attacked first; members of the right wing of the socialist party.* □ **ala**
6 group of squadrons in the air force. □ **ala**
wing commander, rank in the air force below group captain. □ **teniente coronel**
7 ***wings,*** side of the stage in a theatre where actors wait before going on stage. □ **bastidores**
8 *they're waiting* ***in the wings,*** waiting for the right moment to do something. □ **...entre bastidores**
9 side of a football/hockey pitch: *the player took the ball down the left wing.* □ **banda; ala**
10 (*in football/hockey*) forward player on the side of the pitch. □ **extremo**
■ *v.* to fly: *swallows wing their way south in the autumn.* □ **volar**
winged *adj.* with wings. □ **alado**
winger *n.* **1** forward player on the side of the pitch in football/hockey. □ **extremo**
2 person on the right/left of a political party: *a right-winger.* □ **político de derechas/izquierdas**
wingless *adj.* having no wings. □ **sin alas**
wing nut *n.* type of nut with two projecting parts for screwing easily. □ **tuerca mariposa**
wingspan *n.* distance from the tip of one wing to the tip of another (in a bird/aircraft, etc.). □ **envergadura**

wink [wiŋk] *n.* act of quickly shutting and opening one eye: *he gave me a wink as I passed.* □ **guiño**
to have forty winks, (*informal*) to have a short sleep. □ **echarse una siestecita**
to tip someone the wink, (*informal*) to warn someone of something. □ **avisar a tiempo**
■ *v.* **1** to shut one eye and then quickly open it again: *my brother winks at all the pretty girls.* □ **guiñar**
2 (*of lights/stars*) to shine on and off: *I can see the lights of the houses winking in the valley below; the stars winked up above.* □ **...titilando abajo en el valle**
winking *n.* act of shutting and opening one eye. □ **guiño**
as easy as winking, (*informal*) very easy/easily: *he took out the car engine as easy as winking.* □ **con gran facilidad**

winkle ['wiŋkl] *n.* edible snail which lives in salt water. □ **bígaro**
■ *v.* ***to winkle something out,*** to get something out with difficulty. □ **sacar a duras penas**

winnow ['winou] *v.* to separate the grain from chaff, by allowing the wind to blow the chaff away. □ **aventar**

winsome ['winsəm] *adj.* pleasant/charming. □ **encantador**

winter ['wintə] *n.* coldest season of the year: *in winter we wear our warmest clothes.* □ **invierno**
winter sports, sports which are played on snow or ice (like skiing and skating). □ **deportes de invierno**
■ *v.* to spend the cold months of the year: *the cows winter in the barns; some people winter in the South of France.* □ **invernar**
wintry *adj.* **1** like winter: *wintry weather.* □ **invernal**
2 *wintry smile,* unfriendly/cold smile. □ **glacial**

wipe [waip] *n.* act of cleaning or drying with a cloth: *I must give the table a good wipe.* □ **limpieza**
■ *v.* to clean/to dry with a cloth: *I've washed the cups, who will wipe them? here's a handkerchief to wipe your nose! please wipe your shoes on the mat before coming in.* □ **secar; limpiar**
wipe away *v.* to clean away: *the teacher wiped away the little girl's tears.* □ **enjugar; quitar**
wipe out *v.* **1** to clean and dry the inside of something: *I wiped out the bucket after using it.* □ **dejar limpio**

2 to kill/to destroy: *the whole village was wiped out by the enemy; bleach wipes out germs; this money should wipe out all your debts.* □ **destruir**
wiper *n.* something that wipes. □ **trapo**
windscreen wiper, *Amer.* ***windshield wiper,*** device on a car which wipes rain away from the front window, so that the driver can see clearly. □ **limpiaparabrisas**
rear wiper, device for wiping the rain from the rear window of a car. □ **...trasero**

wire ['waiə] *n.* **1** thin metal line or thread: *we tied the rose to the tree with a piece of strong wire.* □ **alambre**
wire netting, pieces of wire twisted together to make a net, used especially along the side of land instead of a fence or hedge: *wire netting around the chicken house stops the foxes getting in.* □ **alambrada**
barbed wire, wire with sharp pieces of metal twisted in at intervals, used to stop animals or people from getting in or out. □ **alambre de espino**
live wire, (i) wire which carries an electrical current. □ **alambre con corriente**
(ii) person who is full of energy. □ **tipo dinámico**
telegraph/telephone wire, wire along which telegraph/telephone messages are sent. □ **hilo telefónico/telegráfico**
wire tapping, listening to other people's telephone conversations with special equipment. □ **intervención de un teléfono**
to get one's wires crossed: *we must have got our wires crossed,* (*informal*) we must have misunderstood each other. □ **ha habido un malentendido (entre nosotros)**
2 (*informal*) telegram: *I'll send him a wire to say we're coming.* □ **telegrama**
■ *v.* **1** to fasten with wires. □ **atar con alambre**
2 to put in wires to carry electricity to a house: *the electrician has wired the new house.* □ **hacer la instalación eléctrica**
3 to send a telegram: *she wired me about his accident.* □ **telegrafiar**
wireless *n.* radio: *I heard the news on the wireless.* □ **radio**
■ *adj.* without wires. □ **inalámbrico**
wiring *n.* system of wires used to carry electricity: *the electrician will remove all the old wiring from the house.* □ **instalación eléctrica**
wiry *adj.* **1** (*of person*) thin but strong. □ **todo nervio**
2 (*of hair*) stiff and strong, not easily combed. □ **tieso**

wisdom ['wizdəm] *n.* intelligence/knowledge/common sense. □ **sabiduría**
wisdom tooth, one of four back teeth which grow when you are an adult. □ **muela del juicio**

wise [waiz] *adj.* having intelligence and common sense/knowing a great deal/prudent: *older people are wiser than younger, because wisdom comes with age; they were wise to take an umbrella because it started to rain later.* □ **juicioso; prudente**
to be none the wiser: *I listened to the lecture but I'm none the wiser,* I know no more than I did before; *if you say nothing, then no one will be any the wiser,* no one will know anything about it. □ **me quedé igual; ...nadie sabrá nada de esto**
wisecrack *n.* clever remark. □ **salida**
■ *v.* to make a joke/a wisecrack. □ **hacer comentarios chistosos/agudos**
wisely *adv.* **1** in a wise way: *he shook his head wisely.* □ **sabiamente**
2 prudently: *he wisely took out an insurance against theft.* □ **prudentemente**

wish [wiʃ] *n.* (*pl. wishes*) **1** want/desire: *the parcel has been sent according to your wishes; her wish came true – she married a millionaire; I haven't the slightest wish to go to the moon.* □ **deseo**
2 kind feelings/greetings: *please give my best wishes to your mother; best wishes for a happy Christmas!* □ **saludos; deseos**
■ *v.* **1** to want/to desire something which is unlikely to happen: *I wish I could live on a Greek island; we wish we were young again; you have everything you could wish for.* □ **desear; ojalá pudiera vivir en una isla...; ojalá fuéramos jóvenes...**
2 to want: *I wish to see the director of the company.* □ **querer**
3 to express a desire or a hope: *I wish you goodnight; wish me good luck before I leave!* □ **desear**
wishbone *n.* V-shaped bone in a chicken's breast, which you are supposed to pull with your partner, the person who holds the larger piece being in luck. □ **espoleta; hueso de la suerte**
wishful *adj.* ***that's wishful thinking!,*** you only believe that because you would like it to happen. □ **¡son ilusiones!**

wishy-washy ['wiʃiwɔʃi] *adj.* watery; not strong (colour/character, etc.). □ **aguado; flojo**

wisp [wisp] *n.* small strand; little piece: *a wisp of straw; a wisp of smoke.* □ **trozo (ramal, hebra); columna (de humo)**
wispy *adj.* (*wispier, wispiest*) thin/slight: *wispy clouds.* □ **delgado**

wistaria [wi'stɛəriə] **wisteria** [wi'stiəriə] *n.* climbing plant with sweet-smelling blue flowers. □ **glicina**

wistful ['wistfəl] *adj.* longing for something, but sad as there is no hope of getting it: *the wistful face of a child staring at the toys in the shop window.* □ **triste; melancólico**
wistfully *adv.* in a sad and longing way. □ **con melancolía**

wit [wit] *n.* **1** (*usually* ***wits***) intelligence: *to find the treasure you must use your wits.* □ **inteligencia; ...tienes que usar la cabeza**
2 *he hadn't the wit to run away,* he didn't have the sense to. □ **no fue lo bastante inteligente como para...**
3 ***to be at your wits' ends,*** not knowing what to do next. □ **no saber a qué carta quedarse**
4 ***to keep your wits about you,*** to keep calm in a difficult situation and think hard what to do next. □ **no perder la cabeza**
5 ability to say clever/funny things: *he's a marvellous speaker because he has such a sharp wit.* □ **ingenio**
6 person who says clever and funny things. □ **ingenioso**
■ *v.* ***to wit,*** (*formal*) namely; that is. □ **a saber/esto es**

witch [witʃ] *n.* (*pl. witches*) woman believed to have evil magic powers. □ **bruja**
witchcraft *n.* art of magic/magic power. □ **brujería**
witch doctor *n.* man in a primitive tribe who appears to cure illnesses by magic. □ **hechicero**
witch hunt *n.* cruel investigation of people who are supposed to be politically unreliable. □ **caza de brujas**

with [wið, wiθ] *prep.* **1** accompanied by/together/beside: *he is coming here with his sister; she is staying with friends; have you a pencil with you?* □ **con**
2 having: *the man came in with his hat on; a girl with blue eyes; with your connections you should find the right sort of job.* □ **con**
3 in spite of: *with all his faults he is still a good husband.* □ **con**

4 using: *he cut the bread with a knife; she can only walk with a stick; fill the cup with water.* □ **con**
it's pouring with rain, it's raining hard. □ **está lloviendo a cántaros**
5 from/because of: *he trembled with fright; my hands are blue with cold.* □ **de**
6 (showing manner): *the orchestra played with feeling; when he returned he was welcomed with open arms.* □ **con**
7 (used after many verbs to show a connection): *to agree with someone; to fight with someone; I can do nothing with him,* I can't change him; *I have nothing to do with him,* I won't talk to him if possible.
□ **estar de acuerdo con; luchar con alguien**
to part with something, to give something away.
□ **ceder algo**
to meet with, to have/to experience unexpectedly: *my father met with an accident on the way to work.*
□ **encontrarse con; sufrir**
I'm with you there!, (i) I agree with you! □ **¡estoy contigo!**
(ii) I understand you. □ **te comprendo**
to be with it, (*informal*) to be fashionable/modern: *she may be old but her clothes are really with it.*
□ **estar a la moda**

withdraw [wiθ'drɔː] *v.* (*he withdrew; he has withdrawn*) to move back/to take back/to pull back: *the general told his army to withdraw to the other side of the river,* to go back; *I withdraw what I said,* I didn't mean it/it wasn't true; *to withdraw some money from a bank,* to take money out of your account. □ **retirar(se)**
withdrawal *n.* taking back; removing of money (from a bank account). □ **retirada**
withdrawal symptoms, symptoms shown by someone who is trying to stop taking a drug/smoking, etc. □ **síndrome de abstinencia**
withdrawn *adj.* shy; (person) who does not like meeting other people. □ **introvertido**

wither ['wiðə] *v.* **1** (*of plants*) to grow weaker and dry up: *plants wither in the strong sun.* □ **marchitarse**
2 to cause to grow weaker and dry up: *strong sun withers some plants.* □ **agostar**
3 ***to wither someone with a look,*** to make someone feel embarrassed by looking disapprovingly at him.
□ **fulminar a uno con la mirada**
withering *adj.* scornful/disapproving: *a withering look.* □ **fulminante**

withers ['wiðəz] *n. pl.* part of a horse's back just below the neck. □ **cruz**

withhold [wiθ'hould] *v.* (*he withheld*) to keep back/to refuse to give: *the bank withheld the money until the account was sorted out.* □ **retener**

within [wi'ðin] *prep.* inside: *the police arrived within five minutes; we live within sight of the sea; I'll fetch you in the car from anywhere within reason.* □ **dentro; ...llegó en 5 minutos; ...se ve el mar**

without [wi'ðaut] *prep.* not having/not with: *I'll come without my sister; after the fire we were without clothes and without money; John passed by without seeing us.* □ **sin**
to go without, not to have (something): *we had no money so we went without food for several days.*
□ **pasarse sin (algo)**
it goes without saying that, it hardly needs to be said that: *it goes without saying that the factory will be closed at Christmas.* □ **ni que decir tiene que...**

withstand [wiθ'stænd] *v.* (*he withstood*) to resist/to endure: *the city withstood three months of bombing.*
□ **resistir**

withy ['wiði] *n.* (*pl. withies*) thin twig of willow used to wind round things to tie them together. □ **mimbre**

witness ['witnəs] *n.* (*pl. witnesses*) **1** person who sees something happening: *there were four witnesses to the accident.* □ **testigo**
2 ***to bear witness to,*** to be evidence of: *the marks on his body bore witness to his terrible tortures.*
□ **dar fe de**
3 person who signs his name on a legal paper to say that another's signature is genuine (because he saw him write it): *when you make a will you must have a witness to your signature.* □ **testigo**
■ *v.* **1** to see (something) happen: *did you witness the accident?* □ **ser testigo de**
2 to sign your name on a legal paper to say that another's signature is genuine. □ **firmar un documento como testigo**
3 to give evidence in court. □ **declarar; atestiguar**
witness-box, *Amer.* **witness stand** *n.* place where a witness stands in a law court. □ **barra de los testigos**

wittingly ['witiŋli] *adv.* on purpose/intentionally.
□ **a sabiendas**

witty ['witi] *adj.* (*wittier, wittiest*) clever and funny: *a witty remark.* □ **ingenioso**
witticism ['witisizəm] *n.* clever/funny remark.
□ **agudeza**

wives [waivz] *n. see* **wife.**

wizard ['wizəd] *n.* **1** man who is believed to have magic powers. □ **brujo; mago**
2 clever person/expert: *a wizard with motorbikes; a wizard with plants; a financial wizard.* □ **fenómeno**

wizened ['wizənd] *adj.* dried up and wrinkled: *the wizened face of a very old man.* □ **apergaminado**

woad [wəud] *n.* wild plant with blue flowers, used to make a blue dye. □ **hierba pastel**

wobble ['wɔbl] *n.* shaking movement. □ **bamboleo**
■ *v.* to shake/to move unsteadily: *the girl has just learnt to ride a bicycle and still wobbles a lot; don't sit on that chair – one of the legs wobbles.* □ **bambolear(se)**
wobbly *adj.* unsteady/shaking: *wobbly chair.*
□ **poco firme**

wodge [wɔdʒ] *n.* (*informal*) thick piece. □ **un buen pedazo**

woe [wou] *n.* sadness/trouble: *a long tale of woe.*
□ **aflicción**
woebegone *adj.* very sad: *the dog gave us a woebegone look as we left him.* □ **desconsolado**
woeful *adj.* full of sadness. □ **afligido**

wog [wɔg] *n.* (*slang*) foreigner. □ **negro; sudaca; moraco; etc.**

woke [wouk] **woken** [woukn] *v. see* **wake.**

wold [would] *n.* (*used in names of places*) area of gently rounded hills. □ **llanura ondulada**

wolf [wulf] *n.* (*pl. wolves*) **1** wild animal like a dog, usually living in a large group in cold northern regions. □ **lobo**
pack of wolves, large group of wolves living together. □ **manada de lobos**
lone wolf, person who prefers to be alone/who does not associate with other people. □ **tipo solitario**
she-wolf, female wolf. □ **loba**
wolf cub, young wolf. □ **lobato**
a wolf in sheep's clothing, someone who seems inoffensive but really is wicked. □ **lobo en piel de cordero**
to keep the wolf from the door: *they have difficulty in keeping the wolf from the door,* in buying enough food to live on. □ **...en evitar caer en la miseria**
2 (*informal*) man who chases women. □ **ligón**
wolf whistle, whistle of admiration given by men as

a pretty woman passes. □ **silbido (a modo de piropo)**
■ *v.* to eat quickly: *the children were so hungry that they wolfed down their food in two minutes.* □ **engullir**
wolfhound *n.* large hunting dog. □ **perro lobo**
wolfish *adj.* like a wolf. □ **lobuno**
woman ['wumən] *n.* (*pl. women*) **1** female adult human being: *there will be ten men and ten women at the dinner.* □ **mujer**
Women's Lib, movement to free women so that they can have equal status in society. □ **movimiento de liberación de la mujer**
2 *he's **an old woman,*** (*informal*) he's very fussy. □ **(él) es como una vieja**
3 female: *woman doctor; woman friend.* □ **doctora; amiga**
womanhood *n.* state of being a woman. □ **condición de mujer**
womanly *adj.* feminine, like a woman. □ **femenino**
womenfolk *n. pl.* all women (in a family, etc.). □ **las mujeres**
womb [wu:m] *n.* uterus/place in a woman or other female mammal where a baby grows before it is born. □ **útero**
wombat ['wɔmbət] *n.* small Australian animal. □ **vombat**
won [wʌn] *v. see* **win.**
wonder ['wʌndə] *n.* **1** something amazing: *the Pyramids of Egypt were one of the Seven Wonders of the World; it's a wonder that he hasn't lost the money as he's always losing things; no wonder there isn't any water — there's a hole in the bucket!* □ **maravilla**
2 astonishment/surprise: *we looked in wonder at the Temple of the Incas.* □ **asombrado**
■ *v.* **1** to be surprised/to marvel: *I don't wonder that he feels angry; I shouldn't wonder if it didn't rain today,* I wouldn't be surprised if it rained. □ **sorprenderse**
2 to want to know/to ask yourself: *I wonder why he always wears a green tie; I wonder who is going to win the race.* □ **preguntarse**
3 (used when asking someone politely to do something): *I wonder if you could open the door for me?* □ **¿no le importaría...?**
wonderful *adj.* marvellous/very good/exciting: *we had a wonderful holiday.* □ **maravilloso**
wonderland *n.* marvellous place. □ **mundo maravilloso**
wonderment *n.* astonishment/wonder. □ **maravilla**
wondrous *adj.* (*formal*) wonderful. □ **maravilloso**
wonky ['wɔŋki] *adj.* (*informal*) unsteady/wobbly: *don't sit on that chair — one of its legs is wonky.* □ **cojo**
wont [wount] *n.* (*formal*) habit: *he went out for a walk after lunch, as is his wont.* □ **costumbre**
wonted *adj.* (*formal*) habitual. □ **acostumbrado**
won't [wount] *v. see* **will.**
woo [wu:] *v.* to try to attract (a woman) to marry you; to try to get (someone) to support you/to vote for you, etc.: *the candidates were wooing the voters with promises of lower taxes.* □ **cortejar a (una mujer); solicitar el apoyo de**
wood [wud] *n.* **1** large group of trees/small forest: *the path goes straight through the wood.* □ **bosque**
2 *he **can't see the wood for the trees,*** he concentrates on the details, and cannot appreciate the main problem. □ **los árboles no le dejan ver el bosque**
3 *we're not **out of the wood** yet,* our problems are not over. □ **todavía no se han acabado las preocupaciones**
4 material that a tree is made of: *our table and chairs are made of wood.* □ **madera**
woodbine *n.* wild climbing plant. □ **madreselva**
woodcarving *n.* art of sculpture in wood. □ **escultura en madera**
woodcock *n.* small brown bird shot for sport or food. □ **becada; chocha**
woodcraft *n.* skill at finding your way about woods and forests and living in them. □ **sentido de la orientación (en el bosque)**
woodcut *n.* made from a carved wooden plate. □ **grabado en madera**
wooded *adj.* covered in trees: *wooded countryside.* □ **arbolado**
wooden *adj.* **1** made of wood: *wooden chair; wooden doll.* □ **de madera**
2 stiff/showing no feeling: *he will never be a dancer — his movements are too wooden.* □ **rígido**
woodland *n.* country covered in woods. □ **monte; bosque**
woodlouse *n.* (*pl. woodlice*) very small animal with a hard shell, which can curl up when attacked, and which lives in rotten wood, etc. □ **cochinilla**
woodpecker *n.* bird with a long sharp beak which finds insects under the bark of trees. □ **pájaro carpintero**
woodshed *n.* small shed/hut used for storing wood. □ **leñera**
woodsman, woodman *n.* (*pl. woodsmen, woodmen*) man who works in woods and forests. □ **guarda forestal; leñador**
woodwind *n.* types of wind instrument in an orchestra which are usually made of wood and not brass. □ **instrumentos (de viento) de madera**
woodwork *n.* **1** carpentry/art of making things out of wood: *he's made a bird-table in woodwork classes.* □ **carpintería**
2 wooden parts of a building: *are you going to paint the woodwork?* □ **maderaje**
woodworm *n.* small grub which bores holes in wood. □ **carcoma**
woody *adj.* (*woodier, woodiest*) like wood: made of wood. □ **leñoso**
woofer ['wu:fə] *n.* loudspeaker which reproduces low sounds. □ **altavoz de graves**
wool [wul] *n.* **1** short, thick hair of a sheep/goat, etc. □ **lana**
2 long threads of spun hair, used to make clothes/carpets, etc.; cloth woven from hair: *how much wool will I need to make this jumper? is the material wool or nylon?* □ **lana**
to pull the wool over someone's eyes, to deceive someone. □ **dar a uno gato por liebre**
3 materials which look a little like sheep's wool: *cotton wool; steel wool; glass wool.* □ **algodón hidrófilo; fibra metálica; lana de vidrio**
wool-gathering *n. **to be wool-gathering,*** to be daydreaming/not thinking of what you are doing. □ **estar en la luna**
woollen *adj.* made of wool: *woollen material.* □ **de lana**
woollens *n. pl.* clothes made of knitted wool. □ **ropa de lana**
woolly *adj.* (*woolier, woolliest*) **1** made of wool/like wool: *woolly clouds in the sky.* □ **lanudo/lanoso; nubes de algodón en...**
2 vague/not clear: *woolly ideas.* □ **ideas confusas**
■ *n.* (*informal*) cardigan/jumper: *put on your woolly as it's cold outside.* □ **jersey**
woozy ['wu:zi] *adj.* (*informal*) dizzy/in a daze. □ **aturdido**

word [wɜːd] *n.* **1** unit of speech either spoken or written: *there are hundreds of words on this page; he saw me but he didn't say a word.* □ **palabra**
to have words with someone, to quarrel with someone. □ **tener unas palabras con...**
to have a word with someone, to have a short talk with someone. □ **hablar con alguien**
to say a good word for someone, to recommend/to speak in favour of someone. □ **dar un buen informe de alguien**
in other words, explaining something in a different way. □ **en otras palabras**
to take the words out of someone's mouth: *you've taken the words out of my mouth,* you've said what I was going to say. □ **me has quitado la palabra de la boca**
without a word, without speaking. □ **sin decir palabra**
word for word, exactly as is said or written: *the secretary wrote down everything word for word.* □ **palabra por palabra; literalmente**
2 *the view is too magnificent for words,* it is beyond description. □ **...para describirlo con palabras**
3 message/news: *the governor sent word of the attack on the city; word came that some people were still alive.* □ **aviso**
by word of mouth, by a spoken message. □ **verbalmente; de palabra**
4 promise: *will you give me your word that you won't run away? he kept his word,* he did what he promised to do. □ **palabra; me das tu palabra...**
5 ***to take someone's word for it:*** *I'll take your word for it,* I'll believe what you said. □ **te creo**
6 *interjection expressing* surprise: *my word! what beautiful flowers!* □ **¡hombre!**
7 *word of command,* order. □ **voz de mando**
■ *v.* to put in a phrase, either written or spoken: *how will you word the telegram to my sister? I wrote a well-worded letter to the manager.* □ **redactar**
wording *n.* choice of words: *I like the wording of the advertisement.* □ **términos**
word-perfect *adj.* able to repeat exactly what has been learnt: *the play was excellent, all the actors were word-perfect.* □ **(que sabe) perfectamente su papel**
word processor *n.* typewriter with a computer memory and a screen on which the text can be displayed. □ **procesador de textos**
wordy *adj.* (*wordier, wordiest*) using too many words. □ **verboso; prolijo**

wore ['wɔː] *v. see* **wear.**

work [wɜːk] *n.* **1** mental or physical activity: *it's hard work; I've lots of work to do; when you've finished that piece of work, you can have a rest.* □ **trabajo**
2 ***it's all in a day's work,*** it's normal for me to do it. □ **son gajes del oficio**
3 *he'll have his work cut out to finish in time,* he will find it difficult. □ **se le va a hacer cuesta arriba**
4 job: *father is at work in his office.* □ **trabajo**
out of work, having no job. □ **sin trabajo**
5 something that has been made by someone: *a work of art; the complete works of Shakespeare.* □ **obra**
6 ***works,*** factory: *gasworks; steelworks; brickworks.* □ **fábrica de gas; acería; fábrica de ladrillos**
7 ***road works ahead!,*** people are working on the road ahead. □ **'obras'**
8 ***works,*** moving parts of a machine: *he was poking around in the works.* □ **mecanismo**
9 ***to give someone the works,*** (*informal*) to give someone everything/the full treatment. □ **tratar a alguien a cuerpo de rey**
■ *v.* **1** to use energy/to make someone use energy in carrying out an activity: *you must work hard to pass your exam; the trainer works his football team hard.* □ **trabajar**
2 (*of machine*) to operate/to move: *the car is working well; can you work a drill? the pump works by electricity.* □ **funcionar (coche, bomba); ¿sabes manejar una fresadora?**
3 to have a job: *he works as a gardener; she wants to work in a factory.* □ **trabajar**
4 to be successful: *do you think my plan will work?* □ **funcionar, salir bien**
5 to embroider/to sew: *she worked the cushion in blue and green.* □ **bordar**
6 to move gradually: *I worked the butter into the flour; we worked our way through the crowd; the prisoner worked his hands free; the rope worked loose.* □ **echar poco a poco (mantequilla); ...se soltó las manos; la cuerda se soltó**
to work oneself into: *he was working himself into a rage,* he was becoming more and more angry. □ **fue montando en cólera**
7 *to work a mine,* to take coal/copper, etc., from a mine: *are they still working the mine?; the next mine is worked out,* all the ore has been extracted from it. □ **explotar una mina**
workable *adj.* able to be worked. □ **explotable; realizable**
worker *n.* **1** someone who works: *he's a hard worker.* □ **trabajador**
blue-collar/white-collar worker, person who has a manual job/person who works in an office. □ **obrero/administrativo**
2 member of the working class: *workers of the world unite!* □ **obrero, trabajador**
3 type of female bee which works to provide the queen with honey, but which is sterile. □ **abeja obrera**
workforce *n.* all the workers (in a factory). □ **mano de obra**
working *adj.* which works; referring to work: *a working model of a train; there are five working days in the week and two rest days; it's in good working order.* □ **un modelo ...que funciona; ...días laborables; ...que funciona**
working class, people who work with their hands/who earn wages and not salaries. □ **clase obrera**
working party, group of experts who investigate a certain problem and report on it. □ **grupo de trabajo**
■ *n.* **1** place where mineral has been dug: *iron ore workings.* □ **explotación**
2 way something works: *I'll never understand the workings of his mind.* □ **funcionamiento**
workman *n.* (*pl. workmen*) man who works with his hands. □ **obrero manual**
workmanlike *adj.* skilful/expert. □ **competente**
workmanship *n.* skill of a good workman: *this cupboard is a fine piece of workmanship.* □ **artesanía**
work off *v.* to get rid of (something) by working: *I worked off my dinner by digging the garden.* □ **ganarse**
work on *v.* **1** to continue to work: *you work on while I tell you a story.* □ **seguir trabajando**
2 to be busy doing something: *he's working on a book about the Vietnam war.* □ **trabajar**
3 to try to influence/to persuade: *John will work on his uncle to see if he'll help us.* □ **trabajarse**
work out *v.* **1** to succeed/to do well: *my plan has worked out.* □ **salir bien**

2 to plan in detail/to find an answer: *father is working out the holiday route; can you work out a solution to this problem?* □ **preparar; encontrar (solución)**
3 to amount to (a price): *how much will the holiday work out at? these oranges work out at 6p each.* □ **ascender a**
workout *n.* exercise/practice before a sports contest: *the horse had a workout on the morning of the big race.* □ **entrenamiento**
workroom *n.* room where work is done. □ **sala de trabajo**
workshop *n.* place where things are made in a small factory or house: *my son makes model trains in the workshop in the garden.* □ **taller**
work to rule *v.* to protest by working strictly according to the rules laid down, in such a way that the work is done excessively slowly. □ **hacer huelga de celo**
work up *v.* **1** to develop/to reach slowly: *he started with a small shop and worked the business up.* □ **desarrollar**
2 to get excited and annoyed: *he gets very worked up about politics.* □ **sulfurarse**
world [wə:ld] *n.* **1** the earth; particular part of the earth: *I'd like to sail right round the world.* □ **mundo**
the Old World, Europe, Asia and Africa. □ **el Viejo Mundo**
the New World, North and South America. □ **el Nuevo Mundo**
the Third World, countries with no strong connections to the superpowers. □ **el Tercer Mundo**
World War, war in which many countries all over the world take part. □ **guerra mundial**
2 people on Earth; everything: *the whole world watched the landing of the first men on the moon.* □ **mundo**
3 ***to come into the world:*** *he came into the world in 1974,* he was born in 1974. □ **vino al mundo...**
4 ***to be all alone in the world,*** to have no family. □ **estar solo en el mundo**
5 ***out of this world,*** magnificent. □ **nunca visto**
6 ***to think the world of someone,*** to think very highly of someone. □ **tener en estima a alguien**
7 *it will do you* ***a world of good,*** it will help you very much. □ **te hará muchísimo bien**
8 people with a particular interest/things which form a particular group: *the theatrical world; the art world; the racing world; the world of books; the world of insects.* □ **mundo**
world-famous *adj.* known everywhere: *Charlie Chaplin was world-famous.* □ **famoso en todo el mundo**
worldliness *n.* being worldly/not being idealistic. □ **mundanería; materialismo**
worldly *adj.* (*worldlier, worldliest*) **1** of the world: *I have very few worldly possessions.* □ **mundano**
2 not idealistic. □ **materialista**
worldwide *adj.* and *adv.* through the whole world: *he travels worldwide; worldwide energy crisis.* □ **por todo el mundo**
worm [wə:m] *n.* **1** small, burrowing creature with no backbone which looks like a very small snake and lives in earth: *birds like to eat worms.* □ **gusano**
2 similar animal which lives in the intestines of human beings or animals: *he's got worms.* □ **lombriz**
3 woodworm: *the old chair has worm in it.* □ **carcoma**
4 spiral thread of a screw. □ **rosca; filete**
■ *v.* **1** to move slowly like a worm: *we wormed our way through the crowd.* □ **deslizarse como un gusano**
2 ***to worm yourself into someone's favour,*** to make someone like you by being especially nice to them. □ **hacer la pelota a alguien**
3 *to worm information out of someone,* to get information by asking many persistent questions. □ **sonsacar un secreto a alguien**
wormeaten *adj.* which has been eaten by woodworms. □ **carcomido**
worn [wɔ:n] *adj.* much used: *he put on his worn old jacket for gardening.* see also **wear.** □ **viejo**
worn out *adj.* **1** used so much that it is now useless: *the battery is old and worn out.* □ **gastado**
2 tired: *I feel worn out when I come home from work.* □ **rendido**
worry ['wʌri] *n.* (*pl. worries*) **1** something which makes you anxious: *tell me your worries.* □ **preocupación**
2 being anxious: *the worry made him ill.* □ **inquietud**
■ *v.* (*worried; worrying*) **1** to be upset/anxious; to make someone upset/anxious: *I worry about my daughter; it worries me when she comes home late; don't worry/(informal) not to worry, she'll be all right!* □ **preocuparse**
2 (*of dogs*) to shake and tear with the teeth. □ **sacudir y morder**
3 *to worry sheep,* to chase and attack sheep. □ **atacar**
worried *adj.* anxious/troubled. □ **preocupado**
worrier *n.* person who worries. □ **aprensivo**
worrisome *adj.* which makes you worried/anxious. □ **preocupante**
worse [wə:s] *adj.* **1** more bad: *Jean's writing is bad but yours is worse* (*than hers*); *things are going from bad to worse; I didn't like the film but I have seen worse.* □ **peor**
2 more ill: *I felt ill yesterday but I feel even worse today.* □ **peor**
■ *n.* something more awful: *there was worse to come.* □ **lo peor**
■ *adv.* more badly: *he plays tennis worse than his sister; the noise went on worse than ever,* louder than before. □ **peor**
worsen *v.* to become or make worse: *the situation in the Middle East is worsening.* □ **empeorar**
worse off *adj.* with less money: *we're worse off now than we were five years ago.* □ **vivir peor**
worship ['wə:ʃip] *n.* **1** praise and honour shown to God: *a church is a place of worship.* □ **culto**
2 praise and honour shown to someone/something. □ **veneración**
3 ***Your Worship,*** title of respect used when speaking to a mayor or a magistrate in a law court. □ **señor alcalde; señor juez/ su señoría**
■ *v.* (*he worshipped*) **1** to praise and love (God). □ **adorar**
2 to take part in a church service. □ **asistir al culto**
3 to praise and love (someone/something). □ **venerar**
worshipper *n.* **1** person who worships. □ **devoto**
2 *sun worshipper,* person who loves sunbathing. □ **amante del sol**
worst [wə:st] *adj.* very bad/worse than anyone/anything else: *it was the worst storm this year.* □ **peor**
■ *n.* most awful thing: *the worst of the storm is over so we can go out again; we saw him before breakfast when he is always at his worst.* □ **lo peor de la tormenta...**
■ *adv.* very badly/worse than anyone/anything else: *most people suffered but he suffered the worst.* □ **...lo peor**
worsted ['wustid] *n.* fine woollen cloth. □ **estambre**
worth [wə:θ] *adj.* **1** having a value/price: *the coat is*

worth $1,000; it's not worth the money! □ **que vale**
2 useful; giving a valuable satisfaction: *a book worth reading; it's well worth knowing something about electricity.* □ **que merece la pena**
3 having riches/money, etc.: *when he died they found he was worth millions.* □ **...que tenía millones**
4 *to run **for all you are worth,*** to run as fast as possible. □ **correr a todo correr**
■ *n.* value: *I'd like five pounds' worth of petrol, please; he had nothing of great worth in the house.* □ **valor**
worthless *adj.* having no worth/no use. □ **sin valor**
worth while *adj.* worth the effort: *it's worth while growing your own vegetables; it would be worth your while to read about Italy before going there.* □ **útil**
worthwhile [wəːθ'wail] *adj.* which is worth doing: *a very worthwhile project.* □ **que vale la pena**
worthy ['wəːði] *adj.* deserving: *he is a worthy winner of the Nobel Prize; she's a good teacher and worthy of respect; to give money to a worthy cause.* □ **meritorio, que merece**

would [wud] *v. see* **will.**

wound [wuːnd] *n.* **1** cut/damage to the skin, usually received in a fight: *the nurse washed the soldier's wounds.* □ **herida**
2 hurt to your feelings. □ **daño**
■ *v.* **1** to hurt: *the police wounded two of the robbers as they escaped with the money.* □ **herir**
2 to hurt your feelings: *none of his family came to the wedding and this wounded his pride.* □ **herir**
3 *see also* **wind.**

wove [wouv] **woven** ['wouvn] *v. see* **weave.**

wow [wau] *n.* (*informal*) great success: *he was a wow at the party.* □ **algo formidable**
■ *v.* (*informal*) (*of a singer, etc.*) to excite (the audience): *he wowed them with his act.* □ **embelesar**

wrack [ræk] *n.* seaweed. □ **fuco; varec**

wraith [raiθ] *n.* ghost. □ **espectro**

wrangle ['ræŋgl] *n.* argument/dispute. □ **altercado**
■ *v.* to argue. □ **reñir**

wrap [ræp] *n.* shawl. □ **chal**
to keep something under wraps, (*informal*) to keep something a secret. □ **guardar algo en el más absoluto secreto**
■ *v.* (*he wrapped*) to cover (something) all round with paper/cloth, etc.: *he was wrapping the book in brown paper before posting it.* □ **envolver**
wrap up *v.* **1** to cover up completely: *we shall wrap up the parcels on Christmas Eve.* □ **envolver**
2 to wear warm clothes: *wrap up warmly as it's freezing cold outside.* □ **arroparse**
3 *to be wrapped up in your work,* to think only of the work and take no notice of other things. □ **estar absorto en el trabajo**
wrapper *n.* piece of paper used to cover something. □ **envoltura**
wrapping *n.* paper/cardboard/plastic, etc., used to wrap things. □ **envoltura**
wrapping paper, paper used to wrap presents. □ **papel de regalo**

wrath [rɔθ] *n.* great anger. □ **ira; furia**
wrathful *adj.* angry. □ **furioso**

wreak [riːk] *v.* to carry out/to do (something violent): *the storm wreaked havoc among the yachts.* □ **ejecutar; la tormenta hizo estragos...**

wreath [riːθ] *n.* **1** circle of flowers or leaves especially given at funerals in memory of the dead person. □ **corona**
2 *wreaths of smoke/mist,* winding clouds of smoke/mist. □ **espiral (de humo); manto (de niebla)**
wreathe [riːð] *v.* **1** to put a circle of flowers on (someone/something). □ **ceñir**
2 to cover with twisting clouds of smoke/mist: *we could see nothing as the building was wreathed in smoke.* □ **envolver**

wreck [rek] *n.* **1** ship which has been sunk/badly damaged on rocks, etc.: *there are many wrecks along this coast.* □ **buque naufragado**
2 action of being wrecked: *the wreck of the liner.* □ **naufragio**
3 anything which has been damaged and is useless: *my car was a total wreck after the accident.* □ **mi coche se quedó hecho una ruina...**
4 person who, because of illness, can do very little: *he's a nervous wreck.* □ **ruina**
■ *v.* to cause severe damage to (something): *fire wrecked the whole house; the accident wrecked our hopes for a happy holiday; the children have wrecked the piano by banging on it.* □ **destruir; arruinar**
wreckage *n.* broken remains of a building/ship, etc., after a disaster: *after the earthquake rats ran about among the wreckage.* □ **escombros (de edificio); pecio (de un barco)**
wrecker *n.* **1** person who destroys a building/train, etc., on purpose, or tries to make a ship crash on to rocks. □ **vándalo (tren, casa, etc.); provocador de naufragios**
2 person whose work it is to destroy old buildings/break up old cars, etc. □ **demoledor de casas**
3 *Amer.* truck which goes to help cars which have broken down on the road; engine which goes to help a train which has broken down on the track. □ **grúa; locomotora de auxilio**

wren [ren] *n.* **1** type of very small brown songbird. □ **reyezuelo**
2 ***Wren,*** woman member of the Royal Navy. □ **mujer perteneciente a la Armada**

wrench [rentʃ] *n.* (*pl. wrenches*) **1** violent twisting movement: *he opened the door with a wrench of the handle.* □ **tirón**
2 large spanner for turning nuts: *adjustable wrench; monkey wrench.* □ **llave inglesa**
3 sadness at leaving someone or something: *it was a wrench to say goodbye to all our friends.* □ **pena**
■ *v.* to turn and pull violently: *he wrenched the lid off the box.* □ **arrancar**

wrest [rest] *v.* (*formal*) to twist/to wrench away: *the soldiers wrested power from the president.* □ **arrebatar**

wrestle ['resl] *v.* **1** to fight with someone in a contest by trying to throw him to the ground. □ **luchar**
2 to fight or struggle with anything: *each week I wrestle with the accounts.* □ **luchar; pelearse**
wrestler *n.* person who wrestles in contests. □ **luchador**
wrestling *n.* ***wrestling match,*** contest of wrestlers watched by crowds of people. □ **lucha**

wretch [retʃ] *n.* (*pl. wretches*) **1** person who looks poor and miserable: *the poor wretch had no coat or shoes in the winter.* □ **desgraciado**
2 naughty/annoying person: *you little wretch – you've eaten all the chocolates!* □ **bandido**
wretched ['retʃid] *adj.* **1** miserable and poor: *poor people live in wretched houses; I feel wretched,* I feel ill. □ **miserable; me siento muy mal**
2 terrible/annoying: *what wretched weather! what's the wretched boy doing?* □ **¡vaya tiempecito!; ¿...ese maldito niño?**
wretchedly *adv.* miserably. □ **lamentablemente**

wriggle ['rigl] *v.* to twist and turn: *the snake wriggled away; sit still and stop wriggling!* □ **culebrear; menearse, moverse**

wring [riŋ] *v.* (*he wrung*) **1** to twist (something), especially to get water out of it: *mother wrings out the washing before hanging it out to dry; if you want to kill a chicken, wring its neck.* □ **escurrir (la ropa); retorcer (el cuello)**
2 *after many days he wrung the information from me,* he managed to get the information with difficulty. □ **...me arrancó la información...**
3 ***to wring your hands,*** to twist and turn your hands, showing sadness and emotion. □ **retorcerse las manos**
wringer *n.* machine for squeezing the water out of wet washing. □ **escurridor**
wringing *adj.* ***wringing wet,*** very wet. □ **empapado**
wrinkle ['riŋkl] *n.* **1** line/fold of the skin: *as she grew older more wrinkles appeared on her face.* □ **arruga**
2 line or crease in cloth: *iron the skirt to take out the wrinkles.* □ **arruga**
■ *v.* to make lines/creases: *when she's thinking she wrinkles her forehead.* □ **fruncir el ceño**
wrist [rist] *n.* joint between the arm and the hand. □ **muñeca**
wrist watch, small watch worn on a strap around the wrist. □ **reloj de pulsera**
writ [rit] *n.* legal paper ordering someone to do/not to do something. □ **orden judicial**
Holy Writ *n.* the Bible. □ **la Sagrada Escritura**
write [rait] *v.* (*he wrote*; *he has written*) **1** to put down words on paper: *have you written your shopping list?* □ **escribir**
2 to be the author of books/music, etc.: *what does your father do? – he writes; she wrote the book in six months; Beethoven wrote nine symphonies.* □ **escribir**
3 to put a letter in writing and send it to someone: *have you written to your mother? write* (*to*) *me when you arrive in Hong Kong.* □ **¿has escrito a...?**
that's nothing to write home about, (*informal*) it's nothing special. □ **eso no tiene nada de particular**
write off *v.* **1** to remove (something) from a written list. □ **borrar**
2 *he couldn't pay so I wrote off his debt,* cancelled it in my accounts. □ **...así que le condoné/cancelé la deuda**
3 *the car was written off after the accident,* the insurance company considered it a total loss. □ **...que fue siniestro total**
write-off *n.* (*informal*) total loss: *our car was a write-off after the accident.* □ **siniestro total**
writer *n.* person who writes, especially to earn money. □ **escritor**
write up *v.* to describe fully in writing: *he wrote up the notes he had taken in the class.* □ **redactar**
write-up *n.* (*informal*) article in a newspaper: *our play had a good write-up in the local paper.* □ **crítica**
writing *n.* something that is written: *please answer in writing; your writing is awful – I can't read it.* □ **escrito**
writing paper, paper used for writing letters. □ **papel de escribir**
writings *n. pl.* books, etc., written by an author: *the writings of Goethe.* □ **escritos; obras**
writhe [raið] *v.* to twist and turn (in agony). □ **retorcerse**
wrong [rɔŋ] *adj.* **1** bad/not right: *it is wrong to steal.* □ **mal/malo**
2 not right; incorrect: *what's the time? – I don't know, my watch is wrong; I'm sorry, I was wrong and you were right; you've come to the wrong house.* □ **equivocado; mi reloj va mal**
3 ***what's wrong?,*** what is the matter? □ **¿qué pasa?**
4 *I hope nothing's wrong,* I hope nothing bad has happened. □ **espero que no haya sucedido nada malo**
■ *n.* something that is bad/incorrect. □ **mal**
to be in the wrong: *he's in the wrong,* he isn't right/he's made a mistake. □ **no tiene razón**
■ *adv.* badly/incorrectly: *I've addressed the letter wrong.* □ **equivocadamente**
to go wrong, to break down; not to work right: *everything has gone wrong this morning.* □ **ir mal**
■ *v.* to treat (someone) unfairly: *he was wronged by the newspaper article.* □ **tratar a (alguien) injustamente**
wrongdoer *n.* person who has committed a crime. □ **delincuente**
wrongdoing *n.* crime/unlawful act. □ **infracción; delito**
wrongful *adj.* unjust/lawful: *wrongful dismissal.* □ **injusto; despido improcedente**
wrongly *adv.* incorrectly/badly: *the letter has been wrongly addressed.* □ **incorrectamente**
wrote [rout] *v. see* **write.**
wrought [rɔːt] *adj.* ***wrought iron,*** hammered, twisted and bent iron used for making decorative gates/balconies, etc. □ **hierro forjado**
wrung [ruŋ] *v. see* **wring.**
wry [rai] *adj.* (*wryer, wryest*) showing dislike by twisting the mouth: *she made a wry face when she tasted the bitter coffee.* □ **torció el gesto**

X,x

X, x [eks] twenty-fourth letter of the alphabet. □ **X, x**

film with an X certificate, film which is not suitable for children. □ **...para mayores de 18 años**

X-ray *n.* **1** ray which will pass through solids and is used especially in hospitals for photographing the inside of the body. □ **rayos X**

2 photograph taken with X-rays: *he has gone to have an X-ray.* □ **radiografía**

■ *v.* to take an X-ray photograph: *she had her ankle X-rayed.* □ **hacer una radiografía**

xenophobe ['zenəfoub] *n.* person who dislikes foreigners. □ **xenófobo**

xenophobia [zenə'foubiə] *n.* hatred of foreigners. □ **xenofobia**

xenophobic *adj.* hating foreigners. □ **xenófobo**

xerox ['ziərɔks] *n.* (*pl. xeroxes*) **1** trademark for a type of photocopier. □ **fotocopiadora**

2 photocopy made with this machine. □ **fotocopia**

■ *v.* to make a photocopy with a xerox machine. □ **fotocopiar**

Xmas ['krisməs, 'eksməs] *n.* (*pl. Xmases*) short for **Christmas.** □ **Navidad**

xylophone ['zailəfoun] *n.* musical instrument consisting of wooden bars of different lengths which make different notes when they are tapped with a hammer. □ **xilófono**

Y,y

Y, y [wai] twenty-fifth letter of the alphabet. □ **Y, y**

yacht [jɔt] *n.* boat used for pleasure and sport. □ **yate**

yacht club, sailing club. □ **club náutico**

yachting *n.* art of sailing a boat. □ **deporte de la vela**

yachtsman *n.* (*pl. yachtsmen*) person who sails a yacht. □ **balandrista**

yack [yæk] *v.* (*informal*) to talk incessantly. □ **hablar por los codos**

yak [jæk] *n.* long-haired ox from Asia. □ **yak**

yam [jæm] *n.* sweet potato/tropical plant with an edible root. □ **batata**

yank [jæŋk] *n.* **1** (*informal*) short sharp pull. □ **tirón**

2 (*informal*) American. □ **yanqui**

■ *v.* (*informal*) to pull hard and sharply: *the dentist yanked out my tooth.* □ **pegar un tirón**

Yank, Yankee *n.* (*informal*) American (especially from the northern states). □ **yanqui**

yap [jæp] *n.* short sharp bark of a dog. □ **ladrido agudo**

■ *v.* (*he yapped*) to make short sharp barks: *the dog was yapping around my feet.* □ **ladrar**

yard [jɑ:d] *n.* **1** measure of length (= .91 metre): *there are three feet in a yard, and 1,760 yards in a mile.* □ **yarda**

2 piece of wood attached to the mast holding a sail. □ **verga**

3 enclosed space (often paved) behind a house or other building: *the washing was blowing on a line across the yard.* □ **patio**

4 *Amer.* small garden round a house. □ **jardincito**

5 enclosed space used for a certain purpose. □ **corral; almacén**

builder's yard, place where a builder keeps stocks of wood/bricks, etc. □ **almacén; depósito**

goods' yard, space where trains are loaded with goods. □ **estación de mercancías**

6 *Scotland Yard*/(*informal*) *the Yard,* headquarters of the London Metropolitan Police. □ **Scotland Yard**

yardage *n.* length in yards or area in square yards. □ **longitud o superficie en yardas**

yardarm *n.* end of the yard or piece of wood holding the sail. □ **penol de verga**

yardstick *n.* standard for measurement: *the opinion polls are the yardstick by which you can test the government's popularity.* □ **criterio**

yarn [yɑ:n] *n.* **1** long thread of wool/fibre used in knitting or weaving: *you need ten balls of yarn for the jumper.* □ **hilo**

2 (*informal*) long story. □ **cuento**

to spin a yarn, to tell a story, often one that is not true. □ **contar un cuento**

■ *v.* (*informal*) to talk at length, especially telling stories. □ **contar historias**

yashmak ['jæʃmæk] *n.* veil worn by Muslim women. □ **velo**

yaw [jɔ:] *v.* (*of ship/aircraft*) to go away from the course. □ **desviarse**

yawl [jɔ:l] *n.* type of two-masted fishing boat. □ **yola**

yawn [jɔ:n] *n.* movement of opening the mouth when tired: *to stifle a yawn,* to try to stop yawning. □ **bostezo**

■ *v.* to open your mouth wide when you are feeling sleepy, and to breathe in and out. □ **bostezar**

to yawn your head off, to yawn again and again. □ **bostezar hasta más no poder**

yawning *adj.* open wide: *a yawning hole,* a deep wide hole. □ **profundo, abierto**

yaws [jɔ:z] *n. pl.* skin disease found in tropical countries. □ **frambesia**

year ['jə:] *n.* **1** period of twelve months starting on 1st January and ending on 31st December: *in the year 1492 Columbus discovered America; last year we went to France, next year we're going to Spain.* □ **año**

the New Year, the first few days of the year. □ **Año Nuevo**

to see the New Year in, to stay up until midnight on 31st December and celebrate with a party the beginning of the next year. □ **festejar la nochevieja**

calendar year, year beginning on 1st January and ending on 31st December. □ **año civil**

leap year, year with 366 days in it, one more than the normal year. □ **año bisiesto**

2 any period of twelve months: *he is five years old.* □ **año**

school year, year starting in September and ending in July of the following year. □ **año escolar**

financial year, (i) twelve month period for a firm's accounts. □ **ejercicio económico**

(ii) period beginning on April 6th and ending on the following April 5th considered for tax purposes. □ **año fiscal**

all (the) year round, through the whole year. □ **durante todo el año**

year in, year out, happening regularly over a long period of time. □ **año tras año**

3 *his earliest years,* his childhood. □ **sus primeros años**

4 *she's getting on in years,* she is quite old. □ **está entradita en años**

5 *I haven't seen him **for** (**donkey's**) **years**,* I haven't seen him for a long time. □ **...en siglos**

yearbook *n.* reference book which comes out each year with up to date information. □ **anuario**

yearling *n.* one year old animal. □ **añal**

yearly *adj.* and *adv.* every year; once a year. □ **anual**

yearn [jə:n] *v.* to long for something/to want something: *I'm yearning to see my brother in Australia again.* □ **anhelar**

yearning *n.* desire/longing. □ **anhelo**

yeast [ji:st] *n.* living fungus used in bread-making and beer-making, etc., causing fermentation: *bread made without yeast is flat and heavy.* □ **levadura**

yell [jel] *n.* loud shout: *he gave a yell and jumped over the side.* □ **grito**

■ *v.* to shout loudly. □ **gritar**

yellow ['jelou] *n.* and *adj.* **1** colour of the sun/of gold: *yellow daffodils.* □ **amarillo**

yellow fever, type of tropical fever. □ **fiebre amarilla**

yellow pages, section of a telephone directory giving a classified list of businesses, etc. □ **páginas amarillas**

2 cowardly: *he has a yellow streak in him,* he is sometimes cowardly/not brave. □ **cobarde**

■ *v.* to turn yellow: *the yellowing pages of a book.* □ **amarillear**

yellowhammer *n.* small bird with a yellow breast. □ **ave tonta; verderón**

yellowish *adj.* rather yellow. □ **amarillento**

yelp [jelp] *n.* cry of pain: *the dog gave a yelp when I touched its leg.* □ **gañido**
■ *v.* (*usually of animals*) to cry out in pain. □ **gañir**

yen [jen] *n.* **1** currency of Japan. □ **yen**
2 (*informal*) strong desire: *he has a yen to go to the States.* □ **tiene ganas de ir...**

yeoman ['jəumən] *n.* **1** formerly, a farmer with his own land. □ **labrador**
2 *he did yeoman service,* he worked long and hard. □ **prestó grandes servicios**

yes [jes] *adv.* and *interjection* expression of agreement: *do you like horses? yes, I do.* □ **sí**
yes man *n.* person who always agrees with a person in authority. □ **pelotillero**

yesterday ['jestədei] *adv.* and *n.* **1** the day before today: *yesterday was June 10th so today is June 11th; yesterday morning we drove to London and came back yesterday afternoon.* □ **ayer**
the day before yesterday, two days before today. □ **anteayer/antes de ayer**
2 recent times. □ **recientemente**
yesteryear *adv.* and *n.* (*formal*) times past: *the carriages of yesteryear.* □ **antaño**

yet [jet] *adv.* **1** up till now/up till this time: *has he come yet? I haven't seen him yet; I have nothing to say as yet.* □ **todavía; aún**
2 in spite of everything: *he's not among the leaders but he could win yet.* □ **pese a todo**
3 even: *yet more people; he ate yet another cake.* □ **todavía más**
■ *conj.* still/but: *she's fat and ugly yet everyone likes her.* □ **sin embargo**

yeti ['jeti] *n.* large animal, like an ape or bear which is supposed to exist in the snows of the Himalyas. □ **yeti**

yew [ju:] *n.* evergreen tree with small cones and poisonous red berries. □ **tejo**

Yiddish ['jidiʃ] *n.* language spoken by European Jews, based on German. □ **yidish**

yield [ji:ld] *n.* crop/product; return on your investment: *a good yield of corn; the company shares give a high yield.* □ **producción (de cereal); beneficio, interés (acciones)**
■ *v.* **1** to give/to produce: *the fields yielded a good harvest.* □ **producir; dar**
2 to produce money: *the money yields 10% interest.* □ **devengar; producir**
3 to give up/to surrender: *the town yielded to the enemy.* □ **rendirse**
4 to give way when pressed: *the wooden bridge began to yield under the lorry's weight.* □ **ceder**
5 (*of traffic*) to allow other vehicles to pass first: *yield to traffic coming from the right.* □ **ceder el paso**

yobbo ['jɔbou] *n.* (*pl. yobbos*) (*slang*) rude/violent young man. □ **macarra**

yodel ['joudl] *v.* to sing with quick changes from low to high notes (typical of Swiss and Austrian folk songs). □ **cantar a la tirolesa**

yoga ['jougə] *n.* system of exercises and meditation practised by Hindu thinkers, and now popular in western countries. □ **yoga**

yoghurt, yogurt ['jɔgət] *n.* fermented milk usually eaten sweetened as a dessert. □ **yogur**

yogi ['jougi] *n.* Hindu thinker who practises yoga. □ **yogui**

yoke [jouk] *n.* **1** piece of wood placed over the neck of a pair of animals when they are used for ploughing or similar work. □ **yugo**
a yoke of oxen, two oxen attached together. □ **una yunta de bueyes**
2 part of a dress which covers the shoulders and upper chest: *her dress was navy blue with a light blue yoke.* □ **canesú**
■ *v.* to join together (with a yoke): *the farmer yoked the oxen to the plough.* □ **uncir**

yokel ['joukl] *n.* stupid man from the country. □ **paleto**

yolk [jouk] *n.* yellow part of an egg. □ **yema**

yon [jɔn] **yonder** ['jɔndə] *adj.* and *adv.* (which is) over there. □ **aquel; allá**

yore [jɔ:] *n.* ***in days of yore,*** (*informal*) in the past. □ **antaño**

Yorkshire pudding ['jɔ:kʃə'pudiŋ] *n.* batter pudding eaten with roast beef. □ **budín de Yorkshire**

you [ju:] *pron.* **1** (referring to the person/persons to whom we are speaking): *you are taller than me; I'll give you my phone number.* □ **tú/vosotros, ustedes; te, os, les**
2 (referring to anybody/people in general): *you can never tell what he will do next.* □ **nunca se podrá decir...**

young [jʌŋ] *adj.* (*younger, youngest*) not old/recently born: *a young man; a young calf; Fred is younger than John but I am the youngest in the family.* □ **joven**
■ *n.* **1** young animals or birds: *the mother bird brought back food for her young in the nest.* □ **crías**
2 *pl.* ***the young,*** young people. □ **los jóvenes**
youngster *n.* young person: *the youngsters have plenty to do after school.* □ **joven**

your ['jɔ:] *adj.* belonging to you: *have you brought your books with you?* □ **tu/tus; vuestro/vuestros**
yours ['jɔ:z] *pron.* belonging to you: *are those books yours? he's a friend of yours.* □ **el tuyo/la tuya**
yourself [jɔ:'self] **yourselves** [jɔ:'selvz] *pron.* (referring to the subject you): *do you do all the cooking yourself? did you both hurt yourselves? a do-it-yourself enthusiast,* person who enjoys repairing and making things for his home. □ **tú mismo/tú misma**

youth [ju:θ] *n.* **1** time when you are young: *in my youth I enjoyed skiing.* □ **juventud**
2 young man: *two youths came towards me.* □ **joven**
3 young people: *people always complain about the youth of today.* □ **la juventud**
youth club, club where young people meet. □ **club juvenil**
youth hostel, building where young walkers, etc., can stay the night cheaply. □ **albergue para jóvenes**
youthful *adj.* young: *he looks youthful but he has four children.* □ **joven**

yowl [jaul] *v.* (*especially of animals*) to howl/to cry out loudly □ **aullar**

yo-yo ['joujou] *n.* trademark for a toy made of a circular piece of wood/metal with a groove round the edge, which can be made to run up and down a piece of string. □ **yoyó**

Yugoslavia [jugou'slɑ:viə] *n.* country in south-east Europe. □ **Yugoslavia**
Yugoslav *adj.* and *n.* (person) from Yugoslavia. □ **yugoslavo**

yule [ju:l] *n.* Christmas. □ **Navidad**
yule log, large piece of wood burnt on the fire at Christmas. □ **leño de Navidad**
Yuletide *n.* the Christmas period. □ **Navidad**

yumyum ['jʌmjʌm] *interjection showing* liking for food: *yumyum, ice cream for pudding.* □ **ñam ñam**

Z,z

Z, z [zed, *Amer.* zi:] twenty-sixth and last letter of the alphabet. □ **Z, z**
Zaire [zɑ:'i:ə] *n.* country in central Africa. □ **Zaire**
Zairean *adj.* and *n.* (person) from Zaire. □ **zaireño**
Zambia ['zæmbiə] *n.* country in central Africa. □ **Zambia**
Zambian *adj.* and *n.* (person) from Zambia. □ **zambiano**
zany ['zeini] *adj.* (*informal*) wildly mad: *zany humour.* □ **estrafalario**
zeal ['zi:l] *n.* keenness/eagerness: *the missionary was full of zeal.* □ **entusiasmo**
zealous ['zeləs] *adj.* eager. □ **entusiasta**
zealot ['zelət] *n.* person who is too enthusiastic about religion or politics. □ **fanático**
zebra ['zebrə] *n.* African animal similar to an ass or a horse, but with a striped coat. □ **cebra**
zebra crossing, path across a road painted with white stripes where people can cross safely as traffic must stop. □ **paso de cebra**
zenith ['zeniθ] *n.* **1** point of the sky directly overhead. □ **cenit**
2 highest point, as in someone's career. □ **apogeo**
zephyr ['zefə] *n.* (*formal*) gentle (often westerly) breeze. □ **céfiro**
zero ['zirou] *n.* (*pl. zeros*) **1** number 0/nothing/nil: *his enthusiasm has sunk to zero.* □ **cero**
2 freezing point of water when measured on a Celsius thermometer. □ **cero (grados)**
zero hour *n.* time fixed to begin something important (launching a satellite/attacking a town, etc.): *there are ten more minutes until zero hour.* □ **la hora H**
zero in on *v.* (*zeroed; zeroing*) to aim at (something)/to go straight to (something). □ **dirigirse derecho a**
zest [zest] *n.* **1** enthusiasm/enjoyment: *we started work with zest.* □ **gusto; ánimo**
2 added pleasure/spice: *the fact that we were rescuing a beautiful blonde girl added zest to the adventure.* □ **regusto**
3 thin piece of orange or lemon peel. □ **cáscara**
zigzag ['zigzæg] *adj.* and *n.* (line) which turns sharply one way, then the opposite way: *a zigzag path led up the mountain.* □ **en zigzag (adj.); zigzag (n.)**
■ *v.* (*he zigzagged*) to move in a zigzag: *we zigzagged across the field.* □ **zigzaguear**
zilch [ziltʃ] *n. Amer. slang* nothing/zero. □ **nada de nada; cero**
Zimbabwe [zim'bɑ:bwi] *n.* country in southern Africa. □ **Zimbabue**
Zimbabwean *adj.* and *n.* (person) from Zimbabwe. □ **zimbabuense**
zinc [ziŋk] *n.* (*chemical element*: Zn) hard bright light-coloured metal. □ **cinc**
zinnia ['zinjə] *n.* garden plant which has bright flowers in the summer. □ **zinnia**
zip [zip] *n.* **1** whistling sound made by a bullet as it goes through the air. □ **silbido**
2 (*informal*) energy: *put a bit of zip into it!* □ **vigor; échale un poco más de salero a...**
3 ***zip (fastener)***, device for closing openings on trousers/dresses, etc., consisting of two rows of metal or nylon teeth which lock together. □ **cremallera**
4 ***zip code, Amer.*** postal code/a code of letters and numbers which quickly shows the town you live in. □ **código postal**
■ *v.* (*he zipped*) **1** to whistle by: *the bullet zipped past my head; a car zipped along the road.* □ **pasar silbando**
2 ***to zip up,*** to close a zip (fastener): *can you zip me up?,* can you close the zip on my dress? □ **subir la cremallera**
zipper *n.* (*informal*) zip (fastener). □ **cremallera**
zippy *adj.* (*zippier, zippiest*) (*informal*) quick and lively. □ **brioso**
zirconium [zə:'kouniəm] *n.* (*chemical element*: Zr) rare metal used in alloys. □ **circonio**
zither ['ziðə] *n.* flat musical instrument played by plucking strings. □ **cítara**
zodiac ['zoudiæk] *n.* part of the sky (divided into twelve imaginary sections) through which the sun and planets are supposed to travel during the year. □ **Zodíaco**
signs of the zodiac, twelve signs named after groups of stars. □ **signos del Zodíaco**
zombie ['zɔmbi] *n.* **1** (West Indian) dead body which is revived and controlled by witchcraft. □ **zombi**
2 (*informal*) person who is half-asleep/moving slowly. □ **zombi**
zone [zoun] *n.* **1** region/area/part (of a country): *danger zone; frontier zone; war zone.* □ **zona**
the Canal Zone, area around the Suez or Panama Canal. □ **la zona del canal**
2 region of the Earth showing a particular type of climate: *Temperate Zone; Torrid Zone.* □ **zona**
■ *v.* to divide into parts for particular purposes: *the middle of the town has been zoned for commercial development.* □ **dividir en zonas**
zonal *adj.* of a zone. □ **zonal**
zoning *n.* the splitting up (of a town or area) into zones. □ **zonificación**
zoo [zu:] *n.* place where wild animals are kept in enclosures and which the public can visit. □ **zoo**
zoology [zu:'ɔlədʒi] *n.* study of animals. □ **zoología**
zoological [zu:ə'lɔdʒikl] *adj.* referring to the study of animals. □ **zoológico**
zoological gardens, zoo/place where wild animals are kept. □ **parque zoológico**
zoologist [zu:'ɔlədʒist] *n.* person who studies animals. □ **zoólogo**
zoom [zu:m] *n.* **1** deep buzzing noise made by something travelling fast. □ **zumbido**
2 sudden steep rise of aircraft/prices. □ **empinadura (avión); subida (precios)**
■ *v.* **1** to make a deep buzzing noise when moving fast: *the cars zoomed past me.* □ **pasar zumbando**
2 to rise suddenly and steeply: *the plane zoomed up into the air.* □ **empinarse**
3 *food prices have zoomed,* food is suddenly much dearer. □ **los precios se han disparado**
4 ***to zoom in on something,*** to focus a camera lens so that it makes a distant object appear to come closer. □ **enfocar**
zoom lens *n.* camera lens which allows you to change quickly from distant to close-up shots while keeping in focus all the time. □ **'zoom'**
zucchini [zu'ki:ni] *n.* (*no pl.*) courgette/small marrow. □ **calabacín**
zwieback ['zwi:bæk] *n. Amer.* type of hard crumbly biscuit. □ **galleta**

Appendix

IRREGULAR VERBS

(The letter (R) after the infinitive indicates that the verb can also be used as a regular verb.)

INFINITIVE	PAST TENSE	PAST PARTICIPLE
abide (R) [ə'baid]	**abode** [ə'boud]	**abode** [ə'boud]
arise [ə'raiz]	**arose** [ə'rouz]	**arisen** [ə'rizn]
awake (R) [ə'weik]	**awoke** [ə'wouk]	**awoken** [ə'woukən]
be [bi:]	**was** [wɔz, wəz] **were** [wə:*, wə*]	**been** [bi:n, bin]
bear [bɛə*]	**bore** [bɔ:*]	**borne** [bɔ:n]
beat [bi:t]	**beat** [bi:t]	**beaten** ['bi:tn]
become [bi'kʌm]	**became** [bi'keim]	**become** [bi'kʌm]
befall [bi'fɔ:l]	**befell** [bi'fel]	**befallen** [bi'fɔlən]
beget [bi'get]	**begot** [bi'gɔt]	**begotten** [bi'gɔtn]
begin [bi'gin]	**began** [bi'gæn]	**begun** [bi'gʌn]
behold [bi'hould]	**beheld** [bi'held]	**beheld** [bi'held]
bend [bend]	**bent** [bent]	**bent** [bent]
bereave (R) [bi'ri:v]	**bereft** [bi'reft]	**bereft** [bi'reft]
beseech (R) [bi'si:tʃ]	**besought** [bi'sɔ:t]	**besought** [bi'sɔ:t]
bet (R) [bet]	**bet** [bet]	**bet** [bet]
bid [bid]	**bid** [bid] **bade** [beid]	**bid** [bid] **bidden** ['bidn]
bind [baind]	**bound** [baund]	**bound** [baund]
bite [bait]	**bit** [bit]	**bitten** ['bitn]
bleed [bli:d]	**bled** [bled]	**bled** [bled]
bless (R) [bles]	**blest** [blest]	**blest** [blest]
blow [blou]	**blew** [blu:]	**blown** [bloun]
break [breik]	**broke** [brouk]	**broken** ['broukən]
breed [bri:d]	**bred** [bred]	**bred** [bred]
bring [briŋ]	**brought** [brɔ:t]	**brought** [brɔ:t]
broadcast ['brɔ:dka:st]	**broadcast** ['brɔ:dka:st]	**broadcast** ['brɔ:dka:st]
build [bild]	**built** [bilt]	**built** [bilt]
burn (R) [bə:n]	**burnt** [bə:nt]	**burnt** [bə:nt]
burst [bə:st]	**burst** [bə:st]	**burst** [bə:st]
buy [bai]	**bought** [bɔ:t]	**bought** [bɔ:t]
cast [ka:st]	**cast** [ka:st]	**cast** [ka:st]
catch [kætʃ]	**caught** [kɔ:t]	**caught** [kɔ:t]
chide (R) [tʃaid]	**chid** [tʃid]	**chidden** ['tʃidən] **chid** [tʃid]
choose [tʃu:z]	**chose** [tʃouz]	**chosen** ['tʃouzn]
cleave (R) [kli:v]	**cleft** [kleft] **clove** [klouv]	**cleft** [kleft] **cloven** ['klouvn]
cling [kliŋ]	**clung** [klʌŋ]	**clung** [klʌŋ]
come [kʌm]	**came** [keim]	**come** [kʌm]
cost [kɔst]	**cost** [kɔst]	**cost** [kɔst]
creep [kri:p]	**crept** [krept]	**crept** [krept]
crow (R) [krou]	**crew** [kru:]	**crowed** [kroud]
cut [kʌt]	**cut** [kʌt]	**cut** [kʌt]
deal [di:l]	**dealt** [delt]	**dealt** [delt]
dig [dig]	**dug** [dʌg]	**dug** [dʌg]
do [du]	**did** [did]	**done** [dʌn]
draw [drɔ:]	**drew** [dru:]	**drawn** [drɔ:n]

dream (R) [dri:m]	**dreamt** [dremt]	**dreamt** [dremt]
drink [driŋk]	**drank** [dræŋk]	**drunk** [drʌŋk]
drive [draiv]	**drove** [drouv]	**driven** ['drivn]
dwell (R) [dwel]	**dwelt** [dwelt]	**dwelt** [dwelt]
eat [i:t]	**ate** [et]	**eaten** ['i:tn]
fall [fɔ:l]	**fell** [fel]	**fallen** ['fɔ:lən]
feed [fi:d]	**fed** [fed]	**fed** [fed]
feel [fi:l]	**felt** [felt]	**felt** [felt]
fight [fait]	**fought** [fɔ:t]	**fought** [fɔ:t]
find [faind]	**found** [faund]	**found** [faund]
flee [fli:]	**fled** [fled]	**fled** [fled]
fling [fliŋ]	**flung** [flʌŋ]	**flung** [flʌŋ]
fly [flai]	**flew** [flu:]	**flown** [floun]
forbear [fɔ:'bɛə*]	**forbore** [fɔ:'bɔ:*]	**forborne** [fɔ:'bɔ:n]
forbid [fə'bid]	**forbade** [fə'beid] **forbad** [fə'bæd]	**forbidden** [fə'bidn]
forecast (R) ['fɔ:ka:st]	**forecast** ['fɔ:ka:st]	**forecast** ['fɔ:ka:st]
forget [fə'get]	**forgot** [fə'gɔt]	**forgotten** [fə'gɔtn]
forgive [fə'giv]	**forgave** [fə'geiv]	**forgiven** [fə'givn]
forsake [fə'seik]	**forsook** [fə'suk]	**forsaken** [fə'seikən]
forswear [fɔ:'swɛə*]	**forswore** [fɔ:'swɔ:*]	**forsworn** [fɔ:'swɔ:n]
freeze [fri:z]	**froze** [frouz]	**frozen** ['frouzn]
get [get]	**got** [gɔt]	**got** [gɔt] **gotten** ['gɔtn] (USA)
gild (R) [gild]	**gilt** [gilt]	**gilt** [gilt]
gird [(R) [gə:d]	**girt** [gə:t]	**girt** [gə:t]
give [giv]	**gave** [geiv]	**given** ['givn]
go [gou]	**went** [went]	**gone** [gɔn]
grind [graind]	**ground** [graund]	**ground** [graund]
grow [grou]	**grew** [gru:]	**grown** [groun]
hang (R) [hæŋ]	**hung** [hʌŋ]	**hung** [hʌŋ]
have [hæv]	**had** [hæd]	**had** [hæd]
hear [hiə*]	**heard** [hə:d]	**heard** [hə:d]
heave (R) [hi:v]	**hove** [houv]	**hove** [houv]
hew (R) [hju:]	**hewed** [hju:d]	**hewn** [hju:n]
hide [haid]	**hid** [hid]	**hidden** ['hidn] **hid** [hid]
hit [hit]	**hit** [hit]	**hit** [hit]
hold [hould]	**held** [held]	**held** [held]
hurt [hə:t]	**hurt** [hə:t]	**hurt** [hə:t]
keep [ki:p]	**kept** [kept]	**kept** [kept]
kneel (R) [ni:l]	**knelt** [nelt]	**knelt** [nelt]
knit (R) [nit]	**knit** [nit]	**knit** [nit]
know [nou]	**knew** [nju:]	**known** [noun]
lay [ley]	**laid** [leid]	**laid** [leid]
lead [li:d]	**led** [led]	**led** [led]
lean (R) [li:n]	**leant** [lent]	**leant** [lent]
leap (R) [li:p]	**leapt** [lept]	**leapt** [lept]
learn (R) [lə:n]	**learnt** [lə:nt]	**learnt** [lə:nt]
leave [li:v]	**left** [left]	**left** [left]
lend [lend]	**lent** [lent]	**lent** [lent]
let [let]	**let** [let]	**let** [let]
lie [lai]	**lay** [lei]	**lain** [lein]
light (R) [lait]	**lit** [lit]	**lit** [lit]
lose [lu:z]	**lost** [lɔst]	**lost** [lɔst]
make [meik]	**made** [meid]	**made** [meid]

mean [mi:n]	**meant** [ment]	**meant** [ment]
meet [mi:t]	**met** [met]	**met** [met]
mistake [mis'teik]	**mistook** [mis'tuk]	**mistaken** [mis'teikn]
misunderstand ['misʌndə'stænd]	**misunderstood** ['misʌndə'stud]	**misunderstood** ['misʌndə'stud]
mow (R) [mou]	**mowed** [moud]	**mown** [moun]
pay [pey]	**paid** [peid]	**paid** [peid]
prove (R) [pru:v]	**proved** ['pru:vəd]	**proven** ['pru:vən]
put [put]	**put** [put]	**put** [put]
quit (R) [kwit]	**quit** [kwit]	**quit** [kwit]
read [(ri:d]	**read** [red]	**read** [red]
rend [rend]	**rent** [rent]	**rent** [rent]
rid (R) [rid]	**rid** [rid]	**rid** [rid]
ride [raid]	**rode** [roud]	**ridden** ['ridn]
ring [riŋ]	**rang** [ræŋ]	**rung** [rʌŋ]
rise [raiz]	**rose** [rouz]	**risen** ['rizn]
run [rʌn]	**ran** [ræn]	**run** [rʌn]
saw (R) [sɔ:]	**sawed** [sɔ:d]	**sawn** [sɔ:n]
say [sei]	**said** [sed]	**said** [sed]
see [si:]	**saw** [sɔ:]	**seen** [si:n]
seek [si:k]	**sought** [sɔ:t]	**sought** [sɔ:t]
sell [sel]	**sold** [sould]	**sold** [sould]
send [send]	**sent** [sent]	**sent** [sent]
set [set]	**set** [set]	**set** [set]
sew (R) [sou]	**sewed** [soud]	**sewn** [soun]
shake [ʃeik]	**shook** [ʃuk]	**shaken** ['ʃeikn]
shave (R) [ʃeiv]	**shaved** [ʃeivd]	**shaven** ['ʃeivn]
shear (R) [ʃiə*]	**sheared** [ʃiəd]	**shorn** [ʃɔ:n]
shed [ʃed]	**shed** [ʃed]	**shed** [ʃed]
shine (R) [ʃain]	**shone** [ʃɔn]	**shone** [ʃɔn]
shoe [ʃu:]	**shod** [ʃɔd]	**shod** [ʃɔd]
shoot [ʃu:t]	**shot** [ʃɔt]	**shot** [ʃɔt]
show (R) [ʃou]	**showed** [ʃoud]	**shown** [ʃoun]
shrink [ʃriŋk]	**shrank** [ʃræŋk]	**shrunk** [ʃrʌŋk]
shrive (R) [ʃraiv]	**shrove** [ʃrouv]	**shriven** [ʃrivn]
shut [ʃʌt]	**shut** [ʃʌt]	**shut** [ʃʌt]
sing [siŋ]	**sang** [sæŋ]	**sung** [sʌŋ]
sink [siŋk]	**sank** [sæŋk]	**sunk** [sʌŋk]
sit [sit]	**sat** [sæt]	**sat** [sæt]
slay [slei]	**slew** [slu:]	**slain** [slein]
sleep [sli:p]	**slept** [slept]	**slept** [slept]
slide [slaid]	**slid** [slid]	**slid** [slid]
sling [sliŋ]	**slung** [slʌŋ]	**slung** [slʌŋ]
slink [sliŋk]	**slunk** [slʌŋk]	**slunk** [slʌŋk]
slit [slit]	**slit** [slit]	**slit** [slit]
smell (R) [smel]	**smelt** [smelt]	**smelt** [smelt]
smite [smait]	**smote** [smout]	**smitten** ['smitn]
sow (R) [sou]	**sowed** [soud]	**sown** [soun]
speak [spi:k]	**spoke** [spouk]	**spoken** ['spoukən]
speed (R) [spi:d]	**sped** [sped]	**sped** [sped]
spell (R) [spel]	**spelt** [spelt]	**spelt** [spelt]
spend [spend]	**spent** [spent]	**spent** [spent]
spill (R) [spil]	**spilt** [spilt]	**spilt** [spilt]
spin [spin]	**spun** [spʌn] **span** [spæn]	**spun** [spʌn]

spit [spit]	**spat** [spæt] **spit** [spit] (USA)	**spat** [spæt] **spit** [spit] (USA)
split [split]	**split** [split]	**split** [split]
spoil (R) [spɔil]	**spoilt** [spɔilt]	**spoilt** [spɔilt]
spread [spred]	**spread** [spred]	**spread** [spred]
spring [spriŋ]	**sprang** [spræŋ]	**sprung** [sprʌŋ]
stand [stænd]	**stood** [stud]	**stood** [stud]
stave (R) [steiv]	**stove** [stouv]	**stove** [stouv]
steal [sti:l]	**stole** [stoul]	**stolen** ['stoulən]
stick [stik]	**stuck** [stʌk]	**stuck** [stʌk]
sting [stiŋ]	**stung** [stʌŋ]	**stung** [stʌŋ]
stink [stiŋk]	**stank** [stæŋk] εstunk [stʌŋk]	**stunk** [stʌŋk]
strew (R) [stru:]	**strewed** [stru:d]	**strewn** [stru:n]
stride [straid]	**strode** [stroud]	**stridden** ['stridn]
strike [straik]	**struck** [strʌk]	**struck** [strʌk]
string [striŋ]	**strung** [strʌŋ]	**strung** [strʌŋ]
strive [straiv]	**strove** [strouv]	**striven** ['strivən]
swear [swεə*]	**swore** [swɔ:*]	**sworn** [swɔ:n]
sweep [swi:p]	**swept** [swept]	**swept** [swept]
swell (R) [swel]	**swelled** [sweld]	**swollen** ['swoulən]
swim [swim]	**swam** [swæm]	**swum** [swʌm]
swing [swiŋ]	**swung** [swʌŋ]	**swung** [swʌŋ]
take [teik]	**took** [tuk]	**taken** ['teikən]
teach [ti:tʃ]	**taught** [tɔ:t]	**taught** [tɔ:t]
tear [tεə*]	**tore** [tɔ:*]	**torn** [tɔ:n]
tell [tel]	**told** [tould]	**told** [tould]
think [θiŋk]	**thought** [θɔ:t]	**thought** [θɔ:t]
thrive (R) [θraiv]	**throve** [θrouv]	**thriven** ['θrivn]
throw [θrou]	**threw** [θru:]	**thrown** [θroun]
thrust [θrʌst]	**thrust** [θrʌst]	**thrust** [θrʌst]
tread [tred]	**trod** [trɔd]	**trodden** ['trɔdn] **trod** [trɔd]
understand ['ʌndə'stænd]	**understood** ['ʌndə'stud]	**understood** ['ʌndə'stud]
wake (R) [weik]	**woke** [wouk]	**woken** ['woukən]
wear [wεə*]	**wore** [wɔ:*]	**worn** [wɔ:n]
weave [wi:v]	**wove** [wouv]	**woven** ['wouvən]
wed (R) [wed]	**wed** [wed]	**wed** [wed]
weep [wi:p]	**wept** [wept]	**wept** [wept]
wet (R) [wet]	**wet** [wet]	**wet** [wet]
win [win]	**won** [wʌn]	**won** [wʌn]
wind [waind]	**wound** [waund]	**wound** [waund]
wring [riŋ]	**wrung** [rʌŋ]	**wrung** [rʌŋ]
write [rait]	**wrote** [rout]	**written** ['ritn]

Weights and Measures

The Metric System

	METRIC	*length*		GB & US
10 millimetres (mm)	=	1 centimetre (cm)	=	0.394 inch (in)
100 centimetres	=	1 metre (m)	=	39.4 inches or 1.094 yards (yd)
1000 metres	=	1 kilometre (km)	=	0.6214 mile or about 5/8 mile
		surface		
100 square metres (m^2)	=	1 are (a)	=	0.025 acre
100 ares	=	1 hectare (ha)	=	2.471 acres
100 hectares	=	1 square kilometre (km^2)	=	0.386 square mile
		weight		
10 milligrams (mg)	=	1 centigram (cg)	=	0.154 grain
100 centigrams	=	1 gram (g)	=	15.43 grains
1000 grams	=	1 kilogram (kg)	=	2.205 pounds
1000 kilograms	=	1 tonne	=	19.688 hundredweight
		capacity		
1000 millilitres (ml)	=	1 litre (l)	=	1.76 pints (2.1 US pints)
10 litres	=	1 decalitre (dl)	=	2.2 gallons (2.63 US gallons)

Avoirdupois Weight

		GB & US		METRIC
		1 grain (gr)	=	0.065 gram (g)
437½ grains	=	1 ounce (oz)	=	28.35 grams
16 drams (dr)	=	1 ounce	=	28.35 grams
16 ounces	=	1 pound (lb)	=	0.454 kilogram (kg)
14 pounds	=	1 stone (st)	=	6.35 kilograms
2 stone	=	1 quarter	=	12.7 kilograms
4 quarters	=	1 hundredweight (cwt)	=	50.8 kilograms
112 pounds	=	1 cwt	=	50.8 kilograms
100 pounds	=	1 short cwt	=	45.4 kilograms
20 cwt	=	1 ton	=	1016.04 kilograms
2000 pounds	=	1 short ton	=	0.907 tonne
2240 pounds	=	1 long ton	=	1.016 tonnes

Linear Measure

		GB & US		METRIC
		1 inch (in)	=	25.4 millimetres (mm)
12 inches	=	1 foot (ft)	=	30.48 centimetres (cm)
3 feet	=	1 yard (yd)	=	0.914 metre (m)
5 1/2 yards	=	1 rod, pole or perch	=	5.029 metres
22 yards	=	1 chain (ch)	=	20.17 metres
220 yards	=	1 furlong (fur)	=	201.17 metres
8 furlongs	=	1 mile	=	1.609 kilometres (km)
1760 yards	=	1 mile	=	1.609 kilometres
3 miles	=	1 league	=	4.828 kilometres

Square Measure

		GB & US		METRIC
		1 square inch	=	6.452 sq centimetres
144 sq inches	=	1 sq foot	=	929.03 sq centimetres
9 sq feet	=	1 sq yard	=	0.836 sq metre
484 sq yards	=	1 sq chain	=	404.62 sq metres
4840 sq yards	=	1 acre	=	0.405 hectare
40 sq rods	=	1 rood	=	10.1168 ares
4 roods	=	1 acre	=	0.405 hectare
640 acres	=	1 sq mile	=	2.59 sq kilometres or 259 hectares

Cubic Measure

	GB & US		METRIC
		1 cubic inch	= 16.4 cu centimetres
1728 cu inches	=	1 cu foot	= 0.028 cu metre
27 cu feet	=	1 cu yard	= 0.765 cu metre

Nautical Measure

used for measuring the depth and surface distance of seas, rivers, etc

	GB & US		METRIC
6 feet	=	1 fathom	= 1.829 metres
608 feet (in the British Navy)	=	1 cable	= 185.31 metres
720 feet (in the US Navy)	=	1 cable	= 219.46 metres
6080 feet	=	sea (or nautical) mile (1.151 statute miles)	= 1.852 kilometres
3 sea miles	=	1 sea league	= 5.55 kilometres
60 sea miles	=	1 degree (69.047 statute miles)	
360 degrees	=	1 circle	

The speed of one sea mile per hour is called a *knot*.

Measure of Capacity

		GB		US		METRIC
4 gills	=	1 pint (pt)	=	1.201 pints	=	0.568 litre
2 pints	=	1 quart (qt)	=	1.201 quarts	=	1.136 litres
4 quarts	=	1 gallon (gal)	=	1.201 gallons	=	4.546 litres

Circular or Angular Measure

60 seconds (")	=	1 minute (')	90 degrees	=	1 quadrant or right angle (∟)
60 minutes	=	1 degree (°)	360 degrees	=	1 circle or circumference

the diameter of a circle	=	the straight line passing through its centre
the radius of a circle	=	1/2 × the diameter
the circumference of a circle	=	22/7 × the diameter

Temperature Equivalents

	FAHRENHEIT (F)	CELSIUS OR CENTIGRADE (C)
Boiling Point	212°	100°
	194°	90°
	176°	80°
	158°	70°
	140°	60°
	122°	50°
	104°	40°
	86°	30°
	68°	20°
	50°	10°
Freezing Point	32°	0°
	14°	–10°
	0°	–17.8°
Absolute Zero	–459.67°	–273.15°

To convert Fahrenheit temperature into Celsius or centigrade: subtract 32 and multiply by 5/9 (five-ninths).

To convert Celsius or centigrade temperature into Fahrenheit: multiply by 9/5 (nine-fifths) and add 32.

Time

60 seconds	=	1 minute (min)	4 weeks, or 28 days	=	1 lunar month (mth)
60 minutes	=	1 hour (hr)	52 weeks, 1 day; or 13 lunar months, 1 day	=	1 year
24 hours	=	1 day	365 days, 6 hours	=	1 (Julian) year (yr)
7 days	=	1 week (wk)			

Table of Chemical Elements

The commonest elements are also given as headwords in the main dictionary.

Name & Symbol	Atomic Number
Actinium (Ac)	89
Aluminium (Al)	13
Americium (Am)	95
Antimony (Sb)	51
Argon (Ar)	18
Arsenic (As)	33
Astatine (At)	85
Barium (Ba)	56
Berkelium (Bk)	97
Beryllium (Be)	4
Bismuth (Bi)	83
Boron (B)	5
Bromine (Br)	35
Cadmium (Cd)	48
Caesium (Cs)	55
Calcium (Ca)	20
Californium (Cf)	98
Cerium (Ce)	58
Chlorine (Cl)	17
Chromium (Cr)	24
Cobalt (Co)	27
Copper (Cu)	29
Curium (Cm)	96
Dysprosium (Dy)	66
Einsteinium (Es)	99
Erbium (Er)	68
Europium (Eu)	63
Fermium (Fm)	100
Fluorine (F)	9
Francium (Fr)	87
Gadolinium (Gd)	64
Gallium (Ga)	31
Germanium (Ge)	32
Gold (Au)	79
Hafnium (Hf)	72
Hahnium (Ha)	105
Helium (He)	2
Holmium (Ho)	67
Hydrogen (H)	1
Indium (In)	49
Iodine (I)	53
Iridium (Ir)	77
Iron (Fe)	26
Krypton (Kr)	36
Lanthanum (La)	57
Lawrencium (Lr)	103
Lead (Pb)	82
Lithium (Li)	3
Lutetium (Lu)	71
Magnesium (Mg)	12
Manganese (Mn)	25
Mendeleevium (Md)	101

Name & Symbol	Atomic Number
Mercury (Hg)	80
Molybdenum (Mo)	42
Neodymium (Nd)	60
Neon (Ne)	10
Neptunium (Np)	93
Nickel (Ni)	28
Niobium (Nb)	41
Nitrogen (N)	7
Nobelium (No)	102
Osmium (Os)	76
Oxygen (O)	8
Palladium (Pd)	46
Phosphorus (P)	15
Platinum (Pt)	78
Plutonium (Pu)	94
Polonium (Po)	84
Potassium (K)	19
Praseodymium (Pr)	59
Promethium (Pm)	61
Protactinium (Pa)	91
Radium (Ra)	88
Radon (Rn)	86
Rhenium (Re)	75
Rhodium (Rh)	45
Rubidium (Rb)	37
Ruthenium (Ru)	44
Rutherfordium (Rf)	104
Samarium (Sm)	62
Scandium (Sc)	21
Selenium (Se)	34
Silicon (Si)	14
Silver (Ag)	47
Sodium (Na)	11
Strontium (Sr)	38
Sulphur (S)	16
Tantalum (Ta)	73
Technetium (Tc)	43
Tellurium (Te)	52
Terbium (Tb)	65
Thallium (Tl)	81
Thorium (Th)	90
Thulium (Tm)	69
Tin (Sn)	50
Titanium (Ti)	22
Tungsten (W)	74
Uranium (U)	92
Vanadium (V)	23
Xenon (Xe)	54
Ytterbium (Yb)	70
Yttrium (Y)	39
Zinc (Zn)	30
Zirconium (Zr)	40

The United States of America: the states (with abbreviations) and their capitals

Alabama	(Ala.)	Montgomery
Alaska		Juneau
Arizona	(Ariz.)	Phoenix
Arkansas	(Ark.)	Little Rock
California	(Cal.)	Sacramento
Colorado	(Colo.)	Denver
Connecticut	(Conn.)	Hartford
Delaware	(Del.)	Dover
Florida	(Fla.)	Tallahassee
Georgia	(Ga.)	Atlanta
Hawaii		Honolulu
Idaho	(Id.)	Boise
Illinois	(Ill.)	Springfield
Indiana	(Ind.)	Indianapolis
Iowa	(Ia.)	Des Moines
Kansas	(Kan.)	Topeka
Kentucky	(Ky.)	Frankfort
Louisiana	(La.)	Baton Rouge
Maine	(Me.)	Augusta
Maryland	(Md.)	Annapolis
Massachusetts	(Mass.)	Boston
Michigan	(Mich.)	Lansing
Minnesota	(Minn.)	St Paul
Mississippi	(Miss.)	Jackson
Missouri	(Mo.)	Jefferson City
Montana	(Mont.)	Helena
Nebraska	(Nebr.)	Lincoln
Nevada	(Nev.)	Carson City
New Hampshire	(N.H.)	Concord
New Jersey	(N.J.)	Trenton
New Mexico	(N.M.)	Santa Fe
New York	(N.Y.)	Albany
North Carolina	(N.C.)	Raleigh
North Dakota	(N.D.)	Bismarck
Ohio		Columbus
Oklahoma	(Okla.)	Oklahoma City
Oregon	(Ore.)	Salem
Pennsylvania	(Pa.)	Harrisburg
Rhode Island	(R.I.)	Providence
South Carolina	(S.C.)	Columbia
South Dakota	(S.D.)	Pierre
Tennessee	(Tenn.)	Nashville
Texas		Austin
Utah		Salt Lake City
Vermont	(Vt.)	Montpelier
Virginia	(Va.)	Richmond
Washington	(Wash.)	Olympia
West Virginia	(W.Va.)	Charleston
Wisconsin	(Wisc.)	Madison
Wyoming	(Wyo.)	Cheyenne
District of Columbia	(D.C.)	Washington

The United Kingdom: counties (with abbreviations) and their county towns

England

Avon		Bristol
Bedfordshire	(Beds.)	Bedford
Berkshire	(Berks.)	Reading
Buckinghamshire	(Bucks.)	Aylesbury
Cambridgeshire	(Cambs.)	Cambridge
Cheshire		Chester
Cleveland		Middlesbrough
Cornwall		Truro
Cumbria		Carlisle
Derbyshire	(Derbys.)	Matlock
Devon		Exeter
Dorset		Dorchester
Durham		Durham
East Sussex	(E. Sussex)	Lewes
Essex		Chelmsford
Gloucesterhire	(Glos.)	Gloucester
Greater London		
Greater Manchester		Manchester
Hampshire	(Hants.)	Winchester
Hereford & Worcester	(Hereford & Worc.)	Worcester
Hertfordshire	(Herts.)	Hertford
Humberside		Hull
Isle of Wight	(I. of Wight)	Newport
Kent		Maidstone
Lancashire	(Lancs.)	Preston
Leicestershire	(Leics.)	Leicester
Lincolnshire	(Linc.)	Lincoln
Merseyside		Liverpool
Norfolk		Norwich
Northamptonshire	(Northants.)	Northampton
Northumberland	(Northd.)	Newcastle-upon-Tyne
North Yorkshire	(N. Yorkshire)	Northallerton
Nottinghamshire	(Notts.)	Nottingham
Oxfordshire	(Oxon.)	Oxford
Shropshire	(Salop)	Shrewsbury
Somerset		Taunton
South Yorkshire	(S. Yorkshire)	Barnsley
Staffordshire	(Staffs.)	Stafford
Suffolk		Ipswich
Surrey		Kingston-upon-Thames
Tyne & Wear		Newcastle-upon-Tyne
Warwickshire	(Warwicks.)	Warwick
West Midlands	(W. Midlands)	Birmingham
West Sussex	(W. Sussex)	Chichester
West Yorkshire	(W. Yorkshire)	Wakefield
Wiltshire	(Wilts.)	Trowbridge

Note: there are 39 non-metropolitan councils
6 metropolitan councils—
Greater Manchester
Merseyside
South Yorkshire
Tyne & Wear
West Midlands
West Yorkshire
and Greater London

Wales

Clwyd		Mold
Dyfed		Carmarthen
Gwent		Cwmbran
Gwynedd		Caenarfon
Mid Glamorgan	(M. Glamorgan)	Cardiff
Powys		Llandrindod Wells
South Glamorgan	(S. Glamorgan)	Cardiff
West Glamorgan	(W. Glamorgan)	Swansea

Scotland

Since 1975 local government in Scotland has not been based on the counties, but on the following regions:

Borders	Newton St Boswells
Central	Stirling
Dumfries & Galloway	Dumfries
Fife	Glenrothes
Grampian	Aberdeen
Highland	Inverness
Lothian	Edinburgh
Orkney	Kirkwall
Shetland	Lerwick
Strathclyde	Glasgow
Tayside	Dundee
Western Isles	Stornoway

Northern Ireland

Since 1973 local government in Northern Ireland has not been based on the counties, but on 23 district councils and 9 area boards.

Australia: the states (with abbreviations) and their capitals

New South Wales	(N.S.W.)	Sydney
Queensland	(Qld.)	Brisbane
South Australia	(S.A.)	Adelaide
Tasmania	(Tas.)	Hobart
Victoria	(Vic.)	Melbourne
Western Australia	(W.A.)	Perth

The Territories

Northern Territory	(N.T.)	Darwin
Australian Capital Territory	(A.C.T.)	Canberra

Canada: the provinces (with abbreviations) and their capitals

Alberta	(Alta.)	Edmonton
British Columbia	(B.C.)	Victoria
Manitoba	(Man.)	Winnipeg
New Brunswick	(N.B.)	Fredericton
Newfoundland	(Nfld.)	St John's
Nova Scotia	(N.S.)	Halifax
Ontario	(Ont.)	Toronto
Prince Edward Island	(P.E.I.)	Charlottetown
Quebec	(Que.)	Quebec
Saskatchewan	(Sask.)	Regina

The Territories

Yukon Territory	(Y.T.)	Whitehorse
Northwest Territories	(N.W.T.)	Yellowknife

A selection of common differences between British English and American English

British English	*American English*
TV aerial	TV antenna
autumn	fall
back garden	back yard
bill	check
bonnet (of a car)	hood
braces	suspenders
candy floss	cotton candy
caravan	trailer
car park	parking lot
chips	French fries
curtains	drapes
dummy	pacifier
estate agent	realtor
from Monday to Friday	Monday through Friday
frying pan	skillet
glandular fever	mononucleosis
green fingers	green thumb
lift	elevator
to go to the loo	to go the john
to meet someone	to meet with someone
minced beef	ground beef
motorway	freeway
nappy	diaper
5 pound note	5 dollar bill
noughts and crosses	tic tac toe
pavement	sidewalk
petrol	gas
post-code	zip-code
to protest against something	to protest something
to reverse the charges	to call collect
silencer	muffler
to stand in a queue	to stand in a line
sweets	candy
tap	faucet
underground	subway
to wash (your face and hands)	to wash up
windscreen	windshield

Numerals

Cardinal numbers

1 one	11 eleven	21 twenty-one	40 forty
2 two	12 twelve	22 twenty-two	50 fifty
3 three	13 thirteen	23 twenty-three	60 sixty
4 four	14 fourteen	24 twenty-four	70 seventy
5 five	15 fifteen	25 twenty-five	80 eighty
6 six	16 sixteen	26 twenty-six	90 ninety
7 seven	17 seventeen	27 twenty-seven	100 a hundred
8 eight	18 eighteen	28 twenty-eight	200 two hundred
9 nine	19 nineteen	29 twenty-nine	1,000 a thousand
10 ten	20 twenty	30 thirty	10,000 ten thousand
			100,000 a hundred thousand
120 a hundred and twenty			1,000,000 a million
1,120 one thousand, one hundred and twenty			

Ordinal numbers

1st first	11th eleventh	21st twenty-first
2nd second	12th twelfth	22nd twenty-second
3rd third	13th thirteenth	23rd twenty-third
4th fourth	14th fourteenth	24th twenty-fourth
5th fifth	15th fifteenth	30th thirtieth
6th sixth	16th sixteenth	40th fourtieth
7th seventh	17th seventeenth	50th fiftieth
8th eighth	18th eighteenth	60th sixtieth
9th ninth	19th nineteenth	70th seventieth
10th tenth	20th twentieth	80th eightieth
		90th ninetieth
		100th hundredth
		thousandth
		millionth

Punctuaction marks and special characters

,	comma
;	semi-colon
:	colon
.	full stop; *(USA)* period
?	question mark
!	exclamation mark; *(USA)* exclamation point
’	apostrophe
“ ”	quotation marks; quotes; inverted commas
( )	brackets; parentheses
-	hyphen
–	en dash
—	em dash
/	solidus; slash; slant; virgule
*	asterisk
%	percent
&	ampersand
´	acute accent
`	grave accent
¨	di(a)eresis; umlaut
ˆ	circumflex
˜	tilde
¸	cedilla